DODS

PARLIAMENTARY COMPANION

2018

DODS

PARLIAMENTARY COMPANION

2018

186th year

ACKNOWLEDGEMENTS

Dods Parliamentary Companion published since 1832

Published by

Dods
Data and Reference Division
11th Floor
The Shard, 32 London Bridge Street
London SE1 9SG

Telephone: 020 7593 5500
E-mail: editor@dods.co.uk
www.dodspeople.com

Editor: Elizabeth Newton
Deputy Editor: Imogen Dale
Editorial Assistants: Ifigenia Balkoura, Hannah Berry
Reference Data Manager: Tom Harris
Digital Typesetter and Data Manager: Kirsty Currie
Publisher (Dods Books): Guy Cleaver

Photo of Richard Drax MP © The Dorset Echo; photo of Lord Liddle © Policy Network; photo of Baroness Young of Hornsey © Eamonn.McCabe@btinternet.com; photo of Lord Giddens © Nigel Stead/LSE; photo of Lord Tyler © Paul Heartfield; photo of Baroness Neuberger ©Derek Tamea.

Typesetting by Dods
Printed in Great Britain by Short Run Press Ltd, Exeter, Devon

ISBN 978-1-908232-27-4 ISSN 0070-7007

CONTENTS

Editor's Introduction viii
Foreword by Rt Hon Damian Green MP, First Secretary of State and Minister for the Cabinet Office ix
Addenda x
Public Legislation 2016–17 xii
Related Politicians xv
Parliaments 1900–2015 xviii
Historical information xix
Prime Ministers since 1721 xx

GOVERNMENT AND OPPOSITION 1
THE GOVERNMENT 2
Cabinet 2
Ministers 3
Lords Spokespeople 7
Parliamentary Private Secretaries 39
Special Advisers 43

THE OPPOSITION 47

Salaried Parliamentarians 57

PARLIAMENT 62
HOUSE OF COMMONS 62
State of the Parties 62
Changes since 2017 general election 62
MPs' Biographies 63
MPs' Political Interests 360
Constituencies 411
Select Committees 447
Officers and Officials 455

GENERAL ELECTION 2017 464
Polling Results by Constituency 465
Analysis 532

HOUSE OF LORDS 548
Membership 548
Changes in membership since last edition 550
Peers' Biographies 551
Peers' Political Interests 988
Hereditary Peers 1032
Bishops 1033
Select Committees 1053
Principal Office Holders and Staff 1059

Joint Select Committees 1062
Privy Counsellors 1066
Political Parties 1069
Parliamentary Press Gallery 1073

DEVOLVED PARLIAMENT AND ASSEMBLIES 1081

Ministerial and Members' Salaries 1082
Scottish Government 1083
MSPs' Directory 1092
Welsh Government 1120
AMs' Directory 1125
Northern Ireland Assembly 1139
MLAs' Directory 1142
Greater London Authority 1159
London Assembly Members' Directory 1160
Police and Crime Commissioners 1165

EUROPEAN UNION 1172

UK MEPs' Directory 1173

GOVERNMENT AND PUBLIC OFFICES 1191

Departments of State 1193
Executive Agencies 1205
Non-Ministerial Departments 1212
Ombudsmen and Complaint-Handling Bodies 1216
Political and Parliamentary Organisations 1221

Diplomatic Representation 1228
Forms of Address 1281
Parliamentary Terms and Procedures 1283
Abbreviations 1297
Index of Members of Parliaments and Assemblies 1308
Index 1315

EDITOR'S INTRODUCTION

On 18 April 2017 Theresa May announced her plan to call an early general election. The motion was put to MPs on 19 April and was approved by 522 to 13. Parliament was then dissolved on 3 May and the election took place on 8 June.

The election turnout was 68.7 per cent – up from 66.1 per cent in 2015. The Conservatives won the largest number of seats but lost their majority – losing 13 seats. However, they increased their number of MPs in Scotland to 13. Labour gained 33, the SNP lost 19, the Liberal Democrats and Sinn Féin gained 3, the DUP gained 2 and Plaid Cymru gained 1. The SDLP, UUP and UKIP all lost their seats. There were 99 new MPs elected, replacing 67 who were defeated and 31 who stood down. The number of women MPs has now increased to 208 – the largest number to be elected ever.

On 26 June Theresa May announced a Confidence and Supply Agreement had been made between the Conservatives and the Democratic Unionist Party, confirming that the DUP will support the Government on votes on the Queen's Speech, the Budget and legislation relating to Brexit and national security.

Following the election May conducted a reshuffle – Damian Green was appointed First Secretary of State and Minister for the Cabinet Office, David Lidington was appointed Lord Chancellor and Secretary of State for Justice, replacing Liz Truss who moved to Chief Secretary to the Treasury. Michael Gove returned to the Cabinet as Secretary of State for Environment, Food and Rural Affairs, replacing Andrea Leadsom who became Leader of the House of Commons and David Gauke was promoted to Secretary of State for Work and Pensions.

Jeremy Corbyn conducted a reshuffle to the Labour Shadow Cabinet in October 2016. Diane Abbott became Shadow Home Secretary, Jon Ashworth Shadow Health Secretary, Keir Starmer joined the Shadow Cabinet as Shadow Brexit Secretary, Nia Griffith returned to the Shadow Cabinet as Shadow Defence Secretary and Baroness Chakrabarti was appointed Shadow Attorney General. Following the election Andrew Gwynne was appointed Shadow Communities Secretary, new MP Lesley Laird was appointed Shadow Scottish Secretary and Owen Smith as Shadow Northern Ireland Secretary.

The SNP's Ian Blackford was elected as leader of the Westminster group, replacing Angus Robertson who lost his seat in the election. Tim Farron was replaced by Sir Vince Cable as leader of the Liberal Democrats.

In Northern Ireland an Assembly election was called following the resignation of Martin McGuinness as Deputy First Minister on 10 January. The election took place on 2 March, with new rules coming into force reducing the number of MLAs from 108 to 90 (five per constituency). The turnout was 64.78 per cent, up from 62.69 in 2016. There were 8 new MLAs elected, 19 MLAs were defeated and seven MLAs retired. Five MLAs were elected to Westminster in June and stood down from their MLA role. The Assembly failed to select a First Minister, Deputy First Minister and other Executive Ministers at the end of March and at the time of going to press a deal had still not been made to restore a devolved government.

In the Scottish Parliament three MSPs stood down after being elected to Westminster, one of which led to a by-election and the seat was held by the Conservatives. Kezia Dugdale resigned as Leader of Scottish Labour in August and the new leader will be announced on 18 November.

Elizabeth Newton, *Editor,*
October 2017

FOREWORD

If the past year has taught us anything it's that politics is unpredictable and anyone who thinks they know what's coming round the corner is kidding themselves. However in this sea of uncertainty and volatility the *Dods Parliamentary Companion* is an island of reliable and essential information.

Since 1832 Dods have produced this comprehensive guide to the who and what of UK politics. Updated annually, the *Parliamentary Companion* is a regular sight on the bookshelves of those working in Westminster. It not only informs, it opens up our democracy so that everyone can participate. Providing this information is a major part of ensuring that elected representatives are available to the people who elect them. For this reason, and all the times I have turned to the *Companion* in an hour of need, I am very pleased to offer Dods my hearty congratulations on this edition and those to come.

Rt Hon Damian Green MP
First Secretary of State and Minister for the Cabinet Office

ADDENDA

PEERAGES PENDING AT THE TIME OF GOING TO PRESS

AGNEW, THEODORE

Parliamentary Under-Secretary of State for the School System and Government Spokesperson, Department for Education

Theodore Thomas More Agnew. Born 17 January 1961; Married Clare (1 son 1 daughter).

Education: Rugby School.

Non-political career: Founder: Town & Country Assistance 1989-2002, WNS Global Services, Somerton Capital LLP 2007-, East Norfolk Academy Trust/Inspiration Trust 2012-.

Political career: Parliamentary Under-Secretary of State for the School System and Government Spokesperson, Department for Education 2017-. Councils and public bodies: Department for Education: Non-executive director 2010-15, Chair, Academies Board 2013-15; Non-executive director, Ministry of Justice 2015-17; DL, Norfolk 2013-.

Other: Board member, Centre Forum; Trustee: Policy Exchange, Education Policy Institute; Vice-patron, Norfolk Community Foundation. Kt 2015.

Sir Theodore Agnew DL, House of Lords, London SW1A 0PW

Tel: 020 7219 3000

FAIRHEAD, RONA

Minister of State and Government Spokesperson, Department for International Trade

Rona Alison Fairhead. Born 28 August 1961; Married Thomas Fairhead 1992 (3 children).

Education: Yarm Grammar School; St Catharine's College, Cambridge (law 1980); Harvard Business School (MBA 1989).

Non-political career: Senior Consultant, Bain & Co 1983-87, 1989-90; Analyst, Morgan Stanley 1988; Industrial Consultant, British Aerospace 1991; Bombardier/Shorts Aerospace 1991-96: Various roles 1991-94, Vice-president, Corporate Strategy and Public Affairs 1994-95, Vice-president UK, Aerospace Services 1995-96; ICI Plc 1996-2001: Director, Planning and Acquisitions 1996-97, Executive Vice-president: Planning and Communications 1997-98, Strategy and Control 1998-2001; Pearson Plc 2001-06: Deputy Finance Director 2001-02, Chief Financial Officer 2002-06; Chair and Chief Executive, Financial Times Group 2006-13.

Political career: Minister of State and Government Spokesperson, Department for International Trade 2017-. Councils and public bodies: Non-executive director, Cabinet Office 2011-14; UKTI Business Ambassador, UK Trade & Investment (UKTI) 2014-15; Chair, BBC Trust 2014-17.

Other: Non-executive director: Langanside Corporation Belfast 1994-2000, HSBC Holdings plc 2004-16, Economist Group 2006-14, PepsiCo Inc; Chair of Board, Interactive Data Corporation 2007-10. Honorary doctorate: Teesside University, Queen's University Belfast. CBE 2012.

Rona Fairhead CBE, House of Lords, London SW1A 0PW

Tel: 020 7219 3000

Public Legislation 2016–17

Dates are of Royal Assent

Broadcasting (Radio Multiplex Services) Act 2017 (27 April 2017)
To make provision about the regulation of small-scale radio multiplex services; and for connected purposes.

Bus Services Act 2017 (27 April 2017)
To make provision about bus services; and for connected purposes.

Children and Social Work Act 2017 (27 April 2017)
To make provision about looked-after children; to make other provision in relation to the welfare of children; and to make provision about the regulation of social workers.

Commonwealth Development Corporation Act 2017 (23 February 2017)
To amend the amount of the limit in section 15 of the Commonwealth Development Corporation Act 1999 on the government's financial assistance.

Criminal Finances Act 2017 (27 April 2017)
To amend the Proceeds of Crime Act 2002; make provision in connection with terrorist property; create corporate offences for cases where a person associated with a body corporate or partnership facilitates the commission by another person of a tax evasion offence; and for connected purposes.

Cultural Property (Armed Conflicts) Act 2017 (23 February 2017)
To enable the United Kingdom to implement the Hague Convention for the Protection of Cultural Property in the Event of Armed Conflict of 1954 and the Protocols to that Convention of 1954 and 1999.

Digital Economy Act 2017 (27 April 2017)
To make provision about electronic communications infrastructure and services; to provide for restricting access to online pornography; to make provision about protection of intellectual property in connection with electronic communications; to make provision about data-sharing; to make provision about functions of OFCOM in relation to the BBC; to provide for determination by the BBC of age-related TV licence fee concessions; to make provision about the regulation of direct marketing; to make other provision about OFCOM and its functions; and for connected purposes.

European Union (Notification of Withdrawal) Act 2017 (16 March 2017)
To confer power on the Prime Minister to notify, under Article 50(2) of the Treaty on European Union, the United Kingdom's intention to withdraw from the EU.

Farriers (Registration) Act 2017 (27 April 2017)
To make provision about the constitution of the Farriers Registration Council and its committees.

Faversham Oyster Fishery Company Act 2017 (27 April 2017)
To provide for the alteration of the objects, powers and constitution of the Faversham Oyster Fishery Company; and for other purposes.

Finance Act 2017 (27 April 2017)
To grant certain duties, to alter other duties, and to amend the law relating to the national debt and the public revenue, and to make further provision in connection with finance.

Guardianship (Missing Persons) Act 2017 (27 April 2017)
To make provision about the property and affairs of missing persons; and for connected purposes.

Health Service Medical Supplies (Costs) Act 2017 (27 April 2017)
To make provision in connection with controlling the cost of health service medicines and other medical supplies; to make provision in connection with the provision of pricing and other information by those manufacturing, distributing or supplying those medicines and supplies, and other related products, and the disclosure of that information; and for connected purposes.

High Speed Rail (London - West Midlands) Act 2017 (23 February 2017)
To make provision for a railway between Euston in London and a junction with the West Coast Main Line at Handsacre in Staffordshire, with a spur from Water Orton in Warwickshire to Curzon Street in Birmingham; and for connected purposes.

Higher Education and Research Act 2017 (27 April 2017)
To make provision about higher education and research; and to make provision about alternative payments to students in higher or further education.

Homelessness Reduction Act 2017 (27 April 2017)
To make provision about measures for reducing homelessness; and for connected purposes.

Intellectual Property (Unjustified Threats) Act 2017 (27 April 2017)
To amend the law relating to unjustified threats to bring proceedings for infringement of patents, registered trademarks, rights in registered designs, design right or Community designs.

Investigatory Powers Act 2016 (29 November 2016)
To make provision about the interception of communications, equipment interference and the acquisition and retention of communications data, bulk personal datasets and other information; to make provision about the treatment of material held as a result of such interception, equipment interference or acquisition or retention; to establish the Investigatory Powers Commissioner and other Judicial Commissioners and make provision about them and other oversight arrangements; to make further provision about investigatory powers and national security; to amend sections 3 and 5 of the Intelligence Services Act 1994; and for connected purposes.

Local Audit (Public Access to Documents) Act 2017 (27 April 2017)
To extend public access to certain local audit documents under section 26 of the Local Audit and Accountability Act 2014.

Merchant Shipping (Homosexual Conduct) Act 2017 (27 April 2017)
To repeal sections 146(4) and 147(3) of the Criminal Justice and Public Order Act 1994.

National Citizen Service Act 2017 (27 April 2017)
To make provision for the national citizen service.

Neighbourhood Planning Act 2017 (27 April 2017)
To make provision about planning and compulsory purchase; and for connected purposes.

Northern Ireland (Ministerial Appointments and Regional Rates) Act 2017 (27 April 2017)
To extend the period of time for making Ministerial appointments following the election of the Northern Ireland Assembly on 2 March 2017, and to make provision about the regional rate in Northern Ireland for the year ending 31 March 2018.

Parking Places (Variation of Charges) Act 2017 (27 April 2017)
To make provision in relation to the procedure to be followed by local authorities when varying the charges to be paid in connection with the use of certain parking places.

Pension Schemes Act 2017 (27 April 2017)
To make provision about pension schemes.

Policing and Crime Act 2017 (31 January 2017)
To make provision for collaboration between the emergency services; to make provision about the handling of police complaints and other matters relating to police conduct and to make further provision about the Independent Police Complaints Commission; to make provision for super-complaints about policing; to make provision for the investigation of concerns about policing raised by whistle-blowers; to make provision about police discipline; to make provision about police inspection; to make provision about the powers of police civilian staff and police volunteers; to remove the powers of the police to appoint traffic wardens; to enable provision to be made to alter police ranks; to make provision about the Police Federation; to make provision in connection with the replacement of the Association of Chief Police Officers with the National Police Chiefs' Council; to make provision about the system for bail after arrest but before charge; to make provision to enable greater use of modern technology at police stations; to make other amendments to the Police and Criminal Evidence Act 1984; to amend the powers of the police under the Mental Health Act 1983; to extend the powers of the police in relation to maritime enforcement; to make provision about deputy police and crime commissioners; to make provision to enable changes to the names of police areas; to make provision about the regulation of firearms; to make provision about the licensing of alcohol; to make provision about the implementation and enforcement of financial sanctions; to amend the Police Act 1996 to make further provision about police collaboration; to make provision about the powers of the National Crime Agency; to make provision for requiring arrested persons to provide details of nationality; to make provision for requiring defendants in criminal proceedings to provide details of nationality and other information; to make provision to combat the sexual exploitation of children; and for connected purposes.

Preventing and Combating Violence Against Women and Domestic Violence (Ratification of Convention) Act 2017 (27 April 2017)
To make provision in connection with the ratification by the United Kingdom of the Council of Europe Convention on preventing and combating violence against women and domestic violence (the Istanbul Convention).

Savings (Government Contributions) Act 2017 (16 January 2017)
To make provision for, and in connection with, government bonuses in respect of additions to savings accounts and other investment plans.

Small Charitable Donations and Childcare Payments Act 2017 (16 January 2017)
To make provision about the payment schemes established by the Small Charitable Donations Act 2012 and the Childcare Payments Act 2014.

Supply and Appropriation (Anticipation and Adjustments) Act 2017 (16 March 2017)
To authorise the use of resources for the years ending with 31 March 2015, 31 March 2016, 31 March 2017 and 31 March 2018; to authorise the issue of sums out of the Consolidated Fund for the years ending 31 March 2017 and 31 March 2018; and to appropriate the supply authorised by this Act for the years ending with 31 March 2015, 31 March 2016 and 31 March 2017.

Supply and Appropriation (Main Estimates) Act 2016 (20 July 2016)
To authorise the use of resources for the year ending with 31 March 2017; to authorise both the issue of sums out of the Consolidated Fund and the application of income for that year; and to appropriate the supply authorised for that year by this Act and by the Supply and Appropriation (Anticipation and Adjustments) Act 2016.

Technical and Further Education Act 2017 (27 April 2017)
To make provision about technical and further education.

Wales Act 2017 (31 January 2017)
To amend the Government of Wales Act 2006 and the Wales Act 2014 and to make provision about the functions of the Welsh Ministers and about Welsh tribunals; and for connected purposes.

Sources:

www.legislation.gov.uk

services.parliament.uk/bills/2016-17.html

Related Politicians

The following lists those who are related and are current members of UK and European legislatures.

Lord Beith and Baroness Maddock
Spouses

Paul Blomfield MP and Linda McAvan MEP
Spouses

Baroness Bonham-Carter of Yarnbury and Lord Razzall
Partners

Lord Boswell of Aynho and Victoria Prentis MP
Father and daughter

Peter Bottomley MP and Baroness Bottomley of Nettlestone
Spouses

Archbishop of Canterbury and Lord Williams of Elvel
Stepson and stepfather

Lord Carrington and Viscount Colville of Culross
Cousins

Lord Chadlington and Lord Deben
Siblings

Jenny Chapman MP and Nick Smith MP
Spouses

Viscount Colville of Culross and Lord Carrington
Cousins

Jon Cruddas MP and Baroness Healy of Primrose Hill
Spouses

John Cryer MP and Ellie Reeves MP
Spouses

John Cryer MP and Rachel Reeves MP
Siblings-in-law

Seb Dance MEP and Lord Livermore
Spouses

Alun Davies AM and Anna McMorrin MP
Partners

Lord Deben and Lord Chadlington
Siblings

Lord Denham and Lord Redesdale
Cousins

Caroline Dinenage MP and Mark Lancaster MP
Spouses

Diane Dodds MEP and Nigel Dodds MP
Spouses

Jack Dromey MP and Harriet Harman MP
Spouses

Angela Eagle MP and Maria Eagle MP
Twins

Baroness Eccles of Moulton and Viscount Eccles
Spouses

Charlie Elphicke MP and Mark Field MP
Brothers-in-law

Annabelle Ewing MSP and Fergus Ewing MSP
Siblings

Mark Field MP and Charlie Elphicke MP
Brothers-in-law

Kenneth Gibson MSP and Patricia Gibson MP
Spouses

Colm Gildernew MLA and Michelle Gildernew MP
Siblings

Viscount Hailsham and Baroness Hogg
Spouses

Baroness Harding of Winscombe and John Penrose MP
Spouses

Harriet Harman MP and Jack Dromey MP
Spouses

Baroness Healy of Primrose Hill and Jon Cruddas MP
Spouses

Baroness Hodgson of Abinger and Lord Hodgson of Astley Abbotts
Spouses

Baroness Hogg and Viscount Hailsham
Spouses

Baroness Hollis of Heigham and Lord Howarth of Newport
Partners

Stewart Hosie MP and Shona Robison MSP
Spouses

Lord Howarth of Newport and Baroness Hollis of Heigham
Partners

Lord Hoyle and Lindsay Hoyle MP
Father and son

Nick Hurd MP and Marquess of Lothian
Son- and father-in-law

Bernard Jenkin MP and Baroness Jenkin of Kennington
Spouses

Boris Johnson MP and Jo Johnson MP
Siblings

Baroness Kennedy of Cradley and Lord Kennedy of Southwark
Spouses

Lord Kinnock and Baroness Kinnock of Holyhead
Spouses

Stephen Kinnock MP and Baroness Kinnock of Holyhead and Lord Kinnock
Son and parents

Mark Lancaster MP and Caroline Dinenage MP
Spouses

Lord Layard and Baroness Meacher
Spouses

Lord Livermore and Seb Dance MEP
Spouses

Marquess of Lothian and Nick Hurd MP
Father- and son-in-law

Linda McAvan MEP and Paul Blomfield MP
Spouses

Baroness McDonagh and Siobhain McDonagh MP
Siblings

Anna McMorrin MP and Alun Davies AM
Partners

Baroness Maddock and Lord Beith
Spouses

Alex Maskey MLA and Paul Maskey MP
Siblings

Baroness Meacher and Lord Layard
Spouses

David Mundell MP and Oliver Mundell MSP
Father and son

Baroness Neuberger and Lord Neuberger of Abbotsbury
Siblings-in-law

Baroness Paisley of St George's and Ian Paisley MP
Mother and son

Lord Palumbo and Lord Palumbo of Southwark
Father and son

Earl Peel and Nicholas Soames MP
Brothers-in-law

John Penrose MP and Baroness Harding of Winscombe
Spouses

Victoria Prentis MP and Lord Boswell of Aynho
Daughter and father

Lord Razzall and Baroness Bonham-Carter of Yarnbury
Partners

Lord Redesdale and Lord Denham
Cousins

Ellie Reeves MP and John Cryer MP
Sibilings-in-law

Ellie Reeves MP and Rachel Reeves MP
Siblings

Rachel Reeves MP and John Cryer MP
Siblings-in-law

Lord Sainsbury of Preston Candover and Lord Sainsbury of Turville
Cousins

Nick Smith MP and Jenny Chapman MP
Spouses

Nicholas Soames MP and Earl Peel
Brothers-in-law

Lord Thomas of Gresford and Baroness Walmsley
Spouses

Tom Tugendhat MP and Lord Tugendhat
Nephew and uncle

Keith Vaz MP and Valerie Vaz MP
Siblings

Baroness Walmsley and Lord Thomas of Gresford
Spouses

Lord Williams of Elvel and Archbishop of Canterbury
Stepfather and stepson

Parliaments of the 20th and 21st centuries

Assembled		Dissolved		Length	Ministries	Took Office	
VICTORIA				yrs. m. d.			
3 Dec	1900	8 Jan	1906	5 1 5	Salisbury (Con)	6 Dec	1900
					Balfour (Con)	12 July	1902
EDWARD VII							
13 Feb	1906	10 Jan	1910	3 10 28	C. Bannerman (Lib)	5 Dec	1905
					Asquith (Lib)	5 April	1908
15 Feb	1910	28 Nov	1910	9 13	Asquith (Lib)	15 Feb	1910
GEORGE V							
31 Jan	1911	25 Nov	1918	7 9 25	Asquith (Lib)	25 May	1915
4 Feb	1919	25 Oct	1922	3 8 21	Lloyd George (Lib) Coalition	6 Dec	1916
20 Nov	1922	16 Nov	1923	11 27	A. Bonar Law (Con)	23 Oct	1922
8 Jan	1924	9 Oct	1924	9 1	J. R. MacDonald (Lab)	22 Jan	1924
2 Dec	1924	10 May	1929	4 5 8	S. Baldwin (Con)	4 Nov	1924
25 June	1929	7 Oct	1931	2 3 12	J. R. MacDonald (Lab)	5 June	1929
3 Nov	1931	25 Oct	1935	3 11 22	J. R. MacDonald (Nat. Govt.)	24 August	1931
					S. Baldwin		
26 Nov	1935				S. Baldwin (Nat. Govt.)	7 June	1935
EDWARD VIII					N. Chamberlain (Nat. Govt.)	28 May	1937
GEORGE VI		15 June	1945	9 6 20	W. Churchill (Nat. Govt.)	10 May	1940
1 Aug	1945	3 Feb	1950	4 6 2	C. R. Attlee (Lab)	26 July	1945
1 Mar	1950	5 Oct	1951	1 7 4	C. R. Attlee (Lab)	25 Feb	1950
31 Oct	1951	6 May	1955	3 6 6	W. Churchill (Con)	26 Oct	1951
					A. Eden (Con)		
ELIZABETH II					A. Eden (Con)	6 April	1955
7 June	1955	18 Sept	1959	4 3 11	H. Macmillan (Con)	10 Jan	1957
					H. Macmillan (Con)	9 Oct	1959
20 Oct	1959	25 Sept	1964	4 11 5	A. Douglas-Home (Con)	9 Oct	1963
27 Oct	1964	10 Mar	1966	1 4 11	H. Wilson (Lab)	16 Oct	1964
18 Apr	1966	29 May	1970	4 1 11	H. Wilson (Lab)	1 April	1966
29 June	1970	8 Feb	1974	3 7 10	E. R. G. Heath (Con)	19 June	1970
6 Mar	1974	20 Sept	1974	6 14	H. Wilson (Lab) (Minority Govt.)	4 Mar	1974
22 Oct	1974	7 April	1979	4 5 15	H. Wilson (Lab)	11 Oct	1974
					J. Callaghan (Lab)	5 April	1976
9 May	1979	13 May	1983	4 0 4	Mrs M. Thatcher (Con)	3 May	1979
15 June	1983	18 May	1987	3 11 3	Mrs M. Thatcher (Con)	9 June	1983
17 June	1987	16 Mar	1992	4 8 28	Mrs M. Thatcher (Con)	11 June	1987
					J. Major (Con)	28 Nov	1990
27 April	1992	8 April	1997	4 11 19	J. Major (Con)	10 April	1992
7 May	1997	14 May	2001	4 0 7	T. Blair (Lab)	1 May	1997
20 June	2001	11 April	2005	3 9 22	T. Blair (Lab)	7 June	2001
17 May	2005	8 April	2010	4 10 22	T. Blair (Lab)	5 May	2005
					G. Brown (Lab)	27 June	2007
13 May	2010	30 March	2015	4 10 18	D. Cameron (Con) (Coalition Govt.)	11 May	2010
18 May	2015	3 May	2017	1 11 15	D. Cameron (Con)	7 May	2015
					T. May (Con)	13 July	2016
13 June	2017				T. May (Con)	8 June	2017

Size of the House of Commons since 1801

With the Union of Great Britain and Ireland in 1801 the number of members of Parliament was fixed at 658. In 1885 the total was increased to 670, and by the Act of 1918 to 707. With the creation of the Irish Free State in 1922, the Irish representation was reduced to 13 members from Ulster, making the membership of the House of Commons 615. In 1945, owing to the division of large constituencies, the number was increased by 25 to 640. Under the Act of 1948 the number was decreased to 625. Orders passed in 1954 and 1955 increased the number to 630. As the result of redistribution and boundary changes, the total number of MPs elected at the 1979 general election was 635. The House of Commons (Redistribution of Seats) Act 1979 and the Boundary Commission reports of 1983 resulted in an increase of 15 seats after the 1983 election to 650 members. At the 1992 election, 651 Members were elected, an extra seat having been created for Milton Keynes. Reports from the Boundary Commission caused an increase to 659 at the 1997 election. The fifth Periodical Review of Westminster constituencies cut the number of seats to 646 at the 2005 general election, with Scotland losing 13 seats as a result of previous over representation and the creation of the Scottish Parliament. The changes to the boundaries in England, Wales and Northern Ireland came into effect at the 2010 election, increasing the number of seats to 650.

General Election Majorities since the Reform Act

(NB *In certain cases, such as the election of* 1910, *the Government Party had a working arrangement with other parties, which ensured them a majority in the House*)

1832	Lib	300
1835	Lib	108
1837	Lib	40
1841	Con	78
1847	Lib	2
1852	Con	8
1857	Lib	92
1859	Lib	40
1865	Lib	62
1868	Lib	106
1874	Con	52
1880	Lib	176
1885	Lib	No majority
1886	Unionist	120
1892	Lib	No majority
1895	Unionist	152
1900	Unionist	135
1906	Lib	130
1910	(Jan) Lib	No majority
1910	(Dec) Lib	No majority
1918	Coalition	249
1922	Con	75
1923	Con	No majority
1924	Con	223
1929	Lab	No majority
1931	Nat Govt	493
1935	Nat Govt	249
1945	Lab	146
1950	Lab	5
1951	Con	17
1955	Con	58
1959	Con	100
1964	Lab	4
1966	Lab	96
1970	Con	30
1974	(Feb) Lab	No majority
1974	(Oct) Lab	3
(3 over all parties, 42 over Cons)		
1979	Con	43
1983	Con	144
1987	Con	101
1992	Con	21
1997	Lab	177
2001	Lab	165
2005	Lab	66
2010	Con/Lib Dem coalition	83
2015	Con	12
2017	Con	No majority

Long Parliaments

The longest lived Parliaments in English history have been the Elizabethan Parliament of 1572–83, the Long Parliament of 1640–53, and the Cavalier Parliament of 1661–79. The First World War Parliament met on 31 January 1911, and was dissolved on 25 November 1918. That of the Second met 26 November 1935, and was dissolved 15 June 1945.

Prime Ministers since 1721

1721–42	Sir Robert Walpole (Whig)
1742–43	Spencer Compton (Whig)
1743–54	Henry Pelham (Whig)
1754–56	Duke of Newcastle (Whig)
1756–57	Duke of Devonshire (Whig)
1757–62	Duke of Newcastle (Whig)
1762–63	Earl of Bute (Tory)
1763–65	George Grenville (Whig)
1765–66	Marquess of Rockingham (Whig)
1766–67	William Pitt (the Elder) (Whig)
1767–70	Duke of Grafton (Whig)
1770–82	Lord North (Tory)
1782	Marquess of Rockingham (Whig)
1782–83	Earl of Shelburne (Whig)
1783	Duke of Portland (Coalition)
1783–1801	William Pitt (the Younger) (Tory)
1801–04	Henry Addington (Tory)
1804–06	William Pitt (the Younger) (Tory)
1806–07	Lord Grenville (Whig)
1807–09	Duke of Portland (Tory)
1809–12	Spencer Perceval (Tory)
1812–27	Earl of Liverpool (Tory)
1827	George Canning (Tory)
1827–28	Viscount Goderich (Tory)
1828–30	Duke of Wellington (Tory)
1830–34	Earl Grey (Whig)
1834	Viscount Melbourne (Whig)
1834–35	Sir Robert Peel (Tory)
1835–41	Viscount Melbourne (Whig)
1841–46	Sir Robert Peel (Tory)
1846–52	Lord John Russell (Whig)
1852	Earl of Derby (Con)
1852–55	Earl of Aberdeen (Lib) (Coalition)
1855–58	Viscount Palmerston (Lib)
1858–59	Earl of Derby (Con)
1859–65	Viscount Palmerston (Lib)
1865–66	Earl Russell (Lib)
1866–68	Earl of Derby (Con)
1868	Benjamin Disraeli (Con)
1868–74	William Gladstone (Lib)
1874–80	Benjamin Disraeli (Con)
1880–85	William Gladstone (Lib)
1885–86	Marquess of Salisbury (Con)
1886	William Gladstone (Lib)
1886–92	Marquess of Salisbury (Con)
1892–94	William Gladstone (Lib)
1894–95	Earl of Rosebery (Lib)
1895–1902	Marquess of Salisbury (Con)
1902–05	Arthur Balfour (Con)
1905–08	Sir Henry Campbell-Bannerman (Lib)
1908–16	Herbert Asquith (Lib)
1916–22	David Lloyd George (Lib) (Coalition)
1922–23	Andrew Bonar Law (Con)
1923–24	Stanley Baldwin (Con)
1924	Ramsay MacDonald (Lab)
1924–29	Stanley Baldwin (Con)
1929–35	Ramsay MacDonald (Lab)
1935–37	Stanley Baldwin (Con) (Nat Govt)
1937–40	Neville Chamberlain (Con) (Nat Govt)
1940–45	Winston Churchill (Con) (Coalition)
1945–51	Clement Attlee (Lab)
1951–55	Winston Churchill (Con)
1955–57	Sir Anthony Eden (Con)
1957–63	Harold Macmillan (Con)
1963–64	Sir Alec Douglas-Home (Con)
1964–70	Harold Wilson (Lab)
1970–74	Edward Heath (Con)
1974–76	Harold Wilson (Lab)
1976–79	James Callaghan (Lab)
1979–90	Margaret Thatcher (Con)
1990–97	John Major (Con)
1997–2007	Tony Blair (Lab)
2007–10	Gordon Brown (Lab)
2010–16	David Cameron (Con) (Coalition 2010-15)
2016–	Theresa May (Con)

GOVERNMENT 2
The Cabinet 2
Departmental Ministers 3
Whips 6
Lords Spokespeople 7
Alphabetical list of Ministers and Whips 8
Ministerial responsibilities and staff 13
Cabinet Committees 38
Implementation Taskforces 38
Parliamentary Private Secretaries 39
Special Advisers 43
Opposition 47
Labour 47
Shadow Cabinet 47
Shadow Ministers 48
Commons Whips 51
Lords Spokespeople 51
Lords Whips 52
Scottish National Party 53
Liberal Democrats 54
Democratic Unionist Party 55
Plaid Cymru (The Party of Wales) 56
Crossbench 56
Salaried Parliamentarians 57

The Government

The Cabinet

Prime Minister, First Lord of the Treasury and Minister for the Civil Service	**Theresa May** MP
First Secretary of State; Minister for the Cabinet Office	**Damian Green** MP
Chancellor of the Exchequer	**Philip Hammond** MP
Secretary of State for the Home Department	**Amber Rudd** MP
Secretary of State for Foreign and Commonwealth Affairs	**Boris Johnson** MP
Secretary of State for Exiting the European Union	**David Davis** MP
Secretary of State for Defence	Sir **Michael Fallon** KCB MP
Secretary of State for Health	**Jeremy Hunt** MP
Lord Chancellor and Secretary of State for Justice	**David Lidington** CBE MP
Secretary of State for Education; Minister for Women and Equalities	**Justine Greening** MP
Secretary of State for International Trade; President of the Board of Trade	Dr **Liam Fox** MP
Secretary of State for Business, Energy and Industrial Strategy	**Greg Clark** MP
Secretary of State for Environment, Food and Rural Affairs	**Michael Gove** MP
Secretary of State for Transport	**Chris Grayling** MP
Secretary of State for Communities and Local Government	**Sajid Javid** MP
Leader of the House of Lords and Lord Privy Seal	**Baroness Evans of Bowes Park**
Secretary of State for Scotland	**David Mundell** MP
Secretary of State for Wales	**Alun Cairns** MP
Secretary of State for Northern Ireland	**James Brokenshire** MP
Secretary of State for International Development	**Priti Patel** MP
Secretary of State for Digital, Culture, Media and Sport	**Karen Bradley** MP
Secretary of State for Work and Pensions	**David Gauke** MP
Chancellor of the Duchy of Lancaster; Chairman of the Conservative Party	Sir **Patrick McLoughlin** MP
Also attending Cabinet	
Chief Secretary to the Treasury	**Elizabeth Truss** MP
Leader of the House of Commons; Lord President of the Council	**Andrea Leadsom** MP
Chief Whip; Parliamentary Secretary to the Treasury	**Gavin Williamson** CBE MP
Attorney General	**Jeremy Wright** QC MP
Minister of State for Immigration, Home Office	**Brandon Lewis** MP
Minister of State for Employment, Department for Work and Pensions	**Damian Hinds** MP

Departmental Ministers

Department for Business, Energy and Industrial Strategy

Secretary of State for Business, Energy and Industrial Strategy	Rt Hon **Greg Clark** MP
Ministers of State	**Claire Perry** MP
	Jo Johnson MP
Parliamentary Under-Secretaries of State	**Margot James** MP
	Richard Harrington MP
	Lord Prior of Brampton

Cabinet Office

First Secretary of State; Minister for the Cabinet Office	Rt Hon **Damian Green** MP
Parliamentary Secretaries	**Chris Skidmore** MP
	Caroline Nokes MP
Chancellor of the Duchy of Lancaster	Rt Hon Sir **Patrick McLoughlin** MP

Department for Communities and Local Government

Secretary of State for Communities and Local Government	Rt Hon **Sajid Javid** MP
Minister of State	**Alok Sharma** MP
Parliamentary Under-Secretaries of State	**Jake Berry** MP
	Marcus Jones MP
	Lord Bourne of Aberystwyth

Ministry of Defence

Secretary of State for Defence	Rt Hon Sir **Michael Fallon** KCB MP
Ministers of State	Rt Hon **Earl Howe**
	Mark Lancaster TD MP
Parliamentary Under-Secretaries of State	**Harriett Baldwin** MP
	Rt Hon **Tobias Ellwood** MP

Department for Digital, Culture, Media and Sport

Secretary of State for Digital, Culture, Media and Sport	Rt Hon **Karen Bradley** MP
Minister of State	Rt Hon **Matt Hancock** MP
Parliamentary Under-Secretaries of State	**Tracey Crouch** MP
	John Glen MP
	Lord Ashton of Hyde

Department for Education

Secretary of State for Education; Minister for Women and Equalities	Rt Hon **Justine Greening** MP
Ministers of State	Rt Hon **Nick Gibb** MP
	Robert Goodwill MP
	Jo Johnson MP
	Rt Hon **Anne Milton** MP
Parliamentary Under-Secretary of State	**Sir Theodore Agnew** (peerage pending)

Department for Environment, Food and Rural Affairs

Secretary of State for Environment, Food and Rural Affairs	Rt Hon **Michael Gove** MP
Minister of State	**George Eustice** MP
Parliamentary Under-Secretaries of State	Dr **Therese Coffey** MP
	Lord Gardiner of Kimble

Department for Exiting the European Union

Secretary of State for Exiting the European Union	Rt Hon **David Davis** MP
Minister of State	Rt Hon **Baroness Anelay of St Johns** DBE
Parliamentary Under-Secretaries of State	**Robin Walker** MP
	Steve Baker MP

Foreign and Commonwealth Office

Secretary of State for Foreign and Commonwealth Affairs (Foreign Secretary)	Rt Hon **Boris Johnson** MP
Ministers of State	Rt Hon Sir **Alan Duncan** KCMG MP
	Rory Stewart OBE MP
	Rt Hon **Alistair Burt** MP
	Lord Ahmad of Wimbledon
	Rt Hon **Mark Field** MP

Department of Health

Secretary of State for Health	Rt Hon **Jeremy Hunt** MP
Minister of State	**Philip Dunne** MP
Parliamentary Under-Secretaries of State	**Jackie Doyle-Price** MP
	Steve Brine MP
	Lord O'Shaughnessy

Home Office

Secretary of State for the Home Department (Home Secretary)	Rt Hon **Amber Rudd** MP
Ministers of State	Rt Hon **Brandon Lewis** MP
	Rt Hon **Ben Wallace** MP
	Nick Hurd MP
	Baroness Williams of Trafford
Parliamentary Under-Secretary of State	**Sarah Newton** MP

Department for International Development

Secretary of State for International Development	Rt Hon **Priti Patel** MP
Ministers of State	**Rory Stewart** OBE MP
	Rt Hon **Alistair Burt** MP
	Rt Hon **Lord Bates**

Department for International Trade

Secretary of State for International Trade; President of the Board of Trade	Rt Hon Dr **Liam Fox** MP
Ministers of State	Rt Hon **Greg Hands** MP
	Rona Fairhead (peerage pending)
Parliamentary Under-Secretary of State	**Mark Garnier** MP

Ministry of Justice

Lord Chancellor and Secretary of State for Justice	Rt Hon **David Lidington** CBE MP
Minister of State	**Dominic Raab** MP
Parliamentary Under-Secretaries of State	**Sam Gyimah** MP
	Dr **Phillip Lee** MP
Spokesperson	Rt Hon **Lord Keen of Elie** QC

Law Officers

Attorney General	Rt Hon **Jeremy Wright** QC MP
Solicitor General	**Robert Buckland** QC MP
Advocate General for Scotland	Rt Hon **Lord Keen of Elie** QC

Leader of the House of Commons

Leader of the House of Commons	Rt Hon **Andrea Leadsom** MP
Deputy Leader	**Michael Ellis** MP

Leader of the House of Lords

Leader of the House of Lords	Rt Hon **Baroness Evans of Bowes Park**
Deputy Leader	Rt Hon **Earl Howe**

Northern Ireland Office

Secretary of State for Northern Ireland	Rt Hon **James Brokenshire** MP
Parliamentary Under-Secretaries of State	**Chloe Smith** MP
	Lord Bourne of Aberystwyth

Privy Council Office

Lord President of the Council	Rt Hon **Andrea Leadsom** MP

Scotland Office

Secretary of State for Scotland	Rt Hon **David Mundell** MP
Parliamentary Under-Secretary of State	**Lord Duncan of Springbank**

Department for Transport

Secretary of State for Transport	Rt Hon **Chris Grayling** MP
Minister of State	Rt Hon **John Hayes** CBE MP
Parliamentary Under-Secretaries of State	**Paul Maynard** MP
	Jesse Norman MP
	Lord Callanan

HM Treasury

Chancellor of the Exchequer	Rt Hon **Philip Hammond** MP
Chief Secretary to the Treasury	Rt Hon **Elizabeth Truss** MP
Financial Secretary	Rt Hon **Mel Stride** MP
Economic Secretary	**Steve Barclay** MP
Exchequer Secretary	**Andrew Jones** MP

Wales Office

Secretary of State for Wales	Rt Hon **Alun Cairns** MP
Parliamentary Under-Secretaries of State	**Guto Bebb** MP
	Lord Duncan of Springbank

Department for Work and Pensions

Secretary of State for Work and Pensions	Rt Hon **David Gauke** MP
Ministers of State	**Damian Hinds** MP
	Penny Mordaunt MP
Parliamentary Under-Secretaries of State	**Guy Opperman** MP
	Caroline Dinenage MP
	Baroness Buscombe

Government Whips

Commons

CHIEF WHIP	
Parliamentary Secretary to the Treasury	Rt Hon **Gavin Williamson** CBE MP
DEPUTY CHIEF WHIP	
Treasurer of HM Household	**Julian Smith** MP
WHIPS	
Comptroller of HM Household	**Christopher Pincher** MP
Vice-Chamberlain of HM Household	**Chris Heaton-Harris** MP
Lords Commissioner of HM Treasury	Rt Hon **David Evennett** MP
	Guto Bebb MP
	Mark Spencer MP
	Heather Wheeler MP
	Andrew Griffiths MP
	David Rutley MP
ASSISTANT WHIPS	**Chloe Smith** MP
	Mike Freer MP
	Rebecca Harris MP
	Stuart Andrew MP
	Graham Stuart MP
	Nigel Adams MP
	Andrew Stephenson MP
	Craig Whittaker MP

Lords

CHIEF WHIP	
Captain of the Honourable Corps of the Gentlemen-at-Arms	Rt Hon **Lord Taylor of Holbeach** CBE
DEPUTY CHIEF WHIP	
Captain of the Queen's Bodyguard of the Yeomen of the Guard	**Earl of Courtown**
WHIPS, BARONESSES IN WAITING	**Baroness Vere of Norbiton**
	Baroness Goldie DL
	Baroness Chisholm of Owlpen
	Baroness Sugg CBE
WHIPS, LORDS IN WAITING	**Viscount Younger of Leckie**
	Rt Hon **Lord Young of Cookham** CH

Government Spokespeople in the Lords

Leader of the House of Lords and Lord Privy Seal	Rt Hon **Baroness Evans of Bowes Park**
Deputy Leader of the House of Lords	Rt Hon **Earl Howe**
Business, Energy and Industrial Strategy	**Lord Prior of Brampton**
Cabinet Office	Rt Hon **Lord Young of Cookham** CH
Communities and Local Government	**Lord Bourne of Aberystwyth**
Defence	Rt Hon **Earl Howe**
Digital, Culture, Media and Sport	**Lord Ashton of Hyde**
Education	Sir **Theodore Agnew** (peerage pending)
Environment, Food and Rural Affairs	**Lord Gardiner of Kimble**
Exiting the European Union	Rt Hon **Baroness Anelay of St Johns** DBE
Foreign and Commonwealth Office	**Lord Ahmad of Wimbledon**
Health	**Lord O'Shaughnessy**
Home Office	**Baroness Williams of Trafford**
International Development	Rt Hon **Lord Bates**
International Trade	**Rona Fairhead** (peerage pending)
Justice	Rt Hon **Lord Keen of Elie** QC
Law Officers	Rt Hon **Lord Keen of Elie** QC
Northern Ireland	**Lord Bourne of Aberystwyth**
Scotland	**Lord Duncan of Springbank**
Transport	**Lord Callanan**
HM Treasury	Rt Hon **Lord Bates**
Wales	**Lord Duncan of Springbank**
Women and Equalities	**Baroness Williams of Trafford**
Work and Pensions	**Baroness Buscombe**

Alphabetical list of Ministers and Whips

ADAMS, Nigel	Assistant Whip
AGNEW, Sir Theodore (peerage pending)	Parliamentary Under-Secretary of State for the School System and Spokesperson, Department for Education
AHMAD OF WIMBLEDON, Lord	Minister of State for the Commonwealth and the UN and Spokesperson, Foreign and Commonwealth Office; Prime Minister's Special Representative on Preventing Sexual Violence in Conflict
ANDREW, Stuart	Assistant Whip
ANELAY OF ST JOHNS, Rt Hon Baroness	Minister of State and Spokesperson, Department for Exiting the European Union
ASHTON OF HYDE, Lord	Parliamentary Under-Secretary of State and Spokesperson, Department for Digital, Culture, Media and Sport
BAKER, Steve	Parliamentary Under-Secretary of State, Department for Exiting the European Union
BALDWIN, Harriett	Parliamentary Under-Secretary of State (Defence Procurement), Ministry of Defence
BARCLAY, Steve	Economic Secretary, HM Treasury
BATES, Rt Hon Lord	Minister of State and Spokesperson, Department for International Development; Spokesperson, HM Treasury
BEBB, Guto	Parliamentary Under-Secretary of State, Wales Office; Whip (Lord Commissioner of HM Treasury)
BERRY, Jake	Parliamentary Under-Secretary of State (Minister for the Northern Powerhouse and Local Growth), Department for Communities and Local Government
BOURNE OF ABERYSTWYTH, Lord	Parliamentary Under-Secretary of State (Minister for Faith) and Spokesperson, Department for Communities and Local Government and Parliamentary Under-Secretary of State and Spokesperson, Northern Ireland Office
BRADLEY, Rt Hon Karen	Secretary of State for Digital, Culture, Media and Sport
BRINE, Steve	Parliamentary Under-Secretary of State (Public Health and Primary Care), Department of Health
BROKENSHIRE, Rt Hon James	Secretary of State for Northern Ireland
BUCKLAND, Robert	Solicitor General
BURT, Rt Hon Alistair	Minister of State for Middle East, Foreign and Commonwealth Office and Minister of State, Department for International Development
BUSCOMBE, Baroness	Parliamentary Under-Secretary of State and Spokesperson, Department for Work and Pensions
CAIRNS, Rt Hon Alun	Secretary of State for Wales
CALLANAN, Lord	Parliamentary Under-Secretary of State for Aviation, International and Security and Spokesperson, Department for Transport
CHISHOLM OF OWLPEN, Baroness	Whip (Baroness in Waiting)
CLARK, Rt Hon Greg	Secretary of State for Business, Energy and Industrial Strategy

COFFEY, Dr Therese	Parliamentary Under-Secretary of State for Environment, Department for Environment, Food and Rural Affairs
COURTOWN, Earl of	Deputy Chief Whip (Captain of the Queen's Bodyguard of the Yeomen of the Guard)
CROUCH, Tracey	Parliamentary Under-Secretary of State for Sport and Civil Society, Department for Digital, Culture, Media and Sport
DAVIS, Rt Hon David	Secretary of State for Exiting the European Union
DINENAGE, Caroline	Parliamentary Under-Secretary of State for Family Support, Housing and Child Maintenance, Department for Work and Pensions
DOYLE-PRICE, Jackie	Parliamentary Under-Secretary of State (Care and Mental Health), Department of Health
DUNCAN, Rt Hon Sir Alan	Minister of State for Europe and the Americas, Foreign and Commonwealth Office
DUNCAN OF SPRINGBANK, Lord	Parliamentary Under-Secretary of State and Spokesperson, Scotland Office and Wales Office
DUNNE, Philip	Minister of State for Health, Department of Health
ELLIS, Michael	Deputy Leader of the House of Commons
ELLWOOD, Rt Hon Tobias	Parliamentary Under-Secretary of State, Ministry of Defence
EUSTICE, George	Minister of State for Agriculture, Fisheries and Food, Department for Environment, Food and Rural Affairs
EVANS OF BOWES PARK, Rt Hon Baroness	Leader of the House of Lords and Lord Privy Seal
EVENNETT, Rt Hon David	Whip (Lord Commissioner of HM Treasury)
FAIRHEAD, Rona (peerage pending)	Minister of State and Spokesperson, Department for International Trade
FALLON, Rt Hon Sir Michael	Secretary of State for Defence
FIELD, Rt Hon Mark	Minister of State for Asia and the Pacific, Foreign and Commonwealth Office
FOX, Rt Hon Dr Liam	Secretary of State for International Trade; President of the Board of Trade
FREER, Mike	Assistant Whip
GARDINER OF KIMBLE, Lord	Parliamentary Under-Secretary of State for Rural Affairs and Biosecurity and Spokesperson, Department for Environment, Food and Rural Affairs
GARNIER, Mark	Parliamentary Under-Secretary of State (Minister for Investment), Department for International Trade
GAUKE, Rt Hon David	Secretary of State for Work and Pensions
GIBB, Rt Hon Nick	Minister of State for School Standards and Minister for Equalities, Department for Education
GLEN, John	Parliamentary Under-Secretary of State for Arts, Heritage and Tourism, Department for Digital, Culture, Media and Sport
GOLDIE, Baroness	Whip (Baroness in Waiting)
GOODWILL, Robert	Minister of State for Children and Families, Department for Education
GOVE, Rt Hon Michael	Secretary of State for Environment, Food and Rural Affairs

GRAYLING, Rt Hon Chris	Secretary of State for Transport
GREEN, Rt Hon Damian	First Secretary of State and Minister for the Cabinet Office
GREENING, Rt Hon Justine	Secretary of State for Education; Minister for Women and Equalities
GRIFFITHS, Andrew	Whip (Lord Commissioner of HM Treasury)
GYIMAH, Sam	Parliamentary Under-Secretary of State for Prisons and Probation, Ministry of Justice
HAMMOND, Rt Hon Philip	Chancellor of the Exchequer
HANCOCK, Rt Hon Matt	Minister of State for Digital, Department for Digital, Culture, Media and Sport
HANDS, Rt Hon Greg	Minister of State for Trade Policy, Department for International Trade; Minister for London
HARRINGTON, Richard	Parliamentary Under-Secretary of State (Minister for Energy and Industry), Department for Business, Energy and Industrial Strategy
HARRIS, Rebecca	Assistant Whip
HAYES, Rt Hon John	Minister of State for Transport Legislation and Maritime, Department for Transport
HEATON-HARRIS, Chris	Whip (Vice-Chamberlain of HM Household)
HINDS, Damian	Minister of State for Employment, Department for Work and Pensions
HOWE, Rt Hon Earl	Deputy Leader of the House of Lords; Minister of State and Spokesperson, Ministry of Defence
HUNT, Rt Hon Jeremy	Secretary of State for Health
HURD, Nick	Minister of State for Policing and the Fire Service, Home Office
JAMES, Margot	Parliamentary Under-Secretary of State (Minister for Small Business, Consumers and Corporate Responsibility), Department for Business, Energy and Industrial Strategy
JAVID, Rt Hon Sajid	Secretary of State for Communities and Local Government
JOHNSON, Rt Hon Boris	Foreign Secretary
JOHNSON, Jo	Minister of State for Universities, Science, Research and Innovation, Department for Business, Energy and Industrial Strategy and Department for Education
JONES, Andrew	Exchequer Secretary, HM Treasury
JONES, Marcus	Parliamentary Under-Secretary of State (Minister for Local Government), Department for Communities and Local Government
KEEN OF ELIE, Rt Hon Lord	Advocate General for Scotland; Spokesperson, Law Officers and Ministry of Justice
LANCASTER, Mark	Minister of State for the Armed Forces, Ministry of Defence
LEADSOM, Rt Hon Andrea	Leader of the House of Commons and Lord President of the Council
LEE, Dr Phillip	Parliamentary Under-Secretary of State for Youth Justice, Victims, Female Offenders and Offender Health, Ministry of Justice
LEWIS, Rt Hon Brandon	Minister of State for Immigration, Home Office

LIDINGTON, Rt Hon David	Lord Chancellor and Secretary of State for Justice
McLOUGHLIN, Rt Hon Sir Patrick	Chancellor of the Duchy of Lancaster; Chairman of Conservative Party
MAY, Rt Hon Theresa	Prime Minister, First Lord of the Treasury and Minister for the Civil Service
MAYNARD, Paul	Parliamentary Under-Secretary of State for Rail, Accessibility and HS2, Department for Transport
MILTON, Rt Hon Anne	Minister of State for Apprenticeships and Skills and Minister for Women, Department for Education
MORDAUNT, Penny	Minister of State for Disabled People, Health and Work, Department for Work and Pensions
MUNDELL, Rt Hon David	Secretary of State for Scotland
NEWTON, Sarah	Parliamentary Under Secretary of State for Crime, Safeguarding and Vulnerability, Home Office
NOKES, Caroline	Parliamentary Secretary (Minister for Resilience and Efficiency), Cabinet Office
NORMAN, Jesse	Parliamentary Under-Secretary of State for Roads, Local Transport and Devolution, Department for Transport
OPPERMAN, Guy	Parliamentary Under-Secretary of State for Pensions and Financial Inclusion, Department for Work and Pensions
O'SHAUGHNESSY, Lord	Parliamentary Under-Secretary of State and Spokesperson, Department of Health
PATEL, Rt Hon Priti	Secretary of State for International Development
PERRY, Claire	Minister of State for Climate Change and Industry, Department for Business, Energy and Industrial Strategy
PINCHER, Christopher	Whip (Comptroller of HM Household)
PRIOR OF BRAMPTON, Lord	Parliamentary Under-Secretary of State and Spokesperson, Department for Business, Energy and Industrial Strategy
RAAB, Dominic	Minister of State, Ministry of Justice
RUDD, Rt Hon Amber	Home Secretary
RUTLEY, David	Whip (Lord Commissioner of HM Treasury)
SHARMA, Alok	Minister of State for Housing and Planning, Department for Communities and Local Government
SKIDMORE, Chris	Parliamentary Secretary (Minister for the Constitution), Cabinet Office
SMITH, Chloe	Parliamentary Under-Secretary of State, Northern Ireland Office; Assistant Whip
SMITH, Julian	Deputy Chief Whip (Treasurer of HM Household)
SPENCER, Mark	Whip (Lord Commissioner of HM Treasury)
STEPHENSON, Andrew	Assistant Whip
STEWART, Rory	Minister of State for Africa, Foreign and Commonwealth Office and Minister of State, Department for International Development
STRIDE, Rt Hon Mel	Financial Secretary; Paymaster General, HM Treasury
STUART, Graham	Assistant Whip
SUGG, Baroness	Whip (Baroness in Waiting)
TAYLOR OF HOLBEACH, Rt Hon Lord	Chief Whip (Captain of the Honourable Corps of the Gentlemen-at-Arms)
TRUSS, Rt Hon Elizabeth	Chief Secretary to the Treasury

VERE OF NORBITON, Baroness	Whip (Baroness in Waiting)
WALKER, Robin	Parliamentary Under-Secretary of State, Department for Exiting the European Union
WALLACE, Rt Hon Ben	Minister of State for Security, Home Office
WHEELER, Heather	Whip (Lord Commissioner of HM Treasury)
WHITTAKER, Craig	Assistant Whip
WILLIAMS OF TRAFFORD, Baroness	Minister of State for Countering Extremism and Spokesperson, Home Office; Spokesperson, Women and Equalities
WILLIAMSON, Rt Hon Gavin	Chief Whip; Parliamentary Secretary to the Treasury
WRIGHT, Rt Hon Jeremy	Attorney General
YOUNG OF COOKHAM, Rt Hon Lord	Spokesperson, Cabinet Office; Whip (Lord in Waiting)
YOUNGER OF LECKIE, Viscount	Whip (Lord in Waiting)

Ministerial Responsibilities and Staff

Prime Minister's Office

10 Downing Street, London SW1A 2AA
Tel: 020 7930 4433
Website: www.gov.uk/number10 Twitter: @number10gov

Prime Minister, First Lord of the Treasury and Minister for the Civil Service Rt Hon **Theresa May** MP

Parliamentary Private Secretaries	George Hollingbery MP Email: george.hollingbery.mp@parliament.uk	020 7219 7109
	Seema Kennedy MP Email: seema.kennedy.mp@parliament.uk	020 7219 4412
Principal Private Secretary	Peter Hill	
Deputy Principal Private Secretary (Economic Affairs and Domestic Policy)	Will Macfarlane	
Chief of Staff (Political)	Rt Hon Gavin Barwell	
Deputy Chief of Staff (Political)	Joanna Penn	
Private Secretaries to the Prime Minister		
(Public Services)	Lorna Gratton	
(Home Affairs)	Alastair Whitehead OBE	
(Speechwriter)	Tim Kiddell	
(Foreign Affairs)	Jonny Hall	
(Europe)	Catherine Page	
Director of Communications (Political)	Robbie Gibb	
Prime Minister's Official Spokesperson	James Slack	
Prime Minister's Legal Adviser	Harry Carter	
Director of Legislative Affairs (Political)	Nikki Da Costa	
Political Secretary to the Prime Minister	Stephen Parkinson	
Head of Operations (Political)	Richard Jackson	
Deputy Director, Events and Visits	Victoria Busby	
Director of Research and Messaging (Political)	Alex Dawson	
Director of Policy (Political)	James Marshall	
Deputy Head of Policy	Natalie Black	
Prime Minister's Special Adviser on Europe (Political)	Denzil Davidson OBE	
Prime Minister's Europe Adviser	Peter Storr CB	

Department for Business, Energy and Industrial Strategy

1 Victoria Street, London SW1H 0ET
Tel: 020 7215 5000 Email: enquiries@beis.gov.uk (Please note: see Private Secretary for Minister's email)
Website: www.gov.uk/beis Twitter: @beisgovuk

Secretary of State for Business, Energy and Industrial Strategy Rt Hon **Greg Clark** MP

Developing and delivering a comprehensive industrial strategy and leading the government's relationship with business; ensuring that the country has secure energy supplies that are reliable, affordable and clean; ensuring the UK remains at the leading edge of science, research and innovation; tackling climate change.

Parliamentary Private Secretaries

Secretary of State	Kelly Tolhurst MP Email: kelly.tolhurst.mp@parliament.uk	020 7219 5387
Ministerial Team	Rishi Sunak MP Email: rishi.sunak.mp@parliament.uk	020 7219 5437
Special Advisers	Jacob Willmer Email: mpst.clarkspad@beis.gov.uk	020 7215 6629
	Glenn Hall Email: mpst.clarkspad@beis.gov.uk	020 7215 6629
Principal Private Secretary	Jacqui Ward Email: mpst.clark@beis.gov.uk	020 7215 5621

Minister of State for Climate Change and Industry **Claire Perry** MP

Industrial strategy; climate change, including carbon budgets; international climate change, including International Climate Fund; climate science and innovation; green finance, energy efficiency and heat, including fuel poverty; industry and enterprise, including advanced manufacturing; materials; automotive.

Senior Private Secretary	Lisa Pearce Email: mpst.perry@beis.gov.uk	020 7215 0967

Minister of State for Universities, Science, Research and Innovation **Jo Johnson** MP

(jointly with Department for Education) Industrial strategy; universities and higher education reform, including implementation of the Higher Education and Research Act and teaching excellence framework and quality; higher education student finance, including Student Loans Company; widening participation and social mobility; education exports, including international students, international research; science and research, including the creation and governance of UK Research and Innovation (UKRI); agri-tech; space; innovation; intellectual property.

Senior Private Secretary	Hannah Nicholls Email: mpst.johnson@beis.gov.uk	020 7215 5568

Parliamentary Under-Secretary of State (Minister for Small Business, Consumers and Corporate Responsibility) **Margot James** MP

Industrial strategy; European Union exit; EU (Approvals) Bill; small business and enterprise, including access to finance; retail sector; consumer and competition, including energy retail markets and competition law; labour markets; corporate governance; local growth; Insolvency Service; postal affairs, including Royal Mail; EU structural funds.

Senior Private Secretary	Sahar Rehman Email: mpst.james@beis.gov.uk	020 7215 5933

Parliamentary Under-Secretary of State (Minister for Energy and Industry) **Richard Harrington** MP

Industrial strategy; energy: nuclear, oil and gas, including shale gas, low carbon generation, security of supply, electricity and gas wholesale markets and networks, smart meters and smart systems, international energy, energy security, including resilience and emergency planning; industrial policy; aerospace.

Senior Private Secretary	Guy Bromley Email: mpst.harrington@beis.gov.uk	020 7215 0971

Parliamentary Under-Secretary of State **Lord Prior of Brampton**

Industrial strategy; Lords lead on all BEIS issues; industrial policy (with the Minister of State for Climate Change and Industry): technology and emerging sectors, infrastructure/construction, professional services, rail supply chain, defence, maritime; life sciences; EU on-going business; better regulation and regulatory reform; Land Registry; Ordnance Survey; Companies House; corporate minister.

Senior Private Secretary	Will Field Email: mpst.prior@beis.gov.uk	020 7215 6011
Head of Parliamentary Unit	Oliver Bennett Email: mpst.parly@beis.gov.uk	020 7215 6630

Cabinet Office

70 Whitehall, London SW1A 2AS
Tel: 020 7276 1234 Email: publiccorrespondence@cabinetoffice.gov.uk (Please note: see Private Secretary for Minister's email) Website: www.gov.uk/cabinet-office

First Secretary of State; Minister for the Cabinet Office Rt Hon **Damian Green** MP

Advising the Prime Minister on developing and implementing Government policy; driving forward government business and implementation, including through chairing and deputy chairing cabinet committees and taskforces; overseeing devolution consequences of EU exit; overseeing constitutional affairs and maintaining the integrity of the Union; oversight of all Cabinet Office policies.

Parliamentary Private Secretaries

First Secretary of State and Minister for the Cabinet Office	James Morris MP Email: james.morris.mp@parliament.uk	020 7219 8715	Fax: 020 7219 1429
Ministerial Team	Will Quince MP Email: will.quince.mp@parliament.uk	020 7219 8049	
Special Advisers	Flora Rose Email: specialadvisers@cabinetoffice.gov.uk	020 7276 7649	
	Dylan Sharpe Email: specialadvisers@cabinetoffice.gov.uk	020 7271 3121	
	Paul Holmes Email: specialadvisers@cabinetoffice.gov.uk	020 7276 0721	
Principal Private Secretary	Athith Shetty Email: psdamiangreen@cabinetoffice.gov.uk	020 7276 2017	
Private Secretary to the Special Adviser Team	Alice Turner Email: specialadvisers@cabinetoffice.gov.uk	020 7271 8933	

Parliamentary Secretary (Minister for the Constitution) **Chris Skidmore** MP

Constitution policy and democracy; FOI/transparency; knowledge management; public appointments; UK Statistics Authority; CO Parliamentary business; CO domestic; fraud, error, debt and grants; Government Communications Service; public bodies reform.

Private Secretary	Frances Clark Email: pschrisskidmore@cabinetoffice.gov.uk	020 7276 1820

Parliamentary Secretary (Minister for Government Resilience and Efficiency) **Caroline Nokes** MP

Efficiency and controls; functions – IPA, CSHR, Digital, Data and Technology, Commercial and CCS, Property, including relocation of ALBs, shared services, commercial models; civil service employment, including pensions, industrial relations and interface with wider public sector; civil service issues; Single Departmental Plans; cyber; resilience.

Acting Private Secretary	Elizabeth Jacobs Email: pscarolinenokes@cabinetoffice.gov.uk	020 7276 2481

Chancellor of the Duchy of Lancaster Rt Hon Sir **Patrick McLoughlin** MP

Conservative Party Chair; administers the estates and rents of the Duchy of Lancaster, Chequers and Dorneywood; attends Cabinet.

Parliamentary Private Secretary	Edward Argar MP Email: edward.argar.mp@parliament.uk	020 7219 8140
Private Secretary	Charles Trew Email: pspatrickmcloughlin@cabinetoffice.gov.uk	020 7276 0656
Parliamentary Clerk	Kevin Candy Email: coparliamentarybranch@cabinetoffice.gov.uk	020 7276 1208

Department for Communities and Local Government

Fry Building, 2 Marsham Street, London SW1P 4DF
Tel: 030 3444 0000
Email: [firstname.lastname]@communities.gsi.gov.uk (Please note: see Private Secretary for Minister's email) Website: www.gov.uk/dclg

Secretary of State for Communities and Local Government Rt Hon **Sajid Javid** MP

Overall leadership of the department, EU Exit and integration; Ministerial Champion for the Midlands Engine.

Parliamentary Private Secretaries		
Secretary of State	Mims Davies MP Email: mims.davies.mp@parliament.uk	020 7219 6853
Ministerial Team	Kevin Foster MP Email: kevin.foster.mp@parliament.uk	020 7219 4711
Special Advisers	Nick King Email: nick.king@communities.gsi.gov.uk	030 3444 3165
	Salma Shah Email: salma.shah@communities.gsi.gov.uk	030 3444 3165
	James Hedgeland Email: james.hedgeland@communities.gsi.gov.uk	030 3444 3165
Principal Private Secretary	Louise Morgan Email: pssajidjavid@communities.gsi.gov.uk	030 3444 3439

Minister of State for Housing and Planning **Alok Sharma** MP

Housing supply policy; home ownership policy; planning policy; planning casework oversight; Homes and Communities Agency sponsorship and performance; building regulations; private rented sector.

Private Secretary	Jennie Taylor Email: psaloksharma@communities.gsi.gov.uk	030 3444 3425

Parliamentary Under-Secretary of State (Minister for the Northern Powerhouse and Local Growth) **Jake Berry** MP

Northern Powerhouse; mayors and devolution; local growth – policy and initiatives (enterprise zones, high streets, coastal communities); place-based initiatives (Thames Estuary Growth Commission); Local Enterprise Partnership (LEP) policy; inward investment and infrastructure, including High Speed 2; European Regional Development Fund and UK Shared Prosperity Fund; resilience and emergencies; community rights, including pubs; Minister for Secondary Legislation.

Private Secretary	Sarah Morgan Email: psjakeberry@communities.gsi.gov.uk	030 3444 3433

Parliamentary Under-Secretary of State (Minister for Local Government) **Marcus Jones** MP

Local government policy, including local government reform; local government finances, including local authority sustainability and business rates retention; adult social care; local government interventions policy and oversight of existing interventions; local government pensions; troubled families; homelessness; supported housing; parks and green spaces.

Private Secretary	Dan Hallam	030 3444 3451
	Email: psmarcusjones@communities.gsi.gov.uk	

Parliamentary Under-Secretary of State (Minister for Faith) **Lord Bourne of Aberystwyth**

(jointly with Northern Ireland Office) Departmental business in the House of Lords; domestic refuges; faith; community cohesion, including Controlling Migration Fund; Race Disparity Audit; Travellers policy.

Private Secretary	Alanna Reid	030 3444 3668
	Email: pslordbourne@communities.gsi.gov.uk	

Parliamentary Clerk	Paul B Smith	030 3444 3407
	Email: paulb.smith@communities.gsi.gov.uk	
Correspondence Manager	Michael Salmon	030 3444 2891
	Email: michael.salmon@communities.gsi.gov.uk	

Ministry of Defence

Floor 5, Main Building, Whitehall, London SW1A 2HB
Tel: 020 7218 9000 Email: defencesecretary-group@mod.uk
Correspondence to parlibranch-mincorrespondence@mod.uk (Please note: see Private Secretary for Minister's email) Website: www.gov.uk/mod

Secretary of State for Defence Rt Hon Sir **Michael Fallon** KCB MP

Strategic operations and operational strategy, including membership of the National Security Council; defence planning, programme and resource allocation; strategic international partnerships: US, France, Germany, Saudi Arabia, NATO; nuclear operations, policy and organisations; strategic communications.

Parliamentary Private Secretaries

Secretary of State	Oliver Dowden CBE MP	020 7219 3415
	Email: oliver.dowden.mp@parliament.uk	
Ministerial Team	Anne-Marie Trevelyan MP	020 7219 4437
	Email: annemarie.trevelyan.mp@parliament.uk	
Special Advisers	James Wild	020 7218 2554
	Email: sofs-specialadvisersgroup@mod.uk	
	Robert Oxley	020 7218 2554
	Email: sofs-specialadvisersgroup@mod.uk	
Principal Private Secretary/ Chief of Staff	Damian Parmenter	020 7218 9000
	Email: defencesecretary-group@mod.uk	

Minister of State and Deputy Leader of the House of Lords Rt Hon **Earl Howe**

Spokesman in the House of Lords on all Defence matters; efficiency programme; EU relations, including Brexit; combat immunity; ceremonial duties, medallic recognition, protocol policy and casework; commemorations; engagement with retired senior defence personnel and wider opinion formers; community engagement; arms control and proliferation, including export licensing; UK Hydrographic Office; Statutory Instrument Programme; Australia, Far East; defence fire and rescue; London Estate; Defence Medical Services; museums and heritage; ministerial correspondence and parliamentary questions.

Private Secretary	George Hutchinson	020 7218 7346
	Email: minlords-privateoffice@mod.uk	

Minister of State for the Armed Forces **Mark Lancaster** TD MP

Operations; operational security and safety; legacy and operational legal issues; Force generation; manning, recruitment and retention of Regulars and Reserves; NATO; space, cyber and intelligence; Permanent Joint Operating Bases; Africa and Latin America; international defence engagement; Northern Ireland; engagement with parliamentarians.

Private Secretary	Dr Victoria Tuke	020 7218 6666
	Email: minaf-privateoffice@mod.uk	

Parliamentary Under-Secretary of State (Defence Procurement) **Harriett Baldwin** MP

Equipment Plan delivery; Nuclear Enterprise; Defence Equipment and Support; defence exports; innovation; science and technology, including Dstl; information computer technology; Gulf and Asia Pacific; Single Source Regulation Office; Scotland and Wales.

Private Secretary	William Johnson	020 7218 6621
	Email: mindp-privateoffice@mod.uk	

Parliamentary Under-Secretary of State (Defence People and Veterans) Rt Hon **Tobias Ellwood** MP

Civilian and service personnel policy; veterans policy, including resettlement, transition, charities and Veterans Board; Armed Forces People Programme; mental health; defence estate; armed forces Pay, pensions and compensation; Armed Forces Covenant; service justice; welfare and service families; youth and cadets; security and safety, including vetting; environment and sustainability; equality, diversity and inclusion.

Private Secretary	Mark Selfridge	020 7218 2452
	Email: mindpv-privateoffice@mod.uk	
Parliamentary Clerk	Teresa Andrews	020 7218 1991
	Email: parlibranch-parliclerk@mod.uk	

Department for Digital, Culture, Media and Sport

Fourth Floor, 100 Parliament Street, London SW1A 2BQ
Tel: 020 7211 6000
Email: enquiries@culture.gov.uk [firstname.surname]@culture.gov.uk (Please note: see Private Secretary for Minister's email) Website: www.gov.uk/dcms Twitter: @DCMS

Secretary of State for Digital, Culture, Media and Sport Rt Hon **Karen Bradley** MP

Overall responsibility for Department; spending review and finance.

Parliamentary Private Secretaries

Secretary of State	Matt Warman MP	020 7219 8643
	Email: matt.warman.mp@parliament.uk	
Ministerial Team	Nigel Huddleston MP	020 7219 5814
	Email: nigel.huddleston.mp@parliament.uk	
Special Adviser	Aidan Corley	
	Email: special.advisers@culture.gov.uk	
Principal Private Secretary	Ben Dean	
	Email: secretary.statesoffice@culture.gov.uk	

Minister of State for Digital Rt Hon **Matt Hancock** MP

Broadband and mobile connectivity; broadcasting; creative industries; cyber security; data; Digital Charter; digital economy; digital skills and inclusion; digital technology; internet governance; media; online safety; spectrum; telecoms markets and resilience.

Private Secretary	Miriam Grigg	
	Email: minister.digital@culture.gov.uk	

Parliamentary Under-Secretary of State for Sport and Civil Society **Tracey Crouch** MP

Gambling; horse racing; Office for Civil Society; sport; National Lottery and society lotteries.

Private Secretary — Cameron Yorston
Email: minister-sportandcivilsociety@culture.gov.uk

Parliamentary Under-Secretary of State for Arts, Heritage and Tourism **John Glen** MP

Arts; culture; heritage; public libraries; museums; National Archives; tourism.

Private Secretary — Emily Mansell
Email: minister-arts-heritage-tourism@culture.gov.uk

Parliamentary Under-Secretary of State **Lord Ashton of Hyde**

Ceremonials; DCMS business in the Lords; First World War commemorations.

Private Secretary — Matt Hiorns
Email: dcmslordsminister@culture.gov.uk

Parliamentary Clerk — Ed Little
Email: parliamentarybranch@culture.gov.uk

Department for Education

Sanctuary Buildings, Great Smith Street, London SW1P 3BT
Tel: 0370 000 2288 (Public Communications Unit) Fax: 0161-600 1332
Email: www.gov.uk/contact-dfe [firstname.surname]@education.gov.uk (Please note: see Private Secretary for Minister's email)
Website: www.gov.uk/dfe Twitter: @educationgovuk
Government Equalities Office, Sanctuary Buildings, Great Smith Street, London SW1P 3BT
Tel: 0370 000 2288 (Public Communications Unit) Website: www.gov.uk/geo
Twitter: @WomenEqualities

Secretary of State for Education; Minister for Women and Equalities Rt Hon **Justine Greening** MP

All the Department's policies, including: social mobility, early years, adoption and child protection, teachers' pay, school curriculum, school improvement, establishment of academies and free schools, further education, higher education, apprenticeships and skills;o verall policy responsibility for policy on women, policy on sexual orientation and transgender equality, cross-government equality strategy and legislation.

Parliamentary Private Secretaries

Secretary of State — Helen Whately MP 020 7219 6472
Email: helen.whately.mp@parliament.uk

Ministerial Team — Luke Hall MP 020 7219 4741
Email: luke.hall.mp@parliament.uk

Special Advisers — Peter Wilson
Email: advisers.ps@education.gov.uk
Victoria Crawford
Email: advisers.ps@education.gov.uk

Principal Private Secretary — Warwick Sharp

Deputy Principal Private Secretaries — Alice Lakeman
John Acland-Hood

Senior Private Secretaries — Emma Hockley
Rebecca Hewstone
Nola Walker
Lynsey Jones
Juliette Cammaerts
Email: sec-of-state.ps@education.gov.uk

Diary Manager — Florence Cooke
Email: sec-of-state-diary.ps@education.gov.uk

Minister of State for School Standards; Minister for Equalities Rt Hon **Nick Gibb** MP

Recruitment and retention of teachers and school leaders, including initial teacher training, qualifications and professional development; supporting a high-quality teaching profession; admissions and school transport; national funding formula for schools and school revenue funding; curriculum; assessment and qualifications, including links with Ofqual; school accountability, including links with Ofsted; personal, social, health and economic education (PSHE), relationships education, relationships and sex education (RSE) and children and young people's mental health; preventing bullying in schools; policy on sexual orientation and transgender equality; cross-government equality strategy and legislation.

Senior Private Secretary — Yuin Chin
Email: gibb.ps@education.gov.uk

Minister of State for Children and Families **Robert Goodwill** MP

Improving social mobility in the 12 opportunity areas; child protection, including protection from child sexual exploitation and safeguarding; care leavers and adoption; childcare policy, including delivery of the 30 hours free childcare offer; early years policy, including inspection, regulation and literacy and numeracy; funding for publicly funded schools in England to raise the attainment of disadvantaged pupils of all abilities (pupil premium and pupil premium plus); free school meals funding and policy; special educational needs and disabilities (SEND); school sports and healthy pupils; cadets and military ethos in the education system.

Senior Private Secretary — Caitlin Devereux
Email: goodwill.ps@education.gov.uk

Minister of State for Universities, Science, Research and Innovation **Jo Johnson** MP

(jointly with Department for Business, Energy and Industrial Strategy) Universities and higher education reform, including implementation of the Higher Education and Research Act and teaching excellence framework; higher education student finance, including Student Loans Company; widening participation and social mobility in higher education; education exports, including international students, international research; science and research, including the creation and governance of UK Research and Innovation; agri-tech; space; innovation; intellectual property.

Senior Private Secretary — Hannah Nicholls
Email: mpst.johnson@beis.gov.uk

Minister of State for Apprenticeships and Skills; Minister for Women Rt Hon **Anne Milton** MP

Apprenticeships, including the apprenticeship levy, traineeships and institutes of technology; technical education and skills, including T-Levels; careers education, information and guidance; post-16 funding, including support for young people and adult learners; further education colleges, sixth-form colleges and local patterns of provision, including area reviews and city deals; adult education, including National Retraining Scheme; reducing the number of young people who are not in education, employment or training; leading on the review of funding across tertiary education; overall responsibility for policy on gender equality.

Senior Private Secretary — Sarah Smith
Email: milton.ps@education.gov.uk

Parliamentary Under-Secretary of State for the School System
Sir **Theodore Agnew** DL *(peerage pending)*

A strong school system, including free schools, academies, multi-academy trusts, university technical colleges, studio schools, faith schools, independent schools, home education, supplementary schools; tackling school underperformance; school improvement, including teaching school alliances, national and local leaders of education and school improvement funds; school governance; school capital investment, including new school places, school maintenance, land and playing fields; tackling extremism in schools and colleges; behaviour and attendance, exclusions and alternative provision.

Senior Private Secretary — Katie Carr
Email: agnew.ps@education.gov.uk

Parliamentary Clerk — Amy Ross
Email: team.parliamentary@education.gov.uk

Department for Environment, Food and Rural Affairs

Nobel House, 17 Smith Square, London SW1P 3JR
Tel: 0345 933 5577 Email: defra.helpline@defra.gsi.gov.uk [firstname.surname]@defra.gsi.gov.uk
(Please note: see Private Secretary for Minister's email) Website: www.gov.uk/defra

Secretary of State for Environment, Food and Rural Affairs Rt Hon **Michael Gove** MP

Oversight of EU exit work and the overall policy programme; international relations; emergencies; departmental administration.

Parliamentary Private Secretaries

Secretary of State	Kevin Hollinrake MP Email: kevin.hollinrake.mp@parliament.uk	020 7219 4746
Ministerial Team	Rebecca Pow MP Email: rebecca.pow.mp@parliament.uk	020 7219 4831
Special Adviser	Henry Cook Email: ps.advisers@defra.gsi.gov.uk	020 8026 9909
Principal Private Secretary	Mike Rowe Email: secretary.state@defra.gsi.gov.uk	020 8026 3732

Minister of State for Agriculture, Fisheries and Food **George Eustice** MP

Food and farming, including CAP (Common Agricultural Policy), apprenticeships, exports, and bovine TB (tuberculosis) policy; fisheries; better regulation; science and innovation.

Private Secretary	Chetal Owens Email: ps.george.eustice@defra.gsi.gov.uk	020 8026 2890

Parliamentary Under-Secretary of State for Environment Dr **Therese Coffey** MP

Natural environment, including biodiversity, marine environment and international wildlife trafficking; floods, water and waterways; air quality; resource and environment management.

Private Secretary	Nuala Carson Email: ps.therese.coffey@defra.gsi.gov.uk	020 8026 3809

Parliamentary Under-Secretary of State for Rural Affairs and Biosecurity **Lord Gardiner of Kimble**

Rural ambassador and rural affairs, covering rural life opportunities, broadband and mobile; biosecurity strategy, including endemic and exotic plant and animal disease, invasive alien species and Kew Gardens; animal health and welfare; commercial projects; landscape, including national parks; climate change adaptation; National Pollinator Strategy; all Defra parliamentary business in the House of Lords.

Private Secretary	Sam Wilson Email: ps.lord.gardiner@defra.gsi.gov.uk	020 8225 7421
Parliamentary Clerk	Deirdre Kennedy MBE Email: parliament.cabinet@defra.gsi.gov.uk	020 8026 3042 Fax: 020 8415 2526

Department for Exiting the European Union

9 Downing Street, London SW1A 2AS
Tel: 020 7276 0432 Email: [firstname.lastname]@dexeu.gov.uk (Please note: see Private Secretary for Minister's email) Website: www.gov.uk/dexeu Twitter: @dexeugov

Secretary of State for Exiting the European Union Rt Hon **David Davis** MP

Policy work to support the UK's negotiations to leave the European Union and to establish the future relationship between the EU and the UK; conducting the negotiations in support of the Prime Minister, including supporting bilateral discussions on EU exit with other European countries; working very closely with the UK's devolved administrations, Parliament and a wide range of other interested parties on what the approach to those negotiations should be; leading and co-ordinating cross-Government work to seize the opportunities and ensure a smooth process of exit on the best possible terms.

Parliamentary Private Secretaries

Secretary of State	Gareth Johnson MP Email: gareth.johnson.mp@parliament.uk	020 7219 7047
Ministerial Team	Jeremy Quin MP Email: jeremy.quin.mp@parliament.uk	020 7219 6341
Special Advisers	Stewart Jackson Tim Smith Raoul Ruparel	
Principal Private Secretary	Jane Walker Email: psdaviddavis@dexeu.gov.uk	

Minister of State Rt Hon **Baroness Anelay of St Johns** DBE

All Departmental business in the Lords.

Private Secretary	Tim Cork Email: psbaronessanelay@dexeu.gov.uk

Parliamentary Under-Secretary of State **Robin Walker** MP

Co-ordinating work to shape the UK's future relationship with the EU Institutions; co-ordinating the development of a negotiation position on market access and trade; co-ordinating cross-Government work to ensure the views of the Overseas Territories and Crown Dependencies, as well as those of stakeholders in network industries, charities and the environmental and services, including Financial Services, sectors are fed into the negotiation strategy.

Private Secretary	Kirsty McVicar Email: psrobinwalker@dexeu.gov.uk

Parliamentary Under-Secretary of State **Steve Baker** MP

Supporting the work of the Department for Exiting the European Union.

Private Secretary	To be appointed Email: psstevebaker@dexeu.gov.uk
Parliamentary Clerk	Bertie Archer Email: bertie.archer@dexeu.gov.uk

Foreign and Commonwealth Office

King Charles Street, Whitehall, London SW1A 2AH
Tel: 020 7008 1500
Email: fcocorrespondence@fco.gsi.gov.uk (Please note: see Private Secretary for Minister's email)
Website: www.gov.uk/fco

Secretary of State for Foreign and Commonwealth Affairs (Foreign Secretary)
Rt Hon **Boris Johnson** MP

Overall responsibility for the work of the Foreign and Commonwealth Office.

Parliamentary Private Secretaries

Foreign Secretary	Conor Burns MP Email: conor.burns.mp@parliament.uk	020 7219 7021
Ministerial Team	Amanda Milling MP Email: amanda.milling.mp@parliament.uk	020 7219 8356

Special Advisers	Ben Gascoigne Email: pospads@fco.gsi.gov.uk	020 7008 2117/020 7008 2312
	David Frost Email: pospads@fco.gsi.gov.uk	020 7008 2117/020 7008 2312
	Liam Parker Email: pospads@fco.gsi.gov.uk	020 7008 2117/020 7008 2312
Principal Private Secretary	Martin Reynolds Email: private.officegsi@fco.gsi.gov.uk	020 7008 6000

Minister of State for Europe and the Americas Rt Hon Sir **Alan Duncan** KCMG MP

The Americas, including Cuba; Europe, including all parts of the Soviet Union and Turkey; NATO and European security; defence and international security; Falklands; polar regions; migration; protocol; human resources; OSCE and Council of Europe; relations with Parliament; Foreign and Commonwealth finance; knowledge and technology.

Private Secretary	Lance Domm Email: psduncan@fco.gsi.gov.uk	020 7008 1280

Minister of State for Africa **Rory Stewart** OBE MP

(jointly with Department for International Development) Africa; consular policy; Foreign and Commonwealth Office representative for cross-Whitehall funds; international crime; stabilisation.

Private Secretary	Iain Griffiths Email: psstewart@fco.gsi.gov.uk	020 7008 3371

Minister of State for the Middle East Rt Hon **Alistair Burt** MP

(jointly with Department for International Development) Middle East and North Africa; estates and security.

Private Secretary	Fleur Willson Email: psministerburtaction@fco.gsi.gov.uk	020 7008 2090

Minister of State for the Commonwealth and the UN **Lord Ahmad of Wimbledon**

All Foreign and Commonwealth Office business in the House of Lords; The Commonwealth (as an institution); UN, peacekeeping, conflict and International Criminal Court; Overseas Territories, excluding Falklands, Sovereign Base Areas and Gibraltar; Caribbean; human rights and modern slavery; Prime Minister's Special Representative on Preventing Sexual Violence in Conflict; national security: counter-terrorism, countering violent extremism and cyber.

Private Secretary	Helen Walker-Fleming Email: psminsiterahmadaction@fco.gsi.gov.uk	020 7008 2356

Minister of State for Asia and the Pacific Rt Hon **Mark Field** MP

Asia, excluding Central Asia; Australasia and Pacific; communications, public diplomacy and scholarships; British Council; economic diplomacy, including climate change, illegal wildlife trade and international energy policy; ministerial oversight of Foreign and Commonwealth Office Services.

Private Secretary	Tom de Fonblanque Email: psfield@fco.gsi.gov.uk	020 7008 3371

Parliamentary Clerk	Nat Dawbarn Email: fcocorrespondence@fco.gsi.gov.uk	020 7008 4005

Department of Health

Richmond House, 79 Whitehall, London SW1A 2NS
Tel: 020 7210 4850
Email: [firstname.surname]@dh.gsi.gov.uk (Please note: see Private Secretary for Minister's email)
Website: www.gov.uk/dh Twitter: @Dhgovuk

Secretary of State for Health Rt Hon **Jeremy Hunt** MP

Business and policies of the department, including financial control; oversight of all NHS delivery and performance; mental health; championing patient safety.

Parliamentary Private Secretaries

Secretary of State	Jo Churchill MP Email: jo.churchill.mp@parliament.uk	020 7219 8487
Ministerial Team	James Cartlidge MP Email: james.cartlidge.mp@parliament.uk	020 7219 4875
Special Adviser	Ed Jones Email: specialadvisors@dh.gsi.gov.uk	020 7210 5945
Principal Private Secretary	Tristan Pedelty Email: tristan.pedelty@dh.gsi.gov.uk	020 7210 5875

Minister of State for Health **Philip Dunne** MP

NHS operations and performance; secondary care commissioning policy; healthcare quality regulation; hospital care quality and patient experience; patient safety; hospitals in special measures; Department of Health expenditure and finances; procurement; hospital productivity; workforce, including pay and pensions, nursing and midwifery and education and training; workforce race equality standard; professional regulation; cosmetic regulation; maternity care; screening in pregnancy; ministerial lead for Care Quality Commission, Health Education England, NHS Improvement, Human Fertilisation and Embryology Authority.

Senior Private Secretary	Andrew Damant Email: andrew.damant@dh.gsi.gov.uk	020 7210 4865

Parliamentary Under-Secretary of State (Care and Mental Health) **Jackie Doyle-Price** MP

Care for the most vulnerable; mental health; adult social care; community care; injustices and vulnerable groups; women and children's health; health and work; blood and transplants; ministerial lead for NHS Blood and Transplant, Human Tissue Authority.

Senior Private Secretary	Georgina Johnson Email: georgina.johnson@dh.gsi.gov.uk pscmh@dh.gsi.gov.uk	020 7972 2848

Parliamentary Under-Secretary of State (Public Health and Primary Care) **Steve Brine** MP

NHS transformation, including out-of-hospital care; primary care; prevention and early intervention; health protection and improvement; sexual health; public health system; international health policy; major diseases; ministerial lead for NHS England, Public Health England, Food Standards Agency.

Senior Private Secretary	Nula Clarke Email: nula.clarke@dh.gsi.gov.uk psphpc@dh.gsi.gov.uk	020 7210 5119

Parliamentary Under-Secretary of State for Health (Lords) **Lord O'Shaughnessy**

Leaving the EU; migrant access to the NHS; devolved administrations; medicines and industry; cancer drugs fund; uptake of new drugs and medical technologies; life sciences industry; data and technology; specialised commissioning; academic health science centres; prescription charging; pathology; death certification; estates and facilities; litigation; NHS security management; NHS income generation; ministerial lead for NHS Litigation Authority, NHS Property Services and Community Health Partnerships, NHS Business Services Authority, NHS Digital, Medicines and Healthcare products Regulatory Agency; all aspects of health in the House of Lords.

Senior Private Secretary	Alex McLaughlin Email: alex.mclaughlin@dh.gsi.gov.uk pslords@dh.gsi.gov.uk	020 7210 6058

Parliamentary Clerk	Tom Powell Email: tom.powell@dh.gsi.gov.uk	

Home Office

Peel Building, 2 Marsham Street, London SW1P 4DF
Tel: 020 7035 4848 Email: public.enquiries@homeoffice.gsi.gov.uk (Please note: see Private Secretary for Minister's email) Website: www.gov.uk/home-office

Secretary of State for the Home Department (Home Secretary) Rt Hon **Amber Rudd** MP

Overall responsibility for work of the Home Office; legislative programmes; expenditure issues; security and terrorism.

Parliamentary Private Secretaries

Home Secretary	Robert Jenrick MP Email: robert.jenrick.mp@parliament.uk	020 7219 7335
Ministerial Team	Nusrat Ghani MP Email: nusrat.ghani.mp@parliament.uk	020 7219 4619
	Simon Hoare MP Email: simon.hoare.mp@parliament.uk	020 7219 5697
Special Advisers	Mo Hussein Email: specialadvisers@homeoffice.gsi.gov.uk	020 7035 0196
	Simon Glasson Email: specialadvisers@homeoffice.gsi.gov.uk	020 7035 0196
	Amy Fisher Email: specialadvisers@homeoffice.gsi.gov.uk	020 7035 0196
Principal Private Secretary	Kenny Bowie Email: privateoffice.external@homeoffice.gsi.gov.uk	020 7035 8813

Minister of State for Immigration Rt Hon **Brandon Lewis** MP

Immigration and border policy, including non-EU migration to the UK, family reunion, border security, detention and removal policy, asylum policy, post-Brexit immigration policy for EU nationals; assisting Secretary of State with all policy on exiting the European Union; international policy, including EU Justice and Home Affairs; border security; foreign national offenders, management in immigration detention and deportation to country of origin; resettlement policy, including operation of Home Office resettlement programmes: Syrian Vulnerable Persons Resettlement Scheme, Gateway, Mandate and Vulnerable Children's Resettlement Scheme; implementation of the Immigration Act 2016; UK Visas and Immigration; Immigration Enforcement; Border Force; Her Majesty's Passport Office; Independent Chief Inspector of Borders and Immigration; Home Office immigration transparency data; net migration statistics.

Parliamentary Private Secretary	James Cleverly MP Email: james.cleverly.mp@parliament.uk	020 7219 8593
Private Secretary	Kieran Watson Email: ministerforimmigration@homeoffice.gsi.gov.uk	020 7035 6767

Minister of State for Security Rt Hon **Ben Wallace** MP

Implementing the strategic defence and security review; counter-terrorism, including CONTEST, counter-terrorism work in prisons, Protect and Prepare, terrorist financing, counter-terrorism policing, international police co-operation, terrorism prevention and investigation measures and individual use of disruptive powers, proscription of terrorist groups; investigatory powers, including Investigatory Powers Bill, Data Retention and Investigatory Powers Act 2014 and Regulation of Investigatory Powers Act legislation; communications data legislation; communications capabilities development; aviation security; chemical biological radiological nuclear defence (CBRNE) and science and technology programme management; serious and organised crime strategy, including foreign national offenders engaged in serious organised crime; criminal finance and asset recovery; cyber security; cyber crime, including fraud; National Crime Agency oversight; UK anti-corruption policy.

Private Secretary	Sidath Wickremasinghe Email: sidath.wickremasinghe@homeoffice.gsi.gov.uk	020 7035 0195

Minister of State for Policing and the Fire Service **Nick Hurd** MP

Police finance and resourcing; police reform and governance; police representative groups; police pay and pensions; police workforce; Independent Police Complaints Commission (IPCC); Policing and Crime Bill; police integrity and transparency, including HM Inspectorate of Constabulary (HMIC), police powers; emergency services collaboration; firearms; single infrastructure policing; crime statistics; national fire policy, including fire safety; Grenfell Tower victims work; Chief Fire and Rescue Adviser; national resilience and fire programmes; localism and reform; workforce pay and pensions and industrial relations; extradition; mutual legal assistance; EU criminal justice, including Europol, Eurojust, Prüm and European Public Prosecutor's Office; Interpol; foreign criminality; security industry engagement.

Private Secretary	Deborah Morrison	020 7035 4848
	Email: policing.minister@homeoffice.gsi.gov.uk	

Minister of State for Countering Extremism **Baroness Williams of Trafford**

All Home Office business in the House of Lords; countering extremism; hate crime; integration; devolution; data strategy; identity and biometrics; Better Regulation; animals in science.

Private Secretary	Lucy Calladine	020 7035 8798
	Email: lucy.calladine@homeoffice.gsi.gov.uk	

Parliamentary Under-Secretary of State for Crime, Safeguarding and Vulnerability **Sarah Newton** MP

Victims of terrorism; Disclosure and Barring Service; drugs; alcohol; countering extremism; crime prevention; anti-social behaviour; gangs, youth crime and youth violence; knife crime; wildlife crime; child sexual exploitation and abuse, including Independent Inquiry into Child Sex Abuse; online child sexual exploitation; mental health; modern slavery; honour-based violence, including forced marriage and honour killings; female genital mutilation (FGM); violence against women and girls; missing people and children; sexual violence, prostitution and lap dancing; domestic violence; WEProtect; internet safety.

Private Secretary	Sean McGarry	020 7035 0202
	Email: sean.mcgarry2@homeoffice.gsi.gov.uk	
Parliamentary Clerk	Benjamin Pugsley	020 7035 8838
	Email: parliamentaryteam@homeoffice.gsi.gov.uk	

Department for International Development

22 Whitehall, London SW1A 2EG
Tel: 020 7023 0000 Email: dfidcorrespondence@dfid.gov.uk [firstinitial-surname]@dfid.gov.uk
(Please note: see Private Secretary for Minister's email) Website: www.gov.uk/dfid

Secretary of State for International Development Rt Hon **Priti Patel** MP

National Security Council; strategy; G7 and G20; World Bank, IMF and other IFIs, including Regional Development Banks; overall delivery and management of 0.7 per cent; communications; Reform: United Nations and multilateral; economic development, including CDC, Trade Policy and private sector; modern day slavery and child exploitation; women and girls.

Parliamentary Private Secretaries

Secretary of State	Wendy Morton MP	020 7219 8784
	Email: wendy.morton.mp@parliament.uk	
Ministerial Team	Michael Tomlinson MP	020 7219 5844
	Email: michael.tomlinson.mp@parliament.uk	
Special Adviser	Richard Parr	020 7023 0114
	Email: special-advisers@dfid.gov.uk	
Principal Private Secretary	Roslayn Eales	020 7023 1340
	Email: privatesecretary@dfid.gsi.gov.uk	

Minister of State **Rory Stewart** OBE MP

(jointly with Foreign and Commonwealth Office) Africa (covering FCO and DFID policy); innovation and research; Ukraine; climate and environment; Corporate Performance Group.

Private Secretary	Oli Sharp	020 7023 0399
	Email: psstewart@dfid.gov.uk	

Minister of State Rt Hon **Alistair Burt** MP

(jointly with Foreign and Commonwealth Office) Middle East and North Africa (covering FCO and DFID policy); Asia; conflict, humanitarian and security; human development, including children, education and youth; Global Funds Department; Cross Government Funds (CSSF, Prosperity, Empowerment).

Private Secretary	Jocelyn Waller	020 7023 0243
	Email: psburt@dfid.gov.uk	

Minister of State Rt Hon **Lord Bates**

Caribbean; Overseas Territories; Europe; United Nations and Commonwealth; global partnerships and emerging powers; education and youth; inclusive societies: disability, ageing, faith, LGBT, VAWG – lead on policy and ensuring consistency with his wider portfolio; supporting Secretary of State on economic development, international finance institutions and international trade; corporate performance within areas of responsibility; Parliamentary champion and House of Lords relations; supporting Rory Stewart engaging on Scotland and with Abercrombie House; supporting on governance, open societies and anti-corruption.

Private Secretary	Nimra Zaheer	020 7023 0218
	Email: psbates@dfid.gov.uk	

Parliamentary Clerk	Ailish McAllister	020 7023 0559
	Email: p-enquiries@dfid.gov.uk	

Department for International Trade

King Charles Street, London SW1A 2AH
Tel: 020 7215 5000 Email: enquiries@trade.gsi.gov.uk (Please note: see Private Secretary for Minister's email) Website: www.gov.uk/dit Twitter: @tradegovuk

Secretary of State for International Trade; President of the Board of Trade Rt Hon Dr **Liam Fox** MP

Overall responsibility for the business of the department; Departmental lead on trade and investment promotion in the defence and security sector.

Parliamentary Private Secretaries		
Secretary of State	Tom Pursglove MP	020 7219 8043
	Email: tom.pursglove.mp@parliament.uk	
Ministerial Team	Mike Wood MP	020 7219 6982
	Email: mikej.wood.mp@parliament.uk	
Special Advisers	David Goss	
	Email: mpst.foxspad@trade.gsi.gov.uk	
	Amy Tinley	
	Email: mpst.foxspad@trade.gsi.gov.uk	
Principal Private Secretary	Oliver Christian	
	Email: mpst.fox@trade.gsi.gov.uk	

Minister of State for Trade Policy Rt Hon **Greg Hands** MP

Leads the Trade Policy Group; trading agreements and arrangements with other countries, UK engagement with the World Trade Organisation, ongoing EU trade business while the UK remains a member of the EU, trade remedies; deputy to the Secretary of State; bill minister; secondary legislation; economic diplomacy, Prosperity Fund, economic horizons markets and Official Development Assistance (ODA).

Senior Private Secretary	Matthew Grainger	
	Email: hands@trade.gsi.gov.uk	

Minister of State **Rona Fairhead** CBE *(peerage pending)*

Responsibilities still to be announced.

Senior Private Secretary — To be appointed
Email: fairhead@trade.gsi.gov.uk

Parliamentary Under-Secretary of State for Investment **Mark Garnier** MP

Investment promotion across all sectors: outward direct investment, foreign direct investment, delivery of trade and investment promotion through overseas partners, policy direction on topics such as mergers and acquisitions, Export Control Organisation (ECO), business planning and forecasting; DIT ministerial lead for the following sectors: financial services, advanced manufacturing and aerospace, automotive, bio-economy, consumer, creative and education.

Senior Private Secretary — Oliver Todd
Email: garnier@trade.gsi.gov.uk

Parliamentary Clerk — Debbie Goodier
Email: parly.unit@trade.gsi.gov.uk

Ministry of Justice

102 Petty France, London SW1H 9AJ
Tel: 020 3334 3555 Fax: 020 3334 4455
Email: general.queries@justice.gov.uk [firstname.surname]@justice.gov.uk (Please note: see Private Secretary for Minister's email) Website: www.gov.uk/moj

Lord Chancellor and Secretary of State for Justice Rt Hon **David Lidington** CBE MP

Overall responsibility for the Department's business; MoJ transformation; resourcing of the department; functions of the Lord Chancellor; EU exit and international business; judicial policy, including pay, pensions and diversity; corporate services.

Parliamentary Private Secretaries

Lord Chancellor and Secretary of State	Lucy Frazer QC MP Email: lucy.frazer.mp@parliament.uk	020 7219 5082
Ministerial Team	Alan Mak MP Email: alan.mak.mp@parliament.uk	020 7219 6266
Special Advisers	Fraser Raleigh Email: advisers@justice.gov.uk Anita Boateng Email: advisers@justice.gov.uk	
Principal Private Secretary	Jerome Glass Email: secofstate@justice.gov.uk	020 3334 3720

Minister of State **Dominic Raab** MP

Court services and reform; supporting the Secretary of State for Justice on EU Exit and international business; legal aid; legal support and fees; admin, tribunals and immigration; criminal justice; family justice; supporting the Secretary of State on departmental finances and transparency; sentencing, including out-of-court disposals; acting as Parliamentary Minister; acting as the Shadow Commons Minister for Lord Keen's portfolio.

Private Secretary — Emma Hindley
Email: emma.hindley1@justice.gov.uk

Parliamentary Under-Secretary of State for Prisons and Probation **Sam Gyimah** MP

Prison operations; prison reform; probation services; probation reform; prison and probation industrial relations; foreign national offenders; extremism; electronic monitoring; public protections, including Parole Board, imprisonment for public protection sentences and serious further offences; Civil Liability Bill.

Private Secretary — Andy Milner
Email: andrew.milner@justice.gov.uk

Parliamentary Under-Secretary of State for Youth Justice, Victims, Female Offenders and Offender Health Dr **Phillip Lee** MP

Victims, including domestic abuse and s.41; female offenders; youth justice; offender health; coroners, burials, inquests and inquiries; Lammy Review; Race Disparity Audit; devolved administrations; devolution (PCCs); human rights; prisoner voting rights; lawfare; mental capacity and Office of the Public Guardian; transgender offenders; veterans.

Private Secretary	Michaela Williamson Email: michaela.williamson@justice.gov.uk	

Spokesperson in the Lords Rt Hon **Lord Keen of Elie** QC

Ministry of Justice business in the Lords; civil justice, including discount rate and whiplash; legal services; Global Britain; relationship with the legal profession; claims management regulation.

Private Secretary	Craig Chalcraft Email: privateoffice@advocategeneral.gsi.gov.uk	
Parliamentary Clerk	Rob Evans Email: robert.evans@justice.gov.uk	

Law Officers

Attorney General's Office, 5-8 The Sanctuary, London SW1P 3JS
Tel: 020 7271 2492 Fax: 020 7271 2430
Email: correspondence@attorneygeneral.gsi.gov.uk privateoffice@attorneygeneral.gsi.gov.uk (Please note: see Private Secretary for Minister's email) Website: www.gov.uk/ago Twitter: @attorneygeneral

Attorney General Rt Hon **Jeremy Wright** QC MP

Overall responsibility for the work of the Attorney General's Office and superintended Departments (the Government Legal Department, the Crown Prosecution Service, the Serious Fraud Office, the Services Prosecuting Authority and HM Crown Prosecution Service Inspectorate).
Specific statutory duty to superintend the discharge of duties by the Director of Public Prosecutions (who heads the Crown Prosecution Service and the Revenue and Customs Prosecution Office) and the Director of the Serious Fraud Office; non-statutory oversight of the Services Prosecuting Authority and government prosecuting departments; Government's principal legal adviser dealing with questions of international law, European Community/Union law, human rights, devolution issues, and public interest functions; questions of law arising on Bills and with issues of legal policy, legal aspects of all major international and domestic litigation involving the Government.

Parliamentary Private Secretary	Michelle Donelan MP Email: michelle.donelan.mp@parliament.uk	020 7219 4451

Solicitor General **Robert Buckland** QC MP

Deputises for Attorney General; provides support to the Attorney General in his superintendence of the Treasury Solicitor's Department, the Crown Prosecution Service, the Service Prosecuting Authority, HM Crown Prosecution Service Inspectorate and the Serious Fraud Office; provides support to the Attorney General on civil litigation and advice on civil law matters and on the public interest function.

Principal Private Secretary	Josh Dodd Email: josh.dodd@attorneygeneral.gsi.gov.uk	020 7271 2405
Deputy Principal Private Secretary	Chris Murphy Email: chris.murphy@attorneygeneral.gsi.gov.uk	020 7271 2452

Advocate General for Scotland Rt Hon **Lord Keen of Elie** QC

Office of the Advocate General for Scotland, Dover House, 66 Whitehall, London SW1A 2AU
Tel: 020 7270 6720 Email: privateoffice@advocategeneral.gsi.gov.uk
[firstname.surname]@advocategeneral.gsi.gov.uk
Website: www.gov.uk/oag

The Advocate General for Scotland is a Minister of the Crown and is one of the three UK Law Officers. Along with the Attorney General and the Solicitor General for England and Wales, the Advocate General provides legal advice to all UK Government departments on a wide range of issues including human rights, European and constitutional law. The Advocate General is also the UK Government's principal legal adviser on Scots law and its senior representative within the Scottish legal community. The Advocate General is the Minister responsible to the UK Parliament for the Office of the Advocate General.

Government Spokesperson in the Lords for the Ministry of Justice.

Private Secretary	Craig Chalcraft Email: privateoffice@advocategeneral.gsi.gov.uk	020 7270 6720

Leader of the House of Commons

70 Whitehall, London SW1A 2AS
Tel: 020 7276 1005 Email: [firstname.surname]@cabinetoffice.gov.uk (Please note: see Private Secretary for Minister's email)
Website: www.gov.uk/government/organisations/the-office-of-the-leader-of-the-house-of-commons
Twitter: @CommonsLeader

Leader of the House of Commons; Lord President of the Council Rt Hon **Andrea Leadsom** MP

Government's Legislative Programme; managing the business of the House; Government's representative in the House (House of Commons Commission); House of Commons representative in Government; House of Commons reform and related issues.

Parliamentary Private Secretary	Victoria Prentis MP Email: victoria.prentis.mp@parliament.uk	020 7219 8756
Special Advisers	Marc Pooler	
	Lucia Hodgson	
Head of Office	Victoria Stott Email: commonsleader@cabinetoffice.gov.uk	020 7276 1005

Deputy Leader of the House of Commons **Michael Ellis** MP

Supports Leader in handling Government's business in the House; monitoring legislative programme; correspondence and freedom of information within Leader's office.

Private Secretary	To be appointed Email: deputycommonsleader@cabinetoffice.gov.uk	020 7276 1005

Leader of the House of Lords

House of Lords, London SW1A 0PW
Tel: 020 7219 3200 Fax: 020 7219 5251 Email: psleaderofthelords@cabinetoffice.gov.uk
Website: www.gov.uk/government/organisations/office-of-the-leader-of-the-house-of-lords

Leader of the House of Lords and Lord Privy Seal Rt Hon **Baroness Evans of Bowes Park**

Principal responsibility for the strategic management and delivery of the Government's legislative programme in the Lords; leading Government benches in the House of Lords; conduct of Government business in the Lords (together with the Lords Chief Whip); repeating in the Lords statements made by the Prime Minister in the Commons; giving guidance to the House on matters of order and procedure; Chair, Board of Trustees for Chevening.

Parliamentary Private Secretary	Victoria Atkins MP	020 7219 5897
Special Advisers	Tom Pretty Email: thomas.pretty@cabinetoffice.gov.uk	020 7219 0267
	Katharine Howell Email: katharine.howell@cabinetoffice.gov.uk	020 7219 1205
	Annabelle Eyre Email: annabelle.eyre@cabinetoffice.gov.uk	020 7219 1046

Principal Private Secretary	Duncan Sagar Email: duncan.sagar@cabinetoffice.gov.uk	020 7219 6961
Private Secretary	Michael Torrance Email: michael.torrance@cabinetoffice.gov.uk	020 7219 6782

Deputy Leader of the House of Lords Rt Hon **Earl Howe**

Support the House of Lords in its job of questioning government ministers, improving legislation and debating topics of national significance.

Private Secretary	George Hutchinson Email: minlords-privateoffice@mod.uk	020 7218 7346

Northern Ireland Office

1 Horse Guards Road, London SW1A 2HQ
Tel: 028 9052 0700 Fax: 028 9052 7040
Email: [firstname.surname]@nio.gov.uk (Please note: see Private Secretary for Minister's email)
Website: www.gov.uk/nio

Secretary of State for Northern Ireland Rt Hon **James Brokenshire** MP

Overall responsibility for all aspects of the department's work; political stability and relations with the Northern Ireland Executive; national security and counter-terrorism; implementation of the Stormont House and Fresh Start Agreements, including legacy of the past; representing Northern Ireland in the Cabinet on EU exit, including new economic opportunities; international interest in Northern Ireland, including relations with the Irish government.

Parliamentary Private Secretary	David Morris MP Email: david.morris.mp@parliament.uk	020 7219 7234
Special Advisers	Lord Caine Email: jonathan.caine@nio.gov.uk	020 7210 0803/028 9052 7007
	Peter Cardwell Email: peter.cardwell@nio.gov.uk	020 7210 6534
Principal Private Secretary	Holly Clark Email: sos.brokenshire@nio.gov.uk	020 7210 6460/028 9052 7860 Fax: 020 7210 6449/028 9052 7040
Private Secretary	Chris Atkinson Email: sos.brokenshire@nio.gov.uk	020 7210 2455/028 9052 7732

Parliamentary Under-Secretary of State **Chloe Smith** MP

EU Exit; security-related issues and casework; legacy stakeholder management; parliamentary liaison with Northern Ireland MPs, the Northern Ireland Affairs Committee and other interested parliamentarians.

Private Secretary	Andy Monaghan Email: min.smith@nio.gov.uk	020 7210 6488/028 9052 7889

Parliamentary Under-Secretary of State **Lord Bourne of Aberystwyth**

(jointly with Department for Communities and Local Government) Engagement and outreach to community groups, including around parading and the business community; electoral services; Armed Forces Covenant; human rights and equality; parliamentary liaison with Peers.

Private Secretary	Una Dumigan Email: min.bourne@nio.gov.uk	020 7210 0206

Parliamentary Clerk	Louise Newby Email: parly.section@nio.gov.uk	020 7210 6575

Scotland Office

Dover House, Whitehall, London SW1A 2AU
Tel: 020 7270 6741 Fax: 020 7270 6815 Email: secretaryofstate@scotlandoffice.gsi.gov.uk
[firstname.surname]@scotlandoffice.gsi.gov.uk (Please note: see Private Secretary for Minister's email)
Website: www.gov.uk/scotland-office Twitter: @UKGovScotland

Secretary of State for Scotland Rt Hon **David Mundell** MP

Leads on: constitutional affairs, including implementation of the Scotland Act 2016; UK Government in Scotland; welfare; foreign affairs, including exiting the EU; culture.

Parliamentary Private Secretary	Alberto Costa MP Email: barronra@parliament.uk	020 7219 4936
Special Advisers	Jenny Donnellan Email: sospecialadvisers@scotlandoffice.gsi.gov.uk	020 7270 6814
	Magnus Gardham Email: sospecialadvisers@scotlandoffice.gsi.gov.uk	020 7270 6814
Principal Private Secretary	Victoria Jones Email: secretaryofstate@scotlandoffice.gsi.gov.uk	020 7270 6741
Senior Private Secretary	Jethro House Email: secretaryofstate@scotlandoffice.gsi.gov.uk	020 7270 6741
Private Secretary	Lauren Newell Email: secretaryofstate@scotlandoffice.gsi.gov.uk	020 7270 6741
Diary Secretary	Bart Williams Email: secretaryofstate@scotlandoffice.gsi.gov.uk	020 7270 6741

Parliamentary Under-Secretary of State **Lord Duncan of Springbank**

(jointly with Wales Office) Agriculture and fisheries; rural and infrastructure issues; stakeholder engagement; economy, energy, climate change and environment; higher education and research; civil contingencies; House of Lords Spokesperson.

Private Secretary	Conal O'Hare Email: pusos@scotlandoffice.gsi.gov.uk	020 7270 6816
Assistant Private Secretary and Diary Secretary	Lara Klopper Email: pusos@scotlandoffice.gsi.gov.uk	020 7270 6816

Parliamentary Clerk	Louise Newby Email: parly.section@nio.gsi.gov.uk	020 7210 6575

Department for Transport

Great Minster House, 33 Horseferry Road, London SW1P 4DR
Tel: 0300 330 3000
Email: [firstname.surname]@dft.gsi.gov.uk (Please note: see Private Secretary for Minister's email)
Website: www.gov.uk/dft

Secretary of State for Transport Rt Hon **Chris Grayling** MP

Overall responsibility for transport strategy, including economic growth and climate change; spending review; transport security; high speed rail (HS2).

Parliamentary Private Secretaries

Secretary of State	James Heappey MP Email: james.heappey.mp@parliament.uk	020 7219 4289
Ministerial Team	Scott Mann MP Email: scott.mann.mp@parliament.uk	020 7219 5744

Special Advisers	Simon Jones	020 7944 4377	
	Email: simon.jones@dft.gsi.gov.uk		
	Emma Boon	020 7944 4377	
	Email: emma.boon@dft.gsi.gov.uk		
Principal Private Secretary	Hannah Newell	020 7944 3011	Fax: 020 7944 4399
	Email: hannah.newell@dft.gsi.gov.uk		

Minister of State for Transport Legislation and Maritime Rt Hon **John Hayes** CBE MP

Maritime policy, including London International Shipping Week; taxi policy; transport legislation and Parliamentary liaison and co-ordination; transport skills.

Private Secretary	Joshua Monahan	020 7944 2637
	Email: joshua.monahan@dft.gsi.gov.uk	

Parliamentary Under-Secretary of State for Rail, Accessibility and HS2 **Paul Maynard** MP

Accessibility across all modes of transport; HS2 policy and legislation; rail; rail security; smart ticketing.

Private Secretary	Hari Rentala	020 7944 4407
	Email: hari.rentala@dft.gsi.gov.uk	

Parliamentary Under-Secretary of State for Roads, Local Transport and Devolution **Jesse Norman** MP

Buses; cycling and walking policy; Highways England and strategic roads; light rail; local roads policy and funding; motoring agencies; road freight; road safety; transport and the environment; transport technology, including digital.

Private Secretary — To be appointed

Parliamentary Under-Secretary of State for Aviation, International and Security **Lord Callanan**

Aviation; corporate issues for the department; international transport; transport legislation in the Lords; transport security.

Private Secretary	Holly Greig	020 7944 4124
	Email: holly.greig2@dft.gsi.gov.uk	

Parliamentary Clerk	James Langston	020 7944 4472	Fax: 020 7944 4466
	Email: james.langston@dft.gsi.gov.uk		

HM Treasury

1 Horse Guards Road, London SW1A 2HQ
Tel: 020 7270 4558 Fax: 020 7270 4861
Email: public.enquiries@hmtreasury.gsi.gov.uk [firstname.surname]@hmtreasury.gsi.gov.uk (Please note: see Private Secretary for Minister's email) Website: www.gov.uk/hm-treasury

Chancellor of the Exchequer Rt Hon **Philip Hammond** MP

Overall responsibility for the work of the Treasury; fiscal policy, including the presenting of the annual Budget; monetary policy, setting inflation targets; ministerial arrangements (in his role as Second Lord of the Treasury).

Parliamentary Private Secretaries

Chancellor of the Exchequer	Kwasi Kwarteng MP	020 7219 4017	Fax: 020 7219 5852
	Email: kwasi.kwarteng.mp@parliament.uk		
Ministerial Team	Suella Fernandes MP	020 7219 8191	
	Email: suella.fernandes.mp@parliament.uk		
	Chris Philp MP	020 7219 8026	
	Email: chris.philp.mp@parliament.uk		

Special Advisers

Duncan McCourt
Email: duncan.mccourt@hmtreasury.gsi.gov.uk

Poppy Trowbridge
Email: poppy.trowbridge@hmtreasury.gsi.gov.uk

Karen Ward
Email: karen.ward@hmtreasury.gsi.gov.uk

Tim Pitt
Email: tim.pitt@hmtreasury.gsi.gov.uk

Jane Ellison
Email: jane.ellison@hmtreasury.gsi.gov.uk

Giles Winn
Email: giles.winn@hmtreasury.gsi.gov.uk

Principal Private Secretary

Stuart Glassborow
Email: action.chancellors@hmtreasury.gsi.gov.uk

Chief Secretary to the Treasury Rt Hon **Elizabeth Truss** MP

Public expenditure, including spending reviews and strategic planning, in-year spending control, public sector pay and pensions, Annually Managed Expenditure (AME) and welfare reform, efficiency and value for money in public service, procurement, capital investment, infrastructure spending, housing and planning, spending issues related to trade, transport policy, including HS2, Crossrail 2, roads, Network Rail, Oxford/Cambridge corridor, Treasury interest in devolution to Scotland, Wales and Northern Ireland; women in the economy; childcare policy, including tax free childcare; tax credits policy; labour market policy.

Private Secretary

Alison Massey
Email: action.cst@hmtreasury.gsi.gov.uk

Financial Secretary; Paymaster General Rt Hon **Mel Stride** MP

Strategic oversight of the UK tax system, including direct, indirect, business, property and personal taxation; corporate and small business taxation; financial services taxation, including bank levy, bank corporation tax surcharge, VAT on financial services, Insurance Premium Tax; European and international tax issues; customs policy, including Customs Bill; National Insurance Bill; departmental minister for HM Revenue and Customs, Valuation Office Agency and Government Actuary's Department; overall responsibility for the Finance Bill; parliamentary deputy on public spending issues.

Private Secretary

Thomas Doherty
Email: fst.action@hmtreasury.gsi.gov.uk

Economic Secretary **Steve Barclay** MP

Banking and financial services reform and regulation: financial stability, including relationship with the PRA, financial conduct, including relationship with the FCA; EU exit financial services; City competitiveness, including Financial Services Trade and Investment Board; retail financial services, including banking competition, consumer finance, financial advice and capability; bank lending and access to finance; personal savings tax and pensions tax policy; insurance; asset management; Women in Finance Charter; UKFI and state owned financial assets (RBS, UKAR); sponsorship of UKGI and sale of government non-financial assets; asset freezing and financial crime; financial inclusion (lead on the government's financial inclusion agenda); Equitable Life; foreign exchange reserves and debt management policy, National Savings and Investments and Debt Management Office; parliamentary deputy on economy issues.

Private Secretary

William Morello
Email: action.est@hmtreasury.gsi.gov.uk

Exchequer Secretary **Andrew Jones** MP

UK growth and productivity: industrial strategy, infrastructure delivery, regional devolution, City deals, Northern Power House and Midlands Engine, promoting UK as a destination for foreign direct investment (non-financial services), better regulation and competition policy, energy policy and climate change, Patient Capital Review, National Infrastructure Commission, Infrastructure and Projects Authority (joint with Cabinet Office); PPPs and PFI; indirect taxes (supporting Financial Secretary to the Treasury as lead tax Minister): excise duties (alcohol, tobacco and gambling), including excise fraud and law enforcement, soft drink industry levy, environment and transport taxation, North Sea oil, gas and shipping; charities, voluntary sector and gift aid; supporting tax legislation in Parliament; Crown Estate and Royal Household; Royal Mint; departmental minister for HM Treasury Group.

Private Secretary	Thea Goodsell Email: action.xst@hmtreasury.gsi.gov.uk	
Parliamentary Clerk	Simon Turrell Email: simon.turrell@hmtreasury.gsi.gov.uk	020 7270 4520

Wales Office

Gwydyr House, Whitehall, London SW1A 2NP
Tel: 020 7270 6137 Email: correspondence@walesoffice.gsi.gov.uk
[firstname.surname]@walesoffice.gsi.gov.uk (Please note: see Private Secretary for Minister's email)
Website: www.gov.uk/wales-office Twitter: @walesoffice/@swyddfacymru

Secretary of State for Wales Rt Hon **Alun Cairns** MP

Overall strategic direction; constitutional and electoral issues; economy and business; budget; infrastructure; foreign affairs; steel; Swansea City Deal/Tidal Lagoon; North Wales Growth Deal/North Wales transport modernisation; broadcasting; exiting the European Union.

Parliamentary Private Secretary	Glyn Davies MP Email: glyn.davies.mp@parliament.uk	020 7219 7112
Special Advisers	Geraint Evans Email: g.evans@walesoffice.gsi.gov.uk	020 7270 0472
	Sophie Traherne Email: sophie.traherne@walesoffice.gsi.gov.uk	020 7270 0535
Principal Private Secretary	Michael Dynan-Oakley Email: secretary.state@walesoffice.gsi.gov.uk	020 7270 0430
Private Secretary	Charis Wilkinson Email: secretary.state@walesoffice.gsi.gov.uk	020 7270 0543

Parliamentary Under-Secretary of State **Guto Bebb** MP

Telecommunications; welfare; Welsh language; heritage and culture; tourism; health; rural affairs; transport; energy; environment.

Private Secretary	Debbie John Email: ukg.ministers@walesoffice.gsi.gov.uk	020 7270 0542

Parliamentary Under-Secretary of State **Lord Duncan of Springbank**

(jointly with Scotland Office) Immigration and social inclusion; defence; local government; localism; education; law and order/justice.

Private Secretary	Debbie John Email: ukg.ministers@walesoffice.gsi.gov.uk	020 7270 0542
Parliamentary Clerk	Louise Newby Email: parly.section@nio.gov.uk	020 7270 0584/020 7210 6551

Department for Work and Pensions

Caxton House, Tothill Street, London SW1H 9DA
Tel: 020 7340 4000
Email: ministers@dwp.gsi.gov.uk (Please note: see Private Secretary for Minister's email)
Website: www.gov.uk/dwp Twitter: @DWP

Secretary of State for Work and Pensions Rt Hon **David Gauke** MP

Overall departmental responsibility.

Parliamentary Private Secretaries

Secretary of State	Peter Heaton-Jones MP Email: peter.heatonjones.mp@parliament.uk	020 7219 5728
Ministerial Team	Huw Merriman MP Email: huw.merriman.mp@parliament.uk	020 7219 1852
Special Advisers	Idil Oyman Email: special-advisers@dwp.gsi.gov.uk	020 3267 5033
	James Dowling Email: special-advisers@dwp.gsi.gov.uk	020 3267 5033
Principal Private Secretary	Robert Specterman-Green Email: secretaryofstate@dwp.gsi.gov.uk	020 3267 5007

Minister of State for Employment **Damian Hinds** MP

Universal Credit, including labour market aspects and overall programme management; employment strategy and labour market interventions, including conditionality and sanctions, youth employment, women's employment, black, Asian and minority ethnic employment, Fuller Working Lives and New Enterprise Allowance; Jobcentre Plus, partnership working and employer engagement; EU and international affairs; support to the Secretary of State on devolution.

Private Secretary	Farhad Chikhalia Email: minister.employment@dwp.gsi.gov.uk	020 3267 5019

Minister of State for Disabled People, Health and Work **Penny Mordaunt** MP

Cross-government disability issues; work and health strategy; disability employment, including Disability Confident, Work Choice, Access to Work, Work and Health Programme and mental health in the workplace; support for those at risk of falling out of work, including occupational health and Statutory Sick Pay; financial support for sick and disabled claimants, including within Universal Credit, Disability Living Allowance, Personal Independence Payment, Employment and Support Allowance, Attendance Allowance, Industrial Injuries Disablement Benefit and Carer's Allowance; specific welfare and health-related issues, including Motability and arms-length compensation schemes; oversight of the Health and Safety Executive and Office for Nuclear Regulation.

Private Secretary	Chris Ramm Email: minister.disabledpeople@dwp.gsi.gov.uk	020 3267 5040

Parliamentary Under-Secretary of State for Pensions and Financial Inclusion **Guy Opperman** MP

Pensioner benefits, including new State Pension, Winter Fuel Payments and Pension Credit; State Pension age review; financial inclusion and guidance, including Single Financial Guidance Body, Credit Union Expansion Project and Post Office Card Accounts; private and occupational pensions, including regulatory powers, Automatic Enrolment and National Employment Savings Trust (NEST); oversight of arms-length bodies, including Pensions Regulator, Pension Protection Fund, Financial Assistance Scheme and Pensions Ombudsman.

Private Secretary	Catherine Hayes Email: minister.pensions@dwp.gsi.gov.uk	020 3267 5027

Parliamentary Under-Secretary of State for Family Support, Housing and Child Maintenance

Caroline Dinenage MP

Cross-DWP Commons spokesperson; family policy issues, including relationship support; childcare and maternity benefits and child maintenance; support for disadvantaged groups; financial support for housing, including within Universal Credit; other social assistance, including supported accommodation, Support for Mortgage Interest, Cold Weather Payments, bereavement benefits and funeral payments; benefit cap implementation and benefit uprating.

Private Secretary	Camilla Thompsell Email: minister.familiesandhousing@dwp.gsi.gov.uk	020 7867 3104

Parliamentary Under-Secretary of State (Lords) **Baroness Buscombe**

Cross-DWP Lords spokesperson; fraud, error and debt strategy; National Insurance number policy; oversight of departmental statutory instruments and managing the relationship with the Social Security Advisory Committee; departmental planning and performance management, including ministerial correspondence; departmental business, including commercial contracting policy, methods of payment policy, transparency and data-sharing, research and trialling, IT security and application of the Military Covenant.

Private Secretary	Mel Sinclair Email: minister.lords@dwp.gsi.gov.uk	020 3267 5035
Parliamentary Clerk	Howard Sargent Email: howard.sargent@dwp.gsi.gov.uk	020 3267 5053

Ministerial Committees of the Cabinet

Economy and Industrial Strategy Committee
Chair: Prime Minister, First Lord of the Treasury and Minister for the Civil Service
Deputy chair: First Secretary of State and Minister for the Cabinet Office

Economy and Industrial Strategy (Airports) Sub-committee
Chair: Prime Minister, First Lord of the Treasury and Minister for the Civil Service

Economy and Industrial Strategy (Economic Affairs) Sub-committee
Chair: Chancellor of the Exchequer

Economy and Industrial Strategy (Reducing Regulation) Sub-committee
Chair: Secretary of State for Business, Energy and Industrial Strategy

European Union Exit and Trade Committee
Chair: Prime Minister, First Lord of the Treasury and Minister for the Civil Service
Deputy chair: First Secretary of State and Minister for the Cabinet Office

European Union Exit and Trade (Negotiations) Sub-Committee
Chair: Prime Minister, First Lord of the Treasury and Minister for the Civil Service

European Union Exit and Trade (International Trade) Sub-Committee
Chair: First Secretary of State and Minister for the Cabinet Office

European Union Exit and Trade (European Affairs) Sub-committee
Chair: First Secretary of State and Minister for the Cabinet Office

National Security Council
Chair: Prime Minister, First Lord of the Treasury and Minister for the Civil Service

NSC (Nuclear Deterrence and Security) Sub-committee
Chair: Prime Minister, First Lord of the Treasury and Minister for the Civil Service

NSC (Threats, Hazards, Resilience and Contingencies) Sub-committee
Chair: First Secretary of State and Minister for the Cabinet Office

NSC (Strategic Defence and Security Review Implementation) Sub-committee
Chair: Secretary of State for the Home Department

Parliamentary Business and Legislation Committee
Chair: Leader of the House of Commons; Lord President of the Council

Social Reform Committee
Chair: Prime Minister, First Lord of the Treasury and Minister for the Civil Service
Deputy chair: First Secretary of State and Minister for the Cabinet Office

Social Reform (Home Affairs) Sub-committee
Chair: First Secretary of State and Minister for the Cabinet Office

Implementation Taskforces

Digital
Chair: First Secretary of State and Minister for the Cabinet Office

Employment and Skills
Chair: First Secretary of State and Minister for the Cabinet Office

Housing
Chair: First Secretary of State and Minister for the Cabinet Office

Immigration
Chair: First Secretary of State and Minister for the Cabinet Office

Tackling Modern Slavery and People Trafficking
Chair: Prime Minister, First Lord of the Treasury and Minister for the Civil Service
Deputy chair: Secretary of State for the Home Department

Parliamentary Private Secretaries

Prime Minister's Office

Theresa May, Prime Minister	George Hollingbery 020 7219 7109 Email: george.hollingbery.mp@parliament.uk Seema Kennedy 020 7219 4412 Email: seema.kennedy.mp@parliament.uk

Business, Energy and Industrial Strategy

Greg Clark, Secretary of State	Kelly Tolhurst 020 7219 5387 Email: kelly.tolhurst.mp@parliament.uk
Ministerial Team	Rishi Sunak 020 7219 5437 Email: rishi.sunak.mp@parliament.uk

Cabinet Office

Damian Green, First Secretary of State	James Morris 020 7219 8715 Fax: 020 7219 1429 Email: james.morris.mp@parliament.uk
Ministerial Team	Will Quince 020 7219 8049 Email: will.quince.mp@parliament.uk
Patrick McLoughlin, Chancellor of the Duchy of Lancaster	Edward Argar 020 7219 8140 Email: edward.argar.mp@parliament.uk

Communities and Local Government

Sajid Javid, Secretary of State	Mims Davies 020 7219 6853 Email: mims.davies.mp@parliament.uk
Ministerial Team	Kevin Foster 020 7219 4711 Email: kevin.foster.mp@parliament.uk

Defence

Michael Fallon, Secretary of State	Oliver Dowden 020 7219 3415 Email: oliver.dowden.mp@parliament.uk
Ministerial Team	Anne-Marie Trevelyan 020 7219 4437 Email: annemarie.trevelyan.mp@parliament.uk

Digital, Culture, Media and Sport

Karen Bradley, Secretary of State	Matt Warman 020 7219 8643 Email: matt.warman.mp@parliament.uk
Ministerial Team	Nigel Huddleston 020 7219 5814 Email: nigel.huddleston.mp@parliament.uk

Education

Justine Greening, Secretary of State

Ministerial Team

Helen Whately
020 7219 6472
Email: helen.whately.mp@parliament.uk
Luke Hall
020 7219 4741
Email: luke.hall.mp@parliament.uk

Environment, Food and Rural Affairs

Michael Gove, Secretary of State

Ministerial Team

Kevin Hollinrake
020 7219 4746
Email: kevin.hollinrake.mp@parliament.uk
Rebecca Pow
020 7219 4831
Email: rebecca.pow.mp@parliament.uk

Exiting the European Union

David Davis, Secretary of State

Ministerial Team

Gareth Johnson
020 7219 7047
Email: gareth.johnson.mp@parliament.uk
Jeremy Quin
020 7219 6341
Email: jeremy.quin.mp@parliament.uk

Foreign and Commonwealth Office

Boris Johnson, Secretary of State

Ministerial Team

Conor Burns
020 7219 7021
Email: conor.burns.mp@parliament.uk
Amanda Milling
020 7219 8356
Email: amanda.milling.mp@parliament.uk

Health

Jeremy Hunt, Secretary of State

Ministerial Team

Jo Churchill
020 7219 8487
Email: jo.churchill.mp@parliament.uk
James Cartlidge
020 7219 4875
Email: james.cartlidge.mp@parliament.uk

Home Office

Amber Rudd, Secretary of State

Robert Jenrick
020 7219 7335
Email: robert.jenrick.mp@parliament.uk

Brandon Lewis, Minister of State

James Cleverly
020 7219 8593
Email: james.cleverly.mp@parliament.uk

Ministerial Team

Nusrat Ghani
020 7219 4619
Email: nusrat.ghani.mp@parliament.uk
Simon Hoare
020 7219 5697
Email: simon.hoare.mp@parliament.uk

International Development

Priti Patel, Secretary of State	Wendy Morton 020 7219 8784 Email: wendy.morton.mp@parliament.uk
Ministerial Team	Michael Tomlinson 020 7219 5844 Email: michael.tomlinson.mp@parliament.uk

International Trade

Liam Fox, Secretary of State	Tom Pursglove 020 7219 8043 Email: tom.pursglove.mp@parliament.uk
Ministerial Team	Mike Wood 020 7219 6982 Email: mikej.wood.mp@parliament.uk

Justice

David Lidington, Lord Chancellor and Secretary of State	Lucy Frazer 020 7219 5082 Email: lucy.frazer.mp@parliament.uk
Ministerial Team	Alan Mak 020 7219 6266 Email: alan.mak.mp@parliament.uk

Law Officers

Jeremy Wright, Attorney General	Michelle Donelan 020 7219 4451 Email: michelle.donelan.mp@parliament.uk

Leader of the House of Commons

Andrea Leadsom, Leader of the House of Commons	Victoria Prentis 020 7219 8756 Email: victoria.prentis.mp@parliament.uk

Leader of the House of Lords

Baroness Evans of Bowes Park, Leader of the House of Lords	Victoria Atkins 020 7219 5897

Northern Ireland Office

James Brokenshire, Secretary of State	David Morris 020 7219 7234 Email: david.morris.mp@parliament.uk

Scotland Office

David Mundell, Secretary of State	Alberto Costa 020 7219 4936 Email: barronra@parliament.uk

Transport

Chris Grayling, Secretary of State

Ministerial Team

James Heappey
020 7219 4289
Email: james.heappey.mp@parliament.uk
Scott Mann
020 7219 5744
Email: scott.mann.mp@parliament.uk

HM Treasury

Philip Hammond, Chancellor of the Exchequer

Ministerial Team

Kwasi Kwarteng
020 7219 4017 Fax: 020 7219 5852
Email: kwasi.kwarteng.mp@parliament.uk
Chris Philp
020 7219 8026
Email: chris.philp.mp@parliament.uk
Suella Fernandes
020 7219 8191
Email: suella.fernandes.mp@parliament.uk

Wales Office

Alun Cairns, Secretary of State

Glyn Davies
020 7219 7112
Email: glyn.davies.mp@parliament.uk

Work and Pensions

David Gauke, Secretary of State

Ministerial Team

Peter Heaton-Jones
020 7219 5728
Email: peter.heatonjones.mp@parliament.uk
Huw Merriman
020 7219 1852
Email: huw.merriman.mp@parliament.uk

Special Advisers

Prime Minister's Office

Theresa May, Prime Minister

Gavin Barwell
Joanna Penn
Robbie Gibb
Nikki Da Costa
Richard Jackson
James Marshall
Alex Dawson
Denzil Davidson

Business, Energy and Industrial Strategy

Greg Clark, Secretary of State

Jacob Willmer
020 7215 6629
mpst.clarkspad@beis.gov.uk
Glenn Hall
020 7215 6629
mpst.clarkspad@beis.gov.uk

Cabinet Office

Damian Green, First Secretary of State

Flora Rose
020 7276 7649
specialadvisers@cabinetoffice.gov.uk
Dylan Sharpe
020 7271 3121
specialadvisers@cabinetoffice.gov.uk
Paul Holmes
020 7276 0721
specialadvisers@cabinetoffice.gov.uk

Communities and Local Government

Sajid Javid, Secretary of State

Nick King
030 3444 3165
nick.king@communities.gsi.gov.uk
Salma Shah
030 3444 3165
salma.shah@communities.gsi.gov.uk
James Hedgeland
030 3444 3165
james.hedgeland@communities.gsi.gov.uk

Defence

Michael Fallon, Secretary of State

Robert Oxley
020 7218 2554
sofs-specialadvisersgroup@mod.uk
James Wild
020 7218 2554
sofs-specialadvisersgroup@mod.uk

Digital, Culture, Media and Sport

Karen Bradley, Secretary of State

Aidan Corley
special.advisers@culture.gov.uk

Education

Justine Greening, Secretary of State

Peter Wilson
advisers.ps@education.gov.uk
Victoria Crawford
advisers.ps@education.gov.uk

Environment, Food and Rural Affairs

Michael Gove, Secretary of State

Henry Cook
020 8026 9909
ps.advisers@defra.gsi.gov.uk

Exiting the European Union

David Davis, Secretary of State

Tim Smith
Raoul Ruparel
Stewart Jackson

Foreign and Commonwealth Office

Boris Johnson, Secretary of State

David Frost
020 7008 2117/020 7008 2312
pospads@fco.gsi.gov.uk
Ben Gascoigne
020 7008 2117/020 7008 2312
pospads@fco.gsi.gov.uk
Liam Parker
020 7008 2117/020 7008 2312
pospads@fco.gsi.gov.uk

Health

Jeremy Hunt, Secretary of State

Ed Jones
020 7210 5945
specialadvisors@dh.gsi.gov.uk

Home Office

Amber Rudd, Secretary of State

Mo Hussein
020 7035 0196
specialadvisers@homeoffice.gsi.gov.uk
Simon Glasson
020 7035 0196
specialadvisers@homeoffice.gsi.gov.uk
Amy Fisher
020 7035 0196
specialadvisers@homeoffice.gsi.gov.uk

International Development

Priti Patel, Secretary of State

Richard Parr
020 7023 0114
special-advisers@dfid.gov.uk

International Trade

Liam Fox, Secretary of State

Amy Tinley
mpst.foxspad@trade.gsi.gov.uk
David Goss
mpst.foxspad@trade.gsi.gov.uk

Justice

David Lidington, Lord Chancellor and Secretary of State

Fraser Raleigh
advisers@justice.gov.uk
Anita Boateng
advisers@justice.gov.uk

Leader of the House of Commons

Andrea Leadsom, Leader of the House of Commons

Marc Pooler
Lucia Hodgson

Leader of the House of Lords

Baroness Evans of Bowes Park, Leader of the House of Lords

Tom Pretty
020 7219 0267
thomas.pretty@cabinetoffice.gov.uk
Katharine Howell
020 7219 1205
katharine.howell@cabinetoffice.gov.uk
Annabelle Eyre
020 7219 1046
annabelle.eyre@cabinetoffice.gov.uk

Northern Ireland Office

James Brokenshire, Secretary of State

Lord Caine
020 7210 0803/028 9052 7007
jonathan.caine@nio.gov.uk
Peter Cardwell
020 7210 6534
peter.cardwell@nio.gov.uk

Scotland Office

David Mundell, Secretary of State

Jenny Donnellan
020 7270 6814
sospecialadvisers@scotlandoffice.gsi.gov.uk
Magnus Gardham
020 7270 6814
sospecialadvisers@scotlandoffice.gsi.gov.uk

Transport

Chris Grayling, Secretary of State

Simon Jones
020 7944 4377
simon.jones@dft.gsi.gov.uk
Emma Boon
020 7944 4377
emma.boon@dft.gsi.gov.uk

HM Treasury

Philip Hammond, Chancellor of the Exchequer

Duncan McCourt
duncan.mccourt@hmtreasury.gsi.gov.uk
Poppy Trowbridge
poppy.trowbridge@hmtreasury.gsi.gov.uk

Karen Ward
karen.ward@hmtreasury.gsi.gov.uk
Tim Pitt
tim.pitt@hmtreasury.gsi.gov.uk
Jane Ellison
jane.ellison@hmtreasury.gsi.gov.uk
Giles Winn
giles.winn@hmtreasury.gsi.gov.uk

Wales Office

Alun Cairns, Secretary of State

Geraint Evans
020 7270 0472
g.evans@walesoffice.gsi.gov.uk
Sophie Traherne
020 7270 0535
sophie.traherne@walesoffice.gsi.gov.uk

Work and Pensions

David Gauke, Secretary of State

Idil Oyman
020 3267 5033
special-advisers@dwp.gsi.gov.uk
James Dowling
020 3267 5033
special-advisers@dwp.gsi.gov.uk

The Opposition

Labour (official opposition)

Shadow Cabinet

Leader of the Opposition	Rt Hon **Jeremy Corbyn** MP
Deputy Leader of the Labour Party; Shadow Secretary of State for Digital, Culture, Media and Sport	**Tom Watson** MP
Shadow Chancellor of the Exchequer	Rt Hon **John McDonnell** MP
Shadow Secretary of State for Foreign and Commonwealth Affairs (Shadow Foreign Secretary)	Rt Hon **Emily Thornberry** MP
Shadow Secretary of State for the Home Department (Shadow Home Secretary)	Rt Hon **Diane Abbott** MP
Shadow Lord President of the Council and Shadow Minister for the Cabinet Office	**Jon Trickett** MP
Shadow Secretary of State for Business, Energy and Industrial Strategy	**Rebecca Long-Bailey** MP
Shadow Secretary of State for Education	**Angela Rayner** MP
Shadow Secretary of State for International Development	**Kate Osamor** MP
Shadow Secretary of State for Exiting the European Union	Rt Hon Sir **Keir Starmer** KCB QC MP
Shadow Lord Chancellor and Secretary of State for Justice	**Richard Burgon** MP
Shadow Secretary of State for Environment, Food and Rural Affairs	**Sue Hayman** MP
Shadow Minister for Voter Engagement and Youth Affairs; Shadow Minister for Transport	**Cat Smith** MP
Shadow Leader of the House of Lords	Rt Hon **Baroness Smith of Basildon**
Shadow Leader of the House of Commons	**Valerie Vaz** MP
Shadow Secretary of State for Housing	Rt Hon **John Healey** MP
Shadow Chief Whip in the House of Lords	Rt Hon **Lord Bassam of Brighton**
Shadow Secretary of State for Work and Pensions	**Debbie Abrahams** MP
Shadow Secretary of State for Health	**Jon Ashworth** MP
Shadow Secretary of State for Communities and Local Government; National Campaign Co-ordinator	**Andrew Gwynne** MP
Shadow Secretary of State for Women and Equalities	**Dawn Butler** MP
Shadow Chief Secretary to the Treasury	**Peter Dowd** MP
Shadow Secretary of State for Wales	**Christina Rees** MP
Shadow Secretary of State for Transport	**Andy McDonald** MP
National Campaign Co-ordinator; Party Chair	**Ian Lavery** MP
Opposition Chief Whip	Rt Hon **Nick Brown** MP
Shadow Secretary of State for Defence	**Nia Griffith** MP
Shadow Attorney General	**Baroness Chakrabarti** CBE

Shadow Secretary of State for International Trade	**Barry Gardiner** MP
Shadow Minister for Mental Health and Social Care	**Barbara Keeley** MP
Shadow Secretary of State for Scotland	**Lesley Laird** MP
Shadow Secretary of State for Northern Ireland	**Owen Smith** MP

Shadow Ministers

Leader's Office

Leader of the Opposition	Rt Hon **Jeremy Corbyn** MP

Business, Energy and Industrial Strategy

Shadow Secretary of State	**Rebecca Long-Bailey** MP
Shadow Ministers	**Barry Gardiner** MP
	Chi Onwurah MP
	Dr **Alan Whitehead** MP
	Bill Esterson MP
	Gill Furniss MP
	Jack Dromey MP
	Lord Mendelsohn
	Baroness Hayter of Kentish Town
	Lord Grantchester

Cabinet Office

Shadow Lord President	**Jon Trickett** MP
Shadow Ministers	**Cat Smith** MP
	Ian Lavery MP
	Rt Hon **Lord Hunt of Kings Heath** OBE

Communities and Local Government

Shadow Secretary of State	**Andrew Gwynne** MP
Shadow Ministers	**Jim McMahon** OBE MP
	Yvonne Fovargue MP
	Lord Kennedy of Southwark
	Lord Beecham

Defence

Shadow Secretary of State	**Nia Griffith** MP
Shadow Ministers	**Fabian Hamilton** MP
	Wayne David MP
	Gerald Jones MP
	Rt Hon **Lord Touhig**
	Lord Tunnicliffe CBE

Digital, Culture, Media and Sport

Shadow Secretary of State	**Tom Watson** MP
Shadow Ministers	**Kevin Brennan** MP
	Dr **Rosena Allin-Khan** MP
	Rt Hon **Liam Byrne** MP
	Steve Reed OBE MP
	Lord Griffiths of Burry Port

Education

Shadow Secretary of State	**Angela Rayner** MP
Shadow Ministers	**Gordon Marsden** MP
	Mike Kane MP
	Emma Lewell-Buck MP
	Tracy Brabin MP
	Lord Watson of Invergowrie
	Rt Hon **Lord Hunt of Kings Heath** OBE

Environment, Food and Rural Affairs

Shadow Secretary of State	**Sue Hayman** MP
Shadow Ministers	Dr **David Drew** MP
	Holly Lynch MP
	Baroness Jones of Whitchurch
	Lord Grantchester

Exiting the European Union

Shadow Secretary of State	Rt Hon Sir **Keir Starmer** KCB QC MP
Shadow Ministers	**Jenny Chapman** MP
	Matthew Pennycook MP
	Paul Blomfield MP
	Baroness Hayter of Kentish Town

Foreign and Commonwealth Office

Shadow Foreign Secretary	Rt Hon **Emily Thornberry** MP
Shadow Ministers	**Fabian Hamilton** MP
	Liz McInnes MP
	Helen Goodman MP
	Khalid Mahmood MP
	Lord Collins of Highbury

Health

Shadow Secretary of State	**Jon Ashworth** MP
Shadow Ministers	**Sharon Hodgson** MP
	Barbara Keeley MP
	Julie Cooper MP
	Justin Madders MP
	Rt Hon **Lord Hunt of Kings Heath** OBE

Home Office

Shadow Home Secretary	Rt Hon **Diane Abbott** MP
Shadow Ministers	**Nick Thomas-Symonds** MP
	Chris Williamson MP
	Afzal Khan MP
	Louise Haigh MP
	Lord Rosser
	Lord Kennedy of Southwark

Housing

Shadow Secretary of State	Rt Hon **John Healey** MP
Shadow Ministers	**Tony Lloyd** MP
	Melanie Onn MP
	Lord Kennedy of Southwark
	Lord Beecham

International Development

Shadow Secretary of State	**Kate Osamor** MP
Shadow Ministers	Dr **Roberta Blackman-Woods** MP
	Lord Collins of Highbury

International Trade

Shadow Secretary of State	**Barry Gardiner** MP
Shadow Ministers	**Bill Esterson** MP
	Lord Mendelsohn

Justice

Shadow Lord Chancellor and Secretary of State	**Richard Burgon** MP
Shadow Ministers	**Yasmin Qureshi** MP
	Gloria De Piero MP
	Imran Hussain MP
	Lord Beecham

Law Officers

Shadow Attorney General	**Baroness Chakrabarti** CBE
Shadow Solicitor General	**Nick Thomas-Symonds** MP
Shadow Advocate General for Scotland	**Lord Davidson of Glen Clova** QC

Leader of the House of Commons

Shadow Leader	**Valerie Vaz** MP
Shadow Deputy Leader	**Karin Smyth** MP

Leader of the House of Lords

Shadow Leader	Rt Hon **Baroness Smith of Basildon**
Shadow Deputy Leader	**Baroness Hayter of Kentish Town**

Northern Ireland

Shadow Secretary of State	**Owen Smith** MP
Shadow Ministers	**Stephen Pound** MP
	Rt Hon **Lord McAvoy**

Scotland

Shadow Secretary of State	**Lesley Laird** MP
Shadow Ministers	**Paul Sweeney** MP
	Rt Hon **Lord McAvoy**

Transport

Shadow Secretary of State	**Andy McDonald** MP
Shadow Ministers	**Cat Smith** MP
	Rachael Maskell MP
	Karl Turner MP
	Lord Rosser

Treasury	
Shadow Chancellor of the Exchequer	Rt Hon **John McDonnell** MP
Shadow Chief Secretary	**Peter Dowd** MP
Shadow Economic Secretary	**Jonathan Reynolds** MP
Shadow Ministers	**Anneliese Dodds** MP Rt Hon **Lord Davies of Oldham** **Lord Tunnicliffe** CBE **Lord Davidson of Glen Clova** QC
Wales	
Shadow Secretary of State	**Christina Rees** MP
Shadow Ministers	**Chris Ruane** MP **Lord Griffiths of Burry Port**
Women and Equalities	
Shadow Secretary of State	**Dawn Butler** MP
Shadow Ministers	**Paula Sherriff** MP **Carolyn Harris** MP **Baroness Gale**
Work and Pensions	
Shadow Secretary of State	**Debbie Abrahams** MP
Shadow Ministers	**Alex Cunningham** MP **Marie Rimmer** CBE MP **Margaret Greenwood** MP **Baroness Sherlock** OBE **Lord McKenzie of Luton**

Opposition Commons Whips

Chief Whip	Rt Hon **Nick Brown**
Deputy Chief Whip	Rt Hon **Alan Campbell**
Assistant Chief Whip	**Mark Tami**
Whips	**Jessica Morden** **Judith Cummins** **Vicky Foxcroft** **Jeff Smith** **Thangam Debbonaire** **Nick Smith** **Chris Elmore** **Nic Dakin** **Colleen Fletcher**

Opposition Lords Spokespeople

Leader of the Opposition	Rt Hon **Baroness Smith of Basildon**
Deputy Leader of the Opposition	**Baroness Hayter of Kentish Town**
Business, Energy and Industrial Strategy	**Baroness Hayter of Kentish Town** **Lord Mendelsohn** **Lord Grantchester**
Cabinet Office	Rt Hon **Lord Hunt of Kings Heath** OBE
Communities and Local Government	**Lord Kennedy of Southwark** **Lord Beecham**

Constitutional Affairs	Rt Hon **Baroness Smith of Basildon** **Baroness Hayter of Kentish Town**
Defence	Rt Hon **Lord Touhig** **Lord Tunnicliffe** CBE
Digital, Culture, Media and Sport	**Lord Griffiths of Burry Port**
Education (Further and Higher Education)	**Lord Watson of Invergowrie** Rt Hon **Lord Hunt of Kings Heath** OBE
Environment, Food and Rural Affairs	**Lord Grantchester** **Baroness Jones of Whitchurch**
Exiting the European Union	**Baroness Hayter of Kentish Town**
Foreign and Commonwealth Office	**Lord Collins of Highbury**
Health	Rt Hon **Lord Hunt of Kings Heath** OBE **Baroness Wheeler** MBE
Home Office	**Lord Rosser** **Lord Kennedy of Southwark**
Housing	**Lord Kennedy of Southwark** **Lord Beecham**
International Development	**Lord Collins of Highbury**
International Trade	**Lord Mendelsohn**
Justice	**Lord Beecham**
Law Officers	**Lord Davidson of Glen Clova** QC **Baroness Chakrabarti** CBE
Northern Ireland	Rt Hon **Lord McAvoy**
Scotland	Rt Hon **Lord McAvoy**
Transport	**Lord Rosser**
Treasury	Rt Hon **Lord Davies of Oldham** **Lord Tunnicliffe** CBE **Lord Davidson of Glen Clova** QC
Wales	**Lord Griffiths of Burry Port**
Women and Equalities	**Baroness Gale**
Work and Pensions	**Baroness Sherlock** OBE **Lord McKenzie of Luton**

Opposition Lords Whips

Chief Whip	Rt Hon **Lord Bassam of Brighton**
Deputy Chief Whips	**Lord Tunnicliffe** CBE Rt Hon **Lord McAvoy**
Senior Whips	**Baroness Wheeler** MBE **Baroness Sherlock** OBE
Whips	**Lord Collins of Highbury** **Lord Kennedy of Southwark** **Lord Stevenson of Balmacara** **Lord Lennie** **Lord Griffiths of Burry Port**

Scottish National Party

Westminster Group Leadership

Group Leader	Rt Hon **Ian Blackford**
Deputy Group Leader; Spokesperson for Economy	**Kirsty Blackman**
Chief Whip	**Patrick Grady**
International Affairs and Europe	**Stephen Gethins**
Trade and Investment	**Hannah Bardell**
Social Justice	**Neil Gray**
Treasury and Cities	**Alison Thewliss**
Business, Energy and Industrial Strategy	**Drew Hendry**
Justice and Home Affairs	**Joanna Cherry QC**
Health	Dr **Philippa Whitford**
Devolved Government Relations; Northern Ireland; Fair Work and Employment	**Deidre Brock**
Culture and Media	**Brendan O'Hara**

Spokespeople

Small Business, Enterprise and Innovation	**Marion Fellows**
Industries for the Future	**Martin Docherty-Hughes**
Pensions and Youth Affairs	**Mhairi Black**
House of Lords; Scotland; Cabinet Office	**Tommy Sheppard**
Equalities, Women and Children, Family Support, Housing, Child Maintenance and Disability	**Angela Crawley**
Europe	**Peter Grant**
Consumer Affairs	**Patricia Gibson**
International Development and Climate Justice	**Chris Law**
Transport, Infrastructure and Energy	**Alan Brown**
Environment and Rural Affairs	**Angus MacNeil**
Immigration, Asylum and Border Control	**Stuart C McDonald**
Education, Armed Forces and Veterans	**Carol Monaghan**
Sport	**Gavin Newlands**
Defence	**Stewart Malcolm McDonald**
Defence Procurement	**Douglas Chapman**
Mental Health	Dr **Lisa Cameron**
Shadow Leader of the House; Spokesperson for Constitution	**Pete Wishart**
Trade Unions and Workers' Rights	**Chris Stephens**

Whips

Chief Whip	**Patrick Grady**
Deputy Whips	**Marion Fellows** **David Linden**

Liberal Democrats

Shadow Cabinet

Leader	Rt Hon Sir **Vince Cable** MP
Deputy Leader; Shadow Foreign Secretary	**Jo Swinson** MP
President	**Baroness Brinton**
Shadow First Secretary of State; Shadow Secretary of State for Exiting the European Union and International Trade	Rt Hon **Tom Brake** MP
Shadow Chancellor of the Exchequer	**To be appointed**
Shadow Home Secretary	Rt Hon Sir **Ed Davey** MP
Shadow Secretary of State for Health	Rt Hon **Norman Lamb** MP
Shadow Secretary of State for Education and Young People	**Layla Moran** MP
Shadow Secretary of State for Communities and Local Government and Refugees	**Wera Hobhouse** MP
Shadow Secretary of State for Culture, Media and Sport	**Christine Jardine** MP
Shadow Secretary of State for Work and Pensions	**Stephen Lloyd** MP
Spokesperson for Exiting the European Union (Lords)	**Baroness Ludford**
Shadow Secretary of State for Scotland	**Jamie Stone** MP
Chief Whip; Shadow Secretary of State for Northern Ireland	Rt Hon **Alistair Carmichael** MP
Lead Spokesperson for Energy and Climate Change	Rt Hon **Baroness Featherstone**
Shadow Secretary of State for Environment, Food and Rural Affairs	**Baroness Parminter**
Shadow Secretary of State for Business, Energy and Industrial Strategy	**Lord Fox**
Shadow Secretary of State for Defence	**Baroness Jolly**
Shadow Secretary of State for Transport	**Baroness Randerson**
Shadow Secretary of State for International Development	**Baroness Sheehan**
Shadow Secretary of State for Equalities	**Baroness Burt of Solihull**
Shadow Lord Chancellor and Secretary of State for Justice	**Lord Marks of Henley-on-Thames** QC
Shadow Secretary of State for Wales	**Baroness Humphreys**
Leader of the House of Lords	Rt Hon **Lord Newby** OBE
Lords Chief Whip	**Lord Stoneham of Droxford**

Lords Spokespeople

Leader	Rt Hon **Lord Newby** OBE
Deputy Leaders	**Baroness Parminter** Rt Hon **Lord Dholakia** OBE DL
Business and Industrial Strategy	**Lord Fox**
Cabinet Office	Rt Hon **Lord Wallace of Saltaire**

Communities and Local Government	**Baroness Pinnock**
Constitutional and Political Reform	Rt Hon **Lord Tyler** CBE
Culture, Media, Sport and Tourism	**Baroness Bonham-Carter of Yarnbury**
Defence	**Baroness Jolly**
Education	**Lord Storey** CBE
Energy and Climate Change	Rt Hon **Baroness Featherstone**
Environment, Food and Rural Affairs	**Baroness Parminter**
Equalities	**Baroness Burt of Solihull**
Exiting the European Union	**Baroness Ludford**
Foreign and Commonwealth Affairs	Rt Hon **Baroness Northover**
Health	**Baroness Walmsley**
Home Affairs	**Lord Paddick**
Housing	**Lord Shipley** OBE
International Development	**Baroness Sheehan**
International Trade	**Lord Purvis of Tweed**
Justice	**Lord Marks of Henley-on-Thames** QC
Law Officers (Shadow Attorney General)	**Lord Thomas of Gresford** OBE QC
Northern Ireland	**Baroness Suttie**
Scotland	Rt Hon **Lord Bruce of Bennachie**
Transport	**Baroness Randerson**
Treasury	Rt Hon **Baroness Kramer**
Wales	**Baroness Humphreys**
Mental Health	**Baroness Tyler of Enfield**
Work and Pensions	**Baroness Bakewell of Hardington Mandeville** MBE

Democratic Unionist Party

Parliamentary Group Leader; Exiting the European Union; Constitutional Issues; Foreign Affairs	Rt Hon **Nigel Dodds** OBE
International Development; Cabinet Office	**Gregory Campbell**
Business in the House of Commons; Chief Whip	Rt Hon Sir **Jeffrey Donaldson**
Education; Transport	**Paul Girvan**
Equality; Justice; International Trade	**Emma Little Pengelly**
Culture Media and Sport; Communities and Local Government	**Ian Paisley**
Defence; Home Affairs	**Gavin Robinson**
Human Rights; Health	**Jim Shannon**
Business, Energy and Industrial Strategy; Environment, Food and Rural Affairs	**David Simpson**
Exiting the European Union; Treasury; Work and Pensions	**Sammy Wilson**

Plaid Cymru (The Party of Wales)

Parliamentary Group Leader; Home Affairs; Justice; Women and Equalities; Business, Energy and Industrial Strategy	**Liz Saville Roberts**
Exiting the European Union; International Trade; Work and Pensions; Cabinet Office	**Hywel Williams**
Treasury; Foreign Affairs; Defence; Transport; International Development; Whip	**Jonathan Edwards**
Education and Skills; Health; Communities and Local Government; Constitutional Affairs; Culture, Media and Sport	**Ben Lake**

Crossbench

Convenor	Rt Hon the **Lord Hope of Craighead** KT

Salaried Parliamentarians 2017–18

The Independent Parliamentary Standards Authority (IPSA) was created in 2009 and has two roles – to regulate the expenses system and to administer and pay MPs' expenses and salaries.

Most Members of the House of Lords do not receive a salary for carrying out their Parliamentary duties. They are entitled to claim a daily allowance of £300 for each qualifying day of attendance at Westminster.

	Annual salary from 1 April 2017 (£)
Member of Parliament	76,011

With effect from 1 April each year, starting with 1 April 2016, the MP salary will be adjusted by the rate of annual change in public sector average earnings.

If an MP holds office, as listed below, they are entitled to receive an additional annual salary.

Office	Annual salary (£)
Prime Minister	77,896

	Salary if a member of the House of Commons (£)	Salary if a member of the House of Lords (no parliamentary salary) (£)
Chancellor of the Exchequer	69,844	
First Secretary of State and Minister for the Cabinet Office	69,844	
Lord Chancellor	69,844	
Secretary of State	69,844	
Chief Secretary to the Treasury	33,490	
Government Deputy Chief Whip	33,490	
Lord President of the Council and Leader of the House of Commons	33,490	
Financial Secretary to the Treasury and Paymaster General	33,490	
Minister of State	33,490	
Parliamentary Secretary to the Treasury (Chief Whip)	33,490	
Economic Secretary	24,048	
Exchequer Secretary	24,048	
Parliamentary Secretary	24,048	
Parliamentary Under-Secretary of State	24,048	
Attorney General	97,186	
Solicitor General	60,122	
Government Whip	19,523	
Assistant Government Whip	19,523	
Leader of the House of Lords, Lord Privy Seal		102,530
Minister of State		80,056
Parliamentary Secretary		69,725
Parliamentary Under-Secretary of State		69,725
Advocate General for Scotland		93,110
Government Lords Chief Whip		80,056
Government Lords Deputy Chief Whip		69,725
Lord/Baroness in Waiting		64,475
Leader of the Opposition	64,030	
Opposition Chief Whip	33,490	
Opposition Deputy Chief Whip	19,532	
Opposition Assistant Whip	19,532	
Speaker	76,886	102,101
Deputy Speaker:		
Chairman of Ways and Means	41,981	
First Deputy Chairman of Ways and Means	36,896	
Second Deputy Chairman of Ways and Means	36,896	
Select Committee Chair	15,235	
Member of Panel of Chairs	15,235	
Chairman of Committees (Senior Deputy Speaker)		84,524
Principal Deputy Chairman of Committees		79,076

The number of paid Ministerial posts is limited to 109. The Government may appoint additional Ministers; however, these will be unpaid appointments.

MP ALLOWANCES

For the full guide see:
http://www.theipsa.org.uk/mp-costs

Accommodation

MPs can claim for accommodation costs either in London or their constituency (but not both), with the exception of those with London area constituencies. Eligible MPs can claim for accommodation in one of three ways: a rental property and associated costs, hotel costs or associated costs only, if they own the property.

The annual London rental accommodation budget is £22,760 for 2017-18.

MPs can claim for budget uplifts for their dependants at a rate of £5,435 per dependant per financial year.

London area MPs can claim a London Area Living Payment (LALP) to help cover the additional costs of living and travelling in London. Non-London area MPs who do not claim accommodation costs can claim the £3,820 LALP instead.

Hotel accommodation is limited to £150 per night in London, or £120 per night elsewhere. In addition MPs may claim £25 for subsistence costs incurred for overnight stays while on parliamentary business.

The annual budget limit for MPs to claim for associated costs, if they own their home, is £5,963 for 2017-18.

Office costs

To maintain a constituency office and provide surgeries London area MPs may claim up to £26,850 and Non-London area MPs up to £24,150 for 2017-18.

Staffing costs

The annual staffing budget is £161,550 for London area MPs and £150,900 for non-London area MPs for 2017-18.

Travel

Non-London area MPs can claim for journeys between their homes or offices in the constituency, and Westminster. London area MPs can only claim for journeys between the constituency office and Westminster.

All MPs can claim for travel within their constituency (and up to 20 miles outside). Mileage rates are set at 45p per mile.

Starting-up budget

Start-up expenditure is available for MPs elected to Parliament for the first time. The budget is set at £6,000 and lasts for 365 days from the day after the MP is elected.

Winding-up budget

The winding-up budget for London area MPs is £57,150 and for non-London area MPs it is £53,950.

When MPs leave Parliament, their staff have to be made redundant. Staff redundancy costs are met from a contingency fund.

Other assistance

Disability assistance and security assistance may be claimed by any MP if they are necessary for MPs to carry out their parliamentary functions.

MPs can apply for contingency funding to deal with exceptional and unpredictable circumstances.

Parliamentary Contributory Pension Fund

A new pension scheme for MPs took effect on 8 May 2015. Benefits provided are on a 'career average revalued earnings' (CARE) basis.

The accrual rate is 1/51st of pensionable earnings, revalued annually in line with the Consumer Prices Index (CPI).

There is now one level of pension contribution for all members: current estimate is 11.09 per cent of pay, but the rate paid will vary in line with the costs of the Scheme. Normal pension age is linked to state pension age.

If an MP was aged 55 or over on 1 April 2013, and re-elected in 2015, they will stay in the previous final salary scheme for as long as you remain an MP.

If an MP was aged between 51 years six months and 55 years on 1 April 2013, and re-elected in 2015, they can choose either to stay in the previous final salary scheme for a limited period before transferring, or to transfer to the new CARE scheme.

If an MP was younger than 51 years and six months on 1 April 2013, and re-elected in 2015, they will automatically move into the new CARE scheme for future service.

Ministerial Pension Scheme
A new pension scheme for Ministers took effect on 8 May 2015.

The accrual rate is 1.775 per cent of pensionable earnings (about 1/56).

The member pension contribution rate is 11.1 per cent.

Normal pension age is linked to state pension age.

Severance pay
Ministers and other paid office holders (with the exception of the Prime Minister and Commons Speaker) are entitled to a severance payment of one-quarter of their final Ministerial salary when they leave office for whatever reason.

Severance payments under £30,000 are tax and National Insurance exempt.

HOUSE OF COMMONS 62
Speaker and Deputy Speakers 62
House of Commons Commission/Members Estimate Committee 62
State of the Parties 62
Changes since 2017 general election 62
MPs' Biographies 63
Analysis of MPs 360
MPs' Political Interests 360
MPs' Countries of Interest 386
MPs by UK Regions 396
Election Statistics by Party, Gender and Region 409
Constituencies, MPs and Majorities 411
Most Vulnerable Constituencies 424
50 Safest Constituencies 428
Women MPs 430
MPs by Age 435
MPs by Party 442
Committees and Offices 447
Select Committees 447
Officers and Officials 455
Political Offices 461
PARLIAMENT
Joint Committees 1062
Statutory Committees 1062
Party Committees 1064
Privy Counsellors 1066
Political Parties 1069
Parliamentary Press Gallery 1073
Parliamentary Agents 1078

HOUSE OF COMMONS

London SW1A 0AA 020 7219 3000 Enquiry Service 020 7219 4272
Website: www.parliament.uk Twitter: @UKParliament @HoCPress

Bulk correspondence to MPs may be delivered to Derby Gate at the Palace of Westminster, but must be stamped or franked or accompanied by a cheque for second-class postage made out to Post Office Counters. A single letter petitioning an individual MP can be delivered without postage payment by hand when the House is sitting.

Speaker and Deputy Speakers

The Speaker is the presiding officer of the Commons, whose main responsibility is to maintain order in debates and apply the rules and traditions of the House. The Chairman of Ways and Means is the principal deputy speaker. By tradition, the Speaker, once elected, renounces party allegiance for the remainder of his or her career.

The Speaker: Rt Hon **John Bercow** MP
Chairman of Ways and Means: Rt Hon **Lindsay Hoyle** MP (Lab)
First Deputy Chairman of Ways and Means and Deputy Speaker: **Eleanor Laing** MP (Con)
Second Deputy Chairman of Ways and Means and Deputy Speaker:
Rt Hon Dame **Rosie Winterton** DBE MP (Lab)
Speaker's Secretary: **Peter Barratt** 020 7219 4111 Email: barrattpf@parliament.uk
Speaker's Chaplain: Rev **Rose Hudson-Wilkin** 020 7219 3768 Email: hudsonwilkinr@parliament.uk

House of Commons Commission/Members Estimate Committee

The House of Commons Commission is responsible for the management of the House, including the employment of its staff and the provision of services by the departments of the House.

Chair: Rt Hon **John Bercow** MP (Speaker)
Members:
Sir **Paul Beresford** MP (Con)
Rt Hon **Tom Brake** MP (Lib Dem)
Stewart Hosie MP (SNP)
Rt Hon **Andrea Leadsom** MP (Con)
Valerie Vaz MP (Lab)
Rt Hon Dame **Rosie Winterton** DBE MP (Lab)
David Natzler
Ian Ailles
Dame **Janet Gaymer** DBE QC
Jane McCall
Secretary: **Marianne Cwynarski** 020 7219 8135 Email: hoccommission@parliament.uk

Members (MPs)

State of the Parties (October 2017)

	Total
Conservative	316
Labour (includes Labour/Co-operative)	262
Scottish National Party	35
Liberal Democrat	12
Democratic Unionist Party	10
Sinn Féin	7
Plaid Cymru	4
Independent	2
Green Party	1
The Speaker	1
	650 seats

Changes since 2017 General Election

CHANGE OF PARTY

Anne Marie Morris	Newton Abbot	Conservative Whip suspended July 2017, now Independent

MPs' BIOGRAPHIES

LABOUR

ABBOTT, DIANE

Hackney North and Stoke Newington *(Majority 35,139)*

Shadow Home Secretary

Diane Julie Abbott. Born 27 September 1953; Daughter of late Reginald Abbott, welder, and late Julie Abbott, psychiatric nurse; Married David Thompson 1991 (divorced 1993) (1 son).

Education: Harrow County Girls' Grammar School; Newnham College, Cambridge (BA history 1976).

Non-political career: Administration trainee, Home Office 1976-78; Race relations officer, National Council for Civil Liberties 1978-80; Journalist: Thames Television 1980-82, TV AM 1982-84, Freelance 1984-85; Principal press officer, Lambeth Council 1986-87. Equality officer, ACTT 1985-86; Member, RMT Parliamentary Campaigning Group 2002-.

Political career: Member for Hackney North and Stoke Newington 1987-2010, for Hackney North and Stoke Newington (revised boundary) since 6 May 2010 general election; Shadow Minister for Public Health 2010-13; Shadow Secretary of State for: International Development 2015-16, Health 2016, Home Department (Shadow Home Secretary) 2016-. *Select committees:* Member: Treasury and Civil Service 1989-97, Foreign Affairs 1997-2001. Member, Labour Party National Executive Committee 1994-97; Contested Labour leadership 2010. *Councils and public bodies:* Westminster City Councillor 1982-86; Former member, advisory cabinet for women and equality, Greater London Assembly.

Political interests: Small businesses, education; Africa, Jamaica.

Other: Founder, Black Women Mean Business 1992-; London Schools and the Black Child. *Spectator* Speech of the Year 2008. PC 2017.

Recreations: Reading, cinema.

Rt Hon Diane Abbott MP, House of Commons, London SW1A 0AA
Tel: 020 7219 4426 *Fax:* 020 7219 4964 *Email:* diane.abbott.office@parliament.uk
Constituency: No constituency office *Website:* www.dianeabbott.org.uk
Twitter: @HackneyAbbott

LABOUR

ABRAHAMS, DEBBIE

Oldham East and Saddleworth *(Majority 8,182)*

Shadow Secretary of State for Work and Pensions

Deborah Angela Elspeth Marie Abrahams. Born 15 September 1960; Married John Abrahams (2 daughters).

Education: Bolton Institute of Technology; Salford University (BA biochemistry and physiology 1984); Liverpool University (MS health and education 1994); Conversational French.

Non-political career: Community worker, charity, Wythenshawe; Head of healthy cities, Knowsley Council 1992-2000; Senior research fellow, IMPACT, University of London 2000-06; Director, International Health Impact Assessment Consortium, Liverpool University 2006-10. Member, Unison.

Political career: Contested Colne Valley 2010 general election. Member for Oldham East and Saddleworth since 13 January 2011 by-election; PPS to Andy Burnham as Shadow Secretary of State for Health 2011-15; Shadow Minister for Work and Pensions 2015-16; Shadow Secretary of State for Work and Pensions 2016-. *Select committees:* Member, Work and Pensions 2011-15. Chair, PLP Departmental Group for Health and Social Services 2011-15. Member, Labour National Policy Forum and Joint Policy Committee. *Councils and public bodies:* Board member, Bury and Rochdale Health Authority 1998-2002; Chair, Rochdale Primary Care NHS Trust 2002-06; School governor.

Political interests: Health, education, child protection, welfare, employment, inequality; Bangladesh, Kashmir, Pakistan.

Other: Co-operative Society; Fellow, Faculty of Public Health; Former Chair, North West Action on Smoking and Health. Hon. President, Greater Manchester and High Peak Ramblers Association.

Recreations: Running, gardening, film.

Debbie Abrahams MP, House of Commons, London SW1A 0AA
Tel: 020 7219 1041 *Fax:* 020 7219 2405 *Email:* abrahamsd@parliament.uk
Constituency: Lord Chambers, 11 Church Lane, Oldham OL1 3AN
Tel: 0161-624 4248 *Website:* www.debbieabrahams.org.uk *Twitter:* @debbie_abrahams

CONSERVATIVE

ADAMS, NIGEL

Selby and Ainsty *(Majority 13,772)*

Assistant Government Whip

Born 30 November 1966; Son of Derek Adams, school caretaker, and late Isabella Adams, home help; Married Claire Robson 1992 (1 son 3 daughters).

Education: Selby High School; French, Spanish.

Non-political career: Member, Armed Forces Parliamentary Scheme (RAF) 2012-. Managing director, Advanced Digital Telecom Ltd 1993-2000; Commercial director, Yorkshire Tourist Board 2005-06; Chairman: NGC Networks Ltd 2006-, NGC Network Services Ltd 2007-.

Political career: Contested Rossendale and Darwen 2005 general election. Member for Selby and Ainsty since 6 May 2010 general election; PPS to Leaders of the House of Lords and Chancellors of the Duchy of Lancaster: Lord Strathclyde 2010-13, Lord Hill of Oareford 2013-14; Assistant Government Whip 2017-. *Select committees:* Member: Environment, Food and Rural Affairs 2010, Culture, Media and Sport 2015-17. Deputy regional chair, Yorkshire and Humber Conservatives 2001-03; President, Selby Conservative Association 2002-04; Board member, North of England Conservative Party 2002-03; President, Conservatives at Work 2012-13; Member, Number 10 Policy Advisory Board (Economic Affairs). *Councils and public bodies:* Governor: Camblesforth Primary School, Selby 2002-04, Selby High School 2007-.

Political interests: Energy, culture, media and sport, business, environment, food and rural affairs.

Other: Member, Yorkshire County Cricket Club Members' Committee 2004-05; Patron, Selby Hands of Hope Charity; Carlton Club, Selby Conservative Club. Member: Yorkshire County Cricket Club, Hovingham Cricket Club, House of Lords and House of Commons Cricket Club.

Recreations: Cricket, golf, football, theatre, shooting.

Nigel Adams MP, House of Commons, London SW1A 0AA
Tel: 020 7219 7141 *Email:* nigel.adams.mp@parliament.uk
Constituency: 17 High Street, Tadcaster, North Yorkshire LS24 9AP
Tel: 01937 838088 *Website:* www.nigeladams.org *Twitter:* @nadams

CONSERVATIVE

AFOLAMI, BIM

Hitchin and Harpenden *(Majority 12,031)*

Abimbola Afolami. Born 11 February 1986; Married (2 children).

Education: Bishopsgate School; Eton College; Oxford University (modern history).

Non-political career: Political Adviser to George Osborne; Corporate Lawyer, Freshfields; Senior Executive, HSBC.

Political career: Contested Lewisham Deptford 2015 general election. Member for Hitchin and Harpenden since 8 June 2017. *Select committees:* Member, Public Accounts 2017-.

Other: Secretary, Bow Publications Ltd 2008-09; Member, Programme Committee, Ditchley Foundation.

Bim Afolami MP, House of Commons, London SW1A 0AA
Tel: 020 7219 3000 *Email:* bim.afolami.mp@parliament.uk
Constituency: 65 High Street, Harpenden AL5 2SL
Tel: 01582 761796 *Email:* tory-herts@btconnect.com *Website:* www.bimafolami.co.uk
Twitter: @BimAfolami

CONSERVATIVE

AFRIYIE, ADAM

Windsor *(Majority 22,384)*

Born 4 August 1965; Married Tracy-Jane Newall 2005 (3 sons 1 daughter 1 stepson).

Education: Addey and Stanhope School, New Cross; Imperial College (Wye), London (BSc agricultural economics 1987).

Non-political career: Managing director (now non-executive chair), Connect Support Services 1993-2016; Chair, DeHavilland Information Services 1998-2005; Board member, Policy Exchange 2003-05; Non-executive chair: Axonn Ltd 2005-, Castleford Media 2010-.

Political career: Member for Windsor 2005-10, for Windsor (revised boundary) since 6 May 2010 general election; Shadow Minister for: Innovation, Universities and Skills 2007-09, Innovation and Science 2009-10; Chair, Parliamentary Office of Science and Technology (POST) 2010-17; Trade Envoy to Ghana and Guinea 2016-. *Select committees:* Member: Science and Technology/Innovation, Universities and Skills 2005-07, Children, Schools and Families 2007-09; Chair, Members' Expenses 2011-15. Chair, Tonbridge Edenbridge and Malling Association constituency branch 1999-2004; President, Conservative Technology Forum 2010-; Founding Member, Conservatives for Britain 2015-16. *Councils and public bodies:* Governor, Museum of London 1999-2005.

Political interests: Mental health, simpler tax and benefits system, public policy, innovation and science.

Other: Chair (London region): Business for Sterling 1999-2004, No to the Euro campaign 2001-04; Trustee, Museum in Docklands 2003-05; Young Enterprise (North Berkshire): Chair 2005-07, Patron 2008-; Windsor and Eton Society.

Recreations: Distance running.

Adam Afriyie MP, House of Commons, London SW1A 0AA
Tel: 020 7219 8023 *Email:* adam.afriyie.mp@parliament.uk
Constituency: No constituency office *Website:* www.adamafriyie.org *Twitter:* @AdamAfriyie

ALDOUS, PETER

Waveney *(Majority 9,215)*

CONSERVATIVE

Peter James Guy Aldous. Born 26 August 1961; Single.

Education: Harrow School; Reading University (BSc land management 1982).

Non-political career: Chartered surveyor, private practice, Norwich and Ipswich 1983-2010.

Political career: Contested Waveney 2005 general election. Member for Waveney since 6 May 2010 general election. *Select committees:* Member, Environmental Audit 2010-17. Member, Conservative Party 1998-; Founding member, Conservatives for Reform in Europe 2016. *Councils and public bodies:* Councillor, Waveney District Council 1999-2002; Suffolk County Council: Councillor 2001-05, Deputy Leader, Conservative Group 2002-05.

Political interests: Employment, transport, broadband, offshore renewables, fishing, agriculture, town planning, urban regeneration; USA.

Other: Member, Royal Institute of Chartered Surveyors; Beccles Conservative Club, Farmers' Club.

Recreations: Squash, Ipswich Town FC, horse racing, cricket.

Peter Aldous MP, House of Commons, London SW1A 0AA
Tel: 020 7219 7182 *Email:* peter.aldous.mp@parliament.uk
Constituency: 15 Surrey Street, Lowestoft, Suffolk NR32 1LJ
Tel: 01502 586568 *Website:* www.peteraldous.com *Twitter:* @peter_aldous

ALEXANDER, HEIDI

Lewisham East *(Majority 21,213)*

LABOUR

Born 17 April 1975; Daughter of Malcolm Alexander, electrician, and Elaine Alexander; Married Martin Ballantyne.

Education: Churchfields Secondary School, Swindon; Durham University (BA geography 1996; MA European urban and regional change 1999); German.

Non-political career: Researcher to Joan Ruddock MP 1999-2005; Campaign manager, Clothes Aid 2006; Director and chair, Greater London Enterprise 2007-09; Director, Lewisham Schools for the Future LEA 2007-09. Member: Unite 2009-13, Community 2013-.

Political career: Member for Lewisham East since 6 May 2010 general election; PPS to Mary Creagh as Shadow Secretary of State for Environment, Food and Rural Affairs 2010-12; Opposition Whip 2012-15; Deputy Shadow Minister for London 2013-15; Shadow Secretary of State for Health 2015-16. *Select committees:* Member: Communities and Local Government 2010-12, Regulatory Reform 2010-15, Selection 2013-16, Health 2016-17. *Councils and public bodies:* London Borough of Lewisham Council: Councillor 2004-10, Deputy Mayor 2006-10, Cabinet Member for Regeneration 2006-10; Vice-President, Local Government Association 2011-.

Political interests: Europe, health, housing, education, home affairs, international development.

Heidi Alexander MP, House of Commons, London SW1A 0AA
Tel: 020 7219 7099 *Email:* heidi.alexander.mp@parliament.uk
Constituency: No constituency office publicised
Tel: 020 8461 4733 *Email:* heidi@heidialexander.org.uk *Website:* www.heidialexander.org.uk
Twitter: @heidi_mp

LABOUR

ALI, RUSHANARA

Bethnal Green and Bow *(Majority 35,393)*

Born 14 March 1975.

Education: Mulberry School; Tower Hamlets College; Oxford University (BA philosophy, politics and economics 1997).

Non-political career: Research assistant to Lord Young of Dartington 1997; Parliamentary assistant to Oona King MP; Research fellow, Institute for Public Policy Research 1999-2001: Seconded to Foreign and Commonwealth Office; Communities Directorate, Home Office 2001-05; Associate director, Young Foundation 2005-10.

Political career: Member for Bethnal Green and Bow since 6 May 2010 general election; Shadow Minister for: International Development 2010-13, Education 2013-14; Trade Envoy to Bangladesh 2016-. *Select committees:* Member: Treasury 2014-15, 2017-, Energy and Climate Change 2015-16, Communities and Local Government 2016-17. *Councils and public bodies:* Governor, Tower Hamlets College.

Other: Commissioner, London Child Poverty Commission; Chair, Tower Hamlets Summer University; Trustee, Paul Hamlyn Foundation; Member, Tate Britain Council.

Rushanara Ali MP, House of Commons, London SW1A 0AA
Tel: 020 7219 7200 *Email:* rushanara.ali.mp@parliament.uk
Constituency: No constituency office publicised
Email: rushanara@rushanaraali.org *Website:* www.rushanaraali.org *Twitter:* @rushanaraali

CONSERVATIVE

ALLAN, LUCY

Telford *(Majority 720)*

Born 2 October 1964; Married Robin (1 son).

Education: Durham University (anthropology); Kingston Law School (Masters employment law); French.

Non-political career: PWC 1987-97; Head of Investment Trusts, Gartmore 1997-2004; UBS Warburg 2004; Owner/Director, Workplace Law 2004-11; Judicial Office Holder, Ministry of Justice 2010-13; Campaign Director, Lobby Family Rights 2011-13.

Political career: Member for Telford since 7 May 2015 general election. *Select committees:* Member: Education 2015-, Education, Skills and the Economy Sub-committee 2016-17, Women and Equalities 2017. Member, management committee, Wandsworth Conservatives; Deputy chair, Putney Conservatives 2007-09. *Councils and public bodies:* Councillor, Wandsworth Council 2006-12; Non-executive director, Wandsworth NHS.

Political interests: Family rights, children in care, broadband, rail links, child protection; Middle East.

Other: Trustee, Women's Aid; ICAEW; ICSA.

Lucy Allan MP, House of Commons, London SW1A 0AA
Tel: 020 7219 4815 *Email:* lucy.allan.mp@parliament.uk
Constituency: Suite 1 Preston House, Hawksworth Road, Central Park, Telford TF2 9TU
Tel: 01952 290039 *Website:* www.lucyallan.com *Twitter:* @lucyallan

CONSERVATIVE

ALLEN, HEIDI

South Cambridgeshire *(Majority 15,952)*

Heidi Suzanne Allen. Born 18 January 1975; Married Phil.

Education: University College London (BSc astrophysics 1996); London Business School; BPP London (DipLaw 2007).

Non-political career: Churchill Insurance; ExxonMobil; Royal Mail; Tubelines; Managing director, RS Bike Paint.

Political career: Member for South Cambridgeshire since 7 May 2015 general election; Board Member, Parliamentary Office of Science and Technology (POST) 2015-. *Select committees:* Member: Work and Pensions 2015-, Public Accounts 2017-. Founding member, Conservatives for Reform in Europe 2016. *Councils and public bodies:* Councillor, St Albans City and District Council 2012-14.

Political interests: Manufacturing, science, UK business.

Heidi Allen MP, House of Commons, London SW1A 0AA
Tel: 020 7219 5091 *Email:* heidi.allen.mp@parliament.uk
Constituency: 82a High Street, Sawston, Cambridge, Cambridgeshire CB22 3HJ
Tel: 01223 830037 *Website:* www.heidisouthcambs.co.uk *Twitter:* @heidiallen75

LABOUR

ALLIN-KHAN, ROSENA

Tooting *(Majority 15,458)*

Shadow Minister for Sport

Rosena Chantelle Allin-Khan. Born 1977; Married Tudor (2 daughters).

Education: Brunel University (BSC medical biochemistry); Cambridge University (medicine): Scholarship: Cancer research, USA, Peace-keeping and conflict-resolution, Switzerland; Polish, Urdu.

Non-political career: NHS doctor 2005-: Royal London Hospital, Homerton Hospital, A&E department, St George's Hospital; Emergency humanitarian assistance, Palestinian refugees in Lebanese camps and with victims of flooding in Pakistan.

Political career: Member for Tooting since 16 June 2016 by-election; Shadow Minister for Culture, Media and Sport/Digital, Culture, Media and Sport (Sport) 2016-; *Councils and public bodies:* Wandsworth Council: Councillor 2014-, Deputy leader, Labour group.

Other: Balham Boxing Club.

Recreations: Boxing.

Dr Rosena Allin-Khan MP, House of Commons, London SW1A 0AA
Tel: 020 7219 0636 *Email:* rosena.allinkhan.mp@parliament.uk
Constituency: No constituency office publicised
Email: rosena@drrosena.co.uk *Website:* www.drrosena.co.uk *Twitter:* @DrRosena

LABOUR

AMESBURY, MIKE

Weaver Vale *(Majority 3,928)*

Michael Lee Amesbury. Born 7 May 1969; Married Amanda (1 son).

Education: BA social science; Postgraduate qualification careers guidance and education.

Non-political career: Convener, Unison; Stakeholder Manager to Andy Burnham, Metro Mayoral election campaign; Parliamentary Adviser to Angela Rayner as Shadow Secretary of State for Education.

Political career: Member for Weaver Vale since 8 June 2017. *Select committees:* Member, Communities and Local Government 2017-. *Councils and public bodies:* Manchester City Council: Councillor 2006-17, Executive Member for Culture and Leisure 2008-17.

Other: Director, Hallé Orchestra; Millennium Quarter Trust Board; Manchester Concert Halls Limited (Bridgewater Hall); Library Theatre Board; Manchester Sport and Leisure Trust; Velodrome Trust; Manchester International Festival.

Mike Amesbury MP, House of Commons, London SW1A 0AA
Tel: 020 7219 2072 *Email:* mike.amesbury.mp@parliament.uk
Constituency: Details still to be confirmed
Tel: 01928 620061 *Website:* www.mikeamesbury.org *Twitter:* @MikeAmesbury

CONSERVATIVE

AMESS, DAVID

Southend West *(Majority 10,000)*

David Anthony Andrew Amess. Born 26 March 1952; Son of late James Amess and Maud Amess; Married Julia Arnold 1983 (1 son 4 daughters).

Education: St Bonaventure's Grammar School, Forest Gate, London; Bournemouth College of Technology (BSc economics and government 1974).

Non-political career: Teacher, St John Baptist Junior School, Bethnal Green, London 1970-71; Underwriter, Leslie Godwin Agency 1974-76; Accountancy personnel 1976-79; Senior consultant, Executemps Company Agency 1979-81; AA Recruitment Co 1981-87; Chair and chief executive: Accountancy Solutions 1987-90, Accountancy Group 1990-96; Parliamentary adviser to Caravan Club.

Political career: Contested Newham North West 1979 general election. Member for Basildon 1983-97, for Southend West 1997-2010, for Southend West (revised boundary) since 6 May 2010 general election; PPS to: Parliamentary Under-Secretaries of State, DHSS: Edwina Currie 1987-88, Lord Skelmersdale 1988, to Michael Portillo: as Minister of State: Department of Transport 1988-90, Department of Environment 1990-92, as Chief Secretary to the Treasury 1992-94, as Secretary of State: for Employment 1994-95, for Defence 1995-97; Contested Deputy Speaker election 2013. *Select committees:* Member: Broadcasting 1994-97, Health 1998-2007, Chairmen's Panel/Panel of Chairs 2001-, Backbench Business 2012-15, Administration 2015-. Chair, Conservative Party Committee on Health 1999; Vice-chair, Conservative Party Committee on Health and Social Services 2001; Member, Executive, 1922 Committee 2004-12. Hon. Secretary, Conservative Friends of Israel 1998-. *Councils and public bodies:* Councillor, London Borough of Redbridge Council 1982-86.

Political interests: Health, education, transport, environment, pro-life movement, animal welfare, foreign affairs; Asia, Far East, Indian Ocean countries, Middle East, Pacific Basin, USA.

Other: Founder member, Wallenberg Appeal Foundation 1996; Industry and Parliament Trust: Fellow 1994, Chair, Fellowship Committee 2007-, Chair, board of trustees 2014-; Chair, 1912 Club 1996-; Fairhaven Hospices, Salvation Army, RSPCA, Southend Fund, Mencap, Age UK, Dogs Trust. Freedom, City of London. Charity Champion awards: Animal Welfare and Environment Champion 2011, Outstanding Achievement (with Stephen Pound MP and Bob Russell MP) 2012. Knighted 2015.

Publications: The Road to Basildon (1993); The Basildon Experience (1995); Basildon 1992: Against All Odds! (2012); Party of Opportunity (2014); Party of Opportunity, The Second Edition (2015).

Recreations: Socialising, reading, writing, sports, modern music, keeping animals, gardening, travel, history.

Sir David Amess MP, House of Commons, London SW1A 0AA
Tel: 020 7219 3452 *Fax:* 020 7219 2245 *Email:* amessd@parliament.uk
Constituency: Iveagh Hall, 67 Leigh Road, Leigh-on-Sea, Essex SS9 1JW
Tel: 01702 472391 *Email:* office@southendwestconservatives.com
Websites: www.southendwestconservatives.com www.davidamess.co.uk

ANDREW, STUART

Pudsey *(Majority 331)*

CONSERVATIVE

Assistant Government Whip

Stuart James Andrew. Born 25 November 1971; Son of James Andrew and Maureen Andrew; Partner.

Education: Ysgol David Hughes, Menai Bridge; Welsh.

Non-political career: British Heart Foundation -1998; Fundraiser, Hope House Children's Hospice 1998-2000; Head of fundraising, East Lancashire Hospice 2000-03; Fundraising manager, Martin House Children's Hospice 2003-10.

Political career: Contested Wrexham 1997 general election. Member for Pudsey since 6 May 2010 general election; PPS: to Francis Maude as Minister for the Cabinet Office and Paymaster General 2012-15, to Patrick McLoughlin: as Secretary of State for Transport 2015-16, as Chancellor of the Duchy of Lancaster, Cabinet Office 2016-17; Assistant Government Whip 2017-. *Select committees:* Member, Welsh Affairs 2010-12. Vice-chairman (Cities), Conservative Party 2016-17. *Councils and public bodies:* Councillor, Leeds City Council 2003-10.

Political interests: Special needs education, transport, planning, charities, health; Commonwealth, USA.

Other: Chair, Yeadon Project; Member, Institute of Fundraising.

Recreations: Walking the Yorkshire Dales, attending the gym.

Stuart Andrew MP, House of Commons, London SW1A 0AA
Tel: 020 7219 7130 *Email:* stuart.andrew.mp@parliament.uk
Constituency: 94a Town Street, Horsforth, Leeds, West Yorkshire LS18 4AP
Tel: 0113-258 5615 *Website:* www.stuartandrew.com *Twitter:* @StuartAndrew

ANTONIAZZI, TONIA

Gower *(Majority 3,269)*

LABOUR

PPS to Owen Smith as Shadow Secretary of State for Northern Ireland

Antonia Louise Antoniazzi. Born 5 October 1971; Divorced (1 son).

Education: St John Lloyd School; Gower College, Swansea; Exeter University (French and Italian); Cardiff University (PGCE).

Non-political career: Head of Languages, Bryngwyn School; Leader of Learning for Foundation, Education through Regional Working (ERW).

Political career: Member for Gower since 8 June 2017; PPS to Owen Smith as Shadow Secretary of State for Northern Ireland 2017-; Contested Mid and West Wales region 2016 National Assembly for Wales election.

Tonia Antoniazzi MP, House of Commons, London SW1A 0AA
Tel: 020 7219 1199 *Email:* tonia.antoniazzi.mp@parliament.uk
Constituency: Ty Newydd Community Centre, 17 West Street, Gorseinon, Swansea SA4 4AA
Tel: 01792 899025 *Website:* www.toniaantoniazzi.co.uk *Twitter:* @ToniaAntoniazzi

CONSERVATIVE

ARGAR, EDWARD

Charnwood *(Majority 16,341)*

PPS to Patrick McLoughlin as Chancellor of the Duchy of Lancaster and Conservative Party Chair

Edward John Comport Argar. Born 9 December 1977.

Education: Harvey Grammar School, Folkestone; Oriel College, Oxford (BA modern history 2000, MA; Masters 2001); French, German.

Non-political career: Political adviser to Rt Hon Michael Ancram MP as Shadow Foreign Secretary 2001-05; Management consultant: Hedra plc 2005-08, Mouchel 2008-11, Serco 2011-14.

Political career: Contested Oxford East 2010 general election. Member for Charnwood since 7 May 2015 general election; Team PPS, Department for Education 2016-17; PPS to Patrick McLoughlin as Chancellor of the Duchy of Lancaster and Conservative Party Chair 2017-. *Select committees:* Member, Procedure 2015-16. *Councils and public bodies:* Westminster City Council: Councillor 2006-15, Cabinet Member for: Health and Adult Services 2008-10, City Management, Transport and Infrastructure 2010-15; Vice-chair, Health and Adult Social Care Forum, London Councils 2008-10; School governor; Board member, NHS trust.

Political interests: Foreign policy, rural affairs, health and social care, particularly dementia care, policing; France, Oman, Norway, USA, Yemen.

Other: RNLI, Alzheimer's Society. Member, Leicestershire County Cricket Club.

Recreations: Travel, reading, skiing, gardening, cricket, tennis.

Edward Argar MP, House of Commons, London SW1A 0AA
Tel: 020 7219 8140 *Email:* edward.argar.mp@parliament.uk
Constituency: Suite 26, Unit 3, Q-Estate, 1487 Melton Road, Queniborough, Leicestershire LE7 3FP
Tel: 0116-269 3789 *Website:* www.edwardargar.org.uk

LAB/CO-OP

ASHWORTH, JON

Leicester South *(Majority 26,261)*

Shadow Secretary of State for Health

Jonathan Michael Graham Ashworth. Born 14 October 1978; Married Emilie Oldknow (2 daughters).

Education: Philips High School, Bury; Bury College; Durham University (BA politics and philosophy 2000).

Non-political career: Special adviser to Chief Secretaries to the Treasury 2004-07: Paul Boateng 2004-05, Des Browne 2005-06, Stephen Timms 2006-07; Deputy Political Secretary to Gordon Brown as Prime Minister 2007-10; Political Secretary to Harriet Harman as Acting Leader of the Opposition 2010; Head of party relations to Ed Miliband as Leader of the Opposition 2010-11. Member: Unite, GMB.

Political career: Member for Leicester South since 6 May 2011 by-election; Opposition Whip 2011-13; Shadow Minister for Cabinet Office 2013-15; Shadow Minister without Portfolio (attending Shadow Cabinet) 2015-16; Shadow Secretary of State for Health 2016-; Labour Party: Political research officer 2001, Economics and welfare policy officer 2002-04, Member, National Executive Committee 2013-16, Campaign Deputy, General Election Strategy 2014-15; Member, Co-operative Party.

Political interests: Health, economy, foreign affairs, international development; Australia, Bangladesh, India, Italy, Middle East, Myanmar, Pakistan, Palestine, Somalia, Syria, USA.

Other: National Association for Children of Alcoholics; Saffron Lane Working Men's Club.

Recreations: Reading, cinema, boxing fan, music.

Jon Ashworth MP, House of Commons, London SW1A 0AA
Tel: 020 7219 0517 *Email:* jon.ashworth.mp@parliament.uk
Constituency: Tenth Floor, 60 Charles Street, Leicester, Leicestershire LE1 1FB
Tel: 0116-251 1927 *Fax:* 0116-262 6329 *Website:* www.jonashworth.org *Twitter:* @JonAshworth

CONSERVATIVE

ATKINS, VICTORIA

Louth and Horncastle *(Majority 19,641)*

PPS to Baroness Evans of Bowes Park as Leader of the House of Lords and Lord Privy Seal

Victoria Mary Atkins. Born March 1976; Married Paul (1 son).

Education: Cambridge University (law).

Non-political career: Called to the Bar, Middle Temple 1998; Barrister, specialising in serious organised crime, fraud and regulatory crime.

Political career: Member for Louth and Horncastle since 7 May 2015 general election; PPS to: Brandon Lewis as Minister of State for Policing and the Fire Service, Home Office 2016-17, Baroness Evans of Bowes Park as Leader of the House of Lords and Lord Privy Seal 2017-. *Select committees:* Member: Home Affairs 2015-16, Joint Committee on the Draft Investigatory Powers Bill 2015-16. Contested Gloucestershire 2012 Police and Crime Commissioner election.

Political interests: Home affairs, agriculture, defence, education.

Other: Associate Member, MCC.

Recreations: Going to concerts, travelling, horse riding.

Victoria Atkins MP, House of Commons, London SW1A 0AA
Tel: 020 7219 5897
Constituency: No constituency office publicised
Email: victoria@victoriaatkins.org.uk *Website:* www.victoriaatkins.org.uk

LABOUR

AUSTIN, IAN

Dudley North *(Majority 22)*

Born 6 March 1965; Son of Alfred and Margaret Austin; Married Catherine Miles 1993 (2 sons 1 daughter).

Education: Dudley School; Essex University (BA government 1987).

Non-political career: Communications manager, Focus Housing 1989-94; Regional press officer, West Midlands Labour Party 1995-98; Deputy director of communications, Scottish Labour Party 1998-99; Special adviser to Gordon Brown as Chancellor of the Exchequer 1999-2005.

Political career: Member for Dudley North 2005-10, for Dudley North (revised boundary) since 6 May 2010 general election; PPS to Gordon Brown: as Chancellor of the Exchequer 2007, as Prime Minister 2007-08; Assistant Government Whip 2008-09; Minister for the West Midlands 2008-10; Parliamentary Under-Secretary of State, Department for Communities and Local Government 2009-10; Shadow Minister for: Communities and Local Government 2010, Sports 2010-11, Work and Pensions 2011-13. *Select committees:* Member: Home Affairs 2013-15, Education 2015-17, Education, Skills and the Economy Sub-committee 2015-16, Foreign Affairs 2017-, Panel of Chairs 2017-. Chair, PLP Departmental Group for Education 2015-. *Councils and public bodies:* Councillor, Dudley Borough Council 1991-95.

Political interests: Housing, training and skills, employment, manufacturing and trade.

Other: Member, UK Delegation, Organisation for Security and Co-operation in Europe Parliamentary Assembly 2015-.

Recreations: Football, cycling, reading.

Ian Austin MP, House of Commons, London SW1A 0AA
Tel: 020 7219 8012 *Fax:* 020 7219 4488 *Email:* austini@parliament.uk
Constituency: St James House, Trinity Road, Dudley, West Midlands DY1 1JB
Tel: 01384 342503/01384 342523 *Website:* www.ianaustin.co.uk *Twitter:* @IanAustinMP

CONSERVATIVE

BACON, RICHARD

South Norfolk *(Majority 16,678)*

Richard Michael Bacon. Born 3 December 1962; Married Victoria Panton 2006 (2 sons).

Education: King's School, Worcester; London School of Economics (BSc (Econ) politics and economics 1986); German.

Non-political career: Investment banker, Barclays de Zoete Wedd 1986-89; Financial journalist, Euromoney Publications plc 1993-94; Deputy director, Management Consultancies Association 1994-96; Brunswick Public Relations 1996-99; Founder, English Word Factory 1999-.

Political career: Contested Vauxhall 1997 general election. Member for South Norfolk 2001-10, for South Norfolk (revised boundary) since 6 May 2010 general election; Member Public Accounts Commission 2005-. *Select committees:* Member: Public Accounts 2001-17, European Scrutiny 2003-07, Unopposed Bills (Panel) 2010-15. Chair, Hammersmith Conservative Association 1995-96; Co-founder, Geneva Conservative general election voluntary agency 2000.

Political interests: Housing, public expenditure, education, health, agriculture, Europe.

Other: Member, Amnesty International; Patron, Elizabeth's Legacy of Hope. Commons Select Committee Member of the Year, *House Magazine* awards 2012.

Publications: Co-author, Conundrum: Why every government gets things wrong and what we can do about it (2013).

Recreations: Music, reading, modern painting.

Richard Bacon MP, House of Commons, London SW1A 0AA
Tel: 020 7219 8301 *Email:* richardbaconmp@parliament.uk
Constituency: Grasmere, Denmark Street, Diss, Norfolk IP22 4LE
Tel: 01379 643728/01379 651979 *Email:* reevet@parliament.uk rigbym@parliament.uk
Website: www.richardbacon.org.uk *Twitter:* @richardbaconmp

CONSERVATIVE

BADENOCH, KEMI

Saffron Walden *(Majority 24,966)*

Olukemi Badenoch. Born 1980; Daughter of Prof Feyi Adegoke and Dr Femi Adegoke; Married (1 daughter).

Education: International School of Lagos; Sussex University (MEng systems engineering 2003); University of London (LLB 2009).

Non-political career: Associate Director, Coutts 2008-15; Head of Digital, *The Spectator* 2015-16.

Political career: Contested (as Kemi Adegoke) Dulwich and West Norwood 2010 general election. Member for Saffron Walden since 8 June 2017. *Select committees:* Member, Justice 2017-. Member, Executive, 1922 Committee 2017-. London Assembly: AM (replacement) for London-wide region 2015-17, Conservative Spokesperson on: Policing and Crime 2015-16, Economy 2016-17. Project Leader, Global Poverty Policy Group 2006-07; Deputy Chair, South London Area Conservatives 2014-.

Political interests: Policing, crime, economy, housing, transport, international development; India, Nigeria, USA.

Other: Member: British Computer Society, Women's Engineering Society.

Recreations: Chess and poker player, reading.

Kemi Badenoch MP, House of Commons, London SW1A 0AA
Tel: 020 7219 1943 *Email:* kemi.badenoch.mp@parliament.uk
Constituency: Details still to be confirmed *Website:* kemibadenoch.org.uk
Twitter: @KemiBadenoch

LAB/CO-OP

BAILEY, ADRIAN

West Bromwich West *(Majority 4,460)*

Adrian Edward Bailey. Born 11 December 1945; Son of Edward Bailey, fitter, and Sylvia Bailey, née Bayliss; Married Jill Millard 1989 (1 stepson).

Education: Cheltenham Grammar School; Exeter University (BA economic history 1967); Loughborough College of Librarianship (Postgraduate Diploma librarianship 1971).

Non-political career: Librarian, Cheshire County Council 1971-82; Political organiser, Co-operative Party 1982-2000. Member, GMBATU 1982-.

Political career: Contested South Worcester 1970 and Nantwich February and October 1974 general elections and Wirral 1976 by-election. Member for West Bromwich West 23 November 2000 by-election to 2010, for West Bromwich West (revised boundary) since 6 May 2010 general election; PPS: to John Hutton: as Chancellor of the Duchy of Lancaster 2005, as Secretary of State for Work and Pensions 2005-06, to Hilary Armstrong as Chancellor of the Duchy of Lancaster 2006, to Ministers of State, Ministry of Defence: Adam Ingram 2006-07, Bob Ainsworth 2007. *Select committees:* Member: Northern Ireland Affairs 2001-05, Unopposed Bills (Panel) 2001-15, Business, Enterprise and Regulatory Reform/Business and Enterprise/Business, Innovation and Skills 2007-09, European Scrutiny 2007-10, Quadripartite (Committees on Strategic Export Controls)/Arms Export Controls 2007-10, West Midlands 2009-10; Chair, Business, Innovation and Skills 2010-15; Member: Liaison 2010-15, Joint Committee on National Security Strategy 2010-15, Panel of Chairs 2015-. Contested Cheshire West 1979 European Parliament election. Secretary, West Bromwich West CLP 1993-2000; Chair, Parliamentary Group 2004. *Councils and public bodies:* Sandwell Borough Council: Councillor 1991-2001, Chair, finance committee 1992-97, Deputy leader 1997-2000.

Political interests: Co-operatives and mutuals, urban regeneration, animal welfare (anti-hunting with dogs), taxation, economic policy, child protection policy; China, India, Pakistan.

Other: Board of trustees, Industry and Parliament Trust 2015-; Action Aid, Redwings Horse Sanctuary, Staffs Bull Terrier Heritage Society, NSPCC.

Recreations: Football, swimming, walking.

Adrian Bailey MP, House of Commons, London SW1A 0AA
Tel: 020 7219 6060 *Fax:* 020 7219 1202 *Email:* baileya@parliament.uk
Constituency: Terry Duffy House, Thomas Street, West Bromwich, West Midlands BR70 6NT
Tel: 0121-569 1926 *Fax:* 0121-569 1936 *Email:* cromptonm@parliament.uk
Twitter: @AdrianBailey4MP

CONSERVATIVE

BAKER, STEVE

Wycombe *(Majority 6,578)*

Parliamentary Under-Secretary of State, Department for Exiting the European Union

Steven John Baker. Born 6 June 1971; Married Beth 1996 (no children).

Education: Poltair Comprehensive School, St Austell; St Austell Sixth Form College; Southampton University (BEng aerospace systems engineering 1992); St Cross College, Oxford (MSc computer science 2000).

Non-political career: Engineer officer, Royal Air Force 1989-99. Head of consulting and product manager, DecisionSoft Ltd, Oxford 2000-01; Principal, Ambriel Consulting Ltd 2001-10; Chief technology officer, BASDA Ltd, Great Missenden 2002-07; Product development director, Core Filing Ltd, Oxford 2005-06; Chief architect, global financing and asset servicing platforms, Lehman Brothers, London 2006-08; Corporate affairs director, Cobden Centre 2009-10; Ambriel Consulting.

Political career: Member for Wycombe since 6 May 2010 general election; Parliamentary Under-Secretary of State, Department for Exiting the European Union 2017-. *Select committees:* Member: Transport 2010-13, Treasury 2014-17, Standing Orders 2015-. Chair, Conservative Party Committee for Public Services 2011-15; Member, Executive, 1922 Committee 2012-17. Chairman, Conservatives for Britain 2015-16.

Political interests: Enterprise, economics, money and banking, health, education, liberty, foreign affairs, defence; Kashmir, Pakistan.

Other: Associate consultant, Centre for Social Justice 2008-10; Member: Speen Baptist Church, Campaign committee, Vote Leave 2016; Chartered aerospace engineer, Royal Aeronautical Society 1999; Member, Institute of Directors; Volunteer, Wycombe Winter Night Shelter 2008-09; Royal Air Force Club.

Recreations: Skydiving, motorcycling, photography, sailing.

Steve Baker MP, House of Commons, London SW1A 0AA
Tel: 020 7219 3547/020 7219 5099 *Fax:* 020 7219 4614 *Email:* steve.baker.mp@parliament.uk
Constituency: 150a West Wycombe Road, High Wycombe, Buckinghamshire HP12 3AE
Tel: 01494 448408 *Email:* sue.hynard@parliament.uk *Website:* www.stevebaker.info
Twitter: @SteveBakerHW

CONSERVATIVE

BALDWIN, HARRIETT

West Worcestershire *(Majority 21,328)*

Parliamentary Under-Secretary of State (Defence Procurement), Ministry of Defence

Harriett Mary Morison Baldwin. Born 2 May 1960; Daughter of Anthony Eggleston OBE and late Jane Eggleston, née Buxton; Married James Stanley Baldwin 2004 (1 son from previous marriage 2 stepdaughters).

Education: Friends' School, Saffron Walden; Marlborough College; Lady Margaret Hall, Oxford (BA French and Russian 1982); McGill University, Montreal, Canada (MBA international finance 1985); French, Russian.

Non-political career: Armed Forces RAF Parliamentary Scheme. Graduate Trainee, Security Pacific National Bank 1982-83; Treasury Analyst, Hewlett-Packard Canada 1985-86; JP Morgan 1986-2008: Various roles/investor 1986-98, Head of Currency Management, Asset Management Division 1998-2006, Managing Director 1998-2008, Senior Adviser -2008.

Political career: Contested Stockton North 2005 general election. Member for West Worcestershire since 6 May 2010 general election; PPS to Minister of State for Employment, Department for Work and Pensions: Mark Hoban 2012-13, Esther McVey 2013-14; Assistant Government Whip 2014; Government Whip 2014-15; Economic Secretary (Minister for the City of London), HM Treasury 2015-16; Parliamentary Under-Secretary of State (Defence Procurement), Ministry of

Defence 2016-. *Select committees:* Member: Work and Pensions 2010-12, Joint Committee on the Draft Care and Support Bill 2013, Administration 2014, Public Accounts 2015-16. *Councils and public bodies:* Associate Governor, Hallow Church of England Primary School.

Political interests: Pensions, economics, social enterprise, financial literacy, micro-finance, welfare reform; Cyprus, Russia.

Other: Member, NATO Parliamentary Assembly 2010-14; Vice-chair, Social Investment Business 2008-12; Centre for Social Justice, Camfed, Opportunity International, Save the Children; Carlton Club.

Publications: Author: Leviathan Is Still At Large (Centre for Policy Studies, 2002), Social Enterprise Zones (Conservative Policy Review, 2007), Growth, Growth, Growth, (Centre for Policy Studies, 2011), Iron Ladies (Demos, 2012).

Recreations: Canal boats, walking, cycling.

Harriett Baldwin MP, House of Commons, London SW1A 0AA
Tel: 020 7219 5487 *Fax:* 020 7219 5151 *Email:* harriett.baldwin.mp@parliament.uk
Constituency: Malvern Hills Science Park, Geraldine Road, Malvern, Worcestershire WR14 3SZ
Tel: 01684 585165 *Website:* www.harriettbaldwin.com *Twitter:* @hbaldwin

BARCLAY, STEVE

North East Cambridgeshire *(Majority 21,270)*

CONSERVATIVE

Economic Secretary, HM Treasury

Stephen Paul Barclay. Born 30 June 1972; Married Karen.

Education: King Edward VII School, Lancashire; Peterhouse, Cambridge (BA history 1994, MA); College of Law, Chester (1996).

Non-political career: 2nd Lieutenant, Royal Regiment of Fusiliers 1991. Trainee solicitor, Lawrence Graham Solicitors 1996-98; Company lawyer, Axa Insurance 1998-2001; Financial Services Authority 2002-06; Barclays Retail Bank 2006-10: Director of regulatory affairs 2006-08, Head of anti-money laundering and sanctions 2008-10.

Political career: Contested Manchester Blackley 1997 and Lancaster and Wyre 2001 general elections. Member for North East Cambridgeshire since 6 May 2010 general election; Assistant Government Whip 2015-16; Government Whip (Lord Commissioner of HM Treasury) 2016-17; Economic Secretary, HM Treasury 2017-. *Select committees:* Member, Public Accounts 2010-14. Member, Conservative Party 1994-.

Recreations: Rugby, skydiving.

Steve Barclay MP, House of Commons, London SW1A 0AA
Tel: 020 7219 7117 *Email:* stephen.barclay.mp@parliament.uk
Constituency: MJS House, Wisbech Road, March, Cambridgeshire PE15 0BA
Tel: 01354 656635 *Website:* www.stevebarclay.net *Twitter:* @SteveBarclay

BARDELL, HANNAH

Livingston *(Majority 3,878)*

SCOTTISH NATIONAL PARTY

SNP Spokesperson for Trade and Investment

Hannah Mary Bardell. Born 1 June 1983.

Education: Broxburn Academy; Stirling University (film, media, politics and English 2005).

Non-political career: STV, Glasgow; Producer and presenter, SNPtv online; Researcher/assistant producer, GMTV 2005-07; Assistant to Ian Hudghton MEP; Office Manager to Alex Salmond MSP 2007-10; Protocol executive and events manager, American Consulate, Edinburgh 2010-12; Communications manager, Subsea 7 2012; Head of communications and marketing (UK, Africa and Norway), Stork Technical Services 2013-15.

Political career: Member for Livingston since 7 May 2015 general election; SNP Spokesperson for: Fair Work and Employment 2015, Business, Innovation and Skills 2015-16, Business and Economy Engagement 2016-17, Trade and Investment 2017-.

Political interests: Anti-trident, anti-austerity, anti-privatisation.

Other: Member: Policy Committee, Grampian Chamber of Commerce, Business for Scotland; Aberdeen Performing Arts Development Committee. Pushkin Prize winner for creative writing.

Recreations: Guitar, singing, creative writing, arts, musical theatre, watching sports, surfing, golf.

Hannah Bardell MP, House of Commons, London SW1A 0AA
Tel: 020 7219 5907 *Email:* hannah.bardell.mp@parliament.uk
Constituency: No constituency office publicised
Tel: 01506 462004 *Twitter:* @HannahB4LiviMP

House of Commons MPs' Biographies

CONSERVATIVE

BARON, JOHN

Basildon and Billericay *(Majority 13,400)*

John Charles Baron. Born 21 June 1959; Son of Raymond Baron and Kathleen Baron, née Whittlestone; Married Thalia Mayson, née Laird 1992 (2 daughters).

Education: Attended nine schools by 16 including: Birmingham Grammar School; Wadham Comprehensive, Crewkerne; Queen's College, Taunton, Somerset; Jesus College, Cambridge (BA history and economics 1982); Royal Military College Sandhurst (1984).

Non-political career: Captain Royal Regiment of Fusiliers 1984-87. Director: Henderson Private Investors Ltd 1987-99, Rothschild Asset Management 1999-2001.

Political career: Contested Basildon 1997 general election. Member for Billericay 2001-10, for Basildon and Billericay since 6 May 2010 general election; Shadow Minister for: Health 2002-03 (resigned over Iraq War), Health 2003-07; Opposition Whip 2007-10. *Select committees:* Member: Education and Skills 2001-02, Foreign Affairs 2010-17. Founding Member, Conservatives for Britain 2015-16.

Political interests: Foreign affairs, economy, civil liberties, defence, cancer.

Other: Chair, Fun Walk Trust; Member, Chartered Institute for Securities and Investment (MCSI); Supports numerous charities. Northern Ireland and UN Medals.

Publications: Regular column for *Financial Times*'s Investors Chronicle; Co-author, The Future of Conservatism: Values Revisited (Biteback, 2011); The FT Guide to Investment Trusts (Pearson, 2013); Time to Recognise the Danger (RUSI, 2015).

Recreations: Tennis, walking, history, cycling, financial journalism.

John Baron MP, House of Commons, London SW1A 0AA
Tel: 020 7219 8138 *Fax:* 020 7219 1743 *Email:* baronj@parliament.uk
Constituency: Suites 2 and 3, Bowden Terminal, Luckyn Lane, Basildon, Essex SS14 3AX
Tel: 01268 520765 *Fax:* 01268 524009 *Email:* turnerja@parliament.uk
Website: www.johnbaron.co.uk

LABOUR

BARRON, KEVIN

Rother Valley *(Majority 3,882)*

Chair, Select Committees on Standards

Kevin John Barron. Born 26 October 1946; Son of late Richard Barron and Edna Barron; Married Carol McGrath 1969 (died 2008) (1 son 2 daughters); married Andrée Deane 2012.

Education: Maltby Hall Secondary Modern, near Rotherham; Sheffield University (day release, social sciences); Ruskin College, Oxford (Diploma labour studies 1977).

Non-political career: Colliery electrician and NUM trade union delegate, Maltby 1962-83; Parliamentary adviser to Japanese Pharmaceutical Group -2015. Member, Unite.

Political career: Member for Rother Valley 1983-2010, for Rother Valley (revised boundary) since 6 May 2010 general election; PPS to Neil Kinnock as Leader of the Opposition 1985-88; Sponsored Private Member's Bills: to ban advertising and promotion of tobacco products 1993, 1994, Energy efficiency stamp duty rebate; Opposition Spokesperson for: Energy 1988-92, Employment 1993-95, Health 1995-97; Member: Intelligence and Security Committee 1997-2005, Speaker's Committee for the Independent Parliamentary Standards Authority 2010-, Speakers' Working Group on All-Party Groups 2011-12. *Select committees:* Chair, Health 2005-10; Member, Liaison 2005-; Standards and Privileges: Member 2005-10, Chair 2010-13; Chair: Privileges 2013- (stood aside from the role when he referred himself to the Parliamentary Commissioner for Standards), Standards 2013- (stood aside from the role when he referred himself to the Parliamentary Commissioner for Standards). Chair, PLP: Yorkshire Regional Group 1987-2010, Departmental Group for Health and Social Services 1997-2001, 2010-11.

Political interests: Energy, environment, home affairs, health, intelligence and security, international development, British film; Bulgaria, Guyana, Tanzania.

Other: Commonwealth Parliamentary Association (UK Branch): Hon. Treasurer 2010-15, Vice-chair 2014-15; Trustee, National Coal Mining Museum 2005; Patron, Safe@last (charity for runaway children and young people) 2008-; Member, General Medical Council 1999-2009; Vice-president, Royal Society of Health 2007; Hon Fellow, Royal College of Physicians; Vice-president, Chartered Institute of Environmental Health 2008-; FRCP 2008; One World Action, British Institute for Brain Injured Children. PC 2001; Knighted 2014.

Recreations: Family life, football, fly fishing, photography, walking, film, lying in bed.

Rt Hon Sir Kevin Barron MP, House of Commons, London SW1A 0AA
Tel: 020 7219 4432/020 7219 6306 *Fax:* 020 7219 5952 *Email:* barronk@parliament.uk
Constituency: 9 Lordens Hill, Dinnington, Sheffield, South Yorkshire S25 2QE
Tel: 01909 568611 *Fax:* 01909 569974 *Email:* woolleys@parliament.uk
Website: www.kevinbarronmp.com *Twitter:* @KevinBarronMP

CONSERVATIVE

BEBB, GUTO

Aberconwy *(Majority 635)*

Parliamentary Under-Secretary of State, Wales Office; Government Whip (Lord Commissioner of HM Treasury)

Guto ap Owain Bebb. Born 9 October 1968; Son of Owain Bebb and Helen Gwyn; Married Esyllt Penri 1993 (3 sons 2 daughters).

Education: Ysgol Syr Hugh Owen, Caernarfon; Aberystwyth University (BA history 1990); Welsh.

Non-political career: Founding partner, Egin Partnership 1993-.

Political career: Contested Ogmore 2002 by-election and Conwy 2005 general election. Member for Aberconwy since 6 May 2010 general election; Parliamentary Under-Secretary of State, Wales Office 2016-; Government Whip (Lord Commissioner of HM Treasury) 2016-. *Select committees:* Member: Welsh Affairs 2010-15, Members' Expenses 2011-15, Public Accounts 2012-15. Member, Executive, 1922 Committee 2012-14. Contested Conwy constituency 2003 National Assembly for Wales election. Founding member, Conservatives for Reform in Europe 2016.

Political interests: Europe, taxation, reform of the welfare state, devolution, economy, rural development, regeneration policy; Eastern Europe, Israel, North America.

Other: Member: British-American Parliamentary Group, UK Delegation, Parliamentary Assembly of the Council of Europe 2015-16; Member, Institute of Business Consultants (IBC) 1993-.

Publications: Various in Welsh language.

Recreations: Wine, reading, music and family.

Guto Bebb MP, House of Commons, London SW1A 0AA
Tel: 020 7219 7002 *Email:* guto.bebb.mp@parliament.uk
Constituency: 1 Ashdown House, Riverside Business Park, Benarth Road, Conwy, Gwynedd LL32 8UB
Tel: 01492 583094 *Email:* office@gutobebbmp.co.uk *Website:* www.gutobebb.org.uk
Twitter: @GutoAberconwy

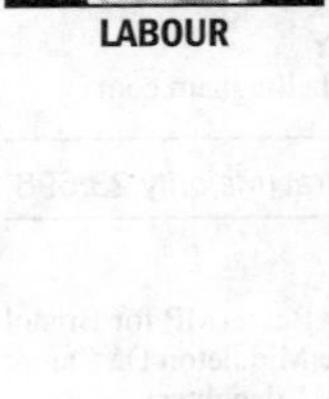

LABOUR

BECKETT, MARGARET

Derby South *(Majority 11,248)*

Margaret Mary Beckett. Born 15 January 1943; Daughter of late Cyril Jackson, carpenter, and Winifred Jackson, teacher; Married Lionel (Leo) Beckett 1979 (2 stepsons).

Education: Notre Dame High School, Manchester and Norwich; Manchester College of Science and Technology; John Dalton Polytechnic.

Non-political career: Student apprentice in metallurgy, AEI Manchester 1961-66; Experimental officer, Department of Metallurgy, Manchester University 1966-70; Industrial policy researcher, Labour Party 1970-74; Political adviser, Ministry of Overseas Development 1974; Principal researcher, Granada Television 1979-83. Member: Transport and General Workers' Union 1964-, National Union of Journalists, BECTU.

Political career: Contested (as Margaret Jackson) Lincoln February 1974 general election. Member for Lincoln October 1974-79. Contested Lincoln 1979 general election. Member (as Margaret Beckett) for Derby South 1983-2010, for Derby South (revised boundary) since 6 May 2010 general election; PPS to Judith Hart as Minister of Overseas Development 1974-75; Assistant Government Whip 1975-76; Parliamentary Under-Secretary of State, Department of Education and Science 1976-79; Shadow Minister, Social Security 1984-89; Shadow Chief Secretary to the Treasury 1989-92; Shadow Leader, House of Commons 1992-94; Deputy Leader, Labour Party and Opposition 1992-94; Leader of Opposition May-July 1994; Shadow Secretary of State for Health 1994-95; Shadow President of the Board of Trade 1995-97; President of the Board of Trade 1997-98; Secretary of State for Trade and Industry 1997-98; President of the Council and Leader of the House of Commons 1998-2001; Secretary of State for: Environment, Food and Rural Affairs 2001-06, Foreign and Commonwealth Affairs (Foreign Secretary) 2006-07; Minister for Housing and Planning (attending Cabinet), Department for Communities and Local Government 2008-09; Chair Intelligence and Security Committee 2008-10; Contested Speaker election 2009. *Select committees:* Chair: Modernisation of the House of Commons 1998-2001; Joint Committee on National Security Strategy 2010-. Labour Party: Member 1963-, Secretary, Trades Council and Labour Party, Swinton and Pendlebury 1968-70, Member, National Executive Committee 1980-81, 1985-86, 1988-97, 2011-, Member: Tribune Group, Socialist Education Committee, Labour Women's Action Committee, Socialist Environment and Resources Association, Chair, Environment, Energy and Culture Policy Commission. *Councils and public bodies:* Member, Committee on Standards in Public Life 2010-.

Political interests: Industry, climate change, nuclear disarmament.

Other: Member: Amnesty International, Anti-Apartheid Movement, Fabian Society, Global Zero, Top Level Group on Nuclear non-proliferation. PC 1993; DBE 2013.

Publications: The Need For Consumer Protection (1972); The National Enterprise Board; The Nationalisation of Shipbuilding, Ship Repair and Marine Engineering; Renewing the NHS (1995); Vision for Growth – A New Industrial Strategy for Britain (1996).

Recreations: Cooking, reading, caravanning.

Rt Hon Dame Margaret Beckett DBE MP, House of Commons, London SW1A 0AA
Tel: 020 7219 5135/020 7219 2088 *Fax:* 020 7219 4780
Email: margaret.beckett.mp@parliament.uk
Constituency: No constituency office publicised
Tel: 01332 345636 *Fax:* 01332 371306 *Email:* james@derbylabourparty.co.uk

CONSERVATIVE

BELLINGHAM, HENRY

North West Norfolk *(Majority 13,788)*

Henry Campbell Bellingham. Born 29 March 1955; Married Emma Whiteley 1993 (1 son).

Education: Eton College; Magdalene College, Cambridge (BA law 1978, MA); Council of Legal Education 1978-79.

Non-political career: Barrister, Middle Temple 1978-87; Company Director and Business Consultant 1997-2001.

Political career: Member for Norfolk North West 1983-97. Contested Norfolk North West 1997 general election. Member for North West Norfolk 2001-10, for North West Norfolk (revised boundary) since 6 May 2010 general election; PPS to Malcolm Rifkind as Secretary of State for Transport and for Defence and as Foreign Secretary 1991-97; Shadow Minister for: Trade and Industry (Small Business and Enterprise) 2002-03, Economic Affairs (Small Business and Enterprise) 2003-05; Opposition Whip 2005-06; Shadow Minister for Constitutional Affairs/Justice 2006-10; Parliamentary Under-Secretary of State, Foreign and Commonwealth Office (Minister for Africa, UN and overseas territories) 2010-12; Contested Deputy Speaker election 2013. *Select committees:* Member: Environment 1988-90, Northern Ireland 2001-02, Trade and Industry 2002-03, High Speed Rail (London-West Midlands) Bill 2014-16, Panel of Chairs 2017-. Chair, Conservative Council on Eastern Europe 1989-93.

Political interests: Small businesses, agriculture, defence, Northern Ireland, foreign policy, legal services; Africa, Caribbean, Overseas Territories.

Other: President, British Resorts Association 1993-97; Non-executive director, Developing Markets Associates (DMA); Non-executive chair: Pontus Marine 2013-, Pathfinder Minerals plc 2013-; Chair: Westminster Foundation for Democracy 2013, Policy Research Unit (PRU) 2013-, Global Law Summit 2015-; Senior Adviser to J Stern & Co LLP 2016-. Kt 2016.

Recreations: Country sports, golf, cricket.

Sir Henry Bellingham MP, House of Commons, London SW1A 0AA
Tel: 020 7219 8234 *Fax:* 020 7219 2844 *Email:* bellinghamh@parliament.uk
Constituency: First Floor, 12 London Road, King's Lynn, Norfolk PE30 5PY
Tel: 01485 600559/01553 692076 *Fax:* 01485 600292 *Website:* www.henrybellingham.com

LABOUR

BENN, HILARY

Leeds Central *(Majority 23,698)*

Chair, Select Committee on Exiting the European Union

Hilary James Wedgwood Benn. Born 26 November 1953; Son of late Tony Benn (MP for Bristol South East 1950-61, 1963-83 and Chesterfield 1984-2001) and late Caroline Middleton De Camp; Married Rosalind Retey 1973 (died 1979); married Sally Clark 1982 (3 sons 1 daughter).

Education: Holland Park Comprehensive School; Sussex University (BA Russian and East European studies 1974).

Non-political career: Research officer and latterly head of policy and communications, MSF 1975-97; Special adviser to David Blunkett as Secretary of State for Education and Employment 1997-99. Member, Unite.

Political career: Contested Ealing North 1983 and 1987 general elections. Member for Leeds Central 10 June 1999 by-election to 2010, for Leeds Central (revised boundary) since 6 May 2010 general election; Parliamentary Under-Secretary of State: Department for International Development 2001-02, Home Office (Community and Custodial Provision) 2002-03; Department for International Development: Minister of State 2003, Secretary of State 2003-07; Secretary of State for Environment, Food and Rural Affairs 2007-10; Shadow Secretary of State for Environment, Food and Rural Affairs 2010; Shadow Leader of the House of Commons 2010-11; Member: House of Commons Commission 2010-11, Speaker's Committee for the Independent Parliamentary Standards Authority 2011-12; Shadow Secretary of State for: Communities and Local Government 2011-15, Foreign and Commonwealth Affairs (Shadow Foreign Secretary) 2015-16. *Select committees:* Member: Environment, Transport and Regional Affairs 1999-2001, Environment, Transport and Regional Affairs (Environment Sub-committee) 1999-2001; Chair, Exiting the European Union 2016-; Member, Liaison 2016-. Joint vice-chair, PLP Departmental Committee for Education and Employment 2000-01. Member, Society – Stronger, Safer Communities Policy Commission. *Councils and public bodies:* London Borough of Ealing: Councillor 1979-99, Deputy Leader 1986-90, Chair, Education Committee 1986-90; Member, Association of Metropolitan Authorities Education Committee 1986-90; Chair, Association of London Authorities Education Committee 1989-90.

Political interests: International development, home affairs, education, employment, trade unions, environment, urban policy; Democratic Republic of the Congo, Sudan, USA.

Other: Minister of the Year *House Magazine* 2006, 2007; Politicians' Politician Channel 4 2006; Parliamentarian of the Year, League Against Cruel Sports 2011; Spectator Parliamentarian of the Year 2016. PC 2003.

Publications: Contributor: Beyond 2002: Long-term policies for Labour (Profile Books, 1999), The Forces of Conservatism (IPPR, 1999), Men who made Labour (Routledge, 2006), Politics for a New Generation (IPPR, 2007), The End of the Peer Show: Responses to the Draft Bill on Lords Reform (2011).

Recreations: Watching sport, gardening.

Rt Hon Hilary Benn MP, House of Commons, London SW1A 0AA
Tel: 020 7219 5770 *Email:* hilary.benn.mp@parliament.uk
Constituency: Unity Business Centre, 26 Roundhay Road, Leeds, West Yorkshire LS7 1AB
Tel: 0113-244 1097 *Email:* boxj@parliament.uk *Website:* www.hilarybennmp.com
Twitter: @HilaryBennMP

CONSERVATIVE

BENYON, RICHARD

Newbury *(Majority 24,380)*

Richard Henry Ronald Benyon. Born 21 October 1960; Son of Sir William Benyon (MP for Buckingham 1970-83 and Milton Kenyes 1983-92) and Lady Benyon; Married Zoe Robinson 2004 (2 sons and 3 sons by previous marriage).

Education: Bradfield College, Reading; Royal Agricultural College (Diploma real estate management, land economy 1987); French, some Swahili.

Non-political career: Army officer, Royal Green Jackets 1980-85. Land agent chartered surveyor 1987-; Farmer 1990-; Chair, Rural and Urban Housing Business 2001-10; Director, Englefield Estate Trust Corporation Limited; Associate director, Sancroft International Ltd 2015-; Director and chair, UK Water Partnership 2015-.

Political career: Contested Newbury 1997 and 2001 general elections. Member for Newbury 2005-10, for Newbury (revised boundary) since 6 May 2010 general election; Opposition Whip 2007-09; Shadow Minister for Environment, Food and Rural Affairs 2009-10; Parliamentary Under-Secretary of State, Department for Environment, Food and Rural Affairs 2010-13 (Natural Environment and Fisheries 2010-12, Natural Environment, Water and Rural Affairs 2012-13); Trade Envoy to: Mozambique and Democratic Republic of Congo 2016-17, Ethiopia 2016-17; Member, Intelligence and Security Committee 2016-. *Select committees:* Member, Home Affairs 2005-07; *Ex-officio* Member, Environmental Audit 2010-13; Member: Defence 2014-16, Arms Export Controls 2014-15. Founding member, Conservatives for Reform in Europe 2016. *Councils and public bodies:* Newbury District Council: Councillor 1991-95, Leader, Conservative group 1994-95.

Political interests: Rural matters, social affairs, defence, health, home affairs; Africa, Middle East, Northern Ireland, Zimbabwe.

Other: UK delegation to NATO Parliamentary Assembly: Member 2014-15, Leader 2015-; Founder patron, Help for Heroes; Vice-chair, Citizens Advice 1994-; Member, Royal Institution of Chartered Surveyors; Berkshire Community Foundation. PC 2017.

Recreations: Walking, tennis, shooting, fishing, cooking.

Rt Hon Richard Benyon MP, House of Commons, London SW1A 0AA
Tel: 020 7219 8319 *Fax:* 020 7219 4509 *Email:* richard.benyon.mp@parliament.uk
Constituency: Park Street Offices, Newbury, Berkshire RG14 1EA
Tel: 01635 551070 *Email:* richard@richardbenyon.com *Website:* www.richardbenyon.com
Twitter: @RichardBenyonMP

THE SPEAKER

BERCOW, JOHN

Buckingham *(Majority 25,725)*

Speaker

John Simon Bercow. Born 19 January 1963; Son of Brenda Bercow, née Bailey, and late Charles Bercow; Married Sally Illman 2002 (2 sons 1 daughter).

Education: Finchley Manorhill School, London; Essex University (BA government 1985).

Non-political career: Credit analyst, Hambros Bank 1987-88; Public affairs consultant, Rowland Sallingbury Casey (public affairs arm of Saatchi & Saatchi Group) 1988-95; Board director, Rowland Company 1994-95; Special adviser to: Jonathan Aitken as Chief Secretary to the Treasury 1995, Virginia Bottomley as Secretary of State for National Heritage 1995-96.

Political career: Contested Motherwell South 1987 and Bristol South 1992 general elections. Member for Buckingham 1997-2010, for Buckingham (revised boundary) since 6 May 2010 general election (Conservative 1997-2009, Speaker since 2009); Opposition Spokesperson for: Education and Employment 1999-2000, Home Affairs 2000-01; Shadow Chief Secretary to the Treasury 2001-02; Opposition Spokesperson for Work and Pensions 2002; Shadow Secretary of State for International Development 2003-04; Speaker 2009-; Ex-officio chair House of Commons Commission 2009-; Chair: Speaker's Committee on the Electoral Commission 2009-, Speaker's Committee for the Independent Parliamentary Standards Authority 2009-, Commons Reference Group on Representation and Inclusion 2017-. *Select committees:* Member: Welsh Affairs 1997-98, Trade and Industry 1998-99, Office of the Deputy Prime Minister 2002-04, Home Affairs 2003, Office of the Deputy Prime Minister (Urban Affairs Sub-Committee) 2003-04, International Development 2004-09, Procedure 2004-05, Chairmen's Panel 2005-09, Joint Committee on Consolidation, Etc, Bills 2005-09, Quadripartite (Committees on Strategic Export Controls)/Arms Export Controls 2006-09. Member, Executive 1922 Committee 1998-99. Chair, Essex University Conservative Association 1984-85; National chair, Federation of Conservative Students 1986; Vice-chair, Conservative Collegiate Forum 1987. *Councils and public bodies:* London Borough of Lambeth: Councillor 1986-90, Deputy Leader, Conservative Opposition 1987-89; Ex-officio chair: Boundary Commission for England 2009-, Boundary Commission for Northern Ireland 2009-, Boundary Commission for Scotland 2009-, Boundary Commission for Wales 2009-.

Political interests: Special educational needs, international development, equality and human rights, constitutional reform; Burma, Sudan, USA, Zimbabwe.

Other: President, Commonwealth Parliamentary Association (UK Branch) 2009-; Hon. President, Inter-Parliamentary Union, British Group 2009-; Hon. President: Armed Forces Parliamentary Scheme 2009-, British-American Parliamentary Group 2009-, Hansard Society for Parliamentary Government 2009-, Parliamentary Press Gallery 2009-; President: Industry and Parliament Trust 2009-, Parliament Choir 2009-. Kaleidoscope Trust; Vice-president, National Autistic Society; Honorary President, Afasic; Ambitious About Autism, Blue Sky Development, Puzzle Centre, Brain Tumour Research, Chiltern MS Centre. Freedom, City of London 2016. Chancellor: Bedfordshire University 2014-, Essex University 2017-. Honorary doctorates: Essex University 2010, Buckingham University 2013, De Montfort University 2014, City University 2014. Backbencher to Watch, *Spectator* awards 1998; Backbencher of the Year *House Magazine* 2005; Opposition Politician of the Year, Channel 4/Hansard Society 2005; Charity Champion, Health, ePolitix/Dods 2006; Disability Champion, ePolitix/Dods 2007; International Champion, ePolitix/Dods 2007; Politician of the Year, Stonewall awards 2010; Politician of the Year, Political Studies Association 2012. PC 2009.

Publications: Turning Scotland Around (1987); Faster Moves Forward for Scotland (1987); Aiming for the Heart of Europe: A Misguided Venture (1998); Subsidiarity and the Illusion of Democratic Control (2003); How Much Common Ground (2004); Incoming Assets: Why Tories Should Change Policy on Immigration and Asylum (2005); Promote Freedom or Protect Oppressors: The Choice at the UN Review Summit (2005); Tennis Maestros: The Twenty Greatest Male Tennis Players of all Time (2014).

Recreations: Tennis (trying to play and watching Roger Federer), football (Arsenal FC supporter), reading, swimming, music.

Rt Hon John Bercow MP, House of Commons, London SW1A 0AA
Tel: 020 7219 4111/020 7219 5300 *Fax:* 020 7219 6901
Email: bercowj@parliament.uk speakersoffice@parliament.uk
Constituency: Speaker's House, House of Commons, London SW1A 0AA
Tel: 020 7219 6346 *Fax:* 020 7219 0981 *Website:* www.johnbercow.co.uk

CONSERVATIVE

BERESFORD, PAUL

Mole Valley *(Majority 24,137)*

Alexander Paul Beresford. Born 6 April 1946; Son of Raymond and Joan Beresford; Married Julie Haynes (3 sons 1 daughter).

Education: Waimea College, New Zealand; Otago University, Dunedin, New Zealand (BDS 1970).

Non-political career: Dental surgeon, Beresford Dental Practice. Member, National Farmers' Union.

Political career: Member for Croydon Central 1992-97, for Mole Valley 1997-2010, for Mole Valley (revised boundary) since 6 May 2010 general election; Parliamentary Under-Secretary of State, Department of the Environment 1994-97; Member, House of Commons Commission 2010-; Board Member, Parliamentary Office of Science and Technology (POST) 2015-16. *Select committees:* Member: Education 1992-94, Procedure 1997-2001, Environment, Transport and Regional Affairs 2000-01, Environment, Transport and Regional Affairs (Environment Sub-Committee) 2001, Environment, Transport and Regional Affairs (Transport Sub-Committee) 2001, Transport, Local Government and the Regions 2001-02, Transport, Local Government and the Regions (Urban Affairs Sub-Committee) 2001-02, ODPM/Communities and Local Government 2002-10, ODPM/Communities and Local Government (Urban Affairs Sub-Committee) 2003-05, Finance and Services 2010-15, Standards and Privileges 2010-13, Joint Committee on Security 2010-15, Standards 2013-, Privileges 2013-, Liaison 2015-; Chair, Administration 2015-. 1922 Committee: Secretary 2002-06, Member, Executive 2006-07. *Councils and public bodies:* London Borough of Wandsworth: Councillor 1978-94, Leader 1983-92.

Political interests: Inner cities, housing, education, health; Australia, Fiji, New Zealand, Samoa.

Other: Fellow, Industry and Parliament Trust 2002; British Dental Association; British Academy/Cosmetic Dentistry; British Endodontic Society. Kt 1990.

Recreations: DIY, reading.

Sir Paul Beresford MP, House of Commons, London SW1A 0AA
Tel: 020 7219 5018 *Email:* annie.winsbury@parliament.uk
Constituency: 212 Barnett Wood Lane, Ashtead, Surrey KT21 2DB
Tel: 01306 883312 *Fax:* 01306 885194 *Email:* office@molevalleyconservatives.org.uk
Website: www.molevalleyconservatives.org.uk

LAB/CO-OP

BERGER, LUCIANA

Liverpool Wavertree *(Majority 29,466)*

Luciana Clare Berger. Born 13 May 1981; Married Alistair Goldsmith 2015 (1 daughter).

Education: Birmingham University (BCom with Spanish 2004); Birkbeck College (MSc government, politics and policy 2005); French, Spanish.

Non-political career: Government strategy unit, Accenture 2005-06; NHS Confederation 2006; Director, Labour Friends of Israel 2007-10. Member: USDAW, UCATT.

Political career: Member for Liverpool Wavertree since 6 May 2010 general election; Shadow Minister for: Climate Change 2010-13, Public Health 2013-15, Mental Health (attending Shadow Cabinet) 2015-16. *Select committees:* Member: Business, Innovation and Skills 2010, Finance and Services 2010, Arms Export Controls 2010, Health 2016-. Vice-chair, PLP Departmental Group for Treasury 2010; Chair, PLP Departmental Groups for Health 2016-. President, Labour Campaign for Mental Health 2016-.

Political interests: Public health, mental health, creative and digital industries, culture; Spain.

Other: Advisory Board Member, Money and Mental Health Policy Institute 2016-; Fellow, Royal Society of Arts; Whizz-Kidz, Sahir House. Alumnus of the Year, Birmingham University 2012; Digital Industries Ambassdor, e-skills UK; Political Supporter of the Year, Anthony Nolan Supporter Awards 2014; No.1 40 under 40, Jewish News 2015; Parliamentarian of the Year, UK Sexual Health Awards 2015.

Recreations: Photography, film, music.

Luciana Berger MP, House of Commons, London SW1A 0AA
Tel: 020 7219 7102 *Email:* luciana.berger.mp@parliament.uk
Constituency: 21 Sandown Lane, Wavertree, Liverpool L15 8HY
Tel: 0151-228 1628 *Email:* luciana4wavertree@hotmail.co.uk *Website:* www.lucianaberger.com
Twitter: @lucianaberger

CONSERVATIVE

BERRY, JAKE

Rossendale and Darwen *(Majority 3,216)*

Parliamentary Under-Secretary of State (Minister for the Northern Powerhouse and Local Growth), Department for Communities and Local Government

James Jacob Gilchrist Berry. Born 29 December 1978; Married Charlotte 2009 (divorced 2016); Partner Alice Robinson (1 son).

Education: Sheffield University (law); Chester College (law finals).

Non-political career: Property lawyer; Consultant to Squire Patton Boggs LLP 2014-15.

Political career: Member for Rossendale and Darwen since 6 May 2010 general election; PPS: to Grant Shapps: as Minister of State for Housing and Local Government 2010-12, as Minister without Portfolio, Cabinet Office and Chairman Conservative Party 2012-15, to Greg Hands as Chief Secretary to the Treasury 2015-16; Parliamentary Under-Secretary of State (Minister for the Northern Powerhouse and Local Growth), Department for Communities and Local Government 2017-. *Select committees:* Member, Finance 2015-17. Member, Number 10 Policy Advisory Board (Housing, Transport and Environment).

Recreations: Walking, water-skiing.

Jake Berry MP, House of Commons, London SW1A 0AA
Tel: 020 7219 7214 *Email:* jake.berry.mp@parliament.uk
Constituency: 4 Mount Terrace, Rawtenstall, Rossendale BB4 8SF
Tel: 01706 215547 *Website:* www.jakeberry.org *Twitter:* @JakeBerry

LABOUR

BETTS, CLIVE

Sheffield South East *(Majority 11,798)*

Chair, Select Committee on Communities and Local Government

Clive James Charles Betts. Born 13 January 1950; Son of late Harold and Nellie Betts; Civil partner James Thomas 2011.

Education: King Edward VII School, Sheffield; Pembroke College, Cambridge (BA economics and politics 1971).

Non-political career: Economist, Trades Union Congress 1971-73; Local government economist: Derbyshire County Council 1973-74, South Yorkshire County Council 1974-86, Rotherham Borough Council 1986-91. Member, TGWU.

Political career: Contested Sheffield Hallam October 1974 and Louth 1979 general elections. Member for Sheffield Attercliffe 1992-2010, for Sheffield South East since 6 May 2010 general election; Opposition Whip 1996-97; Assistant Government Whip 1997-98; Government Whip 1998-2001. *Select committees:* Member: Treasury 1996-97, Selection 1997-2001, Transport, Local Government and the Regions (Urban Affairs Sub-committee) 2001-02, Transport, Local Government and the Regions 2001-02, ODPM/Communities and Local Government 2002-10, ODPM/Communities and Local Government (Urban Affairs Sub-committee) 2003-05, Finance and Services 2005-10, 2010-15, Chairmen's Panel/Panel of Chairs 2009-, Yorkshire and the Humber 2009-10, Reform of the House of Commons 2009-10; Chair, Communities and Local Government 2010-; Member: Liaison 2010-, Liaison (National Policy Statements Sub-committee) 2010-15, Finance 2015-. Member, Labour Leader's Campaign Team, with responsibility for Environment and Local Government 1995-96; Patron, LGBT Labour. *Councils and public bodies:* Sheffield City Council: Councillor 1976-92, Chair: Housing Committee 1980-86, Finance Committee 1986-88, Leader 1987-92; Vice-chair, Association of Metropolitan Authorities 1988-91; Chair, South Yorkshire Pensions Authority 1989-92; Vice-President, Local Government Association 2010-.

Political interests: Local and regional government, housing, planning, regeneration, transport; Bosnia, Iran, Middle East, Netherlands, Portugal, Serbia, Ukraine.

Other: Trustee, Parliamentary Pension Scheme; Fellow, Industry and Parliament Trust 1997; President, South East Sheffield Citizens' Advice Bureau 1998-.

Recreations: Supporting Sheffield Wednesday FC, playing squash, cricket, walking, real ale, scuba diving.

Clive Betts MP, House of Commons, London SW1A 0AA
Tel: 020 7219 5114 *Email:* officeofclivebettsmp@parliament.uk
Constituency: First Floor, Barkers Pool House, Burgess Street, Sheffield, South Yorkshire S1 2HF
Tel: 0114-275 7788 *Website:* www.clivebetts.com

SCOTTISH NATIONAL PARTY

BLACK, MHAIRI

Paisley and Renfrewshire South *(Majority 2,541)*

SNP Spokesperson for Pensions and Youth Affairs

Born 12 September 1994.

Education: Lourdes Secondary School; Glasgow University (BA politics and public policy 2015).

Political career: Member for Paisley and Renfrewshire South since 7 May 2015 general election; SNP Spokesperson for Pensions and Youth Affairs 2017-. *Select committees:* Member, Work and Pensions 2015-17. Member, SNP 2011-.

Political interests: Social justice, powers for Scotland.

Other: Volunteer, Oxfam; Women Against State Pension Inequality (WASPI).

Recreations: Football, Partick Thistle FC supporter.

Mhairi Black MP, House of Commons, London SW1A 0AA
Tel: 020 7219 5558 *Email:* mhairi.black.mp@parliament.uk
Constituency: 9 Wellmeadow Street, Paisley PA1 2EF
Tel: 0141-571 4370 *Website:* www.mhairiblack.scot *Twitter:* @MhairiBlack

SCOTTISH NATIONAL PARTY

BLACKFORD, IAN

Ross, Skye and Lochaber *(Majority 5,919)*

Leader, SNP Westminster Group

Born 14 May 1961; Married Ann.

Non-political career: Director, UBS Philips and Drew 1989-93; Managing director: Natwest Markets 1993-96, Deutsche Bank 1999-2002, First Seer 2003-; Investor relations, CSM 2005-12; Commsworld: Non-executive director 2006-15, Chair 2015-; Golden Charter Trust: Non-executive director 2008-15, Chair 2015-.

Political career: Contested Ayr 1997 general election and Paisley South November 1997 by-election. Member for Ross, Skye and Lochaber since 7 May 2015 general election; SNP: Spokesperson for Pensions 2015-17, Leader, Westminster Group 2017-. *Select committees:* Member, Petitions 2015-16. Scottish National Party: Member 1970s-, Member, National Executive Committee, National treasurer.

Political interests: Connectivity, both digital and transport, anti-austerity.

Other: Chair, North West Skye Recreational Association; Director, Cuillin FM; Non-executive director: Edinburgh Bicycle Cooperative 2008-13, New City Agenda 2017. PC 2017.

Recreations: Hibernian FC supporter.

Rt Hon Ian Blackford MP, House of Commons, London SW1A 0AA
Tel: 020 7219 5292 *Email:* ian.blackford.mp@parliament.uk
Constituency: 29 High Street, Dingwall IV15 9RU
Tel: 01349 866397 *Website:* ianblackford.com *Twitter:* @IanBlackfordMP

CONSERVATIVE

BLACKMAN, BOB

Harrow East *(Majority 1,757)*

Robert John Blackman. Born 26 April 1956; Son of Robert Blackman and Winifred Blackman; Married Nicola 1988 (no children).

Education: Preston Manor High School; Liverpool University (BSc physics and maths) (Union President).

Non-political career: Sales, Unisys 1979-90; British Telecom 1991-2010: Sales 1991-95, Sales tutor, training college 1995-98, Regulatory compliance manager 1998-2010. Member, Connect.

Political career: Contested Brent South 1992, Bedford 1997 and Brent North 2005 general elections. Member for Harrow East since 6 May 2010 general election. *Select committees:* Member: Communities and Local Government 2010-, Backbench Business 2012-, Procedure 2015-. Secretary, 1922 Committee 2015-. AM for Brent and Harrow constituency, London Assembly 2004-08. *Councils and public bodies:* London Borough of Brent Council: Councillor 1986-2010, Conservative Group Leader 1990-2010, Council Leader 1991-96, Deputy Council Leader 2006-10; Governor: Preston Manor High School, Wembley Primary School; Vice-President, Local Government Association 2016-.

Political interests: Local government, science, communications, sport, public expenditure, housing, housing benefit reform and welfare reform; Azerbaijan, Brazil, India, Israel, Italy, Nepal, Sri Lanka, USA.

Other: Member, Executive Committee, Commonwealth Parliamentary Association UK 2015-16; St Luke's Hospice, Cancer Research.

Recreations: Tottenham Hotspur FC, bridge, chess, reading, cricket.

Bob Blackman MP, House of Commons, London SW1A 0AA
Tel: 020 7219 7082 *Email:* bob.blackman.mp@parliament.uk
Constituency: 209 Headstone Lane, Harrow HA2 6ND
Tel: 020 8421 3323 *Website:* www.bobblackmanmp.com *Twitter:* @BobBlackman

SCOTTISH NATIONAL PARTY

BLACKMAN, KIRSTY

Aberdeen North *(Majority 4,139)*

Deputy Leader, SNP Westminster Group; Spokesperson for Economy

Kirsty Ann Blackman. Born 20 March 1986; Married Luke (2 children).

Education: Robert Gordon's College, Aberdeen; Aberdeen University (medicine) (did not complete degree); Open University (mathematics).

Non-political career: Former parliamentary assistant to Nigel Don MSP, Brian Adam MSP and Mark McDonald MSP.

Political career: Member for Aberdeen North since 7 May 2015 general election; SNP Spokesperson for: House of Lords 2015-17, Economy 2017-; Deputy Leader, SNP Westminster Group 2017-; Member, Speaker's Committee on the Electoral Commission 2017-. *Select committees:* Member, Scottish Affairs 2015-16. *Councils and public bodies:* Aberdeen City Council: Councillor 2007-15, Convener, SNP Group 2009-15.

Political interests: Welfare, anti-trident.

Other: Trustee: Aberdeen International Football Festival -2012; Aberdeen Endowment Trust 2007-15; Director, Aberdeen Exhibition and Conference Centre -2013; Representative, Epilepsy Association of Scotland. Granite City Wanderers Hockey Club 2006-11.

Kirsty Blackman MP, House of Commons, London SW1A 0AA
Tel: 020 7219 8791 *Email:* kirsty.blackman.mp@parliament.uk
Constituency: 46 John Street, Aberdeen, Aberdeenshire AB25 1LL
Tel: 01224 633285 *Twitter:* @KirstySNP

LABOUR

BLACKMAN-WOODS, ROBERTA

City of Durham *(Majority 12,364)*

Shadow Minister for International Development

Roberta Carol Blackman-Woods. Born 16 August 1957; Daughter of late Charles and Eleanor Woods; Married Professor Tim Blackman 1986 (1 daughter).

Education: Methodist College, Belfast; Ulster University (BSc social science 1979; PhD 1989).

Non-political career: Welfare rights officer, Newcastle City Council 1982-85; Lecturer in social policy: Ulster University 1985-90, Newcastle University 1990-95; Dean of labour and social studies, Ruskin College, Oxford 1995-2000; Professor of social policy and associate dean, Northumbria University 2000-05. Member: GMB, University and College Union.

Political career: Member for City of Durham since 5 May 2005 general election; PPS to: Hilary Armstrong as Chancellor of the Duchy of Lancaster 2006-07, Des Browne as Secretary of State for Defence 2007-08, David Lammy as Minister of State, Department for Innovation, Universities and Skills/Business, Innovation and Skills 2008-10; Deputy Minister for the North East 2008-10; Shadow Minister, Department of Business, Innovation and Skills May-October 2010; Shadow Minister for: Cabinet Office 2010-11, Communities and Local Government 2011-15, Housing 2015-16; Board Member, Parliamentary Office of Science and Technology (POST) 2015-; Shadow Minister for: Local Government and Housing 2016-17, International Development 2017-. *Select committees:* Member: Joint Committee on Statutory Instruments and Commons Committee on Statutory Instruments 2005-10, Education and Skills 2005-06, Innovation, Universities[, Science] and Skills/Science and Technology 2007-10, Science and Technology 2016-17. Member, PLP Departmental Committees on: Education 2005-10, International Development 2005-10, Communities and Local Government 2005-10; PLP Departmental Group for Women: Honorary Secretary 2007-08, Chair 2008-10, Vice-chair 2010-11. Chair: Newcastle East and Wallsend CLP 1991-95, City of Durham CLP 2003-05. *Councils and public bodies:* Councillor: Newcastle City Council 1992-95, Oxford City Council 1996-2000.

Political interests: Education, housing, international development, regeneration, planning; Afghanistan, Africa, China.

Other: Executive Committee, Commonwealth Parliamentary Association (UK Branch): Vice-chair 2011-17, Honorary Treasurer 2017-.

Recreations: Music, reading, gardening.

Dr Roberta Blackman-Woods MP, House of Commons, London SW1A 0AA
Tel: 020 7219 4258 *Fax:* 020 7219 8018 *Email:* woodsr@parliament.uk
Constituency: The Miners' Hall, Redhills, Flass Street, Durham DH1 4BD
Tel: 0191-374 1915 *Fax:* 0191-374 1916 *Email:* hindmarchc@parliament.uk
Website: www.roberta.org.uk *Twitter:* @robertabwMP

LABOUR

BLOMFIELD, PAUL

Sheffield Central *(Majority 27,748)*

Shadow Minister for Exiting the European Union

Paul Christopher Blomfield. Born 25 August 1953; Son of Henry and Mabel Blomfield; Married Linda McAvan 2000, MEP for Yorkshire and the Humber (1 son from previous marriage).

Education: Abbeydale Boys Grammar School, Sheffield; Tadcaster Grammar School; St John's College, York (theology); Teacher training (CertEd 1976).

Non-political career: Sheffield University 1978-2010: Various posts 1978-2003, General manager, Students' Union 2003-10. Member, National Executive Committee and Vice-President, National Union of Students 1976-78; Former branch secretary, Unison; Member: Amicus/Unite, GMB.

Political career: Member for Sheffield Central since 6 May 2010 general election; PPS to Hilary Benn: as Shadow Leader of the House of Commons 2010-11, as Shadow Secretary of State for Communities and Local Government 2011-15, as Shadow Foreign Secretary 2015-16; Shadow Minister for Exiting the European Union 2016-. *Select committees:* Member: Business, Innovation and Skills 2010-16, Joint Committee on Able Marine Energy Park Development Consent Order 2014 2014-15, Education, Skills and the Economy Sub-committee 2015-16. Chair, Labour for Democracy 2012-. Member: Co-operative Party, Labour Party 1978-; Chair, Sheffield Labour Party 1993-2008. *Councils and public bodies:* Governor, Sheffield City Polytechnic 1982-92; Sheffield City Trust: Board member 1994-2008, Chair 1997-2008.

Political interests: Universities, education, skills, housing, voluntary and community sector, financial inclusion, small businesses; Southern Africa, Burma, Kashmir, Palestine, Somaliland.

Other: Executive committee, Anti-Apartheid Movement 1978-94; Former executive member, Sheffield Race Equality Council.

Recreations: Walking, cycling, Sheffield United FC season ticket holder.

Paul Blomfield MP, House of Commons, London SW1A 0AA
Tel: 020 7219 7142 *Email:* paul.blomfield.mp@parliament.uk
Constituency: Unit 4, Edmund Road Business Centre, 135 Edmund Road, Sheffield S2 4ED
Tel: 0114-272 2882 *Fax:* 0114-272 2442 *Website:* www.paulblomfield.co.uk
Twitter: @paulblomfieldmp

CONSERVATIVE

BLUNT, CRISPIN

Reigate *(Majority 17,614)*

Crispin Jeremy Rupert Blunt. Born 15 July 1960; Son of late Major-General Peter and Adrienne Blunt; Married Victoria Jenkins 1990 (separated) (1 son 1 daughter).

Education: Wellington College, Berkshire; Royal Military Academy, Sandhurst (commissioned 1980); University College, Durham University (BA politics 1984); Cranfield Institute of Technology (MBA 1991).

Non-political career: Army Officer 1979-90; Regimental duty 13th/18th Royal Hussars (QMO) in England, Germany and Cyprus. District agent, Forum of Private Business 1991-92; Political consultant, Politics International 1993; Special adviser to Malcolm Rifkind MP: as Secretary of State for Defence 1993-95, as Foreign Secretary 1995-97; Non-executive director, Social Investment Business Group 2013-17; Consultant to Kamal Exchange Company; Political adviser, CLEAR 2016-.

Political career: Contested West Bromwich East 1992 general election. Member for Reigate 1997-2010, for Reigate (revised boundary) since 6 May 2010 general election; Opposition Spokesperson for Northern Ireland 2001-02; Shadow Minister for Trade and Industry 2002-03; Opposition Whip 2004-09; Shadow Minister for National Security 2009-10; Parliamentary Under-Secretary of State, Ministry of Justice 2010-12. *Select committees:* Member: Defence 1997-2000, 2003-04, Environment, Transport and Regional Affairs 2000-01, Environment, Transport and Regional Affairs (Environment Sub-Committee) 2000-01, Finance and Services 2005-09, Joint Committee on Voting Eligibilty (Prisoners) Bill 2013, Liaison 2015-17; Chair, Foreign Affairs 2015-17; Member: Joint Committee on the National Security Strategy 2015-, Arms Export Controls 2016-17. Secretary, Conservative Party Committees for: Foreign and Commonwealth Affairs 1997-2001, European Affairs 1999-2000. Executive member, 1922 Committee 2000-01; Treasurer, Conservative Parliamentary Friends of India 2001-06; Chair, Conservative Middle East Council 2003-08.

Political interests: Defence, foreign affairs, environment, energy, justice; Middle East, India, USA.

Other: Reigate Priory Cricket, MCC; House of Lords and House of Commons Cricket Club.

Recreations: Cricket, skiing, gardening.

Crispin Blunt MP, House of Commons, London SW1A 0AA
Tel: 020 7219 2254 *Fax:* 020 7219 3373 *Email:* crispinbluntmp@parliament.uk
Constituency: 38-40 Bell Street, Reigate, Surrey RH2 7BA
Tel: 01737 222756 *Website:* www.blunt4reigate.com *Twitter:* @CrispinBlunt

CONSERVATIVE

BOLES, NICK

Grantham and Stamford *(Majority 20,094)*

Nicholas Edward Coleridge Boles. Born 2 November 1965; Civil partner 2011.

Education: Winchester College; Magdalen College, Oxford (BA politics, philosophy and economics 1987); John F Kennedy School of Government, Harvard University (MPP master of public policy 1989); French, German, Spanish.

Non-political career: Longwall Holdings Ltd: Chief Executive 1995-2000, Chair 2000-07; Director, Policy Exchange 2002-07.

Political career: Contested Hove 2005 general election. Member for Grantham and Stamford since 6 May 2010 general election; PPS to Nick Gibb as Minister of State for Schools 2010-12; Parliamentary Under-Secretary of State (Planning), Department for Communities and Local Government 2012-14; Department for Business, Innovation and Skills and Department for Education: Minister of State for: Skills 2014-16, Equalities 2014-15. *Select committees:* Member: Political and Constitutional Reform 2010, Standing Orders 2011-12, 2013-14. *Councils and public bodies:* Westminster City Council: Councillor 1998-2002, Chair, Housing Committee 1999-2001.

Political interests: Education, local government, foreign affairs.

Other: Political fellow, Institute for Government 2010-; Founding supporter, Change Britain 2016-.

Publications: Blue tomorrow (Politicos, 2001); Which Way's Up? – the Future for Coalition Britain (2010).

Recreations: Sailing, skiing, running, playing the piano.

Nick Boles MP, House of Commons, London SW1A 0AA
Tel: 020 7219 7079 *Email:* nick.boles.mp@parliament.uk
Constituency: Office 8, The Old National School, 62 North Street, Bourne PE10 9AJ
Tel: 01778 218120 *Website:* www.nickboles.co.uk *Twitter:* @NickBoles

CONSERVATIVE

BONE, PETER

Wellingborough *(Majority 12,460)*

Peter William Bone. Born 19 October 1952; Son of late William and Marjorie Bone; Married Jeanette Sweeney 1981 (2 sons 1 daughter).

Education: Stewards Comprehensive School, Harlow, Essex; Westcliff High School for Boys, Essex.

Non-political career: Financial director, Essex Electronics and Precision Engineering Group 1977-83; Press secretary to Paul Channon MP 1982-84; Chief executive, High Tech Electronics Company 1983-90; Managing director: Palm Travel (West) Ltd 1990-, AJWB Travel Ltd.

Political career: Contested Islwyn 1992, Pudsey 1997 and Wellingborough 2001 general elections. Member for Wellingborough 2005-10, for Wellingborough (revised boundary) since 6 May 2010 general election. *Select committees:* Member: Joint Committee on Statutory Instruments and Commons Committee on Statutory Instruments 2005-10, Trade and Industry 2005-07, Health 2007-10, Backbench Business 2010-12, 2015-16, Chairmen's Panel/Panel of Chairs 2010-, Exiting the European Union 2017-, Procedure 2017-. Member, Executive, 1922 Committee 2007-12. Contested Mid and West Wales 1994 European Parliament election. Deputy chair, Southend West Conservative Association 1977-84; Member, National Union Executive Committee 1993-96; Founding Member: All Wales Conservative Policy Group (think tank), Conservatives for Britain 2015-16. *Councils and public bodies:* Councillor, Southend-on-Sea Borough Council 1977-86; Former member, Southern Airport Management Committee.

Political interests: European Union parliamentary reform, human trafficking.

Other: Secretary, Parliament First; Founding member, Grassroots Out 2015-16; Fellow, Institute of Chartered Accountants of England and Wales 1976. Wellingborough Golf Club; Wellingborough Old Grammarians.

Publications: Contributor: *Daily Telegraph*, *The Times*, *Daily Express*, *Western Mail*; Numerous TV appearances and radio interviews.

Recreations: Running marathons for charity, cricket.

Peter Bone MP, House of Commons, London SW1A 0AA
Tel: 020 7219 8496 *Fax:* 020 7219 0301 *Email:* bonep@parliament.uk
Constituency: 21 High Street, Wellingborough, Northamptonshire NN8 4JZ
Tel: 01933 279343 *Website:* www.wellingboroughconservatives.org *Twitter:* @PeterBoneUK

BOTTOMLEY, PETER

Worthing West *(Majority 12,090)*

CONSERVATIVE

Peter James Bottomley. Born 30 July 1944; Son of Sir James Bottomley KCMG, HM Diplomatic Service, and Barbara Bottomley, social worker; Married Virginia Garnett 1967 (MP for South West Surrey 1984-2005 as Virginia Bottomley, now Baroness Bottomley of Nettlestone (qv)) (1 son 2 daughters).

Education: Comprehensive school, Washington DC; Westminster School, London; Trinity College, Cambridge (BA economics 1966, MA).

Non-political career: Industrial sales, industrial relations, industrial economics. Former member, TGWU.

Political career: Contested Greenwich, Woolwich West February and October 1974 general elections. Member for Greenwich, Woolwich West 1975 by-election to 1983, for Eltham 1983-97, for Worthing West 1997-2010, for Worthing West (revised boundary) since 6 May 2010 general election; PPS to: Cranley Onslow as Minister of State, Foreign and Commonwealth Office 1982-83, Norman Fowler as Secretary of State for Health and Social Security 1983-84; Parliamentary Under-Secretary of State: Department of Employment 1984-86, Department of Transport (Minister for Roads and Traffic) 1986-89, Northern Ireland Office (Agriculture, Environment) 1989-90; PPS to Peter Brooke as Secretary of State for Northern Ireland 1990. *Select committees:* Member: Standards and Privileges 1997-2002, Unopposed Bills (Panel) 1997-2015, Constitutional Affairs 2003-05, Ecclesiastical Committee, Joint Committee on the Draft Defamation Bill 2011, High Speed Rail (London-West Midlands) Bill 2014-16. President, Conservative Trade Unionists 1978-80; Founding member, Conservatives for Reform in Europe 2016.

Countries of interest: Southern Africa, El Salvador, USA.

Other: Member, UK Delegation: NATO Parliamentary Assembly, Organisation for Security and Co-operation in Europe Parliamentary Assembly; Trustee, Christian Aid 1978-84; Chair: Family Forum 1980-82, Church of England Children's Society 1982-84; Member, Council of Nacro 1997-2003; Fellow, Industry and Parliament Trust; Trustee, Dr Busby's Trustees (Willen) Main Charity; Former Fellow, Institute of Personnel Management; Fellow, Institute of Road Safety Officers. Court Member, Drapers' Company. Gold Medal, Institute of the Motor Industry 1988. Kt 2011. Former Parliamentary swimming and occasional dinghy sailing champion.

Recreations: Children, canoeing.

Sir Peter Bottomley MP, House of Commons, London SW1A 0AA
Tel: 020 7219 5060 *Fax:* 020 7219 1212 *Email:* bottomleyp@parliament.uk
Constituency: No constituency office publicised *Website:* www.sirpeterbottomley.com

BOWIE, ANDREW

West Aberdeenshire and Kincardine *(Majority 7,950)*

CONSERVATIVE

Education: Inverurie Academy; Aberdeen University (MA history and politics 2013).

Non-political career: Junior Warfare Officer, Royal Navy 2007-10; Military Projects Co-ordinator, Divex 2013; North Scotland Campaign Manager, Conservative Party 2014-15; Parliamentary Assistant and Rural Affairs Policy Adviser, European Parliament 2015-16; Head of Office to Liam Kerr MSP 2016-17.

Political career: Member for West Aberdeenshire and Kincardine since 8 June 2017.

Andrew Bowie MP, House of Commons, London SW1A 0AA
Tel: 020 7219 2791 *Email:* andrew.bowie.mp@parliament.uk
Constituency: Westpoint House, Arnhall Business Park, Westhill AB32 6FJ
Tel: 01224 766959 *Twitter:* @AndrewBowieMP

LAB/CO-OP

BRABIN, TRACY
Batley and Spen *(Majority 8,961)*

Shadow Minister for Early Years

Tracy Lynn Brabin. Born 9 May 1961; Married Richard Platt 2005 (2 daughters).

Education: Loughborough University (BA drama); London College of Printing (MA screenwriting 2000).

Non-political career: Actress and screenwriter, Origin Films 2000-2012; Actress: David Pugh (theatre company) 2012-14, ITV 2014, Derby Playhouse 2014; Writer: Tracy Beaker, BBC 2004-06, Shameless, Channel Four 2010, Rollem 2014-, Noon Vision 2015, LAMDA 2015, Bob&Co 2015-.

Political career: Member for Batley and Spen since 20 October 2016 by-election; Shadow Minister for Education (Early Years) 2017-. *Select committees:* Member, Women and Equalities 2016-17.

Other: Trustee, Harinder Veriah Trust.

Tracy Brabin MP, House of Commons, London SW1A 0AA
Tel: 020 7219 4594 *Email:* tracy.brabin.mp@parliament.uk
Constituency: 286 Oxford Road, Gomersal BD19 4PY
Tel: 01924 900036 *Website:* tracybrabinmp.com *Twitter:* @TracyBrabin

CONSERVATIVE

BRADLEY, BEN
Mansfield *(Majority 1,057)*

Benjamin David Bradley. Married Shanade (2 sons).

Education: Nottingham Trent University (BA politics 2013).

Non-political career: Landscape gardener; Administrator, Open University 2009-12; Associate consultant, accountancy and finance, Hays 2013; Office of Mark Spencer MP: Campaign manager 2013-15, Constituency office manager 2015-17; Representing Nick Boles MP and Grantham and Stamford Constituency 2016-17.

Political career: Member for Mansfield since 8 June 2017; Hucknall Conservatives: Deputy Chair 2012-14, Chair 2016-; Deputy Chair, Sherwood Constituency Conservative Association 2016-. *Councils and public bodies:* Ashfield District Council: Councillor 2015-17, Leader, Conservative Group 2015-17; Governor, Holgate Academy; Councillor, Nottingham County Council 2017-.

Ben Bradley MP, House of Commons, London SW1A 0AA
Tel: 020 7219 3594 *Email:* ben.bradley.mp@parliament.uk
Constituency: 36 Church Street, Mansfield, Nottinghamshire NG18 1AE
Tel: 01623 372016 *Website:* www.benbradleymp.com

CONSERVATIVE

BRADLEY, KAREN
Staffordshire Moorlands *(Majority 10,830)*

Secretary of State for Digital, Culture, Media and Sport

Karen Anne Bradley. Born 12 March 1970; Married Neil Bradley 2001 (2 sons).

Education: Buxton Girls School, Buxton; Imperial College, London (BSc mathematics 1991).

Non-political career: Student accountant, then manager, Deloittes 1991-98; Senior manager, KPMG 1998-2004, 2007-14; Self-employed economic and fiscal adviser.

Political career: Contested Manchester Withington 2005 general election. Member for Staffordshire Moorlands since 6 May 2010 general election; Assistant Government Whip 2012-13; Government Whip (Lord Commissioner of HM Treasury) 2013-14; Home Office: Parliamentary Under-Secretary of State: (Modern Slavery and Organised Crime) 2014-15, (Preventing Abuse and Exploitation) 2015-16, (Crime) 2016; Secretary of State for: Culture, Media and Sport 2016-, Digital 2017-. *Select committees:* Member: Work and Pensions 2010-12, Procedure 2011-12, Administration 2012-14. Secretary, 1922 Committee 2012.

Political interests: Economy, rural affairs, home affairs, childcare.

Other: Patron, Foxlowe Arts Centre, Leek; Associate, Institute Chartered Accountants in England and Wales 1994; Member, Chartered Institute of Taxation 1995; Royal British Legion. PC 2016.

Recreations: Walking, cooking.

Rt Hon Karen Bradley MP, House of Commons, London SW1A 0AA
Tel: 020 7219 7215 *Email:* karen.bradley.mp@parliament.uk
Constituency: Unit 24, The Smithfield Centre, Haywood Street, Leek, Staffordshire ST13 5JW
Tel: 01538 382421 *Website:* www.karenbradley.co.uk

LABOUR

BRADSHAW, BEN

Exeter *(Majority 16,117)*

Benjamin Peter James Bradshaw. Born 30 August 1960; Son of late Canon Peter Bradshaw and late Daphne Bradshaw, teacher; Civil partner Neal Dalgleish 2006.

Education: Thorpe St Andrew School, Norwich; Sussex University (BA German 1982); Freiburg University, Germany; German, Italian.

Non-political career: BBC 1986-97: Reporter and presenter 1986-97, Berlin correspondent during fall of Berlin Wall 1989-91, Reporter *World At One* and *World This Weekend*, Radio 4 1991-97. Member: NUJ, GMB, USDAW.

Political career: Member for Exeter 1997-2010, for Exeter (revised boundary) since 6 May 2010 general election; Introduced Pesticides Act (Private Member's Bill) 1998; PPS to John Denham as Minister of State, Department of Health 2000-01; Parliamentary Under-Secretary of State, Foreign and Commonwealth Office 2001-02; Parliamentary Secretary, Privy Council Office 2002-03; Department for Environment, Food and Rural Affairs 2003-07: Parliamentary Under-Secretary of State 2003-06, Minister of State (MoS) 2006-07; MoS for Health Services, Department of Health 2007-09; Minister for the South West 2007-09; Secretary of State for Culture, Media and Sport 2009-10; Shadow Secretary of State for Culture, Olympics, Media and Sport 2010. *Select committees:* Member: European Scrutiny 1998-2001, Ecclesiastical Committee 2010-, Joint Committee on Privacy and Injunctions 2011-12, Culture, Media and Sport 2012-15, Health 2015-. Labour Movement for Europe; Member: Labour Campaign for Electoral Reform, SERA, Christian Socialist Movement/Christians on the Left; Contested Labour deputy leadership election 2015; Patron, LGBT Labour.

Political interests: Foreign affairs, environment, transport, modernisation of Parliament; Europe – particularly Germany and Italy, USA.

Other: Trustee, Terrence Higgins Trust 2011-; Member, Advisory Board, Humboldt University, Berlin. Honorary fellowship, Humboldt University, Berlin. Consumer Journalist of the Year, Argos 1989; Journalist of the Year, Anglo-German Foundation 1990; News Reporter award, Sony 1993; Politician of the Year, Stonewall awards 2009. PC 2009; Whipton Labour Club.

Publications: Numerous for the BBC on domestic and foreign affairs.

Recreations: Cycling, walking, cooking, music, ashtanga yoga.

Rt Hon Ben Bradshaw MP, House of Commons, London SW1A 0AA
Tel: 020 7219 6597 *Fax:* 020 7219 0950 *Email:* ben.bradshaw.mp@parliament.uk
Constituency: Labour HQ, 26b Clifton Hill, Exeter, Devon EX1 2DJ
Tel: 01392 424464 *Fax:* 01392 435523 *Website:* www.benbradshaw.co.uk
Twitter: @BenPBradshaw

CONSERVATIVE

BRADY, GRAHAM

Altrincham and Sale West *(Majority 6,426)*

Graham Stuart Brady. Born 20 May 1967; Son of John Brady, accountant, and Maureen Brady, née Birch, medical secretary; Married Victoria Lowther 1992 (1 son 1 daughter).

Education: Altrincham Grammar School; Durham University (BA law 1989).

Non-political career: Shandwick plc 1989-90; Assistant director of publications, Centre for Policy Studies 1990-92; Public affairs director, The Waterfront Partnership 1992-97.

Political career: Member for Altrincham and Sale West 1997-2010, for Altrincham and Sale West (revised boundary) since 6 May 2010 general election; PPS to Michael Ancram as Conservative Party Chairman 1999-2000; Opposition Whip 2000; Opposition Spokesperson for: Employment 2000-01, Schools 2001-03; PPS to Michael Howard as Leader of the Opposition 2003-04; Shadow Minister for Europe 2004-07. *Select committees:* Member: Education and Employment 1997-2001, Education and Employment (Employment Sub-Committee) 1997-2001, Office of the Deputy Prime Minister 2004-05, Office of the Deputy Prime Minister (Urban Affairs Sub-Committee) 2004-05, Treasury 2007-10, Reform of the House of Commons 2009-10, Chairmen's Panel/Panel of Chairs 2009-. Joint Secretary, Conservative Party Committee for Education and Employment 1997-2000; 1922 Committee: Member, executive 1998-2000, 2007-10, Chairman 2010-. Chair, Durham University Conservative Association 1987-88; National Union Executive Committee 1988; Chair, Northern Area Conservative Collegiate Forum 1987-89; Vice-chair, East Berkshire Conservative Association 1993-95; Council Member, AECR 2015-. *Councils and public bodies:* Independent governor and member, audit committee, Manchester Metropolitan University 2008-11.

Political interests: Education, health, Europe; Commonwealth, Far East, British Overseas Territories.

Other: Vice-Patron, Friends of Rosie (research into children's cancer); Vice-President, Altrincham Chamber of Trade Commerce and Industry 1997-; Patron, Family Contact Line/Counselling and Family Centre; Governor, Westminster Foundation for Democracy 2009-10; Panellist, Medical Practitioners Tribunal Service 2010-; Founding supporter, Change Britain 2016-; Stockdales, Genie Networks, Counselling and Family Centre. Backbencher of the Year, *Spectator*/Threadneedle award 2010; Carlton Club.

Publications: Towards an Employees' Charter – and Away From Collective Bargaining (Centre for Policy Studies, 1991); The Future of Conservatism: Values Revisited (Biteback, 2010); Editor, *House Magazine* 2017-.

Recreations: Family, gardening, reading.

Graham Brady MP, House of Commons, London SW1A 0AA
Tel: 020 7219 1260 *Fax:* 020 7219 1649 *Email:* altsale@parliament.uk
Constituency: Altrincham and Sale West Conservative Association, Thatcher House, Delahays Farm, Green Lane, Timperley, Cheshire WA15 8QW
Tel: 0161-904 8828 *Fax:* 0161-904 8868 *Email:* office@altsaletory.demon.co.uk
Website: www.grahambrady.co.uk

SINN FÉIN

BRADY, MICKEY

Newry and Armagh *(Majority 12,489)*

Michael Brady. Born 7 October 1950.

Non-political career: Project manager and worker, Newry Welfare Rights Centre.

Political career: Member for Newry and Armagh since 7 May 2015 general election; MLA for Newry and Armagh 7 March 2007 to 5 June 2015: Sinn Féin Spokesperson for: Benefits, Older People, Welfare. *Councils and public bodies:* Governor, St Coleman's Abbey Primary School, Newry.

Other: Non-executive member, Committee of the Confederation of Community Groups, Newry.

Mickey Brady MP, House of Commons, London SW1A 0AA
Tel: 020 7219 5775 *Email:* mickey.brady.mp@parliament.uk
Constituency: c/o Newry Sinn Féin Office, 1 Kilmorey Terrace, Newry BT35 8DW
Tel: 028 3026 1693 *Website:* newryarmaghsinnfein.com *Twitter:* @MickeyBradySF

LIBERAL DEMOCRAT

BRAKE, TOM

Carshalton and Wallington *(Majority 1,369)*

Liberal Democrat Shadow First Secretary of State; Shadow Secretary of State for Exiting the European Union and International Trade

Thomas Anthony Brake. Born 6 May 1962; Son of Michael and Judy Brake; Married Candida Goulden 1998 (1 daughter 1 son).

Education: Lycee International, St Germain-en-Laye, France; Imperial College, London (BSc physics 1983); French, Portuguese, Russian.

Non-political career: Principal consultant (IT), Cap Gemini 1983-97.

Political career: Contested Carshalton and Wallington 1992 general election. Member for Carshalton and Wallington 1997-2010, for Carshalton and Wallington (revised boundary) since 6 May 2010 general election; Liberal Democrat: Spokesperson for: Environment, Transport in London and Air Transport 1997-99, Environment, Transport, the Regions, Social Justice and London Transport 1999-2001, Whip 2000-04, Spokesperson for: Transport, Local Government and the Regions 2001-02, Transport 2002-03, Shadow Secretary of State for: International Development 2003-05, Transport 2005-06, Shadow Minister for: Communities and Local Government 2006-07, London and the Olympics 2007-10, Home Office 2008-10, Spokesperson on London 2010-12; Parliamentary Secretary (Deputy Leader of the House of Commons) 2012-15; Assistant Government Whip 2014-15; Liberal Democrat: Spokesperson for Foreign Affairs/Shadow Secretary of State for Foreign and Commonwealth Affairs 2015-17, Chief Whip 2015-17, Shadow Leader of the House 2015-17; Member, House of Commons Commission 2015-17; Liberal Democrat: Shadow First Secretary of State 2017-, Shadow Secretary of State for: Exiting the European Union 2017-, International Trade 2017-; Member, Commons Reference Group on Representation and Inclusion 2017-. *Select committees:* Member: Environment, Transport and Regional Affairs 1997-2001, Environment, Transport and Regional Affairs (Environment Sub-Committee) 1997-2001, Environment, Transport and Regional Affairs (Transport Sub-Committee) 1999-2000, Accommodation and Works 2001-03, Transport 2002-03, Home Affairs 2008-10, Selection 2014-15. Chair, Liberal Democrat Parliamentary Party: Committee on Home Affairs, Justice and Equalities 2010-12, Co-Chairs Committee 2012. *Councils and public bodies:* Councillor: London Borough of Hackney 1988-90, London Borough of Sutton 1994-98.

Political interests: Environment, transport, sport, international development, home affairs; Australia, France, Portugal, Russia.

Other: Member: Amnesty International, Greenpeace; Royal British Legion; Patron, Vote Leave Watch 2016-; Oxfam, Bliss. PC 2011. Collingwood Athletic Club; Wallington Tennis Club.

Publications: Policing paper, 'Trusted, Professional and Effective: British policing at its best' (2012).

Recreations: Sport, film, eating.

Rt Hon Tom Brake MP, House of Commons, London SW1A 0AA
Tel: 020 7219 0924
Constituency: Kennedy House, 5 Nightingale Road, Carshalton, Surrey SM5 2DN
Tel: 020 8255 8155 *Email:* info@tombrake.co.uk *Website:* www.tombrake.co.uk
Twitter: @thomasbrake

LABOUR

BRENNAN, KEVIN

Cardiff West *(Majority 12,551)*

Shadow Minister for Arts and Heritage and Deputy Shadow Secretary of State for Digital, Culture, Media and Sport

Kevin Denis Brennan. Born 16 October 1959; Son of late Michael Brennan, steelworker, and Beryl Brennan, née Evans, school cook/cleaner; Married Amy Wack 1988 (1 daughter).

Education: St Alban's RC Comprehensive, Pontypool; Pembroke College, Oxford (BA philosophy, politics and economics 1982) (President Oxford Union 1982); University College of Wales, Cardiff (PGCE history 1985); Glamorgan University (MSc education management 1992); Welsh.

Non-political career: News editor, volunteer organiser, Cwmbran Community Press 1982-84; Head of economics and business studies, Radyr Comprehensive School 1985-94; Research officer to Rhodri Morgan MP 1995-99; Special adviser to Rhodri Morgan as First Minister, National Assembly for Wales 2000-01. Member: NUT 1984-94, TGWU/Unite 1995-, Musicians' Union 2003-.

Political career: Member for Cardiff West 2001-10, for Cardiff West (revised boundary) since 6 May 2010 general election; PPS to Alan Milburn as Chancellor of the Duchy of Lancaster 2004-05; Assistant Government Whip 2005-06; Government Whip 2006-07; Parliamentary Under-Secretary of State, Department for Children, Schools and Families 2007-08; Parliamentary Secretary, Cabinet Office 2008-09; Minister of State (Further Education, Skills, Apprenticeships and Consumer Affairs), Departments for Business, Innovation and Skills and Children, Schools and Families 2009-10; Shadow Minister for: Business, Innovation and Skills 2010, 2015-16, Education 2010-15; Culture, Media and Sport/Digital, Culture, Media and Sport: Shadow Minister for Arts and Heritage 2016-, Deputy Shadow Secretary of State 2016-. *Select committees:* Member, Public Administration 2001-05, 2010-11. Chair, Cardiff West CLP 1998-2000; Member, Labour Campaign Electoral Reform. *Councils and public bodies:* Cardiff City Council: Councillor, Chair: Finance Committee 1993-96, Economic Scrutiny Committee 1999-2001.

Political interests: Economy, constitutional affairs, creative industries, education; Ireland, USA.

Other: Member, Fabian Society; Chair, Yes for Wales Cardiff 1997; Member, Bevan Foundation.

Recreations: Rugby, golf, reading, cricket, music, member parliamentary rock band 'MP4'.

Kevin Brennan MP, House of Commons, London SW1A 0AA
Tel: 020 7219 8156 *Email:* brennank@parliament.uk
Constituency: 395 Cowbridge Road East, Canton, Cardiff, South Glamorgan CF5 1JG
Tel: 029 2022 3207 *Email:* simmonse@parliament.uk *Website:* www.kevinbrennan.co.uk
Twitter: @KevinBrennanMP

CONSERVATIVE

BRERETON, JACK

Stoke-on-Trent South *(Majority 663)*

Jack Edgar Brereton. Born 3 May 1991; Married Laura.

Education: Keele University (politics); University College London.

Non-political career: Election consultancy; Parliamentary Assistant to Karen Bradley MP.

Political career: Contested Stoke-on-Trent Central 2017 by-election. Member for Stoke-on-Trent South since 8 June 2017; Area Chairman, Conservative Future, Staffordshire Conservatives; Treasurer, Stoke-on-Trent Conservative Federation; Member, Conservative Councillors Association. *Councils and public bodies:* Stoke-on-Trent City Council: Councillor 2011-, Deputy Leader, Conservative Group, Cabinet Member for Regeneration, Transport and Heritage; Chair of governors, Hillside Primary School 2011-.

Other: Member, National Trust; Director, Stoke-on-Trent Regeneration Ltd.

Jack Brereton MP, House of Commons, London SW1A 0AA
Tel: 020 7219 4460 *Email:* jack.brereton.mp@parliament.uk
Constituency: 69 The Strand, Longton, Stoke-on-Trent, Staffordshire ST3 2NS
Tel: 01782 922525 *Website:* www.jackbrereton.co.uk

CONSERVATIVE

BRIDGEN, ANDREW

North West Leicestershire *(Majority 13,286)*

Andrew James Bridgen. Born 28 October 1964; Son of Alan and Ann Bridgen; Married Jacqueline Cremin 2000 (2 sons) (divorced).

Education: Pingle School, Swadlincote; Nottingham University (BSc biological sciences 1986); CPC road haulage operations 1991; French, German.

Non-political career: Royal Marine officer training. AB Produce plc (market gardening business): Managing director 1988-2010, Non-executive chairman -2014.

Political career: Member for North West Leicestershire since 6 May 2010 general election. *Select committees:* Regulatory Reform: Member 2010-15, Chair 2015-; Member: Joint Committee on Draft Deregulation Bill 2013, Liaison 2015-. Member, North West Leicestershire Conservative Association; Founding Member, Conservatives for Britain 2015-16. *Councils and public bodies:* Business member, East Midlands Regional Assembly 1999-2000.

Political interests: Business and enterprise, civil liberties, law and order, armed force, transport, environment, food and rural affairs; Italy, Syria, USA.

Other: Member, British-Irish Parliamentary Assembly 2015-; Regional committee member: Business for Sterling, The 'No' Campaign; Institute of Directors: Member 1992-, Regional chair 1999-2003; Christians Against Poverty, Hospice Hope, National Forest, Action Deafness; Ivanhoe Club Ashby, Carlton Club. Burton Rugby Club.

Recreations: Military history, skiing, fishing, driving, reading, country pursuits.

Andrew Bridgen MP, House of Commons, London SW1A 0AA
Tel: 020 7219 7238 *Fax:* 020 7219 6819 *Email:* andrew.bridgen.mp@parliament.uk
Constituency: Unit 10, The Courtyard, Whitwick Business Park, Coalville, Leicestershire LE67 4JP
Email: andrew@andrewbridgen.com *Website:* www.andrewbridgen.com
Twitter: @Abridgen

CONSERVATIVE

BRINE, STEVE

Winchester *(Majority 9,999)*

Parliamentary Under-Secretary of State (Public Health and Primary Care), Department of Health

Stephen Charles Brine. Born 28 January 1974; Married Susie (1 daughter 1 son).

Education: Bohunt Comprehensive School; Highbury College, Portsmouth; Liverpool Hope University (BA history 2006) (Student Union President).

Non-political career: Journalist: BBC Radio, WGN Radio, Chicago USA; Former director, Azalea Group (public relations and marketing firm).

Political career: Member for Winchester since 6 May 2010 general election; PPS to: Mike Penning as Minister of State for: Disabled People, Department for Work and Pensions 2013-14, Policing, Criminal Justice and Victims, Home Office and Ministry of Justice 2014-15, Jeremy Hunt as Secretary of State for Health 2015-16; Assistant Government Whip 2016-17; Parliamentary Under-Secretary of State (Public Health and Primary Care), Department of Health 2017-. *Select committees:* Member: Justice 2011-14, Joint Committee on Voting Eligibilty (Prisoners) Bill 2013.

Political interests: NHS, media, planning and development, justice, environment; Italy, USA.

Other: Liphook Golf Club, Hampshire.

Recreations: Football, skiing, tennis, golf, live music.

Steve Brine MP, House of Commons, London SW1A 0AA
Tel: 020 7219 7189 *Email:* steve.brine.mp@parliament.uk
Constituency: 9 Stockbridge Road, Winchester, Hampshire SO22 6RN
Tel: 01962 791110 *Website:* www.stevebrine.com *Twitter:* @BrineMinister

SCOTTISH NATIONAL PARTY

BROCK, DEIDRE

Edinburgh North and Leith *(Majority 1,625)*

SNP Spokesperson for Devolved Government Relations, Northern Ireland and Fair Work and Employment

Deidre Leanne Brock. Born 8 December 1961; Partner Dougie (2 daughters).

Education: John Curtin University, Australia (English); WA Academy of Performing Arts, Australia (acting).

Non-political career: Actress; Parliamentary assistant to Rob Gibson MSP.

Political career: Member for Edinburgh North and Leith since 7 May 2015 general election; Member, Public Accounts Commission 2015-16; SNP Spokesperson for: Devolved Government Relations 2015-, Northern Ireland 2017-, Fair Work and Employment 2017-. *Select committees:* Member: Public Accounts 2015-16, Scottish Affairs 2016-. *Councils and public bodies:* City of Edinburgh Council: Councillor 2007-15, Former Deputy Lord Provost.

Political interests: Women in politics, job creation, public services.

Other: Member, British-Irish Parliamentary Assembly 2015-; Board member, Edinburgh International Festival Council; Director, Centre for the Moving Image; Creative Edinburgh.

Recreations: Theatre, netball, cinema, traditional Scottish music and arts.

Deidre Brock MP, House of Commons, London SW1A 0AA
Tel: 020 7219 6647 *Email:* deidre.brock.mp@parliament.uk
Constituency: 166 Great Junction Street, Edinburgh EH6 5LJ
Tel: 0131-555 7009 *Website:* www.dbrockmp.scot *Twitter:* @DeidreBrock

CONSERVATIVE

BROKENSHIRE, JAMES

Old Bexley and Sidcup *(Majority 15,466)*

Secretary of State for Northern Ireland

James Peter Brokenshire. Born 8 January 1968; Son of Joan and Peter Brokenshire; Married Cathrine Anne Mamelok 1999 (2 daughters 1 son).

Education: Davenant Foundation Grammar School; Cambridge Centre for Sixth Form Studies; Exeter University (LLB 1990).

Non-political career: Trainee, solicitor, then partner, Jones Day Gouldens Solicitors 1991-2005.

Political career: Member for Hornchurch 2005-10, for Old Bexley and Sidcup since 6 May 2010 general election; Shadow Minister for Home Affairs 2006-10; Home Office: Parliamentary Under-Secretary of State (Minister for Crime Prevention) 2010-11, Parliamentary Under-Secretary of State for: Crime and Security 2011-14, Security 2014, Minister of State for: Security 2014-15, Immigration 2014-16; Secretary of State for Northern Ireland 2016-. *Select committees:* Member, Constitutional Affairs 2005-06.

Political interests: Health, housing and regeneration, law and order.

Other: Patron, Bexley Borough Neighbourhood Watch Association; Vice-president: Bexleyheath and District Club for the Disabled, Sidcup and Footscray Branch, Royal British Legion. PC 2015.

Recreations: Community radio, watching cricket, hill-walking.

Rt Hon James Brokenshire MP, House of Commons, London SW1A 0AA
Tel: 020 7219 8400 *Fax:* 020 7219 2043 *Email:* james.brokenshire.mp@parliament.uk
Constituency: 19 Station Road, Sidcup, Kent DA15 7EB
Tel: 020 8302 7352 *Website:* www.jamesbrokenshire.com *Twitter:* @Jbrokenshire

SCOTTISH NATIONAL PARTY

BROWN, ALAN

Kilmarnock and Loudoun *(Majority 6,269)*

SNP Spokesperson for Transport, Infrastructure and Energy

Born 12 August 1970; Married Cyndi (2 sons).

Education: Loudoun Academy; Glasgow University (Degree civil engineering).

Non-political career: Civil engineer, private and public sector for 21 years; Principal engineer.

Political career: Member for Kilmarnock and Loudoun since 7 May 2015 general election; SNP Spokesperson for Transport, Infrastructure and Energy 2017-. *Select committees:* Member: European Scrutiny 2016-, Environment, Food and Rural Affairs 2017-. *Councils and public bodies:* East Ayrshire Council: Councillor 2007-15, Spokesperson for: Planning, Housing, Strategic Planning and Resources.

Political interests: Infrastructure, NHS.

Other: Trustee/director: Kilmarnock Leisure Centre, Newmilns Snow and Sports Complex.

Recreations: Attending Kilmarnock FC matches, walking, camping, cooking.

Alan Brown MP, House of Commons, London SW1A 0AA
Tel: 020 7219 6093 *Email:* alan.brown.mp@parliament.uk
Constituency: 31a Titchfield Street, Kilmarnock KA1 1QW
Tel: 01563 501412/01563 501411 *Website:* www.alanbrownmp.scot *Twitter:* @AlanBrownSNP

LABOUR

BROWN, LYN

West Ham *(Majority 36,754)*

Lyn Carol Brown. Born 13 April 1960; Daughter of Joseph and Iris Brown; Married John Cullen 2008.

Education: Plashet Comprehensive School; Whitelands College, Roehampton (BA English and religious studies 1982).

Non-political career: Residential social worker, London Borough of Ealing Council 1984-85; Newham Voluntary Agencies, Newham 1985-87; London Borough of Waltham Forest Council 1988-2005. Member, Unison.

Political career: Contested Wanstead and Woodford general election 1992. Member for West Ham 2005-10, for West Ham (revised boundary) since 6 May 2010 general election; PPS to: Phil Woolas as Minister of State, Department for Communities and Local Government 2006-07, John Denham as Secretary of State for Innovation, Universities and Skills 2007-09; Assistant Government Whip 2009-10; Opposition Whip 2010-13; Shadow Minister for: Communities and Fire 2013-15, Home Office 2015-16, 2016-17. *Select committees:* Member, ODPM/Communities and Local Government 2005-07. Member, Co-operative Party. *Councils and public bodies:* London Borough of Newham: Councillor 1988-2005, Chair, Direct Services Organisation 1989-90, Chair, Leisure 1992-2002, Cabinet Member for Culture and Community 2002-05; Founder Member and Chair, London Library Development Agency 1999-2006; Chair: Cultural Services Executive, Local Government Association 2000-03, Culture and Tourism Panel, Association of London Government 2002-05; Member: London Regional Sports Board -2007, London Arts Board -2007, Museums, Libraries and Archives Council, London -2007: Judge, Golden Dagger Award 2005-07.

Political interests: Poverty, housing, libraries, local government, sexual and reproductive health, foreign affairs; Africa, Bangladesh, China, Pakistan.

Other: Member, Fabian Society.

Recreations: Walking, reading, relaxing with friends.

Lyn Brown MP, House of Commons, London SW1A 0AA
Tel: 020 7219 6999 *Fax:* 020 7219 0864 *Email:* brownl@parliament.uk
Constituency: 306 High Street, London E15 1AJ
Tel: 020 8470 3463 *Email:* lyn@lynbrown.org.uk *Website:* www.lynbrown.org.uk
Twitter: @lynbrownmp

LABOUR

BROWN, NICK

Newcastle upon Tyne East *(Majority 19,261)*

Opposition Chief Whip

Nicholas Hugh Brown. Born 13 June 1950.

Education: Tunbridge Wells Technical High School; Manchester University (BA 1971).

Non-political career: Proctor and Gamble advertising department. Legal adviser for northern region, GMBATU 1978-83.

Political career: Member for Newcastle upon Tyne East 1983-97, for Newcastle upon Tyne East and Wallsend 1997-2010, for Newcastle upon Tyne East since 6 May 2010 general election; Opposition Frontbench Spokesperson for: Legal Affairs 1985-92, Treasury and Economic Affairs 1988-94; Deputy to Margaret Beckett as Shadow Leader of the Commons 1992-94; Opposition Spokesperson for Health 1994-95; Opposition Deputy Chief Whip 1995-97; Government Chief Whip 1997-98; Minister of Agriculture, Fisheries and Food 1998-2001; Minister of State for Work, Department of Work and Pensions 2001-03; Deputy Government Chief Whip 2007-08; Minister for the North East 2007-10; Government Chief Whip 2008-10; Shadow Parliamentary Secretary to the Treasury and Opposition Chief Whip 2010; Member: Speaker's Committee for the Independent Parliamentary Standards Authority 2010-, House of Commons Commission 2015-16, Public Accounts Commission 2015-; Opposition Chief Whip 2016-; Member, Parliamentary and Political Service Honours Committee 2016-. *Select committees:* Member: Broadcasting 1994-95, Selection 1996-97, 2007-08, Administration 2007-09, Joint Committees on the: Draft Financial Services Bill 2011-12, Draft Communications Data Bill 2012-13; Chair, Finance 2015-16; Member, Liaison 2015-16. Patron, LGBT Labour. *Councils and public bodies:* Councillor, Newcastle upon Tyne City Council 1980-83.

Countries of interest: Australia, China, Japan, New Zealand, USA.

Other: Associate Governor, Walker Technology College 1980-; Trustee, Biscuit Factory Foundation 2011-; Non-executive director, Mariinksky Theatre Trust 2012-. Freedom, City of Newcastle 2001. PC 1997.

Rt Hon Nick Brown MP, House of Commons, London SW1A 0AA
Tel: 020 7219 6814 *Email:* nickbrownmp@parliament.uk
Constituency: 1 Mosley Street, Newcastle upon Tyne, Tyne and Wear NE1 1YE
Tel: 0191-261 1408 *Website:* www.nickbrownmp.com

CONSERVATIVE

BRUCE, FIONA

Congleton *(Majority 12,619)*

Fiona Claire Bruce. Born 26 March 1957; Married Richard (2 sons).

Education: Burnley High School; Howell's School, Llandaff; Qualified solicitor 1981.

Non-political career: Senior partner, Fiona Bruce & Co LLP.

Political career: Contested Warrington South 2005 general election. Member for Congleton since 6 May 2010 general election. *Select committees:* Member: Scottish Affairs 2010-13, International Development 2012-17, Joint Committee on the Draft Modern Slavery Bill 2014, Joint Committee on Human Rights 2015-, Ecclesiastical Committee 2015-; Chair, Work of the Independent Commission for Aid Impact Sub-committee 2015-17. Commissioner, Conservative Human Rights Commission 2012-. *Councils and public bodies:* Warrington Borough Council: Councillor 2004-10, Executive Member for Money and Finance 2006-10; Former school governor.

Political interests: Small business, family, community, international aid and development, human rights; North Korea, Rwanda, Tanzania.

Other: Member: Law Society, Specialist Society of Trusts and Estate Practitioners; Prison Fellowship. Overall winner, Women into Business Award 2005.

Publications: Co-author: There is such a thing as society (Politicos, 2002), Freedom, Responsibility and the State: Curbing Over-Mighty Government (Politeia, 2012).

Recreations: Family, countryside, theatre.

Fiona Bruce MP, House of Commons, London SW1A 0AA
Tel: 020 7219 2969 *Email:* fiona.bruce.mp@parliament.uk
Constituency: Riverside, Mountbatten Way, Congleton, Cheshire CW12 1DY
Tel: 01260 274044 *Website:* www.fionabruce.org.uk

LABOUR

BRYANT, CHRIS

Rhondda *(Majority 13,746)*

Christopher John Bryant. Born 11 January 1962; Son of Rees Bryant and Anne Bryant, née Goodwin; Civil partner Jared Cranney 2010.

Education: Cheltenham College; Mansfield College, Oxford (BA English 1983, MA); Ripon College, Cuddesdon (MA CertTheol 1986); French, Spanish.

Non-political career: Church of England: Ordained Deacon 1986, Priest 1987; Curate, All Saints High Wycombe 1986-89; Diocesan youth chaplain, Diocese of Peterborough 1989-91; Local government development officer, Labour Party 1993-94; London manager, Common Purpose 1994-96; Freelance author 1996-98; Head of European Affairs, BBC 1998-2000. Member: GMB 1991-94, MSF 1994-.

Political career: Contested Wycombe 1997 general election. Member for Rhondda since 7 June 2001 general election; PPS to: Lord Falconer of Thoroton as Lord Chancellor 2005-06, Harriet Harman as Leader of the House of Commons 2007-08; Deputy Leader of the House of Commons 2008-09; Parliamentary Under-Secretary of State, Foreign and Commonwealth Office 2009-10; Shadow Minister for: Foreign and Commonwealth Office 2010, Justice (Political and Constitutional Reform) 2010-11; Shadow Minister for: Immigration 2011-13, Work and Pensions 2013-14, Arts 2014-15; Shadow Secretary of State for Culture, Media and Sport 2015; Shadow Leader of the House of Commons 2015-16; Member: House of Commons Commission 2015-16, Speaker's Committee for the Independent Parliamentary Standards Authority 2015-. *Select committees:* Member: Culture, Media and Sport 2001-05, Joint Committee on House of Lords Reform 2002-10, Public Accounts 2007, Modernisation of the House of Commons 2007-10, Joint Committee on the Palace of Westminster 2015-16, Foreign Affairs 2017-. Agent, Holborn and St Pancras Labour Party 1991-93; Chair, Christian Socialist Movement 1993-98; Labour Movement for Europe: Chair 2002-07, Vice-chair 2007-; Patron, LGBT Labour. *Councils and public bodies:* London Borough of Hackney: Councillor 1993-98, Chief Whip 1994-95.

Political interests: Wales, European affairs, broadcasting, information economy; Latin America, Spain.

Other: Associate, National Youth Theatre of Great Britain. Campaigner of the Year, *Wales Yearbook* awards 2011; Politician of the Year, Stonewall awards 2011. Ferndale RFC.

Publications: Reclaiming The Ground (Hodder and Stoughton, 1993); John Smith: An Appreciation (Hodder and Stoughton, 1994); Possible Dreams (Hodder and Stoughton, 1995); Stafford Cripps: The First Modern Chancellor (Hodder and Stoughton, 1997); Glenda Jackson: The Biography (HarperCollins, 1999).

Recreations: Swimming, theatre.

Chris Bryant MP, House of Commons, London SW1A 0AA
Tel: 020 7219 8315 *Fax:* 020 7219 1792 *Email:* bryantc@parliament.uk
Constituency: Oxford House, Dunraven Street, Tonypandy, Mid Glamorgan CF40 1AU
Tel: 01443 687697/01443 687621 *Email:* morganke@parliament.uk
Website: www.chrisbryantmp.org.uk *Twitter:* @RhonddaBryant

LABOUR

BUCK, KAREN

Westminster North *(Majority 11,512)*

Karen Patricia Buck. Born 30 August 1958; Married Barrie Taylor (1 son).

Education: Chelmsford High School; London School of Economics (BSc Econ; MSc Econ; MA social policy and administration).

Non-political career: Research and development worker, Outset (charity specialising in employment for disabled people) 1979-83; London Borough of Hackney: Specialist officer developing services/employment for disabled people 1983-86, Public health officer 1986-87. Member, TGWU.

Political career: Member for Regent's Park and Kensington North 1997-2010, for Westminster North since 6 May 2010 general election; Parliamentary Under-Secretary of State, Department for Transport 2005-06; Parliamentary assistant to Tony McNulty as Minister for London 2008-10; Shadow Minister for: Welfare Reform 2010-11, Education 2011-13; PPS to Leader of the Opposition: Ed Miliband 2013-15, Harriet Harman 2015. *Select committees:* Member: Social Security 1997-2001, Selection 1999-2001, Work and Pensions 2001-05, 2010, Home Affairs 2006-09, Home Affairs Sub-Committee 2008-09, Children, Schools and Families 2009-10; Chair, London 2009-10; Member: Work and Pensions 2015-17, Joint Committee on Human Rights 2015-, Panel of Chairs 2015-, Court of Referees 2016-. Chair, PLP London Regional Group 1999-2010. Labour Party: Policy Directorate (Health) 1987-92, Campaign Strategy Co-ordinator 1992-99. *Councils and public bodies:* Councillor, Westminster City Council 1990-97.

Political interests: Housing, urban regeneration, health care, welfare, children, child poverty, environment and climate change.

Other: EveryChild, Amnesty. MP of the Year, Women in Public Life Awards 2007.

Recreations: Music: rock, soul, jazz, opera.

Karen Buck MP, House of Commons, London SW1A 0AA
Tel: 020 7219 3000 *Fax:* 020 7219 3664 *Email:* buckk@parliament.uk
Constituency: Westminster North Labour Party, 4G Shirland Mews, London W9 3DY
Tel: 020 8968 7999/020 8968 7888 *Fax:* 020 8960 0150 *Email:* buckk@parliament.uk
Website: www.karenbuck.org.uk *Twitter:* @KarenPBuckMP

CONSERVATIVE

BUCKLAND, ROBERT

South Swindon *(Majority 2,464)*

Solicitor General

Robert James Buckland. Born 22 September 1968; Son of Roger and Barbara Buckland; Married Sian Pugh Reed 1997 (twin son and daughter).

Education: St Michael's School, Bryn, Llanelli; Hatfield College, Durham (BA law 1990); Inns of Court School of Law 1991.

Non-political career: Called to the Bar 1991; Barrister, Wales and Chester circuit 1992-: Iscoed Chambers, Swansea -1999, 30 Park Place, Cardiff 1999-2007, Apex Chambers 2007-, Recorder of Crown Court 2009-; Bencher, Inner Temple.

Political career: Contested Islwyn 1995 by-election, Preseli Pembrokeshire 1997 and South Swindon 2005 general elections. Member for South Swindon since 6 May 2010 general election; Solicitor General 2014-. *Select committees:* Member, Justice 2010-13; Member Joint Committees on: Statutory Instruments 2010-14, Consolidation, Etc, Bills 2010-14; Member: Works of Art 2011-12, Joint Committee on Privacy and Injunctions 2011-12, Standards 2013-14, Privileges 2013-14, Joint Committee on Human Rights 2013-15, Justice 2014. Secretary, 1922 Committee 2012-14; Chair, Conservative Party Committee for Home Affairs and Constitution 2014. Society of Conservative Lawyers: Member 1990-, Chair, Executive Committee 2013-; Constituency chair,

Conservative Party: Llanelli 1993-96, Swansea West 1999-2000; Tory Reform Group: Board Member 2000-03, Vice-President; Conservative Group for Europe: Member 2002-, Vice-president 2012-; Conservative Foreign Affairs Forum 2006-; Chair, Conservative Human Rights Commission 2011-. *Councils and public bodies:* Councillor, Dyfed County Council 1993-96.

Political interests: Criminal justice, constitutional affairs, foreign affairs, education; South and East Asia, Europe, Israel, Middle East, North Africa, Russia.

Other: Patron: Swindon Threshold (homelessness charity), Hop Skip and Jump, Swindon Calm, Greatwood; Member, Criminal Bar Association; Llanelli Crossroads Scheme; Carlton Club; Patron, Llanelli Conservative Club; Swindon Conservative Club 2004-. Glamorgan County Cricket Club; Crawshays Welsh RFC.

Recreations: Music, wine, family, church architecture, watching rugby, football and cricket.

Robert Buckland QC MP, House of Commons, London SW1A 0AA
Tel: 020 7219 7168 *Fax:* 020 7219 4849 *Email:* robert.buckland.mp@parliament.uk
Constituency: 29b Wood Street, Swindon SN1 4AN
Tel: 01793 533393 *Website:* www.robertbuckland.co.uk *Twitter:* @robertbuckland

LABOUR

BURDEN, RICHARD

Birmingham, Northfield *(Majority 4,667)*

Richard Haines Burden. Born 1 September 1954; Son of late Kenneth Burden, engineer, and Pauline Burden, secretary; Married Jane Slowey 2001 (divorced 2012) (1 stepson 2 stepdaughters).

Education: Wallasey Technical Grammar School; Bramhall Comprehensive School, Stockport; St John's College of Further Education, Manchester; York University (BA politics 1978); Warwick University (MA industrial relations 1979).

Non-political career: Graduate, Armed Forces Parliamentary Scheme (Royal Navy). President, York University Students' Union 1976-77; NALGO: Branch organiser North Yorkshire 1979-81, West Midlands District Officer 1981-92. Member, TGWU 1979-; Sponsored by TGWU 1989-96.

Political career: Contested Meriden 1987 general election. Member for Birmingham Northfield 1992-2010, for Birmingham, Northfield (revised boundary) since 6 May 2010; PPS to Jeffrey Rooker: as Minister of State and Deputy Minister, Ministry of Agriculture, Fisheries and Food 1997-99, as Minister of State, Department of Social Security 1999-2001; Adviser on motor sports to Richard Caborn, as Minister of State for Sport 2002-07; Shadow Minister for Transport 2013-16, 2016-17. *Select committees:* Member: Trade and Industry 2001-05, International Development 2005-13, Quadripartite (Committees on Strategic Export Controls)/Arms Export Controls 2006-13; Chair, West Midlands 2009-10; Member: International Development 2017-, Work of the Independent Commission for Aid Impact Sub-committee 2017-. Member, Labour Party Departmental Committees for: Trade and Industry/Business, Enterprise and Regulatory Reform 1997-2005, Foreign Affairs 2001-05, International Development 2005-13. Founder member, Bedale Labour Party 1980; Labour Middle East Council: Executive member, Vice-chair 1994-95; Member, Co-operative Party; Labour Campaign for Electoral Reform: Chair 1996-98, Vice-chair 1998-; Labour Friends of Palestine and the Middle East: Policy chair 2009-11, Vice-chair 2011-.

Political interests: Industrial policy – especially motor and motorsport industries, poverty, health, constitution, electoral reform, regeneration, regional government, international development, community empowerment; Middle East, Europe.

Other: Joint Action for Water Services (Jaws) to oppose water privatisation: Founded 1985, Secretary 1985-90; Co-chair, Parliamentary Advisory Council on Transport Safety (PACTS) 1995-98; Fellow, Industry and Parliament Trust 1999; Member, Fabian Society; Macmillan Cancer Support, Medical Aid for Palestinians. Sue Brownson Award, Outstanding Leadership in the Motor Industry, Institute of the Motor Industry 2016; Kingshurst Labour Club, Austin Sports and Social Club, Austin Branch British Legion, Bromsgrove and District MG Owners' Club. 750 Motor.

Publications: Tap Dancing – Water, the Environment and Privatisation (1988).

Recreations: Cinema, motor racing, travel, food.

Richard Burden MP, House of Commons, London SW1A 0AA
Tel: 020 7219 2318 *Email:* richard.burden.mp@parliament.uk
Constituency: No constituency office publicised
Tel: 0121-459 7804 *Website:* www.richardburden.com *Twitter:* @RichardBurdenMP

CONSERVATIVE

BURGHART, ALEX

Brentwood and Ongar *(Majority 24,002)*

Michael Alex Burghart. Born 7 September 1977; Married Hermione Eyre (2 daughters).

Education: Millfield School; Christ Church College, Oxford University (modern history); King's College London (PhD).

Non-political career: Barnardo's; National Children's Bureau; Munro Review for Children and Young People; Adviser to Tim Loughton as Shadow Minister for Children and Young People 2008-10; Director of Policy, Centre for Social Justice; Director of Strategy, Children's Commissioner; Special Adviser, Number 10 Policy Unit 2016-17.

Political career: Contested Islington North 2015 general election. Member for Brentwood and Ongar since 8 June 2017. *Select committees:* Member, Work and Pensions 2017-.

Dr Alex Burghart MP, House of Commons, London SW1A 0AA
Tel: 020 7219 1613 *Email:* alex.burghart.mp@parliament.uk
Constituency: Details still to be confirmed *Website:* www.alexburghart.org.uk
Twitter: @alexburghart

LABOUR

BURGON, RICHARD

Leeds East *(Majority 12,752)*

Shadow Lord Chancellor and Secretary of State for Justice

Born 19 September 1980.

Education: Cardinal Heenan Roman Catholic High School; Cambridge University.

Non-political career: Admitted solicitor 2006; Trade union lawyer, Thompsons Solicitors, Leeds.

Political career: Member for Leeds East since 7 May 2015 general election; Shadow Economic Secretary 2015-16; Shadow Lord Chancellor and Secretary of State for Justice 2016-. *Select committees:* Member, Justice 2015.

Other: Member: East Leeds History and Archaeology Society, Leeds United Supporters' Trust.

Recreations: Live music, Leeds United FC.

Richard Burgon MP, House of Commons, London SW1A 0AA
Tel: 020 7219 5980 *Email:* richard.burgon.mp@parliament.uk
Constituency: Former Presbytery of Our Lady of Good Counsel, Rosgill Drive, Leeds, West Yorkshire LS14 6QY
Tel: 0113-232 3266 *Email:* richard@richardburgon.com *Website:* www.richardburgon.com
Twitter: @RichardBurgon

CONSERVATIVE

BURNS, CONOR

Bournemouth West *(Majority 7,711)*

PPS to Boris Johnson as Foreign Secretary

Born 24 September 1972; Son of Thomas Burns and Kathleen Burns, née Kennedy; Single.

Education: St Columba's College, St Albans; Southampton University (BA modern history and politics with philosophy 1994).

Non-political career: Director, Policy Research Centre for Business Ltd 1997; Company secretary, DeHavilland Global Knowledge Distribution plc 1998; Sales director, insurance company; Associate director, PLMR 2008-10; Consultant to Trant Engineering.

Political career: Contested Eastleigh 2001 and 2005 general elections. Member for Bournemouth West since 6 May 2010 general election; PPS to: Hugo Swire as Minister of State, Northern Ireland Office 2010-11, Owen Paterson as Secretary of State for Northern Ireland (resigned) 2011-12, David Gauke as Financial Secretary, HM Treasury 2015-16, Greg Clark as Secretary of State for Business, Energy and Industrial Strategy 2016-17, Boris Johnson as Foreign Secretary 2017-. *Select committees:* Member: Education 2010, Culture, Media and Sport 2012-15, Administration 2014-15. Member, Executive, 1922 Committee 2014-15. Chair: Southampton University Conservative Association 1992-93, Wessex Area Conservative Students 1993-94. *Councils and public bodies:* Southampton City Council: Councillor 1999-2002, Housing and urban regeneration spokesperson 1999, Education and employment spokesperson 1999, Conservative group leader 2001-02.

Political interests: Mental health, foreign affairs, Northern Ireland, education; China, Latin America, Middle East, USA.

Other: Member, British-Irish Parliamentary Association 2017-; Management team, Homestart.

Recreations: Swimming, snooker, cooking, collecting political biographies.

Conor Burns MP, House of Commons, London SW1A 0AA
Tel: 020 7219 7021 *Email:* conor.burns.mp@parliament.uk
Constituency: Bournemouth West Conservatives, 135 Hankinson Road, Bournemouth, Dorset BH9 1HR
Tel: 01202 534888 *Email:* mail@conorburns.com
Websites: www.bournemouthwestconservatives.com www.conorburns.com
Twitter: @ConorBurnsUK

CONSERVATIVE

BURT, ALISTAIR

North East Bedfordshire *(Majority 20,862)*

Minister of State for Middle East, Foreign and Commonwealth Office and Minister of State, Department for International Development

Alistair James Hendrie Burt. Born 25 May 1955; Son of James Burt, doctor, and Mina Burt, teacher; Married Eve Twite 1983 (1 son 1 daughter).

Education: Bury Grammar School, Lancashire; St John's College, Oxford (BA jurisprudence 1977); French.

Non-political career: Solicitor, Private Practice 1980-98; Executive Search Consultant, Whitehead Mann GKR 1997-2001; Non-executive director, President Energy plc -2015.

Political career: Member for Bury North 1983-97. Contested Bury North 1997 general election. Member for North East Bedfordshire 2001-10, for North East Bedfordshire (revised boundary) since 6 May 2010 general election; PPS to Kenneth Baker as Secretary of State for the Environment, for Education and Science and Chancellor of the Duchy of Lancaster 1985-90; Department of Social Security: Parliamentary Under-Secretary of State 1992-95, Minister of State 1992-97: and Minister for Disabled People 1995-97; Opposition Spokesperson for Education and Skills 2001-02; PPS to Leaders of the Opposition: Iain Duncan Smith 2002-03, Michael Howard 2003-05; Shadow Minister for Communities and Local Government 2005-08; Opposition Assistant Chief Whip 2008-10; Parliamentary Under-Secretary of State, Foreign and Commonwealth Office 2010-13; Minister of State: for Community and Social Care, Department of Health 2015-16, for Middle East, Foreign and Commonwealth Office 2017-, Department for International Development 2017-. *Select committees:* Member: International Development 2001, 2002-03, Procedure 2001-02, Office of the Deputy Prime Minister 2002, Selection 2008-10, Administration 2009-10, Ecclesiastical 2014-15, Exiting the European Union 2016-17. Vice-President, Tory Reform Group 1985-88, 2001-; Deputy Chair, Conservative Party 2007-10: Local Government 2007-08, Development 2008-10. *Councils and public bodies:* Councillor, London Borough of Haringey 1982-84.

Political interests: Church affairs, trade and industry, Third World, foreign affairs, agriculture, rural affairs, disability, sport, poverty, social affairs; North Africa, North America, South Asia, Middle East.

Other: Chair, Inter-Parliamentary Union, British Group 2013-15; Secretary, Parliamentary Christian Fellowship 1985-97; Chair, Bow Group industry committee 1987-92; Patron, Habitat for Humanity UK 1997-; Chair, Enterprise Forum 1998-2001; Vice-president, Headway Bedford 2000-; Chair, Christians in Parliament 2002-06; Fellow, Industry and Parliament Trust 2006; Fellow, Solicitors Part 2 1980. PC 2013. Biggleswade Athletic Club.

Recreations: Football, modern art, walking, outdoor leisure.

Rt Hon Alistair Burt MP, House of Commons, London SW1A 0AA
Tel: 020 7219 8132 *Fax:* 020 7219 1740 *Email:* alistair.burt.mp@parliament.uk
Constituency: Biggleswade Conservative Club, St Andrews Street, Biggleswade, Bedfordshire SG18 8BA
Tel: 01767 313385 *Email:* nebca@northeastbedsconservatives.com
Website: www.alistair-burt.co.uk *Twitter:* @AlistairBurtUK

LABOUR

BUTLER, DAWN

Brent Central *(Majority 27,997)*

Shadow Secretary of State for Women and Equalities

Dawn Petula Butler. Born 3 November 1969; Daughter of Milo and Ambrozene Butler.

Education: Tom Hood Senior High School, Waltham Forest, London; Waltham Forest College; British Sign Language.

Non-political career: Computer programmer, Johnson Matthey 1989-92; Executive officer, Job Centre 1993-96; Recruitment officer and black women's officer, Public and Commercial Services Union 1996-97; GMB 1997-2005: Regional equality officer and regional race officer 1997-2003, National officer 2003-05. Member: GMB, Amicus, Unite.

Political career: Member for Brent South 2005-10. Contested Brent Central 2010 general election. Member for Brent Central since 7 May 2015 general election; PPS to Jane Kennedy as Minister of State, Department of Health 2005-06; Assistant Government Whip 2008-09; Parliamentary Secretary (Minister for Young Citizens and Youth Engagement), Cabinet Office 2009-10; Shadow Minister for Diverse Communities (attends Shadow Cabinet) 2016-17, 2017; Shadow Secretary of State for Women and Equalities 2017-. *Select committees:* Member: Modernisation of the House of Commons 2005-10, Children, Schools and Families 2007-09. Chair, PLP Departmental Group for Women 2015-16. Vice-chair, Labour Friends of India 2006. *Councils and public bodies:* Magistrate (Lay Judge) 2013-15.

Political interests: Poverty, unemployment, crime, children's welfare, equality, employment rights, youth, environment, legal aid; Jamaica.

Other: Member, UK delegation, Parliamentary Assembly of the Council of Europe 2016; Executive Member, Race Equality In Newham 2000-03; Vice-chair, Patient and Public Involvement in Health 2002-05; Chair, Greater London Authority London Black Women's Council 2000-05; Executive member, Black Public Sector Workers GLA think tank 2000-05; Patron: Black Women's Mental Health Project 2006, West Indian Self Effort 2006-; Associate, Westminster Abbey Institute. *New Statesman* Most Promising Feminist Under 35 (2002); Patron's Award, Black Women in Business Awards (2007); MP of the Year Award, Women in Public Life Awards (2009); Community Award, Jamaica National (2009).

Recreations: Salsa dancing.

Dawn Butler MP, House of Commons, London SW1A 0AA
Tel: 020 7219 8591 *Email:* dawn.butler.mp@parliament.uk
Constituency: 156 High Road, Willesden, London NW10 2PB
Tel: 020 8451 6560 *Website:* www.dawnbutler.org.uk *Twitter:* @DawnButlerBrent

LABOUR

BYRNE, LIAM

Birmingham, Hodge Hill *(Majority 31,026)*

Shadow Minister for Digital Economy

Liam Dominic Byrne. Born 2 October 1970; Married Sarah Harnett 1998 (2 sons 1 daughter).

Education: Burnt Mill Comprehensive, Harlow, Essex; Manchester University (BA politics and modern history); Harvard Business School, USA (Fulbright Scholar MBA).

Non-political career: Andersen Consulting 1993-96; Leader of Labour Party's Office 1996-97; N M Rothschild 1997-99; Co-founder eGS Group Ltd 2000-04. Member: National Council, NUS, Amicus.

Political career: Member for Birmingham Hodge Hill 15 July 2004 by-election to 2010, for Birmingham, Hodge Hill (revised boundary) since 6 May 2010 general election; Parliamentary Under-Secretary of State, Department of Health (Care Services) 2005-06; Minister of State, Home Office 2006-08 (Policing, Security and Community Safety 2006, Citizenship, Immigration and Nationality 2006-07, Borders and Immigration 2007-08); Minister for the West Midlands 2007-08; Minister of State, HM Treasury 2008; Minister for the Cabinet Office; Chancellor of the Duchy of Lancaster (attending Cabinet) 2008-09; Chair, Council of Regional Ministers 2008-10; Chief Secretary to the Treasury 2009-10; Shadow Chief Secretary to the Treasury 2010; Shadow Minister for the Cabinet Office 2010-11; Shadow Secretary of State for Work and Pensions 2011-13; Shadow Minister for: Education (Higher Education) 2013-15, Digital, Culture, Media and Sport (Digital Economy) 2017-. *Select committees:* Member: European Scrutiny 2005-10, European Standing B 2005-06, International Trade 2016-17. Adviser 1997 general election campaign; Policy Review Co-ordinator, Labour Party 2011-12.

Political interests: Anti-social behaviour, drugs, social policy, welfare reform, youth policy; Kashmir.

Other: Fellow, Social Market Foundation; Member: Christian Socialist Movement, Fabian Society. PC 2008.

Publications: Local Government transformed (1996); Information Age Government (1997); Cities of Enterprise, New Strategies for Full Employment (2002); A Chance to Serve? (Progress, 2002); Britain in 2020 (2003); The Fate We're In (Progress, 2003); Reinventing Government Again (2004); The Left's Agenda for Science (2004); Why Labour Won: Lessons from 2005 (Fabian Society, 2005); Powered by Politics: Reforming Parties from the Inside (2005); Power to the People, Next Steps for New Labour (Progress); From Free Movement to Fair Movement: The Immigration Debate in the UK (in Rethinking Immigration and Integration: A New Centre-Left Agenda) (Policy Network, 2007); From Choice to Control: Empowering Public Services (in Public Matters: The Renewal of the Public Realm) (2007); A Common Place (Fabian Society, 2007); Contributor, The Purple Book (Progress, 2011); Turning to Face the East (Guardian Books, 2013); Dragons: Ten Entrepreneurs Who Built Britain (Head of Zeus, 2016); Black Flag Down: Counter-extremism, Defeating ISIS and Winning the Battle of Ideas (Biteback Publishing, 2016).

Recreations: Running, music, family.

Rt Hon Liam Byrne MP, House of Commons, London SW1A 0AA
Tel: 020 7219 6953 *Fax:* 020 7219 1431 *Email:* byrnel@parliament.uk
Constituency: No constituency office publicised
Tel: 0121-789 7287 *Fax:* 0121-789 9824 *Website:* www.liambyrne.co.uk
Twitter: @LiamByrneMP

LIBERAL DEMOCRAT

CABLE, VINCE

Twickenham *(Majority 9,762)*

Leader, Liberal Democrats

John Vincent Cable. Born 9 May 1943; Son of late Leonard Cable and Edith Cable; Married Dr Olympia Rebelo (died 2001) (2 sons 1 daughter); married Rachel Wenban Smith 2004.

Education: Nunthorpe Grammar School, York; Fitzwilliam College, Cambridge (BA natural science and economics 1966) (Union President); Glasgow University (PhD international economics 1973).

Non-political career: Finance officer, Kenya Treasury 1966-68; Economics lecturer, Glasgow University 1968-74; Diplomatic Service 1974-76; Deputy director, Overseas Development Institute 1976-83; Special adviser to: John Smith as Secretary of State for Trade 1979, Sir Sonny Ramphal as Commonwealth Secretary-General 1983-90; Adviser to World Commission on Environment and Development (Brundtland Commission) 1985-87; Group planning, Shell 1990-93; Head, economics programme, Chatham House 1993-95; Chief economist, Shell International 1995-97; Former visiting fellow, Nuffield College, Oxford and London School of Economics; Special professor of economics, Nottingham University 1999; Former research fellow, international economics, Royal Institute of International Affairs; Visiting Professor: London School of Economics, Nottingham University, Sheffield University, St Mary's University, Twickenham.

Political career: Contested Glasgow Hillhead (Labour) 1970, York (SDP/Alliance) 1983 and 1987, Twickenham (Liberal Democrat) 1992 general elections. Member for Twickenham 1997-2015. Contested Twickenham 2015 general election. Member for Twickenham since 8 June 2017; Liberal Democrat: Spokesperson for the Treasury (EMU and The City) 1997-99, Principal Spokesperson for Trade and Industry 1999-2003, Shadow Chancellor of the Exchequer 2003-10; Secretary of State for Business, Innovation and Skills; President of the Board of Trade 2010-15; Liberal Democrat Shadow Chancellor of the Exchequer 2017. *Select committees:* Member, Treasury 1998-99. Liberal Democrat Party: Deputy Leader 2006-10, Acting Leader 2007, Leader 2017-. *Councils and public bodies:* Councillor (Labour), Glasgow City Council 1971-74.

Political interests: Economic policy, development, policing, energy, environment; China, India, Kenya, Nigeria, Russia.

Other: Member, Competitiveness Council, Council of the European Union 2010-; Chair: HCT, Hampshire Community Bank -2017; Director, Remind Me Care -2017; Patron: Shooting Star Hospice, Hampton Village Tsunami Appeal, Homelink. Opposition Politician of the Year, *House Magazine* awards 2008; Politician of the Year, *Public Affairs News* awards 2008; Parliamentarian of the Year, CAB 2008; Channel 4 Political awards 2009: Political Impact award, Opposition Politician; 'I Told You So', *The Oldie* awards 2009. PC 2010; Kt 2015; British Legion Club, Twickenham.

Publications: Wide variety of books and pamphlets including: Protectionism and Industrial Decline (1983), The New Giants: China and India (Chatham House, 1994), The World's New Fissures; The Politics of Identity (Demos, 1995), Globalisation and Global Governance (Chatham House, 1999), Multiple Identities (Demos, 2005), Public Services: Reform with a Purpose (Centre for Reform, 2005), The Storm (Atlantic, 2009), Free Radical (Atlantic, 2009), Tackling The Fiscal Crisis (Reform, 2009), Moving from the financial crisis to sustainable growth (Centre Forum, 2011); After the Storm: The World Economy and Britain's Economic Future (Atlantic Books, 2015); Open Arms (2017).

Recreations: Ballroom and Latin dancing, classical music, riding, walking.

Rt Hon Sir Vince Cable MP, House of Commons, London SW1A 0AA
Tel: 020 7219 1950 *Email:* vince.cable.mp@parliament.uk
Constituency: 49 Church Lane, Teddington TW11 8PA
Tel: 020 8977 0606 *Website:* www.vincecable.org *Twitter:* @vincecable

LABOUR

CADBURY, RUTH

Brentford and Isleworth *(Majority 12,182)*

Ruth Margaret Cadbury. Born 14 May 1959; Married Nick Gash (2 sons).

Education: Mount School, York; Bournville FE College; Salford University (BA 1981).

Non-political career: Planning Adviser, Planning Aid for London 1989-96; Policy Planner, Richmond upon Thames Council 1996-2001; Freelance Consultant 2006-10.

Political career: Member for Brentford and Isleworth since 7 May 2015 general election; Shadow Minister for Housing 2016-17. *Select committees:* Member: Women and Equalities 2015-17, Justice 2017-. *Councils and public bodies:* London Borough of Hounslow Council: Councillor 1986-94, 1998-2015, Deputy Leader of Council 2010-12, Cabinet Member for Regeneration and Economic Development and Financial Inclusion 2010-13.

Other: Trustee, Barrow Cadbury Trust -2015. Freedom, London Borough of Hounslow.
Ruth Cadbury MP, House of Commons, London SW1A 0AA
Tel: 020 7219 8590 *Email:* ruthcadburymp@parliament.uk
Constituency: No constituency office publicised
Tel: 020 8581 3646 *Email:* ruth@ruthcadbury.org.uk *Website:* www.ruthcadbury.org.uk
Twitter: @RuthCadbury

CONSERVATIVE

CAIRNS, ALUN

Vale of Glamorgan *(Majority 2,190)*

Secretary of State for Wales

Alun Hugh Cairns. Born 30 July 1970; Son of Hugh Cairns, retired, and Margaret Cairns; Married Emma Turner 1996 (1 son).

Education: Ysgol Gyfun Ddwyieithog Ystalyfera; University of Wales (MBA 2001); Welsh.

Non-political career: Board Member, Reserve and Cadet Forces in Wales. Lloyd's Bank Group 1989-99: Business development consultant 1992-98, Field manager 1998-99.

Political career: Contested Gower 1997 and Vale of Glamorgan 2005 general elections. Member for Vale of Glamorgan since 6 May 2010 general election; Wales Office: Parliamentary Under-Secretary of State 2014-16, Secretary of State for Wales 2016-; Government Whip (Lord Commissioner of HM Treasury) 2014-16. *Select committees:* Member: Welsh Affairs 2010-11, Public Administration 2011-14. Contested Bridgend constituency 1999 and 2003 National Assembly for Wales elections. AM for South Wales West region 1999-2011: Welsh Conservative: Spokesperson for: Economic Development 1999-2000, Economic Development and Europe 2000-03, Economic Development and Transport 2003-07; Chair, Committee on Finance 2007-08; Shadow Minister for: Education and Lifelong Learning 2007-08, Local Government 2008-09, Heritage 2009-10; Spokesperson for the Economy 2009-10; Shadow Chief Whip and Business Manager 2009-10. Member: Vale of Glamorgan Conservative Association, Swansea West Conservative Association 1987-; Deputy Chair, Welsh Young Conservatives 1995-96; Chaired one of William Hague's Policy Advisory Groups 1996-97; Conservative Economic Spokesperson in Wales 1997-98; Regional Policy co-ordinator, South Wales West 1998-99; Member, Number 10 Policy Advisory Board 2013-14.

Political interests: Economy, trade and industry, special educational needs, culture, media and sport, defence; North and South America, South East Asia, Australasia.

Other: Trustee, Ocean Water Sports Trust, Vale of Glamorgan; Motor Neurone Disease Association, Children with Special Needs, MIND in the Vale, Royal British Legion, RAF Association. PC 2016.

Recreations: Running, computing, skiing, gardening, shooting, squash.

Rt Hon Alun Cairns MP, House of Commons, London SW1A 0AA
Tel: 020 7219 7175 *Email:* alun.cairns.mp@parliament.uk
Constituency: 29 High Street, Barry, Vale of Glamorgan CF62 7EB
Tel: 01446 403814 *Fax:* 01446 403861 *Website:* www.aluncairns.com *Twitter:* @AlunCairns

SCOTTISH NATIONAL PARTY

CAMERON, LISA

East Kilbride, Strathaven and Lesmahagow *(Majority 3,866)*

SNP Spokesperson for Mental Health

Born 8 April 1972; Married Mark Horsham (2 daughters).

Education: Duncanrig Secondary; Strathclyde University (MA psychology); Stirling University (MSc psychology and health); Glasgow University (DClinPsy).

Non-political career: NHS Greater Glasgow 1999-2001; Clinical psychologist, NHS Lanarkshire 2001-04; Consultant clinical psychologist, State Hospital 2004-06; Consultant forensic and clinical psychologist, NHS Greater Glasgow and Clyde 2006-; Psychological Services Scotland Ltd 2015-. Member, Unite.

Political career: Member for East Kilbride, Strathaven and Lesmahagow since 7 May 2015 general election; SNP Spokesperson for: Climate Justice 2015-17, Mental Health 2017-; Member, Commons Reference Group on Representation and Inclusion 2017-. *Select committees:* Member: International Development 2015-17, Work of the Independent Commission for Aid Impact Sub-committee 2016-17, Health 2017-.

Political interests: NHS, job creation, infrastructure, fairer society, disability, animal welfare, mental health.

Other: Director, UK Japan 21C Group 2016-.

Dr Lisa Cameron MP, House of Commons, London SW1A 0AA
Tel: 020 7219 6855 *Email:* lisa.cameron.mp@parliament.uk
Constituency: MP Offices, Civic Centre, Andrew Street, East Kilbride G74 1AB
Tel: 01355 587430
Strathaven office, 32 Waterside Street, Strathaven ML10 6AW
Tel: 01357 520879 *Website:* www.lisacameronmp.scot *Twitter:* @lisacameronsnp1

LABOUR

CAMPBELL, ALAN

Tynemouth *(Majority 11,666)*

Opposition Deputy Chief Whip

Born 8 July 1957; Son of Albert Campbell and Marian Campbell, née Hewitt; Married Jayne Lamont 1991 (1 son 1 daughter).

Education: Blackfyne Secondary School, Consett; Lancaster University (BA politics 1978); Leeds University (PGCE 1979); Newcastle Polytechnic (MA history 1984); French (basic).

Non-political career: Whitley Bay High School 1980-89; Hirst High School, Ashington, Northumberland: Teacher 1989-97, Head of sixth form, Head of department.

Political career: Member for Tynemouth 1997-2010, for Tynemouth (revised boundary) since 6 May 2010 general election; PPS to: Lord Macdonald of Tradeston as Minister for the Cabinet Office and Chancellor of the Duchy of Lancaster 2001-03, Adam Ingram as Minister of State, Ministry of Defence 2003-05; Assistant Government Whip 2005-06; Government Whip 2006-08; Parliamentary Under-Secretary of State (Crime Reduction), Home Office 2008-10; Shadow Minister for Home Office 2010; Opposition Deputy Chief Whip 2010-. *Select committees:* Member: Public Accounts 1997-2001, Armed Forces Bill 2005-06, Selection 2006-08, 2010-, Joint Committee on Security 2010-15. Hon. Secretary and Hon. Treasurer, Northern Group of Labour MPs 1999-2005.

Political interests: Crime and policing, shipbuilding and offshore industries, fishing; Colombia, Falkland Islands.

Other: PC 2014.

Recreations: Family.

Rt Hon Alan Campbell MP, House of Commons, London SW1A 0AA
Tel: 020 7219 3000 *Email:* alan.campbell.mp@parliament.uk
Constituency: 99 Howard Street, North Shields, Tyne and Wear NE30 1NA
Tel: 0191-257 1927 *Fax:* 0191-257 6537 *Website:* www.alancampbellmp.co.uk
Twitter: @alancampbellmp

DEMOCRATIC UNIONIST PARTY

CAMPBELL, GREGORY

East Londonderry *(Majority 8,842)*

DUP Spokesperson for International Development and Cabinet Office

Gregory Lloyd Campbell. Born 15 February 1953; Son of James Campbell and Martha Joyce, née Robinson; Married Frances Patterson 1979 (1 son 3 daughters).

Education: Londonderry Technical College; Magee College (Extra-Mural Certificate political studies 1982).

Non-political career: Civil servant 1972-82, 1986-94; Self-employed (set up publishing company) 1994-99; Director, Causeway Press.

Political career: Contested Foyle 1983, 1987, 1992 and East Londonderry 1997 general elections. Member for East Londonderry 2001-10, for East Londonderry (revised boundary) since 6 May 2010 general election; DUP Spokesperson for: Defence 2005-07, Culture, Media and Sport/Culture, Olympics, Media and Sport 2005-12, Work and Pensions 2007-09, 2009-10, Transport 2009, International Development 2010-, Cabinet Office 2012-. *Select committees:* Member: Transport, Local Government and the Regions 2001-02, Transport, Local Government and the Regions (Transport Sub-Committee) 2001-02, Transport 2002-04, Northern Ireland Affairs 2004-09, 2016-. Member: Northern Ireland Assembly 1982-86, Northern Ireland Forum for Political Dialogue 1996-98; MLA for East Londonderry 1998-2011, and for East Londonderry (revised boundary) 2011-16: Minister for Regional Development 2000-01, Chair, Committee on Social Development 2007-08, Minister of Culture, Arts and Leisure 2008-09. DUP: Security Spokesman 1994; Treasurer; Senior Party Officer. *Councils and public bodies:* Councillor, Londonderry City Council 1981-2011.

Political interests: Economic development, tourism, employment, enterprise, trade and industry.

Publications: Discrimination: The Truth (1987); Discrimination: Where Now? (1993); Ulster's Verdict on the Joint Declaration (1994); Working Toward 2000 (1998).

Recreations: Football, music, reading.

Gregory Campbell MP, House of Commons, London SW1A 0AA
Tel: 020 7219 8495 *Fax:* 020 7219 1953 *Email:* fieldingm@parliament.uk
Constituency: 25 Bushmills Road, Coleraine, Co Londonderry BT52 2BP
Tel: 028 7032 7327 *Fax:* 028 7032 7328 *Email:* dupcoleraine@parliament.uk

LABOUR

CAMPBELL, RONNIE

Blyth Valley *(Majority 7,915)*

Ronald Campbell. Born 14 August 1943; Son of Ronnie and Edna Campbell; Married Deirdre McHale 1967 (5 sons including twins 1 daughter).

Education: Ridley High School, Blyth.

Non-political career: Miner 1958-86. NUM Lodge Chairman, Bates Colliery, Blyth 1982-86; NUM Sponsored MP; Unison.

Political career: Member for Blyth Valley since 11 June 1987 general election; Parliamentary Commissioner for Administration 1987-97. *Select committees:* Member: Public Administration 1997-2001, Catering 2001-05, Health 2005-07. Chair, Northern Regional Group of Labour MPs 1999-2000. *Councils and public bodies:* Councillor: Blyth Borough Council 1969-74, Blyth Valley Council 1974-88.

Political interests: Economy, environment, employment; Africa, China, Far East, USA.

Other: Patron, Spartans Supporters Club.

Recreations: Furniture restoration, stamp collecting, antiques.

Ronnie Campbell MP, House of Commons, London SW1A 0AA
Tel: 020 7219 4216 *Email:* ronnie.campbell.mp@parliament.uk
Constituency: 42 Renwick Road, Blyth, Northumberland NE24 2LQ
Tel: 01670 363050 *Website:* www.blythvalleylabour.org *Twitter:* @RCampbellMP

LABOUR

CARDEN, DAN

Liverpool Walton *(Majority 32,551)*

PPS to Rebecca Long-Bailey as Shadow Secretary of State for Business, Energy and Industrial Strategy

Daniel Joseph Carden.

Education: London School of Economics.

Non-political career: Parliamentary Researcher; Aide to Unite General Secretary Len McCluskey. Unite.

Political career: Member for Liverpool Walton since 8 June 2017; PPS to Rebecca Long-Bailey as Shadow Secretary of State for Business, Energy and Industrial Strategy 2017-.

Dan Carden MP, House of Commons, London SW1A 0AA
Tel: 020 7219 2673 *Email:* dan.carden.mp@parliament.uk
Constituency: First Floor, Victoria Building, Bishop Goss Complex, Rose Place, Liverpool L3 3AN
Tel: 0151-298 1383 *Website:* www.dancarden4walton.org *Twitter:* @DanCardenMP

LIBERAL DEMOCRAT

CARMICHAEL, ALISTAIR

Orkney and Shetland *(Majority 4,563)*

Liberal Democrat Chief Whip; Shadow Secretary of State for Northern Ireland

Alexander Morrison Carmichael. Born 15 July 1965; Son of Alexander Carmichael, farmer, and Mina Carmichael, née McKay; Married Kathryn Jane Eastham 1987 (2 sons).

Education: Islay High School, Argyll; Aberdeen University (LLB Scots law 1992; Dip LP 1993); French, German.

Non-political career: Hotel manager 1984-89; Procurator fiscal depute, Procurator Fiscal Service 1993-96; Solicitor, private practice 1996-2001.

Political career: Contested Paisley South 1987 general election. Member for Orkney and Shetland since 7 June 2001 general election; Scottish Liberal Democrat Spokesperson on the Energy Review 2001-02; Liberal Democrat: Deputy Spokesperson for: Northern Ireland 2002-05, Home Affairs 2004-06, Shadow Secretary of State for: Transport 2006-07, Northern Ireland and Scotland 2007-08, 2008-10; Deputy Chief Whip (Comptroller of HM Household) 2010-13; Member, Parliamentary and Political Service Honours Committee 2012-13; Secretary of State for Scotland 2013-15; Liberal Democrat: Spokesperson for Home Affairs 2015-16, Shadow First Secretary of State 2016-17, Chief Whip 2017-, Shadow Secretary of State for Northern Ireland 2017-. *Select committees:* Member: Scottish Affairs 2001-05, 2008-10 International Development 2001-02, Public Accounts 2005-06, Joint Committee on Consolidation, Etc, Bills 2008-10, Members' Allowances 2009-10, Joint Committee on Security 2010-13, Energy and Climate Change 2015-16, Exiting the European Union 2016-17. Liberal Democrat: Member, Federal Policy Committee 2004-, Deputy Leader, Scottish Liberal Democrats 2012-.

Political interests: Transport, agriculture, fishing industry, criminal justice, energy; Burma, Palestine/Israel, Uzbekistan.

Other: Amnesty International; Elder, Church of Scotland 1995-; Director, Solicitors Will Aid (Scotland) Ltd; RNLI, Amicus Lime. PC 2011.

Recreations: Amateur dramatics, music.

Rt Hon Alistair Carmichael MP, House of Commons, London SW1A 0AA
Tel: 020 7219 8181 *Fax:* 020 7219 1787 *Email:* carmichaela@parliament.uk
Constituency: Orkney: 14 Palace Road, Kirkwall, Orkney KW15 1PA
Tel: 01856 876541 *Fax:* 01856 876162 *Email:* flettb@parliament.uk
Shetland: 171 Commercial Street, Lerwick, Shetland ZE1 0EN
Tel: 01595 690044 *Fax:* 01595 690055 *Email:* wishartb@parliament.uk
Website: www.alistaircarmichael.co.uk *Twitter:* @acarmichael4mp

CONSERVATIVE

CARTLIDGE, JAMES

South Suffolk *(Majority 17,749)*

Team PPS, Department of Health

James Roger Cartlidge. Born 30 April 1974; Married Emily (daughter of Sir Gerald Howarth, MP 1983-92, 1997-2017) (4 children).

Education: Queen Elizabeth Boys' School, Barnet; Manchester University (BA economics 1996); Middlesex University (MSc computing 1997).

Non-political career: Researcher: House of Commons, Conservative Research Department; Freelance Journalist; Founder and Director, Share to Buy Ltd 2004-15.

Political career: Contested Lewisham Deptford 2005 general election. Member for South Suffolk since 7 May 2015 general election; Member, Public Accounts Commission 2015-; Team PPS, Department of Health 2017-. *Select committees:* Member, Work and Pensions 2016-17. Vice-chairman, Lewisham Deptford Conservative Association; Founding member, Conservatives for Reform in Europe 2016. *Councils and public bodies:* Councillor, Babergh District Council 2013-15.

Political interests: Housing, economy, employee share ownership, rural services, welfare reform; Hungary, Romania.

Other: St Mungos Broadway.

Recreations: Football, cricket, drummer.

James Cartlidge MP, House of Commons, London SW1A 0AA
Tel: 020 7219 4875 *Email:* james.cartlidge.mp@parliament.uk
Constituency: No constituency office publicised *Website:* www.jamescartlidge.com
Twitter: @jc4southsuffolk

CONSERVATIVE

CASH, BILL

Stone *(Majority 17,495)*

William Nigel Paul Cash. Born 10 May 1940; Son of late Paul Cash MC (killed in action 1944) and Moyra Roberts, née Morrison; Married Bridget Lee 1965 (2 sons 1 daughter).

Education: Stonyhurst College, Clitheroe, Lancashire; Lincoln College, Oxford (MA history); French.

Non-political career: Solicitor 1967-: Solicitor, William Cash & Company 1979-.

Political career: Member for Stafford 1984 by-election to 1997, for Stone 1997-2010, for Stone (revised boundary) since 6 May 2010 general election; Shadow Attorney General 2001-03. *Select committees:* European Scrutiny: Member 1998-2010, Chair 2010-; Member: Joint Committee on Consolidation, Etc, Bills 2005-10, Liaison 2010-, Joint Committee on Parliamentary Privilege 2013. Conservative Backbench Committee for European Affairs: Chair 1989-91, Joint vice-chair 1997-. Vice-President, Conservatives for Britain 2015-16.

Political interests: European Union, trade and industry, media, small businesses, heritage, debt relief; East Africa, Far East, Europe, Malaysia.

Other: Founder and Chair, European Foundation 1993-; Vice-President, Conservative Small Business Bureau 1986-2000. Kt 2014; Beefsteak Club, Carlton Club, Vincent's Club Oxford, Garrick Club.

Publications: Against a Federal Europe (1991); Europe – The Crunch (1992); AEA – The Associated European Area (2000); John Bright: Statesman, Orator, Agitator (I.B.Tauris, 2011).

Recreations: Local history, cricket, jazz.

Sir Bill Cash MP, House of Commons, London SW1A 0AA
Tel: 020 7219 6330 *Fax:* 020 7219 3935 *Email:* mcconaloguej@parliament.uk
Constituency: 50 High Street, Stone, Staffordshire ST15 8AU
Tel: 01785 811000 *Email:* office@stoneconservatives.co.uk *Website:* www.billcashmp.co.uk
Twitter: @BillCashMP

CONSERVATIVE

CAULFIELD, MARIA

Lewes *(Majority 5,508)*

Maria Colette Caulfield. Born 6 August 1973; Partner Steve Bell.

Education: La Retraite High School, Clapham; RGN Dip adult nursing 1994; BSc cancer care 1996; MSc cancer care 2003.

Non-political career: Registered nurse, Royal Marsden Hospital 2004-.

Political career: Contested Caerphilly 2010 general election. Member for Lewes since 7 May 2015 general election. *Select committees:* Member: Women and Equalities 2015-17, Exiting the European Union 2016-17, Northern Ireland Affairs 2017-. Chairman, Conservative Backbench Policy Committee on Health 2015-17. Member, Conservative Councillors Association. *Councils and public bodies:* Brighton and Hove City Council: Councillor 2007-11, Cabinet Member for Housing 2007-11.

Political interests: NHS, housing and homelessness, rural issues and farming.

Other: Owner and shareholder, Lewes Football Club; Member, Nursing and Midwifery Council 1994-; Trustee, BHT Sussex 2013-.

Maria Caulfield MP, House of Commons, London SW1A 0AA
Tel: 020 7219 5946 *Email:* maria.caulfield.mp@parliament.uk
Constituency: Unit 6 Villandry, West Quay, Newhaven, East Sussex BN9 9GB
Website: www.mariacaulfield.co.uk *Twitter:* @mariacaulfield

CONSERVATIVE

CHALK, ALEX

Cheltenham *(Majority 2,569)*

Alexander John Gervase Chalk. Born 8 August 1976; Married Sarah 2011 (2 children).

Education: Winchester College; Magdalen College, Oxford (BA history 1998); City University (Graduate Diploma law 2000); Inns of Court School of Law (Bar Vocational Course 2001); Conversational French and Russian.

Non-political career: Called to the Bar, Middle Temple 2001; Barrister, 6KBW College Hill 2004-.

Political career: Member for Cheltenham since 7 May 2015 general election. *Select committees:* Member, Justice 2015-. *Councils and public bodies:* Councillor, Hammersmith and Fulham Council 2006-14.

Other: Member, South Eastern Circuit; Member, Criminal Bar Association.

Alex Chalk MP, House of Commons, London SW1A 0AA
Tel: 020 7219 8087 *Email:* alex.chalk.mp@parliament.uk
Constituency: 2 Henrietta Street, Cheltenham, Gloucestershire GL50 4AA
Tel: 01242 210473 *Email:* alex@alexchalk.com *Website:* www.alexchalk.com
Twitter: @AlexChalkChelt

LABOUR

CHAMPION, SARAH

Rotherham *(Majority 11,387)*

Sarah Deborah Champion. Born 10 July 1969; Daughter of Ronald Champion and Mary Champion, née Biggs; Divorced.

Education: Prince William Comprehensive School, Oundle; Sheffield University (BA psychology 1991); Derby University (PG Cert; Diploma psychodynamic counselling).

Non-political career: Arts centre manager, Rotherham Metropolitan Borough Council 1992-94; Arts development officer, Ashfield Metropolitan Borough Council 1994-96; Chief executive officer: Chinese Arts Centre, Manchester 1996-2008, Bluebell Wood Children's Hospice, Dinnington 2008-12. Member, Community.

Political career: Member for Rotherham since 29 November 2012 by-election; Shadow Minister for Preventing Abuse and Domestic Violence 2015-June 2016, July 2016; Shadow Secretary of State for Women and Equalities 2016-17. *Select committees:* Member: Transport 2012-15, Environment, Food and Rural Affairs 2015.

Political interests: Welfare, health, education, social care, defence, economy, manufacturing, justice; China, East Asia, Kashmir, Palestine, South East Asia, Sri Lanka, USA.

Other: Various national and constituency based charities. Youth Friendly MP Award.

Publications: Representing the People (1999); Made in China (2001); Vital: International Live Artists of Chinese Descent (2008).

Recreations: Endurance horse riding, gardening, food, travel, film.

Sarah Champion MP, House of Commons, London SW1A 0AA
Tel: 020 7219 5942/2645 *Email:* sarah.champion.mp@parliament.uk
Constituency: Unit 35, Moorgate Crofts Business Centre, South Grove, Rotherham S60 2DH
Tel: 01709 331035/01709 331036 *Website:* www.sarahchampionmp.com
Twitter: @sarahchampionMP

SCOTTISH NATIONAL PARTY

CHAPMAN, DOUGLAS

Dunfermline and West Fife *(Majority 844)*

SNP Spokesperson for Defence Procurement

Born 5 January 1955; Married (2 children).

Education: W Calder High School; Napier College.

Non-political career: TSB Scotland: Branch banking, Personnel management; Gleneagles Hotel; Fife Enterprise; Researcher to Bruce Crawford MSP 1999-2005.

Political career: Contested Dunfermline and West Fife 2005 and Kirkcaldy and Cowdenbeath 2010 general elections. Member for Dunfermline and West Fife since 7 May 2015 general election; SNP Spokesperson for Defence Procurement 2017-. *Select committees:* Member: Defence 2015-17, Arms Export Controls 2016-17. Contested Mid Scotland and Fife region (6) 2011 Scottish Parliament election. Campaign manager, SNP 2006-07. *Councils and public bodies:* Fife Council: Councillor 1997-98, 2007-15, Chair, Education and Children's Services Committee 2007-12.

Douglas Chapman MP, House of Commons, London SW1A 0AA
Tel: 020 7219 6888 *Email:* douglas.chapman.mp@parliament.uk
Constituency: 1 Douglas Street, Dunfermline KY12 7EB
Tel: 01383 730073 *Website:* www.chapman.scot *Twitter:* @DougChapmanSNP

LABOUR

CHAPMAN, JENNY

Darlington *(Majority 3,280)*

Shadow Minister for Exiting the European Union

Jennifer Chapman. Born 25 September 1973; Married Nick Smith (qv) 2014 (MP for Blaenau Gwent).

Education: Hummersknott School, Darlington; Brunel University (BSc psychology 1996); Durham University (MA medieval archaeology 2004).

Non-political career: Member, USDAW.

Political career: Member for Darlington since 6 May 2010 general election; Shadow Minister for: Justice 2011-16, Education 2016, Exiting the European Union 2016-. *Select committees:* Member: Procedure 2010-16, 2016-17, Joint Committee on Consolidation, Etc, Bills 2010-15. *Councils and public bodies:* Darlington Council: Councillor 2007-10, Cabinet Member for Children and Young People; Governor, Branksome School; Member, Darlington Partnership Board.

Political interests: Justice, children, families, employment, transport, economy.

Other: Member, National Trust; Trustee, Darlington Rape Crisis Centre; Vice-chair, Progress 2012-; Chair of trustees, Newblood Live.

Publications: Contributor, The Purple Book (Progress, 2011).

Jenny Chapman MP, House of Commons, London SW1A 0AA
Tel: 020 7219 7046 *Email:* jenny.chapman.mp@parliament.uk
Constituency: 40a Coniscliffe Road, Darlington, Co Durham DL3 7RG
Tel: 01325 382345 *Twitter:* @JennyChapman

LABOUR

CHARALAMBOUS, BAMBOS

Enfield Southgate *(Majority 4,355)*

Charalambos Charalambous. Born 2 December 1967.

Education: Chace School, Enfield; Liverpool Polytechnic (LLB 1990); London South Bank University; Greek.

Non-political career: Trainee solicitor/outdoor clerk, Saunders & Co 1994-97; Housing caseworker, Hodge, Jones & Allen 1998; Solicitor, London Borough of Hackney Council 1998-2017. Member, GMB 1997-.

Political career: Contested Epping Forest 2005 and Enfield Southgate 2010 and 2015 general elections. Member for Enfield Southgate since 8 June 2017. *Select committees:* Member, Justice 2017-. *Councils and public bodies:* Councillor, London Borough of Enfield Council 1994-; Governor, Eversley Primary School 1993-2014.

Political interests: Culture, law and order, local government, child poverty.

Other: Member: Amnesty International 1996-, Fabian Society 2003-; Member, Law Society; Chair, Enfield Law Centre 2002-.

Recreations: Reading, travel, the arts, cinema, sport, walking.

Bambos Charalambous MP, House of Commons, London SW1A 0AA
Tel: 020 7219 3460 *Email:* bambos.charalambous.mp@parliament.uk
Constituency: Details still to be confirmed *Twitter:* @BambosMP

SCOTTISH NATIONAL PARTY

CHERRY, JOANNA

Edinburgh South West *(Majority 1,097)*

SNP Spokesperson for Justice and Home Affairs

Joanna Catherine Cherry. Born 18 March 1966.

Education: Holy Cross School, Edinburgh; St Margaret's Convent School for Girls, Edinburgh; Edinburgh University (LLB 1988; LLM 1989; DipLP 1990); French.

Non-political career: Called to the Bar 1995; Standing Junior Counsel, Scottish Government 2003-09; Advocate Depute 2008-11; National Sex Crimes Unit, Crown Office; QC, Faculty of Advocates 2009-.

Political career: Member for Edinburgh South West since 7 May 2015 general election; SNP Spokesperson for Justice and Home Affairs 2015-. *Select committees:* Member, Exiting the European Union 2016-. Member, SNP 2008-; Co-founder, Lawyers for Yes.

Other: Pro bono work: Women's Aid, Rape Crisis.

Publications: Co-author, Mental Health and Scots Law in Practice.

Joanna Cherry QC MP, House of Commons, London SW1A 0AA
Tel: 020 7219 6646 *Email:* joanna.cherry.mp@parliament.uk
Constituency: 139 Dundee Street, Edinburgh EH11 1BP
Tel: 0131-600 0156 *Twitter:* @joannaccherry

CONSERVATIVE

CHISHTI, REHMAN

Gillingham and Rainham *(Majority 9,430)*

Atta-Ur-Rehman Chishti. Born 4 October 1978.

Education: Fort Luton High School for Boys; Chatham Grammar School for Girls; University of Wales, Aberystwyth (law 2000); Inns of Court School of Law (Bar Vocational Course; Postgraduate Diploma law 2001); Urdu.

Non-political career: Special adviser to Benazir Bhutto 1999-2007; Called to the Bar, Lincoln's Inn 2001; Barrister, Goldsmith Chambers, London 2003-09; Special adviser to Francis Maude MP as Chair of Conservative Party 2006-07; Adviser to King Faisal Center for Research and Islamic Studies 2016-.

Political career: Contested (Labour) Horsham 2005 general election. Member for Gillingham and Rainham since 6 May 2010 general election; PPS to: Nick Gibb as Minister of State for School Reform, Department for Education 2014-15, Jeremy Wright as Attorney General 2015-16; Trade Envoy to Pakistan 2017-. *Select committees:* Member: Joint Committee on Human Rights 2010-14, Joint Committee on the Draft Defamation Bill 2011, Justice 2012-15, Backbench Business 2017-, Petitions 2017-. *Councils and public bodies:* Medway Council: Councillor 2003-, Cabinet Member for Community Safety and Enforcement 2007-10; Governor, Chatham Grammar School for Girls 2001-12.

Political interests: Law and order, criminal justice system, foreign affairs, NHS; Asia, Central America, Middle East, Pakistan, Saudi Arabia, South America, USA.

Other: Bar Council of England and Wales.

Recreations: Cricket, running, reading, squash, tennis.

Rehman Chishti MP, House of Commons, London SW1A 0AA
Tel: 020 7219 7075 *Email:* rehman.chishti.mp@parliament.uk
Constituency: Gillingham and Rainham Conservatives, Burden House, 200a Canterbury Street, Gillingham, Kent ME7 5XG
Tel: 01634 570118 *Website:* www.rehmanchishti.com *Twitter:* @Rehman_Chishti

CONSERVATIVE

CHOPE, CHRISTOPHER

Christchurch *(Majority 25,171)*

Christopher Robert Chope. Born 19 May 1947; Son of late Judge Robert Chope and Pamela Chope, née Durell; Married Christine Hutchinson 1987 (1 son 1 daughter).

Education: St Andrew's School, Eastbourne; Marlborough College; St Andrew's University (LLB 1970).

Non-political career: Barrister, Inner Temple 1972; Consultant, Ernst and Young 1992-98.

Political career: Member for Southampton Itchen 1983-92. Contested Southampton Itchen 1992 general elecion. Member for Christchurch 1997-2010, for Christchurch (revised boundary) since 6 May 2010 general election; PPS to Peter Brooke as Minister of State, HM Treasury 1986; Parliamentary Under-Secretary of State: Department of the Environment 1986-90, Department of Transport (Minister for Roads and Traffic) 1990-92; Opposition Spokesperson for: the Environment,

Transport and the Regions 1997-98, Trade and Industry 1998-99, the Treasury 2001-02; Shadow Minister for: Transport 2002-03, Environment and Transport 2003-05. *Select committees:* Member: Trade and Industry 1999-2002, Chairmen's Panel/Panel of Chairs 2005-, Procedure 2005-10, Administration 2006-10, Political and Constitutional Reform 2010-15, Standards 2013-17, Privileges 2013-17, Justice 2013-15, Scottish Affairs 2015-17, Procedure 2016-, Communities and Local Government 2017, Exiting the European Union 2017-, Home Affairs 2017-. Joint Secretary, Conservative Backbench Environmental Committee 1983-86; 1922 Committee: Executive member 2001-05, 2005-06, Secretary 2006-12. Member, Executive Committee, Society of Conservative Lawyers 1983-86; Vice-chair, Conservative Party 1997-98; Founding Member, Conservatives for Britain 2015-16. *Councils and public bodies:* London Borough Wandsworth Council: Councillor 1974-83, Council Leader 1979-83; Member: Health and Safety Commission 1992-97, Local Government Commission for England 1994-95.

Other: Member, Parliamentary Delegation to Council of Europe -2015: Chair: Migration and Refugees Committee 2011-12, Legal Affairs and Human Rights Committee 2012-; Fellow, Industry and Parliament Trust 2001. OBE 1982.

Christopher Chope OBE MP, House of Commons, London SW1A 0AA
Tel: 020 7219 5808 *Email:* chopec@parliament.uk
Constituency: 37 Bargates, Christchurch, Dorset BH23 1QD
Tel: 01425 541087 *Email:* office@christchurchconservatives.com
Websites: www.christchurchconservatives.com www.chrischope.com

CHURCHILL, JO

Bury St Edmunds *(Majority 18,441)*

CONSERVATIVE

PPS to Jeremy Hunt as Secretary of State for Health

Johanna Peta Churchill. Born 18 March 1964; Daughter of G R Wuidart; Married (4 daughters).

Education: Dame Alice Harpur School, Bedford; BSc business and psychology; MSc business and occupational psychology.

Non-political career: Financial and operational director, SLS Ltd 1998-2015.

Political career: Member for Bury St Edmunds since 7 May 2015 general election; PPS to: Mike Penning as Minister of State for the Armed Forces, Ministry of Defence 2016-17, Jeremy Hunt as Secretary of State for Health 2017-. *Select committees:* Member: Women and Equalities 2015-17, Environmental Audit 2015-16. Founding member, Conservatives for Reform in Europe 2016. *Councils and public bodies:* Lincolnshire County Council: Councillor 2013-15, Executive Support Councillor, Economic and Environmental Portfolio; School governor.

Political interests: Health, business, agritech, life sciences, education.

Other: Member, Executive Committee, Commonwealth Parliamentary Association UK 2016-17; Member: Lincolnshire Economic Action Partnership, Lincolnshire Forum for Agriculture and Horticulture, Breakthrough National Advisory Group; Breakthrough Breast Cancer.

Recreations: Skiing, walking, gardening.

Jo Churchill MP, House of Commons, London SW1A 0AA
Tel: 020 7219 8487 *Email:* jo.churchill.mp@parliament.uk
Constituency: 10 Hatter Street, Bury St Edmunds, Suffolk IP33 1LZ
Tel: 01284 752311 *Email:* lesley.canham@parliament.uk *Website:* www.jochurchill.org.uk
Twitter: @Jochurchill4

CLARK, COLIN

Gordon *(Majority 2,607)*

CONSERVATIVE

Colin James Clark. Born 20 May 1969; Married (1 son).

Education: Heriot-Watt University (1990).

Non-political career: Managing Director and Owner, DGM Growers 1993-2005; Small business investor 2000-12; Owner, R&M Clark Farmers 2005-; Chair, Nessgro Ltd 2005-.

Political career: Contested Gordon 2015 general election. Member for Gordon since 8 June 2017; Contested Aberdeenshire East constituency 2016 Scottish Parliament election. *Councils and public bodies:* Councillor, Aberdeenshire Council 2016-17.

Colin Clark MP, House of Commons, London SW1A 0AA
Tel: 020 7219 1542 *Email:* colin.clark.mp@parliament.uk
Constituency: Details still to be confirmed *Website:* www.colinclark.org.uk
Twitter: @Colin_J_Clark

CONSERVATIVE

CLARK, GREG

Tunbridge Wells *(Majority 16,465)*

Secretary of State for Business, Energy and Industrial Strategy

Gregory David Clark. Born 28 August 1967; Son of John and Patricia Clark; Married Helen Fillingham 1999 (2 daughters 1 son).

Education: St Peter's Comprehensive, Middlesbrough; Magdalene College, Cambridge (BA economics 1989, MA); London School of Economics (PhD 1992).

Non-political career: Consultant, Boston Consulting Group 1991-94; Teaching and research, LSE and Open University Business School 1994-96; Commercial Policy, BBC: Chief adviser 1997-99, Controller 1999-2001; Special adviser to Ian Lang as Secretary of State for Trade and Industry 1996-97; Director of Policy, Conservative Party 2001-05.

Political career: Member for Tunbridge Wells 2005-10, for Tunbridge Wells (revised boundary) since 6 May 2010 general election; Shadow Minister for: Charities, Voluntary Bodies and Social Enterprise 2006-07, Cabinet Office 2007-08; Shadow Secretary of State for Energy and Climate Change 2008-10; Minister of State for: Decentralisation, Department for Communities and Local Government 2010-11, Cities, Departments for Communities and Local Government and Business, Innovation and Skills 2011, Decentralisation and Cities, Departments for Business, Innovation and Skills and Communities and Local Government 2011-12; Financial Secretary, HM Treasury 2012-13; Minister of State for: Cities and Constitution, Cabinet Office 2013-14, Universities, Science and Cities, Department for Business, Innovation and Skills and Cabinet Office 2014-15; Secretary of State for: Communities and Local Government 2015-16, Business, Energy and Industrial Strategy 2016-. *Select committees:* Member, Public Accounts 2005-07. *Councils and public bodies:* Councillor, Westminster City Council 2002-05.

Political interests: Economics, poverty, welfare reform, transport, health, housing development, energy and climate change.

Other: President: Tunbridge Wells Constitutional Club, Hawkhurst Community Hospital League of Friends; Vice-president, Tunbridge Wells Rugby Football Clubs; Patron: Tunbridge Wells Mental Health Resource Centre, Pepenbury, Royal Tunbridge Wells Orpheus Male Voice Choir; Vice-patron, Headway West Kent; Ambassador, Build Africa; Honorary Member, Tunbridge Wells Rotary Club; Honorary Fellow, Nuffield College, Oxford. PC 2010.

Rt Hon Greg Clark MP, House of Commons, London SW1A 0AA
Tel: 020 7219 6977 *Email:* greg.clark.mp@parliament.uk
Constituency: No constituency office publicised
Tel: 01892 519854 *Website:* www.gregclark.org *Twitter:* @GregClarkMP

CONSERVATIVE

CLARKE, KENNETH

Rushcliffe *(Majority 8,010)*

Kenneth Harry Clarke. Born 2 July 1940; Son of late Kenneth Clarke, watchmaker and jeweller, and Doris Clarke; Married Gillian Edwards 1964 (died 2015) (1 son 1 daughter).

Education: Nottingham High School; Gonville and Caius College, Cambridge (BA law 1962; LLB 1963) (President, Cambridge Union 1963).

Non-political career: Called to the Bar 1963; Member, Midland Circuit, practising from Birmingham; QC 1980; Bencher, Gray's Inn; Deputy Chair, British American Tobacco 1998-2007; Director: Independent News and Media (UK), Independent News and Media plc; Member, Advisory Board, Centaurus Capital.

Political career: Contested Mansfield Notts 1964 and 1966 general elections. Member for Rushcliffe 1970-2010, for Rushcliffe (revised boundary) since 6 May 2010 general election; PPS to Sir Geoffrey Howe as Solicitor General 1971-72; Assistant Government Whip 1972-74; Government Whip 1974; Opposition Spokesperson for: Social Services 1974-76, Industry 1976-79; Parliamentary Secretary, Ministry of Transport 1979-80; Parliamentary Under-Secretary of State, Department of Transport 1980-82; Minister for Health 1982-85; Paymaster General and Employment Minister 1985-87; Chancellor, Duchy of Lancaster and Minister of Trade and Industry 1987-88; Secretary of State for: Health 1988-90, Education and Science 1990-92; Home Secretary 1992-93, Chancellor of the Exchequer 1993-97; Shadow Secretary of State for Business, Enterprise and Regulatory Reform/Innovation and Skills 2009-10; Lord Chancellor and Secretary of State for Justice 2010-12; Government Anti-Corruption Champion 2010-12; Minister without Portfolio, Cabinet Office 2012-14; Father of the House 2017-. *Select committees:* Member, Joint Committee on House of Lords Reform 2003-10; Joint Committee on Tax Law Rewrite Bills: Member 2005-09, Chair 2007-09. Chair: Cambridge University Conservative Association 1961, Federation Conservative Students 1963-65; Contested Conservative Party leadership 1997, 2001 and 2005; Chair, Democracy Task Force 2005-; President, Tory Reform Group.

Political interests: Economic policy, National Health Service.

Other: Member, Justice and Home Affairs Council, Council of the European Union 2010-12; President, Industry and Parliament Trust 2010-12. Liveryman, Clockmakers' Company. Three honorary law doctorates; Honorary Fellow, Gonville and Caius College, Cambridge. Double Act of the Year (with Theresa May MP), *Spectator* awards 2011; Oldie of the Year, *Oldie* awards 2012. PC 1984; CH 2014; Garrick Club.

Publications: Kind of Blue: A Political Memoir (Macmillan, 2016).

Recreations: Birdwatching, football, cricket, jazz, Formula 1 motor racing.

Rt Hon Kenneth Clarke CH QC MP, House of Commons, London SW1A 0AA
Tel: 020 7219 3000 *Fax:* 020 7219 4841 *Email:* clarkek@parliament.uk
Constituency: Rushcliffe House, 17/19 Rectory Road, West Bridgford, Nottingham, Nottinghamshire NG2 6BE
Tel: 0115-948 4533 *Website:* www.rushcliffeconservatives.com

CONSERVATIVE

CLARKE, SIMON

Middlesbrough South and East Cleveland *(Majority 1,020)*

Simon Richard Clarke. Born 28 September 1984; Married Hannah (1 son).

Education: Yarm School, Yarm, Stockton on Tees; Oxford University (MA modern history 2006); Oxford Brookes University (Graduate Diploma law 2007); BPP Law School (LPC 2008); French.

Non-political career: Trainee Solicitor, Slaughter and May 2008-10; Senior Parliamentary Assistant to Dominic Raab MP 2010-13; Senior Policy Adviser to Graham Stuart MP 2013-17.

Political career: Contested Middlesbrough 2015 general election. Member for Middlesbrough South and East Cleveland since 8 June 2017.

Political interests: Industrial strategy, economics, energy, education, transport, foreign affairs; China, Iran, Pakistan, Russia.

Simon Clarke MP, House of Commons, London SW1A 0AA
Tel: 020 7219 2674 *Email:* simon.clarke.mp@parliament.uk
Constituency: 11 Rectory Lane, Guisborough TS14 7DJ
Tel: 01287 204709 *Website:* www.simon-clarke.org.uk *Twitter:* @SimonClarkeMP

CONSERVATIVE

CLEVERLY, JAMES

Braintree *(Majority 18,422)*

PPS to Brandon Lewis as Minister of State for Immigration, Home Office

James Spencer Cleverly. Born 4 September 1969; Married Susannah 2000 (2 sons).

Education: Colfe's School for Boys; University of West London (Degree business).

Non-political career: Lt Colonel, Territorial Army: Commanding officer, 266 (Para) Battery Royal Artillery (Volunteers) 2003-05. Sales manager, VNU 1996-2002; International advertising manager, Informa 2002-04; Group advertising manager, Crimson Publishing 2005-06; Online commercial manager, Caspian Publishing 2006-07; Director, Port & Fire Media 2007-11.

Political career: Contested Lewisham East 2005 general election. Member for Braintree since 7 May 2015 general election; PPS to Brandon Lewis as Minister of State for Immigration, Home Office 2017-. *Select committees:* Member: Joint Committee on Consolidation, &c, Bills 2015-, International Trade 2016-17. Member, Executive, 1922 Committee 2015-17. London Assembly: AM for Bexley and Bromley constituency 2008-16, Youth Ambassador to Mayor of London -2010, Conservative Spokesperson for Environment, Chair: London Waste and Recycling Board 2010-12, London Fire and Emergency Planning Authority 2012-15, London Local Resilience Forum 2012-15. Founding Member, Conservatives for Britain 2015-16; Convenor, Free Enterprise Group 2015-.

Political interests: Local business, technology.

Other: President, Bromley District Scouts; Ulysses Trust. Freedom, City of London. Territorial Decoration.

James Cleverly MP, House of Commons, London SW1A 0AA
Tel: 020 7219 8593 *Email:* james.cleverly.mp@parliament.uk
Constituency: No constituency office publicised *Website:* www.cleverly4braintree.com
Twitter: @JamesCleverly

CONSERVATIVE

CLIFTON-BROWN, GEOFFREY

The Cotswolds *(Majority 25,499)*

Geoffrey Robert Clifton-Brown. Born 23 March 1953; Son of Robert Clifton-Brown and late Elizabeth Clifton-Brown; Married Alexandra Peto-Shepherd 1979 (divorced 2003) (1 son 1 daughter).

Education: Eton College; Royal Agricultural College, Cirencester (ARICS); French.

Non-political career: Graduate Estate Surveyor, Property Services Agency, Dorchester 1975; Investment Surveyor, Jones Lang Wootton 1975-79; Managing Director, own farming business in Norfolk 1979-.

Political career: Member for Cirencester and Tewkesbury 1992-97, for Cotswold 1997-2010, for The Cotswolds since 6 May 2010 general election; PPS to Douglas Hogg as Minister of Agriculture, Fisheries and Food 1995-97; Opposition Whip 1999-2001; Opposition Spokesperson for: Environment, Food and Rural Affairs 2001, Transport, Local Government and the Regions 2001-02; Shadow Minister for: Local Government 2002-03, Local and Devolved Government 2003-04; Opposition Whip 2004-05; Assistant Chief Whip 2005; Shadow Minister for: Foreign Affairs 2005-07, Trade 2007, 2009-10, International Development 2007-10. *Select committees:* Member: Public Accounts 1997-99, Broadcasting 2000-01, Administration 2001, 2010-11, Finance and Services 2005-15; Selection: Member 2005-06, Chair 2010-15; Member: Liaison 2010-15, High Speed Rail (London-West Midlands) Bill 2015-16, Finance 2015-, Public Accounts 2017-. 1922 Committee: Member, Executive 2015-16, Treasurer 2016-. Conservative Party: Chair: North Norfolk Constituency Association 1986-91, International Office 2010-15, Vice-chair (international affairs) 2010-15, Board Member 2015-.

Political interests: Economy, taxation, foreign affairs, environment, agriculture; Brazil, China, India.

Other: Fellow, Industry and Parliament Trust 1996; Armed Forces Parliamentary Fellowship 1997; Fellow, Royal Institute of Chartered Surveyors (FRICS) 2002; Fellow: Royal Institute of Chartered Surveyors, Royal Agricultural University. Liveryman, Worshipful Company of Farmers. Freedom, City of London; Farmers' Club.

Publications: Privatisation of the State Pension – Secure Funded Provision For All (Bow Group, 1996).

Recreations: Fishing, other rural pursuits.

Geoffrey Clifton-Brown MP, House of Commons, London SW1A 0AA
Tel: 020 7219 5147 *Fax:* 020 7219 2550 *Email:* cliftonbrowng@parliament.uk
Constituency: Gloucestershire Conservative Association Office, 1143 Regent Court, Gloucester Business Park, Gloucester, Gloucestershire GL3 4AD
Tel: 01452 371630 *Email:* info@gloucestershireconservatives.com
Website: www.cliftonbrown.co.uk

LABOUR

CLWYD, ANN

Cynon Valley *(Majority 13,238)*

Born 21 March 1937; Daughter of Gwilym and Elizabeth Lewis; Married Owen Roberts 1963 (died 2012).

Education: Holywell Grammar School; The Queen's School, Chester; University College of Wales, Bangor; Welsh.

Non-political career: Journalist, *Guardian*; Broadcaster, BBC. Member: NUJ, Unite.

Political career: Contested Denbigh 1970 and Gloucester October 1974 general elections. Member for Cynon Valley 3 May 1984 by-election to 2010, for Cynon Valley (revised boundary) since 6 May 2010 general election; Shadow Minister of Education and Women's Rights 1987-88; Shadow Secretary of State for: International Development 1989-92, Wales 1992, National Heritage 1992-93; Opposition Spokesperson for: Employment 1993-94, Foreign Affairs 1994-95; Assistant to John Prescott as Deputy Leader of Labour Party 1994-95; Special envoy to Iraq on human rights 2003-10. *Select committees:* Member: International Development 1997-2005, Foreign Affairs 2010-, Arms Export Controls 2011-15, 2016-17, Works of Art 2015-. Vice-chair, PLP Departmental Committee for Foreign and Commonwealth Affairs 2002-06; Chair, Parliamentary Labour Party 2005-06. European Parliament: MEP for Mid and West Wales 1979-84. Member, National Executive Committee, Labour Party 1983-84; Chair, Tribune Group 1986-87.

Political interests: Human rights, international development, animal welfare, health, cosmetic surgery; Cambodia, Iran, Iraq, Russia, East Timor, Turkey, Vietnam.

Other: Inter-Parliamentary Union, British Group: Chair 2004-07, Vice-chair 2010-13, 2016-; Member, Arts Council 1975-79; Vice-chair, Welsh Arts Council 1975-79; Royal Commission on NHS 1976-79; Member, White Robe Gorsedd, Royal National Eisteddfod of Wales; MS Charity in Wales. Hon. Fellow: North East Wales Institute of Higher Education 1996, University of Wales,

Bangor 2004; Hon. LLD, University of Wales, Carmarthen 2006. BBC/*House Magazine* Backbencher of the Year 2003; *Spectator* Backbencher of the Year 2003; Channel 4 Campaigning Politician of the Year 2003-04; HTV Communicator of the Year 2005; *House Magazine* Health Campaigner of the Year, Dods Parliamentary Awards 2014. PC 2004.

Publications: Co-author, A Review of the NHS Hospitals Complaints System; Rebel with a Cause: A Memoir (Biteback Publishing, 2017).

Recreations: Walking, boating.

Rt Hon Ann Clwyd MP, House of Commons, London SW1A 0AA
Tel: 020 7219 6609 *Fax:* 020 7219 5943 *Email:* ann.clwyd.mp@parliament.uk
Constituency: Fourth Floor, Crown Buildings, Aberdare, Mid Glamorgan CF44 7HU
Tel: 01685 871394 *Fax:* 01685 883006 *Email:* jean.fitzgerald@parliament.uk
Twitter: @AnnClwyd

LABOUR

COAKER, VERNON

Gedling *(Majority 4,694)*

Vernon Rodney Coaker. Born 17 June 1953; Son of Edwin Coaker; Married Jacqueline Heaton 1978 (1 son 1 daughter).

Education: Drayton Manor Grammar School, London; Warwick University (BA politics 1974); Trent Polytechnic (PGCE 1976).

Non-political career: Humanities teacher, Nottinghamshire: Manvers School 1976-82, Arnold Hill School 1982-89, Bramcote Park School 1989-95, Big Wood School 1995-97. Member: NUT, Unite.

Political career: Contested Gedling 1987 and 1992 general elections. Member for Gedling 1997-2010, for Gedling (revised boundary) since 6 May 2010 general election; PPS: to Stephen Timms: as Minister of State, Department of Social Security 1999, as Financial Secretary, HM Treasury 1999-2001, as Minister of State for Schools and Learners, Department for Education and Skills 2001-02, as Minister of State, Department of Trade and Industry 2002, to Estelle Morris as Secretary of State for Education and Skills 2002, to Tessa Jowell as Secretary of State for Culture, Media and Sport 2002-03; Assistant Government Whip 2003-05; Government Whip 2005-06; Home Office: Parliamentary Under-Secretary of State (Crime Reduction) 2006-08, Minister of State (Policing, Crime and Security) 2008-09; Minister of State, Department of Children, Schools and Families 2009-10; Shadow Minister for: Education 2010, Policing 2010-11; Shadow Secretary of State for: Northern Ireland 2011-13, 2015-16, Defence 2013-15. *Select committees:* Member: Social Security 1998-99, European Standing Committee B 1998. Member, International – Britain's Global Role Policy Commission. *Councils and public bodies:* Councillor, Rushcliffe Borough Council 1983-97.

Political interests: Environment, education, welfare reform, foreign policy, sport; Angola, France, Kosovo, Macedonia.

Other: UNICEF. *House Magazine* Opposition Frontbencher of the Year, Dods Parliamentary Awards 2014.

Recreations: Sport, walking.

Vernon Coaker MP, House of Commons, London SW1A 0AA
Tel: 020 7219 6627 *Email:* vernon.coaker.mp@parliament.uk
Constituency: Arnot Hill House, Arnot Hill Park, Nottingham Road, Arnold, Nottinghamshire NG5 6LU
Tel: 0115-920 4224 *Email:* robertsc@parliament.uk *Website:* www.vernon-coaker-mp.co.uk
Twitter: @Vernon_Coaker

LABOUR

COFFEY, ANN

Stockport *(Majority 14,477)*

Margaret Ann Wishart Coffey. Born 31 August 1946; Daughter of late John Brown MBE, Flight-Lieutenant, RAF, and Marie Brown, nurse; Married 1973 (divorced 1989) (1 daughter); married Peter Saraga 1998 .

Education: Nairn Academy; Bodmin and Bushey Grammar Schools; Polytechnic of South Bank, London (BSc sociology 1967); Walsall College of Education (Postgraduate Certificate education 1971); Manchester University (MSc psychiatric social work 1977).

Non-political career: Trainee social worker, Walsall Social Services 1971-72; Social worker: Birmingham 1972-73, Gwynedd 1973-74, Wolverhampton 1974-75, Stockport 1977-82, Cheshire 1982-88; Team leader, fostering, Oldham Social Services 1988-92. Member, USDAW.

Political career: Contested Cheadle 1987 general election. Member for Stockport 1992-2010, for Stockport (revised boundary) since 6 May 2010 general election; Opposition Whip 1995-96; Opposition Spokeswoman on Health 1996-97; Joint PPS to Tony Blair as Prime Minister 1997-98;

PPS to Alistair Darling as Secretary of State for: Social Security/Work and Pensions 1998-2002, Transport 2002-06, Trade and Industry 2006-07, Chancellor of the Exchequer 2007-10. *Select committees:* Member: Trade and Industry 1993-95, Modernisation of the House of Commons 2000-10, Joint Committee on the Draft House of Lords Reform Bill 2011-12. *Councils and public bodies:* Stockport Metropolitan Borough Council: Councillor 1984-92, Leader, Labour Group 1988-92; Member, District Health Authority 1986-90.

Political interests: Children, health, education, town centres markets.

Other: Fellow, Industry and Parliament Trust 1994.

Recreations: Photography, drawing, cinema, swimming, reading.

Ann Coffey MP, House of Commons, London SW1A 0AA
Tel: 020 7219 4546 *Email:* ann.coffey.mp@parliament.uk
Constituency: 207a Bramhall Lane, Stockport, Cheshire SK2 6JA
Tel: 0161-483 2600 *Email:* dunbarb@parliament.uk *Website:* anncoffeymp.com
Twitter: @anncoffey_MP

CONSERVATIVE

COFFEY, THERESE

Suffolk Coastal *(Majority 16,012)*

Parliamentary Under-Secretary of State for Environment, Department for Environment, Food and Rural Affairs

Therese Anne Coffey. Born 18 November 1971; Daughter of late Tom Coffey and Sally Coffey.

Education: St Mary's College, Rhos-on-Sea; St Mary's College, Crosby; St Edward's College, Liverpool; University College, London (BSc 1993; PhD chemistry 1997).

Non-political career: Chartered management accountant, Mars UK Ltd 1997-2007; Finance director, Mars Drinks UK 2007-09; Property finance manager, BBC 2009-10.

Political career: Contested Wrexham 2005 general election. Member for Suffolk Coastal since 6 May 2010 general election; Board member, Parliamentary Office of Science and Technology (POST) -2014; PPS to Michael Fallon as Minister of State for: Business and Enterprise, Department for Business, Innovation and Skills 2012-13, Energy, Department of Energy and Climate Change 2013-14, Business and Energy, Department for Business, Innovation and Skills 2013-14; Assistant Government Whip 2014-15; Parliamentary Secretary (Deputy Leader of the House of Commons) 2015-16; Department for Environment, Food and Rural Affairs: Parliamentary Under-Secretary of State for: Environment 2016, Rural Life Opportunities 2016-17. *Select committees:* Member: Culture, Media and Sport 2010-12, Environmental Audit 2016-. Contested South East 2004 and 2009 European Parliament elections. Member, Conservative Party 1988-; National deputy chair, Conservative Students 1993-94; Chair, North West Hampshire Conservatives 2006-09; Deputy regional chair, South East 2009; Former member, Conservative Way Forward. *Councils and public bodies:* Councillor, Whitchurch Town Council 1999-2003.

Political interests: Rural affairs, enterprise, energy; EU, Latin America.

Other: Member, CAMRA; Patron: East Coast Hospice, Suffolk Coast Rural Responders, Friends of St Mary's College, Crosby; Life Vice-president, Suffolk Agricultural Association; Member, National Trust; Chair, Suffolk Coast Energy Delivery Board; Water Aid, Dogs Trust.

Recreations: Watching football, gardening, music.

Dr Therese Coffey MP, House of Commons, London SW1A 0AA
Tel: 020 7219 7164 *Email:* therese.coffey.mp@parliament.uk
Constituency: No constituency office publicised *Website:* www.theresecoffey.co.uk
Twitter: @theresecoffey

CONSERVATIVE

COLLINS, DAMIAN

Folkestone and Hythe *(Majority 15,411)*

Chair, Select Committee on Digital, Culture, Media and Sport

Damian Noel Thomas Collins. Born 4 February 1974; Married Sarah Richardson 2004 (1 daughter 1 son).

Education: St Mary's High School, Herefordshire; Belmont Abbey School, Herefordshire; St Benet's Hall, Oxford (BA modern history 1996).

Non-political career: Desk officer, Conservative Party Research Department 1996-98; Press officer, Conservative Party Press Office 1998-99; Account director, M&C Saatchi 1999-2005; Managing director, Influence Communications Ltd 2005-08; Senior counsel, Lexington Communications 2008-10.

Political career: Contested Northampton North 2005 general election. Member for Folkestone and Hythe since 6 May 2010 general election; PPS to: Theresa Villers as Secretary of State for Northern Ireland 2012-14, Philip Hammond as Foreign Secretary 2014-15. *Select committees:*

Culture, Media and Sport/Digital, Culture, Media and Sport: Member 2010-12, 2015-16, Chair 2016-; Member: Joint Committee on Consolidation, Etc, Bills 2010-15, Liaison 2016-. President, Oxford University Conservative Association 1995; Founding member, Conservatives for Reform in Europe 2016.

Political interests: Enterprise, economy, regeneration, social mobility, local food, creative industries, international relations.

Other: Political officer, Bow Group 2003-04; Member, advisory board, Author's Licensing and Collecting Society 2015-; Folkestone Stop Short Project, Folkestone Youth Project; Lord's Taverners Club.

Publications: Conservative Revival (Politicos, 2006); The New Blue (Social Market Foundation, 2008).

Recreations: Sport (football, cricket, rugby union).

Damian Collins MP, House of Commons, London SW1A 0AA
Tel: 020 7219 7072 *Email:* damian.collins.mp@parliament.uk
Constituency: 4 West Cliff Gardens, Folkestone, Kent CT20 1SP
Tel: 01303 253524 *Fax:* 01303 251061 *Email:* shepwayconservatives@btconnect.com
Website: www.damiancollins.com *Twitter:* @DamianCollins

LABOUR

COOPER, JULIE

Burnley *(Majority 6,353)*

Shadow Minister for Community Health

Julie Elizabeth Cooper. Born 20 June 1960; Married Brian (1 son 1 daughter).

Education: Colne Park High School; Edge Hill College, Ormskirk (BA English language and literature).

Non-political career: English teacher, Birkdale High School 1982-84; Librarian, Hagergham High School 1990-92; Director, Cooper's Chemist, Burnley 1992-2010. Member, Unite.

Political career: Contested Burnley 2010 general election. Member for Burnley since 7 May 2015 general election; PPS to Seema Malhotra as Shadow Chief Secretary to the Treasury 2015-16; Shadow Minister for Community Health 2016-. *Select committees:* Member, Health 2015-16. *Councils and public bodies:* Burnley Borough Council: Councillor 2005-16, Leader 2012-14.

Political interests: Healthcare, employment, youth issues, the elderly, affordable housing.

Other: Furniture Education Worldwide.

Julie Cooper MP, House of Commons, London SW1A 0AA
Tel: 020 7219 8521 *Email:* julie.cooper.mp@parliament.uk
Constituency: 8 Keirby Walk, Burnley, Lancashire BB11 2DE
Tel: 01282 425744 *Website:* www.juliecooperforburnley.co.uk *Twitter:* @JulieForBurnley

LABOUR

COOPER, ROSIE

West Lancashire *(Majority 11,689)*

Rosemary Elizabeth Cooper. Born 5 September 1950; Daughter of William and Rose Cooper; Single.

Education: Bellerive Convent Grammar School; Liverpool University.

Non-political career: Concept Design Partnership & W Cooper Limited 1973-80; Littlewoods Organisation 1980-2001: Merchandiser 1980-92, Public relations manager 1994-95, Group corporate communications manager 1995-2000, Seconded as project manager for government task force on equal pay 1999-2001. Member, USDAW.

Political career: Contested (Liberal) Knowsley North 1986 by-election and (Liberal/Alliance) 1987 general election, and (Liberal Democrat) Liverpool Broadgreen 1992 general election. Member (Labour) for West Lancashire since 5 May 2005 general election; PPS to: Lord Rooker as Minister of State, Department for Environment, Food and Rural Affairs 2006-07, Ben Bradshaw: as Minister of State, Department for Health 2007-09, as Secretary of State for Culture, Media and Sport 2009-10. *Select committees:* Member: European Scrutiny 2005-06, Northern Ireland Affairs 2005-10, Justice 2007-08, 2010, North West 2009-10, Health 2010-15, Administration 2010-12, Unopposed Bills (Panel) 2013-15, Health 2016-. Hon. Secretary, PLP Departmental Committee for Northern Ireland 2005-10. Contested North West region 2004 European Parliament election. Member: Liberal Party/Liberal Democrats -1999, Labour Party 1999-. *Councils and public bodies:* Liverpool City Council (Liberal/Liberal Democrat 1973-99, Labour 1999-2000): Councillor 1973-2000, Lord Mayor 1992-93, Labour spokesperson for housing 1999-2000, Honorary Alderman 2011; Member and vice-chair, Liverpool Health Authority 1994-96; Chair, Liverpool Women's Hospital NHS Foundation Trust 1996-2005.

Political interests: Health, disability equality, housing; Dominican Republic, Haiti, Northern Ireland, USA.

Other: Member, British-Irish Parliamentary Assembly; Director, Merseyside Centre for Deaf People 1973-2004; Cosmopolitan Housing Association 1994-2011.

Recreations: Theatre, music, cinema, community affairs.

Rosie Cooper MP, House of Commons, London SW1A 0AA
Tel: 020 7219 3000 *Email:* rosie.cooper.mp@parliament.uk
Constituency: Suite 108, Malthouse Business Centre, 48 Southport Road, Ormskirk, Lancashire L39 1QR
Tel: 01695 570094 *Fax:* 01695 570094 *Email:* rosie@rosiecooper.net
Website: www.rosiecooper.net *Twitter:* @rosie4westlancs

LABOUR

COOPER, YVETTE

Normanton, Pontefract and Castleford *(Majority 14,499)*

Chair, Select Committee on Home Affairs

Born 20 March 1969; Daughter of Tony Cooper, former leader Engineers and Managers Association, and June Cooper; Married Ed Balls 1998 (MP for Normanton 2005-10 and Morley and Outwood 2010-15) (2 daughters 1 son).

Education: Eggars Comprehensive; Balliol College, Oxford (BA philosophy, politics and economics 1990); Harvard University (Kennedy Scholar 1991); London School of Economics (MSc economics 1995).

Non-political career: Economic researcher for John Smith MP 1990-92; Domestic policy specialist, Bill Clinton presidential campaign 1992; Policy adviser to Labour Treasury teams 1992-94; Economic columnist/Leader writer, *The Independent* 1995-97. Member: TGWU, GMB.

Political career: Member for Pontefract and Castleford 1997-2010, for Normanton, Pontefract and Castleford since 6 May 2010 general election; Parliamentary Under-Secretary of State, Department of Health (Public Health) 1999-2002; Parliamentary Secretary, Lord Chancellor's Department 2002-03; Office of the Deputy Prime Minister/Department for Communities and Local Government 2003-08: Parliamentary Under-Secretary of State 2003-05, Minister of State (Minister for Housing and Planning) 2005-07, Minister for Housing (attending cabinet) 2007-08; Chief Secretary to the Treasury 2008-09; Secretary of State for Work and Pensions 2009-10; Shadow Secretary of State for: Work and Pensions 2010, Foreign and Commonwealth Affairs (Shadow Foreign Secretary) 2010-11; Shadow Minister for Women and Equalities 2010-13; Shadow Secretary of State for Home Department (Shadow Home Secretary) 2011-15. *Select committees:* Member: Education and Employment 1997-99, Education and Employment (Employment Sub-Committee) 1997-99; Chair, Home Affairs 2016-; Member: Liaison 2016-, Joint Committee on the National Security Strategy 2016-. Member, Society – Stronger, Safer Communities Policy Commission; Contested Labour leadership election 2015; Chair, Labour's Refugee Taskforce 2015-.

Political interests: Unemployment, coal industry, poverty, equal opportunities; USA.

Other: PC 2007.

Rt Hon Yvette Cooper MP, House of Commons, London SW1A 0AA
Tel: 020 7219 5080 *Email:* coopery@parliament.uk
Constituency: 1 York Street, Castleford, West Yorkshire WF10 1RB
Tel: 01977 553388 *Fax:* 01977 559753 *Website:* www.yvettecooper.com
Twitter: @YvetteCooperMP

LABOUR

CORBYN, JEREMY

Islington North *(Majority 33,215)*

Leader, Labour Party; Leader of the Opposition

Jeremy Bernard Corbyn. Born 26 May 1949; Son of David Corbyn and Naomi Corbyn; Married Laura Alvarez 2015 (3 sons from previous marriage).

Education: Adams Grammar School, Newport, Shropshire; Spanish.

Non-political career: Full-time organiser, National Union of Public Employees (NUPE) 1975-83; Also worked for Tailor and Garment workers and AUEW; NUPE sponsored MP; Member, RMT Parliamentary Campaigning Group.

Political career: Member for Islington North since 9 June 1983 general election; Leader of the Opposition 2015-. *Select committees:* Member: Social Security 1991-97, London 2009-10, Justice 2011-15. Member, Socialist Campaign Group; Leader, Labour Party 2015-. *Councils and public bodies:* Councillor, Haringey Borough Council 1974-84: Chair: Community Development 1975-78, Public Works 1978-79, Planning 1980-81.

Political interests: People of Islington, Stop the War, Liberation, welfare state, NHS, socialism, human rights, anti-racism, anti-imperialism and internationalism, transport safety, environment; Africa, Chagos Islands, Middle East, Latin America.

Other: Member, Executive Committee, Inter-Parliamentary Union, British Group; Vice-president, Campaign for Nuclear Disarmament. PC 2015.

Recreations: Running, railways.

Rt Hon Jeremy Corbyn MP, House of Commons, London SW1A 0AA
Tel: 020 7219 3545 *Fax:* 020 7219 2328 *Email:* jeremy.corbyn.mp@parliament.uk
Constituency: 86 Durham Road, London N7 7DU
Tel: 020 7561 7488 *Email:* leader@labour.org.uk *Website:* www.jeremycorbyn.org.uk
Twitter: @jeremycorbyn

CONSERVATIVE

COSTA, ALBERTO

South Leicestershire *(Majority 18,631)*

PPS to David Mundell as Secretary of State for Scotland

Alberto Castrenze Costa. Born 13 November 1971; Married Maria (1 daughter 1 son).

Education: Glasgow University (MA; LLB) (President SRC 1995-96); Strathclyde University (Postgraduate Diploma legal practice); English law conversion course.

Non-political career: Solicitor, Glasgow, Edinburgh and Aberdeen; International lawyer, commercial law firm, London; Solicitor, HM Treasury; Associate: Bellenden Public Affairs, Brizmo Public Affairs; Consultant solicitor, Nicholas Woolf and Co Solicitors 2015-.

Political career: Contested Angus 2010 general election. Member for South Leicestershire since 7 May 2015 general election; PPS to David Mundell as Secretary of State for Scotland 2017-. *Select committees:* Member, Justice 2015-17. Trustee, Islington Conservative Association.

Political interests: Dementia care, local business, education.

Other: Secretary, Montrose and District Round Table; Associate member, Chartered Institute of Arbitrators; Member: Law Society of England and Wales, Law Society of Scotland; Director, Furniture Recycling Project Angus.

Recreations: Cooking.

Alberto Costa MP, House of Commons, London SW1A 0AA
Tel: 020 7219 4936 *Email:* barronra@parliament.uk
Constituency: Unit 3, 8a Lutterworth Road, Blaby, Leicestershire LE8 4DN
Tel: 0116-278 1924 *Email:* diana.thompson@parliament.uk *Website:* www.albertocosta.org.uk
Twitter: @AlbertoCostaMP

CONSERVATIVE

COURTS, ROBERT

Witney *(Majority 21,241)*

Robert Alexander Courts. Born 21 October 1978; Married Kathryn (1 son).

Education: Berkhamsted School; Sheffield University (law).

Non-political career: Called to the Bar, Lincolns' Inn 2003; Barrister, 3 Paper Buildings 2003-; Crown Law Office, New Zealand.

Political career: Member for Witney since 20 October 2016 by-election. *Select committees:* Member, Backbench Business 2017. Member, Conservative Party 1998-; Chairman, Conservative Future, Meriden; Member, Society of Conservative Lawyers. *Councils and public bodies:* West Oxfordshire District Council: Councillor 2014-17, Deputy Leader and Cabinet Member for Communities and Housing.

Other: Speaker, Thames Valley and Chiltern Air Ambulance Trust 2013-; Member, Federation of Small Businesses; Committee member, Churchill Centre (UK); Member: Personal Injury Bar Association, Criminal Bar Association; Supporter: RAFBF, Combat Stress, Help for Heroes. Pegasus Scholarship to Wellington, New Zealand 2009.

Recreations: Hiking, cycling, playing guitar.

Robert Courts MP, House of Commons, London SW1A 0AA
Tel: 020 7219 5638 *Email:* robert.courts.mp@parliament.uk
Constituency: 58-60 High Street, Witney OX28 6HJ
Tel: 01993 225020 *Email:* robert@robertcourts.co.uk *Website:* www.robertcourts.co.uk
Twitter: @robertcourts

SCOTTISH NATIONAL PARTY

COWAN, RONNIE

Inverclyde *(Majority 384)*

Ronald Jack Cowan. Born 6 September 1959; Son of late James Cowan and May Piggott; 3 children.

Education: Greenock Academy.

Non-political career: Computer Software Consultant; IT Manager; Director, Ronnie Cowan Solutions Ltd 2001-15.

Political career: Member for Inverclyde since 7 May 2015 general election. *Select committees:* Member: Public Administration and Constitutional Affairs 2015-, Transport 2017-, Procedure 2017-.

Political interests: Scotland's independence, inclusive society, universal basic income, anti-trident, renewables, addressing gambling related harm, drugs policy reform.

Other: Leader, Yes Inverclyde -2014; Fellow, RSA; British Red Cross, Amnesty International. Greenock Wanderers Rugby Football Club.

Recreations: Music, art, rugby union.

Ronnie Cowan MP, House of Commons, London SW1A 0AA
Tel: 020 7219 6122 *Email:* ronnie.cowan.mp@parliament.uk
Constituency: 20 Crawfurd Street, Greenock, Inverclyde PA15 1LJ
Tel: 01475 721877 *Website:* www.ronniecowan.com *Twitter:* @ronniecowan

CONSERVATIVE

COX, GEOFFREY

Torridge and West Devon *(Majority 20,686)*

Charles Geoffrey Cox. Born 30 April 1960; Son of Michael and Diane Cox; Married Patricia Macdonald 1985 (1 daughter 2 sons).

Education: King's College, Taunton; Downing College, Cambridge (BA English and law 1981).

Non-political career: Barrister, Thomas More Chambers 1982-2001; Standing counsel to Mauritius 1996-2000; QC 2003. Member, National Farmers' Union.

Political career: Contested Torridge and West Devon 2001 general election. Member for Torridge and West Devon 2005-10, for Torridge and West Devon (revised boundary) since 6 May 2010 general election. *Select committees:* Member: Environment, Food and Rural Affairs 2006-10, Standards and Privileges 2010-13, Standards 2013-15, Privileges 2013-15.

Political interests: Agriculture, education, defence, legal and constitutional issues; Mauritius.

Recreations: Reading, walking dogs, swimming, countryside .

Geoffrey Cox QC MP, House of Commons, London SW1A 0AA
Tel: 020 7219 4719 *Fax:* 020 7219 4307 *Email:* coxg@parliament.uk
Constituency: First Floor, Lockyer House, Paddons Row, Tavistock, Devon PL19 0HF
Tel: 01822 612925 *Website:* www.geoffreycox.co.uk *Twitter:* @Geoffrey_Cox

LABOUR

COYLE, NEIL

Bermondsey and Old Southwark *(Majority 12,972)*

Born 30 December 1978; Son of Alan Coyle and Mary Coyle, née Wesson; Married Sarah 2014 (1 daughter).

Education: Hull University (2001).

Non-political career: Disability Rights Commission 2003-07; Head of Policy, National Centre for Independent Living 2007-09; Director of Policy, Disability Alliance 2009-12; Director of Policy and Campaigns, DRUK 2012-13.

Political career: Member for Bermondsey and Old Southwark since 7 May 2015 general election; PPS to Chris Bryant as Shadow Leader of the House of Commons 2015-16. *Select committees:* Member, Work and Pensions 2016-. *Councils and public bodies:* London Borough of Southwark Council: Councillor 2010-16, Deputy Cabinet Member 2011-13.

Political interests: Disability, welfare, social security, social care, local government.

Other: Board Member, Tower Hamlets Advocacy Network and Community Support; Pecan (charity).

Neil Coyle MP, House of Commons, London SW1A 0AA
Tel: 020 7219 8733 *Email:* neil.coyle.mp@parliament.uk
Constituency: 149-151 Jamaica Road, London SE16 4SH *Website:* www.boslabour.org.uk
Twitter: @coyleneil

CONSERVATIVE

CRABB, STEPHEN

Preseli Pembrokeshire *(Majority 314)*

Born 20 January 1973; Married Béatrice Monnier 1996 (1 son 1 daughter).

Education: Tasker Milward VC School, Haverfordwest; Bristol University (BSc politics 1995); London Business School (MBA 2004); French.

Non-political career: Research assistant to Andrew Rowe MP 1995-96; Parliamentary affairs officer, National Council for Voluntary Youth Services 1996-98; Policy and campaign manager, London Chamber of Commerce 1998-2002; Self-employed marketing consultant 2002-05.

Political career: Contested Preseli Pembrokeshire 2001 general election. Member for Preseli Pembrokeshire 2005-10, for Preseli Pembrokeshire (revised boundary) since 6 May 2010 general election; Assistant Government Whip 2010-12; Parliamentary Under-Secretary of State, Wales Office 2012-14; Government Whip 2012-14; Secretary of State for: Wales 2014-16, Work and Pensions 2016. *Select committees:* Member: Welsh Affairs 2005-07, International Development 2007-09, Treasury 2008-09, Exiting the European Union 2017-. Chair, North Southwark and Bermondsey Conservative Association 1998-2000; Conservative Party: Chair, Human Rights Commission 2007-09, Leader, Social Action Project in Rwanda and Sierra Leone: "Project Umubano" 2010-13.

Political interests: Welfare reform, energy, trade and industry, farming and international development; Africa, France, India, Middle East, USA.

Other: Patron, Haverfordwest Mencap 2005-. PC 2014; Balfour Conservative Club. Haverfordwest County AFC.

Recreations: Rugby, long distance running, cooking, family.

Rt Hon Stephen Crabb MP, House of Commons, London SW1A 0AA
Tel: 020 7219 0907 *Email:* stephen.crabb.mp@parliament.uk
Constituency: Suite 1, 20 Upper Market Street, Haverfordwest, Pembrokeshire SA61 1QA
Tel: 01437 767555 *Email:* jonesad@parliament.uk lattere@parliament.uk
Website: www.stephencrabb.com *Twitter:* @SCrabbPembs

LABOUR

CRAUSBY, DAVID

Bolton North East *(Majority 3,797)*

David Anthony Crausby. Born 17 June 1946; Son of late Thomas Crausby, factory worker/club steward, and Kathleen Crausby, cotton worker; Married Enid Noon 1965 (2 sons).

Education: Derby Grammar School, Bury; Bury Technical College.

Non-political career: Engineer. Shop steward/works convenor, AEEU 1968-97; Full-time works convenor 1978-97; Chair, Amicus (AEEU) Group 2001-; Secretary, Unite Group 2010-.

Political career: Contested Bury North 1987 and Bolton North East 1992 general elections. Member for Bolton North East 1997-2010, for Bolton North East (revised boundary) since 6 May 2010 general election. *Select committees:* Member: Administration 1997-2001, Social Security 1999-2001, Defence 2001-10, Quadripartite (Committees on Strategic Export Controls)/Arms Export Controls 2006-10; Chair, North West 2009-10; Member: Chairmen's Panel/Panel of Chairs 2010-, High Speed Rail (London-West Midlands) Bill 2015-16, Court of Referees 2016-. Member, Labour Party Departmental Committees for: Foreign and Commonwealth Affairs 1997-2001, Social Security 1997-2001, Trade and Industry 1997-2001; North West Regional Group PLP: Vice-chair 2000-01, Chair 2001-02. *Councils and public bodies:* Bury Council: Councillor 1979-92, Chair of Housing 1985-92.

Political interests: Industrial relations, pensions, housing, defence; Bermuda, Canada, New Zealand.

Other: Member, UK Delegation to: NATO Parliamentary Assembly 2014-15, Parliamentary Assembly of the Council of Europe 2015-. Commons Speech of the Year, *House Magazine* awards 2011. Kt 2017.

Recreations: Football, cinema, walking.

Sir David Crausby MP, House of Commons, London SW1A 0AA
Tel: 020 7219 4092 *Fax:* 020 7219 3713 *Email:* crausbyd@parliament.uk
Constituency: 140 Chorley Old Road, Bolton, Greater Manchester BL1 3AT
Tel: 01204 391909 *Website:* www.davidcrausby.co.uk *Twitter:* @DavidCrausby

SCOTTISH NATIONAL PARTY

CRAWLEY, ANGELA

Lanark and Hamilton East *(Majority 266)*

SNP Spokesperson for Equalities, Women and Children, Family Support, Housing, Child Maintenance and Disability

Born 3 June 1987.

Education: John Ogilvie High School; Stirling University (BA politics 2009); Glasgow University (LLB 2015).

Non-political career: Parliamentary Assistant to Bruce Crawford MSP and Clare Adamson MSP 2011-13; Legal assistant, Aamer Anwar & Co 2014.

Political career: Member for Lanark and Hamilton East since 7 May 2015 general election; SNP Spokesperson for: Equalities, Women and Children 2015-, Family Support 2017-, Housing 2017-, Child Maintenance 2017-, Disability 2017-. *Select committees:* Member, Women and Equalities 2015-. National Convener, Young Scots for Independence; Member, National Executive Committee, Scottish National Party. *Councils and public bodies:* Councillor, South Lanarkshire Council 2012-15.

Political interests: Equal rights, social justice.

Angela Crawley MP, House of Commons, London SW1A 0AA
Tel: 020 7219 6044 *Email:* angela.crawley.mp@parliament.uk
Constituency: 12 Campbell Street, Hamilton ML3 6AS
Tel: 01698 200065 *Website:* angelacrawleymp.com *Twitter:* @AngelaCrawley30

LABOUR

CREAGH, MARY

Wakefield *(Majority 2,176)*

Chair, Select Committee on Environmental Audit

Mary Helen Creagh. Born 2 December 1967; Daughter of Thomas and Elizabeth Creagh; Married Adrian Pulham 2001 (1 son 1 daughter).

Education: Bishop Ullathorne RC Comprehensive, Coventry; Pembroke College, Oxford (BA modern languages (French/Italian) 1990); London School of Economics (MSc European studies 1997); French, Italian, Spanish.

Non-political career: Stagiare, Socialist group, European Parliament 1990; Assistant to Stephen Hughes MEP 1991; Press officer: European Youth Forum 1991-95, London Enterprise Agency 1995-97; Lecturer, entrepreneurship, Cranfield School of Management 1997-2005. GMB: Member 1991-95, 2003-05, Chair, Brussels branch 1992-95; Member, Unison 2004-11.

Political career: Member for Wakefield 2005-10, for Wakefield (revised boundary) since 6 May 2010 general election; PPS: to Ministers of State, Department of Health: Andy Burnham 2006-07, Lord Warner 2006, to Andy Burnham: as Chief Secretary to the Treasury 2007-08, as Secretary of State for Culture, Media and Sport 2008-09; Assistant Government Whip 2009-10; Shadow Minister for Public Health 2010; Opposition Whip 2010; Shadow Secretary of State for: Environment, Food and Rural Affairs 2010-13, Transport 2013-14, International Development 2014-15. *Select committees:* Member: Joint Committee on Human Rights 2005-07, Finance and Services 2007-10, Yorkshire and the Humber 2009; Environmental Audit: Member 2015-16, Chair 2016-; Member, Liaison 2016-. Member, Economy – Living Standards and Sustainability Commission 2013-. *Councils and public bodies:* London Borough of Islington: Councillor 1998-2005, Leader, Labour group 2000-04.

Political interests: Europe, employment, social policy, disability issues, Irish community, human rights, children's issues, environment; Burundi, Democratic Republic of Congo, Rwanda, Sudan.

Other: Member, UK delegation to NATO Parliamentary Assembly 2015-; Member: European Movement 1995-, Fabian Society 1995-, Oxfam 1995-, RNID 1996-, Amnesty International 1997-; Trustee, Rathbone Training 1997-2004; Member, Ectopic Pregnancy Trust 2001-; Member Higher Education Academy 2002-; Red Shed Wakefield Club.

Recreations: Family, yoga, cycling, swimming, food.

Mary Creagh MP, House of Commons, London SW1A 0AA
Tel: 020 7219 8766/020 7219 6984 *Fax:* 020 7219 4257 *Email:* creaghm@parliament.uk
Constituency: 20-22 Cheapside, Wakefield, West Yorkshire WF1 2TF
Tel: 01924 386124 *Fax:* 01924 299723 *Email:* mary@marycreagh.co.uk
Website: www.marycreagh.co.uk *Twitter:* @MaryCreaghMP

LAB/CO-OP

CREASY, STELLA

Walthamstow *(Majority 32,017)*

Stella Judith Creasy. Born 5 April 1977.

Education: Colchester County High School; Magdalene College, Cambridge (psychology); London School of Economics (PhD psychology).

Non-political career: Researcher to Douglas Alexander MP, Charles Clarke MP and Ross Cranston MP; Deputy director, Involve; Head of campaigns, Scout Association. Member, Unite.

Political career: Member for Walthamstow since 6 May 2010 general election; Member, Public Accounts Commission 2011-15; PPS to Andy Burnham as Shadow Secretary of State for Education 2011; Shadow Minister for: Crime Prevention 2011-13, Business, Innovation and Skills 2013-15. *Select committees:* Member: Public Accounts 2010-11, Science and Technology 2015-17. Member: SERA, Labour Women's Network, Co-operative Party; Contested Labour deputy leadership election 2015. *Councils and public bodies:* Waltham Forest Council: Councillor 2002-05, Former Deputy Mayor, Interim mayor 2003.

Other: Fabian Society. Campaigner of the Year, *Spectator* awards 2011; Campaign of the Year, *PoliticsHome* awards 2012.

Recreations: Indie music, American TV crime drama, cake, pub quizzes.

Dr Stella Creasy MP, House of Commons, London SW1A 0AA
Tel: 020 7219 6980
Constituency: Walthamstow Labour Party, 23 Orford Road, Walthamstow, London E17 9NL
Tel: 020 8521 1223 *Email:* stella@workingforwalthamstow.org.uk
Website: www.workingforwalthamstow.org.uk *Twitter:* @stellacreasy

CONSERVATIVE

CROUCH, TRACEY

Chatham and Aylesford *(Majority 10,458)*

Parliamentary Under-Secretary of State for Sport and Civil Society, Department for Digital, Culture, Media and Sport

Tracey Elizabeth Anne Crouch. Born 24 July 1975; Partner Steve (1 son).

Education: Folkestone Grammar School for Girls; Hull University (BA law and politics 1996).

Non-political career: Researcher to Michael Howard MP 1996-98; Public affairs manager, Harcourt 1998-2000; Senior public affairs manager, Westminster Strategy 2000-03; Chief of staff to: Damian Green MP 2003, David Davis MP 2003-05; Norwich Union/Aviva 2005-10: Senior political adviser 2005-07, Head of public affairs 2007-10.

Political career: Member for Chatham and Aylesford since 6 May 2010 general election; Member, Speaker's Committee on the Electoral Commission 2013-15; Parliamentary Under-Secretary of State for Sport, Tourism and Heritage, Department for Culture, Media and Sport 2015-17 (on maternity leave January-July 2016); Parliamentary Under-Secretary of State for Sport and Civil Society, Department for Digital, Culture, Media and Sport 2017-. *Select committees:* Member: Culture, Media and Sport 2012-15, Political and Constitutional Reform 2013-15. Member, Executive, 1922 Committee 2010-12. Member, Conservative Co-operative Movement.

Political interests: Sport and wellbeing, health and social care, mental health, constitutional affairs, older people's issues.

Other: Member, UK Delegation, Organisation for Security and Co-operation in Europe Parliamentary Assembly 2011-13; Honorary Member, Royal Engineers; Independent Chair, Medway Council's Physical Disability Partnership Board; President, RSPCA Medway; Vice-president, Campaign to Protect Rural England (Kent Branch); Patron: National Osteoporosis Society (Medway), Peter's Place, Halpern Charitable Foundation, Blenheim CDP; Member, World Anti-Doping Agency Foundation Board 2016-. FA coaching level 1 2006; Manager, Meridian Girls FC.

Recreations: Sport, music, reading.

Tracey Crouch MP, House of Commons, London SW1A 0AA
Tel: 020 7219 7203 *Email:* tracey.crouch.mp@parliament.uk
Constituency: 6-8 Revenge Road, Lordswood, Chatham, Kent ME5 8UD
Tel: 01634 673180 *Website:* www.traceycrouch.org *Twitter:* @tracey_crouch

LABOUR

CRUDDAS, JON

Dagenham and Rainham *(Majority 4,652)*

Jonathan Cruddas. Born 7 April 1962; Son of John Cruddas, sailor, and Pat Cruddas, housewife; Married Anna Healy 1992, now Baroness Healy of Primrose Hill (qv) (1 son).

Education: Oaklands RC Comprehensive, Portsmouth; Warwick University 1981-88 (BSc economics; MA industrial relations; PhD industrial and business studies); Visiting fellow, University of Wisconsin, USA 1987-88.

Non-political career: Policy officer, Labour Party Policy Directorate 1989-94; Chief assistant to General Secretary, Labour Party 1994-97; Deputy political secretary, Prime Minister's political office, Downing Street 1997-2001. TGWU 1989-2001: Branch secretary 1992-94.

Political career: Member for Dagenham 2001-10, for Dagenham and Rainham since 6 May 2010 general election. *Select committees:* Member, Public Accounts 2003-05. Hon. Secretary, PLP London Regional Group 2005-10. Policy Review Co-ordinator, Labour Party 2012-15.

Political interests: Labour law, industrial economy, economic regeneration, housing, the far right, community cohesion.

Other: Dagenham Working Men's Club, Dagenham Royal Naval Association. White Hart Dagenham Angling Society.

Recreations: Golf, angling.

Jon Cruddas MP, House of Commons, London SW1A 0AA
Tel: 020 7219 8161 *Fax:* 020 7219 1756 *Email:* cruddasj@parliament.uk
Constituency: 598 Rainham Road South, Dagenham RM10 8YP
Tel: 020 8984 7854 *Email:* mullanem@parliament.uk *Website:* www.joncruddas.org.uk
Twitter: @JonCruddas_1

LABOUR

CRYER, JOHN

Leyton and Wanstead *(Majority 22,607)*

John Robert Cryer. Born 11 April 1964; Son of late Bob Cryer (MP for Keighley 1974-83 and Bradford South 1987-94) and Ann Cryer, née Place (MP for Keighley 1997-2010); Married Narinder Bains 1994 (divorced 2011) (2 sons 1 daughter); married Ellie Reeves (qv) 2012 (MP for Lewisham West and Penge) (1 son).

Education: Oakbank School, Keighley; Hatfield Polytechnic (BA literature and history 1985); London College of Printing (Postgraduate Certificate print journalism 1988).

Non-political career: Journalist: *Tribune* 1992-96, *Morning Star* 1989-92; Freelance journalist, 1992-97: *Labour Briefing* (editor), *Guardian*, *GPMU Journal*, *T&G Record*; Lloyd's of London Publications; Political officer: ASLEF 2005-06, Unite 2006-10. Member: TGWU 1986-, NUJ 1988-, UCATT 1997-.

Political career: Member for Hornchurch 1997-2005. Contested Hornchurch 2005 general election. Member for Leyton and Wanstead since 6 May 2010 general election. *Select committees:* Member: Deregulation and Regulatory Reform 1997-2002, Treasury 2010-11, Justice 2014-15, Administration 2015-. Member, Labour Party Departmental Committees for: Education and Employment 1997-2001, Parliamentary Affairs 1997-2001, Trade and Industry 1997-2001; Member, PLP Committee 2003-05, 2010-; Secretary, Labour Against the European Superstate 2004-05; Contested PLP chairman election 2012; Chair: Labour for a Referendum, Parliamentary Labour Party 2015-. Member, Executive of Labour Euro Safeguards Committee; Press officer, Defend Clause Four Campaign 1995; Member, Co-operative Party; Secretary, Labour Against the Euro.

Political interests: Employment, social security, education, further education, European Union, health, economic policy, industry, energy policy, transport; Australia, India, USA.

Other: Member: CND, Amnesty International, Transport on Water, Tibet Support Group, Keighley and Worth Valley Railway, RAF Hornchurch Association; Member, British Board of Boxing Control 1997-99; First Step Nursery Hornchurch, St Francis Hospice Havering, Child Poverty Action Group, St Francis Foundation for Animal Welfare, Islamic Relief, East Africa Flood Apeal, Leyton Royal British Legion, Carefree Kids Waltham Forest, Box4Life Leyton, Recovery Resoucres, Foundation Leytonstone. Member: House of Commons Cricket Club, House of Commons Rugby Club, House of Commons Boxing Club.

Publications: Co-author with Ann Cryer, Boldness be my Friend: Remembering Bob Cryer MP (1996); Many articles mainly in political publications.

Recreations: Swimming, reading, sport, old cars, cinema, cycling, triathlons.

John Cryer MP, House of Commons, London SW1A 0AA
Tel: 020 7219 7100 *Email:* john.cryer.mp@parliament.uk
Constituency: 6 Gainsborough Road, Leytonstone, London E11 1HR
Tel: 020 8989 5249 *Website:* www.johncryermp.co.uk *Twitter:* @JohnCryerMP

LABOUR

CUMMINS, JUDITH

Bradford South *(Majority 6,700)*

Opposition Whip

Judith Mary Cummins. Born 26 June 1967; Married Mark (2 children).

Education: Ruskin College; Leeds University.

Non-political career: Benefits adviser; Low Pay Unit. Member: GMB, Unison.

Political career: Member for Bradford South since 7 May 2015 general election; Opposition Whip 2015-. *Select committees:* Member, Armed Forces Bill 2015 2015-16. *Councils and public bodies:* Former Councillor: Bradford District Council, Leeds City Council 2012-16; West Yorkshire Fire and Rescue Authority: Member, Chair, Audit Committee.

Judith Cummins MP, House of Commons, London SW1A 0AA
Tel: 020 7219 8607 *Email:* judith.cummins.mp@parliament.uk
Constituency: Malik House, 29 Manor Row, Bradford, West Yorkshire BD1 4PS
Tel: 01274 924280 *Email:* judith@judithcummins.org.uk *Website:* www.judithcummins.org.uk
Twitter: @JudithCummins

LABOUR

CUNNINGHAM, ALEX

Stockton North *(Majority 8,715)*

Shadow Minister for Pensions

Alexander Cunningham. Born 1 May 1955; Son of John and Jean Cunningham; Married Evaline 1977 (2 sons).

Education: Branksome Comprehensive, Darlington; Queen Elizabeth Sixth Form; Darlington College of Technology (Certificate journalism 1976).

Non-political career: Journalist: *Darlington and Stockton Times* 1974-76, *The Mail*, Hartlepool 1976-77, Radio Tees 1977-79, Radio Clyde 1979, *Evening Gazette* 1979-84; Public relations officer, British Gas 1984-89; Transco: Communications adviser 1995-2000, Head of communications 2000-02; Managing director, Tees Valley Communicators Ltd 2002-10. National Union of Journalists: Member 1974-80, Father of Chapel 1977-79; Member, National Union of Public Employees/ Unison 1980-.

Political career: Member for Stockton North since 6 May 2010 general election; PPS to: Sadiq Khan as Shadow Lord Chancellor and Secretary of State for Justice 2011-15, Lord Falconer as Shadow Lord Chancellor and Secretary of State for Justice 2015; Shadow Minister for: Environment, Food and Rural Affairs 2015-16, Pensions 2016-. *Select committees:* Member: Work and Pensions 2010-11, Armed Forces Bill 2011, Education 2011-15. Stockton North CLP: Press officer 1984-2010, Vice-chair, secretary 1985-95, Chair 1995-2000; Member, Co-operative Party 1986-. *Councils and public bodies:* Cleveland County Council: Councillor 1989-96, Vice-chair, Education Committee 1990-96, Chair, Standing Advisory Council for Religious Education 1989-96; Stockton Borough Council: Councillor 1999-2010, Cabinet Member for Children and Young People 2000-10; Chair, Stockton Children's Trust; Board member, Arts Council England North East 2002-08; Board member and chair, North East Libraries and Archives Council (later MLA North East) 2003-09; Council member, Museums, Libraries and Archives Council 2008-09; Non-executive director, North Tees and Hartlepool NHS Trust 2008-10; Board member, One North East Regional Development Agency 2008-10; Hon Alderman, Stockton on Tees Borough Council 2015.

Political interests: Children's services, education, health, leisure, culture, energy, carers, poverty, pensions; France, Palestine.

Other: Member, Socialist Education Association 1984-; Eastern Ravens Trust, Awayout, Daisychain, Justice First. Patron, Stockton Rugby Club.

Recreations: Sport, reading, travel.

Alex Cunningham MP, House of Commons, London SW1A 0AA
Tel: 020 7219 7157 *Email:* alex.cunningham.mp@parliament.uk
Constituency: Unit 144, Stockton Business Centre, 70-74 Brunswick Street, Stockton on Tees TS18 1DW
Tel: 01642 345291 *Fax:* 01642 345132 *Email:* robert.cook@parliament.uk
Website: www.alexcunninghammp.com *Twitter:* @ACunninghamMP

LABOUR

CUNNINGHAM, JIM

Coventry South *(Majority 7,947)*

James Dolan Cunningham. Born 4 February 1941; Son of Adam and Elizabeth Cunningham; Married Marion Podmore 1985 (1 son 1 daughter 1 stepson 1 stepdaughter).

Education: Columba High School, Coatbridge; Tillycoultry College, Ruskin Courses (Labour movement, industrial law).

Non-political career: Engineer Rolls-Royce 1965-88. Shop steward, MSF 1968-88.

Political career: Member for Coventry South East 1992-97, for Coventry South 1997-2010, for Coventry South (revised boundary) since 6 May 2010 general election; PPS to Mike O'Brien: as Solicitor General 2005-07, as Minister of State: Department for Work and Pensions 2007-08, Department of Energy and Climate Change 2008-09, Department of Health 2009-10. *Select committees:* Member: Home Affairs 1993-97, Trade and Industry 1997-2001, Chairmen's Panel 1998-2001, Constitutional Affairs 2003-05, Office of the Deputy Prime Minister 2005, Procedure 2005-06, Standards and Privileges 2010, Scottish Affairs 2015-17. Chair PLP: Departmental Committee for the Treasury 1999-2010, West Midlands Regional Group 2005-10. Chair, Coventry South East CLP 1977-79. *Councils and public bodies:* Coventry City Council: Councillor 1972-92, Council Leader 1988-92.

Political interests: Economic policy, European Union, industrial relations, NHS; Eastern Europe, Russia, USA.

Recreations: Walking, reading, historical buildings.

Jim Cunningham MP, House of Commons, London SW1A 0AA
Tel: 020 7219 6362 *Fax:* 020 7219 4907 *Email:* eleanorm.connolly@parliament.uk
Constituency: Ground Floor, Rear of Queens House, 16 Queens Road, Coventry, Warwickshire CV1 3EG
Tel: 024 7655 3159 *Email:* jim.cunningham.mp@parliament.uk
Website: www.jimcunningham.org.uk *Twitter:* @jimforcovsouth

LABOUR

DAKIN, NIC

Scunthorpe *(Majority 3,431)*

Opposition Whip

Nicholas Dakin. Born 10 July 1955; Son of Royston and Elsie Dakin; Married Audrey (3 children).

Education: Stonehill High School, Leicestershire; Longslade Upper School, Leicestershire; Hull University (history 1976; MEd 1987); King's College, London (PGCE 1977); French, Swedish.

Non-political career: English teacher, Greatfield High School, Hull 1977-79; Teacher of English as a foreign language in Gävle, Sweden 1979-81; John Leggott College 1982-2010: Vice-principal 2004-07; Principal 2007-10. Member: National Union of Teachers, GMB.

Political career: Member for Scunthorpe since 6 May 2010 general election; Opposition Whip 2011-15, 2016-; Shadow Deputy Leader 2015; Shadow Minister for Education 2015-16. *Select committees:* Member: Education 2010-11, Procedure 2011-. Vice-chair, PLP Departmental Group for DPM/Constitutional Affairs 2010-15. *Councils and public bodies:* North Lincolnshire Council: Councillor, Chair, Education 1996-97, Council Leader 1997-2003, Leader, Labour Group 2003-07.

Political interests: Education, manufacturing, conservation, arts, economic policy, debt advice and support; Finland, Sweden.

Other: Treasurer, Inter-Parliamentary Union, British Group 2016-; Yorkshire Forward: Board member 2003-07, Deputy chair 2004-06. Scunthorpe Squash Club.

Recreations: Scunthorpe United FC, squash, walking, travel.

Nic Dakin MP, House of Commons, London SW1A 0AA
Tel: 020 7219 0446 *Email:* nic.dakin.mp@parliament.uk
Constituency: Suite 3, Limewood Suite, First Floor, 5 Park Square, Laneham Street, Scunthorpe DN15 6JH
Tel: 01724 842000 *Website:* www.nicdakin.com *Twitter:* @NicDakin4MP

LIBERAL DEMOCRAT

DAVEY, ED

Kingston and Surbiton *(Majority 4,124)*

Liberal Democrat Shadow Home Secretary

Edward Jonathon Davey. Born 25 December 1965; Son of late John Davey, solicitor, and late Nina Davey, née Stanbrook, teacher; Married Emily Gasson 2005 (1 son 1 daughter).

Education: Nottingham High School; Jesus College, Oxford (BA philosophy, politics and economics 1988); Birkbeck College, London (MSc economics 1993).

Non-political career: Senior economics adviser to Liberal Democrat MPs 1989-93; Management consultant, Omega Partners 1993-97; Director, Omega Partners Postal 1996-97; Renewable Energy Consultant, Herbert Smith 2015-; Chair, Mongoose Energy.

Political career: Member for Kingston and Surbiton 1997-2010, for Kingston and Surbiton (revised boundary) 2010-15. Contested Kingston and Surbiton 2015 general election. Member for Kingston and Surbiton since 8 June 2017; Liberal Democrat: London Whip 1997-2000; Spokesperson for: the Treasury (Public Spending and Taxation) 1997-99, Economy 1999-2001, London 2000-03; Shadow Chief Secretary to the Treasury 2001-02, Spokesperson for Office of the Deputy Prime Minister 2002-05; Shadow Secretary of State for: Education and Skills 2005-06, Trade and Industry 2006, Chief of Staff to Sir Menzies Campbell as Leader of the Liberal Democrats 2006-07; Shadow Secretary of State for Foreign and Commonwealth Affairs 2007-10; Parliamentary Under-Secretary of State (Minister for Employment Relations, Consumer and Postal Affairs), Department for Business, Innovation and Skills 2010-12; Secretary of State for Energy and Climate Change 2012-15; Liberal Democrat Shadow Home Secretary 2017-. *Select committees:* Member: Procedure 1997-2000, Treasury 1999-2001, Treasury (Treasury Sub-Committee) 1999-2001. Liberal Democrats: Chair, Costing Group (costing all policies for manifesto) 1992 and 1997 general elections, Member: Federal Policy Committee 1994-95, Policy Group (Economics, Tax and Benefits and Transport), Association of Liberal Democrat Councillors, Chair, Campaigns and Communications Committee 2006-09.

Political interests: Taxation, economics, internet, employment, environment, modernisation of Parliament; Latin America.

Other: Patron: Jigsaw, Kingston Special Needs Project; Goodwill Ambassador for Children of Peace; Trustee, Kidsout; Love Kingston; Member, advisory board: Next Energy Capital, Grantham Research Institute; Chair, Fit for the Future. Royal Humane Society Honourable Testimonial; Chief Constable, London Transport Police Commendation 1994; Royal Humane Society 1994; Double Act of the Year (with John Hayes MP), *Spectator* awards 2012. PC 2012; Kt 2016.

Publications: Making MPs Work for our Money: Reforming Budget Scrutiny (Centre for Reform), 2000.

Recreations: Music, walking, swimming.

Rt Hon Sir Ed Davey MP, House of Commons, London SW1A 0AA
Tel: 020 7219 4530 *Email:* edward.davey.mp@parliament.uk
Constituency: 21 Berrylands Road, Surbiton KT5 8QX
Tel: 020 8288 2736 *Email:* contact@eddavey.org *Website:* www.voters4ed.org
Twitter: @EdwardJDavey

LABOUR

DAVID, WAYNE

Caerphilly *(Majority 12,078)*

Shadow Minister for the Armed Forces and Defence Procurement

Born 1 July 1957; Son of David Haydn David, teacher, and Edna David, née Jones, housewife; Married Catherine Thomas 1991 (divorced 2007); married Jayne Edwards 2016.

Education: Cynffig Comprehensive School, Kenfig Hill, Mid Glamorgan; University College, Cardiff (BA history and Welsh history 1979; PGCE further education 1983); University College, Swansea (economic history research 1979-82).

Non-political career: History teacher, Brynteg Comprehensive School 1983-85; Tutor organiser, Workers' Educational Association South Wales District 1985-89; Policy adviser, youth policy, Wales Youth Agency 1999-2001. Member: MSF 1983-2004, AEEU 1998-2004, Amicus 2004-07, Unite 2007-.

Political career: Member for Caerphilly 2001-10, for Caerphilly (revised boundary) since 6 May 2010 general election; Team PPS, Ministry of Defence 2005; PPS to Adam Ingram as Minister of State, Ministry of Defence 2005-06; Assistant Government Whip 2007-08; Parliamentary Under-Secretary of State, Wales Office 2008-10; Shadow Minister for: Wales 2010, Europe 2010-11, Justice (Political and Constitutional Reform) 2011-13; PPS to Leader of the Opposition: Ed Miliband 2013-15, Harriet Harman 2015; Shadow Minister for: Justice 2015-16, Cabinet Office 2015-16, Scotland 2015-16, Armed Forces and Defence Procurement 2016-. *Select committees:* Member: European Scrutiny 2001-07, Standards and Privileges 2004-05, Joint Committee on Conventions 2006, Welsh Affairs 2007. Honorary Secretary PLP: Departmental Committee for Work and Pensions 2002-08, Welsh Regional Group 2003-07. European Parliament: MEP for South Wales 1989-94, for South Wales Central 1994-99: Vice-president, Socialist Group 1994-98, Leader, European Parliamentary Labour Party 1994-98; Contested Rhondda constituency 1999 National Assembly for Wales election. Ex-officio member, NEC, Labour Party 1994-98. *Councils and public bodies:* Cefn Cribwr Community Council: Councillor 1985-91, Chair 1986-87.

Political interests: European affairs, economy, education, devolution, constitution; Belgium, Bulgaria, Poland.

Other: Vice-president, Cardiff UN Association 1989-; President: Aber Valley Male Voice Choir 2001-, Council for Wales of Voluntary Youth Services 2002-, Caerphilly Local History Society 2006-; Fellow, Cardiff University 1995; Bargoed Labour Club.

Publications: Contributor: The Future of Europe, Problems and Issues for the 21st Century (1996); Remaining True (biography of Ness Edwards MP, 2006).

Recreations: Music, playing the oboe.

Wayne David MP, House of Commons, London SW1A 0AA
Tel: 020 7219 8152 *Fax:* 020 7219 1751 *Email:* wayne.david.mp@parliament.uk
Constituency: BTM Community Council Offices, Newport Road, Bedwas, Caerphilly CF83 8YB
Tel: 029 2088 1061 *Fax:* 029 2088 1954 *Email:* jonesli@parliament.uk
Website: www.waynedavid.co.uk *Twitter:* @WayneDavid_MP

CONSERVATIVE

DAVIES, CHRIS

Brecon and Radnorshire *(Majority 8,038)*

Christopher Paul Davies. Born 18 August 1967; Married Liz 2006 (2 daughters).

Education: Morriston Comprehensive.

Non-political career: Rural auctioneer and estate agent; Manager, Hay Veterinary Group 2008-14; Main ring commentator: Royal Welsh Show, Smallholders Show, Winter Fair.

Political career: Member for Brecon and Radnorshire since 7 May 2015 general election. *Select committees:* Member: Environment, Food and Rural Affairs 2015-17, Welsh Affairs 2015-, Environment, Food and Rural Affairs Sub-committee 2016-17. Contested Brecon and Radnorshire constituency 2011 National Assembly for Wales election. *Councils and public bodies:* Councillor, Powys County Council 2012-15; Governor, Gwernyfed High School 2012-.

Chris Davies MP, House of Commons, London SW1A 0AA
Tel: 020 7219 8592 *Email:* chris.davies.mp@parliament.uk
Constituency: 6 Market Street, Builth Wells, Powys LD2 3AG
Tel: 01982 559180 *Website:* www.chrisdavies.org.uk

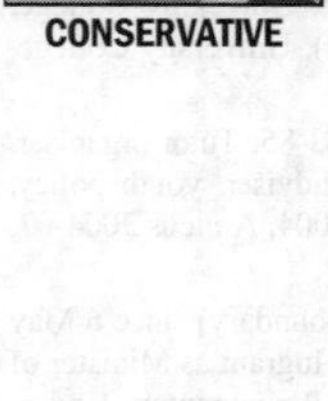

CONSERVATIVE

DAVIES, DAVID

Monmouth *(Majority 8,206)*

Chair, Select Committee on Welsh Affairs

David Thomas Charles Davies. Born 27 July 1970; Son of Peter and Kathleen Davies; Married Aliz Harnisfoger 2003 (2 daughters 1 son).

Education: Bassaleg Comprehensive, Newport; HGV class one; German, Hungarian, Welsh.

Non-political career: Served as a gunner with 104 Air Defence Regiment, Territorial Army, Raglan Barracks, Newport. British Steel Corporation 1988-89; Casual work in Australia 1989-91; Manager, Burrow Heath Ltd (forwarder and tea importers) 1991-99; Special Constable, British Transport Police 2006-15.

Political career: Contested Bridgend 1997 general election. Member for Monmouth since 5 May 2005 general election. *Select committees:* Welsh Affairs: Member 2005-10, Chair 2010-; Member: Home Affairs 2007-10, Home Affairs Sub-Committee 2008-09, Liaison 2010-, Liaison (National Policy Statements Sub-committee) 2010-15. National Assembly for Wales: AM for Monmouth constituency 1999-2007: Deputy Leader/Business Secretary 1999; Chief Whip 1999-2001. Organiser for anti-Assembly 'No' Campaign 1997; Campaign manager for Rod Richards as leader of Welsh Conservative Party 1998.

Political interests: Policing, climate change, Middle East; China, Germany, Hungary.

Other: UK delegation, Parliamentary Assembly of the Council of Europe: Member, Substitute member; Honorary Member: Rotary Club of Usk and District, Institution of Royal Engineers; Former President, Welsh Amateur Boxing Association; Honorary Vice-President, Monmouthshire and District National Eisteddfod 2016; Combat Stress, Richard Hunt Foundation, Chepstow Mencap; Chepstow Conservative Club, Abergavenny Conservative Club, Usk Conservative Club, Monmouth Conservative Club. Torfaen Warriors Boxing Club; Chepstow Amateur Boxing Club.

Recreations: Family, running, surfing, history, boxing.

David Davies MP, House of Commons, London SW1A 0AA
Tel: 020 7219 8360 *Email:* david.davies.mp@parliament.uk
Constituency: The Grange, 16 Maryport Street, Usk, Monmouthshire NP15 1AB
Tel: 01291 672817 *Website:* www.david-daviesmp.co.uk *Twitter:* @davidtcdavies

LAB/CO-OP

DAVIES, GERAINT

Swansea West *(Majority 10,598)*

Geraint Richard Davies. Born 3 May 1960; Son of David Davies, civil servant, and Betty Davies; Married Dr Vanessa Fry 1991 (3 daughters).

Education: Llanishen Comprehensive, Cardiff; JCR President, Jesus College, Oxford (BA philosophy, politics and economics 1982).

Non-political career: Sales and marketing trainee; Group product manager, Unilever 1982-88; Marketing manager, Colgate Palmolive Ltd 1988-89; Managing director, Pure Crete Ltd 1989-97; Chair, Flood Risk Management Wales, Environment Agency 2005-10. Member, GMB.

Political career: Contested Croydon South 1987 and Croydon Central 1992 general elections. Member for Croydon Central 1997-2005. Contested Croydon Central 2005 general election. Member for Swansea West since 6 May 2010 general election; Team PPS, Department for Constitutional Affairs 2003-05. *Select committees:* Member: Public Accounts 1997-2003, Welsh Affairs 2010-15, 2017-, Standing Orders 2011-, Unopposed Bills (Panel) 2011-15, European Scrutiny 2013-, Panel of Chairs 2015-, Environmental Audit 2015-. Chair, PLP Departmental Committee for Environment, Transport and the Regions 1997-2004; Member, PLP Departmental Committees for: National Heritage/Culture, Media and Sport 1997-98, Trade and Industry 1997-2001, Treasury 1998-2001; Vice-chair, PLP Departmental: Committee for Transport 2004-05, Group for Justice 2010-15. Chair, Labour Finance and Industry Group 1998-2005; Member, Co-operative Party. *Councils and public bodies:* Councillor, Croydon Council 1986-97: Chair, Housing Committee 1994-96, Council Leader 1996-97; Governor, Dylan Thomas Community School.

Political interests: Treasury, trade and industry, housing, children's issues, transport, environment, human rights, equality; Crete, Wales.

Other: Member, UK delegation, Parliamentary Assembly of the Council of Europe 2015-; NSPCC, Amnesty International, WWF (UK). Royal Humane Society Award for saving a man's life.

Recreations: Family, singing.

Geraint Davies MP, House of Commons, London SW1A 0AA
Tel: 020 7219 7166 *Email:* geraint.davies.mp@parliament.uk
Constituency: 18 Cradock Street, Swansea SA1 3HE
Tel: 01792 475943 *Website:* www.geraintdavies.org.uk *Twitter:* @GeraintDaviesMP

CONSERVATIVE

DAVIES, GLYN

Montgomeryshire *(Majority 9,285)*

PPS to Alun Cairns as Secretary of State for Wales

Edward Glyn Davies. Born 16 February 1944; Married Bobbie Davies (4 children).

Education: Llanfair Caereinion High School; University College of Wales, Aberyswyth (Diploma international law and relations 1995); Welsh.

Non-political career: Principal, T E Davies & Son (livestock farmers) 1976-. Member: National Farmers' Union, Farmers Union of Wales.

Political career: Contested Montgomeryshire 1997 general election. Member for Montgomeryshire since 6 May 2010 general election; PPS to Secretary of State for Wales: Cheryl Gillan 2010-12, Alun Cairns 2016-. *Select committees:* Member: Welsh Affairs 2010, 2012-15, 2016-, Energy and Climate Change 2015-16, Environmental Audit 2016-17. Chairman, Conservative Backbench Policy Committee on Wales 2015-17. Contested Montgomeryshire constituency 1999 and 2003, and Mid and West Wales region 2007 National Assembly for Wales elections; AM for Mid and West Wales region 1999-2007: Conservative spokesperson for: Agriculture and the Rural Economy 1999, Finance 1999-2001, Culture, Media, Sport and the Welsh Language 2001-03, Local Government, Environment and Planning 2003-05, Finance, Rural Affairs, Environment and Planning/Finance 2005-06. *Councils and public bodies:* Montgomeryshire District Council: Councillor 1979-89, Chair 1985-89, Chair, Planning Committee 1982-87, Chair, Finance Committee 1987-89; Development Board for Rural Wales: Member 1986-99, Chair 1989-94; Member: Welsh Development Agency 1989-94, Welsh Tourist Board 1989-94.

Political interests: Energy policy, Welsh affairs, social care.

Other: Member: RSPB, National Trust, Montgomeryshire Wildlife Trust, Wildfowl and Wetlands Trust, CLA; President, Campaign for the Protection of Rural Wales 2007-10; President: Montgomery Branch, Parkinsons Disease Society 2006-, Montgomeryshire Branch MNDA.

Recreations: Sport and fitness, countryside issues, family, house and garden.

Glyn Davies MP, House of Commons, London SW1A 0AA
Tel: 020 7219 7112 *Email:* glyn.davies.mp@parliament.uk
Constituency: 20 High Street, Welshpool, Powys SY21 7JP
Tel: 01938 552315/01938 554037 *Email:* pamela.williams@parliament.uk
Website: www.glyn-davies.co.uk *Twitter:* @GlynDavies

CONSERVATIVE

DAVIES, MIMS

Eastleigh *(Majority 14,179)*

PPS to Sajid Javid as Secretary of State for Communities and Local Government

Miriam Jane Alice Davies. Born 2 June 1975; Married (2 children).

Education: Croydon Collyers Sixth Form College, Horsham; Swansea University (BA politics and international relations).

Non-political career: Local radio presenter, reporter and producer; Road safety communications officer.

Political career: Member for Eastleigh since 7 May 2015 general election; PPS to: Matt Hancock as Minister of State for Digital and Culture, Department for Culture, Media and Sport 2016-17, Sajid Javid as Secretary of State for Communities and Local Government 2017-; Member, Commons Reference Group on Representation and Inclusion 2017-. *Select committees:* Member: Women and Equalities 2015-16, Joint Committee on Consolidation, &c, Bills 2015-. Chairman, Conservative Backbench Policy Committee on Culture, Media and Sport 2015-16. Chair, Southern Region, Conservative Women's Organisation. *Councils and public bodies:* Councillor: Haywards Heath Town Council, Mid Sussex District Council 2011-15.

Political interests: Carers, sports, equalities, women's rights, transport, road quality and safety.

Other: Haywards Heath Harriers.

Recreations: Running.

Mims Davies MP, House of Commons, London SW1A 0AA
Tel: 020 7219 6853 *Email:* mims.davies.mp@parliament.uk
Constituency: Unit 9, Hedge End Business Centre, Botley Road, Hedge End SO30 2AU
Tel: 01489 786688 *Website:* www.mimsdavies.org.uk *Twitter:* @mimsdavies

CONSERVATIVE

DAVIES, PHILIP

Shipley *(Majority 4,681)*

Philip Andrew Davies. Born 5 January 1972; Son of Peter Davies and Marilyn Lifsey; Married Deborah Hemsley 1994 (divorced) (2 sons).

Education: Old Swinford Hospital School, Stourbridge; Huddersfield University (BA historical and political studies 1993).

Non-political career: Asda Stores: Management training scheme 1995-97, Deputy customer services manager 1997, Customer relations manager 1997-98, Call centre manager 1998-99, Customer service project manager 2000-04, Senior marketing manager 2004-05.

Political career: Contested Colne Valley 2001 general election. Member for Shipley 2005-10, for Shipley (revised boundary) since 6 May 2010 general election. *Select committees:* Member: Culture, Media and Sport 2006-15, Modernisation of the House 2007-10, Backbench Business 2010-12, Chairmen's Panel/Panel of Chairs 2010-, Joint Committee on Privacy and Injunctions 2011-12, Justice 2015-17, Women and Equalities 2016-. Member, Executive, 1922 Committee 2006-12.

Political interests: Law and order, Europe, education; USA.

Other: Readers' Representative of the Year, *Spectator* awards 2011; Parliamentarians of the Year, *Spectator* awards 2013; Champion Award, Internet Telephony Services Providers' Association 2015.

Recreations: Horseracing, cricket, football, rugby league.

Philip Davies MP, House of Commons, London SW1A 0AA
Tel: 020 7219 8264 *Email:* daviesp@parliament.uk
Constituency: First Floor, 3 Manor Lane, Shipley BD18 3EA
Tel: 01274 592248 *Email:* deborah.davies@parliament.uk *Website:* www.philip-davies.org.uk
Twitter: @PhilipDaviesUK

CONSERVATIVE

DAVIS, DAVID

Haltemprice and Howden *(Majority 15,405)*

Secretary of State for Exiting the European Union

David Michael Davis. Born 23 December 1948; Son of late Ronald and Elizabeth Davis; Married Doreen Cook 1973 (1 son 2 daughters).

Education: Bec Grammar School; Warwick University (BSc molecular science, computing science 1971); London Business School (MSc business studies 1973); Harvard Business School (AMP 1985).

Non-political career: Joined Tate & Lyle 1974; Finance director, Manbré & Garton 1976-80; Managing director, Tate & Lyle Transport 1980-82; President, Redpath-Labatt joint venture 1982-84; Tate & Lyle 1984-87: Strategic planning director 1984-87, Non-executive director 1987-90.

Political career: Member for Boothferry 1987-97, for Haltemprice and Howden from 1997 to 18 June 2008 and 11 July 2008 by-election to 2010, for Haltemprice and Howden (revised boundary) since 6 May 2010 general election; PPS to Francis Maude as Financial Secretary to Treasury 1988-90; Assistant Government Whip 1990-93; Parliamentary Secretary, Office of Public Service and Science 1993-94; Minister of State, Foreign and Commonwealth Office 1994-97; Shadow Deputy Prime Minister with responsibility for the Cabinet Office 2002-03; Shadow Secretary of State for Home, Constitutional and Legal Affairs 2003-04; Shadow Home Secretary 2003-08; Secretary of State for Exiting the European Union 2016-. *Select committees:* Chair, Public Accounts 1997-2001; Member, Liaison 1998-2001. Conservative Party: Contested Party leadership 2001, 2005, Chairman 2001-02, Member, Policy Board 2001-03.

Political interests: Health, law and order, industry, agriculture.

Other: Trustee, Special Air Services Association. PC 1997.

Publications: How to Turn Round a Company (1988); The BBC Viewer's Guide to Parliament (1989); Co-author, The Future of Conservatism: Values Revisited (Biteback, 2011).

Recreations: Mountaineering, flying light aircraft, writing.

Rt Hon David Davis MP, House of Commons, London SW1A 0AA
Tel: 020 7219 5900 *Email:* david.davis.mp@parliament.uk
Constituency: No constituency office *Website:* www.daviddavismp.com
Twitter: @DavidDavisMP

SCOTTISH NATIONAL PARTY

DAY, MARTYN

Linlithgow and East Falkirk *(Majority 2,919)*

Born 26 March 1971; Married Debbie.

Non-political career: Former bank worker.

Political career: Member for Linlithgow and East Falkirk since 7 May 2015 general election. *Select committees:* Member: Administration 2015-, Petitions 2016-, Public Accounts 2017-. Election agent 1999-2015. *Councils and public bodies:* West Lothian Council: Councillor 1999-2015, Portfolio holder for Development and Transport.

Political interests: Anti-austerity, anti-Trident.

Other: Member: National Association of Councillors, West Lothian Economic Partnership Forum.

Recreations: Reading, listening to music.

Martyn Day MP, House of Commons, London SW1A 0AA
Tel: 020 7219 5930 *Email:* martyn.day.mp@parliament.uk
Constituency: 62 Hopetoun Street, Bathgate, West Lothian EH48 4PD
Tel: 01506 654415 *Twitter:* @MartynDaySNP

LABOUR

DEBBONAIRE, THANGAM

Bristol West *(Majority 37,336)*

Opposition Whip

Thangam Elizabeth Rachel Debbonaire. Born 3 August 1966; Daughter of late Prabhu Singh, musician, and Eleanor James, musician and teacher; Married Kevin Walton.

Education: Chetham's Music School; Bradford Girls' Grammar School; Bristol University (MSc management, development and social responsibility 1995).

Non-political career: Freelance classical cellist 1976–2000; National Children's Officer, Women's Aid Federation England 1991-98; Director and lead independent practitioner, Domestic Violence Responses 1997-2015; Respect: Accreditation Officer 2006-08, Research Manager 2008-15; Perpetrator Group Worker, Domestic Violence Intervention Project 2008-10. Member: Musicians' Union 1984-2000, Unison (and predecessor union) 1991-.

Political career: Member for Bristol West since 7 May 2015 general election; Shadow Minister for Culture, Media and Sport 2016; Opposition Whip 2016-; Member, South West Regional Labour Party Board 2016. *Councils and public bodies:* Governor, Glenfrome Primary School, Bristol 2011-15.

Political interests: Housing, refugees, autism, violence against women, science and research, climate change and the environment, arts, European Union; Countries in the Horn of Africa, Middle East, Indian sub-continent.

Publications: Numerous articles on domestic violence.

Recreations: Playing the cello.

Thangam Debbonaire MP, House of Commons, London SW1A 0AA
Tel: 020 7219 8559 *Email:* thangam.debbonaire.mp@parliament.uk
Constituency: 16-18 King Square, Bristol BS2 8AZ
Tel: 0117-379 0980 *Website:* www.debbonaire.co.uk *Twitter:* @ThangamMP

LABOUR

DE CORDOVA, MARSHA

Battersea *(Majority 2,416)*

PPS to Debbie Abrahams as Shadow Secretary of State for Work and Pensions

Marsha Chantol De Cordova. Born 23 January 1976.

Education: London South Bank University (law).

Non-political career: Action for Blind People: Welfare rights officer 2005-07, Service Development Manager 2007-10, Policy and Development Manager 2010-12; Welfare Benefit Specialist, Turn2us 2013-14; Thomas Pocklington Trust: Development Manager 2014-15, Engagement and Advocacy Director 2016-17; Chief Executive, South East London Vision 2015-16. Member, Unite.

Political career: Member for Battersea since 8 June 2017; PPS to Debbie Abrahams as Shadow Secretary of State for Work and Pensions 2017-. *Select committees:* Member, Work and Pensions 2017-. *Councils and public bodies:* Councillor, London Borough of Lambeth Council 2014-.

Political interests: Disability, human rights, welfare reform, poverty, employment.

Marsha De Cordova MP, House of Commons, London SW1A 0AA
Tel: 020 7219 0209 *Email:* marsha.decordova.mp@parliament.uk
Constituency: Details still to be confirmed *Website:* marshadecordova.co.uk
Twitter: @Marshadecordova

LABOUR

DENT COAD, EMMA

Kensington *(Majority 20)*

Born 15 November 1954; 3 children.

Education: Royal College of Art (MA design history 1992).

Non-political career: Designer Magazine, Chartered Society of Designers 1980-86; Freelance Writer and Editor 1986-; Visiting Lecturer, University of West England 1986-88; Features Editor, Unique 1987-88; Editor, Docomomo UK Newsletter 2000-; Study Tour Organiser 2000-.

Political career: Member for Kensington since 8 June 2017; *Councils and public bodies:* Councillor, Royal Borough of Kensington and Chelsea Council 2006-.

Publications: Spanish Design and Architecture (1990); Javier Mariscal: Designing the New Spain (1992).

Emma Dent Coad MP, House of Commons, London SW1A 0AA
Tel: 020 7219 4591 *Email:* emma.dentcoad.mp@parliament.uk
Constituency: Details still to be confirmed *Twitter:* @emmadentcoad

LABOUR

DE PIERO, GLORIA

Ashfield *(Majority 441)*

Shadow Minister for Justice

Born 21 December 1972; Married James Robinson 2012.

Education: Yorkshire Martyrs School, Bradford; Bradford and Ilkley College; Westminster University (BA social science 1996); London University (MSc social and political theory 2001).

Non-political career: *Jonathan Dimbleby*, ITV 1997-98; BBC: *On the Record* 1998-2002, *Politics Show* 2002-03; Political correspondent, GMTV 2003-10. Member: Unite, GMB.

Political career: Member for Ashfield since 6 May 2010 general election; Shadow Minister for: Culture 2010-11, Crime Prevention 2011-13, Women and Equalities 2013-15, Young People and Voter Registration (attending Shadow Cabinet) 2015-16, Justice 2017-; Member, Speaker's Committee on the Electoral Commission 2017-; Member, Politics – Better Politics Policy Commission; Campaign Deputy, General Election Strategy 2014-15.

Recreations: Swimming, karaoke.

Gloria De Piero MP, House of Commons, London SW1A 0AA
Tel: 020 7219 7004 *Email:* gloria.depiero.mp@parliament.uk
Constituency: 8 Station Street, Kirkby-in-Ashfield, Nottinghamshire NG17 7AR
Tel: 01623 720399 *Website:* www.gloria-de-piero.co.uk *Twitter:* @GloriaDePiero

DHESI, TANMANJEET SINGH

Slough *(Majority 16,998)*

LABOUR

Born 17 August 1978; Married Manveen 2005 (2 sons).

Education: Sir Joseph Williamson's Mathematical (Grammar) School; Gravesend Grammar School; University College London (mathematics with management studies); Keble College, Oxford (applied statistics); Fitzwilliam College, Cambridge (MPhil history of politics and history of South Asia); Punjabi, Hindi, Urdu, French, German, Italian, Latin.

Non-political career: Family construction business: Worked in a number of entry level roles, including handyman, scabbler, core driller and general labourer, Site Foreman, Site Manager, Project Manager, Project Director; Director, DGP Logistics plc, Edinburgh 2005-11; Consultant, DGP Logistics.

Political career: Contested Gravesham 2015 general election. Member for Slough since 8 June 2017; Chair, Gravesham Constituency Labour Party. *Councils and public bodies:* Gravesham Council: Councillor 2007-15, Mayor 2011, Cabinet Member, Business and Communities 2012-15; Councillor, Kent County Council 2017-.

Other: President, Gatka Federation.

Tanmanjeet Singh Dhesi MP, House of Commons, London SW1A 0AA
Tel: 020 7219 1946 *Email:* tan.dhesi.mp@parliament.uk
Constituency: 52 Chalvey High Street, Slough SL1 2SQ
Tel: 01753 518161 *Website:* www.tsdhesi.com *Twitter:* @TanDhesi

DINENAGE, CAROLINE

Gosport *(Majority 17,211)*

CONSERVATIVE

Parliamentary Under-Secretary of State for Family Support, Housing and Child Maintenance, Department for Work and Pensions

Caroline Julia Dinenage. Born 28 October 1971; Daughter of Fred Dinenage, tv presenter; Married Carlos (divorced) (2 sons); married Mark Lancaster (qv) 2014 (MP for Milton Keynes North).

Education: Wykeham House, Fareham; Oaklands RC Comprehensive, Waterlooville; University of Wales, Swansea (BA English and politics); French.

Non-political career: Member, Armed Forces Parliamentary Scheme. Director, Recognition Express.

Political career: Contested Portsmouth South 2005 general election. Member for Gosport since 6 May 2010 general election; PPS to Nicky Morgan as Secretary of State for Education and Minister for Women and Equalities 2014-15; Parliamentary Under-Secretary of State: for Women, Equalities and Family Justice, Ministry of Justice and Department for Education 2015-16, for Women, Equalities and Early Years, Department for Education 2016-17, for Family Support, Housing and Child Maintenance, Department for Work and Pensions 2017-. *Select committees:* Member: Science and Technology 2012-13, Business, Innovation and Skills 2012-15. *Councils and public bodies:* Councillor, Winchester District Council 1998-2003.

Political interests: Defence (particularly supporting service families), business and industry, sport; China, Falkland Islands, Gibraltar, Hong Kong, India.

Other: Member, NATO Parliamentary Assembly -2015; Parliamentary ambassador, England Netball; Vice-President, RSPCA; Scouting Ambassador; Patron, Daring Club, Gosport; Save the Children.

Recreations: Portsmouth FC, netball, skiing.

Caroline Dinenage MP, House of Commons, London SW1A 0AA
Tel: 020 7219 7078/020 7219 0198 *Fax:* 020 7219 6874
Email: caroline.dinenage.mp@parliament.uk
Constituency: 167 Stoke Road, Gosport, Hampshire PO12 1SE
Tel: 023 9252 2121 *Fax:* 023 9252 0900 *Website:* www.caroline4gosport.co.uk
Twitter: @cj_dinenage

DJANOGLY, JONATHAN

Huntingdon *(Majority 14,475)*

CONSERVATIVE

Jonathan Simon Djanogly. Born 3 June 1965; Son of Sir Harry Djanogly, CBE and Carol Djanogly; Married Rebecca Silk 1991 (1 son 1 daughter).

Education: University College School, London; Oxford Polytechnic (BA law and politics 1987); Guildford College of Law (law finals 1988); ICAEW (corporate finance qualification).

Non-political career: Partner: SJ Berwin LLP Solicitors 1988-2009, Mail order retail business 1994-2002.

Political career: Contested Oxford East 1997 general election. Member for Huntingdon 2001-10, for Huntingdon (revised boundary) since 6 May 2010 general election; Shadow Minister for Home, Constitutional and Legal Affairs 2004-05; Shadow Solicitor General 2005-10; Shadow

Minister for Trade and Industry/Business, Enterprise and Regulatory Reform/Business, Innovation and Skills 2005-10 (Corporate Governance 2006-09, Business 2009-10); Parliamentary Under-Secretary of State, Ministry of Justice 2010-12. *Select committees:* Member: Trade and Industry 2001-05, Joint Committee on Statutory Instruments 2001-02, Exiting the European Union 2017-. Founding member, Conservatives for Reform in Europe 2016. *Councils and public bodies:* Councillor, Westminster City Council 1994-2001.

Political interests: Small businesses, trade, environment, rural affairs, transport, planning, justice.

Other: Chairman: Pembroke VCT plc 2013-, Task Force Europe, British-Swiss Chamber of Commerce 2015-, British Shooting Sports Council 2017-; Law Society.

Recreations: Sport, arts, theatre, reading histories and biographies, Britain's countryside and heritage.

Jonathan Djanogly MP, House of Commons, London SW1A 0AA
Tel: 020 7219 2367 *Fax:* 020 7219 0476 *Email:* jonathan.djanogly.mp@parliament.uk
Constituency: HCCA, Castle Hill House, High Street, Huntingdon, Cambridgeshire PE29 3TE
Tel: 01480 437840 *Fax:* 01480 453012 *Email:* hollandn@parliament.uk
Website: www.jonathandjanogly.com *Twitter:* @JDjanogly

CONSERVATIVE

DOCHERTY, LEO

Aldershot *(Majority 11,473)*

Born 4 October 1976; Married Lucy (2 children).

Education: School of Oriental and African Studies (2000); Royal Military Academy, Sandhurst (2001).

Non-political career: Soldier, 1st Battalion Scots Guards (operational tours in Iraq and Afghanistan) 2001-07. Editor and publisher, Steppe Magazine Ltd; Director, Conservative Middle East Council 2010-17.

Political career: Contested Caerphilly 2015 general election. Member for Aldershot since 8 June 2017. *Select committees:* Member, Defence 2017-. Vice-chairman, Conservative Middle East Council. *Councils and public bodies:* Councillor, South Oxfordshire District Council 2011-15.

Other: Council Member, Chatham House.

Publications: Desert of Death: A Soldier's Journey from Iraq to Afghanistan (2007).

Leo Docherty MP, House of Commons, London SW1A 0AA
Tel: 020 7219 1833/020 7219 6298 *Email:* leo.docherty.mp@parliament.uk
Constituency: Conservative Club, Victoria Road, Aldershot GU11 1JX
Tel: 01252 323637 *Email:* leo4aldershot@leodocherty.org.uk *Website:* www.leodocherty.org.uk
Twitter: @LeoDochertyUK

SCOTTISH NATIONAL PARTY

DOCHERTY-HUGHES, MARTIN

West Dunbartonshire *(Majority 2,288)*

SNP Spokesperson for Industries for the Future

Martin John Docherty-Hughes. Born 21 January 1971; Son of Patrick Anthony Docherty and Eleanor Docherty (née Logan); Married.

Education: Saint Columba High Clydebank; GCFT (HND business administration 1997); Essex University (BA politics 2004); Glasgow School of Art (MPhil).

Non-political career: Policy and research, West Dunbartonshire Community and Volunteering Services; National policy adviser, Volunteer Scotland 2014-15.

Political career: Member for West Dunbartonshire since 7 May 2015 general election; SNP Spokesperson for: Voluntary Sector 2016-17, Industries for the Future 2017-. *Select committees:* Member, Defence 2017-. Scottish National Party: Member 1991-, Former Secretary and Chair, Clydebank SNP, Secretary, Clydebank and Milngavie Constituency, Chair, West Dunbartonshire Liaison Committee. *Councils and public bodies:* Councillor: Clydebank District Council 1992-96, Glasgow City Council 2012-15, Bailie City of Glasgow 2012-15.

Political interests: Scottish independence, child poverty, anti-austerity, disability, technology, defence; Brazil, Denmark, Estonia, Ireland, Latvia, Lithuania, Russia, Ukraine, Venezuela.

Other: Member, UK delegation to NATO Parliamentary Assembly 2015-.

Martin Docherty-Hughes MP, House of Commons, London SW1A 0AA
Tel: 020 7219 4609 *Email:* martin.docherty.mp@parliament.uk
Constituency: Titan Enterprise Centre, Suite 1-11, 1 Aurora Avenue, 1 Queens Quay, Clydebank, Dunbartonshire G81 1BF
Tel: 0141-952 2988 *Website:* www.martindocherty.scot *Twitter:* @MartinJDocherty

DOCKERILL, JULIA (now known as LOPEZ, JULIA)

Hornchurch and Upminster *(Majority 17,723)*

CONSERVATIVE

Julia Louise Lopez. Born 4 June 1984; Married 2017.

Education: Herts and Essex High School; Queens' College, Cambridge (MA social and political science 2005).

Non-political career: Chief of Staff to Mark Field MP 2006-17; Freelance writer 2013-.

Political career: Member for Hornchurch and Upminster since 8 June 2017. *Select committees:* Member, International Trade 2017-. *Councils and public bodies:* Councillor, London Borough of Tower Hamlets Council 2014-.

Other: Trustee, Inspire Malawi 2015-.

Publications: Co-author, The Best of Times and Between the Crashes.

Julia Dockerill MP, House of Commons, London SW1A 0AA
Tel: 020 7219 2631 *Email:* julia.lopez.mp@parliament.uk
Constituency: Details still to be confirmed *Website:* www.julialopez.co.uk
Twitter: @JuliaLopezMP

DODDS, ANNELIESE

Oxford East *(Majority 23,284)*

LAB/CO-OP

Shadow Minister for Treasury

Anneliese Jane Dodds. Born 16 March 1978; Partner (1 son 1 daughter).

Education: Robert Gordon's College, Aberdeen; Oxford University (BA politics, philosophy and economics 2001) (Oxford Union President 1999-2000); Edinburgh University (Masters social policy 2002); London School of Economics (PhD 2006); French.

Non-political career: Economic and Social Research Council postdoctoral fellow, Department of Government, London School of Economics 2006; Public policy lecturer, King's College London 2007-10; Lecturer and Senior Lecturer in Public Policy, Sociology and Public Policy Group, Aston University 2010-14. Member: Universities and College Union 2003-, Unite 2006-.

Political career: Contested Billericay 2005 and Reading East 2010 general elections. Member for Oxford East since 8 June 2017; Shadow Minister for Treasury 2017-; MEP for South East 2014-17. Member: Labour Party 1996-, Co-op Party.

Political interests: Economy, public policy, health.

Other: Member, Higher Education Academy; Volunteer, Oxfam; Member, Political Studies Association 2002-; Research associate, Centre for Analysis of Risk and Regulation, London School of Economics .

Publications: The growth of agencies in Britain and France: EduFrance- transferred from Britain, or an indigenous creation? (2004); The Politicisation Of Trade In Health And Education Services: Black And White Divisions Over A 'Grey Area', Scottish Affairs (2004); The spread of evaluation in international higher education – a uniform phenomenon? (2005); The Core Executive's Approach to Regulation: From `Better Regulation' to `Risk-Tolerant Deregulation', Social Policy and Administration (2006); How does globalization interact with higher education? – The continuing lack of consensus, Comparative Education (2008); Families "at risk" and the Family Nurse Partnership: The intrusion of risk into social exclusion policy, Journal of Social Policy (2009); Liberalization and the public sector: the pre-eminent role of governments in the 'sale' of higher education abroad, Public Administration (2009); The British higher education funding debate: the perils of 'talking economics', London Review of Education (2011); Logics, Thresholds, Strategic Power, and the Promotion of Liberalisation by Governments: A Case Study from British Higher Education, Public Policy and Administration (2011); Comparative Public Policy (2012); Co-author: Can incident reporting improve safety? Healthcare practitioners' views of the effectiveness of incident reporting, (International Journal for Quality in Health Care); Understanding institutional conversion: the case of the National Reporting and Learning System (Journal of Public Policy); Accountability, organisational learning and risks to patient safety in England: conflict or compromise?; Top-down or bottom up: the real choice for public services? (Journal of Poverty and Social Justice); The challenge of improving patient safety in primary care, (British Journal of General Practice 2009); Future of Public Administration (Special edition of the journal Public Policy and Administration); Introduction to Public Administration in an Age of Austerity: The Future of the Discipline within the special edition (2012).

Recreations: Cycling, travelling.

Anneliese Dodds MP, House of Commons, London SW1A 0AA
Tel: 020 7219 2705 *Email:* annaliese.dodds.mp@parliament.uk
Constituency: Unit A, Bishops Mews, Transport Way, Oxford OX4 6HD
Tel: 01865 595790 *Twitter:* @AnnelieseDodds

DEMOCRATIC UNIONIST PARTY

DODDS, NIGEL

Belfast North *(Majority 2,081)*

Leader, DUP Parliamentary Group; Spokesperson for Exiting the European Union, Reform and Constitutional Issues and Foreign Affairs

Nigel Alexander Dodds. Born 20 August 1958; Son of late Joseph Dodds, civil servant, and Doreen Dodds, née McMahon; Married Diane Harris 1985 (MLA for Belfast West 2003-07 as Diane Dodds, now MEP for Northern Ireland) (2 sons 1 daughter).

Education: Portora Royal School, Enniskillen; St John's College, Cambridge (BA law 1980); Queen's University, Belfast Institute of Professional Legal Studies (Cert PLS 1981); French.

Non-political career: Barrister 1981-83; European Parliament Secretariat (non-attached members) 1984-96; Member of Senate, Queen's University, Belfast 1985-93.

Political career: Contested East Antrim 1992 general election. Member for Belfast North 2001-10, for Belfast North (revised boundary) since 6 May 2010 general election; DUP Chief Whip 2001-08; DUP Spokesperson for: Treasury 2005-07, Work and Pensions 2005-07, Business of the House 2005-10, Justice 2007-10, Business, Enterprise and Regulatory Reform 2007-10; DUP Parliamentary Group Leader 2010-; Spokesperson for: Reform and Constitutional Agenda/Constitutional Issues 2010-, Foreign Affairs 2010-, Culture, Olympics, Media and Sport 2012-15, Exiting the European Union 2017-. *Select committees:* Member: Members' Allowances 2009-10, Joint Committee on Statutory Instruments and Commons Committee on Statutory Instruments 2009-10. Member Northern Ireland Forum for Political Dialogue 1996-98; MLA for Belfast North 1998-2010: Minister of: Social Development 1999-2000, 2001-02, Enterprise, Trade and Investment 2007-08, Finance and Personnel 2008-09. DUP: Secretary 1992-2008, Deputy Leader 2008-. *Councils and public bodies:* Belfast City Council: Councillor 1985-2010, Lord Mayor of Belfast 1988-89, 1991-92, Vice-President, Association of Local Authorities of Northern Ireland 1989-90.

Political interests: European affairs, constitution, social policy; The Commonwealth, USA.

Other: Member: Executive Committee, Inter-Parliamentary Union, British Group, UK Delegation to NATO Parliamentary Assembly 2014-; Vote Leave: Board member 2016, Member, Campaign Committee 2016; Founding supporter, Change Britain 2016-. OBE 1997; PC 2010.

Rt Hon Nigel Dodds OBE MP, House of Commons, London SW1A 0AA
Tel: 020 7219 8419 *Fax:* 020 7219 2347 *Email:* nigel.dodds.mp@parliament.uk
Constituency: 39 Shore Road, Belfast BT15 3PG
Tel: 028 9077 4774 *Fax:* 028 9077 7685 *Email:* ndodds@dup-belfast.co.uk
Website: www.nigeldodds.co.uk *Twitter:* @NigelDoddsDUP

DEMOCRATIC UNIONIST PARTY

DONALDSON, JEFFREY

Lagan Valley *(Majority 19,229)*

DUP Spokesperson for Business in the House of Commons; Chief Whip

Jeffrey Mark Donaldson. Born 7 December 1962; Son of James and Sarah Anne Donaldson; Married Eleanor Cousins 1987 (2 daughters).

Education: Kilkeel High School; Castlereagh College (Diploma electrical engineering 1982); French.

Non-political career: Ulster Defence Regiment 1980-85. Agent to Enoch Powell MP 1983-84; Personal assistant to Sir James Molyneaux MP 1984-85; Partner, financial services and estate agency business 1986-96. Former member, AEEU.

Political career: Member for Lagan Valley 1997-2010, for Lagan Valley (revised boundary) since 6 May 2010 general election; Ulster Unionist Spokesperson for: Trade and Industry 1997-2000, Environment, Transport and the Regions 2000-01, Treasury 2001-02, Transport, Local Government and the Regions 2001-02, Work and Pensions 2001-03, Defence 2002-03, Trade and Industry 2002-03; DUP Spokesperson for: Education 2004-05, Defence 2004-05, 2007-17, Transport 2005-07, 2009-10, International Development 2005-07, Home Office 2007-10, Equality 2010-12, Energy and Climate Change 2010-15, Business in the House of Commons 2015-; DUP Chief Whip 2015-; Trade Envoy to Egypt 2015-. *Select committees:* Member: Northern Ireland Affairs 1997-2000, Environment, Transport and Regional Affairs 2000-01, Environment, Transport and Regional Affairs (Transport Sub-Committee) 2000-01, Regulatory Reform 2001-05, Joint Committee on Statutory Instruments 2001-06, Transport 2004-07, 2009-10, Defence 2010-15, Arms Export Controls 2011-12, 2013-15. Member: Northern Ireland Assembly (UUP) 1985-86, Northern Ireland Forum 1996-98; MLA for Lagan Valley 2003-10 (UUP November 2003 to 15 January 2004, DUP 15 January 2004 to 2010): Junior Minister, Office of the First Minister and Deputy First Minister 2008-09; Chair, Assembly Committee on Assembly and Executive Review 2007-08. Ulster Unionist Council: Honorary Secretary 1988-2000, Vice-president 2000-03; Resigned from

UUP 15 January 2004; Democratic Unionist Party: Joined 15 January 2004, Party officer 2004-. *Councils and public bodies:* Alderman, Lisburn City Council 2005-10; Member, Northern Ireland Policing Board 2007-08.

Political interests: Christian values, constitution, transport, defence, international development; Cyprus, Ethiopia, Israel, Moldova, Northern Ireland, South Africa, USA.

Other: Member: UK delegation, Parliamentary Assembly of the Council of Europe 2015-, British-Irish Parliamentary Assembly 2015-; Member: Presbyterian Church, Loyal Orange Order, Constitutional Monarchy Association, Regimental Association of the Ulster Defence Regiment; Trustee, Royal Ulster Rifles Association; Chairman, Causeway Institute for Peace-building and Conflict Resolution; Care and Tear Fund. PC 2007; Kt 2016.

Recreations: Hill-walking, reading, local history, church.

Rt Hon Sir Jeffrey Donaldson MP, House of Commons, London SW1A 0AA
Tel: 020 7219 3407 *Fax:* 020 7219 2347 *Email:* jeffrey.donaldson.mp@parliament.uk
Constituency: The Old Town Hall, 29 Castle Street, Lisburn, Co Antrim BT27 4DH
Tel: 028 9266 8001 *Fax:* 028 9267 1845 *Email:* jeffreydonaldsonmp@laganvalley.net
Website: www.jeffreydonaldson.org *Twitter:* @J_Donaldson_MP

CONSERVATIVE

DONELAN, MICHELLE

Chippenham *(Majority 16,630)*

PPS to Jeremy Wright as Attorney General

Michelle Emma May Elizabeth Donelan. Born 8 April 1984; Daughter of Michael and Kathryn Donelan.

Education: The County High School, Leftwich; York University (BA history and politics).

Non-political career: Marketing, Pacific Magazines, Sydney, Australia 2006-07; Senior partnership marketing, AETN UK 2007-10; International marketing communications manager, WWE 2010-14.

Political career: Contested Wentworth and Dearne 2010 general election. Member for Chippenham since 7 May 2015 general election; PPS to Jeremy Wright as Attorney General 2017-. *Select committees:* Member: Education 2015-, Education, Skills and the Economy Sub-committee 2015-17, Petitions 2017-. Press and media development officer, Conservative Future 2009-15.

Countries of interest: Asia Pacific, Oceania.

Recreations: Travel, history, culture.

Michelle Donelan MP, House of Commons, London SW1A 0AA
Tel: 020 7219 4451 *Email:* michelle.donelan.mp@parliament.uk
Constituency: 61 New Road, Chippenham, Wiltshire SN15 1ES
Tel: 01249 704465 *Email:* michelle@michelledonelan.com *Website:* michelledonelan.co.uk
Twitter: @michelledonelan

CONSERVATIVE

DORRIES, NADINE

Mid Bedfordshire *(Majority 20,983)*

Nadine Vanessa Dorries. Born 21 May 1957; Daughter of Sylvia and George Bargery; 3 daughters.

Education: Halewood Grange Comprehensive, Liverpool; Warrington District School of Nursing.

Non-political career: Former nurse; Businesswoman; Director, BUPA; Adviser to Oliver Letwin MP 2002-05.

Political career: Contested Hazel Grove 2001 general election (as Nadine Bargery). Member for Mid Bedfordshire 2005-10, for Mid Bedfordshire (revised boundary) since 6 May 2010 general election; Contested Deputy Speaker election 2013. *Select committees:* Member: Education and Skills 2005-06, Science and Technology 2007, Innovation, Universities[, Science] and Skills/Science and Technology 2007-10, Energy and Climate Change 2009-10, Health 2010-11, Chairmen's Panel/Panel of Chairs 2010-. Conservative Whip suspended November 2012-May 2013; Founding member, Conservatives for Britain 2015-16.

Political interests: Law and order, social structure, health, rural affairs; Angola, Zambia.

Publications: The Four Streets (2014); Hide Her Name (2015); Ruby Flynn (2015); The Ballymara Road (2016); The Angels of Lovely Lane (2016); The Children of Lovely Lane (2016).

Recreations: Family, friends, walking, reading, dogs.

Nadine Dorries MP, House of Commons, London SW1A 0AA
Tel: 020 7219 5928 *Fax:* 020 7219 6428 *Email:* dorriesn@parliament.uk
Constituency: No constituency office publicised *Website:* www.dorries.org
Twitter: @NadineDorries

DOUBLE, STEVE

St Austell and Newquay *(Majority 11,142)*

CONSERVATIVE

Stephen Daniel Double. Born 19 December 1966; Son of Donald and Heather Double; Married Anne 1986 (3 sons).

Education: Poltair School, St Austell.

Non-political career: Barclay Bank 1983-92; Church Pastor 1992-2002; Director: Bay Director Media 2001-15, Phoenix Corporate Ltd 2011-15.

Political career: Member for St Austell and Newquay since 7 May 2015 general election. *Select committees:* Member: Petitions 2015-, European Scrutiny 2016-, Transport 2017-. Founding member, Conservatives for Britain 2015-16. *Councils and public bodies:* Cornwall Council: Councillor 2009-15, Mayor of St Austell.

Countries of interest: Kenya, Tanzania.

Steve Double MP, House of Commons, London SW1A 0AA
Tel: 020 7219 4408 *Email:* steve.double.mp@parliament.uk
Constituency: 3 Fore Street, St Austell, Cornwall PL25 5PX
Tel: 01726 829379 *Email:* office@stevedouble.org.uk *Website:* www.stevedouble.org.uk
Twitter: @stevedouble

DOUGHTY, STEPHEN

Cardiff South and Penarth *(Majority 14,864)*

LAB/CO-OP

Stephen John Doughty. Born 15 April 1980; Single.

Education: Llantwit Major Comprehensive School, Vale of Glamorgan; Lester B Pearson United World College, Victoria, Canada; Corpus Christi College, Oxford (BA); St Andrews University (MLitt); French, Welsh (basic).

Non-political career: Policy and campaigns adviser, World Vision 2004-06; Head of UK and EU government relations, Oxfam 2006-09; Head of health and education campaign, Oxfam International 2010-11; Head, Oxfam Cymru 2011-12; Special adviser to Douglas Alexander as Secretary of State for International Development 2009-10. Member: GMB, Unison.

Political career: Member for Cardiff South and Penarth since 15 November 2012 by-election; PPS to Rachel Reeves as Shadow Chief Secretary to the Treasury 2013; Opposition Whip 2013-15; Shadow Minister for: Business, Innovation and Skills 2015, Foreign and Commonwealth Office 2015-16. *Select committees:* Member: Welsh Affairs 2012-15, International Development 2016-17, Arms Export Controls 2016-17, Work of the Independent Commission for Aid Impact Sub-committee 2016-17, Home Affairs 2017-. Member: Labour Party, Co-operative Party; Patron, LGBT Labour.

Political interests: Economy and finance, foreign affairs, defence, international development, energy and climate change; Afghanistan, Africa, Argentina, Bangladesh, Canada, EU, India, Israel, Pakistan, Palestine, Somalia/Somaliland, USA, Yemen.

Other: Christian Socialist Movement; Progress; Fabian Society.

Recreations: Cardiff City FC, Welsh rugby union, singing, surfing, sailing, walking.

Stephen Doughty MP, House of Commons, London SW1A 0AA
Tel: 020 7219 5348 *Email:* stephen.doughty.mp@parliament.uk
Constituency: 1 Caspian Point, Cardiff Bay CF10 4DQ
Tel: 029 2044 4055 *Website:* www.stephendoughty.org.uk *Twitter:* @SDoughtyMP

DOWD, PETER

Bootle *(Majority 36,200)*

LABOUR

Shadow Chief Secretary to the Treasury

Peter Christopher Dowd. Born 20 June 1957.

Education: Hugh Baird College, Liverpool; Liverpool University; Lancaster University.

Non-political career: Head of care delivery frameworks, 5 Boroughs NHS Partnership Trust.

Political career: Member for Bootle since 7 May 2015 general election; Shadow Financial Secretary 2016-17; Shadow Chief Secretary to the Treasury 2017-; Agent to Joe Benton MP. *Councils and public bodies:* Councillor, Merseyside County Council 1981-86; Sefton Council: Councillor 1991-, Leader, Labour Group 2008-15, Leader of the Council 2011-15; Former chair, Merseyside Fire and Rescue Service.

Political interests: Health.

Peter Dowd MP, House of Commons, London SW1A 0AA
Tel: 020 7219 8671 *Email:* peter.dowd.mp@parliament.uk
Constituency: No constituency office publicised *Website:* www.peterdowd4bootle.com
Twitter: @Peter_Dowd

CONSERVATIVE

DOWDEN, OLIVER

Hertsmere *(Majority 16,951)*

PPS to Michael Fallon as Secretary of State for Defence

Oliver James Dowden. Born 1 August 1978; Married Blythe (2 children).

Education: Parmiter's School, Watford; Trinity College, Cambridge (BA law); College of London (Legal Practice Course).

Non-political career: Conservative Research Department 2004-07; Hill and Knowlton 2007-09; Conservative Campaign Headquarters 2009-10; Prime Minister's Office: Special Adviser to David Cameron as Prime Minister 2010-12, Deputy Chief of Staff 2012-14, Senior Adviser to David Cameron as Prime Minister 2014-15; Consultant, Policy Exchange 2014-; Policy adviser, Caxton Europe Asset Management 2015-; Political adviser, Association of Independent Professionals and the Self Employed 2015-.

Political career: Member for Hertsmere since 7 May 2015 general election; PPS to Michael Fallon as Secretary of State for Defence 2017-. *Select committees:* Member: Public Administration and Constitutional Affairs 2015-16, Petitions 2015-17.

Political interests: Immigration, welfare, health, criminal justice, education; Canada, India, Israel, Japan.

Other: Conservative Friends of Israel; UK-Japan 21st Century Group; Trustee, Law Family Education Trust 2016-. CBE 2015.

Oliver Dowden CBE MP, House of Commons, London SW1A 0AA
Tel: 020 7219 3415 *Email:* oliver.dowden.mp@parliament.uk
Constituency: 104 High Street, London Colney, Hertfordshire AL2 1QL
Tel: 01727 828221 *Email:* oliver@oliverdowden.com *Website:* www.oliverdowden.com

CONSERVATIVE

DOYLE-PRICE, JACKIE

Thurrock *(Majority 345)*

Parliamentary Under-Secretary of State (Care and Mental Health), Department of Health

Jacqueline Doyle-Price. Born 5 August 1969; Daughter of Brian and Kathleen Doyle-Price; Partner Mark Coxshall.

Education: Notre Dame RC, Sheffield; Durham University (BA economics and politics 1991).

Non-political career: Administrative officer, South Yorkshire Police 1992; Parliamentary officer, City of London Corporation 1993-2000; Assistant private secretary to Rt Hon the Lord Mayor of the City of London 2000-05; Associate, Financial Services Authority 2005.

Political career: Contested Sheffield Hillsborough 2005 general election. Member for Thurrock since 6 May 2010 general election; Assistant Government Whip 2015-17; Parliamentary Under-Secretary of State (Care and Mental Health), Department of Health 2017-. *Select committees:* Member: Public Accounts 2010-14, Selection 2015-17. Treasurer, National Association of Conservative Graduates 1994-97; Chair, Lewisham Deptford Constituency Association 1997-98; Constituency officer, Greenwich and Woolwich Conservatives 2006-07.

Political interests: Welfare, foreign affairs, vocational education, financial services, transport; Bosnia and Herzegovina, Croatia, Serbia.

Other: Patron, Thurrock Male Voice Choir; Member, Tilbury Cruise Terminal and Railway Station Trust. Freedom, City of London; Grays Conservative Club, RAFA Club, Grays Club.

Recreations: Theatre, reading, film, watching soaps.

Jackie Doyle-Price MP, House of Commons, London SW1A 0AA
Tel: 020 7219 7171 *Fax:* 020 7219 4924 *Email:* jackie.doyleprice.mp@parliament.uk
Constituency: 2 Orsett Business Centre, Stanford Road, Grays, Essex RM16 3BX
Tel: 01375 802029 *Website:* www.jackiedoyleprice.com *Twitter:* @JackieDP

CONSERVATIVE

DRAX, RICHARD

South Dorset *(Majority 11,695)*

Richard Grosvenor Plunkett-Ernle-Erle Drax. Born 29 January 1958; Divorced Zara (2 daughters 2 sons); married Elsebet.

Education: Harrow School; Royal Agricultural College, Cirencester (Diploma of Membership rural land management 1990); Westminster Press (Diploma journalism 1995).

Non-political career: Officer, Coldstream Guards 1978-87. Journalist: *Yorkshire Evening Press* 1991-96, *TyneTees*, *Calendar*, *Daily Telegraph* 1996-97; Journalist/Reporter, *BBC South Today*, *BBC Solent* 1997-2006.

Political career: Member for South Dorset since 6 May 2010 general election. *Select committees:* Member: Environment, Food and Rural Affairs 2010-15, European Scrutiny 2015-.

Political interests: Defence.

Other: Patron, Cherry Tree Nursery 2006.

Recreations: Sailing, golf, skiing.

Richard Drax MP, House of Commons, London SW1A 0AA
Tel: 020 7219 7051 *Email:* richard.drax.mp@parliament.uk
Constituency: SDCA, Chesil House, Dorset Green Technology Park, Winfrith Newburgh, Dorchester, Dorset DT2 8ZB
Tel: 01929 462803 *Websites:* www.southdorsetconservatives.com www.richarddrax.com

DREW, DAVID

Stroud *(Majority 687)*

LAB/CO-OP

Shadow Minister for Farming and Rural Affairs

David Elliott Drew. Born 13 April 1952; Son of Ronald Montague Drew, company accountant, and late Maisie Joan Drew, hospital administrator; Married Anne Baker 1990 (2 sons 2 daughters).

Education: Kingsfield School, Gloucestershire; Nottingham University (BA economics 1974); Birmingham University (PGCE 1976); Bristol Polytechnic (MA historical studies 1988); University of the West of England (MEd 1994) (PhD rural policy 2017).

Non-political career: Economics and geography teacher in various schools in Warwickshire, Hertfordshire and Gloucestershire 1976-86; Lecturer in business education, Bristol Polytechnic/University of the West of England 1986-97. NAS/UWT: Member 1976-86, Branch secretary 1984-86; Member: NATFHE/UCU 1986-, UNISON/NUPE 1990-.

Political career: Contested Stroud 1992 general election. Member for Stroud 1997-2010. Contested Stroud 2010 and 2015 general elections. Member for Stroud since 8 June 2017; Shadow Minister for Environment, Food and Rural Affairs (Farming and Rural Affairs) 2017-. *Select committees:* Member: Procedure 1997-2001, Modernisation of the House of Commons 1998-99, Agriculture 1999-2001, Environment, Food and Rural Affairs (Radioactive Waste Policy Sub-Committee) 2001-02, Environment, Food and Rural Affairs 2001-10, South West 2009-10, Reform of the House of Commons 2009-10, Ecclesiastical Committee. Chair PLP Departmental Committee for Agriculture, Fisheries and Food 1997-2001; Vice-chair PLP Departmental Committee for Environmental, Food and Rural Affairs 2002-10, Labour Group of Rural MPs: Chair, Vice-chair 2006-10. Member: Co-op Party 1980-, Christian Socialist Movement, Labour Party Rural Revival, Labour Campaign for Electoral Reform; Treasurer, Gloucestershire County Labour Party 1987-93; Secretary, Stroud Constituency Labour Party 1992-93. *Councils and public bodies:* Councillor: Stevenage Borough Council 1981-82, Stroud District Council 1987-95, 2011-15, Stonehouse Town Council 1987-2015, Gloucestershire County Council 1993-97.

Political interests: Housing, poverty, planning, environment, education, agriculture, rural affairs, small businesses; South Africa, Sudan, Bangladesh, DRC, Rwanda.

Other: Fellow, Industry and Parliament Trust 2002. Bristol Rugby Football Club; Forest Green Football Club.

Publications: Various IT related materials.

Recreations: Reading, watching rugby, football.

Dr David Drew MP, House of Commons, London SW1A 0AA
Tel: 020 7219 4106 *Email:* david.drew.mp@parliament.uk
Constituency: Details still to be confirmed *Twitter:* @DavidEDrew

DROMEY, JACK

Birmingham, Erdington *(Majority 7,285)*

LABOUR

Shadow Minister for Labour

John Eugene Joseph Dromey. Born 29 September 1948; Married Harriet Harman (qv) 1982 (MP for Camberwell and Peckham) (2 sons 1 daughter).

Education: Cardinal Vaughan Grammar School; French.

Non-political career: Chair for 15 years, Joint Industrial Council, Ministry of Defence. Secretary: South East Regional Council, TUC, Brent Trades Council 1976-78; Transport and General Workers' Union 1978-2003: Has served at all levels of the union from district officer to national organiser, Deputy general secretary 2003-08; Deputy general secretary, Unite 2008-10.

Political career: Member for Birmingham, Erdington since 6 May 2010 general election; Shadow Minister for: Communities and Local Government 2010-13, Home Office 2013-16, Labour 2016-. *Select committees:* Member: Business, Innovation and Skills 2010-11, Regulatory Reform 2010-15. Chair, PLP Departmental Group for Business, Innovation and Skills 2010. Treasurer, Labour Party 2004-10. *Councils and public bodies:* Founder member, Greater London Enterprise Board.

Political interests: Workers' rights (including equalities and the Vulnerable Workers' Agenda), manufacturing, housing, transport, international development (including supply chain ethical trading).

Other: Global Organising Alliance; Former executive council member and chair, National Council for Civil Liberties.

Recreations: Music, gym, walking, family.

Jack Dromey MP, House of Commons, London SW1A 0AA
Tel: 020 7219 0903 *Email:* jack.dromey.mp@parliament.uk
Constituency: 77 Mason Road, Birmingham, West Midlands B24 9EH
Tel: 0121-350 6077 *Website:* www.jackdromey.org *Twitter:* @JackDromeyMP

CONSERVATIVE

DUDDRIDGE, JAMES

Rochford and Southend East *(Majority 5,548)*

James Philip Duddridge. Born 26 August 1971; Son of Philip and Jenny Duddridge; Married Kathryn (Katy) Thompson 2004 (2 sons 1 daughter).

Education: Crestwood School, Eastleigh, Hampshire; Huddersfield New College; Wells Blue School; Essex University (BA government 1993).

Non-political career: Research assistant to Bernard Jenkin MP 1991-93; Retail and merchant banking, Barclays Bank 1993-2002: Barclays Bank of Swaziland 1995-96, Barclays Bank Head Office 1996, Sales director, Banque Belgolaise, Ivory Coast 1997-98, National sales manager, Barclays 1998-2001, Service delivery director, Barclays Bank Botswana 2001-02; Account director and consultant, YouGov 2000-05; Director, Okavango Ltd 2002-05; Adviser, Brand Communications Group 2017-.

Political career: Contested Rother Valley 2001 general election. Member for Rochford and Southend East 2005-10, for Rochford and Southend East (revised boundary) since 6 May 2010 general election; Opposition Whip 2008-10; Government Whip 2010-12; Parliamentary Under-Secretary of State, Foreign and Commonwealth Office 2014-June 2015, October 2015-16. *Select committees:* Member: Environment, Food and Rural Affairs 2005-07, International Development 2006-08, 2017-, Strategic Export Controls (Quadripartite Committee)/Arms Export Controls 2007-08; Chair, Regulatory Reform 2012-14; Member: Liaison 2013-14, Joint Committee on Draft Deregulation Bill 2013, Procedures 2016-17, Work of the Independent Commission for Aid Impact Sub-committee 2017-. Member, Executive, 1922 Committee 2013-14. Chair, Wells Young Conservatives 1989-91; Campaigns department, Conservative Central Office 1989-91; Chair, Essex University Conservative Students 1990-91; General election campaign manager to Stephen Shakespeare, Colchester 1997; Adviser, Lady Miller Postal Services Bill 1999; Executive committee member, Conservative Way Forward 2000-01.

Political interests: African politics, pensions; Botswana, Ivory Coast, South Africa, Swaziland, Zimbabwe.

Other: Member, Executive Committee, British Group Inter-Parliamentary Union 2005-06; Chair, Executive Committee, Commonwealth Parliamentary Association United Kingdom 2017-; Student representative, Huddersfield Police Forum 1987-88; Member, Bow Group 1999-; Speaker, Westminster Foundation for Democracy 2003-04; Member, Chartered Institute of Bankers 1993-2002; Associate member, Market Research Society 2003-05.

Recreations: Running, cycling, Southampton FC, Southend United FC.

James Duddridge MP, House of Commons, London SW1A 0AA
Tel: 020 7219 4830
Constituency: Suite 22a, Thamesgate House, 33-41 Victoria Avenue, Southend-on-Sea, Essex SS2 6DF
Tel: 01702 616135 *Email:* james@jamesduddridge.com *Website:* www.jamesduddridge.com
Twitter: @JamesDuddridge

LABOUR

DUFFIELD, ROSIE

Canterbury *(Majority 187)*

Rosemary Clare Duffield. Born 8 June 1971; Single (2 sons).

Non-political career: Teaching Assistant; Political satire writer/comedian. Member, Unison.

Political career: Member for Canterbury since 8 June 2017. *Select committees:* Member, Women and Equalities 2017-. Canterbury Labour Party: Chair 2013-17, Women's Officer 2015-17.

Political interests: Early education, animal rights, healthcare, social care, equalities, LGBTQ+, equal opportunities.

Other: Canterbury Action Network; Amnesty International Canterbury Branch; 50:50 Parliament.

Rosie Duffield MP, House of Commons, London SW1A 0AA
Tel: 020 7219 1183 *Email:* rosie.duffield.mp@parliament.uk
Constituency: 27 Castle Street, Canterbury CT1 2PX
Tel: 01227 467888 *Email:* enquiries@rosieduffieldmp.co.uk *Website:* www.rosieduffieldmp.co.uk
Twitter: @RosieDuffield1

CONSERVATIVE

DUGUID, DAVID

Banff and Buchan *(Majority 3,693)*

David James Duguid. Born 8 October 1970; Son of Norman Morrison Jane Anne Duguid (née Barron); Married Raziya Gasimova 2010 (1 son 1 daughter).

Education: Banff Academy; Robert Gordon University (HND chemistry 1991); Russian, Spanish.

Non-political career: Chemical Sales/Service Engineer, Servo Oilfield Chemicals 1992-93; Production Chemist, SGS 1993-2001; BP: Production Efficiency Engineer/Operationss Excellence Coach 2001-03, Integrity Management/Process Safety Engineer 2003-06, Common Process/Continuous Improvement Coach 2006-11; Project Manager (Management Consulting/Change Management), Hitachi Consulting 2011-16; Managing Director, D&R Duguid Ltd 2016-.

Political career: Member for Banff and Buchan since 8 June 2017. *Select committees:* Member, Scottish Affairs 2017-.

Political interests: Fisheries, agriculture, food and drink production, energy industry, Scottish tourism, Scottish development/regeneration, rural economy, infrastructure and connectivity, exiting the EU with the best deal for Banff and Buchan; Angola, Azerbaijan, Canada, Denmark, Venezuela.

Other: Member, Institute of Asset Management; Member, Institute of Engineering and Technology; Cancer Research, Breast Cancer Now, Parkinsons UK, RNLI.

Recreations: Playing guitar.

David Duguid MP, House of Commons, London SW1A 0AA
Tel: 020 7219 2819 *Email:* david.duguid.mp@parliament.uk
Constituency: Details still to be confirmed *Twitter:* @david_duguid

CONSERVATIVE

DUNCAN, ALAN

Rutland and Melton *(Majority 23,104)*

Minister of State for Europe and the Americas, Foreign and Commonwealth Office

Alan James Carter Duncan. Born 31 March 1957; Son of late Wing-Commander James Duncan OBE, and Anne Duncan, née Carter; Civil partner James Dunseath 2008.

Education: Merchant Taylors' School, Northwood; St John's College, Oxford (BA philosophy, politics and economics 1979) (President, Oxford Union 1979); Harvard University (Kennedy Scholar 1981-82).

Non-political career: Graduate trainee, Shell International Petroleum 1979-81; Marc Rich & Co 1981-88; Oil trader and adviser to governments and companies on oil supply, shipping and refining 1989-92; Visiting Fellow, St Antony's College, Oxford 2002-03; Non-executive chair, Fujairah Refining Ltd 2016-.

Political career: Contested Barnsley West and Penistone 1987 general election. Member for Rutland and Melton 1992-2010, for Rutland and Melton (revised boundary) since 6 May 2010 general election; PPS to Dr Brian Mawhinney as: Minister of State, Department of Health 1993-94, Chairman Conservative Party 1995-97; Parliamentary Political Secretary to William Hague as Leader of the Conservative Party 1997-98; Opposition Spokesperson for: Health 1998-99, Trade and Industry 1999-2001, Foreign and Commonwealth Affairs 2001-03; Shadow Secretary of State for: Constitutional Affairs 2003-04, International Development 2004-05, Transport 2005, Trade and Industry/Business, Enterprise and Regulatory Reform 2005-09, Shadow Leader of the House of Commons 2009; Member, House of Commons Commission 2009; Shadow Minister for Prisons 2009-10; Minister of State, Department for International Development 2010-14; Government's Special Envoy to: Oman -2015, Yemen; Member, Intelligence and Security Committee 2015-16; Minister of State for Europe and the Americas, Foreign and Commonwealth Office 2016-. *Select committees:* Member, Social Security 1992-95. Joint Secretary, Conservative Parliamentary Committee on the Environment 1992-94; Chairman, Conservative Constitutional Affairs Committee 1992-94. Vice-chair, Conservative Party 1997-98. *Councils and public bodies:* Trustee, Uppingham School.

Political interests: International trade, international economics; Middle East, Pakistan.

Other: Trustee and director, Uppingham School 2016-. Liveryman, Merchant Taylors' Company. Freedom, City of London. PC 2010; KCMG 2014; Beefsteak Club.

Publications: Co-author: Bearing the Standard: Themes for a Fourth Term (CPC pamphlet, 1991), Who Benefits? Reinventing Social Security, An End to Illusions (1993), Saturn's Children: How the State Devours Liberty, Prosperity and Virtue (1995); Beware Blair (1997).

Recreations: Shooting, skiing.

Rt Hon Sir Alan Duncan KCMG MP, House of Commons, London SW1A 0AA
Tel: 020 7219 5204 *Email:* alan.duncan.mp@parliament.uk
Constituency: No constituency office publicised *Website:* www.alanduncan.org.uk
Twitter: @AlanDuncanMP

CONSERVATIVE

DUNCAN SMITH, IAIN

Chingford and Woodford Green *(Majority 2,438)*

George Iain Duncan Smith. Born 9 April 1954; Son of late Group Captain W. G. G. Duncan Smith DSO DFC, and late Pamela Duncan Smith, née Summers; Married Hon. Elizabeth Fremantle 1982 (2 sons 2 daughters).

Education: HMS Conway (Cadet School); Universita per Stranieri, Perugia, Italy; RMA Sandhurst; Dunchurch College of Management; Italian.

Non-political career: Commissioned, Scots Guards 1975-81; Active service in: Northern Ireland 1976, Rhodesia/Zimbabwe 1979-80; ADC to Major-General Sir John Acland, KCB, CBE, Commander of Commonwealth Monitoring Force in Zimbabwe 1979-81. GEC Marconi 1981-88; Director: Bellwinch Property 1988-89, Publishing Director Jane's Information Group 1989-92.

Political career: Contested Bradford West 1987 general election. Member for Chingford 1992-97, for Chingford and Woodford Green 1997-2010, for Chingford and Woodford Green (revised boundary) since 6 May 2010 general election; Shadow Secretary of State for: Social Security 1997-99, Defence 1999-2001; Leader of the Opposition 2001-03; Secretary of State for Work and Pensions 2010-16. *Select committees:* Member: Health 1993-95, Administration 1993-97, Standards and Privileges 1995-97. Joint Secretary, Conservative Parliamentary Committees on: Foreign Affairs 1992-97, Defence 1995-96; Former vice-chair, European Affairs Committee; Chair, Conservative Party Committee for Social Security 1997-99. Vice-chair, Fulham Conservative Association 1991; Chair, Conservative Policy Board 2001-03; Leader, Conservative Party 2001-03.

Political interests: Finance, small businesses, transport, defence, environment, social policy.

Other: Member, Employment, Social Affairs, Health and Consumer Affairs Council, Council of the European Union 2010-16; Founder and Patron, Centre for Social Justice 2004-; Patron, Haven House Childrens Hospice; Trustee, Whitefields School Community Trust; Member, Campaign committee, Vote Leave 2016; Haven House Foundation, Whitefields Community Trust. Freedom, City of London 1993. Commons Minister of the Year, *House Magazine* awards 2011. PC 2001; Buck's Club 1919, Pratt's Club.

Publications: Co-author, Who Benefits? Reinventing Social Security; Game, Set and Match? (Maastricht); Facing the Future (Defence and Foreign and Commonwealth Affairs); 1994 and Beyond; A Response to Chancellor Kohl; A Race Against Time, Europe's growing vulnerability to missile attack (2002); The Devil's Tune (Robson Books, 2003).

Recreations: Cricket, rugby, tennis, sport in general, painting, theatre, family, shooting, fishing.

Rt Hon Iain Duncan Smith MP, House of Commons, London SW1A 0AA
Tel: 020 7219 2667 *Email:* olivia.kybett@parliament.uk
Constituency: Chingford and Woodford Green Conservative Association, 64a Station Road, Chingford, London E4 7BA
Tel: 020 8524 4344 *Fax:* 020 8523 9697 *Email:* office@cwgca.org
Website: www.iainduncansmith.org.uk

CONSERVATIVE

DUNNE, PHILIP

Ludlow *(Majority 19,286)*

Minister of State for Health, Department of Health

Philip Martin Dunne. Born 14 August 1958; Son of Sir Thomas Dunne and Henrietta Dunne, née Crawley; Married Domenica Fraser 1989 (2 sons 2 daughters).

Education: Eton College; Keble College, Oxford (BA philosophy, politics and economics 1980, MA).

Non-political career: Graduate trainee to senior manager, S G Warburg & Co Ltd 1980-88; Partner, Gatley Farms 1987-; Ottakar's plc: Co-founder director (non-executive) 1987-2006, Chair (non-executive) 1998-2006; Director of corporate development, James Gulliver Associates 1988-90; Partner, Phoenix Securities and successor 1991-2001; Managing director, Donaldson, Lufkin and Jenette 1997-2001; Chair (non-executive), Baronsmead VCT 4 plc 2001-10; Director, Ruffer Investment Management Limited and Ruffer LLP 2002-09 (non-executive 2005-09). Member, NFU 1987-.

Political career: Member for Ludlow since 5 May 2005 general election; Opposition Whip 2008-10; Assistant Government Whip 2010-12; Ministry of Defence: Parliamentary Under-Secretary of State (Defence Equipment, Support and Technology) 2012-15, Minister of State for Defence Procurement 2015-16; Minister of State for Health, Department of Health 2016-. *Select committees:* Member: Work and Pensions 2005-06, Public Accounts 2006-09; Treasury 2007-08. Deputy chair, International Office and Conservatives Abroad, Conservative Party 2008-10. *Councils and public bodies:* South Shropshire District Council: Councillor 2001-07, Conservative group leader 2003-05.

Political interests: Agriculture, business (especially small business), economy, financial services, health, international affairs, local government; Hong Kong, Middle East, USA.

Other: Non-executive director, Juvenile Diabetes Research Foundation 1998-2005; Director, Moor Park Charitable Trust 2001-07; Governor, Westminster Foundation for Democracy 2008-10; Member, Country Land and Business Association; Trustee: Henry Hewes Almshouse, Ludlow Town Walls, MA Walker Charitable Trust; President, Three Counties Agricultural Society 2016; White's Club. Church Stretton Golf Club.

Recreations: Country sports, skiing, travel.

Philip Dunne MP, House of Commons, London SW1A 0AA
Tel: 020 7219 2388 *Fax:* 020 7219 0788 *Email:* philip.dunne.mp@parliament.uk
Constituency: 54 Broad Street, Ludlow, Shropshire SY8 1GP
Tel: 01584 872187 *Fax:* 01584 876345 *Website:* www.philipdunne.com
Twitter: @Dunne4Ludlow

EAGLE, ANGELA

Wallasey *(Majority 23,320)*

LABOUR

Born 17 February 1961; Daughter of André Eagle, printworker, and late Shirley Eagle, dressmaker; Civil partner Maria Exall 2008.

Education: Formby High School; St John's College, Oxford (BA philosophy, politics and economics 1983).

Non-political career: Researcher, then national press officer, COHSE 1984-92. Member: COHSE, National Union of Journalists, Unison.

Political career: Member for Wallasey 1992-2010, for Wallasey (revised boundary) since 6 May 2010 general election; Opposition Whip 1996-97; Parliamentary Under-Secretary of State: Department of the Environment, Transport and the Regions (Minister for Green Issues and Regeneration) 1997-98, Department of Social Security 1998-2001, Home Office 2001-02; Exchequer Secretary, HM Treasury 2007-09; Minister of State (Minister for Pensions and the Ageing Society), Department for Work and Pensions 2009-10; Shadow Minister for Treasury 2010; Shadow Chief Secretary to the Treasury 2010-11; Shadow Leader of the House of Commons 2011-15; Member: House of Commons Commission 2011-15, Speaker's Committee for the Independent Parliamentary Standards Authority 2012-15; Shadow First Secretary of State and Secretary of State for Business, Innovation and Skills 2015-16. *Select committees:* Member: Public Accounts 1995-97, 2002-03, 2007-09, Treasury 2003-07, Treasury (Treasury Sub-Committee) 2003-10, Joint Committee on the Palace of Westminster 2015. Active at branch, women's section, general committee levels in Crosby Constituency 1978-80; Chair: Oxford University Fabian Club 1980-83, National Conference of Labour Women 1991; Vice-chair, PLP 2005-; Member, Labour Party NEC 2005-16; Chair, National Policy Forum 2012-16; Contested Labour deputy leadership election 2015; Patron, LGBT Labour.

Political interests: Economic policy, NHS, politics of sport.

Other: Member, British Film Institute.

Publications: Columnist and regular contributor to Tribune.

Recreations: Chess, cricket, cinema.

Angela Eagle MP, House of Commons, London SW1A 0AA
Tel: 020 7219 3843/020 7219 5057 *Email:* eaglea@parliament.uk
Constituency: Sherlock House, 6 Manor Road, Liscard, Wallasey, Wirral CH45 4JB
Tel: 0151-637 1979 *Fax:* 0151-638 5861 *Twitter:* @angelaeagle

EAGLE, MARIA

Garston and Halewood *(Majority 32,149)*

LABOUR

Born 17 February 1961; Daughter of André Eagle, printworker, and late Shirley Eagle, dressmaker.

Education: Formby High School; Pembroke College, Oxford (BA philosophy, politics and economics 1983); College of Law, London (Common Professional Exam, Law Society Finals 1990).

Non-political career: Voluntary sector 1983-90; Articles of clerkship, Brian Thompson & Partners, Liverpool 1990-92; Goldsmith Williams, Liverpool 1992-95; Senior Solicitor, Steven Irving & Co, Liverpool 1994-97. Member, GMB.

Political career: Contested Crosby 1992 general election. Member for Liverpool Garston 1997-2010, for Garston and Halewood since 6 May 2010 general election; PPS to John Hutton as Minister of State, Department of Health 1999-2001; Parliamentary Under-Secretary of State: Department for Work and Pensions (Minister for Disabled People) 2001-05, Department for Education and Skills 2005-06 (Minister for Children and Families 2005-06, for Young People 2006), Northern Ireland Office 2006-07; Ministry of Justice 2007-10: Parliamentary Under-Secretary of State 2007-09, Minister of State 2009-10; Government Equalities Office 2008-10: Parliamentary Under-Secretary of State 2008-09, Minister of State (Deputy Minister for Women and Equality) 2009-10; Shadow Solicitor General 2010; Shadow Minister for Justice 2010; Shadow Secretary of State for: Transport 2010-13, Environment, Food and Rural Affairs 2013-15, Defence 2015-16, Culture, Media and Sport 2016. *Select committees:* Member, Public Accounts 1997-99. Campaigns organiser and press officer, Merseyside West Euro CLP 1983-84; CLP secretary, press officer and political education officer 1983-85; Campaigns organiser, Crosby 1993-96; Member, Economy – Living Standards and Sustainability Policy Commission.

Political interests: Transport, housing, employment; Australia, Nicaragua, USA.

Other: Fellow, Industry and Parliament Trust 2001. Played cricket for Lancashire as a Junior; Played chess for England and Lancashire.

Publications: Co-author, High Time or High Tide for Labour Women.

Recreations: Cinema, chess, cricket.

Maria Eagle MP, House of Commons, London SW1A 0AA
Tel: 020 7219 0551 *Email:* eaglem@parliament.uk
Constituency: Unit House, Speke Boulevard, Liverpool, Merseyside L24 9HZ
Tel: 0151-448 1167 *Website:* www.mariaeagle.org.uk *Twitter:* @Meaglemp

EDWARDS, JONATHAN

Carmarthen East and Dinefwr *(Majority 3,908)*

PLAID CYMRU

Plaid Cymru Whip; Spokesperson for Treasury, Transport, Foreign Affairs, Defence and International Development

David Jonathan Edwards. Born 26 April 1976; Married Emma Edwards (2012).

Education: Ysgol Gymraeg Rhydaman; Ysgol Gyfun Maes yr Yrfa; University of Wales, Aberystwyth (history and politics); Postgraduate Degree international history; Welsh.

Non-political career: Chief of staff to Rhodri Glyn Thomas AM and Adam Price MP; National Campaigns Directorate, Plaid Cymru 2005-07; Citizens Advice Cymru 2007-10.

Political career: Member for Carmarthen East and Dinefwr since 6 May 2010 general election; Plaid Cymru: Spokesperson for: Business, Innovation and Skills 2010-16, Communities and Local Government 2010-15, Culture, Olympics, Media and Sport 2010-15, Transport 2010-, Treasury 2010-, Foreign Intervention 2015-16, Leader, Parliamentary group 2015, Spokesperson for: Exiting the European Union 2016-17, International Trade 2016-17, Whip 2017-, Spokesperson for: Foreign Affairs 2017-, Defence 2017-, International Development 2017-. *Select committees:* Member: Welsh Affairs 2010-13, 2014-15, Exiting the European Union 2016-17. *Councils and public bodies:* Councillor, Carmarthen Town Council; Sheriff of Carmarthen Town.

Political interests: Social justice, foreign affairs.

Other: Penygroes cricket team.

Recreations: Cricket, Swansea City FC.

Jonathan Edwards MP, House of Commons, London SW1A 0AA
Tel: 020 7219 3000 *Email:* jonathan.edwards.mp@parliament.uk
Constituency: 37 Wind Street, Ammanford, Carmarthenshire SA18 3DN
Tel: 01269 597677 *Fax:* 01269 591334 *Website:* www.jonathanedwards.org.uk
Twitter: @JonathanPlaid

EFFORD, CLIVE

Eltham *(Majority 6,296)*

LABOUR

Clive Stanley Efford. Born 10 July 1958; Son of Stanley Efford, retired civil servant, and Mary Efford, née Caldwell; Married Gillian Vallins 1981 (3 daughters).

Education: Walworth Comprehensive School; Southwark Further Education College.

Non-political career: Youth and community worker assistant to warden, Pembroke College Mission 1976; Partner family-owned jewellery and watch repair business 1981-85; Taxi driver 1987-97. Member, T&GWU: Member, Passenger Transport Committee of T&G; Represented T&G on London Taxi Board; Member, GMB.

Political career: Contested Eltham 1992 general election. Member for Eltham 1997-2010, for Eltham (revised boundary) since 6 May 2010 general election; Presented two bills in Parliament on energy efficiency and energy conservation; Assistant to Tony McNulty as Minister for London 2008-10; PPS to Ministers of State, Department for Communities and Local Government: Margaret Beckett 2008-09, John Healey 2009; Shadow Minister for: Home Office 2010-11, Culture, Media and Sport 2011-16. *Select committees:* Member: Procedure 1997-2001, Standing Orders 1999-2000, Transport 2002-09, 2016-17, London 2009-10, Communities and Local Government 2010-11. London Group of Labour MPs: Vice-chair 2001-07, Chair 2010-; Hon. Secretary, PLP Departmental Committee for Transport 2006-10. Member, Labour Friends of India. *Councils and public bodies:* London Borough of Greenwich: Councillor 1986-98, Chair: Social Services 1989-90, Health and Environment 1992-96, Secretary Labour Group 1986-87, Chief Whip Labour Group 1990-92; Chair, Eltham area planning and transport committee 1992-97.

Political interests: Welfare state, health, transport, education, environment, local and regional government, energy conservation, energy efficiency, energy from waste, waste management, recycling, social housing.

Other: Chair of trustees, Samuel Montagu Youth Club; Trustee, Greenwich Community College Trust; Eltham Hill CIU Club.

Recreations: Football (FA Preliminary Coachers Club).

Clive Efford MP, House of Commons, London SW1A 0AA
Tel: 020 7219 4057 *Email:* effordc@parliament.uk
Constituency: 132 Westmount Road, Eltham, London SE9 1UT
Tel: 020 8850 5744 *Email:* clive@cliveefford.org.uk *Website:* www.cliveefford.org.uk
Twitter: @Cliveefford

LABOUR

ELLIOTT, JULIE

Sunderland Central *(Majority 9,997)*

Born 29 July 1963; Daughter of late Laura Smith and late Harold Smith; 4 children.

Education: Seaham Northlea Comprehensive; Newcastle Polytechnic (Degree government and public policy).

Non-political career: Organiser, Labour Party 1993-98; Regional officer, National Asthma Campaign 1998-99; Political officer, GMB 1999-2010. Former secretary and treasurer, Northern Trade Union Liaison Organisation.

Political career: Member for Sunderland Central since 6 May 2010 general election; PPS to Caroline Flint as Shadow Secretary of State for: Communities and Local Government 2010-11, Energy and Climate Change 2011-13; Shadow Minister for Energy and Climate Change 2013-15. *Select committees:* Member: European Scrutiny 2010-15, Business, Innovation and Skills 2011-13, Culture, Media and Sport/Digital, Culture, Media and Sport 2015-. Chair, PLP Departmental Group for Housing and Planning 2015-. Member, Labour Party 1984-; Agent, Tynemouth 1997 general election; Former chair, Labour North Board. *Councils and public bodies:* Former governor and chair, Whitburn Comprehensive School.

Political interests: Employment and skills, regeneration, health inequalities, education.

Other: Vice-chair, Progress 2012-.

Recreations: Walking, baking, Rugby Union.

Julie Elliott MP, House of Commons, London SW1A 0AA
Tel: 020 7219 7165 *Fax:* 020 7219 4597 *Email:* julie.elliott.mp@parliament.uk
Constituency: 10 Norfolk Street, Sunderland SR1 1EA
Tel: 0191-565 5327 *Fax:* 0191-565 9848 *Website:* www.julie4sunderland.co.uk
Twitter: @JulieElliottMP

CONSERVATIVE

ELLIS, MICHAEL

Northampton North *(Majority 807)*

Deputy Leader of the House of Commons

Michael Tyrone Ellis. Born 13 October 1967.

Education: Wellingborough School, Northamptonshire; Buckingham University (LLB 1993); Inns of Court School of Law (Bar Vocational Course 1993).

Non-political career: Called to the Bar, Middle Temple 1993; Barrister, Clarendon Chambers, Northampton 1993-2010.

Political career: Member for Northampton North since 6 May 2010 general election; PPS to Theresa May as Home Secretary 2015-16; Deputy Leader of the House of Commons 2016-; Assistant Government Whip 2016-17. *Select committees:* Member: Joint Committee on Statutory Instruments 2010-15, Home Affairs 2011-15, Unopposed Bills (Panel) 2011-15, Joint Committee on the Draft Communications Data Bill 2012-13. *Councils and public bodies:* Councillor, Northamptonshire County Council 1997-2001.

Political interests: Justice, home affairs, constitution, foreign affairs; Israel, USA.

Other: President, Commonwealth Jewish Council 2012-14; Carlton Club.

Recreations: Gym, theatre.

Michael Ellis MP, House of Commons, London SW1A 0AA
Tel: 020 7219 7220 *Email:* michael.ellis.mp@parliament.uk
Constituency: 78 St George's Avenue, Northampton, Northamptonshire NN2 6JF
Tel: 01604 210707 *Website:* www.michaelellis.co.uk *Twitter:* @Michael_Ellis1

ELLMAN, LOUISE

Liverpool Riverside *(Majority 35,947)*

LAB/CO-OP

Louise Joyce Ellman. Born 14 November 1945; Daughter of late Harold and Anne Rosenberg; Married Geoffrey Ellman 1967 (1 son 1 daughter).

Education: Manchester High School for Girls; Hull University (BA sociology 1967); York University (MPhil social administration 1972).

Non-political career: Open University tutor/further education lecturer. Member, TGWU/Unite.

Political career: Member for Liverpool Riverside 1997-2010, for Liverpool Riverside (revised boundary) since 6 May 2010 general election. *Select committees:* Member: Environment, Transport and Regional Affairs 1997-2001, Environment, Transport and Regional Affairs (Environment Sub-Committee) 1997-2001, Transport, Local Government and the Regions 2001-02, Transport, Local Government and the Regions (Transport Sub-Committee) 2001-02, Transport, Local Government and the Regions (Urban Affairs Sub-Committee) 2001-02; Transport: Member 2002-08, Chair 2008-17; Member: Liaison 2008-17, Liaison (National Policy Statements Sub-committee) 2009-15. Member, Co-operative Party; Vice-chair, Labour Friends of Israel. *Councils and public bodies:* Lancashire County Council: Councillor 1970-97, Council Leader 1981-97; Councillor, West Lancashire District Council 1974-87; Vice-chair, Lancashire Enterprises 1982-97; Founder chair, Northwest Regional Association 1991-93; Vice-President, Local Government Association 2011-.

Political interests: Regional policy, local government, transport, public services, arts; Middle East.

Other: Chair, Jewish Labour Movement 2004-.

Louise Ellman MP, House of Commons, London SW1A 0AA
Tel: 020 7219 5210 *Email:* louise.ellman.mp@parliament.uk james.floyd@parliament.uk
Constituency: 212 The Cotton Exchange Building, Old Hall Street, Liverpool, Merseyside L3 9LQ
Tel: 0151-236 2969 *Fax:* 0151-236 4301 *Email:* lloydju@parliament.uk carneyr@parliament.uk
Twitter: @LouiseEllman

ELLWOOD, TOBIAS

Bournemouth East *(Majority 7,937)*

CONSERVATIVE

Parliamentary Under-Secretary of State, Ministry of Defence

Tobias Martin Ellwood. Born 12 August 1966; Son of Peter and Dr Caroline Ellwood; Married Hannah Ryan 2005 (2 sons).

Education: Vienna International School, Austria; Loughborough University of Technology (BA design and technology 1990) (Student Union President); City University Business School (MBA 1998); Kennedy School of Government, Harvard University, USA (Senior Executive Course national and international studies 2009); German.

Non-political career: Member, British Reserve Forces. Army officer, Royal Green Jackets 1991-96, served in Northern Ireland, Cyprus, Kuwait, Germany, Gibraltar and Bosnia; Researcher to Tom King MP 1996-97; Senior business development manager: London Stock Exchange 1998-2002, Allen and Overy 2002-04.

Political career: Contested Worsley 2001 general election. Member for Bournemouth East 2005-10, for Bournemouth East (revised boundary) since 6 May 2010 general election; Opposition Whip 2005-07; Shadow Minister for Culture, Media and Sport 2007-10; PPS to: Liam Fox as Secretary of State for Defence 2010-11, David Lidington as Minister of State, Foreign and Commonwealth Office 2011-13, Jeremy Hunt as Secretary of State for Health 2013-14; Parliamentary Adviser to the Prime Minister for the 2014 NATO Summit; Parliamentary Under-Secretary of State: Foreign and Commonwealth Office 2014-17 (Minister for Middle East and Africa 2016-17), Ministry of Defence 2017-. *Select committees:* Member: Environmental Audit 2005-06, Armed Forces Bill 2011. Chair, Conservative Insight 2000; Branch chair, South West Hertfordshire Conservative Association 1998-2003; Vice-chair, Conservative Middle East Council 2010-. *Councils and public bodies:* Councillor: Aldbury Parish Council 1996-99, Dacorum Borough Council 1999-2003; Governor, Queen's Park Infant School, Bournemouth.

Political interests: Defence, education, environment, tourism; Afghanistan, Iraq, Middle East, USA, Yemen.

Other: Member, UK Delegation to NATO Parliamentary Assembly 2014-15; CBI London Council 2000; Treasurer, Bow Group 2000; Member, Atlantic Council; Patron: Caring Canines, Crumbs Café, Aleevee8, Springbourne Family Centre, ME Support Group. PC 2017.

Publications: Post Conflict Reconstruction – Bridging the Gap Between Military and Civilian Affairs on the Modern Battlefield (2009); Time to Change the Clocks – Arguing the Case for Moving Our Clocks Forward (2010); Upgrading UK Influence in the European Union – A Strategy to Improve Upstreasm Scrutiny of EU Legislation (2012); Stabilizing Afghanistan – Proposals for Improving Security, Governance and Aid/Economic Development (Atlantic Council, 2013); Leveraging UK Carrier Capability (RUSI, 2013); Improving Efficiency, Interoperability and Resilience of our Blue Light Services (Henry Jackson Society, 2013).

Recreations: Volleyball, windsurfing, saxophone, theatre.

Rt Hon Tobias Ellwood MP, House of Commons, London SW1A 0AA
Tel: 020 7219 3596/020 7219 6459 *Email:* tobias.ellwood.mp@parliament.uk
Constituency: Bournemouth East Conservative Association, Haviland Road West, Boscombe, Bournemouth, Dorset BH1 4JW
Tel: 01202 801990/01202 397047 *Websites:* www.bournemoutheastconservatives.com www.tobiasellwood.com *Twitter:* @Tobias_Ellwood

LABOUR

ELMORE, CHRIS

Ogmore *(Majority 13,871)*

Opposition Whip

Christopher Philip James Elmore. Born 23 December 1983.

Education: Cardiff Metropolitan University (BA history and culture 2005).

Non-political career: Trainee butcher; Worked in further education. Member, GMB.

Political career: Contested Vale of Glamorgan 2015 general election. Member for Ogmore since 5 May 2016 by-election; Opposition Whip 2016-. *Select committees:* Member: Justice 2016, Welsh Affairs 2016-17, Procedure 2017-. Member, Co-operative Party. *Councils and public bodies:* Vale of Glamorgan Council: Councillor 2008-17, Youth Champion for the Vale of Glamorgan 2010-11, Cabinet Member for Children's Services and Schools 2012-16; Governor: Holton Primary School 2008-16, Cardiff and Vale College 2009-16; Independent member, Cardiff and Vale University Health Board 2009-16; Governor, Barry Comprehensive School 2012-.

Political interests: Pensions, industry, trade, children and young people, voter engagement; China, France, Ireland, USA.

Other: Board Member, Barry YMCA Hub.

Recreations: Walking, listening to music, watching sport, reading autobiographies.

Chris Elmore MP, House of Commons, London SW1A 0AA
Tel: 020 7219 1165 *Email:* chris.elmore.mp@parliament.uk
Constituency: 44a Penybont Road, Pencoed CF35 5RA
Tel: 01656 860034 *Website:* www.chriselmore.co.uk *Twitter:* @CPJElmore

CONSERVATIVE

ELPHICKE, CHARLIE

Dover *(Majority 6,437)*

Charles Brett Anthony Elphicke. Born 14 March 1971; Married Natalie Ross Pears 1996 (1 son 1 daughter).

Education: Felsted School, Essex; Nottingham University (LLB 1993); Inns of Court School of Law (Bar Finals 1994).

Non-political career: Formerly ran printing business; Called to the Bar, Middle Temple 1994; Solicitor: Supreme Court of England and Wales, Cameron, McKenna and Wilde Sapte 1996-2001; Partner, Reed Smith 2001-05; Partner and head of European tax, Hunton & Williams Solicitors 2006-10.

Political career: Contested St Albans 2001 general election. Member for Dover since 6 May 2010 general election; PPS to: David Lidington as Minister of State for Europe, Foreign and Commonwealth Office 2013-14, Iain Duncan Smith as Secretary of State for Work and Pensions 2014-15; Government Whip (Lord Commissioner of HM Treasury) 2015-16. *Select committees:* Member: Public Administration 2010-13, Joint Committee on Consolidation, Etc, Bills 2010-15, Public Accounts 2016-17, Treasury 2017-. Member, Executive, 1922 Committee 2010-12. Chair, Dulwich and West Norwood Conservatives 1999-2000. *Councils and public bodies:* Councillor, London Borough of Lambeth Council 1994-98.

Political interests: Poverty alleviation, wealth creation, transport, tax fairness.

Other: Research fellow, Centre for Policy Studies; Member, Law Society of England and Wales. Freedom, City of London. Overall Winner, BCS Chartered Institute of IT MP Web Awards 2010.

Publications: Author, Centre for Policy Studies publications: Ending Pensioner Poverty (2003), (with William Norton) SAINTS can get Britain saving again (2005), The Case for Reducing Business Taxes (2006), The Tax Double Whammy: More tax costs more than you think (2006), Robin Hood or Sheriff of Nottingham? Winners and losers from tax and benefit reform over the last 10 years (2006), Where has your pay rise gone? (2006), Are you better off now than you were four years ago? (2007), Why do we feel so broke? (2008), Uh-Oh, We're in trouble (2008), Ten points for growth (2011), Lower, simpler, stronger business taxes (2013).

Recreations: Sailing, walking by the sea, spending time with family.

Charlie Elphicke MP, House of Commons, London SW1A 0AA
Tel: 020 7219 7052 *Email:* charlie.elphicke.mp@parliament.uk
Constituency: c/o Dover and Deal Conservative Association, 54 The Strand, Walmer, Deal, Kent CT14 7DP
Tel: 01304 379669 *Email:* charlie@elphicke.com *Website:* www.elphicke.com
Twitter: @charlieelphicke

LABOUR

ESTERSON, BILL

Sefton Central *(Majority 15,618)*

Shadow Minister for Business, Energy and Industrial Strategy and for International Trade

William Roffen Esterson. Born 27 October 1966; Son of Derek and Joyce Esterson; Married Caroline (1 son 1 daughter).

Education: Rochester Mathematical School; Leeds University (BSc maths and philosophy 1990); French, German.

Non-political career: Director, training consultancy 1995-2010. Member: Unite, USDAW.

Political career: Member for Sefton Central since 6 May 2010 general election; PPS to Stephen Twigg as Shadow Secretary of State for Education 2011-13; Shadow Minister for: Business, Innovation and Skills 2015-16, Business, Energy and Industrial Strategy 2016-, International Trade 2016-. *Select committees:* Member: Environment, Food and Rural Affairs 2010-11, Education 2010-15, Joint Committee on the Draft House of Lords Reform Bill 2011-12, Unopposed Bills (Panel) 2011-15, Communities and Local Government 2011-13, Joint Committee on the Rookery South (Resource Recovery Facility) Order 2012-13, Treasury 2015. Chair, PLP Departmental Group for Education 2010-12. *Councils and public bodies:* Medway Council: Councillor 1995-2010, Labour Spokesperson for Children's Services.

Political interests: Children's service.

Other: Formby Hockey Club.

Recreations: Playing hockey and cricket.

Bill Esterson MP, House of Commons, London SW1A 0AA
Tel: 020 7219 4403 *Email:* bill.esterson.mp@parliament.uk
Constituency: 39 Sefton Lane Industrial Estate, Maghull, Liverpool, Merseyside L31 8BX
Tel: 0151-531 8433 *Email:* bill.estersonmp@gmail.com *Website:* www.billesterson.org.uk
Twitter: @Bill_Esterson

CONSERVATIVE

EUSTICE, GEORGE

Camborne and Redruth *(Majority 1,577)*

Minister of State for Agriculture, Fisheries and Food, Department for Environment, Food and Rural Affairs

Charles George Eustice. Born 28 September 1971; Son of Paul Eustice and Adele Eustice; Married Katy Taylor-Richards 2013.

Education: Truro Cathedral School; Truro School; Cornwall College, Pool; Writtle College, Chelmsford.

Non-political career: Trevaskis Fruit Farm; Conservative Party: Campaign director, anti-Euro 'No Campaign' 1999-2003; Head of press, 2005 general election 2003-05; Press Secretary to Conservative Leader David Cameron 2005-07; External relations co-ordinator, Conservative HQ 2008-09; Associate director, Portland PR 2009-10.

Political career: Member for Camborne and Redruth since 6 May 2010 general election; Department for Environment, Food and Rural Affairs: Parliamentary Under-Secretary of State (Farming, Food and Marine Environment) 2013-15, Minister of State for Farming, Food and the Marine Environment 2015-16, Minister of State for Agriculture, Fisheries and Food 2016-. *Select committees:* Member: Environment, Food and Rural Affairs 2010-13, Joint Committee on

Privacy and Injunctions 2011-12. Member, Executive, 1922 Committee 2012-13. Contested South West region (UKIP) 1999 European Parliament election. Member: UKIP 1998-99, Conservative Party 2003-; Member, Number 10 Policy Advisory Board April-October 2013.

Political interests: Farming, environment, Europe, regeneration.

Other: Redruth 2000; MS Society. Hayle RFC; Camborne RFC; Cornwall Athletic Club.

Publications: Columnist, *PR Week* 2012-13.

George Eustice MP, House of Commons, London SW1A 0AA
Tel: 020 7219 7032 *Email:* george.eustice.mp@parliament.uk
Constituency: 13 Commercial Street, Camborne, Cornwall TR14 8JZ
Tel: 01209 713355 *Email:* camborneredruthconservatives@googlemail.com
Websites: www.camborneredruthconservatives.com www.georgeeustice.org.uk

LAB/CO-OP

EVANS, CHRIS

Islwyn *(Majority 11,412)*

Christopher James Evans. Born 17 June 1977; Son of late Michael Evans and Lynne Evans; Married Julia Ockenden 2013.

Education: Porth County Comprehensive; Pontypridd College; Trinity College, Carmarthen (BA history).

Non-political career: Manager, bookmaker 1998-2001; Lloyds TSB Bank plc 2001-03; Marketing, Glamorgan University 2003-04; Official, Union of Finance Staff 2004-06; Parliamentary researcher to Don Touhig MP 2006-10. Member, Unite.

Political career: Contested Cheltenham 2005 general election. Member for Islwyn since 6 May 2010 general election; PPS to Chris Leslie: as Shadow Chief Secretary to the Treasury 2013-15, as Shadow Chancellor 2015. *Select committees:* Member: Justice 2010-12, Joint Committees on: the Draft Defamation Bill 2011, the Draft Enhanced Terrorism Prevention and Investigation Measures Bill 2012-13; Member: Environmental Audit 2012-14, Public Accounts 2015-. Member, Co-operative Party.

Political interests: Justice, finance, welfare; China, France, Germany, Greece, USA.

Other: Member, Fabian Society; Hon. Fellow. University of Wales Trinity St David.

Publications: Fearless Freddie: The Life and Times of Freddie Mills (2017).

Recreations: Watching sports, running, reading.

Chris Evans MP, House of Commons, London SW1A 0AA
Tel: 020 7219 7091 *Email:* chris.evans.mp@parliament.uk
Constituency: 6 Woodfieldside Business Park, Penmaen Road, Pontllanfraith, Blackwood, Gwent NP12 2DG
Tel: 01495 231990 *Website:* www.chrisevansmp.co.uk *Twitter:* @ChrisEvansMP

CONSERVATIVE

EVANS, NIGEL

Ribble Valley *(Majority 13,199)*

Nigel Martin Evans. Born 10 November 1957; Son of late Albert Evans and Betty Evans; Single.

Education: Dynevor School, Swansea; University College of Wales, Swansea (BA politics 1979); French, Russian (poor).

Non-political career: Management family retail newsagent and convenience store 1979-90; Worked on three US presidential elections in New York, Florida and California.

Political career: Contested Swansea West 1987 general election and Pontypridd 1989 and Ribble Valley 1991 by-elections. Member for Ribble Valley 1992-2010, for Ribble Valley (revised boundary) since 6 May 2010 general election; PPS: to David Hunt: as Secretary of State for Employment 1993-94, as Chancellor of the Duchy of Lancaster 1994-95, to Tony Baldry as Minister of State, Ministry of Agriculture, Fisheries and Food 1995-96, to William Hague as Secretary of State for Wales 1996-97; Opposition Spokesperson for: Scotland and Wales 1997-99, Wales 1999-2001; Shadow Secretary of State for Wales 2001-03; First Deputy Chairman, Ways and Means and Deputy Speaker 2010-13. *Select committees:* Member: Welsh Affairs 2003-05, Trade and Industry 2003-05, Culture, Media and Sport 2005-09, International Development 2009-10, 2015-; Chairmen's Panel/Panel of Chairs: Member 2009-10, 2015-, Ex-officio member 2010-13; Member: Public Administration 2014-15, Backbench Business 2014-15, Administration 2014-15, Northern Ireland Affairs 2015-16, Arms Export Controls 2016-17, Court of Referees 2016-, Work of the Independent Commission for Aid Impact Sub-committee 2016-, International Trade 2016-. 1922 Committee: Member, Executive 2014-15, Secretary 2015-. Chair, Conservative Welsh Parliamentary Candidates Policy Group 1990; President, Conservative North West Parliamentary Candidates Group 1991; North West Conservative MPs: Secretary 1992-97, Chair 2014; Vice-chair, Conservative Party: (Wales) 1999-2001, (Conservatives Abroad) 2004-05; Chair Founding member, Conservatives for Britain 2015-16. *Councils and public bodies:* West Glamorgan County Council: Councillor 1985-91, Deputy Leader, Conservative Group 1990-91.

Political interests: Education, small businesses, US elections, local and regional government, defence, agriculture, international politics, European affairs, telecommunications, space; Australia, Bahrain, Caribbean, Egypt, Europe, Far East, Gibraltar, India, USA.

Other: British Group, Inter-Parliamentary Union: Treasurer 2005-08, Vice-chair 2008-10, Chair 2015-; Executive Committee, Commonwealth Parliamentary Association (United Kingdom branch): Member 2005-17, Hon Treasurer 2010, Vice-chair 2017-; Member: Council of Europe 2006, Western European Union 2006-; UK chair, Technological and Aerospace committee; Member, UK delegation, Parliamentary Assembly of the Council of Europe 2015-; British-Irish Parliamentary Assembly: Member 2015-17, Vice-chair 2017-; Fellow, Industry and Parliament Trust 1998; Adviser, Arensky Chamber Orchestra; Hon. President, British Youth Council; Macmillan Cancer Support. Hon. LLD Swansea University 2012; Carlton Club, CountryClubuk, Royal Automobile Club, Groucho Club.

Recreations: Tennis, swimming, running, theatre, cinema, arts, music.

Nigel Evans MP, House of Commons, London SW1A 0AA
Tel: 020 7219 6939 *Fax:* 020 7219 2568 *Email:* evansn@parliament.uk
Constituency: 9 Railway View, Clitheroe, Lancashire BB7 2HA
Tel: 01200 425939 *Fax:* 01200 422904 *Email:* ribblevalley@tory.org
Website: www.nigel-evans.org.uk *Twitter:* @nigelmp

CONSERVATIVE

EVENNETT, DAVID

Bexleyheath and Crayford *(Majority 9,073)*

Government Whip (Lord Commissioner of HM Treasury)

David Anthony Evennett. Born 3 June 1949; Son of late Norman Evennett and late Irene Evennett, née Turner; Married Marilyn Smith 1975 (2 sons).

Education: Buckhurst Hill County High School; London School of Economics (BSc Econ economics 1971; MSc Econ politics 1972).

Non-political career: Schoolmaster, Ilford County High School 1972-74; Marine insurance broker, Lloyds 1974-81; Member, Lloyds 1976-92; Director, Lloyds Underwriting Agency 1982-91; Commercial liaison manager, Bexley College 1997-2001; Consultant, J&H Marsh and McLennan (UK) then Marsh (UK) Ltd 1998-2000; Freelance lecturer 2001-05.

Political career: Contested Hackney South and Shoreditch 1979 general election. Member for Erith and Crayford 1983-97. Contested Bexleyheath and Crayford 1997 and 2001 general elections. Member for Bexleyheath and Crayford since 5 May 2005 general election; PPS to: Baroness Blatch as Minister of State for Education 1992-93, John Redwood as Secretary of State for Wales 1993-95, Baroness Blatch and David Maclean as Ministers of State, Home Office 1995-96, Gillian Shephard as Secretary of State for Education and Employment 1996-97; Opposition Whip 2005-09; Shadow Minister for: Innovation, Universities and Skills 2009, Universities and Skills 2009-10; PPS to Michael Gove as Secretary of State for Education 2010-12; Government Whip (Lord Commissioner of HM Treasury) 2012-; Parliamentary Under-Secretary of State for Sport, Tourism and Heritage January-July 2016 (maternity cover for Tracey Crouch MP). *Select committees:* Member: Education, Science and the Arts 1986-92, Education and Skills 2005-06, Selection 2012-, Administration 2013-15. *Councils and public bodies:* Councillor, London Borough of Redbridge 1974-78.

Political interests: Education, economy, transport, London, heritage, tourism; Australia, Canada, Italy, New Zealand, USA.

Other: Patron: Townley, Grammar School for Girls, Friends of Christchurch Bexleyheath; Vice-president, Bexleyheath and District Club for the Disabled; Member, National Trust. PC 2015; Bexleyheath Conservative Club.

Recreations: Travel, reading, cinema, family, music.

Rt Hon David Evennett MP, House of Commons, London SW1A 0AA
Tel: 020 7219 8403 *Email:* david.evennett.mp@parliament.uk
Constituency: 17 Church Road, Bexleyheath, Kent DA7 4DD
Websites: www.bexleyheathandcrayford.com www.davidevennett.com
Twitter: @davidevennett

CONSERVATIVE

FABRICANT, MICHAEL

Lichfield *(Majority 18,581)*

Michael Louis David Fabricant. Born 12 June 1950; Son of late Isaac Fabricant and Helena Fabricant, née Freed; Single.

Education: Brighton, Hove and Sussex Grammar School, Brighton; Loughborough University (BSc economics and law 1973); Sussex University (MSc systems and econometrics 1974); Oxford University/London University/University of Southern California, Los Angeles, USA (PhD econometrics and economic forecasting 1975-78); Dutch, French, German, Hebrew (basic), Russian (basic).

Non-political career: Staff, then freelance radio broadcaster and journalist 1968-80; Economist and founder director, leading broadcast and communications group, manufacturing and commissioning electronics equipment to radio stations to 48 countries 1980-91; Adviser, Home Office on broadcasting matters; Adviser to foreign governments on establishment and management of radio stations, including Russian Federation 1980-91; Has lived and worked extensively in Europe, Africa, the Far East, former Soviet Union, and USA.

Political career: Contested South Shields 1987 general election. Member for Mid Staffordshire 1992-97, for Lichfield 1997-2010, for Lichfield (revised boundary) since 6 May 2010 general election; Presented Bills to strengthen economic and political ties between UK, USA, Canada, Australia and New Zealand; Promoted legislation to encourage flying of Union Flag and to force Government to undertake and publish regular financial cost-benefit analyses of Britain's membership of European Union; PPS to Michael Jack as Financial Secretary to the Treasury 1996-97; Shadow Minister for: Trade and Industry 2003, Economic Affairs 2003-05; Opposition Whip 2005-10; Government Whip 2010-12. *Select committees:* Member: Culture, Media and Sport 1997-99, 2001-05, Home Affairs 1999-2001, Catering 1999-2001, Liaison 2001-03; Chair, Information 2001-03; Member: Finance and Services 2001-04, Administration 2009-10, 2014-, Selection 2010-12. Member, Executive, 1922 Committee 2001-03. Chair, Brighton Pavilion Conservative Association 1985-88; Member, Conservative Way Forward; Associate member, European Research Group; Member, Conservative Against a Federal Europe; Chair, Conservative Friends of America 2007-10; Vice-chairman (parliamentary campaigning), Conservative Party 2012-14.

Political interests: Broadcasting and media, business, defence, engineering, enterprise, exports, foreign affairs, heritage, industry, inland waterways, international aid and development, international trade, internet, manufacturing, police and security issues, science and technology, technology, telecommunications, trade and industry; Australia, Eastern Europe, Middle East, USA, Wales.

Other: Member: Inter-Parliamentary Union, Commonwealth Parliamentary Association; Member: Council, Institution of Electrical Engineers 1996-2000, Senate, Engineering Council 1996-2002; Director, Engineering and Technology Board 2002-06; CEng; FIET; FRSA; Cancer Research; Rottingdean Club (Sussex).

Recreations: Reading, music, fell-walking, skiing and listening to the omnibus edition of *The Archers*.

Michael Fabricant MP, House of Commons, London SW1A 0AA
Tel: 020 7219 5022 *Email:* michael.fabricant.mp@parliament.uk
Constituency: No constituency office publicised *Website:* www.michael.fabricant.mp.co.uk
Twitter: @Mike_Fabricant

CONSERVATIVE

FALLON, MICHAEL

Sevenoaks *(Majority 21,917)*

Secretary of State for Defence

Michael Cathel Fallon. Born 14 May 1952; Son of late Martin Fallon OBE FRICS, and Hazel Fallon; Married Wendy Payne 1986 (2 sons).

Education: Epsom College, Surrey; St Andrews University (MA classics and ancient history 1974).

Non-political career: European Educational Research Trust 1974-75; Conservative Research Department 1975-79 (seconded to Opposition Whips Office, House of Lords 1975-77, EEC Desk Officer 1977-79); Secretary, Lord Home's Committee on Future of the House of Lords 1977-78; Joint managing director, European Consultants Ltd 1979-81; Assistant to Baroness Elles MEP 1979-83; Director, Quality Care Homes plc 1992-97; Chief executive, Quality Care Developments Ltd 1996-97; Director: Just Learning Ltd 1996-2009, Bannatyne Fitness Ltd 1999-2000, Just Learning Holdings 2001-09, Just Learning Development Ltd 2001-09, Careshare Ltd 2003-09, Collins Stewart Tullet plc 2004-06, Tullett Prebon plc 2006-12, Attendo AB 2008-12.

Political career: Contested Darlington March 1983 by-election. Member for Darlington 1983-92. Contested Darlington 1992 general election. Member for Sevenoaks 1997-2010, for Sevenoaks (revised boundary) since 6 May 2010 general election; PPS to Cecil Parkinson as Secretary of State for Energy 1987-88; Assistant Government Whip 1988-90; Government Whip May-July 1990; Parliamentary Under-Secretary of State, Department of Education and Science 1990-92; Opposition Frontbench Spokesperson for: Trade and Industry June-December 1997, the Treasury December 1997-98; Department for Business, Innovation and Skills: Minister of State for: Business and Enterprise 2012-13, Business and Energy 2013-14; Minister of State for Energy, Department of Energy and Climate Change 2013-14; Secretary of State for Defence 2014-. *Select committees:* Member, Treasury 1999-2012; Treasury Sub-committee: Member 1999-2001, Chair 2001-10. Member, Executive 1922 Committee 2005-07; Deputy chair, Conservative Party 2010-12. *Councils and public bodies:* Member: Higher Education Funding Council 1992-97, Deregulation Task Force 1994-97.

Political interests: Constitution, public sector, education, Treasury.

Other: Member, Advisory Council, Social Market Foundation 1994-2000; Non-executive director, International Care and Relief 1998-2003; Board member, Centre for Policy Studies 2009-; President, Royal London Society for the Blind 2010-; Ex-officio Chairman, Commonwealth War Graves Commission; President, Friends of St Mary's Church, Sundridge; Patron, Darenth Valley Youth Music. PC 2012; KCB 2016; Academy Club.

Publications: Brighter Schools (Social Market Foundation, 1993); Putting Social Mobility Back Into Britain (NTB, 2007).

Recreations: Skiing, opera, visiting classical sites.

Rt Hon Sir Michael Fallon KCB MP, House of Commons, London SW1A 0AA
Tel: 020 7219 6482 *Fax:* 020 7219 6791 *Email:* michael.fallon.mp@parliament.uk
Constituency: No constituency office publicised *Website:* www.michaelfallonmp.org.uk

LABOUR

FARRELLY, PAUL

Newcastle-under-Lyme *(Majority 30)*

Christopher Paul Farrelly. Born 2 March 1962; Son of late Thomas Farrelly and Anne Farrelly, née King; Married Victoria Perry 1998 (1 son 2 daughters).

Education: Wolstanton County Grammar School; Marshlands Comprehensive, Newcastle-Under-Lyme; St Edmund Hall, Oxford (BA philosophy, politics and economics 1984); French, German, Italian.

Non-political career: Manager, corporate finance division, Barclays De Zoete Wedd Ltd 1984-90; Reuters Ltd 1990-95: Correspondent, News editor; Deputy city and business editor, *Independent on Sunday* 1995-97; City editor, *The Observer* 1997-2001. Member: Unite, Unity.

Political career: Contested Chesham and Amersham 1997 general election. Member for Newcastle-under-Lyme since 7 June 2001 general election. *Select committees:* Member: Joint Committee on Consolidation, Etc, Bills 2001-15, European Standing Committee B 2003-05, Science and Technology 2003-05, Unopposed Bills (Panel) 2004-15, Culture, Media and Sport/Digital, Culture, Media and Sport 2005-, Joint Committee on Privacy and Injunctions 2011-12. Member, Cooperative Party; Vice-chair, Hornsey and Wood Green CLP 1994-95; Newcastle-under-Lyme CLP 1998-2006: Campaign co-ordinator and organiser, Political education officer; Member: Socialist Education Association, Labour Party Irish Society.

Political interests: Education, health, employment, trade and industry, regeneration, investment, European affairs, pensions, crime; Australia, China, France, Germany, Hungary, Iceland, Ireland, Italy, Japan, New Zealand, Norway, Russia.

Other: Member, British-Irish Parliamentary Assembly; Member: Amnesty International, Greenpeace. Trentham RUFC; Finchley RFC; House of Commons and House of Lords RUFC.

Publications: Editor, Hammer of the Left by John Golding (2003).

Recreations: Rugby, football, writing, biography, history, architecture.

Paul Farrelly MP, House of Commons, London SW1A 0AA
Tel: 020 7219 8391 *Fax:* 020 7219 1986 *Email:* paul.farrelly.mp@parliament.uk
Constituency: Waterloo Buildings, 79-81 Dunkirk, Newcastle-under-Lyme, Staffordshire ST5 2SW
Tel: 01782 715033 *Fax:* 01782 613174 *Email:* hopwoodc@parliament.uk
Website: www.paulfarrelly.com

LIBERAL DEMOCRAT

FARRON, TIM

Westmorland and Lonsdale *(Majority 777)*

Timothy James Farron. Born 27 May 1970; Son of Chris Farron and late Susan Farron, née Trenchard; Married Rosie Cantley 2000 (2 daughters 2 sons).

Education: Lostock Hall High School, Preston, Lancashire; Runshaw Tertiary College, Leyland; Newcastle University (BA politics 1991).

Non-political career: Lancaster University: Adult education officer 1992-96, Student support officer 1996-98, Faculty administrator 1998-2002; Head of faculty administration, St Martin's College (Ambleside, Lancaster, Carlisle) 2002-05. Association of University Teachers 1995-.

Political career: Contested North West Durham 1992, South Ribble 1997 and Westmorland and Lonsdale 2001 general elections. Member for Westmorland and Lonsdale 2005-10, for Westmorland and Lonsdale (revised boundary) since 6 May 2010 general election; Liberal Democrat: Spokesperson for Youth Affairs 2005-06; PPS to Sir Menzies Campbell as Leader of the Liberal Democrats 2006-07; Shadow Minister for: Home Affairs 2007, Countryside 2007-08; Shadow Secretary of State for Environment, Food and Rural Affairs 2008-10. *Select committees:* Member: Education and Skills 2005-06, Environmental Audit 2006-07, European Scrutiny 2010-13. Chair, Liberal Democrat Policy Committee on International Affairs 2010-11. Contested North West England 1999 European Parliament election. Liberal Democrats: President 2010-14, Member, Manifesto Working Group 2013-15, Leader 2015-17. *Councils and public bodies:* Councillor: Lancashire County Council 1993-2000, South Ribble Borough Council 1995-99, South Lakeland District Council 2004-08; Vice-president, Local Government Association 2017-.

Political interests: Education, rural affairs, youth work, health, crime and policing, social care.

Other: Member, Amnesty International 1993-; President Kendal and South Westmorland Liberal Club.

Recreations: Fell-walking, running, cycling, football, watching Blackburn Rovers FC, music.

Tim Farron MP, House of Commons, London SW1A 0AA
Tel: 020 7219 8498 *Fax:* 020 7219 2810 *Email:* farront@parliament.uk
Constituency: Acland House, Yard 2, Stricklandgate, Kendal, Cumbria LA9 4ND
Tel: 01539 723403 *Fax:* 01539 740800 *Email:* tim@timfarron.co.uk
Website: www.timfarron.co.uk *Twitter:* @timfarron

SCOTTISH NATIONAL PARTY

FELLOWS, MARION

Motherwell and Wishaw *(Majority 318)*

SNP Spokesperson for Small Business, Enterprise and Innovation; Deputy Whip

Born 5 May 1949.

Education: Heriot Watt University (accountancy and finance).

Non-political career: Accountant; Business studies teacher, West Lothian College. Member, EIS.

Political career: Contested Motherwell and Wishaw 2010 general election. Member for Motherwell and Wishaw since 7 May 2015 general election; SNP: Deputy Whip 2015-, Spokesperson for Small Business, Enterprise and Innovation 2017-. *Select committees:* Member: Education 2015-, Education, Skills and the Economy Sub-committee 2016-17. Contested Motherwell and Wishaw constituency 2007 Scottish Parliament election. *Councils and public bodies:* Councillor, North Lanarkshire Council 2012-15.

Political interests: Home rule for Scotland.

Marion Fellows MP, House of Commons, London SW1A 0AA
Tel: 020 7219 5784 *Email:* marion.fellows.mp@parliament.uk
Constituency: Dalziel Building, 7 Scott Street, Motherwell, North Yorkshire ML1 1PN
Tel: 01698 337191 *Website:* marionfellows.scot *Twitter:* @marionfellows

CONSERVATIVE

FERNANDES, SUELLA

Fareham *(Majority 21,555)*

Team PPS, HM Treasury

Sue-Ellen Cassiana Fernandes. Born 3 April 1980; Daughter of Chris and Uma Fernandes.

Education: Heathfield School, Pinner; Queens' College, Cambridge (MA law 2002); Universite de Paris I, Pantheon-Sorbonne (LLM); Admitted to the New York Bar 2006; French.

Non-political career: Called to the Bar, Middle Temple 2005; Barrister, No 5 Chambers, London, specialising in planning, public and judicial review 2005-15; Treasury Counsel Panel 2010-15.

Political career: Contested Leicester East 2005 general election. Member for Fareham since 7 May 2015 general election; Team PPS, HM Treasury 2017-. *Select committees:* Member: Education 2015-17, Joint Committee on the Draft Investigatory Powers Bill 2015-16, Education, Skills and the Economy Sub-committee 2015-16. Contested Londonwide region 2012 London Assembly election. Chair, European Research Group 2017-. *Councils and public bodies:* Co-founder and Chair of Governors, Michaela Community School, Brent.

Political interests: Education, social mobility, local investment.

Other: Council of Europe UK Delegation: Committee for Legal Affairs and Human Rights; Bar Counsel of England and Wales; New York State Bar; Co-founder and chair, Africa Justice Foundation 2010-14. Middle Temple Scholarship, Bar Vocational Course 2004; Pegasus Scholarship 2010.

Recreations: Cinema, theatre, camping.

Suella Fernandes MP, House of Commons, London SW1A 0AA
Tel: 020 7219 8191 *Email:* suella.fernandes.mp@parliament.uk
Constituency: 14 East Street, Fareham, Hampshire PO16 0BN
Tel: 01329 233573 *Email:* suella@suellafernandes.co.uk *Website:* www.suellafernandes.co.uk
Twitter: @SuellaFernandes

LABOUR

FIELD, FRANK

Birkenhead *(Majority 25,514)*

Chair, Select Committee on Work and Pensions

Born 16 July 1942; Son of late Walter Field.

Education: St Clement Danes Grammar School, London; Hull University (BSc economics 1963).

Non-political career: Teacher in further education 1964-69; Director: Child Poverty Action Group 1969-79, Low Pay Unit 1974-80; Non-executive director, Medicash 2003-.

Political career: Contested Buckinghamshire South 1966 general election. Member for Birkenhead 1979-2010, for Birkenhead (revised boundary) since 6 May 2010 general election; Opposition Spokesperson for Education 1980-81; Minister of State, Department of Social Security (Welfare Reform) 1997-98; Leads Independent Review on Poverty and Life Chances 2010-. *Select committees:* Chair, Social Security 1990-97; Member: Public Accounts 2002-05, Ecclesiastical Committee; Chair: Joint Committee on the Draft Modern Slavery Bill 2014, Work and Pensions 2015-; Member, Liaison 2015-. *Councils and public bodies:* Councillor, Hounslow Borough Council 1964-68; DL 2011.

Political interests: Poverty and income redistribution, church affairs; Poland.

Other: Chair: Churches Conservation Trust 2001-07, King James Bible Trust 2007-12; Chair, Feeding Britain 2015-; Member, Campaign Committee, Vote Leave 2016; Founding Supporter, Change Britain 2016-; Trustee, Cathedral Fabrics Commission for England; Chair, Birkenhead Education Trust. Three honorary doctorates; Two honorary fellowships. *The House Magazine* Home Affairs Campaigner of the Year, Dods Parliamentary Awards 2014. PC 1997.

Publications: Publications on low pay, poverty and social issues 1971-; Neighbours From Hell (2003); Attlee's Great Contemporaries (2009); Saints and Heroes (2010); Contributor, The Purple Book (Progress, 2011); Fixing Broken Britain? An audit of working-age welfare reform since 2010 (2016).

Rt Hon Frank Field MP, House of Commons, London SW1A 0AA
Tel: 020 7219 5193 *Fax:* 020 7219 0601 *Email:* fieldf@parliament.uk
Constituency: No constituency office publicised
Tel: 0800 028 0293 *Email:* edward.beardsley@parliament.uk *Website:* www.frankfield.co.uk
Twitter: @frankfieldteam

CONSERVATIVE

FIELD, MARK

Cities of London and Westminster *(Majority 3,148)*

Minister of State for Asia and the Pacific, Foreign and Commonwealth Office

Mark Christopher Field. Born 6 October 1964; Son of late Major Peter Field and Ulrike Field, née Peipe; Married Michèle Acton 1994 (divorced 2006); married Victoria Elphicke 2007 (1 son 1 daughter).

Education: Reading School; St Edmund Hall, Oxford (BA law 1987, MA) (JCR President); College of Law, Chester (Solicitors' Finals 1988).

Non-political career: Trainee solicitor 1988-90; Solicitor, Freshfields 1990-92; Employment consultant 1992-94; Director and co-owner, Kellyfield Consulting 1994-2001; Member, advisory board, London School of Commerce 2005-; Adviser: Ellwood & Atfield 2011-, Cains (lawyer) 2011-.

Political career: Contested Enfield North 1997 general election. Member for Cities of London and Westminster 2001-10, for Cities of London and Westminster (revised boundary) since 6 May 2010 general election; Opposition Whip 2003-04; Shadow Minister for London 2003-05; Shadow Financial Secretary to the Treasury 2005; Shadow Minister for Culture 2005-06; Member, Intelligence and Security Committee 2010-15; Minister of State for Asia and the Pacific, Foreign and Commonwealth Office 2017-. *Select committees:* Member: Constitutional Affairs 2003-04, Procedure 2008-10. Association/ward officer, Kensington and Chelsea and Islington North Associations 1989-99; Vice-chairman (International Affairs), Conservative Party -2017. *Councils and public bodies:* Councillor, Royal London Borough of Kensington and Chelsea 1994-2002.

Political interests: Economy, financial services, small businesses, foreign affairs, security, employment; Germany, India, USA.

Other: Liveryman, Merchant Taylors' Company. Freedom, City of London. PC 2015; City of London Club, Carlton Club, Royal Automobile Club.

Publications: Contributing Chapters to: A Blue Tomorrow (Politicos, 2001), Reforming the City (Forum Press, 2009); Various and regular articles for national newspapers on financial services, pensions and economic issues; Regular contributor to BBC Radio 4 *Westminster Hour*, Sky News, BBC 2 *Daily Politics*, ITV *Late Debate*; Author, Between the Crashes: Reflections and Insights on UK Politics and Global Economics in the Aftermath of the Financial Crisis (Biteback, 2013).

Recreations: Football, cricket, popular/rock music, walking in London, history of London.

Rt Hon Mark Field MP, House of Commons, London SW1A 0AA
Tel: 020 7219 8155 *Fax:* 020 7219 1980 *Email:* fieldm@parliament.uk
Constituency: 90 Ebury Street, London SW1W 9QD
Tel: 020 7730 8181 *Fax:* 020 7730 4520 *Email:* office@westminsterconservatives.co.uk
Website: www.markfieldmp.com *Twitter:* @MarkFieldUK

LABOUR

FITZPATRICK, JIM

Poplar and Limehouse *(Majority 27,712)*

James Fitzpatrick. Born 4 April 1952; Son of James Fitzpatrick and Jean Fitzpatrick, née Stones; Married Jane Lowe 1980 (divorced) (1 son 1 daughter); married Dr Sheila Hunter 2003.

Education: Holyrood Secondary, Glasgow; Limited French, German, Spanish, Bangla (Sylheti).

Non-political career: Trainee, Tytrak Ltd, Glasgow 1970-73; Driver, Mintex Ltd, London 1973-74; Firefighter, London Fire Brigade 1974-97. Fire Brigades Union: Member 1974-97, Member, National Executive Council 1988-97.

Political career: Member for Poplar and Canning Town 1997-2010, for Poplar and Limehouse since 6 May 2010 general election; PPS to Alan Milburn as Secretary of State for Health 1999-2001; Assistant Government Whip 2001-03; Government Whip (Vice-Chamberlain of HM Household) 2003-05; Parliamentary Under-Secretary of State: Office of the Deputy Prime Minister 2005-06, Department of Trade and Industry (Employment Relations, Postal Services, London) 2006-07, Department for Transport (Minister for Aviation, Shipping and Road Safety) 2007-09; Minister of State, Department for Environment, Food and Rural Affairs (Minister for Food, Farming and the Environment) 2009-10; Shadow Minister for: Environment, Food and Rural Affairs 2010, Transport 2010-13. *Select committees:* Member: Selection 2003-05, Environment, Food and Rural Affairs 2013-17, Transport 2013-15, Environment, Food and Rural Affairs Sub-committee 2015-17. Hon Treasurer, PLP London Regional Group 1999-2001. Member: SNP 1969-70, Labour Party -1977, Socialist Workers' Party 1978, Labour Party 1983-; Agent for Jo Richardson MP 1987; Member, London Labour Executive 1988-97; Chair: Barking Constituency Labour Party 1988-90, Greater London Labour Party 1991-97.

Political interests: Poverty, regeneration, racism, fire, animal welfare, transport, leasehold reform, markets; Bangladesh.

Other: Patron: Richard House Trust, Daneford Trust, Sreeper Village Orphanage, Bangladesh, Neighbours in Poplar, SS Robin, Ragged School Trust; Younger Brother, Trinity House. Worshipful Company of Shipwrights. Freedom, City of London. Fire Brigade Long Service and Good Conduct Medal (HMQ) 1994. Hon President: Millwall Rugby Football Club, Blackwall and District Rowing Club; Hon Vice-president, Poplar Bowls.

Recreations: Reading, TV/film, West Ham United FC.

Jim Fitzpatrick MP, House of Commons, London SW1A 0AA
Tel: 020 7219 5085/6215/020 7219 2776 (media) *Email:* jim.fitzpatrick.mp@parliament.uk
Constituency: Trussler Hall, 78 Grundy Street, London E14 6DR
Tel: 020 7536 0562 *Website:* www.jimfitzpatrickmp.org *Twitter:* @FitzMP

LABOUR

FLETCHER, COLLEEN

Coventry North East *(Majority 15,580)*

Opposition Whip

Colleen Margaret Fletcher. Born 23 November 1954; Daughter of Dot and Bill Dalton; Married (2 sons).

Education: Lyng Hall Comprehensive School; Henley College.

Non-political career: GEC, Coventry; Home Care Assistant, Coventry City Council; Customer Services Officer, Orbit Housing Group.

Political career: Member for Coventry North East since 7 May 2015 general election; PPS to Kerry McCarthy as Secretary of State for Environment, Food and Rural Affairs 2016; Opposition Whip 2017-; Member, National Policy Forum; Officer, West Midlands Regional Board. *Councils and public bodies:* Coventry City Council: Councillor 1992-2000, 2002-04, 2011-15, Former Cabinet Member for Community Safety, Chair: Labour Group, Scrutiny Co-ordination.

Colleen Fletcher MP, House of Commons, London SW1A 0AA
Tel: 020 7219 8036 *Email:* colleen.fletcher.mp@parliament.uk
Constituency: Unite House, Short Street, Coventry, Warwickshire CV1 2LS
Tel: 024 7663 0700 *Email:* smithnb@parliament.uk damian.gannon@parliament.uk
Website: colleenfletchermp.wordpress.com

LABOUR

FLINT, CAROLINE

Don Valley *(Majority 5,169)*

Caroline Louise Flint. Born 20 September 1961; Daughter of late Wendy Flint, née Beasley, clerical/shop employee; Married Saief Zammel (divorced) (1 son 1 daughter); married Phil Cole 2001 (1 stepson).

Education: Twickenham Girls School; Richmond Tertiary College; University of East Anglia (BA American history/literature and film studies 1983).

Non-political career: Graduate, Armed Forces Parliamentary Scheme. Management trainee, Greater London Council/Inner London Education Authority (ILEA) 1984-85; Policy officer, ILEA 1985-87; Head, Women's Unit, National Union of Students 1988-89; Lambeth Council 1989-93: Equal opportunities officer 1989-91, Welfare and staff development officer 1991-93; Senior researcher/political officer, GMB 1994-97. Former shop steward: NALGO at Greater London Council/Inner London Education Authority, GMB at Lambeth Council; Member: GMB, Community.

Political career: Member for Don Valley 1997-2010, for Don Valley (revised boundary) since 6 May 2010 general election; Joint PPS to Ministers of State, Foreign and Commonwealth Office 1999-2001; PPS: to Peter Hain as Minister of State: Department of Trade and Industry 2001, Foreign and Commonwealth Office 2001-02, to John Reid: as Minister without Portfolio and Party Chair 2002-03, as Leader of the House of Commons and President of the Council 2003; Parliamentary Under-Secretary of State (PUSS), Home Office 2003-05; Department of Health 2005-07: PUSS (Public Health) 2005-06, Minister of State (MoS) (Public Health) 2006-07; MoS, Department for Work and Pensions (Minister for Employment and Welfare Reform) 2007-08; Minister for Yorkshire and the Humber 2007-08; Minister for Housing and Planning (attending Cabinet), Department for Communities and Local Government 2008; MoS, Foreign and Commonwealth Office (Europe) 2008-09; Shadow Secretary of State for: Communities and Local Government 2010-11, Energy and Climate Change 2011-15. *Select committees:* Member: Education and Employment 1997-99, Education and Employment (Education Sub-Committee) 1997-99, Administration 2001-05, Modernisation of the House of Commons 2003, Public Accounts 2015-. Chair, PLP Departmental Group for Energy and Climate Change 2015-16. National Women's Officer, Labour Students 1983-85; Executive member, Labour Co-ordinating Committee 1984-85; Chair, Brentford and Isleworth CLP 1991-95; Facilitator, Labour National Policy Forums 1994-97; Associate editor, *Renewal* 1995-2000; Labour Party adviser to Police Federation of England and Wales 1999; Member, Trade Union Group of Labour MPs; Labour Friends of Israel; Friends of Labour Students; Labour Women's Network; Member, Economy – Living Standards and Sustainability Policy Commission; Contested Labour deputy leadership election 2015. *Councils and public bodies:* Governor, Strand on the Green Primary 1992-96.

Political interests: Employment, childcare, welfare to work, crime, education, housing.

Other: Member: Inter-Parliamentary Union 1997-, British American Parliamentary Group 1997-; Chair, Working For Childcare 1991-95; Board member: Sure Start Denaby Main Partnership 2000-03, Doncaster Early Years Development and Childcare Partnership 2001-03; President, Denaby United Football Club 2001-02; Member: Fabian Society, Progress. PC 2008.

Publications: Contributor, The Purple Book (Progress, 2011); The Power Book (LGIU, SERA, The Co-op Party, 2012).

Recreations: Cinema, family and friends.

Rt Hon Caroline Flint MP, House of Commons, London SW1A 0AA
Tel: 020 7219 4407 *Fax:* 020 7219 1277 *Email:* caroline.flint.mp@parliament.uk
Constituency: Meteor House, First Avenue, Auckley, Doncaster, South Yorkshire DN9 3GA
Tel: 01302 623330 *Fax:* 01302 775099 *Website:* www.carolineflint.org *Twitter:* @carolineflintmp

LABOUR

FLYNN, PAUL

Newport West *(Majority 5,658)*

Paul Philip Flynn. Born 9 February 1935; Son of late James and late Kathleen Flynn; Married Samantha Cumpstone 1985 (1 son 1 daughter (deceased) from previous marriage 1 stepson 1 stepdaughter).

Education: St Illtyd's College, Cardiff; University College of Wales, Cardiff; Welsh.

Non-political career: Chemist, steel industry 1962-83; Broadcaster, Gwent Community Radio 1983-84; Research officer to Llewellyn Smith MEP 1984-87.

Political career: Contested Denbigh October 1974 general election. Member for Newport West since 11 June 1987 general election; Opposition Spokesman on: Health and Social Security 1988-89, Social Security 1989-90; Board member, Parliamentary Office of Science and Technology (POST); Shadow Leader of the House of Commons 2016; Shadow Secretary of State for Wales 2016. *Select committees:* Member: Welsh Affairs 1997-98, 2016-, Environmental Audit 2003-05, Public Administration 2005-15, Political and Constitutional Reform 2011-15, Home Affairs 2013-15, Public Administration and Constitutional Affairs 2015-, Petitions 2015-17, Environment, Food and Rural Affairs 2017-. Secretary, Welsh Group of Labour MPs 1997-2000. *Councils and public bodies:* Councillor: Newport Council 1972-81, Gwent County Council 1974-83.

Political interests: Health, medicinal and illegal drugs, social security, pensions, animal welfare, devolution, Welsh affairs, constitutional reform, modernisation of Parliament; Afghanistan, Azerbaijan, Baltic States, Eastern Europe, Hungary, Israel, Romania.

Other: Member, UK Delegation to Council of Europe and Western European Union 1997-; Substitute Member, UK delegation, Parliamentary Assembly of the Council of Europe -2016. Campaign for Freedom of Information award 1991; Backbencher of the Year (jointly), Highland Park/ *The Spectator* 1996; Best Website of an Elected Representative, *New Statesman* 2000; MP Website Awards for Design, BCS 2008; MP of the Year, *Welsh Yearbook* 2009.

Publications: Commons Knowledge. How to be a Backbencher (1997); Baglu Mlaen (Staggering Forward, 1998); Dragons Led by Poodles (1999); The Unusual Suspect (2010); How to be an MP (Biteback, 2012); Clockwinder Who Wouldn't Say No (Biteback, 2012).

Recreations: Local history, photography.

Paul Flynn MP, House of Commons, London SW1A 0AA
Tel: 020 7219 3478 *Fax:* 020 7219 2433
Constituency: No constituency office publicised
Tel: 01633 262348 *Fax:* 01633 760532 *Email:* paulflynnmp@talk21.com
Website: www.paulflynnmp.co.uk *Twitter:* @PaulFlynnMP

CONSERVATIVE

FORD, VICKY

Chelmsford *(Majority 13,572)*

Victoria Grace Ford. Born 21 September 1967; Married Hugo Edward Rawlinson Ford 1996 (1 daughter 2 sons).

Education: St Paul's School, London; Marlborough College, Wiltshire; Trinity College, Cambridge (BA economics 1989, MA).

Non-political career: Vice-president, loans, JP Morgan, London 1988-2000; Managing director, loans, Bear Stearns International, London 2001-03.

Political career: Contested Birmingham Northfield 2005 general election. Member for Chelmsford since 8 June 2017; MEP for Eastern 2009-17: Chair, Internal Market and Consumer Protection Committee 2014-17. Deputy chair: South East Cambridgeshire Conservative Association 2004-08, Cambridgeshire and Bedfordshire Conservatives 2005-07. *Councils and public bodies:* Councillor, South Cambridgeshire District Council 2006-08.

Political interests: Finance, health, family, education, environment.

Other: Chair, Abington Pre-school; Treasurer, Akiki.

Recreations: Music, conservation, gardening, cooking, family.

Vicky Ford MP, House of Commons, London SW1A 0AA
Tel: 020 7219 0138 *Email:* vicky.ford.mp@parliament.uk
Constituency: 88 Rectory Lane, Chelmsford CM1 1RF
Tel: 01245 352872 *Website:* www.vickyford.uk *Twitter:* @vickyford

CONSERVATIVE

FOSTER, KEVIN

Torbay *(Majority 14,283)*

Team PPS, Department for Communities and Local Government

Kevin John Foster. Born 31 December 1978; Married Hazel Noonan 2017.

Education: Hele's School, Plymouth; Warwick University (LLB 2000; LLM international economic law 2001).

Non-political career: Called to the Bar 2002; Assistant to Philip Bradbourn MEP 2002-03; Criminal defence paralegal, Birmingham 2003-04.

Political career: Contested Coventry South 2010 general election. Member for Torbay since 7 May 2015 general election; Team PPS, Department for Communities and Local Government 2017-. *Select committees:* Member: Public Accounts 2015-17, Ecclesiastical Committee 2015-, Backbench Business 2015-17. Chairman, Conservative Backbench Policy Committee on Northern Ireland 2015-17. Member, Conservative Party 1995-; President, Warwick University Conservative Association 1998. *Councils and public bodies:* Coventry City Council: Councillor 2002-14, Deputy Leader of Council 2008-10, Council Leader 2011-13.

Other: Trustee, Coventry Law Centre; Director, Whiteley Community Centre.

Recreations: Coventry City FC.

Kevin Foster MP, House of Commons, London SW1A 0AA
Tel: 020 7219 4711 *Email:* kevin.foster.mp@parliament.uk
Constituency: 5-7 East Street, Torquay TQ2 5SD
Tel: 01803 214989 *Email:* kevin@kevinjfoster.com *Website:* www.kevinjfoster.com
Twitter: @kevin_j_foster

LABOUR

FOVARGUE, YVONNE

Makerfield *(Majority 13,542)*

Shadow Minister for Local Government

Yvonne Helen Fovargue. Born 29 November 1956; Daughter of late Kenneth Gibbon and late Irene Gibbon; Married Paul Kenny 2009 (1 daughter).

Education: Sale Girls Grammar School; Leeds University (BA English 1978); Manchester City College (PGCE English and religious studies 1979); NVQ strategic management level 5 2003.

Non-political career: Housing department, Manchester City Council: Housing information manager 1979-82, Estate manager 1982-86; Newton le Willows Citizens Advice Bureau/St Helen's District Citizens Advice Bureau: Manager 1986-92, Chief executive 1992-2010. Member 1979-: NALGO, NUPE, ASTMS, Amicus, Unite, USDAW.

Political career: Member for Makerfield since 6 May 2010 general election; Opposition Whip 2011-13; Shadow Minister for: Transport 2013, Defence 2013-14, 2015, Education 2014-15, Business, Innovation and Skills 2015-16, Local Government 2017-. *Select committees:* Member: Health 2010-11, Joint Committee on Consolidation, Etc, Bills 2010-15, Selection 2012-13, Procedure 2014-17. Vice-chair, PLP Departmental Group for Work and Pensions 2010-15. Vice-chair, Warrington South CLP 2008-10. *Councils and public bodies:* Councillor, Warrington Borough Council 2004-10.

Political interests: Third sector, consumer credit and debt, employment law, health, legal aid.

Other: Member, Mensa; Trustee and board member, St Helens CVS 2001-10.

Recreations: Reading, theatre, music.

Yvonne Fovargue MP, House of Commons, London SW1A 0AA
Tel: 020 7219 3000 *Email:* yvonne.fovargue.mp@parliament.uk
Constituency: Wigan Investment Centre, Waterside Drive, Wigan WN3 5BA
Tel: 01942 824029 *Website:* www.yvonnefovargue.com *Twitter:* @Y_FovargueMP

CONSERVATIVE

FOX, LIAM

North Somerset *(Majority 17,103)*

Secretary of State for International Trade; President of the Board of Trade

Born 22 September 1961; Son of William Fox, teacher, and Catherine Fox; Married Jesme Baird 2005.

Education: St Bride's High School, East Kilbride; Glasgow University (MB, ChB 1983; MROGP 1989).

Non-political career: Civilian Army Medical Officer. General practitioner, Beaconsfield, Buckinghamshire and Nailsea, North Somerset; Divisional surgeon, St John's Ambulance, Buckinghamshire.

Political career: Contested Roxburgh and Berwickshire 1987 general election. Member for Woodspring 1992-2010, for North Somerset since 6 May 2010 general election; PPS to Michael Howard as Home Secretary 1993-94; Assistant Government Whip 1994-95; Government Whip 1995-96; Parliamentary Under-Secretary of State, Foreign and Commonwealth Office 1996-97; Opposition Spokesperson for: Constitutional Affairs, Scotland and Wales 1997-99; Member Shadow Cabinet 1998-2010: Shadow Secretary of State for Health 1999-2003, Shadow Foreign Secretary 2005, Shadow Secretary of State for Defence 2005-10; Secretary of State for: Defence 2010-11, International Trade 2016-; President of the Board of Trade 2016-. *Select committees:* Member, Scottish Affairs 1992-93. Chair, Conservative Health/Social Services Policy Committee 2001-05. Chair, West of Scotland Young Conservatives 1983; National vice-chair, Scottish Young Conservatives 1983-84; Secretary, West Country Conservative Members' Committee 1992-93; Chair, Conservative Party 2003-05; Contested Conservative Party leadership 2005; Chair, South West Conservative MPs' Group 2015-; Vice-President, Conservatives for Britain 2015-16.

Political interests: Health, mental health, economic policy, foreign affairs, defence; USA.

Other: President, Glasgow University Club 1982-83; Guest of US State Department, involving study of drug abuse problems in USA, and Republican Party campaigning techniques 1985; Member: Central Committee, Families for Defence 1987-89, Campaign committee, Vote Leave 2016; Founder, Give Us Time 2012-. World Debating Competition, Toronto (Individual speaking prize) 1982; Best Speaker's Trophy, Glasgow University 1983. PC 2010.

Publications: Making Unionism Positive (1988); Rising Tides (2013).

Recreations: Tennis, swimming, cinema, theatre.

Rt Hon Dr Liam Fox MP, House of Commons, London SW1A 0AA
Tel: 020 7219 4198 *Email:* ione.douglas@parliament.uk
Constituency: No constituency office publicised *Website:* www.liamfox.co.uk
Twitter: @LiamFox

LABOUR

FOXCROFT, VICKY

Lewisham Deptford *(Majority 34,899)*

Opposition Whip

Victoria Jane Foxcroft. Born 9 March 1977.

Education: De Montfort University (BA 2000); French.

Non-political career: Research officer, AEEU 2002-05; Political officer, Amicus 2005-09; Finance sector officer, Unite 2009-15. Member: Unite, GMB.

Political career: Member for Lewisham Deptford since 7 May 2015 general election; Opposition Whip 2015-. *Select committees:* Member, Joint Committee on Statutory Instruments 2016-. Chair, Labour Students; Member: National Policy Forum, Labour Party; Co-operative Party. *Councils and public bodies:* Lewisham Council: Councillor 2010-14, Chair, Labour Group.

Political interests: Halting the reduction of services at Lewisham Hospital, building more homes and schools.

Vicky Foxcroft MP, House of Commons, London SW1A 0AA
Tel: 020 7219 5934 *Email:* vicky.foxcroft.mp@parliament.uk
Constituency: 82 Tanners Hill, Deptford, London SE8 4PN
Tel: 020 8469 4638 *Website:* www.vickyfoxcroft.org.uk *Twitter:* @vickyfoxcroft

CONSERVATIVE

FRANCOIS, MARK

Rayleigh and Wickford *(Majority 23,450)*

Mark Gino Francois. Born 14 August 1965; Son of Reginald Francois, engineer, and Anna Francois, née Carloni, cook; Married Karen Thomas 2000 (divorced 2006).

Education: St Nicholas Comprehensive School, Basildon; Bristol University (BA history 1986); King's College, London (MA war studies 1987).

Non-political career: TA 1983-89, Commissioned 1985. Management trainee, Lloyds Bank 1987; Market Access International (public affairs consultancy) 1988-95: Consultant, Director; Public affairs consultant, Francois Associates 1996-2001.

Political career: Contested Brent East 1997 general election. Member for Rayleigh 2001-10, for Rayleigh and Wickford since 6 May 2010 general election; Opposition Whip 2002-04; Shadow Economic Secretary 2004-05; Shadow Paymaster General 2005-07; Shadow Minister for Europe 2007-10; Government Whip (Vice-Chamberlain of HM Household) 2010-12; Ministry of Defence: Minister of State for: Defence Personnel, Welfare and Veterans 2012-13, the Armed Forces 2013-15; Minister of State for Communities and Resilience (Minister for Portsmouth), Department for Communities and Local Government 2015-16; Member, Speaker's Committee on the Electoral Commission 2015-16; Chair, Review into the use of Reserves in the Army 2016-. *Select committees:* Member: Environmental Audit 2001-05, European Standing Committee A 2002-05, Selection 2010-12, Administration 2010-12, Armed Forces Bill 2011, Defence 2017-. *Councils and public bodies:* Councillor, Basildon District Council 1991-95.

Political interests: Defence, local and regional government, housing, environment.

Other: Member, Royal United Services Institute for Defence Studies 1991-; President: Friends of Holy Trinity Church, Rayleigh 2002-, Rayleigh Division, St John Ambulance 2002-; Patron, Rayleigh Branch of Royal British Legion 2002-; President: Rayleigh Brass Band 2006-, Wyvern Community Transport 2008-; Patron, Rayleigh Bowls Club 2011-; National Patron, Cruse Bereavement Care. Member, Worshipful Company of Wheelwrights 2003-. Freedom, City of London 2004. PC 2010; Carlton Club, Rayleigh Conservative Club.

Recreations: Reading, sports, military history, travel.

Rt Hon Mark Francois MP, House of Commons, London SW1A 0AA
Tel: 020 7219 8287 *Fax:* 020 7219 1858 *Email:* mark.francois.mp@parliament.uk
Constituency: 25 Bellingham Lane, Rayleigh, Essex SS6 7ED
Tel: 01268 742044 *Fax:* 01268 741833 *Email:* enquiries@rayleighandwickfordconservatives.com
Websites: www.rayleighandwickfordconservatives.com www.markfrancois.com

CONSERVATIVE

FRAZER, LUCY

South East Cambridgeshire *(Majority 16,158)*

PPS to David Lidington as Lord Chancellor and Secretary of State for Justice

Lucy Claire Frazer. Born 17 May 1972; Married David Leigh 2002 (2 children).

Education: Leeds Girls' High School; Newnham College, Cambridge (BA law 1994) (President, Cambridge Union Society 1993).

Non-political career: Called to the Bar, Middle Temple 1996; Barrister, specialising in commercial law, South Square, Gray's Inn 1998-2015; QC 2013.

Political career: Member for South East Cambridgeshire since 7 May 2015 general election; PPS to: Ben Gummer as Minister for the Cabinet Office and Paymaster General 2016-17, David Lidington as Lord Chancellor and Secretary of State for Justice 2017-. *Select committees:* Member: Education 2015-17, Education, Skills and the Economy Sub-committee 2015-16. Deputy chair, Hampstead and Kilburn Conservative Association. *Councils and public bodies:* School governor.

Lucy Frazer QC MP, House of Commons, London SW1A 0AA
Tel: 020 7219 5082 *Email:* lucy.frazer.mp@parliament.uk
Constituency: Alexander House, 38 Forehill, Ely, Cambridgeshire CB7 4AF
Tel: 01353 664407 *Website:* www.lucyfrazer.org.uk *Twitter:* @LucyFrazerUK

CONSERVATIVE

FREEMAN, GEORGE

Mid Norfolk *(Majority 16,086)*

George William Freeman. Born 12 July 1967; Son of Arthur Freeman, National Hunt jockey and trainer, and Joanna Philipson; Married Eleanor Holmes (1 son 1 daughter).

Education: Radley College, Oxfordshire; Girton College, Cambridge (BA geography 1989); French.

Non-political career: Parliamentary officer, National Farmers Union 1990-92; Founder, Local Identity Agency 1992-97; Director, Early Stage Ventures, Merlin Ventures 1997-2001; Chief executive officer, Amedis Pharmaceuticals 2001-03; Director, 4D Biomedical 2003-11; Adviser to Norwich Research Park Venture Fund 2007-10; Non-executive director, Elsoms Seeds Ltd.

Political career: Contested Stevenage 2005 general election. Member for Mid Norfolk since 6 May 2010 general election; PPS to Gregory Barker as Minister of State for Climate Change, Department of Energy and Climate Change 2010-12; Adviser on Life Sciences to David Willetts as Minister of State for Universities and Science 2011-13; Trade Envoy to the Philippines 2014; Parliamentary Under-Secretary of State (Life Sciences), Department for Business, Innovation and Skills and Department of Health 2014-16. *Select committees:* Member, Communities and Local Government 2010. Founding member, 2020 group 2011-14; Chair, Prime Minister's Policy Board 2016-. *Councils and public bodies:* Governor, Bevington Primary School 1995-96; Board member, Greater Cambridge Partnership 2005-10.

Political interests: Constitution, crime, civil society, localism, rural economy, universities and innovation, biotechnology, healthcare reform; France, USA.

Other: Co-founder, Businesswise Learn to Earn 1995-97; Trustee, Cambridge Union Society 2005-09; Norfolk Club. Rob Roy Boat Club.

Recreations: Sailing, horseracing, hill-walking, rowing.

George Freeman MP, House of Commons, London SW1A 0AA
Tel: 020 7219 6502 *Email:* george.freeman.mp@parliament.uk
Constituency: 8 Damgate Street, Wymondham, Norfolk NR18 0BQ
Tel: 01953 600617 *Email:* george@georgefreeman.co.uk *Website:* www.georgefreeman.co.uk
Twitter: @Freeman_george

FREER, MIKE

Finchley and Golders Green *(Majority 1,657)*

CONSERVATIVE

Assistant Government Whip

Michael Whitney Freer. Born 29 May 1960; Married Angelo Crolla 2015.

Education: Chadderton Grammar School, Manchester; St Aidan's School, Carlisle.

Non-political career: Retail catering industry; Retail gaming industry; Relationship director, Barclays Bank plc; Self-employed consultant.

Political career: Contested Harrow West 2005 general election. Member for Finchley and Golders Green since 6 May 2010 general election; PPS: to Department for Communities and Local Government ministerial team 2013-14, to Nick Boles as Minister of State for Skills and Equalities, Department for Business, Innovation and Skills and Department for Education 2014, to Chris Grayling: as Leader of the House of Commons and Lord President of the Council 2015-16, as Secretary of State for Transport 2016-17; Assistant Government Whip 2017-. *Select committees:* Member: Communities and Local Government 2010-11, Scottish Affairs 2010-13, Work and Pensions 2013. Conservative Friends of Cyprus; Conservative Friends of Israel; Friend of British-Asian Conservative Link; Conservative Muslim Forum. *Councils and public bodies:* London Borough of Barnet Council: Councillor 1990-94, 2001-10, Council Leader 2006-09; Non-executive director, London Development Agency 2008-10; Vice-President, Local Government Association 2011-.

Political interests: Breast cancer screening, local government funding, local government reform, dementia, reducing cost of central government; Cyprus, Israel, Middle East, USA.

Other: Member, Friends of Windsor Open Space; Chair, Barnet Multi-faith Forum.

Recreations: Cycling, reading.

Mike Freer MP, House of Commons, London SW1A 0AA
Tel: 020 7219 7071 *Fax:* 020 7219 2211 *Email:* mike.freer.mp@parliament.uk
Constituency: 212 Ballards Lane, Finchley, London N3 2LX
Tel: 020 8445 5875 *Website:* www.mikefreer.com

FRITH, JAMES

Bury North *(Majority 4,375)*

LABOUR

James Richard Frith. Born 23 April 1977; Married Nikki (2 daughters 2 sons).

Education: Monkton Combe School, Bath; Taunton School, Somerset; Manchester Metropolitan University (BA politics and economics 2000).

Non-political career: Senior Finance Recruitment Consultant, Badenoch and Clark 2000-04; Campaign and Communications Manager, Labour Party 2004-05; Business, Education and Skills Policy Manager, Greater Manchester Chamber of Commerce 2005-07; U-Explore Ltd: Interim Managing Director and Head of Strategic Development 2007-10, Managing Director 2010-12; Director, Indicate Online 2013-16; Chief Executive, All Together Ltd 2013-17. Communication Workers Union; GMB.

Political career: Contested Bury North 2015 general election. Member for Bury North since 8 June 2017. *Select committees:* Member, Education 2017-. *Councils and public bodies:* Councillor, Bury Metropolitan Borough Council 2011-15.

Other: Board member, WhatUni.com 2014-; Director (unpaid), All Together Ltd.

James Frith MP, House of Commons, London SW1A 0AA
Tel: 020 7219 2907 *Email:* james.frith.mp@parliament.uk
Constituency: Freepost JAMES FRITH MP
Email: contact@jamesfrith.org *Website:* www.jamesfrith.org *Twitter:* @JamesFrith

FURNISS, GILL

Sheffield, Brightside and Hillsborough *(Majority 19,143)*

LABOUR

Shadow Minister for Steel, Postal Affairs and Consumer Protection

Gillian Furniss. Born 14 March 1957; Married Harry Harpham (died 2016) (MP for Sheffield, Brightside and Hillsborough 2015-16).

Education: Chaucer Comprehensive, Sheffield; Leeds Metropolitan University (BA library and information studies 1998).

Non-political career: Librarian, Firth Park, Parson Cross and Burngreave libraries, Sheffield College 1973-2000; Medical Records Clerk, Northern General Hospital 2008-15; Councillor, Sheffield City Council 1999-2016; Researcher to Harry Harpham MP 2015-16. GMB.

Political career: Contested Sheffield Hallam 2001 general election. Member for Sheffield, Brightside and Hillsborough since 5 May 2016 by-election; Shadow Minister for Steel, Postal Affairs and Consumer Protection 2016-. *Select committees:* Member, Women and Equalities 2016. *Councils and public bodies:* Sheffield City Council: Councillor 1999-2016, Former Cabinet Member for: Planning, Regeneration, Libraries, Parks, Waste management.

Political interests: Industrial strategy, climate change, women and equalities, health.

Other: Ambassador, Hallam FM's Cash for Kids.

Gill Furniss MP, House of Commons, London SW1A 0AA
Tel: 020 7219 0364 *Email:* gill.furniss.mp@parliament.uk
Constituency: Shirecliffe Community Centre, 349 Shirecliffe Road, Sheffield S5 8XJ
Tel: 0114-234 9079 *Website:* www.gillfurniss.com *Twitter:* @GillFurnissMP

FYSH, MARCUS

Yeovil *(Majority 14,723)*

CONSERVATIVE

Marcus John Hudson Fysh. Born 8 November 1970; Married Jenny 2011 (1 daughter).

Education: Oxford University (literature).

Non-political career: Mercury Asset Management 1993-2003; Set up own business in: Australia and India, Healthcare research.

Political career: Member for Yeovil since 7 May 2015 general election. *Select committees:* Member: Standing Orders 2015-, Public Administration and Constitutional Affairs 2016-, International Trade 2016-. *Councils and public bodies:* Councillor: South Somerset District Council 2011-15, Somerset County Council 2013-17.

Political interests: Infrastructure, rail and road transport, healthcare, education, housing.

Recreations: Cinema, playing cricket and tennis, spending time with family.

Marcus Fysh MP, House of Commons, London SW1A 0AA
Tel: 020 7219 4527 *Email:* marcus.fysh.mp@parliament.uk
Constituency: 21-22 High Street, Yeovil BA20 1RF
Tel: 01935 314321 *Email:* marcus@marcusfysh.org.uk *Website:* www.marcusfysh.org.uk
Twitter: @MarcusFysh

GAFFNEY, HUGH

Coatbridge, Chryston and Bellshill *(Majority 1,586)*

LABOUR

Hugh Lawrence Gaffney. Born 10 August 1963; Married Anne (3 children).

Non-political career: Royal Mail Parcelforce 1992-2017. Secretary, North Lanarkshire Trade Union Council; Scottish Political Officer, Communications Workers Union.

Political career: Member for Coatbridge, Chryston and Bellshill since 8 June 2017. *Select committees:* Member, Scottish Affairs 2017-. Contested Central Scotland region 2016 Scottish Parliament election. *Councils and public bodies:* Councillor, North Lanarkshire Council 2017-.

Hugh Gaffney MP, House of Commons, London SW1A 0AA
Tel: 020 7219 1655 *Email:* hugh.gaffney.mp@parliament.uk
Constituency: Municipal Buildings, Kildonan Street, Coatbridge ML5 3QW
Tel: 01236 434565 *Twitter:* @HughGaffneyMP

GALE, ROGER

North Thanet *(Majority 10,738)*

CONSERVATIVE

Roger James Gale. Born 20 August 1943; Son of Richard Gale, solicitor, and Phyllis Gale, née Rowell; Married Wendy Bowman 1964 (divorced 1967); married Susan Sampson 1971 (divorced 1980) (1 daughter); married Susan Marks 1980 (2 sons).

Education: Thomas Hardye School, Dorchester; Guildhall School of Music and Drama (LGSM&D 1963); French (working).

Non-political career: Advanced post-graduate, Parliament and Armed Forces Scheme. Freelance broadcaster 1963-; Programme director, Radio Scotland 1965; Personal assistant to general manager, Universal Films 1971-72; Freelance reporter, BBC Radio London 1972-73; Producer: Radio 1 *Newsbeat*, BBC Radio 4 *Today* 1973-76; Director, BBC Children's Television 1976-79; Senior producer, Children's Television, Thames TV; Editor, Teenage Unit; Producer special projects, Thames TV 1979-83. Member: National Union of Journalists -2005, Equity, BECTU -2005.

Political career: Contested Birmingham Northfield 1982 by-election. Member for North Thanet 1983-2010, for North Thanet (revised boundary) since 6 May 2010 general election; PPS to Ministers of State for the Armed Forces: Archibald Hamilton 1992-93, Jeremy Hanley 1993-94; Temporary Deputy Speaker May-June 2015. *Select committees:* Member: Home Affairs 1990-92, Broadcasting 1997-2005, Chairmen's Panel/Panel of Chairs 1997-, Procedure 2007-15, Ecclesiastical Committee 2015-, Court of Referees 2016-. Vice-chair, Conservative Party Committee for Culture, Media and Sport (Media) 1997-2001. President, Conservative Animal Welfare; Vice-chair: Holborn and St Pancras Conservative Association 1971-72, Conservative Party 2001-03. *Councils and public bodies:* Special constable, British Transport Police 2004-07.

Political interests: Education, animal welfare, media, broadcasting, tourism, leisure industry, licensed trade; Africa (Southern and Western), Cuba, Cyprus, Mongolia, Tunisia.

Other: Delegate: Council of Europe 1987-89, 2011-15, Western European Union 1987-89; International Election Observer: Armenia, Botswana, Gambia, Georgia, Ghana, Kenya, Macedonia, Mongolia, Mozambique, South Africa, Ukraine, Tunisia; Leader, UK Delegation, Council of Europe 2015-; Vice-President, St John (Kent); President, Herne Bay Air Cadets; Hon Member, British Veterinary Association; Lord's Taverners; Fellow, Industry and Parliament Trust; Chair, Try Angle Awards Foundation; Patron, Animals Worldwide; Former Chair and Trustee, Society for the Protection of Animals Abroad; Royal College of Defence Studies; LGSMD; Dogs Trust, Animal Health Trust, Scouts, St John Ambulance, RNLI, Animals Worldwide. Freedom, City of London. RSPCA Richard Martin Award for Outstanding Contribution to Animal Welfare. Kt 2012; Farmers' Club. Royal Temple Yacht.

Recreations: Swimming, sailing.

Sir Roger Gale MP, House of Commons, London SW1A 0AA
Tel: 020 7219 4087 *Email:* galerj@parliament.uk
Constituency: The Old Forge, 215a Canterbury Road, Birchington, Kent CT7 9AH
Tel: 01843 848588 (am) *Email:* suzy@galemail.com *Website:* www.rogergale.co.uk

GAPES, MIKE

Ilford South *(Majority 31,647)*

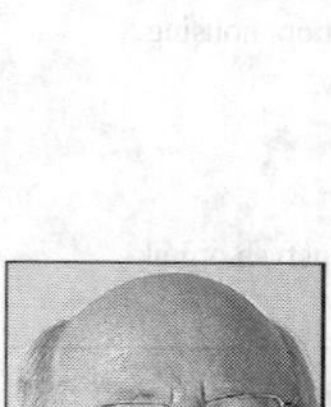

LAB/CO-OP

Michael John Gapes. Born 4 September 1952; Son of late Frank Gapes, postal worker, and Emily Gapes, office worker.

Education: Buckhurst Hill County High School; Fitzwilliam College, Cambridge (MA economics 1975); Middlesex Polytechnic, Enfield (Diploma industrial relations 1976); French.

Non-political career: Voluntary Service Overseas teacher, Swaziland 1971-72; Secretary, Cambridge Students' Union 1973-74; Chair, National Organisation of Labour Students 1976-77; National student organiser, Labour Party 1977-80; Research officer, Labour Party International Department 1980-88; Senior international officer, Labour Party 1988-92. Member, TGWU.

Political career: Contested Ilford North 1983 general election. Member for Ilford South since 9 April 1992 general election; PPS to: Paul Murphy as Minister of State, Northern Ireland Office 1997-99, Lord Rooker as Minister of State, Home Office 2001-02. *Select committees:* Foreign Affairs: Member 1992-97, 2010-, Chair 2005-10; Member: Defence 1999-2001, 2003-05, Liaison 2005-10, Quadripartite (Committees on Strategic Export Controls)/Arms Export Controls 2006-15, Joint Committee on National Security Strategy 2010, Panel of Chairs 2015-. Vice-chair, PLP Departmental Committee for Defence 1992-94, 1996-97; Chair, PLP Departmental: Committee for Children and the Family 1993-95, Group for Foreign Affairs 2010-. Member, Labour National Policy Forum and Joint Policy Committee 1996-2005; Chair, Co-operative Party, Parliamentary Group 2000-01; Trade union liaison officer, London Group of Labour MPs 2001-05.

Political interests: Defence, international affairs, European Union, economic policy, education, mental health.

Other: Vice-President, Council of European National Youth Committees 1977-79; Member: NATO Parliamentary Assembly 2002-05, 2010-, OSCE Parliamentary Assembly 2005-10; Inter-Parliamentary Union, British Group: Treasurer 2010-13, Vice-chair 2013-16; President, Redbridge United Chinese Association 1992-; Vice-President, Redbridge Chamber of Commerce 1992-; Member, Redbridge Racial Equality Council 1992-; Council member: Royal Institute of International Affairs 1996-99, Voluntary Service Overseas 1997-2010; Trustee, Parkside Community Association 1999-2010; Chair, Westminster Foundation for Democracy 2002-05; Fellow, Industry and Parliament Trust 2005; Ilford and Woodford Royal Airforce Association; Webb Memorial Trust; Shelter, Oxfam, Voluntary Service Overseas, Cardiac Risk in the Young. Vice-President, Ilford Football Club; West Ham United Supporters' Club.

Recreations: Watching football at West Ham, blues and jazz music.

Mike Gapes MP, House of Commons, London SW1A 0AA
Tel: 020 7219 6485 *Email:* mike.gapes.mp@parliament.uk
Constituency: No constituency office publicised *Website:* www.mikegapes.org
Twitter: @MikeGapes

LABOUR

GARDINER, BARRY

Brent North *(Majority 17,061)*

Shadow Secretary of State for International Trade; Shadow Minister for International Climate Change

Barry Strachan Gardiner. Born 10 March 1957; Son of late John Flannegan Gardiner, general manager Kelvin Hall, and late Sylvia Strachan, doctor; Married Caroline Smith 1979 (3 sons 1 daughter).

Education: Haileybury College, Hertford; St Andrews University (MA philosophy 1983); Harvard University (JF Kennedy Scholarship 1984); Cambridge University (research 1984-87); French, Russian.

Non-political career: Partner, Mediterranean Average Adjusting Co 1987-97; Occasional lecturer, Academy of National Economy, Moscow, Russia 1992-96. Member: MSF, GMB.

Political career: Member for Brent North 1997-2010, for Brent North (revised boundary) since 6 May 2010 general election; PPS to Beverley Hughes as Minister of State, Home Office 2002-04; Parliamentary Under-Secretary of State: Northern Ireland Office 2004-05, Department of Trade and Industry 2005-06, Minister for Biodiversity, Landscape and Rural Affairs, Department for Environment, Food and Rural Affairs 2006-07; Prime Minister's Special Envoy for Forestry 2007-08; PPS to Lord Mandelson as Secretary of State for Business, Enterprise and Regulatory Reform/Business, Innovation and Skills 2009-10; Leader of the Opposition's Special Envoy for Climate Change and the Environment 2011-15; Shadow Minister for: Natural Environment and Fisheries 2013-15, Water 2015, Energy and Climate Change 2015-16; Shadow Secretary of State for International Trade 2016-; Shadow Minister for International Climate Change 2016-. *Select committees:* Member: Procedure 1997-2001, Broadcasting 1998-2001, Public Accounts 1999-2002, Joint Committee on Consolidation of Bills Etc 2001-10, Energy and Climate Change 2010-13, Environment, Food and Rural Affairs 2011-13. Chair, PLP Departmental Committee for Culture, Media and Sport 2002-04; Vice-chair, PLP Departmental: Committee for the Treasury 2002-04, Group for Energy and Climate Change 2010-15; Chair, PLP Departmental Group for Environment, Food and Rural Affairs 2010-13. Member, Labour Finance and Industry Group; Former vice-chair, Labour Friends of Israel; Chair, Labour Friends of India 1999-2002, 2008-. *Councils and public bodies:* Cambridge City Council: Councillor 1988-94, Chair of Finance, Mayor 1992-93.

Political interests: Chinese community in the UK, economic policy, trade and industry, education, foreign affairs, environment, climate change, India-UK relations; Brazil, China, India, Russia, Sri Lanka.

Other: Former Chair of the Board, GLOBE International Ltd (Global Legislators Organisation); Fellow, Linnean Society; Director, GLOBE International 2016-; Associate, Chartered Insurance Institute; Fellow, The Linnean Society; Move It!, Fryent Country Park. Member, Shipwrights' Company. Freedom, City of London. Environmental Parliamentarian of the Year 2013.

Publications: Articles on: International trade, Brexit, shipping and maritime affairs, energy policy and the environment, science, nature and climate change, Political philosophy in *Philosophical Quarterly*.

Recreations: Walking, music, reading philosophy, bird-watching, singing, opera.

Barry Gardiner MP, House of Commons, London SW1A 0AA
Tel: 020 7219 4046 *Fax:* 020 7219 2495 *Email:* barry.gardiner.mp@parliament.uk
Constituency: No constituency office *Website:* www.barrygardiner.com *Twitter:* @BarryGardiner

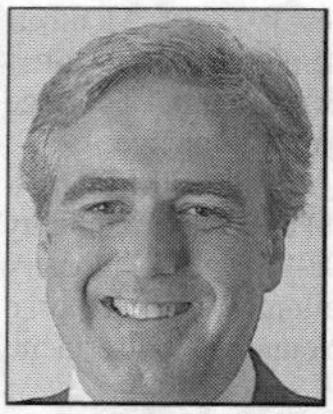

CONSERVATIVE

GARNIER, MARK

Wyre Forest *(Majority 13,334)*

Parliamentary Under-Secretary of State for Investment, Department for International Trade

Mark Robert Timothy Garnier. Born 26 February 1963; Son of late Peter Garnier, motoring writer, and Patricia Garnier, née Dowden, journalist; Married Caroline Joyce 2001 (2 sons 1 daughter).

Education: Charterhouse, Surrey.

Non-political career: Manager, Swiss Bank Corporation 1982-89; Managing director, South China Securities (UK) Ltd 1989-95; Executive director, Daiwa Europe Ltd 1995-96; Executive, LCF Edmond de Rothschild Securities 1996-97; Executive director, Bear Stearns 1998; Self-employed hedge fund adviser 1999-2005; Partner, CGR Capital LLP 2006-09; Senior partner, Severn Capital LLP 2009-.

Political career: Contested Wyre Forest 2005 general election. Member for Wyre Forest since 6 May 2010 general election; Trade Envoy to Burma, Brunei and Thailand 2016; Parliamentary Under-Secretary of State, Department for International Trade 2016- (covering Investment September 2017-). *Select committees:* Member: Treasury 2010-16, Parliamentary Commission on Banking Standards 2012-13, Finance 2015-16. Deputy chair (membership), Forest of Dean Conservative Association 2003-04; Founding member, Conservatives for Reform in Europe 2016. *Councils and public bodies:* Councillor, Forest of Dean District Council 2003-07; Member, Financial Services Trade and Investment Board 2016-.

Political interests: Economic issues, banking and financial regulation reform, financial education, tourism, European Union; China and emerging Asia, Middle East.

Other: Member, Steering Board, Kidderminster College; Fellow, Chartered Institute for Securities and Investment; Royal Society of Arts; Chairman, Investment Committee, Coachmakers of London. Court assistant, Worshipful Company of Coachmakers and Coach Harness Makers of London. Freedom, City of London; Royal Automobile Club, Carlton Club. North London Rifle Club.

Recreations: Historic aviation, historic motorsport, full-bore target rifle, shooting, fishing, photography, writing, skiing, squash.

Mark Garnier MP, House of Commons, London SW1A 0AA
Tel: 020 7219 7198 *Email:* mark.garnier.mp@parliament.uk
Constituency: 9a Lower Mill Street, Kidderminster, Worcestershire DY11 6UU
Tel: 01562 746771 *Website:* www.markgarnier.co.uk *Twitter:* @Mark4wyreForest

CONSERVATIVE

GAUKE, DAVID

South West Hertfordshire *(Majority 19,550)*

Secretary of State for Work and Pensions

David Michael Gauke. Born 8 October 1971; Son of Jim Gauke and Susan Hall; Married Rachel Rank 2000 (3 sons).

Education: Northgate High School, Ipswich; St Edmund Hall, Oxford (BA law 1993); College of Law, Chester (legal practice course 1995).

Non-political career: Parliamentary research assistant to Barry Legg MP 1993-94; Trainee solicitor, then solicitor, Richards Butler 1995-99; Solicitor, Macfarlanes 1999-2005.

Political career: Contested Brent East 2001 general election. Member for South West Hertfordshire 2005-10, for South West Hertfordshire (revised boundary) since 6 May 2010 general election; Shadow Exchequer Secretary to the Treasury 2007-10; HM Treasury: Exchequer Secretary 2010-14, Financial Secretary 2014-16, Chief Secretary to the Treasury 2016-17; Secretary of State for Work and Pensions 2017-. *Select committees:* Member: Procedure 2005-07, Treasury 2006-07, Joint Committee on Tax Law Rewrite Bills 2009. Deputy chair, Brent East Conservative Association 1998-2000; Member: Conservative Friends of Israel 2000-; Centre for Policy Studies 2003-.

Political interests: Education, Europe, tax, economy.

Other: Patron: Three Rivers Museum, Tring Sports Forum, Hospice of St Francis, Berkhamsted, Watford Peace Hospice, Rickmansworth Branch, British Legion; Law Society 1997; Friends of Watersmeet, Iain Rennie Hospice at Home. PC 2016; Rickmansworth Conservative Club, Tring Conservative Club.

Recreations: Football, cricket, country walks.

Rt Hon David Gauke MP, House of Commons, London SW1A 0AA
Tel: 020 7219 4459 *Fax:* 020 7219 4759 *Email:* gauked@parliament.uk
Constituency: South West Hertfordshire Conservative Association, Scots Bridge House, Scots Hill, Rickmansworth, Hertfordshire WD3 3BB
Tel: 01923 771781 *Fax:* 01923 779471 *Email:* david@davidgauke.com
Website: www.davidgauke.com *Twitter:* @DavidGauke

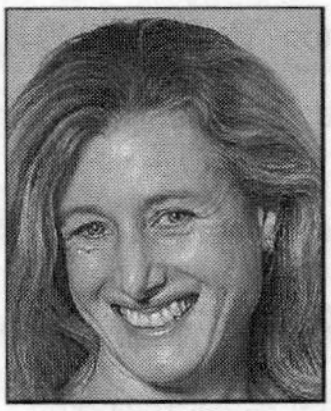

LABOUR

GEORGE, RUTH

High Peak *(Majority 2,322)*

Ruth Stephanie Nicole George. Born 27 November 1969; Married Mark (3 sons 1 daughter).

Education: Millfield School; Manchester University (BA politics and modern history).

Non-political career: Former tax accountant; Parliamentary Officer, Usdaw -2017.

Political career: Member for High Peak since 8 June 2017. *Select committees:* Member, Work and Pensions 2017-.

Other: Member, Whaley Bridge After-School Club Committee; Vice-chair, Chapel Vision.

Ruth George MP, House of Commons, London SW1A 0AA
Tel: 020 7219 1803 *Email:* ruth.george.mp@parliament.uk
Constituency: Details still to be confirmed *Website:* ruthforhighpeak.co.uk
Twitter: @RuthGeorge6

SCOTTISH NATIONAL PARTY

GETHINS, STEPHEN

North East Fife *(Majority 2)*

SNP Spokesperson for International Affairs and Europe

Stephen Patrick Gethins. Born 28 March 1976; Married (1 daughter).

Education: Antwerp University (international law 1997); Dundee University (Scots and international law 1999); Kent University (Research Masters politics and international affairs).

Non-political career: Project co-ordinator, Saferworld 2001-02; Head of Office, SNP Westminster Office 2003-05; Policy adviser, Committee of the Regions 2005-07; Senior executive, Scotland Europa 2007-09; Special adviser to Alex Salmond as First Minister, Scottish Government 2009-12; Independent advocacy and communications consultant and political commentator 2013-15.

Political career: Member for North East Fife since 7 May 2015 general election; SNP Spokesperson for: Europe 2015-, Exiting the European Union 2016-17, International Affairs 2017-. *Select committees:* Member, Foreign Affairs 2015-. Contested Scotland region 2014 European Parliament election. Deputy campaign director, SNP 'In' Europe campaign 2016.

Other: Trustee, Links Trust.

Stephen Gethins MP, House of Commons, London SW1A 0AA
Tel: 020 7219 5671 *Email:* stephen.gethins.mp@parliament.uk
Constituency: 38-40 Bonnygate, Cupar, Fife KY15 4LD
Tel: 01334 657765 *Website:* www.stephengethins.scot *Twitter:* @StephenGethins

CONSERVATIVE

GHANI, NUSRAT

Wealden *(Majority 23,628)*

Team PPS, Home Office

Nusrat Munir Ul-Ghani. Born 1 September 1972; Married.

Education: Bordesley Green Girls School; University of Central England; Leeds University (Masters international relations); Urdu, Hindi, Punjabi.

Non-political career: Age Concern; Breakthrough Breast Cancer; Clerk to All-Party Parliamentary Group on Breast Cancer; BBC World Service Trust.

Political career: Contested Birmingham, Ladywood 2010 general election. Member for Wealden since 7 May 2015 general election; Team PPS, Home Office 2017-; Member, Speaker's Committee on the Electoral Commission 2017-. *Select committees:* Member: Home Affairs 2015-17, Armed Forces Bill 2015 2015-16, Foreign Affairs 2017-. Deputy chair, Brentford and Isleworth Conservative Association; Parliamentary Liaison Officer, Conservative Rural Affairs Group 2016-.

Political interests: Agriculture and farming, security and defence, education and life chances.

Other: Member, Executive Committee, Commonwealth Parliamentary Association United Kingdom 2017-; Supporter: AgeUK, Breakthrough Breast Cancer, Refuge, RNIB, British Heart Foundation, Prostate Cancer UK, Médecins Sans Frontières/Doctors Without Borders.

Nusrat Ghani MP, House of Commons, London SW1A 0AA
Tel: 020 7219 4619 *Email:* nusrat.ghani.mp@parliament.uk
Constituency: No constituency office publicised *Website:* www.nusghani.org.uk
Twitter: @Nus_Ghani

CONSERVATIVE

GIBB, NICK

Bognor Regis and Littlehampton *(Majority 17,494)*

Minister of State for School Standards and Minister for Equalities, Department for Education

Nicolas John Gibb. Born 3 September 1960; Son of late John Gibb, civil engineer, and Eileen Gibb, schoolteacher; Married Michael Simmonds 2015.

Education: Maidstone Boys' Grammar School, Kent; Roundhay School, Leeds; Thornes House School, Wakefield; Durham University (BA law 1981).

Non-political career: Chartered accountant, specialising in taxation, KPMG, London 1984-97.

Political career: Contested Stoke-on-Trent Central 1992 general election and Rotherham 1994 by-election. Member for Bognor Regis and Littlehampton 1997-2010, for Bognor Regis and Littlehampton (revised boundary) since 6 May 2010 general election; Opposition Spokesperson for: the Treasury December 1998-99, Trade and Industry 1999-2001, Transport, Local Government and the Regions 2001; Shadow Minister for: Education and for Young People 2005, Schools 2005-10; Department for Education: Minister of State for: Schools 2010-12, 2015-16, School Reform 2014-15, School Standards 2016-, Minister for Equalities 2017-. *Select committees:* Member: Social Security 1997-98, Treasury 1998, Treasury (Treasury Sub-Committee) 1998, Public Accounts 2001-03, Education and Skills 2003-05; Chair, Joint Committee on Voting Eligibilty (Prisoners) Bill 2013. Member, Number 10 Policy Advisory Board 2013-14.

Political interests: Economics, taxation, education, social security; Israel, USA.

Other: Patron: Bognor Regis Shopmobility, Arun Community Transport, Littlehampton, Sammy Community Transport, Bognor Regis, Arun Sports Association for the Disabled, Littlehampton Sailing and Motorboat Club, West Sussex South Motor Neurone Disease Association, St Barnabas House Hospice, Worthing; Fellow, Institute of Chartered Accountants in England and Wales. PC 2016.

Recreations: Long-distance running, skiing.

Rt Hon Nick Gibb MP, House of Commons, London SW1A 0AA
Tel: 020 7219 6374 *Email:* gibbn@parliament.uk
Constituency: 2 Flansham Business Centre, Hoe Lane, Bognor Regis, West Sussex PO22 8NJ
Tel: 01243 587016/01243 585506 *Website:* www.nickgibb.org.uk *Twitter:* @NickGibbUK

SCOTTISH NATIONAL PARTY

GIBSON, PATRICIA

North Ayrshire and Arran *(Majority 3,633)*

SNP Spokesperson for Consumer Affairs

Born 12 May 1968; Née Duffy. Married Kenneth Gibson 2007 (MSP for Cunninghame North).

Education: Glasgow University (BA English and politics 1991).

Non-political career: English teacher for 20 years, Glasgow, Lanarkshire and East Renfrewshire; Parliamentary adviser to Kenneth Gibson MSP.

Political career: Contested North Ayrshire and Arran 2010 general election. Member for North Ayrshire and Arran since 7 May 2015 general election; SNP Spokesperson for Consumer Affairs 2017-. *Select committees:* Member: Procedure 2015-17, Backbench Business 2017-. *Councils and public bodies:* Glasgow City Council: Councillor 2007-12, SNP Spokesperson for Education.

Political interests: Anti-austerity, anti-Trident, Scottish home rule.

Other: Member, General Teaching Council.

Patricia Gibson MP, House of Commons, London SW1A 0AA
Tel: 020 7219 5748 *Email:* patricia.gibson.mp@parliament.uk
Constituency: 78 Princes Street, Ardrossan, North Ayrshire KA22 8DF
Tel: 01294 603774 *Website:* www.patriciagibson.org *Twitter:* @PGibsonSNP

SINN FÉIN

GILDERNEW, MICHELLE

Fermanagh and South Tyrone *(Majority 875)*

Michelle Angela Grainne Gildernew. Born 28 March 1970; Married Jimmy Taggert (2 sons 1 daughter).

Education: St Catherine's College, Armagh; Ulster University, Coleraine.

Political career: Member for Fermanagh and South Tyrone 2001-15. Contested Fermanagh and South Tyrone 2015 general election. Member for Fermanagh and South Tyrone since 8 June 2017; MLA for Fermanagh and South Tyrone 1998-2012, 2016-17: Sinn Féin Spokesperson for: Social Development, Women's issues, Member, Preparation for Government Committee 2006-07, Minister of Agriculture and Rural Development 2007-11, Sinn Féin Spokesperson for Health 2011-12. Sinn Féin: Member, Inter-Party talks team; Press officer 1997; Head of London office 1997-98.

Political interests: Housing, rural affairs, education.

Other: Aghaloo GFC.

Michelle Gildernew MP, House of Commons, London SW1A 0AA
Tel: 020 7219 3000 *Email:* michelle.gildernew.mp@parliament.uk
Constituency: Details still to be confirmed *Twitter:* @gildernewm

GILL, PREET KAUR

Birmingham, Edgbaston *(Majority 6,917)*

LAB/CO-OP

Born November 1972; Married.

Education: University of East London (Degree sociology and social work).

Non-political career: Team manager, Children Young People and Families Directorate, Birmingham City Council. Member, Unison.

Political career: Member for Birmingham, Edgbaston since 8 June 2017. *Select committees:* Member, Home Affairs 2017-. *Councils and public bodies:* Sandwell Council: Councillor 2012-, Cabinet Member for Public Health and Protection 2016-17; Member, West Midlands Combined Authority.

Other: Non-executive director, Spring Social Housing Board; Bank Inspector, Care Quality Commission; Vice-chair, West Midlands Race and Equality Board; Member: Sikh Network, Jo Cox Women In Leadership.

Preet Kaur Gill MP, House of Commons, London SW1A 0AA
Tel: 020 7219 2879 *Email:* preet.gill.mp@parliament.uk
Constituency: Details still to be confirmed
Tel: 0121-392 8426 *Website:* www.preetkaurgill.com *Twitter:* @PreetKGillMP

GILLAN, CHERYL

Chesham and Amersham *(Majority 22,140)*

CONSERVATIVE

Cheryl Elise Kendall Gillan. Born 21 April 1952; Daughter of late Adam Gillan, company director, and late Mona Gillan; Married John Coates Leeming 1985.

Education: Cheltenham Ladies' College; College of Law; Chartered Institute of Marketing.

Non-political career: International Management Group 1977-84; Director, British Film Year 1984-86; Senior marketing consultant, Ernst and Young 1986-91; Marketing director, Kidsons Impey 1991-93; Consultant, PKF 1999-2005.

Political career: Member for Chesham and Amersham 1992-2010, for Chesham and Amersham (revised boundary) since 6 May 2010 general election; PPS to Viscount Cranborne as Leader of the House of Lords and Lord Privy Seal 1994-95; Parliamentary Under-Secretary of State, Department of Education and Employment 1995-97; Shadow Minister for: Trade and Industry 1997-98, Foreign and Commonwealth Affairs 1998-2001, International Development 1998-2001; Opposition Whip 2001-03; Shadow Minister for Home Affairs 2003-05; Shadow Secretary of State for Wales 2005-10; Secretary of State for Wales 2010-12; Member, Speaker's Committee for the Independent Parliamentary Standards Authority 2015-. *Select committees:* Member: Science and Technology 1992-95, Procedure 1994-95, Public Accounts 2003-04, Public Administration 2014-15, Panel of Chairs 2015-, Public Administration and Constitutional Affairs 2015-. Vice-chairman, 1922 Committee 2015-; Chairman, Conservative Backbench Policy Committee on Business, Innovation and Skills 2015-17. Contested Greater Manchester Central 1989 European Parliament election.

Political interests: Industry, space, international affairs, defence, education, employment; China, Commonwealth, Europe, Hungary, Japan, Pacific Rim, Poland, former Soviet Union, USA.

Other: Member, Executive Committee, Commonwealth Parliamentary Association (CPA) UK Branch 1998-: UK Representative British Islands and Mediterranean region 1999-2004, International treasurer 2004-06; Member: NATO Parliamentary Assembly 2003-05, UK Delegation, Parliamentary Assembly of the Council of Europe 2012-15, 2016-; Chair, Bow Group 1987-88; Trustee, Parliamentary Choir; FCIM. Member, Worshipful Company of Marketors. Freedom, City of London. MP of the Year, *Wales Yearbook* awards 2011. PC 2010; Royal Automobile Club.

Recreations: Golf, music, gardening.

Rt Hon Cheryl Gillan MP, House of Commons, London SW1A 0AA
Tel: 020 7219 4061 *Email:* cheryl.gillan.mp@parliament.uk
Constituency: 7a Hill Avenue, Amersham, Buckinghamshire HP6 5BD
Tel: 01494 721577 *Email:* shawmj@parliament.uk *Website:* www.cherylgillan.co.uk
Twitter: @CherylGillan

GIRVAN, PAUL

South Antrim *(Majority 3,208)*

DEMOCRATIC UNIONIST PARTY

DUP Spokesperson for Education and Transport

William Paul Girvan. Born 6 July 1963; Son of William and Annie Girvan; Married Mandy Girvan (1 son 1 daughter).

Education: Ballyclare Secondary School; Newtownabbey Technical College; Ulster University.

Non-political career: Director, Grow South Antrim Ltd 2009-15.

Political career: Member for South Antrim since 8 June 2017; DUP Spokesperson for Education and Transport 2017-. *Select committees:* Member, Transport 2017-. MLA for South Antrim 2003-07, (replacement) 1 July 2010 to 2011, and for South Antrim (revised boundary) 2011-17: Assembly Private Secretary to Peter Robinson as First Minister 2011-15. *Councils and public bodies:* Newtownabbey Borough Council: Councillor 1997-2013, Deputy Mayor 2001-02, Mayor 2002-03, 2003-04; Member: Newtownabbey District Policing Board, Metropolitan Area Plan Advisory Team; Governor, Ballyclare Secondary School.

Countries of interest: Israel, USA.

Other: Director, Ballyclare Community Concerns; Member, Orange Institution; Chest Heart and Stroke; Action Cancer.

Recreations: Fishing, motorsport, athletics.

Paul Girvan MP, House of Commons, London SW1A 0AA
Tel: 020 7219 3987 *Email:* paul.girvan.mp@parliament.uk
Constituency: 29a The Square, Ballyclare BT39 9BB
Tel: 028 9334 0111 *Twitter:* @PaulGirvanMP

GLEN, JOHN

Salisbury *(Majority 17,333)*

CONSERVATIVE

Parliamentary Under-Secretary of State for Arts, Heritage and Tourism, Department for Digital, Culture, Media and Sport

John Philip Glen. Born 1 April 1974; Son of Philip Glen, nursery man, and Thalia Glen, hairdresser; Married Emma O'Brien 2008 (1 stepson 1 stepdaughter).

Education: King Edward's School, Bath; Mansfield College, Oxford (BA modern history 1996 (Student Union President); Judge Institute, Cambridge (MBA 2003); Royal College of Defence Studies, King's College London (MA International Security and Strategy 2014).

Non-political career: Parliamentary researcher to Michael Bates MP and Gary Streeter MP 1996-97; Strategy consultant, Andersen Consulting 1997-2004: Head of political section, Office of William Hague MP as Leader of the Opposition (on secondment) 2000-01; Research Department, Conservative Party: Deputy director 2004-05, Director 2005-06; Senior adviser to global head of strategy, Accenture 2006-10; Director, Walton Bates 2007-11.

Political career: Contested Plymouth Devonport 2001 general election. Member for Salisbury since 6 May 2010 general election; PPS: to Eric Pickles: as Secretary of State for Communities and Local Government 2012-15, as Minister for Faith 2014-15, to Sajid Javid as Secretary of State for Business, Innovation and Skills and President of the Board of Trade 2015-16, to Philip Hammond as Chancellor of the Exchequer 2016-17; Parliamentary Under-Secretary of State for Arts, Heritage and Tourism, Department for Digital, Culture, Media and Sport 2017-. *Select committees:* Member: Defence 2010-12, Arms Export Controls 2010-12, Work and Pensions 2015-16. Member, Number 10 Policy Advisory Board (Home Affairs and Constitution) 2014-15; Parliamentary Chair, Conservative Christian Fellowship 2015-16. *Councils and public bodies:* JP, Westminster 2006-12.

Political interests: Policy development, youth issues, armed forces, foreign affairs, education, health; Maldives, Uganda, USA.

Other: Board member, Centre for Policy Studies 2009-10; Chippenham Constitutional Club.

Recreations: Church, family, eating out, friends.

John Glen MP, House of Commons, London SW1A 0AA
Tel: 020 7219 7138 *Fax:* 020 7219 3951 *Email:* john.glen.mp@parliament.uk
Constituency: The Morrison Hall, 12 Brown Street, Salisbury, Wiltshire SP1 1HE
Tel: 01722 323050 *Fax:* 01722 327080 *Website:* www.johnglen.org.uk
Twitter: @JohnGlenUK

LABOUR

GLINDON, MARY

North Tyneside *(Majority 19,284)*

Mary Theresa Glindon. Born 13 January 1957; Daughter of Margaret and Cecil Mulgrove; Married Raymond Glindon 2000 (1 daughter 1 stepson 1 stepdaughter).

Education: Sacred Heart Grammar School, Fenham, Newcastle upon Tyne; Newcastle upon Tyne Polytechnic (BSc sociology 1979).

Non-political career: Clerical officer, civil service 1980-85; Administrator, local government 1987-88; Administrator/community development/manager, Centre for Unemployment 1988-2004; Administrator, NHS call centre 2005; Trainee dispenser, NHS 2005-06; Travel sales adviser, call centre 2006; Sales assistant, department store 2006-08; Administration officer, Department for Work and Pensions and Child Maintenance and Enforcement Commission 2008-10. Member: North Tyneside Trades Union Council, GMB.

Political career: Member for North Tyneside since 6 May 2010 general election; Shadow Minister for Farming and Rural Communities 2016-17. *Select committees:* Member: Environment, Food and Rural Affairs 2010-15, Unopposed Bills (Panel) 2011-15, Communities and Local Government 2013-15, Transport 2015-16. Member, Labour Party 1990-; Former constituency chair and vice-chair -2010. *Councils and public bodies:* Councillor, North Tyneside Council 1995-2010; Deputy Mayor 1998-99, Mayor 1999-2000.

Political interests: Employment, housing, health, environment, older people's issues; Middle East.

Other: Founding member and treasurer, Battle Hill Community Development Project 1983-; Kettlewell Education Trust; YMCA, Scouts.

Recreations: Travel, history, walking.

Mary Glindon MP, House of Commons, London SW1A 0AA
Tel: 020 7219 3000 *Fax:* 020 7219 3272 *Email:* mary.glindon.mp@parliament.uk
Constituency: Swans Centre For Innovation, Station Road, Wallsend NE28 6HJ
Tel: 0191-234 2493 *Email:* mary.glindon@maryglindonmp.co.uk
Websites: www.northtynesidelabour.co.uk www.maryglindonmp.co.uk

LABOUR

GODSIFF, ROGER

Birmingham, Hall Green *(Majority 33,944)*

Roger Duncan Godsiff. Born 28 June 1946; Son of late George Godsiff, chargehand/fitter, and Gladys Godsiff; Married Julia Morris 1977 (1 son 1 daughter).

Education: Catford Comprehensive School, London.

Non-political career: Banking 1965-70; Political officer, APEX 1970-88; Senior research officer, GMB 1988-91; Chair (unpaid), South of England Foundation 2001-; Director (unpaid), Syrian Society -2011. Member of, and sponsored by, GMB.

Political career: Contested Birmingham Yardley 1983 general election. Member for Birmingham Small Heath 1992-97, for Birmingham Sparkbrook and Small Heath 1997-2010, for Birmingham, Hall Green since 6 May 2010 general election; Member, Co-operative Party. *Councils and public bodies:* London Borough of Lewisham: Councillor 1971-90, Mayor 1977.

Political interests: European Union, foreign affairs, sport, recreation, immigration; Asia, Middle East, Indian sub-continent, Japan, USA.

Other: Member, Executive Committee, IPU 1999; Fellow, Industry and Parliament Trust 1994; Chair, Charlton Athletic Community Trust 2002-. Japanese Order of the Rising Sun Gold and Silver Star 2014. Member, Charlton Athletic Supporters Club.

Recreations: Sport in general, particularly football.

Roger Godsiff MP, House of Commons, London SW1A 0AA
Tel: 020 7219 5191 *Email:* roger.godsiff.mp@parliament.uk
Constituency: No constituency office publicised *Website:* www.rogergodsiffmp.co.uk
Twitter: @RogerGodsiff

CONSERVATIVE

GOLDSMITH, ZAC

Richmond Park *(Majority 45)*

Frank Zacharias Robin Goldsmith. Born 20 January 1975; Son of Sir James Goldsmith and Lady Annabel Vane-Tempest-Stewart; Married Sheherazade Ventura-Bentley 1999 (divorced 2010) (1 son 2 daughters); married Alice Rothschild 2013 (1 son 1 daughter).

Education: Eton College.

Non-political career: Redefining Progress, San Francisco, USA 1994-95; International Society for Ecology and Culture 1995-97; Editor, *Ecologist* 1997-2007.

Political career: Member (Con) for Richmond Park 2010 to 25 October 2016. Contested (Ind) Richmond Park 2016 by-election. Member (Con) for Richmond Park since 8 June 2017. *Select committees:* Member, Environmental Audit 2010-16, 2017-. Contested 2016 London mayoral election. Deputy Chair, Quality of Life Policy Group, Conservative Party 2005-07.

Political interests: Environment, democratic reform, health, small business.

Other: Trustee, Aspinall Foundation; Director: Countryside Restoration Trust, Rainforest Foundation UK. Beacon Prize for Young Philanthropist of the Year 2003; International Environmental Leadership, Global Green Award 2004; Richmond Green Champion 2010; Politician of the Year, Business Leaders Award 2011; Sustainable National Politician of the Year, Blue & Green Tomorrow 2013; MP of the year, Patchwork 2014, 2015; The Newcomer (Conservative) MP of the Year 2014; Overall MP for Year 2014-15; Backbencher of the year, Asian Voices 2015; Change Opinions (Political) Award, Westbourne 2015.

Publications: Author, The Constant Economy (Atlantic Books, 2009).

Zac Goldsmith MP, House of Commons, London SW1A 0AA
Tel: 020 7219 4578
Constituency: 372 Upper Richmond Road West, London SW14 7JU
Tel: 020 8878 7866 *Email:* zac@zacgoldsmith.com *Website:* www.zacgoldsmith.com
Twitter: @ZacGoldsmith

LABOUR

GOODMAN, HELEN

Bishop Auckland *(Majority 502)*

Shadow Minister for Foreign and Commonwealth Office

Helen Catherine Goodman. Born 2 January 1958; Daughter of Alan and Hanne Goodman; Married Charles Seaford 1988 (2 children).

Education: Lady Manners School, Bakewell; Somerville College, Oxford (BA philosophy, politics and economics 1979).

Non-political career: Research assistant to Phillip Whitehead MP 1979-80; Civil servant, ending as Head of Strategy Unit, HM Treasury 1980-97; Adviser, Czechoslovak Prime Minister's Office 1990-91; Director, Commission on Future of Multi Ethnic Britain 1998; Head of strategy, Children's Society 1998-2002; Chief executive, National Association of Toy and Leisure Libraries 2002-05. FDA branch secretary, HM Treasury 1986-88; Member, GMB.

Political career: Member for Bishop Auckland 2005-10, for Bishop Auckland (revised boundary) since 6 May 2010 general election; PPS to Harriet Harman as Minister of State, Ministry of Justice 2007; Parliamentary Secretary, Office of the Leader of the House of Commons 2007-08; Assistant Government Whip 2008-09; Parliamentary Under-Secretary of State, Department for Work and Pensions 2009-10; Shadow Minister for: Work and Pensions 2010, Justice 2010-11, Culture, Media and Sport 2011-14, Welfare Reform 2014-15, Foreign and Commonwealth Office 2017-. *Select committees:* Member: Public Accounts 2005-07, Joint Committee on the Draft Climate Change Bill 2007, Ecclesiastical Committee 2010-, Procedure 2010-14, 2016-, Treasury 2015-17. Chair, Camden Co-operative Party 1997-98; Member, National Policy Forum 2005-07.

Political interests: Economics, environment, children, international development, human rights; Czech Republic, Denmark.

Recreations: Cooking, family.

Helen Goodman MP, House of Commons, London SW1A 0AA
Tel: 020 7219 4346 *Fax:* 020 7219 0444 *Email:* goodmanh@parliament.uk
Constituency: 1 Cockton Hill Road, Bishop Auckland, Co Durham DL14 6EN
Tel: 01388 603075 *Fax:* 01388 603075 *Website:* www.helengoodman.org.uk
Twitter: @HelenGoodmanMP

CONSERVATIVE

GOODWILL, ROBERT

Scarborough and Whitby *(Majority 3,435)*

Minister of State for Children and Families, Department for Education

Born 31 December 1956; Son of Robert Goodwill and Joan Goodwill; Married Maureen Short 1987 (2 sons 1 daughter).

Education: Bootham School, York; Newcastle University (BSc agriculture 1979); German.

Non-political career: Farmer 1979-; Director, Mowthorpe (UK) Ltd. Member, then branch chairman, National Farmers Union.

Political career: Contested Redcar 1992 and North West Leicestershire 1997 general elections. Member for Scarborough and Whitby since 5 May 2005 general election; Opposition Whip 2006-07; Shadow Minister for Transport 2007-10; Assistant Government Whip 2010-12; Government Whip (Lord Commissioner of HM Treasury) 2012-13; Department for Transport: Parliamentary Under-Secretary of State 2013-15, Minister of State 2015-16; Flooding envoy for Yorkshire 2016-; Minister of State for: Immigration, Home Office 2016-17, Children and Families, Department for Education 2017-. *Select committees:* Member, Transport 2005-06. European Parliament: Contested Cleveland and Richmond 1994 and Yorkshire (South) 1998 elections; MEP for Yorkshire and the Humber 1999-2004: Deputy Conservative leader 2003-04.

Political interests: Agriculture, fisheries, environment, transport; Belarus, Moldova, Ukraine.

Other: Patron, National Traction Engine Trust; Farmers' Club.

Recreations: Steam ploughing, travel.

Robert Goodwill MP, House of Commons, London SW1A 0AA
Tel: 020 7219 8268 *Fax:* 020 7219 8108 *Email:* robert.goodwill.mp@parliament.uk
Constituency: 6 Albemarle Crescent, Scarborough, North Yorkshire YO11 1XS
Tel: 01723 365656 *Website:* www.robertgoodwill.co.uk

CONSERVATIVE

GOVE, MICHAEL

Surrey Heath *(Majority 24,943)*

Secretary of State for Environment, Food and Rural Affairs

Michael Andrew Gove. Born 26 August 1967; Son of Ernest and Christine Gove; Married Sarah Vine 2001 (1 daughter 1 son).

Education: Robert Gordon's College, Aberdeen; Lady Margaret Hall, Oxford (BA English 1988).

Non-political career: Reporter, *Press and Journal*, Aberdeen 1989; Researcher/reporter, Scottish Television 1990-91; Reporter, BBC News and Current Affairs 1991-96; *The Times*: Writer and editor 1996-2005, Writer 2005-. National Union of Journalists 1989-.

Political career: Member for Surrey Heath since 5 May 2005 general election; Shadow Minister for Housing 2005-07; Shadow Secretary of State for Children, Schools and Families 2007-10; Secretary of State for Education 2010-14; Parliamentary Secretary to the Treasury; Chief Whip 2014-15; Member Parliamentary and Political Service Honours Committee 2014-15; Lord Chancellor and Secretary of State for Justice 2015-16; Secretary of State for Environment, Food and Rural Affairs 2017-. *Select committees:* Member: European Scrutiny 2005-07, Exiting the European Union 2016-17.

Political interests: Education, crime, terrorism; Canada, Colombia, Germany, Indonesia, Iraq, Ireland, Israel, Italy, Jordan, Poland, Vietnam.

Other: Member, Education, Youth, Culture and Sport Council, Council of the European Union 2010-14; Chair, Policy Exchange 2003-05; President, Industry and Parliament Trust 2015-16; Co-convenor, Campaign Committee, Vote Leave 2016; Founding supporter, Change Britain 2016-; Public speaker, London Speaker Bureau and Chartwell Speakers 2016-; Member, Advisory Board, Red Tape Initiative 2017. Minister of the Year, *Spectator* awards 2011. PC 2010; Garrick Club.

Publications: Michael Portillo – The Future of the Right (Fourth Estate, 1995); The Price of Peace (CPS, 2000); Celsius 7/7 (Weidenfeld-Nicolson, 2005).

Rt Hon Michael Gove MP, House of Commons, London SW1A 0AA
Tel: 020 7219 3000 *Fax:* 020 7219 4829 *Email:* michael.gove.mp@parliament.uk
Constituency: Curzon House, Church Road, Windlesham, Surrey GU20 6BH
Tel: 01276 472468 *Fax:* 01276 451602 *Email:* office@shca.org.uk
Website: www.michaelgove.com *Twitter:* @michaelgove

SCOTTISH NATIONAL PARTY

GRADY, PATRICK

Glasgow North *(Majority 1,060)*

SNP Chief Whip

Patrick John Grady. Born 5 February 1980.

Education: Inverness Royal Academy; Strathclyde University (BA history 2000).

Non-political career: President, University of Strathclyde Students' Association 2001-02; Scottish Catholic International Aid Fund: Campaigns officer 2002-04, Advocacy Manager 2011-15; Countryside Campaigns Manager, Ramblers' Association 2005-07; Parliamentary Assistant to Jamie Hepburn MSP and Aileen Campbell MSP 2007-11.

Political career: Contested Glasgow North 2010 general election. Member for Glasgow North since 7 May 2015 general election; SNP: Spokesperson for International Development 2015-17, Chief Whip 2017-. *Select committees:* Member: Procedure 2015-17, Selection 2017-. National Secretary, Federation of Student Nationalists 2000-01; Convener, Glasgow Kelvin Constituency Association 2008-11, SNP National Secretary 2012-16.

Political interests: International development, international relations, climate change, transport, arts and creative industries, youth empowerment.

Other: Member, Executive Committee, Commonwealth Parliamentary Association United Kingdom 2015-17.

Recreations: Swimming, hill-walking, reading, music.

Patrick Grady MP, House of Commons, London SW1A 0AA
Tel: 020 7219 6398 *Email:* patrick.grady.mp@parliament.uk
Constituency: Suite 1, Firhill Business Centre, 76 Firhill Road, Glasgow G20 7BA
Tel: 0141-946 3062 *Website:* www.patrickgrady.scot *Twitter:* @GradySNP

CONSERVATIVE

GRAHAM, LUKE

Ochil and South Perthshire *(Majority 3,359)*

Luke Patrick Graham. Born June 1985.

Education: Dorcan Comprehensive School; Sheffield University (Degree economics and social policy).

Non-political career: Finance officer, Sheffield Students' Union; Tesco plc -2012: Central finance, London, Property business, Beijing, China, Finance and business development projects, Tesco Lotus, Thailand, Deputy project manager, first Tesco Extra launch, Thailand; Tough Mudder, USA 2012-14; Marketing and strategy, Marks & Spencer; Seconded to HRH Princes' Accounting for Sustainability Project; Director: Amplecom Ltd 2016-17, Tech & the Beancounters Ltd 2016-.

Political career: Contested Ochil and South Perthshire 2015 general election. Member for Ochil and South Perthshire since 8 June 2017. *Select committees:* Member, Public Accounts 2017-.

Other: Better Together 2014.

Luke Graham MP, House of Commons, London SW1A 0AA
Tel: 020 7219 0274 *Email:* luke.graham.mp@parliament.uk
Constituency: Details still to be confirmed *Website:* www.lukegraham.org.uk
Twitter: @LukeGrahamMP

CONSERVATIVE

GRAHAM, RICHARD

Gloucester *(Majority 5,520)*

Born 4 April 1958; Married Anthea 1989 (1 daughter 2 sons).

Education: Christ Church College, Oxford (BA history 1979); Certificate Investment Management (IMC) 1998; Bahasa Indonesia, Cantonese, French, Malay, Mandarin, Swahili, Tagalog.

Non-political career: Cadet Pilot, Oxford University Air Squadron RAFVR 1977-78. Airline Manager, Cathay Pacific Airways and John Swire & Sons 1980-86; Diplomat, HM Diplomatic Service 1986-92: First Secretary: British High Commission, Nairobi, British Embassy, Beijing 1989-92; Trade Commissioner, China, HM Consul, Macau; Investment manager 1992-2009: Director, Baring Asset Management, Director, Greater China Fund Inc 1994-2004, Head of Institutional and International Business, Baring Asset Management.

Political career: Member for Gloucester since 6 May 2010 general election; PPS to: Lord Howell of Guildford as Minister of State and Government Spokesperson, Foreign and Commonwealth Office 2010-12, Hugo Swire as Minister of State, Foreign and Commonwealth Office 2012-14; Trade Envoy to: Indonesia 2012-, ASEAN Economic Community 2015-, Philippines and Malaysia 2016-. *Select committees:* Member: Work and Pensions 2010, 2015-17, Exiting the European Union 2017-. Chairman, Conservative Backbench Policy Committee on Foreign and

Commonwealth 2015-17. Contested South West England 2004 European Parliament election. *Councils and public bodies:* Cotswold District Council: Councillor 2003-07, Chair, Overview and Scrutiny Committee.

Political interests: Keep calm and carry on regenerating; China, Indonesia.

Other: Chair, British Chamber of Commerce, Shanghai; Vice-chair, Board of Airline Representatives in the Philippines; Former member, Executive Council, China-Britain Business Council; Chair, Pensions Group, International Financial Services Ltd, London; Director, Great Britain China Centre; Trustee, Gloucestershire Community Foundation. Gloucester City Winget Cricket Club; Marylebone Cricket Club.

Recreations: Cricket, squash.

Richard Graham MP, House of Commons, London SW1A 0AA
Tel: 020 7219 7077 *Email:* richard.graham.mp@parliament.uk
Constituency: Second Floor, St Peters House, 2 College Street, Gloucester, Gloucestershire GL1 2NE
Tel: 01452 501167 *Website:* www.richardgraham.org *Twitter:* @RichardGrahamUK

CONSERVATIVE

GRANT, BILL

Ayr, Carrick and Cumnock *(Majority 2,774)*

William Grant. Born 15 August 1951; Married Agnes (2 daughters).

Non-political career: Various posts up to Deputy Commander at retirement, Fire Service 1974-2005.

Political career: Contested Ayr, Carrick and Cumnock 2010 general election. Member for Ayr, Carrick and Cumnock since 8 June 2017. *Select committees:* Member, Science and Technology 2017-. *Councils and public bodies:* Councillor, South Ayrshire Council 2007-17; Justice of the Peace, Ayr District Court.

Other: Kyle and Carrick Civic Society; Alloway Rotary Club; Ayr Classic Motorcycle Club; Ayr Building Preservation Trust.

Recreations: Travel, DIY, motorcycles.

Bill Grant MP, House of Commons, London SW1A 0AA
Tel: 020 7219 1548 *Email:* bill.grant.mp@parliament.uk
Constituency: Details still to be confirmed

CONSERVATIVE

GRANT, HELEN

Maidstone and The Weald *(Majority 17,723)*

Born 28 September 1961; Daughter of Dr Gladys Spedding and Dr Julius Okuboye, both retired; Married Simon Grant 1991 (2 sons).

Education: St Aidans Comprehensive School, Carlisle; Trinity Comprehensive School, Carlisle; Hull University (LLB 1982); College of Law, Guildford (Solicitors Finals 1984).

Non-political career: Articled clerk, Cartmell Mawson & Maine, Carlisle 1985-87; Assistant solicitor, Hempsons, London 1987-88; Fayers & Co, London: Associate solicitor 1988-92, Equity partner 1992-94; Maternity sabbatical 1994-95; Consultant solicitor, T G Baynes & Co, Kent 1995-96; Senior partner/owner, Grants Solicitors LLP 1996-2013.

Political career: Member for Maidstone and The Weald since 6 May 2010 general election; Parliamentary Under-Secretary of State: (Women and Equalities), Department for Culture, Media and Sport and Ministry of Justice 2012-13, (Minister for Victims and the Courts), Ministry of Justice 2012-13, Department for Culture, Media and Sport: (Sport and Tourism) 2013-15, (Equalities) 2013-14. *Select committees:* Member: Justice 2010-11, International Development 2015-16, Arms Export Controls 2016, Work of the Independent Commission for Aid Impact Sub-committee 2015-16. Member, Labour Party 2004-05; Conservative Party: Member 2006-, Deputy Chair, diversity group, Croydon Central and Croydon South Conservative Federation 2006-08, Special adviser to Oliver Letwin MP as Chair of Party Policy Review 2006-10; Member: Social Mobility Task Force 2007-08, Society of Conservative Lawyers. *Councils and public bodies:* Non-executive director, Croydon NHS Primary Care Trust 2005-07.

Political interests: Justice, business and enterprise, women, children and families, social mobility, sport, tourism, gambling, First World War commemorations, international development, equalities; Chagos Islands/Diego Garcia, India, Maldives, Nigeria, Sri Lanka, USA.

Other: Member, Bow Group; Hon Vice-president, MENCAP Trust, Maidstone; Co-president, Maidstone Operatic Society; Centre for Social Justice: Member, Family Division Policy Group 2006-, Member, Family Law Reform Commission 2007-; President, Maidstone Museums Foundation 2008-; Patron, Women in Racing 2015-; Trustee: Human Trafficking Foundation 2016-,

Social Mobility Foundation 2016-; Non-executive director, Cell Therapy Limited 2017-; Law Society: Member 1985-, Member: Resolution 1997-2010, Family Law Panel 2000-12, Equalities and Diversities Committee 2008-09; Tomorrow's People, Maidstone Support Group – National Osteoporosis Society, Advocacy After Fatal Domestic Abuse. Asian Voice Minister of the Year 2014. Kingswood Lawn Tennis Club.

Publications: State of the Nation/Fractured Families (Centre for Social Justice, 2006); Breakthrough Britain (Centre for Social Justice, 2007); Every Family Matters (Centre for Social Justice, 2009).

Recreations: Tennis, movies, family life, sporting events.

Helen Grant MP, House of Commons, London SW1A 0AA
Tel: 020 7219 7107 *Email:* helen.grant.mp@parliament.uk
Constituency: Maidstone East Station, Station Road, Maidstone, Kent ME14 1QN
Website: www.helengrant.org *Twitter:* @HelenGrantMP

SCOTTISH NATIONAL PARTY

GRANT, PETER

Glenrothes *(Majority 3,267)*

SNP Spokesperson for Europe

Married Fiona 1984.

Education: Glasgow University.

Non-political career: Physics teacher in Lanarkshire and Fife; Accountant; Senior local government and NHS finance roles.

Political career: Contested Glenrothes 6 November 2008 by-election. Member for Glenrothes since 7 May 2015 general election; SNP Spokesperson for Europe 2017-. *Select committees:* Member: European Scrutiny 2015-16, Joint Committee on Consolidation, &c, Bills 2015-, Exiting the European Union 2016-. Scottish National Party: Member 1987-, Treasurer 2016-. *Councils and public bodies:* Fife Council: Councillor 1992-2015, Council Leader 2007-12, SNP Group Leader 2007-15; Member: Fife Partnership Group, Joint Health and Social Care Partnership.

Political interests: Welfare, anti-austerity, child poverty.

Other: Member, UK Delegation, Organisation for Security and Co-operation in Europe Parliamentary Assembly 2015-; Member, Chartered Institute of Public Finance and Accountancy. Member, Leslie Bowling Club.

Recreations: Traditional Scottish music, bowls.

Peter Grant MP, House of Commons, London SW1A 0AA
Tel: 020 7219 6349 *Email:* peter.grant.mp@parliament.uk
Constituency: Castleblair Business Centre, Fullerton Road, Glenrothes KY7 5QR
Tel: 01592 759335 *Website:* www.petergrant.scot *Twitter:* @PeterGrantMP

CONSERVATIVE

GRAY, JAMES

North Wiltshire *(Majority 22,877)*

James Whiteside Gray. Born 7 November 1954; Son of late Very Revd John R. Gray, Moderator of General Assembly of Church of Scotland, and Dr Sheila Gray; Married Sarah Ann Beale 1980 (divorced) (2 sons 1 daughter); married Mrs Philippa Mayo 2009 (1 stepson 2 stepdaughters).

Education: Glasgow High School; Glasgow University (MA history 1975); Christ Church, Oxford (history thesis 1975-77); French.

Non-political career: Honourable Artillery Company (TA) 1978-84; Armed Forces Parliamentary Scheme (Army): Member 1998, Post-Graduate Scheme 2000, Chair 2013-; Member, HAC Court of Assistants 2002-07; Royal College of Defence Studies 2003. Management trainee, P&O 1977-78; Anderson Hughes & Co Ltd (Shipbrokers) 1978-84; Baltic Exchange: Member 1978-91, Pro Bono Member 1997-; Managing director, GNI Freight Futures Ltd, Senior Manager, GNI Ltd (Futures Brokers) 1984-92; Special adviser to Secretaries of State for Environment: Michael Howard MP 1992-93, John Gummer MP 1993-95; Director, Westminster Strategy 1995-96. Union of Country Sports Workers.

Political career: Contested Ross, Cromarty and Skye 1992 general election. Member for North Wiltshire 1997-2010, for North Wiltshire (revised boundary) since 6 May 2010 general election; Opposition Whip 2000-01; Opposition Spokesman for Defence 2001-02; Shadow Minister for: Environment, Food and Rural Affairs 2002-03, Environment and Transport 2003-05; Shadow Secretary of State for Scotland May 2005. *Select committees:* Member: Environment, Transport and Regional Affairs 1997-2000, Broadcasting 2001-03, Regulatory Reform 2005-10, Environment, Food and Rural Affairs 2007-10, Chairmen's Panel/Panel of Chairs 2010-, Finance and Services 2010-13, Procedure 2010-15, Defence 2013-17, Arms Export Controls 2014-15, Administration

2015-17. Chair, Conservative Rural Affairs Group 2003-04; Vice-chair, Conservative Backbench Foreign Affairs and Defence Committee 2010-. Deputy Chair, Wandsworth Tooting Conservative Association 1994-96; Board Member, Conservative Party South West.

Political interests: Countryside, agriculture, defence, environment, foreign affairs, polar affairs; Afghanistan, America, Arctic, Antarctica, China, Mongolia, Nepal, Russia, Sri Lanka.

Other: Parliamentary delegate to Council of Europe and Western European Union 2007-10; Member, UK delegation to NATO Parliamentary Assembly 2015-; Vice-President, HAC Saddle Club; President, North Wiltshire Multiple Sclerosis Society; President, Association of British Riding Schools; Younger Brother, Trinity House; Visiting Parliamentary Fellow, St Anthony's College, Oxford; International League for the Protection of Horses, MS Society, RNID. Member, Honourable Artillery Company. Freedom, City of London 1978; President, Chippenham Constitutional Club 2000-, Wootton Bassett Conservative Club, Pratt's Club. Member, Avon Vale Foxhounds.

Publications: Financial Risk Management in the Shipping Industry (1985); Futures and Options for Shipping (1987) (Lloyds of London Book Prize winner); Shipping Futures (1990); Crown v Parliament: Who decides on Going to War (2003); Poles Apart (2013); Who Takes Britain to War? (2014).

Recreations: Riding horses, heritage and local history.

James Gray MP, House of Commons, London SW1A 0AA
Tel: 020 7219 6237 *Email:* jamesgraymp@parliament.uk
Constituency: No constituency office publicised *Website:* www.jamesgray.org *Twitter:* @Jgray

GRAY, NEIL

Airdrie and Shotts *(Majority 195)*

SCOTTISH NATIONAL PARTY

SNP Spokesperson for Social Justice

Neil Charles Gray. Born 16 March 1986; Married (1 daughter 1 son).

Education: Kirkwall Grammar School; Stirling University (BA politics and journalism 2008).

Non-political career: Represented Scotland in 400m athletics; Contract producer and reporter, BBC Radio Orkney 2003-08; Press and research intern, SNP Press Office 2008; Office of Alex Neil MSP 2008-15: Constituency office manager 2011-15.

Political career: Member for Airdrie and Shotts since 7 May 2015 general election; SNP Spokesperson for: Fair Work and Employment 2015-17, Social Justice 2017-. *Select committees:* Member: Joint Committee on the Palace of Westminster 2015-16, Finance 2015-.

Recreations: Running (completed an ultra marathon in 2013).

Neil Gray MP, House of Commons, London SW1A 0AA
Tel: 020 7219 8787 *Email:* neil.gray.mp@parliament.uk
Constituency: Office 15, Airdrie Business Centre, 1 Chapel Lane, Airdrie ML6 6GX
Tel: 01236 439630
Shotts Healthy Living Centre, Kirk Road, Shotts ML7 5ET
Tel: 01501 821821 *Twitter:* @NeilGrayMP

GRAYLING, CHRIS

Epsom and Ewell *(Majority 20,475)*

CONSERVATIVE

Secretary of State for Transport

Christopher Stephen Grayling. Born 1 April 1962; Son of John and Elizabeth Grayling; Married Susan Dillistone 1987 (1 son 1 daughter).

Education: Royal Grammar School, High Wycombe; Sidney Sussex College, Cambridge (BA history 1984); French.

Non-political career: BBC News: Trainee 1985-86, Producer 1986-88; Programme editor, *Business Daily*, Channel 4 1988-91; Business development manager, BBC Select 1991-93; Director: Charterhouse Prods Ltd 1993, Workhouse Ltd 1993-95, SSVC Group 1995-97; Change consultant and European marketing director, Burson Marsteller 1997-2001.

Political career: Contested Warrington South 1997 general election. Member for Epsom and Ewell 2001-10, for Epsom and Ewell (revised boundary) since 6 May 2010 general election; Opposition Whip 2002; Shadow Spokesperson for Health 2002-03; Shadow Minister for: Public Services, Health and Education 2003-04, Higher Education 2004-05, Health 2005; Shadow Leader of the House of Commons 2005; Member, House of Commons Commission 2005, 2015-16; Shadow Secretary of State for: Transport 2005-07, Work and Pensions 2007-09; Shadow Home Secretary 2009-10; Minister of State for Employment, Department for Work and Pensions 2010-12; Lord Chancellor and Secretary of State for Justice 2012-15; Leader of the House of Commons 2015-16;

Lord President of the Council 2015-16; Member: Public Accounts Commission 2015-16, Speaker's Committee on the Electoral Commission 2015, Speaker's Committee for the Independent Parliamentary Standards Authority 2015-16; Secretary of State for Transport 2016-. *Select committees:* Member: Transport, Local Government and the Regions 2001-02, Transport, Local Government and the Regions (Transport Sub-Committee) 2001-02, Transport, Local Government and the Regions (Urban Affairs Sub-Committee) 2001-02, Transport 2002, Modernisation of the House of Commons 2005-06; Joint Committee on the Palace of Westminster: Member 2015, Chair 2015-16. *Councils and public bodies:* Councillor, London Borough of Merton 1998-2002.

Political interests: Transport, welfare reform, pensions, home affairs.

Other: Member, Corporation of Merton College 1999-2001; Chair, Epsom Victim Support 2001-07; President, Industry and Parliament Trust 2012-15; Member, Campaign committee, Vote Leave 2016; Patron: Forces Childrens Trust, Nork Music in the Park. PC 2010.

Publications: The Bridgwater Heritage (1983); A Land Fit for Heroes (1985); Co-author, Just Another Star? (1987).

Recreations: Golf, cricket, football.

Rt Hon Chris Grayling MP, House of Commons, London SW1A 0AA
Tel: 020 7219 8194 *Email:* chris.grayling.mp@parliament.uk
Constituency: PO Box 164, Ashtead, Surrey KT21 9BS
Tel: 01372 271036 *Website:* chrisgrayling.net

CONSERVATIVE

GREEN, CHRIS

Bolton West *(Majority 936)*

Christopher James Green. Born 12 August 1973.

Education: HND applied physics.

Non-political career: Engineer, Micromass, Wythenshawe; AstraZeneca; Waters.

Political career: Contested Manchester Withington 2010 general election. Member for Bolton West since 7 May 2015 general election. *Select committees:* Member, Science and Technology 2015-17.

Political interests: Equal opportunities, investment in science and manufacturing, education, infrastructure.

Other: Deputy Chair, Manchester Federation.

Chris Green MP, House of Commons, London SW1A 0AA
Tel: 020 7219 8685 *Email:* chris.green.mp@parliament.uk
Constituency: 15 Market Street, Westhoughton BL5 3AH
Tel: 01942 409132 *Email:* chris@chris-green.org.uk *Website:* www.chris-green.org.uk
Twitter: @CGreenUK

CONSERVATIVE

GREEN, DAMIAN

Ashford *(Majority 17,478)*

First Secretary of State and Minister for the Cabinet Office

Damian Howard Green. Born 17 January 1956; Son of Howard Green and late Audrey Green; Married Alicia Collinson 1988 (2 daughters).

Education: Reading School; Balliol College, Oxford (BA philosophy, politics and economics 1977, MA) (President, Oxford Union 1977); French.

Non-political career: Financial journalist, BBC Radio 1978-82; *Channel 4 News*: Business producer 1982-84, Business editor 1985-87; News editor, business news, *The Times* 1984-85; Programme presenter and city editor, *Business Daily* 1987-92; Special adviser, Prime Minister's Policy Unit 1992-94; Self-employed public affairs consultant 1995-97.

Political career: Contested Brent East 1992 general election. Member for Ashford 1997-2010, for Ashford (revised boundary) since 6 May 2010 general election; Opposition Spokesperson for: Education and Employment 1998-99, Environment 1999-2001; Shadow Secretary of State for: Education and Skills 2001-03, Transport 2003-04; Shadow Minister for Immigration 2005-10; Minister of State for: Immigration, Home Office 2010-12, Policing, Criminal Justice and Victims, Home Office and Ministry of Justice 2012-14; Secretary of State for Work and Pensions 2016-17; First Secretary of State and Minister for the Cabinet Office 2017-. *Select committees:* Member: Culture, Media and Sport 1997-98, Procedure 1997-98, Home Affairs 2004-05, Treasury 2005-06, European Scrutiny 2015-16, Joint Committee on the National Security Strategy 2015-16. Chairman, Conservative Education Policy Committee 2001-03; Member, Executive, 1922 Committee 2004-05, 2014-15; Chairman, Conservative Backbench Policy Committee on Education 2015-16. Vice-President, Tory Reform Group 1997-; Chair: Conservative Parliamentary Mainstream Group 2003-10, European Mainstream 2014-.

Political interests: Economic policy, foreign affairs, media, education, employment, rural affairs; France, Georgia, Italy, Moldova.

Other: President, Find a Voice; Trustee, Godinton House Preservation Trust; Board member, Britain Stronger in Europe 2015-16. PC 2012.

Publications: ITN Budget Fact Book (1984, 1985, 1986); A Better BBC (1990); The Cross-Media Revolution (1995); Communities in the Countryside (1996); Regulating the Media in the Digital Age (1997); 21st Century Conservatism (1998); The Four Failures of the New Deal (1999); Better Learning (2002); More than Markets (2003); Co-author, Controlling Economic Migration (2006).

Recreations: Football, cricket, opera, cinema.

Rt Hon Damian Green MP, House of Commons, London SW1A 0AA
Tel: 020 7219 3911 *Email:* damian.green.mp@parliament.uk
Constituency: c/o Hardy House, The Street, Bethersden, Ashford, Kent TN26 3AG
Tel: 01233 820454 *Fax:* 01233 820111 *Email:* ashfordconservatives@btconnect.com
Website: www.damiangreenmp.org.uk *Twitter:* @DamianGreen

LABOUR

GREEN, KATE

Stretford and Urmston *(Majority 19,705)*

Katherine Anne Green. Born 2 May 1960; Divorced.

Education: Currie High School; Edinburgh University (LLB 1982).

Non-political career: Various roles, Barclays Bank 1982-97; Whitehall and Industry Group (on secondment), Home Office 1997-99; Director, National Council for One Parent Families 2000-04; Chief executive, Child Poverty Action Group 2004-09. Member: Unite 2000-, GMB 2009-, USDAW 2009-.

Political career: Contested Cities of London and Westminster 1997 general election. Member for Stretford and Urmston since 6 May 2010 general election; Shadow Minister for: Equalities Office 2011-13, Disabled People 2013-15, Women and Equalities (attending Shadow Cabinet) 2015-16. *Select committees:* Member: Work and Pensions 2010-11, European Scrutiny 2016-, Justice 2016-17. Chair, PLP Departmental Group for Women 2011. Member, Labour Party 1990-; Chair, Owen Smith's Labour leadership campaign 2016. *Councils and public bodies:* Magistrate, City of London 1993-2009; Member, National Employment Panel 2001-07; Member, then Chair, London Child Poverty Commission 2006-09; Member, Greater Manchester Poverty Commission 2011-.

Political interests: Employment, exclusion, poverty, criminal justice; United Kingdom.

Other: Trustee: The Avenues Youth Project 1998-2003, End Child Poverty 2000-09, Family and Parenting Institute 2000-07, Institute for Fiscal Studies 2006-09; Member, Fawcett Society 2006-; Trustee, Friends Provident Foundation 2007-09; Fabian Society: Member 2009-, Chair 2016-; Trustee, Webb Memorial Trust 2010-. Freedom, City of London. OBE 2005.

Kate Green OBE MP, House of Commons, London SW1A 0AA
Tel: 020 7219 7162 *Fax:* 020 7219 4561 *Email:* kate.green.mp@parliament.uk
Constituency: Stretford Public Hall, Chester Road, Stretford M32 0LG
Tel: 0161-749 9120 *Website:* www.kategreen.org *Twitter:* @KateGreenSU

CONSERVATIVE

GREENING, JUSTINE

Putney *(Majority 1,554)*

Secretary of State for Education; Minister for Women and Equalities

Born 30 April 1969; Partner Tess.

Education: Oakwood Comprehensive School, Rotherham, Yorkshire; Thomas Rotherham College, Rotherham; Southampton University (BSc business economics and accounting 1990); London Business School (MBA 2000); French.

Non-political career: Audit assistant, PriceWaterhouse 1991-94; Audit assistant manager, Revisuisse PriceWaterhouse 1995-96; Finance manager, SmithKline Beecham 1996-2001; Business strategy manager, GlaxoSmithKline 2001-02; Sales and marketing finance manager, Centrica 2002-05.

Political career: Contested Ealing, Acton and Shepherd's Bush 2001 general election. Member for Putney 2005-10, for Putney (revised boundary) since 6 May 2010 general election; Shadow Minister for: Treasury 2007-09, Communities and Local Government 2009-10; Economic Secretary, HM Treasury 2010-11; Secretary of State for: Transport 2011-12; International Development 2012-16, Education 2016-; Minister for Women and Equalities 2016-. *Select committees:* Member: Work and Pensions 2005-07, Public Accounts 2010-11. Vice-chair (Youth), Conservative Party 2005-10. *Councils and public bodies:* Councillor, Epping Town Council 1998-2002.

Political interests: Social mobility, economy, vocational education, gender equality.

Other: Bow Group: Member 1998-, Political officer 1999-2000; Patron, Wandsworth Arts Society; Associate, Institute of Chartered Accountants in England and Wales 1994. People's Choice Award, Women in Public Life Awards 2011; Patchwork Conservative MP of the Year Award 2015; Patchwork MP of the Year Award 2016. PC 2011.

Publications: A Wholly Healthy Britain in A Blue Tomorrow (2000).

Recreations: Running, swimming, cycling.

Rt Hon Justine Greening MP, House of Commons, London SW1A 0AA
Tel: 020 7219 8300 *Email:* greeningj@parliament.uk
Constituency: 3 Summerstown, London SW17 0BQ
Tel: 020 8946 4557 *Website:* www.justinegreening.co.uk *Twitter:* @JustineGreening

LABOUR

GREENWOOD, LILIAN

Nottingham South *(Majority 15,162)*

Chair, Select Committee on Transport

Lilian Rachel Greenwood. Born 26 March 1966; Daughter of Harry Greenwood, lecturer, and Patricia Greenwood, typist; Married Ravi Subramanian 2008 (3 daughters).

Education: Canon Slade, Bolton; St Catharine's College, Cambridge (BA economics and social and political science 1987); Southbank University, London (MSc sociology and social policy 1991).

Non-political career: Research officer: Local Authority Conditions of Service Advisory Board 1988-89, Civil and Public Services Association 1989-92; Trade union organiser, latterly regional head of campaigns and policy, Unison 1992-2010. Member: NALGO 1988-89, GMB 1989-92, NUPE/Unison 1992-.

Political career: Member for Nottingham South since 6 May 2010 general election; Opposition Assistant Whip 2010-11; Shadow Minister for Transport 2011-15; Shadow Secretary of State for Transport 2015-16. *Select committees:* Transport: Member 2010, Chair 2017-; Member: Regulatory Reform 2010-15, Education 2016-17, Liaison 2017-. Member, Co-operative Party.

Political interests: Transport, employment rights, pensions; Kashmir.

Other: Member: Fabian Society, Compass 2007-. Holme Pierrepont Running Club.

Recreations: Running, walking, cinema, reading.

Lilian Greenwood MP, House of Commons, London SW1A 0AA
Tel: 020 7219 7122 *Email:* lilian.greenwood.mp@parliament.uk
Constituency: First Floor, 12 Regent Street, Nottingham, Nottinghamshire NG1 5BQ
Tel: 0115-711 7000 *Website:* liliangreenwood.co.uk *Twitter:* @LilianGreenwood

LABOUR

GREENWOOD, MARGARET

Wirral West *(Majority 5,365)*

Shadow Minister for Work and Pensions

Born 14 March 1959.

Non-political career: Former English teacher in secondary schools, FE colleges and adult education centres, Liverpool and Wirral; Travel writer; Web consultant.

Political career: Member for Wirral West since 7 May 2015 general election; PPS to Owen Smith as Shadow Secretary of State for Work and Pensions 2015-16; Shadow Minister for Work and Pensions 2016-. *Select committees:* Member, Environmental Audit 2015-16.

Other: Founding member, Defend our NHS.

Recreations: Hill-walking, theatre, music, painting.

Margaret Greenwood MP, House of Commons, London SW1A 0AA
Tel: 020 7219 4608 *Email:* margaret.greenwood.mp@parliament.uk
Constituency: Hilbre House, 35a Market Street, Hoylake, Wirral CH47 2BG
Tel: 0151-792 3416 *Website:* www.margaretgreenwood.org.uk *Twitter:* @MGreenwoodWW

CONSERVATIVE

GRIEVE, DOMINIC

Beaconsfield *(Majority 24,543)*

Dominic Charles Roberts Grieve. Born 24 May 1956; Son of late W P Grieve QC (MP for Solihull 1964-83) and late Evelyn Grieve, née Mijouain; Married Caroline Hutton 1990 (2 sons and 1 son deceased).

Education: Westminster School, London; Magdalen College, Oxford (BA modern history 1978, MA 1989); Central London Polytechnic (Diploma law 1980); French.

Non-political career: Territorial Army 1981-83. Called to the Bar 1980; Bencher, Middle Temple 2004; QC 2008; Honorary Recorder, Royal Borough of Kingston on Thames.

Political career: Contested Norwood 1987 general election. Member for Beaconsfield 1997-2010, for Beaconsfield (revised boundary) since 6 May 2010 general election; Opposition Spokesperson for: Constitutional Affairs and Scotland 1999-2001, Home Office 2001-03; Shadow Attorney General 2003-09; Shadow Home Secretary 2008-09; Shadow Secretary of State for Justice 2009-10; Attorney General 2010-14; Chair, Intelligence and Security Committee 2015-. *Select committees:* Member: Joint Committee on Statutory Instruments 1997-2001, Environmental Audit 1997-2001, Privileges 2014-, Standards 2014-, Joint Committee on the National Security Strategy 2015-. President, Oxford University Conservative Association 1977; Society of Conservative Lawyers: Chair: Research Committee 1992-95, Finance and General Purposes 2006-; Founding member, Conservatives for Reform in Europe 2016. *Councils and public bodies:* Councillor, London Borough of Hammersmith and Fulham 1982-86.

Political interests: Law and order, environment, defence, foreign affairs, European Union, constitution; France, India, Luxembourg.

Other: Vice-chair/director, Hammersmith and Fulham MIND 1986-89; Lay visitor to police stations 1990-96; Council member, Luxembourg Society; Member: London Diocesan Synod of Church of England 1994-2000, John Muir Trust; Governor, Ditchley Foundation 2010-; Vice-chair, Franco-British Council 2011-; President, Franco-British Society 2011-; Vice-President, English Clergy Association 2012-; Member, Council of Management 2016-. Opposition Politician of the Year, *House Magazine* 2005; Politician of the Year, *Spectator* 2005; Politicians' Politician of the Year, Channel 4 2006; Liberty Lifetime Achievement Award 2014. PC 2010.

Recreations: Mountaineering, skiing, scuba diving, fell-walking, architecture and art.

Rt Hon Dominic Grieve QC MP, House of Commons, London SW1A 0AA
Tel: 020 7219 6220 *Email:* dominic.grieve.mp@parliament.uk
Constituency: Disraeli House, 12 Aylesbury End, Beaconsfield, Buckinghamshire HP9 1LW
Tel: 01494 673745 *Fax:* 01494 670428 *Email:* office@beaconsfieldconservatives.co.uk
Websites: www.beaconsfieldconservatives.co.uk www.dominicgrieve.org.uk

LABOUR

GRIFFITH, NIA

Llanelli *(Majority 12,024)*

Shadow Secretary of State for Defence

Nia Rhiannon Griffith. Born 4 December 1956; Daughter of Prof T Gwynfor Griffith, professor of Italian and member of Gorsedd of Bards, and Dr Rhiannon Griffith, née Howell, medical doctor; Married Richard Leggett 1982 (divorced) (no children).

Education: Newland High School, Hull; Somerville College, Oxford (BA modern languages 1979); University College of North Wales, Bangor (PGCE 1980); French, Italian, Spanish, Welsh.

Non-political career: Language teacher 1980-92, 1997-2005; Education adviser 1992-97, Estyn schools inspector 1992-97; Head of modern languages, Morriston Comprehensive School, Swansea 1997-2005; Chair, Carmarthenshire Youth Project 1998-2005. National Union of Teachers; USDAW.

Political career: Member for Llanelli since 5 May 2005 general election; PPS: at Department for Environment, Food and Rural Affairs 2007-08, to Harriet Harman: as Minister for Women and Equality 2008-10, as Acting Leader of the Opposition 2010; Shadow Minister for: Business, Innovation and Skills 2010-11, Wales 2011-15; Shadow Secretary of State for: Wales 2015-16, Defence 2016-. *Select committees:* Member: European Scrutiny 2005-07, 2010-15, Welsh Affairs 2005-10, 2011-15, Joint Committee on Human Rights 2006-07, Joint Committee on the Draft Climate Change Bill 2007. Chair: PLP Welsh Regional Group 2007-08, PLP Departmental Group for Environment, Food and Rural Affairs 2010; Vice-chair, PLP Departmental Group for Energy and Climate Change 2010. Secretary, Carmarthenshire County Labour Party 1994-99, 2004-05; Chair, Carmarthen West and South Pembrokeshire CLP 1999-2000; Patron, LGBT Labour. *Councils and public bodies:* Carmarthen Town Council: Councillor 1987-99, Sheriff 1997, Deputy mayor 1998.

Political interests: Environment, Europe, community issues, cycling, industry, energy, equalities; France, Italy, Spain.

Other: Member, Amnesty International.

Publications: Co-author Ciao BK3 Italian textbook (Nelson, 1990); 100 ideas for teaching languages (Continuum Press, 2005).

Recreations: Arts, European cinema, music, cycling.

Nia Griffith MP, House of Commons, London SW1A 0AA
Tel: 020 7219 6102 *Email:* nia.griffith.mp@parliament.uk
Constituency: 43 Pottery Street, Llanelli SA15 1SU
Tel: 01554 756374 *Website:* niagriffith.org.uk *Twitter:* @NiaGriffithMP

CONSERVATIVE

GRIFFITHS, ANDREW

Burton *(Majority 10,047)*

Government Whip (Lord Commissioner of HM Treasury)

Andrew James Griffiths. Born 19 October 1970; Son of Bob Griffiths and Harriet Griffiths; Married.

Education: High Arcal School, Dudley.

Non-political career: Family engineering business; Manager, Halifax plc; Chief of staff to Jonathan Evans MEP 1999; Farming adviser to Neil Parish MEP -2004; Chief of staff to: Theresa May MP 2004-06, Hugo Swire MP 2006-07, Eric Pickles MP 2007-10.

Political career: Contested Dudley North 2001 general election. Member for Burton since 6 May 2010 general election; PPS to Ministers of State, Department for Communities and Local Government: Brandon Lewis 2015-16, Mark Francois 2015-16; Government Whip (Lord Commissioner of HM Treasury) 2016-. *Select committees:* Member: Political and Constitutional Reform 2010-13, Selection 2017-. Contested West Midlands region 2004 European Parliament election. Secretary, Board of Conservative Party 2009-10.

Political interests: Drugs and alcohol rehabilitation, the brewery and pub industry, manufacturing; China, Kashmir, Pakistan, USA.

Other: Trustee: National Brewery Heritage Trust, Red Lion House; Patron: Victoria Cross Trust, Langan's Tea Rooms; Parliamentary Patron, YMCA England; President, East Staffordshire Citizen's Advice.

Recreations: Sport, architecture, music.

Andrew Griffiths MP, House of Commons, London SW1A 0AA
Tel: 020 7219 7029 *Email:* andrew.griffiths.mp@parliament.uk
Constituency: Gothard House, 9 St Paul's Square, Burton-upon-Trent, Staffordshire DE14 2EF
Tel: 01283 564934 *Website:* www.andrewgriffithsmp.com *Twitter:* @AndrewGriffiths

LABOUR

GROGAN, JOHN

Keighley *(Majority 239)*

John Timothy Grogan. Born 24 February 1961; Son of late John Martin Grogan and late Maureen Grogan.

Education: St Michael's College, Leeds; St John's College, Oxford (BA modern history and economics 1982).

Non-political career: Communications co-ordinator, Leeds City Council 1987-94; Labour Party press officer, European Parliament, Brussels 1995; Self-employed conference organiser 1996-97. Member, GMB.

Political career: Contested Selby 1987 and 1992 general elections. Member for Selby 1997-2010. Contested Keighley 2015 general election. Member for Keighley since 8 June 2017. *Select committees:* Member: Northern Ireland Affairs 1997-2001, 2005-10, Environment, Food and Rural Affairs 2017-. Hon Secretary, PLP Yorkshire Regional Group 2005-10; Chair, PLP Departmental Committee for Health and Social Services 2005-10. Contested York 1989 European Parliament election. Chair, Labour Party Yorkshire and Humber Development Board 2013-.

Political interests: Local and regional government, European Union, economic policy, broadcasting, sport, alcohol licensing reform, small businesses, energy policy, lobbying industry; Albania, Australia, Mongolia, New Zealand, Ukraine.

Other: Fellow, Industry and Parliament Trust 1999; Chair, Mongolian-British Chamber of Commerce. Yorkshire County Cricket Club.

Recreations: Football, running, cinema.

John Grogan MP, House of Commons, London SW1A 0AA
Tel: 020 7219 2642 *Email:* john.grogan.mp@parliament.uk
Constituency: Keighley Civic Centre, 81 North Street, Keighley BD21 3RZ
Tel: 01535 681433

LABOUR

GWYNNE, ANDREW

Denton and Reddish *(Majority 14,077)*

Shadow Secretary of State for Communities and Local Government; National Campaign Co-ordinator

Andrew John Gwynne. Born 4 June 1974; Son of Richard John Gwynne and Margaret Gwynne, née Ridgway; Married Allison Dennis 2003 (2 sons 1 daughter).

Education: Egerton Park Community High School, Denton; North East Wales Institute of Higher Education, Wrexham (HND business and finance 1995); Salford University (BA politics and contemporary history 1998).

Non-political career: Assistant to European Declarative System (EDS) programme manager, ICL 1990-92; National Computing Centre, Y2K team 1999-2000; Researcher for Andrew Bennett MP 2000-05; European co-ordinator for Arlene McCarthy MEP 2000-01. Member, Unite (formerly AEEU and Amicus) 2000-.

Political career: Member for Denton and Reddish 2005-10, for Denton and Reddish (revised boundary) since 6 May 2010 general election; PPS to: Baroness Scotland of Asthal as Minister of State, Home Office 2005-07, Jacqui Smith as Home Secretary 2007-09, Ed Balls as Secretary of State for Children, Schools and Families 2009-10; Shadow Minister for: Transport 2010-11, Health 2011-16 (Public Health 2015-16); Shadow Minister without Portfolio (attends Shadow Cabinet) 2016-17; National Elections and Campaign Co-ordinator/National Campaign Co-ordinator 2017-; Shadow Secretary of State for Communities and Local Government 2017-. *Select committees:* Member: Procedure 2005-10, Court of Referees 2007-10. PLP North West Regional Group: Vice-chair 2008-09, Chair 2009-11. Chair, Denton and Reddish Constituency Labour Party 1998-2004; Member, Co-operative Party 2000-; Member, Christian Socialist Movement/Christians on the Left 2000-; Chair, Labour Friends of Israel 2007-10; Campaign manager to Andy Burnham MP, Labour's mayoral candidate in Greater Manchester 2016-. *Councils and public bodies:* Tameside MBC: Councillor 1996-2008, Chair: Denton and Audenshaw District Assembly 1998-2001, Resources and community services scrutiny panel 2003-04.

Political interests: Education and skills, regeneration, local government, environment, transport; China, Commonwealth, India, Israel/Palestinian Authority, Latin America, USA.

Other: Patron, Tameside and Stockport Homestart; Patron, Friends of Dukinfield Old Hall Chapel; President, Denton and Audenshaw Carnival Association; Honorary Member, XX The Lancashire Fusiliers; President, Denton Brass; Denton Labour Club, Stockport Labour Club.

Recreations: Reading, computing, history, family.

Andrew Gwynne MP, House of Commons, London SW1A 0AA
Tel: 020 7219 4708 *Fax:* 020 7219 4548 *Email:* gwynnea@parliament.uk
Constituency: Town Hall, Market Street, Denton, Greater Manchester M34 2AP
Tel: 0161-320 1504 *Fax:* 0161-320 1503 *Website:* www.andrewgwynne.co.uk
Twitter: @GwynneMP

CONSERVATIVE

GYIMAH, SAM

East Surrey *(Majority 23,914)*

Parliamentary Under-Secretary of State for Prisons and Probation, Ministry of Justice

Samuel Phillip Gyimah. Born 10 August 1976; Married Dr Nicola Black (2 children).

Education: Achimota Secondary School, Ghana; Freman College, Hertfordshire; Somerville College, Oxford (BA philosophy, politics and economics 1999) (Union President 1997).

Non-political career: Investment banker, Goldman Sachs 1999-2003; Entrepreneur 2003-10.

Political career: Member for East Surrey since 6 May 2010 general election; Member, Speaker's Committee on the Electoral Commission 2010-12; PPS to David Cameron as Prime Minister 2012-13; Government Whip (Lord Commissioner of HM Treasury) 2013-14; Parliamentary Secretary (Minister for the Constitution), Cabinet Office 2014-15; Parliamentary Under-Secretary of State for: Childcare and Education, Department for Education 2014-16, Prisons and Probation, Ministry of Justice 2016-. *Select committees:* Member, International Development 2011-12. *Councils and public bodies:* School governor, London 2004-07.

Political interests: Small business, higher education, international development.

Other: Former board member, Nacro; Chair, Bow Group 2007; Member, development board, Somerville College, Oxford; Vice-President, National Centre for Young People with Epilepsy 2010-. CBI Entrepreneur of the Future 2005.

Publications: Editor, From the Ashes... The Future of the Conservative Party (Bow Group, 2005); Co-author with Nesta, Beyond the Banks.

Sam Gyimah MP, House of Commons, London SW1A 0AA
Tel: 020 7219 3504
Constituency: No constituency office publicised
Tel: 01883 715782 *Email:* sam@samgyimah.com *Website:* www.samgyimah.com
Twitter: @SamGyimah

LABOUR

HAIGH, LOUISE

Sheffield Heeley *(Majority 13,828)*

Shadow Minister for Policing

Louise Margaret Haigh. Born 22 July 1987.

Education: Sheffield High School; Nottingham University (politics and economics); Birkbeck School of Law (LLM).

Non-political career: Ant Marketing; Corporate governance policy manager, Aviva Insurance; Parliamentary researcher to Lisa Nandy MP; Youth service training manager, Nottingham Council. Member: Unite, GMB.

Political career: Member for Sheffield Heeley since 7 May 2015 general election; Shadow Minister for: Cabinet Office 2015-16, Culture, Media and Sport (Digital Economy) 2016-17, Home Office (Policing) 2017-.

Political interests: Financial services, investment, education; Kashmir, Palestine, South Africa.

Louise Haigh MP, House of Commons, London SW1A 0AA
Tel: 020 7219 5255 *Email:* louise.haigh.mp@parliament.uk
Constituency: 63 Chesterfield Road, Sheffield S8 0RX
Tel: 0114-250 8113 *Email:* louise@louisehaigh.org.uk *Website:* www.louisehaigh.org.uk
Twitter: @LouHaigh

CONSERVATIVE

HAIR, KIRSTENE

Angus *(Majority 2,645)*

Kirstene Janette Hair.

Education: Brechin High School; Aberdeen University (politics 2011).

Non-political career: Organiser, Scottish Conservatives; Events Manager and Executive Assistant, DC Thomson Publishing.

Political career: Member for Angus since 8 June 2017. *Select committees:* Member, Women and Equalities 2017-. Contested Angus South 2016 Scottish Parliament election.

Kirstene Hair MP, House of Commons, London SW1A 0AA
Tel: 020 7219 0202 *Email:* kirstene.hair.mp@parliament.uk
Constituency: Details still to be confirmed *Twitter:* @kirstene4angus

CONSERVATIVE

HALFON, ROBERT

Harlow *(Majority 7,031)*

Chair, Select Committee on Education

Robert Henry Halfon. Born 22 March 1969; Son of Clement and Jenny Halfon; Partner Vanda Colombo.

Education: Highgate School, London; Exeter University (BA politics 1991; MA Russian and East European politics 1992).

Non-political career: Parliamentary researcher to a number of Conservative MPs; Head of Research, Market Access Ltd 1994-98; Policy Analyst, APCO UK 1998-2000; Political Director, Renewing One Nation, Conservative Central Office 2000-01; Chief of Staff to Oliver Letwin MP 2001-05; Political Director/Consultant, Conservative Friends of Israel 2005-10; Self-employed Consultant 2005-10. Member, Prospect.

Political career: Contested Harlow 2001 and 2005 general elections. Member for Harlow since 6 May 2010 general election; PPS to George Osborne as Chancellor of the Exchequer 2014-15; Minister without Portfolio, Cabinet Office 2015-16; Minister of State, Department for Education 2016-17. *Select committees:* Member, Public Administration 2010-14; Chair, Education 2017-; Member, Liaison 2017-. 1922 Committee: Member, Executive 2010-14, Member, Sub-committee for Campaigning. Chair: Western Area Conservative Students 1987-90, Exeter University Conservative Association 1989-90; Deputy Chair, Vauxhall Conservative Association 1998-2000; Member, Conservative Way Forward; Deputy Chair, Conservative Party 2015-16. *Councils and public bodies:* Councillor, Roydon Parish Council 2005-11.

Political interests: Apprenticeships, community cohesion, education, green belt, housing, information technology, literacy, mobile technology, social action, terrorism, trade unions; Iraq (Kurdistan region), Israel, USA.

Other: Member, Advisory Board, Centre for Social Justice; Great Parndon Community Association President, St Johns Ambulance, Harlow; Patron: Harlow Homestart, St Clare's Hospice, Harlow; Trustee, Parndon Mill, Harlow; Harlow Employability. National Conservative Excellence Award for Social Action 2008; *The Spectator* Campaigning MP of the Year Award 2013; *The House Magazine* Transport Campaigner of the Year, Dods Parliamentary Awards 2014. PC 2015; Harlow Royal British Legion.

Publications: Retreat or Reform (Institute for European Defence and Strategic Studies, 1994); Corporate Irresponsibility (Social Affairs Unit, 1998); Numerous articles in various publications and written chapters for: Encyclopaedia of Soviet Union and Eastern Europe (by Bogdan Szajkowski, 1994), From the Ashes... The Future of the Conservative Party (Bow Group, 2005), The Last Moral Force, The New Blue (Social Market Foundation, 2008), Stop the Union Bashing – Why Conservatives Should Embrace the Trade Union Movement (Demos, 2012).

Recreations: Chelsea FC, countryside, horology, travelling, mobile technology.

Rt Hon Robert Halfon MP, House of Commons, London SW1A 0AA
Tel: 020 7219 7223
Constituency: Harlow Enterprise Hub, Kao-Hockham Building, Edinburgh Way, Harlow, Essex CM20 2NQ
Tel: 01279 311451 *Email:* halfon4harlow@roberthalfon.com *Website:* new.roberthalfon.com
Twitter: @Halfon4Harlow

CONSERVATIVE

HALL, LUKE

Thornbury and Yate *(Majority 12,071)*

Team PPS, Department for Education

Luke Anthony Hall. Born 8 July 1986; Married Roisin Cabry 2016.

Non-political career: Store Manager, Lidl, Yate; South West area manager, Farmfoods -2015.

Political career: Member for Thornbury and Yate since 7 May 2015 general election; Team PPS, Department for Education 2017-. *Select committees:* Member: Environmental Audit 2015-17, Work and Pensions 2016-17, Petitions 2016-17. Constituency chair, South Gloucestershire; Deputy chair, Bristol and South Gloucestershire Conservatives.

Other: Has held an amateur boxing licence.

Luke Hall MP, House of Commons, London SW1A 0AA
Tel: 020 7219 4741 *Email:* luke.hall.mp@parliament.uk
Constituency: 26 High Street, Chipping Sodbury, Gloucestershire BS35 6AH
Tel: 01454 311267 *Email:* luke@lukehall.org.uk *Website:* www.lukehall.org.uk
Twitter: @LukeHall

LABOUR

HAMILTON, FABIAN

Leeds North East *(Majority 16,991)*

Shadow Minister for Foreign Affairs

Fabian Uziell-Hamilton. Born 12 April 1955; Son of late Mario Uziell-Hamilton, solicitor, and late Adrianne Uziell-Hamilton (Her Honour Judge Uziell-Hamilton); Married Rosemary Ratcliffe 1980 (1 son 2 daughters).

Education: Brentwood School, Essex; York University (BA social sciences 1977); French.

Non-political career: Taxi driver 1978-79; Graphic designer 1979-94; Consultant and dealer, Apple Macintosh computer systems 1994-97. Member: SLADE 1978-82, NGA 1982-91, GPMU 1991-2005, Amicus 2005-07, Unite 2007-.

Political career: Contested Leeds North East 1992 general election. Member for Leeds North East 1997-2010, for Leeds North East (revised boundary) since 6 May 2010 general election; PPS to Rachel Reeves as Shadow Chief Secretary to the Treasury 2012-13; Shadow Minister for: Foreign and Commonwealth Office 2016, Foreign Affairs, Foreign and Commonwealth Office and Defence teams 2016-. *Select committees:* Member: Administration 1997-2001, Foreign Affairs 2001-10, Quadripartite (Committees on Strategic Export Controls)/Arms Export Controls 2006-10, Political and Constitutional Reform 2010-15, Joint Committee on National Security Strategy 2010-15, International Development 2013-16, Arms Exports Controls 2013-15, Panel of Chairs 2015-16. Vice-chair, PLP Departmental Group for Home Affairs 2010-15. Member, Co-operative Party 1981-; Member, Labour Friends of Israel 1997-. *Councils and public bodies:* Councillor, Leeds City Council 1987-98: Chair: Race Equality Committee 1988-94, Economic Development Committee 1994-96, Education Committee 1996-97.

Political interests: Education, transport, small businesses, anti-racism, international development, alternative fuels, foreign affairs, holocaust education, prison health, hospices and palliative care; Southern Africa, Caribbean, Cyprus, Europe, Iceland, Indian sub-continent, Iran, Japan, Kashmir, Korea, Middle East, Russia, Tibet, Turkey.

Other: Treasurer, Inter-Parliamentary Union, British Group 2013-16; Member: Fabian Society 1990-, Jewish Labour Movement; St Gemmas Hospice, Childline, Practical Actions, Refugee Education, Training and Advisory Service, St George's Crypt Leeds.

Recreations: Film, opera, cycling, computers, photography.

Fabian Hamilton MP, House of Commons, London SW1A 0AA
Tel: 020 7219 3493 *Fax:* 020 7219 5540 *Email:* fabian.hamilton.mp@parliament.uk
Constituency: 147a Easterly Road, Leeds, West Yorkshire LS8 2RY
Tel: 0113-249 6600 *Website:* www.leedsne.co.uk *Twitter:* @FabianLeedsNE

CONSERVATIVE

HAMMOND, PHILIP

Runnymede and Weybridge *(Majority 18,050)*

Chancellor of the Exchequer

Born 4 December 1955; Son of Bernard Hammond, civil engineer and local government officer; Married Susan Williams-Walker 1991 (2 daughters 1 son).

Education: Shenfield School, Brentwood, Essex; University College, Oxford (MA politics, philosophy and economics 1977).

Non-political career: Assistant to Chair, then marketing manager, Speywood Laboratories Ltd 1977-81; Director, Speywood Medical Ltd 1981-83; Established and ran medical equipment manufacturing and distribution companies 1983-94; Director various medical equipment manufacturing companies 1983-96; Director, Castlemead Ltd 1984-; Partner, CMA Consultants 1993-95; Director, Castlemead Homes Ltd 1994-2004; Consultant to Government of Malawi 1995-97; Director, Consort Resources Ltd 1999-2003.

Political career: Contested Newham North East 1994 by-election. Member for Runnymede and Weybridge since 1 May 1997 general election; Opposition Spokesperson for: Health and Social Services 1998-2001, Trade and Industry 2001-02; Shadow Minister for Local and Devolved Government Affairs 2002-05; Shadow Chief Secretary to the Treasury 2005; Shadow Secretary of State for Work and Pensions 2005-07; Shadow Chief Secretary to the Treasury 2007-10; Secretary of State for: Transport 2010-11, Defence 2011-14, Foreign and Commonwealth Affairs (Foreign Secretary) 2014-16; Chancellor of the Exchequer 2016-. *Select committees:* Member: Unopposed Bills (Panel) 1997-2004, Environment, Transport and Regional Affairs 1998, Environment, Transport and Regional Affairs (Transport Sub-Committee) 1998, Trade and Industry 2002. Secretary, Conservative Party Committee for Health 1997-98. Chair, East Lewisham Conservative Association 1989-96; Member, Executive Council, Greater London Area 1989-96.

Political interests: Economic policy, international trade, European Union, defence, social security, transport, housing and planning, energy, health; Southern and Eastern Africa, Germany, Italy, Latin America.

Other: Joint President, Weybridge Youth Club; Vice-president, Basingstoke Canal Society; Patron, White Lodge, Chertsey. PC 2010; Carlton Club.

Recreations: Travel, cinema, walking.

Rt Hon Philip Hammond MP, House of Commons, London SW1A 0AA
Tel: 020 7219 4055 *Fax:* 020 7219 5851 *Email:* philip.hammond.mp@parliament.uk
Constituency: Runnymede and Weybridge Conservative Association, Curzon House, Church Road, Windlesham, Surrey GU20 6BH
Tel: 01276 472910 *Email:* office@runnymedeweybridgeconservatives.com
Websites: www.runnymedeweybridgeconservatives.com www.rthonphiliphammond.co.uk
Twitter: @PhilipHammondUK

CONSERVATIVE

HAMMOND, STEPHEN

Wimbledon *(Majority 5,622)*

Stephen William Hammond. Born 4 February 1962; Son of Bryan Hammond and Janice Hammond; Married Sally Brodie 1991 (1 daughter).

Education: King Edward VI School, Southampton; Richard Hale School, Hertford; Queen Mary College, London University (BSc Econ 1982).

Non-political career: Trainee analyst, Reed Stenhouse Investment Services 1983-85; Fund manager, Canada Life 1987-88; Stockbroker, UBS Philips and Drew 1987-91; Director: UK equities, Dresdner Kleinwort Benson Securities 1991-98, Pan European research, Commerzbank Securities 1998-2001; Adviser: Inmarsat 2014-, Confederation of Passenger Transport 2016-.

Political career: Contested North Warwickshire 1997 and Wimbledon 2001 general elections. Member for Wimbledon since 5 May 2005 general election; Shadow Minister for Transport 2005-10; PPS to Eric Pickles as Secretary of State for Communities and Local Government 2010-12; Parliamentary Under-Secretary of State, Department for Transport 2012-14. *Select committees:* Member: Regulatory Reform 2005-08, Public Accounts 2014-15, Treasury 2015-, Joint Committee on Statutory Instruments 2015-. Conservative Party: Chair, Stevenage Conservatives 1991-94, Member, Executive, Eastern Area 1992-94, Chair, Wimbledon Conservative Association 2001-03, Member, 2020 Group, Founding member, Conservatives for Reform in Europe 2016, Vice-chairman 2017-. *Councils and public bodies:* Merton Borough Council: Councillor 2002-06, Environment spokesman 2002-04, Deputy group leader 2004-06.

Political interests: Economics, financial affairs, transport, foreign affairs; China, EU, India, Portugal, Sri Lanka, USA.

Other: Member, Executive Committee, Commonwealth Parliamentary Association UK 2016-17; Wimbledon Society; Director (unpaid), South Coast Regeneration and Investment Property 2017-; Associate, Society of Investment Analysts 1985; Macmillan Cancer Support. Royal Wimbledon Golf Club; Wimbledon Hockey Club.

Recreations: Reading, sport, relaxing with family, cooking.

Stephen Hammond MP, House of Commons, London SW1A 0AA
Tel: 020 7219 3401 *Email:* hammonds@parliament.uk
Constituency: Wimbledon Conservative Association, c/o 1 Summerstown, London SW17 0BQ
Tel: 020 8944 2905 *Email:* stephen@stephenhammond.net *Website:* stephenhammond.net
Twitter: @S_Hammond

CONSERVATIVE

HANCOCK, MATT

West Suffolk *(Majority 17,063)*

Minister of State for Digital, Department for Digital, Culture, Media and Sport

Matthew John David Hancock. Born 2 October 1978; Married Martha 2006 (2 sons 1 daughter).

Education: King's School, Chester; West Cheshire College; Exeter College, Oxford (BA politics, philosophy and economics 1999); Christ College, Cambridge (Master's economics 2003).

Non-political career: Border Business Systems, Farndon; Economist, Bank of England 2000-05; Chief of staff to George Osborne MP 2005-10.

Political career: Member for West Suffolk since 6 May 2010 general election; Departments for Business, Innovation and Skills and Education: Parliamentary Under-Secretary of State 2012-13, Minister of State for Skills and Enterprise 2013-14; Minister of State for: Business and Enterprise and Minister for Portsmouth, Department for Business, Innovation and Skills 2014-15, Energy, Department of Energy and Climate Change 2014-15; Minister for the Cabinet Office; Paymaster General (also attending Cabinet) 2015-16; Minister of State for: Digital and Culture, Department for Culture, Media and Sport 2016-17, Digital, Department for Digital, Culture, Media and Sport 2017-. *Select committees:* Member: Public Accounts 2010-12, Standards and Privileges 2010-12. Member, Conservative Party 1999-.

Countries of interest: India, Japan, UK, USA.

Other: Cancer Research UK, Founder Dom Pardey Charitable Trust, Racing Welfare, St Nicholas Hospice, Injured Jockeys Fund. PC 2014; Jockey Club. Bank of England Sports Club.

Publications: Various Bank of England publications; Master of Nothing (with Nadim Zahawi MP) 2011.

Recreations: Walking, cooking, cricket, horse racing.

Rt Hon Matt Hancock MP, House of Commons, London SW1A 0AA
Tel: 020 7219 7186 *Email:* matthew.hancock.mp@parliament.uk
Constituency: Unit 8, Swan Lane Business Park, Exning, Newmarket, Suffolk CB8 7FN
Tel: 01638 576692 *Email:* matt@matt-hancock.com
Websites: www.westsuffolkconservatives.com www.matt-hancock.com *Twitter:* @MattHancock

CONSERVATIVE

HANDS, GREG

Chelsea and Fulham *(Majority 8,188)*

Minister of State for Trade Policy, Department for International Trade; Minister for London

Gregory William Hands. Born 14 November 1965; Son of Edward and Mavis Hands; Married Irina Hundt 2005 (1 daughter 1 son).

Education: Dr Challoner's Grammar School, Amersham; Robinson College, Cambridge (BA modern history 1989); Czech, French, German.

Non-political career: Banker 1989-97.

Political career: Member for Hammersmith and Fulham 2005-10, for Chelsea and Fulham since 6 May 2010 general election; Shadow Minister for the Treasury 2009-10; PPS to George Osborne as Chancellor of the Exchequer 2010-11; Assistant Government Whip 2011-13; Deputy Chief Whip (Treasurer of HM Household) 2013-15; Chief Secretary to the Treasury 2015-16; Department for International Trade: Minister of State for: Trade and Investment 2016-17, Trade Policy 2017-; Minister for London 2017-. *Select committees:* Member: ODPM/Communities and Local Government 2006-08, European Scrutiny 2007-10, Communities and Local Government 2009-10, Selection 2013-15; Chair, Joint Committee on Security 2013-15. *Councils and public bodies:* Hammersmith and Fulham Borough Council: Councillor 1998-2006: Leader, Conservative group 1999-2003; Prison visitor, HMP Wormwood Scrubs 2002-04.

Political interests: Finance, foreign affairs, housing, local government; Central and Eastern Europe, Germany, Ireland, North Korea, Russia and ex-USSR.

Other: Trustee, Brunswick Club for Young People 2003-; Co-Patron, Fulham Boys School. PC 2014; Carlton Club.

Recreations: Playing and watching football, local history, British, German and Soviet history, photography.

Rt Hon Greg Hands MP, House of Commons, London SW1A 0AA
Tel: 020 7219 0809/020 7219 5448 *Email:* handsg@parliament.uk
Constituency: No constituency office publicised *Website:* www.greghands.com
Twitter: @greghands/@UKTradeMinister

LABOUR

HANSON, DAVID

Delyn *(Majority 4,240)*

David George Hanson. Born 5 July 1957; Son of late Brian Hanson, fork lift driver, and Glenda Hanson, wages clerk; Married Margaret Mitchell 1986 (2 sons 2 daughters).

Education: Verdin Comprehensive School, Winsford, Cheshire; Hull University (BA drama 1978; Cert Ed 1980).

Non-political career: Vice-president, Hull University Students' Union 1978-79; Trainee, Co-operative Union 1980-81; Manager, Plymouth Co-operative 1981-82; Various posts with Spastics Society 1982-89; Director, Re-Solv (Society for the Prevention of Solvent Abuse) 1989-92. Member: USDAW, Unite.

Political career: Contested Eddisbury 1983 and Delyn 1987 general elections. Member for Delyn since 9 April 1992 general election; PPS to Alastair Darling as Chief Secretary to the Treasury 1997-98; Assistant Government Whip 1998-99; Parliamentary Under-Secretary of State, Wales Office 1999-2001; PPS to Tony Blair as Prime Minister 2001-05; Minister of State: Northern Ireland Office 2005-07, Ministry of Justice 2007-09, Home Office 2009-10; Shadow Exchequer Secretary 2010-11; Shadow Minister for: Home Office 2011-15: (Policing 2011-13), (Immigration 2013-15), Foreign and Commonwealth Office 2015; Member, Intelligence and Security Committee 2016-. *Select committees:* Member: Welsh Affairs 1992-95, Panel of Chairs 2015-, Justice 2015-, Joint Committee on the Draft Investigatory Powers Bill 2015-16. Contested Cheshire West 1984 European Parliament election. Member, Leadership Campaign Team 1994-97. *Councils and public bodies:* Vale Royal Borough Council: Councillor 1983-91, Leader, Labour group, Council Leader 1989-91; Councillor, Northwich Town Council 1987-91.

Political interests: Foreign affairs, heritage, local and regional government, solvent abuse; South Africa, Cyprus.

Other: Executive Committee, Commonwealth Parliamentary Association (UK Branch): Member 2014-15, Honorary Treasurer 2015-17, Vice-chair 2017-; Fellow, Industry and Parliament Trust 1998; Re-Solv, Flint Life Boats, Flint Abbeyfield Society. PC 2007.

Recreations: Football, cinema, family.

Rt Hon David Hanson MP, House of Commons, London SW1A 0AA
Tel: 020 7219 5064 *Fax:* 020 7219 2671 *Email:* david.hanson.mp@parliament.uk
Constituency: 4 Trelawny Square, Flint, Flintshire CH6 5NN
Tel: 01352 763159 *Fax:* 01352 730140 *Email:* robbinsh@parliament.uk
Website: www.davidhanson.org.uk *Twitter:* @DavidHansonMP

LABOUR

HARDY, EMMA

Kingston upon Hull West and Hessle *(Majority 8,025)*

PPS to Keir Starmer as Shadow Secretary of State for Exiting the European Union

Emma Ann Hardy. 2 children.

Education: Wyke Sixth Form College; Liverpool University (BA politics 2001); Leeds University (PGCE 2003).

Non-political career: Teacher: North East Lincolnshire Council 2003-05, East Riding of Yorkshire Council 2004-11; Organiser, National Union of Teachers Midland Region 2015-17.

Political career: Member for Kingston upon Hull West and Hessle since 8 June 2017; PPS to Keir Starmer as Shadow Secretary of State for Exiting the European Union 2017-. *Select committees:* Member, Education 2017-. Labour Party: Branch secretary 2010, National Policy Forum Representative 2015-, CLP Women's Officer 2016-. *Councils and public bodies:* Councillor, Hessle Town Council 2015-.

Political interests: Education, NHS.

Emma Hardy MP, House of Commons, London SW1A 0AA
Tel: 020 7219 4193 *Email:* emma.hardy.mp@parliament.uk
Constituency: The Octagon, Walker Street, Hull HU3 2RA
Tel: 01482 219211 *Twitter:* @EmmaHardyMP

LABOUR

HARMAN, HARRIET

Camberwell and Peckham *(Majority 37,316)*

Harriet Ruth Harman. Born 30 July 1950; Daughter of late John Bishop Harman and Anna Harman; Married Jack Dromey (qv) 1982 (MP for Birmingham Erdington) (2 sons 1 daughter).

Education: St Paul's Girls' School, London; York University (BA politics 1978).

Non-political career: Legal officer, National Council for Civil Liberties 1978-82; QC 2001. Member, Unite (TGWU sector).

Political career: Member for Peckham 1982 by-election to 1997, for Camberwell and Peckham 1997-2010, for Camberwell and Peckham (revised boundary) since 6 May 2010 general election; Member, Public Accounts Commission; Shadow Minister, Social Services 1984, 1985-87; Spokesperson for Health 1987-92; Shadow Chief Secretary to the Treasury 1992-94; Shadow Secretary of State for: Employment 1994-95, Health 1995-96, Social Security 1996-97; Secretary of State for Social Security and Minister for Women 1997-98; Solicitor General 2001-05; Minister of State, Department for Constitutional Affairs/Ministry of Justice 2005-07; Leader of the House of Commons and Lord Privy Seal 2007-10; Ex-officio member House of Commons Commission 2007-10; Minister for Women and Equality 2007-10; Member Speaker's Committee for the Independent Parliamentary Standards Authority 2009-10; Acting Leader of the Opposition 2010, 2015; Deputy Leader of the Opposition/Shadow Deputy Prime Minister 2010-15; Shadow Secretary of State for: International Development 2010-11, Culture, Media and Sport 2011-15. *Select committees:* Chair: Modernisation of the House of Commons 2007-10; Joint Committee on Human Rights 2015-; Member, Liaison 2015-. Labour Party: Member, National Executive Committee 1993-98, Deputy Leader 2007-15, Chair 2007-15, Acting Leader 2010, 2015. *Councils and public bodies:* Chair, Childcare Commission 1999-2001.

Political interests: Women, social services, provision for under-fives, law, domestic violence, civil liberties.

Other: PC 1997.

Publications: A Woman's Work (Allen Lane, 2017).

Rt Hon Harriet Harman QC MP, House of Commons, London SW1A 0AA
Tel: 020 7219 4218 *Fax:* 020 7219 4877 *Email:* harriet.harman.mp@parliament.uk
Constituency: No constituency office *Website:* www.harrietharman.org *Twitter:* @HarrietHarman

CONSERVATIVE

HARPER, MARK

Forest of Dean *(Majority 9,502)*

Mark James Harper. Born 26 February 1970; Son of James and Jane Harper; Married Margaret Whelan 1999.

Education: Headlands School, Swindon, Wiltshire; Swindon College; Brasenose College, Oxford (BA philosophy, politics and economics 1991).

Non-political career: Auditor, KPMG 1991-95; Intel Corporation (UK) Ltd: Senior finance analyst 1995-97, Finance manager 1997-2000, Operations manager 2000-02; Owned accountancy practice 2002-05; Senior adviser, DWF LLP 2017-.

Political career: Contested Forest of Dean 2001 general election. Member for Forest of Dean since 5 May 2005 general election; Shadow Minister for: Defence 2005-07, Work and Pensions (Disabled People) 2007-10; Parliamentary Secretary (Minister for Political and Constitutional

Reform), Cabinet Office 2010-12; Minister of State for: Immigration, Home Office 2012-14, Disabled People, Department for Work and Pensions 2014-15; Chief Whip; Parliamentary Secretary to the Treasury 2015-16; Member, Parliamentary and Political Service Honours Committee 2015-16. *Select committees:* Member: Administration 2005-06, 2014, Work and Pensions 2009. South Swindon Conservative Association: Treasurer 1993-98, Deputy chair 1998.

Political interests: Education, special needs education, law and order, health, defence; Israel, Turkey, USA.

Other: ACA 1995. PC 2015.

Recreations: Walking the dogs, travel, cinema.

Rt Hon Mark Harper MP, House of Commons, London SW1A 0AA
Tel: 020 7219 5056 *Fax:* 020 7219 0937 *Email:* mark.harper.mp@parliament.uk
Constituency: 35 High Street, Cinderford, Gloucestershire GL14 2SL
Tel: 01594 823482 *Fax:* 01594 823623 *Website:* www.markharper.org
Twitter: @Mark_J_Harper

CONSERVATIVE

HARRINGTON, RICHARD

Watford *(Majority 2,092)*

Parliamentary Under-Secretary of State (Minister for Energy and Industry), Department for Business, Energy and Industrial Strategy

Richard Irwin Harrington. Born 4 November 1957; Married Jessie 1983 (2 sons).

Education: Leeds Grammar School; Keble College, Oxford (MA law and jurisprudence 1979).

Non-political career: Assistant to managing director, Waitrose; Founder, now non-executive director, Harvington Properties 1983-; Managing director, then chairman, holiday resort company 1990-2000.

Political career: Member for Watford since 6 May 2010 general election; Prime Minister's Adviser on Apprentices 2015; Parliamentary Under-Secretary of State: Home Office, Department for Communities and Local Government and Department for International Development 2015-16, for Pensions, Department for Work and Pensions 2016-17, (Minister for Energy and Industry), Department for Business, Energy and Industrial Strategy 2017-. *Select committees:* Member, International Development 2010-12. Conservative Party: Treasurer 2008-10, Vice-chairman (Target Seats) 2012-; Chair, executive board, Conservative Friends of Israel. *Councils and public bodies:* Governor, University College School, Hampstead 2000-15.

Political interests: Youth unemployment, local transport infrastructure, business and enterprise, treasury; Kashmir, Middle East, Pakistan.

Other: Fundraising chair and trustee, Variety Club Children's Society 1998-2001; Trustee, Holocaust Educational Trust; Patron: Watford Workshops, Peace Hospice, Watford, Michael Green Foundation; Oriental Club, Oxhey Conservative Club, Watford Town and Country Club.

Recreations: Cinema, watching football.

Richard Harrington MP, House of Commons, London SW1A 0AA
Tel: 020 7219 7180 *Email:* richard.harrington.mp@parliament.uk
Constituency: No constituency office publicised
Tel: 01923 296790 *Email:* richard@richardharrington.org.uk
Website: www.richardharrington.org.uk *Twitter:* @Richard4Watford

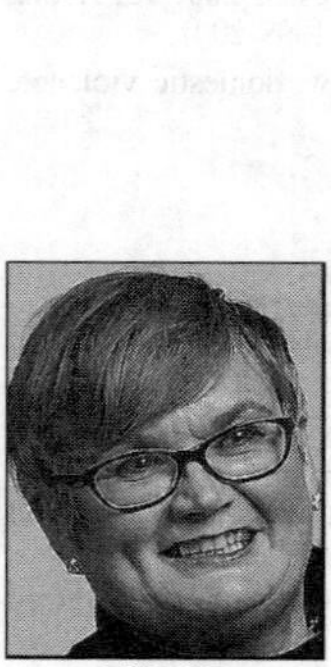

LABOUR

HARRIS, CAROLYN

Swansea East *(Majority 13,168)*

Shadow Minister for Women and Equalities

Born 18 September 1960; Daughter of Don and Pauline Marvelley; 3 sons.

Education: Swansea University (BSc social history 1998).

Non-political career: Project Manager, Guiding Hands Charity 1998-2000; Wales Regional Director, Community Logistics 2000-03; Wales Regional Manager, Children's Cancer Charity 2003-05; Senior Parliamentary Assistant/Constituency Manager to Siân James MP 2005-15. GMB; Unison; Unite; Usdaw.

Political career: Member for Swansea East since 7 May 2015 general election; Shadow Minister for: Home Office 2016-17, Women and Equalities 2017-. *Select committees:* Member: Welsh Affairs 2015-16, Environmental Audit 2015-16. *Councils and public bodies:* School governor.

Political interests: State pension inequality for women, home electrical safety, fixed odds betting terminals, children's funeral fund.

Other: Trustee, Unity Trust Wales; Vice-President, Chartered Institute for Trading Standards. Campaigning MP of the Year, Mirror Politics 2016 Welsh Labour Campaign of the Year 2016.

Carolyn Harris MP, House of Commons, London SW1A 0AA
Tel: 020 7219 4316 *Email:* carolyn.harris.mp@parliament.uk
Constituency: 485 Llangyfelach Road, Brynhyfryd, Swansea SA5 9EA
Tel: 01792 462054 *Website:* www.carolynharris.org.uk *Twitter:* @carolynharris24

CONSERVATIVE

HARRIS, REBECCA Castle Point *(Majority 18,872)*

Assistant Government Whip

Rebecca Elizabeth Scott Harris. Born 22 December 1967; Daughter of Philip and Louise Harris; Married Frank Skelton 1999 (1 son).

Non-political career: Marketing director, Philimore and Co (publisher) 1997-2007; Campaign officer, Conservative Research Department 1998-2001; Special adviser to Tim Yeo MP 2003-10.

Political career: Member for Castle Point since 6 May 2010 general election; PPS to: Theresa Villiers as Secretary of State for Northern Ireland 2015-16, Sajid Javid as Secretary of State for Communities and Local Government 2016-17; Assistant Government Whip 2017-. *Select committees:* Member: Business, Innovation and Skills 2010-15, Joint Committee on the Draft Enhanced Terrorism Prevention and Investigation Measures Bill 2012-13, Regulatory Reform 2012-. Conservative Party: Campaign co-ordinator, Campaign HQ 2000-01, North West London area officer 2007-08, Vice-chairman (Youth) 2013-. *Councils and public bodies:* Chichester District Council: Councillor 1999-2003, Deputy chair, scrutiny committee 1999-2003.

Political interests: Small business, education and skills, planning.

Other: Patron: Cascade Foundation, Danny Green Foundation, Mickey Payne Foundation, Careers Choices; Hadleigh Conservative Club, Canvey Island Conservative Club, Benfleet Conservative Club.

Recreations: Gardening, walking.

Rebecca Harris MP, House of Commons, London SW1A 0AA
Tel: 020 7219 7206 *Email:* rebecca.harris.mp@parliament.uk
Constituency: c/o Castle Point Conservatives, Bernard Braine House, 8 Green Road, Benfleet, Essex SS7 5JT
Tel: 01268 792992 *Fax:* 01268 792992 *Email:* office@castlepointconservatives.com
Websites: www.castlepointconservatives.com www.rebeccaharris.org
Twitter: @RebeccaHarrisMP

CONSERVATIVE

HARRISON, TRUDY Copeland *(Majority 1,695)*

Trudy Lynne Harrison. Born 19 April 1976; Married Keith (4 daughters).

Education: Salford University (FdSc sustainable communities 2013).

Non-political career: Technical clerk, Sellafield Ltd 1993-98; Owner/Director, Sunny Days (childcare business) 2002-06; Copeland Borough Council: Locality officer 2010-13, Community regeneration officer 2013; Project manager, Wellbank Project 2013-17; Programme manager, Bootle2020 2014-17.

Political career: Member for Copeland since 23 February 2017 by-election. *Select committees:* Member, Education 2017-. *Councils and public bodies:* Chair of governors, Captain Shaw's CoE Primary School 2003-; Parish Councillor, Bootle Parish Council.

Other: Director, Pub at Millstones Ltd.

Trudy Harrison MP, House of Commons, London SW1A 0AA
Tel: 020 7219 4002 *Email:* trudy.harrison.mp@parliament.uk
Constituency: Main Street, Bootle, Millom, Cumbria LA19 5TF
Tel: 01229 718333 *Email:* trudy@trudyharrison.co.uk *Website:* www.trudyharrison.co.uk

CONSERVATIVE

HART, SIMON Carmarthen West and South Pembrokeshire *(Majority 3,110)*

Simon Anthony Hart. Born 15 August 1963; Married Abigail Holland 1998 (1 son 1 daughter).

Education: Radley College, Oxfordshire; Royal Agriculture College, Cirencester (Diploma rural estate management 1984).

Non-political career: Territorial Army. Chartered surveyor, Knight, Frank & Rutley 1986-88; Associated to sole principal, Llewellyn Humphreys 1988-98; Associate land agent, Balfour, Burd & Benson 1998-99; Countryside Alliance 1999-2010: Campaigns director 1999-2003, Chief executive 2003-10, Outdoor education consultant -2015, Chair 2015-.

Political career: Member for Carmarthen West and South Pembrokeshire since 6 May 2010 general election; Trade Envoy to Panama, Costa Rica and Dominican Republic 2017-.

Select committees: Member: Political and Constitutional Reform 2010-13, Welsh Affairs 2012-15, Environment, Food and Rural Affairs 2015-17, Environment, Food and Rural Affairs Sub-committee 2015-17, Digital, Culture, Media and Sport 2017-. Member, Executive, 1922 Committee 2012-16. Founding member, Conservatives for Reform in Europe 2016. *Councils and public bodies:* Member, Committee on Standards in Public Life 2017-.

Political interests: Rural affairs, small business; Falkland Islands.

Other: Member, UK Delegation, Organisation for Security and Co-operation in Europe Parliamentary Assembly 2016-; Associate, Royal Institute of Chartered Surveyors 1985; Farmers' Club. Cresselly Cricket Club.

Recreations: Cricket, all aspects of country sports.

Simon Hart MP, House of Commons, London SW1A 0AA
Tel: 020 7219 7228 *Email:* simon.hart.mp@parliament.uk
Constituency: 15 St John Street, Whitland, Carmarthenshire SA34 0AN
Tel: 01994 242002 *Website:* www.simon-hart.com *Twitter:* @Simonhartmp

HAYES, HELEN

Dulwich and West Norwood *(Majority 28,156)*

LABOUR

Helen Elizabeth Hayes. Born 8 August 1974; Married (2 daughters).

Education: Ormskirk Grammar School 1985-92; Balliol College, Oxford (BA politics, philosophy and economics 1996); London School of Economics (MSc social policy and administration 1997).

Non-political career: Joint Managing Director, Urban Practitioners Ltd 1998-2011 Partner, Allies and Morrison 2011-15. Member, GMB.

Political career: Member for Dulwich and West Norwood since 7 May 2015 general election. *Select committees:* Member, Communities and Local Government 2015-. *Councils and public bodies:* Councillor, Southwark Council 2010-16.

Political interests: NHS, local government, housing, planning, climate change, human rights, international development, arts and culture.

Other: Member: Amnesty International, Soil Association, Fabian Society, Compass, Friends of Dulwich Picture Gallery, Friends of Kingswood House, Ramblers; Chartered member, Royal Town Planning Institute; Academician, Academy of Urbanism.

Helen Hayes MP, House of Commons, London SW1A 0AA
Tel: 020 7219 6971 *Email:* helen.hayes.mp@parliament.uk
Constituency: No constituency office publicised *Website:* www.helenhayes.org.uk
Twitter: @helenhayes_

HAYES, JOHN

South Holland and The Deepings *(Majority 24,897)*

CONSERVATIVE

Minister of State for Transport Legislation and Maritime, Department for Transport

John Henry Hayes. Born 23 June 1958; Son of late Henry Hayes and Lily Hayes; Married Susan Hopewell 1997 (2 sons).

Education: Colfe's Grammar School, London; Nottingham University (BA politics 1980; PGCE history/English 1982); Some Italian and Spanish.

Non-political career: Data Base Ltd IT company 1983-99: Director 1986-97, Non-executive director 1997-99; Associate professor, American University in London 2005-10. Associate member, Association of Teachers and Lecturers.

Political career: Contested Derbyshire North East 1987 and 1992 general elections. Member for South Holland and The Deepings 1997-2010, for South Holland and The Deepings (revised boundary) since 6 May 2010 general election; Shadow Minister for Schools 2000-01; Opposition Pairing Whip 2001-02; Shadow Minister for: Agriculture, Fisheries and Food 2002-03, Local and Devolved Government (Housing and Planning) 2003-05, Transport 2005, Vocational Education 2005-09, Lifelong Learning, Further and Higher Education 2009, Universities and Skills 2009-10; Minister of State for: Further Education, Skills and Lifelong Learning, Departments for Business, Innovation and Skills and Education 2010-12, Energy, Department of Energy and Climate Change 2012-13; Minister without Portfolio, Cabinet Office 2013-14; Senior Parliamentary Adviser to the Prime Minister 2013-15; Minister of State: Department for Transport 2014-15, 2016- (for Transport Legislation and Maritime 2017-), for Security, Home Office 2015-16. *Select committees:* Member: Agriculture 1997-99, Education and Employment 1998-99,1999-2000, Education and Employment (Education Sub-Committee) 1999-2000, Selection 2001-02, Administration 2001-

02. Joint vice-chair, Conservative Party Committee for Education and Employment 1997-99; Conservative Party Committee for Agriculture, Fisheries and Food: Joint secretary 1998-99, Secretary 1999-2000. Former chair, Young Conservatives; Vice-chair: Conservatives Against Federal Europe, Conservative Party 1999-2000; Member, 1992 Group; Joint chair, Cornerstone Group 2004-. *Councils and public bodies:* Councillor, Nottinghamshire County Council 1985-98.

Political interests: Education, elections and campaigning, political ideas and philosophy, local government, agriculture, commerce and industry, energy, welfare of elderly and disabled people; England, Italy, Spain, USA.

Other: Countryside member, NFU; Countryside Alliance; SPUC; Patron, Headway Cambridgeshire; Chair, British Caribbean Association 2009-; President: Spalding Parkinson Society, Sneath's Mill; Patron: Headway, Cambridgeshire, Lincolnshire Brain Tumour Support Group, Holbeach Community Vehicle, Spalding Transport Forum; Headway, various local charities in South Lincolnshire. Charity Champion award 2008; Double Act of the Year (with Ed Davey MP), *Spectator* awards 2012; *The House Magazine*: Commons Minister of the Year, Dods Parliamentary Awards 2012, Environmental Campaigner of the Year, Dods Parliamentary Awards 2014. PC 2013; CBE 2016; Carlton Club, Spalding Club, Spalding Gentlemen's Society.

Publications: Representing Rural Britain – Blair's Bogus Claim (Conservative Policy Forum, 2000); Answer the Question: Prime Ministerial Accountability and the Rule of Parliament (Politica, 2000); Tony B. Liar (Conservative Party, 2001); The Right to Own: Conservative Action on Housing (Conservative Party, 2004); The Right Homes in the Right Places (Conservative Party, 2005); Being Conservative: A Cornerstone of Policies to Revive Tory Britain (Cornerstone Group, 2005); Towards a Virtuous Circle of Learning (NIACE, 2006); Towards a Gold Standard for Craft, Guaranteeing Professional Apprenticeships (Centre for Policy Studies, 2007); From Social Engineering to Social Aspiration: Strategies to Broaden Access to Higher Education (UALL/Birkbeck, 2008).

Recreations: The arts (particularly English painting, poetry and prose), good food and wine, many sports (including boxing), studying the past, gardening, making jam, antiques, architecture and aesthetics.

Rt Hon John Hayes CBE MP, House of Commons, London SW1A 0AA
Tel: 020 7219 1389 *Fax:* 020 7219 2273 *Email:* hayesj@parliament.uk
Constituency: 10 Broad Street, Spalding, Lincolnshire PE11 1TB
Tel: 01775 711534 *Fax:* 01775 713905 *Email:* davieshm@parliament.uk

LABOUR

HAYMAN, SUE

Workington *(Majority 3,925)*

Shadow Secretary of State for Environment, Food and Rural Affairs

Susan Mary Hayman. Born 28 July 1962; Married Ross (2 children).

Non-political career: Constituency office manager to: Tess Kingham MP, Michael John Foster MP; Business development director, 3G Communications/Copper Consultancy; Community relations consultant. Former member, Trade and General Workers' Union; Member, GMB.

Political career: Contested Preseli Pembrokeshire 2005 and Halesowen and Rowley Regis 2010 general elections. Member for Workington since 7 May 2015 general election; Opposition Whip 2015-16; Shadow Minister for Flooding and Coastal Communities 2016-17; Shadow Secretary of State for Environment, Food and Rural Affairs 2017-. *Select committees:* Member, Justice 2015. Contested West Midlands region 2004 European Parliament election. *Councils and public bodies:* Cumbria County Council: Councillor 2013-15, Vice-chair, Children and Young People's Scrutiny Committee; Former chair of school governors.

Political interests: Energy, NHS, human rights, local transport, cost of living, arts funding.

Sue Hayman MP, House of Commons, London SW1A 0AA
Tel: 020 7219 4554/020 7219 0584 *Email:* sue.hayman.mp@parliament.uk
Constituency: The Town Hall, Oxford Street, Workington CA14 2RS
Tel: 01900 702929 *Website:* suehayman.org.uk *Twitter:* @SueHayman1

SINN FÉIN

HAZZARD, CHRIS

South Down *(Majority 2,446)*

Christopher John Hazzard. Born 20 August 1984; Son of Brian Hazzard and Teresa Hazzard, née McManus.

Education: Our Lady and St Patrick's College, Belfast; Queen's University, Belfast (BA history and politics 2006; MA Irish politics 2008; PhD political philosophy).

Political career: Contested South Down 2015 general election. Member for South Down since 8 June 2017; MLA (replacement) for South Down 2012-17: Sinn Féin Spokesperson for: Environment 2012, Education 2012-16, Victims and Truth 2014-16; Minister for Infrastructure 2016-17.

Chris Hazzard MP, House of Commons, London SW1A 0AA
Tel: 020 7219 4004 *Email:* chris.hazzard.mp@parliament.uk
Constituency: Details still to be confirmed
Tel: 028 4377 0185 *Twitter:* @chrishazzardsf

CONSERVATIVE

HEALD, OLIVER

North East Hertfordshire *(Majority 16,835)*

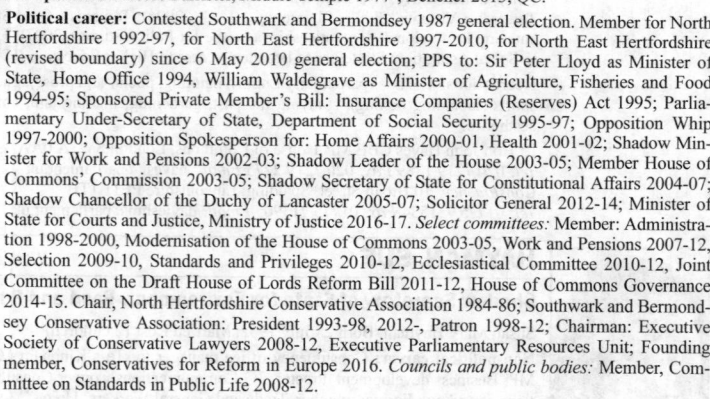

Born 15 December 1954; Son of late J A Heald, chartered engineer, and late Joyce Heald, née Pemberton, teacher; Married Christine Whittle 1979 (1 son 2 daughters).

Education: Reading School; Pembroke College, Cambridge (MA law 1976); French, German.

Non-political career: Barrister, Middle Temple 1977-; Bencher 2013; QC.

Political career: Contested Southwark and Bermondsey 1987 general election. Member for North Hertfordshire 1992-97, for North East Hertfordshire 1997-2010, for North East Hertfordshire (revised boundary) since 6 May 2010 general election; PPS to: Sir Peter Lloyd as Minister of State, Home Office 1994, William Waldegrave as Minister of Agriculture, Fisheries and Food 1994-95; Sponsored Private Member's Bill: Insurance Companies (Reserves) Act 1995; Parliamentary Under-Secretary of State, Department of Social Security 1995-97; Opposition Whip 1997-2000; Opposition Spokesperson for: Home Affairs 2000-01, Health 2001-02; Shadow Minister for Work and Pensions 2002-03; Shadow Leader of the House 2003-05; Member House of Commons' Commission 2003-05; Shadow Secretary of State for Constitutional Affairs 2004-07; Shadow Chancellor of the Duchy of Lancaster 2005-07; Solicitor General 2012-14; Minister of State for Courts and Justice, Ministry of Justice 2016-17. *Select committees:* Member: Administration 1998-2000, Modernisation of the House of Commons 2003-05, Work and Pensions 2007-12, Selection 2009-10, Standards and Privileges 2010-12, Ecclesiastical Committee 2010-12, Joint Committee on the Draft House of Lords Reform Bill 2011-12, House of Commons Governance 2014-15. Chair, North Hertfordshire Conservative Association 1984-86; Southwark and Bermondsey Conservative Association: President 1993-98, 2012-, Patron 1998-12; Chairman: Executive Society of Conservative Lawyers 2008-12, Executive Parliamentary Resources Unit; Founding member, Conservatives for Reform in Europe 2016. *Councils and public bodies:* Member, Committee on Standards in Public Life 2008-12.

Political interests: Industrial relations, environment, law and order, pensions.

Other: Member, Council of Europe 2008-12; Chair, PRU 2010-12. Kt 2014; PC 2016.

Publications: Co-author, Auditing the New Deal: What Figures for the Future (Politeia, 2004); A Reformed Second Chamber: Building a Better House (Society of Conservative Lawyers, 2012).

Recreations: Sport, family.

Rt Hon Sir Oliver Heald QC MP, House of Commons, London SW1A 0AA
Tel: 020 7219 6354 *Email:* oliver.heald.mp@parliament.uk
Constituency: No constituency office publicised
Tel: 01462 486074 *Website:* www.oliverhealdmp.com *Twitter:* @OliverHealdUK

LABOUR

HEALEY, JOHN

Wentworth and Dearne *(Majority 14,803)*

Shadow Secretary of State for Housing

Born 13 February 1960; Son of Aidan Healey, prison service, and Jean Healey, teacher; Married Jackie Bate 1993 (1 son).

Education: Lady Lumley's Comprehensive School, Pickering; St Peter's School, York; Christ's College, Cambridge (Scholar; BA 1982).

Non-political career: Journalist/deputy editor, *House Magazine* 1983-84; Disability campaigner for three national charities 1984-90; Tutor, Open University Business School 1989-92; Campaigns manager, Issue Communications 1990-92; Head of communications, MSF Union 1992-94; Campaigns and communications director, Trades Union Congress 1994-97. Member, GMB.

Political career: Contested Ryedale 1992 general election. Member for Wentworth 1997-2010, for Wentworth and Dearne since 6 May 2010 general election; PPS to Gordon Brown as Chancellor of the Exchequer 1999-2001; Parliamentary Under-Secretary of State, Department for Education and Skills (Adult Skills) 2001-02; HM Treasury 2002-07: Economic Secretary 2002-05, Financial Secretary 2005-07; Minister of State, Department for Communities and Local Government 2007-10: Minister for Local Government 2007-09, Minister for Housing (attending Cabinet) 2009-10; Member Speaker's Committee on the Electoral Commission -2009; Shadow Minister for Housing 2010; Shadow Secretary of State for Health 2010-11; Shadow Minister for Housing and Planning (attending Shadow Cabinet) 2015-16; Shadow Secretary of State for Housing 2016-. *Select committees:* Member: Education and Employment 1997-99, Education and Employment (Employment Sub-Committee) 1997-99, Public Accounts 2005-07, Joint Committee on Tax Law Rewrite Bills 2005-09. Member, Labour Party National Executive Committee 2014-15. *Councils and public bodies:* Vice-President, Local Government Association 2010-11, 2017-.

Political interests: Employment, trade unions, economy, tax, industrial relations, disability, local and regional government; Australia, USA.

Other: Group Board member, Incommunities Housing Association 2013-15; Rotherham Hospice. *The House Magazine* Dods Parliamentary Awards 2014: Constituency Campaigner of the Year, Written Contribution of the Year. PC 2008.

Recreations: Family.

Rt Hon John Healey MP, House of Commons, London SW1A 0AA
Tel: 020 7219 6359 *Fax:* 020 7219 2451 *Email:* john.healey.mp@parliament.uk
Constituency: 79 High Street, Wath-upon-Dearne, Rotherham, South Yorkshire S63 7QB
Tel: 01709 875943 *Fax:* 01709 874207 *Website:* www.johnhealeymp.co.uk
Twitter: @JohnHealey_MP

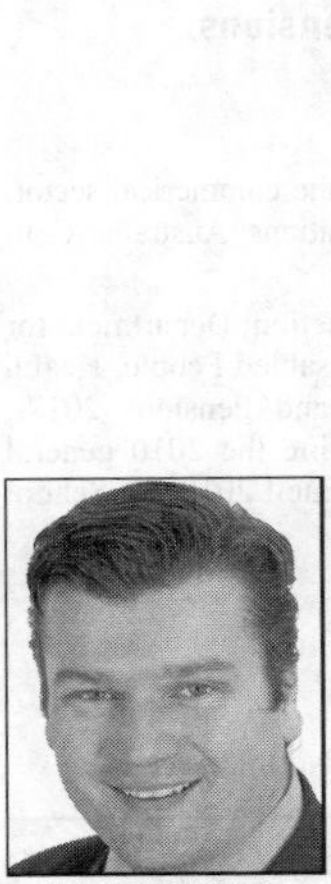

CONSERVATIVE

HEAPPEY, JAMES

Wells *(Majority 7,582)*

PPS to Chris Grayling as Secretary of State for Transport

James Stephen Heappey. Born 30 January 1981; Married Kate (2 children).

Education: Queen Elizabeth's Hospital School, Bristol; Birmingham University (BA political science 2003).

Non-political career: Lieutenant, Royal Gloucestershire, Berkshire and Wiltshire Regiment 2004-06; Captain, the Major, The Rifles 2007-12. British Army: Operations in: Kabul 2005, Northern Ireland 2006, Basra 2007, Sangin, Helmand Province 2009, Executive Office, Army General Staff, Ministry of Defence, London; Parliamentary researcher to Liam Fox MP; Self-employed project manager, specialising in business risk and resilience.

Political career: Member for Wells since 7 May 2015 general election; PPS to Chris Grayling as Secretary of State for Transport 2017-. *Select committees:* Member, Energy and Climate Change 2015-16.

Political interests: Rural affairs, tourism, digital economy, environment, energy, skills.

Recreations: Rugby, golf, tennis, cooking.

James Heappey MP, House of Commons, London SW1A 0AA
Tel: 020 7219 4289 *Email:* james.heappey.mp@parliament.uk
Constituency: 5 Cathedral View Offices, Wookey Hole Road, Wells, Somerset BA5 2BT
Tel: 01749 343255 *Website:* www.jamesheappey.org.uk *Twitter:* @JSHeappey

CONSERVATIVE

HEATON-HARRIS, CHRIS

Daventry *(Majority 21,734)*

Government Whip (Vice-Chamberlain of HM Household)

Christopher Heaton-Harris. Born 28 November 1967; Son of David and Ann Heaton-Harris; Married Jayne Carlow 1990 (2 daughters).

Education: Tiffin Grammar School for Boys, Kingston-upon-Thames, Surrey.

Non-political career: Various positions, What 4 Ltd (wholesale fresh produce company) 1989-99; Owner, Whistle Blower Ltd 2009-10.

Political career: Contested Leicester South 1997 general election and 2004 by-election. Member for Daventry since 6 May 2010 general election; Assistant Government Whip 2016-17; Government Whip (Vice-Chamberlain of HM Household) 2017-. *Select committees:* Member: Public Accounts 2010-15, European Scrutiny 2010-15. European Parliament: MEP for East Midlands 1999-2009: Founder member, Campaign for Parliamentary Reform 2001, Chief Whip, EP Conservatives 2001-04.

Political interests: EU renegotiations, Europe, energy policy, sport, education, disabilities, special olympics, health, neonatal care, selective dorsal rhizotomy; Kenya, Uganda, USA.

Other: Member, Executive Committee, Inter-Parliamentary Union, British Group 2010-12; President, Sports Intergroup 2002-09; Chair, Friends of Football 2003-06; Patron, UKAN2.

Recreations: Football referee, sport.

Chris Heaton-Harris MP, House of Commons, London SW1A 0AA
Tel: 020 7219 7048 *Fax:* 020 7219 1375 *Email:* chris.heatonharris.mp@parliament.uk
Constituency: 78 St George's Avenue, Northampton, Northamptonshire NN2 6JF
Tel: 01604 859721 *Fax:* 01604 859329 *Email:* agent@wnc.uk.com
Websites: www.daventryconservatives.com www.heatonharris.com *Twitter:* @chhcalling

CONSERVATIVE

HEATON-JONES, PETER

North Devon *(Majority 4,332)*

PPS to David Gauke as Secretary of State for Work and Pensions

Born 2 August 1963.

Education: University of London.

Non-political career: Reporter, producer, editor and presenter, BBC and the commerical sector; Media trainer and consultant; Head of marketing, ABC's national radio stations, Australia; Constituency office manager, Robert Buckland MP and Justin Tomlinson MP.

Political career: Member for North Devon since 7 May 2015 general election; Department for Work and Pensions: PPS to: Penny Mordaunt as Minister of State for Disabled People, Health and Work 2016-17, David Gauke as Secretary of State for Work and Pensions 2017-. *Select committees:* Member, Environmental Audit 2015-17. Agent during the 2010 general election. *Councils and public bodies:* Councillor, Swindon Borough Council 2010-14; School governror.

Political interests: Planning.

Peter Heaton-Jones MP, House of Commons, London SW1A 0AA
Tel: 020 7219 5728 *Email:* peter.heatonjones.mp@parliament.uk
Constituency: Church House, Church Lane, Barnstaple, Devon EX31 1DE
Tel: 01271 327990 *Website:* www.peterheatonjones.org.uk *Twitter:* @PeterNorthDevon

CONSERVATIVE

HENDERSON, GORDON

Sittingbourne and Sheppey *(Majority 15,211)*

Gordon Leonard Henderson. Born 27 January 1948; Son of William and Shirley Henderson; Married Louise Crowder 1994 (1 son 2 daughters).

Education: Fort Luton High School for Boys; Rochester Mathematical School.

Non-political career: Manager, Woolworths 1964-79; Self-employed Restaurateur 1979-83; Senior Contracts Officer, GEC Marconi Avionics 1983-93; Operations Manager, Beams UK 1993-2007; Management Consultant 2008-10.

Political career: Contested Luton South 2001 and Sittingbourne and Sheppey 2005 general elections. Member for Sittingbourne and Sheppey since 6 May 2010 general election. *Select committees:* Member, Regulatory Reform 2010-15. Member: Conservative Party, Conservative Friends of Israel. *Councils and public bodies:* Deputy leader, Conservative group, Swale Borough Council 1986-90, 1991-95; Member, Kent Police Authority 1989-93; Councillor, Kent County Council 1989-93.

Political interests: Law and order, defence, business; Southern Africa, India, Israel.

Other: Director, Halfway Conservative Hall Ltd 1989-; Chairman, Litter Angels Ltd 2007-; Freedom Centre Sheerness, Demelza House children's hospice, Litter Angels; Sheerness Conservative Club.

Publications: The Almost Twins and the Litter Angel (2014); Pigeon Pie and Other Tasty Pieces (2014); Operation Seal Island (2016).

Recreations: Reading, writing, football.

Gordon Henderson MP, House of Commons, London SW1A 0AA
Tel: 020 7219 7144 *Email:* gordon.henderson.mp@parliament.uk
Constituency: Top Floor, Unit 10, Periwinkle Court Business Centre, Milton Regis, Sittingbourne, Kent ME10 2JZ
Tel: 01795 423199 *Email:* jess.mcmahon@parliament.uk
Website: www.gordonhendersonmp.org.uk

HENDRICK, MARK

Preston *(Majority 15,723)*

LAB/CO-OP

Mark Phillip Hendrick. Born 2 November 1958; Son of Brian Hendrick, timber worker, and Jennifer Hendrick, née Chapman, clerk/typist; Married Yu Yannan 2008.

Education: Salford Grammar School; Liverpool Polytechnic (BSc electrical and electronic engineering 1982); Manchester University (MSc computer science 1985, CertEd 1992); Volkshochschule, Hanau, Germany ('Zertifikat Deutsch als Fremdsprache'); CEng; German (fluent).

Non-political career: Student engineer, Ministry of Defence 1979; Work student, AEG Telefunken 1981; Science and Engineering Research Council 1982-84, 1985-88; Lecturer in electronics and software design, Stockport college 1990-94. Member, GMB.

Political career: Member for Preston 23 November 2000 by-election to 2010, for Preston (revised boundary) since 6 May 2010 general election; PPS: to Margaret Beckett: as Secretary of State for Environment, Food and Rural Affairs 2003-06, as Foreign Secretary 2006-07, to Jack Straw as Lord Chancellor and Secretary of State for Justice 2007-08, to Ivan Lewis as Minister of State, Foreign and Commonwealth Office 2009-10; Opposition Whip 2010-12. *Select committees:* Member: European Scrutiny 2001-04, International Development 2009-10, Foreign Affairs 2012-17, High Speed Rail (London-West Midlands) Bill 2015-16. European Parliament: MEP for Lancashire Central 1994-99. Chair, Eccles CLP 1990-94; Member, Preston and District Co-operative Party 1994-; Chair, Labour/Co-operative Parliamentary Group 2005-06. *Councils and public bodies:* Salford City Council: Councillor 1987-95, Representative as an alternate director, Manchester Airport plc 1987-94.

Political interests: Foreign affairs, defence, European affairs, economic and industrial affairs, international development; China, Germany, Hungary, Japan, Poland, USA.

Other: Member, UK Delegation, Organisation for Security and Co-operation in Europe Parliamentary Assembly; RSPCA, CAFOD; Deepdale Labour Club. Penwortham Sports and Social.

Publications: Changing States: A Labour Agenda for Europe (Mandarin Paperbacks, 1996); The euro and Co-operative Enterprise: Co-operating with the euro (Co-operative Press Ltd, 1998).

Recreations: Football, boxing, chess, travel, foreign languages.

Mark Hendrick MP, House of Commons, London SW1A 0AA
Tel: 020 7219 4791 *Fax:* 020 7219 5220 *Email:* mark.hendrick.mp@parliament.uk
Constituency: PTMC, Marsh Lane, Preston, Lancashire PR1 8UQ
Tel: 01772 883575 *Fax:* 01772 887188 *Email:* warhurste@parliament.uk
Website: www.prestonmp.co.uk *Twitter:* @MpHendrick

HENDRY, DREW

Inverness, Nairn, Badenoch and Strathspey *(Majority 4,924)*

SCOTTISH NATIONAL PARTY

SNP Spokesperson for Business, Energy and Industrial Strategy

Andrew Egan Henderson Hendry. Born 31 May 1964; Married Jackie (4 children).

Non-political career: Director: Electrolux, AEG; Teclan Ltd: Founder 1999-, Honorary Chairman.

Political career: Member for Inverness, Nairn, Badenoch and Strathspey since 7 May 2015 general election; SNP Spokesperson for: Transport 2015-17, Business, Energy and Industrial Strategy 2017-. *Select committees:* Member, Business, Energy and Industrial Strategy 2017-. Contested Scotland region 2009 European Parliament election and Highlands and Islands region (9) 2011 Scottish Parliament election. Vice-convener, Dingwall and District SNP; Member, SNP CND. *Councils and public bodies:* Highland Council: Councillor 2007-15, Chair, Planning Environment and Development Committee, SNP Group: Finance Spokesperson, Leader 2011-15, Leader of the Council 2012-15.

Political interests: Scottish home rule.

Other: Vice-President, Conference of Maritime Peripheral Regions 2012-; Honorary Consul to Embassy of Romania 2012-.

Recreations: Football, swimming.

Drew Hendry MP, House of Commons, London SW1A 0AA
Tel: 020 7219 6118 *Email:* drew.hendry.mp@parliament.uk
Constituency: 110 Church Street, Inverness IV1 1EP
Tel: 01463 611024 *Website:* www.drewhendrymp.scot *Twitter:* @drewhendrySNP

LABOUR

HEPBURN, STEPHEN

Jarrow *(Majority 17,263)*

Born 6 December 1959; Son of Peter and Margaret Hepburn.

Education: Springfield Comprehensive, Jarrow; Newcastle University (BA politics).

Non-political career: Labourer, South Tyneside Metropolitan Borough Council; Research assistant to Don Dixon MP. Member, UCATT.

Political career: Member for Jarrow 1997-2010, for Jarrow (revised boundary) since 6 May 2010 general election. *Select committees:* Member: Administration 1997-2001, Defence 1999-2001, Accommodation and Works 2003-05, Northern Ireland Affairs 2004-, Administration 2009-10, Scottish Affairs 2015-17. *Councils and public bodies:* South Tyneside Council: Councillor 1985-97, Chair Finance Committee 1989-90, Deputy Leader 1990-97.

Political interests: Small businesses.

Other: Supporter, St Clare's Hospice; Jarrow Neon Social Club, Hebburn Iona Catholic Club. President, Jarrow FC; Patron, Jarrow Roofing FC.

Recreations: Football.

Stephen Hepburn MP, House of Commons, London SW1A 0AA
Tel: 020 7219 4134 *Email:* hepburns@parliament.uk
Constituency: 141 Tedco Business Centre, Viking Industrial Estate, Jarrow, Tyne and Wear NE32 3DT
Tel: 0191-420 0648 *Fax:* 0191-489 7531 *Email:* hepburn4jarrow@btinternet.com
Website: stephenhepburn-mp.org.uk *Twitter:* @jarrowstevemp

CONSERVATIVE

HERBERT, NICK

Arundel and South Downs *(Majority 23,883)*

Nicholas Le Quesne Herbert. Born 7 April 1963; Civil partner Jason Eades 2008.

Education: Haileybury College, Hertford; Magdalene College, Cambridge (BA law and land economy 1985).

Non-political career: British Field Sports Society 1990-96: Director of political affairs 1992-96 (co-founder Countryside Movement); Chief executive, Business for Sterling 1998-2000 (founder of the 'No' Campaign); Director, Reform 2002-05; Member, advisory board, CREST Advisory (UK) Ltd 2015-.

Political career: Contested Berwick-upon-Tweed 1997 general election. Member for Arundel and South Downs 2005-10, for Arundel and South Downs (revised boundary) since 6 May 2010 general election; Shadow Minister for Police Reform 2005-07; Shadow Secretary of State for: Justice 2007-09, Environment, Food and Rural Affairs 2009-10; Minister of State for Policing and Criminal Justice, Home Office and Ministry of Justice 2010-12. *Select committees:* Member, Home Affairs 2005-06.

Political interests: Rural affairs, public services, the economy, international development.

Other: Co-chair, Global TB Caucus. PC 2010; CBE 2016.

Publications: Why Vote Conservative 2015.

Recreations: Watching cricket, racing, country sports, cinema, theatre, opera.

Rt Hon Nick Herbert CBE MP, House of Commons, London SW1A 0AA
Tel: 020 7219 4080
Constituency: No constituency office
Email: nick@nickherbert.com *Website:* www.nickherbert.com *Twitter:* @nickherbertmp

INDEPENDENT

HERMON, SYLVIA

North Down *(Majority 1,208)*

Sylvia Eileen Hermon. Born 11 August 1955; Daughter of Robert and Mary Paisley; Married Sir John Hermon, OBE QPM 1988 (died 2008) (2 sons).

Education: Dungannon High School for Girls; Aberstwyth University, Wales (LLB 1977); Chester College of Law (Part II Solicitors' Qualifying Examinations 1978); French, German.

Non-political career: Lecturer, European, international and constitutional law, Queen's University, Belfast 1978-88.

Political career: Member for North Down since 7 June 2001 general election; UUP Spokesperson for: Home Affairs 2001-05, Trade and Industry 2001-02, Youth and Women's Issues 2001-05, Culture, Media and Sport 2002-05. *Select committees:* Member, Northern Ireland Affairs 2005-. Author and committee member addressing Patten Report, also of Criminal Justice Review 2000; Ulster Unionist Executive 1999; Constituency chair, North Down Unionist Constituency Association 2001-03; Resigned from the UUP March 2010, now sits as an Independent.

Political interests: Policing, human rights, European affairs, health, education; India, Republic of Ireland, Russia.

Other: Honorary member: Donaghadee Rotary Club, Bangor Club of Soroptomists International; Patron, Evergreens; Marie Curie Cancer Care, Alzheimer's Society, RNLI, RUC GC Foundation.

Publications: A Guide to EEC Law in Northern Ireland (SLS Legal Publications (NI), 1986).

Recreations: Swimming, ornithology.

Sylvia Hermon MP, House of Commons, London SW1A 0AA
Tel: 020 7219 0862 *Fax:* 020 7219 1969 *Email:* sylvia.hermon.mp@parliament.uk
Constituency: 17a Hamilton Road, Bangor, Co Down BT20 4LF
Tel: 028 9127 5858 *Fax:* 028 9127 5747 *Email:* jamisons@parliament.uk

LABOUR

HILL, MIKE

Hartlepool *(Majority 7,650)*

Michael Robert Hill. Married Glynis (2 sons).

Education: Lancaster University (BA drama and theatre arts).

Non-political career: Regional Organiser, Unison -2017. Political lead officer, Unison Northern Region; Secretary, Trade Union and Labour Party Liaison Organisation; Former branch secretary, Rochdale Branch, Unison.

Political career: Contested Richmond (Yorkshire) 2015 general election. Member for Hartlepool since 8 June 2017. *Select committees:* Member, Petitions 2017-. Vice-chair, Labour North; Member, Co-operative Party.

Mike Hill MP, House of Commons, London SW1A 0AA
Tel: 020 7219 2543 *Email:* mike.hill.mp@parliament.uk
Constituency: Details still to be confirmed *Twitter:* @MikeHillMP

LAB/CO-OP

HILLIER, MEG

Hackney South and Shoreditch *(Majority 37,931)*

Chair, Select Committee on Public Accounts

Margaret Olivia Hillier. Born 14 February 1969; Married Joe Simpson 1997 (1 son 2 daughters).

Education: Portsmouth High School; St Hilda's College, Oxford (MA philosophy, politics and economics 1990); City University, London (Diploma newspaper journalism 1991).

Non-political career: Reporter, *South Yorkshire Times* 1991; Petty officer, P&O European Ferries 1992; Public relations officer, Newlon Housing Group 1993; *Housing Today*: Reporter 1994-95, Features editor 1995-98; Freelance journalist 1998-2000. Member, TGWU/Unite.

Political career: Member for Hackney South and Shoreditch 2005-10, for Hackney South and Shoreditch (revised boundary) since 6 May 2010 general election; PPS to Ruth Kelly as Secretary of State for Communities and Local Government 2006-07; Parliamentary Under-Secretary of State (Identity), Home Office 2007-10; Shadow Minister for Home Office 2010; Shadow Secretary of State for Energy and Climate Change 2010-11; Member Public Accounts Commission 2015-. *Select committees:* Member, Northern Ireland Affairs 2005-06; Public Accounts: Member 2011-15, Chair 2015-; Member, Liaison 2015-. Vice-chair, PLP Departmental Group for Women 2011-13. AM for North East constituency, London Assembly 2000-04. Co-operative Party: Member, Chair, parliamentary group 2010-11. *Councils and public bodies:* London Borough of Islington: Councillor 1994-2002, Chair, Neighbourhood Services Committee 1995-97, Mayor 1998-99; Board member, Transport for London 2004-05; Vice-president, Local Government Association 2017-.

Political interests: Hackney.

Other: Member, Fabian Society; Trustee, War Memorials Trust 2001-; Ambassador, Healthcare Denmark -2015.

Meg Hillier MP, House of Commons, London SW1A 0AA
Tel: 020 7219 5325 *Fax:* 020 7219 8768 *Email:* meghilliermp@parliament.uk
Constituency: No constituency office *Website:* www.meghillier.com *Twitter:* @Meg_HillierMP

House of Commons MPs' Biographies

CONSERVATIVE

HINDS, DAMIAN

East Hampshire *(Majority 25,852)*

Minister of State for Employment, Department for Work and Pensions

Damian Patrick George Hinds. Born 27 November 1969; Son of Frank Hinds and Bebe Hinds; Married Jacqui Morel 2007 (2 daughters 1 son).

Education: St Ambrose Grammar, Altrincham; Trinity College, Oxford (BA philosophy, politics and economics 1992).

Non-political career: Research analyst, Mercer Management Consulting 1992-95; Various marketing and commercial management roles, Holiday Inn/Bass plc 1995-2003; Freelance adviser to the hotel trade 2003-05, 2007-10; Strategy director, Greene King plc 2005-07.

Political career: Contested Stretford and Urmston 2005 general election. Member for East Hampshire since 6 May 2010 general election; PPS to Mark Francois as Minister of State for: Defence Personnel, Welfare and Veterans, Ministry of Defence 2012-13, the Armed Forces, Ministry of Defence 2013-14; Assistant Government Whip 2014-15; Exchequer Secretary, HM Treasury 2015-16; Minister of State for Employment, Department for Work and Pensions 2016- (also attending Cabinet 2017-). *Select committees:* Member, Education 2010-12.

Political interests: Social mobility, education, welfare, affordable credit, financial inclusion.

Other: Chairman, Bow Group 2001-02; Volunteer, The Prince's Trust 2002-08.

Publications: Co-author, Power to the People (Bow Group, 1998); Editor, The Ideas Book 2000 (Bow Group, 1999); Co-editor, Go Zones: Policies for the Places Politics Forgot (Bow Group, 2004); Co-author, Seven Key Truths About Social Mobility (APPG report on Social Mobility, 2012); Contributor, Unlocking Local Leadership on Climate Change (Green Alliance, 2012).

Recreations: Music.

Damian Hinds MP, House of Commons, London SW1A 0AA
Tel: 020 7219 7057 *Email:* damian.hinds.mp@parliament.uk
Constituency: 14a Butts Road, Alton, Hampshire GU34 1ND
Tel: 01420 84122 *Website:* www.damianhinds.com *Twitter:* @DamianHinds

CONSERVATIVE

HOARE, SIMON

North Dorset *(Majority 25,777)*

Team PPS, Home Office

Simon James Hoare. Born 28 June 1969; Son of Colin and Maria Hoare; Married Kate 2000 (3 daughters).

Education: Bishop Hannon School, Fairwater; Oxford University (BA modern history 1990).

Non-political career: Managing Director, Community Connect 2002-15.

Political career: Contested Cardiff West 1997 and Cardiff South and Penarth 2010 general elections. Member for North Dorset since 7 May 2015 general election; PPS to George Eustice as Minister of State for Agriculture, Fisheries and Food, Department for Environment, Food and Rural Affairs 2016-17; Team PPS, Home Office 2017-. *Select committees:* Member: Procedure 2015-16, Regulatory Reform 2015-, Speaker's Advisory Committee on Works of Art 2015-. Former vice-chair, Wales Young Conservatives. *Councils and public bodies:* West Oxfordshire District Council: Councillor 2004-15, Cabinet Member for Resources and Asset Management 2007-15; Councillor, Oxfordshire County Council 2013-15.

Political interests: Housing, planning, regeneration, farming, education.

Other: Member: Bow Group, Tory Reform Group; Garrick Club. North Dorset Rugby Football Club, Newport (Pembs) Boat Club.

Recreations: Gardening, cooking, walking, family, messing about in boats.

Simon Hoare MP, House of Commons, London SW1A 0AA
Tel: 020 7219 5697 *Email:* simon.hoare.mp@parliament.uk
Constituency: The Stables, Whitecliff Gardens, Blandford Forum, Dorset DT11 7BU
Tel: 01258 452585 *Email:* diana.mogg@parliament.uk *Websites:* www.ndca.org.uk www.simonhoare.org.uk *Twitter:* @Simon4NDorset

LIBERAL DEMOCRAT

HOBHOUSE, WERA

Bath *(Majority 5,694)*

Liberal Democrat Shadow Secretary of State for Communities and Local Government and Refugees

Wera Benedicta Hobhouse. Born 8 February 1960; Married William 1989 (2 daughters 2 sons).

Education: Muenster University, Germany (history 1987); Studied painting, Paris (1989).

Non-political career: Radio Journalist; Artist; Foreign Language Teacher, Audenshaw School; Secretary, Composite Textiles Ltd 2007-17.

Political career: Contested Heywood and Middleton 2010 and North East Somerset 2015 general elections. Member for Bath since 8 June 2017; Liberal Democrat Shadow Secretary of State for: Communities and Local Government 2017-, Refugees 2017-. *Select committees:* Member, Exiting the European Union 2017-. *Councils and public bodies:* Councillor, Rochdale Council 2006-14; Vice-president, Local Government Association 2017-.

Political interests: Waste management, recycling, contaminated land regulations, green agenda.

Other: Trustee, Norden Community Trust; Patron, Bath Festivals.

Wera Hobhouse MP, House of Commons, London SW1A 0AA
Tel: 020 7219 2093 *Email:* wera.hobhouse.mp@parliament.uk
Constituency: 26 Charles Street, Bath BA1 1HU
Tel: 01225 307024 *Email:* office@werahobhouse.co.uk *Twitter:* @Wera_Hobhouse

LABOUR

HODGE, MARGARET

Barking *(Majority 21,608)*

Margaret Eve Hodge. Born 8 September 1944; Daughter of Hans and Lisbeth Oppenheimer; Married Andrew Watson 1968 (divorced 1978) (1 son 1 daughter); married Henry Hodge 1978 (later Mr Justice Hodge) (died 2009) (2 daughters).

Education: Bromley High School; Oxford High School; London School of Economics (BSc economics 1966); German, French, Italian.

Non-political career: Teaching and market research 1966-73; Senior consultant, Price Waterhouse 1992-94. Member, Unison.

Political career: Member for Barking 1994 by-election to 2010, for Barking (revised boundary) since 6 May 2010 general election; Parliamentary Under-Secretary of State, Department for Education and Employment (Employment and Equal Opportunities) 1998-2001; Minister of State: Department for Education and Skills 2001-05: (Lifelong Learning and Higher Education 2001-03, Lifelong Learning, Further and Higher Education 2003, Children, Young People and Families 2003-05), Department for Work and Pensions (Employment and Welfare Reform) 2005-06, Department of Trade and Industry (Industry and the Regions) 2006-07, Department for Culture, Media and Sport 2007-08, 2009-10 (Culture, Creative Industries and Tourism 2007-08, Culture and Tourism 2009-10); Shadow Minister for Culture, Media and Sport 2010; Chair, Public Accounts Commission 2010-15; Member, Commons Reference Group on Representation and Inclusion 2017-. *Select committees:* Member: Education and Employment 1996-97, Deregulation 1996-97, Liaison 1997-98, 2010-15; Chair: Education and Employment (Education Sub-Committee) 1997-98, Public Accounts 2010-15. Progress; Member, Labour Party Local Government Committee 1983-92; Chair, London Group of Labour MPs 1995-98; Labour Women's Network; Chair, Fabian Executive Committee 1997-98. *Councils and public bodies:* London Borough of Islington: Councillor 1973-94, Chair, Housing Committee 1975-79, Leader 1982-92; Chair, Association of London Authorities 1984-92; Member, Home Office Advisory Committee on Race Relations 1988-92.

Political interests: Education, economy, local and regional government, housing, inner cities, democratic reform, London government; Nepal.

Other: Director: University College, Middlesex Hospitals; Governor, London School of Economics 1990-2001; Vice-chair, AMA 1991-92; Fellow, Industry and Parliament Trust 1996; Member, advisory board, GovernUp; Visiting Professor, King's College London 2015-; Chair, board of directors, Theatre Royal Stratford East 2015-; Member, Editorial Board, Political Quarterly 2015-; Visiting Fellow of Practice, Blavatnik School of Government, Oxford University 2016-; Chair, Fawcett Society's Local Government Commission 2016-; Governor, Westminster Foundation for Democracy 2017-. Freedom, City of London. Hon. Fellow, University of North London; Hon. DCL, City University 1993; Hon. Degree, University of South Wales 2014. Inquisitor of the Year, *Spectator* awards 2012, Parliamentarian of the Year Award, Political Studies Association 2012; *The House Magazine* Select Committee Member of the Year, Dods Parliamentary Awards 2014; Tax Personality of the Year Award, Taxation Awards 2014. MBE 1978; PC 2003; DBE 2015.

Publications: Quality, Equality and Democracy; Beyond the Town Hall; Fabian pamphlet on London Government, Not Just the Flower Show; Called to Account: How Corporate Bad Behaviour and Government Waste Combine to Cost us Millions (2016).

Recreations: Family, opera, piano, travel, cooking.

Rt Hon Dame Margaret Hodge DBE MP, House of Commons, London SW1A 0AA
Tel: 020 7219 6666 *Email:* hodgem@parliament.uk
Constituency: Barking Learning Centre, 2 Town Square, Barking, London IG11 7NB
Tel: 020 8594 1333 *Email:* margarethodge@hotmail.co.uk *Website:* margaret-hodge.co.uk
Twitter: @MargaretHodgeBarking

LABOUR

HODGSON, SHARON

Washington and Sunderland West *(Majority 12,940)*

Shadow Minister for Public Health

Born 1 April 1966; Daughter of Joan Cohen, née Wilson; Married Alan Hodgson 1990 (1 son 1 daughter).

Education: Heathfield Senior High School, Gateshead; Newcastle College (HEFC English 1997); TUC, National Education Centre (Open College Network Diploma Labour Party organising 2000).

Non-political career: Team Valley Trading Estate, Gateshead: Payroll/account clerk, Tyneside Safety Glass 1982-88, Payroll administrator, Burgess Microswitch 1992-94; Personnel, Northern Rock Building Society, Gosforth 1988-92; Charity administrator, The Total Learning Challenge (educational charity), Newcastle 1998-99; Regional organiser, Labour North 1999-2000; Constituency organiser, Mitcham and Morden CLP 2000-02; Labour link co-ordinator, London, Unison 2002-05. Member: GMB 1999-2007, Unite 2007-, CWU 2008-.

Political career: Member for Gateshead East and Washington West 2005-10, for Washington and Sunderland West since 6 May 2010 general election; PPS to: Liam Byrne as Minister of State, Home Office 2006-07, Bob Ainsworth as Minister of State, Ministry of Defence 2007-08, Dawn Primarolo as Minister of State, Department of Health 2008-09; Sponsored Special Educational Needs (Information) Act 2008; Assistant Government Whip 2009-10; Opposition Whip 2010; Shadow Minister for: Education 2010-13, 2015, Women and Equalities Office 2013-15, Children 2015-16, Public Health 2016-. *Select committees:* Member: Regulatory Reform 2005-10, European Scrutiny 2006, Court of Referees 2007-10, Children, Schools and Families 2007-10, North East 2009-10, Ecclesiastical Committee 2010-15. Hon. Secretary, PLP Departmental Committee for the Treasury 2006-10; Chair, PLP Northern Group 2015-16. Women's officer, Tyne Bridge CLP 1998-2000; Constituency secretary, Mitcham and Morden CLP 2002-05.

Political interests: North/South divide, employment (especially youth and green jobs), education (especially special educational needs), health (especially cancer issues), child poverty, fuel poverty, free school meals, childcare and early intervention, equality, women's issues, consumer protection (especially secondary ticketing), basketball; Cambodia, China, Japan, New Zealand, Pakistan, Singapore, South Africa, Sri Lanka, USA.

Other: Member: Fabian Society 2004-, Christian Socialist Movement 2005-; Board Member, Basketball Foundation.

Recreations: Reading, cinema, cooking, shopping, travel, family.

Sharon Hodgson MP, House of Commons, London SW1A 0AA
Tel: 020 7219 5160 *Fax:* 020 7219 4493 *Email:* sharon.hodgson.mp@parliament.uk
Constituency: Suites 1 and 1a, Vermont House, Concord, Washington, Tyne and Wear NE37 2SQ
Tel: 0191-417 2000 *Email:* brownjea@parliament.uk *Website:* www.sharonhodgson.org
Twitter: @SharonHodgsonMP

LABOUR

HOEY, KATE

Vauxhall *(Majority 20,250)*

Catharine Letitia Hoey. Born 21 June 1946; Daughter of Thomas and late Letitia Hoey; Single.

Education: Belfast Royal Academy; Ulster College of Physical Education (Diploma teaching 1964); City of London College, London (BSc economics 1968).

Non-political career: Lecturer, Southwark College 1972-76; Senior Lecturer, Kingsway College 1976-85; Educational Adviser to Arsenal Football Club 1985-89; Mayor of London's Commissioner for Sport -2016. Member, GMB; Chair, Fire Brigades Union Parliamentary Group.

Political career: Contested Dulwich 1983 and 1987 general elections. Member for Vauxhall 15 June 1989 by-election to 2010, for Vauxhall (revised boundary) since 6 May 2010; Opposition Spokesperson for Citizen's Charter and Women 1992-93; PPS to Frank Field as Minister of State, Department of Social Security 1997-98; Parliamentary Under-Secretary of State: Home Office (Metropolitan Police, European Union, Judicial Co-operation) 1998-99, Department for Culture,

Media and Sport (Minister for Sport) 1999-2001. *Select committees:* Member: Broadcasting 1991-97, Social Security 1994-97, Science and Technology 2004-05, Northern Ireland Affairs 2007-10, 2010-, Public Administration and Constitutional Affairs 2015-17, European Scrutiny 2015-. Chair, Labour Leave 2016. *Councils and public bodies:* Councillor: Hackney Borough Council 1978-82, Southwark Borough Council 1988-89.

Political interests: Sport, foreign affairs, housing, countryside, European Union; Angola, Bosnia, Oman, Tibet, Zimbabwe.

Other: Chair, Countryside Alliance 2005-14; Hon Vice-President, British Wheelchair Basketball Association; Chair, London Sport; Founding member, Grassroots Out 2016. *The Spectator*/Highland Park Debater of the Year Award 1998; University of Ulster Distinguished Graduate 2000; *The House Magazine* International Campaigner of the Year, Dods Parliamentary Awards 2014. Hon Vice-President, Surrey County Cricket Club; Hon President, British Pistol Club.

Publications: Occasional articles on sport in the press.

Kate Hoey MP, House of Commons, London SW1A 0AA
Tel: 020 7219 5989 *Fax:* 020 7219 5985 *Email:* hoeyk@parliament.uk
Constituency: No constituency office *Website:* www.katehoey.com *Twitter:* @KateHoeyMP

LABOUR

HOLLERN, KATE

Blackburn *(Majority 20,368)*

PPS to Jeremy Corbyn as Leader of the Opposition

Catherine Malloy Hollern. Born 12 April 1955; Partner (2 daughters).

Non-political career: Work study manager, Newman's Footwear; Contracts manager, Blackburn College.

Political career: Member for Blackburn since 7 May 2015 general election; PPS to Maria Eagle as Shadow Secretary of State for Defence 2015-16; Shadow Minister for: Defence 2016, Communities and Local Government 2016-17; PPS to Jeremy Corbyn as Leader of the Opposition 2017-. *Select committees:* Member: Education 2015-16, Armed Forces Bill 2015 2015-16, Education, Skills and the Economy Sub-committee 2015-16. *Councils and public bodies:* Blackburn with Darwen Council: Councillor -2015, Leader, Labour group 2004-15, Council Leader 2004-07, 2010-15.

Kate Hollern MP, House of Commons, London SW1A 0AA
Tel: 020 7219 8692 *Email:* kate.hollern.mp@parliament.uk
Constituency: Richmond Chambers, Richmond Terrace, Blackburn, Lancashire BB1 7AS
Tel: 01254 52317 *Website:* www.katehollern.org *Twitter:* @Kate_HollernMP

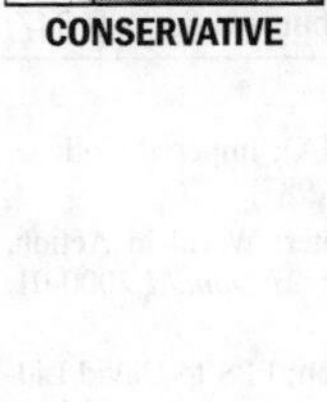

CONSERVATIVE

HOLLINGBERY, GEORGE

Meon Valley *(Majority 25,692)*

PPS to Theresa May as Prime Minister

George Michael Edward Hollingbery. Born 12 October 1963; Married Janette Marie White (1 son 2 daughters).

Education: Radley College, Oxfordshire; Lady Margaret Hall, Oxford (BA human sciences 1985); The Wharton School, Pennsylvania (MBA 1991).

Non-political career: Stockbroker, Robert Fleming Securities 1985-89; Non-executive director and shareholder, Lister Bestcare Ltd 1991-95; Director and founder, Pet Depot Ltd 1994-99; Chairman and founder, Companion Care Veterinary Group 1998-2001.

Political career: Contested Winchester 2005 general election. Member for Meon Valley since 6 May 2010 general election; PPS to Theresa May: as Home Secretary 2012-15, as Prime Minister 2016-; Government Whip (Lord Commissioner of HM Treasury) 2015-16. *Select committees:* Member: Communities and Local Government 2010-12, Works of Art 2011-16. Member, Executive, 1922 Committee February-September 2012. Deputy chairman, Winchester Conservative Association 1999-2001; Chairman, Winchester campaign team 2001 general election. *Councils and public bodies:* Winchester City Council: Councillor 1999-2010, Deputy leader, Conservative group, Council Deputy Leader 2006-08.

Political interests: Countryside issues, entrepreneurship, education, local government; Chile, China, USA.

Other: Founder and chairman: Alresford Golden Jubilee Celebrations, Alresford Millennium Trail Group, A night for Naomi 2000 (local hospice appeal), Another night for Naomi 2005.

Recreations: Field sports, modern garden design, modern crafts.

George Hollingbery MP, House of Commons, London SW1A 0AA
Tel: 020 7219 7109 *Email:* george.hollingbery.mp@parliament.uk
Constituency: No constituency office publicised
Tel: 01962 734076 *Website:* www.georgehollingbery.com

CONSERVATIVE

HOLLINRAKE, KEVIN

Thirsk and Malton *(Majority 19,001)*

PPS to Michael Gove as Secretary of State for Environment, Food and Rural Affairs

Kevin Paul Hollinrake. Born 28 September 1963; Married Nicola Sara Thompson 1994 (1 son 3 daughters).

Education: Easingwold School; Sheffield Polytechnic (physics 1982).

Non-political career: Hunters Property Group Ltd: Managing director 1992-2015, Chairman 2015-.

Political career: Member for Thirsk and Malton since 7 May 2015 general election; PPS to: David Lidington as Leader of the House of Commons and Lord President of the Council 2016-17, Michael Gove as Secretary of State for Environment, Food and Rural Affairs 2017-. *Select committees:* Member: Communities and Local Government 2015-, Armed Forces Bill 2015 2015-16. Treasurer, Conservative Friends of Bangladesh; Founding member, Conservatives for Reform in Europe 2016.

Political interests: Business, crime, housing, immigration.

Other: Member: NAEA 1990, Institute of Directors 2006.

Recreations: Golf, cricket, rugby union, reading.

Kevin Hollinrake MP, House of Commons, London SW1A 0AA
Tel: 020 7219 4746 *Email:* kevin.hollinrake.mp@parliament.uk
Constituency: 9 Hanover House, Market Place, Easingwold, York YO61 3AD
Tel: 01347 666880 *Website:* www.kevinhollinrake.org.uk *Twitter:* @kevinhollinrake

CONSERVATIVE

HOLLOBONE, PHILIP

Kettering *(Majority 10,562)*

Philip Thomas Hollobone. Born 7 November 1964; Son of Thomas and Patricia Hollobone.

Education: Dulwich College, London; Lady Margaret Hall, Oxford University (BA modern history and economics 1987, MA).

Non-political career: Soldier and paratrooper, Territorial Army 1984-93. Industry research analyst 1987-2003.

Political career: Contested Lewisham East 1997 and Kettering 2001 general elections. Member for Kettering 2005-10, for Kettering (revised boundary) since 6 May 2010 general election. *Select committees:* Member: Crossrail Bill 2006-07, Transport 2006-10, Backbench Business 2010-12, 2015-16, Chairmen's Panel/Panel of Chairs 2010-. Chair, Bromley and Chislehurst Conservative Association 1999; Deputy Chair, Kettering Constituency Conservative Association 2002-14, 2017-. *Councils and public bodies:* Councillor: London Borough of Bromley 1990-94, Kettering Borough Council 2003-.

Other: Special Constable, British Transport Police 2008-15.

Philip Hollobone MP, House of Commons, London SW1A 0AA
Tel: 020 7219 8373 *Fax:* 020 7219 8802 *Email:* philip.hollobone.mp@parliament.uk
Constituency: No constituency office publicised

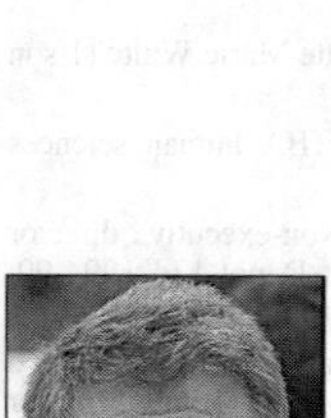

CONSERVATIVE

HOLLOWAY, ADAM

Gravesham *(Majority 9,347)*

Adam James Harold Holloway. Born 29 July 1965; Single.

Education: Cranleigh School, Surrey; Magdalene College, Cambridge (MA); Imperial College, London (MBA 1998); Royal Military Academy Sandhurst (Commissioned 1987).

Non-political career: Commissioned, Grenadier Guards 1987-92. Presenter: World in Action, Granada TV 1992-93; Senior reporter: ITN 1993-97, *Tonight with Trevor McDonald* 2000-01, Contributions to ITN/Sky News, Iraq War 2003.

Political career: Member for Gravesham since 5 May 2005 general election; PPS to David Lidington as Minister of State, Foreign and Commonwealth Office 2010-11. *Select committees:* Member: Defence 2006-10, 2012-14, Arms Export Controls 2009-11, Public Administration 2014-15, Foreign Affairs 2015-17, Public Administration and Constitutional Affairs 2016. Deputy chairman, Conservative Middle East Council 2010-; Founding member, Conservatives for Britain 2015-16.

Political interests: Constituents, defence, foreign, crime.

Other: Trustee: Christian Aid 1997-2001, Map Action 2002-10; Former Parliamentary Chair, Council for Arab British Understanding. Backbencher of the Year, *Spectator* awards 2011; Gravesend Conservative Club, Northfleet Conservative Club, Pratt's Club.

Publications: In Blood Stepp'd in Too Far: Towards a realistic policy for Afghanistan (Centre for Policy Studies, 2009); The Failure of British Political and Military Leadership in Basra (First Defence, 2010).

Adam Holloway MP, House of Commons, London SW1A 0AA
Tel: 020 7219 8402 *Fax:* 020 7219 2871 *Email:* hollowaya@parliament.uk
Constituency: No constituency office *Website:* www.adamholloway.co.uk

HOPKINS, KELVIN

Luton North *(Majority 14,364)*

LABOUR

Kelvin Peter Hopkins. Born 22 August 1941; Son of late Professor Harold Hopkins FRS, physicist and mathematician, and Joan Frost, medical secretary; Married Patricia Langley 1965 (1 son 1 daughter).

Education: Queen Elizabeth's Grammar School, High Barnet; Nottingham University (BA politics, economics and mathematics with statistics); French (basic).

Non-political career: TUC Economic Department 1969-70, 1973-77; Policy and research officer, NALGO/Unison 1977-94. Delegate, Luton Trades Union Council; Member: GMB, CWU.

Political career: Contested Luton North 1983 general election. Member for Luton North 1997-2010, for Luton North (revised boundary) since 6 May 2010 general election; Shadow Secretary of State for Culture, Media and Sport 2016. *Select committees:* Former member, European Standing Committee B; Member: Broadcasting 1999-2001, Public Administration 2002-10, 2011-15, Crossrail Bill 2006-07, European Scrutiny 2007-16, Transport 2010, Joint Committee on Draft Deregulation Bill 2013, Public Administration and Constitutional Affairs 2015-. Chair, PLP Departmental Group for DPM/Constitutional Affairs 2010-15. Vice-chair, Central Region Labour Party 1995-96; Chair, Labour Leave 2016. *Councils and public bodies:* Councillor, Luton Borough Council 1972-76; Governor, Luton Sixth Form College 1993-.

Political interests: Economic policy, employment, transport, European Union, arts; France, Sweden.

Other: Chair of Governors, Luton College of Higher Education 1985-89; Member, Mary Seacole House, Luton; Fellow, Industry and Parliament Trust 2000. Hon. Fellow: Luton University 1993, Bedfordshire University 2010.

Publications: Various NALGO publications.

Recreations: Music, wine, collecting antique glassware.

Kelvin Hopkins MP, House of Commons, London SW1A 0AA
Tel: 020 7219 6670 *Fax:* 020 7219 0957 *Email:* hopkinsk@parliament.uk
Constituency: 3 Union Street, Luton, Bedfordshire LU1 3AN
Tel: 01582 488208 *Fax:* 01582 480990

HOSIE, STEWART

Dundee East *(Majority 6,645)*

SCOTTISH NATIONAL PARTY

Born 3 January 1963; Son of R A Hosie, architectural ironmonger, and E A Hosie, bookkeeper; Married Shona Robison 1997, MSP for Dundee City East (1 daughter) (separated).

Education: Carnoustie High School; Bell Street Tech (HD computer studies 1981); Dundee College of Technology 1981.

Non-political career: Group IS manager, MIH 1988-93; Systems analyst, various organisations 1993-96; Year 2000/EMU project manager, Stakis plc/Hilton 1996-2000; Various project management posts 2000-05. Member, MSF 1992.

Political career: Contested Kirkcaldy 1992 and 1997 general elections. Member for Dundee East since 5 May 2005 general election; SNP: Spokesperson for: Treasury 2005-15, Women 2005-07, Home Affairs 2005-07, Economy 2005-07, 2015-17, Deputy Leader, Westminster Group 2007-17, Chief Whip 2007-13; Member, House of Commons Commission 2015-. *Select committees:* Member: Treasury 2010-15, 2017-, Panel of Chairs 2017-. Contested Kirkcaldy constituency 1999 Scottish Parliament election. Scottish National Party: Youth convener 1986-89, National secretary 1999-2003, Organisation convener 2003-05, Deputy leader 2014-16.

Political interests: Economic development, job creation.

Other: Endorsed by the Save the Scottish Regiments Campaign.

Recreations: Football, hill-walking, rugby.

Stewart Hosie MP, House of Commons, London SW1A 0AA
Tel: 020 7219 8164 *Fax:* 020 7219 6716 *Email:* hosies@parliament.uk
Constituency: 8 Old Glamis Road, Dundee DD3 8HP
Tel: 01382 623200 *Fax:* 01382 903205 *Email:* hosie@dundeesnp.org stewart@stewarthosie.com
95 High Street, Carnoustie, Angus DD7 9EA
Tel: 01241 856489 *Fax:* 01241 856489 *Twitter:* @StewartHosieSNP

LABOUR

HOWARTH, GEORGE

Knowsley *(Majority 42,214)*

George Edward Howarth. Born 29 June 1949; Son of late George Howarth and Eleanor Howarth; Married Julie Rodgers 1977 (2 sons 1 daughter).

Education: Schools in Huyton; Liverpool Polytechnic (BA social sciences 1977).

Non-political career: Engineering apprentice 1966-70; Engineer 1970-75; Teacher 1977-82; Co-operative Development Services 1980-82; Chief executive, Wales Co-operative Centre 1982-86. Member, Unite.

Political career: Member for Knowsley North 13 November 1986 by-election to 1997, for Knowsley North and Sefton East 1997-2010, for Knowsley since 6 May 2010 general election; Opposition Spokesperson for: the Environment 1989-92, Environmental Protection 1993-94, Home Affairs 1994-97; Parliamentary Under-Secretary of State: Home Office 1997-99, Northern Ireland Office 1999-2001; Member, Intelligence and Security Committee 2008-16; Temporary Deputy Speaker May-June 2015. *Select committees:* Member: Public Accounts 2002-03, Modernisation of the House of Commons 2005-10; Chair, Armed Forces Bill 2005-06; Member: Joint Committee on Conventions 2006, Chairmen's Panel/Panel of Chairs 2009-, Finance and Services 2012-15. Labour Party: Chair, Knowsley South 1981-85, Secretary, Knowsley Borough District 1977-80, Member: North West Region Executive 1981-84, National Executive Committee October 2016-. *Councils and public bodies:* Councillor, Huyton Urban District Council 1971-75; Knowsley Borough Council: Councillor 1975-86, Deputy Leader 1982-83.

Political interests: Housing, environment, crime, disorder; Middle East, South Africa.

Other: Chair, Knowsley Skills Academy. PC 2005.

Recreations: Coarse fishing, family, reading.

Rt Hon George Howarth MP, House of Commons, London SW1A 0AA
Tel: 020 7219 6902 *Fax:* 020 7219 0495 *Email:* george.howarth.mp@parliament.uk
Constituency: Lathom House, North Mersey Business Centre, Woodward Road, Kirkby, Merseyside L33 7UY
Tel: 0151-546 9918 *Fax:* 0151-546 9918 *Website:* www.georgehowarth.org.uk

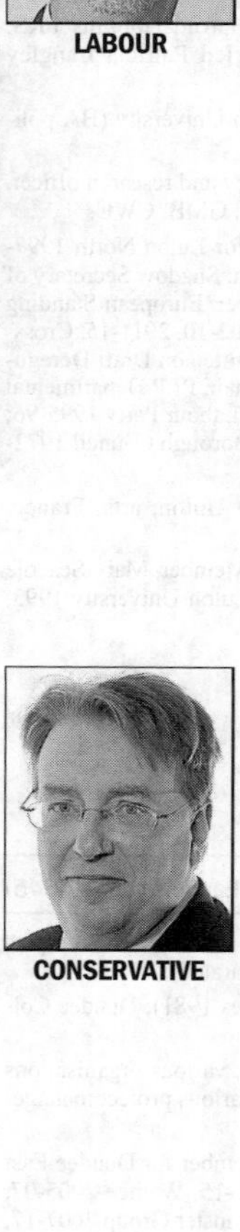

CONSERVATIVE

HOWELL, JOHN

Henley *(Majority 22,294)*

John Michael Howell. Born 27 July 1955; Son of Alexander and Gladys Howell; Married Alison Parker 1987 (1 son 2 daughters).

Education: Battersea Grammar School, London; Edinburgh University (MA archaeology 1978); St John's College, Oxford (DPhil prehistoric archaeology 1981).

Non-political career: Ernst & Young 1987-96; Business presenter, BBC World Service Television 1996-97; Director: Fifth World Productions Ltd 1996-2003, Media Presentation Consultants Ltd 2005-08.

Political career: Member for Henley 26 June 2008 by-election to 2010, for Henley (revised boundary) since 6 May 2010 general election; PPS: to Greg Clark as Minister of State for Decentralisation 2010-11, to Leaders of the House of Commons and Lords Privy Seal: Sir George Young 2010-12, Andrew Lansley 2012-14; Trade Envoy to Nigeria 2016-. *Select committees:* Member: Work and Pensions 2009-10, Justice 2014-, Armed Forces Bill 2015 2015-16. Member, Executive, 1922 Committee 2014-15; Chairman, Conservative Backbench Policy Committee on Communities and Local Government 2015-17. *Councils and public bodies:* Oxfordshire County Council: Councillor 2004-09, Cabinet Member for Change Management 2005-08; Vice-President, Local Government Association 2010-11.

Political interests: Rural issues, social policy, local government, foreign affairs; Central and Eastern Europe, South Asia.

Other: Member, UK delegation, Parliamentary Assembly of the Council of Europe 2015-; Trustee, Industry and Parliament Trust 2010-. OBE 2000; Leander Club Henley.

Publications: Neolithic Northern France (1983); Understanding Eastern Europe: the context of change (1994).

Recreations: Music, theatre.

John Howell OBE MP, House of Commons, London SW1A 0AA
Tel: 020 7219 6676 *Fax:* 020 7219 2606 *Email:* howelljm@parliament.uk
Constituency: PO Box 84, Watlington, Oxfordshire OX49 5XD
Tel: 01491 613072 *Email:* angie.paterson@parliament.uk *Website:* www.johnhowellmp.com
Twitter: @JHowellUK

LABOUR

HOYLE, LINDSAY

Chorley *(Majority 7,512)*

Chairman, Ways and Means and Deputy Speaker

Lindsay Harvey Hoyle. Born 10 June 1957; Son of Doug Hoyle (MP for Nelson and Colne October 1974-79, Warrington 1981-83 and Warrington North 1983-97, now Lord Hoyle (qv)) and late Pauline Hoyle; Married Lynda Fowler (divorced 1982); married Catherine Swindley (2 daughters).

Education: Lords College, Bolton; Horwich FE; Bolton TIC (City & Guilds Construction).

Non-political career: Honorary Colonel, D(64) Medical Squadron, 5 General Services. Company director. Shop steward; Member, Amicus/MSF/Unite.

Political career: Member for Chorley 1997-2010, for Chorley (revised boundary) since 6 May 2010 general election; Parliamentary assistant to Beverley Hughes as Minister for the North West 2008-10; Chairman, Ways and Means and Deputy Speaker 2010-. *Select committees:* Member: Catering 1997-2005, Trade and Industry/Business, Enterprise and Regulatory Reform/Business and Enterprise/Business, Innovation and Skills 1998-2010, European Scrutiny 2005-10, Quadripartite (Committees on Strategic Export Controls) 2006-07; Ex-officio member, Chairmen's Panel/Panel of Chairs 2010-13; Member, Finance and Services 2010-15; Panel of Chairs: Member 2013-15, Chair 2015-, Member, Finance 2015-; Chair, Court of Referees 2016-. Joint vice-chair, PLP Departmental Committee for Defence 1997-2001. *Councils and public bodies:* Councillor, Adlington Town Council 1980-98; Chorley Borough Council: Councillor 1980-98, Chair, Economic Development and Deputy Leader 1994-97, Mayor of Chorley 1997-98.

Political interests: Trade and industry, sport, defence, small businesses, agriculture; British Overseas Territories, Falkland Islands, Gibraltar.

Other: Armed Forces Parliamentary Scheme (Royal Marines) 1998-; Trustee, History of Parliament Trust; Member, Cuerdon Valley Trust; President, Chorley Mencap. PC 2013. Member: Adlington Cricket Club, Chorley Cricket Club.

Recreations: Cricket, Rugby League.

Rt Hon Lindsay Hoyle MP, House of Commons, London SW1A 0AA
Tel: 020 7219 3515 *Fax:* 020 7219 3831 *Email:* gaskillm@parliament.uk
Constituency: 35-39 Market Street, Chorley, Lancashire PR7 2SW
Tel: 01257 271555 *Fax:* 01257 277462 *Email:* goreb@parliament.uk
Websites: www.claytonandwhittlerose.com www.lindsayhoylemp.com
Twitter: @LindsayHoyle_MP

CONSERVATIVE

HUDDLESTON, NIGEL

Mid Worcestershire *(Majority 23,326)*

Team PPS, Department for Digital, Culture, Media and Sport

Nigel Paul Huddleston. Born 13 October 1970; Son of Alan Huddleston, factory worker, and Pauline Huddleston, secretary, sales representative and supermarket checkout operator; Married Melissa Peters 1999 (1 son 1 daughter).

Education: Robert Pattinson Comprehensive School, North Hykeham; Oxford University (BA philosophy, politics and economics 1992) (Vice-President Student Union 1992-93); Anderson Business School, University of California, Los Angeles, USA (MBA 1998).

Non-political career: Management consultant: Arthur Andersen Business Consulting 1993-2002, Deloitte Strategy Consulting 2002-10; Industry Head for Travel, Google 2010-15.

Political career: Contested Luton South 2010 general election. Member for Mid Worcestershire since 7 May 2015 general election; Team PPS, Department for Digital, Culture, Media and Sport 2017-. *Select committees:* Member, Culture, Media and Sport 2015-17. Board Member, Tory Reform Group 2010-15; Founding Member, Conservatives for Reform in Europe 2016. *Councils and public bodies:* Councillor, St Albans City and District Council 2011-14.

Political interests: Business (especially digital sector and the internet), travel and tourism, education; UAE, USA.

Other: Member, National Trust; Chair, Democracy Forum -2017. Freedom, City of Lincoln 1996.

Recreations: Travel, spending time with his children.

Nigel Huddleston MP, House of Commons, London SW1A 0AA
Tel: 020 7219 5814 *Email:* nigel.huddleston.mp@parliament.uk
Constituency: No constituency office *Website:* www.nigelhuddleston.com
Twitter: @HuddlestonNigel

CONSERVATIVE

HUGHES, EDDIE

Walsall North *(Majority 2,601)*

Edmund Francis Hughes. Born 3 October 1968; Married Clare (2 children).

Education: Handsworth Grammar School; Glamorgan University (civil engineering).

Non-political career: YMCA Birmingham: Director of Development and Asset Management 2014-17, Assistant Chief Executive 2017.

Political career: Contested Birmingham Hall Green 2005 general election. Member for Walsall North since 8 June 2017; *Councils and public bodies:* Councillor, Walsall Council 1999-; Governor, St Anne's School, Streetly.

Other: whg Housing Association: Board member 2012-16, Chairperson 2016-; Member, Barr Beacon Trust; Chartered member, Chartered Institute of Building (CIOB) 2011-; Trustee, Walsall Wood Allotment Charity.

Eddie Hughes MP, House of Commons, London SW1A 0AA
Tel: 020 7219 1974 *Email:* eddie.hughes.mp@parliament.uk
Constituency: West Midlands House, Gypsy Lane, Willenhall WV13 2HA
Tel: 01902 585096 *Email:* eddie@eddiehughes.co.uk *Website:* www.eddiehughes.co.uk
Twitter: @EddieHughes4WN

CONSERVATIVE

HUNT, JEREMY

South West Surrey *(Majority 21,590)*

Secretary of State for Health

Jeremy Richard Streynsham Hunt. Born 1 November 1966; Son of late Admiral Sir Nicholas Hunt and Meriel Hunt; Married Lucia Guo 2009 (1 son 2 daughters).

Education: Charterhouse, Surrey; Magdalen College, Oxford (BA philosophy, politics and economics 1988, MA); French, Japanese.

Non-political career: Management consultant, Outram Cullinan and Co 1988-89; English teacher, Japan 1990-91; Founder and managing director, Hotcourses Ltd 1991-2005.

Political career: Member for South West Surrey 2005-10, for South West Surrey (revised boundary) since 6 May 2010 general election; Shadow Minister for Disabled People 2005-07; Shadow Secretary of State for Culture, Media and Sport 2007-10; Secretary of State for: Culture, Olympics, Media and Sport 2010-12, Health 2012-. *Select committees:* Member, International Development 2005-06. *Councils and public bodies:* Ex-officio member, Olympic Board -2012.

Political interests: Education, international development, philanthropy; Africa, Japan.

Other: Member, Education, Youth, Culture and Sport Council, Council of the European Union 2010-12; Founder and trustee, Hotcourses Foundation 2004-; Patron: Haselmere Museum, Meath Art Trust, Brightwells Gostry Community Centre, COINS Foundation, Undershaw School. PC 2010.

Recreations: Latin music and dance.

Rt Hon Jeremy Hunt MP, House of Commons, London SW1A 0AA
Tel: 020 7219 6813 *Email:* huntj@parliament.uk
Constituency: South West Surrey Conservative Association, 2 Royal Parade, Tilford Road, Hindhead, Surrey GU26 6TD
Tel: 01428 609416 *Website:* www.jeremyhunt.org *Twitter:* @Jeremy_Hunt

LABOUR

HUQ, RUPA

Ealing Central and Acton *(Majority 13,807)*

Rupa Asha Huq. Born 2 April 1972; 1 son.

Education: Notting Hill and Ealing High School; Newnham College, Cambridge (BA social and political sciences 1993); University of East London (PhD cultural studies thesis on youth culture 1999).

Non-political career: Assistant to Carole Tongue MEP 1996; Lecturer, School of Education, Manchester University 1998-2004; Senior Lecturer in sociology, Kingston University 2004-15.

Political career: Contested Chesham and Amersham 2005 general election. Member for Ealing Central and Acton since 7 May 2015 general election; Shadow Minister for Home Office 2016-17. *Select committees:* Member: Regulatory Reform 2015-, Justice 2015-16, Public Administration and Constitutional Affairs 2017-. Contested North West region 2004 European Parliament election. Member, Labour Party 1991-. *Councils and public bodies:* Deputy Mayoress of Ealing 2010-11.

Dr Rupa Huq MP, House of Commons, London SW1A 0AA
Tel: 020 7219 6865 *Email:* rupa.huq.mp@parliament.uk
Constituency: No constituency office *Website:* www.rupahuq.co.uk *Twitter:* @RupaHuq

CONSERVATIVE

HURD, NICK

Ruislip, Northwood and Pinner *(Majority 13,980)*

Minister of State for Policing and the Fire Service, Home Office

Nicholas Richard Hurd. Born 13 May 1962; Son of Douglas Hurd (MP for Mid Oxon 1974-83 and Witney 1983-97, now Lord Hurd of Westwell) and Tatiana Hurd, née Eyre; Married Kim Richards 1988 (divorced) (2 sons 2 daughters); married Lady Clare Kerr 2010, daughter of Most Hon the Marquess of Lothian (qv) (1 daughter 1 son).

Education: Eton College; Exeter College, Oxford (BA classics 1984).

Non-political career: Investment manager, Morgan Grenfell 1985-90; Corporate finance executive, Crown Communications 1990-92; Managing director, Passport Magazine Directories 1992-94; Flemings Bank (Brazil-based) 1995-99; Director, Band-X Ltd 2001-06; Founder, Small Business Network 2002; Chief of staff to Tim Yeo MP 2003-05; Non-executive director, Sancroft Ltd 2008-10.

Political career: Member for Ruislip Northwood 2005-10, for Ruislip, Northwood and Pinner since 6 May 2010 general election; Opposition Whip 2007-08; Sponsored Sustainable Communities Act 2007; Shadow Minister for Charities[, Social Enterprise and Volunteering] 2008-10; Parliamentary Secretary (Minister for Civil Society), Cabinet Office 2010-14; Parliamentary Under-Secretary of State, Department for International Development 2015-16; Minister of State: for Climate Change and Industry, Department for Business, Energy and Industrial Strategy 2016-17, for Policing and the Fire Service, Home Office 2017-. *Select committees:* Member: Environmental Audit 2005-10, Joint Committee on the Draft Climate Change Bill 2007, Joint Committee on the Draft Protection of Charities Bill 2014-15, Petitions 2015-16. *Councils and public bodies:* Governor, Coteford Junior School.

Political interests: Environment, community, penal reform, health; Brazil, China.

Other: Member, Vote No to the EU Constitution Campaign; Trustee, Greenhouse Schools Project.

Recreations: Sport, music.

Nick Hurd MP, House of Commons, London SW1A 0AA
Tel: 020 7219 1053 *Fax:* 020 7219 4854 *Email:* nick.hurd.mp@parliament.uk
Constituency: 32 High Street, Northwood, Middlesex HA6 1BN
Tel: 01923 822876 *Fax:* 01923 841514 *Email:* anrnca@aol.com *Website:* www.nickhurd.com
Twitter: @NickHurdUK

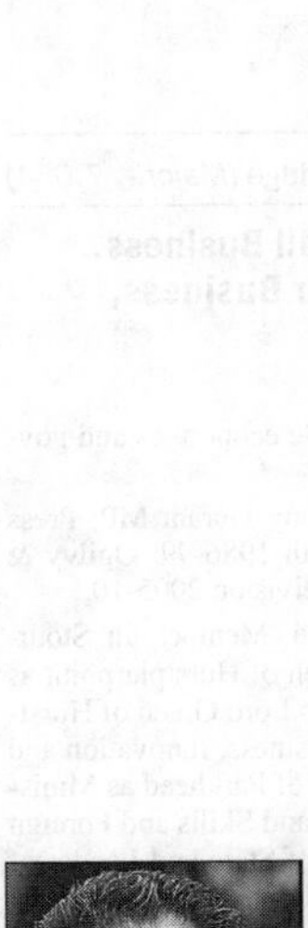

LABOUR

HUSSAIN, IMRAN

Bradford East *(Majority 20,540)*

Shadow Minister for Justice

Born 7 June 1978; Married (2 children).

Education: Rhodesway High School; Huddersfield University (LLB).

Non-political career: Called to the Bar, Lincoln's Inn 2003; Barrister, Altaf Solicitors, Bradford. Member, Unite.

Political career: Contested Bradford West 29 March 2012 by-election. Member for Bradford East since 7 May 2015 general election; PPS to Diane Abbott as Shadow Secretary of State for International Development 2015-16; Shadow Minister for: International Development 2016-17, Justice 2017-. *Select committees:* Member: Regulatory Reform 2015-, Joint Committee on Consolidation, &c, Bills 2015-. Member, Labour Party 1995-; Chair, Bradford West Labour Party. *Councils and public bodies:* Bradford Metropolitan Borough Council: Councillor 2002-, Deputy Leader 2010-15, Portfolio Holder for Safer And Stronger Communities; Governor, Lilycroft Primary School; Chair, Safer Communities Partnership Board; Local Authority Commission on Asylum and Migration; Member, Stronger Communities Partnership Executive Board.

Other: Alternate member, EU Committee of the Regions 2015-; Bradford Centre Regeneration Company.

Imran Hussain MP, House of Commons, London SW1A 0AA
Tel: 020 7219 8636 *Email:* imran.hussain.mp@parliament.uk
Constituency: Karmand Community Centre, Barkerend Road, Bradford, West Yorkshire BD3 9EP
Tel: 01274 231527 *Website:* www.imranhussain.org.uk *Twitter:* @Imran_HussainMP

CONSERVATIVE

JACK, ALISTER

Dumfries and Galloway *(Majority 5,643)*

Alister William Jack. Born 15 July 1963; Married Ann (3 children).

Education: Glenalmond School; Heriot-Watt University.

Non-political career: Founder: Field & Lawn 1987, Aardvark Self-Storage 1992, Armadillo Self-Storage, Alligator Self-Storage; Non-executive chairman and director, Fulling Mill Ltd.

Political career: Contested Tweeddale, Ettrick and Lauderdale 1997 general election. Member for Dumfries and Galloway since 8 June 2017. *Select committees:* Member, Treasury 2017-. Former Vice-chair, Scottish Conservatives.

Other: Chair: River Annan Fishery Board and Trust, Galloway Woodlands.

Alister Jack MP, House of Commons, London SW1A 0AA
Tel: 020 7219 2994 *Email:* alister.jack.mp@parliament.uk
Constituency: 20 Academy Street, Dumfries DG1 1BY
Tel: 01387 216109 *Website:* www.alisterjack.co.uk

CONSERVATIVE

JAMES, MARGOT

Stourbridge *(Majority 7,654)*

Parliamentary Under-Secretary of State (Minister for Small Business, Consumers and Corporate Responsibility), Department for Business, Energy and Industrial Strategy

Margot Cathleen James. Born 28 August 1958; Partner Jay.

Education: Millfield School, Somerset; London School of Economics (BSc economics and government).

Non-political career: Maurice James Industries; Researcher to Sir Anthony Durant MP; Press officer, Conservative Central Office; Co-founder and director, Shire Health 1986-99; Ogilvy & Mather: Head of European healthcare, Regional president, pharmaceutical division 2005-10.

Political career: Contested Holborn and St Pancras 2005 general election. Member for Stourbridge since 6 May 2010 general election; Parliamentary aide to Lord Green of Hurstpierpoint as Minister of State for Trade and Investment January-September 2012; PPS: to Lord Green of Hurstpierpoint as Minister of State for Trade and Investment, Department for Business, Innovation and Skills and Foreign and Commonwealth Office 2012-13, to Lord Livingston of Parkhead as Minister of State for Trade and Investment, Department for Business, Innovation and Skills and Foreign and Commonwealth Office 2013-14, to William Hague as First Secretary of State and Leader of the House of Commons 2014-15; Assistant Government Whip 2015-16; Parliamentary Under-Secretary of State (Minister for Small Business, Consumers and Corporate Responsibility), Department for Business, Energy and Industrial Strategy 2016-. *Select committees:* Member: Business, Innovation and Skills 2010-12, Arms Export Controls 2010-12, Joint Committee on the Draft Care and Support Bill 2013. Chair, London School of Economics Conservative Association; Vice-chair (women's issues), Conservative Party 2005-10; Member, Number 10 Policy Advisory Board (Economic Affairs). *Councils and public bodies:* Non-executive director, Parkside NHS Trust 1998-2003; Councillor, Kensington and Chelsea Borough Council 2006-08; Associate Governor, Redhill School, Stourbridge; Governor, London School of Economics.

Political interests: Business, health, older people, education, prison reform.

Other: Abantu, Prince's Trust, Young Enterprise. Communicator of the Year 1997.

Recreations: Cooking, theatre, travel, opera.

Margot James MP, House of Commons, London SW1A 0AA
Tel: 020 7219 7226 *Fax:* 020 7219 6434 *Email:* margot.james.mp@parliament.uk
Constituency: 1a Worcester Street, Stourbridge DY8 1AH
Tel: 01384 370574 *Website:* www.margotjames.com *Twitter:* @margot_james_mp

LIBERAL DEMOCRAT

JARDINE, CHRISTINE

Edinburgh West *(Majority 2,988)*

Liberal Democrat Shadow Secretary of State for Culture, Media and Sport

Christine Anne Jardine. Born 24 November 1960; Married Calum (1 daughter).

Education: Braidfield High School; Glasgow University (MA 1982); NCTJ (Proficiency Certificate 1985).

Non-political career: Editor, *Deeside Piper*; Senior production journalist, BBC Scotland, Aberdeen 1991-97; Tutor/lecturer in journalism, Strathclyde University 1997-2002; Editor, Scotland, Press Association 2002-04; Project manager, international programme, TRC Media 2009-11; Scotland media adviser 2011-12; Media consultant and political commentator, Scottish Liberal Democrats 2012-17.

Political career: Contested Gordon 2015 general election. Member for Edinburgh West since 8 June 2017; Liberal Democrat Shadow Secretary of State for Culture, Media and Sport 2017-. *Select committees:* Member, Scottish Affairs 2017-. Contested Inverness and Nairn constituency 2011 Scottish Parliament election, Aberdeen Donside constituency 2013 Scottish Parliament by-election and Aberdeenshire East constituency 2016 Scottish Parliament election.

Christine Jardine MP, House of Commons, London SW1A 0AA
Tel: 020 7219 1701 *Email:* christine.jardine.mp@parliament.uk
Constituency: 183 St John's Road, Edinburgh EH12 7SL *Website:* www.christinejardine.com
Twitter: @cajardine

LABOUR

JARVIS, DAN

Barnsley Central *(Majority 15,546)*

Daniel Owen Woolgar Jarvis. Born 30 November 1972; Married Caroline (died 2010) (1 son 2 daughters); Married Rachel 2013.

Education: Rushcliffe Comprehensive, Nottingham; Aberystwyth University (international politics and strategic studies); Royal Military Academy, Sandhurst.

Non-political career: Major, The Parachute Regiment 1996-2011. Member: Unite, Unison.

Political career: Member for Barnsley Central since 3 March 2011 by-election; Shadow Minister for: Culture, Media and Sport 2011-13, Justice 2013-15, Foreign and Commonwealth Office 2015. *Select committees:* Member, Business, Innovation and Skills 2010-11. Chair, PLP Departmental Group for Business, Innovation and Skills 2011. Labour Lead, First World War Centenary 2014.

Political interests: Britain's role in the world, defence, security and international development, child poverty, education and skills, cancer, care for the elderly and the vulnerable, fuel poverty, culture, heritage, sport and the countryside; Afghanistan, Nepal, Pakistan, Iraq.

Other: Vice-chair, Progress 2011-; Honorary Patron, Barnsley Youth Choir. MBE (mil) 2011. Barnsley Harriers; Vice-president, Kexborough Cricket Club.

Recreations: Parliamentary Mountaineering Group; London Marathon (completed five times).

Dan Jarvis MBE MP, House of Commons, London SW1A 0AA
Tel: 020 7219 1082 *Email:* dan.jarvis.mp@parliament.uk
Constituency: Corporate Mailroom, PO Box 634, Barnsley, South Yorkshire S70 9GG
Tel: 01226 787893 *Website:* www.danjarvis.org *Twitter:* @DanJarvisMP

CONSERVATIVE

JAVID, SAJID

Bromsgrove *(Majority 16,573)*

Secretary of State for Communities and Local Government

Born 5 December 1969; Married Laura (4 children).

Education: Downend School, Bristol; Filton Technical College, Bristol; Exeter University (BA economics and politics 1991); Punjabi, Urdu.

Non-political career: Chase Manhattan Bank: Associate and Analyst 1991-95, Vice-president 1995-2000; Deutsche Bank AG: Director 2000-04, Managing director 2004-09; Board member, Deutsche Bank International (Asia) Ltd 2007-09.

Political career: Member for Bromsgrove since 6 May 2010 general election; PPS to: John Hayes as Minister of State for Further Education, Skills and Lifelong Learning 2010-11, George Osborne as Chancellor of the Exchequer 2011-12; HM Treasury: Economic Secretary 2012-13, Financial Secretary 2013-14; Secretary of State for Culture, Media and Sport 2014-15; Minister for Equalities 2014; Secretary of State for: Business, Innovation and Skills and President of the Board of Trade 2015-16, Communities and Local Government 2016-. *Select committees:* Member, Work and Pensions 2010; Ex-officio Member, Public Accounts 2012-13. *Councils and public bodies:* Governor, Normand Croft Community School 2004-05.

Political interests: Civil liberties, free enterprise, defence, welfare policy.

Other: Trustee, London Early Years Foundation 2009-12. PC 2014.

Publications: Contributor, There is Such a Thing as Society (2002).

Recreations: Gym, running, hiking, cricket.

Rt Hon Sajid Javid MP, House of Commons, London SW1A 0AA
Tel: 020 7219 7027 *Email:* sajid.javid.mp@parliament.uk
Constituency: No constituency office publicised *Website:* www.sajidjavid.com
Twitter: @SajidJavid

CONSERVATIVE

JAYAWARDENA, RANIL

North East Hampshire *(Majority 27,772)*

Ranil Malcolm Jayawardena. Born 3 September 1986; Son of Nalin Jayawardena JP, chartered accountant, and Indira, née Daas; Married Alison Lyn Roberts 2011 (2 daughters).

Education: Robert May's School, Odiham; Alton College; London School of Economics; French.

Non-political career: Crown Golf 2003-07; Lloyds Banking Group: Wholesale Banking 2008-10, Group Executive Functions 2010-15.

Political career: Member for North East Hampshire since 7 May 2015 general election. *Select committees:* Member: Home Affairs 2015-17, International Trade 2016-, Procedure 2017-. Contested North Wales region (5) 2011 National Assembly for Wales election. North East Hampshire Conservatives: Member 2003-, Deputy Chair 2009-12; Deputy Chair, South East England Conservatives 2010-12. *Councils and public bodies:* Basingstoke and Deane Borough Council: Councillor 2008-15, Cabinet Member for Finance and Property 2011-12, Cabinet Member for Strategy 2012-15, Deputy Leader of Council 2012-15.

Political interests: Economy, law and order, criminal justice, education, infrastructure, constitution; Commonwealth, USA.

Other: FRSA. Freeman, City of London.

Recreations: Watching cricket and tennis, walks in the local area, shooting, golf, board games, theatre, film, local history.

Ranil Jayawardena MP, House of Commons, London SW1A 0AA
Tel: 020 7219 3637
Constituency: The Office of Ranil Jayawardena MP, The Bury, Odiham, Hampshire RG29 1NB
Tel: 01256 702468 *Email:* ranil@tellranil.com *Website:* www.tellranil.com

CONSERVATIVE

JENKIN, BERNARD

Harwich and North Essex *(Majority 14,356)*

Chair, Select Committee on Public Administration and Constitutional Affairs

Bernard Christison Jenkin. Born 9 April 1959; Son of late Patrick Jenkin (MP for Wanstead and Woodford 1964-87, later Lord Jenkin of Roding) and Alison Graham; Married Anne Strutt 1988 (now Baroness Jenkin of Kennington (qv)) (2 sons).

Education: Highgate School, London; William Ellis School, London; Corpus Christi College, Cambridge (BA English literature 1982) (President, Cambridge Union Society 1982); French (conversational).

Non-political career: Ford Motor Co Ltd 1983-86; Venture capital manager, 3i plc 1986-88; Manager, Legal and General Ventures Ltd 1989-92; Adviser, Legal and General Group plc 1992-95.

Political career: Contested Glasgow Central 1987 general election. Member for North Colchester 1992-97, for North Essex 1997-2010, for Harwich and North Essex since 6 May 2010 general election; PPS to Michael Forsyth as Secretary of State for Scotland 1995-97; Opposition Spokesperson for: Constitutional Affairs, Scotland and Wales 1997-98, Environment, Transport and the Regions (Roads and Environment) 1998; Shadow Minister for Transport 1998-2001; Member, Shadow Cabinet 1999-2003; Shadow Secretary of State for: Defence 2001-03, The Regions 2003-05; Shadow Minister for Energy 2005; Member, Speaker's Committee on the Electoral Commission 2015-17. *Select committees:* Member: European Standing Committee B 1992-97, Social Security 1993-97, Defence 2006-10, Arms Export Controls 2008-10; Chair, Public Administration 2010-15; Member: Liaison 2010-, Unopposed Bills (Panel) 2010-15, Joint Committees on: Parliamentary Privilege 2013, the Draft Protection of Charities Bill 2014-15; Chair, Public Administration and Constitutional Affairs 2015-. Conservative Backbench Committees: Vice-chair, Smaller Businesses 1992-95, Secretary, Foreign Affairs 1994-95; Member, Executive, 1922 Committee 2010-. Deputy chair (candidates), Conservative Party 2005-06; Vice-President, Conservatives for Britain 2015-16. *Councils and public bodies:* Governor, Central Foundation Girls' School 1985-89.

Political interests: Economic policy, trade, European Union, defence, foreign affairs, good governance, the Civil Service; Afghanistan, Chile, France, Georgia, Germany, India, Iraq, New Zealand, Pakistan, Russia, Singapore, USA.

Other: Governor, London Goodenough Trust for Overseas Graduates 1992-2001; Council member, St Paul's Cathedral 2006-; Vice-President, Combat Stress 2009-; Vice-chair and trustee, Parliament Choir; Board member, Vote Leave 2016; Action Aid, BASC, National Trust, British Paralympic Association, Students Partnership Worldwide; Colchester Conservative Constitutional Club.

Publications: Maastricht: Game Set and Match? (1993); Who Benefits: Reinventing Social Security (1993); A Conservative Europe: 1994 and beyond (1994); Fairer Business Rates (1996); A Defence Policy for the UK: Matching Commitments and Resources (2007).

Recreations: Sailing, music (especially opera), fishing, family, DIY.

Bernard Jenkin MP, House of Commons, London SW1A 0AA
Tel: 020 7219 4029 *Fax:* 020 7219 5963 *Email:* bernard.jenkin.mp@parliament.uk
Constituency: Harwich and North Essex Conservatives Association, Unit C2, East Gores Farm, Salmons Lane, Coggeshall, Colchester, Essex CO6 1RZ
Email: info@hneca.co.uk *Website:* www.bernardjenkinmp.com *Twitter:* @bernardjenkin

CONSERVATIVE

JENKYNS, ANDREA

Morley and Outwood *(Majority 2,104)*

Andrea Marie Jenkyns. Born 16 June 1974; Engaged to Jack Lopresti (qv) (MP for Filton and Bradley Stoke) (1 son).

Education: Open University (Diploma economics 2013); Lincoln University (BA international relations and politics 2014).

Non-political career: International business development manager, executive management training company; Music tutor, teaching in three secondary schools.

Political career: Member for Morley and Outwood since 7 May 2015 general election. *Select committees:* Member: Health 2015-17, Exiting the European Union 2016-. *Councils and public bodies:* Councillor, Lincolnshire County Council 2009-13.

Other: Trustee and regional representative, MRSA Action UK 2012-.

Recreations: Soprano singer and songwriter.

Andrea Jenkyns MP, House of Commons, London SW1A 0AA
Tel: 020 7219 5798 *Email:* andrea.jenkyns.mp@parliament.uk
Constituency: 62 Queen Street, Morley, West Yorkshire LS27 9BP
Tel: 0113-345 0380/0113-345 2530 *Website:* www.andreajenkyns.co.uk *Twitter:* @andreajenkyns

CONSERVATIVE

JENRICK, ROBERT

Newark *(Majority 18,149)*

PPS to Amber Rudd as Home Secretary

Robert Edward Jenrick. Born 9 January 1982; Married Michal Berkner (3 daughters).

Education: Wolverhampton Grammar School; St John's College, Cambridge (BA history); Pennsylvania University, Philadelphia, USA (Thouron Fellowship politics); College of Law, Birmingham (law).

Non-political career: Solicitor: Skadden Arps, Sullivan & Cromwell; Senior Executive and International Managing Director, Christie's.

Political career: Contested Newcastle-under-Lyme 2010 general election. Member for Newark since 5 June 2014 by-election; PPS: to Amber Rudd: as Energy Minister 2014-15, as Home Secretary 2017-; to Lord Chancellor and Secretary of State for Justice: Michael Gove 2015-16, Elizabeth Truss 2016-17. *Select committees:* Member, Health 2014-15. Conservative Party: Member 1998-, Chair, North Herefordshire Conservative Association, Member, Conservative Party Board 2017-.

Robert Jenrick MP, House of Commons, London SW1A 0AA
Tel: 020 7219 7335 *Email:* robert.jenrick.mp@parliament.uk
Constituency: 29a London Road, Newark, Nottinghamshire NG24 1TN
Tel: 01636 612837 *Email:* graysj@parliament.uk *Website:* www.robertjenrick.com
Twitter: @RobertJenrick

CONSERVATIVE

JOHNSON, BORIS

Uxbridge and South Ruislip *(Majority 5,034)*

Foreign Secretary

Alexander Boris de Pfeffel Johnson. Born 19 June 1964; Son of Stanley Patrick Johnson and Charlotte Johnson, neé Fawcett; Married Marina Wheeler 1993 (later QC) (2 sons 2 daughters).

Education: Eton College (King's Scholar); Balliol College, Oxford (Brackenbury Scholar in classics) (BA literae humaniores 1987).

Non-political career: Trainee reporter: *The Times*, *Wolverhampton Express*, *Star* 1987-88; *Daily Telegraph*: Leader and feature writer 1988-89, EC correspondent Brussels 1989-94, Assistant editor 1994-99; Political columnist, *Spectator* 1994-95; Chief political commentator, *Daily Telegraph*; Editor, *Spectator* 1999-2005.

Political career: Contested Clwyd South 1997 general election. Member for Henley 7 June 2001 to 4 June 2008, for Uxbridge and South Ruislip since 7 May 2015 general election; Shadow Minister for: the Arts 2004, Higher Education 2005-07; Secretary of State for Foreign and Commonwealth Affairs (Foreign Secretary) 2016-; Mayor of London 2008-16. Conservative Party: Vice-chairman (Campaigning) 2003-04, Member, political cabinet 2015-16.

Other: Patron, Downside UP Moscow; Member, Campaign Committee, Vote Leave 2016; President, Anglo Turkish Society; Patron: Iris Project, Classics for All, Faiths Forum; Honorary Ambassador, KP24 Foundation; Honorary Member, Battle of Britain Historical Society; Honorary Fellow, Royal Institute of British Architects. *What the Papers Say* Political Commentator of the Year 1997; Pagan Federation of Great Britain National Journalist of the Year 1998; Editors' Editor of the Year 2003; British Press Awards Columnist of the Year 2004; Channel 4 News Biggest Impression in Politics 2004, 2005; *What the Papers Say* Columnist of the Year 2005. PC 2016; Beefsteak Club.

Publications: Numerous radio and television broadcasts and publications; Friends, Voters, Countrymen (2001); Lend Me Your Ears (2004); Seventy Two Virgins; Dream of Rome (2006, 2007); Have I Got Views For You (2006); Life in the Fast Lane (2007); Perils of the Pushy Parent (2007); Johnson's Life of London (2011); The Churchill Factor (2015).

Recreations: Painting, poetry, tennis, skiing, rugby, cricket, cycling.

Rt Hon Boris Johnson MP, House of Commons, London SW1A 0AA
Tel: 020 7219 4682 *Email:* boris.johnson.mp@parliament.uk
Constituency: No constituency office publicised *Twitter:* @BorisJohnson

CONSERVATIVE

JOHNSON, CAROLINE

Sleaford and North Hykeham *(Majority 25,237)*

Caroline Elizabeth Johnson. Born 31 December 1977; Married Nik (2 daughters 1 son).

Education: Nunthorpe Comprehensive School; Gordonstoun; Newcastle University (MBBS 2001).

Non-political career: Consultant Paediatrician, Peterborough City Hospital, North West Anglia NHS Foundation Trust.

Political career: Contested Scunthorpe 2010 general election. Member for Sleaford and North Hykeham since 8 December 2016 by-election. *Select committees:* Member: Environment, Food and Rural Affairs 2017-, Health 2017-. Deputy Regional Chairman, Political (East Midlands), Conservative Party 2011-14.

Political interests: Health, education, children, agriculture, defence.

Other: Member: RCPCH, British Medical Association.

Dr Caroline Johnson MP, House of Commons, London SW1A 0AA
Tel: 020 7219 5381 *Email:* caroline.johnson.mp@parliament.uk
Constituency: 6 Market Place, Sleaford, Lincolnshire NG34 7SD
Tel: 01529 419000 *Website:* www.carolinejohnson.co.uk *Twitter:* @drcarolinej

LABOUR

JOHNSON, DIANA

Kingston upon Hull North *(Majority 14,322)*

Diana Ruth Johnson. Born 25 July 1966; Daughter of late Eric and Ruth Johnson; Partner Kevin Morton.

Education: Sir John Deane's Sixth Form College, Cheshire; Northwich County Grammar School for Girls, Cheshire; Queen Mary College, London University (LLB 1989); Council for Legal Education (law finals 1991).

Non-political career: Volunteer/locum lawyer, Tower Hamlets Law Centre 1991-94; Employment, immigration and education lawyer, North Lewisham Law Centre 1995-99; Employment lawyer, Paddington Law Centre 1999-2002; National Officer, FDA Trade Union 2002-03. Member: Unite, Unison.

Political career: Contested Brentwood and Ongar 2001 general election. Member for Hull North 2005-10, for Kingston upon Hull North since 6 May 2010 general election; PPS to Stephen Timms: as Minister of State, Department for Work and Pensions 2005-06, as Chief Secretary to the Treasury 2006-07; Assistant Government Whip 2007-09; Parliamentary Under-Secretary of State for Schools, Department for Children, Schools and Families 2009-10; Shadow Minister for: Health 2010, Home Office 2010-11, Crime and Security 2011-15, Foreign and Commonwealth Office 2015-16. *Select committees:* Member: Public Accounts 2005, Health 2017-. AM for Londonwide region, London Assembly 2003-04. Member: Co-operative Party, Labour Women's Network. *Councils and public bodies:* London Borough of Tower Hamlets: Councillor 1994-2002, Chair: Social services 1997-2000, Social services and health scrutiny panel 2000-02; Legal visiting member, Mental Health Act Commission 1995-98; Member, Metropolitan Police Authority 2003-04; Non-executive director: Newham Healthcare Trust 1998-2001, Tower Hamlets PCT 2001-05.

Political interests: Employment rights, health, education, animal welfare, policing; Colombia, Denmark, Jordan.

Other: Member: Fawcett Society, Amnesty International, Fabian Society.

Recreations: Cinema, theatre, Hull City FC.

Diana Johnson MP, House of Commons, London SW1A 0AA
Tel: 020 7219 5647 *Fax:* 020 7219 0959 *Email:* johnsond@parliament.uk
Constituency: Sycamore Suite, Community Enterprise Centre, Cottingham Road, Hull, Humberside HU5 2DH
Tel: 01482 319135 *Fax:* 01482 319137 *Website:* www.dianajohnson.co.uk
Twitter: @DianaJohnsonMP

CONSERVATIVE

JOHNSON, GARETH

Dartford *(Majority 13,186)*

PPS to David Davis as Secretary of State for Exiting the European Union

Gareth Alan Johnson. Born 12 October 1969; Son of Alan Johnson, retired milkman, and Ruth Johnson; Married Wendy Morris 1997 (1 son 1 daughter).

Education: Dartford Grammar School; University of the West of England (Postgraduate Diploma law); College of Law (legal practice course 1995).

Non-political career: Legal adviser, Magistrates Court Service 1988-98; Solicitor, Gary Jacobs Mehta & Co 1997-2002; Assistant solicitor, then solicitor, Thomas Boyd Whyte 2002-16.

Political career: Contested Lewisham West 2001 and Dartford 2005 general elections. Member for Dartford since 6 May 2010 general election; PPS to: David Gauke as Financial Secretary, HM Treasury 2014-15, Matthew Hancock as Minister for the Cabinet Office; Paymaster General 2015-16, David Davis as Secretary of State for Exiting the European Union 2017-. *Select committees:* Member: Science and Technology 2012, Justice 2013-14, Joint Committee on Human Rights 2014-15. *Councils and public bodies:* London Borough of Bexley Council: Councillor 1998-2002, Cabinet Member for Policy and Resources 1998-2002; Governor, Dartford Grammar Girls School.

Political interests: Home affairs, environment; USA.

Other: Member, Executive Committee, Inter-Parliamentary Union, British Group; Member, Law Society; Dartford Conservative Club.

Recreations: Cricket, rugby.

Gareth Johnson MP, House of Commons, London SW1A 0AA
Tel: 020 7219 7047 *Email:* gareth.johnson.mp@parliament.uk
Constituency: Dartford Civic Offices, Home Gardens, Dartford, Kent DA1 1DR
Tel: 01322 225958 *Website:* www.garethjohnsondartford.co.uk

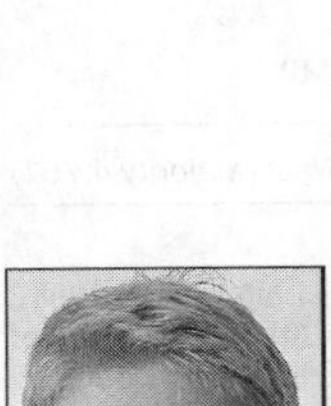

CONSERVATIVE

JOHNSON, JO

Orpington *(Majority 19,461)*

Minister of State for Universities, Science, Research and Innovation, Department for Business, Energy and Industrial Strategy and Department for Education

Joseph Edmund Johnson. Born 23 December 1971; Son of Stanley Johnson and Charlotte Johnson, née Fawcett; Married Amelia Gentleman (2 children).

Education: European School, Uccle, Brussels; Hall School, Hampstead; Eton College; Balliol College, Oxford (BA modern history 1994); INSEAD (MBA 2000); Institut d'Etudes Europennes, Universite Libre de Bruxelles (Licence Speciale 1995); French.

Non-political career: Corporate Finance, Deutsche Bank; *Financial Times*: Lex column 1997, Paris Correspondent 2001-04, Bureau Chief, South Asia 2005-08, Head of Lex 2008-10, Associate Editor.

Political career: Member for Orpington since 6 May 2010 general election; PPS to Mark Prisk as Minister of State for Business and Enterprise 2011-12; Assistant Government Whip 2012-14; Head of Number 10 Policy Unit 2013-15; Cabinet Office: Parliamentary Secretary 2013-14, Minister of State 2014-15; Minister of State for: Universities and Science, Department for Business, Innovation and Skills 2015-16, Universities, Science, Research and Innovation Department for Business, Energy and Industrial Strategy and Department for Education 2016-. *Select committees:* Member, Public Accounts 2010-12. Chair, Number 10 Policy Advisory Board 2013-15.

Political interests: Business, finance; France, India.

Other: President, Orpington Football Club; Honorary Patron, Bromley Community Fund; Trustee, Ditchley Foundation; Member: European Council on Foreign Relations, Prabodhan Steering Committee, UK-India Roundtable, Franco-British Colloque Annual Bilateral Forum.

Publications: Co-author, The Man Who Tried To Buy The World (2003); Co-editor, Reconnecting Britain and India: Ideas for an Enhanced Partnership (2011).

Jo Johnson MP, House of Commons, London SW1A 0AA
Tel: 020 7219 7125 *Email:* jo.johnson.mp@parliament.uk
Constituency: Orpington Conservative Association, 6 Sevenoaks Road, Orpington, Kent BR6 9JJ
Tel: 01689 820347 *Website:* www.jo-johnson.com *Twitter:* @JoJohnsonUK

CONSERVATIVE

JONES, ANDREW

Harrogate and Knaresborough *(Majority 18,168)*

Exchequer Secretary, HM Treasury

Andrew Hanson Jones. Born 28 November 1963; Single.

Education: Bradford Grammar School; Leeds University (BA English 1985).

Non-political career: Kingfisher plc; Going Places plc; Marketing Store; M&C Saatchi; Bettys and Taylors of Harrogate.

Political career: Contested Harrogate and Knaresborough 2001 general election. Member for Harrogate and Knaresborough since 6 May 2010 general election; PPS to: Mark Prisk as Minister of State for Business and Enterprise 2010-11, Justine Greening as Secretary of State for Transport 2011-12, Andrew Mitchell as Parliamentary Secretary to the Treasury and Chief Whip September-October 2012, Department of Health ministerial team 2013-14, Jeremy Hunt as Secretary of State for Health 2014-15; Apprenticeship Ambassador in Parliament 2014-15; Parliamentary Under-Secretary of State, Department for Transport 2015-17; Exchequer Secretary, HM Treasury 2017-. *Select committees:* Member: Regulatory Reform 2010-15, Public Accounts 2017-. Member, Conservative Party 1987-. *Councils and public bodies:* Harrogate Borough Council: Councillor 2003-11, Cabinet Member, Resources 2006-10.

Political interests: Transport, renewable energy.

Other: Chair, Bow Group 1998-99; Patron: Harrogate Gateway FC, Mad4Football, Tewit Youth Band, Harrogate. Member, Yorkshire County Cricket Club.

Recreations: Cricket, walking, music.

Andrew Jones MP, House of Commons, London SW1A 0AA
Tel: 020 7219 3000 *Email:* andrew.jones.mp@parliament.uk
Constituency: 57 East Parade, Harrogate, North Yorkshire HG1 5LQ
Tel: 01423 529614 *Website:* www.andrewjonesmp.co.uk *Twitter:* @AJonesMP

LABOUR

JONES, DARREN

Bristol North West *(Majority 4,761)*

Darren Paul Jones. Born 13 November 1986; Married Lucy Symons.

Education: Portway Community School; Plymouth University (BSc human biosciences 2008); Chartered Management Institute (Certificate leadership and management 2010); University of West of England (Graduate Diploma law 2010); Bristol College of Law (LPC legal practice 2011).

Non-political career: Clinical Auditor, NHS 2002-11; Technology, media and communications solicitor, Bond Dickinson LLP 2009-16; Legal Counsel, British Telecommunications plc 2015-17. Member, Unite.

Political career: Contested Torridge and West Devon 2010 and Bristol North West 2015 general elections. Member for Bristol North West since 8 June 2017. *Select committees:* Member, Science and Technology 2017-. Member, Labour Party 2003-; President, Plymouth Labour Students 2006-08; Member, National Policy Forum, Labour Students; Youth and students officer, Plymouth Sutton and Devonport CLP; South West NEC representative, Co-operative Party (youth) 2008-09. *Councils and public bodies:* Governor: Plymouth University Students' Union 2008-09, Avon Primary School 2009-11, Plymouth NHS Foundation Trust 2009, Hannah More Primary School 2012-13.

Political interests: Brexit, technology, digital, education, NHS; China, EU.

Other: Director, Shirehampton Community Action Forum; Trustee, North Bristol Advice Centre; Chair of Policy and Current Affairs, Bristol Junior Chamber of Commerce; Business Mentor, Prince's Trust; Associate, Chartered Management Institute.

Darren Jones MP, House of Commons, London SW1A 0AA
Tel: 020 7219 2302 *Email:* darren.jones.mp@parliament.uk
Constituency: Details still to be confirmed *Website:* www.darren-jones.co.uk *Twitter:* @darrenpjones

CONSERVATIVE

JONES, DAVID

Clwyd West *(Majority 3,437)*

David Ian Jones. Born 22 March 1952; Son of late Bryn Jones and Elspeth Jones, née Savage-Williams; Married Sara Tudor 1982 (2 sons).

Education: Ruabon Grammar School, Wrexham; University College London (LLB 1973); Chester College of Law; French, Welsh.

Non-political career: Senior partner, David Jones & Company, Llandudno 1985-2005; Director, David Jones (Solicitors) Ltd.

Political career: Contested Conwy 1997 and City of Chester 2001 general elections. Member for Clwyd West 2005-10, for Clwyd West (revised boundary) since 6 May 2010 general election; Shadow Minister for Wales 2006-10; Wales Office: Parliamentary Under-Secretary of State 2010-12, Secretary of State for Wales 2012-14; Minister of State, Department for Exiting the European Union 2016-17. *Select committees:* Member: Welsh Affairs 2005-10, Public Administration and Constitutional Affairs 2015-16, 2017-. Contested North Wales region 1999 National Assembly for Wales election. AM (replacement) for North Wales 2002-03. Chair, Conwy Conservative Association 1998-99; Patron, Chinese Conservative Group; Vice-President, Conservatives for Britain 2015-16.

Political interests: Law and order, constitution, Welsh affairs, countryside; ASEAN, China, Middle East.

Other: Member, UK Delegation, Organisation for Security and Co-operation in Europe Parliamentary Assembly 2015-16; Honorary Life Fellow, Cancer Research UK; Honorary Member, Colwyn Bay Rotary Club; Ambassador, Girlguiding; Member, Law Society. PC 2012.

Recreations: Travel.

Rt Hon David Jones MP, House of Commons, London SW1A 0AA
Tel: 020 7219 8070 *Fax:* 020 7219 0142 *Email:* david.jones.mp@parliament.uk
Constituency: 3 Llewelyn Road, Colwyn Bay, Conwy LL29 7AP
Tel: 01492 535845 *Fax:* 01492 534157 *Email:* bryan.george@parliament.uk
Website: www.davidjones.wales *Twitter:* @DavidJonesMP

LABOUR

JONES, GERALD

Merthyr Tydfil and Rhymney *(Majority 16,334)*

Shadow Minister for Defence

Born 21 August 1970; Partner Tyrone Powell.

Education: Bedwellty Comprehensive School; Ysrad Myncah College.

Non-political career: Grant Liaison Officer, Cardiff County Council 1999-2000; Development Officer, Gwent Association of Voluntary Organisations 2001-05, 2009-15. Member, GMB.

Political career: Member for Merthyr Tydfil and Rhymney since 7 May 2015 general election; PPS to: Nia Griffith as Shadow Secretary of State for Wales 2015-16, Emily Thornbury as Shadow Secretary of State for Defence 2015-16; Shadow Minister for: Wales 2016-17, Defence 2017-. *Select committees:* Member: Public Administration and Constitutional Affairs 2015-17, Welsh Affairs 2015-16. Patron, LGBT Labour. *Councils and public bodies:* Caerphilly County Borough Council: Councillor 1995-2015, Cabinet Member for Policy and Resources 2004-08, Deputy Leader of the Council 2004-08, 2012-15, Cabinet Member for Housing 2012-15, Anti-poverty Champion.

Political interests: Cost of living, job creation, regeneration, housing.

Other: Volunteer director, White Rose Resource Centre.

Gerald Jones MP, House of Commons, London SW1A 0AA
Tel: 020 7219 5874 *Email:* gerald.jones.mp@parliament.uk
Constituency: Oldway House, Castle Street, Merthyr Tydfil, Mid Glamorgan CF47 8UX
Tel: 01685 383739 *Website:* www.geraldjones.co.uk *Twitter:* @GeraldJonesLAB

LABOUR

JONES, GRAHAM

Hyndburn *(Majority 5,815)*

Graham Peter Jones. Born 3 March 1966; Son of Harry Jones, local government officer, and Elaine Taylor, teacher and clerk; Divorced (1 son) Partner Kimberly Whitehead (1 daughter).

Education: St Christopher's CoE High School; Accrington and Rossendale College; University of Central Lancashire (applied social studies 1992); City and Guilds Level 2 graphic design.

Non-political career: Refuge Collector/Parks Department, Blackburn Council 1985-87; Care Assistant, Lancashire County Council 1987-89; University of Central Lancashire 1989-92; Community Transport Driver 1992-96, 1997-99; Voluntary Designing and Publishing 1991-96; Overseas contract (4 months) in Kenya (installation of digital equipment) 1996-97; The Orchard Agency (Pre-press) 1997-99; MEN Manchester/Rochdale working (Pre press/advertising) 1999-2001; Daltons Printers, Accrington (Pre-press) 2001-10. Member, Community.

Political career: Member for Hyndburn since 6 May 2010 general election; Opposition Whip 2010-15. *Select committees:* Member, Defence 2017-. Chair, PLP Departmental Group for Culture, Media and Sport 2015-. *Councils and public bodies:* Hyndburn Borough Council: Councillor 2002-10, Leader, Labour group 2006-10; Councillor, Lancashire County Council 2009-13.

Political interests: Housing, low demand housing, early years education, defence and foreign affairs, consumer rights, communitarianism; Africa, Commonwealth, Europe, Great Lakes Region of Africa, Latin America, Middle East, North America.

Other: Member, British Legion. Baxenden Golf Club.

Recreations: Travel, backpacking, outdoors, walking, football, cricket, golf (handicap of 8), Blackburn Rovers FC, Accrington Stanley FC.

Graham Jones MP, House of Commons, London SW1A 0AA
Tel: 020 7219 7089 *Fax:* 020 7219 2492 *Email:* graham.jones.mp@parliament.uk
Constituency: 50 Abbey Street, Accrington, Lancashire BB5 1EE
Tel: 01254 382283 *Fax:* 01254 398089 *Email:* julie.milligan@parliament.uk
Twitter: @GrahamJones_MP

LABOUR

JONES, HELEN

Warrington North *(Majority 9,582)*

Chair, Select Committee on Petitions

Helen Mary Jones. Born 24 December 1954; Daughter of late Robert Jones and Mary Scanlan; Married Michael Vobe 1988 (1 son).

Education: Ursuline Convent, Chester; University College, London (BA English); Chester College; Liverpool University (MEd); Manchester Metropolitan University; French.

Non-political career: English teacher; Development officer, MIND; Justice and peace officer, Liverpool Archdiocese; Solicitor. Member: USDAW, Unite.

Political career: Contested Shropshire North 1983 and Ellesmere Port and Neston 1987 general elections. Member for Warrington North 1997-2010, for Warrington North (revised boundary) since 6 May 2010 general election; PPS to Dawn Primarolo as Minister of State, Department of Health 2007-08; Assistant Government Whip 2008-09; Government Whip 2009-10; Shadow Minister for Justice 2010; Opposition Whip 2010; Shadow Deputy Leader of the House of Commons 2010-11; Shadow Minister for: Communities and Local Government 2011-13, Home Office 2013-14. *Select committees:* Member: Catering 1997-98, Public Administration 1998-2000, Standing Orders 1999-2000, 2001-10, 2011-13, Education and Employment 1999-2001, Education and Employment (Education sub-committee) 1999-2001, Unopposed Bills (Panel) 1999-2010, Education and Skills 2003-07, Administration 2005-07, Selection 2009-10, Joint Committee on Security 2010-11, Finance 2015-16, Liaison 2015-; Chair, Petitions 2015-. Hon. Secretary, PLP Departmental Committee for Home Affairs 2002-06. Contested Lancashire Central 1984 European Parliament election. *Councils and public bodies:* Councillor, Chester City Council 1984-91.

Political interests: Education, health; Canada, Denmark, Estonia, Finland, Ireland, Sweden.

Other: Member, British-Irish Parliamentary Assembly 2015-.

Publications: How to Be a Government Whip (2016).

Recreations: Gardening, reading, cooking.

Helen Jones MP, House of Commons, London SW1A 0AA
Tel: 020 7219 4048 *Email:* jonesh@parliament.uk
Constituency: Gilbert Wakefield House, 67 Bewsey Street, Warrington, Cheshire WA2 7JQ
Tel: 01925 232480 *Fax:* 01925 232239 *Website:* www.warringtonnorthlabour.com
Twitter: @HelenJonesMP

LABOUR

JONES, KEVAN

North Durham *(Majority 12,939)*

Kevan David Jones. Born 25 April 1964.

Education: Portland Comprehensive, Worksop, Nottinghamshire; Newcastle upon Tyne Polytechnic (BA government and public policy 1985); University of Southern Maine, USA.

Non-political career: Parliamentary assistant to Nick Brown MP 1985-89; GMB: Political officer 1989-2001, Regional organiser 1992-99, Senior organiser 1999-2001. Member, GMB.

Political career: Member for North Durham 2001-10, for North Durham (revised boundary) since 6 May 2010 general election; Parliamentary Under-Secretary of State (Minister for Veterans), Ministry of Defence 2008-10; Shadow Minister for Defence 2010-15. *Select committees:* Member: Defence 2001-09, Armed Forces Bill 2005-06, 2011, Administration 2005-09, 2010-13, Armed Forces Bill 2015 2015-16. Member PLP Parliamentary Affairs Committee 2006-. Northern Region

Labour Party: Chair 1998-2000, Vice-chair 2000-. *Councils and public bodies:* Newcastle City Council: Councillor 1990-2001, Chair, Public Health 1993-97, Chief Whip 1994-2000, Chair, Development and Transport 1997-2001.

Political interests: Regeneration, transport, employment, regional policy, local and regional government, defence; Afghanistan, Iraq, Poland, UAE, USA.

Other: Member, UK Delegation, NATO Parliamentary Assembly 2017-; Patron, Chester Le Street Mind 2001-. Speech of the Year (with Charles Walker MP), *Spectator* awards 2012; Opposition Frontbencher of the Year, *House Magazine* awards 2012; Sacriston Working Men's Club.

Recreations: Golf.

Kevan Jones MP, House of Commons, London SW1A 0AA
Tel: 020 7219 8219 *Fax:* 020 7219 1759 *Email:* kevanjonesmp@parliament.uk
Constituency: Fulforth Centre, Front Street, Sacriston, Co Durham DH7 6JT
Tel: 0191-371 8834 *Fax:* 0191-371 8834 *Website:* www.kevanjonesmp.org.uk
Twitter: @KevanJonesMP

CONSERVATIVE

JONES, MARCUS

Nuneaton *(Majority 4,739)*

Parliamentary Under-Secretary of State (Minister for Local Government), Department for Communities and Local Government

Marcus Charles Jones. Born 5 April 1974; Son of Brian Jones, signwriter, and Jean Jones, legal cashier; Married Suzanne 2004 (1 son 1 daughter).

Education: St Thomas More School, Nuneaton; King Edward VI College.

Non-political career: Conveyancing manager, Tustain Jones & Co. Solicitors 1999-2010.

Political career: Member for Nuneaton since 6 May 2010 general election; PPS to Sajid Javid: as Financial Secretary, HM Treasury 2013-14, as Secretary of State for Culture, Media and Sport 2014-15; Parliamentary Under-Secretary of State (Minister for Local Government), Department for Communities and Local Government 2015-; Member, Speaker's Committee on the Electoral Commission 2017-. *Select committees:* Member: Backbench Business 2012-13, Administration 2012-15. *Councils and public bodies:* Nuneaton and Bedworth Borough Council: Councillor 2005-10, Leader, Conservative group 2006-09, Council Leader 2008-09.

Political interests: Economy, business and skills, local government.

Recreations: Family, watching Coventry City FC, angling.

Marcus Jones MP, House of Commons, London SW1A 0AA
Tel: 020 7219 7123 *Fax:* 020 7219 3483 *Email:* marcus.jones.mp@parliament.uk
Constituency: 13-17 Hollybush House, Bond Gate, Nuneaton, Warwickshire CV11 4AR
Tel: 024 7634 8482 *Fax:* 024 7634 8482 *Website:* www.marcusjones.org.uk
Twitter: @Marcus4Nuneaton

LABOUR

JONES, SARAH

Croydon Central *(Majority 5,652)*

Sarah Ann Jones. Born 20 December 1972; Married Ian Lloyd (3 sons including twins 1 daughter).

Education: Old Palace School; Durham University (history 1995).

Non-political career: Researcher to Mo Mowlam MP 1996-97; Public affairs and campaigns manager, Shelter UK 200-04; Deputy director of communications, NHS Confederation 2004-08; Deputy director, Government Olympic Communications 2008-13; Acting director of campaigns and policy, Bond 2013; Strategic communications adviser, Cambridge University Hospital NHS Foundation Trust 2013-14; Consultant, Inc London 2014-15; Director, Lloyd-Jones Communications 2013-16; Senior consultant, Quiller Consultants 2016-17.

Political career: Contested Croydon Central 2015 general election. Member for Croydon Central since 8 June 2017. *Select committees:* Member, Home Affairs 2017-. *Councils and public bodies:* Governor, Wolsey Junior School; Non-executive director, Wandle Housing Association 2013-.

Sarah Jones MP, House of Commons, London SW1A 0AA
Tel: 020 7219 2963 *Email:* sarah.jones.mp@parliament.uk
Constituency: Details still to be confirmed *Website:* www.sarah-jones.org *Twitter:* @laboursj

LABOUR

JONES, SUSAN ELAN

Clwyd South *(Majority 4,356)*

Born 1 June 1968; Daughter of Richard Jones, retired steelworks costs clerk, and Eirlys Jones, retired medical secretary.

Education: Grango Comprehensive School, Rhosllannerchrugog; Ruabon School Sixth Form; Bristol University (BA English 1989); Cardiff University (MA applied English language studies 1992).

Non-political career: English teacher: Tomakomai English School, Japan 1990-91, Atsuma Board of Education, Japan 1992-94; Corporate development fundraiser, Muscular Dystrophy Campaign 1995-96; Fundraiser, USPG 1997-2002; Director, Caris Haringey 2002-05; Fundraising executive, Housing Justice 2005-10.

Political career: Contested Surrey Heath 1997 general election. Member for Clwyd South since 6 May 2010 general election; PPS to Harriet Harman as Shadow Secretary of State for International Development 2010-11; Opposition Whip 2011-15; Shadow Minister for Wales 2015-16. *Select committees:* Member: Welsh Affairs 2010-12, Standards 2016-, Privileges 2016-, Petitions 2017-. Chair, Bristol University Labour Club 1986-87; Member, National Committee, Labour Students 1989-90. *Councils and public bodies:* London Borough of Southwark Council: Councillor 2006-09, Deputy Labour Group leader 2007-09.

Political interests: Charities, rural communities, economic development, Welsh language, crime.

Other: Member, Church in Wales.

Recreations: Classical music.

Susan Elan Jones MP, House of Commons, London SW1A 0AA
Tel: 020 7219 0920 *Email:* susan.jones.mp@parliament.uk
Constituency: Enterprise Centre, Well Street, Cefn Mawr, Wrexham LL14 3AL
Tel: 01978 824288 *Website:* www.susanelanjones.co.uk *Twitter:* @susanelanjones

LABOUR

KANE, MIKE

Wythenshawe and Sale East *(Majority 14,944)*

Shadow Minister for Schools

Michael Joseph Patrick Kane. Born 9 January 1969; Married Sandra Bracegirdle.

Education: St Paul's School, Newall Green.

Non-political career: Teacher, Springfield Primary School, Sale 2000-08; Parliamentary manager to: James Purnell MP 2008-10, Jonathan Reynolds MP 2010-11; Senior Executive Assistant to Kieran Quinn as Executive Leader, Tameside Council 2011-14; Acting Chief Executive, Movement for Change 2014. Member: Community, Unite.

Political career: Member for Wythenshawe and Sale East since 13 February 2014 by-election; Shadow Minister for: International Development 2015-16, Schools 2016-. *Select committees:* Member: Environmental Audit 2014-15, Treasury 2014-15. Former parliamentary agent to Jonathan Reynolds MP. *Councils and public bodies:* Manchester City Council: Former Councillor, Former executive member for Art and Leisure.

Countries of interest: Chagos Islands, Ireland.

Recreations: Season ticket holder at Manchester City FC, plays flute and bagpipes.

Mike Kane MP, House of Commons, London SW1A 0AA
Tel: 020 7219 7524 *Email:* mike.kane.mp@parliament.uk
Constituency: Unit A, Etrop Court, Wythenshawe, Greater Manchester M22 5RG
Tel: 0161-499 7900 *Fax:* 0161-499 7911 *Website:* www.mikekane.org *Twitter:* @MikeKaneMP

CONSERVATIVE

KAWCZYNSKI, DANIEL

Shrewsbury and Atcham *(Majority 6,627)*

Daniel Robert Kawczynski. Born 24 January 1972; Son of Leonard and Halina Kawczynski; Married Kate Lumb 2000 (divorced) (1 daughter).

Education: St George's College, Weybridge; Stirling University (BA business studies with French 1994); French, Polish.

Non-political career: Sales account manager telecommunications: BT, Cable & Wireless, Xerox 1994-2004; Owner/joint manager, equestrian centre and livery stables.

Political career: Contested Ealing Southall 2001 general election. Member for Shrewsbury and Atcham since 5 May 2005 general election; PPS to: Jim Paice as Minister of State for Agriculture and Food 2010-12, Richard Benyon as Parliamentary Under-Secretary of State (Natural Environment and Fisheries), Department for Environment, Food and Rural Affairs 2010-12, David Jones as Secretary of State for Wales 2012-14. *Select committees:* Member: Environment, Food and Rural Affairs 2005-07, Justice 2007-09, International Development 2008-10, Foreign Affairs 2015-17. Chairman, Stirling University Conservative Association 1991-93.

Political interests: Agriculture, foreign affairs, trade, foreign relations; Libya, Mauritania, Saudi Arabia.

Other: Member, UK Delegation, Organisation for Security and Co-operation in Europe Parliamentary Assembly 2014-; Hon. President, Shrewsbury Parkinson's Society; Fight for Sight.

Publications: Seeking Gadhafi (2010).

Recreations: Golf, vegetable and fruit growing.

Daniel Kawczynski MP, House of Commons, London SW1A 0AA
Tel: 020 7219 6249 *Fax:* 020 7219 1047 *Email:* kawczynskid@parliament.uk
Constituency: 1 Beaconsfield House, 17 Meadow Terrace, Shrewsbury, Shropshire SY1 1PE
Tel: 01743 233646 *Email:* mail@daniel4shrewsbury.co.uk
Website: www.daniel4shrewsbury.co.uk *Twitter:* @DKShrewsbury

CONSERVATIVE

KEEGAN, GILLIAN

Chichester *(Majority 22,621)*

Married Michael (2 stepsons).

Education: Liverpool John Moores University (BA business studies 1990); London Business School (MSc leadership and strategy 2010).

Non-political career: Apprentice, Delco Electronics; Senior Buyer, General Motors 1984-91; Purchasing Manager, National Westminster Bank plc 1992-96; Mondex International Ltd: Head of Strategic Alliances and Partnerships 1996-99, Commercial Director 1999-2001; Amadeus IT Group: Director, Business Travel 2001-02, Group Director, Global Customer Group 2002-07, Group Vice-president, Multinational Customer Group 2007-09; Executive Vice-president and Chief Marketing Officer, Travelport 2011-12.

Political career: Contested St Helens South and Whiston 2015 general election. Member for Chichester since 8 June 2017. *Select committees:* Member, Public Accounts 2017-. Director, Women2Win. *Councils and public bodies:* Chichester District Council: Councillor 2014-, Cabinet Member for Commercial Services; Governor, Western Sussex Hospitals NHS Trust.

Gillian Keegan MP, House of Commons, London SW1A 0AA
Tel: 020 7219 1193 *Email:* gillian.keegan.mp@parliament.uk
Constituency: Details still to be confirmed *Website:* www.gilliankeegan.com
Twitter: @GillianKeegan

LABOUR

KEELEY, BARBARA

Worsley and Eccles South *(Majority 8,379)*

Shadow Minister for Mental Health and Social Care

Barbara Mary Keeley. Born 26 March 1952; Daughter of Edward and Joan Keeley; Married Colin Huggett 1985.

Education: Mount St Mary's College, Leeds; Salford University (BSc politics and contemporary history 1994).

Non-political career: IBM UK Limited: Systems programmer 1983, Field systems engineer 1983-87, Field systems engineering manager 1987-89; Consultant and adviser in community regeneration 1989-94, 1995-2001; Area manager, Business in the Community North West 1994-95; Consultant, Princess Royal Trust for Carers 2001-05; Research on policy issues related to primary health care for Princess Royal Trust 2003-05. Member, GMB.

Political career: Member for Worsley 2005-10, for Worsley and Eccles South since 6 May 2010 general election; PPS: to Jim Murphy: as Parliamentary Secretary, Cabinet Office 2006, as Minister of State, Department for Work and Pensions 2006-07, to Harriet Harman as Minister for Women 2007-08; Assistant Government Whip 2008-09; Deputy Leader of the House of Commons 2009-10; Shadow Deputy Leader of the House of Commons 2010; Shadow Minister for: Health 2010, 2015-16, Communities and Local Government 2010-11; PPS to Ed Balls as Shadow Chancellor of the Exchequer 2011-15; Shadow Financial Secretary 2015; Shadow Minister for Mental Health and Social Care (attends Shadow Cabinet) 2016-. *Select committees:* Member: Constitutional Affairs 2005-06, Finance and Services 2006-10, Health 2011-15, Joint Committee on the Draft Care and Support Bill 2013. PLP Departmental Group for Women: Hon Secretary 2006-07, Chair 2007-08, Vice-chair 2015-. *Councils and public bodies:* Trafford Borough Council: Councillor 1995-2004, Vice-chair, social services 1995-97, Cabinet member 1997-99, 2000-04; Director, Trafford's pathfinder Children's Trust 2002-04.

Political interests: Health and social care, carers, mental health, women in sport; European Union.

Other: Member: Amnesty International, Fabian Society.

Publications: Co-author: Carers Speak Out (2002), Primary Carers (2003).

Recreations: Jogging, swimming, live music.

Barbara Keeley MP, House of Commons, London SW1A 0AA
Tel: 020 7219 8025 *Email:* barbara.keeley.mp@parliament.uk
Constituency: First Floor, 37 Manchester Road, Walkden, Greater Manchester M28 3NS
Tel: 0161-799 4159 *Fax:* 0161-799 5829 *Website:* www.barbarakeeley.co.uk
Twitter: @KeeleyMP

LABOUR

KENDALL, LIZ

Leicester West *(Majority 11,060)*

Elizabeth Louise Kendall. Born 11 June 1971.

Education: Watford Grammar School for Girls; Cambridge University (history).

Non-political career: Special adviser to Harriet Harman MP: as Shadow Secretary of State for Social Security 1996-97, as Secretary of State for Social Security and Minister for Women 1997-98; Research fellow, King's Fund; Associate director, health, social care and children's early years, Institute for Public Policy Research; Director, Maternity Alliance; Special adviser to Patricia Hewitt MP as Secretary of State for: Trade and Industry and Minister for Women and Equality 2004-05, Health 2005-07; Director, Ambulance Service Network 2007-09. Member, Unite.

Political career: Member for Leicester West since 6 May 2010 general election; Shadow Minister for: Health 2010-15, Care and Older People 2011-15. *Select committees:* Member: Education 2010, Communities and Local Government 2015-16. Chair, PLP Departmental Group for Education 2010. Member: Labour Party 1992-, Co-operative Party, Society – Health and Care Policy Commission; Contested Labour leadership election 2015.

Political interests: Employment, care for the elderly, early years services, NHS.

Other: Member, Fabian Society; Vice-chair, Progress.

Publications: Contributor, The Purple Book (Progress, 2011).

Liz Kendall MP, House of Commons, London SW1A 0AA
Tel: 020 7219 3000 *Email:* liz.kendall.mp@parliament.uk
Constituency: 42 Narborough Road, Leicester, Leicestershire LE3 0BQ
Tel: 0116-204 4980 *Fax:* 0116-204 4989 *Website:* www.lizkendall.org *Twitter:* @leicesterliz

CONSERVATIVE

KENNEDY, SEEMA

South Ribble *(Majority 7,421)*

PPS to Theresa May as Prime Minister

Seema Louise Ghiassi Kennedy. Born 6 October 1974; 2 sons.

Education: Westholme School, Blackburn; Cambridge University (oriental studies, French and Persian 1997); College of Law, London (Legal Practice Course international law and legal studies 1999); French, Farsi.

Non-political career: Commercial property solicitor: Slaughter and May 2000-03, Beran Britten 2003-06; Director, Tustin Developments Ltd 2006-15.

Political career: Member for South Ribble since 7 May 2015 general election; Team PPS, Department for Education 2016-17; PPS to Theresa May as Prime Minister 2017-; Chair, St Albans Conservative Association -2009. *Councils and public bodies:* Councillor, St Albans City and District Council -2014.

Political interests: Disability rights, older people; Iran.

Other: Bright Blue; Law Society; St Giles Trust for Children, Friends of Real Lancashire.

Recreations: Cooking, Blackburn Rovers FC.

Seema Kennedy MP, House of Commons, London SW1A 0AA
Tel: 020 7219 4412 *Email:* seema.kennedy.mp@parliament.uk
Constituency: 3 Church Row Chambers, Longton, Preston PR4 5PN
Tel: 01772 619266 *Website:* www.seemakennedy.co.uk *Twitter:* @SeemaKennedy

CONSERVATIVE

KERR, STEPHEN

Stirling *(Majority 148)*

Stephen Charles Kerr. Born 26 September 1960; Son of Charles and Sheila Lillian Kerr; Married Yvonne (4 children).

Education: Forfar Academy; Stirling University (business management 1986).

Non-political career: Bank Officer, Royal Bank of Scotland 1977-79; Missionary, Church of Jesus Christ of Latter-day Saints 1979-81; Sales Representative, Ensign Kitchens 1981-83; Kimberly-Clark Professional UK: Territory Sales Representative 1986-88, Product Manager 1988, Business Development Manager 1988-89, Distributor Account manager 1989-91, Regional Sales Manager 1991-97; Sales Director: Unico Ltd 1997-2004, Montague Lloyd Ltd 2000-04; Managing Director, Stephen Kerr Consultancy 2004-06; Kimberly-Clark Professional UK: District Manager 2006-08, European Distributor Account Manager 2008-10, Regional Sales Leader 2010-15, EMEA Sales Operations Leader 2016-17.

Political career: Contested Stirling 2005 and 2015 general elections. Member for Stirling since 8 June 2017. *Select committees:* Member, Business, Energy and Industrial Strategy 2017-. Chair, Stirling and Clackmannanshire Conservative and Unionist Association 2015-17.

Other: Member, The Chartered Institute of Marketing; Fellow, The Association of Professional Sales.

Stephen Kerr MP, House of Commons, London SW1A 0AA
Tel: 020 7219 2769 *Email:* stephen.kerr.mp@parliament.uk
Constituency: 49 Borestone Crescent, Stirling FK7 9BQ
Website: www.stephenkerr.org *Twitter:* @stephenkerrMP

LABOUR

KHAN, AFZAL

Manchester Gorton *(Majority 31,730)*

Shadow Minister for Immigration

Mohammed Afzal Khan. Born 5 April 1958; Married to Shkeela (2 daughters 1 son).

Education: Manchester Metropolitan University (BA law 1992).

Non-political career: Labourer, Mill; Bus driver; Youth worker; Police Officer, Greater Manchester Police; Senior Partner, Mellor Jackson Solicitors; Solicitor, Khan Solicitors 2014-. Member: GMB, Unite; Campaigner: Unison, USDAW.

Political career: Member for Manchester Gorton since 8 June 2017; Shadow Minister for Home Office (Immigration) 2017-; MEP for North West 2014-17. Labour Party: Member 2000-, North West Regional Board 2005-, Labour Movement for Europe, Co-founder, Black and Minority Ethic Forum. *Councils and public bodies:* Councillor, Manchester City Council 2000-14; Lord Mayor of Manchester 2005-06.

Other: Trustee, British Red Cross; Vice-president, World Mayors for Peace 2005-06. Mayor of the Year, Co-op Bank Award; Commander of the Order of the British Empire (2008).

Afzal Khan MP, House of Commons, London SW1A 0AA
Tel: 020 7219 3570 *Email:* afzal.khan.mp@parliament.uk
Constituency: BMHC, College Road, Whalley Range M16 8BP
Tel: 0161-226 5546 *Email:* contact@afzalkhan.org.uk *Website:* www.afzalkhan.org.uk
Twitter: @Afzal4Gorton

LAB/CO-OP

KILLEN, GERARD

Rutherglen and Hamilton West *(Majority 265)*

Born 15 May 1986; Married.

Education: Trinity High School.

Non-political career: Director, Sennit Construction Ltd 2001-17.

Political career: Member for Rutherglen and Hamilton West since 8 June 2017. *Select committees:* Member, Scottish Affairs 2017-. *Councils and public bodies:* Councillor, South Lanarkshire Council 2013-17.

Gerard Killen MP, House of Commons, London SW1A 0AA
Tel: 020 7219 0049 *Email:* gerard.killen.mp@parliament.uk
Constituency: Details still to be confirmed *Twitter:* @gedk

LABOUR

KINNOCK, STEPHEN

Aberavon *(Majority 16,761)*

Stephen Nathan Kinnock. Born 1 January 1970; Son of Neil Kinnock (MP for Bedwellty 1970-83 and Islwyn 1983-95, Labour Party Leader 1983-92, European Commissioner 1995-2004, now Lord Kinnock (qv)) and Glenys Kinnock (MEP for South East Wales 1994-99 and Wales region 1999-2009, now Baroness Kinnock of Holyhead (qv)); Married Helle Thorning-Schmidt 1996 (former Prime Minister of Denmark) (2 daughters).

Education: Drayton Manor Comprehensive School; Cambridge University (BA modern languages 1992); College of Europe, Bruges (MA European studies 1993); French, Spanish, Russian, Danish.

Non-political career: Research Assistant, European Parliament 1993-94; Consultant, Lancashire Enterprises, Brussels 1994-96; British Council Brussels: Manager 1996-2001, Director 2001-04; Director, British Council: St Petersburg, Russia 2005-08, Sierra Leone 2008-09; Director for Europe and Central Asia, World Economic Forum, Geneva 2009-12; Managing Director, UK office, Xynteo 2012-15. Community Union.

Political career: Member for Aberavon since 7 May 2015 general election; PPS to Angela Eagle as Shadow First Secretary of State and Secretary of State for Business, Innovation and Skills 2015-16. *Select committees:* Member: European Scrutiny 2015-, Welsh Affairs 2016-17, Exiting the European Union 2017-. Chair, Labour Business Parliamentary Group.

Political interests: Workers' rights, employers' responsibility, European Union, steel, industrial strategy; Palestine, Russia.

Other: Member, Advisory Board, Centre for Progressive Capitalism 2016-; Trustee, Radix 2016-; Patron, No Offence! 2014-15. Parliamentary football team.

Publications: A New Nation: building a United Kingdom of purpose, patriotism and resilience; Labour and Business: partners for a new kind of growth; Russia: respect-based realism (Fabians).

Recreations: Rugby, football.

Stephen Kinnock MP, House of Commons, London SW1A 0AA
Tel: 020 7219 8801 *Email:* stephen.kinnock.mp@parliament.uk
Constituency: Unit 7 Water Street Business Centre, Water Street, Port Talbot, West Glamorgan SA12 6LF
Tel: 01639 897660 *Website:* www.stephenkinnock.co.uk *Twitter:* @Skinnock

CONSERVATIVE

KNIGHT, GREG

East Yorkshire *(Majority 15,006)*

Gregory Knight. Born 4 April 1949; Son of Albert Knight, company director, and Isabel Knight, née Bell; Married Janet Knight.

Education: Alderman Newton's Grammar School, Leicester; College of Law, London; College of Law, Guildford (solicitor 1973).

Non-political career: Solicitor 1973-89, 1997-2001; Business consultant 1997-2001.

Political career: Member for Derby North 1983-97. Contested Derby North 1997 general election. Member for Yorkshire East 2001-10, for East Yorkshire (revised boundary) since 6 May 2010 general election; PPS to David Mellor as Minister of State: Foreign and Commonwealth Office 1987-88, Department of Health 1988-89; Assistant Government Whip 1989-90; Government Whip 1990-93; Government Deputy Chief Whip 1993-96; Minister of State, Department of Trade and Industry 1996-97; Deputy Shadow Leader of the House 2002-03; Shadow Minister for: Culture, Media and Sport 2003, Environment and Transport 2003-05, Transport 2005; Government Whip (Vice-Chamberlain of HM Household) 2012-13. *Select committees:* Member: Broadcasting 1993-96, Finance and Services 1993-96, 2013-15, Modernisation of the House of Commons 2001-03, 2005-10, Procedure: Member 2005, Chair 2005-12; Member: Liaison 2006-12, Administration 2006-10, Standards and Privileges 2009-10, Reform of the House of Commons 2009-10, Joint Committee on the Draft Detention of Terrorist Suspects (Temporary Extension) Bills 2011. Chair, Leicester and Leicestershire Young Conservatives 1972-73; Vice-chair, Conservative Parliamentary Candidates Association 1997-2001. *Councils and public bodies:* Councillor: Leicester City Council 1976-79, Leicestershire County Council 1977-83.

Political interests: Consumer issues, information technology, music, arts, home affairs; USA.

Other: British-American Parliamentary Group: Executive Committee Member 2001-08, Treasurer 2008-; The Law Society. PC 1995; Kt 2013; Bridlington Conservative Club.

Publications: Co-author, Westminster Words (1988); Honourable Insults (1990); Parliamentary Sauce (1993); Right Honourable Insults (1998); Naughty Graffiti (2005); Dishonourable Insults (2011).

Recreations: Classic and vintage cars, music, member parliamentary rock band 'MP4'.

Rt Hon Sir Greg Knight MP, House of Commons, London SW1A 0AA
Tel: 020 7219 4077 *Email:* sothcott@parliament.uk
Constituency: 18 Exchange Street, Driffield, East Yorkshire YO25 6LJ
Tel: 0845 090 0203 *Email:* secretary@gregknight.com *Websites:* www.eyorksconservatives.com www.gregknight.com *Twitter:* @GregKnight

CONSERVATIVE

KNIGHT, JULIAN

Solihull *(Majority 20,571)*

Julian Carlton Knight. Born 5 January 1972; Married Philippa.

Education: Chester Catholic High School; Hull University (BA history 1994).

Non-political career: Published author; Consumer journalist, BBC News; Money and property editor, *Independent*.

Political career: Member for Solihull since 7 May 2015 general election. *Select committees:* Member: Communities and Local Government 2015-17, Culture, Media and Sport/Digital, Culture, Media and Sport 2016-.

Countries of interest: Cyprus, Malta, West Indies.

Other: Marie Curie, Troop Aid. Professional Journalist of the Year 2006.

Julian Knight MP, House of Commons, London SW1A 0AA
Tel: 020 7219 3577 *Email:* julian.knight.mp@parliament.uk
Constituency: 631 Warwick Road, Solihull, West Midlands B91 1AR
Tel: 0121-709 0458 *Website:* www.julianknight.org.uk *Twitter:* @julianknight15

CONSERVATIVE

KWARTENG, KWASI

Spelthorne *(Majority 13,425)*

PPS to Philip Hammond as Chancellor of the Exchequer

Kwasi Alfred Addo Kwarteng. Born 26 May 1975; Son of Alfred Kwasi Kwarteng, economist, and Charlotte Kwarteng, barrister; Single.

Education: Eton College (King's Scholar; Newcastle Scholar); Trinity College, Cambridge (BA classics and history 1996, MA; PhD British history 2000); Kennedy Scholar, Harvard University, USA 1997; Birkbeck College, London (Postgraduate Certificate economics 2000); Certificate investment management 2005; Arabic (basic), French, German, Italian.

Non-political career: Financial analyst: Investment banking 2000-04, Fund management 2004-06; Freelance journalist and author 2006-.

Political career: Contested Brent East 2005 general election. Member for Spelthorne since 6 May 2010 general election; PPS to Leader of the House of Lords and Lord Privy Seal: Baroness Stowell of Beeston 2015-16, Baroness Evans of Bowes Park 2016-17; PPS to Philip Hammond as Chancellor of the Exchequer 2017-. *Select committees:* Member: Transport 2010-13, Work and Pensions 2013-15, Finance 2015-17, Public Accounts 2016-17.

Political interests: Economy and finance, transport; Africa, Middle East.

Other: Chair, Bow Group 2005-06; Trustee, History of Parliament Trust.

Publications: Author: Ghosts of Empire (Bloomsbury, 2011), Gridlock Nation (Biteback, 2011); Co-author: (with Chris Skidmore MP), After the Coalition (Biteback, 2011), (with Priti Patel MP, Dominic Raab MP, Chris Skidmore MP and Elizabeth Truss MP) Britannia Unchained: Global Lessons for Growth and Prosperity (Palgrave Macmillan, 2012).

Recreations: Music, foreign languages, travel.

Kwasi Kwarteng MP, House of Commons, London SW1A 0AA
Tel: 020 7219 4017 *Fax:* 020 7219 5852 *Email:* kwasi.kwarteng.mp@parliament.uk
Constituency: Spelthorne Conservative Association, 55 Cherry Orchard, Staines, Middlesex TW18 2DQ
Tel: 01784 453544 *Website:* www.kwasi4spelthorne.org.uk *Twitter:* @KwasiKwarteng

LABOUR

KYLE, PETER

Hove *(Majority 18,757)*

Peter John Kyle. Born 9 September 1970.

Education: Sussex University (BA geography, international development and environmental studies 1999; DPhil community economic development 2003).

Non-political career: Body Shop/Children on the Edge 1989-96: Aid worker, Eastern Europe and the Balkans; Fat Sand Production: Founder 2003-06, Non-executive director 2013-; Special adviser to Hilary Armstrong as Minister for the Cabinet Office and Social Exclusion and Chancellor of the Duchy of Lancaster 2006-07; Deputy chief executive, ACEVO 2007-13; Non-executive director, CAF Bank Ltd 2011-; Chief executive, Working For Youth 2013-15.

Political career: Member for Hove since 7 May 2015 general election. *Select committees:* Member: Business, Innovation and Skills 2015-16, Business, Energy and Industrial Strategy 2016-. Chair, PLP Departmental Group for Business, Innovation and Skills/Business, Energy and Industrial Strategy 2015-. Patron, LGBT Labour. *Councils and public bodies:* Governor, Portslade Aldridge Community College; Chair of governors, Brighton Aldridge Community College.

Dr Peter Kyle MP, House of Commons, London SW1A 0AA
Tel: 020 7219 6133 *Email:* peter.kyle.mp@parliament.uk
Constituency: 99 Church Road, Hove, East Sussex BN3 2BA
Tel: 01273 933380 *Website:* www.peterkyle.co.uk *Twitter:* @peterkyle

CONSERVATIVE

LAING, ELEANOR

Epping Forest *(Majority 18,243)*

First Deputy Chairman, Ways and Means and Deputy Speaker

Eleanor Fulton Laing. Born 1 February 1958; Daughter of late Matthew Pritchard and Betty Pritchard, née McFarlane; Married Alan Laing 1983 (divorced 2003) (1 son).

Education: St Columba's School, Kilmacolm, Renfrewshire; Edinburgh University (BA 1982; LLB) (First woman Union President); French.

Non-political career: Practised law in Edinburgh, City of London and industry 1983-89; Special adviser to John MacGregor MP: as Secretary of State for Education 1989-90, as Leader of the House of Commons 1990-92, as Secretary of State for Transport 1992-94.

Political career: Contested Paisley North 1987 general election. Member for Epping Forest 1997-2010, for Epping Forest (revised boundary) since 6 May 2010 general election; Opposition Whip 1999-2000; Opposition Spokesperson for: Constitutional Affairs and Scotland 2000-01, Education and Skills 2001-03; Shadow Minister for: Children 2003, Women 2004-07; Shadow Secretary of State for Scotland 2005; Shadow Minister for: Women and Equality 2005-07, Justice 2007-10; Special Representative to Gibraltar 2010-; Member: Speakers' Working Group on All-Party Groups 2011-12, Speaker's Committee on the Electoral Commission 2012-13; First Deputy Chairman, Ways and Means and Deputy Speaker 2013-. *Select committees:* Member: Education and Employment 1997-98, Education and Employment (Employment sub-committee) 1997-98, Environment, Transport and Regional Affairs 1998-99, Environment, Transport and Regional Affairs (Transport sub-committee) 1998-99, Office of the Deputy Prime Minister 2004-05, Office of the Deputy Prime Minister (Urban Affairs sub-committee) 2004-05, Political and Constitutional Reform 2010-13, Joint Committee on Human Rights 2010, Joint Committee on the Draft House of Lords Reform Bill 2011-12, Joint Committee on Parliamentary Privilege 2013, Scottish Affairs 2013, Panel of Chairs 2013-, Court of Referees 2016-. Chair, Conservative Party Committee for Home Affairs and Constitution -2013. Chairman, Society of Conservative Lawyers.

Political interests: Education, transport, economic policy, constitution, devolution; Australia, Gibraltar, New Zealand, Uganda, USA.

Recreations: Theatre, music, golf.

Eleanor Laing MP, House of Commons, London SW1A 0AA
Tel: 020 7219 2086 *Email:* eleanor.laing.mp@parliament.uk
Constituency: Thatcher House, 4 Meadow Road, Loughton, Essex IG10 4HX
Tel: 020 8508 6608 *Email:* efca@btinternet.com *Website:* www.eleanorlaing.com
Twitter: @eleanor4epping

LABOUR

LAIRD, LESLEY

Kirkcaldy and Cowdenbeath *(Majority 259)*

Shadow Secretary of State for Scotland

Lesley Margaret Langan Laird. Born 15 November 1958; Married (1 son).

Education: James Watt College; Institute of Personnel Management (1992); Napier University (BA business management and human resources 2002).

Non-political career: Royal Bank of Scotland: Relationship Manager 2007-09, Senior Talent Manager 2009-12; Managing Director, Lesley Laird & Associates Ltd 2012-14. Unison.

Political career: Member for Kirkcaldy and Cowdenbeath since 8 June 2017; Shadow Secretary of State for Scotland 2017-; *Councils and public bodies:* Fife Council: Councillor 2012-, Deputy Leader 2014, Spokesperson for Economy and Planning 2013-14.

Other: Board Member: Fife Economy Partnership, Business Gateway, Fife Coast and Countryside Trust ; Trustee, Muir Dean Trust; Chair, TAYplan; Member: SESplan Planning Committee, East of Scotland Advisory Committee.

Lesley Laird MP, House of Commons, London SW1A 0AA
Tel: 020 7219 3529 *Email:* lesley.laird.mp@parliament.uk
Constituency: Office of Lesley Laird MP, John Smith Business Centre, 1 Begg Road, Kirkcaldy KY2 6HD
Tel: 01592 724129 *Twitter:* @lesleylaird

PLAID CYMRU

LAKE, BEN

Ceredigion *(Majority 104)*

Plaid Cymru Spokesperson for Education and Skills, Health, Communities and Local Government, Constitutional Affairs and Culture, Media and Sport

Ben Morgan Lake. Born 22 January 1993.

Education: Lampeter Comprehensive School; Trinity College, Oxford (BA history and politics 2014; MSt modern European and British history 2015); Welsh.

Non-political career: Press Officer and Caseworker to Elin Jones AM; Research Officer, Plaid Cymru Group in National Assembly for Wales.

Political career: Member for Ceredigion since 8 June 2017; Plaid Cymru Spokesperson for: Education and Skills 2017-, Health 2017-, Communities and Local Government 2017-, Constitutional Affairs 2017-, Culture, Media and Sport 2017-. *Select committees:* Member, Welsh Affairs 2017-.

Political interests: Rural economy and rural development, youth engagement, sustainable development, education, health.

Other: Lampeter RFC, Lampeter AFC.

Ben Lake MP, House of Commons, London SW1A 0AA
Tel: 020 7219 4454 *Email:* ben.lake.mp@parliament.uk
Constituency: Details still to be confirmed *Twitter:* @BenMLake

LIBERAL DEMOCRAT

LAMB, NORMAN

North Norfolk *(Majority 3,512)*

Liberal Democrat Shadow Secretary of State for Health; Chair, Select Committee on Science and Technology

Norman Peter Lamb. Born 16 September 1957; Son of late Hubert Lamb, professor of climatology, and Beatrice Lamb, née Milligan, nurse; Married Mary Green 1984 (2 sons).

Education: George Abbot School, Guildford, Surrey; Wymondham College, Wymondham, Norfolk; Leicester University (LLB 1980); Qualified solicitor 1984.

Non-political career: Norwich City Council: Trainee solicitor 1982-84, Senior assistant solicitor 1984-85; Steele and Company Norfolk: Solicitor 1986-87, Partner 1987-2001; Consultant 2001-06.

Political career: Contested North Norfolk 1992 and 1997 general elections. Member for North Norfolk 2001-10, for North Norfolk (revised boundary) since 6 May 2010 general election; Liberal Democrat Spokesperson for: International Development 2001-02, the Treasury 2002-05, Shadow Secretary of State for Trade and Industry 2005-06; Chief of Staff to Sir Menzies Campbell as Leader of the Liberal Democrats 2006; Liberal Democrat Shadow Secretary of State for Health 2006-10; Chief Parliamentary and Political Adviser to the Deputy Prime Minister 2010-12;

PPS to Nick Clegg as Deputy Prime Minister, Lord President of the Council 2010-12; Assistant Whip 2010-12; Parliamentary Under-Secretary of State (Minister for Employment Relations, Consumer and Postal Affairs), Department for Business, Innovation and Skills 2012; Minister of State for Care and Support, Department of Health 2012-15; Liberal Democrat Spokesperson/Shadow Secretary of State for Health 2015-. *Select committees:* Member: Treasury 2003-05, Treasury (Treasury Sub-committee) 2003-10; Chair, Science and Technology 2017-; Member, Liaison 2017-. Chair, Tottenham Liberals 1980-81; Norwich South Liberals 1985-87; Contested 2015 Liberal Democrats Leadership election. *Councils and public bodies:* Norwich City Council: Councillor 1987-91, Group leader 1989-91; Chair, Mental Health Commission, West Midlands Combined Authority 2016-.

Political interests: Health, employment, social affairs, constitution, environment, international development; South Africa, USA.

Other: Board member, Think Ahead 2016-; Member, advisory board, Money and Mental Health Policy Institute 2016-; Patron, Vote Leave Watch 2016-; Norfolk Air Ambulance, Benjamin Foundation, Norfolk and Norwich Association for the Blind, Wells Hospital, About with Friends. President's Award, Royal College of Psychiatrists 2011. PC 2014.

Publications: Remedies in the Employment Tribunal (Sweet and Maxwell, 1998); The NHS: a liberal blueprint (CentreForum).

Recreations: Walking, football (Norwich City FC), cycling.

Rt Hon Norman Lamb MP, House of Commons, London SW1A 0AA
Tel: 020 7219 0542 *Fax:* 020 7219 1963 *Email:* lambn@parliament.uk
Constituency: Unit 4, North Walsham Garden Centre, Nursery Drive, Norwich Road, North Walsham, Norfolk NR28 0DR
Tel: 01692 403752 *Website:* www.normanlamb.org.uk *Twitter:* @normanlamb

LABOUR

LAMMY, DAVID

Tottenham *(Majority 34,584)*

David Lindon Lammy. Born 19 July 1972; Son of Rosalind Lammy, council officer; Married Nicola Green 2005 (2 children).

Education: The King's School, Peterborough; School of Oriental and African Studies, London University (LLB 1993); Harvard Law School, USA (LLM 1997).

Non-political career: Barrister, 3 Serjeants Inn, Philip Naughton QC 1994-96; Attorney, Howard Rice Nemerovsky Canada Falk & Rabkin 1997-98; Barrister, D J Freeman 1998-2000. Member, Amicus branch of Unite.

Political career: Member for Tottenham since 22 June 2000 by-election; PPS to Estelle Morris as Secretary of State for Education and Skills 2001-02; Parliamentary Under-Secretary of State: Department of Health 2002-03, Department for Constitutional Affairs 2003-05, Department for Culture, Media and Sport 2005-07, Department for Innovation, Universities and Skills (DIUS) (Skills) 2007-08; Minister of State (Higher Education and Intellectual Property) DIUS/Department for Business, Innovation and Skills 2008-10; Shadow Minister for Higher Education 2010; Chair, Lammy Review Leading (review of the treatment of, and outcomes for, Black, Asian and Minority Ethnic individuals in the Criminal Justice System) 2016-. *Select committees:* Member: Public Administration 2001, Procedure 2001, Ecclesiastical Committee 2010-, Works of Art 2011-, Joint Committee on the Draft Defamation Bill 2011. AM for Londonwide region, London Assembly 2000. Member: Society of Labour Lawyers, Christian Socialist Movement. *Councils and public bodies:* Member, Archbishops' Council 1999-2002.

Political interests: Health, Treasury (regeneration), arts and culture, education, international development, gambling, intellectual property, sport; Africa, Latin America, Caribbean, USA.

Other: ActionAid: Trustee 2000-06, Honorary Ambassador 2006-; Patron: Peace Alliance, boys2MEN, Haringey Shed, Oxford Access Scheme, Into University, London Nightline; Honorary president, Haringey Borough Swimming Club; Honorary vice-president, Haringey Advisory Group on Alcohol; President, Tottenham Community Festival; Ovarian Cancer Action; Member, Fabian Society. Honorary Doctorate of Law, University of East London 2004. PC 2008; Honourable Society of Lincoln's Inn.

Publications: Leading Together (2002); Out of the Ashes (2011).

Recreations: Film, live music, Tottenham Hotspur FC.

Rt Hon David Lammy MP, House of Commons, London SW1A 0AA
Tel: 020 7219 0767 *Fax:* 020 7219 0357 *Email:* lammyd@parliament.uk
Constituency: No constituency office *Website:* www.davidlammy.co.uk
Twitter: @DavidLammy

CONSERVATIVE

LAMONT, JOHN

Berwickshire, Roxburgh and Selkirk *(Majority 11,060)*

John Robert Lamont. Born 15 April 1976; Son of Robert Lamont, farmer, and Elizabeth Lamont, née Wilson, teacher.

Education: Kilwinning Academy, Ayrshire; Glasgow University (LLB law 1998); College of Law, Chester (CPD 1999; LPC 2000; qualified solicitor 2002).

Non-political career: Freshfields, London 2000-04: Trainee solicitor 2000-02, Assistant 2002-03; Associate, Bristows, London 2003-05; Solicitor, Brodies, Edinburgh 2005-07.

Political career: Contested Berwickshire, Roxburgh and Selkirk 2005, 2010 and 2015 general elections. Member for Berwickshire, Roxburgh and Selkirk since 8 June 2017. *Select committees:* Member, Scottish Affairs 2017-. Member, Executive, 1922 Committee 2017-. MSP for Roxburgh and Berwickshire constituency 2007-11, and for Ettrick, Roxburgh and Berwickshire constituency 2011-17: Scottish Conservatives: Shadow Minister for Community Safety 2007-10, Shadow Cabinet Secretary for Justice 2010-11, Spokesperson for Justice 2011, Chief Whip 2011-17, Business Manager 2011-17; Member: Scottish Parliamentary Bureau 2011-17, Scottish Commission for Public Audit 2016-17. Member, Conservative Friends of Israel 2011-; National co-ordinator, Conservative Friends of the Union 2012-.

Political interests: Rural affairs, tourism, farming, justice, digital infrastructure; Israel, Taiwan, USA.

Other: Member: East of Scotland Rail Action Group 2005-, Scottish Athletics 2008-, Borders Sport and Leisure Trust 2010-; Trustee, St Abbs Lifeboat Trust; Member, Law Society of England and Wales 2002-; Patron, Borders Osteoporosis Society. College of Law prize for excellence 2002; City of London Company law prize (nominated) 2002. Borders Triathlon Club.

Recreations: Cycling, running, swimming, competing in triathlons.

John Lamont MP, House of Commons, London SW1A 0AA
Tel: 020 7219 1557 *Email:* john.lamont.mp@parliament.uk
Constituency: 25 High Street, Hawick TD9 9BU
Tel: 01450 375948 *Website:* www.johnlamont.org *Twitter:* @john2win

CONSERVATIVE

LANCASTER, MARK

Milton Keynes North *(Majority 1,975)*

Minister of State for the Armed Forces, Ministry of Defence

John Mark Lancaster. Born 12 May 1970; Son of Revd Ron Lancaster MBE and Kath Lancaster; Married Katherine Reader 1995 (divorced) (1 daughter); married Caroline Dinenage (qv) 2014 (MP for Gosport).

Education: Kimbolton School, Huntingdon; Buckingham University (BSc business studies 1991); Exeter University (MBA 1994); French, Nepali.

Non-political career: Officer Royal Engineers 1988-90; Lt Colonel Royal Engineers (TA) 1990-. Director, Kimbolton Fireworks Ltd 1990-2005.

Political career: Contested Nuneaton 2001 general election. Member for Milton Keynes North East 2005-10, for Milton Keynes North since 6 May 2010 general election; Opposition Whip 2006-07; Shadow Minister for International Development 2007-10; PPS to Andrew Mitchell as Secretary of State for International Development 2010-12; Government Whip 2012-15; Ministry of Defence: Parliamentary Under-Secretary of State: Defence Personnel and Veterans 2015-16, Defence Veterans, Reserves and Personnel 2016-17, Minister of State for the Armed Forces 2017-. *Select committees:* Member: Office of the Deputy Prime Minister 2005-06, Defence 2006, Communities and Local Government 2008-09, International Development 2009-10, Armed Forces Bill 2011. *Councils and public bodies:* Huntingdon District Council: Councillor 1995-99, Chair, Leisure Committee 1996-99.

Political interests: Defence, international development, commerce; China, India, Nepal, USA.

Other: Vice-chair: British Fireworks Association 1999-2006, MK SNAP 2004-; Patron, Willen Hospice 2006-; Parliamentary adviser, Royal Society of Chemistry. Member, Worshipful Company of Fanmakers. Hon DSc, Buckingham University 2007. TD 2002; United and Cecil Club, Army and Navy Club. House of Commons and House of Lords Cricket Club; Associate member, MCC.

Publications: Contributor, Fireworks Principles and Practice (Chemical Publishing, 1999).

Recreations: Cricket, football, collecting classic British motorcycles.

Mark Lancaster TD MP, House of Commons, London SW1A 0AA
Tel: 020 7219 8414 *Fax:* 020 7219 6685 *Email:* officeofmarklancaster@parliament.uk
Constituency: Suite 102, Milton Keynes Business Centre, Foxhunter Drive, Linford Wood, Buckinghamshire MK14 6GD
Tel: 01908 686830 *Fax:* 01908 686831 *Website:* lancaster4mk.com *Twitter:* @MarkLancasterMK

CONSERVATIVE

LATHAM, PAULINE

Mid Derbyshire *(Majority 11,616)*

Pauline Elizabeth Latham. Born 4 February 1948; Married Derek Latham 1968 (1 daughter 2 sons).

Education: Bramcote Hills Technical Grammar School.

Non-political career: Proprietor, Humble Pie 1976-87; Director, Michael St Development 1982-95; Founder Member and Chair, Grant Maintained Schools Advisory Committee -2004.

Political career: Contested Broxtowe 2001 general election. Member for Mid Derbyshire since 6 May 2010 general election; PPS to: Hugo Swire as Minister of State, Foreign and Commonwealth Office 2015-16, Alan Duncan as Minister of State for Europe and the Americas, Foreign and Commonwealth Office 2016-17. *Select committees:* Member: International Development 2010-, Work of the Independent Commission for Aid Impact Sub-committee 2017-. Secretary, 1922 Sub-committee on Foreign Affairs, Defence and International Development; Member, Executive, 1922 Committee 2017-. Contested East Midlands 1999 and 2004 European Parliament elections. *Councils and public bodies:* Councillor: Derbyshire County Council 1987-2002, Derby City Council 1992-96, 1998-2010; Mayor of Derby 2007-08; Governor and chair of governors, Ecclesbourne School.

Political interests: International development, health (cancer and type 1 diabetes); Africa.

Other: Commonwealth Parliamentary Association (UK Branch): Vice-chair 2011-14, Member, Executive Committee 2014-15; Free the Children: Trustee, Board Member; Patron, Women's Work. OBE 1995; Carlton Club.

Recreations: Horse riding, walking, travel.

Pauline Latham OBE MP, House of Commons, London SW1A 0AA
Tel: 020 7219 7110 *Email:* pauline.latham.mp@parliament.uk
Constituency: The Old Station, Station Road, Spondon, Derby, Derbyshire DE21 7NE
Tel: 01332 676679 *Website:* www.paulinelatham.co.uk *Twitter:* @Pauline_Latham

LABOUR

LAVERY, IAN

Wansbeck *(Majority 10,435)*

National Campaign Co-ordinator; Labour Party Chair

Born 6 January 1963; Son of John Lavery, miner, and Patricia Lavery; Married Hilary (2 sons).

Education: Ashington High School; New College, Durham (HNC mining engineering).

Non-political career: Miner, National Coal Board: Lynemouth Colliery 1980, Ellington Colliery 1980-92; National Union of Mine Workers: General Secretary, Northumberland Area 1992-2002, National President 2002-10. National Union of Mineworkers: Member 1980-, Representative, Ellington Colliery 1986-92; Member, GMB.

Political career: Member for Wansbeck since 6 May 2010 general election; PPS to Harriet Harman: as Deputy Leader and Chair, Labour Party; Deputy Leader of the Opposition; Shadow Secretary of State for International Development 2010-11, as Shadow Deputy Prime Minister, Chair, Labour Party, and Shadow Secretary of State for Culture, Media and Sport 2011-12; Shadow Minister for Cabinet Office 2015-16; Shadow Minister for the Cabinet Office (attends Shadow Cabinet) 2016-17; National Elections and Campaign Co-ordinator/National Campaign Co-ordinator 2017-. *Select committees:* Member: Northern Ireland Affairs 2010-11, Regulatory Reform 2010-15, Energy and Climate Change 2010-15, Joint Committee on Draft Deregulation Bill 2013. Labour Party: Member, Ashington Town branch, Executive committee member, Wansbeck CLP, Chair, Trade Union Group of MPs, Party Chair 2017-. *Councils and public bodies:* Former councillor, Wansbeck District Council.

Political interests: Local regeneration, employment, energy, climate change, poverty, internationalism, sport, foreign and Commonwealth affairs.

Other: International Energy Miners Organisation; Chair: Ashington Community Football Club, Hirst Welfare Centre, Ashington Group – The Pitmen Painters; Trustee: Northumberland Aged Miners Homes Association, North East Area Miners Trust, Woodhorn Museum, North East CISWO Trust.

Recreations: History, walking, horse and greyhound racing, Newcastle United FC, all sports.

Ian Lavery MP, House of Commons, London SW1A 0AA
Tel: 020 7219 7177 *Email:* ian.lavery.mp@parliament.uk
Constituency: 7 Esther Court, Wansbeck Business Park, Ashington, Northumberland NE63 8AP
Tel: 01670 852494 *Fax:* 01670 818262 *Website:* www.ianlavery.org.uk *Twitter:* @IanLaveryMP

SCOTTISH NATIONAL PARTY

LAW, CHRIS

Dundee West *(Majority 5,262)*

SNP Spokesperson for International Development and Climate Justice

Christopher Murray Alexander Law. Born 21 October 1969.

Education: Dundee College of Further Education (C&G catering); St Andrews University (cultural and social anthropology; Postgraduate Diploma IT).

Non-political career: French chef; Founder and expedition leader, Freewheeling Travels 1997-; Founder, director and writer, Freewheeling Films 2003-; Founder and director, The Mortgage Doctor 2007-.

Political career: Member for Dundee West since 7 May 2015 general election; SNP Spokesperson for International Development and Climate Justice 2017-. *Select committees:* Member: Scottish Affairs 2015-17, International Development 2017-, Work of the Independent Commission for Aid Impact Sub-committee 2017-.

Political interests: Disability benefits, welfare.

Other: Member, Executive Committee, Commonwealth Parliamentary Association (UK Branch) 2017-; Founder and campaigner, Spirit of Independence 2014.

Chris Law MP, House of Commons, London SW1A 0AA
Tel: 020 7219 6917 *Email:* chris.law.mp@parliament.uk
Constituency: 2 Marshall Street, Lochee, Dundee DD2 3BR
Tel: 01382 848906 *Email:* chris@dundeesnp.scot *Twitter:* @ChrisLawSNP

CONSERVATIVE

LEADSOM, ANDREA

South Northamptonshire *(Majority 22,840)*

Leader of the House of Commons and Lord President of the Council

Andrea Jacqueline Leadsom. Born 13 May 1963; Daughter of Judy Crompton and Richard Salmon; Married Ben Leadsom 1993 (2 sons 1 daughter).

Education: Tonbridge Girls Grammar; Warwick University (political science 1984); French.

Non-political career: Various roles, BZW 1987-93; Financial institutions director, Barclays Bank 1991-97; Managing director, De Putron (funds management) 1997-99; Head of corporate governance, Invesco Perpetual 1999-2009.

Political career: Contested Knowsley South 2005 general election. Member for South Northamptonshire since 6 May 2010 general election; Economic Secretary (Minister for the City of London), HM Treasury 2014-15; Minister of State, Department of Energy and Climate Change 2015-16; Secretary of State for Environment, Food and Rural Affairs 2016-17; Leader of the House of Commons and Lord President of the Council (also attending Cabinet) 2017-; Member, House of Commons Commission 2017-. *Select committees:* Member: Treasury 2010-14, Public Accounts 2014-15. Member, Number 10 Policy Advisory Board 2013-14. *Councils and public bodies:* Councillor, South Oxfordshire District Council 2003-07.

Political interests: Economy, early years development, bank reform.

Other: Oxford Parent Infant Project: Chair 2001-09, Patron; Patron: Northamptonshire Parent Infant Project, PIP UK, PSP Association; Member, Campaign committee, Vote Leave 2016. Newcomer of the Year, *Spectator* awards 2012. PC 2016.

Rt Hon Andrea Leadsom MP, House of Commons, London SW1A 0AA
Tel: 020 7219 7149 *Fax:* 020 7219 4045 *Email:* andrea.leadsom.mp@parliament.uk
Constituency: 4a Victoria House, 138 Watling Street East, Towcester NN12 6BT
Tel: 01327 353124 *Website:* www.andrealeadsom.com *Twitter:* @andrealeadsom

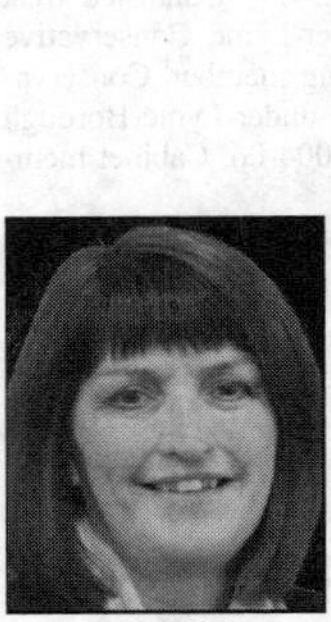

LABOUR

LEE, KAREN

Lincoln *(Majority 1,538)*

PPS to John McDonnell as Shadow Chancellor of the Exchequer

Karen Elizabeth Lee; 4 children.

Education: St Hugh's Roman Catholic School; South Park School; Lincoln College.

Non-political career: Nurse, Lincoln County Hospital. Former Member, Unite; Member, Unison.

Political career: Member for Lincoln since 8 June 2017; PPS to John McDonnell as Shadow Chancellor of the Exchequer 2017-; *Councils and public bodies:* Lincoln City Council: Councillor 2003-, Mayor 2012-13.

Karen Lee MP, House of Commons, London SW1A 0AA
Tel: 020 7219 3569 *Email:* karen.lee.mp@parliament.uk
Constituency: 32 Newland, Lincoln LN1 1XJ *Twitter:* @KarenLeeMP

CONSERVATIVE

LEE, PHILLIP

Bracknell *(Majority 16,016)*

Parliamentary Under-Secretary of State for Youth Justice, Victims, Female Offenders and Offender Health, Ministry of Justice

Phillip James Lee. Born 28 September 1970; Married.

Education: Sir William Borlase's Grammar School, Marlow; King's College, London (BSc human biology 1993); Keble College, Oxford (MSc biological anthropology 1994); St Mary's Hospital Medical School, Imperial College, London (MBBS 1999).

Non-political career: St Mary's Hospital, London; Wexham Park Hospital, Slough; Stoke Mandeville Hospital, Aylesbury; GP, Thames Valley.

Political career: Contested Blaenau Gwent 2005 general election. Member for Bracknell since 6 May 2010 general election; Board member, Parliamentary Office of Science and Technology (POST) -2013; Ministry of Justice: Parliamentary Under-Secretary of State for: Victims, Youth and Family Justice 2016-17, Youth Justice, Victims, Female Offenders and Offender Health 2017-. *Select committees:* Member: Energy and Climate Change 2010-15, Administration 2010-12. Vice-chair, Conservative Middle East Council. *Councils and public bodies:* Councillor, Beaconsfield Town Council 2001-02.

Political interests: Health, science, foreign affairs, energy security policy, space industry; Middle East, Norway.

Other: Member, General Medical Council.

Recreations: Skiing, football, rugby union.

Dr Phillip Lee MP, House of Commons, London SW1A 0AA
Tel: 020 7219 1270 *Email:* phillip.lee.mp@parliament.uk
Constituency: 10 Milbanke Court, Milbanke Way, Western Road, Bracknell, Berkshire RG12 1RP
Tel: 01344 868894 *Email:* leepa@parliament.uk *Website:* www.phillip-lee.com
Twitter: @DrPhillipLeeMP

CONSERVATIVE

LEFROY, JEREMY

Stafford *(Majority 7,729)*

Jeremy John Elton Lefroy. Born 30 May 1959; Married Janet Mackay 1985 (1 son 1 daughter).

Education: Highgate School, London; King's College, Cambridge (BA classics 1980); German, Swahili.

Non-political career: Armed Forces Parliamentary Scheme 2010-11, 2011-12. Foreman, Ford Motor Company 1980-81; Trainee accountant, Arthur Andersen 1981-84; Finance manager/director, Cowan de Groot plc 1984-86; Finance manager, EDM Schluter Ltd 1986-88; General manager/managing director, African Coffee Company Ltd, Tanzania 1989-2000; Director and part-owner, African Speciality Products Ltd 2000-.

Political career: Contested Newcastle-under-Lyme 2005 general election. Member for Stafford since 6 May 2010 general election; Trade Envoy to Ethiopia 2016-. *Select committees:* Member: International Development 2010-17, Joint Committee on Human Rights 2015-, Arms Export Controls 2016-17, Work of the Independent Commission for Aid Impact Sub-committee 2015-17, Exiting the European Union 2016-. Chairman, Conservative Backbench Policy Committee on International Development 2015-17; Member, Executive, 1922 Committee 2017-. Contested West Midlands 2004 European Parliament election. Treasurer, Newcastle-under-Lyme Conservative Association 2003-06; Trustee, Conservative Christian Fellowship; Founding member, Conservatives for Reform in Europe 2016. *Councils and public bodies:* Newcastle-under-Lyme Borough Council: Councillor 2003-07, Shadow finance and resources spokesman 2004-06, Cabinet member for finance and resources 2006-07.

Political interests: Sustainable development and enterprise, urban regeneration, environment, small business, health; Kenya, Switzerland, Tanzania, Uganda.

Other: Director, Tanzania Coffee Board 1997-99; Chair: Tanzania Coffee Association 1997-99, Parliamentary Network of the World Bank and IMF; Trustee, Donald Mackay Trust 1987-; Member and Trustee, Conservative Christian Fellowship 2002-; Chair, Equity for Africa 2003-; Trustee, Liverpool School of Tropical Medicine 2015-; ACA 1984; Institute of Chartered Accountants in England and Wales 1984-.

Recreations: Playing and writing music, hill-walking, sport.

Jeremy Lefroy MP, House of Commons, London SW1A 0AA
Tel: 020 7219 7154 *Email:* jeremy.lefroy.mp@parliament.uk
Constituency: Unit 15, Pearl House, Anson Court, Staffordshire Technology Park, Beaconside, Stafford ST18 0GB
Tel: 01785 252477 *Website:* www.jeremylefroy.org.uk *Twitter:* @JeremyLefroy

CONSERVATIVE

LEIGH, EDWARD

Gainsborough *(Majority 17,023)*

Edward Julian Egerton Leigh. Born 20 July 1950; Son of late Sir Neville Leigh, former Clerk to the Privy Council; Married Mary Goodman 1984 (3 sons 3 daughters).

Education: Oratory School, Reading, Berkshire; French Lycee, London; Durham University (BA history 1972) (Union President); French.

Non-political career: Member, Conservative Research Department 1973-75; Principal correspondence secretary to Margaret Thatcher as Leader of the Opposition 1976-77; Barrister, Inner Temple 1977-.

Political career: Contested Teesside, Middlesbrough October 1974 general election. Member for Gainsborough and Horncastle 1983-97, for Gainsborough 1997-2010, for Gainsborough (revised boundary) since 6 May 2010 general election; PPS to John Patten as Minister of State, Home Office 1990; Parliamentary Under-Secretary of State, Department of Trade and Industry 1990-93; Public Accounts Commission: Member -2010, 2015-, Chair 2011-15; Financial Adviser to the Treasury 2010-11. *Select committees:* Member, Social Security 1997-2000; Public Accounts: Member 2000-01, Chair 2001-10; Member: Liaison 2001-10, Chairmen's Panel/Panel of Chairs 2010-, Members' Expenses 2011-15, Procedure 2015-17, Court of Referees 2016-, International Trade 2016-17. Vice-chair, Conservative Party Committees for: Foreign and Commonwealth Affairs 1997-2001, Social Security 1997-2001; Chair, Conservative Party Committee for Foreign Affairs, Defence and International Development -2015. Member, governing council, Conservative Christian Fellowship; Chair, Cornerstone Group 2004-. *Councils and public bodies:* Councillor: Richmond Borough Council 1974-78, GLC 1977-81; Chair, National Council for Civil Defence 1979-83; Director, Coalition For Peace Through Security 1981-83.

Political interests: Defence, foreign affairs, agriculture, families.

Other: Delegate, Parliamentary Assembly of the Council of Europe -2015; Fellow, Industry and Parliament Trust 1983; Veteran Member, Honourable Artillery Company; President, Catholic Union of Great Britain; Fellow Institute of Arbitrators 1999-; CAFOD, Malteser International, Order of Malta Volunteers. Knight of Honour and Devotion Sovereign Military Order of Malta; Kt 2013; Officier, Légion d'honneur 2015.

Publications: Right Thinking (1982); Onwards from Bruges (1989); Choice and Responsibility – The Enabling State (1990); The Nation that Forgot God (2009); Monastery of the Mind (2012).

Recreations: Walking, reading, swimming.

Sir Edward Leigh MP, House of Commons, London SW1A 0AA
Tel: 020 7219 6480 *Email:* edward.leigh.mp@parliament.uk
Constituency: 1 Rasen Hub, 20 Union Street, Market Rasen, Lincolnshire LN8 3AA
Website: www.edwardleigh.org.uk *Twitter:* @EdwardLeighUK

LAB/CO-OP

LESLIE, CHRIS

Nottingham East *(Majority 19,590)*

Christopher Michael Leslie. Born 28 June 1972; Son of Michael and Dania Leslie; Married Nicola (1 daughter).

Education: Bingley Grammar School; Leeds University (BA politics and parliamentary studies 1994; MA industrial and labour studies 1996).

Non-political career: Office administrator 1994-96; Political research assistant 1996-97; Director, New Local Government Network 2005-10. Member: TGWU, GMB.

Political career: Member for Shipley 1997-2005. Contested Shipley 2005 general election. Member for Nottingham East since 6 May 2010 general election; PPS to Lord Falconer as Minister of State, Cabinet Office 1998-2001; Parliamentary Secretary, Cabinet Office 2001-02; Parliamentary Under-Secretary of State for: Local Government and the Regions, Office of the Deputy Prime Minister 2002-03, Department for Constitutional Affairs 2003-05; Shadow Financial Secretary 2010-13; Shadow Chief Secretary to the Treasury 2013-15; Shadow Chancellor of the Exchequer 2015. *Select committees:* Member: Public Accounts 1997-98, International Trade 2016-. Member, Labour Party Departmental Committees for: Environment, Transport and the Regions 1997-2001, the Treasury 1997-2001; Chair, PLP Departmental Group for Treasury 2015-. Member, Economy – Work and Business Policy Commission. *Councils and public bodies:* Councillor, Bradford City Council 1994-98.

Political interests: Industrial policy, economic policy, environment, local and regional government; Kashmir.

Other: Trustee: Consumer Credit Counselling Service, Credit Action.

Recreations: Travel, tennis, cinema, art.

Chris Leslie MP, House of Commons, London SW1A 0AA
Tel: 020 7219 3000 *Email:* chris.leslie@parliament.uk
Constituency: Ground Floor, 12 Regent Street, Nottingham, Nottinghamshire NG1 5BQ
Tel: 0115-956 9429 *Email:* josie.tanvir@parliament.uk *Website:* www.chrisleslie.org
Twitter: @ChrisLeslieMP

CONSERVATIVE

LETWIN, OLIVER

West Dorset *(Majority 19,091)*

Born 19 May 1956; Son of late Professor William Letwin and late Dr Shirley Robin Letwin; Married Isabel Davidson 1984 (1 son 1 daughter).

Education: Eton College; Trinity College, Cambridge (BA history 1978, MA; PhD philosophy 1982); London Business School; French, Italian.

Non-political career: Visiting fellow (Procter Fellow), Princeton University, USA 1980-81; Research fellow, Darwin College, Cambridge 1981-82; Special adviser to Sir Keith Joseph as Secretary of State for Education 1982-83; Special adviser, Prime Minister's Policy Unit 1983-86; N. M. Rothschild & Son, Merchant Bank: Manager 1986, Assistant director 1987-90, Director 1991-2003, Managing director 2003, Non-executive director 2005-09.

Political career: Contested Hackney North 1987 and Hampstead and Highgate 1992 general elections. Member for West Dorset since 1 May 1997 general election; Opposition Spokesperson for Constitutional Affairs, Scotland and Wales 1998-99; Shadow Financial Secretary 1999-2000; Shadow Chief Secretary to the Treasury 2000-01; Shadow Home Secretary 2001-03; Shadow Secretary of State for Economic Affairs and Shadow Chancellor of the Exchequer 2003-05; Shadow Secretary of State for Environment, Food and Rural Affairs 2005; Cabinet Office: Minister of State 2010-12, Minister for Government Policy 2012-15; Chancellor of the Duchy of Lancaster 2014-16; Member, Speaker's Committee on the Electoral Commission 2015-16. *Select committees:* Member: Deregulation 1998-99, European Standing Committee B 1998. Member, Conservative Disability Group; Chair: Conservative Policy Review 2005-10, Conservative Research Department 2005-10; Conservative Policy Forum 2010-16.

Other: Fellow, Royal Society of Arts; Vice-president, Great Britain-China Centre 2017-; Chair, Red Tape Initiative 2017-; Joseph Weld Hospice. PC 2002; Kt 2016.

Publications: Ethics, Emotion and the Unity of the Self (1985); Aims of Schooling (1986); Privatising the World (1989); Drift to Union (1989); The Purpose of Politics (1999); Plus articles and reviews in learned and popular journals.

Recreations: Skiing, sailing, tennis, reading, writing books.

Rt Hon Sir Oliver Letwin MP, House of Commons, London SW1A 0AA
Tel: 020 7219 0826 *Email:* letwino@parliament.uk
Constituency: No constituency office
Tel: 01308 456891 *Email:* jane.gordonbanks@parliament.uk *Website:* www.oliverletwinmp.com
Twitter: @oletwinofficial

LABOUR

LEWELL-BUCK, EMMA

South Shields *(Majority 14,508)*

Shadow Minister for Children and Families

Emma Louise Lewell-Buck. Born 8 November 1978; Daughter of Linda and David Lewell; Married Simon Buck.

Education: St Joseph's Comprehensive; Northumbria University (BA politics and media studies); Durham University (MSW social work).

Non-political career: Child Protection Social Worker; Cleaner; Bar Worker; Waitress; Salesperson; Shop Assistant; Call Centre Worker; Play Worker. Member, GMB.

Political career: Member for South Shields since 2 May 2013 by-election; PPS to: Ivan Lewis as Shadow Secretary of State for Northern Ireland 2013-15, Andy Burnham as Shadow Home Secretary 2015-16; Shadow Minister for: Communities and Local Government 2016, Children and Families 2016-. *Select committees:* Member: Environment, Food and Rural Affairs 2013-, Joint Committee on the Draft Protection of Charities Bill 2014-15, Work and Pensions 2015-16. Member, Co-operative. *Councils and public bodies:* South Tyneside Council: Councillor 2004-13, Lead Member for Adult Social Care and Support Services.

Political interests: Child protection, children's and adults' social care, welfare, food poverty.

Other: Member, Dyspraxia Foundation; Trustee, Feeding Britain charity.

Emma Lewell-Buck MP, House of Commons, London SW1A 0AA
Tel: 020 7219 4468 *Fax:* 020 7219 0264 *Email:* emma.lewell-buck.mp@parliament.uk
Constituency: 19 Westoe Road, South Shields NE33 4LS
Tel: 0191-427 1240 *Website:* www.emma-lewell-buck.net *Twitter:* @EmmaLewellBuck

CONSERVATIVE

LEWER, ANDREW

Northampton South *(Majority 1,159)*

Andrew Iain Lewer. Born 18 July 1971; Married Gabriela (1 son).

Education: Queen Elizabeth's Grammar School, Ashbourne; Newcastle University (BA history); Cambridge University.

Political career: Member for Northampton South since 8 June 2017. *Select committees:* Member, Communities and Local Government 2017-. MEP for East Midlands 2014-17. *Councils and public bodies:* Councillor, Derbyshire Dales District Council 2003-14; Derbyshire County Council: Councillor 2005-14, Leader, Conservative group 2007-14; Vice-president, Local Government Association 2017-.

Political interests: Regional policy.

Other: UK Delegate, EU Committee of the Regions; Member: Derbyshire Historic Buildings Trust, Ashbourne Gateway Youth Centre; Director, Ashbourne Partnership; Deputy Chair: Local Government Association, LGA Culture, Tourism and Sport Board; Member: East Midlands Museum Service, Derbyshire Museums Forum, Arts Council External Reference Group; Governor, Derby University. MBE 2014.

Andrew Lewer MBE MP, House of Commons, London SW1A 0AA
Tel: 020 7219 3870 *Email:* andrew.lewer.mp@parliament.uk
Constituency: White Lodge, 42 Billing Road, Northampton NN1 5DA
Tel: 01604 978080 *Email:* andrew@andrewlewer.com *Website:* www.andrewlewer.com
Twitter: @ALewerMBE

CONSERVATIVE

LEWIS, BRANDON

Great Yarmouth *(Majority 7,973)*

Minister of State for Immigration, Home Office

Brandon Kenneth Lewis. Born 20 June 1971; Son of Jack and Lynn Lewis; Married Justine Rappolt 1999 (1 son 1 daughter).

Education: Forest School, Snaresbrook; Buckingham University (BSc economics 1993; LLB 1996); King's College, London (LLM commercial law 1998); Inns of Court, School of Law (Bar Vocational Course).

Non-political career: Director: Woodlands Schools Ltd 2001-12, i5 Consulting Ltd -2010.

Political career: Contested Sherwood 2001 general election. Member for Great Yarmouth since 6 May 2010 general election; Department for Communities and Local Government: Parliamentary Under-Secretary of State 2012-14, Minister of State for Housing and Planning 2014-16; Member Speaker's Committee on the Electoral Commission 2013-15; Minister of State, Home Office: for Policing and the Fire Service 2016-17, for Immigration (also attending Cabinet) 2017-. *Select committees:* Member: Regulatory Reform 2010-12, Work and Pensions 2010-12. *Councils and public bodies:* Brentwood Borough Council: Councillor 1998-2009, Leader 2004-09; Associate Governor, Great Yarmouth College; Governor, Felsted School.

Political interests: Tourism, local government, coastal erosion, business, transport; Italy, USA.

Other: Council Member, Buckingham University; Member, Lords Taverner's; Trustee, British Triathlon Trust; Patron, East Coast Hospice; Member, Institute of Directors 2001-07. PC 2016; Carlton Club.

Recreations: Running, cycling, swimming, reading.

Rt Hon Brandon Lewis MP, House of Commons, London SW1A 0AA
Tel: 020 7219 7231 *Email:* toby.willmer@parliament.uk
Constituency: 20 Church Plain, Great Yarmouth, Norfolk NR30 1NE
Tel: 01493 854550 *Email:* office@brandonlewis.co *Website:* www.brandonlewis.co
Twitter: @BrandonLewis

LABOUR

LEWIS, CLIVE

Norwich South *(Majority 15,596)*

Clive Anthony Lewis. Born 11 September 1971; Married Katy Steel 2017.

Education: Bradford University (BSc economics 1993) (Student Union president).

Non-political career: Former Territorial Army reservist, served a tour of duty in Afghanistan 2009. Vice-president, National Union of Students; BBC: News trainee, TV news reporter, Eastern region's chief political reporter.

Political career: Member for Norwich South since 7 May 2015 general election; Shadow Minister for Energy and Climate Change 2015-16; Shadow Secretary of State for: Defence 2016, Business, Energy and Industrial Strategy 2016-17. *Select committees:* Member: Public Accounts 2015, Science and Technology 2017-. *Councils and public bodies:* Associate governor, Thorpe St Andrew School.

Political interests: Social justice, climate change, economics, humanism, progressive alliance, education (academisation), human rights, military personnel, fair banking.

Recreations: Norwich City FC Season ticket holder.

Clive Lewis MP, House of Commons, London SW1A 0AA
Tel: 020 7219 5593 *Email:* clive.lewis.mp@parliament.uk
Constituency: 20 Bank Plain, Norwich, Norfolk NR2 4SF
Tel: 01603 510755 *Website:* www.clivelewis.org *Twitter:* @labourlewis

LABOUR

LEWIS, IVAN

Bury South *(Majority 5,965)*

Born 4 March 1967; Son of Joe Lewis and late Gloria Lewis; Married Juliette Fox 1990 (divorced) (2 sons).

Education: William Hulme Grammar School; Stand College; Bury Further Education College.

Non-political career: Co-ordinator, Contact Community Care Group 1986-89; Community care manager, Jewish Social Services 1989-92; Chief executive, Manchester Jewish Federation 1992-97. Member, Unite.

Political career: Member for Bury South 1997-2010, for Bury South (revised boundary) since 6 May 2010 general election; PPS to Stephen Byers as Secretary of State for Trade and Industry 1999-2001; Parliamentary Under-Secretary of State, Department for Education and Skills 2001-05: for Young People and Learning 2001-02, for Adult Learning and Skills 2002, for Young People and Adult Skills 2002-03, for Skills and Vocational Education 2003-05; Economic Secretary, HM Treasury 2005-06; Parliamentary Under-Secretary of State: Department of Health (Care Services) 2006-08, Department for International Development 2008-09; Minister of State, Foreign and Commonwealth Office 2009-10; Shadow Minister for Foreign and Commonwealth Office 2010; Shadow Secretary of State for: Culture, Media and Sport 2010-11, International Development 2011-13, Northern Ireland 2013-15. *Select committees:* Member: Deregulation 1997-99, Health 1999, International Development 2017-, Work of the Independent Commission for Aid Impact Sub-committee 2017-. Chair, PLP Departmental Group for International Development 2015-. Chair, Bury South Labour Party 1991-96; Vice-chair, Labour Friends of Israel 1997-2001. *Councils and public bodies:* Councillor, Bury Metropolitan Borough Council 1990-98.

Political interests: Health, crime, education, international development, culture, media and sport; Democratic Republic of the Congo, Middle East, Rwanda, USA.

Other: Founder member, Co-ordinator and Chair, Contact Community Care Group 1986-92; Chair, Bury MENCAP 1989-92; Trustee, Holocaust Educational Trust.

Publications: Contributor, The Purple Book (Progress, 2011).

Recreations: Walking, reading, supporting Manchester City FC.

Ivan Lewis MP, House of Commons, London SW1A 0AA
Tel: 020 7219 6404 *Email:* lewisi@parliament.uk
Constituency: 11 Deansgate, Radcliffe, Manchester M26 2SH
Tel: 0161-773 5500 *Email:* ivanlewisburysouth@outlook.com *Website:* www.ivanlewis.org.uk
Twitter: @IvanLewis_MP

CONSERVATIVE

LEWIS, JULIAN

New Forest East *(Majority 21,995)*

Chair, Select Committee on Defence

Julian Murray Lewis. Born 26 September 1951; Son of late Samuel Lewis and late Hilda Lewis.

Education: Dynevor School, Swansea; Balliol College, Oxford (BA philosophy and politics, MA 1977); St Antony's College, Oxford (DPhil strategic studies 1981); Doctoral research (strategic studies) 1975-77, 1978-81.

Non-political career: Seaman, HM Royal Naval Reserve 1979-82. Secretary, Campaign for Representative Democracy 1977-78; Research Director and Director, Coalition for Peace Through Security 1981-85; Director, Policy Research Associates 1985-; Deputy director, Conservative Research Department 1990-96; Visiting Senior Research Fellow, Centre for Defence Studies, Department of War Studies, King's College, London 2010-.

Political career: Contested Swansea West 1983 general election. Member for New Forest East 1997-2010, for New Forest East (revised boundary) since 6 May 2010 general election; Opposition Whip 2001-02; Shadow Minister for: Defence 2002-04, 2005-10, the Cabinet Office 2004-05; Member, Intelligence and Security Committee 2010-15. *Select committees:* Member, Welsh Affairs 1998-2001; Defence: Member 2000-01, 2014-15, Chair 2015-; Member: Arms Export Controls 2014-15, 2016-17, Liaison 2015-, Joint Committee on the National Security Strategy 2015-. Secretary, Conservative Parliamentary Defence Committee 1997-2001; Vice-chair, Conservative Parliamentary Committees for: European Affairs 2000-01, Foreign and Commonwealth Affairs 2000-01; Member Executive, 1922 Committee 2001. Treasurer, Oxford University Conservative Association 1971; Vice-President, Conservatives for Britain 2015-16.

Political interests: Defence, security, foreign affairs, European affairs; Western Europe, Central and Eastern Europe, Russia.

Other: Secretary, Oxford Union 1972; Joint organiser of campaign against militant infiltration of the Labour Party 1977-78; Patron, Pilgrim Bandits. Trench Gascoigne prize winner RUSI 2005, 2007; Royal College of Defence Studies prize winner 2006. PC 2015; Athenæum, Totton Conservative Club. President, Calshot Association.

Publications: Changing Direction: British Military Planning for Post-War Strategic Defence 1942-1947 (1988, 2003, 2008); Who's Left? An Index of Labour MPs and Left-Wing Causes 1985-1992 (1992); Labour's CND Cover-Up (1992); The Liberal Democrats: The Character of Their Politics (1993); What's Liberal? Liberal Democrat Quotations and Facts (1996); Racing Ace – The Fights and Flights of 'Kink' Kinkead DSO, DSC*, DFC* (2011).

Recreations: History, fiction, films, music, photography.

Rt Hon Dr Julian Lewis MP, House of Commons, London SW1A 0AA
Tel: 020 7219 4179
Constituency: 3 The Parade, Southampton Road, Cadnam, Hampshire SO40 2NG
Tel: 023 8081 4817 *Website:* www.julianlewis.net

CONSERVATIVE

LIDDELL-GRAINGER, IAN

Bridgwater and West Somerset *(Majority 15,448)*

Ian Richard Peregrine Liddell-Grainger. Born 23 February 1959; Son of late David Liddell-Grainger, farmer, and Ann Grainger; Married Jill Nesbitt 1985 (1 son 2 daughters).

Education: Millfield School, Somerset; South of Scotland Agricultural College, Edinburgh (National Certificate agriculture 1978).

Non-political career: Major Fusiliers TA. Family farm, Berwickshire 1980-85; Managing director, property management and development companies group 1985-2000.

Political career: Contested Torridge and Devon West 1997 general election. Member for Bridgwater 2001-10, for Bridgwater and West Somerset since 6 May 2010 general election. *Select committees:* Member: Public Administration 2001-10, Scottish Affairs 2002-05, Environment, Food and Rural Affairs 2003-05, Crossrail Bill 2006-07, Environmental Audit 2007-10, Joint Committee on Statutory Instruments 2010-, Works of Art 2011-17, Business, Energy and Industrial Strategy 2017-. Contested Tyne and Wear 1994 European Parliament election. Member, Conservative Agricultural Forum 1992-97; President, Tyne Bridge Conservative Association 1993-96. *Councils and public bodies:* Councillor: Tynedale District Council 1989-95, Northern Area Council 1992-95.

Political interests: Business, economy, defence, rural affairs, farming, taxation, education, health, energy; Africa especially South Africa, China, Hong Kong, Singapore, Switzerland, USA, Vietnam.

Other: Executive Committee, Commonwealth Parliamentary Association: Member -2015, 2017-, Chair 2015-17; Inter-Parliamentary Union, British Group: Member, Executive Committee, Vice-chair 2014-; Member, UK delegation, Parliamentary Assembly of the Council of Europe 2010-; RNLI, Macmillan Cancer Support, Help for Heroes, Royal British Legion, Brainwave.

Recreations: Walking, travel, family, gardening, vigorous debate.

Ian Liddell-Grainger MP, House of Commons, London SW1A 0AA
Tel: 020 7219 8149 *Email:* ianlg@parliament.uk
Constituency: 16 Northgate, Bridgwater, Somerset TA6 3EU
Tel: 01278 458383 *Website:* www.liddellgrainger.org.uk

CONSERVATIVE

LIDINGTON, DAVID

Aylesbury *(Majority 14,656)*

Lord Chancellor and Secretary of State for Justice

David Roy Lidington. Born 30 June 1956; Son of Roy and Rosa Lidington; Married Helen Parry 1989 (4 sons).

Education: Haberdashers' Aske's School, Hertfordshire; Sidney Sussex College, Cambridge (MA history; PhD).

Non-political career: British Petroleum 1983-86; Rio Tinto Zinc 1986-87; Special adviser to Douglas Hurd MP: as Home Secretary 1987-89, as Foreign Secretary 1989-90; Senior consultant, Public Policy Unit 1991-92.

Political career: Contested Vauxhall 1987 general election. Member for Aylesbury since 9 April 1992 general election; Sponsored Chiropractors Act 1994; PPS to: Michael Howard as Home Secretary 1994-97, William Hague as Leader of the Opposition 1997-99; Opposition Spokesperson for Home Affairs 1999-2001; Shadow Financial Secretary 2001-02; Shadow Minister for Agriculture and the Fisheries 2002; Shadow Secretary of State for: Environment, Food and Rural Affairs 2002-03, Northern Ireland 2003-07; Shadow Minister for Foreign and Commonwealth Affairs 2007-10; Minister of State for Europe, Foreign and Commonwealth Office 2010-16; Leader of the House of Commons 2016-17; Lord President of the Council 2016-17; Member: House of Commons Commission 2016-17, Public Accounts Commission 2016-17, Speaker's Committee for the Independent Parliamentary Standards Authority 2016-17; Lord Chancellor and Secretary of State for Justice 2017-. *Select committees:* Member, Education 1992-96. Chair, International Office and Conservatives Abroad -2010.

Other: Honorary Vice-president, Oasis Partnership; Patron: Chilterns Multiple Sclerosis Centre, Halton, New Mozart Orchestra, ABCD (Action for Bethlehem Children with Disabilities), National Paralympic Heritage Trust; Holding Trustee, Age Concern, Buckinghamshire; Trustee, Clare Charity Foundation; Chairman, Standing Committee on Foreign Affairs, International Democratic Union. PC 2011; CBE 2016.

Recreations: History, choral singing, reading.

Rt Hon David Lidington CBE MP, House of Commons, London SW1A 0AA
Tel: 020 7219 3432 *Fax:* 020 7219 2564 *Email:* david.lidington.mp@parliament.uk
Constituency: 100 Walton Street, Aylesbury, Buckinghamshire HP21 7QP
Tel: 01296 482102 *Fax:* 01296 398481 *Email:* office@aylesburyconservatives.com
Website: www.davidlidington.co.uk *Twitter:* @DLidington

SCOTTISH NATIONAL PARTY

LINDEN, DAVID

Glasgow East *(Majority 75)*

SNP Deputy Whip

David Melvyn Linden. Born 14 May 1990; Married Roslyn (1 son).

Education: Bannerman High School; Modern Apprenticeship (Business Administration).

Non-political career: Underwriter, Access Loans and Mortgages; Loan Officer, Glasgow Credit Union; Constituency Caseworker to John Mason MP; SNP campaigns and research in Holyrood, Brussels and Westminster; Office Manager to Alison Thewliss MP.

Political career: Member for Glasgow East since 8 June 2017; SNP Deputy Whip 2017-. *Select committees:* Member, Procedure 2017-.

Political interests: Social security, housing, equal pay, gambling proliferation, inequality.

Other: Member: Bellahouston Road Runners, Airdrieonians Supporters Trust.

Recreations: Badminton, football, angling.

David Linden MP, House of Commons, London SW1A 0AA
Tel: 020 7219 1801 *Email:* david.linden.mp@parliament.uk
Constituency: Room 3, Academy House, 1346 Shettleston Road, Shettleston, Glasgow G32 9AT
Tel: 0141-778 1177 *Website:* www.davidlinden.scot *Twitter:* @davidlinden

DEMOCRATIC UNIONIST PARTY

LITTLE PENGELLY, EMMA

Belfast South *(Majority 1,996)*

DUP Spokesperson for Equality, Justice and International Trade

Mary Emma Jean Little Pengelly. Born 31 December 1979; Married Richard Pengelly.

Education: Queen's University Belfast (LLB 2001; Professional Qualification, Barrister 2003).

Non-political career: Barrister-at-Law, Bar Library Belfast 2003-07; Part-time lecturer and tutor in law, Ulster University 2004-06; Special Adviser to First Minister of Northern Ireland: Ian Paisley 2007-08, Peter Robinson 2008-15.

Political career: Member for Belfast South since 8 June 2017; DUP Spokesperson for Equality, Justice and International Trade 2017-. *Select committees:* Member, International Trade 2017-. MLA (replacement) for Belfast South 2015-17: Junior Minister, Office of the First Minister and Deputy First Minister 2015-16, Chair, Finance Committee 2016-17, Member, Chairpersons' Liaison Group 2016-17; Contested Belfast South 2017 Northern Ireland Assembly election.

Emma Little Pengelly MP, House of Commons, London SW1A 0AA
Tel: 020 7219 1359 *Email:* emma.littlepengelly.mp@parliament.uk
Constituency: 15 Cregagh Road, Belfast BT6 8PX
Tel: 028 9045 5936 *Twitter:* @little_pengelly

LIBERAL DEMOCRAT

LLOYD, STEPHEN

Eastbourne *(Majority 1,609)*

Liberal Democrat Shadow Secretary of State for Work and Pensions

Stephen Anthony Christopher Lloyd. Born 15 June 1957; Son of late John Lloyd, shipping director, and late Nuala Lloyd, nurse; Married Patricia 1993 (divorced 2001); partner Cherine Maskill.

Education: St George's College, Weybridge.

Non-political career: Commodity Broker, Cominco UK Ltd 1977-80; Actor 1981-82; Proprietor, Radio Production Company 1983-90; Membership and Campaigns Manager, Hearing Concern 1990-92; Freelance Campaigns and Business Development Co-ordinator, various leading charities 1992-98; Business Development Director, Grass Roots Group plc 1998-2005; Freelance Business Development Consultant, including Grass Roots Group, Federation of Small Business 2005-10; Business Development Director, West End Studios 2015-16.

Political career: Contested Beaconsfield 2001 and Eastbourne 2005 general elections. Member for Eastbourne 2010-15. Contested Eastbourne 2015 general election. Member for Eastbourne since 8 June 2017; Liberal Democrat Frontbench Spokesperson for Northern Ireland 2011-14; PPS to Edward Davey as Secretary of State for Energy and Climate Change 2014; Liberal Democrat Shadow Secretary of State for Work and Pensions 2017-. *Select committees:* Member, Work and Pensions 2010-14. Maidenhead Liberal Democrats: Chair 2000-02, Membership secretary, Chilterns region 2000-02. *Councils and public bodies:* Member, Hearing Aid Council 1994-97; Vice-president, Local Government Association 2017-.

Political interests: Small business, apprenticeships, employment, disability, microfinance, town centre regeneration.

Other: Electoral Reform Society; Liberal Democrat Business Forum; Greenpeace; Amnesty International; Member, Federation of Small Businesses; Trustee, RNID 1994-98; Patron: Hearing Link, Wellmind, Embrace, Eastbourne Carnival, Eastbourne Bonfire society, Fish4Kidz, Care for the Carers.

Publications: Challenge of Disability (Grass Roots Group, 1998); Age of Opportunity (Liberal Democrats, 2000).

Recreations: Reading, classic film, classic cars, eating out with good food and good company.

Stephen Lloyd MP, House of Commons, London SW1A 0AA
Tel: 020 7219 1298 *Email:* stephen.lloyd.mp@parliament.uk
Constituency: 100 Seaside Road, Eastbourne BN21 3PF
Tel: 01323 733030 *Website:* www.stephenlloyd.org.uk *Twitter:* @StephenLloydEBN

LABOUR

LLOYD, TONY

Rochdale *(Majority 14,819)*

Shadow Minister for Housing

Anthony Joseph Lloyd. Born 25 February 1950; Son of late Sydney Lloyd, lithographic printer, and Ciceley Lloyd, administrative officer; Married Judith Tear 1974 (separated) (1 son 3 daughters).

Education: Stretford Grammar School; Nottingham University (BSc maths); Manchester Business School (Diploma business administration).

Non-political career: Business administration lecturer, Salford university; Police and Crime Commissioner, Greater Manchester 2012-17. GMB; Unite.

Political career: Member for Stretford 1983-97, for Manchester Central 1997-2010, for Manchester Central (revised boundary) 2010-12, and for Rochdale since 8 June 2017; Opposition Whip 1986-87; Opposition Spokesperson for: Transport 1988-89, Employment 1988-92, 1993-94, Education 1992-94, The Environment and London 1994-95, Foreign and Commonwealth Affairs 1995-97; Minister of State, Foreign and Commonwealth Office 1997-99; Shadow Minister for Housing 2017-. *Select committees:* Member: Social Services 1983-84, Home Affairs 1984-86, North West 2009-10, European Scrutiny 2010-11. Chair, Parliamentary Labour Party 2006-12. *Councils and public bodies:* Councillor, Trafford District Council 1979-84.

Political interests: Civil liberties, global security and disarmament, community relations, employment and industrial policy, human rights, overseas aid and development, international relations.

Other: Leader, UK Delegation to Parliamentary Assembly of: Council of Europe/Western European Union 2000-07, OSCE 2005-10; Member, Executive Committee, Inter-Parliamentary Union, British Group. Visiting fellow, St Antony's College, Oxford.

Tony Lloyd MP, House of Commons, London SW1A 0AA
Tel: 020 7219 3000 *Email:* tony.lloyd.mp@parliament.uk
Constituency: Details still to be confirmed *Website:* www.tony4rochdale.com
Twitter: @TonyLloydMP

LABOUR

LONG-BAILEY, REBECCA

Salford and Eccles *(Majority 19,132)*

Shadow Secretary of State for Business, Energy and Industrial Strategy

Born 22 September 1979; Married Stephen (1 son).

Education: Manchester Metropolitan University (politics and sociology).

Non-political career: Solicitor: Halliwells 2003-07, Hill Dickinson LLP 2007-15.

Political career: Member for Salford and Eccles since 7 May 2015 general election; Shadow Exchequer Secretary 2015-16; Shadow Chief Secretary to the Treasury 2016-17; Shadow Secretary of State for Business, Energy and Industrial Strategy 2017-; Member, Labour Party NEC 2015-.

Rebecca Long-Bailey MP, House of Commons, London SW1A 0AA
Tel: 020 7219 5275 *Email:* rebecca.longbailey.mp@parliament.uk
Constituency: 191 Langworthy Road, Salford M6 5PW
Tel: 0161-425 3738 *Website:* www.rebeccalongbailey.com *Twitter:* @RLong_Bailey

LOPEZ, JULIA – please see DOCKERILL, JULIA

CONSERVATIVE

LOPRESTI, JACK

Filton and Bradley Stoke *(Majority 4,190)*

Giacomo Lopresti. Born 23 August 1969; Married Lucy Cope 1992 (divorced 2016) (2 sons 1 daughter); engaged to Andrea Jenkyns (qv) (MP for Morley and Outwood) (1 son).

Education: Brislington Secondary School.

Non-political career: Gunner, 266 Battery, Royal Artillery; Served with 29 Commando Regiment RA in Helmand Province, Afghanistan 2008-09. Estate agent 1998-2001; Independent mortgage broker 2001-05; Regional development manager, Treasurer's Department, Conservative Party 2005-07.

Political career: Contested Bristol East 2001 general election. Member for Filton and Bradley Stoke since 6 May 2010 general election; PPS to Desmond Swayne as Minister of State, Department for International Development 2014-15. *Select committees:* Member: Northern Ireland Affairs 2010-, Armed Forces Bill 2011; Chair, Armed Forces Bill 2015 2015-16; Member, Defence 2016-17. Chairman, Conservative Backbench Policy Committee on Defence 2015-17. Contested South West region 2004 European Parliament election. *Councils and public bodies:* Councillor, Bristol City Council 1999-2007.

Political interests: Defence, security; Afghanistan, Bahrain, Iraq, Israel, USA.

Other: Member: British-Irish Parliamentary Assembly 2015-, UK delegation to NATO Parliamentary Assembly 2015-; Member: International Churchill Society, General George Patton Historical Society; RUSI; Military and Naval Club.

Recreations: Running half-marathons.

Jack Lopresti MP, House of Commons, London SW1A 0AA
Tel: 020 7219 7070 *Email:* jack.lopresti.mp@parliament.uk
Constituency: Office 29, The South Block, The Courtyard, Woodlands, Bradley Stoke, Gloucestershire BS32 4NQ
Tel: 01454 617783 *Website:* www.jacklopresti.com *Twitter:* @JackLopresti

CONSERVATIVE

LORD, JONATHAN

Woking *(Majority 16,724)*

Jonathan George Caladine Lord. Born 17 September 1962; Son of the late His Honour John Lord and Ann Lord, née Caladine; Married Caroline Commander 2000 (1 son 1 daughter).

Education: Shrewsbury School; Kent School, Connecticut, USA; Merton College, Oxford (BA modern history 1985, MA).

Non-political career: Bates Dorland; AP Lintas; Ogilvy and Mather; Director, Saatchi & Saatchi 1998-2000; Marketing consultant.

Political career: Contested Oldham West and Royton 1997 general election. Member for Woking since 6 May 2010 general election; Sponsored: Sports Ground Safety Authority Act 2011, Citizenship (Armed Forces) Act 2014; President, Oxford University Conservative Association 1983; Campaign manager to Anne Milton MP 2005 general election; Chairman, Guildford Conservative Association 2006-10; Deputy chairman, Surrey Area Conservatives 2007-09. *Councils and public bodies:* Westminster City Council: Councillor 1994-2002, Council Deputy Leader 1998-2000; Councillor, Surrey County Council 2009-11.

Political interests: Culture, media and sport, business, health, education; USA.

Other: Patron, Home-Start, Runnymede and Woking.

Recreations: Cricket, theatre, walking.

Jonathan Lord MP, House of Commons, London SW1A 0AA
Tel: 020 7219 6913 *Email:* jonathan.lord.mp@parliament.uk
Constituency: Woking Conservatives, Churchill House, Chobham Road, Woking, Surrey GU21 4AA
Tel: 01483 773384 *Website:* www.jonathanlord.co.uk

CONSERVATIVE

LOUGHTON, TIM

East Worthing and Shoreham *(Majority 5,106)*

Timothy Paul Loughton. Born 30 May 1962; Son of Reverend Michael Loughton and Pamela Loughton; Married Elizabeth MacLauchlan 1992 (1 son 2 daughters).

Education: The Priory School, Lewes; Warwick University (BA classical civilisation 1983); Clare College, Cambridge (Mesopotamian archaeology 1984).

Non-political career: Montagu Loebl Stanley/Flemings London: Fund Manager 1984-, Director 1992-2000. Formerly BIFU.

Political career: Contested Sheffield Brightside 1992 general election. Member for East Worthing and Shoreham 1997-2010, for East Worthing and Shoreham (revised boundary) since 6 May 2010 general election; Opposition Spokesman for: Regeneration, Poverty, Regions, Housing 2000-01, Health 2001-03; Shadow Minister for: Health 2003-07, Children 2003-10; Children's Bill 2004; Childcare Bill 2006; Adoption and Children Bill 2006; Mental Health Bill 2007; Children and Young Person's Bill 2008; Children, Schools and Families Bill 2010; Parliamentary Under-Secretary of State for Children and Families, Department for Education 2010-12. *Select committees:* Member: Environmental Audit 1997-2001, European Standing committee C 1999-2001, Home Affairs 2014-. Chairman, Lewes Young Conservatives 1978; Vice-chairman: Sussex Young Conservatives 1979, Lewes Constituency Conservative Association 1979-81, South East Area Young Conservatives 1980-82; Secretary, Warwick University Conservative Association 1981-82; Member, Cambridge University Conservative Association 1983-84; Vice-chairman, Battersea Conservative Association 1990-93; Member, London Area Conservative Executive Committee 1993-96; Chairman, Conservative Disability Group 1998-2006; President, Shoreham Conservative Club. *Councils and public bodies:* Governor, Battersea Technology College; Governor and Chairman, Finance Committee Latchmere Primary School, Battersea; Local Authority appointee to Wandsworth Community Health Council; Vice-chairman, Wandsworth Alcohol Group; Member, Wandsworth Health Authority Substance Misuse Committee.

Political interests: Finance, foreign affairs, home affairs, education (special needs), environmental taxation, environment and housing, disability, animal welfare, health, children's issues; Indian sub-continent, Latin America, Middle East.

Other: Member: CPA, IPU, British-American Parliamentary Group; Non-executive director, Netlink 1996-99; Member, Securities and Futures Association Working Party on Training; Chair: PIP UK charity trustees (Parent and Infant Partnership), Patron: Positive For Youth Awards, Fatherhood Institute, Grandparents' Association, St Barnabas Hospice, Worthing, Electric Storm Youth, Canadian Roots UK, Guild Care, Worthing, Social Worker of the Year Award, EYE Project, CHAT; Ambassador, Ambition; President: Southwick Camera Club, Lancing Art Club; Member: Sussex Archaeological Society, South Downs Society, Friends of British Museum, Shoreham Society, Southwick Society, Court of East Sussex University; Global Change Ambassador, Round Table Global; Member, Securities Institute MSi; MSi(Dip); Society of Antiquaries 2015; St Barnabas Hospice, Ropetackle Centre Trust, Adur Special Needs Project, Parley Online; President, Shoreham Conservative Club. Patron, Worthing Hockey Club; Captain, Lords and Commons Hockey Team; President, Adur Athletic Football Club; Member: Commons and Lords Ski team, Commons and Lords Tennis team.

Recreations: Archaeology, Sussex Downs, wine, travel, hockey, tennis, skiing.

Tim Loughton MP, House of Commons, London SW1A 0AA
Tel: 020 7219 4471 *Fax:* 020 7219 0461 *Email:* loughtont@parliament.uk
Constituency: 88a High Street, Shoreham by Sea, West Sussex BN43 5DB
Tel: 01273 757182 *Email:* eastworthingandshoreham@tory.org *Website:* www.timloughton.com
Twitter: @timloughton

GREEN PARTY

LUCAS, CAROLINE

Brighton Pavilion *(Majority 14,699)*

Co-leader, Green Party

Caroline Patricia Lucas. Born 9 December 1960; Married Richard Savage 1991 (2 sons).

Education: Malvern Girls' College; Exeter University (BA English literature 1983; PhD English and women's studies 1989); Kansas University, USA (Scholarship 1983-84); Journalism (Diploma 1987); French.

Non-political career: Oxfam: Press officer 1989-91, Communications officer, Asia desk 1991-94, Policy adviser on trade and environment 1994-97, Team leader, Trade and investment, Policy department 1998-99; Policy adviser on trade and investment, Department for International Development 1997-98; Author.

Political career: Contested Oxford East 1992 general election. Member for Brighton Pavilion since 6 May 2010 general election. *Select committees:* Member, Environmental Audit 2010-. European Parliament: MEP for South East 1999-2010: Intergroup on the Welfare and Conservation of Animals: Vice-president 2004-09, President 2009-10. Green Party: National Press Officer 1987-89, Co-chair, Party Council 1989-90, Member, Regional Council 1997-99, Leader 2008-12, Co-leader 2016-. *Councils and public bodies:* Councillor, Oxfordshire County Council 1993-97; Vice-president, Local Government Association 2017-.

Political interests: Animal welfare, environment, social justice, green economy, climate change, drugs policy, equalities and human rights; Burma, Palestine.

Other: Vice-President, Stop the War Coalition -2015; Member, National Council, Campaign for Nuclear Disarmament; Board Member, International Forum on Globalisation; Matron, Women's Environmental Network; Board Member, Britain Stronger in Europe 2015-16; Vice-President, RSPCA. Michael Kay Award for Animal Welfare 2006; Michael Kay Award for Services to European Animal Welfare, RSPCA 2006; *Observer* Ethical Politician of the Year 2007, 2009, 2010; MP of the Year, Women in Public Life Awards 2011.

Publications: Co-author, Writing for Women (Oxford University Press, 1989); Reforming World Trade (Oxfam, 1996); Co-author: With Ruth Mayne: Global Trade and the Rise of New Social Issues (Routledge, 1999), Watchful in Seattle: WTO Threats to Public Services, Food and the Environment (1999); With Mike Woodin: The Euro or a Sustainable Future for Britain (2000); With Colin Hines: From Seattle to Nice: Challenging the Free Trade Agenda at the Heart of Enlargement (2000), Stopping the Great Food Swap: Relocalising Europe's Food Supply (2001); With Mike Woodin: Green Alternatives to Globalisation: A Manifesto (Pluto, 2004); Author, Honourable Friends?: Parliament and the Fight for Change (Portobello Books, 2015); Co-author, with Lisa Nandy MP and Chris Bowers, The Alternative: Towards a New Progressive Politics (Biteback, 2016).

Recreations: Gardening, country walks.

Dr Caroline Lucas MP, House of Commons, London SW1A 0AA
Tel: 020 7219 7025 *Email:* caroline.lucas.mp@parliament.uk
Constituency: Werks Central, 15-17 Middle Street, Brighton, East Sussex BN1 1AL
Tel: 01273 201130 *Email:* brightonoffice@parliament.uk *Website:* www.carolinelucas.com
Twitter: @CarolineLucas

LABOUR

LUCAS, IAN C

Wrexham *(Majority 1,832)*

Ian Colin Lucas. Born 18 September 1960; Son of Colin Lucas, process engineer, and Alice Lucas, cleaner; Married Norah Sudd 1986 (1 daughter 1 son).

Education: Greenwell Comprehensive School, Gateshead; Royal Grammar School, Newcastle upon Tyne; New College, Oxford (BA jurisprudence 1982); College of Law, Christleton law (Solicitor's Final Exam 1983); German.

Non-political career: Russell-Cooke Potter and Chapman Solicitors: Articled clerk, Assistant solicitor 1983-86; Solicitor's Admission 1985; Assistant solicitor: Percy Hughes and Roberts 1986-87, Lees Moore and Price 1987-89, Roberts Moore Nicholas Jones 1989-92, DR Crawford 1992-97; Principal, Crawford Lucas 1997-2000; Partner, Stevens Lucas, Oswestry 2000-01. Member: Amicus/MSF, Unite 1996-.

Political career: Contested Shropshire North 1997 general election. Member for Wrexham since 7 June 2001 general election; PPS to: Bill Rammell as Minister of State, Department for Education and Skills 2005-06, Liam Byrne as Minister of State, Home Office 2007-08; Assistant Government Whip 2008-09; Parliamentary Under-Secretary of State, Department for Business, Innovation and Skills 2009-10; Shadow Minister for the Digital Economy, Departments for: Business, Innovation and Skills 2010-11, Culture, Media and Sport 2011; Shadow Minister for: Foreign and

Commonwealth Office (Africa and Middle East) 2011-14, Defence 2014-15. *Select committees:* Member: Environmental Audit 2001-03, Procedure 2001-02, 2015-16, Transport 2003-05, Public Accounts 2007, Culture, Media and Sport/Digital, Culture, Media and Sport 2015-. Hon. Treasurer, PLP Welsh Regional Group 2005-08. Chair, Wrexham Labour Party 1992-93; Vice-chair, North Shropshire Labour Party 1993-2000; Society of Labour Lawyers 1996-. *Councils and public bodies:* Member, Gresford Community Council 1987-91.

Political interests: Economy, European affairs, health, education, environment, manufacturing; Germany, Japan, Lesotho, USA.

Other: Chair, Committee member, Homeless in Oswestry Action Project 1993-2000; Member, Fabian Society 2000-; Patron: Dynamic Wrexham (for children with disabilities) 2001-, Venture Wrexham (children and young people's charity) 2001-; Fellow, Industry and Parliament Trust 2005.

Recreations: History, film, football, cricket, painting.

Ian C Lucas MP, House of Commons, London SW1A 0AA
Tel: 020 7219 8346 *Fax:* 020 7219 1948 *Email:* lucasi@parliament.uk
Constituency: Vernon House, 41 Rhosddu Road, Wrexham, Clwyd LL11 2NS
Tel: 01978 355743 *Fax:* 01978 310051 *Website:* www.ianlucas.co.uk *Twitter:* @IanCLucas

LABOUR

LYNCH, HOLLY

Halifax *(Majority 5,376)*

Shadow Minister for Flooding and Coastal Communities

Holly Jamie Walker-Lynch. Born 8 October 1986; Daughter of James Lynch and Diane Lynch, née Brophy; Married 2014.

Education: Brighouse High School; Lancaster University (history and politics).

Non-political career: Matrix Technology Solutions; Communications officer to Linda McAvan MEP. Member, GMB.

Political career: Member for Halifax since 7 May 2015 general election; Opposition Whip 2015-16; Shadow Minister for Environment, Food and Rural Affairs (Flooding and Coastal Communities) 2017-. *Select committees:* Member: Environmental Audit 2015, Procedure 2016-17, Women and Equalities 2017.

Political interests: Policing, international development.

Other: Grassroots Diplomat Award 2016.

Holly Lynch MP, House of Commons, London SW1A 0AA
Tel: 020 7219 6277 *Email:* holly.lynch.mp@parliament.uk
Constituency: Elsie Whiteley Innovation Centre, Hopwood Lane, Halifax, West Yorkshire HX1 5ER
Tel: 01422 399515/01422 399516 *Website:* www.hollylynch.org.uk *Twitter:* @HollyLynch5

LABOUR

MCCABE, STEVE

Birmingham, Selly Oak *(Majority 15,207)*

Stephen James McCabe. Born 4 August 1955; Son of James and Margaret McCabe; Married Lorraine Lea Clendon 1991 (divorced) (1 son 1 daughter).

Education: Port Glasgow, Senior Secondary; Moray House College, Edinburgh (Diploma social studies 1977; Certificate Qualification Social Work 1977); Bradford University (MA social work 1986).

Non-political career: Social work with young offenders 1977-85; Lecturer in social work, North East Worcestershire College 1989-91; Part-time researcher, British Association of Social Workers 1989-91; Part-time child protection social worker 1989-91; Central Council for Education in Social Work 1991-97. Member: MSF, Unite; Shop steward, NALGO 1978-82.

Political career: Member for Birmingham Hall Green 1997-2010, for Birmingham, Selly Oak since 6 May 2010 general election; PPS to Charles Clarke: as Secretary of State for Education and Skills 2003-04, as Home Secretary 2004-05; Assistant Government Whip 2006-07; Government Whip 2007-10; Opposition Whip 2010; Shadow Minister for Education 2013-15. *Select committees:* Member: Deregulation 1997-99, Northern Ireland Affairs 1998-2003, Joint Committee on House of Lords Reform 2003-10, Home Affairs 2005-06, 2010-13, Panel of Chairs 2015-, Work and Pensions 2015-. Chair, PLP Departmental Group for Home Affairs 2006, 2010-13, 2015-. *Councils and public bodies:* Birmingham City Council: Councillor 1990-98, Chair, Transportation Committee 1993-96.

Political interests: Community care, transport, economic issues, police and security issues.

Other: Local cricket club.

Recreations: Reading, football, hill-walking.

Steve McCabe MP, House of Commons, London SW1A 0AA
Tel: 020 7219 3509 *Email:* mccabes@parliament.uk
Constituency: No constituency office publicised
Tel: 0121-443 3878 *Website:* www.stevemccabe-mp.org.uk *Twitter:* @steve_mccabe

MCCALLION, ELISHA

Foyle *(Majority 169)*

SINN FÉIN

Born 1982; Married Declan (3 sons).

Non-political career: Community worker; Welfare rights adviser.

Political career: Member for Foyle since 8 June 2017; MLA for Foyle March-June 2017. *Councils and public bodies:* Councillor, Derry City Council 2005-15; Derry City and Strabane District Council: Councillor 2015-, Mayor 2015-16.

Political interests: Mental health, vulnerable people, cross-border investment in health and education, job creation, infrastructural investment.

Other: Director, Greater Shantallow Area Partnership; Member: Outer North Neighbourhood Partnership, Rainbow Child and Family Centre, 'Off the Streets' Initiative.

Elisha McCallion MP, House of Commons, London SW1A 0AA
Tel: 020 7219 2533 *Email:* elisha.mccallion.mp@parliament.uk
Constituency: Details still to be confirmed
Tel: 028 7116 1606 *Twitter:* @ElishaMcC_SF

MCCARTHY, KERRY

Bristol East *(Majority 13,394)*

LABOUR

Kerry Gillian McCarthy. Born 26 March 1965; Daughter of Oliver Haughney and Sheila Rix; Single.

Education: Denbigh High School, Luton; Luton Sixth Form College; Liverpool University (BA Russian, politics and linguistics 1986); Law Society (CPE and final solicitors examinations 1992).

Non-political career: Legal assistant, South Bedfordshire Magistrates Court 1986-88; Litigation assistant, Neves Solicitors, Luton 1988-89; Trainee solicitor, Wilde Sapte 1992-94; Legal manager, Abbey National Treasury Services 1994-96; Senior counsel, debt markets, Merrill Lynch Europe plc 1996-99; Lawyer, Labour Party 2001; Regional director, Britain in Europe campaign 2002-04; Head of public policy, Waterfront Partnership 2004-05. Member: TGWU 1994-2007, Unite 2007-.

Political career: Member for Bristol East 2005-10, for Bristol East (revised boundary) since 6 May 2010 general election; PPS to: Rosie Winterton as Minister of State, Department of Health 2007, Douglas Alexander as Secretary of State for International Development 2007-09; Assistant Government Whip 2009-10; Shadow Minister for Work and Pensions 2010; Opposition Whip 2010; Shadow Economic Secretary 2010-11; Shadow Minister for Foreign and Commonwealth Office 2011-15; Shadow Secretary of State for Environment, Food and Rural Affairs 2015-16. *Select committees:* Member: Treasury 2005-07, South West 2009-10, Environmental Audit 2016-, Environment, Food and Rural Affairs 2016-17. Chair, PLP South West Regional Group 2007-09. Luton North CLP: Chair 1994-96, Secretary 1996-99; National Policy Forum 1998-2005; Economic Policy Commission 1998-2005. *Councils and public bodies:* Luton Borough Council: Councillor 1995-96, 1999-2003, Chair of housing and cabinet member 1999-2001; Director, London Luton Airport 1999-2003.

Political interests: Environment, food policy, poverty, foreign affairs; Latin America, Asia, Jordan, Russia, Somaliland/Somalia.

Other: Substitute Member, UK delegation, Parliamentary Assembly of the Council of Europe 2016-; Member, Labour Animal Welfare Society; Patron, FoodCycle; Vice-President, League Against Cruel Sports; Patron: Music Venue Trust, Attitude is Everything; Honorary Associate, National Secular Society; Member, The Law Society 1994-99. Technology/Social Media User of the Year, *House Magazine* awards 2011; St George Labour.

Recreations: Travel, scuba diving, music.

Kerry McCarthy MP, House of Commons, London SW1A 0AA
Tel: 020 7219 4510 *Email:* kerry.mccarthy.mp@parliament.uk
Constituency: Kings Centre, 16-18 King Square, Bristol BS2 8AZ
Tel: 0117-939 9901 *Website:* www.kerrymccarthymp.org *Twitter:* @kerryMP

LABOUR

MCDONAGH, SIOBHAIN

Mitcham and Morden *(Majority 21,375)*

Siobhain Ann McDonagh. Born 20 February 1960; Daughter of Breda McDonagh, née Doogue, psychiatric nurse, and Cumin McDonagh, building labourer; Single (no children).

Education: Holy Cross Convent, New Malden; Essex University (BA government 1981).

Non-political career: Clerical officer, DHSS 1981-83; Housing benefits assistant 1983-84; Receptionist, Homeless Persons Unit, London Borough of Wandsworth 1984-86; Housing adviser 1986-88; Development co-ordinator, Battersea Church Housing Trust 1988-97. Member, GMB.

Political career: Contested Mitcham and Morden 1987 and 1992 general elections. Member for Mitcham and Morden 1997-2010, for Mitcham and Morden (revised boundary) since 6 May 2010 general election; PPS to John Reid: as Secretary of State for Defence 2005-06, as Home Secretary 2006-07; Assistant Government Whip 2007-08. *Select committees:* Member: Social Security 1997-98, Health 2000-05, Unopposed Bills (Panel) 2004-15, London 2009-10, Education 2012-15, Women and Equalities 2015-16, Panel of Chairs 2017-. *Councils and public bodies:* Councillor, London Borough of Merton 1982-97: Chair, Housing Committee 1990-95.

Political interests: Health, housing, quality of life, welfare reform.

Other: Member: South Mitcham Community Centre, Colliers Wood Community Centre, Grenfell Housing Association, Merton MIND; Vice-President, QUIT (smoking cessation charity); Trustee, Mitcham Garden Village.

Recreations: Travel, friends, music.

Siobhain McDonagh MP, House of Commons, London SW1A 0AA
Tel: 020 7219 4678 *Email:* mcdonaghs@parliament.uk
Constituency: 1 Crown Road, Morden, Surrey SM4 5DD
Tel: 020 8542 4835 *Email:* siobhain@mmlp.org.uk *Website:* www.siobhainmcdonagh.org.uk
Twitter: @Siobhain_MP

LABOUR

MCDONALD, ANDY

Middlesbrough *(Majority 13,873)*

Shadow Secretary of State for Transport

Andrew Joseph McDonald. Born 8 March 1958; Married Sally (children).

Non-political career: Head of office and senior serious injury solicitor, Thompsons Solicitors, Middlesbrough.

Political career: Member for Middlesbrough since 29 November 2012 by-election; PPS to: Chuka Umunna as Shadow Secretary of State for Business, Innovation and Skills 2013-15, John McDonnell as Shadow Chancellor of the Exchequer 2015-16; Shadow Minister for Transport 2016; Shadow Secretary of State for Transport 2016-. *Select committees:* Member, Justice 2012-15, 2015-16. *Councils and public bodies:* Councillor, Middlesbrough Council 1995-99; Governor: Abingdon Primary School 1995-2010, Middlesbrough College 2012-.

Other: Former chair, Davison Trust, Middlesbrough; Chair, Teeside branch, Headway; Former chair and secretary, Military Special Interest Group, Association of Personal Injury Lawyers.

Recreations: Singing, playing the piano, going to Middlesbrough FC matches.

Andy McDonald MP, House of Commons, London SW1A 0AA
Tel: 020 7219 4995 *Email:* andy.mcdonald.mp@parliament.uk
Constituency: Unit 4, Broadcasting House, Newport Road, Middlesbrough, North Yorkshire TS1 5JA
Tel: 01642 246574 *Email:* info@andymcdonaldmp.org *Website:* www.andymcdonaldmp.org
Twitter: @AndyMcDonaldMP

SCOTTISH NATIONAL PARTY

MCDONALD, STEWART MALCOLM

Glasgow South *(Majority 2,027)*

SNP Spokesperson for Defence

Born 24 August 1986.

Education: Govan High School.

Non-political career: Tour guide, Canary Islands, Spain; Caseworker to James Dornan MSP.

Political career: Member for Glasgow South since 7 May 2015 general election; SNP Spokesperson for Defence 2017-. *Select committees:* Member, Transport 2015-17.

Political interests: Poverty, inequality, creating job opportunities, young people.

Stewart Malcolm McDonald MP, House of Commons, London SW1A 0AA
Tel: 020 7219 6388 *Email:* stewart.mcdonald.mp@parliament.uk
Constituency: Suite 5, City Wall House, 32 Eastwood Avenue, Glasgow G41 3NS
Tel: 0141-632 5043 *Website:* www.stewartmcdonald.scot *Twitter:* @StewartMcDonald

SCOTTISH NATIONAL PARTY

MCDONALD, STUART C

Cumbernauld, Kilsyth and Kirkintilloch East *(Majority 4,264)*

SNP Spokesperson for Immigration, Asylum and Border Control

Stuart Campbell McDonald. Born 2 May 1978.

Education: Kilsyth Academy; Edinburgh University (LLB Scots law 2000; Diploma legal practice 2001).

Non-political career: Trainee Solicitor, Simpson and Marwick 2001-03; Solicitor: NHS National Services Scotland 2003-05, Immigration Advisory Service 2005-09; Parliamentary Researcher to Shirley-Anne Somerville MSP and Jim Eadie MSP 2009-13, Senior Researcher, Yes Scotland 2013-14; Parliamentary and public affairs officer, Coalition for Racial Equality and Rights -2015. Member, Unite.

Political career: Member for Cumbernauld, Kilsyth and Kirkintilloch East since 7 May 2015 general election; SNP Spokesperson for Immigration, Asylum and Border Control 2015-. *Select committees:* Member: Home Affairs 2015-, Joint Committee on the Draft Investigatory Powers Bill 2015-16.

Political interests: Anti-fracking, poverty, job creation.

Recreations: Sport, especially football, music, reading.

Stuart C McDonald MP, House of Commons, London SW1A 0AA
Tel: 020 7219 7758 *Email:* stuart.mcdonald.mp@parliament.uk
Constituency: 13 The Wynd, Cumbernauld, North Lanarkshire G67 2ST
Tel: 01236 453969 *Website:* stuartmcdonaldmp.com *Twitter:* @Stuart_McDonald

LABOUR

MCDONNELL, JOHN

Hayes and Harlington *(Majority 18,115)*

Shadow Chancellor of the Exchequer

John Martin McDonnell. Born 8 September 1951; Son of late Robert and Elsie McDonnell; Married Marilyn Cooper 1971 (divorced 1987) (2 daughters); married Cynthia Pinto 1995 (1 son).

Education: Great Yarmouth Grammar School; Burnley Technical College; Brunel University (BSc government and politics); Birkbeck College, London University (MSc politics and sociology); French.

Non-political career: Shopfloor production worker 1968-73; Assistant head, social insurance department, National Union of Mineworkers 1977-78; Researcher, TUC 1978-82; Head of policy unit, London Borough of Camden 1985-87; Chief Executive: Association of London Authorities 1987-95, Association of London Government 1995-97. Former shop steward, Unison; Co-ordinator, RMT Parliamentary Group 2002-; Chair, Bakers and Allied Workers Union Parliamentary Group; PCS Parliamentary Group: Chair -2016, Honorary life chair 2015-; Member: Justice Trade Unions Group, ASLEF Parliamentary Group; Secretary: FBU Group, NUJ Group, Justice Unions Group.

Political career: Contested Hayes and Harlington 1992 general election. Member for Hayes and Harlington 1997-2010, for Hayes and Harlington (revised boundary) since 6 May 2010 general election; Shadow Chancellor of the Exchequer 2015-. *Select committees:* Member: Deregulation and Regulatory Reform 1999-2002, Unopposed Bills (Panel) 1999-2004, Justice 2013-15. Member, Labour Party: Committee on Ireland, CND; Chair: Labour Representation Committee, Socialist Campaign Group of MPs; Member, Unison Group. *Councils and public bodies:* Councillor, GLC 1981-86: Chair, Finance Committee 1982-85, Deputy Leader 1984-85.

Political interests: Economics, local and regional government, Irish affairs, environment, aviation, public administration; Gambia, Iran, Ireland, Kenya, Lango, Nullo Mountains, Punjab, Somalia, Tanzania.

Other: Chair: Britain and Ireland Human Rights Centre, Hands Off Venezuela Group, Hands Off People of Iran; Treasurer Liberation; Chair, Friends of Lake Farm Country Park; Member: Friends of Ireland – Coalition in support of Belfast Agreement, London Wildlife Trust, Hayes Irish Society, Hayes and Harlington History Society, Hayes and Harlington Community Development Forum, Hayes and Harlington Canal Society; Harlington Hospice. PC 2016; Hayes and Harlington Working Men's Club. Hillingdon Outdoor Activities Centre; Wayfarer Sailing Association; Vice-president, Hayes Football Club; Patron, Hayes Cricket Club.

Publications: Editor, Labour Herald; Another World is Possible: a manifesto for 21st century socialism.

Recreations: Sailing, football refereeing, cycling, gardening, theatre, cinema.

Rt Hon John McDonnell MP, House of Commons, London SW1A 0AA
Tel: 020 7219 4100 *Email:* mcdonnellj@parliament.uk
Constituency: Pump Lane, Hayes, Middlesex UB3 3NB
Tel: 020 8569 0010 *Fax:* 020 8569 0109 *Website:* www.john-mcdonnell.net
Twitter: @johnmcdonnellMP

SINN FÉIN

MCELDUFF, BARRY

West Tyrone *(Majority 10,342)*

Columba Barry McElduff. Born 16 August 1966; Son of Donald and late Shiela McElduff; Married Paula (2 daughters 1 son).

Education: Omagh Christian Brothers' Grammar School; Queen's University, Belfast (BA Celtic studies and political science 1988); French, Irish.

Political career: Member for West Tyrone since 8 June 2017; MLA for West Tyrone 1998-2017: Sinn Féin Spokesperson for Culture, Arts and Leisure 2005-09, Member, Assembly Commission 2011-13, Assembly Private Secretary to Carál Ní Chuilín as Minister for Culture, Arts and Leisure 2011-15, Sinn Féin Spokesperson for: Employment and Learning 2011-13, Environment 2013-16. Sinn Féin: Former member, Six County Executive, Former chair, Tyrone branch. *Councils and public bodies:* Omagh District Council: Councillor 2000-10, Council Chair 2001-02.

Political interests: Irish language culture, North/South integration, sport, the arts.

Other: Member, St Colmcille's Gaelic Athletic Club, Carrickmore.

Recreations: Gaelic games.

Barry McElduff MP, House of Commons, London SW1A 0AA
Tel: 020 7219 4118 *Email:* barry.mcelduff.mp@parliament.uk
Constituency: Details still to be confirmed
Tel: 028 8225 3040 *Twitter:* @BarryMcElduff

LABOUR

MCFADDEN, PAT

Wolverhampton South East *(Majority 8,514)*

Patrick Bosco McFadden. Born 26 March 1965; Son of James and Annie McFadden; Married (1 son 1 daughter).

Education: Holyrood Secondary School, Glasgow; Edinburgh University (MA politics 1988).

Non-political career: Adviser to Donald Dewar MP as Scottish Affairs Spokesperson 1988-93; Speechwriter and policy adviser to John Smith MP as Labour Party Leader 1993; Policy adviser to Tony Blair MP as Labour Party Leader and political secretary to him as Prime Minister 1994-2005. Member, Community.

Political career: Member for Wolverhampton South East 2005-10, for Wolverhampton South East (revised boundary) since 6 May 2010 general election; Parliamentary Secretary, Cabinet Office 2006-07; Minister of State (Employment Relations and Postal Affairs 2007-09), Department for Business, Enterprise and Regulatory Reform/Business, Innovation and Skills 2007-10 (attending Cabinet 2009-10); Shadow Secretary of State for Business, Innovation and Skills 2010; Shadow Minister for Foreign and Commonwealth Office (Europe) 2014-16. *Select committees:* Member: Treasury 2011-14, Parliamentary Commission on Banking Standards 2012-13, Exiting the European Union 2016-. Chair, PLP Labour In group 2016.

Other: PC 2008.

Recreations: Reading, sport.

Rt Hon Pat McFadden MP, House of Commons, London SW1A 0AA
Tel: 020 7219 4036 *Email:* mcfaddenp@parliament.uk
Constituency: Crescent House, Broad Street, Bilston, West Midlands WV14 0BZ
Tel: 01902 405762 *Fax:* 01902 402381 *Website:* www.patmcfadden.com
Twitter: @patmcfaddenmp

LABOUR

MCGINN, CONOR

St Helens North *(Majority 18,406)*

Conor Patrick McGinn. Born 31 July 1984; Married Kate 2009 (1 son 1 daughter).

Education: St Paul's High School, Bessbrook; London Metropolitan University (BA history, politics and Irish studies).

Non-political career: Immigrant counselling and psychotherapy; Political Adviser to Vernon Coaker MP as Shadow Secretary of State for Northern Ireland and for Defence.

Political career: Member for St Helens North since 7 May 2015 general election; Opposition Whip 2015-16. *Select committees:* Member: Defence 2015, Northern Ireland Affairs 2017-. Labour Party: Honorary President, Socialist Societies, Member (Socialist Societies), National Executive Committee 2011-15; Political Secretary, National Union of Labour and Socialist Clubs. *Councils and public bodies:* School governor 2005-12; Governor, NHS trust 2011-15.

Political interests: Defence, home affairs; Australia, Brazil, Ireland, South Africa, USA.

Other: Member, British-Irish Parliamentary Assembly 2015-; Alternate Member, UK Delegation, Organisation for Security and Co-operation in Europe Parliamentary Assembly 2016-; Member, Gaelic Athletic Association; Ulster Reform Club.

Conor McGinn MP, House of Commons, London SW1A 0AA
Tel: 020 7219 4367 *Email:* conor.mcginn.mp@parliament.uk
Constituency: Sixth Floor, Century House, Hardshaw Street, St Helens, Merseyside WA10 1QU
Tel: 01744 21336 *Email:* contact@conormcginn.co.uk *Website:* www.conormcginn.co.uk
Twitter: @ConorMcGinn

LABOUR

MCGOVERN, ALISON

Wirral South *(Majority 8,323)*

Born 30 December 1980; Daughter of Mike McGovern, British Rail telecoms engineer, and Ann McGovern, nurse; Married Ashwin Kumar (1 daughter).

Education: Wirral Grammar School; University College, London (BA philosophy); Birkbeck College London (Post Grad Cert economics).

Non-political career: Researcher, House of Commons 2002-06; Public affairs manager: Network Rail 2006-08, The Art Fund 2008-09, Creativity, Culture and Education 2009. Member, Unite.

Political career: Member for Wirral South since 6 May 2010 general election; PPS to Gordon Brown MP 2010-13; Opposition Whip 2013; Shadow Minister for: International Development 2013-14, Children and Families 2014-15; Shadow Economic Secretary 2015. *Select committees:* Member, International Development 2010-13; Works of Art: Member 2011-16, Chair 2016-; Member, Treasury 2017-. *Councils and public bodies:* London Borough of Southwark Council: Councillor 2006-10, Deputy Leader, Labour group -2010.

Political interests: International development, employment, economy, arts and culture, regeneration; Africa, India.

Other: Trustee, South London Gallery 2006-10; Progress: Vice-chair 2012-15, Chair 2015-16.

Publications: The Real Life State (Fabian); Co-editor, Politics of Solutions (Progress); Contributor: Wirral News, Progress Online, Fabian Society.

Alison McGovern MP, House of Commons, London SW1A 0AA
Tel: 020 7219 7190 *Email:* alison.mcgovern.mp@parliament.uk
Constituency: 99 New Chester Road, New Ferry, Wirral, Merseyside CH62 4RA
Tel: 0151-645 6590 *Email:* alison@alisonmcgovern.org.uk *Website:* www.alisonmcgovern.org.uk
Twitter: @Alison_McGovern

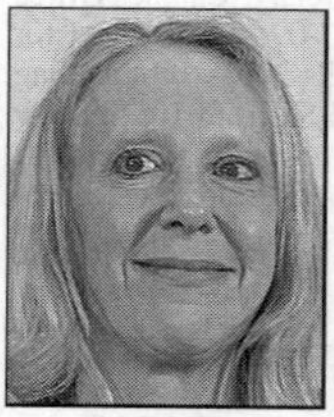

LABOUR

MCINNES, LIZ

Heywood and Middleton *(Majority 7,617)*

Shadow Minister for Foreign and Commonwealth Office

Elizabeth Anne McInnes. Born 30 March 1959; Partner Steve (1 son).

Non-political career: Clinical scientist, Pennine Acute Hospitals NHS Trust. Unite: Member, Secretary, Pennine Acute Unite Brach, Chair, Health Sector National Committee.

Political career: Member for Heywood and Middleton since 9 October 2014 by-election; Shadow Minister for Communities and Local Government 2015-16; Board Member, Parliamentary Office of Science and Technology (POST) 2015-16; Shadow Minister for Foreign and Commonwealth Office 2016-. *Select committees:* Member: Health 2015, Science and Technology 2015. Member, Co-operative Party. *Councils and public bodies:* Rossendale Borough Council: Councillor 2010-14, Chair, Partner Overview and Scrutiny Committee.

Other: Trustee, STAR Centre, Rossendale.

Liz McInnes MP, House of Commons, London SW1A 0AA
Tel: 020 7219 0684 *Email:* liz.mcinnes.mp@parliament.uk
Constituency: 45 York Street, Heywood, Greater Manchester OL10 4NN
Tel: 01706 361135 *Website:* www.lizmcinnesmp.org.uk *Twitter:* @LizMcInnes_MP

CONSERVATIVE

MACKINLAY, CRAIG

South Thanet *(Majority 6,387)*

Born 7 October 1966; Son of Colin and Margaret Mackinlay; Married Katalin 2011.

Education: Rainham Mark Grammar School, Kent; Birmingham University (BSc zoology and comparative physiology); Hungarian.

Non-political career: Parliamentary Armed Forces Scheme 2016-17. Assistant manager, Robson Rhodes Chartered Accountants 1989-93; Partner, Beak Kemmenoe Chartered Accountants and Chartered Tax Advisers 2011-.

Political career: Contested Gillingham (Ind) 1992, Gillingham (UKIP) 1997, Totnes 2001, Gillingham 2005 general elections. Member (Con) for South Thanet since 7 May 2015 general election. *Select committees:* Member: Work and Pensions 2015-17, European Scrutiny 2015-, Exiting the European Union 2016-. Contested (Con) Kent Police and Crime Commissioner 2012 election. UK Independence Party: Founding Member 1993, Acting Leader 1997, Deputy Leader 1997-2000; Member, Conservative Party 2005-; Founding member, Conservatives for Britain 2015-16. *Councils and public bodies:* Councillor, Medway Council 2007-15.

Political interests: Taxation, pensions, European Union, live animal exports, tobacco, fishing, energy, aviation; Hungary, USA.

Other: Trustee, Chatham Historic Dockyard Trust 2007-; Vice-chair, Foord Almshouses, Rochester 2007-; Institute of Chartered Accountants in England and Wales; Chartered Institute of Taxation; Chatham Historic Dockyard Trust, The Foord Almshouses Rochester. Freedom, City of London; Carlton Club, Castle Club. Royal Temple Yacht Club, Ramsgate.

Recreations: Sailing.

Craig Mackinlay MP, House of Commons, London SW1A 0AA
Tel: 020 7219 4442 *Email:* craig.mackinlay.mp@parliament.uk
Constituency: 4 The Broadway, Broadstairs, Kent CT10 2AD
Tel: 01843 603242 *Website:* www.craigmackinlay.com *Twitter:* @cmackinlay

LABOUR

MCKINNELL, CATHERINE

Newcastle upon Tyne North *(Majority 10,349)*

Born 8 June 1976; Daughter of John and Agnes Grady; Married Rhys (3 children).

Education: Sacred Heart Comprehensive School, Fenham, Newcastle upon Tyne; Edinburgh University (MA politics and history 2000); Northumbria University (Postgraduate Diploma law and common professional examination 2002); Italian.

Non-political career: Employment solicitor, Newcastle. Member, GMB.

Political career: Member for Newcastle upon Tyne North since 6 May 2010 general election; Shadow Solicitor General 2010-11; Shadow Minister for Education 2011-12; Shadow Exchequer Secretary 2012-13, 2015; Shadow Economic Secretary 2013-15; Shadow Attorney General 2015-16. *Select committees:* Member: Political and Constitutional Reform 2010, Education 2016-17, Education, Skills and the Economy Sub-committee 2016-17, Petitions 2016-17, 2017-, Treasury 2017-. Chair, PLP Department Group for International Trade 2016-17; Member, PLP Parliamentary Committee 2017-. Chair, Northern Group of Labour MPs 2017-. *Councils and public bodies:* Vice-President, Local Government Association 2016-.

Political interests: Regional development, manufacturing, economy, women and children, international development, justice and legal aid, apprenticeships; Italy.

Other: Northumbrian Association; Tyneside Irish Centre; MS Society, CAFOD. British Military Fitness.

Recreations: Swimming, travel.

Catherine McKinnell MP, House of Commons, London SW1A 0AA
Tel: 020 7219 2231 *Email:* catherine.mckinnell.mp@parliament.uk
Constituency: No constituency office publicised
Tel: 0191-229 0352 *Website:* www.catherinemckinnellmp.co.uk *Twitter:* @CatMcKinnell

CONSERVATIVE

MACLEAN, RACHEL

Redditch *(Majority 7,363)*

Rachel Helen Maclean. Born 3 October 1965; Married David (1 daughter 3 sons).

Education: Oxford University (experimental psychology); Aston University (MSc work and organisational psychology 2006).

Non-political career: International Officer, HSBC 1989-92; Head of Direct Sales, Computer Manuals Ltd 1992-94; Sales and Editorial Manager, Wrox Press Ltd 1994-99; Part-time Post-Natal Teacher, National Childbirth Trust 2000-02; Director of Organisation Development and Human Resources, Packt Publishing 2005-13; Managing Director, ImPackt Publishing 2012-13; Founder and Director, Skilled and Ready 2012-; Head of HR and Organisation Development, Hollywood Monster 2015-16; Co-Founder and COO, Air 2016-17.

Political career: Contested Birmingham, Northfield 2015 general election. Member for Redditch since 8 June 2017. *Select committees:* Member, Business, Energy and Industrial Strategy 2017-. Co-chair, Andy Street West Midlands Mayoral Campaign 2016-16. *Councils and public bodies:* Governor, King Edwards Camp Hill School for Boys, Kings Heath.

Other: Sunday School Teacher; Beaver, Cub and Scout Leader 2004-12; Managing Director, Skills for Birmingham; Ambassador and Volunteer Consultant, LoveBrum 2015-; Regional Council Member, CBI 2015-; Sprint Pirates 2016; National Childbirth Trust.

Recreations: Spending time with family, jogging, long distance walking holidays.

Rachel Maclean MP, House of Commons, London SW1A 0AA
Tel: 020 7219 1848 *Email:* rachel.maclean.mp@parliament.uk
Constituency: Grosvenor House, Prospect Hill, Redditch B97 4DL
Tel: 01527 591334 *Website:* www.rachelmaclean.uk *Twitter:* @redditchrachel

CONSERVATIVE

MCLOUGHLIN, PATRICK

Derbyshire Dales *(Majority 14,327)*

Chancellor of the Duchy of Lancaster; Chairman of Conservative Party

Patrick Allan McLoughlin. Born 30 November 1957; Son of Patrick Alphonsos McLoughlin; Married Lynne Newman 1984 (1 son 1 daughter).

Education: Cardinal Griffin Comprehensive School, Cannock; Staffordshire College of Agriculture.

Non-political career: Agricultural worker 1974-79; Various positions with National Coal Board (including underground) 1979-86.

Political career: Contested Wolverhampton South East 1983 general election. Member for West Derbyshire 8 May 1986 by-election to 2010, for Derbyshire Dales since 6 May 2010 general election; PPS to: Angela Rumbold as Minister of State, Department of Education 1987-88, Lord Young of Graffham as Secretary of State for Trade and Industry 1988-89; Parliamentary Under-Secretary of State, Department of Transport (Minister for Aviation and Shipping) 1989-92; Joint Parliamentary Under-Secretary of State, Department of Employment 1992-93; Parliamentary Under-Secretary of State, Department of Trade and Industry (Trade and Technology) 1993-94; Assistant Government Whip 1995-96; Government Whip 1996-97; Opposition Pairing Whip 1997-98; Opposition Deputy Chief Whip 1998-2005; Opposition Chief Whip 2005-10; Parliamentary Secretary to the Treasury 2010-12; Chief Whip 2010-12; Member, Parliamentary and Political Service Honours Committee 2012; Secretary of State for Transport 2012-16; Chancellor of the Duchy of Lancaster (also attending Cabinet) 2016-. *Select committees:* Member: Broadcasting 1994-95, Selection 1997-2001, Finance and Services 1998-2005, Accommodation and Works 2001-05, Modernisation of the House of Commons 2004-05, Selection 2005, Administration 2005. National vice-chair, Young Conservatives 1982-84; Chairman, Conservative Party 2016-. *Councils and public bodies:* Councillor: Cannock Chase District Council 1980-87, Staffordshire County Council 1981-87.

Political interests: Agriculture, education.

Other: Vice-president, Youth Hostel Association; Chair, board of trustees, Chequers and Dorneywood. PC 2005; Kt 2016.

Rt Hon Sir Patrick McLoughlin MP, House of Commons, London SW1A 0AA
Tel: 020 7219 3511 *Email:* patrick.mcloughlin.mp@parliament.uk
Constituency: No constituency office *Twitter:* @Patrick4Dales

LAB/CO-OP

MCMAHON, JIM

Oldham West and Royton *(Majority 17,198)*

Shadow Minister for Local Government Devolution and Finance

James McMahon. Born 7 July 1980; Son of William McMahon, truck driver, and Alice O'Rourke; Partner Charlene (2 sons).

Education: Oldham College.

Non-political career: Manchester University 1997-2004: Apprentice technician, Senior technician; Programme co-ordinator, Groundwork Trust, Wythenshawe and South Manchester; Town centre manager, Middleton. Member, Unite.

Political career: Member for Oldham West and Royton since 3 December 2015 by-election; PPS to Tom Watson as Deputy Leader, Labour Party, Party Chair and Shadow Minister for the Cabinet Office 2016; Shadow Minister for Communities and Local Government: (Local Government and Devolution) 2016-17, (Local Government Devolution and Finance) 2017-. *Select committees:* Member, Communities and Local Government 2016. Leader, Labour Group, Local Government

Association 2014-15; Member, National Executive Committee, Labour Party 2014-15. *Councils and public bodies:* Oldham Council: Councillor 2003-17, Leader of the Opposition 2008-11, Leader of the Council 2011-16; Representative: Greater Manchester Combined Authority, Association of Greater Manchester Authorities, Police and Crime Panel; Vice-president, Local Government Association 2017-.

Political interests: Finance, local government, regeneration/urban renewal.

Other: Fellow, British American Project 2010-; Co-operative Council Innovation Network; Fellow, Royal Society of Arts 2014; Honorary fellowship, University Campus Oldham 2014. Council Leader of the Year, C'llr Achievement Awards. OBE 2015.

Jim McMahon OBE MP, House of Commons, London SW1A 0AA
Tel: 020 7219 6039 *Email:* jim.mcmahon.mp@parliament.uk
Constituency: Textile House, 108 Union Street, Oldham OL1 1DU
Tel: 0161-652 8485 *Website:* jimmcmahon.co.uk *Twitter:* @JimfromOldham

LABOUR

MCMORRIN, ANNA

Cardiff North *(Majority 4,174)*

PPS to Barry Gardiner as Shadow Secretary of State for International Trade and Shadow Minister for International Climate Change

Anna Rhiannon McMorrin. Born September 1971; Partner Alun Davies (AM for Blaenau Gwent) (2 daughters).

Education: Brecon High School; Southampton University (BA French and politics 1994); Cardiff University (Postgraduate Diploma journalim 1997).

Non-political career: Communications Officer, Labour Party 1997; Account Director: Political Intelligence 1997-99, Hill and Knowlton 1999-2001; Consultant 2001-06; Campaigns and Communications Officer, Friends of the Earth Cymru 2006-08; Specialist Policy Adviser to Minister for Natural Resources, Welsh Government 2008-14; Head of Welsh Office, Invicta Public Affairs 2016-17; Director, Llais Ltd 2016-.

Political career: Member for Cardiff North since 8 June 2017; PPS to Barry Gardiner as Shadow Secretary of State for International Trade and Shadow Minister for International Climate Change 2017-. *Select committees:* Member, Environmental Audit 2017-. Contested South Wales Central region 2016 Welsh Assembly election.

Anna McMorrin MP, House of Commons, London SW1A 0AA
Tel: 020 7219 4307 *Email:* anna.mcmorrin.mp@parliament.uk
Constituency: 13 Llangranog Road, Llanishen, Cardiff CF14 5BL
Tel: 029 2062 4440 *Website:* www.annamcmorrin.co.uk *Twitter:* @annamcmorrin

SCOTTISH NATIONAL PARTY

MCNALLY, JOHN

Falkirk *(Majority 4,923)*

Born 1 February 1951; Married Sandra (1 son 1 daughter).

Education: St Modan's High School.

Non-political career: Self-employed hairdresser/barber, The Barber Shop 1970s-.

Political career: Contested Falkirk 2010 general election. Member for Falkirk since 7 May 2015 general election. *Select committees:* Member, Environmental Audit 2015-. Convener, Denny Branch, SNP. *Councils and public bodies:* Councillor, Falkirk Council 2005-15.

Political interests: Scottish independence.

Other: Local football coach.

John McNally MP, House of Commons, London SW1A 0AA
Tel: 020 7219 6525 *Email:* john.mcnally.mp@parliament.uk
Constituency: 16 Vicar Street, Falkirk FK1 1JL *Twitter:* @JohnMcNallySNP

SCOTTISH NATIONAL PARTY

MACNEIL, ANGUS

Na h-Eileanan An Iar *(Majority 1,007)*

SNP Spokesperson for Environment and Rural Affairs; Chair, Select Committee on International Trade

Angus Brendan MacNeil. Born 21 July 1970; Son of Iain MacNeil, postman and crofter, and late Clare MacNeil, district nurse; Married Jane (3 daughters) (separated).

Education: Castlebay Secondary School, Isle of Barra; Nicolson Institute, Stornoway, Isle of Lewis; Strathclyde University (BEng civil engineering 1992); Jordanhill College (PGCE primary teaching and bilingualism 1996); Gaelic, Irish gaelic.

Non-political career: Civil engineer, Lilley Construction Ltd, Edinburgh 1992-93; Radio reporter, BBC, Inverness 1993-95; Primary teacher, Salen Primary School, Mull 1996-98; Gaelic development officer, Lochaber 1998-99; Education lecturer (part-time), Inverness College.

Political career: Contested Inverness East, Nairn and Lochaber 2001 general election. Member for Na h-Eileanan An Iar since 5 May 2005 general election; SNP Spokesperson for: Transport 2005-15, Environment 2005-07, Tourism 2005-15, Fishing 2005-10, Food and Rural Affairs 2005-10, Work and Pensions 2007-08, Scotland Office 2008-15, Deputy Prime Minister's Portfolio 2013-15, Environment and Rural Affairs 2017-. *Select committees:* Member: Scottish Affairs 2005-09, Liaison 2015-, Joint Committee on the National Security Strategy 2015-; Chair: Energy and Climate Change 2015-16, International Trade 2016-. Convener, Lochaber branch, SNP 1999.

Political interests: Economics of small states; Faroe Islands, Iceland, Norway.

Other: Amnesty International, VSO.

Recreations: Football, sailing, fishing.

Angus MacNeil MP, House of Commons, London SW1A 0AA
Tel: 020 7219 8476 *Fax:* 020 7219 6111 *Email:* macneila@parliament.uk
Constituency: 31 Bayhead Street, Stornoway, Isle of Lewis, Outer Hebrides HS1 2DU
Tel: 01851 702272 *Email:* macdonaldrm@parliament.uk *Twitter:* @AngusMacNeilSNP

CONSERVATIVE

MCPARTLAND, STEPHEN

Stevenage *(Majority 3,386)*

Stephen Anthony McPartland. Born 9 August 1976; Married Emma.

Education: Liverpool College; Liverpool University (BA history 1997); Liverpool John Moores University (MSc technology management 1998).

Non-political career: Agent, North East Hertfordshire Conservative Association 2001-08; Membership director, British American Business (American Chamber of Commerce) 2008-10.

Political career: Member for Stevenage since 6 May 2010 general election; Board Member, Parliamentary Office of Science and Technology (POST) 2013-; PPS to Lord Livingston of Parkhead as Minister of State for Trade and Investment, Department for Business, Innovation and Skills and Foreign and Commonwealth Office 2014-15. *Select committees:* Member: Science and Technology 2011-12, Regulatory Reform 2017-, Finance 2017-. Founding member, Conservatives for Britain 2015-16.

Political interests: Healthcare (particularly cancer treatment and respiratory diseases), education, satellite technology, international trade, policing, addiction treatment, urban regeneration, government procurement of IT projects; China, India, UK, USA.

Other: Asthma UK, The Living Room, Turn the Tide.

Recreations: Reading, keeping fit, cinema.

Stephen McPartland MP, House of Commons, London SW1A 0AA
Tel: 020 7219 7156 *Email:* stephen.mcpartland.mp@parliament.uk
Constituency: No constituency office publicised *Website:* www.stephenmcpartland.co.uk
Twitter: @SMcPartland

CONSERVATIVE

MCVEY, ESTHER

Tatton *(Majority 14,787)*

Esther Louise McVey. Born 24 October 1967; Daughter of James and Barbara McVey.

Education: Belvedere School, Liverpool; Queen Mary and Westfield, London (LLB 1990); City University, London (Postgraduate Course radio journalism 1991); John Moore's University, Liverpool (MSc corporate governance 2009, winner North of England Excellence Award).

Non-political career: Director, JG McVey & Co Ltd 2000-06; Managing director, Making It (UK) Ltd 2002-10; Founder, Winning Women 2003-10.

Political career: Contested Wirral West 2005 general election. MP for Wirral West 2010-15. Contested Wirral West 2015 general election. Member for Tatton since 8 June 2017; PPS to Chris Grayling as Minister of State for Employment 2010-12; Parliamentary Under-Secretary of State (Minister for Disabled People), Department for Work and Pensions 2012-13; Minister of State for Employment, Department for Work and Pensions 2013-15. *Select committees:* Member, Home Affairs 2017-. *Councils and public bodies:* Chair, British Transport Police Authority 2015-17.

Political interests: Law and order and sentencing, transport, education, city regeneration.

Other: Board member: Madeleine McCann Fund 2007-08, North West Women's Enterprise Forum 2008-10; Patron: Wirral Holistic Therapeutic Cancer Care, Full of Life (charity for disabled children and their families); Ambassador, Action Medical Research; Member, NCH. PC 2014.

Recreations: Theatre, cinema, walking.

Rt Hon Esther McVey MP, House of Commons, London SW1A 0AA
Tel: 020 7219 3000 *Email:* esther.mcvey.mp@parliament.uk
Constituency: 84 Chapel Lane, Wilmslow SK9 5JH
Tel: 01625 529922 *Email:* officeofesthermcveymp@parliament.uk
Website: www.esthermcvey.com *Twitter:* @EstherMcVey1

LABOUR

MADDERS, JUSTIN

Ellesmere Port and Neston *(Majority 11,390)*

Shadow Minister for Health

Justin Piers Richard Madders. Born 22 November 1972; Married (3 children).

Education: Sheffield University.

Non-political career: Solicitor. Member, Unite.

Political career: Contested Tatton 2005 general election. Member for Ellesmere Port and Neston since 7 May 2015 general election; Shadow Minister for Health 2015-. *Select committees:* Member, Petitions 2015. Member, Co-operative Party. *Councils and public bodies:* Ellesmere Port and Neston Borough Council: Councillor 1998-2009, Leader 2007-09; Cheshire West and Chester Council: Councillor 2009-15, Leader of the Opposition 2011-14.

Other: Member, Fabian Society; Member: RSPB, Cheshire Wildlife.

Recreations: Football.

Justin Madders MP, House of Commons, London SW1A 0AA
Tel: 020 7219 6584 *Email:* justin.madders.mp@parliament.uk
Constituency: 23 Whitby Road, Ellesmere Port, Cheshire CH65 8AA
Tel: 0151-355 2365 *Website:* www.justinmadders.com *Twitter:* @justinmadders

LABOUR

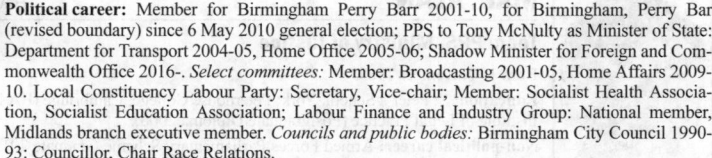

MAHMOOD, KHALID

Birmingham, Perry Barr *(Majority 18,383)*

Shadow Minister for Foreign and Commonwealth Office

Born 13 July 1961.

Non-political career: Former engineer. Member, AEEU; Former adviser, Danish International Trade Union.

Political career: Member for Birmingham Perry Barr 2001-10, for Birmingham, Perry Bar (revised boundary) since 6 May 2010 general election; PPS to Tony McNulty as Minister of State: Department for Transport 2004-05, Home Office 2005-06; Shadow Minister for Foreign and Commonwealth Office 2016-. *Select committees:* Member: Broadcasting 2001-05, Home Affairs 2009-10. Local Constituency Labour Party: Secretary, Vice-chair; Member: Socialist Health Association, Socialist Education Association; Labour Finance and Industry Group: National member, Midlands branch executive member. *Councils and public bodies:* Birmingham City Council 1990-93: Councillor, Chair Race Relations.

Political interests: Community relations, British industry, international trade, terrorism.

Other: Substitute Member, UK delegation, Parliamentary Assembly of the Council of Europe -2016; Adviser to President of Olympic Council Asia; Member, governing body: Neighbourhood forum, South Birmingham CHC.

Khalid Mahmood MP, House of Commons, London SW1A 0AA
Tel: 020 7219 8141 *Fax:* 020 7219 1745 *Email:* mahmoodk@parliament.uk
Constituency: 18 Heathfield Road, Handsworth, Birmingham, West Midlands B19 1HB
Tel: 0121-356 8268 *Fax:* 0121-356 8278 *Twitter:* @khalid4pb

LABOUR

MAHMOOD, SHABANA

Birmingham, Ladywood *(Majority 28,714)*

Born 17 September 1980; Daughter of Zubaida and Mahmood Ahmed.

Education: Small Heath School, Birmingham; King Edward VI Camp Hill School for Girls; Lincoln College, Oxford (BA law 2002); Inns of Court School of Law (Bar Vocational Course 2003); Mirpuri and Urdu (fluent), French (basic).

Non-political career: Barrister: 12 King's Bench Walk 2003-04, Berrymans Lace Mawer 2004-07.

Political career: Member for Birmingham, Ladywood since 6 May 2010 general election; Shadow Minister for: Home Office 2010-11, Business, Innovation and Skills (Higher Education) 2011-13, Business, Innovation and Skills (Universities and Science) 2013; Shadow Exchequer Secretary 2013-15; Shadow Chief Secretary to the Treasury 2015. *Select committees:* Member: Work and Pensions 2010, Joint Committee on the Draft Investigatory Powers Bill 2015-16, International Trade 2016-17, Public Accounts 2017-. Chair, PLP Departmental Group for Justice 2015-. Labour Party: Member, National Executive Committee 2016-, Vice-chair, National Policy Forum.

Shabana Mahmood MP, House of Commons, London SW1A 0AA
Tel: 020 7219 7818 *Email:* shabana.mahmood.mp@parliament.uk
Constituency: No constituency office publicised
Tel: 0121-661 9440 *Website:* www.shabanamahmood.org *Twitter:* @shabanamahmood

MAIN, ANNE

St Albans *(Majority 6,109)*

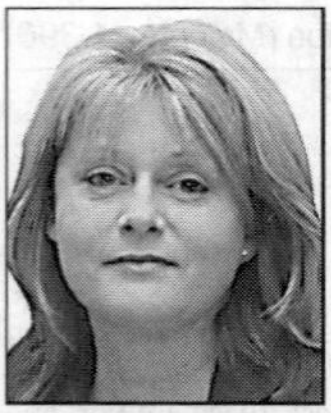

CONSERVATIVE

Anne Margaret Main. Born 17 May 1957; Daughter of Rita and late George Wiseman; Married Stephen Tonks 1978 (died 1991) (1 son 2 daughters); married Andrew Main 1995 (1 son).

Education: Bishop of Llandaff Secondary School, Cardiff; University College of Wales, Swansea (BA English 1978); Sheffield University (PGCE 1979); French.

Non-political career: Teaching and family 1979-80; Home-maker 1980-90; Carer for terminally ill husband 1990-91; Single parent and supply teacher 1991-95. Member, NUT 1979-80.

Political career: Member for St Albans 2005-10, for St Albans (revised boundary) since 6 May 2010 general election. *Select committees:* Member: ODPM/Communities and Local Government 2005-10, Energy and Climate Change 2009-10, Chairmen's Panel/Panel of Chairs 2010-, Court of Referees 2016-. Chair and founder, Conservative Friends of Bangladesh; Founding member, Conservatives for Britain 2015-16.

Political interests: Environment, education, health; Bangladesh.

Other: Member, International League for the Protection of Horses 1999-; St Albans Civic Society 2003-; Fellow, Industry and Parliament Trust 2007; Governor, Westminster Foundation for Democracy 2010-11; Grove House Hospice, Macmillan Cancer Support; Conservative Women's Club, St Albans Conservative Club, Beaconsfield Conservative Club.

Recreations: Dog walking, art, reading, food and wine.

Anne Main MP, House of Commons, London SW1A 0AA
Tel: 020 7219 8270 *Fax:* 020 7219 3058 *Email:* maina@parliament.uk
Constituency: 104 High Street, London Colney, St Albans, Hertfordshire AL2 1QL
Tel: 01727 825100 *Fax:* 01727 828404 *Email:* agent@stalbansconservatives.com
Website: www.annemain.com

MAK, ALAN

Havant *(Majority 15,956)*

CONSERVATIVE

Team PPS, Ministry of Justice

Born 19 November 1983.

Education: St Peter's School, York; Peterhouse College, Cambridge (BA law 2005, MA); Oxford Institute of Legal Practice (Postgraduate Diploma 2006).

Non-political career: Armed Forces Parliamentary Scheme Graduate 2015-16. Solicitor, Clifford Chance LLP; Small business owner and investor; Non-executive board member, Havas Worldwide Group UK; Judge, Wayra UnLtd; Management committee, Enterprise Forum.

Political career: Member for Havant since 7 May 2015 general election; Team PPS, Ministry of Justice 2017-. *Select committees:* Member, Procedure 2015-16. *Councils and public bodies:* Governor, primary school 2008-15.

Political interests: Economy, business, education, defence, foreign policy, social mobility; China, Europe, Israel, South Africa, USA.

Other: Young Global Shaper, World Economic Forum; Former President and Trustee, Magic Breakfast; Founder and President, British Legion's Young Professionals' Branch; Member, Speakers for Schools; Advisory Board Member and Ambassador, One Young World; Former Alumni Advisory Board, Cambridge University; Fellow, Royal Society of Arts; Member, Law Society of England and Wales; Royal British Legion. Freedom, City of London. Vice-President, Havant Rugby Club.

Publications: Next Generation Vision for Financial Services.

Recreations: Playing and watching sports, spending time with family, films, travel.

Alan Mak MP, House of Commons, London SW1A 0AA
Tel: 020 7219 6266 *Email:* alan.mak.mp@parliament.uk
Constituency: Building 6000, Langstone Technology Park, Langstone Road, Havant, Hampshire PO9 1SA
Tel: 023 9241 5620 *Website:* www.alanmak.org.uk *Twitter:* @AlanMakMP

LAB/CO-OP

MALHOTRA, SEEMA

Feltham and Heston *(Majority 15,603)*

Seema Malhotra-Saluja. Born 7 August 1972; Daughter of Sushil Kumar Malhotra, retired engineer and small businessman, and Usha Malhotra, retired teacher; Married Sushil Saluja 2005.

Education: Green School, Isleworth; Warwick University (politics and philosophy 1994) (scholarship, University of Massachusetts, Amhurst, USA 1992-93); Aston University (business IT 1995); German (some), Hindi, Punjabi.

Non-political career: Management consultant, Accenture 1995-2003; Senior manager, PriceWaterhouseCoopers 2003-07; Consultant 2004-05; Adviser: to Liam Byrne MP: as Minister for the West Midlands 2007-08, as Chair of the Council of Regional Ministers 2008-09, to Ian Austin MP as Minister for the West Midlands 2008-09; Adviser to the video games industry on child safety agenda 2008; Programme leader, cross-government programme to increase diversity in public appointments 2009-10; Political adviser to Harriet Harman MP as Acting Leader of the Opposition May-October 2010; Strategic programme adviser, UKIE May-November 2011. Unite: Member, Chair, South Thames Community Branch 2007-11.

Political career: Member for Feltham and Heston since 15 December 2011 by-election; PPS to Yvette Cooper as Shadow Secretary of State for Home Department (Home Secretary); Shadow Minister for Women and Equalities 2012; Opposition Whip 2013-14; Shadow Minister for Preventing Violence Against Women and Girls 2014-15; Shadow Chief Secretary to the Treasury 2015-16; Member, Commons Reference Group on Representation and Inclusion 2017-. *Select committees:* Member: Justice 2012-13, Exiting the European Union 2016-. Chair, PLP Departmental Group for Business, Innovation and Skills 2012-14. Member, Co-operative Party.

Political interests: Business and entrepreneurship, civil and criminal justice, public administration, youth offending, apprenticeships, aviation, gender and equalities, British-American relations, policing, women offenders, community banking, women and business, diversity on public boards; China, India, Middle East.

Other: Chair, Young Fabians 1999-2000; Fabian Society: Executive member 2000-, Chair 2005-06, 2015-16; Founder and director, Fabian Women's Network 2005-; Fellow, British American Project; Fellow, Royal Society of Arts; Trustee, Swanswell 2011-. Shortlisted, Asian Women of Achievement awards 2006.

Publications: Contributor: Dictionary of Labour Biography (Politico's, 2001), From the Workhouse to Welfare (Fabian Society and Webb Memorial Trust, 2009).

Recreations: Running, cinema, music, gardening, playing the guitar.

Seema Malhotra MP, House of Commons, London SW1A 0AA
Tel: 020 7219 8957 *Email:* seema.malhotra.mp@parliament.uk
Constituency: Civic Centre, Lampton Road, Hounslow TW3 4DN
Tel: 020 8814 9786 *Website:* www.seemamalhotra.com *Twitter:* @SeemaMalhotra1

CONSERVATIVE

MALTHOUSE, KIT

North West Hampshire *(Majority 22,679)*

Christopher Laurie Malthouse. Born 27 October 1966; Married (3 children).

Education: Liverpool College; Newcastle University (politics and economics).

Non-political career: Features editor, *The Courier*; Chartered accountant, Deloitte and Touche; Chair, County Finance Group.

Political career: Member for North West Hampshire since 7 May 2015 general election. *Select committees:* Member: Armed Forces Bill 2015 2015-16, Treasury 2016-. London Assembly: AM for West Central constituency 2008-16, Deputy Mayor of London for: Policing and Crime 2008-12, Business and Enterprise 2012-15. *Councils and public bodies:* Westminster City Council: Councillor 1998-2006, Deputy Leader of the Council, Cabinet Member for Finance.

Other: Vice-chair, London Enterprise Panel; Chair, London and Partners.

Recreations: Gardening, reading, writing, watching modern dance, the gym.

Kit Malthouse MP, House of Commons, London SW1A 0AA
Tel: 020 7219 5605 *Email:* kit.malthouse.mp@parliament.uk
Constituency: 2 Church Close, Andover, Hampshire SP10 1DP
Tel: 01264 401401 *Email:* kit@kitmalthouse.com *Website:* kitmalthouse.com
Twitter: @kitmalthouse

House of Commons MPs' Biographies

LABOUR

MANN, JOHN

Bassetlaw *(Majority 4,852)*

Born 10 January 1960; Son of James Mann and Brenda Cleavin; Married Joanna White 1986 (2 daughters 1 son).

Education: Bradford Grammar School; Manchester University (BA Econ 1982); ITD Diploma 1992; French, German.

Non-political career: Head research and education, AEU 1988-90; National training officer, TUC 1990-95; Liaison officer, National Trade Union and Labour Party 1995-2000; Director, Abraxas Communications Ltd 1998-2002. Member, AEEU 1985-.

Political career: Member for Bassetlaw 2001-10, for Bassetlaw (revised boundary) since 6 May 2010 general election; PPS: to Richard Caborn as Minister for Sport 2005-07, to Tessa Jowell as Minister for: the Olympics and London 2007-08, the Olympics 2008, the Olympics and Paymaster General 2009. *Select committees:* Member: Information 2001-05, Treasury 2003-05, 2009-, Treasury (Treasury Sub-committee) 2003-10, Unopposed Bills (Panel) 2004-15. Contested East Midlands 1999 European Parliament election. *Councils and public bodies:* Councillor, London Borough of Lambeth 1986-90.

Political interests: Small businesses, training, economic regeneration, sport, drugs.

Other: Fellow, Industry and Parliament Trust 2003; Founding supporter, Change Britain 2016-; MIPD; Manton Miners Club.

Publications: Labour and Youth: The Missing Generation (Fabian Society, 1985); Heroin in Bassetlaw (2002); The Real Deal (Fabian Society, 2006); The Bassetlaw Anti-Social Behaviour Handbook (2007); Co-Writer, Antisemitism in European Football: A scar on the beautiful game (2008); Miner Compensation – The Legal Complaints Service and the Coal Health Compensation Scheme (2009); What Every Parent and Grandparent Needs to Know about Drugs and Alcohol (2009).

Recreations: Football, cricket, fell-walking, mountaineering.

John Mann MP, House of Commons, London SW1A 0AA
Tel: 020 7219 8345 *Email:* mannj@parliament.uk
Constituency: Stanley Street, Worksop, Nottinghamshire S81 7HX
Tel: 01909 506200 *Website:* www.mann4bassetlaw.com *Twitter:* @johnmannmp

CONSERVATIVE

MANN, SCOTT

North Cornwall *(Majority 7,200)*

Team PPS, Department for Transport

Scott Leslie Mann. Born 24 June 1977; Divorced (1 daughter).

Education: Wadebridge Boys' School.

Non-political career: Gardener; Butcher; Postman, Royal Mail 1995-2015.

Political career: Member for North Cornwall since 7 May 2015 general election; Team PPS, Department for Transport 2017-. *Select committees:* Member, Environmental Audit 2016-17. Founding member, Conservatives for Britain 2015-16. *Councils and public bodies:* Cornwall Council: Councillor 2009-16, Deputy leader, Conservative group -2012.

Recreations: Darts, fly-fishing.

Scott Mann MP, House of Commons, London SW1A 0AA
Tel: 020 7219 5744 *Email:* scott.mann.mp@parliament.uk
Constituency: 10 Market House Arcade, Fore Street, Bodmin, Cornwall PL31 2JA
Tel: 01208 74337 *Website:* www.scottmann.org.uk *Twitter:* @scottmann4NC

LABOUR

MARSDEN, GORDON

Blackpool South *(Majority 2,523)*

Shadow Minister for Education

Born 28 November 1953; Son of late George Henry and Joyce Marsden.

Education: Stockport Grammar School; New College, Oxford (MA history 1976); London University (PhD research in combined historical studies 1976-80); Harvard University (Kennedy Scholarship 1978-79); French, German.

Non-political career: Open University tutor/associate lecturer, arts faculty 1977-97; Public relations consultant 1980-85; Chief public affairs adviser to English Heritage 1984-85; Editor: *History Today* 1985-97, *New Socialist* 1989-90. Member, GMB.

Political career: Contested Blackpool South 1992 general election. Member for Blackpool South 1997-2010, for Blackpool South (revised boundary) since 6 May 2010 general election; PPS to: Lord Irvine of Lairg as Lord Chancellor 2001-03, Tessa Jowell as Secretary of State for Culture,

Media and Sport 2003-05, John Denham as Secretary of State for Communities and Local Government 2009-10; Shadow Minister for: Communities and Local Government 2010, Business, Innovation and Skills 2010-13, 2015-16, Transport 2013-15, Education (Further education and higher education, apprenticeships and skills) 2015-. *Select committees:* Member: Deregulation 1997-99, Ecclesiastical Committee 1997-2015, Education and Employment 1998-2001, Education and Employment (Education Sub-Committee) 1998-2001, Education and Skills 2005-07, Innovation, Universities[, Science] and Skills/Science and Technology 2007-10. Convenor, Labour Seaside Group of MPs 1997-2010; Hon. Secretary, PLP Departmental Committee for Culture, Media and Sport 2005-10; Chair, PLP North West Regional Group 2006-07. Chair, Seaside and Coastal Towns Manifesto Group 2007-10; Patron, LGBT Labour. *Councils and public bodies:* Member, National Skills Commission 2006-10.

Political interests: Heritage, education, international affairs, social affairs, disability, human rights; Caribbean, Eastern Europe, North Africa, Russia, USA.

Other: Member, Fabian Society 1975-: Chair, Young Fabians 1980-81; Judge, Ford Conservation Awards UK 1990-97; Board member, Institute of Historical Research 1996-2001; President, British Resorts and Destinations Association 1998-: Chair, Research and and Public Committee 2000-01; President, Blackpool Disability Services 2000-; Trustee, Dartmouth Street Trust; Board member: History Today Trust, Gareth Butler Trust; Trustee, History of Parliament Trust. Gibbs Prize in History 1975; Parliamentary Fellow, St Antony's College, Oxford 2003; Centenary Fellowship, Historical Association 2006.

Publications: Editor, Victorian Values (1990, 1998); Contributor to The History Debate (1990); Low Cost Socialism (1997); Contributor The English Question (Fabian Society, 2000); International History of Censorship (2001).

Recreations: Theatre, early music and medieval culture, swimming, heritage sites, architecture.

Gordon Marsden MP, House of Commons, London SW1A 0AA
Tel: 020 7219 1262 *Fax:* 020 7219 5859 *Email:* gordonmarsdenmp@parliament.uk
Constituency: 304 Highfield Road, Blackpool, Lancashire FY4 3JX
Tel: 01253 344143 *Fax:* 01253 344940 *Website:* www.gordonmarsden.com
Twitter: @gordonmarsden

LABOUR

MARTIN, SANDY

Ipswich *(Majority 831)*

Alexander Gordon Martin. Born 2 May 1957; Civil Partner.

Education: Merton College, Oxford (PPE) (dropped out 1977).

Political career: Member for Ipswich since 8 June 2017. *Select committees:* Member: Environment, Food and Rural Affairs 2017-, Public Administration and Constitutional Affairs 2017-. Contested Eastern region 2014 European Parliament election. Labour Party National Policy Forum 2015-17. *Councils and public bodies:* Suffolk County Council: Councillor 1997-2017, Leader of the Labour Group 2009-17; Councillor, Ipswich Borough Councillor 2002-14; Former Governor, Copleston High School.

Political interests: Electoral reform, environment, trade unions, poverty, injustice.

Recreations: Walking, cycling, poetry, singing.

Sandy Martin MP, House of Commons, London SW1A 0AA
Tel: 020 7219 1208 *Email:* sandy.martin.mp@parliament.uk
Constituency: 33 Silent Street, Ipswich, IP1 1TF
Tel: 01473 487648 *Twitter:* @sandyofipswich

LAB/CO-OP

MASKELL, RACHAEL

York Central *(Majority 18,575)*

Shadow Minister for Transport

Rachael Helen Maskell. Born 5 July 1972.

Education: University of East Anglia (BSc physiotherapy 1994).

Non-political career: Physiotherapist, NHS; Head of health, Unite. Regional, then National Official, Unite.

Political career: Member for York Central since 7 May 2015 general election; Shadow Minister for Defence 2015-16; Shadow Secretary of State for Environment, Food and Rural Affairs 2016-17; Shadow Minister for Transport 2017-. *Select committees:* Member: Health 2015, Ecclesiastical Committee 2015-.

Rachael Maskell MP, House of Commons, London SW1A 0AA
Tel: 020 7219 4525 *Email:* rachael.maskell.mp@parliament.uk
Constituency: 59 Holgate Road, York YO24 4AA
Tel: 01904 623713 *Website:* www.rachaelmaskell.com *Twitter:* @rachaelmaskell

SINN FÉIN

MASKEY, PAUL

Belfast West *(Majority 21,652)*

Paul John Maskey. Born 10 June 1967; Son of Alex and Teresa Maskey; Married Patricia (2 children).

Education: Edmund Rice College; Irish.

Political career: Member for Belfast West since 9 June 2011 by-election; Northern Ireland Assembly: MLA for Belfast West 2007-11, and for Belfast West (revised boundary) 2011-12: Deputy chair, Enterprise, Trade and Investment Committee 2007-08, Chair, Public Accounts Committee 2008-12; Sinn Féin: Deputy Whip, Spokesperson for: Public Accounts, Governance 2011-12. *Councils and public bodies:* Belfast City Council: Councillor 2001-09, Leader, Sinn Féin Group -2009.

Political interests: Poverty; Basque Country, Italy.

Other: Board member: Upper Andersonstown Community Forum, Greater Andersonstown Neighbourhood Partnership; Fáilte Feirste Thiar.

Recreations: Walking, five-a-side football.

Paul Maskey MP, House of Commons, London SW1A 0AA
Tel: 020 7219 3000 *Email:* paul.maskey.mp@parliament.uk
Constituency: c/o 51-55 Falls Road, Belfast BT12 4PD
Tel: 028 9034 7350 *Fax:* 028 9034 7360 *Email:* westbelfastmp@sinnfein.ie
Website: www.sinnfeinbelfast.com *Twitter:* @PaulMaskeyMP

CONSERVATIVE

MASTERTON, PAUL

East Renfrewshire *(Majority 4,712)*

Born 2 November 1985; Son of John and Mandy Masterton; Married Heather 2012 (1 daughter 1 son).

Education: George Watsons College; Dundee University (LLB 2007).

Non-political career: McGrigors: Trainee solicitor 2008-10, Solicitor 2010-12; Pinsent Mansons: Solicitor 2012-14, Associate 2014-17.

Political career: Member for East Renfrewshire since 8 June 2017. *Select committees:* Member, Scottish Affairs 2017-. Contested Paisley constituency 2016 Scottish Parliament election. Secretary, Renfrewshire and Inverclyde Conservative Association 2016-17.

Recreations: Family, tennis.

Paul Masterton MP, House of Commons, London SW1A 0AA
Tel: 020 7219 2528 *Email:* paul.masterton.mp@parliament.uk
Constituency: Spiersbridge House, 1 Spiersbridge Way, Thornliebank G46 8NG
Tel: 0141-648 8811 *Website:* www.paulmasterton.org.uk *Twitter:* @PM4EastRen

LABOUR

MATHESON, CHRIS

City of Chester *(Majority 9,176)*

PPS to John Healey as Shadow Secretary of State for Housing

Christian John Patrick Matheson. Born 2 January 1968; Married Katherine (2 daughters).

Education: Manchester Grammar School; London School of Economics (Degree).

Non-political career: Manager, electricity industry; Industrial officer, Unite. Member: Unite, GMB.

Political career: Member for City of Chester since 7 May 2015 general election; PPS to: Rachael Maskell as Shadow Secretary of State for Environment, Food and Rural Affairs 2016-17, John Healey as Shadow Secretary of State for Housing 2017-. *Select committees:* Member, Culture, Media and Sport/Digital, Culture, Media and Sport 2015-.

Countries of interest: Argentina, Colombia, Latin America.

Chris Matheson MP, House of Commons, London SW1A 0AA
Tel: 020 7219 8078 *Email:* chris.matheson.mp@parliament.uk
Constituency: Robinson House, 25 Castle Street, Chester, Cheshire CH1 2DS
Tel: 01244 343214 *Email:* chris@chrismatheson.co.uk *Website:* www.chrismatheson.co.uk
Twitter: @chrisM4Chester

CONSERVATIVE

MAY, THERESA

Maidenhead *(Majority 26,457)*

Prime Minister, First Lord of the Treasury and Minister for the Civil Service

Theresa Mary May. Born 1 October 1956; Daughter of late Rev Hubert and Zaidee Brasier; Married Philip May 1980.

Education: Wheatley Park Comprehensive School, Holton, Oxfordshire; St Hugh's College, Oxford (BA geography 1977, MA); French (basic).

Non-political career: Various posts latterly senior adviser, international affairs, Association for Payment Clearing Services 1985-97.

Political career: Contested North West Durham 1992 general election and Barking 1994 by-election. Member for Maidenhead 1997-2010, for Maidenhead (revised boundary) since 6 May 2010 general election; Opposition Spokesperson for Education and Employment (schools, disabled people and women) 1998-99; Member Shadow Cabinet 1999-2010: Spokesperson for Women's Issues 1999-2001, Shadow Secretary of State for: Education and Employment 1999-2001, Transport, Local Government and the Regions 2001-02, Transport 2002, Environment and Transport 2003-04, the Family 2004-05, Culture, Media and Sport 2005; Shadow Leader of the House of Commons 2005-09; Member, House of Commons Commission 2005-09; Shadow Minister for Women 2007-10; Shadow Secretary of State for Work and Pensions 2009-10; Secretary of State for the Home Department (Home Secretary) 2010-16; Minister for Women and Equalities 2010-12; Prime Minister, First Lord of the Treasury and Minister for the Civil Service 2016-. *Select committees:* Member: Education and Employment 1997-98, Education and Employment (Education Sub-Committee) 1997-99, Modernisation of the House of Commons 2006-10. Joint secretary, Conservative Party Committee for Home Affairs 1997-98; Chair, Conservative Transport/Local Government/Planning Policy Committee 2001-02. Conservative Party: Chair, Conservative Disability Group 1997-98, Party Chair 2002-03, Leader 2016-; Patron, Conservative Alumni; President, Conservatives Abroad. *Councils and public bodies:* Councillor, London Borough of Merton 1986-94.

Other: Chair of the Branch, Commonwealth Parliamentary Association (UK Branch) 2016-; President, British Group, Inter-Parliamentary Union; Chairman, British-American Parliamentary Group; Patron: Alexander Devine Children's Hospice, National Rheumatoid Arthritis Society, Electric Eels, Mission Direct, Maidenhead Festival of Music and Dance, Friends of St Andrew's Church (Sonning), Pink Shoe Club, Maidenhead Choral Society, Peel Society, Pure Charity Project, Maidenhead Civic Society League of Friends of St Marks Hospital, Maidenhead, Grandma Flew Spitfires, Stanley Baldwin Statue Appeal; Advisory Board Member, Renewal; Fellow, Royal Geographical Society; Honorary member, Rotary Club of Eastbourne; Joint Patron, St Andrew's Church building appeal, Sonning; Vice-president, Littlewick Green Show Society; Honorary Fellow, Chartered Institute of Marketing. Member, Worshipful Company of Marketors. *Spectator* awards: Double Act of the Year (with Kenneth Clarke MP) 2011, Minister of the Year 2012. PC 2003; Member, Maidenhead Conservative Club; President, United & Cecil Club; Member, Leander Club. President, Wargrave Girls Football Club; Honorary President, Lords and Commons Tennis Club; Honorary member: Maidenhead Golf Club, Ellesborough Golf Club.

Recreations: Walking, cooking.

Rt Hon Theresa May MP, House of Commons, London SW1A 0AA
Tel: 020 7219 5206 *Email:* mayt@parliament.uk
Constituency: c/o Maidenhead Conservative Association, 2 Castle End Farm, Ruscombe, Berkshire RG10 9XQ
Tel: 0118-934 5433 *Email:* office@maidenheadconservatives.com *Websites:* www.tmay.co.uk www.gov.uk/number10 *Twitter:* @theresa_may

CONSERVATIVE

MAYNARD, PAUL

Blackpool North and Cleveleys *(Majority 2,023)*

Parliamentary Under-Secretary of State for Rail, Accessibility and HS2, Department for Transport

Paul Christopher Maynard. Born 16 December 1975.

Education: St Ambrose College, Altrincham; University College, Oxford (BA modern history 1997); French, German.

Non-political career: Researcher, Hodgart Temporal 1997-99; Health policy officer, Conservative Party 1999-2002; Head of home affairs, Conservative Research Department 2001-02; Senior researcher, Reform 2003; Special adviser to Dr Liam Fox MP 2003-07.

Political career: Contested Twickenham 2005 general election. Member for Blackpool North and Cleveleys since 6 May 2010 general election; PPS: to Oliver Letwin: as Minister for Government Policy, Cabinet Office 2012-14, as Chancellor of the Duchy of Lancaster 2014, to Nick Boles as

Minister of State for Skills and Equalities, Departments for Business, Innovation and Skills and for Education 2014-15, to Amber Rudd as Secretary of State for Energy and Climate Change 2015-16; Parliamentary Under-Secretary of State, Department for Transport 2016- (for Rail, Accessibility and HS2 2017-). *Select committees:* Member: Transport 2010-12, Work and Pensions 2014-15. Vice-chair, Weaver Vale Conservative Association 1997-99.

Political interests: Education, social policy; Australia, Bosnia and Herzegovina, Germany, Moldova.

Other: Patron, Blackpool and District Choral Society. Society Champion, Charity Champion awards 2012.

Paul Maynard MP, House of Commons, London SW1A 0AA
Tel: 020 7219 7017 *Email:* paul.maynard.mp@parliament.uk
Constituency: Room 11, Blackpool Technology Management Centre, Faraday Way, Blackpool, Lancashire FY2 0JW
Tel: 01253 473071 *Website:* paulmaynard.co.uk *Twitter:* @PaulMaynardUK

LABOUR

MEARNS, IAN

Gateshead *(Majority 17,350)*

Chair, Select Committee on Backbench Business

James Ian Mearns. Born 21 April 1957; Son of James Mearns and Agnes Mearns, née Watson; Partner Anne (1 son 1 daughter from previous marriage).

Education: St Mary's Technical School, Newcastle upon Tyne.

Non-political career: Northern Gas 1974-85. Member: Unite, Unison.

Political career: Member for Gateshead since 6 May 2010 general election; PPS to Ivan Lewis as Shadow Secretary of State for International Development 2011-13. *Select committees:* Member, Education 2010-; Backbench Business: Member 2010-15, Chair 2015-; Member: High Speed Rail (London-West Midlands) Bill 2014-15, Liaison 2015-, Education, Skills and the Economy Sub-committee 2015-17. Chair PLP Departmental Group for Communities and Local Government 2011-15. *Councils and public bodies:* Gateshead Council: Councillor 1983-2010, Cabinet Member for: Education 1993-2002, Lifelong Learning, Adult Social Care, Jobs and Employment; Council Deputy Leader 2002-10; Local Government Association: Council representative, Vice-President 2010-; Member: Association of North East Councils, North East Regional Authority; Former chair of governors: Kelvin Grove Primary School, Gateshead, Thomas Hepburn Community Comprehensive, Felling.

Political interests: Education, local government, regional development, health, transport; Kurdistan (Iraq).

Other: Patron, Redheugh Boys Club; President, Trinity Community Association, Gateshead; Honorary Member, Royal Engineers; Trustee, Industry and Parliament Trust 2015-; Saltwell Social Club, Gateshead Corporation, Tyneside Irish Centre, Parliamentary Sports and Social Club.

Recreations: Sports – football, cricket.

Ian Mearns MP, House of Commons, London SW1A 0AA
Tel: 020 7219 7074 *Email:* ian.mearns.mp@parliament.uk
Constituency: 12 Regent Terrace, Gateshead NE8 1LU
Tel: 0191-477 0651 *Fax:* 0191-477 7383 *Website:* www.ianmearns.org.uk
Twitter: @IanMearnsMP

CONSERVATIVE

MENZIES, MARK

Fylde *(Majority 11,805)*

Mark Andrew Menzies. Born 18 May 1971; Single (no children).

Education: Keil School, Dumbarton; Glasgow University (MA economic and social history 1994).

Non-political career: Graduate trainee, Marks & Spencer 1994-95; Marketing executive, Asda supermarkets 1995-2008; Senior marketing executive, Morrisons supermarkets 2008-10.

Political career: Contested Glasgow Govan 2001 and Selby 2005 general elections. Member for Fylde since 6 May 2010 general election; PPS to: Charles Hendry as Minister of State, Department of Energy and Climate Change 2010-12, Mark Prisk as Minister of State for Housing, Department for Communities and Local Government 2012-13, Alan Duncan as Minister of State, Department for International Development 2013-14; Trade Envoy to Colombia, Chile and Peru 2017-. *Select committees:* Member: Scottish Affairs 2010, 2014-15, Joint Committee on the Draft Protection of Charities Bill 2014-15, Transport 2015-17, Finance 2016-, Regulatory Reform 2017-. Member, Conservative Party 1987-.

Political interests: Dementia, defence, energy, transport and infrastructure, farming, food retailing; Argentina, Australia, Middle East, USA.

Other: Social innovation marketing award, IGD/Unilever 2007.

Recreations: Skiing, walking, film.

Mark Menzies MP, House of Commons, London SW1A 0AA
Tel: 020 7219 7073 *Fax:* 020 7219 2235 *Email:* mark.menzies.mp@parliament.uk
Constituency: No constituency office publicised
Tel: 01253 739848 *Website:* www.markmenzies.org.uk

CONSERVATIVE

MERCER, JOHNNY

Plymouth, Moor View *(Majority 5,019)*

John Luther Mercer. Born 17 August 1981; Married Felicity Cornelius (2 daughters).

Education: Royal Military Academy, Sandhurst (2002).

Non-political career: British Army, serving at tactical and strategic level, including three combat tours of Afghanistan 2002-14.

Political career: Member for Plymouth, Moor View since 7 May 2015 general election. *Select committees:* Member: Defence 2015-, Health 2017-.

Political interests: Veterans, mental health, inequality, transport.

Publications: We Were Warriors (2017).

Johnny Mercer MP, House of Commons, London SW1A 0AA
Tel: 020 7219 2648 *Email:* johnny.mercer.mp@parliament.uk
Constituency: No constituency office publicised
Tel: 01752 876979 *Website:* johnnyforplymouth.co.uk *Twitter:* @JohnnyMercerUK

CONSERVATIVE

MERRIMAN, HUW

Bexhill and Battle *(Majority 22,165)*

Team PPS, Department for Work and Pensions

Huw William Merriman. Born 13 July 1973.

Education: Buckingham Secondary School; Aylesbury College; Durham University (LLB 1995); Inns of Court School of Law.

Non-political career: Called to the Bar, Inner Temple 1997.

Political career: Member for Bexhill and Battle since 7 May 2015 general election; Team PPS, Department for Work and Pensions 2017-. *Select committees:* Member: Transport 2015-, Procedures 2016-17. *Councils and public bodies:* Councillor, Wealden District Council 2007-15.

Political interests: Transport, education, health, social and economic policy; Ireland.

Other: Member: Parliamentary Delegation to Council of Europe, Legal and Human Rights Committee; Trustee and manager, Accra Crawford Youth Charity, Brixton 1998-2003.

Recreations: Cooking, sport, gardening, family.

Huw Merriman MP, House of Commons, London SW1A 0AA
Tel: 020 7219 1852 *Email:* huw.merriman.mp@parliament.uk
Constituency: 29-31 Sea Road, Bexhill on Sea, East Sussex TN40 1EE
Tel: 01424 736861 *Website:* www.huwmerriman.org.uk *Twitter:* @HuwMerriman

CONSERVATIVE

METCALFE, STEPHEN

South Basildon and East Thurrock *(Majority 11,490)*

Stephen James Metcalfe. Born 9 January 1966; Son of late David Metcalfe and Valerie Metcalfe; Married Angela Giblett 1988 (1 son 1 daughter).

Education: Loughton School; Buckhurst Hill County High School.

Non-political career: Order Clerk, Burrup Mathison, London 1985-86; Metloc Printers Ltd (family business): Sales Executive 1986-87, Studio Manager 1987-92, Director 1992-2011.

Political career: Contested Ilford South 2005 general election. Member for South Basildon and East Thurrock since 6 May 2010 general election; PPS to: Chris Grayling as Lord Chancellor and Secretary of State for Justice 2014-15, Nick Gibb as Minister of State for Schools, Department for Education 2015-16, Edward Timpson as Minister of State for Children and Families, Department for Education 2015-16; Board Member, Parliamentary Office of Science and Technology (POST) 2016-. *Select committees:* Science and Technology: Member 2010-15, 2017-, Chair 2016-17; Member, Liaison 2016-17. Deputy chairman, Essex Area Conservatives 2002-06; Member: Conservative Friends of Israel 2006-, Conservative Christian Fellowship 2006-. *Councils and public bodies:* Epping Forest District Council: Customer service e-government and ICT 2003-06, Customer service including waste management portfolio holder 2006-07.

Political interests: Economy, small business, foreign policy, science and technology, education; Africa, China, Japan, Middle East, USA.

Other: Founder, Wasters Wine Society; President, Northlands Park Community Centre, Basildon 2008-; United and Cecil Club. Woodford Rugby Club.

Recreations: Theatre, wine tasting, travel.

Stephen Metcalfe MP, House of Commons, London SW1A 0AA
Tel: 020 7219 7009 *Fax:* 020 7219 0306 *Email:* stephen.metcalfe.mp@parliament.uk
Constituency: South Basildon and East Thurrock Conservatives, 2 Orsett Business Centre, Stanford Road, Grays, Essex RM16 1BX
Tel: 01268 200430 *Website:* www.stephenmetcalfemp.com *Twitter:* @Metcalfe_SBET

LABOUR

MILIBAND, ED

Doncaster North *(Majority 14,024)*

Edward Samuel Miliband. Born 24 December 1969; Son of Ralph Miliband and Marion Miliband, née Kozak; Married Justine Thornton 2011 (later QC) (2 sons).

Education: Corpus Christi College, Oxford (BA philosophy, politics and economics); London School of Economics (MSc Econ).

Non-political career: Television journalist; Speechwriter and researcher to: Harriet Harman MP 1993, Gordon Brown MP as Shadow Chancellor of the Exchequer 1994-97; HM Treasury: Special adviser to Gordon Brown MP as Chancellor of the Exchequer 1997-2002, Chair, Council of Economic Advisers 2004-05; Fellow and lecturer in government, Harvard University 2002-04. Member, TGWU/USDAW.

Political career: Member for Doncaster North 2005-10, for Doncaster North (revised boundary) since 6 May 2010 general election; Parliamentary Secretary, Cabinet Office 2006-07; Minister for the Cabinet Office; Chancellor of the Duchy of Lancaster 2007-08; Secretary of State for Energy and Climate Change 2008-10; Shadow Secretary of State for Energy and Climate Change 2010; Leader of the Opposition 2010-15; Leader, Labour Party 2010-15.

Other: PC 2007.

Publications: Contributor, The Purple Book (Progress, 2011).

Rt Hon Ed Miliband MP, House of Commons, London SW1A 0AA
Tel: 020 7219 7318 *Email:* ed.miliband.mp@parliament.uk
Constituency: Diamond Business Centre, Bridge Works, Bentley, Doncaster, South Yorkshire DN5 9QP
Tel: 01302 875462 *Twitter:* @Ed_Miliband

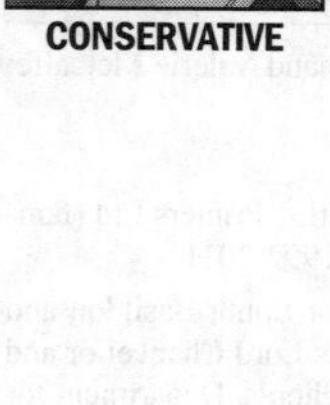

CONSERVATIVE

MILLER, MARIA

Basingstoke *(Majority 9,466)*

Chair, Select Committee on Women and Equalities

Maria Frances Lewis Miller. Born 26 March 1964; Daughter of John and June Lewis; Married Iain Miller 1990 (1 daughter 2 sons).

Education: Brynteg Comprehensive, Bridgend; London School of Economics (BSc economics 1985).

Non-political career: Advertising executive, Grey Advertising Ltd 1985-90; Marketing manager, Texaco 1990-94; Company director: Grey Advertising Ltd 1995-99, The Rowland Company/PR21 1999-2003.

Political career: Contested Wolverhampton North East 2001 general election. Member for Basingstoke 2005-10, for Basingstoke (revised boundary) since 6 May 2010 general election; Shadow Minister for: Education 2005-06, Family Welfare, including Child Support Agency 2006-07, Families 2007-10; Parliamentary Under-Secretary of State (Minister for Disabled People), Department for Work and Pensions 2010-12; Secretary of State for Culture, Media and Sport 2012-14; Minister for Women and Equalities 2012-14; Member, Commons Reference Group on Representation and Inclusion 2017-. *Select committees:* Member: Trade and Industry 2005-06, Children, Schools and Families 2007, Liaison 2015-; Chair, Women and Equalities 2015-. President, Wolverhampton North East Conservative Association 2001-07; Chair, Wimbledon Conservative Association 2002-03.

Political interests: Housing, education, media, UK and international women and equality issues, infrastructure provision, online crime; Belarus, Canada, Nepal, Turkey.

Other: Member, Executive Committee, Commonwealth Parliamentary Association United Kingdom 2017-; Trustee, Belarus Free Theatre. Rising Star, *House Magazine* awards 2012; Pink News MP of the Year 2015. PC 2012.

Recreations: Cycling.

Rt Hon Maria Miller MP, House of Commons, London SW1A 0AA
Tel: 020 7219 5749 *Email:* maria.miller.mp@parliament.uk
Constituency: No constituency office publicised *Website:* www.maria4basingstoke.co.uk
Twitter: @MariaMillerUK

CONSERVATIVE

MILLING, AMANDA

Cannock Chase *(Majority 8,391)*

Team PPS, Foreign and Commonwealth Office

Amanda Anne Milling. Born 12 March 1975; Daughter of Humphrey and Patricia Milling; Divorced.

Education: Moreton Hall; University College London (BSc economics and statistics 1997).

Non-political career: Researcher, SWI Research 1997-99; Director: Quaestor 1999-2009, Optimisa Research Ltd 2010-14.

Political career: Member for Cannock Chase since 7 May 2015 general election; PPS to Baroness Anelay of St Johns as Minister of State for the Commonwealth and the UN: Foreign and Commonwealth Office 2016-17, Department for International Development 2016; Team PPS, Foreign and Commonwealth Office 2017-. *Select committees:* Member: Business, Innovation and Skills 2015-16, Joint Committee on Consolidation, &c, Bills 2015-, Education, Skills and the Economy Sub-committee 2015-17, Arms Export Controls 2016, Business, Energy and Industrial Strategy 2016-17. Deputy Chair, Rossendale and Darwin Conservative Association 2012-14. *Councils and public bodies:* Councillor, Rossendale Borough Council 2009-14; Governor, Helmshore Primary School.

Political interests: Business and skills, economy, education and young people.

Recreations: Running.

Amanda Milling MP, House of Commons, London SW1A 0AA
Tel: 020 7219 8356 *Email:* amanda.milling.mp@parliament.uk
Constituency: 11a Market Street, Hednesford, Cannock, Staffordshire WS11 1AY
Tel: 01543 877142 *Email:* amanda@amandamilling.com *Website:* www.amandamilling.com
Twitter: @amandamilling

CONSERVATIVE

MILLS, NIGEL

Amber Valley *(Majority 8,300)*

Nigel John Mills. Born 28 October 1974; Married Alice 2013.

Education: Loughborough Grammar School; Newcastle University (classics 1996).

Non-political career: Accountant: PriceWaterhouseCoopers 1996-2008, Deloitte LLP 2008-10.

Political career: Member for Amber Valley since 6 May 2010 general election. *Select committees:* Member: Administration 2010-, Northern Ireland Affairs 2011-, Work and Pensions 2012-15, Public Accounts 2015-. Chairman, Conservative Backbench Policy Committee on Work and Pensions 2015-17. Deputy chair, Amber Valley Conservative Association. *Councils and public bodies:* Amber Valley Borough Council: Councillor 2004-11, Chair, scrutiny committee; Councillor, Heanor and Loscoe Town Council 2007-11.

Political interests: Employment, crime, anti-social behaviour, education, taxation.

Other: Member, British-Irish Parliamentary Assembly 2015-; Institute of Chartered Accountants in England and Wales.

Recreations: Sport.

Nigel Mills MP, House of Commons, London SW1A 0AA
Tel: 020 7219 7233 *Email:* nigel.mills.mp@parliament.uk
Constituency: Unicorn House, Wellington Street, Ripley, Derbyshire DE5 3EH
Tel: 01773 744341 *Fax:* 01773 744341 *Email:* nigel@nigelmillsmp.com *Twitter:* @nigelmills

CONSERVATIVE

MILTON, ANNE

Guildford *(Majority 17,040)*

Minister of State for Apprenticeships and Skills and Minister for Women, Department for Education

Anne Frances Milton. Born 3 November 1955; Married Dr Graham Henderson.

Education: Haywards Heath Grammar School, Sussex.

Non-political career: Nurse. Former shop steward, Royal College of Nursing 1970s.

Political career: Member for Guildford 2005-10, for Guildford (revised boundary) since 6 May 2010 general election; Shadow Minister for: Tourism 2006-07, Health 2007-10; Parliamentary Under-Secretary of State (Public Health), Department of Health 2010-12; Government Whip: (Lord Commissioner to HM Treasury) 2012-14, (Vice-Chamberlain of HM Household) 2014-15; Deputy Chief Whip (Treasurer of HM Household) 2015-17; Department for Education: Minister of State for Apprenticeships and Skills 2017-, Minister for Women 2017-; Member, Commons Reference Group on Representation and Inclusion 2017-. *Select committees:* Member: Health 2005-06, Selection 2012-14, 2015-17. *Councils and public bodies:* Reigate Borough Council: Councillor 1999-2004, Leader, Conservative group 2001-03.

Other: Patron: Surrey Law Centre, TALK, Prostrate Cancer Project, Guildford, Rape and Sexual Abuse Support Centre (RASASC), Home-Start Guildford, OG Cancer Project; Warden and member, Nurses Guild; President, Royal British Nurses' Association. PC 2015.

Rt Hon Anne Milton MP, House of Commons, London SW1A 0AA
Tel: 020 7219 8392 *Fax:* 020 7219 5239 *Email:* anne.milton.mp@parliament.uk
Constituency: 17a Home Farm, Loseley Park, Guildford, Surrey GU3 1HS
Tel: 01483 300330 *Fax:* 01483 300321 *Email:* info@guildfordconservatives.com
Twitter: @AnneMilton

CONSERVATIVE

MITCHELL, ANDREW

Sutton Coldfield *(Majority 15,339)*

Andrew John Bower Mitchell. Born 23 March 1956; Son of Sir David Mitchell (MP for Basingstoke 1964-83 and North West Hampshire 1983-97) and Pamela Mitchell; Married Sharon Bennet 1985 (2 daughters).

Education: Rugby School; Jesus College, Cambridge (MA history 1978) (Union President 1978); French.

Non-political career: UN Peacekeeping Forces Cyprus: 1st Royal Tank Regiment (SSLC). International and Corporate Finance, Lazard Brothers and Company Ltd 1979-87; Lazard Brothers: Consultant 1987-92, Director 1997-2009; Director: Miller Insurance Group 1997-2001, Financial Dynamics Holdings 1997-2002; Senior Strategy Adviser: Boots 1997-2000, Andersen Consulting/Accenture 1997-2009; Director, Commer Group 1998-2002; Supervisory Board Member, The Foundation 1999-2009, 2013-16; Senior Adviser: Montrose Associates 2015-, Investec 2015-, EY 2016-.

Political career: Contested Sunderland South 1983 general election. Member for Gedling 1987-97. Contested Gedling 1997 general election. Member for Sutton Coldfield 2001-10, for Sutton Coldfield (revised boundary) since 6 May 2010 general election; PPS to: William Waldegrave as Minister of State, Foreign and Commonwealth Office 1988-90, John Wakeham as Secretary of State for Energy 1990-92; Assistant Government Whip 1992-93; Government Whip 1993-95; Parliamentary Under-Secretary of State, Department of Social Security 1995-97; Shadow Minister for: Economic Affairs 2003-04, Home Affairs 2004-05; Shadow Secretary of State for International Development 2005-10; Secretary of State for International Development 2010-12; Chief Whip; Parliamentary Secretary to the Treasury September-October 2012; Member, Parliamentary and Political Service Honours Committee September-October 2012. *Select committees:* Member: Work and Pensions 2001-03, Modernisation of the House of Commons 2002-04, Parliamentary and Political Service Honours Committee 2012-13. Chair, Cambridge University Conservative Association 1977; Secretary, One Nation Group of Conservative MPs 1989-92, 2005-; Vice-chair, Conservative Party (candidates) 1992-93.

Political interests: International development, health, defence, economy, foreign policy; Africa, Far East, USA.

Other: Council SOS SAHEL 1992-2010; English Speaking Union Council International Debate Council 1998-2010; Council of management, GAP 1999-2006; Alexandra Rose Charity: Vice-chair 1999-2010, Trustee 2010-; Senior Research Fellow, Centre for Rising Powers, Cambridge University; Senior Research Associate, Jesus College, Cambridge University. Liveryman, Vintners' Company. Freedom, City of London. UN Military Medal 1978. PC 2010; Chair, Coningsby Club 1984-85.

Recreations: Music, cycling, skiing, walking.

Rt Hon Andrew Mitchell MP, House of Commons, London SW1A 0AA
Tel: 020 7219 8516 *Email:* andrew.mitchell.mp@parliament.uk
Constituency: Sutton Coldfield Conservative Association, 36 High Street, Sutton Coldfield, West Midlands B72 1UP
Tel: 0121-354 2229 *Fax:* 0121-321 1762 *Email:* info@suttoncoldfieldconservative.com
Websites: www.suttoncoldfieldconservatives.com www.andrew-mitchell-mp.co.uk

SINN FÉIN

MOLLOY, FRANCIE

Mid Ulster *(Majority 12,890)*

Francis Joseph Molloy. Born 16 December 1950; Son of late Arthur Molloy and Annie, née Daly; Married Ann Mulgrew 1971 (2 sons 2 daughters).

Education: St Patrick's Intermediate, Dungannon; FELDEN Government Training Centre (engineering 1967); Ulster University; Newry Further Education College (Foundation Studies humanities).

Non-political career: Trainee fitter welder, Feldon GTC 1966-67; Fitter/welder/sales, Ulster Plant (later Powerscreen) 1967-74; Self-employed welder/light engineer 1978-81. Former member, AEWU.

Political career: Member for Mid Ulster since 7 March 2013 by-election; Contested Northern Ireland region 1994 European Parliament election; Member: Northern Ireland Forum for Political Dialogue 1996, Sinn Féin Talks Team, Castle Buildings Talks 1997-98; MLA for Mid Ulster 1998-2013: Chair Assembly Committee on Finance and Personnel 1999-2002, Deputy Speaker 2006-11, Sinn Féin Spokesperson for: Victims, Families and Poverty 2011-12; Principal Deputy Speaker 2011-13; Sinn Féin Spokesperson for Environment 2012-13. *Councils and public bodies:* Councillor 1985-2011: Dungannon District Council, Dungannon and South Tyrone Borough Council, Mayor 2001, 2005, Deputy mayor 2003.

Political interests: Housing, rural affairs, Lough Neagh, engineering skills development; South Africa.

Other: Member, EU Committee of the Regions 2010-13. Clonmore Robert Emmetts Gaelic FC.

Recreations: Painting, art, mainly water colour, organic gardening, Spanish civil war.

Francie Molloy MP, House of Commons, London SW1A 0AA
Tel: 020 7219 3000
Constituency: 26 Burn Road, Cookstown, Co Tyrone BT80 8DN
Tel: 028 8676 5850 *Fax:* 028 8676 6734 *Email:* sinnfeincookstown@yahoo.com
Twitter: @FrancieMolloy

SCOTTISH NATIONAL PARTY

MONAGHAN, CAROL

Glasgow North West *(Majority 2,561)*

SNP Spokesperson for Education, Armed Forces and Veterans

Carol Frances Monaghan. Born 2 August 1972; Married Feargal Dalton (1 son 2 daughters).

Education: Strathclyde University (BSc laser physics and optoelectronics 1993); PGCE physics and maths.

Non-political career: Hyndland Secondary School: Head of Physics, Head of Science; Lecturer, Glasgow University; Consultant, SQA.

Political career: Member for Glasgow North West since 7 May 2015 general election; Board member, Parliamentary Office of Science and Technology 2015-; SNP Spokesperson for: Public Services and Education 2015-17, Education, Armed Forces and Veterans 2017-. *Select committees:* Member, Science and Technology 2015-17.

Carol Monaghan MP, House of Commons, London SW1A 0AA
Tel: 020 7219 6396 *Email:* carol.monaghan.mp@parliament.uk
Constituency: 500 Dumbarton Road, Glasgow G11 6SL
Tel: 0141-337 2211 *Website:* www.carol.monaghan.scot *Twitter:* @CMonaghanSNP

LABOUR

MOON, MADELEINE

Bridgend *(Majority 4,700)*

Born 27 March 1950; Daughter of Albert Ironside and Hilda Ironside; Married Stephen Moon 1983 (died 2015) (1 son).

Education: Whinney Hill School; Durham Girls Grammar School; Madeley College, Staffordshire (Cert Ed 1971); Keele University (BEd 1972); Cardiff University (CQSW, Dip SW 1980).

Non-political career: Social services directorate, Mid Glamorgan County Council 1980-86; Contracting officer, City and County of Swansea and senior social work practitioner 1996-2002; Residential care home inspector, Care Standards Inspectorate for Wales 2002-05. Member: GMB, Unison.

Political career: Member for Bridgend 2005-10, for Bridgend (revised boundary) since 6 May 2010 general election; PPS to: Jim Knight as Minister of State, Department for Children, Schools and Families 2007-08, Lord Hunt of Kings Heath as Minister of State, Department of Energy and Climate Change 2009-10. *Select committees:* Member: Environment, Food and Rural Affairs 2005-07, Welsh Affairs 2005-06, Defence 2009-, Panel of Chairs 2015-. Vice-chair, PLP Welsh Regional Group 2008-10. *Councils and public bodies:* Porthcawl Town Council 1990-2000: Councillor, Mayor 1992-93, 1995-96; Councillor, Bridgend Borough Council 1991-2004; Bridgend representative: Sports Council for Wales, Tourism South and West Wales; Chair, British Resorts Association 1999-2001.

Political interests: Environment, health and social welfare, care for people with disabilities and old people, police, prisons, suicide, defence, women's role in public life, RAF; Afghanistan, Central Asia, China, Colombia, Israel, MENA, Palestinian Territories, Pakistan, Russia, Turkey.

Other: Member: UK delegation to NATO Parliamentary Assembly 2010-, Executive Committee, Commonwealth Parliamentary Association UK 2015-; RAF Club.

Recreations: Theatre, film, reading, walking.

Madeleine Moon MP, House of Commons, London SW1A 0AA
Tel: 020 7219 0814 *Fax:* 020 7219 6488 *Email:* moonm@parliament.uk
Constituency: 47 Nolton Street, Bridgend, Vale of Glamorgan CF31 3AA
Tel: 01656 750002 *Fax:* 01656 660081 *Website:* www.madeleinemoonmp.com
Twitter: @madeleinemoon

CONSERVATIVE

MOORE, DAMIEN

Southport *(Majority 2,914)*

Born 26 April 1980.

Education: University of Central Lancashire (BA history 2005).

Non-political career: Retail manager, Asda.

Political career: Contested Southport 2015 general election. Member for Southport since 8 June 2017; Chair, Lancashire Conservatives. *Councils and public bodies:* Preston City Council: Councillor 2012-, Deputy Leader, Conservative group.

Damien Moore MP, House of Commons, London SW1A 0AA
Tel: 020 7219 1162 *Email:* damien.moore.mp@parliament.uk
Constituency: Details still to be confirmed *Website:* www.damienmoore.org.uk
Twitter: @moore4southport

LIBERAL DEMOCRAT

MORAN, LAYLA

Oxford West and Abingdon *(Majority 816)*

Liberal Democrat Shadow Secretary of State for Education and Young People

Layla Michelle Moran. Born 12 September 1982.

Education: Imperial College London (BSc physics 2003); Brunel University (PCGE 2006); UCL (MA comparative education 2008); French.

Non-political career: Maths and Physics Teacher, International School of Brussels 2003-07; Physics Teacher, Southbank International School 2007-13; Academic Development Manager, Oxford Study Courses Ltd 2008-17.

Political career: Contested Battersea 2010 and Oxford West and Abingdon 2015 general elections. Member for Oxford West and Abingdon since 8 June 2017; Liberal Democrat Shadow Secretary of State for: Education 2017-, Young People 2017-. *Select committees:* Member, Public Accounts 2017-. Contested West Central constituency 2012 GLA election.

Political interests: Flooding, science innovation, education, taxation, transport.

Layla Moran MP, House of Commons, London SW1A 0AA
Tel: 020 7219 3905 *Email:* layla.moran.mp@parliament.uk
Constituency: Details still to be confirmed *Website:* www.laylamoran.com *Twitter:* @laylamoran

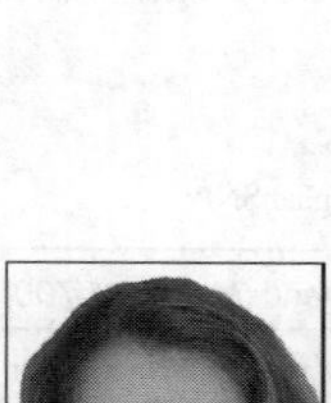

CONSERVATIVE

MORDAUNT, PENNY

Portsmouth North *(Majority 9,965)*

Minister of State for Disabled People, Health and Work, Department for Work and Pensions

Penelope Mary Mordaunt. Born 4 March 1973; Daughter of John Mordaunt and Jennifer Snowden.

Education: Oaklands RC Comprehensive School, Waterlooville; Reading University (philosophy) (President Students' Union).

Non-political career: Royal Navy Reservist on List 6 2015-. Magician's assistant to Will Ayling, President of Magic Circle; Head of foreign press, George W Bush's presidential campaign 2000;

Former communications director: London Borough of Kensington and Chelsea Council, Freight Transport Association, National Lottery; Director of strategy, policy and partnerships, Diabetes UK; Associate, Hanover.

Political career: Contested Portsmouth North 2005 general election. Member for Portsmouth North since 6 May 2010 general election; PPS to Philip Hammond as Secretary of State for Defence 2013-14; Parliamentary Under-Secretary of State, Department for Communities and Local Government 2014-15; Minister of State for: the Armed Forces, Ministry of Defence 2015-16, Disabled People, Health and Work, Department for Work and Pensions 2016-. *Select committees:* Member: European Scrutiny 2010-13, Defence 2010-13, Arms Export Controls 2011-13, Joint Committee on Privacy and Injunctions 2011-12. Member, Executive, 1922 Committee 2012-13. *Councils and public bodies:* Commissioner, Commission on Assisted Dying 2010-12.

Political interests: Care and quality of life for the elderly, healthcare, defence, the arts, space; India, USA.

Other: British Astronomical Association; Trustee, Wymering Manor Trust; Patron: Enable Ability, Portsmouth, The Victoria Cross. Speech of the Year, *Spectator* awards 2014.

Recreations: Painting, astronomy, Burmese cats.

Penny Mordaunt MP, House of Commons, London SW1A 0AA
Tel: 020 7219 3000 *Email:* penny.mordaunt.mp@parliament.uk
Constituency: Ground Floor, 1000 Lakeside, North Harbour, Portsmouth, Hampshire PO6 3EN
Tel: 023 9237 5377 *Website:* www.pennymordaunt.com *Twitter:* @PennyMordaunt

MORDEN, JESSICA

Newport East *(Majority 8,003)*

LABOUR

Opposition Whip

Jessica Elizabeth Morden. Born 29 May 1968; Daughter of Mick and Margaret Morden; Partner Sion Ffrancon Jones (1 daughter 1 son).

Education: Croesyceiliog Comprehensive School; Birmingham University (BA history 1989).

Non-political career: Labour Party organiser; Political assistant to Llew Smith MEP; Constituency assistant to Huw Edwards MP; General Secretary, Welsh Labour Party 1999-2005. Member, GMB.

Political career: Member for Newport East since 5 May 2005 general election; PPS: to Secretaries of State for Wales: Peter Hain 2007-08, 2009-10, Paul Murphy 2008-09; to Shadow Secretaries of State for Wales: Peter Hain 2011-12, Owen Smith 2012-15; Opposition Whip 2015-; Member, Speaker's Committee on the Electoral Commission 2015-17. *Select committees:* Member: Constitutional Affairs/Justice 2005-10, Modernisation of the House of Commons 2005-06, Welsh Affairs 2005-07, 2010-15, Standing Orders 2015-, Selection 2016-.

Political interests: Anti-social behaviour, electoral issues, police, children, steel industry.

Recreations: Cinema, gym.

Jessica Morden MP, House of Commons, London SW1A 0AA
Tel: 020 7219 6213 *Fax:* 020 7219 6196 *Email:* jessica.morden.mp@parliament.uk
Constituency: Room 2, Seventh Floor, Clarence House, Clarence Place, Newport, Gwent NP19 7AA
Tel: 01633 841725 *Fax:* 01633 841727 *Website:* www.jessicamorden.com
Twitter: @jessicamordenmp

MORGAN, NICKY

Loughborough *(Majority 4,269)*

CONSERVATIVE

Chair, Select Committee on Treasury

Nicola Ann Morgan. Born 10 October 1972; Daughter of Peter and Jennifer Griffith; Married Jonathan Morgan 2000 (1 son).

Education: Surbiton High School, Kingston-upon-Thames; St Hugh's College, Oxford (BA law 1993, MA); Legal Practice Course 1994.

Non-political career: Trainee/assistant solicitor, Theodore Goddard 1994-97; Assistant solicitor, Allen & Overy 1998-2002; Corporate professional support lawyer, Travers Smith 2002-10.

Political career: Contested Islington South and Finsbury 2001 and Loughborough 2005 general elections. Member for Loughborough since 6 May 2010 general election; PPS to David Willetts as Minister of State for Universities and Science 2010-12; Assistant Government Whip 2012-13; HM Treasury: Economic Secretary 2013-14, Financial Secretary 2014; Minister for Women, Department for Culture, Media and Sport (attending Cabinet) 2014; Secretary of State for Education and

Minister for Women and Equalities 2014-16. *Select committees:* Member, Business, Innovation and Skills 2010; Ex-officio Member, Public Accounts 2013-14; Chair, Treasury 2017-; Member, Liaison 2017-. Chair, Wessex Young Conservatives 1995-97; Vice-chair, Battersea Conservatives 1997-99.

Political interests: Business, financial services, economy, higher education, mental health; Bangladesh.

Other: Vice-chairman, Indo British Trade Council; Founder, Bluelist Organisation 2002-04; Member, advisory board, Finito Education Ltd 2016-; Member, Law Society; Industry and Parliament Trust; RNIB, Mind, Rethink, Rainbows Hospice, Carpenters Arms, World Vision. PC 2014.

Publications: Ombudsmen – Time for Reform? (Bretwalda Books); The Civil War in Loughborough.

Recreations: Choral singing, cookery, reading, theatre, cinema, running.

Rt Hon Nicky Morgan MP, House of Commons, London SW1A 0AA
Tel: 020 7219 7224 *Email:* nicky.morgan.mp@parliament.uk
Constituency: 18 Pinfold Gate, Loughborough, Leicestershire LE11 1BE
Tel: 01509 262723 *Email:* jane.hunt@parliament.uk *Website:* www.nickymorgan.com
Twitter: @nickymorgan01

LABOUR

MORGAN, STEPHEN

Portsmouth South *(Majority 1,554)*

PPS to Andrew Gwynne as Shadow Secretary of State for Communities and Local Government and National Campaign Co-ordinator

Stephen James Morgan. Born 17 January 1981.

Education: Priory School, Southsea; Portsmouth College, Baffins; Bristol University (BA politics and sociology); Goldsmiths University (MA politics).

Non-political career: Various roles, Portsmouth City Council; Head of community engagement, Kensington and Chelsea Borough Council 2008-15; Chief executive, Basingstoke Voluntary Action 2015-17.

Political career: Contested Orpington 2010 general election. Member for Portsmouth South since 8 June 2017; PPS to Andrew Gwynne as Shadow Secretary of State for Communities and Local Government and National Campaign Co-ordinator 2017-; *Councils and public bodies:* Councillor, Portsmouth City Council 2016-.

Political interests: Education, defence, local government.

Stephen Morgan MP, House of Commons, London SW1A 0AA
Tel: 020 7219 3906 *Email:* stephen.morgan.mp@parliament.uk
Constituency: Details still to be confirmed *Website:* www.stephenjmorgan.org
Twitter: @StephenMorganMP

INDEPENDENT

MORRIS, ANNE MARIE

Newton Abbot *(Con Majority 17,160)*

Born 5 July 1957; Daughter of Margaret Agg and late John Backes.

Education: Bryanston School, Dorset; Hertford College, Oxford (BA jurisprudence 1980); College of Law, London (Law Society finals 1981); Open University (MBA 1997); Harvard University (leadership programme 2004); School of Coaching, Strathclyde University (Diploma executive coaching 2007); French.

Non-political career: Trainee solicitor, Withers, London 1981-83; Corporate finance lawyer, Norton Rose, London 1983-85; Corporate commercial banking lawyer, Crossman Block, London 1985; Asset finance lawyer, Sinclair Roche & Temerley, Singapore 1986-88; Allen & Overy, London: Corporate finance lawyer 1988-90, Head of education and training 1990-93; Director of professional and business development, Baker & McKenzie 1993-95; Director of marketing and business development, Simmons & Simmons 1995-97; Marketing director, tax and legal services, PricewaterhouseCoopers 1997-99; Global marketing director: Ernst & Young 1999-2002, Linklaters 2002-05; Director, Manteion Ltd.

Political career: Member for Newton Abbot since 6 May 2010 general election; PPS to: Nick Boles as Minister of State for Skills, Department for Business, Innovation and Skills and Department for Education 2015-16, Jo Johnson as Minister of State for Universities and Science, Department for Business, Innovation and Skills 2015-16. *Select committees:* Member: Work and Pensions 2012-15, Public Accounts 2016-17. Conservative Whip suspended July 2017-. *Councils and public bodies:* Councillor, West Sussex County Council 2005-07; Associate Governor, Rydon Primary School, Kingsteignton; Governor, Newton Abbot College.

Political interests: Micro and small businesses, health and the NHS, social care, the elderly, education, vocational training and apprenticeships.

Other: Director: LawWorks, Small Business Bureau; Member: Devon and Cornwall Board, Institute of Directors 2001-, Federation of Small Businesses; Fellow, Chartered Institute of Marketing 2002; Member: Law Society of England and Wales, European Mentoring and Coaching Council; Dame Hannah Roger Trust at Seale-Hayne.

Recreations: Horse riding, dog walking.

Anne Marie Morris MP, House of Commons, London SW1A 0AA
Tel: 020 7219 3000 *Fax:* 020 7219 6578 *Email:* annemarie.morris.mp@parliament.uk
Constituency: 2 Salisbury House, Salisbury Road, Newton Abbot, Devon TQ12 2DF
Tel: 01626 368277 *Email:* annemarie@annemariemorris.co.uk
Website: www.annemariemorris.co.uk *Twitter:* @AnneMarieMorris

CONSERVATIVE

MORRIS, DAVID

Morecambe and Lunesdale *(Majority 1,399)*

PPS to James Brokenshire as Secretary of State for Northern Ireland

David Thomas Morris. Born 3 January 1966; Son of Lieutenant Commander Alan Morris, retired Royal Navy, and Vera Morris; Divorced (2 sons); partner Emma Smith.

Education: St Andrews School, Bahamas; Lowton High School.

Non-political career: Honorary Lieutenant Commander, Royal Navy (Armed Forces Parliamentary Scheme). Song writer and session guitar player, music industry; Former managing director, David Morris Hairdressing; Commercial property investor, northern England.

Political career: Contested Blackpool South 2001 and Carmarthen West and South Pembrokeshire 2005 general elections. Member for Morecambe and Lunesdale since 6 May 2010 general election; Self-Employment Ambassador 2014-; PPS: to Secretaries of State for Wales: Stephen Crabb 2014-16, Alun Cairns 2016, to David Mundell as Secretary of State for Scotland 2016-17, to James Brokenshire as Secretary of State for Northern Ireland 2017-. *Select committees:* Member: Science and Technology 2010-12, 2012-14, Administration 2012-14, Political and Constitutional Reform 2014-15, 2017-. Chair, Conservative Friends of Nuclear Energy.

Political interests: Nuclear energy, small business, maritime affairs; Bahamas, Hong Kong.

Other: Government-appointed member, National Hairdressing Council.

Recreations: Playing and collecting guitars, classic cars.

David Morris MP, House of Commons, London SW1A 0AA
Tel: 020 7219 7234 *Email:* david.morris.mp@parliament.uk
Constituency: Office 204, Riverway House, Morecambe Road, Lancaster, Lancashire LA1 2RX
Tel: 01524 841225 *Website:* www.davidmorris.org.uk *Twitter:* @davidmorrisml

LABOUR

MORRIS, GRAHAME

Easington *(Majority 14,892)*

Grahame Mark Morris. Born 13 March 1961; Son of late Richard Morris, colliery electrician, and Constance Morris, pit canteen worker; Married Michelle Hughes 1986 (2 sons).

Education: Peterlee Howletch Secondary School; Newcastle College (BTEC Ordinary National Certificate); Newcastle Polytechnic (BTEC Higher National Certificate medical laboratory sciences).

Non-political career: Medical laboratory scientific officer, Sunderland Royal Infirmary 1980-87; Researcher and constituency caseworker to John Cummings MP 1987-2010. Member, Unite.

Political career: Member for Easington since 6 May 2010 general election; PPS to: Meg Hillier as Shadow Secretary of State for Energy and Climate Change 2010-11, Rachel Reeves as Shadow Chief Secretary to the Treasury 2011-12; Opposition Whip 2015-16; Shadow Secretary of State for Communities and Local Government and for Housing; Shadow Minister for the Constitutional Convention 2016. *Select committees:* Member: Health 2010-15, Joint Committee on the Draft Care and Support Bill 2013, Unopposed Bills (Panel) 2013-15, Joint Committee on Consolidation, &c, Bills 2015-. Member, Labour Party 1976-; Secretary, Easington Constituency Labour Party 1996-2006. *Councils and public bodies:* Councillor, Easington District Council 1987-2003; Non-executive director, City Hospitals Sunderland NHS Trust 1997-2005.

Political interests: NHS, local government, economic regeneration, public health, housing; China, Cuba, Venezuela.

Other: Haswell and District Mencap, Easington Riding for the Disabled, World Vision, Shelter, Dogs Trust; Peterlee Labour Club, Easington Colliery Workingmen's Club CIU, Southside Social Club Easington Village.

Grahame Morris MP, House of Commons, London SW1A 0AA
Tel: 020 7219 1283 *Email:* grahame.morris.mp@parliament.uk
Constituency: The Glebe Centre Annex, Durham Place, Murton, Seaham, Co Durham SR7 9BX
Tel: 0191-526 2828 *Fax:* 0191-526 2828 *Email:* robert.adcock@parliament.uk
Website: www.grahamemorrismp.co.uk *Twitter:* @grahamemorris

CONSERVATIVE

MORRIS, JAMES

Halesowen and Rowley Regis *(Majority 5,253)*

PPS to Damian Green as First Secretary of State and Minister for the Cabinet Office

James George Morris. Born 4 February 1967; Married Anna Mellitt (1 son 1 daughter).

Education: Nottingham High School; Birmingham University (English literature); Oxford University (Postgraduate research); Cranfield School Management (MBA).

Non-political career: Managing director: 1996-2001, Vice-Versa Ltd 2001-06; Director, Mind the Gap 2003-08; Chief executive officer, Localis 2008-10.

Political career: Member for Halesowen and Rowley Regis since 6 May 2010 general election; PPS to: Esther McVey as Minister of State for Employment, Department for Work and Pensions 2014-15, David Lidington as Minister of State for Europe, Foreign and Commonwealth Office 2015-16, Jeremy Hunt as Secretary of State for Health 2016-17, Damian Green as First Secretary of State and Minister for the Cabinet Office 2017-. *Select committees:* Member, Communities and Local Government 2010-14.

Political interests: Localism, local government, foreign affairs.

Publications: Change Starts Small (2004); Big Ideas (2008); Million Vote Mandate (2008); Can Localism Deliver? (2009); The Bottom Line (2009); For Good Measure (2010); Co-author, Freedom, Responsibility and the State: Curbing Over-Mighty Government (Politeia, 2012).

Recreations: Cricket, family, theatre, music.

James Morris MP, House of Commons, London SW1A 0AA
Tel: 020 7219 8715 *Fax:* 020 7219 1429 *Email:* james.morris.mp@parliament.uk
Constituency: Trinity Point, New Road, Halesowen, West Midlands B63 3HY
Tel: 0121-550 6777 *Email:* hadleys@parliament.uk *Website:* www.jamesmorrismp.com
Twitter: @JamesMorris

CONSERVATIVE

MORTON, WENDY

Aldridge-Brownhills *(Majority 14,307)*

PPS to Priti Patel as Secretary of State for International Development

Born 9 November 1967; Daughter of Thomas and Edna Hunter; Married David Morton 1990.

Education: Wensleydale Comprehensive School, Leyburn; Open University (Diploma German; MBA); German.

Non-political career: Executive officer, HM Diplomatic Services, London 1987-89; Sales, marketing and business administration 1989-2015; Director, DM Electronics Ltd 1991-.

Political career: Contested Newcastle upon Tyne Central 2005 and Tynemouth 2010 general elections. Member for Aldridge-Brownhills since 7 May 2015 general election; PPS to: Jo Johnson as Minister of State for Universities, Science, Research and Innovation, Department for Business, Energy and Industrial Strategy 2016-17, Priti Patel as Secretary of State for International Development 2017-. *Select committees:* Member: International Development 2015-17, Regulatory Reform 2015-, Arms Export Controls 2016-17, Backbench Business 2016. Chair, Richmond Conservative Association 2012-14; Vice-chair (Social Action), Conservative Party 2013-14. *Councils and public bodies:* Councillor, Richmondshire District Council 2002-06.

Political interests: EU referendum, communities, local business, local environment, business, enterprise.

Other: Volunteer, Project Umubano; Rotary Club.

Recreations: Running, cooking.

Wendy Morton MP, House of Commons, London SW1A 0AA
Tel: 020 7219 8784 *Email:* wendy.morton.mp@parliament.uk
Constituency: 82 Walsall Road, Aldridge, Walsall WS9 0JW
Tel: 01922 452228 *Website:* wendymorton.co.uk *Twitter:* @morton_wendy

CONSERVATIVE

MUNDELL, DAVID

Dumfriesshire, Clydesdale and Tweeddale *(Majority 9,441)*

Secretary of State for Scotland

David Gordon Mundell. Born 27 May 1962; Son of Dorah Mundell, hotelier; Married Lynda Carmichael 1987 (divorced) (2 sons 1 daughter).

Education: Lockerbie Academy; Edinburgh University (LLB 1984); Strathclyde University Business School (MBA 1991); French, German.

Non-political career: Solicitor, Maxwell Waddell 1987-89; Corporate lawyer, Biggart Baillie & Gifford, Glasgow 1989-91; BT Scotland: Group legal adviser 1991-98, Head of national affairs 1998-99.

Political career: Member for Dumfriesshire, Clydesdale and Tweeddale since 5 May 2005 general election; Shadow Secretary of State for Scotland 2005-10; Parliamentary Under-Secretary of State, Scotland Office 2010-15; Secretary of State for Scotland 2015-. *Select committees:* Member, Scottish Affairs 2005-10. Contested Dumfries constituency 1999 and 2003 Scottish Parliament elections. MSP for South of Scotland region 1999-2005. Chairman, Scottish Conservative and Unionist Party 2011-14. *Councils and public bodies:* Councillor: Annandale and Eskdale District Council 1984-86, Dumfries and Galloway Council 1986-87.

Political interests: Business, commerce, rural affairs; Sierra Leone, USA.

Other: Member: Dyspraxia Foundation, Law Society of Scotland 1986-, Law Society 1992-; Trustee: Lockerbie Trust, Lockerbie Swimming Pool Trust. PC 2010.

Rt Hon David Mundell MP, House of Commons, London SW1A 0AA
Tel: 020 7219 4895 *Fax:* 020 7219 2707 *Email:* david.mundell.mp@parliament.uk
Constituency: Monro House, Duncan Drive, Moffat, Dumfriesshire DG10 9JW
Tel: 01683 222746 *Fax:* 01683 222796 *Email:* david@davidmundell.com
Website: www.davidmundell.com *Twitter:* @DavidMundellDCT

LABOUR

MURRAY, IAN

Edinburgh South *(Majority 15,514)*

Born 10 August 1976; Son of Lena Murray and late James Brownlie Murray; Partner Hannah Woolfson.

Education: Wester Hailes Education Centre; Edinburgh University (MA social policy and law 1997).

Non-political career: Royal Blind Asylum 1996-97; Aegon UK 1998-99; Operations director, Internet TV station 1999-2001; Director, 100mph Events Ltd 2001-; Partner, Alibi Bars 2005-11. Member: USDAW, Community.

Political career: Member for Edinburgh South since 6 May 2010 general election; PPS to Ivan Lewis as Shadow Secretary of State for Culture, Media and Sport 2010-11; Shadow Minister for: Business, Innovation and Skills 2011-13, Trade and Investment 2013-15; Shadow Secretary of State for Scotland 2015-16; Member, Public Accounts Commission 2015-. *Select committees:* Member: Environmental Audit 2010-12, Business, Innovation and Skills 2010-11, Arms Export Controls 2010-12, Scottish Affairs 2016-17, Foreign Affairs 2016-. Vice-chair, PLP Departmental Group for Culture, Olympics, Media and Sport 2010-11. Member: Labour Party, Co-operative Party; Campaign manager, Edinburgh Pentlands, 2001 general election; Westminster Spokesperson for Scottish Labour, Scottish Shadow Cabinet 2016-. *Councils and public bodies:* Councillor, Edinburgh City Council 2003-10.

Political interests: Education, services for disabled people, social justice, equal opportunities, environment, conservation, business; South America, Middle East, Nepal, USA.

Other: Substitute Member, UK delegation, Parliamentary Assembly of the Council of Europe 2016-; Member, Executive Committee, Commonwealth Parliamentary Association United Kingdom 2017-; Member, Fabian Society; Trustee, Great War Memorial Committee; McCrae's Battalion Trust 2007-; Fellow, Industry and Parliament Trust 2011-; Chair, Foundation of Hearts; Director, Heart of Midlothian Football Club plc; Supporter: Care for the Wild, Amnesty International.

Recreations: Sport, reading, cooking, cycling.

Ian Murray MP, House of Commons, London SW1A 0AA
Tel: 020 7219 7064 *Email:* ian.murray.mp@parliament.uk
Constituency: 31 Minto Street, Edinburgh EH9 2BT
Tel: 0131-662 4520 *Email:* ian@ianmurraymp.co.uk *Website:* www.ianmurraymp.co.uk
Twitter: @ianmurraymp

CONSERVATIVE

MURRAY, SHERYLL

South East Cornwall *(Majority 17,443)*

Born 4 February 1956; Married Neil (died 2011) (1 son 1 daughter); partner Robert Davidson.

Education: Torpoint Comprehensive School.

Non-political career: Insurance and NHS.

Political career: Member for South East Cornwall since 6 May 2010 general election; PPS: to Ed Vaizey as Minister of State for Culture and the Digital Economy, Departments for Business, Innovation and Skills and for Culture, Media and Sport 2015-16, to Andrea Leadsom: as Minister of State, Department of Energy and Climate Change 2015-16, as Secretary of State for Environment, Food and Rural Affairs 2016-17. *Select committees:* Member: Environmental Audit 2010-12, Environment, Food and Rural Affairs 2012-15, 2017-. Member, Executive, 1922 Committee 2012-15, 2017-. *Councils and public bodies:* Former councillor, Cornwall County Council; Caradon District Council: Councillor, Leader, Conservative group.

Political interests: Environment, tourism, Royal Navy; America, Middle East, UK.

Other: President, Palace of Westminster Lions Club 2014-; Fishermen's Mission. Animal Welfare Champion, Charity Champion awards 2012.

Recreations: Formula 1.

Sheryll Murray MP, House of Commons, London SW1A 0AA
Tel: 020 7219 3000 *Email:* sheryll.murray.mp@parliament.uk
Constituency: The Parade, Liskeard, Cornwall PL14 6AF
Tel: 01579 344428 *Email:* sheryll@sheryllmurray.com *Website:* www.sheryllmurray.com
Twitter: @sheryllmurray

CONSERVATIVE

MURRISON, ANDREW

South West Wiltshire *(Majority 18,326)*

Chair, Select Committee on Northern Ireland Affairs

Andrew William Murrison. Born 24 April 1961; Son of William Murrison and Marion Murrison, née Horn; Married Jennifer Munden 1994 (5 daughters).

Education: Harwich High School; The Harwich School; Bristol University (MB CHB 1984; MD 1995); Cambridge University (DPH medicine 1996); French.

Non-political career: Surgeon Commander Royal Navy 1981-2000; Royal Naval Reserve 2000-: Served in Iraq (Operation Telic II) 2003. Principal medical officer, HM Naval Base Portsmouth 1996-99; Staff officer, Commander-In-Chief Fleet 1999-2000; Locum consultant occupational physician, Gloucestershire Royal Hospital and GP 2000-01.

Political career: Member for Westbury 2001-10, for South West Wiltshire since 6 May 2010 general election; Shadow Minister for: Public Services, Health and Education 2003-04, Health 2004-07, Defence 2007-10; PPS to Andrew Lansley as Secretary of State for Health 2010-12; Prime Minister's Special Representative for the Centenary Commemoration of the First World War 2011-14; Parliamentary Under-Secretary of State (International Security Strategy), Ministry of Defence 2012-14; Parliamentary Under-Secretary of State, Northern Ireland Office 2014-15; Trade Envoy to Morocco and Tunisia 2016-. *Select committees:* Member: Science and Technology 2001-05, Joint Committee on the Draft Investigatory Powers Bill 2015-16, Joint Committee on the National Security Strategy 2015-, Liaison 2017-; Chair, Northern Ireland Affairs 2017-.

Political interests: Health, defence; Morocco, Iraq.

Other: Royal British Legion. Gilbert Blane Medal 1994; Warminster Conservative Club, Royal British Legion Warminster Branch, Vice-president, Trowbridge White Ensign Association, Westbury Lions Club.

Publications: Tommy This an' Tommy That: The Military Covenant (Biteback, 2011).

Recreations: Sailing, skiing.

Dr Andrew Murrison MP, House of Commons, London SW1A 0AA
Tel: 020 7219 8337 *Email:* murrisona@parliament.uk
Constituency: Suite 1, Holloway House, Epsom Square, White Horse Business Park, Trowbridge, Wiltshire BA14 0XG
Tel: 01225 358584 *Fax:* 01225 358583 *Email:* packerj@parliament.uk
Website: www.andrewmurrison.co.uk *Twitter:* @AWMurrison

LABOUR

NANDY, LISA

Wigan *(Majority 16,027)*

Lisa Eva Nandy. Born 9 August 1979; Daughter of Dipak Nandy, academic and founding director of the Runnymede Trust, and Luise Nandy, television producer.

Education: Parrs Wood Comprehensive School, Manchester; Holy Cross Sixth Form College, Bury; Newcastle University (BA politics 2001); Birkbeck University, London (MSc government, policy and politics 2005).

Non-political career: Parliamentary assistant to Neil Gerrard MP 2001-03; Policy researcher, Centrepoint 2003-05; Policy adviser, Children's Society 2005-10. Member: Unite, CWU.

Political career: Member for Wigan since 6 May 2010 general election; PPS to Tessa Jowell as Shadow Minister for London and the Olympics 2011-12; Shadow Minister for: Children and Families 2012-13, Cabinet Office 2013-15; Shadow Secretary of State for Energy and Climate Change 2015-16. *Select committees:* Member, Education 2010-12. Vice-chair, PLP Departmental Group for Communities and Local Government 2010-11. Member, Wigan Labour Party. *Councils and public bodies:* London Borough of Hammersmith and Fulham Council: Councillor 2006-10, Shadow Cabinet Member for Housing and Regeneration; Governor, Brackenbury Primary School.

Political interests: International corporate responsibility, children, poverty, low pay; Colombia.

Other: Director, Lyric Theatre, Hammersmith 2006-10; Member, Amnesty International.

Publications: Author: Waiting in Line: Young Refugees in the Labour Market (Centrepoint, 2003), Bed and Breakfast: Unfit Housing for Young People (Centrepoint, 2005), Co-author, with: Nicola Clarke, Living on the Edge of Despair (The Children's Society, 2008); Caroline Lucas MP and Chris Bowers, The Alternative: Towards a New Progressive Politics (Biteback, 2016).

Recreations: Rugby league, theatre and the arts.

Lisa Nandy MP, House of Commons, London SW1A 0AA
Tel: 020 7219 7188 *Fax:* 020 7219 5152 *Email:* lisa.nandy.mp@parliament.uk
Constituency: Room S46, Second Floor, Wigan Investment Centre, Waterside Drive, Wigan WN3 5BA
Tel: 01942 242047 *Fax:* 01942 239451 *Website:* www.lisanandy.co.uk *Twitter:* @lisanandy

CONSERVATIVE

NEILL, ROBERT

Bromley and Chislehurst *(Majority 9,590)*

Chair, Select Committee on Justice

Robert James Macgillivray Neill. Born 24 June 1952; Son of John Neill and Elsie Neill, née Coombs; Married Daphne White 2009.

Education: Abbs Cross School, Havering; London School of Economics (LLB 1973); French.

Non-political career: Trainee dealer, London Stock Exchange 1974; Barrister in private practice (specialising in criminal law) 1975-2006; Called to the Irish Bar 1990.

Political career: Contested Dagenham 1983 and 1987 general elections. Member for Bromley and Chislehurst 29 June 2006 by-election to 2010, for Bromley and Chislehusrt (revised boundary) since 6 May 2010 general election; Shadow Minister for Communities and Local Government 2007-10 (Local Government 2009-10); Parliamentary Under-Secretary of State, Department for Communities and Local Government 2010-12. *Select committees:* Member, Constitutional Affairs/Justice 2006-10; Justice: Member 2012-13, Chair 2015-; Member: Political and Constitutional Reform 2013-15, Liaison 2015-, Joint Committee on the National Security Strategy 2015-. Greater London Conservatives: Deputy chairman 1993-96, Chair 1996-99; Conservative Party: Deputy chairman (local government) 2008-10, Vice-chairman (local government) 2012-; Founding member, Conservatives for Reform in Europe 2016. *Councils and public bodies:* London Borough of Havering: Councillor 1974-90, Chief whip and chairman of Environment and Social Services Committees; GLC Councillor for Romford 1985-86; Leader, London Fire and Civil Defence Authority 1985-87; Greater London Authority: Member 2000-08, Leader, Conservative group 2000-02; Non-executive board director, North East London Strategic Health Authority 2002-06; Board member, London Regional Arts Council 2003-07.

Political interests: Policing and criminal justice, local government, environment, arts; France, Hungary, Ireland, Italy, Spain, Switzerland.

Other: Member: EU Committee of the Regions 2002-08, Parliamentary Assembly, Council of Europe 2012-; Member: Royal Opera House Trust, Friends of English National Opera; Carlton Club.

Recreations: Theatre, travel, opera, sailing.

Robert Neill MP, House of Commons, London SW1A 0AA
Tel: 020 7219 8169 *Fax:* 020 7219 8089 *Email:* bob.neill.mp@parliament.uk
Constituency: Bromley and Chislehurst Conservative Association, 5 White Horse Hill, Chislehurst, Kent BR7 6DG
Tel: 020 8295 2639 *Email:* office@bromleyconservatives.com *Website:* www.bobneill.org.uk
Twitter: @neill_bob

SCOTTISH NATIONAL PARTY

NEWLANDS, GAVIN

Paisley and Renfrewshire North *(Majority 2,613)*

SNP Spokesperson for Sport

Gavin Andrew Stuart Newlands. Born 2 February 1980; Son of Gordon and Isabel Newlands; Married Lynn (2 daughters).

Education: Trinity High School, Renfrew.

Non-political career: Business analyst.

Political career: Member for Paisley and Renfrewshire North since 7 May 2015 general election; SNP Spokesperson for Sport 2016-. *Select committees:* Member: Backbench Business 2015-17, Justice 2017-. Fundraiser, Renfrew and Gallowhill SNP. *Councils and public bodies:* Councillor: Renfrew Community Council, Maryhill Community Council.

Political interests: Independence, carers, welfare, Scotland's constitution, CND; Nordic countries, USA.

Other: Brightest Star, Educate the Kids. Paisley Rugby Club: Member, Management Committee, Captain.

Recreations: Sports.

Gavin Newlands MP, House of Commons, London SW1A 0AA
Tel: 020 7219 5583 *Email:* gavin.newlands.mp@parliament.uk
Constituency: 6 Porterfield Road, Renfrew, Renfrewshire PA4 8HG
Tel: 0141-378 0600/0141-378 0601 *Website:* www.gavinnewlands.scot
Twitter: @GavNewlandsSNP

CONSERVATIVE

NEWTON, SARAH

Truro and Falmouth *(Majority 3,792)*

Parliamentary Under Secretary of State for Crime, Safeguarding and Vulnerability, Home Office

Sarah Louise Newton. Born 19 July 1961; Married Alan Newton (1 son 2 daughters).

Education: Falmouth School.

Non-political career: Marketing, Citibank then American Express.

Political career: Member for Truro and Falmouth since 6 May 2010 general election; Board member, Parliamentary Office of Science and Technology (POST); Assistant Government Whip 2015-16; Home Office: Parliamentary Under-Secretary of State: Vulnerability, Safeguarding and Countering Extremism 2016-17, for Crime, Safeguarding and Vulnerability 2017-. *Select committees:* Member: Administration 2010-12, Science and Technology 2012-15, Ecclesiastical Committee 2014-15. Former vice-chair and chair, Wimbledon Conservative Association; Deputy chairman, Conservative Party 2012-15. *Councils and public bodies:* Former councillor, London Borough of Merton Council.

Political interests: Ageing population, rural affairs, sustainable energy.

Other: Director, International Longevity Centre; Fellow, Royal Society of Arts; Patron: Glen Carne, St Angus, Cornwall, Turn to Starboard, Falmouth; Riverside Shelter for Homeless New York City, Age Concern England.

Recreations: Sailing, skiing, bee-keeping.

Sarah Newton MP, House of Commons, London SW1A 0AA
Tel: 020 7219 2931 *Email:* sarah.newton.mp@parliament.uk
Constituency: Office 7, The Palace Buildings, Quay Street, Truro, Cornwall TR1 2HE
Tel: 01872 274760 *Website:* www.sarahnewton.org.uk *Twitter:* @SNewtonUK

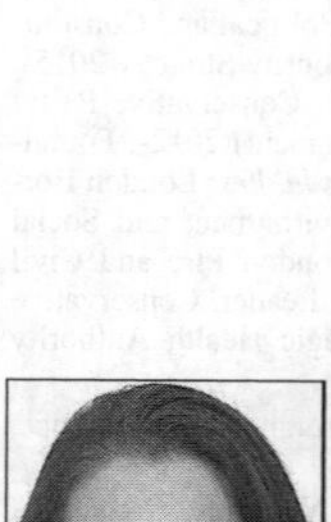

CONSERVATIVE

NOKES, CAROLINE

Romsey and Southampton North *(Majority 18,046)*

Parliamentary Secretary (Minister for Government Resilience and Efficiency), Cabinet Office

Caroline Fiona Ellen Nokes. Born 26 June 1972; Daughter of Roy Perry (MEP for Wight and Hampshire South 1994-99 and South East region 1999-2004) and Veronica Haswell; 1 daughter.

Education: La Sagesse Convent, Romsey; Peter Symonds' College, Winchester; Sussex University (BA government and politics 1994); French.

Non-political career: Political researcher to Roy Perry MEP 1994-2004; Consultant, Euro/Arab affairs 2004; Chief executive, National Pony Society 2008-09.

Political career: Contested Southampton Itchen 2001 and Romsey 2005 general elections. Member for Romsey and Southampton North since 6 May 2010 general election; PPS to: Mark Harper as Minister of State for Disabled People, Department for Work and Pensions 2014-15, Robert Goodwill as Minister of State, Department for Transport 2016; Parliamentary Under-Secretary of State for Welfare Delivery, Department for Work and Pensions 2016-17; Parliamentary Secretary (Minister for Government Resilience and Efficiency), Cabinet Office 2017-. *Select committees:* Member, Environmental Audit 2010-15; Works of Art: Member 2011-15, Chair 2015-16; Member, Education 2014-16. *Councils and public bodies:* Test Valley Borough Council: Councillor 1999-2011, Leisure portfolio holder 2001-10; Governor, Eastleigh College.

Political interests: Agriculture, sport, environment, education.

Other: Member, UK Delegation, Organisation for Security and Co-operation in Europe Parliamentary Assembly 2015-16; Vice-president, Romsey Hospital Appeal 2001; Trustee, World Horse Welfare 2015-.

Recreations: Riding.

Caroline Nokes MP, House of Commons, London SW1A 0AA
Tel: 020 7219 7218 *Email:* caroline.nokes.mp@parliament.uk
Constituency: Room 4, 13 Market Place, Romsey, Hampshire SO51 8NA
Tel: 01794 521155 *Email:* caroline@carolinenokes.com *Website:* www.carolinenokes.com
Twitter: @carolinenokes

CONSERVATIVE

NORMAN, JESSE

Hereford and South Herefordshire *(Majority 15,013)*

Parliamentary Under-Secretary of State for Roads, Local Transport and Devolution, Department for Transport

Alexander Jesse Norman. Born 23 June 1962; Married Kate 1992 (2 sons 1 daughter).

Education: Merton College, Oxford (BA classics 1985); University College, London (MPhil philosophy 1999; PhD 2003).

Non-political career: Project director, educational charity, eastern Europe 1988-91; Director, BZW (Barclays de Zoete Wedd) 1991-97; Teaching fellow and lecturer, University College, London 1999-2003; Conservative Research Department 2004-05; Policy adviser to: George Osborne as Shadow Chancellor of the Exchequer 2005, Philip Hammond as Shadow Secretary of State for Work and Pensions 2005-07; Executive director, Policy Exchange 2005-06.

Political career: Member for Hereford and South Herefordshire since 6 May 2010 general election; Parliamentary Under-Secretary of State: (Minister for Energy and Industry), Department for Business, Energy and Industrial Strategy 2016-17, for Roads, Local Transport and Devolution, Department for Transport 2017-. *Select committees:* Member: Treasury 2010-15, Joint Committees on: Consolidation, Etc, Bills 2010-15, the Draft Enhanced Terrorism Prevention and Investigation Measures Bill 2012-13; House of Commons Governance 2014-15, Liaison 2015-16; Chair, Culture, Media and Sport 2015-16. Chair, Conservative Co-operative Movement; Member, Policy Advisory Board April-September 2013. *Councils and public bodies:* Former school governor.

Political interests: Big Society, economy, public services, PFI, human rights.

Other: Founder, schoolsfirst.org.uk; Member, advisory board, Roundhouse; Vice-President: Ross-on-Wye Horticultural Society, Herefordshire and Gloucestershire Canal Trust, Hereford Musical Theatre Company; Patron: Kindle Centre, Hereford City, Friends of St Mary's, Ross-on-Wye, Herefordshire Mind, Hereford Music Pool, Riding for the Disabled, Herefordshire, St Martin's Church Roof Appeal, Hereford, Friends of Number 1 Ledbury Road, Hereford, Yeleni Trust Cancer Care; Director, Hay Festival of Literature and the Arts; Vice-president, Westfields Football Club. Parliamentarian of the Year, *Spectator* awards 2012; Commons Backbencher of the Year, *House Magazine* awards 2012.

Publications: Author: The Achievements of Michael Oakeshott (Gerald Duckworth & Co, 1993), After Euclid (University of Chicago Press, 2005), Compassionate Conservatism (Policy Exchange, 2006); From Here to Fraternity (Centre Forum, 2007); Compassionate Economics (Policy Exchange, 2008); Churchill's Legacy (Liberty, 2009); The Big Society (University of Buckingham Press, 2010) Edmund Burke: Philosopher, Politician, Prophet (William Collins, 2013).

Recreations: Music, sports, theatre.

Jesse Norman MP, House of Commons, London SW1A 0AA
Tel: 020 7219 7084 *Email:* jesse.norman.mp@parliament.uk
Constituency: Suite 2a, Penn House, Broad Street, Hereford, Herefordshire HR4 9AP
Tel: 01432 276422 *Website:* www.jesse4hereford.com *Twitter:* @jesse_norman

LAB/CO-OP

NORRIS, ALEX

Nottingham North *(Majority 11,160)*

PPS to Jon Ashworth as Shadow Secretary of State for Health

Alexander James Jordan Norris. Born 4 February 1984.

Education: Manchester Grammar; Nottingham University.

Non-political career: Labour Party; Trade Union Representative, GMB and Co-Operative; Organiser, Unison.

Political career: Member for Nottingham North since 8 June 2017; PPS to Jon Ashworth as Shadow Secretary of State for Health 2017-; Former Secretary, East Midlands Regional Co-operative Party. *Councils and public bodies:* Nottingham City Council: Councillor 2011-17, Cabinet Member for Area Working, Cleansing and Community Safety; Chair of governors, Rosslyn Park Primary School.

Other: Member, Society of Union Employees.

Alex Norris MP, House of Commons, London SW1A 0AA
Tel: 020 7219 3899 *Email:* alex.norris.mp@parliament.uk
Constituency: Details still to be confirmed
Tel: 0115-975 2377 *Website:* alexnorrismp.co.uk *Twitter:* @ANorrisMP

CONSERVATIVE

O'BRIEN, NEIL

Harborough *(Majority 12,429)*

Neil John O'Brien. Born 6 November 1978; Married 2012.

Education: Greenhead College, Huddersfield; Christ Church, Oxford (BA politics, philosophy and economics 2000).

Non-political career: Director: Open Europe 2005-08, Policy Exchange 2008-12; Special Adviser: HM Treasury 2013-16, Prime Minister's Office 2016-17.

Political career: Member for Harborough since 8 June 2017. *Select committees:* Member, Science and Technology 2017-.

Neil O'Brien MP, House of Commons, London SW1A 0AA
Tel: 020 7219 1802 *Email:* neil.obrien.mp@parliament.uk
Constituency: 24 Nelson Street, Market Harborough LE16 9AY
Tel: 01858 464146 *Website:* www.neilobrien.org.uk *Twitter:* @neildotobrien

CONSERVATIVE

OFFORD, MATTHEW

Hendon *(Majority 1,072)*

Matthew James Offord. Born 3 September 1969; Married Claire Rowles 2010.

Education: Amery Hill School, Alton; Nottingham Trent University (BA photography 1992); Lancaster University (MA environment, culture and society 2000); King's College London (PhD rural governance and economic redevelopment).

Non-political career: Media analyst, Medialink Communications 1995-96; Political adviser: Conservative Central Office 1996-97, Local Government Association 1997; Political analyst, BBC 2001-10.

Political career: Contested Barnsley East and Mexborough 2001 general election. Member for Hendon since 6 May 2010 general election; PPS to George Eustice as Minister of State for Farming, Food and the Marine Environment, Department for Environment, Food and Rural Affairs 2015-16. *Select committees:* Member: Environmental Audit 2012-15, 2016-, Joint Committee on Able Marine Energy Park Development Consent Order 2014 2014-15. Chair, Hendon Conservative Association 2004-. *Councils and public bodies:* London Borough of Barnet Council: Councillor 2002-10, Council deputy leader 2006-09, Former cabinet member for: Environment and Transport, Community Safety, Community Engagement.

Countries of interest: Sub-Saharan Africa, Cyprus, Israel, Middle East, Sri Lanka.

Other: Fellow, Royal Geographical Society; Member, Association of European Parliamentarians for Africa. Welsh Harp's Seahorse Sailing Club.

Recreations: Sailing, scuba diving.

Dr Matthew Offord MP, House of Commons, London SW1A 0AA
Tel: 020 7219 7083 *Email:* matthew.offord.mp@parliament.uk
Constituency: 120 Bunns Lane, Mill Hill, London NW7 2AS
Tel: 020 3114 2131 *Website:* www.matthewofford.co.uk *Twitter:* @Offord4Hendon

SCOTTISH NATIONAL PARTY

O'HARA, BRENDAN

Argyll and Bute *(Majority 1,328)*

SNP Spokesperson for Culture and Media

Born 27 April 1963; Married Catherine (2 daughters).

Education: St Andrew's, Carntyne; Strathclyde University (economic history and modern history 1992).

Non-political career: Glasgow District Council; Television producer, credits include: *Comedy Connections* and *Movie Connections*, BBC, *The Football Years*, STV, *Scotland's Greatest Album*, STV, *Road To Referendum*, STV, Sky Sports.

Political career: Contested Springburn 1987 and Glasgow Central 1992 general elections. Member for Argyll and Bute since 7 May 2015 general election; SNP Spokesperson for: Defence 2015-17, Culture and Media 2017-. *Select committees:* Member, Digital, Culture, Media and Sport 2017-.

Political interests: Rural issues, transport.

Brendan O'Hara MP, House of Commons, London SW1A 0AA
Tel: 020 7219 8783 *Email:* brendan.ohara.mp@parliament.uk
Constituency: 8 Colquhoun Square, Helensburgh G84 8AD
Tel: 01436 670587 *Website:* www.brendanoharamp.scot *Twitter:* @BrendanOHaraSNP

LABOUR

O'MARA, JARED

Sheffield, Hallam *(Majority 2,125)*

Born 15 November 1981.

Education: Staffordshire University (journalism).

Non-political career: Campaigns Officer, British Council of Disabled People; Owner, West Street Live.

Political career: Member for Sheffield, Hallam since 8 June 2017. *Select committees:* Member, Women and Equalities 2017-. *Councils and public bodies:* Governor, Paces School 2015-.

Other: Governor and Trustee, Paces.

Jared O'Mara MP, House of Commons, London SW1A 0AA
Tel: 020 7219 4298 *Email:* jared.omara.mp@parliament.uk
Constituency: Details still to be confirmed *Twitter:* @ShefHallamLab

LABOUR

ONASANYA, FIONA

Peterborough *(Majority 607)*

PPS to Nia Griffith as Shadow Secretary of State for Defence

Fiona Oluyinka Onasanya. Born August 1983.

Education: Hertfordshire University; College of Law.

Non-political career: Solicitor: Nockolds LLP 2010-12, Eversheds 2013-16, Howes Percival 2016, DC Law 2016-17.

Political career: Member for Peterborough since 8 June 2017; PPS to Nia Griffith as Shadow Secretary of State for Defence 2017-. *Select committees:* Member, Communities and Local Government 2017-. *Councils and public bodies:* Councillor, Cambridge City Council: Cambridgeshire County Council: Councillor 2013-17, Spokesperson for Children, Young People and Families, Deputy Leader.

Other: Trustee, East Hertfordshire YMCA.

Fiona Onasanya MP, House of Commons, London SW1A 0AA
Tel: 020 7219 0837 *Email:* fiona.onasanya.mp@parliament.uk
Constituency: Details still to be confirmed *Twitter:* @FionaOnasanyaMP

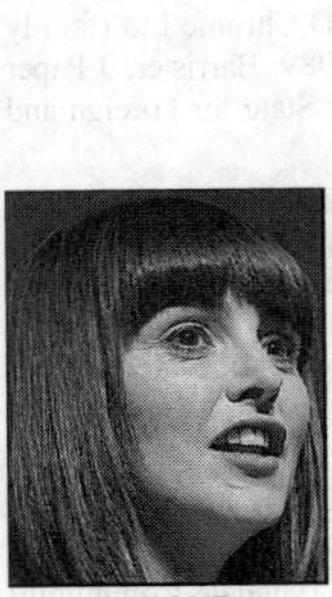

LABOUR

ONN, MELANIE

Great Grimsby *(Majority 2,565)*

Shadow Minister for Housing

Born 19 June 1979; Married Christopher 2014 (1 son).

Education: Middlesex University (BA politics, philosophy and international studies 2000).

Non-political career: Labour Party 2001-10: Communications officer to General Secretary, Head of Compliance Unit; Regional organiser, Yorkshire and Humberside, Unison 2010-15.

Political career: Member for Great Grimsby since 7 May 2015 general election; Shadow Deputy Leader of the House of Commons 2015-16; Shadow Minister for Housing 2017-. *Select committees:* Member: Energy and Climate Change 2015, Joint Committee on Consolidation, &c, Bills

2015-, Communities and Local Government 2016-17, Procedure 2016-. Contested Yorkshire and Humberside region 2009 European Parliament election.

Melanie Onn MP, House of Commons, London SW1A 0AA
Tel: 020 7219 6282 *Email:* melanie.onn.mp@parliament.uk
Constituency: 112 Cleethorpe Road, Grimsby, North East Lincolnshire DN31 3HW
Tel: 01472 359584 *Twitter:* @OnnMel

LABOUR

ONWURAH, CHI

Newcastle upon Tyne Central *(Majority 14,937)*

Shadow Minister for Industrial Strategy

Chinyelu Susan Onwurah. Born 12 April 1965; Daughter of Kathleen Onwurah, née Roche, and Dr Moses Onwurah.

Education: Kenton School; Imperial College, London (BEng electrical engineering 1987); Manchester Business School (MBA 2002); French.

Non-political career: Nortel 1987-95; Cable & Wireless 1995-99; Director of product strategy, Global Telesystems UK 1999-2000; Director of market development, Teligent 2000-01; Partner, Hammatan Ventures 2001-04; Head of telecoms technology, OFCOM 2004-10. Member, Unite.

Political career: Member for Newcastle upon Tyne Central since 6 May 2010 general election; Shadow Minister for Business, Innovation and Skills (Innovation, Science and Digital Infrastructure) 2010-13; Board member, Parliamentary Office of Science and Technology (POST); Shadow Minister for: Cabinet Office 2013-15, Business, Innovation and Skills 2015-16, Culture, Media and Sport 2015-16, Industrial Strategy 2016-. *Select committees:* Member, Business, Innovation and Skills 2010. Member, Labour Party 1981-.

Political interests: Education, technology, manufacturing, international development, trade, social mobility; China, France, Nigeria, South Africa.

Other: Board member, Franco-British Council; Former national executive member, Anti-Apartheid Movement; Member, Chatham House; Open University Business School; Honorary Vice-president, Action for South Africa (ACTSA) 2015-; Institute of Engineering Technology; Fellow: Institute of Engineering and Technology, City and Guilds Institute; Action for South Africa.

Recreations: Reading, music, country walks.

Chi Onwurah MP, House of Commons, London SW1A 0AA
Tel: 020 7219 7114 *Email:* chi.onwurah.mp@parliament.uk
Constituency: Suite 24, 7-15 Pink Lane, Newcastle upon Tyne, Tyne and Wear NE1 5DW
Tel: 0191-232 5838 *Email:* carol.stanners@parliament.uk *Website:* www.chionwurahmp.com
Twitter: @ChiOnwurah

CONSERVATIVE

OPPERMAN, GUY

Hexham *(Majority 9,236)*

Parliamentary Under-Secretary of State for Pensions and Financial Inclusion, Department for Work and Pensions

Guy Thomas Opperman. Born 18 May 1965; Son of Michael and Julie Opperman; Partner Flora Coleman.

Education: Harrow School; Lille University, France (Diploma 1984); Buckingham University (LLB 1987); Bar Vocational Course 1989; French.

Non-political career: Farmer near Arusha, Tanzania 1987-88; Director, TD Chrome Ltd (family engineering business) (unpaid) -2009; Called to the Bar, Middle Temple 1989; Barrister, 3 Paper Buildings 1991-2010; Adviser to Michael Ancram as Shadow Secretary of State for Foreign and Commonwealth Affairs (unpaid) 2001-03.

Political career: Contested North Swindon 1997 and Caernarfon 2005 general elections. Member for Hexham since 6 May 2010 general election; PPS to: Mark Harper as Minister of State for Immigration, Home Office 2012-14, James Brokenshire as Minister of State for Security and Immigration, Home Office 2014-15; Assistant Government Whip 2015-16; Government Whip (Lord Commissioner of HM Treasury) 2016-17; Parliamentary Under-Secretary of State for Pensions and Financial Inclusion, Department for Work and Pensions 2017-; *Councils and public bodies:* Councillor, Marlborough, Wiltshire 1995-99.

Political interests: Prison reform and sentencing, health, fuel poverty, tourism, apprenticeships and youth training, equal pay, Northumberland; Falkland Islands, India, Syria.

Other: Member: Countryside Alliance, Prudhoe Allotments; Co-founder, Tynedale Community Bank; Help for Heroes, Injured Jockeys Fund, Save the Children, Tynedale Hospice at Home,

Children with Leukaemia, Great North Air Ambulance Service. Bar Pro Bono Award for Services to Victim Support 2007; Pro Bono Champion Award for Services to Pro Bono and local community hospital campaign 2009; Albert Edward Club, Hexham.

Publications: 150 journalist articles; Author, Doing Time: Prisons in the 21st Century (Bretwalda Books, 2012).

Recreations: Cricket, amateur steeplechase jockey.

Guy Opperman MP, House of Commons, London SW1A 0AA
Tel: 020 7219 7227 *Fax:* 020 7219 6435 *Email:* guy.opperman.mp@parliament.uk
Constituency: Office 2, Horton Park, Berwick Hill Road, Ponteland, Northumberland NE13 6BU
Tel: 01670 789161 *Email:* teamoppy@gmail.com *Websites:* www.guyopperman.co.uk www.guyopperman.blogspot.com *Twitter:* @GuyOpperman

LAB/CO-OP

OSAMOR, KATE

Edmonton *(Majority 21,115)*

Shadow Secretary of State for International Development

Kate Ofunne Osamor. Born 15 August 1968; 1 son.

Education: Fortismere School; University of East London (BA third world studies and international development 2006).

Non-political career: Executive assistant, Camidoc GP Out Of Hours 2002-10; Practice Manager: Sterndale Surgery, Hammersmith 2012-13, Park Lodge Medical Centre, Enfield 2013-15.

Political career: Member for Edmonton since 7 May 2015 general election; PPS to Jeremy Corbyn as Leader of the Opposition 2015-16; Shadow Minister for Women and Equalities Office 2016; Shadow Secretary of State for International Development 2016-. *Select committees:* Member: Education 2015-16, Petitions 2015-16, Joint Committee on Consolidation, &c, Bills 2015-. Member, Labour: BAME 2012-13, National Executive Committee 2014-15, 2016-.

Other: Member, UK delegation, Parliamentary Assembly of the Council of Europe 2015-16.

Kate Osamor MP, House of Commons, London SW1A 0AA
Tel: 020 7219 6602 *Email:* kate.osamor.mp@parliament.uk
Constituency: 37 Market Square, Edmonton Green Shopping Centre, London N9 0TZ
Tel: 020 8803 0574 *Email:* edmontoncasework@gmail.com *Website:* www.kateosamor.co.uk
Twitter: @KateOsamor

LABOUR

OWEN, ALBERT

Ynys Môn *(Majority 5,259)*

Born 10 August 1959; Son of late William Owen and Doreen, née Wood; Married Angela Margaret Magee 1983 (2 daughters).

Education: Holyhead County Comprehensive School, Anglesey; Coleg Harlech (Diploma industrial relations 1994); York University (BA politics 1997); Welsh.

Non-political career: Merchant seafarer 1976-92; Welfare rights and employment adviser 1995-97; Centre manager, Isle of Anglesey County Council 1997-2001. RMT 1976-92: Health and safety officer 1985-87, Ferry sector national panel 1987-92; NUS 1992-97: Welfare officer 1992-94; Unison 1997-2001.

Political career: Member for Ynys Môn since 7 June 2001 general election. *Select committees:* Member: Welsh Affairs 2001-05, 2006-10, Accommodation and Works 2001-05, Energy and Climate Change 2010-15, Chairmen's Panel/Panel of Chairs 2010-, International Development 2015-17, Work of the Independent Commission for Aid Impact Sub-committee 2015-16, Business, Energy and Industrial Strategy 2016-. Contested Ynys Môn constituency 1999 National Assembly for Wales election. Constituency Labour Party: Treasurer 1991-92, Vice-chair 1992-96, Press officer 1996-2000. *Councils and public bodies:* Councillor, Holyhead Town Council 1997-99.

Political interests: Welsh affairs, welfare, economic development; Ireland, Cyprus, Malta/Gozo.

Other: Director, Homeless project 1998-; Member: Institute of Welsh Affairs 1999-2001, Management committee, WEA North Wales 1999-2001; Chair, Anglesey Regeneration Partnership 2000-01; Cancer Research. Holyhead Sailing Club.

Recreations: Cycling, walking, cooking, gardening.

Albert Owen MP, House of Commons, London SW1A 0AA
Tel: 020 7219 8415 *Fax:* 020 7219 1951 *Email:* albert.owen.mp@parliament.uk
Constituency: 18 Thomas Street, Holyhead, Anglesey LL65 1RR
Tel: 01407 765750 *Fax:* 01407 764336 *Website:* albertowenmp.org *Twitter:* @AlbertOwenMP

DEMOCRATIC UNIONIST PARTY

PAISLEY, IAN

North Antrim *(Majority 20,643)*

DUP Spokesperson for Culture, Media and Sport and Communities and Local Government

Ian Richard Kyle Paisley. Born 12 December 1966; Son of late Ian Paisley (MP for North Antrim 1970-85 and 1986-2010, MEP for Northern Ireland 1979-2004, MLA for North Antrim 1998-2011, later Lord Bannside) and Eileen Paisley, née Cassells (now Baroness Paisley of St George's (qv)); Married Fiona Currie 1990 (2 daughters 2 sons).

Education: Shaftesbury House College; Methodist College, Belfast; Queen's University, Belfast (BA modern history 1989; MSc Irish politics 1992).

Non-political career: Researcher, author and political assistant.

Political career: Member for North Antrim since 6 May 2010 general election; DUP Spokesperson for: Work and Pensions 2010-15, Environment, Food and Rural Affairs 2010-15, Culture, Media and Sport 2015-, Communities and Local Government 2015-, Energy and Climate Change 2015-17. *Select committees:* Member: Northern Ireland Affairs 2010-16, 2017-, House of Commons Governance 2014-15, Joint Committee on the Palace of Westminster 2015-16, Panel of Chairs 2016-. Member Northern Ireland Forum for Political Dialogue 1996-98; MLA for North Antrim 1998-2010: Member, Preparation for Government Committee 2006-07; Junior Minister, Office of First and Deputy First Minister 2007-08; Chair, Agriculture and Rural Development Committee 2009-10. *Councils and public bodies:* Lay visitor, Police Holding Centres for the Police Authority 1996-2001; Member, Northern Ireland Policing Board 2001-07, 2008-10.

Political interests: Justice, Europe, agriculture, policing, foreign policy; Africa, China, Middle East, USA.

Other: Member, Executive Committee: Inter-Parliamentary Union, British Group 2012-14, Commonwealth Parliamentary Association UK 2015-16; British Motorcycle Federation; Fellow, University of Maryland School of Leadership, Washington DC, USA. Royal Humane Society for Life Saving 1999.

Publications: Reasonable Doubt – The Case for the UDR4; Echoes; Peace Deal; Ian Paisley – A Life in Photographs.

Recreations: Rugby, reading, motor racing, collector of 19th century cartoons and political caricatures, motorcycling.

Ian Paisley MP, House of Commons, London SW1A 0AA
Tel: 020 7219 7116 *Fax:* 020 7219 2996 *Email:* ian.paisley.mp@parliament.uk
Constituency: 9-11 Church Street, Ballymena, Co Antrim BT43 6DD
Tel: 028 2564 1421 *Fax:* 028 2564 7296 *Email:* info@ianpaisleymp.co.uk irkpj@yahoo.co.uk
Website: www.ianpaisleymp.co.uk *Twitter:* @ianpaisleymp

CONSERVATIVE

PARISH, NEIL

Tiverton and Honiton *(Majority 19,801)*

Chair, Select Committee on Environment, Food and Rural Affairs

Neil Quentin Gordon Parish. Born 26 May 1956; Married Sue Edwards 1981 (1 son 1 daughter).

Education: Brymore School; Taunton College.

Non-political career: Former farmer and businessman.

Political career: Contested Torfaen 1997 general election. Member for Tiverton and Honiton since 6 May 2010 general election; PPS to John Hayes as Minister of State, Department for Transport 2014-15. *Select committees:* Environment, Food and Rural Affairs: Member 2010-15, Chair 2015-; Member, Liaison 2015-; Chair, Environment, Food and Rural Affairs Sub-committee 2015-17. Chair, Conservative Party Committee for Environment -2015. MEP for South West 1999-2009: Conservative agriculture spokesperson, President, Animal Welfare Intergroup, Chair: Australia and New Zealand Delegation 2004-07, Agriculture and Rural Development Committee 2007-09. Chair, Bridgwater Conservative Assocation 1997-99; Founding member, Conservatives for Reform in Europe 2016. *Councils and public bodies:* Sedgemoor District Council: Councillor 1983-95, Deputy Leader 1989-95; Councillor, Somerset County Council 1989-93.

Political interests: Regional policy, animal welfare, agriculture; China, Israel, Slovenia, Zimbabwe.

Other: Election monitor, Zimbabwe 2000; Founding supporter, Change Britain 2016-; Brains Trust.

Recreations: Swimming, music, country life, debating.

Neil Parish MP, House of Commons, London SW1A 0AA
Tel: 020 7219 7172 *Fax:* 020 7219 5005 *Email:* neil.parish.mp@parliament.uk
Constituency: 9c Mill Park Industrial Estate, White Cross Road, Woodbury Salterton, Exeter, Devon EX5 1EL
Tel: 01884 841497 *Email:* neil@neilparish.co.uk *Website:* www.neilparish.co.uk
Twitter: @neil_parish

CONSERVATIVE

PATEL, PRITI

Witham *(Majority 18,646)*

Secretary of State for International Development

Priti Sushil Patel. Born 29 March 1972; Married Alex Sawyer.

Education: Westfield Girls School, Watford; Keele University (BA economics 1994); Essex University (Diploma British government and politics 1995).

Non-political career: Corporate communications.

Political career: Contested Nottingham North 2005 general election. Member for Witham since 6 May 2010 general election; Prime Minister's Indian Diaspora Champion 2013-; Exchequer Secretary, HM Treasury 2014-15; Minister of State for Employment, Department for Work and Pensions 2015-16; Secretary of State for International Development 2016-. *Select committees:* Member: Members' Expenses 2011-15, Public Administration 2011-14, Joint Committee on Draft Deregulation Bill 2013. Member, Executive, 1922 Committee 2010-14. Elected Member, Conservative Party Board 2010-14; Member, Number 10 Policy Advisory Board 2013-14.

Political interests: Trade, business, the economy, Europe, law and order, immigration; Africa, Asia, India, Middle East.

Other: Member, Campaign committee, Vote Leave 2016; Vice-president, CHAPS; Patron, Dancing Giraffe; Honorary member, Holdfast Credit Union Ltd; Trustee, Crossroads Care Braintree District and Chelmsford; Crossroads Care Braintree and Witham, Brainwave Witham, Homestart Witham, Royal British Legion Witham. PC 2015.

Publications: Co-author (with Kwasi Kwarteng MP, Dominic Raab MP, Chris Skidmore MP and Elizabeth Truss MP), Britannia Unchained: Global Lessons for Growth and Prosperity (Palgrave Macmillan, 2012).

Recreations: Horse racing, cricket, travel, music.

Rt Hon Priti Patel MP, House of Commons, London SW1A 0AA
Tel: 020 7219 3528 *Fax:* 020 7219 5192 *Email:* withammp@parliament.uk
Constituency: No constituency office publicised *Website:* www.priti4witham.com
Twitter: @patel4witham

CONSERVATIVE

PATERSON, OWEN

North Shropshire *(Majority 16,355)*

Owen William Paterson. Born 24 June 1956; Son of late Alfred and Cynthia Paterson; Married Hon. Rose Ridley 1980 (2 sons 1 daughter).

Education: Radley College, Oxfordshire; Corpus Christi College, Cambridge (MA history 1978); French, German.

Non-political career: British Leather Co Ltd: Sales director 1985-93, Managing director 1993-99; Consultant: Randox Laboratories Ltd 2015-, Lynn's Country Foods Ltd 2016-.

Political career: Contested Wrexham 1992 general election. Member for North Shropshire since 1 May 1997 general election; Opposition Whip 2000-01; PPS to Iain Duncan Smith as Leader of the Opposition 2001-03; Shadow Minister for: Environment, Food and Rural Affairs 2003-05, Transport 2005-07; Shadow Secretary of State for Northern Ireland 2007-10; Secretary of State for: Northern Ireland 2010-12, Environment, Food and Rural Affairs 2012-14. *Select committees:* Member: Welsh Affairs 1997-2001, European Standing Committee A 1998-2001, Welsh Grand Committee 1998-2000, European Scrutiny 1999-2000, Agriculture 2000-01. Conservative Party Committees: Joint Vice-chair, Environment, Transport and Regions 1999-2001, Joint Secretary, European Affairs 1999-2001, Secretary, Foreign and Commonwealth Affairs 1999-2001. Member: 92 Group 1997-, Conservative Friends of Israel 1997-, Conservative Way Forward 1997-, Conservative 2000 1997-; Vice-President, Conservatives Against a Federal Europe 1998-2001, Member: No Turning Back Group 1998-, Executive, 1922 Committee 2000; Vice-President, Conservatives for Britain 2015-16.

Political interests: Trade, industry, agriculture, foreign affairs, economy, social justice, Northern Ireland; China, Western and Eastern Europe, India, USA.

Other: President, Cotance (European Tanners' Confederation) 1996-98; Member: Inter-Parliamentary Union 1997-, Commonwealth Parliamentary Association 1997-; Member, Advisory Board, European Foundation 1998-; Director, Orthopaedic Institute Ltd, Oswestry; Member, Countryside Alliance; Royal Irish Regiment Benevolent Fund, Midlands Centre for Spinal Injuries, Ellesmere Community Care Centre Trust. Liveryman, Leathersellers' Company. PC 2010. Patron, Oswestry Cricket Club; Member, Shropshire Cricket Club.

Rt Hon Owen Paterson MP, House of Commons, London SW1A 0AA
Tel: 020 7219 5185 *Fax:* 020 7219 3955 *Email:* patersono@parliament.uk
Constituency: No constituency office publicised
Tel: 01978 710073 *Fax:* 01978 710667 *Email:* rose@repaterson.co.uk
Website: www.owenpaterson.org *Twitter:* @OwenPaterson

CONSERVATIVE

PAWSEY, MARK

Rugby *(Majority 8,212)*

Mark Julian Francis Pawsey. Born 16 January 1957; Son of James Pawsey (MP for Rugby 1979-83 and Rugby and Kenilworth 1983-97) and Cynthia Pawsey; Married Tracy Harris 1984 (2 sons 2 daughters).

Education: Lawrence Sheriff Grammar School, Rugby; Reading University (estate management 1978); French.

Non-political career: Member, Armed Forces Parliamentary Scheme. Trainee Surveyor, Strutt and Parker 1978-79; Account Manager, Autobar Vending Supplies Ltd 1979-82; Managing Director, Central Catering Supplies Ltd 1982-2008.

Political career: Contested Nuneaton 2005 general election. Member for Rugby since 6 May 2010 general election; PPS: to Anna Soubry as Minister of State: for Defence Personnel, Welfare and Veterans, Ministry of Defence 2014-15, for Small Business, Industry and Enterprise, Department for Business, Innovation and Skills 2015-16, to Damian Green as Secretary of State for Work and Pensions 2016-17. *Select committees:* Member: Communities and Local Government 2010-15, Business, Energy and Industrial Strategy 2017-. Member, Executive, 1922 Committee 2017-. *Councils and public bodies:* Councillor, Rugby Borough Council 2002-07.

Political interests: Planning, environment, local government, trade, vaping, business and industrial strategy; China, India, Middle East, Pakistan, Rwanda.

Other: Parkinson's UK; Air Ambulance. FSB Member of Parliament Small Business Friendly Award 2014, 2015. Chairman, Commons and Lords RFC; Old Laurentian RFC.

Recreations: Village life, rugby, wine appreciation.

Mark Pawsey MP, House of Commons, London SW1A 0AA
Tel: 020 7219 7136 *Email:* mark.pawsey.mp@parliament.uk
Constituency: Albert Buildings, 2 Castle Mews, Rugby CV21 2XL
Tel: 01788 579499 *Website:* www.markpawsey.org.uk *Twitter:* @markpawsey

LABOUR

PEACOCK, STEPHANIE

Barnsley East *(Majority 13,283)*

Stephanie Louise Peacock. Born 19 December 1986.

Education: Queen Mary, University of London (modern and contemporary history 2010); Canterbury Christ Church University (PGCE 2011); Institute of Education, University of London (Masters 2013).

Non-political career: Parliamentary Assistant to Sylvia Heal MP 2005-10; Secondary school history and politics teacher 2010-12; Trade union training officer 2012-13; Regional political officer, GMB 2013-17.

Political career: Contested Halesowen and Rowley Regis 2015 general election. Member for Barnsley East since 8 June 2017; Labour Party: Member, NEC, West Midlands representative, National Policy Forum.

Stephanie Peacock MP, House of Commons, London SW1A 0AA
Tel: 020 7219 4129 *Email:* stephanie.peacock.mp@parliament.uk
Constituency: West Bank House, West Street, Hoyland, Barnsley S74 9EE
Tel: 01226 743483 *Website:* www.stephaniepeacock.org.uk *Twitter:* @Steph_Peacock

LABOUR

PEARCE, TERESA

Erith and Thamesmead *(Majority 10,014)*

Born 1 February 1955; Daughter of Arthur Farrington, shoe repairer, and Josephine Farrington, book-keeper/clerk; Married (2 daughters).

Education: St Thomas More; French (basic).

Non-political career: Senior manager, Tax Investigations Team, PriceWaterhouseCoopers 1999-2009. Member, GMB.

Political career: Member for Erith and Thamesmead since 6 May 2010 general election; Shadow Minister for Housing 2015-16; Shadow Secretary of State for Communities and Local Government 2016-17; Shadow Minister for the Constitutional Convention 2016-17. *Select committees:* Member: Work and Pensions 2010-15, Treasury 2011-15, Unopposed Bills (Panel) 2013-15, Public Accounts 2015. Member, National Constitutional Committee 1996-2008. *Councils and public bodies:* Councillor, London Borough of Bexley Council 1998-2002.

Political interests: Tax reform, children in care.

Recreations: Cinema, reading, travel.

Teresa Pearce MP, House of Commons, London SW1A 0AA
Tel: 020 7219 6936 *Fax:* 020 7219 2190 *Email:* teresa.pearce.mp@parliament.uk
Constituency: 315 Bexley Road, Erith DA8 3EX
Tel: 01322 342991 *Website:* www.teresapearce.org.uk *Twitter:* @tpearce003

CONSERVATIVE

PENNING, MIKE

Hemel Hempstead *(Majority 9,445)*

Michael Allan Penning. Born 28 September 1957; Son of Freda and Brian Penning; Married Angela Louden 1988 (2 daughters).

Education: Appleton Comprehensive School, Benfleet, Essex; King Edmund Comprehensive School, Rochford, Essex.

Non-political career: Soldier, Grenadier Guards 1974-80; Royal Army Medical Corps (RAMC) 1980-81; Fire officer, Essex Fire and Rescue Services 1982-88; Freelance political journalist, Express Newspapers and News International 1988-92; Politics and journalism lecturer, UK and USA 1992-2005; Journalist and media adviser to six Shadow Cabinet members 1996-2004; Deputy chief press spokesperson, Conservative Central Office 2000-04; Director, MA Penning Ltd. Member, FBU 1982-.

Political career: Contested Thurrock 2001 general election. Member for Hemel Hempstead 2005-10, for Hemel Hempstead (revised boundary) since 6 May 2010 general election; Shadow Minister for Health 2007-10; Parliamentary Under-Secretary of State, Department for Transport 2010-12; Minister of State, Northern Ireland Office 2012-13; Minister for Disabled People, Department for Work and Pensions 2013-14; Minister of State for: Policing, Crime, Criminal Justice and Victims 2014-16, Fire 2016; Chair, Inter-Ministerial Group on Anti-Corruption 2015-16; Minister of State for the Armed Forces, Ministry of Defence 2016-17. *Select committees:* Member, Health 2005-07. Member, Executive, 1922 Committee 2006-07. Director, Conservatives Against a Federal Europe 1995; General election campaign manager, Rochford and Southend East 1997.

Political interests: Constitution, single currency (against), health, home affairs, defence; Gibraltar.

Other: British Legion; Patron: St Francis Hospice, Ian Rennie Grove Hospice, Paper Trail Heritage Fire Brigade, Herts Hearing Advisory Service; Trustee, Snowbility. GSM (Northern Ireland); PC 2014.

Recreations: Rugby union, football, coarse fishing, golf.

Rt Hon Mike Penning MP, House of Commons, London SW1A 0AA
Tel: 020 7219 3000 *Email:* penningm@parliament.uk
Constituency: The Bury, Queensway, Hemel Hempstead, Hertfordshire HP1 1HR
Tel: 01442 251126 *Email:* mike@penning4hemel.com *Website:* www.mikepenning.com

LABOUR

PENNYCOOK, MATTHEW

Greenwich and Woolwich *(Majority 20,714)*

Shadow Minister for Exiting the European Union

Matthew Thomas Pennycook. Born 29 October 1982; Married Joanna (1 son).

Education: London School of Economics (history and international relations); Balliol College, Oxford (MPhil international relations).

Non-political career: Child Poverty Action Group; Fair Pay Network; Senior Research and Policy Analyst, Resolution Foundation 2012-14. Member: GMB, Unite.

Political career: Member for Greenwich and Woolwich since 7 May 2015 general election; PPS to John Healey as Shadow Minister for Housing and Planning 2015-16; Shadow Minister for Exiting the European Union 2016-. *Select committees:* Member, Energy and Climate Change 2015-16. *Councils and public bodies:* Councillor, Greenwich Council 2010-15; Former governor, James Wolfe Primary School.

Other: Member, Advisory Board, Living Wage Foundation; Trustee, Greenwich Housing Rights.

Matthew Pennycook MP, House of Commons, London SW1A 0AA
Tel: 020 7219 6280 *Email:* matthew.pennycook.mp@parliament.uk
Constituency: No constituency office
Email: matthew@matthewpennycook.com *Website:* www.matthewpennycook.com
Twitter: @mtpennycook

PENROSE, JOHN

Weston-Super-Mare *(Majority 11,544)*

CONSERVATIVE

John David Penrose. Born 22 June 1964; Son of late David Penrose and Anna Penrose, now Lawrie; Married Diana (Dido) Harding 1995, now Baroness Harding of Winscombe (qv) (2 daughters).

Education: Ipswich School, Suffolk; Downing College, Cambridge (BA law 1986); Columbia University, USA (MBA 1991); French, German.

Non-political career: Risk manager, JP Morgan 1986-90; Management consultant, McKinsey and Company 1992-94; Commercial director, academic books division, Thomson Publishing 1995-96; Managing director, schools publishing, Europe, Pearson plc 1996-2000; Non-executive director, Logotron Ltd 2008-11.

Political career: Contested Ealing Southall 1997 and Weston-Super-Mare 2001 general elections. Member for Weston-Super-Mare 2005-10, for Weston-Super-Mare (revised boundary) since 6 May 2010 general election; PPS to Oliver Letwin as Chair, Conservative Policy Review 2006-09; Shadow Minister for: Business, Enterprise and Regulatory Reform 2009, Business 2009-10; Parliamentary Under-Secretary of State (Minister for Tourism and Heritage), Department for Culture, Media and Sport 2010-12; Assistant Government Whip 2013-14; Government Whip (Lord Commissioner of HM Treasury) 2014-16; Parliamentary Secretary, Cabinet Office 2015-16. *Select committees:* Member: Work and Pensions 2005-09, Regulatory Reform 2009-10, Administration 2012-13, Selection 2014-15. Treasurer, Leyton and Wanstead Conservative Association 1993-95.

Political interests: Drug addiction, pensions, environment, education, international development.

Other: Research secretary, Bow Group 1998-99; President, Weston Abbeyfields Nursing (charity); Member, Priory Multi-Academy Trust 2015-; President Weston Conservative Club, President Weston Constitutional Club.

Publications: Members' Rights (The Bow Group, 1997); Better Regulation (Conservative Party, 2009); UK Tourism Policy (UK Government, 2010); We Deserve Better (2013).

Recreations: Fishing, beekeeping.

John Penrose MP, House of Commons, London SW1A 0AA
Tel: 020 7219 5310 *Email:* penrosej@parliament.uk
Constituency: 24-26 Alexandra Parade, Weston-Super-Mare, Somerset BS23 1QX
Tel: 01934 613841 *Fax:* 01934 632955 *Email:* john@johnpenrose.org charlotte@johnpenrose.org
Website: www.johnpenrose.org *Twitter:* @JohnPenroseNews

PERCY, ANDREW

Brigg and Goole *(Majority 12,363)*

CONSERVATIVE

Andrew Theakstone Percy. Born 18 September 1977.

Education: York University.

Non-political career: History teacher; MP's researcher; Part-time primary teacher. Member, NASUWT.

Political career: Contested Normanton 2005 general election. Member for Brigg and Goole since 6 May 2010 general election; Trade Envoy to Canada 2016-; Parliamentary Under-Secretary of State (Minister for the Northern Powerhouse), Department for Communities and Local Government 2016-17. *Select committees:* Member: Procedure 2010-11, Regulatory Reform 2010-17, Standing Orders 2011-15, Northern Ireland Affairs 2012-15, Health 2012-16, Panel of Chairs 2015-16. *Councils and public bodies:* Governor, Goole Academy; Assistant Governor, Bricknell Primary School.

Political interests: Education; Canada, Commonwealth, Far East, Israel, USA.

Other: Member, Executive Committee, Commonwealth Parliamentary Association UK 2015-16; Supporter: Countryside Alliance, Campaign Against Political Correctness; Patron: Save a Child's Heart UK, St Mary's Community Charity, Goole; Ambassador, White Ribbon Campaign; Chair: Imagination Library Goole and Snaith, Imagination Library North Lincolnshire; Community First Responder, Yorkshire Ambulance Service; Chair: Ancholme Flood Strategy Board, Brigg 2020, Humber Flood Strategy Steering Group; President, Northern Association of Drainage Authorities.

Andrew Percy MP, House of Commons, London SW1A 0AA
Tel: 020 7219 7208 *Email:* andrew.percy.mp@parliament.uk
Constituency: 81-83 Pasture Road, Goole, East Yorkshire DN14 6BP
Tel: 01405 767969 *Email:* brigg.goole@gmail.com
2 Morley's Yard, Old Courts Road, Brigg, North Lincolnshire DN20 8JD
Tel: 01624 650094 *Website:* www.andrewpercy.org

PERKINS, TOBY

Chesterfield *(Majority 9,605)*

LABOUR

Matthew Toby Perkins. Born 12 August 1970; Son of V.F Perkins and late Teresa Perkins, both university lecturers; Married Susan Francis 1996 (1 son 1daughter).

Education: Trinity School, Leamington Spa; Silverdale School, Sheffield.

Non-political career: Telephone sales, CCS Media 1991-95; Recruitment consultant/area manager, Prime Time Recruitment 1995-2002; Business owner, Club Rugby (internet sports firm) 2005-. Member, Amicus/Unite 2005-.

Political career: Member for Chesterfield since 6 May 2010 general election; Shadow Minister for: Education 2010-11, Business, Innovation and Skills 2011-15, Defence 2015-16. *Select committees:* Member: Communities and Local Government 2010, Joint Committee on Statutory Instruments 2010-15, International Trade 2016-17. Chair, PLP Departmental Group for Communities and Local Government 2010-11. Member: Labour Party, Co-operative Party; Campaign Deputy, General Election Strategy 2014-15. *Councils and public bodies:* Councillor, Chesterfield Borough Council 2003-11; Director, Families First Nursery 2007-11.

Political interests: Sport and youth involvement, small businesses, crime, jobs and regeneration.

Other: Founder, Chesterfield Flood Victims Appeal 2007-09; Vice-chair, Progress 2012-. Former player, Chesterfield Rugby Club; Coach, Sheffield Tigers Rugby Club.

Recreations: Rugby (qualified coach).

Toby Perkins MP, House of Commons, London SW1A 0AA
Tel: 020 7219 2320 *Email:* toby.perkins.mp@parliament.uk
Constituency: 113 Saltergate, Chesterfield, Derbyshire S40 1NF
Tel: 01246 386286 *Website:* www.tobyperkins.org.uk *Twitter:* @tobyperkinsmp

PERRY, CLAIRE

Devizes *(Majority 21,136)*

CONSERVATIVE

Minister of State for Climate Change and Industry, Department for Business, Energy and Industrial Strategy

Claire Louise Perry. Born 3 April 1964; Daughter of late Joanna and David Richens, retired; Married Clayton Perry 1996 (divorced 2014) (1 son 2 daughters).

Education: Nailsea Comprehensive School; Oxford University (BA geography 1985); Harvard Business School (MBA 1990).

Non-political career: Analyst, Bank of America 1985-88; Consultant, McKinsey and Company 1990-94; Various roles, Credit Suisse First Boston 1994-2000; Volunteer fundraiser 2002-04; Policy adviser to George Osborne MP 2007-09.

Political career: Member for Devizes since 6 May 2010 general election; PPS to Philip Hammond as Secretary of State for Defence 2011-13; Chair, Independent Parliamentary Inquiry into Online Child Protection -2012; Adviser to the Prime Minister on Preventing the Sexualisation and Commercialisation of Childhood 2012-14; Assistant Government Whip 2013-14; Parliamentary Under-Secretary of State, Department for Transport 2014-16; Minister of State for Climate Change and Industry, Department for Business, Energy and Industrial Strategy 2017-. *Select committees:* Member, Justice 2010-11. Member, Conservative Party 2006-; Founding member: 2020 group 2011-, Conservative Women's Forum. *Councils and public bodies:* Governor: Wellington Academy, Tidworth 2010-14, St John's School, Marlborough 2010-14.

Political interests: Economy, education, defence, transport, infrastructure, child protection, climate change, business.

Recreations: Reading, walking, cycling, gardening.

Claire Perry MP, House of Commons, London SW1A 0AA
Tel: 020 7219 7050 *Email:* claire.perry.mp@parliament.uk
Constituency: Renelec House, 46 New Park Street, Devizes, Wiltshire SN10 1DT
Tel: 01380 729358 *Website:* www.claireperry.org.uk

PHILLIPS, JESS

Birmingham, Yardley *(Majority 16,574)*

LABOUR

Jessica Rose Phillips. Born 9 October 1981; Married Tom Phillips (2 sons).

Education: Leeds University (BA economic and social history/social policy 2003); Institute of Local Government, Birmingham University (PGD public sector management 2013).

Non-political career: Project/event manager, Health Links 2008-10; Business development manager, Sandwell Women's Aid 2010-15.

Political career: Member for Birmingham, Yardley since 7 May 2015 general election; PPS to Lucy Powell as Shadow Secretary of State for Education 2015-16; Member, Commons Reference Group on Representation and Inclusion 2017-. *Select committees:* Member: Women and Equalities 2015-, Backbench Business 2015-. Chair, PLP Departmental Group for Women 2016-. *Councils and public bodies:* Victims Champion for Birmingham 2011; Councillor, Birmingham City Council 2012-16.

Publications: Everywoman: One Woman's Truth About Speaking the Truth (Penguin, 2017).

Jess Phillips MP, House of Commons, London SW1A 0AA
Tel: 020 7219 8703 *Email:* jess.phillips.mp@parliament.uk
Constituency: 64 Yardley Road, Acocks Green, West Midlands B27 6LG
Tel: 0121-708 2412 *Website:* www.jessphillips.net *Twitter:* @jessphillips

PHILLIPSON, BRIDGET

Houghton and Sunderland South *(Majority 12,341)*

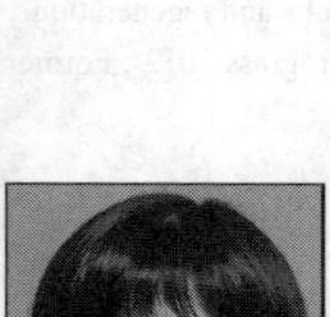

LABOUR

Bridget Maeve Phillipson. Born 19 December 1983; Daughter of Clare Phillipson; Married Lawrence Dimery 2009 (1 daughter 1 son).

Education: St Robert of Newminster School and Sixth Form College, Washington; Hertford College, Oxford (MA modern history 2005); French, Spanish.

Non-political career: Sunderland City Council 2005-07; Women's refuge manager, Wearside Women in Need 2007-10. Member, GMB 2005-.

Political career: Member for Houghton and Sunderland South since 6 May 2010 general election; Member Speaker's Committee on the Electoral Commission 2010-; PPS to Jim Murphy as Shadow Secretary of State for Defence 2010-13; Opposition Whip 2013-15. *Select committees:* Member: Home Affairs 2010-13, Procedure 2010-11, Public Accounts 2015-. Labour Party: Member 1998-, Former chair, Oxford University Labour Club, National Policy Forum: North East representative 2008-10, Vice-chair 2013-.

Political interests: Housing, UK software industry, jobs, economy.

Other: Cancer Research UK, Durham Scouts Association.

Recreations: Running, reading, history, music.

Bridget Phillipson MP, House of Commons, London SW1A 0AA
Tel: 020 7219 7087 *Fax:* 020 7219 2419 *Email:* bridget.phillipson.mp@parliament.uk
Constituency: 106 Newbottle Street, Houghton le Spring, Tyne and Wear DH4 4AJ
Tel: 0191-584 4317 *Email:* bridget@bridgetphillipson.co.uk *Website:* www.bridgetphillipson.com
Twitter: @bphillipsonmp

PHILP, CHRIS

Croydon South *(Majority 11,406)*

Team PPS, HM Treasury

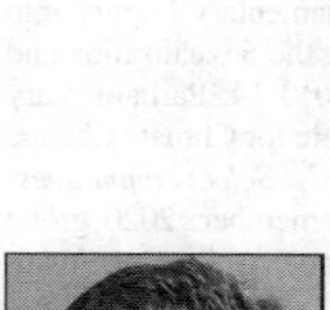

CONSERVATIVE

Chris Ian Brian Mynitt Philp. Born 6 July 1976; Son of Dr Brian Philp MBE, Director of Kent Archaeological Rescue Unit; Married Elizabeth (twin son and daughter).

Education: St Olave's Grammar School, Orpington; University College, Oxford (physics 1998).

Non-political career: McKinsey & Co; Owner, distribution company; Property Investment manager; Director, BP Balkans Pluto (Cyprus) Ltd.

Political career: Contested Hampstead and Kilburn 2010 general election. Member for Croydon South since 7 May 2015 general election; Team PPS, HM Treasury 2017-. *Select committees:* Member, Treasury 2015-17. Co-ordinator, Conservative No2AV Campaign, London; Conservative National No2AV Spokesperson; National Conservatives Treasurers team. *Councils and public bodies:* Councillor, London Borough of Camden Council 2006-10.

Political interests: Economy, creating jobs, state education, housing, road and rail transport.

Other: Former chair, Bow Group; Founder, Next Big Thing 2009-. London's Emerging Entrepreneur, Ernst and Young/*The Times* 2003.

Recreations: Horse riding, skiing, running, football.

Chris Philp MP, House of Commons, London SW1A 0AA
Tel: 020 7219 8026 *Email:* chris.philp.mp@parliament.uk
Constituency: c/o Croydon Conservative Association, 36 Brighton Road, Purley, Surrey CR8 2LG
Tel: 020 8660 0491 *Websites:* www.croydonconservatives.com www.chrisphilp.com
Twitter: @CPhilpOfficial

LABOUR

PIDCOCK, LAURA

North West Durham *(Majority 8,792)*

Education: Manchester Metropolitan University (BA politics).

Non-political career: Mental health support worker; North East Education Manager, Show Racism the Red Card.

Political career: Member for North West Durham since 8 June 2017. *Select committees:* Member, Justice 2017-. Member, Labour National Policy Forum. *Councils and public bodies:* Councillor, Northumberland County Council 2013-17.

Laura Pidcock MP, House of Commons, London SW1A 0AA
Tel: 020 7219 2701 *Email:* laura.pidcock.mp@parliament.uk
Constituency: Details still to be confirmed
Tel: 01207 501782 *Twitter:* @laurapidcockmp

CONSERVATIVE

PINCHER, CHRISTOPHER

Tamworth *(Majority 12,347)*

Government Whip (Comptroller of HM Household)

Christopher John Pincher. Born 24 September 1969; Son of John Pincher and Sandra Pincher; Single.

Education: Ounsdale School, Staffordshire; London School of Economics (BSc (Econ) government and history 1991).

Non-political career: Manager, Accenture 1993-2010.

Political career: Contested Warley 1997 and Tamworth 2005 general elections. Member for Tamworth since 6 May 2010 general election; PPS to Philip Hammond as Foreign Secretary 2015-16; Assistant Government Whip 2016-17; Government Whip (Comptroller of HM Household) 2017-. *Select committees:* Member: Energy and Climate Change 2010-15, Armed Forces Bill 2011, Standing Orders 2011-15, Regulatory Reform 2015-16, Selection 2017-. 1922 Committee: Member, Executive 2014, Secretary 2014-15. Member, Conservative Party 1987-; Treasurer, Conservative Friends of Azerbaijan.

Political interests: Home affairs, defence, education, energy; Azerbaijan, Middle East, Latvia, Russia, USA.

Other: Macmillan Cancer Support, Tamworth in the Community; Travellers' Club.

Recreations: Literature and biographies, golf, the turf, history, Formula 1, horse racing.

Christopher Pincher MP, House of Commons, London SW1A 0AA
Tel: 020 7219 7169 *Email:* christopher.pincher.mp@parliament.uk
Constituency: The White House, 93 Lichfield Street, Tamworth, Staffordshire B79 7QF
Tel: 01827 312778 *Website:* www.christopherpincher.com *Twitter:* @ChrisPincher

LAB/CO-OP

PLATT, JO

Leigh *(Majority 9,554)*

PPS to Angela Rayner as Shadow Secretary of State for Education

Joanne Marie Platt. Born 15 June 1973; 2 children.

Non-political career: Advocacy Worker, Willow 2012-13.

Political career: Member for Leigh since 8 June 2017; PPS to Angela Rayner as Shadow Secretary of State for Education 2017-; Secretary, Leigh CLP. *Councils and public bodies:* Wigan Council: Councillor 2012-17, Cabinet Member for Children and Young People 2014-17; Governor, Boothstown Holy Family School 2011-.

Other: Astley Green Colliery Liaison Panel; Metrofresh Advisory Board.

Jo Platt MP, House of Commons, London SW1A 0AA
Tel: 020 7219 0078 *Email:* joanne.platt.mp@parliament.uk
Constituency: Details still to be confirmed *Website:* www.joplatt.me *Twitter:* @JoPlattMP

LAB/CO-OP

POLLARD, LUKE

Plymouth, Sutton and Devonport *(Majority 6,807)*

PPS to Sue Hayman as Shadow Secretary of State for Environment, Food and Rural Affairs

Luke Jonathan Pollard. Born 10 April 1980; Partner.

Education: Tavistock College, Tavistock; Christleton High School, Chester; Exeter University (BA politics 2001); German.

Non-political career: Researcher to George Foulkes MP 2003-05; Account director, Edelman 2005-09; Association of British Travel Agents: Head of public affairs 2009-13, Head of European development 2013-14; Director, Field Consulting UK 2015-17. Member, Unite (TGWU section) 2003-.

Political career: Contested South West Devon 2010 and Plymouth, Sutton and Devonport 2015 general elections. Member for Plymouth, Sutton and Devonport since 8 June 2017; PPS to Sue Hayman as Shadow Secretary of State for Environment, Food and Rural Affairs 2017-. *Select committees:* Member, Transport 2017-. Member, Co-operative Party 2007-. *Councils and public bodies:* Governor, Millbank Primary School 2008-13.

Political interests: Defence, health, education, housing, agriculture.

Other: Member, Fabian Society 2003-. House of Lords and Commons Hockey Club.

Recreations: Hockey, football (Plymouth Argyle), running.

Luke Pollard MP, House of Commons, London SW1A 0AA
Tel: 020 7219 2749 *Email:* luke.pollard.mp@parliament.uk
Constituency: Office 8, 24-26 The Crescent, Plymouth PL1 3FG
Tel: 01752 717255 *Website:* www.lukepollard.org *Twitter:* @lukepollard

CONSERVATIVE

POULTER, DAN

Central Suffolk and North Ipswich *(Majority 17,185)*

Daniel Leonard James Poulter. Born 30 October 1978.

Education: Bristol University (LLB); Guys and St Thomas' School of Medicine (MBBS); King's College, London (AKC).

Non-political career: Speciality registrar, obstetrics and gynaecology 2008-10; NHS doctor 2010-; Visiting Professor, King's College London 2016-.

Political career: Member for Central Suffolk and North Ipswich since 6 May 2010 general election; Parliamentary Under-Secretary of State, Department of Health 2012-15. *Select committees:* Member: Health 2011-12, Joint Committee on the Draft House of Lords Reform Bill 2011-12, Scottish Affairs 2015-17, Energy and Climate Change 2015-16, Backbench Business 2016-17, Public Administration and Constitutional Affairs 2016-17, Environmental Audit 2017-. *Councils and public bodies:* Councillor, Hastings Borough Council 2006-07; Deputy Leader, Reigate and Banstead Council 2008-10.

Political interests: Health, rural affairs, pensions, older people, voluntary sector, overseas development, energy and climate change; Australasia, Caribbean.

Other: Member, British Medical Association -2012, 2015-; Help the Heroes, Set up medical and lifestyle advice clinics for homeless, raised money for victims of domestic violence, St Elizabeth Hospice Ipswich. Guy's Hospital Rugby Club.

Publications: Published author in field of women's health.

Recreations: Cricket, rugby, golf, fishing.

Dr Dan Poulter MP, House of Commons, London SW1A 0AA
Tel: 020 7219 7038 *Fax:* 020 7219 1192 *Email:* daniel.poulter.mp@parliament.uk
Constituency: Suite Five, The Technology Centre, Framlingham, Suffolk IP13 9EZ
Tel: 01728 726588 *Website:* www.drdanielpoulter.com *Twitter:* @drdanpoulter

LABOUR

POUND, STEPHEN

Ealing North *(Majority 19,693)*

Shadow Minister for Northern Ireland

Stephen Pelham Pound. Born 3 July 1948; Son of late Pelham Pound, journalist, and late Dominica Pound, teacher; Married Maggie Griffiths 1976 (1 son 1 daughter).

Education: Hertford Grammar School; London School of Economics (Diploma industrial relations 1979; BSc economics 1982) (Sabbatical President of Union 1981-82).

Non-political career: Armed Forces Parliamentary Scheme (Navy). Seaman 1964-66; Bus conductor 1966-68; Hospital porter 1969-79; Student 1979-84; Housing officer 1984-97. Branch Secretary, 640 Middlesex Branch, COHSE 1975-79; Branch Officer, TGWU 1990-96; Member: Unite, GMB.

Political career: Member for Ealing North 1997-2010, for Ealing North (revised boundary) since 6 May 2010 general election; PPS: to Hazel Blears: as Minister of State, Home Office 2005-06, as Minister without Portfolio 2006-07, to Stephen Timms: as Minister of State, Department for Business, Enterprise and Regulatory Reform 2007-08, as Minister of State, Department for Work and Pensions 2008, as Financial Secretary, HM Treasury 2008-09, 2010, to Sadiq Khan as Minister of State, Department for Transport 2009; Opposition Assistant Whip 2010; Shadow Minister for Northern Ireland 2010-. *Select committees:* Member: Broadcasting 1997-2001, Northern Ireland Affairs 1999-2010, Standards and Privileges 2003-05. Member, Labour Party Departmental Committee for Environment, Transport and the Regions 1997-2001. *Councils and public bodies:* London Borough of Ealing: Councillor 1982-98, Mayor 1995-96.

Countries of interest: Armenia, Assyria, Ireland, Poland, Ukraine.

Other: Outstanding Achievement (with David Amess MP and Bob Russell MP), Charity Champion awards 2012. Order of Merit (Officer Class), Republic of Poland. Fulham FC Supporters Club.

Recreations: Watching football, playing cricket, snooker, jazz, gardening, collecting comics.

Stephen Pound MP, House of Commons, London SW1A 0AA
Tel: 020 7219 4312 *Fax:* 020 7219 5982 *Email:* steve.pound.mp@parliament.uk
Constituency: No constituency office *Website:* www.stevepound.org.uk

CONSERVATIVE

POW, REBECCA

Taunton Deane *(Majority 15,887)*

Team PPS, Department for Environment, Food and Rural Affairs

Rebecca Faye Pow. Born 10 October 1960; Married Charles Clark (3 children).

Education: Wye College; Imperial College, London (BSc rural environment studies 1982).

Non-political career: Set up PR and communications business, Pow Productions 1988-; Reporter, BBC, ITV and Channel 4, specialising in the environment, farming and gardening 1989-2005; National Farmers Union.

Political career: Member for Taunton Deane since 7 May 2015 general election; PPS to Gavin Barwell as Minister of State for Housing and Planning and Minister for London, Department for Communities and Local Government 2016-17; Team PPS, Department for Environment, Food and Rural Affairs 2017-. *Select committees:* Member: Environment, Food and Rural Affairs 2015-17, Environmental Audit 2015-16, Environment, Food and Rural Affairs Sub-committee 2016-17, Digital, Culture, Media and Sport 2017-. Chairman, Conservative Backbench Policy Committee on Environment, Food and Rural Affairs 2016-17. Parliamentary Liaison Officer, Conservative Rural Affairs Group 2016-. *Councils and public bodies:* Former school governor; Councillor, Stoke St Mary Parish Council.

Other: Trustee, Somerset Wildlife Trust.

Rebecca Pow MP, House of Commons, London SW1A 0AA
Tel: 020 7219 4831 *Email:* rebecca.pow.mp@parliament.uk
Constituency: Masons House, Magdalene Street, Taunton TA1 1SG
Tel: 01823 443062 *Website:* www.rebeccapow.org.uk *Twitter:* @pow_rebecca

LAB/CO-OP

POWELL, LUCY

Manchester Central *(Majority 31,445)*

Lucy Maria Powell. Born 10 October 1974; Married James (1 daughter 1 son 1 stepson).

Education: Parrs Wood High School, Manchester; Xaverian Sixth Form; Oxford University (BSc chemistry); King's College, London.

Non-political career: Labour Party, London, general election campaign 1997; Parliamentary assistant to Beverley Hughes MP; Director, Britain in Europe; Project manager, National Endowment for Science, Technology and the Arts (NESTA) 2007-10; Deputy chief of staff to Ed Miliband MP as Labour Party Leader 2010-12. Member, Unite.

Political career: Contested Manchester Withington 2010 general election. Member for Manchester Central since 15 November 2012 by-election; Shadow Minister for: Childcare and Children 2013-14, the Cabinet Office 2014-15; Shadow Secretary of State for Education 2015-16. *Select committees:* Member: Transport 2012-13, Education 2017-. Chair, PLP Departmental Group for Communities and Local Government 2017-. Member, Co-operative Party; Campaign manager to Ed Miliband MP, Labour Party Leadership Campaign 2010; Vice-chair, General Election Campaign (Operations) 2014-15.

Political interests: Education, health, environment, foreign policy, regeneration, economic development, innovation and skills.

Recreations: Manchester City FC.

Lucy Powell MP, House of Commons, London SW1A 0AA
Tel: 020 7219 4402 *Email:* lucy.powell.mp@parliament.uk
Constituency: No constituency office publicised
Tel: 0161-232 0872 *Email:* contact@lucypowell.org.uk *Website:* lucypowell.org.uk
Twitter: @LucyMPowell

CONSERVATIVE

PRENTIS, VICTORIA

Banbury *(Majority 12,399)*

PPS to Andrea Leadsom as Leader of the House of Commons and Lord President of the Council

Victoria Mary Boswell Prentis. Born 24 March 1971; Daughter of Timothy Boswell (MP for Daventry 1987-2010, now Lord Boswell of Aynho (qv)) and Helen Delahay, née Rees; Married Sebastian Prentis 1996 (2 daughters 1 son deceased).

Education: Malvern St James Girls' School; University of London (BA English literature 1992); Downing College, Cambridge (MA law 1994); French, German.

Non-political career: Called to the Bar, Middle Temple 1995; Government Legal Service 1997-2014.

Political career: Member for Banbury since 7 May 2015 general election; PPS to: John Hayes as Minister of State, Department for Transport 2016-17, Andrea Leadsom as Leader of the House of Commons and Lord President of the Council 2017-. *Select committees:* Member: Justice 2015-, Joint Committee on Statutory Instruments 2015-. Founding member, Conservatives for Reform in Europe 2016.

Political interests: Maternal health, aspirations and education, human rights, justice, especially prison reform, early years, transport; China, France, Germany, Morocco, Russia.

Other: Director, Transport Sense; Member, Benefactors' Board, Oxford Children's Hospital Trust; Hands Up Foundation (Singing for Syrians); Carlton Club, Farmers' Club.

Recreations: Cider making, cooking, detective fiction, charitable fundraising.

Victoria Prentis MP, House of Commons, London SW1A 0AA
Tel: 020 7219 8756 *Email:* victoria.prentis.mp@parliament.uk
Constituency: Heyford Park House, Upper Heyford, Bicester, Oxfordshire OX25 5HD
Tel: 01869 233685 *Website:* victoriaprentis.com *Twitter:* @VictoriaPrentis

CONSERVATIVE

PRISK, MARK

Hertford and Stortford *(Majority 19,035)*

Michael Mark Prisk. Born 12 June 1962; Son of Michael Prisk, chartered surveyor, and Irene Prisk, née Pearce; Married Lesley Titcomb 1989.

Education: Truro School, Cornwall; Reading University (BSc land management 1983).

Non-political career: Graduate surveyor, Knight Frank 1983-85; Derrick Wade & Waters 1985-91: Senior surveyor 1985-89, Director 1989-91; Principal, mp^2, consultancy 1991-2001.

Political career: Contested Newham North West 1992 and Wansdyke 1997 general elections. Member for Hertford and Stortford 2001-10, for Hertford and Stortford (revised boundary) since 6 May 2010 general election; Shadow Financial Secretary 2002-03; Shadow Paymaster General 2003-04; Opposition Whip 2004-05; Shadow Minister for: Business and Enterprise 2005-09, Business 2009-10; Minister of State for: Business and Enterprise, Department for Business, Innovation and Skills 2010-12, Housing, Department for Communities and Local Government 2012-13; Trade Envoy to: Nordic and Baltics 2014-, Brazil 2016-. *Select committees:* Member: Welsh Affairs 2001-05, Regulatory Reform 2008-09, Speaker's Committee on the Electoral Commission 2013, Communities and Local Government 2015-. Secretary, Conservative Defence/Foreign Affairs Policy Committee 2001-02. Chair, Reading University Conservatives 1981-82; National vice-chair, Federation of Conservative Students 1982-83; Deputy chair, Hertfordshire Area Conservatives 1999-2000; Member, Conservative Business Relations Board 2006-; Founding member, Conservatives for Reform in Europe 2016.

Political interests: Defence, education, planning, development, small businesses, trade, foreign direct investment, smart cities; Brazil, China, Estonia, Italy, Latvia, Oman, Russia, Scandinavia, USA.

Other: Member, Prince's Trust; Founding Chair, Youth For Peace Through NATO 1983-86; Chair, Hertfordshire Countryside Partnership; Creator, Charter for Hertfordshire's Countryside; Vice-President, First Defence 2004-10; Trustee: Industry and Parliamentary Trust 2007-10, Parliamentary Choir; Director, Edward Stanford Limited; Fellow, Royal Institute of Chartered Surveyors; Fellow, Royal Institute of Chartered Surveyors.

Publications: Eternal Vigilance, The Defence of a Free Society (First Defence, 2003).

Recreations: Music, piano, rugby, cricket, theatre, architecture, choral singing.

Mark Prisk MP, House of Commons, London SW1A 0AA
Tel: 020 7219 6358 *Email:* natalie.bithell@parliament.uk
Constituency: Room GF31, Harlow Enterprise Hub, Kao Hockham Building, Edinburgh Way, Harlow, Essex CM20 2NQ
Tel: 01279 312197 *Website:* www.markprisk.com *Twitter:* @PriskMark

CONSERVATIVE

PRITCHARD, MARK

The Wrekin *(Majority 9,564)*

Mark Andrew Pritchard. Born 22 November 1966; Son of late Frank Pritchard and Romona Pritchard; Divorced 2013.

Education: St Owen's School, Hereford; Afan Comprehensive School, Cymmer, Glamorgan; Aylestone School, Hereford; Regents Theological College; London Guildhall University (MA marketing management; Postgraduate Diploma marketing); Buckingham University (MA international diplomacy).

Non-political career: Parliamentary researcher 1993-05; Director and founder 1998-2007: Pritchard Communications Ltd, Next Steps Market Research Ltd.

Political career: Contested Warley 2001 general election. Member for The Wrekin 2005-10, for The Wrekin (revised boundary) since 6 May 2010 general election; Trade Envoy to Georgia and Armenia 2017-. *Select committees:* Member: Environmental Audit 2005-07, Work and Pensions 2006-09, Welsh Affairs 2007-10, Transport 2009-10, Joint Committee on National Security Strategy 2010-15, International Development 2012-13, Panel of Chairs 2012-, Joint Committee on Human Rights 2015-, Northern Ireland Affairs 2016-17. Joint secretary, Conservative Parliamentary: Defence Committee -2005, Foreign Affairs Committee -2005; Secretary, 1922 Committee 2010-12. National Board Member, Conservative Councillors Association 2002; Conservative Party Human Rights Commission 2006-; Deputy Chair, International Office, Conservative Party 2010-12. *Councils and public bodies:* Councillor, Harrow Council 1993-94; Woking Borough Council: Councillor 2000-03, Chair, Economic Committee.

Political interests: Defence, cyber-security, homeland security, foreign relations, counter-terrorism, animal welfare and conservation; Africa, Latin America, ASEAN region, India, Israel, USA.

Other: UK Chair, Parliamentarians for Global Action; Member, Executive Committee: Commonwealth Parliamentary Association, Inter-Parliamentary Union; British American Parliamentary Group: Executive Member, Vice-chair 2010-; Member, UK parliamentary delegation to NATO 2010-; Vice-chair, Inter-Parliamentary Union, British Group 2010-11; Member: British Irish Parliamentary Assembly 2013-, UK delegation, Parliamentary Assembly of the Council of Europe 2015-; Bow Group Council 1994; Member, Miniature Schnauzer Club of Great Britain; Oliver Twist Club; Founder, The Music Charity; Member: Chartered Institute of Marketing, Institute of Public Relations, Market Research Society; Great Ormond Street Children's Hospital, Various orphanage charities, Hereford Cathedral Perpetual Trust; Carlton Club.

Recreations: Walking, skiing, writing, animal welfare, tennis, writing comedy.

Mark Pritchard MP, House of Commons, London SW1A 0AA
Tel: 020 7219 8494 *Fax:* 020 7219 5969 *Email:* pritchardm@parliament.uk
Constituency: 25 Church Street, Wellington, Shropshire TF1 1DG
Tel: 01952 256080 *Fax:* 01952 256080 *Website:* www.markpritchard.com
Twitter: @MPritchardUK

CONSERVATIVE

PURSGLOVE, TOM

Corby *(Majority 2,690)*

PPS to Liam Fox as Secretary of State for International Trade and President of the Board of Trade

Thomas Christopher John Pursglove. Born 5 November 1988.

Education: Sir Christopher Hatton School, Wellingborough; Queen Mary College, University of London (BA politics).

Non-political career: Parliamentary Assistant to Christopher Heaton-Harris MP 2010-15; Director, Together Against Wind Ltd.

Political career: Member for Corby since 7 May 2015 general election; PPS to: Robert Goodwill as Minister of State for Immigration, Home Office 2016-17, Liam Fox as Secretary of State for International Trade and President of the Board of Trade 2017-; Chairman, Political, Wellingborough Conservative Association 2011-14; Founding member, Conservatives for Britain 2015-16. *Councils and public bodies:* Councillor, Wellingborough Borough Council 2007-15.

Political interests: Energy policy, EU referendum, constitutional matters, home affairs; USA.

Other: Founding member, Grassroots Out 2015-16; Crazy Hats, Cransley Hospice. Wellingborough Old Grammarians Cricket Club; Welllingborough Golf Club.

Recreations: Cricket (ECB qualified umpire), golf.

Tom Pursglove MP, House of Commons, London SW1A 0AA
Tel: 020 7219 8043 *Email:* tom.pursglove.mp@parliament.uk
Constituency: No constituency office publicised *Website:* www.votepursglove.co.uk
Twitter: @VotePursglove

CONSERVATIVE

QUIN, JEREMY

Horsham *(Majority 23,484)*

Team PPS, Department for Exiting the European Union

Jeremy Mark Quin. Born 24 September 1968; Son of the Revd David Quin and late Elizabeth Quin; Married Joanna.

Education: St Albans School; Hertford College, Oxford (modern history 1990).

Non-political career: NatWest Securities/BT Alex Brown 1990-2000; Deutsche Bank: Managing Director: Corporate Finance (Global Consumer Group) 2001-08, UK Corporate Finance/Regional Management 2009-15; Senior corporate finance adviser, HM Treasury 2008-09.

Political career: Contested Meirionnydd Nant Conwy 1997 general election. Member for Horsham since 7 May 2015 general election; Department for Exiting the European Union: PPS to David Jones as Minister of State 2016-17, Team PPS 2017-. *Select committees:* Member: Work and Pensions 2015-16, Regulatory Reform 2015-. Buckingham Constituency Conservative Association: Chair 2010-13, Vice-President 2013-; Deputy chair, Oxfordshire and Buckinghamshire Conservatives 2013-15. *Councils and public bodies:* Thornborough School: Governor 2010-15, Chair of Finance.

Political interests: Treasury/economic affairs, welfare, financial inclusion; China, India.

Other: Trustee, Mitsubishi UFJ Trust Oxford Foundation; Member, Financial Inclusion Commission 2016-.

Recreations: Countryside, history, cricket.

Jeremy Quin MP, House of Commons, London SW1A 0AA
Tel: 020 7219 6341 *Email:* jeremy.quin.mp@parliament.uk
Constituency: Gough House, Madeira Avenue, Horsham, West Sussex RH12 1AB
Tel: 01403 210600 *Website:* www.jeremyquin.com

CONSERVATIVE

QUINCE, WILL

Colchester *(Majority 5,677)*

Team PPS, Cabinet Office

William James Quince. Born 27 December 1982; Married Elinor Hart (1 daughter).

Education: Windsor Boys' School; University of Wales, Aberystwyth (LLB 2005) (Deputy President Student's Union); University of West of England, Bristol (Postgraduate Diploma legal practice 2012).

Non-political career: Armed Forces Parliamentary Scheme. Marketing developing executive, Concur Technologies 2005-06; Britvic plc: Customer development executive 2006-07, Customer development manager 2007-09, Customer development manager, branded restuarants 2008-10; Trainee solicitor, Asher Prior Bates 2010-13; Solicitor, Thompson Smith and Puxon Solicitors 2013-15.

Political career: Contested Colchester 2010 general election. Member for Colchester since 7 May 2015 general election; Team PPS, Cabinet Office 2017-; Member, Commons Reference Group on Representation and Inclusion 2017-. *Select committees:* Member: Transport 2015-17, Home Affairs 2017-. Member, national executive, Conservative Future 2003-04. *Councils and public bodies:* East Hertfordshire District Council: Councillor 2007-09, Chair, Environmental Scrutiny Committee; Councillor, Colchester Borough Council 2011-16.

Political interests: Health, transport, justice, voluntary sector; China.

Other: Member, Bow Group 2007-; Trustee, Grassroots – Colchester and Tendring Community Trust; Law Society.

Will Quince MP, House of Commons, London SW1A 0AA
Tel: 020 7219 8049 *Email:* will.quince.mp@parliament.uk
Constituency: 37 Layer Road, Colchester, Essex CO2 7JW
Tel: 01206 545990 *Website:* www.willquince.com *Twitter:* @willquince

QURESHI, YASMIN

Bolton South East *(Majority 13,126)*

LABOUR

Shadow Minister for Justice

Born 5 July 1963; Daughter of Mohammad Qureshi, civil engineer, and Sakina Beg, primary school teacher; Married Nadeem Ashraf Butt 2008.

Education: Westfield School; South Bank Polytechnic, London (BA law 1984); Council of Legal Education (Barrister Exams 1985); University College, London (Masters law); Punjabi, Urdu.

Non-political career: Called to the Bar, Lincoln's Inn 1985; Barrister 1987-: Crown prosecutor, Crown Prosecution Service 1987-2000, 2004-08; United Nations Mission in Kosovo, Judicial Affairs Department Co-ordinator, Criminal Law Unit 2000-01, Department director 2001-02; Human rights adviser to Ken Livingstone as Mayor of London 2004-08; Barrister: 2 Kings Bench Walk Chambers, London 2004-08, Kenworthy's Chambers 2008-. Member: First Division Association, USDAW, GMB.

Political career: Contested Brent East 2005 general election. Member for Bolton South East since 6 May 2010 general election; Shadow Minister for Justice 2016-. *Select committees:* Member: Justice 2010-15, Political and Constitutional Reform 2011, Joint Committee on Privacy and Injunctions 2011-12, Home Affairs 2013-15, High Speed Rail (London-West Midlands) Bill 2014-15, Foreign Affairs 2015-16. Vice-chair, PLP Departmental Group for Women 2013-. Watford CLP, Labour Party: Secretary, Treasurer, Regional delegate to area, Delegate to Labour group.

Political interests: Crime, education, young people.

Other: Former chair, Human Rights and Civil Liberties Working Group, Association of Muslim Lawyers; Former president, Pakistan Club (UK); British Institute of Human Rights; Society of Labour Lawyers; Fabian Society: Member, Former chair, Watford and District branch; Voluntary legal work for the Free Representation Unit; Bolton Labour Socialist Club.

Recreations: Reading.

Yasmin Qureshi MP, House of Commons, London SW1A 0AA
Tel: 020 7219 7019 *Fax:* 020 7219 0595 *Email:* yasmin.qureshi.mp@parliament.uk
Constituency: c/o Bolton Labour Party, 60 St Georges Road, Bolton, Lancashire BL1 2DD
Tel: 01204 371202 *Website:* www.yasminqureshi.org.uk *Twitter:* @YasminQureshiMP

RAAB, DOMINIC

Esher and Walton *(Majority 23,298)*

CONSERVATIVE

Minister of State, Ministry of Justice

Dominic Rennie Raab. Born 25 February 1974; Married Erika (1 son).

Education: Dr Challoner's Grammar School, Amersham; Lady Margaret Hall, Oxford (law); Jesus College, Cambridge (Master's law).

Non-political career: Lawyer, Linklaters; Foreign and Commonwealth Office 2000-06: British Embassy, The Hague 2003-06; Chief of staff to: David Davis MP 2006-08, Dominic Grieve MP 2008-10.

Political career: Member for Esher and Walton since 6 May 2010 general election; Parliamentary Under-Secretary of State for Human Rights, Ministry of Justice 2015-16; Minister of State, Ministry of Justice 2017-. *Select committees:* Member: Joint Committee on Human Rights 2010-13, Education 2013-15, Exiting the European Union 2016-17.

Political interests: Civil liberties, human rights, industrial relations, economy; Far East, Latin America, Middle East.

Other: Member, Campaign committee, Vote Leave 2016; Founding supporter, Change Britain 2016-; Member, advisory board, Reliance ACSN Ltd 2017-; Member, Law Society; Esher Neighbourhood Fund. Clive Parry Prize for international law; Newcomer of the Year, *Spectator* awards 2011.

Publications: Author, The Assault on Liberty (Fourth Estate, 2009); Co-author (with Kwasi Kwarteng MP, Priti Patel MP, Chris Skidmore MP and Elizabeth Truss MP), Britannia Unchained: Global Lessons for Growth and Prosperity (Palgrave Macmillan, 2012).

Recreations: Travel, boxing, theatre.

Dominic Raab MP, House of Commons, London SW1A 0AA
Tel: 020 7219 7069 *Email:* dominic.raab.mp@parliament.uk
Constituency: No constituency office publicised
Email: ursula.henry@parliament.uk *Website:* www.dominicraab.com domraab.blogspot.com

LABOUR

RASHID, FAISAL

Warrington South *(Majority 2,549)*

Mian Faisal Rashid. Born 15 September 1972; Married Aleeza.

Education: NCBA&E (MBA business administration).

Non-political career: Team Manager, HBOS 1999-2005; Relationship Manager, Natwest 2006-17.

Political career: Member for Warrington South since 8 June 2017. *Select committees:* Member, International Trade 2017-. *Councils and public bodies:* Warrington Borough Council: Councillor 2011-17, Mayor 2016-17.

Faisal Rashid MP, House of Commons, London SW1A 0AA
Tel: 020 7219 2775 *Email:* faisal.rashid.mp@parliament.uk
Constituency: 1 Wilson Patten Street, Warrington, Cheshire WA1 1PG
Tel: 01925 657600 *Website:* www.faisalrashid.com *Twitter:* @FaisalRashid6

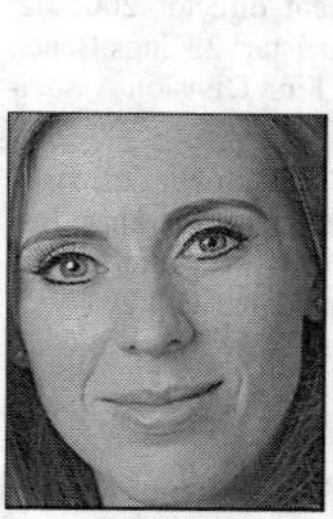

LABOUR

RAYNER, ANGELA

Ashton under Lyne *(Majority 11,295)*

Shadow Secretary of State for Education

Born 28 March 1980; Married Mark (3 children).

Education: Avondale High School.

Non-political career: Care assistant for the elderly 1998-2005; Trade union official, Unison. Unison: Secretary, Stockton branch, Lay official, North West region 2002-15.

Political career: Member for Ashton under Lyne since 7 May 2015 general election; Opposition Whip 2015-16; Shadow Minister for Work and Pensions 2016; Shadow Secretary of State for Education 2016-; Shadow Minister for Women and Equalities 2016. *Select committees:* Member, Communities and Local Government 2015. *Councils and public bodies:* Vice-president, Local Government Association 2017-.

Recreations: Running.

Angela Rayner MP, House of Commons, London SW1A 0AA
Tel: 020 7219 8782 *Email:* angela.rayner.mp@parliament.uk
Constituency: 8 Clarence Arcade, Stamford Street, Ashton-under-Lyne, Greater Manchester OL6 7PT
Email: angela@angelarayner.com *Website:* www.angelarayner.com *Twitter:* @AngelaRayner

CONSERVATIVE

REDWOOD, JOHN

Wokingham *(Majority 18,798)*

John Alan Redwood. Born 15 June 1951; Son of William Redwood and Amy Redwood, née Champion; Married Gail Chippington 1974 (divorced 2004) (1 son 1 daughter).

Education: Kent College, Canterbury; Magdalen College, Oxford (BA modern history 1971, MA); St Antony's College, Oxford (DPhil modern history 1975); French, Spanish.

Non-political career: Fellow, All Souls College, Oxford 1972-87, 2003-05, 2007-; Tutor and lecturer 1972-73; Investment analyst, Robert Fleming & Co. 1974-77; N. M. Rothschild: Bank clerk 1977-78, Manager 1978-79, Assistant director 1979-80, Director, investment division 1980-83, Overseas corporate finance director and head of international (non-UK) privatisation 1986-87; Head, Prime Minister's policy unit 1983-85; Norcros plc: Director 1985-89, Chair 1987-89; Chair, Hare Hatch Holdings 1999-2008; Visiting professor, Middlesex University Business School 2000-16; Chair, Concentric plc 2003-08; Non-executive chair, Evercore Pan-Asset Management Ltd 2008-09.

Political career: Contested Southwark Peckham 1981 by-election. Member for Wokingham 1987-2010, for Wokingham (revised boundary) since 6 May 2010 general election; Department of Trade and Industry: Parliamentary Under-Secretary of State for Corporate Affairs 1989-90, Minister of State 1990-92; Minister for Local Government 1992-93; Secretary of State for Wales 1993-95; Member Shadow Cabinet 1997-2000, 2004-05: Shadow Secretary of State for: Trade and Industry 1997-99, Environment, Transport and the Regions 1999-2000, Deregulation 2004-05; Chair, Conservative Party Committees for: Trade and Industry 1997-99, Environment, Transport and the Regions 1999-2000, Economic Affairs 2010-15, Treasury 2015-17. Contested Conservative Party leadership election 1995, 1997; Chair: No Turning Back Group 2001-, Policy Review on Economic Competitiveness 2005-10; Vice-President, Conservatives for Britain 2015-16. *Councils and public bodies:* Councillor, Oxfordshire County Council 1973-77; Governor, Oxford Polytechnic 1973-77.

Political interests: Popular capitalism, European affairs, constitution, Euro, transport, economy; China, India, USA.

Other: Member, Level 6 Investment Qualification with Distinction 2012, Chartered Institute for Securities and Investment; Various local and educational charities. PC 1993. House of Lords and House of Commons Cricket Club.

Publications: Reason, Ridicule and Religion (Thames & Hudson, 1976); Public Enterprise in Crisis (Blackwell, 1980); Going for Broke (Blackwell, 1984); Popular Capitalism (Routledge, 1987); The Global Marketplace (HarperCollins, 1993); Our Currency, Our Country (Penguin, 1997); Several books and articles, especially on wider ownership and popular capitalism; The Death of Britain (Macmillan, 1999); Stars and Strife (Macmillan, 2001); Just Say No (Politicos, 2001); Third Way Which Way? (Middlesex, 2002); Singing the Blues (Politicos, 2004); Superpower Struggles (Palgrave, 2005); I Want To Make A Difference, But I Don't Like Politics (Politicos, 2006); After the Credit Crisis (Middlesex, 2009).

Recreations: Village cricket, water sports.

Rt Hon John Redwood MP, House of Commons, London SW1A 0AA
Tel: 020 7219 4205 *Fax:* 020 7219 0377 *Email:* john.redwood.mp@parliament.uk
Constituency: 30 Rose Street, Wokingham, Berkshire RG40 1XU
Tel: 0118-304 0200 *Email:* office@wokinghamconservatives.org.uk
Website: www.johnredwoodsdiary.com *Twitter:* @JohnRedwood

LAB/CO-OP

REED, STEVE

Croydon North *(Majority 32,365)*

Shadow Minister for Civil Society

Stephen Mark Ward Reed. Born 12 November 1963.

Education: Sheffield University (English language and literature).

Non-political career: Educational publishing: Routledge, Chapman & Hall, Thomson. Member: Unite, GMB.

Political career: Member for Croydon North since 29 November 2012 by-election; Shadow Minister for: Home Office 2013-15, Communities and Local Government 2015, Local Government 2015-16, Culture, Media and Sport/Digital, Culture, Media and Sport (Civil Society) 2016-. *Select committees:* Member, Public Administration 2012-13. Chair, PLP Departmental Group for Education 2013. Member: Labour Party, Co-operative Party; Patron, LGBT Labour. *Councils and public bodies:* London Borough of Lambeth Council: Councillor 1998-12, Leader 2006-12; Member, London Enterprise Panel 2012-13.

Other: Fellow, Royal Society for the Encouragement of Arts, Manufactures and Commerce. OBE 2013.

Recreations: Cycling, camping, walking, cookery.

Steve Reed OBE MP, House of Commons, London SW1A 0AA
Tel: 020 7219 7297 *Email:* steve.reed.mp@parliament.uk
Constituency: 908 London Road, Thornton Heath CR7 7PE
Tel: 020 8665 1214 *Website:* www.stevereedmp.co.uk *Twitter:* @SteveReedMP

LAB/CO-OP

REES, CHRISTINA

Neath *(Majority 12,631)*

Shadow Secretary of State for Wales

Christina Elizabeth Rees. Born 21 February 1954; Married Ronald Davies 1981 (divorced 2000) (MP for Caerphilly 1983-2001) (1 daughter).

Education: Cynffig Comprehensive School; University of Wales (LLB 1995).

Non-political career: Auditor, South Glamorgan County Council 1979-84; Constituency secretary 1984-96; Called to the Bar 1996; Barrister, 30 Park Place, Cardiff 1997-98; Development officer and national coach, National Governing Body, Squash in Wales 2003-15.

Political career: Member for Neath since 7 May 2015 general election; PPS to Lord Falconer of Thoroton as Shadow Lord Chancellor and Secretary of State for Justice 2015-16; Shadow Minister for Justice Jan-June 2016, October 2016-17; Shadow Secretary of State for Wales 2017-. *Select committees:* Member: Justice 2015, Welsh Affairs 2015-16. Contested Arfon constituency 2011 National Assembly for Wales election and Wales region 2014 European Parliament election. *Councils and public bodies:* Councillor: Mid Glamorgan Council 1988-95, Bridgend Country Borough Council 2012-15, Porthcawl Town Council 2012-15.

Other: Member, UK delegation, Parliamentary Assembly of the Council of Europe 2015-16. Sport Wales National Coach of the Year Award 2008.

Christina Rees MP, House of Commons, London SW1A 0AA
Tel: 020 7219 5783 *Email:* christina.rees.mp@parliament.uk
Constituency: 39 Windsor Road, Neath, West Glamorgan SA11 1NB
Tel: 01639 630152 *Website:* www.christinarees.org *Twitter:* @Rees4Neath

CONSERVATIVE

REES-MOGG, JACOB

North East Somerset *(Majority 10,235)*

Jacob William Rees-Mogg. Born 24 May 1969; Son of late William Rees-Mogg, later Lord Rees-Mogg, and Gillian Rees-Mogg, née Morris; Married Helena de Chair 2007 (5 sons 1 daughter).

Education: Eton College; Trinity College, Oxford (BA history).

Non-political career: *Daily Telegraph* 1989; Conservative Central Office Research Department 1990; J. Rothschild 1991-93; Director: Lloyd George Management 1993-2007, Somerset Capital Management 2007-.

Political career: Contested Central Fife 1997 and the Wrekin 2001 general elections. Member for North East Somerset since 6 May 2010 general election. *Select committees:* Member: Procedure 2010-15, European Scrutiny 2010-, Works of Art 2013-15, House of Commons Governance 2014-15, Treasury 2015-17, Joint Committee on the Palace of Westminster 2015-16, Exiting the European Union 2017-. President, Oxford University Conservative Association 1990; Cities of London and Westminster Conservative Association: Treasurer 1997-2000, Chair 2003-06; Trustee, Conservative Agents' Superannuation Fund.

Political interests: Treasury, Europe (Eurosceptic); China, Far East, India.

Other: Trustee: Mitsubishi UFJ Trust Oxford Foundation, Oxford Literary and Debating Union Trust.

Publications: Co-author, Freedom, Responsibility and the State: Curbing Over-Mighty Government (Politeia, 2012).

Recreations: History, cricket.

Hon Jacob Rees-Mogg MP, House of Commons, London SW1A 0AA
Tel: 020 7219 7118 *Email:* jacob.reesmogg.mp@parliament.uk
Constituency: North East Somerset Conservative Association, Rear of 16 High Street, Keynsham, Bristol BS31 1DQ
Tel: 0117-987 2313 *Fax:* 0117-987 2322 *Email:* jacob@northeastsomersetconservatives.co.uk
Websites: www.northeastsomersetconservatives.co.uk www.jacobreesmogg.com
Twitter: @Jacob_Rees_Mogg

LABOUR

REEVES, ELLIE

Lewisham West and Penge *(Majority 23,162)*

Eleanor Claire Reeves. Born 11 December 1980; Married John Cryer (qv) (MP for Leyton and Wanstead) (1 son).

Education: Oxford University (law).

Non-political career: Called to the Bar 2004; Pupillage, 12 Kings Bench Walk 2004-05; OH Parsons & Partners 2005-07; Senior Executive Solicitor, Thompsons Solicitors 2007-11; Partner, OH Parsons LLPs 2011-16; Barrister, Monaco Solicitors 2016-17.

Political career: Member for Lewisham West and Penge since 8 June 2017. *Select committees:* Member, Justice 2017-. Labour Party: Member, National Executive Committee 2006-16, Vice-chair, London Labour.

Other: Founder, Working Mums Advisory.

Recreations: Travelling, gym, cycling.

Ellie Reeves MP, House of Commons, London SW1A 0AA
Tel: 020 7219 2668 *Email:* ellie.reeves.mp@parliament.uk
Constituency: 43 Sunderland Road, Forest Hill, London SE23 2PS *Website:* www.elliereeves.com
Twitter: @elliereeves

LABOUR

REEVES, RACHEL

Leeds West *(Majority 15,965)*

Chair, Select Committee on Business, Energy and Industrial Strategy

Rachel Jane Reeves. Born 13 February 1979; Daughter of Graham and Sally Reeves, both teachers; Married Dr Nicholas Joicey 2010 (1 daughter 1 son).

Education: Cator Park School; New College, Oxford (BA philosophy, politics and economics 2000); London School of Economics (MSc economics 2004).

Non-political career: Economist: Bank of England 2000-02; British Embassy, Washington DC 2002-03; Bank of England 2004-06, Halifax Bank of Scotland 2006-10. Amicus/MSF/Unite: Member 1998-; Youth representative, Southern Region 1999-2000, Political representative, Southern Region 2001-02, National political committee 2004-06, Yorkshire political committee 2006-.

Political career: Contested Bromley and Chislehurst 2005 general election and 2006 by-election. Member for Leeds West since 6 May 2010 general election; Shadow Minister for Pensions 2010-11; Shadow Chief Secretary to the Treasury 2011-13; Shadow Secretary of State for Work and Pensions 2013-15. *Select committees:* Member: Business, Innovation and Skills 2010, Treasury 2015-17, Liaison 2017-; Chair, Business, Energy and Industrial Strategy 2017-. Vice-chair, PLP Departmental Group for Transport 2010-14. Member, Economy – Work and Business Policy Commission; Labour Friends of Israel. *Councils and public bodies:* Governor: Kirkstall Valley Primary School 2006-10, West Leeds High School 2007-09.

Political interests: Economy, education; China, Japan, USA.

Other: Amnesty International 1996-; Fawcett Society 1998-; Fabian Society 1998-; Board: Leeds Healthy Living Network 2008-, Bramley and Rodley Community Action 2008-10; Patron: Bramley Elderly Action 2010-, June Hancock Mesothelioma Research Fund; Trustee, Bramley and Rodley Community Action 2008-.

Publications: How do Financial Markets React to Central Bank Communication? (Journal of Political Economy, 2006); Why Vote Labour? (2010); Contributor, The Purple Book (Progress, 2011).

Recreations: Tennis, swimming, cycling, reading.

Rachel Reeves MP, House of Commons, London SW1A 0AA
Tel: 020 7219 3000 *Email:* rachel.reeves.mp@parliament.uk
Constituency: 8a Bramley Shopping Centre, Bramley, Leeds, West Yorkshire LS13 2ET
Tel: 0113-255 2311 *Email:* rreevesmp@gmail.com *Website:* www.rachelreevesmp.co.uk
Twitter: @RachelReevesMP

LABOUR

REYNOLDS, EMMA

Wolverhampton North East *(Majority 4,587)*

Emma Elizabeth Reynolds. Born 2 November 1977; Married Richard Stevens 2016 (1 son).

Education: Codsall High School; Wulfrun College; Wadham College, Oxford (BA politics, philosophy and economics 2000); French, Italian, Spanish.

Non-political career: Intern, British High Commission, Pakistan summer 1999; English teacher, France, Spain and Argentina; Information officer, Enlargement Information Centre, European Commission 2000-01; Policy researcher, Small Business Europe, Brussels 2001-04; Political adviser, Party of European Socialists, Brussels 2004-06; Special adviser to Geoff Hoon MP: as Minister for Europe 2006-07, as Chief Whip 2007-08; Senior consultant (part-time), Cogitamus Ltd 2009-10. Member, GMB 2002.

Political career: Member for Wolverhampton North East since 6 May 2010 general election; Shadow Minister for: Foreign and Commonwealth Office 2010-13, Housing 2013-15; Shadow Secretary of State for Communities and Local Government 2015. *Select committees:* Member: Foreign Affairs 2010, Arms Export Controls 2010-11, Health 2015-16, Exiting the European Union 2016-. Chair PLP Departmental Groups for: Health 2015-16, Exiting the European Union 2016-. Member, Joint Policy Committee, Labour Party 2016-.

Political interests: Foreign affairs, public services, economy, welfare state, manufacturing, skills; EU, India, Latin America, Pakistan, USA.

Other: Patron, Vote Leave Watch 2016-.

Recreations: Running, cinema, reading, swimming, tennis.

Emma Reynolds MP, House of Commons, London SW1A 0AA
Tel: 020 7219 6919 *Email:* emma.reynolds.mp@parliament.uk
Constituency: 492a Stafford Road, Wolverhampton, West Midlands WV10 6AN
Tel: 01902 397698 *Fax:* 01902 397538 *Website:* www.emmareynolds.org.uk
Twitter: @EmmaReynoldsMP

LAB/CO-OP

REYNOLDS, JONATHAN

Stalybridge and Hyde *(Majority 8,084)*

Shadow Economic Secretary

Jonathan Neil Reynolds. Born 28 August 1980; Son of Keith Reynolds, fireman, and Judith Reynolds, civil servant; Married Claire (3 sons 1 daughter).

Education: Houghton Kepier Comprehensive School; Sunderland City College; Manchester University (BA politics and modern history 2001); BPP Law School, Manchester (2009).

Non-political career: Honorary Army, Major, Armed Forces Parliamentary Scheme 2010-11. Political Assistant: to Stockport Labour Group 2001-02, to James Purnell MP 2002-08; Trainee Solicitor, Addleshaw Goddard 2009-10; Columnist, Progress Online Magazine 2010-11. Member: Unite, USDAW.

Political career: Member for Stalybridge and Hyde since 6 May 2010 general election; Opposition Assistant Whip 2010-11; PPS to Ed Miliband as Leader of the Opposition 2011-13; Shadow Minister for: Energy and Climate Change 2013-15, Transport 2015-16; Shadow Economic Secretary 2016-. *Select committees:* Member: Science and Technology 2010-12, Finance and Services 2010-12, Standing Orders 2011-15, Business, Innovation and Skills 2016, Education, Skills and the Economy Sub-committee 2016. Member: National Executive Committee, Labour Party 2003-05, Co-operative Party; Labour Friends of Israel; Fabian Society Democratic Reform. *Councils and public bodies:* Tameside Council: Councillor 2007-11, Cabinet Secretary Without Portfolio (Policy and Corporate Performance), Deputy chair, Longdendale and Hattersley District Assembly; Governor: Hollingworth Primary School, Longdendale Language College.

Political interests: Democratic reform, faith issues, transport, defence, economy, manufacturing, climate change, autism, devolution; China, Germany, Middle East, Turkey.

Other: Vice-chair, Progress -2012; Chair, Christians on the Left 2016-; National Autistic Society.

Publications: Contributor, Making the Progressive Case for Israel.

Recreations: Football, history, music, gardening.

Jonathan Reynolds MP, House of Commons, London SW1A 0AA
Tel: 020 7219 7155 *Email:* jonathan.reynolds.mp@parliament.uk
Constituency: Hyde Town Hall, Market Street, Hyde, Greater Manchester SK14 1AL
Tel: 0161-367 8077 *Email:* jonathan@jonathanreynolds.org.uk
Website: www.jonathanreynolds.org.uk *Twitter:* @jreynoldsmp

LABOUR

RIMMER, MARIE

St Helens South and Whiston *(Majority 24,343)*

Shadow Minister for Disabled People

Marie Elizabeth Rimmer. Born 27 April 1947.

Non-political career: Pilkington Glass 1962-99: Statistics and accounts, Procurement/buyer of engineering equipment for glass production lines, Health and safety adviser in float glass manufacturing. Member, Unite.

Political career: Member for St Helens South and Whiston since 7 May 2015 general election; Shadow Minister for Disabled People 2017-. *Select committees:* Member, Justice 2015-17. *Councils and public bodies:* St Helens Council: Councillor 1978-2016, Council Leader 1985-93, 1999-2013.

Other: Trustee, Hope Centre, St Helens.

Marie Rimmer CBE MP, House of Commons, London SW1A 0AA
Tel: 020 7219 4847 *Email:* marie.rimmer.mp@parliament.uk
Constituency: Century House, Hardshaw Street, St Helens WA10 1QU
Tel: 01744 752075 *Website:* www.marierimmer.org.uk *Twitter:* @MarieRimmer

CONSERVATIVE

ROBERTSON, LAURENCE

Tewkesbury *(Majority 22,574)*

Laurence Anthony Robertson. Born 29 March 1958; Son of James Robertson, former colliery electrician, and late Jean Robertson, née Larkin; Married Susan Lees 1989 (marriage dissolved) (2 stepdaughters); married Anne Marie, née Adams 2015.

Education: St James' Church of England Secondary School; Farnworth Grammar School; Bolton Institute of Higher Education (Diploma management services 1979).

Non-political career: Warehouse assistant 1976-77; Work study engineer 1977-83; Industrial management consultant 1983-89; Factory owner 1987-88; Charity fundraising, public relations and special events consultant 1988-.

Political career: Contested Makerfield 1987 and Ashfield 1992 general elections. Member for Tewkesbury 1997-2010, for Tewkesbury (revised boundary) since 6 May 2010 general election; Opposition Whip 2001-03; Shadow Minister for: Trade and Industry 2003, Economic Affairs 2003-05, Northern Ireland 2005-10. *Select committees:* Member: Environmental Audit 1997-99, Joint Committee on Consolidation of Bills Etc 1997-2001, Social Security 1999-2001, European Scrutiny 1999-2002, Education and Skills 2001, Liaison 2010-17; Chair, Northern Ireland Affairs 2010-17; Member, Panel of Chairs 2017-. Vice-chair, Association of Conservative Clubs 1997-2000; Chair, Westminster Africa Business Group 2001-.

Political interests: International development, constitutional affairs, countryside, Northern Ireland; Africa, particularly Ethiopia, UK, USA.

Other: Co-chairman, British-Irish Parliamentary Association 2011-17; Member: Executive Committee, Commonwealth Parliamentary Association UK 2015-17, UK Delegation, Organisation for Security and Co-operation in Europe Parliamentary Assembly 2015-; Fellow, Industry and Parliament Trust 2001; Overseas aid charities, charities linked to horse racing.

Publications: Europe: The Case Against Integration (1991); The Right Way Ahead (1995).

Recreations: Horses and horseracing, golf, other sports (completed six marathons), reading, writing, countryside.

Laurence Robertson MP, House of Commons, London SW1A 0AA
Tel: 020 7219 4196 *Fax:* 020 7219 2325 *Email:* robertsonl@parliament.uk
Constituency: 22 High Street, Tewkesbury, Gloucestershire GL20 5AL
Tel: 01684 291640 *Fax:* 01684 291759 *Website:* www.laurencerobertson.org.uk
Twitter: @lrobertsonTewks

DEMOCRATIC UNIONIST PARTY

ROBINSON, GAVIN

Belfast East *(Majority 8,474)*

DUP Spokesman for Defence and Home Affairs

Gavin James Robinson. Born 22 November 1984; Married Lindsay (1 son).

Education: Greenwood, Strandtown and Grosvenor Grammar school; Ulster University (law); Queens University Belfast (MA politics).

Non-political career: Barrister 2007-11; Special Adviser to Peter Robinson MLA as First Minister 2011.

Political career: Member for Belfast East since 7 May 2015 general election; DUP Spokesperson for: Justice 2015-17, Home Affairs 2015-, Human Rights 2015-17, Defence 2017-. *Select committees:* Member: Northern Ireland Affairs 2015-16, Ecclesiastical Committee 2015-, Defence 2016-. *Councils and public bodies:* Belfast City Council: Councillor 2010-15, Lord Mayor 2012-13, Alderman 2012-15.

Political interests: Economy, benefits, schools, healthcare.

Other: Ulster Orchestra Board; World Police and Fire Games; Board member: iESE, Craigavon House Preservation Trust.

Recreations: Art, sport.

Gavin Robinson MP, House of Commons, London SW1A 0AA
Tel: 020 7219 8746 *Email:* gavin.robinson.mp@parliament.uk
Constituency: Strandtown Hall, 96 Belmont Avenue, Belfast BT4 3DE
Tel: 028 9047 3111 *Twitter:* @GRobinsonDUP

LABOUR

ROBINSON, GEOFFREY

Coventry North West *(Majority 8,580)*

Born 25 May 1938; Son of late Robert Robinson and late Dorothy Robinson, née Skelly; Married Marie Elena Giorgio 1967 (1 daughter 1 son).

Education: Emanuel School, London; Clare College, Cambridge; Yale University, USA; French, German, Italian.

Non-political career: Research assistant, Labour Party 1965-68; Senior executive, Industrial Reorganisation Corporation 1968-70; Financial controller, British Leyland 1970-72; Managing director, Leyland Innocenti 1972-73; Chief executive, Jaguar Cars Coventry 1974-75; Chief executive (unpaid), Triumph Motorcycles (Meriden) Ltd 1978-80; Director, West Midlands Enterprise Board 1982-85; Chief executive, TransTec plc 1986-97. Member, T&G.

Political career: Member for Coventry North West 4 March 1976 by-election to 2010, for Coventry North West (revised boundary) since 6 May 2010 general election; Opposition Frontbench Spokesperson for: Science 1982-83, Trade and Industry and Regional Affairs 1983-87; Paymaster General, HM Treasury 1997-98.

Political interests: Industry, economic policy, new technology; France, Germany, Italy, USA.

Publications: The Unconventional Minister: My Life in New Labour.

Recreations: Motorcars, gardens, architecture, football.

Geoffrey Robinson MP, House of Commons, London SW1A 0AA
Tel: 020 7219 4083 *Email:* robinsong@parliament.uk
Constituency: Transport House, Short Street, Coventry, Warwickshire CV1 2LS
Tel: 024 7625 7870 *Twitter:* @Geoffrey4CovNW

CONSERVATIVE

ROBINSON, MARY

Cheadle *(Majority 4,507)*

Mary Josephine Robinson. Born 23 August 1955; Married Stephen (4 children).

Education: Degree law.

Non-political career: Founder, Robinson Rose Accountants -2008; Mary Felicity Design.

Political career: Member for Cheadle since 7 May 2015 general election. *Select committees:* Member: Communities and Local Government 2015-, Administration 2017-. Chair, South Ribble Conservative Association. *Councils and public bodies:* Councillor, South Ribble Borough Council -2013; School governor.

Other: Member, Healthwatch Stockport.

Mary Robinson MP, House of Commons, London SW1A 0AA
Tel: 020 7219 8091 *Email:* mary.robinson.mp@parliament.uk
Constituency: 8a Station Road, Cheadle Hulme, Cheadle SK8 5AE
Tel: 0161-672 6855 *Website:* www.mary-robinson.org.uk *Twitter:* @MaryRobinson01

LABOUR

RODDA, MATT

Reading East *(Majority 3,749)*

PPS to Andy McDonald as Shadow Secretary of State for Transport

Matthew Richard Allen Rodda. Born 15 December 1966; Married (2 children).

Education: Sussex University.

Non-political career: Journalist: *Coventry Telegraph*, *The Independent*; Civil Servant, Department for Education; Educational Charity Project Manager. Usdaw, GMB.

Political career: Contested East Surrey 2010 and Reading East 2015 general elections. Member for Reading East since 8 June 2017; PPS to Andy McDonald as Shadow Secretary of State for Transport 2017-; *Councils and public bodies:* Councillor, Reading Borough Council 2011-.

Political interests: Fairness for all, high quality public services, economy.

Matt Rodda MP, House of Commons, London SW1A 0AA
Tel: 020 7219 3980 *Email:* matt.rodda.mp@parliament.uk
Constituency: Details still to be confirmed
Email: mattroddampoffice@gmail.com *Website:* www.mattrodda.net *Twitter:* @MattRodda

CONSERVATIVE

ROSINDELL, ANDREW

Romford *(Majority 13,778)*

Andrew Richard Rosindell. Born 17 March 1966; Son of Frederick Rosindell, tailor, and Eileen Clark, pianist; Single.

Education: Marshalls Park Comprehensive School, Romford.

Non-political career: Armed Forces Parliamentary Scheme: Royal Marines 2002-03, RAF 2004-06, Army 2009-13. Central Press Features London 1984-86; Freelance journalist 1986-97; Parliamentary researcher to Vivian Bendall MP 1986-97; Director and international director, European Foundation 1997-2001.

Political career: Contested Glasgow Provan 1992 and Thurrock 1997 general elections. Member for Romford 2001-10, for Romford (revised boundary) since 6 May 2010 general election; Opposition Whip 2005-07; Shadow Minister for Home Affairs (Animal Welfare) 2007-10. *Select committees:* Member: Regulatory Reform 2001-05, Joint Committee on Statutory Instruments 2002-03, Constitutional Affairs 2004-05, Foreign Affairs 2010-, Panel of Chairs 2010-. Member, National Union Executive Committee, Conservative Party 1986-88, 1992-94; Chairman, Greater London Young Conservatives 1987-88; International secretary, Young Conservatives United Kingdom 1991-98; Chairman: National Young Conservatives 1993-94, Romford Conservative Association 1998-2001, Conservative Friends of Gibraltar 2002-; Member, Conservative Christian Fellowship; Vice-chair (campaigning), Conservative Party 2004-05; Chairman, Conservative Friends of Australia and New Zealand 2010-; Founding member, Conservatives for Britain 2015-16. *Councils and public bodies:* London Borough of Havering: Councillor 1990-2002, Alderman 2007-; Chairman, North Romford Community Area Forum 1998-2002.

Political interests: Foreign and international relations, European affairs, law and order, defence, local and regional government, animal welfare; Australia, British Overseas Territories and Crown Dependencies, Canada, Eastern Europe, Gulf States, Liechtenstein, New Zealand, Nordic countries, Switzerland, USA.

Other: Chairman, European Young Conservatives 1993-97; Executive member, International Democrat Union 1994-2002; Chair, International Young Democrat Union 1998-2002; Executive Committee, Commonwealth Parliamentary Association: Member 2010-15, 2017-, Vice-chair 2015-17; Member, Executive Committee, Inter-Parliamentary Union, British Group 2010-; British-Irish Parliamentary Association: Vice-chair 2015-17, Chair 2017-; Member, UK delegation to NATO Parliamentary Assembly 2015-; Westminster Foundation for Democracy: Governor 2010, Board Member 2010-; Fellow, Industry and Parliament Trust. Freedom, City of London; Romford Conservative and Constitutional Club, Royal Air Forces Association, Romford Royal British Legion Club.

Publications: Co-author, Defending Our Great Heritage (1993).

Recreations: Staffordshire bull terrier named Buster, travel, philately, history.

Andrew Rosindell MP, House of Commons, London SW1A 0AA
Tel: 020 7219 8475/020 7219 5228 *Email:* andrew.rosindell.mp@parliament.uk
Constituency: Margaret Thatcher House, 85 Western Road, Romford RM1 3LS
Tel: 01708 766700 *Email:* andrew@rosindell.com *Website:* www.rosindell.com
Twitter: @AndrewRosindell

CONSERVATIVE

ROSS, DOUGLAS

Moray *(Majority 4,159)*

Born 27 January 1983; Son of Alexander and Lesley Ross; Married Krystle Bentley 2015.

Education: Forres Academy; Scottish Agricultural College, Ayr (BTech agriculture 2004).

Non-political career: Dairy farm worker 2004-07; Parliamentary Assistant to MSP 2007-16.

Political career: Contested Moray 2010 and 2015 general elections. Member for Moray since 8 June 2017; Contested Moray constituency 2011 and 2016 Scottish Parliament elections. MSP for Highlands and Islands region 2016 to 11 June 2017: Shadow Cabinet Secretary for Justice 2016-17. *Councils and public bodies:* Councillor, Moray Council 2007-17.

Recreations: Scottish FA qualified referee.

Douglas Ross MP, House of Commons, London SW1A 0AA
Tel: 020 7219 3648 *Email:* douglas.ross.mp@parliament.uk
Constituency: 63 High Street, Forres, Moray IV36 1PB
Tel: 01309 679253 *Twitter:* @douglas4moray

LABOUR

ROWLEY, DANIELLE

Midlothian *(Majority 885)*

PPS to Emily Thornberry as Shadow Foreign Secretary

Education: Dalkeith High School; Edinburgh Telford College (HNC radio broadcasting 2010); Edinburgh Napier University (BA journalism 2014).

Non-political career: Press Officer, Dalkeith Festival Committee 2008-11; Producer and Presenter, Black Diamond FM 2008-11; Social Media Officer, Scottish Youth Parliament 2011; Page Editor, *Edinburgh Now*, *Scottish Daily Record* and *Sunday Mail* 2013; Local Digital Content, STV Group plc 2013; Constituency Media Manager to Gordon Brown MP 2014-15; E-Communications Officer, Scottish Parliament 2015; Communications and Marketing Officer, ACOSVO 2015-16; Campaigns and Public Affairs Officer, Shelter Scotland 2016-17. Unison.

Political career: Member for Midlothian since 8 June 2017; PPS to Emily Thornberry as Shadow Foreign Secretary 2017-. *Select committees:* Member, Scottish Affairs 2017-. Campaigns Co-ordinator, Midlothian 2013-15.

Other: Volunteer, Midlothian Youth Platform 2008-10; Trustee Director, Scottish Youth Parliament 2009-11.

Danielle Rowley MP, House of Commons, London SW1A 0AA
Tel: 020 7219 3619 *Email:* danielle.rowley.mp@parliament.uk
Constituency: 97 High Street, Dalkeith, Midlothian EH22 1AX
Tel: 0131-663 9675 *Website:* www.daniellerowleymp.uk *Twitter:* @danirowley

CONSERVATIVE

ROWLEY, LEE

North East Derbyshire *(Majority 2,860)*

Lee Benjamin Rowley. Born 11 September 1980; Son of Linda Rowley, teacher, and Malcolm Rowley, milkman.

Education: St Mary's High School, Chesterfield; Lincoln College, Oxford (BA modern history 2002); Manchester University (MA history 2004).

Non-political career: Senior Energy Analyst, Clarkson 2004-07; Strategy Analyst, Barclays 2007-08; Senior Consultant, Santander 2008-11; Manager, KPMG 2011-12; Santander: Senior Manager Corporate Change 2012-14, Head of Risk Change Management and Processes 2014-17; Head of Change and Portfolio, Co-op Insurance 2017.

Political career: Contested Bolsover 2010 and North East Derbyshire 2015 general elections. Member for North East Derbyshire since 8 June 2017; *Councils and public bodies:* Councillor, City of Westminster Council 2006-14.

Political interests: Housing, economy, finance, transport; Australia, USA.

Recreations: Travel, local history, fitness.

Lee Rowley MP, House of Commons, London SW1A 0AA
Tel: 020 7219 4197 *Email:* lee.rowley.mp@parliament.uk
Constituency: Details still to be confirmed *Website:* www.lee4ned.com *Twitter:* @Lee4NED

LABOUR

RUANE, CHRIS

Vale of Clwyd *(Majority 2,379)*

Shadow Minister for Wales Office

Christopher Shaun Ruane. Born 18 July 1958; Son of late Michael Ruane, labourer, and Esther Ruane; Married Gill Roberts 1994 (2 daughters).

Education: Blessed Edward Jones Comprehensive, Rhyl; University College of Wales, Aberystwyth (BSc (Econ) history and politics 1979); Liverpool University (PGCE 1980); Welsh (learner).

Non-political career: Ysgol Mair, Rhyl: Primary school teacher 1982-97, Deputy head 1991-97. National Union of Teachers: School Rep 1982-97, President, West Clwyd 1991, Vale of Clwyd 1997.

Political career: Contested Clwyd North West 1992 general election. Member for Vale of Clwyd 1997-2010, for Vale of Clwyd (revised boundary) 2010-15. Contested Vale of Clwyd 2015 general election. Member for Vale of Clwyd since 8 June 2017; PPS: to Peter Hain as Secretary of State for Wales 2002-07, to Caroline Flint: as Minister of State, Department for Work and Pensions 2007-08, as Minister for Housing, Department for Communities and Local Government 2008, to David Miliband as Foreign Secretary 2009-10; PPS to Ed Balls: as Shadow Home Secretary 2010-11, as Shadow Chancellor 2011; Opposition Whip 2011-13; PPS to Caroline Flint as Shadow Secretary of State for Energy and Climate Change 2013-15; Shadow Minister for Wales Office 2017-. *Select committees:* Member: Welsh Affairs 1999-2002, Joint Committee on Statutory Instruments and Commons Committee on Statutory Instruments 2009-10, Home Affairs 2013, Political and Constitutional Reform 2014-15. PLP Welsh Regional Group: Vice-chair 2007-08, Chair 2008-15. Chair, North Wales Group of Labour MPs 2002-15. *Councils and public bodies:* Councillor, Rhyl Town Council 1988-99.

Political interests: Regeneration of seaside towns, housing, electoral registration, anti-poverty, environment, tourism, mindfulness; Belize, Ireland, Vietnam.

Other: Member, British-Irish Parliamentary Assembly; Member, Steering Group forming Vale of Clwyd Credit Union; Founder member, Rhyl Anti Apartheid 1987; Rhyl Environmental Association: Founder member 1988, President; Founder member, Rhyl and District Amnesty International Group 1989; Chair, Rhyl City Strategy Consortium; Fellow, Industry and Parliament Trust 2001; President, North Wales Ramblers Association 2008-.

Recreations: Cooking, walking, reading, humour.

Chris Ruane MP, House of Commons, London SW1A 0AA
Tel: 020 7219 3000 *Email:* chris.ruane.mp@parliament.uk
Constituency: Details still to be confirmed *Twitter:* @ChrisRuane2017

CONSERVATIVE

RUDD, AMBER

Hastings and Rye *(Majority 346)*

Home Secretary

Amber Augusta Rudd. Born 1 August 1963; Divorced (1 son 1 daughter).

Education: Queen's College, London; Edinburgh University (MA history 1986); French, German, Italian.

Non-political career: JP Morgan, London 1986-87; Director: Lawnstone Ltd 1988-97, MacArthur and Co 1997-99; Chief executive officer, Investors Noticeboard Ltd 1999-2001; Consultant, I-Search Ltd 2001-03; Columnist, *Corporate Financier* 2003-; Managing director and senior consultant, Lawnstone Ltd 2003-10; Director, Hastings Academies Trust.

Political career: Contested Liverpool Garston 2005 general election. Member for Hastings and Rye since 6 May 2010 general election; PPS to George Osborne as Chancellor of the Exchequer 2012-13; Assistant Government Whip 2013-14; Parliamentary Under-Secretary of State for Climate Change, Department of Energy and Climate Change 2014-15; Secretary of State for: Energy and Climate Change 2015-16, the Home Department (Home Secretary) 2016-. *Select committees:* Member, Environment, Food and Rural Affairs 2010-12.

Political interests: Welfare, transport, economy.

Other: Substitute member, Parliamentary Assembly of the Council of Europe 2010-12; Trustee, Snowdon Awards Scheme; Director, Susan Smith Blackburn Prize. PC 2015; Carlton Club.

Recreations: Theatre, cinema.

Rt Hon Amber Rudd MP, House of Commons, London SW1A 0AA
Tel: 020 7219 7229 *Email:* amber.rudd.mp@parliament.uk
Constituency: Swallow House, Theaklen Drive, St Leonards-on-Sea, East Sussex TN38 9AZ
Tel: 01424 716756 *Email:* louisem.sargent@parliament.uk *Website:* www.amberrudd.co.uk
Twitter: @AmberRuddHR

LAB/CO-OP

RUSSELL-MOYLE, LLOYD

Brighton Kemptown *(Majority 9,868)*

PPS to Richard Burgon as Shadow Lord Chancellor and Secretary of State for Justice

Born 14 September 1986.

Education: Priory School, Lewes; Sussex Downs College; Bradford University (BA peace studies 2012); Sussex University (LLM international law 2016).

Non-political career: Young trainer and consultant, National Youth Agency 2003-06; Union Secretary/Treasurer, Bradford University 2007-09; Consultant, United Nations 2015; Sussex University Branch, University and College Union. Member: GMB, Unite.

Political career: Contested Lewes 2015 general election. Member for Brighton Kemptown since 8 June 2017; PPS to Richard Burgon as Shadow Lord Chancellor and Secretary of State for Justice 2017-. *Select committees:* Member: International Development 2017-, Work of the Independent Commission for Aid Impact Sub-committee 2017-. Chair, Brighton and Hove Labour Party 2016-; Member: LGBT Labour, Labour Campaign for International Development. *Councils and public bodies:* Councillor, Brighton and Hove City Council 2016-.

Other: Woodcraft Folk 2004-13; British Youth Council: Trustee 2006-07, Vice-chair (participation and development) 2007-08; Woodcraft Folk: Member, General Council 2004-13, Chair 2009-12; European Volunteer, International Falcon Movement 2010-11; European Youth Forum: Board member 2011-14, Vice-president 2012-14; Member: Campaign for Nuclear Disarmament, Royal Society of Arts, British Humanist Association.

Lloyd Russell-Moyle MP, House of Commons, London SW1A 0AA
Tel: 020 7219 2280 *Email:* lloyd.russellmoyle.mp@parliament.uk
Constituency: 11 Hunns Mere Way, Woodingdean BN2 6AH
Tel: 01273 550121 *Website:* www.russell-moyle.co.uk *Twitter:* @lloyd_rm

CONSERVATIVE

RUTLEY, DAVID

Macclesfield *(Majority 8,608)*

Government Whip (Lord Commissioner of HM Treasury)

David Henry Rutley. Born 7 March 1961; Son of John Rutley and Birthe Anderson; Married Rachel (4 children).

Education: The Priory School, Lewes; London School of Economics (BSc (Econ) 1985); Harvard Business School (MBA 1989).

Non-political career: Business development director, PepsiCo International 1991-94; Special adviser 1994-96: Cabinet Office, Ministry of Agriculture, HM Treasury; Director of business effectiveness, Safeway Stores 1996-2000; ASDA stores 2000-05: Director of Financial Services, Director of E-commerce; Sales and marketing director, Halifax General Insurance 2005-07; Barclays Bank 2008-10: Business consultant 2008-09, Marketing director 2009-10.

Political career: Contested St Albans 1997 general election. Member for Macclesfield since 6 May 2010 general election; PPS: to Damian Green as Minister of State: for Immigration, Home Office 2010-12, for Policing, Criminal Justice and Victims, Home Office and Ministry of Justice 2012-14, to David Lidington as Minister of State for Europe, Foreign and Commonwealth Office 2014-15, to Secretary of State for Work and Pensions: Iain Duncan Smith 2015-16, Stephen Crabb 2016, to Amber Rudd as Home Secretary 2016-17; Government Whip (Lord Commissioner of HM Treasury) 2017-. *Select committees:* Member, Treasury 2010.

Political interests: Economy, business, home affairs, rural issues, community groups; China, Denmark, Slovenia, USA.

Other: Trustee, Kids Count 1988; Member: British Mountaineering Council, RSPB, National Trust; Many charities in Macclesfield including: NSPCC (East Cheshire Branch), East Cheshire Hospice, Macclesfield Silk Museum Trust, Just Drop In, Macclesfield Community Garden Centre, Poynton Royal British Legion Concert Band.

Recreations: Spending time with family, walking and climbing in the Peak District, mountaineering, fishing, ornithology.

David Rutley MP, House of Commons, London SW1A 0AA
Tel: 020 7219 7106 *Email:* david.rutley.mp@parliament.uk
Constituency: c/o Macclesfield Conservative Association, West Bank Road, Macclesfield, Cheshire SK10 3BT
Tel: 01625 422848 *Websites:* www.macclesfieldconservatives.com www.davidrutley.org.uk
Twitter: @DavidRutley

LABOUR

RYAN, JOAN

Enfield North *(Majority 10,247)*

Joan Marie Ryan. Born 8 September 1955; Daughter of Michael Joseph Ryan and Dolores Marie, neé Joyce; Married Martin Hegarty 1998 (1 son 1 daughter from previous marriage 1 stepson 1 stepdaughter).

Education: St Josephs Secondary School, Notre Dame High School; City of Liverpool College (BA history, sociology 1979); South Bank Polytechnic (MSc sociology 1981).

Non-political career: Oral history interviewer, Imperial War Museum, London 1985-90. Member: USDAW, Unite, NUT.

Political career: Member for Enfield North 1997-2010. Contested Enfield North 2010 general election. Member for Enfield North since 7 May 2015 general election; PPS to Andrew Smith: as Minister of State, Department for Education and Employment 1998-99, as Chief Secretary to the Treasury 1999-2002; Assistant Government Whip 2002-03; Government Whip 2003-06; Parliamentary Under-Secretary of State, Home Office 2006-07; Special Representative to Cyprus 2007-08. *Select committees:* Member: Selection 2001-06, Panel of Chairs 2016-, Environmental Audit

2016-. Chair: Finchley CLP 1992-96, London North European Constituency 1994-97; Vice-chair, Labour Party 2007-08; Chair, Labour Friends of Israel. *Councils and public bodies:* Barnet Council: Councillor 1990-98, Deputy Leader 1994-98.

Political interests: Employment, education, health services, environment, crime reduction; Cyprus, Ireland, Israel, Turkey.

Other: Guide Ambassador, Girl Guide Association; Trustee, Riders For Health -2015; Patron: Nightingale Community Hospice Trust, North London Lupus. PC 2007.

Recreations: Swimming, reading, music, visiting historic buildings.

Rt Hon Joan Ryan MP, House of Commons, London SW1A 0AA
Tel: 020 7219 2442 *Email:* joan.ryan.mp@parliament.uk
Constituency: 542 Hertford Road, Enfield EN3 5ST
Tel: 020 8804 4543 *Email:* joan@joanryan.org.uk *Website:* www.joanryan.org.uk
Twitter: @joanryanEnfield

CONSERVATIVE

SANDBACH, ANTOINETTE

Eddisbury *(Majority 11,942)*

Antoinette Geraldine Mackeson-Sandbach. Born 1969; Married Matt Sherratt (1 daughter 1 son deceased).

Education: West Heath and Haileybury College; Nottingham University (LLB; LLM environmental and humanitarian law 1992).

Non-political career: Called to the Bar, Lincoln's Inn 1993; Barrister, 9 Bedford Row 1995-2006; Farmer 2006-11; Parliamentary aide to David Jones MP 2008-10.

Political career: Contested Delyn 2010 general election. Member for Eddisbury since 7 May 2015 general election. *Select committees:* Member: Energy and Climate Change 2015-16, Welsh Affairs 2015-16, Business, Energy and Industrial Strategy 2017-. Member, Executive, 1922 Committee 2015-. Contested Delyn constituency 2007 National Assembly for Wales election. AM for North Wales region 5 May 2011 to 12 May 2015: Welsh Conservatives Shadow Minister for: Rural Affairs 2011-14, Environment 2014-15. Special adviser on health, Welsh Conservative Party.

Political interests: Rural affairs, health, child bereavement, energy, climate change; Indonesia, Middle East, Netherlands.

Other: Medecins sans Frontiers, RNLI, Save the Rhino, FSID, Chrysalis. Grocer's Company. Freedom, City of London.

Recreations: Walking, cycling, art projects, skiing.

Antoinette Sandbach MP, House of Commons, London SW1A 0AA
Tel: 020 7219 6671 *Email:* antoinette.sandbach.mp@parliament.uk
Constituency: Units 24 and 25, The Verdin Exchange, Winsford, Cheshire CW7 2AN
Tel: 01606 861300 *Website:* www.antoinettesandbach.org.uk *Twitter:* @Sandbach

PLAID CYMRU

SAVILLE ROBERTS, LIZ

Dwyfor Meirionnydd *(Majority 4,850)*

Plaid Cymru Parliamentary Group Leader; Spokesperson for Home Affairs, Justice, Women and Equalities and Business, Energy and Industrial Strategy

Born 16 December 1964; Married Dewi Wyn Roberts 1994 (twin daughters).

Education: Blackheath High School; Avery Hill College, Eltham; Aberystwyth University (BA Celtic studies 1987); WJEC Postgraduate Certificate (1988); National Council for Training of Journalists (1992); PGCE (1996); Welsh, Irish, French, some Russian.

Non-political career: Secretary, Russian and French departments, Queen Mary College, London 1988-89; Staff reporter, Retail Journalist 1989-90; News Reporter 1990-93: *Holyhead and Anglesey Mail, Caernarfon Herald, Herald Môn, Herald Cymraeg*; Lecturer, Manager and Director, Coleg Meirion-Dwyfor/Grwp Llandrillo Menai 1993-2014. Member, UCAC (Welsh teachers' union) 1993-.

Political career: Member for Dwyfor Meirionnydd since 7 May 2015 general election; Plaid Cymru: Spokesperson for: Home Affairs 2015-, Education 2015-17, Health 2015-16, Environment, Food and Rural Affairs 2015-17, Women and Equalities 2015-, Communities and Local Government 2015-17, Energy and Natural Resources 2015-16, Business, Energy and Industrial Strategy 2016-, Justice 2016-, Constitutional Affairs 2016-17, Parliamentary Group Leader 2017-. *Select committees:* Member, Welsh Affairs 2015-17. Contested North Wales region 2003, Mid and West Wales (4) region 2007 and North Wales (4) region 2011 National Assembly for Wales elections. *Councils and public bodies:* Councillor, Gwynedd Council 2004-15; Vice-president, Local Government Association 2017-.

Political interests: Economic development of Wales, rural affairs, social justice, sustainability; Wales.

Other: Member, Amnesty 2008-; Trustee, Canolfan Iaith Nant Gwrtheyrn -2016; Barddas, Cymdeithas Hanes Uwchgwyrfai, Cymdeithas Marchogaeth Llyn Club.

Recreations: Horse riding, hill-walking, agricultural shows, languages, folk music, poetry and eisteddfodau.

Liz Saville Roberts MP, House of Commons, London SW1A 0AA
Tel: 020 7219 6876 *Email:* liz.savilleroberts.mp@parliament.uk
Constituency: Angorfa, Heol Meurig, Dolgellau, Gwynedd LL40 1LN
Tel: 01341 422661 *Website:* lizsavilleroberts.org *Twitter:* @LSRPlaid

CONSERVATIVE

SCULLY, PAUL

Sutton and Cheam *(Majority 12,698)*

Paul Stuart Scully. Born 29 April 1968; Married Emma Scully.

Education: Bedford School; Reading University (chemistry and food science).

Non-political career: Parliamentary Assistant to Alok Sharma MP 2010-12; Partner, Nudge Factory Ltd 2011-.

Political career: Member for Sutton and Cheam since 7 May 2015 general election; Trade Envoy to Burma, Brunei and Thailand 2017-. *Select committees:* Member: Petitions 2015-, Standing Orders 2015-, International Development 2016-; Work of the Independent Commission for Aid Impact Sub-committee: Member 2016-17, Chair 2017-. Member, Conservative Party's Project Maja. *Councils and public bodies:* Sutton Borough Council: Councillor -2010, Former Leader of the Opposition; Governor: Sutton College of Learning for Adults, Manor Park Primary School.

Political interests: Small business, local government, education; Bangladesh, Burma, India.

Paul Scully MP, House of Commons, London SW1A 0AA
Tel: 020 7219 4837 *Email:* paul.scully.mp@parliament.uk
Constituency: c/o Sutton and Cheam Conservatives, Donnington House, 2a Sutton Court Road, Sutton SM1 4SY
Tel: 020 8642 3791 *Email:* info@scully.org.uk *Website:* www.scully.org.uk *Twitter:* @scullyp

CONSERVATIVE

SEELY, BOB

Isle of Wight *(Majority 21,069)*

Robert William Henry Seely; Son of Richard and Helga Seely; Divorced.

Education: Birkbeck University (MA); Oxford University (Research Associate, Changing Character of War Programme); Russian.

Non-political career: Mobilised or on FTRS 2008-17. Journalist 1990-2000: *The Times* Kiev Correspondent, *Washington Post* Kiev Special Correspondent, Associated Press London; Adviser, CCHQ 2000-05; Public relations team, MTV 2005-08.

Political career: Contested Broxtowe 2005 general election. Member for Isle of Wight since 8 June 2017; *Councils and public bodies:* Councillor, Isle of Wight Council 2013-.

Political interests: The Isle of Wight, UK Islands, overseas policy: foreign, defence and aid, housing and land use, education; States of the former Soviet Union, the Middle Eas.

Other: Military MBE 2016. Island Sailing Club, Yarmouth Sailing Club.

Publications: Russo-Chechen Conflict 1800-2000: A Deadly Embrace (2001, 2004); Co-Author, War and Humanitarian Action in Chechnya (2002).

Bob Seely MBE MP, House of Commons, London SW1A 0AA
Tel: 020 7219 1840 *Email:* bob.seely.mp@parliament.uk
Constituency: Northwood House, Ward Avenue, Cowes PO31 8AZ
Tel: 01983 220220 *Website:* www.bobseely.org.uk *Twitter:* @iowbobseely

CONSERVATIVE

SELOUS, ANDREW

South West Bedfordshire *(Majority 14,168)*

Andrew Edmund Armstrong Selous. Born 27 April 1962; Son of Commander Gerald Selous and Miranda Selous, née Casey; Married Harriet Marston 1993 (3 daughters).

Education: Eton College; London School of Economics (BSc (Econ) industry and trade 1984); French, German.

Non-political career: TA officer, Honourable Artillery Company, Royal Regiment of Fusiliers 1981-94. Director, CNS Electronics Ltd 1988-94; Underwriter, Great Lakes Re (UK) plc 1991-2001.

Political career: Contested Sunderland North 1997 general election. Member for South West Bedfordshire since 7 June 2001 general election; PPS to Michael Ancram as Shadow Foreign Secretary 2004; Opposition Whip 2004-06; Shadow Minister for Work and Pensions 2006-10; PPS to

Iain Duncan Smith as Secretary of State for Work and Pensions 2010-14; Assistant Government Whip 2014-16; Ministry of Justice: Parliamentary Under-Secretary of State: (Minister for Prisons, Probation and Rehabilitation) 2014-15, for Prisons, Probation, Rehabilitation and Sentencing 2015-16; Trade Envoy to South Africa 2017-. *Select committees:* Member: Work and Pensions 2001-05, Ecclesiastical Committee 2010-14, Health 2016-. Chair, Conservative Christian Fellowship 2001-06.

Political interests: Trade and industry, families, defence, homelessness; Australia, Nicaragua, USA.

Other: ACII 1993; Chartered Insurer 1998; Parkinsons UK, Homestart, Leighton Linslade Homeless, Brain Tumour Action; Leighton Buzzard Conservative Club, Dunstable Conservative Club.

Recreations: Family, walking, tennis, bridge.

Andrew Selous MP, House of Commons, London SW1A 0AA
Tel: 020 7219 8134 *Fax:* 020 7219 1741 *Email:* andrew.selous.mp@parliament.uk
Constituency: Rooms 26/27, Wentworth House, 83 High Street North, Dunstable, Bedfordshire LU6 1JJ
Tel: 01582 662821 *Fax:* 01582 476619 *Website:* www.andrewselous.org.uk
Twitter: @AndrewSelous

SHAH, NAZ

Bradford West *(Majority 21,902)*

LABOUR

Naseem Akhter Shah. Born 13 November 1973; 1 daughter 2 sons.

Urdu, Punjabi.

Non-political career: Social worker, Bradford Council 1998-99; Senior advocate, Bradnet 2000-03; Commissioner, Bradford and Airedale Primary Care Trust 2003-07; Programme director, Local Government Yorkshire and Humber 2009-10; Chief executive, Monster Fun and Listers Ladies Gym 2010-13.

Political career: Member for Bradford West since 7 May 2015 general election; PPS to John McDonnell as Shadow Chancellor of the Exchequer 2016. *Select committees:* Member, Home Affairs 2015-. Suspended from Labour Party April-July 2016. *Councils and public bodies:* Executive board member, Nashayman Housing Association 2001-03.

Other: Chair, Sharing Voices Bradford 2012-15. Emma Humphries Memorial Prize (1999).

Naz Shah MP, House of Commons, London SW1A 0AA
Tel: 020 7219 8603 *Email:* naz.shah.mp@parliament.uk
Constituency: West Riding House, 41 Cheapside, Bradford, West Yorkshire BD1 4HR
Tel: 01274 725171 *Website:* nazshah.org.uk *Twitter:* @NazShahBfd

SHANNON, JIM

Strangford *(Majority 18,343)*

DEMOCRATIC UNIONIST PARTY

DUP Spokesperson for Human Rights and Health

Richard James Shannon. Born 25 March 1955; Son of Richard and Moira Shannon, both retired; Married Sandra George 1987 (3 sons).

Education: Coleraine Academical Institution (1971); Ulster-Scots.

Non-political career: Ulster Defence Regiment 1973-75, 1976-77; Royal Artillery, TA 1977-88. Self-employed pork retailer 1985-. Member: Mid Ards Branch, Ulster Farmers' Union, TGWU 1976-85.

Political career: Member for Strangford since 6 May 2010 general election; DUP Spokesperson for: Health 2010-, Transport 2010-17, Equality 2012-17, Human Rights 2012-15, 2017-. *Select committees:* Member: Defence 2015-16, Arms Export Controls 2016-17, Northern Ireland Affairs 2016-. Member Northern Ireland Forum for Political Dialogue 1996-98; MLA for Strangford 1998-2010. *Councils and public bodies:* Ards Borough Council: Councillor 1985-2010, Mayor 1991-92.

Political interests: Farming, fishing, environment, Ulster-Scots; Scotland, USA.

Other: Secretary, Loyal Orange Institution, Kircubbin LOL 1900; Registrar, Royal Black Perceptory Ballywater No 675; Comber, Apprentice Boys of Derry; Member: British Association Shooting and Conservation, Countryside Alliance NI, Royal British Legion, Greyabbey Branch, National Trust; NSPCC, Action Cancer. General Service Medal, Ulster Defence Regiment. Carrowdore Shooting Club.

Recreations: Fieldsports, football.

Jim Shannon MP, House of Commons, London SW1A 0AA
Tel: 020 7219 7160 *Fax:* 020 7219 2347 *Email:* jim.shannon.mp@parliament.uk
Constituency: 34a Frances Street, Newtownards, Co Down BT23 7DN
Tel: 028 9182 7990 *Fax:* 028 9182 7991 *Twitter:* @JimShannonMP

CONSERVATIVE

SHAPPS, GRANT

Welwyn Hatfield *(Majority 7,369)*

Grant V Shapps. Born 14 September 1968; Son of Tony and Beryl Shapps; Married Belinda Goldstone 1997 (1 son twin son and daughter).

Education: Watford Boys' Grammar School; Cassio College, Watford (OND business and finance 1987); Manchester Polytechnic (HND business and finance 1989).

Non-political career: Sales executive, Nashua Gestetner 1989-90; Printhouse Corporation: Founder 1990-, Chairman 2000-.

Political career: Contested North Southwark and Bermondsey 1997 and Welwyn Hatfield 2001 general elections. Member for Welwyn Hatfield since 5 May 2005 general election; Shadow Minister for Housing (attending Shadow Cabinet) 2007-10; Minister of State for Housing and Local Government, Department for Communities and Local Government 2010-12; Member Speaker's Committee on the Electoral Commission 2010-12; Minister without Portfolio, Cabinet Office 2012-15; Minister of State: Department for International Development 2015, Foreign and Commonwealth Office 2015. *Select committees:* Member, Public Administration 2005-07. Branch chair, Barnhill, Brent North 1995-99; Member: Conservative Friends of Israel 1995, Selsdon Group 1996, Conservative Foreign Affairs Forum 1996; Vice-President, North Southwark and Bermondsey Association 1997; Conservative Party: Vice-chair (Campaigning) 2005-09, Chairman 2012-15.

Political interests: Health, education, home affairs, foreign affairs.

Other: Isabel Hospice, Resolve, Hertfordshire Action on Disability, Mixed Group. MP Contribution to Central Lobby, *PoliticsHome* awards 2012. PC 2010.

Rt Hon Grant Shapps MP, House of Commons, London SW1A 0AA
Tel: 020 7219 8497 *Email:* shappsg@parliament.uk
Constituency: Welwyn Hatfield Conservative Association, Maynard House, The Common, Hatfield, Hertfordshire AL10 0NF
Tel: 01707 262632 *Fax:* 01707 263892 *Email:* sandra@welhatconservatives.com
Website: www.shapps.com *Twitter:* @grantshapps

CONSERVATIVE

SHARMA, ALOK

Reading West *(Majority 2,876)*

Minister of State for Housing and Planning, Department for Communities and Local Government

Alok Kumar Sharma. Born 7 September 1967; Married (2 daughters).

Education: Blue Coat School, Reading; Salford University (BSc applied physics with electronics 1988); Institute of Chartered Accountants in England and Wales (ACA 1991).

Non-political career: Chartered accountant; Accountancy and corporate finance advicer.

Political career: Member for Reading West since 6 May 2010 general election; PPS to: Mark Hoban as Financial Secretary 2010-12, Oliver Letwin as Chancellor of the Duchy of Lancaster 2015-16; Parliamentary Under-Secretary of State (Minister for Asia and the Pacific), Foreign and Commonwealth Office 2016-17; Minister of State for Housing and Planning, Department for Communities and Local Government 2017-. *Select committees:* Member: Science and Technology 2010-11, Treasury 2014-15. Conservative Party: Member 1978-, Vice-chairman (BME communities); Chair, Conservative Friends of India.

Political interests: Trade, industry, finance; India, Pakistan, Sweden.

Other: Former chair, economic affairs committee, Bow Group; Fellow, Royal Society for the Encouragement of Arts, Manufacturing and Commerce; Patron: Wren Free School, Bengali Cultural Society of Reading; Member, Institute of Chartered Accountants in England and Wales.

Alok Sharma MP, House of Commons, London SW1A 0AA
Tel: 020 7219 7131 *Email:* alok.sharma.mp@parliament.uk
Constituency: 16c Upton Road, Tilehurst, Reading, Berkshire RG30 4BJ
Tel: 0118-941 3803 *Website:* www.aloksharma.co.uk *Twitter:* @AlokSharma_RDG

LABOUR

SHARMA, VIRENDRA

Ealing Southall *(Majority 22,090)*

Virendra Kumar Sharma. Born 5 April 1947; Married Nirmala (1 son 1 daughter).

Education: London School of Economics (MA 1979); Punjabi, Hindi, Urdu.

Non-political career: Day services manager, London Borough of Hillingdon 1996-2007. Member, TGWU/Unite.

Political career: Member for Ealing Southall 17 July 2007 by-election to 2010, for Ealing Southall (revised boundary) since 6 May 2010 general election; PPS to Phil Woolas as Minister of State, Home Office and HM Treasury 2008-09. *Select committees:* Member: Joint Committee on Human Rights 2007-10, 2010-15, Justice 2007-09, International Development 2009-10, 2015-, Health 2010-15, Arms Export Controls 2016-17, Work of the Independent Commission for Aid Impact Sub-committee 2017-, Panel of Chairs 2017-. Labour Party National Ethnic Minorities Officer 1986-92. *Councils and public bodies:* Councillor, London Borough of Ealing 1982-2010: Former Mayor.

Political interests: Health, international development, human rights; Bangladesh, Canada, Cyprus, India, Mauritius, Nepal, Pakistan, Sri Lanka, USA.

Other: Member, UK delegation, Parliamentary Assembly of the Council of Europe 2016-; Member, Indian Workers Association; Age UK.

Virendra Sharma MP, House of Commons, London SW1A 0AA
Tel: 020 7219 6080 *Fax:* 020 7219 3969 *Email:* sharmav@parliament.uk
Constituency: 112a The Green, Southall, Middlesex UB2 4BQ
Tel: 020 8571 1003 *Fax:* 020 8571 9991 *Website:* www.virendrasharma.com
Twitter: @VirendraSharma

LAB/CO-OP

SHEERMAN, BARRY

Huddersfield *(Majority 12,005)*

Barry John Sheerman. Born 17 August 1940; Son of late Albert Sheerman and Florence Sheerman, née Pike; Married Pamela Brenchley 1965 (1 son 3 daughters).

Education: Hampton Grammar School; Kingston Technical College (economics and politics); London School of Economics (BSc economics 1965); London University (MSc political sociology 1967); French.

Non-political career: Lecturer, University College of Wales, Swansea 1966-79. Member: AUT, Amicus.

Political career: Contested Taunton October 1974 general election. Member for Huddersfield East 1979-83, for Huddersfield 1983-2010, for Huddersfield (revised boundary) since 6 May 2010 general election; Opposition Spokesperson for: Employment and Education 1983-88, Home Affairs 1988-92, Disabled People's Rights 1992-94; Chair, Cross-Party Advisory Group on Preparation for EMU; Vice-chair, Joint Pre-Legislative Committee Investigating the Financial Services and Markets Bill; Chair, Cross-Party Advisory Group to Chancellor of the Exchequer on European Economic Reform. *Select committees:* Chair, Education and Employment (Education Sub-committee) 1999-2001; Member: Liaison 1999-2010, Education and Employment (Employment Sub-committee) 2000-01; Chair, Education and Skills/Children, Schools and Families 2001-10; Member, Liaison (Liaison Sub-committee) 2002-10. Chair, PLP Departmental Group for Environment, Food and Rural Affairs 2015-. Member, Co-operative Party; Chair, Labour Forum for Criminal Justice. *Councils and public bodies:* Councillor, Loughor and Lliw Valley Unitary District Council 1972-79; Emeritus Governor, London School of Economics 1995-.

Political interests: Trade, industry, finance, further education, education, economy, social enterprise and entrepreneurship; European Union, Kenya, South America, USA.

Other: World Bank Business Partnership for Development Global Road Safety Partnership (GRSP); Chair: Parliamentary Advisory Council on Transport Safety 1981-, National Educational Research and Development Trust; Fellow, Industry and Parliament Trust 1982, 1996; Chair: Urban Mines 1995-, Networking for Industry/Policy Connect 1995-, Schools to Work; Director and trustee, National Children's Centre; Chair: John Clare Education and Environment Trust 2004-, Sutton Trust Education Advisory Group 2015-; FRSA, FRGS, City and Guilds Institute; National Children's Centre, John Clare Trust, Dominic Rogers Trust. Two honorary doctorates. Member, Royal Commonwealth Club.

Publications: Co-author, Harold Laski: A Life on the Left (1993).

Recreations: Walking, biography, films, social entrepreneurship.

Barry Sheerman MP, House of Commons, London SW1A 0AA
Tel: 020 7219 5037 *Fax:* 020 7219 2404 *Email:* sheermanb@parliament.uk
Constituency: Office F18, The Media Centre, 7 Northumberland Street, Huddersfield, West Yorkshire HD1 1RL
Tel: 01484 487970 *Twitter:* @BarrySheerman

CONSERVATIVE

SHELBROOKE, ALEC

Elmet and Rothwell *(Majority 9,805)*

Alec Edward Shelbrooke. Born 10 January 1976; Son of Cllr Derek Shelbrooke and Patricia Shelbrooke JP, both retired teachers; Married Susan Shelbrooke.

Education: St George's CoE Comprehensive School, Gravesend; Brunel University (BSc mechanical engineering 1998).

Non-political career: Project Manager, Leeds University 1999-2010. Member, MSF/Unite 1999-2010.

Political career: Contested Wakefield 2005 general election. Member for Elmet and Rothwell since 6 May 2010 general election; PPS to: Theresa Villiers as Minister of State, Department for Transport 2010-12, Mike Penning as Minister of State, Northern Ireland Office 2012-13, Hugo Swire as Minister of State, Foreign and Commonwealth Office 2014-15, Priti Patel as Minister of State for Employment, Department for Work and Pensions 2015-16. *Select committees:* Member: Backbench Business 2013-14, Communities and Local Government 2014-15, European Scrutiny 2015-16. Member, Executive, 1922 Committee 2016-. Conservative Party: Deputy chair, Elmet Conservative Association 2001-04, Vice-chairman 2017-. *Councils and public bodies:* Councillor, Leeds City Council 2004-10.

Political interests: Foreign affairs, transport, welfare, international aid; Middle East, USA.

Other: Member, UK delegation to NATO Parliamentary Assembly 2015-; Member: Institute of Mechanical Engineers 1994-, Association of Project Managers 2001-11; Martin House, Lee's Smile; Carlton Club.

Recreations: Football, motor racing, cricket, music, reading.

Alec Shelbrooke MP, House of Commons, London SW1A 0AA
Tel: 020 7219 3000 *Email:* alec.shelbrooke.mp@parliament.uk
Constituency: First Floor, 43 Market Place, Wetherby, Leeds, West Yorkshire LS22 6LN
Tel: 01937 589002 *Email:* conservatives@elmetandrothwell.com
Websites: www.elmetandrothwell.com www.alecshelbrooke.co.uk
Twitter: @AlecShelbrooke

SCOTTISH NATIONAL PARTY

SHEPPARD, TOMMY

Edinburgh East *(Majority 3,425)*

SNP Spokesperson for House of Lords, Scotland and Cabinet Office

Thomas Sheppard. Born 6 March 1959; Partner Kate.

Education: Aberdeen University (Degree sociology and politics 1982).

Non-political career: Vice-president, National Union of Students; Public Relations; Founder, Stand Comedy Club 1995-.

Political career: Contested (Labour) Bury St Edmunds 1992 general election. Member (SNP) for Edinburgh East since 7 May 2015 general election; SNP Spokesperson for: Cabinet Office 2015-, House of Lords 2017-, Scotland 2017-. *Select committees:* Member: Standards 2015-, Privileges 2015-, Scottish Affairs 2017-. Assistant general secretary, Labour Party 1993-96. *Councils and public bodies:* Former Labour Councillor, London Borough of Hackney Council.

Other: Member, national council, Scottish Independence Convention.

Tommy Sheppard MP, House of Commons, London SW1A 0AA
Tel: 020 7219 6653 *Email:* tommy.sheppard.mp@parliament.uk
Constituency: 94 Portobello High Street, Portobello, Edinburgh EH15 1AN
Tel: 0131-661 8023 *Website:* tommysheppardmp.scot *Twitter:* @TommySheppard

LABOUR

SHERRIFF, PAULA

Dewsbury *(Majority 3,321)*

Shadow Minister for Women and Equalities

Paula Michelle Sherriff. Born 16 April 1975.

Non-political career: Crime management/victim support roles 1993-2003; Community healthcare, NHS 2003-13; Service co-ordinator, Virgin Care 2013-15. Member, GMB.

Political career: Member for Dewsbury since 7 May 2015 general election; PPS to Jon Trickett as Shadow Secretary of State for Communities and Local Government 2015-16; Shadow Minister for Women and Equalities 2016-. *Select committees:* Member, Health 2015-16. *Councils and public bodies:* Councillor, Wakefield Council 2012-15.

Other: Member, UK delegation, Parliamentary Assembly of the Council of Europe 2016.

Paula Sherriff MP, House of Commons, London SW1A 0AA
Tel: 020 7219 6987 *Email:* paula.sherriff.mp@parliament.uk
Constituency: The Old Dewsbury Reporter Building, 17 Wellington Road, Dewsbury, West Yorkshire WF13 1HQ
Tel: 01924 565450 *Email:* paula@paulasherriff.org.uk *Website:* www.paulasherriff.org.uk
Twitter: @paulasherriff

LAB/CO-OP

SHUKER, GAVIN

Luton South *(Majority 13,925)*

Gavin Paul Shuker. Born 10 October 1981; Married Lucie 2007 (1 daughter).

Education: Icknield High School; Luton Sixth Form College; Girton College, Cambridge (BA social and political science 2003).

Non-political career: Associate Pastor, City Life Church, Cambridge 2003-06; Charity Worker, Fusion UK 2003-08; Endis Ltd 2008-10; Church Leader, City Life Church, Luton 2006-10. Member, USDAW.

Political career: Member for Luton South since 6 May 2010 general election; PPS to Sadiq Khan as Shadow Lord Chancellor and Secretary of State for Justice 2010-11; Shadow Minister for: Environment, Food and Rural Affairs 2011-13, International Development 2013-15; Member, Commons Reference Group on Representation and Inclusion 2017-. *Select committees:* Member: Transport 2010-11, Armed Forces Bill 2015 2015-16, Women and Equalities 2015-, Environmental Audit 2016-17. Chair, PLP Departmental Group for Transport 2015-. Co-operative Party: Member, Chair, Parliamentary Group 2014-.

Political interests: Political engagement, electoral reform, child poverty, student funding, transport policy, international development, debt reduction, civil liberties, freedom of religion and belief; Bangladesh, Israel, New Zealand, Norway, Pakistan, Palestine.

Other: Member, UK Delegation, Organisation for Security and Co-operation in Europe Parliamentary Assembly 2015-; Member: Evangelical Alliance, Campaign for Real Ale.

Recreations: Cooking, real ale, church, Formula 1.

Gavin Shuker MP, House of Commons, London SW1A 0AA
Tel: 020 7219 1130 *Email:* gavin.shuker.mp@parliament.uk
Constituency: 3 Union Street, Luton, Bedfordshire LU1 3AN
Tel: 01582 457774 *Email:* office@gavinshuker.org *Website:* www.gavinshuker.org
Twitter: @gavinshuker

LABOUR

SIDDIQ, TULIP

Hampstead and Kilburn *(Majority 15,560)*

Tulip Rizwana Siddiq. Born 16 September 1982; Married Chris Percy 2013 (1 daughter).

Education: University College London (BA); King's College London (MA); University of London, Birkbeck (MSc).

Non-political career: Policy adviser to Dame Tessa Jowell MP; Researcher: Philip Gould Association, Greater London Authority; Caseworker for Harry Cohen MP. Member, Unite.

Political career: Member for Hampstead and Kilburn since 7 May 2015 general election; PPS to Michael Dugher as Shadow Secretary of State for Culture, Media and Sport 2015-16; Shadow Minister for Early Years 2016-17. *Select committees:* Member, Women and Equalities 2015, 2017-. Member, Co-operative Party; Deputy field director to Ed Miliband MP, Labour Party Leadership Campaign 2010. *Councils and public bodies:* Camden Council: Councillor 2010-14, Cabinet Member for Culture and Communities 2010-14; Governor: Richard Cobden Primary School, Working Men's College, Camden and Islington NHS Trust.

Other: Member, Royal Society of Arts; Chair: Camden Library Network, Camden Faith Leaders' Forum.

Tulip Siddiq MP, House of Commons, London SW1A 0AA
Tel: 020 7219 6276 *Email:* tulip.siddiq.mp@parliament.uk
Constituency: 21 Winchester Road, London NW3 3NR
Tel: 020 8127 5525 *Email:* tulip@tulipsiddiq.com *Website:* www.tulipsiddiq.com
Twitter: @TulipSiddiq

DEMOCRATIC UNIONIST PARTY

SIMPSON, DAVID

Upper Bann *(Majority 7,992)*

DUP Spokesperson for Business, Energy and Industrial Strategy and Environment, Food and Rural Affairs

Thomas David Simpson. Born 16 February 1959; Married Elaine Elizabeth (1 adopted son 2 adopted daughters).

Education: Killicomaine High School; College of Business Studies, Belfast.

Non-political career: Food manufacturing industry; Senior partner, Universal Meat Company.

Political career: Contested Upper Bann 2001 general election. Member for Upper Bann since 5 May 2005 general election; DUP Spokesperson for: Trade and Industry 2005-07, Young People 2007-10, Transport 2007-09, International Development 2007-10, Business, Innovation and Skills 2009-17, Communities and Local Government 2010-15, Education 2012-15, Environment, Food and Rural Affairs 2015-, Business, Energy and Industrial Strategy 2017-. *Select committees:* Member: Joint Committee on Statutory Instruments and Commons Committee on Statutory Instruments 2006-09, Transport 2007-09, Northern Ireland Affairs 2009-15, Environment, Food and Rural Affairs 2015-, Environment, Food and Rural Affairs Sub-committee 2016. Northern Ireland Assembly: MLA for Upper Bann 2003-10, Chair, Committee on Social Development 2008-09. DUP: Vice-President, Vice-Chairman: Victims Committee, Council Association, Chairman, Upper Bann Constituency Association. *Councils and public bodies:* Craigavon Borough Council: Councillor 2001-10, Deputy Mayor 2003-04, Mayor 2004-05; Member, Northern Ireland Policing Board 2007-08.

Political interests: History of politics; Africa, Israel.

Other: Deputy Master, Loughall District Loyal Orange Order.

David Simpson MP, House of Commons, London SW1A 0AA
Tel: 020 7219 8533 *Fax:* 020 7219 2347 *Email:* simpsond@parliament.uk
Constituency: 13 Thomas Street, Portadown, Co Armagh BT62 3NP
Tel: 028 3833 2234 *Fax:* 028 3833 2123 *Email:* davidsimpson@upperbanndup.co.uk
Twitter: @DavidSimpsonDUP

CONSERVATIVE

SIMPSON, KEITH

Broadland *(Majority 15,816)*

Keith Robert Simpson. Born 29 March 1949; Son of Harry Simpson and Jean Simpson, née Day; Married Pepita Hollingsworth 1984 (1 son).

Education: Thorpe Grammar School, Norfolk; Hull University (BA history 1970); King's College, University of London.

Non-political career: Honorary Colonel Royal Military Police TA 1998-2007. Senior lecturer in war studies, RMA Sandhurst 1973-86; Head of foreign affairs and defence section, Conservative Research Department 1987-88; Special adviser to George Younger MP and Tom King MP as Secretaries of State for Defence 1988-90; Director, Cranfield Security Studies Institute, Cranfield University 1991-97.

Political career: Contested Plymouth Devonport 1992 general election. Member for Mid Norfolk 1997-2010, for Broadland since 6 May 2010 general election; Opposition Spokesperson for Defence 1998-99; Opposition Whip 1999-2001; Opposition Spokesperson for Environment, Food and Rural Affairs 2001-02; Shadow Minister for: Defence 2002-05, Foreign Affairs 2005-10; PPS to William Hague as First Secretary of State, Secretary of State for Foreign and Commonwealth Affairs 2010-14; Member: Prime Minister's advisory board on commemorating the First World War 2014-15, Intelligence and Security Committee 2015-. *Select committees:* Member: European Standing Committee A 1998, Environment, Food and Rural Affairs 2001-02. Joint Secretary Conservative Party Committee for Defence 1997-99. National vice-chair, Federation of Conservative Students 1971-72; Chair, Conservative History Group 2003-; Founding member, Conservatives for Reform in Europe 2016. *Councils and public bodies:* Member: Royal United Services Institute for Defence Studies, British Commission for Military History, Parliamentary Commissioner, Commonwealth War Graves Commission 2008-.

Political interests: Foreign affairs, defence, education, farming, countryside; France, Germany, Gulf States, Israel, Jordan, Poland, Saudi Arabia, Syria, USA.

Other: Council member, SSAFA 1997-2002; Trustee, History of Parliament Trust 2005-10; Macmillan Cancer Support. PC 2015.

Publications: The Old Contemptibles (1981); Joint editor, A Nations in Arms (1985); History of the German Army (1985); Editor, The War the Infantry Knew 1914-1919 (1986).

Recreations: Stroking cats, reading, restaurants, cinema, malt whiskies, observing ambitious people.

Rt Hon Keith Simpson MP, House of Commons, London SW1A 0AA
Tel: 020 7219 4053 *Email:* keithsimpsonmp@parliament.uk
Constituency: Broadland Conservative Association, The Stable, Church Farm, Attlebridge, Norfolk NR9 5ST
Tel: 01603 865763 *Fax:* 01603 865762 *Email:* organiser@broadlandconservatives.org.uk
Website: www.keithsimpson.com

CONSERVATIVE

SKIDMORE, CHRIS

Kingswood *(Majority 7,500)*

Parliamentary Secretary (Minister for the Constitution), Cabinet Office

Christopher James Skidmore. Born 17 May 1981; Married Lydia (1 son 1 daughter).

Education: Bristol Grammar School; Oxford University (history).

Non-political career: *Western Daily Press*; *People* magazine; Researcher, *Great Tales of English History*; University tutor, Bristol University; Author.

Political career: Member for Kingswood since 6 May 2010 general election; PPS to George Osborne as First Secretary of State and Chancellor of the Exchequer 2015-16; Parliamentary Secretary (Minister for the Constitution), Cabinet Office 2016-. *Select committees:* Member: Health 2010-13, Education 2012-14. Conservative Party: Member 1996-, Adviser on education, Director, Public Services Improvement Group; Number 10 Policy Advisory Board: Member (Public Services and Family), Deputy Chair.

Political interests: Health, education, social care, disability.

Other: Chair, Bow Group; Fellow, Royal Society of Arts; Fellow, Royal Historical Society.

Publications: Author: Edward VI: The Lost King of England (Weidenfeld, 2007), Death and the Virgin (Weidenfeld, 2010); Co-author: (with Kwasi Kwarteng MP) After the Coalition (BiteBack, 2011), (with Kwasi Kwarteng MP, Priti Patel MP, Dominic Raab MP and Elizabeth Truss MP) Britannia Unchained: Global Lessons for Growth and Prosperity (Palgrave Macmillan, 2012); Bosworth: The Birth of the Tudors (Weidenfeld and Nicolson, 2013).

Chris Skidmore MP, House of Commons, London SW1A 0AA
Tel: 020 7219 7094 *Email:* chris.skidmore.mp@parliament.uk
Constituency: 60 High Street, Hanham BS15 3DR
Tel: 0117-908 1524 *Email:* chris@chrisskidmore.com *Website:* www.chrisskidmore.com
Twitter: @CSkidmoreUK

LABOUR

SKINNER, DENNIS

Bolsover *(Majority 5,288)*

Dennis Edward Skinner. Born 11 February 1932; Son of Edward Skinner; Married Mary Parker 1960 (died) (1 son 2 daughters); partner Lois Blasenheim.

Education: Tupton Hall Grammar School, Clay Cross, Derbyshire; Ruskin College, Oxford.

Non-political career: Miner 1949-70. President, Derbyshire Miners 1966-70.

Political career: Member for Bolsover 1970-2010, for Bolsover (revised boundary) since 6 May 2010 general election; President, North East Derbyshire Constituency Labour Party 1968-71; National Executive Committee, Labour Party: Member 1978-92, 1994-98, 1999-2014, 2015-16, Vice-chair 1987-88, Chair 1988-89. *Councils and public bodies:* Councillor: Clay Cross UDC 1960-70, Derbyshire County Council 1964-70; Former President, Derbyshire UDC Association.

Political interests: Inland waterways, energy, economic policy, environment, anti-Common Market, Third World.

Other: Parliamentarian of the Year 2010, Political Studies Association.

Publications: Sailing Close to the Wind (Quercus, 2014).

Recreations: Cycling, tennis, athletics (watching).

Dennis Skinner MP, House of Commons, London SW1A 0AA
Tel: 020 7219 5107 *Fax:* 020 7219 0028 *Email:* skinnerd@parliament.uk
Constituency: 1 Elmhurst Close, South Normanton, Alfreton, Derbyshire DE55 3NF
Tel: 01773 581027 *Website:* www.eastmidslabour.org.uk

LABOUR

SLAUGHTER, ANDY

Hammersmith *(Majority 18,651)*

Andrew Francis Slaughter. Born 29 September 1960; Son of Alfred Slaughter and Marie Slaughter; Single.

Education: Latymer Upper School, London; Exeter University (BA English 1982); Qualified as a Barrister 1993.

Non-political career: Barrister, specialising in housing and personal injury law 1993-. Member: GMB, Unite.

Political career: Contested Uxbridge 1997 by-election. Member for Ealing, Acton and Shepherd's Bush 2005-10, for Hammersmith since 6 May 2010 general election; PPS to: Stephen Ladyman as Minister of State, Department for Transport 2005-07, Lord Jones of Birmingham as Minister of State, Foreign and Commonwealth Office and Department for Business, Enterprise and Regulatory Reform 2007-08, Lord Malloch-Brown as Minister of State, Foreign and Commonwealth Office 2007-09; Shadow Minister for: Justice 2010-16, Housing 2016-17, London 2016-17. *Select committees:* Member: Regulatory Reform 2005-07, Children, Schools and Families 2007-09, Court of Referees 2007-10, Communities and Local Government 2009-10, London 2009-10, Joint Committee on Human Rights 2010. Vice-chair, PLP London Regional Group 2007-. *Councils and public bodies:* Governor, William Morris Sixth Form 1994-; London Borough of Hammersmith and Fulham: Councillor 1986-2006, Council leader 1996-2005.

Political interests: International affairs, housing, education, health, transport; Bahrain, Caribbean, Egypt, Middle East, Palestine, Spain, Tunisia.

Other: Management committee, Hammersmith and Fulham Community Law Centre 1990-.

Andy Slaughter MP, House of Commons, London SW1A 0AA
Tel: 020 7219 4990 *Email:* andy.slaughter.mp@parliament.uk
Constituency: 28 Greyhound Road, London W6 8NX
Tel: 020 7610 1950 *Fax:* 020 7381 5074 *Email:* andy@andyslaughter.com
Website: www.andyslaughter.co.uk *Twitter:* @hammersmithandy

LABOUR

SMEETH, RUTH

Stoke-on-Trent North *(Majority 2,359)*

PPS to Tom Watson as Deputy Leader, Labour Party and Shadow Secretary of State for Digital, Culture, Media and Sport

Ruth Lauren Smeeth. Born 29 June 1979; Daughter of Lucy Kelly, retired trade union officer; Married Michael Smeeth 2004.

Education: Downend Comprehensive, Bristol; Filton Sixth Form College, Bristol; Birmingham University (BSocSci politics and international relations 2000); Chartered Institute of Public Relations (Postgraduate Diploma public relations 2005).

Non-political career: Senior Research and Policy Officer, AMICUS-AEEU 2000-03; Head of government relations, Sodexho 2004-05; Director of Campaigns, British-Israel Communications Centre (BICOM) 2005-07; Public Affairs Manager, Nestlé 2007; Anti-racism Campaigns Co-ordinator, CST 2008-10; Deputy Director, Hope not Hate Educational Ltd 2010-15. Member: Unite 1998-, GMB 2007-.

Political career: Contested Burton 2010 general election. Member for Stoke-on-Trent North since 7 May 2015 general election; PPS to: Vernon Coaker as Shadow Secretary of State for Northern Ireland 2015-16, Ian Murray as Shadow Secretary of State for Scotland 2015-16, Tom Watson as Deputy Leader, Labour Party and Shadow Secretary of State for Digital, Culture, Media and Sport 2017-. *Select committees:* Member: Defence 2015-, Armed Forces Bill 2015 2015-16. Various posts at constituency party level 1996-.

Political interests: British manufacturing, public services, community cohesion, British brewing, child food poverty; Kashmir, USA.

Other: Member, Chartered Institute of Public Relations 2004-08; Royal Society of Arts; Victory Working Men's Club and Institute, Naval and Military Club.

Recreations: Reading, cinema, socialising with family and friends.

Ruth Smeeth MP, House of Commons, London SW1A 0AA
Tel: 020 7219 4844 *Email:* ruth.smeeth.mp@parliament.uk
Constituency: PO Box 3663, Stoke-on-Trent ST6 9EP
Tel: 01782 454370 *Website:* www.ruthsmeeth.org.uk *Twitter:* @RuthSmeeth

LABOUR

SMITH, ANGELA

Penistone and Stocksbridge *(Majority 1,322)*

Angela Christine Smith. Born 16 August 1961; Daughter of Tom and Pat Smith; Married Steven Wilson 2005 (1 stepson 1 stepdaughter).

Education: Toll Bar Secondary School, Waltham; Nottingham University (BA English studies 1990); Newnham College, Cambridge (PhD 1994).

Non-political career: Medical secretary, NHS 1979-84; Secretary, Barclays Bank 1984-87; English lecturer, Dearne Valley College 1994-2003. Member: Unison, GMB.

Political career: Member for Sheffield Hillsborough 2005-10, for Penistone and Stocksbridge since 6 May 2010 general election; PPS to Yvette Cooper: as Minister of State, ODPM/Department for Communities and Local Government 2005-08, as Chief Secretary to the Treasury 2008; Opposition Assistant Whip 2010-11; Shadow Deputy Leader of the House of Commons 2011-14; Shadow Minister for Environment, Food and Rural Affairs 2014-15. *Select committees:* Member: Regulatory Reform 2005-07, Transport 2009-10, Administration 2010-12, Environment, Food and Rural Affairs 2015-, Environment, Food and Rural Affairs Sub-committee 2016-17. Member, Labour Party National Executive Committee 2010-11. *Councils and public bodies:* Sheffield City Council: Councillor 1996-2005, Chair of Finance 1998-99, Cabinet Member for Education 2002-05; Member, Regional Education and Skills Commission 2002-05; Chair, 14-19 Board, Sheffield First for Learning and Work 2002-05.

Political interests: Education, skills agenda, environment and conservation, transport, manufacturing; Balkans, Finland.

Other: Substitute Member, UK delegation, Parliamentary Assembly of the Council of Europe 2016-; Honorary life member, BVA; Trustee, IPT; IPT; RSPB, Wildlife Trust, Woodland Trust, Ramblers Association, IFAW, League Against Cruel Sports. Constituency MP of the Year, *House Magazine* awards 2011.

Recreations: Hill-walking, cooking.

Angela Smith MP, House of Commons, London SW1A 0AA
Tel: 020 7219 6713 *Fax:* 020 7219 8598 *Email:* officeofangelasmithmp@parliament.uk
Constituency: 2 Maria House, 3 Fox Valley Way, Stocksbridge, Sheffield S36 2AA
Tel: 0114-283 1855 *Website:* www.angelasmith-mp.org.uk *Twitter:* @angelasmithmp

LABOUR

SMITH, CAT

Lancaster and Fleetwood *(Majority 6,661)*

Shadow Minister for Voter Engagement and Youth Affairs; Shadow Minister for Transport

Catherine Jane Smith. Born 16 June 1985; Married Ben Soffa 2016.

Education: Parkview School, Barrow-in-Furness; Barrow Sixth Form College; Lancaster University (BA gender and sociology 2006).

Non-political career: Campaign and policy officer, British Association of Social Workers 2011-15.

Political career: Contested Wyre and Preston North 2010 general election. Member for Lancaster and Fleetwood since 7 May 2015 general election; Shadow Minister for: Women and Equalities Office 2015-16, Voter Engagement and Youth Affairs (attends Shadow Cabinet) 2016-; Shadow Deputy Leader of the House of Commons 2016-17; Shadow Minister for Transport 2017-. *Select committees:* Member, Women and Equalities 2015. Patron, LGBT Labour.

Other: Former chair, Compass Youth Organising Committee; Trustee, Empowerment (formed by merger of Lancaster and Blackpool Women's Aids).

Cat Smith MP, House of Commons, London SW1A 0AA
Tel: 020 7219 6001 *Email:* cat.smith.mp@parliament.uk
Constituency: No constituency office publicised *Website:* www.catsmith.co.uk
Twitter: @CatSmithMP

CONSERVATIVE

SMITH, CHLOE

Norwich North *(Majority 507)*

Parliamentary Under-Secretary of State, Northern Ireland Office; Assistant Government Whip

Chloe Rebecca Smith. Born 17 May 1982; Daughter of David Smith, furniture designer and maker, and Claire Smith, teacher; Married Sandy McFadzean (1 son).

Education: Methwold High School, Norfolk; Swaffham Sixth Form College, Norfolk; York University (BA English literature 2004); French.

Non-political career: Business consultant, Deloitte 2004-09.

Political career: Member for Norwich North 23 July 2009 by-election to 2010, for Norwich North (revised boundary) since 6 May 2010 general election; Assistant Government Whip 2010-11, 2017-; Economic Secretary, HM Treasury 2011-12; Parliamentary Secretary (Minister for Political and Constitutional Reform), Cabinet Office 2012-13; Parliamentary Adviser to Lord Feldman as Chairman, Conservative and Unionist Party 2015-16; Parliamentary Under-Secretary of State, Northern Ireland Office 2017-. *Select committees:* Member: Work and Pensions 2009-10, Public Accounts 2011-12, Transport 2013-15. Member: Conservative Friends of Israel 2001-, Conservative Party Implementation Team 2008-09, Tory Reform Group 2009-; Conservative Party: Board member 2015-17, Member, Organisational Review Panel 2015-17. *Councils and public bodies:* Governor, Heartsease Primary School, Norwich 2010-12; Member: Hellesdon High School Academy Trust/Wesum Trust 2012-, Advisory Board, Norwich Business School.

Political interests: Transport, skills, youth engagement, work and pensions, modern slavery, public services, efficiency, electoral engagement.

Other: Patron, YMCA Norfolk 2009-; Honorary Vice-President, Norfolk and Norwich Novi Sad Association 2009-; Patron, Blue Ribbon Foundation; Chair, National Youth Agency's Commission into Young People and Enterprise 2014-15; Commissioner, Industry and Parliament Trust's Youth Skills Commission 2014-15; Patron: Eating Matters, Surviving Together; Trustee, Chill4Us. Youth Friendly MP, Youth Employment UK 2014; Business Driver, Grassroots Diplomat Initiative 2014.

Recreations: Arts, including theatre and drawing; sports, including cycling, badminton.

Chloe Smith MP, House of Commons, London SW1A 0AA
Tel: 020 7219 8449
Constituency: No constituency office publicised
Tel: 01603 414756 *Email:* chloe@chloesmith.org.uk *Website:* www.chloesmith.org.uk
Twitter: @NorwichChloe

LABOUR

SMITH, ELEANOR

Wolverhampton South West *(Majority 2,185)*

PPS to Diane Abbott as Shadow Home Secretary

Eleanor Patricia Smith. Born 5 July 1957; Married (2 daughters).

Non-political career: Register Theatre Nurse, Birmingham Women's and Children's NHS Foundation Trust. Unison: Branch Secretary 1999-, Member, National Executive, President 2011-12; Chair: Unison National Labour Link, Midlands TUC.

Political career: Member for Wolverhampton South West since 8 June 2017; PPS to Diane Abbott as Shadow Home Secretary 2017-.

Other: Non-executive Director, UIA Mutual Insurance; Senior Staff Side Convener, Birmingham Women's Hospital Trust.

Eleanor Smith MP, House of Commons, London SW1A 0AA
Tel: 020 7219 0634 *Email:* eleanor.smith.mp@parliament.uk
Constituency: 8 Tettenhall Road, Wolverhampton WV1 4SA
Tel: 01902 422344 *Website:* www.eleanor4wolves.net *Twitter:* @Eleanor_SmithMP

CONSERVATIVE

SMITH, HENRY

Crawley *(Majority 2,457)*

Henry Edward Millar Smith. Born 14 May 1969; Son of late John Smith and late Josephine Smith; Married Jennifer Ricks 1994 (divorced 2015) (1 son 1 daughter 1 son deceased).

Education: Frensham Heights, Farnham; University College London (BA philosophy 1991).

Non-political career: Property investment business.

Political career: Contested Crawley 2001 and 2005 general elections. Member for Crawley since 6 May 2010 general election; PPS to: Greg Clark as Secretary of State for Communities and Local Government 2015-16, Justine Greening as Secretary of State for Education and Minister for Women and Equalities 2016-17. *Select committees:* Member: European Scrutiny 2010-15, International Development 2017-, Work of the Independent Commission for Aid Impact Sub-committee

2017-. Founding member, Conservatives for Britain 2015-16. *Councils and public bodies:* West Sussex County Council: Councillor 1997-2010, Council leader 2003-10; Councillor, Crawley Borough Council 2002-04; Vice-President, Local Government Association 2011-15.

Political interests: Local government, foreign policy; British Overseas Territories, USA.

Other: Member, Pilgrim Society; Flag Institute.

Publications: Co-author, Direct Democracy: An Agenda for a New Model Party (2005).

Recreations: Vexillology, skiing.

Henry Smith MP, House of Commons, London SW1A 0AA
Tel: 020 7219 7043 *Email:* henry.smith.mp@parliament.uk
Constituency: Crawley Business Centre, Stephenson Way, Three Bridges, Crawley, West Sussex RH10 1TN
Tel: 01293 934554 *Email:* steve.aldridge@parliament.uk *Website:* www.henrysmith.info
Twitter: @HenrySmithUK

LABOUR

SMITH, JEFF

Manchester Withington *(Majority 29,875)*

Opposition Whip

Jeffrey Smith. Born 26 January 1963; Son of Alan and Deirdre Smith; Unmarried.

Education: Manchester Grammar School; Manchester University (BA economics).

Non-political career: Self-employed event manager and DJ 1985-2011. Member, USDAW.

Political career: Member for Manchester Withington since 7 May 2015 general election; Opposition Whip 2015-. *Select committees:* Member, Environmental Audit 2015. Former Chair, Secretary and Agent, Withington CLP; Member, Co-operative Party. *Councils and public bodies:* Manchester City Council: Councillor 1997-2015, Executive Member for: Children's Services, Finance, Housing and Regeneration.

Other: Former Board Member, Southway Housing Trust; Former Governor: Parrs Wood High School, Old Moat School, Mauldeth Road Primary.

Jeff Smith MP, House of Commons, London SW1A 0AA
Tel: 020 7219 5878 *Email:* jeff.smith.mp@parliament.uk
Constituency: Unit 1, Withington Fire Station, 505-507 Wilmslow Road, Withington, Manchster M20 4AW
Tel: 0161-445 0678 *Website:* www.jeffsmith.org.uk *Twitter:* @JeffSmithetc

CONSERVATIVE

SMITH, JULIAN

Skipton and Ripon *(Majority 19,985)*

Deputy Chief Whip (Treasurer of HM Household)

Julian Richard Smith. Born 30 August 1971; Married Amanda.

Education: Balfron High School; Millfield School, Somerset; Birmingham University (BA English and history 1993); French.

Non-political career: Squash Coach, Perpignan; The Bird Moore Partnership 1994-99; Arq International Ltd, London: Founder and Managing Director 1999-2010, Non-executive Director 2010-11.

Political career: Member for Skipton and Ripon since 6 May 2010 general election; PPS to: Alan Duncan as Minister of State, Department for International Development 2010-12, Justine Greening as Secretary of State for International Development 2012-15; Assistant Government Whip 2015-16; Government Whip (Vice-Chamberlain of HM Household) 2016-17; Deputy Chief Whip (Treasurer of HM Household) 2017-. *Select committees:* Member: Scottish Affairs 2010, Selection 2015-. Deputy chair, Bethnal Green and Bow Conservatives 2008-09.

Political interests: Business, education, welfare, universities and skills, agriculture.

Other: Junior international squash player.

Recreations: Violin and piano.

Julian Smith MP, House of Commons, London SW1A 0AA
Tel: 020 7219 7145 *Email:* julian.smith.mp@parliament.uk
Constituency: 7 Gargrave Road, Broughton, Skipton BD23 3AQ
Tel: 01756 795898 *Website:* www.juliansmith.org.uk *Twitter:* @JulianSmithUK

LABOUR

SMITH, LAURA

Crewe and Nantwich *(Majority 48)*

PPS to Jon Trickett as Shadow Minister for the Cabinet Office

Partner Steve (1 daughter 1 son 1 stepson).

Education: Brine Leas School; South Cheshire College; Manchester Metropolitan University.

Non-political career: Primary school teacher; Founder, One-to-one Tutoring 2013-.

Political career: Member for Crewe and Nantwich since 8 June 2017; PPS to Jon Trickett as Shadow Minister for the Cabinet Office 2017-. *Select committees:* Member, Transport 2017-.

Political interests: Education.

Laura Smith MP, House of Commons, London SW1A 0AA
Tel: 020 7219 4571 *Email:* laura.smith.mp@parliament.uk
Constituency: Suite 3a, Breeden House, Edleston Road, Crewe CW2 7EA
Tel: 01270 617645 *Twitter:* @LauraSmithMP

LABOUR

SMITH, NICK

Blaenau Gwent *(Majority 11,907)*

Opposition Whip

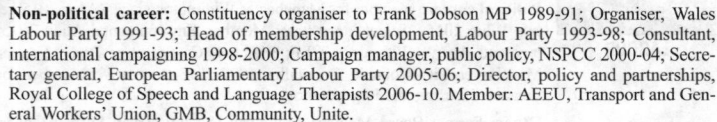

Nicholas Desmond John Smith. Born 14 January 1960; Son of William and Alma Smith; Married (2 daughters); married Jenny Chapman (qv) 2014 (MP for Darlington).

Education: Tredegar Comprehensive School; Coventry University (BA history, politics and international relations 1981); Birkbeck College, London (MSc economic change 1991).

Non-political career: Constituency organiser to Frank Dobson MP 1989-91; Organiser, Wales Labour Party 1991-93; Head of membership development, Labour Party 1993-98; Consultant, international campaigning 1998-2000; Campaign manager, public policy, NSPCC 2000-04; Secretary general, European Parliamentary Labour Party 2005-06; Director, policy and partnerships, Royal College of Speech and Language Therapists 2006-10. Member: AEEU, Transport and General Workers' Union, GMB, Community, Unite.

Political career: Member for Blaenau Gwent since 6 May 2010 general election; PPS to Douglas Alexander as Shadow Secretary of State for: Work and Pensions 2010-11, Foreign and Commonwealth Office 2011-15; Shadow Minister for Environment, Food and Rural Affairs 2015-16; Opposition Whip 2016-. *Select committees:* Member, Public Accounts 2010-15. Election agent to Emily Thornberry MP 2005. *Councils and public bodies:* London Borough of Camden Council: Former councillor, Member, then Executive Member for Education 2003-05.

Political interests: Economic development, health, children; China, India, Nepal, USA.

Other: Alternate Member, UK Delegation, Organisation for Security and Co-operation in Europe Parliamentary Assembly -2016; Member: Aneurin Bevan Society, Tribune, Fabian Society; Fellow, Royal Geographical Society.

Recreations: Hiking, singing, reading, chess.

Nick Smith MP, House of Commons, London SW1A 0AA
Tel: 020 7219 7018 *Fax:* 020 7219 0565 *Email:* nick.smith.mp@parliament.uk
Constituency: 23 Beaufort Street, Brynmawr, Blaenau Gwent, Gwent NP23 4AQ
Tel: 01495 313167 *Website:* www.nick-smith.net *Twitter:* @BlaenauGwentMP

LABOUR

SMITH, OWEN

Pontypridd *(Majority 11,448)*

Shadow Secretary of State for Northern Ireland

Born 2 May 1970; Married Liz (2 sons 1 daughter).

Education: Coed-y-Lan Comprehensive, Pontypridd; Barry Boys Comprehensive, Barry; Sussex University (history and French); French.

Non-political career: BBC Radio and TV Producer, including BBC Radio 4 *Today* and BBC Wales *Dragon's Eye* 1992-2002; Special adviser to Paul Murphy MP as Secretary of State for: Wales 2002, Northern Ireland 2002-05; Head of policy and government affairs, Pfizer 2005-08; Director of health economic and corporate affairs, Amgen UK & Ireland 2008-10. Member: Unite, GMB.

Political career: Contested Blaenau Gwent 2006 by-election. Member for Pontypridd since 6 May 2010 general election; Shadow Minister for Wales 2010-11; Shadow Exchequer Secretary 2011-12; Shadow Secretary of State for: Wales 2012-15, Work and Pensions 2015-16, Northern Ireland 2017-. *Select committees:* Member, Welsh Affairs 2010-11. Contested Labour leadership election 2016.

Political interests: Economic affairs, industrial policy, equality, health, constitutional reform; France, Ireland, Wales.

Other: Llantrisant Working Men's Club.

Recreations: Family, reading, fishing, Pontyclun RFC.

Owen Smith MP, House of Commons, London SW1A 0AA
Tel: 020 7219 1287 *Email:* owen.smith.mp@parliament.uk
Constituency: 10 Market Street, Pontypridd CF37 2ST
Tel: 01443 401122 *Website:* www.owensmithmp.co.uk *Twitter:* @OwenSmith_MP

SMITH, ROYSTON

Southampton Itchen *(Majority 31)*

CONSERVATIVE

Royston Matthew Smith. Born 13 May 1964.

Education: Bitterne Park Secondary School; Royal Air Force School of Technical Training (aeronautical engineering 1980).

Non-political career: Aeronautical engineer: Royal Air Force 1980-90, British Airways 1990-2006.

Political career: Contested Southampton Itchen 2010 general election. Member for Southampton Itchen since 7 May 2015 general election. *Select committees:* Member: Work and Pensions 2016-17, Foreign Affairs 2017-. *Councils and public bodies:* Southampton City Council: Councillor 2000-15, Deputy Leader; Vice-chair, Hampshire Fire and Rescue Authority 2000-15.

Political interests: Economic development, defence.

Other: Member, UK Delegation, Organisation for Security and Co-operation in Europe Parliamentary Assembly 2015-; Director, Blue Lamp Trust; Member, Institute of British Engineers.

Recreations: Walking, climbing, tennis, gym.

Royston Smith MP, House of Commons, London SW1A 0AA
Tel: 020 7219 5226 *Email:* royston.smith.mp@parliament.uk
Constituency: 70 Dean Road, Bitterne, Southampton SO18 6AN
Tel: 023 8047 3309 *Email:* royston@roystonsmith.co.uk *Website:* www.roystonsmith.co.uk
Twitter: @Royston_Smith

SMYTH, KARIN

Bristol South *(Majority 15,987)*

LABOUR

Shadow Deputy Leader of House of Commons

Karin Marguerite Smyth. Born 8 September 1964; Married (3 children).

Education: Bishopshalt School; University of East Anglia (Degree economics and social studies 1988); Bath University (MBA 1995).

Non-political career: Political Assistant to Valerie Davey MP 1997-2001; Non-executive director, Bristol North PCT 2002-06; Independent Project and Interim Manager 2008-10; Locality Manager, South Bristol Consortium 2010-15.

Political career: Member for Bristol South since 7 May 2015 general election; PPS to: Heidi Alexander as Shadow Secretary of State for Health 2015-16, Keir Starmer as Shadow Secretary of State for Exiting the European Union 2016-17; Shadow Deputy Leader of House of Commons 2017-. *Select committees:* Member, Public Accounts 2015-17. Member, Labour Party 1985-. *Councils and public bodies:* School governor; Non-executive director, NHS Trust.

Other: Vice-chair, British-Irish Parliamentary Association 2017-.

Karin Smyth MP, House of Commons, London SW1A 0AA
Tel: 020 7219 3000 *Email:* karin.smyth.mp@parliament.uk
Constituency: No constituency office publicised
Tel: 0117-953 3575 *Website:* karinsmyth.com *Twitter:* @karinsmyth

SNELL, GARETH

Stoke-on-Trent Central *(Majority 3,897)*

LAB/CO-OP

Gareth Craig Snel; Married Sophia.

Education: Keele University (history).

Non-political career: Office of Tristram Hunt MP; Central services manager, Unison (West Midlands).

Political career: Member for Stoke-on-Trent Central since 23 February 2017 by-election. *Select committees:* Member: Science and Technology 2017, Public Accounts 2017-. *Councils and public bodies:* Newcastle-under-Lyme Borough Council: Councillor 2010-14, 2016-, Council Leader 2012-14.

Other: Director, Staffordshire Credit Union.

Gareth Snell MP, House of Commons, London SW1A 0AA
Tel: 020 7219 1276 *Email:* gareth.snell.mp@parliament.uk
Constituency: Ceramics House, Garth Street, Hanley, Stoke-on-Trent ST1 2AB
Tel: 01782 272897 *Twitter:* @gareth_snell

CONSERVATIVE

SOAMES, NICHOLAS

Mid Sussex *(Majority 19,673)*

Arthur Nicholas Winston Soames. Born 12 February 1948; Son of late Christopher Soames (MP for Bedford 1950-66, later Lord Soames) and late Lady Soames; Married Catherine Weatherall 1981 (divorced 1988) (1 son); married Serena Smith 1993 (1 daughter 1 son).

Education: Eton College; Mons Officer Cadet School 1966; French.

Non-political career: Lieutenant, 11th Hussars 1967-72; Hon Colonel: Bristol University Officers Training Corps 2006-11, The Kent and Sharpshooters Yeomanry 2012-. Equerry to Prince of Wales 1970-72; Stockbroker 1972-74; PA to: Sir James Goldsmith 1974-76, US Senator Mark Hatfield 1976-78; Assistant director, Sedgwick Group 1979-81; Senior adviser, MARSH.

Political career: Contested Dumbartonshire Central 1979 general election. Member for Crawley 1983-97, for Mid Sussex 1997-2010, for Mid Sussex (revised boundary) since 6 May 2010 general election; PPS to: John Gummer as Minister of State for Employment and Chairman of the Conservative Party 1984-86, Nicholas Ridley as Secretary of State for the Environment 1987-89; Joint Parliamentary Secretary, Ministry of Agriculture, Fisheries and Food 1992-94; Minister of State for the Armed Forces, Ministry of Defence 1994-97; Shadow Secretary of State for Defence 2003-05: Member Shadow Cabinet 2004-05. *Select committees:* Member: Public Administration 1999, Joint Committee on Consolidation of Bills Etc 2001-10, Standards and Privileges 2006-10, Administration 2013-14. Secretary, Conservative Foreign Affairs Committee 1986-87; Member, Executive, 1922 Committee 2000-03, 2005-06, 2010-12. President, Conservative Middle East Council 2007-; Patron, Tory Reform Group; Founding member, Conservatives for Reform in Europe 2016.

Political interests: Defence, foreign affairs, trade and industry, aerospace, aviation, agriculture and countryside matters; Europe, Middle East, USA.

Other: Trustee, Amber Foundation; Senior Adviser, Marsh; Member, International Advisory Board of GardaWorld. Vintners' Company. PC 2011; Kt 2014; White's Club, Turf Club, Pratt's Club. President, Haywards Heath Rugby Football Club.

Recreations: Country pursuits, racing.

Rt Hon Sir Nicholas Soames MP, House of Commons, London SW1A 0AA
Tel: 020 7219 4143 *Email:* nicholas.soames.mp@parliament.uk
Constituency: 5 Hazelgrove Road, Haywards Heath, West Sussex RH16 3PH
Tel: 01444 452590 *Email:* info@msca.org.uk *Websites:* www.midsussexconservatives.com
www.nicholassoames.org.uk *Twitter:* @Nsoames

LAB/CO-OP

SOBEL, ALEX

Leeds North West *(Majority 4,224)*

Alexander David Sobel. Born 26 April 1975; Married Susan (2 sons).

Education: Leeds University (BSc information systems 1997).

Non-political career: Community relations officer, Leeds University Union 2000-01; Community participation co-ordinator, Leeds Voice 2001-02; Senior development officer, Bradford University 2004-06; Development manager, UnLtd 2006-08; Centre manager, Urban Biz 2008-09; General manager, Social Enterprise Yorkshire and the Humber 2009-17.

Political career: Contested Beaconsfield 2005 and Leeds North West 2015 general elections. Member for Leeds North West since 8 June 2017. *Select committees:* Member: Backbench Business 2017-, Environmental Audit 2017-. Member, Labour Party 1997-; Regional organiser, Yorkshire and Humber, Ed Miliband's Leadership campaign 2010; Operations manager, Labour Yes to Fairer Votes 2011. *Councils and public bodies:* Councillor, Leeds City Council 2012-.

Alex Sobel MP, House of Commons, London SW1A 0AA
Tel: 020 7219 3568 *Email:* alex.sobel.mp@parliament.uk
Constituency: Details still to be confirmed *Website:* www.alexsobel.org *Twitter:* @alexsobel

CONSERVATIVE

SOUBRY, ANNA

Broxtowe *(Majority 863)*

Anna Mary Soubry. Born 7 December 1956; 2 daughters.

Education: Hartland Comprehensive School, Worksop; Birmingham University (law); Bar Finals.

Non-political career: Trainee reporter, Alloa; Presenter and reporter, *North Tonight*, Grampian TV; Presenter and reporter, Central TV: *Central News East*, *Central Weekend*, *Heart of the Country*; Barrister 1995-. Former shop steward, National Union of Journalists.

Political career: Contested Gedling 2005 general election. Member for Broxtowe since 6 May 2010 general election; PPS to Simon Burns as Minister of State for Health 2010-12; Parliamentary Under-Secretary of State (Public Health), Department of Health 2012-13; Ministry of Defence: Parliamentary Under-Secretary of State (Defence Personnel, Welfare and Veterans) 2013-14, Minister of State for Defence Personnel, Welfare and Veterans 2014-15; Minister of State for Small Business, Industry and Enterprise, Department for Business, Innovation and Skills 2015-16. *Select committees:* Member: Justice 2010, Scottish Affairs 2016-17.

Political interests: Justice, home affairs, health.

Other: Rector, Stirling University. PC 2015.

Recreations: Gardening, cooking, watching cricket, rugby and football.

Anna Soubry MP, House of Commons, London SW1A 0AA
Tel: 020 7219 3000 *Email:* anna.soubry.mp@parliament.uk
Constituency: Barton House, 61 High Road, Chilwell, Nottingham, Nottinghamshire NG9 4AJ
Tel: 0115-943 6507 *Fax:* 0115-943 0950 *Website:* www.annasoubry.org.uk
Twitter: @Anna_Soubry

LABOUR

SPELLAR, JOHN

Warley *(Majority 16,483)*

John Francis Spellar. Born 5 August 1947; Son of late William Spellar and Phyllis Spellar; Married Anne Wilmot 1981 (died 2003) (1 daughter).

Education: Dulwich College, London; St Edmund's Hall, Oxford (BA philosophy, politics and economics 1969).

Non-political career: National officer, Electrical, Electronic, Telecommunication and Plumbing Union 1969-97.

Political career: Contested Bromley 1970 general election. Member for Birmingham Northfield 28 October 1982 by-election to June 1983. Contested Birmingham Northfield 1983 and 1987 general elections. Member for Warley West 1992-97, for Warley 1997-2010, for Warley (revised boundary) since 6 May 2010 general election; Opposition Whip 1992-94; Opposition Spokesperson for: Northern Ireland 1994-95, Defence, Disarmament and Arms Control 1995-97; Ministry of Defence: Parliamentary Under-Secretary of State 1997-99, Minister of State for the Armed Forces 1999-2001; Minister for Transport: Department of Transport, Local Government and the Regions 2001-02, Department for Transport 2002-03; Minister of State, Northern Ireland Office 2003-05; Government Whip 2008-10; Opposition Deputy Chief Whip 2010; Shadow Minister for Foreign and Commonwealth Office 2010-15. *Select committees:* Member: Joint Committee on Conventions 2006, Finance and Services 2009-10, Selection 2010, Joint Committee on Security 2010, Administration 2010-13, Defence 2015-, Arms Export Controls 2016-17.

Political interests: Energy, electronics industry, motor industry, construction industry, defence; Australia, Israel, USA.

Other: Member, Executive Committee, Commonwealth Parliamentary Association UK 2015-17. PC 2001; Rowley Regis and Blackheath Labour Club, Brand Hall Labour Club.

Recreations: Gardening.

Rt Hon John Spellar MP, House of Commons, London SW1A 0AA
Tel: 020 7219 0674 *Fax:* 020 7219 2113 *Email:* john.spellar.mp@parliament.uk
Constituency: Brandhall Labour Club, Tame Road, Oldbury, West Midlands B68 0JT
Tel: 0121-423 2933 *Fax:* 0121-423 2933 *Email:* john.spellar@btconnect.com
Website: www.johnspellar.org.uk *Twitter:* @spellar

CONSERVATIVE

SPELMAN, CAROLINE

Meriden *(Majority 19,198)*

Caroline Alice Spelman. Born 4 May 1958; Daughter of late Marshall Cormack and Helen Cormack; Married Mark Spelman 1987 (2 sons 1 daughter).

Education: Herts and Essex Grammar School for Girls, Bishops Stortford; Queen Mary College, London (BA European studies 1980); French, German.

Non-political career: Sugar beet commodity secretary, National Farmers Union 1981-84; Deputy director, International Confederation of European Beetgrowers, Paris 1984-89; Research fellow, Centre for European Agricultural Studies 1989-93; Director, Spelman, Cormack and Associates 1989-2010.

Political career: Contested Bassetlaw 1992 general election. Member for Meriden 1997-2010, for Meriden (revised boundary) since 6 May 2010 general election; Opposition Whip 1998-99; Board member Parliamentary Office of Science and Technology (POST) 1997-2001; Opposition Spokesperson for: Health 1999-2001, Women's Issues 1999-2001; Shadow Secretary of State for International Development 2001-03; Shadow Minister for Women 2001-04; Shadow Secretary of State for: the Environment 2003-04, Local and Devolved Government Affairs 2004-05, Office of the Deputy Prime Minister/Communities and Local Government 2005-07, 2009-10; Secretary of State for Environment, Food and Rural Affairs 2010-12; Second Church Estates Commissioner 2015-. *Select committees:* Member: Science and Technology 1997-98, Environmental Audit 2013-15, Joint Committee on the Draft Modern Slavery Bill 2014, Ecclesiastical Committee 2014-. Member, Conservative Agriculture Policy Committee 2001-04. Co-opted member, executive committee, Conservative Women's National Council; Member, board of directors, governing council, Conservative Christian Fellowship; Advisory board member, Women2Win; Chair, Conservative Party 2007-09; Patron, Conservatives for Reform in Europe 2016.

Political interests: Environment, agriculture, international development, religion; Brazil, France, Germany, Portugal.

Other: Council of the European Union: Member: Agriculture and Fisheries Council 2010-12, Environment Council 2010-12; Patron, Drug Rehabilitation Charity (WELCOME); Member, Parliamentary Choir; Ambassador, Tearfund; National Trust, Wildlife Trust, Canal and River Trust, Member Royal British Legion. PC 2010; DBE 2016. Member: Lords and Commons Tennis Group, Lords and Commons ski team.

Publications: The non-food uses of agricultural raw materials (CABI, 1991); A Green and Pleasant Land (Bow Group, 1994).

Recreations: Tennis, cooking, gardening.

Rt Hon Dame Caroline Spelman DBE MP, House of Commons, London SW1A 0AA
Tel: 020 7219 2886
Constituency: 631 Warwick Road, Solihull, West Midlands B91 1AR
Tel: 0121-711 7029 *Email:* caroline@carolinespelman.com *Website:* www.carolinespelman.com
Twitter: @spelmanc

CONSERVATIVE

SPENCER, MARK

Sherwood *(Majority 5,198)*

Government Whip (Lord Commissioner of HM Treasury)

Mark Steven Spencer. Born 20 January 1970; Son of Cyril and Dorothy Spencer; Married Claire (1 son 1 daughter).

Education: Colonel Frank Seeley School, Calverton; Shuttleworth Agricultural College, Bedfordshire (farming course; National Certificate agriculture).

Non-political career: Farmer; Proprietor: Spring Lane Farm Shop, Floralands Garden Village, Lambley.

Political career: Member for Sherwood since 6 May 2010 general election; PPS to: Baroness Stowell of Beeston as Leader of the House of Lords and Lord Privy Seal 2014-15, Elizabeth Truss as Secretary of State for Environment, Food and Rural Affairs 2015-16; Assistant Government Whip 2016-17; Government Whip (Lord Commissioner of HM Treasury) 2017-. *Select committees:* Member: Environmental Audit 2010-15, Backbench Business 2013, Environment, Food and Rural Affairs 2013-15. *Councils and public bodies:* Councillor, Gedling District Council 2003-11; Nottinghamshire County Council: Councillor 2005-13, Shadow Spokesperson for Community Safety and Partnerships 2006-13; Member, East Midlands Regional Assembly 2009-10.

Political interests: Rural affairs, education, health, employment, business; UK.

Other: Chair, National Federation of Young Farmers' Clubs 2000; Royal Agricultural Society of England: Trustee, Associate 2005, Honorary show director 2007-09, Fellow 2010; Trustee, Core Centre, Calverton; Council member, Royal Agricultural Society; Fellow, Royal Agricultural Societies; Nottingham Breast Institute, NORSACA.

Recreations: Family, farming, socialising.

Mark Spencer MP, House of Commons, London SW1A 0AA
Tel: 020 7219 7143 *Email:* mark.spencer.mp@parliament.uk
Constituency: Sherwood Constituency Office, Room 3, Under One Roof, 3a Vine Terrace, Hucknall, Nottingham, Nottinghamshire NG15 7HN
Tel: 0115-968 1186 *Website:* www.markspencermp.co.uk *Twitter:* @mark_spencer

LABOUR

STARMER, KEIR

Holborn and St Pancras *(Majority 30,509)*

Shadow Secretary of State for Exiting the European Union

Born 2 September 1962; Married Victoria (1 son 1 daughter).

Education: Reigate Grammar School; Leeds University (LLB); Oxford University (BCL).

Non-political career: Called to the Bar 1987; Legal officer, Liberty -1990; Doughty Street Chambers: Barrister 1990-2008, Associate tenant 2015-; QC 2002; Consultant, Association of Chief Police Officers; Human rights adviser, Northern Ireland Policing Board 2003-07; Director of Public Prosecutions and Head of the Crown Prosecution Service 2008-13.

Political career: Member for Holborn and St Pancras since 7 May 2015 general election; Shadow Minister for Home Office 2015-16; Shadow Secretary of State for Exiting the European Union 2016-. *Select committees:* Member, Home Affairs 2015. *Councils and public bodies:* Member: Sentencing Guidelines Council 2008-10, Sentencing Council 2010-13.

Other: Chair, advisory board, Kids Company taskforce 'See the child, change the system' -2015; Member, advisory board, Youth Justice Legal Centre; Advisory board, Leeds University Law Faculty; Director, Death Penalty Project; Member, advisory board, European Institute, University College, London 2015-; Patron, Sante Refugee Mental Health Project 2015-; Fellow, Human Rights Centre, Essex University. Honorary doctorate: Leeds University, Essex University, University of East London, London School of Economics. KCB 2014; PC 2017.

Publications: The Three Pillars of Liberty: Political Rights and Freedoms in the UK (Routledge); European Human Rights Law (LAG); Human Rights Manual for Africa (BIICL).

Recreations: Playing football, Arsenal FC.

Rt Hon Sir Keir Starmer KCB QC MP, House of Commons, London SW1A 0AA
Tel: 020 7219 6234 *Email:* keir.starmer.mp@parliament.uk
Constituency: 110 Gloucester Avenue, London NW1 8HX *Website:* www.keirstarmer.com
Twitter: @Keir_Starmer

SCOTTISH NATIONAL PARTY

STEPHENS, CHRIS

Glasgow South West *(Majority 60)*

SNP Spokesperson for Trade Unions and Workers' Rights

Christopher Charles Stephens. Born 20 March 1973; Married Aileen Colleran.

Education: Trinity High School.

Non-political career: Strathclyde Regional Council/Glasgow City Council: Senior Unison activist and lead negotiator. Member, Unison; Chair, PCS Parliamentary Group 2016-.

Political career: Contested Hamilton North and Bellshill 2001 and Glasgow South West 2010 general elections. Member for Glasgow South West since 7 May 2015 general election; SNP Spokesperson for Trade Unions and Workers' Rights 2017-. *Select committees:* Member: European Scrutiny 2017-, Work and Pensions 2017-. Contested Glasgow Pollock constituency 2007 and 2011 Scottish Parliament elections. Member, SNP National Executive Committee; Convener, Glasgow Pollock Constituency Association; Secretary, SNP Trade Union Group.

Political interests: Equal pay, disability discrimination, pensions, social justice, Scottish independence.

Recreations: Partick Thistle FC supporter.

Chris Stephens MP, House of Commons, London SW1A 0AA
Tel: 020 7219 6381 *Email:* chris.stephens.mp@parliament.uk
Constituency: 1612-1614 Paisley Road West, Glasgow G52 3QN
Tel: 0141-883 0875 *Website:* www.chrisstephens.scot *Twitter:* @ChrisStephens

CONSERVATIVE

STEPHENSON, ANDREW

Pendle *(Majority 1,279)*

Assistant Government Whip

Andrew George Stephenson. Born 17 February 1981; Son of Malcolm Stephenson and Ann Stephenson.

Education: Poynton County High School; Royal Holloway, University of London (BSc business management 2002).

Non-political career: Partner, Stephenson and Threader Insurances 2002-10.

Political career: Member for Pendle since 6 May 2010 general election; PPS to: Robert Halfon as Minister without portfolio, Cabinet Office 2015-16, Mike Penning as Minister for Policing, Fire and Criminal Justice and Victims, Home Office and Ministry of Justice 2015-16, John Hayes as Minister for Security, Home Office 2015-16, Boris Johnson as Foreign Secretary 2016-17; Assistant Government Whip 2017-; Chair, Royal Holloway Conservative Students 2000-02; National Deputy Chair, Conservative Future 2001-02; Area Officer, Cheshire & the Wirral Area Management Executive 2005-07; Chair, Tatton Conservative Association 2006-07; Vice-chair, Conservative Party (Youth) 2010-13; Parliamentary Co-Chair, Conservative Friends of Pakistan 2012-; Member, Conservative Trade Unionists Advisory Panel 2015-; Copeland By-Election Campaign Coordinator 2017. *Councils and public bodies:* Macclesfield Borough Council: Councillor 2003-07, Chair, Housing Policy Development Committee 2005-07; School Governor, Whitefield Infant School (Nelson) 2009-.

Political interests: Foreign affairs, health, small business, apprenticeships, economy, manufacturing, aerospace, domestic violence, democracy and elections, dementia, community cohesion, charities and volunteering, enterprise, employment, engineering, home affairs, NHS, Northern Ireland, tourism; America, Bangladesh, Canada, China, Commonwealth, Kashmir, Middle East, Montenegro, Pakistan, Saudi Arabia, Sierra Leone.

Other: Vice-President, Trawden Agricultural Show 2007-; Member, Friends of the Pendle Hippodrome Theatre 2008-; Patron, SELRAP (Skipton East Lancashire Railway Action Partnership) 2010-; President: Nelson Brass Band 2010-13, North East Lancashire Ramblers 2014-; Executive Committee Member, John Adams Society 2012-; Community First Responder, North West Ambulance Service 2014-; Life Member, Friends of Pendle Heritage 2016-; Colne British Legion, Earby Conservative Club, Barnoldswick Conservative Club. Honorary Vice-president, Pendle Phoenix RUFC 2011-; Member, House of Commons Tug of War Team 2010-14.

Recreations: Manchester City FC, walking, food and drink.

Andrew Stephenson MP, House of Commons, London SW1A 0AA
Tel: 020 7219 7222 *Fax:* 020 7219 6385 *Email:* andrew.stephenson.mp@parliament.uk
Constituency: 9 Cross Street, Nelson, Lancashire BB9 7EN
Tel: 01282 614748 *Website:* www.pendleconservatives.com *Twitter:* @Andrew4Pendle

LABOUR

STEVENS, JO

Cardiff Central *(Majority 17,196)*

Joanna Meriel Stevens. Born 6 September 1966.

Education: Elfed High School; Manchester University (Degree law 1988); Manchester Polytechnic (Law Society Professional Examination).

Non-political career: Solicitor and director, Thompsons Solicitors LLP -2015. Member: GMB, Unison.

Political career: Member for Cardiff Central since 7 May 2015 general election; PPS to Tom Watson as Deputy Leader, Labour Party, Party Chair and Shadow Minister for the Cabinet Office 2015-16; Shadow Solicitor General and Shadow Minister for Justice 2016; Shadow Secretary of State for Wales 2016-17. *Select committees:* Member: Business, Innovation and Skills 2015-16, Standards 2015-16, Privileges 2015-16, Justice 2017, Digital, Culture, Media and Sport 2017-. Member, Co-operative Party; Vice-chair, Welsh Parliamentary Labour Party; Secretary, Trade Union Group of MPs; Vice-chair, Parliamentary Friends of Colombia.

Political interests: Civil and criminal justice, employment rights, sport, women and equalities; Colombia.

Other: Member: Fabian Society, Haldane Society of Socialist Lawyers; Member, Law Society of England and Wales; Show Racism the Red Card. Member, Glamorgan County Cricket Club.

Recreations: Football (Cardiff City FC season ticket holder), cricket (Glamorgan member), rugby, darts, theatre and the arts.

Jo Stevens MP, House of Commons, London SW1A 0AA
Tel: 020 7219 8290 *Email:* jo.stevens.mp@parliament.uk
Constituency: 116 Albany Road, Cardiff, South Glamorgan CF24 3RU
Tel: 029 2132 9736 *Website:* www.jostevens.co.uk *Twitter:* @JoStevensLabour

CONSERVATIVE

STEVENSON, JOHN

Carlisle *(Majority 2,599)*

Andrew John Stevenson. Born 4 July 1963; Married Tracy Nixon 2013.

Education: Aberdeen Grammar School; Dundee University (BA history and politics); College of Law, Chester.

Non-political career: Trainee solicitor, Dickinson Dees, Newcastle upon Tyne 1990; Solicitor, now partner, Bendles, Carlisle.

Political career: Member for Carlisle since 6 May 2010 general election. *Select committees:* Member: Joint Committee on the Draft House of Lords Reform Bill 2011-12, Communities and Local Government 2012-15, Scottish Affairs 2015-17, Public Administration and Constitutional Affairs 2016-17. Member, Executive, 1922 Committee 2017-. Chair: Carlisle Conservative Association, Penrith and the Border Conservative Association, North Cumbria Conservatives. *Councils and public bodies:* Councillor, Carlisle City Council 1999-2010.

Countries of interest: Israel.

Other: Member, Law Society; Eden Valley Hospice. Committee member, Chatsworth Tennis Club.

Publications: Co-author, Freedom, Responsibility and the State: Curbing Over-Mighty Government (Politeia, 2012).

Recreations: Golf, running, sport.

John Stevenson MP, House of Commons, London SW1A 0AA
Tel: 020 7219 3000 *Email:* john.stevenson.mp@parliament.uk
Constituency: 2 Currie Street, Carlisle, Cumbria CA1 1HH
Tel: 01228 550684 *Email:* office@johnstevensonmp.co.uk *Website:* www.johnstevensonmp.co.uk
Twitter: @John4Carlisle

CONSERVATIVE

STEWART, BOB

Beckenham *(Majority 15,087)*

Robert Alexander Stewart. Born 7 July 1949; Son of Jock Stewart MC and Joan Stewart; Married Claire Podbielski 1994 (4 children 2 children from first marriage).

Education: Chigwell School; Royal Military Academy Sandhurst 1969; Wales University (international politics 1977); Army Staff College 1980-81; Joint Services Staff College 1987-88.

Non-political career: Regular officer (infantry officer-colonel) British Army, Cheshire Regiment 1969-96: Served in Northern Ireland, British UN Commander, Bosnia 1992-93, Policy chief, Supreme HQ Allied Powers Europe, Belgium -1996; Senior consultant, Hill & Knowlton 1997-98; Managing director, WorldSpace 1999-2001; Freelance writer and lecturer 2002-.

Political career: Member for Beckenham since 6 May 2010 general election. *Select committees:* Member: Defence 2010-17, Arms Export Controls 2011-14, Northern Ireland Affairs 2016-17.

Political interests: Defence, veteran service personnel, disabled children; Eastern Europe, Middle East, Northern Ireland.

Other: Member, UK Delegation to: Organisation for Security and Co-operation in Europe Parliamentary Assembly, NATO Parliamentary Assembly 2015-; President, Action for Armed Forces; Vice-president, UKNDA; Patron, ELIFAR. DSO 1993; Army and Navy Club.

Publications: Broken Lives (1993); Leadership Under Pressure (2009).

Bob Stewart MP, House of Commons, London SW1A 0AA
Tel: 020 7219 7011 *Email:* bob.stewart.mp@parliament.uk
Constituency: No constituency office *Website:* www.bobstewart.org.uk

CONSERVATIVE

STEWART, IAIN

Milton Keynes South *(Majority 1,665)*

Iain Aitken Stewart. Born 18 September 1972; Son of James Stewart and Leila Stewart.

Education: Hutchesons' Grammar School, Glasgow; Exeter University (BA politics 1993); Chartered Management Institute (Diploma management 2006).

Non-political career: Trainee chartered accountant, Coopers and Lybrand 1993-94; Head of research, Scottish Conservative Party 1994-98; Parliamentary Resources Unit, House of Commons: Deputy director 1998-2001, Director 2001-06; Associate, Odgers Berndtson 2006-10.

Political career: Contested Milton Keynes South West 2001 and 2005 general elections. Member for Milton Keynes South since 6 May 2010 general election; PPS to: Patrick McLoughlin as Secretary of State for Transport 2013-15, David Mundell as Secretary of State for Scotland 2015-16, Liam Fox as Secretary of State for International Trade and President of the Board of

Trade 2016-17. *Select committees:* Member, Transport 2010-13, 2015-. Chairman, Conservative Backbench Policy Committee on Transport 2015-16. Contested Glasgow Rutherglen constituency 1999 Scottish Parliament election. *Councils and public bodies:* Councillor, Shenley Brook End and Tattenhoe Parish Council 2005-11.

Political interests: Constitution, economy, transport, energy security, education.

Other: Founder member, Atlantic Bridge 1999; Patron, Milton Keynes City Orchestra; Bletchley Conservative Club, President, Stony Stratford Conservative 2007-.

Publications: It's Our Money! Who Spends it? (London Scottish Tory Club, 2004) The Scottish Constitution – In Search of a New Settlement (Policy Institute, 2007).

Recreations: Opera, good food, wine and whisky, gym, running marathons.

Iain Stewart MP, House of Commons, London SW1A 0AA
Tel: 020 7219 7230 *Email:* iain.stewart.mp@parliament.uk
Constituency: Suite 102, Milton Keynes Business Centre, Foxhunter Drive, Linford Wood, Buckinghamshire MK14 6GD
Tel: 01908 686830 *Fax:* 01908 686831 *Website:* www.iainstewartmp.co.uk
Twitter: @iainastewart

CONSERVATIVE

STEWART, RORY

Penrith and The Border *(Majority 15,910)*

Minister of State for Africa, Foreign and Commonwealth Office and Minister of State, Department for International Development

Roderick James Nugent Stewart. Born 3 January 1973; Son of Mr and Mrs Brian Thomas Webster Stewart; Married Shoshana Clark 2012.

Education: Eton College; Balliol College, Oxford (BA politics, philosophy and economics, MA); French, Indonesian, Persian (Dari), conversational Urdu and Serbo-Croatian.

Non-political career: 2nd Lieutenant, Black Watch. Foreign and Commonwealth Office 1995-2000: Second Secretary, British Embassy, Jakarta, Indonesia 1997, British Representative, Montenegro 1999-2000; Walked across Pakistan, Iran, Afghanistan, India and Nepal 2000-02; Deputy governorate co-ordinator, Amara, Iraq 2003; Senior adviser, Nasiriyah, Iraq 2004; Founder and chief executive, Turquoise Mountain 2006-10; Ryan Family professor, practice of human rights and director, Carr Centre for Human Rights Policy, Harvard University 2008-10.

Political career: Member for Penrith and The Border since 6 May 2010 general election; Parliamentary Under-Secretary of State, Department for Environment, Food and Rural Affairs 2015-16; Minister of State: Department for International Development 2016-, for Africa, Foreign and Commonwealth Office 2017-. *Select committees:* Member: Foreign Affairs 2010-14, Liaison 2014-15; Chair, Defence 2014-15; Member: Joint Committee on National Security Strategy 2014-15, Environmental Audit 2015-16.

Political interests: Local democracy, rural affairs, broadband, foreign affairs; Asia, EU, Middle East.

Other: Member, UK Delegation, Organisation for Security and Co-operation in Europe Parliamentary Assembly; Member, advisory board, Brenthurst Foundation -2015; Director, Cumbria Broadband Rural and Community Projects Limited -2016; Patron, Vindolanda; Executive chairman, Turquoise Mountain Foundation 2006-10. Royal Society of Literature Oondaatje Award 2004; Camino del Cid 2008; Radio France Award 2009; Livingstone Medal, Royal Scottish Geographical Society 2010. OBE 2004.

Publications: Author: The Places in Between (Picador, 2004), The Prince of the Marshes (Harcourt, 2006), Occupational Hazards: My Time Governing in Iraq (Picador, 2006); The Marches (2016).

Recreations: Walking.

Rory Stewart OBE MP, House of Commons, London SW1A 0AA
Tel: 020 7219 7127 *Email:* rory.stewart.mp@parliament.uk
Constituency: New Rent Cottage, Hutton in the Forest, Penrith CA1 9TJ
Tel: 01768 484114 *Email:* rory@rorystewart.co.uk *Website:* www.rorystewart.co.uk
Twitter: @RoryStewartUK

LIBERAL DEMOCRAT

STONE, JAMIE

Caithness, Sutherland and Easter Ross *(Majority 2,044)*

Liberal Democrat Shadow Secretary of State for Scotland

Born 16 June 1954; Son of late Edward Reginald Stone, farmer, and Susannah Gladys (née Waddell-Dudley) company director; Married Flora Armstrong 1981 (1 son 2 daughters).

Education: Tain Royal Academy; Gordonstoun School; St Andrews University (MA history and geology 1977); French, Italian.

Non-political career: Territorial Army 1979-80. Cleaner/kitchen porter, Grandmet 1977; English teacher, Catania, Sicily 1977-78; Fish gutting, Faroe Islands 1978; Stores clerk, Wimpey 1979-81; Site administrator, Bechtel Great Britain Ltd 1981-84; Administrative manager, Odfjell Drilling (UK) Ltd 1984-86; Director, Highland Fine Cheeses Ltd 1986-94.

Political career: Member for Caithness, Sutherland and Easter Ross since 8 June 2017; Liberal Democrat Shadow Secretary of State for Scotland 2017-; MSP for Caithness, Sutherland and Easter Ross constituency 1999-2011; Contested Caithness, Sutherland and Ross constituency and the Highlands and Islands region 2016 Scottish Parliament election; Spokesperson for: Highlands and Islands and Fisheries 2000-01, Equal Opportunities 2001, Fisheries 2001-02, Finance 2002-03, Enterprise, Lifelong Learning and Tourism 2003-05, Justice 2005, Enterprise and Lifelong Learning (including Tourism) 2005-07; Shadow Minister for Public Health 2007-08; Deputy Spokesperson on Health 2008-11. Chair, Ross, Cromarty and Skye Scottish Liberal Democrats 1992-93; Secretary, Scottish Liberal Democrat Parliamentary Party 2003-. *Councils and public bodies:* Councillor, Ross and Cromarty District Council 1986-96; Chair, Tain Community Council 1983-84; Councillor, Highland Council 1995-99, 2012-17.

Countries of interest: France, Germany, Italy, Poland.

Other: Director, Grey Coast Theatre; Trustee, Tain Museum Trust; FRSA; New (Edinburgh), Armagh (Armagh City).

Recreations: Singing, gardening, golf, reading, classical music.

Jamie Stone MP, House of Commons, London SW1A 0AA
Tel: 020 7219 1654 *Email:* jamie.stone.mp@parliament.uk
Constituency: Details still to be confirmed *Twitter:* @Jamie4North

CONSERVATIVE

STREETER, GARY

South West Devon *(Majority 15,816)*

Gary Nicholas Streeter. Born 2 October 1955; Son of Kenneth Streeter, farmer, and Shirley Streeter; Married Janet Stevens 1978 (1 son 1 daughter).

Education: Tiverton Grammar School; King's College, London (LLB 1977).

Non-political career: Solicitor; Partner, specialising in company and employment law, Foot and Bowden, Plymouth 1984-98.

Political career: Member for Plymouth Sutton 1992-97, for South West Devon 1997-2010, for South West Devon (revised boundary) since 6 May 2010 general election; PPS to: Sir Derek Spencer as Solicitor General 1993-95, Sir Nicholas Lyell as Attorney General 1994-95; Assistant Government Whip 1995-96; Parliamentary Secretary, Lord Chancellor's Department 1996-97; Opposition Spokesperson for: Foreign Affairs 1997-98, Europe 1997-98; Shadow Secretary of State for International Development 1998-2001; Shadow Minister for Foreign Affairs 2003-04; Member, Speaker's Committee on the Electoral Commission 2010-17; Contested Deputy Speaker election 2013. *Select committees:* Member: Office of the Deputy Prime Minister 2002-04, Office of the Deputy Prime Minister (Urban Affairs Sub-Committee) 2003-04, Home Affairs 2005-10, Chairmen's Panel/Panel of Chairs 2009-, Joint Committee on Security 2010-15, Ecclesiastical Committee 2010-, Court of Referees 2016-. Chair, board of directors, governing council, Conservative Christian Fellowship; Conservative Party: Vice-chair 2001-02 Chair: Human Rights Commission 2005-07, International Office 2005-08; Founding member, Conservatives for Reform in Europe 2016. *Councils and public bodies:* Plymouth City Council: Councillor 1986-92, Chair, Housing Committee 1989-91.

Political interests: Law and order, family moral and social affairs, developing world; Middle East, North Korea.

Other: Chair: Westminster Foundation for Democracy 2010-, Christians in Parliament 2010-.

Recreations: Watching cricket and rugby, family.

Gary Streeter MP, House of Commons, London SW1A 0AA
Tel: 020 7219 5033 *Fax:* 020 7219 2414 *Email:* deans@parliament.uk
Constituency: Old Newnham Farm, Plymouth, Devon PL7 5BL
Tel: 01752 335666 *Fax:* 01752 338401 *Email:* mail@garystreeter.co.uk
Website: www.garystreeter.co.uk *Twitter:* @garystreeterSWD

LABOUR

STREETING, WES

Ilford North *(Majority 9,639)*

Wesley Paul William Streeting. Born 21 January 1983; Son of Mark Streeting, car salesman, and Corrina, cleaner and shopworker; Partner Joseph Dancey.

Education: Westminster City School; Selwyn College, Cambridge (BA history 2004) (President Students' Union 2004-05); Limited French.

Non-political career: National Union of Students: National executive member 2005-06, Vice-President (Education) 2006-08, National President 2008-10; Membership assistant, Progress 2005-06; Chief Executive, Helena Kennedy Foundation 2010-12; Member, Widening Participation Strategic Advisory Committee, Higher Education Funding Council of England 2011-; Head of Education, Stonewall 2012-13; Self-employed campaigns consultant 2014-16. Member, Community 2012-.

Political career: Member for Ilford North since 7 May 2015 general election. *Select committees:* Member, Treasury 2015-. National Committee, Labour Students 2006-10; Member, Co-operative Party 2006-; Patron, LGBT Labour 2006-; Chair, London Group of Labour MPs 2016-; Member, London Regional Board 2016-. *Councils and public bodies:* London Borough of Redbridge Council: Councillor 2010-, Deputy Leader of the Opposition 2011-14, Deputy Leader of Council and Cabinet Member for Health and Wellbeing 2014-15; Governor, Grove Primary School.

Political interests: Social mobility, education, further education, higher education, creative industries, foreign policy, London; Bangladesh, China, European Union, India, Israel and the Occupied Palestine Territories, Pakistan, Sri Lanka, USA.

Other: Member, Progress 2000-; Fellow, RSA 2008-; Shelter, Great Ormond Street Hospital.

Recreations: Reading, walking, arts, film.

Wes Streeting MP, House of Commons, London SW1A 0AA
Tel: 020 7219 6132 *Email:* wes.streeting.mp@parliament.uk
Constituency: 12a Highview Parade, Woodford Avenue, Ilford IG4 5EP
Tel: 020 3475 7901 *Email:* wes@redbridgelabour.org.uk *Website:* www.wesstreeting.org
Twitter: @wesstreeting

CONSERVATIVE

STRIDE, MEL

Central Devon *(Majority 15,680)*

Financial Secretary; Paymaster General, HM Treasury

Melvyn John Stride. Born 30 September 1961; Son of Mel Stride and Barbara Stride; Married Michelle King Hughes 2006 (3 daughters).

Education: Portsmouth Grammar School; St Edmund Hall, Oxford (BA politics, philosophy and economics 1984) (President, Oxford Union 1984).

Non-political career: Founder and ex-director, Venture Marketing Group 1987-2007. Member, Amicus 2006-10.

Political career: Member for Central Devon since 6 May 2010 general election; PPS to John Hayes as Minister: of State for Further Education, Skills and Lifelong Learning 2011-12, of State for Energy, Department of Energy and Climate Change 2012-13, without Portfolio, Cabinet Office 2013-14; Assistant Government Whip 2014-15; Government Whip: (Lord Commissioner of HM Treasury) 2015-16, (Comptroller of HM Household) 2016-17; Financial Secretary; Paymaster General, HM Treasury 2017-. *Select committees:* Member, Northern Ireland Affairs 2010-11. Oxford University Conservative Association: Member 1981-84, President 1982. *Councils and public bodies:* Community Governor, Okehampton College.

Political interests: Economy, education, welfare reform, social justice; USA.

Other: Oxford Union Society: Member 1981-, President 1984; Pilot's licence 1990; Registered blue badge guide 2005; Commission for Social Justice Working Group 2006-07; President, Tarka Railway Association; Member, Association of Professional Tourist Guides 2006. Guide of the Year 2005. PC 2017.

Recreations: History, walking, spending time with family.

Rt Hon Mel Stride MP, House of Commons, London SW1A 0AA
Tel: 020 7219 7037 *Email:* mel.stride.mp@parliament.uk
Constituency: 2a Manaton Court, Manaton Close, Matford Business Park, Exeter, Devon EX2 8PF
Tel: 01392 823306 *Website:* www.melstridemp.com *Twitter:* @MelJStride

LABOUR

STRINGER, GRAHAM

Blackley and Broughton *(Majority 19,601)*

Graham Eric Stringer. Born 17 February 1950; Son of late Albert Stringer, railway clerk, and late Brenda Stringer, shop assistant; Married Kathryn Carr 1999 (1 son 1 stepson 1 stepdaughter).

Education: Moston Brook High School; Sheffield University (BSc chemistry 1971).

Non-political career: Analytical chemist; Chair of Board, Manchester Airport plc 1996-97. Branch officer and shop steward, MSF; Member, Amicus/Unite.

Political career: Member for Manchester Blackley 1997-2010, for Blackley and Broughton since 6 May 2010 general election; Parliamentary Secretary, Cabinet Office 1999-2001; Government Whip 2001-02. *Select committees:* Member: Environment, Transport and Regional Affairs 1997-99, Environment, Transport and Regional Affairs (Transport Sub-Committee) 1997-99, Transport 2002-10, 2011-, Modernisation of the House of Commons 2006, Science and Technology 2006-07, 2010-, Innovation, Universities[, Science] and Skills 2007-10, Justice 2013-14, Energy and Climate Change 2013-15, Panel of Chairs 2015-, European Scrutiny 2015-. Vice-chair, PLP Departmental Committee for Transport 2006-10. Chair, Labour Leave 2016. *Councils and public bodies:* Manchester City Council: Councillor 1979-98, Leader 1984-96.

Political interests: Urban regeneration, House of Lords reform, revitalising local democracy, aviation and airports, bus regulation, science policy, justice policy.

Other: Trustee, Global Warming Policy Foundation; Vote Leave: Board member 2016, Member, Campaign Committee 2016; Founding supporter, Change Britain 2016-. Hon. RNCM. Member: Manchester Tennis and Racquet Club, Cheetham Hill Cricket Club.

Recreations: Real tennis, squash.

Graham Stringer MP, House of Commons, London SW1A 0AA
Tel: 020 7219 5235 *Email:* graham.stringer.mp@parliament.uk
Constituency: North Manchester Sixth Form College, Rochdale Road, Manchester M9 4AF
Tel: 0161-202 6600 *Fax:* 0161-202 6626

CONSERVATIVE

STUART, GRAHAM

Beverley and Holderness *(Majority 14,042)*

Assistant Government Whip

Graham Charles Stuart. Born 12 March 1962; Son of late Dr Peter Stuart and Joan Stuart; Married Anne Crawshaw 1989 (2 daughters).

Education: Glenalmond College, Perthshire; Selwyn College, Cambridge (law/philosophy 1985).

Non-political career: Sole proprietor, Go Enterprises 1984-2010; Director, CSL Publishing Ltd 1987-.

Political career: Contested Cambridge 2001 general election. Member for Beverley and Holderness 2005-10, for Beverley and Holderness (revised boundary) since 6 May 2010 general election; Assistant Government Whip 2016-. *Select committees:* Member: Environmental Audit 2006-10, Joint Committee on the Draft Climate Change Bill 2007, Education and Skills/Children, Schools and Families 2007-10; Chair, Education 2010-15; Member, Liaison 2010-15. Chairman, Cambridge University Conservative Association 1985; Board member, Conservative Party 2006-10. *Councils and public bodies:* Cambridge City Council: Councillor 1998-2004, Leader, Conservative Group 2000-04.

Political interests: Education, older people, mental health, welfare, economics, rural funding, climate change; China, Latin America.

Other: Chair: CHANT (Community Hospitals Acting Nationally Together) 2005-10, East Riding Health Action Group 2007-09, Globe International 2007-, Rural Fair Share Campaign -2011; Vice-chair, f40 Group 2015-; Vice-president: Northern branch, Association of Drainage Authorities, Beverley and District Civic Society; Patron: St Augustine's Church, Hedon, Beverley War Memorial Hall Trust; Member, River Hull Board.

Recreations: Sailing, cricket, motor cycling, triathlon.

Graham Stuart MP, House of Commons, London SW1A 0AA
Tel: 020 7219 4340 *Email:* graham.stuart.mp@parliament.uk
Constituency: 9 Cross Street, Beverley, East Yorkshire HU17 9AX
Tel: 01482 679687 *Fax:* 01482 861667 *Email:* graham@grahamstuart.com
Website: www.grahamstuart.com *Twitter:* @grahamstuart

CONSERVATIVE

STURDY, JULIAN

York Outer *(Majority 8,289)*

Julian Charles Sturdy. Born 3 June 1971; Son of Robert Sturdy (MEP for Cambridgeshire 1994-99 and Eastern region 1999-2014), and Elizabeth Hommes; Married Victoria (1 son 1 daughter).

Education: Harper Adams University (agriculture).

Non-political career: Farming and property business.

Political career: Contested Scunthorpe 2005 general election. Member for York Outer since 6 May 2010 general election; PPS to: Simon Burns as Minister of State, Department for Transport 2012-13, Department for Transport ministerial team 2013-14, Brandon Lewis as Minister of State, Department for Communities and Local Government 2014-15. *Select committees:* Member: Transport 2010-12, Energy and Climate Change 2015-16, Standing Orders 2015-, Joint Committee on Consolidation, &c, Bills 2015-, Environment, Food and Rural Affairs 2017-. *Councils and public bodies:* Councillor, Harrogate Borough Council 2002-07; Governor, educational foundation of local school.

Other: Director, Harrogate District Community Transport.

Julian Sturdy MP, House of Commons, London SW1A 0AA
Tel: 020 7219 7199 *Email:* julian.sturdy.mp@parliament.uk
Constituency: York Conservatives, 1 Ash Street, York YO26 4ZB
Tel: 01904 784847 *Website:* www.juliansturdy.co.uk

CONSERVATIVE

SUNAK, RISHI

Richmond (Yorkshire) *(Majority 23,108)*

Team PPS, Department for Business, Energy and Industrial Strategy

Born 12 May 1980; Married Akshatha Murthy 2009 (2 daughters).

Education: Winchester College; Oxford University (BA philosophy, politics and economics 2001); Stanford University (Fulbright Scholar, MBA 2006).

Non-political career: Principal Investment Area, Goldman Sachs; The Children's Investment Fund; Theleme Fund; Head of Black and Minority Ethnic (BME) Research Unit, Policy Exchange; Catamaran Ventures UK.

Political career: Member for Richmond (Yorkshire) since 7 May 2015 general election; Team PPS, Department for Business, Energy and Industrial Strategy 2017-. *Select committees:* Member, Environment, Food and Rural Affairs 2015-17.

Political interests: Rural affairs, economy and enterprise, defence; India, USA.

Recreations: Southampton FC supporter, Yorkshire County Cricket Club supporter.

Rishi Sunak MP, House of Commons, London SW1A 0AA
Tel: 020 7219 5437 *Email:* rishi.sunak.mp@parliament.uk
Constituency: Unit 1, Omega Business Village, Northallerton, North Yorkshire DL6 2NJ
Tel: 01609 765330 *Website:* www.rishisunak.com

CONSERVATIVE

SWAYNE, DESMOND

New Forest West *(Majority 23,431)*

Desmond Angus Swayne. Born 20 August 1956; Son of George Swayne and Elisabeth Swayne, née Gibson; Married Moira Teek 1987 (1 son 2 daughters).

Education: Bedford School; St Mary's College, St Andrews University (MA theology 1980); Spanish and French (rusty).

Non-political career: Major, Territorial Army. Schoolmaster, A-level economics: Charterhouse 1980-81, Wrekin College 1982-87; Risk management systems manager, Royal Bank of Scotland 1988-96.

Political career: Contested Pontypridd 1987 and West Bromwich West 1992 general elections. Member for New Forest West 1997-2010, for New Forest West (revised boundary) since 6 May 2010 general election; Opposition Whip 2002-03; Opposition Spokesperson for: Health 2001, Defence 2001-02; Shadow Minister for: International Affairs 2003-04, Northern Ireland 2004; PPS to: Michael Howard as Leader of the Opposition 2004-05, David Cameron: as Leader of the Opposition 2005-10, as Prime Minister 2010-12; Government Whip 2012-13; Government Whip (Vice-Chamberlain of HM Household) 2013-14; Minister of State, Department for International Development 2014-16. *Select committees:* Member: Scottish Affairs 1997-2001, Social Security 1999-2001, Procedure 2002-05, Defence 2005-06, Ecclesiastical Committee -2010, Administration 2012-13, International Trade 2016-17.

Other: Member, Countryside Alliance. TD; PC 2011; Kt 2016; Cavalry and Guards Club. Serpentine Swimming Club.

Recreations: Territorial Army.

Rt Hon Sir Desmond Swayne TD MP, House of Commons, London SW1A 0AA
Tel: 020 7219 4886 *Fax:* 020 7219 0901 *Email:* swayned@parliament.uk
Constituency: 4 Cliff Crescent, Marine Drive, Barton-on-Sea, New Milton, Hampshire BH25 7EB
Tel: 01425 629844 *Fax:* 01425 621898 *Email:* desmondswayne@hotmail.com
Website: www.desmondswaynemp.com *Twitter:* @desmondswayne

LAB/CO-OP

SWEENEY, PAUL

Glasgow North East *(Majority 242)*

Shadow Minister for Scotland Office

Paul John Sweeney.

Education: Turnbull High School; Glasgow University (MA economic history and politics 2011); Stirling University (CertHE, economics and politics 2008).

Non-political career: Army Reservist, Territorial Army 2006-. BAE Systems: Manufacturing and Production Operations Graduate Programme 2011-13, Operations Strategy Coordinator 2013-15; Senior Executive Account Manager, Scottish Enterprise 2015-17.

Political career: Member for Glasgow North East since 8 June 2017; Shadow Minister for Scotland Office 2017-.

Other: Member, Fairfield Heritage Centre 2012-; STEM Ambassador, STEMNET 2012-; Trustee and Secretary, Springburn Winter Gardens Trust 2013-; Board of Management Member, Glasgow University Union 2013-; Medal Ceremonies Team Member, Glasgow 2014 Ltd 2014; Adviser, Better Together Ltd 2014; Councillor, Institution of Engineers and Shipbuilders in Scotland 2016-; Member, Board of Directors, Glasgow Building Preservation Trust 2017-.

Paul Sweeney MP, House of Commons, London SW1A 0AA
Tel: 020 7219 0486 *Email:* paul.sweeney.mp@parliament.uk
Constituency: Details still to be confirmed *Twitter:* @PaulJSweeney

LIBERAL DEMOCRAT

SWINSON, JO

East Dunbartonshire *(Majority 5,339)*

Deputy Leader, Liberal Democrats; Liberal Democrat Shadow Foreign Secretary

Joanne Kate Swinson. Born 5 February 1980; Daughter of Peter and Annette Swinson; Married Duncan Hames 2011 (MP for Chippenham 2010-15) (1 son).

Education: Douglas Academy, Milngavie; London School of Economics (BSc management 2000); French.

Non-political career: Marketing executive and manager, Emap's Viking FM 2000-02; Marketing manager, Spaceandpeople Ltd 2002-04; Development officer, UK Public Health Association Scotland 2004-05.

Political career: Contested Hull East 2001 general election. Member for East Dunbartonshire 2005-15. Contested East Dunbartonshire 2015 general election. Member for East Dunbartonshire since 8 June 2017; Liberal Democrat: Spokesperson for Culture, Media and Sport 2005-06; Whip 2005-06; Shadow Secretary of State for Scotland 2006-07; Shadow Minister for: Women and Equalities 2007, Foreign and Commonwealth Office 2008-10; PPS: to Vincent Cable as Secretary of State for Business, Innovation and Skills and President of the Board of Trade 2010-12, to Nick Clegg as Deputy Prime Minister, Lord President of the Council 2012; Parliamentary Under-Secretary of State (Minister for Employment Relations and Consumer Affairs), Department for Business, Innovation and Skills 2012-15; Parliamentary Under-Secretary of State for Women and Equalities: Department for Culture, Media and Sport 2012-14, Department for Education 2014-15; Liberal Democrat Shadow Foreign Secretary 2017-. *Select committees:* Member, Environmental Audit 2007-10. Contested Strathkelvin and Bearsden constituency 2003 Scottish Parliament election. Liberal Democrat Youth and Students: Secretary 1998-99, Vice-chair 1999-2000, Vice-chair, Campaigns 2000-01; Liberal Democrats: Vice-chair, Haltemprice and Howden Liberal Democrats 2000, Member, Federal Executive 2002, Vice-chair, Gender Balance Taskforce 2003-06, Chair: Campaign for Gender Balance 2007-08, Women's Policy Working Group 2008-09; Deputy leader, Scottish Liberal Democrats 2010-12; Liberal Democrats: Chair, Federal Polcy Committee 2012-, Member, Manifesto Working Group 2013-, Deputy Leader 2017-.

Political interests: Quality of life and wellbeing, climate change, allergy, foreign affairs, corporate social responsibility; Chechnya, India, Kosovo, Romania, Sierra Leone.

Other: Member: Amnesty International 1998-, New Economics Foundation 2003-, Friends of the Earth, Unlock Democracy; Trustee, Help a Local Child 2001-02; Ran Great North Run for Diabetes UK 2006; Ran Loch Ness Marathon for Anaphylaxis Campaign 2007; Moonwalk for breast cancer charity walk the walk 2008; Glasgow half-marathon for Beatson Pebble Appeal 2009; Ran London Marathon for Leukaemia and Lymphoma Research 2011.

Recreations: Hiking, reading, running.

Jo Swinson MP, House of Commons, London SW1A 0AA
Tel: 020 7219 3000 *Email:* jo.swinson.mp@parliament.uk
Constituency: Unit 44c, 100-102 Crowhill Road, Bishopbriggs, Glasgow G64 1RP
Tel: 0141-370 6226 *Website:* www.joswinson.org.uk *Twitter:* @joswinson

CONSERVATIVE

SWIRE, HUGO

East Devon *(Majority 8,036)*

Hugo George William Swire. Born 30 November 1959; Son of late Humphrey Swire and Dowager Marchioness Townshend, née Montgomerie; Married Sasha Nott 1996 (2 daughters).

Education: Eton College; St Andrews University (1978-79); Royal Military Academy Sandhurst.

Non-political career: Lt, 1st Btn Grenadier Guards. Commissioned, 1st Battalion Grenadier Guards 1980-83; Joint managing director, International News Services and Prospect Films 1983-85; Financial consultant, Streets Financial Ltd 1985-87; Head of development, National Gallery 1988-92; Sotheby's: Deputy director 1992-97, Director 1997-2003; Non-executive director, then non-executive chair, PhotoMe International plc 2005-10; Non-executive director, Symphony Environmental Technologies plc 2008-10; Adviser, KIS (France) 2016-.

Political career: Contested Greenock and Inverclyde 1997 general election. Member for East Devon 2001-10, for East Devon (revised boundary) since 6 May 2010 general election; PPS to Theresa May as chairman of the Conservative Party 2003; Opposition Whip 2003-04; Shadow Minister for the Arts 2004-05; Shadow Secretary of State for Culture, Media and Sport 2005-07; Chair, Speakers' Advisory Committee on Works of Art 2005-10; Minister of State: Northern Ireland Office 2010-12, Foreign and Commonwealth Office 2012-16. *Select committees:* Member, Northern Ireland Affairs 2002-05.

Other: Council member, RNLI; Fund for Refugees in Slovenia; Jurassic Coast Trust; Fellow, Royal Society of Arts; Deputy Chair, Commonwealth Enterprise and Investment Council 2016-. PC 2011; KCMG 2016.

Rt Hon Sir Hugo Swire KCMG MP, House of Commons, London SW1A 0AA
Tel: 020 7219 8173 *Fax:* 020 7219 1895 *Email:* hugo.swire.mp@parliament.uk
Constituency: Currently moving offices *Website:* www.hugoswire.org.uk *Twitter:* @hugoswire

CONSERVATIVE

SYMS, ROBERT

Poole *(Majority 14,209)*

Robert Andrew Raymond Syms. Born 15 August 1956; Son of Raymond Syms, builder, and Mary Syms, teacher; Married Nicola Guy 1991 (divorced 1999); married Fiona Mellersh 2000 (divorced 2009) (1 daughter 1 son).

Education: Colston's School, Bristol.

Non-political career: Director, family building, plant hire and property group, Chippenham, Wiltshire 1978-.

Political career: Contested Walsall North 1992 general election. Member for Poole 1997-2010, for Poole (revised boundary) since 6 May 2010 general election; PPS to Michael Ancram as Chair Conservative Party 1999-2000; Opposition Spokesperson for Environment, Transport and Regions 1999-2001; Opposition Whip 2003; Shadow Minister for: Local and Devolved Government Affairs 2003-05, Local Government 2005-07; Assistant Government Whip 2012-13; Government Whip (Lord Commissioner of HM Treasury) 2016-17. *Select committees:* Member: Health 1997-2000, 2007-10, Procedure 1998-99, Transport 2002-03, Liaison 2010-13; Chair, Regulatory Reform 2010-12; Member: Joint Committee on the Draft Detention of Terrorist Suspects (Temporary Extension) Bills 2011, Administration 2013-14, 2016-, Finance and Services 2013-15, Standing Orders 2014-15; Chair, High Speed Rail (London-West Midlands) Bill 2014-16. Joint Vice-chair, Conservative Party Committee for Constitutional Affairs, Scotland and Wales 1997-99. North Wiltshire Conservative Association: Treasurer 1982-84, Deputy chair 1983-84, Chair 1984-86; Vice-chair, Conservative Party 2001-03. *Councils and public bodies:* Councillor: North Wiltshire District Council 1983-87, Wiltshire County Council 1985-97; Member, Wessex Regional Health Authority 1988-90.

Political interests: Economic policy, constitution, local and regional government; USA, most of English speaking world.

Other: Member: North Wiltshire Enterprise Agency 1986-90, Calne Development Project Trust 1986-97; Fellow, Chartered Institute of Building.

Recreations: Reading, music.

Robert Syms MP, House of Commons, London SW1A 0AA
Tel: 020 7219 4601 *Fax:* 020 7219 6867 *Email:* symsr@parliament.uk
Constituency: Poole Conservative Association, 38 Sandbanks Road, Poole, Dorset BH14 8BX
Tel: 01202 739922 *Fax:* 01202 739944 *Email:* symsr@pooleconservatives.org
Website: www.pooleconservatives.org *Twitter:* @RobertSyms

LABOUR

TAMI, MARK

Alyn and Deeside *(Majority 5,235)*

Opposition Assistant Chief Whip

Mark Richard Tami. Born 3 October 1962; Son of Michael Tami and Patricia Tami; Married Sally Ann Daniels 1994 (2 sons).

Education: Enfield Grammar School; Swansea University (BA history 1985).

Non-political career: AEEU: Head of research and communications 1992-99, Head of policy 1999-2001. Member: AEEU/Amicus 1986-, TUC General Council 1999-2001.

Political career: Member for Alyn and Deeside since 7 June 2001 general election; PPS to John Healey as Financial Secretary to the Treasury 2005-06; Assistant Government Whip 2007-10; Opposition Whip 2010-11; Opposition Assistant Chief Whip 2011-. *Select committees:* Member: Northern Ireland Affairs 2001-05, European Standing Committee B 2003-05, Joint Committee on Tax Law Rewrite Bills 2005-07, Joint Committee on Human Rights 2007, Selection 2010-, Works of Art 2011-12, Joint Committee on Security 2011-15, Administration 2012-, Joint Committee on the Palace of Westminster 2015-16. Vice-chair PLP Welsh Regional Group 2005-07. Treasurer, Labour Friends of Australia.

Political interests: Manufacturing, aerospace, animal welfare.

Other: Glamorgan County Cricket.

Recreations: Football (Norwich City FC), cricket, fishing, antiques.

Mark Tami MP, House of Commons, London SW1A 0AA
Tel: 020 7219 8174 *Email:* tamim@parliament.uk
Constituency: 70 High Street, Connah's Quay, Flintshire CH5 4DD
Tel: 01244 819854 *Website:* www.marktami.co.uk *Twitter:* @MarkTamiMP

SCOTTISH NATIONAL PARTY

THEWLISS, ALISON

Glasgow Central *(Majority 2,267)*

SNP Spokesperson for Treasury and Cities

Alison Emily Thewliss. Born 13 September 1982; Married (2 children).

Education: Aberdeen University.

Non-political career: Part-time parliamentary assistant to Bill Kidd MSP.

Political career: Member for Glasgow Central since 7 May 2015 general election; SNP Spokesperson for: Cities 2015-, Treasury 2017-. *Select committees:* Member, Communities and Local Government 2015-17. *Councils and public bodies:* Glasgow City Council: Councillor 2007-15, SNP Spokesperson for Land and Environmental Services.

Political interests: Local government, democracy, anti-nuclear weapons.

Other: Member: Scottish CND, Glasgow Greenspace Partnership.

Alison Thewliss MP, House of Commons, London SW1A 0AA
Tel: 020 7219 6447 *Email:* alison.thewliss.mp@parliament.uk
Constituency: 33 London Road, Glasgow G1 5NW
Tel: 0141-552 7117 *Website:* www.alisonthewliss.scot *Twitter:* @alisonthewliss

CONSERVATIVE

THOMAS, DEREK

St Ives *(Majority 312)*

Derek Gordon Thomas. Born 20 July 1972; Married 1998 (2 sons).

Education: Camborne Comprehensive.

Non-political career: Cornish mason (including apprenticeship), Trethowan Builders, West Cornwall 1988-93; Outreach worker, Church of England, Wallington 1993-96; Youth and community manager, Methodist Church, Penzance 1996-99; Self-employed craftsman 1999-2002; Former Community development manager, Mustard Seed Helston; Businessman.

Political career: Contested St Ives 2010 general election. Member for St Ives since 7 May 2015 general election. *Select committees:* Member, Science and Technology 2015-17. Deputy chair (political), St Ives Conservative Association. *Councils and public bodies:* Penwith District Council: Councillor 2005-09, Chair, Overview and Scrutiny 2007-09, Champion, Children and Young People 2006-09.

Political interests: Health, education.

Recreations: Sport, sea kayaking.

Derek Thomas MP, House of Commons, London SW1A 0AA
Tel: 020 7219 4435 *Email:* derek.thomas.mp@parliament.uk
Constituency: Wharfside Shopping Centre, Wharf Road, Penzance, Cornwall TR18 2GB
Tel: 01736 363038 *Website:* derekthomas.org *Twitter:* @DerekThomasUK

LAB/CO-OP

THOMAS, GARETH

Harrow West *(Majority 13,314)*

Gareth Richard Thomas. Born 15 July 1967.

Education: Hatch End High School; Lowlands College; University College of Wales, Aberystwyth (BSc (Econ) politics 1988); Greenwich University (PGCE 1992); King's College, London (MA imperial and Commonwealth studies 1996).

Non-political career: Teacher. Member, Amicus.

Political career: Member for Harrow West 1997-2010, for Harrow West (revised boundary) since 6 May 2010 general election; PPS to Charles Clarke: as Minister of State, Home Office 1999-2001, as Minister without Portfolio and Party Chair 2001-02, as Secretary of State for Education and Skills 2002-03; Sponsored Private Member's Bill, Industrial and Provident Societies Act 2002; Parliamentary Under-Secretary of State: Department for International Development 2003-08, Department for Business, Enterprise and Regulatory Reform (Trade and Consumer Affairs) 2007-08; Minister of State (Trade, Investment and Consumer Affairs/Trade, Development and Consumer Affairs), Departments for: Business, Enterprise and Regulatory Reform 2008-09, International Development 2008-10; Shadow Minister for: International Development 2010, Treasury 2010, Business, Innovation and Skills 2010-11, Cabinet Office 2011-13; Shadow Deputy Minister for London 2013; Shadow Minister for Foreign and Commonwealth Office: Europe 2013-14, North Africa and Middle East 2014-15; Shadow Minister for Communities and Local Government 2016-17. *Select committees:* Member, Environmental Audit 1997-99. Vice-chair, PLP Departmental Committee for Culture, Media and Sport 2000-04; Hon. Secretary, PLP Departmental Committee for Trade and Industry 2000-04. Member, SERA; Chair, Co-operative Party 2000-. *Councils and public bodies:* London Borough of Harrow: Councillor 1990-97, Labour Group Whip 1996; Vice-chair, Association of Local Government Social Services Committee.

Political interests: Energy, mutuals, health, environment; Europe, India, Norway, Pakistan, Sri Lanka.

Other: Member, Fabian Society; Fellow, Industry and Parliament Trust 2003; Pinner United Services Club.

Publications: At the Energy Crossroads Policies for a Low Carbon Economy (Fabian Society, 2001); From Margins to Mainstream – Making Social Responsibility Part of Corporate Culture (2002).

Recreations: Canoeing, running, rugby union.

Gareth Thomas MP, House of Commons, London SW1A 0AA
Tel: 020 7219 4243 *Fax:* 020 7219 1154 *Email:* gareth.thomas.mp@parliament.uk
Constituency: 132 Blenheim Road, West Harrow, Middlesex HA2 7AA
Tel: 020 8861 6300 *Email:* gareth.thomas@harrowlabour.org *Website:* www.garethomas.org
Twitter: @GarethThomasMP

LABOUR

THOMAS-SYMONDS, NICK

Torfaen *(Majority 10,240)*

Shadow Solicitor General; Shadow Minister for Security

Nicklaus Thomas-Symonds. Born 26 May 1980; Married Rebecca (2 daughters 1 son).

Education: St Alban's RC High School, Pontypool; Oxford University (BA politics, philosophy and economics 2001); Glamorgan University (DipLaw); Cardiff University (BVC).

Non-political career: Lecturer, Oxford University 2002-15; Called to the Bar, Lincoln's Inn 2004; Barrister, Civitas Law 2004-15.

Political career: Member for Torfaen since 7 May 2015 general election; Shadow Minister for Work and Pensions 2015-16; Shadow Solicitor General 2016-; Shadow Minister for Home Office (Security) 2017-. *Select committees:* Member, Justice 2015. Secretary, Torfaen CLP 2009-15.

Political interests: NHS.

Other: Fellow, Royal Historical Society 2012.

Publications: Attlee: A Life in Politics (2010); Nye: The Political Life of Aneurin Bevan (2014).

Nick Thomas-Symonds MP, House of Commons, London SW1A 0AA
Tel: 020 7219 4294 *Email:* nick.thomassymonds.mp@parliament.uk
Constituency: 73 Upper Trosnant Street, Pontypool, Torfaen NP4 8AU
Tel: 01495 740498 *Website:* www.nickthomassymonds.uk *Twitter:* @NickTorfaenMP

CONSERVATIVE

THOMSON, ROSS

Aberdeen South *(Majority 4,752)*

Born 21 September 1987; Son of John and Rosalind Thomson; Civil Partner Douglas.

Education: Bridge of Don Academy; Aberdeen University (MA politics and international relations 2009).

Non-political career: Customer Adviser, Bank of Scotland 2010-11; Store Trainer, Debenhams 2011-12.

Political career: Contested Gordon 2010 and Aberdeen South 2015 general elections. Member for Aberdeen South since 8 June 2017. *Select committees:* Member, Scottish Affairs 2017-. Contested Coatbridge and Chryston constituency 2007 and Aberdeen Donside constituency 2011 Scottish Parliament elections, Aberdeen Donside constituency 2013 Scottish Parliament by-election and Aberdeen South and North Kincardine constituency 2016 Scottish Parliament election. MSP for North East Scotland region 2016 to 12 June 2017: Shadow Minister for Further Education, Higher Education and Science 2016-17. Vice-president: University of Aberdeen Conservatives 2005, Conservative Future Scotland; Chair, Aberdeen City Conservative Association 2013-14. *Councils and public bodies:* Aberdeen City Council: Councillor 2012-17, Vice-Convener, Education, Culture and Sport Committee 2012-14, Vice-Convener, Finance, Policy and Resources 2014-16, Convener, Property Sub-Committee 2014-16; Governor, Robert Gordons College.

Political interests: Scotland, international relations, defence, education, equality issues, international trade, European Union, energy, security, crime and policing; Australia, Canada, Iran, Israel, Japan, North Korea, South Korea, Spain, UK, UK Overseas Territories, USA.

Other: Trustee: Aberdeen International Youth Festival, Chris Anderson Trust; Spokesperson for Scottish Vote Leave campaign, EU Referendum 2016. Rotary Youth Leadership Award.

Recreations: Films, friends and family, going out for dinner, going on walks, reading, scuba diving, dogs.

Ross Thomson MP, House of Commons, London SW1A 0AA
Tel: 020 7219 1538 *Email:* ross.thomson.mp@parliament.uk
Constituency: 192 Holburn Street, Aberdeen AB10 6DA
Tel: 01224 592229 *Website:* www.rossthomson.org.uk *Twitter:* @RossThomson_MP

LABOUR

THORNBERRY, EMILY

Islington South and Finsbury *(Majority 20,263)*

Shadow Foreign Secretary

Born 27 July 1960; Daughter of late Sallie Thornberry and late Cedric Thornberry; Married Christopher Nugee 1992 (1 daughter 2 sons).

Education: Church of England Secondary Modern, Guildford; Burlington Danes, Shepherd's Bush, London; Kent University, Canterbury (BA law 1982).

Non-political career: Member, Mike Mansfield's Chambers: Tooks Court 1985. Member, Unite (TGWU sector) 1985-.

Political career: Member for Islington South and Finsbury since 5 May 2005 general election; PPS to Joan Ruddock as Minister of State, Department of Energy and Climate Change 2009-10; Shadow Minister for: Energy and Climate Change 2010, Health 2010-11; Shadow Attorney General 2011-14; Shadow Minister for Employment 2015-16; Shadow Secretary of State for: Defence 2016, Foreign and Commonwealth Affairs (Shadow Foreign Secretary) 2016-, Exiting the European Union 2016. *Select committees:* Member: Environmental Audit 2005-07, Joint Committee on the Draft Legal Services Bill 2006, Communities and Local Government 2006-09, Health 2015.

Political interests: Housing, environment, poverty, equality; Middle East.

Other: Society of Labour Lawyers 1983; Friends of the Earth 1990; Fawcett Society; Fabian Society. PC 2017.

Recreations: Family, cycling, travel.

Rt Hon Emily Thornberry MP, House of Commons, London SW1A 0AA
Tel: 020 7219 5676 *Fax:* 020 7219 5955 *Email:* emily.thornberry.mp@parliament.uk
Constituency: 65 Barnsbury Street, Islington, London N1 1EJ
Tel: 020 7697 9307 *Fax:* 020 7697 4587 *Website:* www.emilythornberry.com
Twitter: @emilythornberry

CONSERVATIVE

THROUP, MAGGIE

Erewash *(Majority 4,534)*

Margaret Ann Throup. Born 27 January 1957; Divorced.

Education: Bradford Girls' Grammar School; Manchester University (BSc biology 1978); Diploma marketing 1987; Fellowship biomedical sciences 1980.

Non-political career: Medical laboratory scientist, Calderdale Health Authority 1978-85; Nycomed (UK) Ltd: Sales executive 1985-86, Product manager 1986-90, Sales and marketing manager 1990-93, Business development manager 1993-96; Director, Maggie Throup Marketing Ltd 1996-.

Political career: Contested Colne Valley 2005 and Solihull 2010 general elections. Member for Erewash since 7 May 2015 general election. *Select committees:* Member: Scottish Affairs 2015-16, Health 2015-.

Political interests: Healthcare, small business, environment; Rwanda.

Other: Trustee, Industry and Parliament Trust 2017-; Fellow, Institute of Biomedical Sciences 1978-85; Chartered Institute of Marketing 1987-96; Trustee: Solihull Community Foundation 2003-, Solihull Carers Centre 2007-.

Recreations: Skiing, sailing, walking.

Maggie Throup MP, House of Commons, London SW1A 0AA
Tel: 020 7219 6571 *Email:* maggie.throup.mp@parliament.uk
Constituency: Unit 2, The Old Co-Op, South Street, Ilkeston, Derbyshire DE7 5SG
Tel: 0115-930 0521 *Website:* www.maggiethroup.com

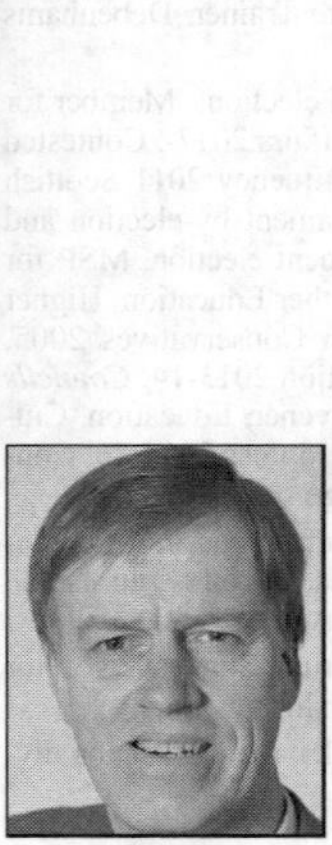

LABOUR

TIMMS, STEPHEN

East Ham *(Majority 39,883)*

Stephen Creswell Timms. Born 29 July 1955; Son of late Ronald Timms, engineer, and Margaret Timms, retired school teacher; Married Hui-Leng Lim 1986.

Education: Farnborough Grammar School, Hampshire; Emmanuel College, Cambridge (MA mathematics 1977; MPhil operational research 1978); German.

Non-political career: Computer and telecommunications industry; Logica Ltd 1978-86; Ovum Ltd 1986-94. Member, Unite.

Political career: Member for Newham North East from 9 June 1994 by-election to 1997, for East Ham 1997-2010, for East Ham (revised boundary) since 6 May 2010 general election; PPS to Andrew Smith as Minister of State, Department for Education and Employment 1997-98; Joint PPS to Mo Mowlam as Secretary of State for Northern Ireland 1998; Department of Social Security 1998-99: Parliamentary Under-Secretary of State 1998-99, Minister of State 1999; Financial Secretary, HM Treasury 1999-2001, 2004-05, 2008-10; Minister of State: Department for Education and Skills (School Standards) 2001-02, Department of Trade and Industry (Energy, E-Commerce and Postal Services) 2002-04, Department for Work and Pensions (Pensions Reform) 2005-06; Chief Secretary to the Treasury 2006-07; Minister of State: Department for Business, Enterprise and Regulatory Reform (Competitiveness) 2007-08, Department for Work and Pensions 2008; Parliamentary Under-Secretary of State, Department for Business, Innovation and Skills (Digital Britain) 2009-10; Shadow Financial Secretary 2010; Shadow Minister for: Business, Innovation and Skills 2010, Employment 2010-15. *Select committees:* Member: Treasury 1996-97, Public Accounts 2004-05, Joint Committee on Tax Law Rewrite Bills 2009-10, Education 2016, Education, Skills and the Economy Sub-committee 2016, Exiting the European Union 2016-. Chair, PLP Departmental Group for Work and Pensions 2015-. Christian Socialist Movement/Christians on the Left: Joint Vice-chair 1995-98, Chair 2012-16; Labour Party Faith Envoy 2007-. *Councils and public bodies:* London Borough of Newham: Councillor 1984-97, Leader of the Council 1990-94; Board Member, East London Partnership (now East London Business Alliance) 1990-2006; Stratford Development Partnership 1992-94.

Political interests: Economic policy, urban regeneration, telecommunications, employment, Christian socialism; Germany, Singapore.

Other: Fellow, Industry and Parliament Trust 1997; Trustee, Traidcraft Foundation 2011-. Honorary doctorate. PC 2006.

Publications: Broadband Communications: The Commercial Impact (1987).

Recreations: Cycling, walking.

Rt Hon Stephen Timms MP, House of Commons, London SW1A 0AA
Tel: 020 7219 4000 *Fax:* 020 7219 2949 *Email:* timmss@parliament.uk
Constituency: No constituency office
Email: stephen@stephentimms.org.uk *Website:* www.stephentimms.org.uk
Twitter: @stephenctimms

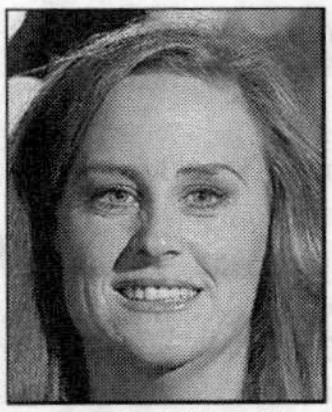

CONSERVATIVE

TOLHURST, KELLY

Rochester and Strood *(Majority 9,850)*

PPS to Greg Clark as Secretary of State for Business, Energy and Industrial Strategy

Kelly Jane Tolhurst. Born 23 August 1978; Daughter of Morris and Christine Tolhurst.

Education: Chapter High School; Italian.

Non-political career: Account Manager, New Zealand Farmers 1996-99; Sales and Marketing Director, Masion Mer Seafood 1999-2001; Business Development Manager, Lactalis UK 2001-02; Director, Skipper (UK) Ltd 2002-; Yacht Surveyor, Tolhurst Associated 2008; Contact Supervisor, Supported Fostering Services 2007-15.

Political career: Contested Rochester and Strood 20 November 2014 by-election. Member for Rochester and Strood since 7 May 2015 general election; PPS to: Priti Patel as Secretary of State for International Development 2016-17, Greg Clark as Secretary of State for Business, Energy and Industrial Strategy 2017-. *Select committees:* Member: Business, Innovation and Skills 2015-16, European Scrutiny 2015-16, Business, Energy and Industrial Strategy 2016-17. *Councils and public bodies:* Medway Council: Councillor 2011-, Portfolio Holder for Educational Improvement 2013-15.

Other: Trustee, Chatham Maritime Trust; Trustee and Director, Action for Borstal Community Project; Association of Dunkirk Little Ships; International Institute of Marine Surveyors; British Marine Federation; RSPB. Medway Yacht Club.

Kelly Tolhurst MP, House of Commons, London SW1A 0AA
Tel: 020 7219 5387 *Email:* kelly.tolhurst.mp@parliament.uk
Constituency: No constituency office publicised
Tel: 01634 840411 *Website:* www.kelly4rochesterandstrood.com *Twitter:* @KellyTolhurst

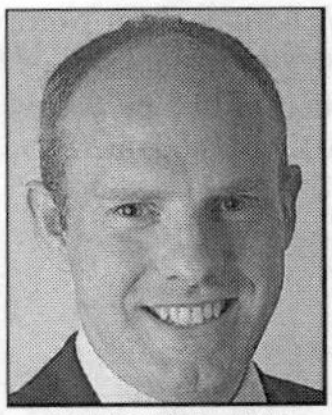

CONSERVATIVE

TOMLINSON, JUSTIN

North Swindon *(Majority 8,335)*

Justin Paul Tomlinson. Born 5 November 1976; Son of Vera and Paul Tomlinson; Married Jo Wheeler 2012.

Education: Harry Cheshire High School, Kidderminster; Oxford Brookes University (BA business 1999).

Non-political career: Sales and marketing manager, First Leisure 1999-2000; Marketing executive, Point to Point 2000; Director, TB Marketing Solutions Ltd 2000-10.

Political career: Contested North Swindon 2005 general election. Member for North Swindon since 6 May 2010 general election; PPS to Ed Vaizey as Minister of State for Culture and the Digital Economy, Departments for Business, Innovation and Skills and Culture, Media and Sport 2014-15; Parliamentary Under-Secretary of State for Disabled People, Department for Work and Pensions 2015-16. *Select committees:* Member: Joint Committee on Consolidation, Etc, Bills 2010-15, Unopposed Bills (Panel) 2011-15, Public Accounts 2012-14. Chair, Oxford Brookes University Conservative Students' Association 1995-99; Deputy chair, North Swindon Conservative Association 2000-04; National chair, Conservative Future 2002-03. *Councils and public bodies:* Swindon Borough Council: Councillor 2000-10, Cabinet member 2003-08.

Political interests: Business, financial education, development, local government, sport, consumer issues, young entrepreneurs.

Other: Honorary President, Swindon British Heart Foundation. Swindon Town Supporters Trust; Swindon Supermarine Football Club.

Recreations: Football, cricket, cinema, video games.

Justin Tomlinson MP, House of Commons, London SW1A 0AA
Tel: 020 7219 7167 *Email:* justin.tomlinson.mp@parliament.uk
Constituency: Customer Service Hub, Orbital Shopping Park, Swindon SN25 4AN
Tel: 01793 533393 *Website:* www.justintomlinson.com *Twitter:* @JustinTomlinson

CONSERVATIVE

TOMLINSON, MICHAEL

Mid Dorset and North Poole *(Majority 15,339)*

Team PPS, Department for International Development

Michael James Tomlinson-Mynors. Born 1 October 1977; Married Frances Mynors 2000 (3 children).

Education: University of London (BA classics).

Non-political career: Called to the Bar, Middle Temple 2002; Barrister, specialising in housing and property related work, 3PB.

Political career: Member for Mid Dorset and North Poole since 7 May 2015 general election; Team PPS, Department for International Development 2017-. *Select committees:* Member, European Scrutiny 2016-. Deputy chair, political, Mid Dorset and North Poole Conservative Association; Campaign manager to Nick King, 2010 general election.

Other: Member: Poole Hockey Club, Hamworthy Cricket Club.

Recreations: Spending time with family, walking, playing sport.

Michael Tomlinson MP, House of Commons, London SW1A 0AA
Tel: 020 7219 5844 *Email:* michael.tomlinson.mp@parliament.uk
Constituency: The Office, Race Farm, Huntick Road, Lytchett Matravers, Poole BH16 6BB
Tel: 01202 624216 *Website:* www.michaeltomlinson.org.uk *Twitter:* @Michael4MDNP

CONSERVATIVE

TRACEY, CRAIG

North Warwickshire *(Majority 8,510)*

Craig Paul Tracey. Born 21 August 1974; Married Karen 2014.

Education: Framwellgate Moor Comprehensive School.

Non-political career: Senior Partner, Dunelm Insurance Brokers, Lichfield 1996-2015; Director, Politically Correct 2014-.

Political career: Member for North Warwickshire since 7 May 2015 general election. *Select committees:* Member: Business, Innovation and Skills 2015-16, Education, Skills and the Economy Sub-committee 2015-16, Business, Energy and Industrial Strategy 2016-17. Former chair, North Warwickshire Conservative Association; West Midlands Co-ordinator, Conservative Voice 2012-.

Other: Member, UK Delegation, Organisation for Security and Co-operation in Europe Parliamentary Assembly 2016-; Founder trustee, Lichfield Garrick Theatre 2012-; Board member, Southern Staffordshire Employment and Skills Board 2014-.

Craig Tracey MP, House of Commons, London SW1A 0AA
Tel: 020 7219 5646 *Email:* craig.tracey.mp@parliament.uk
Constituency: 76 Station Street, Atherstone, Warwickshire CV9 1BU
Tel: 01827 715243 *Website:* www.craigtracey.co.uk *Twitter:* @craig4nwarks

CONSERVATIVE

TREDINNICK, DAVID

Bosworth *(Majority 18,351)*

David Arthur Stephen Tredinnick. Born 19 January 1950; Son of late Stephen Tredinnick and late Evelyn Tredinnick, née Wates; Married Rebecca Shott 1983 (divorced 2008) (1 son 1 daughter).

Education: Eton College; Mons Officer Cadet School; Graduate School of Business Cape Town University (MBA 1975); St John's College, Oxford (MLitt 1987).

Non-political career: 2nd Lieutenant Grenadier Guards 1968-71. Trainee, E. B. Savory Milln & Co. (Stockbrokers) 1972-73; Account executive, Quadrant Int. 1974; Salesman, Kalle Infotech UK 1976; Sales manager, Word Right Word Processing 1977-78; Consultant, Baird Communications NY 1978-79; Marketing manager, QI Europe Ltd 1979-81; Malden Mitcham Properties: Manager 1981-87, Director.

Political career: Contested Cardiff South and Penarth 1983 general election. Member for Bosworth 1987-2010, for Bosworth (revised boundary) since 6 May 2010 general election; PPS to Sir Wyn Roberts as Minister of State, Wales Office 1991-94. *Select committees:* Member, Liaison 1997-2005; Chair, Joint Committee on Statutory Instruments 1997-2005; Member: Health 2010-15, Science and Technology 2013-15. Member, Executive, 1922 Committee 2002-05.

Political interests: Complementary and alternative medicine, health care, diet and nutrition, foreign affairs, home affairs, police, law and order, environment; Eastern Europe.

Other: Chair, British Atlantic Group of Young Politicians 1989-91; Future of Europe Trust 1991-95.

Recreations: Golf, skiing, tennis, windsurfing, sailing.

David Tredinnick MP, House of Commons, London SW1A 0AA
Tel: 020 7219 4514 *Fax:* 020 7219 4901 *Email:* tredinnickd@parliament.uk
Constituency: Bosworth Conservative Association, 10a Priory Walk, Hinckley, Leicestershire LE10 1HU
Tel: 01455 635741 *Fax:* 01455 612023 *Websites:* www.bosworthconservatives.com www.davidtredinnickmp.com

CONSERVATIVE

TREVELYAN, ANNE-MARIE

Berwick-upon-Tweed *(Majority 11,781)*

Team PPS, Ministry of Defence

Anne-Marie Belinda Trevelyan. Born 6 April 1969; Married John Trevelyan 1998 (1 daughter 1 son).

Education: St Pauls Girls School, London; Oxford Polytechnic (mathematics 1990); ACA 1993; French.

Non-political career: PricewaterhouseCoopers, London 1990-94; European financial controller, Blenheim Exhibitions, London 1994-97; Corporate finance, PricewaterhouseCoopers, Newcastle 1997-99; Self-employed consultant 1999-2008.

Political career: Contested Berwick-upon-Tweed 2010 general election. Member for Berwick-upon-Tweed since 7 May 2015 general election; Team PPS, Ministry of Defence 2017-. *Select committees:* Member, Public Accounts 2015-17. Founding member, Conservatives for Britain 2015-16.

Political interests: Education, health, finance.

Other: Member, UK Delegation, Organisation for Security and Co-operation in Europe Parliamentary Assembly 2015-; Board member, Vote Leave 2016; Treasurer, Action Research Medical 1997-2006; Carlton Club.

Recreations: Tennis, reading, cooking for friends.

Anne-Marie Trevelyan MP, House of Commons, London SW1A 0AA
Tel: 020 7219 4437 *Email:* annemarie.trevelyan.mp@parliament.uk
Constituency: 21a The Hotspur, Bondgate Without, Alnwick, Northumberland NE66 1PR
Tel: 01665 517512 *Email:* trevelyanoffice@gmail.com *Website:* www.teamtrevelyan.co.uk
Twitter: @annietrev

LABOUR

TRICKETT, JON

Hemsworth *(Majority 10,174)*

Shadow Lord President of the Council and Shadow Minister for the Cabinet Office

Jon Hedley Trickett. Born 2 July 1950; Son of Laurence and Rose Trickett; Married Sarah Balfour 1993 (1 son 2 daughters).

Education: Roundhay School, Leeds; Hull University (BA politics); Leeds University (MA political sociology); French.

Non-political career: Plumber/builder 1974-86. Member: GMB, RMT Parliamentary Campaigning Group 2002-.

Political career: Member for Hemsworth 1 February 1996 by-election to 2010, for Hemsworth (revised boundary) since 6 May 2010 general election; PPS: to Peter Mandelson: as Minister without Portfolio 1997-98, as Secretary of State for Trade and Industry July-December 1998; to Gordon Brown as Prime Minister 2008-10; Shadow Minister of State for Cabinet Office 2010-11; Shadow Minister for the Cabinet Office 2011-13, 2017-; Shadow Minister without Portfolio 2013-15; Shadow Secretary of State for Communities and Local Government 2015-16; Shadow Minister for the Constitutional Convention 2015-16; Shadow Secretary of State for Business, Innovation and Skills/Business and Industrial Strategy 2016; Shadow Lord President of the Council 2016-; National Elections and Campaigns Co-ordinator 2016-17. *Select committees:* Member: Unopposed Bills (Panel) 1997-2013, Education and Employment 2001, Education and Employment (Employment Sub-Committee) 2001, Public Accounts 2001-06, Public Administration 2010. Secretary PLP Departmental Committee for Health and Social Services 2005-08. Labour Party: Deputy Chair 2013-15, Senior Adviser, Office of the Leader 2014-15, Election co-ordinator 2015-, Member, NEC 2016-. *Councils and public bodies:* Leeds City Council: Councillor 1984-96, Leader of the Council 1989-96.

Political interests: Economic policy, finance, industry, sport; Middle East, France, USA.

Other: Member: British Cycling Federation, West Riding Sailing Club; Hon Life Member, Cyclists' Touring Club.

Recreations: Cycle racing, windsurfing.

Jon Trickett MP, House of Commons, London SW1A 0AA
Tel: 020 7219 5074 *Fax:* 020 7219 2133 *Email:* jon.trickett.mp@parliament.uk
Constituency: Ground Floor, Moorthorpe Railway Station, Barnsley Road, South Kirkby WF9 3AT
Tel: 01977 655695 *Email:* jtrickett@jontrickett.org.uk *Website:* www.jontrickett.org.uk
Twitter: @jon_trickett

CONSERVATIVE

TRUSS, ELIZABETH

South West Norfolk *(Majority 18,312)*

Chief Secretary to the Treasury

Elizabeth Mary Truss. Born 26 July 1975; Daughter of John Truss and Priscilla Truss; Married Hugh O'Leary 2000 (2 daughters).

Education: Roundhay School, Leeds; Merton College, Oxford (BA philosophy, politics and economics 1996).

Non-political career: Commercial analyst, Shell International 1996-2000; Director, financial analysis, Cable and Wireless 2000-05; Managing director, political division, Communication Group 2006-07; Deputy director, Reform 2007-09.

Political career: Contested Hemsworth 2001 and Calder Valley 2005 general elections. Member for South West Norfolk since 6 May 2010 general election; Parliamentary Under-Secretary of State, Department for Education 2012-14; Secretary of State for Environment, Food and Rural Affairs 2014-16; Lord Chancellor and Secretary of State for Justice 2016-17; Chief Secretary to the Treasury 2017-. *Select committees:* Member, Justice 2010-12. Member, Conservative Party 1996-; Chair, Lewisham Deptford Conservative Association 1998-2000. *Councils and public bodies:* Councillor, London Borough of Greenwich Council 2006-10.

Political interests: Economy, education, environment, food.

Other: President, Industry and Parliament Trust 2016-17; Member, Chartered Institute of Management Accountants. Minister to Watch, *Spectator* awards 2012. PC 2014.

Publications: Co-author (with Kwasi Kwarteng MP, Priti Patel MP, Dominic Raab MP and Chris Skidmore MP), Britannia Unchained: Global Lessons for Growth and Prosperity (Palgrave Macmillan, 2012).

Recreations: Film, food, design.

Rt Hon Elizabeth Truss MP, House of Commons, London SW1A 0AA
Tel: 020 7219 7151 *Email:* elizabeth.truss.mp@parliament.uk
Constituency: No constituency office publicised
Tel: 01842 766155 *Website:* www.elizabethtruss.com *Twitter:* @trussliz

CONSERVATIVE

TUGENDHAT, TOM

Tonbridge and Malling *(Majority 23,508)*

Chair, Select Committee on Foreign Affairs

Thomas Georg John Tugendhat. Born 27 June 1973; Son of Michael and Blandine Tugendhat; Married Anissia Morel 2013 (1 son).

Education: St Paul's School, London; Bristol University (BA theology and religious studies 1995); Cambridge University (MPhil Islamic studies 1996); French, Italian, Arabic, Pashto, Dari.

Non-political career: Commissioned Territorial Army Officer 2003; British Army: Army officer 2003, 2007-09, Army Strategy Team 2009-10. Journalist 1997-99; Management consultant, First Consulting 1999-2000; Energy analyst, Bloomberg 2000-03; Consultant 2003-05; Foreign and Commonwealth Office: Adviser to: National Security Adviser of Afghanistan 2005-06, Governor of Helmand 2006-07; Military assistant to the Chief of Defence Staff, Ministry of Defence 2010-13.

Political career: Member for Tonbridge and Malling since 7 May 2015 general election. *Select committees:* Member: Public Administration and Constitutional Affairs 2015-16, Joint Committee on Consolidation, &c, Bills 2015-, Speaker's Advisory Committee on Works of Art 2016-, Liaison 2017-; Chair, Foreign Affairs 2017-.

Political interests: Localism, business, economic development, defence, foreign affairs; North Africa, Southern Africa, West Africa, Central Asia, Europe, Middle East, USA.

Other: MBE (Military) 2010; Special Forces Club.

Publications: The Fog of Law (Policy Exchange, 2013).

Recreations: Walking, conversation, family.

Tom Tugendhat MBE MP, House of Commons, London SW1A 0AA
Tel: 020 7219 3000 *Email:* tom.tugendhat.mp@parliament.uk
Constituency: 130 Vale Road, Tonbridge, Kent TN9 1SP
Tel: 01732 441563 *Website:* www.tomtugendhat.org.uk *Twitter:* @TomTugendhat

LAB/CO-OP

TURLEY, ANNA

Redcar *(Majority 9,485)*

Anna Catherine Turley. Born 9 October 1978.

Education: Ashford School, Kent; Oxford University (BA history).

Non-political career: Home Office 2001-05; Special adviser to David Blunkett MP and Hilary Armstrong MP 2005-07; Deputy director, New Local Government Network 2007-10; Senior research fellow, IPPR North; Co-ordinator, Co-operative Councils Network. Member, Community.

Political career: Member for Redcar since 7 May 2015 general election; Shadow Minister for Cabinet Office 2015-16. *Select committees:* Member: Home Affairs 2015, Business, Energy and Industrial Strategy 2016-. Member, Co-operative Party; Vice-Chair, Co-operative Party Parliamentary Group 2015-. *Councils and public bodies:* School governor.

Anna Turley MP, House of Commons, London SW1A 0AA
Tel: 020 7219 5441 *Email:* anna.turley.mp@parliament.uk
Constituency: 10 Milbank Terrace, Redcar TS10 1ED
Tel: 01642 485138 *Email:* anna@anna4redcar.org.uk *Website:* www.anna4redcar.org.uk
Twitter: @annaturley

LABOUR

TURNER, KARL

Kingston upon Hull East *(Majority 10,396)*

Shadow Minister for Shipping, Aviation and Road Safety

Born 15 April 1971; Son of Ken Turner, trade unionist, and Pat Turner; Married Leanne (1 daughter).

Education: Bransholme High School; Hull College; Hull University (law 2004).

Non-political career: Youth training scheme, Hull City Council; Self-employed antiques dealer; Called to the Bar, Middle Temple 2005; Barrister: Max Gold Partnership, Hull 2005-09, Wilberforce Chambers, Hull 2009-10. Member: Unison, GMB.

Political career: Member for Kingston upon Hull East since 6 May 2010 general election; Opposition Whip 2013-15, 2016-17; Shadow Solicitor General 2014-16; Shadow Minister for Justice (Legal Aid) 2015-16; Shadow Attorney General 2016; Shadow Minister for Transport (Shipping, Aviation and Road Safety) 2017-. *Select committees:* Member: Justice 2010-13, Home Affairs 2012-13.

Political interests: Justice, jobs, welfare, home affairs, animal welfare; Sri Lanka.

Karl Turner MP, House of Commons, London SW1A 0AA
Tel: 020 7219 0971 *Email:* karl.turner.mp@parliament.uk
Constituency: 430 Holderness Road, Hull, East Yorkshire HU9 3DW
Tel: 01482 781019 *Website:* www.karlturnermp.org.uk *Twitter:* @KarlTurnerMP

LABOUR

TWIGG, DEREK

Halton *(Majority 25,405)*

John Derek Twigg. Born 9 July 1959; Son of Kenneth and Irene Twigg; Married Mary Cassidy 1988 (1 son 1 daughter).

Education: Bankfield High School, Widnes; Halton College of Further Education (1978).

Non-political career: Civil servant, Department for Education and Employment 1975-96. Member, GMB.

Political career: Member for Halton 1997-2010, for Halton (revised boundary) since 6 May 2010 general election; PPS: to Helen Liddell as Minister of State: Department of the Environment, Transport and the Regions 1999, Department of Trade and Industry 1999-2001, to Stephen Byers as Secretary of State for Transport, Local Government and the Regions 2001-02; Assistant Government Whip 2002-03, Government Whip 2003-04; Parliamentary Under-Secretary of State: Department for Education and Skills 2004-05, Department for Transport 2005-06; Parliamentary Under-Secretary of State (Minister for Veterans), Ministry of Defence 2006-08; Shadow Minister for Health 2010-11. *Select committees:* Member: Public Accounts 1998-99, Children, Schools and Families 2009-10, Joint Committee on Voting Eligibilty (Prisoners) Bill 2013, Defence 2013-15, Arms Export Controls 2014, Liaison 2015-; Chair, Joint Committee on Statutory Instruments 2015-. *Councils and public bodies:* Councillor: Cheshire County Council 1981-85, Halton Borough Council 1983-97.

Political interests: Economy, education, health and poverty, defence; Greece.

Recreations: Various sporting activities, hill-walking, military history.

Derek Twigg MP, House of Commons, London SW1A 0AA
Tel: 020 7219 1039 *Email:* derek.twigg.mp@parliament.uk
Constituency: Bridge Buisness Centre, Suite E, Cheshire House, Gorsey Lane, Widnes, Cheshire WA8 0RP
Tel: 0151-424 7030 *Website:* www.derektwigg.org *Twitter:* @DerekTwiggMP

LAB/CO-OP

TWIGG, STEPHEN

Liverpool West Derby *(Majority 32,908)*

Chair, Select Committee on International Development

Born 25 December 1966; Son of Ian David Twigg and late Jean Barbara Twigg; Civil Partner.

Education: Southgate Comprehensive; Balliol College, Oxford (BA politics and economics 1988); French.

Non-political career: President, National Union of Students; Parliamentary officer: Amnesty International UK, NCVO; Research assistant to Margaret Hodge MP; Political consultant, Rowland Sallingbury Casey; General Secretary, Fabian Society 1996-97; Director: Foreign Policy Centre 2005-, Special projects, Aegis Trust 2005-. Member, Amicus-MSF.

Political career: Member for Enfield Southgate 1997-2005. Contested Enfield Southgate 2005 general election. Member for Liverpool West Derby since 6 May 2010 general election; Parliamentary Secretary, Privy Council Office 2001-02; Department for Education and Skills 2002-05: Parliamentary Under-Secretary of State 2002-04: for Young People and Learning 2002, for Schools 2002-04, Minister of State 2004-05; Shadow Minister for Foreign Commonwealth Office 2010-11; Shadow Secretary of State for Education 2011-13; Shadow Minister for Justice 2013-15. *Select committees:* Member: Modernisation of the House of Commons 1998-2000, Education and Employment 1999-2001, Education and Employment (Employment Sub-Committee) 1999-2001, Liaison 2015-; Chair, International Development 2015-; Member: Joint Committee on the National Security Strategy 2015-, Work of the Independent Commission for Aid Impact Sub-committee 2016-. Hon. Secretary, Labour Party Departmental Committee for Foreign and Commonwealth Affairs 1997-99; Member, Labour Party Departmental Committees for: Education and Employment 1997-2001, Home Affairs 1997-2001; Member, Departmental Committee for Education and Skills 2001-05. Chair: Labour Campaign for Electoral Reform -2001, Labour Friends of Israel -2001; Patron, LGBT Labour. *Councils and public bodies:* London Borough of Islington Council: Councillor 1992-97, Chief Whip 1994-96, Deputy Leader 1996; Governor: Merryhills Primary School, Southgate School, Middlesex University Court.

Political interests: Education, electoral reform, local and regional government, foreign affairs; Africa, Middle East.

Other: Member: Amnesty International, Stonewall, Holocaust Educational Trust, League Against Cruel Sports; Hon. President, British Youth Council; Patron, Principal Theatre Company; Hon. President, Progress 2011-; Chicken Shed Theatre Company; National Liberal Club. Southgate Cricket.

Publications: Co-author, The Cross We Bear: Electoral Reform in Local Government (1997); Contributor, The Purple Book (Progress, 2011).

Stephen Twigg MP, House of Commons, London SW1A 0AA
Tel: 020 7219 4158 *Email:* stephen.twigg.mp@parliament.uk
Constituency: 229 Eaton Road, Liverpool, Merseyside L12 2AG
Tel: 0151-230 0853 *Website:* www.stephentwiggmp.co.uk *Twitter:* @StephenTwigg

LABOUR

TWIST, LIZ

Blaydon *(Majority 13,477)*

Mary Elizabeth Twist. Born February 1944.

Non-political career: Constituency Staff Member to Dave Anderson MP; Regional Head of Health, Unison. Unison.

Political career: Member for Blaydon since 8 June 2017. *Select committees:* Member: Communities and Local Government 2017-, Petitions 2017-. *Councils and public bodies:* Gateshead Council: Councillor, Cabinet Member for Housing.

Other: Stargate and Crookhill Community Centre Association; Ryton Community Library Volunteers Association; Tyneside Samaritans.

Liz Twist MP, House of Commons, London SW1A 0AA
Tel: 020 7219 2221 *Email:* liz.twist.mp@parliament.uk
Constituency: St Cuthbert's Community Hall, Shibdon Road, Blaydon NE21 5PT
Tel: 0191-414 2488 *Website:* liztwist.co.uk *Twitter:* @LizTwistMP

LABOUR

UMUNNA, CHUKA

Streatham *(Majority 26,285)*

Chuka Harrison Umunna. Born 17 October 1978; Son of Patricia Umunna and late Ben Umunna; Married Alice Sullivan 2016.

Education: St Dunstan's College, Catford; Manchester University (LLB English and French law 2001); Nottingham Law School 2002.

Non-political career: Trainee solicitor/solicitor, Herbert Smith LLP 2002-06; Solicitor, Rochman Landau 2006-10. Member: GMB, Unite.

Political career: Member for Streatham since 6 May 2010 general election; PPS to Ed Miliband as Leader of the Opposition 2010-11; Shadow Minister for Business, Innovation and Skills 2011; Shadow Secretary of State for Business, Innovation and Skills 2011-15. *Select committees:* Member: Treasury 2010-11, Home Affairs 2015-17. Member, Labour Party 1997-; Vice-chair, Streatham Labour Party 2004-08; Member: BAME Labour 2006-, Economy – Work and Business Policy Commission.

Political interests: Economy, employment, equality, education, home affairs and justice, climate change, community and youth engagement.

Other: Member, Fabian Society 1998-; Management committee member, Compass 2003-; Trustee, Generation Next Foundation; Member, advisory board, Centre for Progressive Capitalism 2016-; Chair, Vote Leave Watch 2016-; Member: Law Society Roll of Solicitors 2004-, Employment Lawyers Association 2004-; Trustee, Anthony Bourne Foundation.

Publications: Founder and former editor, TMP Online 2007-08.

Chuka Umunna MP, House of Commons, London SW1A 0AA
Tel: 020 7219 2115 *Email:* chuka.umunna.mp@parliament.uk
Constituency: Hideaway Workspace, 1 Empire Mews, Streatham, London SW16 2BF
Tel: 020 8835 7062 *Website:* www.chuka.org.uk *Twitter:* @ChukaUmunna

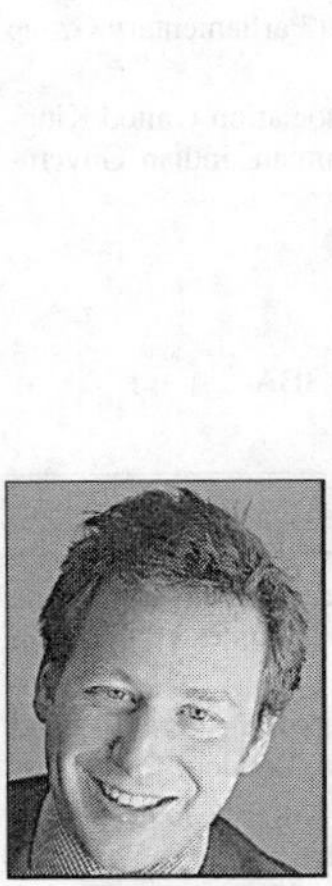

CONSERVATIVE

VAIZEY, ED

Wantage *(Majority 17,380)*

Edward Henry Butler Vaizey. Born 5 June 1968; Son of late Lord Vaizey of Greenwich and Marina Vaizey CBE; Married Alexandra Holland 2005 (1 son 1 daughter).

Education: St Paul's School, London; Merton College, Oxford (BA modern history 1989, MA); City University (Diploma law 1992); Inns of Court School of Law.

Non-political career: Desk officer, Conservative Research Department 1989-91; Called to the Bar, Middle Temple 1993; Barrister specialising in family law and child care 1994-96; Director: Public Policy Unit 1996-97, Politics International 1997-98; Director and partner, Consolidated Communications 1998-2003; Freelance journalist 2001-; Speechwriter to Michael Howard MP as Leader of the Opposition 2003-05; Consultant, LionTree Europe 2016-.

Political career: Contested Bristol East 1997 general election. Member for Wantage 2005-10, for Wantage (revised boundary) since 6 May 2010 general election; Shadow Minister for the Arts 2006-10; Parliamentary Under-Secretary of State (Minister for Culture, Communications and Creative Industries), Departments for: Business, Innovation and Skills 2010-11, Culture, Media and Sport 2010-14; Minister of State for Culture and the Digital Economy, Departments for Business, Innovation and Skills and Culture, Media and Sport 2014-16; Trade Envoy to Vietnam, Cambodia and Laos 2017-. *Select committees:* Member: Modernisation of the House of Commons 2005-07, Environmental Audit 2006-07, Works of Art 2016-. Election aide to Iain Duncan Smith MP 2001 general election; Deputy chair, Conservative Globalisation and Global Poverty Policy Group 2006.

Political interests: Arts, architecture, energy, science and technology, environment; India, Israel, Middle East, USA.

Other: Hon. Fellow, Royal Institute of British Architects 2011; Trustee: BRITDOC Charitable Trust 2016-, National Youth Theatre of Great Britain 2016-; Chair, advisory board: Creative Fuse North East 2016-, International eGames Committee 2017-; Member, advisory board, *The Sunday Times* Short Story Award 2017-; President, advisory board, British Esports Association Ltd 2017-; Adviser, International Group Management 2017-; Judge, Indigo Index Prize 2017-; Samaritans, Didcot Train. PC 2016.

Publications: Editor: A Blue Tomorrow (Politicos, 2001), The Blue Book on Health (Politicos, 2002), The Blue Book on Transport (Politicos, 2002).

Recreations: Horse riding, football.

Rt Hon Ed Vaizey MP, House of Commons, London SW1A 0AA
Tel: 020 7219 6350 *Email:* ed.vaizey.mp@parliament.uk
Constituency: Vale and Downland Museum, Church Street, Wantage, Oxfordshire OX12 8BL
Tel: 01235 768888 *Email:* dicksonce@parliament.uk
Websites: www.oxfordshireconservatives.com www.vaizey.com *Twitter:* @edvaizey

CONSERVATIVE

VARA, SHAILESH

North West Cambridgeshire *(Majority 18,008)*

Shailesh Lakhman Vara. Born 4 September 1960; Son of Lakhman Arjan Vara and Savita, née Gadher; Married Beverley Fear 2002 (2 sons).

Education: Aylesbury Grammar School; Brunel University (LLB).

Non-political career: Articled: Richards Butler 1988-90 (in Hong Kong 1989-90), Solicitor: Crossman Block 1991-92, Payne Hicks Beach 1992-93, CMS Cameron McKenna 1994-2001.

Political career: Contested Birmingham Ladywood 1997 and Northampton South 2001 general elections. Member for North West Cambridgeshire 2005-10, for North West Cambridgeshire (revised boundary) since 6 May 2010 general election; Shadow Deputy Leader of the House 2006-10; Assistant Government Whip 2010-12; Parliamentary Under-Secretary of State: for the Courts and Legal Aid, Ministry of Justice 2013-16, Department for Work and Pensions 2015-16. *Select committees:* Member: Environment, Food and Rural Affairs 2005-06, Administration 2010-11, Finance and Services 2011-13. Society of Conservative Lawyers: Treasurer 2001-04, Vice-chair, Executive Committee 2006-09; Vice-chair, Conservative Party 2001-05; Chair, Conservative Parliamentary Friends of India 2008-10; Vice-chair, Conservative China Parliamentary Group 2009-10.

Other: Member, Executive Committee, Commonwealth Parliamentary Association United Kingdom 2017-. Hon. Fellow, Brunel University 2010-. Pravasi Bharatiya Samman, Indian Government 2014. Vice-president, Huntingdonshire County Cricket Club 2007-.

Recreations: Cricket, theatre, taekwondo.

Shailesh Vara MP, House of Commons, London SW1A 0AA
Tel: 020 7219 6050 *Email:* shailesh.vara.mp@parliament.uk
Constituency: The Old Barn, Hawthorn Farm, Ashton, Cambridgeshire PE9 3BA
Tel: 01733 380089 *Website:* www.shaileshvara.com

LABOUR

VAZ, KEITH

Leicester East *(Majority 22,428)*

Nigel Keith Anthony Standish Vaz. Born 26 November 1956; Son of late Merlyn Verona Vaz, teacher, and late Anthony Xavier Vaz, personnel manager; Married Maria Fernandes 1993 (1 son 1 daughter).

Education: St Joseph's Convent, Aden; Latymer Upper School, Hammersmith; Gonville and Caius College, Cambridge (BA law 1979, MA, MCFI 1988); College of Law, London.

Non-political career: London Borough of Richmond: Articled Clerk 1980-82, Solicitor 1982; Senior solicitor, London Borough of Islington 1982-85; Solicitor: Highfields and Belgrave Law Centre 1985-87, North Leicester Advice Centre 1986-87. Member, Unison 1985-.

Political career: Contested Richmond and Barnes 1983 general election. Member for Leicester East 1987-2010, for Leicester East (revised boundary) since 6 May 2010 general election; Opposition Frontbench Spokesperson for the Environment 1992-97; Promoter Race Relations Remedies Act 1994; PPS: to John Morris as Attorney General 1997-99, to Solicitors General Lord Falconer of Thoroton 1997-98, Ross Cranston 1998-99; Parliamentary Secretary, Lord Chancellor's Department 1999; Minister of State, Foreign and Commonwealth Office (Minister for Europe) 1999-2001. *Select committees:* Home Affairs: Member 1987-92, Chair 2007-16; Member: Constitutional Affairs 2003-07, Liaison 2007-16, Joint Committee on National Security Strategy 2010-16, Administration 2012-, Justice 2016-17, International Trade 2017-. Joint vice-chair, PLP Departmental Committee for International Development 1997-2000. Contested Surrey West 1984 and 1994 European Parliament elections. Labour Party Race Action Group: Chair 1983-2000, Patron 2000-; Chair, Unison Group 1990-99; Vice-chair, Tribune Group 1992; Labour Party Regional Executive 1994-96; Chair, National Ethnic Minority Taskforce 2006-; Member, Labour Party National Executive Committee 2007-; Vice-chair, Women's, Race and Equality Committee; Trustee, Labour Party Pensions Regulator 2008-. *Councils and public bodies:* Vice-chair, British Council 1998-99; Governor, Commonwealth Institute 1998-99.

Political interests: Education, legal services, local and regional government, race relations, urban policy, small businesses; Bangladesh, India, Oman, Pakistan, Yemen.

Other: Member, Executive Committee Inter-Parliamentary Union 1993-94; EU Ambassador for Year of Inter-Cultural Dialogue 2008; Member, Executive Committee, Commonwealth Parliamentary Association United Kingdom 2017-; President, Leicester and South Leicestershire RSPCA 1988-99; Member, National Advisory Committee, Crime Concern 1989-93; Patron, Gingerbread 1990-; Fellow, Industry and Parliament Trust 1993; Joint patron, UN Year of Tolerance 1995; Founder patron, Naz Project, London 1999-; Patron, Asian Donors Appeal 2000-; Founder patron, Silver Star Appeal 2006. Medal of Honour, President of Yemen on behalf of the people of Yemen 2004; PC 2006; Safari Club (Leicester).

Publications: Columnist: Tribune, Catholic Herald; Co-author, Law Reform Now (1996).
Recreations: Tennis.

Rt Hon Keith Vaz MP, House of Commons, London SW1A 0AA
Tel: 020 7219 4605 *Email:* vazk@parliament.uk
Constituency: 123 Belgrave Road, Leicester, Leicestershire LE4 6AS
Tel: 0116-267 9144 *Fax:* 0116-212 2121 *Email:* casework@live.co.uk
Website: www.keithvazmp.com

LABOUR

VAZ, VALERIE

Walsall South *(Majority 8,892)*

Shadow Leader of the House of Commons

Valerie Carol Marian Vaz. Born 7 December 1954; Daughter of late Merlyn Verona Vaz, teacher, and late Anthony Xavier Vaz, personnel manager; Married Paul Townsend 1992 (1 daughter).

Education: Twickenham County Grammar School; Bedford College, London University (BSc biochemistry 1978); Sidney Sussex College, Cambridge (Research animal nutrition 1978-79); College of Law, London (CPE 1981; SFE 1982); French (basic).

Non-political career: Trainee solicitor, Herbert Smith; Lawyer: London Borough of Brent, London Borough of Hammersmith and Fulham; Presenter, Network East, BBC; Townsend Vaz Solicitors; Deputy district judge (part-time), Midlands and Oxford Circuits; Solicitor, Government Legal Service, Treasury Solicitors Department 2001-10; On secondment, Ministry of Justice 2008-09. Member, USDAW.

Political career: Contested Twickenham 1987 general election. Member for Walsall South since 6 May 2010 general election; Shadow Leader of the House of Commons 2016-; Member, House of Commons Commission 2016-. *Select committees:* Member: Health 2010-15, Regulatory Reform 2010-15, House of Commons Governance 2014-15, Panel of Chairs 2015-16, Science and Technology 2015-16, Environment, Food and Rural Affairs 2016. Vice-chair, PLP Departmental Group for Business, Innovation and Skills 2010-14. Contested East Midlands 1999 European Parliament election. *Councils and public bodies:* London Borough of Ealing Council: Councillor 1986-90, Deputy Council Leader 1988-89; Member, Ealing Health Authority 1986-89; School governor 1986-90.

Political interests: Health, science and technology, legal and constitutional affairs, music; South Asia, Burma, Yemen.

Other: Member, Executive Committee, Commonwealth Parliamentary Association UK 2015-; Member, National Trust; Friend, Kew Gardens; Law Society; Association of Women Solicitors.

Publications: Author, Obesity and Diabetes Programmes in England: Capturing the State of Play (2011); Instruments on Planes (compiled and prepared with the Incorporated Society of Musicians) (2012); Author, The Use of Higher Rate Telephone Numbers by Government Departments (2014).

Recreations: Music – playing piano, gardening, walking.

Valerie Vaz MP, House of Commons, London SW1A 0AA
Tel: 020 7219 2237/020 7219 5054 *Email:* valerie.vaz.mp@parliament.uk
Constituency: 16a Lichfield Street, Walsall WS1 1TJ
Tel: 01922 635835 *Website:* www.valerievazmp.co.uk *Twitter:* @Valerie_VazMP

CONSERVATIVE

VICKERS, MARTIN

Cleethorpes *(Majority 10,400)*

Martin John Vickers. Born 13 September 1950; Son of Norman and Winifred Vickers, née Watson; Married Ann 1981 (1 daughter).

Education: Havelock School; Grimsby College; Lincoln University (BA politics 2004).

Non-political career: Printing industry; Retail industry.

Political career: Contested Cleethorpes 2005 general election. Member for Cleethorpes since 6 May 2010 general election. *Select committees:* Member: Procedure 2012-15, Transport 2013-. Constituency agent to Edward Leigh MP 1994-2010. *Councils and public bodies:* Councillor, Great Grimsby Borough Council 1980-94; North East Lincolnshire Council: Councillor 1999-2011, Cabinet Member for Environmental Services 2003-08.

Political interests: Constitution, local government, regeneration issues, energy policy, transport.

Publications: Contributor: Freedom, Responsibility and the State: Curbing Over-Mighty Government (Politeia, 2012), Unlocking Local Leadership on Climate Change (Green Alliance, 2012).

Recreations: Reading, football, cricket, travel, railways, music, religion.

Martin Vickers MP, House of Commons, London SW1A 0AA
Tel: 020 7219 7212 *Email:* martin.vickers.mp@parliament.uk
Constituency: 62 St Peter's Avenue, Cleethorpes, North East Lincolnshire DN35 8HP
Tel: 01472 603554 *Email:* mvickersmp@gmail.com *Website:* www.martinvickers.org.uk
Twitter: @MartinVickers

CONSERVATIVE

VILLIERS, THERESA

Chipping Barnet *(Majority 353)*

Theresa Anne Villiers. Born 5 March 1968; Daughter of Virginia Villiers and late George Villiers; Married Sean Wilken 1999 (divorced).

Education: Francis Holland School, London; Bristol University (LLB 1990); Jesus College, Oxford (BCL 1991); Inns of Court School of Law (1992).

Non-political career: Barrister Lincoln's Inn 1994-95; Lecturer in law King's College, London University 1995-99.

Political career: Member for Chipping Barnet 2005-10, for Chipping Barnet (revised boundary) since 6 May 2010 general election; Shadow Chief Secretary to the Treasury 2005-07; Shadow Secretary of State for Transport 2007-10; Minister of State, Department for Transport 2010-12; Secretary of State for Northern Ireland 2012-16. *Select committees:* Member: Environmental Audit 2005-06, Joint Committee on the National Security Strategy 2016-. European Parliament: MEP for London 1999-2005: Deputy leader, Conservatives group 2001-02.

Political interests: Economic policy, business, transport, animal welfare, financial services, environment; Cyprus, Israel.

Other: President: Friends of Barnet Hospital, Barnet Borough Talking Newspapers, Barnet Old People's Welfare; Member: Campaign committee, Vote Leave 2016, Board Member, Red Tape Initiative 2017-; North London Hospice, Cherry Lodge Cancer Care. Freedom, City of London. PC 2010. Middlesex County Cricket Club.

Publications: European Tax harmonisation: The Impending Threat; Co-author, Waiver, Variation and Estoppel (Chancery Wiley Law Publications, 1998).

Recreations: Cycling.

Rt Hon Theresa Villiers MP, House of Commons, London SW1A 0AA
Tel: 020 7219 3000
Constituency: 163 High Street, Barnet, Hertfordshire EN5 5SU
Tel: 020 8449 7345 *Email:* theresa@theresavilliers.co.uk *Website:* www.theresavilliers.co.uk

CONSERVATIVE

WALKER, CHARLES

Broxbourne *(Majority 15,792)*

Chair, Select Committee on Procedure

Charles Ashley Rupert Walker. Born 11 September 1967; Son of Carola Chataway, née Ashton, and late Timothy Walker; Married Fiona Newman 1995 (1 daughter 2 sons).

Education: American School of London; University of Oregon, USA (BSc politics and American history 1990).

Non-political career: Communications director, CSG (Corporate Services Group) plc 1997-2001; Director: Blue Arrow Ltd 1999-2001, LSM Processing Ltd 2002-04, Debitwise 2004. Member, Amicus.

Political career: Contested Ealing North 2001 general election. Member for Broxbourne since 5 May 2005 general election; Member, Speaker's Committee for the Independent Parliamentary Standards Authority 2010-. *Select committees:* Member: Scottish Affairs 2005-10, Public Administration 2007-11, Chairmen's Panel/Panel of Chairs 2010-, Standing Orders 2011-15; Chair, Prodecure 2012-; Member, Liaison 2012-. 1922 Committee: Member, Executive 2006-10, 2014-15, Vice-chairman 2010-14, 2015-; Chairman, Conservative Backbench Policy Committee on Scotland 2015-17. Vice-chair: Lewisham East Conservatives 1992-93, Battersea Conservatives 2002-03; Member, Conservative Party Board 2010-. *Councils and public bodies:* Councillor, Wandsworth Borough Council 2002-06; Vice-President, Local Government Association 2010-.

Political interests: Employment, taxation, the economy, mental health.

Other: Patron, Isabelle Hospice. *Spectator* awards: Speech of the Year 2011, Speech of the Year (with Kevan Jones MP) 2012; Best Contribution to the *House Magazine*, *House Magazine* awards 2012. OBE 2015.

Recreations: Fishing, watching cricket.

Charles Walker OBE MP, House of Commons, London SW1A 0AA
Tel: 020 7219 0338 *Fax:* 020 7219 0505 *Email:* charles.walker.mp@parliament.uk
Constituency: 57-59 High Street, Hoddesdon, Hertfordshire EN11 8TQ
Tel: 01992 479972 *Fax:* 01992 479973 *Email:* broxbourne@tory.org
Website: www.charleswalker.org

CONSERVATIVE

WALKER, ROBIN

Worcester *(Majority 2,508)*

Parliamentary Under-Secretary of State, Department for Exiting the European Union

Robin Caspar Walker. Born 12 April 1978; Son of late Peter Walker (MP for Worcester 1961-92, later Lord Walker of Worcester) and Tessa Pout; Married Charlotte Keenan 2011.

Education: St Paul's School, London; Balliol College, Oxford (BA ancient and modern history 2000).

Non-political career: Member, Armed Forces Parliamentary Scheme (RAF). Intern, Office of the chairman of the House Ways and Means Committee, Washington DC September 2000; Chief executive, Property Map Ltd 2000-01; Research executive, i-Search Ltd 2001-03; Finsbury Group (Financial Communications): Executive 2003-04, Senior executive 2004-06, Associate partner 2006-09, Partner 2009-10.

Political career: Member for Worcester since 6 May 2010 general election; PPS to: Andrew Robathan as Minister of State, Northern Ireland Office 2013-14, Elizabeth Truss as Secretary of State for Environment, Food and Rural Affairs 2014-15, Nicky Morgan as Secretary of State for Education and Minister for Women and Equalities 2015-16; Parliamentary Under-Secretary of State, Department for Exiting the European Union 2016-. *Select committees:* Member: Welsh Affairs 2011-12, Business, Innovation and Skills 2012-15, Arms Export Controls 2013, Administration 2015-16. Volunteer assistant to: Stephen Dorrell MP, 1997 general election campaign, Worcester Conservative Association, 2001 general election campaign; Press officer to Oliver Letwin MP, 2005 general election; Member: Conservative Middle East Council, Tory Reform Group.

Political interests: Education, health, police, foreign affairs, defence, business; Canada, India, Italy, Latin America, Middle East, South Africa, USA, Zambia.

Other: Commonwealth Parliamentary Association; Inter-Parliamentary Union; Member, British-Irish Parliamentary Assembly 2015-17; Member, TRG 1997-; Honorary Board Member, Worcester Live; St Richard's Hospice Worcester, New Hope Worcester, Acorns Children's Hospice; Carlton Club. Worcester County Cricket Club; Worcester Warriors RFC.

Recreations: Walking, reading, travel, writing, watching cricket and rugby.

Robin Walker MP, House of Commons, London SW1A 0AA
Tel: 020 7219 7196 *Email:* robin.walker.mp@parliament.uk
Constituency: Office of Robin Walker MP, Guildhall, High Street, Worcester WR1 2EY
Tel: 01905 22401 *Website:* www.walker4worcester.com *Twitter:* @WalkerWorcester

LABOUR

WALKER, THELMA

Colne Valley *(Majority 915)*

Thelma Doris Walker. Born 7 April 1957; Married Rob Walker (2 sons).

Education: Marple Hall Grammar School; Manchester Polytechnic (BEd education 1978).

Non-political career: Headteacher: Flockton First School 2001-06, Overthorpe C of E School 2006-12; Independent Educational Consultant 2012-17.

Political career: Member for Colne Valley since 8 June 2017. *Select committees:* Member, Education 2017-.

Political interests: Education, health, social care, environment.

Other: Vice-Chair, Kirkless Leadership Development Group; Chair, Kirklees Primary Heads; Member, Kirklees Safeguarding Board.

Thelma Walker MP, House of Commons, London SW1A 0AA
Tel: 020 7219 4137 *Email:* thelma.walker.mp@parliament.uk
Constituency: Civic Hall, 15a New Street, Slaithwaite, Huddersfield HD7 5AB
Tel: 01484 843068 *Website:* www.thelmawalker4cv.co.uk *Twitter:* @Thelma_WalkerMP

CONSERVATIVE

WALLACE, BEN

Wyre and Preston North *(Majority 12,246)*

Minister of State for Security, Home Office

Robert Ben Lobban Wallace. Born 15 May 1970; Married Liza Cooke 2001 (2 sons 1 daughter).

Education: Millfield School, Somerset; Royal Military Academy, Sandhurst (Commission 1991); French, German.

Non-political career: Army officer, Scots Guards 1991-98: Mentioned in Despatches 1991, Service in Northern Ireland, Central America, Cyprus, Germany; Intelligence 1994-95. RGS&H advertising agency, Boston, USA 1988; Ski instructor, Austrian National Ski School 1988-89; EU and overseas director, Qinetiq 2003-05.

Political career: Member for Lancaster and Wyre 2005-10, for Wyre and Preston North since 6 May 2010 general election; Shadow Minister for Scotland 2007-10; PPS to Kenneth Clarke: as Lord Chancellor and Secretary of State for Justice 2010-12, as Minister without portfolio, Cabinet Office 2012-14; Assistant Government Whip 2014-15; Parliamentary Under-Secretary of State, Northern Ireland Office 2015-16; Minister of State for Security, Home Office 2016-. *Select committees:* Member: Scottish Affairs 2005-10, Administration 2014-15. Contested West Aberdeenshire and Kincardine constituency 1999 Scottish Parliament election. MSP for North East Scotland region 1999-2003: Scottish Conservative Spokesperson for Health.

Political interests: Foreign policy, intelligence, home affairs, health, security, sport; Iran, Italy, Middle East, Romania, Russia, USA.

Other: Member, Queen's Bodyguard of Scotland, Royal Archers 2007-; President, Lancashire branch, Scots Guards Association. PC 2017.

Recreations: Sailing, skiing, racing, motorsport.

Rt Hon Ben Wallace MP, House of Commons, London SW1A 0AA
Tel: 020 7219 5804 *Fax:* 020 7219 5901 *Email:* wallaceb@parliament.uk
Constituency: Great Eccleston Village Centre, 59 High Street, Great Eccleston, Lancashire PR3 0YB
Tel: 01995 672977 *Website:* www.benwallace.org.uk *Twitter:* @BWallaceMP

WARBURTON, DAVID

Somerton and Frome *(Majority 22,906)*

CONSERVATIVE

David John Warburton. Born 28 October 1965; Son of John and Erica Warburton; Married Harriet (1 daughter 1 son).

Education: Reading School; Waingel's College; Royal College of Music (Masters classical music composition and piano); King's College London (Doctorate studies).

Non-political career: Pianist, London hotels and restaurants 1987-95; Shop assistant, Our Price Records, King's Road and Selfridges London 1992-94; Cleaner, delivery van driver, sandwich seller office-to-office, carpet cleaner 1993-96; Teacher: Junior department, Royal College of Music 1995-98, Hurlingham and Chelsea School, London 1995-98; Founder, chief executive and chairman: The Music Solution Ltd/Pitch Entertainment Group Ltd 1999-2008, Oflang Partners LLP and Oflang Ltd 2008-15, MyHigh.St Ltd 2012-15; Forex Trader 2007-12.

Political career: Member for Somerton and Frome since 7 May 2015 general election. *Select committees:* Member, European Scrutiny 2016-. Wells Conservative Associations 2009-12: Treasurer, Deputy Chair. *Councils and public bodies:* Chair, Parents Association, Wells Cathedral School.

Political interests: Business, education, arts, culture and media, rural affairs, foreign affairs; India, Japan, USA.

Other: Member: Mensa 1993-, Royal Bath and West Society, Mendip Decorative and Fine Arts Society, Rectory Society, Bow Group, Arts Theatre Club, English Speaking Union, Taxpayers' Alliance, National Trust, Campaign to Protect Rural England, Frome Festival, Frome Society for Local Study, Somerset Historic Buildings Preservation Trust; Member, capital executive committee and commercial working group, Shakespeare Globe Trust 2007-09; Founder, The Pulse 2008-11; Volunteer business mentor, Working Knowledge Group 2011-13; Volunteer advocate, Age UK Somerset 2012-13; Trustee, Ups and Downs Southwest; Royal Society of Arts. Elgar Memorial Prize; United Music Publishers Prize; Octavia Scholarship; Ralph Vaughan Williams Trust Scholarship; Major van Someron Godfrey Prize; Sir Richard Stapley Educational Trust Scholarship; Dartington International Scholarship.

Recreations: Occasional organist at two Somerset churches on the Mendips, keen reader, particularly history, music, politics and finance.

David Warburton MP, House of Commons, London SW1A 0AA
Tel: 020 7219 5229 *Email:* david.warburton.mp@parliament.uk
Constituency: Unit G9, Woodside Court, Dairy House Yard, Sparkford BA22 7LH
Tel: 01373 580500 *Email:* david@davidwarburton.org.uk *Website:* www.davidwarburton.org.uk
Twitter: @DJWarburton

CONSERVATIVE

WARMAN, MATT

Boston and Skegness *(Majority 16,572)*

PPS to Karen Bradley as Secretary of State for Digital, Culture, Media and Sport

Matthew Robert Warman. Born 1 September 1981; Married Rachel.

Education: Salcombe Preparatory School; Haberdashers' Aske's Boys School; Durham University (BA English literature 2004).

Non-political career: Telegraph Media Group: Journalist 1999-15, Writer 2004-09, Consumer Technology Editor 2008-13, Technology Editor (Head of Technology) 2013-15.

Political career: Member for Boston and Skegness since 7 May 2015 general election; Board Member, Parliamentary Office of Science and Technology (POST) 2015-17; PPS to Karen Bradley as Secretary of State for Digital, Culture, Media and Sport 2017-. *Select committees:* Member: Science and Technology 2015-17, Joint Committee on the Draft Investigatory Powers Bill 2015-16.

Matt Warman MP, House of Commons, London SW1A 0AA
Tel: 020 7219 8643 *Email:* matt.warman.mp@parliament.uk
Constituency: 63 Wide Bargate, Boston, Lincolnshire PE21 6SG
Tel: 01205 809110 *Website:* www.mattwarman.co.uk *Twitter:* @mattwarman

CONSERVATIVE

WATLING, GILES

Clacton *(Majority 15,828)*

Giles Francis Watling. Son of late Jack Watling and late Patricia Hicks; Married Vanda (2 daughters).

Non-political career: Actor, in shows including: *Gideon's Way*, *How's Your Father*, *You're Only Young Twice*, *Keep It In The Family*, *Allo Allo*, *Bread*, *Upstairs Downstairs*, *Grange Hill*, *Melissa*, *The Tutankhamun Conspiracy*; Producer and director.

Political career: Contested Clacton 2014 by-election and 2015 general election. Member for Clacton since 8 June 2017. *Select committees:* Member, Digital, Culture, Media and Sport 2017-. *Councils and public bodies:* Tendring District Council: Councillor 2007-, Chair, Education and Skills Committee.

Other: Variety Club's BBC TV Personality of the Year award (1988). Essex Junior Champion Archer.

Recreations: Sailing, horse-riding, scuba-diving.

Giles Watling MP, House of Commons, London SW1A 0AA
Tel: 020 7219 0795 *Email:* giles.watling.mp@parliament.uk
Constituency: 84 Station Road, Clacton-on-Sea CO15 1SP
Tel: 01255 474395 *Email:* giles@gileswatling.co.uk *Website:* www.gileswatling.co.uk
Twitter: @GilesWatling

LABOUR

WATSON, TOM

West Bromwich East *(Majority 7,713)*

Deputy Leader, Labour Party; Shadow Secretary of State for Digital, Culture, Media and Sport

Thomas Anthony Watson. Born 8 January 1967; Son of Anthony Watson, trade union official, and Linda Watson, née Pearce, social worker; Married Siobhan Corby 2000 (separated) (1 son 1 daughter).

Education: King Charles I School, Kidderminster.

Non-political career: Marketing officer, Save the Children 1987-88; Account executive, advertising agency 1988-90; Development officer, Labour Party 1993-97; Political officer, AEEU 1997-2001. Member, AEEU 1995-.

Political career: Member for West Bromwich East 2001-10, for West Bromwich East (revised boundary) since 6 May 2010 general election; PPS to Dawn Primarolo as Paymaster General, HM Treasury 2003-04; Assistant Government Whip 2004-05, 2007-08; Government Whip 2005-06; Parliamentary Under-Secretary of State, Ministry of Defence (Minister for Veterans) 2006; Parliamentary Secretary, Cabinet Office 2008-09; Deputy Leader of the Opposition 2015-; Shadow Minister for the Cabinet Office 2015-16; Shadow Secretary of State for Culture, Media and Sport/Digital, Culture, Media and Sport 2016-. *Select committees:* Member: Home Affairs 2001-03, Culture, Media and Sport 2009-12. Labour Party: National Development Officer (Youth) 1993-97, Member, NEC, Deputy Chair 2011-13, Campaign Co-ordinator 2011-13, Deputy Leader 2015-, Chair 2015-17.

Political interests: Culture, media, manufacturing, digital policy; Australia, Japan, USA.

Other: Fellow, Industry and Parliament Trust 2006; Cystic Fibrosis Trust. Commons Select Committee Member of the Year, *House Magazine* awards 2011; MP of the Year, *PoliticsHome* awards 2012; West Bromwich Labour Club, Friar Park Labour Club.

Publications: Co-author: Votes for All (Fabian Society pamphlet, 2000), Dial M for Murdoch (2012).

Recreations: Supporter West Bromwich Albion FC, gardening, film.

Tom Watson MP, House of Commons, London SW1A 0AA
Tel: 020 7219 8123 *Email:* tom.watson.mp@parliament.uk
Constituency: Terry Duffy House, 1 Thomas Street, West Bromwich, West Midlands B70 6NT
Tel: 0121-569 1904 *Website:* www.tom-watson.com *Twitter:* @tom_watson

LABOUR

WEST, CATHERINE

Hornsey and Wood Green *(Majority 30,738)*

Catherine Elizabeth West. Born 14 September 1966; Married (2 children).

Education: Degree social science and languages; School of Oriental and African Studies (Masters Chinese studies 2004); French, Italian, German, Mandarin.

Non-political career: Teacher of English as a second language, Nanjing, China 1996-97; Caseworker to David Lammy MP 2000-03; Publisher; Local government social worker with asylum seekers. Member: Unite, GMB.

Political career: Member for Hornsey and Wood Green since 7 May 2015 general election; Shadow Minister for Foreign and Commonwealth Office 2015-17. *Select committees:* Member, International Trade 2017-. *Councils and public bodies:* London Borough of Islington Council: Councillor 2000-14, Leader of the Opposition 2004-10, Leader of the Council 2010-13; Chair, London Councils Transport and Environment Committee 2010-14.

Political interests: Housing infrastructure, economy, health, communities, human rights, affordable housing, local government, hospitals, GP provision, mental health, living wage, legal aid, London, education, climate change; Algeria, Australia, Bangladesh, China, Cyprus, Greece, Somalia, Turkey.

Other: Fabian Society. Local Authority Leader of the Year, Local Government Information Unit 2013.

Recreations: Walking, cycling, swimming.

Catherine West MP, House of Commons, London SW1A 0AA
Tel: 020 7219 6141 *Email:* catherine.west.mp@parliament.uk
Constituency: No constituency office publicised *Website:* www.catherinewest.org.uk
Twitter: @CatherineWest1

LABOUR

WESTERN, MATT

Warwick and Leamington *(Majority 1,206)*

Matthew Raymond Western. Married Rebecca Earle.

Education: St Albans School; Bristol University (BSc geography 1984).

Non-political career: Peugeot Motor Company: Fleet Sales Manager 1992-95, Advertising and Media Manager 1997-2002, Manager International Communications Strategy 2002-03, Regional Manager 2003-04, Purchasing Manager 2004-08; Owner, Oxygency 2008-.

Political career: Member for Warwick and Leamington since 8 June 2017. *Select committees:* Member, International Trade 2017-. *Councils and public bodies:* Councillor, Warwickshire County Council 2013-.

Political interests: Housing, transport, education.

Recreations: Cycling.

Matt Western MP, House of Commons, London SW1A 0AA
Tel: 020 7219 2051 *Email:* matt.western.mp@parliament.uk
Constituency: Details still to be confirmed *Twitter:* @MattWestern_

CONSERVATIVE

WHATELY, HELEN

Faversham and Mid Kent *(Majority 17,413)*

PPS to Justine Greening as Secretary of State for Education and Minister for Women and Equalities

Helen Olivia Bicknell Whately. Born 23 June 1976; Married Marcus Whately 2005 (3 children).

Education: Woldingham School; Westminster School (sixth form); Lady Margaret Hall, Oxford (BA philosophy, politics and economics 1998).

Non-political career: Consultant, PricewaterhouseCoopers 1998-2001; AOL Europe: Senior analyst 2001-02, Manager 2003-05, Senior manager 2005-06; Adviser on media/new media to Hugo Swire MP as Shadow Secretary of State for Culture, Media and Sport 2006-07; Consultant, McKinsey & Co 2007-15.

Political career: Contested Kingston and Surbiton 2010 general election. Member for Faversham and Mid Kent since 7 May 2015 general election; PPS to: Greg Hands as Minister of State for Trade and Investment, Department for International Trade 2016-17, Justine Greening as Secretary of State for Education and Minister for Women and Equalities 2017-. *Select committees:* Member: Health 2015-17, Standing Orders 2015-.

Political interests: Housing, NHS.

Recreations: Riding, running, skiing.

Helen Whately MP, House of Commons, London SW1A 0AA
Tel: 020 7219 6472 *Email:* helen.whately.mp@parliament.uk
Constituency: Alexander Centre, Preston Street, Faversham, Kent ME13 8NZ
Website: www.helenwhately.co.uk *Twitter:* @helen_whately

CONSERVATIVE

WHEELER, HEATHER

South Derbyshire *(Majority 11,970)*

Government Whip (Lord Commissioner of HM Treasury)

Heather Kay Wheeler. Born 14 May 1959; Daughter of Mr C.P.C. Wilkinson, retired civil servant, and Mrs F.M. Wilkinson, retired primary teacher; Married Bob Wheeler 1986 (1 daughter).

Education: Grey Coat Hospital Secondary School, London.

Non-political career: Manager, Rics Ins Brokers 1979-87; Company secretary and director, Bretby Inns Ltd 1997-2006; Professional indemnity insurance broker, Lloyd's.

Political career: Contested Coventry South 2001 and 2005 general elections. Member for South Derbyshire since 6 May 2010 general election; PPS to: Jeremy Wright as Attorney General 2014-15, John Whittingdale as Secretary of State for Culture, Media and Sport 2015-16; Assistant Government Whip 2016-17; Government Whip (Lord Commissioner of HM Treasury) 2017-. *Select committees:* Member: Standards and Privileges 2010-13, Communities and Local Government 2011-15, Standards 2013-14, Privileges 2013-14, European Scrutiny 2015-16. Member, Executive, 1922 Committee 2012-14. Various posts, Putney and South Derbyshire Conservative Association 1976-99. *Councils and public bodies:* Councillor, London Borough of Wandsworth Council 1982-86; South Derbyshire District Council: Councillor 1995-2011, Leader, Conservative group 2002-10, Council Leader 2007-10; Vice-President, Local Government Association 2011-16.

Political interests: Affordable housing, economic regeneration; China, Japan, Taiwan.

Other: Trustee, Industry and Parliament Trust 2015- (suspended while Government Whip); Patron, Leaside Singers; Association of Chartered Insurance Institute 1985.

Recreations: Watching sport, DIY, the Archers.

Heather Wheeler MP, House of Commons, London SW1A 0AA
Tel: 020 7219 1184 *Email:* heather.wheeler.mp@parliament.uk
Constituency: Room 1/24, Repton House, Bretby Business Park, Bretby, Derbyshire DE15 0YZ
Tel: 01283 225365 *Email:* heather@heatherwheeler.org.uk *Website:* www.heatherwheeler.org.uk
Twitter: @HeatherWheeler

LABOUR

WHITEHEAD, ALAN

Southampton Test *(Majority 11,503)*

Shadow Minister for Energy and Climate Change

Alan Patrick Vincent Whitehead. Born 15 September 1950; Married Sophie Wronska 1979 (1 son 1 daughter).

Education: Isleworth Grammar School, Middlesex; Southampton University (BA politics and philosophy 1973; PhD political science 1976); French.

Non-political career: Outset: Deputy director 1976-79, Director 1979-83; Director, BIIT 1983-92; Professor of public policy, Southampton Institute 1992-97. Member, Unison (formerly NUPE).

Political career: Contested Southampton Test 1983, 1987 and 1992 general elections. Member for Southampton Test 1997-2010, for Southampton Test (revised boundary) since 6 May 2010 general election; Joint PPS to David Blunkett as Secretary of State for Education and Employment 1999-2000; PPS to Baroness Blackstone as Minister for Education and Employment 1999-2001; Parliamentary Under-Secretary of State, Department for Transport, Local Government and the Regions 2001-02; Shadow Minister for Energy and Climate Change 2015-16, 2016-; Board Member, Parliamentary Office of Science and Technology (POST) 2015-. *Select committees:* Member: Environment, Transport and Regional Affairs 1997-99, Environment, Transport and Regional Affairs (Environment Sub-committee) 1997-99, Constitutional Affairs/Justice 2003-10, Standards and Privileges 2005-13, Joint Committee on the Draft Climate Change Bill 2007, Energy and Climate Change 2009-15 Environmental Audit 2010-15, 2016, Standards 2013-15, Privileges 2013-15. Chair: PLP Departmental Committee for Local Government 1998-2001, PLP Departmental Group for Energy and Climate Change 2010-15; Vice-chair, PLP Departmental Group for Environment, Food and Rural Affairs 2010-15. Member, Labour Party National Policy Forum 1999-2001, 2010-; Chair, Manifesto Group Local Government 2007-; Sustainable Communities Policy Commission, National Policy Forum. *Councils and public bodies:* Southampton City Council: Councillor 1980-92, Leader 1984-92.

Political interests: Environment, local and regional government, higher education, education, constitution, transport, energy; France, Lithuania, Poland.

Other: Director/board member: Southampton Environment Centre, Third Age Centre, Southampton. Visiting professor, Southampton Institute 1997-.

Recreations: Football (playing and watching), writing, tennis.

Dr Alan Whitehead MP, House of Commons, London SW1A 0AA
Tel: 020 7219 5517 *Fax:* 020 7219 0918 *Email:* whiteheada@parliament.uk
Constituency: Unit 39, Basepoint Centres, Anderson's Road, Southampton SO14 5FE
Tel: 023 8068 2086 *Email:* alan@alan-whitehead.org.uk *Website:* www.alan-whitehead.org.uk
alansenergyblog.wordpress.com *Twitter:* @alanwhiteheadmp

LABOUR

WHITFIELD, MARTIN

East Lothian *(Majority 3,083)*

Martin David Whitfield.

Non-political career: Personal Injury Lawyer; Teacher, Prestonpans Primary School.

Political career: Member for East Lothian since 8 June 2017. *Select committees:* Member, Science and Technology 2017-. *Councils and public bodies:* Chair, Prestonpans Community Council.

Other: Member, General Teaching Council of Scotland.

Martin Whitfield MP, House of Commons, London SW1A 0AA
Tel: 020 7219 2510 *Email:* martin.whitfield.mp@parliament.uk
Constituency: 65 High Street, Tranent EH33 1LN
Tel: 01875 824779 *Twitter:* @MartWhitfieldMP

SCOTTISH NATIONAL PARTY

WHITFORD, PHILIPPA

Central Ayrshire *(Majority 1,267)*

SNP Spokesperson for Health

Born 24 December 1958; Married Hans 1987 (1 son).

Education: Glasgow University (MB ChB 1982; MD 1991); German.

Non-political career: Medical volunteer in Gaza and Lebanon 1991-93; Senior registrar, Aberdeen Royal Infirmary 1994-96; Consultant breast surgeon, Crosshouse Hospital 1996-2014; Lead Clinician: Ayrshire and Arran Health Board 1996-2010, West of Scotland Managed Clinical Network 2006-09; Locum consultant breast cancer surgeon, Ayrshire and Arran Health Board 2015-.

Political career: Member for Central Ayrshire since 7 May 2015 general election; SNP Spokesperson for Health 2015-. *Select committees:* Member, Health 2015-17.

Political interests: NHS and health, breast cancer, Trident; Palestine.

Other: Chair, breast cancer project groups, Clinical Standards Board for Scotland.

Dr Philippa Whitford MP, House of Commons, London SW1A 0AA
Tel: 020 7219 8158 *Email:* philippa.whitford.mp@parliament.uk
Constituency: 14 Eglinton Street, Irvine KA12 8AS
Tel: 01294 311160 *Website:* whitford.scot *Twitter:* @Dr_PhilippaW

CONSERVATIVE

WHITTAKER, CRAIG

Calder Valley *(Majority 609)*

Assistant Government Whip

Born 30 August 1962; Son of late Frank Whittaker and Marjorie Whittaker; Divorced (1 son 2 daughters).

Education: Belmont High School, New South Wales, Australia; Tighes Hill College, New South Wales, Australia.

Non-political career: Armed Forces Parliamentary Scheme 2010-11. Director, Kezdem PTY Ltd, New South Wales, Australia 1991; Branch manager, Wilkinsons Home and Garden Stores 1992-98; General manager, PC World Dixons Store Group 1998-2009.

Political career: Member for Calder Valley since 6 May 2010 general election; PPS to: James Brokenshire as Minister for Immigration, Home Office 2015-16, Karen Bradley as Secretary of State for Culture, Media and Sport 2016-17; Assistant Government Whip 2017-. *Select committees:* Member: Education 2010-15, Unopposed Bills (Panel) 2011-15, Joint Committee on the Draft Communications Data Bill 2012-13, Joint Committee on Able Marine Energy Park Development Consent Order 2014 2014-15. Constituency agent 2005 general election; Chair, Calder Valley Conservative Association 2005-06; Founding member, Conservatives for Reform in Europe 2016. *Councils and public bodies:* Councillor, Heptonstall Parish Council 1998-2003; Calderdale Metropolitan Borough Council: Councillor 2003-04, 2007-11, Cabinet member, Children and Young Peoples Services 2007-10.

Political interests: Education, children, aged care; Australia, Kenya, New Zealand, Tanzania.

Other: Member, Executive Committee, Commonwealth Parliamentary Association (UK Branch) 2014-15; Treasurer, Heptonstall Festival Committee 1996-2000; Chair, TLC (Together for Looked-After Children) 2010-.

Publications: Co-author, Freedom, Responsibility and the State: Curbing Over-Mighty Government (Politeia, 2012).

Recreations: Sailing, reading.

Craig Whittaker MP, House of Commons, London SW1A 0AA
Tel: 020 7219 7031 *Fax:* 020 7219 1054 *Email:* craig.whittaker.mp@parliament.uk
Constituency: Unit 7 Brookfoot Business Park, Elland Road, Brighouse, West Yorkshire HD6 2SD
Tel: 01484 711260 *Fax:* 01484 718288 *Email:* office@craigwhittakermp.co.uk
Website: www.craigwhittakermp.co.uk *Twitter:* @CWhittakerMP

CONSERVATIVE

WHITTINGDALE, JOHN

Maldon *(Majority 23,430)*

John Flasby Lawrance Whittingdale. Born 16 October 1959; Son of late John Whittingdale and Margaret Whittingdale; Married Ancilla Murfitt 1990 (divorced 2008) (1 son 1 daughter).

Education: Winchester College; University College, London (BSc economics 1982).

Non-political career: Head of Political Section, Conservative Research Department 1982-84; Special Sdviser to Secretaries of State for Trade and Industry 1984-87: Norman Tebbit MP, Leon Brittan MP and Paul Channon MP; Manager, N M Rothschild & Sons 1987; Political Secretary to Margaret Thatcher MP as Prime Minister 1988-90; Private Secretary to Margaret Thatcher MP 1990-92.

Political career: Member for South Colchester and Maldon 1992-97, for Maldon and Chelmsford East 1997-2010, for Maldon since 6 May 2010 general election; PPS to Eric Forth as Minister of State for: Education 1994-95, Education and Employment 1994-96; Opposition Whip 1997-98; Opposition Spokesperson for the Treasury 1998-99; PPS to William Hague as Leader of Opposition 1999-2001; Shadow Secretary of State for: Trade and Industry 2001-02, Culture, Media and Sport 2002-03, 2004-05, Agriculture, Fisheries and Food 2003-04; Secretary of State for Culture, Media and Sport 2015-16. *Select committees:* Member: Health 1993-97, Information 1997-98, Trade and Industry 2001; Chair, Culture, Media and Sport 2005-15; Member, Liaison 2005-15; Joint Committee on Privacy and Injunctions: Member 2011, Chair 2011-12; Member, Exiting the European Union 2016-. 1922 Committee: Member, Executive 2005-06, Vice-chair 2006-15. Member: 92 Group, No Turning Back Group; Member: Executive, Conservative Way Forward 2005-10, Conservative Party Board 2006-10.

Political interests: Broadcasting and media; Armenia, China, Georgia, Israel, Japan, Korea, Malaysia, Russia, Ukraine, USA.

Other: Member, Executive Committee, Inter-Parliamentary Union, British Group 2010-15, 2016-; Fellow: Industry and Parliament Trust 1996, Royal Society of Arts 2008-; Council Member, Freedom Association 2008-15; Member, Campaign committee, Vote Leave 2016; Consultant, Authors Licensing and Collecting Society 2017-; Member, advisory board, SWNS Media Group 2017-. Inquisitor of the Year, *The Spectator* awards 2011. OBE 1990; PC 2015; Essex Club. Captain, House of Commons Rifle Team 2010-15.

Publications: New Policies for the Media (1995).

Recreations: Cinema, music.

Rt Hon John Whittingdale OBE MP, House of Commons, London SW1A 0AA
Tel: 020 7219 3557 *Fax:* 020 7219 2522 *Email:* john.whittingdale.mp@parliament.uk
Constituency: 19 High Street, Maldon, Essex CM9 5PE
Tel: 01621 855663 *Email:* m.c.c.a@btconnect.com *Website:* www.johnwhittingdale.org.uk
Twitter: @Jwhittingdale

CONSERVATIVE

WIGGIN, BILL

North Herefordshire *(Majority 21,602)*

William David Wiggin. Born 4 June 1966; Son of Sir Jerry Wiggin (MP for Weston-super-Mare 1969-97) and Mrs Rosie Dale Harris; Married Camilla Chilvers 1999 (2 sons 1 daughter).

Education: Eton College; University College of North Wales (BA economics 1988).

Non-political career: Trader, UBS 1991-93; Associate director, currency options sales, Dresdner Kleinwort Benson 1994-98; Manager, structured products, Commerzbank 1998-2001; Managing director, Emerging Asset Management Ltd 2015-.

Political career: Contested Burnley 1997 general election. Member for Leominster 2001-10, for North Herefordshire since 6 May 2010 general election; Shadow Minister for Environment, Food and Rural Affairs 2003, 2005-09; Shadow Secretary of State for Wales 2003-05; Opposition Whip 2009-10; Assistant Government Whip 2010-12. *Select committees:* Member: Welsh Affairs 2001-03, Transport, Local Government and the Regions 2001-02, Environment, Food and Rural Affairs 2002-05, Liaison 2015-; Chair, Selection 2015-. Secretary, Conservative Agricultural/Rural Affairs Policy Committee 2001-03; Member, Executive, 1922 Committee 2002-03, 2015-. Contested North West region 1999 European Parliament election. Vice-chair, Hammersmith and Fulham Conservative Association 1995-97. *Councils and public bodies:* Governor, Hammersmith and West London College 1995-98.

Political interests: Defence, agriculture, Treasury, environment.

Other: Trustee, Violet Eveson Charitable Trust; Non-executive director: Philip T English International Financial Services Ltd, Allpay Ltd. Goldsmiths' Company. Freedom, City of London; Hurlingham Club, Annabel's Club, Pratt's Club, Rankin Club.

Recreations: Motorcycles, country sports, Hereford cattle.

Bill Wiggin MP, House of Commons, London SW1A 0AA
Tel: 020 7219 8175/020 7219 2394 *Fax:* 020 7219 1893 *Email:* bill.wiggin.mp@parliament.uk
Constituency: North Herefordshire Conservative Association Office, 8 Corn Square, Leominster, Herefordshire HR6 8LR
Tel: 01568 612565 *Fax:* 01568 610320 *Website:* www.billwiggin.com

PLAID CYMRU

WILLIAMS, HYWEL

Arfon *(Majority 92)*

Plaid Cymru Spokesperson Exiting the European Union, International Trade, Work and Pensions and Cabinet Office

Born 14 May 1953; Son of Robert Williams and Jennie Page Williams, shopkeepers; Divorced (3 daughters); married Dr Myfanwy Davies 2010 (1 son 1 daughter).

Education: Glan y Môr School, Pwllheli; University of Wales: Cardiff (BSc psychology 1974), Bangor (CQSW social work 1979); Welsh.

Non-political career: Social Worker: Mid Glamorgan County Council 1974-76, Gwynedd County Council 1976-84; North Wales Social Work Practice Centre, University of Wales, Bangor 1985-94: Project Worker 1985-94, Head of Centre 1991-94; Freelance Lecturer, Consultant and Author social work and social policy 1994-2001. Member: NALGO 1974-84, NUPE 1974-84, UCAC 1984-94.

Political career: Member for Caernarfon 2001-10, for Arfon since 6 May 2010 general election; Plaid Cymru Spokesperson for: Work and Pensions 2001-, Health 2001-15, 2016-17, Disability 2001-05, International Development 2004-17, Culture, Media and Sport 2005-06, 2015-17, Education and Skills/Children, Schools and Families 2005-10, Treasury 2006-07, Defence 2007-09, 2015-17, Transport 2007-09, Cabinet Office 2010-15, 2016-, Energy and Climate Change 2010-14, Education 2010-15, Foreign and Commonwealth Office 2015-17, Europe 2015-16, Leader, Parliamentary Group 2015-17, Spokesperson for: Exiting the European Union 2017-, International Trade 2017-. *Select committees:* Member: European Standing Committee B 2002-04, Welsh Affairs 2004-05, 2014, Chairmen's Panel/Panel of Chairs 2005-15, Science and Technology 2012-14, Works of Art 2012-, Exiting the European Union 2017-. Contested Clwyd South constituency 1999 National Assembly for Wales election. Plaid Cymru: Policy developer (social security and policy for older people) 1999-2001, Policy cabinet 1999-2001.

Political interests: Social affairs, social security, social work, language issues, international development; France, Turkey.

Publications: Geirfa Gwaith Cymdeithasol/A Social Work Vocabulary (University of Wales Press, 1988); General editor Geirfa Gwaith Plant/Child Care Terms (UWP, 1993); Gwaith Cymdeithasol a'r Iaith Gymraeg/Social Work and the Welsh Language (UWP/CCETSW); Llawlyfr Hyfforddi a Hyfforddwyr/An Index of Trainers and Training (AGWC, 1994); Gofal – Pecyn Adnoddau a Hyfforddi Gofal yn y Gymuned yng Nghymru/A Training and Resource Pack for Community Care in Wales (CCETSW Cymru, 1998).

Recreations: Reading, walking, cooking.

Hywel Williams MP, House of Commons, London SW1A 0AA
Tel: 020 7219 8150 *Email:* hywel.williams.mp@parliament.uk
Constituency: 8 Castle Street, Caernarfon, Gwynedd LL55 1SE
Tel: 01286 672076
70 High Street, Bangor, Gwynedd LL57 1NR
Tel: 01248 372948 *Twitter:* @HywelPlaidCymru

LABOUR

WILLIAMS, PAUL

Stockton South *(Majority 888)*

Paul Daniel Williams. Born 23 August 1972; Son of William and Susan Ann Williams (née Burtenshaw); Partner Vicky (2 daughters).

Education: Queens School, Wisbech; Neale Wade Community College, March; Newcastle University (Medicine and Surgery 1996); Newcastle University (Masters, Health Sciences, Public Health 2004).

Non-political career: GP, Arrival Practice 2002-06; Medical Superintendent, Bwindi Community Hospital, Uganda 2006-10; GP: A&B Medical Practice 2012-15, Tennant Street Medical Practice 2015-17; Chief Executive, Hartlepool and Stockton-on-Tees GP Federation 2015-17. GMB.

Political career: Member for Stockton South since 8 June 2017. *Select committees:* Member, Health 2017-.

Political interests: Health, international development; Kashmir, South Africa, Uganda.

Other: Governing Body Member, Hartlepool and Stockton-on-Tees Clinical Commissioning Group 2012-16; Board Member: Catalyst 2012-17, Arc (Stockton Arts Centre) 2011-17; Patron, Justice First 2006-; Member, Royal College of General Practitioners. Cleveland Wheelers; Cleveland Triathlon Club.

Recreations: Cycling, swimming, running, triathlon, live music.

Dr Paul Williams MP, House of Commons, London SW1A 0AA
Tel: 020 7219 0372 *Email:* paul.williams.mp@parliament.uk
Constituency: Details still to be confirmed
Tel: 01642 345291 *Email:* office@paulwilliamsmp.co.uk *Twitter:* @PaulWilliamsMP

LABOUR

WILLIAMSON, CHRIS

Derby North *(Majority 2,015)*

Shadow Minister for Fire and Emergency Services

Christopher Williamson. Born 16 September 1956; Son of late George and Eileen Williamson.

Education: Castle Donington High School; Sir Thomas More School, Allenton; Leicester Polytechnic (CQSW).

Non-political career: Bricklayer 1973-78; Market trader 1978-79; Social worker 1981-87; Welfare rights officer 1987-2002.

Political career: Member for Derby North 2010-15. Contested Derby North 2015 general election. Member for Derby North since 8 June 2017; Shadow Minister for: Communities and Local Government 2010-13, Home Office (Fire and Emergency Services) 2017-. *Select committees:* Member: Communities and Local Government 2010, 2013-15, Joint Committee on the Draft Protection of Charities Bill 2014-15. Member, Labour Party 1976-. *Councils and public bodies:* Derby City Council: Councillor 1991-2011, Council Leader; Member: General Assembly, Local Government Association 2006-10, State of the City Forum, Derby City Partnership 2009-10.

Political interests: Poverty, animal welfare, urban regeneration, environment, climate change, local government community empowerment; Cuba, Ecuador, Scandinavian countries, Venezuela.

Other: League Against Cruel Sports: Member 1976-, Chair 1984-94, Trustee.

Recreations: Cycling, walking, watching Derby County.

Chris Williamson MP, House of Commons, London SW1A 0AA
Tel: 020 7219 3000 *Email:* chris.williamson.mp@parliament.uk
Constituency: 9a Theatre Walk, Eagle Centre, Derby DE1 2NG
Tel: 01332 343261 *Twitter:* @DerbyChrisW

CONSERVATIVE

WILLIAMSON, GAVIN

South Staffordshire *(Majority 22,733)*

Chief Whip; Parliamentary Secretary to the Treasury

Gavin Alexander Williamson. Born 25 June 1976; Married Joanne (2 daughters).

Education: Raincliffe Comprehensive School; Bradford University (BSc social sciences 1997).

Non-political career: Businessman; Managing director, architecture design company; Ran and owned a pottery company.

Political career: Contested Blackpool North and Fleetwood 2005 general election. Member for South Staffordshire since 6 May 2010 general election; PPS to Hugo Swire as Minister of State, Northern Ireland Office 2011-12; Acting PPS to Owen Paterson as Secretary of State for Northern Ireland July-September 2012; PPS: to Patrick McLoughlin as Secretary of State for Transport 2012-13, to David Cameron as Prime Minister 2013-16; Chief Whip; Parliamentary Secretary to the Treasury 2016-; Member Parliamentary and Political Service Honours Committee 2016-. *Select committees:* Member, Northern Ireland Affairs 2010-11. Former chair, Conservative Students; Deputy chair, Staffordshire Conservatives; Chair, Stoke-on-Trent Conservative Association; Vice-chair, Derbyshire Dales Conservative Association. *Councils and public bodies:* Councillor, North Yorkshire County Council 2001-05; Governor, St Thomas More RC Primary School.

Political interests: Manufacturing and industry, design, Ministry of Defence, Commonwealth affairs, green belt, fair funding for schools; China, Japan, Korea, Sierra Leone.

Other: Member, British Irish Parliamentary Assembly; Executive member, Commonwealth Parliamentary Association; Patron: South Staffordshire Community and Voluntary Action, World Owl Trust. PC 2015; CBE 2016.

Recreations: Pottery, time with family, books, architecture, cars.

Rt Hon Gavin Williamson CBE MP, House of Commons, London SW1A 0AA
Tel: 020 7219 7150 *Email:* gavin.williamson.mp@parliament.uk
Constituency: Jubilee House, 59 Wolverhampton Road, Codsall, South Staffordshire, Staffordshire WV8 1PL
Tel: 01902 846616 *Email:* gavin@gavinwilliamson.org *Website:* www.gavinwilliamson.org
Twitter: @GavinWilliamson

LABOUR

WILSON, PHIL

Sedgefield *(Majority 6,059)*

Philip Wilson. Born 31 May 1959; Son of late Ivy and late Bernard Wilson; Married Kerrin Smith 2016.

Education: Trimdon Secondary Modern; Sedgefield Comprehensive School.

Non-political career: Shop assistant; Civil Service clerical worker; Aide to Tony Blair MP 1987-94; Researcher to Stephen Hughes MEP 1989; Labour Party organiser and assistant general secretary 1994-99; Public relations consultant: Brunswick 1999-2002, Fellows Associates 2002-07. Member: USDAW 1977-78, CPSA 1978-87, TGWU 1986-, GMB 1994-.

Political career: Member for Sedgefield 19 July 2007 by-election to 2010, for Sedgefield (revised boundary) since 6 May 2010 general election; PPS: to Vernon Coaker as Minister of State: Home Office 2008-09, Department for Children, Schools and Families 2009, to Andy Burnham as Secretary of State for Health 2009-10; Opposition Whip 2010-15. *Select committees:* Member: Public Accounts 2007-10, Regulatory Reform 2007-10, North East 2009-10, Panel of Chairs 2015-, Defence 2015-. Hon. secretary/treasurer, PLP Northern Regional Group 2007-10. Chair: Labour Yes 2015-16, PLP Labour In group 2016.

Political interests: Regional development, sustainable communities, education; USA.

Recreations: Reading, jazz, history.

Phil Wilson MP, House of Commons, London SW1A 0AA
Tel: 020 7219 4966 *Email:* phil.wilson.mp@parliament.uk
Constituency: 4 Beveridge Walkway, Newton Aycliffe, Co Durham DL5 4EE
Tel: 01325 321603 *Email:* trippettp@parliament.uk *Twitter:* @PhilWilsonMP

DEMOCRATIC UNIONIST PARTY

WILSON, SAMMY

East Antrim *(Majority 15,923)*

DUP Spokesperson for Exiting the European Union, Treasury and Work and Pensions

Samuel Wilson. Born 4 April 1953; Son of Alexander and Mary Wilson.

Education: Methodist College, Belfast; Queen's University, Belfast (BA economics and politics 1975); Stranmillis College, Belfast (DipEd 1976).

Non-political career: Head of economics, Grosvenor Grammar School, Belfast 1975-83.

Political career: Contested Strangford 1992 and East Antrim 2001 general elections. Member for East Antrim 2005-10, for East Antrim (revised boundary) since 6 May 2010 general election; DUP Spokesperson for: Education and Skills 2003-07, Housing 2005-07, Communities and Local Government 2007-09, Children, Schools and Families 2007-10, Innovation, Universities and Skills 2007-09, Treasury 2009-, Education 2010-12, 2015-17, Work and Pensions 2015-, Exiting the European Union 2017-. *Select committees:* Member: Northern Ireland Affairs 2005-09, Transport 2009, Exiting the European Union 2016-. Northern Ireland Assembly: Member Northern Ireland Forum for Political Dialogue 1996, MLA for Belfast East 1998-2003, for East Antrim 2003-11, and for East Antrim (revised boundary) 2011 to 29 July 2015: Education Committee: Deputy chair 1999-2003, Chair 2007-08; Minister of: Environment 2008-09, Finance and Personnel 2009-13. DUP press officer 1982-96. *Councils and public bodies:* East Belfast City Council: Councillor 1981-2010, Lord Mayor 1986-87, 2000-01; Member, Northern Ireland Policing Board 2001-06.

Political interests: Social issues, policing, education; America, China.

Publications: The Carson Trail (1982); The Unionist Case – The Forum Report Answered (1984); Data Response Questions in Economics (1995).

Recreations: Gardening, motorbikes.

Sammy Wilson MP, House of Commons, London SW1A 0AA
Tel: 020 7219 8523 *Fax:* 020 7219 3671 *Email:* barronj@parliament.uk
Constituency: East Antrim DUP, 116 Main Street, Larne, Co Antrim BT40 1RG
Tel: 028 2826 7722 *Twitter:* @eastantrimmp

LABOUR

WINTERTON, ROSIE

Doncaster Central *(Majority 10,131)*

Second Deputy Chairman of Ways and Means and Deputy Speaker

Rosalie Winterton. Born 10 August 1958; Daughter of late Gordon and Valerie Winterton, teachers.

Education: Doncaster Grammar School; Hull University (BA history 1979).

Non-political career: Member, Armed Forces Parliamentary Scheme. Constituency personal assistant to John Prescott MP 1980-86; Parliamentary officer: Southwark Council 1986-88, Royal College of Nursing 1988-90; Managing director, Connect Public Affairs 1990-94; Head of private office, John Prescott MP as Deputy Leader of Labour Party 1994-97. Transport and General Workers' Union: Branch officer 1998-99, Chair, Parliamentary Group 1998-99; Member, Unite.

Political career: Member for Doncaster Central 1997-2010, for Doncaster Central (revised boundary) since 6 May 2010 general election; Parliamentary Secretary, Lord Chancellor's Department 2001-03; Minister of State: Department of Health 2003-07, Department for Transport 2007-08; Minister for Yorkshire and the Humber 2008-10; Minister of State: (Pensions and the Ageing Society), Department for Work and Pensions 2008-09, (Regional Economic Development and Coordination) Departments for Business, Innovation and Skills and for Communities and Local Government 2009-10; Member, Speaker's Committee on the Electoral Commission 2009-10; Shadow Leader of the House of Commons and Lord Privy Seal 2010; Shadow Minister for Women 2010; Member: House of Commons Commission 2010, 2016-, Speaker's Committee for the Independent Parliamentary Standards Authority 2010-11; Opposition Chief Whip 2010-16; Member, Parliamentary and Political Service Honours Committee 2012-16; Second Deputy Chairman of Ways and Means and Deputy Speaker 2017-. *Select committees:* Member: Transport Bill January 2000, Finance Bill April 2000, Liaison 2016-17; Chair, Finance 2016-17; Member, Panel of Chairs 2017-. Led Labour Party's work on the Boundary Review 2015-16; Labour Party envoy to the Party of European Socialists 2016-.

Political interests: Regional policy, employment, transport, housing, home affairs.

Other: Member, UK delegation, Parliamentary Assembly of the Council of Europe 2016-; Member, Amnesty International; Patron: Doncaster Housing for Young People (DHYP), Darts Doncaster Community Arts, South Yorkshire Centre for Inclusive Living (SYCIL). PC 2006; DBE 2016; Doncaster Trades and Labour Club, Intake Social Club, Doncaster Catholic Club. Green Wyvern Sailing Club.

Recreations: Sailing, reading.

Rt Hon Dame Rosie Winterton DBE MP, House of Commons, London SW1A 0AA
Tel: 020 7219 3000 *Email:* rosie.winterton.mp@parliament.uk
Constituency: Doncaster Trades, 19 South Mall, Frenchgate, Doncaster, South Yorkshire DN1 1LL
Tel: 01302 326297 *Fax:* 01302 342921 *Website:* www.rosiewinterton.co.uk

SCOTTISH NATIONAL PARTY

WISHART, PETE

Perth and North Perthshire *(Majority 21)*

SNP Shadow Leader of the House of Commons; Spokesperson for Constitution; Chair, Select Committee on Scottish Affairs

Peter Wishart. Born 9 March 1962; Son of late Alex Wishart, former dockyard worker, and Nan Irvine, retired teacher; Married Carrie Lindsay 1990 (separated 2003) (1 son).

Education: Queen Anne High School, Dunfermline; Moray House College of Education (Dip CommEd 1984).

Non-political career: Musician, Big Country 1981; Community worker, Central Region 1984-85; Musician, Runrig 1985-2001. Member, Musicians' Union 1985-.

Political career: Member for North Tayside 2001-05, for Perth and North Perthshire since 5 May 2005 general election; SNP: Chief Whip 2001-07, 2013-15, Spokesperson for: Transport 2001-05, Rural Affairs 2001-05, Culture, Media and Sport 2001-15, Constitution 2005-07, 2012-15, 2017-, Overseas Aid 2005-07, Home Affairs 2007-15, Justice 2007-15, International Development 2007-10, Shadow Leader of the House of Commons 2015-; Member: Speaker's Committee on the Electoral Commission 2015-17, Speaker's Committee for the Independent Parliamentary Standards Authority 2015-; SNP MP Group Secretary 2017-. *Select committees:* Member: Catering 2004-05, Administration 2005-08; Scottish Affairs: Member 2009-10, Chair 2015-; Member: Works of Art 2011-12, Liaison 2015-. SNP: Member: National Council 1997-, NEC 1999-2006, Executive vice-convener, fundraising 1999-2001, Group executive member 2015-.

Political interests: Arts and culture, international development, justice and equality; Southern Africa, Germany, Scandinavia.

Other: Member, Executive Committee, Commonwealth Parliamentary Association (UK Branch) 2014-15; Director, Fast Forward Positive Lifestyle 1992-2001; Campaign Committee, Scotland Against Drugs 1997-99.

Recreations: Music, hill-walking, travel, member parliamentary rockband 'MP4'.

Pete Wishart MP, House of Commons, London SW1A 0AA
Tel: 020 7219 8303 *Email:* pete.wishart.mp@parliament.uk
Constituency: 17-19 Leslie Street, Blairgowrie, Perthshire PH10 6AH
Tel: 01250 876576
63 Glasgow Road, Perth, Perthshire PH2 0PE
Tel: 01738 639598 *Website:* www.petewishartmp.com *Twitter:* @PeteWishart

CONSERVATIVE

WOLLASTON, SARAH

Totnes *(Majority 13,477)*

Chair, Select Committee on Health

Born 17 February 1962; Married Adrian (1 son 2 daughters).

Education: Tal Handaq Service Children's School, Malta; Watford Grammar School for Girls; Guys Hospital Medical School (BSc pathology 1983; MB 1986).

Non-political career: Forensic medical examiner, police 1996-2001; GP, Chagford Health Centre 1999-2010; Trainer, Peninsula Medical School 2001-10; Teacher, Exeter Postgraduate Centre -2010; Examiner, Royal College of General Practitioners.

Political career: Member for Totnes since 6 May 2010 general election. *Select committees:* Health: Member 2010-14, Chair 2014-; Member: Joint Committee on the Draft Care and Support Bill 2013, Liaison 2014-.

Political interests: NHS, alcohol related problems, obesity, bovine TB, rural communities.

Other: Patron, Devon Rape Crisis Centre; Member, Royal College of General Practitioners 1992; Fellow, Higher Education Academy 2007; Children and Families in Grief. Backbencher of the Year, *Spectator* Awards 2014; Parliamentarian of the Year, Political Studies Association Awards 2015.

Recreations: Cross-country running, tandeming.

Dr Sarah Wollaston MP, House of Commons, London SW1A 0AA
Tel: 020 7219 5129 *Fax:* 020 7219 5019 *Email:* sarah.wollaston.mp@parliament.uk
Constituency: Constituency Office, Station Road, Totnes, Devon TQ9 5HW
Tel: 01803 868378 *Fax:* 01803 868378 *Email:* nina.smith@parliament.uk
Website: www.drsarah.org.uk *Twitter:* @sarahwollaston

CONSERVATIVE

WOOD, MIKE

Dudley South *(Majority 7,730)*

Team PPS, Department for International Trade

Michael Jon Wood. Born 17 March 1976; Married Laura (1 daughter 1 son).

Education: Old Swinford Hospital School; University of Wales, Aberystwyth (BScEcon economics and law 1997); Cardiff University (Postgraduate Diploma Bar Vocational Course 1999).

Non-political career: Assistant to Earl of Stockton MEP, Brussels 1999-2002; Policy adviser, internal market legislation and environmental regulation, European Parliament 2002-06; Senior researcher, JDS Associates 2006-08; Constituency organiser, Stourbridge, Halesowen and Rowley Regis 2009-10; Caseworker to Andrew Griffiths MP 2010-11; Parliamentary assistant to James Morris MP 2011-14.

Political career: Member for Dudley South since 7 May 2015 general election; Team PPS, Department for International Trade 2017-. *Select committees:* Member, European Scrutiny 2016-. *Councils and public bodies:* Dudley Metropolitan Borough Council: Councillor 2014-16, Spokesperson for Finance; School governor.

Other: Member, UK delegation, Parliamentary Assembly of the Council of Europe 2015-.

Mike Wood MP, House of Commons, London SW1A 0AA
Tel: 020 7219 6982 *Email:* mikej.wood.mp@parliament.uk
Constituency: 111a High Street, Wordsley, Stourbridge DY8 5QR
Tel: 01384 913123 *Email:* mike@mikewood.mp *Website:* www.mikewood.mp
Twitter: @mikejwood

LAB/CO-OP

WOODCOCK, JOHN

Barrow and Furness *(Majority 209)*

John Zak Woodcock. Born 14 October 1978; Married Mandy Telford (2 daughters).

Education: Tapton Secondary School, Sheffield; Edinburgh University (MA English literature and history).

Non-political career: Journalist, *Scotsman*; Head, safeguarding vulnerable people, Crime and Policing Group, Home Office 2003-07; Special adviser: to John Hutton MP: as Chancellor of the Duchy of Lancaster and Minister for the Cabinet Office 2005, as Secretary of State for Work and Pensions 2005-07, as Secretary of State for Business, Enterprise and Regulatory Reform 2007-08, to Gordon Brown MP as Prime Minister (on political press issues) 2009.

Political career: Member for Barrow and Furness since 6 May 2010 general election; Shadow Minister for: Transport 2010-13, Education 2015. *Select committees:* Member: Defence 2010, 2013-15, Arms Export Controls 2010. PLP Departmental Group for Defence: Vice-chair 2010-11, Chair 2015-. Former chair, Labour Friends of Israel. *Councils and public bodies:* Governor, Walney School.

Political interests: Civil nuclear power, manufacturing industry.

Other: Member, UK Delegation, Organisation for Security and Co-operation in Europe Parliamentary Assembly 2014-; Former chair, Progress. Sports Parliamentarian of the Year, Sport and Recreation Alliance 2011.

Publications: Columnist, *PR Week*; Contributor, The Purple Book (Progress, 2011).

Recreations: Barrow Athletic FC, Barrow Raiders RLFC, Sheffield Wednesday FC.

John Woodcock MP, House of Commons, London SW1A 0AA
Tel: 020 7219 7008 *Fax:* 020 7219 0170 *Email:* john.woodcock.mp@parliament.uk
Constituency: 22 Hartington Street, Barrow-in-Furness, Cumbria LA14 5SL
Tel: 01229 431204 *Website:* www.johnwoodcock.org *Twitter:* @JWoodcockMP

CONSERVATIVE

WRAGG, WILLIAM

Hazel Grove *(Majority 5,514)*

William Peter Wragg. Born 11 December 1987.

Education: Poynton High School; Manchester University (BA history 2010); Liverpool John Moores University (PGCE 2013).

Non-political career: Teacher: Hulme Hall Grammer School, 2011-12, St Mary's CofE Primary School 2012-14. Member, Association of Teachers and Lecturers.

Political career: Member for Hazel Grove since 7 May 2015 general election. *Select committees:* Member: Education 2016-, Backbench Business 2016-, Education, Skills and the Economy Sub-committee 2016, Finance 2017-, Procedure 2017-. Member, Executive, 1922 Committee 2016-. Member, Conservative Councillors Association 2011-15; Founding Member, Conservatives for Britain 2015-16. *Councils and public bodies:* Councillor, Stockport Council 2011-15; Governor, Hazel Grove Primary School 2008-15.

Other: Hazel Grove Conservative Club.

William Wragg MP, House of Commons, London SW1A 0AA
Tel: 020 7219 6258
Constituency: 13 Stockport Road, Marple, Stockport SK6 6BD
Tel: 0161-427 0660 *Email:* william@williamwragg.org.uk *Website:* www.williamwragg.org.uk
Twitter: @William_Wragg

CONSERVATIVE

WRIGHT, JEREMY

Kenilworth and Southam *(Majority 18,076)*

Attorney General

Jeremy Paul Wright. Born 24 October 1972; Son of John and Audrey Wright; Married Yvonne Salter 1998 (1 daughter 1 son).

Education: Taunton School, Somerset; Trinity School, New York City, USA; Exeter University (LLB 1995); Inns of Court School of Law (Bar Vocational Course 1996).

Non-political career: Barrister, specialising in criminal law 1996-; Called to the Bar of Northern Ireland 2016.

Political career: Member for Rugby and Kenilworth 2005-10, for Kenilworth and Southam since 6 May 2010 general election; Opposition Whip 2007-10; Government Whip 2010-12; Parliamentary Under-Secretary of State (Minister for Prisons and Rehabilitation), Ministry of Justice 2012-14; Attorney General 2014-. *Select committees:* Member, Constitutional Affairs 2005-07. Chair, Warwick and Leamington Conservative Association 2002-03.

Political interests: Criminal justice, education, foreign affairs, dementia; USA.

Other: PC 2014.

Recreations: Travel, golf, James Bond films.

Rt Hon Jeremy Wright QC MP, House of Commons, London SW1A 0AA
Tel: 020 7219 2008 *Email:* jeremy.wright.mp@parliament.uk
Constituency: Jubilee House, Smalley Place, Kenilworth, Warwickshire CV8 1QG
Tel: 01926 853650 *Fax:* 01926 854615 *Email:* jeremy@jeremywright.org.uk
Website: www.jeremywright.org.uk

LABOUR

YASIN, MOHAMMAD

Bedford *(Majority 789)*

Born 15 October 1971; Married Shakila (4 children).

Non-political career: Private hire driver (Milton Keynes area).

Political career: Member for Bedford since 8 June 2017; *Councils and public bodies:* Bedford Borough Council: Councillor 2006-, Speaker, Portfolio Holder for Adult Services and Housing -2017.

Other: Trustee: Bedford Freemen's Common Charity, Bedford Tree Fund, Mayor of Bedford's Charity.

Mohammad Yasin MP, House of Commons, London SW1A 0AA
Tel: 020 7219 1513 *Email:* mohammad.yasin.mp@parliament.uk
Constituency: 2a Duke Street, Bedford MK40 3HR
Tel: 01234 346525 *Email:* office@mohammadyasin.org *Website:* mohammadyasin.org

CONSERVATIVE

ZAHAWI, NADHIM

Stratford-on-Avon *(Majority 21,958)*

Born 2 June 1967; Married Lana (2 sons 1 daughter).

Education: King's College School, Wimbledon; University College, London (BSc chemical engineering).

Non-political career: European marketing director, Smith and Brooks Ltd; Co-founder and chief executive officer, YouGov 2000-10; Chief strategy officer, Gulf Keystone Petroleum 2015-.

Political career: Contested Erith and Thamesmead 1997 general election. Member for Stratford-on-Avon since 6 May 2010 general election; Prime Minister's Adviser on Apprentices 2015-. *Select committees:* Member: Business, Innovation and Skills 2010-15, Arms Export Controls 2010-15, Joint Committee on Privacy and Injunctions 2011-12, Foreign Affairs 2014-, Speaker's Advisory Committee on Works of Art 2015-. Founding member, 2020 group 2011-; Member, Number 10 Policy Advisory Board (Economic Affairs); Founding member, Conservatives for Reform in Europe 2016. *Councils and public bodies:* Councillor, London Borough of Wandsworth Council 1994-2006; Governor: Chartfield Delicate School 2002-04, Brandlehow Primary School.

Political interests: Business, foreign affairs; Middle East.

Other: Chair: Police Consultative Committee, Putney, Apprenticeship Delivery Board 2015-; Patron, Peace One Day.

Recreations: Horseriding and show jumping.

Nadhim Zahawi MP, House of Commons, London SW1A 0AA
Tel: 020 7219 7159 *Fax:* 020 7219 4462 *Email:* nadhim.zahawi.mp@parliament.uk
Constituency: First Floor, 3 Trinity Street, Stratford-upon-Avon, Warwickshire CV37 6BL
Tel: 01789 264362 *Email:* constituents@zahawi.com *Websites:* www.stratfordconservatives.com www.zahawi.com *Twitter:* @nadhimzahawi

LABOUR

ZEICHNER, DANIEL

Cambridge *(Majority 12,661)*

Daniel Stephen Zeichner. Born 9 November 1956; Partner Barbara.

Education: King's College, Cambridge (history).

Non-political career: Computer programmer, Perkins Engines, Peterborough; Red and Green Nurseries 1983-91; Parliamentary assistant to MP 1992-97; Assistant to MEP 1995-99; National political officer, Unison 2002-15.

Political career: Contested Mid Norfolk 2005 and Cambridge 2010 general elections. Member for Cambridge since 7 May 2015 general election; Shadow Minister for Transport 2015-17. *Select committees:* Member: Science and Technology 2015, Transport 2017-. Member: National Policy Forum, SERA. *Councils and public bodies:* Councillor, South Norfolk Council 1995-2003.

Recreations: Cycling, walking, music, international cinema, gardening.

Daniel Zeichner MP, House of Commons, London SW1A 0AA
Tel: 020 7219 8462 *Email:* daniel.zeichner.mp@parliament.uk
Constituency: Alex Wood Hall, Norfolk Street, Cambridge CB1 2LD
Tel: 01223 500515 *Email:* daniel@danielzeichner.co.uk *Website:* www.danielzeichner.co.uk
Twitter: @DanielZeichner

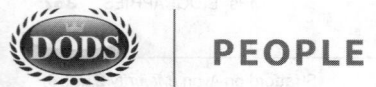

DODS | PEOPLE

FIND YOUR KEY POLITICAL STAKEHOLDERS

Dods People is the contact tool and reference guide to key parliamentarians and their advisers, institutions, and public affairs professionals.

Dods People provides you with an unparalleled service which is updated daily and enables you to:

- View contact details and full biographies of all Members of Parliament, the House of Lords, the Scottish Parliament, the National Assembly for Wales and the Northern Ireland Assembly.
- Search, filter and compile your own list of key parliamentarians for effective communications.
- Download records of your recent contacts.

To find out more visit:
www.dodsinformation.com/dodspeople

ANALYSIS OF MPs 360

MPs' Political Interests 360
MPs' Countries of Interest 386
MPs by UK Regions 396
Constituencies, MPs and Majorities 411
Most Vulnerable Constituencies 424
50 Safest Constituencies 428
Women MPs 430
MPs by Age 435
MPs by Party 442
Committees and Offices 447
Select Committees 447
Officers and Officials 455
Political Offices 461

MPs' Political Interests

For precise details of individuals' stated interests, see relevant biography. The interests listed are supplied by MPs themselves.

Animals

See also:
- Animal health
- Animal rights and welfare

Benefits

See also:
- Benefits payment systems

Business and industry

See also:
- Business
- Economics and finance
- Economy
- Enterprise
- Finance
- Financial services
- Personal finance
- Tax
- Trade

Children and Families

See also:
- Childcare
- Children
- Family

Communities, planning and local government

See also:
- Communities
- Construction industry
- Housing
- Local government
- Planning
- Urban renewal

Culture, media and sport

See also:
- Alcohol licensing
- Architecture
- Arts
- Broadcasting
- Creative industries
- Culture
- Culture, Media and Sport
- Gambling and lotteries
- Heritage
- Media
- Music
- Tourism

Defence and security

See also:
- Armed Forces
- Defence
- Security

Disability

See also:
- Disability equality
- Disability rights
- Disabled children
- Learning disabilities

Education and skills

See also:
- Education
- Further and higher education
- Schools
- Skills
- Student finance

Employment and welfare

See also:
- Employment
- Employment Law
- Employment rights
- Equal opportunities and diversity
- Unemployment and jobseeking
- Welfare

Energy and Utilities

See also:
- Electricity
- Energy
- Energy Industry
- Energy Security
- Energy sources
- Telecommunications

Environment, agriculture and rural affairs

See also:
- Agriculture
- Countryside
- Environment
- Farming
- Fisheries
- Recycling
- Rural affairs
- Rural communities
- Sustainable development
- Waste management

European affairs

See also:
- European Union
- Internal Market
- Justice and Home Affairs
- Regional policy

Government, politics and public administration
See also:
Civil Service
Constitutional Affairs
Democracy and elections
Ireland
Public administration
Scotland

Health, wellbeing and care
See also:
Addiction
Care
Cosmetic surgery
Food and drink
Health
Mental health
National Health Service

Home affairs
See also:
Charities and volunteers
Consumer affairs
Counter-terrorism
Crime
Human rights
Immigration and nationality
Justice system
Law
Police
Prisons
Security
Sentencing
Social affairs
Social inclusion
Social justice
Youth justice

Information and communication
See also:
Communications
Information and communication technology
Intellectual property

International affairs
See also:
Foreign policy
International development and aid
Terrorism
Third World

Religion
See also:
Church Affairs

Science, technology and research
See also:
Biotechnology
Engineering
Research and development
Science
Technology

Transport
See also:
Aviation
Infrastructure
Road safety
Road transport

Abortion

David Amess	*Con*	p67

Academies

Clive Lewis	*Lab*	p231

Addiction

Stephen McPartland	*Con*	p248

Affordable housing

Catherine West	*Lab*	p346
Heather Wheeler	*Con*	p347

Agriculture

Nigel Adams	*Con*	p64
Peter Aldous	*Con*	p65
Victoria Atkins	*Con*	p70
Richard Bacon	*Con*	p70
Henry Bellingham	*Con*	p76
Alistair Burt	*Con*	p97
Alistair Carmichael	*Lib Dem*	p102
Geoffrey Clifton-Brown	*Con*	p110
Geoffrey Cox	*Con*	p116
David Davis	*Con*	p126
David Drew	*Lab/Co-op*	p136
David Duguid	*Con*	p138
Philip Dunne	*Con*	p139
Nigel Evans	*Con*	p146
Nusrat Ghani	*Con*	p163
Robert Goodwill	*Con*	p169
James Gray	*Con*	p172
John Hayes	*Con*	p188
Lindsay Hoyle	*Lab*	p203
Caroline Johnson	*Con*	p210
Daniel Kawczynski	*Con*	p216
Edward Leigh	*Con*	p229
Patrick McLoughlin	*Con*	p246
Caroline Nokes	*Con*	p270
Ian Paisley	*DUP*	p276
Neil Parish	*Con*	p276
Owen Paterson	*Con*	p277
Luke Pollard	*Lab/Co-op*	p284
Julian Smith	*Con*	p313
Nicholas Soames	*Con*	p316
Caroline Spelman	*Con*	p318
Bill Wiggin	*Con*	p350

Airports
Graham Stringer *Lab* p325
Alcohol licensing
John Grogan *Lab* p178
Allergies
Jo Swinson *Lib Dem* p327
Alternative fuels
Fabian Hamilton *Lab* p181
Animal health
Craig Mackinlay *Con* p245
Animal rights and welfare
David Amess *Con* p67
Adrian Bailey *Lab/Co-op* p71
Lisa Cameron *SNP* p100
Ann Clwyd *Lab* p110
Rosie Duffield *Lab* p137
Jim Fitzpatrick *Lab* p152
Paul Flynn *Lab* p154
Roger Gale *Con* p160
Diana Johnson *Lab* p210
Tim Loughton *Con* p237
Caroline Lucas *Green* p238
Neil Parish *Con* p276
Mark Pritchard *Con* p287
Andrew Rosindell *Con* p297
Karl Turner *Lab* p337
Theresa Villiers *Con* p342
Animal welfare
Caroline Lucas *Green* p238
Anti-social behaviour
Liam Byrne *Lab* p98
Nigel Mills *Con* p259
Jessica Morden *Lab* p263
Apprenticeships
Robert Halfon *Con* p180
Stephen Lloyd *Lib Dem* p235
Catherine McKinnell *Lab* p245
Seema Malhotra *Lab/Co-op* p251
Anne Marie Morris *Ind* p264
Guy Opperman *Con* p274
Andrew Stephenson *Con* p320
Architecture
Ed Vaizey *Con* p339
Armed Forces
Andrew Bridgen *Con* p90
Caroline Dinenage *Con* p129
John Glen *Con* p166
Clive Lewis *Lab* p231
Arts
John Bercow *Speaker* p78
Nic Dakin *Lab* p122
Thangam Debbonaire *Lab* p127
Louise Ellman *Lab/Co-op* p143
Patrick Grady *SNP* p170
Helen Hayes *Lab* p188
Sue Hayman *Lab* p189
Kelvin Hopkins *Lab* p201
Greg Knight *Con* p220
David Lammy *Lab* p224
Barry McElduff *Sinn Féin* p243
Alison McGovern *Lab* p244
Robert Neill *Con* p269
Ed Vaizey *Con* p339
David Warburton *Con* p344
Pete Wishart *SNP* p354
Autism
Thangam Debbonaire *Lab* p127
Jonathan Reynolds *Lab/Co-op* p294
Aviation
John McDonnell *Lab* p242
Craig Mackinlay *Con* p245
Seema Malhotra *Lab/Co-op* p251
Nicholas Soames *Con* p316
Andrew Stephenson *Con* p320
Graham Stringer *Lab* p325
Banking and finance
Steve Baker *Con* p72
Mark Garnier *Con* p162
Banking services
Adrian Bailey *Lab/Co-op* p71
Clive Lewis *Lab* p231
Benefits
Gavin Robinson *DUP* p295
Benefits payment systems
Adam Afriyie *Con* p64
Big Society
Jesse Norman *Con* p271
Biotechnology
George Freeman *Con* p157
Bovine TB
Sarah Wollaston *Con* p354
Breast cancer
Philippa Whitford *SNP* p348
Breast cancer screening
Mike Freer *Con* p158
Brewing industry
Ruth Smeeth *Lab* p310
British film
Kevin Barron *Lab* p74
Broadband
Peter Aldous *Con* p65
Lucy Allan *Con* p66
Rory Stewart *Con* p322
Broadcasting
Chris Bryant *Lab* p93
Michael Fabricant *Con* p148

Roger Gale *Con* p160
John Grogan *Lab* p178
Alison McGovern *Lab* p244
John Whittingdale *Con* p349

Building schools for the future

Vicky Foxcroft *Lab* p156

Buses

Graham Stringer *Lab* p325

Business

Nigel Adams *Con* p64
Heidi Allen *Con* p66
Andrew Bridgen *Con* p90
Jo Churchill *Con* p107
James Cleverly *Con* p109
Alberto Costa *Con* p115
Caroline Dinenage *Con* p129
Michael Fabricant *Con* p148
Helen Grant *Con* p171
Gordon Henderson *Con* p192
Nigel Huddleston *Con* p203
Margot James *Con* p206
Jo Johnson *Con* p211
Marcus Jones *Con* p215
Brandon Lewis *Con* p231
Ian Liddell-Grainger *Con* p233
Jonathan Lord *Con* p236
Alan Mak *Con* p250
Seema Malhotra *Lab/Co-op* p251
Nicky Morgan *Con* p263
Wendy Morton *Con* p266
David Mundell *Con* p267
Ian Murray *Lab* p267
Priti Patel *Con* p277
Claire Perry *Con* p281
David Rutley *Con* p300
Julian Smith *Con* p313
Mark Spencer *Con* p318
Justin Tomlinson *Con* p333
Tom Tugendhat *Con* p336
Theresa Villiers *Con* p342
Robin Walker *Con* p343
David Warburton *Con* p344
Nadhim Zahawi *Con* p357

Business and industry

Caroline Dinenage *Con* p129
Chris Elmore *Lab* p144
Michael Fabricant *Con* p148
Michael Gove *Con* p169
Nia Griffith *Lab* p177
David Hanson *Lab* p184
John Hayes *Con* p188
Oliver Heald *Con* p190
Lindsay Hoyle *Lab* p203
Khalid Mahmood *Lab* p249
Owen Paterson *Con* p277
Mark Pawsey *Con* p278
Dominic Raab *Con* p289
Geoffrey Robinson *Lab* p296
Andrew Selous *Con* p302
Alok Sharma *Con* p304
Barry Sheerman *Lab/Co-op* p305
Owen Smith *Lab* p314
Nicholas Soames *Con* p316
Jon Trickett *Lab* p335
Gavin Williamson *Con* p352

Cancer

John Baron *Con* p74
Sharon Hodgson *Lab* p198
Dan Jarvis *Lab* p207
Pauline Latham *Con* p226
Stephen McPartland *Con* p248

Care

Sarah Champion *Lab* p104
John Cryer *Lab* p120
Tim Farron *Lib Dem* p150
Emma Lewell-Buck *Lab* p230
Jonathan Reynolds *Lab/Co-op* p294
Joan Ryan *Lab* p300
Chris Skidmore *Con* p309
Caroline Spelman *Con* p318
Maggie Throup *Con* p332

Care for the disabled

Mims Davies *Con* p126
Dan Jarvis *Lab* p207

Care for the elderly

Mims Davies *Con* p126
Mary Glindon *Lab* p167
Margot James *Con* p206
Dan Jarvis *Lab* p207
Liz Kendall *Lab* p218
Seema Kennedy *Con* p218
Penny Mordaunt *Con* p262
Anne Marie Morris *Ind* p264
Sarah Newton *Con* p270
Dan Poulter *Con* p284
Graham Stuart *Con* p325
Craig Whittaker *Con* p349

Carer's allowance

Gavin Newlands *SNP* p270

Charities and volunteers

Stuart Andrew *Con* p68
Paul Blomfield *Lab* p83
Yvonne Fovargue *Lab* p155
Jeremy Hunt *Con* p204
Susan Elan Jones *Lab* p216
Dan Poulter *Con* p284
Will Quince *Con* p288
Andrew Stephenson *Con* p320

Child poverty

Karen Buck *Lab* p94
Bambos Charalambous *Lab* p105

Martin Docherty-Hughes *SNP* p130
Peter Grant *SNP* p172
Sharon Hodgson *Lab* p198
Dan Jarvis *Lab* p207
Gavin Shuker *Lab/Co-op* p307
Ruth Smeeth *Lab* p310

Child protection

Debbie Abrahams *Lab* p63
Lucy Allan *Con* p66
Adrian Bailey *Lab/Co-op* p71
Emma Lewell-Buck *Lab* p230
Claire Perry *Con* p281

Childcare

Karen Bradley *Con* p86
Caroline Flint *Lab* p153
Harriet Harman *Lab* p185
Sharon Hodgson *Lab* p198

Children

Karen Buck *Lab* p94
Dawn Butler *Lab* p97
Jenny Chapman *Lab* p105
Ann Coffey *Lab* p111
Mary Creagh *Lab* p118
Geraint Davies *Lab/Co-op* p125
Chris Elmore *Lab* p144
Helen Goodman *Lab* p168
Helen Grant *Con* p171
Caroline Johnson *Con* p210
Tim Loughton *Con* p237
Stewart Malcolm McDonald *SNP* p241
Catherine McKinnell *Lab* p245
Jessica Morden *Lab* p263
Lisa Nandy *Lab* p269
Victoria Prentis *Con* p286
Yasmin Qureshi *Lab* p289
Nick Smith *Lab* p314
Craig Whittaker *Con* p349

Children's services

Alex Cunningham *Lab* p121

Church Affairs

Alistair Burt *Con* p97
Frank Field *Lab* p151

Civil Service

Bernard Jenkin *Con* p208

Climate change

Margaret Beckett *Lab* p75
Karen Buck *Lab* p94
Greg Clark *Con* p108
David Davies *Con* p124
Thangam Debbonaire *Lab* p127
Stephen Doughty *Lab/Co-op* p134
Gill Furniss *Lab* p159
Barry Gardiner *Lab* p161
Patrick Grady *SNP* p170
Helen Hayes *Lab* p188
Ian Lavery *Lab* p226
Clive Lewis *Lab* p231
Caroline Lucas *Green* p238
Claire Perry *Con* p281
Dan Poulter *Con* p284
Jonathan Reynolds *Lab/Co-op* p294
Antoinette Sandbach *Con* p301
Graham Stuart *Con* p325
Jo Swinson *Lib Dem* p327
Chuka Umunna *Lab* p339
Catherine West *Lab* p346
Chris Williamson *Lab* p351

Coal

Yvette Cooper *Lab* p114

Commonwealth

Ranil Jayawardena *Con* p208
Ian Lavery *Lab* p226
Gavin Williamson *Con* p352

Communications

Ian Blackford *SNP* p81
Bob Blackman *Con* p81

Communities

Fiona Bruce *Con* p93
Richard Burden *Lab* p95
Nia Griffith *Lab* p177
Nick Hurd *Con* p205
Khalid Mahmood *Lab* p249
Wendy Morton *Con* p266
David Rutley *Con* p300
Chuka Umunna *Lab* p339
Catherine West *Lab* p346

Communities, planning and local government

Hilary Benn *Lab* p76
Richard Burden *Lab* p95
John Grogan *Lab* p178
John Healey *Lab* p190
George Howarth *Lab* p202
Edward Leigh *Con* p229
Mark Prisk *Con* p286
Robert Syms *Con* p328

Community Cohesion

Jon Cruddas *Lab* p120
Robert Halfon *Con* p180
Ruth Smeeth *Lab* p310
Andrew Stephenson *Con* p320

Conservation areas

Nic Dakin *Lab* p122
Mark Pritchard *Con* p287

Constitutional Affairs

Kevin Brennan *Lab* p89
Robert Buckland *Con* p94
Richard Burden *Lab* p95
Tracey Crouch *Con* p119

Wayne David *Lab* p123
Nigel Dodds *DUP* p132
Jeffrey Donaldson *DUP* p132
Michael Ellis *Con* p142
Michael Fallon *Con* p148
George Freeman *Con* p157
Dominic Grieve *Con* p177
David Jones *Con* p213
Eleanor Laing *Con* p222
Norman Lamb *Lib Dem* p223
Mike Penning *Con* p279
Tom Pursglove *Con* p288
John Redwood *Con* p290
Laurence Robertson *Con* p295
Iain Stewart *Con* p321
Robert Syms *Con* p328
Valerie Vaz *Lab* p341
Martin Vickers *Con* p341
Alan Whitehead *Lab* p348

Constitutional reform

John Bercow *Speaker* p78
Geoffrey Cox *Con* p116
Paul Flynn *Lab* p154
Ranil Jayawardena *Con* p208
Owen Smith *Lab* p314

Construction industry

John Spellar *Lab* p317

Consumer affairs

Greg Knight *Con* p220
Justin Tomlinson *Con* p333

Consumer debt

Yvonne Fovargue *Lab* p155

Consumer rights

Sharon Hodgson *Lab* p198
Graham Jones *Lab* p213

Corporate Social Responsibility

Jo Swinson *Lib Dem* p327

Cosmetic surgery

Ann Clwyd *Lab* p110

Counter-terrorism

Mark Pritchard *Con* p287

Countryside

James Gray *Con* p172
Kate Hoey *Lab* p198
George Hollingbery *Con* p199
Dan Jarvis *Lab* p207
David Jones *Con* p213
Laurence Robertson *Con* p295
Keith Simpson *Con* p308
Nicholas Soames *Con* p316

Creative industries

Luciana Berger *Lab/Co-op* p79
Kevin Brennan *Lab* p89
Damian Collins *Con* p112
Patrick Grady *SNP* p170
Wes Streeting *Lab* p324

Crime

Kemi Badenoch *Con* p71
Dawn Butler *Lab* p97
Paul Farrelly *Lab* p149
Tim Farron *Lib Dem* p150
Caroline Flint *Lab* p153
George Freeman *Con* p157
Michael Gove *Con* p169
Adam Holloway *Con* p200
George Howarth *Lab* p202
Susan Elan Jones *Lab* p216
Ivan Lewis *Lab* p232
Maria Miller *Con* p258
Nigel Mills *Con* p259
Toby Perkins *Lab* p281
Yasmin Qureshi *Lab* p289
Ross Thomson *Con* p331

Crime reduction

Joan Ryan *Lab* p300

Culture

Nigel Adams *Con* p64
Luciana Berger *Lab/Co-op* p79
Bambos Charalambous *Lab* p105
Alex Cunningham *Lab* p121
Helen Hayes *Lab* p188
Dan Jarvis *Lab* p207
David Lammy *Lab* p224
Ivan Lewis *Lab* p232
Jonathan Lord *Con* p236
Alison McGovern *Lab* p244
David Warburton *Con* p344
Tom Watson *Lab* p345
Pete Wishart *SNP* p354

Culture, media and sport

Nigel Adams *Con* p64
Clive Betts *Lab* p80
Alun Cairns *Con* p100
Jim Cunningham *Lab* p122
Ivan Lewis *Lab* p232
Jonathan Lord *Con* p236
Penny Mordaunt *Con* p262

Cycling

Nia Griffith *Lab* p177

Debt advice

Bill Cash *Con* p103
Nic Dakin *Lab* p122
Gavin Shuker *Lab/Co-op* p307

Defence

Victoria Atkins *Con* p70
Steve Baker *Con* p72

John Baron *Con* p74
Henry Bellingham *Con* p76
Richard Benyon *Con* p77
Crispin Blunt *Con* p83
Alun Cairns *Con* p100
Sarah Champion *Lab* p104
Geoffrey Cox *Con* p116
David Crausby *Lab* p117
Caroline Dinenage *Con* p129
Martin Docherty-Hughes *SNP* p130
Jeffrey Donaldson *DUP* p132
Stephen Doughty *Lab/Co-op* p134
Richard Drax *Con* p135
Iain Duncan Smith *Con* p139
Tobias Ellwood *Con* p143
Nigel Evans *Con* p146
Michael Fabricant *Con* p148
Liam Fox *Con* p155
Mark Francois *Con* p156
Mike Gapes *Lab/Co-op* p160
Nusrat Ghani *Con* p163
Cheryl Gillan *Con* p165
James Gray *Con* p172
Dominic Grieve *Con* p177
Philip Hammond *Con* p182
Mark Harper *Con* p185
Chris Heaton-Harris *Con* p191
Gordon Henderson *Con* p192
Mark Hendrick *Lab/Co-op* p193
Adam Holloway *Con* p200
Lindsay Hoyle *Lab* p203
Dan Jarvis *Lab* p207
Sajid Javid *Con* p207
Bernard Jenkin *Con* p208
Caroline Johnson *Con* p210
Graham Jones *Lab* p213
Kevan Jones *Lab* p214
Mark Lancaster *Con* p225
Edward Leigh *Con* p229
Julian Lewis *Con* p232
Ian Liddell-Grainger *Con* p233
Jack Lopresti *Con* p236
Conor McGinn *Lab* p243
Alan Mak *Con* p250
Mark Menzies *Con* p256
Andrew Mitchell *Con* p260
Madeleine Moon *Lab* p261
Stephen Morgan *Lab* p264
Andrew Murrison *Con* p268
Mike Penning *Con* p279
Claire Perry *Con* p281
Christopher Pincher *Con* p283
Luke Pollard *Lab/Co-op* p284
Mark Prisk *Con* p286
Mark Pritchard *Con* p287
Jonathan Reynolds *Lab/Co-op* p294
Andrew Rosindell *Con* p297
Bob Seely *Con* p302
Andrew Selous *Con* p302
Keith Simpson *Con* p308
Royston Smith *Con* p315
Nicholas Soames *Con* p316
John Spellar *Lab* p317
Bob Stewart *Con* p321
Rishi Sunak *Con* p326
Ross Thomson *Con* p331
Tom Tugendhat *Con* p336
Derek Twigg *Lab* p337
Robin Walker *Con* p343
Bill Wiggin *Con* p350
Gavin Williamson *Con* p352

Defence and security
Dan Jarvis *Lab* p207

Dementia
Alberto Costa *Con* p115
Mike Freer *Con* p158
Mark Menzies *Con* p256
Andrew Stephenson *Con* p320
Jeremy Wright *Con* p356

Democracy and elections
Zac Goldsmith *Con* p168
John Hayes *Con* p188
Jonathan Reynolds *Lab/Co-op* p294
Andrew Stephenson *Con* p320
Alison Thewliss *SNP* p329

Devolved government
Guto Bebb *Con* p75
Paul Flynn *Lab* p154
Jonathan Reynolds *Lab/Co-op* p294

Diabetes
Pauline Latham *Con* p226

Disability
Alistair Burt *Con* p97
Lisa Cameron *SNP* p100
Rosie Cooper *Lab* p113
Neil Coyle *Lab* p116
Mary Creagh *Lab* p118
Marsha De Cordova *Lab* p128
Martin Docherty-Hughes *SNP* p130
John Hayes *Con* p188
John Healey *Lab* p190
Chris Heaton-Harris *Con* p191
Tim Loughton *Con* p237
Gordon Marsden *Lab* p252
Madeleine Moon *Lab* p261
Chris Skidmore *Con* p309

Disability equality
Seema Kennedy *Con* p218

Disability rights
Chris Law *SNP* p227

Disabled children

Bob Stewart	*Con*	p321

Doctors

Catherine West	*Lab*	p346

Domestic violence

Thangam Debbonaire	*Lab*	p127
Harriet Harman	*Lab*	p185
Andrew Stephenson	*Con*	p320

Drugs use and abuse

Liam Byrne	*Lab*	p98
Ronnie Cowan	*SNP*	p116

Economic development

Gregory Campbell	*DUP*	p101
Stewart Hosie	*SNP*	p201
Susan Elan Jones	*Lab*	p216
John Mann	*Lab*	p252
Albert Owen	*Lab*	p275
Lucy Powell	*Lab/Co-op*	p286
Nick Smith	*Lab*	p314
Royston Smith	*Con*	p315
Tom Tugendhat	*Con*	p336

Economics and finance

Simon Clarke	*Con*	p109
John Cryer	*Lab*	p120
Nic Dakin	*Lab*	p122
John Grogan	*Lab*	p178
Stephen Hammond	*Con*	p182
Clive Lewis	*Lab*	p231
John McDonnell	*Lab*	p242
Huw Merriman	*Con*	p257
Graham Stuart	*Con*	p325

Economy

Jon Ashworth	*Lab/Co-op*	p69
Kemi Badenoch	*Con*	p71
Adrian Bailey	*Lab/Co-op*	p71
Steve Baker	*Con*	p72
Harriett Baldwin	*Con*	p72
John Baron	*Con*	p74
Guto Bebb	*Con*	p75
Karen Bradley	*Con*	p86
Kevin Brennan	*Lab*	p89
Alun Cairns	*Con*	p100
Ronnie Campbell	*Lab*	p102
James Cartlidge	*Con*	p103
Sarah Champion	*Lab*	p104
Jenny Chapman	*Lab*	p105
Greg Clark	*Con*	p108
Kenneth Clarke	*Con*	p108
Geoffrey Clifton-Brown	*Con*	p110
Damian Collins	*Con*	p112
Jon Cruddas	*Lab*	p120
John Cryer	*Lab*	p120
Jim Cunningham	*Lab*	p122
Nic Dakin	*Lab*	p122
Wayne David	*Lab*	p123
Geraint Davies	*Lab/Co-op*	p125
Anneliese Dodds	*Lab/Co-op*	p131
Stephen Doughty	*Lab/Co-op*	p134
Alan Duncan	*Con*	p138
Philip Dunne	*Con*	p139
Angela Eagle	*Lab*	p140
David Evennett	*Con*	p147
Michael Fallon	*Con*	p148
Mark Field	*Con*	p151
Liam Fox	*Con*	p155
Mike Gapes	*Lab/Co-op*	p160
Barry Gardiner	*Lab*	p161
Mark Garnier	*Con*	p162
David Gauke	*Con*	p162
Nick Gibb	*Con*	p164
Helen Goodman	*Lab*	p168
Justine Greening	*Con*	p175
Philip Hammond	*Con*	p182
John Healey	*Lab*	p190
Mark Hendrick	*Lab/Co-op*	p193
Nick Herbert	*Con*	p194
Margaret Hodge	*Lab*	p197
Kelvin Hopkins	*Lab*	p201
Ranil Jayawardena	*Con*	p208
Bernard Jenkin	*Con*	p208
Marcus Jones	*Con*	p215
Kwasi Kwarteng	*Con*	p221
Eleanor Laing	*Con*	p222
David Lammy	*Lab*	p224
Andrea Leadsom	*Con*	p227
Chris Leslie	*Lab/Co-op*	p229
Ian Liddell-Grainger	*Con*	p233
Ian C Lucas	*Lab*	p238
Steve McCabe	*Lab*	p239
Alison McGovern	*Lab*	p244
Catherine McKinnell	*Lab*	p245
Alan Mak	*Con*	p250
Stephen Metcalfe	*Con*	p257
Andrew Mitchell	*Con*	p260
Nicky Morgan	*Con*	p263
Grahame Morris	*Lab*	p265
Jesse Norman	*Con*	p271
Priti Patel	*Con*	p277
Owen Paterson	*Con*	p277
Claire Perry	*Con*	p281
Bridget Phillipson	*Lab*	p282
Chris Philp	*Con*	p282
Jeremy Quin	*Con*	p288
Dominic Raab	*Con*	p289
John Redwood	*Con*	p290
Rachel Reeves	*Lab*	p293
Emma Reynolds	*Lab*	p293
Jonathan Reynolds	*Lab/Co-op*	p294
Gavin Robinson	*DUP*	p295
Geoffrey Robinson	*Lab*	p296
Matt Rodda	*Lab*	p296
Lee Rowley	*Con*	p298
Amber Rudd	*Con*	p299

David Rutley	*Con*	p300
Barry Sheerman	*Lab/Co-op*	p305
Dennis Skinner	*Lab*	p309
Owen Smith	*Lab*	p314
Andrew Stephenson	*Con*	p320
Iain Stewart	*Con*	p321
Mel Stride	*Con*	p324
Rishi Sunak	*Con*	p326
Robert Syms	*Con*	p328
Stephen Timms	*Lab*	p332
Jon Trickett	*Lab*	p335
Elizabeth Truss	*Con*	p336
Derek Twigg	*Lab*	p337
Chuka Umunna	*Lab*	p339
Theresa Villiers	*Con*	p342
Charles Walker	*Con*	p342
Catherine West	*Lab*	p346
Heather Wheeler	*Con*	p347
Bill Wiggin	*Con*	p350

Economy and enterprise

Rishi Sunak	*Con*	p326

Education

Diane Abbott	*Lab*	p63
Debbie Abrahams	*Lab*	p63
Nigel Adams	*Con*	p64
Peter Aldous	*Con*	p65
Heidi Alexander	*Lab*	p65
David Amess	*Con*	p67
Victoria Atkins	*Con*	p70
Richard Bacon	*Con*	p70
Steve Baker	*Con*	p72
Hilary Benn	*Lab*	p76
Paul Beresford	*Con*	p79
Roberta Blackman-Woods	*Lab*	p82
Paul Blomfield	*Lab*	p83
Nick Boles	*Con*	p84
Graham Brady	*Con*	p87
Kevin Brennan	*Lab*	p89
Robert Buckland	*Con*	p94
Conor Burns	*Con*	p96
Sarah Champion	*Lab*	p104
Simon Clarke	*Con*	p109
Vernon Coaker	*Lab*	p111
Ann Coffey	*Lab*	p111
Alberto Costa	*Con*	p115
Geoffrey Cox	*Con*	p116
John Cryer	*Lab*	p120
Alex Cunningham	*Lab*	p121
Nic Dakin	*Lab*	p122
Wayne David	*Lab*	p123
Philip Davies	*Con*	p126
Oliver Dowden	*Con*	p135
Jackie Doyle-Price	*Con*	p135
David Drew	*Lab/Co-op*	p136
Rosie Duffield	*Lab*	p137
Clive Efford	*Lab*	p141
Julie Elliott	*Lab*	p142
Tobias Ellwood	*Con*	p143
Nigel Evans	*Con*	p146
David Evennett	*Con*	p147
Michael Fallon	*Con*	p148
Paul Farrelly	*Lab*	p149
Tim Farron	*Lib Dem*	p150
Suella Fernandes	*Con*	p150
Caroline Flint	*Lab*	p153
Marcus Fysh	*Con*	p159
Roger Gale	*Con*	p160
Mike Gapes	*Lab/Co-op*	p160
Barry Gardiner	*Lab*	p161
David Gauke	*Con*	p162
Nusrat Ghani	*Con*	p163
Nick Gibb	*Con*	p164
Michelle Gildernew	*Sinn Féin*	p164
Cheryl Gillan	*Con*	p165
John Glen	*Con*	p166
Michael Gove	*Con*	p169
Chris Green	*Con*	p174
Damian Green	*Con*	p174
Justine Greening	*Con*	p175
Andrew Gwynne	*Lab*	p179
Louise Haigh	*Lab*	p180
Robert Halfon	*Con*	p180
Fabian Hamilton	*Lab*	p181
Mark Harper	*Con*	p185
Rebecca Harris	*Con*	p187
John Hayes	*Con*	p188
Chris Heaton-Harris	*Con*	p191
Sylvia Hermon	*Ind*	p194
Damian Hinds	*Con*	p196
Simon Hoare	*Con*	p196
Margaret Hodge	*Lab*	p197
Sharon Hodgson	*Lab*	p198
George Hollingbery	*Con*	p199
Nigel Huddleston	*Con*	p203
Jeremy Hunt	*Con*	p204
Margot James	*Con*	p206
Ranil Jayawardena	*Con*	p208
Caroline Johnson	*Con*	p210
Diana Johnson	*Lab*	p210
Darren Jones	*Lab*	p212
Graham Jones	*Lab*	p213
Helen Jones	*Lab*	p214
Eleanor Laing	*Con*	p222
Ben Lake	*PlC*	p223
David Lammy	*Lab*	p224
Clive Lewis	*Lab*	p231
Ivan Lewis	*Lab*	p232
Ian Liddell-Grainger	*Con*	p233
Jonathan Lord	*Con*	p236
Tim Loughton	*Con*	p237
Ian C Lucas	*Lab*	p238
Elisha McCallion	*Sinn Féin*	p240
Patrick McLoughlin	*Con*	p246
Esther McVey	*Con*	p248
Anne Main	*Con*	p250

Alan Mak	*Con*	p250
Gordon Marsden	*Lab*	p252
Paul Maynard	*Con*	p255
Ian Mearns	*Lab*	p256
Huw Merriman	*Con*	p257
Stephen Metcalfe	*Con*	p257
Maria Miller	*Con*	p258
Nigel Mills	*Con*	p259
Layla Moran	*Lib Dem*	p262
Stephen Morgan	*Lab*	p264
Anne Marie Morris	*Ind*	p264
Ian Murray	*Lab*	p267
Caroline Nokes	*Con*	p270
Chi Onwurah	*Lab*	p274
John Penrose	*Con*	p280
Andrew Percy	*Con*	p280
Claire Perry	*Con*	p281
Christopher Pincher	*Con*	p283
Luke Pollard	*Lab/Co-op*	p284
Lucy Powell	*Lab/Co-op*	p286
Victoria Prentis	*Con*	p286
Mark Prisk	*Con*	p286
Yasmin Qureshi	*Lab*	p289
Rachel Reeves	*Lab*	p293
Joan Ryan	*Lab*	p300
Paul Scully	*Con*	p302
Bob Seely	*Con*	p302
Grant Shapps	*Con*	p304
Barry Sheerman	*Lab/Co-op*	p305
Keith Simpson	*Con*	p308
Chris Skidmore	*Con*	p309
Andy Slaughter	*Lab*	p310
Angela Smith	*Lab*	p311
Julian Smith	*Con*	p313
Mark Spencer	*Con*	p318
Iain Stewart	*Con*	p321
Wes Streeting	*Lab*	p324
Mel Stride	*Con*	p324
Graham Stuart	*Con*	p325
Derek Thomas	*Con*	p329
Ross Thomson	*Con*	p331
Anne-Marie Trevelyan	*Con*	p335
Elizabeth Truss	*Con*	p336
Derek Twigg	*Lab*	p337
Stephen Twigg	*Lab/Co-op*	p338
Chuka Umunna	*Lab*	p339
Keith Vaz	*Lab*	p340
Robin Walker	*Con*	p343
Thelma Walker	*Lab*	p343
David Warburton	*Con*	p344
Catherine West	*Lab*	p346
Matt Western	*Lab*	p346
Alan Whitehead	*Lab*	p348
Craig Whittaker	*Con*	p349
Gavin Williamson	*Con*	p352
Phil Wilson	*Lab*	p352
Sammy Wilson	*DUP*	p353
Jeremy Wright	*Con*	p356

Education and skills

Diane Abbott	*Lab*	p63
Nigel Adams	*Con*	p64
Robert Buckland	*Con*	p94
Paul Flynn	*Lab*	p154
Vicky Ford	*Con*	p154
Michael Gove	*Con*	p169
Andrew Gwynne	*Lab*	p179
Rebecca Harris	*Con*	p187
Dan Jarvis	*Lab*	p207
Norman Lamb	*Lib Dem*	p223
Ivan Lewis	*Lab*	p232
Caroline Spelman	*Con*	p318
Jon Trickett	*Lab*	p335

Electoral reform

Richard Burden	*Lab*	p95
Sandy Martin	*Lab*	p253
Gavin Shuker	*Lab/Co-op*	p307
Stephen Twigg	*Lab/Co-op*	p338

Electoral registration

Chris Ruane	*Lab*	p298

Electoral services

Chloe Smith	*Con*	p312

Electricity

Carolyn Harris	*Lab*	p186

Employment

Debbie Abrahams	*Lab*	p63
Peter Aldous	*Con*	p65
Ian Austin	*Lab*	p70
Hilary Benn	*Lab*	p76
Deidre Brock	*SNP*	p91
Gregory Campbell	*DUP*	p101
Ronnie Campbell	*Lab*	p102
Jenny Chapman	*Lab*	p105
Mary Creagh	*Lab*	p118
John Cryer	*Lab*	p120
Ed Davey	*Lib Dem*	p122
Marsha De Cordova	*Lab*	p128
Maria Eagle	*Lab*	p140
Julie Elliott	*Lab*	p142
Paul Farrelly	*Lab*	p149
Mark Field	*Con*	p151
Caroline Flint	*Lab*	p153
Cheryl Gillan	*Con*	p165
Mary Glindon	*Lab*	p167
Michael Gove	*Con*	p169
Damian Green	*Con*	p174
Kate Green	*Lab*	p175
John Healey	*Lab*	p190
Margaret Hodge	*Lab*	p197
Sharon Hodgson	*Lab*	p198
Kelvin Hopkins	*Lab*	p201
Gerald Jones	*Lab*	p213
Kevan Jones	*Lab*	p214
Liz Kendall	*Lab*	p218

Norman Lamb *Lib Dem* p223
Ian Lavery *Lab* p226
Stephen Lloyd *Lib Dem* p235
Alison McGovern *Lab* p244
Nigel Mills *Con* p259
Bridget Phillipson *Lab* p282
Joan Ryan *Lab* p300
Chloe Smith *Con* p312
Mark Spencer *Con* p318
Andrew Stephenson *Con* p320
Stephen Timms *Lab* p332
Karl Turner *Lab* p337
Chuka Umunna *Lab* p339
Charles Walker *Con* p342
Rosie Winterton *Lab* p353

Employment and welfare

Gerald Jones *Lab* p213
Chloe Smith *Con* p312
Graham Stringer *Lab* p325

Employment Law

Yvonne Fovargue *Lab* p155

Employment rights

Dawn Butler *Lab* p97
Lilian Greenwood *Lab* p176
Diana Johnson *Lab* p210
Stephen Kinnock *Lab* p220
Jo Stevens *Lab* p320

Energy

Nigel Adams *Con* p64
Kevin Barron *Lab* p74
Crispin Blunt *Con* p83
Vince Cable *Lib Dem* p99
Alistair Carmichael *Lib Dem* p102
Greg Clark *Con* p108
Simon Clarke *Con* p109
Therese Coffey *Con* p112
Stephen Crabb *Con* p117
John Cryer *Lab* p120
Alex Cunningham *Lab* p121
Stephen Doughty *Lab/Co-op* p134
Clive Efford *Lab* p141
Nia Griffith *Lab* p177
John Grogan *Lab* p178
Philip Hammond *Con* p182
John Hayes *Con* p188
Sue Hayman *Lab* p189
James Heappey *Con* p191
Chris Heaton-Harris *Con* p191
Ian Lavery *Lab* p226
Ian Liddell-Grainger *Con* p233
Craig Mackinlay *Con* p245
Mark Menzies *Con* p256
Christopher Pincher *Con* p283
Dan Poulter *Con* p284
Tom Pursglove *Con* p288
Antoinette Sandbach *Con* p301
Dennis Skinner *Lab* p309
John Spellar *Lab* p317
Gareth Thomas *Lab/Co-op* p330
Ross Thomson *Con* p331
Ed Vaizey *Con* p339
Martin Vickers *Con* p341
Alan Whitehead *Lab* p348

Energy and Utilities

Barry Gardiner *Lab* p161

Energy Industry

David Duguid *Con* p138

Energy Security

Phillip Lee *Con* p228
Iain Stewart *Con* p321

Energy sources

David Duguid *Con* p138

Engineering

Michael Fabricant *Con* p148
Francie Molloy *Sinn Féin* p261
Andrew Stephenson *Con* p320

Enterprise

Steve Baker *Con* p72
Andrew Bridgen *Con* p90
Gregory Campbell *DUP* p101
Therese Coffey *Con* p112
Damian Collins *Con* p112
Michael Fabricant *Con* p148
Helen Grant *Con* p171
Sajid Javid *Con* p207
Wendy Morton *Con* p266
Andrew Stephenson *Con* p320
Rishi Sunak *Con* p326

Environment

Nigel Adams *Con* p64
David Amess *Con* p67
Kevin Barron *Lab* p74
Hilary Benn *Lab* p76
Crispin Blunt *Con* p83
Ben Bradshaw *Lab* p87
Tom Brake *Lib Dem* p88
Andrew Bridgen *Con* p90
Steve Brine *Con* p90
Karen Buck *Lab* p94
Dawn Butler *Lab* p97
Vince Cable *Lib Dem* p99
Ronnie Campbell *Lab* p102
Geoffrey Clifton-Brown *Con* p110
Vernon Coaker *Lab* p111
Jeremy Corbyn *Lab* p114
Mary Creagh *Lab* p118
Ed Davey *Lib Dem* p122
Geraint Davies *Lab/Co-op* p125

Analysis of MPs
House of Commons

Thangam Debbonaire	*Lab*	p127
Jonathan Djanogly	*Con*	p129
David Drew	*Lab/Co-op*	p136
Iain Duncan Smith	*Con*	p139
Clive Efford	*Lab*	p141
Tobias Ellwood	*Con*	p143
George Eustice	*Con*	p145
Mark Francois	*Con*	p156
Barry Gardiner	*Lab*	p161
Mary Glindon	*Lab*	p167
Zac Goldsmith	*Con*	p168
Helen Goodman	*Lab*	p168
Robert Goodwill	*Con*	p169
James Gray	*Con*	p172
Dominic Grieve	*Con*	p177
Nia Griffith	*Lab*	p177
Andrew Gwynne	*Lab*	p179
Oliver Heald	*Con*	p190
James Heappey	*Con*	p191
George Howarth	*Lab*	p202
Nick Hurd	*Con*	p205
Gareth Johnson	*Con*	p211
Norman Lamb	*Lib Dem*	p223
Jeremy Lefroy	*Con*	p228
Chris Leslie	*Lab/Co-op*	p229
Tim Loughton	*Con*	p237
Caroline Lucas	*Green*	p238
Ian C Lucas	*Lab*	p238
Kerry McCarthy	*Lab*	p240
John McDonnell	*Lab*	p242
Anne Main	*Con*	p250
Sandy Martin	*Lab*	p253
Madeleine Moon	*Lab*	p261
Wendy Morton	*Con*	p266
Ian Murray	*Lab*	p267
Sheryll Murray	*Con*	p268
Robert Neill	*Con*	p269
Caroline Nokes	*Con*	p270
Mark Pawsey	*Con*	p278
John Penrose	*Con*	p280
Lucy Powell	*Lab/Co-op*	p286
Chris Ruane	*Lab*	p298
Amber Rudd	*Con*	p299
Joan Ryan	*Lab*	p300
Jim Shannon	*DUP*	p303
Dennis Skinner	*Lab*	p309
Angela Smith	*Lab*	p311
Gareth Thomas	*Lab/Co-op*	p330
Emily Thornberry	*Lab*	p331
Maggie Throup	*Con*	p332
David Tredinnick	*Con*	p334
Elizabeth Truss	*Con*	p336
Ed Vaizey	*Con*	p339
Theresa Villiers	*Con*	p342
Thelma Walker	*Lab*	p343
Alan Whitehead	*Lab*	p348
Bill Wiggin	*Con*	p350
Chris Williamson	*Lab*	p351

Environment, agriculture and rural affairs

Nigel Adams	*Con*	p64
Ben Bradshaw	*Lab*	p87
Barry Gardiner	*Lab*	p161
John Healey	*Lab*	p190
Chris Ruane	*Lab*	p298

Equal opportunities and diversity

Debbie Abrahams	*Lab*	p63
John Bercow	*Speaker*	p78
Deidre Brock	*SNP*	p91
Dawn Butler	*Lab*	p97
Lisa Cameron	*SNP*	p100
Rosie Cooper	*Lab*	p113
Yvette Cooper	*Lab*	p114
Ronnie Cowan	*SNP*	p116
Angela Crawley	*SNP*	p118
Geraint Davies	*Lab/Co-op*	p125
Mims Davies	*Con*	p126
Rosie Duffield	*Lab*	p137
Gill Furniss	*Lab*	p159
Nusrat Ghani	*Con*	p163
Helen Grant	*Con*	p171
Chris Green	*Con*	p174
Justine Greening	*Con*	p175
Nia Griffith	*Lab*	p177
Harriet Harman	*Lab*	p185
Sharon Hodgson	*Lab*	p198
David Linden	*SNP*	p234
Caroline Lucas	*Green*	p238
Stewart Malcolm McDonald	*SNP*	p241
Seema Malhotra	*Lab/Co-op*	p251
Johnny Mercer	*Con*	p257
Maria Miller	*Con*	p258
Ian Murray	*Lab*	p267
Victoria Prentis	*Con*	p286
Owen Smith	*Lab*	p314
Jo Stevens	*Lab*	p320
Ross Thomson	*Con*	p331
Emily Thornberry	*Lab*	p331
Chuka Umunna	*Lab*	p339
Pete Wishart	*SNP*	p354

Equal pay

David Linden	*SNP*	p234
Guy Opperman	*Con*	p274

European affairs

Heidi Alexander	*Lab*	p65
Richard Bacon	*Con*	p70
Guto Bebb	*Con*	p75
Graham Brady	*Con*	p87
Chris Bryant	*Lab*	p93
Mary Creagh	*Lab*	p118
Wayne David	*Lab*	p123
Philip Davies	*Con*	p126
Nigel Dodds	*DUP*	p132
George Eustice	*Con*	p145
Nigel Evans	*Con*	p146

Paul Farrelly	*Lab*	p149
David Gauke	*Con*	p162
Nia Griffith	*Lab*	p177
Mark Hendrick	*Lab/Co-op*	p193
Sylvia Hermon	*Ind*	p194
Julian Lewis	*Con*	p232
Ian C Lucas	*Lab*	p238
Ian Paisley	*DUP*	p276
Priti Patel	*Con*	p277
John Redwood	*Con*	p290
Andrew Rosindell	*Con*	p297

European Constitution

Chris Heaton-Harris	*Con*	p191

European Union

Bill Cash	*Con*	p103
John Cryer	*Lab*	p120
Jim Cunningham	*Lab*	p122
Thangam Debbonaire	*Lab*	p127
David Duguid	*Con*	p138
Mike Gapes	*Lab/Co-op*	p160
Mark Garnier	*Con*	p162
Roger Godsiff	*Lab*	p167
Dominic Grieve	*Con*	p177
John Grogan	*Lab*	p178
Philip Hammond	*Con*	p182
Chris Heaton-Harris	*Con*	p191
Kate Hoey	*Lab*	p198
Kelvin Hopkins	*Lab*	p201
Bernard Jenkin	*Con*	p208
Stephen Kinnock	*Lab*	p220
Craig Mackinlay	*Con*	p245
Wendy Morton	*Con*	p266
Tom Pursglove	*Con*	p288
Ross Thomson	*Con*	p331

European Union affairs

Nia Griffith	*Lab*	p177

Exports

Michael Fabricant	*Con*	p148

Family

Lucy Allan	*Con*	p66
Fiona Bruce	*Con*	p93
Jenny Chapman	*Lab*	p105
Edward Leigh	*Con*	p229
Andrew Selous	*Con*	p302
Gary Streeter	*Con*	p323

Farming

Maria Caulfield	*Con*	p104
Stephen Crabb	*Con*	p117
George Eustice	*Con*	p145
Nusrat Ghani	*Con*	p163
Simon Hoare	*Con*	p196
John Lamont	*Con*	p225
Ian Liddell-Grainger	*Con*	p233
Mark Menzies	*Con*	p256
Jim Shannon	*DUP*	p303
Keith Simpson	*Con*	p308

Finance

Harriett Baldwin	*Con*	p72
John Cryer	*Lab*	p120
Nic Dakin	*Lab*	p122
Stephen Doughty	*Lab/Co-op*	p134
Iain Duncan Smith	*Con*	p139
Chris Evans	*Lab/Co-op*	p146
Greg Hands	*Con*	p184
Jo Johnson	*Con*	p211
Kwasi Kwarteng	*Con*	p221
Tim Loughton	*Con*	p237
Jim McMahon	*Lab/Co-op*	p246
Lee Rowley	*Con*	p298
Alok Sharma	*Con*	p304
Barry Sheerman	*Lab/Co-op*	p305
Anne-Marie Trevelyan	*Con*	p335
Jon Trickett	*Lab*	p335

Financial services

Jackie Doyle-Price	*Con*	p135
Philip Dunne	*Con*	p139
Mark Field	*Con*	p151
Louise Haigh	*Lab*	p180
Nicky Morgan	*Con*	p263
Theresa Villiers	*Con*	p342

Financial services regulation

Mark Garnier	*Con*	p162

Fire and rescue services

Jim Fitzpatrick	*Lab*	p152

Fisheries

Peter Aldous	*Con*	p65
Alistair Carmichael	*Lib Dem*	p102
David Duguid	*Con*	p138
Robert Goodwill	*Con*	p169
Craig Mackinlay	*Con*	p245

Food and drink

Andrew Bridgen	*Con*	p90
Kerry McCarthy	*Lab*	p240
David Tredinnick	*Con*	p334
Elizabeth Truss	*Con*	p336

Food industry

Damian Collins	*Con*	p112
Mark Menzies	*Con*	p256

Food supply

Emma Lewell-Buck	*Lab*	p230
Ruth Smeeth	*Lab*	p310

Foreign policy

David Amess	*Con*	p67
Jon Ashworth	*Lab/Co-op*	p69
Steve Baker	*Con*	p72
John Baron	*Con*	p74
Henry Bellingham	*Con*	p76

Crispin Blunt	*Con*	p83
Nick Boles	*Con*	p84
Ben Bradshaw	*Lab*	p87
Lyn Brown	*Lab*	p92
Robert Buckland	*Con*	p94
Conor Burns	*Con*	p96
Alistair Burt	*Con*	p97
Rehman Chishti	*Con*	p106
Simon Clarke	*Con*	p109
Geoffrey Clifton-Brown	*Con*	p110
Vernon Coaker	*Lab*	p111
Stephen Doughty	*Lab/Co-op*	p134
Jackie Doyle-Price	*Con*	p135
Jonathan Edwards	*PlC*	p141
Michael Ellis	*Con*	p142
Liam Fox	*Con*	p155
Barry Gardiner	*Lab*	p161
John Glen	*Con*	p166
James Gray	*Con*	p172
Dominic Grieve	*Con*	p177
Greg Hands	*Con*	p184
David Hanson	*Lab*	p184
Mark Hendrick	*Lab/Co-op*	p193
Kate Hoey	*Lab*	p198
Adam Holloway	*Con*	p200
John Howell	*Con*	p202
Bernard Jenkin	*Con*	p208
Daniel Kawczynski	*Con*	p216
Phillip Lee	*Con*	p228
Edward Leigh	*Con*	p229
Tim Loughton	*Con*	p237
Alan Mak	*Con*	p250
Stephen Metcalfe	*Con*	p257
James Morris	*Con*	p266
Ian Paisley	*DUP*	p276
Owen Paterson	*Con*	p277
Lucy Powell	*Lab/Co-op*	p286
Emma Reynolds	*Lab*	p293
Bob Seely	*Con*	p302
Henry Smith	*Con*	p312
Andrew Stephenson	*Con*	p320
Wes Streeting	*Lab*	p324
Tom Tugendhat	*Con*	p336
Ben Wallace	*Con*	p343
David Warburton	*Con*	p344
Jeremy Wright	*Con*	p356

Fostering

Lucy Allan	*Con*	p66

Fuel poverty

Sharon Hodgson	*Lab*	p198
Dan Jarvis	*Lab*	p207
Guy Opperman	*Con*	p274

Further and higher education

Paul Blomfield	*Lab*	p83
John Cryer	*Lab*	p120
George Freeman	*Con*	p157
Andrew Gwynne	*Lab*	p179
Sam Gyimah	*Con*	p179
Nicky Morgan	*Con*	p263
Barry Sheerman	*Lab/Co-op*	p305
Julian Smith	*Con*	p313
Wes Streeting	*Lab*	p324
Alan Whitehead	*Lab*	p348

Gambling and lotteries

Ronnie Cowan	*SNP*	p116
Helen Grant	*Con*	p171
Carolyn Harris	*Lab*	p186
David Lammy	*Lab*	p224
David Linden	*SNP*	p234

Gender identity

Caroline Lucas	*Green*	p238

General economy

Vicky Ford	*Con*	p154

Government, politics and public administration

Ben Bradshaw	*Lab*	p87
Ed Davey	*Lib Dem*	p122
Wayne David	*Lab*	p123
Nigel Evans	*Con*	p146
Bernard Jenkin	*Con*	p208
John McDonnell	*Lab*	p242
Paul Maynard	*Con*	p255
Penny Mordaunt	*Con*	p262
Robert Neill	*Con*	p269

Green belts

Robert Halfon	*Con*	p180
Gavin Williamson	*Con*	p352

Greenbelt development

Wendy Morton	*Con*	p266

Health

Debbie Abrahams	*Lab*	p63
Heidi Alexander	*Lab*	p65
David Amess	*Con*	p67
Stuart Andrew	*Con*	p68
Jon Ashworth	*Lab/Co-op*	p69
Richard Bacon	*Con*	p70
Steve Baker	*Con*	p72
Kevin Barron	*Lab*	p74
Richard Benyon	*Con*	p77
Paul Beresford	*Con*	p79
Luciana Berger	*Lab/Co-op*	p79
Graham Brady	*Con*	p87
James Brokenshire	*Con*	p91
Karen Buck	*Lab*	p94
Richard Burden	*Lab*	p95
Sarah Champion	*Lab*	p104
Jo Churchill	*Con*	p107
Greg Clark	*Con*	p108
Ann Clwyd	*Lab*	p110
Ann Coffey	*Lab*	p111

Analysis of MPs
House of Commons

Rosie Cooper	*Lab*	p113
Tracey Crouch	*Con*	p119
John Cryer	*Lab*	p120
Alex Cunningham	*Lab*	p121
David Davis	*Con*	p126
Anneliese Dodds	*Lab/Co-op*	p131
Nadine Dorries	*Con*	p133
Peter Dowd	*Lab*	p134
Oliver Dowden	*Con*	p135
Rosie Duffield	*Lab*	p137
Philip Dunne	*Con*	p139
Clive Efford	*Lab*	p141
Julie Elliott	*Lab*	p142
Paul Farrelly	*Lab*	p149
Tim Farron	*Lib Dem*	p150
Paul Flynn	*Lab*	p154
Yvonne Fovargue	*Lab*	p155
Liam Fox	*Con*	p155
George Freeman	*Con*	p157
Gill Furniss	*Lab*	p159
Marcus Fysh	*Con*	p159
John Glen	*Con*	p166
Mary Glindon	*Lab*	p167
Zac Goldsmith	*Con*	p168
Philip Hammond	*Con*	p182
Mark Harper	*Con*	p185
Chris Heaton-Harris	*Con*	p191
Sylvia Hermon	*Ind*	p194
Sharon Hodgson	*Lab*	p198
Nick Hurd	*Con*	p205
Margot James	*Con*	p206
Caroline Johnson	*Con*	p210
Diana Johnson	*Lab*	p210
Helen Jones	*Lab*	p214
Barbara Keeley	*Lab*	p217
Ben Lake	*PlC*	p223
Norman Lamb	*Lib Dem*	p223
David Lammy	*Lab*	p224
Pauline Latham	*Con*	p226
Phillip Lee	*Con*	p228
Jeremy Lefroy	*Con*	p228
Emma Lewell-Buck	*Lab*	p230
Ivan Lewis	*Lab*	p232
Ian Liddell-Grainger	*Con*	p233
Jonathan Lord	*Con*	p236
Tim Loughton	*Con*	p237
Ian C Lucas	*Lab*	p238
Elisha McCallion	*Sinn Féin*	p240
Siobhain McDonagh	*Lab*	p241
Stephen McPartland	*Con*	p248
Anne Main	*Con*	p250
Ian Mearns	*Lab*	p256
Huw Merriman	*Con*	p257
Andrew Mitchell	*Con*	p260
Madeleine Moon	*Lab*	p261
Anne Marie Morris	*Ind*	p264
Grahame Morris	*Lab*	p265
Andrew Murrison	*Con*	p268
Guy Opperman	*Con*	p274
Mike Penning	*Con*	p279
Luke Pollard	*Lab/Co-op*	p284
Dan Poulter	*Con*	p284
Lucy Powell	*Lab/Co-op*	p286
Will Quince	*Con*	p288
Gavin Robinson	*DUP*	p295
Joan Ryan	*Lab*	p300
Antoinette Sandbach	*Con*	p301
Grant Shapps	*Con*	p304
Virendra Sharma	*Lab*	p305
Chris Skidmore	*Con*	p309
Andy Slaughter	*Lab*	p310
Nick Smith	*Lab*	p314
Owen Smith	*Lab*	p314
Anna Soubry	*Con*	p317
Mark Spencer	*Con*	p318
Andrew Stephenson	*Con*	p320
Derek Thomas	*Con*	p329
Gareth Thomas	*Lab/Co-op*	p330
Maggie Throup	*Con*	p332
David Tredinnick	*Con*	p334
Anne-Marie Trevelyan	*Con*	p335
Derek Twigg	*Lab*	p337
Valerie Vaz	*Lab*	p341
Robin Walker	*Con*	p343
Thelma Walker	*Lab*	p343
Ben Wallace	*Con*	p343
Catherine West	*Lab*	p346
Philippa Whitford	*SNP*	p348
Paul Williams	*Lab*	p351

Health, wellbeing and care

John Cryer	*Lab*	p120
Paul Farrelly	*Lab*	p149
Vicky Ford	*Con*	p154
Harriet Harman	*Lab*	p185
Kelvin Hopkins	*Lab*	p201
David Lammy	*Lab*	p224
Ian C Lucas	*Lab*	p238
Joan Ryan	*Lab*	p300
Caroline Spelman	*Con*	p318
Graham Stringer	*Lab*	p325
Maggie Throup	*Con*	p332

Heritage

Bill Cash	*Con*	p103
David Evennett	*Con*	p147
Michael Fabricant	*Con*	p148
David Hanson	*Lab*	p184
Dan Jarvis	*Lab*	p207
Gordon Marsden	*Lab*	p252

Home affairs

Heidi Alexander	*Lab*	p65
Victoria Atkins	*Con*	p70
Kevin Barron	*Lab*	p74
Hilary Benn	*Lab*	p76
Richard Benyon	*Con*	p77

Karen Bradley	*Con*	p86
Tom Brake	*Lib Dem*	p88
Michael Ellis	*Con*	p142
Chris Grayling	*Con*	p173
Gareth Johnson	*Con*	p211
Greg Knight	*Con*	p220
Norman Lamb	*Lib Dem*	p223
Tim Loughton	*Con*	p237
Conor McGinn	*Lab*	p243
Mike Penning	*Con*	p279
Christopher Pincher	*Con*	p283
Tom Pursglove	*Con*	p288
Will Quince	*Con*	p288
David Rutley	*Con*	p300
Grant Shapps	*Con*	p304
Anna Soubry	*Con*	p317
Andrew Stephenson	*Con*	p320
David Tredinnick	*Con*	p334
Karl Turner	*Lab*	p337
Chuka Umunna	*Lab*	p339
Ben Wallace	*Con*	p343
Rosie Winterton	*Lab*	p353

Homelessness

Maria Caulfield	*Con*	p104
Andrew Selous	*Con*	p302

Hospices

Fabian Hamilton	*Lab*	p181

Hospitals

Catherine West	*Lab*	p346

Housing

Heidi Alexander	*Lab*	p65
Ian Austin	*Lab*	p70
Richard Bacon	*Con*	p70
Kemi Badenoch	*Con*	p71
Paul Beresford	*Con*	p79
Clive Betts	*Lab*	p80
Bob Blackman	*Con*	p81
Roberta Blackman-Woods	*Lab*	p82
Paul Blomfield	*Lab*	p83
James Brokenshire	*Con*	p91
Lyn Brown	*Lab*	p92
Karen Buck	*Lab*	p94
James Cartlidge	*Con*	p103
Maria Caulfield	*Con*	p104
Greg Clark	*Con*	p108
Rosie Cooper	*Lab*	p113
David Crausby	*Lab*	p117
Jon Cruddas	*Lab*	p120
Geraint Davies	*Lab/Co-op*	p125
Thangam Debbonaire	*Lab*	p127
David Drew	*Lab/Co-op*	p136
Jack Dromey	*Lab*	p136
Maria Eagle	*Lab*	p140
Clive Efford	*Lab*	p141
Jim Fitzpatrick	*Lab*	p152
Caroline Flint	*Lab*	p153
Vicky Foxcroft	*Lab*	p156
Mark Francois	*Con*	p156
Marcus Fysh	*Con*	p159
Michelle Gildernew	*Sinn Féin*	p164
Mary Glindon	*Lab*	p167
Robert Halfon	*Con*	p180
Philip Hammond	*Con*	p182
Greg Hands	*Con*	p184
Helen Hayes	*Lab*	p188
Simon Hoare	*Con*	p196
Margaret Hodge	*Lab*	p197
Kate Hoey	*Lab*	p198
George Howarth	*Lab*	p202
Gerald Jones	*Lab*	p213
Graham Jones	*Lab*	p213
David Linden	*SNP*	p234
Tim Loughton	*Con*	p237
Siobhain McDonagh	*Lab*	p241
Maria Miller	*Con*	p258
Francie Molloy	*Sinn Féin*	p261
Grahame Morris	*Lab*	p265
Bridget Phillipson	*Lab*	p282
Chris Philp	*Con*	p282
Luke Pollard	*Lab/Co-op*	p284
Lee Rowley	*Con*	p298
Chris Ruane	*Lab*	p298
Bob Seely	*Con*	p302
Andy Slaughter	*Lab*	p310
Emily Thornberry	*Lab*	p331
Catherine West	*Lab*	p346
Matt Western	*Lab*	p346
Helen Whately	*Con*	p347
Rosie Winterton	*Lab*	p353

Human rights

Steve Baker	*Con*	p72
John Baron	*Con*	p74
John Bercow	*Speaker*	p78
Andrew Bridgen	*Con*	p90
Fiona Bruce	*Con*	p93
Ann Clwyd	*Lab*	p110
Jeremy Corbyn	*Lab*	p114
Mary Creagh	*Lab*	p118
Geraint Davies	*Lab/Co-op*	p125
Marsha De Cordova	*Lab*	p128
Helen Goodman	*Lab*	p168
Harriet Harman	*Lab*	p185
Helen Hayes	*Lab*	p188
Sue Hayman	*Lab*	p189
Sylvia Hermon	*Ind*	p194
Sajid Javid	*Con*	p207
Clive Lewis	*Lab*	p231
Caroline Lucas	*Green*	p238
Gordon Marsden	*Lab*	p252
Jesse Norman	*Con*	p271
Victoria Prentis	*Con*	p286
Dominic Raab	*Con*	p289
Virendra Sharma	*Lab*	p305
Catherine West	*Lab*	p346

Immigration and nationality

Oliver Dowden	*Con*	p135
Priti Patel	*Con*	p277

Information and communication technology

Greg Knight	*Con*	p220

Infrastructure

Alan Brown	*SNP*	p91
Lisa Cameron	*SNP*	p100
David Duguid	*Con*	p138
Marcus Fysh	*Con*	p159
Chris Green	*Con*	p174
Ranil Jayawardena	*Con*	p208
Darren Jones	*Lab*	p212
Elisha McCallion	*Sinn Féin*	p240
Mark Menzies	*Con*	p256
Maria Miller	*Con*	p258
Claire Perry	*Con*	p281

Innovation

Adam Afriyie	*Con*	p64

Intellectual property

David Lammy	*Lab*	p224

Intelligence Services

Kevin Barron	*Lab*	p74
Ben Wallace	*Con*	p343

Internal Market

Michael Gove	*Con*	p169

International affairs

Damian Collins	*Con*	p112
Jeremy Corbyn	*Lab*	p114
Philip Dunne	*Con*	p139
Cheryl Gillan	*Con*	p165
Roger Godsiff	*Lab*	p167
Patrick Grady	*SNP*	p170
Fabian Hamilton	*Lab*	p181
Stephen Hammond	*Con*	p182
Dan Jarvis	*Lab*	p207
Graham Jones	*Lab*	p213
Kerry McCarthy	*Lab*	p240
Gordon Marsden	*Lab*	p252
Andrew Mitchell	*Con*	p260
Andrew Rosindell	*Con*	p297
Grant Shapps	*Con*	p304
Alec Shelbrooke	*Con*	p306
Keith Simpson	*Con*	p308
Andy Slaughter	*Lab*	p310
Nicholas Soames	*Con*	p316
Rory Stewart	*Con*	p322
Ross Thomson	*Con*	p331
David Tredinnick	*Con*	p334
Stephen Twigg	*Lab/Co-op*	p338
Robin Walker	*Con*	p343

International and European affairs

Vernon Coaker	*Lab*	p111
Jeremy Corbyn	*Lab*	p114
Roger Godsiff	*Lab*	p167
John Grogan	*Lab*	p178
Kate Hoey	*Lab*	p198
Ben Wallace	*Con*	p343
Tom Watson	*Lab*	p345

International development and aid

Heidi Alexander	*Lab*	p65
Jon Ashworth	*Lab/Co-op*	p69
Kemi Badenoch	*Con*	p71
Kevin Barron	*Lab*	p74
Hilary Benn	*Lab*	p76
John Bercow	*Speaker*	p78
Roberta Blackman-Woods	*Lab*	p82
Tom Brake	*Lib Dem*	p88
Fiona Bruce	*Con*	p93
Richard Burden	*Lab*	p95
Ann Clwyd	*Lab*	p110
Stephen Crabb	*Con*	p117
Jeffrey Donaldson	*DUP*	p132
Stephen Doughty	*Lab/Co-op*	p134
Jack Dromey	*Lab*	p136
Michael Fabricant	*Con*	p148
Helen Goodman	*Lab*	p168
Patrick Grady	*SNP*	p170
Helen Grant	*Con*	p171
Sam Gyimah	*Con*	p179
Fabian Hamilton	*Lab*	p181
Helen Hayes	*Lab*	p188
Mark Hendrick	*Lab/Co-op*	p193
Nick Herbert	*Con*	p194
Jeremy Hunt	*Con*	p204
Dan Jarvis	*Lab*	p207
Norman Lamb	*Lib Dem*	p223
David Lammy	*Lab*	p224
Mark Lancaster	*Con*	p225
Pauline Latham	*Con*	p226
Ivan Lewis	*Lab*	p232
Holly Lynch	*Lab*	p239
Alison McGovern	*Lab*	p244
Catherine McKinnell	*Lab*	p245
Chi Onwurah	*Lab*	p274
John Penrose	*Con*	p280
Dan Poulter	*Con*	p284
Mark Prisk	*Con*	p286
Laurence Robertson	*Con*	p295
Bob Seely	*Con*	p302
Virendra Sharma	*Lab*	p305
Alec Shelbrooke	*Con*	p306
Gavin Shuker	*Lab/Co-op*	p307
Caroline Spelman	*Con*	p318
Hywel Williams	*PlC*	p350
Paul Williams	*Lab*	p351
Pete Wishart	*SNP*	p354

International trade

Caroline Lucas	*Green*	p238

Internet

Ed Davey	*Lib Dem*	p122
Michael Fabricant	*Con*	p148
Nigel Huddleston	*Con*	p203

Investment

Paul Farrelly	*Lab*	p149
Louise Haigh	*Lab*	p180

Ireland

Mary Creagh	*Lab*	p118

Job vacancies

Lisa Cameron	*SNP*	p100
Stewart Hosie	*SNP*	p201
Elisha McCallion	*Sinn Féin*	p240
Stewart Malcolm McDonald	*SNP*	p241
Toby Perkins	*Lab*	p281

Justice and Home Affairs

Liam Byrne	*Lab*	p98
John Lamont	*Con*	p225
Will Quince	*Con*	p288

Justice system

Crispin Blunt	*Con*	p83
Steve Brine	*Con*	p90
Robert Buckland	*Con*	p94
Alistair Carmichael	*Lib Dem*	p102
Sarah Champion	*Lab*	p104
Jenny Chapman	*Lab*	p105
Rehman Chishti	*Con*	p106
Jonathan Djanogly	*Con*	p129
Michael Ellis	*Con*	p142
Chris Evans	*Lab/Co-op*	p146
Helen Grant	*Con*	p171
Ranil Jayawardena	*Con*	p208
Catherine McKinnell	*Lab*	p245
Seema Malhotra	*Lab/Co-op*	p251
Robert Neill	*Con*	p269
Ian Paisley	*DUP*	p276
Victoria Prentis	*Con*	p286
Will Quince	*Con*	p288
Anna Soubry	*Con*	p317
Jo Stevens	*Lab*	p320
Graham Stringer	*Lab*	p325
Karl Turner	*Lab*	p337
Chuka Umunna	*Lab*	p339
Pete Wishart	*SNP*	p354
Jeremy Wright	*Con*	p356

Law

Oliver Dowden	*Con*	p135
Harriet Harman	*Lab*	p185

Law and order

Andrew Bridgen	*Con*	p90
James Brokenshire	*Con*	p91
Bambos Charalambous	*Lab*	p105
Rehman Chishti	*Con*	p106
Philip Davies	*Con*	p126
David Davis	*Con*	p126
Nadine Dorries	*Con*	p133
Dominic Grieve	*Con*	p177
Mark Harper	*Con*	p185
Oliver Heald	*Con*	p190
Gordon Henderson	*Con*	p192
Ranil Jayawardena	*Con*	p208
David Jones	*Con*	p213
Priti Patel	*Con*	p277
Andrew Rosindell	*Con*	p297
Gary Streeter	*Con*	p323
David Tredinnick	*Con*	p334

Learning disabilities

Stuart Andrew	*Con*	p68
John Bercow	*Speaker*	p78
Alun Cairns	*Con*	p100

Legal affairs

Henry Bellingham	*Con*	p76
Geoffrey Cox	*Con*	p116
Valerie Vaz	*Lab*	p341

Legal aid

Dawn Butler	*Lab*	p97
Yvonne Fovargue	*Lab*	p155
Catherine McKinnell	*Lab*	p245
Catherine West	*Lab*	p346

Legal services

Keith Vaz	*Lab*	p340

Leisure centres

Roger Gale	*Con*	p160

Libraries

Lyn Brown	*Lab*	p92

Lobbying

John Grogan	*Lab*	p178

Local elections

Rory Stewart	*Con*	p322
Graham Stringer	*Lab*	p325

Local government

Clive Betts	*Lab*	p80
Bob Blackman	*Con*	p81
Nick Boles	*Con*	p84
Lyn Brown	*Lab*	p92
Bambos Charalambous	*Lab*	p105
Neil Coyle	*Lab*	p116
Philip Dunne	*Con*	p139
Clive Efford	*Lab*	p141
Louise Ellman	*Lab/Co-op*	p143
Nigel Evans	*Con*	p146
Mark Francois	*Con*	p156
Mike Freer	*Con*	p158
John Grogan	*Lab*	p178
Andrew Gwynne	*Lab*	p179
Greg Hands	*Con*	p184
David Hanson	*Lab*	p184
Helen Hayes	*Lab*	p188
John Hayes	*Con*	p188
George Hollingbery	*Con*	p199
John Howell	*Con*	p202
Marcus Jones	*Con*	p215
Brandon Lewis	*Con*	p231

Jim McMahon	*Lab/Co-op*	p246
Ian Mearns	*Lab*	p256
Stephen Morgan	*Lab*	p264
Grahame Morris	*Lab*	p265
James Morris	*Con*	p266
Robert Neill	*Con*	p269
Mark Pawsey	*Con*	p278
Andrew Rosindell	*Con*	p297
Paul Scully	*Con*	p302
Henry Smith	*Con*	p312
Alison Thewliss	*SNP*	p329
Justin Tomlinson	*Con*	p333
Stephen Twigg	*Lab/Co-op*	p338
Keith Vaz	*Lab*	p340
Martin Vickers	*Con*	p341
Catherine West	*Lab*	p346
Alan Whitehead	*Lab*	p348

Local government funding

Mike Freer	*Con*	p158

Local government reform

Mike Freer	*Con*	p158

London economy

David Evennett	*Con*	p147
Catherine West	*Lab*	p346

Manufacturing

Heidi Allen	*Con*	p66
Ian Austin	*Lab*	p70
Sarah Champion	*Lab*	p104
Nic Dakin	*Lab*	p122
Jack Dromey	*Lab*	p136
Michael Fabricant	*Con*	p148
Chris Green	*Con*	p174
Andrew Griffiths	*Con*	p178
Ian C Lucas	*Lab*	p238
Catherine McKinnell	*Lab*	p245
Madeleine Moon	*Lab*	p261
Chi Onwurah	*Lab*	p274
Emma Reynolds	*Lab*	p293
Jonathan Reynolds	*Lab/Co-op*	p294
Ruth Smeeth	*Lab*	p310
Angela Smith	*Lab*	p311
Andrew Stephenson	*Con*	p320
Mark Tami	*Lab*	p329
Tom Watson	*Lab*	p345
Gavin Williamson	*Con*	p352

Maternity services

Victoria Prentis	*Con*	p286

Media

Nigel Adams	*Con*	p64
Steve Brine	*Con*	p90
Bill Cash	*Con*	p103
Michael Fabricant	*Con*	p148
Roger Gale	*Con*	p160
Ivan Lewis	*Lab*	p232
Jonathan Lord	*Con*	p236
Maria Miller	*Con*	p258
David Warburton	*Con*	p344
Tom Watson	*Lab*	p345
John Whittingdale	*Con*	p349

Mental health

Adam Afriyie	*Con*	p64
Luciana Berger	*Lab/Co-op*	p79
Conor Burns	*Con*	p96
Lisa Cameron	*SNP*	p100
Tracey Crouch	*Con*	p119
Liam Fox	*Con*	p155
Mike Gapes	*Lab/Co-op*	p160
Barbara Keeley	*Lab*	p217
Elisha McCallion	*Sinn Féin*	p240
Johnny Mercer	*Con*	p257
Nicky Morgan	*Con*	p263
Graham Stuart	*Con*	p325
Charles Walker	*Con*	p342
Catherine West	*Lab*	p346

Mental health services

Adam Afriyie	*Con*	p64

Mental health support

Conor Burns	*Con*	p96

Middle East

John Grogan	*Lab*	p178

Motor industry

John Spellar	*Lab*	p317

Music

Greg Knight	*Con*	p220
Valerie Vaz	*Lab*	p341

National Health Service

Steve Brine	*Con*	p90
Alan Brown	*SNP*	p91
Lisa Cameron	*SNP*	p100
Maria Caulfield	*Con*	p104
Rehman Chishti	*Con*	p106
Kenneth Clarke	*Con*	p108
Jeremy Corbyn	*Lab*	p114
Jim Cunningham	*Lab*	p122
Angela Eagle	*Lab*	p140
Helen Hayes	*Lab*	p188
Sue Hayman	*Lab*	p189
Darren Jones	*Lab*	p212
Liz Kendall	*Lab*	p218
Anne Marie Morris	*Ind*	p264
Grahame Morris	*Lab*	p265
Andrew Stephenson	*Con*	p320
Nick Thomas-Symonds	*Lab*	p330
Helen Whately	*Con*	p347
Philippa Whitford	*SNP*	p348
Sarah Wollaston	*Con*	p354

Northern Ireland

Henry Bellingham	*Con*	p76
Owen Paterson	*Con*	p277

Laurence Robertson *Con* p295
Andrew Stephenson *Con* p320

Nuclear power

David Morris *Con* p265

Nuclear weapons

Margaret Beckett *Lab* p75
Kirsty Blackman *SNP* p82
Gavin Newlands *SNP* p270
Alison Thewliss *SNP* p329
Philippa Whitford *SNP* p348

Obesity

Sarah Wollaston *Con* p354

Palliative care

Fabian Hamilton *Lab* p181

Pensions

Harriett Baldwin *Con* p72
David Crausby *Lab* p117
Alex Cunningham *Lab* p121
James Duddridge *Con* p137
Chris Elmore *Lab* p144
Paul Farrelly *Lab* p149
Paul Flynn *Lab* p154
Mary Glindon *Lab* p167
Chris Grayling *Con* p173
Lilian Greenwood *Lab* p176
Carolyn Harris *Lab* p186
Oliver Heald *Con* p190
Margot James *Con* p206
Seema Kennedy *Con* p218
Craig Mackinlay *Con* p245
Penny Mordaunt *Con* p262
Anne Marie Morris *Ind* p264
Sarah Newton *Con* p270
John Penrose *Con* p280
Dan Poulter *Con* p284
Chloe Smith *Con* p312
Graham Stuart *Con* p325

Personal finance

Sue Hayman *Lab* p189
Gerald Jones *Lab* p213

PFI/PPP

Jesse Norman *Con* p271

Planning

Stuart Andrew *Con* p68
Clive Betts *Lab* p80
Roberta Blackman-Woods *Lab* p82
Steve Brine *Con* p90
Jonathan Djanogly *Con* p129
David Drew *Lab/Co-op* p136
Philip Hammond *Con* p182
Rebecca Harris *Con* p187
Helen Hayes *Lab* p188
Peter Heaton-Jones *Con* p192
Simon Hoare *Con* p196
Mark Pawsey *Con* p278
Mark Prisk *Con* p286

Police

Kemi Badenoch *Con* p71
David Davies *Con* p124
Michael Fabricant *Con* p148
Tim Farron *Lib Dem* p150
Sylvia Hermon *Ind* p194
Diana Johnson *Lab* p210
Steve McCabe *Lab* p239
Stephen McPartland *Con* p248
Seema Malhotra *Lab/Co-op* p251
Madeleine Moon *Lab* p261
Jessica Morden *Lab* p263
Robert Neill *Con* p269
Ian Paisley *DUP* p276
Ross Thomson *Con* p331
David Tredinnick *Con* p334
Robin Walker *Con* p343
Sammy Wilson *DUP* p353

Poverty

Lyn Brown *Lab* p92
Richard Burden *Lab* p95
Alistair Burt *Con* p97
Dawn Butler *Lab* p97
Greg Clark *Con* p108
Yvette Cooper *Lab* p114
Alex Cunningham *Lab* p121
Marsha De Cordova *Lab* p128
Martin Docherty-Hughes *SNP* p130
David Drew *Lab/Co-op* p136
Charlie Elphicke *Con* p144
Frank Field *Lab* p151
Jim Fitzpatrick *Lab* p152
Kate Green *Lab* p175
Ian Lavery *Lab* p226
Kerry McCarthy *Lab* p240
Stewart Malcolm McDonald *SNP* p241
Stuart C McDonald *SNP* p242
Sandy Martin *Lab* p253
Paul Maskey *Sinn Féin* p254
Lisa Nandy *Lab* p269
Emily Thornberry *Lab* p331
Derek Twigg *Lab* p337
Chris Williamson *Lab* p351

Pregnancy

Chris Heaton-Harris *Con* p191

Prison health

Fabian Hamilton *Lab* p181

Prison reform

Nick Hurd *Con* p205
Margot James *Con* p206
Guy Opperman *Con* p274
Victoria Prentis *Con* p286

Prisons

Madeleine Moon *Lab* p261

Procurement
Stephen McPartland *Con* p248

Public administration
John McDonnell *Lab* p242
Seema Malhotra *Lab/Co-op* p251

Public services
Adam Afriyie *Con* p64
Deidre Brock *SNP* p91
Louise Ellman *Lab/Co-op* p143
Nick Herbert *Con* p194
Jesse Norman *Con* p271
Emma Reynolds *Lab* p293
Matt Rodda *Lab* p296
Ruth Smeeth *Lab* p310
Chloe Smith *Con* p312

Racial discrimination
Jeremy Corbyn *Lab* p114

Rail transport
Lucy Allan *Con* p66
Marcus Fysh *Con* p159
Chris Philp *Con* p282

Recreation
Roger Godsiff *Lab* p167

Recycling
Clive Efford *Lab* p141

Refugees and asylum seekers
Thangam Debbonaire *Lab* p127

Regeneration
Guto Bebb *Con* p75
Clive Betts *Lab* p80
Roberta Blackman-Woods *Lab* p82
James Brokenshire *Con* p91
Richard Burden *Lab* p95
Damian Collins *Con* p112
Julie Elliott *Lab* p142
George Eustice *Con* p145
Paul Farrelly *Lab* p149
Jim Fitzpatrick *Lab* p152
Andrew Gwynne *Lab* p179
Simon Hoare *Con* p196
Gerald Jones *Lab* p213
Kevan Jones *Lab* p214
Stephen Lloyd *Lib Dem* p235
Alison McGovern *Lab* p244
Jim McMahon *Lab/Co-op* p246
Toby Perkins *Lab* p281
Lucy Powell *Lab/Co-op* p286

Regional assemblies
Richard Burden *Lab* p95

Regional government and policy
Clive Betts *Lab* p80
Kevin Brennan *Lab* p89
Vince Cable *Lib Dem* p99
Ed Davey *Lib Dem* p122
Wayne David *Lab* p123
Mark Field *Con* p151
Liam Fox *Con* p155
Mark Garnier *Con* p162
Nick Gibb *Con* p164
John Grogan *Lab* p178
Kelvin Hopkins *Lab* p201
Eleanor Laing *Con* p222
Chris Leslie *Lab/Co-op* p229
Tony Lloyd *Lab* p235
John McDonnell *Lab* p242
Angus MacNeil *SNP* p247
Albert Owen *Lab* p275
Graham Stuart *Con* p325
Robert Syms *Con* p328
Stephen Timms *Lab* p332
Theresa Villiers *Con* p342

Regional policy
Louise Ellman *Lab/Co-op* p143
Neil Parish *Con* p276
Rachel Reeves *Lab* p293
Phil Wilson *Lab* p352
Rosie Winterton *Lab* p353

Religion
Jonathan Reynolds *Lab/Co-op* p294
Gavin Shuker *Lab/Co-op* p307
Caroline Spelman *Con* p318

Renewables
Peter Aldous *Con* p65
Ronnie Cowan *SNP* p116
Andrew Jones *Con* p212
Sarah Newton *Con* p270

Research and development
Thangam Debbonaire *Lab* p127
Vicky Ford *Con* p154
Stephen Metcalfe *Con* p257
Ed Vaizey *Con* p339
Valerie Vaz *Lab* p341

Road accidents
Mims Davies *Con* p126

Road building
Mims Davies *Con* p126
Marcus Fysh *Con* p159

Road safety
Mims Davies *Con* p126

Road transport
Chris Philp *Con* p282

Royal Air Force
Madeleine Moon *Lab* p261

Royal Navy
Sheryll Murray *Con* p268

Rural affairs

Nigel Adams	*Con*	p64
Guto Bebb	*Con*	p75
Richard Benyon	*Con*	p77
Karen Bradley	*Con*	p86
Andrew Bridgen	*Con*	p90
Alistair Burt	*Con*	p97
James Cartlidge	*Con*	p103
Maria Caulfield	*Con*	p104
Therese Coffey	*Con*	p112
Jonathan Djanogly	*Con*	p129
Nadine Dorries	*Con*	p133
David Drew	*Lab/Co-op*	p136
Tim Farron	*Lib Dem*	p150
Michelle Gildernew	*Sinn Féin*	p164
Damian Green	*Con*	p174
Simon Hart	*Con*	p187
James Heappey	*Con*	p191
Nick Herbert	*Con*	p194
John Howell	*Con*	p202
John Lamont	*Con*	p225
Ian Liddell-Grainger	*Con*	p233
Francie Molloy	*Sinn Féin*	p261
David Mundell	*Con*	p267
Sarah Newton	*Con*	p270
Brendan O'Hara	*SNP*	p273
Dan Poulter	*Con*	p284
Amber Rudd	*Con*	p299
David Rutley	*Con*	p300
Antoinette Sandbach	*Con*	p301
Liz Saville Roberts	*PlC*	p301
Mark Spencer	*Con*	p318
Rory Stewart	*Con*	p322
Rishi Sunak	*Con*	p326
David Warburton	*Con*	p344

Rural communities

Susan Elan Jones	*Lab*	p216
Sarah Wollaston	*Con*	p354

Rural economy

David Duguid	*Con*	p138
George Freeman	*Con*	p157
Ben Lake	*PlC*	p223
Graham Stuart	*Con*	p325

School meals

Sharon Hodgson	*Lab*	p198

Schools

Gavin Robinson	*DUP*	p295

Science

Adam Afriyie	*Con*	p64
Heidi Allen	*Con*	p66
Bob Blackman	*Con*	p81
Thangam Debbonaire	*Lab*	p127
Michael Fabricant	*Con*	p148
Chris Green	*Con*	p174
Phillip Lee	*Con*	p228
Stephen Metcalfe	*Con*	p257
Graham Stringer	*Lab*	p325
Ed Vaizey	*Con*	p339
Valerie Vaz	*Lab*	p341

Science and technology

Adam Afriyie	*Con*	p64
Jon Cruddas	*Lab*	p120
Sylvia Hermon	*Ind*	p194
David Lammy	*Lab*	p224
Jon Trickett	*Lab*	p335
Tom Watson	*Lab*	p345

Science, technology and research

Stephen Metcalfe	*Con*	p257
Ed Vaizey	*Con*	p339
Valerie Vaz	*Lab*	p341

Scotland

David Duguid	*Con*	p138
Ross Thomson	*Con*	p331

Scotland economy

David Duguid	*Con*	p138

Scottish Government

Gavin Newlands	*SNP*	p270

Scottish home rule

Mhairi Black	*SNP*	p81
Ronnie Cowan	*SNP*	p116
Martin Docherty-Hughes	*SNP*	p130
Marion Fellows	*SNP*	p150
Patricia Gibson	*SNP*	p164
Drew Hendry	*SNP*	p193
Gavin Newlands	*SNP*	p270

Security

Kevin Barron	*Lab*	p74
Michael Fabricant	*Con*	p148
Mark Field	*Con*	p151
Nusrat Ghani	*Con*	p163
Dan Jarvis	*Lab*	p207
Julian Lewis	*Con*	p232
Jack Lopresti	*Con*	p236
Steve McCabe	*Lab*	p239
Ben Wallace	*Con*	p343

Security

Ross Thomson	*Con*	p331

Sentencing

Guy Opperman	*Con*	p274

Skills

Diane Abbott	*Lab*	p63
Nigel Adams	*Con*	p64
Ian Austin	*Lab*	p70
Paul Blomfield	*Lab*	p83
Julie Elliott	*Lab*	p142
Andrew Gwynne	*Lab*	p179
Rebecca Harris	*Con*	p187
James Heappey	*Con*	p191

Marcus Jones	*Con*	p215
Lucy Powell	*Lab/Co-op*	p286
Emma Reynolds	*Lab*	p293
Chloe Smith	*Con*	p312
Julian Smith	*Con*	p313

Slavery

Chloe Smith	*Con*	p312

Small businesses

Diane Abbott	*Lab*	p63
Henry Bellingham	*Con*	p76
Paul Blomfield	*Lab*	p83
Fiona Bruce	*Con*	p93
Bill Cash	*Con*	p103
Jonathan Djanogly	*Con*	p129
David Drew	*Lab/Co-op*	p136
Iain Duncan Smith	*Con*	p139
Philip Dunne	*Con*	p139
Nigel Evans	*Con*	p146
Mark Field	*Con*	p151
Zac Goldsmith	*Con*	p168
John Grogan	*Lab*	p178
Sam Gyimah	*Con*	p179
Fabian Hamilton	*Lab*	p181
Rebecca Harris	*Con*	p187
Simon Hart	*Con*	p187
Stephen Hepburn	*Lab*	p194
Lindsay Hoyle	*Lab*	p203
Jeremy Lefroy	*Con*	p228
Stephen Lloyd	*Lib Dem*	p235
John Mann	*Lab*	p252
Stephen Metcalfe	*Con*	p257
Anne Marie Morris	*Ind*	p264
David Morris	*Con*	p265
Toby Perkins	*Lab*	p281
Mark Prisk	*Con*	p286
Paul Scully	*Con*	p302
Andrew Stephenson	*Con*	p320
Maggie Throup	*Con*	p332
Keith Vaz	*Lab*	p340

Social affairs

Richard Benyon	*Con*	p77
Alistair Burt	*Con*	p97
Liam Byrne	*Lab*	p98
Mary Creagh	*Lab*	p118
Iain Duncan Smith	*Con*	p139
Michael Gove	*Con*	p169
Paul Maynard	*Con*	p255
Huw Merriman	*Con*	p257
Madeleine Moon	*Lab*	p261
Gary Streeter	*Con*	p323
Sammy Wilson	*DUP*	p353

Social inclusion

Damian Collins	*Con*	p112
Nadine Dorries	*Con*	p133
Justine Greening	*Con*	p175
Damian Hinds	*Con*	p196
Chi Onwurah	*Lab*	p274
Wes Streeting	*Lab*	p324

Social justice

Mhairi Black	*SNP*	p81
Angela Crawley	*SNP*	p118
Jonathan Edwards	*PlC*	p141
Suella Fernandes	*Con*	p150
Clive Lewis	*Lab*	p231
Caroline Lucas	*Green*	p238
Alan Mak	*Con*	p250
Ian Murray	*Lab*	p267
Owen Paterson	*Con*	p277
Liz Saville Roberts	*PlC*	p301
Mel Stride	*Con*	p324

Social workers

Neil Coyle	*Lab*	p116
Tracey Crouch	*Con*	p119
Alex Cunningham	*Lab*	p121
Rosie Duffield	*Lab*	p137
Anne Marie Morris	*Ind*	p264
Hywel Williams	*PlC*	p350

Socialism

Jeremy Corbyn	*Lab*	p114

Software

Bridget Phillipson	*Lab*	p282

Solvent abuse

David Hanson	*Lab*	p184

Special schools

Stuart Andrew	*Con*	p68
Alun Cairns	*Con*	p100

Sport

Nigel Adams	*Con*	p64
Bob Blackman	*Con*	p81
Tom Brake	*Lib Dem*	p88
Alistair Burt	*Con*	p97
Vernon Coaker	*Lab*	p111
Tracey Crouch	*Con*	p119
Mims Davies	*Con*	p126
Caroline Dinenage	*Con*	p129
Angela Eagle	*Lab*	p140
Roger Godsiff	*Lab*	p167
Helen Grant	*Con*	p171
John Grogan	*Lab*	p178
Chris Heaton-Harris	*Con*	p191
Sharon Hodgson	*Lab*	p198
Kate Hoey	*Lab*	p198
Lindsay Hoyle	*Lab*	p203
Dan Jarvis	*Lab*	p207
Barbara Keeley	*Lab*	p217
David Lammy	*Lab*	p224
Ian Lavery	*Lab*	p226
Ivan Lewis	*Lab*	p232
Jonathan Lord	*Con*	p236
Barry McElduff	*Sinn Féin*	p243

John Mann	*Lab*	p252
Caroline Nokes	*Con*	p270
Toby Perkins	*Lab*	p281
Jo Stevens	*Lab*	p320
Justin Tomlinson	*Con*	p333
Jon Trickett	*Lab*	p335
Ben Wallace	*Con*	p343

State schools

Chris Philp	*Con*	p282

Steel industry

Stephen Kinnock	*Lab*	p220
Jessica Morden	*Lab*	p263

Student finance

Gavin Shuker	*Lab/Co-op*	p307

Suicide

Madeleine Moon	*Lab*	p261

Sustainable communities

Phil Wilson	*Lab*	p352

Sustainable development

Ben Lake	*PlC*	p223
Liz Saville Roberts	*PlC*	p301

Tax

Adam Afriyie	*Con*	p64
Adrian Bailey	*Lab/Co-op*	p71
Guto Bebb	*Con*	p75
Geoffrey Clifton-Brown	*Con*	p110
Ed Davey	*Lib Dem*	p122
Charlie Elphicke	*Con*	p144
David Gauke	*Con*	p162
Nick Gibb	*Con*	p164
John Healey	*Lab*	p190
Ian Liddell-Grainger	*Con*	p233
Craig Mackinlay	*Con*	p245
Nigel Mills	*Con*	p259
Layla Moran	*Lib Dem*	p262
Charles Walker	*Con*	p342

Technology

Adam Afriyie	*Con*	p64
James Cleverly	*Con*	p109
Martin Docherty-Hughes	*SNP*	p130
Michael Fabricant	*Con*	p148
James Heappey	*Con*	p191
Darren Jones	*Lab*	p212
Stephen Metcalfe	*Con*	p257
Chi Onwurah	*Lab*	p274
Geoffrey Robinson	*Lab*	p296
Ed Vaizey	*Con*	p339
Valerie Vaz	*Lab*	p341

Telecommunications

Nigel Evans	*Con*	p146
Michael Fabricant	*Con*	p148
Stephen Timms	*Lab*	p332

Terrorism

Michael Gove	*Con*	p169
Robert Halfon	*Con*	p180
Khalid Mahmood	*Lab*	p249

Third World

Dennis Skinner	*Lab*	p309
Gary Streeter	*Con*	p323

Tourism

Gregory Campbell	*DUP*	p101
David Duguid	*Con*	p138
Tobias Ellwood	*Con*	p143
David Evennett	*Con*	p147
Roger Gale	*Con*	p160
Mark Garnier	*Con*	p162
Helen Grant	*Con*	p171
James Heappey	*Con*	p191
Nigel Huddleston	*Con*	p203
John Lamont	*Con*	p225
Brandon Lewis	*Con*	p231
Sheryll Murray	*Con*	p268
Guy Opperman	*Con*	p274
Chris Ruane	*Lab*	p298
Andrew Stephenson	*Con*	p320

Town planning

Peter Aldous	*Con*	p65
Ann Coffey	*Lab*	p111

Trade

Ian Austin	*Lab*	p70
Alistair Burt	*Con*	p97
Alun Cairns	*Con*	p100
Gregory Campbell	*DUP*	p101
Bill Cash	*Con*	p103
Stephen Crabb	*Con*	p117
Geraint Davies	*Lab/Co-op*	p125
Jonathan Djanogly	*Con*	p129
Alan Duncan	*Con*	p138
Chris Elmore	*Lab*	p144
Michael Fabricant	*Con*	p148
Paul Farrelly	*Lab*	p149
Barry Gardiner	*Lab*	p161
Philip Hammond	*Con*	p182
Lindsay Hoyle	*Lab*	p203
Bernard Jenkin	*Con*	p208
Daniel Kawczynski	*Con*	p216
Stephen McPartland	*Con*	p248
Khalid Mahmood	*Lab*	p249
Chi Onwurah	*Lab*	p274
Priti Patel	*Con*	p277
Owen Paterson	*Con*	p277
Mark Pawsey	*Con*	p278
Mark Prisk	*Con*	p286
Andrew Selous	*Con*	p302
Alok Sharma	*Con*	p304
Barry Sheerman	*Lab/Co-op*	p305
Nicholas Soames	*Con*	p316
Ross Thomson	*Con*	p331

Trade Unions

Hilary Benn	*Lab*	p76
David Crausby	*Lab*	p117
Jon Cruddas	*Lab*	p120
Jim Cunningham	*Lab*	p122
Jack Dromey	*Lab*	p136
Robert Halfon	*Con*	p180
John Healey	*Lab*	p190
Sandy Martin	*Lab*	p253

Transport

Peter Aldous	*Con*	p65
David Amess	*Con*	p67
Stuart Andrew	*Con*	p68
Kemi Badenoch	*Con*	p71
Clive Betts	*Lab*	p80
Ian Blackford	*SNP*	p81
Ben Bradshaw	*Lab*	p87
Tom Brake	*Lib Dem*	p88
Andrew Bridgen	*Con*	p90
Alistair Carmichael	*Lib Dem*	p102
Jenny Chapman	*Lab*	p105
Greg Clark	*Con*	p108
Simon Clarke	*Con*	p109
Jeremy Corbyn	*Lab*	p114
John Cryer	*Lab*	p120
Geraint Davies	*Lab/Co-op*	p125
Jonathan Djanogly	*Con*	p129
Jeffrey Donaldson	*DUP*	p132
Jackie Doyle-Price	*Con*	p135
Jack Dromey	*Lab*	p136
Iain Duncan Smith	*Con*	p139
Maria Eagle	*Lab*	p140
Clive Efford	*Lab*	p141
Louise Ellman	*Lab/Co-op*	p143
Charlie Elphicke	*Con*	p144
David Evennett	*Con*	p147
Michael Fabricant	*Con*	p148
Jim Fitzpatrick	*Lab*	p152
Robert Goodwill	*Con*	p169
Patrick Grady	*SNP*	p170
Chris Grayling	*Con*	p173
Lilian Greenwood	*Lab*	p176
Andrew Gwynne	*Lab*	p179
Fabian Hamilton	*Lab*	p181
Philip Hammond	*Con*	p182
Stephen Hammond	*Con*	p182
Sue Hayman	*Lab*	p189
Kelvin Hopkins	*Lab*	p201
Andrew Jones	*Con*	p212
Kevan Jones	*Lab*	p214
Kwasi Kwarteng	*Con*	p221
Eleanor Laing	*Con*	p222
Brandon Lewis	*Con*	p231
Steve McCabe	*Lab*	p239
Esther McVey	*Con*	p248
Ian Mearns	*Lab*	p256
Mark Menzies	*Con*	p256
Johnny Mercer	*Con*	p257
Huw Merriman	*Con*	p257
Layla Moran	*Lib Dem*	p262
Brendan O'Hara	*SNP*	p273
Claire Perry	*Con*	p281
Victoria Prentis	*Con*	p286
Will Quince	*Con*	p288
John Redwood	*Con*	p290
Jonathan Reynolds	*Lab/Co-op*	p294
Lee Rowley	*Con*	p298
Amber Rudd	*Con*	p299
Alec Shelbrooke	*Con*	p306
Gavin Shuker	*Lab/Co-op*	p307
Andy Slaughter	*Lab*	p310
Angela Smith	*Lab*	p311
Chloe Smith	*Con*	p312
Iain Stewart	*Con*	p321
Martin Vickers	*Con*	p341
Theresa Villiers	*Con*	p342
Matt Western	*Lab*	p346
Alan Whitehead	*Lab*	p348
Rosie Winterton	*Lab*	p353

Unemployment and jobseeking

Dawn Butler	*Lab*	p97
Yvette Cooper	*Lab*	p114
Stuart C McDonald	*SNP*	p242

Urban renewal

Peter Aldous	*Con*	p65
Adrian Bailey	*Lab/Co-op*	p71
Stephen McPartland	*Con*	p248
Graham Stringer	*Lab*	p325

Veterans

Johnny Mercer	*Con*	p257
Bob Stewart	*Con*	p321

Wales economy

Liz Saville Roberts	*PlC*	p301

Waste management

Clive Efford	*Lab*	p141

Welfare

Debbie Abrahams	*Lab*	p63
Harriett Baldwin	*Con*	p72
Guto Bebb	*Con*	p75
Bob Blackman	*Con*	p81
Kirsty Blackman	*SNP*	p82
Karen Buck	*Lab*	p94
Liam Byrne	*Lab*	p98
James Cartlidge	*Con*	p103
Sarah Champion	*Lab*	p104
Greg Clark	*Con*	p108
Vernon Coaker	*Lab*	p111
Jeremy Corbyn	*Lab*	p114
Neil Coyle	*Lab*	p116
Stephen Crabb	*Con*	p117
Marsha De Cordova	*Lab*	p128
Oliver Dowden	*Con*	p135

Jackie Doyle-Price	*Con*	p135
Clive Efford	*Lab*	p141
Chris Evans	*Lab/Co-op*	p146
Caroline Flint	*Lab*	p153
Peter Grant	*SNP*	p172
Chris Grayling	*Con*	p173
Damian Hinds	*Con*	p196
Sajid Javid	*Con*	p207
Gerald Jones	*Lab*	p213
Chris Law	*SNP*	p227
Emma Lewell-Buck	*Lab*	p230
Siobhain McDonagh	*Lab*	p241
Madeleine Moon	*Lab*	p261
Gavin Newlands	*SNP*	p270
Albert Owen	*Lab*	p275
Jeremy Quin	*Con*	p288
Emma Reynolds	*Lab*	p293
Amber Rudd	*Con*	p299
Alec Shelbrooke	*Con*	p306
Chloe Smith	*Con*	p312
Julian Smith	*Con*	p313
Mel Stride	*Con*	p324
Graham Stuart	*Con*	p325
Karl Turner	*Lab*	p337

Wind farms planning

Peter Aldous	*Con*	p65

Youth justice

Seema Malhotra	*Lab/Co-op*	p251

Youth services

Liam Byrne	*Lab*	p98
John Glen	*Con*	p166
Patrick Grady	*SNP*	p170

Youth training schemes

Guy Opperman	*Con*	p274

MPs' Countries of Interest

For precise details of individuals' stated interests, see relevant biography. The interests listed are supplied by MPs themselves.

Afghanistan

Roberta Blackman-Woods	*Lab*	p82
Stephen Doughty	*Lab/Co-op*	p134
Tobias Ellwood	*Con*	p143
Paul Flynn	*Lab*	p154
James Gray	*Con*	p172
Dan Jarvis	*Lab*	p207
Bernard Jenkin	*Con*	p208
Kevan Jones	*Lab*	p214
Jack Lopresti	*Con*	p236
Madeleine Moon	*Lab*	p261

Albania

John Grogan	*Lab*	p178

Algeria

Catherine West	*Lab*	p346

Angola

Vernon Coaker	*Lab*	p111
Nadine Dorries	*Con*	p133
David Duguid	*Con*	p138
Kate Hoey	*Lab*	p198

Antarctica

James Gray	*Con*	p172

Argentina

Stephen Doughty	*Lab/Co-op*	p134
Chris Matheson	*Lab*	p254
Mark Menzies	*Con*	p256

Armenia

Stephen Pound	*Lab*	p285
John Whittingdale	*Con*	p349

Australia

Jon Ashworth	*Lab/Co-op*	p69
Paul Beresford	*Con*	p79
Tom Brake	*Lib Dem*	p88
Nick Brown	*Lab*	p92
John Cryer	*Lab*	p120
Maria Eagle	*Lab*	p140
Nigel Evans	*Con*	p146
David Evennett	*Con*	p147
Michael Fabricant	*Con*	p148
Paul Farrelly	*Lab*	p149
John Grogan	*Lab*	p178
John Healey	*Lab*	p190
Eleanor Laing	*Con*	p222
Conor McGinn	*Lab*	p243
Paul Maynard	*Con*	p255
Mark Menzies	*Con*	p256
Andrew Rosindell	*Con*	p297
Lee Rowley	*Con*	p298
Andrew Selous	*Con*	p302
John Spellar	*Lab*	p317
Ross Thomson	*Con*	p331
Tom Watson	*Lab*	p345
Catherine West	*Lab*	p346
Craig Whittaker	*Con*	p349

Azerbaijan

Bob Blackman	*Con*	p81
David Duguid	*Con*	p138
Paul Flynn	*Lab*	p154
Christopher Pincher	*Con*	p283

Bahamas

David Morris	*Con*	p265

Bahrain

Nigel Evans	*Con*	p146
Jack Lopresti	*Con*	p236
Andy Slaughter	*Lab*	p310

Bangladesh

Debbie Abrahams	*Lab*	p63
Jon Ashworth	*Lab/Co-op*	p69
Lyn Brown	*Lab*	p92
Stephen Doughty	*Lab/Co-op*	p134
David Drew	*Lab/Co-op*	p136
Jim Fitzpatrick	*Lab*	p152
Anne Main	*Con*	p250
Nicky Morgan	*Con*	p263
Paul Scully	*Con*	p302
Virendra Sharma	*Lab*	p305
Gavin Shuker	*Lab/Co-op*	p307
Andrew Stephenson	*Con*	p320
Keith Vaz	*Lab*	p340
Catherine West	*Lab*	p346

Belarus

Robert Goodwill	*Con*	p169
Maria Miller	*Con*	p258

Belgium

Wayne David	*Lab*	p123

Belize

Chris Ruane	*Lab*	p298

Bermuda

David Crausby	*Lab*	p117

Bosnia/Herzegovina

Clive Betts	*Lab*	p80
Jackie Doyle-Price	*Con*	p135
Kate Hoey	*Lab*	p198
Paul Maynard	*Con*	p255
Andrew Stephenson	*Con*	p320

Botswana

James Duddridge	*Con*	p137

Brazil

Bob Blackman	*Con*	p81
Geoffrey Clifton-Brown	*Con*	p110

Martin Docherty-Hughes	*SNP*	p130
Barry Gardiner	*Lab*	p161
Nick Hurd	*Con*	p205
Conor McGinn	*Lab*	p243
Mark Prisk	*Con*	p286
Caroline Spelman	*Con*	p318

Bulgaria

Kevin Barron	*Lab*	p74
Wayne David	*Lab*	p123

Burma

John Bercow	*Speaker*	p78
Paul Blomfield	*Lab*	p83
Alistair Carmichael	*Lib Dem*	p102
Caroline Lucas	*Green*	p238
Paul Scully	*Con*	p302
Valerie Vaz	*Lab*	p341

Burundi

Mary Creagh	*Lab*	p118

Cambodia

Ann Clwyd	*Lab*	p110
Sharon Hodgson	*Lab*	p198

Canada

David Crausby	*Lab*	p117
Stephen Doughty	*Lab/Co-op*	p134
Oliver Dowden	*Con*	p135
David Duguid	*Con*	p138
David Evennett	*Con*	p147
Michael Gove	*Con*	p169
Helen Jones	*Lab*	p214
Maria Miller	*Con*	p258
Andrew Percy	*Con*	p280
Andrew Rosindell	*Con*	p297
Virendra Sharma	*Lab*	p305
Andrew Stephenson	*Con*	p320
Ross Thomson	*Con*	p331
Robin Walker	*Con*	p343

Chile

George Hollingbery	*Con*	p199
Bernard Jenkin	*Con*	p208

China

Adrian Bailey	*Lab/Co-op*	p71
Roberta Blackman-Woods	*Lab*	p82
Lyn Brown	*Lab*	p92
Nick Brown	*Lab*	p92
Conor Burns	*Con*	p96
Vince Cable	*Lib Dem*	p99
Ronnie Campbell	*Lab*	p102
Sarah Champion	*Lab*	p104
Simon Clarke	*Con*	p109
Geoffrey Clifton-Brown	*Con*	p110
David Davies	*Con*	p124
Caroline Dinenage	*Con*	p129
Chris Evans	*Lab/Co-op*	p146
Paul Farrelly	*Lab*	p149
Barry Gardiner	*Lab*	p161
Mark Garnier	*Con*	p162
Cheryl Gillan	*Con*	p165
Richard Graham	*Con*	p170
James Gray	*Con*	p172
Andrew Griffiths	*Con*	p178
Andrew Gwynne	*Lab*	p179
Stephen Hammond	*Con*	p182
Mark Hendrick	*Lab/Co-op*	p193
Sharon Hodgson	*Lab*	p198
George Hollingbery	*Con*	p199
Nick Hurd	*Con*	p205
David Jones	*Con*	p213
Mark Lancaster	*Con*	p225
Ian Liddell-Grainger	*Con*	p233
Stephen McPartland	*Con*	p248
Alan Mak	*Con*	p250
Seema Malhotra	*Lab/Co-op*	p251
Stephen Metcalfe	*Con*	p257
Madeleine Moon	*Lab*	p261
Grahame Morris	*Lab*	p265
Chi Onwurah	*Lab*	p274
Ian Paisley	*DUP*	p276
Neil Parish	*Con*	p276
Owen Paterson	*Con*	p277
Mark Pawsey	*Con*	p278
Victoria Prentis	*Con*	p286
Mark Prisk	*Con*	p286
Jeremy Quin	*Con*	p288
Will Quince	*Con*	p288
John Redwood	*Con*	p290
Jacob Rees-Mogg	*Con*	p292
Rachel Reeves	*Lab*	p293
Jonathan Reynolds	*Lab/Co-op*	p294
David Rutley	*Con*	p300
Nick Smith	*Lab*	p314
Andrew Stephenson	*Con*	p320
Wes Streeting	*Lab*	p324
Graham Stuart	*Con*	p325
Catherine West	*Lab*	p346
Heather Wheeler	*Con*	p347
John Whittingdale	*Con*	p349
Gavin Williamson	*Con*	p352
Sammy Wilson	*DUP*	p353

Colombia

Alan Campbell	*Lab*	p101
Michael Gove	*Con*	p169
Diana Johnson	*Lab*	p210
Chris Matheson	*Lab*	p254
Madeleine Moon	*Lab*	p261
Lisa Nandy	*Lab*	p269
Jo Stevens	*Lab*	p320

Croatia

Jackie Doyle-Price	*Con*	p135

Cuba

Roger Gale	*Con*	p160
Grahame Morris	*Lab*	p265
Chris Williamson	*Lab*	p351

Cyprus
Harriett Baldwin *Con* p72
Jeffrey Donaldson *DUP* p132
Mike Freer *Con* p158
Roger Gale *Con* p160
Fabian Hamilton *Lab* p181
David Hanson *Lab* p184
Julian Knight *Con* p221
Matthew Offord *Con* p272
Albert Owen *Lab* p275
Joan Ryan *Lab* p300
Virendra Sharma *Lab* p305
Theresa Villiers *Con* p342
Catherine West *Lab* p346

Czech Republic
Helen Goodman *Lab* p168

Democratic Republic of Congo
Hilary Benn *Lab* p76
Mary Creagh *Lab* p118
David Drew *Lab/Co-op* p136
Ivan Lewis *Lab* p232

Denmark
Martin Docherty-Hughes *SNP* p130
David Duguid *Con* p138
Helen Goodman *Lab* p168
Diana Johnson *Lab* p210
Helen Jones *Lab* p214
David Rutley *Con* p300

Dominican Republic
Rosie Cooper *Lab* p113

East Timor
Ann Clwyd *Lab* p110

Ecuador
Chris Williamson *Lab* p351

Egypt
Nigel Evans *Con* p146
Andy Slaughter *Lab* p310

El Salvador
Peter Bottomley *Con* p85

Estonia
Martin Docherty-Hughes *SNP* p130
Helen Jones *Lab* p214
Mark Prisk *Con* p286

Ethiopia
Jeffrey Donaldson *DUP* p132
Laurence Robertson *Con* p295

Falkland Islands
Alan Campbell *Lab* p101
Caroline Dinenage *Con* p129
Simon Hart *Con* p187
Lindsay Hoyle *Lab* p203
Guy Opperman *Con* p274

Faroe Islands
Angus MacNeil *SNP* p247

Fiji
Paul Beresford *Con* p79

Finland
Nic Dakin *Lab* p122
Helen Jones *Lab* p214
Angela Smith *Lab* p311

France
Edward Argar *Con* p69
Tom Brake *Lib Dem* p88
Vernon Coaker *Lab* p111
Stephen Crabb *Con* p117
Alex Cunningham *Lab* p121
Chris Elmore *Lab* p144
Chris Evans *Lab/Co-op* p146
Paul Farrelly *Lab* p149
George Freeman *Con* p157
Damian Green *Con* p174
Dominic Grieve *Con* p177
Nia Griffith *Lab* p177
Kelvin Hopkins *Lab* p201
Bernard Jenkin *Con* p208
Jo Johnson *Con* p211
Robert Neill *Con* p269
Chi Onwurah *Lab* p274
Victoria Prentis *Con* p286
Geoffrey Robinson *Lab* p296
Keith Simpson *Con* p308
Owen Smith *Lab* p314
Caroline Spelman *Con* p318
Jamie Stone *Lib Dem* p323
Jon Trickett *Lab* p335
Alan Whitehead *Lab* p348
Hywel Williams *PlC* p350

Gambia
John McDonnell *Lab* p242

Georgia
Damian Green *Con* p174
Bernard Jenkin *Con* p208
John Whittingdale *Con* p349

Germany
Ben Bradshaw *Lab* p87
David Davies *Con* p124
Chris Evans *Lab/Co-op* p146
Paul Farrelly *Lab* p149
Mark Field *Con* p151
Michael Gove *Con* p169
Philip Hammond *Con* p182
Greg Hands *Con* p184
Mark Hendrick *Lab/Co-op* p193
Bernard Jenkin *Con* p208
Ian C Lucas *Lab* p238
Paul Maynard *Con* p255
Victoria Prentis *Con* p286

Jonathan Reynolds *Lab/Co-op* p294
Geoffrey Robinson *Lab* p296
Keith Simpson *Con* p308
Caroline Spelman *Con* p318
Jamie Stone *Lib Dem* p323
Stephen Timms *Lab* p332
Pete Wishart *SNP* p354

Gibraltar

Caroline Dinenage *Con* p129
Nigel Evans *Con* p146
Lindsay Hoyle *Lab* p203
Eleanor Laing *Con* p222
Mike Penning *Con* p279

Greece

Chris Elmore *Lab* p144
Chris Evans *Lab/Co-op* p146
Derek Twigg *Lab* p337
Catherine West *Lab* p346

Guyana

Kevin Barron *Lab* p74

Haiti

Rosie Cooper *Lab* p113

Hong Kong

Caroline Dinenage *Con* p129
Philip Dunne *Con* p139
Ian Liddell-Grainger *Con* p233
David Morris *Con* p265

Hungary

James Cartlidge *Con* p103
David Davies *Con* p124
Paul Farrelly *Lab* p149
Paul Flynn *Lab* p154
Cheryl Gillan *Con* p165
Mark Hendrick *Lab/Co-op* p193
Craig Mackinlay *Con* p245
Robert Neill *Con* p269

Iceland

Paul Farrelly *Lab* p149
Fabian Hamilton *Lab* p181
Angus MacNeil *SNP* p247

India

Jon Ashworth *Lab/Co-op* p69
Kemi Badenoch *Con* p71
Adrian Bailey *Lab/Co-op* p71
Bob Blackman *Con* p81
Crispin Blunt *Con* p83
Vince Cable *Lib Dem* p99
Geoffrey Clifton-Brown *Con* p110
Stephen Crabb *Con* p117
John Cryer *Lab* p120
Caroline Dinenage *Con* p129
Stephen Doughty *Lab/Co-op* p134
Oliver Dowden *Con* p135
Nigel Evans *Con* p146
Mark Field *Con* p151
Barry Gardiner *Lab* p161
Helen Grant *Con* p171
Dominic Grieve *Con* p177
Andrew Gwynne *Lab* p179
Stephen Hammond *Con* p182
Matt Hancock *Con* p183
Gordon Henderson *Con* p192
Sylvia Hermon *Ind* p194
Bernard Jenkin *Con* p208
Jo Johnson *Con* p211
Mark Lancaster *Con* p225
Alison McGovern *Lab* p244
Stephen McPartland *Con* p248
Seema Malhotra *Lab/Co-op* p251
Penny Mordaunt *Con* p262
Guy Opperman *Con* p274
Priti Patel *Con* p277
Owen Paterson *Con* p277
Mark Pawsey *Con* p278
Mark Pritchard *Con* p287
Jeremy Quin *Con* p288
John Redwood *Con* p290
Jacob Rees-Mogg *Con* p292
Emma Reynolds *Lab* p293
Paul Scully *Con* p302
Alok Sharma *Con* p304
Virendra Sharma *Lab* p305
Nick Smith *Lab* p314
Rishi Sunak *Con* p326
Jo Swinson *Lib Dem* p327
Gareth Thomas *Lab/Co-op* p330
Ed Vaizey *Con* p339
Keith Vaz *Lab* p340
Robin Walker *Con* p343
David Warburton *Con* p344

Indonesia

Michael Gove *Con* p169
Richard Graham *Con* p170
Antoinette Sandbach *Con* p301

Iran

Clive Betts *Lab* p80
Simon Clarke *Con* p109
Ann Clwyd *Lab* p110
Fabian Hamilton *Lab* p181
Seema Kennedy *Con* p218
John McDonnell *Lab* p242
Ross Thomson *Con* p331
Ben Wallace *Con* p343

Iraq

Ann Clwyd *Lab* p110
Tobias Ellwood *Con* p143
Michael Gove *Con* p169
Robert Halfon *Con* p180
Dan Jarvis *Lab* p207
Bernard Jenkin *Con* p208
Kevan Jones *Lab* p214
Jack Lopresti *Con* p236
Andrew Murrison *Con* p268

Ireland

Kevin Brennan	*Lab*	p89
Rosie Cooper	*Lab*	p113
Martin Docherty-Hughes	*SNP*	p130
Jeffrey Donaldson	*DUP*	p132
Chris Elmore	*Lab*	p144
Paul Farrelly	*Lab*	p149
Michael Gove	*Con*	p169
Greg Hands	*Con*	p184
Sylvia Hermon	*Ind*	p194
Helen Jones	*Lab*	p214
Mike Kane	*Lab*	p216
David Linden	*SNP*	p234
John McDonnell	*Lab*	p242
Conor McGinn	*Lab*	p243
Huw Merriman	*Con*	p257
Robert Neill	*Con*	p269
Albert Owen	*Lab*	p275
Stephen Pound	*Lab*	p285
Chris Ruane	*Lab*	p298
Joan Ryan	*Lab*	p300
Owen Smith	*Lab*	p314
Bob Stewart	*Con*	p321

Israel

Guto Bebb	*Con*	p75
Bob Blackman	*Con*	p81
Robert Buckland	*Con*	p94
Alistair Carmichael	*Lib Dem*	p102
Jeffrey Donaldson	*DUP*	p132
Stephen Doughty	*Lab/Co-op*	p134
Oliver Dowden	*Con*	p135
Michael Ellis	*Con*	p142
Paul Flynn	*Lab*	p154
Mike Freer	*Con*	p158
Nick Gibb	*Con*	p164
Paul Girvan	*DUP*	p166
Michael Gove	*Con*	p169
Andrew Gwynne	*Lab*	p179
Robert Halfon	*Con*	p180
Mark Harper	*Con*	p185
Gordon Henderson	*Con*	p192
John Lamont	*Con*	p225
Jack Lopresti	*Con*	p236
Alan Mak	*Con*	p250
Madeleine Moon	*Lab*	p261
Matthew Offord	*Con*	p272
Neil Parish	*Con*	p276
Andrew Percy	*Con*	p280
Mark Pritchard	*Con*	p287
Joan Ryan	*Lab*	p300
Gavin Shuker	*Lab/Co-op*	p307
David Simpson	*DUP*	p308
Keith Simpson	*Con*	p308
John Spellar	*Lab*	p317
John Stevenson	*Con*	p321
Wes Streeting	*Lab*	p324
Ross Thomson	*Con*	p331
Ed Vaizey	*Con*	p339
Theresa Villiers	*Con*	p342
John Whittingdale	*Con*	p349

Italy

Jon Ashworth	*Lab/Co-op*	p69
Bob Blackman	*Con*	p81
Ben Bradshaw	*Lab*	p87
Andrew Bridgen	*Con*	p90
Steve Brine	*Con*	p90
David Evennett	*Con*	p147
Paul Farrelly	*Lab*	p149
Michael Gove	*Con*	p169
Damian Green	*Con*	p174
Nia Griffith	*Lab*	p177
Philip Hammond	*Con*	p182
John Hayes	*Con*	p188
Brandon Lewis	*Con*	p231
Catherine McKinnell	*Lab*	p245
Paul Maskey	*Sinn Féin*	p254
Robert Neill	*Con*	p269
Mark Prisk	*Con*	p286
Geoffrey Robinson	*Lab*	p296
Jamie Stone	*Lib Dem*	p323
Robin Walker	*Con*	p343
Ben Wallace	*Con*	p343

Jamaica

Diane Abbott	*Lab*	p63
Dawn Butler	*Lab*	p97

Japan

Nick Brown	*Lab*	p92
Oliver Dowden	*Con*	p135
Paul Farrelly	*Lab*	p149
Cheryl Gillan	*Con*	p165
Roger Godsiff	*Lab*	p167
Fabian Hamilton	*Lab*	p181
Matt Hancock	*Con*	p183
Mark Hendrick	*Lab/Co-op*	p193
Sharon Hodgson	*Lab*	p198
Jeremy Hunt	*Con*	p204
Ian C Lucas	*Lab*	p238
Stephen Metcalfe	*Con*	p257
Rachel Reeves	*Lab*	p293
Ross Thomson	*Con*	p331
David Warburton	*Con*	p344
Tom Watson	*Lab*	p345
Heather Wheeler	*Con*	p347
John Whittingdale	*Con*	p349
Gavin Williamson	*Con*	p352

Jordan

Michael Gove	*Con*	p169
Diana Johnson	*Lab*	p210
Keith Simpson	*Con*	p308

Kenya

Vince Cable	*Lib Dem*	p99
Steve Double	*Con*	p134
Chris Heaton-Harris	*Con*	p191
Jeremy Lefroy	*Con*	p228
John McDonnell	*Lab*	p242
Barry Sheerman	*Lab/Co-op*	p305
Craig Whittaker	*Con*	p349

Korea, North

Fiona Bruce	*Con*	p93
Fabian Hamilton	*Lab*	p181
Greg Hands	*Con*	p184
Gary Streeter	*Con*	p323
Ross Thomson	*Con*	p331
John Whittingdale	*Con*	p349
Gavin Williamson	*Con*	p352

Korea, South

Fabian Hamilton	*Lab*	p181
Ross Thomson	*Con*	p331
John Whittingdale	*Con*	p349
Gavin Williamson	*Con*	p352

Kosovo

Vernon Coaker	*Lab*	p111
Jo Swinson	*Lib Dem*	p327

Latvia

Martin Docherty-Hughes	*SNP*	p130
Christopher Pincher	*Con*	p283
Mark Prisk	*Con*	p286

Lesotho

Ian C Lucas	*Lab*	p238

Libya

Daniel Kawczynski	*Con*	p216

Liechtenstein

Andrew Rosindell	*Con*	p297

Lithuania

Martin Docherty-Hughes	*SNP*	p130
Alan Whitehead	*Lab*	p348

Luxembourg

Dominic Grieve	*Con*	p177

Malaysia

Bill Cash	*Con*	p103
John Whittingdale	*Con*	p349

Maldives

John Glen	*Con*	p166
Helen Grant	*Con*	p171

Malta

Julian Knight	*Con*	p221
Albert Owen	*Lab*	p275

Mauritania

Daniel Kawczynski	*Con*	p216

Mauritius

Geoffrey Cox	*Con*	p116
Virendra Sharma	*Lab*	p305

Moldova

Jeffrey Donaldson	*DUP*	p132
Robert Goodwill	*Con*	p169
Damian Green	*Con*	p174
Paul Maynard	*Con*	p255

Mongolia

Roger Gale	*Con*	p160
James Gray	*Con*	p172
John Grogan	*Lab*	p178

Montenegro

Andrew Stephenson	*Con*	p320

Morocco

Andrew Murrison	*Con*	p268
Victoria Prentis	*Con*	p286

Myanmar

Jon Ashworth	*Lab/Co-op*	p69

Nepal

Bob Blackman	*Con*	p81
James Gray	*Con*	p172
Margaret Hodge	*Lab*	p197
Dan Jarvis	*Lab*	p207
Mark Lancaster	*Con*	p225
Maria Miller	*Con*	p258
Ian Murray	*Lab*	p267
Virendra Sharma	*Lab*	p305
Nick Smith	*Lab*	p314

Netherlands

Clive Betts	*Lab*	p80
Antoinette Sandbach	*Con*	p301

New Zealand

Paul Beresford	*Con*	p79
Nick Brown	*Lab*	p92
David Crausby	*Lab*	p117
David Evennett	*Con*	p147
Paul Farrelly	*Lab*	p149
John Grogan	*Lab*	p178
Sharon Hodgson	*Lab*	p198
Bernard Jenkin	*Con*	p208
Eleanor Laing	*Con*	p222
Andrew Rosindell	*Con*	p297
Gavin Shuker	*Lab/Co-op*	p307
Craig Whittaker	*Con*	p349

Nicaragua

Maria Eagle	*Lab*	p140
Andrew Selous	*Con*	p302

Nigeria

Kemi Badenoch	*Con*	p71
Vince Cable	*Lib Dem*	p99
Helen Grant	*Con*	p171
Chi Onwurah	*Lab*	p274

Norway

Edward Argar	*Con*	p69
Paul Farrelly	*Lab*	p149
Phillip Lee	*Con*	p228
Angus MacNeil	*SNP*	p247
Gavin Shuker	*Lab/Co-op*	p307
Gareth Thomas	*Lab/Co-op*	p330

Oman

Edward Argar	*Con*	p69
Kate Hoey	*Lab*	p198
Mark Prisk	*Con*	p286
Keith Vaz	*Lab*	p340

Pakistan

Debbie Abrahams	*Lab*	p63
Jon Ashworth	*Lab/Co-op*	p69
Adrian Bailey	*Lab/Co-op*	p71
Steve Baker	*Con*	p72
Lyn Brown	*Lab*	p92
Rehman Chishti	*Con*	p106
Simon Clarke	*Con*	p109
Stephen Doughty	*Lab/Co-op*	p134
Alan Duncan	*Con*	p138
Andrew Griffiths	*Con*	p178
Richard Harrington	*Con*	p186
Sharon Hodgson	*Lab*	p198
Dan Jarvis	*Lab*	p207
Bernard Jenkin	*Con*	p208
Madeleine Moon	*Lab*	p261
Mark Pawsey	*Con*	p278
Emma Reynolds	*Lab*	p293
Alok Sharma	*Con*	p304
Virendra Sharma	*Lab*	p305
Gavin Shuker	*Lab/Co-op*	p307
Andrew Stephenson	*Con*	p320
Gareth Thomas	*Lab/Co-op*	p330
Keith Vaz	*Lab*	p340

Poland

Wayne David	*Lab*	p123
Frank Field	*Lab*	p151
Cheryl Gillan	*Con*	p165
Michael Gove	*Con*	p169
Mark Hendrick	*Lab/Co-op*	p193
Kevan Jones	*Lab*	p214
Stephen Pound	*Lab*	p285
Keith Simpson	*Con*	p308
Jamie Stone	*Lib Dem*	p323
Alan Whitehead	*Lab*	p348

Portugal

Clive Betts	*Lab*	p80
Tom Brake	*Lib Dem*	p88
Stephen Hammond	*Con*	p182
Caroline Spelman	*Con*	p318

Romania

James Cartlidge	*Con*	p103
Paul Flynn	*Lab*	p154
Jo Swinson	*Lib Dem*	p327
Ben Wallace	*Con*	p343

Russia

Harriett Baldwin	*Con*	p72
Tom Brake	*Lib Dem*	p88
Robert Buckland	*Con*	p94
Vince Cable	*Lib Dem*	p99
Simon Clarke	*Con*	p109
Ann Clwyd	*Lab*	p110
Jim Cunningham	*Lab*	p122
Martin Docherty-Hughes	*SNP*	p130
Paul Farrelly	*Lab*	p149
Barry Gardiner	*Lab*	p161
James Gray	*Con*	p172
Fabian Hamilton	*Lab*	p181
Greg Hands	*Con*	p184
Sylvia Hermon	*Ind*	p194
Bernard Jenkin	*Con*	p208
Stephen Kinnock	*Lab*	p220
Julian Lewis	*Con*	p232
Kerry McCarthy	*Lab*	p240
Gordon Marsden	*Lab*	p252
Madeleine Moon	*Lab*	p261
Christopher Pincher	*Con*	p283
Victoria Prentis	*Con*	p286
Mark Prisk	*Con*	p286
Ben Wallace	*Con*	p343
John Whittingdale	*Con*	p349

Rwanda

Fiona Bruce	*Con*	p93
Mary Creagh	*Lab*	p118
David Drew	*Lab/Co-op*	p136
Ivan Lewis	*Lab*	p232
Mark Pawsey	*Con*	p278
Maggie Throup	*Con*	p332

Samoa

Paul Beresford	*Con*	p79

Saudi Arabia

Rehman Chishti	*Con*	p106
Daniel Kawczynski	*Con*	p216
Keith Simpson	*Con*	p308
Andrew Stephenson	*Con*	p320

Scotland

Jim Shannon	*DUP*	p303

Serbia

Clive Betts	*Lab*	p80
Jackie Doyle-Price	*Con*	p135

Sierra Leone

David Mundell	*Con*	p267
Andrew Stephenson	*Con*	p320
Jo Swinson	*Lib Dem*	p327
Gavin Williamson	*Con*	p352

Singapore

Sharon Hodgson	*Lab*	p198
Bernard Jenkin	*Con*	p208
Ian Liddell-Grainger	*Con*	p233
Stephen Timms	*Lab*	p332

Slovenia

Neil Parish	*Con*	p276
David Rutley	*Con*	p300

Somalia

Jon Ashworth	*Lab/Co-op*	p69
Paul Blomfield	*Lab*	p83
Stephen Doughty	*Lab/Co-op*	p134
Kerry McCarthy	*Lab*	p240
John McDonnell	*Lab*	p242
Catherine West	*Lab*	p346

South Africa

Jeffrey Donaldson	*DUP*	p132
David Drew	*Lab/Co-op*	p136
James Duddridge	*Con*	p137
Louise Haigh	*Lab*	p180
David Hanson	*Lab*	p184
Sharon Hodgson	*Lab*	p198
George Howarth	*Lab*	p202
Norman Lamb	*Lib Dem*	p223
Ian Liddell-Grainger	*Con*	p233
Conor McGinn	*Lab*	p243
Alan Mak	*Con*	p250
Francie Molloy	*Sinn Féin*	p261
Chi Onwurah	*Lab*	p274
Robin Walker	*Con*	p343
Paul Williams	*Lab*	p351

Spain

Luciana Berger	*Lab/Co-op*	p79
Chris Bryant	*Lab*	p93
Nia Griffith	*Lab*	p177
John Hayes	*Con*	p188
Robert Neill	*Con*	p269
Andy Slaughter	*Lab*	p310
Ross Thomson	*Con*	p331

Sri Lanka

Bob Blackman	*Con*	p81
Sarah Champion	*Lab*	p104
Barry Gardiner	*Lab*	p161
Helen Grant	*Con*	p171
James Gray	*Con*	p172
Stephen Hammond	*Con*	p182
Sharon Hodgson	*Lab*	p198
Matthew Offord	*Con*	p272
Virendra Sharma	*Lab*	p305
Gareth Thomas	*Lab/Co-op*	p330
Karl Turner	*Lab*	p337

Sudan

Hilary Benn	*Lab*	p76
John Bercow	*Speaker*	p78
Mary Creagh	*Lab*	p118
David Drew	*Lab/Co-op*	p136

Swaziland

James Duddridge	*Con*	p137

Sweden

Nic Dakin	*Lab*	p122
Kelvin Hopkins	*Lab*	p201
Helen Jones	*Lab*	p214
Alok Sharma	*Con*	p304

Switzerland

Jeremy Lefroy	*Con*	p228
Ian Liddell-Grainger	*Con*	p233
Robert Neill	*Con*	p269
Andrew Rosindell	*Con*	p297

Syria

Jon Ashworth	*Lab/Co-op*	p69
Andrew Bridgen	*Con*	p90
Guy Opperman	*Con*	p274
Keith Simpson	*Con*	p308

Taiwan

John Lamont	*Con*	p225
Heather Wheeler	*Con*	p347

Tanzania

Kevin Barron	*Lab*	p74
Fiona Bruce	*Con*	p93
Steve Double	*Con*	p134
Jeremy Lefroy	*Con*	p228
David Linden	*SNP*	p234
John McDonnell	*Lab*	p242
Craig Whittaker	*Con*	p349

Tunisia

Roger Gale	*Con*	p160
Andy Slaughter	*Lab*	p310

Turkey

Ann Clwyd	*Lab*	p110
Fabian Hamilton	*Lab*	p181
Mark Harper	*Con*	p185
Maria Miller	*Con*	p258
Madeleine Moon	*Lab*	p261
Jonathan Reynolds	*Lab/Co-op*	p294
Joan Ryan	*Lab*	p300
Catherine West	*Lab*	p346
Hywel Williams	*PlC*	p350

Uganda

John Glen	*Con*	p166
Chris Heaton-Harris	*Con*	p191
Eleanor Laing	*Con*	p222
Jeremy Lefroy	*Con*	p228
Paul Williams	*Lab*	p351

Ukraine

Clive Betts	*Lab*	p80
Martin Docherty-Hughes	*SNP*	p130
Robert Goodwill	*Con*	p169
John Grogan	*Lab*	p178
Stephen Pound	*Lab*	p285
John Whittingdale	*Con*	p349

United Arab Emirates

Nigel Huddleston	*Con*	p203
Kevan Jones	*Lab*	p214

United Kingdom

Kate Green	*Lab*	p175
Matt Hancock	*Con*	p183
John Hayes	*Con*	p188
Stephen McPartland	*Con*	p248
Sheryll Murray	*Con*	p268
Laurence Robertson	*Con*	p295
Mark Spencer	*Con*	p318
Ross Thomson	*Con*	p331

USA

Peter Aldous	*Con*	p65
David Amess	*Con*	p67
Stuart Andrew	*Con*	p68
Edward Argar	*Con*	p69
Jon Ashworth	*Lab/Co-op*	p69
Kemi Badenoch	*Con*	p71
Hilary Benn	*Lab*	p76
John Bercow	*Speaker*	p78
Bob Blackman	*Con*	p81
Crispin Blunt	*Con*	p83
Peter Bottomley	*Con*	p85
Ben Bradshaw	*Lab*	p87
Kevin Brennan	*Lab*	p89
Andrew Bridgen	*Con*	p90
Steve Brine	*Con*	p90
Nick Brown	*Lab*	p92
Conor Burns	*Con*	p96
Ronnie Campbell	*Lab*	p102
Sarah Champion	*Lab*	p104
Rehman Chishti	*Con*	p106
Rosie Cooper	*Lab*	p113
Yvette Cooper	*Lab*	p114
Stephen Crabb	*Con*	p117
John Cryer	*Lab*	p120
Jim Cunningham	*Lab*	p122
Philip Davies	*Con*	p126
Nigel Dodds	*DUP*	p132
Jeffrey Donaldson	*DUP*	p132
Stephen Doughty	*Lab/Co-op*	p134
Philip Dunne	*Con*	p139
Maria Eagle	*Lab*	p140
Michael Ellis	*Con*	p142
Tobias Ellwood	*Con*	p143
Chris Elmore	*Lab*	p144
Chris Evans	*Lab/Co-op*	p146
Nigel Evans	*Con*	p146
David Evennett	*Con*	p147
Michael Fabricant	*Con*	p148
Mark Field	*Con*	p151
Liam Fox	*Con*	p155
George Freeman	*Con*	p157
Mike Freer	*Con*	p158
Nick Gibb	*Con*	p164
Cheryl Gillan	*Con*	p165
Paul Girvan	*DUP*	p166
John Glen	*Con*	p166
Roger Godsiff	*Lab*	p167
Helen Grant	*Con*	p171
James Gray	*Con*	p172
Andrew Griffiths	*Con*	p178
Andrew Gwynne	*Lab*	p179
Robert Halfon	*Con*	p180
Stephen Hammond	*Con*	p182
Matt Hancock	*Con*	p183
Mark Harper	*Con*	p185
John Hayes	*Con*	p188
John Healey	*Lab*	p190
Chris Heaton-Harris	*Con*	p191
Mark Hendrick	*Lab/Co-op*	p193
Sharon Hodgson	*Lab*	p198
George Hollingbery	*Con*	p199
Nigel Huddleston	*Con*	p203
Ranil Jayawardena	*Con*	p208
Bernard Jenkin	*Con*	p208
Gareth Johnson	*Con*	p211
Kevan Jones	*Lab*	p214
Greg Knight	*Con*	p220
Eleanor Laing	*Con*	p222
Norman Lamb	*Lib Dem*	p223
David Lammy	*Lab*	p224
John Lamont	*Con*	p225
Mark Lancaster	*Con*	p225
Brandon Lewis	*Con*	p231
Ivan Lewis	*Lab*	p232
Ian Liddell-Grainger	*Con*	p233
Jack Lopresti	*Con*	p236
Jonathan Lord	*Con*	p236
Ian C Lucas	*Lab*	p238
Conor McGinn	*Lab*	p243
Craig Mackinlay	*Con*	p245
Stephen McPartland	*Con*	p248
Alan Mak	*Con*	p250
Gordon Marsden	*Lab*	p252
Mark Menzies	*Con*	p256
Stephen Metcalfe	*Con*	p257
Andrew Mitchell	*Con*	p260
Penny Mordaunt	*Con*	p262
David Mundell	*Con*	p267
Ian Murray	*Lab*	p267
Sheryll Murray	*Con*	p268
Gavin Newlands	*SNP*	p270
Ian Paisley	*DUP*	p276
Owen Paterson	*Con*	p277
Andrew Percy	*Con*	p280
Christopher Pincher	*Con*	p283
Mark Prisk	*Con*	p286
Mark Pritchard	*Con*	p287
Tom Pursglove	*Con*	p288
John Redwood	*Con*	p290
Rachel Reeves	*Lab*	p293
Emma Reynolds	*Lab*	p293
Laurence Robertson	*Con*	p295
Geoffrey Robinson	*Lab*	p296
Andrew Rosindell	*Con*	p297
Lee Rowley	*Con*	p298
David Rutley	*Con*	p300
Andrew Selous	*Con*	p302
Jim Shannon	*DUP*	p303
Virendra Sharma	*Lab*	p305
Barry Sheerman	*Lab/Co-op*	p305
Alec Shelbrooke	*Con*	p306
Keith Simpson	*Con*	p308
Ruth Smeeth	*Lab*	p310
Henry Smith	*Con*	p312
Nick Smith	*Lab*	p314

Nicholas Soames	*Con*	p316
John Spellar	*Lab*	p317
Andrew Stephenson	*Con*	p320
Wes Streeting	*Lab*	p324
Mel Stride	*Con*	p324
Rishi Sunak	*Con*	p326
Robert Syms	*Con*	p328
Ross Thomson	*Con*	p331
Jon Trickett	*Lab*	p335
Tom Tugendhat	*Con*	p336
Ed Vaizey	*Con*	p339
Robin Walker	*Con*	p343
Ben Wallace	*Con*	p343
David Warburton	*Con*	p344
Tom Watson	*Lab*	p345
John Whittingdale	*Con*	p349
Phil Wilson	*Lab*	p352
Sammy Wilson	*DUP*	p353
Jeremy Wright	*Con*	p356

Uzbekistan

Alistair Carmichael	*Lib Dem*	p102

Venezuela

Martin Docherty-Hughes	*SNP*	p130
David Duguid	*Con*	p138
Grahame Morris	*Lab*	p265
Chris Williamson	*Lab*	p351

Vietnam

Ann Clwyd	*Lab*	p110
Michael Gove	*Con*	p169
Ian Liddell-Grainger	*Con*	p233
Chris Ruane	*Lab*	p298

Wales

Geraint Davies	*Lab/Co-op*	p125
Michael Fabricant	*Con*	p148
Liz Saville Roberts	*PlC*	p301
Owen Smith	*Lab*	p314

Yemen

Edward Argar	*Con*	p69
Stephen Doughty	*Lab/Co-op*	p134
Tobias Ellwood	*Con*	p143
Keith Vaz	*Lab*	p340
Valerie Vaz	*Lab*	p341

Zambia

Nadine Dorries	*Con*	p133
Robin Walker	*Con*	p343

Zimbabwe

Richard Benyon	*Con*	p77
John Bercow	*Speaker*	p78
James Duddridge	*Con*	p137
Kate Hoey	*Lab*	p198
David Linden	*SNP*	p234
Neil Parish	*Con*	p276

MPs by UK Regions

England

Eastern

Basildon and Billericay	John Baron	Con
South Basildon and East Thurrock	Stephen Metcalfe	Con
Bedford	Mohammad Yasin	Lab
Mid Bedfordshire	Nadine Dorries	Con
North East Bedfordshire	Alistair Burt	Con
South West Bedfordshire	Andrew Selous	Con
Braintree	James Cleverly	Con
Brentwood and Ongar	Alex Burghart	Con
Broadland	Keith Simpson	Con
Broxbourne	Charles Walker	Con
Bury St Edmunds	Jo Churchill	Con
Cambridge	Daniel Zeichner	Lab
North East Cambridgeshire	Steve Barclay	Con
North West Cambridgeshire	Shailesh Vara	Con
South Cambridgeshire	Heidi Allen	Con
South East Cambridgeshire	Lucy Frazer	Con
Castle Point	Rebecca Harris	Con
Chelmsford	Vicky Ford	Con
Clacton	Giles Watling	Con
Colchester	Will Quince	Con
Epping Forest	Eleanor Laing	Con
Great Yarmouth	Brandon Lewis	Con
Harlow	Robert Halfon	Con
Harwich and North Essex	Bernard Jenkin	Con
Hemel Hempstead	Mike Penning	Con
Hertford and Stortford	Mark Prisk	Con
North East Hertfordshire	Oliver Heald	Con
South West Hertfordshire	David Gauke	Con
Hertsmere	Oliver Dowden	Con
Hitchin and Harpenden	Bim Afolami	Con
Huntingdon	Jonathan Djanogly	Con
Ipswich	Sandy Martin	Lab
Luton North	Kelvin Hopkins	Lab
Luton South	Gavin Shuker	Lab/Co-op
Maldon	John Whittingdale	Con
Mid Norfolk	George Freeman	Con
North Norfolk	Norman Lamb	Lib Dem
North West Norfolk	Henry Bellingham	Con
South Norfolk	Richard Bacon	Con
South West Norfolk	Elizabeth Truss	Con
Norwich North	Chloe Smith	Con
Norwich South	Clive Lewis	Lab
Peterborough	Fiona Onasanya	Lab
Rayleigh and Wickford	Mark Francois	Con
Rochford and Southend East	James Duddridge	Con
Saffron Walden	Kemi Badenoch	Con
St Albans	Anne Main	Con
Southend West	David Amess	Con
Stevenage	Stephen McPartland	Con
Central Suffolk and North Ipswich	Dan Poulter	Con

Suffolk Coastal	Therese Coffey	Con
South Suffolk	James Cartlidge	Con
West Suffolk	Matt Hancock	Con
Thurrock	Jackie Doyle-Price	Con
Watford	Richard Harrington	Con
Waveney	Peter Aldous	Con
Welwyn Hatfield	Grant Shapps	Con
Witham	Priti Patel	Con

East Midlands

Amber Valley	Nigel Mills	Con
Ashfield	Gloria De Piero	Lab
Bassetlaw	John Mann	Lab
Bolsover	Dennis Skinner	Lab
Boston and Skegness	Matt Warman	Con
Bosworth	David Tredinnick	Con
Broxtowe	Anna Soubry	Con
Charnwood	Edward Argar	Con
Chesterfield	Toby Perkins	Lab
Corby	Tom Pursglove	Con
Daventry	Chris Heaton-Harris	Con
Derby North	Chris Williamson	Lab
Derby South	Margaret Beckett	Lab
Derbyshire Dales	Patrick McLoughlin	Con
Mid Derbyshire	Pauline Latham	Con
North East Derbyshire	Lee Rowley	Con
South Derbyshire	Heather Wheeler	Con
Erewash	Maggie Throup	Con
Gainsborough	Edward Leigh	Con
Gedling	Vernon Coaker	Lab
Grantham and Stamford	Nick Boles	Con
Harborough	Neil O'Brien	Con
High Peak	Ruth George	Lab
Kettering	Philip Hollobone	Con
Leicester East	Keith Vaz	Lab
Leicester South	Jon Ashworth	Lab/Co-op
Leicester West	Liz Kendall	Lab
North West Leicestershire	Andrew Bridgen	Con
South Leicestershire	Alberto Costa	Con
Lincoln	Karen Lee	Lab
Loughborough	Nicky Morgan	Con
Louth and Horncastle	Victoria Atkins	Con
Mansfield	Ben Bradley	Con
Newark	Robert Jenrick	Con
Northampton North	Michael Ellis	Con
Northampton South	Andrew Lewer	Con
South Northamptonshire	Andrea Leadsom	Con
Nottingham East	Chris Leslie	Lab/Co-op
Nottingham North	Alex Norris	Lab/Co-op
Nottingham South	Lilian Greenwood	Lab
Rushcliffe	Kenneth Clarke	Con
Rutland and Melton	Alan Duncan	Con
Sherwood	Mark Spencer	Con
Sleaford and North Hykeham	Caroline Johnson	Con
South Holland and The Deepings	John Hayes	Con
Wellingborough	Peter Bone	Con

London

Barking	Margaret Hodge	Lab
Battersea	Marsha De Cordova	Lab
Beckenham	Bob Stewart	Con
Bermondsey and Old Southwark	Neil Coyle	Lab
Bethnal Green and Bow	Rushanara Ali	Lab
Old Bexley and Sidcup	James Brokenshire	Con
Bexleyheath and Crayford	David Evennett	Con
Brent Central	Dawn Butler	Lab
Brent North	Barry Gardiner	Lab
Brentford and Isleworth	Ruth Cadbury	Lab
Bromley and Chislehurst	Robert Neill	Con
Camberwell and Peckham	Harriet Harman	Lab
Carshalton and Wallington	Tom Brake	Lib Dem
Chelsea and Fulham	Greg Hands	Con
Chingford and Woodford Green	Iain Duncan Smith	Con
Chipping Barnet	Theresa Villiers	Con
Croydon Central	Sarah Jones	Lab
Croydon North	Steve Reed	Lab/Co-op
Croydon South	Chris Philp	Con
Dagenham and Rainham	Jon Cruddas	Lab
Dulwich and West Norwood	Helen Hayes	Lab
Ealing Central and Acton	Rupa Huq	Lab
Ealing North	Stephen Pound	Lab
Ealing Southall	Virendra Sharma	Lab
East Ham	Stephen Timms	Lab
Edmonton	Kate Osamor	Lab/Co-op
Eltham	Clive Efford	Lab
Enfield North	Joan Ryan	Lab
Enfield Southgate	Bambos Charalambous	Lab
Erith and Thamesmead	Teresa Pearce	Lab
Feltham and Heston	Seema Malhotra	Lab/Co-op
Finchley and Golders Green	Mike Freer	Con
Greenwich and Woolwich	Matthew Pennycook	Lab
Hackney North and Stoke Newington	Diane Abbott	Lab
Hackney South and Shoreditch	Meg Hillier	Lab/Co-op
Hammersmith	Andy Slaughter	Lab
Hampstead and Kilburn	Tulip Siddiq	Lab
Harrow East	Bob Blackman	Con
Harrow West	Gareth Thomas	Lab/Co-op
Hayes and Harlington	John McDonnell	Lab
Hendon	Matthew Offord	Con
Holborn and St Pancras	Keir Starmer	Lab
Hornchurch and Upminster	Julia Dockerill	Con
Hornsey and Wood Green	Catherine West	Lab
Ilford North	Wes Streeting	Lab
Ilford South	Mike Gapes	Lab/Co-op
Islington North	Jeremy Corbyn	Lab
Islington South and Finsbury	Emily Thornberry	Lab
Kensington	Emma Dent Coad	Lab
Kingston and Surbiton	Ed Davey	Lib Dem
Lewisham Deptford	Vicky Foxcroft	Lab
Lewisham East	Heidi Alexander	Lab
Lewisham West and Penge	Ellie Reeves	Lab
Leyton and Wanstead	John Cryer	Lab

Cities of London and Westminster	Mark Field	Con
Mitcham and Morden	Siobhain McDonagh	Lab
Orpington	Jo Johnson	Con
Poplar and Limehouse	Jim Fitzpatrick	Lab
Putney	Justine Greening	Con
Richmond Park	Zac Goldsmith	Con
Romford	Andrew Rosindell	Con
Ruislip, Northwood and Pinner	Nick Hurd	Con
Streatham	Chuka Umunna	Lab
Sutton and Cheam	Paul Scully	Con
Tooting	Rosena Allin-Khan	Lab
Tottenham	David Lammy	Lab
Twickenham	Vince Cable	Lib Dem
Uxbridge and South Ruislip	Boris Johnson	Con
Vauxhall	Kate Hoey	Lab
Walthamstow	Stella Creasy	Lab/Co-op
West Ham	Lyn Brown	Lab
Westminster North	Karen Buck	Lab
Wimbledon	Stephen Hammond	Con

North East

Berwick-upon-Tweed	Anne-Marie Trevelyan	Con
Bishop Auckland	Helen Goodman	Lab
Blaydon	Liz Twist	Lab
Blyth Valley	Ronnie Campbell	Lab
Darlington	Jenny Chapman	Lab
City of Durham	Roberta Blackman-Woods	Lab
North Durham	Kevan Jones	Lab
North West Durham	Laura Pidcock	Lab
Easington	Grahame Morris	Lab
Gateshead	Ian Mearns	Lab
Hartlepool	Mike Hill	Lab
Hexham	Guy Opperman	Con
Houghton and Sunderland South	Bridget Phillipson	Lab
Jarrow	Stephen Hepburn	Lab
Middlesbrough	Andy McDonald	Lab
Middlesbrough South and East Cleveland	Simon Clarke	Con
Newcastle upon Tyne Central	Chi Onwurah	Lab
Newcastle upon Tyne East	Nick Brown	Lab
Newcastle upon Tyne North	Catherine McKinnell	Lab
Redcar	Anna Turley	Lab/Co-op
Sedgefield	Phil Wilson	Lab
South Shields	Emma Lewell-Buck	Lab
Stockton North	Alex Cunningham	Lab
Stockton South	Paul Williams	Lab
Sunderland Central	Julie Elliott	Lab
Tynemouth	Alan Campbell	Lab
North Tyneside	Mary Glindon	Lab
Wansbeck	Ian Lavery	Lab
Washington and Sunderland West	Sharon Hodgson	Lab

North West

Altrincham and Sale West	Graham Brady	Con
Ashton under Lyne	Angela Rayner	Lab
Barrow and Furness	John Woodcock	Lab/Co-op

Birkenhead	Frank Field	Lab
Blackburn	Kate Hollern	Lab
Blackley and Broughton	Graham Stringer	Lab
Blackpool North and Cleveleys	Paul Maynard	Con
Blackpool South	Gordon Marsden	Lab
Bolton North East	David Crausby	Lab
Bolton South East	Yasmin Qureshi	Lab
Bolton West	Chris Green	Con
Bootle	Peter Dowd	Lab
Burnley	Julie Cooper	Lab
Bury North	James Frith	Lab
Bury South	Ivan Lewis	Lab
Carlisle	John Stevenson	Con
Cheadle	Mary Robinson	Con
City of Chester	Chris Matheson	Lab
Chorley	Lindsay Hoyle	Lab
Congleton	Fiona Bruce	Con
Copeland	Trudy Harrison	Con
Crewe and Nantwich	Laura Smith	Lab
Denton and Reddish	Andrew Gwynne	Lab
Eddisbury	Antoinette Sandbach	Con
Ellesmere Port and Neston	Justin Madders	Lab
Fylde	Mark Menzies	Con
Garston and Halewood	Maria Eagle	Lab
Halton	Derek Twigg	Lab
Hazel Grove	William Wragg	Con
Heywood and Middleton	Liz McInnes	Lab
Hyndburn	Graham Jones	Lab
Knowsley	George Howarth	Lab
West Lancashire	Rosie Cooper	Lab
Lancaster and Fleetwood	Cat Smith	Lab
Leigh	Jo Platt	Lab/Co-op
Liverpool Riverside	Louise Ellman	Lab/Co-op
Liverpool Walton	Dan Carden	Lab
Liverpool Wavertree	Luciana Berger	Lab/Co-op
Liverpool West Derby	Stephen Twigg	Lab/Co-op
Macclesfield	David Rutley	Con
Makerfield	Yvonne Fovargue	Lab
Manchester Central	Lucy Powell	Lab/Co-op
Manchester Gorton	Afzal Khan	Lab
Manchester Withington	Jeff Smith	Lab
Morecambe and Lunesdale	David Morris	Con
Oldham East and Saddleworth	Debbie Abrahams	Lab
Oldham West and Royton	Jim McMahon	Lab/Co-op
Pendle	Andrew Stephenson	Con
Penrith and The Border	Rory Stewart	Con
Preston	Mark Hendrick	Lab/Co-op
South Ribble	Seema Kennedy	Con
Ribble Valley	Nigel Evans	Con
Rochdale	Tony Lloyd	Lab
Rossendale and Darwen	Jake Berry	Con
St Helens North	Conor McGinn	Lab
St Helens South and Whiston	Marie Rimmer	Lab
Salford and Eccles	Rebecca Long-Bailey	Lab
Sefton Central	Bill Esterson	Lab
Southport	Damien Moore	Con

Stalybridge and Hyde	Jonathan Reynolds	Lab/Co-op
Stockport	Ann Coffey	Lab
Stretford and Urmston	Kate Green	Lab
Tatton	Esther McVey	Con
Wallasey	Angela Eagle	Lab
Warrington North	Helen Jones	Lab
Warrington South	Faisal Rashid	Lab
Weaver Vale	Mike Amesbury	Lab
Westmorland and Lonsdale	Tim Farron	Lib Dem
Wigan	Lisa Nandy	Lab
Wirral South	Alison McGovern	Lab
Wirral West	Margaret Greenwood	Lab
Workington	Sue Hayman	Lab
Worsley and Eccles South	Barbara Keeley	Lab
Wyre and Preston North	Ben Wallace	Con
Wythenshawe and Sale East	Mike Kane	Lab

South East

Aldershot	Leo Docherty	Con
Arundel and South Downs	Nick Herbert	Con
Ashford	Damian Green	Con
Aylesbury	David Lidington	Con
Banbury	Victoria Prentis	Con
Basingstoke	Maria Miller	Con
Beaconsfield	Dominic Grieve	Con
Bexhill and Battle	Huw Merriman	Con
Bognor Regis and Littlehampton	Nick Gibb	Con
Bracknell	Phillip Lee	Con
Brighton Kemptown	Lloyd Russell-Moyle	Lab/Co-op
Brighton Pavilion	Caroline Lucas	Green
Buckingham	John Bercow	Speaker
Canterbury	Rosie Duffield	Lab
Chatham and Aylesford	Tracey Crouch	Con
Chesham and Amersham	Cheryl Gillan	Con
Chichester	Gillian Keegan	Con
Crawley	Henry Smith	Con
Dartford	Gareth Johnson	Con
Dover	Charlie Elphicke	Con
Eastbourne	Stephen Lloyd	Lib Dem
Eastleigh	Mims Davies	Con
Epsom and Ewell	Chris Grayling	Con
Esher and Walton	Dominic Raab	Con
Fareham	Suella Fernandes	Con
Faversham and Mid Kent	Helen Whately	Con
Folkestone and Hythe	Damian Collins	Con
Gillingham and Rainham	Rehman Chishti	Con
Gosport	Caroline Dinenage	Con
Gravesham	Adam Holloway	Con
Guildford	Anne Milton	Con
East Hampshire	Damian Hinds	Con
North East Hampshire	Ranil Jayawardena	Con
North West Hampshire	Kit Malthouse	Con
Hastings and Rye	Amber Rudd	Con
Havant	Alan Mak	Con

Henley	John Howell	Con
Horsham	Jeremy Quin	Con
Hove	Peter Kyle	Lab
Isle of Wight	Bob Seely	Con
Lewes	Maria Caulfield	Con
Maidenhead	Theresa May	Con
Maidstone and The Weald	Helen Grant	Con
Meon Valley	George Hollingbery	Con
Milton Keynes North	Mark Lancaster	Con
Milton Keynes South	Iain Stewart	Con
Mole Valley	Paul Beresford	Con
New Forest East	Julian Lewis	Con
New Forest West	Desmond Swayne	Con
Newbury	Richard Benyon	Con
Oxford East	Anneliese Dodds	Lab/Co-op
Oxford West and Abingdon	Layla Moran	Lib Dem
Portsmouth North	Penny Mordaunt	Con
Portsmouth South	Stephen Morgan	Lab
Reading East	Matt Rodda	Lab
Reading West	Alok Sharma	Con
Reigate	Crispin Blunt	Con
Rochester and Strood	Kelly Tolhurst	Con
Romsey and Southampton North	Caroline Nokes	Con
Runnymede and Weybridge	Philip Hammond	Con
Sevenoaks	Michael Fallon	Con
Sittingbourne and Sheppey	Gordon Henderson	Con
Slough	Tanmanjeet Singh Dhesi	Lab
Southampton Itchen	Royston Smith	Con
Southampton Test	Alan Whitehead	Lab
Spelthorne	Kwasi Kwarteng	Con
East Surrey	Sam Gyimah	Con
Surrey Heath	Michael Gove	Con
South West Surrey	Jeremy Hunt	Con
Mid Sussex	Nicholas Soames	Con
North Thanet	Roger Gale	Con
South Thanet	Craig Mackinlay	Con
Tonbridge and Malling	Tom Tugendhat	Con
Tunbridge Wells	Greg Clark	Con
Wantage	Ed Vaizey	Con
Wealden	Nusrat Ghani	Con
Winchester	Steve Brine	Con
Windsor	Adam Afriyie	Con
Witney	Robert Courts	Con
Woking	Jonathan Lord	Con
Wokingham	John Redwood	Con
East Worthing and Shoreham	Tim Loughton	Con
Worthing West	Peter Bottomley	Con
Wycombe	Steve Baker	Con

South West

Bath	Wera Hobhouse	Lib Dem
Bournemouth East	Tobias Ellwood	Con
Bournemouth West	Conor Burns	Con
Bridgwater and West Somerset	Ian Liddell-Grainger	Con
Bristol East	Kerry McCarthy	Lab

Bristol North West	Darren Jones	Lab
Bristol South	Karin Smyth	Lab
Bristol West	Thangam Debbonaire	Lab
Camborne and Redruth	George Eustice	Con
Cheltenham	Alex Chalk	Con
Chippenham	Michelle Donelan	Con
Christchurch	Christopher Chope	Con
North Cornwall	Scott Mann	Con
South East Cornwall	Sheryll Murray	Con
The Cotswolds	Geoffrey Clifton-Brown	Con
Devizes	Claire Perry	Con
Central Devon	Mel Stride	Con
East Devon	Hugo Swire	Con
North Devon	Peter Heaton-Jones	Con
South West Devon	Gary Streeter	Con
Mid Dorset and North Poole	Michael Tomlinson	Con
North Dorset	Simon Hoare	Con
South Dorset	Richard Drax	Con
West Dorset	Oliver Letwin	Con
Exeter	Ben Bradshaw	Lab
Filton and Bradley Stoke	Jack Lopresti	Con
Forest of Dean	Mark Harper	Con
Gloucester	Richard Graham	Con
Kingswood	Chris Skidmore	Con
Newton Abbot	Anne Marie Morris	Ind*
Plymouth, Moor View	Johnny Mercer	Con
Plymouth, Sutton and Devonport	Luke Pollard	Lab/Co-op
Poole	Robert Syms	Con
St Austell and Newquay	Steve Double	Con
St Ives	Derek Thomas	Con
Salisbury	John Glen	Con
North Somerset	Liam Fox	Con
North East Somerset	Jacob Rees-Mogg	Con
Somerton and Frome	David Warburton	Con
Stroud	David Drew	Lab/Co-op
North Swindon	Justin Tomlinson	Con
South Swindon	Robert Buckland	Con
Taunton Deane	Rebecca Pow	Con
Tewkesbury	Laurence Robertson	Con
Thornbury and Yate	Luke Hall	Con
Tiverton and Honiton	Neil Parish	Con
Torbay	Kevin Foster	Con
Torridge and West Devon	Geoffrey Cox	Con
Totnes	Sarah Wollaston	Con
Truro and Falmouth	Sarah Newton	Con
Wells	James Heappey	Con
Weston-Super-Mare	John Penrose	Con
North Wiltshire	James Gray	Con
South West Wiltshire	Andrew Murrison	Con
Yeovil	Marcus Fysh	Con

West Midlands

Aldridge-Brownhills	Wendy Morton	Con
Birmingham, Edgbaston	Preet Kaur Gill	Lab/Co-op
Birmingham, Erdington	Jack Dromey	Lab

*Elected as Conservative

Analysis of MPs
House of Commons

Birmingham, Hall Green	Roger Godsiff	Lab
Birmingham, Hodge Hill	Liam Byrne	Lab
Birmingham, Ladywood	Shabana Mahmood	Lab
Birmingham, Northfield	Richard Burden	Lab
Birmingham, Perry Barr	Khalid Mahmood	Lab
Birmingham, Selly Oak	Steve McCabe	Lab
Birmingham, Yardley	Jess Phillips	Lab
Bromsgrove	Sajid Javid	Con
Burton	Andrew Griffiths	Con
Cannock Chase	Amanda Milling	Con
Coventry North East	Colleen Fletcher	Lab
Coventry North West	Geoffrey Robinson	Lab
Coventry South	Jim Cunningham	Lab
Dudley North	Ian Austin	Lab
Dudley South	Mike Wood	Con
Halesowen and Rowley Regis	James Morris	Con
Hereford and South Herefordshire	Jesse Norman	Con
North Herefordshire	Bill Wiggin	Con
Kenilworth and Southam	Jeremy Wright	Con
Lichfield	Michael Fabricant	Con
Ludlow	Philip Dunne	Con
Meriden	Caroline Spelman	Con
Newcastle-under-Lyme	Paul Farrelly	Lab
Nuneaton	Marcus Jones	Con
Redditch	Rachel Maclean	Con
Rugby	Mark Pawsey	Con
Shrewsbury and Atcham	Daniel Kawczynski	Con
North Shropshire	Owen Paterson	Con
Solihull	Julian Knight	Con
Stafford	Jeremy Lefroy	Con
Staffordshire Moorlands	Karen Bradley	Con
South Staffordshire	Gavin Williamson	Con
Stoke-on-Trent Central	Gareth Snell	Lab/Co-op
Stoke-on-Trent North	Ruth Smeeth	Lab
Stoke-on-Trent South	Jack Brereton	Con
Stone	Bill Cash	Con
Stourbridge	Margot James	Con
Stratford-on-Avon	Nadhim Zahawi	Con
Sutton Coldfield	Andrew Mitchell	Con
Tamworth	Christopher Pincher	Con
Telford	Lucy Allan	Con
Walsall North	Eddie Hughes	Con
Walsall South	Valerie Vaz	Lab
Warley	John Spellar	Lab
Warwick and Leamington	Matt Western	Lab
North Warwickshire	Craig Tracey	Con
West Bromwich East	Tom Watson	Lab
West Bromwich West	Adrian Bailey	Lab/Co-op
Wolverhampton North East	Emma Reynolds	Lab
Wolverhampton South East	Pat McFadden	Lab
Wolverhampton South West	Eleanor Smith	Lab
Worcester	Robin Walker	Con
Mid Worcestershire	Nigel Huddleston	Con
West Worcestershire	Harriett Baldwin	Con
The Wrekin	Mark Pritchard	Con
Wyre Forest	Mark Garnier	Con

Yorkshire and Humberside

Barnsley Central	Dan Jarvis	Lab
Barnsley East	Stephanie Peacock	Lab
Batley and Spen	Tracy Brabin	Lab/Co-op
Beverley and Holderness	Graham Stuart	Con
Bradford East	Imran Hussain	Lab
Bradford South	Judith Cummins	Lab
Bradford West	Naz Shah	Lab
Brigg and Goole	Andrew Percy	Con
Calder Valley	Craig Whittaker	Con
Cleethorpes	Martin Vickers	Con
Colne Valley	Thelma Walker	Lab
Dewsbury	Paula Sherriff	Lab
Don Valley	Caroline Flint	Lab
Doncaster Central	Rosie Winterton	Lab
Doncaster North	Ed Miliband	Lab
Elmet and Rothwell	Alec Shelbrooke	Con
Great Grimsby	Melanie Onn	Lab
Halifax	Holly Lynch	Lab
Haltemprice and Howden	David Davis	Con
Harrogate and Knaresborough	Andrew Jones	Con
Hemsworth	Jon Trickett	Lab
Huddersfield	Barry Sheerman	Lab/Co-op
Kingston upon Hull East	Karl Turner	Lab
Kingston upon Hull North	Diana Johnson	Lab
Kingston upon Hull West and Hessle	Emma Hardy	Lab
Keighley	John Grogan	Lab
Leeds Central	Hilary Benn	Lab
Leeds East	Richard Burgon	Lab
Leeds North East	Fabian Hamilton	Lab
Leeds North West	Alex Sobel	Lab/Co-op
Leeds West	Rachel Reeves	Lab
Morley and Outwood	Andrea Jenkyns	Con
Normanton, Pontefract and Castleford	Yvette Cooper	Lab
Penistone and Stocksbridge	Angela Smith	Lab
Pudsey	Stuart Andrew	Con
Richmond (Yorkshire)	Rishi Sunak	Con
Rother Valley	Kevin Barron	Lab
Rotherham	Sarah Champion	Lab
Scarborough and Whitby	Robert Goodwill	Con
Scunthorpe	Nic Dakin	Lab
Selby and Ainsty	Nigel Adams	Con
Sheffield, Brightside and Hillsborough	Gill Furniss	Lab
Sheffield Central	Paul Blomfield	Lab
Sheffield, Hallam	Jared O'Mara	Lab
Sheffield Heeley	Louise Haigh	Lab
Sheffield South East	Clive Betts	Lab
Shipley	Philip Davies	Con
Skipton and Ripon	Julian Smith	Con
Thirsk and Malton	Kevin Hollinrake	Con
Wakefield	Mary Creagh	Lab
Wentworth and Dearne	John Healey	Lab
York Central	Rachael Maskell	Lab/Co-op
York Outer	Julian Sturdy	Con
East Yorkshire	Greg Knight	Con

Northern Ireland

East Antrim	Sammy Wilson	DUP
North Antrim	Ian Paisley	DUP
South Antrim	Paul Girvan	DUP
Belfast East	Gavin Robinson	DUP
Belfast North	Nigel Dodds	DUP
Belfast South	Emma Little Pengelly	DUP
Belfast West	Paul Maskey	Sinn Féin
North Down	Sylvia Hermon	Ind
South Down	Chris Hazzard	Sinn Féin
Fermanagh and South Tyrone	Michelle Gildernew	Sinn Féin
Foyle	Elisha McCallion	Sinn Féin
Lagan Valley	Jeffrey Donaldson	DUP
East Londonderry	Gregory Campbell	DUP
Newry and Armagh	Mickey Brady	Sinn Féin
Strangford	Jim Shannon	DUP
West Tyrone	Barry McElduff	Sinn Féin
Mid Ulster	Francie Molloy	Sinn Féin
Upper Bann	David Simpson	DUP

Scotland

Aberdeen North	Kirsty Blackman	SNP
Aberdeen South	Ross Thomson	Con
West Aberdeenshire and Kincardine	Andrew Bowie	Con
Airdrie and Shotts	Neil Gray	SNP
Angus	Kirstene Hair	Con
Argyll and Bute	Brendan O'Hara	SNP
Ayr, Carrick and Cumnock	Bill Grant	Con
Central Ayrshire	Philippa Whitford	SNP
North Ayrshire and Arran	Patricia Gibson	SNP
Banff and Buchan	David Duguid	Con
Berwickshire, Roxburgh and Selkirk	John Lamont	Con
Caithness, Sutherland and Easter Ross	Jamie Stone	Lib Dem
Coatbridge, Chryston and Bellshill	Hugh Gaffney	Lab
Cumbernauld, Kilsyth and Kirkintilloch East	Stuart C McDonald	SNP
Dumfries and Galloway	Alister Jack	Con
Dumfriesshire, Clydesdale and Tweeddale	David Mundell	Con
East Dunbartonshire	Jo Swinson	Lib Dem
West Dunbartonshire	Martin Docherty-Hughes	SNP
Dundee East	Stewart Hosie	SNP
Dundee West	Chris Law	SNP
Dunfermline and West Fife	Douglas Chapman	SNP
East Kilbride, Strathaven and Lesmahagow	Lisa Cameron	SNP
Edinburgh East	Tommy Sheppard	SNP
Edinburgh North and Leith	Deidre Brock	SNP
Edinburgh South	Ian Murray	Lab
Edinburgh South West	Joanna Cherry	SNP
Edinburgh West	Christine Jardine	Lib Dem
Falkirk	John McNally	SNP
North East Fife	Stephen Gethins	SNP
Glasgow Central	Alison Thewliss	SNP
Glasgow East	David Linden	SNP

Glasgow North	Patrick Grady	SNP
Glasgow North East	Paul Sweeney	Lab/Co-op
Glasgow North West	Carol Monaghan	SNP
Glasgow South	Stewart Malcolm McDonald	SNP
Glasgow South West	Chris Stephens	SNP
Glenrothes	Peter Grant	SNP
Gordon	Colin Clark	Con
Inverclyde	Ronnie Cowan	SNP
Inverness, Nairn, Badenoch and Strathspey	Drew Hendry	SNP
Kilmarnock and Loudoun	Alan Brown	SNP
Kirkcaldy and Cowdenbeath	Lesley Laird	Lab
Lanark and Hamilton East	Angela Crawley	SNP
Linlithgow and East Falkirk	Martyn Day	SNP
Livingston	Hannah Bardell	SNP
East Lothian	Martin Whitfield	Lab
Midlothian	Danielle Rowley	Lab
Moray	Douglas Ross	Con
Motherwell and Wishaw	Marion Fellows	SNP
Na h-Eileanan An Iar	Angus MacNeil	SNP
Ochil and South Perthshire	Luke Graham	Con
Orkney and Shetland	Alistair Carmichael	Lib Dem
Paisley and Renfrewshire North	Gavin Newlands	SNP
Paisley and Renfrewshire South	Mhairi Black	SNP
Perth and North Perthshire	Pete Wishart	SNP
East Renfrewshire	Paul Masterton	Con
Ross, Skye and Lochaber	Ian Blackford	SNP
Rutherglen and Hamilton West	Gerard Killen	Lab/Co-op
Stirling	Stephen Kerr	Con

Wales

Aberavon	Stephen Kinnock	Lab
Aberconwy	Guto Bebb	Con
Alyn and Deeside	Mark Tami	Lab
Arfon	Hywel Williams	PlC
Blaenau Gwent	Nick Smith	Lab
Brecon and Radnorshire	Chris Davies	Con
Bridgend	Madeleine Moon	Lab
Caerphilly	Wayne David	Lab
Cardiff Central	Jo Stevens	Lab
Cardiff North	Anna McMorrin	Lab
Cardiff South and Penarth	Stephen Doughty	Lab/Co-op
Cardiff West	Kevin Brennan	Lab
Carmarthen East and Dinefwr	Jonathan Edwards	PlC
Carmarthen West and South Pembrokeshire	Simon Hart	Con
Ceredigion	Ben Lake	PlC
Clwyd South	Susan Elan Jones	Lab
Vale of Clwyd	Chris Ruane	Lab
Clwyd West	David Jones	Con
Cynon Valley	Ann Clwyd	Lab
Delyn	David Hanson	Lab
Dwyfor Meirionnydd	Liz Saville Roberts	PlC
Vale of Glamorgan	Alun Cairns	Con
Gower	Tonia Antoniazzi	Lab
Islwyn	Chris Evans	Lab/Co-op

Llanelli	Nia Griffith	Lab
Merthyr Tydfil and Rhymney	Gerald Jones	Lab
Monmouth	David Davies	Con
Montgomeryshire	Glyn Davies	Con
Neath	Christina Rees	Lab/Co-op
Newport East	Jessica Morden	Lab
Newport West	Paul Flynn	Lab
Ogmore	Chris Elmore	Lab
Pontypridd	Owen Smith	Lab
Preseli Pembrokeshire	Stephen Crabb	Con
Rhondda	Chris Bryant	Lab
Swansea East	Carolyn Harris	Lab
Swansea West	Geraint Davies	Lab/Co-op
Torfaen	Nick Thomas-Symonds	Lab
Wrexham	Ian C Lucas	Lab
Ynys Môn	Albert Owen	Lab

Election statistics by party, gender and region

The following tables list all members in the House of Commons following the 2017 General Election by the year they were elected. If an MP had a period out of parliament, ie are a retread MP, the newly-elected year has been used. An exception to this rule is David Davis MP – he is allocated to 1987 rather than the 2008 by-election.

Political party

	By-election*	%	1970	%	1979	%	1983	%	1987	%	1992	%	1997	%	2001	%	2005	%	2010	%	2015	%	2017	%	Total
Con	10	3.16	1	0.32	0	0.00	4	1.27	3	0.95	13	4.11	21	6.65	17	5.38	44	13.92	108	34.18	63	19.94	32	10.13	316
Lab/Lab Co-op	33	12.60	1	0.38	2	0.76	4	1.53	4	1.53	9	3.44	29	11.07	12	4.58	20	7.63	47	17.94	50	19.08	51	19.47	262
SNP	0	0.00	0	0.00	0	0.00	0	0.00	0	0.00	0	0.00	0	0.00	0	0.00	3	8.57	0	0.00	31	88.57	1	2.86	35
Lib Dem	0	0.00	0	0.00	0	0.00	0	0.00	0	0.00	0	0.00	1	8.33	2	16.67	1	8.33	0	0.00	0	0.00	8	66.67	12
DUP	0	0.00	0	0.00	0	0.00	0	0.00	0	0.00	0	0.00	1	10.00	2	20.00	2	20.00	2	20.00	1	10.00	2	20.00	10
Sinn Féin	2	28.57	0	0.00	0	0.00	0	0.00	0	0.00	0	0.00	0	0.00	0	0.00	0	0.00	0	0.00	1	14.29	4	57.14	7
PlC	0	0.00	0	0.00	0	0.00	0	0.00	0	0.00	0	0.00	0	0.00	1	25.00	0	0.00	1	25.00	1	25.00	1	25.00	4
Ind	0	0.00	0	0.00	0	0.00	0	0.00	0	0.00	0	0.00	0	0.00	1	50.00	0	0.00	1	50.00	0	0.00	0	0.00	2
Green	0	0.00	0	0.00	0	0.00	0	0.00	0	0.00	0	0.00	0	0.00	0	0.00	0	0.00	1	100.00	0	0.00	0	0.00	1
Speaker	0	0.00	0	0.00	0	0.00	0	0.00	0	0.00	0	0.00	1	100.00	0	0.00	0	0.00	0	0.00	0	0.00	0	0.00	1
Total	**45**	**6.92**	**2**	**0.31**	**2**	**0.31**	**8**	**1.23**	**7**	**1.08**	**22**	**3.38**	**53**	**8.15**	**35**	**5.38**	**70**	**10.77**	**160**	**24.62**	**147**	**22.62**	**99**	**15.23**	**650**

Gender

	By-election*	%	1970	%	1979	%	1983	%	1987	%	1992	%	1997	%	2001	%	2005	%	2010	%	2015	%	2017	%	Total
Male	29	6.56	2	0.45	2	0.45	7	158	6	1.36	19	4.30	42	9.50	34	7.69	49	11.09	110	24.89	79	17.87	63	14.25	442
Female	16	7.69	0	0.00	0	0.00	1	048	1	0.48	3	1.44	11	5.29	1	0.48	21	10.10	50	24.04	68	32.69	36	17.31	208
Total	**45**	**6.92**	**2**	**0.31**	**2**	**0.31**	**8**	**1.23**	**7**	**1.08**	**22**	**3.38**	**53**	**8.15**	**35**	**5.38**	**70**	**10.77**	**160**	**24.62**	**147**	**22.62**	**99**	**15.23**	**650**

UK Region

	By-election*	%	1970	%	1979	%	1983	%	1987	%	1992	%	1997	%	2001	%	2005	%	2010	%	2015	%	2017	%	Total
Eastern	1	1.72	0	0.00	0	0.00	1	1.72	0	0.00	3	5.17	3	5.17	9	15.52	8	13.79	16	27.59	9	15.52	8	13.79	58
East Midlands	4	8.70	2	4.35	0	0.00	2	4.35	2	4.35	1	2.17	2	4.35	1	2.17	2	4.35	16	34.78	6	13.04	8	17.39	46
London	10	13.70	0	0.00	0	0.00	1	1.37	1	1.37	2	2.74	9	12.33	3	4.11	11	15.07	11	15.07	16	21.92	9	12.33	73
North East	3	10.34	0	0.00	0	0.00	1	3.45	1	3.45	0	0.00	2	6.90	1	3.45	3	10.34	11	37.93	2	6.90	5	17.24	29
North West	8	10.67	0	0.00	1	1.33	0	0.00	0	0.00	3	4.00	10	13.33	0	0.00	5	6.67	20	26.67	18	24.00	10	13.33	75
South East	3	3.57	0	0.00	0	0.00	2	2.38	1	1.19	3	3.57	12	14.29	1	1.19	11	13.10	24	28.57	16	19.05	11	13.10	84
South West	0	0.00	0	0.00	0	0.00	0	0.00	0	0.00	3	5.45	6	10.91	3	5.45	5	9.09	17	30.91	17	30.91	4	7.27	55
West Midlands	5	8.47	0	0.00	0	0.00	0	0.00	0	0.00	5	8.47	3	5.08	5	8.47	6	10.17	19	32.20	10	16.95	6	10.17	59
Yorkshire and Humberside	6	11.11	0	0.00	1	1.85	1	1.85	1	1.85	1	1.85	5	9.26	1	1.85	7	12.96	13	24.07	12	22.22	6	11.11	54
Northern Ireland	2	11.11	0	0.00	0	0.00	0	0.00	0	0.00	0	0.00	1	5.56	3	16.67	2	11.11	2	11.11	2	11.11	6	33.33	18
Scotland	0	0.00	0	0.00	0	0.00	0	0.00	0	0.00	0	0.00	0	0.00	1	1.69	4	6.78	1	1.69	31	52.54	22	37.29	59
Wales	3	7.50	0	0.00	0	0.00	0	0.00	1	2.50	1	2.50	0	0.00	7	17.50	6	15.00	10	25.00	8	20.00	4	10.00	40
Total	**45**	**6.92**	**2**	**0.31**	**2**	**0.31**	**8**	**1.23**	**7**	**1.08**	**22**	**3.38**	**53**	**8.15**	**35**	**5.38**	**70**	**10.77**	**160**	**24.62**	**147**	**22.62**	**99**	**15.23**	**650**

*Earliest by-election that returned a sitting MP was in 1975.

N.B. No current Members were elected in the general elections of February and October 1974.

Constituencies, MPs and Majorities

ENGLAND	533
SCOTLAND	59
WALES	40
NORTHERN IRELAND	18
	TOTAL 650

England

			Majority	*%*
Aldershot	Leo Docherty	Con	11,473	23.39
Aldridge-Brownhills	Wendy Morton	Con	14,307	35.48
Altrincham and Sale West	Graham Brady	Con	6,426	12.14
Amber Valley	Nigel Mills	Con	8,300	18.08
Arundel and South Downs	Nick Herbert	Con	23,883	39.53
Ashfield	Gloria De Piero	Lab	441	0.88
Ashford	Damian Green	Con	17,478	29.12
Ashton under Lyne	Angela Rayner	Lab	11,295	28.34
Aylesbury	David Lidington	Con	14,656	24.88
Banbury	Victoria Prentis	Con	12,399	20.1
Barking	Margaret Hodge	Lab	21,608	45.22
Barnsley Central	Dan Jarvis	Lab	15,546	39.71
Barnsley East	Stephanie Peacock	Lab	13,283	32.5
Barrow and Furness	John Woodcock	Lab/Co-op	209	0.44
Basildon and Billericay	John Baron	Con	13,400	29.75
South Basildon and East Thurrock	Stephen Metcalfe	Con	11,490	24.35
Basingstoke	Maria Miller	Con	9,466	16.87
Bassetlaw	John Mann	Lab	4,852	9.26
Bath	Wera Hobhouse	Lib Dem	5,694	11.46
Batley and Spen	Tracy Brabin	Lab/Co-op	8,961	16.62
Battersea	Marsha De Cordova	Lab	2,416	4.38
Beaconsfield	Dominic Grieve	Con	24,543	43.72
Beckenham	Bob Stewart	Con	15,087	29.12
Bedford	Mohammad Yasin	Lab	789	1.62
Mid Bedfordshire	Nadine Dorries	Con	20,983	33.14
North East Bedfordshire	Alistair Burt	Con	20,862	32.42
South West Bedfordshire	Andrew Selous	Con	14,168	25.39
Bermondsey and Old Southwark	Neil Coyle	Lab	12,972	22.11
Berwick-upon-Tweed	Anne-Marie Trevelyan	Con	11,781	27.86
Bethnal Green and Bow	Rushanara Ali	Lab	35,393	58.89
Beverley and Holderness	Graham Stuart	Con	14,042	25.15
Bexhill and Battle	Huw Merriman	Con	22,165	37.21
Old Bexley and Sidcup	James Brokenshire	Con	15,466	32.13
Bexleyheath and Crayford	David Evennett	Con	9,073	20.04
Birkenhead	Frank Field	Lab	25,514	58.29
Birmingham, Edgbaston	Preet Kaur Gill	Lab/Co-op	6,917	15.82
Birmingham, Erdington	Jack Dromey	Lab	7,285	19.52
Birmingham, Hall Green	Roger Godsiff	Lab	33,944	62.29
Birmingham, Hodge Hill	Liam Byrne	Lab	31,026	66.65

			Majority	*%*
Birmingham, Ladywood	Shabana Mahmood	Lab	28,714	69.25
Birmingham, Northfield	Richard Burden	Lab	4,667	10.49
Birmingham, Perry Barr	Khalid Mahmood	Lab	18,383	41.44
Birmingham, Selly Oak	Steve McCabe	Lab	15,207	30.96
Birmingham, Yardley	Jess Phillips	Lab	16,574	37.16
Bishop Auckland	Helen Goodman	Lab	502	1.16
Blackburn	Kate Hollern	Lab	20,368	42.7
Blackley and Broughton	Graham Stringer	Lab	19,601	48.74
Blackpool North and Cleveleys	Paul Maynard	Con	2,023	4.93
Blackpool South	Gordon Marsden	Lab	2,523	7.21
Blaydon	Liz Twist	Lab	13,477	27.99
Blyth Valley	Ronnie Campbell	Lab	7,915	18.6
Bognor Regis and Littlehampton	Nick Gibb	Con	17,494	34
Bolsover	Dennis Skinner	Lab	5,288	11.34
Bolton North East	David Crausby	Lab	3,797	8.39
Bolton South East	Yasmin Qureshi	Lab	13,126	30.94
Bolton West	Chris Green	Con	936	1.83
Bootle	Peter Dowd	Lab	36,200	71.75
Boston and Skegness	Matt Warman	Con	16,572	38.57
Bosworth	David Tredinnick	Con	18,351	32.58
Bournemouth East	Tobias Ellwood	Con	7,937	16.29
Bournemouth West	Conor Burns	Con	7,711	17.27
Bracknell	Phillip Lee	Con	16,016	28.58
Bradford East	Imran Hussain	Lab	20,540	44.95
Bradford South	Judith Cummins	Lab	6,700	16.3
Bradford West	Naz Shah	Lab	21,902	47.87
Braintree	James Cleverly	Con	18,422	35.16
Brent Central	Dawn Butler	Lab	27,997	53.33
Brent North	Barry Gardiner	Lab	17,061	30.12
Brentford and Isleworth	Ruth Cadbury	Lab	12,182	19.72
Brentwood and Ongar	Alex Burghart	Con	24,002	45.27
Bridgwater and West Somerset	Ian Liddell-Grainger	Con	15,448	26.45
Brigg and Goole	Andrew Percy	Con	12,363	27.4
Brighton Kemptown	Lloyd Russell-Moyle	Lab/Co-op	9,868	19.99
Brighton Pavilion	Caroline Lucas	Green	14,699	25.41
Bristol East	Kerry McCarthy	Lab	13,394	26.3
Bristol North West	Darren Jones	Lab	4,761	8.78
Bristol South	Karin Smyth	Lab	15,987	29.34
Bristol West	Thangam Debbonaire	Lab	37,336	52.01
Broadland	Keith Simpson	Con	15,816	28.21
Bromley and Chislehurst	Robert Neill	Con	9,590	20.5
Bromsgrove	Sajid Javid	Con	16,573	30.55
Broxbourne	Charles Walker	Con	15,792	33.19
Broxtowe	Anna Soubry	Con	863	1.55
Buckingham	John Bercow	Speaker	25,725	47.08
Burnley	Julie Cooper	Lab	6,353	15.74
Burton	Andrew Griffiths	Con	10,047	20.07
Bury North	James Frith	Lab	4,375	9.1
Bury South	Ivan Lewis	Lab	5,965	11.67
Bury St Edmunds	Jo Churchill	Con	18,441	29.59
Calder Valley	Craig Whittaker	Con	609	1.05
Camberwell and Peckham	Harriet Harman	Lab	37,316	64.73
Camborne and Redruth	George Eustice	Con	1,577	3.25

			Majority	*%*
Cambridge	Daniel Zeichner	Lab	12,661	22.58
North East Cambridgeshire	Steve Barclay	Con	21,270	39.86
North West Cambridgeshire	Shailesh Vara	Con	18,008	28.08
South Cambridgeshire	Heidi Allen	Con	15,952	24.51
South East Cambridgeshire	Lucy Frazer	Con	16,158	25.56
Cannock Chase	Amanda Milling	Con	8,391	17.5
Canterbury	Rosie Duffield	Lab	187	0.33
Carlisle	John Stevenson	Con	2,599	6.02
Carshalton and Wallington	Tom Brake	Lib Dem	1,369	2.69
Castle Point	Rebecca Harris	Con	18,872	42.13
Charnwood	Edward Argar	Con	16,341	29.55
Chatham and Aylesford	Tracey Crouch	Con	10,458	23.26
Cheadle	Mary Robinson	Con	4,507	8.24
Chelmsford	Vicky Ford	Con	13,572	23.83
Chelsea and Fulham	Greg Hands	Con	8,188	19.38
Cheltenham	Alex Chalk	Con	2,569	4.5
Chesham and Amersham	Cheryl Gillan	Con	22,140	39.97
City of Chester	Chris Matheson	Lab	9,176	16.22
Chesterfield	Toby Perkins	Lab	9,605	20.01
Chichester	Gillian Keegan	Con	22,621	37.67
Chingford and Woodford Green	Iain Duncan Smith	Con	2,438	5.17
Chippenham	Michelle Donelan	Con	16,630	29
Chipping Barnet	Theresa Villiers	Con	353	0.63
Chorley	Lindsay Hoyle	Lab	7,512	13.47
Christchurch	Christopher Chope	Con	25,171	49.55
Clacton	Giles Watling	Con	15,828	35.8
Cleethorpes	Martin Vickers	Con	10,400	21.7
Colchester	Will Quince	Con	5,677	10.58
Colne Valley	Thelma Walker	Lab	915	1.51
Congleton	Fiona Bruce	Con	12,619	22.4
Copeland	Trudy Harrison	Con	1,695	3.94
Corby	Tom Pursglove	Con	2,690	4.48
North Cornwall	Scott Mann	Con	7,200	14.1
South East Cornwall	Sheryll Murray	Con	17,443	32.69
The Cotswolds	Geoffrey Clifton-Brown	Con	25,499	42.62
Coventry North East	Colleen Fletcher	Lab	15,580	33.41
Coventry North West	Geoffrey Robinson	Lab	8,580	17.18
Coventry South	Jim Cunningham	Lab	7,947	16.86
Crawley	Henry Smith	Con	2,457	4.87
Crewe and Nantwich	Laura Smith	Lab	48	0.09
Croydon Central	Sarah Jones	Lab	5,652	9.88
Croydon North	Steve Reed	Lab/Co-op	32,365	54.16
Croydon South	Chris Philp	Con	11,406	18.58
Dagenham and Rainham	Jon Cruddas	Lab	4,652	10.13
Darlington	Jenny Chapman	Lab	3,280	7.31
Dartford	Gareth Johnson	Con	13,186	24.27
Daventry	Chris Heaton-Harris	Con	21,734	38.97
Denton and Reddish	Andrew Gwynne	Lab	14,077	35.48
Derby North	Chris Williamson	Lab	2,015	4.13
Derby South	Margaret Beckett	Lab	11,248	24.77
Derbyshire Dales	Patrick McLoughlin	Con	14,327	28.81
Mid Derbyshire	Pauline Latham	Con	11,616	23
North East Derbyshire	Lee Rowley	Con	2,860	5.67

			Majority	*%*
South Derbyshire	Heather Wheeler	Con	11,970	22.69
Devizes	Claire Perry	Con	21,136	41.69
Central Devon	Mel Stride	Con	15,680	27.07
East Devon	Hugo Swire	Con	8,036	13.3
North Devon	Peter Heaton-Jones	Con	4,332	7.77
South West Devon	Gary Streeter	Con	15,816	29.87
Dewsbury	Paula Sherriff	Lab	3,321	5.86
Don Valley	Caroline Flint	Lab	5,169	11.22
Doncaster Central	Rosie Winterton	Lab	10,131	23.48
Doncaster North	Ed Miliband	Lab	14,024	33.08
Mid Dorset and North Poole	Michael Tomlinson	Con	15,339	31.69
North Dorset	Simon Hoare	Con	25,777	46.12
South Dorset	Richard Drax	Con	11,695	22.49
West Dorset	Oliver Letwin	Con	19,091	31.95
Dover	Charlie Elphicke	Con	6,437	12.37
Dudley North	Ian Austin	Lab	22	0.06
Dudley South	Mike Wood	Con	7,730	20.19
Dulwich and West Norwood	Helen Hayes	Lab	28,156	50.01
City of Durham	Roberta Blackman-Woods	Lab	12,364	25.54
North Durham	Kevan Jones	Lab	12,939	29.83
North West Durham	Laura Pidcock	Lab	8,792	18.33
Ealing Central and Acton	Rupa Huq	Lab	13,807	24.86
Ealing North	Stephen Pound	Lab	19,693	37.39
Ealing Southall	Virendra Sharma	Lab	22,090	48.74
Easington	Grahame Morris	Lab	14,892	40.89
East Ham	Stephen Timms	Lab	39,883	70.2
Eastbourne	Stephen Lloyd	Lib Dem	1,609	2.8
Eastleigh	Mims Davies	Con	14,179	24.7
Eddisbury	Antoinette Sandbach	Con	11,942	23.23
Edmonton	Kate Osamor	Lab/Co-op	21,115	48.22
Ellesmere Port and Neston	Justin Madders	Lab	11,390	22.33
Elmet and Rothwell	Alec Shelbrooke	Con	9,805	16.43
Eltham	Clive Efford	Lab	6,296	13.6
Enfield North	Joan Ryan	Lab	10,247	21.05
Enfield Southgate	Bambos Charalambous	Lab	4,355	8.98
Epping Forest	Eleanor Laing	Con	18,243	35.83
Epsom and Ewell	Chris Grayling	Con	20,475	34.43
Erewash	Maggie Throup	Con	4,534	9.09
Erith and Thamesmead	Teresa Pearce	Lab	10,014	22.48
Esher and Walton	Dominic Raab	Con	23,298	38.9
Exeter	Ben Bradshaw	Lab	16,117	29.01
Fareham	Suella Fernandes	Con	21,555	37.72
Faversham and Mid Kent	Helen Whately	Con	17,413	34.95
Feltham and Heston	Seema Malhotra	Lab/Co-op	15,603	29.36
Filton and Bradley Stoke	Jack Lopresti	Con	4,190	8.24
Finchley and Golders Green	Mike Freer	Con	1,657	3.15
Folkestone and Hythe	Damian Collins	Con	15,411	26.13
Forest of Dean	Mark Harper	Con	9,502	18.33
Fylde	Mark Menzies	Con	11,805	25.34
Gainsborough	Edward Leigh	Con	17,023	33.01
Garston and Halewood	Maria Eagle	Lab	32,149	59.91
Gateshead	Ian Mearns	Lab	17,350	41.14
Gedling	Vernon Coaker	Lab	4,694	9.07

			Majority	*%*
Gillingham and Rainham	Rehman Chishti	Con	9,430	19.26
Gloucester	Richard Graham	Con	5,520	10.19
Gosport	Caroline Dinenage	Con	17,211	34.76
Grantham and Stamford	Nick Boles	Con	20,094	35.44
Gravesham	Adam Holloway	Con	9,347	19.03
Great Grimsby	Melanie Onn	Lab	2,565	7.21
Great Yarmouth	Brandon Lewis	Con	7,973	17.98
Greenwich and Woolwich	Matthew Pennycook	Lab	20,714	38.86
Guildford	Anne Milton	Con	17,040	30.62
Hackney North and Stoke Newington	Diane Abbott	Lab	35,139	62.21
Hackney South and Shoreditch	Meg Hillier	Lab/Co-op	37,931	68.26
Halesowen and Rowley Regis	James Morris	Con	5,253	11.81
Halifax	Holly Lynch	Lab	5,376	11.11
Haltemprice and Howden	David Davis	Con	15,405	29.86
Halton	Derek Twigg	Lab	25,405	51.22
Hammersmith	Andy Slaughter	Lab	18,651	35.61
East Hampshire	Damian Hinds	Con	25,852	46.52
North East Hampshire	Ranil Jayawardena	Con	27,772	48.09
North West Hampshire	Kit Malthouse	Con	22,679	38.52
Hampstead and Kilburn	Tulip Siddiq	Lab	15,560	26.57
Harborough	Neil O'Brien	Con	12,429	21.53
Harlow	Robert Halfon	Con	7,031	15.65
Harrogate and Knaresborough	Andrew Jones	Con	18,168	31.94
Harrow East	Bob Blackman	Con	1,757	3.45
Harrow West	Gareth Thomas	Lab/Co-op	13,314	26.37
Hartlepool	Mike Hill	Lab	7,650	18.25
Harwich and North Essex	Bernard Jenkin	Con	14,356	28.03
Hastings and Rye	Amber Rudd	Con	346	0.63
Havant	Alan Mak	Con	15,956	34.4
Hayes and Harlington	John McDonnell	Lab	18,115	37.8
Hazel Grove	William Wragg	Con	5,514	12.46
Hemel Hempstead	Mike Penning	Con	9,445	18.01
Hemsworth	Jon Trickett	Lab	10,174	22.1
Hendon	Matthew Offord	Con	1,072	2.05
Henley	John Howell	Con	22,294	38.96
Hereford and South Herefordshire	Jesse Norman	Con	15,013	29.7
North Herefordshire	Bill Wiggin	Con	21,602	42.95
Hertford and Stortford	Mark Prisk	Con	19,035	31.61
North East Hertfordshire	Oliver Heald	Con	16,835	30.2
South West Hertfordshire	David Gauke	Con	19,550	32.16
Hertsmere	Oliver Dowden	Con	16,951	32.36
Hexham	Guy Opperman	Con	9,236	19.95
Heywood and Middleton	Liz McInnes	Lab	7,617	15.25
High Peak	Ruth George	Lab	2,322	4.3
Hitchin and Harpenden	Bim Afolami	Con	12,031	20.42
Holborn and St Pancras	Keir Starmer	Lab	30,509	51.56
Hornchurch and Upminster	Julia Dockerill	Con	17,723	31.56
Hornsey and Wood Green	Catherine West	Lab	30,738	49.22
Horsham	Jeremy Quin	Con	23,484	37.82
Houghton and Sunderland South	Bridget Phillipson	Lab	12,341	29.7
Hove	Peter Kyle	Lab	18,757	32.5
Huddersfield	Barry Sheerman	Lab/Co-op	12,005	27.32
Kingston upon Hull East	Karl Turner	Lab	10,396	28.33

			Majority	%
Kingston upon Hull North	Diana Johnson	Lab	14,322	38.5
Kingston upon Hull West and Hessle	Emma Hardy	Lab	8,025	23.18
Huntingdon	Jonathan Djanogly	Con	14,475	24.18
Hyndburn	Graham Jones	Lab	5,815	12.83
Ilford North	Wes Streeting	Lab	9,639	18.17
Ilford South	Mike Gapes	Lab/Co-op	31,647	54.75
Ipswich	Sandy Martin	Lab	831	1.62
Isle of Wight	Bob Seely	Con	21,069	28.25
Islington North	Jeremy Corbyn	Lab	33,215	60.34
Islington South and Finsbury	Emily Thornberry	Lab	20,263	42.04
Jarrow	Stephen Hepburn	Lab	17,263	40.05
Keighley	John Grogan	Lab	239	0.46
Kenilworth and Southam	Jeremy Wright	Con	18,076	35.15
Kensington	Emma Dent Coad	Lab	20	0.05
Kettering	Philip Hollobone	Con	10,562	21.33
Kingston and Surbiton	Ed Davey	Lib Dem	4,124	6.62
Kingswood	Chris Skidmore	Con	7,500	15.35
Knowsley	George Howarth	Lab	42,214	75.99
West Lancashire	Rosie Cooper	Lab	11,689	21.45
Lancaster and Fleetwood	Cat Smith	Lab	6,661	14.45
Leeds Central	Hilary Benn	Lab	23,698	49.59
Leeds East	Richard Burgon	Lab	12,752	30.71
Leeds North East	Fabian Hamilton	Lab	16,991	32
Leeds North West	Alex Sobel	Lab/Co-op	4,224	9.11
Leeds West	Rachel Reeves	Lab	15,965	37.74
Leicester East	Keith Vaz	Lab	22,428	42.57
Leicester South	Jon Ashworth	Lab/Co-op	26,261	51.8
Leicester West	Liz Kendall	Lab	11,060	29.39
North West Leicestershire	Andrew Bridgen	Con	13,286	24.74
South Leicestershire	Alberto Costa	Con	18,631	32.8
Leigh	Jo Platt	Lab/Co-op	9,554	20.34
Lewes	Maria Caulfield	Con	5,508	10.14
Lewisham Deptford	Vicky Foxcroft	Lab	34,899	63.09
Lewisham East	Heidi Alexander	Lab	21,213	44.84
Lewisham West and Penge	Ellie Reeves	Lab	23,162	43.41
Leyton and Wanstead	John Cryer	Lab	22,607	48.81
Lichfield	Michael Fabricant	Con	18,581	34.62
Lincoln	Karen Lee	Lab	1,538	3.15
Liverpool Riverside	Louise Ellman	Lab/Co-op	35,947	74.61
Liverpool Walton	Dan Carden	Lab	32,551	76.95
Liverpool Wavertree	Luciana Berger	Lab/Co-op	29,466	67.34
Liverpool West Derby	Stephen Twigg	Lab/Co-op	32,908	72.68
Cities of London and Westminster	Mark Field	Con	3,148	8.12
Loughborough	Nicky Morgan	Con	4,269	7.87
Louth and Horncastle	Victoria Atkins	Con	19,641	37.16
Ludlow	Philip Dunne	Con	19,286	38.49
Luton North	Kelvin Hopkins	Lab	14,364	30.73
Luton South	Gavin Shuker	Lab/Co-op	13,925	30.12
Macclesfield	David Rutley	Con	8,608	15.81
Maidenhead	Theresa May	Con	26,457	45.34
Maidstone and The Weald	Helen Grant	Con	17,723	34.21
Makerfield	Yvonne Fovargue	Lab	13,542	28.79
Maldon	John Whittingdale	Con	23,430	46.58

			Majority	%
Manchester Central	Lucy Powell	Lab/Co-op	31,445	63.05
Manchester Gorton	Afzal Khan	Lab	31,730	68.83
Manchester Withington	Jeff Smith	Lab	29,875	55.6
Mansfield	Ben Bradley	Con	1,057	2.1
Meon Valley	George Hollingbery	Con	25,692	47.31
Meriden	Caroline Spelman	Con	19,198	35.07
Middlesbrough	Andy McDonald	Lab	13,873	38.87
Middlesbrough South and East Cleveland	Simon Clarke	Con	1,020	2.14
Milton Keynes North	Mark Lancaster	Con	1,975	3.08
Milton Keynes South	Iain Stewart	Con	1,665	2.57
Mitcham and Morden	Siobhain McDonagh	Lab	21,375	44.31
Mole Valley	Paul Beresford	Con	24,137	42.45
Morecambe and Lunesdale	David Morris	Con	1,399	3.06
Morley and Outwood	Andrea Jenkyns	Con	2,104	4
New Forest East	Julian Lewis	Con	21,995	42.71
New Forest West	Desmond Swayne	Con	23,431	47.12
Newark	Robert Jenrick	Con	18,149	32.89
Newbury	Richard Benyon	Con	24,380	39.97
Newcastle-under-Lyme	Paul Farrelly	Lab	30	0.07
Newcastle upon Tyne Central	Chi Onwurah	Lab	14,937	40.18
Newcastle upon Tyne East	Nick Brown	Lab	19,261	46.17
Newcastle upon Tyne North	Catherine McKinnell	Lab	10,349	21.4
Newton Abbot	Anne Marie Morris	Ind*	17,160	33.15
Mid Norfolk	George Freeman	Con	16,086	28.85
North Norfolk	Norman Lamb	Lib Dem	3,512	6.72
North West Norfolk	Henry Bellingham	Con	13,788	28.2
South Norfolk	Richard Bacon	Con	16,678	27.21
South West Norfolk	Elizabeth Truss	Con	18,312	34.83
Normanton, Pontefract and Castleford	Yvette Cooper	Lab	14,499	29.43
Northampton North	Michael Ellis	Con	807	2
Northampton South	Andrew Lewer	Con	1,159	2.82
South Northamptonshire	Andrea Leadsom	Con	22,840	35.07
Norwich North	Chloe Smith	Con	507	1.1
Norwich South	Clive Lewis	Lab	15,596	30.28
Nottingham East	Chris Leslie	Lab/Co-op	19,590	49.67
Nottingham North	Alex Norris	Lab/Co-op	11,160	29.07
Nottingham South	Lilian Greenwood	Lab	15,162	31.41
Nuneaton	Marcus Jones	Con	4,739	10.27
Oldham East and Saddleworth	Debbie Abrahams	Lab	8,182	17.36
Oldham West and Royton	Jim McMahon	Lab/Co-op	17,198	37.48
Orpington	Jo Johnson	Con	19,461	38.49
Oxford East	Anneliese Dodds	Lab/Co-op	23,284	43.12
Oxford West and Abingdon	Layla Moran	Lib Dem	816	1.36
Pendle	Andrew Stephenson	Con	1,279	2.85
Penistone and Stocksbridge	Angela Smith	Lab	1,322	2.65
Penrith and The Border	Rory Stewart	Con	15,910	34.18
Peterborough	Fiona Onasanya	Lab	607	1.27
Plymouth, Moor View	Johnny Mercer	Con	5,019	11.03
Plymouth, Sutton and Devonport	Luke Pollard	Lab/Co-op	6,807	13.27
Poole	Robert Syms	Con	14,209	28.43
Poplar and Limehouse	Jim Fitzpatrick	Lab	27,712	46.9
Portsmouth North	Penny Mordaunt	Con	9,965	21.07
Portsmouth South	Stephen Morgan	Lab	1,554	3.48

* Elected as Conservative

			Majority	%
Preston	Mark Hendrick	Lab/Co-op	15,723	44.09
Pudsey	Stuart Andrew	Con	331	0.61
Putney	Justine Greening	Con	1,554	3.31
Rayleigh and Wickford	Mark Francois	Con	23,450	42.31
Reading East	Matt Rodda	Lab	3,749	6.77
Reading West	Alok Sharma	Con	2,876	5.54
Redcar	Anna Turley	Lab/Co-op	9,485	22.25
Redditch	Rachel Maclean	Con	7,363	16.25
Reigate	Crispin Blunt	Con	17,614	32.62
South Ribble	Seema Kennedy	Con	7,421	13.51
Ribble Valley	Nigel Evans	Con	13,199	23.84
Richmond Park	Zac Goldsmith	Con	45	0.07
Richmond (Yorkshire)	Rishi Sunak	Con	23,108	40.44
Rochdale	Tony Lloyd	Lab	14,819	29.55
Rochester and Strood	Kelly Tolhurst	Con	9,850	18.3
Rochford and Southend East	James Duddridge	Con	5,548	11.72
Romford	Andrew Rosindell	Con	13,778	27.52
Romsey and Southampton North	Caroline Nokes	Con	18,046	35.92
Rossendale and Darwen	Jake Berry	Con	3,216	6.39
Rother Valley	Kevin Barron	Lab	3,882	7.83
Rotherham	Sarah Champion	Lab	11,387	29.96
Rugby	Mark Pawsey	Con	8,212	15.95
Ruislip, Northwood and Pinner	Nick Hurd	Con	13,980	26.12
Runnymede and Weybridge	Philip Hammond	Con	18,050	34.88
Rushcliffe	Kenneth Clarke	Con	8,010	13.7
Rutland and Melton	Alan Duncan	Con	23,104	40.03
Saffron Walden	Kemi Badenoch	Con	24,966	40.86
St Albans	Anne Main	Con	6,109	10.69
St Austell and Newquay	Steve Double	Con	11,142	20.47
St Helens North	Conor McGinn	Lab	18,406	36.58
St Helens South and Whiston	Marie Rimmer	Lab	24,343	45.96
St Ives	Derek Thomas	Con	312	0.61
Salford and Eccles	Rebecca Long-Bailey	Lab	19,132	40.08
Salisbury	John Glen	Con	17,333	32.46
Scarborough and Whitby	Robert Goodwill	Con	3,435	6.8
Scunthorpe	Nic Dakin	Lab	3,431	8.52
Sedgefield	Phil Wilson	Lab	6,059	14.55
Sefton Central	Bill Esterson	Lab	15,618	29.92
Selby and Ainsty	Nigel Adams	Con	13,772	24.5
Sevenoaks	Michael Fallon	Con	21,917	42.67
Sheffield, Brightside and Hillsborough	Gill Furniss	Lab	19,143	45.64
Sheffield Central	Paul Blomfield	Lab	27,748	57.79
Sheffield, Hallam	Jared O'Mara	Lab	2,125	3.72
Sheffield Heeley	Louise Haigh	Lab	13,828	31.21
Sheffield South East	Clive Betts	Lab	11,798	27.01
Sherwood	Mark Spencer	Con	5,198	9.72
Shipley	Philip Davies	Con	4,681	8.74
Shrewsbury and Atcham	Daniel Kawczynski	Con	6,627	11.36
North Shropshire	Owen Paterson	Con	16,355	29.34
Sittingbourne and Sheppey	Gordon Henderson	Con	15,211	29.56
Skipton and Ripon	Julian Smith	Con	19,985	34.27
Sleaford and North Hykeham	Caroline Johnson	Con	25,237	38.29
Slough	Tanmanjeet Singh Dhesi	Lab	16,998	31.21

			Majority	%
Solihull	Julian Knight	Con	20,571	36.17
North Somerset	Liam Fox	Con	17,103	27.53
North East Somerset	Jacob Rees-Mogg	Con	10,235	18.9
Somerton and Frome	David Warburton	Con	22,906	35.79
South Holland and The Deepings	John Hayes	Con	24,897	49.4
South Shields	Emma Lewell-Buck	Lab	14,508	35.52
Southampton Itchen	Royston Smith	Con	31	0.07
Southampton Test	Alan Whitehead	Lab	11,503	24.46
Southend West	David Amess	Con	10,000	21.15
Southport	Damien Moore	Con	2,914	6.07
Spelthorne	Kwasi Kwarteng	Con	13,425	26.73
Stafford	Jeremy Lefroy	Con	7,729	14.85
Staffordshire Moorlands	Karen Bradley	Con	10,830	24.21
South Staffordshire	Gavin Williamson	Con	22,733	44.32
Stalybridge and Hyde	Jonathan Reynolds	Lab/Co-op	8,084	18.98
Stevenage	Stephen McPartland	Con	3,386	6.84
Stockport	Ann Coffey	Lab	14,477	34.77
Stockton North	Alex Cunningham	Lab	8,715	20.36
Stockton South	Paul Williams	Lab	888	1.65
Stoke-on-Trent Central	Gareth Snell	Lab/Co-op	3,897	11.73
Stoke-on-Trent North	Ruth Smeeth	Lab	2,359	5.63
Stoke-on-Trent South	Jack Brereton	Con	663	1.59
Stone	Bill Cash	Con	17,495	34.9
Stourbridge	Margot James	Con	7,654	16.21
Stratford-on-Avon	Nadhim Zahawi	Con	21,958	40.9
Streatham	Chuka Umunna	Lab	26,285	46.97
Stretford and Urmston	Kate Green	Lab	19,705	39.19
Stroud	David Drew	Lab/Co-op	687	1.07
Central Suffolk and North Ipswich	Dan Poulter	Con	17,185	30.34
Suffolk Coastal	Therese Coffey	Con	16,012	27.47
South Suffolk	James Cartlidge	Con	17,749	32.66
West Suffolk	Matt Hancock	Con	17,063	32.91
Sunderland Central	Julie Elliott	Lab	9,997	22.12
East Surrey	Sam Gyimah	Con	23,914	40.31
Surrey Heath	Michael Gove	Con	24,943	42.97
South West Surrey	Jeremy Hunt	Con	21,590	35.64
Mid Sussex	Nicholas Soames	Con	19,673	31.86
Sutton and Cheam	Paul Scully	Con	12,698	24.38
Sutton Coldfield	Andrew Mitchell	Con	15,339	28.94
North Swindon	Justin Tomlinson	Con	8,335	15.15
South Swindon	Robert Buckland	Con	2,464	4.8
Tamworth	Christopher Pincher	Con	12,347	26.11
Tatton	Esther McVey	Con	14,787	30.04
Taunton Deane	Rebecca Pow	Con	15,887	25.16
Telford	Lucy Allan	Con	720	1.61
Tewkesbury	Laurence Robertson	Con	22,574	38.13
North Thanet	Roger Gale	Con	10,738	22.18
South Thanet	Craig Mackinlay	Con	6,387	12.81
Thirsk and Malton	Kevin Hollinrake	Con	19,001	33.92
Thornbury and Yate	Luke Hall	Con	12,071	23.77
Thurrock	Jackie Doyle-Price	Con	345	0.68
Tiverton and Honiton	Neil Parish	Con	19,801	34.15
Tonbridge and Malling	Tom Tugendhat	Con	23,508	41.23

			Majority	%
Tooting	Rosena Allin-Khan	Lab	15,458	26.51
Torbay	Kevin Foster	Con	14,283	27.87
Torridge and West Devon	Geoffrey Cox	Con	20,686	34.69
Totnes	Sarah Wollaston	Con	13,477	26.77
Tottenham	David Lammy	Lab	34,584	69.89
Truro and Falmouth	Sarah Newton	Con	3,792	6.69
Tunbridge Wells	Greg Clark	Con	16,465	30.32
Twickenham	Vince Cable	Lib Dem	9,762	14.69
Tynemouth	Alan Campbell	Lab	11,666	20.48
North Tyneside	Mary Glindon	Lab	19,284	37.1
Uxbridge and South Ruislip	Boris Johnson	Con	5,034	10.76
Vauxhall	Kate Hoey	Lab	20,250	36.68
Wakefield	Mary Creagh	Lab	2,176	4.69
Wallasey	Angela Eagle	Lab	23,320	48.15
Walsall North	Eddie Hughes	Con	2,601	6.81
Walsall South	Valerie Vaz	Lab	8,892	20.12
Walthamstow	Stella Creasy	Lab/Co-op	32,017	66.29
Wansbeck	Ian Lavery	Lab	10,435	24.55
Wantage	Ed Vaizey	Con	17,380	27.26
Warley	John Spellar	Lab	16,483	40.88
Warrington North	Helen Jones	Lab	9,582	19.71
Warrington South	Faisal Rashid	Lab	2,549	4.1
Warwick and Leamington	Matt Western	Lab	1,206	2.23
North Warwickshire	Craig Tracey	Con	8,510	17.99
Washington and Sunderland West	Sharon Hodgson	Lab	12,940	31.83
Watford	Richard Harrington	Con	2,092	3.56
Waveney	Peter Aldous	Con	9,215	17.47
Wealden	Nusrat Ghani	Con	23,628	39
Weaver Vale	Mike Amesbury	Lab	3,928	7.74
Wellingborough	Peter Bone	Con	12,460	23.36
Wells	James Heappey	Con	7,582	12.43
Welwyn Hatfield	Grant Shapps	Con	7,369	14.23
Wentworth and Dearne	John Healey	Lab	14,803	33.47
West Bromwich East	Tom Watson	Lab	7,713	19.66
West Bromwich West	Adrian Bailey	Lab/Co-op	4,460	12.33
West Ham	Lyn Brown	Lab	36,754	60.38
Westminster North	Karen Buck	Lab	11,512	26.47
Westmorland and Lonsdale	Tim Farron	Lib Dem	777	1.5
Weston-Super-Mare	John Penrose	Con	11,544	20.43
Wigan	Lisa Nandy	Lab	16,027	33.64
North Wiltshire	James Gray	Con	22,877	42.52
South West Wiltshire	Andrew Murrison	Con	18,326	33.38
Wimbledon	Stephen Hammond	Con	5,622	10.88
Winchester	Steve Brine	Con	9,999	17.46
Windsor	Adam Afriyie	Con	22,384	41.39
Wirral South	Alison McGovern	Lab	8,323	18.38
Wirral West	Margaret Greenwood	Lab	5,365	12.18
Witham	Priti Patel	Con	18,646	37.74
Witney	Robert Courts	Con	21,241	34.79
Woking	Jonathan Lord	Con	16,724	30.2
Wokingham	John Redwood	Con	18,798	31.39
Wolverhampton North East	Emma Reynolds	Lab	4,587	12.53
Wolverhampton South East	Pat McFadden	Lab	8,514	23.4

			Majority	%
Wolverhampton South West	Eleanor Smith	Lab	2,185	5.15
Worcester	Robin Walker	Con	2,508	4.87
Mid Worcestershire	Nigel Huddleston	Con	23,326	42.26
West Worcestershire	Harriett Baldwin	Con	21,328	37.69
Workington	Sue Hayman	Lab	3,925	9.41
Worsley and Eccles South	Barbara Keeley	Lab	8,379	18.31
East Worthing and Shoreham	Tim Loughton	Con	5,106	9.6
Worthing West	Peter Bottomley	Con	12,090	22.14
The Wrekin	Mark Pritchard	Con	9,564	19.27
Wycombe	Steve Baker	Con	6,578	12.26
Wyre and Preston North	Ben Wallace	Con	12,246	23.21
Wyre Forest	Mark Garnier	Con	13,334	26.03
Wythenshawe and Sale East	Mike Kane	Lab	14,944	32.55
Yeovil	Marcus Fysh	Con	14,723	24.75
York Central	Rachael Maskell	Lab/Co-op	18,575	34.85
York Outer	Julian Sturdy	Con	8,289	14.4
East Yorkshire	Greg Knight	Con	15,006	27.76

Scotland

			Majority	%
Aberdeen North	Kirsty Blackman	SNP	4,139	11.24
Aberdeen South	Ross Thomson	Con	4,752	10.67
West Aberdeenshire and Kincardine	Andrew Bowie	Con	7,950	15.38
Airdrie and Shotts	Neil Gray	SNP	195	0.51
Angus	Kirstene Hair	Con	2,645	6.57
Argyll and Bute	Brendan O'Hara	SNP	1,328	2.76
Ayr, Carrick and Cumnock	Bill Grant	Con	2,774	5.99
Central Ayrshire	Philippa Whitford	SNP	1,267	2.81
North Ayrshire and Arran	Patricia Gibson	SNP	3,633	7.65
Banff and Buchan	David Duguid	Con	3,693	8.86
Berwickshire, Roxburgh and Selkirk	John Lamont	Con	11,060	21.08
Caithness, Sutherland and Easter Ross	Jamie Stone	Lib Dem	2,044	6.61
Coatbridge, Chryston and Bellshill	Hugh Gaffney	Lab	1,586	3.52
Cumbernauld, Kilsyth and Kirkintilloch East	Stuart C McDonald	SNP	4,264	9.72
Dumfries and Galloway	Alister Jack	Con	5,643	10.93
Dumfriesshire, Clydesdale and Tweeddale	David Mundell	Con	9,441	19.26
East Dunbartonshire	Jo Swinson	Lib Dem	5,339	10.29
West Dunbartonshire	Martin Docherty-Hughes	SNP	2,288	5.18
Dundee East	Stewart Hosie	SNP	6,645	15.46
Dundee West	Chris Law	SNP	5,262	13.57
Dunfermline and West Fife	Douglas Chapman	SNP	844	1.65
East Kilbride, Strathaven and Lesmahagow	Lisa Cameron	SNP	3,866	7.14
Edinburgh East	Tommy Sheppard	SNP	3,425	7.85
Edinburgh North and Leith	Deidre Brock	SNP	1,625	2.87
Edinburgh South	Ian Murray	Lab	15,514	32.38
Edinburgh South West	Joanna Cherry	SNP	1,097	2.22
Edinburgh West	Christine Jardine	Lib Dem	2,988	5.65
Falkirk	John McNally	SNP	4,923	9.14
North East Fife	Stephen Gethins	SNP	2	0
Glasgow Central	Alison Thewliss	SNP	2,267	6.28

			Majority	%
Glasgow East	David Linden	SNP	75	0.21
Glasgow North	Patrick Grady	SNP	1,060	3.16
Glasgow North East	Paul Sweeney	Lab/Co-op	242	0.76
Glasgow North West	Carol Monaghan	SNP	2,561	6.58
Glasgow South	Stewart Malcolm McDonald	SNP	2,027	4.54
Glasgow South West	Chris Stephens	SNP	60	0.17
Glenrothes	Peter Grant	SNP	3,267	8.08
Gordon	Colin Clark	Con	2,607	4.85
Inverclyde	Ronnie Cowan	SNP	384	0.98
Inverness, Nairn, Badenoch and Strathspey	Drew Hendry	SNP	4,924	9.31
Kilmarnock and Loudoun	Alan Brown	SNP	6,269	13.46
Kirkcaldy and Cowdenbeath	Lesley Laird	Lab	259	0.56
Lanark and Hamilton East	Angela Crawley	SNP	266	0.53
Linlithgow and East Falkirk	Martyn Day	SNP	2,919	5.2
Livingston	Hannah Bardell	SNP	3,878	7.37
East Lothian	Martin Whitfield	Lab	3,083	5.51
Midlothian	Danielle Rowley	Lab	885	1.95
Moray	Douglas Ross	Con	4,159	8.73
Motherwell and Wishaw	Marion Fellows	SNP	318	0.76
Na h-Eileanan An Iar	Angus MacNeil	SNP	1,007	6.78
Ochil and South Perthshire	Luke Graham	Con	3,359	6.19
Orkney and Shetland	Alistair Carmichael	Lib Dem	4,563	19.57
Paisley and Renfrewshire North	Gavin Newlands	SNP	2,613	5.6
Paisley and Renfrewshire South	Mhairi Black	SNP	2,541	6.08
Perth and North Perthshire	Pete Wishart	SNP	21	0.04
East Renfrewshire	Paul Masterton	Con	4,712	8.76
Ross, Skye and Lochaber	Ian Blackford	SNP	5,919	15.37
Rutherglen and Hamilton West	Gerard Killen	Lab/Co-op	265	0.52
Stirling	Stephen Kerr	Con	148	0.3

Wales

			Majority	%
Aberavon	Stephen Kinnock	Lab	16,761	50.3
Aberconwy	Guto Bebb	Con	635	1.97
Alyn and Deeside	Mark Tami	Lab	5,235	11.67
Arfon	Hywel Williams	PlC	92	0.33
Blaenau Gwent	Nick Smith	Lab	11,907	36.73
Brecon and Radnorshire	Chris Davies	Con	8,038	19.42
Bridgend	Madeleine Moon	Lab	4,700	10.85
Caerphilly	Wayne David	Lab	12,078	29.19
Cardiff Central	Jo Stevens	Lab	17,196	42.51
Cardiff North	Anna McMorrin	Lab	4,174	8.01
Cardiff South and Penarth	Stephen Doughty	Lab/Co-op	14,864	29.24
Cardiff West	Kevin Brennan	Lab	12,551	26.87
Carmarthen East and Dinefwr	Jonathan Edwards	PlC	3,908	9.51
Carmarthen West and South Pembrokeshire	Simon Hart	Con	3,110	7.35
Ceredigion	Ben Lake	PlC	104	0.26
Clwyd South	Susan Elan Jones	Lab	4,356	11.61
Vale of Clwyd	Chris Ruane	Lab	2,379	6.14
Clwyd West	David Jones	Con	3,437	8.44

			Majority	%
Cynon Valley	Ann Clwyd	Lab	13,238	41.53
Delyn	David Hanson	Lab	4,240	10.74
Dwyfor Meirionnydd	Liz Saville Roberts	PlC	4,850	15.95
Vale of Glamorgan	Alun Cairns	Con	2,190	4.07
Gower	Tonia Antoniazzi	Lab	3,269	7.16
Islwyn	Chris Evans	Lab/Co-op	11,412	31.55
Llanelli	Nia Griffith	Lab	12,024	29.76
Merthyr Tydfil and Rhymney	Gerald Jones	Lab	16,334	48.59
Monmouth	David Davies	Con	8,206	16.48
Montgomeryshire	Glyn Davies	Con	9,285	26.55
Neath	Christina Rees	Lab/Co-op	12,631	32.92
Newport East	Jessica Morden	Lab	8,003	21.7
Newport West	Paul Flynn	Lab	5,658	13
Ogmore	Chris Elmore	Lab	13,871	37.21
Pontypridd	Owen Smith	Lab	11,448	28.62
Preseli Pembrokeshire	Stephen Crabb	Con	314	0.74
Rhondda	Chris Bryant	Lab	13,746	41.66
Swansea East	Carolyn Harris	Lab	13,168	37.39
Swansea West	Geraint Davies	Lab/Co-op	10,598	28.36
Torfaen	Nick Thomas-Symonds	Lab	10,240	26.6
Wrexham	Ian C Lucas	Lab	1,832	5.21
Ynys Môn	Albert Owen	Lab	5,259	14.06

Northern Ireland

			Majority	%
East Antrim	Sammy Wilson	DUP	15,923	41.61
North Antrim	Ian Paisley	DUP	20,643	42.49
South Antrim	Paul Girvan	DUP	3,208	7.41
Belfast East	Gavin Robinson	DUP	8,474	19.71
Belfast North	Nigel Dodds	DUP	2,081	4.51
Belfast South	Emma Little Pengelly	DUP	1,996	4.55
Belfast West	Paul Maskey	Sinn Féin	21,652	53.03
North Down	Sylvia Hermon	Ind	1,208	3.08
South Down	Chris Hazzard	Sinn Féin	2,446	4.79
Fermanagh and South Tyrone	Michelle Gildernew	Sinn Féin	875	1.63
Foyle	Elisha McCallion	Sinn Féin	169	0.37
Lagan Valley	Jeffrey Donaldson	DUP	19,229	42.69
East Londonderry	Gregory Campbell	DUP	8,842	21.42
Newry and Armagh	Mickey Brady	Sinn Féin	12,489	23.17
Strangford	Jim Shannon	DUP	18,343	47.24
West Tyrone	Barry McElduff	Sinn Féin	10,342	23.68
Mid Ulster	Francie Molloy	Sinn Féin	12,890	27.44
Upper Bann	David Simpson	DUP	7,992	15.54

Most Vulnerable Constituencies

Constituencies have been classed as vulnerable if their majority is less than 15 per cent following the 2017 general election.

				Majority	*%*
1	North East Fife	Stephen Gethins	SNP	2	0
2	Perth and North Perthshire	Pete Wishart	SNP	21	0.04
3	Kensington	Emma Dent Coad	Lab	20	0.05
4	Dudley North	Ian Austin	Lab	22	0.06
5	Newcastle-under-Lyme	Paul Farrelly	Lab	30	0.07
6	Southampton Itchen	Royston Smith	Con	31	0.07
7	Richmond Park	Zac Goldsmith	Con	45	0.07
8	Crewe and Nantwich	Laura Smith	Lab	48	0.09
9	Glasgow South West	Chris Stephens	SNP	60	0.17
10	Glasgow East	David Linden	SNP	75	0.21
11	Ceredigion	Ben Lake	PlC	104	0.26
12	Stirling	Stephen Kerr	Con	148	0.3
13	Arfon	Hywel Williams	PlC	92	0.33
14	Canterbury	Rosie Duffield	Lab	187	0.33
15	Foyle	Elisha McCallion	Sinn Féin	169	0.37
16	Barrow and Furness	John Woodcock	Lab/Co-op	209	0.44
17	Keighley	John Grogan	Lab	239	0.46
18	Airdrie and Shotts	Neil Gray	SNP	195	0.51
19	Rutherglen and Hamilton West	Gerard Killen	Lab/Co-op	265	0.52
20	Lanark and Hamilton East	Angela Crawley	SNP	266	0.53
21	Kirkcaldy and Cowdenbeath	Lesley Laird	Lab	259	0.56
22	St Ives	Derek Thomas	Con	312	0.61
23	Pudsey	Stuart Andrew	Con	331	0.61
24	Hastings and Rye	Amber Rudd	Con	346	0.63
25	Chipping Barnet	Theresa Villiers	Con	353	0.63
26	Thurrock	Jackie Doyle-Price	Con	345	0.68
27	Preseli Pembrokeshire	Stephen Crabb	Con	314	0.74
28	Glasgow North East	Paul Sweeney	Lab/Co-op	242	0.76
29	Motherwell and Wishaw	Marion Fellows	SNP	318	0.76
30	Ashfield	Gloria De Piero	Lab	441	0.88
31	Inverclyde	Ronnie Cowan	SNP	384	0.98
32	Calder Valley	Craig Whittaker	Con	609	1.05
33	Stroud	David Drew	Lab/Co-op	687	1.07
34	Norwich North	Chloe Smith	Con	507	1.1
35	Bishop Auckland	Helen Goodman	Lab	502	1.16
36	Peterborough	Fiona Onasanya	Lab	607	1.27
37	Oxford West and Abingdon	Layla Moran	Lib Dem	816	1.36
38	Westmorland and Lonsdale	Tim Farron	Lib Dem	777	1.5
39	Colne Valley	Thelma Walker	Lab	915	1.51
40	Broxtowe	Anna Soubry	Con	863	1.55
41	Stoke-on-Trent South	Jack Brereton	Con	663	1.59
42	Telford	Lucy Allan	Con	720	1.61
43	Bedford	Mohammad Yasin	Lab	789	1.62
44	Ipswich	Sandy Martin	Lab	831	1.62
45	Fermanagh and South Tyrone	Michelle Gildernew	Sinn Féin	875	1.63
46	Dunfermline and West Fife	Douglas Chapman	SNP	844	1.65
47	Stockton South	Paul Williams	Lab	888	1.65
48	Bolton West	Chris Green	Con	936	1.83
49	Midlothian	Danielle Rowley	Lab	885	1.95
50	Aberconwy	Guto Bebb	Con	635	1.97

				Majority	*%*
51	Northampton North	Michael Ellis	Con	807	2
52	Hendon	Matthew Offord	Con	1,072	2.05
53	Mansfield	Ben Bradley	Con	1,057	2.1
54	Middlesbrough South and East Cleveland	Simon Clarke	Con	1,020	2.14
55	Edinburgh South West	Joanna Cherry	SNP	1,097	2.22
56	Warwick and Leamington	Matt Western	Lab	1,206	2.23
57	Milton Keynes South	Iain Stewart	Con	1,665	2.57
58	Penistone and Stocksbridge	Angela Smith	Lab	1,322	2.65
59	Carshalton and Wallington	Tom Brake	Lib Dem	1,369	2.69
60	Argyll and Bute	Brendan O'Hara	SNP	1,328	2.76
61	Eastbourne	Stephen Lloyd	Lib Dem	1,609	2.8
62	Central Ayrshire	Philippa Whitford	SNP	1,267	2.81
63	Northampton South	Andrew Lewer	Con	1,159	2.82
64	Pendle	Andrew Stephenson	Con	1,279	2.85
65	Edinburgh North and Leith	Deidre Brock	SNP	1,625	2.87
66	Morecambe and Lunesdale	David Morris	Con	1,399	3.06
67	North Down	Sylvia Hermon	Ind	1,208	3.08
68	Milton Keynes North	Mark Lancaster	Con	1,975	3.08
69	Lincoln	Karen Lee	Lab	1,538	3.15
70	Finchley and Golders Green	Mike Freer	Con	1,657	3.15
71	Glasgow North	Patrick Grady	SNP	1,060	3.16
72	Camborne and Redruth	George Eustice	Con	1,577	3.25
73	Putney	Justine Greening	Con	1,554	3.31
74	Harrow East	Bob Blackman	Con	1,757	3.45
75	Portsmouth South	Stephen Morgan	Lab	1,554	3.48
76	Coatbridge, Chryston and Bellshill	Hugh Gaffney	Lab	1,586	3.52
77	Watford	Richard Harrington	Con	2,092	3.56
78	Sheffield, Hallam	Jared O'Mara	Lab	2,125	3.72
79	Copeland	Trudy Harrison	Con	1,695	3.94
80	Morley and Outwood	Andrea Jenkyns	Con	2,104	4
81	Vale of Glamorgan	Alun Cairns	Con	2,190	4.07
82	Warrington South	Faisal Rashid	Lab	2,549	4.1
83	Derby North	Chris Williamson	Lab	2,015	4.13
84	High Peak	Ruth George	Lab	2,322	4.3
85	Battersea	Marsha De Cordova	Lab	2,416	4.38
86	Corby	Tom Pursglove	Con	2,690	4.48
87	Cheltenham	Alex Chalk	Con	2,569	4.5
88	Belfast North	Nigel Dodds	DUP	2,081	4.51
89	Glasgow South	Stewart Malcolm McDonald	SNP	2,027	4.54
90	Belfast South	Emma Little Pengelly	DUP	1,996	4.55
91	Wakefield	Mary Creagh	Lab	2,176	4.69
92	South Down	Chris Hazzard	Sinn Féin	2,446	4.79
93	South Swindon	Robert Buckland	Con	2,464	4.8
94	Gordon	Colin Clark	Con	2,607	4.85
95	Crawley	Henry Smith	Con	2,457	4.87
96	Worcester	Robin Walker	Con	2,508	4.87
97	Blackpool North and Cleveleys	Paul Maynard	Con	2,023	4.93
98	Wolverhampton South West	Eleanor Smith	Lab	2,185	5.15
99	Chingford and Woodford Green	Iain Duncan Smith	Con	2,438	5.17
100	West Dunbartonshire	Martin Docherty-Hughes	SNP	2,288	5.18

				Majority	%
101	Linlithgow and East Falkirk	Martyn Day	SNP	2,919	5.2
102	Wrexham	Ian C Lucas	Lab	1,832	5.21
103	East Lothian	Martin Whitfield	Lab	3,083	5.51
104	Reading West	Alok Sharma	Con	2,876	5.54
105	Paisley and Renfrewshire North	Gavin Newlands	SNP	2,613	5.6
106	Stoke-on-Trent North	Ruth Smeeth	Lab	2,359	5.63
107	Edinburgh West	Christine Jardine	Lib Dem	2,988	5.65
108	North East Derbyshire	Lee Rowley	Con	2,860	5.67
109	Dewsbury	Paula Sherriff	Lab	3,321	5.86
110	Ayr, Carrick and Cumnock	Bill Grant	Con	2,774	5.99
111	Carlisle	John Stevenson	Con	2,599	6.02
112	Southport	Damien Moore	Con	2,914	6.07
113	Paisley and Renfrewshire South	Mhairi Black	SNP	2,541	6.08
114	Vale of Clwyd	Chris Ruane	Lab	2,379	6.14
115	Ochil and South Perthshire	Luke Graham	Con	3,359	6.19
116	Glasgow Central	Alison Thewliss	SNP	2,267	6.28
117	Rossendale and Darwen	Jake Berry	Con	3,216	6.39
118	Angus	Kirstene Hair	Con	2,645	6.57
119	Glasgow North West	Carol Monaghan	SNP	2,561	6.58
120	Caithness, Sutherland and Easter Ross	Jamie Stone	Lib Dem	2,044	6.61
121	Kingston and Surbiton	Ed Davey	Lib Dem	4,124	6.62
122	Truro and Falmouth	Sarah Newton	Con	3,792	6.69
123	North Norfolk	Norman Lamb	Lib Dem	3,512	6.72
124	Reading East	Matt Rodda	Lab	3,749	6.77
125	Na h-Eileanan An Iar	Angus MacNeil	SNP	1,007	6.78
126	Scarborough and Whitby	Robert Goodwill	Con	3,435	6.8
127	Walsall North	Eddie Hughes	Con	2,601	6.81
128	Stevenage	Stephen McPartland	Con	3,386	6.84
129	East Kilbride, Strathaven and Lesmahagow	Lisa Cameron	SNP	3,866	7.14
130	Gower	Tonia Antoniazzi	Lab	3,269	7.16
131	Blackpool South	Gordon Marsden	Lab	2,523	7.21
132	Great Grimsby	Melanie Onn	Lab	2,565	7.21
133	Darlington	Jenny Chapman	Lab	3,280	7.31
134	Carmarthen West and South Pembrokeshire	Simon Hart	Con	3,110	7.35
135	Livingston	Hannah Bardell	SNP	3,878	7.37
136	South Antrim	Paul Girvan	DUP	3,208	7.41
137	North Ayrshire and Arran	Patricia Gibson	SNP	3,633	7.65
138	Weaver Vale	Mike Amesbury	Lab	3,928	7.74
139	North Devon	Peter Heaton-Jones	Con	4,332	7.77
140	Rother Valley	Kevin Barron	Lab	3,882	7.83
141	Edinburgh East	Tommy Sheppard	SNP	3,425	7.85
142	Loughborough	Nicky Morgan	Con	4,269	7.87
143	Cardiff North	Anna McMorrin	Lab	4,174	8.01
144	Glenrothes	Peter Grant	SNP	3,267	8.08
145	Cities of London and Westminster	Mark Field	Con	3,148	8.12
146	Filton and Bradley Stoke	Jack Lopresti	Con	4,190	8.24
147	Cheadle	Mary Robinson	Con	4,507	8.24
148	Bolton North East	David Crausby	Lab	3,797	8.39
149	Clwyd West	David Jones	Con	3,437	8.44
150	Scunthorpe	Nic Dakin	Lab	3,431	8.52

				Majority	%
151	Moray	Douglas Ross	Con	4,159	8.73
152	Shipley	Philip Davies	Con	4,681	8.74
153	East Renfrewshire	Paul Masterton	Con	4,712	8.76
154	Bristol North West	Darren Jones	Lab	4,761	8.78
155	Banff and Buchan	David Duguid	Con	3,693	8.86
156	Enfield Southgate	Bambos Charalambous	Lab	4,355	8.98
157	Gedling	Vernon Coaker	Lab	4,694	9.07
158	Erewash	Maggie Throup	Con	4,534	9.09
159	Bury North	James Frith	Lab	4,375	9.1
160	Leeds North West	Alex Sobel	Lab/Co-op	4,224	9.11
161	Falkirk	John McNally	SNP	4,923	9.14
162	Bassetlaw	John Mann	Lab	4,852	9.26
163	Inverness, Nairn, Badenoch and Strathspey	Drew Hendry	SNP	4,924	9.31
164	Workington	Sue Hayman	Lab	3,925	9.41
165	Carmarthen East and Dinefwr	Jonathan Edwards	PlC	3,908	9.51
166	East Worthing and Shoreham	Tim Loughton	Con	5,106	9.6
167	Sherwood	Mark Spencer	Con	5,198	9.72
168	Cumbernauld, Kilsyth and Kirkintilloch East	Stuart C McDonald	SNP	4,264	9.72
169	Croydon Central	Sarah Jones	Lab	5,652	9.88
170	Dagenham and Rainham	Jon Cruddas	Lab	4,652	10.13
171	Lewes	Maria Caulfield	Con	5,508	10.14
172	Gloucester	Richard Graham	Con	5,520	10.19
173	Nuneaton	Marcus Jones	Con	4,739	10.27
174	East Dunbartonshire	Jo Swinson	Lib Dem	5,339	10.29
175	Birmingham, Northfield	Richard Burden	Lab	4,667	10.49
176	Colchester	Will Quince	Con	5,677	10.58
177	Aberdeen South	Ross Thomson	Con	4,752	10.67
178	St Albans	Anne Main	Con	6,109	10.69
179	Delyn	David Hanson	Lab	4,240	10.74
180	Uxbridge and South Ruislip	Boris Johnson	Con	5,034	10.76
181	Bridgend	Madeleine Moon	Lab	4,700	10.85
182	Wimbledon	Stephen Hammond	Con	5,622	10.88
183	Dumfries and Galloway	Alister Jack	Con	5,643	10.93
184	Plymouth, Moor View	Johnny Mercer	Con	5,019	11.03
185	Halifax	Holly Lynch	Lab	5,376	11.11
186	Don Valley	Caroline Flint	Lab	5,169	11.22
187	Aberdeen North	Kirsty Blackman	SNP	4,139	11.24
188	Bolsover	Dennis Skinner	Lab	5,288	11.34
189	Shrewsbury and Atcham	Daniel Kawczynski	Con	6,627	11.36
190	Bath	Wera Hobhouse	Lib Dem	5,694	11.46
191	Clwyd South	Susan Elan Jones	Lab	4,356	11.61
192	Alyn and Deeside	Mark Tami	Lab	5,235	11.67
193	Bury South	Ivan Lewis	Lab	5,965	11.67
194	Rochford and Southend East	James Duddridge	Con	5,548	11.72
195	Stoke-on-Trent Central	Gareth Snell	Lab/Co-op	3,897	11.73
196	Halesowen and Rowley Regis	James Morris	Con	5,253	11.81
197	Altrincham and Sale West	Graham Brady	Con	6,426	12.14
198	Wirral West	Margaret Greenwood	Lab	5,365	12.18
199	Wycombe	Steve Baker	Con	6,578	12.26
200	West Bromwich West	Adrian Bailey	Lab/Co-op	4,460	12.33
201	Dover	Charlie Elphicke	Con	6,437	12.37

				Majority	%
202	Wells	James Heappey	Con	7,582	12.43
203	Hazel Grove	William Wragg	Con	5,514	12.46
204	Wolverhampton North East	Emma Reynolds	Lab	4,587	12.53
205	South Thanet	Craig Mackinlay	Con	6,387	12.81
206	Hyndburn	Graham Jones	Lab	5,815	12.83
207	Newport West	Paul Flynn	Lab	5,658	13
208	Plymouth, Sutton and Devonport	Luke Pollard	Lab/Co-op	6,807	13.27
209	East Devon	Hugo Swire	Con	8,036	13.3
210	Kilmarnock and Loudoun	Alan Brown	SNP	6,269	13.46
211	Chorley	Lindsay Hoyle	Lab	7,512	13.47
212	South Ribble	Seema Kennedy	Con	7,421	13.51
213	Dundee West	Chris Law	SNP	5,262	13.57
214	Eltham	Clive Efford	Lab	6,296	13.6
215	Rushcliffe	Kenneth Clarke	Con	8,010	13.7
216	Ynys Môn	Albert Owen	Lab	5,259	14.06
217	North Cornwall	Scott Mann	Con	7,200	14.1
218	Welwyn Hatfield	Grant Shapps	Con	7,369	14.23
219	York Outer	Julian Sturdy	Con	8,289	14.4
220	Lancaster and Fleetwood	Cat Smith	Lab	6,661	14.45
221	Sedgefield	Phil Wilson	Lab	6,059	14.55
222	Twickenham	Vince Cable	Lib Dem	9,762	14.69
223	Stafford	Jeremy Lefroy	Con	7,729	14.85

50 Safest Constituencies

50 safest constituencies are calculated on the 2017 General Election.

				Majority	%
1	Liverpool Walton	Dan Carden	Lab	32,551	76.95
2	Knowsley	George Howarth	Lab	42,214	75.99
3	Liverpool Riverside	Louise Ellman	Lab/Co-op	35,947	74.61
4	Liverpool West Derby	Stephen Twigg	Lab/Co-op	32,908	72.68
5	Bootle	Peter Dowd	Lab	36,200	71.75
6	East Ham	Stephen Timms	Lab	39,883	70.2
7	Tottenham	David Lammy	Lab	34,584	69.89
8	Birmingham, Ladywood	Shabana Mahmood	Lab	28,714	69.25
9	Manchester Gorton	Afzal Khan	Lab	31,730	68.83
10	Hackney South and Shoreditch	Meg Hillier	Lab/Co-op	37,931	68.26
11	Liverpool Wavertree	Luciana Berger	Lab/Co-op	29,466	67.34
12	Birmingham, Hodge Hill	Liam Byrne	Lab	31,026	66.65
13	Walthamstow	Stella Creasy	Lab/Co-op	32,017	66.29
14	Camberwell and Peckham	Harriet Harman	Lab	37,316	64.73
15	Lewisham Deptford	Vicky Foxcroft	Lab	34,899	63.09
16	Manchester Central	Lucy Powell	Lab/Co-op	31,445	63.05
17	Birmingham, Hall Green	Roger Godsiff	Lab	33,944	62.29
18	Hackney North and Stoke Newington	Diane Abbott	Lab	35,139	62.21
19	West Ham	Lyn Brown	Lab	36,754	60.38
20	Islington North	Jeremy Corbyn	Lab	33,215	60.34
21	Garston and Halewood	Maria Eagle	Lab	32,149	59.91
22	Bethnal Green and Bow	Rushanara Ali	Lab	35,393	58.89
23	Birkenhead	Frank Field	Lab	25,514	58.29
24	Sheffield Central	Paul Blomfield	Lab	27,748	57.79
25	Manchester Withington	Jeff Smith	Lab	29,875	55.6
26	Ilford South	Mike Gapes	Lab/Co-op	31,647	54.75

				Majority	*%*
27	Croydon North	Steve Reed	Lab/Co-op	32,365	54.16
28	Brent Central	Dawn Butler	Lab	27,997	53.33
29	Belfast West	Paul Maskey	Sinn Féin	21,652	53.03
30	Bristol West	Thangam Debbonaire	Lab	37,336	52.01
31	Leicester South	Jon Ashworth	Lab/Co-op	26,261	51.8
32	Holborn and St Pancras	Keir Starmer	Lab	30,509	51.56
33	Halton	Derek Twigg	Lab	25,405	51.22
34	Aberavon	Stephen Kinnock	Lab	16,761	50.3
35	Dulwich and West Norwood	Helen Hayes	Lab	28,156	50.01
36	Nottingham East	Chris Leslie	Lab/Co-op	19,590	49.67
37	Leeds Central	Hilary Benn	Lab	23,698	49.59
38	Christchurch	Christopher Chope	Con	25,171	49.55
39	South Holland and The Deepings	John Hayes	Con	24,897	49.4
40	Hornsey and Wood Green	Catherine West	Lab	30,738	49.22
41	Leyton and Wanstead	John Cryer	Lab	22,607	48.81
42	Blackley and Broughton	Graham Stringer	Lab	22,090	48.74
43	Ealing Southall	Virendra Sharma	Lab	19,601	48.74
44	Merthyr Tydfil and Rhymney	Gerald Jones	Lab	16,334	48.59
45	Edmonton	Kate Osamor	Lab/Co-op	21,115	48.22
46	Wallasey	Angela Eagle	Lab	23,320	48.15
47	North East Hampshire	Ranil Jayawardena	Con	27,772	48.09
48	Bradford West	Naz Shah	Lab	21,902	47.87
49	Meon Valley	George Hollingbery	Con	25,692	47.31
50	Strangford	Jim Shannon	DUP	18,343	47.24

Analysis of MPs
House of Commons

Women MPs 1945–2017 general elections

	Conservative	Labour*	Liberal/ Liberal Democrat	SNP†	Others	Total
1945	1	21	1	–	1	24
1950	6	14	1	–	0	21
1951	6	11	0	–	0	17
1955	10	14	0	–	0	24
1959	12	13	0	–	0	25
1964	11	18	0	–	0	29
1966	7	19	0	–	0	26
1970	15	10	0	–	1	26
1974 (Feb)	9	13	0	–	1	23
1974 (Oct)	7	18	0	–	2	27
1979	8	11	0	–	0	19
1983	13	10	0	–	0	23
1987	17	21	2	–	1	41
1992	20	37	2	–	1	60
1997	13	101	3	–	3	120
2001	14	95	5	–	4	118
2005	17	98	9	–	3	128
2010	49	81	7	1	5	143
2015	68	99	0	19	5	191
2017	66	119	4	12	7	208

* Includes Labour/Co-operative

† SNP have been included in the analysis since the 2010 General Election

Women MPs (208)

ABBOTT Diane	*Lab*	Hackney North and Stoke Newington
ABRAHAMS Debbie	*Lab*	Oldham East and Saddleworth
ALEXANDER Heidi	*Lab*	Lewisham East
ALI Rushanara	*Lab*	Bethnal Green and Bow
ALLAN Lucy	*Con*	Telford
ALLEN Heidi	*Con*	South Cambridgeshire
ALLIN-KHAN Rosena	*Lab*	Tooting
ANTONIAZZI Tonia	*Lab*	Gower
ATKINS Victoria	*Con*	Louth and Horncastle
BADENOCH Kemi	*Con*	Saffron Walden
BALDWIN Harriett	*Con*	West Worcestershire
BARDELL Hannah	*SNP*	Livingston
BECKETT Margaret	*Lab*	Derby South
BERGER Luciana	*Lab/Co-op*	Liverpool Wavertree
BLACK Mhairi	*SNP*	Paisley and Renfrewshire South
BLACKMAN Kirsty	*SNP*	Aberdeen North
BLACKMAN-WOODS Roberta	*Lab*	City of Durham
BRABIN Tracy	*Lab/Co-op*	Batley and Spen
BRADLEY Karen	*Con*	Staffordshire Moorlands
BROCK Deidre	*SNP*	Edinburgh North and Leith
BROWN Lyn	*Lab*	West Ham
BRUCE Fiona	*Con*	Congleton

Analysis of MPs
House of Commons

BUCK Karen	*Lab*	Westminster North
BUTLER Dawn	*Lab*	Brent Central
CADBURY Ruth	*Lab*	Brentford and Isleworth
CAMERON Lisa	*SNP*	East Kilbride, Strathaven and Lesmahagow
CAULFIELD Maria	*Con*	Lewes
CHAMPION Sarah	*Lab*	Rotherham
CHAPMAN Jenny	*Lab*	Darlington
CHERRY Joanna	*SNP*	Edinburgh South West
CHURCHILL Jo	*Con*	Bury St Edmunds
CLWYD Ann	*Lab*	Cynon Valley
COFFEY Ann	*Lab*	Stockport
COFFEY Therese	*Con*	Suffolk Coastal
COOPER Julie	*Lab*	Burnley
COOPER Rosie	*Lab*	West Lancashire
COOPER Yvette	*Lab*	Normanton, Pontefract and Castleford
CRAWLEY Angela	*SNP*	Lanark and Hamilton East
CREAGH Mary	*Lab*	Wakefield
CREASY Stella	*Lab/Co-op*	Walthamstow
CROUCH Tracey	*Con*	Chatham and Aylesford
CUMMINS Judith	*Lab*	Bradford South
DAVIES Mims	*Con*	Eastleigh
DEBBONAIRE Thangam	*Lab*	Bristol West
DE CORDOVA Marsha	*Lab*	Battersea
DENT COAD Emma	*Lab*	Kensington
DE PIERO Gloria	*Lab*	Ashfield
DINENAGE Caroline	*Con*	Gosport
DOCKERILL Julia	*Con*	Hornchurch and Upminster
DODDS Anneliese	*Lab/Co-op*	Oxford East
DONELAN Michelle	*Con*	Chippenham
DORRIES Nadine	*Con*	Mid Bedfordshire
DOYLE-PRICE Jackie	*Con*	Thurrock
DUFFIELD Rosie	*Lab*	Canterbury
EAGLE Angela	*Lab*	Wallasey
EAGLE Maria	*Lab*	Garston and Halewood
ELLIOTT Julie	*Lab*	Sunderland Central
ELLMAN Louise	*Lab/Co-op*	Liverpool Riverside
FELLOWS Marion	*SNP*	Motherwell and Wishaw
FERNANDES Suella	*Con*	Fareham
FLETCHER Colleen	*Lab*	Coventry North East
FLINT Caroline	*Lab*	Don Valley
FORD Vicky	*Con*	Chelmsford
FOVARGUE Yvonne	*Lab*	Makerfield
FOXCROFT Vicky	*Lab*	Lewisham Deptford
FRAZER Lucy	*Con*	South East Cambridgeshire
FURNISS Gill	*Lab*	Sheffield, Brightside and Hillsborough
GEORGE Ruth	*Lab*	High Peak
GHANI Nusrat	*Con*	Wealden
GIBSON Patricia	*SNP*	North Ayrshire and Arran
GILDERNEW Michelle	*Sinn Féin*	Fermanagh and South Tyrone
GILL Preet Kaur	*Lab/Co-op*	Birmingham, Edgbaston
GILLAN Cheryl	*Con*	Chesham and Amersham
GLINDON Mary	*Lab*	North Tyneside
GOODMAN Helen	*Lab*	Bishop Auckland
GRANT Helen	*Con*	Maidstone and The Weald

GREEN Kate	*Lab*	Stretford and Urmston
GREENING Justine	*Con*	Putney
GREENWOOD Lilian	*Lab*	Nottingham South
GREENWOOD Margaret	*Lab*	Wirral West
GRIFFITH Nia	*Lab*	Llanelli
HAIGH Louise	*Lab*	Sheffield Heeley
HAIR Kirstene	*Con*	Angus
HARDY Emma	*Lab*	Kingston upon Hull West and Hessle
HARMAN Harriet	*Lab*	Camberwell and Peckham
HARRIS Carolyn	*Lab*	Swansea East
HARRIS Rebecca	*Con*	Castle Point
HARRISON Trudy	*Con*	Copeland
HAYES Helen	*Lab*	Dulwich and West Norwood
HAYMAN Sue	*Lab*	Workington
HERMON Sylvia	*Ind*	North Down
HILLIER Meg	*Lab/Co-op*	Hackney South and Shoreditch
HOBHOUSE Wera	*Lib Dem*	Bath
HODGE Margaret	*Lab*	Barking
HODGSON Sharon	*Lab*	Washington and Sunderland West
HOEY Kate	*Lab*	Vauxhall
HOLLERN Kate	*Lab*	Blackburn
HUQ Rupa	*Lab*	Ealing Central and Acton
JAMES Margot	*Con*	Stourbridge
JARDINE Christine	*Lib Dem*	Edinburgh West
JENKYNS Andrea	*Con*	Morley and Outwood
JOHNSON Caroline	*Con*	Sleaford and North Hykeham
JOHNSON Diana	*Lab*	Kingston upon Hull North
JONES Helen	*Lab*	Warrington North
JONES Sarah	*Lab*	Croydon Central
JONES Susan Elan	*Lab*	Clwyd South
KEEGAN Gillian	*Con*	Chichester
KEELEY Barbara	*Lab*	Worsley and Eccles South
KENDALL Liz	*Lab*	Leicester West
KENNEDY Seema	*Con*	South Ribble
LAING Eleanor	*Con*	Epping Forest
LAIRD Lesley	*Lab*	Kirkcaldy and Cowdenbeath
LATHAM Pauline	*Con*	Mid Derbyshire
LEADSOM Andrea	*Con*	South Northamptonshire
LEE Karen	*Lab*	Lincoln
LEWELL-BUCK Emma	*Lab*	South Shields
LITTLE PENGELLY Emma	*DUP*	Belfast South
LONG-BAILEY Rebecca	*Lab*	Salford and Eccles
LUCAS Caroline	*Green*	Brighton Pavilion
LYNCH Holly	*Lab*	Halifax
McCALLION Elisha	*Sinn Féin*	Foyle
McCARTHY Kerry	*Lab*	Bristol East
McDONAGH Siobhain	*Lab*	Mitcham and Morden
McGOVERN Alison	*Lab*	Wirral South
McINNES Liz	*Lab*	Heywood and Middleton
McKINNELL Catherine	*Lab*	Newcastle upon Tyne North
MACLEAN Rachel	*Con*	Redditch
McMORRIN Anna	*Lab*	Cardiff North
McVEY Esther	*Con*	Tatton
MAHMOOD Shabana	*Lab*	Birmingham, Ladywood

MAIN Anne	*Con*	St Albans
MALHOTRA Seema	*Lab/Co-op*	Feltham and Heston
MASKELL Rachael	*Lab/Co-op*	York Central
MAY Theresa	*Con*	Maidenhead
MILLER Maria	*Con*	Basingstoke
MILLING Amanda	*Con*	Cannock Chase
MILTON Anne	*Con*	Guildford
MONAGHAN Carol	*SNP*	Glasgow North West
MOON Madeleine	*Lab*	Bridgend
MORAN Layla	*Lib Dem*	Oxford West and Abingdon
MORDAUNT Penny	*Con*	Portsmouth North
MORDEN Jessica	*Lab*	Newport East
MORGAN Nicky	*Con*	Loughborough
MORRIS Anne Marie	*Ind**	Newton Abbot
MORTON Wendy	*Con*	Aldridge-Brownhills
MURRAY Sheryll	*Con*	South East Cornwall
NANDY Lisa	*Lab*	Wigan
NEWTON Sarah	*Con*	Truro and Falmouth
NOKES Caroline	*Con*	Romsey and Southampton North
ONASANYA Fiona	*Lab*	Peterborough
ONN Melanie	*Lab*	Great Grimsby
ONWURAH Chi	*Lab*	Newcastle upon Tyne Central
OSAMOR Kate	*Lab/Co-op*	Edmonton
PATEL Priti	*Con*	Witham
PEACOCK Stephanie	*Lab*	Barnsley East
PEARCE Teresa	*Lab*	Erith and Thamesmead
PERRY Claire	*Con*	Devizes
PHILLIPS Jess	*Lab*	Birmingham, Yardley
PHILLIPSON Bridget	*Lab*	Houghton and Sunderland South
PIDCOCK Laura	*Lab*	North West Durham
PLATT Jo	*Lab/Co-op*	Leigh
POW Rebecca	*Con*	Taunton Deane
POWELL Lucy	*Lab/Co-op*	Manchester Central
PRENTIS Victoria	*Con*	Banbury
QURESHI Yasmin	*Lab*	Bolton South East
RAYNER Angela	*Lab*	Ashton under Lyne
REES Christina	*Lab/Co-op*	Neath
REEVES Ellie	*Lab*	Lewisham West and Penge
REEVES Rachel	*Lab*	Leeds West
REYNOLDS Emma	*Lab*	Wolverhampton North East
RIMMER Marie	*Lab*	St Helens South and Whiston
ROBINSON Mary	*Con*	Cheadle
ROWLEY Danielle	*Lab*	Midlothian
RUDD Amber	*Con*	Hastings and Rye
RYAN Joan	*Lab*	Enfield North
SANDBACH Antoinette	*Con*	Eddisbury
SAVILLE ROBERTS Liz	*PlC*	Dwyfor Meirionnydd
SHAH Naz	*Lab*	Bradford West
SHERRIFF Paula	*Lab*	Dewsbury
SIDDIQ Tulip	*Lab*	Hampstead and Kilburn
SMEETH Ruth	*Lab*	Stoke-on-Trent North
SMITH Angela	*Lab*	Penistone and Stocksbridge
SMITH Cat	*Lab*	Lancaster and Fleetwood

* Elected as Conservative

SMITH Chloe	*Con*	Norwich North
SMITH Eleanor	*Lab*	Wolverhampton South West
SMITH Laura	*Lab*	Crewe and Nantwich
SMYTH Karin	*Lab*	Bristol South
SOUBRY Anna	*Con*	Broxtowe
SPELMAN Caroline	*Con*	Meriden
STEVENS Jo	*Lab*	Cardiff Central
SWINSON Jo	*Lib Dem*	East Dunbartonshire
THEWLISS Alison	*SNP*	Glasgow Central
THORNBERRY Emily	*Lab*	Islington South and Finsbury
THROUP Maggie	*Con*	Erewash
TOLHURST Kelly	*Con*	Rochester and Strood
TREVELYAN Anne-Marie	*Con*	Berwick-upon-Tweed
TRUSS Elizabeth	*Con*	South West Norfolk
TURLEY Anna	*Lab/Co-op*	Redcar
TWIST Liz	*Lab*	Blaydon
VAZ Valerie	*Lab*	Walsall South
VILLIERS Theresa	*Con*	Chipping Barnet
WALKER Thelma	*Lab*	Colne Valley
WEST Catherine	*Lab*	Hornsey and Wood Green
WHATELY Helen	*Con*	Faversham and Mid Kent
WHEELER Heather	*Con*	South Derbyshire
WHITFORD Philippa	*SNP*	Central Ayrshire
WINTERTON Rosie	*Lab*	Doncaster Central
WOLLASTON Sarah	*Con*	Totnes

MPs by Age

(Ages as at 1 October 2017)

	Conservative	%	Labour	%	SNP	%	Other	%	Total	%
Under 30	3	1.0	0	0.0	2	5.9	1	2.7	6	0.9
30–39	36	11.6	46	18.3	9	26.5	6	16.2	97	15.3
40–49	113	36.5	56	22.3	10	29.4	3	8.1	182	28.8
50–59	98	31.6	72	28.7	10	29.4	15	40.5	195	30.9
60–69	53	17.1	55	21.9	3	8.8	11	29.7	122	19.3
70–79	7	2.3	19	7.6	0	0.0	1	2.7	27	4.3
Over 80	0	0.0	3	1.2	0	0.0	0	0.0	3	0.5
	310		251		34		37		632*	
Average age	**50.4**		**52.7**		**45.9**		**52.5**		**51.2**	

* The average age has been calculated on supplied dates of birth only.

MPs who have not supplied date of birth

Andrew Bowie (Con)
Ben Bradley (Con)
Dan Carden (Lab)
Peter Grant (SNP)
Kirstene Hair (Con)
Emma Hardy (Lab)
Mike Hill (Lab)
Gillian Keegan (Con)
Karen Lee (Lab)
Laura Pidcock (Lab)
Danielle Rowley (Lab)
Bob Seely (Con)
Laura Smith (Lab)
Gareth Snell (Lab/Co-op)
Paul Sweeney (Lab/Co-op)
Giles Watling (Con)
Matt Western (Lab)
Martin Whitfield (Lab)

Mhairi Black	23	*SNP*
Ben Lake	24	*PlC*
Jack Brereton	26	*Con*
David Linden	27	*SNP*
Tom Pursglove	28	*Con*
William Wragg	29	*Con*
Angela Crawley	30	*SNP*
Louise Haigh	30	*Lab*
Darren Jones	30	*Lab*
Holly Lynch	30	*Lab*
Stephanie Peacock	30	*Lab*
Ross Thomson	30	*Con*
Bim Afolami	31	*Con*
Kirsty Blackman	31	*SNP*
Neil Gray	31	*SNP*
Luke Hall	31	*Con*
Ranil Jayawardena	31	*Con*
Gerard Killen	31	*Lab/Co-op*
Stewart Malcolm McDonald	31	*SNP*
Paul Masterton	31	*Con*
Lloyd Russell-Moyle	31	*Lab/Co-op*
Luke Graham	32	*Con*
Gavin Robinson	32	*DUP*
Cat Smith	32	*Lab*
Simon Clarke	33	*Con*
Julia Dockerill	33	*Con*
Michelle Donelan	33	*Con*
Chris Elmore	33	*Lab*
Chris Hazzard	33	*Sinn Féin*
Conor McGinn	33	*Lab*
Alan Mak	33	*Con*
Alex Norris	33	*Lab/Co-op*
Bridget Phillipson	33	*Lab*
Hannah Bardell	34	*SNP*
Elisha McCallion	34/35	*Sinn Féin*
Fiona Onasanya	34	*Lab*
Matthew Pennycook	34	*Lab*
Will Quince	34	*Con*
Douglas Ross	34	*Con*
Wes Streeting	34	*Lab*
Robert Jenrick	35	*Con*
Layla Moran	35	*Lib Dem*
Jared O'Mara	35	*Lab*
Jess Phillips	35	*Lab*
Gavin Shuker	35	*Lab/Co-op*
Tulip Siddiq	35	*Lab*
Chloe Smith	35	*Con*
Alison Thewliss	35	*SNP*

Kemi Badenoch	36/37	*Con*	Robin Walker	39	*Con*
Luciana Berger	36	*Lab/Co-op*	Alex Burghart	40	*Con*
James Heappey	36	*Con*	Stella Creasy	40	*Lab/Co-op*
Alison McGovern	36	*Lab*	Leo Docherty	40	*Con*
Johnny Mercer	36	*Con*	Chris Evans	40	*Lab/Co-op*
Stephen Morgan	36	*Lab*	Vicky Foxcroft	40	*Lab*
Ellie Reeves	36	*Lab*	James Frith	40	*Lab*
Chris Skidmore	36	*Con*	Scott Mann	40	*Con*
Andrew Stephenson	36	*Con*	Andrew Percy	40	*Con*
Matt Warman	36	*Con*	Justin Tomlinson	40	*Con*
Richard Burgon	37	*Lab*	Michael Tomlinson	40	*Con*
Stephen Doughty	37	*Lab/Co-op*	Victoria Atkins	41	*Con*
Suella Fernandes	37	*Con*	Alex Chalk	41	*Con*
Patrick Grady	37	*SNP*	Marsha De Cordova	41	*Lab*
Emma Little Pengelly	37	*DUP*	Jonathan Edwards	41	*PlC*
Jim McMahon	37	*Lab/Co-op*	Stephen Gethins	41	*SNP*
Shabana Mahmood	37	*Lab*	Sam Gyimah	41	*Con*
Damien Moore	37	*Con*	Trudy Harrison	41	*Con*
Gavin Newlands	37	*SNP*	John Lamont	41	*Con*
Luke Pollard	37	*Lab/Co-op*	Catherine McKinnell	41	*Lab*
Angela Rayner	37	*Lab*	Stephen McPartland	41	*Con*
Jonathan Reynolds	37	*Lab/Co-op*	Paul Maynard	41	*Con*
Lee Rowley	37	*Con*	Ian Murray	41	*Lab*
Rishi Sunak	37	*Con*	Chris Philp	41	*Con*
Jo Swinson	37	*Lib Dem*	Alec Shelbrooke	41	*Con*
Nick Thomas-Symonds	37	*Lab*	Helen Whately	41	*Con*
Jon Ashworth	38	*Lab/Co-op*	Gavin Williamson	41	*Con*
Jake Berry	38	*Con*	Mike Wood	41	*Con*
Rehman Chishti	38	*Con*	Heidi Alexander	42	*Lab*
Robert Courts	38	*Con*	Rushanara Ali	42	*Lab*
Neil Coyle	38	*Lab*	Heidi Allen	42	*Con*
Kevin Foster	38	*Con*	Tracey Crouch	42	*Con*
Matt Hancock	38	*Con*	Mims Davies	42	*Con*
Emma Lewell-Buck	38	*Lab*	Zac Goldsmith	42	*Con*
Rebecca Long-Bailey	38	*Lab*	Seema Kennedy	42	*Con*
Lisa Nandy	38	*Lab*	Kwasi Kwarteng	42	*Con*
Neil O'Brien	38	*Con*	Amanda Milling	42	*Con*
Melanie Onn	38	*Lab*	Nigel Mills	42	*Con*
Dan Poulter	38	*Con*	Lucy Powell	42	*Lab/Co-op*
Rachel Reeves	38	*Lab*	Paula Sherriff	42	*Lab*
Ruth Smeeth	38	*Lab*	Alex Sobel	42	*Lab/Co-op*
Anna Turley	38	*Lab/Co-op*	Elizabeth Truss	42	*Con*
Chuka Umunna	38	*Lab*	Steve Brine	43	*Con*
John Woodcock	38	*Lab/Co-op*	James Cartlidge	43	*Con*
Rosena Allin-Khan	39/40	*Lab*	Damian Collins	43	*Con*
Edward Argar	39	*Con*	John Glen	43	*Con*
Tanmanjeet Singh Dhesi	39	*Lab*	Andrew Gwynne	43	*Lab*
Anneliese Dodds	39	*Lab/Co-op*	Helen Hayes	43	*Lab*
Oliver Dowden	39	*Con*	Andrea Jenkyns	43	*Con*
Imran Hussain	39	*Lab*	Marcus Jones	43	*Con*
Caroline Johnson	39	*Con*	Dominic Raab	43	*Con*
Stuart C McDonald	39	*SNP*	Naz Shah	43	*Lab*
Emma Reynolds	39	*Lab*	Craig Tracey	43	*Con*
Kelly Tolhurst	39	*Con*	Maria Caulfield	44	*Con*

Analysis of MPs
House of Commons

Jenny Chapman	44	*Lab*	Andrew Griffiths	46	*Con*
Stephen Crabb	44	*Con*	Nigel Huddleston	46	*Con*
Gloria De Piero	44	*Lab*	Liz Kendall	46	*Lab*
Preet Kaur Gill	44	*Lab/Co-op*	Andrew Lewer	46	*Con*
Chris Green	44	*Con*	Brandon Lewis	46	*Con*
Dan Jarvis	44	*Lab*	Clive Lewis	46	*Lab*
Sarah Jones	44	*Lab*	Anna McMorrin	46	*Lab*
Justin Madders	44	*Lab*	Mark Menzies	46	*Con*
Huw Merriman	44	*Con*	Victoria Prentis	46	*Con*
Penny Mordaunt	44	*Con*	Julian Smith	46	*Con*
Nicky Morgan	44	*Con*	Julian Sturdy	46	*Con*
Jo Platt	44	*Lab/Co-op*	Karl Turner	46	*Lab*
Chris Stephens	44	*SNP*	Karen Bradley	47	*Con*
Rory Stewart	44	*Con*	Alan Brown	47	*SNP*
Tom Tugendhat	44	*Con*	Dawn Butler	47	*Lab*
Jeremy Wright	44	*Con*	Alun Cairns	47	*Con*
Stuart Andrew	45	*Con*	David Davies	47	*Con*
Tonia Antoniazzi	45	*Lab*	Tim Farron	47	*Lib Dem*
Steve Barclay	45	*Con*	Ruth George	47	*Lab*
Conor Burns	45	*Con*	Michelle Gildernew	47	*Sinn Féin*
Lisa Cameron	45	*SNP*	Mark Harper	47	*Con*
Therese Coffey	45	*Con*	Damian Hinds	47	*Con*
Alberto Costa	45	*Con*	Sajid Javid	47	*Con*
Philip Davies	45	*Con*	Gareth Johnson	47	*Con*
Caroline Dinenage	45	*Con*	Gerald Jones	47	*Lab*
Lucy Frazer	45	*Con*	Stephen Kinnock	47	*Lab*
David Gauke	45	*Con*	Peter Kyle	47	*Lab*
Nusrat Ghani	45	*Con*	Mark Lancaster	47	*Con*
Rupa Huq	45	*Lab*	Chris Law	47	*SNP*
Jo Johnson	45	*Con*	Phillip Lee	47	*Con*
Daniel Kawczynski	45	*Con*	Angus MacNeil	47	*SNP*
Julian Knight	45	*Con*	Ed Miliband	47	*Lab*
David Lammy	45	*Lab*	Toby Perkins	47	*Lab*
Chris Leslie	45	*Lab/Co-op*	Antoinette Sandbach	47/48	*Con*
Seema Malhotra	45	*Lab/Co-op*	Owen Smith	47	*Lab*
Rachael Maskell	45	*Lab/Co-op*	Mark Spencer	47	*Con*
Carol Monaghan	45	*SNP*	Ben Wallace	47	*Con*
Caroline Nokes	45	*Con*	Mike Amesbury	48	*Lab*
Priti Patel	45	*Con*	Guto Bebb	48	*Con*
Faisal Rashid	45	*Lab*	Sarah Champion	48	*Lab*
Iain Stewart	45	*Con*	Colin Clark	48	*Con*
Derek Thomas	45	*Con*	James Cleverly	48	*Con*
Paul Williams	45	*Lab*	Yvette Cooper	48	*Lab*
Mohammad Yasin	45	*Lab*	Jackie Doyle-Price	48	*Con*
Steve Baker	46	*Con*	Justine Greening	48	*Con*
Liam Byrne	46	*Lab*	Robert Halfon	48	*Con*
Martyn Day	46	*SNP*	Meg Hillier	48	*Lab/Co-op*
Martin Docherty-Hughes	46	*SNP*	Simon Hoare	48	*Con*
James Duddridge	46	*Con*	Eddie Hughes	48	*Con*
Rosie Duffield	46	*Lab*	Mike Kane	48	*Lab*
David Duguid	46	*Con*	Jack Lopresti	48	*Con*
Charlie Elphicke	46	*Con*	Matthew Offord	48	*Con*
George Eustice	46	*Con*	Christopher Pincher	48	*Con*
Marcus Fysh	46	*Con*	Jacob Rees-Mogg	48	*Con*

Henry Smith	48	*Con*
Anne-Marie Trevelyan	48	*Con*
James Brokenshire	49	*Con*
Robert Buckland	49	*Con*
Bambos Charalambous	49	*Lab*
Mary Creagh	49	*Lab*
Michael Ellis	49	*Con*
Patricia Gibson	49	*SNP*
Rebecca Harris	49	*Con*
Chris Heaton-Harris	49	*Con*
Susan Elan Jones	49	*Lab*
Esther McVey	49	*Con*
Chris Matheson	49	*Lab*
Jessica Morden	49	*Lab*
Wendy Morton	49	*Con*
Kate Osamor	49	*Lab/Co-op*
Jeremy Quin	49	*Con*
Paul Scully	49	*Con*
Grant Shapps	49	*Con*
Ed Vaizey	49	*Con*
Theresa Villiers	49	*Con*
Nigel Adams	50	*Con*
Graham Brady	50	*Con*
Greg Clark	50	*Con*
Judith Cummins	50	*Lab*
Chris Davies	50	*Con*
Steve Double	50	*Con*
Bill Esterson	50	*Lab*
Vicky Ford	50	*Con*
George Freeman	50	*Con*
Michael Gove	50	*Con*
Jeremy Hunt	50	*Con*
Ivan Lewis	50	*Lab*
Craig Mackinlay	50	*Con*
Kit Malthouse	50	*Con*
Paul Maskey	50	*Sinn Féin*
James Morris	50	*Con*
Ian Paisley	50	*DUP*
Mark Pritchard	50	*Con*
Matt Rodda	50	*Lab*
Alok Sharma	50	*Con*
Gareth Thomas	50	*Lab/Co-op*
Stephen Twigg	50	*Lab/Co-op*
Charles Walker	50	*Con*
Tom Watson	50	*Lab*
Nadhim Zahawi	50	*Con*
Nick Boles	51	*Con*
Joanna Cherry	51	*SNP*
Ed Davey	51	*Lib Dem*
Thangam Debbonaire	51	*Lab*
Tobias Ellwood	51	*Con*
Lilian Greenwood	51	*Lab*
Greg Hands	51	*Con*
Sharon Hodgson	51	*Lab*
Diana Johnson	51	*Lab*
Graham Jones	51	*Lab*
Barry McElduff	51	*Sinn Féin*
Rachel Maclean	51	*Con*
Stephen Metcalfe	51	*Con*
David Morris	51	*Con*
Andrew Rosindell	51	*Con*
Jo Stevens	51	*Lab*
David Warburton	51	*Con*
Catherine West	51	*Lab*
Bill Wiggin	51	*Con*
Adam Afriyie	52	*Con*
Lucy Allan	52	*Con*
Ian Austin	52	*Lab*
Andrew Bridgen	52	*Con*
Alistair Carmichael	52	*Lib Dem*
Jonathan Djanogly	52	*Con*
Mark Field	52	*Con*
Mark Francois	52	*Con*
Philip Hollobone	52	*Con*
Adam Holloway	52	*Con*
Kerry McCarthy	52	*Lab*
Pat McFadden	52	*Lab*
Chi Onwurah	52	*Lab*
Guy Opperman	52	*Con*
Liz Saville Roberts	52	*PlC*
Jo Churchill	53	*Con*
John Cryer	53	*Lab*
Drew Hendry	53	*SNP*
George Hollingbery	53	*Con*
Boris Johnson	53	*Con*
Andrew Jones	53	*Con*
Kevan Jones	53	*Lab*
Maria Miller	53	*Con*
John Penrose	53	*Con*
Claire Perry	53	*Con*
Steve Reed	53	*Lab/Co-op*
Royston Smith	53	*Con*
Karin Smyth	53	*Lab*
Richard Bacon	54	*Con*
John Bercow	54	*Speaker*
Jeffrey Donaldson	54	*DUP*
Julie Elliott	54	*Lab*
Hugh Gaffney	54	*Lab*
Mark Garnier	54	*Con*
Paul Girvan	54	*DUP*
Simon Hart	54	*Con*
Peter Heaton-Jones	54	*Con*
Nick Herbert	54	*Con*
Kevin Hollinrake	54	*Con*
Stewart Hosie	54	*SNP*
Alister Jack	54	*Con*
Ian Lavery	54	*Lab*
Andrea Leadsom	54	*Con*

Brendan O'Hara	54	*SNP*	Geraint Davies	57	*Lab/Co-op*
Yasmin Qureshi	54	*Lab*	Mike Freer	57	*Con*
Amber Rudd	54	*Con*	Nick Gibb	57	*Con*
Jeff Smith	54	*Lab*	Kate Green	57	*Lab*
John Stevenson	54	*Con*	Carolyn Harris	57	*Lab*
Mark Tami	54	*Lab*	John Healey	57	*Lab*
Tom Brake	55	*Lib Dem*	Stephen Hepburn	57	*Lab*
Deidre Brock	55	*SNP*	Wera Hobhouse	57	*Lib Dem*
Chris Bryant	55	*Lab*	Stephen Kerr	57	*Con*
Jon Cruddas	55	*Lab*	Ian C Lucas	57	*Lab*
Paul Farrelly	55	*Lab*	Siobhain McDonagh	57	*Lab*
Chris Grayling	55	*Con*	John Mann	57	*Lab*
Stephen Hammond	55	*Con*	Andy Slaughter	57	*Lab*
Sue Hayman	55	*Lab*	Nick Smith	57	*Lab*
Nick Hurd	55	*Con*	Hugo Swire	57	*Con*
Jonathan Lord	55	*Con*	Emily Thornberry	57	*Lab*
Tim Loughton	55	*Con*	Shailesh Vara	57	*Con*
David Mundell	55	*Con*	John Whittingdale	57	*Con*
Jesse Norman	55	*Con*	John Baron	58	*Con*
Mark Prisk	55	*Con*	Ruth Cadbury	58	*Lab*
Andrew Selous	55	*Con*	Ronnie Cowan	58	*SNP*
Keir Starmer	55	*Lab*	Margaret Greenwood	58	*Lab*
Graham Stuart	55	*Con*	Mark Hendrick	58	*Lab/Co-op*
Craig Whittaker	55	*Con*	Bernard Jenkin	58	*Con*
Pete Wishart	55	*SNP*	Lesley Laird	58	*Lab*
Sarah Wollaston	55	*Con*	Jeremy Lefroy	58	*Con*
Peter Aldous	56	*Con*	Ian Liddell-Grainger	58	*Con*
Richard Benyon	56	*Con*	Liz McInnes	58	*Lab*
Ian Blackford	56	*SNP*	Albert Owen	58	*Lab*
Tracy Brabin	56	*Lab/Co-op*	Tommy Sheppard	58	*SNP*
Angela Eagle	56	*Lab*	David Simpson	58	*DUP*
Maria Eagle	56	*Lab*	Derek Twigg	58	*Lab*
Caroline Flint	56	*Lab*	Heather Wheeler	58	*Con*
Liam Fox	56	*Con*	Philippa Whitford	58	*SNP*
Helen Grant	56	*Con*	Phil Wilson	58	*Lab*
John Grogan	56	*Lab*	Karen Buck	59	*Lab*
Christine Jardine	56	*Lib Dem*	Nigel Dodds	59	*DUP*
Caroline Lucas	56	*Green*	Richard Drax	59	*Con*
Khalid Mahmood	56	*Lab*	Philip Dunne	59	*Con*
Grahame Morris	56	*Lab*	Clive Efford	59	*Lab*
Andrew Murrison	56	*Con*	Nigel Evans	59	*Con*
Sarah Newton	56	*Con*	Helen Goodman	59	*Lab*
Rebecca Pow	56	*Con*	Richard Graham	59	*Con*
David Rutley	56	*Con*	Richard Harrington	59	*Con*
Angela Smith	56	*Lab*	John Hayes	59	*Con*
Mel Stride	56	*Con*	Margot James	59	*Con*
Debbie Abrahams	57	*Lab*	Afzal Khan	59	*Lab*
Harriett Baldwin	57	*Con*	Eleanor Laing	59	*Con*
Crispin Blunt	57	*Con*	Andy McDonald	59	*Lab*
Ben Bradshaw	57	*Lab*	Patrick McLoughlin	59	*Con*
Kevin Brennan	57	*Lab*	Laurence Robertson	59	*Con*
Lyn Brown	57	*Lab*	Chris Ruane	59	*Lab*
Julie Cooper	57	*Lab*	Caroline Spelman	59	*Con*
Geoffrey Cox	57	*Con*	Rosie Winterton	59	*Lab*

Roberta Blackman-Woods	60	*Lab*	Oliver Heald	62	*Con*
Fiona Bruce	60	*Con*	Sylvia Hermon	62	*Ind*
Alan Campbell	60	*Lab*	Kate Hollern	62	*Lab*
Wayne David	60	*Lab*	John Howell	62	*Con*
Nadine Dorries	60	*Con*	Helen Jones	62	*Lab*
Peter Dowd	60	*Lab*	Steve McCabe	62	*Lab*
Alan Duncan	60	*Con*	Teresa Pearce	62	*Lab*
Yvonne Fovargue	60	*Lab*	Mary Robinson	62	*Con*
Gill Furniss	60	*Lab*	Joan Ryan	62	*Lab*
Barry Gardiner	60	*Lab*	Jim Shannon	62	*DUP*
Mary Glindon	60	*Lab*	Stephen Timms	62	*Lab*
Robert Goodwill	60	*Con*	Valerie Vaz	62	*Lab*
Nia Griffith	60	*Lab*	Hilary Benn	63	*Lab*
David Hanson	60	*Lab*	Richard Burden	63	*Lab*
Lindsay Hoyle	60	*Lab*	Iain Duncan Smith	63	*Con*
Norman Lamb	60	*Lib Dem*	Gordon Marsden	63	*Lab*
Stephen Lloyd	60	*Lib Dem*	Christina Rees	63	*Lab/Co-op*
Anne Main	60	*Con*	Jamie Stone	63	*Lib Dem*
Sandy Martin	60	*Lab*	Diane Abbott	64	*Lab*
Ian Mearns	60	*Lab*	Paul Blomfield	64	*Lab*
Anne Marie Morris	60	*Ind*	Peter Bone	64	*Con*
Mark Pawsey	60	*Con*	Gregory Campbell	64	*DUP*
Mike Penning	60	*Con*	Geoffrey Clifton-Brown	64	*Con*
Eleanor Smith	60	*Lab*	Vernon Coaker	64	*Lab*
Anna Soubry	60	*Con*	Hywel Williams	64	*PlC*
Maggie Throup	60	*Con*	Sammy Wilson	64	*DUP*
Keith Vaz	60	*Lab*	David Amess	65	*Con*
Thelma Walker	60	*Lab*	David Drew	65	*Lab/Co-op*
Daniel Zeichner	60	*Lab*	Michael Fallon	65	*Con*
Bob Blackman	61	*Con*	Jim Fitzpatrick	65	*Lab*
Damian Green	61	*Con*	Mike Gapes	65	*Lab/Co-op*
Dominic Grieve	61	*Con*	Cheryl Gillan	65	*Con*
Philip Hammond	61	*Con*	David Jones	65	*Con*
Oliver Letwin	61	*Con*	Barbara Keeley	65	*Lab*
David Lidington	61	*Con*	Robert Neill	65	*Con*
Theresa May	61	*Con*	Mickey Brady	66	*Sinn Féin*
Anne Milton	61	*Con*	Bill Grant	66	*Con*
Andrew Mitchell	61	*Con*	Julian Lewis	66	*Con*
Sheryll Murray	61	*Con*	John McDonnell	66	*Lab*
Neil Parish	61	*Con*	John McNally	66	*SNP*
Owen Paterson	61	*Con*	Francie Molloy	66	*Sinn Féin*
Gary Streeter	61	*Con*	John Redwood	66	*Con*
Desmond Swayne	61	*Con*	Clive Betts	67	*Lab*
Robert Syms	61	*Con*	Nick Brown	67	*Lab*
Chris Williamson	61	*Lab*	Rosie Cooper	67	*Lab*
Henry Bellingham	62	*Con*	Michael Fabricant	67	*Con*
Alistair Burt	62	*Con*	Harriet Harman	67	*Lab*
Douglas Chapman	62	*SNP*	Edward Leigh	67	*Con*
Alex Cunningham	62	*Lab*	Tony Lloyd	67	*Lab*
Nic Dakin	62	*Lab*	Madeleine Moon	67	*Lab*
Emma Dent Coad	62	*Lab*	Graham Stringer	67	*Lab*
Colleen Fletcher	62	*Lab*	David Tredinnick	67	*Con*
James Gray	62	*Con*	Jon Trickett	67	*Lab*
Fabian Hamilton	62	*Lab*	Martin Vickers	67	*Con*

Alan Whitehead	67	*Lab*
Jeremy Corbyn	68	*Lab*
David Davis	68	*Con*
David Evennett	68	*Con*
Marion Fellows	68	*SNP*
George Howarth	68	*Lab*
Greg Knight	68	*Con*
Keith Simpson	68	*Con*
Bob Stewart	68	*Con*
Jack Dromey	69	*Lab*
Gordon Henderson	69	*Con*
Pauline Latham	69	*Con*
Stephen Pound	69	*Lab*
Nicholas Soames	69	*Con*
Kevin Barron	70	*Lab*
Christopher Chope	70	*Con*
Marie Rimmer	70	*Lab*
Virendra Sharma	70	*Lab*
John Spellar	70	*Lab*
Adrian Bailey	71	*Lab/Co-op*
Paul Beresford	71	*Con*
Ann Coffey	71	*Lab*
David Crausby	71	*Lab*
Louise Ellman	71	*Lab/Co-op*
Roger Godsiff	71	*Lab*
Kate Hoey	71	*Lab*
Peter Bottomley	73	*Con*
Glyn Davies	73	*Con*
Margaret Hodge	73	*Lab*
Liz Twist	73	*Lab*
Margaret Beckett	74	*Lab*
Vince Cable	74	*Lib Dem*
Ronnie Campbell	74	*Lab*
Roger Gale	74	*Con*
Frank Field	75	*Lab*
Jim Cunningham	76	*Lab*
Kelvin Hopkins	76	*Lab*
Bill Cash	77	*Con*
Kenneth Clarke	77	*Con*
Barry Sheerman	77	*Lab/Co-op*
Geoffrey Robinson	79	*Lab*
Ann Clwyd	80	*Lab*
Paul Flynn	82	*Lab*
Dennis Skinner	85	*Lab*

MPs by Party

Conservative

ADAMS Nigel
AFOLAMI Bim
AFRIYIE Adam
ALDOUS Peter
ALLAN Lucy
ALLEN Heidi
AMESS David
ANDREW Stuart
ARGAR Edward
ATKINS Victoria
BACON Richard
BADENOCH Kemi
BAKER Steve
BALDWIN Harriett
BARCLAY Steve
BARON John
BEBB Guto
BELLINGHAM Henry
BENYON Richard
BERESFORD Paul
BERRY Jake
BLACKMAN Bob
BLUNT Crispin
BOLES Nick
BONE Peter
BOTTOMLEY Peter
BOWIE Andrew
BRADLEY Ben
BRADLEY Karen
BRADY Graham
BRERETON Jack
BRIDGEN Andrew
BRINE Steve
BROKENSHIRE James
BRUCE Fiona
BUCKLAND Robert
BURGHART Alex
BURNS Conor
BURT Alistair
CAIRNS Alun
CARTLIDGE James
CASH Bill
CAULFIELD Maria
CHALK Alex
CHISHTI Rehman
CHOPE Christopher
CHURCHILL Jo
CLARK Colin
CLARK Greg
CLARKE Kenneth
CLARKE Simon
CLEVERLY James
CLIFTON-BROWN Geoffrey
COFFEY Therese
COLLINS Damian
COSTA Alberto
COURTS Robert
COX Geoffrey
CRABB Stephen
CROUCH Tracey
DAVIES Chris
DAVIES David
DAVIES Glyn
DAVIES Mims
DAVIES Philip
DAVIS David
DINENAGE Caroline
DJANOGLY Jonathan
DOCHERTY Leo
DOCKERILL Julia
DONELAN Michelle
DORRIES Nadine
DOUBLE Steve
DOWDEN Oliver
DOYLE-PRICE Jackie
DRAX Richard
DUDDRIDGE James
DUGUID David
DUNCAN Alan
DUNCAN SMITH Iain
DUNNE Philip
ELLIS Michael
ELLWOOD Tobias
ELPHICKE Charlie
EUSTICE George
EVANS Nigel
EVENNETT David
FABRICANT Michael
FALLON Michael
FERNANDES Suella
FIELD Mark
FORD Vicky
FOSTER Kevin
FOX Liam
FRANCOIS Mark
FRAZER Lucy
FREEMAN George
FREER Mike
FYSH Marcus
GALE Roger
GARNIER Mark
GAUKE David
GHANI Nusrat
GIBB Nick
GILLAN Cheryl
GLEN John
GOLDSMITH Zac
GOODWILL Robert
GOVE Michael
GRAHAM Luke
GRAHAM Richard
GRANT Bill
GRANT Helen
GRAY James
GRAYLING Chris
GREEN Chris
GREEN Damian
GREENING Justine
GRIEVE Dominic
GRIFFITHS Andrew
GYIMAH Sam
HAIR Kirstene
HALFON Robert
HALL Luke
HAMMOND Philip
HAMMOND Stephen
HANCOCK Matt
HANDS Greg
HARPER Mark
HARRINGTON Richard
HARRIS Rebecca
HARRISON Trudy
HART Simon
HAYES John
HEALD Oliver
HEAPPEY James
HEATON-HARRIS Chris
HEATON-JONES Peter
HENDERSON Gordon
HERBERT Nick
HINDS Damian
HOARE Simon
HOLLINGBERY George
HOLLINRAKE Kevin
HOLLOBONE Philip
HOLLOWAY Adam
HOWELL John
HUDDLESTON Nigel
HUGHES Eddie
HUNT Jeremy
HURD Nick
JACK Alister
JAMES Margot

JAVID Sajid
JAYAWARDENA Ranil
JENKIN Bernard
JENKYNS Andrea
JENRICK Robert
JOHNSON Boris
JOHNSON Caroline
JOHNSON Gareth
JOHNSON Jo
JONES Andrew
JONES David
JONES Marcus
KAWCZYNSKI Daniel
KEEGAN Gillian
KENNEDY Seema
KERR Stephen
KNIGHT Greg
KNIGHT Julian
KWARTENG Kwasi
LAING Eleanor
LAMONT John
LANCASTER Mark
LATHAM Pauline
LEADSOM Andrea
LEE Phillip
LEFROY Jeremy
LEIGH Edward
LETWIN Oliver
LEWER Andrew
LEWIS Brandon
LEWIS Julian
LIDDELL-GRAINGER Ian
LIDINGTON David
LOPRESTI Jack
LORD Jonathan
LOUGHTON Tim
MACKINLAY Craig
MACLEAN Rachel
McLOUGHLIN Patrick
McPARTLAND Stephen
McVEY Esther
MAIN Anne
MAK Alan
MALTHOUSE Kit
MANN Scott
MASTERTON Paul
MAY Theresa
MAYNARD Paul
MENZIES Mark
MERCER Johnny
MERRIMAN Huw
METCALFE Stephen
MILLER Maria
MILLING Amanda
MILLS Nigel
MILTON Anne
MITCHELL Andrew
MOORE Damien
MORDAUNT Penny
MORGAN Nicky
MORRIS David
MORRIS James
MORTON Wendy
MUNDELL David
MURRAY Sheryll
MURRISON Andrew
NEILL Robert
NEWTON Sarah
NOKES Caroline
NORMAN Jesse
O'BRIEN Neil
OFFORD Matthew
OPPERMAN Guy
PARISH Neil
PATEL Priti
PATERSON Owen
PAWSEY Mark
PENNING Mike
PENROSE John
PERCY Andrew
PERRY Claire
PHILP Chris
PINCHER Christopher
POULTER Dan
POW Rebecca
PRENTIS Victoria
PRISK Mark
PRITCHARD Mark
PURSGLOVE Tom
QUIN Jeremy
QUINCE Will
RAAB Dominic
REDWOOD John
REES-MOGG Jacob
ROBERTSON Laurence
ROBINSON Mary
ROSINDELL Andrew
ROSS Douglas
ROWLEY Lee
RUDD Amber
RUTLEY David
SANDBACH Antoinette
SCULLY Paul
SEELY Bob
SELOUS Andrew
SHAPPS Grant
SHARMA Alok
SHELBROOKE Alec
SIMPSON Keith
SKIDMORE Chris
SMITH Chloe
SMITH Henry
SMITH Julian
SMITH Royston
SOAMES Nicholas
SOUBRY Anna
SPELMAN Caroline
SPENCER Mark
STEPHENSON Andrew
STEVENSON John
STEWART Bob
STEWART Iain
STEWART Rory
STREETER Gary
STRIDE Mel
STUART Graham
STURDY Julian
SUNAK Rishi
SWAYNE Desmond
SWIRE Hugo
SYMS Robert
THOMAS Derek
THOMSON Ross
THROUP Maggie
TOLHURST Kelly
TOMLINSON Justin
TOMLINSON Michael
TRACEY Craig
TREDINNICK David
TREVELYAN Anne-Marie
TRUSS Elizabeth
TUGENDHAT Tom
VAIZEY Ed
VARA Shailesh
VICKERS Martin
VILLIERS Theresa
WALKER Charles
WALKER Robin
WALLACE Ben
WARBURTON David
WARMAN Matt
WATLING Giles
WHATELY Helen
WHEELER Heather
WHITTAKER Craig
WHITTINGDALE John
WIGGIN Bill
WILLIAMSON Gavin
WOLLASTON Sarah
WOOD Mike
WRAGG William
WRIGHT Jeremy
ZAHAWI Nadhim

Labour

ABBOTT Diane
ABRAHAMS Debbie
ALEXANDER Heidi
ALI Rushanara
ALLIN-KHAN Rosena
AMESBURY Mike
ANTONIAZZI Tonia
AUSTIN Ian
BARRON Kevin
BECKETT Margaret
BENN Hilary
BETTS Clive
BLACKMAN-WOODS Roberta
BLOMFIELD Paul
BRADSHAW Ben
BRENNAN Kevin
BROWN Lyn
BROWN Nick
BRYANT Chris
BUCK Karen
BURDEN Richard
BURGON Richard
BUTLER Dawn
BYRNE Liam
CADBURY Ruth
CAMPBELL Alan
CAMPBELL Ronnie
CARDEN Dan
CHAMPION Sarah
CHAPMAN Jenny
CHARALAMBOUS Bambos
CLWYD Ann
COAKER Vernon
COFFEY Ann
COOPER Julie
COOPER Rosie
COOPER Yvette
CORBYN Jeremy
COYLE Neil
CRAUSBY David
CREAGH Mary
CRUDDAS Jon
CRYER John
CUMMINS Judith
CUNNINGHAM Alex
CUNNINGHAM Jim
DAKIN Nic
DAVID Wayne
DEBBONAIRE Thangam
DE CORDOVA Marsha
DENT COAD Emma
DE PIERO Gloria
DHESI Tanmanjeet Singh
DOWD Peter
DROMEY Jack
DUFFIELD Rosie
EAGLE Angela
EAGLE Maria
EFFORD Clive
ELLIOTT Julie
ELMORE Chris
ESTERSON Bill
FARRELLY Paul
FIELD Frank
FITZPATRICK Jim
FLETCHER Colleen
FLINT Caroline
FLYNN Paul
FOVARGUE Yvonne
FOXCROFT Vicky
FRITH James
FURNISS Gill
GAFFNEY Hugh
GARDINER Barry
GEORGE Ruth
GLINDON Mary
GODSIFF Roger
GOODMAN Helen
GREEN Kate
GREENWOOD Lilian
GREENWOOD Margaret
GRIFFITH Nia
GROGAN John
GWYNNE Andrew
HAIGH Louise
HAMILTON Fabian
HANSON David
HARDY Emma
HARMAN Harriet
HARRIS Carolyn
HAYES Helen
HAYMAN Sue
HEALEY John
HEPBURN Stephen
HILL Mike
HODGE Margaret
HODGSON Sharon
HOEY Kate
HOLLERN Kate
HOPKINS Kelvin
HOWARTH George
HOYLE Lindsay
HUQ Rupa
HUSSAIN Imran
JARVIS Dan
JOHNSON Diana
JONES Darren
JONES Gerald
JONES Graham
JONES Helen
JONES Kevan
JONES Sarah
JONES Susan Elan
KANE Mike
KEELEY Barbara
KENDALL Liz
KHAN Afzal
KINNOCK Stephen
KYLE Peter
LAIRD Lesley
LAMMY David
LAVERY Ian
LEE Karen
LEWELL-BUCK Emma
LEWIS Clive
LEWIS Ivan
LLOYD Tony
LONG-BAILEY Rebecca
LUCAS Ian C
LYNCH Holly
McCABE Steve
McCARTHY Kerry
McDONAGH Siobhain
McDONALD Andy
McDONNELL John
McFADDEN Pat
McGINN Conor
McGOVERN Alison
McINNES Liz
McKINNELL Catherine
McMORRIN Anna
MADDERS Justin
MAHMOOD Khalid
MAHMOOD Shabana
MANN John
MARSDEN Gordon
MARTIN Sandy
MATHESON Chris
MEARNS Ian
MILIBAND Ed
MOON Madeleine
MORDEN Jessica
MORGAN Stephen
MORRIS Grahame
MURRAY Ian

Analysis of MPs
House of Commons

NANDY Lisa
O'MARA Jared
ONASANYA Fiona
ONN Melanie
ONWURAH Chi
OWEN Albert
PEACOCK Stephanie
PEARCE Teresa
PENNYCOOK Matthew
PERKINS Toby
PHILLIPS Jess
PHILLIPSON Bridget
PIDCOCK Laura
POUND Stephen
QURESHI Yasmin
RASHID Faisal
RAYNER Angela
REEVES Ellie
REEVES Rachel
REYNOLDS Emma
RIMMER Marie
ROBINSON Geoffrey
RODDA Matt
ROWLEY Danielle
RUANE Chris
RYAN Joan
SHAH Naz
SHARMA Virendra
SHERRIFF Paula
SIDDIQ Tulip
SKINNER Dennis
SLAUGHTER Andy
SMEETH Ruth
SMITH Angela
SMITH Cat
SMITH Eleanor
SMITH Jeff
SMITH Laura
SMITH Nick
SMITH Owen
SMYTH Karin
SPELLAR John
STARMER Keir
STEVENS Jo
STREETING Wes
STRINGER Graham
TAMI Mark
THOMAS-SYMONDS Nick
THORNBERRY Emily
TIMMS Stephen
TRICKETT Jon
TURNER Karl
TWIGG Derek
TWIST Liz
UMUNNA Chuka
VAZ Keith
VAZ Valerie
WALKER Thelma
WATSON Tom
WEST Catherine
WESTERN Matt
WHITEHEAD Alan
WHITFIELD Martin
WILLIAMS Paul
WILLIAMSON Chris
WILSON Phil
WINTERTON Rosie
YASIN Mohammad
ZEICHNER Daniel

Labour/Co-operative

ASHWORTH Jon
BAILEY Adrian
BERGER Luciana
BRABIN Tracy
CREASY Stella
DAVIES Geraint
DODDS Anneliese
DOUGHTY Stephen
DREW David
ELLMAN Louise
EVANS Chris
GAPES Mike
GILL Preet Kaur
HENDRICK Mark
HILLIER Meg
KILLEN Gerard
LESLIE Chris
McMAHON Jim
MALHOTRA Seema
MASKELL Rachael
NORRIS Alex
OSAMOR Kate
PLATT Jo
POLLARD Luke
POWELL Lucy
REED Steve
REES Christina
REYNOLDS Jonathan
RUSSELL-MOYLE Lloyd
SHEERMAN Barry
SHUKER Gavin
SNELL Gareth
SOBEL Alex
SWEENEY Paul
THOMAS Gareth
TURLEY Anna
TWIGG Stephen
WOODCOCK John

Scottish National Party

BARDELL Hannah
BLACK Mhairi
BLACKFORD Ian
BLACKMAN Kirsty
BROCK Deidre
BROWN Alan
CAMERON Lisa
CHAPMAN Douglas
CHERRY Joanna
COWAN Ronnie
CRAWLEY Angela
DAY Martyn
DOCHERTY-HUGHES Martin
FELLOWS Marion
GETHINS Stephen
GIBSON Patricia
GRADY Patrick
GRANT Peter
GRAY Neil
HENDRY Drew
HOSIE Stewart
LAW Chris
LINDEN David
McDONALD Stewart Malcolm
McDONALD Stuart C
McNALLY John
MacNEIL Angus
MONAGHAN Carol
NEWLANDS Gavin
O'HARA Brendan
SHEPPARD Tommy
STEPHENS Chris
THEWLISS Alison
WHITFORD Philippa
WISHART Pete

Liberal Democrat

BRAKE Tom
CABLE Vince
CARMICHAEL Alistair
DAVEY Ed
FARRON Tim
HOBHOUSE Wera
JARDINE Christine
LAMB Norman
LLOYD Stephen
MORAN Layla
STONE Jamie
SWINSON Jo

Democratic Unionist Party

CAMPBELL Gregory
DODDS Nigel
DONALDSON Jeffrey
GIRVAN Paul
LITTLE PENGELLY Emma
PAISLEY Ian
ROBINSON Gavin
SHANNON Jim
SIMPSON David
WILSON Sammy

Sinn Féin

BRADY Mickey
GILDERNEW Michelle
HAZZARD Chris
McCALLION Elisha
McELDUFF Barry
MASKEY Paul
MOLLOY Francie

Plaid Cymru

EDWARDS Jonathan
LAKE Ben
SAVILLE ROBERTS Liz
WILLIAMS Hywel

Independent

HERMON Sylvia
*MORRIS Anne Marie

Green Party

LUCAS Caroline

The Speaker

BERCOW John

*Elected as Conservative

Select Committees

Each Department of State is shadowed by a Select Committee. In addition to these departmentally related select committees there are committees with responsibilities cutting across government departments (Public Accounts, Public Administration and Constitutional Affairs, Environmental Audit, Human Rights, Statutory Instruments, European Scrutiny, Regulatory Reform, etc.) and a number of committees which concern themselves with the running of the House.

Departmental Committees

Business, Energy and Industrial Strategy

Tel: 020 7219 5777
Email: beiscom@parliament.uk
www.parliament.uk/beis
Twitter: @CommonsBEIS

Rachel Reeves (Chair)	*Lab*
Drew Hendry	*SNP*
Stephen Kerr	*Con*
Dr Peter Kyle	*Lab*
Ian Liddell-Grainger	*Con*
Rachel Maclean	*Con*
Albert Owen	*Lab*
Mark Pawsey	*Con*
Antoinette Sandbach	*Con*
Anna Turley	*Lab/Co-op*

Staff: Chris Shaw (Clerk), Ben Sneddon (Second Clerk), Ian Cruse, Jeanne Delebarre, Becky Mawhood (Committee Specialists), Gary Calder (Media Officer), James McQuade (Senior Committee Assistant), Jonathan Olivier-Wright (Committee Assistant)

Communities and Local Government

Tel: 020 7219 4972/020 7219 1353
Email: clgcom@parliament.uk
www.parliament.uk/clg
Twitter: @CommonsCLG

Clive Betts (Chair)	*Lab*
Mike Amesbury	*Lab*
Bob Blackman	*Con*
Helen Hayes	*Lab*
Kevin Hollinrake	*Con*
Andrew Lewer	*Con*
Fiona Onasanya	*Lab*
Mark Prisk	*Con*
Mary Robinson	*Con*
Liz Twist	*Lab*

Staff: Ed Beale (Clerk), Craig Bowdery, Tamsin Maddock, Nick Taylor (Committee Specialists), Gary Calder (Media Officer), Tony Catinella (Senior Committee Assistant), Eldon Gallagher (Committee Support Assistant)

Defence

Tel: 020 7219 5857
Email: defcom@parliament.uk
www.parliament.uk/defcom
Twitter: @CommonsDefence

Dr Julian Lewis (Chair)	*Con*
Leo Docherty	*Con*
Martin Docherty-Hughes	*SNP*
Mark Francois	*Con*
Graham Jones	*Lab*
Johnny Mercer	*Con*
Madeleine Moon	*Lab*
Gavin Robinson	*DUP*
Ruth Smeeth	*Lab*
John Spellar	*Lab*
Phil Wilson	*Lab*

Staff: Mark Etherton (Clerk), Anna Dickson (Second Clerk), David Nicholas, Eleanor Scarnell, Ian Thomson (Committee Specialists), Alex Paterson (Media Officer), Sarah Williams (Senior Committee Assistant), Carolyn Bowes, Arvind Gunnoo (Committee Assistants)

Digital, Culture, Media and Sport

Tel: 020 7219 6188
Email: cmscom@parliament.uk
www.parliament.uk/cmscom
Twitter: @CommonsCMS

Damian Collins (Chair)	*Con*
Julie Elliott	*Lab*
Paul Farrelly	*Lab*
Simon Hart	*Con*
Julian Knight	*Con*
Ian C Lucas	*Lab*
Chris Matheson	*Lab*
Brendan O'Hara	*SNP*
Rebecca Pow	*Con*
Jo Stevens	*Lab*
Giles Watling	*Con*

Staff: Elizabeth Flood (Clerk), Joe Watt (Second Clerk), Josephine Willows (Committee Specialist), Estelle Currie (Media Officer), Andy Boyd (Senior Committee Assistant), Keely Bishop (Committee Assistant)

Education
Tel: 020 7219 1376
Email: educom@parliament.uk
www.parliament.uk/education-committee
Twitter: @CommonsEd

Robert Halfon (Chair)	*Con*
Lucy Allan	*Con*
Michelle Donelan	*Con*
Marion Fellows	*SNP*
James Frith	*Lab*
Emma Hardy	*Lab*
Trudy Harrison	*Con*
Ian Mearns	*Lab*
Lucy Powell	*Lab/Co-op*
Thelma Walker	*Lab*
William Wragg	*Con*

Staff: Richard Ward (Clerk), Katya Cassidy (Second Clerk), Anna Connell-Smith (Committee Specialist), Gary Calder (Senior Media Officer), Jonathan Arkless (Senior Committee Assistant), Simon Armitage (Committee Assistant)

Environment, Food and Rural Affairs
Tel: 020 7219 7341
Email: efracom@parliament.uk
www.parliament.uk/efracom
Twitter: @CommonsEFRA

Neil Parish (Chair)	*Con*
Alan Brown	*SNP*
Paul Flynn	*Lab*
John Grogan	*Lab*
Dr Caroline Johnson	*Con*
Sandy Martin	*Lab*
Sheryll Murray	*Con*
David Simpson	*DUP*
Angela Smith	*Lab*
Julian Sturdy	*Con*

Staff: Eliot Barrass, Sîan Woodward (Clerks), Danielle Nash (Second Clerk), Sarah Coe (Senior Committee Specialist), Anwen Rees (Committee Specialist), Shagufta Hailes (Media Officer), Caitriona Fleming (Senior Committee Assistant), Zainab Balogun (Committee Assistant (Tuesday and Wednesday))

Exiting the European Union
Tel: 020 7219 7568/020 7219 5430
Email: exeucom@parliament.uk
www.parliament.uk/exeucom
Twitter: @CommonsEUexit

Hilary Benn (Chair)	*Lab*
Peter Bone	*Con*
Joanna Cherry	*SNP*
Christopher Chope	*Con*
Stephen Crabb	*Con*
Jonathan Djanogly	*Con*
Richard Graham	*Con*
Peter Grant	*SNP*
Wera Hobhouse	*Lib Dem*
Andrea Jenkyns	*Con*
Stephen Kinnock	*Lab*
Jeremy Lefroy	*Con*
Pat McFadden	*Lab*
Craig Mackinlay	*Con*
Seema Malhotra	*Lab/Co-op*
Hon Jacob Rees-Mogg	*Con*
Emma Reynolds	*Lab*
Stephen Timms	*Lab*
John Whittingdale	*Con*
Hywel Williams	*PlC*
Sammy Wilson	*DUP*

Staff: James Rhys (Clerk), Claire Cozens (Second Clerk), Shakera Ali (Inquiry Manager), Ariella Huff (Senior Committee Specialist), Judy Goodall, Duma Langton (Committee Specialists), Nick Davies (Media Officer), Hannah Finer, Jamie Mordue (Senior Committee Assistants), Henry Ayi-Hyde (Committee Assistant)

Foreign Affairs
Tel: 020 7219 6105
Email: fac@parliament.uk
www.parliament.uk/facom
Twitter: @CommonsForeign

Tom Tugendhat (Chair)	*Con*
Ian Austin	*Lab*
Chris Bryant	*Lab*
Ann Clwyd	*Lab*
Mike Gapes	*Lab/Co-op*
Stephen Gethins	*SNP*
Nusrat Ghani	*Con*
Ian Murray	*Lab*
Andrew Rosindell	*Con*
Royston Smith	*Con*
Nadhim Zahawi	*Con*

Staff: Chris Stanton (Clerk), Zoe Oliver-Watts (Second Clerk), Areilla Huff (Senior Committee Specialist), Ashlee Godwin, Eoin Martin, Nicholas Wade (Committee Specialists), Estelle Currie (Media Officer), Clare Genis (Senior Committee Assistant), James Hockaday, Su Panchanathan (Committee Assistants)

Health
Tel: 020 7219 6182
Email: healthcom@parliament.uk
www.parliament.uk/healthcom
Twitter: @CommonsHealth

Dr Sarah Wollaston (Chair)	*Con*
Luciana Berger	*Lab/Co-op*
Ben Bradshaw	*Lab*
Dr Lisa Cameron	*SNP*
Rosie Cooper	*Lab*
Dr Caroline Johnson	*Con*
Diana Johnson	*Lab*
Johnny Mercer	*Con*
Andrew Selous	*Con*
Maggie Throup	*Con*
Dr Paul Williams	*Lab*

Staff: Huw Yardley (Clerk), Laura Daniels (Senior Committee Specialist), Stephen Aldhouse (Committee Specialist), Charlotte Refsum (Clinical Fellow), Alex Paterson (Media Officer), Cecilia Santi O Desanti (Senior Committee Assistant), Lucy Hale (Committee Assistant)

Home Affairs
Tel: 020 7219 2049
Email: homeaffcom@parliament.uk
www.parliament.uk/homeaffairscom
Twitter: @CommonsHomeAffs

Yvette Cooper (Chair)	*Lab*
Christopher Chope	*Con*
Stephen Doughty	*Lab/Co-op*
Preet Kaur Gill	*Lab/Co-op*
Sarah Jones	*Lab*
Tim Loughton	*Con*
Stuart C McDonald	*SNP*
Esther McVey	*Con*
Will Quince	*Con*
Naz Shah	*Lab*

Staff: Carol Oxborough (Clerk), Phil Jones (Second Clerk), Harriet Deane (Committee Specialist), George Perry (Senior Media and Communications Officer), David Gardner (Senior Committee Assistant), Mandy Sullivan (Committee Assistant)

International Development
Tel: 020 7219 1223
Email: indcom@parliament.uk
www.parliament.uk/indcom
Twitter: @CommonsIDC

Stephen Twigg (Chair)	*Lab/Co-op*
Richard Burden	*Lab*
James Duddridge	*Con*
Nigel Evans	*Con*
Pauline Latham	*Con*
Chris Law	*SNP*
Ivan Lewis	*Lab*
Lloyd Russell-Moyle	*Lab/Co-op*
Paul Scully	*Con*
Virendra Sharma	*Lab*
Henry Smith	*Con*

Staff: Fergus Reid (Clerk), Rob Page (Second Clerk), Jake Barker, Faten Hussein (Committee Specialists), Louise Whitley (Committee Specialist (Tuesday-Thursday)), Estelle Currie (Senior Media Officer), Zac Mead (Senior Committee Assistant), Paul Hampson (Committee Assistant), Zainab Balogun (Committee Assistant (Monday and Friday))

Work of the Independent Commission for Aid Impact Sub-committee

Paul Scully (Chair)	*Con*
Richard Burden	*Lab*
James Duddridge	*Con*
Nigel Evans	*Con*
Pauline Latham	*Con*
Chris Law	*SNP*
Ivan Lewis	*Lab*
Lloyd Russell-Moyle	*Lab/Co-op*
Virendra Sharma	*Lab*
Henry Smith	*Con*
Stephen Twigg	*Lab/Co-op*

International Trade
Email: tradecom@parliament.uk
www.parliament.uk/tradecom
Twitter: @CommonsIntTrade

Angus MacNeil (Chair)	*SNP*
Nigel Evans	*Con*
Marcus Fysh	*Con*
Ranil Jayawardena	*Con*
Chris Leslie	*Lab/Co-op*
Emma Little Pengelly	*DUP*
Julia Lopez	*Con*
Faisal Rashid	*Lab*
Keith Vaz	*Lab*
Catherine West	*Lab*
Matt Western	*Lab*

Staff: Lydia Menzies (Clerk), Joanna Welham (Second Clerk), Karlene Agard, Stephen Habberley, David Turner, Luke Villiers (Committee Specialists), George Perry (Media Officer), Andrew Wallace (Senior Committee Assistant), Ian Blair, Mariam Keating (Committee Assistants)

Justice
Tel: 020 7219 8196
Email: justicecom@parliament.uk
www.parliament.uk/business/committees/committees-a-z/commons-select/justice-committee Twitter: @CommonsJustice

Robert Neill (Chair)	*Con*
Kemi Badenoch	*Con*
Ruth Cadbury	*Lab*
Alex Chalk	*Con*
Bambos Charalambous	*Lab*
David Hanson	*Lab*
John Howell	*Con*
Gavin Newlands	*SNP*
Laura Pidcock	*Lab*
Victoria Prentis	*Con*
Ellie Reeves	*Lab*

Staff: Nick Walker (Clerk), Gavin O'Leary (Second Clerk), Gemma Buckland (Senior Committee Specialist), Nony Ardill (Legal Specialist), Liz Parratt (Media Officer), Christine Randall (Senior Committee Assistant), Anna Browning (Committee Assistant)

Northern Ireland Affairs
Tel: 020 7219 2173
Email: northircom@parliament.uk
www.parliament.uk/niacom
Twitter: @CommonsNIAC

Dr Andrew Murrison (Chair)	*Con*
Gregory Campbell	*DUP*
Maria Caulfield	*Con*
Stephen Hepburn	*Lab*
Sylvia Hermon	*Ind*
Kate Hoey	*Lab*
Jack Lopresti	*Con*
Conor McGinn	*Lab*
Nigel Mills	*Con*
Ian Paisley	*DUP*
Jim Shannon	*DUP*

Staff: Margaret McKinnon (Clerk), Elektra Garvie-Adams (Committee Specialist), George Perry (Media Officer), John Hitchcock (Senior Committee Assistant)

Science and Technology
Tel: 020 7219 2793 Fax: 020 7219 0896
Email: scitechcom@parliament.uk
www.parliament.uk/science
Twitter: @CommonsSTC

Norman Lamb (Chair)	*Lib Dem*
Bill Grant	*Con*
Darren Jones	*Lab*
Clive Lewis	*Lab*
Stephen Metcalfe	*Con*
Neil O'Brien	*Con*
Graham Stringer	*Lab*
Martin Whitfield	*Lab*

Staff: Simon Fiander (Clerk), To be appointed (Second Clerk), Harry Beeson, Elizabeth Rough, Martin Smith (Committee Specialists), Sean Kinsey (Media Officer), Sonia Draper (Senior Committee Assistant), Julie Storey (Committee Assistant)

Scottish Affairs
Tel: 020 7219 8204
Email: scotaffcom@parliament.uk
www.parliament.uk/scotaffcom
Twitter: @CommonsScotAffs

Pete Wishart (Chair)	*SNP*
Deidre Brock	*SNP*
David Duguid	*Con*
Hugh Gaffney	*Lab*
Christine Jardine	*Lib Dem*
Gerard Killen	*Lab/Co-op*
John Lamont	*Con*
Paul Masterton	*Con*
Danielle Rowley	*Lab*
Tommy Sheppard	*SNP*
Ross Thomson	*Con*

Staff: Ben Williams (Clerk), Laura-Jane Tiley (Second Clerk), Edward Faulkner (Committee Specialist), George Perry (Media Officer), Pansy Barrett (Senior Committee Assistant), Chloe Freeman (Committee Assistant)

Transport
Tel: 020 7219 3266
Email: transcom@parliament.uk
www.parliament.uk/transcom
Twitter: @CommonsTrans

Lilian Greenwood (Chair)	*Lab*
Ronnie Cowan	*SNP*
Steve Double	*Con*
Paul Girvan	*DUP*
Huw Merriman	*Con*
Luke Pollard	*Lab/Co-op*
Laura Smith	*Lab*
Iain Stewart	*Con*
Graham Stringer	*Lab*
Martin Vickers	*Con*
Daniel Zeichner	*Lab*

Staff: Gordon Clarke (Clerk), Nehal Bradley-Depani (Second Clerk), James Clarke, Andrew Haylen (Committee Specialists), Estelle Currie (Media Officer), Daniel Moeller (Senior Committee Assistant), Michelle Owens (Committee Assistant)

Treasury
Tel: 020 7219 5769
Email: treascom@parliament.uk
www.parliament.uk/treascom

Nicky Morgan (Chair)	*Con*
Rushanara Ali	*Lab*
Charlie Elphicke	*Con*
Stephen Hammond	*Con*
Stewart Hosie	*SNP*
Alister Jack	*Con*
Alison McGovern	*Lab*
Catherine McKinnell	*Lab*
Kit Malthouse	*Con*
John Mann	*Lab*
Wes Streeting	*Lab*

Staff: Sarah Rees (Clerk), Peter Stam (Second Clerk), Dan Lee, Gavin Thompson, Marcus Wilton (Senior Economists), Adam Wales (Chief Policy Adviser), Matt Panteli (Senior Media and Policy Officer), George James (Senior Committee Assistant), Nick Berry (Committee Support Assistant)

Welsh Affairs
Tel: 020 7219 3264
Email: welshcom@parliament.uk
www.parliament.uk/welshcom
Twitter: @CommonsWelshAff

David Davies (Chair)	*Con*
Chris Davies	*Con*
Geraint Davies	*Lab/Co-op*
Glyn Davies	*Con*
Paul Flynn	*Lab*
Ben Lake	*PlC*

Staff: Sarah Thatcher (Clerk), Elin Jones (Committee Specialist), George Perry (Media Officer), Louise Glen (Senior Committee Assistant), Chloe Freeman (Committee Assistant)

Women and Equalities
Tel: 020 7219 6123
Email: womeqcom@parliament.uk
www.parliament.uk/business/committees/committees-a-z/commons-select/women-and-equalities-committee
Twitter: @Commonswomequ

Maria Miller (Chair)	*Con*
Angela Crawley	*SNP*
Philip Davies	*Con*
Rosie Duffield	*Lab*
Kirstene Hair	*Con*
Jared O'Mara	*Lab*
Jess Phillips	*Lab*
Gavin Shuker	*Lab/Co-op*
Tulip Siddiq	*Lab*

Staff: Judith Boyce, Sharmini Selvarajah (Clerks), Holly Dustin, Tansy Hutchinson, Shai Jacobs (Committee Specialists), Aaron Huang, Asaad Qadri (Inquiry Managers), Liz Parratt (Media Officer), Alexandra Hunter-Wainwright (Senior Committee Assistant), Mandy Sullivan (Committee Assistant)

Work and Pensions
Tel: 020 7219 8976
Email: workpencom@parliament.uk
www.parliament.uk/workpencom
Twitter: @CommonsWorkPen

Frank Field (Chair)	*Lab*
Heidi Allen	*Con*
Dr Alex Burghart	*Con*
Neil Coyle	*Lab*
Marsha De Cordova	*Lab*
Ruth George	*Lab*
Steve McCabe	*Lab*
Chris Stephens	*SNP*

Staff: Adam Mellows-Facer (Clerk), Libby McEnhill, Rod McInnes, Tom Tyson (Committee Specialists), Jess Bridges Palmer (Senior Media and Policy Officer), Alison Pickard (Senior Committee Assistant), Michelle Garratty (Committee Assistant)

Joint Committees
See Lords and Commons Joint Select Committees on p1062

Committees on Private Bills

Court of Referees
The Court of Referees is a committee of senior backbenchers, assisted by the Speaker's Counsel, which decides on cases involving the right of any petitioner to make a challenge to a Private Bill (known as locus standi). The three Deputy Speakers and the Counsel to the Speaker are ex-officio members.

Email: hamlynm@parliament.uk
www.parliament.uk/business/committees/committees-a-z/other-committees/court-of-referees

Members still to be appointed

Staff: Matthew Hamlyn (Clerk)

Standing Orders

When the Examiners of Petitions for Private Bills decide that Standing Orders relating to Private Business have not been complied with in relation to an individual bill, the Standing Orders Committee (appointed for the duration of a Parliament) decides whether or not to dispense with the Standing Order(s) under question. The three Deputy Speakers are ex-officio members.

Tel: 020 7219 3771
www.parliament.uk/business/committees/committees-a-z/commons-select/standing-orders

Members still to be appointed

Other Committees

Environmental Audit

Tel: 020 7219 5776
Email: eacom@parliament.uk
www.parliament.uk/eacom
Twitter: @Commonseac

Mary Creagh (Chair)	*Lab*
Dr Therese Coffey	*Con*
Geraint Davies	*Lab/Co-op*
Zac Goldsmith	*Con*
Dr Caroline Lucas	*Green*
Kerry McCarthy	*Lab*
Anna McMorrin	*Lab*
John McNally	*SNP*
Dr Matthew Offord	*Con*
Dr Dan Poulter	*Con*
Joan Ryan	*Lab*
Alex Sobel	*Lab/Co-op*
Michelle Donelan	*Con*
Steve Double	*Con*
Mike Hill	*Lab*
Susan Elan Jones	*Lab*
Catherine McKinnell	*Lab*
Paul Scully	*Con*
Liz Twist	*Lab*

Staff: David Slater (Clerk), Nina Foster (Second Clerk), Tom Leveridge (Senior Committee Specialist), Ian Cruse (Committee Specialist), Nick Davies (Media Officer), Ameet Chudasama (Senior Committee Assistant), Baris Tufekci (Committee Assistant (Tuesdays and Thursdays))

Staff: Anne-Marie Griffiths (Clerk)

European Scrutiny

Tel: 020 7219 3292
Email: escom@parliament.uk
www.parliament.uk/escom
Twitter: @CommonsESC

Members still to be appointed

Staff: Eve Samson (Clerk), Sarah Crandall (Senior Committee Assistant)

Petitions

Tel: 020 7219 7614
Email: petitionscommittee@parliament.uk
www.parliament.uk/petitions-committee
Twitter: @HoCpetitions

Helen Jones (Chair)	*Lab*
Rehman Chishti	*Con*
Martyn Day	*SNP*

Privileges

Tel: 020 7219 3259/3310 Fax: 020 7219 6864
Email: privileges@parliament.uk
www.parliament.uk/business/committees/committees-a-z/commons-select/privileges

Members still to be appointed

Staff: Lynn Gardner (Clerk), Jennifer Burch (Second Clerk), Jim Camp (Committee Assistant)

Procedure

Tel: 020 7219 3351 Fax: 020 7219 2269
Email: proccom@parliament.uk
www.parliament.uk/business/committees/committees-a-z/commons-select/procedure-committee
Twitter: @commonsproccom

Charles Walker (Chair)	*Con*
Bob Blackman	*Con*
Peter Bone	*Con*
Christopher Chope	*Con*
Ronnie Cowan	*SNP*
Nic Dakin	*Lab*
Chris Elmore	*Lab*
Helen Goodman	*Lab*
Ranil Jayawardena	*Con*
David Linden	*SNP*
Melanie Onn	*Lab*
William Wragg	*Con*

Staff: Martyn Atkins (Clerk), Leoni Kurt (Second Clerk), Alasdair Rendall (Media Officer), Jim Lawford (Committee Assistant)

Analysis of MPs
House of Commons

Public Accounts

Tel: 020 7219 4099 Fax: 020 7219 2782
Email: pubaccom@parliament.uk
www.parliament.uk/pac
Twitter: @CommonsPAC

Meg Hillier (Chair)	*Lab/Co-op*
Bim Afolami	*Con*
Heidi Allen	*Con*
Geoffrey Clifton-Brown	*Con*
Martyn Day	*SNP*
Chris Evans	*Lab/Co-op*
Caroline Flint	*Lab*
Luke Graham	*Con*
Andrew Jones	*Con*
Gillian Keegan	*Con*
Shabana Mahmood	*Lab*
Nigel Mills	*Con*
Layla Moran	*Lib Dem*
Bridget Phillipson	*Lab*
Gareth Snell	*Lab/Co-op*

Staff: Richard Cooke (Clerk), Dominic Stockbridge (Senior Clerk), Tim Bowden (Media Officer), Ruby Radley (Senior Committee Assistant)

Public Administration and Constitutional Affairs

Tel: 020 7219 3268
Email: pacac@parliament.uk
www.parliament.uk/pacac
Twitter: @CommonsPACAC

Bernard Jenkin (Chair)	*Con*
Ronnie Cowan	*SNP*
Paul Flynn	*Lab*
Marcus Fysh	*Con*
Cheryl Gillan	*Con*
Kelvin Hopkins	*Lab*
Dr Rupa Huq	*Lab*
David Jones	*Con*
Sandy Martin	*Lab*
David Morris	*Con*

Staff: Rebecca Davies, Rhiannon Hollis (Clerks)

Regulatory Reform

Tel: 020 7219 5908
Email: regrefcom@parliament.uk
www.parliament.uk/regrefcom

Members still to be appointed

Staff: To be appointed (Clerk), James McQuade (Senior Committee Assistant), Jonathan Olivier-Wright (Committee Assistant)

Selection

To nominate or propose Members to serve on General and Select Committees of the House of Commons. The Committee's decisions are recorded in the Votes and Proceedings on a daily basis.

Tel: 020 7219 3123
www.parliament.uk/business/committees/committees-a-z/other-committees/committee-of-selection

Bill Wiggin (Chair)	*Con*
Alan Campbell	*Lab*
David Evennett	*Con*
Patrick Grady	*SNP*
Andrew Griffiths	*Con*
Jessica Morden	*Lab*
Christopher Pincher	*Con*
Julian Smith	*Con*
Mark Tami	*Lab*

Staff: Gail Bartlett, Clementine Brown (Clerks), Christine McGrane (Committee Assistant)

Standards

Tel: 020 7219 3259
Email: standards@parliament.uk
www.parliament.uk/business/committees/committees-a-z/commons-select/standards

MPs and Lay Members still to be appointed

Staff: Dr Lynn Gardner (Clerk), Jennifer Burch (Second Clerk), Jim Camp (Committee Assistant)

Internal Committees

Administration

Tel: 020 7219 2471
Email: ac@parliament.uk
www.parliament.uk/ac

Members still to be appointed

Staff: Sarah Heath (Clerk), Anikka Weerasinghe (Media Officer), Amy Vistuer (Senior Committee Assistant)

Backbench Business

The Committee gives an opportunity to backbench Members to bring forward debates of their choice.

Tel: 020 7219 5084
Email: bbcom@parliament.uk
www.parliament.uk/bbcom
Twitter: @CommonsBBCom

Analysis of MPs
House of Commons

Ian Mearns (Chair) *Lab*
Bob Blackman *Con*
Rehman Chishti *Con*
Patricia Gibson *SNP*
Jess Phillips *Lab*
Alex Sobel *Lab/Co-op*
William Wragg *Con*
Staff: Ed Beale (Clerk), Sharon Maddix (Second Clerk), Alasdair Rendall (Media Officer), Aleksandra Perisik-Green (Committee Assistant)

Finance

Tel: 020 7219 3275
Email: financecommittee@parliament.uk
www.parliament.uk/business/committees/committees-a-z/commons-select/finance-committee

Members still to be appointed

Staff: Helen Wood (Clerk), Ronnie Jefferson (Committee Assistant)

Liaison

Tel: 020 7219 5675 Fax: 020 7219 6952
Email: liaisoncommittee@parliament.uk
www.parliament.uk/liaisoncom

Members still to be appointed

Staff: Sarah Hartwell-Naguib (Clerk), Liz Parratt (Media Officer), Anita Fuki (Senior Committee Assistant)

Panel of Chairs

The Panel of Chairs comprises the Chairman of Ways and Means, the Deputy Chairmen of Ways and Means, and not fewer than ten Members nominated by the Speaker. Members of the Panel chair debates in Westminster Hall and act as the chairs of Public Bill Committees and other general committees. They may also act as temporary chairs of committees of the whole House when requested by the Chairman of Ways and Means.

Tel: 020 7219 3257
Email: pbohoc@parliament.uk
www.parliament.uk/business/committees/committees-a-z/other-committees/panel-of-chairs

Lindsay Hoyle (Chair) *Lab*
Sir David Amess *Con*
Ian Austin *Lab*
Adrian Bailey *Lab/Co-op*
Sir Henry Bellingham *Con*
Clive Betts *Lab*
Peter Bone *Con*
Graham Brady *Con*
Karen Buck *Lab*
Christopher Chope *Con*
Sir David Crausby *Lab*
Geraint Davies *Lab/Co-op*
Philip Davies *Con*
Nadine Dorries *Con*
Nigel Evans *Con*
Sir Roger Gale *Con*
Mike Gapes *Lab/Co-op*
Cheryl Gillan *Con*
James Gray *Con*
David Hanson *Lab*
Philip Hollobone *Con*
Stewart Hosie *SNP*
George Howarth *Lab*
Eleanor Laing *Con*
Sir Edward Leigh *Con*
Steve McCabe *Lab*
Siobhain McDonagh *Lab*
Anne Main *Con*
Madeleine Moon *Lab*
Albert Owen *Lab*
Ian Paisley *DUP*
Mark Pritchard *Con*
Laurence Robertson *Con*
Andrew Rosindell *Con*
Joan Ryan *Lab*
Virendra Sharma *Lab*
Gary Streeter *Con*
Graham Stringer *Lab*
Charles Walker *Con*
Phil Wilson *Lab*
Rosie Winterton *Lab*
Staff: Colin Lee (Secretary)

Commons Reference Group on Representation and Inclusion

Tel: 020 7219 7458
Email: petits@parliament.uk
www.parliament.uk/business/committees/committees-a-z/other-committees/reference-group-representation-inclusion

John Bercow (Chair) *Speaker*
Tom Brake *Lib Dem*
Dr Lisa Cameron *SNP*
Mims Davies *Con*
Margaret Hodge *Lab*
Seema Malhotra *Lab/Co-op*
Maria Miller *Con*
Anne Milton *Con*
Jess Phillips *Lab*
Will Quince *Con*
Gavin Shuker *Lab/Co-op*
Staff: Sarah Petit (Secretary to the Executive Committee and the Board)

Analysis of MPs
House of Commons

Officers and Officials

Governance Office

Tel: 020 7219 1707
Email: governanceoffice@parliament.uk

Clerk of the House: David Natzler
Director-General, House of Commons: Ian Ailles
Head of Office and Secretary to the Commission: Marianne Cwynarski
Secretary to the Executive Committee: Sarah Petit
Private Secretary to the Clerk: John-Paul Flaherty
Private Secretary to the Director-General: James Mirza Davies
Head of Internal Audit: To be appointed
Corporate Risk Management Facilitator: Rachel Harrison
Clerk of Domestic Committees: Helen Wood
Head of Parliamentary Safety: Marianne McDougall
Head of Team Services and Projects: Vasilis Gialias

Chamber and Committees Team

Tel: 020 7219 8232

Clerk Assistant and Managing Director: Dr John Benger 020 7219 3311
PA to the Clerk Assistant: Charlotte Every 020 7219 8232
Head of Team Services: Gosia McBride 020 7219 8428

Media and Communications Service (Select Committees)

Head: Liz Parratt 07917 488978
Media and Communications Officers: Tim Bowden 07917 488162 Email: bowdent@parliament.uk, Jess Bridges Palmer 07917 488489 Email: bridgespalmerj@parliament.uk, Gary Calder 07917 488622 Email: calderg@parliament.uk, Estelle Currie 07834 171965 Email: curriee@parliament.uk, Lucy Dargahi 07921 293636 Email: dargahil@parliament.uk, Nick Davies 07917 488141 Email: daviesnick@parliament.uk, Simon Horswell 07703 800004 Email: horswells@parliament.uk, Sean Kinsey 07917 488791 Email: kinseys@parliment.uk, Matt Panteli 07720 205645 Email: pantelim@parliament.uk, Alex Paterson 07917 488488 Email: patersona@parliament.uk, George Perry 07834 172099 Email: perryg@parliament.uk, Ben Shave 07917 488183 Email: shaveb@parliment.uk

Overseas Office

Tel: 020 7219 3728
Email: overseasoffice@parliament.uk

Principal Clerk: Matthew Hamlyn 020 7219 3728
Delegation Secretary: Nick Wright 020 7219 3293

National Parliament Office, Brussels

Tel: +32 2 284 3703/+32 2 284 4656

National Parliament Representative: Alison Groves
Deputy National Parliament Representative: Fraser McIntosh

Chamber Business Team

Clerk of Legislation: Liam Laurence Smyth 020 7219 3255
Clerk of Bills, Examiner of Petitions for Private Bills and Taxing Officer: Colin Lee 020 7219 3257

Public Bill Office

Tel: 020 7219 6758/020 7219 3251

Clerks: Clemmie Brown, Kenneth Fox, Dr Mark Everett

Private Bill Office
Tel: 020 7219 6008/020 7219 4975
Clerk of Private Bills: Dr Farah Bhatti

Journal Office
Tel: 020 7219 3318/020 7219 3361
Email: journaloffice@parliament.uk
Clerk of the Journals: Mark Hutton 020 7219 3315
Clerks: Martyn Atkins, Mems Ayinla, Elizabeth Hunt, Dr Robin James, Leoni Kurt, Dr Stephen McGuiness

Table Office
Tel: 020 7219 3305
Email: tableoffice@parliament.uk
Principal Clerk: Philippa Helme
Senior Executive Officer: Francene Graham
Clerks: Nick Beech, James Davies, Dr Anna Dickson, Gini Griffin, Mike Hennessy, Libby Kurien, Catherine Meredith, Jessica Mulley, David Weir

Vote Office
Tel: 020 7219 3631 Email: vote_office@parliament.uk
Deliverer of the Vote: Catherine Fogarty 020 7219 4220
Head of Distribution Services: Barry Underwood
Head of Procedural Publishing: Tom McVeagh

Committee Office
Tel: 020 7219 4300/020 7219 5675
Clerk of Committees: Paul Evans
Principal Clerks: Crispin Poyser 020 7219 4355, Tom Goldsmith 020 7219 0447, Sarah Davies 020 7219 1365
Head of Scrutiny Unit: David Lloyd 020 7219 8370
Head of Media and Communications (Select Committees): Liz Parratt 020 7219 1708
Head of the Web and Publications Unit: Miranda Olivier-Wright 020 7219 7589

Official Report (Hansard)
Tel: 020 7219 4786/020 7219 5290
Website: hansard.parliament.uk
Editor: Alex Newton 020 7219 3388
Deputy Editor: Jack Homer 020 7219 5291

Parliamentary Audio Visual
Parliamentary Press Gallery enquiries: 020 7219 4700
Tel: 020 7219 4975/020 7219 6758
Director: John Angeli 020 7219 5848

Office of Speaker's Counsel
Reporting directly to the Clerk of the House
Tel: 020 7219 3877
Speaker's Counsel: Saira Salimi
Counsel for European Legislation: Arnold Ridout
Counsel for Domestic Legislation: Daniel Greenberg
Deputy Counsel: Peter Brooksbank, Vanessa Macnair, Philip Davies, Francoise Spencer, Samantha Godec, Helen Kinghorn
Deputy Speaker's Counsel: Helen Emes
Assistant Counsel: Klara Banaszak, Joanne Dee, Andrew Burrow, Natasha Osei

Communications Office

Tel: 020 7219 0969 (media general enquiries)/020 7219 7395 (media out of hours)/
020 7219 4801 (central communications) Email: communications@parliament.uk

Head of Communications: Lee Bridges
Marketing Communications Specialist: Owen Burdekin 020 7219 4483
Deputy Director of Media Relations: Pippa Lansdell 020 7219 1123
Media Relations Managers: Alasdair Rendall 020 7219 0771, To be appointed
Deputy Director of Central Communications: Amanda Saunders
Head of Internal Communications: Alex Noonoo 020 7219 0532

In-House Services

Tel: 020 7219 6551
Email: inhouseservices@parliament.uk

Managing Director: Carlos C. Bamford MBE 020 7219 6551
Executive Officer: Katie Phelan-Molloy 020 7219 4755
Director of Business Management: Della Herd 020 7219 1488
Acting Head of In-House Services Finance: David Laryea 020 7219 2873

Serjeant at Arms Office

Tel: 020 7219 3030

Serjeant at Arms: Kamal El-Hajji BEM
Principal Doorkeeper (Assistant Serjeant at Arms): Phil Howse
Access Manager (Assistant Serjeant at Arms): Emily Cathcart
Clerk in Charge (Associate Serjeant at Arms): Laura Blake
Admission Order Office Manager: Sarah Dinsdale

Parliamentary Maintenance Services Team

Tel: 020 7219 3202/020 7219 4747 (Parliamentary Maintenance Helpdesk)

Head of Maintenance: Mike McCann 020 7219 6493
Business Compliance Manager: Martin Wittekind 020 7219 6301
Operations Manager: Phil Sturgeon 020 7219 5334
Reactive and Ceremonial Maintenance Manager: Steve Jaggs 020 7219 4762
Small Works Maintenance Manager: Len Thorogood 020 7219 4814
Contracts Manager: John Taylor 020 7219 4785
Fire Safety Manager: John Bradbury 020 7219 8451

Catering Services

Tel: 020 7219 3686
Email: csfeedback@parliament.uk

Director of Catering Services: Richard Tapner-Evans 020 7219 3686
Executive Chef: Mark Hill 020 7219 1444
Operations Manager: Robert Gibbs 020 7219 0355

Curator's Office

Tel: 020 7219 3157
Email: curator@parliament.uk

Curator of Works of Art: Malcolm Hay 020 7219 3157
Deputy Curator and Head of Interpretation: Emma Gormley 020 7219 0182
Assistant Curator: To be appointed
Collections Care Manager: Caroline Babington 020 7219 5069
Collections Information Manager: Therese Crawley 020 7219 2812
Registrar: Emily Green 020 7219 5503

Historic Collections Team
Email: historicfurniture@parliament.uk

Keeper of Historic Collection (Furniture and Decorative Arts): Mary-Jane Tsang 020 7219 4798
Collections Manager: Emma Traherne 020 7219 1543
Conservation Manager: Patrick Walsh 020 7219 5321

Accommodation and Logistics Services
Tel: 020 7219 1319 Email: accommodationservices@parliament.uk

Director: Fiona Channon 020 7219 3060
Head of Service Delivery: Brendon Mulvihill 020 7219 2393
Members' Accommodation Manager: Lis Gerhold 020 7219 3080
Parliamentary Logistics Manager: Wes Auvache 020 7219 7525
Parliamentary Facilities Performance and Contract Manager: Ryan Auvache 020 7219 5412
Deputy Accommodation Manager: Dawn Brown 020 7219 4190

Corporate Services
Tel: 020 7219 8001

Managing Director: Myfanwy Barrett
Deputy Head of Corporate Services, Director of Efficiencies and Joint Working: Martin Trott
Director of People: Alix Langley
Acting Head of Diversity and Inclusion: Maxine Albert
Director of Financial Planning and Performance: Philip Collins
Head of Enterprise Portfolio Management Office: Charlotte Simmonds
Head of Members' Hub: Lucy Tindal

Parliamentary Digital Service
Director: Tracey Jessup
Deputy Director: David Smith
Director of Live Services: Rob Sanders
Chief Technology Officer: Ray Cross
Digital Portfolio Director: Rebecca Elton
Director of Digital Development: Emma Allen
Head of Cyber Security: Mark Harbord
Director of Cyber Security Programme: Steven Mark
Director of Transformation: Tori Baker
Head of Human Resources: Jonathan Seller

Parliamentary Security Department
Tel: 020 7219 2244

Director of Security for Parliament: Eric Hepburn CBE
Deputy Director of Security (Delivery): Chloe Challender
Deputy Director of Security (Operations) and Head of Security Operations: Fay Tennet

Participation Team
House of Commons Librarian and Managing Director: Penny Young
Head of Education and Engagement: David Clark
Head of Public Information and Resources: Matthew Ringer
Head of Visitor and Retail Services: Amy Pitts
Head of Team Services: John Owen

House of Commons Enquiry Service
Tel: 020 7219 4272
Email: hcenquiries@parliament.uk Website: www.parliament.uk/hcio

Public Enquiries Manager: Fiona Green

Houses of Parliament Shop

Tel: 020 7219 3890 Email: shop@parliament.uk

Head of Retail Operations: Andrew Bailey (maternity cover)
Senior Retail Operations: Sheila Mitchell

Research and Information Team

House of Commons Librarian and Managing Director: Penny Young
Director of Information: Steve Wise
Director of Research: Edward Wood
Director of Research Development: Bryn Morgan
Head of Information Rights and Information Security (IRIS): Victoria Payne
Acting Director of Parliamentary Office of Science and Technology: Dr Chandrika Nath
Head of SPIRE Benefits Realisation: Anne Thompson
Head of Team Services: John Owen
Head of Evaluation and Insight: Clare Bamberger
Head of Research Communications: Grace Rowley
Head of Research Information Service: David Beales
Head of Customer Service, House of Commons Library: Hannah Roberts
Head of Operations and Engagement, House of Commons Library: Hannah Russell
Head of Team Services: John Owen

House of Commons Library

Tel: 020 7219 3666
Email: hclibrary@parliament.uk

Research Sections

Tel: 020 7219 3666
Email: papers@parliament.uk

Head of Business and Transport Section: Timothy Edmonds
Library Clerks: Louise Butcher, Frederico Mor, Douglas Pyper, Antony Seely, Djuna Thurley
Head of Economic Policy and Statistics Section: Lorna Booth
Library Clerks: Daniel Harari, Matthew Keep, Feargal McGuinness, Andrew Powell, Chris Rhodes, Dominic Webb
Head of Home Affairs Section: Pat Strickland
Library Clerks: Jacqueline Beard, Lorraine Conway, Joanna Dawson, Jack Dent, Catherine Fairbairn, Melanie Gower, Sally Lipscombe, Terry McGuinness
Head of International Affairs and Defence Section: Vaughne Miller
Library Clerks: John Curtis, Louisa Brooke-Holland, Arabella Lang, Jon Lunn, Clare Mills, Ben Smith
Parliament and Constitution Centre: Lucinda Maer
Library Clerks: Dr Paul Bowers, Neil Johnston, Richard Kelly, Mark Sandford, Dr Jack Simson Caird
Head of Science and Environment Section: Edward Potton
Library Clerks: Dr Elena Ares, Dr Sarah Barber, Emma Downing, Gabrielle Garton Grimwood, David Hirst, Gergina Hutton, Sarah Priestley, Louise Smith
Head of Social and General Statistics Section: Richard Cracknell
Library Clerks: Grahame Allen, Dr Carl Baker, Cassie Barton, Paul Bolton, Noel Dempsey, Dr Rachael Harker, Oliver Hawkins, Richard Keen, Tom Rutherford, Dr Elise Uberoi
Head of Social Policy Section: Wendy Wilson
Library Clerks: Alex Bate, Hannah Cromarty, David Foster, Majit Gheera, Susan Hubble, Tim Jarrett, Steven Kennedy, Robert Long, Elizabeth Parkin, Nerys Roberts

Parliamentary Office of Science and Technology (POST)

Tel: 020 7219 2840 Email: post@parliament.uk Website: www.parliament.uk/post

Acting Director of POST: Dr Chandrika Nath
Advisers: Dr Peter Border, Dr Sarah Bunn, Dr Lydia Harriss, Dr Abbi Hobbs, Dr Caroline Kenny, Dr Jack Miller, Dr Jonathan Wentworth

Parliamentary Office of Science and Technology Board

Chair: To be appointed
Vice-chair: Professor Lord Winston
Acting Director of POST: Dr Chandrika Nath
Board Members: Professor Frances Balkwill, Lord Haskel, Professor Jim Norton, Lord Oxburgh, Lord Patel, Professor Bernard Silverman, Professor Sarah Whatmore

Strategic Estates

Tel: 020 7219 6896
Email: strategicestates@parliament.uk
Managing Director, Strategic Estates: Brian Finnimore 020 7219 3944
Director, Project Delivery: Victor Akinbile 020 7219 2154
Director, Estates Investment: David Hemming 020 7219 1407
Director, Property, Planning and Design: Donald Grant 020 7219 3815
Programme Director, Palace of Westminster Restoration and Renewal: Tom Healey 020 7219 0531
Programme Director, Northern Estates: John Cryer 020 7219 1341
Director, Portfolio Management Office: Jonathan Lewsey 020 7219 5327
Business Management Director: Jo Regan 020 7219 5911
Head of Finance: Abiola Babalola 020 7219 6598

Associated Offices

Parliamentary Commissioner for Standards

Office of the Parliamentary Commissioner for Standards, House of Commons, London SW1A 0AA
Tel: 020 7219 0320
Email: standardscommissioner@parliament.uk Website: www.parliament.uk/pcs
Parliamentary Commissioner for Standards: Kathryn Hudson
Registrar of Members' Financial Interests: Heather Wood

Political Offices

Government

Leader of the House of Commons' Office 020 7219 4040
Chief Whip's Office 020 7219 4400

Whips' Assistants Office

Chief Clerk: Joe Pearce 020 7219 0057/020 7219 4333
Whips' Assistants:
Alexander Steele 020 7219 3612
Owen Davies 020 7219 5964
Michael McCarthy 020 7219 6570
Emma McEwan 020 7219 0058

Official Opposition

Leader's Office 020 7219 3000
Opposition Chief Whip's Office 020 7219 4770

Head of Parliamentary Support: Elaine Theophil 020 7219 0009
Email: elaine.theophil@parliament.uk
Deputy Head of Parliamentary Support: Sam Clark 020 7219 2786 Email: clarksb@parliament.uk
Whips' Assistants:
Millie Wright 020 7219 4770 Email: wrightml@parliament.uk
Kadisha Llewelyn Auguste 020 7219 1225 Email: llewelynaugustek@parliament.uk

Scottish National Party

Leader's Office 020 7219 8259

Chief of Staff: Ian Donaldson 020 7219 6025 Email: donaldsoni@parliament.uk
Head of Group Leader's Office: Lynsey-Anne Marwick 020 7219 3494
Email: lynsey-anne.marwick@parliament.uk
Principal Assistant to the Chief Whip: Anne Harvey 020 7219 3020
Email: anne.harvey@parliament.uk
Head of Communications: Catriona Matheson 020 7219 1602
Email: catriona.matheson@parliament.uk
Head of Research: Paul Robertson 020 7219 7422 Email: robertsonp@parliament.uk

Liberal Democrats

Chief Whip's Office 020 7219 1415

Democratic Unionist Party

Group Leader's Office 020 7219 8419

Whip's Office Manager: Camilla Toogood 020 7219 8525 Email: camilla.toogood@parliament.uk

Plaid Cymru

Leader's Office 020 7219 8150

Whip's Office and Researchers:
Heledd Brooks-Jones 020 7219 6883 Email: heledd.brooksjones@parliament.uk
Ben O'Keeffe 020 7219 1867 Email: ben.okeeffe@parliament.uk
Press Officer: Osian Lewis 020 7219 1900 Email: osian.lewis@parliament.uk

GENERAL ELECTION 2017

GENERAL ELECTION 2017 464

Electoral Information 464

Parties standing 465

Polling Results by Constituency 465

State of the Parties 532

Share of the Vote 532

Share of the Vote by Region 532

- England 532
- Northern Ireland 535
- Scotland 536
- Wales 536

Seats which changed Parties 536

Results in vulnerable seats 537

New MPs 543

Defeated MPs 544

Retired MPs 546

Electoral Information

The Fixed-Term Parliaments Act 2011 set the polling day of the first general election following its enactment as Thursday 7 May 2015, and set each subsequent parliamentary general election to the first Thursday in May in the fifth calendar year following the polling day the previous parliamentary general election fell on. There are two provisions that could be used to trigger an earlier election – a motion of no confidence is passed in Her Majesty's Government by a simple majority and 14 days elapses without the House passing a confidence motion in any new Government formed or a motion for a general election is agreed by two thirds of the total number of seats in the Commons including vacant seats (currently 434 out of 650). This second provision was used in 2017 to call an early general election, which took place on Thursday 8 June 2017.

Parliament dissolves at the beginning of the 25th working day before the polling day for the parliamentary general election. The last day for the delivery of nomination papers is the sixth day after the date of dissolution. The poll is held in every constituency on the 19th day after the last day for delivery of nomination papers.

In the case of a by-election, the last day for the delivery of nomination papers and the date the polling day takes place is fixed by the Returning Officer and are stated on the notice of election. There is a limit of £100,000 on the total amount that a candidate can spend on campaigning in the run-up to a parliamentary by-election.

In calculating election timetables Saturdays, Sundays, Christmas Eve, Christmas Day, Good Friday, bank holidays and days appointed for public thanksgiving or mourning are disregarded.

Parliamentary Franchise

A person resident in the United Kingdom is entitled to be entered on the register of electors if he or she is:

- resident in the constituency
- not subject to any legal incapacity to vote (age apart)
- a British or other qualifying Commonwealth citizen or a citizen of the Republic of Ireland
- is at least 18 years of age (or will become 18 during the currency of the register)
- applies to vote to the Registration Officer no later than 11 working days before polling day.

British citizens resident abroad may also register and vote in parliamentary elections for up to 15 years after leaving the UK. HM Forces can register while serving.

Since 1999 hereditary peers, who were previously barred from voting in general elections, have been allowed to do so if they no longer sit in the Lords.

Parliamentary Candidates

A candidate must be at least 18 years old and a citizen of the United Kingdom, Commonwealth or Republic of Ireland and have indefinite leave to remain in the UK.

Since 1999 hereditary peers who no longer sit in the House of Lords have been allowed to stand as candidates for the Commons.

Each candidate must deposit £500 with the Returning Officer at the time of nomination, refunded if elected, or polls over 5 per cent of votes cast.

Rules on candidate spending apply during the 'regulated period', this is made up of the Long campaign and Short campaign:

Long campaign – the fixed amount is £30,700 plus, 6p per registered parliamentary elector in a borough constituency, or 9p per registered parliamentary elector in a county constituency.

Short campaign – the fixed amount is £8,700 plus, 6p per registered parliamentary elector in a borough constituency, or 9p per registered parliamentary elector in a county constituency.

Number of Voters

In December 2016 there was a total of 45,766,000 names on the electoral registers for the United Kingdom.

England	38,386,900
Scotland	3,930,000
Wales	2,243,900
Northern Ireland	1,205,700

Parties with seats in the House of Commons

Con	Conservative	**Lib Dem**	Liberal Democrat
DUP	Democratic Unionist Party	**PlC**	Plaid Cymru
Green	Green Party	**Sinn Féin**	Sinn Féin
Ind	Independent	**SNP**	Scottish National Party
Lab	Labour	**Speaker**	The Speaker
Lab/Co-op	Labour/Co-operative		

Parties with candidates in the General Election

All Alliance; **Apol Dem** Apolitical Democrats; **Ashfield Ind** Ashfield Independents; **AWP** Animal Welfare Party; **BFB** Better for Bradford; **Blue Rev** Blue Revolution; **BNP** British National Party; **Christian** Christian Party; **cista** Citizens Independent Social Thought Alliance; **Comm League** Communist League; **Common Good** Common Good; **Compass** Compass Party; **Con** Conservative; **Concordia** Concordia; **CPA** Christian Peoples Alliance; **DDIP** Demos Direct Initiative Party; **DUP** Democratic Unionist Party; **Elvis** Church of the Militant Elvis Party; **Eng Dem** English Democrats; **Friends** Friends Party; **GMHV** Greater Manchester Homeless Voice; **Green** Green Party; **Green Soc** Alliance for Green Socialism; **Humanity** Humanity; **Ind** Independent; **Ind Sov Dem Britain** Independent Sovereign Democratic Britain; **ISWSL** Independent Save Withybush Save Lives; **JACP** Justice and Anti-Corruption Party; **Just** Just Party; **Lab** Labour; **Lab/Co-op** Labour/Co-operative; **Lib** Liberal; **Lib Dem** Liberal Democrat; **Libertarian** Libertarian Party; **Loony** Official Monster Raving Loony Party; **Money Free** Money Free Party; **MAD** Movement for Active Democracy; **NECA** North of England Community Alliance; **NEP** North East Party; **New Society of Worth** New Society of Worth; **NHA** National Health Action Party; **Open Borders** Open Borders Party; **Patria** Patria; **PBPA** People Before Profit Alliance; **Peace Party** Peace Party; **Pirate** Pirate Party; **PlC** Plaid Cymru; **Populist** Populist Party; **Radical** Radical Party; **Realists** Realists' Party; **Reboot** Rebooting Democracy; **SDLP** Social Democratic and Labour Party; **SDP** Social Democratic Party; **Sinn Féin** Sinn Féin; **SIRP** Scotland's Independence Referendum Party; **SLP** Socialist Labour Party; **SN** Something New; **SNP** Scottish National Party; **Southampton Ind** Southampton Independents; **Southend Ind Ass** Southend Independent Association; **SP** Socialist Party; **Space Navies** Space Navies Party; **Speaker** The Speaker; **TUV** Traditional Unionist Voice; **UKIP** UK Independence Party; **UUP** Ulster Unionist Party; **WEP** Women's Equality Party; **Wessex Reg** Wessex Regionalists; **WP** Workers Party; **WRP** Workers Revolutionary Party; **WVPTFP** War Veteran's Pro-Traditional Family Party; **YP** Yorkshire Party; **YPP** Young People's Party.

ABERAVON

		%	+/-%
Kinnock, S. Lab*	22,662	68.0	19.2
Vidal, S. Con	5,901	17.7	5.9
Bennison, A. PlC	2,761	8.3	-3.3
Jones, C. UKIP	1,345	4.0	-11.7
Phillips, C. Lib Dem	599	1.8	-2.6
Lab majority	16,761	50.3	
Electorate	49,892		
Turnout	33,325	66.79	

Lab hold (6.66% from Con to Lab)

ABERCONWY

		%	+/-%
Bebb, G. Con*	14,337	44.5	3.1
Owen, E. Lab	13,702	42.5	14.3
Jones, W. PlC	3,170	9.8	-1.9
Lesiter-Burgess, S. Lib Dem	941	2.9	-1.7
Con majority	635	1.97	
Electorate	45,251		
Turnout	32,228	71.22	

Con hold (5.63% from Con to Lab)

ABERDEEN NORTH

		%	+/-%
Blackman, K. SNP*	15,170	41.2	-15.1
Vinegold, O. Lab	11,031	30.0	4.1
O'Keeffe, G. Con	8,341	22.7	10.6
Davidson, I. Lib Dem	1,693	4.6	-0.1
Durkin, R. Ind	522	1.4	
SNP majority	4,139	11.24	
Electorate	62,130		
Turnout	36,812	59.25	

SNP hold (9.6% from SNP to Lab)

ABERDEEN SOUTH

		%	+/-%
Thomson, R. Con	18,746	42.1	19.3
McCaig, C. SNP*	13,994	31.4	-10.2
O'Dwyer, C. Lab	9,143	20.5	-6.2
Wilson, J. Lib Dem	2,610	5.9	1.2
Con majority	4,752	10.67	
Electorate	64,964		
Turnout	44,556	68.59	

Con gain (14.73% from SNP to Con)

WEST ABERDEENSHIRE AND KINCARDINE

		%	+/-%
Bowie, A. Con	24,704	47.8	19.0
Donaldson, S. SNP*	16,754	32.4	-9.1
Black, B. Lab	5,706	11.0	6.5
Waddell, J. Lib Dem	4,461	8.6	-12.8
Con majority	7,950	15.38	
Electorate	72,477		
Turnout	51,674	71.3	

Con gain (14.06% from SNP to Con)

AIRDRIE AND SHOTTS

		%	+/-%
Gray, N. SNP*	14,291	37.6	-16.3
Mcfarlane, H. Lab	14,096	37.0	3.0
Donnellan, J. Con	8,813	23.2	15.5
McRobert, E. Lib Dem	802	2.1	0.6
SNP majority	195	0.51	
Electorate	64,146		
Turnout	38,049	59.32	

SNP hold (9.65% from SNP to Lab)

ALDERSHOT

		%	+/-%
Docherty, L. Con	26,950	54.9	4.5
Puffett, G. Lab	15,477	31.6	13.3
Hilliar, A. Lib Dem	3,637	7.4	-1.4
Swales, R. UKIP	1,796	3.7	-14.2
Wallace, D. Green	1,090	2.2	-2.2
Con majority	11,473	23.39	
Electorate	76,205		
Turnout	49,052	64.37	

Con hold (4.4% from Con to Lab)

ALDRIDGE-BROWNHILLS

		%	+/-%
Morton, W. Con*	26,317	65.3	13.4
Fisher, J. Lab	12,010	29.8	7.5
Garrett, I. Lib Dem	1,343	3.3	0.0
Beech, M. Loony	565	1.4	0.9
Con majority	14,307	35.48	
Electorate	60,363		
Turnout	40,322	66.8	

Con hold (2.94% from Lab to Con)

ALTRINCHAM AND SALE WEST

		%	+/-%
Brady, G. Con*	26,933	50.9	-1.9
Western, A. Lab	20,507	38.8	12.1
Brophy, J. Lib Dem	4,051	7.7	-0.7
Coggins, G. Green	1,000	1.9	-2.0
Taylor, N. Lib	299	0.6	
Con majority	6,426	12.14	
Electorate	73,227		
Turnout	52,922	72.27	

Con hold (7.05% from Con to Lab)

ALYN AND DEESIDE

		%	+/-%
Tami, M. Lab*	23,315	52.0	12.0
Knightly, L. Con	18,080	40.3	8.4
Hurst, J. PIC	1,171	2.6	-1.3
Griffiths, D. UKIP	1,117	2.5	-15.1
Williams, P. Lib Dem	1,077	2.4	-1.8
Lab majority	5,235	11.67	
Electorate	63,012		
Turnout	44,844	71.17	

Lab hold (1.8% from Con to Lab)

*Member of last Parliament

AMBER VALLEY

		%	+/-%
Mills, N. Con*	25,905	56.4	12.6
Dawson, J. Lab	17,605	38.4	3.7
Smith, K. Lib Dem	1,100	2.4	-0.6
McGuinness, M. Green	650	1.4	-0.9
Bamford, D. Ind	551	1.2	
Con majority	8,300	18.08	
Electorate	68,065		
Turnout	45,910	67.45	

Con hold (4.45% from Lab to Con)

ANGUS

		%	+/-%
Hair, K. Con	18,148	45.1	16.1
Weir, M. SNP*	15,503	38.5	-15.7
Campbell, W. Lab	5,233	13.0	4.2
Sneddon, C. Lib Dem	1,308	3.3	0.5
Con majority	2,645	6.57	
Electorate	63,840		
Turnout	40,257	63.06	

Con gain (15.9% from SNP to Con)

EAST ANTRIM

		%	+/-%
Wilson, S. DUP*	21,873	57.2	21.2
Dickson, S. All	5,950	15.6	0.6
Stewart, J. UUP	4,524	11.8	-6.9
McMullan, O. Sinn Féin	3,555	9.3	2.4
McKillop, M. SDLP	1,278	3.3	-1.5
Logan, M. Con	963	2.5	0.9
DUP majority	15,923	41.61	
Electorate	62,908		
Turnout	38,269	60.83	

DUP hold (10.29% from All to DUP)

NORTH ANTRIM

		%	+/-%
Paisley, I. DUP*	28,521	58.7	15.7
McShane, C. Sinn Féin	7,878	16.2	4.0
Minford, J. UUP	3,482	7.2	-4.8
Gaston, T. TUV	3,282	6.8	-8.8
O'Lynn, P. All	2,723	5.6	0.0
O'Loan, D. SDLP	2,574	5.3	-1.6
DUP majority	20,643	42.49	
Electorate	75,657		
Turnout	48,580	64.21	

DUP hold (5.86% from Sinn Féin to DUP)

SOUTH ANTRIM

		%	+/-%
Girvan, P. DUP	16,508	38.1	8.2
Kinahan, D. UUP*	13,300	30.7	-1.8
Kearney, D. Sinn Féin	7,797	18.0	5.2
Kelly, N. All	3,203	7.4	-2.3
Lynch, R. SDLP	2,362	5.5	-2.7
DUP majority	3,208	7.41	
Electorate	68,244		
Turnout	43,292	63.44	

DUP gain (5% from UUP to DUP)

ARFON

		%	+/-%
Williams, H. PIC*	11,519	40.7	-3.0
Griffiths Clarke, M. Lab	11,427	40.4	10.3
Parry, P. Con	4,614	16.3	3.3
Davies, C. Lib Dem	648	2.3	-0.4
PIC majority	92	0.33	
Electorate	41,367		
Turnout	28,275	68.35	

PIC hold (6.65% from PIC to Lab)

ARGYLL AND BUTE

		%	+/-%
O'Hara, B. SNP*	17,304	36.0	-8.3
Mulvaney, G. Con	15,976	33.2	18.3
Reid, A. Lib Dem	8,745	18.2	-9.7
Kelly, M. Lab	6,044	12.6	2.2
SNP majority	1,328	2.76	
Electorate	67,230		
Turnout	48,138	71.6	

SNP hold (13.28% from SNP to Con)

ARUNDEL AND SOUTH DOWNS

		%	+/-%
Herbert, N. Con*	37,573	62.2	1.7
Fife, C. Lab	13,690	22.7	11.5
Kapadia, S. Lib Dem	4,783	7.9	0.8
Prior, J. Green	2,542	4.2	-2.2
Wallace, J. UKIP	1,668	2.8	-11.6
Con majority	23,883	39.53	
Electorate	79,478		
Turnout	60,410	76.01	

Con hold (4.92% from Con to Lab)

ASHFIELD

		%	+/-%
De Piero, G. Lab*	21,285	42.6	1.7
Harper, T. Con	20,844	41.7	19.4
Turner, G. Ashfield Ind	4,612	9.2	
Young, R. UKIP	1,885	3.8	-17.5
Charlesworth, B. Lib Dem	969	1.9	-12.8
Rangi, A. Green	398	0.8	
Lab majority	441	0.88	
Electorate	78,076		
Turnout	50,055	64.11	

Lab hold (8.82% from Lab to Con)

ASHFORD

		%	+/-%
Green, D. Con*	35,318	58.9	6.6
Gathern, S. Lab	17,840	29.7	11.4
Gee-Turner, A. Lib Dem	3,101	5.2	-0.8
O'Brien, G. UKIP	2,218	3.7	-15.1
Rossi, M. Green	1,402	2.3	-2.0
Con majority	17,478	29.12	
Electorate	87,387		
Turnout	60,014	68.68	

Con hold (2.4% from Con to Lab)

ASHTON UNDER LYNE

		%	+/-%
Rayner, A. Lab*	24,005	60.2	10.7
Rankin, J. Con	12,710	31.9	9.9
Jackson, M. UKIP	1,878	4.7	-16.9
Hicks, C. Lib Dem	646	1.6	-0.8
Hunter-Rossall, A. Green	534	1.3	-2.6
Lab majority	11,295	28.34	
Electorate	67,674		
Turnout	39,854	58.89	

Lab hold (0.42% from Con to Lab)

AYLESBURY

		%	+/-%
Lidington, D. Con*	32,313	54.9	4.4
Bateman, M. Lab	17,657	30.0	14.9
Lambert, S. Lib Dem	5,660	9.6	-1.0
Srao, V. UKIP	1,296	2.2	-17.4
Simpson, C. Green	1,237	2.1	-1.7
Michael, K. Ind	620	1.1	
Con majority	14,656	24.88	
Electorate	82,546		
Turnout	58,905	71.36	

Con hold (5.25% from Con to Lab)

AYR, CARRICK AND CUMNOCK

		%	+/-%
Grant, B. Con	18,550	40.1	20.3
Wilson, C. SNP*	15,776	34.1	-14.7
Mochan, C. Lab	11,024	23.8	-3.4
Leslie, C. Lib Dem	872	1.9	0.2
Con majority	2,774	5.99	
Electorate	71,241		
Turnout	46,296	64.99	

Con gain (17.48% from SNP to Con)

CENTRAL AYRSHIRE

		%	+/-%
Whitford, P. SNP*	16,771	37.1	-16.0
Hollins Martin, C. Con	15,504	34.3	17.0
McDonald, N. Lab	11,762	26.0	-0.3
Inglis, T. Lib Dem	1,050	2.3	0.5
SNP majority	1,267	2.81	
Electorate	68,999		
Turnout	45,162	65.45	

SNP hold (16.49% from SNP to Con)

NORTH AYRSHIRE AND ARRAN

		%	+/-%
Gibson, P. SNP*	18,451	38.8	-14.3
Rocks, D. Con	14,818	31.2	16.4
Rimicans, C. Lab	13,040	27.4	-0.5
Dickson, M. Lib Dem	1,124	2.4	0.7
SNP majority	3,633	7.65	
Electorate	73,176		
Turnout	47,515	64.93	

SNP hold (15.34% from SNP to Con)

BANBURY

		%	+/-%
Prentis, V. Con*	33,388	54.1	1.5
Woodcock, S. Lab	20,989	34.0	12.9
Howson, J. Lib Dem	3,452	5.6	-0.3
Bird, D. UKIP	1,581	2.6	-11.2
Middleton, I. Green	1,225	2.0	-2.6
Edwards, R. Ind	927	1.5	
Con majority	12,399	20.1	
Electorate	83,824		
Turnout	61,677	73.58	

Con hold (5.69% from Con to Lab)

BANFF AND BUCHAN

		%	+/-%
Duguid, D. Con	19,976	47.9	19.2
Whiteford, E. SNP*	16,283	39.1	-21.0
Stott, C. Lab	3,936	9.4	3.7
Milne, G. Lib Dem	1,448	3.5	-1.7
Con majority	3,693	8.86	
Electorate	67,601		
Turnout	41,689	61.67	

Con gain (20.11% from SNP to Con)

BARKING

		%	+/-%
Hodge, M. Lab*	32,319	67.6	10.1
Talati, M. Con	10,711	22.4	6.2
Gravett, R. UKIP	3,031	6.3	-15.8
Butterfield, S. Green	724	1.5	-0.6
Pearce, P. Lib Dem	599	1.3	-0.1
Falvey, N. Ind	295	0.6	
Lab majority	21,608	45.22	
Electorate	77,022		
Turnout	47,782	62.04	

Lab hold (1.98% from Con to Lab)

BARNSLEY CENTRAL

		%	+/-%
Jarvis, D. Lab*	24,982	63.8	8.2
Ford, A. Con	9,436	24.1	9.1
Felton, G. UKIP	3,339	8.5	-13.1
Trotman, R. Green	570	1.5	-1.1
Ridgway, D. Lib Dem	549	1.4	-0.7
Morris, S. Eng Dem	211	0.5	-0.8
Lab majority	15,546	39.71	
Electorate	64,204		
Turnout	39,153	60.98	

Lab hold (0.45% from Lab to Con)

BARNSLEY EAST

		%	+/-%
Peacock, S. Lab	24,280	59.4	4.9
Lloyd, A. Con	10,997	26.9	12.4
Dalton, J. UKIP	3,247	8.0	-15.4
Devoy, T. YP	1,215	3.0	
Turner, N. Lib Dem	750	1.8	-1.3
Riddiough, K. Eng Dem	287	0.7	-0.4
Lab majority	13,283	32.5	
Electorate	69,214		
Turnout	40,867	59.04	

Lab hold (3.72% from Lab to Con)

BARROW AND FURNESS

		%	+/-%
Woodcock, J. Lab/Co-op*	22,592	47.4	5.2
Fell, S. Con	22,383	47.0	6.6
Birchall, L. Lib Dem	1,278	2.7	0.0
Piper, A. UKIP	962	2.0	-9.6
O'Hara, R. Green	375	0.8	-1.6
Lab/Co-op majority	209	0.44	
Electorate	69,474		
Turnout	47,650	68.59	

Lab/Co-op hold (0.7% from Lab/Co-op to Con)

BASILDON AND BILLERICAY

		%	+/-%
Baron, J. Con*	27,381	60.8	8.4
Block, K. Lab	13,981	31.0	7.5
Hughes, T. UKIP	2,008	4.5	-15.3
Harrison, A. Lib Dem	1,548	3.4	-0.3
Con majority	13,400	29.75	
Electorate	69,149		
Turnout	45,039	65.13	

Con hold (0.44% from Lab to Con)

SOUTH BASILDON AND EAST THURROCK

		%	+/-%
Metcalfe, S. Con*	26,811	56.8	13.5
Taylor, B. Lab	15,321	32.5	7.3
Whittle, P. UKIP	3,193	6.8	-19.7
Banerji, R. Lib Dem	732	1.6	-1.4
Harman, S. Green	680	1.4	
Borg, P. BNP	383	0.8	
Con majority	11,490	24.35	
Electorate	73,537		
Turnout	47,195	64.18	

Con hold (3.1% from Lab to Con)

BASINGSTOKE

		%	+/-%
Miller, M. Con*	29,510	52.6	4.3
Bridgeman, T. Lab	20,044	35.7	8.1
Shaw, J. Lib Dem	3,406	6.1	-1.3
Stone, A. UKIP	1,681	3.0	-12.6
Winter, R. Green	1,106	2.0	
Neville, S. Libertarian	213	0.4	
Con majority	9,466	16.87	
Electorate	81,875		
Turnout	56,098	68.52	

Con hold (1.95% from Con to Lab)

BASSETLAW

		%	+/-%
Mann, J. Lab*	27,467	52.6	4.1
Simpson, A. Con	22,615	43.3	12.7
Duveen, L. Lib Dem	1,154	2.2	-0.5
Turner, N. Ind	1,014	1.9	
Lab majority	4,852	9.26	
Electorate	78,540		
Turnout	52,377	66.69	

Lab hold (4.3% from Lab to Con)

*Member of last Parliament

BATH

		%	+/-%
Hobhouse, W. Lib Dem	23,436	47.2	17.6
Howlett, B. Con*	17,742	35.7	-2.0
Rayment, J. Lab	7,279	14.7	1.5
Field, E. Green	1,126	2.3	-9.6
Lib Dem majority	5,694	11.46	
Electorate	66,778		
Turnout	49,695	74.42	

Lib Dem gain (9.78% from Con to Lib Dem)

BATLEY AND SPEN

		%	+/-%
Brabin, T. Lab/Co-op*	29,844	55.4	12.3
Myatt, A. Con	20,883	38.7	7.6
Lawson, J. Lib Dem	1,224	2.3	-2.5
Lukic, A. Ind	1,076	2.0	
Freeman, A. Green	695	1.3	-1.1
Hanif, M. Ind	58	0.1	
Lab/Co-op majority	8,961	16.62	
Electorate	80,161		
Turnout	53,908	67.25	

Lab/Co-op hold (2.3% from Con to Lab/Co-op)

BATTERSEA

		%	+/-%
De Cordova, M. Lab	25,292	45.8	9.1
Ellison, J. Con*	22,876	41.5	-10.8
Davis, R. Lib Dem	4,401	8.0	3.6
Coghlan, C. Ind	1,234	2.2	
Davis, L. Green	866	1.6	-1.7
Power, E. UKIP	357	0.7	-2.5
Lambert, D. SP	32	0.1	
Lab majority	2,416	4.38	
Electorate	77,574		
Turnout	55,170	71.12	

Lab gain (9.95% from Con to Lab)

BEACONSFIELD

		%	+/-%
Grieve, D. Con*	36,559	65.1	2.2
English, J. Lab	12,016	21.4	10.0
Chapman, P. Lib Dem	4,448	7.9	0.6
Conway, J. UKIP	1,609	2.9	-10.8
Secker, R. Green	1,396	2.5	-1.7
Con majority	24,543	43.72	
Electorate	77,524		
Turnout	56,137	72.41	

Con hold (3.92% from Con to Lab)

BECKENHAM

		%	+/-%
Stewart, B. Con*	30,632	59.1	2.0
Ahmad, M. Lab	15,545	30.0	10.6
Ireland, J. Lib Dem	4,073	7.9	1.0
Fabricant, R. Green	1,380	2.7	-1.2
Con majority	15,087	29.12	
Electorate	67,925		
Turnout	51,812	76.28	

Con hold (4.32% from Con to Lab)

BEDFORD

		%	+/-%
Yasin, M. Lab	22,712	46.7	6.7
Fuller, R. Con*	21,923	45.1	2.7
Vann, H. Lib Dem	2,837	5.8	1.6
Bywater, L. Green	1,008	2.1	-1.0
Lab majority	789	1.62	
Electorate	71,829		
Turnout	48,656	67.74	

Lab gain (2% from Con to Lab)

MID BEDFORDSHIRE

		%	+/-%
Dorries, N. Con*	38,936	61.5	5.7
Meades, R. Lab	17,953	28.4	12.5
French, L. Lib Dem	3,788	6.0	-1.2
Ellis, G. Green	1,794	2.8	-1.4
Kelly, A. Loony	667	1.1	0.6
Con majority	20,983	33.14	
Electorate	84,161		
Turnout	63,323	75.24	

Con hold (3.44% from Con to Lab)

NORTH EAST BEDFORDSHIRE

		%	+/-%
Burt, A. Con*	39,139	60.8	1.5
Vaughan, J. Lab	18,277	28.4	12.7
Rutherford, S. Lib Dem	3,693	5.7	-0.1
Strachan, D. UKIP	1,896	3.0	-11.6
Fleming, P. Green	1,215	1.9	-2.4
Con majority	20,862	32.42	
Electorate	87,505		
Turnout	64,354	73.54	

Con hold (5.57% from Con to Lab)

SOUTH WEST BEDFORDSHIRE

		%	+/-%
Selous, A. Con*	32,961	59.1	4.3
Scott, D. Lab	18,793	33.7	13.5
Norton, D. Lib Dem	2,630	4.7	-0.4
Rennie, M. Green	950	1.7	-2.4
Mafoh, M. CPA	301	0.5	
Con majority	14,168	25.39	
Electorate	79,658		
Turnout	55,798	70.05	

Con hold (4.59% from Con to Lab)

BELFAST EAST

		%	+/-%
Robinson, G. DUP*	23,917	55.6	6.5
Long, N. All	15,443	35.9	-6.7
Legge, H. UUP	1,408	3.3	
O'Donnell, M. Sinn Féin	894	2.1	0.0
Milne, G. Green	561	1.3	-1.4
Bodel, S. Con	446	1.0	-1.8
de Faoite, S. SDLP	167	0.4	0.1
Beck, B. Ind	54	0.1	
DUP majority	8,474	19.71	
Electorate	63,495		
Turnout	42,994	67.71	

DUP hold (6.6% from All to DUP)

BELFAST NORTH

		%	+/-%
Dodds, N. DUP*	21,240	46.1	-0.6
Finucane, J. Sinn Féin	19,159	41.5	7.9
Nelson, S. All	2,475	5.4	-1.8
McAuley, M. SDLP	2,058	4.5	-3.7
O'Hara, M. Green	644	1.4	
Weir, G. WP	360	0.8	-1.5
DUP majority	2,081	4.51	
Electorate	68,249		
Turnout	46,107	67.56	

DUP hold (4.25% from DUP to Sinn Féin)

BELFAST SOUTH

		%	+/-%
Little Pengelly, E. DUP	13,299	30.3	8.2
McDonnell, A. SDLP*	11,303	25.8	1.4
Bradshaw, P. All	7,946	18.1	1.0
Ó Muilleoir, M. Sinn Féin	7,143	16.3	2.5
Bailey, C. Green	2,241	5.1	-0.6
Henderson, M. UUP	1,527	3.5	-5.6
Salier, C. Con	246	0.6	-0.9
DUP majority	1,996	4.55	
Electorate	66,105		
Turnout	43,851	66.34	

DUP gain (3.44% from SDLP to DUP)

BELFAST WEST

		%	+/-%
Maskey, P. Sinn Féin*	27,107	66.4	12.6
McCoubrey, F. DUP	5,455	13.4	5.6
Carroll, G. PBPA	4,132	10.1	-9.0
Attwood, T. SDLP	2,860	7.0	-2.8
Eastwood, S. All	731	1.8	
Campbell, C. WP	348	0.9	-0.8
Sinn Féin majority	21,652	53.03	
Electorate	62,423		
Turnout	40,830	65.41	

Sinn Féin hold (3.51% from DUP to Sinn Féin)

BERMONDSEY AND OLD SOUTHWARK

		%	+/-%
Coyle, N. Lab*	31,161	53.1	10.2
Hughes, S. Lib Dem	18,189	31.0	-3.2
Baillie, S. Con	7,581	12.9	1.2
Jones, E. UKIP	838	1.4	-4.9
Tyson, J. Green	639	1.1	-2.8
Clarke, J. Ind	113	0.2	
Lab majority	12,972	22.11	
Electorate	87,282		
Turnout	58,669	67.22	

Lab hold (6.71% from Lib Dem to Lab)

BERWICK-UPON-TWEED

		%	+/-%
Trevelyan, A. Con*	22,145	52.4	11.4
Dickinson, S. Lab	10,364	24.5	9.6
Pörksen, J. Lib Dem	8,916	21.1	-7.8
Stewart, T. Green	787	1.9	-1.8
Con majority	11,781	27.86	
Electorate	58,807		
Turnout	42,291	71.91	

Con hold (0.89% from Lab to Con)

BERWICKSHIRE, ROXBURGH AND SELKIRK

		%	+/-%
Lamont, J. Con	28,213	53.8	17.8
Kerr, C. SNP*	17,153	32.7	-3.9
Davidson, I. Lab/Co-op	4,519	8.6	3.7
Burgess, C. Lib Dem	2,482	4.7	-13.9
Con majority	11,060	21.08	
Electorate	73,191		
Turnout	52,463	71.68	

Con gain (10.84% from SNP to Con)

BETHNAL GREEN AND BOW

		%	+/-%
Ali, R. Lab*	42,969	71.5	10.6
Chirico, C. Con	7,576	12.6	-2.6
Masroor, A. Ind	3,888	6.5	
Dyer, W. Lib Dem	2,982	5.0	0.5
Polson, A. Green	1,516	2.5	-6.7
De Wulverton, I. UKIP	894	1.5	-4.6
Lab majority	35,393	58.89	
Electorate	86,075		
Turnout	60,100	69.82	

Lab hold (6.59% from Con to Lab)

BEVERLEY AND HOLDERNESS

		%	+/-%
Stuart, G. Con*	32,499	58.2	10.2
Boal, J. Lab	18,457	33.1	8.1
Healy, D. Lib Dem	2,808	5.0	-0.5
Walton, L. YP	1,158	2.1	
Howarth, R. Green	716	1.3	-2.1
Con majority	14,042	25.15	
Electorate	80,657		
Turnout	55,826	69.21	

Con hold (1.03% from Lab to Con)

BEXHILL AND BATTLE

		%	+/-%
Merriman, H. Con*	36,854	61.9	7.4
Bayliss, C. Lab	14,689	24.7	10.6
Kemp, J. Lib Dem	4,485	7.5	0.0
Bastin, G. UKIP	2,006	3.4	-14.9
Kent, J. Green	1,438	2.4	-2.7
Con majority	22,165	37.21	
Electorate	81,331		
Turnout	59,574	73.25	

Con hold (1.62% from Con to Lab)

BEXLEYHEATH AND CRAYFORD

		%	+/-%
Evennett, D. Con*	25,113	55.5	8.3
Borella, S. Lab	16,040	35.4	9.3
Ferro, M. UKIP	1,944	4.3	-16.7
Reynolds, S. Lib Dem	1,201	2.6	-0.3
Lobo, I. Green	601	1.3	-0.8
Finch, P. BNP	290	0.6	
Con majority	9,073	20.04	
Electorate	65,315		
Turnout	45,281	69.33	

Con hold (0.48% from Con to Lab)

*Member of last Parliament

BIRKENHEAD

		%	+/-%
Field, F. Lab*	33,558	76.7	9.3
Gardiner, S. Con	8,044	18.4	3.6
Brame, A. Lib Dem	1,118	2.5	-1.0
Clough, J. Green	943	2.1	-2.0
Lab majority	25,514	58.29	
Electorate	64,484		
Turnout	43,771	67.88	

Lab hold (2.85% from Con to Lab)

BIRMINGHAM, EDGBASTON

		%	+/-%
Gill, P. Lab/Co-op	24,124	55.2	10.5
Squire, C. Con	17,207	39.4	1.2
Green, C. Lib Dem	1,564	3.6	0.7
Kiff, A. Green	562	1.3	-2.0
Rodgers, D. Common Good	155	0.4	
Lab/Co-op majority	6,917	15.82	
Electorate	71,476		
Turnout	43,720	61.17	

Lab/Co-op hold (4.65% from Con to Lab/Co-op)

BIRMINGHAM, ERDINGTON

		%	+/-%
Dromey, J. Lab*	21,571	57.8	12.3
Alden, R. Con	14,286	38.3	7.5
Holtom, A. Lib Dem	750	2.0	-0.8
Lovatt, J. Green	610	1.6	-1.1
Lab majority	7,285	19.52	
Electorate	69,158		
Turnout	37,329	53.98	

Lab hold (2.39% from Con to Lab)

BIRMINGHAM, HALL GREEN

		%	+/-%
Godsiff, R. Lab*	42,143	77.3	17.9
Ranger, R. Con	8,199	15.0	-2.6
Evans, J. Lib Dem	3,137	5.8	-5.8
Cox, P. Green	831	1.5	-3.1
Lab majority	33,944	62.29	
Electorate	81,389		
Turnout	54,497	66.96	

Lab hold (10.21% from Con to Lab)

BIRMINGHAM, HODGE HILL

		%	+/-%
Byrne, L. Lab*	37,606	80.8	12.8
Reza, A. Con	6,580	14.1	2.7
Khan, M. UKIP	1,016	2.2	-9.1
Bennion, P. Lib Dem	805	1.7	-4.6
Thomas, C. Green	387	0.8	-1.2
Lab majority	31,026	66.65	
Electorate	79,379		
Turnout	46,553	58.65	

Lab hold (5.05% from Con to Lab)

BIRMINGHAM, LADYWOOD

		%	+/-%
Mahmood, S. Lab*	34,166	82.4	9.3
Browning, A. Con	5,452	13.2	0.5
Dargue, L. Lib Dem	1,156	2.8	-1.0
Dennis, K. Green	533	1.3	-2.9
Lab majority	28,714	69.25	
Electorate	77,499		
Turnout	41,462	53.5	

Lab hold (4.4% from Con to Lab)

BIRMINGHAM, NORTHFIELD

		%	+/-%
Burden, R. Lab*	23,596	53.0	11.5
Powell-Chandler, M. Con	18,929	42.5	6.9
Harmer, R. Lib Dem	959	2.2	-1.0
Masters, E. Green	864	1.9	-0.8
Lab majority	4,667	10.49	
Electorate	73,881		
Turnout	44,499	60.23	

Lab hold (2.3% from Con to Lab)

BIRMINGHAM, PERRY BARR

		%	+/-%
Mahmood, K. Lab*	30,109	67.9	10.8
Hodivala, C. Con	11,726	26.4	5.1
Singh, H. Lib Dem	1,080	2.4	-2.4
Bhatoe, S. SLP	592	1.3	
Rana, V. Green	591	1.3	-1.9
Singh, H. Open Borders	99	0.2	
Lab majority	18,383	41.44	
Electorate	73,980		
Turnout	44,361	59.96	

Lab hold (2.87% from Con to Lab)

BIRMINGHAM, SELLY OAK

		%	+/-%
McCabe, S. Lab*	30,836	62.8	15.3
Shrubsole, S. Con	15,629	31.8	2.9
Radcliffe, D. Lib Dem	1,644	3.4	-2.2
Pritchard, J. Green	876	1.8	-3.3
Lab majority	15,207	30.96	
Electorate	76,440		
Turnout	49,123	64.26	

Lab hold (6.19% from Con to Lab)

BIRMINGHAM, YARDLEY

		%	+/-%
Phillips, J. Lab*	25,398	56.9	15.5
Afzal, M. Con	8,824	19.8	5.8
Hemming, J. Lib Dem	7,984	17.9	-7.6
Clayton, P. UKIP	1,916	4.3	-11.8
Garghan, C. Green	280	0.6	-1.1
Nowshed, A. Ind	100	0.2	
Lab majority	16,574	37.16	
Electorate	75,829		
Turnout	44,605	58.82	

Lab hold (4.82% from Con to Lab)

BISHOP AUCKLAND

		%	+/-%
Goodman, H. Lab*	20,808	48.0	6.7
Adams, C. Con	20,306	46.8	14.4
Morrissey, C. Lib Dem	1,176	2.7	-1.7
Walker, A. BNP	991	2.3	
Lab majority	502	1.16	
Electorate	67,661		
Turnout	43,359	64.08	

Lab hold (3.87% from Lab to Con)

BLACKBURN

		%	+/-%
Hollern, K. Lab*	33,148	69.5	13.6
Eastwood, B. Con	12,780	26.8	-0.3
Miller, D. Ind	878	1.8	
Ahmed, I. Lib Dem	709	1.5	-0.7
Lab majority	20,368	42.7	
Electorate	70,664		
Turnout	47,702	67.51	

Lab hold (6.96% from Con to Lab)

BLACKLEY AND BROUGHTON

		%	+/-%
Stringer, G. Lab*	28,258	70.3	8.7
Goss, D. Con	8,657	21.5	6.6
Power, M. UKIP	1,825	4.5	-11.8
Gadsden, R. Lib Dem	737	1.8	-0.5
Jones, D. Green	462	1.1	-3.0
Ajoku, A. CPA	174	0.4	
Lab majority	19,601	48.74	
Electorate	71,648		
Turnout	40,214	56.13	

Lab hold (1.05% from Con to Lab)

BLACKPOOL NORTH AND CLEVELEYS

		%	+/-%
Maynard, P. Con*	20,255	49.3	5.1
Webb, C. Lab	18,232	44.4	8.6
White, P. UKIP	1,392	3.4	-11.3
Close, S. Lib Dem	747	1.8	-0.6
Royle, D. Green	381	0.9	-1.3
Con majority	2,023	4.93	
Electorate	63,967		
Turnout	41,066	64.2	

Con hold (1.76% from Con to Lab)

BLACKPOOL SOUTH

		%	+/-%
Marsden, G. Lab*	17,581	50.2	8.7
Anthony, P. Con	15,058	43.0	9.4
Matthews, N. UKIP	1,339	3.8	-13.4
Greene, B. Lib Dem	634	1.8	-0.5
Warnock, J. Green	341	1.0	-1.6
Lab majority	2,523	7.21	
Electorate	58,470		
Turnout	34,997	59.85	

Lab hold (0.36% from Lab to Con)

BLAENAU GWENT

		%	+/-%
Smith, N. Lab*	18,787	58.0	0.1
Copner, N. PlC	6,880	21.2	12.3
West, T. Con	4,783	14.8	4.0
May, D. UKIP	973	3.0	-14.9
Browning, V. Ind	666	2.0	
Sullivan, C. Lib Dem	295	0.9	-1.0
Lab majority	11,907	36.73	
Electorate	51,227		
Turnout	32,419	63.28	

Lab hold (6.09% from Lab to PlC)

*Member of last Parliament

BLAYDON

		%	+/-%
Twist, L. Lab	26,979	56.0	7.0
Smith, T. Con	13,502	28.0	10.6
Wallace, J. Lib Dem	4,366	9.1	-3.1
Tolley, R. UKIP	2,459	5.1	-12.4
McNally, P. Green	583	1.2	-2.5
Marchetti, M. Libertarian	114	0.2	
Marschild, L. Space Navies	81	0.2	
Lab majority	13,477	27.99	
Electorate	68,459		
Turnout	48,148	70.33	

Lab hold (1.83% from Lab to Con)

BLYTH VALLEY

		%	+/-%
Campbell, R. Lab*	23,770	55.9	9.6
Levy, I. Con	15,855	37.3	15.6
Reid, J. Lib Dem	1,947	4.6	-1.3
Furness, D. Green	918	2.2	-1.6
Lab majority	7,915	18.6	
Electorate	63,415		
Turnout	42,560	67.11	

Lab hold (3% from Lab to Con)

BOGNOR REGIS AND LITTLEHAMPTON

		%	+/-%
Gibb, N. Con*	30,276	58.9	7.8
Butcher, A. Lab	12,782	24.8	11.1
Oppler, F. Lib Dem	3,352	6.5	-2.4
Sanderson, P. Ind	2,088	4.1	
Lowe, P. UKIP	1,861	3.6	-18.0
Bishop, A. Green	993	1.9	-2.2
Con majority	17,494	34	
Electorate	75,827		
Turnout	51,450	67.85	

Con hold (1.67% from Con to Lab)

BOLSOVER

		%	+/-%
Skinner, D. Lab*	24,153	51.9	0.9
Harrison, H. Con	18,865	40.5	16.2
Rose, P. UKIP	2,129	4.6	-16.3
Shipman, R. Lib Dem	1,372	3.0	-0.4
Lab majority	5,288	11.34	
Electorate	73,429		
Turnout	46,626	63.5	

Lab hold (7.64% from Lab to Con)

BOLTON NORTH EAST

		%	+/-%
Crausby, D. Lab*	22,870	50.5	7.7
Daly, J. Con	19,073	42.1	9.4
Lamb, H. UKIP	1,567	3.5	-15.3
Fox, W. Lib Dem	1,316	2.9	0.1
Spencer, L. Green	357	0.8	-1.8
Lab majority	3,797	8.39	
Electorate	67,233		
Turnout	45,273	67.34	

Lab hold (0.86% from Lab to Con)

BOLTON SOUTH EAST

		%	+/-%
Qureshi, Y. Lab*	25,676	60.5	10.2
Pochin, S. Con	12,550	29.6	9.3
Armstrong, J. UKIP	2,779	6.5	-17.0
Harasiwka, F. Lib Dem	781	1.8	-0.8
Johnson, A. Green	537	1.3	-1.7
Lab majority	13,126	30.94	
Electorate	68,886		
Turnout	42,420	61.58	

Lab hold (0.47% from Con to Lab)

BOLTON WEST

		%	+/-%
Green, C. Con*	24,459	47.8	7.4
Hilling, J. Lab	23,523	46.0	7.2
Tighe, M. UKIP	1,587	3.1	-12.1
Forrest, R. Lib Dem	1,485	2.9	-1.1
Con majority	936	1.83	
Electorate	72,797		
Turnout	51,135	70.24	

Con hold (0.09% from Lab to Con)

BOOTLE

		%	+/-%
Dowd, P. Lab*	42,259	83.8	9.6
Fifield, C. Con	6,059	12.0	4.0
Newman, D. Lib Dem	837	1.7	-0.5
Gibbon, A. Green	709	1.4	-1.9
Bryan, K. SLP	424	0.8	
Lab majority	36,200	71.75	
Electorate	72,872		
Turnout	50,451	69.23	

Lab hold (2.79% from Con to Lab)

BOSTON AND SKEGNESS

		%	+/-%
Warman, M. Con*	27,271	63.6	20.0
Kenny, P. Lab	10,699	24.9	8.5
Nuttall, P. UKIP	3,308	7.7	-25.9
Smith, P. Lib Dem	771	1.8	-0.5
Percival, V. Green	547	1.3	-0.6
Gilbert, M. Blue Rev	283	0.7	
Con majority	16,572	38.57	
Electorate	68,402		
Turnout	42,971	62.82	

Con hold (5.72% from Lab to Con)

BOSWORTH

		%	+/-%
Tredinnick, D. Con*	31,864	56.6	13.9
Kealey, C. Lab	13,513	24.0	6.6
Mullaney, M. Lib Dem	9,744	17.3	-4.9
Gregg, M. Green	1,047	1.9	
Con majority	18,351	32.58	
Electorate	80,620		
Turnout	56,323	69.86	

Con hold (3.66% from Lab to Con)

BOURNEMOUTH EAST

		%	+/-%
Ellwood, T. Con*	25,221	51.8	2.7
Semple, M. Lab	17,284	35.5	18.9
Nicholas, J. Lib Dem	3,168	6.5	-1.8
Hughes, D. UKIP	1,405	2.9	-13.6
Keddie, A. Green	1,236	2.5	-4.7
Wilson, K. Ind	304	0.6	
Con majority	7,937	16.29	
Electorate	74,591		
Turnout	48,733	65.33	

Con hold (8.1% from Con to Lab)

BOURNEMOUTH WEST

		%	+/-%
Burns, C. Con*	23,812	53.3	5.3
Stokes, D. Lab	16,101	36.1	18.5
Dunn, P. Lib Dem	2,929	6.6	-1.3
Bull, S. Green	1,247	2.8	-4.6
Halsey, J. Pirate	418	0.9	
Con majority	7,711	17.27	
Electorate	73,195		
Turnout	44,654	61.01	

Con hold (6.58% from Con to Lab)

BRACKNELL

		%	+/-%
Lee, P. Con*	32,882	58.7	3.1
Bidwell, P. Lab	16,866	30.1	13.3
Smith, P. Lib Dem	4,186	7.5	
Amos, L. UKIP	1,521	2.7	-12.9
Barreto, O. Ind	437	0.8	
Con majority	16,016	28.58	
Electorate	79,199		
Turnout	56,038	70.76	

Con hold (5.08% from Con to Lab)

BRADFORD EAST

		%	+/-%
Hussain, I. Lab*	29,831	65.3	18.9
Trafford, M. Con	9,291	20.3	9.1
Ward, D. Ind	3,576	7.8	
Barras, J. UKIP	1,372	3.0	-6.9
Jewell, M. Lib Dem	843	1.8	-27.5
Parkins, P. BFB	420	0.9	
Stanford, A. Green	289	0.6	-1.5
Lab majority	20,540	44.95	
Electorate	70,389		
Turnout	45,700	64.92	

Lab hold (4.9% from Con to Lab)

BRADFORD SOUTH

		%	+/-%
Cummins, J. Lab*	22,364	54.4	11.1
Graham, T. Con	15,664	38.1	11.9
Place, S. UKIP	1,758	4.3	-19.7
Thomas, S. Lib Dem	516	1.3	-1.6
Hirst, T. Eng Dem	377	0.9	
Parkinson, D. Green	370	0.9	-2.4
Lab majority	6,700	16.3	
Electorate	67,752		
Turnout	41,111	60.68	

Lab hold (0.4% from Lab to Con)

General Election 2017

BRADFORD WEST

		%	+/-%
Shah, N. Lab*	29,444	64.4	15.1
Grant, G. Con	7,542	16.5	1.3
Yaqoob, S. Ind	6,345	13.9	
Hodgson, D. UKIP	885	1.9	-5.8
Griffiths, A. Lib Dem	712	1.6	-1.3
Hickson, C. Green	481	1.1	-1.6
Hussain, K. Ind	65	0.1	
Hijazi, M. Ind	54	0.1	
Lab majority	21,902	47.87	
Electorate	67,568		
Turnout	45,749	67.71	

Lab hold (6.89% from Con to Lab)

BRAINTREE

		%	+/-%
Cleverly, J. Con*	32,873	62.7	9.1
Fincken, M. Lab	14,451	27.6	9.2
Turner, P. Lib Dem	2,251	4.3	-0.6
Bingley, R. UKIP	1,835	3.5	-15.2
Pashby, T. Green	916	1.8	-1.4
Con majority	18,422	35.16	
Electorate	75,316		
Turnout	52,400	69.57	

Con hold (0.03% from Con to Lab)

BRECON AND RADNORSHIRE

		%	+/-%
Davies, C. Con*	20,081	48.5	7.5
Gibson-Watt, J. Lib Dem	12,043	29.1	0.8
Lodge, D. Lab	7,335	17.7	3.0
Heneghan, K. PlC	1,299	3.1	-1.3
Gilbert, P. UKIP	576	1.4	-6.9
Con majority	8,038	19.42	
Electorate	56,010		
Turnout	41,397	73.91	

Con hold (3.36% from Lib Dem to Con)

BRENT CENTRAL

		%	+/-%
Butler, D. Lab*	38,208	72.8	11.0
Bhansali, R. Con	10,211	19.4	-0.8
Georgiou, A. Lib Dem	2,519	4.8	-3.5
Lish, S. Green	802	1.5	-2.5
North, J. UKIP	556	1.1	-2.8
Lab majority	27,997	53.33	
Electorate	80,499		
Turnout	52,495	65.21	

Lab hold (5.89% from Con to Lab)

BRENT NORTH

		%	+/-%
Gardiner, B. Lab*	35,496	62.7	8.7
Jogia, A. Con	18,435	32.5	-0.8
Lorber, P. Lib Dem	1,614	2.9	-2.1
Lichten, M. Green	660	1.2	-1.8
Jeffers, E. Ind	239	0.4	0.0
Lab majority	17,061	30.12	
Electorate	82,567		
Turnout	56,647	68.61	

Lab hold (4.75% from Con to Lab)

*Member of last Parliament

BRENTFORD AND ISLEWORTH

		%	+/-%
Cadbury, R. Lab*	35,364	57.2	13.6
Macleod, M. Con	23,182	37.5	-5.3
Bourke, J. Lib Dem	3,083	5.0	1.0
Lab majority	12,182	19.72	
Electorate	85,164		
Turnout	61,785	72.55	

Lab hold (9.46% from Con to Lab)

BRENTWOOD AND ONGAR

		%	+/-%
Burghart, A. Con	34,811	65.7	7.0
Barrett, G. Lab	10,809	20.4	7.9
Chilvers, K. Lib Dem	4,426	8.3	-0.4
McGough, M. UKIP	1,845	3.5	-13.3
Jeater, P. Green	915	1.7	-0.9
Kousoulou, L. Ind	104	0.2	
Con majority	24,002	45.27	
Electorate	75,067		
Turnout	53,017	70.63	

Con hold (0.47% from Con to Lab)

BRIDGEND

		%	+/-%
Moon, M. Lab*	21,913	42.5	5.5
Robson, K. Con	17,213	33.4	1.3
Watkins, R. PlC	1,783	3.5	-3.6
Pratt, J. Lib Dem	919	1.8	-2.4
Williams, A. UKIP	781	1.5	-13.4
Robson, I. Ind	646	1.3	
Lab majority	4,700	10.85	
Electorate	62,185		
Turnout	43,310	69.65	

Lab hold (2.12% from Con to Lab)

BRIDGWATER AND WEST SOMERSET

		%	+/-%
Liddell-Grainger, I. Con*	32,111	55.0	9.2
Hinckes, W. Lab	16,663	28.5	11.0
Kravis, M. Lib Dem	6,332	10.8	-1.5
Smedley, S. UKIP	2,102	3.6	-15.5
Powell, K. Green	1,059	1.8	-3.0
Con majority	15,448	26.45	
Electorate	89,294		
Turnout	58,397	65.4	

Con hold (0.89% from Con to Lab)

BRIGG AND GOOLE

		%	+/-%
Percy, A. Con*	27,219	60.3	7.5
Smith, T. Lab	14,856	32.9	5.8
Jeffreys, D. UKIP	1,596	3.5	-11.9
Lonsdale, J. Lib Dem	836	1.9	0.1
Pires, I. Green	550	1.2	-0.9
Con majority	12,363	27.4	
Electorate	66,069		
Turnout	45,117	68.29	

Con hold (0.84% from Lab to Con)

General Election 2017

BRIGHTON KEMPTOWN

		%	+/-%
Russell-Moyle, L. Lab/Co-op	28,703	58.1	19.1
Kirby, S. Con*	18,835	38.2	-2.4
Tester, E. Lib Dem	1,457	3.0	-0.1
Haze, D. Ind	212	0.4	
Lab/Co-op majority	9,868	19.99	
Electorate	67,893		
Turnout	49,361	72.7	

Lab/Co-op gain (10.76% from Con to Lab/Co-op)

BRIGHTON PAVILION

		%	+/-%
Lucas, C. Green*	30,149	52.1	10.4
Curtis, S. Lab	15,450	26.7	-0.5
Warman, E. Con	11,082	19.2	-3.5
Buchanan, I. UKIP	630	1.1	-3.9
Yeomans, N. Ind	376	0.7	0.4
Green majority	14,699	25.41	
Electorate	75,486		
Turnout	57,841	76.62	

Green hold (5.45% from Lab to Green)

BRISTOL EAST

		%	+/-%
McCarthy, K. Lab*	30,847	60.6	21.4
Clarke, T. Con	17,453	34.3	3.7
Lucas, C. Lib Dem	1,389	2.7	-3.1
Francis, L. Green	1,110	2.2	-6.1
Lab majority	13,394	26.3	
Electorate	72,415		
Turnout	50,932	70.33	

Lab hold (8.86% from Con to Lab)

BRISTOL NORTH WEST

		%	+/-%
Jones, D. Lab	27,400	50.5	16.2
Leslie, C. Con*	22,639	41.8	-2.1
Downie, C. Lib Dem	2,814	5.2	-1.0
Bousa, S. Green	1,243	2.3	-3.4
Lab majority	4,761	8.78	
Electorate	75,434		
Turnout	54,228	71.89	

Lab gain (9.16% from Con to Lab)

BRISTOL SOUTH

		%	+/-%
Smyth, K. Lab*	32,666	59.9	21.7
Weston, M. Con	16,679	30.6	6.3
Nutland, B. Lib Dem	1,821	3.3	-5.3
Kealey, I. UKIP	1,672	3.1	-13.4
Dyer, T. Green	1,428	2.6	-8.9
Langley, J. Ind	116	0.2	
Lab majority	15,987	29.34	
Electorate	83,012		
Turnout	54,494	65.65	

Lab hold (7.68% from Con to Lab)

BRISTOL WEST

		%	+/-%
Debbonaire, T. Lab*	47,213	65.8	30.2
Tall, A. Con	9,877	13.8	-1.4
Scott Cato, M. Green	9,216	12.8	-13.9
Williams, S. Lib Dem	5,201	7.3	-11.5
Rodgers, J. Money Free	101	0.1	
Lab majority	37,336	52.01	
Electorate	93,003		
Turnout	71,782	77.18	

Lab hold (15.8% from Con to Lab)

BROADLAND

		%	+/-%
Simpson, K. Con*	32,406	57.8	7.5
Simpson, I. Lab	16,590	29.6	10.9
Riley, S. Lib Dem	4,449	7.9	-1.8
Moreland, D. UKIP	1,594	2.8	-13.8
Boswell, A. Green	932	1.7	-2.6
Con majority	15,816	28.21	
Electorate	77,334		
Turnout	56,075	72.51	

Con hold (1.7% from Con to Lab)

BROMLEY AND CHISLEHURST

		%	+/-%
Neill, R. Con*	25,175	53.8	1.0
Hyde, S. Lab	15,585	33.3	11.2
Webber, S. Lib Dem	3,369	7.2	0.8
Jenner, E. UKIP	1,383	3.0	-11.3
Robertson, R. Green	1,150	2.5	-1.7
Con majority	9,590	20.5	
Electorate	65,117		
Turnout	46,781	71.84	

Con hold (5.1% from Con to Lab)

BROMSGROVE

		%	+/-%
Javid, S. Con*	33,493	61.7	8.1
Thompson, M. Lab	16,920	31.2	9.1
Lewis, N. Lib Dem	2,488	4.6	-0.4
Esposito, S. Green	1,139	2.1	-1.2
Con majority	16,573	30.55	
Electorate	73,571		
Turnout	54,246	73.73	

Con hold (0.49% from Con to Lab)

BROXBOURNE

		%	+/-%
Walker, C. Con*	29,515	62.0	6.1
Norgrove, S. Lab	13,723	28.8	10.5
Faulkner, T. UKIP	1,918	4.0	-15.6
Graham, A. Lib Dem	1,481	3.1	-0.1
Evans, T. Green	848	1.8	-0.9
Con majority	15,792	33.19	
Electorate	73,502		
Turnout	47,587	64.74	

Con hold (2.19% from Con to Lab)

BROXTOWE

		%	+/-%
Soubry, A. Con*	25,983	46.8	1.8
Marshall, G. Lab	25,120	45.3	8.2
Hallam, T. Lib Dem	2,247	4.0	0.1
Loi, F. UKIP	1,477	2.7	-7.9
Morton, P. Green	681	1.2	-1.6
Con majority	863	1.55	
Electorate	74,013		
Turnout	55,628	75.16	

Con hold (3.22% from Con to Lab)

BUCKINGHAM

		%	+/-%
Bercow, J. Speaker*	34,299	62.8	-0.2
Sheppard, M. Green	8,574	15.7	2.2
Raven, S. Ind	5,638	10.3	
Mapletoft, B. UKIP	4,168	7.6	-13.6
Speaker majority	25,725	47.08	
Electorate	79,615		
Turnout	54,646	68.64	

Speaker hold (1.21% from Speaker to Green)

BURNLEY

		%	+/-%
Cooper, J. Lab*	18,832	46.7	9.2
White, P. Con	12,479	30.9	17.5
Birtwistle, G. Lib Dem	6,046	15.0	-14.4
Commis, T. UKIP	2,472	6.1	-11.1
Fisk, L. Green	461	1.1	-1.0
Lab majority	6,353	15.74	
Electorate	64,709		
Turnout	40,353	62.36	

Lab hold (4.13% from Lab to Con)

BURTON

		%	+/-%
Griffiths, A. Con*	28,936	57.8	8.2
McKiernan, J. Lab	18,889	37.7	10.3
Hardwick, D. Lib Dem	1,262	2.5	0.0
Hales, S. Green	824	1.6	-0.8
Con majority	10,047	20.07	
Electorate	73,960		
Turnout	50,054	67.68	

Con hold (1.05% from Con to Lab)

BURY NORTH

		%	+/-%
Frith, J. Lab	25,683	53.4	12.5
Nuttall, D. Con*	21,308	44.3	2.6
Baum, R. Lib Dem	912	1.9	-0.2
Lab majority	4,375	9.1	
Electorate	67,580		
Turnout	48,059	71.11	

Lab gain (4.97% from Con to Lab)

*Member of last Parliament

BURY SOUTH

		%	+/-%
Lewis, I. Lab*	27,165	53.1	8.3
Largan, R. Con	21,200	41.5	7.0
Henderson, I. UKIP	1,316	2.6	-10.7
Page, A. Lib Dem	1,065	2.1	-1.5
Wright, P. Ind	244	0.5	
Lab majority	5,965	11.67	
Electorate	73,715		
Turnout	51,113	69.34	

Lab hold (0.65% from Con to Lab)

BURY ST EDMUNDS

		%	+/-%
Churchill, J. Con*	36,794	59.0	5.7
Edwards, B. Lab	18,353	29.4	11.8
Korfanty, H. Lib Dem	3,565	5.7	-0.3
Geake, H. Green	2,596	4.2	-3.7
Byrne, L. Ind	852	1.4	
Con majority	18,441	29.59	
Electorate	86,071		
Turnout	62,312	72.4	

Con hold (3.08% from Con to Lab)

CAERPHILLY

		%	+/-%
David, W. Lab*	22,491	54.4	10.1
Pratt, J. Con	10,413	25.2	8.6
Whittle, L. PlC	5,962	14.4	-0.2
Wilks, L. UKIP	1,259	3.0	-16.3
David, K. Lib Dem	725	1.8	-0.6
Creak, A. Green	447	1.1	-1.2
Lab majority	12,078	29.19	
Electorate	64,381		
Turnout	41,380	64.27	

Lab hold (0.75% from Con to Lab)

CAITHNESS, SUTHERLAND AND EASTER ROSS

		%	+/-%
Stone, J. Lib Dem	11,061	35.8	0.7
Monaghan, P. SNP*	9,017	29.1	-17.1
Mackie, S. Con	6,990	22.6	15.8
Bell, O. Lab	3,833	12.4	3.5
Lib Dem majority	2,044	6.61	
Electorate	46,868		
Turnout	30,936	66.01	

Lib Dem gain (8.92% from SNP to Lib Dem)

CALDER VALLEY

		%	+/-%
Whittaker, C. Con*	26,790	46.1	2.6
Fenton-Glynn, J. Lab	26,181	45.0	9.8
Battye, J. Lib Dem	1,952	3.4	-1.6
Rogan, P. UKIP	1,466	2.5	-8.6
Holden, R. Ind	1,034	1.8	
Turner, K. Green	631	1.1	-2.8
Con majority	609	1.05	
Electorate	79,045		
Turnout	58,169	73.59	

Con hold (3.59% from Con to Lab)

CAMBERWELL AND PECKHAM

		%	+/-%
Harman, H. Lab*	44,665	77.5	14.5
Spencer, B. Con	7,349	12.8	-0.4
Bukola, M. Lib Dem	3,413	5.9	0.9
Margolies, E. Green	1,627	2.8	-7.2
Towey, R. CPA	227	0.4	
Sellu, A. WRP	131	0.2	0.0
Lab majority	37,316	64.73	
Electorate	85,613		
Turnout	57,648	67.34	

Lab hold (7.43% from Con to Lab)

CAMBORNE AND REDRUTH

		%	+/-%
Eustice, G. Con*	23,001	47.4	7.2
Winter, G. Lab	21,424	44.1	19.2
Williams, G. Lib Dem	2,979	6.1	-6.2
Garbett, G. Green	1,052	2.2	-3.5
Con majority	1,577	3.25	
Electorate	68,419		
Turnout	48,549	70.96	

Con hold (6% from Con to Lab)

CAMBRIDGE

		%	+/-%
Zeichner, D. Lab*	29,032	51.8	15.9
Huppert, J. Lib Dem	16,371	29.2	-5.5
Hayward, J. Con	9,133	16.3	0.7
Tuckwood, S. Green	1,265	2.3	-5.7
Garrett, K. Reboot	133	0.2	-0.1
Lab majority	12,661	22.58	
Electorate	78,544		
Turnout	56,069	71.39	

Lab hold (10.71% from Lib Dem to Lab)

NORTH EAST CAMBRIDGESHIRE

		%	+/-%
Barclay, S. Con*	34,340	64.3	9.5
Rustidge, K. Lab	13,070	24.5	10.1
Fower, D. Lib Dem	2,383	4.5	0.0
Talbot, R. UKIP	2,174	4.1	-18.3
Johnson, R. Green	1,024	1.9	-1.6
Goldspink, S. Eng Dem	293	0.6	
Con majority	21,270	39.86	
Electorate	84,413		
Turnout	53,365	63.22	

Con hold (0.31% from Con to Lab)

NORTH WEST CAMBRIDGESHIRE

		%	+/-%
Vara, S. Con*	37,529	58.5	6.2
Ramsbottom, I. Lab	19,521	30.4	12.6
Smith, B. Lib Dem	3,168	4.9	-0.7
Whitby, J. UKIP	2,518	3.9	-16.1
Guthrie, G. Green	1,255	2.0	-1.6
Con majority	18,008	28.08	
Electorate	93,221		
Turnout	64,123	68.79	

Con hold (3.21% from Con to Lab)

SOUTH CAMBRIDGESHIRE

		%	+/-%
Allen, H. Con*	33,631	51.7	0.8
Greef, D. Lab	17,679	27.2	9.6
Van De Ven, S. Lib Dem	12,102	18.6	3.4
Saggers, S. Green	1,512	2.3	-3.9
Con majority	15,952	24.51	
Electorate	85,257		
Turnout	65,090	76.35	

Con hold (4.41% from Con to Lab)

SOUTH EAST CAMBRIDGESHIRE

		%	+/-%
Frazer, L. Con*	33,601	53.1	4.8
Jones, H. Lab	17,443	27.6	12.5
Nethsingha, L. Lib Dem	11,958	18.9	-1.2
Con majority	16,158	25.56	
Electorate	86,121		
Turnout	63,228	73.42	

Con hold (3.84% from Con to Lab)

CANNOCK CHASE

		%	+/-%
Milling, A. Con*	26,318	54.9	10.9
Dadge, P. Lab	17,927	37.4	3.8
Allen, P. UKIP	2,018	4.2	-13.2
Woodhead, P. Green	815	1.7	-0.2
Green, N. Lib Dem	794	1.7	-1.0
Con majority	8,391	17.5	
Electorate	74,540		
Turnout	47,950	64.33	

Con hold (3.54% from Lab to Con)

CANTERBURY

		%	+/-%
Duffield, R. Lab	25,572	44.9	20.4
Brazier, J. Con*	25,385	44.5	1.8
Flanagan, J. Lib Dem	4,561	8.0	-3.6
Stanton, H. Green	1,282	2.3	-4.7
Lab majority	187	0.33	
Electorate	78,182		
Turnout	56,978	72.88	

Lab gain (9.3% from Con to Lab)

CARDIFF CENTRAL

		%	+/-%
Stevens, J. Lab*	25,193	62.3	22.4
Stafford, G. Con	7,997	19.8	5.1
Parrott, E. Lib Dem	5,415	13.4	-13.6
Hooper, M. PlC	999	2.5	-2.5
Smith, B. Green	420	1.0	-5.3
Sarul-Islam, M. UKIP	343	0.9	-5.6
Lab majority	17,196	42.51	
Electorate	59,288		
Turnout	40,447	68.22	

Lab hold (8.64% from Con to Lab)

CARDIFF NORTH

		%	+/-%
McMorrin, A. Lab	26,081	50.0	11.8
Williams, C. Con*	21,907	42.0	-0.3
Webb, S. PlC	1,738	3.3	-1.2
Hemsley, M. Lib Dem	1,714	3.3	-0.5
Oldfield, G. UKIP	582	1.1	-6.6
Lab majority	4,174	8.01	
Electorate	67,221		
Turnout	52,120	77.54	

Lab gain (6.09% from Con to Lab)

CARDIFF SOUTH AND PENARTH

		%	+/-%
Doughty, S. Lab/Co-op*	30,182	59.4	16.7
Rees, B. Con	15,318	30.1	3.4
Titherington, I. PlC	2,162	4.3	-3.1
Sands, E. Lib Dem	1,430	2.8	-2.1
Bevan, A. UKIP	942	1.9	-11.9
Slaughter, A. Green	532	1.1	-2.7
Hedges, J. Pirate	170	0.3	
Lab/Co-op majority	14,864	29.24	
Electorate	76,499		
Turnout	50,843	66.46	

Lab/Co-op hold (6.65% from Con to Lab/Co-op)

CARDIFF WEST

		%	+/-%
Brennan, K. Lab*	26,425	56.6	16.0
Smith, M. Con	13,874	29.7	4.6
Deem, M. PlC	4,418	9.5	-4.4
Meredith, A. Lib Dem	1,214	2.6	-2.1
Lewis, R. UKIP	698	1.5	-9.7
Lab majority	12,551	26.87	
Electorate	66,775		
Turnout	46,718	69.96	

Lab hold (5.7% from Con to Lab)

CARLISLE

		%	+/-%
Stevenson, J. Con*	21,472	49.8	5.6
Alcroft, R. Lab	18,873	43.7	6.0
Mills, F. UKIP	1,455	3.4	-9.0
Thornton, P. Lib Dem	1,256	2.9	0.4
Con majority	2,599	6.02	
Electorate	62,294		
Turnout	43,144	69.26	

Con hold (0.23% from Con to Lab)

CARMARTHEN EAST AND DINEFWR

		%	+/-%
Edwards, J. PlC*	16,127	39.3	0.9
Darkin, D. Lab	12,219	29.8	5.6
Hughes, H. Con	10,778	26.2	5.1
Hamilton, N. UKIP	985	2.4	-8.7
Prosser, L. Lib Dem	920	2.2	-0.1
PlC majority	3,908	9.51	
Electorate	56,720		
Turnout	41,074	72.42	

PlC hold (2.34% from PlC to Lab)

CARMARTHEN WEST AND SOUTH PEMBROKESHIRE

		%	+/-%
Hart, S. Con*	19,771	46.8	3.1
Tierney, M. Lab	16,661	39.4	10.8
Thomas, A. PlC	3,933	9.3	-1.1
Cameron, A. Lib Dem	956	2.3	-0.1
Edwards, P. UKIP	905	2.1	-9.5
Con majority	3,110	7.35	
Electorate	58,565		
Turnout	42,291	72.21	

Con hold (3.82% from Con to Lab)

CARSHALTON AND WALLINGTON

		%	+/-%
Brake, T. Lib Dem*	20,819	40.9	6.2
Maxwell Scott, M. Con	19,450	38.3	6.6
Ibrahim, E. Lab	9,360	18.4	3.4
Khan, S. Green	501	1.0	-2.1
Mattey, N. Ind	434	0.9	
Dickenson, A. CPA	189	0.4	
Lib Dem majority	1,369	2.69	
Electorate	70,849		
Turnout	50,850	71.77	

Lib Dem hold (0.24% from Lib Dem to Con)

CASTLE POINT

		%	+/-%
Harris, R. Con*	30,076	67.1	16.4
Cooke, J. Lab	11,204	25.0	11.2
Kurten, D. UKIP	2,381	5.3	-25.8
Holder, T. Lib Dem	1,049	2.3	0.6
Con majority	18,872	42.13	
Electorate	69,470		
Turnout	44,797	64.48	

Con hold (2.6% from Lab to Con)

CENTRAL AYRSHIRE – see under Ayrshire

CENTRAL DEVON – see under Devon

CENTRAL SUFFOLK AND NORTH IPSWICH – see under Suffolk

CEREDIGION

		%	+/-%
Lake, B. PlC	11,623	29.2	1.6
Williams, M. Lib Dem*	11,519	28.9	-6.8
Mulholland, D. Lab	8,017	20.1	10.5
Davis, R. Con	7,307	18.4	7.4
Harrison, T. UKIP	602	1.5	-8.7
Ham, G. Green	542	1.4	-4.2
The Crazed, S. Loony	157	0.4	
PlC majority	104	0.26	
Electorate	54,262		
Turnout	39,819	73.38	

PlC gain (4.22% from Lib Dem to PlC)

*Member of last Parliament

General Election 2017

CHARNWOOD

		%	+/-%
Argar, E. Con*	33,318	62.7	8.6
Kelly-Walsh, S. Lab	16,977	32.0	10.1
Sansome, S. Lib Dem	2,052	3.9	-3.0
Connor, V. UKIP	1,471	2.8	-13.1
Cox, N. Green	1,036	2.0	
Denham, S. BNP	322	0.6	-0.3
Con majority	16,341	29.55	
Electorate	78,071		
Turnout	55,291	70.82	

Con hold (0.76% from Con to Lab)

CHATHAM AND AYLESFORD

		%	+/-%
Crouch, T. Con*	25,587	56.9	6.9
Maple, V. Lab	15,129	33.6	10.2
Bushill, N. UKIP	2,225	5.0	-14.9
Quinton, T. Lib Dem	1,116	2.5	-0.7
Hyde, B. Green	573	1.3	-1.3
Gibson, J. CPA	260	0.6	0.3
Con majority	10,458	23.26	
Electorate	70,419		
Turnout	44,963	63.85	

Con hold (1.62% from Con to Lab)

CHEADLE

		%	+/-%
Robinson, M. Con*	24,331	44.5	1.5
Hunter, M. Lib Dem	19,824	36.3	5.4
Miller, M. Lab	10,417	19.1	2.8
Con majority	4,507	8.24	
Electorate	73,406		
Turnout	54,689	74.5	

Con hold (1.94% from Con to Lib Dem)

CHELMSFORD

		%	+/-%
Ford, V. Con	30,525	53.6	2.2
Vince, C. Lab	16,953	29.8	12.2
Robinson, S. Lib Dem	6,916	12.1	0.3
Carter, N. UKIP	1,645	2.9	-11.3
Hossain, R. Green	821	1.4	-2.1
Con majority	13,572	23.83	
Electorate	83,661		
Turnout	56,963	68.09	

Con hold (4.98% from Con to Lab)

CHELSEA AND FULHAM

		%	+/-%
Hands, G. Con*	22,179	52.5	-10.3
De'Ath, A. Lab	13,991	33.1	10.1
Rowntree, L. Lib Dem	4,627	10.9	5.8
Cashmore, B. Green	807	1.9	-1.7
Seton-Marsden, A. UKIP	524	1.2	-3.8
Con majority	8,188	19.38	
Electorate	63,728		
Turnout	42,254	66.3	

Con hold (10.16% from Con to Lab)

CHELTENHAM

		%	+/-%
Chalk, A. Con*	26,615	46.6	0.6
Horwood, M. Lib Dem	24,046	42.1	8.2
White, K. Lab	5,408	9.5	2.2
Van Coevorden, A. Green	943	1.6	-3.3
Con majority	2,569	4.5	
Electorate	78,878		
Turnout	57,119	72.41	

Con hold (3.8% from Con to Lib Dem)

CHESHAM AND AMERSHAM

		%	+/-%
Gillan, C. Con*	33,514	60.5	1.7
Dluzewska, N. Lab	11,374	20.5	7.9
Jones, P. Lib Dem	7,179	13.0	4.0
Booth, A. Green	1,660	3.0	-2.5
Meacock, D. UKIP	1,525	2.8	-10.9
Con majority	22,140	39.97	
Electorate	71,654		
Turnout	55,388	77.3	

Con hold (3.07% from Con to Lab)

CITY OF CHESTER

		%	+/-%
Matheson, C. Lab*	32,023	56.6	13.6
Gallagher, W. Con	22,847	40.4	-2.5
Jewkes, L. Lib Dem	1,551	2.7	-2.8
Lab majority	9,176	16.22	
Electorate	72,859		
Turnout	56,565	77.64	

Lab hold (8.02% from Con to Lab)

CHESTERFIELD

		%	+/-%
Perkins, T. Lab*	26,266	54.7	7.0
Pitfield, S. Con	16,661	34.7	16.7
Snowdon, T. Lib Dem	2,612	5.4	-8.3
Bent, S. UKIP	1,611	3.4	-13.1
Wadsworth, D. Green	777	1.6	-1.3
Lab majority	9,605	20.01	
Electorate	80,220		
Turnout	47,993	59.83	

Lab hold (4.86% from Lab to Con)

CHICHESTER

		%	+/-%
Keegan, G. Con	36,032	60.0	2.5
Farwell, M. Lab	13,411	22.3	10.2
Brown, J. Lib Dem	6,749	11.2	2.8
Barrie, H. Green	1,992	3.3	-3.2
Moncreiff, A. UKIP	1,650	2.8	-12.1
Emerson, A. Patria	84	0.1	0.0
Con majority	22,621	37.67	
Electorate	84,991		
Turnout	60,047	70.65	

Con hold (3.85% from Con to Lab)

CHINGFORD AND WOODFORD GREEN

		%	+/-%
Duncan Smith, I. Con*	23,076	49.0	1.2
Mahmood, B. Lab	20,638	43.8	15.1
Unger, D. Lib Dem	2,043	4.3	-1.1
King, S. Green	1,204	2.5	-1.7
Con majority	2,438	5.17	
Electorate	65,958		
Turnout	47,131	71.46	

Con hold (6.96% from Con to Lab)

CHIPPENHAM

		%	+/-%
Donelan, M. Con*	31,267	54.5	7.0
Belcher, H. Lib Dem	14,637	25.5	-3.8
Newman, A. Lab	11,236	19.6	11.4
Con majority	16,630	29	
Electorate	76,431		
Turnout	57,350	75.03	

Con hold (5.43% from Lib Dem to Con)

CHIPPING BARNET

		%	+/-%
Villiers, T. Con*	25,679	46.2	-2.3
Whysall, E. Lab	25,326	45.5	11.5
Ray, M. Lib Dem	3,012	5.4	0.9
Fletcher, P. Green	1,406	2.5	-2.2
Con majority	353	0.63	
Electorate	77,218		
Turnout	55,627	72.04	

Con hold (6.89% from Con to Lab)

CHORLEY

		%	+/-%
Hoyle, L. Lab*	30,745	55.1	10.1
Moon, C. Con	23,233	41.7	5.4
Fenn, S. Lib Dem	1,126	2.0	-0.6
Lageard, P. Green	530	1.0	-1.2
Lab majority	7,512	13.47	
Electorate	76,404		
Turnout	55,768	72.99	

Lab hold (2.37% from Con to Lab)

CHRISTCHURCH

		%	+/-%
Chope, C. Con*	35,230	69.4	11.5
Canavan, P. Lab	10,059	19.8	10.3
Cox, M. Lib Dem	4,020	7.9	1.4
Rigby, C. Green	1,325	2.6	-1.7
Con majority	25,171	49.55	
Electorate	70,309		
Turnout	50,795	72.25	

Con hold (0.61% from Lab to Con)

CITIES OF LONDON AND WESTMINSTER – see under London

CITY OF CHESTER – see under Chester

CITY OF DURHAM – see under Durham

*Member of last Parliament

CLACTON

		%	+/-%
Watling, G. Con	27,031	61.1	24.6
Osben, T. Lab	11,203	25.3	11.0
Oakley, P. UKIP	3,357	7.6	-36.7
Grace, D. Lib Dem	887	2.0	0.2
Southall, C. Green	719	1.6	-1.0
Shearer, C. Ind	449	1.0	
Tilbrook, R. Eng Dem	289	0.7	
Martin, N. Ind	210	0.5	
Con majority	15,828	35.8	
Electorate	68,566		
Turnout	44,218	64.49	

Con gain (6.81% from Lab to Con)

CLEETHORPES

		%	+/-%
Vickers, M. Con*	27,321	57.0	10.5
Keith, P. Lab	16,921	35.3	6.3
Blake, T. UKIP	2,022	4.2	-14.3
Horobin, R. Lib Dem	1,110	2.3	-0.7
Emmerson, L. Green	470	1.0	-1.3
Con majority	10,400	21.7	
Electorate	73,047		
Turnout	47,923	65.61	

Con hold (2.12% from Lab to Con)

CLWYD SOUTH

		%	+/-%
Jones, S. Lab*	19,002	50.6	13.5
Baynes, S. Con	14,646	39.0	8.7
Allen, C. PlC	2,293	6.1	-4.2
Bassford-Barton, J. UKIP	802	2.1	-13.5
Roberts, B. Lib Dem	731	2.0	-1.9
Lab majority	4,356	11.61	
Electorate	54,266		
Turnout	37,530	69.16	

Lab hold (2.39% from Con to Lab)

VALE OF CLWYD

		%	+/-%
Ruane, C. Lab	19,423	50.1	11.8
Davies, J. Con*	17,044	44.0	5.0
Wyatt, D. PlC	1,551	4.0	-3.0
Williams, G. Lib Dem	666	1.7	-0.9
Lab majority	2,379	6.14	
Electorate	56,890		
Turnout	38,775	68.16	

Lab gain (3.4% from Con to Lab)

CLWYD WEST

		%	+/-%
Jones, D. Con*	19,541	48.0	4.8
Thomas, G. Lab	16,104	39.5	14.0
Roberts, D. PlC	3,918	9.6	-2.6
Babu, V. Lib Dem	1,091	2.7	-1.0
Con majority	3,437	8.44	
Electorate	58,263		
Turnout	40,733	69.91	

Con hold (4.62% from Con to Lab)

COATBRIDGE, CHRYSTON AND BELLSHILL

		%	+/-%
Gaffney, H. Lab	19,193	42.5	8.7
Boswell, P. SNP*	17,607	39.0	-17.5
Halbert, R. Con	7,318	16.2	9.9
Bennie, D. Lib Dem	922	2.0	1.0
Lab majority	1,586	3.52	
Electorate	71,198		
Turnout	45,119	63.37	

Lab gain (13.09% from SNP to Lab)

COLCHESTER

		%	+/-%
Quince, W. Con*	24,565	45.8	6.9
Young, T. Lab	18,888	35.2	19.1
Russell, B. Lib Dem	9,087	16.9	-10.4
Goacher, M. Green	828	1.5	-3.6
Rennie, R. CPA	177	0.3	0.1
Con majority	5,677	10.58	
Electorate	79,996		
Turnout	53,657	67.07	

Con hold (6.07% from Con to Lab)

COLNE VALLEY

		%	+/-%
Walker, T. Lab	28,818	47.6	12.7
McCartney, J. Con*	27,903	46.1	1.7
Burke, C. Lib Dem	2,494	4.1	-1.9
King, S. Green	892	1.5	-1.9
Sadio, P. Ind	313	0.5	
Lab majority	915	1.51	
Electorate	84,387		
Turnout	60,578	71.79	

Lab gain (5.48% from Con to Lab)

CONGLETON

		%	+/-%
Bruce, F. Con*	31,830	56.5	3.4
Corcoran, S. Lab	19,211	34.1	13.8
Hirst, P. Lib Dem	2,902	5.2	-3.9
Davies, M. UKIP	1,289	2.3	-11.2
Heath, A. Green	999	1.8	-1.9
Con majority	12,619	22.4	
Electorate	76,694		
Turnout	56,329	73.45	

Con hold (5.19% from Con to Lab)

COPELAND

		%	+/-%
Harrison, T. Con*	21,062	49.0	13.3
Troughton, G. Lab	19,367	45.0	2.9
Hanson, R. Lib Dem	1,404	3.3	-0.2
Crossman, H. UKIP	1,094	2.5	-12.9
Con majority	1,695	3.94	
Electorate	61,751		
Turnout	43,012	69.65	

Con gain (5.19% from Lab to Con)

CORBY

		%	+/-%
Pursglove, T. Con*	29,534	49.1	6.5
Miller, B. Lab	26,844	44.7	6.3
Stanbra, C. Lib Dem	1,545	2.6	0.0
Watts, S. UKIP	1,495	2.5	-11.2
Scrutton, S. Green	579	1.0	-1.5
Con majority	2,690	4.48	
Electorate	83,020		
Turnout	60,091	72.38	

Con hold (0.09% from Lab to Con)

NORTH CORNWALL

		%	+/-%
Mann, S. Con*	25,835	50.6	5.7
Rogerson, D. Lib Dem	18,635	36.5	5.3
Bassett, J. Lab	6,151	12.1	6.6
Allman, J. CPA	185	0.4	
Hawkins, R. SLP	138	0.3	
Con majority	7,200	14.1	
Electorate	68,844		
Turnout	51,047	74.15	

Con hold (0.2% from Lib Dem to Con)

SOUTH EAST CORNWALL

		%	+/-%
Murray, S. Con*	29,493	55.3	4.8
Derrick, G. Lab	12,050	22.6	13.3
Hutty, P. Lib Dem	10,346	19.4	2.5
Corney, M. Green	1,335	2.5	-2.9
Con majority	17,443	32.69	
Electorate	71,880		
Turnout	53,357	74.23	

Con hold (4.24% from Con to Lab)

COVENTRY NORTH EAST

		%	+/-%
Fletcher, C. Lab*	29,499	63.3	11.3
Mayer, T. Con	13,919	29.9	6.9
Taggar, A. UKIP	1,350	2.9	-11.9
Field, R. Lib Dem	1,157	2.5	-2.3
Handley, M. Green	502	1.1	-1.9
Mahmood, A. Ind	81	0.2	
Lab majority	15,580	33.41	
Electorate	75,759		
Turnout	46,636	61.56	

Lab hold (2.23% from Con to Lab)

COVENTRY NORTH WEST

		%	+/-%
Robinson, G. Lab*	26,894	53.9	13.0
Kotecha, R. Con	18,314	36.7	5.7
Gee, M. UKIP	1,525	3.0	-12.6
Hilton, A. Lib Dem	1,286	2.6	-1.4
Norris, C. Ind	1,164	2.3	
Gray, S. Green	666	1.3	-3.0
Lab majority	8,580	17.18	
Electorate	75,196		
Turnout	49,937	66.41	

Lab hold (3.63% from Con to Lab)

COVENTRY SOUTH

		%	+/-%
Cunningham, J. Lab*	25,874	54.9	12.8
Lowe, M. Con	17,927	38.0	3.2
Judge, G. Lib Dem	1,343	2.9	-1.2
Rogers, I. UKIP	1,037	2.2	-10.8
Challenor, A. Green	604	1.3	-2.6
Findlay, S. Ind	224	0.5	
Lab majority	7,947	16.86	
Electorate	70,736		
Turnout	47,123	66.62	

Lab hold (4.8% from Con to Lab)

CRAWLEY

		%	+/-%
Smith, H. Con*	25,426	50.4	3.5
Lunnon, T. Lab	22,969	45.5	12.0
Scepanovic, M. Lib Dem	1,878	3.7	1.0
Con majority	2,457	4.87	
Electorate	73,425		
Turnout	50,454	68.72	

Con hold (4.27% from Con to Lab)

CREWE AND NANTWICH

		%	+/-%
Smith, L. Lab	25,928	47.0	9.5
Timpson, E. Con*	25,880	47.0	2.2
Stanley, M. UKIP	1,885	3.4	-11.1
Crowther, D. Lib Dem	1,334	2.4	-0.3
Lab majority	48	0.09	
Electorate	78,895		
Turnout	55,128	69.88	

Lab gain (3.65% from Con to Lab)

CROYDON CENTRAL

		%	+/-%
Jones, S. Lab	29,873	52.2	9.6
Barwell, G. Con*	24,221	42.3	-0.6
Hickson, G. Lib Dem	1,083	1.9	-0.3
Staveley, P. UKIP	1,040	1.8	-7.3
Hague, T. Green	626	1.1	-1.6
Boadu, J. CPA	177	0.3	
Locke, D. Ind	71	0.1	
Lab majority	5,652	9.88	
Electorate	80,045		
Turnout	57,200	71.46	

Lab gain (5.11% from Con to Lab)

CROYDON NORTH

		%	+/-%
Reed, S. Lab/Co-op*	44,213	74.0	11.6
Kasumu, S. Con	11,848	19.8	-2.8
Pindar, J. Lib Dem	1,656	2.8	-0.8
Underwood, P. Green	983	1.6	-3.0
Swadling, M. UKIP	753	1.3	-4.1
Berks, L. Ind	170	0.3	0.0
Lab/Co-op majority	32,365	54.16	
Electorate	87,461		
Turnout	59,754	68.32	

Lab/Co-op hold (7.19% from Con to Lab/Co-op)

CROYDON SOUTH

		%	+/-%
Philp, C. Con*	33,334	54.3	-0.3
Brathwaite, J. Lab	21,928	35.7	11.3
Jones, A. Lib Dem	3,541	5.8	-0.2
Shelley, C. Green	1,125	1.8	-1.9
Garner, K. UKIP	1,116	1.8	-8.7
Omamogho, D. CPA	213	0.4	
Con majority	11,406	18.58	
Electorate	83,518		
Turnout	61,380	73.49	

Con hold (5.82% from Con to Lab)

CUMBERNAULD, KILSYTH AND KIRKINTILLOCH EAST

		%	+/-%
McDonald, S. SNP*	19,122	43.6	-16.2
Fisher, E. Lab	14,858	33.9	3.9
Johnston, S. Con	8,010	18.3	10.4
Ackland, R. Lib Dem	1,238	2.8	0.6
Pearson, C. UKIP	605	1.4	
SNP majority	4,264	9.72	
Electorate	66,554		
Turnout	43,883	65.94	

SNP hold (10.05% from SNP to Lab)

CYNON VALLEY

		%	+/-%
Clwyd, A. Lab*	19,404	60.9	13.3
Dewhurst, K. Con	6,166	19.4	7.3
Walters, L. PIC	4,376	13.7	-3.0
McLean, I. UKIP	1,271	4.0	-12.3
Knight, N. Lib Dem	585	1.8	-0.9
Lab majority	13,238	41.53	
Electorate	51,334		
Turnout	31,873	62.09	

Lab hold (3% from Con to Lab)

DAGENHAM AND RAINHAM

		%	+/-%
Cruddas, J. Lab*	22,958	50.0	8.7
Marson, J. Con	18,306	39.9	15.6
Harris, P. UKIP	3,246	7.1	-22.7
Breading, D. Green	544	1.2	-0.7
Fryer, J. Lib Dem	465	1.0	-0.6
Sturdy, P. BNP	239	0.5	0.2
London, T. Concordia	85	0.2	
Lab majority	4,652	10.13	
Electorate	70,616		
Turnout	45,916	65.02	

Lab hold (3.45% from Lab to Con)

DARLINGTON

		%	+/-%
Chapman, J. Lab*	22,681	50.5	7.9
Cuthbertson, P. Con	19,401	43.2	8.2
Brack, K. UKIP	1,180	2.6	-10.4
Curry, A. Lib Dem	1,031	2.3	-2.5
Snedker, M. Green	524	1.2	-2.3
Lab majority	3,280	7.31	
Electorate	66,341		
Turnout	44,896	67.67	

Lab hold (0.16% from Lab to Con)

*Member of last Parliament

General Election 2017

DARTFORD

		%	+/-%
Johnson, G. Con*	31,210	57.4	8.6
Kaini, B. Lab	18,024	33.2	7.8
Fryer, B. UKIP	2,544	4.7	-15.1
Beard, S. Lib Dem	1,428	2.6	-0.1
Blatchford, A. Green	807	1.5	-1.0
Adewunmi, O. Ind	211	0.4	
Con majority	13,186	24.27	
Electorate	77,495		
Turnout	54,341	70.12	

Con hold (0.4% from Lab to Con)

DAVENTRY

		%	+/-%
Heaton-Harris, C. Con*	35,464	63.6	5.6
Ramsey, A. Lab	13,730	24.6	6.6
Simpson, A. Lib Dem	4,015	7.2	2.7
Gibbins, I. UKIP	1,497	2.7	-13.1
Wildman, J. Green	957	1.7	-1.8
Con majority	21,734	38.97	
Electorate	75,268		
Turnout	55,765	74.09	

Con hold (0.51% from Con to Lab)

DELYN

		%	+/-%
Hanson, D. Lab*	20,573	52.1	11.6
Wright, M. Con	16,333	41.4	8.7
Rowlinson, P. PlC	1,481	3.8	-1.1
Rippeth, T. Lib Dem	1,031	2.6	-1.1
Lab majority	4,240	10.74	
Electorate	54,090		
Turnout	39,487	73	

Lab hold (1.47% from Con to Lab)

DENTON AND REDDISH

		%	+/-%
Gwynne, A. Lab*	25,161	63.4	12.8
Kana, R. Con	11,084	27.9	4.4
Seddon, J. UKIP	1,798	4.5	-14.1
Ankers, L. Lib Dem	853	2.1	-0.3
Hayes, G. Green	486	1.2	-2.5
Dave, F. Loony	217	0.6	
Lab majority	14,077	35.48	
Electorate	65,751		
Turnout	39,671	60.34	

Lab hold (4.21% from Con to Lab)

DERBY NORTH

		%	+/-%
Williamson, C. Lab	23,622	48.4	12.0
Solloway, A. Con*	21,607	44.3	7.8
Care, L. Lib Dem	2,262	4.6	-3.9
Piper, B. UKIP	1,181	2.4	-12.1
Lab majority	2,015	4.13	
Electorate	69,919		
Turnout	48,781	69.77	

Lab gain (2.11% from Con to Lab)

DERBY SOUTH

		%	+/-%
Beckett, M. Lab*	26,430	58.2	9.4
Williams, E. Con	15,182	33.4	6.2
Graves, A. UKIP	2,011	4.4	-11.0
Naitta, J. Lib Dem	1,229	2.7	-1.5
Sleeman, I. Green	454	1.0	-2.0
Lab majority	11,248	24.77	
Electorate	69,918		
Turnout	45,411	64.95	

Lab hold (1.62% from Con to Lab)

DERBYSHIRE DALES

		%	+/-%
McLoughlin, P. Con*	29,744	59.8	7.6
Botham, A. Lab	15,417	31.0	8.4
Hollyer, A. Lib Dem	3,126	6.3	-2.1
Buckler, M. Green	1,002	2.0	-2.6
Greenwood, R. Humanity	282	0.6	0.3
Con majority	14,327	28.81	
Electorate	64,430		
Turnout	49,722	77.17	

Con hold (0.38% from Con to Lab)

MID DERBYSHIRE

		%	+/-%
Latham, P. Con*	29,513	58.4	6.4
Martin, A. Lab	17,897	35.4	10.1
Wain, A. Lib Dem	1,793	3.5	-1.2
MacFarlane, S. Green	1,168	2.3	-1.7
Con majority	11,616	23	
Electorate	67,466		
Turnout	50,507	74.86	

Con hold (1.85% from Con to Lab)

NORTH EAST DERBYSHIRE

		%	+/-%
Rowley, L. Con	24,783	49.1	12.5
Engel, N. Lab*	21,923	43.5	2.9
Bush, J. UKIP	1,565	3.1	-12.8
Lomax, D. Lib Dem	1,390	2.8	-1.4
Kesteven, D. Green	719	1.4	-0.8
Con majority	2,860	5.67	
Electorate	72,097		
Turnout	50,458	69.99	

Con gain (4.8% from Lab to Con)

SOUTH DERBYSHIRE

		%	+/-%
Wheeler, H. Con*	30,907	58.6	9.4
Pearson, R. Lab	18,937	35.9	9.2
Johnson, L. Lib Dem	1,870	3.5	-0.2
Kats, M. Green	917	1.7	-0.6
Con majority	11,970	22.69	
Electorate	76,380		
Turnout	52,751	69.06	

Con hold (0.09% from Lab to Con)

DEVIZES

		%	+/-%
Perry, C. Con*	31,744	62.6	5.0
Shaikh, I. Lab	10,608	20.9	8.0
Coleman, C. Lib Dem	4,706	9.3	1.2
Page, T. UKIP	1,706	3.4	-12.0
Dawnay, E. Green	1,606	3.2	-2.6
Gunter, J. Wessex Reg	223	0.4	
Con majority	21,136	41.69	
Electorate	72,185		
Turnout	50,700	70.24	

Con hold (1.48% from Con to Lab)

CENTRAL DEVON

		%	+/-%
Stride, M. Con*	31,278	54.0	2.0
Robillard Webb, L. Lab	15,598	26.9	14.1
White, A. Lib Dem	6,770	11.7	-0.5
Williamson, A. Green	1,531	2.6	-6.3
Matthews, T. UKIP	1,326	2.3	-10.8
Dean, J. NHA	871	1.5	
Knight, L. Lib	470	0.8	
Con majority	15,680	27.07	
Electorate	74,370		
Turnout	57,928	77.89	

Con hold (6.1% from Con to Lab)

EAST DEVON

		%	+/-%
Swire, H. Con*	29,306	48.5	2.3
Wright, C. Ind	21,270	35.2	11.3
Ross, J. Lab	6,857	11.3	1.2
Eden, A. Lib Dem	1,468	2.4	-4.3
Graham, B. UKIP	1,203	2.0	-10.5
Faithfull, P. Ind	150	0.3	
Val Davies, M. Ind	128	0.2	
Con majority	8,036	13.3	
Electorate	82,369		
Turnout	60,443	73.38	

Con hold (4.51% from Con to Ind)

NORTH DEVON

		%	+/-%
Heaton-Jones, P. Con*	25,517	45.8	3.2
Harvey, N. Lib Dem	21,185	38.0	8.6
Cann, M. Lab	7,063	12.7	5.6
Crowther, S. UKIP	1,187	2.1	-12.6
Knight, R. Green	753	1.4	-4.4
Con majority	4,332	7.77	
Electorate	75,801		
Turnout	55,771	73.58	

Con hold (2.73% from Con to Lib Dem)

SOUTH WEST DEVON

		%	+/-%
Streeter, G. Con*	31,634	59.7	3.3
Davey, P. Lab/Co-op	15,818	29.9	13.3
Voaden, C. Lib Dem	2,732	5.2	-2.3
Ross, I. UKIP	1,540	2.9	-11.6
Scutt, W. Green	1,133	2.1	-2.6
Con majority	15,816	29.87	
Electorate	71,260		
Turnout	52,954	74.31	

Con hold (4.99% from Con to Lab/Co-op)

*Member of last Parliament

DEWSBURY

		%	+/-%
Sherriff, P. Lab*	28,814	50.8	9.2
Prescott, B. Con	25,493	45.0	6.1
Hussain, E. Lib Dem	1,214	2.1	-1.4
Cope, S. Green	1,024	1.8	-0.7
Lab majority	3,321	5.86	
Electorate	81,343		
Turnout	56,700	69.7	

Lab hold (1.59% from Con to Lab)

DON VALLEY

		%	+/-%
Flint, C. Lab*	24,351	52.8	6.8
Bell, A. Con	19,182	41.6	16.5
Manion, S. YP	1,599	3.5	
Smith, A. Lib Dem	856	1.9	-1.6
Lab majority	5,169	11.22	
Electorate	73,990		
Turnout	46,083	62.28	

Lab hold (4.81% from Lab to Con)

DONCASTER CENTRAL

		%	+/-%
Winterton, R. Lab*	24,915	57.8	8.9
Hunt, T. Con	14,784	34.3	13.6
Whitwood, C. YP	1,346	3.1	
Todd, E. Ind	1,006	2.3	
Brelsford, A. Lib Dem	973	2.3	-2.0
Lab majority	10,131	23.48	
Electorate	71,718		
Turnout	43,146	60.16	

Lab hold (2.36% from Lab to Con)

DONCASTER NORTH

		%	+/-%
Miliband, E. Lab*	25,711	60.7	8.5
Adoh, S. Con	11,687	27.6	9.3
Parkinson, K. UKIP	2,738	6.5	-16.0
Bridges, C. YP	741	1.8	
Adamson, R. Lib Dem	706	1.7	-0.9
Calladine, F. Ind	366	0.9	
Allen, D. Eng Dem	363	0.9	-0.3
Lab majority	14,024	33.08	
Electorate	72,377		
Turnout	42,388	58.57	

Lab hold (0.44% from Lab to Con)

MID DORSET AND NORTH POOLE

		%	+/-%
Tomlinson, M. Con*	28,585	59.1	8.4
Slade, V. Lib Dem	13,246	27.4	-0.7
Brew, S. Lab	6,423	13.3	7.3
Con majority	15,339	31.69	
Electorate	65,050		
Turnout	48,399	74.4	

Con hold (4.56% from Lib Dem to Con)

General Election 2017

NORTH DORSET

		%	+/-%
Hoare, S. Con*	36,169	64.7	8.3
Osborne, P. Lab	10,392	18.6	9.6
Panton, T. Lib Dem	7,556	13.5	1.9
Tutton, J. Green	1,607	2.9	-2.8
Con majority	25,777	46.12	
Electorate	76,324		
Turnout	55,891	73.23	

Con hold (0.7% from Con to Lab)

SOUTH DORSET

		%	+/-%
Drax, R. Con*	29,135	56.0	7.3
Warr, T. Lab	17,440	33.5	9.4
Legg, H. Lib Dem	3,053	5.9	-0.1
Orrell, J. Green	2,278	4.4	-0.3
Con majority	11,695	22.49	
Electorate	72,323		
Turnout	52,009	71.91	

Con hold (1.06% from Con to Lab)

WEST DORSET

		%	+/-%
Letwin, O. Con*	33,081	55.4	5.4
Canning, A. Lib Dem	13,990	23.4	1.9
Rhodes, L. Lab	10,896	18.2	8.3
Clayton, K. Green	1,631	2.7	-3.0
Con majority	19,091	31.95	
Electorate	82,277		
Turnout	59,750	72.62	

Con hold (1.75% from Lib Dem to Con)

DOVER

		%	+/-%
Elphicke, C. Con*	27,211	52.3	9.2
Blair, S. Lab	20,774	39.9	9.3
Wauchope, P. UKIP	1,722	3.3	-16.9
Dodd, S. Lib Dem	1,336	2.6	-0.6
Sawbridge, B. Green	923	1.8	-0.8
Con majority	6,437	12.37	
Electorate	74,564		
Turnout	52,042	69.8	

Con hold (0.06% from Con to Lab)

NORTH DOWN

		%	+/-%
Hermon, S. Ind*	16,148	41.1	-8.0
Easton, A. DUP	14,940	38.0	14.5
Muir, A. All	3,639	9.3	0.7
Agnew, S. Green	2,549	6.5	1.1
Shivers, F. Con	941	2.4	-2.0
McCartney, T. Sinn Féin	531	1.4	0.6
McNeill, C. SDLP	400	1.0	0.0
Reynolds, G. Ind	37	0.1	
Ind majority	1,208	3.08	
Electorate	64,334		
Turnout	39,268	61.04	

Ind hold (11.23% from Ind to DUP)

SOUTH DOWN

		%	+/-%
Hazzard, C. Sinn Féin	20,328	39.8	11.4
Ritchie, M. SDLP*	17,882	35.0	-7.0
Forsythe, D. DUP	8,867	17.4	9.3
McKee, H. UUP	2,002	3.9	-5.3
McMurray, A. All	1,814	3.5	-0.2
Sinn Féin majority	2,446	4.79	
Electorate	75,685		
Turnout	51,082	67.49	

Sinn Féin gain (9.24% from SDLP to Sinn Féin)

DUDLEY NORTH

		%	+/-%
Austin, I. Lab*	18,090	46.4	4.7
Jones, L. Con	18,068	46.4	15.6
Etheridge, B. UKIP	2,144	5.5	-18.4
France, B. Lib Dem	368	0.9	-0.3
Nixon, A. Green	240	0.6	-0.7
Lab majority	22	0.06	
Electorate	62,042		
Turnout	38,983	62.83	

Lab hold (5.46% from Lab to Con)

DUDLEY SOUTH

		%	+/-%
Wood, M. Con*	21,588	56.4	12.7
Millward, N. Lab	13,858	36.2	3.7
Bolton, M. UKIP	1,791	4.7	-14.2
Brammall, J. Lib Dem	625	1.6	-0.5
Maxwell, J. Green	382	1.0	-1.5
Con majority	7,730	20.19	
Electorate	61,324		
Turnout	38,295	62.45	

Con hold (4.52% from Lab to Con)

DULWICH AND WEST NORWOOD

		%	+/-%
Hayes, H. Lab*	39,096	69.4	15.6
Wolf, R. Con	10,940	19.4	-3.2
Kent, G. Lib Dem	4,475	8.0	-1.9
Nix, R. Green	1,408	2.5	-6.9
Lambert, R. Ind	121	0.2	0.0
Chong, Y. Ind	103	0.2	
Lab majority	28,156	50.01	
Electorate	78,037		
Turnout	56,305	72.15	

Lab hold (9.37% from Con to Lab)

DUMFRIES AND GALLOWAY

		%	+/-%
Jack, A. Con	22,344	43.3	13.4
Arkless, R. SNP*	16,701	32.3	-9.0
Goodare, D. Lab	10,775	20.9	-3.8
Mitchell, J. Lib Dem	1,241	2.4	0.7
Hongmei Jin, Y. Ind	538	1.0	
Con majority	5,643	10.93	
Electorate	74,206		
Turnout	51,644	69.6	

Con gain (11.21% from SNP to Con)

DUMFRIESSHIRE, CLYDESDALE AND TWEEDDALE

		%	+/-%
Mundell, D. Con*	24,177	49.3	9.5
McAllan, M. SNP	14,736	30.1	-8.2
Beattie, D. Lab	8,102	16.5	1.8
Ferry, J. Lib Dem	1,949	4.0	1.3
Con majority	9,441	19.26	
Electorate	67,672		
Turnout	49,024	72.44	

Con hold (8.87% from SNP to Con)

EAST DUNBARTONSHIRE

		%	+/-%
Swinson, J. Lib Dem	21,023	40.5	4.3
Nicolson, J. SNP*	15,684	30.2	-10.0
Mechan, S. Con	7,563	14.6	6.0
McNally, C. Lab	7,531	14.5	2.2
Lib Dem majority	5,339	10.29	
Electorate	66,300		
Turnout	51,869	78.23	

Lib Dem gain (7.12% from SNP to Lib Dem)

WEST DUNBARTONSHIRE

		%	+/-%
Docherty-Hughes, M. SNP*	18,890	42.8	-16.2
Mitchell, J. Lab	16,602	37.6	6.3
Hutton, P. Con	7,582	17.2	10.1
Plenderleith, R. Lib Dem	1,009	2.3	0.7
SNP majority	2,288	5.18	
Electorate	67,602		
Turnout	44,169	65.34	

SNP hold (11.25% from SNP to Lab)

DUNDEE EAST

		%	+/-%
Hosie, S. SNP*	18,391	42.8	-16.9
Price, E. Con	11,746	27.3	12.4
Brennan, L. Lab	11,176	26.0	6.1
McIntyre, C. Lib Dem	1,615	3.8	0.9
SNP majority	6,645	15.46	
Electorate	65,854		
Turnout	42,985	65.27	

SNP hold (14.65% from SNP to Con)

DUNDEE WEST

		%	+/-%
Law, C. SNP*	18,045	46.5	-15.4
Cowan, A. Lab	12,783	33.0	9.3
Cormack, D. Con	6,257	16.1	7.5
Blain, J. Lib Dem	1,189	3.1	0.7
Dobson, S. Ind	403	1.0	
SNP majority	5,262	13.57	
Electorate	62,644		
Turnout	38,776	61.9	

SNP hold (12.33% from SNP to Lab)

*Member of last Parliament

DUNFERMLINE AND WEST FIFE

		%	+/-%
Chapman, D. SNP*	18,121	35.5	-14.7
Hilton, C. Lab/Co-op	17,277	33.8	2.1
Hacking, B. Con	12,593	24.6	12.8
Calder, J. Lib Dem	3,019	5.9	1.9
SNP majority	844	1.65	
Electorate	75,672		
Turnout	51,083	67.51	

SNP hold (8.43% from SNP to Lab/Co-op)

CITY OF DURHAM

		%	+/-%
Blackman-Woods, R. Lab*	26,772	55.3	8.1
Lawrie, R. Con	14,408	29.8	7.6
Hopgood, A. Lib Dem	4,787	9.9	-1.4
Bint, M. UKIP	1,116	2.3	-9.1
Elmer, J. Green	797	1.6	-4.2
Clark, J. Ind	399	0.8	0.4
Collings, J. YPP	45	0.1	
Lab majority	12,364	25.54	
Electorate	71,132		
Turnout	48,410	68.06	

Lab hold (0.27% from Con to Lab)

NORTH DURHAM

		%	+/-%
Jones, K. Lab*	25,917	59.8	4.9
Glossop, L. Con	12,978	29.9	9.0
Rollings, K. UKIP	2,408	5.5	-10.4
Martin, C. Lib Dem	1,981	4.6	-0.5
Lab majority	12,939	29.83	
Electorate	66,970		
Turnout	43,372	64.76	

Lab hold (2.05% from Lab to Con)

NORTH WEST DURHAM

		%	+/-%
Pidcock, L. Lab	25,308	52.8	6.0
Hart, S. Con	16,516	34.4	11.1
Temple, O. Lib Dem	3,398	7.1	-2.0
Breeze, A. UKIP	2,150	4.5	-12.4
Horsman, D. Green	530	1.1	-2.5
Lab majority	8,792	18.33	
Electorate	71,918		
Turnout	47,973	66.71	

Lab hold (2.56% from Lab to Con)

DWYFOR MEIRIONNYDD

		%	+/-%
Saville Roberts, L. PlC*	13,687	45.0	4.2
Fairlamb, N. Con	8,837	29.1	6.4
Norman, M. Lab	6,273	20.6	7.2
Churchman, S. Lib Dem	937	3.1	-0.9
Wykes, F. UKIP	614	2.0	-8.8
PlC majority	4,850	15.95	
Electorate	44,699		
Turnout	30,415	68.04	

PlC hold (1.11% from PlC to Con)

General Election 2017

EALING CENTRAL AND ACTON

		%	+/-%
Huq, R. Lab*	33,037	59.5	16.4
Morrissey, J. Con	19,230	34.6	-7.9
Ball, J. Lib Dem	3,075	5.5	-0.5
Lab majority	13,807	24.86	
Electorate	74,200		
Turnout	55,533	74.84	

Lab hold (12.16% from Con to Lab)

EALING NORTH

		%	+/-%
Pound, S. Lab*	34,635	65.8	10.9
Grant, I. Con	14,942	28.4	-1.2
Sanders, H. Lib Dem	1,275	2.4	-0.8
Mcilvenna, P. UKIP	921	1.8	-6.3
Hans, M. Green	743	1.4	-2.0
Lab majority	19,693	37.39	
Electorate	74,764		
Turnout	52,668	70.45	

Lab hold (6.04% from Con to Lab)

EALING SOUTHALL

		%	+/-%
Sharma, V. Lab*	31,720	70.0	5.3
Conti, F. Con	9,630	21.3	-0.3
Bakhai, N. Lib Dem	1,892	4.2	0.6
Ward, P. Green	1,037	2.3	-2.3
Poynton, J. UKIP	504	1.1	-3.0
Thiara, A. WRP	362	0.8	
Lab majority	22,090	48.74	
Electorate	65,188		
Turnout	45,318	69.52	

Lab hold (2.81% from Con to Lab)

EASINGTON

		%	+/-%
Morris, G. Lab*	23,152	63.6	2.6
Campbell, B. Con	8,260	22.7	9.8
McDonnell, S. NEP	2,355	6.5	4.1
Roberts, A. UKIP	1,727	4.7	-14.0
Hancock, T. Lib Dem	460	1.3	-1.1
Warin, M. Green	410	1.1	-1.0
Lab majority	14,892	40.89	
Electorate	62,385		
Turnout	36,421	58.38	

Lab hold (3.57% from Lab to Con)

EAST ANTRIM – see under Antrim

EAST DEVON – see under Devon

EAST DUNBARTONSHIRE – see under Dunbartonshire

EAST HAM

		%	+/-%
Timms, S. Lab*	47,124	83.0	5.7
Finlayson, K. Con	7,241	12.8	0.7
Oxley, D. UKIP	697	1.2	-3.8
Williams, G. Lib Dem	656	1.1	-0.5
Oti-Obihara, C. Green	474	0.8	-1.6
Afzal, C. Friends	311	0.6	
Rahman, M. Ind	130	0.2	
Lab majority	39,883	70.2	
Electorate	83,928		
Turnout	56,812	67.69	

Lab hold (2.48% from Con to Lab)

EAST HAMPSHIRE – see under Hampshire

EAST KILBRIDE, STRATHAVEN AND LESMAHAGOW

		%	+/-%
Cameron, L. SNP*	21,023	38.8	-16.8
McAdams, M. Lab	17,157	31.7	3.4
McGeever, M. Con	13,704	25.3	13.5
McGarry, P. Lib Dem	1,590	2.9	1.2
MacKay, J. UKIP	628	1.2	-0.9
SNP majority	3,866	7.14	
Electorate	80,442		
Turnout	54,183	67.36	

SNP hold (10.07% from SNP to Lab)

EAST LONDONDERRY – see under Londonderry

EAST LOTHIAN – see under Lothian

EAST RENFREWSHIRE – see under Renfrewshire

EAST SURREY – see under Surrey

EAST WORTHING AND SHOREHAM – see under Worthing

EAST YORKSHIRE – see under Yorkshire

EASTBOURNE

		%	+/-%
Lloyd, S. Lib Dem	26,924	46.8	8.8
Ansell, C. Con*	25,315	44.0	4.6
Lambert, J. Lab	4,671	8.1	0.3
Hough, A. Green	510	0.9	-1.7
Lib Dem majority	1,609	2.8	
Electorate	78,754		
Turnout	57,511	73.03	

Lib Dem gain (2.09% from Con to Lib Dem)

EASTLEIGH

		%	+/-%
Davies, M. Con*	28,889	50.3	8.2
Thornton, M. Lib Dem	14,710	25.6	-0.1
Payne, J. Lab	11,454	19.9	7.1
Jones, M. UKIP	1,477	2.6	-13.2
Meldrum, R. Green	750	1.3	-1.4
Con majority	14,179	24.7	
Electorate	81,212		
Turnout	57,416	70.7	

Con hold (4.14% from Lib Dem to Con)

EDDISBURY

		%	+/-%
Sandbach, A. Con*	29,192	56.8	5.9
Reynolds, C. Lab	17,250	33.6	10.0
Priestner, I. Lib Dem	2,804	5.5	-3.6
Bickley, J. UKIP	1,109	2.2	-10.0
Green, M. Green	785	1.5	-1.9
Hill, M. Pirate	179	0.4	
Con majority	11,942	23.23	
Electorate	70,272		
Turnout	51,404	73.15	

Con hold (2.04% from Con to Lab)

EDINBURGH EAST

		%	+/-%
Sheppard, T. SNP*	18,509	42.4	-6.7
King, P. Lab	15,084	34.6	4.7
Mackie, K. Con	8,081	18.5	8.6
Gray, T. Lib Dem	1,849	4.2	1.4
SNP majority	3,425	7.85	
Electorate	65,896		
Turnout	43,623	66.2	

SNP hold (5.73% from SNP to Lab)

EDINBURGH NORTH AND LEITH

		%	+/-%
Brock, D. SNP*	19,243	34.0	-6.9
Munro, G. Lab/Co-op	17,618	31.1	-0.1
McGill, I. Con	15,385	27.2	11.0
Veart, M. Lib Dem	2,579	4.5	0.0
Slater, L. Green	1,727	3.0	-2.4
SNP majority	1,625	2.87	
Electorate	79,473		
Turnout	56,624	71.25	

SNP hold (3.38% from SNP to Lab/Co-op)

EDINBURGH SOUTH

		%	+/-%
Murray, I. Lab*	26,269	54.8	15.7
Eadie, J. SNP	10,755	22.4	-11.3
Smith, S. Con	9,428	19.7	2.2
Beal, A. Lib Dem	1,388	2.9	-0.8
Lab majority	15,514	32.38	
Electorate	64,553		
Turnout	47,913	74.22	

Lab hold (13.52% from SNP to Lab)

EDINBURGH SOUTH WEST

		%	+/-%
Cherry, J. SNP*	17,575	35.5	-7.4
Briggs, M. Con	16,478	33.3	13.1
Choudhury, F. Lab	13,213	26.7	-0.4
Mir, A. Lib Dem	2,124	4.3	0.6
SNP majority	1,097	2.22	
Electorate	71,178		
Turnout	49,464	69.49	

SNP hold (10.24% from SNP to Con)

EDINBURGH WEST

		%	+/-%
Jardine, C. Lib Dem	18,108	34.3	1.2
Giugliano, T. SNP	15,120	28.6	-10.3
Batho, S. Con	11,559	21.9	9.6
Telford, M. Lab	7,876	14.9	3.2
Whittet, M. SIRP	132	0.3	
Lib Dem majority	2,988	5.65	
Electorate	71,500		
Turnout	52,866	73.94	

Lib Dem gain (5.75% from SNP to Lib Dem)

*Member of last Parliament

EDMONTON

		%	+/-%
Osamor, K. Lab/Co-op*	31,221	71.3	10.1
Daniels, G. Con	10,106	23.1	-0.9
Sussman, N. UKIP	860	2.0	-6.2
Schmitz, D. Lib Dem	858	2.0	-0.2
Gill, B. Green	633	1.5	-1.8
Lab/Co-op majority	21,115	48.22	
Electorate	65,777		
Turnout	43,791	66.57	

Lab/Co-op hold (5.53% from Con to Lab/Co-op)

ELLESMERE PORT AND NESTON

		%	+/-%
Madders, J. Lab*	30,137	59.1	11.5
Jones, N. Con	18,747	36.8	2.5
Gough, E. Lib Dem	892	1.8	-1.6
Fricker, F. UKIP	821	1.6	-10.3
Baker, S. Green	342	0.7	-1.4
Lab majority	11,390	22.33	
Electorate	68,666		
Turnout	51,008	74.28	

Lab hold (4.47% from Con to Lab)

ELMET AND ROTHWELL

		%	+/-%
Shelbrooke, A. Con*	32,352	54.2	5.9
Nagle, D. Lab	22,547	37.8	4.2
Golton, S. Lib Dem	2,606	4.4	-0.2
Clover, M. YP	1,042	1.8	
Brown, D. Green	995	1.7	-0.5
Con majority	9,805	16.43	
Electorate	80,291		
Turnout	59,676	74.32	

Con hold (0.89% from Lab to Con)

ELTHAM

		%	+/-%
Efford, C. Lab*	25,128	54.3	11.8
Hartley, M. Con	18,832	40.7	4.4
Hall-Matthews, D. Lib Dem	1,457	3.1	0.1
Clarke, J. BNP	738	1.6	
Lab majority	6,296	13.6	
Electorate	64,474		
Turnout	46,305	71.82	

Lab hold (3.69% from Con to Lab)

ENFIELD NORTH

		%	+/-%
Ryan, J. Lab*	28,177	57.9	14.2
de Bois, N. Con	17,930	36.8	-4.5
da Costa, N. Lib Dem	1,036	2.1	-0.2
Cairns, D. UKIP	848	1.7	-7.2
Linton, B. Green	574	1.2	-1.6
Lab majority	10,247	21.05	
Electorate	68,076		
Turnout	48,690	71.52	

Lab hold (9.35% from Con to Lab)

ENFIELD SOUTHGATE

		%	+/-%
Charalambous, B. Lab	24,989	51.5	12.6
Burrowes, D. Con*	20,634	42.6	-6.7
Morgan, P. Lib Dem	1,925	4.0	0.7
Flint, D. Green	780	1.6	-2.1
Lab majority	4,355	8.98	
Electorate	65,210		
Turnout	48,486	74.35	

Lab gain (9.66% from Con to Lab)

EPPING FOREST

		%	+/-%
Laing, E. Con*	31,462	61.8	7.2
Preston, L. Lab	13,219	26.0	9.9
Whitehouse, J. Lib Dem	2,884	5.7	-1.3
O'Flynn, P. UKIP	1,871	3.7	-14.6
Heap, S. Green	1,233	2.4	-1.2
Hall, T. YPP	110	0.2	0.1
Con majority	18,243	35.83	
Electorate	74,737		
Turnout	50,909	68.12	

Con hold (1.35% from Con to Lab)

EPSOM AND EWELL

		%	+/-%
Grayling, C. Con*	35,313	59.4	1.3
Mayne, E. Lab	14,838	24.9	9.5
Gee, S. Lib Dem	7,401	12.4	3.7
Baker, J. Green	1,714	2.9	-0.8
Con majority	20,475	34.43	
Electorate	80,029		
Turnout	59,468	74.31	

Con hold (4.11% from Con to Lab)

EREWASH

		%	+/-%
Throup, M. Con*	25,939	52.0	9.4
Atkinson, C. Lab	21,405	42.9	7.7
Garnett, M. Lib Dem	1,243	2.5	-0.9
Hierons, R. Green	675	1.4	-1.1
Dunn, R. Ind	519	1.0	
Con majority	4,534	9.09	
Electorate	72,995		
Turnout	49,867	68.32	

Con hold (0.85% from Lab to Con)

ERITH AND THAMESMEAD

		%	+/-%
Pearce, T. Lab*	25,585	57.4	7.8
Baxter, E. Con	15,571	35.0	7.6
Johnson, R. UKIP	1,728	3.9	-13.4
Waddington, S. Lib Dem	750	1.7	-0.6
Letsae, C. Green	507	1.1	-1.1
Olodu, T. CPA	243	0.6	-0.1
Oddiri, D. Ind	80	0.2	
Lab majority	10,014	22.48	
Electorate	69,724		
Turnout	44,543	63.88	

Lab hold (0.09% from Con to Lab)

ESHER AND WALTON

		%	+/-%
Raab, D. Con*	35,071	58.6	-4.1
Hylands, L. Lab	11,773	19.7	7.0
Davis, A. Lib Dem	10,374	17.3	7.9
Palmer, O. Green	1,074	1.8	-2.3
Ions, D. UKIP	1,034	1.7	-8.0
Badger, B. Loony	318	0.5	
Reynolds, D. Ind	198	0.3	-0.1
Con majority	23,298	38.9	
Electorate	80,938		
Turnout	59,894	74	

Con hold (5.58% from Con to Lab)

EXETER

		%	+/-%
Bradshaw, B. Lab*	34,336	61.8	15.6
Taghdissian, J. Con	18,219	32.8	-0.2
Newcombe, V. Lib Dem	1,562	2.8	-1.5
Levy, J. Green	1,027	1.9	-4.6
West, J. Ind	212	0.4	
Bishop, J. Ind	67	0.1	
Lab majority	16,117	29.01	
Electorate	77,330		
Turnout	55,554	71.84	

Lab hold (7.89% from Con to Lab)

FALKIRK

		%	+/-%
McNally, J. SNP*	20,952	38.9	-18.8
Martin, C. Lab	16,029	29.8	4.7
Laidlaw, C. Con	14,088	26.1	14.0
Reid, A. Lib Dem	1,120	2.1	0.1
Pickering, D. Green	908	1.7	
Martin, S. UKIP	712	1.3	-1.7
SNP majority	4,923	9.14	
Electorate	82,240		
Turnout	53,867	65.5	

SNP hold (11.74% from SNP to Lab)

FAREHAM

		%	+/-%
Fernandes, S. Con*	35,915	62.9	6.9
Randall, M. Lab	14,360	25.1	10.9
Winnington, M. Lib Dem	3,896	6.8	-2.0
Blewett, T. UKIP	1,541	2.7	-12.7
Grindey, M. Green	1,302	2.3	-1.6
Con majority	21,555	37.72	
Electorate	78,837		
Turnout	57,138	72.48	

Con hold (2.01% from Con to Lab)

FAVERSHAM AND MID KENT

		%	+/-%
Whately, H. Con*	30,390	61.0	6.8
Desmond, M. Lab	12,977	26.0	9.9
Naghi, D. Lib Dem	3,249	6.5	-0.1
McGiffin, M. UKIP	1,702	3.4	-14.5
Gould, A. Green	1,431	2.9	-1.0
Con majority	17,413	34.95	
Electorate	72,205		
Turnout	49,826	69.01	

Con hold (1.58% from Con to Lab)

FELTHAM AND HESTON

		%	+/-%
Malhotra, S. Lab/Co-op*	32,462	61.1	8.9
Jassal, S. Con	16,859	31.7	2.7
Agnew, S. UKIP	1,510	2.8	-9.7
Malik, H. Lib Dem	1,387	2.6	-0.6
Firkins, T. Green	809	1.5	-1.3
Lab/Co-op majority	15,603	29.36	
Electorate	81,714		
Turnout	53,138	65.03	

Lab/Co-op hold (3.12% from Con to Lab/Co-op)

FERMANAGH AND SOUTH TYRONE

		%	+/-%
Gildernew, M. Sinn Féin	25,230	47.0	1.9
Elliott, T. UUP*	24,355	45.3	-0.8
Garrity, M. SDLP	2,587	4.8	-0.5
Campbell, N. All	886	1.6	0.4
Jones, T. Green	423	0.8	-0.8
Sinn Féin majority	875	1.63	
Electorate	70,601		
Turnout	53,714	76.08	

Sinn Féin gain (1.33% from UUP to Sinn Féin)

NORTH EAST FIFE

		%	+/-%
Gethins, S. SNP*	13,743	32.8	-8.0
Riches, E. Lib Dem	13,741	32.8	1.5
Miklinski, T. Con	10,088	24.1	7.8
Garton, R. Lab	4,026	9.6	2.0
Scott-Hayward, M. Ind Sov Dem Britain	224	0.5	-0.2
SNP majority	2	0	
Electorate	58,685		
Turnout	41,848	71.31	

SNP hold (4.8% from SNP to Lib Dem)

FILTON AND BRADLEY STOKE

		%	+/-%
Lopresti, J. Con*	25,339	49.8	3.3
Rylatt, N. Lab	21,149	41.6	15.0
Fielding, E. Lib Dem	3,052	6.0	-1.3
Warner, D. Green	1,162	2.3	-2.3
Con majority	4,190	8.24	
Electorate	72,483		
Turnout	50,866	70.18	

Con hold (5.87% from Con to Lab)

FINCHLEY AND GOLDERS GREEN

		%	+/-%
Freer, M. Con*	24,599	46.8	-3.9
Newmark, J. Lab	22,942	43.7	4.0
Davies, J. Lib Dem	3,463	6.6	3.3
Ward, A. Green	919	1.8	-0.9
Price, A. UKIP	462	0.9	-2.5
Con majority	1,657	3.15	
Electorate	73,329		
Turnout	52,544	71.66	

Con hold (3.98% from Con to Lab)

*Member of last Parliament

FOLKESTONE AND HYTHE

		%	+/-%
Collins, D. Con*	32,197	54.6	7.0
Davison, L. Lab	16,786	28.5	14.1
Beaumont, L. Lib Dem	4,222	7.2	-1.7
Priestley, S. UKIP	2,565	4.3	-18.3
Whybrow, M. Green	2,498	4.2	-1.1
Plumstead, D. Ind	493	0.8	
Slade, N. Ind	114	0.2	
Con majority	15,411	26.13	
Electorate	86,272		
Turnout	58,972	68.36	

Con hold (3.56% from Con to Lab)

FOREST OF DEAN

		%	+/-%
Harper, M. Con*	28,096	54.2	7.5
Stammers, S. Lab	18,594	35.9	11.3
Ellard, J. Lib Dem	2,029	3.9	-1.4
Greenwood, J. Green	1,241	2.4	-3.1
Warrender, E. UKIP	1,237	2.4	-15.3
Burrett, J. Ind	570	1.1	
Con majority	9,502	18.33	
Electorate	70,898		
Turnout	51,848	73.13	

Con hold (1.9% from Con to Lab)

FOYLE

		%	+/-%
McCallion, E. Sinn Féin	18,256	39.6	8.4
Durkan, M. SDLP*	18,087	39.2	-8.0
Middleton, G. DUP	7,398	16.0	3.8
Harkin, S. PBPA	1,377	3.0	
Doherty, J. All	847	1.8	-0.4
Sinn Féin majority	169	0.37	
Electorate	70,324		
Turnout	46,136	65.6	

Sinn Féin gain (8.24% from SDLP to Sinn Féin)

FYLDE

		%	+/-%
Menzies, M. Con*	27,334	58.7	9.7
Sullivan, J. Lab	15,529	33.3	14.6
van Mierlo, F. Lib Dem	2,341	5.0	1.3
Rothery, T. Green	1,263	2.7	-0.4
Con majority	11,805	25.34	
Electorate	65,937		
Turnout	46,594	70.66	

Con hold (2.45% from Con to Lab)

GAINSBOROUGH

		%	+/-%
Leigh, E. Con*	31,790	61.6	9.2
Tite, C. Lab	14,767	28.6	7.4
Rollings, L. Lib Dem	3,630	7.0	0.4
Pearson, V. Green	1,238	2.4	-0.2
Con majority	17,023	33.01	
Electorate	75,893		
Turnout	51,575	67.96	

Con hold (0.88% from Lab to Con)

GARSTON AND HALEWOOD

		%	+/-%
Eagle, M. Lab*	41,599	77.5	8.7
Marsden, A. Con	9,450	17.6	4.0
Martin, A. Lib Dem	1,723	3.2	-1.4
Brown, L. Green	750	1.4	-2.0
Lab majority	32,149	59.91	
Electorate	75,248		
Turnout	53,665	71.32	

Lab hold (2.36% from Con to Lab)

GATESHEAD

		%	+/-%
Mearns, I. Lab*	27,426	65.0	8.4
Hankinson, L. Con	10,076	23.9	9.4
Bell, M. UKIP	2,281	5.4	-12.4
Hindle, F. Lib Dem	1,709	4.0	-2.7
Redfern, A. Green	611	1.5	-2.6
Lab majority	17,350	41.14	
Electorate	65,186		
Turnout	42,174	64.7	

Lab hold (0.52% from Lab to Con)

GEDLING

		%	+/-%
Coaker, V. Lab*	26,833	51.8	9.7
Abbott, C. Con	22,139	42.8	6.8
Waters, L. UKIP	1,143	2.2	-12.2
Swift, R. Lib Dem	1,052	2.0	-1.9
Connick, R. Green	515	1.0	-2.2
Lab majority	4,694	9.07	
Electorate	71,223		
Turnout	51,765	72.68	

Lab hold (1.44% from Con to Lab)

GILLINGHAM AND RAINHAM

		%	+/-%
Chishti, R. Con*	27,091	55.3	7.6
Stamp, A. Lab	17,661	36.1	10.6
Cook, M. UKIP	2,097	4.3	-15.2
Chaplin, P. Lib Dem	1,372	2.8	-0.8
Gregory, C. Green	520	1.1	-1.3
Peacock, R. CPA	127	0.3	
Con majority	9,430	19.26	
Electorate	72,903		
Turnout	48,958	67.15	

Con hold (1.51% from Con to Lab)

VALE OF GLAMORGAN

		%	+/-%
Cairns, A. Con*	25,501	47.4	1.5
Beaven, C. Lab	23,311	43.3	10.8
Johnson, I. PlC	2,295	4.3	-1.3
Geroni, J. Lib Dem	1,020	1.9	-0.6
Hunter-Clarke, M. UKIP	868	1.6	-9.1
Davis-Barker, S. Green	419	0.8	-1.3
Lovell, S. WEP	177	0.3	
Elston, D. Pirate	127	0.2	
Con majority	2,190	4.07	
Electorate	73,959		
Turnout	53,781	72.72	

Con hold (4.66% from Con to Lab)

GLASGOW CENTRAL

		%	+/-%
Thewliss, A. SNP*	16,096	44.6	-7.9
Hameed, F. Lab	13,829	38.3	5.3
Fairbanks, C. Con	5,014	13.9	7.9
Nelson, I. Lib Dem	1,045	2.9	1.3
SNP majority	2,267	6.28	
Electorate	64,346		
Turnout	36,098	56.1	

SNP hold (6.59% from SNP to Lab)

GLASGOW EAST

		%	+/-%
Linden, D. SNP	14,024	38.7	-18.1
Watson, K. Lab	13,949	38.5	6.2
Kerr, T. Con	6,816	18.8	12.8
Clark, M. Lib Dem	567	1.6	0.8
Ferguson, J. UKIP	504	1.4	-1.2
Finegan, K. Ind	158	0.4	
Marshall, S. SDP	148	0.4	
SNP majority	75	0.21	
Electorate	66,242		
Turnout	36,222	54.68	

SNP hold (12.14% from SNP to Lab)

GLASGOW NORTH

		%	+/-%
Grady, P. SNP*	12,597	37.6	-15.5
Duncan-Glancy, P. Lab	11,537	34.4	6.5
Cullen, S. Con	4,935	14.7	6.9
Harvie, P. Green	3,251	9.7	3.5
Shepherd, C. Lib Dem	1,153	3.4	0.7
SNP majority	1,060	3.16	
Electorate	53,862		
Turnout	33,534	62.26	

SNP hold (10.99% from SNP to Lab)

GLASGOW NORTH EAST

		%	+/-%
Sweeney, P. Lab/Co-op	13,637	42.8	9.2
McLaughlin, A. SNP*	13,395	42.1	-15.8
Wyllie, J. Con	4,106	12.9	8.2
Donaldson, D. Lib Dem	637	2.0	1.2
Lab/Co-op majority	242	0.76	
Electorate	59,931		
Turnout	31,832	53.11	

Lab/Co-op gain (12.54% from SNP to Lab/Co-op)

GLASGOW NORTH WEST

		%	+/-%
Monaghan, C. SNP*	16,508	42.4	-12.0
Shanks, M. Lab	13,947	35.8	5.0
Land, C. Con	7,002	18.0	9.6
Speirs, J. Lib Dem	1,387	3.6	0.8
SNP majority	2,561	6.58	
Electorate	63,773		
Turnout	38,933	61.05	

SNP hold (8.5% from SNP to Lab)

GLASGOW SOUTH

		%	+/-%
McDonald, S. SNP*	18,312	41.0	-13.8
Dinning, E. Lab	16,285	36.5	6.8
Muir, T. Con	8,506	19.1	9.3
Hoyle, E. Lib Dem	1,447	3.2	1.1
SNP majority	2,027	4.54	
Electorate	69,126		
Turnout	44,633	64.57	

SNP hold (10.29% from SNP to Lab)

GLASGOW SOUTH WEST

		%	+/-%
Stephens, C. SNP*	14,386	40.6	-16.5
Kerr, M. Lab/Co-op	14,326	40.4	7.6
Haddow, T. Con	5,524	15.6	10.6
Denton-Cardew, B. Lib Dem	661	1.9	0.9
Hemy, S. UKIP	481	1.4	-1.0
SNP majority	60	0.17	
Electorate	62,991		
Turnout	35,444	56.27	

SNP hold (12.06% from SNP to Lab/Co-op)

GLENROTHES

		%	+/-%
Grant, P. SNP*	17,291	42.8	-17.0
Craik, A. Lab	14,024	34.7	4.1
Brown, A. Con	7,876	19.5	11.8
Bell, R. Lib Dem	1,208	3.0	1.1
SNP majority	3,267	8.08	
Electorate	66,378		
Turnout	40,440	60.92	

SNP hold (10.54% from SNP to Lab)

GLOUCESTER

		%	+/-%
Graham, R. Con*	27,208	50.3	5.0
Kirby, B. Lab	21,688	40.0	8.6
Hilton, J. Lib Dem	2,716	5.0	-0.3
Woolf, D. UKIP	1,495	2.8	-11.5
Hartley, G. Green	754	1.4	-1.4
Ridgeon, G. Loony	210	0.4	0.0
Con majority	5,520	10.19	
Electorate	82,964		
Turnout	54,147	65.27	

Con hold (1.78% from Con to Lab)

GORDON

		%	+/-%
Clark, C. Con	21,861	40.7	29.0
Salmond, A. SNP*	19,254	35.8	-11.8
Muat, K. Lab	6,340	11.8	5.9
Evans, D. Lib Dem	6,230	11.6	-21.1
Con majority	2,607	4.85	
Electorate	78,531		
Turnout	53,740	68.43	

Con gain (20.38% from SNP to Con)

*Member of last Parliament

GOSPORT

		%	+/-%
Dinenage, C. Con*	30,647	61.9	6.7
Durrant, A. Lab	13,436	27.1	12.6
Tennent, B. Lib Dem	2,328	4.7	-2.2
Palmer, C. UKIP	1,790	3.6	-15.8
Cassidy, M. Green	1,024	2.1	-1.5
Roberts, J. Ind	256	0.5	0.3
Con majority	17,211	34.76	
Electorate	74,152		
Turnout	49,509	66.77	

Con hold (2.98% from Con to Lab)

GOWER

		%	+/-%
Antoniazzi, T. Lab	22,727	49.8	12.8
Davies, B. Con*	19,458	42.6	5.6
Roberts, H. PlC	1,669	3.7	-3.5
Evans, H. Lib Dem	931	2.0	-1.6
Ford, R. UKIP	642	1.4	-9.7
Winstanley, J. Pirate	149	0.3	
Lab majority	3,269	7.16	
Electorate	62,163		
Turnout	45,629	73.4	

Lab gain (3.62% from Con to Lab)

GRANTHAM AND STAMFORD

		%	+/-%
Boles, N. Con*	35,090	61.9	9.3
Fairbairn, B. Lab	14,996	26.4	9.6
Day, A. Lib Dem	3,120	5.5	-0.5
King, M. UKIP	1,745	3.1	-14.4
Mahmood, T. Ind	860	1.5	
Thackray, B. Green	782	1.4	-2.1
Con majority	20,094	35.44	
Electorate	81,740		
Turnout	56,699	69.37	

Con hold (0.18% from Con to Lab)

GRAVESHAM

		%	+/-%
Holloway, A. Con*	27,237	55.5	8.8
Garford, M. Lab	17,890	36.4	6.4
Feyisetan, E. UKIP	1,742	3.5	-14.9
Willis, J. Lib Dem	1,210	2.5	0.3
Gilligan, M. Green	723	1.5	-0.8
Rogan, M. Ind	195	0.4	
Con majority	9,347	19.03	
Electorate	72,954		
Turnout	49,106	67.31	

Con hold (1.21% from Lab to Con)

GREAT GRIMSBY

		%	+/-%
Onn, M. Lab*	17,545	49.3	9.7
Gideon, J. Con	14,980	42.1	15.9
Hookem, M. UKIP	1,648	4.6	-20.3
Beasant, S. Lib Dem	954	2.7	-2.3
McGilligan-Fell, C. Ind	394	1.1	
Lab majority	2,565	7.21	
Electorate	61,743		
Turnout	35,581	57.63	

Lab hold (3.11% from Lab to Con)

GREAT YARMOUTH

		%	+/-%
Lewis, B. Con*	23,901	53.9	11.1
Smith-Clare, M. Lab	15,928	35.9	6.9
Blaiklock, C. UKIP	2,767	6.2	-16.8
Joyce, J. Lib Dem	987	2.2	-0.1
Webb, H. Green	563	1.3	-0.9
Con majority	7,973	17.98	
Electorate	71,408		
Turnout	44,349	62.11	

Con hold (2.09% from Lab to Con)

GREENWICH AND WOOLWICH

		%	+/-%
Pennycook, M. Lab*	34,215	64.2	12.2
Attfield, C. Con	13,501	25.3	-1.2
Adams, C. Lib Dem	3,785	7.1	1.5
Garrun, D. Green	1,605	3.0	-3.4
Lab majority	20,714	38.86	
Electorate	77,190		
Turnout	53,306	69.06	

Lab hold (6.69% from Con to Lab)

GUILDFORD

		%	+/-%
Milton, A. Con*	30,295	54.4	-2.4
Franklin, Z. Lib Dem	13,255	23.8	8.4
Smith, H. Lab	10,545	18.9	6.9
Bray-Parry, M. Green	1,152	2.1	-2.7
Morris, J. Peace Party	205	0.4	-0.1
Essessi, S. Ind	57	0.1	
Con majority	17,040	30.62	
Electorate	75,455		
Turnout	55,656	73.76	

Con hold (5.42% from Con to Lib Dem)

HACKNEY NORTH AND STOKE NEWINGTON

		%	+/-%
Abbott, D. Lab*	42,265	74.8	12.2
Gray, A. Con	7,126	12.6	-2.0
Richards, J. Lib Dem	3,817	6.8	1.8
Binnie-Lubbock, A. Green	2,606	4.6	-9.9
Homan, J. AWP	222	0.4	-0.1
Spielmann, A. Ind	203	0.4	
Khan, S. Friends	59	0.1	
Lab majority	35,139	62.21	
Electorate	85,058		
Turnout	56,485	66.41	

Lab hold (7.14% from Con to Lab)

HACKNEY SOUTH AND SHOREDITCH

		%	+/-%
Hillier, M. Lab/Co-op*	43,974	79.1	15.0
Parker, L. Con	6,043	10.9	-2.6
Raval, D. Lib Dem	3,168	5.7	1.1
Johnson, R. Green	1,522	2.7	-8.8
Hudson, V. AWP	226	0.4	
Higgs, R. Ind	143	0.3	0.1
Watt, A. CPA	113	0.2	-0.3
Leff, J. WRP	86	0.2	0.0
Sugg, H. Ind	50	0.1	
Kalamazad, D. Ind	29	0.1	
Lab/Co-op majority	37,931	68.26	
Electorate	83,099		
Turnout	55,569	66.87	

Lab/Co-op hold (8.77% from Con to Lab/Co-op)

HALESOWEN AND ROWLEY REGIS

		%	+/-%
Morris, J. Con*	23,012	51.8	8.7
Cooper, I. Lab	17,759	39.9	3.9
Henley, S. UKIP	2,126	4.8	-11.8
Scott, J. Lib Dem	859	1.9	-0.1
Robertson, J. Green	440	1.0	-0.9
Weller, T. Ind	183	0.4	
Con majority	5,253	11.81	
Electorate	66,766		
Turnout	44,469	66.6	

Con hold (2.4% from Lab to Con)

HALIFAX

		%	+/-%
Lynch, H. Lab*	25,507	52.7	12.9
Pearson, C. Con	20,131	41.6	2.8
Weedon, M. UKIP	1,568	3.2	-9.5
Baker, J. Lib Dem	1,070	2.2	-1.5
Lab majority	5,376	11.11	
Electorate	71,224		
Turnout	48,375	67.92	

Lab hold (5.08% from Con to Lab)

HALTEMPRICE AND HOWDEN

		%	+/-%
Davis, D. Con*	31,355	60.8	6.8
Devanney, H. Lab	15,950	30.9	10.0
Nolan, D. Lib Dem	2,482	4.8	-1.4
Wallis, D. YP	942	1.8	
Needham, C. Green	711	1.4	-2.3
Con majority	15,405	29.86	
Electorate	71,519		
Turnout	51,599	72.15	

Con hold (1.62% from Con to Lab)

HALTON

		%	+/-%
Twigg, D. Lab*	36,115	72.8	10.2
Lloyd, M. Con	10,710	21.6	3.9
Redican, G. UKIP	1,488	3.0	-11.0
Bate, R. Lib Dem	896	1.8	-0.6
Turton, V. Ind	309	0.6	0.0
Lab majority	25,405	51.22	
Electorate	73,457		
Turnout	49,603	67.53	

Lab hold (3.17% from Con to Lab)

HAMMERSMITH

		%	+/-%
Slaughter, A. Lab*	33,375	63.7	13.9
Dewhirst, C. Con	14,724	28.1	-8.2
Onstad, J. Lib Dem	2,802	5.3	0.7
Horn, A. Green	800	1.5	-2.8
Bovill, J. UKIP	507	1.0	-3.4
Hauzaree, J. Ind	44	0.1	
Lab majority	18,651	35.61	
Electorate	72,803		
Turnout	52,383	71.95	

Lab hold (11.03% from Con to Lab)

EAST HAMPSHIRE

		%	+/-%
Hinds, D. Con*	35,263	63.5	3.0
Dasgupta, R. Lab	9,411	16.9	6.9
Robinson, R. Lib Dem	8,403	15.1	4.1
Knight, R. Green	1,760	3.2	-3.0
Jerrard, S. JACP	571	1.0	
Con majority	25,852	46.52	
Electorate	74,151		
Turnout	55,567	74.94	

Con hold (1.92% from Con to Lab)

NORTH EAST HAMPSHIRE

		%	+/-%
Jayawardena, R. Con*	37,754	65.4	-0.3
Jones, B. Lab	9,982	17.3	7.5
Cockarill, G. Lib Dem	6,987	12.1	1.7
Spradbery, C. Green	1,476	2.6	-1.8
Gascoigne, M. UKIP	1,061	1.8	-6.9
Blay, R. Ind	367	0.6	
Con majority	27,772	48.09	
Electorate	75,476		
Turnout	57,748	76.51	

Con hold (3.9% from Con to Lab)

NORTH WEST HAMPSHIRE

		%	+/-%
Malthouse, K. Con*	36,471	61.9	4.1
Fitchet, A. Lab	13,792	23.4	10.2
Payton, A. Lib Dem	5,708	9.7	0.4
Clark, R. UKIP	1,467	2.5	-12.1
Hill, D. Green	1,334	2.3	-2.3
Con majority	22,679	38.52	
Electorate	81,430		
Turnout	58,880	72.31	

Con hold (3.05% from Con to Lab)

HAMPSTEAD AND KILBURN

		%	+/-%
Siddiq, T. Lab*	34,464	58.8	14.6
Leyland, C. Con	18,904	32.3	-9.9
Allan, K. Lib Dem	4,100	7.0	1.4
Mansook, J. Green	742	1.3	-3.1
Easterbrook, H. Ind	136	0.2	
Weiss, ". Ind	61	0.1	
Lab majority	15,560	26.57	
Electorate	82,957		
Turnout	58,572	70.61	

Lab hold (12.24% from Con to Lab)

HARBOROUGH

		%	+/-%
O'Brien, N. Con	30,135	52.2	-0.3
Thomas, A. Lab	17,706	30.7	15.4
Haq, Z. Lib Dem	7,286	12.6	-0.7
Khong, T. UKIP	1,361	2.4	-11.9
Woodiwiss, D. Green	1,110	1.9	-2.2
Con majority	12,429	21.53	
Electorate	78,810		
Turnout	57,716	73.23	

Con hold (7.87% from Con to Lab)

*Member of last Parliament

HARLOW

		%	+/-%
Halfon, R. Con*	24,230	53.9	5.2
Waite, P. Lab	17,199	38.3	8.4
Gough, M. UKIP	1,787	4.0	-12.3
Seeff, G. Lib Dem	970	2.2	0.1
Clare, H. Green	660	1.5	-0.7
Con majority	7,031	15.65	
Electorate	67,699		
Turnout	44,921	66.35	

Con hold (1.59% from Con to Lab)

HARROGATE AND KNARESBOROUGH

		%	+/-%
Jones, A. Con*	31,477	55.3	2.7
Flynn, H. Lib Dem	13,309	23.4	1.4
Sewards, M. Lab	11,395	20.0	9.9
Fraser, D. Ind	559	1.0	
Con majority	18,168	31.94	
Electorate	77,280		
Turnout	56,879	73.6	

Con hold (0.68% from Lib Dem to Con)

HARROW EAST

		%	+/-%
Blackman, B. Con*	25,129	49.3	-0.9
Shah, N. Lab	23,372	45.8	5.3
Bernard, A. Lib Dem	1,573	3.1	1.0
Wallace, E. Green	771	1.5	-0.2
Con majority	1,757	3.45	
Electorate	71,755		
Turnout	50,987	71.06	

Con hold (3.12% from Con to Lab)

HARROW WEST

		%	+/-%
Thomas, G. Lab/Co-op*	30,640	60.7	13.9
David, H. Con	17,326	34.3	-7.8
Noyce, C. Lib Dem	1,267	2.5	-0.8
Langley, R. Green	652	1.3	-1.5
Alagaratnam, R. UKIP	470	0.9	-3.5
Lab/Co-op majority	13,314	26.37	
Electorate	69,797		
Turnout	50,483	72.33	

Lab/Co-op hold (10.83% from Con to Lab/Co-op)

HARTLEPOOL

		%	+/-%
Hill, M. Lab	21,969	52.4	16.9
Jackson, C. Con	14,319	34.2	13.3
Broughton, P. UKIP	4,801	11.4	-16.5
Hagon, A. Lib Dem	746	1.8	-0.1
Lab majority	7,650	18.25	
Electorate	71,718		
Turnout	41,921	58.45	

Lab hold (1.78% from Con to Lab)

HARWICH AND NORTH ESSEX

		%	+/-%
Jenkin, B. Con*	29,921	58.4	7.5
Scott, R. Lab	15,565	30.4	10.7
Graham, D. Lib Dem	2,787	5.4	-1.9
Hammond, A. UKIP	1,685	3.3	-14.1
Roberts, B. Green	1,042	2.0	-2.3
Todd, S. CPA	141	0.3	
Con majority	14,356	28.03	
Electorate	71,294		
Turnout	51,224	71.85	

Con hold (1.6% from Con to Lab)

HASTINGS AND RYE

		%	+/-%
Rudd, A. Con*	25,668	46.8	2.3
Chowney, P. Lab	25,322	46.1	11.1
Perry, N. Lib Dem	1,885	3.4	0.3
Phillips, M. UKIP	1,479	2.7	-10.6
Wilson, N. Ind	412	0.8	
Con majority	346	0.63	
Electorate	78,319		
Turnout	54,863	70.05	

Con hold (4.38% from Con to Lab)

HAVANT

		%	+/-%
Mak, A. Con*	27,676	59.7	8.2
Giles, G. Lab	11,720	25.3	9.4
Gray, P. Lib Dem	2,801	6.0	-0.5
Perry, J. UKIP	2,011	4.3	-16.2
Dawes, T. Green	1,122	2.4	-2.8
Buckley, A. Ind	984	2.1	
Con majority	15,956	34.4	
Electorate	72,470		
Turnout	46,390	64.01	

Con hold (0.6% from Con to Lab)

HAYES AND HARLINGTON

		%	+/-%
McDonnell, J. Lab*	31,796	66.3	7.0
Smith, G. Con	13,681	28.6	3.9
Dixon, C. UKIP	1,153	2.4	-9.5
Newton Dunn, B. Lib Dem	601	1.3	-0.7
Bowman, J. Green	571	1.2	-0.6
Lab majority	18,115	37.8	
Electorate	73,267		
Turnout	47,920	65.4	

Lab hold (1.53% from Con to Lab)

HAZEL GROVE

		%	+/-%
Wragg, W. Con*	20,047	45.3	4.1
Smart, L. Lib Dem	14,533	32.9	6.7
Mishra, N. Lab	9,036	20.4	2.9
Lee, R. Green	516	1.2	-1.5
Con majority	5,514	12.46	
Electorate	63,166		
Turnout	44,246	70.05	

Con hold (1.33% from Con to Lib Dem)

HEMEL HEMPSTEAD

		%	+/-%
Penning, M. Con*	28,735	54.8	2.1
Tattershall, M. Lab	19,290	36.8	13.1
Symington, S. Lib Dem	3,233	6.2	1.4
Hassan, S. Green	1,024	2.0	-1.4
Con majority	9,445	18.01	
Electorate	74,415		
Turnout	52,433	70.46	

Con hold (5.47% from Con to Lab)

HEMSWORTH

		%	+/-%
Trickett, J. Lab*	25,740	55.9	4.8
Jordan, M. Con	15,566	33.8	11.1
Dews, D. UKIP	2,591	5.6	-14.5
Roberts, M. YP	1,135	2.5	
MacQueen, M. Lib Dem	912	2.0	-1.2
Lab majority	10,174	22.1	
Electorate	71,870		
Turnout	46,027	64.04	

Lab hold (3.14% from Lab to Con)

HENDON

		%	+/-%
Offord, M. Con*	25,078	47.9	-1.0
Katz, M. Lab	24,006	45.9	4.5
Hill, A. Lib Dem	1,985	3.8	1.6
Legarda, C. Green	578	1.1	-0.9
Warsame, S. UKIP	568	1.1	-4.1
Con majority	1,072	2.05	
Electorate	76,522		
Turnout	52,330	68.39	

Con hold (2.72% from Con to Lab)

HENLEY

		%	+/-%
Howell, J. Con*	33,749	59.0	0.7
Kavanagh, O. Lab	11,455	20.0	7.5
Coyle, L. Lib Dem	8,485	14.8	3.6
Bennett, R. Green	1,864	3.3	-3.6
Scott, T. UKIP	1,154	2.0	-8.8
Gray, P. Radical	392	0.7	
Con majority	22,294	38.96	
Electorate	74,997		
Turnout	57,218	76.29	

Con hold (3.42% from Con to Lab)

HEREFORD AND SOUTH HEREFORDSHIRE

		%	+/-%
Norman, J. Con*	27,004	53.4	1.1
Coda, A. Lab	11,991	23.7	11.0
Kenyon, J. Ind	5,560	11.0	
Hurds, L. Lib Dem	3,556	7.0	-3.5
Toynbee, D. Green	1,220	2.4	-4.8
Price, G. UKIP	1,153	2.3	-14.5
Con majority	15,013	29.7	
Electorate	71,088		
Turnout	50,555	71.12	

Con hold (4.96% from Con to Lab)

NORTH HEREFORDSHIRE

		%	+/-%
Wiggin, B. Con*	31,097	61.8	6.4
Page, R. Lab	9,495	18.9	7.5
Falconer, J. Lib Dem	5,874	11.7	-0.3
Chowns, E. Green	2,771	5.5	-1.4
Norris, S. Ind	577	1.1	
Devine, A. Ind	363	0.7	
Con majority	21,602	42.95	
Electorate	67,751		
Turnout	50,293	74.23	

Con hold (0.55% from Con to Lab)

HERTFORD AND STORTFORD

		%	+/-%
Prisk, M. Con*	36,184	60.1	4.2
Chibah, K. Lab	17,149	28.5	10.6
Argent, M. Lib Dem	4,845	8.1	0.3
Woollcombe, D. Green	1,814	3.0	-1.7
Con majority	19,035	31.61	
Electorate	82,339		
Turnout	60,222	73.14	

Con hold (3.22% from Con to Lab)

NORTH EAST HERTFORDSHIRE

		%	+/-%
Heald, O. Con*	32,587	58.5	3.3
Swanney, D. Lab	15,752	28.3	9.5
Shepard, N. Lib Dem	4,276	7.7	0.1
Lee, T. Green	2,965	5.3	0.0
Con majority	16,835	30.2	
Electorate	75,965		
Turnout	55,748	73.39	

Con hold (3.09% from Con to Lab)

SOUTH WEST HERTFORDSHIRE

		%	+/-%
Gauke, D. Con*	35,128	57.8	1.0
Wakely, R. Lab	15,578	25.6	9.4
Townsend, C. Lib Dem	7,078	11.6	1.4
de Hoest, P. Green	1,576	2.6	-1.9
Anderson, M. UKIP	1,293	2.1	-9.4
Con majority	19,550	32.16	
Electorate	81,087		
Turnout	60,791	74.97	

Con hold (4.18% from Con to Lab)

HERTSMERE

		%	+/-%
Dowden, O. Con*	31,928	60.9	2.0
Smith, F. Lab	14,977	28.6	6.3
Jordan, J. Lib Dem	2,794	5.3	-0.2
Hoy, D. UKIP	1,564	3.0	-9.7
Summerhayes, S. Green	990	1.9	
Con majority	16,951	32.36	
Electorate	73,561		
Turnout	52,389	71.22	

Con hold (2.14% from Con to Lab)

*Member of last Parliament

HEXHAM

		%	+/-%
Opperman, G. Con*	24,996	54.0	1.4
Powers, S. Lab/Co-op	15,760	34.0	9.2
Hall, F. Lib Dem	3,285	7.1	0.3
Foot, W. Green	1,253	2.7	-2.9
Miles, S. UKIP	930	2.0	-7.9
Con majority	9,236	19.95	
Electorate	61,053		
Turnout	46,303	75.84	

Con hold (3.88% from Con to Lab/Co-op)

HEYWOOD AND MIDDLETON

		%	+/-%
McInnes, L. Lab*	26,578	53.2	10.2
Clarkson, C. Con	18,961	38.0	18.9
Seville, L. UKIP	3,239	6.5	-25.6
Winlow, B. Lib Dem	1,087	2.2	-1.1
Lab majority	7,617	15.25	
Electorate	79,901		
Turnout	49,962	62.53	

Lab hold (4.35% from Lab to Con)

HIGH PEAK

		%	+/-%
George, R. Lab	26,753	49.5	14.3
Bingham, A. Con*	24,431	45.2	0.4
Lawley, C. Lib Dem	2,669	4.9	0.3
Lab majority	2,322	4.3	
Electorate	73,248		
Turnout	54,013	73.74	

Lab gain (6.96% from Con to Lab)

HITCHIN AND HARPENDEN

		%	+/-%
Afolami, B. Con	31,189	52.9	-3.9
Hayes, J. Lab	19,158	32.5	11.9
Annand, H. Lib Dem	6,236	10.6	2.5
Cano, R. Green	1,329	2.3	-3.3
Blake, R. Ind	629	1.1	
Cordle, S. CPA	242	0.4	
Con majority	12,031	20.42	
Electorate	75,916		
Turnout	58,921	77.61	

Con hold (7.9% from Con to Lab)

HOLBORN AND ST PANCRAS

		%	+/-%
Starmer, K. Lab*	41,343	69.9	17.2
Barnes, T. Con	10,834	18.3	-3.5
Crosher, S. Lib Dem	4,020	6.8	0.3
Berry, S. Green	1,980	3.4	-9.4
Game, G. UKIP	727	1.2	-3.7
Polenceus, J. Eng Dem	93	0.2	
Lab majority	30,509	51.56	
Electorate	88,088		
Turnout	59,175	67.18	

Lab hold (10.32% from Con to Lab)

General Election 2017

HORNCHURCH AND UPMINSTER

		%	+/-%
Dockerill, J. Con	33,750	60.1	11.2
Gill, R. Lab	16,027	28.5	8.5
Webb, L. UKIP	3,502	6.2	-19.0
Mitchell, J. Lib Dem	1,371	2.4	-0.3
Caton, P. Green	1,077	1.9	-0.6
Furness, D. BNP	318	0.6	0.2
Con majority	17,723	31.56	
Electorate	80,802		
Turnout	56,155	69.5	

Con hold (1.37% from Lab to Con)

HORNSEY AND WOOD GREEN

		%	+/-%
West, C. Lab*	40,738	65.2	14.5
Barnes, D. Lib Dem	10,000	16.0	-15.7
Lane, E. Con	9,246	14.8	5.6
Hall, S. Green	1,181	1.9	-3.5
Ali, N. WEP	551	0.9	
Price, R. UKIP	429	0.7	-1.5
Spiby-Vann, H. CPA	93	0.2	-0.1
Athow, A. WRP	55	0.1	-0.1
Lab majority	30,738	49.22	
Electorate	79,946		
Turnout	62,451	78.12	

Lab hold (15.07% from Lib Dem to Lab)

HORSHAM

		%	+/-%
Quin, J. Con*	36,906	59.4	2.4
Brady, S. Lab	13,422	21.6	10.3
Millson, M. Lib Dem	7,644	12.3	0.7
Ross, C. Green	1,844	3.0	-0.9
Arthur, R. UKIP	1,533	2.5	-11.5
Smith, J. SN	375	0.6	-0.1
Duggan, J. Peace Party	263	0.4	-0.1
Con majority	23,484	37.82	
Electorate	82,772		
Turnout	62,093	75.02	

Con hold (3.95% from Con to Lab)

HOUGHTON AND SUNDERLAND SOUTH

		%	+/-%
Phillipson, B. Lab*	24,665	59.4	4.5
Howell, P. Con	12,324	29.7	11.3
Joyce, M. UKIP	2,379	5.7	-15.7
Edgeworth, P. Lib Dem	908	2.2	0.1
Bradley, R. Green	725	1.7	-1.1
Watson, M. Ind	479	1.1	
Lab majority	12,341	29.7	
Electorate	68,123		
Turnout	41,557	61	

Lab hold (3.41% from Lab to Con)

HOVE

		%	+/-%
Kyle, P. Lab*	36,942	64.0	21.9
Adams, K. Con	18,185	31.5	-8.2
Hynds, C. Lib Dem	1,311	2.3	-1.3
Mac Cafferty, P. Green	971	1.7	-5.1
Sabel, C. Ind	187	0.3	
Lab majority	18,757	32.5	
Electorate	74,236		
Turnout	57,716	77.75	

Lab hold (15.08% from Con to Lab)

HUDDERSFIELD

		%	+/-%
Sheerman, B. Lab/Co-op*	26,470	60.2	15.5
Benton, S. Con	14,465	32.9	6.2
Cooper, A. Green	1,395	3.2	-3.7
Ali, Z. Lib Dem	1,155	2.6	-3.2
Katenga, B. YP	274	0.6	
Thokkudubiyyapu, M. Ind	75	0.2	
Lab/Co-op majority	12,005	27.32	
Electorate	67,037		
Turnout	43,950	65.56	

Lab/Co-op hold (4.63% from Con to Lab/Co-op)

KINGSTON UPON HULL EAST

		%	+/-%
Turner, K. Lab*	21,355	58.2	6.6
Burton, S. Con	10,959	29.9	14.0
Fox, M. UKIP	2,573	7.0	-15.3
Marchington, A. Lib Dem	1,258	3.4	-3.1
Brown, J. Green	493	1.3	-0.9
Lab majority	10,396	28.33	
Electorate	65,959		
Turnout	36,698	55.64	

Lab hold (3.69% from Lab to Con)

KINGSTON UPON HULL NORTH

		%	+/-%
Johnson, D. Lab*	23,685	63.7	11.1
Nici-Townend, L. Con	9,363	25.2	10.2
Ross, M. Lib Dem	1,869	5.0	-3.9
Kitchener, J. UKIP	1,601	4.3	-11.9
Deane, M. Green	604	1.6	-4.2
Lab majority	14,322	38.5	
Electorate	64,665		
Turnout	37,198	57.52	

Lab hold (0.43% from Con to Lab)

KINGSTON UPON HULL WEST AND HESSLE

		%	+/-%
Hardy, E. Lab	18,342	53.0	3.9
Mackay, C. Con	10,317	29.8	12.4
Thomas, C. Lib Dem	2,210	6.4	-3.6
Dewberry, M. Ind	1,898	5.5	
Shores, G. UKIP	1,399	4.0	-15.8
Lammiman, M. Green	332	1.0	-2.0
Taylor, W. Libertarian	67	0.2	
Lab majority	8,025	23.18	
Electorate	60,181		
Turnout	34,613	57.51	

Lab hold (4.23% from Lab to Con)

HUNTINGDON

		%	+/-%
Djanogly, J. Con*	32,915	55.0	2.1
Johnson, N. Lab	18,440	30.8	12.5
Cantrill, R. Lib Dem	5,090	8.5	0.7
Bullen, P. UKIP	2,180	3.6	-13.2
MacLennan, T. Green	1,095	1.8	-2.0
Con majority	14,475	24.18	
Electorate	84,273		
Turnout	59,856	71.03	

Con hold (5.2% from Con to Lab)

General Election 2017

HYNDBURN

		%	+/-%
Jones, G. Lab*	24,120	53.2	11.3
Horkin, K. Con	18,305	40.4	8.6
Brown, J. UKIP	1,953	4.3	-17.0
Jones, L. Lib Dem	824	1.8	-0.2
Lab majority	5,815	12.83	
Electorate	71,608		
Turnout	45,307	63.27	

Lab hold (1.32% from Con to Lab)

ILFORD NORTH

		%	+/-%
Streeting, W. Lab*	30,589	57.7	13.9
Scott, L. Con	20,950	39.5	-3.1
Clare, R. Lib Dem	1,034	2.0	-0.3
Osen, D. Ind	368	0.7	0.5
Lab majority	9,639	18.17	
Electorate	70,791		
Turnout	53,052	74.94	

Lab hold (8.49% from Con to Lab)

ILFORD SOUTH

		%	+/-%
Gapes, M. Lab/Co-op*	43,724	75.6	11.8
Chapman, C. Con	12,077	20.9	-4.9
Ahmed, F. Lib Dem	772	1.3	-0.6
Warrington, R. Green	542	0.9	-2.0
Saeed, T. UKIP	477	0.8	-4.4
Khan, K. Friends	65	0.1	
Lab/Co-op majority	31,647	54.75	
Electorate	82,487		
Turnout	57,803	70.08	

Lab/Co-op hold (8.39% from Con to Lab/Co-op)

INVERCLYDE

		%	+/-%
Cowan, R. SNP*	15,050	38.4	-16.6
McCluskey, M. Lab	14,666	37.5	7.2
Wilson, D. Con	8,399	21.4	11.5
Stevens, D. Lib Dem	978	2.5	0.0
SNP majority	384	0.98	
Electorate	58,853		
Turnout	39,150	66.52	

SNP hold (11.9% from SNP to Lab)

INVERNESS, NAIRN, BADENOCH AND STRATHSPEY

		%	+/-%
Hendry, D. SNP*	21,042	39.8	-10.2
Tulloch, N. Con	16,118	30.5	24.6
Robb, M. Lab	8,552	16.2	8.7
Cunningham, R. Lib Dem	6,477	12.3	-19.3
Boyd, D. Christian	612	1.2	0.4
SNP majority	4,924	9.31	
Electorate	76,844		
Turnout	52,868	68.8	

SNP hold (17.4% from SNP to Con)

*Member of last Parliament

IPSWICH

		%	+/-%
Martin, S. Lab	24,224	47.3	10.3
Gummer, B. Con*	23,393	45.7	1.0
Gould, T. UKIP	1,372	2.7	-9.0
Hyyrylainen-Trett, A. Lib Dem	1,187	2.3	-0.6
Armstrong, C. Green	840	1.6	-1.9
Tabane, D. Ind	121	0.2	
Lab majority	831	1.62	
Electorate	75,668		
Turnout	51,237	67.71	

Lab gain (4.64% from Con to Lab)

ISLE OF WIGHT

		%	+/-%
Seely, B. Con	38,190	51.2	10.6
Critchley, J. Lab	17,121	23.0	10.2
Lowthion, V. Green	12,915	17.3	4.0
Belfitt, N. Lib Dem	2,740	3.7	-3.8
Pitcher, D. UKIP	1,921	2.6	-18.6
Jones-Evans, J. Ind	1,592	2.1	
Con majority	21,069	28.25	
Electorate	110,683		
Turnout	74,574	67.38	

Con hold (0.2% from Lab to Con)

ISLINGTON NORTH

		%	+/-%
Corbyn, J. Lab*	40,086	72.8	12.8
Clark, J. Con	6,871	12.5	-4.6
Angus, K. Lib Dem	4,946	9.0	0.9
Russell, C. Green	2,229	4.0	-6.2
Fraser, K. UKIP	413	0.8	-3.2
Foster, M. Ind	208	0.4	
Knapp, K. Loony	106	0.2	
Cameron-Blackie, S. Ind	41	0.1	
Martin, B. SP	21	0.0	-0.2
Mendoza, A. Comm League	7	0.0	
Lab majority	33,215	60.34	
Electorate	74,831		
Turnout	55,050	73.57	

Lab hold (8.73% from Con to Lab)

ISLINGTON SOUTH AND FINSBURY

		%	+/-%
Thornberry, E. Lab*	30,188	62.6	11.9
Charalambous, J. Con	9,925	20.6	-1.6
Desmier, A. Lib Dem	5,809	12.1	1.2
Hamdache, B. Green	1,198	2.5	-5.1
Muswell, P. UKIP	929	1.9	-5.7
Lab majority	20,263	42.04	
Electorate	69,536		
Turnout	48,196	69.31	

Lab hold (6.72% from Con to Lab)

ISLWYN

		%	+/-%
Evans, C. Lab/Co-op*	21,238	58.7	9.8
Thomas, D. Con	9,826	27.2	12.0
Jones, D. PlC	2,739	7.6	-3.1
Smyth, J. UKIP	1,605	4.4	-15.1
Kidner, M. Lib Dem	685	1.9	-0.8
Lab/Co-op majority	11,412	31.55	
Electorate	56,256		
Turnout	36,171	64.3	

Lab/Co-op hold (1.11% from Lab/Co-op to Con)

JARROW

		%	+/-%
Hepburn, S. Lab*	28,020	65.0	9.5
Gwynn, R. Con	10,757	25.0	7.9
Askwith, J. UKIP	2,338	5.4	-14.2
Maughan, P. Lib Dem	1,163	2.7	-0.5
Herbert, D. Green	745	1.7	-1.7
Lab majority	17,263	40.05	
Electorate	64,778		
Turnout	43,100	66.53	

Lab hold (0.79% from Con to Lab)

KEIGHLEY

		%	+/-%
Grogan, J. Lab	24,056	46.4	8.5
Hopkins, K. Con*	23,817	46.0	1.8
Latham, P. UKIP	1,291	2.5	-9.0
Walker, M. Lib Dem	1,226	2.4	-0.3
Brown, R. Green	790	1.5	-1.9
Crabtree, D. Ind	534	1.0	
Lab majority	239	0.46	
Electorate	71,429		
Turnout	51,805	72.53	

Lab gain (3.33% from Con to Lab)

KENILWORTH AND SOUTHAM

		%	+/-%
Wright, J. Con*	31,207	60.7	2.5
Singh, B. Lab	13,131	25.5	10.3
Dickson, R. Lib Dem	4,921	9.6	-0.5
Ballantyne, R. Green	1,133	2.2	-1.8
Cottam, H. UKIP	929	1.8	-9.4
Con majority	18,076	35.15	
Electorate	66,319		
Turnout	51,420	77.53	

Con hold (3.9% from Con to Lab)

KENSINGTON

		%	+/-%
Dent Coad, E. Lab	16,333	42.1	11.1
Borwick, V. Con*	16,313	42.0	-10.0
Mullin, A. Lib Dem	4,724	12.2	6.6
Nadel, J. Green	767	2.0	-3.1
Torrance, J. Ind	393	1.0	
Marshall, P. Ind	98	0.3	
Lloyd, J. Green Soc	49	0.1	-0.2
Lab majority	20	0.05	
Electorate	60,588		
Turnout	38,795	64.03	

Lab gain (10.56% from Con to Lab)

KETTERING

		%	+/-%
Hollobone, P. Con*	28,616	57.8	6.1
Scrimshaw, M. Lab	18,054	36.5	11.4
Austin, S. Lib Dem	1,618	3.3	0.1
Reeves, R. Green	1,116	2.3	-1.2
Con majority	10,562	21.33	
Electorate	71,440		
Turnout	49,524	69.32	

Con hold (2.63% from Con to Lab)

KILMARNOCK AND LOUDOUN

		%	+/-%
Brown, A. SNP*	19,690	42.3	-13.3
Dover, L. Lab	13,421	28.8	-1.5
Harper, A. Con	12,404	26.6	14.1
Lang, I. Lib Dem	994	2.1	0.7
SNP majority	6,269	13.46	
Electorate	73,327		
Turnout	46,590	63.54	

SNP hold (5.91% from SNP to Lab)

KINGSTON AND SURBITON

		%	+/-%
Davey, E. Lib Dem	27,810	44.7	10.3
Berry, J. Con*	23,686	38.0	-1.1
South, L. Lab	9,203	14.8	0.3
Matthews, G. UKIP	675	1.1	-6.2
Walker, C. Green	536	0.9	-3.0
Chinnery, J. Loony	168	0.3	
Basman, M. Ind	100	0.2	
Lib Dem majority	4,124	6.62	
Electorate	81,588		
Turnout	62,265	76.32	

Lib Dem gain (5.7% from Con to Lib Dem)

KINGSTON UPON HULL EAST – see under Hull

KINGSTON UPON HULL NORTH – see under Hull

KINGSTON UPON HULL WEST AND HESSLE – see under Hull

KINGSWOOD

		%	+/-%
Skidmore, C. Con*	26,754	54.8	6.6
Threlfall, M. Lab	19,254	39.4	9.9
Wilkinson, K. Lib Dem	1,749	3.6	-0.2
Furey-King, M. Green	984	2.0	-0.8
Con majority	7,500	15.35	
Electorate	69,368		
Turnout	48,857	70.43	

Con hold (1.66% from Con to Lab)

KIRKCALDY AND COWDENBEATH

		%	+/-%
Laird, L. Lab	17,016	36.8	3.5
Mullin, R. SNP*	16,757	36.2	-15.9
Dempsey, D. Con	10,762	23.3	13.4
Wood, M. Lib Dem	1,118	2.4	0.3
Coburn, D. UKIP	540	1.2	-1.2
Lab majority	259	0.56	
Electorate	72,721		
Turnout	46,250	63.6	

Lab gain (9.7% from SNP to Lab)

KNOWSLEY

		%	+/-%
Howarth, G. Lab*	47,351	85.2	7.4
Spencer, J. Con	5,137	9.3	2.6
Miney, N. UKIP	1,285	2.3	-7.5
Cashman, C. Lib Dem	1,189	2.1	-0.8
Baines, S. Green	521	0.9	-1.5
Lab majority	42,214	75.99	
Electorate	81,760		
Turnout	55,551	67.94	

Lab hold (2.39% from Con to Lab)

LAGAN VALLEY

		%	+/-%
Donaldson, J. DUP*	26,762	59.4	11.8
Butler, R. UUP	7,533	16.7	1.6
McIntyre, A. All	4,996	11.1	-2.8
Catney, P. SDLP	3,384	7.5	1.3
Russell, J. Sinn Féin	1,567	3.5	0.6
Nickels, I. Con	462	1.0	-0.6
Orr, J. Ind	222	0.5	-1.4
DUP majority	19,229	42.69	
Electorate	72,380		
Turnout	45,044	62.23	

DUP hold (5.09% from UUP to DUP)

LANARK AND HAMILTON EAST

		%	+/-%
Crawley, A. SNP*	16,444	32.5	-16.2
Corbett, P. Con	16,178	32.0	16.2
Hilland, A. Lab	16,084	31.8	1.3
Robb, C. Lib Dem	1,214	2.4	0.2
MacKay, D. UKIP	550	1.1	-1.5
SNP majority	266	0.53	
Electorate	77,313		
Turnout	50,527	65.35	

SNP hold (16.2% from SNP to Con)

WEST LANCASHIRE

		%	+/-%
Cooper, R. Lab*	32,030	58.8	9.6
Currie, S. Con	20,341	37.3	5.0
Barton, J. Lib Dem	1,069	2.0	-0.6
Higgins, N. Green	680	1.3	-1.9
Braid, D. WVPTFP	269	0.5	0.2
Lab majority	11,689	21.45	
Electorate	73,257		
Turnout	54,503	74.4	

Lab hold (2.33% from Con to Lab)

LANCASTER AND FLEETWOOD

		%	+/-%
Smith, C. Lab*	25,342	55.0	12.9
Ollerenshaw, E. Con	18,681	40.5	1.5
Long, R. Lib Dem	1,170	2.5	-0.8
Novell, R. Green	796	1.7	-3.3
Lab majority	6,661	14.45	
Electorate	67,154		
Turnout	46,082	68.62	

Lab hold (5.72% from Con to Lab)

LEEDS CENTRAL

		%	+/-%
Benn, H. Lab*	33,453	70.0	15.3
Davies, G. Con	9,755	20.4	3.2
Palfreman, B. UKIP	2,056	4.3	-11.4
Carlisle, E. Green	1,189	2.5	-5.4
Nash, A. Lib Dem	1,063	2.2	-1.2
Coetzee, A. CPA	157	0.3	
Lab majority	23,698	49.59	
Electorate	89,537		
Turnout	47,789	53.37	

Lab hold (6.05% from Con to Lab)

LEEDS EAST

		%	+/-%
Burgon, R. Lab*	25,428	61.2	7.7
Robinson, M. Con	12,676	30.5	9.7
Spivey, P. UKIP	1,742	4.2	-14.7
Sanderson, E. Lib Dem	739	1.8	-1.6
Moran, J. Green	434	1.1	-1.9
Otley, J. YP	422	1.0	
Lab majority	12,752	30.71	
Electorate	65,950		
Turnout	41,530	62.97	

Lab hold (0.97% from Lab to Con)

LEEDS NORTH EAST

		%	+/-%
Hamilton, F. Lab*	33,436	63.0	15.3
Stephenson, R. Con	16,445	31.0	-1.8
Hannah, J. Lib Dem	1,952	3.7	-1.6
Forsaith, A. Green	680	1.3	-4.0
Seddon, T. YP	303	0.6	
Foote, C. Green Soc	116	0.2	-0.7
Mutamiri, T. CPA	67	0.1	
Lab majority	16,991	32	
Electorate	70,112		
Turnout	53,102	75.74	

Lab hold (8.53% from Con to Lab)

LEEDS NORTH WEST

		%	+/-%
Sobel, A. Lab/Co-op	20,416	44.0	14.1
Mulholland, G. Lib Dem*	16,192	34.9	-1.7
Lamb, A. Con	9,097	19.6	1.0
Hemingway, M. Green	582	1.3	-5.7
Lab/Co-op majority	4,224	9.11	
Electorate	68,152		
Turnout	46,384	68.06	

Lab/Co-op gain (7.9% from Lib Dem to Lab/Co-op)

LEEDS WEST

		%	+/-%
Reeves, R. Lab*	27,013	63.9	16.0
Metcalfe, Z. Con	11,048	26.1	6.1
Thackray, M. UKIP	1,815	4.3	-14.1
Pointon, A. Green	1,023	2.4	-5.9
McGregor, A. Lib Dem	905	2.1	-1.7
Jones, E. YP	378	0.9	
Davies, M. Green Soc	47	0.1	
Lab majority	15,965	37.74	
Electorate	67,955		
Turnout	42,301	62.25	

Lab hold (4.97% from Con to Lab)

LEICESTER EAST

		%	+/-%
Vaz, K. Lab*	35,116	66.7	6.2
He, E. Con	12,688	24.1	1.4
Barot, S. Ind	1,753	3.3	
Dave, N. Lib Dem	1,343	2.5	0.0
Wakley, M. Green	1,070	2.0	-1.0
Fox, I. Ind	454	0.9	
Lab majority	22,428	42.57	
Electorate	77,792		
Turnout	52,682	67.72	

Lab hold (2.41% from Con to Lab)

*Member of last Parliament

LEICESTER SOUTH

		%	+/-%
Ashworth, J. Lab/Co-op*	37,157	73.3	14.0
Sonecha, M. Con	10,896	21.5	0.7
Bisnauthsing, H. Lib Dem	1,287	2.5	-2.0
Lewis, M. Green	1,177	2.3	-3.2
Lab/Co-op majority	26,261	51.8	
Electorate	75,534		
Turnout	50,699	67.12	

Lab/Co-op hold (6.65% from Con to Lab/Co-op)

LEICESTER WEST

		%	+/-%
Kendall, L. Lab*	22,823	60.6	14.5
Hickey, J. Con	11,763	31.3	5.8
Young, S. UKIP	1,406	3.7	-13.4
Bradwell, I. Lib Dem	792	2.1	-2.2
Gould, M. Green	607	1.6	-3.8
Bowley, D. Ind	121	0.3	
Lab majority	11,060	29.39	
Electorate	64,836		
Turnout	37,634	58.04	

Lab hold (4.33% from Con to Lab)

NORTH WEST LEICESTERSHIRE

		%	+/-%
Bridgen, A. Con*	31,153	58.0	8.7
Sheahan, S. Lab	17,867	33.3	5.9
Wyatt, M. Lib Dem	3,420	6.4	2.4
Woolley, M. Green	1,101	2.0	-0.2
Con majority	13,286	24.74	
Electorate	75,362		
Turnout	53,694	71.25	

Con hold (1.38% from Lab to Con)

SOUTH LEICESTERSHIRE

		%	+/-%
Costa, A. Con*	34,795	61.4	8.4
Aslam, S. Lab	16,164	28.5	6.6
Webb, G. Lib Dem	2,403	4.2	-3.1
Helmer, R. UKIP	2,235	3.9	-13.3
Morgan, M. Green	1,092	1.9	
Con majority	18,631	32.8	
Electorate	78,985		
Turnout	56,801	71.91	

Con hold (0.92% from Lab to Con)

LEIGH

		%	+/-%
Platt, J. Lab/Co-op	26,347	56.1	2.4
Grundy, J. Con	16,793	35.8	13.2
Bradley, M. UKIP	2,783	5.9	-13.7
Kilpatrick, R. Lib Dem	951	2.0	-0.5
Lab/Co-op majority	9,554	20.34	
Electorate	76,202		
Turnout	46,979	61.65	

Lab/Co-op hold (5.39% from Lab/Co-op to Con)

LEWES

		%	+/-%
Caulfield, M. Con*	26,820	49.4	11.5
Blundell, K. Lib Dem	21,312	39.2	3.5
Chapman, D. Lab	6,060	11.2	1.3
Con majority	5,508	10.14	
Electorate	70,941		
Turnout	54,328	76.58	

Con hold (4% from Lib Dem to Con)

LEWISHAM DEPTFORD

		%	+/-%
Foxcroft, V. Lab*	42,461	76.8	16.8
McLean, M. Con	7,562	13.7	-1.1
Dean, B. Lib Dem	2,911	5.3	0.0
Coughlin, J. Green	1,640	3.0	-9.5
Martin, M. CPA	252	0.5	-0.2
McAnea, L. AWP	225	0.4	
Lawrence, J. Realists	61	0.1	
Lab majority	34,899	63.09	
Electorate	78,468		
Turnout	55,320	70.5	

Lab hold (8.97% from Con to Lab)

LEWISHAM EAST

		%	+/-%
Alexander, H. Lab*	32,072	67.8	12.3
Fortune, P. Con	10,859	22.9	0.7
Frith, E. Lib Dem	2,086	4.4	-1.3
Poorun, S. Green	803	1.7	-3.9
Forster, K. UKIP	798	1.7	-7.3
Winston, W. Ind	355	0.8	
Martin, M. CPA	228	0.5	-0.2
Lab majority	21,213	44.84	
Electorate	68,124		
Turnout	47,312	69.45	

Lab hold (5.78% from Con to Lab)

LEWISHAM WEST AND PENGE

		%	+/-%
Reeves, E. Lab	35,411	66.4	15.9
Bailey, S. Con	12,249	23.0	-1.1
Russell, J. Lib Dem	3,317	6.2	-1.5
Wheller, K. Green	1,144	2.1	-6.3
Cheah, H. UKIP	700	1.3	-6.5
Hortense, K. CPA	325	0.6	
White, R. Populist	50	0.1	
Lab majority	23,162	43.41	
Electorate	72,899		
Turnout	53,352	73.19	

Lab hold (8.54% from Con to Lab)

LEYTON AND WANSTEAD

		%	+/-%
Cryer, J. Lab*	32,234	69.6	11.2
Farris, L. Con	9,627	20.8	-1.1
Sims, B. Lib Dem	2,961	6.4	0.8
Gunstock, A. Green	1,351	2.9	-4.4
Lab majority	22,607	48.81	
Electorate	65,149		
Turnout	46,312	71.09	

Lab hold (6.16% from Con to Lab)

LICHFIELD

		%	+/-%
Fabricant, M. Con*	34,018	63.4	8.4
Worsey, C. Lab	15,437	28.8	9.0
Ray, P. Lib Dem	2,653	4.9	-0.3
Pass, R. Green	1,416	2.6	-1.2
Con majority	18,581	34.62	
Electorate	74,430		
Turnout	53,671	72.11	

Con hold (0.31% from Con to Lab)

LINCOLN

		%	+/-%
Lee, K. Lab	23,333	47.8	8.4
McCartney, K. Con*	21,795	44.7	2.2
Smith, N. UKIP	1,287	2.6	-9.5
Kenyon, C. Lib Dem	1,284	2.6	-1.6
Loryman, B. Green	583	1.2	-1.4
Gray, P. Ind	312	0.6	
Scott-Burdon, I. Ind	124	0.3	
Lab majority	1,538	3.15	
Electorate	73,111		
Turnout	48,797	66.74	

Lab gain (3.11% from Con to Lab)

LINLITHGOW AND EAST FALKIRK

		%	+/-%
Day, M. SNP*	20,388	36.3	-15.7
Coombes, J. Lab	17,469	31.1	0.1
Kennedy, C. Con	16,311	29.0	17.1
Pattle, S. Lib Dem	1,926	3.4	1.4
SNP majority	2,919	5.2	
Electorate	86,186		
Turnout	56,186	65.19	

SNP hold (7.88% from SNP to Lab)

LIVERPOOL RIVERSIDE

		%	+/-%
Ellman, L. Lab/Co-op*	40,599	84.3	17.2
Hall, P. Con	4,652	9.7	0.1
Pitchers, S. Green	1,582	3.3	-8.8
Sebire, T. Lib Dem	1,187	2.5	-1.4
Lab/Co-op majority	35,947	74.61	
Electorate	76,332		
Turnout	48,178	63.12	

Lab/Co-op hold (8.56% from Con to Lab/Co-op)

LIVERPOOL WALTON

		%	+/-%
Carden, D. Lab	36,175	85.5	4.5
Evans, L. Con	3,624	8.6	3.9
May, T. Ind	1,237	2.9	
Brown, K. Lib Dem	638	1.5	-0.8
Feeley, C. Green	523	1.2	-1.2
Lab majority	32,551	76.95	
Electorate	62,738		
Turnout	42,300	67.42	

Lab hold (0.32% from Con to Lab)

LIVERPOOL WAVERTREE

		%	+/-%
Berger, L. Lab/Co-op*	34,717	79.3	10.3
Haddad, D. Con	5,251	12.0	2.0
Kemp, R. Lib Dem	2,858	6.5	0.6
Grant, T. Green	598	1.4	-3.8
Heatherington, A. Ind	216	0.5	
Lab/Co-op majority	29,466	67.34	
Electorate	62,411		
Turnout	43,759	70.11	

Lab/Co-op hold (4.13% from Con to Lab/Co-op)

LIVERPOOL WEST DERBY

		%	+/-%
Twigg, S. Lab/Co-op*	37,371	82.5	7.6
Richardson, P. Con	4,463	9.9	3.3
Radford, S. Lib	2,150	4.8	-0.2
Parr, P. Lib Dem	545	1.2	-1.1
Ward, W. Green	329	0.7	-1.7
Hughes, G. Ind	305	0.7	
Lab/Co-op majority	32,908	72.68	
Electorate	65,164		
Turnout	45,275	69.48	

Lab/Co-op hold (2.17% from Con to Lab/Co-op)

LIVINGSTON

		%	+/-%
Bardell, H. SNP*	21,036	40.0	-16.8
Wolfson, R. Lab	17,158	32.6	5.1
Timson, D. Con	12,799	24.3	14.1
Dundas, C. Lib Dem	1,512	2.9	0.7
SNP majority	3,878	7.37	
Electorate	81,208		
Turnout	52,589	64.76	

SNP hold (10.93% from SNP to Lab)

LLANELLI

		%	+/-%
Griffith, N. Lab*	21,568	53.4	12.1
Davies, S. Con	9,544	23.6	9.3
Arthur, M. PlC	7,351	18.2	-4.7
Rees, K. UKIP	1,331	3.3	-12.9
Daniels, R. Lib Dem	548	1.4	-0.6
Lab majority	12,024	29.76	
Electorate	60,186		
Turnout	40,398	67.12	

Lab hold (1.4% from Con to Lab)

CITIES OF LONDON AND WESTMINSTER

		%	+/-%
Field, M. Con*	18,005	46.4	-7.4
Dogus, I. Lab	14,857	38.3	11.1
Fox, B. Lib Dem	4,270	11.0	4.1
McNally, L. Green	821	2.1	-3.3
Bhatti, A. UKIP	426	1.1	-4.1
Lord, T. Ind	173	0.5	
The Maharaja of Kashmir, A. Ind	59	0.2	
Weenen, B. YPP	43	0.1	
Con majority	3,148	8.12	
Electorate	61,533		
Turnout	38,787	63.03	

Con hold (9.24% from Con to Lab)

*Member of last Parliament

EAST LONDONDERRY

		%	+/-%
Campbell, G. DUP*	19,723	47.8	5.8
Nicholl, D. Sinn Féin	10,881	26.4	6.7
Quigley, S. SDLP	4,423	10.7	-1.5
Holmes, R. UUP	3,135	7.6	-7.7
McCaw, C. All	2,538	6.2	-1.4
St Clair-Legge, L. Con	330	0.8	-0.4
DUP majority	8,842	21.42	
Electorate	67,038		
Turnout	41,278	61.57	

DUP hold (0.45% from DUP to Sinn Féin)

EAST LOTHIAN

		%	+/-%
Whitfield, M. Lab	20,158	36.0	5.1
Kerevan, G. SNP*	17,075	30.5	-12.0
Low, S. Con	16,540	29.6	10.1
Wilson, E. Lib Dem	1,738	3.1	0.5
Allan, M. Ind	367	0.7	0.4
Lab majority	3,083	5.51	
Electorate	79,093		
Turnout	55,935	70.72	

Lab gain (8.52% from SNP to Lab)

LOUGHBOROUGH

		%	+/-%
Morgan, N. Con*	27,022	49.8	0.5
Miah, J. Lab	22,753	41.9	10.2
Walker, D. Lib Dem	1,937	3.6	-0.5
McWilliam, A. UKIP	1,465	2.7	-8.2
Leicester, P. Green	971	1.8	-1.7
Con majority	4,269	7.87	
Electorate	79,607		
Turnout	54,258	68.16	

Con hold (4.86% from Con to Lab)

LOUTH AND HORNCASTLE

		%	+/-%
Atkins, V. Con*	33,733	63.8	12.9
Speed, J. Lab	14,092	26.7	8.7
Noble, J. UKIP	2,460	4.7	-16.7
Gabriel, L. Lib Dem	1,990	3.8	-0.7
Arty-Pole, T. Loony	496	0.9	0.4
Con majority	19,641	37.16	
Electorate	79,007		
Turnout	52,855	66.9	

Con hold (2.09% from Lab to Con)

LUDLOW

		%	+/-%
Dunne, P. Con*	31,433	62.7	8.6
Buckley, J. Lab	12,147	24.2	12.0
Kidd, H. Lib Dem	5,336	10.7	-2.8
Wendt, H. Green	1,054	2.1	-3.0
Con majority	19,286	38.49	
Electorate	68,034		
Turnout	50,110	73.65	

Con hold (1.71% from Con to Lab)

LUTON NORTH

		%	+/-%
Hopkins, K. Lab*	29,765	63.7	11.8
Kerswell, C. Con	15,401	33.0	3.2
Martins, R. Lib Dem	808	1.7	-1.3
Hall, S. Green	648	1.4	-0.9
Lab majority	14,364	30.73	
Electorate	66,811		
Turnout	46,742	69.96	

Lab hold (4.28% from Con to Lab)

LUTON SOUTH

		%	+/-%
Shuker, G. Lab/Co-op*	28,804	62.3	18.5
Russell, D. Con	14,879	32.2	1.8
Strange, A. Lib Dem	1,056	2.3	-5.2
UB, U. UKIP	795	1.7	-10.3
Scheimann, M. Green	439	1.0	-2.0
Ali, A. Ind	160	0.4	
Lab/Co-op majority	13,925	30.12	
Electorate	67,188		
Turnout	46,233	68.81	

Lab/Co-op hold (8.37% from Con to Lab/Co-op)

MACCLESFIELD

		%	+/-%
Rutley, D. Con*	28,595	52.5	0.2
Puttick, N. Lab	19,987	36.7	14.1
Flowers, R. Lib Dem	3,350	6.2	-1.6
Booth, J. Green	1,213	2.2	-2.6
Johnson, M. Ind	1,162	2.1	
Con majority	8,608	15.81	
Electorate	75,228		
Turnout	54,444	72.37	

Con hold (6.96% from Con to Lab)

MAIDENHEAD

		%	+/-%
May, T. Con*	37,718	64.6	-1.0
McDonald, P. Lab	11,261	19.3	7.5
Hill, T. Lib Dem	6,540	11.2	1.3
Wall, D. Green	907	1.6	-2.0
Batten, G. UKIP	871	1.5	-6.9
Knight, A. AWP	282	0.5	
Buckethead, L. Ind	249	0.4	
Smith, G. Ind	152	0.3	
Hope, H. Loony	119	0.2	
Victor, E. CPA	69	0.1	
Reid, J. Just	52	0.1	
Hailemariam, Y. Ind	16	0.0	
Smith, B. Ind	3	0.0	
Con majority	26,457	45.34	
Electorate	76,076		
Turnout	58,347	76.7	

Con hold (4.22% from Con to Lab)

MAIDSTONE AND THE WEALD

		%	+/-%
Grant, H. Con*	29,156	56.3	10.9
Simpson, A. Lab	11,433	22.1	11.6
Fermor, E. Lib Dem	8,455	16.3	-7.7
Watts, P. UKIP	1,613	3.1	-12.7
Jeffery, S. Green	888	1.7	-1.1
Kenward, Y. Ind	172	0.3	
Con majority	17,723	34.21	
Electorate	75,334		
Turnout	51,803	68.76	

Con hold (0.33% from Con to Lab)

MAKERFIELD

		%	+/-%
Fovargue, Y. Lab*	28,245	60.0	8.4
Carney, A. Con	14,703	31.3	11.8
Brierley, B. Ind	2,663	5.7	
Skipworth, J. Lib Dem	1,322	2.8	-0.8
Lab majority	13,542	28.79	
Electorate	74,259		
Turnout	47,037	63.34	

Lab hold (1.7% from Lab to Con)

MALDON

		%	+/-%
Whittingdale, J. Con*	34,111	67.8	7.4
Edwards, P. Lab	10,681	21.2	9.4
O'Connell, Z. Lib Dem	2,181	4.3	-0.1
Pryke, J. UKIP	1,899	3.8	-10.8
Betteridge, S. Green	1,073	2.1	-1.0
Perry, R. BNP	257	0.5	
Con majority	23,430	46.58	
Electorate	71,470		
Turnout	50,301	70.38	

Con hold (0.99% from Con to Lab)

MANCHESTER CENTRAL

		%	+/-%
Powell, L. Lab/Co-op*	38,490	77.2	16.2
Wang, X. Con	7,045	14.1	0.7
Bridges, J. Lib Dem	1,678	3.4	-0.7
Chapman, K. UKIP	1,469	3.0	-8.1
Shah, R. Green	846	1.7	-6.7
Blackburn, N. Pirate	192	0.4	-0.4
Lab/Co-op majority	31,445	63.05	
Electorate	90,261		
Turnout	49,870	55.25	

Lab/Co-op hold (7.78% from Con to Lab/Co-op)

MANCHESTER GORTON

		%	+/-%
Khan, A. Lab	35,085	76.1	9.5
Jaradat, S. Con	3,355	7.3	-2.3
Galloway, G. Ind	2,615	5.7	
Pearcey, J. Lib Dem	2,597	5.6	1.4
Mayo, J. Green	1,038	2.3	-7.5
Eckersley, P. UKIP	952	2.1	-6.1
Abidogun, K. CPA	233	0.5	
Hopkins, D. Ind	51	0.1	
Clifford, P. Comm League	27	0.1	
Lab majority	31,730	68.83	
Electorate	75,362		
Turnout	46,098	61.17	

Lab hold (5.9% from Con to Lab)

MANCHESTER WITHINGTON

		%	+/-%
Smith, J. Lab*	38,424	71.5	18.1
Leech, J. Lib Dem	8,549	15.9	-7.9
Heald, S. Con	5,530	10.3	0.6
Bannister, L. Green	865	1.6	-6.4
Carr, S. WEP	234	0.4	
Lab majority	29,875	55.6	
Electorate	74,654		
Turnout	53,736	71.98	

Lab hold (13% from Lib Dem to Lab)

*Member of last Parliament

MANSFIELD

		%	+/-%
Bradley, B. Con	23,392	46.5	18.5
Meale, A. Lab*	22,335	44.4	5.1
Pepper, S. UKIP	2,654	5.3	-19.8
Shields, P. Ind	1,079	2.1	
Prabhakar, A. Lib Dem	697	1.4	-2.1
Con majority	1,057	2.1	
Electorate	77,811		
Turnout	50,256	64.59	

Con gain (6.67% from Lab to Con)

MEON VALLEY

		%	+/-%
Hollingbery, G. Con*	35,624	65.6	4.7
King, S. Lab	9,932	18.3	7.4
Tod, M. Lib Dem	5,900	10.9	1.2
Bailey, P. UKIP	1,435	2.6	-12.1
Hayward, A. Green	1,301	2.4	-1.1
Con majority	25,692	47.31	
Electorate	74,246		
Turnout	54,307	73.14	

Con hold (1.36% from Con to Lab)

MERIDEN

		%	+/-%
Spelman, C. Con*	33,873	61.9	7.3
McNeil, T. Lab	14,675	26.8	7.9
Rogers, A. Lib Dem	2,663	4.9	-0.1
Kaye, L. UKIP	2,016	3.7	-13.2
Gavin, A. Green	1,416	2.6	-1.5
Con majority	19,198	35.07	
Electorate	81,443		
Turnout	54,740	67.21	

Con hold (0.28% from Con to Lab)

MERTHYR TYDFIL AND RHYMNEY

		%	+/-%
Jones, G. Lab*	22,407	66.7	13.0
Jorgensen, P. Con	6,073	18.1	8.0
Kitcher, A. PlC	2,740	8.2	-1.3
Rowlands, D. UKIP	1,484	4.4	-14.2
Griffin, B. Lib Dem	841	2.5	-1.6
Lab majority	16,334	48.59	
Electorate	55,463		
Turnout	33,616	60.61	

Lab hold (2.46% from Con to Lab)

MID BEDFORDSHIRE – see under Bedfordshire

MID DERBYSHIRE – see under Derbyshire

MID DORSET AND NORTH POOLE – see under Dorset

MID NORFOLK – see under Norfolk

MID SUSSEX – see under Sussex

MID ULSTER – see under Ulster

MID WORCESTERSHIRE – see under Worcestershire

MIDDLESBROUGH

		%	+/-%
McDonald, A. Lab*	23,404	65.6	9.1
Young, J. Con	9,531	26.7	10.3
Hodgson, D. UKIP	1,452	4.1	-14.5
Lawton, T. Ind	632	1.8	
Islam, D. Lib Dem	368	1.0	-2.7
Martinez, C. Green	250	0.7	-3.6
Lab majority	13,873	38.87	
Electorate	61,059		
Turnout	35,694	58.46	

Lab hold (0.63% from Lab to Con)

MIDDLESBROUGH SOUTH AND EAST CLEVELAND

		%	+/-%
Clarke, S. Con	23,643	49.5	12.6
Harvey, T. Lab	22,623	47.4	5.5
Foote-Wood, C. Lib Dem	1,354	2.8	-0.6
Con majority	1,020	2.14	
Electorate	72,336		
Turnout	47,764	66.03	

Con gain (3.54% from Lab to Con)

MIDLOTHIAN

		%	+/-%
Rowley, D. Lab	16,458	36.3	6.1
Thompson, O. SNP*	15,573	34.3	-16.2
Donnelly, C. Con	11,521	25.4	13.5
Laird, R. Lib Dem	1,721	3.8	1.5
Lab majority	885	1.95	
Electorate	68,328		
Turnout	45,344	66.36	

Lab gain (11.18% from SNP to Lab)

MILTON KEYNES NORTH

		%	+/-%
Lancaster, M. Con*	30,367	47.4	0.4
Pullen, C. Lab	28,392	44.3	14.1
Shepherd-DuBey, I. Lib Dem	2,499	3.9	-2.3
Wyatt, J. UKIP	1,390	2.2	-9.7
Francis, A. Green	1,107	1.7	-2.2
Sams, V. CPA	169	0.3	
Con majority	1,975	3.08	
Electorate	89,207		
Turnout	64,039	71.79	

Con hold (6.88% from Con to Lab)

MILTON KEYNES SOUTH

		%	+/-%
Stewart, I. Con*	30,652	47.4	0.8
O'Neill, H. Lab	28,987	44.8	12.8
Maher, T. Lib Dem	1,895	2.9	-1.0
Peddle, V. UKIP	1,833	2.8	-10.4
Findlay, G. Green	1,179	1.8	-1.5
Con majority	1,665	2.57	
Electorate	92,417		
Turnout	64,668	69.97	

Con hold (6.04% from Con to Lab)

MITCHAM AND MORDEN

		%	+/-%
McDonagh, S. Lab*	33,039	68.5	8.0
Kearns, A. Con	11,664	24.2	1.1
Mathys, C. Lib Dem	1,494	3.1	0.1
Hilton, R. UKIP	1,054	2.2	-7.3
Collins, L. Green	644	1.3	-1.8
Coke, D. CPA	223	0.5	0.0
Lab majority	21,375	44.31	
Electorate	68,705		
Turnout	48,244	70.22	

Lab hold (3.47% from Con to Lab)

MOLE VALLEY

		%	+/-%
Beresford, P. Con*	35,092	61.7	1.3
Kennedy, P. Lib Dem	10,955	19.3	4.8
Green, M. Lab	7,864	13.8	5.6
Fewster, J. Green	1,463	2.6	-2.8
Moore, J. UKIP	1,352	2.4	-8.8
Con majority	24,137	42.45	
Electorate	74,545		
Turnout	56,866	76.28	

Con hold (1.78% from Con to Lib Dem)

MONMOUTH

		%	+/-%
Davies, D. Con*	26,411	53.0	3.2
Jones, R. Lab	18,205	36.6	9.8
German, V. Lib Dem	2,064	4.1	-1.1
Damon, C. PIC	1,338	2.7	-1.3
Chandler, I. Green	954	1.9	-1.5
Neale, R. UKIP	762	1.5	-8.9
Con majority	8,206	16.48	
Electorate	64,909		
Turnout	49,798	76.72	

Con hold (3.31% from Con to Lab)

MONTGOMERYSHIRE

		%	+/-%
Davies, G. Con*	18,075	51.7	6.7
Dodds, J. Lib Dem	8,790	25.1	-4.1
Jones, I. Lab	5,542	15.8	10.2
Hughes, A. PIC	1,960	5.6	0.4
Chaloner, R. Green	524	1.5	-2.2
Con majority	9,285	26.55	
Electorate	50,755		
Turnout	34,966	68.89	

Con hold (5.4% from Lib Dem to Con)

MORAY

		%	+/-%
Ross, D. Con	22,637	47.5	16.4
Robertson, A. SNP*	18,478	38.8	-10.7
Kirby, J. Lab	5,208	10.9	1.0
Linklater, A. Lib Dem	1,078	2.3	-0.6
Glen, A. Ind	204	0.4	
Con majority	4,159	8.73	
Electorate	70,649		
Turnout	47,667	67.47	

Con gain (13.56% from SNP to Con)

MORECAMBE AND LUNESDALE

		%	+/-%
Morris, D. Con*	21,773	47.6	2.2
Singleton, V. Lab	20,374	44.5	9.7
Severn, M. Lib Dem	1,699	3.7	
Gillespie, R. UKIP	1,333	2.9	-9.4
Sinclair, C. Green	478	1.1	-2.2
Con majority	1,399	3.06	
Electorate	66,818		
Turnout	45,729	68.44	

Con hold (3.76% from Con to Lab)

MORLEY AND OUTWOOD

		%	+/-%
Jenkyns, A. Con*	26,550	50.5	11.7
Dawson, N. Lab/Co-op	24,446	46.5	8.6
Dobson, C. Lib Dem	1,361	2.6	-0.4
Con majority	2,104	4	
Electorate	76,495		
Turnout	52,555	68.7	

Con hold (1.57% from Lab/Co-op to Con)

MOTHERWELL AND WISHAW

		%	+/-%
Fellows, M. SNP*	16,150	38.5	-18.0
Feeney, A. Lab	15,832	37.7	5.9
Gallacher, M. Con	8,490	20.2	12.6
Finlayson, Y. Lib Dem	920	2.2	0.9
Wilson, N. UKIP	534	1.3	-1.4
SNP majority	318	0.76	
Electorate	68,215		
Turnout	41,984	61.55	

SNP hold (11.94% from SNP to Lab)

NA H-EILEANAN AN IAR

		%	+/-%
MacNeil, A. SNP*	6,013	40.5	-13.7
MacDonald, E. Lab	5,006	33.7	5.2
McCroskrie, D. Con	2,441	16.4	8.8
Cormack, J. Christian	1,108	7.5	0.9
Paterson, J. Lib Dem	250	1.7	-1.2
SNP majority	1,007	6.78	
Electorate	21,301		
Turnout	14,853	69.73	

SNP hold (9.45% from SNP to Lab)

NEATH

		%	+/-%
Rees, C. Lab/Co-op*	21,713	56.6	12.9
Lowe, O. Con	9,082	23.7	8.4
Williams, D. PlC	5,339	13.9	-4.1
Pritchard, R. UKIP	1,419	3.7	-12.7
Little, F. Lib Dem	732	1.9	-1.2
Lab/Co-op majority	12,631	32.92	
Electorate	55,862		
Turnout	38,368	68.68	

Lab/Co-op hold (2.26% from Con to Lab/Co-op)

NEW FOREST EAST

		%	+/-%
Lewis, J. Con*	32,162	62.5	6.4
Renyard, J. Lab	10,167	19.7	7.6
Harrison, D. Lib Dem	7,786	15.1	5.8
Mellor, H. Green	1,251	2.4	-2.3
Con majority	21,995	42.71	
Electorate	72,602		
Turnout	51,493	70.93	

Con hold (0.6% from Con to Lab)

NEW FOREST WEST

		%	+/-%
Swayne, D. Con*	33,170	66.7	7.0
Graham, J. Lab	9,739	19.6	8.8
Scriven, T. Lib Dem	4,781	9.6	2.7
Richards, J. Green	1,454	2.9	-2.8
Hjerling, D. Pirate	483	1.0	
Con majority	23,431	47.12	
Electorate	68,786		
Turnout	49,725	72.29	

Con hold (0.91% from Con to Lab)

NEWARK

		%	+/-%
Jenrick, R. Con*	34,493	62.5	5.7
Lee, C. Lab	16,344	29.6	8.0
Watts, D. Lib Dem	2,786	5.0	0.5
Arundel, X. UKIP	1,419	2.6	-9.4
Con majority	18,149	32.89	
Electorate	75,510		
Turnout	55,179	73.08	

Con hold (1.16% from Con to Lab)

NEWBURY

		%	+/-%
Benyon, R. Con*	37,399	61.3	0.5
Bunting, J. Lib Dem	13,019	21.4	6.4
Skirvin, A. Lab	8,596	14.1	5.7
Field, P. Green	1,531	2.5	-1.5
Yates, D. Apol Dem	304	0.5	0.1
Con majority	24,380	39.97	
Electorate	82,924		
Turnout	60,993	73.55	

Con hold (2.95% from Con to Lib Dem)

NEWCASTLE UPON TYNE CENTRAL

		%	+/-%
Onwurah, C. Lab*	24,071	64.8	9.7
Kyte, S. Con	9,134	24.6	5.7
Cott, N. Lib Dem	1,812	4.9	-1.5
Muat, D. UKIP	1,482	4.0	-10.9
Thomson, P. Green	595	1.6	-3.3
Lab majority	14,937	40.18	
Electorate	55,368		
Turnout	37,173	67.14	

Lab hold (2.03% from Con to Lab)

*Member of last Parliament

General Election 2017

NEWCASTLE UPON TYNE EAST

		%	+/-%
Brown, N. Lab*	28,127	67.4	18.0
Kitchen, S. Con	8,866	21.3	3.7
Taylor, W. Lib Dem	2,574	6.2	-4.9
Sanderson, T. UKIP	1,315	3.1	-9.4
Ford, A. Green	755	1.8	-6.9
Lab majority	19,261	46.17	
Electorate	61,989		
Turnout	41,721	67.3	

Lab hold (7.16% from Con to Lab)

NEWCASTLE UPON TYNE NORTH

		%	+/-%
McKinnell, C. Lab*	26,729	55.3	9.2
Crute, D. Con	16,380	33.9	10.4
Lower, A. Lib Dem	2,533	5.2	-4.5
Marron, T. UKIP	1,780	3.7	-12.9
Whalley, A. Green	513	1.1	-2.3
Moore, B. NECA	353	0.7	
Lab majority	10,349	21.4	
Electorate	66,073		
Turnout	48,371	73.21	

Lab hold (0.61% from Lab to Con)

NEWCASTLE-UNDER-LYME

		%	+/-%
Farrelly, P. Lab*	21,124	48.0	9.7
Meredith, O. Con	21,094	47.9	11.1
Jones, N. Lib Dem	1,624	3.7	-0.5
Lab majority	30	0.07	
Electorate	65,598		
Turnout	44,014	67.1	

Lab hold (0.73% from Lab to Con)

NEWPORT EAST

		%	+/-%
Morden, J. Lab*	20,804	56.4	15.8
Asghar, N. Con	12,801	34.7	7.4
Gorman, I. UKIP	1,180	3.2	-15.2
Brown, P. Lib Dem	966	2.6	-3.8
Wixcey, C. PlC	881	2.4	-1.1
Ahmed, N. Ind	188	0.5	
Lab majority	8,003	21.7	
Electorate	57,233		
Turnout	36,888	64.45	

Lab hold (4.17% from Con to Lab)

NEWPORT WEST

		%	+/-%
Flynn, P. Lab*	22,723	52.2	11.1
Jones-Evans, A. Con	17,065	39.2	6.8
Edwards, S. UKIP	1,100	2.5	-12.6
Bowler-Brown, M. PlC	1,077	2.5	-1.5
Lockyer, S. Lib Dem	976	2.2	-1.7
Bartolotti, P. Green	497	1.1	-2.0
Lab majority	5,658	13	
Electorate	64,399		
Turnout	43,518	67.58	

Lab hold (2.16% from Con to Lab)

NEWRY AND ARMAGH

		%	+/-%
Brady, M. Sinn Féin*	25,666	47.6	6.9
Irwin, W. DUP	13,177	24.4	
McNulty, J. SDLP	9,055	16.8	-7.1
Nicholson, S. UUP	4,425	8.2	-24.2
Coade, J. All	1,256	2.3	0.7
Sinn Féin majority	12,489	23.17	
Electorate	78,266		
Turnout	53,900	68.87	

Sinn Féin hold (8.79% from Sinn Féin to DUP)

NEWTON ABBOT

		%	+/-%
Morris, A. Con*	28,635	55.3	8.3
Osben, J. Lab	11,475	22.2	12.4
Chadwick, M. Lib Dem	10,601	20.5	-3.4
Driscoll, K. Green	926	1.8	-2.8
Con majority	17,160	33.15	
Electorate	71,714		
Turnout	51,768	72.19	

Con hold (2.07% from Con to Lab)

MID NORFOLK

		%	+/-%
Freeman, G. Con*	32,828	58.9	7.0
Simpson, S. Lab	16,742	30.0	11.8
Tod, F. Lib Dem	2,848	5.1	-1.2
Knowles, T. UKIP	2,092	3.8	-15.2
Lester, H. Green	1,158	2.1	-2.1
Con majority	16,086	28.85	
Electorate	80,027		
Turnout	55,764	69.68	

Con hold (2.38% from Con to Lab)

NORTH NORFOLK

		%	+/-%
Lamb, N. Lib Dem*	25,260	48.3	9.4
Wild, J. Con	21,748	41.6	10.8
Burke, S. Lab	5,180	9.9	-0.3
Lib Dem majority	3,512	6.72	
Electorate	69,271		
Turnout	52,279	75.47	

Lib Dem hold (0.72% from Lib Dem to Con)

NORTH WEST NORFOLK

		%	+/-%
Bellingham, H. Con*	29,408	60.1	8.2
Rust, J. Lab	15,620	31.9	9.3
Stone, M. UKIP	1,539	3.1	-14.5
Moss-Eccardt, R. Lib Dem	1,393	2.9	-0.7
de Whalley, M. Green	851	1.7	-2.0
Con majority	13,788	28.2	
Electorate	77,082		
Turnout	48,891	63.43	

Con hold (0.55% from Con to Lab)

SOUTH NORFOLK

		%	+/-%
Bacon, R. Con*	35,580	58.0	4.0
Glavin, D. Lab	18,902	30.8	12.5
Brown, C. Lib Dem	5,074	8.3	0.1
Rowett, C. Green	1,555	2.5	-2.8
Con majority	16,678	27.21	
Electorate	83,055		
Turnout	61,293	73.8	

Con hold (4.27% from Con to Lab)

SOUTH WEST NORFOLK

		%	+/-%
Truss, E. Con*	32,894	62.6	11.9
Smith, P. Lab	14,582	27.7	10.6
Williams, D. UKIP	2,575	4.9	-18.3
Gordon, S. Lib Dem	2,365	4.5	0.1
Con majority	18,312	34.83	
Electorate	77,874		
Turnout	52,570	67.51	

Con hold (0.65% from Lab to Con)

NORMANTON, PONTEFRACT AND CASTLEFORD

		%	+/-%
Cooper, Y. Lab*	29,268	59.4	4.7
Lee, A. Con	14,769	30.0	9.2
Thompson, L. UKIP	3,030	6.2	-15.1
Gascoigne, D. YP	1,431	2.9	
Roberts, C. Lib Dem	693	1.4	-1.5
Lab majority	14,499	29.43	
Electorate	81,641		
Turnout	49,274	60.35	

Lab hold (2.26% from Lab to Con)

NORTH ANTRIM – see under Antrim

NORTH AYRSHIRE AND ARRAN – see under Ayrshire

NORTH CORNWALL – see under Cornwall

NORTH DEVON – see under Devon

NORTH DORSET – see under Dorset

NORTH DOWN – see under Down

NORTH DURHAM – see under Durham

NORTH EAST BEDFORDSHIRE – see under Bedfordshire

NORTH EAST CAMBRIDGESHIRE – see under Cambridgeshire

NORTH EAST DERBYSHIRE – see under Derbyshire

*Member of last Parliament

NORTH EAST FIFE – see under Fife

NORTH EAST HAMPSHIRE – see under Hampshire

NORTH EAST HERTFORDSHIRE – see under Hertfordshire

NORTH EAST SOMERSET – see under Somerset

NORTH HEREFORDSHIRE – see under Herefordshire

NORTH NORFOLK – see under Norfolk

NORTH SHROPSHIRE – see under Shropshire

NORTH SOMERSET – see under Somerset

NORTH SWINDON – see under Swindon

NORTH THANET – see under Thanet

NORTH TYNESIDE – see under Tyneside

NORTH WARWICKSHIRE – see under Warwickshire

NORTH WEST CAMBRIDGESHIRE – see under Cambridgeshire

NORTH WEST DURHAM – see under Durham

NORTH WEST HAMPSHIRE – see under Hampshire

NORTH WEST LEICESTERSHIRE – see under Leicestershire

NORTH WEST NORFOLK – see under Norfolk

NORTH WILTSHIRE – see under Wiltshire

NORTHAMPTON NORTH

		%	+/-%
Ellis, M. Con*	19,065	47.1	4.9
Keeble, S. Lab	18,258	45.1	11.1
Bullock, J. UKIP	1,404	3.5	-12.6
Smid, G. Lib Dem	1,015	2.5	-1.0
Miller, S. Green	636	1.6	-2.2
Con majority	807	2	
Electorate	58,861		
Turnout	40,441	68.71	

Con hold (3.11% from Con to Lab)

General Election 2017

NORTHAMPTON SOUTH

		%	+/-%
Lewer, A. Con	19,231	46.8	5.4
McKeever, K. Lab	18,072	44.0	12.3
Gibbins, R. UKIP	1,630	4.0	-14.3
Hope, J. Lib Dem	1,405	3.4	-0.9
Mabbutt, S. Green	696	1.7	-1.9
Con majority	1,159	2.82	
Electorate	61,766		
Turnout	41,105	66.55	

Con hold (3.45% from Con to Lab)

SOUTH NORTHAMPTONSHIRE

		%	+/-%
Leadsom, A. Con*	40,599	62.3	2.4
Johnson, S. Lab	17,759	27.3	10.6
Lofts, C. Lib Dem	3,623	5.6	-0.4
Wickens, N. UKIP	1,363	2.1	-11.4
Donaldson, D. Green	1,357	2.1	-1.6
Phillips, J. Ind	297	0.5	
Con majority	22,840	35.07	
Electorate	85,759		
Turnout	65,123	75.94	

Con hold (4.1% from Con to Lab)

NORWICH NORTH

		%	+/-%
Smith, C. Con*	21,900	47.6	4.1
Jones, C. Lab	21,393	46.5	13.2
Lanham, H. Lib Dem	1,480	3.2	-1.1
Holmes, A. Green	782	1.7	-2.7
Matthews, L. Pirate	340	0.7	
Con majority	507	1.1	
Electorate	66,924		
Turnout	45,977	68.7	

Con hold (4.55% from Con to Lab)

NORWICH SOUTH

		%	+/-%
Lewis, C. Lab*	31,311	60.8	21.7
Hempsall, L. Con	15,715	30.5	7.1
Wright, J. Lib Dem	2,841	5.5	-8.1
Bearman, R. Green	1,492	2.9	-11.0
Lab majority	15,596	30.28	
Electorate	74,182		
Turnout	51,501	69.43	

Lab hold (7.28% from Con to Lab)

NOTTINGHAM EAST

		%	+/-%
Leslie, C. Lab/Co-op*	28,102	71.3	17.1
Murray, S. Con	8,512	21.6	1.0
Holliday, B. Lib Dem	1,003	2.5	-1.6
Hall-Palmer, R. UKIP	817	2.1	-7.8
Boettge, K. Green	698	1.8	-8.0
Bishop, D. Elvis	195	0.5	
Lab/Co-op majority	19,590	49.67	
Electorate	61,760		
Turnout	39,441	63.86	

Lab/Co-op hold (8.06% from Con to Lab/Co-op)

NOTTINGHAM NORTH

		%	+/-%
Norris, A. Lab/Co-op	23,067	60.1	5.6
Tinley, J. Con	11,907	31.0	10.0
Crosby, S. UKIP	2,133	5.6	-12.9
Jones, T. Lib Dem	674	1.8	-0.6
Jones, K. Green	538	1.4	-1.7
Lab/Co-op majority	11,160	29.07	
Electorate	66,886		
Turnout	38,390	57.4	

Lab/Co-op hold (2.24% from Lab/Co-op to Con)

NOTTINGHAM SOUTH

		%	+/-%
Greenwood, L. Lab*	30,013	62.2	14.8
Hunt, J. Con	14,851	30.8	-0.7
Sutton, T. Lib Dem	1,564	3.2	-0.3
Hollas, D. UKIP	1,103	2.3	-8.9
McGregor, A. Green	598	1.2	-4.1
Lab majority	15,162	31.41	
Electorate	71,182		
Turnout	48,266	67.81	

Lab hold (7.77% from Con to Lab)

NUNEATON

		%	+/-%
Jones, M. Con*	23,755	51.5	6.0
Johnson, P. Lab	19,016	41.2	6.4
Carpenter, C. UKIP	1,619	3.5	-10.9
Brighton-Knight, R. Lib Dem	914	2.0	0.2
Brookes, C. Green	763	1.6	-1.1
Con majority	4,739	10.27	
Electorate	69,201		
Turnout	46,138	66.67	

Con hold (0.19% from Con to Lab)

OCHIL AND SOUTH PERTHSHIRE

		%	+/-%
Graham, L. Con	22,469	41.4	20.7
Ahmed-Sheikh, T. SNP*	19,110	35.2	-10.7
Ross, J. Lab	10,847	20.0	-8.4
Stefanov, I. Lib Dem	1,742	3.2	0.6
Con majority	3,359	6.19	
Electorate	76,767		
Turnout	54,245	70.66	

Con gain (15.72% from SNP to Con)

OGMORE

		%	+/-%
Elmore, C. Lab*	23,225	62.3	9.5
Wallis, J. Con	9,354	25.1	9.2
Marshall, H. PlC	2,796	7.5	-2.6
Davies, G. UKIP	1,235	3.3	-12.0
Francis, G. Lib Dem	594	1.6	-1.4
Lab majority	13,871	37.21	
Electorate	57,125		
Turnout	37,276	65.25	

Lab hold (0.15% from Con to Lab)

OLD BEXLEY AND SIDCUP

		%	+/-%
Brokenshire, J. Con*	29,545	61.4	8.7
Hackett, D. Lab	14,079	29.3	10.3
Vachha, F. UKIP	1,619	3.4	-14.8
Heffernan, D. Lib Dem	1,572	3.3	-0.2
Moran, D. Green	820	1.7	-1.1
Jones, M. BNP	324	0.7	0.2
Nwadikeduruibe, C. CPA	83	0.2	
Con majority	15,466	32.13	
Electorate	66,005		
Turnout	48,141	72.94	

Con hold (0.81% from Con to Lab)

OLDHAM EAST AND SADDLEWORTH

		%	+/-%
Abrahams, D. Lab*	25,629	54.4	15.1
Ali, K. Con	17,447	37.0	11.2
Bond, I. UKIP	2,278	4.8	-14.3
Smith, J. Lib Dem	1,683	3.6	-9.2
Lab majority	8,182	17.36	
Electorate	72,557		
Turnout	47,141	64.97	

Lab hold (1.96% from Con to Lab)

OLDHAM WEST AND ROYTON

		%	+/-%
McMahon, J. Lab/Co-op*	29,846	65.0	10.5
Glenny, C. Con	12,648	27.6	8.7
Keating, R. UKIP	1,899	4.1	-16.4
Harkness, G. Lib Dem	956	2.1	-1.6
King, A. Green	439	1.0	-1.0
Lab/Co-op majority	17,198	37.48	
Electorate	72,359		
Turnout	45,887	63.42	

Lab/Co-op hold (0.93% from Con to Lab/Co-op)

ORKNEY AND SHETLAND

		%	+/-%
Carmichael, A. Lib Dem*	11,312	48.5	7.3
Brett, M. SNP	6,749	28.9	-8.7
Barton, R. Lab	2,664	11.4	4.3
Halcro Johnston, J. Con	2,024	8.7	-0.2
Smith, R. UKIP	283	1.2	-3.5
Hill, S. Ind	245	1.1	
Lib Dem majority	4,563	19.57	
Electorate	34,164		
Turnout	23,320	68.26	

Lib Dem hold (8% from SNP to Lib Dem)

ORPINGTON

		%	+/-%
Johnson, J. Con*	31,762	62.8	5.5
de Gruchy, N. Lab	12,301	24.3	8.8
Feakes, A. Lib Dem	3,315	6.6	-0.2
Philp, B. UKIP	2,023	4.0	-12.6
Galloway, T. Green	1,060	2.1	-1.4
Con majority	19,461	38.49	
Electorate	67,902		
Turnout	50,565	74.47	

Con hold (1.64% from Con to Lab)

*Member of last Parliament

OXFORD EAST

		%	+/-%
Dodds, A. Lab/Co-op	35,118	65.0	15.2
Bartington, S Con	11,834	21.9	2.1
Johnson, K. Lib Dem	4,904	9.1	-1.6
Sanders, L. Green	1,785	3.3	-8.3
Artwell, C. Ind	255	0.5	0.2
Lab/Co-op majority	23,284	43.12	
Electorate	78,353		
Turnout	54,002	68.92	

Lab/Co-op hold (6.54% from Con to Lab/Co-op)

OXFORD WEST AND ABINGDON

		%	+/-%
Moran, L. Lib Dem	26,256	43.7	14.8
Blackwood, N. Con*	25,440	42.3	-3.3
Tidball, M. Lab	7,573	12.6	-0.1
Harris, A. UKIP	751	1.3	-5.7
Lib Dem majority	816	1.36	
Electorate	75,574		
Turnout	60,134	79.57	

Lib Dem gain (9.02% from Con to Lib Dem)

PAISLEY AND RENFREWSHIRE NORTH

		%	+/-%
Newlands, G. SNP*	17,455	37.4	-13.3
Taylor, A. Lab	14,842	31.8	-0.9
Gardiner, D. Con	12,842	27.5	15.3
Boyd, J. Lib Dem	1,476	3.2	1.1
SNP majority	2,613	5.6	
Electorate	67,436		
Turnout	46,666	69.2	

SNP hold (6.18% from SNP to Lab)

PAISLEY AND RENFREWSHIRE SOUTH

		%	+/-%
Black, M. SNP*	16,964	40.6	-10.3
Dowling, A. Lab	14,423	34.5	-4.1
Thomson, A. Con	8,122	19.4	11.8
McCartin, E. Lib Dem	1,327	3.2	1.0
Mack, P. Ind	876	2.1	
SNP majority	2,541	6.08	
Electorate	61,344		
Turnout	41,771	68.09	

SNP hold (3.1% from SNP to Lab)

PENDLE

		%	+/-%
Stephenson, A. Con*	21,986	48.9	1.9
Blackburn, W. Lab	20,707	46.1	11.3
Lishman, G. Lib Dem	941	2.1	-1.2
Parker, B. BNP	718	1.6	
Barnett, I. Green	502	1.1	-1.2
Con majority	1,279	2.85	
Electorate	64,962		
Turnout	44,936	69.17	

Con hold (4.69% from Con to Lab)

General Election 2017

PENISTONE AND STOCKSBRIDGE

		%	+/-%
Smith, A. Lab*	22,807	45.7	3.9
Wilson, N. Con	21,485	43.0	15.5
Booker, J. UKIP	3,453	6.9	-15.9
Baker, P. Lib Dem	2,042	4.1	-2.2
Lab majority	1,322	2.65	
Electorate	71,293		
Turnout	49,910	70.01	

Lab hold (5.82% from Lab to Con)

PENRITH AND THE BORDER

		%	+/-%
Stewart, R. Con*	28,078	60.3	0.9
McEvoy, L. Lab	12,168	26.1	11.8
Hughes, N. Lib Dem	3,641	7.8	-0.7
Wilde, K. UKIP	1,142	2.5	-9.7
Lawson, D. Green	1,029	2.2	-3.0
Davies, J. Ind	412	0.9	
Con majority	15,910	34.18	
Electorate	65,139		
Turnout	46,548	71.46	

Con hold (5.48% from Con to Lab)

PERTH AND NORTH PERTHSHIRE

		%	+/-%
Wishart, P. SNP*	21,804	42.2	-8.2
Duncan, I. Con	21,783	42.2	9.5
Roemmele, D. Lab	5,349	10.4	2.2
Barrett, P. Lib Dem	2,589	5.0	1.2
SNP majority	21	0.04	
Electorate	71,762		
Turnout	51,624	71.94	

SNP hold (8.87% from SNP to Con)

PETERBOROUGH

		%	+/-%
Onasanya, F. Lab	22,950	47.9	12.5
Jackson, S. Con*	22,343	46.7	7.1
Sellick, B. Lib Dem	1,597	3.3	-0.4
Radic, F. Green	848	1.8	-0.8
Lab majority	607	1.27	
Electorate	71,522		
Turnout	47,883	66.95	

Lab gain (2.67% from Con to Lab)

PLYMOUTH, MOOR VIEW

		%	+/-%
Mercer, J. Con*	23,567	51.8	14.3
Dann, S. Lab	18,548	40.8	5.7
Noble, W. UKIP	1,849	4.1	-17.4
Reed, G. Lib Dem	917	2.0	-0.9
Pope, J. Green	536	1.2	-1.2
Con majority	5,019	11.03	
Electorate	69,342		
Turnout	45,487	65.6	

Con hold (4.31% from Lab to Con)

PLYMOUTH, SUTTON AND DEVONPORT

		%	+/-%
Pollard, L. Lab/Co-op	27,283	53.2	16.6
Colvile, O. Con*	20,476	39.9	2.3
Ellison, R. UKIP	1,364	2.7	-11.3
Bewley, H. Lib Dem	1,244	2.4	-1.7
Sheaff, D. Green	604	1.2	-5.9
Bamping, D. Ind	237	0.5	
Lab/Co-op majority	6,807	13.27	
Electorate	76,584		
Turnout	51,291	66.97	

Lab/Co-op gain (7.18% from Con to Lab/Co-op)

PONTYPRIDD

		%	+/-%
Smith, O. Lab*	22,103	55.3	14.3
Ash, J. Con	10,655	26.6	9.4
Elin, F. PlC	4,102	10.3	-1.2
Powell, M. Lib Dem	1,963	4.9	-8.0
Hunter-Clarke, R. UKIP	1,071	2.7	-10.7
Lab majority	11,448	28.62	
Electorate	60,564		
Turnout	40,000	66.05	

Lab hold (2.48% from Con to Lab)

POOLE

		%	+/-%
Syms, R. Con*	28,888	57.8	7.8
Taylor, K. Lab	14,679	29.4	16.5
Plummer, M. Lib Dem	4,433	8.9	-2.8
Oliver, A. Green	1,299	2.6	-2.0
Caine, M. DDIP	551	1.1	
Con majority	14,209	28.43	
Electorate	73,796		
Turnout	49,976	67.72	

Con hold (4.35% from Con to Lab)

POPLAR AND LIMEHOUSE

		%	+/-%
Fitzpatrick, J. Lab*	39,558	66.9	8.6
Wilford, C. Con	11,846	20.1	-5.2
Bagshaw, E. Lib Dem	3,959	6.7	2.5
Rahman, O. Ind	1,477	2.5	
Lant, B. Green	989	1.7	-3.1
McQueen, N. UKIP	849	1.4	-4.7
Barker, D. Ind	136	0.2	
Lab majority	27,712	46.9	
Electorate	87,331		
Turnout	59,091	67.66	

Lab hold (6.93% from Con to Lab)

PORTSMOUTH NORTH

		%	+/-%
Mordaunt, P. Con*	25,860	54.7	7.8
Khan, R. Lab	15,895	33.6	9.9
Sanders, D. Lib Dem	2,608	5.5	-0.7
Fitzgerald, M. UKIP	1,926	4.1	-14.9
Hawkins, K. Green	791	1.7	-1.5
Jenkins, J. Libertarian	130	0.3	
Con majority	9,965	21.07	
Electorate	71,374		
Turnout	47,287	66.25	

Con hold (1.03% from Con to Lab)

PORTSMOUTH SOUTH

		%	+/-%
Morgan, S. Lab	18,290	41.0	21.5
Drummond, F. Con*	16,736	37.5	2.8
Vernon-Jackson, G. Lib Dem	7,699	17.2	-5.0
Chippindall-Higgin, K. UKIP	1,129	2.5	-10.8
McCulloch, I. Green	712	1.6	-5.9
Lab majority	1,554	3.48	
Electorate	69,785		
Turnout	44,660	64	

Lab gain (9.35% from Con to Lab)

PRESELI PEMBROKESHIRE

		%	+/-%
Crabb, S. Con*	18,302	43.3	3.0
Thompson, P. Lab	17,988	42.6	14.5
Williams, O. PlC	2,711	6.4	0.2
Overton, C. ISWSL	1,209	2.9	
Kilmister, B. Lib Dem	1,106	2.6	0.7
Bale, S. UKIP	850	2.0	-8.5
Maile, R. New Society of Worth	31	0.1	0.0
Con majority	314	0.74	
Electorate	58,554		
Turnout	42,256	72.17	

Con hold (5.75% from Con to Lab)

PRESTON

		%	+/-%
Hendrick, M. Lab/Co-op*	24,210	67.9	12.1
Beaty, K. Con	8,487	23.8	3.9
Platt, S. UKIP	1,348	3.8	-11.5
Darby, N. Lib Dem	1,204	3.4	-0.3
Power, A. Green	348	1.0	-3.9
Lab/Co-op majority	15,723	44.09	
Electorate	56,164		
Turnout	35,660	63.49	

Lab/Co-op hold (4.1% from Con to Lab/Co-op)

PUDSEY

		%	+/-%
Andrew, S. Con*	25,550	47.3	1.0
McCargo, I. Lab/Co-op	25,219	46.6	9.2
Nixon, A. Lib Dem	1,761	3.3	-0.5
Buxton, B. YP	1,138	2.1	
Wharton, M. Ind	291	0.5	
Con majority	331	0.61	
Electorate	72,622		
Turnout	54,077	74.46	

Con hold (4.1% from Con to Lab/Co-op)

PUTNEY

		%	+/-%
Greening, J. Con*	20,679	44.0	-9.6
Patil, N. Lab	19,125	40.7	10.8
Mercer, R. Lib Dem	5,448	11.6	5.3
Fletcher, B. Green	1,107	2.4	-2.5
Ward, P. UKIP	477	1.0	-3.6
Quizeen, L. Ind	58	0.1	
Con majority	1,554	3.31	
Electorate	65,031		
Turnout	47,006	72.28	

Con hold (10.21% from Con to Lab)

RAYLEIGH AND WICKFORD

		%	+/-%
Francois, M. Con*	36,914	66.6	12.1
Daniels, M. Lab	13,464	24.3	11.7
Smith, P. UKIP	2,326	4.2	-18.0
Tindall, R. Lib Dem	1,557	2.8	-0.2
Hill, P. Green	1,062	1.9	-0.9
Con majority	23,450	42.31	
Electorate	78,556		
Turnout	55,419	70.55	

Con hold (0.18% from Lab to Con)

READING EAST

		%	+/-%
Rodda, M. Lab	27,093	48.9	16.0
Wilson, R. Con*	23,344	42.2	-3.7
Woods, J. Lib Dem	3,378	6.1	-1.2
Johannessen, K. Green	1,093	2.0	-4.4
Turberville, M. Ind	188	0.3	
Kirkwood, A. MAD	142	0.3	
Lab majority	3,749	6.77	
Electorate	75,537		
Turnout	55,370	73.3	

Lab gain (9.82% from Con to Lab)

READING WEST

		%	+/-%
Sharma, A. Con*	25,311	48.8	1.2
Bailey, O. Lab	22,435	43.2	9.4
O'Connell, M. Lib Dem	3,041	5.9	1.0
Whitham, J. Green	979	1.9	-1.0
Con majority	2,876	5.54	
Electorate	74,523		
Turnout	51,913	69.66	

Con hold (4.09% from Con to Lab)

REDCAR

		%	+/-%
Turley, A. Lab/Co-op*	23,623	55.4	11.7
Gibson, P. Con	14,138	33.2	17.0
Mason, J. Lib Dem	2,849	6.7	-11.7
Gallacher, C. UKIP	1,950	4.6	-13.7
Lab/Co-op majority	9,485	22.25	
Electorate	66,836		
Turnout	42,626	63.78	

Lab/Co-op hold (2.65% from Lab/Co-op to Con)

REDDITCH

		%	+/-%
Maclean, R. Con	23,652	52.2	5.2
Blake, R. Lab	16,289	36.0	4.9
Stote, N. NHA	2,239	4.9	
Swansborough, P. UKIP	1,371	3.0	-13.1
Juned, S. Lib Dem	1,173	2.6	-0.5
White, K. Green	380	0.8	-1.3
Woodhall, S. Ind	99	0.2	
Con majority	7,363	16.25	
Electorate	64,413		
Turnout	45,298	70.32	

Con hold (0.15% from Lab to Con)

*Member of last Parliament

REIGATE

		%	+/-%
Blunt, C. Con*	30,896	57.2	0.6
Brampton, T. Lab	13,282	24.6	11.8
Tarrant, A. Lib Dem	5,889	10.9	0.5
Essex, J. Green	2,214	4.1	-2.6
Fox, J. UKIP	1,542	2.9	-10.4
Con majority	17,614	32.62	
Electorate	74,628		
Turnout	53,993	72.35	

Con hold (5.6% from Con to Lab)

EAST RENFREWSHIRE

		%	+/-%
Masterton, P. Con	21,496	40.0	18.0
Oswald, K. SNP*	16,784	31.2	-9.3
McDougall, B. Lab	14,346	26.7	-7.3
Morton, A. Lib Dem	1,112	2.1	0.2
Con majority	4,712	8.76	
Electorate	70,067		
Turnout	53,805	76.79	

Con gain (13.66% from SNP to Con)

RHONDDA

		%	+/-%
Bryant, C. Lab*	21,096	63.9	13.4
Cennard, B. PlC	7,350	22.3	-4.7
Crosbie, V. Con	3,333	10.1	3.4
Kenrick, J. UKIP	880	2.7	-10.0
Roberts, K. Lib Dem	277	0.8	-0.7
Lab majority	13,746	41.66	
Electorate	50,514		
Turnout	32,996	65.32	

Lab hold (9.04% from PlC to Lab)

SOUTH RIBBLE

		%	+/-%
Kennedy, S. Con*	28,980	52.8	6.5
Gibson, J. Lab	21,559	39.3	4.3
Wright, J. Lib Dem	2,073	3.8	-0.6
Smith, M. UKIP	1,387	2.5	-11.5
Wight, A. Green	494	0.9	
Jarnell, M. NHA	341	0.6	
Con majority	7,421	13.51	
Electorate	75,752		
Turnout	54,926	72.51	

Con hold (1.1% from Lab to Con)

RIBBLE VALLEY

		%	+/-%
Evans, N. Con*	31,919	57.6	9.2
Hinder, D. Lab	18,720	33.8	11.3
Knox, A. Lib Dem	3,247	5.9	0.6
Sowter, G. Green	1,314	2.4	-1.8
Con majority	13,199	23.84	
Electorate	77,968		
Turnout	55,363	71.01	

Con hold (1.06% from Con to Lab)

RICHMOND (YORKSHIRE)

		%	+/-%
Sunak, R. Con*	36,458	63.8	12.6
Perry, D. Lab	13,350	23.4	10.2
Abel, T. Lib Dem	3,360	5.9	-0.5
Pearson, C. YP	2,106	3.7	
Yorke, F. Green	1,739	3.0	-1.2
Con majority	23,108	40.44	
Electorate	80,905		
Turnout	57,148	70.64	

Con hold (1.19% from Lab to Con)

RICHMOND PARK

		%	+/-%
Goldsmith, Z. Con*	28,588	45.0	-13.0
Olney, S. Lib Dem*	28,543	45.0	25.8
Tuitt, C. Lab	5,773	9.1	-3.2
Jewell, P. UKIP	426	0.7	-3.5
Con majority	45	0.07	
Electorate	80,025		
Turnout	63,461	79.3	

Con hold (19.39% from Con to Lib Dem)

ROCHDALE

		%	+/-%
Lloyd, T. Lab	29,035	57.9	12.0
Howard, J. Con	14,216	28.4	11.4
Kelly, A. Lib Dem	4,027	8.0	-2.2
Baksa, C. UKIP	1,641	3.3	-15.4
Danczuk, S. Ind*	883	1.8	
Littlewood, A. GMHV	242	0.5	
Lab majority	14,819	29.55	
Electorate	78,064		
Turnout	50,147	64.24	

Lab hold (0.3% from Con to Lab)

ROCHESTER AND STROOD

		%	+/-%
Tolhurst, K. Con*	29,232	54.3	10.4
Murray, T. Lab	19,382	36.0	16.3
Allen, D. UKIP	2,893	5.4	-25.0
Ricketts, B. Lib Dem	1,189	2.2	-0.2
Hyner, S. Green	781	1.5	-1.4
Benson, S. CPA	163	0.3	
Chiguri, P. Ind	129	0.2	
Con majority	9,850	18.3	
Electorate	82,702		
Turnout	53,839	65.1	

Con hold (2.95% from Con to Lab)

ROCHFORD AND SOUTHEND EAST

		%	+/-%
Duddridge, J. Con*	23,013	48.6	2.4
Dalton, A. Lab	17,465	36.9	12.3
Woodley, R. Ind	2,924	6.2	
Hookway, N. UKIP	1,777	3.8	-16.7
Gwizdala, P. Lib Dem	1,265	2.7	-0.7
Cross, S. Green	804	1.7	-3.3
Con majority	5,548	11.72	
Electorate	73,501		
Turnout	47,323	64.38	

Con hold (4.97% from Con to Lab)

ROMFORD

		%	+/-%
Rosindell, A. Con*	29,671	59.3	8.4
Leatherbarrow, A. Lab	15,893	31.7	10.9
Beadle, A. UKIP	2,350	4.7	-18.0
Sanderson, I. Lib Dem	1,215	2.4	-0.4
Hughes, D. Green	815	1.6	-0.9
Con majority	13,778	27.52	
Electorate	73,493		
Turnout	50,070	68.13	

Con hold (1.24% from Con to Lab)

ROMSEY AND SOUTHAMPTON NORTH

		%	+/-%
Nokes, C. Con*	28,668	57.1	2.9
Royce, C. Lib Dem	10,622	21.1	3.5
Paffey, D. Lab	9,614	19.1	7.3
Callaghan, I. Green	953	1.9	-2.8
Jerrard, D. JACP	271	0.5	
Con majority	18,046	35.92	
Electorate	67,186		
Turnout	50,245	74.78	

Con hold (0.28% from Con to Lib Dem)

ROSS, SKYE AND LOCHABER

		%	+/-%
Blackford, I. SNP*	15,480	40.2	-7.9
Mackenzie, R. Con	9,561	24.8	18.6
Davis, J. Lib Dem	8,042	20.9	-14.9
Ó Donnghaile, P. Lab	4,695	12.2	7.3
Campbell, R. Ind	499	1.3	0.8
Sturrock, S. SN	177	0.5	
SNP majority	5,919	15.37	
Electorate	53,638		
Turnout	38,503	71.78	

SNP hold (13.25% from SNP to Con)

ROSSENDALE AND DARWEN

		%	+/-%
Berry, J. Con*	25,499	50.7	4.2
Barnes, A. Lab	22,283	44.3	9.3
Bonner, S. Lib Dem	1,550	3.1	1.4
Payne, J. Green	824	1.6	-0.5
Con majority	3,216	6.39	
Electorate	72,486		
Turnout	50,290	69.38	

Con hold (2.56% from Con to Lab)

ROTHER VALLEY

		%	+/-%
Barron, K. Lab*	23,821	48.0	4.6
Eddy, B. Con	19,939	40.2	17.0
Hunter, L. UKIP	3,704	7.5	-20.5
Pruszynski, K. Lib Dem	1,155	2.3	-1.9
Martin, P. Green	869	1.8	
Lab majority	3,882	7.83	
Electorate	75,230		
Turnout	49,595	65.92	

Lab hold (6.21% from Lab to Con)

ROTHERHAM

		%	+/-%
Champion, S. Lab*	21,404	56.3	4.0
Bellis, J. Con	10,017	26.4	14.1
Cowles, A. UKIP	3,316	8.7	-21.3
Carter, A. Lib Dem	1,754	4.6	1.7
Bower, M. YP	1,432	3.8	
Lab majority	11,387	29.96	
Electorate	63,237		
Turnout	38,006	60.1	

Lab hold (5.04% from Lab to Con)

RUGBY

		%	+/-%
Pawsey, M. Con*	27,872	54.1	5.2
Edwards, C. Lab	19,660	38.2	10.3
Roodhouse, J. Lib Dem	2,851	5.5	-0.1
Bliss, G. Green	953	1.9	-1.0
Con majority	8,212	15.95	
Electorate	72,175		
Turnout	51,479	71.33	

Con hold (2.56% from Con to Lab)

RUISLIP, NORTHWOOD AND PINNER

		%	+/-%
Hurd, N. Con*	30,555	57.1	-2.3
Lury, R. Lab	16,575	31.0	10.9
Cunliffe, A. Lib Dem	3,813	7.1	2.2
Green, S. Green	1,268	2.4	-1.1
Braine, R. UKIP	1,171	2.2	-8.7
Con majority	13,980	26.12	
Electorate	73,427		
Turnout	53,528	72.9	

Con hold (6.63% from Con to Lab)

RUNNYMEDE AND WEYBRIDGE

		%	+/-%
Hammond, P. Con*	31,436	60.8	1.2
Dent, F. Lab	13,386	25.9	10.4
Vincent, J. Lib Dem	3,765	7.3	0.6
Wood, N. UKIP	1,675	3.2	-10.6
Lawrance, L. Green	1,347	2.6	-1.5
Con majority	18,050	34.88	
Electorate	74,888		
Turnout	51,749	69.1	

Con hold (4.59% from Con to Lab)

RUSHCLIFFE

		%	+/-%
Clarke, K. Con*	30,223	51.7	0.6
Mellen, D. Lab	22,213	38.0	11.8
Phoenix, J. Lib Dem	2,759	4.7	-0.3
Mallender, R. Green	1,626	2.8	-3.6
Faithfull, M. UKIP	1,490	2.5	-8.2
Con majority	8,010	13.7	
Electorate	74,738		
Turnout	58,468	78.23	

Con hold (5.62% from Con to Lab)

*Member of last Parliament

General Election 2017

RUTHERGLEN AND HAMILTON WEST

		%	+/-%
Killen, G. Lab/Co-op	19,101	37.5	2.3
Ferrier, M. SNP*	18,836	37.0	-15.5
Le Blond, A. Con	9,941	19.5	12.0
Brown, R. Lib Dem	2,158	4.2	2.4
Santos, C. UKIP	465	0.9	-1.4
Dixon, A. Ind	371	0.7	
Lab/Co-op majority	265	0.52	
Electorate	80,089		
Turnout	50,929	63.59	

Lab/Co-op gain (8.91% from SNP to Lab/Co-op)

RUTLAND AND MELTON

		%	+/-%
Duncan, A. Con*	36,169	62.7	7.2
Peto, H. Lab	13,065	22.6	7.3
Reynolds, E. Lib Dem	4,711	8.2	0.1
Scutter, J. UKIP	1,869	3.2	-12.6
McQuillan, A. Green	1,755	3.0	-1.2
Con majority	23,104	40.03	
Electorate	78,463		
Turnout	57,710	73.55	

Con hold (0.05% from Con to Lab)

SAFFRON WALDEN

		%	+/-%
Badenoch, K. Con	37,629	61.6	4.6
Berney, J. Lab	12,663	20.7	9.0
Hibbs, M. Lib Dem	8,528	14.0	3.4
Howe, L. UKIP	2,091	3.4	-10.3
Con majority	24,966	40.86	
Electorate	83,072		
Turnout	61,108	73.56	

Con hold (2.19% from Con to Lab)

SALFORD AND ECCLES

		%	+/-%
Long-Bailey, R. Lab*	31,168	65.3	16.1
Sugarman, J. Con	12,036	25.2	4.9
Barnes, C. UKIP	2,320	4.9	-13.1
Reid, J. Lib Dem	1,286	2.7	-1.0
Olsen, W. Green	809	1.7	-3.5
Lab majority	19,132	40.08	
Electorate	78,080		
Turnout	47,730	61.13	

Lab hold (5.61% from Con to Lab)

SALISBURY

		%	+/-%
Glen, J. Con*	30,952	58.0	2.4
Corbin, T. Lab	13,619	25.5	10.2
Sample, P. Lib Dem	5,982	11.2	1.2
Palethorpe, D. UKIP	1,191	2.2	-9.9
Oubridge, B. Green	1,152	2.2	-3.3
Pendragon, K. Ind	415	0.8	-0.7
Con majority	17,333	32.46	
Electorate	72,891		
Turnout	53,399	73.26	

Con hold (3.88% from Con to Lab)

SCARBOROUGH AND WHITBY

		%	+/-%
Goodwill, R. Con*	24,401	48.3	5.3
Broadbent, E. Lab	20,966	41.5	11.4
Cross, S. UKIP	1,682	3.3	-13.7
Lockwood, G. Lib Dem	1,354	2.7	-1.8
Malone, D. Green	915	1.8	-2.8
Freeman, J. Ind	680	1.4	
Black, B. YP	369	0.7	
Johnson, G. Ind	82	0.2	
Con majority	3,435	6.8	
Electorate	73,599		
Turnout	50,523	68.65	

Con hold (3.07% from Con to Lab)

SCUNTHORPE

		%	+/-%
Dakin, N. Lab*	20,916	51.9	10.4
Mumby-Croft, H. Con	17,485	43.4	10.4
Talliss, A. UKIP	1,247	3.1	-14.0
Downes, R. Lib Dem	554	1.4	-0.7
Lab majority	3,431	8.52	
Electorate	61,578		
Turnout	40,274	65.4	

Lab hold (0.03% from Con to Lab)

SEDGEFIELD

		%	+/-%
Wilson, P. Lab*	22,202	53.3	6.2
Davison, D. Con	16,143	38.8	9.3
Grant, J. UKIP	1,763	4.2	-12.3
Psallidas, S. Lib Dem	797	1.9	-1.6
Wilson, M. Green	686	1.6	-1.5
Lab majority	6,059	14.55	
Electorate	63,889		
Turnout	41,653	65.2	

Lab hold (1.55% from Lab to Con)

SEFTON CENTRAL

		%	+/-%
Esterson, B. Lab*	32,830	62.9	9.3
Marsden, J. Con	17,212	33.0	3.5
Lewis, D. Lib Dem	1,381	2.6	-1.6
Carter, M. Green	656	1.3	-1.1
Lab majority	15,618	29.92	
Electorate	69,019		
Turnout	52,207	75.64	

Lab hold (2.93% from Con to Lab)

SELBY AND AINSTY

		%	+/-%
Adams, N. Con*	32,921	58.6	6.2
Bowgett, D. Lab	19,149	34.1	7.3
Delhoy, C. Lib Dem	2,293	4.1	0.5
Pycroft, T. UKIP	1,713	3.0	-10.9
Con majority	13,772	24.5	
Electorate	75,918		
Turnout	56,221	74.05	

Con hold (0.55% from Con to Lab)

General Election 2017

SEVENOAKS

		%	+/-%
Fallon, M. Con*	32,644	63.5	6.9
Clark, C. Lab	10,727	20.9	8.1
Bullion, A. Lib Dem	4,280	8.3	0.5
Cushway, G. UKIP	1,894	3.7	-14.1
Dodd, P. Green	1,673	3.3	-1.2
Con majority	21,917	42.67	
Electorate	71,565		
Turnout	51,364	71.77	

Con hold (0.59% from Con to Lab)

SHEFFIELD CENTRAL

		%	+/-%
Blomfield, P. Lab*	33,963	70.7	16.0
Roe, S. Con	6,215	12.9	1.9
Bennett, N. Green	3,848	8.0	-7.8
Mohammed, S. Lib Dem	2,465	5.1	-4.5
Cook, D. UKIP	1,060	2.2	-5.2
Carrington, J. YP	197	0.4	
Moran, R. Pirate	91	0.2	-0.1
Westnidge, J. SDP	38	0.1	
Lab majority	27,748	57.79	
Electorate	77,560		
Turnout	48,014	61.91	

Lab hold (7.05% from Con to Lab)

SHEFFIELD, HALLAM

		%	+/-%
O'Mara, J. Lab	21,881	38.3	2.6
Clegg, N. Lib Dem*	19,756	34.6	-5.4
Walker, I. Con	13,561	23.8	10.2
Thurley, J. UKIP	929	1.6	-4.8
Robin, L. Green	823	1.4	-1.8
Winstone, S. SDP	70	0.1	
Lab majority	2,125	3.72	
Electorate	73,455		
Turnout	57,109	77.75	

Lab gain (3.98% from Lib Dem to Lab)

SHEFFIELD HEELEY

		%	+/-%
Haigh, L. Lab*	26,524	59.9	11.8
Gregory, G. Con	12,696	28.7	12.6
Otten, J. Lib Dem	2,022	4.6	-6.7
Denby, H. UKIP	1,977	4.5	-12.9
Walsh, D. Green	943	2.1	-4.0
Oberoi, J. SDP	64	0.1	
Lab majority	13,828	31.21	
Electorate	68,040		
Turnout	44,305	65.12	

Lab hold (0.37% from Lab to Con)

SHEFFIELD SOUTH EAST

		%	+/-%
Betts, C. Lab*	25,520	58.4	7.1
Cawrey, L. Con	13,722	31.4	14.1
Dawson, D. UKIP	2,820	6.5	-15.4
Ross, C. Lib Dem	1,432	3.3	-2.0
Oberoi, I. SDP	102	0.2	
Lab majority	11,798	27.01	
Electorate	68,945		
Turnout	43,686	63.36	

Lab hold (3.48% from Lab to Con)

*Member of last Parliament

SHEFFIELD, BRIGHTSIDE AND HILLSBOROUGH

		%	+/-%
Furniss, G. Lab*	28,193	67.2	10.9
Naughton, M. Con	9,050	21.6	10.6
Harper, S. UKIP	2,645	6.3	-15.7
Clement-Jones, S. Lib Dem	1,061	2.5	-2.0
Gilligan Kubo, C. Green	737	1.8	-2.5
Driver, M. WRP	137	0.3	
Rahman, M. SDP	47	0.1	
Lab majority	19,143	45.64	
Electorate	70,344		
Turnout	41,940	59.62	

Lab hold (0.12% from Con to Lab)

SHERWOOD

		%	+/-%
Spencer, M. Con*	27,492	51.4	6.5
Pringle, M. Lab	22,294	41.7	5.9
Bestwick, S. UKIP	1,801	3.4	-11.2
Thomas, B. Lib Dem	1,113	2.1	-0.1
Findley, M. Green	664	1.2	-0.9
Con majority	5,198	9.72	
Electorate	76,196		
Turnout	53,462	70.16	

Con hold (0.29% from Lab to Con)

SHIPLEY

		%	+/-%
Davies, P. Con*	27,417	51.2	1.3
Clapcote, S. Lab	22,736	42.5	11.6
Jones, C. Lib Dem	2,202	4.1	0.3
Walker, S. WEP	1,040	1.9	
Con majority	4,681	8.74	
Electorate	73,133		
Turnout	53,533	73.2	

Con hold (5.13% from Con to Lab)

SHREWSBURY AND ATCHAM

		%	+/-%
Kawczynski, D. Con*	29,073	49.9	4.4
Davies, L. Lab	22,446	38.5	10.7
Fraser, H. Lib Dem	4,254	7.3	-0.6
Higginbottom, E. UKIP	1,363	2.3	-12.1
Bullard, E. Green	1,067	1.8	-2.3
Con majority	6,627	11.36	
Electorate	79,043		
Turnout	58,312	73.77	

Con hold (3.14% from Con to Lab)

NORTH SHROPSHIRE

		%	+/-%
Paterson, O. Con*	33,642	60.4	9.0
Currie, G. Lab	17,287	31.0	11.0
Thornhill, T. Lib Dem	2,948	5.3	-0.7
Kerr, D. Green	1,722	3.1	-1.8
Con majority	16,355	29.34	
Electorate	80,535		
Turnout	55,745	69.22	

Con hold (0.98% from Con to Lab)

SITTINGBOURNE AND SHEPPEY

		%	+/-%
Henderson, G. Con*	30,911	60.1	10.8
Rolfe, M. Lab	15,700	30.5	11.0
Baldock, M. Ind	2,133	4.1	
Nevols, K. Lib Dem	1,392	2.7	-0.4
Lindop, M. Green	558	1.1	-1.3
Young, M. Loony	403	0.8	0.2
McCall, L. Ind	292	0.6	
Con majority	15,211	29.56	
Electorate	81,717		
Turnout	51,466	62.98	

Con hold (0.11% from Con to Lab)

SKIPTON AND RIPON

		%	+/-%
Smith, J. Con*	36,425	62.5	7.2
Woodhead, A. Lab	16,440	28.2	10.9
Brown, A. Green	3,734	6.4	0.7
Render, J. YP	1,539	2.6	
Con majority	19,985	34.27	
Electorate	78,104		
Turnout	58,324	74.67	

Con hold (1.83% from Con to Lab)

SLEAFORD AND NORTH HYKEHAM

		%	+/-%
Johnson, C. Con*	42,245	64.1	8.1
Clarke, J. Lab	17,008	25.8	8.6
Pepper, R. Lib Dem	2,722	4.1	-1.5
Chadd, S. UKIP	1,954	3.0	-12.7
McKenna, F. Green	968	1.5	
Coyne, P. Ind	900	1.4	
Con majority	25,237	38.29	
Electorate	90,929		
Turnout	65,904	72.48	

Con hold (2.46% from Con to Lab)

SLOUGH

		%	+/-%
Dhesi, T. Lab	34,170	62.7	14.5
Vivis, M. Con	17,172	31.5	-1.6
McCann, T. Lib Dem	1,308	2.4	-0.2
Perez, K. UKIP	1,228	2.3	-10.7
Janik, P. Ind	417	0.8	
Lab majority	16,998	31.21	
Electorate	81,062		
Turnout	54,463	67.19	

Lab hold (8.05% from Con to Lab)

SOLIHULL

		%	+/-%
Knight, J. Con*	32,985	58.0	8.9
Knowles, N. Lab	12,414	21.8	11.5
Adeyemo, A. Lib Dem	8,901	15.7	-9.9
Garcarz, A. UKIP	1,291	2.3	-9.3
McLoughlin, M. Green	1,157	2.0	-0.9
Con majority	20,571	36.17	
Electorate	77,789		
Turnout	56,868	73.11	

Con hold (1.27% from Con to Lab)

NORTH SOMERSET

		%	+/-%
Fox, L. Con*	33,605	54.1	0.8
Chambers, G. Lab	16,502	26.6	12.3
Foord, R. Lib Dem	5,982	9.6	-3.0
Davies, D. Ind	3,929	6.3	
Pattison, C. Green	1,976	3.2	-3.3
Con majority	17,103	27.53	
Electorate	80,529		
Turnout	62,114	77.13	

Con hold (5.76% from Con to Lab)

NORTH EAST SOMERSET

		%	+/-%
Rees-Mogg, J. Con*	28,992	53.5	3.9
Moss, R. Lab	18,757	34.6	9.9
Rigby, M. Lib Dem	4,461	8.2	0.4
Calverley, S. Green	1,245	2.3	-3.2
Hughes, S. Ind	588	1.1	
Con majority	10,235	18.9	
Electorate	71,355		
Turnout	54,147	75.88	

Con hold (2.99% from Con to Lab)

SOMERTON AND FROME

		%	+/-%
Warburton, D. Con*	36,231	56.6	3.8
Blackburn, M. Lib Dem	13,325	20.8	1.5
Dromgoole, S. Lab	10,998	17.2	9.9
Simon, T. Green	2,347	3.7	-5.3
Hadwin, R. Ind	991	1.6	
Con majority	22,906	35.79	
Electorate	84,437		
Turnout	63,996	75.79	

Con hold (1.14% from Lib Dem to Con)

SOUTH ANTRIM – see under Antrim

SOUTH BASILDON AND EAST THURROCK – see under Basildon

SOUTH CAMBRIDGESHIRE – see under Cambridgeshire

SOUTH DERBYSHIRE – see under Derbyshire

SOUTH DORSET – see under Dorset

SOUTH DOWN – see under Down

SOUTH EAST CAMBRIDGESHIRE – see under Cambridgeshire

SOUTH EAST CORNWALL – see under Cornwall

SOUTH HOLLAND AND THE DEEPINGS

		%	+/-%
Hayes, J. Con*	35,179	69.8	10.4
Kowalewski, W. Lab	10,282	20.4	8.0
Smith, J. UKIP	2,185	4.3	-17.4
Cambridge, J. Lib Dem	1,433	2.8	-0.1
Wilshire, D. Green	894	1.8	-1.4
Stringer, R. Ind	342	0.7	
Con majority	24,897	49.4	
Electorate	76,374		
Turnout	50,399	65.99	

Con hold (1.22% from Lab to Con)

General Election 2017

SOUTH LEICESTERSHIRE – see under Leicestershire

SOUTH NORFOLK – see under Norfolk

SOUTH NORTHAMPTONSHIRE – see under Northamptonshire

SOUTH RIBBLE – see under Ribble

SOUTH SHIELDS

		%	+/-%
Lewell-Buck, E. Lab*	25,078	61.4	10.2
Buchan, F. Con	10,570	25.9	9.3
Elvin, R. UKIP	3,006	7.4	-14.6
Ford, S. Green	1,437	3.5	-0.9
Gordon, G. Lib Dem	681	1.7	-0.1
Lab majority	14,508	35.52	
Electorate	63,433		
Turnout	40,849	64.4	

Lab hold (0.47% from Con to Lab)

SOUTH STAFFORDSHIRE – see under Staffordshire

SOUTH SUFFOLK – see under Suffolk

SOUTH SWINDON – see under Swindon

SOUTH THANET – see under Thanet

SOUTH WEST BEDFORDSHIRE – see under Bedfordshire

SOUTH WEST DEVON – see under Devon

SOUTH WEST HERTFORDSHIRE – see under Hertfordshire

SOUTH WEST NORFOLK – see under Norfolk

SOUTH WEST SURREY – see under Surrey

SOUTH WEST WILTSHIRE – see under Wiltshire

SOUTHAMPTON ITCHEN

		%	+/-%
Smith, R. Con*	21,773	46.5	4.8
Letts, S. Lab	21,742	46.4	9.9
Bell, E. Lib Dem	1,421	3.0	-0.5
Rose, K. UKIP	1,122	2.4	-11.0
Pearce, R. Green	725	1.6	-2.6
Con majority	31	0.07	
Electorate	71,722		
Turnout	46,875	65.36	

Con hold (2.55% from Con to Lab)

*Member of last Parliament

SOUTHAMPTON TEST

		%	+/-%
Whitehead, A. Lab*	27,509	58.5	17.4
Holmes, P. Con	16,006	34.0	1.6
Gravatt, T. Lib Dem	1,892	4.0	-0.8
Pope, A. Southampton Ind	816	1.7	
Morrell, K. Ind	680	1.5	
Lab majority	11,503	24.46	
Electorate	70,199		
Turnout	47,022	66.98	

Lab hold (7.88% from Con to Lab)

SOUTHEND WEST

		%	+/-%
Amess, D. Con*	26,046	55.1	5.4
Ware-Lane, J. Lab	16,046	33.9	15.7
Salek, L. Lib Dem	2,110	4.5	-4.8
Stansfield, J. UKIP	1,666	3.5	-13.9
Ellis, D. Green	831	1.8	-2.9
Callaghan, T. Southend Ind Ass	305	0.6	
Pilley, J. Ind	187	0.4	
Con majority	10,000	21.15	
Electorate	67,677		
Turnout	47,292	69.88	

Con hold (5.13% from Con to Lab)

SOUTHPORT

		%	+/-%
Moore, D. Con	18,541	38.6	10.8
Savage, L. Lab	15,627	32.5	13.4
McGuire, S. Lib Dem	12,661	26.4	-4.5
Durrance, T. UKIP	1,127	2.4	-14.4
Con majority	2,914	6.07	
Electorate	69,400		
Turnout	48,019	69.19	

Con gain (1.33% from Con to Lab)

SPELTHORNE

		%	+/-%
Kwarteng, K. Con*	28,692	57.1	7.6
Geach, R. Lab	15,267	30.4	11.9
Shimell, R. Lib Dem	2,755	5.5	-0.9
Cunningham, R. UKIP	2,296	4.6	-16.2
Jacobs, P. Green	1,105	2.2	-1.3
Con majority	13,425	26.73	
Electorate	72,641		
Turnout	50,221	69.14	

Con hold (2.13% from Con to Lab)

ST ALBANS

		%	+/-%
Main, A. Con*	24,571	43.0	-3.7
Cooper, D. Lib Dem	18,462	32.3	13.8
Pollard, K. Lab	13,137	23.0	-0.3
Easton, J. Green	828	1.5	-2.3
Con majority	6,109	10.69	
Electorate	72,811		
Turnout	57,140	78.48	

Con hold (8.73% from Con to Lib Dem)

ST AUSTELL AND NEWQUAY

		%	+/-%
Double, S. Con*	26,856	49.3	9.2
Neil, K. Lab	15,714	28.9	18.6
Gilbert, S. Lib Dem	11,642	21.4	-2.6
Con majority	11,142	20.47	
Electorate	78,609		
Turnout	54,443	69.26	

Con hold (4.73% from Con to Lab)

ST HELENS NORTH

		%	+/-%
McGinn, C. Lab*	32,012	63.6	6.8
Ng, J. Con	13,606	27.0	7.5
Peers, P. UKIP	2,097	4.2	-10.9
Morrison, T. Lib Dem	1,287	2.6	-1.8
Parkinson, R. Green	1,220	2.4	-1.4
Lab majority	18,406	36.58	
Electorate	76,088		
Turnout	50,312	66.12	

Lab hold (0.32% from Lab to Con)

ST HELENS SOUTH AND WHISTON

		%	+/-%
Rimmer, M. Lab*	35,879	67.7	8.1
McRandal, E. Con	11,536	21.8	5.9
Spencer, B. Lib Dem	2,101	4.0	-1.7
Hitchen, M. UKIP	1,953	3.7	-10.2
Northey, J. Green	1,417	2.7	-1.9
Lab majority	24,343	45.96	
Electorate	79,036		
Turnout	52,965	67.01	

Lab hold (1.11% from Con to Lab)

ST IVES

		%	+/-%
Thomas, D. Con*	22,120	43.1	4.9
George, A. Lib Dem	21,808	42.5	9.4
Drew, C. Lab	7,298	14.2	4.9
Con majority	312	0.61	
Electorate	67,451		
Turnout	51,335	76.11	

Con hold (2.25% from Con to Lib Dem)

STAFFORD

		%	+/-%
Lefroy, J. Con*	28,424	54.6	6.4
Williams, D. Lab	20,695	39.8	10.3
Tinker, C. Lib Dem	1,540	3.0	0.2
Pearce, T. Green	1,265	2.4	-0.4
Con majority	7,729	14.85	
Electorate	69,957		
Turnout	52,046	74.4	

Con hold (1.95% from Con to Lab)

STAFFORDSHIRE MOORLANDS

		%	+/-%
Bradley, K. Con*	25,963	58.0	7.1
Mazzocchi-Jones, D. Lab	15,133	33.8	6.7
Sheldon, N. Ind	1,524	3.4	
Jebb, H. Lib Dem	1,494	3.3	-0.8
Shone, M. Green	541	1.2	-1.7
Con majority	10,830	24.21	
Electorate	63,260		
Turnout	44,739	70.72	

Con hold (0.19% from Lab to Con)

SOUTH STAFFORDSHIRE

		%	+/-%
Williamson, G. Con*	35,656	69.5	10.3
Freeman, A. Lab	12,923	25.2	6.9
Myers, H. Lib Dem	1,348	2.6	-0.3
McIlvenna, C. Green	1,182	2.3	-0.3
Con majority	22,733	44.32	
Electorate	73,441		
Turnout	51,296	69.85	

Con hold (1.69% from Lab to Con)

STALYBRIDGE AND HYDE

		%	+/-%
Reynolds, J. Lab/Co-op*	24,277	57.0	12.3
Dowse, T. Con	16,193	38.0	9.5
Ankers, P. Lib Dem	996	2.3	-0.7
Wood, J. Green	991	2.3	-2.2
Lab/Co-op majority	8,084	18.98	
Electorate	71,409		
Turnout	42,584	59.63	

Lab/Co-op hold (1.38% from Con to Lab/Co-op)

STEVENAGE

		%	+/-%
McPartland, S. Con*	24,798	50.1	5.7
Taylor, S. Lab/Co-op	21,412	43.3	9.2
Gibson, B. Lib Dem	2,032	4.1	0.8
Snelling, V. Green	1,085	2.2	-0.7
Con majority	3,386	6.84	
Electorate	70,765		
Turnout	49,468	69.9	

Con hold (1.75% from Con to Lab/Co-op)

STIRLING

		%	+/-%
Kerr, S. Con	18,291	37.0	13.9
Paterson, S. SNP*	18,143	36.7	-8.8
Kane, C. Lab	10,902	22.1	-3.4
Chamberlain, W. Lib Dem	1,683	3.4	0.7
Rummery, K. WEP	337	0.7	
Con majority	148	0.3	
Electorate	66,415		
Turnout	49,428	74.42	

Con gain (11.39% from SNP to Con)

STOCKPORT

		%	+/-%
Coffey, A. Lab*	26,282	63.1	13.4
Hamilton, D. Con	11,805	28.4	3.9
Hawthorne, D. Lib Dem	1,778	4.3	-3.4
Kelly, J. UKIP	1,088	2.6	
Lawson, G. Green	591	1.4	-3.0
Lab majority	14,477	34.77	
Electorate	64,236		
Turnout	41,641	64.83	

Lab hold (4.74% from Con to Lab)

STOCKTON NORTH

		%	+/-%
Cunningham, A. Lab*	24,304	56.8	7.9
Fletcher, M. Con	15,589	36.4	8.6
Strike, T. UKIP	1,834	4.3	-14.8
Brown, S. Lib Dem	646	1.5	-0.7
Robson, E. Green	358	0.8	
Lab majority	8,715	20.36	
Electorate	66,285		
Turnout	42,805	64.58	

Lab hold (0.34% from Lab to Con)

STOCKTON SOUTH

		%	+/-%
Williams, P. Lab	26,102	48.4	11.5
Wharton, J. Con*	25,214	46.8	0.1
Outterside, D. UKIP	1,186	2.2	-8.4
Durning, D. Lib Dem	951	1.8	-0.9
Fitzgerald, J. Green	371	0.7	-1.1
Lab majority	888	1.65	
Electorate	75,625		
Turnout	53,906	71.28	

Lab gain (5.69% from Con to Lab)

STOKE-ON-TRENT CENTRAL

		%	+/-%
Snell, G. Lab/Co-op*	17,083	51.4	12.3
Jellyman, D. Con	13,186	39.7	17.3
Harold, M. UKIP	1,608	4.8	-17.7
Andras, P. Lib Dem	680	2.0	-2.1
Colclough, A. Green	378	1.1	-2.5
Fielding, B. Ind	210	0.6	
Lab/Co-op majority	3,897	11.73	
Electorate	56,915		
Turnout	33,209	58.35	

Lab/Co-op hold (2.48% from Lab/Co-op to Con)

STOKE-ON-TRENT NORTH

		%	+/-%
Smeeth, R. Lab*	21,272	50.8	11.0
Adams, B. Con	18,913	45.1	17.8
Whelan, R. Lib Dem	916	2.2	-0.7
Rouxel, D. Green	685	1.6	-1.2
Lab majority	2,359	5.63	
Electorate	71,558		
Turnout	41,909	58.57	

Lab hold (3.41% from Lab to Con)

STOKE-ON-TRENT SOUTH

		%	+/-%
Brereton, J. Con	20,451	48.9	16.4
Flello, R. Lab*	19,788	47.4	8.3
Wilkes, I. Lib Dem	808	1.9	-1.4
Zablocki, J. Green	643	1.5	-1.1
Con majority	663	1.59	
Electorate	66,057		
Turnout	41,791	63.27	

Con gain (4.03% from Lab to Con)

STONE

		%	+/-%
Cash, B. Con*	31,614	63.1	8.5
Hale, S. Lab/Co-op	14,119	28.2	8.1
Lewis, M. Lib Dem	2,222	4.4	-0.8
Whitfield, E. UKIP	1,370	2.7	-13.4
Pancheri, S. Green	707	1.4	-1.1
Con majority	17,495	34.9	
Electorate	67,994		
Turnout	50,131	73.73	

Con hold (0.23% from Lab/Co-op to Con)

*Member of last Parliament

STOURBRIDGE

		%	+/-%
James, M. Con*	25,706	54.5	8.5
Lowe, P. Lab	18,052	38.2	6.8
Wilson, G. UKIP	1,801	3.8	-13.0
Bramall, C. Lib Dem	1,083	2.3	-1.0
Mohr, A. Green	493	1.0	-1.2
Con majority	7,654	16.21	
Electorate	70,220		
Turnout	47,207	67.23	

Con hold (0.85% from Lab to Con)

STRANGFORD

		%	+/-%
Shannon, J. DUP*	24,036	61.9	17.8
Armstrong, K. All	5,693	14.7	0.9
Nesbitt, M. UUP	4,419	11.4	-2.9
Boyle, J. SDLP	2,404	6.2	-0.7
Murphy, C. Sinn Féin	1,083	2.8	0.2
Bamford, R. Green	607	1.6	
Hiscott, C. Con	507	1.3	-5.0
DUP majority	18,343	47.24	
Electorate	64,327		
Turnout	38,826	60.36	

DUP hold (8.43% from All to DUP)

STRATFORD-ON-AVON

		%	+/-%
Zahawi, N. Con*	33,657	62.7	5.2
Kenner, J. Lab	11,699	21.8	8.9
Adams, E. Lib Dem	6,357	11.8	-0.1
Giles, D. Green	1,345	2.5	-1.6
Spurway, J. Ind	255	0.5	
Darwood, T. Ind	219	0.4	
Con majority	21,958	40.9	
Electorate	72,572		
Turnout	53,684	73.97	

Con hold (1.83% from Con to Lab)

STREATHAM

		%	+/-%
Umunna, C. Lab*	38,212	68.3	15.4
Caddy, K. Con	11,927	21.3	-3.7
Davies, A. Lib Dem	3,611	6.5	-2.5
Griffiths, N. Green	1,696	3.0	-5.8
Stephenson, R. UKIP	349	0.6	-2.6
Lab majority	26,285	46.97	
Electorate	78,649		
Turnout	55,956	71.15	

Lab hold (9.59% from Con to Lab)

STRETFORD AND URMSTON

		%	+/-%
Green, K. Lab*	33,519	66.7	13.8
Cooke, L. Con	13,814	27.5	-0.3
Beaumont, A. UKIP	1,094	2.2	-8.7
Fryer, A. Lib Dem	1,001	2.0	-0.9
Ingleson, M. Green	641	1.3	-3.4
Doman, R. CPA	122	0.2	
Lab majority	19,705	39.19	
Electorate	71,834		
Turnout	50,286	70	

Lab hold (7.05% from Con to Lab)

STROUD

		%	+/-%
Drew, D. Lab/Co-op	29,994	46.9	9.3
Carmichael, N. Con*	29,307	45.9	0.2
Wilkinson, M. Lib Dem	2,053	3.2	-0.2
Lunnon, S. Green	1,423	2.2	-2.3
Gogerly, G. UKIP	1,039	1.6	-6.3
Lab/Co-op majority	687	1.07	
Electorate	82,839		
Turnout	63,913	77.15	

Lab/Co-op gain (4.53% from Con to Lab/Co-op)

CENTRAL SUFFOLK AND NORTH IPSWICH

		%	+/-%
Poulter, D. Con*	33,992	60.0	4.1
Hughes, E. Lab	16,807	29.7	10.9
Van de Weyer, A. Lib Dem	2,431	4.3	-1.8
Scott, R. Green	1,659	2.9	-2.0
Searle, S. UKIP	1,635	2.9	-10.9
Con majority	17,185	30.34	
Electorate	78,116		
Turnout	56,637	72.5	

Con hold (3.4% from Con to Lab)

SUFFOLK COASTAL

		%	+/-%
Coffey, T. Con*	33,713	57.8	6.1
Matthews, C. Lab	17,701	30.4	12.4
Sandbach, J. Lib Dem	4,048	7.0	-1.6
O'Nolan, E. Green	1,802	3.1	-2.8
Young, P. Ind	810	1.4	
Con majority	16,012	27.47	
Electorate	79,366		
Turnout	58,284	73.44	

Con hold (3.16% from Con to Lab)

SOUTH SUFFOLK

		%	+/-%
Cartlidge, J. Con*	32,829	60.4	7.5
Bishton, E. Lab	15,080	27.8	8.6
Aalders-Dunthorne, A. Lib Dem	3,154	5.8	-2.0
Lindsay, R. Green	1,723	3.2	-1.2
Powlesland, A. UKIP	1,449	2.7	-12.5
Con majority	17,749	32.66	
Electorate	75,485		
Turnout	54,351	72	

Con hold (0.52% from Con to Lab)

WEST SUFFOLK

		%	+/-%
Hancock, M. Con*	31,649	61.0	9.1
Jefferys, M. Lab	14,586	28.1	10.7
Flood, J. UKIP	2,396	4.6	-17.0
Tealby-Watson, E. Lib Dem	2,180	4.2	-0.8
Allwright, D. Green	935	1.8	-1.8
Con majority	17,063	32.91	
Electorate	77,348		
Turnout	51,850	67.03	

Con hold (0.82% from Con to Lab)

SUNDERLAND CENTRAL

		%	+/-%
Elliott, J. Lab*	25,056	55.5	5.5
Oliver, R. Con	15,059	33.3	10.0
Leighton, G. UKIP	2,209	4.9	-14.2
Hodson, N. Lib Dem	1,777	3.9	1.3
Featherstone, R. Green	705	1.6	-2.5
Cockburn, S. Ind	305	0.7	
Lab majority	9,997	22.12	
Electorate	72,728		
Turnout	45,187	62.13	

Lab hold (2.27% from Lab to Con)

EAST SURREY

		%	+/-%
Gyimah, S. Con*	35,310	59.5	2.3
Tailor, H. Lab	11,396	19.2	7.4
Lee, D. Lib Dem	6,197	10.4	1.2
Parr, A. Ind	2,973	5.0	
Windsor, H. UKIP	2,227	3.8	-13.2
Southworth, B. Green	1,100	1.9	-2.0
Con majority	23,914	40.31	
Electorate	82,004		
Turnout	59,324	72.34	

Con hold (2.58% from Con to Lab)

SURREY HEATH

		%	+/-%
Gove, M. Con*	37,118	63.9	4.4
Atroshi, L. Lab	12,175	21.0	9.8
Barker, A. Lib Dem	6,271	10.8	1.8
Galliford, S. Green	2,258	3.9	-0.5
Con majority	24,943	42.97	
Electorate	80,766		
Turnout	58,048	71.87	

Con hold (2.73% from Con to Lab)

SOUTH WEST SURREY

		%	+/-%
Hunt, J. Con*	33,683	55.6	-4.0
Irvine, L. NHA	12,093	20.0	11.5
Black, D. Lab	7,606	12.6	3.1
Purkiss, O. Lib Dem	5,967	9.8	3.6
Webber, M. UKIP	1,083	1.8	-8.1
Con majority	21,590	35.64	
Electorate	78,042		
Turnout	60,583	77.63	

Con hold (7.76% from Con to NHA)

MID SUSSEX

		%	+/-%
Soames, N. Con*	35,082	56.8	0.9
Mountain, G. Lab	15,409	25.0	11.1
Osborne, S. Lib Dem	7,855	12.7	1.3
Jerrey, C. Green	1,571	2.5	-1.7
Brothers, T. UKIP	1,251	2.0	-9.9
Thunderclap, B. Loony	464	0.8	0.2
Con majority	19,673	31.86	
Electorate	84,170		
Turnout	61,745	73.36	

Con hold (5.1% from Con to Lab)

SUTTON AND CHEAM

		%	+/-%
Scully, P. Con*	26,567	51.0	9.6
Ahmad, A. Lib Dem	13,869	26.6	-7.0
Craven, B. Lab	10,663	20.5	9.4
Jackson-Prior, C. Green	871	1.7	-0.4
Con majority	12,698	24.38	
Electorate	70,404		
Turnout	52,093	73.99	

Con hold (8.27% from Lib Dem to Con)

SUTTON COLDFIELD

		%	+/-%
Mitchell, A. Con*	32,224	60.8	6.3
Pocock, R. Lab	16,885	31.9	9.6
Wilkinson, J. Lib Dem	2,302	4.3	-0.8
Ratcliff, D. Green	965	1.8	-1.0
Sophia, H. Ind	482	0.9	
Con majority	15,339	28.94	
Electorate	77,094		
Turnout	52,999	68.75	

Con hold (1.62% from Con to Lab)

SWANSEA EAST

		%	+/-%
Harris, C. Lab*	22,307	63.4	10.6
Boucher, D. Con	9,139	25.9	10.7
Phillips, S. PlC	1,689	4.8	-5.6
Johnson, C. UKIP	1,040	3.0	-14.2
Hasted, C. Lib Dem	625	1.8	-2.4
Evans, C. Green	359	1.0	
Lab majority	13,168	37.39	
Electorate	58,521		
Turnout	35,215	60.17	

Lab hold (0.07% from Lab to Con)

SWANSEA WEST

		%	+/-%
Davies, G. Lab/Co-op*	22,278	59.6	17.2
Lawton, C. Con	11,680	31.3	8.8
Fitter, R. PlC	1,529	4.1	-2.3
O'Carroll, M. Lib Dem	1,269	3.4	-5.6
Whittall, M. Green	434	1.2	-3.9
Johnson, B. SP	92	0.3	0.1
Lab/Co-op majority	10,598	28.36	
Electorate	56,892		
Turnout	37,365	65.68	

Lab/Co-op hold (4.21% from Con to Lab/Co-op)

NORTH SWINDON

		%	+/-%
Tomlinson, J. Con*	29,431	53.5	3.3
Dempsey, M. Lab	21,096	38.4	10.7
Webster, L. Lib Dem	1,962	3.6	0.3
Halden, S. UKIP	1,564	2.8	-12.4
Bentley, A. Green	858	1.6	-1.7
Con majority	8,335	15.15	
Electorate	80,168		
Turnout	55,015	68.62	

Con hold (3.68% from Con to Lab)

*Member of last Parliament

SOUTH SWINDON

		%	+/-%
Buckland, R. Con*	24,809	48.3	2.2
Church, S. Lab/Co-op	22,345	43.5	9.1
Pajak, S. Lib Dem	2,079	4.0	0.4
Costello, M. UKIP	1,291	2.5	-9.5
Kimberley-Fairbourn, T. Green	747	1.5	-2.1
Con majority	2,464	4.8	
Electorate	72,372		
Turnout	51,358	70.96	

Con hold (3.46% from Con to Lab/Co-op)

TAMWORTH

		%	+/-%
Pincher, C. Con*	28,748	60.8	10.9
Hammond, A. Lab	16,401	34.7	8.7
Pinkett, J. Lib Dem	1,961	4.2	1.1
Con majority	12,347	26.11	
Electorate	71,308		
Turnout	47,290	66.32	

Con hold (1.1% from Lab to Con)

TATTON

		%	+/-%
McVey, E. Con	28,764	58.4	0.1
Rushworth, S. Lab	13,977	28.4	10.1
Wilson, G. Lib Dem	4,431	9.0	0.5
Hennerley, N. Green	1,024	2.1	-1.7
Abel, Q. Ind	920	1.9	
Con majority	14,787	30.04	
Electorate	67,874		
Turnout	49,220	72.52	

Con hold (5.04% from Con to Lab)

TAUNTON DEANE

		%	+/-%
Pow, R. Con*	33,333	52.8	4.8
Amos, G. Lib Dem	17,446	27.6	6.3
Jevon, M. Lab	9,689	15.3	6.1
Dimmick, A. UKIP	1,434	2.3	-9.6
Martin, C. Green	1,151	1.8	-2.7
Con majority	15,887	25.16	
Electorate	85,457		
Turnout	63,152	73.9	

Con hold (0.77% from Con to Lib Dem)

TELFORD

		%	+/-%
Allan, L. Con*	21,777	48.6	9.2
Sahota, K. Lab	21,057	47.0	9.4
King, S. Lib Dem	954	2.1	-0.1
Shirley, L. Green	898	2.0	-0.3
Con majority	720	1.61	
Electorate	68,106		
Turnout	44,832	65.83	

Con hold (0.09% from Con to Lab)

TEWKESBURY

		%	+/-%
Robertson, L. Con*	35,448	59.9	5.5
Kang, M. Lab	12,874	21.8	7.0
Clucas, C. Lib Dem	7,981	13.5	-0.3
Cody, C. Green	1,576	2.7	-1.3
Collins, S. UKIP	1,205	2.0	-10.8
Con majority	22,574	38.13	
Electorate	81,440		
Turnout	59,199	72.69	

Con hold (0.72% from Con to Lab)

NORTH THANET

		%	+/-%
Gale, R. Con*	27,163	56.1	7.3
Rehal, F. Lab	16,425	33.9	16.1
Egan, C. UKIP	2,198	4.5	-21.1
Pennington, M. Lib Dem	1,586	3.3	-0.2
Targett, E. Green	825	1.7	-1.9
White, I. CPA	128	0.3	
Con majority	10,738	22.18	
Electorate	72,651		
Turnout	48,407	66.63	

Con hold (4.41% from Con to Lab)

SOUTH THANET

		%	+/-%
Mackinlay, C. Con*	25,262	50.7	12.7
Ara, R. Lab	18,875	37.9	14.2
Piper, S. UKIP	2,997	6.0	-26.3
Williams, J. Lib Dem	1,514	3.0	1.2
Roper, T. Green	809	1.6	-0.6
Garbutt, T. Ind	181	0.4	
Fisher, F. CPA	115	0.2	
Con majority	6,387	12.81	
Electorate	72,334		
Turnout	49,845	68.91	

Con hold (0.75% from Con to Lab)

THE COTSWOLDS

		%	+/-%
Clifton-Brown, G. Con*	36,201	60.5	4.2
Huband, M. Lab	10,702	17.9	8.7
Gant, A. Lib Dem	9,748	16.3	-2.3
Poole, S. Green	1,747	2.9	-1.7
Harlow, C. UKIP	1,197	2.0	-8.9
Steel, S. Ind	107	0.2	
Con majority	25,499	42.62	
Electorate	80,449		
Turnout	59,829	74.37	

Con hold (2.26% from Con to Lab)

THE WREKIN – see under Wrekin

THIRSK AND MALTON

		%	+/-%
Hollinrake, K. Con*	33,572	59.9	7.5
Avery, A. Lab	14,571	26.0	10.6
Keal, D. Lib Dem	3,859	6.9	-2.1
Horton, T. UKIP	1,532	2.7	-12.1
Brampton, M. Green	1,100	2.0	-2.6
Clark, J. Lib	753	1.3	-0.8
Tate, P. Ind	542	1.0	-0.3
Con majority	19,001	33.92	
Electorate	78,670		
Turnout	56,023	71.21	

Con hold (1.56% from Con to Lab)

THORNBURY AND YATE

		%	+/-%
Hall, L. Con*	28,008	55.1	14.3
Young, C. Lib Dem	15,937	31.4	-6.4
Mead, B. Lab	6,112	12.0	4.3
Hamilton, I. Green	633	1.3	-1.5
Con majority	12,071	23.77	
Electorate	67,892		
Turnout	50,791	74.81	

Con hold (10.35% from Lib Dem to Con)

THURROCK

		%	+/-%
Doyle-Price, J. Con*	19,880	39.4	5.8
Kent, J. Lab	19,535	38.7	6.2
Aker, T. UKIP	10,112	20.1	-11.6
McNamara, K. Lib Dem	798	1.6	0.3
Con majority	345	0.68	
Electorate	78,154		
Turnout	50,422	64.52	

Con hold (0.2% from Con to Lab)

TIVERTON AND HONITON

		%	+/-%
Parish, N. Con*	35,471	61.2	7.6
Kolek, C. Lab	15,670	27.0	14.4
Wilson, M. Lib Dem	4,639	8.0	-2.4
Westcott, G. Green	2,035	3.5	-2.8
Con majority	19,801	34.15	
Electorate	80,731		
Turnout	57,987	71.83	

Con hold (3.43% from Con to Lab)

TONBRIDGE AND MALLING

		%	+/-%
Tugendhat, T. Con*	36,218	63.5	4.3
Jones, D. Lab	12,710	22.3	8.2
Miller, K. Lib Dem	3,787	6.6	-0.2
Clark, A. Green	2,335	4.1	-0.3
Bullen, C. UKIP	1,857	3.3	-11.9
Con majority	23,508	41.23	
Electorate	77,417		
Turnout	57,015	73.65	

Con hold (1.94% from Con to Lab)

TOOTING

		%	+/-%
Allin-Khan, R. Lab*	34,694	59.5	12.5
Watkins, D. Con	19,236	33.0	-8.7
Glassbrook, A. Lib Dem	3,057	5.2	1.3
Obiri-Darko, E. Green	845	1.5	-2.7
Coshall, R. UKIP	339	0.6	-2.3
Lab majority	15,458	26.51	
Electorate	77,971		
Turnout	58,304	74.78	

Lab hold (10.62% from Con to Lab)

TORBAY

		%	+/-%
Foster, K. Con*	27,141	53.0	12.4
Brewer, D. Lib Dem	12,858	25.1	-8.6
Raybould, P. Lab	9,310	18.2	9.5
McIntyre, T. UKIP	1,213	2.4	-11.2
Moss, S. Green	652	1.3	-2.0
Con majority	14,283	27.87	
Electorate	75,931		
Turnout	51,249	67.49	

Con hold (10.53% from Lib Dem to Con)

TORFAEN

		%	+/-%
Thomas-Symonds, N. Lab*	22,134	57.5	12.9
Smith, G. Con	11,894	30.9	7.8
Rees, J. PIC	2,059	5.3	-0.4
Williams, I. UKIP	1,490	3.9	-15.1
Best, A. Lib Dem	852	2.2	-1.1
Lab majority	10,240	26.6	
Electorate	61,839		
Turnout	38,491	62.24	

Lab hold (2.55% from Con to Lab)

TORRIDGE AND WEST DEVON

		%	+/-%
Cox, G. Con*	33,612	56.4	5.7
Barry, V. Lab/Co-op	12,926	21.7	11.1
Chalmers, D. Lib Dem	10,526	17.6	4.5
Jordan, C. Green	1,622	2.7	-4.2
Julian, R. Ind	794	1.3	
Con majority	20,686	34.69	
Electorate	80,524		
Turnout	59,624	74.05	

Con hold (2.7% from Con to Lab/Co-op)

TOTNES

		%	+/-%
Wollaston, S. Con*	26,972	53.6	0.8
Messer, G. Lab	13,495	26.8	14.1
Brazil, J. Lib Dem	6,466	12.8	3.0
Hodgson, J. Green	2,097	4.2	-6.1
Harvey, S. UKIP	1,240	2.5	-11.6
Con majority	13,477	26.77	
Electorate	68,914		
Turnout	50,352	73.06	

Con hold (6.67% from Con to Lab)

TOTTENHAM

		%	+/-%
Lammy, D. Lab*	40,249	81.3	14.3
Stacey, M. Con	5,665	11.4	-0.4
Haley, B. Lib Dem	1,687	3.4	-0.7
Francis, J. Green	1,276	2.6	-6.6
Rumble, P. UKIP	462	0.9	-2.6
Lab majority	34,584	69.89	
Electorate	72,884		
Turnout	49,486	67.9	

Lab hold (7.4% from Con to Lab)

TRURO AND FALMOUTH

		%	+/-%
Newton, S. Con*	25,123	44.3	0.4
Kirkham, J. Lab	21,331	37.6	22.5
Nolan, R. Lib Dem	8,465	14.9	-1.9
Odgers, D. UKIP	897	1.6	-10.0
Pennington, A. Green	831	1.5	-7.2
Con majority	3,792	6.69	
Electorate	74,683		
Turnout	56,717	75.94	

Con hold (11.06% from Con to Lab)

*Member of last Parliament

TUNBRIDGE WELLS

		%	+/-%
Clark, G. Con*	30,856	56.8	-1.7
Woodgate, C. Lab	14,391	26.5	12.3
Sadler, R. Lib Dem	5,355	9.9	1.4
Hoare, C. UKIP	1,464	2.7	-9.9
Bisdee, T. Green	1,441	2.6	-2.5
Thomas, C. WEP	702	1.3	
Con majority	16,465	30.32	
Electorate	74,782		
Turnout	54,308	72.62	

Con hold (7.01% from Con to Lab)

TWICKENHAM

		%	+/-%
Cable, V. Lib Dem	34,969	52.6	14.7
Mathias, T. Con*	25,207	37.9	-3.2
Dunne, K. Lab	6,114	9.2	-2.3
Lib Dem majority	9,762	14.69	
Electorate	83,362		
Turnout	66,433	79.69	

Lib Dem gain (8.97% from Con to Lib Dem)

TYNEMOUTH

		%	+/-%
Campbell, A. Lab*	32,395	56.9	8.8
Varley, N. Con	20,729	36.4	3.7
Appleby, J. Lib Dem	1,724	3.0	0.1
Houghton, S. UKIP	1,257	2.2	-10.0
Erskine, J. Green	629	1.1	-2.7
The Durham Cobbler, A. Ind	124	0.2	
Lab majority	11,666	20.48	
Electorate	77,434		
Turnout	56,964	73.56	

Lab hold (2.56% from Con to Lab)

NORTH TYNESIDE

		%	+/-%
Glindon, M. Lab*	33,456	64.4	8.6
Newman, H. Con	14,172	27.3	8.1
Legg, G. UKIP	2,101	4.0	-12.2
Stone, G. Lib Dem	1,494	2.9	-1.5
Collins, M. Green	669	1.3	-1.8
Lab majority	19,284	37.1	
Electorate	78,914		
Turnout	51,984	65.87	

Lab hold (0.24% from Con to Lab)

WEST TYRONE

		%	+/-%
McElduff, B. Sinn Féin	22,060	50.5	7.4
Buchanan, T. DUP	11,718	26.8	9.5
McCrossan, D. SDLP	5,635	12.9	-3.6
Clarke, A. UUP	2,253	5.2	-10.6
Donnelly, S. All	1,000	2.3	0.1
McClean, C. Green	427	1.0	-1.0
Brown, B. cista	393	0.9	
Sinn Féin majority	10,342	23.68	
Electorate	64,009		
Turnout	43,675	68.23	

Sinn Féin hold (1.06% from Sinn Féin to DUP)

General Election 2017

MID ULSTER

		%	+/-%
Molloy, F. Sinn Féin*	25,455	54.2	5.9
Buchanan, K. DUP	12,565	26.8	13.5
Quinn, M. SDLP	4,563	9.7	-2.5
Glasgow, M. UUP	3,017	6.4	-8.9
Watson, F. All	1,094	2.3	0.4
Sinn Féin majority	12,890	27.44	
Electorate	68,485		
Turnout	46,975	68.59	

Sinn Féin hold (3.79% from Sinn Féin to DUP)

UPPER BANN

		%	+/-%
Simpson, D. DUP*	22,317	43.4	10.9
O'Dowd, J. Sinn Féin	14,325	27.9	3.4
Beattie, D. UUP	7,900	15.4	-12.4
McAlinden, D. SDLP	4,397	8.6	-0.4
Doyle, T. All	2,319	4.5	0.8
DUP majority	7,992	15.54	
Electorate	80,168		
Turnout	51,431	64.15	

DUP hold (3.73% from Sinn Féin to DUP)

UXBRIDGE AND SOUTH RUISLIP

		%	+/-%
Johnson, B. Con*	23,716	50.7	0.6
Lo, V. Lab	18,682	39.9	13.6
Robson, R. Lib Dem	1,835	3.9	-1.0
Kemp, E. UKIP	1,577	3.4	-10.8
Keir, M. Green	884	1.9	-1.3
Con majority	5,034	10.76	
Electorate	69,938		
Turnout	46,778	66.88	

Con hold (6.53% from Con to Lab)

VALE OF CLWYD – see under Clwyd

VALE OF GLAMORGAN – see under Glamorgan

VAUXHALL

		%	+/-%
Hoey, K. Lab*	31,576	57.2	3.7
Turner, G. Lib Dem	11,326	20.5	13.6
Theis, D. Con	10,277	18.6	-8.5
Hasnain, G. Green	1,152	2.1	-5.5
Iyengar, H. WEP	539	1.0	
Chapman, M. Pirate	172	0.3	-0.1
Lab majority	20,250	36.68	
Electorate	82,055		
Turnout	55,206	67.28	

Lab hold (4.98% from Lab to Lib Dem)

WAKEFIELD

		%	+/-%
Creagh, M. Lab*	22,987	49.5	9.4
Calvert, A. Con	20,811	44.9	10.8
Brown, L. YP	1,176	2.5	
Cronin, F. Lib Dem	943	2.0	-1.4
Ali, W. Ind	367	0.8	
Lab majority	2,176	4.69	
Electorate	70,340		
Turnout	46,396	65.96	

Lab hold (0.68% from Lab to Con)

WALLASEY

		%	+/-%
Eagle, A. Lab*	34,552	71.3	11.2
Livsey, A. Con	11,232	23.2	0.6
Caplin, D. UKIP	1,160	2.4	-9.2
Childs, P. Lib Dem	772	1.6	-0.7
Clough, L. Green	637	1.3	-1.6
Lab majority	23,320	48.15	
Electorate	67,454		
Turnout	48,430	71.8	

Lab hold (5.31% from Con to Lab)

WALSALL NORTH

		%	+/-%
Hughes, E. Con	18,919	49.5	15.9
Winnick, D. Lab*	16,318	42.7	3.8
Hazell, L. UKIP	2,295	6.0	-15.9
Parasram, I. Lib Dem	586	1.5	-0.7
Con majority	2,601	6.81	
Electorate	67,308		
Turnout	38,196	56.75	

Con gain (6.03% from Lab to Con)

WALSALL SOUTH

		%	+/-%
Vaz, V. Lab*	25,286	57.2	10.3
Bird, J. Con	16,394	37.1	4.4
Bennett, D. UKIP	1,805	4.1	-11.5
Wellings Purvis, A. Lib Dem	587	1.3	-0.3
Lab majority	8,892	20.12	
Electorate	67,417		
Turnout	44,189	65.55	

Lab hold (2.92% from Con to Lab)

WALTHAMSTOW

		%	+/-%
Creasy, S. Lab/Co-op*	38,793	80.3	11.8
Samuel-Leport, M. Con	6,776	14.0	0.7
Obasi, U. Lib Dem	1,384	2.9	-1.1
Johns, A. Green	1,190	2.5	-3.9
Lab/Co-op majority	32,017	66.29	
Electorate	67,957		
Turnout	48,302	71.08	

Lab/Co-op hold (5.51% from Con to Lab/Co-op)

WANSBECK

		%	+/-%
Lavery, I. Lab*	24,338	57.3	7.3
Galley, C. Con	13,903	32.7	11.0
Tebbutt, J. Lib Dem	2,015	4.7	-1.5
Hurst, M. UKIP	1,483	3.5	-14.7
Leyland, S. Green	715	1.7	-2.1
Lab majority	10,435	24.55	
Electorate	62,151		
Turnout	42,511	68.4	

Lab hold (1.82% from Lab to Con)

WANTAGE

		%	+/-%
Vaizey, E. Con*	34,459	54.1	0.9
Eden, R. Lab/Co-op	17,079	26.8	10.8
Carrigan, C. Lib Dem	9,234	14.5	1.5
Ap-Roberts, S. Green	1,546	2.4	-2.7
McLeod, D. UKIP	1,284	2.0	-10.4
Con majority	17,380	27.26	
Electorate	85,786		
Turnout	63,748	74.31	

Con hold (4.95% from Con to Lab/Co-op)

WARLEY

		%	+/-%
Spellar, J. Lab*	27,004	67.0	9.1
Mangnall, A. Con	10,521	26.1	6.9
Magher, D. UKIP	1,349	3.4	-13.1
Manley-Green, B. Lib Dem	777	1.9	-0.2
Redding, M. Green	555	1.4	-2.5
Lab majority	16,483	40.88	
Electorate	63,739		
Turnout	40,322	63.26	

Lab hold (1.12% from Con to Lab)

WARRINGTON NORTH

		%	+/-%
Jones, H. Lab*	27,356	56.3	8.7
Allen, V. Con	17,774	36.6	8.5
Ashington, J. UKIP	1,561	3.2	-13.8
Krizanac, S. Lib Dem	1,207	2.5	-1.6
McAteer, L. Green	619	1.3	-1.5
Lab majority	9,582	19.71	
Electorate	71,918		
Turnout	48,616	67.6	

Lab hold (0.08% from Con to Lab)

WARRINGTON SOUTH

		%	+/-%
Rashid, F. Lab	29,994	48.3	9.4
Mowat, D. Con*	27,445	44.2	0.6
Barr, B. Lib Dem	3,339	5.4	-0.2
Boulton, J. Ind	1,217	2.0	
Lab majority	2,549	4.1	
Electorate	85,617		
Turnout	62,115	72.55	

Lab gain (4.37% from Con to Lab)

WARWICK AND LEAMINGTON

		%	+/-%
Western, M. Lab	25,227	46.6	11.9
White, C. Con*	24,021	44.3	-3.3
Solman, N. Lib Dem	2,810	5.2	0.1
Chilvers, J. Green	1,198	2.2	-1.7
Dhillon, B. UKIP	799	1.5	-6.8
Lab majority	1,206	2.23	
Electorate	74,237		
Turnout	54,180	72.98	

Lab gain (7.61% from Con to Lab)

*Member of last Parliament

NORTH WARWICKSHIRE

		%	+/-%
Tracey, C. Con*	26,860	56.8	14.6
Jackson, J. Lab	18,350	38.8	2.9
Cox, J. Lib Dem	1,028	2.2	0.1
Kondakor, K. Green	940	2.0	0.1
Con majority	8,510	17.99	
Electorate	72,277		
Turnout	47,315	65.46	

Con hold (5.87% from Lab to Con)

WASHINGTON AND SUNDERLAND WEST

		%	+/-%
Hodgson, S. Lab*	24,639	60.6	5.9
Gullis, J. Con	11,699	28.8	10.0
Foster, B. UKIP	2,761	6.8	-12.8
Appleby, T. Lib Dem	961	2.4	-0.3
Chantkowski, M. Green	514	1.3	-1.6
Lab majority	12,940	31.83	
Electorate	67,280		
Turnout	40,648	60.42	

Lab hold (2.04% from Lab to Con)

WATFORD

		%	+/-%
Harrington, R. Con*	26,731	45.5	2.0
Ostrowski, C. Lab	24,639	42.0	15.9
Stotesbury, I. Lib Dem	5,335	9.1	-9.0
Green, I. UKIP	1,184	2.0	-7.8
Murray, A. Green	721	1.2	-1.1
Con majority	2,092	3.56	
Electorate	86,507		
Turnout	58,723	67.88	

Con hold (6.96% from Con to Lab)

WAVENEY

		%	+/-%
Aldous, P. Con*	28,643	54.3	12.1
Barker, S. Lab	19,428	36.8	-0.8
Poole, B. UKIP	1,933	3.7	-10.8
Brambley-Crawshaw, E. Green	1,332	2.5	-0.8
Howe, J. Lib Dem	1,012	1.9	-0.1
Barron, A. Ind	326	0.6	
Con majority	9,215	17.47	
Electorate	80,763		
Turnout	52,742	65.3	

Con hold (6.44% from Lab to Con)

WEALDEN

		%	+/-%
Ghani, N. Con*	37,027	61.1	4.3
Smith, A. Lab	13,399	22.1	11.3
Bowers, C. Lib Dem	6,281	10.4	
Stocks, C. Green	1,959	3.2	-3.1
Burton, N. UKIP	1,798	3.0	-13.7
Con majority	23,628	39	
Electorate	81,425		
Turnout	60,577	74.4	

Con hold (3.53% from Con to Lab)

WEAVER VALE

		%	+/-%
Amesbury, M. Lab	26,066	51.4	10.1
Evans, G. Con*	22,138	43.6	0.6
Roberts, P. Lib Dem	1,623	3.2	0.2
Copeman, C. Green	786	1.6	-1.0
Lab majority	3,928	7.74	
Electorate	69,016		
Turnout	50,721	73.49	

Lab gain (4.73% from Con to Lab)

WELLINGBOROUGH

		%	+/-%
Bone, P. Con*	30,579	57.3	5.5
Watts, A. Lab	18,119	34.0	14.6
Shipham, A. UKIP	1,804	3.4	-16.1
Nelson, C. Lib Dem	1,782	3.3	-1.1
Hornett, J. Green	956	1.8	-2.6
Con majority	12,460	23.36	
Electorate	79,254		
Turnout	53,340	67.3	

Con hold (4.53% from Con to Lab)

WELLS

		%	+/-%
Heappey, J. Con*	30,488	50.0	4.0
Munt, T. Lib Dem	22,906	37.6	4.9
Merryfield, A. Lab	7,129	11.7	5.1
Corke, L. CPA	320	0.5	
Con majority	7,582	12.43	
Electorate	82,451		
Turnout	60,974	73.95	

Con hold (0.43% from Con to Lib Dem)

WELWYN HATFIELD

		%	+/-%
Shapps, G. Con*	26,374	50.9	0.8
Miah, A. Lab	19,005	36.7	10.6
Quinton, N. Lib Dem	3,836	7.4	1.2
Milliken, D. UKIP	1,441	2.8	-10.2
Sayers, C. Green	835	1.6	-1.9
Jones, M. Ind	178	0.3	
Con majority	7,369	14.23	
Electorate	72,888		
Turnout	51,778	71.04	

Con hold (4.94% from Con to Lab)

WENTWORTH AND DEARNE

		%	+/-%
Healey, J. Lab*	28,547	64.5	7.9
Jackson, S. Con	13,744	31.1	16.2
Middleton, J. Lib Dem	1,656	3.7	1.1
Lab majority	14,803	33.47	
Electorate	74,890		
Turnout	44,227	59.06	

Lab hold (4.18% from Lab to Con)

WEST ABERDEENSHIRE AND KINCARDINE
– see under Aberdeenshire

WEST BROMWICH EAST

		%	+/-%
Watson, T. Lab*	22,664	57.8	7.8
Crane, E. Con	14,951	38.1	13.3
Trench, K. Lib Dem	625	1.6	-0.4
Macefield, J. Green	533	1.4	-0.3
Rankine, C. Ind	325	0.8	
Lab majority	7,713	19.66	
Electorate	63,846		
Turnout	39,236	61.45	

Lab hold (2.76% from Lab to Con)

WEST BROMWICH WEST

		%	+/-%
Bailey, A. Lab/Co-op*	18,789	51.9	4.8
Hardie, A. Con	14,329	39.6	15.8
Anderton, S. UKIP	2,320	6.4	-18.7
Clucas, F. Lib Dem	333	0.9	-0.6
Buckman, R. Green	323	0.9	-1.1
Lab/Co-op majority	4,460	12.33	
Electorate	65,967		
Turnout	36,184	54.85	

Lab/Co-op hold (5.52% from Lab/Co-op to Con)

WEST DORSET – see under Dorset

WEST DUNBARTONSHIRE – see under Dunbartonshire

WEST HAM

		%	+/-%
Brown, L. Lab*	46,591	76.5	8.4
Spencer, P. Con	9,837	16.2	0.8
Reynolds, P. Lib Dem	1,836	3.0	0.3
Beattie, R. UKIP	1,134	1.9	-5.6
Spracklin, M. Green	957	1.6	-3.4
Shedowo, K. CPA	353	0.6	-0.1
Lab majority	36,754	60.38	
Electorate	92,418		
Turnout	60,869	65.86	

Lab hold (3.8% from Con to Lab)

WEST LANCASHIRE – see under Lancashire

WEST SUFFOLK – see under Suffolk

WEST TYRONE – see under Tyrone

WEST WORCESTERSHIRE – see under Worcestershire

WESTMINSTER NORTH

		%	+/-%
Buck, K. Lab*	25,934	59.6	13.0
Hall, L. Con	14,422	33.2	-8.5
Harding, A. Lib Dem	2,253	5.2	1.5
Tandy, E. Green	595	1.4	-2.0
Dharamsey, A. Ind	91	0.2	
Lab majority	11,512	26.47	
Electorate	63,846		
Turnout	43,487	68.11	

Lab hold (10.75% from Con to Lab)

WESTMORLAND AND LONSDALE

		%	+/-%
Farron, T. Lib Dem*	23,686	45.8	-5.6
Airey, J. Con	22,909	44.3	11.1
Aldridge, E. Lab	4,783	9.2	3.8
Fishfinger, M. Ind	309	0.6	
Lib Dem majority	777	1.5	
Electorate	66,391		
Turnout	51,768	77.97	

Lib Dem hold (8.37% from Lib Dem to Con)

WESTON-SUPER-MARE

		%	+/-%
Penrose, J. Con*	29,982	53.0	5.3
Taylor, T. Lab	18,438	32.6	14.4
Bell, M. Lib Dem	5,175	9.2	-1.2
Hims, H. UKIP	1,932	3.4	-14.3
Basu, S. Green	888	1.6	-3.3
Con majority	11,544	20.43	
Electorate	82,136		
Turnout	56,512	68.8	

Con hold (4.58% from Con to Lab)

WIGAN

		%	+/-%
Nandy, L. Lab*	29,575	62.1	10.1
Williams, A. Con	13,548	28.4	7.8
Ryding, N. UKIP	2,750	5.8	-13.6
Clayton, M. Lib Dem	916	1.9	-0.8
Patterson, W. Green	753	1.6	-1.2
Lab majority	16,027	33.64	
Electorate	75,359		
Turnout	47,638	63.21	

Lab hold (1.15% from Con to Lab)

NORTH WILTSHIRE

		%	+/-%
Gray, J. Con*	32,398	60.2	3.1
Mathew, B. Lib Dem	9,521	17.7	2.1
Baldrey, P. Lab	9,399	17.5	7.7
Chamberlain, P. Green	1,141	2.1	-2.5
Singh, P. UKIP	871	1.6	-9.9
Tweedie, L. Ind	376	0.7	
Con majority	22,877	42.52	
Electorate	71,410		
Turnout	53,797	75.34	

Con hold (0.5% from Lib Dem to Con)

SOUTH WEST WILTSHIRE

		%	+/-%
Murrison, A. Con*	32,841	59.8	7.3
Pictor, L. Lab	14,515	26.4	13.0
Carbin, T. Lib Dem	5,360	9.8	-0.8
Walford, C. Green	1,445	2.6	-3.1
Silcocks, L. Ind	590	1.1	
Con majority	18,326	33.38	
Electorate	76,898		
Turnout	54,897	71.39	

Con hold (2.88% from Con to Lab)

*Member of last Parliament

WIMBLEDON

		%	+/-%
Hammond, S. Con*	23,946	46.4	-5.6
Uddin, I. Lab	18,324	35.5	9.5
Quilliam, C. Lib Dem	7,472	14.5	1.9
Barraball, C. Green	1,231	2.4	-1.7
McDonald, S. UKIP	553	1.1	-4.0
Con majority	5,622	10.88	
Electorate	66,780		
Turnout	51,653	77.35	

Con hold (7.55% from Con to Lab)

WINCHESTER

		%	+/-%
Brine, S. Con*	29,729	51.9	-2.9
Porter, J. Lib Dem	19,730	34.5	10.1
Chaloner, M. Lab	6,007	10.5	2.2
Wainwright, A. Green	846	1.5	-3.3
Lyon, M. UKIP	695	1.2	-6.2
Skelton, T. JACP	149	0.3	
Con majority	9,999	17.46	
Electorate	72,497		
Turnout	57,256	78.98	

Con hold (6.52% from Con to Lib Dem)

WINDSOR

		%	+/-%
Afriyie, A. Con*	34,718	64.2	1.0
Shearman, P. Lab	12,334	22.8	9.5
Tisi, J. Lib Dem	5,434	10.1	1.5
McKeown, F. Green	1,435	2.6	-1.0
Con majority	22,384	41.39	
Electorate	73,595		
Turnout	54,085	73.49	

Con hold (4.22% from Con to Lab)

WIRRAL SOUTH

		%	+/-%
McGovern, A. Lab*	25,871	57.1	13.9
Sykes, A. Con	17,548	38.8	5.3
Carubia, C. Lib Dem	1,322	2.9	-0.2
Roberts, M. Green	454	1.0	-0.9
Lab majority	8,323	18.38	
Electorate	57,670		
Turnout	45,279	78.51	

Lab hold (4.26% from Con to Lab)

WIRRAL WEST

		%	+/-%
Greenwood, M. Lab*	23,866	54.2	9.2
Caldeira, T. Con	18,501	42.0	-2.0
Reisdorf, P. Lib Dem	1,155	2.6	-0.8
Coyne, J. Green	429	1.0	
Lab majority	5,365	12.18	
Electorate	55,995		
Turnout	44,034	78.64	

Lab hold (5.6% from Con to Lab)

WITHAM

		%	+/-%
Patel, P. Con*	31,670	64.1	6.8
Barlow, P. Lab	13,024	26.4	10.6
Hayes, J. Lib Dem	2,715	5.5	-0.6
Abbott, J. Green	1,832	3.7	-0.6
Con majority	18,646	37.74	
Electorate	69,137		
Turnout	49,400	71.45	

Con hold (1.89% from Con to Lab)

WITNEY

		%	+/-%
Courts, R. Con*	33,839	55.4	-4.6
Carter, L. Lab	12,598	20.6	3.5
Leffman, L. Lib Dem	12,457	20.4	13.7
Lasko, C. Green	1,053	1.7	-3.3
Craig, A. UKIP	980	1.6	-7.5
Con majority	21,241	34.79	
Electorate	82,727		
Turnout	61,051	73.8	

Con hold (4.05% from Con to Lab)

WOKING

		%	+/-%
Lord, J. Con*	29,903	54.0	-2.0
Colley, F. Lab	13,179	23.8	7.7
Forster, W. Lib Dem	9,711	17.5	5.9
De Leon, T. UKIP	1,161	2.1	-9.2
Brierley, J. Green	1,092	2.0	-2.1
Akberali, H. Ind	200	0.4	
Con majority	16,724	30.2	
Electorate	76,170		
Turnout	55,373	72.7	

Con hold (4.87% from Con to Lab)

WOKINGHAM

		%	+/-%
Redwood, J. Con*	33,806	56.5	-1.1
Croy, A. Lab	15,008	25.1	10.6
Jones, C. Lib Dem	9,512	15.9	2.4
Seymour, R. Green	1,364	2.3	-1.4
Con majority	18,798	31.39	
Electorate	79,112		
Turnout	59,889	75.7	

Con hold (5.85% from Con to Lab)

WOLVERHAMPTON NORTH EAST

		%	+/-%
Reynolds, E. Lab*	19,282	52.7	6.8
Macken, S. Con	14,695	40.2	10.4
Eardley, G. UKIP	1,479	4.0	-15.1
Jenkins, I. Lib Dem	570	1.6	-1.2
Wood, C. Green	482	1.3	-0.7
Lab majority	4,587	12.53	
Electorate	60,770		
Turnout	36,594	60.22	

Lab hold (1.79% from Lab to Con)

WOLVERHAMPTON SOUTH EAST

		%	+/-%
McFadden, P. Lab*	21,137	58.1	5.0
Mullan, K. Con	12,623	34.7	12.4
Hodgson, B. UKIP	1,675	4.6	-15.6
Mathis, B. Lib Dem	448	1.2	-1.1
Bertaut, A. Green	421	1.2	-0.6
Lab majority	8,514	23.4	
Electorate	60,301		
Turnout	36,390	60.35	

Lab hold (3.75% from Lab to Con)

WOLVERHAMPTON SOUTH WEST

		%	+/-%
Smith, E. Lab	20,899	49.2	6.2
Uppal, P. Con	18,714	44.1	3.0
Jones, R. UKIP	1,012	2.4	-8.3
Quarmby, S. Lib Dem	784	1.9	-0.2
Cantrill, A. Green	579	1.4	-1.3
Singh, J. Ind	358	0.8	
Lab majority	2,185	5.15	
Electorate	59,971		
Turnout	42,461	70.8	

Lab hold (1.59% from Con to Lab)

WORCESTER

		%	+/-%
Walker, R. Con*	24,731	48.0	2.8
Squires, J. Lab	22,223	43.1	9.3
Kearney, S. Lib Dem	1,757	3.4	0.1
Hickling, P. UKIP	1,354	2.6	-10.2
Stephen, L. Green	1,211	2.4	-1.7
Rugg, A. Ind	109	0.2	0.1
Shuker, M. Compass	38	0.1	
Con majority	2,508	4.87	
Electorate	73,893		
Turnout	51,515	69.72	

Con hold (3.23% from Con to Lab)

MID WORCESTERSHIRE

		%	+/-%
Huddleston, N. Con*	35,967	65.2	8.4
Grindrod, F. Lab	12,641	22.9	8.5
Rowley, M. Lib Dem	3,450	6.3	-0.9
Greenwood, D. UKIP	1,660	3.0	-14.6
Whitfield, F. Green	1,371	2.5	-1.2
Con majority	23,326	42.26	
Electorate	76,057		
Turnout	55,191	72.57	

Con hold (0.05% from Con to Lab)

WEST WORCESTERSHIRE

		%	+/-%
Baldwin, H. Con*	34,703	61.3	5.4
Charles, S. Lab	13,375	23.6	10.3
McMillan-Scott, E. Lib Dem	5,307	9.4	-0.3
McVey, N. Green	1,605	2.8	-3.6
Savage, M. UKIP	1,481	2.6	-11.7
Con majority	21,328	37.69	
Electorate	74,375		
Turnout	56,583	76.08	

Con hold (2.43% from Con to Lab)

WORKINGTON

		%	+/-%
Hayman, S. Lab*	21,317	51.1	9.0
Vasey, C. Con	17,392	41.7	11.7
Kemp, G. UKIP	1,556	3.7	-15.8
Roberts, P. Lib Dem	1,133	2.7	-1.7
Ivinson, R. Ind	278	0.7	0.2
Lab majority	3,925	9.41	
Electorate	60,265		
Turnout	41,731	69.25	

Lab hold (1.36% from Lab to Con)

WORSLEY AND ECCLES SOUTH

		%	+/-%
Keeley, B. Lab*	26,046	56.9	12.8
Lindley, I. Con	17,667	38.6	8.6
Clarkson, K. Lib Dem	1,087	2.4	-0.2
Dylan, T. Green	842	1.8	-1.1
Lab majority	8,379	18.31	
Electorate	73,689		
Turnout	45,757	62.09	

Lab hold (2.11% from Con to Lab)

EAST WORTHING AND SHOREHAM

		%	+/-%
Loughton, T. Con*	25,988	48.9	-0.4
Cook, S. Lab	20,882	39.3	19.8
Henman, O. Lib Dem	2,523	4.7	-2.0
Glennon, M. UKIP	1,444	2.7	-13.8
Groves Williams, L. Green	1,273	2.4	-2.8
Walker, C. NHA	575	1.1	-1.4
Lutwyche, A. Ind	432	0.8	
Con majority	5,106	9.6	
Electorate	75,525		
Turnout	53,187	70.42	

Con hold (10.12% from Con to Lab)

WORTHING WEST

		%	+/-%
Bottomley, P. Con*	30,181	55.3	4.0
Cooper, B. Lab	18,091	33.1	17.5
Thorpe, H. Lib Dem	2,982	5.5	-3.3
Withers, M. UKIP	1,635	3.0	-15.2
Cornish, B. Green	1,614	3.0	-2.8
Con majority	12,090	22.14	
Electorate	77,757		
Turnout	54,614	70.24	

Con hold (6.77% from Con to Lab)

THE WREKIN

		%	+/-%
Pritchard, M. Con*	27,451	55.3	5.8
Harrison, D. Lab	17,887	36.0	10.1
Allen, D. UKIP	1,656	3.3	-13.4
Keyes, R. Lib Dem	1,345	2.7	-1.6
McCarthy, P. Green	804	1.6	-1.5
Easton, F. Ind	380	0.8	
Con majority	9,564	19.27	
Electorate	68,604		
Turnout	49,638	72.35	

Con hold (2.14% from Con to Lab)

WREXHAM

		%	+/-%
Lucas, I. Lab*	17,153	48.8	11.6
Atkinson, A. Con	15,321	43.6	12.0
Harper, C. PlC	1,753	5.0	-2.6
O'Toole, C. Lib Dem	865	2.5	-2.8
Lab majority	1,832	5.21	
Electorate	50,425		
Turnout	35,160	69.73	

Lab hold (0.19% from Lab to Con)

WYCOMBE

		%	+/-%
Baker, S. Con*	26,766	49.9	-1.2
Raja, R. Lab	20,188	37.6	15.3
Guy, S. Lib Dem	4,147	7.7	-1.0
Phoenix, R. UKIP	1,210	2.3	-7.8
Sims, P. Green	1,182	2.2	-3.8
Con majority	6,578	12.26	
Electorate	77,087		
Turnout	53,637	69.58	

Con hold (8.22% from Con to Lab)

WYRE AND PRESTON NORTH

		%	+/-%
Wallace, B. Con*	30,684	58.1	5.2
Heaton-Bentley, M. Lab	18,438	34.9	10.2
Potter, J. Lib Dem	2,551	4.8	-0.6
Norbury, R. Green	973	1.8	-1.5
Con majority	12,246	23.21	
Electorate	72,319		
Turnout	52,772	72.97	

Con hold (2.53% from Con to Lab)

WYRE FOREST

		%	+/-%
Garnier, M. Con*	29,859	58.3	13.1
Lamb, M. Lab	16,525	32.3	13.0
Miah, S. Lib Dem	1,943	3.8	1.3
Connolly, G. UKIP	1,777	3.5	-12.6
Caulfield, B. Green	1,025	2.0	-0.3
Con majority	13,334	26.03	
Electorate	77,758		
Turnout	51,219	65.87	

Con hold (0.03% from Lab to Con)

WYTHENSHAWE AND SALE EAST

		%	+/-%
Kane, M. Lab*	28,525	62.1	12.2
Green, F. Con	13,581	29.6	4.0
Jones, W. Lib Dem	1,504	3.3	-1.2
Bayley-Sanderson, M. UKIP	1,475	3.2	-11.4
Jerrome, D. Green	576	1.3	-2.6
Francis Augustine, L. Ind	185	0.4	
Lab majority	14,944	32.55	
Electorate	76,361		
Turnout	45,917	60.13	

Lab hold (4.1% from Con to Lab)

*Member of last Parliament

YEOVIL

		%	+/-%
Fysh, M. Con*	32,369	54.4	12.1
Roundell Greene, J. Lib Dem	17,646	29.7	-3.4
Martin, I. Lab	7,418	12.5	5.4
Wood, R. Green	1,052	1.8	-2.1
Pritchard, K. Ind	919	1.5	
Con majority	14,723	24.75	
Electorate	82,916		
Turnout	59,498	71.76	

Con hold (7.72% from Lib Dem to Con)

YNYS MÔN

		%	+/-%
Owen, A. Lab*	15,643	41.8	10.8
Davies, T. Con	10,384	27.8	6.6
Jones, I. PlC	10,237	27.4	-3.0
Turner, J. UKIP	624	1.7	-13.0
Jackson, S. Lib Dem	479	1.3	-0.9
Lab majority	5,259	14.06	
Electorate	52,921		
Turnout	37,407	70.68	

Lab hold (2.06% from Con to Lab)

YORK CENTRAL

		%	+/-%
Maskell, R. Lab/Co-op*	34,594	64.9	22.7
Young, E. Con	16,019	30.1	1.9
Love, N. Lib Dem	2,475	4.6	-3.3
Lab/Co-op majority	18,575	34.85	
Electorate	77,315		
Turnout	53,301	68.94	

Lab/Co-op hold (10.41% from Con to Lab/Co-op)

YORK OUTER

		%	+/-%
Sturdy, J. Con*	29,356	51.0	2.0
Charters-Reid, L. Lab	21,067	36.6	11.9
Blanchard, J. Lib Dem	5,910	10.3	-1.3
Vincent, B. Green	1,094	1.9	-2.8
Con majority	8,289	14.4	
Electorate	75,856		
Turnout	57,573	75.9	

Con hold (4.95% from Con to Lab)

EAST YORKSHIRE

		%	+/-%
Knight, G. Con*	31,442	58.2	7.8
Clark, A. Lab	16,436	30.4	9.8
Minns, C. Lib Dem	2,134	4.0	-2.0
Dennis, A. UKIP	1,986	3.7	-14.2
Norman, T. YP	1,015	1.9	
Jackson, M. Green	943	1.7	-1.7
Con majority	15,006	27.76	
Electorate	81,065		
Turnout	54,053	66.68	

Con hold (0.98% from Con to Lab)

General Election 2017

State of the parties

	2017 General Election	2015 General Election
Conservative	317	330
Labour*	262	232
Scottish National Party	35	56
Liberal Democrat	12	8
Democratic Unionist Party	10	8
Sinn Fein	7	4
Plaid Cymru	4	3
Green	1	1
Independent	1	1
The Speaker	1	1
Social Democratic Labour Party	0	3
Ulster Unionist Party	0	2
UK Independence Party	0	1
TOTAL	**650**	**650**

*Includes Labour/Co-operative MPs.

Share of the vote

	Total Seats	Total Votes	% of votes
Con	317	13636684	42.3
Lab	262	12877918	40.0
Lib Dem	12	2371861	7.4
SNP	35	977568	3.0
UKIP	0	594068	1.8
Green	1	525665	1.6
DUP	10	292316	0.9
Sinn Féin	7	238915	0.7
PlC	4	164466	0.5
Ind	1	151471	0.5
SDLP	0	95419	0.3
UUP	0	83280	0.3
All	0	64553	0.2
Speaker	1	34299	0.1
Other	0	95701	0.3
TOTAL	**650**	**32204184**	**68.7**

Share of the vote by region

England

EASTERN

	Total Seats	Total Votes	% of Votes
Con	50	1690813	54.6
Lab	7	1012357	32.7
Lib Dem	1	244054	7.9
UKIP	0	77793	2.5
Green	0	58704	1.9
Ind	0	6950	0.2
CPA	0	861	0.0
Loony	0	667	0.0
BNP	0	640	0.0
Eng Dem	0	582	0.0
Pirate	0	340	0.0
Southend Ind Ass	0	305	0.0
Reboot	0	133	0.0
YPP	0	110	0.0
TOTAL	**58**	**3094309**	**69.7**

EAST MIDLANDS

	Total Seats	*Total Votes*	*% of Votes*
Con	31	1195982	50.7
Lab	15	954635	40.5
Lib Dem	0	101612	4.3
UKIP	0	56358	2.4
Green	0	34355	1.5
Ind	0	8326	0.4
Ashfield Ind	0	4612	0.2
Loony	0	496	0.0
BNP	0	322	0.0
Blue Rev	0	283	0.0
Humanity	0	282	0.0
Elvis	0	195	0.0
TOTAL	**46**	**2357458**	**68.9**

LONDON

	Total Seats	*Total Votes*	*% of Votes*
Lab	49	2086595	54.5
Con	21	1268800	33.1
Lib Dem	3	336725	8.8
Green	0	67561	1.8
UKIP	0	49369	1.3
Ind	0	11101	0.3
CPA	0	2719	0.1
BNP	0	1909	0.0
WEP	0	1090	0.0
AWP	0	673	0.0
WRP	0	634	0.0
Friends	0	435	0.0
Loony	0	274	0.0
Pirate	0	172	0.0
Eng Dem	0	93	0.0
Concordia	0	85	0.0
Realists	0	61	0.0
SP	0	53	0.0
Populist	0	50	0.0
Green Soc	0	49	0.0
YPP	0	43	0.0
Comm League	0	7	0.0
TOTAL	**73**	**3828498**	**70.1**

NORTH EAST

	Total Seats	*Total Votes*	*% of Votes*
Lab	26	709738	55.4
Con	3	440613	34.4
Lib Dem	0	58409	4.6
UKIP	0	49348	3.9
Green	0	16080	1.3
NEP	0	2355	0.2
Ind	0	1939	0.2
BNP	0	991	0.1
NECA	0	353	0.0
Libertarian	0	114	0.0
Space Navies	0	81	0.0
YPP	0	45	0.0
TOTAL	**29**	**1280066**	**66.0**

NORTH WEST

	Total Seats	*Total Votes*	*% of Votes*
Lab	54	1972632	54.9
Con	20	1301562	36.2
Lib Dem	1	193053	5.4
UKIP	0	68946	1.9
Green	0	39608	1.1
Ind	0	13884	0.4
Lib	0	2449	0.1
BNP	0	718	0.0
CPA	0	529	0.0
SLP	0	424	0.0
Pirate	0	371	0.0
NHA	0	341	0.0
WVPTFP	0	269	0.0
GMHV	0	242	0.0
WEP	0	234	0.0
Loony	0	217	0.0
Comm League	0	27	0.0
TOTAL	**75**	**3595506**	**67.8**

SOUTH EAST

	Total Seats	*Total Votes*	*% of Votes*
Con	72	2495350	53.8
Lab	8	1326380	28.6
Lib Dem	2	487203	10.5
Green	1	143873	3.1
UKIP	0	104509	2.3
Speaker	1	34299	0.7
Ind	0	23836	0.5
NHA	0	12668	0.3
Loony	0	1304	0.0
CPA	0	1031	0.0
JACP	0	991	0.0
Southampton Ind	0	816	0.0
WEP	0	702	0.0
Pirate	0	483	0.0
Peace Party	0	468	0.0
Radical	0	392	0.0
SN	0	375	0.0
Libertarian	0	343	0.0
Apol Dem	0	304	0.0
AWP	0	282	0.0
MAD	0	142	0.0
Patria	0	84	0.0
Just	0	52	0.0
TOTAL	**84**	**4635887**	**71.2**

SOUTH WEST

	Total Seats	*Total Votes*	*% of Votes*
Con	47	1542296	51.4
Lab	7	875213	29.1
Lib Dem	1	448730	14.9
Green	0	68010	2.3
UKIP	0	33160	1.1
Ind	0	31763	1.1
NHA	0	871	0.0
DDIP	0	551	0.0
CPA	0	505	0.0

SOUTH WEST CONT.	*Total Seats*	*Total Votes*	*% of Votes*
Lib	0	470	0.0
Pirate	0	418	0.0
Wessex Reg	0	223	0.0
Loony	0	210	0.0
SLP	0	138	0.0
Money Free	0	101	0.0
TOTAL	**55**	**3002659**	**71.8**

WEST MIDLANDS

	Total Seats	*Total Votes*	*% of Votes*
Con	35	1356486	49.0
Lab	24	1175095	42.5
Lib Dem	0	122287	4.4
UKIP	0	50106	1.8
Green	0	46347	1.7
Ind	0	12213	0.4
NHA	0	2239	0.1
SLP	0	592	0.0
Loony	0	565	0.0
Common Good	0	155	0.0
Open Borders	0	99	0.0
Compass	0	38	0.0
TOTAL	**59**	**2766222**	**66.4**

YORKSHIRE AND HUMBERSIDE

	Total Seats	*Total Votes*	*% of Votes*
Lab	37	1276912	49.0
Con	17	1054099	40.5
Lib Dem	0	129687	5.0
UKIP	0	67801	2.6
Green	0	32661	1.3
YP	0	20958	0.8
Ind	0	19315	0.7
Eng Dem	0	1238	0.0
WEP	0	1040	0.0
Lib	0	753	0.0
BFB	0	420	0.0
SDP	0	321	0.0
CPA	0	224	0.0
Green Soc	0	163	0.0
WRP	0	137	0.0
Pirate	0	91	0.0
Libertarian	0	67	0.0
TOTAL	**54**	**2605887**	**66.4**

Northern Ireland

	Total Seats	*Total Votes*	*% of Votes*
DUP	10	292316	36.0
Sinn Féin	7	238915	29.4
SDLP	0	95419	11.7
UUP	0	83280	10.3
All	0	64553	7.9
Ind	1	16461	2.0
Green	0	7452	0.9
PBPA	0	5509	0.7
Con	0	3895	0.5
TUV	0	3282	0.4
WP	0	708	0.1
cista	0	393	0.0
TOTAL	**18**	**812183**	**65.4**

Scotland

	Total Seats	Total Votes	% of Votes
SNP	35	977568	36.9
Con	13	757949	28.6
Lab	7	717007	27.1
Lib Dem	4	179062	6.8
Green	0	5886	0.2
UKIP	0	5302	0.2
Ind	0	4183	0.2
Christian	0	1720	0.1
WEP	0	337	0.0
Ind Sov Dem Britain	0	224	0.0
SN	0	177	0.0
SDP	0	148	0.0
SIRP	0	132	0.0
TOTAL	**59**	**2649695**	**66.4**

Wales

	Total Seats	Total Votes	% of Votes
Lab	28	771354	48.9
Con	8	528839	33.6
PlC	4	164466	10.4
Lib Dem	0	71039	4.5
UKIP	0	31376	2.0
Green	0	5128	0.3
Ind	0	1500	0.1
ISWSL	0	1209	0.1
Pirate	0	446	0.0
WEP	0	177	0.0
Loony	0	157	0.0
SP	0	92	0.0
New Society of Worth	0	31	0.0
TOTAL	**40**	**1575814**	**68.5**

Seats which changed parties

	2015	2017
Aberdeen South	SNP	Con
West Aberdeenshire and Kincardine	SNP	Con
Angus	SNP	Con
South Antrim	UUP	DUP
Ayr, Carrick and Cumnock	SNP	Con
Banff and Buchan	SNP	Con
Bath	Con	Lib Dem
Battersea	Con	Lab
Bedford	Con	Lab
Belfast South	SDLP	DUP
Berwickshire, Roxburgh and Selkirk	SNP	Con
Brighton Kemptown	Con	Lab/Co-op
Bristol North West	Con	Lab
Bury North	Con	Lab
Caithness, Sutherland and Easter Ross	SNP	Lib Dem
Canterbury	Con	Lab
Cardiff North	Con	Lab
Ceredigion	Lib Dem	PlC
Clacton	UKIP	Con
Vale of Clwyd	Con	Lab

	2015	2017
Coatbridge, Chryston and Bellshill	SNP	Lab
Colne Valley	Con	Lab
Copeland	Lab	Con
Crewe and Nantwich	Con	Lab
Croydon Central	Con	Lab
Derby North	Con	Lab
North East Derbyshire	Lab	Con
South Down	SDLP	Sinn Féin
Dumfries and Galloway	SNP	Con
East Dunbartonshire	SNP	Lib Dem
Eastbourne	Con	Lib Dem
Edinburgh West	SNP	Lib Dem
Enfield Southgate	Con	Lab
Fermanagh and South Tyrone	UUP	Sinn Féin
Foyle	SDLP	Sinn Féin
Glasgow North East	SNP	Lab/Co-op
Gordon	SNP	Con
Gower	Con	Lab
High Peak	Con	Lab
Ipswich	Con	Lab
Keighley	Con	Lab
Kensington	Con	Lab
Kingston and Surbiton	Con	Lib Dem
Kirkcaldy and Cowdenbeath	SNP	Lab
Leeds North West	Lib Dem	Lab/Co-op
Lincoln	Con	Lab
East Lothian	SNP	Lab
Mansfield	Lab	Con
Middlesbrough South and East Cleveland	Lab	Con
Midlothian	SNP	Lab
Moray	SNP	Con
Ochil and South Perthshire	SNP	Con
Oxford West and Abingdon	Con	Lib Dem
Peterborough	Con	Lab
Plymouth, Sutton and Devonport	Con	Lab/Co-op
Portsmouth South	Con	Lab
Reading East	Con	Lab
East Renfrewshire	SNP	Con
Rutherglen and Hamilton West	SNP	Lab/Co-op
Sheffield, Hallam	Lib Dem	Lab
Southport	Lib Dem	Con
Stirling	SNP	Con
Stockton South	Con	Lab
Stoke-on-Trent South	Lab	Con
Stroud	Con	Lab/Co-op
Twickenham	Con	Lib Dem
Walsall North	Lab	Con
Warrington South	Con	Lab
Warwick and Leamington	Con	Lab
Weaver Vale	Con	Lab

Results in vulnerable Conservative seats

	% majority 2015	*Result*	*Swing*
Gower	0.06	Lab Gain	3.62% from Con to Lab
Derby North	0.09	Lab Gain	2.11% from Con to Lab
Croydon Central	0.31	Lab Gain	5.11% from Con to Lab
Vale of Clwyd	0.67	Lab Gain	3.4% from Con to Lab

General Election 2017

	% majority 2015	*Result*	*Swing*
Bury North	0.83	Lab Gain	4.97% from Con to Lab
Morley and Outwood	0.87	Con Hold	1.57% from Lab/Co-op to Con
Thurrock	1.08	Con Hold	0.2% from Con to Lab
Plymouth, Sutton and Devonport	1.09	Lab/Co-op Gain	7.18% from Con to Lab/Co-op
Eastbourne	1.38	Lib Dem Gain	2.09% from Con to Lib Dem
Brighton Kemptown	1.52	Lab/Co-op Gain	10.76% from Con to Lab/Co-op
Dumfriesshire, Clydesdale and Tweeddale	1.53	Con Hold	8.87% from SNP to Con
Bolton West	1.64	Con Hold	0.09% from Lab to Con
Weaver Vale	1.71	Lab Gain	4.73% from Con to Lab
Telford	1.79	Con Hold	0.09% from Con to Lab
Lewes	2.13	Con Hold	4% from Lib Dem to Con
Bedford	2.37	Lab Gain	2% from Con to Lab
Plymouth, Moor View	2.4	Con Hold	4.31% from Lab to Con
Lincoln	3.07	Lab Gain	3.11% from Con to Lab
Thornbury and Yate	3.07	Con Hold	10.35% from Lib Dem to Con
Twickenham	3.25	Lib Dem Gain	8.97% from Con to Lib Dem
Peterborough	4.07	Lab Gain	2.67% from Con to Lab
Cardiff North	4.17	Lab Gain	6.09% from Con to Lab
Corby	4.28	Con Hold	0.09% from Lab to Con
Waveney	4.6	Con Hold	6.44% from Lab to Con
Warrington South	4.62	Lab Gain	4.37% from Con to Lab
Kingston and Surbiton	4.77	Lib Dem Gain	5.7% from Con to Lib Dem
St Ives	5.1	Con Hold	2.25% from Con to Lib Dem
Southampton Itchen	5.17	Con Hold	2.55% from Con to Lab
South Thanet	5.67	Con Hold	0.75% from Con to Lab
Keighley	6.19	Lab Gain	3.33% from Con to Lab
North Warwickshire	6.26	Con Hold	5.87% from Lab to Con
Carlisle	6.5	Con Hold	0.23% from Con to Lab
Torbay	6.82	Con Hold	10.53% from Lib Dem to Con
Halesowen and Rowley Regis	7.01	Con Hold	2.4% from Lab to Con
Crewe and Nantwich	7.22	Lab Gain	3.65% from Con to Lab
Erewash	7.39	Con Hold	0.85% from Lab to Con
Hendon	7.48	Con Hold	2.72% from Con to Lab
Ipswich	7.64	Lab Gain	4.64% from Con to Lab
Sutton and Cheam	7.84	Con Hold	8.27% from Lib Dem to Con
Stroud	7.98	Lab/Co-op Gain	4.53% from Con to Lab/Co-op
Broxtowe	7.99	Con Hold	3.22% from Con to Lab
Bath	8.09	Lib Dem Gain	9.78% from Con to Lib Dem
Northampton North	8.21	Con Hold	3.11% from Con to Lab
Calder Valley	8.23	Con Hold	3.59% from Con to Lab
Blackpool North and Cleveleys	8.43	Con Hold	1.76% from Con to Lab
Pudsey	8.81	Con Hold	4.1% from Con to Lab/Co-op
Sherwood	9.14	Con Hold	0.29% from Lab to Con
Amber Valley	9.18	Con Hold	4.45% from Lab to Con
Yeovil	9.31	Con Hold	7.72% from Lib Dem to Con
Hastings and Rye	9.39	Con Hold	4.38% from Con to Lab
Colne Valley	9.44	Lab Gain	5.48% from Con to Lab
Bristol North West	9.52	Lab Gain	9.16% from Con to Lab
High Peak	9.61	Lab Gain	6.96% from Con to Lab
Harrow East	9.68	Con Hold	3.12% from Con to Lab
Northampton South	9.71	Con Hold	3.45% from Con to Lab
Stockton South	9.71	Lab Gain	5.69% from Con to Lab
Boston and Skegness	9.96	Con Hold	5.72% from Lab to Con
Norwich North	10.2	Con Hold	4.55% from Con to Lab
Stevenage	10.34	Con Hold	1.75% from Con to Lab/Co-op
Enfield Southgate	10.35	Lab Gain	9.66% from Con to Lab

	% majority 2015	Result	Swing
Cannock Chase	10.42	Con Hold	3.54% from Lab to Con
Morecambe and Lunesdale	10.58	Con Hold	3.76% from Con to Lab
Nuneaton	10.65	Con Hold	0.19% from Con to Lab
Finchley and Golders Green	11.13	Con Hold	3.98% from Con to Lab
Dudley South	11.15	Con Hold	4.52% from Lab to Con
Worcester	11.32	Con Hold	3.23% from Con to Lab
South Ribble	11.32	Con Hold	1.1% from Lab to Con
Colchester	11.45	Con Hold	6.07% from Con to Lab
Rossendale and Darwen	11.5	Con Hold	2.56% from Con to Lab
South Swindon	11.71	Con Hold	3.46% from Con to Lab/Co-op
Cheltenham	12.1	Con Hold	3.8% from Con to Lib Dem
Cheadle	12.12	Con Hold	1.94% from Con to Lib Dem
Berwick-upon-Tweed	12.13	Con Hold	0.89% from Lab to Con
Pendle	12.21	Con Hold	4.69% from Con to Lab
Preseli Pembrokeshire	12.23	Con Hold	5.75% from Con to Lab
Portsmouth South	12.45	Lab Gain	9.35% from Con to Lab
Dover	12.48	Con Hold	0.06% from Con to Lab
Brecon and Radnorshire	12.71	Con Hold	3.36% from Lib Dem to Con
Reading East	12.86	Lab Gain	9.82% from Con to Lab
Scarborough and Whitby	12.94	Con Hold	3.07% from Con to Lab
Warwick and Leamington	12.99	Lab Gain	7.61% from Con to Lab
North Devon	13.22	Con Hold	2.73% from Con to Lib Dem
Aberconwy	13.24	Con Hold	5.63% from Con to Lab
Wells	13.29	Con Hold	0.43% from Con to Lib Dem
Vale of Glamorgan	13.39	Con Hold	4.66% from Con to Lab
Crawley	13.41	Con Hold	4.27% from Con to Lab
Rochester and Strood	13.54	Con Hold	2.95% from Con to Lab
Reading West	13.7	Con Hold	4.09% from Con to Lab
North Cornwall	13.71	Con Hold	0.2% from Lib Dem to Con
Gloucester	13.76	Con Hold	1.78% from Con to Lab
Great Yarmouth	13.79	Con Hold	2.09% from Lab to Con
Chipping Barnet	14.4	Con Hold	6.89% from Con to Lab
Stourbridge	14.51	Con Hold	0.85% from Lab to Con
Elmet and Rothwell	14.65	Con Hold	0.89% from Lab to Con
Milton Keynes South	14.66	Con Hold	6.04% from Con to Lab
Carmarthen West and South Pembrokeshire	14.98	Con Hold	3.82% from Con to Lab

Results in vulnerable Labour seats

	% majority 2015	Result	Swing
City of Chester	0.18	Lab Hold	8.02% from Con to Lab
Ealing Central and Acton	0.54	Lab Hold	12.16% from Con to Lab
Ynys Môn	0.65	Lab Hold	2.06% from Con to Lab
Brentford and Isleworth	0.81	Lab Hold	9.46% from Con to Lab
Halifax	0.97	Lab Hold	5.08% from Con to Lab
Wirral West	0.99	Lab Hold	5.6% from Con to Lab
Cambridge	1.15	Lab Hold	10.71% from Lib Dem to Lab
Ilford North	1.2	Lab Hold	8.49% from Con to Lab
Newcastle-under-Lyme	1.51	Lab Hold	0.73% from Lab to Con
Wolverhampton South West	1.99	Lab Hold	1.59% from Con to Lab
Hampstead and Kilburn	2.1	Lab Hold	12.24% from Con to Lab
Enfield North	2.35	Lab Hold	9.35% from Con to Lab
Hove	2.36	Lab Hold	15.08% from Con to Lab
Dewsbury	2.69	Lab Hold	1.59% from Con to Lab
Lancaster and Fleetwood	3.02	Lab Hold	5.72% from Con to Lab

	% majority 2015	Result	Swing
North East Derbyshire	3.92	Con Gain	4.8% from Lab to Con
Bridgend	4.88	Lab Hold	2.12% from Con to Lab
Middlesbrough South and East Cleveland	4.95	Con Gain	3.54% from Lab to Con
Westminster North	4.98	Lab Hold	10.75% from Con to Lab
Walsall North	5.23	Con Gain	6.03% from Lab to Con
Tooting	5.29	Lab Hold	10.62% from Con to Lab
Edinburgh South	5.34	Lab Hold	13.52% from SNP to Lab
Wrexham	5.59	Lab Hold	0.19% from Lab to Con
Birmingham, Northfield	5.9	Lab Hold	2.3% from Con to Lab
Wakefield	6.07	Lab Hold	0.68% from Lab to Con
Gedling	6.2	Lab Hold	1.44% from Con to Lab
Eltham	6.23	Lab Hold	3.69% from Con to Lab
Copeland	6.45	Con Gain	5.19% from Lab to Con
Stoke-on-Trent South	6.47	Con Gain	4.03% from Lab to Con
Birmingham, Edgbaston	6.53	Lab/Co-op Hold	4.65% from Con to Lab/Co-op
Clwyd South	6.84	Lab Hold	2.39% from Con to Lab
Coventry South	7.27	Lab Hold	4.8% from Con to Lab
Hartlepool	7.64	Lab Hold	1.78% from Con to Lab
Darlington	7.65	Lab Hold	0.16% from Lab to Con
Delyn	7.81	Lab Hold	1.47% from Con to Lab
Blackpool South	7.92	Lab Hold	0.36% from Lab to Con
Alyn and Deeside	8.08	Lab Hold	1.8% from Con to Lab
Burnley	8.13	Lab Hold	4.13% from Lab to Con
Scunthorpe	8.45	Lab Hold	0.03% from Con to Lab
Bristol East	8.58	Lab Hold	8.86% from Con to Lab
Newport West	8.68	Lab Hold	2.16% from Con to Lab
Bermondsey and Old Southwark	8.69	Lab Hold	6.71% from Lib Dem to Lab
Southampton Test	8.7	Lab Hold	7.88% from Con to Lab
Chorley	8.74	Lab Hold	2.37% from Con to Lab
Bristol West	8.81	Lab Hold	15.8% from Con to Lab
Bishop Auckland	8.89	Lab Hold	3.87% from Lab to Con
Wirral South	9.87	Lab Hold	4.26% from Con to Lab
Coventry North West	9.93	Lab Hold	3.63% from Con to Lab
Bolton North East	10.11	Lab Hold	0.86% from Lab to Con
Hyndburn	10.22	Lab Hold	1.32% from Con to Lab
Bury South	10.38	Lab Hold	0.65% from Con to Lab
Heywood and Middleton	10.89	Lab Hold	4.35% from Lab to Con
Dudley North	10.98	Lab Hold	5.46% from Lab to Con
Mansfield	11.23	Con Gain	6.67% from Lab to Con
Dagenham and Rainham	11.55	Lab Hold	3.45% from Lab to Con
Batley and Spen	11.95	Lab/Co-op Hold	2.3% from Con to Lab/Co-op
Workington	12.11	Lab Hold	1.36% from Lab to Con
Stoke-on-Trent North	12.46	Lab Hold	3.41% from Lab to Con
Cardiff Central	12.85	Lab Hold	8.64% from Con to Lab
Exeter	13.25	Lab Hold	7.89% from Con to Lab
Newport East	13.37	Lab Hold	4.17% from Con to Lab
Ellesmere Port and Neston	13.38	Lab Hold	4.47% from Con to Lab
Great Grimsby	13.42	Lab Hold	3.11% from Lab to Con
Oldham East and Saddleworth	13.44	Lab Hold	1.96% from Con to Lab
Hammersmith	13.54	Lab Hold	11.03% from Con to Lab
Bristol South	13.97	Lab Hold	7.68% from Con to Lab
Worsley and Eccles South	14.1	Lab Hold	2.11% from Con to Lab
Walsall South	14.29	Lab Hold	2.92% from Con to Lab
Penistone and Stocksbridge	14.29	Lab Hold	5.82% from Lab to Con
Birmingham, Erdington	14.74	Lab Hold	2.39% from Con to Lab
Leeds North East	14.94	Lab Hold	8.53% from Con to Lab

Results in vulnerable Labour/Co-operative seats

	% majority 2015	Result	Swing
Barrow and Furness	1.83	Lab/Co-op Hold	0.7% from Lab/Co-op to Con
Harrow West	4.72	Lab/Co-op Hold	10.83% from Con to Lab/Co-op
Luton South	13.39	Lab/Co-op Hold	8.37% from Con to Lab/Co-op
York Central	14.02	Lab/Co-op Hold	10.41% from Con to Lab/Co-op

Results in vulnerable SNP seats

	% majority 2015	Result	Swing
Berwickshire, Roxburgh and Selkirk	0.6	Con Gain	10.84% from SNP to Con
East Dunbartonshire	3.95	Lib Dem Gain	7.12% from SNP to Lib Dem
Edinburgh West	5.85	Lib Dem Gain	5.75% from SNP to Lib Dem
East Renfrewshire	6.54	Con Gain	13.66% from SNP to Con
North East Fife	9.59	SNP Hold	4.8% from SNP to Lib Dem
Edinburgh North and Leith	9.64	SNP Hold	3.38% from SNP to Lab/Co-op
Caithness, Sutherland and Easter Ross	11.23	Lib Dem Gain	8.92% from SNP to Lib Dem
Dumfries and Galloway	11.5	Con Gain	11.21% from SNP to Con
East Lothian	11.52	Lab Gain	8.52% from SNP to Lab
Ross, Skye and Lochaber	12.24	SNP Hold	13.25% from SNP to Con
Paisley and Renfrewshire South	12.28	SNP Hold	3.1% from SNP to Lab
West Aberdeenshire and Kincardine	12.73	Con Gain	14.06% from SNP to Con
Aberdeen South	14.87	Con Gain	14.73% from SNP to Con
Gordon	14.92	Con Gain	20.38% from SNP to Con

Results in vulnerable DUP seats

	% majority 2015	Result	Swing
Upper Bann	4.77	DUP Hold	3.73% from Sinn Féin to DUP
Belfast East	6.52	DUP Hold	6.6% from All to DUP
Belfast North	13.03	DUP Hold	4.25% from DUP to Sinn Féin

Results in vulnerable Liberal Democrat seats

	% majority 2015	Result	Swing
Southport	2.99	Con Gain	1.33% from Con to Lab
Carshalton and Wallington	3.16	Lib Dem Hold	0.24% from Lib Dem to Con
Orkney and Shetland	3.58	Lib Dem Hold	8% from SNP to Lib Dem
Sheffield, Hallam	4.23	Lab Gain	3.98% from Lib Dem to Lab
Leeds North West	6.68	Lab/Co-op Gain	7.9% from Lib Dem to Lab/Co-op
North Norfolk	8.16	Lib Dem Hold	0.72% from Lib Dem to Con
Ceredigion	8.18	PlC Gain	4.22% from Lib Dem to PlC

Results in vulnerable PlC seats

	% majority 2015	Result	Swing
Arfon	13.62	PlC Hold	6.65% from PlC to Lab
Carmarthen East and Dinefwr	14.19	PlC Hold	2.34% from PlC to Lab

Result in vulnerable SDLP seat

	% majority 2015	Result	Swing
Belfast South	2.31	DUP Gain	3.44% from SDLP to DUP
South Down	13.7	Sinn Féin Gain	9.24% from SDLP to Sinn Féin

Results in vulnerable UUP seats

	% majority 2015	*Result*	*Swing*
Fermanagh and South Tyrone	1.04	Sinn Féin Gain	1.33% from UUP to Sinn Féin
South Antrim	2.58	DUP Gain	5% from UUP to DUP

Result in vulnerable Green seat

	% majority 2015	*Result*	*Swing*
Brighton Pavilion	14.52	Green Hold	5.45% from Lab to Green

Result in vulnerable Sinn Féin seat

	% majority 2015	*Result*	*Swing*
Newry and Armagh	8.31	Sinn Féin Hold	8.79% from Sinn Féin to DUP

Result in vulnerable UKIP seat

	% majority 2015	*Result*	*Swing*
Clacton	7.75	Con Gain	6.81% from Lab to Con

New MPs (99)

* served in previous Parliaments.

AFOLAMI, Bim	*Con*	Hitchin and Harpenden
AMESBURY, Mike	*Lab*	Weaver Vale
ANTONIAZZI, Tonia	*Lab*	Gower
BADENOCH, Kemi	*Con*	Saffron Walden
BOWIE, Andrew	*Con*	West Aberdeenshire and Kincardine
BRADLEY, Ben	*Con*	Mansfield
BRERETON, Jack	*Con*	Stoke-on-Trent South
BURGHART, Alex	*Con*	Brentwood and Ongar
CABLE, Vince*	*Lib Dem*	Twickenham
CARDEN, Dan	*Lab*	Liverpool Walton
CHARALAMBOUS, Bambos	*Lab*	Enfield Southgate
CLARK, Colin	*Con*	Gordon
CLARKE, Simon	*Con*	Middlesbrough South and East Cleveland
DAVEY, Ed*	*Lib Dem*	Kingston and Surbiton
DE CORDOVA, Marsha	*Lab*	Battersea
DENT COAD, Emma	*Lab*	Kensington
DHESI, Tanmanjeet Singh	*Lab*	Slough
DOCHERTY, Leo	*Con*	Aldershot
DOCKERILL, Julia	*Con*	Hornchurch and Upminster
DODDS, Anneliese	*Lab/Co-op*	Oxford East
DREW, David*	*Lab/Co-op*	Stroud
DUFFIELD, Rosie	*Lab*	Canterbury
DUGUID, David	*Con*	Banff and Buchan
FORD, Vicky	*Con*	Chelmsford
FRITH, James	*Lab*	Bury North
GAFFNEY, Hugh	*Lab*	Coatbridge, Chryston and Bellshill
GEORGE, Ruth	*Lab*	High Peak
GILDERNEW, Michelle*	*Sinn Féin*	Fermanagh and South Tyrone
GILL, Preet Kaur	*Lab/Co-op*	Birmingham, Edgbaston
GIRVAN, Paul	*DUP*	South Antrim
GOLDSMITH, Zac*	*Con*	Richmond Park
GRAHAM, Luke	*Con*	Ochil and South Perthshire
GRANT, Bill	*Con*	Ayr, Carrick and Cumnock
GROGAN, John*	*Lab*	Keighley
HAIR, Kirstene	*Con*	Angus
HARDY, Emma	*Lab*	Kingston upon Hull West and Hessle
HAZZARD, Chris	*Sinn Féin*	South Down
HILL, Mike	*Lab*	Hartlepool
HOBHOUSE, Wera	*Lib Dem*	Bath
HUGHES, Eddie	*Con*	Walsall North
JACK, Alister	*Con*	Dumfries and Galloway
JARDINE, Christine	*Lib Dem*	Edinburgh West
JONES, Darren	*Lab*	Bristol North West
JONES, Sarah	*Lab*	Croydon Central
KEEGAN, Gillian	*Con*	Chichester
KERR, Stephen	*Con*	Stirling
KHAN, Afzal	*Lab*	Manchester Gorton
KILLEN, Gerard	*Lab/Co-op*	Rutherglen and Hamilton West
LAIRD, Lesley	*Lab*	Kirkcaldy and Cowdenbeath
LAKE, Ben	*PlC*	Ceredigion
LAMONT, John	*Con*	Berwickshire, Roxburgh and Selkirk

LEE, Karen	*Lab*	Lincoln
LEWER, Andrew	*Con*	Northampton South
LINDEN, David	*SNP*	Glasgow East
LITTLE PENGELLY, Emma	*DUP*	Belfast South
LLOYD, Stephen*	*Lib Dem*	Eastbourne
LLOYD, Tony*	*Lab*	Rochdale
MCCALLION, Elisha	*Sinn Féin*	Foyle
MCELDUFF, Barry	*Sinn Féin*	West Tyrone
MACLEAN, Rachel	*Con*	Redditch
MCMORRIN, Anna	*Lab*	Cardiff North
MCVEY, Esther*	*Con*	Tatton
MARTIN, Sandy	*Lab*	Ipswich
MASTERTON, Paul	*Con*	East Renfrewshire
MOORE, Damien	*Con*	Southport
MORAN, Layla	*Lib Dem*	Oxford West and Abingdon
MORGAN, Stephen	*Lab*	Portsmouth South
NORRIS, Alex	*Lab/Co-op*	Nottingham North
O'BRIEN, Neil	*Con*	Harborough
O'MARA, Jared	*Lab*	Sheffield, Hallam
ONASANYA, Fiona	*Lab*	Peterborough
PEACOCK, Stephanie	*Lab*	Barnsley East
PIDCOCK, Laura	*Lab*	North West Durham
PLATT, Jo	*Lab/Co-op*	Leigh
POLLARD, Luke	*Lab/Co-op*	Plymouth, Sutton and Devonport
RASHID, Faisal	*Lab*	Warrington South
REEVES, Ellie	*Lab*	Lewisham West and Penge
RODDA, Matt	*Lab*	Reading East
ROSS, Douglas	*Con*	Moray
ROWLEY, Danielle	*Lab*	Midlothian
ROWLEY, Lee	*Con*	North East Derbyshire
RUANE, Chris*	*Lab*	Vale of Clwyd
RUSSELL-MOYLE, Lloyd	*Lab/Co-op*	Brighton Kemptown
SEELY, Bob	*Con*	Isle of Wight
SMITH, Eleanor	*Lab*	Wolverhampton South West
SMITH, Laura	*Lab*	Crewe and Nantwich
SOBEL, Alex	*Lab/Co-op*	Leeds North West
STONE, Jamie	*Lib Dem*	Caithness, Sutherland and Easter Ross
SWEENEY, Paul	*Lab/Co-op*	Glasgow North East
SWINSON, Jo*	*Lib Dem*	East Dunbartonshire
THOMSON, Ross	*Con*	Aberdeen South
TWIST, Liz	*Lab*	Blaydon
WALKER, Thelma	*Lab*	Colne Valley
WATLING, Giles	*Con*	Clacton
WESTERN, Matt	*Lab*	Warwick and Leamington
WHITFIELD, Martin	*Lab*	East Lothian
WILLIAMS, Paul	*Lab*	Stockton South
WILLIAMSON, Chris*	*Lab*	Derby North
YASIN, Mohammad	*Lab*	Bedford

Defeated MPs (67)

AHMED-SHEIKH, Tasmina	*SNP*	Ochil and South Perthshire
ANSELL, Caroline	*Con*	Eastbourne
ARKLESS, Richard	*SNP*	Dumfries and Galloway
BARWELL, Gavin	*Con*	Croydon Central
BERRY, James	*Con*	Kingston and Surbiton

General Election 2017

BINGHAM, Andrew	*Con*	High Peak
BLACKWOOD, Nicola	*Con*	Oxford West and Abingdon
BORWICK, Victoria	*Con*	Kensington
BOSWELL, Philip	*SNP*	Coatbridge, Chryston and Bellshill
BRAZIER, Julian	*Con*	Canterbury
BURROWES, David	*Con*	Enfield Southgate
CARMICHAEL, Neil	*Con*	Stroud
CLEGG, Nick	*Lib Dem*	Sheffield, Hallam
COLVILE, Oliver	*Con*	Plymouth, Sutton and Devonport
DANCZUK, Simon	*Ind*	Rochdale
DAVIES, Byron	*Con*	Gower
DAVIES, James	*Con*	Vale of Clwyd
DONALDSON, Stuart Blair	*SNP*	West Aberdeenshire and Kincardine
DRUMMOND, Flick	*Con*	Portsmouth South
DURKAN, Mark	*SDLP*	Foyle
ELLIOTT, Tom	*UUP*	Fermanagh and South Tyrone
ELLISON, Jane	*Con*	Battersea
ENGEL, Natascha	*Lab*	North East Derbyshire
EVANS, Graham	*Con*	Weaver Vale
FERRIER, Margaret	*SNP*	Rutherglen and Hamilton West
FLELLO, Robert	*Lab*	Stoke-on-Trent South
FULLER, Richard	*Con*	Bedford
GUMMER, Ben	*Con*	Ipswich
HOPKINS, Kris	*Con*	Keighley
HOWLETT, Ben	*Con*	Bath
JACKSON, Stewart	*Con*	Peterborough
KEREVAN, George	*SNP*	East Lothian
KERR, Calum	*SNP*	Berwickshire, Roxburgh and Selkirk
KINAHAN, Danny	*UUP*	South Antrim
KIRBY, Simon	*Con*	Brighton Kemptown
LESLIE, Charlotte	*Con*	Bristol North West
MCCAIG, Callum	*SNP*	Aberdeen South
MCCARTNEY, Jason	*Con*	Colne Valley
MCCARTNEY, Karl	*Con*	Lincoln
MCDONNELL, Alasdair	*SDLP*	Belfast South
MCLAUGHLIN, Anne	*SNP*	Glasgow North East
MATHIAS, Tania	*Con*	Twickenham
MEALE, Alan	*Lab*	Mansfield
MONAGHAN, Paul	*SNP*	Caithness, Sutherland and Easter Ross
MOWAT, David	*Con*	Warrington South
MULHOLLAND, Greg	*Lib Dem*	Leeds North West
MULLIN, Roger	*SNP*	Kirkcaldy and Cowdenbeath
NICOLSON, John	*SNP*	East Dunbartonshire
NUTTALL, David	*Con*	Bury North
OLNEY, Sarah	*Lib Dem*	Richmond Park
OSWALD, Kirsten	*SNP*	East Renfrewshire
PATERSON, Steven	*SNP*	Stirling
RITCHIE, Margaret	*SDLP*	South Down
ROBERTSON, Angus	*SNP*	Moray
SALMOND, Alex	*SNP*	Gordon
SOLLOWAY, Amanda	*Con*	Derby North
THOMPSON, Owen	*SNP*	Midlothian
TIMPSON, Edward	*Con*	Crewe and Nantwich
WEIR, Mike	*SNP*	Angus

WHARTON, James	*Con*	Stockton South
WHITE, Chris	*Con*	Warwick and Leamington
WHITEFORD, Eilidh	*SNP*	Banff and Buchan
WILLIAMS, Craig	*Con*	Cardiff North
WILLIAMS, Mark	*Lib Dem*	Ceredigion
WILSON, Corri	*SNP*	Ayr, Carrick and Cumnock
WILSON, Robert	*Con*	Reading East
WINNICK, David	*Lab*	Walsall North

Retired MPs (31)

ALLEN, Graham	*Lab*	Nottingham North
ANDERSON, David	*Lab*	Blaydon
BLENKINSOP, Tom	*Lab*	Middlesbrough South and East Cleveland
BURNHAM, Andy	*Lab*	Leigh
BURNS, Simon	*Con*	Chelmsford
CARSWELL, Douglas	*Ind*	Clacton
CARSWELL, Douglas	*Ind*	Clacton
DOHERTY, Pat	*Sinn Féin*	West Tyrone
DOWD, Jim	*Lab*	Lewisham West and Penge
DUGHER, Michael	*Lab*	Barnsley East
GARNIER, Edward	*Con*	Harborough
GLASS, Patricia	*Lab*	North West Durham
HASELHURST, Alan	*Con*	Saffron Walden
HOWARTH, Gerald	*Con*	Aldershot
JOHNSON, Alan	*Lab*	Kingston upon Hull West and Hessle
LILLEY, Peter	*Con*	Hitchin and Harpenden
LUMLEY, Karen	*Con*	Redditch
MCGARRY, Natalie	*Ind*	Glasgow East
MACKINTOSH, David	*Con*	Northampton South
MACTAGGART, Fiona	*Lab*	Slough
MARRIS, Rob	*Lab*	Wolverhampton South West
OSBORNE, George	*Con*	Tatton
PICKLES, Eric	*Con*	Brentwood and Ongar
PUGH, John	*Lib Dem*	Southport
ROTHERAM, Steve	*Lab*	Liverpool Walton
SMITH, Andrew	*Lab*	Oxford East
STUART, Gisela	*Lab*	Birmingham, Edgbaston
THOMSON, Michelle	*Ind*	Edinburgh West
TURNER, Andrew	*Con*	Isle of Wight
TYRIE, Andrew	*Con*	Chichester
WATKINSON, Angela	*Con*	Hornchurch and Upminster
WRIGHT, Iain	*Lab*	Hartlepool

General Election 2017

HOUSE OF LORDS 548
Membership 548
Speaker and Deputies 548
House of Lords Commission 549
House of Lords Appointments Commission 549
Party affiliation 549
Changes since last edition 550
Peers' Biographies 551
Analysis of Peers 988
Peers' Political Interests 988
Peers' Countries of Interest 1015
MPs who are now Peers 1028
Hereditary Peers 1032
Bishops 1033
Law Lords 1033
Peers on leave of absence 1034
Women Members 1034
Peers by Party 1045
Select Committees 1053
Principal Office Holders and Staff 1059
Political Offices 1060
PARLIAMENT
Joint Committees 1062
Statutory Committees 1062
Party Committees 1064
Privy Counsellors 1066
Political Parties 1069
Parliamentary Press Gallery 1073
Parliamentary Agents 1078

House of Lords

London SW1A 0PW 020 7219 3000 Peers' message service: 020 7219 5353
Communications Team: 020 7219 3107 Website: www.parliament.uk Twitter: @UKHouseofLords

Bulk correspondence to Members may be delivered to Derby Gate at the Palace of Westminster, but must be stamped or franked or accompanied by a cheque for second-class postage made out to Post Office Counters.

Membership

Since the passing of the House of Lords Act, 1999, the majority of members, around 700, are life peers. The minority of life peers who are Lords of Appeal in Ordinary became Justices of the Supreme Court of the United Kingdom from October 2009, forfeiting their right to participate in the Lords. The Archbishops of Canterbury and York and the Bishops of London, Durham and Winchester are ex-officio members of the Lords, while the remaining 21 Bishops who are members sit by rotation according to seniority; these are known as Lords Spiritual.

Ninety hereditary peers still sit by virtue of election by their fellow peers. In addition, some hereditary peers have been created life peers, of whom 8 remain.

There are two hereditary office holders who are members of the House under the House of Lords Act,1999: the Duke of Norfolk as Earl Marshal, and the Marquess of Cholmondeley as Lord Great Chamberlain.

Speaker and Deputies

Lord Speaker

Lord Fowler

Deputy Speakers

Several Lords are appointed to act as Speaker of the House of Lords in the absence of the Lord Speaker. Last Commission: 29 November 2010.

Baroness Anelay of St Johns (Con)
Lord Bassam of Brighton (Lab/Co-op)
Lord Brabazon of Tara (Con)
Lord Brougham and Vaux (Con)
Lord Faulkner of Worcester (Lab)
Baroness Fookes (Con)
Lord Geddes (Con)
Baroness Gibson of Market Rasen (Lab)
Baroness Gould of Potternewton (Lab)
Baroness Harris of Richmond (Lib Dem)
Lord Haskel (Lab)
Baroness Hooper (Con)
Baroness McIntosh of Hudnall (Lab)
Countess of Mar (CB)
Baroness Morris of Bolton (Con)
Baroness Pitkeathley (Lab)
Viscount Simon (Lab)
Lord Skelmersdale (Con)
Viscount Ullswater (Con)

Chairman and Deputy Chairmen

Lords are appointed by the House to fill the offices of Chairman and Principal Deputy Chairman of Committees. The Chairman [now known as Senior Deputy Speaker] is chairman *ex-officio* of all committees of the House.

Senior Deputy Speaker and Chairman of Committees:
Lord McFall of Alcluith (NA)
Principal Deputy Chairman of Committees:
Lord Boswell of Aynho (NA)
Deputy Chairmen:
Baroness Andrews (Lab)
Lord Brougham and Vaux (Con)
Lord Dear (CB)
Lord Faulkner of Worcester (Lab)
Baroness Fookes (Con)
Baroness Garden of Frognal (Lib Dem)
Lord Geddes (Con)
Baroness Harris of Richmond (Lib Dem)
Lord Haskel (Lab)
Baroness Henig (Lab)
Baroness Hooper (Con)
Baroness McIntosh of Hudnall (Lab)
Countess of Mar (CB)
Baroness Morris of Bolton (Con)
Baroness Pitkeathley (Lab)
Viscount Simon (Lab)
Baroness Stedman-Scott (Con)
Viscount Ullswater (Con)

House of Lords Commission

House of Lords, London SW1A 0PW
Tel: 020 7219 6644
Email: milnerp@parliament.uk
Website: www.parliament.uk/business/committees/committees-a-z/lords-select/house-of-lords-commission
Senior Committee to provide high-level strategic and political direction for the House of Lords.
Chair: Rt Hon **Lord Fowler** (Lord Speaker)
Members: **Baroness Doocey** OBE (Lib Dem), Rt Hon **Baroness Evans of Bowes Park** (Con), Rt Hon **Lord Hope of Craighead** KT (CB), Rt Hon **Lord Laming** CBE DL (CB), Rt Hon **Lord McFall of Alcluith** (Non-Affiliated), **Baroness McIntosh of Hudnall** (Lab), Rt Hon **Lord Newby** OBE (Lib Dem), Rt Hon **Baroness Smith of Basildon** (Lab/Co-op), Rt Hon **Lord Wakeham** DL (Con)
External Members: **Matthew Duncan, Liz Hewitt**
Clerk: **Patrick Milner**

House of Lords Appointments Commission

Room G8, Ground Floor, 1 Horse Guards Road, London SW1A 2HQ
Tel: 020 7271 0848
Email: enquiry@lordsappointments.gov.uk Website: lordsappointments.independent.gov.uk
The Appointments Commission is a non-statutory advisory non-departmental public body. It has two functions: to make recommendations for non-party-political peers and to vet for propriety nominations for peerages, including those from the political parties.
Chair: Rt Hon Professor **Lord Kakkar** (CB)
Independent Members: **Lord Low of Dalston** CBE (CB), Prof **Gillian Peele**, Lt Col Sir **Malcom Ross** GVO OBE
Political Party Nominees: Rt Hon **Lord Clark of Windermere** (Lab), Rt Hon **Lord Howard of Lympne** CH QC (Con), **Baroness Scott of Needham Market** (Lib Dem)
Secretary: **Peter Lawrence** OBE

Members (Peers)

Party Affiliation (October 2017)

	Total
Conservative	257
Labour	204*
Crossbench	179
Liberal Democrat	101
Other	71†
Democratic Unionist Party	4
UK Independence Party	3
Ulster Unionist Party	2
Green Party	1
Plaid Cymru	1
	824 seats

* Includes 15 Labour/Co-operative peers.
† Includes the Lord Speaker, Lords Spiritual, independents and peers who have not declared any party affiliation.

Summary (October 2017)

Life Peers	707
Hereditary Peers	92
Archbishops and Bishops	25*

* The new Bishop of London is likely to be appointed by the end of 2017.

Changes since last edition

NEW MEMBERS

Lord Colgrain (*Con*)	27 March 2017
Baroness Wyld (*Con*)	22 June 2017
Lord Duncan of Springbank (*Con*)	14 July 2017
Lord Vaux of Harrowden (*CB*)	19 July 2017
Bishop of Lincoln (*NA*)	14 Septmber 2017

DEATHS

Lord Taylor of Blackburn (*Lab*)	25 November 2016
Lord Prior (*Con*)	12 December 2016
Lord Lyell (*Con*)	11 January 2017
Baroness Heyhoe Flint (*Con*)	18 January 2017
Baroness Wall of New Barnet (*Lab*)	25 January 2017
Lord McCluskey (*CB*)	20 July 2017
Lord Williams of Baglan (*CB*)	23 April 2017
Lord Thomas of Swynnerton (*CB*)	7 May 2017
Lord Hart of Chilton (*Lab*)	3 August 2017

CHANGE OF PARTY

Lord Carlile of Berriew	previously Lib Dem, now Non-Affiliated
Lord Carter of Barnes	previously Lab, now Non-Affiliated
Baroness Cavendish of Little Venice	previously Con, now Non-Affiliated
Lord Collins of Mapesbury	previously Non-Affiliated, now CB
Lord Davies of Abersoch	previously Lab, now Non-Affiliated
Lord Gadhia	previously Con, now Non-Affiliated
Lord Loomba	previously Lib Dem, now Non-Affiliated
Lord Rana	previously CB, now Con
Baroness Tonge	previously Ind Lib Dem, now Non-Affiliated
Baroness Worthington	previously Lab, now Non-Affiliated

RETIREMENTS

Lord Wade of Chorlton *(Con)*	1 November 2016
Lord Scott of Foscote *(CB)*	21 December 2016
Lord Mackay of Drumadoon *(CB)*	17 January 2017
Lord Nicholls of Birkenhead *(CB)*	3 April 2017
Lord Macdonald of Tradeston *(Lab)*	27 April 2017
Lord May of Oxford *(CB)*	2 May 2017
Lord Millett *(CB)*	4 May 2017
Baroness Lockwood *(Lab)*	18 May 2017
Lord Hattersley *(Lab)*	19 May 2017
Marquess of Salisbury *(Con)*	8 June 2017
Lord Simon of Highbury *(NA)*	9 June 2017
Lord Walpole *(CB)*	13 June 2017
Lord Feldman *(Con)*	30 June 2017
Earl of Mar and Kellie *(Lib Dem)*	30 June 2017
Baroness Trumpington *(Con)*	24 October 2017

PEERAGES PENDING

Bishop of Chichester *(NA)*
Sir Theodore Agnew *(Con)*
Rona Fairhead CBE *(Con)*

CEASED TO BE MEMBERS DUE TO NON-ATTENDANCE DURING 2016-17 SESSION

Baroness Turner of Camden *(Lab)*	13 June 2017
Lord Wolfson of Sunningdale *(Con)*	13 June 2017

Peers' Biographies

CROSSBENCH

ABERDARE, LORD

ABERDARE (5th Baron, UK), Alastair John Lyndhurst Bruce; cr. 1873. Born 2 May 1947; Son of Morys George Lyndhurst Bruce, 4th Baron Aberdare, and Sarah, née Dashwood; Married Elizabeth Foulkes 1971 (1 son 1 daughter).

Education: Eton College; Christ Church, Oxford (MA literae humaniores 1972); French.

Non-political career: IBM UK 1969-91; Partner, Bruce Naughton Wade (public affairs management consultants) 1991-99; Director: ProbusBNW Ltd (corporate reputation consultants) 1999-2009, WALTZ Programmes Ltd, learning to work 2009-12.

Political career: *House of Lords:* Elected hereditary peer 2009-. Member: Information 2012-15, Digital Skills 2014-15, EU Internal Market Sub-committee 2015-. *Councils and public bodies:* Trustee: National Botanic Garden of Wales 1994-2006, National Library of Wales 2012-; DL, Dyfed 2009.

Political interests: Arts, culture and heritage, education and skills, trade and technology, small businesses and entrepreneurship; China, Kenya, Russia, USA, Wales.

Other: Trustee, St John Cymru-Wales 2008-; Vice-President, Public Monuments and Sculpture Association 2011-; Chair, Berlioz Society 2014-; FRSA; FRGS. Hon Fellow, Cardiff University 2008. KStJ 2015. MCC.

Publications: Translator and Editor, Hector Berlioz: The Musical Madhouse (University of Rochester Press, 2003); Contributor, Berlioz: Scenes from the Life and Work (University of Rochester Press, 2008).

Recreations: Wales, classical music – especially Berlioz, crosswords, family.

The Lord Aberdare, House of Lords, London SW1A 0PW
Tel: 020 7219 6861 *Email:* aberdarea@parliament.uk
Email: alastair@aberdares.co.uk

LABOUR

ADAMS OF CRAIGIELEA, BARONESS

ADAMS OF CRAIGIELEA (Life Baroness), (Katherine Patricia) Irene Adams; cr 2005. Born 27 December 1947; Married Allen Adams 1968 (MP 1979-90, died 1990) (1 son 2 daughters).

Education: Stanley Green High School, Paisley.

Political career: *House of Commons:* MP (Labour) for Paisley North 29 November 1990 by-election to 2005. Member, Chairmen's Panel 1998-2005; Chair, Scottish Affairs 2001-05. *House of Lords:* Raised to the peerage as Baroness Adams of Craigielea, of Craigielea in Renfrewshire 2005. *Councils and public bodies:* Councillor: Paisley Town Council 1970, Renfrew District Council 1974-78, Strathclyde Regional Council 1979-84; JP.

Other: Member, UK delegation to NATO Parliamentary Assembly 2015-.

Recreations: Reading, walking.

The Baroness Adams of Craigielea, House of Lords, London SW1A 0PW
Tel: 020 7219 6536

LIBERAL DEMOCRAT

ADDINGTON, LORD

ADDINGTON (6th Baron, UK), Dominic Bryce Hubbard; cr. 1887. Born 24 August 1963; Son of 5th Baron; Married Elizabeth Ann Morris 1999.

Education: The Hewett School, Norwich; Aberdeen University (MA history 1988).

Non-political career: Charity fundraiser and counsellor, Apex Trust 1991-94; Consultant, Milton Broadway, Events Company 1996-99; Chair, Microlink plc 2012-.

Political career: *House of Lords:* First entered House of Lords 1986; Liberal Democrat Spokesperson for: Work and Social Services/Pensions (Disability) 1994-2009, Culture, Media and Sport (Sport) 1995-2015; Elected hereditary peer 1999-; Liberal Democrat: Whip 2002-13, Deputy Chief Whip 2005-13, Spokesperson for: Defence 2007-10, Sport 2015. Member: Merits of Statutory Instruments 2003-05, Procedure 2005-08, Hybrid Instruments 2011-, Olympic and Paralympic Legacy 2013-14, The Arctic 2014-15.

Political interests: Education, prison reform, disabilities, sport.

Other: Vice-President: British Dyslexia Association, UK Sports Association (Sport for those with learning disabilities); President, Apex Trust; Patron: Cascade Foundation, X-Forces 2015-; Aberdeen University Student Hardship Fund; *Clubs:* National Liberal Club. Lakenham Hewett Rugby Club; Playing Captain, Commons and Lords RFC.

Recreations: Rugby football, portrait painting.

The Lord Addington, House of Lords, London SW1A 0PW
Tel: 020 7219 4443 *Email:* addingtond@parliament.uk

ADEBOWALE, LORD

CROSSBENCH

ADEBOWALE (Life Baron), Victor Olufemi Adebowale; cr 2001. Born 21 July 1962; Son of Grace Adebowale and Ezekiel Adebowale; Married Tracey Jones (1 son 1 daughter).

Education: Thornes House School, Wakefield; Tavistock Institute (Postgraduate Diploma advanced organisational consulting); City University (MA advanced organisational consulting 2008).

Non-political career: Housing administration, London Borough of Newham 1983-86; Management posts, housing associations 1986-90; Director, alcohol recovery project 1990-95; Chief executive, Centre Point (youth social exclusion charity) 1995-2001; Member: Social Exclusion Unit Policy Action, National Employment Panel, New Deal Task Force 1997-2007; Chief executive, Turning Point 2001-; Visiting Professor, Lincoln University. Member, Unison.

Political career: *House of Lords:* Raised to the peerage as Baron Adebowale, of Thornes in the County of West Yorkshire 2001. *Councils and public bodies:* Commission Employment and Skills 2007; Board member, Audit Commission -2012; President, Community Practitioners' and Health Visitors' Association; Council member, Social Enterprise Coalition -2009; Non-executive director, NHS England; Vice-President, Local Government Association.

Political interests: Poverty, regeneration, arts; Italy, Nigeria, USA.

Other: Director: Leadership in Mind Ltd, THP Ltd, 360 action Ltd; Patron: Tomorrow's Project, Nursing Council on Alcohol, CARE International Foundation, National College for School Leadership, ROTA, International Philosophy and Psychiatry, Social Enterprise UK; Centre for Inclusion and Diversity, Bradford University, Equalities National Council; Urban Development (Music); Hon. Fellow, Royal College of Psychiatry; Sunningdale fellow. Chancellor, Lincoln University. Four honorary doctorates; Three honorary fellowships; Honorary degree, Nottingham University 2017. CBE 2000.

Recreations: Poetry writing, reading, music, kites.

The Lord Adebowale CBE, House of Lords, London SW1A 0PW
Tel: 020 7219 8704 *Email:* adebowalev@parliament.uk
Tel: 020 7481 7600 *Fax:* 020 7481 7620 *Email:* victor@leadershipinmind.co.uk
Twitter: @Voa1234

ADONIS, LORD

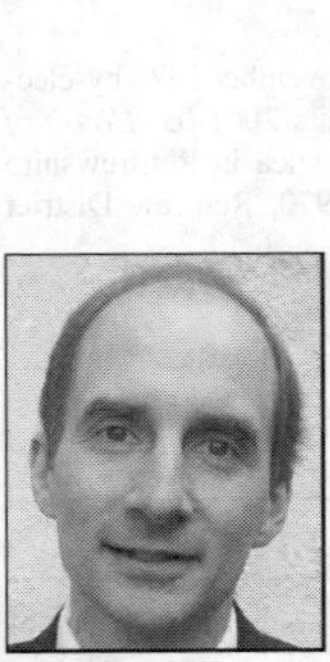

LABOUR

ADONIS (Life Baron), Andrew Adonis; cr 2005. Born 22 February 1963; Married Kathryn Davies 1994 (1 son 1 daughter).

Education: Kingham Hill School, Oxford; Keble College, Oxford (BA modern history 1984); Christ Church, Oxford (DPhil 1988).

Non-political career: Headquarters Secretariat, British Gas Corporation 1984-85; Research student, Nuffield College, Oxford 1985-86; Fellow, politics, Nuffield College, Oxford 1988-91; Journalist, *Financial Times* 1991-96: Political columnist, *Observer* 1996-98; Prime Minister's Policy Unit 1998-2005: Head of Policy 2001-03; Non-executive director, Dods Group plc 2011-; Non-executive board member, HS2 Ltd 2015-17.

Political career: *House of Lords:* Raised to the peerage as Baron Adonis, of Camden Town in the London Borough of Camden 2005. Parliamentary Under-Secretary of State and Government Spokesperson for Department for Education and Skills/Children, Schools and Families (Schools and Learners) 2005-08; Department for Transport 2008-10: Minister of State and Government Spokesperson 2008-09, Secretary of State 2009-10; Opposition Spokesperson for Treasury 2012-15; Shadow Minister for the Treasury 2013-15. *Other:* Adviser to Policy Review on Industrial Strategy, Labour Party 2012-15; Resigned Labour Party Whip October 2015-June 2017. *Councils and public bodies:* Councillor, Oxford City Council 1987-91; Chair, National Infrastructure Commission 2015-.

Other: Director, Institute for Government 2010-; Chair, Progress 2012-; Director, English National Ballet. Peer of the Year, Channel 4 Political awards 2009. PC 2009.

Publications: Parliament Today (1990); Making Aristocracy Work: the peerage and the political system in Britain 1884-1914 (1993); Co-Author, A Conservative Revolution?: the Thatcher-Reagan decade in perspective (1994); Failure in British Government: the politics of the poll tax (1994); A Class Act: the myth of Britain's classless society (1997); Co-editor, Roy Jenkins: a retrospective (2004); Contributor, The Purple Book (Progress, 2011); Five Days in May: The Coalition and Beyond (Biteback, 2013).

Rt Hon the Lord Adonis, House of Lords, London SW1A 0PW
Tel: 020 7219 5353 *Email:* adonisa@parliament.uk *Twitter:* @Andrew_Adonis

AFSHAR, BARONESS

CROSSBENCH

AFSHAR (Life Baroness), Haleh Afshar; cr 2007. Born 21 May 1944; Daughter of Pouran Afshar and Prof Hassan Afshar; Married Maurice, later Professor, Dodson 1974 (1 daughter 1 son).

Education: Ecole Jeanne d'Arc Theran, Iran; St Martin's School, Solihull; Davis College, Brighton; York University (BA social sciences 1967); Strasbourg University (Diploma comparative European Community law 1972); Department of Land Economy, Cambridge (PhD 1974); French, Persian.

Non-political career: Researcher, Rural Research Centre, Tehran; Journalist, *Kayhan International* daily newspaper, Tehran 1971-74; Lecturer in development, Bradford University 1976-85; York University 1985-: Deputy Director and Lecturer in health economics 1985-87, Department of Politics and Centre for Women's Studies 1987-: Professor 1999-, Emeritus Professor 2012; Visiting Professor, Strasbourg University International Faculty of Comparative Law 1986-; Founder Member, Women Living Under Muslim Laws 1987-; Visiting Professor, Women's studies, Strathclyde University 1993-98; Muslim Women's Network: Founder Member and Chair 2002-10, Honorary President 2010-. Member, AUT 1975-.

Political career: *House of Lords:* Raised to the peerage as Baroness Afshar, of Heslington in the County of North Yorkshire 2007. *Councils and public bodies:* Commissioner, UK Drug Policy Commission 2006-13; Member, Education Honours Committee 2007-13; Commissioner, National Commission for Women 2008-10.

Political interests: Islam, feminism; France, India, Iran, Middle East, North Africa.

Other: Member and various posts numerous organisations, concerned with women, particularly ethnic minority women, and education, including: Deputy chair, British Council's Gender and Development Task Force 2001-03, UN Associations' Services: Chair, board of trustees 2001-04, President 2004-; Fellow, Academy of Social Sciences; Political Studies Association; British Association for Middle Eastern Studies; Development Studies Association; Fellow, Academy of Social Sciences 2009; Oxfam, NSPCC, Samaritans, Friends of the Earth, National Trust, Scope, Shelter, CAF/Mind, Cancer Research, Centrepoint, Camphill Village, Medecins sans Frontiers, Refugee Action, Action Aid. Hon doctorate: Exeter University 2011, York St John University 2013. OBE 2005.

Publications: Books: (as Homa Omid) Islam and the Post-Revolutionary State in Iran (Macmillan, 1994), Islam and Feminisms, an Iranian case study (Macmillan, 1998), Co-author, Women in Later Life: Exploring Race and Ethnicity (Open University Press, 2008); Reports: 'Women and poverty' in Women and Development (International Development Committee, Seventh Report, 1999), Pamphlet, Democracy and Islam (Hansard Society, 2006); Edited volumes: Iran, A Revolution in Turmoil (Macmillan, 1985, reprinted 1989), Women, Work and Ideology In The Third World (Tavistock, 1985), Women, State and Ideology (Macmillan, 1987), Co-editor, Women, Poverty and Ideology (Macmillan, 1989), Women Development and Survival in the Third World (Longman, 1991), Co-editor, Women and Adjustment Policies in The Third World (Macmillan, 1992), Women in the Middle East: Perceptions, Realities and Struggles for Liberation (Macmillan, 1993), Co-editor, The Dynamics of Race and Gender: some Feminist Interventions (Taylor and Francis 1994, reprinted 1995), Women and Politics in the Third World (Routledge, 1996), Co-editor, Empowering Women for Development (Booklinks Corporation, Hyderabad, 1997), Women and Empowerment, Illustrations from the Third World (Macmillan, 1998), Co-editor: Women and Globalization and Fragmentation in the Developing World (Macmillan, 1999), Development, Women, and War (Oxfam, 2004); Authored many papers in academic journals and contributed chapters to books, mainly on women, feminism, politics and Iran.

Recreations: Reading, opera.

The Baroness Afshar OBE, House of Lords, London SW1A 0PW
Tel: 020 7219 5353 *Email:* afsharh@parliament.uk
Department of Politics, York University, York YO10 5DD

AGNEW, THEODORE –
(Peer name still to be announced) **see Addenda page x**

AHMAD OF WIMBLEDON, LORD

CONSERVATIVE

Minister of State for the Commonwealth and the UN and Government Spokesperson, Foreign and Commonwealth Office; Prime Minister's Special Representative on Preventing Sexual Violence in Conflict

AHMAD OF WIMBLEDON (Life Baron), Tariq Mahmood Ahmad; cr 2011. Born 3 April 1968; Son of Ch. Mansoor Ahmad and Amtul Matin Ahmad, nee Mir; Married Siddiquea Masud 2011 (2 sons 1 daughter).

Education: Rutlish School, London; London South Bank University/South Bank Polytechnic (BA business, corporate finance 1990); Chartered Institute of Bankers (ACIB 1995); Hindi, Punjabi, Urdu.

Non-political career: NatWest Group 1991-2000: Corporate Banking Executive 1991-94, Manager: Market Intelligence 1994-97, European Strategy 1997-99, Senior manager, Corporate Banking and Financial Markets 1999-2000; Alliance Bernstein: Vice-president, Marketing director 2000-04; Strategy and marketing director and head of Russia and CIS, Sucden Financial 2004-12.

Political career: *House of Commons:* Contested (Conservative) Croydon North 2005 general election. *House of Lords:* Raised to the peerage as Baron Ahmad of Wimbledon, of Wimbledon in the London Borough of Merton 2011. Party Whip 2012; Government Whip 2012-14; Department for Communities and Local Government: Government Spokesperson 2012-15, Parliamentary Under-Secretary of State 2014-15; Government Spokesperson for: International Development 2012-13, Justice 2012-14, Business, Innovation and Skills (Universities and Science) 2013-14, Home Office 2013-14; Parliamentary Under-Secretary of State and Government Spokesperson: Home Office 2015-16, Department for Transport 2015-17; Minister of State for the Commonwealth and the UN and Government Spokesperson, Foreign and Commonwealth Office 2017-. Member, Inheritance and Trustees' Powers Bill 2013. *Other:* Deputy chairman, Wimbledon Conservative Association 1997-2002; Member, Conservative Friends of India 2003-; Vice-chairman (Cities), Conservative Party 2008-10; Parliamentary chairman, Conservative Friends of Pakistan 2011-. *Councils and public bodies:* Member, Merton Racial Equality Council 1994-97; London Borough of Merton Council: Councillor 2002-12, Opposition Spokesperson on Environment and Regeneration 2002-06, Cabinet Member: Environment and Transport 2006-08, Community Safety and Engagement 2008-09; Governor, Wimbledon Park School 2003-06; Deputy chairman, London Councils Transport and Environment Committee 2006-08.

Political interests: Foreign affairs, EU, international development, city and financial affairs; Bangladesh, China, India, Indonesia, Israel, Middle East, Pakistan, Russia, USA.

Other: National Vice-president, AMYA-UK 2000-09; Patron: Humanity First, MDS UK Patient Support Group; Associate, Institute of Financial Services; Member, Institute of Directors; Associate, Chartered Institute of Bankers 1995; Conservative Friends of Bangladesh, Save the Children. Glory of India Award 2010.

Recreations: Gym, tennis, voluntary work.

The Lord Ahmad of Wimbledon, House of Lords, London SW1A 0PW
Tel: 020 7219 2807 *Email:* ahmadt@parliament.uk *Twitter:* @tariqahmadbt

AHMED, LORD

NON-AFFILIATED

AHMED (Life Baron), Nazir Ahmed; cr. 1998. Born 24 April 1957; Son of late Haji Sain Mohammed and Rashem Bibi; Married Sakina Bibi 1974 (2 sons 1 daughter).

Education: Spurley Hey Comprehensive School, Rotherham; Thomas Rotherham College, Rotherham; Sheffield Hallam University (BA public administration 1992); Punjabi, Urdu.

Non-political career: Ran chain of fish and chip shops and mini-markets 1978-85; Marble mining in Kashmir 1985-87; Business development manager, Kilnhurst Business Park 1991-; Property development 2007-; Chairman, Blackhorn Properties Ltd; Non-executive director of international relations, Midcost Ltd. Member, USDAW: Chair, Sheffield Private Branch 1996-98, Member, Political Committee 1996-98.

Political career: *House of Lords:* Raised to the peerage as Baron Ahmed, of Rotherham in the County of South Yorkshire 1998. *Other:* Chair, South Yorkshire Labour Party 1994-98; Vice-chair, South Yorkshire Euro-constituency Party 1996-98; Administrative suspension from Labour Party April-June 2012; Labour Whip suspended March 2013; Resigned from the Labour Party May 2013. *Councils and public bodies:* Councillor, Rotherham Metropolitan Borough Council 1990-2000; JP, Rotherham 1992-2000; Founder, British Muslim Councillors Forum 1992-98.

Political interests: Human rights, Kashmiri right of self-determination, conflict resolution, race relations, relations with Muslim countries, dialogue of civilisation, education, immigration, minorities' rights, private diplomacy; China, Middle East, North Africa, Pakistan, Russia, South Asia, USA.

Other: Member: Inter-Parliamentary Union 1998-, Commonwealth Parliamentary Association 1998-; Patron, Jammu and Kashmir Human Rights Commission 1998, Al-Shifa, Pakistan 1999-2013; Head of British Muslim Peace and Recognition Initiative in Darfur 2007-11; FACE Advice Centre, Rotherham 1992-2000; Al-Hamd Trust-International Disabled Network 1994-98; Member, Kashmir Policy Group 1995-2008; Unity Centre, Rotherham 1996-98; Alma Hospital Trust 1998-; Patron: British Hujjaj Association 1999-, SAARC Foundation 1999-2008, Kashmiri Journalist Association Mirpur 1999-2008, Mirpur Friendship Association 2000-07, Khattak Medical College, Pakistan 2000-06, Yemeni Development Foundation, UK 2000-06, Layton Rehmatula Trust, Pakistan 2002-13, Chinese Muslim Charity, Kuwait 2002-08; Trustee, Fazaldad Human Rights Organisation 2002-10; Patron: SAHARA, Pakistan 2002-11, Al-Hijrah School; Board member, Board of Trustees, Jinnah Institute (London) 2003-06; President, South Yorkshire Victim Support 2003-08; Trustee, Zindagi Trust (charity for underprivileged children) 2005-08; Patron, Response International 2005-11; British Institute of Technology and E-commerce: Board member 2006-, Chancellor 2010-13; Chair, Joseph Interfaith Foundation 2006-13; Patron: Concordis International 2006-13; UK Consultative, Maimonides Foundation 2007-09; Board member, British Heart Foundation 2007-10; Muslim Chaplains Association 2010-13; Rehab UK Trust 2010-13; Magistrates Association 1992-2000; Young Pakistani Doctors' Association 1999-2009; Patron, Kashmiri and Pakistani Professional Association 2000-08; Muslim Aid, Islamic Relief, SAARC Foundation UK, Human Appeal International, Sahara Foundation, Muslim Hands, A Better Tomorrow School in Mirpur Pakistan. Honorary doctorate, Ukraine 2004; *Clubs:* Commonwealth Club 2009-13.

Publications: Peace and reconcilliation in Darfur.

Recreations: Reading, travel, volleyball.

The Lord Ahmed, House of Lords, London SW1A 0PW
Tel: 020 7219 1396 *Fax:* 020 7219 1384 *Email:* ahmedn@parliament.uk
Room 318, Fielden House, Little College Street, London SW1P 3SH *Twitter:* @nazir_lord

LIBERAL DEMOCRAT

ALDERDICE, LORD

ALDERDICE (Life Baron), John Thomas Alderdice; cr. 1996. Born 28 March 1955; Son of late Reverend David Alderdice and Helena Alderdice, née Shields; Married Joan Hill 1977 (2 sons 1 daughter).

Education: Ballymena Academy, County Antrim; Queen's University, Belfast (MB BCh BAO 1978).

Non-political career: Consultant psychiatrist in psychotherapy, Belfast Health and Social Care Trust 1988-2010; Executive medical director, South and East Belfast Health and Social Services Trust 1993-97; President, ARTIS (Europe) Ltd 2009-; Senior research fellow, Harris Manchester College, Oxford 2012-; Research associate, School of Anthropology and Museum Ethnography, Oxford University 2013-; Director, Centre for the Resolution of Intractable Conflict, Oxford University 2013-; Chairman, Centre for Democracy and Peace Building 2014-; Research associate, Department of Politics and International Relations, Oxford University 2014-; Clinical Professor, Department of Psychiatry, Maryland University, USA 2016-.

Political career: *House of Commons:* Contested (Alliance) Belfast East 1987 and 1992 general elections. *House of Lords:* Raised to the peerage as Baron Alderdice, of Knock in the City of Belfast 1996. Convener of the Liberal Democrat Peers 2010-14; Liberal Democrat Spokesperson for: Health 2010, Northern Ireland 2015-16. Member: Procedure 2003-05, House 2010-14, Liaison 2010-14, Mental Capacity Act 2005 2013-14, Administration and Works 2015-16. Chair, Liberal Democrat: Policy Committee on Health and Social Care 2010-11, Parliamentary Party Committee on Northern Ireland 2011-15. *Other:* Leader, Alliance Delegation, Forum for Peace and Reconciliation, Dublin Castle 1994-97; Member, Northern Ireland Forum 1996-98; Leader, Alliance Delegation to Northern Ireland Multiparty Talks 1996-98; Northern Ireland Assembly: MLA (Alliance) for Belfast East 1998-2004: Speaker 1998-2004. Alliance Party: Executive Committee 1984-98: Chair, Policy Committee 1985-87; Party Vice-chair 1987, Party Leader 1987-98; European Liberal Democrat and Reform Party: Executive Committee 1987-2003, Treasurer 1995-99, Vice-President 1999-2003; Liberal International: Deputy President 2000-05, President 2005-09, Presidente D'Honneur 2015-. *Councils and public bodies:* Councillor, Belfast City Council 1989-97; Member: Belfast Education and Library Board 1993-97, UK Committee on Standards in Public Life 2010-16.

Political interests: Northern Ireland, psychoanalysis, fundamentalism, radicalisation, terrorism and political conflict resolution, theology, mental health, problems of First Nation peoples; Colombia, Middle East.

Other: Member, Commonwealth Parliamentary Association (President Northern Ireland Assembly Branch) 2000-04; Commissioner: Independent Monitoring Commission 2003-11, Commonwealth Commission on Respect and Understanding 2006-07; Patron, Northern Ireland Institute of Human Relations; President, Westminster Pastoral Foundation; Trustee, Ulster Museum 1993-97; Chair, World Education of Scientists Permanent Monitoring Panel on Motivations for Terrorism 2004-17; Vice-President, International Dialogue Initiative 2009-; Chair of trustees, National Liberal Club, London 2012-14; President, Westminster Pastoral Foundation; Patron, Youth Access UK; FRCPsych 1997. Freedom, City of Baltimore, USA 1991. Faculty of Medicine, Queen's University, Belfast: Hon. Lecturer 1991-99, Hon. Senior Lecturer 1999; Hon. Fellow, Royal College of Physicians of Ireland 1997; Hon. Professor, Faculty of Medicine, University of San Marcos, Peru 1999; Hon. Fellow, Royal College of Psychiatrists 2001; Hon. Affiliate, British Psychoanalytical Society 2001; Visiting Professor, Department of Psychiatry, University of Virginia, USA 2006-; Four honorary doctorates. Galloway Medal (National Schizophrenia Fellowship, NI) 1987; John F Kennedy Profiles in Courage Award 1998; W Averell Harriman Democracy Award 1998; Silver Medal Congress of Peru 1999, 2004; Medal of Honour College of Medicine, Peru 1999; KCFO (Knight Commander Royal Order of Francis I) 2002; World Federation of Scientists Ettore Majorana Erice Prize 2005; International Psychoanalytic Association's 2005 Award for Extraordinarily Meritorious Service to Psychoanalysis; Prize for Freedom, Liberal International 2015; Global Thinkers Forum Award for Excellence in Promoting Peace and Collaboration, London 2016; Dr Whitney Holland Rose Memorial Award for Cultural Diversity in Psychiatry, University of Maryland and Sheppard Pratt Psychiatry Program 2017; *Clubs:* National Liberal, Ulster Reform (Belfast) Club.

Publications: Various professional articles on eating disorders, psychotherapy and ethics, the psychology of fundamentalism, radicalisation and intractable conflict and terrorism, the problems of First Nation peoples, many political papers, articles and book chapters.

Recreations: Reading, music, gastronomy.

The Lord Alderdice, House of Lords, London SW1A 0PW
Tel: 020 7219 5050 *Email:* alderdicej@parliament.uk
Email: john.alderdice@hmc.ox.ac.uk
Website: www.lordalderdice.com *Twitter:* @AlderdiceLord

ALLAN OF HALLAM, LORD

LIBERAL DEMOCRAT

ALLAN OF HALLAM (Life Baron), Richard Beecroft Allan; cr 2010. Born 11 February 1966; Son of John Allan, retired, and Elizabeth Allan, doctor's receptionist; Married Louise Netley 1991 (1 daughter) (divorced).

Education: Oundle School, Northamptonshire; Pembroke College, Cambridge (BA archaeology and anthropology 1988); Bristol Polytechnic (MSc information technology 1990); French, Spanish.

Non-political career: Field archaeologist in: Britain, France and Netherlands 1984-85, Ecuador 1988-89; Computer manager: Avon FHSA 1991-95, FHS 1995-97; Director of government affairs, Europe, Cisco 2005-09; Director of policy, Europe, Facebook 2009-.

Political career: *House of Commons:* MP (Liberal Democrat) for Sheffield Hallam 1997-2005. Board member, Parliamentary Office of Science and Technology (POST) 1997-2001; Liberal Democrat Spokesperson for: Home and Legal Affairs (Community Relations and Urban Affairs) 1997-99, Education and Employment (Employment and Information Technology) 1999-2001, Trade and Industry (Information Technology) 2001-02, Cabinet Office (Information Technology) 2002-05. Member: Home Affairs 1997-98, Liaison 1998-2005, Finance and Services 1998-2001; Chair, Information 1998-2001; Member: Education and Employment 2000-01, Education and Employment (Employment Sub-Committee) 2001, Information 2001-05, Liaison (Liaison Sub-Committee) 2002-05, Public Accounts 2003-05. *House of Lords:* Raised to the peerage as Baron Allan of Hallam, of Ecclesall in the County of South Yorkshire 2010. *Councils and public bodies:* Avon County Council: Councillor 1993-95, Deputy Leader, Liberal Democrats group; Councillor, Bath City Council 1994-95.

Political interests: Information technology, heritage, home affairs, education; Kenya, Latin America especially Ecuador and Colombia, USA.

Other: Board member, Sheffield City Trust 1999-2005.

Recreations: Visiting sites of natural beauty and historical interest, walking.

The Lord Allan of Hallam, House of Lords, London SW1A 0PW
Tel: 020 7219 5353 *Email:* allanr@parliament.uk

House of Lords
Peers' Biographies

ALLEN OF KENSINGTON, LORD

LABOUR

ALLEN OF KENSINGTON (Life Baron), Charles Lamb Allen; cr 2013. Born 4 January 1957; Son of John and Helen Allen.

Education: Bellshill Academy, Bellshill; Bell College, Hamilton.

Non-political career: Accountant, British Steel 1974-79; Deputy audit manager, Gallaghers plc 1979-82; Director, Management Services, Grandmet International Services Ltd 1982-85; Group managing director, Compass Vending, Grandmet Innovations Ltd 1986-87; Managing director, Compass Group Ltd 1988-91; Granada Group: Chief executive, Leisure Division 1991-92, Chief executive 1996-2000; Granada TV: Chief executive 1992-96, Chair 1996-2006; LWT: Chief executive 1994-96, Chair 1996-2006; Executive chair, Granada Media/Granada plc 2000–04; Chief executive, ITV plc 2004-06; Chief adviser, Home Office 2006-08.

Political career: *House of Lords:* Raised to the peerage as Baron Allen of Kensington, of Kensington in the Royal Borough of Kensington and Chelsea 2013. Member, Communications 2016-. *Other:* Chairman, Labour Party management board; Patron, LGBT Labour.

Political interests: Business and the economy, humanitarian and development aid, culture, media and sport, third sector, home affairs; Europe, Middle East, USA.

Other: Chair: Granada Leisure and Services 1993-2000, Boxclever 1994-2000; GMTV: Deputy chair 1994-96, Chair 1996-2000; Vice-President, RTS 1996-2010; Member, International Academy of Television Arts and Sciences 1996; Deputy chair, Business in the Community 1997-2007; Chair: Tyne Tees TV 1997-2006, Yorkshire TV 1997-2006, Creative Industries Advisory Group 1999-2002; Non-executive director, Tesco plc 1999-2010; Chair: Anglia TV 2000-06, Meridian TV 2000-06, ITV Digital 2001-02; Chair: British Commonwealth Games 2000-02, Manchester 2002 Ltd 2000-02; Vice-chair, London 2012 Olympic Bid 2004-05; Director, London Organising Committee of the Olympic Games 2005-13; Member, Talent and Enterprise Taskforce Advisory Group 2006-08; Chair, Global Radio Group 2007-; Senior adviser, Goldman Sachs Equity Partners 2008-; Chair, Endemol 2008-14; Non-executive director, Virgin Media 2008-12; Get AS 2009-; EMI Music: Non-executive chair 2009-10, Executive chair 2010-11; Chair: 2 Sisters Food Group 2011-, Red Cross 2012-13, ISS A/S 2013; Advisory chair, Moelis and Company 2016-; ACMA; FRSA; FCMA 1989; British Red Cross, Seagulls Reuse, Simon on the Streets, Gipton Together, Happy Faces in South Africa. Freedom, City of London. Hon. Doctor of Business Administration, Manchester Metropolitan University 1999; Hon. Doctor of Letters, Salford University 2002; Hon. Doctor of Education, Southampton Solent University 2006. CBE 2003; Kt 2012; *Clubs:* Garrick Club, The Ivy Club.

Recreations: Walking, boating, travel.

The Lord Allen of Kensington CBE, House of Lords, London SW1A 0PW
Tel: 020 7219 5353 *Email:* charles.allen@parliament.uk
Global Radio, 30 Leicester Square, London WC2H 7LA *Tel:* 020 7766 6065
Email: charles.allen@thisisglobal.com

ALLI, LORD

LABOUR

ALLI (Life Baron), Waheed Alli; cr. 1998. Born 16 November 1964; Partner.

Education: Norbury Manor School, south London; Stanley Technical High School.

Non-political career: Research Wootton Publications Ltd 1982-85; Head of investment research, Save and Prosper Investment 1985-88; United Trade Press Ltd 1988-91: Marketing director 1988-89, Publisher 1989-91; Management consultant, Bacon and Woodrow 1991-92; Managing director, Planet 24 Productions Ltd 1992-99; Director, Carlton Media Group 1999-2000; Non-executive director, ShineLimited 2000-; Chairman, Chorion plc 2002-11.

Political career: *House of Lords:* Raised to the peerage as Baron Alli, of Norbury in the London Borough of Croydon 1998. *Other:* Patron, LGBT Labour.

Other: Patron: Skillset (national training organisation for broadcast, film, video and multimedia), Family Planning Association, Naz Foundation, Albert Kennedy Trust; Director, Elton John Aids Foundation; Vice-President, Unicef UK; President, National Youth Theatre London Academy; Trustee: Crimestoppers -2016, Charlie Parsons Foundation.

The Lord Alli, House of Lords, London SW1A 0PW
Tel: 020 7219 8537 *Email:* alliw@parliament.uk

ALLIANCE, LORD

LIBERAL DEMOCRAT

ALLIANCE (Life Baron), David Alliance; cr. 2004. Born 15 June 1932; Son of Eliyahou Alliance and Ashouri Sarehi; Divorced (2 sons 1 daughter).

Education: Etahad School, Iran.

Non-political career: Chair, N Brown Group plc 1968-2012; Founder, Coats Viyella plc (now Coats plc) 1986: Group chief executive 1975-90, Chair 1989-99; Chair, Tootal Group 1991-99.

Political career: *House of Lords:* Raised to the peerage as Baron Alliance, of Manchester in the County of Greater Manchester 2004. *Councils and public bodies:* Board member, UK Holocaust Memorial Foundation 2015-.

Other: CBIM 1985. Three honorary doctorates; Two honorary fellowships. CBE 1984; Kt 1989.

Publications: Co-author, A Bazaar Life (autobiography) (The Robson Press, 2015).

Recreations: Art, persian poetry, music.

The Lord Alliance CBE, House of Lords, London SW1A 0PW
Tel: 020 7219 5353

ALTMANN, BARONESS

CONSERVATIVE

ALTMANN (Life Baroness), Rosalind Miriam Altmann; cr 2015. Born 8 April 1956; Daughter of Leo and Renate Altmann; Married Paul Richer (1 son 2 daughters).

Education: Henrietta Barnett Grammar School; University College London (BScEcon); Harvard University, USA (Kennedy Scholarship economics and government); London School of Economics (PhD economics of pensions and pensioner incomes 1981); French, German.

Non-political career: Fund Manager, Prudential Assurance 1981-84; Head, international equities, Chase Manhattan Bank 1984-89; Director: Rothschild Asset Management 1989-91, Natwest Investment Management 1991-93; Consultant on pension fund investment to HM Treasury 2000; Independent Policy Adviser on pensions, investments and savings to Number 10 Policy Unit 2000-05; Director-General, Saga 2010-13; Chair, Office of Public Guardian and Official Solicitor Strategic Investment Board 2014-15.

Political career: *House of Lords:* Raised to the peerage as Baroness Altmann, of Tottenham in the London Borough of Haringey 2015. Minister of State for Pensions and Government Spokesperson, Department for Work and Pensions 2015-16.

Political interests: Personal finance, consumer protection, pensions policy, social care policy, economic policy, financial markets, intergenerational equity, demographics, climate change, sustainable investment; European Union.

Other: Non-Executive Director: Trafalgar House Trust 2007-10, 2013-15, Green Deal Finance Co 2014-2015 IPSO, 2014-15; Non-Executive Board Member, Lord Chancellor's Strategic Investment Board; Governor: Pensions Policy Institute, London School of Economics; Teenage Cancer Trust, Nightingale Home for the Elderly, Jewish Care, OneFamilyUK. Hon. DLitt, Westminster University 2010; Hon Doctor of Civil Law, Newcastle University 2015. Women in Public Life Award; Pensions Personality of the Year. CBE 2014.

The Baroness Altmann CBE, House of Lords, London SW1A 0PW
Tel: 020 7219 3000 *Email:* altmannr@parliament.uk
Website: www.rosaltmann.com *Twitter:* @rosaltmann

ALTON OF LIVERPOOL, LORD

CROSSBENCH

ALTON OF LIVERPOOL (Life Baron), David Patrick Paul Alton; cr. 1997. Born 15 March 1951; Son of late Frederick Alton, car worker, and Bridget Mulroe; Married Elizabeth Bell 1988 (3 sons 1 daughter).

Education: Edmund Campion School, Hornchurch; Christ's College, Liverpool (Teaching Certificate history and divinity 1972).

Non-political career: Primary school teacher 1972-74, then with children with special needs 1974-79; Liverpool John Moores University: Professor of citizenship 1997-2016, Director, Roscoe Foundation for Citizenship 1997-2016. Former member, National Union of Teachers.

Political career: *House of Commons:* Contested Liverpool Edge Hill February and October 1974 general elections. MP for Liverpool Edge Hill 1979-83, and for Liverpool Mossley Hill 1983-97 (Liberal 1979-88, Liberal Democrat 1988-97). Liberal Chief Whip 1985-87; Party Spokesperson on several portfolios. *House of Lords:* Raised to the peerage as Baron Alton of Liverpool, of Mossley Hill in the County of Merseyside 1997. *Other:* National President, National League of Young

Liberals 1976; Chair: Liberal Policy Committee 1981-83, Candidates Committee 1984-87. *Councils and public bodies:* Liverpool City Council: Councillor 1972-80, Chair, Housing Committee 1977, Deputy Leader of Council 1978; Merseyside County Council: Councillor 1973-77, Chief Whip (Liberal); Vice-President, Local Government Association 2010-.

Political interests: Pro-life, environment, housing, inner cities, refugees, human rights, freedom of religion or belief, Northern Ireland, citizenship; Burma, China, Congo, Egypt, Indian sub-continent, Iraq, Kenya, North Korea, Sudan, Syria, Tibet, Uganda.

Other: Member: Inter-Parliamentary Union, Commonwealth Parliamentary Association; Board Member, US Institute on Religion and Public Policy; Former Chair, Council for Education in the Commonwealth; Sages international advisory group on North Korea; International Catholic Legislators Network; Patron, vice-president, chair numerous charities, especially those concerned with children, ethics and human rights; Trustee, Chesterton Institute; Chair, Christian Heritage Centre; Trustee, Arise Foundation (on human trafficking); Patron, Pyongyang University of Science and Technology, North Korea; Board Member, Aid to the Church in Need 2014; Former Director and Chair, Merseyside Special Investment Fund and Banner Ethical Investment Fund; Bernard Braine Memorial Fund; Visiting Fellowship, Philosophy and Theology, St Andrew's University 1996-97; Trustee, ACN; Vice President: Liverpool School of Tropical Medicine, Crisis; Patron, Karen Aid; Member, Korean Sages; Trustee, Arise; Life hospice for dying children, Zoe's Place, NSPCC, St Francis House, Jubilee Action, Jospice, CAFOD, Aid to the Church In Need. Hon. Professor, Yanbian University of Science and Technology, China 2012; Hon. Fellowship, Liverpool John Moores University 2016. Knights of St Columba Michael Bell award for services to the life cause 1997; Advocates International award for human rights work 2004; Mystery of Life award for human rights work 2009; 2014 Coptic Solidarity Leadership award presented at the US Congress; St. Thomas More Religious Freedom Award, presented in Rome, for work on Article 18 of the Universal declaration of Human Rights 2016. Knight of the Sacred Military Constantinian Order of St George 2002; Knight Commander Order of St Gregory 2008; Commander's Cross of the Order of Merit, Hungary 2017.

Publications: Author of numerous human rights reports for Jubilee Campaign of which he was a co-founder 1987-; What Kind of Country (1987); Whose Choice Anyway – the Right to Life (1988); Faith in Britain (1991); Signs of Contradiction (1996); Life After Death (1997); Citizen Virtues (1998); Citizen 2000 (2000); Pilgrim Ways (2001); Passion and Pain (2003); Abortion: Heart of the Matter (2005); Euthanasia: Heart of the Matter (2005); Building Bridges: Is There Hope for North Korea? (2013).

Recreations: Walking, reading, theatre, gardening, Liverpool FC supporter.

The Lord Alton of Liverpool, House of Lords, London SW1A 0PW
Tel: 020 7219 3551 *Email:* altond@parliament.uk
Website: www.davidalton.net

AMOS, BARONESS

NON-AFFILIATED

AMOS (Life Baroness), Valerie Ann Amos; cr. 1997. Born 13 March 1954; Daughter of Michael and Eunice Amos.

Education: Townley Grammar School for Girls; Warwick University (BA sociology 1976); Birmingham University (MA cultural studies 1977); University of East Anglia (doctoral research).

Non-political career: London Boroughs of: Lambeth 1981-82, Camden 1983-85, Hackney 1985-89: Head of training, Head of management services; Chief executive, Equal Opportunities Commission 1989-94; Director, Amos Fraser Bernard 1995-98; Non-executive director: Travant Capital Partners 2007-09, Titanium Resources Group 2008-09; High Commissioner to Australia 2009-11; Under-Secretary-General, Office of the Co-ordination of Humanitarian Affairs, United Nations 2010-15; Director of SOAS, London University 2015-.

Political career: *House of Lords:* Raised to the peerage as Baroness Amos, of Brondesbury in the London Borough of Brent 1997. Government Whip 1998-2001; Government Spokesperson for: Social Security 1998-2001, International Development 1998-2007, Women's Issues 1998-2001; Parliamentary Under-Secretary of State and Government Spokesperson, Foreign and Commonwealth Office 2001-03; Secretary of State for International Development 2003; Government Spokesperson for Northern Ireland Office 2003-05; Leader of the House of Lords and Lord President of the Council 2003-07; On leave of absence 2009-. Member: Selection 2000-07, House 2003-07, Liaison 2003-07, Privileges 2003-07, Procedure 2003-07. *Councils and public bodies:* Council member, Institute of Employment Studies 1993-98; Chair, board of governors, Royal College of Nursing Institute 1994-98.

Countries of interest: Sub-Saharan Africa, Caribbean, China, India.

Other: Deputy chair, Runnymede Trust 1990-98; Trustee, Institute of Public Policy Research 1994-98; Non-executive director, UCLH Trust; Director, Hampstead Theatre 1995-98; Chair, Afiya Trust 1996-98; Trustee: VSO 1997-98, Project Hope 1997-98; Chair, Royal African Society 2008-09; Amos Bursary. Honorary professorship; 12 honorary doctorates. Peer of the Year award, Women in Public Life Awards 2007. PC 2003; CH 2016.

Rt Hon the Baroness Amos CH, House of Lords, London SW1A 0PW
Tel: 020 7219 5353 *Email:* amosv@parliament.uk *Twitter:* @ValerieAmos

LABOUR

ANDERSON OF SWANSEA, LORD

ANDERSON OF SWANSEA (Life Baron), Donald Anderson; cr 2005. Born 17 June 1939; Son of late David Anderson, fitter, and late Eva Anderson, née Mathias; Married Dr Dorothy Trotman 1963 (3 sons).

Education: Bishop Gore Grammar School, Swansea; University College of Wales, Swansea (BA modern history and politics 1960); Inns of Court School of Law 1966-69; French, German.

Non-political career: HM Diplomatic Service 1960-64; Lecturer in US and comparative government, University College of Wales, Swansea 1964-66; Director, Campaign for a Politcal Europe 1966-67; Called to the Bar, Inner Temple 1969-; Barrister, South Eastern Circuit 1970-97. Former member: TGWU, NUR/RMT, AUT, FDA, FSBAA, Bar.

Political career: *House of Commons:* MP (Labour) for Monmouth 1966-70, for Swansea East October 1974-2005. PPS: to Minister of Defence (Administration) 1969-70, to Sam Silkin as Attorney General 1974-79; Opposition Frontbench Spokesperson for: Foreign and Commonwealth Affairs 1983-92, Defence, Disarmament and Arms Control 1993-94, Shadow Solicitor General 1994-96. Chair, Welsh Affairs 1981-83; Member, Chairman's Panel 1994-97; Chair, Foreign Affairs 1997-2005. *House of Lords:* Raised to the peerage as Baron Anderson of Swansea, of Swansea in the County of West Glamorgan 2005. Co-opted Member, EU Sub-committee C (Foreign Affairs, Defence and Development Policy) 2006-10; Member EU Sub-committee E: (Justice and Institutions) 2011-12, (Justice, Institutions and Consumer Protection) 2012-15; Member, EU Justice Sub-committee 2017-. Vice-chair, PLP Departmental Group for Foreign and Commonwealth Affairs 2010-15. *Other:* Welsh Labour Group: Vice-chair 1969-70, Chair 1977-78. *Councils and public bodies:* Councillor, Royal Borough of Kensington and Chelsea 1970-75; Vice-President, Institute of Environmental Health Officers 1984-95; DL, West Glamorgan 2006-.

Political interests: Wales, foreign affairs, law, transport; Africa, particularly South Africa, Central Europe and Balkans, EU, France, Germany, Norway.

Other: Commonwealth Parliamentary Association (CPA) UK Branch: Member, Executive Committee 1983-2012, Vice-chair 1987-88, 2007-08, 2010-11, Treasurer 1990-93, Special Representative 1989-90, Chair 1997-2001; Co-founder and Senior Vice-President, Association of European Parliamentarians for Africa (AWEPA) (Southern) 1984-97; Inter-Parliamentary Union: Member, Vice-chair 1985-88, Treasurer 1988-90, 1993-95; UK Delegation to North Atlantic Assembly: Member 1992-2005, Leader 1997-2001, Leader, Socialist Group 1997-2001; Organisation for Security and Co-operation in Europe: Member 1997-2001, Leader, UK delegation 1997-98; Inter-Parliamentary Union British Group: Executive Committee Member:1983-2001, 2005-06, 2007-, Vice-chair 2016-; Executive Committee Member: British-American Parliamentary Group 2006-, UK Delegation to Council of Europe and WEU Assembly 2008-; Former board member, World Vision; Former president, Swansea Association for the Single Homeless 1975-81; President, Gower Society 1976-78; Chair, Parliamentary Campaign for the Homeless and Rootless 1984-90; Chair: Parliamentary Christian Fellowship 1993-95, National Prayer Breakfast 1994, Anglo-Israel Association 2005-08; Board member, Mercy Ships 2005-12; President: Swansea Male Choir 1990-2007, Morriston Big Band; Patron, Morriston Ladies Choir; Vice-President, Morriston Orpheus Choir; Swansea Harriers; President: HAFOD Brotherhood, 32nd Rhyddings Scout Group; Vice-president: Morriston Rotary Club, Swansea Business Club; Hon. Fellow: Sussex University 1985, Swansea Metropolitan University 2005; Hon. Parliamentary Fellow, St Antony's College, Oxford 1999-2000; Churches in London and Swansea. Freedom: City and County of Swansea 2000, City of London 2006. Honorary Fellow, Swansea University 1985-2000; Visiting Parliamentary Fellow, St Antony's College, Oxford 1999-2000; Honorary Fellow, Swansea Metropolitan University 2006. Commander's Cross, Order of Merit (Federal Republic of Germany) 1986; PC 2001; Medal of the Foreign Minister of Slovakia 2004; Chevalier de la Légion d'Honneur (France) 2005; Order of Merit of Republic of Hungary 2007. Bonymaen RFC; Ospreys RFC.

Recreations: Walking, church work.

Rt Hon the Lord Anderson of Swansea, House of Lords, London SW1A 0PW
Tel: 020 7219 6562/020 7219 2870 *Fax:* 020 7219 8602 *Email:* trotmang@parliament.uk

ANDREWS, BARONESS

LABOUR

ANDREWS (Life Baroness), Elizabeth Kay Andrews; cr. 2000. Born 16 May 1943; Married Professor Roy MacLeod 1970 (divorced 1992).

Education: Lewis School for Girls, Hengoed, Ystradmynach; University College of Wales, Aberystwyth (BA international politics 1964); Sussex University (MA political sociology 1966; DPhil history and social studies of science 1975).

Non-political career: Fellow, Science Policy Research Unit, Sussex University 1968-70; Parliamentary Clerk 1970-85; Policy adviser to Neil Kinnock MP as Leader of the Opposition 1985-92; Founder and director, Education Extra 1992-2002; Adviser on culture and heritage to the Welsh Government 2013-15.

Political career: *House of Lords:* Raised to the peerage as Baroness Andrews, of Southover in the County of East Sussex 2000. Government Whip 2002-05; Government Spokesperson for: Health 2002-05, Work and Pensions 2002-05, Education and Skills 2003-05, Parliamentary Under-Secretary of State and Government Spokesperson, Office of the Deputy Prime Minister/Department for Communities and Local Government 2005-09; Deputy Chair of Committees 2012-, Deputy Speaker 2012. Member: Delegated Powers and Regulatory Reform 2010-15, Leader's Group on the Working Practices of the House of Lords 2010-11, Joint Committee on the Draft House of Lords Reform Bill 2011-12, Mental Capacity Act 2005 2013-14, Joint Committee on the Draft Deregulation Bill 2013, Secondary Legislation Scrutiny 2014-17, Built Environment 2015-16, Joint Committee on Consolidation, &c, Bills 2015-. *Councils and public bodies:* Deputy Chair and Trustee for Wales, National Heritage Memorial Fund/Heritage Lottery Fund.

Political interests: Education and social policy, international development, cultural policy, science policy, heritage, housing and planning; Latin America.

Other: Chair, English Heritage 2009-13; Trustee: Kids in Museums 2013-16, National Literacy Trust 2014-16; President, Friends of Lewes 2014; Trustee, National Museum of Wales 2015-; Hon. Fellow, Aberystwyth University; ContinYou. Hon. Doctor of Laws, Sussex University 2012. OBE 1998.

Publications: Articles and books on science and education policy, social policy and out of school learning; Extra Learning (Kogan Page, 2001).

Recreations: Music, mountains, museums.

The Baroness Andrews OBE, House of Lords, London SW1A 0PW
Tel: 020 7219 8656 *Email:* andrewsk@parliament.uk

ANELAY OF ST JOHNS, BARONESS

CONSERVATIVE

Minister of State and Government Spokesperson, Department for Exiting the European Union

ANELAY OF ST JOHNS (Life Baroness) Joyce Anne Anelay; cr. 1996. Born 17 July 1947; Daughter of late Stanley and Annette Clarke; Married Richard Anelay QC 1970.

Education: Enfield County School; Bristol University (BA history 1968); London University Institute of Education (CertEd 1969); Brunel University (MA public and social administration 1982).

Non-political career: History teacher, St David's School, Ashford, Middlesex 1969-74.

Political career: *House of Lords:* Raised to the peerage as Baroness Anelay of St Johns, of St Johns in the County of Surrey 1996. Opposition Whip 1997-98; Opposition Spokesperson for: Agriculture 1997-98, Social Security 1997-99, Home Affairs 1997-98, 2002-07, Culture, Media and Sport 1998-2002, Legal Affairs 2003-04, Opposition Chief Whip 2007-10; Deputy Speaker 2008-14; Deputy Chairman of Committees 2008-14; Government Chief Whip 2010-14; Minister of State and Government Spokesperson, Foreign and Commonwealth Office 2014-16 (also attending Cabinet 2014-16); Prime Minister's Special Representative on Preventing Sexual Violence in Conflict 2015-17; Acting Minister of State for Trade and Investment and Government Spokesperson, Department for Business, Innovation and Skills 2016; Minister of State for the Commonwealth and the UN and Government Spokesperson: Foreign and Commonwealth Office 2016-17, Department for International Development 2016; Minister of State and Government Spokesperson, Department for Exiting the European Union 2017-. Member: Procedure 1997-2000, 2007-14, Selection 2007-14, Administration and Works 2007-14, Privileges/Privileges and Conduct 2007-14, Sub-committee on Leave of Absence 2011-13. *Other:* Chair, South East Area Conservative Women's Committee 1987-90; Member, National Union Executive Committee Conservative Party 1987-97, Vice-chair, South East Area Executive Committee 1990-93; Chair, Women's National

Committee 1993-96; Vice-President, National Union 1996-97. *Councils and public bodies:* Member, Social Security Appeal Tribunal 1983-96; JP, North West Surrey 1985-97; Member: Social Security Advisory Committee for Great Britain and Northern Ireland 1989-96, Women's National Commission 1991-94, Child Support Appeal Tribunal 1993-96; President, World Travel Market 2003-08.

Political interests: Social security, home affairs.

Other: President, Woking Citizens' Advice Bureau 1996-2010; Trustee, UNICEF UK 2004-07; Patron: St John's Memorial Hall Appeal Fund, Talking about Cannabis; Trustee, 1949 Conservative and Unionist Trust. Hon. DSocSci, Brunel University 1997. OBE 1990; DBE 1995; PC 2009; *Clubs:* Carlton Club. Woking Golf.

Recreations: Golf, reading.

Rt Hon the Baroness Anelay of St Johns DBE, House of Lords, London SW1A 0PW
Tel: 020 7219 5353 *Twitter:* @JoyceAnelay

ARBUTHNOT OF EDROM, LORD

CONSERVATIVE

ARBUTHNOT OF EDROM (Life Baron), James Norwich Arbuthnot; cr 2015. Born 4 August 1952; Son of late Sir John Sinclair-Wemyss Arbuthnot (MP for Dover 1950-64) and Lady Arbuthnot; Married Emma Broadbent 1984 (1 son 3 daughters).

Education: Eton College; Trinity College, Cambridge (BA law 1974).

Non-political career: Called to the Bar: Inner Temple 1975, Lincoln's Inn 1977.

Political career: *House of Commons:* Contested Cynon Valley 1983 general election and 1984 by-election. MP (Conservative) for Wanstead and Woodford 1987-97, for North East Hampshire 1997-2010, for North East Hampshire (revised boundary) 2010-15. PPS to: Archie Hamilton as Minister of State for the Armed Forces 1988-90, Peter Lilley as Secretary of State for Trade and Industry 1990-92; Assistant Government Whip 1992-94; Parliamentary Under-Secretary of State, Department of Social Security 1994-95; Minister of State for Procurement, Ministry of Defence 1995-97; Member, Shadow Cabinet 1997-2001: Opposition Chief Whip 1997-2001; Member, Intelligence and Security Committee 2001-05; Shadow Secretary of State for Trade 2003-05; Shadow Minister for Trade 2005. Member, Joint Committee on House of Lords Reform 2002-03; Chair, Defence 2005-14; Member: Liaison 2005-14, Joint Committee on National Security Strategy 2010-14; Chair, Armed Forces Bill 2011. *House of Lords:* Raised to the peerage as Baron Arbuthnot of Edrom, of Edrom in the County of Berwick 2015. *Other:* Branch chair, Putney Conservative Association 1975-77; Joint deputy chair, Chelsea Conservative Association 1980-82; President, Cynon Valley Conservative Association 1983-92; Chairman, Conservative Friends of Israel 2005-13; President, North East Hampshire Conservative Association 2015-. *Councils and public bodies:* Councillor, Royal Borough of Kensington and Chelsea 1978-87.

Political interests: Defence, security, foreign affairs, law, taxation; Afghanistan, Australia, France, Germany, India, Israel, Italy, Pakistan, Russia, Spain, Taiwan, USA.

Other: Member, Advisory Board, Electric Infrastucture Security Council (USA); Fellow, Industry and Parliament Trust 1989; Chair (UK), UK-Spain Tertulias 2012-15; Senior associate fellow, RUSI 2014-; Chair: Nuffield Trust for the Forces of the Crown 2017-, Advisory Board, Thalles (UK), NeuroBio Ltd; Director: SC Strategy Ltd, Astute Strategy Ltd, Gusbourne Estates Ltd; Adviser, Pure Storage Inc. Freedom, City of London 1974-. PC 1998; *Clubs:* Pratt's Club.

Recreations: Playing guitar, skiing, cooking.

Rt Hon the Lord Arbuthnot of Edrom, House of Lords, London SW1A 0PW
Tel: 020 7219 3000 *Email:* arbuthnotj@parliament.uk

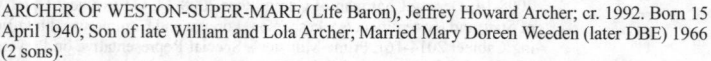

ARCHER OF WESTON-SUPER-MARE, LORD

NON-AFFILIATED

ARCHER OF WESTON-SUPER-MARE (Life Baron), Jeffrey Howard Archer; cr. 1992. Born 15 April 1940; Son of late William and Lola Archer; Married Mary Doreen Weeden (later DBE) 1966 (2 sons).

Education: Wellington School, Somerset; Brasenose College, Oxford (Dip Ed 1963).

Non-political career: Athletics Blues 1963-65; Gymnastics Blue 1963; Represented Great Britain in athletics 1966; Author, playwright and amateur auctioneer.

Political career: *House of Commons:* MP (Conservative) for Louth 1969-74. Contested Louth February 1974 general election. *House of Lords:* Raised to the peerage as Baron Archer of Weston-Super-Mare, of Mark in the County of Somerset 1992. *Other:* Deputy chair, Conservative Party 1985-86; President, Conservative Party London Clubs 1998-99. *Councils and public bodies:* Councillor, Greater London Council 1966-70.

Political interests: Art, sport, 2012 Olympics; Australia, India, Kurdistan.

Other: The Archer Charitable Trust. President, Somerset AAA 1973-99; Vice-President, Cambridge City RFU; President, World Snooker Association 1997-99.

Publications: Plays: Beyond Reasonable Doubt (1987), Exclusive (1990), The Accused (2000); Novels/short stories: Not a Penny More, Not a Penny Less (1975); Shall We Tell the President? (1977); Kane and Abel (1979); A Quiver Full of Arrows (short stories, 1980); The Prodigal Daughter (1982); First Among Equals (1984); A Matter of Honour (1986); A Twist in the Tale (short stories, 1988); As the Crow Flies (1991); Honour Among Thieves (1993); Twelve Red Herrings (short stories, 1994); The Fourth Estate (1996); Collected Short Stories (1997); The Eleventh Commandment (1998); To Cut a Long Story Short (short stories, 2000); A Prison Diary – Volume I: Hell (2002); Sons of Fortune (2003); A Prison Diary – Volume II: Purgatory (2003); A Prison Diary – Volume III: Heaven (2004); False Impression (2006); Cat O'Nine Tales (short stories, 2006); The Gospel According to Judas (2007); A Prisoner of Birth (2008); Paths of Glory (2009); Rewrite of Kane and Abel (2009); And Thereby Hangs a Tale (short stories, 2010); Only Time Will Tell (2011); The Sins of the Father (2012); Best Kept Secret (2013); Be Careful What You Wish For (2014); Mightier Than The Sword (2015); Cometh The Hour (2016); This Was A Man (2016); Tell Tale (2017).

Recreations: Theatre, cricket, auctioneering, art.

The Lord Archer of Weston-Super-Mare, House of Lords, London SW1A 0PW
Tel: 020 7219 5353
The Penthouse, Peninsula Heights, 93 Albert Embankment, London SE1 7TY
Website: www.jeffreyarcher.com *Twitter:* @Jeffrey_Archer

LABOUR

ARMSTRONG OF HILL TOP, BARONESS

ARMSTRONG OF HILL TOP (Life Baroness), Hilary Jane Armstrong; cr 2010. Born 30 November 1945; Daughter of late Ernest Armstrong (MP for Durham North West 1966-87) and Hannah Armstrong; Married Dr Paul Corrigan 1992.

Education: Monkwearmouth Comprehensive School, Sunderland; West Ham College of Technology (BSc sociology 1967); Birmingham University (Diploma social work 1970); Swahili (rusty).

Non-political career: VSO teaching in Kenya 1967-69; Social worker, Newcastle Social Services 1970-73; Community worker, Southwick Neighbourhood Action Project 1973-75; Lecturer in community and youth work, Sunderland Polytechnic 1975-86; Secretary/researcher for Ernest Armstrong MP 1986-87. Chair ASTMS Northern Division Council 1981-88.

Political career: *House of Commons:* MP (Labour) for North West Durham 1987-2010. Opposition Spokesperson for Education 1988-92; PPS to John Smith as Leader of the Opposition 1992-94; Opposition Spokesperson for: Treasury and Economic Affairs 1994-95, The Environment and London 1995-97; Minister of State, Department of the Environment, Transport and the Regions 1997-2001; Government Chief Whip 2001-06; Minister for the Cabinet Office and Social Exclusion; Chancellor of the Duchy of Lancaster 2006-07. Member, Education 1998. Chair, PLP Northern Regional Group 2009-10. *House of Lords:* Raised to the peerage as Baroness Armstrong of Hill Top, of Crook in the County of Durham 2010. Member: Adoption Legislation 2012-13, Soft Power and the UK's Influence 2013-14, European Union 2015-, EU External Affairs Sub-Committee 2015-. *Other:* Member, Labour Party National Executive Committee 1992-94, 1996-2006. *Councils and public bodies:* Councillor, Durham County Council 1985-88; Vice-chair, British Council 1994-97; Non-executive director, Co. Durham and Darlington Foundation Hospital Trust.

Political interests: Regional development, world development, education, environment, social exclusion and social enterprise; Central Africa, Kenya, South Africa, Tanzania, Uganda.

Other: NCH Action for Children: Member, NCH Board 1985-91, Vice-president 1991-97; Member, UNICEF National Committee 1995-97; Patron, Revolving Doors 2007-; Chair, Tony Blair Sports Foundation 2007, Trustee, Africa Governance Initiative 2008-, Board member, Emmaus 2008-11; The Cyrenians (Tyneside): Board member 2008-, Chair 2010-; Ambassador Action for Children 2008-; Board member, VSO International 2008-11; Chair, Community Energy Solutions 2009-13 Board member, VSO UK 2011-; Chair, VSO Federation Council 2011-. Honorary degree, Sunderland University. PC 1999.

Recreations: Theatre, reading, football.

Rt Hon the Baroness Armstrong of Hill Top, House of Lords, London SW1A 0PW
Tel: 020 7219 5353 *Email:* armstrongh@parliament.uk

House of Lords Peers' Biographies

CROSSBENCH

ARMSTRONG OF ILMINSTER, LORD

ARMSTRONG OF ILMINSTER (Life Baron), Robert Temple Armstrong; cr. 1988. Born 30 March 1927; Son of late Sir Thomas Armstrong, musician, and late Hester Muriel, née Draper; Married Serena Chance 1953 (divorced 1985, died 1994) (2 daughters); married (Mary) Patricia Carlow 1985.

Education: Dragon School, Oxford; Eton College (King's Scholar); Christ Church, Oxford (Scholar) (BA classical mods 1947, literae humaniores 1949, MA); Hon. Student, Christ Church, Oxford 1985; French.

Non-political career: HM Treasury: Assistant principal 1950-55, Private secretary to: Reginald Maudling MP as Economic Secretary 1953-54, Rab Butler MP as Chancellor of the Exchequer 1954-55; Principal 1955-57, 1959-64, Assistant secretary 1967-68, Principal Private Secretary to Roy Jenkins MP as Chancellor of the Exchequer 1968, Under-Secretary (Home Finance) 1968-70; Secretary: Radcliffe Committee on Working of Monetary System 1957-59, Armitage Committee on Pay of Postmen 1964; Assistant Secretary, Cabinet Office 1964-66; Principal Private Secretary to Edward Heath MP and Harold Wilson MP as Prime Minister 1970-75; Home Office: Deputy Under-Secretary of State 1975-77, Permanent Under-Secretary of State 1977-79; Secretary of the Cabinet 1979-87; Head of the Home Civil Service 1981-87; Lucas Industries PLC 1985-92; Inchcape PLC 1988-95; NM Rothschild and Sons 1988-97; Shell Transport and Trading PLC 1988-97; British-American Tobacco PLC 1988-97; RTZ PLC 1988-97; Director, Royal Opera House 1988-93; Carlton Television Ltd 1991-95; IAM Gold Ltd 1996-2003; Chair: Biotechnology Investments Ltd 1989-2000, Bristol and West plc (formerly Building Society) 1993-97; Forensic Investigative Associates plc 1997-2003; Director: Bank of Ireland 1997-2001, 3i Bioscience Investment Trust plc 2000-01; Member, Advisory Panel, E-Clear (UK) plc 2007-08.

Political career: *House of Lords:* Raised to the peerage as Baron Armstrong of Ilminster, of Ashill in the County of Somerset 1988. Member: EU Sub-committee A (Economic and Financial Affairs) 2000-03, Merits of Statutory Instruments 2003-07, Review of the BBC Charter 2005-06, Delegated Powers and Regulatory Reform 2007-10, Joint Committees on: Pre-legislative Scrutiny of Constitutional Renewal Bill 2008, the Draft Detention of Terrorist Suspects (Temporary Extension) Bills 2011, the Draft Communications Data Bill 2012-13, Able Marine Energy Park Development Consent Order 2014 2014-15; Member: Administration and Works 2014-16, Joint Committee on Consolidation, &c, Bills 2015-.

Political interests: Arts, museums and galleries, public service, constitutional matters; Canada, France, USA.

Other: Council member, Musicians Benevolent Fund; Royal United Kingdom Benevolent Association; Council of Honour, Royal Academy of Music; Trustee, RVW Trust 1956-; Fellow, Eton College 1979-94; Chair: Board of Trustees, V&A Museum 1988-98, Hestercombe Gardens Trust 1996-2007, Leeds Castle Foundation 2001-07; Trustee, Derek Hill Foundation 2002-; Chair, Sir Edward Heath Charitable Foundation 2005-13; Trustee, Wells Cathedral School Foundation 2007-12; Musicians Benevolent Fund. Honorary Member, Salters' Company. Freedom, City of London. Chancellor, Hull University 1994-2006. Honorary LLD, Hull University. CB 1974; CVO 1975; KCB 1978; GCB 1983; *Clubs:* Brooks's, Garrick Club.

Recreations: Music.

The Lord Armstrong of Ilminster GCB CVO, House of Lords, London SW1A 0PW
Tel: 020 7219 4983 *Email:* armstrongr@parliament.uk

CONSERVATIVE

ARRAN, EARL OF

ARRAN (9th Earl of, I), Arthur Desmond Colquhoun Gore; cr. 1762; 9th Viscount Sudley and Baron Saunders (I) 1758; 5th Baron Sudley (UK) 1884; 11th Bt of Castle Gore (I) 1662. Born 14 July 1938; Son of 8th Earl; Married Eleanor Van Cutsem 1974 (2 daughters).

Education: Eton College; Balliol College, Oxford (BA English literature 1960, MA).

Non-political career: Served Grenadier Guards, national service, commissioned 1958-60. Assistant manager, *Daily Mail* 1972-73; Managing director, Clark Nelson 1973-74; Assistant general manager, *Daily Express* and *Sunday Express* 1974; Director, Waterstone & Co Ltd 1984-87; Parliamentary consultant to the waste industry 1995-; Non-executive director: HMV (EMI) 1995-98, SWEL (the Economy and Inward Investment of the West Country), Bonham's (Auctioneers) 1998-2001, Weather World 2005-.

Political career: *House of Lords:* First entered House of Lords 1983. Sits as Baron Sudley; Government Whip 1987-89; Government Spokesperson for: Home Office, Department for Education and Science and Department of Health and Social Security 1987-89, Department of the Environment 1988-89; Parliamentary Under-Secretary of State: Ministry of Defence (Armed Forces)

1989-92, Northern Ireland Office 1992-94, Department of the Environment 1994; Government Deputy Chief Whip 1994-95; Elected hereditary peer 1999-. EU Sub-committee D (Environment and Agriculture): Member 2007-08, Co-opted member 2008-10; Member: EU Sub-committee D (Agriculture, Fisheries and Environment) 2010-12, Olympic and Paralympic Legacy 2013-14, Communications 2015-16, Natural Environment and Rural Communities Act 2006 2017-.

Political interests: Media, charity, sport, foreign affairs.

Other: President, Children's Country Holidays Fund 1999; Trustee, Chelsea Physic Garden; *Clubs:* Turf, Beefsteak, Pratt's, White's Club.

Recreations: Tennis, golf, croquet, shooting, gardening.

The Earl of Arran, House of Lords, London SW1A 0PW
Tel: 020 7219 5353

ASHDOWN OF NORTON-SUB-HAMDON, LORD

LIBERAL DEMOCRAT

ASHDOWN OF NORTON-SUB-HAMDON (Life Baron), Jeremy John (Paddy) Ashdown; cr. 2001. Born 27 February 1941; Son of late Lieutenant Colonel John W. R. D. Ashdown; Married Mary Jane Donne Courtenay 1961 (1 son 1 daughter).

Education: Bedford School; Hong Kong Language School (Chinese (Mandarin) 1967-70).

Non-political career: Royal Marines Officer (Captain) 1959-72 with Commando Units in Far East, Middle East and Belfast; Commanded Unit of Special Boat Service in Far East. 1st class interpreter, Chinese; First secretary (Foreign Office), UK Mission to UN in Geneva 1971-76; Westland Helicopters, Yeovil 1976-78; Morlands, Yeovil 1978-81; Youth officer, Dorset County Council 1981-83; UN High Representative for Bosnia and Herzegovina 2002-06.

Political career: *House of Commons:* Contested (Liberal) Yeovil 1979 general election. MP for Yeovil 1983-2001 (Liberal/All 1983-88, Liberal Democrat 1988-2001). Liberal Spokesperson for: Trade and Industry 1985-87, Education and Science 1987-88; Liberal Democrats Spokesperson for Northern Ireland 1988-92. *House of Lords:* Raised to the peerage as Baron Ashdown of Norton-sub-Hamdon, of Norton-sub-Hamdon in the County of Somerset 2001. *Other:* Liberal Democrats: Leader 1988-99, Chair, 2015 general election campaign 2012-15, Local and general election co-ordinator 2015.

Political interests: Youth affairs, foreign affairs, defence, industry, new technology, nation building; Western Balkans.

Other: President, UNICEF UK 2009-15; Convenor, MoreUnited.uk 2016-; Hope and Homes for Children. Officier de la Legion d'Honneur 2017. PC 1989; KBE 2000; GCMG 2006; CH 2015; Officier de la Legion d'Honneur 2017; *Clubs:* National Liberal Club.

Publications: Citizens' Britain: A Radical Agenda for the 1990s (1989); Beyond Westminster: Finding Hope in Britain (1992); The Ashdown Diaries (2000, 2001); Swords and Ploughshares – bringing peace to the 21st century (Orion, 2007); A Fortunate Life (autobiography) (2009); A Brilliant Little Operation (2013); The Cruel Victory (2014); Game of Spies (2016).

Recreations: Gardening, classical music, hillwalking, wine-making.

Rt Hon the Lord Ashdown of Norton-sub-Hamdon GCMG CH KBE, House of Lords, London SW1A 0PW
Tel: 020 7219 8726 *Email:* ashdownp@parliament.uk *Twitter:* @paddyashdown

ASHTON OF HYDE, LORD

CONSERVATIVE

Parliamentary Under-Secretary of State and Government Spokesperson, Department for Digital, Culture, Media and Sport

ASHTON OF HYDE (4th Baron, UK), Thomas Henry Ashton; cr. 1911. Born 18 July 1958; Son of late 3rd Baron and Pauline Trewlove Ashton, née Brackenbury; Married Emma Allinson 1987 (4 daughters).

Education: Eton College; Trinity College, Oxford (BA 1980, MA).

Non-political career: Lieutenant: Royal Hussars, Royal Wessex Yeomanry. Barclays Bank 1981-82; CT Bowring Reinsurance Ltd 1982-90; Vice-President, Guy Carpenter & Company 1990-92; Director: C.T Bowring Reinsurance Ltd 1992-93, D.P Mann Ltd 1996-99; Faraday Underwriting Ltd: Director 1999-2013, Chief Executive Officer 2005-13; Faraday Reinsurance Company Ltd: Director 2002-13, Chief Executive Officer 2005-13; Council Member, Lloyd's 2010-13; Non-executive Director, Aegis Managing Agency Ltd 2014.

Political career: *House of Lords:* Elected hereditary peer 2011-; Government Whip (Lord in Waiting) 2014-17; Government Spokesperson for: Business, Innovation and Skills 2014-15, Home Office 2014-16, Justice 2014-15, Defence 2015-16, Treasury 2015-16; Parliamentary Under-Secretary of State and Government Spokesperson, Department for Culture, Media and Sport/Digital, Culture, Media and Sport 2016-. Member: The Arctic 2014, Insurance Bill 2014-15.

Other: Joint master, Heythrop Hunt 2007-09.

The Lord Ashton of Hyde, House of Lords, London SW1A 0PW
Email: ashtont@parliament.uk

ASHTON OF UPHOLLAND, BARONESS

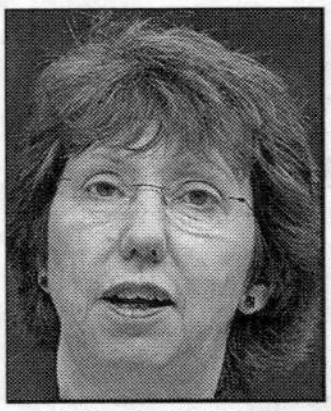

NON-AFFILIATED

ASHTON OF UPHOLLAND (Life Baroness), Catherine Margaret Ashton; cr 1999. Born 20 March 1956; Daughter of late Harold and Clare Ashton; Married Peter Kellner 1988 (1 son 1 daughter 1 stepson 2 stepdaughters).

Education: Upholland Grammar School; Bedford College, London University (BSc (Econ) 1977); French.

Non-political career: Administrative officer, CND 1977-79; The Coverdale Organisation 1979-81; Central Council for Education and Training in Social Work 1981-83; Director of community development and public affairs, Business in the Community 1983-89; Public policy adviser 1989-, seconded by London First to Home Office 1998-99; Director, Political Context 1996-98; Adviser, Lattice Foundation 2000-01; European Commission: Commissioner for Trade 2008-09, High Representative for Foreign Affairs and Security Policy, and Vice-President and External Relations Commissioner 2009-14; Chair, steering board, European Defence Agency 2009-14; Visiting Professor, King's College London.

Political career: *House of Lords:* Raised to the peerage as Baroness Ashton of Upholland, of St Albans in the County of Hertfordshire 1999. Parliamentary Under-Secretary of State and Government Spokesperson, Department for Education and Skills 2001-04 (also Department for Work and Pensions 2002-04); Government Spokesperson for Children 2003-04; Parliamentary Under-Secretary of State and Government Spokesperson, Department for Constitutional Affairs/Ministry of Justice 2004-07; Leader of the House of Lords and Lord President of the Council 2007-08; Government Spokesperson for: Cabinet Office 2008, Equality 2008; On leave of absence 2008-15, March 2016-. Member: Selection 2007-08, Liaison 2007-08, Privileges 2007-08, House 2007-08, Procedure 2007-08. *Councils and public bodies:* Chair, Hertfordshire Health Authority 1998-2001.

Other: Vice-president, National Council for One Parent Families 1998-2001; Trustee, Verulamium Museum 2000-. Chancellor, Warwick University 2017-. *House Magazine* Minister of the Year 2005; Channel 4 Peer of the Year 2005; Stonewall Politician of the Year 2006. PC 2006; GCMG 2015; *Clubs:* Royal Commonwealth Society Club.

Rt Hon the Baroness Ashton of Upholland GCMG, House of Lords, London SW1A 0PW
Tel: 020 7219 5353

ASTOR, VISCOUNT

CONSERVATIVE

ASTOR (4th Viscount, UK), William Waldorf Astor; cr. 1917; 4th Baron Astor (UK) 1916. Born 27 December 1951; Son of 3rd Viscount and Hon. Sarah Norton, daughter of 6th Baron Grantley; Married Annabel Sheffield, née Jones 1976 (2 sons 1 daughter).

Education: Eton College.

Non-political career: Silvergate Media 2011-.

Political career: *House of Lords:* First entered House of Lords 1972; Government Whip 1990-93; Government Spokesperson for: Department of Environment 1990-91, Home Office 1991-92, Department of National Heritage 1992-93; Parliamentary Under-Secretary of State: Department of Social Security 1993-94, Department of National Heritage 1994-95; Opposition Spokesperson for: Home Office 1997-2001; Elected hereditary peer 1999-; Opposition Spokesperson for: Education and Employment 1999-2001, Transport, Local Government and the Regions 2001-02, Transport 2002-05, Culture, Media and Sport 2005-06.

Other: Trustee, Stanley Spencer Gallery, Cookham; *Clubs:* White's Club.

The Viscount Astor, House of Lords, London SW1A 0PW
Tel: 020 7219 4139 *Email:* astorw@parliament.uk
44 Grosvenor Gardens Mews South, London SW1W 0LB

CONSERVATIVE

ASTOR OF HEVER, LORD

ASTOR OF HEVER (3rd Baron, UK), John Jacob Astor; cr. 1956. Born 16 June 1946; Son of 2nd Baron and late Lady Irene Haig; Married Fiona Harvey 1970 (divorced 1990) (3 daughters); married Hon. Elizabeth Mackintosh 1990 (1 son 1 daughter).

Education: Eton College; French.

Non-political career: Lieutenant, Life Guards 1966-70; Honorary Colonel 101 (City of London) Engineer Regiment 2005-10. Chair, Newwaves Solutions Ltd 2016-.

Political career: *House of Lords:* First entered House of Lords 1984; Opposition Whip 1998-2010; Elected hereditary peer 1999-; Opposition Spokesperson for: Defence 2003-10, Foreign and Commonwealth Office 2003-10, International Development 2003-10; Parliamentary Under-Secretary of State and Government Spokesperson, Ministry of Defence 2010-15; Government Whip 2010-11; Trade Envoy to: Kazakhstan 2015-17, Oman 2016-; Secretary of State for Defence's Adviser on Oman 2016-. *Other:* Member of Executive, Association of Conservative Peers 1996-98. *Councils and public bodies:* DL Kent 1996-.

Political interests: France, motorsport industry, defence; Belgium, France, USA.

Other: Trustee, Astor of Hever Trust 1986-; Chair, Council of the Order of St John for Kent 1987-97; Trustee: Astor Foundation 1988-2008, Rochester Cathedral Trust 1988-2010; Patron, Edenbridge Music and Arts Trust 1989-2010; Trustee, Canterbury Cathedral Trust 1992-2007; Patron, Kent Youth Trust 1994-2010; President: Earl Haig Branch, Royal British Legion 1994-2010, Motorsport Industry Association 1995-2010, RoSPA 1996-99, Eden Valley Museum Trust 1998-2010; Patron, Aquarian Opera 1999-2010; Royal British Legion, Kent 2002-07; President, Kent County Agricultural Society 2006-10; Patron, Conservatives in Paris; President: Tunbridge Wells International Music Festival 2009-10, Motorsport Industry Association 2016-. Member, Goldsmiths' Company. PC 2015; *Clubs:* White's Club.

Rt Hon the Lord Astor of Hever DL, House of Lords, London SW1A 0PW
Tel: 020 7219 5475 *Email:* astorjj@parliament.uk

CONSERVATIVE

ATTLEE, EARL

ATTLEE (3rd Earl, UK), John Richard Attlee; cr. 1955; Viscount Prestwood. Born 3 October 1956; Son of 2nd Earl; Married Celia Plummer 1993 (divorced); married Terese Ahern 2008.

Education: Stowe School, Buckinghamshire.

Non-political career: Major, REME TA, All Arms Pool of Watchkeepers; Operation Lodestar 1997-98; Operation Telic (Iraq) 2003. Materials Management, Smith Industries; In-Country director (Rwanda), British Direct Aid 1995-96.

Political career: *House of Lords:* First entered House of Lords 1994; Opposition Whip 1997-99, 2002-05, 2007-10; Opposition Spokesperson for: Defence June-Oct 1997, 1998-2001, 2002-03, Transport 1997, 1999-2001, 2002-03, 2007-10, Northern Ireland 1997, 1998-99, Trade and Industry 1998-99; Elected hereditary peer 1999-; Opposition Spokesperson for: Energy 2003-04, Office of the Deputy Prime Minister 2004-05, Maritime and Shipping 2007-10; Government Whip 2010-14; Government Spokesperson for: International Development 2010, Northern Ireland 2010-14, Transport 2010-13, Communities and Local Government 2010-12, 2013-14, Home Office 2010-14, Wales 2012-14, Law Officers 2013-14, Scotland 2013-14, Immigration 2013-14. Member: Statutory Instruments Joint Committee 2007-08, Partnerships (Prosecution) (Scotland) Bill 2013, Administration and Works 2015-16, Services 2016-17.

Political interests: Overseas aid and development, engineering, defence, transport.

Other: President, Heavy Transport Association 1994-2008. TD.

Recreations: Restoration and operation of classic commericial and military vehicles.

The Earl Attlee TD, House of Lords, London SW1A 0PW
Tel: 020 7219 6071 *Fax:* 020 7219 5979 *Email:* attleej@parliament.uk

LABOUR

BACH, LORD

BACH (Life Baron), William Stephen Goulden Bach; cr. 1998. Born 25 December 1946; Son of late Stephen Bach CBE and late Joan Bach; Married Caroline Jones 1984 (1 daughter and 2 children from previous marriage).

Education: Westminster School; New College, Oxford (BA English 1968).

Non-political career: Called to the Bar, Middle Temple 1972, Tenant Barristers' Chambers 1975-2000, Head of Chambers 1996-99; Served on a number of circuit and local court and bar committees over many years. Member, TGWU/Unite 1977-.

Political career: *House of Commons:* Contested (Labour) Gainsborough 1979 and Sherwood 1983 and 1987 general elections. *House of Lords:* Raised to the peerage as Baron Bach, of Lutterworth in the County of Leicestershire 1998. Government Whip 1999-2000, 2007-08; Government Spokesperson for: Home Office 1999-2000, Lord Chancellor's Department 1999-2000, Education and Employment 1999-2000; Parliamentary Secretary, Lord Chancellor's Department 2000-01; Parliamentary Under-Secretary of State (Minister for Defence Procurement) and Government Spokesperson, Ministry of Defence 2001-05; Parliamentary Under-Secretary of State and Government Spokesperson, Department for Environment, Food and Rural Affairs 2005-06; Government Spokesperson for: Business, Enterprise and Regulatory Reform 2007-08, Justice 2007-10, HM Treasury 2007-08, Foreign and Commonwealth Office 2008; Parliamentary Under-Secretary of State, Ministry of Justice 2008-10; Opposition Spokesperson for: Justice 2010-12, 2015-16, Foreign and Commonwealth Office 2013-15, Law Officers 2014-15; Shadow Attorney General 2014-15. Member: European Communities Sub-committee E (Laws and Institutions) 1998-99, Draft Legal Services Bill Joint Committee 2006; Co-opted Member, EU Sub-committee D (Environment and Agriculture) 2006-07. *Other:* Police and Crime Commissioner for Leicestershire 2016-. Society of Labour Lawyers: Executive committee member, Chair and co-founder, Society of Labour Lawyers, East Midlands; Elected member, Labour Party: National Policy Forum 1998-99, Economic Policy Commission 1998-99; Member, Co-operative Party; Chair: Harborough District Labour Party 1989-95, 2007-, Northants and Blaby Euro Constituency GC 1992-99, South Leicestershire CLP 2007-. *Councils and public bodies:* Leicester City Council: Councillor 1976-87, Chief Whip, Labour Group 1981-83; Councillor, Lutterworth Town Council 1991-99; Mayor of Lutterworth 1993-94; Harborough District Council: Councillor 1995-99, Chair, Contracts Services Committee 1995-97; Chief Whip, Labour Group 1995-98.

Political interests: Crime and criminal justice, local government, sport, foreign affairs, defence and security, social welfare law; Latin America, Chile, India, Italy, Portugal, Spain, USA.

Other: Leicester University: Council member 1980-99, Court member 1980-; Member, Fabian Society; Vice-chair, Cotesbach Education Trust; Trustee, LawWorks; Patron, Coventry Law Centre. Honorary degree, Leicester University. Peer of the Year, *House Magazine* awards 2012. Leicestershire CCC; Founder Member and President, Walcote Cricket Club.

Recreations: Playing and watching football and cricket, supporting Leicester City FC, American crime writing.

The Lord Bach, House of Lords, London SW1A 0PW
Tel: 020 7219 6389 *Fax:* 020 7219 2146 *Email:* bachw@parliament.uk *Twitter:* @FightBach

CONSERVATIVE

BAKER OF DORKING, LORD

BAKER OF DORKING (Life Baron), Kenneth Wilfred Baker; cr. 1997. Born 3 November 1934; Son of late Wilfred Baker, OBE; Married Mary Gray-Muir 1963 (1 son 2 daughters).

Education: St Paul's School, London; Magdalen College, Oxford (BA history 1958) (Union Secretary 1958).

Non-political career: National service 1953-55 (Lieutenant in Gunners). Non-executive director, Stanley Leisure plc (now called Genting UK) 2001-.

Political career: *House of Commons:* Contested (Conservative) Poplar 1964 and Acton 1966 general elections. MP for Acton 1968-70, for St Marylebone 1970-83, for Mole Valley 1983-97. PPS to Minister of State, Department of Employment 1970-72; Parliamentary Secretary, Civil Service Department 1972-74; Minister of State for Industry and Information Technology 1981-84; Minister for Local Government 1984-85; Secretary of State for: Environment 1985-86, Education and Science 1986-89; Chancellor of the Duchy of Lancaster 1989-90; Home Secretary 1990-92. *House of Lords:* Raised to the peerage as Baron Baker of Dorking, of Iford in the County of East Sussex 1997. Chair, Information 2003-07; Member, House 2007-12. *Other:* Chairman, Conservative Party 1989-90; Hon. Life member, Tory Reform Group. *Councils and public bodies:* Councillor, Twickenham Borough Council 1960-62.

Political interests: Education, history, information technology; UK.

Other: Chair: Hansard Society 1978-81, Museum of British History 1995-2005; President, Royal London Society for the Blind 2000-10; Trustee: Cartoon AG Trust 2003-, Booker Prize Foundation 2005-; President, Old Pauline Club 2007-09; Chair, Edge Foundation 2008-; Trustee, Baker Dearing Educational Trust 2003-; City & Guilds Fellowship Diploma 2012; Cartoon Museum. Hon degree, Richmond College, American University in London; Hon fellowship diploma, City and Guilds; Hon DSc, Aston University; Hon doctorate of education, Plymouth University; DLitt, Chester University. PC 1984; CH 1992; *Clubs:* Athenæum, Garrick Club.

Publications: I Have No Gun But I Can Spit (1980); London Lines (1982); The Faber Book of English History in Verse (1988); Unauthorised Versions: Poems and their Parodies (1990); The Faber Book of Conservatism (1993); The Turbulent Years: My Life in Politics (1993); The Prime Ministers – An Irreverent Political History in Cartoons (1995); Kings and Queens: An Irreverent Cartoon History of the British Monarchy (1996); The Faber Book of War Poetry (1996); Children's English History in Verse (2000); The Faber Book of Landscape Poetry (2000); George IV: A Life in Caricature (2005); George III: A Life in Caricature (2007); GK Chesterton Poems (2007); George Washington's War in Contemporary Caricature and Print (2009); 14-18: A New Vision for Secondary Education (2013).

Recreations: Collecting books, collecting political cartoons.

Rt Hon the Lord Baker of Dorking CH, House of Lords, London SW1A 0PW
Tel: 020 7219 4434 *Email:* bakerk@parliament.uk

BAKEWELL, BARONESS

LABOUR

BAKEWELL (Life Baroness), Joan Dawson Bakewell; cr 2011. Born 16 April 1933; Daughter of John Rowlands and Rose Bland; Married Michael Bakewell 1955 (divorced 1972) (1 daughter 1 son); married Jack Emery (divorced 2001).

Education: Stockport High School for Girls; Newnham College, Cambridge (BA history and economics).

Non-political career: TV presenter: *Sunday Break* 1962, *Home at 4.30* 1964, *Meeting Point* 1964, *The Second Sex* 1964, *Late Night Line Up* 1965-72, *The Youthful Eye* 1968, *Moviemakers at the National Film Theatre* 1971, *Film 72* 1972, *Film 73* 1973, *For the Sake of Appearance, Where is Your God?, Who Cares?, and the Affirmative Way* (series) 1973, *Holiday* (series) 1974-78, *Thank You, Ron* (documentary) 1974, *What's it All About?* (series) 1974, *Fairest Fortune and Edinburgh Festival Report* 1974, *Time Running Out* (series) 1974, *The Shakespeare Business* (series) 1976, *The Brontë Business* (series) 1976, *Generation to Generation* (series) 1976, *Reports Action* (series) 1976-79, *My Dad with the Children* 1977, *Arts UK: OK?* 1980, *The Heart of the Matter* 1988-2000, *Travels with Persner* 1998, *My Generation* 2000, *Taboo* (series) 2001; TV critic, *The Times* 1978-81; Radio presenter: *Away From it All* 1978-79, *PM* 1979-81, *Artist of the Week* 1998-2000, *Belief* 2001-, *Midsummer Sins* 2004, *There and Back* (play); *Brontës: The Private Faces* (theatre), Edinburgh Festival 1979; Arts correspondent, BBC 1981-87; Columnist, *Sunday Times* 1988-90; Chair, *The Brains Trust*, BBC 1998-2001; Columnist: *Guardian* 2003-05, *Independent* 2006-.

Political career: *House of Lords:* Raised to the peerage as Baroness Bakewell, of Stockport in the County of Greater Manchester 2011. Member: Communications 2012-15, Works of Art 2015-16, Lord Speaker's Advisory Panel on Works of Art 2017-, Artificial Intelligence 2017-.

Political interests: Women's rights, the elderly, the arts; Brazil, India, Turkey.

Other: President, Society of Arts Publicists 1984-90; Council member, Aldeburgh Foundation 1985-99; British Film Institute: Governor 1994-2003, Deputy chair 1997-99, Chair 1999-2003; Board member, Royal National Theatre 1996-2003; Chair, Shared Experience 2004-12; National chair, Campaign for the Arts 2004-12; President, Birkbeck College 2013-; Hon. FRCA 1994; Breast Cancer Care, Women for Refugee Women, British Humanist Association, English Pen, Fawcett Society, Amnesty International. Newnham College, Cambridge: Associate 1980-91, Associate fellow 1984-87; Hon. Fellow, Royal Holloway and Bedford New College 1997; Hon. DLitt, Queen Margaret University College, Edinburgh 2005; Honorary professor, Department of Film and Media, Stirling University 2006-; Hon. DLitt: Chester 2007, University of Arts, London 2008, Staffordshire University 2009, Lancaster University 2010, Newcastle University 2011, Open University 2010, Essex University 2011, Manchester Metropolitan University 2013. Richard Dimbleby Award, BAFTA 1994; Journalist of the Year, Stonewall awards 2009. CBE 1999; DBE 2008.

Publications: Co-author, The New Priesthood: British Television Today (1970); A Fine and Private Place (1977); The Complete Traveller (1977); The Heart of Heart of the Matter (1996); The Centre of the Bed (autobiography, 2003); Belief (2005); The View from Here (2006); All the Nice Girls (2009).

Recreations: Cinema, theatre, travel.

The Baroness Bakewell DBE, House of Lords, London SW1A 0PW
Tel: 020 7219 2921
Email: joanbakewell@googlemail.com *Website:* joanbakewell.com *Twitter:* @JDBakewell

LIBERAL DEMOCRAT

BAKEWELL OF HARDINGTON MANDEVILLE, BARONESS

Liberal Democrat Lords Spokesperson for Work and Pensions

BAKEWELL OF HARDINGTON MANDEVILLE (Life Baroness), Catherine Mary Bakewell; cr 2013. Born 7 March 1949; Married David Bakewell 1979 (1 daughter 1 son).

Non-political career: Assistant to Leader of Liberal Democrats 1983-95, 1997-98.

Political career: *House of Lords:* Raised to the peerage as Baroness Bakewell of Hardington Mandeville, of Hardington Mandeville in the County of Somerset 2013. Liberal Democrat: Spokesperson for: Housing 2015, Communities and Local Government 2016, Shadow Secretary of State/Lords Spokesperson for Work and Pensions 2016-. Member, Personal Service Companies 2013-14; Alternate Member, Procedure 2014-17; Member, EU Energy and Environment Sub-Committee 2015. *Other:* Member, Liberal Party/Liberal Democrats 1974-; Yeovil Liberal Democrats: Chair 2008-11, Vice-chair 2011-13. *Councils and public bodies:* Somerset County Council: Councillor 1993-2013, Leader 2001-07; Member: Somerset Strategic Partnership 2013-16, County Council Network 2001-08, South West Regional Assembly; Non-executive director, South West Regional Development Agency 2004-12; Member: Councillors Commission 2007, Avon and Somerset Police Authority 2008-09; Councillor, South Somerset District Council 2009-; Governor, Yeovil College Corporation 2010-13; Member, Devon and Somerset Fire and Rescue Service 2012-13; Vice-president, Local Government Association 2017-.

Political interests: Local government, rural affairs and agriculture, housing, children and young people.

Other: Non-executive Director, Somerset Rural Youth Project 1997-2009; Board Member, Equality South West 2009-13; Chair, South Somerset Together 2013-16. MBE 1999.

The Baroness Bakewell of Hardington Mandeville MBE, House of Lords, London SW1A 0PW
Tel: 020 7219 8310 *Email:* bakewellc@parliament.uk

CROSSBENCH

BALDWIN OF BEWDLEY, EARL

BALDWIN OF BEWDLEY (4th Earl, UK), Edward Alfred Alexander Baldwin; cr. 1937; Viscount Corvedale. Born 3 January 1938; Son of 3rd Earl and late Joan Elspeth, née Tomes; Married Sarah James 1970 (died 2001) (3 sons).

Education: Eton College; Trinity College, Cambridge (BA modern languages and law 1961, MA; CertEd 1970); French, German.

Non-political career: Army national service 1956-58; 2nd Lieutenant, Intelligence Corps 1957-58. German and French teacher: Christ's Hospital 1970-74, Hemel Hempstead School 1974-77; Education officer: Leicestershire 1978-80, Oxfordshire 1980-87.

Political career: *House of Lords:* First entered House of Lords 1976; Elected hereditary peer 1999-. Co-opted Member, Science and Technology Sub-committee I (Complementary and Alternative Medicine) 2000. *Councils and public bodies:* Member, Research Council for Complementary Medicine 1989-91; Chair, British Acupuncture Accreditation Board 1990-98.

Political interests: Health, environment, integrated medicine, education.

Other: *Clubs:* MCC.

Publications: Co-editor Baldwin Papers: A Conservative Statesman, 1908-1947 (2004).

Recreations: Mountains, tennis, music.

The Earl Baldwin of Bewdley, House of Lords, London SW1A 0PW
Tel: 020 7219 5353
2 Scholar Place, Cumnor Hill, Oxford OX2 9RD *Tel:* 01865 865318

CONSERVATIVE

BALFE, LORD

BALFE (Life Baron), Richard Andrew Balfe; cr 2013. Born 14 May 1944; Son of Dr Richard Balfe and Dorothy Balfe; Married Susan Jane Honeyford (2 sons 1 daughter).

Education: Brook Secondary Modern School, Sheffield; London School of Economics (BSc social policy and administration 1971); French.

Non-political career: 1st Battalion Irish Rifles (TA) 1961-67. Civil Servant: Crown Agents for Overseas Governments 1961-65, Foreign Office 1965-70 (1967-70 on sabbatical at LSE); Research Officer, Finer Committee on One Parent Families 1970-73; Political Secretary, Royal Arsenal Co-operative Society 1973-79; Director: Co-operative Wholesale Society 1978-80, Royal Arsenal Co-operative Society and associated companies 1987-96. AUEW TASS/Unite.

Political career: *House of Commons:* Contested (Labour) Paddington South 1970 and Southwark and Bermondsey 1992 general elections. *House of Lords:* Raised to the peerage as Baron Balfe, of Dulwich in the London Borough of Southwark 2013. Member: European Union Sub-committee A (Economic and Financial Affairs) 2014-15, EU External Affairs Sub-Committee 2015-17, International Relations 2017-. *Other:* European Parliament: MEP for: London South Inner 1979-99, London region 1999-2004: Quaestor 1994-2004, Member: PES bureau 1994-99, European Parliament Bureau 1994-2004. Labour Party 1963-64, 1967-2001: London Executive 1973-95, Chair, Policy Committee 1983-85, Labour Whip removed 2001; Conservative Party: Member 2002-, Envoy to the Trades Union Movement 2007-15. *Councils and public bodies:* Greater London Council: Member for Southwark Dulwich 1973-77, Chair, Housing Development Committee 1975-77; Member, Court of Governors, London School of Economics 1973-91; Chair, Thamesmead New Town 1973-75.

Political interests: Defence, foreign policy, trade union affairs; Turkey, all EU countries, Commonwealth, USA.

Other: Member, European Economic and Social Committee 2012-13; Election Monitor in: Ukraine 2004, 2007, 2014, Turkey 2015; Member, Executive Committee, Fabian Society 1981-82; President, European Parliament Members Pension Fund 2004-; Chair, Anglia Community Leisure 2008-13; Director, CERN Pension Fund 2009-15; Trustee, Royal Statistical Society Pension Fund 2011-13; Vice-President, European Parliament Former Members' Association; Executive Committee Member, Global Democracy Initiative; Honorary President, British Dietetic Association; Member, CERN Actuarial and Technical Committee 2015-; Honorary Adviser, BALPA 2015-; Royal Statistical Society; Fellow, Royal Statistical Society 1973-; *Clubs:* Reform Club.

Recreations: Walking, reading, opera.

The Lord Balfe, House of Lords, London SW1A 0PW
Tel: 020 7219 8710 *Email:* richard.balfe@parliament.uk

BAMFORD, LORD

CONSERVATIVE

BAMFORD (Life Baron), Anthony Paul Bamford; cr 2013. Born 23 October 1945; Son of late Joseph Cyril Bamford CBE; Married Carole Gray Whitt 1974 (2 sons 1 daughter).

Education: Ampleforth College; Grenoble University.

Non-political career: Chair, J C Bamford Group/JCB 1975-; Director, Tarmac plc 1988-94.

Political career: *House of Lords:* Raised to the peerage as Baron Bamford, of Daylesford in the County of Gloucestershire and of Wootton in the County of Staffordshire 2013. *Other:* President, Burton on Trent Conservative Association 1987-90. *Councils and public bodies:* Staffordshire: High Sheriff 1985-86, DL 1989.

Other: Member: President's committee, CBI 1986-88, Design Council 1987-89; President, Staffordshire Agricultural Society 1987-88; Hon. Fellow: City and Guilds Institute 1993, Chartered Society of Designers 1994; Fellow, Institute of Agricultural Engineers 2003; Hon. Fellow: Institution of Engineering Designers 2008, Royal Academy of Engineering 2014, Institution of Mechanical Engineers 2015; NSPCC. Hon. MA engineering, Birmingham University 1987; Hon. doctorate in science, Cranfield University 1994; Hon. degree of business administration, Robert Gordon University, Aberdeen 1996; Hon. doctorates in: Technology, Staffordshire University 1998, Technology, Loughborough University 2002, Science, Harper Adams University College 2010. Chevalier de l'Ordre National du Mérite, France 1989; Commendatore al merito della Republica Italiana 1995. Kt 1990.

Recreations: Farming, gardening.

The Lord Bamford, House of Lords, London SW1A 0PW
Tel: 020 7219 5353
J C Bamford Excavators Ltd, Rocester, Staffordshire ST14 5JP *Tel:* 01889 590312
Email: jane.cornwall@jcb.com

BARKER, BARONESS

LIBERAL DEMOCRAT

BARKER (Life Baroness); Elizabeth Jean Barker; cr. 1999. Born 31 January 1961; Married Caroline Downie 2016.

Education: Dalziel High School, Motherwell; Broadway School, Oldham; Southampton University (BSc (SocSci) psychology 1982).

Non-political career: Age Concern England 1982-2008: Project co-ordinator, Opportunities for Volunteering Programme 1983-88, Grants officer 1988-92, Field officer 1992-2008; Management consultant to Age Concern organisations; Director: Third Sector Business (management consultancy) 2008-, B&W Consulting 2008-; Head of business development, SeeTheDifference.org 2010-11; Development Adviser, Charity Checkout 2014-.

Political career: *House of Lords:* Raised to the peerage as Baroness Barker, of Anagach in Highland 1999. Liberal Democrat Spokesperson for: Pensions 2000-02, Social Services 2000-04, Health 2004-10, Voluntary Sector and Social Enterprise 2015-16. Member: Mental Capacity Act 2005 2013-14, Joint Committee on the Draft Protection of Charities Bill 2014-15, Charities 2016-17, Citizenship and Civic Engagement 2017-. *Other:* Union of Liberal Students: Member 1979-83, Chair 1982-83; Member: Liberal Party National Executive 1982-83, Liberal Assembly Committee 1984-97; Liberal Democrats: Member, Federal Policy Committee 1997-2003, Chair, Federal Conference Committee 1997-2004, Member, Policy Working Groups on: Future of Social Services, Freedom and Fairness for Women, An Age of Opportunity, It's About Freedom, Member, Federal Executive 2004, Chair, Policy Working Groups on: Poverty and Inequality 2006-07, Future of the Voluntary Sector 2010-11. *Councils and public bodies:* Vice-President, Local Government Association 2010-.

Political interests: Health, social services, ageing, LGBT equality, equality for women and girls, social enterprise, HIV/AIDS; India, Morocco, Nigeria, South Africa.

Other: Patron, Spare Tyre Theatre Company 2010-; Ambassador, FreeFormers; Trustee, Andy Lawson Memorial Fund; Patron, Opening Doors London 2016-; Chair, Parliamentary Gender Identity Forum; Map Action, Albert Kennedy Trust, Lesbian and Gay Foundation.

The Baroness Barker, House of Lords, London SW1A 0PW
Tel: 020 7219 2955 *Email:* barkere@parliament.uk *Twitter:* @LizBarkerLords

BARKER OF BATTLE, LORD

CONSERVATIVE

BARKER OF BATTLE (Life Baron), Gregory Leonard George Barker; cr 2015. Born 8 March 1966; Married Celeste Harrison 1992 (divorced 2008) (1 daughter 2 sons).

Education: Steyning Grammar School; Lancing College, West Sussex; Royal Holloway College, London University (BA modern history, economic history, politics 1987); London Business School (corporate finance programme 1992).

Non-political career: Researcher, Centre for Policy Studies 1987-89; Equity analyst, Gerrard Vivian Gray 1988-90; Director, International Pacific Securities 1990-97; Associate partner, Brunswick Group Ltd 1997-98; Head, investor communications, Siberian Oil Company 1998-2000; Director, Daric plc (Bartlett Merton) 1998-2001; Chair, London Sustainable Development Commission 2014-; Non-executive director: Lightsource Renewable Energy Ltd 2015-, Dragon Harvest Group 2015-, Ilioss Group 2015-; Chair, international advisory board, Innasol Group Ltd 2015-; Director, Pont Street Capital 2015-; Senior adviser: Powerhive Ltd 2015-, Equinox Energy Capital 2015-; International adviser, SolarCity Corp USA 2015-; Chair, Global Sustainability Practice, Gyro Ltd 2016-.

Political career: *House of Commons:* Contested Eccles 1997 general election. MP (Conservative) for Bexhill and Battle 2001-10, for Bexhill and Battle (revised boundary) 2010-15. Opposition Whip 2003-05; Shadow Minister for: the Environment 2005-08, Climate Change 2008-10; Minister of State, Department of Energy and Climate Change 2010-14. Member: Environmental Audit 2001-05, 2007-10, Broadcasting 2003-05. *House of Lords:* Raised to the peerage as Baron Barker of Battle, of Battle in the County of East Sussex 2015. *Other:* Chair: Shoreham Young Conservatives 1982-83, Royal Holloway Conservative Society 1986-87; Vice-chair: Hammersmith Conservative Association 1993-95, Wandsworth and Tooting Conservative Association 1997-98; Founding Member, 2020 group 2011.

Political interests: Environment, education, overseas development; Australia, Germany, Russia, USA.

Other: Associate, Centre for Policy Studies 1988-89; Director of European Board, Environmental Defense Fund; Trustee: De La Warr Pavilion, Bexhill-on-Sea, Climate Group. Honourable Artillery Company. PC 2012; *Clubs:* Pratt's Club. Bexhill Rowing Club.

Recreations: Skiing, hunting, horse racing.

Rt Hon the Lord Barker of Battle, House of Lords, London SW1A 0PW
Tel: 020 7219 3000
Email: office@gregorybarker.com
Website: www.gregorybarker.com *Twitter:* @GregBarkerUK

LAB/CO-OP

BASSAM OF BRIGHTON, LORD

Shadow Chief Whip in the House of Lords

BASSAM OF BRIGHTON (Life Baron), John Steven Bassam; cr. 1997. Born 11 June 1953; Son of late Sydney Stevens and Enid Bassam; Partner Jill Whittaker (1 son 2 daughters 1 son deceased).

Education: Clarton Secondary Modern School for Boys; Sussex University (BA history 1975); Kent University (MA social work 1979).

Non-political career: Social worker, East Sussex County Council 1976-77; Legal adviser, North Lewisham Law Centre 1979-83; Research officer, Camden Council 1983-84; Head of environmental health, Trading Standards AMA 1988-97; Consultant adviser, KPMG Capital 1997-99. Member, Unison.

Political career: *House of Commons:* Contested (Labour) Brighton Kemptown 1987 general election. *House of Lords:* Raised to the peerage as Baron Bassam of Brighton, of Brighton in the County of East Sussex 1997. Parliamentary Under-Secretary of State, Home Office 1999-2001; Government Spokesperson for: Home Office 1999-2008, Cabinet Office 2001-07; Government Whip 2001-08; Government Spokesperson for: Lord Chancellor's Department 2001-04, Office of the Deputy Prime Minister/Communities and Local Government 2002-04, 2005-07, 2008, Attorney General's Office 2005-08, Transport 2007-08, Culture, Media and Sport 2008; Government Chief Whip 2008-10; Deputy Speaker 2008-; Deputy Chairman of Committees 2008-17; Opposition Chief Whip 2010-. Member: Administration and Works 2008-12, 2015-16, Procedure 2008-, Selection 2008-, Privileges/Privileges and Conduct 2009-, Sub-committee on Leave of Absence 2011-13, Services 2016-. *Councils and public bodies:* Brighton Borough Council: Councillor 1983-97, Leader 1987-96; Brighton and Hove Council: Councillor 1996-99, Leader 1996-99; Head of Environmental Health and Consumer Issues, Local Government Association 1997-99.

Political interests: Local government, housing, home affairs, culture, education, political strategy, environment; Australia, India, Spain, USA.

Other: Laura Martin Trust (Homelessness Charity). Fellow, Brighton College 2002. Alumni Fellow, Sussex University 2001. PC 2009. Preston Village Cricket Club.

Recreations: Cricket, walking, running.

Rt Hon the Lord Bassam of Brighton, House of Lords, London SW1A 0PW
Tel: 020 7219 4918 *Fax:* 020 7219 6837 *Email:* bassams@parliament.uk
Longstone, 25 Church Place, Brighton BN2 5JN *Tel:* 01273 609473 *Twitter:* @SteveTheQuip

CONSERVATIVE

BATES, LORD

Minister of State and Government Spokesperson, Department for International Development; Government Spokesperson, HM Treasury

BATES (Life Baron), Michael Walton Bates; cr 2008. Born 26 May 1961; Son of John MacLennan Bates and Ruth Bates, née Walton; Married Carole Whitfield 1983 (divorced 2008) (2 sons); married Xuelin 2012.

Education: Heathfield Senior High School, Gateshead; Gateshead College (Diploma business studies 1982); Saïd Business School, Oxford (MBA Wadham College 1998).

Non-political career: Trainee Salesman, Gresham Life Assurance 1983; Agency Inspector, Clerical Medical Investment Group 1983-87; Investment Adviser: Hogg Robinson (benefit consultants) 1986-87, Joseph Nelson (fund management) 1987-91; Assistant Director, Godwins (pension consultants and actuaries) 1991; Oxford Analytica International Group 1998-2007: Senior Vice-president 1998-99, Director of Consultancy and Research 1999-2005, Head of Operations 2004-05, Director 2004-06, Senior Adviser 2006-07; Managing Director, Walton Bates (management consultants) Ltd 2006-11; Non-executive Director, Vardy Group 2006-10; Non-executive Chair: Scholes & Brown Asset Management 2008-11, 55 Plus Ltd 2010-11; Chair, International Property Awards 2013.

Political career: *House of Commons:* Contested Tynebridge 1987 general election and Langbaurgh 1991 by-election. MP (Conservative) for Langbaurgh 1992-97. Contested Middlesbrough South and Cleveland East 1997 general election. PPS to Ministers of State: Nicholas Scott, Department of Social Security 1992-93, Sir John Wheeler, Northern Ireland Office 1994; Assistant Government Whip 1994-95; Government Whip 1995-96; Paymaster General, Office of Public Services 1996-97. *House of Lords:* Raised to the peerage as Baron Bates, of Langbaurgh in the County of North Yorkshire 2008. Opposition Whip 2009-10; Opposition Spokesperson for: Cabinet Office 2009-10, Communities and Local Government 2009-10, Energy and Climate Change

2009, Children, Schools and Families 2009-10; Deputy Chair of Committees 2013-14; Government Whip 2013-14; Government Spokesperson for: Culture, Media and Sport (Broadcasting) 2013-14, International Development 2013-14, Work and Pensions 2013-14, Business, Innovation and Skills (Universities and Science) 2014; Home Office: Government Spokesperson 2014-16, Parliamentary Under-Secretary of State 2014-15, Minister of State 2015-16; Leave of absence April-September 2016; Minister of State and Government Spokesperson, Department for International Development 2016-; Government Spokesperson, HM Treasury 2017-. Member: Leader's Group on the Working Practices of the House of Lords 2010-11, Partnerships (Prosecution) (Scotland) Bill 2013, Olympic and Paralympic Legacy 2013. *Other:* Young Conservatives: Member, National Advisory Committee 1984-87, Chair, Northern Area 1984-87; Deputy chair, Conservative Party 2007-10; Project director, Campaign North 2007-10.

Political interests: Education, foreign policy, sport for development and peace; Albania, China, Croatia, Greece, Japan, Korea, USA.

Other: International Olympic Truce Foundation; Fellow: 48 Group Club, Industry and Parliament Trust, Royal Geographical Society, Caux Round Table; Board member, International Olympic Truce Foundation; Trustee, Walk for Peace Foundation -2016. Open Fields Awards, Olympic Truce Foundation 2012; Order of Skanderbeg, Albania 2014. PC 2015; *Clubs:* Northern Counties Club.

Recreations: Cinema, walking, Newcastle United FC.

Rt Hon the Lord Bates, House of Lords, London SW1A 0PW
Tel: 020 7219 5353 *Email:* batesm@parliament.uk
Website: lordsoftheblog.net/category/lord-bates *Twitter:* @bateslord

LABOUR

BEECHAM, LORD

Opposition Spokesperson for Communities and Local Government, Housing and Justice

BEECHAM (Life Baron), Jeremy Hugh Beecham; cr 2010. Born 17 November 1944; Son of Lawrence Beecham and Florence Beecham; Married Brenda Woolf 1968 (died 2010) (1 son 1 daughter).

Education: Royal Grammar School, Newcastle upon Tyne; University College, Oxford (BA jurisprudence 1965, MA).

Non-political career: Solicitor 1968; Partner, Allan Henderson Beecham & Peacock/Beecham Peacock 1968-2002; Director, Northern Development Company 1986-91; Consultant, Beecham Peacock 2002-11.

Political career: *House of Commons:* Contested (Labour) Tynemouth 1970 general election. *House of Lords:* Raised to the peerage as Baron Beecham, of Benwell and Newcastle upon Tyne in the County of Tyne and Wear 2010. Opposition Spokesperson for: Communities and Local Government 2010-, Health 2010-12, Justice 2012-, Housing 2015-. Member, Inheritance and Trustees' Powers Bill 2013. *Other:* Chair, Oxford University Labour Club 1964; Labour Party: Member: National Executive Committee/Shadow Cabinet Working Party on Future of Local Government 1984-87, Joint Policy Committee 1992-; National Executive Committee: Member 1998-2010, Chair 2005-06. *Councils and public bodies:* Newcastle upon Tyne City Council: Councillor 1967-, Leader 1977-2006; Commissioner, English Heritage 1983-87; Association of Metropolitan Authorities: Deputy chair 1984-86, Vice-chair 1986-91, Chair 1991-97; Vice-chair, Northern Regional Councils Association 1986-91; DL, Tyne and Wear 1995; Local Government Association: Chair 1995-2004, Vice-chair 2004-10, Vice-President 2010-.

Political interests: Local government, social policy, health, criminal justice, legal aid, regional policy, environment; Israel.

Other: President: Bura 1995-2009, Age Concern Newcastle 1995-2017, Newcastle Choral Society 1995; Vice-President, Newcastle CVS; Trustee, Trusthouse Charitable Foundation 1999-2012; Vice-President, Community Foundation 2000-; Member, advisory board, Harold Hartog School of Government, Tel Aviv 2005-; New Israel Fund: Vice-chair 2006-, Board member 2007-. Hon. Freedom, Newcastle upon Tyne 1995. Hon. Fellow, Northumbria University 1989; Hon. DCL, Newcastle University 1992. Kt 1994.

Recreations: Reading, music.

The Lord Beecham, House of Lords, London SW1A 0PW
Tel: 020 7219 5353 *Email:* beechamj@parliament.uk *Twitter:* @JeremyBeecham

LIBERAL DEMOCRAT

BEITH, LORD

BEITH (Life Baron), Alan James Beith; cr 2015. Born 20 April 1943; Son of late James Beith, foreman packer, and Joan Beith; Married Barbara Ward 1965 (died 1998) (1 son deceased 1 daughter); married Baroness Maddock (qv) 2001.

Education: King's School, Macclesfield; Balliol College, Oxford (BA philosophy, politics and economics 1964); Nuffield College, Oxford (BLitt, MA 1966); Welsh, French, Norwegian.

Non-political career: Politics lecturer, Newcastle University 1966-73. Member, Association of University Teachers.

Political career: *House of Commons:* Contested Berwick-upon-Tweed 1970 general election. MP for Berwick-upon-Tweed 8 November 1973 by-election to 2010, for Berwick-upon-Tweed (revised boundary) 2010-15 (Liberal 1973-83, Liberal/All 1983-88, Liberal Democrat 1988-2015). Chief Whip, Liberal Party 1976-87; Member House of Commons Commission 1979-97; Liberal Spokesperson for: Foreign Affairs 1985-87, Treasury 1987; SLD Spokesperson for Treasury 1988-89; Liberal Democrat Spokesperson for: Treasury 1989-94, Home Affairs 1994-95; Member, Intelligence and Security Committee 1994-2008; Liberal Democrat Spokesperson for: Police, Prison and Security Matters 1995-97, Home and Legal Affairs (Home Affairs) 1997-99; Contested Speaker election 2000, 2009; Member, Speaker's Committee on the Electoral Commission 2001-10; Deputy Chair, Review Committee of Privy Counsellors of the Anti-terrorism, Crime and Security Act 2002-04 Member, Advisory Group of Privy Counsellors on use of Intercept as Evidence 2007-12. Member: Procedure 2000-01; Liaison: Member 2003-10, Chair 2010-15; Chair, Constitutional Affairs/Justice 2003-15; Member: Liaison (Liaison Sub-Committee) 2006-10, Joint Committee on National Security Strategy 2010-15; Liaison (National Policy Statements Sub-committee): Member 2010-12, Chair 2012-15. *House of Lords:* Raised to the peerage as Baron Beith, of Berwick upon Tweed in the County of Northumberland 2015. Member: Constitution 2016-, Lord Speaker's Committee on the Size of the House 2016-. *Other:* Deputy Leader: Liberal Party 1985-88, Liberal Democrat Party 1993-2003. *Councils and public bodies:* Councillor: Hexham RDC 1969-74, Tynedale DC 1974-75.

Political interests: Parliamentary and constitutional affairs, justice and the legal system, architectural and artistic heritage; Canada, Scandinavia, Zimbabwe.

Other: Local preacher, Methodist Church 1965-; Historic Chapels Trust: Trustee 1995-, Chair 2002-15, President 2015-; President, North of England Civic Trust 2005-; Member, Committee of Privy Councillors to Review Use of Intercept as Evidence 2008-14; Vice-President, Northumberland and Newcastle Society 2009-; Honorary Bencher, Middle Temple 2014-; Diabetes UK, Hospice Care North Northumberland. Honorary DCL: Newcastle University 1998, Northumbria University 2010; Honorary doctorate, Earlham College, Indiana 2013. PC 1992; Kt 2008; *Clubs:* President, National Liberal Club 2009-, Athenæum, Northern Counties, Newcastle upon Tyne Club.

Publications: Co-author, Case for Liberal Party and Alliance (1983); Faith and Politics (1987); A View From the North (2008).

Recreations: Music, walking, boating.

Rt Hon the Lord Beith, House of Lords, London SW1A 0PW
Tel: 020 7219 3540
Email: beithalanj@gmail.com

CONSERVATIVE

BELL, LORD

BELL (Life Baron), Timothy John Leigh Bell; cr. 1998. Born 18 October 1941; Son of late Arthur Bell and Greta Bell; Married 2nd Virginia Wallis Hornbrook 1988 (1 son 1 daughter).

Education: Queen Elizabeth's Grammar School, Barnet.

Non-political career: ABC Television 1959-61; Colman Prentis and Varley 1961-63; Hobson Bates 1963-66; Geers Gross 1966-70; Managing director, Saatchi & Saatchi 1970-75; Chair and managing director, Saatchi & Saatchi Compton 1975-85; Special adviser: to Chairman, National Coal Board 1984-86, to South Bank Board 1985-86; Group chief executive, Lowe Howard-Spink Campbell Ewald 1985-87; Deputy chair, Lowe Hoard-Spink and Bell 1987-89; Chair: Lowe Bell Communications 1987-94, Chime Communications plc 1994-, Bell Pottinger Private 2011-16.

Political career: *House of Lords:* Raised to the peerage as Baron Bell, of Belgravia in the City of Westminster 1998. *Other:* Chair, Conservative Party Keep the Pound Campaign. *Councils and public bodies:* Governor, British Film Institute 1983-86.

Other: Council member, Royal Opera House 1982-85; Charity Projects: Chair 1984-93, President 1993-; Director, Centre for Policy Studies 1989-92; FIPA, FIPR; Save The Children Fund, BACUP Living with Cancer. Kt 1990. Prince Edward Yacht Club Sydney, RAC.

Publications: Right or Wrong (2014).

Recreations: Golf, music.

The Lord Bell, House of Lords, London SW1A 0PW
Tel: 020 7219 5353
Email: lordtbell@gmail.com

LIBERAL DEMOCRAT

BENJAMIN, BARONESS

BENJAMIN (Life Baroness), Floella Karen Yunies Benjamin; cr 2010. Born 23 September 1949; Daughter of Roy and Veronica Benjamin; Married Keith Taylor 1980 (1 son 1 daughter).

Education: Penge Girls' School.

Non-political career: Chief Accountant's Office, Barclays Bank 1967-69; Founder, Crystalrowe Ltd 1987-; Actress: Appeared in a number of productions on the stage including: *Hair* 1970-72, *Jesus Christ Superstar* 1972-74, *Black Mikado* 1974-75, *The Husband-in-Law* 1976; Television appearances include: *Within These Walls* 1973-75, *Playschool* 1976-88, *PlayAway* 1976-82, *Angels* 1978-80, *Gentle Touch* 1980, *Bergerac* 1980, *Fast Forward* 1983-85, *Sarah Jane Adventures* 2007-10, *Mama Mirabelle's Home Movies* 2007-09, *Chuggington* 2010-13; *CBeebies Bedtime Stories* 2010-; Film appearances include: *Black Joy* 1977, *Run Fatboy Run* 2007, *Rendition* 2008; Floella Benjamin Productions Ltd: Founder 1987, Chief Executive 1998-2013, Chair 2002-12; Floella Food and Drink Ltd 2004-12. Equity.

Political career: *House of Lords:* Raised to the peerage as Baroness Benjamin, of Beckenham in the County of Kent 2010. Member: EU Sub-committee F (Home Affairs, Health and Education) 2013-15, Communications 2015-. Chair, Liberal Democrat Parliamentary Party Committee on Culture, Media and Sport 2012. *Councils and public bodies:* Millenium Commission 1999-2004; Governor, Dulwich College 2001-11; Member, Content Board, Ofcom 2003-06; DL, Greater London 2008-; Chair of Governors, Isle of Sheppey Academy 2009-11.

Political interests: Children and young people, media, culture and arts, sport, education, diversity, equality; All Caribbean countries, France, Ghana, South Korea, South Africa, USA.

Other: Patron, Sickle Cell Society 1985-; BAFTA: Council member 1990-2001, Vice-chair 1998-99, Chair, Television 1999-2000; President, Elizabeth R Commonwealth Broadcasting Fund 1995-2015; Governor: National Film and Television School 1995-2015, Commonwealth Institute 1998-2006; Vice-president, Barnardo's 2000-; President, Ramblers' Association 2008-10; Patron, British Association of Play Therapists 2009-; Trustee, Sparks 2009-2013; Vice-president, Royal Television Society; Patron: Transplant Links 2013-, Finding Rhythms 2015-; President, Society of Women Writers & Journalists 2017-; NSPCC. Chancellor, Exeter University 2006-16. DLitt Exeter University; Doctor of Education, York University. RTS award 2004; Special Lifetime Achievement award, BAFTA 2004; J.M. Barrie Award, Action for Children's Arts 2012. OBE 2001.

Publications: Author of numerous children's books; Written over 25 books including: Autobiographies: Coming to England (1995), 20th Anniversary edition (2016); The Arms of Britannia (2010), Sea of Tears (2011); My Two Grandads (2011).

Recreations: Running, golf, singing, photography, walking, cooking.

The Baroness Benjamin OBE, House of Lords, London SW1A 0PW
Tel: 020 7219 8901 *Email:* benjaminf@parliament.uk
Website: www.floellabenjamin.com *Twitter:* @FloellaBenjamin

LABOUR

BERKELEY, LORD

BERKELEY (18th Baron, E), Anthony Fitzhardinge Gueterbock; cr. 1421; (Life) Baron Gueterbock 2000. Born 20 September 1939; Son of late Brigadier Ernest Adolphus Leopold Gueterbock and late Hon. Cynthia Ella Gueterbock; Married Diana (Dido) Townsend 1965 (2 sons 1 daughter); married Rosalind Clarke 1999 (divorced 2011); married Marian Bennett 2017.

Education: Eton College; Trinity College, Cambridge (MA mechanical sciences 1961); French, German.

Non-political career: Civil engineer, Sir Alexander Gibb and Partners 1961-67; George Wimpey plc 1967-87; Public affairs manager, Eurotunnel 1987-95; Chair: Piggyback Consortium 1995-98, Rail Freight Group 1997-; European Rail Freight Association: Board member 2007-, President 2009-11.

Political career: *House of Lords:* Created a life peer as Baron Gueterbock, of Cranford in the London Borough of Hillingdon 2000. First entered House of Lords 1992; Opposition Spokesperson for Transport 1996-97; Opposition Whip 1996-97. Member, European Union 1997-2001. *Councils and public bodies:* President, UK Maritime Pilots' Association.

Political interests: Transport, environment; European Union member states.

Other: MICE; FRSA; FCILT; Honorary FIMechE. Honorary degree, Brighton University. OBE 1989.

Recreations: Sailing, skiing.

The Lord Berkeley OBE, House of Lords, London SW1A 0PW
Tel: 020 7219 0611 *Email:* berkeleyafg@parliament.uk *Twitter:* @tonyberkeley1

BERKELEY OF KNIGHTON, LORD

CROSSBENCH

BERKELEY of KNIGHTON (Life Baron), Michael Fitzhardinge Berkeley; cr 2013. Born 29 May 1948; Son of Sir Lennox and Freda Berkeley; Married Deborah Coltman-Rogers (died 2012) (1 daughter); Married Elizabeth Jane West 2014.

Education: Westminster Cathedral Choir School; The Oratory School; Royal Academy of Music.

Non-political career: Phlebotomist, St Bartholomew's Hospital 1969-71; Presentation Assistant, LWT 1973; Announcer, BBC Radio 3 1974-79; Associate Composer, Scottish Chamber Orchestra 1979; Joint Artistic Director, Spitalfields Festival 1994-97; Artistic Director, Cheltenham Festival 1995-2004; Associate Composer, BBC National Orchestra of Wales 2001-08; Radio Presenter.

Political career: *House of Lords:* Raised to the peerage as Baron Berkeley of Knighton, of Knighton in the County of Powys 2013. *Councils and public bodies:* General Advisory Council, BBC 1990-95.

Other: Member: Executive committee, Association of Professional Composers 1982-84, New music sub-committee, Arts Council of Great Britain 1984-86, Central music advisory committee, BBC 1986-90; Music panel adviser, Arts Council 1986-90; Visiting professor, Huddersfield University 1991-94; Governor, National Youth Orchestra 1994-96; Director, Britten-Pears Foundation 1996-2009; Member, Board of Directors, Royal Opera House, Covent Garden 1996-2001; Chair, Royal Ballet 2003-; Fellow: Royal Academy of Music, Royal Northern College of Music, Royal Welsh College of Music and Drama. Hon DMus, University of East Anglia. CBE 2012. Campden Hill Tennis Club; Holland Park Tennis Club.

Publications: The Music Pack (1994).

Recreations: Walking, tennis.

The Lord Berkeley of Knighton CBE, House of Lords, London SW1A 0PW
Tel: 020 7219 5353 *Email:* berkeleym@parliament.uk
Website: www.michaelberkeley.co.uk *Twitter:* @MichaelBerkele2

BERRIDGE, BARONESS

CONSERVATIVE

BERRIDGE (Life Baroness), Elizabeth Rose Berridge; cr 2011. Born 22 March 1972.

Education: Catmose College, Rutland; Emmanuel College (BA law 1995).

Non-political career: Barrister, Kings Chambers 1996-2005; Project Director, Commonwealth Initiative for Freedom of Religion or Belief 2015-.

Political career: *House of Commons:* Contested (Conservative) Stockport 2005 general election. *House of Lords:* Raised to the peerage as Baroness Berridge, of the Vale of Catmose in the County of Rutland 2011. Member: Joint Committee on Statutory Instruments 2010-12, Joint Committee on Human Rights 2011-15, Social Mobility 2015-16, Ecclesiastical Committee 2015-. Member, Joint Committee on Statutory Instruments 2011-. *Other:* Director, Conservative Christian Fellowship, CCHQ 2005-11.

Political interests: Religious freedom, multiculturalism, policing, human rights; Central African Republic, Commonwealth, Egypt, Iraq.

Other: Member: International Panel, Parliamentarians for Freedom of Religion or Belief, Executive Committee, Commonwealth Parliamentary Association United Kingdom 2017-.

Recreations: Tennis, Swimming.

The Baroness Berridge, House of Lords, London SW1A 0PW
Tel: 020 7219 8943 *Email:* brotennoblej@parliament.uk
Website: www.baronessberridge.com *Twitter:* @BaronessEB

BERTIN, BARONESS

CONSERVATIVE

BERTIN (Life Baroness), Gabrielle Louise Bertin; cr 2016. Born 14 March 1978; Married Chris Glenny 2007 (divorced); married Michael Grist (2 daughters).

Non-political career: Press Officer to Liam Fox; Researcher, Atlantic Bridge; Press Secretary to David Cameron: as Leader of the Opposition 2005-10, as Prime Minister 2010-12; Director of External Relations, Prime Minister's Office 2013-16; Director of Strategic Communications and Campaigns, BT 2017-.

Political career: *House of Lords:* Raised to the peerage as Baroness Bertin, of Battersea in the London Borough of Wandsworth 2016. Member, Communications 2017-.

Other: Trustee, KIDS (disabled children charity) 2013-.

The Baroness Bertin, House of Lords, London SW1A 0PW
Tel: 020 7219 3000

BEST, LORD

CROSSBENCH

BEST (Life Baron), Richard Stuart Best; cr. 2001. Born 22 June 1945; Son of late Walter Best, DL, JP and late Frances Best, née Chignell; Married Belinda Stemp 1978 (2 daughters 2 sons).

Education: Shrewsbury School; Nottingham University (BA social administration 1967).

Non-political career: Chief executive: British Churches Housing Trust 1970-73, National Federation of Housing Associations 1973-88, Joseph Rowntree Foundation 1988-2006, Joseph Rowntree Housing Trust 1988-2006.

Political career: *House of Lords:* Raised to the peerage as Baron Best, of Godmanstone in the County of Dorset 2001. Chair, House of Lords Audit Committee 2004-09; Member: Joint Committee on the Charities Bill 2004, Economic Affairs 2007-12, Economic Affairs Finance Bill Sub Committee 2009-, Information 2013-14, Olympic and Paralympic Legacy 2013-14; Chair, Communications 2014-17. *Councils and public bodies:* Commissioner, Rural Development Commission 1989-98; Chair, Hull Partnership Liaison Board 2003-05; Member, Audit Commission's Advisory Board on Housing, Communities and Environment 2003-10; Local Government Association: President 2005-15, Vice-president 2016-; Chair: Westminster Housing Commission 2005-06, Hanover Housing Association 2006-15, Office of Public Management's Public Interest Council 2007-12; Deputy chair, Standards Committee, Westminster City Council 2008-12; Chair: Commission on Housing in Northern Ireland 2009-10, Property Ombudsman 2009-17, Housing for an Ageing Population 2009, CLG/LGA Housing Commission 2010; DL, North Yorkshire 2012-.

Political interests: Housing, regeneration, social policy.

Other: Chair, International Board, South East European Research Centre; Royal Society of Arts: Trustee 2006-12, Treasurer 2009-12; Patron, Housing Associations Charitable Trust 2007-; Chair, Hanover Housing Group 2006-15; Joint Chair of the Judges, International Property Awards 2013-; Vice-President, Town and Country Planning Association 2013-; Hon. Fellow RIBA 2001; Hon. Life Member, Chartered Institute of Housing 2003; Fellow, Academy of Social Sciences. Honorary degrees: Sheffield University 2006, York University 2008. Parliamentarian of the Year, CAB 2010; UK Social Policy Association Award 2012. OBE 1988; *Clubs:* Travellers Club, Farmers Club.

Publications: Contributor to various books and numerous articles for magazines and journals.

The Lord Best OBE, House of Lords, London SW1A 0PW
Tel: 020 7219 6799 *Email:* best@parliament.uk

BEW, LORD

CROSSBENCH

BEW (Life Baron), Paul Anthony Elliott; cr 2007. Born 22 January 1950; Son of Dr Kenneth Bew and Dr Mary Bew, née Leahy; Married Dr Greta Jones 1977 (1 son).

Education: Campbell College, Belfast; Pembroke College, Cambridge (BA modern history, MA; PhD 1974).

Non-political career: Humanities Lecturer, Ulster College 1975-79; Queen's University, Belfast 1979-: European and American History Lecturer 1979-84, Politics Lecturer 1984-87, Reader, Politics 1987-91, Professor of Politics 1991-, Emeritus Professor 2014-; Visiting Professor, King's College London 2015-.

Political career: *House of Lords:* Raised to the peerage as Baron Bew, of Donegore in the County of Antrim 2007. Member Joint Committees on: the Draft Defamation Bill 2011, Parliamentary Privilege 2013. *Councils and public bodies:* Chair, Committee on Standards in Public Life 2013-.

Political interests: Nationalism, foreign policy, education.

Other: Chairman: British-Irish Association 2007-13, Anglo-Israel Association 2007-; Member, British-Irish Parliamentary Assembly 2013-; Chairman, Key Stage 2 Assessment Review 2010-11; President, Airey Neave Trust 2013-; MRIA. Honorary Fellow, Pembroke College, Cambridge.

Recreations: Five-a-side football.

The Lord Bew, House of Lords, London SW1A 0PW
Tel: 020 7219 5353
GC05, 1 Horse Guards Road, London SW1A 0PW *Tel:* 020 7271 2948
Email: paul.bew@public-standards.gov.uk

NON-AFFILIATED

BHATIA, LORD

BHATIA (Life Baron), Amirali Alibhai Bhatia; cr. 2001. Born 18 March 1932; Married Nurbanu Amersi Kanji 1954 (3 daughters).

Education: Schools in Tanzania and India.

Non-political career: Chair and managing director, Forbes Campbell International Ltd 1980-2001; Director, Casley Finance Ltd 1985-2001.

Political career: *House of Lords:* Raised to the peerage as Baron Bhatia, of Hampton in the London Borough of Richmond upon Thames 2001. Suspended from membership October 2010-June 2011, April-December 2016. Member, Religious Offences 2002-03.

Countries of interest: Africa, Bangladesh, India, Middle East, Pakistan, Sri Lanka.

Other: Chair, Forbes Trust 1985-; Chair and Co-founder, Ethnic Minority Foundation 1999-2009; British Muslim Research Centre; British Edutrust Foundation; Vice-chair, India800 Foundation; FRSA; Oxfam, Ethnic Minority Foundation. UK Charity Awards Personality of the Year 2001; Beacon Prize 2003. OBE 1997; *Clubs:* Commonwealth Club, Institute of Directors.

Recreations: Swimming, walking, reading, music.

The Lord Bhatia OBE, House of Lords, London SW1A 0PW
Tel: 020 7219 5652 *Email:* bhatiaa@parliament.uk
Forbes House, 9 Artillery Lane, London E1 7LP *Tel:* 020 7377 8484 *Fax:* 020 7377 0032
Email: abhatia@casley.co.uk

LABOUR

BHATTACHARYYA, LORD

BHATTACHARYYA (Life Baron), Sushantha Kumar Bhattacharyya; cr. 2004. Born 6 June 1940; Son of Sudhir Bhattacharyya and Hemanalini, née Chakraborty; Married Brigid Carmel Rabbitt 1981 (3 daughters).

Education: IIT, Kharagpur (BTech mechanical engineering 1960); Birmingham University (MSc engineering production and management 1965; PhD engineering production 1970).

Non-political career: Production/industrial management, Lucas Industries Ltd 1961-67; Department of engineering, Birmingham University 1967-80; Professor of manufacturing and director, Warwick Manufacturing Group, Warwick University 1980-; Non-executive director, Technology Rover Group 1986-92; Member: National Consumer Council 1990-93, Council for Science and Technology 1993-2003.

Political career: *House of Lords:* Raised to the peerage as Baron Bhattacharyya, of Moseley in the County of West Midlands 2004. Co-opted Member, Science and Technology Sub-committee I (Waste Reduction) 2007-08. *Councils and public bodies:* West Midlands Regional Development Agency 1999-2003.

Political interests: Manufacturing, education, industry, innovation; China, India, Singapore, Turkey.

Other: Trustee, Institute for Public Policy Research 1997; Advisory Council, Nurse Review of UK Research Councils 2015; Fellow, RSA; FIEE 1975; FREng 1991; FILT 1996; CCMI 2003; Fellow, Royal Society 2014-. Hon. Freedom, City of Coventry 2015. Hon DUniv, Surrey University 1992; Hon DSc, UTM Malaysia 1997; Hon Doctor of Business Administration, Hong Kong Polytechnic University 2003; Hon DSc: Birmingham University 2004, IIT Kharagpur 2008, IIT Bhubaneswar 2013; Hon LLD, Monash University 2015. IEE Mensforth Gold Medal 1998; Sir Robert Lawrence Award, Institute of Logistics and Transport 1999; President of India Padma Bhusan 2002; IIT Kharagpur Distinguished Alumnus Award 2005. CBE 1997; Kt 2003; *Clubs:* Athenæum Club.

Recreations: Family, flying, cricket.

Professor the Lord Bhattacharyya CBE, House of Lords, London SW1A 0PW
Tel: 020 7219 2363 *Email:* senhn@parliament.uk
Warwick Manufacturing Group, Warwick University, Coventry CV4 7AL *Tel:* 024 7652 3155
Fax: 024 7652 4827 *Email:* wmgchairmanpa@warwick.ac.uk
Website: www2.warwick.ac.uk/fac/sci/wmg/people/chairman

CROSSBENCH

BICHARD, LORD

BICHARD (Life Baron), Michael George Bichard; cr 2010. Born 31 January 1947; Son of George and Nora Bichard; Married Gillian Guy 2008.

Education: King Edward VI Grammar School, Southampton; Manchester University (LLB, Hon Fellow 1968); Birmingham University (Master's social science 1973).

Non-political career: Solicitor; Chief executive: London Borough of Brent Council 1980-86, Gloucestershire County Council 1986-90, Social Security Benefits Agency 1990-95; Permanent secretary: Department for Employment 1995, Department for Education and Employment 1995-2001; Rector, London Institute/University of the Arts, London 2001-08; Chair, Rathbone Training Ltd 2001-08; Non-executive director, Reed Executive plc 2002-04; Director, River and Rowing Museum Foundation 2002-; Non-executive chair, RSe Consulting 2003-08; Chair: Soham Murders Inquiry 2004, Legal Services Commission 2005-08, Design Council 2008-12; Institute for Government: Director 2008-10, Senior fellow 2010-12; Chair: Social Care Institute for Excellence 2013-17, National Audit Office 2015-.

Political career: *House of Lords:* Raised to the peerage as Baron Bichard, of Nailsworth in the County of Gloucestershire 2010. Member, Leader's Group Reforming Working Practices 2010-11; Deputy Chair of Committees 2012-16. Member: Leader's Group on the Working Practices of the House of Lords 2010-11, Secondary Legislation Scrutiny 2012-15, Public Service and Demographic Change 2012-13, Charities 2016-17. *Councils and public bodies:* Vice-President, Local Government Association 2011-.

Political interests: Social policy, education, public service reform, child protection.

Other: Member, Economic and Social Research Council 1989-92; Chair, Film Club 2007; Henley Business School Strategy Board 2008-13; Chair: Shakespeare's Globe 2015-, Bristol Business School 2016-; Non-executive Director, The Key. Honorary Doctorates: Leeds Metropolitan University, Birmingham University, Bradford University, Middlesex University, Southampton Solent University, Cranfield University, Gloucestershire University, University of the West of England. KCB 1999.

Recreations: Food, gardening, Manchester United FC.

The Lord Bichard KCB, House of Lords, London SW1A 0PW
Tel: 020 7219 5353 *Email:* m.bichard@btinternet.com

CROSSBENCH

BILIMORIA, LORD

BILIMORIA (Life Baron), Karan Faridoon Bilimoria; cr 2006. Born 26 November 1961; Son of late Lt General Faridoon Noshir Bilimoria PVSM ADC and Yasmin Bilimoria; Married Heather Walker 1993 (2 sons 2 daughters).

Education: Hebron School, Lushington Hall, Ooty, India; Indian Institute of Management and Commerce, Osmania University, Hyderabad, India (BComm 1981); School of Business Studies, City of London Polytechnic (Diploma accounting 1982); ACA 1986; Sidney Sussex College, Cambridge (BA law 1988, MA) (Vice-president, Cambridge Union 1988); Cranfield University School of Management 1998; London Business School 2008; Harvard Business School 2011; French, Hindi.

Non-political career: Trainee and qualified chartered accountant, Ernst & Young 1982-86; Consulting accountant, Crevsale Ltd, London 1988; Sales and marketing director, European Accounting Focus magazine 1989; Cobra Beer: Founder 1989, Chief executive 1989-2007, Chair 2007-09; Founder, General Bilimoria Wines 1989-; Founder and publishing director, *Tandoori Magazine* 1994-2003; UK Chair, Indo British Partnership 2003-09; Non-executive director, Brake Brothers Ltd 2004-07; Visiting entrepreneur, Cambridge University 2004-; Member, advisory board, Boston Analytics, Boston, USA 2005-10; Senior independent director and non-executive director, Booker Group plc 2007-16; Visiting Professor, London Metropolitan University 2009; Chairman: Cobra Beer Partnership Limited 2009-, Molson Coors Cobra India Pvt Ltd 2011-; Vice-chair, Asian Business Association 2003-08; Chair: Faridoon Wines 2015-, PictoSo 2015-.

Political career: *House of Lords:* Raised to the peerage as Baron Bilimoria, of Chelsea in the Royal Borough of Kensington and Chelsea 2006. Member, Economic Affairs Finance Bill Subcommittee 2012-13, 2014, 2015-16, 2016-17. *Councils and public bodies:* Member: New Deal Task Force, Department for Education and Employment 1999-2001, National Employment Panel 2001-07; DL, Greater London 2001-; Representative DL, Hounslow 2005-10; Deputy President, London Chamber of Commerce 2008-10.

Political interests: Manufacturing and industry, armed forces, defence, economic affairs, business and finance, banking, higher education and universities, inter faith, capital and financial markets, culture and creativity, SMEs, EU; Commonwealth, EU, India, USA.

Other: Member, Prime Minister of India's Global Advisory Council 2009-; Chair, advisory board, Loomba Foundation 2001-; President's Committee, London First 2002-06; Vice-chair, Asian Business Association 2003-08; Patron, Rethink Severe Mental Illness 2003-; Ditchley Foundation: Governor 2004-11, Council member 2011-; Member: UK-India Round Table 2005-, Asia Task Force 2005-10, Advisory board, Birmingham Business School 2005-; Trustee, British Cardiac Research Trust 2006-; Commissioner, Royal Hospital, Chelsea 2006-12; Member, HRH The Duke of York's Business Advisory Council 2006-09; Adab Trust 2007-; UK-India Business Council: Chair 2007-09, President 2009-11; Trustee, British Cardiac Research Trust 2006-; Patron, Child in Need India (CINI) UK 2008-; Roundhouse Trust 2008-; Enterprise Leader, Princes Trust 2008-; Patron, Pratham UK 2008-; Deputy President, London Chamber of Commerce and Industry 2008-10; Advisory board, Judge Business School, Cambridge University: Member 2008-16, Chair 2016-; Member, advisory board, Cranfield School of Management 2009-; Chair, University of Cambridge India Partnership 2009-12; Trustee, St Paul's Cathedral Foundation 2011-; Member, World President's Organization 2012-; Vice Chancellor's Circle of Advisors for India, Cambridge University 2012-; Seven Hills 2013-; President, UKCISA 2015-; Chair, Manufacturing Commission 2016-; Ambassador, SkillForce 2016-; FCA 2002; Fellow, Institute of Directors 2005-; Companion, Chartered Management Institute 2005-; Hon. Life Fellow, RSA 2004; Hon. Fellow, Sidney Sussex College, Cambridge 2009-. Liveryman: Drapers' Company City of London 2008-, Brewers' Company City of London 2008-, Worshipful Company of Chartered Accountants in England and Wales 2010-. Freedom: City of London, Guild of Entrepreneurs 2015. Chancellor: Thames Valley University 2005-10, Birmingham University 2014-. Nine honorary doctorates; Hon. Fellow, Sidney Sussex College, Cambridge 2007. India Link International Indian of the Year Award. Non-resident Indian Millennium Honour 2001; CBE 2004; *Clubs:* Secunderabad Club, Hawks' Club, Cambridge, University Pitt Club, Cambridge, Kelvin Grove Club, Cape Town, South Africa, Carlton Club. Delhi Gymkhana; Delhi Golf Club; Guards Polo Club, Ascot.

Publications: Bottled for Business (Capstone, 2007); Against the Grain (Capstone, 2009).

Recreations: Reading, current affairs, travel, art, music, theatre, tennis, horse riding, golf, scuba diving, sailing.

The Lord Bilimoria CBE DL, House of Lords, London SW1A 0PW
Tel: 020 7219 6040 *Fax:* 020 7219 5979 *Email:* bilimoria@parliament.uk
Cobra Beer Partnership Limited, Welken House, 10-11 Charterhouse Square, London EC1M 6EH
Tel: 020 7788 2880 *Fax:* 020 7788 2895 *Email:* karan.bilimoria@cobrabeerpartnership.com
Website: www.lordbilimoria.co.uk *Twitter:* @Lord_Bilimoria

BILLINGHAM, BARONESS

LABOUR

BILLINGHAM (Life Baroness), Angela Theodora Billingham; cr. 2000. Born 31 July 1939; Daughter of late Theodore and Eva Case; Married Peter Billingham 1962 (died 1992) (2 daughters).

Education: Aylesbury Grammar School; College of Education (London); Department of Education, Oxford University (MEd).

Non-political career: Teacher 1960-90; Examiner for Education Board 1990-95; Chair, Catalyst Corby urban regeneration company 2001-07. Member: NUT, GMB.

Political career: *House of Commons:* Contested (Labour) Banbury 1992 general election. *House of Lords:* Raised to the peerage as Baroness Billingham, of Banbury in the County of Oxfordshire 2000. Opposition Spokesperson for Culture, Media and Sport 2010-13. Member: European Union 2000-05, EU Sub-committee D (Environment, Agriculture, Public Health and Consumer Protection/Environment and Agriculture) 2000-05, Draft Climate Change Bill Joint Committee 2007, Information 2008-10; Co-opted member, EU Sub-committee F (Home Affairs) 2009-10, Member: Olympic and Paralympic Legacy 2013-14, EU Sub-committee C: External Affairs 2014-16. Vice-chair PLP Departmental Committee for Culture, Media and Sport 2005-06. *Other:* European Parliament: MEP for Northamptonshire and Blaby 1994-99: Chief Whip, Socialist Group. *Councils and public bodies:* Councillor: Banbury Borough Council 1970-74, Cherwell District Council 1974-84: Leader of Labour Group; Mayor of Banbury 1976; JP 1976-; Councillor, Oxfordshire County Council 1993-94.

Political interests: Europe, education, health, sport, urban regeneration, planning; European Union, India, USA.

Other: Patron: Supporters Direct (football and all professional sport), CSCS (Centre for supporting comprehensive education in the UK); Chair: Banbury and District Sport for the Disabled, Early Education; Member, advisory board, Save the Children; Chair: Northampton Osteoporosis, Council for the Advancement of Arts, Recreation and Education (CAARE); One World, Oxfam, Imperial Cancer.

Recreations: Family, tennis, cinema, bridge, gardening.

The Baroness Billingham, House of Lords, London SW1A 0PW
Tel: 020 7219 5481 *Email:* a.billingham77@btinternet.com

CROSSBENCH

BIRD, LORD

BIRD (Life Baron), John Anthony Bird; cr 2015. Born 30 January 1946; Married 3rd Parveen Sodhi 2004 (1 son 1 daughter) (1 son 2 daughters from previous marriages).

Education: St Thomas More's Secondary Modern School; BA humanities.

Non-political career: Printer: Pictorial Charts Educational Trust 1974-75, Broadoak Press 1978-83; Print and publishing consultant 1983-91; Homelessness campaigner; Founder and Editor-in-Chief, *The Big Issue* 1991-; Founder: International Network of Street Papers 1994-, Big Issue Foundation 2005-; Director, The Big Issue Group 2005-; Social Enterprise Ambassador, Cabinet Office 2010-; Visiting Professor, Lincoln University 2015-.

Political career: *House of Lords:* Raised to the peerage as Baron Bird, of Notting Hill in the Royal Borough of Kensington and Chelsea 2015. Member, Lord Speaker's Advisory Panel on Works of Art 2017-.

Political interests: Arts and culture, economic empowerment, poverty alleviation.

Other: Director: Wedge Card Ltd, The Big Issue Digital Ltd, Burgeon Creative Ideas Ltd; Senior Fellow, Ashoka UK. MBE 1995.

Publications: Some Luck (autobiography, 2003).

The Lord Bird MBE, House of Lords, London SW1A 0PW
Tel: 020 7219 3000 *Email:* birdja@parliament.uk
Website: johnbird.co.uk *Twitter:* @johnbirdswords

NON-AFFILIATED

BIRMINGHAM, LORD BISHOP OF

BIRMINGHAM (9th Bishop of), David Andrew Urquhart. Born 14 April 1952.

Education: Croftinloan School, Perthshire; Rugby School; Ealing Business School (BA 1977); Wycliffe Hall, Oxford (1984).

Non-political career: Volunteer, Uganda 1971; BP plc 1972-82; Ordained Deacon 1984; Priest 1985; Curate, St Nicholas, Kingston-upon-Hull 1984-87; Vicar: Drypool 1987-92, Holy Trinity, Coventry 1992-2000; Hon. Canon, Coventry Cathedral 1999-2000; Bishop Suffragen of Birkenhead 2000-06; Prelate of the Most Distinguished Order of St Michael and St George 2005-; Archbishop of Canterbury's Envoy to China 2005-; Bishop of Birmingham 2006-.

Political career: *House of Lords:* Entered House of Lords 2010; Convenor of the Lords Spiritual 2015-. Member, Financial Exclusion 2016-17. *Councils and public bodies:* Governor, Rugby School 2001-; Chair, Ridley Hall Council, Cambridge 2011-.

Political interests: Local government, economy, foreign affairs; China, DR Congo, Malawi.

Other: Chair: Church Mission Society 1994-2008, Chester Diocese Education Board 2001-06; Trustee, Hippodrome Theatre, Birmingham 2009-; Church Mission Society, Institut Pan-Africain deSanté Communitaire, DR Congo. Hon Freedom, Metropolitan Borough of Wirral 2006. Hon DD, Birmingham University 2009; Hon DUniv, Birmingham City University 2014; *Clubs:* Athenæum Club. Jesters.

Recreations: Rugby fives, Scottish hill-walking.

Rt Rev the Lord Bishop of Birmingham, House of Lords, London SW1A 0PW
Tel: 020 7219 5353
Bishop's Croft, Old Church Road, Harborne, Birmingham B17 0BG *Tel:* 0121-427 1163
Fax: 0121-426 1322 *Email:* bishop@cofebirmingham.com *Website:* www.cofebirmingham.com
Twitter: @David_Urq

CROSSBENCH

BIRT, LORD

BIRT (Life Baron), John Birt; cr. 2000. Born 10 December 1944; Son of late Leo and Ida Birt; Married Jane Lake 1965 (divorced 2006) (1 son 1 daughter); married Eithne Wallis, CB 2006.

Education: St Mary's College, Liverpool; St Catherine's College, Oxford (BA engineering science 1966, MA).

Non-political career: Granada TV 1968-70: Producer, *Nice Time* 1968-69, Joint editor, *World in Action* 1969-70; London Weekend Television 1971-87: Producer, *The Frost Programme* 1971-72, Executive producer, *Weekend World* 1972-74, Head of current affairs 1974-77, Producer, *The Nixon Interviews* 1977, Controller of features and current affairs 1977-81, Director of programmes 1981-87; BBC 1987-2000: Deputy Director-General 1987-92, Director-General 1992-2000; Visiting Fellow, Nuffield College, Oxford 1991-99; Chairman, Lynx Capital Ventures 2000-04; Strategy adviser to Tony Blair as Prime Minister 2000-05; Adviser, McKinsey's Global Media Practice

2000-05; Member: Cabinet Office Strategy Board 2003-05, Civil Service Reform Programme Board 2004-05 PayPal (Europe) Ltd, an eBay subsidiary: Non-executive director 2004-10, Chair 2010-14; Non-executive director, Infinis 2006-13; Eutelsat: Non-executive director 2006-12, Vice-chairman 2012-; Adviser: Terra Firma 2006, Capgemini 2006-10; Chairman: Waste Recycling Group 2006, Maltby Capital (EMI Holding Company) 2007-10; Non-executive director, Shopcade 2011-17; Chairman: Host Europe Group 2013-17, CPA Global 2015-.

Political career: *House of Lords:* Raised to the peerage as Baron Birt, of Liverpool in the County of Merseyside 2000.

Political interests: Broadcasting, digital Britain, crime, transport, constitution, humanism, energy, public sector management, London; China, France, Japan, South Africa, USA.

Other: Member, Wilton Park Academic Council 1980-83; Royal Television Society: Fellow 1989, Vice-president 1994-2001; Member, Advisory Board, GovernUp 2014. Two honorary university fellowships, three honorary doctorates. Emmy Award, US National Academy of Television, Arts and Sciences 1995. Kt 1998; *Clubs:* Groucho Club, Ivy Club.

Publications: The Harder Path (2002).

Recreations: Walking, cinema, football.

The Lord Birt, House of Lords, London SW1A 0PW
Tel: 020 7219 8723 *Email:* gomesd@parliament.uk birtj@parliament.uk
Fielden House, 13 Little College Street, London SW1P 3SH

BLACK OF BRENTWOOD, LORD

CONSERVATIVE

BLACK OF BRENTWOOD (Life Baron), Guy Vaughan Black; cr 2010. Born 6 August 1964; Son of late Thomas and late Monica Black; Married Mark Bolland 2015.

Education: Brentwood School, Essex; Peterhouse, Cambridge (BA history 1985, MA).

Non-political career: Graduate trainee, corporate banking division, BZW 1985-86; Desk officer, Conservative Research Department 1986-89; Special adviser to Rt Hon John Wakeham MP as Secretary of State for Energy 1989-92; Account director, Westminster Strategy 1992-94; Associate director, Lowe Bell Good Relations 1994-96; Director, Press Complaints Commission 1996-2003; Press secretary to Rt Hon Michael Howard MP as Leader of the Opposition 2004-05; Director of Media, Conservative Central Office 2004-05; Telegraph Media Group: Corporate affairs director 2005-09, Executive director 2009-.

Political career: *House of Lords:* Raised to the peerage as Baron Black of Brentwood, of Brentwood in the County of Essex 2010. Member: Information 2011-15, Joint Committee on Privacy and Injunctions 2011-12, Sexual Violence in Conflict 2015-16. *Other:* Member, Association of Conservative Peers. *Councils and public bodies:* Councillor, Brentwood District Council 1988-92.

Political interests: Media and creative industries, health, education, energy, animal welfare; Commonwealth, Italy.

Other: Director, Advertising Standards Board of Finance 2005-; Press Standards Board of Finance: Director 2006-, Chair 2009-; Trustee: Sir Edward Heath's Charitable Foundation 2006-10, Imperial War Museum 2007-, Royal College of Music 2009-; Chair, Commonwealth Press Union Media Trust 2009-; Fellow, Royal Society of Arts; President: London Press Club 2012-, The Printing Charity 2013-; Member, Chartered Institute of Public Relations; Cats Protection, National Osteoporosis Society.

Recreations: Music, history.

The Lord Black of Brentwood, House of Lords, London SW1A 0PW
Tel: 020 7219 5353 *Email:* blackgv@parliament.uk
Website: www.guyblack.org.uk

BLACK OF CROSSHARBOUR, LORD

NON-AFFILIATED

BLACK OF CROSSHARBOUR (Life Baron), Conrad Moffat Black; cr 2001. Born 25 August 1944; Son of George M Black and Jean Elizabeth Riley; Married Shirley Gail Hishon 1978 (divorced 1992) (2 sons 1 daughter); married Barbara Amiel 1992.

Education: Carleton University, Canada (BA history and political science 1965); Laval University, Canada (LLL law 1970); McGill University, Canada (MA history 1973).

Non-political career: Co-founded, Sterling Newspapers Ltd 1971; Argus Corporation Ltd: President 1978-79, Chair 1979-2005; Chair: Telegraph Group Ltd, London 1985-2003, Hollinger Inc, USA 1985-2003, Hollinger Inc, Canada 1986-2004.

Political career: *House of Lords:* Raised to the peerage as Baron Black of Crossharbour, of Crossharbour in the London Borough of Tower Hamlets 2001. On leave of absence June 2012-.

Countries of interest: Canada.

Other: Hudson Institute; International Institute of Strategic Studies; Trilateral Commission on Foreign Relations (New York); National Interest (Washington); Nixon Centre (Washington); Member, Advisory Committee, Jubilee Appeal for Veterans; Honorary Chairman, Black Family Foundation. Four honorary doctorates from Canadian universities. Knight Commander of the Order of St Gregory the Great (Holy See) 2001; *Clubs:* Athenæum, Beefsteak, Garrick, Whites, Century (New York), Everglades (Palm Beach, Florida), Beach (Palm Beach, Florida), Toronto (Toronto), York (Toronto), Mount Royal (Montreal), University Club (Montreal).

Publications: Duplessis (1976) revised as Render unto Caesar (1998); A Life in Progress (1993); Franklin Delano Roosevelt, Champion of Freedom (2003); The Invincible Quest: The Life of Richard Milhous Nixon (2007); A Matter of Principle (2011); Flight of the Eagle: A Strategic History of the United States (2013).

The Lord Black of Crossharbour OC, House of Lords, London SW1A 0PW
Tel: 020 7219 5353
c/o 9 Montague Gardens, London W3 9PT ,
3044 Bloor St West, Suite 296, Toronto Ontario M8X 2Y8, Canada *Tel:* +1 416 241 7758
Fax: +1 416 241 5026 *Email:* dconnors@blackam.net *Twitter:* @ConradMBlack

BLACKSTONE, BARONESS

LABOUR

BLACKSTONE (Life Baroness), Tessa Ann Vosper Blackstone; cr. 1987. Born 27 September 1942; Daughter of late Geoffrey Blackstone and late Joanna Blackstone, née Vosper; Married Tom Evans 1963 (divorced 1975) (1 son 1 daughter).

Education: Ware Grammar School; London School of Economics (BScSoc sociology 1964; PhD 1969); Some French and German.

Non-political career: Associate Lecturer, Enfield College 1965-66; Assistant Lecturer then Lecturer, Department of Social Administration, London School of Economics 1966-75; Fellow, Centre for Studies in Social Policy 1972-74; Adviser, Central Policy Review Staff, Cabinet Office 1975-78; Professor of Educational Administration, University of London Institute of Education 1978-83; Deputy Education Officer (Resources), Inner London Education Authority 1983-86; Fellow, Policy Studies Institute 1987; Master, Birkbeck College, London University 1987-97; Vice-chancellor, Greenwich University 2004-11; Non-executive Director: Thames Television, VT Group 2004-10, Mott MacDonald 2005-08.

Political career: *House of Lords:* Raised to the peerage as Baroness Blackstone, of Stoke Newington in the County of Greater London 1987. Opposition Spokesperson for: Education and Science 1988-96, Treasury Matters 1990-91; Principal Opposition Spokesperson for Education and Science 1990-92; Opposition Spokesperson for Trade and Industry 1992-96; Principal Opposition Spokesperson for Foreign Affairs 1992-97; Minister of State and Government Spokesperson for: Department for Education and Employment (Minister of State for Education and Employment) 1997-2001, Department for Culture, Media and Sport (Minister of State for the Arts) 2001-03. Member: Public Service and Demographic Change 2012-13, Economic Affairs 2013-16, Sub-committee on Economic Affairs Finance Bill 2014-15, Long-Term Sustainability of the NHS 2016-17. *Councils and public bodies:* Chair, BBC General Advisory Council 1987-91; Chair and founder member, Institute for Public Policy Research 1988-97; Chair, British Library 2010-.

Political interests: Education, social policy, foreign affairs, arts; France, India, Palestine, USA.

Other: Royal Opera House: Board member 1987-97, 2009-14, Chair, Ballet Board 1991-97, Chair, Education and Access Committee 2011-; Trustee, Natural History Museum 1992-97; Chair: Royal Institute of British Architects Trust 2003-10, Great Ormond Street Hospital Trust 2009-17, Orbit Group 2013-, of trustees, Franco-British Council 2013-, British Lung Foundation 2017-; Vice-president VSO, Patron Why Me?. Twelve honorary doctorates; Three honorary fellowships. Lifetime Award for Higher Education, *The Times* Higher Education awards 2011. PC 2001; Legion d'Honneur 2016.

Publications: A Fair Start (1971); Co-author: Students in Conflict (1967), The Academic Labour Market (1974), Educational Policy and Educational Inequality (1982), Disadvantage and Education (1982), Response to Adversity (1983), Inside the Think Tank: Advising the Cabinet 1971-84 (1988); Author, Prison and Penal Reform (1992); Co-edited, Race Relations in Britain (1998).

Recreations: Tennis, walking, ballet, opera, cinema.

Rt Hon the Baroness Blackstone, House of Lords, London SW1A 0PW
Tel: 020 7219 5409 *Email:* blackstonet@parliament.uk
The British Library, 96 Euston Road, London NW1 2DB *Tel:* 020 7412 7262

CONSERVATIVE

BLACKWELL, LORD

BLACKWELL (Life Baron), Norman Roy Blackwell; cr. 1997. Born 29 July 1952; Son of Albert and Frances Blackwell; Married Brenda Clucas 1974 (3 sons 2 daughters).

Education: Latymer Upper School, London; Royal Academy of Music (Junior Exhibitioner); Trinity College, Cambridge (BA natural sciences 1973, MA); Wharton Business School, University of Pennsylvania (AM, MBA 1975; PhD finance and economics 1976).

Non-political career: Plessey Company 1976-78; McKinsey & Co 1978-95: Partner 1984-95; Prime Minister's Policy Unit: Special adviser 1986-87, Head 1995-97; Director: Group Development, NatWest Group 1997-2000, Dixons Group 2000-03; Special adviser, KPMG Corporate Finance 2000-08; Director: Corporate Services Group 2000-06, SEGRO plc (formerly Slough Estates) 2001-10, SmartStream Technologies Ltd 2001-06; Chair, Akers Biosciences Inc 2002-03; Director, Standard Life Assurance 2003-12; Chair, Interserve plc 2006-16; Director: Halma plc 2010-14; Lloyds Banking Group plc: Director 2012-, Chairman 2014-; Chair, Scottish Widows Group Ltd 2012-14.

Political career: *House of Lords:* Raised to the peerage as Baron Blackwell, of Woodcote in the County of Surrey 1997. Member: Joint Committee on Tax Simplification 2001-, EU Sub-committee A (Economic and Financial Affairs) 2003-07, Economic Affairs Sub-committee on the Finance Bill 2004–10, European Union 2005-08, Joint Committee on Tax Law Rewrite Bills 2005-10; EU Sub-committee E (Law and Institutions): Member 2007-08, Co-opted member 2008-10; Member: Delegated Powers and Regulatory Reform 2008-13, EU Sub-committee E (Justice and Institutions) 2010-12, Secondary Legislation Scrutiny 2013-14. *Councils and public bodies:* Board member, Office of Fair Trading 2003-10; Office of Communications (Ofcom): Non-executive board member 2009-14, Member, content board 2012-14.

Political interests: Economic policy and taxation, public services, European Union.

Other: Chair: Centre for Policy Studies 2000-09, Global Vision 2007-09; Governor, Yehudi Menuhin School 2016-; *Clubs:* Carlton, Royal Automobile Club.

Publications: Funding the Basic State Pension (CPS, 2001); Towards Smaller Government (CPS, 2001); Better Healthcare for all (CPS, 2002); A defining moment? – the European Constitutional Convention (CPS, 2003); Freedom annd Responsibility: A manifesto for a smaller state, bolder nation! (CPS, 2003); What if Britain says No to the EU Constitution? (CPS, 2004); Better Schools and Hospitals – Why parent and patient choice will work (CPS, 2004); Sleepwalking into an EU Legal System (CPS, 2006); From principle to policy – an outline manifesto (CPS, 2006); Three cheers for selection – How Grammar Schools help the poor (CPS, 2007).

Recreations: Classical music, walking.

The Lord Blackwell, House of Lords, London SW1A 0PW
Tel: 020 7219 8672 *Email:* blackwelln@parliament.uk
Tel: 020 7356 1390 *Fax:* 020 7356 2323 *Email:* blackwelln@parliament.uk

CROSSBENCH

BLAIR OF BOUGHTON, LORD

BLAIR OF BOUGHTON (Life Baron), Ian Warwick Blair; cr 2010. Born 19 March 1953; Married Felicity White 1980 (1 son 1 daughter).

Education: Wrekin College, Shropshire; Harvard High School, Los Angeles, USA; Christ Church, Oxford (BA English language and literature 1974, MA).

Non-political career: Metropolitan Police: Police Constable, Sergeant, then Inspector (uniform and CID) 1974-85, Detective Chief Inspector, CID, Kentish Town 1985-88, Manager, Crime Investigation Project 1988-89, Superintendent, Kensington Division 1989-91, Chief Superintendent and Staff Officer to HM Chief Inspector of Constabulary, Home Office 1991-93, Officer in charge of Operation Gallery 1993-96, Deputy Commissioner 2000-05, Commissioner 2005-08; Thames Valley Police: Assistant Chief Constable 1994-97, Deputy Chief Constable 1997-98; Chief Constable, Surrey Police 1998-2000.

Political career: *House of Lords:* Raised to the peerage as Baron Blair of Boughton, of Boughton in the County of Cheshire 2010. Member: EU Sub-committee E (Justice, Institutions and Consumer Protection) 2013-15, European Union 2015-16, EU Justice Sub-committee 2015-16, Licensing Act 2003 2016-17. *Councils and public bodies:* Commissioner, Commission on Assisted Dying 2010-.

Countries of interest: India.

Other: Visiting fellow: International Centre for Advanced Studies, New York University 1998, Nuffield College, Oxford 2001; Visiting Professor, John Jay College, New York 2010; Chairman: Thames Valley Partnership, Woolf Foundation for the Study of Abrahamic Faiths; Trustee:

Michael Sieff Foundation, Shakespeare's Globe, Longford Trust; Chair, Woolf Institute for the Study of Relationships Between Jews, Christians and Muslims 2015-. Hon. LLD, Lincoln University 2013. QPM 1998; Kt 2003; *Clubs:* MCC, Athenæum Club.

Publications: Author: Investigating Rape: A New Approach for Police (1985); Policing Controversy (Profile Books, 2009).

Recreations: Theatre, opera, tennis.

The Lord Blair of Boughton QPM, House of Lords, London SW1A 0PW
Tel: 020 7219 5353

BLENCATHRA, LORD

CONSERVATIVE

BLENCATHRA (Life Baron), David John Maclean; cr 2011. Born 16 May 1953.

Education: Fortrose Academy; Aberdeen University.

Non-political career: Director, Cayman Islands Government Office, London 2011-14.

Political career: *House of Commons:* MP (Conservative) for Penrith and The Border 1983 by-election to 2010. Assistant Government Whip 1987-89; Government Whip 1988-89; Parliamentary Secretary, Ministry of Agriculture, Fisheries and Food 1989-92; Minister of State: Department of the Environment 1992-93, Home Office 1993-97; Opposition Chief Whip 2001-03, 2003-05; Member House of Commons Commission 2006. Chair, Joint Committee on Statutory Instruments 2006; Member, Liaison 2006. *House of Lords:* Raised to the peerage as Baron Blencathra, of Penrith in the County of Cumbria 2011. Member: EU Sub-committee F: (Home Affairs) 2011-12, (Home Affairs, Health and Education) 2012-15, Procedure 2012-15; Chair: Joint Committee on the Draft Communications Data Bill 2012-13, Delegated Powers and Regulatory Reform 2017-. *Other:* Vice-President, Conservatives for Britain 2015-16.

Other: PC 1995.

Rt Hon the Lord Blencathra, House of Lords, London SW1A 0PW
Tel: 020 7219 5353

BLOOD, BARONESS

LABOUR

BLOOD (Life Baroness), May Blood; cr. 1999. Born 26 May 1938; Daughter of late William and Mary Blood.

Education: Linfield Secondary, Belfast.

Non-political career: Cutting supervisor, Blackstaff Mill 1952-90; Community worker, Great Shankill Partnership 1990-98. Member, TGWU: Shop steward 1968-90, Senior steward 1980-90, Regional committee 1980, 1990.

Political career: *House of Lords:* Raised to the peerage as Baroness Blood, of Blackwatertown in the County of Armagh 1999. Member, Social Mobility 2015-16. *Councils and public bodies:* Member of Senate, Queen's University Belfast 2000-07.

Political interests: Women's issues, low pay, working class issues, family, children.

Other: Member, British-Irish Parliamentary Assembly; Chair: Impact Training 1994-2014, Shankill Sure Start 1997-, Barnados Northern Ireland 2000-09; Trustee, Barnados UK 2000-09; Chair, Integrated Education Fund 2002-; Trustee, Ulster Historical Society 2010-; Citizen's Global Circle, Boston; Centre Point, Art Ability (NI). Honorary doctorates: Ulster University 1998, Queens University, Belfast 2001, Open University 2002; Fellow, National College Dublin 2004. Catherine Dunpfy Peace Global Citizens Awards 1997; Frank Cousins Peace Award 1999; Irish Woman of the Year 2006; Grassroots Diplomat Award 2012. MBE 1995.

Publications: Autobiography, Watch My Lips, I'm Speaking (Gill & Macmillan, 2008).

Recreations: Reading, gardening.

The Baroness Blood MBE, House of Lords, London SW1A 0PW
Tel: 020 7219 8700 *Email:* bloodm@parliament.uk
Alessie Centre, 60 Shankhill Road, Belfast BT13 2BD *Tel:* 028 9087 4000 *Fax:* 028 9087 4009
Email: wendy@earlyyears.org.uk

CONSERVATIVE

BLOOMFIELD OF HINTON WALDRIST, BARONESS

BLOOMFIELD OF HINTON WALDRIST (Life Baroness), Olivia Caroline Bloomfield; cr 2016. Born 30 June 1960; Married Andrew 1984 (1 son 2 daughters).

Education: Atlantic College; St Hugh's college, Oxford (BA philosophy, politics and economics 1982).

Non-political career: Bank of America 1982-86; Russell Reynolds Associates 1986-93; Chief of Staff to Michael Spencer as Treasurer of CCHQ 2006-10; Partner: Atlantic Superconnection Corporation -2016, Partner of Disruptive Capital Finance 2010-.

Political career: *House of Lords:* Raised to the peerage as Baroness Bloomfield of Hinton Waldrist, of Hinton Waldrist in the County of Oxfordshire 2016. Conservative Party Whip 2017-. Member, Joint Committee on Statutory Instruments 2017-. *Other:* Chairman, Wantage Conservative Group 2002-15. *Councils and public bodies:* Governor, Cheltenham Ladies College 2003-09.

Other: Chair, Pump House Project 2013-.

The Baroness Bloomfield of Hinton Waldrist, House of Lords, London SW1A 0PW
Tel: 020 7219 3000 *Email:* bloomfieldo@parliament.uk

LABOUR

BLUNKETT, LORD

BLUNKETT (Life Baron), David Blunkett; cr 2015. Born 6 June 1947; Son of late Arthur and Doris Blunkett; Married Ruth Gwynneth Mitchell 1970 (divorced 1990) (3 sons); (1 son); married Dr Margaret Williams 2009 (3 stepdaughters).

Education: Royal National Normal College for the Blind; Shrewsbury Technical College; Sheffield Richmond College of Further Education (day release and evening courses); Sheffield University (BA political theory and institutions 1972); Huddersfield College of Education (PGCE 1973); Esperanto.

Non-political career: Office work, East Midlands Gas Board 1967-69; Tutor in industrial relations and politics, Barnsley College of Technology 1973-81. Shop steward, GMB EMGB 1967-69; Member: NATFHE 1973-87, Unison 1973-.

Political career: *House of Commons:* Contested (Labour) Sheffield Hallam February 1974 general election. MP for Sheffield Brightside 1987-2010, for Sheffield Brightside and Hillsborough 2010-15. Opposition Spokesperson for Local Government 1988-92; Shadow Secretary of State for: Health 1992-94, Education 1994-95, Education and Employment 1995-97; Secretary of State for Education and Employment 1997-2001; Home Secretary 2001-04; Secretary of State for Work and Pensions 2005. *House of Lords:* Raised to the peerage as Baron Blunkett, of Brightside and Hillsborough in the City of Sheffield 2015. Member, Citizenship and Civic Engagement 2017-. *Other:* Labour Party: Member, National Executive Committee 1983-98, Vice-chair 1992-93, Chair 1993-94. *Councils and public bodies:* Councillor, Sheffield City Council 1970-88, Chair, Social Services Committee 1976-80, Leader 1980-87; Councillor, South Yorkshire County Council 1973-77; Former chair, Race Relations Forum.

Political interests: Local government, employment and welfare to work, citizenship and civil renewal; France, USA.

Other: Former Council Member, Guide Dogs for the Blind Association; Former Trustee, Community Service Volunteers; Fellow, Industry and Parliament Trust 1991; Vice-president, Alzheimer's Society 2009; Patron, Society of Occupational Medicine; Board Member, National Citizens Service; Guide Dogs for the Blind. Honorary Doctorate: Haifa University, Israel 2005, Sheffield University 2016; Fellow, Sheffield Hallam University. PC 1997.

Publications: Building from the Bottom (1983); Democracy in Crisis – the Town Halls Respond (1987); On a Clear Day (autobiography) (1995, 2002); Politics and Progress (2001); The Blunkett Tapes – My Life in the Bear Pit (2006).

Recreations: Walking, sailing, music, poetry.

Rt Hon the Lord Blunkett, House of Lords, London SW1A 0PW
Tel: 020 7219 3000

BLYTH OF ROWINGTON, LORD

CONSERVATIVE

BLYTH OF ROWINGTON (Life Baron), James Blyth; cr. 1995. Born 8 May 1940; Son of Daniel and Jane Blyth; Married Pamela Campbell Dixon 1967 (1 daughter and 1 son deceased).

Education: Spiers School; Glasgow University (BA history 1963, MA); Competent French.

Non-political career: Mobil Oil Company 1963-69; General Foods Ltd 1969-71; Mars Ltd 1971-74; General manager: Lucas Batteries Ltd 1974-77, Lucas Aerospace Ltd 1977-81; Head of defence sales, Ministry of Defence 1981-85; Non-executive director, Imperial Group plc 1984-86; Managing director, Plessey Electronic Systems 1985-86; Chief Executive, Plessey Co plc 1986-87; Non-executive director, Cadbury-Schweppes plc 1986-90; Boots Company plc: Director and chief executive 1987-2000, Deputy Chair 1994-98, Chair 1998-2000; Non-executive director: British Aerospace 1990-94, Anixter Inc 1995-; Director, NatWest Group 1998-2000; Diageo plc: Director 1999-, Chair 2000-08; Greenhill and Company: Senior adviser 2000-02, 2007-15, Partner 2002-07; Vice-chair, Middlebrook Pharmaceuticals Inc 2008-10; Chair, GreyCastle Holdings 2014-.

Political career: *House of Lords:* Raised to the peerage as Baron Blyth of Rowington, of Rowington in the County of Warwickshire 1995. On leave of absence March 2013-. *Councils and public bodies:* Governor, London Business School 1987-96; Chair, Advisory panel on Citizen's Charter 1991-97.

Political interests: Business, economics, pensions; Central and Latin America, Middle East, USA.

Other: President, Middle East Association 1988-93; Patron, Combined Services Winter Sports Association 1997-2002. Liveryman, Coachmakers' and Coach Harness Makers' Company. Hon. LLD, Nottingham University 1992; Hon. Fellow, London Business School 1997. Kt 1985; *Clubs:* East India Club, Devonshire, Sports and Public Schools, RAC, Caledonian Club. Blackwell Golf Club.

Recreations: Skiing, tennis, paintings, theatre, horses, golf.

The Lord Blyth of Rowington, House of Lords, London SW1A 0PW
Tel: 020 7219 5353
Email: blyth08@googlemail.com

BOATENG, LORD

LABOUR

BOATENG (Life Baron), Paul Yaw Boateng; cr 2010. Born 14 June 1951; Son of Kwaku Boateng, barrister, and Eleanor Boateng, teacher; Married Janet Alleyne 1980 (2 sons 3 daughters).

Education: Achimota School, Ghana; Accra Academy, Ghana; Apsley Grammar School, Ghana; Bristol University (LLB 1972); College of Law (solicitor 1975); French (colloquial).

Non-political career: Solicitor 1975; Barrister-at-law; High Commissioner, South Africa 2005-09; Advisory Board, Aegis; Chair, advisory board, Aventa Capital Partners; Member: Health policy advisory board, Gilead Sciences Inc, Non-executive director, 4G Africa AG; Director, Akyen Law and Advisory Science Ltd. Member, GMB.

Political career: *House of Commons:* Contested Hertfordshire West 1983 general election. MP (Labour) for Brent South 1987-2005. Opposition Frontbench Spokesperson on: Treasury and Economic Affairs 1989-92, Lord Chancellor's Department 1992-97; Parliamentary Under-Secretary of State, Department of Health 1997-98; Home Office: Minister of State (Minister for Criminal Policy) 1998-99, Minister of State and Deputy Home Secretary 1999-2001; Minister for Young People 2000-01; HM Treasury 2001-05: Financial Secretary 2001-02, Chief Secretary 2002-05. Member, Public Accounts 2001-02. *House of Lords:* Raised to the peerage as Baron Boateng, of Akyem in the Republic of Ghana and of Wembley in the London Borough of Brent 2010. Member, Joint Committee on National Security Strategy 2014-. *Other:* Member: Labour Party NEC Human Rights sub-committee 1979-83, Labour Party Joint Committee on Crime and Policing 1984-86. *Councils and public bodies:* Member Greater London Council 1981-86: Chair, Police Committee 1981-86, Vice-chair, Ethnic Minority Committee 1981-86; Governor: Museum of London 2009-, London School of Economics 2011.

Political interests: Home affairs, housing, inner cities, overseas aid and development, environment, children and young people's policy; Africa, Caribbean, Southern Africa, USA.

Other: Chair: Afro-Caribbean Education Resource Project 1978-84, Westminster Community Relations Council 1979-81; Legal adviser, Scrap Sus Campaign 1977-81; Home Office Advisory Council on Race Relations 1981-86; World Council of Churches Commission on programme to combat racism 1984-91; Vice-Moderator 1984-91; Police Training Council 1981-85; Executive NCCL 1980-86; Governor, Police Staff College Bramshill 1981-84; Board of English National

Opera 1984-97; Governor, Ditchley Park 2007-11; Board of Governors, English Speaking Union 2009-; Board member, Food for the Hungry 2009-; Trustee, Duke of Edinburgh International Youth Award 2009-; Non-executive director, Ghana International Bank plc London; Member, Gray's Inn. DL, Lincoln College, Philadelphia, USA; LLD, Bristol University. PC 1999.

Publications: Contributor, Reclaiming the Ground; Introduction to Sense and Sensibility: The Complete Jane Austen.

Recreations: Family, swimming, opera.

Rt Hon the Lord Boateng, House of Lords, London SW1A 0PW
Tel: 020 7219 5353 *Email:* boatengp@parliament.uk

BONHAM-CARTER OF YARNBURY, BARONESS

LIBERAL DEMOCRAT

Liberal Democrat Lords Spokesperson for Digital, Culture, Media and Sport

BONHAM-CARTER OF YARNBURY (Life Baroness), Jane Bonham Carter; cr. 2004. Born 20 October 1957; Daughter of Mark Bonham Carter and Leslie Nast; Partner Lord Razzall (qv).

Education: St Paul's Girls' School, London; University College, London (BA philosophy).

Non-political career: Producer, BBC Television's *Panorama* and *Newsnight* 1988-93; Editor, *A Week in Politics*, Channel Four 1993-96; Director of communications, Liberal Democrat Party 1996-98; Independent television producer, Brook Lapping Productions 1998-2004; Associate, Brook Lapping Productions, Ten Alps plc 2004-09.

Political career: *House of Lords:* Raised to the peerage as Baroness Bonham-Carter of Yarnbury, of Yarnbury in the County of Wiltshire 2004. Liberal Democrat Spokesperson for Culture, Media and Sport (Broadcasting and the Arts) 2004-10; Deputy Convener of the Liberal Democrat Peers 2010-15; Prime Minister's Trade Envoy to Mexico 2012-; Liberal Democrat: Principal Spokesperson for Culture, Media and Sport 2010-15, Shadow Secretary of State/Lords Spokesperson for: Culture, Media and Sport 2015-, Digital 2017-. Member: EU Sub-committee F (Home Affairs) 2004-07, Review of the BBC Charter 2005-06, Communications 2007-10, 2015-, Joint Committee on Privacy and Injunctions 2011-12, EU Sub-committee C: (Foreign Affairs, Defence and Development Policy) 2010-12, (External Affairs) 2012-15. Chair, Liberal Democrat Parliamentary Party Committee on Culture, Media and Sport 2010-15. *Other:* Member, Liberal Democrats Campaigns and Communications Committee 1998-2006.

Countries of interest: America, Ethiopia, Italy, Mexico, Zimbabwe.

Other: Advisory committee, Centre Forum 1998-2015; Council member, Britain in Europe 1998-2005; Member: RAPt Rehabilitation of Addicted Prisoners Trust 1999-, Referendum Campaign team 2004-05; Trustee, The Lowry 2011-; Board member, National Campaign for the Arts 2010-12. Visiting Parliamentary Fellow of St Antony's College, Oxford 2013-14; *Clubs:* Academicians' Room Royal Academy of Arts, Groucho Club.

The Baroness Bonham-Carter of Yarnbury, House of Lords, London SW1A 0PW
Tel: 020 7219 2717 *Email:* bonhamcarterj@parliament.uk *Twitter:* @jbonham_carter

BOOTHROYD, BARONESS

CROSSBENCH

BOOTHROYD (Life Baroness), Betty Boothroyd; cr. 2001. Born 8 October 1929; Daughter of late Archibald and Mary Boothroyd.

Education: Dewsbury College of Commerce and Art.

Non-political career: Personal/political assistant to: Barbara Castle MP 1956-58, Lord Walston as Minister of State, Foreign and Commonwealth Office 1962-73; Legislative assistant, US congressman Silvio O Conte 1960-62.

Political career: *House of Commons:* Contested Leicester South East 1957 by-election, Peterborough 1959 general election, Nelson and Colne 1968 by-election and Rossendale 1970 general election. MP for West Bromwich 1973-74, for West Bromwich West 1974-2000 (Labour 1973-92, Speaker 1992-2000). Assistant Government Whip 1974-76; Second Deputy Chairman of Ways and Means and Deputy Speaker 1987-92; Speaker 1992-2000; Chairman, House of Commons Commission 1992-2000. *House of Lords:* Raised to the peerage as Baroness Boothroyd, of Sandwell in the County of West Midlands 2001. *Other:* European Parliament: MEP 1975-77. Member, National Executive Committee, Labour Party 1981-87. *Councils and public bodies:* Councillor, Hammersmith Borough Council 1965-68.

Political interests: Constitutional affairs; Commonwealth.

Other: Patron: London International Orchestra 2000-, National Benevolent Fund for the Aged 2009-, Commonwealth Countries League 2011-14, CHICKS (Country Holidays for Inner City Kids) 2012-, David Nott Foundation 2016-; Memorial to the Women of World War Two, Friends of the Elderly, London Trust, Silver Trust. Worshipful Company of: Feltmakers 1994, Glovers of London 2001 (Special Member), Lightmongers 2001 (Special Member), Grocers 2005 (Honorary Member). Freedom: Metropolitan Borough of Sandwell, Metropolitan Borough of Kirklees, City of London. Chancellor, Open University 1994-2006. Ten honorary degrees, including Oxford, Cambridge and St Andrews; Honorary Master of the Bench, Middle Temple 2011. *The Spectator*: Parliamentarian of the Year Award 1992, Personality of the Year 1993, Communicator of the Year 1994; Lifetime Achievement, *House Magazine* awards 2012. PC 1992; OM 2005; *Clubs:* Reform Club, University Women's Club.

Publications: The Autobiography Betty Boothroyd (2001).

Recreations: Gardening.

Rt Hon the Baroness Boothroyd OM, House of Lords, London SW1A 0PW
Tel: 020 7219 3000 *Email:* boothroyd@parliament.uk

CONSERVATIVE

BORWICK, LORD

BORWICK (5th Baron, UK) Geoffrey Robert James (Jamie) Borwick; cr 1922; 5th Bt of Eden Lacy (UK) 1916. Born 7 March 1955; Son of late Hon. Robin Sandbach Borwick; Married Victoria Lorne Peta Borwick 1981, London Assembly Member 2008-15, Deputy Mayor of London 2012-15, MP for Kensington 2015-17 (3 sons 1 daughter).

Education: Eton College.

Non-political career: Sir Robert McAlpine & Sons Ltd 1972-81; Non-executive director, Hansa Trust plc 1984-2012; Manganese Bronze Holdings plc: Chief executive officer 1987-2001, Chair 2001-03; Chair, Federated Trust Corporation Ltd 1987-.

Political career: *House of Lords:* Elected hereditary peer 2013-. Member: Secondary Legislation Scrutiny 2014-15, European Union 2015-16, EU Financial Affairs Sub-committee 2015-16, Science and Technology 2016-.

Political interests: Business, economy, planning, transport; USA.

Other: Trustee: Federated Foundation 1985-, Ewing Foundation 1985-, British Lung Foundation 2001-08, 2011-16, Royal Brompton and Harefield Charity 2012-; Fellow, Ewing Foundation; *Clubs:* Garrick Club.

Recreations: Travel, swimming, walking.

The Lord Borwick, House of Lords, London SW1A 0PW
Email: borwickgr@parliament.uk

NON-AFFILIATED

BOSWELL OF AYNHO, LORD

Principal Deputy Chairman of Committees

BOSWELL OF AYNHO (Life Baron), Timothy Eric Boswell; cr 2010. Born 2 December 1942; Son of late Eric Boswell and Joan Boswell; Married Helen Delahay 1969, née Rees (3 daughters, including Victoria Prentis (qv) MP for Banbury).

Education: Marlborough College, Wiltshire; New College, Oxford (BA classics 1965, MA; Diploma agricultural economics 1966); French, German, Italian.

Non-political career: Conservative Research Department 1966-73: Head, economic section 1970-73; Farmer 1974-87; Part-time special adviser to Minister of Agriculture 1984-86. Chair, Leicestershire, Northamptonshire and Rutland NFU County Branch 1983.

Political career: *House of Commons:* Contested Rugby February 1974 general election. MP (Conservative) for Daventry 1987-2010. PPS to Peter Lilley as Financial Secretary to Treasury 1989-90; Assistant Government Whip 1990-92; Government Whip 1992; Parliamentary Under-Secretary of State, Department for Education 1992-95; Parliamentary Secretary, Ministry of Agriculture, Fisheries and Food 1995-97; Opposition Spokesperson for: the Treasury 1997, Trade and Industry 1997-99, Education 1999-2001, Work and Pensions (People with Disabilities) 2001; Shadow Minister for: Education and Skills (People with Disabilities) 2002-03, Home, Constitutional and Legal Affairs 2003-04, Home Affairs 2004, Work and Pensions 2004-06, Welfare Reform 2004-05; PPS to Francis Maude as Chairman, Conservative Party 2005-07. Member: Innovation, Universities[, Science] and Skills/Science and Technology 2007-10. Member, Executive, 1922 Committee 2007-10. *House of Lords:* Raised to the peerage as Baron Boswell of Aynho, of Aynho in the County of Northamptonshire 2010. Principal Deputy Chairman of Committees

2012-. Chair, European Union 2012-. *Other:* Chair, Daventry Constituency Conservative Association 1979-83; Acting Chairman, Milton Keynes Conservatives 2009-10. *Councils and public bodies:* Member, Agriculture and Food Research Council 1988-90; DL, Northamptonshire 2010-.

Political interests: Agriculture, finance, European Union, education, equalities; Europe.

Other: Perry Foundation: Council member 1967-90, President 1984-90; Governor: University of Wales Institute, Cardiff 2007-12, Northampton University 2010-12; Fellow: City and Guilds Institutes, Society of Antiquaries of London; *Clubs:* Farmers Club.

Recreations: Shooting.

The Lord Boswell of Aynho, House of Lords, London SW1A 0PW
Tel: 020 7219 7291 *Email:* boswellte@parliament.uk

BOTTOMLEY OF NETTLESTONE, BARONESS

CONSERVATIVE

BOTTOMLEY OF NETTLESTONE (Life Baroness), Virginia Hilda Brunette Maxwell Bottomley; cr 2005. Born 12 March 1948; Daughter of late W. John Garnett, CBE; Married Peter Bottomley (qv) 1967 (later Sir Peter, MP for Worthing West) (1 son 2 daughters).

Education: Putney High School; Essex University (BA sociology); London School of Economics (MSc social administration 1975).

Non-political career: Behavioural scientist 1971-84; Executive director, Odgers Berndston (executive search) 2000-; Member, Supervisory Board, Akzo Nobel NV 2000-12; NED; BUPA 2007-13; Non-executive director, Smith & Nephew 2012-.

Political career: *House of Commons:* Contested Isle of Wight 1983 general election. MP (Conservative) for South West Surrey 1984 by-election to 2005. PPS: to Chris Patten as Minister of State: Department of Education and Science 1985-86, Overseas Development Administration 1986-87, to Sir Geoffrey Howe as Foreign Secretary 1987-88; Parliamentary Under-Secretary of State, Department of Environment 1988-89; Department of Health: Minister of State 1989-92, Secretary of State 1992-95; Secretary of State for National Heritage 1995-97. *House of Lords:* Raised to the peerage as Baroness Bottomley of Nettlestone, of St Helens in the County of Isle of Wight 2005. *Councils and public bodies:* Magistrate, Inner London Juvenile Courts 1975-84; Chairman, Lambeth Juvenile Court 1980-84; Governor, London School of Economics 1985-; Chair, Millennium Commission 1995-97; Government Co-chair, Women's National Commission 1991-92; Vice-chair, British Council 1997-2001; Governor, University of the Arts, London 1999-2004; DL, Surrey 2006; Sheriff of Hull 2013-; Member, State Honours Committee.

Political interests: Health, universities, prison reform, diversity, business enterprise, regulatory reform, children and family policy; China, India, Japan, Netherlands.

Other: Fellow, Industry and Parliament Trust 1987; Council member: Ditchley Foundation 1991-, Prince of Wales International Business Leaders Forum 2002-09; Lay Canon, Guildford Cathedral 2002-; President: Farnham Castle (Centre for International Briefing) 2003-, Abbeyfield Society 2004-09; International Chamber of Commerce, UK Advisory Council 2004-; Advisory Council, Cambridge Judge Business School 2004-09; Trustee, *The Economist* 2005-. Freedom, City of London 1988. Pro-chancellor, Surrey University 2005-15; Chancellor, Hull University 2006-. Honorary LLD, Portsmouth University 1993; Honorary doctorate, Aston University. PC 1992; *Clubs:* Athenæum Club.

Publications: Various articles on criminal justice, poverty, children and corporate governance.

Recreations: Grandchildren.

Rt Hon the Baroness Bottomley of Nettlestone DL, House of Lords, London SW1A 0PW
Tel: 020 7219 5060 *Email:* bottomleyv@parliament.uk

BOURNE OF ABERYSTWYTH, LORD

CONSERVATIVE

Parliamentary Under-Secretary of State (Minister for Faith) and Government Spokesperson, Department for Communities and Local Government and Parliamentary Under-Secretary of State and Government Spokesperson, Northern Ireland Office

BOURNE OF ABERYSTWYTH (Life Baron), Nicholas Henry Bourne; cr 2013. Born 1 January 1952; Son of late John Morgan Bourne, systems engineer, and late Joan Mary Bourne, housewife.

Education: King Edward VI School, Chelmsford; University College of Wales, Aberystwyth (LLB law 1973; LLM 1976); Trinity College, Cambridge (LLM 1975); Honourable Society of Gray's Inn (Barrister-at-Law 1976); French.

Non-political career: Supervisor in law: Corpus Christi College, Cambridge 1974-82, St Catharine's College, Cambridge 1974-82, London School of Economics 1975-77; Principal, Chart University Tutors Ltd 1979-88; Company secretary, Chart Foulks Lynch plc 1984-88; Director of studies, Holborn Law Tutors Ltd 1988-91; Senior lecturer in law, South Bank University 1991-92; Dean, Swansea Law School 1992-96; Assistant principal, Swansea Institute 1996-98; Visiting lecturer, Hong Kong University 1996-. Former member, NATFHE.

Political career: *House of Commons:* Contested (Conservative) Chesterfield 1983 general election and 1984 by-election and Worcester 1997 general election. *House of Lords:* Raised to the peerage as Baron Bourne of Aberystwyth, of Aberystwyth in the County of Ceredigion and of Wethersfield in the County of Essex 2013. Government Whip (Lord in Waiting) 2014-16; Government Spokesperson for: Culture, Media and Sport (Broadcasting) 2014-15, International Development 2014-15, Work and Pensions 2014-15, Wales Office 2014-17, Energy and Climate Change 2015-16, Communities and Local Government 2016-; Parliamentary Under-Secretary of State: Wales Office 2015-17, Department of Energy and Climate Change 2015-16; Department for Communities and Local Government: Parliamentary Under-Secretary of State: for Faith and Integration 2016-17, Minister for Faith 2017-; Parliamentary Under-Secretary of State, Northern Ireland Office 2017-. Member, Delegated Powers and Regulatory Reform 2014. *Other:* National Assembly for Wales: Contested Brecon and Radnorshire constituency 1999, 2003, 2007 and 2011 elections, AM for Mid and West Wales region 1999-2011, Leader, Conservative Group in the National Assembly 1999-2011, Welsh Conservative Spokesperson for: Finance 1999, 2001-02, 2006-07, Europe and Constituional Affairs 2007-09, Leader of the Official Opposition 2007-11, Shadow Minister for: Finance 2008-11, Heritage 2010, Contested Mid and West Wales region 2011 election. *Councils and public bodies:* Member: North East Thames Regional Health Authority 1990-92, West Glamorgan Health Authority 1994-97, Doctor and Dentist Review Body 1998-99, Silk Commission 2011-13, Commission on Public Service Governance and Delivery 2013.

Political interests: Foreign affairs, economy, education, health, constitutional issues; France, Greece, India, Italy, Malaysia, Singapore.

Other: Patron: Kidney Wales, Heart of Wales Line Association; Member, Advisory Committee: British Council, Wales Governance Centre; Member, Honourable Society of Gray's Inn; BHF, NSPCC; *Clubs:* Society of Authors, United Oxford and Cambridge University Club.

Publications: Various company law and business law text books; Editor of a series of legal text books; Business Law Review, editorial board.

Recreations: Badminton, squash, tennis, walking, theatre, cinema.

The Lord Bourne of Aberystwyth, House of Lords, London SW1A 0PW
Tel: 020 7219 8758 *Email:* bournen@parliament.uk *Twitter:* @lordnickbourne

BOWLES OF BERKHAMSTED, BARONESS

LIBERAL DEMOCRAT

BOWLES OF BERKHAMSTED (Life Baroness), Sharon Margaret Bowles; cr 2015. Born 12 June 1953; Daughter of late Percy Bowles and late Florence Bowles; Married Andrew Horton (2 sons).

Education: Our Lady's Convent, Abingdon; Reading University (BSc chemical physics and mathematics 1974); Lady Margaret Hall, Oxford (research 1974-77).

Non-political career: Chartered Patent Attorney, Registered Trademark Agent and European Patent Attorney 1981-; Professional Representative, Office for Harmonisation of the Single Market; Partner, Bowles Horton partnership 1981-2005; Non-executive Director: London Stock Exchange Group 2014-16, London Stock Exchange plc 2014-.

Political career: *House of Lords:* Raised to the peerage as Baroness Bowles of Berkhamsted, of Bourne End in the County of Hertfordshire 2015. Member: Economic Affairs 2016-, Economic Affairs Finance Bill Sub-committee 2016-17, Intellectual Property (Unjustified Threats) Bill 2016. *Other:* European Parliament: MEP for South East 2005-14: Bureau member, ALDE group 2009-14, Chair, Economic and Monetary Affairs Committee 2009-14. Liberal Democrats: Secretary, Chilterns region 1990-95, Member, federal executive and federal finance committee 2000-03; Co-founder, Association of Liberal Democrat Engineers and Scientists; Vice-president and bureau member, ELDR group 2004-14; Chair, Liberal Democrat International Relations Committee.

Political interests: Financial services, science and technology, intellectual property, company law.

Other: Vice-president, Liberal International; Member, advisory board, Centre for Progressive Capitalism 2016-; Anti-Slavery International; *Clubs:* National Liberal Club.

The Baroness Bowles of Berkhamsted, House of Lords, London SW1A 0PW
Tel: 020 7219 3000 *Email:* bowless@parliament.uk *Twitter:* @SharonBowlesUK

CONSERVATIVE

BOWNESS, LORD

BOWNESS (Life Baron), Peter Spencer Bowness; cr. 1996. Born 19 May 1943; Son of late Hubert Bowness and Doreen Bowness; Married Marianne Hall 1969 (divorced 1983) (1 daughter); married Patricia Cook 1984 (1 stepson).

Education: Whitgift School, Croydon; Law Society School of Law, College of Law.

Non-political career: Hon. Colonel 151 (Greater London) RCT Regiment (V) 1988-93. Admitted Solicitor 1966; Partner, Weightman Sadler, Solicitors, Purley, Surrey 1970-2002; Notary Public 1977; Consultant, Streeter Marshall Solicitors, Warlingham/Purley/Croydon 2002-11.

Political career: *House of Lords:* Raised to the peerage as Baron Bowness, of Warlingham in the County of Surrey and of Croydon in the London Borough of Croydon 1996. Opposition Spokesperson for Local Government 1997-98; House of Lords representative to Convention to Draft an EU Charter of Fundamental Rights 1999-2000. Chair, Draft Local Government (Organisation and Standards) Bill Joint Committee 1999; Member: EU Sub-committee C (Common Foreign and Security Policy) 2000-03, Chinook ZD567 2001-02, Joint Committee on Human Rights 2002-06, 2008-12, European Union 2003-07; Chair, EU Sub-committee C (Foreign Affairs, Defence and Development Policy) 2003-06; EU Sub-committee E (Law and Institutions): Co-opted Member 2006-09, Co-opted Chair 2009-10; Member, European Union 2009-14; Chair, EU Sub-committee E: (Justice and Institutions) 2010-12, (Justice, Institutions and Consumer Protection) 2012-13; Member: EU Sub-committee D (Agriculture, Fisheries, Environment and Energy) 2013-15, Secondary Legislation Scrutiny 2014-17, EU Energy and Environment Sub-Committee 2015-16. *Councils and public bodies:* London Borough of Croydon Council: Councillor 1968-98, Leader 1976-94, Mayor 1979-80; Deputy Chair, Association of Metropolitan Authorities 1978-80; Chair, London Boroughs Association 1978-94; DL, Greater London 1981-; Member: Audit Commission 1983-95, London Residuary Body 1985-93, National Training Task Force 1989-92.

Political interests: European Union, local government, London; Europe, particularly Balkans and Baltics, Caucasus.

Other: Member, UK Delegation to: Congress of Regional and Local Authorities of Europe, Council of Europe 1990-98, EU Committee of the Regions 1994-98; Member, Inter-Parliamentary Union; UK Delegation, Organisation for Security and Co-operation in Europe Parliamentary Assembly: Member 2007-, Leader 2014-, Vice-President 2015-. Freedom, City of London 1984; Honorary Freedom, London Borough of Croydon 2002. CBE 1981; Kt 1987.

Recreations: Travel, gardening.

The Lord Bowness CBE DL, House of Lords, London SW1A 0PW
Tel: 020 7219 2575 *Email:* bownessp@parliament.uk

CROSSBENCH

BOYCE, LORD

BOYCE (Life Baron), Michael Cecil Boyce; cr. 2003. Born 2 April 1943; Son of late Commander Hugh Boyce DSC RN and late Madeleine Boyce, née Manley; Married Harriette Fletcher 1971 (separated 1994, divorced 2005) (1 son 1 daughter); married Fleur Rutherford, née Smith 2006 (died 2016).

Education: Hurstpierpoint College; Britannia Royal Naval College, Dartmouth; Royal College of Defence Studies.

Non-political career: Royal Navy 1961-2003: Served HM Submarines Anchorite, Valiant and Conqueror 1965-72; Commanded HM Submarines: Oberon 1973-74, Opossum 1974-75, Superb 1979-81, HMS Brilliant 1983-84; Captain Submarine Sea Training 1984-86; Royal College of Defence Studies 1988; Senior Naval Officer, Middle East 1989; Director, Naval Staff Duties 1989-91; Flag Officer Sea Training 1991-92, Surface Flotilla 1992-95; Commander Anti-Submarine Warfare Striking Force 1992-94; Second Sea Lord and Commander-in-Chief Naval Home Command 1995-97; Commander-in-Chief Fleet and Eastern Atlantic Area and Commander Naval Forces North Western Europe 1977-98; First Sea Lord and Chief of Naval Staff 1988-2001; Chief of the Defence Staff 2001-03; Colonel Commandant Special Boat Service 2003-. Non-executive Director: WS Atkins plc 2004-13, VT Group plc 2004-10.

Political career: *House of Lords:* Raised to the peerage as Baron Boyce, of Pimlico in the City of Westminster 2003. European Union Sub-committee C (Foreign Affairs, Defence and Development Policy): Member 2005-06, Co-opted member 2006-08. *Councils and public bodies:* DL, Greater London.

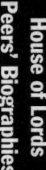

Other: Officers Association: President 2003-11, Senior President 2009-11; President, St John Ambulance (London District) 2003-11; Patron: Sail 4 Cancer 2003-, Submarine Association 2003-, Trafalgar Woods 2004-; Lord Warden and Admiral of the Cinque Ports and Constable of Dover

Castle 2004-; UK Defence Forum; Vice-Patron, Tall Ships Youth Trust; Forces in Mind Trust; Historic Dockyard Chatham; President, Royal Navy Submarine Museum 2005-; Vice-President, Forces Pension Society 2006-; Elder Brother, Trinity House 2007-; Chair, Council White Ensign Association 2007-10; Chair and trustee, RNLI 2008-13; Chair, HMS Victory Preservation Company 2012-; Honorary Bencher, Middle Temple 2012-; Chair, RBL Centre for Blast Injury Studies Advisory Board. Draper's Company: Master 2013-14. Freedom, City of London. Honorary doctorates: Portsmouth University 2005, Canterbury Christ Church University 2011, Kent University 2013. King of Arms Order of the Bath. OBE 1982; KCB 1995; GCB 1999; KStJ 2002; Commander, Legion of Merit (USA) 2003; King of Arms Order of the Bath 2009-; KG 2011; *Clubs:* Naval and Military, Garrick Club. RNSA; RYA; Jester; West Withering Windsurfing Club; Queen's.

Recreations: Tennis, real tennis, squash, windsurfing, opera.

Admiral of the Fleet the Lord Boyce KG GCB OBE DL, House of Lords, London SW1A 0PW
Tel: 020 7219 8714 *Email:* boycem@parliament.uk

NON-AFFILIATED

BOYD OF DUNCANSBY, LORD

BOYD OF DUNCANSBY (Life Baron), Colin David Boyd; cr 2006. Born 7 June 1953; Son of Dr David Boyd and Bette Boyd, née Mutch; Married Fiona McLeod 1979 (2 sons 1 daughter).

Education: Wick High School; George Watson's College, Edinburgh; Manchester University (BA Econ 1974); Edinburgh University (LLB 1976).

Non-political career: Solicitor 1978-82, 2007-12; Advocate, Scotland 1983-2007; Legal associate, Royal Town Planning Institute 1990; Advocate depute 1993-95; QC (Scotland) 1995; Scottish Executive: Solicitor General for Scotland 1997-2000, Lord Advocate for Scotland 2000-06; Commissioner, Northern Lighthouse Board 1997-2006; Consultant and head of public law, Dundas & Wilson CS LLP 2007-12; Honorary Professor of Law, Glasgow University 2007-12; Senator of the College of Justice in Scotland 2012-.

Political career: *House of Lords:* Raised to the peerage as Baron Boyd of Duncansby, of Duncansby in Caithness 2006. As a senior member of the judiciary, disqualified from participation 2012-. Member: Delegated Powers and Regulatory Reform 2007-10, EU Sub-committee E (Justice and Institutions) 2010-12. *Councils and public bodies:* Member, Commission on Scottish Devolution 2008-09.

Political interests: Constitutional affairs, criminal justice, planning and built environment.

Other: Fellow: Legal Associate Royal Town Planning Institute; Writer to the Signet. PC 2000.

Recreations: Watching rugby, reading, walking.

Rt Hon the Lord Boyd of Duncansby QC, House of Lords, London SW1A 0PW
Tel: 020 7219 5353

CONSERVATIVE

BRABAZON OF TARA, LORD

BRABAZON OF TARA (3rd Baron, UK), Ivon Anthony Moore-Brabazon; cr. 1942. Born 20 December 1947; Son of 2nd Baron, CBE; Married Harriet Frances de Courcy Hamilton 1979 (1 son 1 daughter).

Education: Harrow School.

Non-political career: Member, Stock Exchange 1972-84.

Political career: *House of Lords:* First entered House of Lords 1977; Government Whip 1984-86; Government Spokesperson for: Transport 1984-85, Trade and Industry, Treasury and Energy 1985-86; Parliamentary Under-Secretary of State, Department of Transport 1986-89; Minister of State: Foreign and Commonwealth Office 1989-90, Department of Transport 1990-92; Opposition Spokesperson for Transport 1998-2000; Elected hereditary peer 1999-; Principal Deputy Chairman of Committees 2001-02; Chairman of Committees 2002-12; Deputy Speaker 2002-. House of Lords' Offices/House: Member 2001-03, 2006-12, Chair 2003-06; Procedure: Member 2001-03, 2010-11, 2015-, Chair 2003-10, 2011-12; Chair: European Union 2001-02, Hybrid Instruments 2003-12, Liaison 2003-12, Personal Bills 2003-09, Privileges/Privileges and Conduct 2003-12, Selection 2003-12, Standing Orders (Private Bills) 2003-12, 2013, Administration and Works 2003-10, 2011-12, Refreshment 2008-12, Sub-committee on Leave of Absence 2011-12, Joint Committee on Parliamentary Privilege 2013, Hybrid Instruments 2013-14; Member: Affordable Childcare 2014-15, High Speed Rail (London-West Midlands) Bill 2016. *Councils and public bodies:* DL, Isle of Wight 1993-.

Political interests: Transport; Switzerland.

Other: President, United Kingdom Warehousing Association 1992-; Deputy chair, Foundation for Sport and the Arts 1992-2012; Shipwrecked Mariners' Society: Council member 1993-2011, Vice-President 2011-; President, Natural Gas Vehicles Association 1995-97; Institute of the Motor Industry: Deputy President 1997-98, Fellow 1997-, President 1998-2004, Vice-President 2008-; President, British International Freight Association 1997-98; Shipwrecked Mariners' Society. PC 2013; *Clubs:* Royal Yacht Squadron (Cowes) Club.

Recreations: Sailing, golf.

Rt Hon the Lord Brabazon of Tara DL, House of Lords, London SW1A 0PW
Tel: 020 7219 6796 *Email:* brabazoni@parliament.uk

LABOUR

BRADLEY, LORD

BRADLEY (Life Baron), Keith John Charles Bradley; cr 2006. Born 17 May 1950; Son of late John Bradley and late Mrs Beatrice Harris; Married Rhona Graham 1987 (2 sons 1 daughter).

Education: Bishop Vesey's Grammar School, Sutton Coldfield; Manchester Polytechnic (BA social science 1976); York University (MPhil social policy 1978).

Non-political career: Charles Impey and Co, chartered accountants 1969-73; Research Officer, Manchester City Council Housing Department 1978-81; Secretary, Stockport Community Health Council 1981-87; Manchester University: Special Adviser to President and Vice-chancellor 2005-10, 2013-, Associate Vice-president 2010-13. Member, Unite.

Political career: *House of Commons:* MP (Labour) for Manchester Withington 1987-2005. Opposition Spokesperson for: Social Security 1991-96, Transport 1996-97; Parliamentary Under-Secretary of State, Department of Social Security 1997-98; Deputy Chief Whip 1998-2001; Minister of State, Home Office 2001-02. *House of Lords:* Raised to the peerage as Baron Bradley, of Withington in the County of Greater Manchester 2006. Opposition Spokesperson for: Health 2013-15, Work and Pensions 2013-15. Member: House 2007-10, Long-Term Sustainability of the NHS 2016-17. *Other:* Member: Co-operative Party, Labour Party. *Councils and public bodies:* Manchester City Council: Councillor 1983-88, Chair, Environment and Consumer Services Committee 1984-88; City Council Director: Manchester Ship Canal Co 1984-87, Manchester Airport plc 1984-87; Non-executive Chair, Manchester, Salford and Trafford Lift Company 2007-; Council Member, Medical Protection Society 2007-15; Non-executive Chair: Christie Hospital NHS Foundation Trust 2011-, Bury Tameside and Glossop Lit Company 2014-; Non-executive Director, Pennine Care NHS Foundation Trust 2015-.

Political interests: Local and regional government, housing, health, pensions, poverty, sport; China, France, USA.

Other: Trustee: Centre for Mental Health 2011-, Prison Reform Trust 2011-. PC 2001.

Publications: The Bradley Report [a review of people with mental health problems or learning disabilities in the criminal justice system] (Department of Health, 2009).

Recreations: All sports, theatre, cinema.

Rt Hon the Lord Bradley, House of Lords, London SW1A 0PW
Tel: 020 7219 4207 *Email:* bradleykj@parliament.uk
Tel: 0161-275 3963 *Fax:* 0161-275 8863 *Email:* keith.bradley@manchester.ac.uk

LIBERAL DEMOCRAT

BRADSHAW, LORD

BRADSHAW (Life Baron), William Peter Bradshaw; cr. 1999. Born 9 September 1936; Son of late Leonard Bradshaw and Ivy Bradshaw; Married Jill Hayward 1957 (died 2002) (1 son 1 daughter); married Diana Ayris 2003.

Education: Slough Grammar School; Reading University (BA political economy 1957, MA 1960); Little French.

Non-political career: National Service 1957-59. British Railways/Rail 1959-85: Management trainee, Western Region 1959-62, Various appointments, London and West of England Division 1962-73, Divisional manager, Liverpool 1973-75, Chief operating manager, London Midland (LM) Region, Crewe 1976, Deputy general manager, LM Region 1977, Chief operations manager, BR Headquarters 1978-80, Director, Policy Unit 1980-83, General manager, Western Region 1983-85, Professor of transport management, Salford University 1986-92; Chair, Ulsterbus and Citybus Ltd Belfast 1987-93; Special adviser to Transport Select Committee 1992-97. Transport Salaried Staffs Association 1961-77.

Political career: *House of Lords:* Raised to the peerage as Baron Bradshaw, of Wallingford in the County of Oxfordshire 1999. Liberal Democrat Spokesperson for: Transport 2001-15 (and Industry Contact 2015). Co-opted Member, EU Sub-committee B (Internal Market) 2007-10; Member,

EU Sub-committee B (Internal Market, Energy and Transport) 2010-12. Chair, Liberal Democrat Parliamentary Party Committee on Transport 2010-15. *Councils and public bodies:* Councillor, Oxfordshire County Council 1993-2008, Thames Valley Police Authority: Member 1993-95, 1997-2008, Vice-chair 1999-2003; Member: Commission for Integrated Transport -2001, British Railways Board (Shadow Strategic Rail Authority) 1999-2001.

Political interests: Transport, environment, planning, police.

Other: President, Friends of the Ridgeway; National Trust, Salvation Army. Honorary Fellow, Wolfson College, Oxford; *Clubs:* National Liberal Club.

Publications: Many chapters and articles on transport issues.

Recreations: Growing hardy perennial plants.

Professor the Lord Bradshaw, House of Lords, London SW1A 0PW
Tel: 020 7219 8621 *Email:* bradshaww@parliament.uk

BRADY, BARONESS

CONSERVATIVE

BRADY (Life Baroness), Karren Rita Brady; cr 2014. Born 4 April 1969; Daughter of Terry and Rita Brady; Married Paul Peschisolido 1995 (1 daughter 1 son).

Non-political career: Saatchi & Saatch 1987-88; Sales executive, London Broadcasting Company 1988-89; Sport Newspapers Ltd 1989-93; Managing director, Birmingham Football Club 1993-2010; Vice-chair, West Ham Football Club 2010-; Management consultant, Syco Entertainment; Appears on BBC The Apprentice TV show; Member, women and sport advisory board, Department for Culture, Media and Sport; Chairman, Taveta Investments Ltd; Director, BKB Media Ltd.

Political career: *House of Lords:* Raised to the peerage as Baroness Brady, of Knightsbridge in the City of Westminster 2014. *Other:* Small business ambassador, Conservative Party.

Other: Board member: Mothercare plc, Channel 4 Television, Sport England, Britain Stronger in Europe 2015-16; Stroke Association, Wellchild, Teenage Cancer Trust. Hon. doctorate (business), Birmingham University. Business Woman of the Year; Cosmopolitan Woman of the Year; Spirit of Everywoman Award; Britain's Most Influential Woman Award. CBE 2013.

Publications: Playing to Win: 10 Steps to Achieving Your Goals (2004); Strong Woman: The Truth About Getting To The Top (2013).

Recreations: Football, family.

The Baroness Brady CBE, House of Lords, London SW1A 0PW
Tel: 020 7219 5353
West Ham United Football Club, London Stadium, Queen Elizabeth Olympic Park, London E20 2ST
Website: www.karrenbrady.com *Twitter:* @karren_brady

BRAGG, LORD

LABOUR

BRAGG (Life Baron), Melvyn Bragg; cr. 1998. Born 6 October 1939; Son of Stanley and Mary Bragg; Married Marie-Elisabeth Roche 1961 (died 1971) (1 daughter); married Catherine Haste 1973 (1 son 1 daughter).

Education: Nelson-Thomlinson Grammar School, Wigton; Wadham College, Oxford (BA modern history 1961, MA); French.

Non-political career: BBC radio and TV producer 1961-67; Novelist 1964-; Writer and broadcaster 1967-; Presenter, BBC TV series: *Melvyn Bragg on Class and Culture*, BBC 2012, *2nd House* 1973-77, *Read All About It* 1975-77; *The Mystery of Mary Magdalene* 2013, *The Most Dangerous Man in Tudor England* 2013; Presenter and editor: *The South Bank Show*, ITV 1978-2010, *The South Bank Show*, Sky Arts 2012-, *Start the Week*, Radio 4 1988-98; London Weekend Television: Controller of Arts 1990-2010, Head of Arts 1982-90; Border Television: Chair 1990-95, Deputy Chair 1985-90; Radio 4: *In Our Time* 1998-, *Rates of English* 1999-2001, *The Value of Culture* 2013; Director, Directors Cut Productions 2010-.

Political career: *House of Lords:* Raised to the peerage as Baron Bragg, of Wigton in the County of Cumbria 1998. Member, Communications 2010-13. *Councils and public bodies:* Governor, London School of Economics 1997; DL, Cumbria 2003.

Political interests: Broadcasting, universities, the arts, countryside; France, USA.

Other: Chair, Literature Panel of Arts Council 1977-80; President: Cumbrians for Peace 1982-86, Northern Arts 1983-87, National Campaign for the Arts 1986-2005, MIND 2001-11; Chair, RNIB Talking Books Appeal 2000-05; Fellow: Royal Society of Literature, Royal Television Society;

Hon. fellow: Royal Society, British Academy; BAFTA; MIND, RNIB, St. Mungo's. Chancellor, Leeds University 1999-2017. Twelve honorary doctorates; Four honorary fellowships. Royal Television Society Gold Medal; John Llewllyn-Rhys Memorial Award for *Without a City Wall*; PEN Awards for Fiction for *The Hired Man*; Outstanding Contribution to Television, Richard Dimbleby award 1987; Best Musical (*The Hired Man*), Ivor Novello award 1985; Numerous prizes for *The South Bank Show* including four Prix Italias; Television and Radio Industries Club (TRIC) award: Radio Programme of the Year for *Start the Week* 1990, Radio Personality of the Year for *Start the Week* 1991; WHS Literary award for *The Soldier's Return*; Viewers and Listeners Broadcaster of the Year 2007-08; Bafta Fellowship 2010; Media Brief Award 2010; Outstanding Achievement South Bank Show Awards 2010; Sandford St. Martin Personal Award 2014; *Clubs:* Garrick Club.

Publications: For Want of a Nail (1965); The Second Inheritance (1966); Without a City Wall (1968); The Hired Man (1969); A Place in England (1970); The Nerve (1971); Josh Lawton (1972); The Silken Net (1974); A Christmas Child (1976); Speak for England (1976); Mardi Gras (musical 1976); Orion (TV play 1977); Autumn Manoeuvres (1978); Kingdom Come (1980); Love and Glory (1983); Land of the Lakes (1983); Laurence Olivier (1984); The Hired Man (musical 1984); The Maid of Buttermere (1987); Rich: The Life of Richard Burton (1988); A Time to Dance (1990); Crystal Rooms (1992); King Lear in New York (play 1992); The Seventh Seal: a study of Ingmar Bergman (1993); Credo (1996); On Giants' Shoulders (1998); The Soldier's Return (1999); A Son of War (2001); Crossing the Lines (2003); The Adventure of English (2003); 12 Books that Changed the World; Remember Me (2008); In Our Time (2009); Final Cut: The South Bank Show (2010); The Book of Books: The Radical Impact of the King James Bible 1611-2011 (Hodder & Stoughton, 2011); Screenplays: Isadora, Jesus Christ Superstar, Clouds of Glory, Grace and Mary.

Recreations: Walking, books.

The Lord Bragg, House of Lords, London SW1A 0PW
Tel: 020 7219 8741
12 Hampstead Hill Gardens, London NW3 2PL *Tel:* 020 3475 5571 *Fax:* 020 3475 5572
Email: melvyn.bragg@dcptv.co.uk

LABOUR

BRENNAN, LORD

BRENNAN (Life Baron), Daniel Joseph Brennan; cr. 2000. Born 19 March 1942; Son of late Daniel and Mary Brennan; Married Pilar Sanchez 1968 (4 sons).

Education: St Bede's Grammar School, Bradford; Manchester University (LLB 1964).

Non-political career: Called to the Bar, Gray's Inn 1967 (Bencher 1993); Crown Court Recorder 1982-; QC 1985; Member, Criminal Injuries Compensation Board 1989-97; Deputy High Court Judge 1994-; Chair, General Council of the Bar 1999; Independent assessor to Home Office on Miscarriages of Justice 2001-.

Political career: *House of Lords:* Raised to the peerage as Baron Brennan, of Bibury in the County of Gloucestershire 2000. Member, Constitution 2014-17.

Other: Councillor, International Bar Association; President: Catholic Union of Great Britain 2001-, Consortium for Street Children; FRSA. Two honorary doctorates. QC 1985; Cruz de Honor of the Order of St Raimond de Penafort (Spain) 2000; *Clubs:* Garrick Club.

Publications: General editor, Bullen and Leake on Pleadings (2003).

The Lord Brennan QC, House of Lords, London SW1A 0PW
Tel: 020 7219 5353
Matrix Chambers, Griffin Building, Gray's Inn, London WC1R 5LN *Tel:* 020 7404 3447
Fax: 020 7404 3448 *Email:* danbrennan@matrixlaw.co.uk

CONSERVATIVE

BRIDGEMAN, VISCOUNT

BRIDGEMAN (3rd Viscount, UK), Robin John Orlando Bridgeman; cr. 1929. Born 5 December 1930; Son of late Brigadier Hon. Geoffrey Bridgeman, MC, FRCS, second son of 1st Viscount; Married Victoria Turton (CBE 2014) 1966 (3 sons 1 son deceased).

Education: Eton College.

Non-political career: 2nd Lieutenant, The Rifle Brigade 1950-51. Partner, Henderson Crosthwaite and Co., Stockbrokers 1973-86; Director: The Bridgeman Art Library Limited 1972-, Guinness Mahon and Co. Ltd 1988-90, Nestor-BNA plc 1988-2000.

Political career: *House of Lords:* First entered House of Lords 1982; Opposition Whip 1998-2010; Elected hereditary peer 1999-; Opposition Spokesperson for: Home Affairs 2001-10, Northern Ireland 2001-07, 2009-10. Member: Information 2010-11, EU Sub-committees: G (Social Policies and Consumer Protection) 2011-12, F (Home Affairs, Health and Education) 2012-15, Joint Committee on Consolidation, &c, Bills 2015-. *Councils and public bodies:* Reed's School: Chair of Governors 1994-2002, Joint life president 2002-.

Political interests: Health, social services, environment, home affairs, local government.

Other: Member, British-Irish Parliamentary Assembly; Chairman, Friends of Lambeth Palace Library 1992-2008; Special Trustee, Hammersmith and Queen Charlotte's Hospital Authority 1992-2000; Trustee, Music at Winchester 1995-2006; Treasurer: Florence Nightingale Aid in Sickness Trust 1995-2006, New England Company 1996-2006; Chairman: Hospital of St John and St Elizabeth 1999-2007, CORESS 2006-12; Trustee, Parliament Choir 2011-; MCC. Sovereign Military Order of Malta, Knight, 1995; *Clubs:* Beefsteak, Pitt Club.

Recreations: Gardening, music, shooting.

The Viscount Bridgeman, House of Lords, London SW1A 0PW
Tel: 020 7219 0663 *Fax:* 020 7219 0753 *Email:* bridgemanr@parliament.uk
19 Chepstow Road, London W2 5BP *Tel:* 020 7727 5400 *Fax:* 020 7792 9178

BRIDGES OF HEADLEY, LORD

CONSERVATIVE

BRIDGES OF HEADLEY (Life Baron), James George Robert Bridges; cr 2015. Born 15 July 1970; Married Alice Hickman (1 son 2 daughters).

Education: Eton College; Exeter College, Oxford (modern history); University of Pennsylvania (government administration).

Non-political career: Assistant political secretary to John Major as Prime Minister 1994-97; Director of communications, British Digital Consultants 1997-98; Lead writer, *The Times* 1998-2000; Quiller Consultants: Consultant 2000-04, 2007-09, Chief executive 2010-13; Chairman, Conservative Research Department 2004-05; Senior adviser to UK Chief Executive, Santander 2014-15.

Political career: *House of Lords:* Raised to the peerage as Baron Bridges of Headley, of Headley Heath in the County of Surrey 2015. Parliamentary Secretary and Government Spokesperson, Cabinet Office 2015-16; Parliamentary Under-Secretary of State and Government Spokesperson, Department for Exiting the European Union 2016-17. *Other:* Campaign Director, Conservative Party 2006-07.

Other: Freedom, City of London. MBE 1997.

The Lord Bridges of Headley MBE, House of Lords, London SW1A 0PW
Tel: 020 7219 3000 *Email:* bridgesg@parliament.uk

BRINTON, BARONESS

LIBERAL DEMOCRAT

BRINTON (Life Baroness), Sarah (Sal) Virginia Brinton; cr 2011. Born 1 April 1955; Daughter of late Tim Brinton (MP 1979-87) and late Jane-Mari Shearing, née Coningham; Married Tim Whittaker 1983 (2 sons 1 daughter 2 wards – 1 male 1 female).

Education: Benenden, Cranbrook; Central School of Speech and Drama (1973); London College of Secretaries (1974); Churchill College, Cambridge (BA 1984, MA); Conversational French.

Non-political career: Floor manager, BBC radio and television 1974-81; Venture capitalist 1984-90; Bursar: Lucy Cavendish College, Cambridge 1992-97, Selwyn College, Cambridge 1997-2002; Consultant, IDeA 2003-06; Director, Association of Universities in the East of England 2006-11.

Political career: *House of Commons:* Contested (Liberal Democrat) Cambridgeshire South East 1997 and 2001 and Watford 2005 and 2010 general elections. *House of Lords:* Raised to the peerage as Baroness Brinton, of Kenardington in the County of Kent 2011. Member, Equality Act 2010 and Disability 2015-16. *Other:* Liberal Democrat Party: Education and Higher Education Working Group 1993-97, Federal Conference Committee: Member 2004-08, Vice-chair 2010-; Federal Policy Committee: Member 2004-08, 2010-, Vice-chair 2006-08; Schools Working Group 2008-, Member, Manifesto Working Group 2013-15, Chair, Diversity Engagement Group 2011-14, President 2015- (attends Shadow Cabinet 2016-). *Councils and public bodies:* Cambridgeshire County Council 1993-2004: Councillor 1993-2004, Education portfolio holder 1993-97, Leader, Liberal Democrat group 1997-2004; East of England Development Agency: Board Member 1999-2004, Deputy Chair 2002-04; Chair, Cambridgeshire Learning and Skills Council 2000-06.

Political interests: Education, including further and higher education and skills, health and social care, economic development, disability; France, Palestine.

House of Lords
Peers' Biographies

Other: St Johns Innovation Centre, Cambridge 1992-2010; Director and trustee, Christian Blind Mission 2003-13; Director: UFI Charitable Trust 2003-, East of England International 2006-11; Trustee, Unicef UK 2013-; Director, Joseph Rowntree Reform Trust 2013-; Member: Institute of Directors, RSA; Fellow, Birkbeck College 2013. Honorary Doctorate Anglia Ruskin University (for services to education and skills) 2003. East Anglian Entrepreneurial Businesswoman of the Year 1997.

Recreations: Theatre, football, cooking, swimming.

The Baroness Brinton, House of Lords, London SW1A 0PW
Tel: 020 7219 3234 *Email:* brintons@parliament.uk
Liberal Democrats, 8-10 Great George Street, London SW1P 3AE *Twitter:* @SalBrinton

CROSSBENCH

BROERS, LORD

BROERS (Life Baron), Alec Nigel Broers; cr. 2004. Born 17 September 1938; Son of late Alec Broers and Constance Broers, née Cox; Married Marie Phelan 1964 (2 sons).

Education: Geelong Church of England Grammar School, Australia; Melbourne University, Australia (BSc physics 1959, electronics 1960); Gonville and Caius College, Cambridge (BA mechanical sciences 1962; PhD electrical engineering 1965; ScD 1991).

Non-political career: IBM 1965-84: Research staff, TJ Watson Research Center 1965-81, Manager: Photon and electron optics 1977-81, Advanced development East Fishkill Laboratory 1982-84, Member, corporate technical committee, corporate headquarters 1984; Cambridge University: Professor of electrical engineering 1984-96, Professor emeritus 1996-, Fellow, Trinity College 1985-90, Churchill College: Fellow 1990-, Master 1990-96, Vice-chancellor 1996-2003.

Political career: *House of Lords:* Raised to the peerage as Baron Broers, of Cambridge in the County of Cambridgeshire 2004. Chair, Science and Technology 2004-07; Member, Science and Technology Sub-committees: II (Energy Efficiency) 2004-08, I (Scientific Aspects of Ageing) 2005-07; Co-opted Member, Science and Technology Sub-committee II (Genomic Medicine) 2008-09; Member, Science and Technology 2009-13; Chair, Science and Technology Sub-committee I (Radioactive Waste Management: a further update) 2010; Member, Science and Technology Sub-committee I 2012-13. *Councils and public bodies:* President, Royal Academy of Engineering 2001-06; Member: Board of Trustees, American University of Shaijah, Singapore, One-North Resource Advisory Board, AIST (Japanese Instutite of Advanced Industrial Science and Technology); Chair, Board of Diamond Light Source.

Political interests: Energy, industry, education; Australia, USA.

Other: Trustee: British Museum, Needham Research Institute; Foreign associate, US National Academy of Engineering; Foreign member: Chinese Academy of Engineering, American Philosophical Society; Honorary Fellow, Australian Academy of Technological Sciences and Engineering; FIEE 1984; FREng 1985; FRS 1986; FIME; FInstP; FMedSci 2004. Numerous honorary doctorates and fellowships. American Institute of Physics Prize for Industrial Applications of Physics 1981; IEEE Cledo Brunetti Award 1985; Prince Philip Medal of Royal Academy of Engineering 2001. Kt 1998; *Clubs:* Athenæum Club.

Publications: Numerous papers and book chapters on electron microscopy, micro-electronics and nanotechnology; Reith Lectures – Triumph of Technology (Cambridge University Press, 2005).

Recreations: Sailing, skiing, listening to music.

Professor the Lord Broers, House of Lords, London SW1A 0PW
Tel: 020 7219 5353
Email: anb1000@cam.ac.uk

LABOUR

BROOKE OF ALVERTHORPE, LORD

BROOKE OF ALVERTHORPE (Life Baron), Clive Brooke; cr. 1997. Born 21 June 1942; Son of John and Mary Brooke; Married Lorna Roberts 1967.

Education: Thornes House School, Wakefield.

Non-political career: Inland Revenue Staff Federation: Assistant Secretary 1964-82, Deputy General Secretary 1982-88, General Secretary 1988-95; Joint General Secretary, Public Services Tax and Commerce Union 1996-98; Member, TUC: General Council 1989-96, Executive Committee 1993-96; Senior strategic adviser, Accenture plc 1997-2010; Self-employed consultant 1997-2010. Member, Public and Commercial Services Union.

Political career: *House of Lords:* Raised to the peerage as Baron Brooke of Alverthorpe, of Alverthorpe in the County of West Yorkshire 1997. Chair, European Communities Sub-committee B (Energy, Industry and Transport) 1999-2002; Member, Information 2005-09, 2015-16; EU Sub-committee D (Environment and Agriculture): Member 2007, Co-opted member 2008-10; Member: Crossrail Bill 2008, EU Sub-committee B: (Internal Market, Energy and Transport) 2010-12, (Internal Market, Infrastructure and Employment) 2012-15, Licensing Act 2003 2016-17. Vice-chair, PLP Departmental Groups for: Cabinet Office 1998-2010, Home Affairs 2010, Transport 2010-15. *Councils and public bodies:* Member: House of Commons Speaker's Commission on Citizenship 1988, Council of Churches for Britain and Ireland Enquiry into Unemployment and the Future of Work 1995-97, Pensions Compensation Board 1996-2005; Government Partner Director, NATS Limited 2001-06.

Political interests: Public health and wellbeing, particularly related to alcohol and sugar abuse; Sweden.

Other: Member: Inter-Parliamentary Union, Commonwealth Parliamentary Association; Trustee: Community Service Volunteers 1989-2008, Duke of Edinburgh's Study Conference 1993-2007; Institute for Public Policy Research: Trustee 1997-2010, Policy advisory council 2010-; Member, Fabian Society; Patron, Sparrow Foundation 2002-; Trustee, Action on Addiction 2002-13; Patron: Kenward Trust 2008-, Everyman Project 2010-, British Liver Trust 2013-; FRSA; Cancer Research UK, Royal Marsden Hospital, Trinity Hospice Clapham, Sparrow Foundation, Woodland Trust.

Recreations: Spiritual pursuits, meditation, painting, association football, Chelsea FC.

The Lord Brooke of Alverthorpe, House of Lords, London SW1A 0PW
Tel: 020 7219 0478 *Fax:* 020 7219 5979 *Email:* brookec@parliament.uk

BROOKEBOROUGH, VISCOUNT

CROSSBENCH

BROOKEBOROUGH (3rd Viscount, UK), Alan Henry Brooke; cr. 1952; 7th Bt of Colebrooke (UK) 1822. Born 30 June 1952; Son of 2nd Viscount, PC; Married Janet Cooke 1980.

Education: Harrow School; Millfield School, Somerset; Royal Agricultural College, Cirencester 1978.

Non-political career: Commission, 17th/21st Lancers 1971; Ulster Defence Regiment 1977, Royal Irish Regiment 1992; Lieutenant-Colonel 1993; Hon. Colonel, 4th/5th Battalion, Royal Irish Rangers 1997-2008. Owner, Colebrooke Estate 1973-; Non-executive director: Green Park Health Care Trust 1993-2001, Basel International (Jersey); Personal Lord in Waiting to HM The Queen 1997-.

Political career: *House of Lords:* First entered House of Lords 1987; Elected hereditary peer 1999-. Member: EU Sub-committee D 1988-92, 1993-97, European Communities 1998-2002, Procedure 2003-05; Co-opted member, EU Sub-committee D (Environment and Agriculture) 2006-10; Member: EU Sub-committee A (Economic and Financial Affairs) 2012-15, Financial Exclusion 2016-17. *Councils and public bodies:* County Fermanagh: DL 1987-2012, High Sheriff 1995, Lord Lieutenant 2012-; Board member, Northern Ireland Policing Board 2001-06.

Political interests: Northern Ireland, agriculture, tourism, defence, health; Europe, UK.

Other: Vice-President, Somme Association 1990-; President, Army Benevolent Fund, Northern Ireland 1995-; Fellow, Industry and Parliament Trust 1999; Member, Duke of Edinburgh Award Advisory Council, Northern Ireland; President, Northern Ireland Outward Bound Association; Military, cancer and disabled charities; *Clubs:* Cavalry and Guards, Pratt's, Farmers' Club.

Recreations: Shooting, fishing, gardening, sailing.

The Viscount Brookeborough, House of Lords, London SW1A 0PW
Tel: 020 7219 1668
Colebrooke Park, Brookeborough, Enniskillen, Co. Fermanagh BT94 4DW *Tel:* 028 8953 1402
Fax: 028 8953 1312 *Email:* ahb@colebrooke.info *Website:* www.colebrooke.info

BROOKMAN, LORD

LABOUR

BROOKMAN (Life Baron), David Keith Brookman; cr. 1998. Born 3 January 1937; Son of George Brookman MM and Blodwin Brookman; Married Patricia Worthington 1958 (3 daughters).

Education: Nantyglo Grammar School, Gwent.

Non-political career: RAF national service 1955-57. Steel worker, Richard Thomas and Baldwin, Ebbw Vale 1953-55, 1957-73; Iron and Steel Trades Confederation 1953-: Divisional organiser 1973-85, Assistant General Secretary 1985-93, General Secretary 1993-99; Board Member, British Steel (Industry)/UK Steel Enterprise 1993-2015. Member: Iron and Steel Trades Confederation/Community 1953-, Trades Union Congress Educational Advisory Committee for Wales 1976-82, Trades Union Congress 1992-99; National TU Steel Co-ordinating Committee: Member 1991-99, Chair 1993-99.

Political career: *House of Lords:* Raised to the peerage as Baron Brookman, of Ebbw Vale in the County of Gwent 1998. *Other:* Member, Labour Party 1957-: Executive Committee, Wales 1982-85, National Constitutional Committee 1987-91, NEC 1991-92. *Councils and public bodies:* Governor, Gwent College of Higher Education 1980-84; Member: Joint Industrial Council for Slag Industry 1985-93, British Steel: Joint Accident Prevention Advisory Committee 1985-93, Advisory Committee on Education and Training 1986-93, Joint Secretary British Steel: Strip Trade Board 1993-98, Joint Standing Committee 1993-98, European Works Council 1996-99.

Political interests: Employment law, manufacturing, sport.

Other: Executive Council, European Metalworkers Federation 1985-95; International Metalworkers' Federation: Honorary Secretary (British Section) 1993-99, President, Iron, Steel and Non-Ferrous Metals Department 1993-99; Member, European Coal and Steel Community Consultative Committee 1993-2002; World Cancer Research Fund, NSPCC, British Heart Foundation; *Clubs:* Union Jack Club.

The Lord Brookman, House of Lords, London SW1A 0PW
Tel: 020 7219 8633 *Fax:* 020 7219 5979

CONSERVATIVE

BROUGHAM AND VAUX, LORD

BROUGHAM AND VAUX (5th Baron, UK), Michael John Brougham; cr. 1860. Born 2 August 1938; Son of 4th Baron; Married Olivia Gray 1963 (divorced 1967, died 1986) (1 daughter); married Catherine Gulliver 1969 (divorced 1981) (1 son).

Education: Lycée Jaccard, Lausanne, Switzerland; Millfield School, Somerset; Northampton Institute of Agriculture.

Political career: *House of Lords:* First entered House of Lords 1968; Deputy Chair of Committees 1993-97, 1997-; Deputy Speaker 1995-; Elected hereditary peer 1999-. Member: Statutory Instruments Joint Committee 2001-07, Information 2003-07, Standing Orders (Private Bills) 2003-06, Refreshment 2007-12, Administration and Works 2009-14. *Other:* Vice-chair Association of Conservative Peers 1998-2002, 2003-10.

Political interests: Road safety, transport, motor industry, aviation; France, Spain.

Other: Royal Society for the Prevention of Accidents: President 1986-89, Vice-President 1999-; Chair, Tax Payers' Society 1989-91; Fellow, Industry and Parliament Trust 1990, 1993; Chair, European Secure Vehicle Alliance 1992-2015; President, National Health Safety Groups Council/Safety Groups UK 1994-; Honorary Vice-President, Institute of Occupational Safety and Health 2008-. CBE 1995.

Recreations: Photography, bridge, shooting.

The Lord Brougham and Vaux CBE, House of Lords, London SW1A 0PW
Tel: 020 7219 5353 *Fax:* 020 7219 5979
11 Westminster Gardens, Marsham Street, London SW1P 4JA

CROSSBENCH

BROWN OF CAMBRIDGE, BARONESS

BROWN OF CAMBRIDGE (Life Baroness), Julia Elizabeth King; cr 2015. Born 11 July 1954; Daughter of Jane King and Derrick King; Married Dr Colin Brown 1984.

Education: Godolphin and Latymer Girls' School, London; New Hall, Cambridge (BA natural sciences (metallurgy) 1975; MA 1978; PhD 1979); French.

Non-political career: Rolls-Royce Research Fellow, Girton College Cambridge, 1978-80; University Lecturer, Nottingham University 1980-87; Cambridge University: British Gas/Fellowship of Engineering Senior Research Fellow 1987-92, University Lecturer, Department of Materials Science and Metallurgy 1992-94; Fellow, Churchill College, Cambridge 1987-94; Rolls-Royce plc 1994-2002: Head of Materials, Director of Advanced Engineering, Rolls-Royce Industrial Power Group, Managing Director, Rolls-Royce Fan Systems; Director, Engineering and Technology, Rolls-Royce Marine Business; Chief Executive, Institute of Physics 2002-04; Principal, Engineering Faculty, Imperial College London 2004-06; Vice-Chancellor, Aston University 2006-16; Chair: Henry Royce Institute for Advanced Materials, Manchester University 2015-, STEM Learning Ltd 2016-.

Political career: *House of Lords:* Raised to the peerage as Baroness Brown of Cambridge, of Cambridge in the County of Cambridgeshire 2015. Member: European Union 2016-, EU External Affairs Sub-committee 2016-. *Councils and public bodies:* Non-executive director, Department of Business, Innovation and Skills; Chair, Defence Scientific Advisory Council; Member, National Security Forum; Board member, Technology Strategy Board 2004-09; Committee on Climate Change: Member 2008-, Deputy chair 2017-, Chair, Adaptation Sub-Committee 2017-; Member: UK Airports Commission, Science and Technology Honours Committee; UK Low Carbon Business Ambassador 2009-; Non-executive director, UK Green Investment Bank 2012-17.

Political interests: Science and engineering, climate change, higher education, diversity; China, Europe, India, Vietnam.

Other: World Economic Forum Automotive Council 2008-12; World Economic Forum Global Agenda Council on Decarbonizing Energy 2014-; Non-executive director: Birmingham Technology Limited (Innovation Birmingham) 2007-16, Higher Education Statistics Agency 2007-11; Member, Governing Board, European Institute of Innovation and Technology (EIT) 2008-12; Non-executive director: UniversitiesUK 2011-15, Angel Trains 2012-15, National Centre for Universities and Business 2013-15, Marketing Birmingham 2015-16; Trustee: Rolls-Royce Pension Fund 1997-2000, Institute of Physics Pension Fund 2002-04, Forum for the Future, 2011-13, Cumberland Lodge 2013-15; Fellow: Institute of Materials, Mining and Metallurgy, Royal Aeronautical Society, Institute of Marine Engineering, Science and Technology, Institute of Physics, Energy Institute; Member, Women's Engineering Society; Fellow: Royal Academy of Engineering (FREng) 1997, Royal Society of London 2017; Honorary Fellow: Murray Edwards College, Cambridge, Cardiff University, Society for the Environment, British Science Association, Polymer Processing Academy India, Institute of Engineering and Technology; Oxfam, Murray Edwards College, Cambridge, Aston University, RSPB, WWF. Liveryman, Goldsmiths' Company. Freedom, City of London 1998. Honorary DSc: Queen Mary, University of London, Manchester University, Exeter University, Brunel University, Aston University. Grunfeld Medal 1992; Bengough Medal 1995; Kelvin Medal 2001; John Collier Medal 2009; Lunar Society Medal 2011; President's Prize, Engineering Professors' Council 2012; Constance Tipper Silver Medal (International Congress on Fracture) 2013; Erna Hamburger Prize (WISH Foundation, EPFL, Switzerland) 2013; Leonardo Da Vinci Medal (European Society for Engineering Education) 2014; LowCVP Low Carbon Champion Award 'Outstanding Individual in Promoting Low Carbon Transport' 2014. CBE 1999; DBE 2012.

Publications: Over 160 papers on fatigue and fracture in structural materials and developments in aerospace and marine propulsion technology.

Recreations: Walking, growing orchids, gardening, collecting modern prints and sculpture.

Professor the Baroness Brown of Cambridge DBE, House of Lords, London SW1A 0PW
Tel: 020 7219 3000 *Email:* julia.king@parliament.uk

BROWN OF EATON-UNDER-HEYWOOD, LORD

CROSSBENCH

BROWN OF EATON-UNDER-HEYWOOD (Life Baron), Simon Denis Brown; cr. 2004. Born 9 April 1937; Son of late Denis Baer Brown and Edna Brown, née Abrahams; Married Jennifer Buddicom 1963 (2 sons 1 daughter).

Education: Stowe School, Buckinghamshire; Worcester College, Oxford (BA law 1960).

Non-political career: Army national service 1955-57. Barrister 1961; Recorder 1979-84; First Junior Treasury Counsel, Common Law 1979-84; Judge of the High Court of Justice Queen's Bench Division 1984-92; President, Security Service Tribunal 1989-2000; Lord Justice of Appeal 1992-2004; President, Intelligence Services Tribunal 1995-2000; Intelligence Services Commissioner 2000-06; Vice-president, Court of Appeal Civil Division 2001-03; Lord of Appeal in Ordinary 2004-09; Justice of the Supreme Court of the United Kingdom 2009-12.

Political career: *House of Lords:* Raised to the peerage as Baron Brown of Eaton-under-Heywood, of Eaton-under-Heywood in the County of Shropshire 2004. Lord of Appeal in Ordinary 2004-09; As Justice of the Supreme Court, disqualified from participation 2009-12. Member, European Union 2005-07; Chair, European Union Sub-committee E (Law and Institutions) 2005-07; Member, Privileges and Conduct 2013-; Chair, Sub-committee on Lords' Conduct 2013-; Member, Extradition Law 2014-15; Alternate member, Procedure 2015-.

Political interests: The law and constitution.

Other: Butcher's Company. Honorary Fellow, Worcester College, Oxford 1993-; Visitor, Pembroke College, Cambridge 2010; High Steward, Oxford University 2011-12; Visitor, St Hugh's College, Oxford 2011-. Kt 1984; PC 1992; *Clubs:* Garrick Club. Denham Golf Club; Church Stretton Golf Club.

Recreations: Golf, reading, theatre.

Rt Hon the Lord Brown of Eaton-under-Heywood, House of Lords, London SW1A 0PW
Tel: 020 7219 1639
Email: sdbrown@blueyonder.co.uk

DEMOCRATIC UNIONIST PARTY

BROWNE OF BELMONT, LORD

BROWNE OF BELMONT (Life Baron), Wallace Hamilton Browne; cr 2006. Born 29 October 1947; Son of Gerald Browne and Phyllis Hamilton Browne; Married.

Education: Campbell College, Belfast; Queen's University, Belfast (BSc zoology 1970).

Non-political career: A-level biology teacher, Rainey Endowed School, Magherafelt 1970-2000. Member, NASUWT (retirement association).

Political career: *House of Lords:* Raised to the peerage as Baron Browne of Belmont, of Belmont in the County of Antrim 2006. *Other:* Northern Ireland Assembly: MLA for East Belfast 2007-11, Chair, Committee on Procedures 2010-11. *Councils and public bodies:* Belfast City Council: Councillor 1985-2011, Alderman 1993, Lord Mayor 2005-06; High Sheriff of Belfast 2002-.

Political interests: Education, Northern Ireland affairs, Balkan affairs; Brazil, Canada, Croatia, France, Germany, Italy, Montenegro, Serbia.

Other: Trustee, Somme Association, Northern Ireland.

Recreations: Golf, football, cricket, rugby.

The Lord Browne of Belmont, House of Lords, London SW1A 0PW
Tel: 020 7219 5353 *Fax:* 020 7219 2347 *Email:* brownew@parliament.uk

LABOUR

BROWNE OF LADYTON, LORD

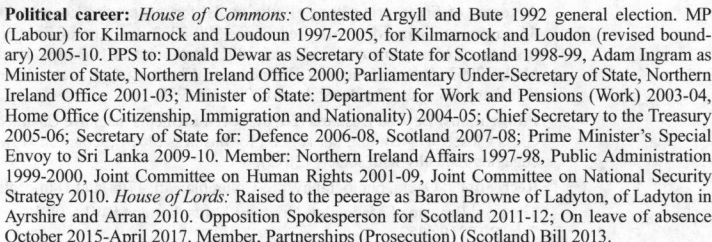

BROWNE OF LADYTON (Life Baron), Desmond Henry Browne; cr 2010. Born 22 March 1952; Son of late Peter Browne, process worker, and Maureen Browne, catering manageress; Married Maura Taylor 1983 (2 sons).

Education: Saint Michael's Academy, Kilwinning; Glasgow University (LLB 1973).

Non-political career: Qualified as solicitor 1976; Solicitor, Jas Campbell & Co, WS Ross Haper & Murphy and McCluckey Browne 1976-93; Called to Scottish Bar 1993; Advocate, Faculty of Advocates 1993-. Member, Unison.

Political career: *House of Commons:* Contested Argyll and Bute 1992 general election. MP (Labour) for Kilmarnock and Loudoun 1997-2005, for Kilmarnock and Loudon (revised boundary) 2005-10. PPS to: Donald Dewar as Secretary of State for Scotland 1998-99, Adam Ingram as Minister of State, Northern Ireland Office 2000; Parliamentary Under-Secretary of State, Northern Ireland Office 2001-03; Minister of State: Department for Work and Pensions (Work) 2003-04, Home Office (Citizenship, Immigration and Nationality) 2004-05; Chief Secretary to the Treasury 2005-06; Secretary of State for: Defence 2006-08, Scotland 2007-08; Prime Minister's Special Envoy to Sri Lanka 2009-10. Member: Northern Ireland Affairs 1997-98, Public Administration 1999-2000, Joint Committee on Human Rights 2001-09, Joint Committee on National Security Strategy 2010. *House of Lords:* Raised to the peerage as Baron Browne of Ladyton, of Ladyton in Ayrshire and Arran 2010. Opposition Spokesperson for Scotland 2011-12; On leave of absence October 2015-April 2017. Member, Partnerships (Prosecution) (Scotland) Bill 2013.

Political interests: Legal affairs, human rights, disability, education, Northern Ireland, constitution, international affairs; Afghanistan, Burundi, Colombia, Rwanda, South Africa.

Other: Member, Scottish Council for Civil Liberties 1976-; Council member, Law Society of Scotland 1988-92; Chair, Scottish Child Law Centre 1988-92; Fellow, Industry and Parliament Trust 2002. PC 2005.

Publications: Report for Lord MacAulay's Working Party on the Prison System (1990).

Recreations: Sports, football, tennis, swimming, reading, computing.

Rt Hon the Lord Browne of Ladyton, House of Lords, London SW1A 0PW
Tel: 020 7219 4501 *Email:* browned@parliament.uk

CROSSBENCH

BROWNE OF MADINGLEY, LORD

BROWNE OF MADINGLEY (Life Baron), Edmund John Phillip Browne; cr 2001. Born 20 February 1948.

Education: King's School, Ely; St John's College, Cambridge (BA physics 1969, MA); Stanford University, USA (MS business 1980).

Non-political career: BP plc 1966-2007: Exploration and production posts in USA, UK and Canada 1969-83, Group treasurer and chief executive, BP Finance International 1984-86, Executive vice-president and chief financial officer, BP America and chief executive officer (CEO), Standard Oil Production Company 1986-89, CEO, BP Exploration, London 1989-91, Managing director, British Petroleum Company plc 1991-95, Group chief executive 1995-2007; Numerous non-executive directorships, including Intel Corporation -2006 and Goldman Sachs -2007; Partner, Riverstone LLC 2007-15; Chair: Mubadala International Oil and Gas Advisory Board -2014, Accenture Global Energy Board, Cuadrilla Resource Holdings Ltd -2015, Stanhope Capital Advisory Board; Member: Deutsche Bank Advisory Board for Climate Change -2014, Deutsche Bank Europe Advisory Board -2014; Letterone Petroleum Ltd/L1 Energy Advisory Board: Former member, Chair; Schlumberger Business Consulting Advisory Group; PCCW Group of Advisers -2016; Former adviser, Fidelity International; Chair: L1 Energy 2015-, Huawei Technologies UK Ltd 2015-.

Political career: *House of Lords:* Raised to the peerage as Baron Browne of Madingley, of Cambridge in the County of Cambridgeshire 2001. Lead Non-Executive Director, Cabinet Office Board 2010-15. EU Sub-committee A (Economic and Financial Affairs and International Trade): Co-opted member 2008-10, Member 2010-11. *Councils and public bodies:* Board of trustees, Tate Galleries: Trustee 2007-17, Chair 2009-17; Non-executive director, Cabinet Office 2010-14.

Political interests: Arts, culture, education, energy, environment.

Other: Trustee: British Museum 1995-2005, Eisenhower Fellowships; Vice-President, Prince of Wales Business Leaders Forum 1997-2007; Council member, Foundation for Science and Technology; President, British Association for Advancement of Science -2008; Chair: International Advisory Board, Blavatnik School of Government, Performance Theatre Advisory Group, Queen Elizabeth Prize for Enginneering Foundation, Donmar Theatre; Vice-president, Flora and Fauna International; Senior fellow, St Anthony's College, Oxford; Elder Brother, Corporation of Trinity House; President, Royal Academy of Engineering 2006-11; Chair: Independent Review of Higher Education Funding and Student Finance 2009-10, Advisory board, Judge Business School, Cambridge -2010; Emeritus chairman, Graduate School of Business, Stanford University; Fellow, American Academy of Arts and Sciences; Honorary member, School of Economics and Management, Tsinghua University, Beijing; Co-chair, International Advisory Board, Russian Museum; Chair: Queen Elizabeth prize Foundation, John Browne Charitable Trust; Member: Blavatinik School of Government Foundation, Needham Resarch Institute, Cambridge China Development Trust, Cambridge Foundation, Jewish Museum and Tolerance Centre, Russia, Francis Crick Institute 2017-, Courtauld Institute 2017-; FREng; FRS; FIMM; FInstP; FInstPet. 19 honorary doctorates from UK, western European, Russian and US universities; 9 honorary fellowships. Royal Academy of Engineering Prince Philip medal for outstanding contribution to engineering 1999; *Management Today* Most Admired CEO 1999-2002; Institute of Energy Melchett Medal 2001; Institute of Management Gold Medal 2001; Institution of Chemical Engineers Commemorative Medal 2003; British American Business Inc Channing Corporate Citizen Award 2004; World Petroleum Congress Dewhurst Award 2005. Kt 1998.

Publications: Beyond Business (2010); Seven Elements that have Changed the World (2013); The Glass Closet: why coming out is good for business (2014); Connect: How companies succeed by engaging radically with society (2015).

Recreations: Opera, photography, pre-Columbian art, 17th- and 18th-century printed works.

The Lord Browne of Madingley, House of Lords, London SW1A 0PW
Tel: 020 7219 5353
Email: spaynter@l1energy.co.uk *Twitter:* @lordjohnbrowne

CONSERVATIVE

BROWNING, BARONESS

BROWNING (Life Baroness), Angela Frances Browning; cr 2010. Born 4 December 1946; Daughter of late Thomas Pearson and late Linda Chamberlain; Married David Browning 1968 (2 sons).

Education: Westwood Grammar School; Reading College of Technology; Bournemouth College of Technology.

Non-political career: Teacher, home economics, adult education 1968-74; Auxiliary nurse 1976-77; Self-employed consultant, manufacturing industry 1977-85; Management consultant specialising in training, corporate communications and finance 1985-94; Director, Small Business Bureau 1985-94; Chair, Women Into Business 1988-92; Member, Department of Employment Advisory Committee for Women's Employment 1989-92.

Political career: *House of Commons:* Contested Crewe and Nantwich 1987 general election. MP (Conservative) for Tiverton 1992-97, for Tiverton and Honiton 1997-2010. PPS to Michael Forsyth as Minister of State, Department of Employment 1993-94; Parliamentary Secretary, Ministry of Agriculture, Fisheries and Food 1994-97; Opposition Spokesperson on Education and Employment (Education and Disability) 1997-98; Member, Shadow Cabinet 1999-2001: Shadow Secretary of State for Trade and Industry 1999-2000, Shadow Leader of the House 2000-01. Member: Agriculture 1992-93, Modernisation of the House of Commons 2000-01, Public Accounts 2004-06, 2007-10, Standards and Privileges 2004-06. *House of Lords:* Raised to the peerage as Baroness

Browning, of Whimple in the County of Devon 2010. Government Spokesperson, Home Office 2011; Minister of State for Crime Prevention and Anti-Social Behaviour Reduction, Home Office 2011. Member: Liaison 2012-15, Mental Capacity Act 2005 2013-14, The Arctic 2014-15; Alternate member, Procedure 2015-; Member: Equality Act 2010 and Disability 2015-16, Joint Committee on the Draft Investigatory Powers Bill 2015-16, European Union 2016-, EU Home Affairs Sub-committee 2016-, Lord Speaker's Committee on the Size of the House 2016-. *Other:* Conservative Party: Vice-chair 2001-05, Deputy chair (organisation and campaigning) 2005-07. *Councils and public bodies:* Government co-chair, Women's National Commission 1995-97; Electoral Commissioner 2010-12; Advisory Committee on Business Appointments: Member 2014, Chair 2015-.

Political interests: Small businesses, education (special needs), mental health, learning disabilities.

Other: Vice-president: National Autistic Society, Institute of Sales and Marketing Management 1997-; National vice-president, Alzheimer's Society 1997-; Patron: Research Autism, Action on Elder Abuse; Fellow, Institute of Sales and Marketing Management.

Recreations: Theatre, cooking.

The Baroness Browning, House of Lords, London SW1A 0PW
Tel: 020 7219 5353

BRUCE OF BENNACHIE, LORD

Liberal Democrat Lords Spokesperson for Scotland

LIBERAL DEMOCRAT

BRUCE OF BENNACHIE (Life Baron), Malcolm Gray Bruce; cr 2015. Born 17 November 1944; Son of David Bruce, agricultural merchant and hotelier, and Kathleen Bruce; Married Veronica Wilson 1969 (divorced 1992) (1 son 1 daughter); married Rosemary Vetterlein 1998 (2 daughters 1 son).

Education: Wrekin College, Shropshire; St Andrews University (MA economics and political science 1966); Strathclyde University (MSc marketing 1971); CPE and Inns of Court School of Law, Gray's Inn 1995; French, German (a little).

Non-political career: Trainee journalist, *Liverpool Post* 1966-67; Boots section buyer 1968-69; Research and information officer, NE Scotland Development Authority 1971-75; Director, Noroil Publishing House (UK) Ltd 1975-81; Joint editor/publisher, Aberdeen Petroleum Publishing 1981-84. Member, NUJ.

Political career: *House of Commons:* Contested Angus North and Mearns October 1974 and Aberdeenshire West 1979 general elections. MP (Liberal Democrat) for Gordon 1983-97, for Gordon (revised boundary) 1997-2005, for Gordon (revised boundary) 2005-15. Liberal Spokesperson for Energy 1985-87; Scottish Liberal Spokesperson for Education 1986-87; Alliance Spokesperson for Employment 1987; Liberal Spokesperson for Trade and Industry 1987-88; SLD Spokesperson for Natural Resources (energy and conservation) 1988-89; Liberal Democrat Spokesperson for: the Environment and Natural Resources 1989-90, Scottish Affairs 1990-92, Trade and Industry 1992-94, the Treasury 1994-99; Chair, Liberal Democrat Parliamentary Party 1999-2001; Liberal Democrat Shadow Secretary of State for: Environment, Food and Rural Affairs 2001-02, Trade and Industry 2003-05. Member: Scottish Affairs 1990-92, Trade and Industry 1992-94, Treasury 1997-99, Standards and Privileges 1999-2001; Chair: International Development 2005-15; Member: Liaison 2005-15, Quadripartite (Committees on Strategic Export Controls)/Arms Export Controls 2006-15, Joint Committee on National Security Strategy 2010-15. *House of Lords:* Raised to the peerage as Baron Bruce of Bennachie, of Torphins in the County of Aberdeen 2015. Liberal Democrat Shadow Minister/Lords Spokesperson for Scotland 2016-. Member, EU Financial Affairs Sub-committee 2017-. *Other:* Leader, Scottish Social and Liberal Democrats 1988-89; Scottish Liberal Democrats: Leader 1989-92, President 2000-15; Deputy Leader, Liberal Democrats 2014-15. *Councils and public bodies:* Rector, Dundee University 1986-89.

Political interests: Energy, gas industry, oil industry, industrial policy, trade policy, deaf children, Scottish home rule and federalism; Balkans, Baltic States, Canada, Czech Republic, Eastern Europe, Hungary, Russia, Scandinavia, South Africa, USA, Zimbabwe.

Other: Member: UK Delegation Parliamentary Assembly of the Council of Europe/Western European Union 2000-05, Executive Committee, Inter-Parliamentary Union, British Group 2010-15, Executive Committee, Commonwealth Parliamentary Association (UK Branch) 2014-15; Hon. Vice-President, National Deaf Children's Society; Hon. President, Grampian Branch; Hon. Vice-President: Combined Heat and Power Association, Action on Hearing Loss; Council member, Overseas Development Institute; National Deaf Children's Society. PC 2006; Kt 2012.

Recreations: Golf, cycling, walking, theatre and music.

Rt Hon the Lord Bruce of Bennachie, House of Lords, London SW1A 0PW
Tel: 020 7219 3000 *Twitter:* @malcolmbruce

LIBERAL DEMOCRAT

BURNETT, LORD

BURNETT (Life Baron), John Patrick Aubone Burnett; cr 2006. Born 19 September 1945; Son of late Lt-Col Aubone Burnett OBE and Joan Burnett, née Bolt; Married Elizabeth Sherwood, née de la Mare 1971 (2 sons 2 daughters).

Education: Ampleforth College, Yorkshire; Royal Marines Commando Training Centre; Britannia Royal Naval College, Dartmouth; College of Law, London.

Non-political career: Royal Marines 1964-70: Troop Commander, 42 Commando in Borneo and Singapore, Troop Commander and Company Second-in-Command, 40 Commando in Far East and Middle East. Farmer 1976-98; Solicitor 1975; Partner, senior partner Burd Pearse solicitors, Okehampton, Devon 1976-97. Member, NFU.

Political career: *House of Commons:* Contested Torridge and West Devon 1987 general election. MP (Liberal Democrat) for Torridge and West Devon 1997-2005. Spokesperson for: Home and Legal Affairs 1997-2004, Solicitor General's Department 2004-05. *House of Lords:* Raised to the peerage as Baron Burnett, of Whitchurch in the County of Devon 2006. Liberal Democrat Spokesperson for: Planning 2007-09, Environment, Food and Rural Affairs 2009-10. Co-opted Member, EU Sub-committee E (Law and Institutions) 2006-10.

Political interests: Economic policy, defence, agriculture.

Other: Member: Law Society, Devon and Exeter Law Society, Law Society's Revenue (Tax) Law Committee 1984-96, Council of Devon Cattle Breeders' Association, Royal Marine Association, Royal British Legion.

Recreations: Breeding Devon cattle, walking, sport.

The Lord Burnett, House of Lords, London SW1A 0PW
Tel: 020 7219 8730

CROSSBENCH

BURNS, LORD

BURNS (Life Baron), Terence Burns; cr. 1998. Born 13 March 1944; Son of Patrick and Doris Burns; Married Anne Powell 1969 (1 son 2 daughters).

Education: Houghton-le-Spring Grammar School; Manchester University (BA economics 1965).

Non-political career: London Business School (LBS): Research posts 1965-70, Lecturer in economics 1970-74, Senior lecturer in economics 1974-79, Director, LBS Centre for Economic Forecasting 1976-79, Professor of economics 1979, Fellow 1989; Member, HM Treasury Academic Panel 1976-79; Chief Economic Adviser to HM Treasury and Head of Government Economic Service 1980-91; Visiting Fellow, Nuffield College, Oxford 1989-97; Permanent Secretary, HM Treasury 1991-98; Non-executive director: Legal and General Group plc 1999-2001, Pearson plc 1999-2010; British Land Company plc 2000-05; Chair: Glas Cymru (Welsh Water) 2001-10, Santander UK plc (formerly Abbey National plc) 2002-15; Marks and Spencer plc: Deputy chair 2005-06, Chair 2006-07; Channel 4 Television Corporation: Chairman Designate 2009-10, Chair 2010-16.

Political career: *House of Lords:* Raised to the peerage as Baron Burns, of Pitshanger in the London Borough of Ealing 1998. Chair: Financial Services and Markets Joint Committee 1999, Trade Union and Party Funding 2016; Member, Economic Affairs 2016-; Chair, Lord Speaker's Committee on the Size of the House 2016-. *Councils and public bodies:* Non-executive member, Office for Budget Responsibility 2012-; Chair, Freedom of Information Commission 2015-16.

Other: Society of Business Economists: Vice-President 1985-98, President 1998-; Fellow, London Business School 1989-; Vice-President, Royal Economic Society 1992-; Board Member, Manchester Business School 1992-98; Non-executive director, Queens Park Rangers FC 1996-2001; Royal Academy of Music: Governor 1998-2002, Chair of governing body 2002-; Monteverdi Choir and Orchestra: Trustee 1998-2001, Chair of trustees 2001-07; Chair, National Lottery Commission 2000-01; Member, Hansard Society Commission on Scrutiny Role of Parliament 1999-; Chair, Committee of Inquiry into Hunting with Dogs in England and Wales 2000; Governor, National Institute of Economic and Social Research; Chair, Independent Adviser on BBC Charter Review 2003-04. Four honorary degrees. Kt 1983; GCB 1995; *Clubs:* Reform Club.

Recreations: Watching football, music, golf.

The Lord Burns GCB, House of Lords, London SW1A 0PW
Tel: 020 7219 0312 *Email:* burnst@parliament.uk

LIBERAL DEMOCRAT

BURT OF SOLIHULL, BARONESS

Liberal Democrat Shadow Secretary of State for Equalities

BURT OF SOLIHULL (Life Baroness), Lorely Jane Burt; cr 2015. Born 10 September 1954; Daughter of Hazel Baker, née Abbiss, and Raymond Baker; Married Richard Burt 1992 (1 daughter from previous marriage 1 stepson).

Education: High Arcal Grammar School, Dudley; University College of Wales, Swansea (BSc Econ economics 1975); Open University (MBA 1997); Financial Times Non-executive Director Diploma.

Non-political career: Assistant governor, Pucklechurch Remand Centre and HMP Holloway 1975-78; Personnel and training posts, Beecham, Eurocar, Forte and Mercers 1978-84; Managing director, Kudos Leisure Ltd training company 1984-97; Director: Ace Creative Enterprises Ltd marketing company 1994-99, Mansion House Group 1999-2002; Self-employed estate planning consultant 2002-05; Board adviser: Total Training 2015-, DBS Law 2016-; Non-executive director, DBS Heart CIC 2016-.

Political career: *House of Commons:* Contested Dudley South 2001 general election. MP (Liberal Democrat) for Solihull 2005-10, for Solihull (revised boundary) 2010-15. Contested Solihull 2015 general election. Liberal Democrat: Whip 2005-06, Shadow Minister for: Northern Ireland 2005-06, Small Business, Women and Equality 2006-07, Business, Enterprise and Regulatory Reform 2007-09, Business, Innovation and Skills 2009-10; PPS to Danny Alexander as Chief Secretary to the Treasury 2012-14; Government Ambassador for Women and Enterprise 2014-15; Assistant Government Whip 2014-15. Member: Treasury 2005-06, Regulatory Reform 2006-10, Joint Committee on Voting Eligibilty (Prisoners) Bill 2013. Chair, Liberal Democrat Parliamentary Party Committee on Business, Innovation and Skills 2010-12. *House of Lords:* Raised to the peerage as Baroness Burt of Solihull, of Solihull in the County of West Midlands 2015. Liberal Democrat: Spokesperson for Business, Innovation and Skills 2015-16, Shadow Secretary of State for Equalities 2016-. *Other:* Contested West Midlands region 2004 European Parliament election. Liberal Democrats: Member: Federal Policy Committee 2002-03, West Midlands regional executive 2002-, Chair, Liberal Democrat Parliamentary Party 2007-12, Member, Federal Executive, President, West Midlands Liberal Democrats 2016-. *Councils and public bodies:* Councillor, Dudley Metropolitan Borough Council 1998-2003.

Political interests: Industry, manufacturing, equalities, planning, women in enterprise, osteoporosis, funerals and bereavement, personal and company debt, management, prisons; Guinea-Bissau, Israel, Japan, Palestine, Papua New Guinea, Tunisia.

Other: Fellow, Institute of Sales and Marketing Management 1998. Small Business Friendly Award, Federation of Small Businesses 2008; International Luminary Award, Women's Business Enterprise National Council 2009; Small Business Friendly Award, Federation of Small Businesses Warwickshire and Coventry region 2009; Community Inspiration Award, Community Foundation 2014. President, Colebridge Table Tennis Club 2013-.

Recreations: Theatre, cinema, socialising, food, keeping fit.

The Baroness Burt of Solihull, House of Lords, London SW1A 0PW
Tel: 020 7219 8269 *Email:* burtl@parliament.uk *Twitter:* @lorelyburt

CONSERVATIVE

BUSCOMBE, BARONESS

Parliamentary Under-Secretary of State and Government Spokesperson, Department for Work and Pensions

BUSCOMBE (Life Baroness), Peta Jane Buscombe; cr. 1998. Born 12 March 1954; Married Philip John Buscombe 1980 (twin sons 1 daughter).

Education: Hinchley Wood School, Surrey; Rosebery Grammar School, Epsom; Inns of Court School of Law; Columbia Law School, New York; French.

Non-political career: Called to the Bar, Inner Temple 1977; Director, R Buxton textile marketing company 1977-79; Legal adviser, Dairy Trade Federation 1979-80; Barclays Bank 1980-84: Legal counsel, New York, Head office lawyer and inspector, London; Legal adviser and assistant secretary, Institute of Practitioners in Advertising 1984-87; Non-executive director, Affinity Water plc 2006-; Chief executive, Advertising Association 2007-; Director: Advertising Standards Board of Finance 2007-, Committee of Advertising Practice 2007-; Non-executive Director, Local World Ltd 2013-.

Political career: *House of Commons:* Contested (Conservative) Slough 1997 general election. *House of Lords:* Raised to the peerage as Baroness Buscombe, of Goring in the County of Oxfordshire 1998. Opposition Spokesperson for: Law Officers and Lord Chancellor's Department/Legal

Affairs 1999-2005, Social Security 1999-2001, Trade and Industry 1999-2000, 2001, Cabinet Office 2000-01, Home Office 2001-02, Culture, Media and Sport 2002-05, Education and Skills 2005-07; Government Whip (Baroness in Waiting) 2016-; Parliamentary Under-Secretary of State and Government Spokesperson, Department for Work and Pensions 2017-. Member: EU Sub-committee B (Internal Market, Infrastructure and Employment) 2012-13, Inquiries Act 2005 2013-14, Joint Committee on Human Rights 2014-16, Joint Committee on the National Security Strategy 2015-. *Other:* Vice-chair, Conservative Party 1997-99; President, Slough Conservative Association 1997-2001; Patron, Inns of Court School of Law Conservative Association; President, Henley Constituency Association 2015-. *Councils and public bodies:* Councillor, South Oxfordshire District Council 1995-99; Chair, Press Complaints Commission 2009-11.

Political interests: Law and order, legal affairs, defence, media.

Other: Member, Inter-Parliamentary Union; Patron, PALS (Partnership for Active Leisure Scheme); Vice-president, Henley Society; Ambassador, Guide Association; Chair, Samaritans Advisory Board; Foundation for International and Commercial Arbitration and Alternative Dispute Resolution.

Recreations: Gardening, riding, tennis, theatre, cinema, shooting.

The Baroness Buscombe, House of Lords, London SW1A 0PW
Tel: 020 7219 5353 *Email:* buscombep@parliament.uk
Website: petabuscombe.com

BUTLER OF BROCKWELL, LORD

CROSSBENCH

BUTLER OF BROCKWELL (Life Baron), Frederick Edward Robin Butler; cr. 1998. Born 3 January 1938; Son of late Bernard and Nora Butler; Married Gillian Galley 1962 (1 son 2 daughters).

Education: Harrow School; University College, Oxford (BA literae humaniores 1961, MA).

Non-political career: Civil Service 1961-98: HM Treasury (HMT) 1961-72: Private secretary to Niall MacDermot as Financial Secretary to Treasury 1964-65; Secretary Budget Committee 1965-69; Seconded to Cabinet Office as Member Central Policy Review Staff 1971-72; Private Secretary to Prime Ministers: Edward Heath 1972-74, Harold Wilson 1974-75; HMT 1975-82: Assistant Secretary-General, Expenditure Intelligence Division 1975-77, Under Secretary, General Expenditure Policy Group 1977-80, Principal Establishment Officer 1980-82; Principal Private Secretary to Rt Hon Margaret Thatcher as Prime Minister 1982-85; Second Permanent Secretary, Public Expenditure, HMT 1985-87; Secretary of the Cabinet and Head of the Home Civil Service 1988-98; Master, University College, Oxford 1998-2008; Non-executive director: ICI plc 1998-2008, HSBC Holdings plc 1998-2008; Member, Marsh and McLennan International Advisory Board 2005-09; Kings Health Partners Academic Health Science Centre: Chair 2009-15, Board Member 2015-.

Political career: *House of Lords:* Raised to the peerage as Baron Butler of Brockwell, of Herne Hill in the London Borough of Lambeth 1998. Member: Intelligence and Security Committee 2010-15, Parliamentary and Political Service Honours Committee 2012-. Member: Delegated Powers and Regulatory Reform 2009-13, Leader's Group on the Working Practices of the House of Lords 2010-11, Procedure 2012-15, EU Financial Affairs Sub-committee 2015-, Joint Committee on the Draft Investigatory Powers Bill 2015-16. *Councils and public bodies:* Member, Royal Commission on the Reform of the House of Lords 1999; Chair, Review of Intelligence on Weapons of Mass Destruction 2004.

Political interests: Higher education, civil service, constitutional matters.

Other: Chair of Governors: Harrow School 1988-91, Dulwich College 1997-2003; Visitor, Ashmolean Museum 2001-08; Trustee, Rhodes Trust 2002-09. The Salters' Company: Hon. Member, Master 2011-12. Six honorary degrees from UK and US universities; Hon. Fellow, King's College, London. CVO 1986; KCB 1988; GCB 1992; KG 2003; PC 2004; *Clubs:* Athenæum, Brooks's, Beefsteak, Anglo-Belgian Club. MCC; Dulwich and Sydenham Golf Club; St Enodoc Golf Club.

Recreations: Competitive games.

Rt Hon the Lord Butler of Brockwell KG GCB CVO, House of Lords, London SW1A 0PW
Tel: 020 7219 5353

CROSSBENCH

BUTLER-SLOSS, BARONESS

BUTLER-SLOSS (Life Baroness), (Ann) Elizabeth Oldfield Butler-Sloss; cr 2006. Born 10 August 1933; Daughter of Sir Cecil Havers, High Court Judge Queen's Bench Division and Lady Havers, née Enid Snelling; Married Joseph Butler-Sloss 1958 (2 sons 1 daughter).

Education: Wycombe Abbey School; French.

Non-political career: Barrister, Inner Temple 1955; Practising barrister 1955-70; Registrar Principal Registry of Probate/Family Division 1970-79; High Court Judge Family Division 1979-88; Lord Justice of Appeal 1988-99; President Family Division 1999-2005.

Political career: *House of Commons:* Contested (Conservative) Lambeth, Vauxhall 1959 general election. *House of Lords:* Raised to the peerage as Baroness Butler-Sloss, of Marsh Green in the County of Devon 2006. Member: Merits of Statutory Instruments 2007-12, Ecclesiastical Committee 2010-, Statutory Instruments Committee 2010; Chair, Adoption Legislation 2012-13; Member, Joint Committee on the Draft Modern Slavery Bill 2014. *Councils and public bodies:* Chair: Cleveland Child Abuse Inquiry 1987-88, Security Commission 1995-2005; Commission on Appointment of Archbishop of Canterbury 2002.

Political interests: Education, children, family, intelligence/security, Commonwealth, legal issues, human trafficking, interfaith relations, Forced Marriages Commission 2013; Hong Kong, India, Kenya, Malaysia, Pakistan, Singapore.

Other: Former chair, St Paul's Cathedral Council; Governor, Coram and Merchant Taylors School; Inner Temple: Bencher, Treasurer 1998; Vice-President, Devon Hospice Care; President, Devon Branch National Trust; Patron, Grandparents' Association; Visitor, St Hilda's College, Oxford; Trustee: Muzaffarabad Earthquake Appeal, Human Trafficking Foundation; Chair, Commission on Religion and Belief in British Public Life; Honorary FCP; FCPaed; FCPsych; FSM. Honorary Freeman, Merchant Taylors. Freedom, City of London. Chancellor, University of West of England 1993-2011. 18 honorary degrees; Honorary fellow: King's College, London, St Hilda's College, Oxford, Peterhouse Cambridge, Corpus Christi College, Cambridge. DBE 1979; PC 1988; GBE 2005; *Clubs:* RSM, Landsdowne Club.

Rt Hon the Baroness Butler-Sloss GBE, House of Lords, London SW1A 0PW
Tel: 020 7219 4044 *Email:* butlerslosse@parliament.uk

CONSERVATIVE

BYFORD, BARONESS

BYFORD (Life Baroness), Hazel Byford; cr. 1996. Born 14 January 1941; Daughter of late Sir Cyril Osborne (MP for Louth 1945-69) and Lady Osborne CBE; Married Charles Byford 1962 (died 2013) (1 daughter and 1 son deceased).

Education: St Leonard's School, St Andrews; Moulton Agricultural College, Northampton.

Non-political career: Former poultry farmer.

Political career: *House of Lords:* Raised to the peerage as Baroness Byford, of Rothley in the County of Leicestershire 1996. Opposition Whip 1997-98; Opposition Spokesperson for: Agriculture December 1998-2002, Environment 1998-2003, Food, Farming and Rural Affairs 1998-2007. Member EU Sub-committee D: (Agriculture, Fisheries and Environment) 2010-12, (Agriculture, Fisheries, Environment and Energy) 2012-13, 2013-15; Member: Information 2015-16, Natural Environment and Rural Communities Act 2006 2017-. *Other:* Chairman, National Committee, Conservative Women 1990-93; President, National Union of Conservative and Unionist Associations 1996-97. *Councils and public bodies:* Member: Transport Users' Consultative Committee 1989-94, Rail Users' Consultative Committee 1994-95; Associate member, Royal Agricultural Society 2003-.

Political interests: Agriculture, countryside and rural issues; Suffolk.

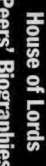

Other: WRVS Leicestershire 1961-96, County Organiser 1972-76; Patron: VIRSA 1998-2003, Institute of Agricultural Secretaries and Administrators 2000-09, Rural Stress Information Network 2001-06, National Farm Attractions Network 2002-08; Fellow, Industry and Parliament Trust 2002; Lay Canon of Leicester Cathedral 2003-; Honorary associate, British Veterinary Association 2003; President: Concordia 2004-09, Guild of Agricultural Journalists 2004-07; Honorary associate, Royal College of Veterinary Surgeons 2006; President: Lincolnshire Agricultural Society 2006, Leicestershire Clubs for Young People/Young Leicestershire 2006-, Royal Association of Dairy Farmers 2007-10; Patron, Women's Farming Union 2007-15; President: LEAF, Royal Smithfield Club 2010; Fellow, Royal Agricultural Society of England. Worshipful Company of Farmers 2013-14. Honorary Doctorate (business administration) Lincoln University 2007; Doctor of Science, Nottingham Trent University 2008; Honorary Doctor of Laws, Leicester University 2010. DBE 1994; *Clubs:* Farmers Club.

Recreations: Golf, reading, bridge.

The Baroness Byford DBE, House of Lords, London SW1A 0PW
Tel: 020 7219 3095 *Email:* byfordh@parliament.uk

CONSERVATIVE

CAINE, LORD

CAINE (Life Baron), Jonathan Michael Caine; cr 2016. Born 11 April 1966.

Education: Temple Moor High School; Leicester University (history).

Non-political career: Research Department, Conservative Central Office; Special Adviser to Secretaries of State for Northern Ireland: Tom King 1988-89, Peter Brooke 1989-92, Patrick Mayhew 1992-97, Owen Paterson 2010-12, Theresa Villiers 2012-16, James Brokenshire 2016-.

Political career: *House of Lords:* Raised to the peerage as Baron Caine, of Temple Newsam in the City of Leeds 2016.

Recreations: Leeds Rhinos RLFC, Yorkshire County Cricket Club.

The Lord Caine, House of Lords, London SW1A 0PW
Tel: 020 7219 3000

CONSERVATIVE

CAITHNESS, EARL OF

CAITHNESS (20th Earl of, S), Malcolm Ian Sinclair; cr. 1455; Lord Berriedale; 15th Bt of Canisbay (NS) 1631. Born 3 November 1948; Son of 19th Earl; Married Diana Caroline Coke 1975 (died 1994) (1 son 1 daughter); married Leila Jenkins 2004 (divorced); married Diana Penelope Wilson 2015.

Education: Marlborough College, Wiltshire; Royal Agricultural College, Cirencester.

Non-political career: Savills 1972-78; Brown and Mumford 1978-80; Director of various companies 1980-84; Consultant, Rickett Tinne Property Consultants, and other companies 1994-.

Political career: *House of Lords:* First entered House of Lords 1969; Government Spokesperson for DHSS 1984-85; Government Whip 1984-85; Government Spokesperson for Scotland 1984-86; Parliamentary Under-Secretary of State, Department of Transport 1985-86; Minister of State: Home Office 1986-88, Department of Environment 1988-89; Paymaster General and Treasury Minister 1989-90; Minister of State: Foreign and Commonwealth Office 1990-92, Department of Transport 1992-94; Elected hereditary peer 1999-. Member: EU Sub-committee G 1979, EU Sub-committee D 1979-82, Consolidation Bills (Joint Committee) 1979-84, Procedure Committee 1997-2004, House of Lords Offices Committee 1997-2000, EU Sub-committee F (Home Affairs) 2003-07, Draft Climate Change Bill Joint Committee 2007; Co-opted member, EU Sub-committee D (Environment and Agriculture) 2008-10; Member: EU Sub-committee D: (Agriculture, Fisheries and Environment) 2010-12, (Agriculture, Fisheries, Environment and Energy) 2012-13, EU Sub-committee A (Economic and Financial Affairs) 2013-15, European Union 2014-16, EU Financial Affairs Sub-committee 2015-16, Communications 2016-17, Natural Environment and Rural Communities Act 2006 2017-. *Other:* Chair, West Oxfordshire Conservative Association 1985-2001.

Other: Trustee: Queen Elizabeth Castle of Mey Trust 1996-2016, Clan Sinclair Trust 1998-; Chair, Caithness Archaeological Trust 2002-2011; FRICS. PC 1990.

Rt Hon the Earl of Caithness, House of Lords, London SW1A 0PW
Tel: 020 7219 5442 *Email:* caithness@parliament.uk

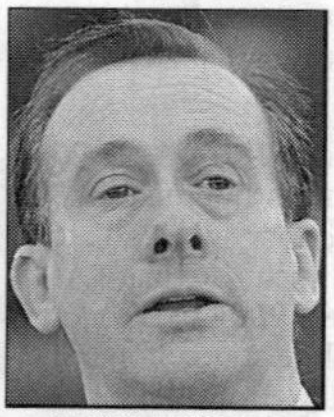

CONSERVATIVE

CALLANAN, LORD

Parliamentary Under-Secretary of State for Aviation, International and Security and Government Spokesperson, Department for Transport

CALLANAN (Life Baron), Martin John Callanan; cr 2014. Born 8 August 1961; Married Jayne Burton 1997 (1 son).

Education: Heathfield Senior High School; Newcastle Polytechnic (BSc electrical and electronic engineering 1995).

Non-political career: Project engineer, Scottish and Newcastle Breweries 1986-98.

Political career: *House of Lords:* Raised to the peerage as Baron Callanan, of Low Fell in the County of Tyne and Wear 2014. Parliamentary Under-Secretary of State for Aviation, International and Security and Government Spokesperson, Department for Transport 2017-. Member: Information 2015-16, Trade Union and Party Funding 2016, EU Financial Affairs Sub-committee 2016-17. *Other:* European Parliament: MEP for North East 1999-2014: PPS to Leader of Conservative MEPs 2003-05, Chief whip, European Conservatives and Reformists group 2009-14, Conservative Spokesperson for Transport 2009-14, Leader, Conservative Delegation 2010-14. Conservative

Party: Member, Gateshead East and Washington West constituency party 1989-, President, Newcastle University Conservative Future 1999-. *Councils and public bodies:* Member: Tyne and Wear County Council 1981-85, Gateshead Metropolitan Borough Council 1987-96.

Recreations: Squash, restoring vintage cars.

The Lord Callanan, House of Lords, London SW1A 0PW
Tel: 020 7219 5353

CAMERON OF DILLINGTON, LORD

CROSSBENCH

CAMERON OF DILLINGTON (Life Baron), Ewen James Hanning Cameron; cr. 2004. Born 24 November 1949; Son of Major Allan and Elizabeth Cameron; Married Caroline Ripley 1975 (3 sons 1 daughter).

Education: Harrow School; Oxford University (BA modern history 1972, MA).

Non-political career: Manager, Dillington Estate, Somerset 1971-; Chair, Orchard Media Ltd 1989-99; President, Somerset Young Farmers 1990-91; Director, Village Retail Services Association 1992-99; National president, Country Land and Business Association 1995-97; Member, Round Table for Sustainable Development 1997-2000; Chair: Let's Go Travel Ltd 1998-2006, Countryside Agency 1999-2004, Government's rural advocate for England 2000-04, Airport Direct Travel Ltd 2006-; Royal Bath and West Society: President 2006-07, Director 2008-15.

Political career: *House of Lords:* Raised to the peerage as Baron Cameron of Dillington, of Dillington in the County of Somerset 2004. Member: EU Sub-committee D (Environment and Agriculture) 2005-09, Administration and Works 2009-14, EU Sub-committee D: (Agriculture, Fisheries and Environment) 2010-12, (Agriculture, Fisheries, Environment and Energy) 2012-15, European Union 2012-15, Science and Technology 2015-17; Chair, Natural Environment and Rural Communities Act 2006 2017-. *Councils and public bodies:* High Sheriff of Somerset 1986-87; DL, Somerset 1989.

Political interests: Countryside, agriculture, environment, food and rural affairs, fisheries, housing, international development and aid, Africa, food and agriculture in developing world; (Agriculture in) Sub-Saharan Africa.

Other: Fellow, Royal Agricultural Societies 1995; Chair, Somerset Strategic Partnership 2004-11; Trustee, Lawes Agricultural Trust 2005-; President, British Guild of Agricultural Journalists 2010-15; Chair: Strategic Advisory Board of the Governments' Global Food Security Programme 2012-, Advisory Council, Centre for Ecology and Hydrology 2015-; FRICS 1992-. Hon. LLD Exeter 2004; Hon. degree Royal Agricultural University, Cirencester 2015. Kt 2003.

Recreations: Golf, windsurfing, shooting.

The Lord Cameron of Dillington, House of Lords, London SW1A 0PW
Tel: 020 7219 2530 *Email:* camerone@parliament.uk
Clouds, Golf Hill Road, Rock, Cornwall TA19 9EG

CAMPBELL OF LOUGHBOROUGH, BARONESS

CROSSBENCH

CAMPBELL OF LOUGHBOROUGH (Life Baroness), Susan Catherine Campbell; cr 2008. Born 10 October 1948.

Education: Long Eaton Grammar School, Derbyshire; Bedford College of Further Education; Leicester University (Advanced DipEd, MEd 1975).

Non-political career: Physical Education Teacher, Whalley Range High School, Manchester 1970-72; Director of PE, Leicester University 1972-76; Lecturer, Department of PE and Sports Science, Loughborough University 1976-80; East Midlands Regional Officer, Sports Council 1980-84; National Coaching Foundation 1984-95: Deputy Chief Executive 1984, Chief Executive 1985-95; Youth Sport Trust 1995-: Chief Executive 1995-2005, Chair 2005-; PE Adviser to Departments for Culture, Media and Sport and for Education and Science 2000-04; UK Sport 2003-13: Reform Chair 2003-05, Chair 2005-13; Head of Women's Football, Football Association 2016-.

Political career: *House of Lords:* Raised to the peerage as Baroness Campbell of Loughborough, of Loughborough in the County of Leicestershire 2008.

Countries of interest: Africa, Asia.

Other: Chair, Commonwealth Advisory Board on Sport 2004-08; Trustee, International Development through Sport; Hon. Fellow: Leeds Polytechnic 1990, Sheffield Polytechnic 1991; UK Sport Fellowship 2015. Hon DEd: Leicester University, Council for National Academic Awards 1992, De Montfort University 1996; Hon DSc, Brighton University 1993; Hon DTech, Loughborough

University 1997; Hon doctorate: Bedford University, Leeds Metropolitan University 2006, City and Guilds 2010, Exeter University 2010, Endicott College Boston, USA 2011, Queen's University 2013, Nottingham Trent University 2016. MBE 1991; CBE 2003.

Recreations: Competitive squash and hockey, kayaking, golf, tennis, cycling.

The Baroness Campbell of Loughborough CBE, House of Lords, London SW1A 0PW
Tel: 020 7219 5353 *Website:* www.youthsporttrust.org

LIBERAL DEMOCRAT

CAMPBELL OF PITTENWEEM, LORD

CAMPBELL OF PITTENWEEM (Life Baron), Walter Menzies Campbell; cr 2015. Born 22 May 1941; Son of late George and Elizabeth Campbell; Married Elspeth Urquhart 1970.

Education: Hillhead High School, Glasgow; Glasgow University (MA arts 1962; LLB law 1965); Stanford University, California (Postgraduate Studies international law 1966-67).

Non-political career: Competed: 1964 (Tokyo) Olympics, 1966 Commonwealth Games (Jamaica); UK Athletics Team Captain 1965-66; UK 100 metres record holder 1967-74; Called to the Bar (Scotland) 1968; QC (Scotland) 1982; Chair, Royal Lyceum Theatre Company, Edinburgh 1984-87.

Political career: *House of Commons:* Contested Greenock and Port Glasgow February and October 1974, East Fife 1979, and North East Fife 1983 general elections. MP for North East Fife 1987-2005, for North East Fife (revised boundary) 2005-15 (Liberal/All 1987-88, Liberal Democrat 1988-2015). Liberal Spokesperson for Arts, Broadcasting and Sport 1987-88; Liberal Democrat Spokesperson for: Scotland (Legal Affairs, Lord Advocate) 1988-99, Defence and Sport 1988-89, Defence and Disarmament and Sport 1989-94, Foreign Affairs and Defence and Sport 1994-97, Foreign Affairs (Defence and Europe) 1997-99, Liberal Democrat Principal Spokesperson for Defence and Foreign Affairs 1999-2001; Contested Speaker election 2000; Liberal Democrat Shadow Secretary of State for Foreign and Commonwealth Affairs 2001-06; Member, Intelligence and Security Committee 2010-15. Member: Trade and Industry 1990-92, Defence 1992-97, 1997-99, Foreign Affairs 2008-15, Joint Committees on: Intelligence and Security 2008-15, the Draft Detention of Terrorist Suspects (Temporary Extension) Bills 2011, Parliamentary Privilege 2013. *House of Lords:* Raised to the peerage as Baron Campbell of Pittenweem, of Pittenweem in the County of Fife 2015. *Other:* Chair, Scottish Liberal Party 1975-77; Liberal Democrats: Deputy Leader 2003-06, Leader 2006-07, Chair, Home Rule Commission 2011-.

Political interests: Defence, foreign affairs, legal affairs, sport, arts; North America, Middle East.

Other: North Atlantic Assembly (now NATO Parliamentary Assembly): Member 1989-, Leader, UK Delegation 2010-15; Parliamentary Assembly of OSCE: Member, UK Delegation 1992-97, 1999-2001, Vice-President 2017-; Member: Board of the British Council 1998-2002, Council of the Air League 1999-2006, Olympic Board 2010-12; President, European Movement in Scotland 2016-; Member, Faculty of Advocates; Patron, Lymphoma Association 2016-. Chancellor, St Andrews University 2006-. Three honorary doctorates: Glasgow University, Strathclyde University, St Andrews University. Member to Watch, Highland Park/*Spectator* 1996; Opposition Politician of the Year, Channel 4 2004; Opposition Politician of the Year, *House Magazine* 2004; Westminster Politician of the Year, *Herald*/Diageo 2004; Politician of the Year, *Oldie* magazine 2005; Parliamentarian of the Year, Political Studies Association 2005; Lifetime Achievement Award, *Herald* 2016. CBE 1987; PC 1999; Kt 2004; CH 2013; *Clubs:* Reform, National Liberal Club.

Publications: Menzies Campbell: My Autobiography (2008).

Recreations: All sports, theatre, music.

Rt Hon the Lord Campbell of Pittenweem CH CBE QC, House of Lords, London SW1A 0PW
Tel: 020 7219 6910 *Email:* campbellm@parliament.uk

CROSSBENCH

CAMPBELL OF SURBITON, BARONESS

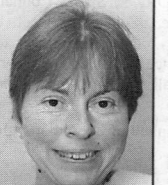

CAMPBELL OF SURBITON (Life Baroness), Jane Susan Campbell; cr 2007. Born 19 April 1959; Daughter of Ronald Campbell, engineer, and Jessie Campbell, nursery nurse; Married Roger Symes 2000.

Education: Hereward College, Coventry; Hatfield Polytechnic (BA history 1979); Sussex University (MA political history 1982).

Non-political career: Equal opportunities liaison officer, Greater London Council 1984-86; Disability training development officer, London Boroughs Joint Disability Committee 1986-87; Principal disability adviser, Hounslow Council 1987-88; Director of training, London Boroughs Disability Resource Team 1988-94; Freelance consultant 1994-96; Co-director, National Centre for Independent Living 1996-2000; Chair: Social Care Institute for Excellence 2001-05, Independent Living Strategy Group 2016-.

Political career: *House of Lords:* Raised to the peerage as Baroness Campbell of Surbiton, of Surbiton in the Royal Borough of Kingston upon Thames 2007. Independent member, House of Lords Appointments Commission 2008-13; Disability adviser, Department for Work and Pensions and Department of Health 2007-12. Member: Joint Committee on Human Rights 2010-12, Equality Act 2010 and Disability 2015-16. *Councils and public bodies:* Chair, British Council of Disabled People 1991-95; Governor, National Institute for Social Work 1995-2001; Commissioner, Disability Rights Commission 2000-06; Chair, Disability Committee and Commissioner, Commission for Equality and Human Rights 2006-09.

Political interests: Health and social care, social policy, medical ethics, independent living, equality and human rights, disability rights, end of life issues; Sweden.

Other: Founder and co-director, Not Dead Yet UK 2006-; President, National Disability Archive (Shape, London) 2013-; Patron: National Disability Arts Collection and Archive 2013-, Just Fair (UK) 2014-; Member, Justice Advisory Group (justice.org.uk) 2015-; Disability Rights UK, Power International. Honorary LLD, Bristol University 2002; Honorary Doctorate: Sheffield Hallam University 2003, Birmingham University 2009. Lifetime Achievement Award, Liberty Human Rights Awards (2012); Lifetime Achievement Award, Bevan Prize for Health and Wellbeing (2015). MBE 2000; DBE 2006.

Publications: With Mike Oliver, Disability Politics (Routledge, 1996); Contributor, Disabled People and the Right to Life (Routledge, 2008).

Recreations: Theatre, cinema, reading, gardening.

The Baroness Campbell of Surbiton DBE, House of Lords, London SW1A 0PW
Tel: 020 7219 5124 *Email:* campbelljs@parliament.uk
Website: www.baronesscampbellofsurbiton.com *Twitter:* @BnsJaneCampbell

CAMPBELL-SAVOURS, LORD

LABOUR

CAMPBELL-SAVOURS (Life Baron), Dale Norman Campbell-Savours; cr 2001. Born 23 August 1943; Son of late John Lawrence and Cynthia Lorraine Campbell-Savours; Married Gudrun Kristin Runolfsdottir 1970 (3 sons).

Education: Keswick School; Sorbonne, Paris.

Non-political career: Company director, clock and metal component manufacturing company.

Political career: *House of Commons:* Contested Darwen February and October 1974 general elections and Workington 1976 by-election. MP (Labour) for Workington 1979-2001. Opposition Frontbench Spokesperson for: Development and Co-operation 1991-92, Food, Agriculture and Rural Affairs 1992-94 (resigned from frontbench because of ill health). *House of Lords:* Raised to the peerage as Baron Campbell-Savours, of Allerdale in the County of Cumbria 2001. Member: Administration and Works 2007-12, Liaison 2010-15, Procedure 2010-15, House 2012-16, Services 2016-. *Councils and public bodies:* Councillor, Ramsbottom Urban District Council 1972-74.

Political interests: Investigative political and social work, education and health reform, industrial democracy.

Other: Patron: Cumbria Deaf Association, The Rural Academy Cumbria; President: Allerdale Mind, Cumberland County League.

Publications: The Case for the Supplementary Vote (1990); The Case for a Cattle Traceability Scheme (1993); The Case for The University of the Lakes (1995).

Recreations: Trout fishing, music.

The Lord Campbell-Savours, House of Lords, London SW1A 0PW
Tel: 020 7219 3513

CANTERBURY, LORD ARCHBISHOP OF

NON-AFFILIATED

CANTERBURY (105th Archbishop of), Justin Portal Welby. Born 6 January 1956; Son of late Gavin Welby and Jane Welby (now Lady Williams of Elvel); Married Caroline 1979 (2 sons 3 daughters 1 daughter deceased).

Education: Eton College; Trinity College, Cambridge (BA 1978); St John's College, Durham (BA 1991); French.

Non-political career: Project finance manager, Société Nationale Elf Aquitaine, Paris 1978-83; Treasurer, Elf UK 1983-84; Group Treasurer, Enterprise Oil plc 1984-89; Ordained: Deacon 1992, Priest 1993; Curate, All Saints, Chilvers Coton, Nuneaton 1992-95; Rector: St James', Southam 1995-2002, St Michael and All Angels, Ufton 1996-2002; Coventry Cathedral: Co-director, International Ministry and Canon Residentiary 2002-05, Sub-Dean and Canon for Reconciliation Ministry 2005-07; Dean of Liverpool 2007-11; Bishop of Durham 2011-13; Archbishop of Canterbury 2013-.

Political career: *House of Lords:* Entered House of Lords 2011. Member, Parliamentary Commission on Banking Standards 2012-13. *Councils and public bodies:* Southam College: Parent governor 1996-2002, Chair of governors 1998-2002; South Warwickshire General Hospitals NHS Trust: Non-executive director 1998-2000, Chair 2000-02.

Countries of interest: Burundi, DR Congo, France, Israel, Kenya, Nigeria, Palestine.

Other: Association Internationale pour l'Enseignement Social Chrétien; Diocesan Trust; Pershaw, Nashdom and Elmore Trust; Hon. Fellow, Association of Corporate Treasurers. Skinners. Chancellor, Canterbury Christ Church University. Peer of the Year, *Spectator* awards 2012. PC 2013; *Clubs:* Athenæum, Liverpool Club.

Publications: Can Companies Sin? (Grove Books, 1992); Various articles in The Treasurer magazine, and numerous other articles on risk management, finance, and on reconciliation; Various chapters in books on reconciliation, conflict management.

Recreations: Sailing, reading, travel.

Most Rev and Rt Hon the Archbishop of Canterbury, House of Lords, London SW1A 0PW
Tel: 020 7219 5353
Lambeth Palace, London SE1 7JU *Tel:* 020 7898 1472 *Email:* jack.palmer@churchofengland.org
Website: www.archbishopofcanterbury.org *Twitter:* @JustinWelby

CROSSBENCH

CAREY OF CLIFTON, LORD

CAREY OF CLIFTON (Life Baron), George Leonard Carey; cr 2002. Born 13 November 1935; Son of late George and Ruby Carey; Married Eileen Harmsworth Hood 1960 (2 sons 2 daughters).

Education: Bifrons School, Barking; King's College, London (PhD); London College of Divinity (ALCD, BD, MTh).

Non-political career: Royal Air Force 1954-56. Curate of St Mary's, Islington 1962-66; Lecturer: Oakhill Theological College 1966-70, St John's College, Nottingham; Occasional teacher at Nottingham University 1970-75; Vicar of St Nicholas Church, Durham 1975-82; Principal, Trinity Theological College, Bristol 1982-87; Bishop of Bath and Wells 1987-91; Archbishop of Canterbury 1991-2002.

Political career: *House of Lords:* Raised to the peerage as Baron Carey of Clifton, of Clifton in the City and Council of Bristol 2002. First entered the House of Lords as Archbishop of Canterbury 1991.

Countries of interest: Israel, Palestine, Sudan.

Other: President, World Conference for Religion and Peace; Honorary President, International Council for Christians and Jews; Chairman, World Faiths Development Dialogue; International Sports Promotion Society; Vice-President, Tearfund; Fellow: King's College, London, Christchurch University College, Canterbury, Library of Congress; Chair: United Church Schools Trust, Foundation for Reconciliation in the Middle East; Tearfund. Honorary Liveryman, Scriveners' Company. Freedom: City of London, Bath, Wells. 12 honorary doctorates. PC 1991; Royal Victorian Chain 2002; *Clubs:* Athenæum, ROSL Club.

Publications: I Believe in Man (1975); God Incarnate (1976); Co-author, The Great Acquittal (1980); The Church in the Market Place (1984); The Meeting of the Waters (1985); The Gate of Glory (1986); The Message of the Bible (1986); The Great God Robbery (1989); I Believe (1991); Sharing a Vision (1993); Spiritual Journey (1994); Co-author, My Journey, Your Journey (1996); Canterbury Letters to the Future (1998); Jesus 2000 (1999); Know The Truth (memoirs, 2004); We Don't Do God (2012).

Recreations: Family life, music, poetry, reading, walking.

Rt Rev and Rt Hon the Lord Carey of Clifton, House of Lords, London SW1A 0PW
Tel: 020 7219 5353
Email: carey.george01@gmail.com
Website: www.glcarey.co.uk

NON-AFFILIATED

CARLILE OF BERRIEW, LORD

CARLILE OF BERRIEW (Life Baron), Alexander Charles Carlile; cr. 1999. Born 12 February 1948; Married Frances Soley 1968 (divorced) (3 daughters); married Alison Levitt QC 2007 (2 stepdaughters).

Education: Epsom College; King's College, London University (LLB, AKC 1969); Council of Legal Education.

Non-political career: Called to the Bar, Gray's Inn 1970; QC 1984; Crown Court Recorder 1986-2014; Bencher 1992; Honorary Recorder of City of Hereford 1996-2009; Deputy High Court Judge 1998-2014; Independent Reviewer of Terrorism Legislation 2001-11; Chair: Competition Appeals Tribunal 2005-13, Lloyd's Enforcement Board.

Political career: *House of Commons:* Contested (Liberal) Flint East, February 1974 and 1979 general elections. MP for Montgomery 1983-97 (Liberal 1983-88, Liberal Democrat 1988-97). Liberal Spokesperson for Home Affairs, Law 1985-88; Alliance Spokesperson for Legal Affairs 1987; SLD Spokesperson for Foreign Affairs 1988-89; Liberal Democrat Spokesperson for: Legal Affairs 1989-90, Trade and Industry 1990-92, Wales 1992-97, Employment 1992-94, Health 1994-95, Justice, Home Affairs and Immigration 1995-97. *House of Lords:* Raised to the peerage as Baron Carlile of Berriew, of Berriew in the County of Powys 1999. Liberal Democrat Spokesperson for Mental Health and Disability 2007-10. Chair, Mental Health Bill Joint Committee 2005-06; Member, Delegated Powers and Regulatory Reform 2010-12. *Other:* Chair, Welsh Liberal Party 1980-82; Leader, Welsh Liberal Democrat Party 1992-97; President, Liberal Democrats Wales 1997-99; Joined Non-affiliated group in the Lords 2017-. *Councils and public bodies:* Lay member, General Medical Council 1989-99; Member, Advisory Council on Public Records 1989-95; Chairman (part-time), Competition Appeals Tribunal 2005-13; Deputy Chief Steward, City of Hereford 2009-; Commissioner, Independent Commission on Freedom of Information 2015-16.

Political interests: Home affairs, agriculture, legal affairs, United Nations, arts, Wales, mental health, medical profession; Central and Eastern Europe, Middle East, South Asia.

Other: Patron: National Depression Campaign, Concord Prison Trust, No Panic; Council member, White Ensign Association; Fellow: Institute of Advanced Legal Studies, Industry and Parliament Trust 1989; President, Howard League for Penal Reform 2006-13; Board member, Royal Medical Benevolent Institution (Epsom College); Fellow, Royal Society of Arts; Hope House Children's Hospice, NACRO, Unicef, Rekindle, Howard League for Penal Reform, Addaction. Fellow, King's College, London 2003; Hon. LLD: Glamorgan University 2009, Hungarian Institute of Criminology 2010, Manchester Metropolitan University 2011; Hon Professor, Swansea University 2017. QC 1984; CBE 2012; *Clubs:* Athenæum Club. President, Berriew FC.

Publications: Too Serious a Thing (National Assembly for Wales review of safety of children in the NHS, 2002); Various articles and reports on Terrorism; If all do their duty they need not fear harm (Report for the Howard League on Children in Custody, 2006).

Recreations: Family, politics, theatre, food, association football.

The Lord Carlile of Berriew CBE QC, House of Lords, London SW1A 0PW
Tel: 020 7219 5535 *Email:* carlilea@parliament.uk

NON-AFFILIATED

CARLISLE, LORD BISHOP OF

CARLISLE (67th Bishop of), James William Scobie Newcome. Born 24 July 1953; Son of Major John Newcome and Jane Newcome; Married Alison Clarke (2 sons 2 daughters).

Education: Marlborough College; Trinity College, Oxford (BA modern history 1974, MA); Selwyn College, Cambridge (BA theology 1977, MA).

Non-political career: Territorial Army Commission 1973. Ordained deacon 1978; Assistant curate, All Saints, Leavesden 1978-82; Priest 1979; Minister, Bar Hill 1982-94; Tutor, Ridley Hall, Cambridge 1983-88; Rural dean 1993-94; Residentiary Canon, Chester Cathedral 1994-2002; Diocesan Director of: Ordinands 1994-2000, Ministry 1996-2002; Bishop Suffragan of Penrith 2002-09; Bishop of Carlisle 2009-; Lead Bishop on Health 2010-; Clerk of the Closet 2014-.

Political career: *House of Lords:* Entered House of Lords 2013. Member, Long-Term Sustainability of the NHS 2016-17. *Councils and public bodies:* DL, Cumbria 2013-.

Political interests: Healthcare, defence, social care; Africa, Argentina, Norway.

Other: Member, Society for Study for Christian Ethics 1985-; President, St John's College, Durham 2012-; Vice-president, Cumbria Community Foundation; Director, Cumbria University; National chaplain, Royal British Legion 2016-; Chair, Rose Castle Foundation; Fellow, Royal Society of Arts; Christian Aid; *Clubs:* Athenæum Club.

Publications: Contributor, Setting the Church of England Free (2003); Great Ideas for Growing Healthy Churches (2012); At the End of the Day (2014); Facing Disappointment (Grove 2016).

Recreations: Film, contemporary novels, sport, furniture restoration.

Rt Rev the Lord Bishop of Carlisle, House of Lords, London SW1A 0PW
Tel: 020 7219 5353
Bishop's House, Ambleside, Keswick, Cumbria CA12 4DD *Tel:* 01768 773430
Email: bishop.carlisle@carlislediocese.org.uk *Website:* www.carlislediocese.org.uk

CARRINGTON, LORD

CONSERVATIVE

CARRINGTON (6th Baron, I), Peter Alexander Rupert Carington; cr. 1796; 6th Baron Carrington (GB) 1797; (Life) Baron Carington of Upton 1999. Born 6 June 1919; Son of 5th Baron, DL, and late Hon. Sybil Marion Colville, daughter of 2nd Viscount Colville of Culross; Married Iona McClean 1942 (died 2009) (1 son 2 daughters).

Education: Eton College; RMC, Sandhurst 1937-38.

Non-political career: Major, Grenadier Guards, served North West Europe 1940-46. UK High Commissioner in Australia 1956-59; Chairman, GEC 1983-84; Hon. Bencher, Middle Temple 1983-; Secretary-General, NATO 1984-88; Chairman, Christies International plc 1988-93; Director, The Telegraph plc 1990-2004; Chairman, EC Peace Conference on Yugoslavia 1991-92.

Political career: *House of Lords:* Created a life peer as Baron Carington of Upton, of Upton in the County of Nottinghamshire 1999. Succeeded his father 1938; Eligible to take his seat 1940; First entered House of Lords 1945; Joint Parliamentary Secretary, Ministry of Agriculture and Fisheries 1951-54; Parliamentary Secretary, Ministry of Defence 1954-56; First Lord of the Admiralty 1959-63; Minister without Portfolio and Leader of the House of Lords 1963-64; Leader of Opposition 1964-70, 1974-79; Secretary of State for Defence 1970-74; Minister of Aviation Supply 1971-74; Opposition Whip 1947-51; Secretary of State for: Energy January-February 1974, Foreign and Commonwealth Affairs 1979-82. *Other:* Chairman, Conservative Party 1972-74. *Councils and public bodies:* JP, Bucks 1948; DL, Bucks 1951.

Other: Vice-President, Commonwealth Parliamentary Association (UK Branch); Trustee: Dulverton Trust 1981-, Cambridge Commonwealth Trust 1982-; Chairman of trustees, Victoria and Albert Museum 1983-88; President, The Pilgrims 1983-2002; Elder Brother, Trinity House 1984; Trustee: Royal Fine Art Commission 1987-, Daiwa Anglo Japanese Foundation 1989, Winston Churchill Memorial Trust -2001; President, VSO 1993-98; Hope and Homes for Children, Treloar Trust. Chancellor, Reading University 1992-. Hon. LLD, Cambridge University 1981; Hon. fellow, St Antony's College, Oxford 1982; 12 honorary degrees from universities in the UK and abroad. MC 1945; PC 1959; CH 1983; Chancellor of the Order of St Michael and St George 1984-94; KG 1985; GCMG 1988; Chancellor of the Most Noble Order of the Garter 1994-2013; *Clubs:* Pratt's, White's Club.

Publications: Reflect on Things Past (autobiography, 1988).

Rt Hon the Lord Carrington KG GCMG CH MC DL, House of Lords, London SW1A 0PW
Tel: 020 7219 5353
The Courtyard, Manor Farm, Church End, Bledlow, Buckinghamshire HP27 9PD *Tel:* 01844 273508 *Fax:* 01844 274991 *Email:* lordc@carington.co.uk

CARRINGTON OF FULHAM, LORD

CONSERVATIVE

CARRINGTON (Life Baron), Matthew Hadrian Marshall Carrington; cr 2013. Born 19 October 1947; Son of Walter and Dilys Carrington; Married Mary Lou 1975 (1 daughter); married Margaret Millward 2012.

Education: Lycee, London; Imperial College, London; London Business School; French.

Non-political career: Production foreman, GKN Ltd 1969-72; Banker: First National Bank of Chicago 1974-78, Saudi International Bank 1978-87; Chair, Outdoor Advertising Association 1998-2002; Chief executive, Retail Motor Industry Federation 2002-06.

Political career: *House of Commons:* Contested Tottenham 1979 general election and Fulham 1986 by-election. MP (Conservative) for Fulham 1987-97. Contested Hammersmith and Fulham 1997 and 2001 general elections. PPS to: Lord Trefgarne as Minister of State, Department for Trade and Industry 1988-90, John Patten: as Minister of State, Home Office 1990-92, as Secretary of State for Education 1992-94; Assistant Whip 1996-97. Member, Treasury and Civil Service 1994-96; Chair, Treasury 1996. *House of Lords:* Raised to the peerage as Baron Carrington of Fulham, of Fulham in the London Borough of Hammersmith and Fulham 2013. Member: Economic Affairs 2014-15, Insurance Bill 2014-15. *Other:* Conservative Party: Chair: London Region 2005-08, North West London Area 2002-05, 2008-10.

Political interests: Economy, international affairs, business and industry; Middle East, USA.

Other: Gatehouse Bank plc: Director 2007-, Deputy chair 2008-; Director, Arab British Chamber of Commerce 2011-.

Recreations: Political history, cooking.

The Lord Carrington, House of Lords, London SW1A 0PW
Tel: 020 7219 5353 *Email:* carringtonm@parliament.uk

CARSWELL, LORD

CROSSBENCH

CARSWELL (Life Baron), Robert Douglas Carswell; cr. 2004. Born 28 June 1934; Son of late Alan Carswell and Nance Carswell; Married Romayne Ferris 1961 (2 daughters).

Education: Royal Belfast Academical Institution; Pembroke College, Oxford (BA classics and law 1956, MA); Chicago University Law School (Doctor of Jurisprudence 1958).

Non-political career: Barrister, Northern Ireland 1957; QC (NI) 1971; Barrister, Gray's Inn 1972; Counsel to Attorney General for Northern Ireland 1970-71; Senior Crown Counsel in Northern Ireland 1979-84; Judge of the High Court of Justice Northern Ireland 1984-93; Lord Justice of Appeal Supreme Court of Judicature Northern Ireland 1993-97; Lord Chief Justice of Northern Ireland 1997-2004.

Political career: *House of Lords:* Raised to the peerage as Baron Carswell, of Killeen in the County of Down 2004. Lord of Appeal in Ordinary 2004-09. Joint Committee on Consolidation, Etc, Bills: Chair 2009-11, 2012-, Member 2011-12.

Political interests: Legal and constitutional matters, Northern Ireland.

Other: Chancellor, Dioceses of Armagh, Down and Dromore 1990-97. Honorary doctorate; Hon Fellow, Pembroke College, Oxford 1984. Kt 1988; PC 1993; *Clubs:* Ulster Reform Club, Belfast.

Publications: Trustee Acts (Northern Ireland) (1964).

Recreations: Golf, hillwalking.

Rt Hon the Lord Carswell QC, House of Lords, London SW1A 0PW
Tel: 020 7219 5353 *Email:* carswellr@parliament.uk

CARTER OF BARNES, LORD

NON-AFFILIATED

CARTER OF BARNES (Life Baron), Stephen Andrew Carter; cr 2008. Born 12 February 1964; Married Anna Maria Gorman 1992 (1 son 1 daughter).

Education: Currie High School, Edinburgh; Aberdeen University (LLB 1987); Harvard University (AMP 1997).

Non-political career: Managing director and chief executive, J Walter Thompson Ltd 1992-2000; Chief operating officer and managing director, ntl UK and Ireland 2000-02; Chief executive officer, Office of Communications (Ofcom) 2003-07; Group chief executive, Brunswick Group LLP 2007-08; Chief of strategy and principal adviser to Prime Minister 2008; Chief marketing, strategy and communications officer, EVP solutions division, Alcatel-Lucent, Paris 2010-13; Group chief executive, Informa plc 2013-.

Political career: *House of Lords:* Raised to the peerage as Baron Carter of Barnes, of Barnes in the London Borough of Richmond upon Thames 2008. Parliamentary Under-Secretary of State and Government Spokesperson: Department for Business, Enterprise and Regulatory Reform/ Business, Innovation and Skills (Minister for Communications, Technology and Broadcasting) 2008-09, Department for Culture, Media and Sport 2008-09; On leave of absence July 2011-13. *Other:* Sat with Labour Party in the Lords until February 2017, now sits as Non-Affiliated.

Other: Vice-President, Unicef 2005-; Governor and Chairman, Ashridge Business Management School 2005-. CBE 2007.

The Lord Carter of Barnes CBE, House of Lords, London SW1A 0PW
Tel: 020 7219 5353 *Email:* carterst@parliament.uk
Informa plc, 5 Howick Place, London SW1P 1WG *Tel:* 020 7017 5771

CARTER OF COLES, LORD

LABOUR

CARTER OF COLES (Life Baron), Patrick Robert Carter; cr. 2004. Born 9 February 1946; Married Julia Bourne 1969 (2 daughters).

Education: Brentwood School, Essex; Durham University (BA economics, economic history 1967).

Non-political career: Hambros Bank Ltd 1967-70; Director: Whitecross Equipment Ltd 1970-75, MAI Ltd 1975-85, Westminster Healthcare plc 1975-99; Chair, Sport England 2002-06.

Political career: *House of Lords:* Raised to the peerage as Baron Carter of Coles, of Westmill in the County of Hertfordshire 2004. EU Sub-committee D (Environment and Agriculture): Co-opted member 2009, Chair 2009-10; Member, European Union 2010-13; Chair, EU Sub-committee D: (Agriculture, Fisheries and Environment) 2010-12, (Agriculture, Fisheries, Environment and Energy) 2012-13; Member: EU Sub-committee A (Economic and Financial Affairs) 2013-15, Audit 2013-, Joint Committee on the Palace of Westminster 2015-16. *Councils and public bodies:* Non-executive member: Prisons Board/Strategy Board for Correctional Services 1998-2002, Home Office General Board 2002-06; Chair: National Athletics Review, Review of Payroll Services, Criminal Records Bureau, Review of Offender Services 2006, Review of Pathology 2008, Review of Courts Estate 2009, Competition and Co-operation Panel -2014, Chair, NHS Procurement and Efficiency Board.

Other: Member, Productivity Panel 2000-; Chair: Commonwealth Games 2002, English National Stadium 2002.

Recreations: Reading, walking, skiing, gardening, opera.

The Lord Carter of Coles, House of Lords, London SW1A 0PW
Tel: 020 7219 3342

CASHMAN, LORD

LABOUR

CASHMAN (Life Baron), Michael Maurice Cashman; cr 2014. Born 17 December 1950; Son of John and Mary Cashman; Civil partner Paul Cottingham 2006 (died 2014).

Education: Cardinal Griffin Secondary Modern School; Gladys Dare's Stage School; French.

Non-political career: Actor in theatre, musical theatre, TV films and radio; Associate artist, Birmingham Repertory Theatre 1963-99. Member, Equity.

Political career: *House of Lords:* Raised to the peerage as Baron Cashman, of Limehouse in the London Borough of Tower Hamlets 2014. Member, EU Justice Sub-committee 2017-. *Other:* European Parliament: MEP for West Midlands 1999-2014: Vice-chair, Petitions Committee 2004-09, Chair: Lesbian, Gay, Bisexual and Transgender Rights Intergroup 2004-14, South Africa Delegation 2009-14. Labour Party: Member: National Executive Committee 1998-2012, Conference Arrangements Committee 2015-17, LGBT global envoy -2016; Patron, LGBT Labour.

Political interests: Human rights, civil liberties, poverty, freedom of information, development, LGBTI; South Africa, Turkey, USA.

Other: Stonewall Group: Founder member, Chair 1988-96; Councillor/honorary treasurer, Equity 1994-98; Sarcoma Unit Royal Marsden Hospital, Peter Tatchell Foundation. Honorary doctorate, Staffordshire University (2007). Special service award, American Association Physicians for Human Rights; Lifetime achievement award, EDA 2012; Lifetime achievement award, *Pink News* 2014; Politican of the Year, Stonewall 2014. CBE 2013.

Recreations: Travel, photography, ceramics.

The Lord Cashman CBE, House of Lords, London SW1A 0PW
Tel: 020 7219 6533 *Email:* cashmanm@parliament.uk *Twitter:* @mcashmanCBE

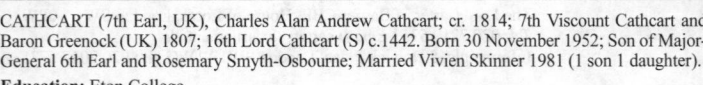

CATHCART, EARL

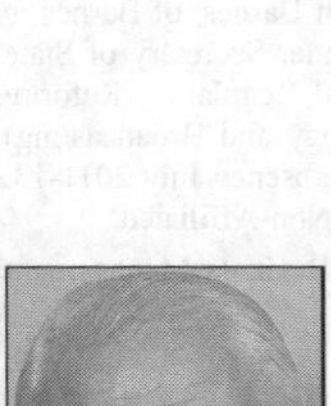

CONSERVATIVE

CATHCART (7th Earl, UK), Charles Alan Andrew Cathcart; cr. 1814; 7th Viscount Cathcart and Baron Greenock (UK) 1807; 16th Lord Cathcart (S) c.1442. Born 30 November 1952; Son of Major-General 6th Earl and Rosemary Smyth-Osbourne; Married Vivien Skinner 1981 (1 son 1 daughter).

Education: Eton College.

Non-political career: Command Scots Guards 1972-75. Chartered accountant: Whinney Murray 1976-79, Ernst and Whinney 1979-83 (ICAEW 1981); Director and Lloyd's underwriter: Gardner Mountain and Capel-cure Agencies 1983-94, Murray Lawrence Members Agencies 1995-96; Director, Reinsurance Group of America (UK) 1996-2011; Chairman, Equator Films plc (now Handmade Films Ltd) 1998-2004; Finance director, Vivien Greenock Ltd 2001-; Director, Spring Gardens Eggs Ltd.

Political career: *House of Lords:* First entered House of Lords 1999; Elected hereditary peer 2007-; Opposition Whip 2007-10; Opposition Spokesperson for: Communities and Local Government 2007-10, Environment, Food and Rural Affairs 2007-10, Northern Ireland 2007-09, Scotland 2009-10. Member: Administration and Works 2015-16, Privileges and Conduct 2016-. *Other:* President: Mid Norfolk Conservative Association 2009-11, Mid Norfolk Patrons Club 2010-; Executive Committee of Association of Conservative Peers 2010-13. *Councils and public bodies:* Councillor, Breckland District Council 1998-2007.

Political interests: Rural affairs, environment, energy, farming, housing; UK.

Other: Member, Queen's Bodyguards for Scotland, Royal Company of Archers; ICAEW.

Recreations: Skiing, sailing, country pursuits.

The Earl Cathcart, House of Lords, London SW1A 0PW
Tel: 020 7219 5422 *Email:* cathcartc@parliament.uk

CONSERVATIVE

CAVENDISH OF FURNESS, LORD

CAVENDISH OF FURNESS (Life Baron), Richard Hugh Cavendish; cr. 1990. Born 2 November 1941; Son of late Captain Richard Edward Osborne Cavendish, DL; Married Grania Caulfeild 1970 (1 son 2 daughters).

Education: Eton College.

Non-political career: International merchanting and banking in London 1961-71; Chairman, Holker Estate Group of Companies 1971-2015; Commissioner for the Historic Buildings and Monuments Commission (English Heritage) 1992-98; Director, UK Nirex Ltd 1993-99.

Political career: *House of Lords:* Raised to the peerage as Baron Cavendish of Furness, of Cartmel in the County of Cumbria 1990. Government Whip 1990-92. Member: Croydon Tramlink Bill 1992-93, European Union Sub Committee B (Energy, Industry and Transport) 2001-04, European Union 2002-. *Other:* Chair, Morecambe and Lonsdale Conservative Association 1975-78; Member, Association of Conservative Peers. *Councils and public bodies:* Councillor, Cumbria County Council 1985-90; High Sheriff of Cumbria 1978; DL, Cumbria 1988; Chairman of Governors, St Anne's School, Windermere 1983-89.

Political interests: Environment, local issues, industry, foreign affairs, drug and alcohol rehabilitation, agriculture, forestry, palliative care, national hunt racing.

Other: Co-founder and Trustee, St Mary's Hospice, Ulverston 1987-2012; Chair, Lancashire and Cumbria Foundation for Medical Research 1994-96; President, Dry Stone Walling Association; Fellow, Royal Society of Arts 1988; Hospice movement. Liveryman, Fishmongers' Company. Hon. Fellow, Cumbria University; *Clubs:* Brooks's, White's, Pratt's, Beefsteak Club.

Publications: A Time To Plant (2012).

Recreations: Gardening, National Hunt racing, shooting, reading, travel, fishing.

The Lord Cavendish of Furness DL, House of Lords, London SW1A 0PW
Tel: 020 7219 5353
Low Frith, Cark-in-Cartmel, Cumbria LA11 7PP *Tel:* 01539 558123
Email: cavendish@holker.co.uk

NON-AFFILIATED

CAVENDISH OF LITTLE VENICE, BARONESS

CAVENDISH OF LITTLE VENICE (Life Baroness), Hilary Camilla Cavendish; cr 2016. Born 20 August 1968; Married 1999 (3 children).

Education: Putney High School; Brasenose College, Oxford (BA philosophy, politics and economics 1989); Harvard School of Government (Kennedy Scholar, MPA 1991).

Non-political career: Business analyst, McKinsey & Co 1991-93; Director of Programmes, London First 1993-95; Chief executive, South Bank Employers Group 1995-99; Adviser to chief executive, Pearsons plc 1999-2002; Columnist, *The Times* 2002-13; Columnist and associate editor, *Sunday Times* 2013-15; Director of Policy Unit, Prime Minister's Office 2015-16.

Political career: *House of Lords:* Raised to the peerage as Baroness Cavendish of Little Venice, of Mells in the County of Somerset 2016. *Other:* Resigned from Conservative Party December 2016; now sits as Non-affiliated. *Councils and public bodies:* Commissioner, Care Quality Commission 2013-15.

Other: Trustee: Policy Exchange 2002-, Foundation Years Trust 2013-15; Non-executive director, Care Quality Commission 2013-15; Chair, Frontline 2017-. Paul Foot Award for Campaigning Journalism 2008.

The Baroness Cavendish of Little Venice, House of Lords, London SW1A 0PW
Tel: 020 7219 3000 *Twitter:* @camcavendish

CONSERVATIVE

CHADLINGTON, LORD

CHADLINGTON (Life Baron), Peter Selwyn Gummer; cr. 1996. Born 24 August 1942; Son of late Rev Canon Selwyn Gummer and late Sybille Selwyn Gummer, née Mason; Married Lucy Dudley-Hill 1982 (3 daughters 1 son).

Education: King's School, Rochester; Selwyn College, Cambridge (BA moral sciences tripos 1964, MA).

Non-political career: Portsmouth and Sunderland Newspaper Group Ltd 1964-65; Viyella International 1965-66; Hodgkinson and Partners 1966-67; Industrial and Commercial Finance Corporation 1967-74; Shandwick International plc 1974-2000: Founder and chief executive 1974-94, Chairman 1994-2000; Non-executive director, CIA Group plc 1990-94; Chairman, Marketing Group of GB 1993-95; Halifax Building Society/plc: Non-executive director, London Bonds 1990-94, Non-executive director 1994-2001; Chairman, International Public Relations 1998-2000; Director: Black Box Music Ltd 1999-2001, Walbrook Club 1999-2004; Chairman, Hotcourses Ltd 2000-04; Huntsworth plc: Chief executive 2000-05, Sept 2005-, Executive chairman May-Sept 2005; Director, Hill Hay Saddle Ltd 2002-; Non-executive director, Britax Childcare Holdings Ltd 2005-11.

Political career: *House of Lords:* Raised to the peerage as Baron Chadlington, of Dean in the County of Oxfordshire 1996. Member: European Union Sub-committee B (Energy, Industry and Transport) 2000-03, Information 2005-06, Charities 2016-17. *Councils and public bodies:* Member: NHS Policy Board 1991-95, Arts Council of England 1991-96; Chairman: National Lottery Advisory Board for Arts and Film 1994-96, Royal Opera House 1996-97; Council member, Cheltenham Ladies College 1998-2003; Non-executive director, Oxford Resources 1999-2002; Non-executive chairman, guideforlife.com 2000-02.

Other: Chairman, Understanding Industry Trust 1991-96; Trustee, Atlantic Partnership 1999-; Board of Trustees, American University 1999-2001; Action on Addiction: Trustee 1999-2000, Chairman 2000-07; Governor, Ditchley Foundation 2008; Committee member, British Heart Foundation Mending Broken Hearts Appeal 2010-; Chairman, LAPADA (professional art and antique dealers' trade association) 2011-; FRSA; FIPR. Freedom, City of London. Honorary Fellow, Bournemouth University 1999-. *PR Week* Award for outstanding individual contribution to public relations 1984; Institute of Public Relations Presidents' Medal 1988; Ernst & Young Entrepreneur of the Year, Master Entrepreneur London Region 2008; *Clubs:* White's, Garrick, Carlton, Walbrook Club. MCC.

Publications: Various articles and booklets on public relations.

Recreations: Opera, rugby, cricket.

The Lord Chadlington, House of Lords, London SW1A 0PW
Tel: 020 7219 5172

LABOUR

CHAKRABARTI, BARONESS

Shadow Attorney General

CHAKRABARTI (Life Baroness), Sharmishta Chakrabarti; cr 2016. Born 16 June 1969; Married Martyn Hopper 1995 (divorced 2014) (1 son).

Education: Harrow Weald Sixth Form College; London School of Economics (LLB).

Non-political career: Called to the Bar, Middle Temple 1994; Associate Tenant, 39 Essex Chambers; Legal Adviser's Branch, Home Office 1996-2001; Liberty: Lawyer 2001-03, Director 2003-15; Leveson Inquiry 2011-12.

Political career: *House of Lords:* Raised to the peerage as Baroness Chakrabarti, of Kennington in the London Borough of Lambeth 2016. Shadow Attorney General 2016-. *Councils and public bodies:* Governor, London School of Economics 2005-11.

Other: Governor, British Film Institute 2006-13. Chancellor: Oxford Brookes University 2008-15, Essex University 2014-17. Channel 4 News Most Inspiring Political Figure 2006. CBE 2007.

The Baroness Chakrabarti CBE, House of Lords, London SW1A 0PW
Tel: 020 7219 3000

CONSERVATIVE

CHALKER OF WALLASEY, BARONESS

CHALKER OF WALLASEY (Life Baroness), Lynda Chalker; cr. 1992. Born 29 April 1942; Daughter of late Sidney Bates and late Marjorie Randell; Married Eric Chalker 1967 (divorced 1973); married Clive Landa 1981 (divorced 2003).

Education: Roedean School, Sussex; Heidelberg University (technical German 1961); London University; Central London Polytechnic (statistics 1965).

Non-political career: Hon. Colonel, Royal Logistic Corps (156 Transport Regiment NW) 1995-2001. Statistician, Unilever's Research Bureau Ltd 1963-69; Market researcher, Shell Mex and BP 1969-72; Executive director (International), Opinion Research International Ltd 1972-74; Adviser, Barclays Bank International 1976-79; Independent Consultant on Africa and Development 1997-; Africa Matters Limited: Chair 1997-16, President 2016-; Director: Unilever plc 1998-2007, Ashanti Goldfields Ltd 1998-2007, Group Five Construction Pty (SA) 2001-12.

Political career: *House of Commons:* MP (Conservative) for Wallasey February 1974-92. Contested Wallasey 1992 general election. Parliamentary Under-Secretary of State, Department of Health and Social Security 1979-82, Department of Transport: Parliamentary Under-Secretary of State 1982-83, Minister of State 1983-86; Foreign and Commonwealth Office: Minister of State 1986-97, Deputy to Foreign Secretary 1987-97, Minister for Overseas Development 1989-92. *House of Lords:* Raised to the peerage as Baroness Chalker of Wallasey, of Leigh-on-Sea in the County of Essex 1992. Minister of Overseas Development and Minister for Africa and Commonwealth, Foreign and Commonwealth Office 1992-97. *Other:* National vice-chair, Young Conservatives 1970-71; Hon. Life member, Tory Reform Group. *Councils and public bodies:* Member, BBC Advisory Committee 1974-76.

Political interests: Voluntary sector, European co-operation, Africa, overseas development, trade, transport, construction; Sub-Saharan Africa, Egypt, Jordan.

Other: Adviser, World Bank 1997-2005; Co-ordinator, Presidential International Investment Council for Nigeria 2001-; Member: Kenyan National Economic and Social Council 2004-09, Ugandan Presidential Investment Round Table 2004-, Tanzania National Business Council 2004-; Chair: London School of Hygiene and Tropical Medicine 1998-2006, Medicines for Malaria Venture 2006-11; Trustee: Global Leadership Foundation, Investment Climate Facility for Africa; Fellow: Royal Geographical Society, London School of Hygiene and Tropical Medicine, Institute of Highways and Transportation, Royal Statistical Society; British Executive Services Overseas, Intermediate Technology Development Group, African Medical Research Foundation, British Red Cross, Red R, Water Aid. Nine honorary degrees. PC 1987; *Clubs:* Royal Overseas League, St James Club.

Publications: Police in Retreat (1968); Unhappy Families (1972); We're Richer than We Think (1978); Africa – Turning the Tide (1989).

Recreations: Theatre, cooking, gardening, jazz.

Rt Hon the Baroness Chalker of Wallasey, House of Lords, London SW1A 0PW
Tel: 020 7219 3000
13-15 Carteret Street, London SW1H 9DJ *Tel:* 020 7976 6850 *Email:* pa@africamatters.com
Twitter: @BaronessChalker

LABOUR

CHANDOS, VISCOUNT

CHANDOS (3rd Viscount, UK), Thomas Orlando Lyttelton; cr. 1954; (Life) Baron Lyttelton of Aldershot 2000. Born 12 February 1953; Son of 2nd Viscount; Married Arabella Sarah Bailey 1985 (2 sons 1 daughter).

Education: Eton College; Worcester College, Oxford (BA).

Non-political career: Director: Kleinwort Benson 1985-93, Botts & Company Limited 1993-98, Capital and Regional Properties plc 1993-, Cine-UK Limited 1995-, Video Networks Limited 1996-99, Chair: Lopex plc 1997-99, Mediakey plc 1998-2000, Capital and Regional plc 2000-; Director: Global Natural Energy plc 2000-, Northbridge (UK) Limited 2001-.

Political career: *House of Lords:* Created a life peer as Baron Lyttelton of Aldershot, of Aldershot in the County of Hampshire 2000. First entered House of Lords 1982; Formerly SDP Spokesperson for Finance and Trade; Opposition Spokesperson on Treasury and Economic Affairs 1995-97. Member: Works of Art 2003-07, Information 2015-16.

Other: Director, English National Opera 1995-; Trustee: 21st Century Learning Initiative 1995-, Education Low-Priced Sponsored Texts 1996-99; Governor, National Film and Television School 1996-2001; President, National Kidney Research Fund 2001-; Director, Social Market Foundation 2001-.

The Viscount Chandos, House of Lords, London SW1A 0PW
Tel: 020 7219 6307
Northbridge UK Ltd, 9 Park Place, London SW1A 1LP

NON-AFFILIATED

CHELMSFORD, LORD BISHOP OF

CHELMSFORD (10th Bishop of), Stephen Geoffrey Cottrell. Born 31 August 1958; Son of John and Eileen Cottrell; Married Rebecca Stirling 1984 (3 sons).

Education: Belfairs High School for Boys; Polytechnic of Central London (BA media studies 1979); St Stephen's House, Oxford.

Non-political career: Ordained deacon 1984; Curate, Christ Church, Forest Hill 1984-88; Priest 1985; Priest-in-charge, St Wilfrid's Chichester 1988-93; Assistant director, Pastoral Studies, Chichester Theological College 1988-93; Diocesan missioner, Wakefield 1993-98; Springboard missioner 1998-2001; Canon Pastor, Peterborough Cathedral 2001-04; Area Bishop of Reading 2004-10; Bishop of Chelmsford 2010-.

Political career: *House of Lords:* Entered House of Lords 2014. Member, Communications 2015-.

Other: Visitor, Society of the Precious Blood; Chair, Church Army.

Publications: Many publications including: I Thirst (2003), The Adventures of Naughty Nora (2008), Hit the Ground Kneeling: seeing leadership differently (2008), The Things He Said: the story of the first Easter Day (2009), How to Pray (2011), The Nail: being part of the Passion (2011), Christ in the Wilderness: reflecting on the paintings by Stanley Spencer (2012).

Recreations: Writing, reading, cooking, music, football.

Rt Rev the Lord Bishop of Chelmsford, House of Lords, London SW1A 0PW
Tel: 020 7219 5353 *Email:* cottrells@parliament.uk
Bishopscourt, Main Road, Margaretting, Ingatestone, Essex CM4 0HD *Tel:* 01277 352001
Fax: 01277 355374 *Email:* bishopscourt@chelmsford.anglican.org
Websites: www.chelmsford.anglican.org www.stephencottrell.org
Twitter: @cottrellstephen

NON-AFFILIATED

CHESTER, LORD BISHOP OF

CHESTER (40th Bishop of), Peter Robert Forster. Born 16 March 1950; Son of Thomas and Edna Forster; Married Elisabeth Stevenson 1978 (2 sons 2 daughters).

Education: Tudor Grange Grammar School for Boys, Solihull; Merton College, Oxford (MA chemistry 1973); Edinburgh University (BD theology 1977; PhD 1985).

Non-political career: Assistant Curate, Mossley Hill Parish Church, Liverpool 1980-82; Senior Tutor, St John's College, Durham 1983-91; Vicar, Beverley Minster 1991-96; Bishop of Chester 1996-.

Political career: *House of Lords:* Entered House of Lords 2001. Member: Joint Committee on Privacy and Injunctions 2011-12, Administration and Works 2013-16, Joint Committee on the Draft Investigatory Powers Bill 2015-16. *Councils and public bodies:* Chair, Council, Chester University 1997-; Former Chair, Board of governors, Ellesmere Port Academy.

Countries of interest: The Congo, Solomon Islands, Vanuatu.

Recreations: Gardening, crafts, hens.

Rt Rev Dr the Lord Bishop of Chester, House of Lords, London SW1A 0PW
Tel: 020 7219 5353
Bishop's House, Abbey Square, Chester CH1 2JD *Tel:* 01244 350864
Email: bpchester@chester.anglican.org *Website:* www.chester.anglican.org

NON-AFFILIATED

CHICHESTER, LORD BISHOP OF – Peerage pending at time of going to press

CHICHESTER (104th Bishop of), Martin Clive Warner. Born 24 December 1958.

Education: King's School; Maidstone Grammar School; King's School; Maidstone Grammar School; St Chad's College, Durham; St Stephen's House, Oxford; St Chad's College, Durham; St Stephen's House, Oxford.

Non-political career: Ordained Deacon 1984, Priest 1985; Curate, St Peter's Plymouth 1984-88; Team Vicar, Parish of the Resurrection, Leicester 1988-93; Priest Administrator, Shrine of Our Lady of Walsingham 1993-2002; Priest-in-charge, Hempton and Pudding Norton 1998-2000; Honorary Canon of Norwich 2000-02; Canon, St Paul's Cathedral, London 2003-10; Suffragan Bishop of Whitby 2010-12; Bishop of Chichester 2012-. Ordained Deacon 1984, Priest 1985; Curate, St Peter's Plymouth 1984-88; Team Vicar, Parish of the Resurrection, Leicester 1988-93; Priest Administrator, Shrine of Our Lady of Walsingham 1993-2002; Priest-in-charge, Hempton and Pudding Norton 1998-2000; Honorary Canon of Norwich 2000-02; Canon, St Paul's Cathedral, London 2003-10; Suffragan Bishop of Whitby 2010-12; Bishop of Chichester 2012-.

Publications: Walsingham, an Ever-circling Year (1996); Say Yes to God (1999); The Habit of Holiness (2004); Known to the Senses (2004); Between Heaven and Charing Cross (2009); Contributor, *Church Times*; Walsingham, an Ever-circling Year (1996); Say Yes to God (1999); The Habit of Holiness (2004); Known to the Senses (2004); Between Heaven and Charing Cross (2009); Contributor, *Church Times*.

Recreations: Cycling, the arts.

Rt Rev Dr the Lord Bishop of Chichester, House of Lords, London SW1A 0PW
Tel: 020 7219 3000
The Palace, Chichester, West Sussex PO19 1PY
Tel: 01243 782161 *Email:* bishop@chichester.anglican.org *Website:* www.chichester.anglican.org

LIBERAL DEMOCRAT

CHIDGEY, LORD

CHIDGEY (Life Baron), David William George Chidgey; cr 2005. Born 9 July 1942; Son of Major Cyril and Winifred Chidgey; Married April Idris-Jones 1964 (1 son 2 daughters).

Education: Brune Park County High School, Gosport; Portsmouth Polytechnic (Dip CivilEng 1965, CEng); Portsmouth Naval College; Graduate, Institute of Mechanical Engineers; French.

Non-political career: Consulting civil engineer; Senior civil engineer, Hampshire County Council 1964-73; Brian Colquhoun and Partners 1973-93: Associate partner 1988-93, Projects director, West Africa and South East Asia 1978-87, Managing director, Ireland 1981-88; Chief consultant to Dublin Transport Authority 1987-88; Associate director and projects director, Central Southern England Thorburn Colquhoun 1994.

Political career: *House of Commons:* Contested Eastleigh 1992 general election. MP (Liberal Democrat) for Eastleigh 1994 by-election to 2005. Liberal Democrat Spokesperson for: Employment 1994-95, Transport 1995-97, Trade and Industry 1997-99, Foreign Affairs 1999-2005. Member: Accomodation and Works 1998-2001, Standards and Privileges 2001, Foreign Affairs 1999-2005, Chairman's Panel 2001-05, Joint Committee on Human Rights 2003-05. *House of Lords:* Raised to the peerage as Baron Chidgey, of Hamble-le-Rice in the County of Hampshire 2005. Liberal Democrat Spokesperson for: Defence (Royal Navy, Defence Procurement) 2005-06, International Development and Foreign and Commonwealth Office (Africa) -2010, International Development 2015. Co-opted Member, EU Sub-committee C (Foreign Affairs, Defence and Development Policy) 2006-10. Chair, Liberal Democrat Parliamentary Party Committee on International Affairs (International Development) 2010-15. *Other:* Contested (SLD) Hampshire Central 1988 by-election and 1989 European Parliament election. Regional chair, Hampshire and Wight Liberal Democrats 1992-94; Joint founder and president, Association of Liberal Democrat Engineers and Applied Scientists. *Councils and public bodies:* Councillor, Winchester City Council 1987-91.

Political interests: Foreign affairs, international development, transport, built environment; Africa, Pacific Rim and South East Asia, Indian sub-continent, Middle East, Europe.

Other: AWEPA (European Parliamentarians with Africa): UK Parliament Representative 2007-, Director, Governing Council 2010-, Political co-ordinator for aid effectiveness, SADC region 2011-; Member, advisory board, UK Transatlantic Leadership Academy SLLF/Europe 2007-12; Chair, international advisory board, CPSU (Commonwealth Policy Studies Unit) 2008-12; Member, advisory board, TI (UK) 2008-; Delegate, Parliamentary Assembly Council of Europe and Western European Union 2009-11; Member, Chartered Institute of Transport; Companion, Royal Aeronautical Society; Fellow, Industry and Parliament Trust 1999; Fellow: Institution of Civil Engineers, Institution of Engineers of Ireland, Institution of Highways and Transportation, Association of Consulting Engineers of Ireland; Save The Children. Liveryman Worshipful Company of Carmen. Freedom: City of London 1997, Borough of Eastleigh 2005; *Clubs:* National Liberal Club.

Recreations: Reading, walking, following cricket.

The Lord Chidgey, House of Lords, London SW1A 0PW
Tel: 020 7219 6944 *Fax:* 020 7219 5436 *Email:* chidgeyd@parliament.uk

CONSERVATIVE

CHISHOLM OF OWLPEN, BARONESS

Government Whip (Baroness in Waiting)

CHISHOLM OF OWLPEN (Life Baroness), Caroline (Carlyn) Elizabeth Chisholm; cr 2014. Born 23 December 1951; Daughter of Baron Egremont MBE; Married Colin Chisholm 1976 (2 sons 1 daughter).

Non-political career: Nurse.

Political career: *House of Lords:* Raised to the peerage as Baroness Chisholm of Owlpen, of Owlpen in the County of Gloucestershire 2014. Government Whip (Baroness in Waiting) 2015-16, 2017-; Government Spokesperson for Cabinet Office 2015-16. *Other:* Senior volunteer, Conservative Party; Chair, Conservative Candidates Committee; President, Stroud Conservative Association.

Other: Trustee, National Osteoporosis Society.

The Baroness Chisholm of Owlpen, House of Lords, London SW1A 0PW *Tel:* 020 7219 5353

NON-AFFILIATED

CHOLMONDELEY, MARQUESS OF

CHOLMONDELEY (7th Marquess of, UK), David George Philip Cholmondeley; cr. 1815; 10th Earl of Cholmondeley (E) 1706; 7th Earl of Rocksavage (UK) 1815; 10th Viscount Malpas (E) 1706; 11th Viscount Cholmondeley (I) 1661; 10th Baron Cholmondeley (E) 1689; 10th Baron Newburgh (GB) 1716; 10th Baron Newborough (I) 1715. Born 27 June 1960; Son of 6th Marquess, GCVO, MC, DL; Married Rose Hanbury 2009 (twin sons 1 daughter).

Education: Eton College; Sorbonne.

Non-political career: Page of Honour to HM The Queen 1974-76; Joint Hereditary Lord Great Chamberlain of England (acting for the reign of Queen Elizabeth II) 1990-.

Political career: *House of Lords:* First entered House of Lords 1990; On leave of absence.

Other: KCVO 2007.

Most Hon the Marquess of Cholmondeley KCVO, House of Lords, London SW1A 0PW
Tel: 020 7219 5353
Houghton Hall, King's Lynn, Norfolk PE31 6UA *Tel:* 01829 720202

LABOUR

CHRISTOPHER, LORD

CHRISTOPHER (Life Baron), Anthony (Tony) Martin Grosvenor Christopher; cr. 1998. Born 25 April 1925; Son of late George and Helen Christopher; Married Adela Thompson 1962.

Education: Cheltenham Grammar School; Westminster College of Commerce.

Non-political career: RAF 1944-48. Articled Pupil Agricultural Valuers, Gloucester 1941-44; Inland Revenue 1948-57; Civil Service Building Society: Director 1958-87, Chair 1978-87; General Secretary, Inland Revenue Staff Federation 1976-88; TUC General Council: Member 1976-89, Chair 1988-89; TU Fund Managers Ltd: Director 1981-2013, Chair 1983-2013; Director, Birmingham Midshires Building Society 1987-88; Industrial and Public Affairs Consultant 1988-.

Political career: *House of Lords:* Raised to the peerage as Baron Christopher, of Leckhampton in the County of Gloucestershire 1998. Member: Consolidation, Etc, Bills Joint Committee 2000-16, Audit 2003-06, European Union Sub-committee D (Environment and Agriculture) 2003-06, Tax Law Rewrite Bills Joint Committee 2007-09. *Councils and public bodies:* Member, Inner London Probation and After-care Committee 1966-79; Chair, NACRO 1973-98; Member: Tax Reform Committee 1974-80, Royal Commission on Distribution of Income and Wealth 1978-79, Independent Broadcasting Authority 1978-83; Chair, Tyre Industry Economic Development Council 1983-86; Member: Council of Institute of Manpower Studies 1984-89, Economic and Social Research Council 1985-88; Vice-President, Building Societies Association 1985-90; Member: General Medical Council 1989-94, Audit Commission 1989-95, Broadcasting Complaints Commission 1989-97.

Political interests: Agriculture, financial services, pensions, penal affairs and policy, economics, industry, the elderly; Africa, China, Egypt.

Other: Members' Auditor, International Confederation of Free Trades Unions 1983-2007; Trustee: Trades Union Unit Trust Charitable Trust 1981-, Commonwealth Trades Union Council Charitable Trust 1985-89, Save The Children Fund 1985-90; Institute for Public Policy Research: Trustee 1989-94, Treasurer 1990-94; Trustee, Douglas Houghton Memorial Fund 1998-; Hon. Fellow, Association of Taxation Technicians 2015; FRSA 1989. CBE 1984; *Clubs:* Beefsteak, Wig and Pen Club.

Publications: Co-author: Policy for Poverty (1970); The Wealth Report (1979); The Wealth Report 2 (1982).

Recreations: Gardening, dog walking.

The Lord Christopher CBE, House of Lords, London SW1A 0PW
Tel: 020 7219 6162
TU Fund Managers Ltd, Congress House, Great Russell Street, London WC1B 3LQ
Tel: 020 7637 7114 *Fax:* 020 7637 7057

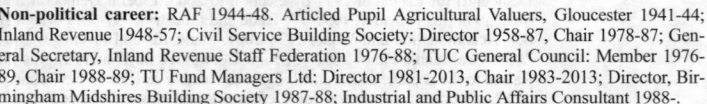

CLANCARTY, EARL OF

CROSSBENCH

CLANCARTY (9th Earl of, I), Nicholas Power Richard Le Poer Trench; cr. 1803; 9th Viscount Dunlo (I), 1800; 8th Viscount Clancarty (UK) 1823; 9th Baron Kilconnel (I) 1797; 8th Baron Trench (UK) 1815; 8th Marquess of Heusden in the Netherlands 1818. Born 1 May 1952; Son of late Hon Power Edward Ford Le Poer (Terry) Trench and late Jocelyn Louise (Joy) Courtney; Married Victoria Frances Lambert 2005 (1 daughter).

Education: Westminster School; Ashford County Grammar School; Plymouth Polytechnic (BA geography and geology 1975); University of Colorado, USA (MA geography 1978); Sheffield Polytechnic (BA fine art 1987); French, German.

Non-political career: Artist and writer; Company secretary, Dysart Press.

Political career: *House of Lords:* First entered House of Lords 1995. Sits as Viscount Clancarty; Elected hereditary peer 2010-.

Political interests: Arts and cultural issues, welfare, education; France, Germany, Netherlands.

The Earl of Clancarty, House of Lords, London SW1A 0PW
Tel: 020 7219 8929 *Email:* clancartyn@parliament.uk *Twitter:* @NickClancarty

CLARK OF CALTON, BARONESS

NON-AFFILIATED

CLARK OF CALTON (Life Baroness), Lynda Margaret Clark; cr 2005. Born 26 February 1949.

Education: Queen's College, St Andrews University (LLB 1970); Edinburgh University (PhD 1975).

Non-political career: Dundee University: Part-time tutor 1971-73, Lecturer in jurisprudence 1973-76; Advocate, Scots Bar 1977-89; QC 1989-99 in practice at Scots Bar; Called to the English Bar 1990; Governing bencher, Inner Temple 2000; Senator of the College of Justice in Scotland 2006-.

Political career: *House of Commons:* Contested North East Fife 1992 general election. MP (Labour) for Edinburgh Pentlands 1997-2005. Advocate General for Scotland 1999-2005. *House of Lords:* Raised to the peerage as Baroness Clark of Calton, of Calton in the City of Edinburgh 2005. Advocate General for Scotland 2005-06; Lord of Appeal 2006-08; As a senior member of the judiciary, disqualified from participation 2006-.

Political interests: Constitutional reform, justice system, health, education, pensions.

Other: Former member: Scottish Legal Aid Board, Edinburgh University Court. QC (Scot) 1989; PC 2013.

Rt Hon the Baroness Clark of Calton QC, House of Lords, London SW1A 0PW
Tel: 020 7219 5353

CLARK OF WINDERMERE, LORD

LABOUR

CLARK OF WINDERMERE (Life Baron), David George Clark; cr. 2001. Born 19 October 1939; Son of George Clark; Married Christine Kirkby 1970 (1 daughter).

Education: Windermere Grammar School; Manchester University (BA economics 1963, MSc 1965) Sheffield University (PhD 1978).

Non-political career: Forester 1956-57; Laboratory worker in textile mill 1957-59; Student teacher, Salford 1959-60; President, Manchester University Union 1963-64; Lecturer in public administration, Salford University 1965-70; Chair, Forestry Commission 2001-10; Visiting Professor, History and Politics, Huddersfield University 2013-. Member, Unison.

Political career: *House of Commons:* Contested Manchester Withington 1966 general election. MP (Labour) for Colne Valley 1970-74, for South Shields 1979-2001. Opposition Spokesperson for: Agriculture, Fisheries and Food 1972-74, Defence 1980-81, Environment 1981-87, Food, Agricultural and Rural Affairs 1987-92, Defence, Disarmament and Arms Control 1992-97; Chancellor of the Duchy of Lancaster 1997-98. *House of Lords:* Raised to the peerage as Baron Clark of Windermere, of Windermere in the County of Cumbria 2001. Member, Joint Committee on National Security Strategy 2013-16. Vice-chair, PLP Departmental Group for Defence 2010-15. *Councils and public bodies:* DL, Cumbria 2006; Member, House of Lords Appointments Commission 2017-.

Political interests: Open spaces, forestry, defence, security.

Other: UK Delegation of the North Atlantic Assembly 1980-2005: Member 1980-97, 1998-2005, Leader 2001-05; Executive member, National Trust 1980-94; Patron, Vindolanda Trust 1983-; Trustee, History of Parliament Trust 1986-. Freedom, Borough of South Tyneside 1998. Hon. Fellow, Cumbria University 2009. PC 1997. Director, Carlisle United AFC 2002-.

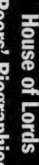

Publications: Industrial Manager (1966); Colne Valley: Radicalism to Socialism (1981); Victor Grayson: Labour's Lost Leader (1985); We Do Not Want The Earth (1992); The Labour Movement in Westmorland (2012); Voices from Labour's Past (2015); Victor Grayson: The Man and the Mystery (2016).

Recreations: Gardening, fell-walking, reading, watching football.

Rt Hon the Lord Clark of Windermere DL, House of Lords, London SW1A 0PW
Tel: 020 7219 2558 *Email:* clarkd@parliament.uk

LABOUR

CLARKE OF HAMPSTEAD, LORD

CLARKE OF HAMPSTEAD (Life Baron), Anthony James Clarke; cr. 1998. Born 17 April 1932; Son of Henry Clarke and Elizabeth Clarke; Married Josephine Turner 1954 (1 son 1 daughter).

Education: St Dominic's Roman Catholic School, Kentish Town; Ruskin College, Oxford (Correspondence course trade union studies).

Non-political career: National Service, Royal Signals 1950-52; TA and Army Emergency Reserve 1952-68. Post Office: Telegraph boy, Postman, Postman higher grade (sorter); Union of Postal Workers (UPW): Full-time trade union officer 1979-93, Editor, UPW journal *The Post* 1979, Deputy General Secretary 1981-93. Branch Secretary, UPW 1962-69; Member: London Trades Council 1965-69 (EC Member 1967-68), TUC Disputes Panel 1972-93, TUC South East Regional Council 1974-79, London Council of Post Office Unions 1975-79, Midlands Council of Post Office Unions 1975-79; President, TU Friends of Israel.

Political career: *House of Commons:* Contested (Labour) Camden Hampstead February and October 1974 general elections. *House of Lords:* Raised to the peerage as Baron Clarke of Hampstead, of Hampstead in the London Borough of Camden 1998. *Other:* Member, Executive Committee, Labour Friends of Israel 1972-2001; Labour Party: Member, National Executive Committee 1983-93, St Albans Labour Party 1986-2013, Chair 1992-93. *Councils and public bodies:* Councillor, London Borough of Camden 1971-78.

Political interests: Overseas aid and development, industrial relations.

Other: Organiser and Lecturer, Postal and Telegraph International, Malaysia and India; Trustee, Post Office Pension Funds 1991-97; Governor, Westminster Foundation for Democracy 1992-98; Founder member, One World Action; RAF Museum. Knight of St Gregory (Papal Order) 1994; CBE 1998.

Recreations: Arsenal FC, *The Archers*, reading.

The Lord Clarke of Hampstead CBE, House of Lords, London SW1A 0PW
Tel: 020 7219 1379 *Email:* clarkeaj@parliament.uk

NON-AFFILIATED

CLARKE OF STONE-CUM-EBONY, LORD

CLARKE OF STONE-CUM-EBONY (Life Baron), Anthony Peter Clarke; cr 2009. Born 13 May 1943; Son of late Harry Clarke and Isobel Clarke, née Kay; Married Rosemary Adam 1968 (2 sons 1 daughter).

Education: Oakham School, Rutland; King's College, Cambridge (BA economics, law, MA).

Non-political career: Called to the Bar, Middle Temple 1965; QC 1979; Recorder 1985-92; Bencher Middle Temple 1987; Judge Queen's Bench Division High Court of Justice 1993-98; Admiralty Judge 1993-98; Lord Justice of Appeal 1998-2005; Head of Civil Justice 2005-09; Master of the Rolls 2005-09; Justice of the Supreme Court of the United Kingdom 2009-17.

Political career: *House of Lords:* Raised to the peerage as Baron Clarke of Stone-cum-Ebony, of Stone-cum-Ebony in the County of Kent 2009. As Justice of the Supreme Court, disqualified from participation 2009-17.

Other: Hon. Doctor of Laws: Exeter University 2006, Kent University 2009, Hull University 2009. Kt 1993; PC 1998.

Recreations: Bridge, tennis, golf, holidays.

Rt Hon the Lord Clarke of Stone-cum-Ebony, House of Lords, London SW1A 0PW
Tel: 020 7219 5353

LIBERAL DEMOCRAT

CLEMENT-JONES, LORD

CLEMENT-JONES (Life Baron), Timothy Francis Clement-Jones; cr. 1998. Born 26 October 1949; Son of late Maurice Clement-Jones and late Margaret Clement-Jones, née Hudson; Married Dr Vicky Yip 1973 (died 1987); married Jean Whiteside 1994 (1 son).

Education: Haileybury College, Hertford; Trinity College, Cambridge (MA economics and law 1971); French, German.

Non-political career: Solicitor; Head of legal services, London Weekend Television 1980-83; Legal director, Grand Metropolitan Retailing 1984-86; Group company secretary and legal adviser, Kingfisher plc 1986-95; Chair: Context Group Ltd 1997-2009, Upstream (government and media relation practice of DLA Piper Rudick Gray Cary) 1999-2006; Partner, DLA Piper The Global Law Firm 1999-; Co-chair, DLA Piper Global Government Relations 2006-09; London Managing Partner, DLA Piper 2011-.

Political career: *House of Lords:* Raised to the peerage as Baron Clement-Jones, of Clapham in the London Borough of Lambeth 1998. Liberal Democrat Spokesperson for: Health 1998-2004, Culture, Media and Sport 2004-10; Member, Speakers' Working Group on All-Party Groups 2011-12; Liberal Democrat Spokesperson for: Business, Innovation and Skills 2015, Culture, Media, Sport and Tourism 2015. Member: Communications 2010-15, Built Environment 2015-16, Licensing Act 2003 2016; Chair, Artificial Intelligence 2017-. *Other:* Chair, Association of Liberal Lawyers 1981-86; Liberal Democrats: Member, National Executive 1988-98, Chair, Federal Finance Committee 1991-98, Director, Campaign for the European Parliamentary elections 1994, Chair, London mayoral and Assembly campaign 2000, 2004, Federal Treasurer 2005-10; Chair, Liberal Democrats in Communications.

Political interests: Cancer, inner cities, autism, crime prevention, creative industries, intellectual property, higher education; Central Asia, China, Iraq, Turkey, UAE.

Other: Trustee, Cancerbackup 1986-2008; Chairman and director, Crime Concern 1988-99; Council member, London Lighthouse 1989-93; Director, Brixton City Challenge 1994-98; Patron, Tymes Trust; Director, British America Business Inc; Member, 48 Group Club (promotion of relations with China); Chair: Treehouse (charity for autistic children) 2001-08, Lambeth Crime Prevention Trust 2004-09, Council, School of Pharmacy, London University 2008-12; President, Ambitious About Autism 2011-; Member of Council, University College London 2012-; Trustee: Space for Giants, Barbican Centre Trust 2012-; Council Member, Heart of the City 2013-; Chair, Ombudsman Services 2016-; Fellow, Public Relations Consultants Association; Law Society of England and Wales (City Ambassador); Fellow, Chartered Institute of Public Relations; FIPR; FCPRA; Ambitious About Autism, Macmillan Cancer Support, Target Ovarian Cancer, Learning Skills Foundation. Freedom, City of London. Hon. Fellow, UCL School of Pharmacy. CBE 1988; *Clubs:* Arts Club.

Recreations: Travelling, eating, talking, reading, walking, the arts.

The Lord Clement-Jones CBE, House of Lords, London SW1A 0PW
Tel: 020 7219 5353 *Email:* clementjonest@parliament.uk
DLA Piper UK LLP, 3 Noble Street, London EC2V 7EE *Tel:* 020 7796 6169
Email: tim.clement-jones@dlapiper.com
Website: www.lordclementjones.org

LABOUR

CLINTON-DAVIS, LORD

CLINTON-DAVIS (Life Baron), Stanley Clinton Clinton-Davis; cr. 1990. Born 6 December 1928; Son of Sidney and Lily Davis; Married Frances Lucas 1954 (1 son 3 daughters).

Education: Hackney Downs School, London; Mercers' School, London; King's College, London University (LLB 1950).

Non-political career: Admitted solicitor 1953; Senior Partner Clintons/Clinton Davis & Co; European Commissioner for Environment Policy, Nuclear Safety and Transport 1985-89; Chairman, UNEP Sasakawa Award Committee 1989-2005; Member, panel of judges, Seatrade Awards; Former consultant on European law and affairs with S. J. Berwin & Co. solicitors. Member, GMB; Former trustee, NUMAST.

Political career: *House of Commons:* Contested Portsmouth, Langstone 1955 and Yarmouth 1959 and 1964 general elections. MP (Labour) for Hackney Central 1970-83. Parliamentary Under-Secretary of State, Department of Trade 1974-79; Opposition Spokesperson for: Trade, Prices and Consumer Protection 1979-81, Foreign Affairs 1981-83. *House of Lords:* Raised to the peerage as Baron Clinton-Davis, of Hackney in the London Borough of Hackney 1990. Opposition Spokesperson for Transport 1990-97; Supporting Spokesperson for: Trade and Industry 1990-96, Foreign Affairs 1990-97; Minister of State, Department of Trade and Industry (Minister for Trade) 1997-

98; On leave of absence July 2017-. Member: Liaison 2001-05, EU Sub-committee E (Law and Institutions) 2003-07, Joint Committee on Statutory Instruments 2009-13, EU Sub-committee B: (Internal Market, Energy and Transport) 2010-12, (Internal Market, Infrastructure and Employment) 2012-15, Inquiries Act 2005 2013. Vice-chair, Labour Party Departmental Committee for Legal and Constitutional Affairs 2004-10. *Other:* Member, executive council, National Association of Labour Student Organisations 1949-50; Former Joint President, Society of Labour Lawyers. *Councils and public bodies:* London Borough of Hackney: Councillor 1959-71, Mayor 1968-69, Former chair of social services.

Political interests: Transport, environment, foreign affairs, law, civil liberties, international trade; Commonwealth, Europe, Israel, South Africa, USA.

Other: Member, Parliamentary Assembly of Council of Europe and Assembly of Western European Union 2000-02; Former president: Hackney branch, Multiple Sclerosis Society, Aviation Environment Federation, UK Pilots (Marine Association); Former vice-president, Chartered Institute of Environmental Health; Former chair, Packaging Council; Former member: Royal Overseas League, Board of Deputies of British Jews; Former president, London Maritime Association; Vice-president, Institute of Export; British Airline Pilots Association: President 1980-2011, Honorary Life President 2011-; Chair: Advisory Committee on Protection of the Sea 1984-85, 1989-97, Refugee Council 1989-97; President, Association of Municipal Authorities 1992-97; Fellow, Chartered Institution of Water and Environmental Management; Fellow: Queen Mary and Westfield College, University of London 1992, King's College London, Queen Mary College 2003. Hon. Doctorate, Polytechnic University of Bucharest 1993; Hon. ACA Degree; Hon. Doctorate, University of North London/Metropolitan University 2000. First Eurogroup medal for Animal Welfare 1988. Grand Cross, Order of Leopold II (Belgium) for services to the EC 1990; PC 1998. Hendon Golf Club.

Recreations: Association football, golf, reading political biographies.

Rt Hon the Lord Clinton-Davis, House of Lords, London SW1A 0PW
Tel: 020 7219 5353 *Fax:* 020 7219 5979
35 Regency House, 269 Regents Park Road, London N3 3JZ *Tel:* 020 8343 2249
Email: clintondavis200@btinternet.com

COE, LORD

CONSERVATIVE

COE (Life Baron), Sebastian Newbold Coe; cr. 2000. Born 29 September 1956; Son of late Peter and Angela Coe; Married Nicola McIrvine 1990 (2 sons 2 daughters); married Carole Annett, née Smith 2011.

Education: Tapton Secondary Modern School, Sheffield; Abbeydale Grange School; Loughborough University (BSc economics and social history 1979).

Non-political career: Athlete; Associate member, Academy of Sport (France) 1982; Sports Council: Member 1983-89, Vice-chair 1986-89; Member, Health Education Authority 1987-92; Steward, British Boxing Board of Control; Member, Athletes and Medical Commission of International Olympic Committee 1997; Private Secretary to William Hague MP as Leader of the Opposition 1997-2001; President, Amateur Athletics Association 2000-03; Sports columnist, *Daily Telegraph*; Founding member, Laureus World Sports Academy 2000; Global adviser to Nike 2001-15; Athletics commentator, Channel 7, Australia; London 2012 Olympic Bid: Vice-chair 2003-04, Chair 2004-05; Chair, LOCOG (London Organising Committee of the Olympic Games and Paralympic Games) 2005-13; International Association of Athletics Federations (IAAF): Vice-president 2007-15, President 2015-, Ex-officio member, Olympic Board; Chair: British Olympic Association 2012-16; Complete Leisure Group Ltd; Executive chair, CSM Sport and Entertainment LLP 2013-.

Political career: *House of Commons:* MP (Conservative) for Falmouth and Camborne 1992-97. PPS: to Roger Freeman: as Minister of State for Defence Procurement 1994-95, as Chancellor of the Duchy of Lancaster and Minister of Public Service 1995-96, to Nicholas Soames as Minister of State for the Armed Forces 1994-95, to Michael Heseltine as First Secretary of State and Deputy Prime Minister 1995-96; Assistant Government Whip 1996-97. *House of Lords:* Raised to the peerage as Baron Coe, of Ranmore in the County of Surrey 2000. Olympics legacy ambassador 2012-; On leave of absence October 2016-June 2017. *Councils and public bodies:* Member, UK Government Honours Main Committee and chair, Sports Honours Committee.

Political interests: Health, foreign affairs, education, environment, economy, voluntary movement.

Other: Progressive Supranucleur Palsy Association. Pro-Chancellor, Loughborough University. Hon. DSc, Hull University 1988; Hon. LLD, Sheffield University; Honorary Fellow, UWIC; Hon. D Tech, Loughborough University 1985; Hon. DSc, University of East London; Hon. DLetters, Sunderland University 2011; Honorary Fellow, RIBA 2010. Gold 1,500m and silver 800m medals at Moscow Olympic Games 1980 and Los Angeles Olympic Games 1984; European Champion for 800m Stuttgart 1986; Set nine world records; BBC Sports Personality of the Year 1979; Sportswriters' Sportsman of the Year: 1979, 1980, 1981, 1984; Lifetime Achievement Award, BBC Sports Personality of the Year 2012. MBE 1982; OBE 1990; KBE 2006; CH 2013; *Clubs:* Carlton Club, East India Club.

Publications: Autobiography, Running My Life (Hodder & Stoughton, 2012).

Recreations: Jazz, theatre, reading.

The Lord Coe CH KBE, House of Lords, London SW1A 0PW
Tel: 020 7219 5353 *Twitter:* @sebcoe

LABOUR

COHEN OF PIMLICO, BARONESS

COHEN OF PIMLICO (Life Baroness), Janet Cohen; cr. 2000. Born 4 July 1940; Daughter of late George Neel and Mary Isabel Neel; Married James Lionel Cohen 1971 (2 sons 1 daughter).

Education: South Hampstead High School, London; Newnham College, Cambridge (BA law 1962) (Associate Fellow 1988-91); Good French, some German.

Non-political career: Articled clerk, Frere Cholmeley 1963-65; Admitted solicitor 1965; Consultant: ABT Associates, USA 1965-67, John Laing Construction 1968-69; Department of Trade and Industry: Principal 1969-78, Assistant secretary 1978-82; Charterhouse Bank Ltd: Assistant director 1982-88, Director 1988-2000; Chair, Café Pelican Ltd 1984-90; Yorkshire Building Society: Director 1991-94, Vice-chair 1994-99; BPP Holdings: Non-executive director 1994-2002, Non-executive chair 2002-06; Non-executive director: Waddington plc 1994-97, London and Manchester Assurance 1997-98, ISI Ltd 1998-2002, United Assurance 1999-2000, Defence Logistics Organisation 1999-2005, London Stock Exchange 2001-13; Vice-chair, Borsa Italiana 2001-14; Non-executive director: Management Consulting Group plc 2003-10, Freshwater UK plc 2007-09, Inviseo Media Holdings 2007-09. Member, First Division Association 1969-82.

Political career: *House of Lords:* Raised to the peerage as Baroness Cohen of Pimlico, in the City of Westminster 2000. Member: Tax Law Rewrite Bills Joint Committee 2001-07, EU Sub-committee B (Internal Market, Energy and Transport) 2002-06, European Union 2006-10; Chair, EU Sub-committee A (Economic and Financial Affairs) 2006-10; Member: Small- and Medium-Sized Enterprises 2012-13, Joint Committee on the Draft Communications Data Bill 2012-13; Audit: Member 2013-15, 2016-, Chair 2015-16. *Councils and public bodies:* Sheffield Development Corporation 1993-97; Governor, BBC 1994-99; Board Member, Parkside Federation Academies Trust 2016-; Governor, University Technical College Cambridge 2016-.

Political interests: Finance, City affairs, education; France, Germany, Italy, New Zealand.

Other: Chair, Cambridge Arts Theatre 2007-15; BPP University College: President 2008-13, Chancellor 2013-; Hon President, Cambridge Arts Theatre Trust 2015-; Law Society; Hon. Fellow: Lucy Cavendish College Cambridge, St Edmund's College Cambridge; Cambridge Arts Theatre Trust, Arthur Rank Hospice Trust. Chancellor, BPP University 2013-. Hon. DLitt, Humberside 1995.

Publications: As Janet Neel: Death's Bright Angel (1988); Death on Site (1989); Death of a Partner (1991); Death among the Dons (1993); A Timely Death (1999); To Die For (1998); O Gentle Death (2000); Ticket to Ride (2005); As Janet Cohen: The Highest Bidder (1992); Children of a Harsh Winter (1994).

Recreations: Writing, theatre.

The Baroness Cohen of Pimlico, House of Lords, London SW1A 0PW
Tel: 020 7219 5353
Email: janet@bnsjcohen.com

CONSERVATIVE

COLGRAIN, LORD

COLGRAIN (4th Baron, UK), Alastair Colin Leckie Campbell; cr 1946. Born 16 September 1951; Son of David Colin Campbell, 3rd Baron Colgrain, and Veronica Webster; Married Annabel (Bella) Warrender 1979 (2 sons).

Education: Eton College; Trinity College, Cambridge (MA English 1973); Royal Agricultural College, Cirencester.

Non-political career: J Henry Schroder Wagg & Co; Welbeck Group Ltd; Managing Director, Webster and Partners 2002-; Partner, Campbell Brothers (farming partnership).

Political career: *House of Lords:* Elected hereditary peer 2017-. Member, Finance 2017-. *Councils and public bodies:* High Sherriff of Kent 2013-14; Governor, Sevenoaks School; DL, Kent 2017-.

Political interests: Environment, agriculture, armed forces and police, employment.

Other: Special Constable, London; Trustee: Belmont House, Arvon Foundation, Belnor Farms, Rochester Cathedral; Non-executive director, Cripps 2014-; President, Kent County Agricultural Society 2015-; *Clubs:* Brooks's Club.

The Lord Colgrain DL, House of Lords, London SW1A 0PW
Tel: 020 7219 3000

LABOUR

COLLINS OF HIGHBURY, LORD

Opposition Spokesperson for International Development and Foreign and Commonwealth Office; Opposition Whip

COLLINS OF HIGHBURY (Life Baron), Raymond Edward Harry Collins; cr 2011. Born 21 December 1954; Son of late Harry and Isobel Collins; Married Rafael Ballesteros 2005.

Education: Matthew Arnold School, Staines; Richmond College; Kent University, Canterbury (BA industrial relations and politics 1980); Conversational Spanish.

Non-political career: Transport and General Workers' Union/Unite: Assistant librarian 1972-74, Specialist assistant, Education 1974-77, Policy adviser and special assistant to General Secretary 1980-84, National administrative officer 1984-99, Assistant General Secretary 1999-2008. Member: TGWU/Unite 1972-, Branch Committee, Staff Negotiating Committee.

Political career: *House of Lords:* Raised to the peerage as Baron Collins of Highbury, of Highbury in the London Borough of Islington 2011. Opposition Whip 2011-; Opposition Spokesperson for: Work and Pensions 2012-13, International Development 2013-, Foreign and Commonwealth Office 2015-. Member, Finance 2016-. *Other:* Labour Party: Member 1970-, Member, National Policy Forum 1997-2003, Elected Member, National Constitution Committee 2001-08, General Secretary 2008-11, Patron, LGBT Labour. *Councils and public bodies:* Governing Body, Ruskin College, Oxford.

Political interests: Equality, international affairs, justice and opportunity; South America, Spain.

Other: Director, Lionel Cook Memorial Fund 2008-; Stonewall, Positive East, Human Dignity Trust.

Recreations: Arsenal FC, cinema, reading, swimming.

The Lord Collins of Highbury, House of Lords, London SW1A 0PW
Tel: 020 7219 1675 *Fax:* 020 7219 0699 *Email:* collinsr@parliament.uk *Twitter:* @Lord_Collins

CROSSBENCH

COLLINS OF MAPESBURY, LORD

COLLINS OF MAPESBURY (Life Baron), Lawrence Antony Collins; cr 2009. Born 7 May 1941; Son of Sol and Phoebe Collins; Married Sara Shamni 1982 (divorced 2003) (1 son 1 daughter); married Patti Langton 2012.

Education: City of London School; Downing College, Cambridge (BA 1963; LLB 1964); Columbia University, New York (LLM 1965); Cambridge University (LLD 1994).

Non-political career: Solicitor 1968; Herbert Smith Solicitors: Partner 1971-2000, Head of Litigation and Arbitration Department 1995-98; Visiting Professor, Queen Mary College, London 1982-; QC 1997; Deputy High Court Judge 1997-2000; High Court Judge Chancery Division, High Court of Justice 2000-07; Bencher Inner Temple 2001; Lord Justice of Appeal 2007-09; Justice of the Supreme Court of the United Kingdom 2009-11; Professor of law, Faculty of Laws, University College London 2011-; Non-Permanent Judge, Hong Kong Court of Final Appeal 2011-; Arbitrator member, Essex Court Chambers 2012-; Visiting Professor, New York University Law School 2014-.

Political career: *House of Lords:* Raised to the peerage as Baron Collins of Mapesbury, of Hampstead Town in the London Borough of Camden 2009. Lord of Appeal in Ordinary 2009; As Justice of the Supreme Court, disqualified from participation 2009-11. *Councils and public bodies:* Member, Department for Constitutional Affairs/Ministry of Justice Advisory Committee on Private International Law 2004-.

Other: Member, Institut de Droit International 1989; Hon. Member, Society of Legal Scholars 1993; Fellow, British Academy 1994; Hon. Life Member, Law Society 2000; Vice-President, British Institute of International and Comparative Law 2011-; Takeover Appeal Board: Deputy Chair 2013-14, Chair 2014-. Wolfson College, Cambridge: Fellow 1975-, Hon Fellow 2009-; Hon Fellow, Downing College, Cambridge 2000; Hon LLD, College of Law 2008. Kt 2000; PC 2007; *Clubs:* Athenæum, Ronnie Scott's Club.

Publications: General editor, Dicey & Morris/Dicey, Morris & Collins Conflict of Laws 1987-; Essays in International Litigation and the Conflict of Laws (1994); European Community Law in the United Kingdom (1st ed 1975, 4th ed 1990).

Rt Hon the Lord Collins of Mapesbury QC, House of Lords, London SW1A 0PW
Tel: 020 7219 5353
24 Lincoln's Inn Fields, London WC2A 3EG *Tel:* 020 7813 8000 *Email:* lcollins@essexcourt.net

CROSSBENCH

COLVILLE OF CULROSS, VISCOUNT

COLVILLE OF CULROSS (5th Viscount, UK), Charles Mark Townshend Colville; cr. 1902; 14th Lord Colville of Culross (S) 1604; 5th Baron Colville of Culross (UK) 1885. Born 5 September 1959; Son of late 4th Viscount and Mary Colville, née Webb-Bowen.

Education: Rugby School; Durham University (BA history 1981); French, Russian.

Non-political career: Former reporter: *Ludlow Advertiser*, *Worcester Evening News*, *Weekend World*, LWT; BBC -2016: *Newsnight*, *Money Programme*, Senior director of science and history documentaries, including: *Mutant Mouse* (also wrote) 2004, *Incredible Human Journey* 2009, *How The Earth Made Us* (also produced) 2010, *Horizon*, *Normans*, *Orbit*. BECTU.

Political career: *House of Lords:* Elected hereditary peer 2011-. Member, Communications 2017-.

Political interests: Media, science, foreign affairs; China, Japan, Russia.

Other: Trustee, Tree Council.

Recreations: Theatre, trees, learning Russian.

The Viscount Colville of Culross, House of Lords, London SW1A 0PW
Tel: 020 7219 3000 *Email:* colvillec@parliament.uk

CONSERVATIVE

COLWYN, LORD

COLWYN (3rd Baron, UK), Ian Anthony Hamilton-Smith; cr. 1917; 3rd Bt of Colwyn Bay (UK) 1912. Born 1 January 1942; Son of 2nd Baron; Married Sonia Morgan 1964 (divorced 1976) (1 son 1 daughter); married Nicola Tyers 1977 (2 daughters).

Education: Cheltenham College; St Bartholomew's Hospital and Royal Dental Hospital, London University (BDS London University 1966, LDS, RCS (England) 1966).

Non-political career: Dental practice 1965-2005; Non-executive director, Medical Protection Society 1989-2002; Chair, Dental Protection Ltd 1995-2001; Non-executive director, Project Hope 1996-2001; Bandleader, Lord Colwyn Organisation; Chair: RAW FM (Radio) 1998-99, Banbury Local Radio 2003-05, Campbell, Montague International 2005-08, Dental Sedation Practice 2005-08. Member, Musicians' Union 1966-.

Political career: *House of Lords:* First entered House of Lords 1967; Elected hereditary peer 1999-; Deputy Chairman of Committees 2007-16; Deputy Speaker 2008-16; Contested Lord Speaker election 2011. Member: Administration and Works Sub-committee 1997-2003, Finance and Staff Sub-committee 1997-2003; Chair, Refreshment Sub-committee 1997-2003; Co-opted member: Science and Technology Sub-committee I (Complementary and Alternative Medicine) 2000, EU Sub-committee G (Social Policy and Consumer Affairs) 2003-07; Member: Science and Technology 2006-10, Science and Technology Sub-committees: I (Allergy) 2007, II (Genomic Medicine) 2008-09, Refreshment 2012-15. *Other:* Member, Conservative Medical Society; Executive member, Association of Conservative Peers 2004-10.

Political interests: Health, dentistry, complementary medicine, arts, sport, cycling.

Other: FDI Federation Dentaire International; Member, Royal Society of Medicine; President, Natural Medicines Society 1988-2005; Member, Eastman Research Institute Trust 1990-2001; President: Huntington's Disease Association 1991-98, Society for Advancement of Anaesthesia in Dentistry 1993-98, Arterial Health Foundation 1993-2004, Metropolitan Branch, British Dental Association 1994-95; Council member, Medical Protection Society 1994-2001; Fellow, Industry and Parliament Trust 2000; Trustee, Portman Estates 2004-08; Fellow, Institute of Directors 1999-2001; Fellowship, British Dental Association 2005; Macmillan, Fight for Sight, AF Foundation. CBE 1989; *Clubs:* Ronnie Scott's, 606 Club. Life member: Cheltenham Rugby Club, Colwyn Bay Rugby Club, Hennerton Golf Club, Leander.

Recreations: Bandleader, music, riparian pursuits, golf, rugby.

The Lord Colwyn CBE, House of Lords, London SW1A 0PW
Tel: 020 7219 3184 *Fax:* 020 7219 0318 *Email:* colwyna@parliament.uk

CROSSBENCH

CONDON, LORD

CONDON (Life Baron) Paul Leslie Condon; cr 2001. Born 10 March 1947; Son of late Patrick and Beryl Condon; Married Janet Workman 1969 (2 sons 1 daughter).

Education: Summerbee Secondary Modern School, Bournemouth; St Peter's College, Oxford (BA jurisprudence 1972, MA).

Non-political career: Police service 1967-2000: Kent Police: Assistant Chief Constable 1984-87, Chief Constable 1989-93, Metropolitan Police: Deputy Assistant Commissioner 1987-88, Assistant Commissioner 1988-89, Commissioner 1993-2000; Director, anti-corruption unit, International Cricket Council 2000-10.

Political career: *House of Lords:* Raised to the peerage as Baron Condon, of Langton Green in the County of Kent 2005. Member, EU Home Affairs Sub-committee 2015-. *Councils and public bodies:* DL, Kent 2000-.

Other: QPM 1989; Knighthood 1994.

Recreations: Swimming, walking, reading, cricket.

The Lord Condon QPM DL, House of Lords, London SW1A 0PW
Tel: 020 7219 3617 *Email:* condonp@parliament.uk

CONSERVATIVE

COOPER OF WINDRUSH, LORD

COOPER OF WINDRUSH (Life Baron), Andrew Timothy Cooper; cr 2014. Born 9 June 1963; Married Elizabeth Campbell 2000 (3 daughters).

Education: Reigate Grammar School, Surrey; London School of Economics.

Non-political career: Head of research, Social Market Foundation 1994-96; Conservative Party: Deputy director of research 1996-97, Director of strategy 1997-99, Director, Political Operations 2011-13; Populus: Founder 2003-, Board Director.

Political career: *House of Lords:* Raised to the peerage as Baron Cooper of Windrush, of Chipping Norton in the County of Oxfordshire 2014. Member, Information 2015-16.

Political interests: Political reform, elections, economy, health, human rights; Australia, Middle East, North and South America.

Other: Member, advisory board, Centre for Progressive Capitalism 2016-.

The Lord Cooper of Windrush, House of Lords, London SW1A 0PW
Tel: 020 7219 5353 *Email:* cooperac@parliament.uk
Populus, 10 Northburgh Street, London EC1V 0AT *Tel:* 020 7253 9900
Twitter: @AndrewCooper__

CONSERVATIVE

COPE OF BERKELEY, LORD

COPE OF BERKELEY (Life Baron), John Ambrose Cope; cr. 1997. Born 13 May 1937; Son of late George Cope, MC, FRIBA; Married Djemila Payne 1969 (2 daughters).

Education: Oakham School, Rutland.

Non-political career: National Service (Commissioned RA) 1955-57, subsequently TA. Chartered accountant.

Political career: *House of Commons:* Contested Woolwich East 1970 general election. MP (Conservative) for Gloucestershire South February 1974-83, for Northavon 1983-97. Government Whip 1979-83; Deputy Chief Whip 1983-87; Minister of State for: Employment with special responsibility for Small Firms 1987-89, Northern Ireland Office 1989-90; Paymaster General, HM Treasury 1992-94. *House of Lords:* Raised to the peerage as Baron Cope of Berkeley, of Berkeley in the County of Gloucestershire 1997. Opposition Spokesperson for: Northern Ireland 1997-98, Home Affairs 1998-2001; Opposition Chief Whip 2001-07; Deputy Chairman of Committees 2001-07; Deputy Speaker 2002-08. Member: Procedure 2000-02, House of Lords Offices 2001-02, House of Lords Offices Administration and Works Sub-committee/Committee 2001-07, Liaison 2003-09, Privileges 2005-07, Sub-committee on Lords' Interests 2008-10, Joint Committee on National Security Strategy 2010-12, Sub-committee on Lords' Conduct 2010-; Chair, Small- and Medium- Sized Enterprises 2012-13; Member: House 2013-16, Finance 2016-. *Other:* Conservative Party: Deputy Chair 1990-92, Hon. Joint Treasurer 1991-92; Trustee, Conservative Party Archive at Bodleian Library 2008-15.

Political interests: Small businesses; Palestine.

Other: Member, UK Parliamentary Delegation to Council of Europe and Western European Union 1995-97; British-Irish Parliamentary Assembly: UK Member 2008-11, British co-chair 2010-11; Commissioner, Royal Hospital Chelsea 1992-94; Patron, Friends of Royal National Hospital for Rheumatic Diseases; Vice-President, Royal Society of St George 1998-; Trustee, War Memorials Trust 1997-, Chair, UK Friends of Edward Said National Conservatory of Music 2013-; Institute of Chartered Accountants in England and Wales; FCA. PC 1988; Kt 1991; *Clubs:* Carlton; Pratts; Tudor House (Chipping Sodbury) Club. Bentley Drivers' Club, Rolls-Royce Enthusiasts Club.

Recreations: A 1939 Bentley motor car, church bell ringing.

Rt Hon the Lord Cope of Berkeley, House of Lords, London SW1A 0PW
Tel: 020 7219 2249 *Fax:* 020 7219 0753 *Email:* copej@parliament.uk

CROSSBENCH

CORK AND ORRERY, EARL OF

CORK AND ORRERY (15th Earl of, I), John Richard Boyle; cr 1620 and 1660; 15th Viscount Dungarvan (I) 1620; 16th Viscount Boyle of Kinalmeaky and Baron of Bandon Bridge (I) 1627; 15th Baron Boyle of Youghal (I) 1616; 15th Baron Boyle of Broghill (I) 1621; 12th Baron Boyle of Marston (GB) 1711. Born 3 November 1945; Married Hon Rebecca Noble 1973 (1 son 2 daughters).

Education: Harrow School; RNC Dartmouth.

Non-political career: Officer, Royal Navy 1963-79; E D and F Man Sugar Ltd: Employee 1979-94, Director 1994-2014; Chair, Commodity Handling Ltd 1986-2014.

Political career: *House of Lords:* Elected hereditary peer 2016-. Member, Ecclesiastical Committee 2017-.

Political interests: Maritime affairs, disaster relief, financial services, charity governance, trading with Commonwealth countries.

Other: Chair, Society for the Advancement of the Christian Faith 2003-; Trustee, MapAction 2007-14; Council member, International Dendrology Society 2008-; Trustee, Chichester Cathedral Trusts 2009-; Chair, Chichester Cathedral Restoration and Development Trust 2009-15.

Recreations: Dendrology, sailing, cathedrals.

The Earl of Cork and Orrery, House of Lords, London SW1A 0PW
Tel: 020 7219 5353 *Email:* corkj@parliament.uk

CONSERVATIVE

CORMACK, LORD

CORMACK (Life Baron), Patrick Thomas Cormack; cr 2010. Born 18 May 1939; Son of late Thomas Cormack, local government officer; Married Kathleen McDonald 1967 (2 sons).

Education: St James' Choir School, Grimsby; Havelock School, Grimsby; Hull University (BA English and history 1961); French (basic).

Non-political career: Industrial consultant; Second master, St James' Choir School, Grimsby 1961-66; Training and education officer, Ross Group Ltd 1966-67; Assistant housemaster, Wrekin College, Shropshire 1967-69; Head of history, Brewood Grammar School, Staffordshire 1969-70; Associate editor, *Time and Tide* 1977-79; *The House Magazine*: Chairman editorial board 1976-, Editor 1979-2005, Life president 2005-; Company director, Historic House Hotels 1980-88, Aitken Dott 1984-90; Visiting lecturer, University of Texas 1984; St Antony's College, Oxford: Visiting parliamentary fellowship 1994, Senior member 1995-; Visiting senior lecturer, Hull University 1994-; *First* magazine: International president 1994-, President 2004-.

Political career: *House of Commons:* Contested Bolsover 1964 and Grimsby 1966 general elections. MP (Conservative) for Cannock 1970-74, for South West Staffordshire 1974-83, for South Staffordshire 1983-2010. PPS to Joint Parliamentary Secretaries, Department of Health and Social Security 1970-73; Deputy Shadow Leader of the House of Commons 1997-2000; Contested Speaker election 2000, 2009; Opposition Spokesperson for Constitutional Affairs 1997-2000; Member, House of Commons Commission 2002-05. Member: Ecclesiastical Committee 1970-2010, Lord Chancellor's Advisory Committee on Public Records 1982-87, Accommodation and Works 1987-2001, Modernisation of the House of Commons 1997-98, Joint Committee on Parliamentary Privilege 1997-2000, Foreign Affairs 2001-03, Standing Orders 2001-10, Joint Committee on Human Rights 2001, Joint Committee on Consolidation Etc Bills 2001-09; Chair: Northern Ireland Affairs 2005-10; Member: Liaison 2005-10. Chairman: Conservative Parliamentary Arts and Heritage Committee 1979-83, Conservative Party's Advisory Committee on Arts and Heritage 1987-99; Member, Executive, 1922 Committee 2002-05. *House of Lords:* Raised to the peerage as Baron Cormack, of Enville in the County of Staffordshire 2010. Member: Works of Art 2012-13, 2014-15, Ecclesiastical Committee 2015-, EU Home Affairs Sub-committee 2015-17. *Councils* *and public bodies:* Member, Council of Historical Association 1963-66; Founder and vice-chairman, Heritage in Danger 1974-97; Member, Historic Buildings Council 1979-84; Chairman, Council for Independent Education 1980-95; Royal Commission on Historical Manuscripts/National Archives 1981-2004; Member, General Synod of the Church of England 1995-2005; Governor, English Speaking Union 1999-2006; DL, Staffordshire 2011.

Political interests: Arts, heritage, defence and NATO, Parliamentary history, education, constitutional affairs, industrial relations, human rights; Bosnia, Croatia, Finland, Lithuania, Netherlands, former Soviet Union, USA.

Other: Vice-chairman, De Burght Conference; Commonwealth Parliamentary Association (CPA) UK Branch 1970: Member, executive committee 1997-99, Joint vice-chairman 1999-2000, Treasurer 2000-03; Member, Council for Peace in the Balkans 1992-2000; Historic Churches Preservation Trust/National Churches Trust: Trustee 1973-, Vice-President 2004-; Society of Antiquaries: Fellow 1978-, Vice-President 1994-98; History of Parliament Trust: Member 1979-, Trustee 1983-, Chairman 2001-16, Patron 2016-; Member, Institute of Journalists 1979-89; Museum of Garden History 1980-2000; Member, Council of Winston Churchill Memorial Trust 1983-93; President, Staffordshire Historic Buildings Trust 1992-; Vice-President, Lincolnshire Historic Churches Trust 1997-; Director, Parliamentary Broadcasting Unit 1997-2010; President, Staffordshire Historic Churches Trust 1998-2012; Chairman, Campaign for an Effective Second Chamber 2001-; President, Staffordshire Parks and Gardens Trust 2006-15; Vice-President, Tennyson Society 2009-; President, Prayer Book Society 2011-; Chairman, Historic Lincoln Trust 2012; Fellow, Royal Historical Society 2010-; Hon. Fellow, Historical Association 2010-; Save The Children, Historic Churches Preservation Trust, RNLI, Aid to the Church in Need. Member, Worshipful Company of Glaziers; Company of Art Scholars. Freedom, City of London 1980. Hon Fellow: Historical Association 2010, Golden Jubilee Parliamentarians, the Political Studies Association 2010; Hon DLitt, Hull University 2011, Hon Doctor of Laws, Catholic University of America 2011. Political Studies Jubilee Award 2011. Hon. Citizen of Texas 1985; Kt 1995; Commander of the Order of the Lion (Finland) 1998; *Clubs:* Athenæum.

Publications: Heritage in Danger (1976); Right Turn (1978); Westminster: Palace and Parliament (1981); Castles of Britain (1982); Wilberforce – The Nation's Conscience (1983); English Cathedrals (1984); Responsible Capitalism (2009).

Recreations: Walking, talking, fighting Philistines.

The Lord Cormack, House of Lords, London SW1A 0PW
Tel: 020 7219 5353

CORSTON, BARONESS

LABOUR

CORSTON (Life Baroness), Jean Ann Corston; cr 2005. Born 5 May 1942; Daughter of late Laurie Parkin, trade union official, and late Eileen Parkin; Married Christopher Corston 1961 (1 son 1 daughter 1 daughter stillborn); married Professor Peter Townsend 1985 (died 2009).

Education: Yeovil Girls' High School; Open University; London School of Economics (LLB 1989); Inns of Court School of Law 1989-90.

Non-political career: Barrister. Former Member, Unite.

Political career: *House of Commons:* MP (Labour) for Bristol East 1992-2005. PPS to David Blunkett as Secretary of State for Education and Employment 1997-2000. Chair, Joint Committee on Human Rights 2001-05; Member: Agriculture 1992-95, Home Affairs 1995-97. Co-chair, Parliamentary Labour Party Women's Group 1992-97; Chair: PLP Children and Family Group 1995-97, PLP Civil Liberties Group 1997-2001. *House of Lords:* Raised to the peerage as Baroness Corston, of St George in the County and City of Bristol 2005. Member: Liaison 2009-13, Joint Committee on Privacy and Injunctions 2011-12; EU Sub-committee E (Justice, Institutions and Consumer Protection): Member 2012-13, Chair 2013-14; Member, European Union 2013-14; Chair, Social Mobility 2015-16; Member, Constitution 2017-. *Other:* Labour Party: Regional organiser, South West Region 1981-85, Assistant national agent, London 1985-86, Secretary, Annual Conference Arrangements 1985-86, Parliamentary Labour Party: Deputy chair 1997-2001, Chair 2001-05, Vice-chair, Labour Peers 2012-.

Political interests: Equal opportunities, human rights, complementary medicine, women in prison; India, Kenya, USA.

Other: Member, Executive Committee, Commonwealth Parliamentary Association (UK Branch) 1999-2005, 2010-; Chair, Commonwealth Women Parliamentarians 2000; Member, British-Irish Parliamentary Assembly 2015-; Fellow, Royal Society of Arts; Chair, Fawcett Society Commission on Women in the Criminal Justice System 2007-08; Vice-chair and Trustee, Parliament Choir 2011-17; Patron: Women in Prison, Working Chance, Award Scheme Development Accreditation Network; Honorary Fellow, Royal College of Chiropractors; Fellow, Royal Society of Arts; Addiction Recovery Agency, Battle Against Tranquilisers, Organisation for Sickle Cell Anaemia Research, Elizabeth Fry Approved Premises, Bristol Children's Playhouse, Meningitis Trust. PC 2003.

Publications: The Corston Report (Home Office, 2007).

Recreations: Gardening, reading.

Rt Hon the Baroness Corston, House of Lords, London SW1A 0PW
Tel: 020 7219 4575 *Email:* corstonj@parliament.uk

LIBERAL DEMOCRAT

COTTER, LORD

COTTER (Life Baron), Brian Joseph Cotter; cr 2006. Born 24 August 1936; Son of late Michael Cotter and late Mary Cotter; Married Eyleen Wade 1963 (2 sons 1 daughter).

Education: Downside School, Somerset; London Polytechnic (business studies).

Non-political career: National Service 1956-58. Plasticable Ltd 1990-2003: Sales manager, Managing director.

Political career: *House of Commons:* Contested Weston-Super-Mare 1992 general election. MP (Liberal Democrat) for Weston-Super-Mare 1997-2005. Liberal Democrat Spokesperson for Small Businesses 1997-2005. *House of Lords:* Raised to the peerage as Baron Cotter, of Congresbury in the County of Somerset 2006. Liberal Democrat Spokesperson for: Small Business 2006-10, Skills 2007-10. Co-opted Member, EU Sub-committee G (Social Policy and Consumer Affairs) 2008-10; Member EU Sub-committees: G (Social Policies and Consumer Protection) 2010-12, B (Internal Market, Infrastructure and Employment) 2013-15, Internal Market 2015. *Councils and public bodies:* Councillor, Woking Borough Council 1986-90.

Political interests: Business, tourism, foreign affairs, youth affairs, apprenticeships and skills; China, Ireland, Rwanda.

Other: MIND, Oxfam, Cafod, Survivors' Fund (Rwandan Widows Charity).

Publications: Creating an Entrepreneurial Culture (2001).

Recreations: Reading, walking, gardening, films.

The Lord Cotter, House of Lords, London SW1A 0PW
Tel: 020 7219 8271 *Email:* cotterb@parliament.uk

CONSERVATIVE

COURTOWN, EARL OF

Deputy Chief Whip (Captain of the Queen's Bodyguard of the Yeomen of the Guard)

COURTOWN (9th Earl of, I), James Patrick Montagu Burgoyne Winthrop Stopford; cr. 1762; Viscount Stopford; 9th Baron Courtown (I) 1758; 8th Baron Saltersford (GB) 1796. Born 19 March 1954; Son of 8th Earl, OBE, TD; Married Elisabeth Dunnett 1985 (1 son 2 daughters).

Education: Eton College; Berkshire College of Agriculture; Royal Agricultural College, Cirencester.

Non-political career: Land agent: Bruton Knowles, Gloucester 1987-90, John German, Shrewsbury 1990-93; Landscape Contractor 2001-10.

Political career: *House of Lords:* First entered House of Lords 1975. Sits as Baron Saltersford; Government Spokesperson for the Home Office, Scotland and Transport 1995-97; Government Whip 1995-97; Opposition Whip 1997-2000; Elected hereditary peer 1999-; Government Whip (Lord in Waiting) 2015-16; Government Spokesperson for: Business, Innovation and Skills 2015-16, Culture, Media and Sport 2015-16, International Development 2015-16, Foreign and Commonwealth Office 2015-16; Deputy Chief Whip, Captain of the Queen's Bodyguard of the Yeomen of the Guard 2016-. Member: Bodmin Moor Commons Bill 1994, EU Sub-committees: G (Social Policies and Consumer Protection) 2011-12, D (Agriculture, Fisheries, Environment and Energy) 2012-13; Member: Inheritance and Trustees' Powers Bill 2013, Digital Skills 2014-15, Finance 2016-.

Political interests: Agriculture, environment, property, landscape industry, West Country; Ireland, Switzerland.

Other: Patron, Stroud Court Community Trust.

Recreations: Skiing, gardening.

The Earl of Courtown, House of Lords, London SW1A 0PW
Tel: 020 7219 3129 *Email:* courtownp@parliament.uk *Twitter:* @LordCourtown

CROSSBENCH

COUSSINS, BARONESS

COUSSINS (Life Baroness), Jean Elizabeth Coussins; cr 2007. Born 26 October 1950; Daughter of Jessica Coussins, née Hughes, and Walter Coussins; Divorced (1 son 2 daughters).

Education: Godolphin and Latymer Girls' School, London; Newnham College, Cambridge (BA modern and medieval languages 1973, MA); French, Spanish, basic Arabic.

Non-political career: Secretary, United Nations Association 1973-75; Women's rights officer, National Council for Civil Liberties 1975-80; Deputy director, Child Poverty Action Group 1980-83; Senior education officer, Inner London Education Authority 1983-88; Commission for Racial Equality 1988-96: Director: Social policy 1988-94, Equality assurance 1994-96; Chief executive officer, Portman Group 1996-2006; Independent consultant on corporate responsibility 2006-.

Political career: *House of Lords:* Raised to the peerage as Baroness Coussins, of Whitehall Park in the London Borough of Islington 2007. Member: Information 2007-12, EU Sub-committee C (External Affairs) 2013-16, International Relations 2016-. *Councils and public bodies:* Member: DTI Crime Prevention Panel 1999, Scottish Ministerial Advisory Group on Alcohol Problems 2001-06, Advisory council, British Board of Film Classification 2002-05, Advertising Standards Authority 2003-09, Alcohol Education and Research Council 2004-07, Better Regulation Commission 2004-07; Governor, Channing School 2007-12.

Political interests: Modern languages and linguists, corporate social responsibility, regulation, social justice and equal opportunity, international affairs, UN; Latin America, especially Chile, Peru and Colombia, Cuba, EU, France, South Africa, Spain.

Other: President, Money Advice Trust 2010-; Vice-President, Chartered Institute of Linguists 2010-; President: Peru Support Group 2012-, Speak to the Future 2015-; Member, MOD's LEC Assurance Committee 2016-; President, Speak to the Future 2016-; Newnham College, Cambridge: Associate Fellow 2003-05, Hon Fellow 2015-; Hon Fellow: University College London 2010-, Chartered Institute of Linguists 2010-. British Academy President's Medal 2013.

Recreations: Family, travel, food, swimming, football, Fulham FC, crosswords.

The Baroness Coussins, House of Lords, London SW1A 0PW
Tel: 020 7219 5353 *Email:* coussinsj@parliament.uk

CONSERVATIVE

COUTTIE, BARONESS

COUTTIE (Life Baroness), Philippa Marion Roe; cr 2016. Born 25 September 1962; Daughter of Dame Marion Roe (former MP for Broxbourne) and James Roe; Married Stephen Couttie 2002 (twin son and daughter).

Education: Roedean School, Brighton; St Andrews University (BSc psychology 1984); French.

Non-political career: Various PR roles 1984-90; Managing director, Cornerstone Communications and CPP Brussels 1990-92; Chief executive, PR Consultants 1992-99; Associate director, J Henry Schroder 1999-2000; Director, Citigroup 2000-06; Non-executive Senior Adviser, FTI Consulting 2014-17.

Political career: *House of Lords:* Raised to the peerage as Baroness Couttie, of Downe in the County of Kent 2016. Member, Political Polling and Digital Media 2017-. *Other:* Conservative Party: Private Finance Panel, Treasury Team, James Committee; Executive board member, Conservative Group, Local Government Association 2012-. *Councils and public bodies:* Westminster City Council: Councillor 2006-, Cabinet Member for: Housing 2008-11, Finance 2011-12, Council Leader 2012-17; Board member, Royal Parks 2012-17.

Political interests: Local government, economy, business, welfare; Europe, Middle East.

Other: Council member, Imperial College London 2006-14; Member, London Crime Reduction Board 2012-14; Board member, Canal and River Trust 2013-14; Chair, West End Partnership 2013-17; Board member, London Local Enterprise Partnership 2014-16; Deputy Leader: London Councils 2013-17, Local Government Association 2014-17; Breast Cancer Haven, Macmillan. Freedom, City of London.

Recreations: Skiing, antiquities, theatre, opera, gardening.

The Baroness Couttie, House of Lords, London SW1A 0PW
Tel: 020 7219 3000

NON-AFFILIATED

COVENTRY, LORD BISHOP OF

COVENTRY (9th Bishop of), Christopher John Cocksworth. Born 12 January 1959; Son of late Stanley Cocksworth and Auriol Cocksworth; Married Charlotte Pytches 1979 (5 sons).

Education: Forest School for Boys, Horsham; Manchester University (BA theology 1980; PhD 1989); Didsbury School of Education, Manchester Polytechnic (PGCE 1981); German.

Non-political career: Teacher, King Edward's School, Witley 1981-84; Doctoral research 1986-88; Ordained deacon 1988; Assistant curate, Christ Church, Epsom 1988-92; Ordained priest 1989; Chaplain, Royal Holloway and Bedford New College 1992-97; Director, Southern Theological Education and Training Scheme 1997-2001; Hon. Canon, Guildford Cathedral 2000-01; Principal, Ridley Hall, Cambridge 2001-08; Bishop of Coventry 2008-.

Political career: *House of Lords:* Entered House of Lords 2013.

Political interests: Education, international affairs, reconciliation, beginning and end of life issues; Egypt, Germany, Israel, Jordan, Nigeria, Palestine, Syria.

Other: Member, House of Bishops' Standing Committee; Co-chair, Joint Implementation Commission for the Anglican Methodist Covenant; Chair, Faith and Order Commission of the Church of England; Chair of Trustees: Coventry 2020 Educational Trust 2008-, Dudley Lodge Family Assessment Centre, Coventry 2008-; Trustee: Frauenkirche Foundation, Dresden 2008-, Shakespeare Birthplace Trust 2008-; Society for the Study of Theology; Society for the Study of Liturgy. Doctor of Divinity, University of London; *Clubs:* Farmers Club.

Publications: Numerous theological articles in journals, chapters in books and book reviews; Evangelical Eucharistic Thought in the Church of England (CUP, 1993); Co-author, An Anglican Companion (CHP/SPCK, 1996); Holy, Holy, Holy: Worshipping the Trinitarian God (DLT, 1997); Co-author, Being a Priest Today (Cantebury Press-SCM, 2004); Holding Together: Gospel, Church and Spirit – the Essentials of Christian Identity (Canterbury Press-SCM, 2008); Seeing Jesus and Being Seen by Him (SPCK, 2014).

Recreations: Organic fruit and vegetable growing.

Rt Rev Dr the Lord Bishop of Coventry, House of Lords, London SW1A 0PW
Tel: 020 7219 5353 *Email:* cocksworthc@parliament.uk
Bishop's House, 23 Davenport Road, Coventry CV5 6PW *Tel:* 024 7667 2244
Fax: 024 7671 3271 *Email:* bishop@bishop-coventry.org *Websites:* www.dioceseofcoventry.org
www.bishop-coventry.org

CROSSBENCH

COX, BARONESS

COX (Life Baroness), Caroline Anne Cox; cr. 1983. Born 6 July 1937; Daughter of late Robert McNeill Love and Dorothy Borland; Married Dr Murray Cox 1959 (died 1997) (2 sons 1 daughter).

Education: Channing School, Highgate, London; London Hospital (SRN 1958); London University external student (BScSoc 1967; MSc(Econ) 1969); French (basic); Italian; Russian (basic).

Non-political career: Staff nurse, Edgware General Hospital 1960; North London Polytechnic: Lecturer, senior lecturer and principal lecturer 1969-74, Head, Department of Sociology 1974-77; Director, Nursing Education Research Unit, Chelsea College, London University 1977-84; Royal College of Nursing: Fellow, Vice-President 1990-; Humanitarian Aid Relief Trust (HART): Chief executive officer 2005-16, 2017- President 2016-17.

Political career: *House of Lords:* Raised to the peerage as Baroness Cox, of Queensbury in Greater London 1983. Government Whip 1985; Deputy Speaker 1986-2005; Deputy Chair of Committees 1986-2004.

Political interests: Human rights, humanitarian aid, education, health, nursing; Armenia, Burma, Nigeria, North Korea, Poland, Sudan, South Sudan, Syria, East Timor, Uganda.

Other: Patron: Medical Aid for Poland Fund 1983-, Physicians for Human Rights, UK 1990-; Standing Conference on Women's Organisations 1990-; Vice-President, Girl Guides Association 1995-; Hon. vice-chair, International Islamic Christian Organisation for Reconciliation and Reconstruction 2002-; Patron, Christian Solidarity Worldwide UK 2006-; Vice-President, Liverpool School of Tropical Medicine 2006-; Hon. FRCN; Hon. FRCS 1997. Honorary Freeman, Worshipful Society of Apothecaries. Chancellor: Bournemouth University 1992-2001, Liverpool Hope University 2006-13. 14 honorary doctorates and fellowships. Wilberforce Award 1995; Fridej of Nansen International Foundation Award 2004; International Mother Teresa Award 2005. Commander Cross of the Order of Merit of the Republic of Poland 1990; Mkhitar Gosh Medal (Armenia) 2005; Polish Solidarity Movement Medal 2005; *Clubs:* Royal Over-Seas League Club.

Publications: Author of numerous publications on education and health care, including: Co-editor, A Sociology of Medical Practice (1975); Co-author, The Rape of Reason: The Corruption of the Polytechnic of North London (1975); The Right to Learn (1982); Sociology: A Guide for Nurses, Midwives and Health Visitors (1983); Editor, Trajectories of Despair: Misdiagnosis and Maltreatment of Soviet Orphans (1991); Co-author: Ethnic Cleansing in Progress: War in Nagorno Karabakh (1993), Made to Care: The Case for Residential and Village Communities for People with a Mental Handicap (1995), The 'West', Islam and Islamism: Is Ideological Islam Compatible With Liberal Democracy? (2003, 2006); Cox's Book of Modern Saints and Martyrs (Continuum, 2006); This Immoral Trade: Slavery in the 21st Century (Monarch, 2006, revised edition 2013); The Very Stones Cry Out: The Persecuted Church: Pain, Passion and Praise (Continuum, 2011).

Recreations: Campanology, hill-walking, tennis.

The Baroness Cox, House of Lords, London SW1A 0PW
Tel: 020 7219 8638 *Email:* coxc@parliament.uk
Unit 1, Jubilee Business Centre, 213 Kingsbury Road, London NW9 8AQ *Tel:* 020 8205 4608
Email: caroline.cox@hart-uk.org *Websites:* www.hart-uk.org www.carolinecox.org

CRAIG OF RADLEY, LORD

CROSSBENCH

CRAIG OF RADLEY (Life Baron), David Brownrigg Craig; cr. 1991. Born 17 September 1929; Son of late Major Francis Brownrigg Craig and Hannah Olivia (Olive) Craig; Married June Derenburg 1955 (1 son 1 daughter).

Education: Radley College; Lincoln College, Oxford (BA pure maths 1951, MA).

Non-political career: Commissioned into RAF 1951; Flying instructor on Meteors and Hunter pilot in Fighter Command 1953-55; CO, No. 35 Squadron 1963-65; Military Assistant to Chief of the Defence Staff 1965-68; Group Captain 1968; Station CO, RAF College, Cranwell 1968-70; ADC to HM The Queen 1969-71; Director, Plans and Operations, HQ Far East Command 1970-71; OC, RAF Akrotiri (Cyprus) 1972-73; Assistant Chief of Air Staff (Operations), Ministry of Defence 1975-78; Air Officer Commanding No 1 Group 1978-80; Vice-Chief of Air Staff 1980-82; Air Officer Commanding-in-Chief Strike Command and Commander-in-Chief UK Air Forces 1982-85; Chief of the Air Staff 1985-88; Air ADC to HM The Queen 1985-88; Marshal of the Royal Air Force 1988; Chief of the Defence Staff 1988-91.

Political career: *House of Lords:* Raised to the peerage as Baron Craig of Radley, of Helhoughton in the County of Norfolk 1991. Convenor of Crossbench Peers 1999-2004. Member: Privileges 2000-04, Liaison 2000-04, 2013-16, Procedure 2000-04, Selection 2000-04, 2016-, House 2002-04, 2007-13, Administration and Works 2002-04, Information 2004-07. *Councils and public bodies:* Chairman of Council, King Edward VII's Hospital 1998-2004.

Political interests: Defence, foreign and Commonwealth affairs.

Other: Vice-chair, RAF Benevolent Fund 1991-2013; President: (RAF) The "Not Forgotten" Association 1993-2014, RAF Club 2002-12; FRAeS; King Edward VII's Hospital for Officers; RAF Benevolent Fund. Hon. Fellow, Lincoln College, Oxford 1984; Hon. DSc, Cranfield Institute of Technology 1988. OBE (Mil) 1967; CB 1978; KCB 1981; GCB (Mil) 1984.

Recreations: Fishing, shooting, woodwork.

Marshal of the Royal Air Force the Lord Craig of Radley GCB OBE, House of Lords, London SW1A 0PW
Tel: 020 7219 2200 *Fax:* 020 7219 0147 *Email:* craigd@parliament.uk

CRAIGAVON, VISCOUNT

CROSSBENCH

CRAIGAVON (3rd Viscount, UK), Janric Fraser Craig; cr. 1927; 3rd Bt of Craigavon (UK) 1918. Born 9 June 1944; Son of 2nd Viscount.

Education: Eton College; London University (BA; BSc).

Non-political career: Chartered accountant.

Political career: *House of Lords:* First entered House of Lords 1974; Elected hereditary peer 1999-. Member, Hybrid Instruments 1993-97, 1999-2005; Alternate member, Procedure 2010-15.

Countries of interest: Netherlands, Nordic countries.

Other: Commander of the Order of the Lion (Finland) 1998; Commander of the Royal Order of the Polar Star (Sweden) 1999; Knight of the Order of Dannebrog (Denmark) 2006; Commander of the Royal Norwegian Order of Merit 2010.

The Viscount Craigavon, House of Lords, London SW1A 0PW
Tel: 020 7219 3881 *Email:* craigavonj@parliament.uk
54 Westminster Mansions, 1 Little Smith Street, London SW1P 3DQ *Tel:* 020 7222 1949

CONSERVATIVE

CRATHORNE, LORD

CRATHORNE (2nd Baron, UK), (Charles) James Dugdale; cr. 1959; 2nd Bt of Crathorne (UK) 1945. Born 12 September 1939; Son of 1st Baron, PC, TD; Married Sylvia Montgomery 1970 (died 2009) (1 son 2 daughters).

Education: Eton College; Trinity College, Cambridge (MA fine arts 1963).

Non-political career: Impressionist painting department, Sotheby & Co. 1963-66; Assistant to president, Parke-Bernet Galleries, New York 1966-69; Independent fine art consultancy, James Dugdale & Associates/James Crathorne & Associates 1969-; Lecture tours to the USA 1969-99; Director, Blakeney Hotels Ltd 1979-96; Lecture series *Aspects of England*, in Metropolitan Museum, New York 1981; Australian bicentennial lecture tour 1988; Director: Woodhouse Securities Ltd 1988-99, Cliveden plc 1996-99, Cliveden Ltd 1999-2002, Hand Picked Hotels 2000-01.

Political career: *House of Lords:* First entered House of Lords 1977; Elected hereditary peer 1999-. Works of Art: Member 1983-2004, 2012-13, 2014-15, Chair 2003-07. *Other:* Member, Conservative Advisory Group on Arts and Heritage 1988-99. *Councils and public bodies:* DL, County of Cleveland 1983-96; Member of Court, Leeds University 1985-97; President, Cleveland and North Yorkshire Magistrates' Association 1997-2003; County of North Yorkshire: DL 1996-98, Lord Lieutenant 1999-2014; JP 1999-; Member of Court: York University 1999-, Hull University 1999-.

Political interests: Visual and performing arts, country houses; India, USA.

Other: Trustee, Georgian Theatre Royal, Richmond, Yorkshire 1970-; Fellow, Royal Society of Arts 1972; Captain Cook Birthplace Museum Trust: Trustee 1978-, Chair 1993-; Editorial Board, *House Magazine* 1983-; Council, RSA 1982-88; Georgian Group: Executive Committee 1985-, Chair 1990-99, President 1999-; President: Cleveland Family History Society 1988-, Cleveland Sea Cadets 1988-2014; Hambleton District, Council for the Protection of Rural England 1988-; Trustee, Yorkshire Regional Committee, National Trust 1988-94; Vice-President, Cleveland Wildlife Trust 1989-; Patron: Attingham Trust for Study of British Country House 1990-, Cleveland Community Foundation 1990-2004; Trustee, National Heritage Memorial Fund 1992-95; Joint Committee of National Amenity Societies: Deputy chair 1993-96, Chair 1996-99; Vice-President, Public Monuments and Sculpture Association 1997-; President, Cleveland Search and Rescue Team 1998-; Patron, Friends of Public Record Office 1998-; President: North Yorkshire County Scout Council 1999-2014, St John Ambulance North Yorkshire and Teesside 1999-; Yorkshire and Humberside Reserve Forces and Cadets' Association (RFCA): Vice-President 1999-2014, President 2006-09; Patron, British Red Cross, North Yorkshire Branch 1999-2014; Vice-President, North of England (RFCA) 2001-; Patron, Tees Valley Community Foundation 2004-; Fellow, Society of Antiquaries 2009, Patron, Middlesbrough Institute of Modern Art (MIMA); Chair, Sylvia Crathorne Memorial Trust; Marie Curie Cancer Care, Georgian Theatre Royal. Freedom, Richmond, North Yorkshire 2014. Hon. LLD: Teeside University 2013, York University. KStJ 1999; Queen's Golden Jubilee Medal 2002; Queen's Diamond Jubilee Medal 2012; KCVO 2013; *Clubs:* Pratts, Garrick Club.

Publications: Articles in The Connoisseur and Apollo; Edouard Vuillard (1967); Co-author: Tennant's Stalk (1973), A Present from Crathorne (1989); Cliveden, the Place and the People (1995); The Royal Crescent Book of Bath (1998); Co-Photographer, Parliament in Pictures (1999).

Recreations: Photography, jazz, collecting, country pursuits, travel.

The Lord Crathorne KCVO, House of Lords, London SW1A 0PW
Tel: 020 7219 5224 *Email:* crathornej@parliament.uk
Crathorne House, Yarm, North Yorkshire TS15 0AT *Tel:* 01642 700431
Email: james.crathorne@btconnect.com

CONSERVATIVE

CRAWFORD AND BALCARRES, EARL OF

CRAWFORD (29th Earl of, S), cr. 1398, AND BALCARRES (12th Earl of, S), cr. 1651; Robert Alexander Lindsay; Lord Lindsay of Crawford before 1143. Lord Lindsay (S) 1633; Lord Balniel (S) 1651; 5th Baron Wigan (UK) 1826; (Life) Baron Balniel 1974. Born 5 March 1927; Son of 28th Earl, KT, GBE; Married Ruth Meyer-Bechtler 1949 (2 sons 2 daughters).

Education: Eton College; Trinity College, Cambridge.

Non-political career: Grenadier Guards 1945-48. Director, National Westminster Bank 1975-89; Vice-chair, Sun Alliance & London Insurance 1975-91; Director, Scottish American Investment Trust 1978-88; Lord Chamberlain to HM Queen Elizabeth the Queen Mother 1992-2002.

Political career: *House of Commons:* MP (Conservative) for Hertford 1955-74, for Welwyn and Hatfield March-October 1974. Contested Welwyn and Hatfield October 1974 general election. PPS to Henry Brooke: as Financial Secretary to the Treasury 1955-56, as Minister of Housing and

Local Government 1956-59; Principal Opposition Frontbench Spokesperson for Health and Social Security 1967-70; Minister of State: Defence 1970-72, Ministry of Foreign and Commonwealth Affairs 1972-74. *House of Lords:* Created a life peer as Baron Balniel, of Pitcorthie in the County of Fife 1974. First entered House of Lords 1975; On leave of absence 2013-. *Councils and public bodies:* President, Rural District Council Association for England and Wales 1959-65; Chair, National Association for Mental Health 1963-70; DL, Fife 1976-2002; Chair, Historic Buildings Council for Scotland 1976-83; First Commissioner of the Crown Estate 1980-85; Chair: Royal Commission on the Ancient and Historical Monuments of Scotland 1985-95, National Library of Scotland Board 1991-2000.

Other: Hon. Fellow: Royal Incorporation of Architects in Scotland 1993, National Library of Scotland 2012. Premier Earl of Scotland on Union Roll; Head of the House of Lindsay; PC 1972; KT 1996; GCVO 2002.

Rt Hon the Earl of Crawford and Balcarres KT GCVO, House of Lords, London SW1A 0PW
Tel: 020 7219 5353

CRAWLEY, BARONESS

LABOUR

CRAWLEY (Life Baroness), Christine Mary Crawley; cr. 1998. Born 9 January 1950; Daughter of Thomas Louis Quinn and Joan Ryan; Married (1 son 2 daughters, including twins).

Education: Notre Dame Girls School, Plymouth; Digby Stuart Teacher Training College, Roehampton, London.

Non-political career: Former teacher and youth theatre leader, Oxfordshire. Member: MSF, Unison.

Political career: *House of Commons:* Contested (Labour) Staffordshire South East 1983 general election. *House of Lords:* Raised to the peerage as Baroness Crawley, of Edgbaston in the County of West Midlands 1998. Government Whip 2002-08, 2009-10; Government Spokesperson for: Defence 2002-08, Foreign and Commonwealth Office 2002-05, International Development 2002-04, 2008, Transport 2004-05, 2007-08, Education and Skills/Children, Schools and Families and for Innovation, Universities and Skills 2005-08, Northern Ireland 2007-08; Opposition Spokesperson for: Communities and Local Government 2010, Foreign and Commonwealth Office 2010, Health 2010; Opposition Deputy Chief Whip 2010-12. Member: European Union -2000, European Union Sub-committee A (Economic and Financial Affairs, Trade and External Relations) 2000-01, Refreshment 2011-12, Lord Speaker's Committee on the Size of the House 2016-. *Other:* European Parliament: MEP for Birmingham East 1984-99: Chair, Women's Rights Committee 1989-94. Member: Co-operative Party, Labour Movement in Europe. *Councils and public bodies:* Former Town and District Councillor in South Oxfordshire; Chair: Women's National Commission 1999-2002, West Midlands Regional Cultural Consortium 1999-2002; President, Chartered Trading Standards Institute 2009-17.

Political interests: Women's rights, equal opportunities, European Union.

Other: Member: Amnesty International, Fabian Society; Fellow, Royal Society of Arts.

Recreations: Latin American literature, amateur dramatics, attending local football matches in Birmingham.

The Baroness Crawley, House of Lords, London SW1A 0PW
Tel: 020 7219 4650 *Fax:* 020 7219 6837 *Email:* crawleyc@parliament.uk
Email: ccrawley@enterprise.net

CRICKHOWELL, LORD

CONSERVATIVE

CRICKHOWELL (Life Baron), Roger Nicholas Edwards; cr. 1987. Born 25 February 1934; Son of late Ralph Edwards, CBE, FSA; Married Ankaret Healing 1963 (1 son 2 daughters).

Education: Westminster School; Trinity College, Cambridge (BA history 1952, MA).

Non-political career: National service (Second Lieutenant), Royal Welch Fusiliers; Lieutenant, TA. Chief executive, William Brandt's Insurance 1960-76; Member of Lloyds 1963-2002; Director: A L Sturge Holdings Ltd 1970-76, PA International & Sturge Underwriting Agency Ltd 1971-79, Globtik Tankers Ltd 1976-79, William Brandt's Ltd 1977-79, Associated British Ports Holdings plc 1988-99, Vice-chair, Anglesey Mining 1988-2000; Member, Committee of Automobile Association 1988-98; Chair: ITNET plc 1996-2004, HTV Group Ltd 1997-2002.

Political career: *House of Commons:* MP (Conservative) for Pembroke 1970-87. Secretary of State for Wales 1979-87. *House of Lords:* Raised to the peerage as Baron Crickhowell, of Pont Esgob in the Black Mountains and County of Powys 1987. Member, Procedure 2000-03; Co-opted Member, EU Sub-committee D (Environment, Agriculture, Public Health and Consumer Protection/Environment and Agriculture) 2000-05; Member, Joint Committees on: Draft Communications Bill 2002, Constitutional Reform Bill (HL); Co-opted Member, EU Sub-committee C (Foreign Affairs, Defence and Development Policy) 2006-10; Member: Draft Climate Change Bill Joint Committee 2007, Science and Technology 2007-12, Science and Technology Sub-committee I 2007-10 (Waste Reduction 2007-08, Nanotechnologies and food 2008-10), Constitution 2010-15, Hybrid Instruments 2015-. *Councils and public bodies:* Chair: National Rivers Authority Advisory Committee 1988-89, National Rivers Authority 1989-96.

Political interests: Environment, economic policy, urban policies, arts, broadcasting.

Other: President: Cardiff University of Wales 1988-98, South East Wales Arts Association 1988-94; Chair, Cardiff Bay Opera House Trust 1993-97; Fellow, RSA. Fishmongers' Company. Hon. Fellow, Cardiff University; Hon. Doctor of Law, Glamorgan University. PC 1979; *Clubs:* Brooks's Club.

Publications: Opera House Lottery – Zaha Hadid and The Cardiff Bay Opera House (1997); Westminster, Wales and Water (1999); The Rivers Join (2009).

Rt Hon the Lord Crickhowell, House of Lords, London SW1A 0PW
Email: crickhowelln@parliament.uk
4 Henning Street, London SW11 3DR

CROSSBENCH

CRISP, LORD

CRISP (Life Baron), (Edmund) Nigel Ramsay Crisp; cr. 2006. Born 14 January 1952; Married Siân Jenkins 1976 (1 daughter 1 son).

Education: Uppingham School, Rutland; St John's College, Cambridge (BA moral sciences 1973, MA).

Non-political career: Deputy director, Halewood Community Council 1973-77; Production manager, Trebor plc 1977-81; Director, Cambridgeshire Community Council 1981-86; General manager, East Berkshire Health Authority 1986-88; Wexham Park Hospital and Heatherwood Hospital 1988-93: Chief executive 1992-93; Chief executive, Oxford Radcliffe Hospital 1993-97; Regional director: South Thames Regional Office 1997-98, London Regional Office 1999-2000; Permanent Secretary for Health and Chief Executive, NHS, Department of Health 2000-06.

Political career: *House of Lords:* Raised to the peerage as Baron Crisp, of Eaglescliffe in the County of Durham 2006. Member: Merits of Statutory Instruments 2007-09, European Union 2017-, EU Home Affairs Sub-committee 2017-.

Countries of interest: Developing world.

Other: Honorary Professor, London School of Hygiene and Tropical Medicine; Senior Fellow, Institute for Health Care Improvement. KCB 2003.

Recreations: Countryside.

The Lord Crisp KCB, House of Lords, London SW1A 0PW
Tel: 020 7219 3873 *Email:* crisp@parliament.uk
Website: www.nigelcrisp.com

CROSSBENCH

CROMWELL, LORD

CROMWELL (7th Baron, E), Godfrey John Bewicke-Copley; cr 1375. Born 4 March 1960; Son of 6th Baron Cromwell and Vivian de Lisle Penfold; Married Elizabeth Hawksley 1990 (3 sons 1 daughter).

Education: Eton College; Selwyn College, Cambridge (BA 1982).

Non-political career: Director/economist, international development NGOs 1987-2006; Director, British East-West Centre 2000-; Executive director, Russo-British Chamber of Commerce 2003-07; Director, British-Georgian Chamber of Commerce 2007-09; Vice-president, Barclays Wealth and Investment Management 2007-16; Divisional Director, Brewin Dolphin 2017-.

Political career: *House of Lords:* Elected hereditary peer 2014-. Member: EU Justice Sub-committee 2015-, Finance 2016-, European Union 2017-.

Political interests: Business education; Africa, Russia and CIS Countries.

The Lord Cromwell, House of Lords, London SW1A 0PW
Tel: 020 7219 6899 *Email:* cromwellg@parliament.uk

CROSSBENCH

CULLEN OF WHITEKIRK, LORD

CULLEN OF WHITEKIRK (Life Baron), William Douglas Cullen; cr. 2003. Born 18 November 1935; Son of late Sheriff K D Cullen and G M Cullen; Married Rosamond Downer 1961 (2 sons 2 daughters).

Education: Dundee High School; St Andrews University (MA classics 1957); Edinburgh University (LLB 1960).

Non-political career: Called to Scottish Bar 1960; Standing junior counsel to HM Customs and Excise 1970-73; QC (Scotland) 1973; Advocate-Depute 1978-81; Senator College of Justice in Scotland 1986-2005; Lord Justice Clerk and President of the Second Division of Court of Session 1997-2001; Lord Justice General of Scotland and Lord President of the Court of Session 2001-05; Justice of the Civil and Commercial Court of Qatar 2007-15.

Political career: *House of Lords:* Raised to the peerage as Baron Cullen of Whitekirk, of Whitekirk in East Lothian 2003. Lord of Appeal 2003-08. Chair, Partnerships (Prosecution) (Scotland) Bill 2013; Member, Constitution 2013-16. *Councils and public bodies:* Chair, Medical Appeal Tribunal 1977-86; Court of Inquiry into Piper Alpha disaster 1988-90; Review of Business of Outer House of Court of Session 1995; Tribunal of Inquiry into shootings at Dunblane Primary School 1996; Ladbroke Grove Rail Inquiry 1999-2001; Review of Fatal Accident Inquiry Legislation 2008-09.

Other: President: Sacro 2000-, Saltire Society 2005-11; Faculty of Advocates; Honorary FRCS, Edinburgh; FRCP, Edinburgh. Chancellor, University of Abertay Dundee 2009-. Six honorary doctorates; Hon FREng 1995; Hon Bencher, Inner Temple 2001; Inn of Northern Ireland 2002. FRSE 1993. PC 1997; KT 2008; *Clubs:* Caledonian, New Club (Edinburgh).

Recreations: Gardening, natural history.

Rt Hon the Lord Cullen of Whitekirk KT, House of Lords, London SW1A 0PW
Tel: 020 7219 5353

CONSERVATIVE

CUMBERLEGE, BARONESS

CUMBERLEGE (Life Baroness), Julia Frances Cumberlege; cr. 1990. Born 27 January 1943; Daughter of Dr LU Camm and MGG Camm; Married Patrick Cumberlege 1961 (3 sons).

Education: Convent of the Sacred Heart, Tunbridge Wells.

Non-political career: Executive director, MJM Healthcare Solutions 1997-2001; Non-executive director, Huntsworth plc 2001-03; Consultant, Quo Health 2001-05; Founded Cumberlege Connections 2001; Founder, Cumberlege Eden and Partners Ltd 2013, Director: Assuring Better Practice (UK) Ltd 2004-07, South East Water plc 2006-08.

Political career: *House of Lords:* Raised to the peerage as Baroness Cumberlege, of Newick in the County of East Sussex 1990. Joint Parliamentary Under-Secretary of State, Department of Health 1992-97; Opposition Spokesperson for Health 1997. Member, Draft Mental Health Bill Joint Committee 2004-05. *Councils and public bodies:* Lewes District Council: Councillor 1966-79, Leader 1977-78; Councillor, East Sussex County Council 1974-85: Chair, Social Services Committee 1979-82; Chair, Brighton Health Authority 1981-88; Member, Press Council 1984-90; Chair, Review of Community Nursing for England (Report: Neighbourhood Nursing) 1985, DL, East Sussex 1986-; Member, DHSS Expert Advisory Group on AIDS 1987-89, Chair, South West Thames Regional Health Authority 1988-92; Vice-President, Royal College of Nursing 1989-; Member, NHS Policy Board for England 1989-97; Council Member, UK Central Council for Nursing, Midwifery and Health Visiting 1989-92; Vice-Lord Lieutenant, East Sussex 1992; Chair: Review of Maternity Services for England (Report: Changing Childbirth) 1993, St George's Medical School Council 2000-06; Council Member, Sussex University 2001-09; Vice-President, Royal College of Midwives; Chair, Review of National Maternity Services 2016.

Political interests: Local government, NHS, media, education.

Other: Patron, National Childbirth Trust; Fellow, Royal Society of Arts 1989; Trustee: Chailey Heritage Foundation School 1990-2014; Leeds Castle Foundation 2005-16; Governor, Lancing College 2013-; Chair, National Association of Health Authorities 1987-88; Fellow: Royal College of Physicians 2006, Royal College of General Practioners 2006, Royal College of Nursing 2010, Royal College of Obstetrics and Gynaecology 2012; Royal Society of Medicine, Rural College of Midwives; Fellow: RCM, RCN. Ten honorary doctorates. CBE 1985.

Recreations: Other people's gardens, bicycling.

The Baroness Cumberlege CBE DL, House of Lords, London SW1A 0PW
Email: cumberlegej@parliament.uk

CUNNINGHAM OF FELLING, LORD

LABOUR

CUNNINGHAM OF FELLING (Life Baron), John Anderson (Jack) Cunningham; cr 2005. Born 4 August 1939; Son of late Andrew and Freda Cunningham; Married Maureen Appleby 1964 (1 son 2 daughters).

Education: Jarrow Grammar School; Bede College, Durham University (BSc chemistry 1962; PhD 1966).

Non-political career: Research fellow, Durham University 1966-68; Executive Chairman and Director, Navitas Resources (UK) Ltd. Full-time officer, GMWU 1969-70.

Political career: *House of Commons:* MP (Labour) for Whitehaven 1970-83, for Copeland 1983-2005. PPS to James Callaghan as Foreign Secretary and Prime Minister 1974-76; Parliamentary Under-Secretary for Energy 1976-79; Shadow Environment Secretary 1983-89; Shadow Leader of the House 1989-92; Shadow Secretary of State for: Foreign and Commonwealth Affairs 1992-94, Trade and Industry 1994-95, National Heritage 1995-97; Minister of Agriculture, Fisheries and Food 1997-98; Minister for the Cabinet Office, and Chancellor of the Duchy of Lancaster 1998-99. Chair, Joint Committee on House of Lords Reform 2002-05. *House of Lords:* Raised to the peerage as Baron Cunningham of Felling, of Felling in the County of Tyne and Wear 2005. Chair, Conventions Joint Committee 2006; Member: Science and Technology Sub-committee I: (Nanotechnologies and food) 2008-10, (Radioactive Waste Management: a further update) 2010, Science and Technology 2009-13, Science and Technology Sub-committee I 2012-13, EU Sub-committee D: Agriculture, Fisheries, Environment and Energy 2014-15, EU Energy and Environment Sub-Committee 2015-17, Finance 2016-. *Other:* General Election Campaign Co-ordinator 1989-92; Labour Whip withdrawn June 2013-January 2014. *Councils and public bodies:* DL, Cumbria 1991; Commissioner, Millennium Commission 1998-99.

Political interests: Regional policy, environment, foreign affairs, industry, energy; China, Europe, Japan, South Africa, USA.

Other: Chairman, UK-Japan 21 Century Group 2004-11; Fellow, Industry and Parliament Trust 1981. PC 1993.

Recreations: Fell-walking, gardening, music, reading, fishing, theatre.

Rt Hon the Lord Cunningham of Felling DL, House of Lords, London SW1A 0PW
Tel: 020 7219 5222

CURRIE OF MARYLEBONE, LORD

CROSSBENCH

CURRIE OF MARYLEBONE (Life Baron), David Anthony Currie; cr. 1996. Born 9 December 1946; Son of late Kennedy Currie and Marjorie Currie; Married Shaziye Gazioglu 1975 (divorced 1992) (2 sons); married Angela Dumas 1995 (1 stepson).

Education: Battersea Grammar School; Manchester University (BSc maths 1968); Birmingham University (MSocSci Econs 1971); London University (PhD economics 1978).

Non-political career: Economist, Hoare Govett 1971-72; Lecturer, reader and professor of economics, Queen Mary College, London University 1972-88; Visiting scholar, International Monetary Fund 1987; London Business School: Professor of economics 1988-2000, Research dean 1989-92, Governor 1989-95, 1999-2000, Deputy principal 1992-95, Deputy dean, External Relations 1999-2000; Director: Joseph Rowntree Reform Trust 1991-2002, International Schools of Business Management 1992-95; Visiting professor, European University Institute 1992-95; Director: Charter 88 1994-98, Gas and Electricity Markets Authority 2000-02; Member, Terra Firma, Advisory Board of Nomura Private Finance Group 2000-02; Dean, City University Business School/Cass Business School, City of London 2001-08; Director, Abbey National plc 2001-02; Member, advisory board, Terra Firma Capital Partners 2002-05; Director: Dubai Financial Services Authority 2005-, London Philharmonic Orchestra 2007-12; Chair, Semperian PPP Investment Partners 2007-12; Director: BDO 2008-12, Royal Mail 2009-12; Chair, International Centre for Financial Regulation 2009-12; Director, IG Group 2010-12.

Political career: *House of Lords:* Raised to the peerage as Baron Currie of Marylebone, of Marylebone in the City of Westminster 1996. Member, Economic Affairs 2008-12. *Councils and public bodies:* Houblon-Norman resident fellow, Bank of England 1985-86; Member: Retail Price Index Advisory Committee 1992-95, Treasury's Panel of Independent Forecasters 1992-95, Management Board, OFGEM 1999-2000; Chairman, Ofcom 2002-09; Panel member, Leveson Inquiry 2011-12; Chair, Competition and Markets Authority 2012-.

Political interests: Economic policy, media and communications, regulation.

Other: Research Fellow, Centre for Economic Policy Research 1983-98; Governor, Institute for Government 2008-; Council of Essex University: Member 2008-13, 2015-, Chair 2011-13, 2016-;

Chair, Alacrity Foundation 2010-13. Honorary fellowship and doctorate: Queen Mary, University of London 1997, Glasgow University 1998, Birmingham University 2003, City University, London 2012, Essex University 2014.

Publications: Advances in Monetary Economics (1985); Co-author: The Operation and Regulation of Financial Markets (1986), Macroeconomic Interactions Between North and South (1988), Rules, Reputation and Macroeconomic Policy Co-ordination (1993), EMUs Problems in the Transition to a Single European Currency (1995), North-South Linkages and International Macroeconomic Policy (1995); The Pros and Cons of EMU (1997); Will the Euro Work? (1998); Articles in journals.

Recreations: Music, literature, swimming.

Professor the Lord Currie of Marylebone, House of Lords, London SW1A 0PW
Tel: 020 7219 5353
Competitition and Markets Authority, Victoria House, Southampton Row, London WC1B 4AD
Tel: 020 3738 6286 *Email:* david.currie@cma.gsi.gov.uk

CROSSBENCH

CURRY OF KIRKHARLE, LORD

CURRY OF KIRKHARLE (Life Baron); Donald Thomas Younger Curry cr. 2011. Born 4 April 1944; Married Rhoda Murdie 1966 (2 sons 1 daughter).

Education: Northumberland College of Agriculture.

Non-political career: Farmer, Northumberland 1971-; Founder and chairman: North Country Primestock 1990-2001, At Home in the Community 1992-; NFU Mutual Insurance Society: Non-executive director 1997-2011, Vice-chairman 2000-03, Chairman 2003-11; Chair: Leckford Estate Management Committee, Waitrose Farm 2009-16, Better Regulation Executive, Department for Business, Innovation and Skills 2009-15, Cawood Scientific Group 2014-.

Political career: *House of Lords:* Raised to the peerage as Baron Curry of Kirkharle, of Kirkharle in the County of Northumberland 2011. Member: Refreshment 2014-16, EU Energy and Environment Sub-Committee 2015-. *Councils and public bodies:* Commissioner, Crown Estate 2000-07; Chair, Commission on the Future of Farming and Food 2001-02; Government Strategy for Sustainable Farming and Food 2002-09.

Political interests: Agriculture and food, social care; South Sudan.

Other: Fellow: Royal Agricultural Society 1995, British Veterinary Association 1998, Myerscough College 2000, Scottish Agricultural College 2006; Trustee: NFU Mutual Charitable Trust 2002-, Lawes Agricultural Trust 2009-, Clinton Devon Estate 2009-, The Prince's Countryside Fund 2010-, Anglican International Development 2010-; Chair: Centre of Excellence for UK Farming 2010-, Royal Veterinary College 2012-, National Land Based College; Anglican International Development. Hon. BSc, Cranfield University 2004; Hon. doctorate, Gloucester University 2005; Hon. DCL, Newcastle University 2008. CBE 1997; Kt 2001; *Clubs:* Farmers Club.

Recreations: Church, Newcastle United FC.

The Lord Curry of Kirkharle CBE, House of Lords, London SW1A 0PW
Tel: 020 7219 8952 *Email:* curryd@parliament.uk

CROSSBENCH

DANNATT, LORD

DANNATT (Life Baron), Francis Richard Dannatt; cr 2011. Born 23 December 1950; Son of Mary Dannatt, née Chilvers, and Anthony Dannatt; Married Philippa Gurney 1977 (3 sons 1 daughter).

Education: St Lawrence College, Ramsgate; Royal Military Academy, Sandhurst; Durham University (BA economic history 1976).

Non-political career: British Army/Ministry of Defence (MoD) 1969-2009: Chief of Staff, 20th Armoured Brigade 1983-84, Military Assistant to Minister of State for Armed Forces 1986-89, Commanding Officer, 1 Green Howards 1989-91, Colonel, Higher Command and Staff Course, Camberley 1992-94, Commander, 4th Armoured Brigade 1994-96, Director, Defence Programmes, MoD 1996-98, General Officer Commanding, 3rd UK Division 1999-2000, Deputy Commander, Operations, HQ Stabilisation Force 2000-01, Assistant Chief of the General Staff 2001-02, Commander, Allied Rapid Reaction Corps 2003-05, Commander in Chief, Land Command 2005-06, Chief of the General Staff 2006-09; Constable, HM Tower of London 2009-16.

Political career: *House of Lords:* Raised to the peerage as Baron Dannatt, of Keswick in the County of Norfolk 2011. *Councils and public bodies:* DL: Greater London 2010, Norfolk 2011; Trustee, Royal Armouries.

Political interests: Defence, security, agriculture, human rights; Africa, South Asia, Middle East.

Other: Patron, Military Mission International 2010-; President, Royal Norfolk Agricultural Association 2008; Trustee: Windsor Leadership Trust, Historic Royal Palaces; Vice-President, Officers Christian Union 1998-, President: Army Rifle Association 2000-08, Army Winter Sports Association 2003-09, Army Rugby Union 2003-09, The Soldiers' and Airmen's Scripture Readers Association 2003-; Chairman, Strategic Advisory Board, Durham Global Security Institute, Durham University; Help for Heroes, Street Child of Sierra Leone, The Soldier's Charity, Combat Stress, Blind Veterans UK, Royal British Legion, Haig Housing Trust. Hon. Freeman, Merchant Taylors; Hon. Liveryman, Security Professionals. Honorary Doctorate of Civil Law: Durham University 2009, Kent University 2009; Honorary Doctorate of Technology, Anglia Ruskin University 2010. Military Cross 1973; CBE 1996; KCB 2004; GCB 2009; *Clubs:* Army & Navy; Cavalry and Guards Club. Norfolk County Cricket Club.

Publications: Autobiography, Leading from the Front (Bantam Press, 2010); Boots on the Ground: Britain and her Army since 1945 (Profile Books, 2016).

Recreations: Sport, reading.

General the Lord Dannatt GCB CBE MC, House of Lords, London SW1A 0PW
Tel: 020 7219 8949 *Email:* dannattr@parliament.uk

LABOUR

DARLING OF ROULANISH, LORD

DARLING OF ROULANISH (Life Baron), Alistair Maclean Darling; cr 2015. Born 28 November 1953; Married Margaret McQueen Vaughan 1986 (1 son 1 daughter).

Education: Loretto School; Aberdeen University (LLB 1976).

Non-political career: Solicitor 1978-82; Advocate 1984-2009.

Political career: *House of Commons:* MP (Labour) for Edinburgh Central 1987-2005, for Edinburgh South West 2005-15. Opposition Spokesperson for: Home Affairs 1988-92, Treasury, Economic Affairs and the City 1992-96; Sponsored Solicitors (Scotland) Act 1988 (Private Member's Bill); Shadow Chief Secretary to the Treasury 1996-97; Chief Secretary to the Treasury 1997-98; Secretary of State for: Social Security/Work and Pensions 1998-2002, Transport 2002-06, Scotland 2003-06, Trade and Industry 2006-07; Chancellor of the Exchequer 2007-10; Shadow Chancellor of the Exchequer 2010. *House of Lords:* Raised to the peerage as Baron Darling of Roulanish, of Great Bernera in the County of Ross and Cromarty 2015. Member, Economic Affairs 2016-. *Other:* Member, Labour Party's Economic Commission 1994-97. *Councils and public bodies:* Lothian Regional Council: Councillor 1982-87, Chair, Lothian Region Transport Committee 1986-87.

Political interests: Transport, education, health, economic policy, constitution.

Other: Governor, European Investment Bank 2007-10; Chair, Better Together Campaign 2012-14; Member, Board of Directors, Morgan Stanley 2016-; Chair, Standard Life Foundation 2017-; Hon. President, Chatham House 2017-. Backbencher of the Year, *Spectator* awards 2012. PC 1997.

Publications: Back from the Brink: 1,000 days at No. 11 (2011).

Rt Hon the Lord Darling of Roulanish, House of Lords, London SW1A 0PW
Tel: 020 7219 3000

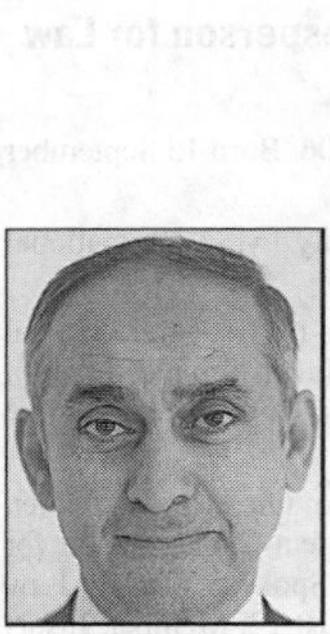

LABOUR

DARZI OF DENHAM, LORD

DARZI OF DENHAM (Life Baron), Ara Warkes Darzi; cr 2007. Born 7 May 1960; Married Wendy Hutchinson 1991 (1 son 1 daughter).

Education: Royal College of Surgeons of Ireland (MB BCh BAO 1984); Trinity College, Dublin (MD 1992).

Non-political career: Consultant surgeon and senior lecturer, Central Middlesex Hospital 1993-94; Consultant, St Mary's Hospital, Paddington 1994-98; Honorary consultant surgeon: Imperial College Healthcare NHS Trust 1994-, Royal Marsden Hospital NHS Foundation Trust 1994-, Great Ormond Street Hospital 1995-, Central Middlesex Hospital 1995-; Imperial College, London: Professor of surgery 1998-, Head of surgery, oncology, reproductive biology and anaesthesia 2002-07, Head of surgery division 2009-12; Adviser on surgery, Department of Health 2001-07; Professor of surgery, Institute of Cancer Research 2005-; Paul Hamlyn chair of surgery 2005-; Director, Institute of Global Health Innovation 2010-; Chair, Imperial College Healthcare Partners 2012-13; Executive Chair, World Innovation Summit for Health 2013-; Vice-Dean, Health Policy and Engagement, Imperial College London 2013-17; Chair, London Health Commission 2013-14; Director, Imperial CRUK Centre 2016-.

Political career: *House of Lords:* Raised to the peerage as Baron Darzi of Denham, of Gerrards Cross in the County of Buckinghamshire 2007. Department of Health: Parliamentary Under-Secretary of State 2007-09, Government Spokesperson 2007-09; UK Business Ambassador, Department of Business, Innovation and Skills 2009-13. *Councils and public bodies:* Non-executive director, NHS Improvement, NHS England 2015-; Member, Council, Engineering and Physical Sciences Research Council.

Other: Member, advisory board, Helen Hamlyn Centre for Design, Royal College of Arts; Royal Society of Medicine; Surgical Research Society; Irish Society of Gastroenterology; American Society of Colon and Rectal Surgeons; Society of Minimally Invasive Therapy; European Association of Endoscopic Surgery; Association of Endoscopic Surgeons of Great Britain and Ireland; Association of Surgeons of Great Britain and Ireland; Association of Coloproctology of Great Britain and Ireland; Society of American Gastrointestinal Endoscopic Surgeons; Société Internationale de Chirurgie; World Association of Hepato-Pancreato-Biliary Surgery; American College of Surgeons; Association for Surgical Education; International Surgical Group; International Society of Surgery; Society of Laparoscopic Surgery; American Surgical Association; Numerous fellowships including: Hon. Fellowship, American Surgical Association, USA, Visiting Professor, London School of Economics and Political Science, Foreign Associate Member, Institute of Medicine of the National Academies, USA, Hon. Fellowship, American Society for Colon and Rectal Surgeons, FRS Fellow, Royal Society, Hon. Membership, Japan Society for Endoscopic Surgery, Hon. Professor, Department of Surgery, University of Hong Kong, Hon. Fellow, American College of Surgeons, Fellow, Royal College of Physicians, Hon. Fellow, Royal Academy of Engineering; Beating Bowel Cancer, Meningitis Now, Barrett's Oesophagus Campaign, Chordoma UK, National Competitiveness Foundation of Armenia, Lord Leonard and Lady Estelle Wolfson of Marylebone Charitable Trust for Preventative Medicine, Rangoon Hospital Reinvigoration Charitable Trust, Cyberbullying Foundation, N Sethia Foundation, Smile Support and Care, Pathway Charity. Numerous honorary academic degrees, including: Hon FRCSI, Royal College of Surgeons, Ireland, Hon LLD, Trinity College Dublin, Hon DSc, De Montfort University, Hon DEng, Bath University, Hon DSc, Cranfield University. Queen's Anniversary Prize in Higher and Further Education 2001; Hamdan Award for Medical Research Excellence 2004; Scientific Achievement Award, Armenian Medical World Congress, New York 2009; Distinguished Graduates Medal, Royal College of Surgeons, Ireland 2009; Qatari Sash of Independence 2014. KBE 2002; PC 2009; OM 2016.

Publications: Over 1000 peer reviewed articles in academic journals.

Rt Hon Professor the Lord Darzi of Denham OM KBE, House of Lords, London SW1A 0PW
Tel: 020 7219 5416
Department of Surgery and Cancer, Tenth Floor QEQM Building, St Mary's Hospital Campus, Imperial College London, Praed Street, London W2 1NY *Tel:* 020 3312 1310 *Fax:* 020 3312 6309
Email: n.kurek@imperial.ac.uk *Website:* www.imperial.ac.uk/people/a.darzi

DAVIDSON OF GLEN CLOVA, LORD

LABOUR

Shadow Advocate General for Scotland; Opposition Spokesperson for Law Officers and Treasury

DAVIDSON OF GLEN CLOVA (Life Baron), Neil Forbes Davidson; cr 2006. Born 13 September 1950; Son of John and Flora Davidson; Married Regina Sprissler 1980.

Education: Stirling University (BA economics 1971); Bradford University (MSc international business 1972); Edinburgh University (LLB 1977; LLM 1979).

Non-political career: Faculty of Advocates 1979; Standing Junior Counsel to: Registrar General 1982-88, Departments of Health and Social Security 1988-93; Barrister Inner Temple, London 1990; QC (Scot) 1993; Solicitor General for Scotland 2000-01; Director City Disputes Panel 1993-2000; Advocate, Axiom Advocates.

Political career: *House of Lords:* Raised to the peerage as Baron Davidson of Glen Clova, of Glen Clova in Angus 2006. Advocate General for Scotland 2006-10; Government Spokesperson for Scotland 2008-10; Shadow Advocate General for Scotland and Opposition Spokesperson for Law Officers 2010-; Opposition Spokesperson for: Treasury 2010-, Scotland 2010-12. Member, Insurance Bill 2014-15.

Countries of interest: China.

Other: Chair, Human Rights Committee, Faculty of Advocates 1997-2000. DUniv, Stirling University 2012.

The Lord Davidson of Glen Clova QC, House of Lords, London SW1A 0PW
Tel: 020 7219 5353
Email: lord.davidson@axiomadvocates.com

NON-AFFILIATED

DAVIES OF ABERSOCH, LORD

DAVIES OF ABERSOCH (Life Baron), (Evan) Mervyn Davies; cr 2009. Born 21 November 1952; Son of late Richard Davies and Margaret Davies; Married Jeanne Gammie 1979 (1 son 1 daughter).

Education: Rydal School, Colwyn Bay; Harvard Business School (PMD 1989); Welsh.

Non-political career: Senior credit officer, Citibank 1983-93; Standard Chartered plc and predecessors 1993-2009: Director 1997-2009, Director, Hong Kong 1997-2001, Group chief executive 2001-06, Chair 2006-09; Chair and partner, Corsair Capital 2010-; Non-executive chairman, Pine-Bridge Investments Ltd 2010-; Moelis & Co: Chair, advisory board 2010-15, Senior adviser to CEO 2015-16; Non-executive director: Bharti Airtel Ltd 2010-12, Diageo plc 2010-; Chairman, Chime Communications 2012-15; Director, Glyndebourne Productions Ltd 2012-; Chair, Jack Wills 2014-; Deputy Chair, LetterOne Holdings 2015-.

Political career: *House of Lords:* Raised to the peerage as Baron Davies of Abersoch, of Abersoch in the County of Gwynedd 2009. Minister of State and Government Spokesperson, Department for Business, Enterprise and Regulatory Reform/Business, Innovation and Skills and Foreign and Commonwealth Office (Minister for Trade, Investment and Small Business) 2009-10. *Other:* Resigned from Labour 2016; now sits as Non-affiliated. *Councils and public bodies:* Chair, Council, University of Wales, Bangor -2014; JP, Hong Kong.

Political interests: Labour, free trade, equality; Africa, Asia, Middle East.

Other: Former chair: British Chamber of Commerce, Hong Kong, Hong Kong Association of Banks; Chair: Royal Academy of Arts Trustees 2012-, Garden Bridge Trust 2013-17; Member, International Advisory Board, Discovery Insurance; Fellow, Institute of Bankers; Breakthrough Breast Cancer, Hope House Children's Hospice. CBE 2002; *Clubs:* Shek O, Arts/Alfred's Club. Abersoch GC; Morla Nefyn GC.

Recreations: Soccer, skiing, golf, music, Welsh art.

The Lord Davies of Abersoch CBE, House of Lords, London SW1A 0PW
Tel: 020 7219 3000

LAB/CO-OP

DAVIES OF COITY, LORD

DAVIES OF COITY (Life Baron), David Garfield Davies; cr. 1997. Born 24 June 1935; Son of late David and Lizzie Davies; Married Marian Jones 1960 (4 daughters).

Education: Heolgam Secondary Modern School; Bridgend Technical College (part-time).

Non-political career: RAF national service 1956-58. Junior operative, electrical apprentice and electrician, British Steel Corporation, Port Talbot 1950-69; Union of Shop, Distributive and Allied Workers: Area organiser, Ipswich 1969-73, Deputy division officer, London/Ipswich 1973-78, National officer, Manchester 1978-85, General Secretary 1986-97. TUC: Member, General Council 1986-97, Chairman, International Committee 1992-94; Spokesperson on International Affairs 1994-97.

Political career: *House of Lords:* Raised to the peerage as Baron Davies of Coity, of Penybont in the County of Mid Glamorgan 1997. Member, Ecclesiastical Committee 2005-15. *Councils and public bodies:* Councillor, Penybont RDC 1966-69; JP, Ipswich 1972-78; Member, Employment Appeal Tribunal 1990-2006; Governor, Birmingham College of Food, Tourism and Creative Studies 1995-99.

Political interests: Health service, education, industrial relations; British Overseas Territories, Central America.

Other: Member: Executive Board, International Confederation of Free Trade Unions 1992-97, Executive Committee, European Trade Union Confederation 1992-97, Inter-Parliamentary Union 1997-, Commonwealth Parliamentary Association 1997-; Trustee, People's National Museum -2009; Vice-President, Commercial Travellers Benevolent Institute -2007; President: Sea Shell Trust, Manchester East Scout Council, Stockport County FC Independent Supporters Club, (Wales) UK Kidney Research, Royal School for the Deaf, Manchester, Kidney Research UK; Christian Aid, NCH. CBE 1996; *Clubs:* Reform Club. Lancashire CCC; Stockport County AFC.

Recreations: Most sports, swimming, family, reading.

The Lord Davies of Coity CBE, House of Lords, London SW1A 0PW
Tel: 020 7219 6932
64 Dairyground Road, Bramhall, Stockport, Cheshire SK7 2QW *Tel:* 0161-439 9548

LABOUR

DAVIES OF OLDHAM, LORD

Opposition Spokesperson for Treasury

DAVIES OF OLDHAM (Life Baron), Bryan Davies; cr. 1997. Born 9 November 1939; Son of late George and Beryl Davies; Married Monica Shearing 1963 (2 sons 1 daughter).

Education: Redditch High School; University College, London (BA history 1961); Institute of Education (PGCE 1962); London School of Economics (BSc economics 1968).

Non-political career: History teacher, Latymer School, London 1962-65; History and social science lecturer, Middlesex Polytechnic, Enfield 1965-74. Divisional executive officer, NATFHE 1967-74; Member, Transport and General Workers' Union/Unite 1979-.

Political career: *House of Commons:* Contested Norfolk Central 1966 general election. MP (Labour) for Enfield North 1974-79. Contested Enfield North 1979 and Newport West 1983 general elections. MP for Oldham Central and Royton 1992-97. Assistant Government Whip 1978-79; Opposition Spokesperson for: Education 1993-95, Education and Employment 1995-97. *House of Lords:* Raised to the peerage as Baron Davies of Oldham, of Broxbourne in the County of Hertfordshire 1997. Government Whip 2000-03; Government Spokesperson for: Home Office 2000-02, Education and Skills 2001-03, Culture, Media and Sport 2001-08, Transport 2002-07, Trade and Industry 2003-04; Deputy Chief Whip (Captain, the Queen's Body Guard of the Yeomen of the Guard) 2003-10; Government Spokesperson for: Cabinet Office 2007-08, Treasury 2007-08, Environment, Food and Rural Affairs 2008, Scotland 2008, Wales 2008-10; Parliamentary Under-Secretary of State and Government Spokesperson, Department for Environment, Food and Rural Affairs 2009-10; Opposition Spokesperson for: Transport 2010-15, Treasury 2010-, Wales 2010-13. Member: Refreshment 2005-08, 2009-11, Joint Committee on Security 2010. *Other:* Secretary, Parliamentary Labour Party and Shadow Cabinet 1979-92. *Councils and public bodies:* Member, Medical Research Council 1977-79; Chair, Further Education Funding Council 1998-2000.

Political interests: Economic policy, employment, training, education, arts, transport; Nepal, Sri Lanka.

Other: President, Royal Society for the Prevention of Accidents 1999-2000; Oxfam. Honorary Doctorate, Middlesex University 1996. PC 2007.

Recreations: Sport, literature.

Rt Hon the Lord Davies of Oldham, House of Lords, London SW1A 0PW
Tel: 020 7219 1475 *Email:* daviesb@parliament.uk
Email: bm.davies@ntlworld.com

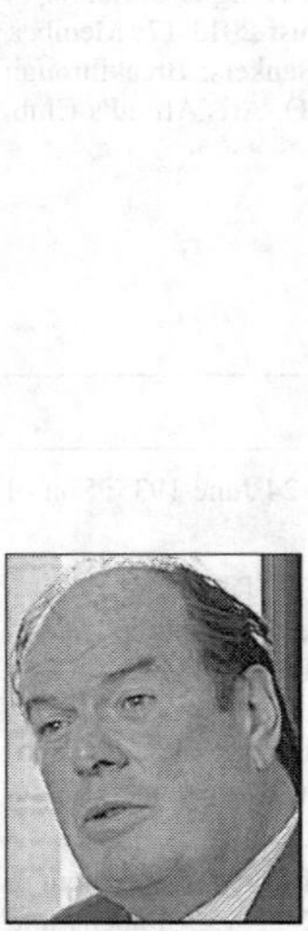

LABOUR

DAVIES OF STAMFORD, LORD

DAVIES OF STAMFORD (Life Baron), John Quentin Davies; cr 2010. Born 29 May 1944; Son of late Dr M I Davies, general practitioner, and Thelma Davies; Married Chantal Tamplin 1983 (2 sons).

Education: Leighton Park School, Reading; Gonville and Caius College, Cambridge (BA history 1966, MA); Harvard University, USA (Frank Knox Fellow); French, German, Italian, Russian.

Non-political career: HM Diplomatic Service 1967-74: Third Secretary, FCO 1967-69, Second Secretary, Moscow 1969-72, First Secretary, FCO 1972-74; Manager then assistant director, Morgan Grenfell & Co Ltd 1974-78; Director-general and President, Morgan Grenfell France 1978-81; Morgan Grenfell Co Ltd and certain group subsidiaries: Director, main board 1981-87, Consultant 1987-93; Consultant, National Westminster Securities plc 1993-99; Dewe Rogerson International 1987-94; Société Genérale d'Entreprises 1999-2000; Consultant, Royal Bank of Scotland 1999-2002; Director: Vinci 2003-08, Vinci UK 2003-08; Lloyd's of London: Director, Member of the Council 2004-07.

Political career: *House of Commons:* Contested Birmingham Ladywood 1977 by-election. MP (Conservative) for Stamford and Spalding 1987-97, for Grantham and Stamford 1997-2010 (Labour June 2007-10). PPS to Angela Rumbold as Minister of State: Department of Education and Science 1988-90, Home Office 1990-91; Shadow Minister for Pensions 1998-99; Shadow Paymaster General 1999-2000; Shadow Minister for Defence 2000-01; Shadow Secretary of State for Northern Ireland 2001-03; Parliamentary Under-Secretary of State (Minister for Defence Equipment and Support), Ministry of Defence 2008-10. Member: Standards and Privileges 1995-97, 1997-98, Treasury 1997-98, European Scrutiny 1998, International Development 2003-07, Joint Committee on Tax Law Rewrite Bills 2007-09, Regulatory Reform 2007-10. Secretary, Conservative Parliamentary Committees on: Finance 1991-97, Trade and Industry 1991-95; Vice-chair, Conservative Party Committee for Trade and Industry 1995-98; Chair, Conservative Group for Europe 2006-07. *House of Lords:* Raised to the peerage as Baron Davies of Stamford, of Stamford in the County of Lincolnshire 2010. Member: Selection 2011, Joint Committee on the Draft Detention of Terrorist Suspects (Temporary Extension) Bills 2011, Consumer Insurance (Disclosure and Representations) Bill 2011-12, Joint Committee on Parliamentary Privilege 2013, EU Sub-committee A (Economic and Financial Affairs) 2013-15, European Union 2015-16, EU Financial Affairs Sub-committee 2015-16, Joint Committee on Statutory Instruments 2016, Licensing Act 2003 2016-17.

Political interests: Defence, trade and industry, finance, agriculture, health, welfare, pensions, overseas development; EU, Russia, USA.

Other: Parliamentary adviser, Chartered Institute of Taxation 1993-2008; Fellow, Industry and Parliament Trust 1995; Trustee and member, Executive Committee, Council for Economic Policy Research 1996-2008. Liveryman, Goldsmiths' Company; *Clubs:* Beefsteak, Brooks's, Travellers, RAF Club.

Publications: Britain and Europe: A Conservative View (1996); Co-author, Report of Inquiry into National Recognition of our Armed Forces (2008).

Recreations: Reading, walking, skiing, travel.

The Lord Davies of Stamford, House of Lords, London SW1A 0PW
Tel: 020 7219 5353 *Email:* daviesq@parliament.uk

DEAN OF THORNTON-LE-FYLDE, BARONESS

LABOUR

DEAN OF THORNTON-LE-FYLDE (Life Baroness), Brenda Dean; cr. 1993. Born 29 April 1943; Daughter of Hugh and Lillian Dean; Married Keith McDowall CBE 1988 (2 stepdaughters).

Education: Stretford High School for Girls.

Non-political career: SOGAT: Administrative secretary 1959-72, Assistant secretary, Manchester Branch 1972-76, Secretary, Manchester Branch 1976-83, Member, National Executive Council 1977-83, President, SOGAT '82 1983-91; Deputy general secretary, Graphical, Paper and Media Union 1991-92; Non-executive director: George Wimpey plc 2003-07, Dawson Holdings plc 2003-10; Chair, Covent Garden Market Authority 2005-13; Partnership director, National Air Traffic Services 2006-; Non-executive director, Taylor Wimpey plc 2007-13. Member: TUC General Council 1985-92, Graphical, Paper and Media Union 1959-.

Political career: *House of Lords:* Raised to the peerage as Baroness Dean of Thornton-le-Fylde, of Eccles in the County of Greater Manchester 1993. Opposition Spokesperson for: Employment 1994-96, National Heritage 1996-97; Opposition Whip 1996-97; Member, Committee of Inquiry into Future of Higher Education 1996-97; House of Lords Appointments Commission 2000-10. Co-opted Member, European Communities Sub-committee B (Energy, Industry and Transport) 1995-97, 1997-98; Member: Constitution 2014-17, Trade Union and Party Funding 2016, Delegated Powers and Regulatory Reform 2017-. *Councils and public bodies:* Council member: Association for Business Sponsorship of the Arts 1990-96, City University 1991-96; Governor, Ditchley Foundation 1992-; Member: Armed Forces Pay Review Body 1993-94, Press Complaints Commission 1993-98, Broadcasting Complaints Commission 1993-94; Board member, Council, London School of Economics 1994-99; Council member, Open University 1995-98; Chair: Housing Corporation 1997-2003, Armed Forces Pay Review Body 1999-2004; Member: Senior Salaries Review Body 1999-2004, Royal Commission on the Reform of the House of Lords 1999; Council member, Nottingham University 2012-.

Political interests: Industry, media, women's issues, pensions, housing, defence; Australia, China, South Africa, USA.

Other: Industry and Parliament Trust: Trustee 1997-2009, Fellow 1998; Member, General Insurance Standards Council 1999-2005, Chair, Freedom to Fly Coalition 2002-04; President, Abbeyfield Society 2012-; Trustee, Thomson Foundation; FRSA. Liveryman, Worshipful Company of Stationers and Newspaper Makers. Freedom, City of London. Ten honorary degrees; Honorary Fellow, Preston Polytechnic, Lancashire 1991. PC 1998; *Clubs:* Reform Club. Royal Cornwall Yacht Club.

Recreations: Watching cricket and rugby.

Rt Hon the Baroness Dean of Thornton-le-Fylde, House of Lords, London SW1A 0PW
Tel: 020 7219 6907 *Fax:* 020 7219 0549 *Email:* deanb@parliament.uk

CROSSBENCH

DEAR, LORD

DEAR (Life Baron), Geoffrey James Dear; cr 2006. Born 20 September 1937; Son of late Cecil Dear and Violet Dear, née Mackney; Married Judith Stocker 1958 (died 1996) (1 son 2 daughters); married Alison Martin Jones 1998.

Education: Fletton Grammar School, Huntingdonshire; University College, London (Bramshill Scholarship, LLB 1968).

Non-political career: Mid-Anglia Constabulary 1965; Assistant Chief Constable (operations), Nottinghamshire 1972-80; Seconded as director of command training, Bramshill Police College 1975-77; Metropolitan Police 1980-85: Personnel and training 1981-84, Operations 1984-85; Chief Constable, West Midlands Police 1985-90; HM Inspector of Constabulary 1990-97; Hon. Bencher Gray's Inn 2008; Non-executive chair, Blaythorne Group plc.

Political career: *House of Lords:* Raised to the peerage as Baron Dear, of Willersey in the County of Gloucestershire 2006. Deputy Chairman of Committees 2015-. EU Sub-committee F (Home Affairs): Co-opted member 2007-09, Member 2009-12; Member: European Union 2009-14, EU Sub-committee A (Economic and Financial Affairs) 2012-15, Joint Committee on the Rookery South (Resource Recovery Facility) Order 2012-13, Works of Art 2015-16, Privileges and Conduct 2015-, Lord Speaker's Advisory Panel on Works of Art 2017-. *Councils and public bodies:* DL, West Midlands 1985-96; Worcestershire: DL 1996-, Vice-Lord Lieutenant 1998-2001.

Countries of interest: Egypt, India, Middle East, USA.

Other: Trustee: The Country Trust 1987-2012, Police Rehabilitation Trust 1991-; Police Foundation 2008-13; World Horse Welfare 2010-15; Fellow, University College, London; Hon. fellow, Birmingham University. Freedom, City of London 2004. Queen's Commendation for Bravery 1979; QPM 1982; Kt 1997; *Clubs:* East India Club, Special Forces Club. Vice-President, Warwickshire County Cricket Club.

Recreations: Country sports, cricket, rugby football, gardening, music, literature.

The Lord Dear QPM, House of Lords, London SW1A 0PW
Email: deargj@parliament.uk

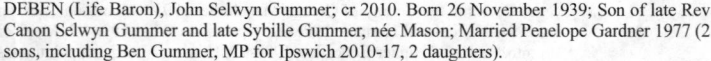

CONSERVATIVE

DEBEN, LORD

DEBEN (Life Baron), John Selwyn Gummer; cr 2010. Born 26 November 1939; Son of late Rev Canon Selwyn Gummer and late Sybille Gummer, née Mason; Married Penelope Gardner 1977 (2 sons, including Ben Gummer, MP for Ipswich 2010-17, 2 daughters).

Education: King's School, Rochester; Selwyn College, Cambridge (BA history 1961, MA 1971) (Union President 1962); French (reasonable).

Non-political career: Editor, Business Publications 1962-64; Editor-in-Chief, Max Parrish & Oldbourne Press 1964-66; Director, Shandwick Publishing Co 1966-81; BPC Publishing: Special assistant to chairman 1967, Publisher, special projects 1967-69, Editorial co-ordinator 1969-70; Siemssen Hunter Ltd: Director 1973-80, Chairman 1979-80; Chairman: Selwyn Shandwick International 1976-81, Sancroft International Ltd (corporate responsibility consultants) 1997-, Marine Stewardship Council 1997-2006; Vivendi UK/Veolia Water UK: Director 1997-2013, Chairman 2004-13; Chairman, Valpak Ltd 1998-; International Commission on Consumption 1998-2005; Association of Professional Financial Advisers (formerly Association of Independent Financial Advisers) 2003-17; President, Association of Mortgage Intermediaries; Chairman, Zero C Holdings Ltd 2008-14; Non-executive directorships, including: Catholic Herald, Castle Trust 2011-; Personal Investment Management & Financial Advice Association 2017-.

Political career: *House of Commons:* Contested Greenwich 1964 and 1966 general elections. MP (Conservative) for Lewisham West 1970-February 1974. Contested Lewisham West February 1974 general election. MP for Eye 1979-83, for Suffolk Coastal 1983-2010. PPS: to Jim Prior as Minister of Agriculture, Fisheries and Food 1971-72, to Patrick Jenkin as Secretary of State for Social Services 1979-81; Government Whip 1981-83; Department of Employment: Parliamentary Under-Secretary of State 1983, Minister of State 1983-84; Paymaster General 1984-85; Minister of State, Ministry of Agriculture, Fisheries and Food 1985-88; Minister for Local Government, Department of Environment 1988-89; Minister of Agriculture, Fisheries and Food 1989-93; Secretary of State for the Environment 1993-97. *House of Lords:* Raised to the peerage as Baron Deben, of Winston in the County of Suffolk 2010. *Other:* Chairman, Cambridge University Conservative Association 1961; Conservative Party: Vice-chairman 1972-74, Chairman 1983-85; Chairman, Conservative Group for Europe 1997-2000. *Councils and public bodies:* Councillor, Inner London Education Authority 1967-70; Chairman, Committee on Climate Change 2012-.

Political interests: Energy, environment, European affairs, business, industry, consumers.

Other: Member, General Synod of Church of England for St Edmundsbury and Ipswich Diocese 1978-92. Hon. Doctorate, Westminster University 2014. PC 1985.

Publications: When the Coloured People Come (1966); The Permissive Society (1971); Co-author, The Christian Calendar (1974); Faith in Politics (1987).

Recreations: Architecture, walking.

Rt Hon the Lord Deben, House of Lords, London SW1A 0PW
Tel: 020 7219 5353
46 Queen Anne's Gate, London SW1H 9AP *Tel:* 020 7960 7900 *Email:* office@sancroft.com
Twitter: @lordddeben

CROSSBENCH

DEECH, BARONESS

DEECH (Life Baroness), Ruth Lynn Deech; cr 2005. Born 29 April 1943; Daughter of Josef Fraenkel and Dora, née Rosenfeld; Married Dr John Deech 1967 (1 daughter).

Education: Christ's Hospital, Hertford; St Anne's College, Oxford (BA law 1965, MA); Brandeis University, USA (MA Jewish studies 1966).

Non-political career: Called to the Bar Inner Temple 1967 (later Hon. Bencher); St Anne's College, Oxford: Fellow and law tutor 1970-91, Principal 1991-2004; Appointed Queen's Counsel 2013.

Political career: *House of Lords:* Raised to the peerage as Baroness Deech, of Cumnor in the County of Oxfordshire 2005. Member: Merits of Statutory Instruments 2007-10, Draft Human Tissue and Embryos Bill Joint Committee 2007, Communications 2010-15; Chair, Equality Act 2010 and Disability 2015-16. *Councils and public bodies:* Chair, Human Fertilisation and Embryology Authority 1994-2002; BBC Governor 2002-06; Independent Adjudicator for Higher Education 2004-08; Gresham Professor of Law 2008-12; Chair, Bar Standards Board 2009-14.

Political interests: Higher education, family law, broadcasting, reproductive technology; Israel, Poland, USA.

Other: Advisory Council, Oxford Philharmonic; Fellow: Royal Society of Medicine, International Society of Family Law. Liveryman, Drapers' Company. Pro-vice-chancellor, Oxford University 2001-04. Honorary LLD: Strathclyde University 2003, Richmond American International University 2006, Ben Gurion University, Israel 2012. DBE 2002; *Clubs:* Royal Society of Medicine Club.

Publications: Co-editor, Biomedicine, the Family and Human Rights (Kluwer, 2002); From IVF to Immortality (OUP, 2007).

Recreations: Opera, travel, after-dinner speaking.

The Baroness Deech DBE, House of Lords, London SW1A 0PW
Tel: 020 7219 3000 *Email:* deechr@parliament.uk
Email: ruth.deech@st-annes.ox.ac.uk
Websites: www.lordsoftheblog.net/category/baroness-deech
www.law.ox.ac.uk/people/baroness-ruth-deech *Twitter:* @BaronessDeech

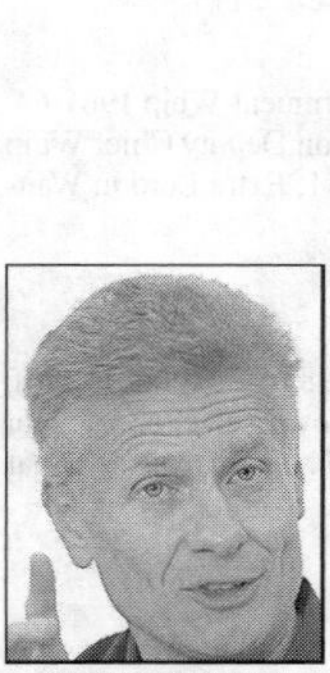

CONSERVATIVE

DEIGHTON, LORD

DEIGHTON (Life Baron), Paul Clive Deighton; cr 2012. Born 18 January 1956; Son of late Walter Deighton and late Mabel King; Married Alison Klebanoff 1985 (2 sons).

Education: Wallington County Grammar School for Boys; Trinity College, Cambridge (BA economics 1978).

Non-political career: Bank of America 1978-81; Security Pacific 1981-83; Goldman Sachs 1983-2006; Chief executive officer, LOCOG 2006-12; Non-executive chair, Heathrow Airport Holdings Ltd 2016-.

Political career: *House of Lords:* Raised to the peerage as Baron Deighton, of Carshalton in the County of Surrey 2012. Commercial Secretary and Government Spokesperson, HM Treasury 2013-15. Member, Joint Committee on the Palace of Westminster 2015-16. *Councils and public bodies:* Governor, King's College School, Wimbledon.

Other: Board member, England Rugby 2015 (organising body for the Rugby World Cup) 2013-15; International Association of Athletics Federations: Head, Reform Task Force 2015-16, Chair, Audit and Finance Commission 2016-; Non-executive director: Holdingham Group 2015-, Square 2016-; Honorary fellow, Institution of Civil Engineers. Honorary doctorate, Sheffield Hallam University. KBE 2013.

The Lord Deighton KBE, House of Lords, London SW1A 0PW
Tel: 020 7219 5353

DE MAULEY, LORD

CONSERVATIVE

DE MAULEY (7th Baron, UK), Rupert Charles Ponsonby; cr. 1838. Born 30 June 1957; Son of late Colonel Hon Thomas Maurice Ponsonby, TD, DL, younger son of 5th Baron; Married Hon Lucinda Royle 2002.

Education: Eton College.

Non-political career: Royal Wessex Yeomanry: Lt Col (Commanded) 2003-04, Honorary Colonel 2015-; Colonel Commandant, The Yeomanry 2011-. Director, Samuel Montagu & Co Ltd 1990-93; Standard Chartered Merchant Bank Asia Ltd 1994-99.

Political career: *House of Lords:* Elected hereditary peer 2005-; Opposition Whip 2005-10; Opposition Spokesperson for: Trade and Industry/Business, Enterprise and Regulatory Reform/Business, Innovation and Skills 2005-10, Cabinet Office 2006-09, Energy and Climate Change 2008-09, Innovation, Universities and Skills 2008-09, Children, Schools and Families 2008-09, Treasury 2009-10; Government Whip 2010-12; Government Spokesperson for: Business, Innovation and Skills 2010-12, Home Office 2010, HM Treasury 2010-12, Environment, Food and Rural Affairs 2010-15, Work and Pensions 2011-12; Department for Environment, Food and Rural Affairs: Parliamentary Under-Secretary of State: (Resource Management, the Local Environment and Environmental Science) 2012-13, (Natural Environment and Science) 2013-15. Member: Joint Committee on Security 2010-12, Consumer Insurance (Disclosure and Representations) Bill 2011-12, Trade Union and Party Funding 2016, EU Financial Affairs Sub-committee 2016-. *Other:* President, Conservative Rural Affairs Group 2016-.

Countries of interest: South east Asia, China, Europe.

Other: President: UK Council, Reserve Forces and Cadets Associations 2010-, Society for the Protection of Animals Abroad 2010-; Panel member, Youd Andrews 2016-; Trustee, Horse Trust 2016-; Institute of Chartered Accountants in England and Wales; FCA 1990. TD.

Recreations: Country sports, woodland management.

The Lord de Mauley TD, House of Lords, London SW1A 0PW
Tel: 020 7219 3000 *Email:* demauley@parliament.uk

DENHAM, LORD

CONSERVATIVE

DENHAM (2nd Baron, UK), Bertram Stanley Mitford Bowyer; cr. 1937; 10th Bt of Denham (E) 1660; 2nd Bt of Weston Underwood (UK) 1933. Born 3 October 1927; Son of 1st Baron, MC; Married Jean McCorquodale 1956 (3 sons 1 daughter).

Education: Eton College; King's College, Cambridge (BA English literature 1951).

Non-political career: Countryside Commissioner 1993-99.

Political career: *House of Lords:* First entered House of Lords 1948; Government Whip 1961-64, 1970-72; Opposition Whip 1964-70; Deputy Chief Whip 1972-74; Opposition Deputy Chief Whip 1974-78; Opposition Chief Whip 1978-79; Government Chief Whip 1979-91; Extra Lord in Waiting to HM The Queen 1998-; Elected hereditary peer 1999-.

Political interests: Machinery of Government.

Other: PC 1981; KBE 1991; *Clubs:* Pratt's, Garrick Club.

Publications: The Man Who Lost His Shadow (1979); Two Thyrdes (1983); Foxhunt (1988); Black Rod (1997); A Thing of Shreds and Patches (a read anthology of own selection of light verse, 2000); Victorian Plums (CD including The Hunting of the Snark, The Rubaiyat of Omar Khayyam and the Ballad of Reading Gaol).

Recreations: Field sports.

Rt Hon the Lord Denham KBE, House of Lords, London SW1A 0PW
Tel: 020 7219 6056 *Fax:* 020 7219 6056
The Laundry Cottage, Weston Underwood, Olney, Buckinghamshire MK46 5JZ
Tel: 01234 711535

DERBY, LORD BISHOP OF

NON-AFFILIATED

DERBY (7th Bishop of) Alastair Llewellyn John Redfern. Born 1 September 1948; Son of Victor and Audrey Redfern; Married Jane Straw 1974 (died 2004) (2 daughters); married Caroline Boddington 2006.

Education: Bicester School; Christ Church College, Oxford (BA modern history 1970, MA 1974); Trinity College, Cambridge (BA theology 1974, MA 1979); Westcott House, Cambridge; Queen's College, Birmingham; Bristol University (PhD theology 2001).

Non-political career: Curate, Wolverhampton 1976-79; Ripon College, Cuddesdon: Lecturer, church history 1979-87, Vice-principal 1985-87; Director, Oxford Institute for Church and Society 1979-83; Curate, All Saints, Cuddesdon 1983-87; Canon Theologian, Bristol Cathedral 1987-97; Diocesan Director of Training 1991-97; Bishop Suffragan of Grantham 1997-2005; Dean of Stamford 1997-2005; Canon and Prebendary, Lincoln Cathedral 2000-05; Bishop of Derby 2005-.

Political career: *House of Lords:* Entered House of Lords 2010. Member: Joint Committee on the Draft Modern Slavery Bill 2014, Sexual Violence in Conflict 2015-16.

Countries of interest: Diocesan links with church of North India.

Other: Global Sustainability Network; Chair, Multi-Faith Centre, Derby 2005-; Derbyshire Community Foundation: Trustee 2005-13, Vice-president 2013-; Member, Community and Cohesion Group, Derby 2005-; Vice-President, Arkwright Society 2008-; Patron, Derby Arts Festival 2008-; Co-chair, Interfaith Network 2009-12; House of Bishops; General Synod; Trustee, Christian Aid 2005-15; Chair, Churches' Legislation Advisory Service 2013-; Vice-chair, Anglican Alliance 2016-.

Publications: Ministry and Priesthood (1999); Being Anglican (2000); Growing the Kingdom: The Letter to the Hebrews as a Resource for Mission (2009); Thomas Hobbes and the Limits of Democracy (2009); Public Space and Private Faith: A Challenge to the Churches (2009); Community and Conflict (2011); Out of the Depths (2012); The Leadership of the People of God (2013); Discipleship: A Call and a Commission (2013); Editor, Sacrificed Remembered (2014); Mission in Action (2014); Living in Love (2014); The Word on the Street (2015); Peace that Passes Understanding (2015); The Church: A Workshop of Salvation (2016); The Challenge of our Christian Calling (2016); Shaping the Spiritual Life (2017).

Recreations: Walking, reading, published author, cycling.

Rt Rev Dr the Lord Bishop of Derby, House of Lords, London SW1A 0PW
Tel: 020 7219 5353 *Email:* redferna@parliament.uk
The Bishop's House, 6 King Street, Duffield, Belper DE56 4EU *Tel:* 01332 840132
Email: bishop@bishopofderby.org *Website:* www.derby.anglican.org

DESAI, LORD

LABOUR

DESAI (Life Baron), Meghnad Jagdishchandra Desai; cr. 1991. Born 10 July 1940; Son of late Jagdishchandra and Mandakini Desai; Married Gail Wilson 1970 (1 son 2 daughters) (divorced 2004); married Kishwar Ahluwalia, née Rosha 2004.

Education: Sayaji High School, Baroda; Premier High School, Bombay; University of Bombay (BA economics 1958, MA 1960); University of Pennsylvania (PhD economics 1964); French, Gujarati, Hindi, Marathi, Sanskrit.

Non-political career: Associate specialist, Department of Agricultural Economics, University of California, Berkeley 1963-65; London School of Economics 1965-2003: Lecturer in economics 1965-77, Senior lecturer 1977-80, Reader 1980-83, Professor 1983-2004, Convenor, Economics Department 1987-90, Head, Development Studies Institute 1990-95, Director, Centre for the Study of Global Governance 1992-2003; Chair, Cape Claims Services 2007-.

Political career: *House of Lords:* Raised to the peerage as Baron Desai, of St Clement Danes in the City of Westminster 1991. Opposition Whip 1991-94; Opposition Spokesperson for: Health 1991-93, Treasury and Economic Affairs 1992-93; Contested Lord Speaker election 2011. Member: Science and Technology 1991-92, European Community, Sub Committee A (Economic and Financial Affairs, Trade and External Relations) 1995-99, Delegated Powers Scrutiny 2001-05, Speakership of the House 2003, Merits of Statutory Instruments 2003-04, Intergovernmental Organisations 2007-08, EU Financial Affairs Sub-committee 2016-. *Other:* Chair, Islington South and Finsbury CLP 1986-92.

Political interests: Economic policy, education, development; Australia, Bangladesh, Brazil, Canada, China, India, Malaysia, Mauritius, Pakistan, Sierra Leone, Singapore, Sri Lanka, USA.

Other: Member: Executive Committee, Inter-Parliamentary Union British Group 1995-2003, Marshall Aid Commission 1998-2002; Member of Senate, London University 1980-88; Chair, City Life (drug rehabilitation charity) 1992-2000; Member: One World Action, Association of University Teachers; FRSA. Five honorary doctorates; Honorary Fellow, London School of Economics 2005. Pravasi Bharatiya Purnskar Award for Overseas Indians of Distinction granted by Indian Government 2004; Padma Bhushan awarded by the Government of India 2008.

Publications: Several on economics.

Recreations: Reading, writing, cricket.

Professor the Lord Desai, House of Lords, London SW1A 0PW
Tel: 020 7219 5066 *Fax:* 020 7219 5787 *Email:* desaim@parliament.uk

LIBERAL DEMOCRAT

DHOLAKIA, LORD

Deputy Leader, Liberal Democrat Peers

DHOLAKIA (Life Baron), Navnit Dholakia; cr. 1997. Born 4 March 1937; Son of Permananddas Mulji Dholakia and Shantabai Permananddas Dholakia; Married Ann McLuskie 1967 (2 daughters).

Education: Indian public schools in Moshi, Arusha, Tabora and Morogoro in Tanzania; Institute of Science, Bhavnager, Gujarat, India; Brighton Technical College; Gujarari, Hindi, Swahili.

Non-political career: Medical laboratory technician, Southlands Hospital, Shoreham-by-Sea 1960-66; Development officer, National Committee for Commonwealth Immigrants 1966-68; Community Relations Commission: Senior development officer 1968-74, Principal officer and secretary 1974-76; Commission for Racial Equality 1976-94: Head, administration of justice section 1984-94; Member, Police Complaints Authority 1994-98.

Political career: *House of Lords:* Raised to the peerage as Baron Dholakia, of Waltham Brooks in the County of West Sussex 1997. Liberal Democrat: Spokesperson for Home Affairs 1998-2007, Deputy Chief Whip 1998-2002; Member, House of Lords Appointments Commission 2000-10; Deputy Leader, Liberal Democrat Peers 2004-; Liberal Democrat Spokesperson for Communities 2007-10. Co-opted Member, European Communities Sub-committee F (Social Affairs, Education and Home Affairs) 1997-2000; Member: House of Lords Offices, Sub-committee on Lords' Interests 2008-10, Sub-committee on Lords' Conduct 2010-, Joint Committee on Voting Eligibilty (Prisoners) Bill 2013. *Other:* Chair: Brighton Young Liberals 1959-62, Brighton Liberal Association 1962-64; Secretary, Race and Community Relations Panel, Liberal Party 1969-74; Member: Liberal Democrat Federal Policy Committee 1996-97, Federal Executive Committee; President: Liberal Democrat Party 2000-04, Liberal Democrat Federal Conference Committee 2001-; Chair, Diversity Engagement Group 2014-. *Councils and public bodies:* Councillor, County Borough of Brighton 1961-64; Member: Lord Hunt's Committee on Immigration and Youth Service 1967-69, Board of Visitors, HM Prison Lewes 1978-95; JP, Mid Sussex 1978; Member: Home Office Interdepartmental Committee on Racial Attacks and Harassment 1987-92, Sussex Police Authority 1991-94, Ethnic Minority Advisory Committee of Judicial Studies Board 1992-96; DL, West Sussex 1999-; Member: Lord Carlisle's Committee on Parole Systems Review, Home Secretary's Race Forum 1999-; Vice-chair, Policy Research Institute on Ageing and Ethnicity; Member, Governing Body, Commonwealth Institute 1999-; Trustee, Police Foundation 2004-; Member, Prime Minister's Advisory Committee on Business Appointments.

Political interests: Home affairs; East Africa, South East Asia, India.

Other: Member, Executive Committee: Inter-Parliamentary Union, British Group, Commonwealth Parliamentary Association; Patron, vice-patron and trustee numerous organisations, particularly those concerned with ethnic minorities; National Association of Care and Resettlement of Offenders: Council member 1984-, Chairman 1998-, President, Chair, Race Issues Advisory Committee 1989-; Council member: Save The Children Fund 1986-99, Howard League of Penal Reform 1992-2002; Editorial Board, *The Howard Journal of Criminology* 1993-; President, Nacro; Vice-President, Mental Health Foundation; Governor, Commonwealth Institute 1998-2005; Melvin Jones Fellowship, Lions Club. Hon. Doctor of Laws: Hertfordshire University 2009, York University 2010, East London University 2010. Asian of the Year 2000; Pravasi Bharatiya Samman Award (Government of India) 2003; Pride of India Award 2004, 2005. OBE 1994; PC 2010.

Publications: Various articles on criminal justice matters.

Recreations: Photography, travel, gardening, cooking exotic dishes.

Rt Hon The Lord Dholakia OBE DL, House of Lords, London SW1A 0PW
Tel: 020 7219 5203 *Email:* dholakian@parliament.uk

CONSERVATIVE

DIXON-SMITH, LORD

DIXON-SMITH (Life Baron), Robert William Dixon-Smith; cr. 1993. Born 30 September 1934; Son of late Dixon and Alice Smith; Married Georgina Cook 1960 (1 son 1 daughter).

Education: Oundle School, Northamptonshire; Writtle Agricultural College, Essex.

Non-political career: Second Lieutenant, King's Dragoon Guards (National Service) 1956-57. Farmer.

Political career: *House of Lords:* Raised to the peerage as Baron Dixon-Smith, of Bocking in the County of Essex 1993. Opposition Spokesperson for: Environment, Transport and the Regions (Local Government) December 1998-2001, Home Affairs 2001-02, Environment 2003-07, Communities and Local Government 2007-09. Member: Science and Technology 1994-97, 2012-15, European Communities 1994-97, Communications 2010-11. *Councils and public bodies:* Essex County Council: Councillor 1965-93, Chair 1986-89; DL, Essex 1986; Chair, Association of County Councils 1992-93.

Political interests: Agriculture, environment, transport.

Other: Writtle Agricultural College: Governor 1967-94, Chair 1973-85, Fellow; Anglia Polytechnic University (formerly Anglia Polytechnic): Governor 1973-2000, Chair of Governors 1993-94; Fellow, Industry and Parliament Trust 1998. Liveryman, Farmers' Company 1990. Honorary Doctorate, Anglia Polytechnic University.

Recreations: Country sports, golf.

The Lord Dixon-Smith DL, House of Lords, London SW1A 0PW
Tel: 020 7219 5351
Houchins, Coggeshall, Colchester, Essex CO6 1RT *Tel:* 01376 561448

CONSERVATIVE

DOBBS, LORD

DOBBS (Life Baron), Michael John Dobbs; cr 2010. Born 14 November 1948; Son of Eric and Eileen Dobbs.

Education: Hertford Grammar School; Christ Church, Oxford (BA); Fletcher School of Law and Diplomacy (MA, MALD, PhD).

Non-political career: Government special adviser 1981-87; Deputy chairman, Saatchi & Saatchi 1983-86, 1988-91; Presenter, *Despatch Box*, BBC 1999-2001.

Political career: *House of Lords:* Raised to the peerage as Baron Dobbs, of Wylye in the County of Wiltshire 2010. Member: Joint Committee on Privacy and Injunctions 2011-12, Communications 2015. *Other:* Conservative Party: Chief of Staff 1986-87, Joint deputy chairman 1994-95.

Political interests: Constitution, foreign affairs, arts; China, Middle East, USA.

Other: *Clubs:* Royal Automobile Club.

Publications: House of Cards (1989); Wall Games (1990); Last Man to Die (1991); To Play the King (1992); The Touch of Innocents (1994); The Final Cut (1995); Goodfellowe MP (1996); The Buddha of Brewer Street (1998); Whispers of Betrayal (2000); Winston's War (2002); Never Surrender (2003); Churchill's Hour (2004); Churchill's Triumph (2005); First Lady (2006); The Lord's Day (2007); The Edge of Madness (2008); The Reluctant Hero (2009); Old Enemies (2010); A Sentimental Traitor (2012); A Ghost at the Door (2013).

The Lord Dobbs, House of Lords, London SW1A 0PW
Tel: 020 7219 5353 *Email:* dobbsm@parliament.uk
Website: www.michaeldobbs.com *Twitter:* @dobbs_michael

LABOUR

DONAGHY, BARONESS

DONAGHY (Life Baroness), Rita Margaret Donaghy; cr 2010. Born 9 October 1944; Married James Donaghy 1968 (died 1986); married Ted Easen-Thomas 2000.

Education: Leamington College for Girls; Durham University (BA English language and literature 1967).

Non-political career: Technical assistant, National Union of Teachers 1967-68; Institute of Education, London University: Assistant registrar 1968-84, Permanent secretary, Students' Union 1984-2000; Chair, Advisory, Conciliation and Arbitration Service 2000-07. Member: National Executive Committee, NALGO/Unison 1973-2000, General council, Trades Union Congress 1987-2000; President: NALGO 1989-90, Trades Union Congress 2000.

Political career: *House of Lords:* Raised to the peerage as Baroness Donaghy, of Peckham in the London Borough of Southwark 2010. Member, Personal Service Companies 2013-14; Chair, Information 2014-16; Member, EU Internal Market Sub-committee 2015-. *Councils and public* *bodies:* Member, Low Pay Commission 1997-2000; Committee on Standards in Public Life: Member 2001-07, Interim chair 2007; Chair, Department of Work and Pensions Inquiry into Fatal Construction Accidents 2009.

Other: Non-executive director, King's College Hospital NHS Trust 2005-; Fellow, Chartered Institute of Personnel and Development 2002. OBE 1998; CBE 2005.

The Baroness Donaghy CBE, House of Lords, London SW1A 0PW
Tel: 020 7219 5353 *Email:* donaghyr@parliament.uk

LABOUR

DONOUGHUE, LORD

DONOUGHUE (Life Baron), Bernard Donoughue; cr. 1985. Born 8 September 1934; Son of late Thomas Donoughue; Married Carol Goodman 1959 (divorced 1989) (2 sons 2 daughters); married The Hon. Sarah, Lady Berry 2009.

Education: Campbell Secondary Modern School, Northampton; Northampton Grammar School; Lincoln College, Oxford (BA history 1957); Harvard University, USA (1958-59); Nuffield College, Oxford (DPhil 1963).

Non-political career: Editorial staff, *The Economist* 1959-60; Senior research officer, Political and Economic Planning Institute 1960-63; Senior lecturer, London School of Economics 1963-74; Senior policy adviser to Prime Ministers: Harold Wilson 1974-76, James Callaghan 1976-79; Development director, Economist Intelligence Unit 1979-81; Assistant editor, *The Times* 1981-82; Head of research and investment policy, Grieveson Grant and Co. 1982-86; Head of international research and director, Kleinwort Grieveson Securities Ltd 1986-88; Executive vice-chair, LBI 1988-91; Director, Towcester Racecourse Ltd 1992-97; Visiting Professor of Government, LSE 2000-01. Member, GMBW.

Political career: *House of Lords:* Raised to the peerage as Baron Donoughue, of Ashton in the County of Northamptonshire 1985. Opposition Spokesperson for: Energy 1991-92, Treasury Affairs 1991-92, National Heritage 1992-97; Parliamentary Secretary, Ministry of Agriculture, Fisheries and Food (Minister for Farming and the Food Industry) 1997-99. *Councils and public bodies:* Member: Sports Council 1965-71, Commission of Enquiry into Association Football 1966-68, LSE Court of Governors 1968-97; Consultant member, Horse Industry Confederation 1999-2003; British Horseracing Board: Member, Committee on VAT 2000-03, Commission of Enquiry into Stable and Stud Staff 2003-04; Member, London Arts Board 1992-97; Vice-President, Comprehensive Schools Association 2000-08; Chair: Starting Price Regulatory Board 2003-, Future Funding of Racing Group 2005-, Review of Regulation of Greyhound Racing 2007-08.

Political interests: Arts, finance, sport; France, Ireland, Italy.

Other: London Symphony Orchestra: Chair Executive 1979-91, Patron 1989-95, Associate 2000-; Member: Dorneywood Trust 1998-2015, Victoria County History of Northamptonshire; World Horse Welfare, Trustee Global Warming Policy Foundation 2010-. Hon. Fellow, Lincoln College, Oxford; Hon. LLD, Leicester; Hon. Fellow: LSE, Northampton University; *Clubs:* Beefsteak, Pratt's, Farmers', 1795 Club.

Publications: Books on history and politics including: Trade Unions in a Changing Society (1963); British Politics and the American Revolution (1964); Herbert Morrison (1973); Prime Minister (1987); The Heat of the Kitchen (2003); Downing Street Diaries, Vol 1, Harold Wilson (2005); Downing Street Diaries, Vol 2, James Callaghan (2008); Westminster Diaries 1995-98 (2010).

Recreations: Music, theatre, sport.

The Lord Donoughue, House of Lords, London SW1A 0PW
Tel: 020 7219 5353

LIBERAL DEMOCRAT

DOOCEY, BARONESS

DOOCEY (Life Baroness), Elizabeth Dee Doocey; cr 2010. Born 2 May 1948; Daughter of Joseph and Sheila O'Keefe; Married James Doocey (1 son).

Non-political career: Liberal Democrat Party: Finance director, Financial adviser; Group managing director, international fashion company; Management consultant.

Political career: *House of Lords:* Raised to the peerage as Baroness Doocey, of Hampton in the London Borough of Richmond upon Thames 2010. Coalition representative, Criminal Justice Board, Home Office; Liberal Democrat Principal Spokesperson for Culture, Media, Sport and Tourism 2015; Member, House of Lords Commission 2016-. Member: Refreshment 2012-15, Joint Committee on the Draft Enhanced Terrorism Prevention and Investigation Measures Bill 2012-13, Joint Committee on the Draft Modern Slavery Bill 2014, Leader's Group on Governance 2015; Chair, Finance 2016-. *Other:* Election Agent to Dr Vincent Cable, Twickenham 1992-2015. *Councils and public bodies:* Richmond-upon-Thames Borough Council: Councillor 1986-94,

Chair, Housing Committee; London Assembly: Member 2004-12, Chair, Economy, Culture and Sport Committee 2004-10, 2011-12, Chair 2010-11, Deputy Chair 2011-12; Metropolitan Police Authority: Member 2005-12, Chair, Finances and Resources Committee 2011-12; Member, Home Office Olympic Security Board 2008-12.

Political interests: Police, economic development, housing, people with disabilities, ending child trafficking, culture, sport, tourism, Olympic legacy; Ireland, USA.

Other: Member, British-Irish Parliamentary Assembly. OBE.

The Baroness Doocey OBE, House of Lords, London SW1A 0PW
Tel: 020 7219 0926 *Email:* dooceyd@parliament.uk

DRAKE, BARONESS

LABOUR

DRAKE (Life Baroness), Jean Lesley Patricia Drake; cr 2010. Born 16 January 1948.

Non-political career: Research officer, NUPE; Assistant general secretary, Civil and Public Services Association 1978-85; Deputy general secretary, National Communications Union 1985-95; Deputy general secretary (telecommunications and financial services), Communication Workers' Union 1996-2008. Trades Union Congress: Member, general council and executive committee 1986-2008, President 2004-05.

Political career: *House of Lords:* Raised to the peerage as Baroness Drake, of Shene in the County of Surrey 2010. Member: Joint Committee on the Draft Financial Services Bill 2011-12, Small-and Medium-Sized Enterprises 2012-13, Delegated Powers and Regulatory Reform 2014-17, Economic Affairs Finance Bill Sub-committee 2014, 2015-16, 2016-17, Trade Union and Party Funding 2016, Constitution 2017-. Vice-chair, PLP Departmental Group for Work and Pensions 2010-15. *Councils and public bodies:* Member, Employment Tribunal 1988-2001; Commissioner, Equal Opportunities Commission 2000-07; Member, Employment Appeals Tribunal 2001-; Board member, Sector Skills Development Agency 2001-08; Member, Pensions Commission 2002-06; Non-executive board member, Pension Protection Fund 2004-; Supervisory board member, Union Moderation Fund (BERR) 2005-; Commissioner, Equal and Human Rights Commission 2006-09; Chair, Railway Pensions Commission 2006-08; Personal Accounts Delivery Authority: Member 2007-08, Acting chair 2008-; Governor, Pensions Policy Institute; Non-executive director, Pensions Advisory Service.

Other: Trustee: Alliance and Leicester Group Pension Fund 1991-, O2 Pension Trustee Company 2003-; Non-executive director, Communication Workers' Friendly Society -2010. OBE; CBE.

The Baroness Drake CBE, House of Lords, London SW1A 0PW
Tel: 020 7219 5353

DRAYSON, LORD

LABOUR

DRAYSON (Life Baron), Paul Rudd Drayson; cr. 2004. Born 5 March 1960; Son of Michael Rudd and Ruth Irene Drayson; Married Elspeth Jane Bellhouse 1994 (2 daughters 3 sons).

Education: St Dunstan's College, London; Aston University (BSc production engineering 1982; PhD robotics 1985).

Non-political career: Undergraduate engineer, BL Cars 1978-82; Development engineer, Trebor Group 1982-86; Managing director, Lambourn Food Co 1986-91; Founder and managing director, Genisys Development Ltd 1991-95; Chief executive, Powerject Pharmaceuticals plc 1993-2003; Chairman, BioIndustry Association 2001-02; Entrepreneur in Residence, Saïd Business School, Oxford University 2003-05.

Political career: *House of Lords:* Raised to the peerage as Baron Drayson, of Kensington in the Royal Borough of Kensington and Chelsea 2004. Ministry of Defence: Government Spokesperson 2005-07, Parliamentary Under-Secretary of State 2005-07, Minister of State (MoS) (Minister for Defence Equipment and Support) 2007; MoS (Business and Regulatory Reform), Department for Business, Enterprise and Regulatory Reform 2007; MoS (Science and Innovation) and Government Spokesperson, Department for Innovation, Universities and Skills/Business, Innovation and Skills (attending Cabinet) 2008-10; MoS (Strategic Defence Acquisition Reform) and Government Spokesperson, Ministry of Defence 2009-10. Member: Science and Technology Committee 2004-05, Information 2005-09, Science and Technology Sub-committee I (Scientific Aspects of Ageing) 2005.

Political interests: Science, business innovation, entrepreneurship; France.

Other: Trustee, Drayson Foundation; Oxford Children's Hospital (Chairman Campaign 2002-05). PC 2008; *Clubs:* Salle d'Armes Club.

Recreations: Motor racing, sword fencing.

Rt Hon the Lord Drayson, House of Lords, London SW1A 0PW
Tel: 020 7219 4147 *Email:* draysonp@parliament.uk
Nether Lypiatt Manor, Nether Lypiatt, Nr Stroud, Gloucestershire GL6 7LS
Twitter: @lorddrayson

CROSSBENCH

D'SOUZA, BARONESS

D'SOUZA (Life Baroness), Frances Gertrude Claire D'Souza; cr. 2004. Born 18 April 1944; Daughter of Robert Russell and Pauline Russell, née Parmet; Married Stanislaus D'Souza 1959 (divorced 1974) (2 daughters); married Martin Griffiths 1985 (divorced 1994); remarried Stanislaus D'Souza 2003 (died 2011).

Education: University College, London (BSc anthropology 1970); Lady Margaret Hall, Oxford (DPhil evolutionary models 1976).

Non-political career: Ford Foundation research fellow in comparative reproductive physiology, Nuffield Institute of Comparative Medicine 1973-77; Part-time lecturer, London School of Economics 1973-80; Senior lecturer, department of humanities, Oxford Polytechnic 1977-80; Founder director and research director, International Relief and Development Institute 1977-85; Independent research consultant for UN, Save the Children Fund, Ford Foundation 1985-88; Research fellow, Overseas Development Administration 1988-89; Executive director, Article 19 anti-censorship organisation 1989-98; Redress Trust: Director 2003-04, Consultant 2004-06.

Political career: *House of Lords:* Raised to the peerage as Baroness D'Souza, of Wychwood in the County of Oxfordshire 2004. Convenor of the Crossbench Peers 2007-11; Lord Speaker 2011-16. Member, Procedure 2005-;16 Co-opted Member, European Union Sub-committee F (Home Affairs) 2006-07; Member: Selection 2007-11, Liaison 2007-11, Administration and Works 2007-11, Privileges/Privileges and Conduct 2007-11, 2011-12; House: Member 2007-11, Chair 2011-16; Member, Joint Committee on Security 2010-11.

Political interests: Human rights and development, House of Lords Reform; Afghanistan, Japan, India, Jordan, Nordic countries, Southern Africa (SADC countries).

Other: Commonwealth Parliamentary Association (UK Branch): President 2011-16, Member, Executive Committee 2016-; Inter-Parliamentary Union, British Group: Hon. President 2011-16, Executive Committee Member 2016-; BIFG 2011-16; Co-founder, Marefat High School, Kabul, Afghanistan 2002-; President: Hansard Society 2011-16, Industry and Parliament Trust 2011-16, Parliament Choir 2011-16, PICTFOR 2011-16; Chair, David Nott Foundation 2016-; Hazara Charitable Trust. CMG 1999; PC 2009.

Recreations: Music (opera, string quartets, jazz and flamenco).

Rt Hon the Baroness D'Souza CMG, House of Lords, London SW1A 0PW
Tel: 020 7219 3670 *Email:* dsouzaf@parliament.uk

LABOUR

DUBS, LORD

DUBS (Life Baron), Alfred Dubs; cr. 1994. Born 5 December 1932; Married (1 son 1 daughter).

Education: London School of Economics (BSc Econ).

Non-political career: Former local government officer; Chief executive, Refugee Council 1988-95; Deputy chair, ITC 2000; Chair: Broadcasting Standards Commission 2001-03, Appeals Panel, Association of Energy Suppliers 2004-. Member, TGWU.

Political career: *House of Commons:* Contested Cities of London and Westminster 1970 and Hertfordshire South February and October 1974 general elections. MP (Labour) for Battersea South 1979-83, for Battersea 1983-87. Contested Battersea 1987 and 1992 general elections. Opposition Spokesperson for Home Affairs 1983-87. *House of Lords:* Raised to the peerage as Baron Dubs, of Battersea in the London Borough of Wandsworth 1994. Opposition Whip 1995-97; Opposition Spokesperson for: The Environment (Health and Safety) 1996-97, Energy 1996-97; Parliamentary Under-Secretary of State, Northern Ireland Office (Minister for Environment and Agriculture) 1997-99; Chair, Labour Party in Lords 2000-05. Member, European Union 2003-06; Procedure: Member 2005-07, Alternate member 2007-10; Co-opted member, European Union Sub-committee F (Home Affairs) 2006-07; Member: Human Rights Joint Committee 2007-12, Communications 2012-15, EU External Affairs Sub-Committee 2015-. Vice-chair: PLP Departmental Committee for Culture, Media and Sport -2005, PLP Departmental Groups for: Justice 2010-15, Northern Ireland 2010-15, DPM/Constitutional Affairs 2011-15. *Other:* Member, Co-operative Party. *Councils and public bodies:* Councillor, Westminster City Council 1971-78; Chair, Westminster Community Relations Council 1972-77; Member, Kensington, Chelsea and Westminster Area Health Authority 1975-78; Broadcasting Standards Council: Member 1988-94, Deputy Chairman 1994-97; Non-executive director, Pathfinder NHS Trust 1995-97.

Political interests: Civil liberties, penal reform, race relations, immigration, health service, Ireland, human rights.

Other: Member: Executive Committee, British Group, Inter-Parliamentary Union, UK Delegation, Organisation for Security and Co-operation in Europe Parliamentary Assembly, British-Irish

Parliamentary Assembly; Trustee, Action Aid 1989-97; Chair, Liberty 1990-92; Trustee, Immigration Advisory Service 1992-97; Chair, Fabian Society 1993-94; Fellow, Industry and Parliament Trust 2003; Trustee, Open University 2004-09; Patron, Naz Project London.

Publications: Lobbying: An Insider's Guide to the Parliamentary Process (1989).

Recreations: Walking in the Lake District.

The Lord Dubs, House of Lords, London SW1A 0PW
Tel: 020 7219 3590 *Fax:* 020 7219 3981 *Email:* dubsa@parliament.uk

CONSERVATIVE

DUNCAN OF SPRINGBANK, LORD

Parliamentary Under-Secretary of State and Government Spokesperson, Scotland Office and Wales Office

DUNCAN OF SPRINGBANK (Life Baron), Ian James Duncan; cr 2017. Born 13 February 1973; Son of Robert Duncan and Audrey Duncan, née Doig; Married Benjamin Neal Brust 2012.

Education: Alyth High School; St Andrews University (BSc geology 1994); Bristol University (PhD palaeontology 1997); French.

Non-political career: Analyst, BP 1998-99; Deputy Chief Executive/Secretary, Scottish Fishermen's Federation 1999-2003; Policy and Communication, Scottish Refugee Council 2004-05; Scottish Parliament Office, Brussels 2005-11; Clerk, Scottish Parliament 2011-14; EU Adviser, European Committee, Scottish Parliament 2011-14.

Political career: *House of Commons:* Contested (Con) Perth and North Perthshire 2017 general election. *House of Lords:* Raised to the peerage as Baron Duncan of Springbank, of Springbank in the County of Perth 2017. Parliamentary Under-Secretary of State and Government Spokesperson: Scotland Office 2017-, Wales Office 2017-. *Other:* Contested Aberdeen constituency South 2003 Scottish Parliament election. MEP for Scotland 2014-17; Chief Whip, UK Conservative Delegation, European Parliament 2014-17.

Political interests: Energy and climate change policy, fisheries management, constitutional affairs.

Other: Secretary-general, Foundation for European Reform 2014-17; Chair, English Speaking Union (Scotland) 2014-; Board member, Schwarzenegger Institute, University of Southern California 2016-; Fellow, Geological Society of London; *Clubs:* The New Club, Edinburgh.

Recreations: Oil painting, hill walking, carpentry.

The Lord Duncan of Springbank, House of Lords, London SW1A 0PW
Tel: 020 7219 3000
1 Melville Crescent, Edinburgh EH3 7HW *Tel:* 020 7270 6806 *Twitter:* @IanDuncanHMG

CONSERVATIVE

DUNDEE, EARL OF

DUNDEE (12th Earl of, S), Alexander Henry Scrymgeour; cr. 1660; Viscount Dudhope (S) 1641; Lord Scrymgeour (S) 1641; Lord Inverkeithing (S) 1660; Baron Glassary (UK) 1954. Born 5 June 1949; Son of 11th Earl, PC, DL; Married Siobhan Mary Llewellyn 1979 (1 son 3 daughters).

Education: Eton College; St Andrews University.

Political career: *House of Commons:* Contested (Conservative) Hamilton 1978 by-election. *House of Lords:* First entered House of Lords 1983; Government Whip 1986-89; Government Spokesperson for: Education 1986-88, Scottish Affairs 1986-89, Home Affairs and for Energy 1987-89; Elected hereditary peer 1999-. Member: Joint Committee on Consolidation, Etc, Bills 2000-05, 2006-15, EU Sub-committee G (Social Policy and Consumer Affairs) 2003-07; EU Sub-committee D (Environment and Agriculture): Member 2007-08, Co-opted member 2008-10; Member: EU Sub-committee D (Agriculture, Fisheries and Environment) 2010-12, Public Service and Demographic Change 2012-13. *Councils and public bodies:* DL, Fife.

Other: Member: UK delegation, Organisation for Security and Co-operation in Europe 1992-97, Council of Europe parliament 1992-99, Western European parliament 1992-99, UK delegation, Parliamentary Assembly of the Council of Europe 2015-; Fellow, Industry and Parliament Trust 2002. Hereditary Banner Bearer for Scotland; *Clubs:* White's, New (Edinburgh) Club.

The Earl of Dundee, House of Lords, London SW1A 0PW
Tel: 020 7219 6781 *Email:* dundeea@parliament.uk

CONSERVATIVE

DUNLOP, LORD

DUNLOP (Life Baron), Andrew James Dunlop; cr 2015. Born 21 June 1959; Married (3 daughters).

Education: Glasgow Academy; Trinity College, Glenalmond; Edinburgh University (MA political science and government 1981); King's College, London (Postgraduate Diploma European competition law).

Non-political career: Midland Bank International 1981-82; Special Adviser: to Defence Secretary, Ministry of Defence 1986-88, Prime Minister's Policy Unit 1988-90; Founder and Managing Director, Politics International Ltd 1991-2008; Interel Consulting UK: Managing Director 2008-10, Executive Chairman 2010-11; Member, Management Board, Interel Group, Brussels 2008-11; Special Adviser to the Prime Minister 2012-15; Government Communications Service Board 2016-17.

Political career: *House of Lords:* Raised to the peerage as Baron Dunlop, of Helensburgh in the County of Dunbarton 2015. Parliamentary Under-Secretary of State and Government Spokesperson, Scotland Office 2015-17; Government Spokesperson for Northern Ireland 2015-17; Parliamentary Under-Secretary of State, Northern Ireland Office 2016-17. Member, Constitution 2017-. *Other:* Head of Policy and Research, Scottish Conservative and Unionist Party 1982-84; Conservative Research Department 1984-86; Prime Minister's Policy Unit 1988-90. *Councils and public bodies:* Councillor, Horsham District Council 2011-13.

Political interests: Scotland, Northern Ireland, devolution, constitutional issues, economy, business, sport and culture; Central Asia, China, Russia, USA.

Other: *Clubs:* Horsham Reform Club. Chair, Atlantis Swimming Club, Horsham 2007-12; Managing committee member, Sussex Amateur Swimming Association 2009-11; Management committee member, South East Region Amateur Swimming Association 2011-12.

Recreations: Reading, tennis, skiing, swimming, sailing, gardening, watching football, walking.

The Lord Dunlop, House of Lords, London SW1A 0PW
Tel: 020 7219 0645 *Email:* dunlopa@parliament.uk *Twitter:* @ScotlandDunlop

NON-AFFILIATED

DURHAM, LORD BISHOP OF

DURHAM (76th Bishop of), Paul Roger Butler. Born 18 September 1955; Son of Denys and Jean Butler; Married Rosemary Johnson 1982 (2 sons 2 daughters).

Education: Kingston Grammar School; Nottingham University (BA English and history 1977); Wycliffe Hall, Oxford (BA theology 1982).

Non-political career: Ordained deacon 1983; Curate, Holy Trinity, Wandsworth 1983-87; Priest 1984; Scripture Union: Inner London Evangelist 1987-92, Deputy head of missions 1992-94; St Paul, East Ham 1988-94; Priest-in-charge: St Mary with St Stephen, and St Luke, Walthamstow 1994-97, St Gabriel, Walthamstow 1997; Team rector, Parish of Walthamstow 1997-2004; Area dean, Waltham Forest 2000-04; Honorary Canon, St Paul's Cathedral, Rwanda 2001-; Bishop Suffragan of Southampton 2004-09; Bishop of: Southwell and Nottingham 2009-14, Durham 2014-.

Political career: *House of Lords:* Entered House of Lords 2014.

Countries of interest: Burundi, Iran, Israel, Lesotho, Palestine, Russia, Rwanda, South Africa, Uganda.

Other: Chair, Friends of Byumba Trust 2001-; Advocate for Children on behalf of Bishops 2004-; Chair, Church Mission Society 2007-10; President, Scripture Union 2011-17; Trustee: Safe Families for Children 2016-, Child Theology Movement 2017-; Christian Aid, Tearfund, Church Mission Society. Doctor of Divinity, Nottingham University 2016; *Clubs:* Farmers Club.

Publications: Reaching Children (1992); Reaching Families (1994); God's Friends (1994); Following Jesus (1994); Want to be in God's Family? (1998); Growing Up in God's Family (1998); Temptation and Testing (2007); Contributor: Through the Eyes of a Child (2009), Offering the Best Children's Ministry (2011); Co-author, Living Your Confirmation (2012); Contributor: On Being a Curate (2014), Clergy in a Complex Age (2016); Co-author with Sandra Millar, We Welcome You (2016).

Rt Rev the Lord Bishop of Durham, House of Lords, London SW1A 0PW
Tel: 020 7219 5353
Auckland Castle, Bishop Auckland DL14 7NR *Tel:* 01388 602576
Email: bishop.of.durham@durham.anglican.org *Website:* www.durham.anglican.org
Twitter: @BishopPaulB

CROSSBENCH

DYKES, LORD

DYKES (Life Baron), Hugh John Maxwell Dykes; cr. 2004. Born 17 May 1939; Son of Richard and Doreen Dykes; Married Susan Smith 1965 (divorced 2000) (2 sons and 1 son deceased); partner Sarah.

Education: Weston-Super-Mare Grammar School; College de Normandie, France; Pembroke College, Cambridge (MA economics 1963); Speaks many European languages.

Non-political career: Assistant to Edward Heath MP as Leader of the Conservative Party 1965-66; Partner, Simon and Coates stockbrokers 1968-78; Founder shareholder, Dewe Rogerson Ltd 1972-98; Associate member, Quilter Goodison stockbrokers 1978-87; Group director, Far East Division of Dixons plc 1985-90; EU special adviser to Rogers and Wells 1990-97; Member, Securities Institute (MSI) 1993-2003.

Political career: *House of Commons:* Contested Tottenham 1966 and Harrow East 1997 general elections. MP (Conservative) for Harrow East 1970-97. PPS to: Lord Lambton at Ministry of Defence 1971-72, Kenneth Baker as Civil Service Minister in Cabinet Office 1972-74; Chief Sponsor, Heavy Commercial Vehicles Act (Dykes Act) 1973. *House of Lords:* Raised to the peerage as Baron Dykes, of Harrow Weald in the London Borough of Harrow 2004. Liberal Democrat Spokesperson for: Foreign and Commonwealth Affairs (Europe) 2005-10, Environment, Food and Rural Affairs (CAP Reform) 2006-10. Member, Statutory Instruments Joint Committee 2005-09; Co-opted member, EU Sub-committee C (Foreign Affairs, Defence and Development Policy) 2005-06; EU Sub-committee B (Internal Market): Co-opted member 2006-07, Member 2007-10; Member: European Union 2007-12, EU Sub-committee E: (Justice and Institutions) 2010-12, (Justice, Institutions and Consumer Protection) 2012-15, Hybrid Instruments 2017-. *Other:* European Parliament: MEP (Conservative) 1974-76; Contested (Lib Dem) London region 1999 European Parliament election. Joined Liberal Democrat Party after 1997 election; joined Crossbenches July 2015. *Councils and public bodies:* Governor, North London Collegiate School 1981-97.

Political interests: EU, economics, taxation, transport; China, Europe, South Africa, USA.

Other: Chair, UK-European Movement 1990-96; Official International EU Observer to first South African Elections 1994; Chair, Mid-Atlantic Club 2002-05; European-Atlantic Group: Chair 2005-08, President 2008-10; Vice-president, British German Association; President, League of Friends, Royal National Orthopaedic Hospital 1986-97; Visiting Fellow, European Institution, London School of Economics 1998-2003. Freedom, City of London 1979. Order of Merit (Germany) 1991; Medaille pour l'Europe (Luxembourg) 1993; Légion d'Honneur (France) 2004; *Clubs:* Garrick, Beefsteak Club. Harrow Rugby Club.

Publications: Many articles and pamphlets on foreign affairs and Europe; Co-author, Britain on the Edge (2012).

Recreations: Music, theatre, swimming, travel, languages.

The Lord Dykes, House of Lords, London SW1A 0PW
Tel: 020 7219 2729 *Email:* dykesh@parliament.uk

CROSSBENCH

EAMES, LORD

EAMES (Life Baron), Robert (Robin) Henry Alexander Eames; cr. 1995. Born 27 April 1937; Son of Revd. William and Mary Eames; Married Ann Christine Daly OBE 1966 (2 sons).

Education: Belfast Royal Academy; Methodist College, Belfast; Queen's University, Belfast (LLB 1957, PhD ecclesiastical and constitutional law 1963, LLD 1990); Trinity College, Dublin (divinity test 1963).

Non-political career: Research scholar and tutor, Faculty of Laws, Queen's University, Belfast 1960-63; Curate assistant, Bangor Parish Church 1963-66; Rector of St Dorothea's, Belfast 1966-74; Examining Chaplain to Bishop of Down 1973; Rector St Mark's, Dundela 1974-75; Bishop of Derry and Raphoe 1975-80; Bishop of Down and Dromore 1980-86; Archbishop of Armagh and Primate of All Ireland and Metropolitan 1986-2006; Hon. Bencher, Lincoln's Inn 1998; Senior Primate of Anglican Communion 2000-06.

Political career: *House of Lords:* Raised to the peerage as Baron Eames, of Armagh in the County of Armagh 1995. Member: Works of Art 2006-07, Privileges/Privileges and Conduct 2007-, Consolidation of Private/Public Bills 2007-; Co-opted member, EU Sub-committee G (Social Policy and Consumer Affairs) 2007-10; Chair, Leader's Group on the Code of Conduct 2009; Member: Joint Committee on Consolidation, Etc, Bills 2009-, EU Sub-committee G (Social Policies and Consumer Protection) 2010-12, Merits of Statutory Instruments/Secondary Legislation Scrutiny 2010-15. *Councils and public bodies:* Select Preacher, Oxford University 1987; Chair: Commission on Communion and Women in the Episcopate (Eames Commission) 1988-, Commission on

Inter-Anglican Relations (Virginia Report) 1988-; Select Preacher, Cambridge University 1990; Chair, Inter-Anglican Theological and Doctrinal Commission 1991; Select Preacher, Edinburgh University 1993; Chair, Inter-Anglican Finance Committee 1997-2005; Select Preacher, St Andrews University 2001-; Chair, Lambeth Commission Communion (Windsor Report) 2003-04; Co-chair: Consultative Commission on Northern Ireland's Past 2007-08, Consultative Group on Legacy of Northern Ireland Conflict 2008-09 (Co-chairman, Report 2009); Member, Independent Police Commission in England and Wales 2012-.

Political interests: Northern Ireland, social issues, community care, broadcasting; Middle and Far East, North Korea, South Korea, USA.

Other: Member, Anglican International Consultative Council; Member, Institute of Advanced Motorists 1965-; Life Member, Royal Yachting Association 1973-; Governor, Church Army 1985-88; Chair: Board of Governors, Royal School, Armagh 1986-2006, Armagh Observatory and Planetarium 1986-2006; Council member, St George's House, Windsor 2008-; Christian Aid, Save the Children, RNLI. Member, Livery Company of Carmen. Freedom: City of London 1989, City of Armagh 2007. Eleven honorary doctorates from British, Irish and US universities, including Hon LLD Queen's University, Belfast 1990. Archbishop of Canterbury's award for Outstanding Service to the International Anglican Communion 2006. OM 2007; *Clubs:* Kildare Street and University (Dublin), Athenæum Club. Member, Strangford Lough Yacht Club, Co Down; Carrickfergus Marina, Co Antrim.

Publications: A Form of Worship for Teenagers (1965); The Quiet Revolution – Irish Disestablishment (1970); Through Suffering (1973); Thinking through Lent (1978); Through Lent (1984); Chains to be Broken (1992); Biography Nobody's Fool (McCreery, 2004); Contributor to: Irish Legal Quarterly, Criminal Law Review, New Divinity, Cambridge Law Review, Conflict, Freedom and Religion (2008); Unfinished Search (2017).

Recreations: Sailing, rugby union, reading, travel.

Rt Rev the Lord Eames OM, House of Lords, London SW1A 0PW
Tel: 020 7219 5353
Email: robin.eames@yahoo.co.uk

EATON, BARONESS

CONSERVATIVE

EATON (Life Baroness), (Ellen) Margaret Eaton; cr 2010. Born 1 June 1942; Daughter of John and Evelyn Midgley; Married John Eaton 1969 (1 son 1 daughter).

Education: Hanson Grammar School; Balls Park Teacher Training College; German.

Non-political career: Former teacher.

Political career: *House of Lords:* Raised to the peerage as Baroness Eaton, of Cottingley in the County of West Yorkshire 2010. Member: Merits of Statutory Instruments/Secondary Legislation Scrutiny 2011-13, Adoption Legislation 2012-13, Joint Committee on the Draft Care and Support Bill 2013, Refreshment 2015-16, Licencing Act 2003 2016-17. *Other:* Conservative Party Local Government Committee. *Councils and public bodies:* Bradford Metropolitan Borough Council: Councillor 1986-2016, Leader, Conservative Group 1995-2006, Council Leader 2000-06; Former chair: Bradford Local Strategic Partnership Board, Bradford Cultural Consortium, Bradford Safer Communities Partnership; Director: Bradford Centre Regeneration Company, Leeds Bradford International Airport; Member, Yorkshire and Humber Assembly; Local Government Association: Vice-chair, Conservative Group, Chair, Conservative Group, Chair 2008-11, Vice-President 2011-; DL, West Yorkshire 2008.

Political interests: Education, children's services; Eastern Europe, Germany.

Other: Member, EU Committee of the Regions 2003-06; Substitute member, UK delegation, Parliamentary Assembly of the Council of Europe 2012-; FRSA; Hon Lay Canon, Bradford Cathedral; Member, Beckfoot Multi-Academy Trust, Bingley 2016-; Near Neighbours, Angelus Foundation, Candlelighters. Fellow, Bradford College; Hon. degree, Bradford University. Lifetime Achievement Award, Variety Club. OBE; DBE 2010; *Clubs:* United, Cecil Club.

The Baroness Eaton DBE, House of Lords, London SW1A 0PW
Tel: 020 7219 6380 *Email:* eatonm@parliament.uk

House of Lords
Peers' Biographies

NON-AFFILIATED

EATWELL, LORD

EATWELL (Life Baron), John Leonard Eatwell; cr. 1992. Born 2 February 1945; Son of late Harold Eatwell and Mary Eatwell; Married Hélène Seppain 1970 (divorced 2002) (2 sons 1 daughter); married Mrs Susan Digby 2006.

Education: Headlands Grammar School, Swindon; Queens' College, Cambridge (BA economics 1967, MA 1971); Harvard University (PhD economics 1975).

Non-political career: Teaching fellow, Graduate School of Arts and Sciences, Harvard University 1968-69; Research fellow, Queens' College, Cambridge 1969-70; Fellow, Trinity College, Cambridge 1970-96; Faculty of Economics and Politics, Cambridge University: Assistant lecturer 1975-77, Lecturer 1977-2002; Visiting professor of economics, New School for Social Research, New York 1982-96; Economic adviser to Neil Kinnock as Leader of the Labour Party 1985-92; Chair, Extemporary Dance Theatre 1990; Non-executive director: Anglia Television Group Ltd 1994-2001, Cambridge Econometrics Ltd 1996-2007; President, Queens' College, Cambridge 1997-; Director: Cambridge Endowment for Research in Finance, and Professor of Financial Policy, Cambridge University 2002-12, SAV Credit Ltd (now NewDay Ltd) 2007-16; Professor of Economics, University of Southern California 2012-. Member, Association of University Teachers.

Political career: *House of Lords:* Raised to the peerage as Baron Eatwell, of Stratton St Margaret in the County of Wiltshire 1992. Opposition Spokesperson for: Trade and Industry 1992-96, Treasury and Economic Affairs 1992-93; Principal Opposition Spokesperson for Treasury and Economic Affairs 1993-97; Opposition Spokesperson for Treasury 2010-14. Member: Economic Affairs 2008-10, Consumer Insurance (Disclosure and Representations) Bill 2011-12. *Councils and public bodies:* Director, Securities and Futures Authority 1997-2002; Chair: British Screen 1997-2000, British Library 2001-06; Commissioner, Jersey Financial Services Commission 2010-.

Political interests: Economics, trade and industry, arts.

Other: Institute for Public Policy Research: Trustee 1988-, Secretary 1988-97, Chair 1997-2001, 2016-; Governor, Contemporary Dance Trust 1991-95; Director, Arts Theatre Trust, Cambridge 1991-98; Chair, Crusaid, the national fundraiser for AIDS 1993-98; Director, Royal Opera House 1998-2006; Chair: Commercial Radio Companies Association 2000-04, British Library 2001-06; Director, Cambridge Endowment for Research in Finance 2002-12; Governor, Royal Ballet School 2003-06; Chair, Royal Opera House Pension Fund Trustees 2007-; Jersey Financial Services Commission: Commissioner 2010-, Chair 2014-; *Clubs:* Harvard Club of New York City, Bohemian Club, San Francisco. House of Lords and House of Commons RUFC.

Publications: Co-author An Introduction to Modern Economics (1973); Whatever happened to Britain? (1982); Co-author Keynes's Economics and the Theory of Value and Distribution (1983); The New Palgrave: A Dictionary of Economics, 4 vols (1987); The New Palgrave Dictionary of Money and Finance, 3 vols (1992); Editor Global Unemployment: Loss of Jobs in the '90s (1996); Co-author Not Just Another Accession: The Political Economy of EU Enlargement to the East (1997); Understanding Globalisation: The Nation-State, Democracy and Economic Policies in the New Epoch (1998); Global Finance at Risk: The Case for International Regulation (2000); Hard Budgets and Soft States: Social Policy Choices in Central and Eastern Europe (2000); Articles in scientific journals and other collected works.

Recreations: Classical and contemporary dance, rugby union football.

The Lord Eatwell, House of Lords, London SW1A 0PW
Tel: 020 7219 6947
The President's Lodge, Queens' College, Cambridge CB3 9ET *Tel:* 01223 335532/01223 335556
Fax: 01223 335555 *Email:* president@queens.cam.ac.uk je24@cam.ac.uk

CONSERVATIVE

ECCLES, VISCOUNT

ECCLES (2nd Viscount, UK), John Dawson Eccles; cr. 1964; 2nd Baron Eccles (UK) 1962. Born 20 April 1931; Son of 1st Viscount and late Hon. Sybil Dawson, daughter of 1st Viscount Dawson of Penn; Married Diana Sturge 1955, now Baroness Eccles of Moulton (qv) (1 son 3 daughters).

Education: Winchester College; Magdalen College, Oxford (BA philosophy, politics and economics 1954).

Non-political career: National service 1st Battalion KRRC (60th Rifles) 2nd Lieutenant. Head Wrightson 1954; Director, Nuclear Power Group 1968-74; Head Wrightson & Co Ltd: Managing director 1968-77, Chair 1976-77; Director: Glynwed International plc 1972-96, Investors in Industry plc (3i) 1974-88, Davy International Ltd 1977-81; Commonwealth Development Corporation: Member 1982-85, General manager and subsequently chief executive 1985-94; Chair, Chamberlin & Hill plc 1982-2004; Member, Industrial Development Advisory Board 1989-93; Courtaulds Textiles plc: Director 1992-2000, Chair 1995-2000; Chair, Acker Deboeck corporate psychologists 1994-2004.

Political career: *House of Lords:* First entered House of Lords 1999; Elected hereditary peer 2005-. Member: Information 2005-07, Merits of Statutory Instruments 2005-09, Delegated Powers and Regulatory Reform 2007-10, Adoption Legislation 2012-13, EU Sub-committee E (Justice, Institutions and Consumer Protection) 2012-15, Joint Committee on Consolidation, &c, Bills 2015-. *Councils and public bodies:* Monopolies and Mergers Commission: Member 1976-85, Deputy chair 1981-85.

Political interests: Economy, education, Third World development, museums and the arts, secondary legislation, local government; Third World.

Other: Chair: Board of Trustees, Royal Botanical Gardens, Kew 1983-91, Hospital for Tropical Diseases Foundation 2000-, Bowes Museum Trust, Co Durham 2000-08; Council member, Eccles Centre for American Studies, British Library 2003-. Hon. DSc, Cranfield Institute of Technology 1989. CBE 1985; *Clubs:* Brooks's Club.

Recreations: Arts, gardening, bridge.

The Viscount Eccles CBE, House of Lords, London SW1A 0PW
Tel: 020 7219 5353 *Email:* ecclesj@parliament.uk

CONSERVATIVE

ECCLES OF MOULTON, BARONESS

ECCLES OF MOULTON (Life Baroness), Diana Catherine Eccles; cr. 1990. Born 4 October 1933; Daughter of late Raymond and Margaret Sturge; Married Hon John Eccles 1955, now 2nd Viscount Eccles (qv) (1 son 3 daughters).

Education: St James's School, West Malvern; Open University (BA 1978).

Non-political career: Voluntary work, Middlesbrough Community Council 1955-58; Partner in graphic design business 1963-77; Vice-chair, National Council for Voluntary Organisations 1981-87; Director: Tyne Tees Television 1986-94, J. Sainsbury plc 1986-95, Yorkshire Electricity Group plc 1990-97, National and Provincial Building Society 1991-96, Times Newspapers Holdings Ltd 1998-, Opera North 1998-2011, London Clinic 2003-08.

Political career: *House of Lords:* Raised to the peerage as Baroness Eccles of Moulton, of Moulton in the County of North Yorkshire 1990. Member: Animals in Scientific Procedures 2001-02, EU Sub-committee B (Internal Market) 2003-07, Pre-legislative Scrutiny on Mental Health Bill 2005, Communications 2007-10, Intergovernmental Organisations 2007-08, EU Sub-committee F (Home Affairs) 2010-12, Joint Committee on Statutory Instruments 2010-12, European Union 2012-15, EU Sub-committees: C (External Affairs) 2012-13, E (Justice, Institutions and Consumer Protection) 2013-15, EU Justice Sub-committee 2015-16, Liaison 2016-17. *Councils and public bodies:* Member, North Eastern Electricity Board 1974-85; Durham University Council: Lay Member 1981-, Vice-chair 1985-2004; Chair, Tyne Tees Television Programme Consultative Council 1982-84; Member: Advisory Council on Energy Conservation (Department of Energy) 1982-84, Widdicombe Inquiry into Local Government 1985-86, Home Office Advisory Panel on Licences for Experimental Community Radio 1985-86, British Rail Eastern Board 1986-92, Teesside Urban Development Corporation 1987-98; Chair, Ealing District Health Authority 1988-93; Member, Unrelated Live Transplant Regulatory Authority 1990-99; Chair, Ealing, Hammersmith and Hounslow Health Authority 1993-2000; DL, North Yorkshire 1998-2008.

Other: Member, UK delegation, Parliamentary Assembly of the Council of Europe 2010-; Trustee: Charities Aid Foundation 1982-89, York Minster Trust Fund 1989-99, 2006-09; Member, British Heart Foundation 1989-98. Hon. DCL, Durham 1995.

The Viscountess Eccles, Lady Eccles of Moulton DL, House of Lords, London SW1A 0PW
Tel: 020 7219 5353 *Email:* ecclesd@parliament.uk

LABOUR

ELDER, LORD

ELDER (Life Baron), Thomas Murray Elder; cr. 1999. Born 9 May 1950.

Education: Kirkcaldy High School; Edinburgh University (MA economic history).

Non-political career: Bank of England 1972-80; Research assistant to Shadow Secretary of State for Trade and Industry 1980-84; Labour Party Scotland 1984-92, General Secretary 1988-92; Chief of Staff to John Smith MP as Leader of the Labour Party 1992-94; Special adviser, Scottish Office 1997-99.

Political career: *House of Commons:* Contested (Labour) Ross, Cromarty and Skye 1983 general election. *House of Lords:* Raised to the peerage as Baron Elder, of Kirkcaldy in Fife 1999. Member: Monetary Policy of the Bank of England/Economic Affairs 2000-05, Refreshment 2008-13, High Speed Rail (London-West Midlands) Bill 2016.

Recreations: Walking, reading, opera.

The Lord Elder, House of Lords, London SW1A 0PW
Tel: 020 7219 8512

NON-AFFILIATED

ELIS-THOMAS, LORD

ELIS-THOMAS (Life Baron), Dafydd Elis-Thomas; cr. 1992. Born 18 October 1946; Son of Rev William Ellis Thomas and Eirlys Thomas; Married Elen Williams 1970 (divorced) (3 sons); married Mair Parry Jones 1993.

Education: Ysgol Dyffryn Conwy; University College of Wales (PhD); Welsh.

Non-political career: Tutor in Welsh studies, Coleg Harlech 1971-74; Lecturer: University College of North Wales, Bangor, Aberystwyth, Cardiff, Open University; Broadcaster on BBC Wales, HTV, S4C, Radio Wales; Consultant to: S4C, Welsh Development Agency, Rural Initiative Programme, Assembly of European Regions, Government of Catalonia; Chairman, Screen Wales; Director and deputy chair, Cynefin Environmental; Director and chair, New Media Agency; Director: Oriel Mostyn, National Botanical Gardens, MFM Marcher.

Political career: *House of Commons:* Contested Conway 1970 general election. MP (Plaid Cymru) for Meirionnydd February 1974-83, for Meirionnydd Nant Conwy 1974-92. *House of Lords:* Raised to the peerage as Baron Elis-Thomas, of Nant Conwy in the County of Gwynedd 1992. Member: European Communities 1997-98, European Communities Sub-committee C (Environment, Public Health and Consumer Protection) 1997-98. *Other:* National Assembly for Wales: AM for Meirionnydd Nant Conwy constituency 1999-2007, for Dwyfor Meirionnydd constituency since 3 May 2007: Presiding Officer 1999-2011, Chair, Assembly Committee on Environment and Sustainability 2011-14, Plaid Cymru: Spokesperson for: Environment, Energy and Planning 2011-12, Rural Affairs, Fisheries and Food 2012-13, Transport 2013-14, Society 2013-14, Shadow Minister for Wales Bill, Government Liaison and Constitution 2016. Plaid Cymru: President 1984-91, Contested leadership election 2012, Whip withdrawn 18-20 July 2012, Resigned from Party October 2016.

Political interests: Rural affairs, environment, constitutional affairs; Wales.

Other: President, Commonwealth Parliamentary Association (Wales Branch) 1999-2011; President: Hay-on-Wye Literature Festival, Ramblers Association in Wales -1999, Snowdonia National Park Society -1999, Abbeyfield -1999; Member: Welsh Arts Council -1999, Welsh Film Council -1999, Welsh Film Board -1999, Wales Committee of National Trust; BBC General Consultative Council -1999; Chair, Welsh Language Board 1993-96, 1996-99; Trustee: Big Issue Foundation -1999, Theatr Bara Caws -1999; Fellow, International Centre for Intercultural Studies, Institute of Education, London; Patron, Prince of Wales Trust – Bro; Surname changed from Thomas to Elis-Thomas by deed poll 1992. Chancellor, Bangor University 2001-17. Welsh Politician of the Year 2008, ITV Wales. PC 2004.

Recreations: Welsh literature and art, music, theatre, films, hill- and mountain-walking, jogging.

Rt Hon the Lord Elis-Thomas, House of Lords, London SW1A 0PW
Tel: 020 7219 8701 *Email:* elisthomasd@parliament.uk
7 Bank Place, Porthmadog, Gwynedd LL49 9AA *Tel:* 01766 515028
Email: dafydd.elis-thomas@assembly.wales
Website: www.dafyddelisthomas.org *Twitter:* @ElisThomasD

CONSERVATIVE

ELTON, LORD

ELTON (2nd Baron, UK), Rodney Elton; cr. 1934. Born 2 March 1930; Son of Godfrey 1st Baron and Dedi Hartmann; Married Anne Tilney 1958 (divorced 1979) (1 son 3 daughters); married Richenda Gurney 1979 (Lady in Waiting to HM the Queen 1987-, DCVO 2010).

Education: Eton College; New College, Oxford (MA modern history 1953).

Non-political career: 2nd Lieutenant, The Queens Bays 1950; Captain, Queen's Own Warwickshire and Worcestershire Yeomanry 1959; Major, Leicestershire and Derbyshire Yeomanry 1970. Farming 1957-73; Assistant mastership (history): Loughborough Grammar School 1962-67, Fairham Comprehensive School for Boys 1967-69; Lecturer, Bishop Lonsdale College of Education 1969-72; Director: Overseas Exhibitions Ltd 1977-79, Building Trades Exhibition Ltd 1977-79; Director and deputy chair, Andry Montgomery Ltd 1987-2002; DIVERT Trust: Founder and chair 1993-99, President 1999-2001; Licensed Lay Minister, Church of England 1998-. Assistant Masters Association 1962-69.

Political career: *House of Commons:* Contested (Conservative) Loughborough 1966 and 1970 general elections. *House of Lords:* First entered House of Lords 1973; Opposition Whip 1974-76; Opposition Spokesperson 1976-79; Parliamentary Under-Secretary of State for: Northern Ireland 1979-81, Department of Health and Social Security 1981-82, Home Office 1982-84; Minister of State: Home Office 1984-85, Department of the Environment 1985-86; Deputy Chairman of Committees 1997-2007; Elected hereditary peer 1999-; Deputy Speaker 1999-2008; Contested Lord Speaker election 2006. Member: Scrutiny of Delegated Powers 1994-97, Ecclesiastical Committee

2001-, Constitution 2003-07, Procedure 2005-09, Conventions Joint Committee 2006, EU Sub-committee B: Internal Market, Infrastructure and Employment 2013. *Other:* Vice-chair, Association of Conservative Peers 1988-93. *Councils and public bodies:* Member, Boyd Commission (South Rhodesia Independence Elections) 1979; Chair, Financial Intermediaries Managers and Brokers Regulatory Association 1987-90; Member, Panel on Takeovers and Mergers 1988-90; Chair, Inquiry into Discipline in Schools (Elton Report) 1988; Vice-President, Institute of Trading Standards Administration 1990-; Chair, Quality and Standards Committee, City and Guilds of London Institute 1999-2004.

Political interests: Juvenile justice, education; Norway.

Other: Chair, Intermediate Treatment Fund 1990-93; Trustee: The Airey Neave Trust 1991-96, City Parochial Foundation and Trust for London 1991-97; RSA. Hon. Fellow, City and Guilds of London 2000. TD 1970; Lord of the Manor of Adderbury; *Clubs:* Beefsteak, Pratt's, Cavalry and Guards Club.

Recreations: Painting.

The Lord Elton TD, House of Lords, London SW1A 0PW
Tel: 020 7219 3165 *Fax:* 020 7219 0785

NON-AFFILIATED

ELY, LORD BISHOP OF

ELY (69th Bishop of), Stephen David Conway. Born 22 December 1957; Son of late David Conway and Dorothy Lambert.

Education: Archbishop Tenison's Grammar School, London; Keble College, Oxford (BA modern history 1980); Selwyn College, Cambridge (BA theology 1985).

Non-political career: Assistant master, Glenalmond College 1981-83; Ordained deacon 1986; Priest 1987; Curate: Heworth 1986-89, Bishopwearmouth 1989-90, St Margaret, Durham 1990-94; Diocesan director of ordinands, Durham 1989-94; Priest then Vicar, Cockerton 1994-98; Senior chaplain to Bishop of Durham and Diocesan communications officer 1998-2002; Archdeacon of Durham 2002-06; Area Bishop of Ramsbury 2006-10; Bishop of Ely 2010-.

Political career: *House of Lords:* Entered House of Lords 2014. *Councils and public bodies:* Member, General Synod of Church of England 1995-2000, 2011-.

Political interests: Mental health, education, rural affairs, disability; Germany, India, Rwanda.

Other: Chair: National Society Council, Development and Appointments Group, House of Bishops 2013-15, Westcott House Council; Faith and Order Commission, World Council of Churches; Honorary Fellow, Harris Manchester College, Oxford 2017-; L'Arche Community, Arthur Rank Hospice, Romsey Mill, Arts and Minds, National Youth Arts Trust.

Publications: Editor, Living the Eucharist (2001); Contributor: This is Our Calling (2004), The Vicar's Guide (2005), 'Generous Episcopacy' in Generous Ecclesiology (SCM, 2013); 'A Good Easter' in Mark Oakley's "A Good Year" (2016).

Recreations: Reading detective fiction, biographies and history, film, travel.

Rt Rev the Lord Bishop of Ely, House of Lords, London SW1A 0PW
Tel: 020 7219 5353 *Email:* bishopofely@parliament.uk
The Bishop's House, Ely, Cambridgeshire CB7 4DW *Tel:* 01353 662749
Email: bishop@elydiocese.org *Website:* www.elydiocese.org *Twitter:* @Bishop_S_Conway

CROSSBENCH

ELYSTAN-MORGAN, LORD

ELYSTAN-MORGAN (Life Baron), Dafydd Elystan Elystan-Morgan; cr. 1981. Born 7 December 1932; Son of late Dewi, journalist, and Olwen Morgan; Married Alwen Roberts 1959 (died 2006) (1 son 1 daughter).

Education: Ardwyn Grammar School, Aberystwyth; University of Wales, Aberystwyth (LLB 1953).

Non-political career: Solicitor 1957; Partner in North Wales firm of solicitors 1958-68; Called to the Bar 1971 (Gray's Inn); Wales and Chester Circuit 1983-2003: Recorder 1983-87, Judge 1987-2003; Deputy High Court Judge 1989-2003; President, School of Welsh Legal Studies 2001-.

Political career: *House of Commons:* MP (Labour) for Cardigan 1966-74. Joint Under-Secretary of State, Home Office 1968-70; Deputy Opposition Spokesperson for: Home Affairs 1970-72, Welsh Affairs 1972-74. *House of Lords:* Raised to the peerage as Baron Elystan-Morgan, of Aberteifi in the County of Dyfed 1981. Opposition Spokesperson for Home Affairs and Legal Affairs 1983-87. Member EU Sub-committee E: (Justice and Institutions) 2012, (Justice, Institutions and Consumer Protection) 2012-15. *Other:* Chair, Welsh Parliamentary Party 1974. *Councils and pub-*

lic bodies: Chair, Welsh Local Government Association 1966-74; President, Association of Welsh Local Authorities 1970-74; University of Wales, Aberystwyth: Vice-President 1990-97, President 1997-2007; President, School of Welsh Legal Studies 2001-.

Other: Honorary Fellow, University of Wales Aberystwyth 1989. Doctor of Laws, University of Wales 2015. Welsh Politician of the Year 2013.

The Lord Elystan-Morgan, House of Lords, London SW1A 0PW
Tel: 020 7219 5353
Carreg Afon, Dolau, Bow Street, Ceredigion SY24 5AE

CROSSBENCH

EMERTON, BARONESS

EMERTON (Life Baroness), Audrey Caroline Emerton; cr. 1997. Born 10 September 1935; Daughter of late George Emerton and Lily Emerton.

Education: Tunbridge Wells Grammar School for Girls; St George's Hospital; Battersea College of Technology.

Non-political career: Senior tutor, St George's Hospital, London 1965-68; St John Ambulance: Kent County nursing officer 1967-85, County Commissioner 1985-88; Principal nursing officer, Education, Bromley Hospital Management Committee 1968-70; Chief nursing officer, Tunbridge Wells and Leybourne Hospital Management Committee 1970-73; Regional nursing officer, South East Thames RHA 1973-91; St John Ambulance: Chief nursing officer 1988-96, Chair, Medical Board 1993-96, Chief Officer, Care in the Community 1996-98, Chancellor, Chief Commander 1998-2002.

Political career: *House of Lords:* Raised to the peerage as Baroness Emerton, of Tunbridge Wells in the County of Kent and of Clerkenwell in the London Borough of Islington 1997. On leave of absence December 2016-June 2017. Member Science and Technology Sub-committees: I (Fighting Infection) 2003, I (Scientific Aspects of Ageing) 2005; Member, Refreshment 2010-12. *Councils and public bodies:* DL, Kent 1992-2010; Chair, Brighton Health Care NHS Trust 1994-2000 Commissioner, Prime Minister's Commission on the Future of Nursing and Midwifery.

Political interests: Health – social care, voluntary services, defence medical welfare service, Jerusalem.

Other: President, chair several nursing, midwifery and health visiting organisations 1983-99; Trustee, Kent Community Housing Trust 1993-98; Hon Vice-president, Royal College of Nursing 1994-99; Member, Court of Sussex University 1996-98; Lay Member, General Medical Council 1996-2001; Member, Burdett Nursing Trust 2001-03; Defence Medical Welfare Service: Trustee 2001-12, Patron 2013-; Chair, Association of Hospital and Community Friends 2003-06; President, Florence Nightingale Foundation 2004-; Fellow: Royal Society of Arts, Kings College London, Brighton University, Kingston University, Christ Church Canterbury, Royal College of Nursing; St John Ambulance, Order of St John of Jerusalem, Ophthalmic Hospital Jerusalem. Seven honorary doctorates. CStJ 1978; DBE 1989; DStJ 1993, Dame Grand Cross 2004.

Recreations: Walking, travel, reading.

The Baroness Emerton DBE, House of Lords, London SW1A 0PW
Tel: 020 7219 5035
Email: audrey.emerton@gmail.com

ULSTER UNIONIST PARTY

EMPEY, LORD

EMPEY (Life Baron), Reginald Norman Morgan Empey; cr 2011. Born 26 October 1947; Son of late Samuel Empey and late Emily Empey, née Morgan; Married Stella Donnan 1977 (1 son 1 daughter).

Education: Royal School, Armagh; Queen's University, Belfast (BSc (Econ) 1969).

Non-political career: 1970-86: Industrial rubber products division, Goodyear International Corporation; House of Fraser/Switzer and Company; McMahon Co; Self-employed clothing retailer 1986-.

Political career: *House of Commons:* Contested (UUP) Belfast East 1997 and 2005 and (UCUNF) South Antrim 2010 general elections. *House of Lords:* Raised to the peerage as Baron Empey, of Shandon in the City and County of Belfast 2011. Member: Small- and Medium-Sized Enterprises 2012-13, Personal Service Companies 2013-14, Extradition Law 2014-15, Information 2015-16, Financial Exclusion 2016-17. *Other:* Member: Northern Ireland Convention 1975, UUP Talks Team: Brooke/Mayhew Talks 1991, Castle Buildings Talks 1996-98; Northern Ireland Assembly: MLA for Belfast East 1998-2011, Minister for Enterprise, Trade and Investment 1999-2002, Acting First Minister 2001, Minister for Employment and Learning 2007-10. Vice-president, Ulster

Unionist Council 1996-2004; Ulster Unionist Party: Leader 2005-10, Chair 2012-. *Councils and public bodies:* Belfast City Council: Councillor 1985-2010, Mayor 1989, 1993; Member, Police Authority of Northern Ireland 1992-2001.

Political interests: Economic policy, education, UK-US relations, EU, small- and medium-sized enterprises; Canada, India, USA.

Other: Member: EU Committee of the Regions 1994-2002, British-Irish Parliamentary Assembly; Vice-president, Institute of Export. OBE 1994; Kt 1999; *Clubs:* Army and Navy Club.

Recreations: Walking, gardening.

The Lord Empey OBE, House of Lords, London SW1A 0PW
Tel: 020 7219 8482 *Email:* empeyr@parliament.uk
Room 501, Millbank House, 1 Millbank, London SW1A 0PW

ERROLL, EARL OF

CROSSBENCH

ERROLL (24th Earl of, S), Merlin Sereld Victor Gilbert Hay; cr. 1452. 25th Lord Hay (S) 1429, 24th Lord Slains (S) 1452; 12th Bt (NS) 1685; 28th Hereditary Lord High Constable of Scotland, 1314; 32nd Chief of The Hays since 1160 (Celtic Title) Mac Garadh Mhor. Born 20 April 1948; Son of Sir Iain Moncreiffe of that Ilk, 11th Bt and Diana Denyse, Countess of Erroll (23rd in line); Married Isabelle Jacqueline Laline Astell 1982 (2 sons 2 daughters).

Education: Eton College; Trinity College, Cambridge.

Non-political career: Lieutenant, Atholl Highlanders 1974; TA 1975-90; Hon. Colonel, RMPTA 1992-97. Hayway Partners (Marketing) 1991-; Computer consultant -1993; Group director, Applications and Development, Girovend Holdings plc 1993-94; Chair: CRC Ltd 1995-, Fonem Ltd 2004-.

Political career: *House of Lords:* First entered House of Lords 1978; Elected hereditary peer 1999-. Board Member, Parliamentary Office of Science and Technology 2000-; Council Member, PITCOM 2000-; Member, Information 2003-05, 2007-08, 2009-12.

Political interests: Defence, ICT, science, Scotland, environment.

Other: Member, Queen's Body Guard for Scotland, Royal Company of Archers; Fishmongers Company Charitable Trust; Billingsgate Christian Mission; Trustee, Mar Estate Trust; Royal Caledonian Ball. Member, Court of Assistants of Fishmongers' Company, Prime Warden 2000-01. Freedom, City of London. Page to the Lord Lyon 1956; OStJ 1977; *Clubs:* White's, Pratt's, Puffin's (Edinburgh) Club.

Recreations: Country pursuits.

The Earl of Erroll, House of Lords, London SW1A 0PW
Tel: 020 7219 3885 *Email:* errollm@parliament.uk
Woodbury Hall, Everton, Sandy, Bedfordshire SG19 2HR *Tel:* 01767 650251

EVANS OF BOWES PARK, BARONESS

CONSERVATIVE

Leader of the House of Lords and Lord Privy Seal

EVANS OF BOWES PARK (Life Baroness), Natalie Jessica Evans; cr 2014. Born 29 November 1975; Married James Wild 2010.

Education: Henrietta Barnett School; Cambridge University (social and political sciences).

Non-political career: Head of policy, British Chambers of Commerce; Deputy director, Policy Exchange 2008-11; New Schools Network: Chief operating officer 2011-13 Director 2013-15.

Political career: *House of Lords:* Raised to the peerage as Baroness Evans of Bowes Park, of Bowes Park in the London Borough of Haringey 2014. Government Whip (Baroness in Waiting) 2015-16; Government Spokesperson for: Education 2015-16, Justice 2015-16, Work and Pensions 2015-16; Leader of the House of Lords and Lord Privy Seal 2016-; Member, House of Lords Commission 2016-. Member: House 2016, Liaison 2016-, Privileges and Conduct 2016-, Procedure 2016-, Selection 2016-. *Other:* Deputy director, research department, Conservative Party 2000-02.

Political interests: Education, crime and justice, sport.

Other: Chair, board of trustees, Chevening House. PC 2016.

Rt Hon the Baroness Evans of Bowes Park, House of Lords, London SW1A 0PW
Tel: 020 7219 3200
Email: psleaderofthelords@cabinetoffice.gov.uk

LABOUR

EVANS OF WATFORD, LORD

EVANS OF WATFORD (Life Baron), David Charles Evans; cr. 1998. Born 30 November 1942; Son of Arthur Charles Evans and Phyllis Connie Evans; Married June Scaldwell 1966 (divorced) (2 sons 1 daughter).

Education: Hampden Secondary School; Watford College of Technology (Full Tech 1962).

Non-political career: Apprentice Printer, Stone and Cox Ltd 1957; Sales Executive and Sales Director at various printers; Centurion Press: Founder 1971, Chair, and of subsidiary companies in UK, Netherlands and the USA -2002; Former Chair: Personnel Publications Ltd, Redactive Publishing Ltd, Indigo Publishing Ltd, Iconic Images Ltd, Advanced Oncotherapy plc, Newsdesk Media Ltd; Chair: Senate Publishing Ltd, TU Ink Ltd, Evans Mitchell Books, Kennedy Scott Ltd; Stormount Energy Ltd; Non-executive Chair, Institute for Collaborative Working. Unite.

Political career: *House of Lords:* Raised to the peerage as Baron Evans of Watford, of Chipperfield in the County of Hertfordshire 1998. Departmental Liaison Peer for Department of Trade and Industry 1999-2004. Member, Small-and Medium-Sized Enterprises 2012-13.

Political interests: Trade and industry, industrial relations, current affairs, education, travel, voluntary sector; Europe, Far East, Middle East, USA.

Other: Honorary Fellow, Cancer Research UK; Assisted in creation of One World group/One World Action; Voluntary lecturer for Postal Telegraph and Telephone International in trade union studies and media public relations; Non-executive director, Hendon Museum Enterprises Ltd; Patron: Watford Peace Hospice, VITAL, Alma Hospital Trust, Eliminating Domestic Violence; Fellow: Chartered Institute of Marketing, City and Guilds Institute; Cancer Research UK, Royal British Legion, British Red Cross, Peace Hospice Care, Prostate Cancer UK. Member, Worshipful Company of Marketors; *Clubs:* George, 5 Hertford Street Club.

Recreations: Theatre, the arts, reading, travel.

The Lord Evans of Watford, House of Lords, London SW1A 0PW
Tel: 020 7219 6184 *Fax:* 020 7219 1733
Senate Publishing, 5 Wythburn Place, London W1H 7BU *Tel:* 020 7723 9825
Email: lordevans@senatepublishing.co.uk *Website:* www.senatepublishing.co.uk

CROSSBENCH

EVANS OF WEARDALE, LORD

EVANS OF WEARDALE (Life Baron), Jonathan Douglas Evans; cr 2014. Born 17 February 1958.

Education: Sevenoaks School, Kent; Bristol University (Degree classical studies); Institute of Directors (Certificate company direction).

Non-political career: Security Service 1980-2013: Roles including counter-espionage investigations, protective security policy, international and domestic counter-terrorism, Secondment to the Home Office, Director of international counter-terrorism, Security Service's Management Board, Deputy Director-General 2005-07, Director-General 2007-13; Non-executive director: HSBC 2013-, Ark Data Centres Ltd.

Political career: *House of Lords:* Raised to the peerage as Baron Evans of Weardale, of Toys Hill in the County of Kent 2014. *Councils and public bodies:* Governor, Skinners' Kent Academy, Tunbridge Wells; DL, Kent 2015; Member, Parliamentary and Political Service Honours Committee 2017-.

Other: Non-executive Director: HSBC Holdings plc, Ark Data Centres Ltd; Senior Adviser, Accenture plc -2015; Member, Advisory Board: Darktrace Ltd, Facewatch Ltd; Patron: West Kent YMCA, Sevenoaks School, Member, Council of Reference, Westminster Abbey Institute; Senior associate fellow, Royal United Services Institute; Honorary professor, St Andrews University. Freedom, City of London. Hon LLD, Bristol University. KCB 2013.

Recreations: Classic cars, town and country walks.

The Lord Evans of Weardale KCB DL, House of Lords, London SW1A 0PW
Tel: 020 7219 5353

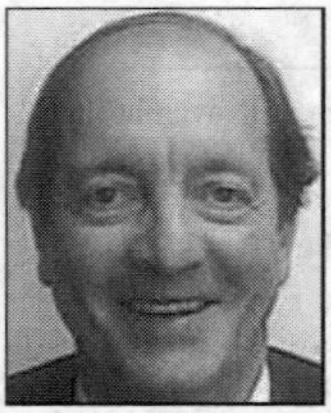

CONSERVATIVE

FAIRFAX OF CAMERON, LORD

FAIRFAX OF CAMERON (14th Lord, S), Nicholas John Albert Fairfax; cr 1627. Born 4 January 1956; Son of 13th Lord and late Sonia Gunston; Married Annabel Morriss 1982 (3 sons).

Education: Eton College; Downing College, Cambridge (Postgraduate LLB international law subjects 1981); French, German, Italian, Russian.

Non-political career: Called to the Bar, Gray's Inn 1977; Director: Thomas Miller P&I and Thomas Miller Defence 1987-90, Sedgwick Marine and Cargo Ltd 1995-96, Sovcomflot (UK) Ltd 2005-, North of England P&I Association Ltd 2012-; Chair: SCF Overseas Holding Ltd 2012-, SCF Management Services Ltd 2012-, Advisory board, Hawk-i Worldwide Ltd 2015-, Consultant, Burford Capital 2014-.

Political career: *House of Lords:* First entered House of Lords 1977; Elected hereditary peer 2015-.

Political interests: Shipping, marine insurance and law, exiting the European Union, artificial intelligence, security, motorcycling, choice at end of life, mental health, homelessness; Eastern Europe, Russia, former Soviet Union, USA.

Other: Patron, Downside Up; Patron: Wildlife Vets International, Downside Up, Warm House, Friends of Fairfax House. Liveryman, Shipwrights' Company. Freedom, City of London; *Clubs:* Royal Yacht Squadron Club.

Recreations: Sailing, motorcycling, astronomy, photography.

The Lord Fairfax of Cameron, House of Lords, London SW1A 0PW
Tel: 020 7219 3000 *Email:* fairfaxn@parliament.uk

FAIRHEAD, RONA –
(Peer name still to be announced) see Addenda page x

LABOUR

FALCONER OF THOROTON, LORD

FALCONER OF THOROTON (Life Baron), Charles Leslie Falconer; cr. 1997. Born 19 November 1951; Son of late John Leslie Falconer and Anne Mansel Falconer; Married Marianna Catherine Thoroton Hildyard (later QC) 1985 (3 sons 1 daughter).

Education: Trinity College, Glenalmond; Queens' College, Cambridge.

Non-political career: Called to the Bar, Inner Temple 1974; QC 1991; Elected Master, Bench of the Inner Temple 1997; Senior Counsel, Gibson Dunn and Crutcher LLP.

Political career: *House of Lords:* Raised to the peerage as Baron Falconer of Thoroton, of Thoroton in the County of Nottinghamshire 1997. Solicitor General 1997-98; Minister of State and Government Spokesperson for: Cabinet Office 1998-2001, Department for Transport, Local Government and the Regions (Minister for Housing, Planning and Regeneration) 2001-02, Home Office (Criminal Justice, Sentencing and Law Reform) 2002-03; Secretary of State and Government Spokesperson for Constitutional Affairs/Justice and Lord Chancellor 2003-07; Opposition Spokesperson for Justice (Constitutional Affairs) 2010-16; Shadow Lord Chancellor and Secretary of State for Justice 2015-16. Member, Procedure 2003-07. *Other:* Adviser on Planning and Transition into Government 2013-. *Councils and public bodies:* Chair, Commission on Assisted Dying 2010-.

Other: Vice-President, Commonwealth Parliamentary Association (UK Branch). Peer of the Year, *Spectator* awards 2014. PC 2003.

Rt Hon the Lord Falconer of Thoroton QC, House of Lords, London SW1A 0PW
Tel: 020 7219 5159
Email: cfalconer@gibsondunn.com

LABOUR

FALKENDER, BARONESS

FALKENDER (Life Baroness), Marcia Matilda Falkender; cr. 1974. Born 10 March 1932; Daughter of late Harry Field; Married George Williams 1955 (divorced 1961) (2 sons).

Education: Northampton High School for Girls; Queen Mary College, London University (BA history).

Non-political career: Secretary to General Secretary, Labour Party HQ 1955-56; Private secretary to Harold Wilson MP 1956-64; Political secretary and head of political office to Harold Wilson as Leader of the Labour Party and Prime Minister 1964-70, 1974-76; Columnist, *Mail on Sunday* 1983-88; Local director, Cheltenham and Gloucester Building Society, Peckham; Director: South London Investment Mortgage Corporation 1986-91, Canvasback Productions 1988-91, Regent (GM) Laboratories 1996-.

Political career: *House of Lords:* Raised to the peerage as Baroness Falkender, of West Haddon in the County of Northamptonshire 1974.

Political interests: Exports, health, breast cancer, British film industry.

Other: Member: Film Industry Working Party 1975, Film Industry Action Committee 1977-85, British Screen Advisory Council 1985-, Royal Society of Arts; Former President, UN Unifem UK Trust; Lay Governor, Queen Mary and Westfield College, London University 1987-93; Silver Trust, Imperial Cancer Research. CBE 1983; *Clubs:* Reform Club.

Publications: Inside No. 10 (1972); Perspective on Downing Street (1983).

Recreations: Films, reading, music.

The Baroness Falkender CBE, House of Lords, London SW1A 0PW
Tel: 020 7219 3156

FALKLAND, VISCOUNT OF

CROSSBENCH

FALKLAND (15th Viscount of, S), Lucius Edward William Plantagenet Cary; cr. 1620; Lord Cary 1620. Born 8 May 1935; Son of 14th Viscount; Married Caroline Butler 1962 (divorced 1990) (1 son 2 daughters and 1 daughter deceased); married Nicole Mackey 1990 (1 son).

Education: Wellington College, Berkshire; French, German.

Non-political career: 2nd Lieutenant, 8th Hussars. Journalist, Theatrical agent, Chartered shipbroker; Chief executive, C T Bowring Trading (Holdings) Ltd 1974-80; Marketing consultant 1980-86.

Political career: *House of Lords:* First entered House of Lords 1984; Liberal Democrat: Deputy Chief Whip 1988-2001, Spokesperson for: National Heritage 1995-97, Culture, Media and Sport 1997-2005; Elected hereditary peer 1999-; Former Deputy Chair of Committees. Member: Overseas Trade 1984-85, Pre-legislative Gambling Joint Committee 2004-05; Works of Art: Member 2005-07, 2014-16, Chair 2007-13; Member, Lord Speaker's Advisory Panel on Works of Art 2017-. *Other:* Resigned Liberal Democrat Whip March 2011, now sits as Crossbench.

Political interests: Theatre, Europe, film industry, alcohol and drug addiction, transport (particularly motorcycling), racing and bloodstock; France, Sub-Saharan Africa.

Other: Tower Hamlets Mission, U Can Do It; *Clubs:* Brooks's Club. Sunningdale Golf.

Recreations: Golf, cinema, motorcycling, reading, racing.

The Viscount of Falkland, House of Lords, London SW1A 0PW
Tel: 020 7219 3230
Email: lordfalkland@aol.com

FALKNER OF MARGRAVINE, BARONESS

LIBERAL DEMOCRAT

FALKNER OF MARGRAVINE (Life Baroness), Kishwer Falkner; cr. 2004. Born 9 March 1955; Daughter of Ahsan Mohammad Khan and Saeeda Ahsan; Married Robert Falkner 1996 (1 daughter).

Education: St Joseph's Convent School, Karachi, Pakistan; London School of Economics (BSc (Econ) international relations 1992); Kent University (MA international relations and European studies 1994).

Non-political career: Deputy manager, Saudi Arabian Airlines, France and USA 1982-86; Senior researcher, Liberal Democrats, House of Commons 1992-93; Liberal Democrats: Director: International Affairs 1993-99, Policy 1997-98; Chief programme officer, Political Affairs Division, Commonwealth Secretariat 1999-2003; Chief executive, Student Partnerships Worldwide 2003-04. Commonwealth Secretariat Staff Association: Member 1999-2003, Vice-chair 2000-03.

Political career: *House of Commons:* Contested (Liberal Democrat) Kensington and Chelsea 2001 general election. *House of Lords:* Raised to the peerage as Baroness Falkner of Margravine, of Barons Court in the London Borough of Hammersmith and Fulham 2004. Liberal Democrat Spokesperson for: Home Affairs 2004-05, 2009-10, Communities and Local Government 2005-06, Children, Schools and Families 2007-08, Justice 2008-09, Foreign and Commonwealth Affairs 2009-10, 2015. Member, Human Rights Joint Committee 2005; Co-opted Member, EU Sub-committee C (Foreign Affairs, Defence and Development Policy) 2005-06; Member: Draft Legal Services Bill Joint Committee 2006, Intergovernmental Organisations 2007-08, Human Rights Joint Committee 2009-10, Constitution 2010-11, 2012-15, Joint Committee on National Security Strategy 2014-, European Union 2015-; Chair, EU Financial Affairs Sub-committee 2015-. Chair, Liberal Democrat Parliamentary Party Committee on International Affairs (FCO) 2010-15. *Other:* Contested London region 2004 European Parliament election. Liberal Democrat: Member, Federal Policy Committee 1999-2001, Chair, policy, London Liberal Democrats 2000-04, Member, Federal Executive 2010-.

Political interests: European and foreign affairs, political Islam, diversity and equality, constitution, governance, transitional democracies; Middle East, USA.

Other: Fellow: Kennedy School of Government, Harvard University 2006, St Antony's College, Oxford 2008. Chancellor, Northampton University 2008-16. Hon. Doc, Northampton University 2008.

Recreations: Travel, reading, cooking, running, cinema.

The Baroness Falkner of Margravine, House of Lords, London SW1A 0PW
Tel: 020 7219 2809 *Email:* falknerk@parliament.uk *Twitter:* @KishwerFalkner

FALL, BARONESS

CONSERVATIVE

FALL (Life Baroness), Catherine Susan Fall; cr 2015. Born 2 October 1967; Daughter of Sir Brian Fall, diplomat, and Delmar Alexandra Roos; Married Ralph Ward-Jackson 1996 (divorced 2010) (1 son 1 daughter).

Education: King's School, Canterbury (music scholar); St Hilda's College, Oxford (philosophy, politics, economics 1986).

Non-political career: Research assistant to Patricia Rawlings MEP; Special adviser to the Deputy Director-general, Confederation of British Industry; Conservative Research Department: Desk officer for Europe and agriculture, Head of Home Affairs Section; Assistant to: Michael Howard MP as Shadow Foreign Secretary, John Maples MP as Shadow Health Secretary; Political adviser, 1999 European Parliament election; Director, Atlantic Partnership; Deputy Chief of Staff to David Cameron MP as: Leader of the Opposition 2005-10, Prime Minister 2010-16; Senior Adviser, Brunswick Group LLP 2016-.

Political career: *House of Lords:* Raised to the peerage as Baroness Fall, of Ladbroke Grove in the Royal Borough of Kensington and Chelsea 2015. Member, Political Polling and Digital Media 2017-.

Other: Trustee, Atlantic Partnership.

The Baroness Fall, House of Lords, London SW1A 0PW
Tel: 020 7219 3000

FARMER, LORD

CONSERVATIVE

FARMER (Life Baron), Michael Stahel Farmer; cr 2014. Born 17 December 1944; Married Jenny (3 children).

Non-political career: Head of base metal trading, Phibro Salomon 1987-89; Chief executive, Metal & Commodity Company Ltd 1989-99; Managing Director: Merchanting, MG plc 1999-2000, Base metal trading, Enron Europe Ltd 2000-01; Senior partner, RK Capital Management 2005-.

Political career: *House of Lords:* Raised to the peerage as Baron Farmer, of Bishopsgate in the City of London 2014. Member, Social Mobility 2015-16. *Other:* Treasurer, Conservative and Unionist Party 2011-15. *Councils and public bodies:* Council member, Oakhill Theological College 2001-14; Sponsor governor, Ark All Saints Camberwell 2013-.

Other: Chair, Great St Helen's Trust 1996-2015; Trustee, Kingham Hill Trust 2001-14.

The Lord Farmer, House of Lords, London SW1A 0PW
Tel: 020 7219 3000 *Email:* callans@parliament.uk

FARRINGTON OF RIBBLETON, BARONESS

LABOUR

FARRINGTON OF RIBBLETON (Life Baroness), Josephine Farrington; cr. 1994. Born 29 June 1940; Daughter of late Ernest Joseph Cayless and Dorothy Cayless; Married Michael James Farrington 1960 (3 sons).

Political career: *House of Commons:* Contested (Labour) West Lancashire 1983 general election. *House of Lords:* Raised to the peerage as Baroness Farrington of Ribbleton, of Fulwood in the County of Lancashire 1994. Opposition Whip 1995-97; Government Whip 1997-2007, 2008-10; Government Spokesperson for: Local Government 1997-2001, Northern Ireland 1997-2007, Wales Office -2002, Environment and Rural Affairs 2001-07, Cabinet Office 2001-02, Women's Issues/Equality Agenda -2003. Member: Leader's Group on Members Leaving the House 2010-15, Delegated Powers and Regulatory Reform 2013-15, Procedure 2015-. *Councils and public bodies:* Councillor, Preston Borough Council 1973-76; Lancashire County Council: Councillor 1977-97, Chair, Education Committee 1981-91, Council Chair 1992-93; Association of County

Councils: Leader, Labour Group 1987-94, Chair, Policy Committee 1993-94, Chair 1994-96; Member: Burnham Primary and Secondary and Further Education Committees, National Advisory Body for Public Sector Higher Education.

Other: Council member, Europe Standing Conference of Local and Regional Authorities 1981-94; Chair, Council of Europe Culture, Education, Media and Sport Committee 1988-94; International observer at local elections in Poland, Ukraine and Albania; EU Committee of the Regions: Member 1994, Chair, Education and Training Committee 1994. UK Woman of Europe (1994).

Recreations: Reading.

The Baroness Farrington of Ribbleton, House of Lords, London SW1A 0PW
Tel: 020 7219 3104

FAULKNER OF WORCESTER, LORD

LABOUR

FAULKNER OF WORCESTER (Life Baron), Richard Oliver Faulkner; cr. 1999. Born 22 March 1946; Son of late Harold and Mabel Faulkner; Married Susan Heyes 1968 (2 daughters).

Education: Merchant Taylors' School, Northwood; Worcester College, Oxford (BA philosophy, politics and economics 1967, MA).

Non-political career: Graduate Armed Forces Parliamentary Scheme, attached to Royal Navy 2002-07. Research assistant and journalist, Labour Party 1967-69; Public relations officer, Construction Industry Training Board 1969-70; Editor, *Steel News* 1971; Account director, F J Lyons (Public Relations) Ltd 1971-73; Director, PPR International 1973-76; Government relations adviser to various companies, unions, councils and bodies 1973-99; *The House Magazine*: Co-founder, Member, Editorial Board 2003-; Communications adviser to Leader of the Opposition and Labour Party (unpaid) in general elections 1987, 1992, 1997; Communications adviser to Bishop at Lambeth 1990; Deputy chair, Citigate Westminster 1997-99 (Joint Managing Director, Westminster Communications Group 1989-97); Cardiff Millennium Stadium plc: Director 1997-2004, Deputy chair 2004-08; Strategy adviser, Littlewoods Leisure 1999-2009; Alderney Gambling Control Commission: Adviser 2005-08, Commissioner 2013-, Chairman 2014; Adviser on Railway Heritage, New South Wales Government 2012.

Political career: *House of Commons:* Contested (Labour) Devizes 1970, February 1974, Monmouth October 1974, Huddersfield West 1979 general elections. *House of Lords:* Raised to the peerage as Baron Faulkner of Worcester, of Wimbledon in the London Borough of Merton 1999. Departmental Liaison Peer: Department of the Environment, Transport and the Regions 2000-01, Cabinet Office 2001-05; Deputy Chairman of Committees 2007-09, 2010-; Deputy Speaker 2008-09, 2010-; Government Whip 2009-10; Trade Envoy to Taiwan 2016-. Chair, London Local Authorities Private Bill 2006; Member: Draft Gambling Bill Joint Scrutiny Committee 2003-04, London Local Authorities Private Bill 2006, Delegated Powers and Regulatory Reform 2007-09; Co-opted Member, European Union Sub-committee F (Home Affairs) 2009; Member: Administration and Works 2011-15, Joint Committee on the Rookery South (Resource Recovery Facility) Order 2012-13, Selection 2013-17, Olympic and Paralympic Legacy 2013-14, Sub-committee F: Home Affairs, Health and Education 2013-15; Alternate Member, Procedure 2014-15; Member: Equality Act 2010 and Disability 2015-16, Information 2015-16, EU Home Affairs Sub-committee 2015-16, Ecclesiastical Committee 2015-, Lord Speaker's Advisory Panel on Works of Art 2017-, Secondary Legislation Scrutiny 2017-, Natural Environment and Rural Communities Act 2006 2017-. *Other:* Member, National Policy Commission 2014. *Councils and public bodies:* Councillor, Merton Borough Council 1971-78; Member of Court, Bedfordshire University 1999-2009; ROSPA: President 2001-04, Vice-president 2004-; Science Museum Group: Trustee 2007-09, 2011-, Deputy Chair 2015-; President, College of Fellows, Worcester University 2014-.

Political interests: Transport, sport, human rights, smoking and health, sex equality; Argentina, Australia, Canada, Jamaica, Namibia, New Zealand, Norway, South Africa, Taiwan.

Other: Member: Inter-Parliamentary Union, Executive committee, Commonwealth Parliamentary Association UK 2003-05; Various posts numerous sports, especially football, including directorships of four football clubs; Patron, Roy Castle Lung Cancer Foundation 1999-2003, 2006-; Trustee Foundation for Sports and the Arts 2000-12; Vice-president, Campaign for Better Transport (Formerly Transport 2000 Ltd) 2001-; Director, West Somerset Railway 2004-05; Chair, Railway Heritage Committee 2004-09; Trustee: Gamcare 2005-09, National Football Museum 2007-09, 2012-16; Vice-president, Level Playing Field 2007-09, 2010-; President, Cotswold Line Promotion Group 2007-09, 2010-; Science Museum Group: Trustee 2008-09, 2011-, Deputy Chair 2014-; First Great Western Trains Advisory Board (now Great Western Railway Advisory Board): Member 2010-, Chair 2014-; President, Heritage Railway Association 2011-; Vice-President, Football Conference 2011-15; President, Old Merchant Taylors' Society 2011-12; Worcester Live: Patron and director 2011, Chairman 2014-; Patron, Myriad Centre 2012-; Chair, Railway Heritage

Designation Advisory Board 2013-; Patron, Guild of Battlefield Guides 2013-; President, Worcester College Oxford Society 2014-; Vice-President, National League 2015-; Chair, Museum of Science and Industry Advisory Board 2017-. Hon. Fellow, Worcester College, Oxford 2002; Hon. Doctor of Law, Luton University 2003; Fellow, Worcester University 2008. Diplomatic Medal of Honour, Government of Taiwan 2004; Order of the Brilliant Star with Grand Cordon, Government of Taiwan 2008.

Publications: Co-author, Holding the Line – How Britain's Railways Were Saved (Oxford Publishing Company, 2012); Disconnected! – Broken Links in Britain's Rail Policy (Oxford Publishing Company, 2015).

Recreations: Travelling by railway, collecting Lloyd George memorabilia, tinplate trains, watching Association Football.

The Lord Faulkner of Worcester, House of Lords, London SW1A 0PW
Tel: 020 7219 8503 *Fax:* 020 7219 1460 *Email:* faulknerro@parliament.uk
Website: www.lordfaulkner.net

FAULKS, LORD

CONSERVATIVE

FAULKS (Life Baron), Edward Peter Lawless Faulks; cr 2010. Born 19 August 1950; Son of His Honour Peter Faulks MC and Pamela Faulks, née Lawless; Married Catherine Turner 1990 (2 sons).

Education: Wellington College, Berkshire; Jesus College, Oxford; French.

Non-political career: Called to the Bar, Middle Temple 1973; Literary agent, Curtis Brown 1980-81; QC 1996; Assistant recorder 1996-2000; Recorder 2000-; Bencher 2002; Chair, Professional Negligence Bar Association 2002-04; Special adviser to Department for Constitutional Affairs on compensation culture 2005-06.

Political career: *House of Lords:* Raised to the peerage as Baron Faulks, of Donnington in the Royal County of Berkshire 2010. Ministry of Justice: Government Spokesperson 2013-16, Minister of State for: Civil Justice 2013-16, Legal Policy 2013-15. Member: Selection 2011, Joint Committees on: the Draft Detention of Terrorist Suspects (Temporary Extension) Bills 2011, Human Rights 2012-14, the Draft Communications Data Bill 2012-13; Member, Mental Capacity Act 2005 2013.

Political interests: Legal issues, constitution, education, medicine, conservation, human rights; India, Sri Lanka, USA.

Publications: Contributing editor, Local Authority Liability (2012).

Recreations: Sports, the arts.

The Lord Faulks QC, House of Lords, London SW1A 0PW
Tel: 020 7219 5353
1 Chancery Lane, London WC2A 1LF *Tel:* 020 7092 2900 *Email:* efaulks@1chancerylane.com

FEARN, LORD

LIBERAL DEMOCRAT

FEARN (Life Baron), Ronnie Cyril Fearn; cr. 2001. Born 6 February 1931; Son of late James Fearn and late Martha Fearn; Married Joyce Dugan 1955 (1 son 1 daughter).

Education: Norwood School; King George V Grammar School, Southport.

Non-political career: Royal Navy national service 1950-51. Banker, Royal Bank of Scotland 1947-87. Member, Association of Liberal Democrat Trade Unionists.

Political career: *House of Commons:* MP for Southport 1987-92 (Liberal/All 1987-88, Liberal Democrat 1988-92). Contested Southport 1992 general election. MP (Liberal Democrat) for Southport 1997-2001. Liberal Democrat: Deputy Chief Whip 1988-90, Spokesperson for: Tourism 1997-2001, Civil Service 1997-99, Constitution 1997. *House of Lords:* Raised to the peerage as Baron Fearn, of Southport in the County of Merseyside 2001. Co-opted Member, EU Sub-committee B (Energy, Industry and Transport/Internal Market) 2003-06; Member EU Sub-committee B: (Internal Market, Energy and Transport) 2010-12, (Internal Market, Infrastructure and Employment) 2012-15. *Councils and public bodies:* Councillor and Leader of Liberal Democrat Group: Southport Borough Council 1963-74, Merseyside Metropolitan County Council 1974-86; Councillor, Sefton Metropolitan Borough Council 1974-2016.

Political interests: Tourism, health, transport, leisure, local government.

Other: Member: Inter-Parliamentary Union, Commonwealth Parliamentary Association, Liberal International; Voluntary Youth Leader in Southport 1960-81; President, Local Carers' Association 1974-80; Local President, Sue Ryder Association 1975-85; Hon. Member, LIFE; Vice-president,

British Resorts Association 1987-; Southport Offshore Rescue Trust; Member, Institute of Bankers 1970; Fellow, Chartered Institute of Bankers. OBE 1985; *Clubs:* National Liberal, Southport Gladstone Liberal Club. Southport and Waterloo Athletic Club.

Recreations: Amateur dramatics, badminton, athletics, community work.

The Lord Fearn OBE, House of Lords, London SW1A 0PW
Tel: 020 7219 5116

LIBERAL DEMOCRAT

FEATHERSTONE, BARONESS

Liberal Democrat Lead Spokesperson for Energy and Climate Change

FEATHERSTONE (Life Baroness), Lynne Choona Featherstone; cr 2015. Born 20 December 1951; Daughter of late Joseph Woolf and Gladys Ryness; Married Stephen Featherstone 1982 (divorced 2002) (2 children).

Education: South Hampstead High School, London; Oxford Polytechnic (Diploma communications and design 1974); French.

Non-political career: Graphic designer, London and Australia 1974-77; Freelance designer 1977-80; Managing director, Inhouse Outhouse Design 1980-87; Strategic design consultant 1987-97; Director, Ryness Electrical Supplies Ltd 1991-2002.

Political career: *House of Commons:* Contested Hornsey and Wood Green 1997 and 2001 general elections. MP for Hornsey and Wood Green 2005-15. Contested Hornsey and Wood Green 2015 general election. Liberal Democrat: Spokesperson for: Home Affairs 2005-06, London 2006-07, Shadow Secretary of State for International Development 2006-07; Shadow Minister for Youth and Equalities 2008-10; Parliamentary Under-Secretary of State: (Minister for Equalities), Home Office and Government Equalities Office 2010-12, Department for International Development 2012-14; Minister of State for Crime Prevention, Home Office 2014-15. Member, Environmental Audit 2005-06. *House of Lords:* Raised to the peerage as Baroness Featherstone, of Highgate in the London Borough of Haringey 2015. Liberal Democrat Lead Spokesperson for Energy and Climate Change 2015-. *Other:* Member, Human Rights Committee, Liberal International 2016-. *Councils and public bodies:* London Borough of Haringey Council: Councillor 1998-2006, Leader of Opposition 1998-2003; London Assembly: Member 2000-05, Chair, Assembly Committee on Transport 2000-05; Member, Metropolitan Police Authority 2000-05.

Political interests: Energy and climate change, female genital mutilation, gay rights in Africa and Asia, disability in the Developing World, contaminated blood scandal; Africa, Asia.

Other: Member, Human Rights Committee Liberal International 2016-17. Unsung Hero award, *Daily Mail* 2002; Best Campaign Website, Orange Digital award 2010; Politician of the Year, *Attitude Magazine* 2012; Ally of the Year, *PinkNews* 2014; Politician of the Year, Stonewall 2014. PC 2014.

Publications: Marketing and Communications Techniques for Architects (Longman, 1992); Equal Ever After (Biteback, 2016).

Recreations: Writing poetry, film.

Rt Hon the Baroness Featherstone, House of Lords, London SW1A 0PW
Tel: 020 7219 3000 *Email:* featherstonel@parliament.uk *Twitter:* @lfeatherstone

CONSERVATIVE

FELDMAN OF ELSTREE, LORD

FELDMAN OF ELSTREE (Life Baron), Andrew Simon Feldman; cr 2010. Born 25 February 1966; Son of Malcolm and Marcia Feldman; Married Gabrielle Gourgey (2 sons 1 daughter).

Education: Haberdashers' Aske's School, Elstree; Brasenose College, Oxford (BA jurisprudence 1988).

Non-political career: Management consultant, Bain & Company 1988-90; Barrister, 1 Essex Court 1991-95; Chief executive, Jayroma 1995-.

Political career: *House of Lords:* Raised to the peerage as Baron Feldman of Elstree, of Elstree in the County of Hertfordshire 2010. *Other:* Conservative Party: Deputy treasurer 2005-08, Chief executive 2008-10, Co-chairman 2010-16, Chairman, party board 2010-16. *Councils and public bodies:* Board member, UK Holocaust Memorial Foundation 2015-.

Other: PC 2015.

Recreations: Tennis, golf.

Rt Hon the Lord Feldman of Elstree, House of Lords, London SW1A 0PW
Tel: 020 7219 5353

CROSSBENCH

FELLOWES, LORD

FELLOWES (Life Baron), Robert Fellowes; cr. 1999. Born 11 December 1941; Son of late Sir William Fellowes, KCVO and Lady Fellowes; Married Lady Jane Spencer, daughter of 8th Earl Spencer, LVO, and Hon. Mrs Shand Kydd 1978 (1 son 2 daughters).

Education: Eton College.

Non-political career: Short Service Commission, Scots Guards 1960-63. Director, Allen Harvey & Ross Ltd 1968-77; Private Office of HM The Queen: Assistant Private Secretary 1977-86, Deputy Private Secretary 1986-90, Private Secretary 1990-99; Barclays Private Bank: Vice-chair 1999-2000, Chair 2000-09; Non-executive director, SAB Miller 1999-2010; Secretary and registrar, Order of Merit 2003-.

Political career: *House of Lords:* Raised to the peerage as Baron Fellowes, of Shotesham in the County of Norfolk 1999. Member: Constitution 2001-04, Liaison 2009-13, Joint Committee on National Security Strategy 2010-14, Financial Exclusion 2016-17, Standing Orders (Private Bills) 2017-. *Councils and public bodies:* Board member, British Library 2007-16.

Political interests: Prison reform, constitution; USA.

Other: Winston Churchill Memorial Trust: Trustee 2001-16, Chair 2009-16; Rhodes Trust 2001-10; Chair, Prison Reform Trust 2001-08; Mandela-Rhodes Foundation 2003-10; Scots Guards 2006-; Vice-chair, Commonwealth Education Trust 2007-16; Goodenough College: President, Advisory Council 2008-13, Governor Emeritus 2014-; Trustee, King Edward VII Hospital, Sister Agnes 2010-13. Liveryman, Goldsmith's Company. LVO 1983; CB 1987; KCVO 1989; PC 1990; KCB 1991; GCVO 1996; GCB 1998; QSO 1999; *Clubs:* White's, Pratt's, Royal Overseas League Club. MCC.

Recreations: Golf, watching cricket, reading.

Rt Hon the Lord Fellowes GCB GCVO QSO, House of Lords, London SW1A 0PW
Tel: 020 7219 8754 *Email:* fellowesr@parliament.uk

CONSERVATIVE

FELLOWES OF WEST STAFFORD, LORD

FELLOWES OF WEST STAFFORD (Life Baron), Julian Alexander Kitchener-Fellowes; cr 2011. Born 17 August 1949; Son of late Peregrine Fellowes and Olwen Fellowes, née Stuart-Jones; Married Emma Kitchener LVO 1990 (1 son).

Education: Ampleforth College, Yorkshire; Magdalene College, Cambridge (BA); Webber Douglas Academy.

Non-political career: Actor: Joking Apart, Queen's Theatre 1978, Present Laughter, Vaudeville Theatre 1981, Futurists, Royal National Theatre, For the Greater Good 1991, Shadowlands 1993, Damage 1993, Our Friends in the North 1996, Tomorrow Never Dies 1997, Place Vendôme 1998, Aristocrats 1999, Monarch of the Glen 1999-2005; Producer, A Married Man 1982; Writer, Little Lord Fauntleroy 1994; Writer and co-producer, The Prince and the Pauper 1997; Writer, Gosford Park 2001; Writer and director, Separate Lies 2005; Writer: Vanity Fair 2005, The Young Victoria 2009; Writer and director, From Time to Time 2010; Writer and creator, Downton Abbey 2010-15. Member, Equity.

Political career: *House of Lords:* Raised to the peerage as Baron Fellowes of West Stafford, of West Stafford in the County of Dorset 2011. *Councils and public bodies:* DL, Dorset 2008; Member, Arts and Media Honours Committee.

Other: Chairman, Talking Books Appeal, RNIB 2003-; Vice-President, Weldmar Hospicecare Trust 2006-; President, Thomas Hardy Society 2007-; Ambassador: The Haven 2007-, Alzheimer's Society 2008-; Member, Appeal Council, National Memorial Arboretum 2009-; Vice-President, Catholic Association of Performing Arts 2010-; Member, National Advisory Council, RicNic Trust 2011-; Vice-Patron, Priory of England and the Islands, of the Order of St. John; Patron: Rainbow Trust 2005-, Help the Aged/Age UK 2007-, Changing Faces 2007-, Moviola 2008-, Lewiston School Appeal 2009-, AdLib, Association of Friends of Dorset Libraries 2010-, Bay Theatre, Weymouth College 2010-; Honorary Patron, Sleaford Playhouse 2011-. Hon. DLitt, Bournemouth 2007; Hon. DArts, Southampton Solent 2010. Best Screenplay, New York Film Critics' Award 2001; Best Screenplay, National Film Critics' Award 2001; Screenwriter of the Year, ShoWest 2002; Best Original Screenplay, Writer's Guild Award 2002; Best Original Screenplay, Academy Award 2002; Best Directorial Debut, National Board of Review 2006; Best Writer, British Press Guild Awards 2011; Outstanding Writing for a Mini-series, Emmy Awards 2011; *Clubs:* Boodle's, Pratt's, Annabel's Club.

Publications: Author: Snobs (2004), Past Imperfect (2008).

The Lord Fellowes of West Stafford, House of Lords, London SW1A 0PW
Tel: 020 7219 5353

NON-AFFILIATED

FILKIN, LORD

FILKIN (Life Baron), David Geoffrey Nigel Filkin; cr. 1999. Born 1 July 1944; Son of late Donald and Winifred Filkin; Married Elizabeth Tompkins 1974 (divorced 1994) (3 daughters); married Brigitte Paupy 2005.

Education: King Edward VI School, Birmingham; Clare College, Cambridge (MA history 1966); Manchester University (DipTP 1972); Birmingham University (management in local government); French.

Non-political career: Teacher on VSO, Ghana 1966-67; Town planner, Redditch Development Corporation (New Town) 1969-72; Manager, Brent Housing Aid Centre, London Borough of Brent 1972-75; Deputy chief executive, Merseyside Improved Housing 1975-79; Borough housing officer, Ellesmere Port and Neston Borough Council 1979-82; Director of housing, London Borough of Greenwich 1982-88; Chief executive: Reading Borough Council 1988-91, Association of District Councils 1991-97; Local government adviser, Joseph Rowntree Foundation 1997-2001; Director, New Local Government Network 1997-2001; Policy analyst and writer 1997-2001; Adviser, Capgemini plc 2005-12; Non-executive director, Accord plc 2005-07; Adviser: Serco 2006-, NCP 2006-; Chair: Public Sector Reform Group 2005-08, St Alban's Cathedral Music Trust 2006-10; Founder chair, 2020 Public Services Trust 2008-11; Chair, Centre for Ageing Better 2014-.

Political career: *House of Lords:* Raised to the peerage as Baron Filkin, of Pimlico in the City of Westminster 1999. Government Spokesperson for: Transport, Local Government and the Regions 2001-02, Health 2001-02; Government Whip 2001-02; Parliamentary Under-Secretary of State and Government Spokesperson for: Home Office 2002-03, Department for Constitutional Affairs 2003-04, Department for Education and Skills and Department for Work and Pensions 2004-05. Chair, Merits of Statutory Instruments 2005-09; Member, Leader's Group on the Working Practices of the House of Lords 2010-11; Alternate member, Procedure 2011-13; Chair, Public Service and Demographic Change 2012-13; Member, Procedure 2012-13.

Political interests: Policy development, policy implementation, housing; Southern Africa, West Africa.

Other: Parliament Choir: Founder chair 2000-, Trustee; Trustee, Southbank Sinfonia; Former member, Royal Town Planning Institute; Former associate member, Institute of Housing; Honorary Fellow, Chartered Institute of Purchasing and Supplies. CBE 1997.

Publications: Best Value for the Public; Political Leadership of Best Value; Partnerships for Best Value; Modernising Local Government; Starting to Modernise; Achieving Best Value; Towards a New Localism; Winning the e-Revolution; Strategic Partnering for Local Services; Co-author: Public Matters – Renewing the Public Realm (Methuen, 2007), Better Outcomes (2009).

Recreations: Music, walking, swimming, singing, church.

The Lord Filkin CBE, House of Lords, London SW1A 0PW
Tel: 020 7219 0640 *Email:* filking@parliament.uk
Email: gfilkin1@aol.com

CONSERVATIVE

FINK, LORD

FINK (Life Baron), Stanley Fink; cr 2011. Born 15 September 1957; Married Barbara Paskin (2 sons 2 daughters).

Education: Manchester Grammar School; Trinity Hall, Cambridge (LLB 1976).

Non-political career: Chartered accountancy training, Arthur Andersen 1980-82; Financial planning team, Mars Confectionery 1982-83; Vice-President, Citibank 1983-87; Man Group plc: Director, mergers acquisitions and treasury 1987-2000, Chief executive officer 2000, Deputy chairman 2008; Chief executive officer, International Standard Asset Management 2008-.

Political career: *House of Lords:* Raised to the peerage as Baron Fink, of Northwood in the County of Middlesex 2011. Member: Refreshment 2014, Audit 2014-, EU Financial Affairs Sub-committee 2016. *Other:* Treasurer, Conservative Party 2010-12, 2012-13.

Other: Member, Institute of Chartered Accountants 1982. Hon. Fellow, King's College London 2011.

Recreations: Skiing, golf.

The Lord Fink, House of Lords, London SW1A 0PW
Tel: 020 7219 5353

FINKELSTEIN, LORD

CONSERVATIVE

FINKELSTEIN (Life Baron), Daniel William Finkelstein; cr 2013. Born 30 August 1962; Son of late Prof Ludwik Finkelstein OBE and Mirjam Emma Weiner; Married Dr Nicola Ruth 1993 (3 sons).

Education: Hendon Preparatory School; University College School; London School of Economics (BSc economics 1984); City University (MSc 1986).

Non-political career: Political adviser to Dr David Owen MP as Leader of the Social Democrat Party 1986-91; Journalist, *Network* Magazine 1987-89; Editor, Connexion 1989-92; Associate editor, *New Moon* Magazine 1990-97; Director: Social Market Foundation 1992-95, Conservative Party Research Department 1995-98, Policy Unit, Conservative Central Office 1999-2001; *The Times*: Associate editor 2001-10, Comment editor 2004-08, Chief leader writer 2008-, Executive editor 2010-; Columnist, *Jewish Chronicle* 2004-; Editor, Comment Central, *Times* Online 2006-; Chair, Policy Exchange 2012-14.

Political career: *House of Commons:* Contested (SDP/All) Brent East 1987 and (Conservative) Harrow West 2001 general elections. *House of Lords:* Raised to the peerage as Baron Finkelstein, of Pinner in the County of Middlesex 2013. Member: Works of Art 2014-16, Lord Speaker's Advisory Panel on Works of Art 2017-, Communications 2017-. *Other:* Member, national committee, SDP 1986-90.

Other: Enterprise Europe: Chair 1990-95, Board member 1990-; Non-executive director, Equitable Life Assurance Society. OBE 1997.

The Lord Finkelstein OBE, House of Lords, London SW1A 0PW
Tel: 020 7219 5353 *Twitter:* @Dannythefink

FINLAY OF LLANDAFF, BARONESS

CROSSBENCH

FINLAY OF LLANDAFF (Life Baroness), Ilora Gillian Finlay; cr 2001. Born 23 February 1949; Daughter of Charles Beaumont Benoy Downman and Thaïs Helène, née Barakan; Married Andrew Yule Finlay CBE 1972 (1 son 1 daughter).

Education: Wimbledon High School, London; St Mary's Hospital, London University (MB BS 1972); French.

Non-political career: General practitioner 1981-86; Palliative medicine 1987-; Member, Expert Advisory Group on Cancers 1993-97, Chair, Association for Palliative Medicine 1995-98; Velindre NHS Trust Cancer Centre, Cardiff 1994-; National Cancer Forum 1997-2000; Vice-dean, School of Medicine, University of Wales College of Medicine 2000-05; President: Medical Women's Federations 2001-02, Chartered Society of Physiotherapy 2002-; Vice-president, Marie Curie Cancer Care 2004-; President, Royal Society of Medicine 2006-08; Chair: Palliative Care Strategy (Wales) Implementation Board 2008-14, Palliative Care Implementation Group Wales 2009-, Royal College of General Practitioners' Inquiry into Generalism 2011; President, British Medical Association 2014-15; Chair: UK Bioethics Program (UNESCO) 2015-, National Council for Palliative Care 2015-.

Political career: *House of Lords:* Raised to the peerage as Baroness Finlay of Llandaff, of Llandaff in the County of South Glamorgan 2001. Contested Crossbench Convener election 2011. Member: Science and Technology 2003-08, Science and Technology Sub-committees: I (Fighting Infection) 2003, II (Science and the Regional Development Agencies) 2003, I (Science and International Agreements) 2003-04, I (Ageing) 2004-05, Assisted Dying for the Terminally Ill Bill 2004-05, Mental Health Bill 2004-05, Science and Technology Sub-committees: I (Avian Flu) 2005-06, II (Conservation Science) 2005-06; Chair, Science and Technology Sub-committee I (Allergy) 2006-07; Co-opted member: Science and Technology Sub-committee II (Genomic Medicine) 2008-09, Science and Technology (Pandemic Influenza) 2008-09; Member: Public Service and Demographic Change 2012-13, Built Environment 2015-16. *Councils and public bodies:* Non-executive director, Gwent Health Authority 1995-2001; Member: Cancer Research UK Science Committee 2002-04, Cancer Strategy Board, National Assembly for Wales 2006-07, End of Life Care Strategy Board, Department of Health 2007-09, UK Drugs Policy Commission 2008-; Chair, National Mental Capacity Forum 2015-.

Political interests: Women's careers, medical ethics, Welsh affairs, health and medicine; China (Hong Kong), France, Netherlands, Spain.

Other: President, vice-president, patron of several organisations, especially concerned with palliative care, end of life care, multiple sclerosis, music and Foodbanks Cymru; Associate, Girls' Day School Trust 2005-; Member, BMA Medical Ethics Committee 2009-; Royal College of Physicians; Royal College of General Practitioners; Royal Society of Medicine; Association for Palliative Medicine, Great Britain & Ireland; FRCP, FRCGP, F Med Sci; Fellow, Academy of Medical

Sciences 2014; Honorary Fellow: Royal Society of Medicine 2009, Royal College of Surgeons Faculty of Dentistry 2009; Learned Society of Wales 2010; College of Emergency Medicine 2014; Faculty of Public Health 2015; Marie Curie Cancer Care, Changing Faces, MNDA, MS Society, Trussell Trust, National Council for Palliative Care, NSPCC. Honorary Doctor of Science: Glamorgan University, University of Wales, Worcester University; Honorary Fellow: Cardiff University, University of Wales Institute, Cardiff; Johanna Bijtel Professor, Gröningen University, Netherlands 2000-02; Honorary Professorial Associate, University of Melbourne 1996-2001. Welsh Woman of the Year 1996-97; Peer of the Year, Women in Public Life Awards 2008; Lifetime Achievement, Livery Company of Wales 2014 Innovator, Grassroots Diplomat 2015. Patron, Llandaff Rowing Club.

Publications: Co-author Care of the Dying – a clinical handbook (Churchill Livingstone, 1984); Co-editor: Medical Humanities, (BMJ Press, 2001), The Effective Management of Cancer Pain (Aesculapius Medical Press, 2000, 2001); Oral Care in Advanced Disease (Oxford University Press, 2005); Communication in Cancer (Oxford University Press, 2010); Many chapters in books and papers on palliative medicine, medical education, ethics and service provision.

Recreations: Cycling, family events.

The Baroness Finlay of Llandaff, House of Lords, London SW1A 0PW
Tel: 020 7219 6693 *Fax:* 020 7219 1991 *Email:* finlayi@parliament.uk
Email: finlayig@cardiff.ac.uk

CONSERVATIVE

FINN, BARONESS

FINN (Life Baroness), Simone Jari Finn; cr 2015. Born 10 June 1968; Daughter of Professor Jan Kubes and Morwenna Talfan Davies; Married Alex 1996 (1 son 1 daughter).

Education: Lady Margaret Hall, Oxford (BA history); French.

Non-political career: Manager, Coopers & Lybrand/PricewaterhouseCoopers 1991-98; Senior accountant, Financial Service Authority 1998-2001; Adviser on industrial relations to Cabinet Office 2010-11; Special adviser: to Francis Maude MP as Minister for the Cabinet Office and Paymaster General, Cabinet Office 2012-15, to Lord Maude of Horsham as Minister of State for Trade and Investment, Foreign and Commonwealth Office and Department for Business, Innovation and Skills 2015-16, to Sajid Javid MP as Secretary of State for Business, Innovation and Skills 2016; Partner, Francis Maude Associates.

Political career: *House of Lords:* Raised to the peerage as Baroness Finn, of Swansea in the County of West Glamorgan 2015. Member, Secondary Legislation Scrutiny 2017-. *Other:* Member, Conservative Party's Implementation Team 2009-10.

Political interests: Industrial relations, efficiency, Civil Service reform and diversity; China, Czech Republic, Hong Kong, India, Indonesia, Japan, Singapore, USA.

Other: Member, advisory board, Centre for Politics, Philosophy and Law, King's College London; ACA; ICAEW.

The Baroness Finn, House of Lords, London SW1A 0PW
Tel: 020 7219 3000 *Email:* finns@parliament.uk

CROSSBENCH

FLATHER, BARONESS

FLATHER (Life Baroness), Shreela Flather; cr. 1990. Born 13 February 1934; Daughter of Aftab and Krishna Rai; Married Gary Flather 1965 (2 sons).

Education: Attended schools in Buenos Aires, Delhi and Rio de Janerio; University College, London (LLB 1956); Hindi, some Spanish.

Non-political career: Called to the Bar, Inner Temple 1962; Infant teacher, ILEA 1965-67; Teacher of English as second language: Altwood Comprehensive School, Maidenhead 1968-74, Broadmoor Hospital 1974-78; Member, Committee of Management, Servite Houses Ltd 1987-94; Director: Meridian Broadcasting (MAI) Ltd 1990-2000, Marie Stopes International 1996-2017, Cable Corporation 1997-2000; Director, Kiss FM and Magic FM 1999-2002; Chair and Director, Club Asia 2002-06; Member, LWT Advisory Board 1993-2000; Chair, Star FM.

Political career: *House of Lords:* Raised to the peerage as Baroness Flather, of Windsor and Maidenhead in the Royal County of Berkshire 1990. Member: European Communities Sub-committee C 1990-95, Medical Ethics 1993-94, Intergovernmental Organisations 2007-08. *Other:* Member: Conservative Women's National Committee 1978-88, Anglo-Asian Conservative Society 1979-83, National Union Executive Committee, Conservative Party 1989-90; Resigned the Conservative Whip December 1998, rejoined November 1999, moved to Crossbenches 2008. *Councils and public bodies:* JP, Maidenhead 1971-90; Royal Borough of Windsor and Maidenhead: Councillor 1976-91, Mayor 1986-87; Senior posts in numerous organisations involved in refugee, community, carer, race relations and prison work, including: Member: Commission for Racial Equality 1980-86, BBC South and East Regional Advisory Council 1987-89, Social Security Advisory Committee 1987-90; Vice-chair, Refugee Council 1991-94; Governor, Commonwealth Institute 1993-98; President, Ethics Committee Broadmoor Hospital 1993-97; DL, Berkshire 1994-2009; Chair, Alcohol Education and Research Council 1995-2001; Joint President, Family Planning Association 1995-98; Member, Council of University College London 2000-06.

Political interests: Role of four million Indians in two World Wars, empowerment of women in South Asia and Africa, assisting family planning financially and with advocacy, negative impact of sharia law, disability of children from first cousin marriages; Africa, Indian sub-continent, including Burma.

Other: UK Representative, EU Advisory Commission on Racism and Xenophobia 1995-97; UK Member, Economic and Social Committee, European Community 1987-90; Trustee: Hillingdon Hospital 1990-98, Rajiv Gandhi (UK) Foundation 1993-2002; Member, Council, Winston Churchill Memorial Trust 1993-2008; Patron, Cedar Centre (community centre Isle of Dogs) 1994-2007; Member, Council of St George's House, Windsor Castle 1996-2002; Chair, Memorial Gates Trust (memorial on Constitution Hill) 1998-2009; Fellow, Industry and Parliament Trust 1998; Bookpower (providing low priced educational texts in developing countries) 2001-07; Pan African Health Foundation (auto disable syringe factory in Nigeria) 2004-; Member, Advisory Council, American Intercontinental University 2004-06; Patron: Population Matters 2011-, L'orchestre du Monde 2014-, Asian Women's Resource Centre 2014-, Commonwealth Countries League Education Fund, Corona Worldwide; Vice-president, Townswomen's Guilds; Associate Member, National Secular Society; Patron, Women's Council; Chair and Founder, Women Matter 2015-; Fellow: University College London, Royal Society of Arts; Memorial Gates, Fistula Hospital Addis Ababa, Trustee Friends of Seva Mandir. Honorary DUniv, Open University 1994; Honorary LLD, Leeds University 2008; Honorary Doctorate, Northampton University 2010. Asian of the Year, *Asian Who's Who* 1996; Asian Jewel Award 2003; Lifetime Achievement Award, Global NRI Institute 2011; Lifetime Achievement Award, GG2 2012. Pravasi Diwas Samman by President of India 2009.

Publications: Woman: Acceptable Exploitation for Profit (2010).

Recreations: Reading, cinema, travel.

The Baroness Flather DL, House of Lords, London SW1A 0PW
Tel: 020 7219 5353 *Fax:* 020 7219 5979

FLIGHT, LORD

CONSERVATIVE

FLIGHT (Life Baron), Howard Emerson Flight; cr 2011. Born 16 June 1948; Son of late Bernard Flight and late Doris Flight; Married Christabel Norbury 1973 (1 son 3 daughters).

Education: Brentwood School, Essex; Magdalene College, Cambridge (MA economics 1969); University of Michigan, USA (Power exchange scholar, MBA 1971); French.

Non-political career: Investment adviser, N M Rothschild 1970-73; Manager: Cayzer Ltd 1973-76, Wardley Ltd (HSBC) Hong Kong 1976-78, Merchant banking division, Hong Kong Bank, Bombay, India 1978-79; Director, investment division, Guinness Mahon 1979-86; Joint managing director, Guinness Flight Global Asset Management Ltd 1986-99; Investec Asset Management Ltd: Director 1987-, Chairman 1999-2003; Director, Panmure Gordon & Co 2002-07; Chairman, EIS Association 2005-; Commissioner, Guernsey Financial Services Commission 2006-; Chairman: CIM Investment Management Ltd 2006-, Flight and Partners 2007-; Director, Marechale Capital 2007-; Chairman: Downing Structured Opportunities VCT 1 plc 2009-; Director, Metrobank plc 2010-; Chairman, Aurora Investment Trust plc 2011-; Director: Edge Performance VCT plc 2011-, R5FX; Consultant: TISA, Kinetic Partners, Arden Partners plc; Member, advisory board: Financial Services Forum, Guinness Renewable Energy EIS Fund.

Political career: *House of Commons:* Contested Southwark (Bermondsey) February and October 1974 general elections. MP (Conservative) for Arundel and South Downs 1997-2005; Whip withdrawn March 2005. Shadow Economic Secretary, HM Treasury 1999-2001; Shadow Paymaster General 2001-02; Shadow Chief Secretary to the Treasury 2002-04; Special envoy to City of London 2004-05. Member: Environment, Transport and Regional Affairs 1997-98, Environment, Transport and Regional Affairs (Environment Sub-Committee) 1997-98, Social Security 1998-99. Joint Secretary, Conservative Party Committee for International Development 1997-98; Joint Chairman, Conservative Party Committee for Hong Kong 1997-2005; Secretary, Conservative Party Committees for: Finance 1999-2005, Social Security 1999-2005. *House of Lords:* Raised to the peerage as Baron Flight, of Worcester in the County of Worcestershire 2011. Member, EU Sub-committee A: (Economic and Financial Affairs and International Trade) 2011-12, (Economic and Financial Affairs) 2012-15; Member: Delegated Powers and Regulatory Reform 2015-, Economic Affairs Finance Bill Sub-committee 2017. *Other:* Chair, Cambridge University Conservative

Association 1968-69; Vice-chair, Federation of Conservative Students 1969; Conservative City Circle: Chairman 2002-05, President 2006-10; Deputy Chairman, Conservative Party 2004-05; Vice-President, Conservatives for Britain 2015-16. *Councils and public bodies:* Member, HMG Tax Consultative Committee to HM Treasury 1985-92; Commissioner, Guernsey Financial Services Commission 2005-; Governor and trustee, Brentwood School.

Political interests: Taxation, pensions, economic policy, farming, charities, venture capital, EMU, private finance initiative; China, India, South East Asia, USA.

Other: Trustee, Elgar Foundation 1979-; Fellow, Royal Society of Arts; Advisory Board, Institute for Economic Affairs; Chairman, Enterprise Investment Scheme Association 2005-; Trustee, Africa Research Institute 2006-; Council Member, Centre for Policy Studies 2008-; Chairman: 1900 Club 2008-, National Trust Croome Court Appeal Committee 2009-; Worcester Porcelein Museum, Wedgewood Collection Trust, Magdalene College Cambridge. Liveryman, Carpenters' Company. Freedom, City of London 1999; *Clubs:* Carlton, Pratt's, Boodles Club. Marden (Skiing).

Publications: All You Need to Know About Exchange Rates (1988).

Recreations: Skiing, classical music, antique collecting, gardening.

The Lord Flight, House of Lords, London SW1A 0PW
Tel: 020 7219 5353 *Email:* flighth@parliament.uk
Tel: 020 7222 7559 *Fax:* 020 7976 7059 *Email:* hflight@btinternet.com

CONSERVATIVE

FOOKES, BARONESS

FOOKES (Life Baroness), Janet Evelyn Fookes; cr. 1997. Born 21 February 1936; Daughter of late Lewis Fookes, company director, and late Evelyn Fookes, née Holmes.

Education: Hastings and St Leonards Ladies' College; Hastings High School for Girls; Royal Holloway College, London University (BA history 1957).

Non-political career: History and English teacher in independent schools 1958-70.

Political career: *House of Commons:* MP (Conservative) for Merton and Morden 1970-74, for Plymouth Drake 1974-97. Deputy Speaker and Second Deputy Chairman of Ways and Means 1992-97; Sponsored as Private Member's Bill: Sexual Offences Act 1985, Dangerous Dogs Act 1989. Chair, Education, Arts and Home Affairs sub-committee 1975-79; Member: Panel of Chairs 1976-92, Home Affairs 1984-92. *House of Lords:* Raised to the peerage as Baroness Fookes, of Plymouth in the County of Devon 1997. Member, Armed Forces Parliamentary Scheme 2001-; Deputy Chair of Committees 2002-; Deputy Speaker 2002-; Contested Lord Speaker election 2006. Member: Consolidation, Etc, Bills Joint Committee 2000-10, Hybrid Instruments 2002-10; Chair, Refreshments 2003-07; Member: Crossrail Bill 2008, Communications 2010-15; Delegated Powers and Regulatory Reform: Member 2013-15, Chair 2015-17. *Other:* Member, Association of Conservative Peers. *Councils and public bodies:* County Borough of Hastings: Councillor 1960-61, 1963-70, Chair, Education Committee 1967-70; DL, East Sussex -2001; Governor, Kelly College 2002-14.

Political interests: Health, defence, animal welfare, equal opportunities; Canada, New Zealand.

Other: Fellow, Industry and Parliament Trust 1978; Member: Commonwealth War Graves Commission 1987-97, Council of Management, College of St Mark and St John 1989-2004, Art Fund; Chair, ambassadors group, Tomorrow's People; Governor, Kelly College, Tavistock 2002-; President, War Widows Association of Great Britain; Hon. Fellow, Royal Holloway; RSPCA, SSAFA, Fellowship of St Nicholas, NSPCC. Worshipful Company of Gardeners 2005-. Hon. Freedom, City of Plymouth 2000; Freedom, City of London 2005. Honorary DLitt, Plymouth University; Honorary fellow, Royal Holloway College. DBE 1989.

Recreations: Swimming, gardening, theatre, yoga, opera.

The Baroness Fookes DBE, House of Lords, London SW1A 0PW
Tel: 020 7219 5899 *Email:* fookesj@parliament.uk

CROSSBENCH

FORD, BARONESS

FORD (Life Baroness), Margaret Anne Ford; cr 2006. Born 16 December 1957; Daughter of Edward Garland and Susan Garland, née Townsley; Married David Bolger 1990 (1 son 1 daughter from previous marriage 1 stepson).

Education: St Michael's Academy, Kilwinning; Glasgow University (MA arts 1979, MPhil economics 1984).

Non-political career: Local government officer, Cunninghame District Council 1979-82; Scottish organiser, Banking Insurance and Finance Union 1982-87; Management consultant, Price Waterhouse & Co 1987-90; Director, Scottish Homes 1990-93; Founder and managing director, Eglinton Management Centre 1993-99; Founder and chief executive, Good Practice Ltd 2000-07; Managing director, Royal Bank of Canada Capital Markets 2007-09; Non-executive director: Thus plc 2002-05, Serco plc 2003-10, Segro plc 2013-, Taylor Wimpey plc 2013-; Non-executive Chairman, Grainger plc 2008-, May Gurney Integrated Services plc 2011-13, Barchester Healthcare Ltd 2011-15, STV plc 2013. Branch secretary, NALGO 1979-82; Scottish organiser, BIFU 1982-87.

Political career: *House of Lords:* Raised to the peerage as Baroness Ford, of Cunninghame in North Ayrshire 2006. Member, Political Polling and Digital Media 2017-. *Other:* Resigned Labour Whip February 2013; Joined Crossbenches October 2016. *Councils and public bodies:* Non-executive director, Scottish Prison Service 1993-97; Chair, Lothian Health Board 1997-2000; Non-executive director, Gas and Electrical Markets Authority (Ofgem) 2000-04; Chair: English Partnerships 2002-07, Olympic Park Legacy Company 2009-12.

Political interests: Regeneration, housing, planning, energy, public sector reform; Australia, USA.

Other: President, British Epilepsy Association 2008-; Chairman, STV Appeal 2013-; Trustee, Tennis Foundation 2013-; Member, Scottish Economic Council 1997-2000; Chairman, Irvine Bay Urban Regeneration Company 2006-10; Hon. Member, Royal Institute of Chartered Surveyors; Member, Royal Television Society; Fellow, Royal Society of Edinburgh 2015-; Epilepsy Action. D.BA, Napier University; D.Univ, Stirling University.

Publications: Contributor, Anatomy of New Scotland (Mainstream Publishing, 2002); Leadership Development: How Government Works (Audit Scotland, 2005).

Recreations: Family, fine art, music, gardening, sport (all kinds).

The Baroness Ford, House of Lords, London SW1A 0PW
Tel: 020 7219 5439 *Email:* fordm@parliament.uk

FORSYTH OF DRUMLEAN, LORD

CONSERVATIVE

FORSYTH OF DRUMLEAN (Life Baron), Michael Bruce Forsyth; cr. 1999. Born 16 October 1954; Son of John T. Forsyth; Married Susan Clough 1977 (1 son 2 daughters).

Education: Arbroath High School; St Andrews University (MA).

Non-political career: Director, Robert Fleming & Co Ltd 1997-2000; J P Morgan 2000-: Vice-chair, investment banking Europe 2000-02, Deputy chair (UK) 2002-05; Non-executive director: J & J Denholm 2005-, Denholm Industrial Service (Holdings) Ltd 2006-; Evercore Partners: Senior adviser 2006-07, Senior managing director 2007-.

Political career: *House of Commons:* MP (Conservative) for Stirling 1983-97. PPS to Geoffrey Howe as Foreign Secretary 1986-87; Parliamentary Under-Secretary of State, Scottish Office 1987-90; Minister of State: Scottish Office with responsibility for Health, Education, Social Work and Sport 1990-92, Department of Employment 1992-94, Home Office 1994-95; Secretary of State for Scotland 1995-97. *House of Lords:* Raised to the peerage as Baron Forsyth of Drumlean, of Drumlean in Stirling 1999. Member: Monetary Policy of the Bank of England 2000-01, House of Lords Reform Joint Committee 2002-05, Barnett Formula 2008-09, Economic Affairs 2008-13, 2015-17, Soft Power and the UK's Influence 2013-14, Joint Committee on National Security Strategy 2014-15, Economic Affairs Finance Bill Sub-committee 2015-16; Chair, Economic Affairs 2017-. *Other:* President, St Andrews University Conservative Association 1973-76; Member, Executive Committee, National Union of Conservative and Unionist Associations 1975-77; Chair: Federation of Conservative Students 1976-77, Scottish Conservative Party 1989-90; Vice-President, Conservatives for Britain 2015-16. *Councils and public bodies:* Councillor, Westminster City Council 1978-83; Member: Commission on Strengthening Parliament 1999-2000, Development Board, National Portrait Gallery 2000-03; Chair, Tax Reform Commission 2005-06.

Political interests: Local government, privatisation, economics, healthcare, education, environment, constitution.

Other: Director, Centre for Policy Studies 2006-; Patron: Craighalbent Centre for Children with motor impairments, Children in Need Institute (UK), working in India 2008-; Vote Leave: Board member 2016, Member, Campaign committee 2016; President, Steam Boat Association of Great Britain; Save the Children, Debra, St Mungus. Highland Park/*The Spectator*: Member to Watch 1993, Parliamentarian of the Year 1996. PC 1995; KB 1997.

Publications: Various pamphlets on privatisation and local government.

Recreations: Mountaineering, photography, gardening, fly-fishing, astronomy.

Rt Hon the Lord Forsyth of Drumlean, House of Lords, London SW1A 0PW
Tel: 020 7219 3000 *Email:* forsythm@parliament.uk

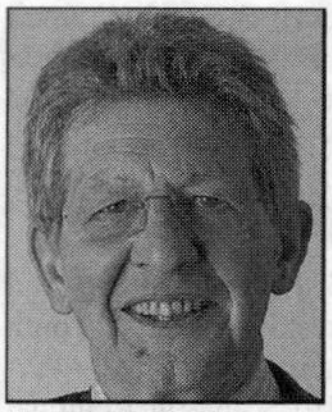

LIBERAL DEMOCRAT

FOSTER OF BATH, LORD

FOSTER OF BATH (Life Baron), Donald Michael Ellison Foster; cr 2015. Born 31 March 1947; Son of late John Foster, vicar, and late Iris Foster, née Ellison; Married Victoria Pettegree 1968 (1 son 1 daughter).

Education: Lancaster Royal Grammar School; Keele University (BSc physics and psychology 1969; CEd 1969); Bath University (MEd 1981); French (enthusiastic).

Non-political career: Science teacher, Sevenoaks School, Kent 1969-75; Science project director, Resources for Learning Development Unit, Avon LEA 1975-80; Education lecturer, Bristol University 1980-89; Management consultant, Pannell Kerr Forster 1989-92; Associate, Global Partners Governance 2016-.

Political career: *House of Commons:* Contested (Liberal/All) Bristol East 1987 general election. MP (Liberal Democrat) for Bath 1992-2010, for Bath (revised boundary) 2010-15. Liberal Democrat: Spokesperson for: Education 1992-95, Education and Employment 1995-97; Principal Spokesperson for: Environment, Transport, the Regions and Social Justice 1999-2001, Transport, Local Government and the Regions 2001-02, Shadow Secretary of State for: Transport 2002-03, Culture, Media and Sport 2003-10; Sponsored Live Music Act 2012; Parliamentary Under-Secretary of State, Department for Communities and Local Government 2012-13; Member, Parliamentary and Political Service Honours Committee 2013-15; Deputy Chief Whip (Comptroller of HM Household) 2013-15. Member: Education and Employment 1996-99, Education and Employment (Education Sub-Committee) 1997-99, Joint Committee on Security 2013-15. Chair, Liberal Democrat Parliamentary Party Committee on Culture, Media and Sport 2010-12. *House of Lords:* Raised to the peerage as Baron Foster of Bath, of Bath in the County of Somerset 2015. Liberal Democrat Shadow Secretary of State for Business and Industrial Strategy 2016-17. Member, Licensing Act 2003 2016-17. *Other:* President, Liberal Democrat Youth and Students 1993-95. *Councils and public bodies:* Councillor, Avon County Council 1981-89; Executive, Association of County Councils 1985-89; Joint Hon. President, British Youth Council 1992-99.

Political interests: Education, local and regional government, transport, culture, media, sport and tourism, international development; Africa, Iraq.

Other: Vice-chair, British Association for Central and Eastern Europe 1994-97; Trustee, Open School and Education Extra 1993-99; National Campaign for Nursery Education: Vice-chair 1993-99, President 1999-2001; President, British Association for Early Childhood Education 1998-2002; Governor, Westminster Foundation for Democracy 2010-; Member, Olympic Board 2010-12; CPhys; MInstP; Water Aid, Patron, Designability. Honorary Fellow, Bath College of High Education 1995; Honorary Doctor of Letters, Bath University 2016. Sports Parliamentarian of the Year 2011. PC 2010.

Publications: Resource-based Learning in Science (1979); Science With Gas (1981); Co-author: Aspects of Science (1984), Reading About Science (1984), Nuffield Science (1986); Teaching Science 11-13 (1987); From the Three Rs to the Three Cs (2003); Numerous educational and political articles and pamphlets.

Recreations: Classical music, travel, sport, modern ballet.

Rt Hon the Lord Foster of Bath, House of Lords, London SW1A 0PW
Tel: 020 7219 6332 *Email:* fosterdon@parliament.uk *Twitter:* @TheDon_Foster

LABOUR

FOSTER OF BISHOP AUCKLAND, LORD

FOSTER OF BISHOP AUCKLAND (Life Baron), Derek Foster; cr 2005. Born 25 June 1937; Son of Joseph Foster, shipyard worker; Married Florence Anne Bulmer 1972 (3 sons 1 daughter).

Education: Bede Grammar School, Sunderland; Oxford University (BA philosophy, politics and economics 1960); French, German.

Non-political career: Private sector marketing 1960-70; Durham County Council: Youth and community worker 1970-73, Further education organiser 1973-74; Assistant director of education, Sunderland Borough Council 1974-79. Member, National Union of Teachers.

Political career: *House of Commons:* MP (Labour) for Bishop Auckland 1979-2005. Opposition Whip 1981-82; Opposition Frontbench Spokesperson for Social Security 1982-83; PPS to Neil Kinnock as Leader of Opposition 1983-85; Opposition Chief Whip 1985-95; Shadow Chancellor of the Duchy of Lancaster 1995-97. Chair: Education and Employment 1994-2001, Employment Sub-Committee 1997-2001. *House of Lords:* Raised to the peerage as Baron Foster of Bishop Auckland, of Bishop Auckland in the County of Durham 2005. Member: Equality Act 2010 and Disability 2015-16, Natural Environment and Rural Communities Act 2006 2017-. *Other:* Ex-officio member, Labour Party National Executive Committee 1985-95; Chair, Labour Manufacturing

Industry Group. *Councils and public bodies:* Councillor: Sunderland County Borough Council 1972-74, Tyne and Wear County Council 1973-77; Chair: North of England Development Council 1974-76, National Prayer Breakfast 1998-99; Member, Advisory Committee for the Registration of Political Parties 1998; DL, Durham 2001-.

Political interests: Youth affairs, education and training, regional policy, socialist enterprise, transport, economics, finance, small businesses, education; Africa, Japan, USA.

Other: Uniformed member, Salvation Army; Vice-chair, Youthaid 1979-83; Fellow, Industry and Parliament Trust 1983; Vice-chair, Youth Affairs Lobby 1984-86; Hon President, British Youth Council 1984-86; Vice-President, Christian Socialist Movement 1985-; Member, National Advisory Board, Salvation Army 1995-; Chair: Pioneering Care Partnership 1997-, North Regional Information Society Initiative 1997-2000; Non-executive director, Northern Informatics 1998-; Chair: Regional Electronics Economy Project 2000-, Bishop Auckland Development Company Ltd; President, South West Durham Training; Chair, e-Learning Foundation North East; Trustee: Auckland Castle, National e-Learning Foundation; Member: Fabian Society, Christian Socialists Society; Companion of the Institution of Lighting Engineers 2001; Salvation Army, Fabian Society. Doctor of Civil Law, Durham University. PC 1993. Durham County Cricket.

Recreations: Brass bands, male voice choirs, cricket, soccer.

Rt Hon the Lord Foster of Bishop Auckland DL, House of Lords, London SW1A 0PW
Tel: 020 7219 6500 *Email:* fosterderek@parliament.uk

FOULKES OF CUMNOCK, LORD

LAB/CO-OP

FOULKES OF CUMNOCK (Life Baron), George Foulkes; cr 2005. Born 21 January 1942; Son of late George Horace Foulkes, engineer, and late Jessie Foulkes, principal nursing officer; Married Elizabeth Hope 1970 (2 sons 1 daughter).

Education: Keith Grammar School, Banff; Haberdashers' Aske's School; Edinburgh University (BSc psychology 1964) (President, Edinburgh University SRC 1963-64); Conversational Spanish.

Non-political career: Territorial Army 1961-64. President, Scottish Union of Students 1964-66; Director, European League for Economic Co-operation 1966-68; Scottish organiser, European Movement 1968-69; Director: Enterprise Youth 1969-73, Age Concern Scotland 1973-79; Chairman, advisory committee, GovNet 2008-. Member, GMB.

Political career: *House of Commons:* Contested Edinburgh West 1970 and Edinburgh Pentlands October 1974 general elections. MP (Labour) for South Ayrshire 1979-83, for Carrick, Cumnock and Doon Valley 1983-2005. Opposition Frontbench Spokesperson for: Europe 1983-85, Foreign and Commonwealth Affairs 1985-92, Defence, Disarmament and Arms Control 1992-93, Overseas Development 1994-97; Parliamentary Under-Secretary of State, Department of International Development 1997-2001; Minister of State, Scotland Office 2001-02. *House of Lords:* Raised to the peerage as Baron Foulkes of Cumnock, of Cumnock in East Ayrshire 2005. Member, Intelligence and Security Committee 2007-10. Co-opted Member, European Union Sub-committee F (Home Affairs) 2006-07; Member: Joint Committee on National Security Strategy 2010-13, EU Sub-Committee G (Social Policies and Consumer Protection) 2011-12, European Union 2011-15, EU Sub-committee C (External Affairs) 2012-15, Soft Power and the UK's Influence 2013-14, Liaison 2015-; Alternate Member, Procedure 2015-; Member: Charities 2016-17, Political Polling and Digital Media 2017-. *Other:* Scottish Parliament: MSP for Lothians region 2007-11 (as George Foulkes). Chair, Labour Campaign for a Scottish Parliament -1997; Member, Co-operative Party; Chair, Scottish Group PLP 2015-17. *Councils and public bodies:* Councillor: Edinburgh Corporation 1970-75, Lothian Regional Council 1974-79; Chair: Lothian Region Education Committee 1974-79, Education Committee, Convention of Scottish Local Authorities 1975-78; JP, Edinburgh 1975.

Political interests: International development, foreign affairs, devolution, energy, human rights, defence, Scotland, financial regulation; Latin America, Caribbean, China, EU, Russia.

Other: Delegate, Parliamentary Assemblies of the Council of Europe and Western European Union 1979-80; Executive Committee, Commonwealth Parliamentary Association (UK Branch): Member 1989-97, 2011-15, Vice-chair 2015-; Executive member: British Section of Inter-Parliamentary Union 1989-97, Socialist International 2004-08; Delegate, Parliamentary Assembly of the Council of Europe 2016-; Rector's assessor, Edinburgh University 1968-71; Director, Co-operative Press 1990-97; Chair, John Wheatley Centre 1990-97; Trustee, Commonwealth Parliamentary Association Funds 1998-2008; Chair, Heart of Midlothian FC 2004-05; President, Caribbean Council 2011-16, Treasurer, Climate Parliament 2015-16; Chair, Age Scotland 2016-; Age Scotland, Ayrshire Hospice, Garvald Edinburgh. Wilberforce Medal 1998; Order of Merit of Duarte, Sanchez & Mella (Dominican Republic). PC 2000; *Clubs:* Royal Scots Club.

Publications: Editor, 80 Years On (History of Edinburgh University SRC); Chapters in: Scotland – A Claim of Right, Football and the Commons People.

Recreations: Boating, Heart of Midlothian FC season ticket holder and shareholder.

Rt Hon the Lord Foulkes of Cumnock, House of Lords, London SW1A 0PW
Tel: 020 7219 3474 *Email:* foulkesg@parliament.uk
Website: lordgeorgefoulkes.wordpress.com *Twitter:* @GeorgeFoulkes

LORD SPEAKER

FOWLER, LORD

Lord Speaker

FOWLER (Life Baron), Peter Norman Fowler; cr. 2001. Born 2 February 1938; Son of late N F and Katherine Fowler; Married Fiona Poole, née Donald 1979 (2 daughters).

Education: King Edward VI School, Chelmsford; Trinity Hall, Cambridge (BA economics and law 1961, MA).

Non-political career: Commissioned national service, Essex Regiment 1956-58. *The Times*: Special correspondent 1961-66, Home affairs correspondent 1966-70; Non-executive director, NFC plc 1990-97; Non-executive chair: Midland Independent Newspapers 1991-98, National House Building Council 1992-98, Regional Independent Media 1998-2002, Numark plc 1998-2005, Aggregate Industries plc 2000-06; Non-executive director, Holcim Ltd 2006-09; Member, Advisory Council, Electra QMC Europe Development Capital Fund plc 2006-08; Non-executive director: ABTA 2009-16.

Political career: *House of Commons:* MP (Conservative) for Nottingham South 1970-74, for Sutton Coldfield February 1974-2001. PPS to Minister of State for Northern Ireland 1972-74; Opposition Spokesperson for Home Affairs 1974-75; Chief Opposition Spokesperson for: Social Services 1975-76, Transport 1976-79; Minister of Transport 1979-81; Secretary of State for: Transport 1981, Social Services 1981-87, Employment 1987-90; Shadow Secretary of State for: Environment, Transport and the Regions 1997-98, the Home Department 1998-99. *House of Lords:* Raised to the peerage as Baron Fowler, of Sutton Coldfield in the County of West Midlands 2001. Lord Speaker 2016-; Chair, House of Lords Commission 2016-. Chair: Review of the BBC Charter 2005-06, Communications 2007-10, HIV and AIDS in the UK 2010-11; Member, Procedure 2016-. *Other:* Chair, Cambridge University Conservative Association 1960; Editorial board, *Crossbow* 1962-70; Vice-chair, North Kensington Conservative Association 1967-68; Chair: East Midlands Conservative Political Centre 1970-73, Conservative Party 1992-94; Member, Executive Association of Conservative Peers 2001-04; Vice-chairman, Association of Conservative Peers 2005-10.

Political interests: HIV/AIDS, media; Middle East.

Other: President, Commonwealth Parliamentary Association (UK Branch) 2016-; Hon. President, Inter-Parliamentary Union, British Group 2016-; Council member, Bow Group 1967-69; Chairman: Thomson Foundation, Hansard Society 2015-. Honorary Doctorate, City of Birmingham University 2011. PC 1979; Kt 1990; *Clubs:* Garrick, Hurlingham, Seaview Yacht Club.

Publications: After the Riots (1979); Ministers Decide (1991); A Political Suicide (2008).

Rt Hon the Lord Fowler, House of Lords, London SW1A 0PW
Tel: 020 7219 6444 *Email:* lordspeaker@parliament.uk fowlern@parliament.uk

LIBERAL DEMOCRAT

FOX, LORD

Liberal Democrat Shadow Secretary of State for Business, Energy and Industrial Strategy

FOX (Life Baron), Christopher Francis Fox; cr 2014. Born 27 September 1957; Son of Andrew and Elizabeth Fox; Married Sarah (1 daughter).

Education: Minster School, Leominster; Imperial College (BSc analytical chemistry and geology) (President, Imperial College Students' Union 1980).

Non-political career: Field engineer 1981-85; Editor, offshore engineer 1985-90; Communications manager, Schlumberger Inc 1990-98; Director of corporate relations, Tate & Lyle 1998-2005; Director of communications, Smiths Group 2005-09; Director of group communications, GKN Plc 2012-17; Director, Vulpes Advisory Ltd.

Political career: *House of Lords:* Raised to the peerage as Baron Fox, of Leominster in the County of Herefordshire 2014. Liberal Democrat Shadow Secretary of State for Business, Energy and Industrial Strategy 2017-. Member, Science and Technology 2015-. *Other:* Chief executive, Liberal Democrats 2009-11. *Councils and public bodies:* Councillor, Hounslow Borough Council 1994-98.

Political interests: Engineering, manufacturing, technology, education, business.

Other: Ambassador, Wave Trust; *Clubs:* MCC Club.

Recreations: Season ticket holder, Arsenal FC.

The Lord Fox, House of Lords, London SW1A 0PW
Tel: 020 7219 3215 *Email:* foxc@parliament.uk

FRAMLINGHAM, LORD

CONSERVATIVE

FRAMLINGHAM (Life Baron), Michael Nicholson Lord; cr 2011. Born 17 October 1938; Son of late John Lord, headmaster; Married Jennifer Childs 1965 (1 son 1 daughter).

Education: William Hulme's Grammar School, Manchester; Christ's College, Cambridge (MA agriculture 1962) (Cambridge Rugby Blue).

Non-political career: Farmer and agriculture tutor 1962-66; Director, Power Line Maintenance Ltd 1966-68; Founded Lords Tree Services Ltd 1968; Aboricultural Consultant 1983.

Political career: *House of Commons:* Contested Manchester Gorton 1979 general election. MP (Conservative) for Central Suffolk 1983-97, for Central Suffolk and North Ipswich 1997-2010. PPS to John MacGregor: as Minister of Agriculture, Fisheries and Food 1984-85, as Chief Secretary to the Treasury 1985-87; Second Deputy Chairman, Ways and Means and Deputy Speaker 1997-2010; Contested Speaker elections 2000, 2009. Member: Chairmen's Panel 1997-2010, Court of Referees 1997-2010, Standing Orders 1998-2010, Unopposed Bills (Panel) 2000-10. *House of Lords:* Raised to the peerage as Baron Framlingham, of Eye in the County of Suffolk 2011. *Councils and public bodies:* North Bedfordshire Borough Council: Councillor 1974-77, Chair, Policy Committee 1974-77; Bedfordshire County Council: Councillor 1981-83, Chair, Further Education Committee 1981-83.

Political interests: Agriculture, forestry, environment.

Other: Parliamentary delegate, Council of Europe and Western European Union 1987-91; Member, Executive Committee, Inter-Parliamentary Union British Group 1995-97; President, Arboricultural Association 1989-95; Captain, Parliamentary Golfing Society 1999-2002; FArbA. Kt 2001. Hawks Club.

Recreations: Golf, sailing, gardening.

The Lord Framlingham, House of Lords, London SW1A 0PW
Tel: 020 7219 5353

FRASER OF CORRIEGARTH, LORD

CONSERVATIVE

FRASER OF CORRIEGARTH (Life Baron), Alexander Andrew Macdonell Fraser; cr 2016. Born 2 December 1946; Son of Lord Fraser of Tullybelton; Married Sarah Joanna Jones 1982 (divorced); Married Rebecca Shaw-Mackenzie 2010.

Education: Eton College; St John's College, Oxford (MA philosophy, politics and economics); French.

Non-political career: Worked in the City, including Vickers da Costa, Sun Hung Kai Securities; Director, Barings Bank; Chief executive, Baring Securities; Director, Asia Frontier Capital Ltd.

Political career: *House of Lords:* Raised to the peerage as Baron Fraser of Corriegarth, of Corriegarth in the County of Inverness 2016. Member, EU Financial Affairs Sub-committee 2017-. *Other:* Treasurer, Conservative Party 2015-16.

Political interests: Financial affairs, defence, Scotland; China, North Korea, Scotland, Vietnam.

Other: Treasurer, Better Together Campaign 2013-14; New Foundation Fellow, Eton College; Member, Court of Benefactors, Oxford University; *Clubs:* White's, Brooks's, Leander Club.

The Lord Fraser of Corriegarth, House of Lords, London SW1A 0PW
Tel: 020 7219 3000
Email: andrewfraser1946@gmail.com

CONSERVATIVE

FREEMAN, LORD

FREEMAN (Life Baron), Roger Norman Freeman; cr. 1997; PC 1993. Born 27 May 1942; Son of Norman Freeman CBE and Marjorie Freeman; Married Jennifer Watson OBE 1969 (1 son 1 daughter).

Education: Whitgift School, Croydon; Balliol College, Oxford (BA philosophy, politics and economics 1964); Institute of Chartered Accountants, England and Wales (ACA 1968).

Non-political career: Managing director, Bow Publications Ltd 1968-69; Partner, Lehman Bros 1969-86; Director, Martini & Rossi UK Ltd and Baltic Leasing Group plc -1986; PricewaterhouseCoopers (PWC): Partner, Corporate Finance Division 1997-98, Adviser 1999-, Chair, UK Advisory Board, PWC 2000-17; Chair, advisory board, Thales UK plc 1999-2013; Director, Thales SA 1999-2012; Chair, Cambridge Enterprise Ltd 2006-10; Director: Chemring Group plc 2006-14, Global Energy Development plc 2006-10; Director and former chair, Parity Group plc 2007-17; Chair: Security Innovation and Technology Consortium Ltd (Public Sector Sponsored) 2008-11, Big DNA Ltd 2008-14; Director: Saville Group plc 2008-13, ITM Energy plc 2010-.

Political career: *House of Commons:* Contested Don Valley 1979 general election. MP (Conservative) for Kettering 1983-97. Parliamentary Under-Secretary of State: for the Armed Forces 1986-88, Department of Health 1988-90; Minister of State for: Public Transport, Department of Transport 1990-94, Defence Procurement, Ministry of Defence 1994-95; Chancellor of the Duchy of Lancaster and Cabinet Minister for Public Service 1995-97. *House of Lords:* Raised to the peerage as Baron Freeman, of Dingley in the County of Northamptonshire 1997. Co-opted Member, Science and Technology Sub-committee II (Innovations in Computer Processors/Microprocessing/ Science and the Regional Development Agencies) 2002-03; Member, Speakership of the House 2003, 2005; Co-opted Member, EU Sub-committee C (Foreign Affairs, Defence and Development Policy) 2005-06; Member, European Union 2006-10; Chair, EU Sub-committee B (Internal Market) 2006-10; Member: Selection 2011, Joint Committee on the Draft Detention of Terrorist Suspects (Temporary Extension) Bills 2011, EU Sub-committee B (Internal Market, Infrastructure and Employment) 2013-15, Built Environment 2015-16, EU Internal Market Sub-committee 2015-16, High Speed Rail (London-West Midlands) Bill 2016-17. *Other:* President, Oxford University Conservative Association 1964; Chief financial officer, Conservative Central Office 1984-86; Special adviser on Candidates, Conservative Party 1997-2001; Association of Conservative Peers: Member Executive 2005-09, Vice-chair 2017-.

Political interests: International development, defence reservists, pensions, technology investment; Africa, in particular Sierra Leone, Uganda.

Other: Treasurer, Bow Group 1967-68; President: Council of the UK Reserve Forces and Cadets Association 1999-2011, British International Freight Association 1999-2002; Chair: Busoga Trust 2000-10, Skill Force Development 2004-; Trustee, National Army Museum 2005-11; Co-chair, UK-Sierra Leone Business Forum 2005-07; Fellow, Institute of Chartered Accountants, England and Wales; Busoga Trust. PC 1993; *Clubs:* Chairman, Carlton Club 2010-13.

Publications: Fair Deal for Water (1986); Democracy in the Digital Age (1997); All Change, British Railway Privatisation (2000); Spin out Companies (2004).

Rt Hon the Lord Freeman, House of Lords, London SW1A 0PW
Tel: 020 7219 6364 *Email:* freemanr@parliament.uk

CONSERVATIVE

FREUD, LORD

FREUD (Life Baron), David Anthony Freud; cr 2009. Born 24 June 1950; Son of late Anton Freud and late Annette Freud, née Krarup; Married Priscilla Dickinson 1978 (1 son 2 daughters).

Education: Whitgift School, Croydon; Merton College, Oxford (BA philosophy, politics and economics 1972).

Non-political career: Journalist 1972-83: *Western Mail* 1972-75, *Financial Times* 1976-83; Investment banker, Rowe and Pitman and successors, ultimately UBS AG 1984-2003; Chief executive, Portland Trust 2005-08; Adviser on welfare reform to Secretary of State for Work and Pensions 2008-09. Member, National Union of Journalists 1972-83.

Political career: *House of Lords:* Raised to the peerage as Baron Freud, of Eastry in the County of Kent 2009. Shadow Minister for Welfare Reform and Opposition Spokesperson for Work and Pensions 2009-10; Department for Work and Pensions: Parliamentary Under-Secretary of State (Minister for Welfare Reform) 2010-15, Government Spokesperson 2010-16, Minister of State for Welfare Reform 2015-16.

Political interests: Welfare reform.

Other: Trustee, Jecda Foundation. PC 2015.

Publications: Freud in the City (Bene Factum Publishing, 2006); Reducing Dependency, Increasing Opportunity: Options for the Future of Welfare to Work (Independent Report to DWP).

Recreations: Cycling, swimming, skiing, tennis, history.

Rt Hon the Lord Freud, House of Lords, London SW1A 0PW
Tel: 020 7219 4907 *Email:* freudd@parliament.uk

CROSSBENCH

FREYBERG, LORD

FREYBERG (3rd Baron, UK), Valerian Bernard Freyberg; cr. 1951. Born 15 December 1970; Son of Colonel 2nd Baron, and Ivry Perronelle Katharine Guild; Married Dr Harriet Atkinson 2002 (1 son 2 daughters).

Education: Eton College; Camberwell College of Arts (BA 1994); Slade School of Fine Art (MA 2006).

Non-political career: Artist.

Political career: *House of Lords:* First entered House of Lords 1994; Elected hereditary peer 1999-. Member House of Lords Offices Sub-committees: House of Lords Library and Computers 1995-98, Advisory Panel on Works of Art 1999-2002. *Councils and public bodies:* Member, Design Council 2001-04.

Political interests: Visual arts; New Zealand.

The Lord Freyberg, House of Lords, London SW1A 0PW
Tel: 020 7219 5101 *Email:* freybergv@parliament.uk

CROSSBENCH

FRITCHIE, BARONESS

FRITCHIE (Life Baroness), Irene Tordoff Fritchie; cr 2005. Born 29 April 1942; Daughter of Charles Fennell and Eva, née Tordoff; Married Don Fritchie 1960 (1 son 1 son deceased).

Education: Ribston Hall Grammar School for Girls.

Non-political career: Insurance 1970-76; Training posts Food and Drink Industry Training Board 1976-80; Consultant, Social Ecology Associates 1980-81; Director: Transform Ltd 1981-85, Rennie Fritchie Consultancy 1985-89; Managing director, Working Choices Ltd 1989-91; Consultant, Mainstream Development 1991-; Vice-chair, Stroud and Swindon Building Society 2004-08; Chair, Nominet 2010-; Non-executive, UK SBS 2013.

Political career: *House of Lords:* Raised to the peerage as Baroness Fritchie, of Gloucester in the County of Gloucestershire 2005. Member: Delegated Powers and Regulatory Reform 2007-09, Refreshment 2008-12, Audit 2015-. *Councils and public bodies:* Chair: Gloucester Health Authority 1988-92, South Western Regional Health Authority 1992-94, South and West Regional Health Authority 1994-96; Civil Service Commissioner 1999-2005; Commissioner for Public Appointments 1999-2005; Chair, Independent Appointments Selection Board, Royal Institution of Chartered Surveyors 2007-10; Board member and deputy chair, Scottish Public Services Ombudsman Audit Advisory Board 2007-10; Chair, 2gether NHS Mental Health Foundation Trust 2008-12.

Countries of interest: China, New Zealand, Turkey, USA.

Other: President and Founder Member, Pennell Initiative, focusing on the health of women in later life 1997-2006; Gloucestershire Ambassador 2000-; Patron: Pied Piper Appeal 2002-, Winston's Wish (grief support for children) 2002-; St Andrew's Ambassador 2004-; Vice-president, British Lung Foundation 2005-10; President, Chronic Pain Policy Coalition 2005-08; Chair, Advisory Board, Web Science Research Initiative 2006-09; Patron, Women in Banking and Finance 2008-12; President, Hospital Caterers Association 2009-10; Chair, Lloyds Bank Foundation England and Wales 2015-; Companion, Institute of Management; Member, Royal Society of Medicine. Pro-chancellor, Southampton University 1998-2007; Chancellor, Gloucestershire University 2012-. Seven honorary doctorates; Two fellowships. DBE 1996.

Publications: Working Choices (Dent, 1988), Co-author: The Business of Assertiveness (BBC Books, 1991), Resolving Conflicts in Organisations (Lemos & Crane, 1998), Career Life Planning – a tutor's guide (Manpower Services Commission), Interpersonal Skills for Managers, a tutor's guide (Manpower Services Commission), Women, Work and Training (Manpower Services Commission); Articles in training and management journals; Member, editorial board, Whitehall & Westminster World.

Recreations: Gardening, writing, reading, babysitting, *The Archers*.

The Baroness Fritchie DBE, House of Lords, London SW1A 0PW
Tel: 020 7219 5353 *Email:* fritchiei@parliament.uk
Tel: 01452 414542/01452 301266 *Fax:* 01452 414542/01452 304685
Email: renniefritchie@hotmail.com

NON-AFFILIATED

GADHIA, LORD

GADHIA (Life Baron), Jitesh Kishorekumar Gadhia; cr 2016. Born 27 May 1971; Married Angeli, née Saujani (1 daughter 1 son).

Education: Cambridge University (BA economics 1991); London Business School (MSc management 2000).

Non-political career: Director, Baring Brothers 1991-98; Managing Director, ABN AMRO 2001-08; Managing Director and Head of Advisory, Barclays Capital 2008-10; Senior Managing Director, Blackstone Group 2010-15.

Political career: *House of Lords:* Raised to the peerage as Baron Gadhia, of Northwood in the County of Middlesex 2016. *Other:* Co-Founder, Conservative Friends of India; Joined House of Lords as Conservative; now sits as Non-affiliated. *Councils and public bodies:* Non-executive board member: UK Financial Investments Ltd 2014-, UK Government Investments Ltd 2016-.

Countries of interest: Brazil, Russia, India, China, South Africa.

Other: Young Global Leader, World Economic Forum; Trustee: Guy's & St Thomas' Charity 1999-2009, Nesta 2007-13; Advisory Board, City Hindus Network; Vice-Chancellor's Circle of Advisors on India, Cambridge University; Member, UK-India CEO Council 2015-; Board member, BGL Group 2016-.

The Lord Gadhia, House of Lords, London SW1A 0PW
Tel: 020 7219 3000 *Twitter:* @JiteshGadhia

LABOUR

GALE, BARONESS

Opposition Spokesperson for Women and Equalities

GALE (Life Baroness), Anita Gale; cr. 1999. Born 28 November 1940; Daughter of late Arthur Gale, coalminer, and late Lillian Gale, housewife; Married Morcom Holmes 1959 (divorced 1983) (2 daughters).

Education: Treherbert Secondary Modern School; Pontypridd Technical College 1970-73; University College of Wales, Cardiff (BSc Econ politics 1976).

Non-political career: Sewing machinist, clothing factory 1956-57; Shop assistant 1957-59; Sewing machinist 1965-69; Wales Labour Party: Women's Officer and Assistant Organiser 1976-84, General Secretary 1984-99. Shop steward, Tailors and Garment Workers' Union 1967-70; GMB Labour Organisers' Branch 1976-: Chair, Wales and South West Section 1986-99, Equal opportunities officer 1991-99.

Political career: *House of Lords:* Raised to the peerage as Baroness Gale, of Blaenrhondda in the County of Mid Glamorgan 1999. Opposition Whip 2010-13; Assistant Opposition Whip 2015-; Opposition Spokesperson for Women and Equalities 2016-. Member, Statutory Instruments Joint Committee 2003-07; Co-opted member, EU Sub-Committee G (Social Policy and Consumer Affairs) 2006-09; Member: Works of Art 2009-11, 2013, 2014-16, Refreshment 2012-13, Charities 2016-17, Lord Speaker's Advisory Panel on Works of Art 2017-. Vice-chair, PLP Departmental Group for Women 2006-10, 2014-. *Other:* Vice-chair, Labour Animal Welfare Society 1995-; Member: Wales Labour Women's Committee 2000-; Labour Women's Network National Committee 2001-09; Joint Vice-chair, Parliamentary Labour Party Women's Committee 2013-. *Councils and public bodies:* Commissioner for Wales, Women's National Commission 2004-09.

Political interests: Animal welfare, women's equality, children's rights, Wales, devolution, smoking and health, environment; India, Rwanda, Taiwan, USA.

Other: Member: Inter-Parliamentary Union 1999-, Parliamentary Assembly of Council of Europe 2008-10, CPA 2005-; President, Royal British Legion Treherbert and District Branch 2003-; Patron, Kidney Wales Foundation 2008-; President, National Association of Old Age Pensioners in Wales 2010-; Hon. Vice-President, James Whale Fund for Kidney Cancer 2010-; Patron, Bees for Development 2013-; President, Cardiff and District Rhondda Society 2013-; NSPCC, Parkinson's UK, Royal British Legion, AFASIC. Welsh Woman of the Year, Val Feld award 2005.

Recreations: Swimming, walking, travel.

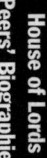

The Baroness Gale, House of Lords, London SW1A 0PW
Tel: 020 7219 8511 *Email:* galea@parliament.uk *Twitter:* @BaronessGale

LIBERAL DEMOCRAT

GARDEN OF FROGNAL, BARONESS

GARDEN OF FROGNAL (Life Baroness), Susan (Sue) Elizabeth Garden; cr 2007. Born 22 February 1944; Daughter of late Henry Button and Peggy, née Heslop; Married Timothy Garden (later Air Marshal Lord Garden KCB, died 2007) 1965 (2 daughters).

Education: Westonbirt School, Gloucestershire; St Hilda's College, Oxford (BA modern and medieval languages 1965, MA); French, Spanish.

Non-political career: Schoolteacher, various posts in England and Germany 1966-84; City & Guilds: Administrator/manager 1988-2000, Consultant 2000-08.

Political career: *House of Commons:* Contested (Liberal Democrat) Finchley and Golders Green 2005 general election. *House of Lords:* Raised to the peerage as Baroness Garden of Frognal, of Hampstead in the London Borough of Camden 2007. Liberal Democrat: Whip 2008-10, Spokesperson for: Children, Schools and Families 2008-09, Innovation, Universities and Skills 2009-10; Government Whip 2010-13, 2014-15; Government Spokesperson for: Business, Innovation and Skills (Higher Education) 2010-13, Culture, Olympics Media and Sport: (Olympics, Sport, Tourism and Lottery) 2010-12, (Women and Equalities) 2014-15, Education 2010-13, 2014-15, Defence 2012-13 Environment, Food and Rural Affairs 2014-15; Liberal Democrat Spokesperson for Higher and Further Education and Skills 2015; Deputy Chairman of Committees 2015-. EU Sub-committee F (Home Affairs): Co-opted Member 2008-10, Member 2010; Member: Digital Skills 2014, Liaison 2015-. *Other:* Member, Liberal Democrat Federal Conference Committee 2004-08; President, Camden Liberal Democrats 2007-.

Political interests: Education and skills.

Other: Director, UK-Japan 21st Century Group; St Hilda's College Association 1965-: Chairman 1996-2000; President, Relate central Middlesex 1997-2001; Caseworker, SSAFA Forces Help 2000-05; Vice-chairman: Oxford University Society 2005-07; Council member, Air League 2012-; FRSA 1993; Fellow, City & Guilds 2010; Hon. FCIL 2012. Master World Traders' Livery Company 2008-09. PC 2015; *Clubs:* National Liberal, Royal Air Force Club.

Rt Hon the Baroness Garden of Frognal, House of Lords, London SW1A 0PW
Tel: 020 7219 2747 *Email:* gardens@parliament.uk
Email: sue.garden@blueyonder.co.uk

CONSERVATIVE

GARDINER OF KIMBLE, LORD

Parliamentary Under-Secretary of State for Rural Affairs and Biosecurity and Government Spokesperson, Department for Environment, Food and Rural Affairs

GARDINER OF KIMBLE (Life Baron), John Eric Gardiner; cr 2010. Born 17 March 1956; Son of Anthony Gardiner and Heather Gardiner, née Robarts; Married Olivia Musgrave 2004.

Education: Uppingham School, Rutland; Royal Holloway College, London University (BA modern history and politics 1977).

Non-political career: Partner, family farm, Kimble, Buckinghamshire; Private secretary to Chairmen of Conservative Party 1989-95: Kenneth Baker MP 1989-90, Chris Patten MP 1990-92, Sir Norman Fowler MP 1992-94, Jeremy Hanley MP 1994-95, Brian Mawhinney MP 1995; British Field Sports Society/Countryside Alliance: Director of political affairs 1995-2004, Deputy chief executive 2004-10, Executive director and board member 2010-12.

Political career: *House of Lords:* Raised to the peerage as Baron Gardiner of Kimble, of Kimble in the County of Buckinghamshire 2010. Party Whip 2010-12; Government Whip 2012-15; Government Spokesperson for: Cabinet Office 2012-15, Business, Innovation and Skills 2012-13, Energy and Climate Change 2012-15, Culture, Media and Sport 2013-15, Justice (Criminal Justice and Courts Bill) 2014, Environment, Food and Rural Affairs 2015-; Deputy Chief Whip (Captain of the Queen's Bodyguard of the Yeomen of the Guard) 2015-16; Parliamentary Under-Secretary of State Rural Affairs and Biosecurity, Department for Environment, Food and Rural Affairs 2016-. Member: HIV and AIDS in the UK 2010-11, Joint Committee on Security 2013-15, Refreshment 2015-16. *Other:* Member, Quality of Life Commission Rural Affairs Group, Conservative Party.

Political interests: Agriculture, rural affairs, housing, conservation, heritage; Australia, Greece, Ireland, Zimbabwe.

Other: Chair, Vale of Aylesbury with Garth and South Berks Hunt 1992-2006; Federation of Associations for Hunting and Conservation of the European Union: Chair (UK) 1998-2012, Treasurer (Europe) 2003-; Vice-President: Buckinghamshire Agricultural Association, Suffolk Agricultural Association; President, Buckinghamshire County Show 2007; Vice-president,

Peterborough Royal Foxhound Show; Member: Easton Harriers Hunt, British Horse Society, Countryside Alliance, National Farmers' Union, National Trust, Royal Horticultural Society; Honorary Member, Kimblewick Hunt; *Clubs:* Pratt's Club.

Recreations: Hunting, gardening.

The Lord Gardiner of Kimble, House of Lords, London SW1A 0PW
Tel: 020 7219 3000 *Email:* gardinerj@parliament.uk

CONSERVATIVE

GARDNER OF PARKES, BARONESS

GARDNER OF PARKES (Life Baroness), Rachel Trixie Anne Gardner; cr. 1981. Born 17 July 1927; Daughter of late Hon. J. J. Gregory McGirr and late Rachel McGirr, OBE, LC; Married Kevin Gardner 1956 (died 2007) (3 daughters).

Education: Monte Sant Angelo College, north Sydney, Australia; East Sydney Technical College; Sydney University (BDS 1954); Cordon Bleu de Paris (Diploma 1956).

Non-political career: Came to UK 1954; Dentist in general practice 1955-90; Director: Gateway Building Society 1987-88, Woolwich Building Society 1988-93; Chair (UK), Plan International 1989-2003.

Political career: *House of Commons:* Contested (Conservative) Blackburn 1970 and North Cornwall February 1974 general elections. *House of Lords:* Raised to the peerage as Baroness Gardner of Parkes, of Southgate in Greater London and of Parkes in the State of New South Wales and Commonwealth of Australia 1981. Deputy Chair of Committees 1999-2002; Deputy Speaker 1999-2002. Member: Information 2003-05, Delegated Powers and Regulatory Reform 2005-09, 2010-13. *Councils and public bodies:* Member: Inner London Executive Council NHS 1966-71, Standing Dental Advisory Committee for England and Wales 1968-76, Industrial Tribunal Panel for London 1974-97; Councillor, Westminster City Council 1968-78: Lady Mayoress of Westminster 1987-88; Councillor, GLC 1970-86; JP, North Westminster 1971-97; Member, Westminster, Kensington and Chelsea Area Health Authority 1974-81; Department of Employment's Advisory Committee on Women's Employment 1980-89; North Thames Gas Consumer Council 1980-82; Member: General Dental Council 1984-86, 1987-91, London Electricity Board 1984-90; Vice-chair, North East Thames Regional Health Authority 1990-94; Trustee, Parliamentary Advisory Council on Transport Safety 1992-98; Vice-President, National House Building Council 1992-99; Chair, Royal Free Hampstead NHS Trust 1994-97.

Political interests: Transport, housing, health, planning, energy; Commonwealth, Latin America, Scandinavia.

Other: British chair, European Union of Women 1978-82; UK representative on the UN Status of Women Commission 1982-88; Member, Executive Committee, Inter-Parliamentary Union, British Group -1997, 2008-11; UK representative to Euro-Mediterranean Women's Forum 2000-02; Governor: Eastman Dental Hospital 1971-80, National Heart Hospital 1974-90; Hon. President, War Widows' Association of Great Britain 1984-87; Sydney University UK Alumni Association: President 1990-2012, Patron 2012; President, British Fluoridation Society 1990-93; Chair, Suzy Lamplugh Trust 1993-96; President, Women's Guild of Friendship 1995-2011; Chair, Cook Society 1996; President, Married Women's Association 1998-2010; Honorary Vice-President, British Legion, Women's Section 2001-06; PLAN International UK, Multiple Sclerosis Trust. Freedom, City of London 1992. DU, Middlesex 1997; Fellow, University of Sydney, Australia 2005. International Achievement award, Sydney University; Peer Contribution to Central Lobby, *PoliticsHome* awards 2012. AM (Order of Australia) 2003.

Recreations: Family life, gardening, needlework, travel.

The Baroness Gardner of Parkes AM, House of Lords, London SW1A 0PW
Tel: 020 7219 6611 *Email:* gardnert@parliament.uk

CONSERVATIVE

GAREL-JONES, LORD

GAREL-JONES (Life Baron), William Armand Thomas Tristan Garel-Jones; cr. 1997. Born 28 February 1941; Son of Bernard Garel-Jones and Meriel Williams; Married Catalina Garrigues 1966 (4 sons 1 daughter).

Education: King's School, Canterbury; Madrid University (Spanish).

Non-political career: In business on the Continent 1960-70; Personal assistant to Michael Roberts MP at Cardiff North 1970 general election; Merchant banker 1971-74; Personal Assistant to Lord Thorneycroft 1978-79; Managing director, UBS.

Political career: *House of Commons:* Contested Caernarvon February 1974 and Watford October 1974 general elections. MP (Conservative) for Watford 1979-97. PPS to Barney Hayhoe as Minister of State, Civil Service Department 1981-82; Assistant Government Whip 1982-83; Government Whip 1983-89; Deputy Chief Whip 1989-90; Minister of State, Foreign and Commonwealth Office 1990-93. *House of Lords:* Raised to the peerage as Baron Garel-Jones, of Watford in the County of Hertfordshire 1997.

Political interests: European Union; Latin America, Spain.

Other: Canning House. PC 1992.

Recreations: Book collecting.

Rt Hon the Lord Garel-Jones, House of Lords, London SW1A 0PW
Tel: 020 7219 1855
Tel: 020 7568 1379 *Fax:* 020 7568 1468 *Email:* tristan.garel-jones@ubs.com

GEDDES, LORD

CONSERVATIVE

GEDDES (3rd Baron, UK), Euan Michael Ross Geddes; cr. 1942. Born 3 September 1937; Son of 2nd Baron, KBE, DL; Married Gillian Butler 1966 (died 1995) (1 son 1 daughter); married Susan Hunter, née Carter 1996.

Education: Rugby School; Gonville and Caius College, Cambridge (BA history 1961, MA); Harvard Business School 1969.

Non-political career: Royal Navy 1956-58; Lieutenant-Commander, RNR (Rtd). Trinity College London: Chair 1992-2009, Life President.

Political career: *House of Lords:* First entered House of Lords 1975; Elected hereditary peer 1999-; Deputy Chair of Committees 2000-; Deputy Speaker 2002-. Member: European Union 1994-2000, EU Sub-committee A 1985-90, 2000-03; EU Sub-committee B: Member 1990-94, 1995-99, Chair 1996-99; Member: Science and Technology Sub-committee I 1990-92, Refreshment Sub-committee 2000-03, Procedure 2003-05, 2017-, European Union 2003-07, EU Sub-committee B (Internal Market) 2003-07, Personal Bills 2003-09, Standing Orders (Private Bills) 2003-, Liaison 2003-08, Refreshment 2007-12, Intergovernmental Organisations 2007-08, Joint Committees on: Statutory Instruments 2012, the Rookery South (Resource Recovery Facility) Order 2012-13. *Other:* Executive of Association of Conservative Peers: Member 1999-, Treasurer 2000-.

Political interests: Shipping, Anglo-Chinese relations, immigration, energy, transport, industry, tourism; South East Asia, Hong Kong.

Other: Trustee, Portman. Hon. FTCL; *Clubs:* Brooks's, Hong Kong, Noblemen and Gentlemen's Catch Club. Hong Kong Golf.

Recreations: Golf, music, bridge, gardening, shooting.

The Lord Geddes, House of Lords, London SW1A 0PW
Tel: 020 7219 4633 *Fax:* 020 7219 0034 *Email:* geddese@parliament.uk

GERMAN, LORD

LIBERAL DEMOCRAT

GERMAN (Life Baron), Michael James German; cr 2010. Born 8 May 1945; Son of Arthur Ronald German, retired, and Molly German, retired; Divorced (2 daughters); married Veronica Watkins (later AM as Veronica German 2010-11) 2006 (3 stepchildren).

Education: St Illtyd's College, Cardiff; St Mary's College London; Open University (BA educational studies 1972); Bristol Polytechnic (Postgraduate Diploma education management 1974); French.

Non-political career: Primary school teacher 1966-97; Secondary school teacher, Mostyn High School 1967-70; Head of music: Lady Mary High School, Cardiff 1970-86, Corpus Christi High School, Cardiff 1986-91; European director, Welsh Joint Education Committee 1991-99.

Political career: *House of Commons:* Contested (Liberal) Cardiff North October 1974 and 1979, Cardiff Central (Liberal/All) 1983 and 1987 general elections. *House of Lords:* Raised to the peerage as Baron German, of Llanfrechfa in the County Borough of Torfaen 2010. Liberal Democrat Principal Spokesperson for Work and Pensions 2015. Member, EU Internal Market Sub-committee 2015-. Chair, Liberal Democrat Parliamentary Party Committee on Work and Pensions 2010-15. *Other:* National Assembly for Wales: Contested Caerphilly constituency 1999 and Torfaen constituency 2003 elections, AM for South Wales East region 1999-2010: Welsh Liberal Democrat Spokesperson for Economic Development 1999-2001, Deputy First Minister 2000-01, 2002-03, Minister for: Economic Development 2000-01, Rural Development and Wales Abroad 2002-03, Welsh Liberal Democrat Spokesperson for: Local Government 2004-05, Local Government and European Affairs 2005-07, Europe 2007-10, Shadow Minister for Environment 2010. Liberal Party/Welsh Liberal Democrats: Member 1974-, Federal Executive Committee 1989-91; Welsh

Liberal Democrats: General election director 1992-97, Leader, Welsh Liberal Democrats in the National Assembly 1998-2008, Leader, Welsh Liberal Democrats 2007-08; Liberal Democrats: Member: Federal Executive Committee 2001-03, Federal Policy Committee 2010-, Treasurer 2016-. *Councils and public bodies:* Cardiff City Council: Councillor 1983-96, Group Leader 1983-96, Joint Leader 1987-91; Member, Advisory Committee on Business Appointments.

Political interests: Small businesses, education and skills, governance and constitutional affairs; European Union, Oman, Moldova, Sub-Saharan Africa.

Other: Executive member, Wales branch, Commonwealth Parliamentary Association 2004-10; Member, British-Irish Parliamentary Assembly; President, Dolen Cymru (The Wales-Lesotho Link) 2008-; Parliament Choir: Chair and trustee 2011-13, Vice-chair 2013-; President, Monmouth, Brecon and Abergavenny Canals Trust 2011-. OBE 1996; *Clubs:* National Liberal Club.

Recreations: Reading, music, travel.

The Lord German OBE, House of Lords, London SW1A 0PW
Tel: 020 7219 6942 *Email:* germanm@parliament.uk *Twitter:* @mjgerman

GIBSON OF MARKET RASEN, BARONESS

LABOUR

GIBSON OF MARKET RASEN (Life Baroness), Anne Gibson; cr. 2000. Born 10 December 1940; Daughter of Harry and Jessie Tasker; Married John Gibson 1962 (1 daughter); married John Bartell 1988 (1 stepdaughter).

Education: Caistor Grammar School, Lincolnshire; Chelmsford College of Further Education; Essex University (BA government 1976).

Non-political career: Secretary 1956-59; Bank cashier 1959-62; Organiser, Saffron Walden Labour Party 1966-70; Political researcher and advertising administrator, *House Magazine* 1976-77; Assistant secretary, Organisation and Industrial Relations Department, TUC 1977-87; National secretary, MSF (now Unite) 1987-2000. Member: AMICUS/Unite, TUC General Council 1989-2000.

Political career: *House of Lords:* Raised to the peerage as Baroness Gibson of Market Rasen, of Market Rasen in the County of Lincolnshire 2000. Deputy Speaker 2008-. Member: EU Sub-committee F (Social Affairs, Education and Home Affairs/Home Affairs) 2001-05, Joint Committee on House of Lords Reform 2002-03, Constitutional Reform Bill 2004, Review of the BBC Charter 2005-06, Information 2007-11, Constitutional Renewal Bill 2008-09, Joint Committees on: the Draft Enhanced Terrorism Prevention and Investigation Measures Bill 2012-13, Voting Eligibilty (Prisoners) Bill 2013. *Other:* Member: Labour Party National Constitutional Committee 1997-2000, PLP Women's Committee 2000-, Labour Animal Welfare Society 2000-; Chair, BERR: Bullying at Work Partnership Committee 2003-08. *Councils and public bodies:* Member: Equal Opportunities Commission 1991-98, Department of Employment Advisory Group for Older Workers 1993-96, Health and Safety Commission 1996-2000, Occupational Health and Safety Commission 1996-2000; President, Royal Society for Prevention of Accidents 2004-08; Hon President, Dispensing Doctors Association 2009-.

Political interests: Industrial relations, equality issues, women's issues, health and safety at work, adoption, foreign affairs (especially Latin America), penal policy; China, France, Portugal, Spain.

Other: ETUC Women's Committee 1977-2000: Chair, EC Committee on Violence at Work 1996-2000; ICFTU Women's Committee 1977-2000: Member: EC Committee on Health and Safety 1996-2000, Bilbao Agency 1996-2000; Member: Fawcett Society, Fabian Society, Air League Council 2006-, Air Cadet Council 2007-; Rare Breeds Society, National Asthma Campaign, National Osteoporosis Campaign, Action for Prisoners Families, End Child Poverty. Honorary Doctorate of Laws, Portsmouth University 2007. Distinguished service award for work in health and safety, Royal Society for Prevention of Accidents 2001. OBE 1998.

Publications: Numerous pamphlets on trade unions, workplace rights, equal pay, equal opportunities.

Recreations: Embroidery, reading, theatre.

The Baroness Gibson of Market Rasen OBE, House of Lords, London SW1A 0PW
Tel: 020 7219 5737 *Email:* gibsonan@parliament.uk

GIDDENS, LORD

LABOUR

GIDDENS (Life Baron), Anthony Giddens; cr. 2004. Born 18 January 1938; Son of Thomas George and Nell Maude Giddens; Married Alena Ledeneva 2005 (divorced).

Education: Minchenden Grammar School, London; Hull University (BA sociology and psychology 1959); London School of Economics (MA sociology 1961); Cambridge University (PhD 1976); French, some German.

Non-political career: Lecturer in sociology, Leicester University 1961-70; Cambridge University: Sociology lecturer 1970-84, Reader/professor of sociology 1984-96, Fellow, King's College; Former chair and director, Polity Press Ltd; London School of Economics: Director 1997-2004, Emeritus professor.

Political career: *House of Lords:* Raised to the peerage as Baron Giddens, of Southgate in the London Borough of Enfield 2004. Co-opted Member, EU Sub-committee A (Economic and Financial Affairs) 2006-08; Member EU Sub-committee D: (Agriculture, Fisheries and Environment) 2010-12, (Agriculture, Fisheries, Environment and Energy) 2012-13; Member: Digital Skills 2014-15, Artificial Intelligence 2017-.

Political interests: Welfare, social policy, foreign policy, global issues; Latin America, China, EU, Russia.

Other: BBC Reith Lecturer 1998; Member, Academy of Social Sciences. 22 honorary doctorates from Europe, South America and China. Asturias Prize for Social Sciences 2002; Fellow American Academy of Arts and Sciences; Academician of the Russian Academy of Sciences. Order of the Southern Cross (Brazil); Order of the Finnish Lion (Finland). Queen's Club.

Publications: Over 40 books on sociology, politics and psychology.

Recreations: Watching Spurs, tennis, travel.

The Lord Giddens, House of Lords, London SW1A 0PW
Tel: 020 7219 6710 *Email:* giddensa@parliament.uk

GILBERT OF PANTEG, LORD

CONSERVATIVE

GILBERT OF PANTEG (Life Baron), Stephen Gilbert; cr 2015. Born 24 July 1963.

Non-political career: Political Secretary to David Cameron as Prime Minister 2010-15; Director, Stephen Gilbert Consulting; Consultant, Populus 2015-.

Political career: *House of Lords:* Raised to the peerage as Baron Gilbert of Panteg, of Panteg in the County of Monmouthshire 2015. Member, Communications 2016-. *Other:* Deputy Chair (Campaigning) and Member, Party Board, Conservative Party 2015-16.

Other: *Clubs:* Carlton Club.

The Lord Gilbert of Panteg, House of Lords, London SW1A 0PW
Tel: 020 7219 3000

GLASGOW, EARL OF

LIBERAL DEMOCRAT

GLASGOW (10th Earl of, S), Patrick Robin Archibald Boyle; cr. 1703; Viscount of Kelburn; 10th Lord Boyle (S) 1699/1703; 4th Baron Fairlie (UK) 1897. Born 30 July 1939; Son of Rear-Admiral 9th Earl, CB, DSC; Married Isabel James 1975 (1 son 1 daughter).

Education: Eton College; Sorbonne, Paris.

Non-political career: Royal Navy national service 1959-60; Sub-Lieutenant, RNR 1960. Television and film production: Assistant film director 1962-67, Documentary producer/director, Yorkshire TV 1968-70, Freelance television documentary producer 1971-86; Owner/manager, Kelburn Country Centre country park and visitor attraction. Former member, ACTT.

Political career: *House of Lords:* First entered House of Lords 1990; Elected hereditary peer 2005-; Liberal Democrat Spokesperson for: Transport 2005-10, Culture, Media and Sport 2008-10. Member: Works of Art 2005-09, 2015-16, Lord Speaker's Advisory Panel on Works of Art 2017-. *Councils and public bodies:* DL, Ayrshire and Arran 1995.

Political interests: Tourism, television, performing arts, small businesses, assisted dying.

Other: Arthritis Care.

Publications: Occasional articles for the *Spectator* and other magazines.

Recreations: Theatre, cinema, skiing.

The Earl of Glasgow DL, House of Lords, London SW1A 0PW
Tel: 020 7219 5419 *Email:* glasgowp@parliament.uk
Kelburn Country Centre, Fairlie, Ayrshire KA29 0BE *Tel:* 01475 568685
Email: admin@kelburncountrycentre.com
Websites: www.kelburncastle.com www.kelburncountrycentre.com

LABOUR

GLASMAN, LORD

GLASMAN (Life Baron), Maurice Mark Glasman; cr 2011. Born 8 March 1961; Married Catherine (3 sons 1 daughter).

Education: JFS Comprehensive School; St Katherine's College, Cambridge (BA modern history); York University (MA political philosophy); European University Institute, Florence (PhD unnecessary suffering 1989).

Non-political career: Senior lecturer in political theory, London Guildhall University; Senior lecturer in political theory and director of faith and citizenship programme, London Metropolitan University.

Political career: *House of Lords:* Raised to the peerage as Baron Glasman, of Stoke Newington and of Stamford Hill in the London Borough of Hackney 2011.

Other: London Citizens; Patron, Change Britain 2016-.

Publications: Unnecessary Suffering: Managing Market Utopia (Verso, 1996).

The Lord Glasman, House of Lords, London SW1A 0PW
Tel: 020 7219 5353

CONSERVATIVE

GLENARTHUR, LORD

GLENARTHUR (4th Baron, UK), Simon Mark Arthur; cr. 1918; 4th Bt of Carlung (UK) 1903. Born 7 October 1944; Son of 3rd Baron, OBE, DL; Married Susan Barry 1969 (1 son 1 daughter).

Education: Eton College.

Non-political career: Commissioned 10th Royal Hussars (PWO) 1963; ADC to High Commissioner, Aden 1964-65; Retired 1975 as Major; Major, The Royal Hussars (PWO) TAVR 1976-80; Honorary Colonel, 306 Hospital Support Medical Regiment (Volunteers) 2001-11; Honorary Air Commodore, 612 (County of Aberdeen) Squadron, Royal Auxiliary Air Force 2004-14. Captain, British Airways Helicopters Ltd 1976-82; Director: Aberdeen and Texas Corporate Finance Ltd 1977-82, ABTEX Computer Systems Ltd 1979-82; Senior executive, Hanson plc 1989-96; Deputy chair, Hanson Pacific Ltd 1994-98; Director, Whirly Bird Services Ltd 1995-2004; Consultant, British Aerospace 1989-99; Director, Lewis Group plc 1993-94; Consultant, Chevron UK Ltd 1994-97; Director, Millennium Chemicals Inc 1996-2004; Consultant: Hanson plc 1996-99, Imperial Tobacco Group plc 1996-98; Audax Trading Ltd: Consultant 2001-02, Director 2003-05; Director: Medical Defence Union 2002-06, Audax Global S.à.r.l. 2005-; Non-executive Chair, British European Aviation Group Ltd 2015-.

Political career: *House of Lords:* First entered House of Lords 1976; Government Whip 1982-83; Government Spokesperson for: the Treasury 1982-85, Home Office, Employment and Industry 1982-83, Defence 1983-89; Parliamentary Under-Secretary of State: Department of Health and Social Security 1983-85, Home Office 1985-86; Minister of State: Scottish Office 1986-87, Foreign and Commonwealth Office 1987-89; Elected hereditary peer 1999-. Member: Refreshment 2007-10, Ecclesiastical Committee 2010-. *Councils and public bodies:* DL, Aberdeenshire 1988-; Chair, St Mary's Hospital, Paddington, NHS Trust 1991-98; President, National Council for Civil Protection 1991-2003; Member, National Employers Liaison Committee for HM Reserve Forces 1996-2002; Governor, Nuffield Hospitals (now Nuffield Health) 2000-09; Commissioner, Royal Hospital, Chelsea 2001-07; Chair, National Employer Advisory Board for Britain's Reserve Forces 2002-09; King Edward VII's Hospital, Sister Agnes: Governor 2010-13, Chairman of council 2012-13; Governor, Sutton's Hospital, Charterhouse 2011-.

Political interests: Aviation, foreign affairs, defence, penal policy, health, Scotland; South Pacific.

Other: Member, Queen's Bodyguard for Scotland (Royal Company of Archers); Trustee, Hanson Research Trust 1990-; Fellow, Royal Aeronautical Society 1992-2010; British Helicopter Association: Chair 1992-2004, President 2004-; Special Trustee, St Mary's Hospital, Paddington 1991-2000; Scottish Patron, Butler Trust 1994-2014; Council member, Air League 1994-2009; Chair: European Helicopter Association 1996-2003, International Federation of Helicopter Associations 1997-2004; Trustee, Philip Alison Foundation 2000-; Royal College of Organists: Member 2003, Co-opted Council Trustee 2014-; Chartered Institute of Transport (now Chartered Institute of Logistics and Transport): Member 1978-2011, Fellow 1999-2011. Guild of Air Pilots and Air Navigators: Freeman 1992, Liveryman 1996-2011. Freedom, City of London 1996. Grand Cross, Order of Crown of Tonga; Royal Military Order of St George, Tonga; *Clubs:* Cavalry and Guards Club.

Recreations: Field sports, gardening, choral singing, organ playing, antique barometers.

The Lord Glenarthur DL, House of Lords, London SW1A 0PW
Tel: 020 7219 5429
Northbrae Farmhouse, Crathes, Banchory, Kincardineshire AB31 6JQ *Tel:* 01330 844467
Email: glenarthur@northbrae.co.uk

CONSERVATIVE

GLENDONBROOK, LORD

GLENDONBROOK (Life Baron), Michael David Bishop; cr 2011. Born 10 February 1942; Son of Clive Bishop.

Education: Mill Hill School.

Non-political career: Mercury Airlines, Manchester 1963; Chair: British Midland Airways 1964-2009, Airlines of Britain Holdings/British Midland plc 1978-2009, British Regional Air Lines Group plc 1982-2001, Manx Airlines 1982-2001; Airtours plc: Director 1987-2001, Deputy Chairman 1996-2001; Chairman, D'Oyly Carte Opera Trust Ltd 1989-2008; Channel 4 Television: Deputy Chairman 1991-93, Chairman 1993-97; Director, Williams Holdings plc 1993-2000; Non-executive director, Kidde plc 2000-02.

Political career: *House of Lords:* Raised to the peerage as Baron Glendonbrook, of Bowdon in the County of Cheshire 2011. *Councils and public bodies:* Member, East Midlands Electricity Board 1980-83.

Other: Member, East Midlands Regional Board, Central Television 1981-89; Honorary member, Royal Society of Musicians of Great Britain 1989; Chair of Trustees, Michael Bishop Foundation 1989-; Trustee and director, Friends in the UK, Royal Flying Doctor Service of Australia 2005. Liveryman, Guild of Air Pilots and Air Navigators. CBE 1986; Kt 1991; *Clubs:* Brooks's Club.

The Lord Glendonbrook CBE, House of Lords, London SW1A 0PW
Tel: 020 7219 5353

CONSERVATIVE

GLENTORAN, LORD

GLENTORAN (3rd Baron, UK), Thomas Robin Valerian Dixon; cr. 1939; 5th Bt of Ballymenoch (UK) 1903. Born 21 April 1935; Son of 2nd Baron, PC, KBE, and late Lady Diana Wellesley, daughter of 3rd Earl Cowley; Married Rona Colville 1959 (divorced 1975) (3 sons); married Alwyn Mason 1979 (divorced 1988); married Mrs Margaret Rainey 1990.

Education: Eton College; Grenoble University, France; French.

Non-political career: Grenadier Guards 1954-66, retired as Major. Redland (NI) Ltd: Managing director 1971-95, Chair 1995-98; Chair, Roofing Industry Alliance 1997-2003; Non-executive director, NHBC 2001-07; Betonsports plc 2004-07.

Political career: *House of Lords:* First entered House of Lords 1995; Elected hereditary peer 1999-; Opposition Spokesperson for: Northern Ireland 1999-2010, Industry 2004-05, Sport 2005-06, Olympics 2007-10, Wales 2007-10. *Councils and public bodies:* DL, Co. Antrim 1995-.

Political interests: Sport, environment, Northern Ireland, army, maritime affairs; India, Ireland, Nepal.

Other: Alternate Member, UK Delegation, OSCE Parliamentary Assembly; Member, British-Irish Parliamentary Assembly; Member, chair, president numerous organisations, especially related to sport, including: Member: Commission for Irish Lights 1985-2010, Millennium Commission 1994-2005; Chair: 'Paralympic World Cup' 2006-, BSSC 2006-; Royal Society of Ulster Architects; Parkinsons Society, Ocean Youth Club. Liveryman, Worshipful Company of Tylers and Bricklayers. Gold medal bobsleigh at Innsbruck Winter Olympic Games 1964. MBE 1969; CBE 1992; *Clubs:* Royal Yacht Squadron (Cowes) Club. Royal Portrush Golf; Irish Cruising.

Recreations: Sailing, travel, music, arts.

The Lord Glentoran CBE DL, House of Lords, London SW1A 0PW
Tel: 020 7219 5123 *Email:* glentoranr@parliament.uk

NON-AFFILIATED

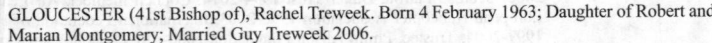

GLOUCESTER, LORD BISHOP OF

GLOUCESTER (41st Bishop of), Rachel Treweek. Born 4 February 1963; Daughter of Robert and Marian Montgomery; Married Guy Treweek 2006.

Education: Broxbourne School; Reading University (BA linguistics and language pathology 1985); Wycliffe Hall, Oxford (BTh theology 1994).

Non-political career: Paediatric speech and language therapist, Hampstead Heath Authority 1985-91; Manager of Paediatric Speech and Language Therapists in Health Centres across three Health Authorities (Bloomsbury, Hampstead and Islington) 1989-91; Assistant Curate, St George's, Tufnell Park 1994-97 (Ordained deacon 1994; Priest 1995); Associate Vicar, St George's, Tufnell Park 1997-99; Vicar, St James-the-Less, Bethnal Green 1999-2006; Continuing Ministerial Education Officer 1999-2001; Archdeacon of Northolt 2006-11; Archdeacon of Hackney 2011-15; Bishop of Gloucester 2015-.

Political career: *House of Lords:* Entered House of Lords 2015; First female Bishop to enter the House of Lords. *Councils and public bodies:* Governor: Tufnell Park Primary School 1996-99, Bonner Primary School, Tower Hamlets 1999-2006; Member: Church Commissioners' Pastoral Committee 2007-11, General Synod 2010-; Adviser to the House of Bishop's Working Group on Human Sexuality 2011-13.

Political interests: Conflict resolution, education, gospel transformation in society, justice, gender equality, overseas aid, young people, children and families; India, Mozambique, South Africa, Sweden, Tanzania, USA.

Other: Member, Management Committee, Whittington Community Centre 1995-99; Trustee: RADICLE 1999-2003, Ignite Trust 2007-11; Chair, Board of Reference for Heathrow Multi-faith Chaplaincy 2008-11; Member, Bridge Builders' Council of Reference 2012-; Trustee: Gloucester Magdalen Charity 2015-, Children's Society 2015-, Church of England Foundation for Educational Leadership 2017-; Ambassador, RESTORED; Patron, Gloucestershire Action for Refugees and Asylum Seekers. Honorary Degree of Doctor of Letters, Reading University 2016.

Recreations: Walking, canoeing, reading and writing.

Rt Rev the Lord Bishop of Gloucester, House of Lords, London SW1A 0PW
Tel: 020 7219 3000
2 College Green, Gloucester GL1 2LR *Tel:* 01452 835511 *Email:* bgloucester@glosdioc.org.uk
Website: www.gloucester.anglican.org *Twitter:* @BishGloucester

LIBERAL DEMOCRAT

GODDARD OF STOCKPORT, LORD

GODDARD OF STOCKPORT (Life Baron), David Goddard; cr 2014. Born 2 October 1952; Married Helen (1 son).

Education: Brinnington Secondary Modern.

Non-political career: Taxi driver; British Gas.

Political career: *House of Lords:* Raised to the peerage as Baron Goddard of Stockport, of Stockport in the County of Greater Manchester 2014. Member: Refreshment 2015-16, Secondary Legislation Scrutiny 2015-. *Councils and public bodies:* Stockport Metropolitan Council: Member 1990-2012, 2014-, Leader of the Council 2007-12; Member, Greater Manchester Police Authority; Governor, Stockport School; Non-executive director, Manchester International Airport.

Political interests: Liberal Democrat history, House of Lords history; China, USA.

Other: Environment commissioner, Great Manchester Combined Authority; Age Concern.

The Lord Goddard of Stockport, House of Lords, London SW1A 0PW
Tel: 020 7219 6563 *Email:* goddardd@parliament.uk *Twitter:* @davegoddardsk2

CONSERVATIVE

GOLD, LORD

GOLD (Life Baron), David Laurence Gold; cr 2011. Born 1 March 1951; Son of Michael and Betty Gold; Married Sharon Levy 1978 (1 daughter 2 sons).

Education: Westcliff High School for Boys; London School of Economics (LLB 1972).

Non-political career: Admitted solicitor 1975; Herbert Smith: Head of litigation 2003-05, Senior partner 2005-10; Corporate Monitor BAE Systems plc 2010-; Principal, David Gold and Associates 2011-.

Political career: *House of Lords:* Raised to the peerage as Baron Gold, of Westcliffe-on-Sea in the County of Essex 2011. Member: Joint Committee on Privacy and Injunctions 2011-12, EU Justice Sub-committee 2017-. *Other:* Chairman, Conservative Party Disciplinary Committee 2010-12.

Other: Governor, London School of Economics 2010-; Law Society of England and Wales.

Recreations: Theatre, cinema, travel, family.

The Lord Gold, House of Lords, London SW1A 0PW
Tel: 020 7219 5353 *Email:* goldd@parliament.uk
3 Fitzhardinge Street, London W1H 6EF *Tel:* 020 3535 8989
Email: david.gold@davidgoldassociates.com *Website:* www.davidgoldassociates.com

CONSERVATIVE

GOLDIE, BARONESS

Government Whip (Baroness in Waiting)

GOLDIE (Life Baroness), Annabel MacNicoll Goldie; cr 2013. Born 27 February 1950; Daughter of Alexander and Margaret Goldie.

Education: Greenock Academy, Greenock; Strathclyde University (LLB law 1971).

Non-political career: Admitted Solicitor 1974; Apprentice Solicitor, McClure Naismith Brodie & Co, Glasgow 1971-73; Assitant Solicitor, Haddow & McLay/Dickson, Haddow & Co 1973-77; Partner, Dickson, Haddow & Co/Donaldson, Alexander, Russell & Haddow, Glasgow 1978-2006.

Political career: *House of Commons:* Contested (Conservative) Renfrew West and Inverclyde 1992 general election. *House of Lords:* Raised to the peerage as Baroness Goldie, of Bishopton in the County of Renfrewshire 2013. Government Whip (Baroness in Waiting) 2016-. Member, Communications 2016. *Other:* Scottish Parliament: Contested West Renfrewshire constituency 1999, 2003 and 2007 and Renfrewshire North and West constituency 2011 elections, MSP (as Annabel Goldie) for: West of Scotland region 1999-2011, West Scotland region 2011-16, Scottish Conservative Spokesperson for: Economy, Industry and Finance 1999-2001, Enterprise and Lifelong Learning 2001-03, Justice and Home Affairs 2003-05, Home Affairs 2005-06, Leader, Conservatives in the Scottish Parliament 2005-11, Scottish Conservative Spokesperson for: Culture and Communities 2011-13, Constitution 2013-16. Scottish Conservatives: Vice-chair 1992-95, Deputy Chair 1995-97, 1997-98, Chair March-July 1997, Deputy Leader 1998-2005. *Councils and public bodies:* DL, Renfrewshire 1993-.

Other: Notary Public 1978-2007; Elder, Church of Scotland, Bishopton; Member: Glasgow Charing Cross Rotary Club, RSPB, West Scotland advisory board, Salvation Army; Director, Prince's Scottish Youth Business Trust 1995-2010; Honorary Fellow, Royal Incorporation of Architects in Scotland. Honorary fellow, Strathclyde University.

Recreations: Countryside, walking, bird-watching, wildlife, music.

The Baroness Goldie DL, House of Lords, London SW1A 0PW
Tel: 020 7219 5353

LABOUR

GOLDING, BARONESS

GOLDING (Life Baroness), Llinos Golding; cr. 2001. Born 21 March 1933; Daughter of late Ness Edwards (MP for Caerphilly 1939-68); Married Dr Roland Lewis 1957 (1 son 2 daughters); married John Golding 1980 (MP 1969-86) (died 1999).

Education: Caerphilly Girls Grammar School; Cardiff Royal Infirmary School of Radiography (1952).

Non-political career: Radiographer; Secretary and assistant to John Golding MP 1972-86. Former branch secretary, NUPE; Secretary, Newcastle Staffs and District Trades Council 1976-86.

Political career: *House of Commons:* MP (Labour) for Newcastle-under-Lyme 1986-2001. Opposition Whip 1987-92; Opposition Spokesperson for: Social Security 1992-93, Children and Families 1993-95, Food, Agriculture and Rural Affairs 1995-97. *House of Lords:* Raised to the peerage as Baroness Golding, of Newcastle-under-Lyme in the County of Staffordshire 2001. *Councils and public bodies:* Member: BBC Advisory Committee 1989-92, Commonwealth War Graves Commission 1992-2001; Administrative steward, British Boxing Board of Control 2004.

Political interests: Health service, trade unions, children, racing, gambling, fishing; Spain.

Other: Executive Committee Member, Inter-Parliamentary Union British Group 1996-99; Trustee, NSPCC 1988-2001; Chair: Second Chance 1988-, Citizencard; Member, Board of Countryside Alliance 2002-: Vice-President; Chair, Countryside Alliance Fishing Committee 2004.

Recreations: Fishing.

The Baroness Golding, House of Lords, London SW1A 0PW
Tel: 020 7219 4209 *Email:* goldingll@parliament.uk

LABOUR

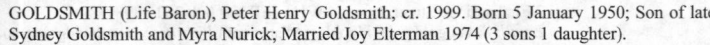

GOLDSMITH, LORD

GOLDSMITH (Life Baron), Peter Henry Goldsmith; cr. 1999. Born 5 January 1950; Son of late Sydney Goldsmith and Myra Nurick; Married Joy Elterman 1974 (3 sons 1 daughter).

Education: Quarry Bank High School, Liverpool; Gonville and Caius College, Cambridge (MA law 1971); University College, London (LLM 1972); French, German.

Non-political career: Called to the Bar, Gray's Inn 1972; In practice 1972-; QC 1987; Assistant Recorder, then Recorder of the Crown Court 1987-; Member, Paris Bar (Avocat a la Cour) 1997; Fellow, American Law Institute; European and Asian chair, Litigation Debevoise & Plimpton LLP 2007-.

Political career: *House of Lords:* Raised to the peerage as Baron Goldsmith, of Allerton in the County of Merseyside 1999. Attorney General and Government Spokesperson for Law Officers' Departments 2001-07. Member: Procedure 2009-12, Constitution 2010-15. *Councils and public bodies:* Chair, Financial Reporting Review Panel 1997-2000.

Other: Prime Minister's Representative on Convention for a Charter of Fundamental Rights of the EU 1999-2000; Executive committee member, Great Britain China Centre 1996-2001; Council member, Public Concern at Work 1996-2001; Bar Pro Bono Unit: Founder 1996, President 2001-; Various offices international law organisations, including American Law Institute 1996-; Chairman, Access to Justice Foundation; Council member: Hong Kong International Arbitration Centre, CEELI (Central and Eastern European Law Initiative); Chair: Bar Council of England and Wales 1995, Bar Council International Relations Committee 1996, IBA Standing Committee on Globalisation 1996-98; Co-chair, IBA Human Pro Rights Institute 1998-2001; Fellow, University College London. Freedom, City of London. PC 2002.

Rt Hon the Lord Goldsmith QC, House of Lords, London SW1A 0PW
Tel: 020 7219 7500 *Email:* goldsmithp@parliament.uk
Debevoise & Plimpton LLP, 65 Gresham Street, London EC2V 7NQ *Tel:* 020 7786 9088
Fax: 020 7588 4180 *Email:* phgoldsmith@debevoise.com *Website:* www.debevoise.com

GOODLAD, LORD

CONSERVATIVE

GOODLAD (Life Baron), Alastair Robertson Goodlad; cr 2005. Born 4 July 1943; Son of late Dr. John Goodlad and Isabel Goodlad, née Sinclair; Married Cecilia Hurst 1968 (2 sons).

Education: Marlborough College, Wiltshire; King's College, Cambridge (BA 1966, MA, LLB).

Non-political career: Former director, Bowater Overseas Holdings Ltd; President, Water Companies Association 1989; High Commissioner to Australia 2000-05.

Political career: *House of Commons:* Contested Crewe 1970 general election. MP (Conservative) for Northwich February 1974-83, for Eddisbury 1983-99. Government Whip 1981-84; Parliamentary Under-Secretary of State, Department of Energy 1984-87; Government Whip 1989-92; Minister of State, Foreign and Commonwealth Office 1992-95; Government Chief Whip 1995-97; Member, Shadow Cabinet 1997-98: Shadow Secretary of State for International Development 1997-98. Chairman, Conservative Party Committee for International Development 1997-98. *House of Lords:* Raised to the peerage as Baron Goodlad, of Lincoln in the County of Lincolnshire 2005. Contested Lord Speaker election 2011. Constitution: Member 2007, Chair 2007-10; Chair: Merits of Statutory Instruments/Secondary Legislation Scrutiny 2010-15, Leader's Group on the Working Practices of the House of Lords 2010-11; Member: Standing Orders (Private Bills) 2015-, Communications 2015-16.

Other: PC 1992; KCMG 1997; *Clubs:* Brooks's, Beefsteak, Pratt's Club.

Rt Hon the Lord Goodlad KCMG, House of Lords, London SW1A 0PW
Tel: 020 7219 3427

GORDON OF STRATHBLANE, LORD

LABOUR

GORDON OF STRATHBLANE (Life Baron), James Stuart Gordon; cr. 1997. Born 17 May 1936; Son of late James and Elsie Gordon, née Riach; Married Margaret Anne Stevenson 1971 (1 daughter 2 sons).

Education: St Aloysius' College, Glasgow; Glasgow University (MA classics 1958).

Non-political career: Political editor, Scottish Television 1965-73; Managing director, Radio Clyde 1973-96; Scottish Advisory Board, BP 1990-2002; Scottish Radio Holdings: Chief executive 1991-96, Chair 1996-2005; Vice-chair, Melody Radio 1991-97; Director: Clydeport Holdings 1992-98, Johnston Press plc 1996-2007, AIM Trust plc (now Active Capital Trust) 1996-2009; Chair, RAJAR (Radio Audience Research) 2003-06.

Political career: *House of Commons:* Contested (Labour) East Renfrewshire 1964 general election. *House of Lords:* Raised to the peerage as Baron Gordon of Strathblane, of Deil's Craig in Stirling 1997. Member, Communications 2009-13. *Councils and public bodies:* Member, Scottish Development Agency 1981-90; Chair, Scottish Exhibition Centre 1983-89; Member of Court, Glasgow University 1984-97; Committee member, Inquiry into Teacher's Pay 1986; Chair, Advisory Group on Listed Events on TV 1997-98; Member, Independent Review Panel on Funding of BBC 1998-99; Board member, British Tourist Authority 1998-2001.

Political interests: Broadcasting, tourism, constitutional affairs, Scotland; China, India, Middle East.

Other: Trustee: John Smith Memorial Trust 1995-2007, National Galleries of Scotland 1998-2001; Scottish Tourist Board: Board member 1997-2001, Chair 1998-2001. Hon. DLitt, Glasgow Caledonian 1994; DUniv, Glasgow University 1998. Sony Award for outstanding services to radio 1984; Fellow, Radio Academy 1994; Lord Provost's Award for Public Service in Glasgow 1994. CBE 1984; *Clubs:* New (Edinburgh), Glasgow Art Club. Prestwick Golf.

Recreations: Skiing, walking, genealogy.

The Lord Gordon of Strathblane CBE, House of Lords, London SW1A 0PW
Tel: 020 7219 1452 *Fax:* 020 7219 1993 *Email:* gordonj@parliament.uk

GOSCHEN, VISCOUNT

CONSERVATIVE

GOSCHEN (4th Viscount, UK), Giles John Harry Goschen; cr. 1900. Born 16 November 1965; Son of 3rd Viscount, KBE; Married Sarah Penelope Horsnail 1991 (2 daughters 1 son).

Education: Eton College.

Non-political career: Deutsche Bank 1997-2000; Director: Barchester Advisory 2000-02, Korn/Ferry International 2005-.

Political career: *House of Lords:* First entered House of Lords 1986; Government Whip (Lord-in-Waiting to HM The Queen) 1992-94; Government Spokesperson for Environment, Employment, Social Security, Transport and Trade and Industry 1992-94; Parliamentary Under-Secretary of State, Department of Transport 1994-97; Opposition Spokesperson for Environment, Transport and the Regions (Transport) 1997; Elected hereditary peer 1999-.

Countries of interest: Sub-Saharan Africa.

Other: Chair, Kasanka Trust; *Clubs:* Air Squadron, Pratt's Club.

The Viscount Goschen, House of Lords, London SW1A 0PW
Tel: 020 7219 3198

GOUDIE, BARONESS

LABOUR

GOUDIE (Life Baroness), Mary Teresa Goudie; cr. 1998. Born 2 September 1946; Daughter of Martin and Hannah Brick; Married James Goudie QC 1969 (2 sons).

Education: Our Lady of The Visitation, Greenford; Our Lady of St Anselm, Hayes.

Non-political career: Assistant director, Brent People's Housing Association 1977-81; Director: The Hansard Society for Parliamentary Government 1985-90, *The House Magazine* 1989-90; European director of public affairs, World Wide Fund for Nature (UK) 1990-95; Independent public affairs consultant 1995-98; Strategic and management consultant 1998-; Member, global advisory board, WEConnect International 2012-; Director, Center for Talent Innovations 2012-. Member: APEX, GMB.

Political career: *House of Lords:* Raised to the peerage as Baroness Goudie, of Roundwood in the London Borough of Brent 1998. Co-opted Member, European Union Sub-committee E (Law and Institutions) 1998-2000; Member: Procedure 2001-04, House of Lords' Offices Finance and Staff Sub-committee 2002-03, Information Committee 2003-05, Statutory Instruments Joint Committee 2005-06, Selection 2008-13, Joint Committee on Tax Law Rewrite Bills 2009-10, Soft Power and the UK's Influence 2013-14, Insurance Bill 2014-15, Sexual Violence in Conflict 2015-16, Licensing Act 2003 2016-17, Finance 2016-. Vice-chair, PLP Departmental Group for International Development 2010-15. *Other:* Secretary, Labour Solidarity Campaign 1981-87; Campaign manager to Roy Hattersley MP, Labour Party Deputy leadership election 1983; Member, Labour Parliamentary general election campaign team 1998-2001; Vice-chair, Labour Peers 2001-03; Member: Society of Labour Lawyers, Labour Movement in Europe. *Councils and public bodies:* London Borough of Brent: Councillor 1971-78, Chair, Housing and Planning Committees, Deputy Whip.

Political interests: Women and children, regional development, human rights, charity law, human trafficking, sexual violence and conflict, women on boards, European Commission and Parliament; Azerbaijan, Europe, India, Ireland, Middle East, Northern Ireland, Scotland, USA.

Other: Member, Inter-Parliamentary Union, British-Irish Inter-Parliamentary Committee; Chair, Women Leaders' Council to Fight Human Trafficking, UN; Member: Fabian Society, Smith Institute; Trustee: Piggybank Kids, Share Gift; Patron: National Childbirth Trust, Northern Ireland Community Foundation; Ambassador, World Wildlife Federation; Member, executive and board of directors, Vital Voices Global Partnership; Founding member, 30% Club 2010-; Trustee, El-Hibri Charitable Foundation 2012-. Honorary doctorate, Napier University 2000. Global Power award, Centre for Women Policy Studies 2012. SBCC Tennis Club.

Recreations: Family, travelling, gardening, food and wine, art.

The Baroness Goudie, House of Lords, London SW1A 0PW
Tel: 020 7219 5880
Website: www.baronessgoudie.com *Twitter:* @BaronessGoudie

LABOUR

GOULD OF POTTERNEWTON, BARONESS

GOULD OF POTTERNEWTON (Life Baroness), Joyce Brenda Gould; cr. 1993. Born 29 October 1932; Daughter of late Sydney and Fanny Manson; Married Kevin Gould 1952 (died) (1 daughter).

Education: Roundhay High School for Girls, Leeds; Bradford Technical College (pharmacy).

Non-political career: Pharmaceutical dispenser 1952-65; Organiser, Pioneer Women 1965; Clerical worker 1966-69; Labour Party 1969-93: Assistant regional organiser 1969-75, Assistant national agent and chief women's officer 1975-85, Director of organisation 1985-93. Member: TGWU, GMW.

Political career: *House of Lords:* Raised to the peerage as Baroness Gould of Potternewton, of Leeds in the County of West Yorkshire 1993. Opposition Whip 1994-97; Opposition Spokesperson for: Citizen's Charter 1994-96, Women 1996-97; Government Whip 1997; Deputy Chair of Committees 2002-12; Deputy Speaker 2002-. Member: Finance and Staffing 1994-97, EU Sub-committee C (Environmental Affairs) 1994-97, Constitution 2001-05, Speakership of the House 2003, Standing Orders (Private Bills) 2005-, Refreshment 2005-08, 2012-15, Procedure 2008-12, 2012-13, HIV and AIDS in the UK 2010-11, Inquiries Act 2005 2013-14, Affordable Childcare 2014-15, Administration and Works 2015-16, Delegated Powers and Regulatory Reform 2015-17, Secondary Legislation Scrutiny 2017-. Vice-chair: Labour Party Departmental Committee/Group for Women 2001-06, 2011-15, Labour Party Departmental Committee Office of the Deputy Prime Minister 2003-04, 2004-07. *Other:* Member: Regional Women's Advisory Committee 1960-69, National Labour Women's Committee 1960-69, Plant Committee on Electoral Systems 1990-92; Chair, Computing for Labour 1993-2002; Member: Labour Electoral Reform Association, Bevan Society, Labour, Arts and Heritage. *Councils and public bodies:* Member: Jenkins Commission 1977-98, Commission on Conduct of Referendums 1990-94, Independent Commission on Electoral System 1997-98; Vice-chair and executive member, Hansard Society 1999-2007; Council member, Constitution Unit 2001-07; Chair: Independent Advisory Group on Sexual Health and HIV 2003-10, Women's National Commission 2007-10; Co-Chair, Sexual Health Forum, Department of Health 2011-15.

Political interests: Women's equality, constitutional affairs, electoral affairs, race relations, population and development, disabled, sexual health; Bulgaria, China, USA.

Other: Vice-President, Socialist International Women 1978-85; Member: Inter-Parliamentary Union 1993-, Commonwealth Parliamentary Association 1993-; Member, secretary several anti-racist, women's and civil liberties bodies 1965-85; Member Fawcett Society; Fabian Society: Member, President Brighton and Hove branch; President and Trustee, Mary MacArthur Holiday Trust 1993-2007; Fellow, Industry and Parliamentary Trust 1996, 2001; Epilepsy Action: President 1996-2008, Honorary life member; Chair, H Chapman Society 1999-; Patron: Brighton and Hove Women's Centre 1999-2016, Forward 2000-; Vice-President, Speakability 2000-; President, fpa (formerly Family Planning Association) 2000-; Vice-president, Electoral Reform Society 2003-06; Patron: Yorkshire MESMAC (gay and bisexual men's health charity) 2008-, Sussex Beacon, HIVsport; Trustee, Brighton and Hove Age UK 2011-17; Patron: Martin Fisher Foundation, Sussex Beacon; Fellow, Faculty for Reproductive Health; Brighton and South Downs Women's Refuge, Red Card Appeal, Hangleton and knoll project. Hon. Doctorate, Bradford University 1997; Hon. Fellow: Faculty of Sexual and Reproductive Healthcare (RCOG) 2006, British Association for Sexual Health and HIV 2007; Hon. Doctorates: Birmingham City University 2009, Greenwich University 2012. Health Champion Award, Charity Champion Awards 2007.

Publications: Editor, Include Women and Health (1989); Pamphlets on feminism, socialism and sexism, women's right to work, violence in society; Articles and reports on women's rights, electoral systems; The Witchfinder General: A Political Odyssey (autobiography) (Biteback Publishing, 2016).

Recreations: Theatre, cinema, reading.

The Baroness Gould of Potternewton, House of Lords, London SW1A 0PW
Tel: 020 7219 3138 *Fax:* 020 7219 1372 *Email:* gouldj@parliament.uk

CROSSBENCH

GRABINER, LORD

GRABINER (Life Baron), Anthony Stephen Grabiner; cr. 1999. Born 21 March 1945; Son of late Ralph and Freda Grabiner, née Cohen; Married Jane Portnoy 1983 (3 sons 1 daughter).

Education: Central Foundation Boys' Grammar School, London; London School of Economics (LLB 1966; LLM 1967); Lincoln's Inn (Hardwicke Scholar 1966, Droop Scholar 1968).

Non-political career: Called to the Bar, Lincoln's Inn 1968; Standing Junior Counsel to Department of Trade, Export Credits Guarantee Department 1976-81; Junior Counsel to the Crown 1978-81; QC 1981; Bencher 1989; Recorder of the Crown Court 1990-99; Deputy High Court Judge 1994-; Non-executive director, Next plc 2002; Non-executive chair, Arcadia Group Limited 2002-; Bank of England Financial Services Law Committee 2002-05.

Political career: *House of Lords:* Raised to the peerage as Baron Grabiner, of Aldwych in the City of Westminster 1999. Member, Religious Offences 2002-03; Co-opted Member, European Union Sub-committee E (Law and Institutions) 2003-06; Member, Joint Committee on Privacy and Injunctions 2011-12. *Other:* Resigned Labour whip October 2015; now sits on Cross-benches.

Political interests: Law reform, commercial and company law, city, pensions, higher education.

Other: Chair: Court of Governors, LSE 1998-2007, Management and Standards Committee, News Corporation 2011-; *Clubs:* Garrick Club. Brocket Hall Golf; Non-executive director Wentworth Golf Club 2005-.

Publications: Co-editor, Sutton and Shannon on Contract (7th edition, 1970); The Informal Economy (Report to Chancellor of the Exchequer, March 2000).

Recreations: Golf, theatre, reading.

The Lord Grabiner QC, House of Lords, London SW1A 0PW
Tel: 020 7219 5353
1 Essex Court, Temple, London EC4Y 9AR *Tel:* 020 7583 2000 *Fax:* 020 7583 0118
Email: agrabiner@oeclaw.co.uk

GRADE OF YARMOUTH, LORD

CONSERVATIVE

GRADE OF YARMOUTH (Life Baron), Michael Ian Grade; cr 2011. Born 8 March 1943; Son of Leslie Grade; Married Penelope Levinson 1967 (divorced 1981) (1 son 1 daughter); married Hon Sarah Lawson 1982 (divorced 1991); Married Francesca Leahy 1998 (1 son).

Education: St Dunstan's College, London; French.

Non-political career: *Daily Mirror*: Trainee journalist 1960s, Sports columnist 1964-66; Theatrical agent, Grade Organisation 1966; London Management and Representation: Joint managing director -1973, London Weekend Television: Deputy controller of programmes (entertainment) 1973, Director of programmes 1977-81; President, Embassy Television 1981-84; Controller, BBC1 1984-86; Director of programmes, BBC TV 1986-87; Chief executive, Channel Four 1988-97; Director: ITN 1989-93, Delfont Macintosh Theatres Ltd 1994-99, New Millennium Experience Co 1997-2001; Former director, Charlton Athletic Football Club; Pinewood-Shepperton plc: Chair 2000-16, Senior Consultant 2016-; Camelot Group: Director 2000-04, Chair 2002-04; Director: Reel Enterprises Ltd 2002-04, SMG 2003-04, Television Corporation 2003-04; Chair, Ocado 2006-13; Executive chair and chief executive, ITV 2007-09; Chair, James Grant Group 2010-12; Director, WRG Group 2011-14; Chair, Infinity Creative Media 2014-; Director: Grade Linnit Company, Performing Right Society for Music 2015-.

Political career: *House of Lords:* Raised to the peerage as Baron Grade of Yarmouth, of Yarmouth in the County of Isle of Wight 2011. Member: Joint Committee on the Draft Defamation Bill 2011, Small- and Medium-Sized Enterprises 2012-13. *Councils and public bodies:* Chairman, Fear of Crime Working Group 1989; Member, National Committee of Inquiry into Prevention of Child Abuse 1994-96; Chairman: Index on Censorship 2000-04, Board of Governors, BBC 2004-06; Member, Panel on Fair Access to the Professions 2009; Lay member, Press Complaints Commission 2011-14; Trustee, Science Museum 2011-; Chair: Media Museum, Bradford 2011-, Charity Fundraising Regulator 2015-.

Political interests: Media, arts, business; Middle East.

Other: Council member: LAMDA 1981-93, RADA 1996-2004; BAFTA: Council member 1981-82, 1986-88, Fellowship 1994, Vice-President 2004-; Member, British Screen Advisory Council 1986-97; Fellow, Royal Television Society 1991; Council member, Royal Albert Hall 1997-2004; Chair advisory board, National Science and Media Museum; The Healing Foundation, Samaritans, Royal National Lifeboat Institute, Tall Ships Trust, Royal National Mission for Deep Sea Fishermen. Honorary Professor, Thames Valley University (1994); Hon. LLD, Nottingham University (1997). CBE 1998. Royal Thames Yacht Club; Royal Solent Yacht Club.

Publications: It Seemed Like a Good Idea at the Time (autobiography, 1999).

Recreations: Sailing, theatre, opera, cricket.

The Lord Grade of Yarmouth CBE, House of Lords, London SW1A 0PW
Tel: 020 7219 5353
GradeLinnit Company Ltd, 17 Old Park Lane, London W1K 1QT *Tel:* 020 3150 2471
Email: ros@mgrade.com

GRAHAM OF EDMONTON, LORD

LAB/CO-OP

GRAHAM OF EDMONTON (Life Baron), Thomas Edward Graham; cr. 1983. Born 26 March 1925; Son of Thomas Edward Graham; Married Margaret Golding 1950 (2 sons).

Education: Westgate Hill; WEA Co-operative College (Secretarial Diploma 1962; Managerial Diploma 1964); Open University (BA 1976).

Non-political career: Corporal, Royal Marines 1943-46. Various posts within Co-operative Movement 1939-74. Member, National Association of Co-operative Officials; Life member Prison Officers Association.

Political career: *House of Commons:* Contested Enfield West 1966 general election. MP (Labour) for Enfield, Edmonton 1974-83. PPS to Alan Williams as Minister of State, Department of Prices and Consumer Affairs 1974-76; Government Whip 1976-79; Opposition Whip 1979-81; Opposition Spokesperson for the Environment 1981-83. Member, Refreshments Committee 1990-. *House of Lords:* Raised to the peerage as Baron Graham of Edmonton, of Edmonton in Greater London 1983. Opposition Spokesperson for the Environment, Northern Ireland and Defence 1983-90; Opposition Whip 1983-90; Opposition Spokesperson for National Heritage (Tourism) 1990-95; Opposition Chief Whip 1990-97; Deputy Speaker 1990-97; Deputy Chair of Committees 1997-2000; On Leave of absence September 2017-. Member: Privileges/Privileges and Conduct 2000-12, Merits of Statutory Instruments 2003-05. *Other:* Member, Co-operative Party 1997-2000; Chair, Labour Peers' Group 1997-2000. *Councils and public bodies:* Councillor and Labour leader, Enfield Borough Council 1961-68: Chair, Housing and Redevelopment Committee 1961-68; President, Co-operative Congress 1987-.

Political interests: Local government, consumer affairs, environment; Israel, USA.

Other: President, Institute of Meat; Patron, Ancient Order of Foresters; Fellow: Institute of British Management, Royal Society of Arts; Senate, Open University; National Association of Co-operative Officials; Charis (deals with drug and alcohol abuse), League Against Cruel Sports. Freeman, Worshipful Company of Butchers. Freedom, London Borough of Enfield. Honorary MA Open University 1989. PC 1998.

Publications: From Tyne to Thames via the Usual Channels (2005).

Recreations: Gardening, reading, relaxing.

Rt Hon the Lord Graham of Edmonton, House of Lords, London SW1A 0PW
Tel: 020 7219 6704
2 Clerks Piece, Loughton, Essex IG10 1NR *Tel:* 020 8508 9801

GRANTCHESTER, LORD

LABOUR

Opposition Spokesperson for Environment, Food and Rural Affairs and Business, Energy and Industrial Strategy

GRANTCHESTER (3rd Baron, UK), Christopher John Suenson-Taylor; cr. 1953. Born 8 April 1951; Son of 2nd Baron, CBE, QC and Betty, née Moores; Married Jacqueline Jaffé 1973 (divorced) (2 sons 2 daughters).

Education: Winchester College; London School of Economics (BSc economics 1973).

Non-political career: Dairy farmer and cattle breeder; Director: Littlewoods Organisation various companies 1993-97, Everton Football Club Company 1994-2000, Dairy Farmers of Britain 2003-09, Cheshire and Warrington Economic Alliance 2005-10.

Political career: *House of Lords:* First entered House of Lords 1995; Elected hereditary peer 2003-; Opposition Whip 2010-15; Opposition Spokesperson for: Environment, Food and Rural Affairs 2014-, Energy and Climate Change 2015-16, Business, Energy and Industrial Strategy 2016-. Member: EU Sub-Committee D Agriculture, Fisheries and Food 1996-99, Hybrid Instruments 2005-.

Political interests: Rural economy, the environment, sport, Merseyside, Cheshire and the North West; China, Denmark, Taiwan.

Other: Member of the Executive Council, Cheshire Agricultural Society 1986-99; Cheshire Representative to The Royal Agricultural Society of England 1994-97; Trustee, Foundation for Sports and the Arts 1997-; President: Western Holstein Breeders Club 1999-2000, President, Royal Association of British Dairy Farmers 2001-03; Chair: Cheshire County Country Lane and Business Association 2002-04, Local Football Partnership, Liverpool County FA 2001-06; Chairman, Everton Collection Charitable Trust 2005-; Vice-president, Wingate Special Children's Trust 2008. Vice-president, Oulton Park Cricket Club 2006.

Recreations: Sport (football, cricket, tennis), Everton FC, countryside and gardens, the arts.

The Lord Grantchester, House of Lords, London SW1A 0PW
Tel: 020 7219 5421 *Fax:* 020 7219 5979 *Email:* grantchesterj@parliament.uk

GREAVES, LORD

LIBERAL DEMOCRAT

GREAVES (Life Baron), Anthony Robert Greaves; cr. 2000. Born 27 July 1942; Son of late Geoffrey Lawrence and Moyra Louise Greaves; Married Heather Ann Baxter 1968 (2 daughters).

Education: Queen Elizabeth Grammar School, Wakefield; Hertford College, Oxford (BA geography 1963); French.

Non-political career: Teacher 1969-74; Organising secretary, Association of Liberal Councillors 1977-85; Manager, Liberal Party Publications 1985-90; Book dealer.

Political career: *House of Commons:* Contested (Liberal) Nelson and Colne February and October 1974 and (Liberal Democrat) Pendle 1997 general elections. *House of Lords:* Raised to the peerage as Baron Greaves, of Pendle in the County of Lancashire 2000. Liberal Democrat Spokesperson for: Environment, Food and Rural Affairs 2001-03, Deputy Prime Minister, Regional and Local Government 2003, Environment, Food and Rural Affairs 2005-10, Communities and Local Government 2007-10. Member: Standing Orders (Private Bills) 2000-05, Personal Bills 2005-09; Co-opted member, European Union Sub-committee D (Environment and Agriculture) 2006-08; Member, Procedure 2014-17. Chair, Liberal Democrat Parliamentary Party Committee on Energy and Climate Change; Environment, Food and Rural Affairs (Environment, Food and Rural Affairs) 2010-12. *Other:* Chairman: Union of Liberal Students 1965-66, National League of Young Liberals 1970-71; Member, Liberal Democrat Federal Policy Committee. *Councils and public bodies:* Councillor: Colne Borough Council 1971-74, Pendle Borough Council 1973-92, 1994-98, 2004-, Lancashire County Council 1973-97; Vice-President, Local Government Association 2011-16.

Political interests: Local government and democracy, environment, railways, elections, human rights, asylum seekers and refugees, countryside access; Bosnia-Herzegovina, Croatia, France.

Other: Vice-President, Open Spaces Society.

Publications: Co-author, Merger: The Inside Story (1989).

Recreations: Climbing, mountaineering, botany, cycling.

The Lord Greaves, House of Lords, London SW1A 0PW
Tel: 020 7219 8620 *Email:* greavesa@parliament.uk
3 Hartington Street, Colne BB8 8DB *Tel:* 01282 864346 *Email:* tonygreaves@cix.co.uk
Website: liberallord.com

GREEN OF DEDDINGTON, LORD

CROSSBENCH

GREEN OF DEDDINGTON (Life Baron), Andrew Fleming Green; cr 2014. Born 6 August 1941; Married Jane Churchill (1 son 1 daughter).

Education: Cambridge University (natural sciences and economics); Arabic.

Non-political career: Short Service Commission in the Royal Green Jackets 1962-65. Diplomatic Service 1965-2000: Ambassador to Syria 1991-94, Director for Middle East, Foreign and Commonwealth Office 1994-96, Ambassador to Saudi Arabia 1996-2000; Founder chair, Migration Watch 2001-.

Political career: *House of Lords:* Raised to the peerage as Baron Green of Deddington, of Deddington in the County of Oxfordshire 2014.

Political interests: Immigration, Christian persecution; Middle East.

Other: Former chair, Medical Aid for Palestinians; Former member, advisory board, Concordis; Former board member, Christian Solidarity Worldwide. CMG 1991; KCMG 1998.

Recreations: Tennis, bridge.

The Lord Green of Deddington KCMG, House of Lords, London SW1A 0PW
Tel: 020 7219 3000 *Email:* greena@parliament.uk

GREEN OF HURSTPIERPOINT, LORD

CONSERVATIVE

GREEN OF HURSTPIERPOINT (Life Baron), Stephen Keith Green; cr 2010. Born 7 November 1948; Son of late Dudley and Rosamund Green; Married Janian Joy (1971) (2 daughters).

Education: Lancing College, West Sussex; Exeter College, Oxford (BA philosophy, politics and economics); Massachusetts Institute of Technology, USA (MSc political science); French, German.

Non-political career: Overseas Development Agency, Foreign and Commonwealth Office 1970-77; McKinsey & Co Inc. 1977-82; HSBC plc 1982-2010: Chief executive officer, Group Chairman 2006-10; Ordained deacon 1987; Priest 1988; Member, board of directors, BASF 2009-10.

Political career: *House of Lords:* Raised to the peerage as Baron Green of Hurstpierpoint, of Hurstpierpoint in the County of West Sussex 2010. Minister of State for Trade and Investment and Government Spokesperson, Department for Business, Innovation and Skills and Foreign and Commonwealth Office 2011-13. Member: European Union 2015-17, EU Internal Market Sub-committee 2015-17. *Councils and public bodies:* Chair, Natural History Museum 2014-.

Countries of interest: Asia, France, Germany.

Other: Advisory Council, Centre for Anglo-German Cultural Relations, Queen Mary University; Member, Steering Group, Centre for Excellence in Finance, Sabanci University; Trustee: Archbishop of Canterbury's Anglican Communion Fund, Wintershall Charitable Trust; Member, advisory board, Centre for Progressive Capitalism 2016-; Chair, Asia House 2017-; President, Institute of Export. Freedom, City of London; *Clubs:* Athenæum Club.

Publications: Serving God? Serving Mammon? (1996); Good Value: reflections on money, morality and an uncertain world (2009); Reluctant Meister: How Germany's Past is Shaping its European Future (2014); The European Identity: Historical and Cultural Realities we Cannot Deny (2015).

Recreations: Art, European literature, opera.

The Lord Green of Hurstpierpoint, House of Lords, London SW1A 0PW
Tel: 020 7219 3000 *Email:* bullena@parliament.uk

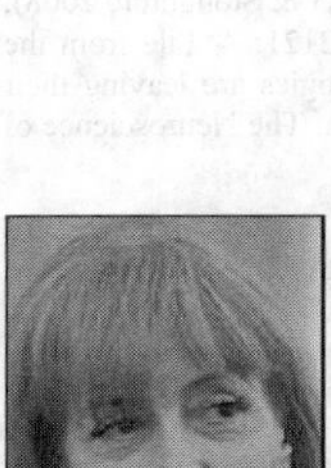

CROSSBENCH

GREENFIELD, BARONESS

GREENFIELD (Life Baroness) Professor Susan Adele Greenfield; cr 2001. Born 1 October 1950; Daughter of Reginald Greenfield and Doris Thorpe; Married Professor Peter Atkins 1991 (divorced 2003).

Education: Godolphin and Latymer Girls' School, London; St Hilda's College, Oxford (BA experimental psychology 1973, MA; DPhil pharmacology 1977); French.

Non-political career: Medical Research Council (MRC) research scholarship, pharmacology department, Oxford 1973-76; MRC-INSERM exchange fellowship, College de France, Paris 1979-80; Junior research fellowship, Green College, Oxford 1981-84; Lecturer in synaptic pharmacology, Oxford 1985-96; Tutorial fellowship in medicine, Lincoln College, Oxford 1985-98; Deputy director, Squibb Projects 1988-95; Gresham Chair of Physics, Gresham College, London 1995-99; Professor of synaptic pharmacology, Oxford University and Director, Institute for the Future of the Mind 1996-2013; Distinguished visiting scholar, Queen's University, Belfast 1996; Senior research fellowship, Lincoln College 1998-2016; Director: Royal Institution of Great Britain 1998-2010, Synaptica Ltd 1998-2003, BrainBoost Ltd 2003-06, Neurodiagnostics Ltd 2004-05; Thinker in Residence, Adelaide, South Australia 2004-05; Director: Enkephala 2005-13, MindWeavers 2006-09; Chair of Innovation, Queen's University, Belfast 2006; Director: Greenfield PPS Ltd 2007-, Mind Change 2011-13, Neuro-Bio Ltd 2013-.

Political career: *House of Lords:* Raised to the peerage as Baroness Greenfield, of Ot Moor in the County of Oxfordshire 2001. Member, Information 2005-08.

Political interests: Science, education, women's rights, biotech; Australia, France, Israel, Middle East.

Other: Science Museum: Trustee 1998-2003, Fellow 2010-; Vice-President, Association of Woman in Science and Engineering 2001; Chair, Women in Science Group 2002; Board of Governors, Weizmann Institute of Science 2004-; President, Classical Association 2004-05; Fellow, James Martin Institute 2004-; Editorial Board, Common Knowledge 2004-; Trustee: 'Plants and us' Charity 2004, Carnegie Mellon University Proposal 2004, John Porter National Trust 2004, Alexandria Library, Egypt 2006; Board of Trustees, Cyprus Research Institute 2006; Fellow: Royal Society of Edinburgh 2007-, Australian Davos Connection 2007-; Trustee: Institute for Food, Brain and Behaviour (formerly National Justice) 2007-, Science for Humanities 2007-; Science Media Centre Board, Australia 2007-, Royal Institution Australia 2008-; Governor, Florey Institute for Neuroscience and Mental Health 2012; Various posts in numerous organisations, particularly in fields of neurological illnesses and promotion of science; Royal Society of South Australia 2005; British Association for the Advancement of Science 2006; Senior Research Fellow, Department of Pharmacology, Lincoln College, Oxford; Honorary Fellow: St Hildas College, Oxford 1999, Royal College of Physicians 2000, Cardiff University 2000, College of Teachers 2001, Royal Society of South Australia 2005; Honorary Senior Fellow, Higher Education Academy 2007; Fellow, Royal Society of Edinburgh 2007; Honorary Fellow, Science Museum 2010; Alzheimer's Research UK. Chancellor, Heriot-Watt University 2005-12. 32 honorary doctorates from UK, US, Israeli and Australian universities; Honorary Fellowship, Royal College of Physicians 2000; Honorary Fellow, Institute of Risk Management 2012; Honorary Professor, Melbourne Medical School 2014. Dame Catherine Fulford Senior Scholarship, St Hugh's College, Oxford

1974; J.H. Burn Trust Scholarship, pharmacology department, Oxford 1977; MRC training fellowship, physiology department, Oxford 1977-81; Royal Society study visit award, College de France, Paris 1978; Woman of Distinction of the Year (Jewish Care) 1998; Royal Society Michael Faraday Award 1998; *Observer* Woman of the Year 2000; Golden Plate Award, American Academy of Achievement 2003; Honorary Australian of the Year 2006; British Inspiration Award – Science and Technology 2010; Australian Society for Medical Research Medal 2010. CBE 2000; Ordre National de la Légion d'Honneur (France) 2003; *Clubs:* Hospital Club.

Publications: Co-editor, Mindwaves: Thoughts on Intelligence, Identity and Consciousness (Basil Blackwell, 1987); Co-author, Journey to the Centres of the Brain (BBC Education Publishers, 1994); Editor, The Human Mind Explained (Reader's Digest, USA; Cassell UK, 1994); Author, The Human Brain: A Guided Tour (Weidenfield & Nicolson/Basic Books, 1997, Paperback Phoenix Press, 1998); Editor, Brainpower (Ivy Press, 1999); Author: The Private Life of the Brain (Penguin, 2000), Brain Story (BBC Books, 2000), Set Fair; a report on Women in Science, Engineering and Technology to the Secretary of State for Trade and Industry (2002), Tomorrow's People (Penguin, 2003); 'ID' The Quest for Identity in the 21st Century (Hodder & Stoughton, 2008); You and Me: Neuroscience and Identity (Notting Hill Education, 2011); 2121: A Tale from the Next Century (Head of Zeus, 2013); Mind Change: How digital technologies are leaving their mark on our Brains (Random House, 2014), A Day in the Life of the Brain: The Neuroscience of Consciousness from Dawn 'til Dusk (Penguin, 2016).

Recreations: Squash, dancing.

Professor the Baroness Greenfield CBE, House of Lords, London SW1A 0PW
Tel: 020 7219 6451 *Email:* greenfieldsu@parliament.uk
Building F5, Culham Science Centre, Abingdon OX14 3DB *Tel:* 01865 407158
Email: sagpa@susangreenfield.com
Website: www.susangreenfield.com *Twitter:* @SusanGreenfie10

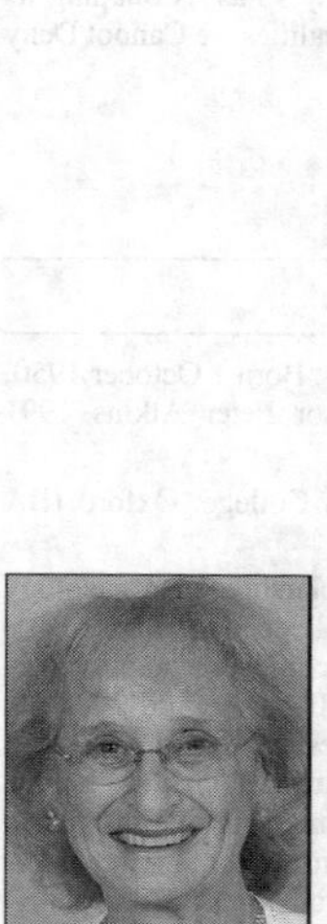

CROSSBENCH

GREENGROSS, BARONESS

GREENGROSS (Life Baroness), Sally Ralea Greengross; cr. 2000. Born 29 June 1935; Married Sir Alan Greengross 1959 (1 son 3 daughters).

Education: Brighton and Hove High School; London School of Economics (BA 1972); French, Spanish.

Non-political career: Formerly a linguist, executive in industry, lecturer and researcher; Age Concern England: Assistant director 1977-82, Deputy director 1982-87, Director-General (formerly director) 1987-2000; International Federation on Ageing: Secretary General 1982-87, Vice-President (Europe) 1987-2001; Joint chair, Age Concern Institute of Gerontology, King's College London 1987-2000; Chair, Experience Corps 2001-04; International Longevity Centre UK: Executive chair 2000-04, Chief executive 2004-; Co-president, ILC Global Alliance 2007-17.

Political career: *House of Lords:* Raised to the peerage as Baroness Greengross, of Notting Hill in the Royal Borough of Kensington and Chelsea 2000. Co-opted Member, European Union Sub-committee F (Social Affairs, Education and Home Affairs) 2000-03; Member: European Union Sub-committee G (Social Policy and Consumer Affairs) 2003-07, Joint Committee on the Draft Care and Support Bill 2013. *Councils and public bodies:* Commissioner, Equality and Human Rights Commission 2006-12; Vice-President, Local Government Association 2010-.

Other: Independent member, UN and WHO Networks on Ageing 1983-2000; Member, advisory council, European Movement 1992-; Vice-chair, Britain in Europe 2000-; Past and current member of several advisory bodies concerned with older people; Founder and Patron, Action on Elder Abuse 1994-; Vice-President, EXTEND 1996; Patron, Family Planning Association; President: Pensions Policy Institute, Association of Retirement Housing Managers; Royal Society for Public Health; Royal Society of Medicine; FRSH 1994; FRSA 1994; Patron to various charities. Eight honorary doctorates. UK Woman of Europe 1990; Outstanding achievement awards from the British Society of Gerontology and the British Geriatrics Society Medal. OBE 1993; *Clubs:* Hurlingham, Reform Club.

Publications: Consultant, Journal of Educational Gerontology 1987-; Editor, Ageing: an adventure in living (1985); Has edited and contributed to other publications on ageing issues and social policy.

Recreations: Countryside, music.

The Baroness Greengross OBE, House of Lords, London SW1A 0PW
Tel: 020 7219 5494 *Email:* greengrosss@parliament.uk

CROSSBENCH

GREENWAY, LORD

GREENWAY (4th Baron, UK), Ambrose Charles Drexel Greenway; cr. 1927; 4th Bt of Stanbridge Earls (UK) 1919. Born 21 May 1941; Son of 3rd Baron; Married Rosalynne Peta Schenk, née Fradgley 1985.

Education: Winchester College; Working French and German.

Non-political career: Marine photographer; Shipping consultant, Eurolist International Ltd -2017.

Political career: *House of Lords:* First entered House of Lords 1975; Elected hereditary peer 1999-. Member, Statutory Instruments Joint Committee 2000-07.

Political interests: Shipping, marine industry.

Other: Trinity House: Younger Brother 1987, Elder Brother 2007; Chair, Marine Society 1994-2000; Vice-President, Sail Training Association 1995-2004; President, Cruise Europe 1996-2003; Chair, World Ship Trust 2003-13; Hon. Fellow: Institute of Marine Engineering, Science and Technology, Nautical Institute; Mission to Seafarers, RNLI, Tall Ships Youth Trust; *Clubs:* House of Lords Yacht Club.

Publications: Soviet Merchant Ships (1976); Comecon Merchant Ships (1978); A Century of Cross-Channel Passenger Ferries (1981); A Century of North Sea Passenger Steamers (1986); Cargo Liners (2009).

Recreations: Sailing, swimming.

The Lord Greenway, House of Lords, London SW1A 0PW
Tel: 020 7219 4943 *Email:* greenwaya@parliament.uk

LIBERAL DEMOCRAT

GRENDER, BARONESS

GRENDER (Life Baroness), Rosalind (Olly) Grender; cr 2013. Born 19 August 1962; Married (1 child).

Non-political career: Office of Paddy Ashdown MP: Speechwriter and responsible for housing and transport policy, Head of communication as Leader of Liberal Democrats 1990-95; Director of Communications, Shelter; Deputy Director of Communications, Number 10; Political co-ordinator and director for special projects to Lord Ashdown of Norton-sub-Hamdon as Chair of the Liberal Democrat's 2015 general election campaign 2012-15.

Political career: *House of Lords:* Raised to the peerage as Baroness Grender, of Kingston upon Thames, in the London Borough of Kingston upon Thames 2013. Member: Licensing Act 2003 2016-17, Artificial Intelligence 2017-. *Other:* Member, Liberal Party/Liberal Democrats 1981-; Deputy Local and General Election Co-ordinator 2015.

Other: Trustee: Homeless Link, Wandle Housing Association. MBE 1996.

The Baroness Grender MBE, House of Lords, London SW1A 0PW
Tel: 020 7219 5353 *Twitter:* @OllyGrender

CROSSBENCH

GREY-THOMPSON, BARONESS

GREY-THOMPSON (Life Baroness), Carys Davina (Tanni) Grey-Thompson; cr 2010. Born 26 July 1969; Daughter of Peter Grey and Sulwen Grey, née Jones; Married Dr Ian Thompson 1999 (1 daughter).

Education: St Cyres School, Penarth; Loughborough University (BA politics and administration 1991).

Non-political career: Paralympic Athlete, GB Paralympic Team 1988-2004; Development officer, UK Athletics 1996-2000; Director: TGT International Limited 2002-, Tanni Grey-Thompson Ltd 2006-.

Political career: *House of Lords:* Raised to the peerage as Baroness Grey-Thompson, of Eaglescliffe in the County of Durham 2010. *Councils and public bodies:* Member: Sports Council for Wales 1996-2002, UK Sport 1998-2003, Sport Honours Committee 2006-17; Board member: Transport for London 2008-, London Legacy Development Corporation 2012-; Vice-president, Local Government Association; Non-executive member, BBC Board 2017-.

Political interests: Sport, women's issues, disability rights; Developing countries.

Other: Council member, Winston Churchill Memorial Trust 2006-; Trustee and vice-chair, Laureus Sport for Good Foundation; Chair, Commission of the Future of Women's Sport; Non-executive director, UK Athletics 2007-12; Board member, London Marathon 2007-; President, Sports Leaders UK; Ambassador, International Inspiration; Trustee: Jane Tomlinson Trust, Tony Blair Sports Foundation, Snowdon Award Scheme 2012-; President, National Council for Voluntary Organisations;

Member, executive committee, British Wheelchair Sports Foundation; Trustee: Spirit of 2012 Trust, Wembley National Stadium Trust; V Charity. Freedom: City of Cardiff, Borough of Redcar and Cleveland. Pro-chancellor, Staffordshire University 2005-13; Chancellor, Northumbria University 2015-. 28 honorary degrees. Bronze 400m medal Seoul Paralympics 1988; Gold 100m, 200m, 400m, 800m medals Barcelona Paralympics 1992; Gold 800m and Silver 100m, 200m, 400m medals Atlanta Paralympics 1996; Gold 100m, 200m, 400m, 800m medals Sydney Paralympics 2000; Gold 100m, 400m medals Athens Paralympics 2004. MBE 1993; OBE 2000; DBE 2005. Cardiff Amateur Athletics Club; New Marske Harriers; Cleveland Wheelers Cycling Club.

Publications: Seize the Day (autobiography, 2001); Aim High (2007).

Recreations: Handcycling, wheelchair sports.

The Baroness Grey-Thompson DBE, House of Lords, London SW1A 0PW
Tel: 020 7219 3143 *Email:* greythompsont@parliament.uk
Website: www.tanni.co.uk *Twitter:* @Tanni GT

GRIFFITHS OF BURRY PORT, LORD

LABOUR

Opposition Spokesperson for Digital, Culture, Media and Sport and Wales; Opposition Whip

GRIFFITHS OF BURRY PORT (Life Baron), Leslie John Griffiths; cr. 2004. Born 15 February 1942; Son of Olwen Griffiths, née Thomas, and Sidney Griffiths; Married Margaret Rhodes 1969 (1 daughter 2 sons).

Education: Llanelli Grammar School; University College of Wales, Cardiff (BA medieval English 1963); Fitzwilliam College, Cambridge (MA theology 1969); School of Oriental and African Studies, London University (PhD 1987); French, Haitian Créole.

Non-political career: Assistant lecturer in English, University of Wales 1964-67; Methodist minister: Port-au-Prince, Haiti 1970-74, Reading, Berkshire 1974-77, Cap Haitien, Haiti 1997-80, Loughton, Essex 1980-86, West London Mission 1986-91, Golders Green 1991-96; President, Methodist Conference 1994-95; Methodist minister, Wesley's Chapel, City of London 1996-; Canon, St Paul's Cathedral 2000-. Member Association of University Teachers 1964-67.

Political career: *House of Lords:* Raised to the peerage as Baron Griffiths of Burry Port, of Pembrey and Burry Port in the County of Dyfed 2004. Opposition Whip 2017-. Opposition Spokesperson for: Digital, Culture, Media and Sport 2017-, Wales 2017-. Member, Ecclesiastical Committee 2010-17.

Political interests: Education, international affairs, urban affairs, ethical issues; Cambodia, Dominican Republic, Fiji, Ghana, Haiti.

Other: Addiction Recovery Foundation 1989-2004, Patron 2004-; Christian Aid 1991-99; Birnbeck Housing Association 1991-96; Trustee, Sir Halley Stewart Trust 1999-; Art and Christianity Enquiry 1999-2008; Wesley House, Cambridge 2001-05; Central Foundation Schools of London 2002-; Abraham Path Initiative; Chairman, Central Foundation Schools of London; Paul Harris fellow, Rotary International 2008; Associate member, Learned Society of Wales; President, Boys' Brigade 2011-; Chair of Trustees, Central Foundation Schools of London 2011-; Patron, Waldensian Society in Britain 2012-; Christian Aid, Shelter. Freedom, City of London 1997. Fellow: Sarum College, Salisbury 2001, Sion College 2003, Cardiff University 2005, University of Wales, Lampeter 2006. Knight of the Order of St John of Jerusalem 1989; Office of the Order of Christopher Columbus (Dominican Republic) 2011; *Clubs:* Graduate Centre Club, Cambridge.

Publications: History of Haitian Methodism (1991); Letters Home (Methodist Publishing House, 1995); The Aristide Factor (1996); Worship in Our Diverse World (1998); Voices from the Desert (Canterbury Press, 2003); World Without End? (Epworth Press, 2007); A View from the Edge (Continuum, 2010).

Recreations: Cricket, rugby union, the post-colonial world, poetry.

The Lord Griffiths of Burry Port, House of Lords, London SW1A 0PW
Tel: 020 7219 5353 *Email:* griffithslj@parliament.uk
26 Stroud Road, Croydon London

CONSERVATIVE

GRIFFITHS OF FFORESTFACH, LORD

GRIFFITHS OF FFORESTFACH (Life Baron), Brian Griffiths; cr. 1991. Born 27 December 1941; Son of Ivor and Phyllis Griffiths; Married Rachel Jones 1965 (1 son 2 daughters).

Education: Dynevor Grammar School; London School of Economics (BScEcon 1963; MScEcon 1965).

Non-political career: Lecturer in economics, London School of Economics 1965-76; Professor of banking and Director of Centre, Banking and International Finance, City University 1977-82; Dean, Business School, City University 1982-85; Director, Bank of England 1983-85; Head, Prime Minister's Policy Unit and special adviser to Margaret Thatcher 1985-90; Director: Thorn EMI 1990-96, Herman Miller Inc. 1991-2011, Times Newspapers Ltd 1991-; International adviser, Goldman Sachs 1991; Director: Servicemaster 1992-2007, HTV 1992-93, Telewest 1995-98, English, Welsh, Scottish Railway 1996-2007; Chair: Trillium 1998-2000, Westminster Health Care 1999-2002, Trillium Land Securities 2000-08; Vice-chair, Goldman Sachs (International) 2007; Adviser, Telereal Trillium 2009-.

Political career: *House of Lords:* Raised to the peerage as Baron Griffiths of Fforestfach, of Fforestfach in the County of West Glamorgan 1991. Member: European Union Sub-committee F (Social Affairs, Education and Home Affairs) 1999-2003, Religious Offences 2002-03, Economic Affairs 2007-10, Economic Affairs Finance Bill Sub-Committee 2011, Public Service and Demographic Change 2012-13, Sub-committee on Economic Affairs Finance Bill 2012-13, Economic Affairs 2013-16, Science and Technology 2017-. *Other:* Chairman, Centre for Policy Studies 1991-2001; Member, board of directors Conservative Christian Fellowship 2000-02. *Councils and public bodies:* Chair, Schools Examinations and Assessment Council 1991-93.

Political interests: Economic policy, education, broadcasting, social policy; China, Eastern and Central Europe.

Other: Freedom, City of London. Honorary doctorates: City University, University of Wales; Richmond University; Fellow: Trinity College, Carmarthen 1996, Swansea Institute of Higher Education 2003, Swansea University 2006; *Clubs:* Garrick Club.

Publications: Several books on economics including: The Creation of Wealth (1984); Morality and the Market Place (1989).

The Lord Griffiths of Fforestfach, House of Lords, London SW1A 0PW
Tel: 020 7219 5353
Email: brian.griffiths@gs.com

LABOUR

GROCOTT, LORD

GROCOTT (Life Baron), Bruce Joseph Grocott; cr. 2001. Born 1 November 1940; Son of late Reginald and Helen Grocott; Married Sally Ridgway 1965 (2 sons).

Education: Hemel Hempstead Grammar School; Leicester University (BA politics 1962); Manchester University (MA economics 1966).

Non-political career: Administrative officer, London County Council 1963-64; Tutor in politics, Manchester University 1964-65; Lecturer then senior lecturer in politics, Birmingham Polytechnic 1965-72; Principal lecturer, North Staffs Polytechnic 1972-74; Presenter then producer, Central Television 1979-87. Member: National Union of Journalists, Unite.

Political career: *House of Commons:* Contested South West Hertfordshire 1970 and Lichfield and Tamworth February 1974 general elections. MP (Labour) for Lichfield and Tamworth October 1974-79. Contested Lichfield and Tamworth 1979 and The Wrekin 1983 general elections. MP for The Wrekin 1987-97, for Telford 1997-2001. PPS to John Silkin: as Minister for Planning and Local Government 1975-76, as Minister of Agriculture 1976-78; Deputy Shadow Leader of the House and Deputy Campaigns Co-ordinator 1987-92; Opposition Frontbench Spokesperson for Foreign and Commonwealth Affairs 1992-93; PPS to Tony Blair: as Leader of the Labour Party 1994-2001, as Prime Minister 1997-2001. *House of Lords:* Raised to the peerage as Baron Grocott, of Telford in the County of Shropshire 2001. Government Spokesperson for: Defence 2001-02, Foreign and Commonwealth Office 2001-02, International Development 2001-02, Work and Pensions 2001-02; Government Whip 2001-02; Chief Whip 2002-08; Deputy Chair of Committees 2002-08; Deputy Speaker 2002-08. Member: Privileges 2002-08, Procedure 2002-08, Selection 2002-08, House of Lords' Offices Administration and Works Sub-committee 2002-08, Refreshment 2003-05, Communications 2008, Leader's Group on the Working Practices of the House of Lords 2010-11, International Relations 2016-. *Councils and public bodies:* Councillor, Bromsgrove Urban District Council 1971-74; Governor, Birmingham City University.

Political interests: Foreign affairs, media, health service, machinery of government.

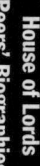

Other: Chairman, Hansard Society 2012-15. Chancellor, Leicester University 2013-. Hon. Doctorates: Birmingham City University 2006, Leicester University 2011. PC 2002; *Clubs:* Trench Labour Club.

Recreations: Steam railways, sport.

Rt Hon the Lord Grocott, House of Lords, London SW1A 0PW
Tel: 020 7219 5058 *Email:* grocottb@parliament.uk

CROSSBENCH

GUTHRIE OF CRAIGIEBANK, LORD

GUTHRIE OF CRAIGIEBANK (Life Baron), Charles Ronald Llewelyn Guthrie; cr 2001. Born 17 November 1938; Son of Ronald Guthrie and Nina Guthrie, née Llewelyn; Married Catherine Worrall 1971 (2 sons).

Education: Harrow School; Royal Military Academy, Sandhurst (Commission 1959).

Non-political career: Colonel: Life Guards and Gold Stick 1999-, SAS 2001-10. 2nd lieutenant to captain, Welsh Guards 1959-65; Captain, 22 Special Air Service 1965-69; Lieutenant colonel, Welsh Guards 1977-80; Brigadier, 4th Armoured Brigade 1982-84; Major General, 2 Infantry Division 1986-87; Lieutenant General, 1 (BR) Corps 1987-91; Commander-in-chief, British Army of the Rhine 1992-94; Ministry of Defence: Chief of the General Staff 1994-97, Chief of the Defence Staff 1997-2001; Non-executive director, Gulf Keystone Petroleum 2000-; Consultant, NM Rothschild 2001-09; Non-executive director, Colt Defense (US) 2002-; Director: Petropavlovsk plc 2008-, Gulf Keystone 2011-; Non-executive director, Rivada 2011-.

Political career: *House of Lords:* Raised to the peerage as Baron Guthrie of Craigiebank, of Craigiebank in the City of Dundee 2001. *Councils and public bodies:* DL 2008.

Political interests: Defence, international relations, youth, medical ethics; India, Oman, Pakistan, Russia.

Other: International Institute of Strategic Studies; Institute of Strategic Dialogue; President: Federation of London Youth Clubs, Action Medical Research, Progressive Supranuclear Palsy Association; Chair: Hospital of St John and St Elizabeth, Advisory board, London School of Hygiene and Tropical Medicine; King's College London: Visiting Professor 2001-, Fellow 2002; Board member, Moscow School of Political Studies; Patron, Change Britain 2016-; Hon. Fellow, King's College; Hon. Bencher, Middle Temple; Hon. Fellow, Cranfield; St Johns Hospice, Army Benevolent Fund, London Ferderation of Youth Clubs. Painter Stainers. Freedom, City of London. Liverpool Hope University. LVO 1977; OBE 1980; KCB 1990; GCB 1994; Commander Legion of Merit (USA) 2001; *Clubs:* White's Club. All-England Lawn Tennis.

Publications: Co-author, Just War (Bloomsbury, 2007).

Recreations: Tennis, opera, travel.

Field Marshal the Lord Guthrie of Craigiebank GCB LVO OBE DL, House of Lords, London SW1A 0PW
Tel: 020 7219 5353
Email: crlguthrie@gmail.com

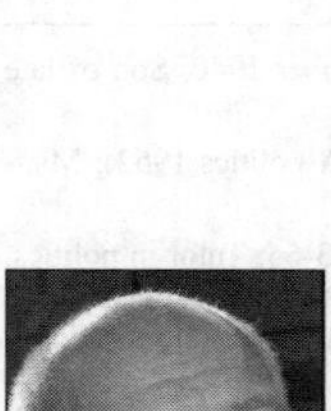

CONSERVATIVE

HAGUE OF RICHMOND, LORD

HAGUE OF RICHMOND (Life Baron), William Jefferson Hague; cr 2015. Born 26 March 1961; Son of Nigel and Stella Hague; Married Ffion Jenkins 1997.

Education: Wath-upon-Dearne Comprehensive School, Yorkshire; Magdalen College, Oxford (BA philosophy, politics and economics 1982) (President, Oxford Union 1981); INSEAD Business School, France 1985-86.

Non-political career: Shell UK 1982-83; McKinsey and Company 1983-88; Political adviser to Sir Geoffrey Howe as Chancellor of the Exchequer and Leon Brittan as Chief Secretary to the Treasury 1983; Political and economic adviser, JCB 2001-; Non-executive director, AES Engineering 2001-09; Member, Political Council of Terra Firma Capital Partners 2001-; Columnist, *News of the World* 2003-05; Non-executive director: AMT Sybex 2003-09, Intercontinental Exchange 2015-; Chair, International Advisory Group, Linklaters 2015-; Senior adviser, Teneo Holdings 2015-; Columnist, *Daily Telegraph* 2015-; Consultant, Citigroup 2017-.

Political career: *House of Commons:* Contested Wentworth 1987 general election. MP (Conservative) for Richmond (Yorkshire) 23 February 1989 by-election to 2010, for Richmond (Yorkshire) (revised boundary) 2010-15. PPS to Norman Lamont as Chancellor of the Exchequer 1990-93; Department of Social Security: Joint Parliamentary Under-Secretary of State 1993-94, Minister of State for Social Security and Disabled People 1994-95; Secretary of State for Wales 1995-97; Leader of the Opposition 1997-2001; Shadow Foreign Secretary and Senior Member of the

Shadow Cabinet 2005-10; First Secretary of State 2010-15; Secretary of State for Foreign and Commonwealth Affairs (Foreign Secretary) 2010-14; Leader of the House of Commons 2014-15; Member: House of Commons Commission 2014-15, Speaker's Committee for the Independent Parliamentary Standards Authority 2014-15, Public Accounts Commission 2014-15. Member, Joint Committee on House of Lords Reform 2002-05. *House of Lords:* Raised to the peerage as Baron Hague of Richmond, of Richmond in the County of North Yorkshire 2015. *Other:* President Oxford University Conservative Association 1981; Leader Conservative Party June 1997-2001.

Political interests: Agriculture, economic policy.

Other: International Democrat Union, Global Alliance of Conservative, Christian Democrat and like-minded parties: Chair 1999-2002, Deputy Chair 2002-05, Assistant chair 2005-; Vice-President, Commonwealth Parliamentary Association (UK Branch) 2010-14; Member, Foreign Affairs Council, Council of the European Union 2010-14; Chairman: United for Wildlife Transport Task-force 2014-, Royal United Services Institute 2015-; Fellow, Royal Society of Literature. *The Spectator*/Highland Park Parliamentarian of the Year 1998; National Book Awards History Book of the Year for biography of Pitt the Younger 2005; Threadneedle/*Spectator* Speech of the Year 2007; Lifetime Achievement Award, *Spectator* awards 2014. PC 1995; *Clubs:* Beefsteak, Carlton, Buck's, Pratt's, Budokwai Club.

Publications: Speaking with Conviction (Conservative Policy Forum, 1998); I Will Give you Back your Country (Conservative Policy Forum, 2000); Biography of William Pitt the Younger (2004); Biography of William Wilberforce (2007).

Recreations: Walking, sailing, cross country, skiing, judo.

Rt Hon the Lord Hague of Richmond, House of Lords, London SW1A 0PW
Tel: 020 7219 3000
Email: general@williamjhague.com
Website: www.williamhague.com *Twitter:* @WilliamJHague

HAILSHAM, VISCOUNT

CONSERVATIVE

HAILSHAM (3rd Viscount, UK), Douglas Martin Hogg; cr 1929; 3rd Baron Hailsham (UK) 1928; (Life) Baron Hailsham of Kettlethorpe 2015. Born 5 February 1945; Son of late Baron Hailsham of St Marylebone, former Lord Chancellor who disclaimed his hereditary honours for life 1963 and was subsequently created a life peer; succeeded his father 2001 as 3rd Viscount Hailsham and 3rd Baron Hailsham; Married Hon Sarah Boyd-Carpenter 1968 (now Baroness Hogg (qv)) (1 son 1 daughter).

Education: Eton College; Christ Church, Oxford (MA history 1968) (President, Oxford Union 1966).

Non-political career: Called to the Bar, Lincoln's Inn 1968 (Kennedy Law Scholar); QC 1990.

Political career: *House of Commons:* MP (Conservative) for Grantham 1979-97, for Sleaford and North Hykeham 1997-2010. PPS to Leon Brittan as Chief Secretary to the Treasury 1982-83; Government Whip 1983-84; Parliamentary Under-Secretary, Home Office 1986-89; Minister of State: Department of Trade and Industry (Minister for Industry and Enterprise) 1989-90, Foreign and Commonwealth Office 1990-95; Minister of Agriculture, Fisheries and Food 1995-97. Member: Home Affairs 1997-98, Justice 2009-10. *House of Lords:* Created a life peer as Baron Hailsham of Kettlethorpe, of Kettlethorpe in the County of Lincolnshire 2015.

Other: PC 1992.

Rt Hon the Viscount Hailsham QC, House of Lords, London SW1A 0PW
Tel: 020 7219 3000

HAIN, LORD

LABOUR

HAIN (Life Baron), Peter Gerald Hain; cr 2015. Born 16 February 1950; Son of Walter and Adelaine Hain; Married Patricia Western 1975 (divorced 2002) (2 sons); married Elizabeth Haywood 2003.

Education: Pretoria Boys High School, South Africa; Emanuel School, Wandsworth, London; Queen Mary College, London University (BSc economics and political science 1973); Sussex University (MPhil political science 2000).

Non-political career: Head of research, Union of Communication Workers 1976-91. Member, GMB.

Political career: *House of Commons:* Contested Putney 1983 and 1987 general elections. MP (Labour) for Neath 4 April 1991 by-election to 2010, for Neath (revised boundary) 2010-15. Opposition Whip 1995-96; Opposition Spokesperson for Employment 1996-97; Parliamentary

Under-Secretary of State, Welsh Office 1997-99; Minister of State: Foreign and Commonwealth Office 1999-2001, Department of Trade and Industry (Energy and Competitiveness) 2001, Foreign and Commonwealth Office (Europe) 2001-02; Government representative European Union Convention 2002-03; Secretary of State for Wales 2002-08; Leader of the House of Commons and Lord Privy Seal 2003-05; Secretary of State for: Northern Ireland 2005-07, Work and Pensions 2007-08, Wales 2009-10; Shadow Secretary of State for Wales 2010-12. Chair, Modernisation of the House of Commons 2003-05. *House of Lords:* Raised to the peerage as Baron Hain, of Neath in the County of West Glamorgan 2015. *Other:* Leader, Young Liberals 1971-73; Member: Labour Party 1977-, Labour Party NEC 2011-12; Chair, National Policy Forum 2010-12.

Political interests: Social justice, democratic renewal, including Lords reform, electoral reform and devolution, environmental policy, including renewable energy, foreign affairs; Southern Africa, Spain.

Other: Former Member, Anti-Apartheid Movement; Chair, 'Stop the Seventy Tour' (which disrupted the South African rugby tour, and stopped the South African cricket tour to Britain) 1969-70; Founder, *Anti-Nazi League* 1977; Director, *Tribune* Newspaper 1991-97; Founder, Unite Against Fascism 2005; Honorary President, Unite Against Fascism, Wales 2009-; Non-executive Director, Amara Mining PCC 2013-16; Visiting Professor, University of South Wales 2014-; Strategic adviser, Developing Markets Associates 2014-; Chair, Board of Trustees, Donald Woods Foundation 2014-; Non-executive director, African Potash 2015-; Ambassador, Desmond Tutu Foundation 2015-; Trustee, Listen Charity 2015-; Global and Governmental adviser, Gordon Dadds LLP 2016-; Strategic adviser, Cyrus IM LLP 2016-; Visiting Adjunct Professor, University of Witwatersrand 2016-; Fellow: Sussex University, Queen Mary University 2017. Hon. doctorate, University of South Wales 2013. Welsh Politician of the Year, *am.pm* 2006; Welsh MP of the Year, BBC 2007. PC 2001; OR Tambo Presidential National Award (South Africa) 2015. Ynysygerwn Cricket Club; Resolven Rugby Club.

Publications: 21 books including: Ayes to the Left: A future for socialism (Lawrence and Wishart, 1995), Mandela (Spruce, 2010), Outside In (autobiography) (Biteback, 2012), Ad & Wal (Biteback, 2014), Back to the Future of Socialism (Policy Press, 2015) The Hain Diaries 1998-2007 (Biteback Publishing, 2015).

Recreations: Rugby, soccer, cricket, motor racing, rock and folk music.

Rt Hon the Lord Hain, House of Lords, London SW1A 0PW
Tel: 020 7219 3000 *Email:* peter.hain@parliament.uk
Website: www.peterhain.org.uk *Twitter:* @peterhain

HALE OF RICHMOND, BARONESS

NON-AFFILIATED

HALE OF RICHMOND (Life Baroness), Brenda Marjorie Hale; cr. 2004. Born 31 January 1945; Daughter of Cecil Hale and Marjorie Hale, née Godfrey; Married Anthony Hoggett 1968 (divorced 1992) (1 daughter); married Dr Julian Farrand QC 1992 (1 stepson 2 stepdaughters).

Education: Richmond High School for Girls, Yorkshire; Girton College, Cambridge (BA law 1966, MA 1969); Gray's Inn (Barrister 1969).

Non-political career: Manchester University law faculty 1966-89: Assistant lecturer, Lecturer, Senior lecturer, Reader, Professor; Barrister 1969-72; On leave 1984-89; Commissioner, Law Commission 1984-93; QC 1989; High Court judge 1994-99; Lord Justice of Appeal 1999-2004; Visitor, Girton College, Cambridge 2004-; Supreme Court of the United Kingdom: Justice 2009-13, Deputy President 2013-17, President 2017-.

Political career: *House of Lords:* Raised to the peerage as Baroness Hale of Richmond, of Easby in the County of North Yorkshire 2004. Lord of Appeal in Ordinary 2004-09; Disqualified from participation as: Justice of the Supreme Court 2009-13, Deputy President of the Supreme Court 2013-17, President of the Supreme Court 2017-. *Councils and public bodies:* Member, Council on Tribunals 1980-84; Chair then President, National Family Mediation 1989-; Governor, Centre for Policy on Ageing 1990-93; Member: Human Fertilisation and Embryology Authority 1990-93, Judicial Studies Board, Civil and Family Committee 1990-94; Chair, Royal Courts of Justice Advice Bureau 2001-03.

Other: Managing trustee, Nuffield Foundation 1987-2002; Patron: Richmond Open Spaces Appeal 2004-, Hammersmith and Fulham Law Centre 2010-; President: Association of Women Barristers 1997-2005; UK Association of Women Judges 2003-; International Association of Women Judges: President-elect 2008-10, President 2010-12. Fellmongers Company of Richmond, North Yorkshire. Chancellor, Bristol University 2004-16. Twenty honorary law doctorates; Hon. FBA; Hon. FRC Psych; Honorary degree, Bristol University 2017. DBE 1994; PC 1999; *Clubs:* Athenæum Club.

Publications: Women and the Law (Blackwell, 1984); Parents and Children (Sweet and Maxwell, 4th edition 1993); From the Test Tube to the Coffin (Stevens, 1996); The Family, Law and Society (Butterworth, 6th edition 2008); Mental Health Law (Sweet and Maxwell, 5th edition 2010).

Recreations: Domesticity, drama, duplicate bridge.

Rt Hon the Baroness Hale of Richmond DBE, House of Lords, London SW1A 0PW
Tel: 020 7219 5353
Supreme Court of the United Kingdom, Parliament Square, London SW1P 3BD
Tel: 020 7960 1960 *Fax:* 020 7960 1961 *Email:* justices@supremecourt.gsi.gov.uk

CROSSBENCH

HALL OF BIRKENHEAD, LORD

HALL OF BIRKENHEAD (Life Baron), Anthony (Tony) William Hall; cr 2010. Born 3 March 1951; Son of late Donald Hall and Mary Hall; Married Cynthia Davis 1977 (1 son 1 daughter).

Education: King Edward's School, Birmingham; Birkenhead School; Keble College, Oxford (BA philosophy, politics and economics).

Non-political career: BBC 1973-2001: News trainee 1973, Producer, *World Tonight* 1976, Senior producer, *World at One* 1978, Output editor, *Newsnight* 1980, Senior producer, *Six O'Clock News* 1984, Assistant editor, *Nine O'Clock News* 1985, Editor, news and 1987 general election 1987, News and Current Affairs Department: Editor 1988-90, Director 1990-93, Managing director 1993-96, Chief executive, BBC News 1996-2001, Director-General, BBC 2013-; Chief executive, Royal Opera House 2001-13; Non-executive director: HM Customs and Excise 2002-05, University for Industry 2003-06, Channel 4 Television 2005-.

Political career: *House of Lords:* Raised to the peerage as Baron Hall of Birkenhead, of Birkenhead in the County of Cheshire 2010. *Councils and public bodies:* Chair, Creative and Culture Skills 2004-09; Member, Olympics Cultural Advisory Board, Department for Culture, Media and Sport 2006-08; Board member, London Organising Committee of the Olympic Games 2009-13; Chair, Cultural Olympiad Board 2009-13; Mayor of London's Cultural Forum.

Political interests: Arts, culture, broadcasting, skills; China, Italy.

Other: Fellow, Royal Society of Arts 1997; Chair, Theatre Royal, Stratford 2001-09; Trustee, British Council 2008-13. Honorary DLitt, London University 2009. CBE 2006.

Recreations: Ballet, TV and radio, gardening, walking, books, opera.

The Lord Hall of Birkenhead CBE, House of Lords, London SW1A 0PW
Tel: 020 7219 5353 *Email:* halla@parliament.uk
NBH 04A Director-General's Office, BBC Broadcasting House, Portland Place, London W1A 1AA *Tel:* 020 3614 2255 *Email:* tony.hall@bbc.co.uk

CROSSBENCH

HAMEED, LORD

HAMEED (Life Baron), Khalid Hameed; cr 2007. Born 1 July 1941; Son of late Prof Dr M Abdul Hameed and Rashida Abdul Hameed; Married Dr Ghazala Afzal 1989 (3 daughters 3 sons).

Education: Colvin Taluqdars College, Lucknow, India; Lucknow University (BSc, DPA, MBBS 1966); London University (Diploma tropical medicine and hygiene 1972); Hindi, Urdu.

Non-political career: Clinical assistant, University College Hospital, London; Senior house officer, St George's Hospital, London; Registrar, St Mary's Hospital, London; Private and corporate medicine, London 1980-90; Chief executive officer, Cromwell Hospital, London 1990-2005; Chair, Alpha Hospitals 2003-17; Director, London International Hospital 2005-15.

Political career: *House of Lords:* Raised to the peerage as Baron Hameed, of Hampstead in the London Borough of Camden 2007. *Councils and public bodies:* Chair, Commonwealth Youth Exchange Council 1997-; High Sheriff of Greater London 2006-07; DL, Greater London 2007-.

Countries of interest: Commonwealth.

Other: Parliament of the World Religions, Brussels; Chair, Woolf Institute; President: Little Foundation, Friends of British Library; Trustee, International Students House; Member: Royal Society of Medicine, Medical Defence Union, General Medical Council; Honorary Fellow, Royal College of Physicians; Save the Children, MacMillan Cancer Research, Royal Academy School of Art, British Red Cross, MENCAP. Freedom, City of London. DSc Lucknow University 1999; Honorary Fellow, Royal College of Physicians, London 2006; Honorary doctorates: Middlesex University 2008, Metropolitan University 2009. Several awards from UK and overseas organisations and universities. Padma Shri (India) 1992; Sitare Qaide Azam (Pakistan) 1996; Hilali-Quaid-i-Azam (Pakistan) 1999; PGDB (Nepal) 1999; Order of the Burning Spear (Kenya) 2001; CBE 2004; Padma Bhushan (India) 2009; *Clubs:* Athenæum, Marks, Mossiman Dining Club. Member, Guards Polo Club; Life Member: MCC, Lucknow Golf Club.

Publications: Published speeches on Interfaith Harmony.

Recreations: Chess, bridge, cricket, poetry, polo.

The Lord Hameed CBE DL, House of Lords, London SW1A 0PW
Email: hameed@parliament.uk
94 Harley Street, London W1G 7HX *Tel:* 020 7935 5012 *Fax:* 020 7486 6174

HAMILTON OF EPSOM, LORD

CONSERVATIVE

HAMILTON OF EPSOM (Life Baron), Archibald (Archie) Gavin Hamilton; cr 2005. Born 30 December 1941; Son of late 3rd Baron Hamilton of Dalzell, GCVO, MC; Married Anne Napier 1968 (3 daughters).

Education: Eton College.

Non-political career: Lieutenant, Coldstream Guards 1960-62. Director, Tower Assets 1971-73; Managing Director, British Quadruplex 1974; Director, Jupiter Dividend & Growth Trust plc 1998-.

Political career: *House of Commons:* Contested Dagenham February and October 1974 general elections. MP (Conservative) for Epsom and Ewell 1978 by-election to 2001. PPS to David Howell as Secretary of State for: Energy 1979-81, Transport 1981-82; Assistant Government Whip 1982-84; Government Whip 1984-86; Ministry of Defence: Parliamentary Under-Secretary of State for Defence Procurement 1986-87, Minister of State for the Armed Forces 1988-93; PPS to Margaret Thatcher as Prime Minister 1987-88; Member, Committee on Intelligence and Security 1994-97. 1922 Committee: Member, Executive 1995-97, Chair 1997-2001; Member, Conservative Ethics and Integrity Committee 1999. *House of Lords:* Raised to the peerage as Baron Hamilton of Epsom, of West Anstey in the County of Devon 2005. Co-opted Member, EU Sub-committee C (Foreign Affairs, Defence and Development Policy) 2006-10; Member: EU Sub-committee A: (Economic and Financial Affairs and International Trade) 2010-12, (Economic and Financial Affairs) 2012-15, Joint Committee on the National Security Strategy 2015-. *Other:* Vice-President, Conservatives for Britain 2015-16. *Councils and public bodies:* Councillor, Royal Borough of Kensington and Chelsea 1968-71; Trustee, National Army Museum 2012-.

Political interests: Finance, tax, economic policy, trade and industry, defence.

Other: Member, UK Delegation to NATO Parliamentary Assembly 2014-; Governor, Westminster Foundation for Democracy 1993-97; President, Lest We Forget. PC 1991; Knighted 1994; *Clubs:* White's Club.

Rt Hon the Lord Hamilton of Epsom, House of Lords, London SW1A 0PW
Tel: 020 7219 3000 *Email:* hamiltona@parliament.uk

HAMWEE, BARONESS

LIBERAL DEMOCRAT

HAMWEE (Life Baroness), Sally Rachel Hamwee; cr. 1991. Born 12 January 1947; Daughter of late Alec and Dorothy Hamwee.

Education: Manchester High School for Girls; Girton College, Cambridge (BA law 1969, MA).

Non-political career: Admitted Solicitor 1972; Clintons Solicitors: Partner 1984-2004, Consultant 2004-10.

Political career: *House of Lords:* Raised to the peerage as Baroness Hamwee, of Richmond upon Thames in the London Borough of Richmond upon Thames 1991. Liberal Democrat Spokesperson for: Local Government 1991-98, Housing and Planning 1993-98, Local Government and Planning 1998-2000, Environment, Transport and the Regions 1999-2000, Local Government and the Regions 2001-04, ODPM/Communities and Local Government 2004-10, Regional and Local Government 2006-09, Home Affairs 2009-10, 2015, Immigration 2017-. Member, Economic Affairs 2008-10; Alternate member, Procedure 2009-14; Member: Leader's Group on Code of Conduct 2009, Merits of Statutory Instruments/Secondary Legislation Scrutiny 2010-15, Leader's Group on the Working Practices of the House of Lords 2010-11, Adoption Legislation 2012-13, Inquiries Act 2005 2013-14, Inheritance and Trustees' Powers Bill 2013, Extradition Law 2014-15, Joint Committee on Human Rights 2015-. Chair, Liberal Democrat Parliamentary Party Committee on Home Affairs, Justice and Equalities (Home Office) 2010-15. *Other:* Member, National Executive, Liberal Party 1987-88; Liberal Democrats, Member: Federal Executive 1989-91, General election team 1992, 1997, Federal Policy Committee 1996-98. *Councils and public bodies:* Councillor, London Borough of Richmond upon Thames 1978-98: Chair: Planning Committee 1983-94, London Planning Advisory Committee 1986-94; Joint President, Association of London Government; London Assembly: Member 2000-08, Deputy chair 2000-01, 2002-03, 2004-05, 2006-07, Chair 2001-02, 2003-04, 2005-06, 2007-08; Joint President, London Councils.

Political interests: Local government, planning, London, arts, home affairs, immigration and asylum, penal policy.

Other: Council Member, Parents for Children 1977-86; Legal Adviser, Simon Community 1980-; Council Member, Refuge 1991-2005; Member: Joseph Rowntree Foundation Inquiry, Planning for Housing 1991, Advisory Board, Compact Advocacy Advisory Group, NCVO; Family Policy Studies Centre: Governing Council -2000, Council Member 1994-2001; Town and Country Planning Association: President 1995-2002, Vice-president 2002-; Chair, Xfm Ltd 1996-98; Member, Advisory Board, Centre for Public Scrutiny 2000-; Board Member: Arts Council London 2006-08, Rose Theatre Kingston 2009-; Vice-President, Chartered Institute of Environmental Health; Member, Advisory Board, Equality and Diversity Forum, Human Rights Project; Trustee, Safer London 2014-; Member, Missing People, Policy and Research Advisory group 2014-.

The Baroness Hamwee, House of Lords, London SW1A 0PW
Tel: 020 7219 5353 *Email:* hamwees@parliament.uk

HANHAM, BARONESS

CONSERVATIVE

HANHAM (Life Baroness), Joan Brownlow Hanham; cr. 1999. Born 23 September 1939; Daughter of late Alfred Spark and Mary Spark, née Mitchell; Married Dr Iain Hanham FRCP FRCR 1964 (died 2011) (1 son 1 daughter).

Education: Hillcourt School, Dublin.

Political career: *House of Lords:* Raised to the peerage as Baroness Hanham, of Kensington in the Royal Borough of Kensington and Chelsea 1999. Opposition Whip 2000-09; Opposition Spokesperson for: Transport, Local Government and the Regions 2001-02, Local Government and the Regions 2002, Office of the Deputy Prime Minister/Communities and Local Government 2003-07, Scotland 2003-07, Transport 2005-07, Home Affairs 2007-09, Health 2007-09, Transport 2009-10; Department for Communities and Local Government: Parliamentary Under-Secretary of State 2010-13, Government Spokesperson 2010-13. Member: Procedure -2002, Joint Committee on the Draft Modern Slavery Bill 2014, Communications 2014-16. *Councils and public bodies:* Royal Borough of Kensington and Chelsea: Councillor 1970-2011, Mayor 1983-84, Chair: Town Planning Committee 1984-86, Social Services Committee 1987-89, Policy and Resources Committee 1989-2000, Leader of the Council 1989-2000; Member, Mental Health Act Commission 1983-90; Non-executive member, North West Thames Regional Health Authority 1983-94; JP: City of London Commission 1984-2009, Inner London Family Proceedings Court 1992-2009; Governor: Sir John Cass Foundation 1996-99, Sir John Cass Primary School 1997-99; Member, Policy Committee, London Government Association 1999-2001; Chair, St Mary's Hospital NHS Trust 2000-07.

Political interests: Local government, health, justice, environment, communities and families, housing and planning; Europe, USA.

Other: Member/alternate member, EU Committee of the Regions 1998-2010; Director, London First 1996-99; Vice-President, Commonwealth Institute 1999-2006; Friend, University of Grenada 2000-; Trustee, St Mary's Paddington Charitable Trust 2001-08; Chair, England Volunteering Development Council 2004-11; President, Volunteering England 2009-10; In Deep. Freedom: City of London 1984, Royal Borough of Kensington and Chelsea 2011. CBE 1997; *Clubs:* Hurlingham Club.

Recreations: Music, travel.

The Baroness Hanham CBE, House of Lords, London SW1A 0PW
Tel: 020 7219 5609 *Email:* hanhamj@parliament.uk

HANNAY OF CHISWICK, LORD

CROSSBENCH

HANNAY OF CHISWICK (Life Baron), David Hugh Alexander Hannay; cr 2001. Born 28 September 1935; Son of late Julian Hannay and late Eileen Hannay; Married Gillian Rex 1961 (died 2015) (4 sons).

Education: Craigflower School; Winchester College; New College, Oxford (BA modern history 1959); French.

Non-political career: National Service 1954-56 (2nd Lieutenant 8th King's Royal Irish Hussars). Foreign Office (FCO) 1959-95: London 1959-60, Language student, Tehran 1960-61, Oriental secretary, Kabul 1961-63, Second secretary, FCO 1963-65, First secretary, Brussels (EC) 1965-70, Brussels negotiating team 1970-72, Chef de Cabinet to Vice-President EC Commission 1973-77, FCO 1977-84: Head of: Energy, science and space department 1977-79, Middle East department 1979, Assistant under-secretary, EC 1979-84; Minister, Washington 1984-85, Ambassador, perma-

House of Lords Peers' Biographies

nent representative to: EC 1985-90, UN, New York 1990-95; Special Representative for Cyprus 1996-2003; Non-executive director: Chime Communications 1999-2006, Aegis 2000-03; Member, advisory board, GPW 2011-. First Division Association 1959-95.

Political career: *House of Lords:* Raised to the peerage as Baron Hannay of Chiswick, of Bedford Park in the London Borough of Ealing 2001. Member: EU Sub-committee A (Economic and Financial Affairs, Trade and External Relations/Economic and Financial Affairs) 2001-05, European Union 2003-06, 2008-14; EU Sub-committee C (Foreign Affairs, Defence and Development Policy): Member 2005-06, Co-opted member 2006-08; Member, Intergovernmental Organisations 2007-08, EU Sub-committee F (Home Affairs) 2008-12: Chair, EU Sub-committee F (Home Affairs, Health and Education) 2012-14; Member: The Arctic 2014-15, Sexual Violence in Conflict 2015-16, International Relations 2016-. *Councils and public bodies:* Council Member: Birmingham University 1997-2006, Kent University 2009-15; Council Chair and Pro-Chancellor, Birmingham University 2001-06.

Political interests: Foreign and development policy, EU, energy policy and climate change, higher education.

Other: Adviser to Executive Committee, World Federation of United Nations Associations 1995-2000; Member, UN Secretary-General High Level Panel on Threats, Challenges and Change 2003-04; Chair, United Nations Association, UK 2006-11; Member: Top Level Group for Nuclear Disarmament and Non-proliferation 2011-, Future of Europe Forum 2013-16; Advisory Board: Prospect 1995-2005, Centre for European Reform 1996-, European Foreign Affairs Review 1996-; Salzburg Seminar 2001-05; Chair, International Advisory Board, EDHEC Business School, France 2002-09; TANGGUH Independent Advisory Panel 2002-09; Judge, School of Management, Cambridge 2004-10; Governor, Ditchley Foundation 2005-; Chair of Board, Soil Association UK 2006-11; Fellow, New College, Oxford; Children at Risk Foundation (UK). Honorary Fellow, New College, Oxford; Hon DLitt, Birmingham University. Sir Brian Urquhart Award for Distinguished Service to the United Nations 2015. CMG 1981; KCMG 1986; GCMG 1995; CH 2003; *Clubs:* Travellers Club.

Publications: Editor, Britain's Entry into the European Community, Report on the Negotiations (1970-72); Cyprus: The Search for a Solution (2004); New World Disorder – The UN after the Cold War, an Insider's View (2008); Britain's Quest for a Role: A Diplomatic Memoir from Europe to the UN (I.B. Tauris, 2012).

Recreations: Travel, photography, gardening, grandchildren.

The Lord Hannay of Chiswick GCMG CH, House of Lords, London SW1A 0PW
Tel: 020 7219 1358
3 The Orchard, London W4 1JZ *Tel:* 020 8987 9052 *Fax:* 020 8987 9012
Email: d.h.a.hannay@gmail.com

NON-AFFILIATED

HANNINGFIELD, LORD

HANNINGFIELD (Life Baron), Paul Edward Winston White; cr. 1998. Born 16 September 1940; Son of late Edward Ernest William White and Irene Joyce Gertrude, née Williamson.

Education: King Edward VI Grammar School, Chelmsford; Nuffield Scholarship for Agriculture (research in USA specialising in marketing in farming).

Non-political career: Farmer.

Political career: *House of Lords:* Raised to the peerage as Baron Hanningfield, of Chelmsford in the County of Essex 1998. Opposition Whip 2003-07; Opposition Spokesperson for: Office of the Deputy Prime Minister/Communities and Local Government 2003-07, Education and Skills 2004-05, Transport 2005-09, Business, Innovation and Skills 2009-10; Suspended from membership: July 2011-May 2012, May 2014-May 2015. *Other:* Chair: Conservative Party National Local Government Advisory Committee, Board of Conservative Party 1997-2001; Conservative Whip suspended February 2010. *Councils and public bodies:* Essex County Council: Councillor 1970-2010, Council Leader 1998-99, 2001-10, Leader, Conservative Group 2001-10; DL, Essex 1991-; Deputy Chair and Conservative Group Leader, Local Government Association 1997-2001.

Political interests: Local government, education, transport and infrastructure, agriculture, constitutional affairs, foreign policy.

Other: President, Assembly of European Regions Sub-Commission 1990-2005; EU Committee of the Regions: Leader, Conservative Group, UK Delegation -2005, Chair: Enlargement Group 1998-2005, Bulgarian Joint Consultative Committee 2002-05; Vice-President, Commission on Transport and the Information Society 1998-2000; Board member, Commonwealth Local Government Forum 2007-; Association of County Councils: Member 1981-97, Conservative Leader 1995-97; Chair: Council of Local Education Authorities 1990-92; Eastern Region Further Education Funding Council 1992-97; Chair and co-founder, Localis 2001-; Member of Court, Essex University; President, Society of Emergency Planning Officers 2003-; Vice-Patron, Helen Rollason Cancer Centre Appeal. Two honorary doctorates: Essex University, Anglia Ruskin University.

Publications: Several contributions to local government journals.

Recreations: Botany, politics and current affairs, travel, food and wine.

The Lord Hanningfield DL, House of Lords, London SW1A 0PW
Tel: 020 7219 5353

LABOUR

HANWORTH, VISCOUNT

HANWORTH (3rd Viscount, UK), David Stephen Geoffrey Pollock; cr. 1936; 3rd Baron Hanworth (UK) 1926; 3rd Bt of Hanworth (UK) 1922. Born 16 February 1946; Son of 2nd Viscount Hanworth; Married Elizabeth 1968 (2 daughters).

Education: Wellington College, Berkshire; Guildford Technical College; Sussex University (BSc economics 1969); Southampton University (MSc economics and statistics 1970); Amsterdam University (PhD 1988); French.

Non-political career: University of London 1972-2007: Lecturer, Reader; Professor, Leicester University 2007-.

Political career: *House of Lords:* First entered House of Lords 1996; Elected hereditary peer 2011-. Member: Joint Committee on Consolidation, Etc, Bills 2013-, Inheritance and Trustees' Powers Bill 2013, Partnerships (Prosecution) (Scotland) Bill 2013, The Arctic 2014-15, EU Energy and Environment Sub-Committee 2015-, Intellectual Property (Unjustified Threats) Bill 2016.

Political interests: Economic policy, financial regulation, energy, transport, environment, foreign affairs; Austria, France, Germany, Italy, Netherlands.

Publications: The Algebra of Econometrics (1979); Handbook of Time Series Analysis Signal Processing and Dynamics (1999); Co-author, Innovations in Multivariate Statistical Analysis (2000).

The Viscount Hanworth, House of Lords, London SW1A 0PW
Tel: 020 7219 5353 *Email:* pollockd@parliament.uk
Department of Economics, Astley Clarke Building, A108, University of Leicester, Leicester LE1 7RH *Website:* www.le.ac.uk/users/dsgp1

CROSSBENCH

HARDIE, LORD

HARDIE (Life Baron), Andrew Rutherford Hardie; cr 1997. Born 8 January 1946; Son of late Andrew Rutherford and late Elizabeth Currie Hardie; Married Catherine Storrar Elgin 1971 (2 sons 1 daughter).

Education: St Modan's High School, Stirling; Edinburgh University (MA French and German 1966; LLB 1969).

Non-political career: Solicitor 1971; Member, Faculty of Advocates 1973; Advocate Depute 1979-83; QC (Scot) 1985; Treasurer, Faculty of Advocates 1989-94, Dean 1994-97; Lord Advocate 1997-2000; Senator of the College of Justice in Scotland 2000-13; Honorary Bencher, Lincoln's Inn.

Political career: *House of Lords:* Raised to the peerage as Baron Hardie, of Blackford in the City of Edinburgh 1997. As a senior member of the judiciary, disqualified from participation 2009-13; On leave of absence July 2016-. Chair, Mental Capacity Act 2005 2013-14.

Political interests: Law and the constitution, human rights, issues relating to families and children, care and rehabilitation of prisoners (particularly young offenders), disability issues, asylum and immigration, energy and environment; China, India, Sri Lanka, Taiwan.

Other: Non-practising member, Faculty of Advocates; Capability (Scotland), Children's Charities, Christian Aid. PC 1997.

Recreations: Cricket, travel, grandchildren.

Rt Hon the Lord Hardie, House of Lords, London SW1A 0PW
Tel: 020 7219 5353 *Email:* hardiera@parliament.uk

CONSERVATIVE

HARDING OF WINSCOMBE, BARONESS

HARDING OF WINSCOMBE (Life Baroness), Diana (Dido) Mary Harding; cr 2014. Born 9 November 1967; Daughter of Lord and Lady Harding of Petherton; Married John Penrose (qv) 1995 (MP for Weston-Super-Mare) (2 daughters).

Education: St Antony's Leweston School, Dorset; Oxford University (BA philosophy, politics and economics 1988); Harvard Business School (MBA 1992).

Non-political career: Consultant, McKinsey & Co 1988-90; Marketing Director, Thomas Cook 1995-98; Global Sourcing Director, Kingfisher plc 1998-2000; Commercial Director, Woolworths 1998-99; Commercial Director and International Support Director, Tesco plc 2000-08; Convenience Director, Sainsbury's 2008-10; Chief Executive, TalkTalk Telecom Group plc 2010-17.

Political career: *House of Lords:* Raised to the peerage as Baroness Harding of Winscombe, of Nether Compton in the County of Dorset 2014. Member, Economic Affairs 2017-. *Councils and public bodies:* Non-executive director, Bank of England 2014-; Board member, UK Holocaust Memorial Foundation 2015-.

Political interests: Business, digital economic and social issues; China, India.

Other: Non-executive director: British Land Company plc 2010-14, Cheltenham Racecourse 2011-14; Trustee: Go-On, Digital Skills Alliance 2013-, Doteveryone 2016-. Liveryman, Worshipful Company of Goldsmiths. Honorary Doctor of Business Administration, Anglia Ruskin University. Member, Jockey Club.

Recreations: Horse racing, hunting.

The Baroness Harding of Winscombe, House of Lords, London SW1A 0PW
Tel: 020 7219 5353 *Email:* hardingd@parliament.uk

CROSSBENCH

HARRIES OF PENTREGARTH, LORD

HARRIES OF PENTREGARTH (Life Baron), Richard Douglas Harries; cr 2006. Born 2 June 1936; Son of late Brigadier W. D. J. Harries, CBE; Married Josephine Bottomley, MB, BChir, DCH 1963 (1 son 1 daughter).

Education: Wellington College, Berkshire; RMA, Sandhurst; Selwyn College, Cambridge (MA theology 1965); Cuddesdon College, Oxford.

Non-political career: Lieutenant, Royal Corps of Signals 1955-58. Curate, Hampstead Parish Church 1963-69; Chaplain, Westfield College 1966-69; Lecturer, Wells Theological College 1969-72; Vicar, All Saints, Fulham 1972-81; Dean, King's College, London 1981-87; 41st Bishop of Oxford 1987-2006; Visiting Professor, Liverpool Hope University College 2002; Nuffield Council on Bioethics 2002-08; Hon. Professor of Theology, Kings College, London 2006-; Gresham College: Professor of Divinity 2008-12, Fellow and Emeritus Professor 2012-.

Political career: *House of Lords:* Raised to the peerage as Baron Harries of Pentregarth, of Ceinewydd in the County of Dyfed 2006. First entered House of Lords as Bishop of Oxford 1993; Convener of Bench of Bishops 1998-2006. Member, House of Lords' Offices 1997-2001; Chair, Stem Cell Research 2001-02; Member: Procedure 2007-12, Joint Committee on Privacy and Injunctions 2011-12, Works of Art 2012-13, 2014-15, Charities 2016-17, Citizenship and Civic Engagement 2017-. *Councils and public bodies:* General Ordination examiner in Christian Ethics 1972-76; Director, Post Ordination Training, Kensington Jurisdiction 1973-79; Member, Home Office Advisory Committee for reform of sexual offences law 1981-85; Chair, Southwark Ordination Course 1982-87; Vice-chair, Council for Arms Control 1982-87; Chair: Council of Christians and Jews 1992-2001, Board of Social Responsibility for Church of England 1996-2001; Member, Royal Commission on Reform of House of Lords 1999-2000; Nuffield Council on Bioethics 2002-07; Human Fertilisation and Embryo Authority 2003-09.

Political interests: Dalits, religion and belief in British public life, ethics in relation to end of life issues, use of armed forces, poverty, human rights; Georgia, India, West Papua.

Other: Member, Anglican Consultative Council 1994-2003; Consultant, Anglican Peace and Justice Network 1984-94; Vice-chair, Council for Christian Action 1979-87; President, Johnson Society 1988-89; Board member, Christian Aid 1994-2000. Five honorary doctorates; Two honorary Oxbridge fellowships; Fellow, King's College, London; Hon. Fellow: Academy of Medical Sciences, Institute of Biology; Fellow: Learned Society of Wales, Royal Society of Literature. President's Medal, British Academy 2012.

Publications: Prayers of Hope (1975); Turning to Prayer (1978); Prayers of Grief and Glory (1979); Being a Christian (1981); Should Christians Support Guerillas? (1982); The Authority of Divine Love (1983); Praying Round the Clock (1983); Prayer and the Pursuit of Happiness (1985); Morning Has Broken (1985); Christianity and War in a Nuclear Age (1986); C. S. Lewis: the man and his God (1987); Christ is Risen (1988); Is There a Gospel for the Rich (1992); Art and the Beauty of God (1993); The Real God: A Response to Anthony Freeman (1994); Questioning Belief (1995); A Gallery of Reflections – The Nativity in Art (1995); Co-editor, Two Cheers For Secularism (1998); In The Gladness of Today (2000); Co-editor, Christianity: Two Thousand Years (2001); God outside the Box: Why spiritual people object to Christianity (2002); After the Evil: Christianity and Judaism in the Shadow of the Holocaust (2003); The Passion in Art (2004); Praying the Eucharist (2004); The Re-enchantment of Morality (2008); Faith in Politics? Rediscovering the Christian Roots of our Political Values (2010, 2014); Issues of Life and Death: Christian Faith and Medical Intervention (2010); Co-editor, Reinhold Niebuhr and Contemporary Politics (2010); Reinhold Niebuhr Considered (2011); The Image of Christ in Modern Art (2013); Has edited and contributed to other Christian publications as well as articles in the press and periodicals.

Recreations: Theatre, literature, the visual arts, sport.

Rt Rev the Lord Harries of Pentregarth, House of Lords, London SW1A 0PW
Tel: 020 7219 2910 *Email:* harriesr@parliament.uk

LABOUR

HARRIS OF HARINGEY, LORD

HARRIS OF HARINGEY (Life Baron), Jonathan Toby Harris; cr. 1998. Born 11 October 1953; Son of late Professor Harry and Muriel Harris; Married Ann Herbert 1979 (2 sons 1 daughter).

Education: Haberdashers' Aske's School, Elstree; Trinity College, Cambridge (BA natural sciences and economics 1975) (Union President 1974).

Non-political career: Economics division, Bank of England 1975-79; Electricity Consumers' Council 1979-86: Deputy director 1983-86; Director, Association of Community Health Councils for England and Wales 1987-98; Senior associate, The King's Fund 1998-2004; Chair, Toby Harris Associates 1998-; Consultant adviser to: Harrogate Management Centre 1998-2004, Infolog Training 1998-2005, Vantage Point 1998-2001, KPMG 1999-2013, DEMSA 2001-03. Member, Unite.

Political career: *House of Lords:* Raised to the peerage as Baron Harris of Haringey, of Hornsey in the London Borough of Haringey 1998. Member: House of Lords Offices Finance and Staff Sub-committee 2000-02, Science and Technology Sub-committee on Personal Internet Security 2006-07, Joint Committee on National Security Strategy 2010-14; Chair, Olympic and Paralympic Legacy 2013-14; Member, Joint Committee on the National Security Strategy 2016-. Member, Labour Peers' Co-ordinating Committee 2004-. *Other:* Chair: Cambridge University Labour Club 1973, Hornsey Labour Party 1978, 1979, 1980, Labour Group of Local Government Association 1995-2004; Member: Labour Party National Policy Forum 1992-2004, Labour Party Local Government Committee 1993-2004, Greater London Labour Party Regional Board 1993-2004, Labour Peers Co-ordinating Committee 2004-; Labour Peers: Vice-chair 2008-12, Chair 2012-. *Councils and public bodies:* London Borough of Haringey: Councillor 1978-2002, Council Leader 1987-99; Deputy chair, National Fuel Poverty Forum 1981-86; Governor, National Institute for Social Work 1986-94; Member, London Drug Policy Forum 1990-98; Deputy chair, Association of Metropolitan Authorities 1991-97; Member: National Nursery Examination Board 1992-94, Home Office Advisory Council on Race Relations 1992-97; Chair: Association of London Authorities 1993-95, Local Government Anti-Poverty Unit 1994-97, Association of London Government 1995-2000; Member: Court of Middlesex University 1995-, Joint London Advisory Panel 1996-97, London Ambulance Service NHS Trust 1998-2006, London Pension Fund Authority 1998-2000, Metropolitan Police Committee 1998-2000; Local Government Association: Member, Executive 1999-2003, Vice-President 2005-10; Association of Police Authorities: Member, Executive 2000-06, Vice-President 2007-12; Member: Greater London Authority for Brent and Harrow 2000-04; Metropolitan Police Authority: Chair 2000-04, Member (representing the Home Secretary) 2004-12; Special adviser to Board, Transport for London 2004-08; Founding chair, Institute of Commissioning Professionals 2007-08; Member: Police Counter-Terrorism Board 2007-12, Police Counter-Terrorism Ministerial Advisory Group 2008-10; Chair: Independent Advisory Panel on Deaths in Custody 2009-15, Audit Panel, Metropolitan Police and Mayor's Office for Policing and Crime 2012, National Trading Standards Board 2013-; Independent Review into Self-Inflicted Deaths in NOMS Custody of 18-24 year olds 2014-15; Reviewer, Independent Review of London's Preparedness to deal with a Major Terrorist Attack 2016; Chair, Independent Reference Group, National Crime Agency 2017-.

Political interests: Local government, health, policing, information technology, homeland security, consumer protection; Australia, Canada, Cyprus, France, Greece, Italy, USA.

Other: EU Committee of the Regions: Member 1994-98, Alternate member 1998-2002; Chair, Young Fabian Group 1976-77; Board member, London First 1993-2002; Executive council member, RNIB 1993-94; Trustee: *Evening Standard* Blitz Memorial Appeal 1995-99, Help for Health Trust 1995-97, Learning Agency 1996-98; Chair, Wembley National Stadium Trust 1996-; Vice-patron: Artificial Heart Fund 2004, Vocaleyes 2004; Trustee, Safer London Foundation 2004-08;

London Ambassador, Community Service Volunteers 2005-10; Member, Public Sector Advisory Council, Anite 2005-06; Burned Children's Club 2007; Trustee, Bilimankhwe Arts 2008-15; Chair: Freedom Trust 2010-15, Advisory Council, Cities Security and Resilience Network 2011-; Fellow, British Computer Society 2011-; Member, Trading Standards Institute 2013-; FRSA. Freedom, City of London 1998. Honorary doctorate, Middlesex University 1999.

Publications: Co-author, Why Vote Labour? (1979); Contributor to Economics of Prosperity (1980); Co-editor, Energy and Social Policy (1983).

Recreations: Reading, theatre, classical music, opera.

The Lord Harris of Haringey, House of Lords, London SW1A 0PW
Tel: 020 7219 8513
Email: toby@lordtobyharris.org.uk
Website: www.lordtobyharris.org.uk *Twitter:* @LordTobySays

HARRIS OF PECKHAM, LORD

CONSERVATIVE

HARRIS OF PECKHAM (Life Baron), Philip Charles Harris; cr. 1996. Born 15 September 1942; Son of Charles Harris, MC and Ruth Harris; Married Pauline Chumley (later DBE) 1960 (3 sons 1 daughter).

Education: Streatham Grammar School.

Non-political career: Harris Queensway plc: Chairman 1964-88, Chief executive 1987-88; Non-executive director: Great Universal Stores 1986-2004, Fisons plc 1986-94; Chairman: Harris Ventures Ltd 1988-, C. W. Harris Properties 1988-97; Non-executive director, Molyneux Estates 1990-95; Carpetright plc: Chairman 1993-2014, Non-executive chair 2014-; Non-executive director: Matalan 2004-06, Arsenal FC 2005-; Consultant, Tapi Carpets and Floors Ltd 2015-.

Political career: *House of Lords:* Raised to the peerage as Baron Harris of Peckham, of Peckham in the London Borough of Southwark 1996. Member, Works of Art 2005-09. *Other:* Deputy Chairman, Conservative Party Treasurers 1993. *Councils and public bodies:* Governor, United Medical and Dental School of Guy's and St Thomas's Hospitals 1983-98; Member, Court of Patrons, Royal College of Gynaecologists 1984-; Chair, Guy's and Lewisham NHS Trust 1991-93; Deputy chair, Lewisham NHS Trust 1993-97; Council member, University of London Court 1994-96; University College London Council 1996-99.

Other: British Showjumping Association 1974-; Chair: Prostate Cancer Charity: Investing in Life Campaign, Generation Trust, Guy's Hospital 1984-2004; Trustee: National Hospital for Neurology and Neurosurgery Development Foundation 1984-92, Westminster Abbey Trust 1987-96; Sponsor, Harris Federation of Schools 1989-; Director and co-sponsor, Bacon's City Technology College 1990-; Trustee, Tavistock Trust for Aphasia 1993-2003; NSPCC National Appeal Board and Executive Committee 1998-2008; Deputy chair, Full-Stop Campaign 1998-2008; President, Friends of Guy's Hospital 1999-; Trustee: Royal Academy of Arts 1999-2005, Outward Bound Trust 2001-03; Sponsor, Harris HospisCare, Orpington 2002-; Bowel Cancer and Research Trust: Trustee 2005-10, Patron 2010-; Non-executive Director, Arsenal Holdings plc 2005-; Trustee, Westminster Abbey Campaign Development Board 2011-; Hon. Fellow, Royal College of Radiologists 1992; Great Ormond Street Hospital, Wellbeing of Women, Prostate Cancer Charity. Liveryman: Broderers' Company 1992, Clockmakers Company 2003. Freedom, City of London 1992. Three honorary doctorates; Four honorary University Fellowships. Hambro Business Man of the Year 1983; Ernst and Young Entrepreneur of the Year 2007; Beacon Award 2015. Kt 1985; *Clubs:* Mosimanns, Mark's Club. Queens Club.

Recreations: Football, cricket, show jumping, tennis.

The Lord Harris of Peckham, House of Lords, London SW1A 0PW
Tel: 020 7219 5353
Harris Ventures Ltd, Philip Harris House, 1a Spur Road, Orpington, Kent BR6 0PH
Tel: 01689 886886 *Fax:* 01689 886887 *Email:* judy.willett@harrisventures.co.uk

HARRIS OF RICHMOND, BARONESS

LIBERAL DEMOCRAT

HARRIS OF RICHMOND (Life Baroness), Angela Felicity Harris; cr. 1999. Born 4 January 1944; Daughter of late Rev. G H Hamilton Richards and Eva Richards; Married 2nd John Harris 1976 (1 son from previous marriage).

Education: Canon Slade Grammar School, Bolton; Ealing Hotel and Catering College.

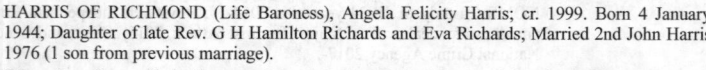

Political career: *House of Lords:* Raised to the peerage as Baroness Harris of Richmond, of Richmond in the County of North Yorkshire 1999. Liberal Democrat: Whip 2000-08, Spokesperson for: Northern Ireland 2003-10, Home Office (police) 2005-10; Deputy Speaker 2008-; Deputy Chairman of Committees 2008-; Contested Lord Speaker election 2011. Member: European Union 2000-04, European Union Sub-committee F (Social Affairs, Education and Home Affairs/Home Affairs) 2000-04 (Chair 2000-04), Refreshment 2003-07, Administration and Works 2007-12,

Ecclesiastical Committee 2013-. *Other:* Contested Yorkshire and the Humber region 1999 European Parliament election. *Councils and public bodies:* Richmond Town Council (Yorkshire): Councillor 1978-81, 1991-99, Mayor 1993-94; Richmondshire District Council: Councillor 1979-89, Chair 1987-88; North Yorkshire County Council: Councillor 1981-2001, Chair 1991-92, Honorary Alderman 2002; JP 1982-98; Non-executive director, Northallerton NHS Trust 1989-97; DL, North Yorkshire 1994-; Chair, North Yorkshire Police Authority 1994-2001; Deputy Chair, National Association of Police Authorities 1997-2001; High Steward, Ripon Cathedral 2012-.

Political interests: Police, Northern Ireland; Canada, Ireland, Nepal, Qatar.

Other: Member: British-American Parliamentary Group 1999-, Inter-Parliamentary Union 2003-, British-Irish Parliamentary Assembly 2005-17; York University: Member, Court 1995-, Member, Nominations Committee 2012-; Patron, Herriot Hospice Homecare, Northallerton 1999-; Police Rehabilitation Trust (Flint House) 2003-; Industry and Parliament Trust: Fellow 2003, Trustee 2006-14, Chair of Trustees 2010-14; President, National Association of Chaplains to the Police 2005-16; Patron, Northern Ireland Hospice; Trustee, Fellowship of St John Trust. Freedom, City of London; Honorary Freedom, Richmond, North Yorkshire 2004; *Clubs:* RAF Club, Civil Service Club.

Recreations: Music, political biographies.

The Baroness Harris of Richmond DL, House of Lords, London SW1A 0PW
Tel: 020 7219 6709 *Email:* harrisa@parliament.uk

HARRISON, LORD

LABOUR

HARRISON (Life Baron), Lyndon Henry Arthur Harrison; cr. 1999. Born 28 September 1947; Son of late Charles and Edith Harrison; Married Hilary Plank 1980 (1 son 1 daughter).

Education: Oxford School; Warwick University (BA English and American studies 1970); Sussex University (MA American studies 1971); Keele University (MA American studies 1978).

Non-political career: Research officer, UMIST Union, Manchester 1975-78; Manager, North East Wales Institute Student Union, Clwyd 1978-89. Member, GMB.

Political career: *House of Lords:* Raised to the peerage as Baron Harrison, of Chester in the County of Cheshire 1999. Departmental Liaison Peer for Northern Ireland 1999-2001. Member: EU Sub-committee C (Common Foreign and Security Policy) 1999-2003, Delegated Powers and Regulatory Reform 2003-07, EU Sub-committee G (Social Policy and Consumer Affairs) 2003-07, Hybrid Instruments 2003-, European Union 2004-08, 2010-15; EU Sub-committee F (Home Affairs): Member 2006-08, Co-opted member 2008-10; Chair, EU Sub-committee A: (Economic and Financial Affairs and International Trade) 2010-12, (Economic and Financial Affairs) 2012-15; Member: Equality Act 2010 and Disability 2015-16, Financial Exclusion 2016-17, Natural Environment and Rural Communities Act 2006 2017-. *Other:* European Parliament: MEP for: Cheshire West 1989-94: Cheshire West and Wirral 1994-99; Secretary, European Parliamentary Labour Party 1991-94. *Councils and public bodies:* Councillor, Cheshire County Council 1981-90; Deputy Chair, North West Tourist Board 1986-89; Vice-President, Association of County Councils 1990-97.

Political interests: Small businesses, tourism, monetary union, children, European Union; Commonwealth, EU member and applicant countries, USA.

Other: Member: Inter-Parliamentary Union 1999-, Commonwealth Parliamentary Association 2007-; Vice-President, Cheshire Landscape Trust 1999-; President, Chester and District Parkinson's Disease Society 2005-; Honorary Council Member NSPCC.

Publications: Everything you wanted to know about the Euro...and were afraid to ask; Tourism means Jobs.

Recreations: Chess, the arts, sport, bridge.

The Lord Harrison, House of Lords, London SW1A 0PW
Tel: 020 7219 6424 *Fax:* 020 7219 5979 *Email:* harrisonlh@parliament.uk

HASKEL, LORD

LABOUR

HASKEL (Life Baron), Simon Haskel; cr. 1993. Born 8 October 1934; Son of late Isaac and Julia Haskel; Married Carole Lewis 1962 (1 son 1 daughter).

Education: Sedbergh School; Salford College of Advanced Technology (ARTCS textile technology 1955); French, Spanish.

Non-political career: National service commission, Royal Artillery 1957. Joined Perrotts Ltd 1961; Chairman, Perrotts Group plc and associated companies 1973-97.

Political career: *House of Lords:* Raised to the peerage as Baron Haskel, of Higher Broughton in the County of Greater Manchester 1993. Opposition Spokesperson for Trade and Industry 1994-97; Opposition Whip 1994-97; Government Whip (Lord in Waiting) 1997-98; Government Spokesperson for: Social Security 1997-98, Trade and Industry 1997-98, the Treasury 1997-98; Deputy Chair of Committees 2002-; Deputy Speaker 2002-; Board member, Parliamentary Office of Science and Technology (POST). Member: Science and Technology 1994-97, 1999-2002, 2005-10, Procedure 2002-05, Science and Technology Sub-committee I (Fighting Infection) 2002-03, EU Sub-committee B (Internal Market) 2003-07, Information 2003-07, Joint Committee on Tax Law Rewrite Bills 2005-10, Science and Technology Sub-Committee I 2007-10 (Allergy/Waste Reduction 2007-08, Nanotechnologies and food 2008-10), Information 2009-14, Delegated Powers and Regulatory Reform 2009-14, EU Sub-committee B: (Internal Market, Energy and Transport) 2010-12, (Internal Market, Infrastructure and Employment) 2012-15, Small- and Medium-Sized Enterprises 2012-13, Digital Skills 2014-15, Secondary Legislation Scrutiny 2015-, Built Environment 2015, Financial Exclusion 2016-17. *Other:* Labour Party 1972 Industry Group: Founder Member, Secretary 1976-81; Chair, Labour Finance and Industry Group 1980-92.

Political interests: Trade and industry, science and technology, overseas development; Europe, USA.

Other: Chair, Thames Concerts Society 1982-90; Trustee, Smith Institute 1998-2008; Patron, Chronic Disease Research Foundation 1999-2006; Trustee, Haskel Family Foundation 2000-; President, Environment Industries Commission 2000-; Patron, Society of Operations Engineers 2000-04; President, Institute for Jewish Policy Research 2002-; International President, Textile Institute 2002-05; Hon. President, Materials UK 2006-. Hon. Doctorate, Bolton University 2007. Cyclists' Touring Club; Tandem Club.

Recreations: Music, cycling.

The Lord Haskel, House of Lords, London SW1A 0PW
Tel: 020 7219 4076 *Email:* haskels@parliament.uk

CROSSBENCH

HASKINS, LORD

HASKINS (Life Baron), Christopher Robin Haskins; cr. 1998. Born 30 May 1937; Son of Robin and Margaret Haskins; Married Gilda Horsley 1959 (3 sons 2 daughters).

Education: St Columba's College, Dublin; Trinity College, Dublin (BA modern history 1959).

Non-political career: Ford Motor Company, Dagenham 1960-62; Northern Foods 1962-, Chairman 1986-2002; Chair, Express Dairies 1998-2002; Director, Yorkshire Television 2002-06; Adviser, Montrose Associates 2003-; Chair, Airtrack Railways Ltd 2004-09; Director, JSR Farms 1991-.

Political career: *House of Lords:* Raised to the peerage as Baron Haskins, of Skidby in the County of the East Riding of Yorkshire 1998. Member, EU Sub-committee D (Environment, Agriculture, Public Health and Consumer Protection/Environment and Agriculture) 2003-06; EU Sub-committee A (Economic and Financial Affairs and International Trade): Co-opted member 2007-10, Member 2010-12; Member: Small- and Medium-Sized Enterprises 2012-13, EU Financial Affairs Sub-committee 2015-. *Councils and public bodies:* Member: Commission for Social Justice 1992-94, UK Round Table on Sustainable Development 1995-97, Hampel Committee on Corporate Governance 1996-97, New Deal Advisory Task Force 1997-2001; Chairman, Better Regulation Task Force 1997-2002; Board member Yorkshire Forward Regional Development Agency 1998-2008; Chair Council, Open University 2005-14; Member, Equality and Reform Group Board, Cabinet Office 2010-; Chair, Humber Local Enterprise Partnership 2011-.

Political interests: Europe, food and agriculture, countryside, regulation, universities, regionalism/devolution; France, Ireland, Italy, USA.

Other: Trustee: Runnymede Trust 1989-98, Demos 1993-2000, Civil Liberties Trust 1997-99, Legal Assistance Trust 1998-04, Lawes Agricultural Trust 2000-, Business Dynamics 2002-07; Oxfam, Unicef, Medical Aid for Palestine, Samaritans, One World, Médecins Sans Frontières, Safer World, Citizens Advice Bureau. Honorary doctorates: Trinity College, Dublin, Bradford University, Essex University, Cranfield University, Huddersfield University, Leeds Metropolitan University, Hull University, Lincoln University.

Recreations: Walking, writing.

The Lord Haskins, House of Lords, London SW1A 0PW
Tel: 020 7219 5353
Quarryside Farm, 46 Main Street, Skidby, Nr Cottingham, East Yorkshire HU16 5TG
Tel: 01482 842692 *Fax:* 01482 845249 *Email:* gshaskins@aol.com

HASTINGS OF SCARISBRICK, LORD

CROSSBENCH

HASTINGS OF SCARISBRICK (Life Baron), Michael John Hastings; cr 2005. Born 29 January 1958; Son of late Petain Hastings and Olive Hastings; Married Jane 1990 (2 daughters 1 son).

Education: Scarisbrick Hall School, Ormskirk; Cornwall College, Montego Bay, Jamaica; London School of Theology (BA theology and sociology 1979); Westminster College, Oxford (PGCE).

Non-political career: BBC 1994-2006: Political and parliamentary affairs department, Head of public affairs 1995-2006, Head of corporate social responsibility 2003-06; Chair, Crime Concern 1995-2008; Board member, Responsible and Sustainable Business Committee, BT 2004-; KPMG: International Director for Corporate Citizenship 2006-, Global Head, Citizenship and Diversity 2007-.

Political career: *House of Lords:* Raised to the peerage as Baron Hastings of Scarisbrick, of Scarisbrick in the County of Lancashire 2005. Member, Communications 2007-09. *Councils and public bodies:* Commissioner, Commission for Racial Equality 1993-2001; Member, Government Social Security Advisory Committee 1993-95; Founding member, Metropolitan Police Advisory Committee 1995-97.

Other: Patron: Zane, Child Brain Injury Trust; Founding chair: Childnet International, Springboard for Children; Trustee, Vodafone Group Foundation 2008-; Vice-President, Unicef; Chairman, Millenium Promise UK; Council member, Overseas Development Institute. Chancellor, Regent's University London 2017-. Unicef award 2005. CBE 2002.

The Lord Hastings of Scarisbrick CBE, House of Lords, London SW1A 0PW
Tel: 020 7219 3781 *Email:* hastingsm@parliament.uk

HAUGHEY, LORD

LABOUR

HAUGHEY (Life Baron), William Haughey; cr 2013. Born 2 July 1956; Married Susan 1978.

Education: St Francis; Holyrood Secondary; Springburn College.

Non-political career: Engineering supervisor, Turner Refrigeration 1973-83; Head of engineering, UTS Carrier, UAE 1983-85; Founder, City Refrigeration 1985-.

Political career: *House of Lords:* Raised to the peerage as Baron Haughey, of Hutchesontown in the City of Glasgow 2013.

Other: Chair: Scottish Enterprise Glasgow, Asset Skills; Non-executive: Dunedin Enterprise Trust, Glasgow Culture and Leisure; Charter member, Duke of Edinburgh Awards Scheme; Member, Growth Fund Panel, Prince's Trust Youth Business Scotland; Director, Celtic Football Club; Founder, City Charitable Trust. Honorary doctorate, Glasgow Caledonian University. The Loving Cup 2001; St Mungo Prize 2006. OBE 2003; Kt 2012.

The Lord Haughey OBE, House of Lords, London SW1A 0PW
Tel: 020 7219 5353
Website: www.williehaughey.com

HAWORTH, LORD

LABOUR

HAWORTH (Life Baron), Alan Robert Haworth; cr. 2004. Born 26 April 1948; Son of late John Haworth, retail grocer, and Hilma Haworth, née Westhead; Married Gill Cole 1973 (divorced); married Maggie Rae 1991.

Education: Blackburn Technical and Grammar School; Barking Regional College of Technology (BSc Soc London University external 1971).

Non-political career: North East London Polytechnic 1972-75: Registrar, Faculty of Art and Design 1972-73, Assistant to director of course development 1973-75; Parliamentary Labour Party: Committee Officer 1975-85, Senior Committee Officer 1985-92, Secretary 1992-2004. Member, Transport and General Workers' Union 1975-2005.

Political career: *House of Lords:* Raised to the peerage as Baron Haworth, of Fisherfield in Ross and Cromarty 2004.

Political interests: Energy, environment, transport, health, Royal Navy; Azerbaijan, Cambodia, Georgia, Iran, Kazakhstan, Kyrgyzstan, Laos, Russia, Tibet, Vietnam.

Other: Member: Munro Society, Mountain Bothies Association, Marine Conservation Society, Scottish Wild Land Group, National Trust for Scotland, RSPB, John Muir Trust, Mountaineering Council of Scotland, Wildfowl and Wetlands Trust, Ramblers.

Publications: Co-editor (with Baroness Hayter of Kentish Town), Men Who Made Labour (Routledge, 2006).

Recreations: Hillwalking, mountaineering, first member of Lords to have climbed all the Munros.

The Lord Haworth, House of Lords, London SW1A 0PW
Tel: 020 7219 6620 *Email:* hawortha@parliament.uk

HAY OF BALLYORE, LORD

DEMOCRATIC UNIONIST PARTY

HAY OF BALLYORE (Life Baron), William Alexander Hay; cr 2014. Born 16 April 1950; Divorced (3 sons 2 daughters); married 2010.

Education: Faughen Valley High School.

Non-political career: Haulage contractor.

Political career: *House of Commons:* Contested (DUP) Foyle 1997, 2001 and 2005 general elections. *House of Lords:* Raised to the peerage as Baron Hay of Ballyore, of Ballyore in the City of Londonderry 2014. *Other:* Northern Ireland Assembly: MLA for: Foyle 1998-2011, Foyle (revised boundary) 2011 to 13 October 2014, Speaker 2007-14, Chair: Assembly Commission 2007-14, Business Committee 2007-14. *Councils and public bodies:* Londonderry City Council: Councillor 1981-2010, Deputy Mayor 1992, Mayor 1993; Member: Western Education and Library Board 1998, Northern Ireland Housing Council 1998, Northern Ireland Policing Board 2001-07.

Other: President, Commonwealth Parliamentary Association (Northern Ireland Assembly Branch); Member: Loyal Orders, Londonderry Port and Harbour Commission 1998-; Spokesperson, Apprentice Boys.

The Lord Hay of Ballyore, House of Lords, London SW1A 0PW
Tel: 020 7219 5353

HAYMAN, BARONESS

CROSSBENCH

HAYMAN (Life Baroness), Helene Valerie Hayman; cr. 1996. Born 26 March 1949; Daughter of late Maurice and Maude Middleweek; Married Martin Hayman 1974 (4 sons).

Education: Wolverhampton High School for Girls; Newnham College, Cambridge (BA law 1969) (Union President 1969).

Non-political career: Shelter, National Campaign for the Homeless 1969-71; Social Services Department, London Borough of Camden 1971-74; Deputy director, National Council for One Parent Families 1974.

Political career: *House of Commons:* Contested Wolverhampton South West February 1974 general election. MP (Labour) for Welwyn and Hatfield October 1974-79. Contested Welwyn and Hatfield 1979 general election. *House of Lords:* Raised to the peerage as Baroness Hayman, of Dartmouth Park in the London Borough of Camden 1996. Opposition Spokesperson for Health 1996-97; Parliamentary Under-Secretary of State: Department of the Environment, Transport and the Regions (Minister for Roads) 1997-98, Department of Health 1998-99; Minister of State, Ministry of Agriculture, Fisheries and Food 1999-2001; Lord Speaker 2006-11; Member, Parliamentary and Political Service Honours Committee 2012-. Member: Constitution 2005-06, Liaison 2005-06, Procedure 2006-11; Chair, House 2006-11. *Councils and public bodies:* Member, Royal College of Gynaecologists Ethics Committee 1982-97; Committee on Ethics of Clinical Investigation, University College London/University College Hospital: Member 1987-97, Vice-chair 1990-97; Vice-chair: Bloomsbury Health Authority 1988-90, Bloomsbury and Islington Health Authority 1991-92; Council member, University College, London 1992-97; Chair, Whittington Hospital NHS Trust 1992-97; Member: Review Committee of Privy Counsellors of the Anti-terrorism, Crime and Security Act 2002-04, General Medical Council 2013-.

Political interests: Health, education, overseas development; Sub-Saharan Africa.

Other: Commonwealth Parliamentary Association (UK Branch): President 2006-11, Vice-President 2011-14, Member, Executive Committee 2014-16; Hon. President, Inter-Parliamentary Union, British Group 2006-11; Chair, Cancer Research UK 2001-04; Roadsafe: Board member 2001-05, Patron 2006-; Board of Trustees, Royal Botanical Gardens, Kew 2002-06; Chair: Specialised Health Care Alliance 2004-06, Human Tissue Authority 2005-06; Trustee, Tropical Health and Education Trust 2005-06; Patron, Anne Frank Trust UK 2009-; President: Hansard Society 2010-11, Industry and Parliament Trust -2011, Parliament Choir -2011; Trustee: Sabin Vaccine Institute 2013-17, Malaria Consortium 2013-16, Disaster Emergency Committee 2014-; Chair: Cambridge University Health Partners 2014-, Ethics and Governance Council UK Biobank 2015-; Fellow, Newnham College, Cambridge. Honorary degree: University of North London, Hertfordshire University, Wolverhampton University, Birmingham University, Brunel University. PC 2001; GBE 2012.

Rt Hon the Baroness Hayman GBE, House of Lords, London SW1A 0PW
Tel: 020 7219 5083 *Email:* haymanh@parliament.uk

HAYTER OF KENTISH TOWN, BARONESS

LAB/CO-OP

Shadow Deputy Leader of the House of Lords; Opposition Spokesperson for Business, Energy and Industrial Strategy, Exiting the European Union and Constitutional Affairs

HAYTER OF KENTISH TOWN (Life Baroness); Dianne Hayter; cr 2010. Born 7 September 1949; Daughter of late Alec Hayter and late Nancy Hayter; Married Prof. David Caplin 1994.

Education: Penrhos College, Colwyn Bay; Aylesbury High School; Durham University (BA sociology and social administration 1970); London University (PhD 2004); French (basic).

Non-political career: Research assistant: General and Municipal Workers Union 1970-72, European Trade Union Confederation, Brussels 1973; Research officer, Trade Union Advisory Committee to OECD, Paris 1973-74; Fabian Society: Assistant general secretary 1974-76, General secretary 1976-82, Member, executive committee 1986-95, Chair 1992-93; Journalist, *A Week in Politics*, Channel 4 1982-84; Director, Alcohol Concern 1984-90; Chief executive, European Parliamentary Labour Party 1990-96; Director of corporate affairs, Wellcome Trust 1996-99; Chief executive, Pelican Centre 1999-2001; Member, Board for Actuarial Standards 2006-11; Chair: Consumer panel, Bar Standards Board 2006-09, Property Standards Board 2008-10, Legal Services Consumer Panel 2009-11; Visiting Professor, Westminster University 2012-. GMB.

Political career: *House of Lords:* Raised to the peerage as Baroness Hayter of Kentish Town, of Kentish Town in the London Borough of Camden 2010. Opposition Whip 2011-15; Opposition Spokesperson for: Business, Innovation and Skills (Consumer Affairs) 2012-16, Cabinet Office 2012-17, Women and Equalities Office 2015-16, Business, Energy and Industrial Strategy 2016-, Exiting the European Union 2016-, Constitutional Affairs 2017-; Shadow Deputy Leader of the House of Lords 2017-. Member: Joint Committee on the Draft Defamation Bill 2011, Liaison 2017-. *Other:* Member: Executive committee, London Labour Party 1977-83, National Constitution Committee, Labour Party 1987-98; National Executive Committee, Labour Party: Member 1998-2010, Vice-chair 2006-07, Chair 2007-08; Chair, Holborn and St Pancras Labour Party 1990-93.

Political interests: Trade unions, consumer affairs, women; France, New Zealand, Sri Lanka.

Other: Member, Royal Commission on Criminal Procedure 1978-80; Vice-chair, Webb Memorial Trust 1997-; Member: National board, Patient Safety Agency 2001-04, Dr Foster Ethics Committee 2001-10; Financial Services Consumer Panel: Member 2001-05, Vice-chair 2003-05; Board member, National Consumer Council 2001-08; Member: Determinations Panel, Pensions Regulator 2005-10, Insolvency Practices Council 2006-10; Blenheim, Pelican Cancer Trust, Dartmouth Street Trust, Webb Memorial Trust. Hon. Doctor of Letters, Westminster University 2015.

Publications: Author, Fightback! Labour's Traditional Right in the 1970s and 1980s (2005); Co-editor (with Lord Haworth), Men Who Made Labour (2006); Contributor, The Prime Ministers Who Never Were (2011).

Recreations: Reading, travel.

The Baroness Hayter of Kentish Town, House of Lords, London SW1A 0PW
Tel: 020 7219 8926 *Email:* hayterd@parliament.uk *Twitter:* @HayteratLords

HAYWARD, LORD

CONSERVATIVE

HAYWARD (Life Baron), Robert Antony Hayward; cr 2015. Born 11 March 1949; Son of late Ralph and Mary Hayward.

Education: Abingdon School; Maidenhead Grammar School; University College of Rhodesia (BSc (Econ) 1970).

Non-political career: Personnel Manager: Esso Petroleum 1971-75, Coca Cola Bottlers 1975-79, GEC Large Machines 1979-82; Director-General, British Soft Drink Association 1993-99; Director, British Beer and Pub Association 1999-2009.

Political career: *House of Commons:* Contested Carmarthen October 1974 general election. MP (Conservative) for Kingswood 1983-92. PPS: to Minister for: Corporate and Consumer Affairs 1985-87, Industry 1986-87, to Secretary of State for Transport 1987-89. *House of Lords:* Raised to the peerage as Baron Hayward, of Cumnor in the County of Oxfordshire 2015. Member: Licensing Act 2003 2016, Political Polling and Digital Media 2017-. *Other:* National vice-chairman, Young Conservatives 1975. *Councils and public bodies:* Councillor, Coventry City Council 1976-78.

Political interests: Economics, transport, defence.

Other: Director, Stonewall 1997-2003; Board Member and Treasurer, Dignity in Dying 2012-16; Director, Portcullis Public Affairs 2012-14; Chair, Public Sector Equality Duty Review 2012-13; Deputy Chair, Central YMCA 2014-17; Board Member, YMCA Training 2013-; Business Breakfast Presenter, Colourful Radio 2014-15. OBE 1991. Founder Chairman, Kings Cross Steelers RFC 1996-99.

Recreations: Former RFU rugby referee.

The Lord Hayward OBE, House of Lords, London SW1A 0PW
Tel: 020 7219 7058
Email: robertahayward11@gmail.com

LABOUR

HEALY OF PRIMROSE HILL, BARONESS

HEALY OF PRIMROSE HILL (Life Baroness), Anna Mary Healy; cr 2010. Born 10 May 1955; Daughter of late Martin Healy and Kathleen Healy; Married Jon Cruddas (qv) 1992 (MP for Dagenham and Rainham) (1 son).

Education: St Aloysius Convent; Royal Holloway College, London (BA modern history/economic history/politics 1976); Birkbeck College, London (MSc politics 1982); City University, London (Diploma journalism 1982-83).

Non-political career: Labour Party HQ 1978-88: Personal assistant to the international secretary 1978-81, Personal assistant to director of communications 1981-85; Press officer, later campaigns press officer 1985-88; Press office, Parliamentary Labour Party 1988-96; Press officer to Tony Blair MP as Leader of the Opposition 1996-97; Special adviser to: Mo Mowlam MP as Secretary of State for Northern Ireland 1997-98, Jack Cunningham MP as Minister for the Cabinet Office and Chancellor of the Duchy of Lancaster 1998-99; Communications strategist, Carlton TV 2000; Senior consultant, GPC 2000-01; Special adviser to Lord Macdonald of Tradeston as: Minister for Transport 2001, Minister for the Cabinet Office 2001-03; Head of office of Jon Cruddas MP 2003-07; Special adviser to Harriet Harman MP as Leader of the House of Commons and Lord Privy Seal 2007-10; Chief of staff to Harriet Harman MP as Leader of the Opposition 2010. Former Member: NUJ, Unite.

Political career: *House of Lords:* Raised to the peerage as Baroness Healy of Primrose Hill, of Primrose Hill in the London Borough of Camden 2010. Member: HIV and AIDS in the UK 2010-11, Joint Committee on Parliamentary Privilege 2013, Communications 2013-16.

Political interests: Labour Party, health and welfare policies, penal reform; China, Ireland, Italy, Middle East, Spain, USA.

Other: Commonwealth Parliamentary Association; Anaphylaxis Campaign.

Recreations: Music, film, literature.

The Baroness Healy of Primrose Hill, House of Lords, London SW1A 0PW
Tel: 020 7219 8912 *Email:* healyab@parliament.uk

CONSERVATIVE

HELIC, BARONESS

BARONESS HELIC (Life Baroness), Arminka Helic; cr 2014. Born 20 April 1968.

Education: High school, Gracanica, Bosnia and Herzegovina; University of Sarajevo; London School of Economics.

Non-political career: Defence adviser to Conservative Shadow Secretaries of State for Defence 1999-2005; Senior adviser to William Hague as Shadow Foreign Secretary 2005-10; Special adviser to William Hague as: Foreign Secretary 2010-14, Leader of the House of Commons 2014-15; Co-author, Preventing Sexual Violence Initiative (PSVI) 2012-; Director, JP.D.H. London Ltd 2015- .

Political career: *House of Lords:* Raised to the peerage as Baroness Helic, of Millbank in the City of Westminster 2014. Member, International Relations 2016-.

Political interests: Foreign policy, defence and international security, human rights, post-conflict issues.

The Baroness Helic, House of Lords, London SW1A 0PW
Tel: 020 7219 5353 *Twitter:* @arminkahelic

LABOUR

HENIG, BARONESS

HENIG (Life Baroness), Ruth Beatrice Henig; cr. 2004. Born 10 November 1943; Daughter of Kurt and Elfrieda Munzer; Married Stanley Henig 1966 (divorced 1993) (2 sons); married Jack Johnstone 1994 (died 2013).

Education: Wyggeston Girls' Grammar School, Leicester; Bedford College, London (BA history 1965); Lancaster University (PhD history 1978); French, German.

Non-political career: Lancaster University 1968-2002: History lecturer 1968-93, Senior history lecturer 1993-2002, Head of department 1995-97, Dean of arts and humanities 1997-2000; Chair, Security Industry Authority 2007-13. Member, AUT 1968-2002.

Political career: *House of Commons:* Contested (Labour) Lancaster 1979 and 1992 general elections. *House of Lords:* Raised to the peerage as Baroness Henig, of Lancaster in the County of Lancashire 2004. Deputy Chairman of Committees 2015-. Member: EU Sub-committee F (Home Affairs) 2005-09, Draft Legal Services Bill Joint Committee 2006, Refreshment 2009-10, 2011-14; Co-opted member, EU Sub-committee G (Social Policy and Consumer Affairs) 2009-10; Member EU Sub-committees: G (Social Policies and Consumer Protection) 2010-12, C (External Affairs) 2012-15; Member: European Union 2014-15, Licensing Act 2003 2016-17. Vice-chair, PLP Departmental: Committee for Home Affairs 2006-10, Group for Home Affairs 2010-15. *Other:* Vice-chair, PLP Departmental Group for Home Affairs 2006-09, 2011-. *Councils and public bodies:* Lancashire County Council: Councillor 1981-2005, Chair 1999-2000; Magistrate, Lancaster Bench 1984-2005; Chair, Lancashire Police Authority 1995-2005; Member, Lawrence Steering Group (Home Office) 1998-2005; Association of Police Authorities: Chair 1997-2005, President 2005-12; DL, Lancashire 2002; Member: Street Crime Action Group 2002-04, National Criminal Justice Board 2003-05.

Political interests: Policing and private security, criminal justice system, foreign affairs, Europe; China, Japan, Malaysia, Thailand.

Other: Chair, Storey Creative Industries Centre, Lancaster 2006-10; Royal National Lifeboat Institute, Save the Children, International Red Cross, Well-being of Women, Prince's Trust, Be Your Best Foundation. Member, Worshipful Company of Security Professionals. Hon. Fellow, Lancaster University. Outstanding Contribution to Industry, Security Excellence Awards 2012; Imbert Prize for Security Industry Professional of the Year, ASC 2013. CBE 2000.

Publications: The League of Nations (Oliver and Boyd, 1973); Versailles and After (Routledge, 1984, 1995); Origins of the Second World War (Routledge, 1985); The Weimer Republic 1919-33 (Routledge, 1988); Origins of the First World War (Routledge, 1989, 1993, 2002); Co-author: Europe 1870-1945 (Longmans, 1997), Women and Political Power (Routledge, 2000); History of the League of Nations (Haus, 2010).

Recreations: Bridge, fell-walking, gardening, wine.

The Baroness Henig CBE, House of Lords, London SW1A 0PW
Tel: 020 7219 5133 *Email:* henigr@parliament.uk
Email: ruthhenig@gmail.com
Website: ruthhenigassociates.co.uk

CONSERVATIVE

HENLEY, LORD

HENLEY (8th Baron, I), Oliver Michael Robert Eden; cr. 1799; 6th Baron Northington (UK) 1885. Born 22 November 1953; Son of 7th Baron; Married Caroline Patricia Sharp 1984 (3 sons 1 daughter).

Education: Dragon School, Oxford; Clifton College, Bristol; Durham University (BA modern history 1975).

Non-political career: Called to the Bar, Middle Temple 1977.

Political career: *House of Lords:* First entered House of Lords 1977. Sits as Baron Northington; Government Whip 1989; Government Spokesperson for Health 1989; Joint Parliamentary Under-Secretary of State: Department of Social Security 1989-93, Department of Employment 1993-94, Ministry of Defence 1994-95; Minister of State, Department of Education and Employment 1995-97; Opposition Spokesperson for: Defence 1997, Education and Employment 1997, Treasury 1997-98, Home Affairs 1997-98, Constitutional Affairs 1998-99; Opposition Chief Whip 1998-2001; Elected hereditary peer 1999-; Deputy Speaker 1999-2001; Deputy Chairman of Committees 1999-2001; Opposition Spokesperson for: Cabinet Office June 1999-2000, Legal Affairs 2003-07, Constitutional Affairs 2005-07, Home Affairs 2006-07, Justice 2007-10; Parliamentary Under-Secretary of State and Government Spokesperson, Department for Environment, Food and Rural Affairs 2010-11; Government Spokesperson for: Business, Innovation and Skills 2011,

House of Lords Peers' Biographies

Home Office 2011-12; Minister of State for Crime Prevention and Anti-Social Behaviour Reduction, Home Office 2011-12; Government Whip (Lord in Waiting) 2016-17; Parliamentary Under-Secretary of State and Government Spokesperson, Department for Work and Pensions 2016-17. Member: House of Lords Offices Administration and Works Sub-committee 1998-2001, Procedure 1998-2001, Privileges 1998-2002, Selection 1999-2001, House of Lords Offices -2001; Co-opted Member, European Union Sub-committee E (Law and Institutions) 2003-06; Member: Inheritance and Trustees' Powers Bill 2013, Extradition Law 2014-15, Joint Committee on Human Rights 2015-16, Joint Committee on the Draft Investigatory Powers Bill 2015-16; Chair, Communications 2017-. *Other:* Penrith and the Border Conservative Association: Chair 1987-89, President 1989-94. *Councils and public bodies:* President, Cumbria Association of Local Councils 1981-89; Councillor, Cumbria County Council 1986-89.

Other: PC 2013; *Clubs:* Brooks's Club.

Rt Hon the Lord Henley, House of Lords, London SW1A 0PW
Tel: 020 7219 3108 *Email:* henleyo@parliament.uk

HENNESSY OF NYMPSFIELD, LORD

CROSSBENCH

HENNESSY OF NYMPSFIELD (Life Baron), Peter John Hennessy; cr 2010. Born 28 March 1947; Son of William Gerald and Edith Hennessy; Married Enid Candler 1969 (2 daughters).

Education: Marling School, Stroud; St John's College, Cambridge (BA 1969; PhD 1990); London School of Economics; Harvard University, USA.

Non-political career: Reporter, *Times Higher Education Supplement* 1972-74, *The Times*: Reporter 1974-76, Whitehall Correspondent 1976-82, Home leader writer and columnist 1982-84; Lobby Correspondent, *Financial Times* 1976; Journalist, *The Economist* 1982; Columnist: *New Statesman* 1986-87, *The Independent* 1987-91; Visiting professor of government, Strathclyde University 1989-94; Professor of contemporary history, Queen Mary University, London 1992-2000; Professor of rhetoric, Gresham College 1994-97; Member, Steering group, Sharman Review of Audit and Accountability for Central Government 2001-01; Attlee professor of contemporary British history 2001-; Member, Cabinet Office advisory group on security and intelligence records 2004-10; Mile End Institute of Contemporary British Government, Intelligence and Society, Queen Mary University, London: Director 2006-11, Patron 2011-.

Political career: *House of Lords:* Raised to the peerage as Baron Hennessy of Nympsfield, of Nympsfield in the County of Gloucestershire 2010. Member: Joint Committee on the Draft House of Lords Reform Bill 2011-12, Science and Technology 2014-17.

Other: Vice-President, Politics Association 1985-90; Trustee, Attlee Foundation 1985-98; Institute of Contemporary British History: Founder and co-director 1986-89, Board member 1989-98; Board member, Institute of Historical Research 1992-97; President, Johnian Society 1995; Chairman, Kennedy Memorial Trust 1995-2000; Vice-President, RHists 1996-2000; Governor, Ditchley Foundation 2001-; Trustee: Geffrye Museum 2002-04, Orwell Memorial Trust 2002-04; Director, The Tablet 2003-; Fellow, British Academy 2003-; Patron, Bletchley Park Trust 2011-; Visiting fellow: Policy Studies Institute 1986-91, Reading University 1988-94, Nottingham University 1989-95; Honorary research fellow, Department of Politics and Sociology, Birkbeck College, London 1990-91; Visiting scholar, Centre for Australian Public Sector Management, Griffith University, Brisbane 1991; Honorary fellow, Institute of Contemporary British History 1995; Fellow, Gresham College 1997. Hon. DLitt, Universities of: West of England 1995, Westminster 1996, Kingston 1998, Strathclyde 2005; Hon. Fellow, St Benet's Hall, Oxford 2008; DUniv, Open University 2009; Hon. DLitt, Reading University 2011; Hon. Master of the Bench, Middle Temple 2012. Duff Cooper Prize 1993; NCR Prize 1994; Orwell Prize for Political Writing 2007.

Publications: What the Papers Never Said (1985); Never Again: Britain 1945-51 (1992); The Hidden Wiring: Unearthing the British Constitution (1995); Muddling Through (1996); The Prime Minister: the office and its holders since 1945 (2000); The Secret State (2002, 2nd edn 2010); Having it So Good: Britain in the Fifties (2006); Editor, The New Protective State: Government, Intelligence and Terrorism (Continuum, 2007); Cabinets and the Bomb (2007); Distilling the Frenzy: Writing the History of One's Own Times (Biteback, 2012).

Professor the Lord Hennessy of Nympsfield, House of Lords, London SW1A 0PW
Tel: 020 7219 5790 *Email:* hennessyp@parliament.uk

HESELTINE, LORD

CONSERVATIVE

HESELTINE (Life Baron), Michael Ray Dibdin Heseltine; cr. 2001. Born 21 March 1933; Son of late Colonel R. D. Heseltine; Married Anne Williams 1962 (1 son 2 daughters).

Education: Shrewsbury School; Pembroke College, Oxford (BA philosophy, politics and economics 1954) (Union President).

Non-political career: Chair: Haymarket Press (Magazine Publishers) 1964-70, Haymarket Media Group 1999-2010, Haymarket Group 1997-, Advisory Committee, Regional Growth Fund 2010-17; Chair: Thames Estuary 2050 Commission 2016-17, Regeneration Advisory Panel 2016-17; Commissioner, National Infrastructure Commission 2015-17.

Political career: *House of Commons:* Contested Gower 1959 and Coventry North 1964 general elections. MP (Conservative) for Tavistock 1966-74, for Henley February 1974-2001. Parliamentary Secretary, Ministry of Transport June-October 1970; Parliamentary Under-Secretary of State, Department of the Environment 1970-72; Minister for Aerospace and Shipping, Department of Trade and Industry 1972-74; Opposition Spokesperson for: Industry 1974-76, Environment 1976-79; Secretary of State for: Environment 1979-83, 1990-92, Defence 1983-86, President of the Board of Trade and Secretary of State for Trade and Industry 1992-95; Deputy Prime Minister and First Secretary of State 1995-97. *House of Lords:* Raised to the peerage as Baron Heseltine, of Thenford in the County of Northamptonshire 2001. Government Adviser on Local Growth 2015-17. *Other:* Chair, Conservative Mainstream Group; President, Conservative Group for Europe; Contested Conservative Party leadership November 1990; Patron, Tory Reform Group. *Councils and public bodies:* Commissioner, National Infrastructure Commission 2015-.

Other: Member, Millennium Commission 1994-2001; Chair, Anglo/Chinese Forum 1998-2004; Vice-President, Royal Horticultural Society 2009-; Chair, Tees Valley Inward Investment Initiative 2015-; Royal Institute of British Architects 1991; The 48 Group Club 2003. Honorary Liveryman of the Worshipful Company of Marketers 2015. Freedom: City of Liverpool 2012, City of London 2012. Hon fellow, Pembroke College 1986; Hon degree, Leeds Metropolitan University 1989; Hon LLD, Liverpool University 1990; Hon degree: Swansea University 2001, Aston University 2013; Hon doctorate, University of South Wales 2013; Hon fellow: Northampton University 2013, Liverpool John Moores University 2013; Birmingham City University 2014. PPA Marcus Morris Award 2003; Publicity Club of London Cup 2005; Lifetime Achievment, National Business Awards 2005; Goldie Oldie of the Year, *The Oldie* awards 2013. PC 1979; CH 1997; *Clubs:* Carlton, Pratt's, Brooks's, White's, Beefsteak Club.

Publications: Where There's a Will (1987); The Challenge of Europe: Can Britain Win? (1989); Life in the Jungle (autobiography) (2000); No Stone Unturned (2012); Co-author with Lady Heseltine, Thenford: The Creation of an English Garden (2016).

Recreations: Gardening.

Rt Hon the Lord Heseltine CH, House of Lords, London SW1A 0PW

HIGGINS, LORD

CONSERVATIVE

HIGGINS (Life Baron), Terence Langley Higgins; cr. 1997. Born 18 January 1928; Son of late Reginald and Rose Higgins; Married Rosalyn Cohen 1961 (later QC and DBE and HE Judge Rosalyn Higgins, President of the International Court of Justice) (1 son 1 daughter).

Education: Alleyn's School, Dulwich, London; Gonville and Caius College, Cambridge (BA economics 1958, MA) (Union President 1958); Yale University, USA 1958-59.

Non-political career: Served in the RAF 1946-48. British Olympic Games Team 1948, 1952; New Zealand Shipping Co., in UK and New Zealand 1948-55; Commonwealth Games Team 1950; Economic specialist, Unilever Ltd 1958-64; Economic consultant, Lex Services Group plc 1975-80; Director: Warne Wright Group 1976-84, Lex Service Group 1980-92; First Choice Holidays plc (formerly Owners Abroad plc) 1991-97; Chair and trustee, Lex Services Pension Fund 1994-2003; Member, Claims Resolution Tribunal for Dormant Accounts in Switzerland 1998-2002.

Political career: *House of Commons:* MP (Conservative) for Worthing 1964-97. Minister of State, Treasury 1970-72; Financial Secretary, Treasury 1972-74. Chair: Procedure 1980-83, Treasury 1983-92, Liaison 1984-97. Member, Executive, 1922 Committee 1980-97. *House of Lords:* Raised to the peerage as Baron Higgins, of Worthing in the County of West Sussex 1997. Opposition Spokesperson for: Social Security/Work and Pensions 1997-2005, the Treasury 1997-2001. Member: Speakership 2005, Conventions Joint Committee 2006, Personal Service Companies 2013-14. *Councils and public bodies:* Governor, Dulwich College 1980-95; DL, West Sussex 1988; Governor, Alleyn's School, Dulwich 1995-99.

Political interests: Finance, social security, transport, sport, horse welfare; Netherlands, New Zealand, USA.

Other: Hon. member, Keynes College, Kent University 1976-; Council, Royal Institute of International Affairs, Chatham House 1980-85; Institute of Advanced Motorists: Council 1980-97, Fellow 1997; Council, National Institute for Economic and Social Research: Council member 1980-, Governor 1988-; Trustee, Industry and Parliament Trust 1987-92. Freedom, Worthing 1997. PC 1979; KBE 1993; *Clubs:* Hawk's (Cambridge), Reform, Yale Club of London. Koninklijke Haagsche Golf, Netherlands; Patron Herne Hill Harriers.

Recreations: Golf, boating.

Rt Hon the Lord Higgins KBE DL, House of Lords, London SW1A 0PW
Tel: 020 7219 4164 *Fax:* 020 7219 6012 *Email:* higginst@parliament.uk

CONSERVATIVE

HILL OF OAREFORD, LORD

HILL OF OAREFORD (Life Baron), Jonathan Hopkin Hill; cr 2010. Born 24 July 1960; Son of Rowland Hill and Paddy Henwood; Married Alexandra Nettelfield 1988 (1 son 2 daughters).

Education: Highgate School, London; Trinity College, Cambridge (BA history 1982).

Non-political career: RIT & Northern 1983; Hamish Hamilton 1984-85; Conservative Research Department 1985-86; Special adviser to Rt Hon Kenneth Clarke MP: as Paymaster General and Employment Minister 1986-87, as Chancellor of the Duchy of Lancaster and Minister of Trade and Industry 1987-88, as Secretary of State for Health 1988-89; Lowe Bell Communications 1989-91; Number 10 Policy Unit 1991-92; Political Secretary to Rt Hon John Major MP as Prime Minister 1992-94; Senior consultant, Bell Pottinger Consultants 1994-98; Founding director, Quiller Consultants 1998-2010; Commissioner for Financial Stability, Financial Services and Capital Markets Union, European Commission 2014-16; Independent National Director, Times Newspapers 2017-; Senior Adviser, Freshfields Bruckhaus Deringer 2017-.

Political career: *House of Lords:* Raised to the peerage as Baron Hill of Oareford, of Oareford in the County of Somerset 2010. Parliamentary Under-Secretary of State for Schools and Government Spokesperson, Department for Education 2010-13; Leader of the House of Lords 2013-14; Chancellor of the Duchy of Lancaster 2013-14; On leave of absence October 2014-October 2016. Member: House 2013-14, Liaison 2013-14, Privileges and Conduct 2013-14, Procedure 2013-14, Selection 2013-14. *Councils and public bodies:* Governor: Highgate School 1995-2010, Hanford School 2004-10.

Other: Trustee, National Literacy Trust 1995-2009; Member, advisory board, Reform 2004-10; Trustee, Teach First; Member, Council of Management, Ditchley Foundation. Resignation of the Year, *Spectator* awards 2012. CBE 1995; PC 2013.

Publications: Co-author, Too Close to Call: John Major, Power and Politics in No.10 (1995).

Recreations: Reading, gardening, walking on Exmoor.

Rt Hon the Lord Hill of Oareford CBE, House of Lords, London SW1A 0PW
Tel: 020 7219 5353

LABOUR

HILTON OF EGGARDON, BARONESS

HILTON OF EGGARDON (Life Baroness), Jennifer Hilton; cr. 1991. Born 12 January 1936; Daughter of late John Hilton, CMG and Margaret Hilton.

Education: Bedales School, Hampshire; Manchester University (BA psychology 1970; MA (police scholarship) 1971); London University (Diploma criminology 1973; Diploma history of art 1980); French.

Non-political career: Metropolitan Police 1956-90; Directing staff, National Police Staff College; Metropolitan Police Management Services 1975-76; Superintendent/Chief Superintendent 1977-83; Senior Command Course, National Staff College 1979; New Scotland Yard 1983-87; North West London, responsible for Complaints/Discipline, Personnel, Community Relations 1987-88; Peel Centre, Hendon, responsible for all Metropolitan Police training 1988-90; Member: ACPOs Executive Committee, Equal Opportunities, Extended Interview Panel, Various Home Office Committees.

Political career: *House of Lords:* Raised to the peerage as Baroness Hilton of Eggardon, of Eggardon in the County of Dorset 1991. Opposition Whip 1991-95; Opposition Spokesperson for: the Environment 1991-97, Home Affairs 1994-97. EU Sub-committee D (Environment): Member 1991-97, Chair 1995-97; Member: Science and Technology 1992-95, 2010-15, European Union 1997-99; Chair: EU Sub-committee C (Environment, Public Health and Consumer Protection) 1997-99, Advisory Panel on Works of Art 1998-2003, EU Sub-committee C (Foreign Affairs and

Defence): Member 2000-03, Chair 2000-01; Member: House of Lords Offices 2000-03, Science and Technology Sub-committees: I (Science and International Agreements) 2003-04, I (Scientific Aspects of Ageing) 2004-05, Works of Art 2007-09, Science and Technology Sub-committee I 2012-14, Sexual Violence in Conflict 2015-16, International Relations 2016-. *Other:* Patron, LGBT Labour.

Political interests: Environment, race relations, criminal justice; All countries of the old Russian empire.

Other: Member, UK Delegation, Organisation for Security and Co-operation in Europe Parliamentary Assembly. QPM 1989.

Publications: The Gentle Arm of the Law (1967); Co-author, Individual Development and Social Experience (1974).

Recreations: Gardening, travel, art.

The Baroness Hilton of Eggardon QPM, House of Lords, London SW1A 0PW
Tel: 020 7219 3182 *Email:* hiltonj@parliament.uk

HODGSON OF ABINGER, BARONESS

CONSERVATIVE

BARONESS HODGSON OF ABINGER (Life Baroness), Fiona Ferelith Hodgson; cr 2013. Born 7 November 1954; Daughter of Keith Allom and Jean Allom, née Robertson; Married Robin Granville Hodgson 1982 (MP Walsall North 1976-79, now Lord Hodgson of Astley Abbotts (qv)) (3 sons 1 daughter 1 twin son deceased).

Education: Queen Anne's School Caversham; Guildford High School.

Non-political career: Personal Secretary to Prime Minister's Private Secretary 1973-76; Research executive, Reader's Digest Association Ltd 1980-83; Managing director, Kensington Carnival Co Ltd 1984-87; Director: Johnson Brothers Design 1991-2006, Johnson Bros & Co. Ltd. 1991-.

Political career: *House of Lords:* Raised to the peerage as Baroness Hodgson of Abinger, of Abinger in the County of Surrey 2013. Member, Sexual Violence in Conflict 2015-16. *Other:* Conservative Women's Organisation: Deputy chair 2002-05, Chair 2005-08, President 2008-11, Honorary vice-president 2011-; Conservative National Convention: Vice-president 2009-11, President 2011-12; Chair, 2011 Conservative Party Conference; Member, Conservative Human Rights Commission 2009-; Vice-chair, Conservative Policy Forum 2010-13; Patron, Conservative Friends of International Development 2012-. *Councils and public bodies:* Member, Farm Animal Welfare Council 1989-97; Non-executive director, Barnet Health Authority 1992-94; Member, Advisory Committee on Animal Food Stuffs, Food Standards Agency 2001-04.

Political interests: International development, international women's rights, foreign affairs, equality; Afghanistan, Middle East, conflict and post-conflict countries.

Other: Member, Wellbeing general council and appeals committee, Royal College of Obstetricians and Gynaecologists 1993-2006; Member, International Social Services UK 2003-04; Delegate, Commission on the Status of Women 2008-; Chair, GAPS (Gender Action in Peace and Security) advisory group 2009-; Member, Oxfam Association 2009-15; Trustee, Chalker Foundation 2010-; Women's Justice Task Force 2010-; Independent Doctors Federation (ISAAC Group) 2010-13; Patron, Afghan Connection 2011-; Chair, governance board, Independent Sector Complaints and Adjudication Service 2012-; Member, steering board, Preventing Sexual Violence Initiative in Conflict and Post Conflict Countries; Founder member, Afghan Women's Support Forum in the UK 2012-. CBE 2012.

Recreations: Cooking, reading, riding, walking.

The Baroness Hodgson of Abinger CBE, House of Lords, London SW1A 0PW
Tel: 020 7219 8283 *Email:* hodgsonf@parliament.uk *Twitter:* @hodgsonfiona

HODGSON OF ASTLEY ABBOTTS, LORD

CONSERVATIVE

HODGSON OF ASTLEY ABBOTTS (Life Baron), Robin Granville Hodgson; cr. 2000. Born 25 April 1942; Son of late Henry and Natalie Hodgson; Married Fiona Ferelith Allom 1982, now Baroness Hodgson of Abinger (qv) (3 sons 1 daughter 1 twin son deceased).

Education: Shrewsbury School; Oxford University (BA modern history 1964); Wharton School of Finance, Pennsylvania University (MBA 1969).

Non-political career: Investment banker, New York and Montreal 1964-67; Industry in Birmingham 1969-72; Director, Johnson Brothers & Co Ltd, Walsall 1970-; Granville Baird Group: Director 1972-2003, Group chief executive 1979-95, Chair 1995-2002; Director: Domnick Hunter plc 1989-2002, Staffordshire Building Society 1995-2005, Community Hospitals plc 1995-2001; Chair: Market Touch plc 2001-02, Nova Capital Management 2002-15, Carbo plc 2002-05; Director, Marstons plc (formerly Wolverhampton and Dudley Breweries plc) 2002-14; Chair: RFIB Group Limited 2007-15, Tenet Group Ltd 2007-12, EIS Optics Ltd 2009-11, CMS Group Ltd 2014-.

Political career: *House of Commons:* Contested Walsall North February and October 1974 general elections. MP (Conservative) for Walsall North November 1976 by-election to 1979. *House of Lords:* Raised to the peerage as Baron Hodgson of Astley Abbotts, of Nash in the County of Shropshire 2000. Opposition Spokesperson for: Home Office 2002-06, Trade and Industry 2002-06. EU Sub-committee F (Home Affairs): Co-opted member 2007-10, Member 2010-12; Member: Consumer Insurance (Disclosure and Representations) Bill 2011-12, EU Sub-committee E (Justice, Institutions and Consumer Protection) 2012-15, Soft Power and the UK's Influence 2013-14, Joint Committee on Draft Protection of Charities Bill 2014-15; Member, Secondary Legislation Scrutiny 2015-17; Chair, Citizenship and Civic Engagement 2017-. *Other:* Chairman: National Union of Conservative Associations 1996-98, National Conservative Convention 1998-2000; Deputy Chairman, Conservative Party 1998-2000. *Councils and public bodies:* Member: Council for Securities Industry 1980-85, Securities and Investment Board 1985-89, West Midlands Industrial Development Board 1989-97, Securities and Futures Authority 1993-2001; President, National Council for Voluntary Organisation (NCVO) 2007-12; Official Reviewer of: The Charities Act 2011-12, Transparency in Lobbying Act 2015-16.

Other: Chair, Armed Forces Charity Advisory Committee 2008-; Trustee, Fair Trials International 2012-; Salvation Army, Fair Trials International, Freedom from Torture, Howard League. Liveryman, Goldsmith's Company 1983. Trustee and Honorary Fellow, St Peter's College, Oxford. CBE 1992.

Publications: Britain's Home Defence Gamble (1978); Unshackling Good Neighbours (2011).

Recreations: Squash, fishing, theatre.

The Lord Hodgson of Astley Abbotts CBE, House of Lords, London SW1A 0PW
Tel: 020 7219 8526 *Fax:* 020 7219 1903 *Email:* hodgsonr@parliament.uk

HOFFMANN, LORD

CROSSBENCH

HOFFMANN (Life Baron), Leonard Hubert Hoffmann; cr. 1995. Born 8 May 1934; Married Gillian Lorna Sterner 1957 (2 daughters).

Education: South African College School, Cape Town; University of Cape Town (BA); Queen's College, Oxford (Rhodes Scholar, MA, BCL, Vinerian Law Scholar).

Non-political career: Advocate of Supreme Court of South Africa 1958-60; Stowell Civil Law Fellow, University College, Oxford 1961-73; Called to the Bar, Gray's Inn 1964; QC 1977; Judge of the Courts of Appeal of Jersey and Guernsey 1980-85; Bencher 1984; Judge of the High Court of Justice, Chancery Division 1985-92; Lord Justice of Appeal 1992-95; Judge, Hong Kong Court of Final Appeal, 1998-; Chair, Financial Market Law Committee 2009-.

Political career: *House of Lords:* Raised to the peerage as Baron Hoffmann, of Chedworth in the County of Gloucestershire 1995. Lord of Appeal in Ordinary 1995-2009; Leave of absence October 2013-November 2016. Chair, European Communities Sub-committee E (Law and Institutions) 1997-2000. *Councils and public bodies:* Member, Royal Commission on Gambling 1976-78; Council of Legal Education: Member 1983-92, Chair 1989-92.

Other: President, British-German Jurists Association 1991-2009; Director, English National Opera 1985-90, 1991-94. Three honorary doctorates; Hon. fellow: Queen's College, Oxford 1992, University College, Oxford 1995. Kt 1985; PC 1992.

Publications: The South African Law of Evidence (1963).

Recreations: Music, cycling.

Rt Hon the Lord Hoffmann, House of Lords, London SW1A 0PW
Tel: 020 7219 6067
Surrey Lodge, 23 Keats Grove, London NW3 2RS

HOGG, BARONESS

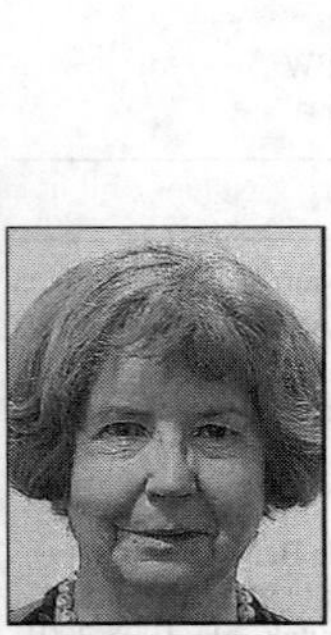

CROSSBENCH

HOGG (Life Baroness), Sarah Elizabeth Mary Hogg; cr. 1995. Born 14 May 1946; Daughter of late Rt Hon Baron Boyd-Carpenter; Married Douglas Martin Hogg 1968 (MP for Grantham 1979-97 and for Sleaford and North Hykeham 1997-2001, QC, 3rd Viscount Hailsham (qv)) (1 son 1 daughter).

Education: St Mary's Convent, Ascot; Lady Margaret Hall, Oxford (BA philosophy, politics and economics 1967).

Non-political career: *The Economist* 1967-81: Literary editor 1970-77, Economics editor 1977-81; Economics editor, *The Sunday Times* 1981-82; Presenter, *Channel 4 News* 1982-83; Director, London Broadcasting Company 1982-90; Economics editor and deputy executive editor, finance and industry, *The Times* 1984-86; Assistant editor and business and city editor, *The Independent* 1986-89; Economics editor, *Daily Telegraph* and *Sunday Telegraph* 1989-90; Head, Prime Minister's Policy Unit, with rank of Second Permanent Secretary 1990-95; Director, London School of Economics 1995-97; Chairman: Chair, London Economics 1997-99, Frontier Economics Ltd 1999-2013; Foreign and Colonial Smaller Companies Trust: Non-executive director 1995-2002, Chairman 1997-2002; International advisory board, National Westminster Bank 1995-98; Advisory board, Bankinter 1995-98; NPI 1996-99; Non-executive director, Energy Group 1996-98; GKN: Non-executive director 1996-2006, Deputy Chair 2003-06; 3i: Director 1997-, Deputy Chair 2000-01, Chair 2002-10; Non-executive director: Scottish Eastern Investment Trust 1998-99, Martin Currie Portfolio Trust 1999-2002, P&O 1999-2000, P&O Princess Cruises 2000-03, Carnival Corporation and Carnival plc 2003-08, BG Group plc 2005-; Cadbury plc 2008-10; Chairman, Financial Reporting Council 2010-14, Non-executive director, John Lewis Partnership 2011-.

Political career: *House of Lords:* Raised to the peerage as Baroness Hogg, of Kettlethorpe in the County of Lincolnshire 1995. Member: Science and Technology Committee 1996-99, Monetary Policy of the Bank of England/Economic Affairs 2000-03. *Councils and public bodies:* Governor, BBC 2000-04; Non-executive director, HM Treasury Board 2010-; Non-executive board member, Financial Conduct Authority 2016-.

Other: Governor, Centre for Economic Policy Research 1985-92; Director, Royal National Theatre 1988-91; Trustee, St Mary's School, Ascot 1994-; Fellow, Eton College 1996-2008; Council Member: Royal Economic Society 1996-2004, Institute for Fiscal Studies 1996-2005, 2010-, Hansard Society for Parliamentary Government 1996-2000, Lincolnshire Foundation 1996-98, Lincoln University 2002-05; Trustee, Trusthouse Charitable Foundation 2003-; Governor, London Business School 2004-10; Trustee: Cicely Saunders International 2009-10, Historic Lincoln Trust 2013-, Queen Elizabeth Jubilee Memorial Trust 2013-; Governor, NIESR 2014-; Member, Mentoring Foundation. Honorary MA, Open University, 1987; Honorary DLitt, Loughborough, 1992; Honorary Fellow, Lady Margaret Hall, 1994; Honorary LLD, Lincoln, 2001; Honorary DPhil: City University, 2002, Cranfield, 2006. Wincott Foundation Financial Journalist of the Year 1985; CBI First Women Lifetime Award 2005.

Publications: Co-author, Too Close to Call (1995).

Viscountess Hailsham, The Baroness Hogg, House of Lords, London SW1A 0PW
Tel: 020 7219 5353

HOLLICK, LORD

LABOUR

HOLLICK (Life Baron), Clive Richard Hollick; cr. 1991. Born 20 May 1945; Son of late Leslie Hollick and Olive Hollick; Married Susan Woodford 1977 (3 daughters).

Education: Taunton's School, Southampton; Nottingham University (BA sociology 1966).

Non-political career: Hambros Bank: Joined 1967, Director 1973-96; Managing director, MAI plc 1974-96; Director, Mills and Allen Ltd 1975-89; Chair, Shepperton Studios Ltd 1976-84; Member, National Bus Company 1984-91; Director: Logica plc 1987-91, Avenir Havas Media SA (France) 1988-92, National Opinion Polls Ltd 1989-97, Satellite Information Services 1990-94; Chair, Meridian Broadcasting 1991-96; Director, British Aerospace 1992-97; Member, Financial Law Panel 1993-97; Director, Anglia Television 1994-97; Member, Commission on Public Policy and British Business 1995-97; Chair, United Broadcasting and Entertainment Ltd 1995-2000; Chief executive, United Business Media plc 1996-2005; Special adviser to Margaret Beckett MP as President of the Board of Trade 1997-98; Director: Express Newspapers plc 1998-2000, TRW Inc 2000-02, Diageo plc 2001-12; Chair, South Bank Centre 2002-08; Director, Honeywell International Inc 2003-; Kohlberg Kravis Roberts: Partner 2005-09, Senior adviser 2009-10; Partner, GP Bullhound 2010-; Senior adviser, Jefferies Inc 2011-.

Political career: *House of Lords:* Raised to the peerage as Baron Hollick, of Notting Hill in the Royal Borough of Kensington and Chelsea 1991. Trade Envoy to Kenya and Tanzania 2014-. Economic Affairs: Member 2010-14, Chair 2014-17; Member, Joint Committee on Privacy and Injunctions 2011-12; Economic Affairs Finance Bill Sub-committee: Member 2012-13, 2014, 2015-16, Chair 2016-17; Member, Artificial Intelligence 2017-.

Political interests: Business, economic policy, constitutional affairs, transport, media.

Other: Founder, Institute for Public Policy Research 1988-; Governor, London School of Economics and Political Science 1997-2002; Trustee: Dorneywood, Heart of England Forest. Hon. LLD, Nottingham University 1993.

Recreations: Reading, countryside, cinema, theatre, tennis, golf.

The Lord Hollick, House of Lords, London SW1A 0PW
Tel: 020 7219 8942 *Email:* hollickrc@parliament.uk *Twitter:* @clivehollick

CROSSBENCH

HOLLINS, BARONESS

HOLLINS (Life Baroness), Sheila Clare Hollins; cr 2010. Born 22 June 1946; Daughter of late Captain Adrian Kelly and late Monica Kelly, née Edwards; Married Martin Prior Hollins 1969 (1 son 3 daughters).

Education: Notre Dame High School, Sheffield; St Thomas' Hospital Medical School, London (MB BS medicine 1970); French.

Non-political career: Senior registrar in child psychiatry, Earl's Court Child Guidance Unit and Westminster Child's Hospital 1979-81; Senior lecturer in psychiatry of learning disability 1981-90; Honorary Consultant Psychiatrist 1981-2011: Wandsworth Community Health Trust, Richmond, Twickenham and Roehampton Healthcare Trust, South West London and St George's Mental Health Trust; St George's, University of London: Professor of psychiatry of disability 1990-2011, Chair, Academic Division of Mental Health 2002-05; Policy adviser on learning disability, Department of Health (on secondment) 1992-93, 2001-03; Member, Minister's Advisory Group on Learning Disability 1999-2001; Chair, NHS Working Party on Breast and Cervical Screening in Learning Disability 1999-2000; Deputy chair, National Specialist Commissioning Advisory Group 2006-08; Chair, WHO Europe Steering and Drafting Groups on developing a declaration about children with intellectual disabilities for agreement by Ministers of Health across Europe 2008-10; Chair, External Advisory Group, National Confidential Inquiry into Suicides and Homicides 2007-11; Honorary Professor, Department of Theology and Religion, Durham University 2013-; Chair, Scientific Advisory Group, Centre for Child Protection, Pontifical Gregorian University, Rome 2014-; Chair, Expert Reference Group on workforce for Transforming Care programme, Health Education England 2015-17. President, BMA 2012-13; Chair, Board of Science 2013-16.

Political career: *House of Lords:* Raised to the peerage as Baroness Hollins, of Wimbledon in the London Borough of Merton and of Grenoside in the County of South Yorkshire 2010. Member, Mental Capacity Act 2005 2013-14.

Political interests: Health and social care (especially mental health and learning disability), welfare reform, special education (long term conditions), human rights abuses of disabled people.

Other: Member, Pontifical Commission for the Protection of Minors Rome 2014-; Member: Community Care and Disability Sub-committee, Joseph Rowntree Foundation 1989-93, Academy of Medical Royal Colleges 2005-08; Founder and Chair, Books Beyond Word CIC; Patron, Respond 2011-; Honorary fellow and vice-president, Institute of Psychotherapy and Disability; Patron: Wimbledon Bookfest 2010-, Living and Dying Well 2012, St Teresa's School, Effingham 2014-; Royal College of Psychiatrists: Vice-President 2003-04, President 2005-08; President, Royal College of Occupational Therapists 2015-; MRCPsych 1978; FRCPsych 1988; FRCPCH 1990; Honorary FRCP 2007; FHEA; Honorary Fellow, Medical Women's Federation; FIPD 2009; Fellow, City Lit 2015; Books Beyond Words, Respond, Lay Community of St Benedict. Honorary fellow, Colleges of Medecine, South Africa 2005; DD, University of London 2013; MD, Sheffield University 2014; DL, Bath University 2014; DS, Worcester University 2014; Doctor of the University, Australian Catholic University, Melbourne 2016; *Clubs:* Farmers Club, RSM.

Publications: Over 200 academic and professional articles on mental health and learning disability; 50 books in the Books Beyond Words series for adults with intellectual disabilities.

Recreations: Walking, music.

Professor the Baroness Hollins, House of Lords, London SW1A 0PW
Tel: 020 7219 0520 *Email:* hollinss@parliament.uk *Twitter:* @baronesshollins

LABOUR

HOLLIS OF HEIGHAM, BARONESS

HOLLIS OF HEIGHAM (Life Baroness), Patricia Lesley Hollis; cr. 1990. Born 24 May 1941; Daughter of Harry Lesley George and Queenie Rosalyn Wells; Married James Martin Hollis 1965 (later Professor, FBA) (died 1998) (2 sons); partner Lord Howarth of Newport (qv).

Education: Plympton Grammar School; Cambridge University (BA history 1962, MA); University of California and Columbia University, New York (Harkness Fellow 1962-64); Nuffield College, Oxford (MA, DPhil 1967).

Non-political career: University of East Anglia: Modern history: Lecturer 1967, Senior lecturer 1979, Reader 1985, Dean School of English and American Studies 1988-90; Founder-director, Radio Broadland 1983-97. Member, AUT.

Political career: *House of Commons:* Contested (Labour) Great Yarmouth February and October 1974 and 1979 general elections. *House of Lords:* Raised to the peerage as Baroness Hollis of Heigham, of Heigham in the City of Norwich 1990. Opposition Whip 1990-95; Opposition Spokesperson for Environment and Social Security 1990-97; Parliamentary Under-Secretary of

State and Government Spokesperson for: Department of Social Security 1997-2001, (Minister for Children and the Family), Department for Work and Pensions 2001-05. Member: Administration and Works 2006-07, 2015-16, Draft Human Tissue and Embryos Bill Joint Committee 2007, House 2007-13, Barnett Formula 2008-09, Procedure 2013-16, Services 2016-. *Councils and public bodies:* Norwich City Council: Councillor 1968-91, Leader 1983-88; Member: BBC Regional Advisory Council 1973-79, East Anglian Planning Council 1975-79, Regional Health Authority 1979-83; Councillor, Norfolk County Council 1981-85; Member, Press Council 1988-90, Commissioner, English Heritage 1988-91; Vice-President: Association of District Councils 1990-97, Association of Metropolitan Authorities 1990-97, Association of Environmental Health Officers 1992-97, National Federation of Housing Associations 1993-97; DL, Norfolk 1994-; Vice-President: Local Government Association 2005-10, Board, Pensions Advisory Service 2006-14; President, Women's Local Government Society 2007-; Chair, Broadland Housing Association 2009-; Governor, Pensions Policy Institute 2010-.

Political interests: Local government, heritage, pensions, women's issues, housing.

Other: Patron: Norfolk Millennium Carers, St Martin's Housing Trust; Trustee, History of Parliament Trust; Fellow, Royal Historical Society. Freedom, City of Norwich. Three honorary doctorates; Honorary fellow, Girton College, Cambridge. Wolfson prize for History 1998; George Orwell prize for political biography 1998; Peer of the Year, Women in Public Life Awards 2009; Campaigining Politician, Channel 4 Political awards 2009. PC 1999.

Publications: The Pauper Press (1970); Class and Class Conflict 1815-50 (1973); Pressure from Without (1974); Women in Public, 1850-1900 (1979); Robert Lowry, Radical and Chartist (1979); Ladies Elect: women in English Local Government 1865-1914 (1987); Jennie Lee: a Life (1997); A new State Pension (2010).

Recreations: Boating, singing, domesticity.

Rt Hon the Baroness Hollis of Heigham DL, House of Lords, London SW1A 0PW
Tel: 020 7219 6784 *Email:* hollisp@parliament.uk
30 Park Lane, Norwich, Norfolk NR2 3EE *Tel:* 01603 621990

HOLMES OF RICHMOND, LORD

CONSERVATIVE

HOLMES OF RICHMOND (Life Baron), Christopher Holmes; cr 2013. Born 15 October 1971; Son of Michael and Margaret Holmes.

Education: Harry Cheshire High School, Kidderminster; King's College, Cambridge (BA 1994).

Non-political career: Paralympic swimmer; Public Speaker 1992-; Ashurst 2002-07; Admitted solicitor 2004.

Political career: *House of Lords:* Raised to the peerage as Baron Holmes of Richmond, of Richmond in the London Borough of Richmond upon Thames 2013. Member: Digital Skills 2014-15, Social Mobility 2015-16, Financial Exclusion 2016-17, Artificial Intelligence 2017-. *Councils and public bodies:* Non-executive director: Disability Rights Commission 2002-07, UK Sport 2005-13; Director, Paralympic integration, London Organising Committee of 2012 Olympic and Paralympic Games 2009-13; Non-executive Director, Equality and Human Rights Commission (Disability Commissioner) 2013-17; Diversity adviser, Cabinet Office 2015-.

Political interests: Economy, pensions, education, employment, diversity and inclusion, digital, foreign affairs, broadcasting, media, sport, culture; Australia, Canada, Japan, Malawi, Middle East, Singapore, South Korea, USA.

Other: Patron, Help for Heroes 2008-; Solicitors Regulation Authority; Nick Webber Trust, Queen Elizabeth Diamond Jubilee Trust, Duke of Edinburgh Award. Deputy Chancellor, BPP. Honorary LLD, Bath University 2012. Six Paralympic gold medals at Barcelona Games 1992; Sports Personality of the Year 1992; Bass Midlander of the Year 1992; Three Paralympic gold medals at Atlanta Games 1996; Saf Paul Zetter Award 1996; Sports Personality of the Year, Variety Club of GB 1997. MBE 1993; *Clubs:* Hawks' Club, Cambridge University.

Recreations: Skiing, theatre, reading, music.

The Lord Holmes of Richmond MBE, House of Lords, London SW1A 0PW
Tel: 020 7219 8617 *Email:* holmesc@parliament.uk
Website: chrisholmes.co.uk *Twitter:* @LordCHolmes

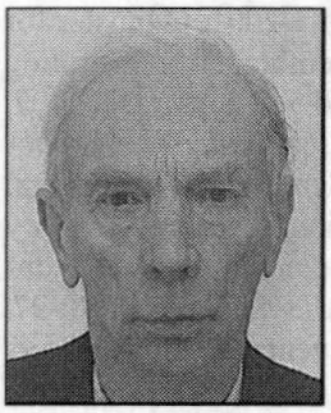

CONSERVATIVE

HOME, EARL OF

HOME (15th Earl of, S), David Alexander Cospatrick Douglas-Home; cr. 1604; Lord Dunglass; 20th Lord Home (S) 1473; 5th Baron Douglas (UK) 1875. Born 20 November 1943; Son of 14th Earl, KT, PC, DL, who disclaimed the earldom 1963 to become Prime Minister as Sir Alec Douglas-Home, and who was subsequently made a life peer as Baron Home of the Hirsel 1974; Married Jane Williams-Wynne 1972 (1 son 2 daughters).

Education: Eton College; Christ Church, Oxford (BA philosophy, politics and economics 1966).

Non-political career: Douglas and Angus Estates: Director 1966-, Chair 1995-; Director: Morgan Grenfell & Co Ltd 1974-99, Arab-British Chamber of Commerce 1975-84; Morgan Grenfell (Asia) Ltd: Director 1978-82, Deputy chair 1979-82; Director: Arab Bank Investment Co 1979-87, Agricultural Mortgage Corporation plc 1979-93; Tandem Group plc (formerly EFG plc): Director 1981-96, Chair 1993-96; Chair: Morgan Grenfell Export Services 1984-98, Morgan Grenfell (Scotland) 1986-98, Committee for Middle East Trade 1986-92, Morgan Grenfell International Ltd 1987-98; Director: Morgan Grenfell Asia (Hong Kong) Ltd/Deutsche Morgan Grenfell Hong Kong Ltd 1989-99, Morgan Grenfell Asia Holdings Pte Ltd/Deutsche Morgan Grenfell Asia Holdings Pte Ltd 1989-99, K & N Kenanga Holdings Bhd 1993-99; Non-executive director, Grosvenor Estate Holdings 1993-2000; Director: Kenanga DMG Futures Sdn Bhd/Kenanga Deutsche Futures Sdn Bhd 1995-99, Deutsche Morgan Grenfell Group plc 1996-99; Board member: Deva Group/Wheatsheaf Investments Ltd 1999-, Deva Holding Ltd/Deva Group 1999-2010; Chair: Coutts and Company 1999-2012, Coutts Switzerland Ltd/RBS Coutts/Coutts & Co Ltd 2000-17, MAN Ltd 2000-09; Board member: Oryx Fund 2004-07, Dubai Financial Services Authority 2005-12; Grosvenor Group Ltd: Board member 2005-10, Chair 2007-10.

Political career: *House of Lords:* First entered House of Lords 1995; Opposition Frontbench Spokesperson for: Trade 1997-98, the Treasury 1997-98; Elected hereditary peer 1999-. *Councils and public bodies:* Member, Export Guarantee Advisory Council, ECGD 1988-93.

Political interests: Foreign affairs, Scottish affairs, industry, agriculture; Australia, Middle and Far East.

Other: President, British Malaysian Society 2006-; Trustee: Grosvenor Estate 1993-2010, Royal Agricultural Society of England 1999-2003; Chairman: Coutts Charitable Trust -2017, Coutts Foundation -2017; Fellow, Chartered Institute of Bankers 1999-; Lymphoma Association. CBE 1991; CVO 1997; KT 2014; *Clubs:* Turf Club.

Recreations: Outdoor sports.

The Earl of Home KT CVO CBE, House of Lords, London SW1A 0PW
Tel: 020 7219 3168

CONSERVATIVE

HOOPER, BARONESS

HOOPER (Life Baroness), Gloria Dorothy Hooper; cr. 1985. Born 25 May 1939; Daughter of late Frederick Hooper and late Frances Hooper, née Maloney.

Education: La Sainte Union Convent; Royal Ballet School; Southampton University (BA law 1960); Universidad Central, Ecuador (Rotary Foundation Fellow 1965-66); French, Spanish.

Non-political career: Assistant to chief registrar, John Lewis Partnership 1960-61; Editor, Current Law, Sweet & Maxwell, Law Publishers 1961-62; Information officer, Winchester City Council 1962-67; Assistant solicitor, Taylor and Humbert 1967-72; Legal adviser, Slater Walker France S.A. 1972-73; Partner, Taylor and Humbert (Solicitors), now Taylor Wessing 1974-84.

Political career: *House of Lords:* Raised to the peerage as Baroness Hooper, of Liverpool and St James's in the City of Westminster 1985. Government Whip 1985-87; Parliamentary Under-Secretary of State, Department of: Education and Science 1987-88, Energy 1988-89, Health 1989-92; Deputy Speaker 1993-; Deputy Chairman of Committees 1993-; PPS to William Hague as Leader of the Opposition 1999-2001. Member, Intergovernmental Organisations 2008; EU Sub-committee A (Economic and Financial Affairs and International Trade): Co-opted member 2008-10, Member 2010-12; Member EU Sub-committees: A (Economic and Financial Affairs) 2012-13, B (Internal Market, Infrastructure and Employment) 2013-15; Member, European Union 2014-15. *Other:* European Parliament: MEP for Liverpool 1979-84: Deputy chief whip, European Democratic Group. Member, Association of Conservative Peers 1985-; President, Greater London Women's Conservative Association 2006-.

Political interests: European Union, cultural heritage, education, energy, international relations; Mercosur countries, Andean Pact countries, CAFTA countries, Commonwealth countries, NAFTA countries, Council of Europe countries, Overseas Territories.

Other: Member: Parliamentary Delegation to Council of Europe and to Western European Union 1992-97, 2001-09, Executive Committee, Commonwealth Parliamentary Association (UK Branch) 2008-17, Executive Committee, Inter-Parliamentary Union, British Group 2010-; Member, Law Society; President, British Educational Equipment and Supplies Association; Vice-President, Canning House (Hispanic and Luso Brazilian Council); President: Good Guy's Cancer Appeal, Friends of Colombia for Social Aid, European Foundation For Heritage Skills, Friends of Gibraltar; Chair: Institute of the Americas UCL, Dance Teachers Benevolent Fund; Trustee/Governor, Centre for Global Energy Studies; Industry and Parliament Trust: Fellow 1983, Trustee 1996-2012; Trustee: Tablet Trust 2004-, St George's House, Windsor Castle 2007-13; Fellow: Royal Geographical Society, RSA. Hon. LLD, Southampton University 2009. Order of Francisco de Miranda (Venezuela) 1999; CMG 2003; Order of Boyaca Gran Cruz (Colombia) 2004; Order of Merit (Ecuador) 2004; Order of Bernardo O'Higgins (Chile) 2004; Dame of the Order of St Gregory the Great 2005; *Clubs:* In and Out Club.

Recreations: Theatre, travel, gardening.

The Baroness Hooper CMG, House of Lords, London SW1A 0PW
Tel: 020 7219 5489 *Email:* hooperg@parliament.uk

CROSSBENCH

HOPE OF CRAIGHEAD, LORD

Convenor of the Crossbench Peers

HOPE OF CRAIGHEAD (Life Baron), James Arthur David Hope; cr. 1995. Born 27 June 1938; Son of late Arthur Hope, OBE, WS; Married Mary Kerr 1966 (twin sons 1 daughter).

Education: Edinburgh Academy; Rugby School; St John's College, Cambridge (Scholarship 1956, BA classics 1962, MA); Edinburgh University (LLB 1965).

Non-political career: National service, Seaforth Highlanders 1957-59. Admitted Faculty of Advocates 1965; Standing Junior Counsel in Scotland to Board of Inland Revenue 1974-78; Advocate-Depute 1978-82; QC (Scotland) 1978; Legal Chairman, Pensions Appeal Tribunal 1985-86; Chairman, Medical Appeal Tribunals 1985-86; Dean, Faculty of Advocates 1986-89; Lord Justice General of Scotland and Lord President of the Court of Session 1989-96; Hon. Bencher: Gray's Inn 1989, Inn of Court of Northern Ireland 1995; Deputy President, Supreme Court of the United Kingdom 2009-13; HM Lord High Commissioner to the General Assembly of the Church of Scotland 2015-16.

Political career: *House of Lords:* Raised to the peerage as Baron Hope of Craighead, of Bamff in the District of Perth and Kinross 1995. Lord of Appeal in Ordinary 1996-2009: Second Senior Law Lord 2009; As Deputy President of the Supreme Court, disqualified from participation 2009-13; Convenor of the Crossbench Peers 2015-; Member, House of Lords Commission 2016-. Member, European Communities 1998-2001; Chair, European Communities Sub-committee E (Law and Institutions) 1998-2001; Member: Personal Service Companies 2013-14, Privileges and Conduct 2014-; Chair, Joint Committee on the Draft Protection of Charities Bill 2014-15; Member: Administration and Works 2015-16, House 2015-16, Liaison 2015-, Procedure 2015-, Selection 2015-, Services 2016-.

Countries of interest: Scotland.

Other: Board of Trustees, National Library of Scotland 1989-96; Member, University of Strathclyde Charitable Foundation 1998-2001; Chair, Advisory Council, Institute of Advanced Legal Studies 1998-2013; President: Stair Society 1993-2013, International Criminal Law Association 2000-13; Fellow: Strathclyde University 2000, Royal Society of Edinburgh 2003; Commonwealth Magistrates' and Judges' Association: President 2003-06, Life Vice-President; Chair, Botanic Cottage Trust, Edinburgh 2009-12. Chancellor, Strathclyde University 1998-2013. Hon. LLD: Aberdeen 1991, Strathclyde 1993, Edinburgh 1995; Hon. Fellow, St John's College, Cambridge 1995; Hon. DUniv, Strathclyde 2013; Hon. LLD: Glasgow 2013, BPP (London) 2014, Abertay 2014. PC 1989; KT 2010; *Clubs:* New Club (Edinburgh).

Publications: Co-editor, Gloag and Henderson's Introduction to the Law of Scotland (6th-9th eds 1956-87); Armour on Valuation for Rating (4th-5th eds, 1971, 1985); Co-author, The Rent (Scotland) Act (1984, 1986); Contributor, Stair Memorial Encyclopaedia of Scots Law; Gloag and Henderson's The Law of Scotland (11th ed, 2002); Court of Session Practice (2005) with regular updates.

Recreations: Walking, ornithology, music.

Rt Hon the Lord Hope of Craighead KT, House of Lords, London SW1A 0PW
Tel: 020 7219 1414/8054 *Email:* hopejad@parliament.uk

HORAM, LORD

CONSERVATIVE

HORAM (Life Baron), John Rhodes Horam; cr 2013. Born 7 March 1939; Son of Sydney and Catherine Horam; Married Judith Jackson 1987 (2 sons from previous marriage).

Education: Silcoates School, Wakefield; St Catharine's College, Cambridge (MA economics 1960).

Non-political career: Market research officer, Rowntree & Co 1960-62; Leader and feature writer: *Financial Times* 1962-65, *The Economist* 1965-68; Managing director: Commodities Research Unit Ltd 1968-70, 1983-87, CRU Holdings Ltd 1988-92; CRU International Ltd: Deputy chair 1992-95, Non-executive director 1997-.

Political career: *House of Commons:* Contested Folkstone and Hythe 1966 general election. MP for Gateshead West 1970-83 (Labour 1970-81, SDP 1981-83). Contested Newcastle upon Tyne Central (SDP/All) 1983 general election. MP (Conservative) for Orpington 1992-2010. Parliamentary Under-Secretary of State, Department of Transport 1976-79; Labour Spokesperson for Economic Affairs 1979-81; SDP Spokesperson for Economic Affairs 1981-83; Parliamentary Secretary, Office of Public Service 1995; Parliamentary Under-Secretary of State, Department of Health 1995-97. Member: Public Accounts 1992-95, Liaison 1997-2003; Environmental Audit: Chair 1997-2003, Member 2003-05, Member: Foreign Affairs 2005-10. *House of Lords:* Raised to the peerage as Baron Horam, of Grimsargh in the County of Lancashire 2013. Member: Delegated Powers and Regulatory Reform 2013-14, Communications 2014-15, EU External Affairs Sub-Committee 2015-. *Other:* Member, Executive, 1922 Committee 2004-07. *Councils and public bodies:* Electoral Commissioner 2012-.

Political interests: Economic policy, transport, health, foreign affairs; France, Germany, USA.

Other: St Catharine's Society Cambridge: Chair 2006-13, President 2014; Fellow Commoner, St Catherine's College Cambridge 2010-.

Publications: Making Britain Competitive (1993).

Recreations: Opera, gardening, walking, golf, cooking.

The Lord Horam, House of Lords, London SW1A 0PW
Tel: 020 7219 8759
Tel: 020 7736 8521 *Fax:* 020 7736 7795 *Email:* jrhoram@gmail.com

HOWARD OF LYMPNE, LORD

CONSERVATIVE

HOWARD OF LYMPNE (Life Baron), Michael Howard; cr 2010. Born 7 July 1941; Son of late Bernard and Hilda Howard; Married Sandra Paul 1975 (1 son 1 daughter 1 stepson).

Education: Llanelli Grammar School; Peterhouse, Cambridge (MA economics and law; LLB 1963).

Non-political career: Called to the Bar, Inner Temple 1964; Junior Counsel to the Crown 1980-82; QC 1982.

Political career: *House of Commons:* Contested Liverpool Edge Hill 1966 and 1970 general elections. MP (Conservative) for Folkestone and Hythe 1983-2010. PPS to Sir Patrick Mayhew as Solicitor-General 1984-85; Parliamentary Under-Secretary of State, Department of Trade and Industry 1985-87; Minister of State, Department of the Environment 1987-90; Secretary of State for: Employment 1990-92, the Environment 1992-93; Home Secretary 1993-97; Member, Shadow Cabinet 1997-99, 2001-05: Shadow Foreign Secretary 1997-99, Shadow Chancellor of the Exchequer 2001-03, Leader of the Opposition 2003-05. Chair, Conservative Policy Committee for Economic Affairs/Enterprise/Pensions/Social Affairs 2001-03. *House of Lords:* Raised to the peerage as Baron Howard of Lympne, of Lympne in the County of Kent 2010. *Other:* Chair, Coningsby Club 1972-73; Member, Conservative Policy Board 2001-03; Contested Conservative Party leadership June 1997; Leader, Conservative Party 2003-05; Patron, Tory Reform Group. *Councils and public bodies:* Member, House of Lords Appointments Commission 2010-; Commissioner, Independent Commission on Freedom of Information 2015-.

Political interests: Home affairs, foreign affairs; USA.

Other: Chair, Bow Group 1970; President and founding chair, Atlantic Partnership 2003-; Chair, Hospice UK. *Spectator* Parliamentarian of the Year 2003. PC 1990; CH 2011; *Clubs:* Carlton, Pratt's, Buck's Club.

Recreations: Football, baseball.

Rt Hon the Lord Howard of Lympne CH QC, House of Lords, London SW1A 0PW
Tel: 020 7219 3964 *Fax:* 0207 219 4551 *Email:* howardm@parliament.uk
Website: www.michaelhoward.org

CONSERVATIVE

HOWARD OF RISING, LORD

HOWARD OF RISING (Life Baron), Greville Patrick Charles Howard; cr. 2004. Born 22 April 1941; Son of Lt Col H R G Howard; Married Mary Cortland Culverwell 1981 (2 sons 1 daughter).

Education: Eton College.

Non-political career: Private secretary to J Enoch Powell MP 1968-70; Director: Keep Trust 1980-87, Fortress Trust 1989-93, Fortress Holdings 1993-2008.

Political career: *House of Lords:* Raised to the peerage as Baron Howard of Rising, of Castle Rising in the County of Norfolk 2004. Opposition Whip 2005-09; Opposition Spokesperson for: Treasury 2005-09, Work and Pensions 2005-06, Constitutional Affairs 2006, Cabinet Office 2006-09, Culture, Media and Sport 2006-10. Member: Joint Committee on Statutory Instruments 2005-07, Refreshment 2012-14. *Other:* Vice-President, Conservatives for Britain 2015-16. *Councils and public bodies:* Councillor, King's Lynn and West Norfolk 2003-.

Other: Vice-president, National Playing Fields Association. Captain, Lords and Commons tennis team.

Publications: Editor, Enoch at 100 (Biteback, 2012).

The Lord Howard of Rising, House of Lords, London SW1A 0PW
Tel: 020 7219 5353 *Email:* howardgr@parliament.uk

CROSSBENCH

HOWARTH OF BRECKLAND, BARONESS

HOWARTH OF BRECKLAND (Life Baroness), Valerie Georgina Howarth OBE; cr 2001. Born 5 September 1940; Daughter of George Howarth and Edith Steele.

Education: Abbeydale Girls Grammar School, Sheffield; Leicester University (Diploma social studies 1963; Certificate applied social studies); Home Office Certificate childcare.

Non-political career: Caseworker, Family Welfare Association 1963-68; London Borough of Lambeth 1968-82: Senior child care worker and training officer 1968-70, Area co-ordinator 1970-72, Chief co-ordinator of social work 1972-76, Assistant director of personal services 1976-82; Director of social services, London Borough of Brent 1982-86; Chief executive, ChildLine charity 1987-2001.

Political career: *House of Lords:* Raised to the peerage as Baroness Howarth of Breckland, of Parson Cross in the County of South Yorkshire 2001. EU Sub-committee G (Social Policy and Consumer Affairs): Member 2003-07, Chair 2007-10; Member: European Union 2007-12, EU Sub-committee D: (Agriculture, Fisheries and Environment) 2010-12, (Agriculture, Fisheries, Environment and Energy) 2012-15, Adoption Legislation, 2012-13, Ecclesiastical Committee 2015-. *Councils and public bodies:* UK Representative, European Forum for Child Welfare 1994-97; Chair, UK Group on Child Exploitation (linked with EFCW); Board member: Food Standards Agency 2000-07, National Care Standards Commission 2001-04, Meat Hygiene Services Board 2004-07; Cafcass (Children and Families Advisory and Support Services): Board member 2004-08, Chair 2008-12; Vice-President, Local Government Association 2010-; Director and committee member, ICSTIS (Independent Committee for the Supervision of Television Information Systems) 1988-2000.

Political interests: Social care, children, consumer affairs, energy, animal welfare, environment; Canada, Europe.

Other: Founder and first chair, King's Cross Homeless Project 1986-87; Founder member, London Homeless Forum 1986-87; Trustee and vice-chair, National Council for Voluntary Child Care Organisations 1990-95, Member NCH Commission considering Children as Abusers 1991-92; Trustee and vice-chair, Lucy Faithfull Foundation 1992-; Chair, 'Stop it Now' Steering Group 2009-11; Trustee, National Children's Bureau 1993-94; Member, NSPCC Professional Advisory Panel 1993-95; Adviser and trustee, Sieff Foundation 1994-2004; Founder member and first chair, Telephone Helplines Association 1995-96; Resident, John Grooms Association for Disabled People and Chair of Care and Development Committee 2000-07; Patron and trustee, Little Hearts Matter 2002-; Chair, Children's International Helplines Association 2003-07; Patron: Voice 2006-, TRACKS 2011-; Senior Vice-President, Livability 2013-; British Association of Social Workers; Association of Directors of Adult Social Care; President, Child Helpline International. Honorary Doctorate, Open University 2007. Children's Champion, Charity Champion awards 2012. OBE 1999.

Recreations: People, gardening, reading, walking dog, church.

The Baroness Howarth of Breckland OBE, House of Lords, London SW1A 0PW
Tel: 020 7219 8744 *Fax:* 020 7219 0269 *Email:* howarthv@parliament.uk

LABOUR

HOWARTH OF NEWPORT, LORD

HOWARTH OF NEWPORT (Life Baron), Alan Thomas Howarth; cr 2005. Born 11 June 1944; Son of late T. E. B. Howarth MC, TD, and Margaret Howarth, née Teakle; Married Gillian Chance 1967 (divorced 1996) (2 sons 2 daughters); partner Baroness Hollis of Heigham (qv).

Education: Rugby School; King's College, Cambridge (BA history 1965); French.

Non-political career: Senior research assistant to Field-Marshal Montgomery on *A History of Warfare* 1965-67; English and history teacher, Westminster School 1968-74; Private secretary to Conservative Party Chairmen William Whitelaw and Lord Thorneycroft 1975-79; Vice-chair and chief executive, Conservative Central Office 1979-81; Co-ordinated campaign planning for 1979 election; Director, Conservative Research Department 1979-81; Investment department, Baring Brothers 1982-87.

Political career: *House of Commons:* MP for Stratford-on-Avon 1983-97, for Newport East 1997-2005 (Conservative 1983-95, Labour 1995-2005). PPS to Sir Rhodes Boyson as Minister of State, Northern Ireland Office and Department of Environment 1985-87; Assistant Government Whip 1987-88; Government Whip 1988-89; Parliamentary Under-Secretary of State, Department for Education and Science 1989-92, Minister for Schools 1989-90, Minister for Higher Education and Science 1990-92; Resigned from Conservative Party and joined Labour Party, October 1995; Parliamentary Under-Secretary of State: Department for Education and Employment, Employment Minister and Minister for Disabled People 1997-98, Department for Culture, Media and Sport (Minister for the Arts) 1998-2001; Member, Intelligence and Security Committee 2001-05. *House of Lords:* Raised to the peerage as Baron Howarth of Newport, of Newport in the County of Gwent 2005. Member: Intergovernmental Organisations 2007-08, Political Polling and Digital Media 2017-. Vice-chair PLP Departmental Committee for Culture, Media and Sport 2006-15. *Other:* Vice-chair, Conservative Party 1980-81. *Councils and public bodies:* Vice-President, Local Government Association 2001-.

Political interests: Economic policy, education, disability, charities, voluntary sector, social security, arts, heritage, constituencies; Brazil, South Africa, Uganda, Vietnam.

Other: Leader, UK Parliamentary Trade Delegation to Washington 2003; Governor, Royal Shakespeare Company 1984-97; Founder and chair, Friends of the Huntington's Disease Association 1985-87; Board member: Retirement Security Ltd 1987, Institute of Historical Research 1992-97; Member, Constitution Unit Advisory Committee 1992-97; Vice-president, British Dyslexia Association 1992-97; Patron, Neurological Alliance 1992-97; Trustee, Employment Policy Institute 1992-97; Member, Executive Committee, Fabian Society 1995-96; Chair, Trustees and Governors, Friends of the Royal Pavilion, Brighton 2006-11; Board member, Norwich Heritage and Economic Regeneration Trust 2006-; Trustee: Poetry Archive 2006-13, Foundation for International Cultural Diplomacy 2006-11; Chair, Working Group on UK Literary Heritage 2006-12; Patron, Tourism for All UK 2006-; Vice-President, Victorian Society 2009-; Hon Fellow, Royal Institute of British Architects 2004; Fellow, Society of Antiquaries 2007. CBE 1982; PC 2000.

Publications: Co-author: Changing Charity (1984), Monty at Close Quarters (1985), Save Our Schools (1986), The Arts: The Next Move Forward (1987); Articles in the *Guardian*, *Independent*, *Observer*, *Daily Telegraph*.

Recreations: The arts, heritage, reading, walking.

Rt Hon the Lord Howarth of Newport CBE, House of Lords, London SW1A 0PW
Tel: 020 7219 5077 *Email:* howartha@parliament.uk

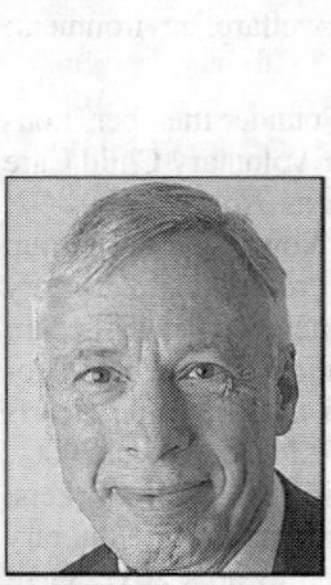

CONSERVATIVE

HOWE, EARL

Deputy Leader of the House of Lords; Minister of State and Government Spokesperson, Ministry of Defence

HOWE (7th Earl, UK), Frederick Richard Penn Curzon; cr. 1821; 8th Viscount Curzon (UK) 1802; 9th Baron Howe (GB) 1788; 8th Baron Curzon (GB) 1794. Born 29 January 1951; Son of late Commander Chambré George William Penn Curzon, RN, grandson of 3rd Earl, GCVO, CB, and late Mrs Jane Curzon, née Fergusson; Married Elizabeth Stuart 1983 (1 son 3 daughters).

Education: Rugby School; Christ Church, Oxford (MA literae humaniores 1973).

Non-political career: Arable farmer; Director: Adam & Company plc 1987-90, Provident Life Association Ltd 1988-91; Barclays Bank plc 1973-87, Senior manager 1984-87; Chair, LAPADA 1999-2010; Director, Andry Montgomery Ltd 2000-10; Trustee, Kedleston and Portman Estates 2006-. Member, National Farmers' Union.

Political career: *House of Lords:* First entered House of Lords 1984; Government Whip 1991-92; Parliamentary Secretary, Ministry of Agriculture, Fisheries and Food 1992-95; Parliamentary Under-Secretary of State, Ministry of Defence 1995-97; Elected hereditary peer 1999-; Opposition Spokesperson for: Defence May-October 1997, Health October 1997-2010, the Family 2004-05; Parliamentary Under-Secretary of State (Quality) and Government Spokesperson, Department of Health 2010-15; Minister of State and Government Spokesperson, Ministry of Defence 2015-; Deputy Leader of the House of Lords 2015-.

Political interests: Agriculture, penal affairs and policy, healthcare.

Other: Governor, King William IV Naval Foundation 1984-; National Society for Epilepsy: Vice-President 1984-86, President 1986-2010; President: South Bucks Association for the Disabled 1984-, Chilterns Branch, RNLI 1985-; Governor, Trident Trust 1985-2008; President, CPRE (Penn Country Branch) 1986-92; Trustee, Milton's Cottage 1986-2012; Member, RNLI Council 1997-2014; Trustee: Sir William Borlase's Grammar School, Marlow 1998-2010, Restoration of Appearance and Function Trust (RAFT) 1999-2010; Patron: Demand 1999-2010, Chiltern Society 2001-; President, Institute of Clinical Research 2008-10; Chairman, Patrons of Buckinghamshire County Museum and Art Gallery; Associate, Chartered Institute of Bankers 1976-; Hon FRCP 2008-. Lords Minister of the Year, *House Magazine* awards 2012. PC 2013.

Recreations: Old films.

Rt Hon the Earl Howe, House of Lords, London SW1A 0PW
Tel: 020 7219 5353 *Email:* howef@parliament.uk

HOWE OF IDLICOTE, BARONESS

CROSSBENCH

BARONESS HOWE OF IDLICOTE (Life Baroness), Elspeth Rosamund Morton Howe; cr 2001. Born 8 February 1932; Daughter of late Philip Shand and Sybil Shand; Married Geoffrey Howe (later Sir Geoffrey, then Lord Howe of Aberavon) (died 2015) 1953 (2 daughters 1 son).

Education: Bath High School; Wycombe Abbey; London School of Economics (BSc social science and administration 1985).

Non-political career: JP 1964-90; Chair, Inner London Juvenile Court 1970-90; Member: Briggs Committee on the Future of the Nursing Profession 1970-72, Parole Board for England and Wales 1972-75; Deputy chair, Equal Opportunities Commission 1975-79; President, Federation of Recruitment and Employment Services 1980-94; Governor, London School of Economics 1985-2007; Chair, BOC Foundation for the Environment 1990-2003; Institute of Business Ethics' Advisory Council: Member 1990-, Advisory Council Vice-President 2002-; Business in the Community: Chair, BITC's opportunity 2000 Target Team 1990-99, Board member 1992-98; Chair, Archbishop's Commission on Cathedrals 1992-94; Member, Department of Employment working group on women's issues 1992-97; Chair, Broadcasting Standards Commission 1993-99; President, UK Committee of Unicef 1993-2002; Council of the Open University: Member 1996-2003, Vice-chair 2001-03; Board member, Veolia (formerly Onyx) Environmental Trust plc 2003-.

Political career: *House of Lords:* Raised to the peerage as Baroness Howe of Idlicote, of Shipston-on-Stour in the County of Warwickshire 2001. Member: Review of the BBC Charter 2005-06, Communications 2007-10. *Councils and public bodies:* Co-opted member, Inner London Education Authority 1967-70; Vice-president, Institute of Business Ethics Advisory Council 2002-.

Political interests: Equal opportunities, education, environment, law, third age, communications.

Other: President, Peckham Settlement; Member, NCVO Advisory Council; Patron, Mary Ward Legal Centre; Trustee: Architectural Association, Ann Driver Trust; President, National Governors' Association 2007-; Unicef and other children's charities. Seven honorary doctorates; Honorary Fellow London School of Economics 2001. CBE 1999; *Clubs:* Royal Society of Arts Club.

Publications: Under Five (CPC, 1966); Women and Credit (Equal Opportunities Commission, 1978); Women at the Top (Hansard Society, 1990).

Recreations: Bridge, theatre, grandchildren.

The Baroness Howe of Idlicote CBE, House of Lords, London SW1A 0PW
Tel: 020 7219 6581 *Email:* howee@parliament.uk
Old Rectory, Idlicote, Shipston-On-Stour CV36 5DT

CONSERVATIVE

HOWELL OF GUILDFORD, LORD

HOWELL OF GUILDFORD (Life Baron), David Arthur Russell Howell; cr. 1997. Born 18 January 1936; Son of late Arthur Howell, retired army officer and businessman; Married Davina Wallace 1967 (1 son 2 daughters).

Education: Eton College; King's College, Cambridge (BA economics 1959, MA).

Non-political career: Second Lieutenant, 2nd Btn Coldstream Guards 1954-56. Economic section, HM Treasury 1959-60; Leader writer, *Daily Telegraph* 1960-64; Editor, *Crossbow* 1962-64; Chair, UK-Japan 21st Century Group 1990-2000; Director, Trafalgar House 1990-2006; Visiting Fellow, Nuffield College, Oxford 1992-2000; Director: Monks Investment Trust 1993-2004, Jardine Insurance 1994-97; Advisory director, UBS-Warburg 1997-2000; Director, John Laing 2000-03; Financial advisory board, Kuwait Investment Authority 2003-10, 2012-.

Political career: *House of Commons:* Contested Dudley 1964 general election. MP (Conservative) for Guildford 1966-97. Parliamentary Secretary, Civil Service Department 1970-72; Parliamentary Under-Secretary of State: Department of Employment 1971-72, Northern Ireland Office March-November 1972; Minister of State: Northern Ireland Office 1972-74, Department of Energy 1974; Secretary of State for: Energy 1979-81, Transport 1981-83. Chair, Foreign and Commonwealth Affairs 1987-97. Chairman, One Nation Group of Conservative MPs 1988-97. *House of Lords:* Raised to the peerage as Baron Howell of Guildford, of Penton Mewsey in the County of Hampshire 1997. Opposition Spokesperson for Foreign and Commonwealth Affairs 2000-10; Deputy Leader of the Opposition 2005-10; Minister of State and Government Spokesperson, Foreign and Commonwealth Office 2010-12. Member, European Communities Sub-committee B (Energy, Industry and Transport) 1997-99; Chair: European Communities Sub-committee C (Defence and Foreign Policy) 1999-2000, Soft Power and the UK's Influence 2013-14, International Relations 2016-. *Other:* Director, Conservative Political Centre 1964-66.

Political interests: Economics, international finance, energy, oil, foreign affairs; All Central European countries, China, India, Japan, Middle East.

Other: Chair, Bow Group 1962; Director, Shakespeare Globe Theatre 2008-10; Chair, Council of Commonwealth Societies; Trustee, 800th Anniversary Magna Carta Trust; Chair, Windsor Energy Group; President, Royal Commonwealth Society 2012-; President, Energy Industries Council 2013-16. Liveryman, Clothworkers' Company. Grand Cordon of Order of Sacred Treasure (Japan) 2002. PC 1979; *Clubs:* Beefsteak Club.

Publications: Co-author, Principles in Practice (1960); The Conservative Opportunity (1965); Freedom and Capital (1981); Blind Victory: a study in income, wealth and power (1986); The Edge of Now (2000); Out of the Energy Labyrinth (2007); Old Links and New Ties (2013); Empires in Collision – the green versus black struggle for our energy future (2016).

Recreations: Writing, travel, do-it-yourself.

Rt Hon the Lord Howell of Guildford, House of Lords, London SW1A 0PW
Tel: 020 7219 5414 *Email:* howelld@parliament.uk
Website: www.lorddavidhowell.com *Twitter:* @Lordhowell

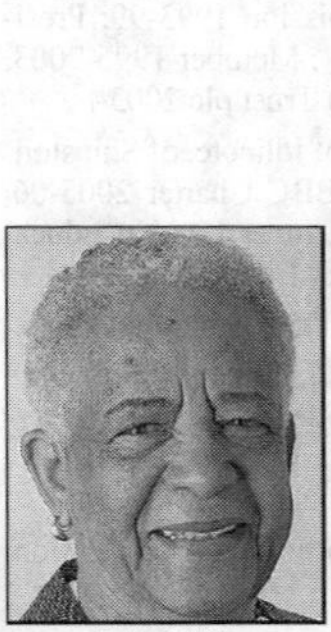

LABOUR

HOWELLS OF ST DAVIDS, BARONESS

HOWELLS OF ST DAVIDS (Life Baroness), Rosalind Patricia-Anne Howells; cr 1999. Born 10 January 1931; Married John Charles Howells 1955 (died) (2 daughters).

Education: St Joseph's Convent, Grenada; South West London College (Certificate welfare and counselling); City University, Washington DC (community and race relations); La Readille de la Ville de Paris (Echelon Vermeil).

Non-political career: Former community and equal opportunities worker: Moonshot Youth Club, Community industry; Equal opportunities director, Greenwich Racial Equality Council (until retirement).

Political career: *House of Lords:* Raised to the peerage as Baroness Howells of St Davids, of Charlton in the London Borough of Greenwich 1999. Member: Works of Art 2009-11, 2012-13, Social Mobility 2015-16. *Councils and public bodies:* Member, Court of Governors, Greenwich University.

Political interests: Community relations, international affairs (Africa/Caribbean), education, health; Algeria, China/Taiwan, Grenada, Nigeria, Saudi Arabia.

Other: St George's University, Grenada West Indies: Trustee 2005-, President 2014-; Has been an active campaigner for justice in the field of race relations: New Cross Fire, Roland Adams Campaign, Stephen Lawrence Family Campaign, SUS Campaign; Vice-chair, London Voluntary Services Council 1978-83; Former chair: Charlton Consortium, Carnival Liaison Committee, Greater

London Action on Race Equality; Chair, Lewisham Racial Equality Council 1994-97, Director, Smithville Associates; President, Grenada Convent Past Pupils Association; Patron: Grenada Arts Council, Mediation Service; Has served on various committees including: Advisory Committee to the Home Secretary, Commonwealth Countries League, Greenwich Police/Community Consultative Group; Trustee: West Indian Standing Conference, Museum of Ethnic Arts, Women of the Year Committee, Stephen Lawrence Charitable Trust, City Parochial Foundation; Chair, Talawa Theatre Company 2004-06; Hon. fellow, International Slavery Museum 2007-; Fellow, Bedfordshire University 2014; Sickle Cell Anemia, Cancer Research. Chancellor, Bedfordshire University 2009-14. Hon. DUniv, Greenwich University 1998; Hon. Doctorate of Civil Law, Northumbria University. Hansib Publications Award; The Voice Newspaper Community Award. OBE 1993.

Recreations: Food, music of all kinds, cricket, football.

The Baroness Howells of St Davids OBE, House of Lords, London SW1A 0PW
Tel: 020 7219 8655 *Fax:* 020 7219 8652 *Email:* howellsr@parliament.uk

HOWIE OF TROON, LORD

LABOUR

HOWIE OF TROON (Life Baron), William Howie; cr. 1978. Born 2 March 1924; Son of late Peter and Annie Howie; Married Mairi Sanderson 1951 (died 2005) (2 daughters 2 sons).

Education: Marr College, Troon; Royal Technical College, Glasgow (BSc, DRTC civil engineering 1944).

Non-political career: Civil engineer 1944-63, 1970-73; Journalist and publisher 1973-96; Director: Internal relations of Thomas Telford Ltd, publishers 1976-95, SETO 1996-2001; Consultant: George S Hall Ltd, building services engineer 1999-2007, PMS 1995-2007, Parliamentary Perceptions: Consultant 2007-11, Chair 2011-14. Life member, National Union of Journalists.

Political career: *House of Commons:* Contested Cities of London and Westminster 1959 general election. MP (Labour) for Luton 1963 by-election to 1970. *House of Lords:* Raised to the peerage as Baron Howie of Troon, of Troon, Kyle and Carrick 1978. Member: Science and Technology 1992-95, 1997-2001, 2005-09, European Communities 1995-97; Member: Science and Technology Sub-committees: II (Science and Society) 1999-2000, I (Complementary and Alternative Medicine) 2000; European Union 2003-05, European Union Sub-committees: B (Energy, Industry and Transport) 2003, G (Social Policy and Consumer Affairs) 2003-06; Science and Technology Sub-committee I (Waste Reduction) 2007-08. *Councils and public bodies:* Member, Committee of Inquiry into Engineering Profession 1977-79.

Political interests: Construction industry, professional engineers, higher education.

Other: Member: Council of Institution of Civil Engineers 1965-68, Council of City University 1968-91; Vice-President, Periodical Publishers Association; Fellow, Industry and Parliamentary Trust 1983; Fellow, Institution of Civil Engineers; Member, Society of Engineers and Scientists (France); Hon Fellow: Institution of Structural Engineers, Association of Building Engineers; Register of Engineers for Disaster Relief (RedR). Pro-Chancellor, City University 1984-91. Hon DSc, City University; Hon LLD, Strathclyde University. Institution of Civil Engineers Garth Watson Medal; *Clubs:* St Stephens Club, Lighthouse Club.

Publications: Co-author, Public Sector Purchasing (1968); Trade Unions and the Professional Engineer (1977); Trade Unions in Construction (1981); Co-editor, Thames Tunnel to Channel Tunnel (1987).

Recreations: Opera.

The Lord Howie of Troon, House of Lords, London SW1A 0PW
Tel: 020 7219 3238
34 Temple Fortune Lane, London NW11 7UL *Tel:* 020 8455 0492 *Fax:* 020 8455 0492

HOYLE, LORD

LABOUR

HOYLE (Life Baron), Eric Douglas Harvey Hoyle; cr. 1997. Born 17 February 1930; Son of late William Hoyle; Married Pauline Spencer 1952 (died 1991) (1 son, Lindsay Hoyle (qv) MP for Chorley).

Education: Adlington School; Horwich Technical College (HNC mechanical engineering).

Non-political career: British Rail 1945-51; AEI 1951-53; Sales engineer, C. Weston Ltd, Salford 1953-74; Warrington Rugby League plc: Chair 1999-2009, President 2009-. ASTMS: Vice-President 1972-74, 1981-85, President 1977-81, 1985-88; Merged with TASS 1988; MSF: Joint President 1988-90, President 1990-91; Unite: Member, Chair, Lords Parliamentary Group.

Political career: *House of Commons:* Contested Clitheroe 1964, Nelson and Colne 1970 and February 1974 general elections. MP (Labour) for Nelson and Colne October 1974-79, for Warrington 1981 by-election to 1983, for Warrington North 1983-97. Member Shadow Cabinet 1992-97. Chair: PLP Trade and Industry Committee 1987-92, PLP 1992-97; Member, PLP Parliamentary

Committee 2001-05. *House of Lords:* Raised to the peerage as Baron Hoyle, of Warrington in the County of Cheshire 1997. Government Spokesperson for: Defence 1997-99, Home Office 1997-99, Agriculture 1997-99; Government Whip 1997-99. Member, Procedure 2003-05. *Other:* Member, Labour Party National Executive 1978-82, 1983-85. *Councils and public bodies:* JP 1958; Member, North West Regional Health Authority 1968-74.

Political interests: Trade, employment, industrial relations, health, immigration, arts, sport; Australia, Europe, Gibraltar, New Zealand, South Africa.

Other: Freedom: Gibraltar, Warrington. Hon Doctorate, Chester University; *Clubs:* Reform Club. President: Adlington Cricket Club 1974-, Chorley Rugby League Club 1989-96; Warrington Wolves RLFC: Chair 1999-2009, President 2010-.

Recreations: Cricket, rugby league, theatre, cinema, sport.

The Lord Hoyle, House of Lords, London SW1A 0PW
Tel: 020 7219 3196 *Fax:* 020 7219 3831

HUGHES OF STRETFORD, BARONESS

LABOUR

HUGHES OF STRETFORD (Life Baroness), Beverley June Hughes; cr 2010. Born 30 March 1950; Daughter of late Norman Hughes and late Doris Hughes; Married Thomas McDonald 1973 (1 son 2 daughters).

Education: Ellesmere Port Girls' Grammar School; Manchester University (BSc 1971; MSc 1978); Liverpool University (Diploma applied social studies 1974).

Non-political career: Trainee probation officer, Merseyside 1971; Probation officer, Merseyside 1972-76; Manchester University: Research associate 1976-81; Lecturer 1981-93, Senior lecturer and head of department 1993-97. Member, USDAW.

Political career: *House of Commons:* MP (Labour) for Stretford and Urmston 1997-2010. PPS to Hilary Armstrong as Minister of State, Department of the Environment, Transport and the Regions (DETR) 1998-99; Parliamentary Under-Secretary of State, DETR 1999-2001; Home Office 2001-04: Parliamentary Under-Secretary of State 2001-02, Minister of State 2002-04: (for Citizenship, Immigration and Community Cohesion 2002-03, (Citizenship, Immigration and Counter Terrorism 2003-04); Minister of State, Department for Education and Skills/Children, Schools and Families 2005-09 (Children, Young People and Families 2005-07, Children and Youth Justice 2007-09) (attending cabinet 2008-09); Minister for the North West 2007-09. Member, Home Affairs 1997-98. Joint Vice-chair, PLP Departmental Committee for Women 1999-2000. *House of Lords:* Raised to the peerage as Baroness Hughes of Stretford, of Ellesmere Port in the County of Cheshire 2010. Opposition Spokesperson for Education 2010-15. Member, EU Justice Sub-committee 2015-17. *Councils and public bodies:* Trafford Metropolitan Borough Council: Councillor 1986-97, Labour Group Leader 1992-97, Council Leader 1995-97; Director: Trafford Park Development Corporation 1992-97, Manchester Airport plc 1995-97; Chair of Governing Council, Salford University 2014-17; Deputy Mayor (Police and Crime) for Greater Manchester 2017-.

Political interests: Economic regeneration, investment, local and regional government, health and community care, families, regional development, education, criminal justice, child protection and safety; Commonwealth countries, USA.

Other: Member, Executive Committee, Commonwealth Parliamentary Association (UK Branch) 2014-15; Strategic Policy Adviser, Greater Manchester Chamber of Commerce 2010-17; Trustee, Lowry Theatre 2011-. PC 2004.

Publications: Older People and Community Care: Critical Theory and Practice (1995); Numerous academic and professional publications.

Recreations: Jazz, fell-walking.

Rt Hon the Baroness Hughes of Stretford, House of Lords, London SW1A 0PW
Tel: 020 7219 0956 *Email:* hughesb@parliament.uk

HUGHES OF WOODSIDE, LORD

LABOUR

HUGHES OF WOODSIDE (Life Baron), Robert Hughes; cr. 1997. Born 3 January 1932; Son of Mitchell Hughes and Jessie Anderson; Married Ina Miller 1957 (2 sons 3 daughters).

Education: Robert Gordon's College, Aberdeen; Benoni High School, Transvaal, South Africa; Pietermaritzburgh Technical College, Natal, South Africa; Pietermaritzburg Technical College South Africa (Higher National Diploma engineering 1953).

Non-political career: Emigrated to South Africa 1947; Returned UK 1954; CF Wilson and Co (1932) Ltd, Aberdeen: Draughtsman 1954-64, Chief draughtsman 1964-70. Member, Unite.

Political career: *House of Commons:* Contested North Angus and Mearns 1959 general election. MP (Labour) for Aberdeen North 1970-97. Parliamentary Under-Secretary of State, Scottish

Office 1974-75; Piloted the Rating (Disabled Persons) Act 1978 as Private Member's Bill. Chair, Scottish Affairs 1991-94. *House of Lords:* Raised to the peerage as Baron Hughes of Woodside, of Woodside in the City of Aberdeen 1997. *Other:* Chairman, Aberdeen City Labour Party 1963-69. *Councils and public bodies:* Councillor, Aberdeen Town Council 1962-71; Member: North East Scotland Regional Hospital Board 1964-70, General Medical Council 1976-81.

Political interests: Agriculture, fishing industry, transport, health service, overseas aid and development; Countries in Southern Africa.

Other: Founder member, CND; Anti-Apartheid Movement: Vice-chair 1976, Chair 1977-94; Action for Southern Africa: Chair 1994-98, Hon. President 1998-; Hon. President, Mozambique, Angola Committee 2001-. South African Government National Order, Grand Companion of Oliver Tambo 2004.

Recreations: Fishing.

The Lord Hughes of Woodside, House of Lords, London SW1A 0PW
Tel: 020 7219 1451 *Fax:* 020 7219 2772/020 7219 5979 *Email:* hughesr@parliament.uk

LIBERAL DEMOCRAT

HUMPHREYS, BARONESS

Liberal Democrat Shadow Secretary of State for Wales

HUMPHREYS (Life Baroness), Christine Mary Humphreys; cr 2013. Born 26 May 1947.

Languages: Welsh.

Non-political career: Former teacher and head of vocational education, Welsh Medium School; Part-time tutor, Welsh for adults courses, Bangor University.

Political career: *House of Lords:* Raised to the peerage as Baroness Humphreys, of Llanrwst in the County of Conwy 2013. Liberal Democrat: Deputy Chief Whip 2015-16, Shadow Minister/Shadow Secretary of State for Wales 2016-. Member: Joint Committee on Statutory Instruments 2013-16, Secondary Legislation Scrutiny 2014-17, Procedure 2015-, Services 2016-. *Other:* National Assembly for Wales: AM for North Wales region 1999-2001: Liberal Democrats Spokesperson on Economics and Environment. Welsh Liberal Democrats: Member, National Executive Committee, President 2007-. *Councils and public bodies:* Councillor, Colwyn Bay Borough Council 1984-88, 1990-94.

Other: Chair of trustees, Llanrwst Almshouse Museum; President, Conwy Valley Rotary Club 2011-.

The Baroness Humphreys, House of Lords, London SW1A 0PW
Tel: 020 7219 5353

LABOUR

HUNT OF CHESTERTON, LORD

HUNT OF CHESTERTON (Life Baron), Julian Charles Roland Hunt; cr. 2000. Born 5 September 1941; Son of Roland Hunt CMG and Pauline Hunt, née Garnett; Married Marylla Shephard 1965 (1 son, Tristram Hunt, MP for Stoke-on-Trent Central 2010-17, 2 daughters).

Education: Westminster School; Trinity College, Cambridge (BA engineering 1963; PhD engineering 1967); Warwick University (engineering on secondment from Cambridge); French.

Non-political career: Cambridge University: Fellow 1966-, Senior research fellow 1998-99; Post-doctoral research, Cornell University, USA 1967; Research officer, Central Electricity Research Laboratories 1968-70; Trinity College: Lecturer in applied mathematics and in engineering 1970-78, Reader in fluid mechanics 1978-90, Professor 1990-92, Hon. Professor 1992-; Visiting professor: Colorado State University, USA 1975, National Center for Atmospheric Research, Boulder, Colorado, USA 1983; Cambridge Environmental Research Consultants Ltd: Founder director 1986-91, Director 1997-, Chair 2000-; Chief executive, Meteorological Office 1992-97; Visiting scientist, Cerfacs, Toulouse, France 1997, 1998, 2007, 2008; Visiting professor: Arizona State University, USA 1997-98, 2007-11, Stanford University, USA 1998, Delft University of Technology 1998-; Professor in climate modelling, and director, Lighthill Institute for Mathematical Science, University College, London 1999-2008, Emeritus 2008-; Visiting professor, Cornell University 2003-06; Pierre Fermat Visiting Professor, Toulouse 2007-08; Visiting fellow, Malaysian Commonwealth Studies Centre, Cambridge; Visiting professor, Hong Kong University 2011-; Chair, Advisory Committee Tokamak Solutions Ltd. Electrical Power Engineers Association: Member 1968-70, Branch secretary 1970; Member: AUT 1970-91, 1999-2008, IPCS 1992-97.

Political career: *House of Lords:* Raised to the peerage as Baron Hunt of Chesterton, of Chesterton in the County of Cambridgeshire 2000. Member: Animals in Scientific Procedures 2001-02, Science and Technology Sub-committees: II (Innovations in Microprocessing) 2002-03, I (Science and International Agreements) 2003-04; Member: The Arctic 2014-15, Science and Technology 2015-. *Councils and public bodies:* Cambridge City Council: Councillor 1971-74, Leader, Labour Group 1972; President, National Society of Clean Air 2006-09.

Political interests: Environment, science, government – civil service issues, informational aspects; France, India, USA.

Other: Member, Management board, European Research Community for Flow Turbulence and Combustion 1988-95; Member, Executive council, World Meteorological Organisation 1992-97; President, Institute of Mathematics and its Applications 1993-95; Council member, Royal Society 1998-99; ACOPS (Advisory Committee on Protection of the Sea): Chair 2001-04, President 2004-; Vice-President, Globe International 2009; Hon. Fellow: Institution of Civil Engineers, Institute of Mathematics and its applications, Royal Meteorological Society; FRS 1989; Oxfam, Unipal. Eight honorary doctorates from England, Scotland, France and Sweden. European Geophysical Society, LF Richardson Medal 2001. CB 1998; *Clubs:* Meteorological Club.

Publications: Editor four volumes including London's Environment (Imperial College Press, 2005); Articles in mathematical and scientific publications, and newspapers.

Recreations: Swimming, history, rough gardening.

Professor the Lord Hunt of Chesterton CB, House of Lords, London SW1A 0PW
Tel: 020 7219 6193
Department of Earth Sciences, University College London, Gower Street, London WC1E 6BT

LAB/CO-OP

HUNT OF KINGS HEATH, LORD

Opposition Spokesperson for Health, Further and Higher Education and Cabinet Office

HUNT OF KINGS HEATH (Life Baron), Philip Alexander Hunt; cr. 1997. Born 19 May 1949; Son of late Rev. Philip Hunt and Muriel Hunt; Married 1974 (divorced) (1 daughter); married Selina Stewart 1988 (3 sons 1 daughter).

Education: City of Oxford High School; Oxford School; Leeds University (BA political studies 1970).

Non-political career: Oxford Regional Hospital Board 1972-74; Nuffield Orthopaedic Centre 1974-75; Secretary, Edgware/Hendon Community Health Council 1975-78; National Association of Health Authorities: Assistant secretary 1978-79, Assistant director 1979-84, Director 1984-90; Director, National Association of Health Authorities and Trusts 1990-96; Chief executive, NHS Confederation 1996-97. Member, Unison.

Political career: *House of Lords:* Raised to the peerage as Baron Hunt of Kings Heath, of Birmingham in the County of West Midlands 1997. Government Spokesperson for Education and Employment 1998-99; Government Whip 1998-99; Parliamentary Under-Secretary of State and Government Spokesperson for: Department of Health 1999-2003, Department for Work and Pensions 2005-06; Minister of State for Quality, Department of Health and Government Spokesperson for Health 2006-07; Parliamentary Under-Secretary of State and Government Spokesperson, Ministry of Justice 2007-08; Minister of State and Government Spokesperson: Department for Environment, Food and Rural Affairs 2008-09, Department of Energy and Climate Change 2008-10; Deputy Leader of the House of Lords 2008-10; Opposition Spokesperson for: Cabinet Office 2010-12, Energy and Climate Change 2010, Home Office 2010-12; Shadow Deputy Leader of the House of Lords 2010-17; Opposition Spokesperson for: Health 2012-, Constitutional Affairs 2015-17, Further and Higher Education 2017-, Cabinet Office 2017-. Member, Consolidation, Etc, Bills Joint Committee 1998; Chair, Merits of Statutory Instruments 2003-05; Member: Leader's Group on Members Leaving the House 2010-15, House 2015-16, Liaison 2015-17. *Councils and public bodies:* Councillor, Oxford City Council 1973-79; Member, Oxfordshire Area Health Authority 1975-77; Councillor, Birmingham City Council 1980-82; Chair, National Patient Safety Agency 2004-05; Chairman, Heart of England NHS Foundation Trust, Birmingham 2011-14.

Political interests: Transport, constitutional affairs, energy and climate change.

Other: Council, International Hospital Federation 1986-91; Association for Public Health: Council 1992, Co-chair 1994-98; President: Family Planning Association 1997-98, Royal Society for Public Health 2010-; Oxfam, Living Streets, St Mary's Hospice Birmingham, Birmingham Contemporary Music Group, City of Birmingham Symphony Orchestra. Honorary Doctorate: Birmingham University, Birmingham City University, Aston University. OBE 1993; PC 2009. Warwickshire CCC.

Recreations: Cycling, swimming, Birmingham City FC, music.

Rt Hon the Lord Hunt of Kings Heath OBE, House of Lords, London SW1A 0PW
Tel: 020 7219 2030 *Email:* huntp@parliament.uk *Twitter:* @LordPhilofBrum

HUNT OF WIRRAL, LORD

CONSERVATIVE

HUNT OF WIRRAL (Life Baron), David James Fletcher Hunt; cr. 1997. Born 21 May 1942; Son of late Alan Hunt, OBE, shipping agent, and late Jessie Ellis Hunt; Married Paddy Orchard 1973 (2 sons 2 daughters).

Education: Liverpool College; Montpellier University, France (1962); Bristol University (LLB 1965); Guildford College of Law (1968).

Non-political career: Solicitor; Beachcroft LLP: Partner 1968-, Senior Partner 1996-2005, Chair, Financial Services Division 2005-; Director, BET Omnibus Services Ltd 1980-81; Chair, Beachcroft Regulatory Consulting 2002-08.

Political career: *House of Commons:* Contested Bristol South 1970 and Kingswood 1974 general elections. MP (Conservative) for Wirral 1976-83, for Wirral West 1983-97. Opposition Spokesperson for Shipping and Shipbuilding 1977-97; PPS to John Nott as Secretary of State for: Trade 1979-81, Defence 1981; Assistant Whip 1981-83; Government Whip 1983-84; Parliamentary Under-Secretary of State, Department of Energy 1984-87; Deputy Chief Whip (Treasurer of HM Household) 1987-89; Minister for Local Government and Inner Cities 1989-90; Secretary of State: for Wales 1990-93, for Employment 1993-94; Chancellor of the Duchy of Lancaster and Minister for Public Service and Science 1994-95. *House of Lords:* Raised to the peerage as Baron Hunt of Wirral, of Wirral in the County of Merseyside 1997. Opposition Spokesperson for Business, Enterprise and Regulatory Reform/Business, Innovation and Skills 2008-10. Member: Offices 1999-2001, European Communities Sub-committee E (Law and Institutions) 1999-2002, House 2003-07; Chair, Draft Legal Services Bill Joint Committee 2006; Alternate member, Procedure 2007-08, 2008-11; Member, EU Sub-committee G (Social Policies and Consumer Protection) 2010-12; Chair, Leader's Group on Members Leaving the House 2010-15; Member, Constitution 2015-. *Other:* Vice-chair, Bristol Conservative Association 1970; Chair, National Young Conservatives 1972-73; Vice-President, European Conservative and Christian Democratic Youth Community 1974-76; Vice-chair, Conservative Party 1983-84; Tory Reform Group: President 1991-97, Patron 1997-; Chairman, Association of Conservative Peers 2016-. *Councils and public bodies:* Chair, British Youth Council 1971-74; Member: South West Economic Planning Council 1972-76, Government Advisory Committee on Pop Festivals 1972-75; President, British Youth Council 1978-80; English Speaking Union: Governor 1998-2011, Deputy chair 2000-05, Chair 2005-11, International chair 2008-11; Board of the Chartered Insurance Institute: Professional Standards Board: Chair 2004-06, President 2007-08; Chair: McEdCo 2009-15, Lending Standards Board 2011-17, Press Complaints Commission 2011-14, British Insurance Brokers' Association 2014-.

Political interests: Europe, business and economy, skills; Commonwealth, European Union, USA.

Other: Governor, European Youth Foundation at Strasbourg 1972-75; Chair, British Atlantic Group of Young Politicians 1979-81; President, Atlantic Association for Young Political Leaders 1981-83; Vice-President and trustee, Holocaust Educational Trust 1995-; Honorary Fellow: International Institute of Risk and Safety Management 2000, Institute of Actuaries 2003, Chartered Insurance Institute 2004; Member, Law Society of England and Wales 1968-; Fellow: Chartered Insurance Institute, Institute of Chartered Secretaries and Administrators, International Risk and Safety Management, Institute of Actuaries. Honorary Freedom, Worshipful Company of Insurers 2009-. Hon LLD, Bristol University 2008; Doctor of Letters, Chester University 2013. MBE 1973; PC 1990; *Clubs:* Hurlingham Club.

Recreations: Cricket, walking.

Rt Hon the Lord Hunt of Wirral MBE, House of Lords, London SW1A 0PW
Tel: 020 7219 6688 *Email:* huntd@parliament.uk
DAC Beachcroft LLP, 100 Fetter Lane, London EC4A 1BN *Tel:* 020 7831 6630
Email: lordhunt@dacbeachcroft.com *Website:* www.dacbeachcroft.com

HUSSAIN, LORD

LIBERAL DEMOCRAT

HUSSAIN (Life Baron), Qurban Hussain; cr 2011. Born 27 March 1956; Married (6 children).

Education: Rochdale College; Bedford College; Luton University.

Non-political career: Secretary, Luton TUC 1994-96.

Political career: *House of Commons:* Contested (Liberal Democrat) Luton South 2005 and 2010 general elections. *House of Lords:* Raised to the peerage as Baron Hussain, of Luton in the County of Bedfordshire 2011. Member, Extradition Law 2014-15. *Other:* Member: Labour Party 1996-2003, Liberal Democrats 2003-. *Councils and public bodies:* Luton Borough Council: Councillor 2003-11, Deputy leader 2005-07.

Political interests: Luton.

Other: Member: Luton Law Centre, Justice Foundation, Islamic Cultural Society.

Recreations: Badminton, swimming, walking, writing.

The Lord Hussain, House of Lords, London SW1A 0PW
Tel: 020 7219 3159 *Email:* hussainq@parliament.uk

HUSSEIN-ECE, BARONESS

LIBERAL DEMOCRAT

HUSSEIN-ECE (Life Baroness), Meral Hussein Ece; cr 2010. Born 10 October 1953; Daughter of late Hasan Nihet Hussein and Ayshe Hussein, née Abdullah; 3 children.

Education: Edith Cavell Secondary School, Hackney; Art school (BA); Turkish.

Non-political career: Special adviser to Nick Clegg MP on community cohesion and minority ethnic communities 2006-12; Member, Government BME Women Councillors' Task Force 2008-10.

Political career: *House of Lords:* Raised to the peerage as Baroness Hussein-Ece, of Highbury in the London Borough of Islington 2010. Liberal Democrat Spokesperson for Equalities 2015-16. Member: HIV and AIDS in the UK 2010-11, Soft Power and the UK's Influence 2013-14, Sexual Violence in Conflict 2015-16. *Other:* Liberal Democrats: Member: Executive, London Liberal Democrats 1998-2003, Federal Policy Committee 2005-06, Federal Executive 2005-10, Chair, Ethnic Minority Liberal Democrats 2006-10. *Councils and public bodies:* London Borough of Hackney Council: Councillor 1994-2002, Deputy Leader 1995-96; London Borough of Islington Council: Councillor 2002-10, Cabinet Member for Health and Social Care 2002-06; Board member, Islington Primary Care Trust 2002-06; Non-executive director, Camden and Islington Mental Health and Social Care Trust 2004-06; Chair, Islington Health Partnership Board 2004-06; Commissioner, Equality and Human Rights Commission 2009-12.

Political interests: Local government, health, equality and diversity, women, youth, community cohesion, European and foreign affairs; Cyprus, Middle East, Turkey.

Other: Hon DLitt Coventry University 2012. OBE 2009.

The Baroness Hussein-Ece OBE, House of Lords, London SW1A 0PW
Tel: 020 7219 5353 *Email:* ecem@parliament.uk *Twitter:* @meralhece

HUTTON, LORD

CROSSBENCH

HUTTON (Life Baron), James Brian Edward Hutton; cr. 1997. Born 29 June 1931; Son of late James and Mabel Hutton; Married Mary Murland 1975 (died 2000) (2 daughters); married Rosalind Nickols 2001 (2 stepsons 1 stepdaughter).

Education: Shrewsbury School; Balliol College, Oxford (BA jurisprudence 1953); Queen's University, Belfast 1954.

Non-political career: Called to Northern Ireland Bar 1954; Junior Counsel to Attorney-General for Northern Ireland 1969; QC (NI) 1970; Called to English Bar 1972; Legal Adviser to Ministry of Home Affairs (NI) 1973; Senior Crown Counsel in NI 1973-79; Bencher, Inn of Court of Northern Ireland 1974; Judge of the High Court of Justice (NI) 1979-88; Hon. Bencher: Inner Temple 1988, King's Inn, Dublin 1988; Lord Chief Justice of Northern Ireland 1988-97; Visitor, Ulster University 1999-2003; Chair, Hutton Inquiry 2003-04.

Political career: *House of Lords:* Raised to the peerage as Baron Hutton, of Bresagh in the County of Down 1997. Lord of Appeal in Ordinary 1997-2004; On leave of absence March 2015-June 2017. *Councils and public bodies:* Member, Joint Law Enforcement Commission 1974; President, Northern Ireland Association for Mental Health 1983-90; Deputy chair, Boundary Commission (NI) 1985-88.

Other: Hon. Fellow, Balliol College, Oxford 1988; Two honorary law doctorates from NI universities. PC 1988; Kt 1988.

Rt Hon the Lord Hutton, House of Lords, London SW1A 0PW
Tel: 020 7219 5353

LABOUR

HUTTON OF FURNESS, LORD

HUTTON OF FURNESS (Life Baron), John Matthew Patrick Hutton; cr 2010. Born 6 May 1955; Son of late George Hutton, salesman and general labourer, and Rosemary Hutton, orthoptist; Married Rosemary Caroline Little 1978 (divorced 1993) (3 sons 1 daughter and 1 son deceased); married Heather Rogers 2004.

Education: Westcliffe High School, Southend; Magdalen College, Oxford (BA law 1976; BCL 1978).

Non-political career: Legal assistant, CBI 1978-80; Research fellow, Templeton College, Oxford 1980-81; Senior law lecturer, Newcastle Polytechnic 1981-92; Adviser, Bechtel 2011-; Special Adviser, PWC LLP 2013-17; Consultant, Lockheed Martin 2014-.

Political career: *House of Commons:* Contested Penrith and the Border 1987 general election. MP (Labour) for Barrow and Furness 1992-2010. PPS to Margaret Beckett: as President of the Board of Trade and Secretary of State for Trade and Industry 1997-98, as President of the Council and Leader of the House of Commons 1998; Department of Health: Parliamentary Under-Secretary of State 1998-99, Minister of State for Health 1999-2005; Chancellor of the Duchy of Lancaster and Minister for the Cabinet Office 2005; Secretary of State for: Work and Pensions 2005-07, Business, Enterprise and Regulatory Reform 2007-08, Defence 2008-09. Member, Home Affairs 1994-97. Chair PLP Departmental Committees for: Defence 1992-94, Home Affairs 1994-97. *House of Lords:* Raised to the peerage as Baron Hutton of Furness, of Aldingham in the County of Cumbria 2010. Member, Public Service and Democratic Change 2012-13. *Other:* Contested Cumbria and North Lancashire 1989 European Parliament election. *Councils and public bodies:* Chair, Independent Public Service Pensions Commission 2010-.

Political interests: Defence, welfare state, home affairs, legal affairs.

Other: Chair: Royal United Services Institute 2010-, Nuclear Industry Association 2011-, Cuba Initiative 2011-; Trustee, RAF Museum 2012-; Non-executive director: Sirius Minerals 2012-, Circle Holdings plc, Total Decom Ltd; Terence Higgins Trust. PC 2001.

Publications: Kitchener's Men (2008); August 1914 – Surrender at St Quentin (2010); A Doctor on the Western Front (2013).

Recreations: Cricket, football, films, music, history.

Rt Hon the Lord Hutton of Furness, House of Lords, London SW1A 0PW
Tel: 020 7219 5353

CROSSBENCH

HYLTON, LORD

HYLTON (5th Baron, UK), Raymond Hervey Jolliffe; cr. 1866; 5th Bt of Merstham (UK) 1821. Born 13 June 1932; Son of 4th Baron; Married Joanna de Bertodano 1966 (4 sons 1 daughter).

Education: Eton College; Trinity College, Oxford (MA history 1955); French, some Italian.

Non-political career: National Service, commissioned Coldstream Guards 1951-52. Assistant Private Secretary to the Governor-General of Canada 1960-62; Farmer (organic), forester and land-owner.

Political career: *House of Lords:* First entered House of Lords 1971; Private Member's Bills: Sexual Offences (Amendment) Bill, Overseas Domestic Workers (Protection) Bill; Elected hereditary peer 1999-. Member, Selection 2008-13. *Councils and public bodies:* Councillor, Frome RDC 1968-72; Govenor: Kilmersdon Primary School 1967-87, Writhlington Comprehensive School 1969-75; DL, Somerset 1970-90; President, Northern Ireland Association for Care and Resettlement of Offenders 1988-2009; Chair, Advisory Council Foundation for Reconciliation and Relief in Middle East (Iraq) 2006.

Political interests: Northern Ireland, housing, British-Irish relations, human rights, prisons, penal affairs and policy, conflict resolution, peace building, inter-faith relations, foreign affairs and policy, asylum issues; Caucasus (North and South), Europe, Iraq, Israel, Middle East, Moldova, Palestine, Russia, South East Europe, former Soviet Union.

Other: Member, Chatham House; Associated in various capacities 1962-: Abbeyfield Society, Catholic Housing Aid Society, London Housing Aid Centre, National Federation of Housing Associations 1970-73, Age Concern, L'Arche Ltd, Royal MENCAP, Foundation for Alternatives, Mendip Wansdyke Local Enterprise Group, Action around Bethlehem Children with Disability (ABCD); Trustee and governor, Ammerdown Centre Ltd, near Bath 1970-; Housing Associations Charitable Trust; Trustee, Forward Thinking (Re Israel and Palestine etc); Acorn Christian Healing Trust 1976-99; Chair, St Francis and St Sergius Trust Fund (for the churches and youth in Russia) 1993-2001; Chair, MICOM – Moldova Initiatives Committee of Management 1994; Soul of Europe (Kosovo); Associate, Royal Institute of Chartered Surveyors; ARICS 1960; Fellow, Land Agency. Hon. DSocSci, Southampton University 1994; *Clubs:* Lansdowne Club.

Publications: Numerous articles.

The Lord Hylton, House of Lords, London SW1A 0PW
Tel: 020 7219 3883 *Fax:* 020 7219 5979 *Email:* hyltonr@parliament.uk
Website: lordsoftheblog.net/category/lord-hylton

CROSSBENCH

IMBERT, LORD

IMBERT (Life Baron), Peter Michael Imbert; cr. 1999. Born 27 April 1933; Son of late William Imbert and Frances Imbert, née Hodge; Married Iris Dove 1956 (1 son 2 daughters).

Education: Harvey Grammar School, Folkestone; Holborn College of Law, Languages and Commerce; Russian (basic).

Non-political career: Joined Metropolitan Police 1953; Metropolitan Police Anti-Terrorist Squad 1973-75; Police negotiator at Balcombe Street siege December 1975; Surrey Constabulary: Assistant Chief Constable 1976, Deputy Chief Constable 1977; Chief Constable, Thames Valley Police 1979-85; National Crime Committee-ACPO Council: Secretary 1980-83, Chair 1983-85; Metropolitan Police: Deputy Commissioner 1985-87, Commissioner 1987-93; Non-executive director: Securicor 1994-2000, Camelot plc 1994-2001; Non-executive chair, Retainagroup 1995-2002; Has lectured on terrorism and siege situations in UK, Europe, Australia and Canada; Chair, Capital Eye Ltd 1997-2014; Strategic adviser, Inkerman Group 2009-13.

Political career: *House of Lords:* Raised to the peerage as Baron Imbert, of New Romney in the County of Kent 1999. *Councils and public bodies:* Member: General Advisory Council, BBC 1980-87, Criminal Justice Consultative Committee 1992-93, Ministerial Advisory Group, Royal Parks 1993-99, Public Policy Committee, RAC 1993-2000; Leader, International Criminal Justice Delegation to Russia 1993; Visiting International Fellow, Australian Police Staff College 1994, 1997; Member, Mental Health Foundation, Committee of Inquiry into Care in the Community for the Severely Mentally Ill 1994; JP 1998-2005; Greater London: Lord Lieutenant 1998-2008, DL 2008-.

Political interests: Police, criminal justice; Russia.

Other: Life member, Association of Chief Police Officers; Trustee, Queen Elizabeth Foundation of St Catharine's 1988-2001; Chair, Surrey CCC Youth Trust 1993-96; Trustee: Police Foundation 1994-, Crimestoppers Trust 1994-; Vice-president, Friends of Guys' and St Thomas' Hospitals 1995-; Member, International Police Association; CIMgt (CBIM 1982); John Grooms, Crimestoppers, Police Foundation, Stroke Association. Security Professionals. Freedom: City of London, New Romney, Kent. Hon. DLitt, Reading University 1987; DBA, Buckingham University. QPM 1980; Kt 1988; CVO 2008; *Clubs:* RAC, Saints and Sinners Club. Life Vice-President, Surrey County CC 1995-; President, Littlestone Golf Club 2013-17.

Recreations: Bad bridge, coarse golf, talking about grandchildren.

The Lord Imbert CVO QPM DL, House of Lords, London SW1A 0PW
Tel: 020 7219 5353

CONSERVATIVE

INGLEWOOD, LORD

INGLEWOOD (2nd Baron, UK), William Richard Fletcher-Vane; cr. 1964. Born 31 July 1951; Son of 1st Baron, TD, DL and Mary, neé Proby; Married Cressida Pemberton-Pigott 1986 (1 son 2 daughters).

Education: Eton College; Trinity College, Cambridge (BA English/land economy 1973, MA); Cumbria College of Agriculture and Forestry (City and Guilds Levels III and IV 1982); French, German.

Non-political career: Called to the Bar, Lincoln's Inn 1975; CN Group: Non-executive director 1997-, Chair 2002-16; Chair, Reviewing Committee on Export of Works of Art and Objects of Cultural Interest 2003-14; Carrs Milling Industries plc: Non-executive director 2004-05, Chair 2005-13; Chair, Gen2 2016-.

Political career: *House of Commons:* Contested (Conservative) Houghton and Washington 1983 general election. *House of Lords:* First entered House of Lords 1989; Government Whip 1994-95; Government Deputy Chief Whip 1995; Parliamentary Under-Secretary of State and Government Spokesperson, Department of National Heritage 1995-97; Opposition Spokesperson for Environment, Transport and the Regions 1997-98; Elected hereditary peer 1999-. Member: EU Sub-committee E 1997-99, EU Sub-committee A 2004-07, Communications 2007-10; Co-opted member, EU Sub-committee G (Social Policy and Consumer Affairs) 2008-10; Member, EU Sub-committee G (Social Policies and Consumer Protection) 2010-11; Chair: Communications 2010-14, Extradition Law 2014-15; Member: Works of Art 2015-16, Built Environment 2015-16, International Relations 2016-17, Lord Speaker's Advisory Panel on Works of Art 2017-. *Other:* European Parliament: Contested Durham 1984 election, MEP for Cumbria and Lancashire North 1989-94, Contested Cumbria and Lancashire North 1994 election, MEP for North West region 1999-2004, Vice-President, EP-China Delegation 1999-2004. *Councils and public bodies:* Member, Lake District Special Planning Board 1984-90; Chair, Development Control Committee 1985-89; Member, North West Water Authority 1987-89; DL, Cumbria 1993; Chair, Reviewing Committee Export of Works of Art 2003-14; Governor, Skinners' Academy, Hackney 2008-11; Vice Lord-Lieutenant, Cumbria 2013-; Chair, Cumbria Local Nature Partnership 2013-; President, Uplands Alliance 2015-.

Political interests: Rural affairs, agriculture, environment, Europe, local and regional government, regional policy, legal affairs, media, arts, constitutional affairs; China, Egypt, EU, Iceland, Turkey.

Other: Adviser and Member of the Advisory Board, Knowledge City Cairo 2015-; President, Cumbria Tourist Board 2004-; Visiting Parliamentary Fellow, St Antony's College Oxford 2014-15; President: British Art Market Federation 2014-, Uplands Alliance 2015-, Ancient Monuments Society 2015-; Member, Advisory Board, Reuters' Institute, Oxford University 2015-; President, National Sheep Association 2017-; Member, Royal Institution of Chartered Surveyors; Barrister, Lincolns Inn; Fellow, Society of Antiquaries of London; FSA. Liveryman, Skinners' Company; *Clubs:* Travellers Club, Pratt's Club.

The Lord Inglewood, House of Lords, London SW1A 0PW
Tel: 020 7219 3190 *Email:* inglewoodw@parliament.uk
Hutton-in-the-Forest, Penrith, Cumbria CA11 9TH *Tel:* 01768 484500 *Fax:* 01768 484571
Email: inglewood@hutton-in-the-forest.co.uk *Website:* www.hutton-in-the-forest.co.uk

IRVINE OF LAIRG, LORD

LABOUR

IRVINE OF LAIRG (Life Baron), Alexander Andrew Mackay Irvine; cr. 1987. Born 23 June 1940; Son of Alexander and Margaret Christina Irvine; Married Alison Mary McNair 1974 (2 sons).

Education: Inverness Royal Academy; Hutchesons' Boys' Grammar School, Glasgow; Glasgow University (MA, LLB); Christ's College, Cambridge (Scholar, BA, LLB).

Non-political career: University lecturer, London School of Economics 1965-69; Called to the Bar, Inner Temple 1967; QC 1978; Head, 11 King's Bench Walk Chambers 1981-97; Bencher of the Inner Temple, 1985; Recorder 1985-88; Deputy High Court Judge 1987-97.

Political career: *House of Commons:* Contested (Labour) Hendon North 1970 general election. *House of Lords:* Raised to the peerage as Baron Irvine of Lairg, of Lairg in the District of Sutherland 1987. Opposition Spokesperson for Legal Affairs and Home Affairs 1987-92; Shadow Lord Chancellor 1992-97; Lord Chancellor and Government Spokesperson for Legal Affairs and Lord Chancellor's Department 1997-2003; Lord of Appeal -2008. Member: Privileges/Privileges and Conduct 2008-, Sub-committee on Lords' Interests 2008-10, Constitution 2009-14, Sub-committee on Lords' Conduct 2010-. *Councils and public bodies:* Church Commissioner.

Political interests: Legal affairs, home affairs, constitutional affairs.

Other: Vice-Patron, World Federation of Mental Health; Joint President: Inter-Parliamentary Union, Commonwealth Parliamentary Association; Vice-President, Commonwealth Parliamentary Association (UK Branch); President, Magistrates Association; Chair, Glasgow 2001 Committee; Member, Committee of the Slade School of Fine Art 1990-; Foundation trustee, Whitechapel Art Gallery 1990-97; Trustee: John Smith Memorial Trust 1992-97, Hunterian Collection 1997-; Joint President, Industry and Parliament Trust 1997-; Hon. Fellow, Society for Advanced Legal Studies; Fellow, US College of Trial Lawyers 1998-. Hon. Fellow, Christ's College, Cambridge 1996; Hon. LLD, Glasgow 1997; Hon. Bencher, Inn of Court of Northern Ireland 1998; Hon. Doctorate, Siena 2000; Fellowship, LSE 2000; Member, Polish Bar 2000. George and Thomas Hutchison Award 1998. PC 1997; Knight Commander of the Order of Merit of the Republic of Poland, with Star 2004; *Clubs:* Garrick Club.

Publications: Articles on constitutional and legal topics in legal journals.

Recreations: Collecting paintings, travel, reading, cinema and theatre.

Rt Hon the Lord Irvine of Lairg, House of Lords, London SW1A 0PW
Tel: 020 7219 1446

CONSERVATIVE

JAMES OF BLACKHEATH, LORD

JAMES OF BLACKHEATH (Life Baron), David Noel James; cr 2006. Born 7 December 1937; Son of Captain Francis James and Alsina James, née Burdett; Married Caroline Webster 2004.

Education: Christ's College, Blackheath.

Non-political career: Lloyds Bank 1959-64; Ford Motor Co (UK) 1964-73; Rank Organisation plc 1974-81; Chairman: Central and Sherwood plc 1984-88, Eagle Trust 1989-97; LFP Group plc 1991-95, Henleys Group plc 1991-96, Robinson Group plc 1997-2001, New Millennium Experience Co 2000-01, Litigation Control Group Ltd 2002-06, Vidapulse Ltd 2003-.

Political career: *House of Lords:* Raised to the peerage as Baron James of Blackheath, of Wildbrooks in the County of West Sussex 2006. Co-opted Member, EU Sub-committee B (Internal Market) 2007-10; Member: Merits of Statutory Instruments 2007-10, Crossrail Bill 2008, EU Sub-committee B (Internal Market, Energy and Transport) 2010-12. *Other:* James Review of Taxpayer Value 2004-05.

Political interests: Horseracing industry, NHS finances, MoD procurement, funding and organisation of 2012 Olympics, renewable energy; Libya.

Other: Fellow, Institute of Directors; Trustee, David James Musical charity, Aphasia Society. Lifetime Achievement, Society of Turnaround Practitioners 2003. CBE 1992; *Clubs:* Savile, Jockey Club Rooms. MCC, Lords' Taverners.

Publications: Future Capital Structure of Lloyd's of London (1996); James Report on Public Expenditure (2005).

Recreations: Opera, ballet, cricket, rugby, tennis, horseracing, golf.

The Lord James of Blackheath CBE, House of Lords, London SW1A 0PW
Tel: 020 7219 4954

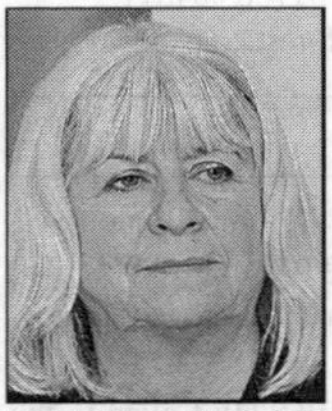

LIBERAL DEMOCRAT

JANKE, BARONESS

JANKE (Life Baroness), Barbara Lilian Janke; cr 2014. Born 5 June 1947; Daughter of Esther and Alfred Kearns; Married John (1 son 1 daughter).

Education: Waterloo Park Girls Grammar School; College St Matteas, Bristol (Cert. Ed. 1968); Open University (economic and politics 1981); French.

Non-political career: Languages and economics teacher 1968-95; Caseworker to Don Foster MP 1994.

Political career: *House of Commons:* Contested (Liberal Democrat) Surbiton 1992 general election. *House of Lords:* Raised to the peerage as Baroness Janke, of Clifton in the City and County of Bristol 2014. Liberal Democrat Spokesperson for: Communities and Local Government 2015, Treasury 2015. Member: EU Home Affairs Sub-committee 2015-, Political Polling and Digital Media 2017-. *Other:* Member, Liberal Party 1978; Leader, Bristol Liberal Democrats 1997-. *Councils and public bodies:* Councillor, London Borough of Kingston-upon-Thames 1986; Bristol City Council: Councillor 1995-2015, Leader of the Council 2003-04, 2005-07, 2009-12; Vice-President, Local Government Association 2016-.

Political interests: Local government, health, care, treasury, finance, constitutional reform.

The Baroness Janke, House of Lords, London SW1A 0PW
Tel: 020 7219 5353 *Email:* jankeb@parliament.uk

CROSSBENCH

JANVRIN, LORD

JANVRIN (Life Baron), Robin Berry Janvrin; cr 2007. Born 20 September 1946; Married Isabelle de Boissonneaux de Chevigny 1977 (2 sons 2 daughters).

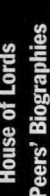

Education: Marlborough College, Wiltshire; Brasenose College, Oxford (BA philosophy, politics and economics 1969).

Non-political career: Various positions, Royal Navy 1964-75. HM Diplomatic Service 1975-87: First secretary, UK delegation to NATO 1976-78, New Delhi High Commission 1981-84, Counsellor 1985; HM the Queen: Press secretary to 1987-90, Assistant private secretary to 1990-95, Deputy private secretary to 1996-99, Private secretary to and Keeper of the Queen's Archives 1999-2007, Permanent Lord-in-waiting 2007-; Senior adviser, HSBC Private Bank (UK) 2008-.

Political career: *House of Lords:* Raised to the peerage as Baron Janvrin, of Chalford Hill in the County of Gloucestershire 2007. Trade Envoy to Turkey; Member, Intelligence and Security Committee 2015-. Member: Joint Committee on Privacy and Injunctions 2011-12, Soft Power and the UK's Influence 2013-14, Digital Skills 2014-15, Secondary Legislation Scrutiny 2015-. *Councils and public bodies:* Trustee, National Portrait Gallery 2008-16; Board member, British Library 2017-.

Political interests: Constitutional issues, foreign and commonwealth affairs, philanthropy; France, India.

Other: Chair, Royal Foundation 2010-16; Trustee, Gurkha Welfare Trust 2010-16. LVO 1983; CVO 1994; CB 1997; PC 1998; KCVO 1998; KCB 2003; GCB 2007; GCVO 2007; QSO 2008.

Recreations: Family, painting.

Rt Hon the Lord Janvrin GCB GCVO QSO, House of Lords, London SW1A 0PW
Tel: 020 7219 6989 *Email:* janvrinr@parliament.uk

CROSSBENCH

JAY OF EWELME, LORD

JAY OF EWELME (Life Baron), Michael Hastings Jay; cr 2006. Born 19 June 1946; Son of late Alan Jay and Vera Effa Vickery; Married Sylvia Mylroie 1975.

Education: Winchester College; Magdalen College, Oxford (BA philosophy, politics and economics 1968, MA); School of Oriental and African Studies, London University (MSc economic development 1969); French.

Non-political career: Volunteer teacher, Zambia 1965; Assistant principal, Ministry of Overseas Development (ODM) 1969-73; Technical assistant, UK delegation to International Monetary Fund and International Bank for Reconstruction and Development (World Bank), Washington DC 1973-75; Principal, ODM 1976-78; First Secretary (Development), New Delhi High Commission 1978-81; Foreign and Commonwealth Office (FCO), London 1981-85: Deputy Head, FCO Policy Planning Staff 1981-82, Private Secretary to Permanent Under Secretary 1982-85; Counsellor, European Secretariat, Cabinet Office 1985-87; Financial and Commercial Counsellor, British Embassy, Paris 1987-90; FCO 1990-96: Assistant Under-Secretary for European Affairs 1990-94, Deputy Under-Secretary of State for Economic and Economic Affairs 1994-96; Ambassador to France 1996-2001; Permanent Under-Secretary, FCO and Head of the Diplomatic Service 2002-06; Prime Minister's Personal Representative for G8 Presidency and Summits 2005-06; Non-executive director: Associated British Foods 2006-, Valeo SA 2007-, Credit Agricole SA 2007-11, Candover Investments plc 2008-, EDF 2009-; Trustee, Thomson Reuters Founders Share Company 2013-.

Political career: *House of Lords:* Raised to the peerage as Baron Jay of Ewelme, of Ewelme in the County of Oxfordshire 2006. Co-opted Member, EU Sub-committee E (Law and Institutions) 2006-08; Member: Draft Climate Change Bill Joint Committee 2007, Intergovernmental Organisations 2007-08; EU Sub-committee C (Foreign Affairs, Defence and Development Policy): Co-opted Member 2008-10, Member 2010-12; Member: EU Sub-committee C (External Affairs) 2012-13, Joint Committee on the Draft Enhanced Terrorism Prevention and Investigation Measures Bill 2012-13, EU Sub-committee F (Home Affairs, Health and Education) 2014-15, European Union 2015-; EU Home Affairs Sub-committee: Member 2015-17, Chair 2017-. *Councils and public bodies:* Chair, House of Lords Appointments Commission 2008-13.

Political interests: Foreign and European policy, energy policy, environment and climate change, development; Africa, EU, India.

Other: Vice-chair, Business for New Europe 2006-; Chair: Merlin (international medical charity) 2007-13, British Library Advisory Council: Member 2011-, Chair 2014-; Hon. Fellow, Magdalen College, Oxford; Francis Crick Institute, Friends of Ewelme Church. Senior associate member, St Antony's College, Oxford 1996; Honorary Fellow, Magdalen College, Oxford 2004. CMG 1992; KCMG 1997; GCMG 2006; *Clubs:* Special Forces Club.

The Lord Jay of Ewelme GCMG, House of Lords, London SW1A 0PW
Tel: 020 7219 3941/020 7219 3156 *Email:* jaymh@parliament.uk

LABOUR

JAY OF PADDINGTON, BARONESS

JAY OF PADDINGTON (Life Baroness), Margaret Ann Jay; cr. 1992. Born 18 November 1939; Daughter of late James Callaghan, former Prime Minister, and late Audrey Moulton; Married Hon Peter Jay 1961 (divorced 1986) (1 son 2 daughters); married Professor Michael Adler CBE 1994.

Education: Blackheath High School, London; Somerville College, Oxford (BA philosophy, politics and economics 1961).

Non-political career: Various production posts with BBC Television in current affairs and further education 1965-77; Former reporter for: BBC Television's *Panorama*, Thames Television's *This Week*; Founder director, National AIDS Trust 1988-92; Non-executive director: Carlton Television 1996-97, Scottish Power 1996-97, Independent News and Media UK 2001-12, BT 2002-08; Political consultant to Currie and Brown 2004-07; Non-executive director, British Telecom Committee for Responsible and Sustainable Business 2008-17. Member, National Union of Journalists.

Political career: *House of Lords:* Raised to the peerage as Baroness Jay of Paddington, of Paddington in the City of Westminster 1992. Opposition Spokesperson for Health 1992-97, Minister of State, Department of Health 1997-98; Deputy Leader, House of Lords 1997-98; Leader of the House of Lords and Lord Privy Seal; Minister for Women 1998-2001; Opposition Whip 1992-95. Member: House of Lords Offices 1997-2001, Assisted Dying 2004-05, Leader's Group on Code of Conduct 2009; Constitution: Member 2009-10, Chair 2010-14; Member: Extradition Law 2014-15, Communications 2015-16, Privileges and Conduct 2016-, Political Polling and Digital Media 2017-. *Other:* Member, Labour Party Donations Committee 2002-05; President, One Thousand Club 2002-06; Member, Lionel Cooke Memorial Fund Trust 2008-. *Councils and public bodies:* Member, Kensington and Chelsea and Westminster Health Authority 1993-97; Former Member, Central Research and Development Committee for NHS.

Political interests: Health, overseas aid and development, media, broadcasting, constitution; China, India, South Africa, USA.

Other: Former Member, President World Bank International Advisory Group on Health; Member, International Advisory Board Independent News and Media 2002-; Associate member, InterAction Council; Former Governor, South Bank University; Former Member, Governing Board: Queen Charlotte's Maternity Hospital, Chelsea Hospital for Women; Chair: Overseas Development Institute 2002-10; Bringing Research to Life Development Board, Great Ormond Street Hospital 2010-; Overseas Development Institute: Chair 2002-10, Council member; Trustee, Hansard Society 2012-; Member, Court of Governors, South Bank University 2012-. Two honorary degrees; Senior Honorary Fellow, Somerville College, Oxford; Honorary Fellow: Sunderland University, South Bank University, Greenwich University. PC 1998.

Publications: How Rich Can We Get? (1972); Co-author, Battered – The Story of Child Abuse (1986).

Rt Hon the Baroness Jay of Paddington, House of Lords, London SW1A 0PW
Tel: 020 7219 4912 *Email:* jaym@parliament.uk

CONSERVATIVE

JENKIN OF KENNINGTON, BARONESS

JENKIN OF KENNINGTON (Life Baroness), Anne Caroline Jenkin; cr 2011. Born 8 December 1955; Daughter of late Hon. Charles Strutt and Hon. Jean Strutt, née Davidson; Married Bernard Jenkin (qv) 1988 (MP for Harwich and North Essex) (2 sons).

Political career: *House of Lords:* Raised to the peerage as Baroness Jenkin of Kennington, of Hatfield Peverel in the County of Essex 2011. Member: Refreshment 2012-15, Equality Act 2010 and Disability 2015-16, Charities 2016-17. *Other:* Founder and co-chair, Women2Win; Chair, Conservative Friends of International Development.

Other: Patron, Restless Development; Trustee: Unicef UK, Sir Simon Milton Foundation -2015, Cool Earth, WRAP 2016-.

The Baroness Jenkin of Kennington, House of Lords, London SW1A 0PW
Tel: 020 7219 5353 *Twitter:* @BaronessJenkin

LIBERAL DEMOCRAT

JOLLY, BARONESS

Liberal Democrat Lord Spokesperson for Defence

JOLLY (Life Baroness), Judith Anne Jolly; cr 2010. Born 27 April 1951; Married (2 sons).

Education: The King's High School for Girls, Warwick; Leeds University (BSc engineering); Nottingham University (PGCE).

Non-political career: Maths teacher 1974-97; Chief of staff to Robin Teverson MEP 1997-99; Taught English as a foreign language, British Council, Oman 1990s.

Political career: *House of Lords:* Raised to the peerage as Baroness Jolly, of Congdon's Shop in the County of Cornwall 2010. Government Whip 2013-15; Government Spokesperson for: Culture, Media and Sport (Arts, Tourism and Sport; Women and Equalities) 2013-15, Defence 2013-15, Health 2013-15; Liberal Democrat Spokesperson/Shadow Secretary of State for Defence 2015-. Member: Ecclesiastical Committee 2012-13, Joint Committee on the Draft Care and Support Bill 2013. Chair, Liberal Democrat Parliamentary Party Committee on Health and Social Care 2011-15. *Other:* Member, Liberal Party/Liberal Democrats 1984-; Election Agent to Paul Tyler MP 1997; Vice-chair, Parliamentary Candidates' Assocation 1999-2008; Member, Federal Policy Committee 2002-10; Chair, Devon and Cornwall Regional Executive 2007-10. *Councils and public bodies:* Non-executive director, Mental Health and Learning Disability NHS Trust 1997-2007; Former chair, North and East Cornwall NHS Primary Care Trust; Former lay member, Commission for Health Improvement; President, Society of Chiropodists and Podiatrists 2013-; Chair, Digital Services Cornwall CIC.

Political interests: Defence, international affairs, poverty, rural affairs, global health, music; Middle East, Oman.

Other: Trustee: Help Musicians UK, Focus on Labour Exploitation; Chair, HFT WEF 2016-.

Recreations: Singing, reading modern novels.

The Baroness Jolly, House of Lords, London SW1A 0PW
Tel: 020 7219 1286 *Email:* jollyj@parliament.uk *Twitter:* @jollyjudith

JONES, LORD

LABOUR

JONES (Life Baron), Stephen Barry Jones; cr. 2001. Born 26 June 1937; Son of late Stephen Jones, steelworker, and late Grace Jones; Married Janet Davies (1 son).

Education: Hawarden Grammar School; Teacher training, Normal College, UCNW Bangor.

Non-political career: Head of English department, Deeside Secondary School, Flintshire; Regional officer, National Union of Teachers. Member, Transport and General Workers Union.

Political career: *House of Commons:* Contested Northwich, Cheshire 1966 general election. MP (Labour) for East Flint 1970-83, for Alyn and Deeside 1983-2001. PPS to Denis Healey as Chancellor of the Exchequer 1972-74; Parliamentary Under-Secretary of State for Wales 1974-79; Member, Public Accounts Committee 1979-80; Opposition Frontbench Spokesperson for Employment 1980-83; Member: Shadow Cabinet 1983-92, Prime Minister's Intelligence and Security Committee 1994-97, 1997-2001; Madam Speaker's Chairman Panel 1997-2001; Chairman: Welsh Grand Committee 1997-2001, Advisory Committee on Registration of Political Parties 1999-2001; Deputy Speaker, Westminster Hall 2000-01. *House of Lords:* Raised to the peerage as Baron Jones, of Deeside in the County of Clwyd 2001. Member, EU Sub-committee A (Economic and Financial Affairs, Trade and External Relations/Economic and Financial Affairs) 2003-06; EU Sub-committee C (Foreign Affairs, Defence and Development Policy): Co-opted member 2008-10, Member 2010-12; Member: Joint Committee on the Draft Communications Data Bill 2012-13, Inheritance and Trustees' Powers Bill 2013, Extradition Law 2014-15, Delegated Powers and Regulatory Reform 2015-. *Other:* Chair, Flint East Constituency Labour Party 1964-66; Member, Executive of Labour Party, Wales 1966-70. *Councils and public bodies:* Governor: National Museum of Wales, National Library of Wales.

Political interests: Manufacturing industries, regional policy, NHS, education, aerospace; Austria, Germany.

Other: Member, Delegation of Council of Europe and Western European Union 1971-74; Hon. Life Member, Royal Liverpool Philharmonic Society 1980-; Chair, Diocesan Board of Continuing Education, St Asaph 2004-; Trustee: Friends of Africa Foundation, Winnicot Clinic, Bodelwyddan Castle Trust (NPG Wales); President: Deeside Hospital League of Friends, North East Wales Institute of Higher Education 2007-09, North Wales Exporters Club, Neighbourhood Watch, Flintshire 2008-, Hawarden Singers, Saltney History Society; Vice-President, Federation of Economic Development Authorities; Chair, Diocesan Education Board (St Asaph); Dementia Champion Wales 2012-; President: Army Cadet Forces Association Wales 2013, Royal Buckley Town Band, Wrexham and Bidston Rail Users Association, Chester and East Clwyd Advanced Motorists, Deeside Business Forum, Arthritis Care, Flintshire, Flintshire County Business Week 2014; Sain Clwyd Sound (Talking Newspaper); Patron: Brain Injury Rehabilitation and Development Learning Centre, Chester, Neuro Centre, Chester and North Wales; President: Mersey Dee Alliance, Cornerstone Flintshire (L'Arche UK); Hon. Fellow: Bangor University 2012, Gladstone's Library, Hawarden; Alzheimer's Disease Society, Wales Ambassador and Dementia Friend, Royal Academy, Tate Galleries, Merseyside Museum and Gallery, Patron, Welsh Association of ME and CFS Support (Wales Neurological Alliance). Founding Chancellor, Glyndwr University 2009-12. PC 1999. Patron, GAP Connah's Quay Nomads Football Club.

Recreations: Soccer, cricket, watching tennis.

Rt Hon the Lord Jones, House of Lords, London SW1A 0PW
Tel: 020 7219 3556

JONES OF BIRMINGHAM, LORD

CROSSBENCH

JONES OF BIRMINGHAM (Life Baron), Digby Marritt Jones; cr 2007. Born 28 October 1955; Son of late Derek Jones and of Bernice Jones; Married Patricia Moody 1990.

Education: Bromsgrove School, Worcestershire; University College, London (LLB 1977); College of Law, Chester; French.

Non-political career: University cadetship, Royal Navy 1974-77. Edge & Ellison, Solicitors 1978-98: Articled clerk 1978-80, Solicitor 1980-98, Partner 1984-98, Deputy senior partner 1990-95, Senior partner 1995-98; Vice-chair, corporate finance, KPMG Business Advisers 1998-2000; Director-general, Confederation of British Industry 2000-06; Director, Business in the Community 2000-06; Chair: Tourism Alliance 2001-06, Extrinsic plc 2003-05; Non-executive director: Alba plc 2004-

07; Mhl plc 2004-06, Iclean Systems plc 2005-07, Leicester Tigers plc 2005-; UK Skills Envoy 2006-07; Adviser: Wragge & Co, Solicitors 2006-07, Hugh James, Solicitors 2006-07; Senior adviser: Ford of Europe 2006-07, Barclays Capital 2006-07, Deloitte 2006-07, JCB 2006-07, Computer Science Corporation Inc 2006-07; Member, advisory board, Thales 2006-07; Chairman: International Business Advisory Board, HSBC 2009-11, International Business Advisory Board, British Airways 2009-12, Grove Indistries 2012-16, Triumph Motorcycles Limited 2009-, Neutrino Concepts Limited 2009-; Corporate Ambassador to Jaguar Cars 2009-; Corporate adviser to JCB 2009-; Senior Global Adviser Monitise plc 2009-; Business adviser to: ISeeU Limited 2009-10, Grove Industries Limited 2009-11, Barberry Developments Ltd 2009-, Business Ambassador for UK Trade & Investment 2008-; Adviser to: Duke of York as Special Representative to UK Trade & Investment 2009-10, BP plc 2012-, SHP Limited 2013; Chairman: International business advisory board, British Airways 2009-12, Emergency services advisory board, Babcock International Group plc; Senior adviser, Harvey Nash plc; Chairman, advisory board: Jaguar academy of sport 2017, Argentex Ltd 2012-; Non-executive director: Flybe plc 2012-, Spicers Ltd 2012-; Non-executive deputy chair, Unipart Expert Practices 2013-17; Corporate Ambassador Ravenscroft 2015-17; Chair, G-Labs Ltd 2016-.

Political career: *House of Lords:* Raised to the peerage as Baron Jones of Birmingham, of Alvechurch and of Bromsgrove in the County of Worcestershire 2007. Minister of State (Trade and Investment) and Government Spokesperson, Foreign and Commonwealth Office and Department for Business, Enterprise and Regulatory Reform 2007-08. *Councils and public bodies:* Member, Commission for Racial Equality 2002-07; Director, VisitBritain 2003-05; Member, National Learning and Skills Council 2003-06; President, Diversity Works Initiative 2004-07; Chairman of Governors, Stratford upon Avon College 2015-17.

Countries of interest: Australia, India, New Zealand, Singapore, South Africa, USA.

Other: Corporate ambassador, Cancer Research UK 2004-; Chairman, Corporate Advisory Board, Sense 2004-07; Vice-President, Birmingham Hospice; Member, Development Trust CBSO; Vice-President, Birmingham Civic Society; Trustee, Millenium Point, Birmingham 2006-11; Corporate ambassador and member, Royal British Legion; Vice-President, Industrial Trust; Chairman, advisory board, Birmingham University Business School 2003-16; Guardian, Birmingham Assay Office; Chairman, London Board, Sportaccord 2010-11; Founding supporter, Change Britain 2016-; Member: Bromsgrove School Foundation Board, Artists' Circle at The Royal Shakespeare Company; Honorary Vice-Patron, National Museum of the Royal Navy; Member, Law Society 1980; Honorary Fellow, Institute of Mechanical Engineers; Hon. Fellow: University College, London 2004, Cardiff University 2006, Cardiff Metropolitan University 2013; Visiting Professor, Hull University Business School 2004-13; Get-a-Head Charitable Trust, Sense, Ovarian Cancer Action, Matt Hampson Foundation, Ladies Fighting Breast Cancer, Hospice of Hope (Romania), Help for Heroes, Birmingham St Mary's Hospice, Flying for Freedom, Avon River Trust, Birmingham Foundation, Royal Navy & Royal Marines Charity, Ovarian Cancer Action. Freedom, City of London. Fifteen UK honorary doctorates: University of Central England 2002, Birmingham University 2002, Manchester University Institute of Science and Technology 2003, Hertfordshire University 2004, Middlesex University 2005, Sheffield Hallam University 2005, Aston University 2006, Hull University 2006, Queen University Belfast 2006, Warwick University 2006, Bradford University 2006, Thames Valley University 2006, Wolverhampton University 2006, Loughborough University 2007, Nottingham University 2007. UK Speaker of the Year 2008; EVCOM Fellowship Award for Services to the Communications and Marketing Sector 2014. Kt 2005; *Clubs:* Reform Club.

Publications: Fixing Britain: The Business of Reshaping Our Nation (2011); Fixing Business; Making Profitable Business Work for All (2017).

Recreations: Rugby (especially Leicester Tigers), Aston Villa, skiing, theatre, military history.

The Lord Jones of Birmingham, House of Lords, London SW1A 0PW
Tel: 020 7219 3232
78 York Street, London, London W1H 1DP
Website: www.digbylordjones.com *Twitter:* @digbylj

LIBERAL DEMOCRAT

JONES OF CHELTENHAM, LORD

JONES OF CHELTENHAM (Life Baron), Nigel David Jones; cr 2005. Born 30 March 1948; Son of late A J and Nora Jones; Married Katy Grinnell 1981 (1 son twin daughters).

Education: Prince Henry's Grammar School, Evesham; Arabic, French, German, Swedish.

Non-political career: Clerk; Computer operator, Westminster Bank 1965-67; Computer programmer, ICL Computers 1967-70; Systems analyst, Vehicle and General Insurance 1970-71; Systems programmer, Atkins Computing 1971; Systems designer; Consultant; Project manager, ICL Computers 1971-92.

Political career: *House of Commons:* Contested Cheltenham 1979 general election. MP (Liberal Democrat) for Cheltenham 1992-2005. Liberal Democrat Spokesperson for: England, Local Government and Housing 1992-93, Science and Technology 1993-2005, Consumer Affairs 1995-97, Sport 1997-99, Science and Technology 1997-99, International Development 1999-2002. *House of Lords:* Raised to the peerage as Baron Jones of Cheltenham, of Cheltenham in the County of Gloucestershire 2005. Member: Information 2007-09, Crossrail Bill 2008, High Speed Rail (London-West Midlands) Bill 2016. *Councils and public bodies:* Councillor, Gloucestershire County Council 1989-93.

Political interests: Trade and industry, transport, restructuring of defence industries, information technology, sport, international development; Africa, Bahrain, Botswana, Gambia, Ghana, Kenya, Kuwait, Lesotho, Malawi, Middle East, St Helena, Sierra Leone, Swaziland, Tanzania, Turks and Caicos Islands, Uganda, UAE, Zambia, Zimbabwe.

Other: Member, Executive Committee: Governing Body British Association for Central and Eastern Europe 1996-2001, Inter-Parliamentary Union British Group 1997-2005, Commonwealth Parliamentary Association UK Branch 1999-2005; NSPCC, Help the Aged, WWF, Smile Train; *Clubs:* National Liberal, Reform Club. Gloucestershire County Cricket Club; Cheltenham Town FC Season Ticket Holder.

Recreations: Watching Swindon Town FC and Cheltenham Town FC, playing cricket, gardening.

The Lord Jones of Cheltenham, House of Lords, London SW1A 0PW
Tel: 020 7219 4415 *Email:* jonesn@parliament.uk

GREEN PARTY

JONES OF MOULSECOOMB, BARONESS

JONES OF MOULSECOOMB (Life Baroness), Jennifer Helen Jones; cr 2013. Born 23 December 1949; 2 daughters.

Education: Westlain Grammar, Brighton; University College, London (BSc environmental archaeology 1994); Arabic (a little), French, German.

Non-political career: Housewife, Secretary, Office Manager with some political activism 1970-90; Archaeologist/Political Activist 1991-99; Financial Controller, Metro Inspection Services (a fire safety company) 1999-2000.

Political career: *House of Commons:* Contested (Green) Dulwich and West Norwood 2001 and 2005 and Camberwell and Peckham 2010 general elections. *House of Lords:* Raised to the peerage as Baroness Jones of Moulsecoomb, of Moulsecoomb in the County of East Sussex 2013. *Other:* Contested London region 1999 European Parliament election. London Assembly: AM for Londonwide region 2000-16, Chair, Standards Committee 2000-03, Mayor of London's Road Safety Ambassador 2002-08, Deputy Mayor of London 2003-04, Chair: Mayor of London's Walking Advisory Panel 2003-08, Mayor of London's Green Transport Adviser 2006-08, Planning and Housing Committee 2009-10, 2011-12, Economy Committee 2014-16; Contested London Mayoral 2012 election. Chair, Green Party 1996-98. *Councils and public bodies:* Member, Metropolitan Police Authority 2000-12; Chair, London Food 2004-08; Councillor, London Borough of Southwark Council 2006-10.

Political interests: Sustainability, social justice; Middle East.

Other: WWF, Southwark Day Centre for Asylum Seekers, Green Gathering Charity.

Recreations: Yoga, films, walking.

The Baroness Jones of Moulsecoomb, House of Lords, London SW1A 0PW
Tel: 020 7219 3000
Email: contact@jennyjones.org
Website: jennyjones.org *Twitter:* @GreenJennyJones

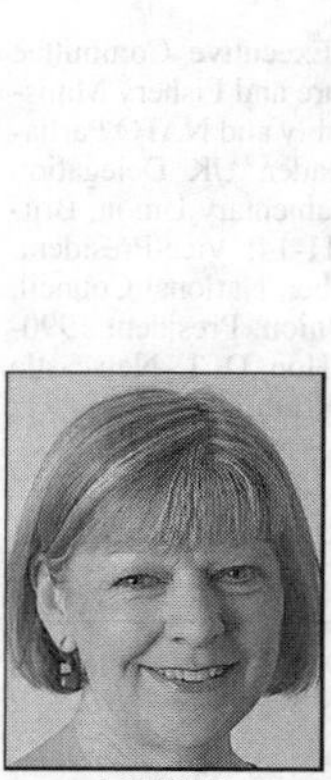

LABOUR

JONES OF WHITCHURCH, BARONESS

Opposition Spokesperson for Environment, Food and Rural Affairs

JONES OF WHITCHURCH (Life Baroness), Margaret (Maggie) Beryl Jones; cr 2006. Born 22 May 1955; Daughter of Bill and Audrey Jones.

Education: Whitchurch High School, Cardiff; Sussex University (BA sociology 1976).

Non-political career: Inland Revenue Staff Federation 1977-78; National Union of Bank Employees 1978-79; National Union of Public Employees/Unison 1979-2006: Regional official 1979-89, National officer 1989-95, Director, policy and public affairs 1995-2006; Chair, Circle 33 Housing Association 2006-12; Non-executive board member: Circle Housing 2006-16, WRAP (Waste and Resources Action Programme) 2006-15, Ombudsman Services 2013-. Unison.

Political career: *House of Commons:* Contested (Labour) Blaenau Gwent 2005 general election. *House of Lords:* Raised to the peerage as Baroness Jones of Whitchurch, of Whitchurch in the County of South Glamorgan 2006. Opposition Whip 2010-11; Opposition Spokesperson for: Culture, Media and Sport 2010-14, Education 2011-15, Environment, Food and Rural Affairs 2015-,

Energy and Climate Change 2016. Co-opted Member, EU Sub-committee D (Environment and Agriculture) 2006-09; Member, Statutory Instruments Joint Committee 2007-10; Co-opted Member, EU Sub-committee G (Social Policy and Consumer Affairs) 2009-10. *Other:* Labour Party: Member, National Executive Committee trade union section 1993-2005, Chair: Local Government Committee 1996-2004, Housing, Transport and the Regions Commission 1999-2004, Labour Party 2000-01, Labour's Joint Policy Committee 2003-05. *Councils and public bodies:* General Medical Council, Fitness to Practice Panel 2006-13; Chair, Ombudsman Services: Property 2007-13.

Political interests: Housing, public service reform, food and nutrition, education, culture and media; Burma, China.

Other: Trustee, Shelter 2003-09; Deputy chair, School Food Trust 2005-09; Farming and Countryside Education Strategy Group 2007-11; Member, Fabian Society; Patron, Empty Homes Agency 2010-; Fundraising Committee, Passage Homeless Centre 2011-15; Chair, Surveyors Ombudsman Service 2007-13; ClientEarth Development Board 2016–; Q Bot energy saving 2017-; Shelter, Passage Homeless Centre, ClientEarth.

Recreations: Walking, sailing, horse riding.

The Baroness Jones of Whitchurch, House of Lords, London SW1A 0PW
Tel: 020 7219 8272 *Email:* jonesmag@parliament.uk *Twitter:* @WhitchurchGirl

JOPLING, LORD

CONSERVATIVE

JOPLING (Life Baron), Thomas Michael Jopling; cr. 1997. Born 10 December 1930; Son of Mark Jopling; Married Gail Dickinson 1958 (2 sons).

Education: Cheltenham College; King's College, Newcastle upon Tyne (BSc agriculture 1952).

Non-political career: Farmer 1955-.

Political career: *House of Commons:* Contested Wakefield 1959 general election. MP (Conservative) for Westmorland 1964-83, for Westmorland and Lonsdale 1983-97. Sponsored Private Member's Bill on Parish Councils 1969; PPS to James Prior as Minister of Agriculture, Fisheries and Food 1970-71; Government: Assistant Whip 1971-73, Whip 1973-74; Opposition Spokesperson for Agriculture 1974-79; Shadow Minister for Agriculture 1975-76; Government Chief Whip 1979-83; Minister of Agriculture, Fisheries and Food 1983-87; Sponsored Private Member's Bills on: Children's Seat Belts 1990, Antarctica 1994. Member, Foreign Affairs 1989-97; Chair, Sittings of the House (Jopling Report) 1991-92. *House of Lords:* Raised to the peerage as Baron Jopling, of Ainderby Quernhow in the County of North Yorkshire 1997. Member, European Union 1999-2003, 2007-12; EU Sub-committee C (Common Foreign and Security Policy): Member 1999-2003, Chair 2000-03, Member: Procedure 2003-06, 2010-12, Merits of Statutory Instruments 2003-07; EU Sub-committee F (Home Affairs): Co-opted Member 2006-07, Chair 2007-10; Member EU Sub-committee C: (Foreign Affairs, Defence and Development Policy) 2010-12, (External Affairs) 2012-15; Member, International Relations 2016-. *Other:* Committee member, Association of Conservative Peers 1997-2000. *Councils and public bodies:* Councillor, Thirsk Rural District Council 1958-64; DL: Cumbria 1991-97, North Yorkshire 1998-2005.

Other: UK branch, Commonwealth Parliamentary Association (CPA): Executive Committee 1974-79, 1987-97, Vice-chair 1977-78; President, EU Councils of Agriculture and Fishery Ministers 1986; Executive, CPA HQ 1988-89; UK delegate, North Atlantic Assembly and NATO Parliamentary Assembly 1987-97, 2001-; OSCE Parliamentary Assembly: Leader, UK Delegation 1991-97, UK delegate 2000-01; Member, Executive Committee, Inter-Parliamentary Union, British Group 1999-; Chair, Committee on Civilian Aspects of Security 2011-14; Vice-President, North Atlantic Assembly and NATO Parliamentary Assembly 2014-; Member, National Council, NFU 1962-65; Fellow, Industry and Parliament Trust 1979; Auto Cycle Union: President 1990-2004, President Emeritus 2004-; President, Despatch Association 2002-07. Hon. DCL, Newcastle 1992. PC 1979; *Clubs:* Honorary Member, Royal Automobile Club, Buck's Club.

Rt Hon the Lord Jopling DL, House of Lords, London SW1A 0PW
Tel: 020 7219 0801

JORDAN, LORD

LABOUR

JORDAN (Life Baron), William Brian Jordan; cr. 2000. Born 28 January 1936; Son of Walter and Alice Jordan; Married Jean Ann Livesey 1958 (3 daughters).

Education: Barford Road Secondary Modern School, Birmingham.

Non-political career: Royal Air Force 1954-56. Machine Toolmaker; Convener of shop stewards, Guest, Keen and Nettlefold 1966; Full-time AUEW divisional organiser 1976; President, AEU then AEEU 1986-95; Member, TUC General Council 1986-95; General Secretary, ICFTU (International Confederation of Free Trade Unions) 1995-2002. Member: AEEU England, Amicus, Unite.

Political career: *House of Lords:* Raised to the peerage as Baron Jordan, of Bournville in the County of West Midlands 2000. Member EU Sub-committee A: (Economic and Financial Affairs)

2005-07, 2008-09, 2012-13, (Economic and Financial Affairs and International Trade) 2010-12. *Councils and public bodies:* Member, National Economic Development Council 1986-92; Governor, Henley College; Member, Council, Industrial Society 1987-; Manchester Business School 1987-92; Governor, BBC 1988-98; Engineering Industry Training Board 1986-91; Governor, LSE 1987-2002; Victim Support Advisory Committee 1990-2007; Council Winston Churchill Trust 1990-; Governor, Ashridge Management College 1992-2015; Board Member, English Partnerships 1993-2002; Chair, Housing and Communities Agency Pension Scheme 2004-; UK National Contact Point (NCP) Steering Board 2007-.

Political interests: Labour Party; Bahrain, India, Jordan.

Other: President: European Metal Workers Federation 1986-95, International Metal Workers Federation 1986-95; UN High Panel on Youth Employment 2001-; UN Global Compact Advisory Council 2001; Fellow, World Economic Forum; President, RoSPA; FRSA 1996; City and Guilds London Institute (Honoris Causa). DUniv, Central England 1993; Hon. DSc, Cranfield 1995. Silver Medal, Institute of Sheet Metal Engineering. CBE 1992.

Recreations: Reading, watching football.

The Lord Jordan CBE, House of Lords, London SW1A 0PW
Tel: 020 7219 5648 *Email:* jordanw@parliament.uk
352 Heath Road South, Northfield, Birmingham, West Midlands B31 2BH *Tel:* 0121-475 7319
Email: lordjordan@btinternet.com

JOWELL, BARONESS

LABOUR

JOWELL (Life Baroness), Tessa Jane Helen Douglas Jowell; cr 2015. Born 17 September 1947; Daughter of Dr Kenneth Palmer and Rosemary Palmer, radiographer; Married Roger Jowell 1970 (divorced 1977); married David Mills 1979 (1 son 1 daughter 3 stepchildren).

Education: St Margaret's School, Aberdeen; Aberdeen University (MA); Edinburgh University; Goldsmith's College, London University; French.

Non-political career: Child care officer, London Borough of Lambeth 1969-71; Psychiatric social worker, Maudsley Hospital 1972-74; Assistant director, MIND 1974-86; Director: Community care special action project, Birmingham 1987-90, Joseph Rowntree Foundation, Community Care Programme 1990-92; Senior visiting research fellow: Policy Studies Institute 1987-90, King's Fund Institute 1990-92; Visiting Fellow, Nuffield College, Oxford 1993-2000. Member, Unison.

Political career: *House of Commons:* Contested Ilford North 1978 by-election and 1979 general election. MP (Labour) for Dulwich 1992-97, for Dulwich and West Norwood 1997-2010, for Dulwich and West Norwood (revised boundary) 2010-15. Opposition Whip 1994-95; Opposition Spokesperson for: Women 1995-96, Health 1994-95, 1996-97; Minister of State: Department of Health (Minister for Public Health) 1997-99, Department for Education and Employment (Minister for Employment, Welfare to Work and Equal Opportunities) 1999-2001; Minister for Women 1999-2001, 2005-06; Secretary of State for Culture, Media and Sport 2001-07; Minister for: Olympics 2005-10, London 2007-08, 2009-10; Paymaster General (also attending Cabinet, reporting to Prime Minister, based in Cabinet Office) 2007-10, Minister for the Cabinet Office 2009-10; Shadow Minister for: Cabinet Office 2010, 2011, London and Olympics 2010-12. Member: Social Security 1992, Health 1992-94. *House of Lords:* Raised to the peerage as Baroness Jowell, of Brixton in the London Borough of Lambeth 2015. *Councils and public bodies:* Councillor, London Borough of Camden Council 1971-86; Vice-chair, then chair, Social Services Committee, Association of Metropolitan Authorities 1978-86; Central Council for Training and Education in Social Work (CCETSW) 1980s; Mental Health Act Commission 1985-90; Chair, Millennium Commission.

Political interests: Early childhood development, governance, public health, sport; China, India, Malawi, Vietnam.

Other: Governor, National Institute for Social Work 1985-97; Ditchley Park: Trustee 2011, Council of Management 2013; Chair, City Safe Foundation London Citizens 2012; Member, Olympic Board; Trustee: Amelia Ward Prize Fund, Tennis Foundation 2013; Vice-President, Royal Television Society 2013; Member, Harvard School for Public Health, Ministerial Health Leaders' Forum: Expert Resource Group 2013, Advisory Board 2014; Adviser, IOC Olympic Agenda Working Group on Bidding Procedure 2014; Associate fellow, Institute for Government; Chair, Gatwick Growth Board 2016-; International Women's Forum; Senior Fellow, Institute for Government 2012; Hon. Fellow, Faculty of Public Health 2014; Menschel Senior Fellow, Policy Translation and Leadership, Harvard School for Public Health 2014; Homestart, Magic Bus India, Dulwich Helpline and Southwark Churches Care, London Citizens. Freedom: London Borough of Southwark 2012, City of London 2014. Hon. LLD, Aberdeen University 2016. PC 1998; DBE 2012; *Clubs:* Hon. Member, Crystal Palace and Norwood Rotary Club 2014.

Publications: Various articles on social policy; Contributor, The Purple Book (Progress, 2011).

Recreations: Family, reading, walking.

Rt Hon the Baroness Jowell DBE, House of Lords, London SW1A 0PW
Tel: 020 7219 3000
Email: tessa@jowell.co.uk *Twitter:* @TessaJowell

JUDD, LORD

LABOUR

JUDD (Life Baron), Frank Ashcroft Judd; cr. 1991. Born 28 March 1935; Son of late Charles Judd, CBE, and late Helen Judd, JP; Married Christine Willington 1961 (2 daughters).

Education: City of London School; London School of Economics (BSc economics 1956).

Non-political career: Short Service Commission, RAF 1957-59. General Secretary, International Voluntary Service 1960-66; Private Secretary to: Anthony Greenwood, Minister for Housing and Local Government 1967-70, Harold Wilson as Leader of the Opposition 1970-72; Associate director, International Defence and Aid Fund for Southern Africa 1979-80; Director: Voluntary Service Overseas 1980-85, Oxfam 1985-91; Chair, International Council of Voluntary Agencies 1986-90; Consultant (professional) to De Montfort University (Faculty of Health and Life Sciences and Scholarship Board) 1993-2012; Adviser to: Forbes Trust 1992-2000, Saferworld 1992-2002; Non-executive director, Portsmouth Harbour Renaissance 1998-2006. Member: Unite, GMB.

Political career: *House of Commons:* Contested Sutton and Cheam 1959 and Portsmouth West 1964 general elections. MP (Labour) for Portsmouth West 1966-74, for Portsmouth North 1974-79. PPS to: Anthony Greenwood as Minister of Housing 1967-70, Harold Wilson as Leader of Opposition 1970-72; Shadow Defence Team 1972-74; Parliamentary Under-Secretary of State (Navy), Ministry of Defence 1974-76; Minister of State: Overseas Development 1976-77, Foreign and Commonwealth Office 1977-79. *House of Lords:* Raised to the peerage as Baron Judd, of Portsea in the County of Hampshire 1991. Opposition Spokesperson for Foreign Affairs 1991-92; Principal Opposition Spokesperson for: Development and Co-operation 1992-97, Education 1992-94; Opposition Spokesperson for Defence 1995-97. Member: Procedure 2001-04, Ecclesiastical Committee 2002-, Joint Committee on Human Rights 2003-07, EU Sub-committee F: (Home Affairs) 2010-12, (Home Affairs, Health and Education) 2012-15; Member, EU Justice Sub-committee 2015-. *Councils and public bodies:* LSE: Member of the Court 1982-2012, Member, advisory board, Centre for Human Rights 2007-, Emeritus governor 2012-, Member, Commission on Diplomacy 2014-15; Vice-President, Campaign for National Parks 1998-; Lancaster University Court: Member 2002-11, Life member 2011-; Newcastle University Court: Member 2004-13, Life member 2013-.

Political interests: Foreign affairs, Third World, defence, education, refugees, migration, race relations, penal affairs, environment policy, human rights.

Other: Member, Parliamentary Delegation to Council of Europe and WEU 1969-72, 1997-2005: Chair: Sub-committee on Refugees 1998-2001, Rapporteur and Co-chair, Ad Hoc Committee on the conflict in Chechnya, Council of Europe 1999-2003; Chair, Conference on the Future of Southern Africa, World Economic Forum 1990, 1991; Member, Commission on Global Governance 1992-2001; Vice-President, United Nations Association; Member: WHO Task Force on Health and Development 1994-98, Justice Richard Goldstone's Commission on Human Duties and Responsibilities 1997-99; President, Middle East Committee, Inter-Parliamentary Union 2012-15; President, YMCA (England) 1996-2005; Trustee: Saferworld 2002-15, Ruskin Foundation 2002-11; Member: British Council, Royal Institute for International Affairs; Fellow, Royal Society of Arts; Member and Former Chair, Fabian Society; Member: Christians on the Left, Advisory board, Institute for Global Challenges, Rutgers University, New Jersey, USA Member, Advisory Panel, UNA-K; Friends of the Royal Naval Museum: President 2002-12, Honorary Vice-President 2012-; Friends of the Lake District: President 2005-12, Patron 2012-; Hospice at Home, West Cumbria: President 2008-15, Vice-President 2015-. Freedom, City of Portsmouth 1995. Hon. DLitt, Bradford University 1987; Hon. Fellow: Portsmouth University 1995, Selly Oak Colleges, Birmingham 1997; Hon. DLitt, Portsmouth University 1997; Hon. LLD, Greenwich University 1999; Hon. DLitt, De Montfort University 2006; Hon. Fellow, Lancaster University 2015; *Clubs:* Royal Overseas League Club.

Publications: Co-author: Radical Future (1967); Purpose in Socialism (1973); Imagining Tomorrow (2000).

Recreations: Enjoying the countryside, family holidays, music, theatre.

The Lord Judd, House of Lords, London SW1A 0PW
Fax: 020 7219 5979/020 7630 7135

JUDGE, LORD

CROSSBENCH

JUDGE (Life Baron), Igor Judge; cr 2008. Born 19 May 1941; Son of Raymond Judge and Rosa Judge, née Micallef; Married Judith Robinson 1965 (1 son 2 daughters).

Education: St Edward's College, Malta; Oratory School, Woodcote; Magdalene College, Cambridge (BA 1962); Middle Temple, London; Maltese.

Non-political career: Called to the Bar, Middle Temple 1963; Recorder 1976-88; QC 1979; Bencher Middle Temple 1987; Midland and Oxford Circuit: Leader 1988, High Court Judge, Queens Bench Division 1988-96, Presiding Judge 1993-96; Lord Justice of Appeal 1996-2005; Senior Presiding Judge for England and Wales 1998-2003; Deputy Chief Justice of England and Wales 2003-05; President, QBD 2005-08; Lord Chief Justice of England and Wales 2008-13; Treasurer, Middle Temple 2014; Visiting Professor, King's College, London 2014-; Commissary, Cambridge University 2017-.

Political career: *House of Lords:* Raised to the peerage as Baron Judge, of Draycote in the County of Warwickshire 2008. As a senior member of the judiciary, disqualified from participation 2008-13. Member, Constitution 2015-. *Councils and public bodies:* Surveillance Commissioner 2015; Chief Surveillance Commissioner 2015-17.

Countries of interest: Malta.

Other: Commissary, Cambridge University. Hon. LLD: Cambridge University, Kings College London, Aberystwyth University, Swansea University, Nottingham Trent University, Northampton University, Kingston University; Buckingham University. Kt 1988; PC 1996; *Clubs:* Athenæum Club.

Publications: Co-author, Magna Carter Uncovered (2014); The Safest Shield (2015).

Recreations: History, music, cricket.

Rt Hon the Lord Judge, House of Lords, London SW1A 0PW
Tel: 020 7219 5353

KAKKAR, LORD

CROSSBENCH

KAKKAR (Life Baron), Ajay Kumar Kakkar; cr 2010. Born 28 April 1964; Son of Prof. Vijay Vir Kakkar and Dr Savitri Kakkar; Married Nicola Lear 1993 (2 daughters).

Education: Alleyn's School, Dulwich, London; King's College School of Medicine and Dentistry (BSc 1985; MBBS 1988); Imperial College, London (PhD 1998).

Non-political career: House surgeon and physician, King's College Hospital 1988-89; Junior surgical trainee 1989-92; Hammersmith Hospital/Royal Postgraduate Medical School (Medical Research Council): Clinical training fellow 1993-96, Clinical scientist fellow 1996-99; Senior lecturer in surgery and consultant surgeon, Hammersmith Hospital 1999-2004; Professor of surgical sciences, St Barts and the London School of Medicine and Dentistry, Queen Mary University, London 2004-; Consultant surgeon: St Barts and the London NHS Trust 2004-, University College Hospitals NHS Foundation Trust 2006-; Director, Thrombosis Research Institute 2008-; Professor of surgery, University College, London 2011-; Chair, UCL Partners 2014-.

Political career: *House of Lords:* Raised to the peerage as Baron Kakkar, of Loxbeare in the County of Devon 2010. Member: EU Sub-committee B (Internal Market, Infrastructure and Employment) 2012-15, Science and Technology 2015-16, 2017-, Long-Term Sustainability of the NHS 2016-17. *Councils and public bodies:* Chair: House of Lords Appointments Commission 2013-, UK Business Ambassador for Pharmaceutical and Healthcare 2013-; Member, UK Government Honours Main Committee and chair, Health Honours Committee 2013-; Chair, Judicial Appointments Commission 2016-.

Countries of interest: India, USA.

Other: Fellow, Royal College of Surgeons 1992; Trustee: Dulwich Estate, Thrombosis Research Institute; Wellcome lecturer, Royal Society of Medicine 2009; Vice-Patron: Smile, Power International; Patron, Partners Staff College, University College London; Trustee: London Pathway, Frederick Hugh House; Association of Surgeons of Great Britain and Ireland; General Medical Council; Royal College of Surgeons. Worshipful Company of Barbers. Hon. Fellow, Harris Manchester College, Oxford. James VI Association of Surgeons Fellow 1992; Hunterian Professor, Royal College of Surgeons of England 1996; David Patey Prize, Surgical Research Society of Great Britain and Ireland 1996; Knoll William Harvey Prize, International Society on Thrombosis and Haemostasis 1997. PC 2014; *Clubs:* Athenæum Club.

Publications: Numerous academic publications.

Rt Hon Professor the Lord Kakkar, House of Lords, London SW1A 0PW
Tel: 020 7219 8933 *Email:* kakkara@parliament.uk

KALMS, LORD

NON-AFFILIATED

KALMS (Life Baron), Harold Stanley Kalms; cr. 2004. Born 21 November 1931; Son of Charles and Cissie Kalms; Married Pamela Jimack 1954 (3 sons).

Education: Christ's College, Finchley.

Non-political career: Dixons Group/DSG International plc 1948-: Managing director 1962-72, Chair 1972-2002, President 2002-; Director, British Gas 1987-97; Chair, Volvere 2001-11.

Political career: *House of Lords:* Raised to the peerage as Baron Kalms, of Edgware in the London Borough of Barnet 2004. Member: Review of the BBC Charter 2005-06, Information 2006-09. *Other:* Treasurer, Conservative Party 2001-03. *Councils and public bodies:* Governor, Dixons Bradford City Technology College 1988-2002; Chair, Kings Healthcare NHS Trust 1993-96; Member, Funding Agency for Schools 1994-97.

Political interests: Islamism, reforming EU, dignity in dying; Europe, Israel.

Other: Director, Centre for Policy Studies 1991-2001; Trustee: Economic Trust 1993-2002, Industry in Education 1993-; Member, Business for Sterling 1998-2001. Five honorary doctorates; Honorary fellow London Business School 1995. Kt 1996; *Clubs:* Saville, Portland Club.

Publications: A Time for Change (1996).

Recreations: Opera, ballet, bridge.

The Lord Kalms, House of Lords, London SW1A 0PW
Tel: 020 7219 5353
39-40 St James's Place, London SW1A 1NS *Tel:* 020 7629 1427
Email: stanley.kalms@btinternet.com

KEEN OF ELIE, LORD

CONSERVATIVE

Advocate General for Scotland; Government Spokesperson, Law Officers and Ministry of Justice

KEEN OF ELIE (Life Baron), Richard Sanderson Keen; cr 2015. Born 29 March 1954; Married (1 son 1 daughter).

Education: King's School, Rochester; Dollar Academy; Edinburgh University (LLB 1976).

Non-political career: Faculty of Advocates: Admitted 1980, Dean 2007-14; Standing junior counsel to the DTI in Scotland 1986-93; QC 1993; Chairman: Appeal Committee, Institute of Chartered Accountants in Scotland 2000-04, Police Appeals Tribunal 2004-10; Member: Bar of England and Wales, Blackstone Chambers (non-practising); Bencher, Middle Temple 2013.

Political career: *House of Lords:* Raised to the peerage as Baron Keen of Elie, of Elie in Fife 2015. Advocate General for Scotland 2015-; Government Spokesperson: Law Officers 2015-, Home Office 2016, Justice 2016-. *Other:* Chairman, Scottish Conservative Party 2014-15.

Other: Member, Scottish Public Law Group. Hon. Company of Edinburgh Golfers, Muirfield; Golf Home Club, Elie; New Club, Edinburgh.

The Lord Keen of Elie QC, House of Lords, London SW1A 0PW
Tel: 020 7219 3000

KENNEDY OF CRADLEY, BARONESS

LABOUR

KENNEDY OF CRADLEY (Life Baroness), Alicia Pamela Kennedy; cr 2013. Born 22 March 1969; Daughter of Mary and Frank Chater; Married Roy Kennedy 2004, now Lord Kennedy of Southwark (qv).

Education: King Edward VI College; Warwick University (BSc pychology 1991).

Non-political career: Labour Party: Regional organiser 1995-97, Policy officer, Partnership in Power February 2000, Head of General Secretary's Office 2000-01, Chief of Staff 2001-05, Field of Operation, Task Force Leader 2003-05, 2009-10, Director of Campaigns, Organisation, Membership and Equalities 2005-06, Deputy General Secretary 2006-11; Political adviser to Joan Ruddock MP as Parliamentary Under-Secretary of State for Women 1997-98; Policy analyst, Leader's Office, London Borough of Lambeth 1998-2000; Strategic adviser to Ed Miliband MP as Leader of the Opposition 2011-13. GMB.

Political career: *House of Lords:* Raised to the peerage as Baroness Kennedy of Cradley, of Cradley in the Metropolitan Borough of Dudley 2013. Member: Joint Committee on the Draft Modern Slavery Bill 2014, Affordable Childcare 2014-15. *Other:* Chief of Staff to Tom Watson as Deputy Leader of the Labour Party 2015-. *Councils and public bodies:* Councillor, London Borough of Lewisham Council 2014-.

Political interests: International development, home affairs, community development, consumer protection; South Asia, Sub-Saharan Africa.

Other: Trustee, APT Action on Poverty -2017; Board member, Marsha Phoenix Trust; Member: Black Country Society, Institute of Marketing, Amnesty International, Child Poverty Action Group.

The Baroness Kennedy of Cradley, House of Lords, London SW1A 0PW
Tel: 020 7219 6495 *Email:* alicia.kennedy@parliament.uk *Twitter:* @aliciakennedy07

LAB/CO-OP

KENNEDY OF SOUTHWARK, LORD

Opposition Spokesperson for Communities and Local Government, Housing and Home Office; Opposition Whip

KENNEDY OF SOUTHWARK (Life Baron), Roy Francis Kennedy; cr 2010. Born 9 November 1962; Son of John and Frances Kennedy; Married Alicia 2004, now Baroness Kennedy of Cradley (qv) (no children).

Education: St Thomas the Apostle School, Peckham.

Non-political career: Member, GMB; President, Society of Chiropodists and Podiatrists.

Political career: *House of Lords:* Raised to the peerage as Baron Kennedy of Southwark, of Newington in the London Borough of Southwark 2010. Opposition Whip 2011-12, 2014-; Opposition Spokesperson for: Communities and Local Government 2015-, Housing 2015-, Home Office 2015-. Member: Joint Committee on Statutory Instruments 2010-15, Refreshment 2013-16. *Other:* Contested East Midlands region 2009 European Parliament election. Labour Party: Regional director, East Midlands 1997-2005, Director of Finance and Compliance 2005-10; Co-operative Party: Member, House of Lords Parliamentary Group Representative. *Councils and public bodies:* London Borough of Southwark Council: Councillor 1986-94, Former deputy leader, Former chair, Highways Committee; Commissioner, Electoral Commission 2010-13; Councillor, London Borough of Lewisham Council 2014-; Vice-President, Local Government Association 2016-.

Political interests: Low pay, credit unions, diabetes, co-operatives, mutuals; EU, Ireland.

Other: Member: Fabian Society, Diabetes UK, Ramblers Association, Amnesty International; Trustee, National Association of Stable Staff. Hon. Alderman, London Borough of Southwark. Member, Surrey County Cricket Club; Season ticket holder at Millwall FC.

Recreations: Reading, walking, theatre, football.

The Lord Kennedy of Southwark, House of Lords, London SW1A 0PW
Tel: 020 7219 1772 *Fax:* 020 7219 1506 *Email:* kennedyro@parliament.uk
Email: lordroykennedy@gmail.com *Twitter:* @LordRoyKennedy

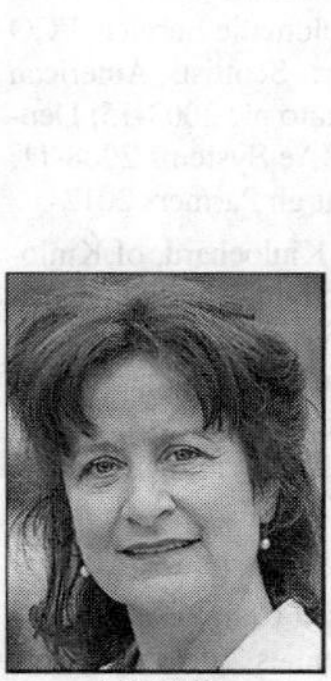

LABOUR

KENNEDY OF THE SHAWS, BARONESS

KENNEDY OF THE SHAWS (Life Baroness), Helena Ann Kennedy; cr. 1997. Born 12 May 1950; Daughter of late Joshua Kennedy and Mary Kennedy; Partner Roger Mitchell 1977-84 (1 son); married Dr Iain Hutchison 1986 (1 son 1 daughter).

Education: Holyrood Secondary School, Glasgow; Council of Legal Education.

Non-political career: Called to the Bar, Gray's Inn 1972; Established Chambers at: Garden Court 1974, Tooks Court 1984, Doughty Street 1990; Broadcaster: First female moderator, Hypotheticals (Granada) on surrogate motherhood and artificial insemination; Presenter: *Heart of the Matter*, BBC 1987, *Putting Women in the Picture*, BBC2 1987, *Time Gentlemen Please*, BBC Scotland 1994; QC 1991; Bencher of Gray's Inn 1999; Investigating Commissioner, Inquiry into Human Trafficking in Scotland, Equality and Human Rights Commission 2011.

Political career: *House of Lords:* Raised to the peerage as Baroness Kennedy of The Shaws, of Cathcart in the City of Glasgow 1997. Member: Joint Committee on Human Rights 2012-15, European Union 2015-, EU Justice Sub-committee 2015-.

Other: IBA's International Task Force on Terrorism 2001-02; Haldane Society: Chair 1983-86, Vice-President 1986-; Member, National Board, Women's Legal Defence Fund 1989-91; Council member, Howard League for Penal Reform 1989-; Board Member: *New Statesman* 1990-96, *Counsel Magazine* 1990-; Committee member, Association of Women Barristers 1991-92; Chair: Charter '88 1992-97, Standing Committee for Youth Justice, NACRO 1993-, London International Festival of Theatre 1993-2002, British Council 1998-, Human Genetics Commission 2000-07, Advisory Council, World Bank Institute; Member, Independent Newspaper Board; Chair of council, JUSTICE; Vice-President, Haldane Society; Patron, Liberty; President, National Children's Bureau; Member, Bar Council 1990-93; Fellow, Royal Society of Arts; Hon. Fellow: Institute of

Advanced Legal Studies 1997, City and Guilds London Institute, Institute of Advanced Legal Studies; Hon. Member, Paris-based Academie Universelle des Cultures. Chancellor, Oxford Brookes University 1994-2001. Eighteen honorary law doctorates; Honorary degree: City University London 2016, Essex University 2017. Women's Network Award for her work on women and justice 1992; UK Woman of Europe Award 1995; National Federation of Women's Institutes Making a World of Difference Award Institutes for her work on equal rights 1996; *The Times* (Joint) Lifetime Achievement Award 1997.

Publications: Co-author: The Bar on Trial (1978), Child Abuse Within the Family (1984), Balancing Acts (1989); Eve was Framed (1992); Leader of enquiry into health, environmental and safety aspects of Atomic Weapons Establishment Secrecy Versus Safety (1994); Inquiry into Violence in Penal Institutions for Young People (1995); Learning Works Official report for the FEFC on widening participation in Further Education (1997); Lectures; Has contributed articles on law, civil liberties and women.

Recreations: Theatre, spending time with family and friends.

The Baroness Kennedy of The Shaws QC, House of Lords, London SW1A 0PW
Tel: 020 7219 5353
c/o Hilary Hard, 12 Athelstan Close, Harold Wood RM3 0QJ
Website: www.helenakennedy.co.uk

CROSSBENCH

KERR OF KINLOCHARD, LORD

KERR OF KINLOCHARD (Life Baron), John Olav Kerr; cr. 2004. Born 22 February 1942; Son of Dr and Mrs J D O Kerr; Married Elizabeth Kalaugher 1965 (2 sons 3 daughters).

Education: Glasgow Academy; Pembroke College, Oxford (BA modern history 1963); French, Russian.

Non-political career: HM Diplomatic Service 1966-2002: Foreign Office, Moscow embassy, Rawalpindi, Pakistan High Commission, Foreign and Commonwealth Office (FCO), Private secretary to Permanent Under Secretary FCO 1974-79, Seconded to HM Treasury 1979-84: Principal private secretary to Sir Geoffrey Howe MP and Nigel Lawson MP as Chancellors of Exchequer 1981-84, Head of chancery, Washington DC, USA embassy 1984-87, Assistant Under-Secretary FCO 1987-90, Ambassador and UK Permanent Representative to EC/EU Brussels 1990-95, Ambassador to USA 1995-97, Permanent Under-Secretary and Head of Diplomatic Service, FCO 1997-2002; Secretary-General, European Convention 2002-03; Director: Scottish American Investment Trust 2002-, Shell Transport and Trading Co plc 2002-05, Rio Tinto plc 2003-15; Deputy chairman, Royal Dutch Shell plc 2005-12; Member, Advisory Board, BAe Systems 2008-11; Scottish Power: Director 2009-12, Deputy Chairman 2012-; Adviser, Edinburgh Partners 2012-.

Political career: *House of Lords:* Raised to the peerage as Baron Kerr of Kinlochard, of Kinlochard in Perth and Kinross 2004. Member EU Sub-committee A: (Economic and Financial Affairs) 2006-08, 2012-15, (Economic and Financial Affairs and International Trade) 2011-12; Member: European Union 2007-10, 2014-15, EU Sub-committee E: (Law and Institutions) 2008-10, (Justice and Institutions) 2010-11, Economic Affairs 2015-, Economic Affairs Finance Bill Sub-committee 2015-16. *Councils and public bodies:* Trustee and Deputy Chair, National Gallery 2002-10; Member, Scottish Government's Standing Council of Europe 2016-.

Political interests: International affairs, economic affairs; China, EU, Korea, Russia, USA.

Other: Trustee: Rhodes Trust 1997-2010, National Gallery 2002-10, Fulbright Commission 2004-09; Hon President, Universities Association for Contemporary European Studies 2004-07; Carnegie Trust for the Universities of Scotland: Trustee 2005-, Deputy Chair 2013-; Chairman of Court/Council, Imperial College, London 2005-11; Centre for European Reform: Member of Council 2005-, Chair 2008-; Member of Council, European Policy Centre 2007-; President, UK-Korea Forum for the Future 2007-14; Hon President, St Andrews Clinics for Children 2010-; Advisory Board Member, Burrell Collection Glasgow 2011-; Deputy Chair, Scottish Power 2012-; Member of Council, British Influence in Europe 2014-15; Trustee, Refugee Council 2016-; Scottish Centre on European Relations 2017-; Hon. Fellow: Pembroke College, Oxford 1991, Royal Society of Edinburgh 2006, Imperial College, London 2012. Honorary LLD: St Andrews 1996, Glasgow University 1999; Honorary DLitt, Aston University 2010. CMG 1987; KCMG 1991; GCMG 2001; *Clubs:* Garrick Club.

Publications: Various articles.

Recreations: Travel, books, film, following Queen's Park Rangers FC.

The Lord Kerr of Kinlochard GCMG, House of Lords, London SW1A 0PW
Tel: 020 7219 5353

NON-AFFILIATED

KERR OF TONAGHMORE, LORD

KERR OF TONAGHMORE (Life Baron), Brian Francis Kerr; cr 2009. Born 22 February 1948; Son of James Kerr and Kathleen Kerr, née Murray; Married Gillian Widdowson 1970 (2 sons).

Education: St Colman's College, Newry; Queen's University, Belfast (LLB 1969).

Non-political career: Called to Bar: Northern Ireland (NI) 1970, Gray's Inn 1974; Junior Crown Counsel, common law 1978-83; QC (NI) 1983; Senior Crown Counsel 1988-93; High Court Judge NI 1993-2004; Hon. Bencher, Gray's Inn 1997; Lord Chief Justice NI 2004-09; Hon. Bencher, King's Inn 2004; Justice of the Supreme Court of the United Kingdom 2009-.

Political career: *House of Lords:* Raised to the peerage as Baron Kerr of Tonaghmore, of Tonaghmore in the County of Down 2009. Lord of Appeal in Ordinary 2009; As Justice of the Supreme Court, disqualified from participation 2009-. *Councils and public bodies:* Chair, Mental Health Commission for NI 1988; Member: Judicial Studies Board NI 1995-2004, Franco-British Judicial Co-operation Committee 1995-2001; Chair, Distinction and Meritorious Service Awards Committee NI 1997-2001.

Other: Eisenhower Exchange Fellow 1999; Hon. Fellow, American Board of Trial Advocates 2004. Honorary law doctorate: Queen's University, Belfast 2009, Ulster University. Kt 1993; PC 2003.

Recreations: Family, friends, France.

Rt Hon the Lord Kerr of Tonaghmore, House of Lords, London SW1A 0PW
Tel: 020 7219 5353
Supreme Court of the United Kingdom, Parliament Square, London SW1P 3BD *Tel:* 020 7960 1956

CROSSBENCH

KERSLAKE, LORD

KERSLAKE (Life Baron), Robert Walter Kerslake. Born 24 February 1955; Son of Robert James Kerslake and Maura Kerslake; Married Anne (1 son 1 daughter).

Education: Blue School, Somerset; Warwick University (BSc mathematics).

Non-political career: Greater London Council: CIPFA trainee 1979-82, Transport Finance 1982-85, Inner London Education Authority 1985-89, Director, Finance 1989-90; Chief Executive: London Borough of Hounslow 1990-97, Sheffield City Council 1997-2008, Homes and Communities Agency 2008-10; Permanent Secretary, Department for Communities and Local Government 2010-15; Head of the Civil Service 2012-14; Endcliffe Services 2015-.

Political career: *House of Lords:* Raised to the peerage as Baron Kerslake, of Endcliffe in the City of Sheffield 2015. Member: Administration and Works 2015-16, Finance 2016-. *Councils and public bodies:* President, Local Government Association 2015-; Chair, King's College Hospital Foundation Trust 2015-.

Political interests: Local government, housing, local growth and regeneration, devolution.

Other: Chair: Peabody 2015-, Centre for Public Scrutiny 2015-, IPPR London Housing Commission 2015-; Member, CIPFA. Honorary degree: Sheffield University, Sheffield Hallam University. Kt 2005.

Recreations: Music, walking.

The Lord Kerslake, House of Lords, London SW1A 0PW
Tel: 020 7219 3000 *Email:* kerslakeb@parliament.uk *Twitter:* @sirbobkerslake

LABOUR

KESTENBAUM, LORD

KESTENBAUM (Life Baron) Jonathan Andrew Kestenbaum; cr 2011. Born 5 August 1959; Son of Ralph and Gaby Kestenbaum; Married Deborah Zackon 1984 (3 sons 1 daughter).

Education: London School of Economics (BA 1982); Wolfson College, Cambridge; Hebrew University (MA 1989); Cass Business School (MBA 1994).

Non-political career: Chief executive: Office of Chief Rabbi 1991-96, UJIA 1996-2002, Portland Trust 2002-06; Chief of staff to Sir Ronald Cohen, chairman of Apax Partners 2002-06; Chief executive, National Endowment for Science, Technology and the Arts 2005-10; Chairman, Five Arrows Ltd 2010-; Chief operating officer, RIT Capital Partners plc 2011-.

Political career: *House of Lords:* Raised to the peerage as Baron Kestenbaum, of Foxcote in the county of Somerset 2011.

Other: Governing Board, Royal Shakespeare Company; Rowley Lane Recreational Trust. Chancellor, Plymouth University. Honorary Doctorate of Technology, Plymouth University 2010; Honorary Fellowship, Royal College of Art 2011; *Clubs:* MCC Club.

The Lord Kestenbaum, House of Lords, London SW1A 0PW
Tel: 020 7219 5353
RIT Capital Partners, 27 St James' Place, London SW1A 1NR *Tel:* 020 7647 8565
Email: jkestenbaum@ritcap.co.uk *Website:* www.ritcap.com

CROSSBENCH

KIDRON, BARONESS

KIDRON (Life Baroness), Beeban Tania Kidron; cr 2012. Born 2 May 1961; Daughter of Nina Kidron and late Michael Kidron; Married Lee Hall (1 son 1 daughter from previous marriage).

Education: Camden School for Girls, London; National Film and Television School (1981-85).

Non-political career: Director: *Carry Greenham Home* 1983, *Oranges Are Not the Only Fruit* 1989, *Antonia and Jane* 1990, *Vroom* 1990, *Itch* 1991, *Used People* 1992, *Great Moments in Aviation* 1993, *Hookers, Hustlers, Pimps and their Johns* 1993, *To Wong Foo Thanks for Everything, Julie Newmar* 1995, *Eve Arnold in Retrospect* 1996, *Swept from the Sea* 1997, *Texarkana* 1998, *Cinderella* 2000, *Murder* 2002, *Bridget Jones: The Edge of Reason* 2004, *Antony Gormley: Making Space* 2007, *Storyville: Sex, Death and the Gods* 2011, *In Real Life* 2013; Producer, Cross Street Films.

Political career: *House of Lords:* Raised to the peerage as Baroness Kidron, of Angel in the London Borough of Islington 2012. Member, Communications 2015-.

Political interests: Justice, arts, education, media, children, young people, internet; China, India, Liberia, Somalia, USA.

Other: Founder, IntoFilm (previously Film Club) 2007-; Co-founder and Vice-chair, Film Club Educational Charity 2007-; Trustee, UK Film Council 2008-10; Governor, British Film Institute 2010-12; Council member, Institute of Contemporary Art 2011-; Trustee, Paul Hamlyn Foundation 2012-; President, Voluntary Arts 2013-; Patron: Legal Aid Worldwide, Artangel; ICA; Directors' Guild of America 1990-; Directors UK; Academy of Motion Picture Sciences 1992-; Fellow, National Film and Television School. Honorary doctorate, Kingston University 2010. OBE 2012.

The Baroness Kidron OBE, House of Lords, London SW1A 0PW
Tel: 020 7219 5353 *Email:* kidronb@parliament.uk
Email: nicola@crosstreefilms.com

CROSSBENCH

KILCLOONEY, LORD

KILCLOONEY (Life Baron), John David Taylor; cr. 2001. Born 24 December 1937; Son of late George David Taylor, architect, and Georgina Taylor, née Baird; Married Mary Todd 1970 (1 son 5 daughters).

Education: Royal School, Armagh; Queen's University, Belfast (BSc applied science and technology 1950); French.

Non-political career: Company director; Chairman: West Ulster Estates Ltd 1965-, Alpha Newspaper Group 1977-, Sovereign Properties (NI) Ltd 1981-, Midland Tribune Ltd 2002-, Alpha Publications (Ireland) Ltd 2002-, Northern Media Group Ltd 2006-14, Northern Newspapers Ltd, Bramley Apples Restaurant Ltd.

Political career: *House of Commons:* MP (UUP) for Strangford 1983-2001. Spokesperson for: Trade and Industry 1992-97, Foreign and Commonwealth Affairs 1997-2001. *House of Lords:* Raised to the peerage as Baron Kilclooney, of Armagh in the County of Armagh 2001. *Other:* MP for South Tyrone, Northern Ireland Parliament 1965-73: Parliamentary Secretary, Ministry of Home Affairs 1969-70, Minister of State, Home Affairs 1970-72, Member for: Fermanagh and South Tyrone, Northern Ireland Assembly 1973-75, North Down, Northern Ireland Constitutional Convention 1976-77, North Down, Northern Ireland Assembly 1982-86; European Parliament: MEP for Northern Ireland 1979-89; Member Northern Ireland Forum for Political Dialogue 1996-98; Northern Ireland Assembly: MLA for Strangford 1998-2007. Chair: Queen's University Conservative and Unionist Association 1959-60, Ulster Young Unionist Council 1961-62; Ulster Unionist Party: Hon. Secretary 1994-96, Deputy Leader 1995-2001. *Councils and public bodies:* Governor, Royal School, Armagh City 1973-; Castlereagh Borough Council: Councillor 1989-97, Leader, UUP 1989-94; Member, Northern Ireland Policing Board 2001-06.

Political interests: Irish politics, European Union, regional policy, agriculture; Asia, Cyprus, Gibraltar, Ireland, Latin America, Middle East, Taiwan, Turkey.

Other: Member: Council of Europe Assembly 1997-2005, Western European Union 1997-2011; Member: Charles Sheils Charity Homes Board 1973-, Royal Horticultural Society; Elder, Presbyterian Church in Ireland; Member, Loyal Orange Institution of Ireland; AMICEI; AMInstHE; Tear Fund. Eastern Mediterranean University, Famagusta (PhD international relations 1999). PC (Northern Ireland) 1970; *Clubs:* Farmers Club, County Club, Armagh. City of Armagh Cricket Club.

Publications: Ulster – The Economic Facts (1974).

Recreations: Antiques, Irish art, travelling, horticulture.

Rt Hon the Lord Kilclooney, House of Lords, London SW1A 0PW
Tel: 020 7219 6443

KING OF BOW, BARONESS

LABOUR

KING OF BOW (Life Baroness), Oona Tamsyn King; cr 2011. Born 22 October 1967; Daughter of Preston King, professor of political science, and Hazel King, teacher; Married Tiberio Santomarco 1994 (1 adopted son 2 adopted daughters 1 son).

Education: Haverstock Comprehensive Secondary School, London; York University (BA politics 1990); Berkeley-University of California, USA (Scholarship); French, Italian.

Non-political career: Researcher, Socialist Group, European Parliament 1990; Political assistant to Glyn Ford MEP 1991-93; John Smith's Labour Party leadership campaign team 1992; Freelance speech-writer/ghost writer 1993-94; Political assistant to Glenys Kinnock MEP 1994-95; Trade union organiser, GMB Southern Region 1995-97; Diversity executive, Channel 4 2009-16; Director of diversity, YouTube 2016-. Southern region equality officer, GMB.

Political career: *House of Commons:* MP (Labour) for Bethnal Green and Bow 1997-2005. Contested Bethnal Green and Bow 2005 general election. PPS to: Stephen Timms as Minister of State, Department of Trade and Industry 2002-03, Patricia Hewitt as Secretary of State for Trade and Industry 2003-05; Senior Policy Adviser on equalities to Gordon Brown as Prime Minister 2007-09. Member: International Development 1997-2001, Transport, Local Government and the Regions 2001-02, Transport, Local Government and the Regions (Urban Affairs Sub-Committee) 2001-02. Member, Labour Party Departmental Committees for: Education and Employment 1997-99, Home Affairs 1997-2001. *House of Lords:* Raised to the peerage as Baroness King of Bow, of Bow in the London Borough of Tower Hamlets 2011. Opposition Whip 2014-15; Opposition Spokesperson for: Culture, Media and Sport 2015, Equalities 2015; On leave of absence November 2016-. Member: Adoption Legislation 2012-13, Olympic and Paralympic Legacy 2013-14. *Other:* Joint vice-chair, London Regional Group of Labour MPs 1997-2005; Chair, Labour Campaign for Electoral Reform; Contested Labour Party London Mayor candidacy 2010. *Councils and public bodies:* Governor, British Film Institute.

Political interests: Race relations, employment, education, health, development, equal opportunities, housing, European affairs, electoral reform, poverty; Bangladesh, France, Great Lakes Region, Italy, Nicaragua, Rwanda, South Africa, USA.

Other: Member: Oxfam, Amnesty International, Jewish Council for Racial Equality, One World Action, Fabian Society, Unicef; Member, 1990 Trust, Toynbee Hall; Vice-chair, British Council 1999-; Patron, Dane Ford Trust; Vice-chair, British Council 2001-; Patron: Positive Care Link, Council for Education in the World, Riverside Gallery; Associate fellow, Chatham House; Chair: Institute for Community Cohesion, Rich Mix Cultural Foundation. Hon. degree, Sussex University 2013.

Publications: Oona King Diaries (Bloomsbury, 2007).

Recreations: Ice skating, cycling, pilates, cinema, history.

The Baroness King of Bow, House of Lords, London SW1A 0PW
Tel: 020 7219 5353 *Email:* miahr@parliament.uk
Website: www.oonaking.com *Twitter:* @oona_king

KING OF BRIDGWATER, LORD

CONSERVATIVE

KING OF BRIDGWATER (Life Baron), Thomas Jeremy King; cr. 2001. Born 13 June 1933; Son of John H King, JP; Married Jane Tilney 1960 (1 son 1 daughter).

Education: Rugby School; Emmanuel College, Cambridge (MA classics, archaeology and anthropology 1956).

Non-political career: Army national service 1952-53; Service in East Africa; TA 1953-56. E. S. and A. Robinson Ltd, Bristol 1956-69: Divisional General Manager 1964-69; Chair, Sale, Tilney & Co Ltd industrial holding company 1971-79; Non-executive director, Electra Investment Trust 1992-2008; London International Exhibition Centre plc: Chair 1994-2008, Non-executive director 2008-.

Political career: *House of Commons:* MP (Conservative) for Bridgwater 3 March 1970 by-election to 2001. PPS to Christopher Chataway: as Minister of Posts and Telecommunications 1970-72, as Minister for Industrial Development 1972-74; Opposition Spokesperson for: Industry 1975-76, Energy 1976-79; Minister for Local Government and Environmental Services 1979-83; Secretary of State for: Environment January-June 1983, Transport June-October 1983, Employment 1983-85, Northern Ireland 1985-89, Defence 1989-92; Chair, Intelligence and Security Committee 1994-2001. *House of Lords:* Raised to the peerage as Baron King of Bridgwater, of Bridgwater in the County of Somerset 2001. Trade Envoy to Saudi Arabia 2014-. Member: Review of the BBC

Charter 2005-06, Communications 2007-10, Joint Committee on the Draft Enhanced Terrorism Prevention and Investigation Measures Bill 2012-13, Inquiries Act 2005 2013-14, Joint Committee on the National Security Strategy 2017-.

Other: PC 1979; CH 1992.

Recreations: Cricket, skiing.

Rt Hon the Lord King of Bridgwater CH, House of Lords, London SW1A 0PW
Tel: 020 7219 4467

CROSSBENCH

KING OF LOTHBURY, LORD

KING OF LOTHBURY (Life Baron), Mervyn Allister; cr. 2013. Born 30 March 1948; Son of Eric King and Kathleen Passingham; Married Barbara Melander.

Education: Wolverhampton Grammar School; King's College, Cambridge (BA 1969); Harvard University (Kennedy Scholar 1971-72); French.

Non-political career: Lecturer, Faculty of Economics, Cambridge 1976-77; Esmée Fairbairn professor of investment, Birmingham University 1977-84; Managing editor, Review of Economic Studies 1978-83; Associate editor, Journal of Public Economics 1982-98; Professor of economics, London School of Economics 1984-95; Associate editor, American Economic Review 1985-88; Bank of England: Non-executive director 1990-91, Chief economist and executive director 1991-98, Deputy Governor 1998-2003, Governor 2003-13.

Political career: *House of Lords:* Raised to the peerage as Baron King of Lothbury, of Lothbury in the City of London 2013. *Councils and public bodies:* Trustee, National Gallery 2005-09, 2014-.

Other: Member, Meade Committee 1975-78; Council and executive, Royal Economic Society 1981-86, 1992-97; Visiting professor of economics: Harvard University 1982-83, 1990, Massachusetts Institute of Technology 1983-84; Board member, Securities Association 1987-89; London School of Economics: Co-director, Financial Markets Group 1987-91, Visiting professor of economics 1996-2015, School professor of economics 2015-; Member, City Capital Markets Committee 1989-91; Trustee, Kennedy Memorial Trust 1990-2000; President, European Economic Association 1993; Member, Group of Thirty 1997-; Monetary Policy Committee: Founder member 1997, Chair 2003-13; President, Institute for Fiscal Studies 1999-2003; Member, Advisory Council, London Symphony Orchestra 2001-; Chair, Interim Financial Policy Committee 2011-13; Vice-chair, European Systematic Risk Board 2011-13; Visiting professor of economics, New York University 2014-; President, Chance to Shine; Fellow, St John's College, Cambridge 1972-77; Honorary fellow, King's College, Cambridge; Fellow, Econometric Society 1982; FBA. Honorary degree: London Guildhall 2001, Birmingham University 2002, City University, London 2002, London School of Economics 2003, Wolverhampton University 2003, Edinburgh University 2005, Helsinki Univeristy 2006; Honorary LLD, Cambridge Univeristy 2006, Honorary degree: Worcestershire University 2008, Kent University 2012, Abertay University 2013. GBE 2011; KG 2014; *Clubs:* Athenæum, Brook's Club, Garrick Club. MCC; AELTC Club; Honorary President, Ekenäs Cricket Club, Finland; President, Worcestershire County Cricket Club 2015-.

Publications: Public Policy and the Corporation (1977); The British Tax System (1978); The Taxation of Income from Capital (1984); The End of Alchemy (2016).

The Lord King of Lothbury KG GBE, House of Lords, London SW1A 0PW
Tel: 020 7219 5353

LABOUR

KINGSMILL, BARONESS

KINGSMILL (Life Baroness), Denise Patricia Byrne Kingsmill; cr 2006. Born 24 April 1947; Daughter of Patrick Henry and Hester Jean Byrne; Married David Kingsmill 1970 (divorced 2002) (2 children); married Richard Wheatly 2006.

Education: Croesy Ceiliog Grammar School, Wales; Girton College, Cambridge (BA economics and anthropology 1968); Solicitor 1980.

Non-political career: ICI, International Wool Secretariat 1968-75; Robin Thompson & Partners 1979-82; Russell Jones and Walker 1982-85; Denise Kingsmill & Co 1985-90; Partner, D J Freeman 1990-93; Consultant, Denton Hall 1994-2000; Non-executive director, British Airways 2004-10; Chair, advisory forum, Laing O'Rourke 2004-06; Senior adviser, Royal Bank of Scotland 2005-08; Non-executive director: E.ON AG, Betfair plc 2011-12, APR Energy plc; Member, European Advisory Council, Microsoft 2007-12; Non-executive director, Korn/Ferry International 2009-12; Independent non-executive director, International Consolidated Airlines Group SA; Columnist, *Management Today*; Chair, European Advisory Board.

Political career: *House of Lords:* Raised to the peerage as Baroness Kingsmill, of Holland Park in the Royal Borough of Kensington and Chelsea 2006. Co-opted Member, European Union Sub-committee E (Law and Institutions) 2006-09; Member: Merits of Statutory Instruments 2007-09, Economic Affairs 2008-13, 2017-, EU Financial Affairs Sub-committee 2015-16, Economic Affairs Finance Bill Sub-committee 2016-17. *Councils and public bodies:* Deputy chair, Monopolies and Mergers/Competition Commission 1997-2003.

Political interests: International business, women; Australia, China, India, New Zealand, USA.

Other: Member, advisory board, IESE Business School. Pro-Chancellor, Brunel University 2002-06. Fellow, University of Wales 2000; Hon. LLD: Brunel University 2001, Stirling University 2003, Cranfield University 2007. CBE 2000.

Recreations: Fly-fishing, walking.

The Baroness Kingsmill CBE, House of Lords, London SW1A 0PW
Tel: 020 7219 4537 *Email:* kingsmilldp@parliament.uk
Tel: 020 7221 1700 *Fax:* 020 7727 8304 *Email:* tess@dkingsmill.com *Twitter:* @denisekingsmill

LABOUR

KINNOCK, LORD

KINNOCK (Life Baron), Neil Gordon Kinnock; cr 2005. Born 28 March 1942; Son of late Gordon H Kinnock, steelworker and coalminer, and Mary, née Howells, district nurse; Married Glenys Elizabeth Parry 1967 (MEP for South East Wales 1994-99 and Wales region 1999-2009, now Baroness Kinnock of Holyhead (qv)) (1 son, Stephen Kinnock (qv) MP for Aberavon, 1 daughter).

Education: Lewis School, Pengam; University College of Wales, Cardiff (BA industrial relations and history 1966).

Non-political career: University College of Wales, Cardiff: President: Socialist Society 1963-65, Students' Union 1965-66; Tutor and organiser, Workers' Educational Association 1966-70; European Commission: Commissioner 1995-2004: Commissioner for Transport 1995-99, Vice-president for Administrative Reform, Internal Audit, Personnel, Language Services and Logistics 1999-2004. Member, Transport and General Workers Union 1966-.

Political career: *House of Commons:* MP (Labour) for Bedwellty 1970-83, for Islwyn 1983-95. PPS to Michael Foot as Secretary of State for Employment 1974-75; Principal Opposition Spokesperson for Education 1979-83; Leader of the Opposition 1983-92. *House of Lords:* Raised to the peerage as Baron Kinnock, of Bedwellty in the County of Gwent 2005. *Other:* Labour Party: NEC: Member 1978-94, Chair 1987-88; Leader 1983-92. *Councils and public bodies:* Member, BBC Advisory Council 1976-79; Chair, British Council 2004-09.

Other: President of the Council (Chancellor), Cardiff University 1998-2009. PC 1983.

Publications: Making Our Way – Investing in Britain's Future (1986); Thorns and Roses (1992).

Recreations: Opera, male choral music, theatre, rugby, soccer, cricket, grandchildren.

Rt Hon the Lord Kinnock, House of Lords, London SW1A 0PW
Tel: 020 7219 8304 *Email:* kinnockn@parliament.uk

LABOUR

KINNOCK OF HOLYHEAD, BARONESS

KINNOCK OF HOLYHEAD (Life Baroness); Glenys Elizabeth Kinnock; cr 2009. Born 7 July 1944; Daughter of Cyril Parry, railway signalman, and Elizabeth Parry; Married Neil Kinnock 1967 (MP for Bedwellty 1970-83 and Islwyn 1983-95, Labour Party Leader 1983-92, European Commissioner 1995-2004, now Lord Kinnock (qv)) (1 son, Stephen Kinnock (qv) MP for Aberavon, 1 daughter).

Education: Holyhead Comprehensive School, Anglesey; University College of Wales, Cardiff (Degree history and education 1964; DipEd 1965); Welsh.

Non-political career: Primary and secondary school teacher 1965-93. Member: GMB, National Union of Teachers.

Political career: *House of Lords:* Raised to the peerage as Baroness Kinnock of Holyhead, of Holyhead in the County of Ynys Môn 2009. Minister of State and Government Spokesperson, Foreign and Commonwealth Office 2009-10: Minister for Europe 2009, Minister for Africa and UN 2009-10; Opposition Spokesperson for: Foreign and Commonwealth Office 2011, International Development 2011-12. Member, Sexual Violence in Conflict 2015-16. *Other:* European Parliament: MEP for: South East Wales 1994-99, Wales 1999-2009, Labour Spokesperson for International Development, Co-President, ACP-EU Joint Parliamentary Assembly. Co-president, Labour Campaign for International Development.

Political interests: International development, regions, gender issues, children's rights, education; African countries, Burma, Sudan, South Sudan.

Other: Board member, Burma Campaign UK -2017; Council member, Overseas Development Institute -2017; Patron: Saferworld, Womankind, Waging Peace; Various charities supported. Honorary Fellow: University of Wales, Newport, University of Wales, Bangor; Honorary Doctorate: Thames Valley University, Brunel University, Kingston University.

Publications: Voices for One World (Fontana, 1988); Eritrea – Images of War and Peace (Chatto and Windus, 1988); Namibia: Birth of a Nation (Quartet, 1990); By Faith and Daring (Virago, 1993); Changing States (Heinemann, 1996); Could do Better (1996); Zimbabwe on the Brink (Centurion, 2003).

Recreations: Grandchildren, cooking, theatre, cinema, reading.

The Baroness Kinnock of Holyhead, House of Lords, London SW1A 0PW
Tel: 020 7219 1297 *Email:* kinnockg@parliament.uk *Twitter:* @GlenysKinnock

CROSSBENCH

KINNOULL, EARL OF

KINNOULL (16th Earl of, S), Charles William Harley Hay; cr. 1633; Viscount Dupplin and Lord Hay of Kinfauns, 1627, 1633, 1697; Baron Hay (GB), 1711. Born 20 December 1962; Son of 15th Earl; Married Clare (1 son 3 daughters).

Education: Eton College; Christ Church, Oxford; City University (Diploma law); Inns of Court School of Law; French, German.

Non-political career: Associate, Credit Suisse First Boston 1985-88; Called to the Bar, Middle Temple 1990; Underwriter, Roberts & Hiscox/Hiscox Syndicates Ltd 1990-95; Hiscox Insurance Company: Managing director, Europe 1995-2000, Chief executive officer 2009-12; Director of mergers and acquisitions, Hiscox Ltd 2000-14; Company secretary, Hiscox Group 2009-12.

Political career: *House of Lords:* Elected hereditary peer 2015-. Member: Social Mobility 2015-16, Trade Union and Party Funding 2016, European Union 2016-, EU Justice Sub-committee 2016-.

Political interests: Science and technology, insurance and financial services, art and the art market, red squirrels, rural issues, Scotland, constitutional issues, Post Office; Austria, Bermuda.

Other: Member: Association of Bermuda Insurers and Reinsurers 2009-12, Reinsurance Association of America 2009-12; President, Royal Caledonian Charities Trust 2013-; Chair, Red Squirrel Survival Trust 2013-; Director, Horsecross Arts Ltd 2014-; Chair, Culture Perth & Kinross. Freedom, City of London 2008; *Clubs:* Whites, Turf Club, Pratt's, Royal Perth, Jockey Club (Vienna). MCC.

Recreations: Real tennis, lawn tennis, philately, skiing.

The Earl of Kinnoull, House of Lords, London SW1A 0PW
Tel: 020 7219 3000 *Email:* kinnoull@parliament.uk

CONSERVATIVE

KIRKHAM, LORD

KIRKHAM (Life Baron), Graham Kirkham; cr. 1999. Born 14 December 1944; Son of Tom and Elsie Kirkham; Married Pauline Fisher 1965 (1 son and 1 daughter).

Education: Maltby Grammar School.

Non-political career: Founder, DFS Furniture Company Ltd 1969-2010: Director, Iceland Frozen Foods 2012-14.

Political career: *House of Lords:* Raised to the peerage as Baron Kirkham, of Old Cantley in the County of South Yorkshire 1999. Member: Administration and Works 2003-05, Leader's Group on Governance 2015. *Other:* Chairman, Conservative Party Treasurers 1997.

Political interests: Business, children.

Other: Chair of trustees, Duke of Edinburgh's Award Scheme; Deputy patron, Outward Bound Trust; Deputy president, Animal Health Trust. Honorary Liveryman Worshipful Company of Furniture Makers 2007. Hon. Member, Emmanuel College, Cambridge 1995; Hon. Doctorate, Bradford University 1997. Kt 1995; CVO 2001.

The Lord Kirkham CVO, House of Lords, London SW1A 0PW
Tel: 020 7219 5353
Black Diamond Investments LP, Redhouse Interchange, Adwick-le-Street, Doncaster DN6 7FE
Tel: 01302 337215 *Fax:* 01302 573308 *Email:* lord.kirkham@bdinvestments.co.uk

LABOUR

KIRKHILL, LORD

KIRKHILL (Life Baron), John Farquharson Smith; cr. 1975. Born 7 May 1930; Son of late Alexander Findlay Smith and Ann Farquharson; Married Frances Reid 1965.

Non-political career: Lord Provost, Aberdeen 1971-75; Chairman, North of Scotland Hydro-Electric Board 1979-82.

Political career: *House of Lords:* Raised to the peerage as Baron Kirkhill, in the District of the City of Aberdeen 1975. Minister of State, Scottish Office 1975-78.

Other: Member, Parliamentary Assembly, Western European Union 1987-91; Parliamentary Assembly, Council of Europe: Member 1987-91, Chairman, Legal Affairs and Human Rights Committee 1991-95. Hon. LLD, Aberdeen University 1974.

The Lord Kirkhill, House of Lords, London SW1A 0PW
Tel: 020 7219 3128
3 Rubislaw Den North, Aberdeen AB15 4AL

CONSERVATIVE

KIRKHOPE OF HARROGATE, LORD

KIRKHOPE OF HARROGATE (Life Baron), Timothy John Robert Kirkhope; cr 2016. Born 29 April 1945; Son of late John Kirkhope and late Dorothy Kirkhope; Married Caroline Maling 1969 (4 sons).

Education: Royal Grammar School, Newcastle; College of Law, Guildford (1969-70).

Non-political career: Solicitor 1973-: Principal, Timothy J R Kirkhope Solicitors 1973-79, 1997-, Partner, Wilkinson Maughan Solicitors 1977-87; Director, Newcastle International Airport 1983-86; Business consultant on central and eastern Europe 1997-99; Director, Bournemouth and West Hampshire Water Company plc 1999-2011.

Political career: *House of Commons:* MP for Leeds North East 1987-97. Assistant Government Whip 1990-92; Government Whip: Lord Commissioner of HM Treasury 1992-95, Vice-Chamberlain of HM Household 1995; Parliamentary Under-Secretary of State, Home Office 1995-97. *House of Lords:* Raised to the peerage as Baron Kirkhope of Harrogate, of Harrogate in the County of North Yorkshire 2016. Member, EU Home Affairs Sub-committee 2017-. *Other:* MEP for Yorkshire and the Humber 1999-2016: Conservative Spokesperson on Citizens' Freedoms and Rights, Justice and Home Affairs 1999-2009, Chief Whip 1999-2001, Member, Convention on the Future of Europe 2002-04, Leader, UK Conservative Party delegation in European Parliament 2004-07, 2008-10; Vice-President, EPP-ED Group 2007-08; ECR Group: Deputy Chair 2009-11, Interim First Chair 2009; ECR Spokesperson on Justice and Home Affairs 2009-14, 2014-16. Treasurer, Hexham Association 1982-85; Member, Conservative Party Board 2005-07, 2008-10. *Councils and public bodies:* Member: Northumberland County Council 1981-85, Northern Regional Health Authority 1982-86; Founder member, Mental Health Act commission 1983-86; Governor, Newcastle Royal Grammar School 1989-99.

Political interests: Defence, home affairs, environment, broadcasting, health, aviation, Trans-atlantic relations, immigration; Germany, United States.

Other: Vice-chair, Governing Bodies Association for Independent Schools 1990-98; Member: Fountain Society (for restoration of water features), Bentley Drivers Club, Porsche Owners Club; Trustee, Biwater Retirement and Security Scheme Pension Trust 2011-; Member: Institute of Directors, The Law Society; Dunstaburgh Castle Golf Club; *Clubs:* Northern Counties Club, Newcastle-upon-Tyne. Dunstanburgh Castle Golf Club, Northumberland.

Recreations: Tennis, swimming, flying, golf, holds a private pilot's licence.

The Lord Kirkhope of Harrogate, House of Lords, London SW1A 0PW
Tel: 020 7219 3107
Email: timothy@kirkhope.org.uk
Website: www.kirkhope.org.uk *Twitter:* @LordKirkhope

LIBERAL DEMOCRAT

KIRKWOOD OF KIRKHOPE, LORD

KIRKWOOD OF KIRKHOPE (Life Baron), Archibald Johnstone Kirkwood; cr 2005. Born 22 April 1946; Son of David Kirkwood; Married Rosemary Chester 1972 (1 son 1 daughter).

Education: Cranhill School, Glasgow; Heriot-Watt University (BSc pharmacy 1971).

Non-political career: Aide to David Steel MP 1971-75, 1977-78; Solicitor.

Political career: *House of Commons:* MP (Liberal Democrat) for Roxburgh and Berwickshire 1983-2005. Liberal Spokesperson for: Health, Social Services and Social Security 1985-87, Scotland 1987-88; Alliance Spokesperson for Overseas Development 1987; Sponsored: Access to Personal Files Act 1987 (Private Member's Bill), Access to Medical Reports Act 1988 (Private Member's Bill); Convenor and Spokesperson for Welfare and Social Security 1989-94; Liberal

Democrat: Deputy Chief Whip 1989-92, Chief Whip 1992-97, Shadow Leader of the House 1994-97, Spokesperson for Community Care 1994-97; Member, House of Commons Commission 1997-2005; Chair, Select Committee on Work and Pensions 2001-05. Chair, Social Security 1997-2001. *House of Lords:* Raised to the peerage as Baron Kirkwood of Kirkhope, of Kirkhope in Scottish Borders 2005. Liberal Democrat Spokesperson for: Work and Pensions 2007-10, Welfare 2015. Co-opted Member, EU Sub-committee G (Social Policy and Consumer Affairs) 2007-10; Information: Member 2009-10, Chair 2010-14; Member: EU Sub-committee G (Social Policies and Consumer Protection) 2010-11, Digital Skills 2014-15, Financial Exclusion 2016-17, Services 2016-, Secondary Legislation Scrutiny 2017-. *Other:* Social and Liberal Democrat Convenor on Welfare, Health and Education 1988-89.

Political interests: Freedom of information, health, social security, human rights.

Other: Joseph Rowntree Reform Trust: Trustee 1985-2007, Chair 1999-2006. Rowntree Political Fellow 1971. Kt 2003.

Publications: Co-author, Long Term Care – a Framework for Reform.

Recreations: Music, gardening.

The Lord Kirkwood of Kirkhope, House of Lords, London SW1A 0PW
Tel: 020 7219 4217 *Email:* kirkwooda@parliament.uk

KNIGHT OF WEYMOUTH, LORD

LAB/CO-OP

KNIGHT OF WEYMOUTH (Life Baron), James Philip Knight; cr 2010. Born 6 March 1965; Son of Philip John Knight, accountant, and Hilary Jean Howlett, neé Harper, craftswoman; Married Anna Wheatley 1989 (1 daughter 1 son).

Education: Eltham College, London; Fitzwilliam College, Cambridge (BA geography, social and political sciences 1987); French.

Non-political career: Works Theatre Co-operative 1986-88; Manager, Central Studio Basingstoke 1988-90; Director, West Wiltshire Arts Centre Ltd 1990-91; Dentons Directories Ltd 1991-2001: Sales Executive 1991-96, General Manager 1997-98, Director 1998-2000, Production Manager 2000-01; Board Member, Arsenal Fanshare Society Ltd 2010-13; Chief Education Adviser, TES Global 2015-; Founder and Chair, XRapid Ltd 2015-. Member: Unite 1995-2010, GMB 2001-.

Political career: *House of Commons:* Contested South Dorset 1997 general election. MP (Lab/Co-op) for South Dorset 2001-10. Contested South Dorset 2010 general election. PPS at Department of Health 2003-05: to Rosie Winterton as Minister of State 2003-04, Team PPS 2004-05; Parliamentary Under-Secretary of State, Department for Environment, Food and Rural Affairs 2005-06; Minister of State: Department for Education and Skills/Children, Schools and Families (Schools and Learners) 2006-09, Department for Work and Pensions 2009-10; Minister for the South West 2009-10. Member, Defence 2001-03. *House of Lords:* Raised to the peerage as Baron Knight of Weymouth, of Weymouth in the County of Dorset 2010. Opposition Spokesperson for: Work and Pensions 2010-11, Environment, Food and Rural Affairs 2011-14. *Other:* Contested South West region 1999 European Parliament election. Various posts local constituency party 1990-. *Councils and public bodies:* Frome Town Council: Councillor 1993-2001, Mayor 1998-2001; Mendip District Council: Councillor 1997-2001, Deputy leader 1999-2001, Labour group leader 1999-2001; Vice-President, Local Government Association 2010-13.

Political interests: International development, families, arts, sport, housing, rural affairs.

Other: Nominet Trust: Deputy Chair, Chair -2015; Chair and trustee, Tinder Foundation -2017; Director, Whole Education Ltd; Hon. Fellow, Institute of Employability Professionals. Visiting Professor, Institute of Education, University of London. Campaigner of the Year, *House Magazine* 2006. PC 2008.

Recreations: Football, tennis, cooking, cycling.

Rt Hon the Lord Knight of Weymouth, House of Lords, London SW1A 0PW
Tel: 020 7219 3000 *Email:* knightja@parliament.uk
Website: www.jimknight.uk *Twitter:* @LordJimKnight

LIBERAL DEMOCRAT

KRAMER, BARONESS

Liberal Democrat Lords Spokesperson for Treasury

KRAMER (Life Baroness), Susan Veronica Kramer; cr 2010. Born 21 July 1950; Daughter of Harry Victor (Bill) Richards and Elisabeth Richards; Married John Kramer 1972 (died 2006) (1 daughter 1 son).

Education: St Paul's Girls' School, London; St Hilda's College, Oxford (BA philosophy, politics and economics 1972, MA); Illinois University, USA (MBA business/finance 1982).

Non-political career: Staff associate, National Academy of Engineering 1972-73; Second vice-president, Continental Bank, USA 1982-88; Vice-president, corporate finance, Citibank/Citicorp, USA 1988-92; Chief operating officer, Future Water International 1992-95; Partner, Kramer and Associates 1995-99; Board member, CAIB Infrastructure Project Advisers 1997-99; Director, Infrastructure Capital Partners Ltd 1999-2006; Board member, Transport for London 2000-05; Director, Speciality Scanners plc 2001-11.

Political career: *House of Commons:* Contested Dulwich and West Norwood 1997 general election. MP (Liberal Democrat) for Richmond Park 2005-10. Contested Richmond Park 2010 general election. Liberal Democrat: Spokesperson for the Treasury 2005-06, Shadow Secretary of State for: International Development 2006, Trade and Industry 2006-07, Transport 2007, Shadow Minister for the Cabinet Office and Shadow Chancellor of the Duchy of Lancaster 2007-09. Member, Treasury 2005-06. *House of Lords:* Raised to the peerage as Baroness Kramer, of Richmond Park in the London Borough of Richmond upon Thames 2010. Minister of State and Government Spokesperson, Department for Transport 2013-15; Liberal Democrat: Lords Spokesperson for Economy/Treasury 2015-, Shadow Chancellor of the Exchequer 2015-17. Member: Economic Affairs Finance Bill Sub-Committee 2011, Consumer Insurance (Disclosure and Representations) Bill 2011-12, Small- and Medium-Sized Enterprises 2012-13, Parliamentary Commission on Banking Standards 2012-13, Sub-committee on Economic Affairs Finance Bill 2012-13. Chair, Liberal Democrat Parliamentary Party Committee on Treasury 2012-15. *Other:* Contested London region 1999 European Parliament election and London mayoral 2000 election. Liberal Democrats: Member: Women executive 1997-2000, London Region executive 1997-2003, Federal executive 2001-04, Chair, Twickenham and Richmond Liberal Democrats 2001-02.

Political interests: Environment, finance, transport; Eastern Europe, USA.

Other: President, Oxford Union Trinity term 1971; Advisory board member, Centre for Reform 2001-04; Holly Lodge, Richmond Park Charitable Trust, Orange Tree Theatre. PC 2014; *Clubs:* National Liberal Club.

Publications: Orange Book chapter 'Harnessing the Markets to Achieve Environmental Goals' (Profile Books, 2004).

Recreations: Theatre, reading, walking.

Rt Hon the Baroness Kramer, House of Lords, London SW1A 0PW
Tel: 020 7219 1492 *Email:* kramers@parliament.uk

CROSSBENCH

KREBS, LORD

KREBS (Life Baron), John Richard Krebs; cr 2007. Born 11 April 1945; Son of Sir Hans Adolf Krebs FRCP FRS, Nobel Prize winning scientist, and Margaret Cicely Krebs; Married Katharine Fullerton 1968 (divorced 2012) (2 daughters); married Sarah Margaret Phibbs 2013.

Education: City of Oxford High School; Pembroke College, Oxford (BA zoology 1966, MA; DPhil 1970); German.

Non-political career: Oxford University: Departmental demonstrator in ornithology, Edward Grey Institute 1969-70, Research officer, Animal Behaviour Research Group 1975-76, Zoology lecturer, Edward Grey Institute 1976-88, Fellow, Wolfson College 1976-81, Pembroke College: EP Abraham Fellow 1981-88, Official Fellow 1988-2005; Royal Society Research Professor 1988-2005: Seconded as Chief executive, National Environment Research Council 1994-99; Principal, Jesus College 2005-15, Emeritus Professor of Zoology 2015-; Assistant professor of animal resource ecology, University of British Columbia, Canada 1970-73; Zoology lecturer, University College of North Wales, Bangor 1973-75; Chair, Food Standards Agency 2000-05.

Political career: *House of Lords:* Raised to the peerage as Baron Krebs, of Wytham in the County of Oxfordshire 2007. Board member, Parliamentary Office of Science and Technology (POST) -2014. Science and Technology: Member 2007, 2008-10, Chair 2010-14, Co-opted member 2015-16; Chair, Science and Technology Sub-committee I (Nanotechnologies and food) 2008-10; Member, Science and Technology Sub-committees: II (Genomic Medicine) 2008-09, I 2012-13; Member, EU Energy and Environment Sub-Committee 2015-. *Councils and public bodies:* Chair, Adaptation Sub-Committee 2009-17; Member, Committee on Climate Change 2010-17.

Political interests: Science, environment, food, education.

Other: Trustee and Deputy Chair, Nuffield Foundation 2013-; President, Campden BRI 2010-14; Chair, Wellcome Trust Advisory Group on Sustaining Health 2014-; Scientific Adviser to: Marks and Spencer plc 2015-, Ajinomoto Co Inc 2015-. Tesco plc 2017-; FRS 1984; FMedSci 2004; Foreign member: US National Academy of Science, American Philosophical Society, American Academy of Arts and Science; German National Academy of Sciences, Leopoldina 2013-. 14 honorary fellowships; 17 honorary doctorates. Numerous awards, including: Linnean Society Bicentenary Medal 1983, Frink medal, Zoological Society 1997, Harben Gold Medal, Royal Institute of Public Health 2006. Kt 1999.

Publications: 250-plus books and articles on ecology and animal behaviour.

Recreations: Running, tennis, walking, food including cooking, music, gardening, family.

Professor the Lord Krebs, House of Lords, London SW1A 0PW
Tel: 020 7219 5353
The Zoology Department, University of Oxford, South Parks Road, Oxford OX1 3PS

NON-AFFILIATED

LAIRD, LORD

LAIRD (Life Baron), John Dunn Laird; cr. 1999. Born 23 April 1944; Son of late Dr Norman Laird OBE (Northern Ireland MP) and late Margaret Laird; Married Caroline Ferguson 1971 (1 son 1 daughter).

Education: Royal Belfast Academical Institution; Ulster Scots.

Non-political career: Bank official 1963-67; Bank inspector 1967-68; Computer programmer 1968-73; Public relations consultant 1973-2005; Chair, John Laird Public Relations 1976-2005; Visiting professor of public relations, Ulster University. National Union of Journalists.

Political career: *House of Lords:* Raised to the peerage as Baron Laird, of Artigarvan in the County of Tyrone 1999. Suspended from membership December 2013-April 2014. *Other:* MP (UUP) for St Annes, Belfast, Northern Ireland Parliament 1970-73; Member for West Belfast: Northern Ireland Assembly 1973-75, Northern Ireland Convention 1975-76. Resigned from Ulster Unionist Party June 2013. *Councils and public bodies:* Member, North/South Language Implementation Board 1999-2004; Chair, Ulster/Scots Agency 1999-2004.

Political interests: Transport, dyslexia, Ulster Scots activity, new energy, new thinking.

Other: Chairman, advisory board, European Azerbaijan Society 2009-; Fellow, Royal Society of Arts 2012; Fellow, Chartered Institute of Public Relations 1991; Combat Cancer, NI Hospice. Freedom, City of London 2012. Lifetime Achievement Award, Certified Institute of Public Relations. Member Instonians, Belfast.

Publications: Videos and DVDs: Trolley Bus Day in Belfast (1992), Swansong of Steam in Ulster (1994), Twilight of Steam in Ulster (1995); Book: A Struggle to be Heard: By a True Ulster Liberal (Global & Western Publishing, 2010).

Recreations: Local history, railways, cricket.

The Lord Laird, House of Lords, London SW1A 0PW
Tel: 020 7219 8626 *Fax:* 020 7219 1657 *Email:* lairdj@parliament.uk
13 Little College Street, London SW1P 3SH

CROSSBENCH

LAMING, LORD

LAMING (Life Baron), (William) Herbert Laming; cr. 1998. Born 19 July 1936; Son of William and Lillian Laming; Married Aileen Pollard 1962 (died 2010).

Education: Durham University (Diploma applied social sciences 1960); Rainer House (probation training 1960-61); London School of Economics (mental health course 1964-65).

Non-political career: Royal Navy 1954-56. Nottingham Probation Service: Probation officer 1961-66, Senior probation officer 1966-68; Assistant chief probation Officer, Nottingham City and County Probation Service 1968-71; Hertfordshire County Council Social Services: Deputy Director 1971-75, Director 1975-91; Chair, Independent Inquiry for Somerset Health Authority 1989; Chief Inspector, Social Services Inspectorate, Department of Health 1991-98; Chair: Review of Management of the Prison Service 1999-2000, Independent Statutory Inquiry following the murder of Victoria Climbié 2001-03, Review of Protection of Children in England 2010, In Care, Out of Trouble 2016.

Political career: *House of Lords:* Raised to the peerage as Baron Laming, of Tewin in the County of Hertfordshire 1998. Convener of the Crossbench Peers 2011-15; Chairman of Committees 2015-16; Member, House of Lords Commission 2016-. Member: Ecclesiastical Committee 2003-15, House 2011-16, Joint Committee on Security 2011-15; Administration and Works: Member 2011-15, Chair 2015-16; Liaison: Member 2011-15, Chair 2015-16; Procedure: Member 2011-15, Chair 2015-16; Selection: Member 2011-15, Chair 2015-16; Member: Privileges and Conduct 2011-16, Sub-committee on Leave of Absence 2011; Member, Joint Committee on the Palace of Westminster 2015-16; Chair: Refreshment 2015-16, Standing Orders (Private Bills) 2015-16, Hybrid Instruments 2015-16, Privileges and Conduct 2015-16; Chair, Services 2016-. *Councils and public bodies:* DL, Hertfordshire 1999-; Vice-President, Local Government Association 2012-15.

Political interests: Public services; China, Europe.

Other: President, Association of Directors of Social Services 1982-83; President and Patron of social care charities. Freedom, City of London 1996. Five honorary doctorates. CBE 1985; Kt 1996; PC 2014.

Publications: Lessons from America: the balance of services in social care (1985).

Rt Hon the Lord Laming CBE DL, House of Lords, London SW1A 0PW
Tel: 020 7219 8907 *Email:* lamingh@parliament.uk

LAMONT OF LERWICK, LORD

CONSERVATIVE

LAMONT OF LERWICK (Life Baron), Norman Stewart Hughson Lamont; cr. 1998. Born 8 May 1942; Son of late Daniel Lamont and Helen Irene Lamont; Married Rosemary White 1971 (divorced) (1 son 1 daughter).

Education: Loretto School, Musselburgh (Scholar); Fitzwilliam College, Cambridge (BA economics 1965) (Union President 1964).

Non-political career: NM Rothschild and Sons Ltd 1968-79, 1993-95; Director: Rothschild Asset Management 1978-79, NM Rothschild and Sons 1993-95; Consultant to Monsanto Corporation 1994-99; Director, Balli Group plc 1995-2012; Adviser to Romanian Government 1995-97; Chair, East European Food Fund 1995-2006; Director: Cie International de Participations Bancaires et Financieres 1999-, Banca Commerciala Robank 2000-05; President, British Romanian Chamber of Commerce 2002-16; Director, Scottish Re 2002-07; Chair, British Iranian Chamber of Commerce 2004-; Director: RAB Capital 2004-11, Jupiter Second Split 2005-; Chair, Jupiter Adria 2006-; Consultant to Western Union Company 2006-08; Chair: Advisory board, Uniastrum Bank 2006-08, Smaller Companies Dividend Trust 2008-; Director, Phorm plc.

Political career: *House of Commons:* Contested Kingston-upon-Hull East 1970 general election. MP (Conservative) for Kingston-upon-Thames 1972 by-election to 1997. Contested Harrogate and Knaresborough 1997 general election. PPS to Norman St John Stevas as Minister for the Arts 1974; Parliamentary Under-Secretary of State, Department of Energy 1979-81; Minister of State, Department of Trade and Industry 1981-85; Minister for Defence Procurement, Ministry of Defence 1985-86; HM Treasury 1986-93: Financial Secretary 1986-89, Chief Secretary 1989-90, Chancellor of the Exchequer 1990-93. *House of Lords:* Raised to the peerage as Baron Lamont of Lerwick, of Lerwick in the Shetland Islands 1998. Trade Envoy to Iran 2016-. Member: Economic Affairs 2005-08, 2015-, Economic Affairs Taxation Sub-committee 2005-08, EU Sub-committee C: (Foreign Affairs, Defence and Development Policy) 2010-12, (External Affairs) 2012-15. *Other:* Bruges Group: Vice-President 1994-2003, Co-chair 2003-07; Vice-President, Conservatives for Britain 2015-16.

Political interests: Economics, European Union, foreign affairs; Chile, Iran, Middle East, Romania.

Other: Chair, Bow Group 1971-72; Trustee, Romanian Orthodox Church in London 2005-08; Chair: Clan Lamont Society 2006-08, Le Cercle 2007-08; Member, advisory board, Iran Heritage Foundation 2008-; President, Economic Research Council 2009-. Honorary Fellow, Fitzwilliam College, Cambridge. PC 1986; Order of Faithful Service (Romania) 2010; *Clubs:* Garrick, Beefsteak, White's Club.

Publications: Sovereign Britain (1995); In Office (1999).

Recreations: Theatre, history, ornithology.

Rt Hon the Lord Lamont of Lerwick, House of Lords, London SW1A 0PW
Tel: 020 7219 5353
Seventh Floor, 33 Cavendish Square, London W1G OPW *Tel:* 020 7306 2138
Email: beverley.gaynor@lhcap.co.uk

LANE-FOX OF SOHO, BARONESS

CROSSBENCH

LANE-FOX OF SOHO (Life Baroness), Martha Lane Fox; cr 2013. Born 10 February 1973; Partner Chris Gorell Barnes (twin sons).

Education: Oxford High School; Westminster School; Oxford University (BA ancient and modern history).

Non-political career: Co-founder: lastminute.com 1998-2003, Lucky Voice 2005-; Founder and chair: Antigone Foundation 2007-15, Go On UK 2012-16, Doteveryone 2015-; Chair, MakieLab 2012-17; Non-executive director: Marks and Spencer 2007-15, Women's Prize for Fiction 2011-, Twitter Inc 2016-.

Political career: *House of Lords:* Raised to the peerage as Baroness Lane-Fox of Soho, of Soho in the City of Westminster 2013. Member, Joint Committee on National Security Strategy. *Councils and public bodies:* Board member, Channel 4 2007-11; Government Digital Champion 2009-13; Non-executive director, Efficiency and Reform Board, Cabinet Office 2010-12; Member, advisory board, Government Digital Service 2016-.

Political interests: Entrepreneurship, government policy, open data, women, security, cyber.

Other: Patron: AbilityNet, Reprieve, Just for Kids Law, Camfed; Convenor, MoreUnited.uk 2016-; Founder and chair, Doteveryone. Chancellor, Open University 2014-. CBE 2013.

The Baroness Lane-Fox of Soho CBE, House of Lords, London SW1A 0PW
Tel: 020 7219 5353
Email: martha@marthalanefox.com
Website: marthalanefoxblog.wordpress.com *Twitter:* @Marthalanefox

LANG OF MONKTON, LORD

CONSERVATIVE

LANG OF MONKTON (Life Baron), Ian Bruce Lang; cr. 1997. Born 27 June 1940; Son of late James Lang, DSC; Married Sandra Montgomerie 1971 (2 daughters).

Education: Lathallan School, Montrose; Rugby School; Sidney Sussex College, Cambridge (BA history 1962).

Non-political career: Marsh and McLennan Companies Inc: Director 1997-2016, Chair 2011-16; Executive Adviser, Aquiline Capital LLC 2016-.

Political career: *House of Commons:* Contested Ayrshire Central 1970 and Glasgow Pollok February 1974 general elections. MP (Conservative) for Galloway 1979-83, for Galloway and Upper Nithsdale 1983-97. Assistant Government Whip 1981-83; Government Whip 1983-86; Parliamentary Under-Secretary of State, Department of Employment 1986; Scottish Office: Parliamentary Under-Secretary of State 1986-87, Minister of State 1987-90, Secretary of State for Scotland 1990-95; President of the Board of Trade and Secretary of State for Trade and Industry 1995-97. *House of Lords:* Raised to the peerage as Baron Lang of Monkton, of Merrick and the Rhinns of Kells in Dumfries and Galloway 1997. Constitution: Member 2001-05, 2012-14, Chair 2014-17; Member, Barnett Formula 2008-09; Member, Liaison 2017-. *Councils and public bodies:* Governor, Rugby School 1997-2007; DL, Ayrshire and Arran 1998-; Prime Minister's Advisory Committee on Business Appointments: Member 2009-14, Chairman 2009-14.

Political interests: Constitutional, economic.

Other: Member, Queen's Bodyguard for Scotland, Royal Company of Archers 1974-; President, Association for the Protection of Rural Scotland 1998-2001; Chair, Patrons of the National Galleries of Scotland 1999-2007. Officer of the Order of St John 1974; PC 1990; *Clubs:* Pratt's Club. Prestwick Golf Club.

Publications: Blue Remembered Years (2002).

Rt Hon the Lord Lang of Monkton DL, House of Lords, London SW1A 0PW
Tel: 020 7219 5792

LANSLEY, LORD

CONSERVATIVE

LANSLEY (Life Baron), Andrew David Lansley; cr 2015. Born 11 December 1956; Son of Thomas Lansley, OBE, and Irene Lansley; Married Marilyn Biggs 1985 (divorced 2001) (3 daughters); married Sally Low 2001 (1 daughter 1 son).

Education: Brentwood School, Essex; Exeter University (BA politics 1979) (President, Guild of Students 1977-78).

Non-political career: Department of [Trade and] Industry 1979-87: Private Secretary to Norman Tebbit as Secretary of State for Trade and Industry 1984-85; Principal Private Secretary to Norman Tebbit as Chancellor of the Duchy of Lancaster 1985-87; British Chambers of Commerce 1987-90: Policy Director 1987-89, Deputy Director-General 1989-90; Director: Conservative Research

Department 1990-95, Public Policy Unit 1995-97; Speaker, Dods Training 2015-; Consultant, Bain & Company 2015-; Adviser, UK Active 2015-; Associate, Low Associates 2015-.

Political career: *House of Commons:* MP (Conservative) for South Cambridgeshire 1997-2010, for South Cambridgeshire (revised boundary) 2010-15. Member Shadow Cabinet 1999-2001: Shadow Minister for the Cabinet Office and Policy Renewal 1999-2001; Shadow Chancellor of the Duchy of Lancaster 1999-2001; Member Shadow Cabinet 2003-10: Shadow Secretary of State for Health 2003-10; Secretary of State for Health 2010-12; Leader of the House of Commons, Lord Privy Seal 2012-14; Member: House of Commons Commission 2012-14, Speaker's Committee for the Independent Parliamentary Standards Authority 2012-14, Public Accounts Commission 2012-14. Member: Health 1997-98, Trade and Industry 2001-04. *House of Lords:* Raised to the peerage as Baron Lansley, of Orwell in the County of Cambridgeshire 2015. Member, EU Internal Market Sub-committee 2016-. *Other:* Vice-chair, Conservative Party (with responsibility for policy renewal) 1998-99.

Political interests: Health, local and regional government, economic policy, trade and industry; Egypt, France, Germany, Israel, Japan, South Africa, USA.

Other: Patron: ASPIRE (Spinal injury), Headway (Acquired Brain injury); Member, National Union Executive Committee 1990-95; Chair, UK-Japan 21st Century Group 2015-; Trustee, Radix (think tank) 2016-. CBE 1996; PC 2010.

Publications: A Private Route (1988); Co-author Conservatives and the Constitution (1997); Do the right thing – Why Conservatives must achieve greater fairness and diversity in candidate selection (2002); Extending the Reach (2003).

Recreations: Spending time with my children, films, biography, history, cricket.

Rt Hon the Lord Lansley CBE, House of Lords, London SW1A 0PW
Tel: 020 7219 3000 *Email:* lansleya@parliament.uk *Twitter:* @andrewdlansley

LABOUR

LAWRENCE OF CLARENDON, BARONESS

LAWRENCE OF CLARENDON (Life Baroness), Doreen Delceita Lawrence; cr 2013. Born 24 October 1952.

Education: Greenwich University (BA humanities 1995; Postgraduate counselling skills 1997).

Non-political career: Campaigner for justice, race equality and better policing; Stephen Lawrence Charitable Trust: Founder 1998, Director 2002-15.

Political career: *House of Lords:* Raised to the peerage as Baroness Lawrence of Clarendon, of Clarendon in the Commonwealth Realm of Jamaica 2013. Member, Joint Committee on Human Rights 2015-.

Other: Trustee, Liberty -2017; Honorary Fellow: Royal Institute of British Architects 2010, Goldsmith's University of London 2012; Stop Hate UK, MOSAIC, EKAYA Housing. Freedom: Royal Borough of Greenwich, London Borough of Lewisham. Chancellor, De Montfort University, Leicester. Hon. doctorate (Civil Law), University of East Anglia 1999; Hon. LLD, Bradford University 2000; Hon. doctorate: Staffordshire University 2001, Greenwich University 2006; Bishop Grosseteste University College Lincoln 2008, University of East London 2012, York University 2013, Sheffield Hallam University 2013, Oxford Brookes University 2014, Exeter University 2014. Special award for the Legal Aid Lawyer of the Year 2012; Lifetime Achievement at Pride of Britain Awards 2012; Londoner of the Year at London Press Club Awards 2013. OBE 2003.

Publications: And Still I Rise (2006).

The Baroness Lawrence of Clarendon OBE, House of Lords, London SW1A 0PW
Tel: 020 7219 5353 *Twitter:* @DLawrenceOBE

CONSERVATIVE

LAWSON OF BLABY, LORD

LAWSON OF BLABY (Life Baron), Nigel Lawson; cr. 1992. Born 11 March 1932; Son of late Ralph Lawson and late Joan Lawson, née Davis; Married Vanessa Salmon 1955 (divorced 1980, died 1985) (1 son 2 daughters 1 daughter deceased); married Thérèse Maclear 1980 (divorced 2012) (1 son 1 daughter).

Education: Westminster School; Christ Church, Oxford (Scholar, BA philosophy, politics and economics 1954).

Non-political career: Royal Navy national service 1954-56; Sub-Lt RNVR, CO HMMTB Gay Charger. Member editorial staff, *Financial Times* 1956-60; City editor, *Sunday Telegraph* 1961-63; Special assistant to Sir Alec Douglas-Home as Prime Minister 1963-64; *Financial Times* columnist and BBC broadcaster 1965; Editor, *The Spectator* 1966-70; Director, Barclays Bank plc 1990-

98; Chair: Central Europe Trust Co Ltd 1990-2012; Oxford Investment Partners 2006-13; Founding Chair: Global Warming Policy Foundation 2009-, Global Warming Policy Forum 2014-; Mousquetaire d'Armagnac 2010-.

Political career: *House of Commons:* Contested Eton and Slough 1970 general election. MP (Conservative) for Blaby February 1974-92. Opposition Whip 1976-77; Opposition Spokesperson on Treasury and Economic Affairs 1977-79; Financial Secretary to the Treasury 1979-81; Secretary of State for Energy 1981-83; Chancellor of the Exchequer 1983-89. *House of Lords:* Raised to the peerage as Baron Lawson of Blaby, of Newnham in the County of Northamptonshire 1992. Member: Economic Affairs 2004-08, 2010-15, Barnett Formula 2008-09, Parliamentary Commission on Banking Standards 2012-13, EU Financial Affairs Sub-committee 2015-16. *Other:* President, Conservatives for Britain 2015-16.

Political interests: Climate change, economics, finance, banking, Europe.

Other: President, British Institute of Energy Economics 1995-2004; Member, Governing Body, Westminster School 1999-2005; Vote Leave: Interim chair 2016, Member, Campaign Committee 2016; Founding supporter, Change Britain 2016-; Fellow, Nuffield College, Oxford 1972-73. Hon. Student, Christ Church, Oxford 1996; Fellow, Westminster School 2005; Hon. DSc, Buckingham University 2011. IEA National Free Enterprise Award 2008; *The House Magazine* Lifetime Achievement Award, Dods Parliamentary Awards 2014. PC 1981; *Clubs:* Beefsteak, Garrick, Pratt's Club.

Publications: Co-author, The Power Game (1976); The View from Number 11: (Memoirs 1992) [abridged and updated as Memoirs of a Tory Radical, 2010]; Co-author, The Nigel Lawson Diet Book (1996); An Appeal to Reason: A Cool Look at Global Warming (2008).

Rt Hon the Lord Lawson of Blaby, House of Lords, London SW1A 0PW
Tel: 020 7219 4464/020 7219 5582 *Email:* lawsonn@parliament.uk rathbonea@paerliament.uk

LAYARD, LORD

LABOUR

LAYARD (Life Baron) (Peter) Richard Grenville Layard; cr. 2000. Born 15 March 1934; Son of Dr John Layard and Doris Layard; Married Molly Meacher 1991, née Reid, now Baroness Meacher (qv).

Education: Eton College; King's College, Cambridge (BA history 1957); London School of Economics (MSc economics 1967).

Non-political career: History master, London comprehensive secondary schools 1959-61; Senior research officer, Robbins Committee on Higher Education 1961-63; London School of Economics 1964-: Deputy director, Higher Education Research Unit 1964-74, Lecturer in economics 1968-75, Reader in economics of labour 1975-80, Head, Centre for Labour Economics 1974-90, Professor of Economics 1980-99, Emeritus Professor of Economics 1999-; Director, Centre for Economic Performance 1990-2003; Economic Consultant to the Russian Government 1991-97; Consultant: Department for Education and Employment 1997-2001, Cabinet Office 2001; Programme director, Well-Being Programme, LSE Centre for Economic Performance 2003-; Adviser, Improved Access to Psychological Therapy Programme, Department of Health 2006-. Member, Association of University Teachers.

Political career: *House of Lords:* Raised to the peerage as Baron Layard, of Highgate in the London Borough of Haringey 2000. Member: European Union Sub-Committee A (Economic and Financial Affairs, Trade and External Relations) 2001-02, Economic Affairs 2005-08, 2015-.

Political interests: Economic policy, employment, inequality, well-being, mental health; Bhutan.

Other: Member, UGC 1985-89; Chair, Employment Institute 1987-92; Member, Good Childhood Inquiry Panel 2007-09; Fellow: Econometric Society 1986, British Academy 2003, European Economics Association 2004, Society of Labour Economists 2007. Honorary Fellow, London School of Economics 2000. WW Leontief Medal of the Russian Academy of Natural Sciences 2005; 12A Prize (Joint) in Labour Economics 2008; Royal College of Psychiatrists Medal 2010.

Publications: Co-author: The Causes of Graduate Unemployment in India (1969), The Impact of Robbins: Expansion in Higher Education (1969), Qualified Manpower and Economic Performance (1971); Editor, Cost-Benefit Analysis (1973, 1994); Co-author: Microeconomic Theory (1978), The Causes of Poverty (1978); Author: More Jobs, Less Inflation (1982), How to Beat Unemployment (1986); Co-author: Handbook of Labour Economics (1986), The Performance of the British Economy (1988), Unemployment: Macroeconomic Performance and the Labour Market (1991), Reform in Eastern Europe (1991), East-West Migration: the alternatives (1992), Post-Communist Russia: pain and progress (1993), Macroeconomics: a text for Russia (1994), The Coming Russian Boom (1996); Author, What Labour Can Do (1997); Co-author, Emerging from Communism: Lessons from Russia, China and Eastern Europe (1998); Author: Tackling Unemployment (1999), Tackling Inequality (1999); Co-author, What the Future Holds (2001); Author,

Happiness (2005, 2011); Co-author: A Good Childhood: Searching for Values in a Competitive Age (2009), Combatting Unemployment (2011); Thrive: The Power of Evidence-based Psychological Therapies (2014).

Recreations: Tennis, sailing.

Professor the Lord Layard, House of Lords, London SW1A 0PW
Tel: 020 7219 5353
Centre for Economic Performance, London School of Economics, Houghton Street, London WC2A 2AE *Tel:* 020 7955 7048 *Email:* r.layard@lse.ac.uk *Website:* cep.lse.ac.uk/layard

LEA OF CRONDALL, LORD

LABOUR

LEA OF CRONDALL (Life Baron), David Edward Lea; cr. 1999. Born 2 November 1937; Son of late Edward and Lilian Lea.

Education: Farnham Grammar School, Surrey; Christ's College, Cambridge (MA economics 1961) (Inaugural chair Cambridge University Students Representative Council 1961); French.

Non-political career: National Service, Royal Horse Artillery 1955-57. Economist Intelligence Unit 1961-63; Trades Union Congress: Research/Economic Department 1964-67, Assistant secretary, Economic and Social Affairs 1968-70, Head, Economic and Social Affairs 1970-77, Assistant general secretary 1978-99. Member, TGWU 1962-; TUC: Member, Mission to Study Employment and Technology in the USA 1980, Secretary: Nuclear Energy Review Body 1986-88, Task Force on Representation at Work 1994-99; European TUC: Chair, Economic Committee 1980-90, Member, Executive Committee and Steering Group 1991-99, Vice-President 1997-99.

Political career: *House of Lords:* Raised to the peerage as Baron Lea of Crondall, of Crondall in the County of Hampshire 1999. Member: European Communities Sub-committees: A (Economic and Financial Affairs, Trade and External Relations) 2000-03, C (Foreign Affairs, Defence and Development Policy) 2003-07, G (Social Policy and Consumer Affairs) 2007-09, Insurance Bill 2014-15. *Other:* President, Cambridge University Liberal Club 1960-61; Secretary, TUC-Labour Party: Liaison Committee 1972-86, Contact Group 1987-96. *Councils and public bodies:* Member: DTI Investment Mission in Japan 1974, Channel Tunnel Advisory Committee 1974-75, Bullock Committee on Industrial Democracy 1975-77, Royal Commission on the Distribution of Income and Wealth 1975-79, Delors Committee on Economic and Social Concepts in the Community 1977-79, Energy Commission 1977-79, UN Commission on Transnational Corporations 1977-82, NEDC Committee on Finance for Industry 1978-82, Franco-British Council 1982-99; Governor, National Institute of Economic and Social Research; Member: Retail Prices Index Advisory Committee 1985-99, Kreisky Commission on Employment Issues in Europe 1987-89, Tripartite Mission EU, Japan 1990, European Social Dialogue Joint Steering Committee 1992-, UK Delegation Earth Summit, Rio 1992, Round Table on Sustainable Development 1995-99, Advisory Committee on Vehicle Emissions 1998-99, EU High Level Group on Benchmarking 1998-99, Treasury Advisory Committee on EMU 1998-99, Central Arbitration Committee 2000-10; Council member, Britain in Europe 2000-05; Election monitor: Congo (DRC) 2007, Nepal 2008.

Political interests: European Union, employment, energy, economy, constitution; Africa, Bolivia, Madagascar, Nepal.

Other: Chair, Hammarskjold Inquiry Trust 2012-13; Editorial board member, New Economy (IPPR) 1991-99. OBE 1978. Bourne Club, Farnham, Lords/Commons Tennis and Ski Clubs.

Publications: Trade Unionism (1966); Co-author, Europe and Your Rights at Work (2006).

Recreations: Tennis, music, theatre, skiing.

The Lord Lea of Crondall OBE, House of Lords, London SW1A 0PW
Tel: 020 7219 8518 *Email:* lead@parliament.uk

LEE OF TRAFFORD, LORD

LIBERAL DEMOCRAT

LEE OF TRAFFORD (Life Baron), John Robert Louis Lee; cr 2006. Born 21 June 1942; Son of Basil Lee, doctor; Married Anne Bakirgian 1975 (2 daughters).

Education: William Hulme's Grammar School, Manchester; Chartered accountant 1964.

Non-political career: Founding director, Chancery Consolidated Ltd (investment bankers), Manchester; Various non-executive directorships.

Political career: *House of Commons:* Contested Manchester Moss-side October 1974. MP (Conservative) for Nelson and Colne 1979-83, for Pendle 1983-92. Contested Pendle 1992 general election. PPS to: Kenneth Baker as Minister of State for Industry 1981-83, Cecil Parkinson as Secretary of State for Industry 1983; Parliamentary Under-Secretary of State: Ministry of Defence

1983-86, Department of Employment 1986-89; Minister for Tourism 1987-89. *House of Lords:* Raised to the peerage as Baron Lee of Trafford, of Bowdon in the County of Cheshire 2006. Liberal Democrat: Spokesperson for: Trade and Industry 2006-07, Culture, Media and Sport (Tourism) 2006-10, Defence 2007-10, Whip 2007-10. Co-opted Member, EU Sub-committee B (Internal Market) 2006-07; Member: Refreshment 2007-12, 2015-16, Joint Committee on National Security Strategy 2010-14. Chair, Liberal Democrat Parliamentary Party Committee on International Affairs (Defence) 2010-12. *Other:* Joined Liberal Democrats 2001; Chairman, Liberal Democrat Friends of Armed Forces 2010-12. *Councils and public bodies:* Chair, Association of Leading Visitor Attractions 1990-; Member, English Tourist Board 1992-99; Chair: Museum of Science and Industry, Manchester 1992-99, Christie Hospital NHS Trust 1992-98; DL, Greater Manchester 1995; High Sheriff, Greater Manchester 1998-99.

Political interests: Defence, tourism, trade and industry, investment; UK.

Other: Chairman, Association of Leading Visitor Attractions; Trustee and Deputy Chair, Museum of Richmond.

Publications: Portfolio Man (Willow Publishing, 2005); How to Make a Million – Slowly (2014).

Recreations: Golf, stock market, salmon fishing, antiques.

The Lord Lee of Trafford, House of Lords, London SW1A 0PW
Tel: 020 7219 3949 *Email:* leej@parliament.uk

NON-AFFILIATED

LEEDS, LORD BISHOP OF

LEEDS (1st Bishop of), Nicholas Baines. Born 13 November 1957; Son of Frank and Beryl Baines; Married Linda Higgins 1980 (2 sons 1 daughter).

Education: Holt Comprehensive School, Liverpool; Bradford University (BA modern languages); Trinity College, Bristol (BA theological studies); German, French, Russian.

Non-political career: Linguist specialist, GCHQ, Cheltenham 1980-84; Ordained deacon 1987; Assistant curate, St Thomas, Kendal 1987-91; Priest 1988; Assistant Priest, Holy Trinity with St John, Leicester 1991-92; Vicar, St Mary and St John, Leicester 1992-2000; Archdeacon of Lambeth 2000-03; Bishop of: Croydon 2003-11, Bradford 2011-14, Leeds 2014-.

Political career: *House of Lords:* Entered House of Lords as the Bishop of Leeds 2014. *Councils and public bodies:* Member, General Synod 1995-2005.

Political interests: The common good, Europe; Germany, Kazakhstan, Russia, Sri Lanka, Sudan, Tanzania.

Other: Anglican co-chair, Meissen Commission 2007-17; Chair, Sandford St Martin Trust 2008-17. Honorary doctorate: Bradford University, Friedrich-Schiller-University Jena, Germany; Honorary fellow, Bradford College.

Publications: Hungry for Hope (1991, 2007); Speedbumps and Potholes (2003); Jesus and People Like Us (2004); Marking Time: 47 Reflections on Mark's Gospel for Lent, Holy Week and Easter (2005); Finding Faith: Stories of Music and Life (2008); Scandal of Grace: The Danger of Following Jesus (2008); Why Wish You a Merry Christmas?: What Matters (and What Doesn't) in the Festive Season (2009).

Recreations: Sport, literature, music, theatre.

Rt Rev the Lord Bishop of Leeds, House of Lords, London SW1A 0PW
Tel: 020 7219 5353 *Email:* bainesn@parliament.uk
Hollin House, Weetwood Avenue, Leeds LS16 5NG *Tel:* 0113-284 4301
Email: bishop.nick@leeds.anglican.org *Website:* www.leeds.anglican.org
Website: nickbaines.wordpress.com *Twitter:* @nickbaines

CONSERVATIVE

LEIGH OF HURLEY, LORD

LEIGH OF HURLEY (Life Baron), Howard Darryl Leigh; cr 2013. Born 3 April 1959; Married Jennifer Peach 1998 (2 daughters).

Education: Clifton College, Bristol; Southampton Univeristy (BSc Soc Sci Economics 1980); Chartered Accountant 1983.

Non-political career: Deloitte Haskins & Sells 1981-88: Chartered Accountant, Corporate Tax Department, Mergers and Acquisitions Group; Cavendish Corporate Finance: Founder 1988, Senior Partner 2010-.

Political career: *House of Lords:* Raised to the peerage as Baron Leigh of Hurley, of Hurley in the Royal County of Berkshire 2013. Member: Economic Affairs Finance Bill Sub-committee 2014, 2016-17, Administration and Works 2014-15, Finance 2016-. *Other:* Conservative Party: Treasurer 2000-05, Chair, Leader's Group 2010-, Senior treasurer 2005-; Member, executive board, Conservative Friends of Israel; Westminster North Conservative Association: President 2010-17, Patron 2017-.

Other: Member: Chartered Institute of Taxation 1985, Deregulation Taskforce, DTI 1994-97; ICAEW: Council Member 1998-2004, Chair, Corporate Finance Faculty 1998-2004, Member: Takeover Panel Appeal Committee 1998-, Jewish Care Business Group 2000-; Vice-President, Jewish Leadership Council 2010-; President, Westminster Synagogue 2010-; Member, Deliver Life Board Wateraid 2015-16; President, Institute for Jewish Policy Research 2016-; Member Advisory Board, Metro Bank plc 2017-; ICAEW; Chartered Institute of Taxation; Jewish Care, Wateraid. Member of Court, Worshipful Company of Chartered Accountants 2003-15. Freedom, City of London. Lifetime Achievement Award, Corporate Finance Faculty ICAEW; *Clubs:* Carlton Club.

Publications: Lecturer, author and broadcaster on mergers and acquisitions; Good Practice Guideline: Selling a Business (Institute of Chartered Accountants).

Recreations: Running.

The Lord Leigh of Hurley, House of Lords, London SW1A 0PW
Tel: 020 7219 5353
Cavendish Corporate Finance LLP, 40 Portland Place, London W1B 1NB *Tel:* 020 7908 6000

LEITCH, LORD

LABOUR

LEITCH (Life Baron), Alexander Park Leitch; cr. 2004. Born 20 October 1947; Son of Donald Leitch and Agnes Smith, née Park; Married (3 daughters); married Noelle Kristin Dowd 2003 (1 daughter).

Education: Dunfermline High School.

Non-political career: Chief systems designer, National Mutual Life/Hambro Life 1969-75; Allied Dunbar plc: Chief executive 1993-96, Chair 1996-2001; Chair: Dunbar Bank 1994-2001, Eagle Star 1996-2004, Threadneedle Asset Management 1996-2004; Director, BAT Industries 1997-98; Chief executive, Zurich Financial Services (UKISA Asia Pacific) 1998-2004; Chair: Association of British Insurers 1998-2000, National Employment Panel 2000-07; Intrinsic FS 2005; Director: Lloyds TSB plc 2005, UBM plc 2005-09, Paternoster 2006-10, BUPA 2006; Scottish Widows plc: Director 2007-13, Chair 2008-13; Deputy chair, Lloyds Banking Group plc 2011-13; FNZ 2013; Adviser, Guggenheim Investments 2014; Director, Old Mutal Wealth 2014.

Political career: *House of Lords:* Raised to the peerage as Baron Leitch, of Oakley in Fife 2004.

Political interests: Skills and education, pensions, financial services, charity, Scotland; Africa, China, France, India, Italy, Latin America, Spain, Switzerland, USA.

Other: Deputy chair, BITC 1996-2004; Chair, SANE 1999-2000; Trustee, National Galleries of Scotland 1999-2003; Deputy chair, Commonwealth Education Fund 2001-06; Vice-President, UK Cares 2004; Chair: Balance Foundation 2004-05, Leitch Review of UK Skills 2005-07, Medical Aid Films 2010; Trustee, Lloyds TSB Foundation 2011; Fellow, Carnegie College. Member, Worshipful Company of Insurers 2002. Freedom, City of London 2002. Chancellor, Carnegie College, Dunfermline 2010. Hon. Doctorate, Sunderland University; City and Guilds. Prince of Wales Ambassador's Award for Charitable Work 2001; *Clubs:* Caledonia Club.

Recreations: Antiquarian books, antiques, poetry, malt whisky, art, painting.

The Lord Leitch, House of Lords, London SW1A 0PW
Tel: 020 7219 2929
Tel: 020 7222 3180 *Fax:* 020 7222 7913 *Email:* sandy.leitch@bupa.com

LENNIE, LORD

LABOUR

Opposition Whip

LENNIE (Life Baron), Christopher (Chris) John Lennie; cr 2014. Born 22 February 1953; Son of Magnus and Elizabeth Lennie; Partner Anne (2 children).

Education: West Kent College; Newcastle University (history and English literature 1976).

Non-political career: National campaigns manager and Northern political officer, Unison; Labour Party: Regional director (Northern England) 1999-2001, Deputy Secretary-general, Acting Secretary-general 2008-09, External relations adviser. Member, Unison.

Political career: *House of Lords:* Raised to the peerage as Baron Lennie, of Longsands Tynemouth in the County of Tyne and Wear 2014. Opposition Whip 2016-.

Political interests: Social mobility, economic security, North East region of England; Europe, USA.

Other: *Clubs:* Tynemouth CIU Club.

Recreations: Newcastle United FC.

The Lord Lennie, House of Lords, London SW1A 0PW
Tel: 020 7219 5353 *Email:* lenniec@parliament.uk

LESTER OF HERNE HILL, LORD

LIBERAL DEMOCRAT

LESTER OF HERNE HILL (Life Baron), Anthony Paul Lester; cr. 1993. Born 3 July 1936; Son of late Harry and Kate Lester; Married Catherine Wassey 1971 (1 son 1 daughter).

Education: City of London School; Trinity College, Cambridge (MA history and law 1962); Harvard Law School (LLM 1964); French.

Non-political career: 2nd Lieutenant, Royal Artillery 1955-57 (national service). Called to Bar, Lincoln's Inn 1963; Special adviser to: Home Secretary 1974-76, Standing Advisory Commission on Human Rights in Northern Ireland 1975-77; QC 1975; Hon. Visiting Professor, University College London 1983-; Irish Bar 1983; Called to Bar of Northern Ireland 1984; QC (NI) 1984; Bencher 1985; Recorder of the Crown Court 1987-93; Independent adviser to Jack Straw as Secretary of State for Justice on aspects of constitutional reform 2007-08.

Political career: *House of Lords:* Raised to the peerage as Baron Lester of Herne Hill, of Herne Hill in the London Borough of Southwark 1993. Liberal Democrat Spokesperson for: Discrimination Law Reform 2008-09, Women and Equality 2009-10, Human Rights Legislation 2015. Member: Procedure 1995-97, European Communities Sub-committees E: Law and Institutions 1995-97, 1999-2003, 2005-06, 1996 Inter-Governmental Conference 1995-97, European Communities Sub-committee F (Social Affairs, Education and Home Affairs) 1997-99, Human Rights Joint Committee 2001-05, 2005-09, 2010-15; Co-opted Member, EU Sub-committee E (Law and Institutions) 2006-08; Member, Constitution 2013-16. *Other:* Founder member, Social Democrat Party 1981; President, Liberal Democrat Lawyers' Association. *Councils and public bodies:* Governor, British Institute of Human Rights; Member, Council of Justice 1977-; President, Interights (International Centre for the Legal Protection of Human Rights) 1991-; European Roma Rights Centre: Executive Committee, Co-chair 1998-2001; Member, board of directors, Salzburg Seminar 1996-2000; Open Society Justice Initiative Board 2000-; Chair, Equal Rights Trust 2006-07; Vice-president, English PEN 2010; Commissioner, Bill of Rights Commission 2011-.

Political interests: Human rights, constitutional reform, law reform, equality and non-discrimination, media, European political integration; India, Ireland, South Africa, USA.

Other: Board member, Open Society Institute Justice Initiative 2000-; Overseas member, American Law Institute 1985-; Member, Bar Council of England and Wales; Hon. Fellow, Society for Advanced Legal Studies 1998-; Hon. Member, American Academy of Arts and Sciences 2002; Hon. Fellow, American Philosophical Society 2003; Hon. Member, Society of Legal Scholars 2008; Interights, Justice, Liberty. Seven honorary doctorates; Hon. Life Fellow, University College London 1998; Adj. Prof. of Law, University College Cork, Ireland 2006. Human Rights Lawyer of the Year, Liberty 1997; Lifetime Achievement Award, The Lawyer 2004; Peer of the Year, *House Magazine* 2006; Lifetime Achievement in Service of Human Rights, Liberty Judges Award 2008; Lifetime Achievement Award, Association of Muslim Lawyers 2008. Chevalier de la Légion d'Honneur (France) 2009; *Clubs:* Royal Automobile Club.

Publications: Justice in the American South (Amnesty International, 1964); Co-editor, Shawcross and Beaumont on Air Law (3rd edition, 1964); Co-author, Race and Law (1972); Numerous articles on human rights law and constitutional reform; Contributor to other legal publications; Editor-in-Chief, Butterworths Human Rights Cases; Member, Editorial Board of Public Law; Consultant editor and contributor on 'Constitutional Law and Human Rights', Halsbury's Laws of England (4th edition, reissued 1996); Co-editor, Butterworths Human Rights Law and Practice (1999, 2004, 2009).

Recreations: Walking, sailing, watercolours.

The Lord Lester of Herne Hill QC, House of Lords, London SW1A 0PW
Tel: 020 7219 2999 *Email:* lestera@parliament.uk
The Odysseus Trust, 193 Fleet Street, London EC4A 2AH *Tel:* 020 7404 4712
Fax: 020 7405 7314 *Email:* info@odysseustrust.org *Website:* www.odysseustrust.org
Twitter: @Odysseus_Trust

CROSSBENCH

LEVENE OF PORTSOKEN, LORD

LEVENE OF PORTSOKEN (Life Baron), Peter Keith Levene; cr. 1997. Born 8 December 1941; Son of late Maurice and Rose Levene; Married Wendy Fraiman 1966 (2 sons 1 daughter).

Education: City of London School; Manchester University (BA economics 1963); French, German, Italian.

Non-political career: Hon. Col. Comdt, Royal Logistic Corps 1993-2006. United Scientific Holdings 1963-85: Managing director 1968-85, Chair 1982-85; Member, South East Asia Trade Advisory Group 1979-83; Defence Manufacturers' Association: Council member 1982-85, Chair 1984-85, President 2005-09; Personal adviser to Michael Heseltine as Secretary of State for Defence 1984; Chief of Defence Procurement, Ministry of Defence 1985-91; UK National Armaments Director 1988-91; Chair, European National Armaments Directors 1989-90; Personal adviser to Michael Heseltine as Secretary of State for the Environment 1991-92; Chair, Docklands Light Railway Ltd 1991-94; Deputy chair, Wasserstein Perella & Co Ltd 1991-94; Personal adviser on competition and purchasing to Norman Lamont as Chancellor of the Exchequer 1992; Member, Citizen's Charter Advisory Panel 1992-93; Personal adviser to the President of the Board of Trade 1992-95; Adviser on efficiency and effectiveness to John Major as Prime Minister 1992-97; Chair and chief executive, Canary Wharf Ltd 1993-96; Senior adviser, Morgan Stanley & Co Ltd 1996-98; Director, Haymarket Group Ltd 1997-; Chair: Bankers Trust International plc 1998-99, Investment Banking Europe Deutsche Bank 1999-2001; Vice-chair, Deutsche Bank AG London 2001-02; Director, J Sainsbury plc 2001-04; Chair: General Dynamics UK Ltd 2001-, World Trade Centre Disaster Fund (UK) 2001-03, Lloyd's 2002-11; Member, supervisory board, Deutsche Boerse ag 2004-05; Board member, TOTAL SA 2005-11; Director, China Construction Bank 2006-12; Chair: Ministry of Defence Reform Group 2010-16, NBNK Investments plc 2011-12; Vice-chair, Starr International Company Inc 2012-; Chair, Starr Underwriting Agents Ltd 2012-; Board member, Eurotunnel SA 2012-; Chair, Tikehau Investments Ltd 2013-; Director, China Construction Bank (Asia) 2013-.

Political career: *House of Lords:* Raised to the peerage as Baron Levene of Portsoken, of Portsoken in the City of London 1997. Member: Economic Affairs 2008-13, Joint Committee on National Security Strategy 2013-16, Personal Service Companies 2013-14, Artificial Intelligence 2017-. *Councils and public bodies:* Court of Common Council, City of London: Member 1983-84, Alderman 1984-2012; JP, City of London 1984-2002; Governor, City of London School 1986-; Sheriff, City of London 1995-96; Lord Mayor of London 1998-99.

Other: Chair: Board of management, London Homes for the Elderly 1990-93, Bevis Marks Trust; CIMgt; FCIPS; LEUKA 2000. Carmen's Company: Liveryman 1984-, Master 1992-93; Liveryman: Information Technologists 1992-, Management Consultant (Honorary) 2004-. Chancellor, City University 1998-99. Fellow, Queen Mary and Westfield College 1995; Two honorary doctorates. KBE 1989; KStJ 1998; Commandeur, Ordre National du Merite (France) 1996; Knight Commander Order of Merit (Germany) 1998; Middle Cross Order of Merit (Hungary) 1999; *Clubs:* Guildhall, Royal Automobile Club, Walbrook Club.

Recreations: Skiing, watching football, travel.

The Lord Levene of Portsoken KBE, House of Lords, London SW1A 0PW
Tel: 020 7219 5353
Fourth Floor, 30 Fenchurch Avenue, London EC3M 5AD *Tel:* 020 7398 5087
Email: barbara.addison@starrcompanies.com

LABOUR

LEVY, LORD

LEVY (Life Baron), Michael Abraham Levy; cr. 1997. Born 11 July 1944; Son of Samuel and Annie Levy; Married Gilda Altbach 1967 (1 son 1 daughter).

Education: Hackney Downs Grammar School, London; FCA 1966.

Non-political career: Lubbock Fine (Chartered Accountants) 1961-66; Principal, M Levy & Co 1966-69; Partner, Wagner Prager Levy & Partners 1969-73; Chair, Magnet Group of Companies 1973-88; Vice-chair: Phonographic Performance Ltd 1979-84, British Phonographic Industry Ltd 1984-87; Chair: D & J Securities Ltd 1988-92, M & G Records Ltd 1992-97, Chase Music Ltd (formerly M & G Music Ltd) 1992-2008, Wireart Ltd 1992-2008; Principal, Global Consultancy Services 2005-; Chair, International Standard Asset Management 2008-2011.

Political career: *House of Lords:* Raised to the peerage as Baron Levy, of Mill Hill in the London Borough of Barnet 1997. Personal Envoy to the Prime Minister and Special Adviser on the Middle East 1998-2007. *Other:* Member, Labour Party Donations Committee 2002-07. *Councils and public bodies:* JFS (Jews Free School): Governor 1990-95, Hon. President 1995-2001, President 2001; President, Barnet and Southgate College 2017-.

Political interests: Voluntary sector, social welfare, education, Middle East; European countries, North Africa, Latin and Central America, Middle East.

Other: International Peace Institute; United Joint Israel Appeal: National Campaign Chair 1982-85, Honorary Vice-President 1994-2000, Honorary President 2000-; Member, World Board of Governors: Jewish Agency 1990-95, Keren Hayesod 1991-95; World Chair, Youth Aliyah Committee, Jewish Agency Board of Governors 1991-95; Chair: British Music Industry Trust Awards Committee 1992-95, Jewish Care 1992-97, Chief Rabbinate Awards for Excellence 1992-2007, Foundation for Education 1993-2006; Vice-chair, Central Council for Jewish Social Services 1994-2006; Patron, British Music Industry Trust Awards 1995; Chair, Jewish Care Community Foundation 1995-2010; Member: World Commission on Israel-Diaspora Relations 1995-, International Board of Governors, Peres Centre for Peace 1997-2009, Advisory Council, Foreign Policy Centre 1997-2006; Patron, Prostate Cancer Charitable Trust 1997-2011; President, Volunteering Matters 1998-; Patron, Friends of Israel Educational Trust 1998-2001; Member: National Council for Voluntary Organisations Advisory Committee 1998-2011, Community Legal Service Champions Panel 1999-2010; Patron, Save A Child's Heart Foundation 2000-04; Member, Honorary Committee, Israel Britain and the Commonwealth Association 2000-04; Chair, Board of Trustees, New Policy Network Foundation 2000-07; Executive Committee Member, Chai-Lifeline 2001-02; Hon. Patron, Cambridge University Jewish Society 2002-; Patron, Simon Marks Jewish Primary School Trust 2002-; Former Trustee and Co-chair, Academy Sponsors Trust; President, Specialist Schools and Academics Trust 2005-08; Trustee and Member, executive committee, Jewish Leadership Council (JLC) 2006-11; President, Jewish Lads' and Girls' Brigade (JLGB) 2006-; Member, Development Board, British Library 2008-11; Patron: Mathilda Marks-Kennedy Jewish Primary School 2011-, Etz Chaim Jewish Primary School 2011; Member: Advisory Council, "Step Up to Serve Campaign" under the patronage of HRH The Princes of Wales 2014-, Board, International Peace Institute 2015-; President, Barnet and Southgate College 2017-; Fellow, Institute of Chartered Accountants; FCA 1966. Honorary Doctorate, Middlesex University 1999. B'nai B'rith First Lodge Award 1994; Friends of the Hebrew University of Jerusalem Scopus Award 1998; Israel Policy Forum (USA) Special Recognition Award 2003; *Jewish Chronicle* Award 2016; Who's Who Marquis Lifetime Achievement Award 2017.

Publications: A Question of Honour (2008).

Recreations: Tennis, swimming.

The Lord Levy, House of Lords, London SW1A 0PW
Tel: 020 7219 5353

3 Marylebone Mews, London W1G 8PU *Tel:* 020 7487 5174 *Fax:* 020 7486 7919
Email: ml@lordlevy.com

LEXDEN, LORD

CONSERVATIVE

LEXDEN (Life Baron), Alistair Basil Cooke; cr 2010. Born 20 April 1945; Son of Dr Basil and Nancy Cooke.

Education: Framlingham College, Suffolk; Peterhouse, Cambridge (BA, MA 1970); Queen's University, Belfast (PhD 1979).

Non-political career: Lecturer and tutor in modern history, Queen's University, Belfast 1971-77; Political adviser to Shadow Minister for Northern Ireland 1977-79; Conservative Research Department: Desk officer 1977-83, Assistant director 1983-85, Deputy director 1985-97; Director, Conservative Political Centre 1988-97; Official historian of the Conservative Party 2009-.

Political career: *House of Lords:* Raised to the peerage as Baron Lexden, of Lexden in the County of Essex and of Strangford in the County of Down 2010. Member: EU Sub-committee G (Social Policies and Consumer Protection) 2012, Constitution 2012-15, Joint Committee on Statutory Instruments 2015-, Ecclesiastical Committee 2017-. *Other:* Co-chairman, Conservative History Group 2012-. *Councils and public bodies:* General Secretary, Independent Schools Council 1997-2004.

Political interests: Northern Ireland, education, constitutional and electoral affairs; All countries of the United Kingdom.

Other: President, Northern Ireland Schools Debating Competition 2001-; Co-Chairman, London Friends of the Belfast Buildings Preservation Trust 2006-; Vice-President, Council of British International Schools 2011-; President: Independent Schools Association 2013-, Council for Independent Education 2013-. OBE 1988; *Clubs:* Carlton Club.

Publications: Joint-editor, Lord Carlingford's Journal (1971); Co-author, The Governing Passion: Cabinet Government and Party Politics in Britain 1885-86 (1974); Editor: The Ashbourne Papers 1869-1913 (1974), The Conservative Party's Campaign Guides, Seven Volumes (1987-2005), The Conservative Party: Seven Historical Studies (1997), The Conservative Research Department

1929-2004 (2004); Co-author, The Carlton Club 1832-2007 (2007); Tory Heroine: Dorothy Brant and the Rise of Conservative Women (2008); A Party of Change: A Brief History of the Conservatives (2008); Contributor, Between the Thin Blue Lines (2008); Editor and co-author, Tory Policy Making: The Conservative Research Department 1929-2009 (2009); A Gift from the Churchills: The Primrose League 1883-2004 (2010); Contributor, Enoch at 100: A Re-evaluation of Enoch Powell (2012).

Recreations: Writing letters to the press (and getting them published), collecting royal and political memorabilia, book reviewing.

The Lord Lexden OBE, House of Lords, London SW1A 0PW
Tel: 020 7219 8216 *Email:* lexdena@parliament.uk
Website: www.alistairlexden.org.uk

LIDDELL OF COATDYKE, BARONESS

LABOUR

LIDDELL OF COATDYKE (Life Baroness), Helen Lawrie Liddell; cr 2010. Born 6 December 1950; Daughter of Hugh and Bridget Reilly; Married Dr Alistair Liddell 1972 (1 son 1 daughter).

Education: St Patrick's High School, Coatbridge; Strathclyde University (BA economics 1972); French.

Non-political career: Head, Economic Department, Scottish TUC 1971-76; Economics correspondent, BBC Scotland 1976-77; General secretary, Labour Party in Scotland 1977-88; Director, personnel and public affairs, Scottish Daily Record and Sunday Mail (1986) Ltd 1988-92; Chief executive, Business Venture Programme 1993-94; High Commissioner to Australia 2005-09. GMB; NUJ.

Political career: *House of Commons:* Contested Fife East October 1974 general election. MP (Labour) for Monklands East 30 June 1994 by-election to 1997, and for Airdrie and Shotts 1997-2005. Opposition Spokesperson on Scotland 1995-97; Economic Secretary, HM Treasury 1997-98; Minister of State: Scottish Office (Minister for Education) 1998-99, Department of the Environment, Transport and the Regions (Minister for Transport) 1999, Department of Trade and Industry (Minister for Energy and Competitiveness in Europe) 1999-2001; Secretary of State for Scotland 2001-03. Member, Labour Party Departmental Committee for the Treasury 1997-2001. *House of Lords:* Raised to the peerage as Baroness Liddell of Coatdyke, of Airdrie in Lanarkshire 2010. Member: Selection 2011, Joint Committee on the Draft Detention of Terrorist Suspects (Temporary Extension) Bills 2011, EU Sub-committee E: Justice, Institutions and Consumer Protection 2013-15, Partnerships (Prosecution) (Scotland) Bill 2013, EU Financial Affairs Sub-committee 2016-. *Councils and public bodies:* Commissioner, BBC Privacy Commission 2011; Member: Inquiry into the Mull of Kintyre Helicopter Accident 2010-11, Advisory Committee on Business Appointments.

Political interests: Media, foreign affairs, economic policy, trade and industry, small businesses, energy and climate change, defence and security; Australia, China, Europe, USA.

Other: Vice-chair, Rehab Scotland 1990-92; Chair, Independent Review into the future of the Scottish Symphony Orchestra and Orchestra of Scottish Opera 1993-94; Chair, UN5O: Scotland 1994; Associate member, BUPA 2010; Director, British-Australia Society 2011-; Cook Society 2011-; Trustee: Northcote Educational Trust, Arthur Philip Trust; St Andrew's Hospice Airdrie, Maggie's Centres. Honorary Doctor of Laws, Strathclyde University 2005. PC 1998.

Publications: Elite (1990).

Recreations: Cooking, hill-walking, music, writing.

Rt Hon the Baroness Liddell of Coatdyke, House of Lords, London SW1A 0PW
Tel: 020 7219 6960 *Email:* liddellh@parliament.uk

LIDDLE, LORD

LABOUR

LIDDLE (Life Baron), Roger John Liddle; cr 2010. Born 14 June 1947; Son of late John Thwaites Liddle, railway clerk, and late Elizabeth Liddle, née Temple; Married Caroline Thomson 1983 (1 son).

Education: Carlisle Grammar School; Queen's College, Oxford (BA modern history 1968, MA; MPhil management studies 1970).

Non-political career: Oxford School of Social and Administrative Studies 1970-74; Industrial relations officer, Electricity Council 1974-76; Special adviser to William Rodgers MP 1976-81: as Secretary of State for Transport 1976-79; Director, Public Policy Centre 1982-87; Managing director, Prima Europe Ltd 1987-97; Special adviser to Tony Blair MP as Prime Minister 1997-2004; European Commission: Member of cabinet of Peter Mandelson as Trade Commissioner

2004-06, Principal adviser to the President of the European Commission 2006-07; Chair, advisory board, New Industry New Jobs Panel, Department for Business, Innovation and Skills 2008-10. Member, GMB.

Political career: *House of Lords:* Raised to the peerage as Baron Liddle, of Carlisle in the County of Cumbria 2010. Opposition Whip 2011-13; Opposition Spokesperson for: Foreign and Commonwealth Office (Europe) 2012-14, Business, Innovation and Skills 2013-14. Member: European Union 2010, 2015-, EU Sub-committee G (Social Policies and Consumer Protection) 2011, EU Internal Market Sub-committee 2015-. *Other:* Member, National committee, Social Democratic Party 1981-86; Labour Campaign for Electoral Reform; Labour Movement for Europe. *Councils and public bodies:* Oxford City Council: Councillor 1971-76, Deputy Leader 1973-76; Councillor, Lambeth Borough Council 1982-86, 1994-95; Chair, Cumbria Vision 2007-10; Councillor, Cumbria County Council 2013-.

Political interests: Future of European Union, European social democracy, industrial economic questions, regional policy, future of welfare state, universities; France, Germany, Italy, Sweden, USA.

Other: Member: Fabian Society, Progress; Policy Network: Vice-chair 2007-09, Chair 2009-. Pro-Chancellor, Lancaster University 2013-; *Clubs:* Reform Club.

Publications: Co-author (with Peter Mandelson), The Blair Revolution (1996); Author, The New Case for Europe (2005); Co-author: Global Europe, Social Europe (2006), Beyond New Labour (2009).

Recreations: Tennis, opera, reading history and politics, walking.

The Lord Liddle, House of Lords, London SW1A 0PW
Tel: 020 7219 2132 *Email:* liddler@parliament.uk
Policy Network, 11 Tufton Street, London SW1P 3QB *Tel:* 020 7340 2205

LINCOLN, LORD BISHOP OF

NON-AFFILIATED

LINCOLN (72nd Bishop of), Christopher Lowson. Born 3 February 1953; Married Susan Osborne 1976 (1 son 1 daughter).

Education: Newcastle Cathedral School; Consett Grammar School; Newcastle Cathedral School; Consett Grammar School; King's College London.

Non-political career: Ordained 1978; Assistant Curate, Richmond, Surrey 1977-82; Holy Trinity, Eltham: Priest-in-charge 1982-83, Vicar 1983-91; Chaplain: Avery Hill College 1982-85, Thames Polytechnic 1985-91; Vicar of Petersfield and Rector of Buriton 1991-99; Rural Dean of Petersfield 1995-99; Archdeacon of Portsmouth/Archdeacon of Portsdown 1999-2006; Director, Ministry Division, Archbishops' Council and Priest Vicar, Westminster Abbey 2006-11; Bishop of Lincoln 2011-. Ordained 1978; Assistant Curate, Richmond, Surrey 1977-82; Holy Trinity, Eltham: Priest-in-charge 1982-83, Vicar 1983-91; Chaplain: Avery Hill College 1982-85, Thames Polytechnic 1985-91; Vicar of Petersfield and Rector of Buriton 1991-99; Rural Dean of Petersfield 1995-99; Archdeacon of Portsmouth/Archdeacon of Portsdown 1999-2006; Director, Ministry Division, Archbishops' Council and Priest Vicar, Westminster Abbey 2006-11; Bishop of Lincoln 2011-.

Political career: *House of Lords:* Entered House of Lords 2017.

Rt Rev the Lord Bishop of Lincoln, House of Lords, London SW1A 0PW
Tel: 020 7219 3000
The Old Palace, Minster Yard, Lincoln LN2 1PU
Tel: 01522 504090 *Email:* bishop.lincoln@lincoln.anglican.org
Website: www.lincoln.anglican.org

LINDSAY, EARL OF

CONSERVATIVE

LINDSAY (16th Earl of, S), James Randolph Lindesay-Bethune; cr. 1633; Viscount Garnock (S) 1703; Lord Lindsay of the Byres (S) 1445; Lord Parbroath (S) 1633; Lord Kilbirnie, Kingsburn and Drumry (S) 1703. Born 19 November 1955; Son of 15th Earl and Hon. Mary-Clare Douglas Scott Montagu, daughter of 2nd Baron Montagu of Beaulieu, KCIE, CSI, DL; Married Diana Mary Chamberlayne-Macdonald 1982 (2 sons 3 daughters inc. twins).

Education: Eton College; Edinburgh University (MA economic history 1978); University of California, Davis (land use).

Non-political career: Chair, Assured British Meat Ltd 1997-2001; Non-executive director, UA Group plc 1998-2005; Chair: Scottish Quality Salmon 1999-2006, UA Properties Ltd 1999-2000, UA Forestry Ltd 1999-2000, Genesis Quality Assurance Ltd 2001-02, Elmwood College Board of Management 2001-09; Managing director, Marine Stewardship Council International 2001-04; Non-executive director, Mining (Scotland) Ltd/Scottish Resources Group Ltd 2001-13; British Polythene Industries plc: Non-executive director 2006-15, Adviser; Associate director, National

Non-Food Crops Centre 2007-12; Chair: Scottish Agricultural College Ltd/SRUC-Scotland's Rural College 2007-15, British Polythene Pension Scheme 2009-; Non-executive director, Hargreaves Energy Projects 2015-17; Adviser, Hargreaves (UK) Services 2015-17; Non-executive Director, Brockwell Energy Ltd 2017-.

Political career: *House of Lords:* First entered House of Lords 1989; Government Whip 1995; Parliamentary Under-Secretary of State, Scottish Office 1995-97; Opposition Spokesperson for Green Issues June-October 1997; Elected hereditary peer 1999-. Member: European Communities Sub-committee C (Environment and Social Affairs) 1993-95, 1997-98, Sustainable Development 1994-95, Science and Technology Sub-committee II (Energy Efficiency) 2004-, Partnerships (Prosecution) (Scotland) Bill 2013, EU Financial Affairs Sub-committee 2015-. *Councils and public bodies:* Board member, Cairngorms Partnership 1998-2003; Member: Secretary of State's Advisory Group on Sustainable Development 1998-99, UK Round Table on Sustainable Development 1998-99; Chair: United Kingdom Accreditation Service 2002-; Better Regulation Commission: Member 2006-08, Deputy chair 2007-08; DL, Fife 2007-; Member: Advisory board, Business and a Sustainable Environment 2007-15, Commission on Scottish Devolution 2008-09, Risk and Regulation Advisory Council 2008-10, Better Regulation Strategy Group 2013-15.

Political interests: Environment, agriculture, rural affairs, energy, food industry, Scotland, risk regulation, accreditation, standards.

Other: Inter-Parliamentary Union Committee on Environment: Member 1993-95, Vice-chair 1994-95; Chair, Landscape Foundation 1992-95; International Tree Foundation: President 1995-2005, Vice-President 2005-; Vice-President, Royal Smithfield Club 1998-; Director, West Highland Rail Heritage Trust Ltd 1998-2006; RSPB: Chair, Scotland 1998-2003, UK vice-president 2004-; Royal Scottish Geographical Society: President 2005-12, Vice-President 2012-; President, Royal Highland Agriculture Society of Scotland 2005-06; Chair, Moorland Forum 2007-; Director and trustee, Leven Valley Development Trust 2009-; President, National Trust (Scotland) 2012-; Hon. Fellow, Institute of Wastes Management 1998-; Fellow, Royal Agricultural Societies 2003. Freedom, City of London 2015. Honorary doctorate, Glasgow University 2012. Green Ribbon Political Award 1995; *Clubs:* New Club (Edinburgh).

The Earl of Lindsay, House of Lords, London SW1A 0PW
Tel: 020 7219 5353 *Fax:* 020 7219 5979 *Email:* lindsayj@parliament.uk
Lahill, Upper Largo, Fife KY8 6JE

LINGFIELD, LORD

CONSERVATIVE

LINGFIELD (Life Baron), Robert George Alexander Balchin; cr 2010. Born 31 July 1942; Son of late Leonard George and Elizabeth Balchin; Married Jennifer Kinlay 1970 (twin sons, 1 deceased).

Education: Bec School; London University; Hull University.

Non-political career: Honorary Colonel, Humberside & South Yorkshire ACF 2004-12. Teacher 1964-69; Researcher, Institute of Education, Hull University 1969-71; Chairman, HSW Ltd 1972-2000; St John Ambulance: Assistant director-general 1982-84, Director-general 1984-90, Member, Chapter-General, Order of St John 1984-99; Joint founder and treasurer, Catch 'em Young Project Trust 1984-98; Chairman: Grant-Maintained Schools Foundation 1989-99, Pardoe-Blacker (Publishing) Ltd 1989-99, CEFM Ltd 1994-; Imperial Society of Knights Bachelor: Council Member 1995-, Knight Registrar 1998-2006, Knight Principal and Chairman of Knight Bachelors' Council 2006-12, Knight President 2012-; President: English Schools Orchestra 1998-, League of Mercy 1999-; Chairman: Blacker-Publishing Ltd 2003-09, Education Commission 2003-10, Government Review, Professionalism in Further Education 2012; Chartered Institution for Further Education 2014-.

Political career: *House of Lords:* Raised to the peerage as Baron Lingfield, of Lingfield in the County of Surrey 2010. Member, EU Sub-committee F (Home Affairs, Health and Education) 2012-13. *Councils and public bodies:* Councillor, Surrey County Council 1981-85; Member, Funding Agency for Schools 1994-97; DL, Greater London 2001.

Political interests: Education, stroke rehabilitation; UK.

Other: Chairman, Balchin Family Society 1993-; Member of Court, Leeds University 1995-2000; Goldsmith' College, London: Council member 1997-2005, Deputy chair of council 1999-2005; Deputy patron, National Association for Gifted Children 1999-2014; Patron, Gateway Training Centre for Homeless 1999-2010; Chairman: ARNI Institute 2008-, Maritime Heritage Foundation 2011-; CVQO 2012-; FCP 1971; Honorary FHS 1987; Honorary FCP 1987; Honorary FCGI 1998. Goldsmiths' Company 1980; Broderers' Company 2004-12; Apothecaries' Society 2014. Freedom, City of London 1980. Pro-chancellor, Brunel University 2008-13. DLitt, Hull University; EdD, Brunel University. KStJ 1984; SMOM 1987; Kt 1993; GCFO 2014; GCEO 2014; Grand Officer of Merit SMOM 2017; *Clubs:* Athenæum Club.

Publications: Emergency Aid in Schools (1984); Choosing a State School (1989); Many articles on politics and education.

Recreations: Restoration of ancient house.

The Lord Lingfield DL, House of Lords, London SW1A 0PW
Tel: 020 7219 5353

LABOUR

LIPSEY, LORD

LIPSEY (Life Baron), David Lawrence Lipsey; cr. 1999. Born 21 April 1948; Son of late Lawrence Lipsey and Penelope Lipsey; Married Margaret Robson 1982 (1 daughter 2 stepsons).

Education: Bryanston School, Dorset; Magdalen College, Oxford (BA philosophy, politics and economics 1970).

Non-political career: Research assistant, GMWU 1970-72; Political adviser to Anthony Crosland (in Opposition, DoE and FCO) 1972-77; Adviser to 10 Downing Street 1977-79; *New Society*: Journalist 1979-80, Editor 1986-88; Journalist, then economics editor, *Sunday Times* 1980-86; Founder/deputy editor, *Sunday Correspondent* 1988-90; Associate (acting deputy) editor, *The Times* 1990-92; Journalist, political editor, public policy editor, *The Economist* 1992-99; Visiting professor, Ulster University 1993-98; Public interest director, Personal Investment Authority 1994-2000; Chairman: Impower 2001-03, Shadow Racing Trust 2002-07, British Greyhound Racing Board 2004-08; Non-executive director, LWT/ITV London 2004-06; Visiting professor, Salford University 2008-12; Visiting fellow, Centre for European Studies, Havard University, USA 2011.

Political career: *House of Lords:* Raised to the peerage as Baron Lipsey, of Tooting Bec in the London Borough of Wandsworth 1999. Member, Speakers' Working Group on All-Party Groups 2011-12. Member: Economic Affairs 2009-14, Sub-committee on Economic Affairs Finance Bill 2012-13, Information 2013-15, Long-Term Sustainability of the NHS 2016-17; Chair, Political Polling and Digital Media 2017-. *Other:* Secretary, Streatham Labour Party 1970-72. *Councils and public bodies:* Member: Jenkins Commission on Electoral Reform 1998, Royal Commission on Long-term Care of the Elderly 1998-99, Davies Panel on BBC Licence Fee 1999; Council member, Advertising Standards Authority 1999-2005; Chair, Financial Services' Consumers Panel 2008.

Political interests: Elderly people, electoral reform, psephology, machinery of government, greyhound welfare, racing, music.

Other: Chair: Fabian Society 1982-83, Make Votes Count 1999-2006, Social Market Foundation 2000-10; Member, advisory council, Constitution Unit; President, British Harness Racing Club 2015; Patron, Glasbury Arts Festival; Trustee, Mid Wales Music Trust; Chair, Straight Statistics 2008-11; President, Society of Later Life Advisers 2009-; Chair, Trinity Laban Conservatoire of Music and Dance 2012-17; Sidney Nolan Trust: Chair, President 2017-.

Publications: Labour and Land (1972); Editor, The Socialist Agenda (1981); The Name of the Rose (1992); The Secret Treasury (2000); In the Corridors of Power (autobiography) (Biteback, 2012); Counter Coup (2014).

Recreations: Music, golf, harness, point-to-point and greyhound racing, National Trust, opera, walking, cooking.

The Lord Lipsey, House of Lords, London SW1A 0PW
Tel: 020 7219 5353

LABOUR

LISTER OF BURTERSETT, BARONESS

LISTER OF BURTERSETT (Life Baroness), Margot Ruth Aline Lister; cr 2011. Born 3 May 1949; Daughter of Dr Werner Bernard and Daphne Lister.

Education: Moreton Hall, Shropshire; Essex University (BA sociology 1970); Sussex University (MA multi-racial studies 1971); Rusty French and German.

Non-political career: Child Poverty Action Group: Legal research officer 1971-75, Assistant director 1975-77, Deputy director 1977-79, Director 1979-87; Professor of Applied Social Studies, Bradford University 1987-93; Loughborough University: Professor of Social Policy 1994-2010, Emeritus Professor of Social Policy 2010-; Donald Dewar Visiting Professor of Social Justice, Glasgow University 2005-06. University and College Union (when employed).

Political career: *House of Lords:* Raised to the peerage as Baroness Lister of Burtersett, of Nottingham in the County of Nottinghamshire 2011. Member: Joint Committee on Human Rights 2012-15, Citizenship and Civic Engagement 2017-. Vice-chair, PLP Departmental Group for Women 2015-.

Political interests: Poverty, social security, welfare reform, gender, children, refugees and asylum seekers; Australia, Japan, Nordic countries, USA.

House of Lords
Peers' Biographies

Other: Vice-chair, NVCO 1991-93; Founding Academician, Academy of Social Sciences 1999; Member: Opsahl Commission 1992-93, Commission for Social Justice 1992-94, Commission on Poverty, Participation and Power 1999-2000; Trustee, Community Development Foundation (Government appointment) 2000-10; Member: Fabian Commission on Life Chances and Child Poverty 2004-06, National Equality Panel (Government appointment) 2009-10; Fellow, British Academy 2009; Honorary President, Child Poverty Action Group 2010-; Board Member, Smith Institute; Chair, Management Committee, Compass 2011-; Patron, Just Fair 2012-; Honorary President, Social Policy Association 2016-. Hon LLD, Manchester University 1987; Hon DLitt, Glasgow Caledonian University 2011; Hon LLD, Brighton University 2012; DUniv, Essex University 2012; Hon DSc, Lincoln University; Hon LLD, Bath University 2014. Lifetime Achievement Award, Social Policy Association. CBE 1999.

Publications: Supplementary Benefit Rights (1974); Welfare Benefits (1981); The Exclusive Society (1990); Women's Economic Dependency and Social Security (1992); Citizenship: feminist perspectives (1997, 2003); Poverty (2004); Co-author, Gendering Citizenship in Western Europe (2007); Co-editor, Why Money Matters (2008); Understanding Theories and Concepts in Social Policy (2010).

Recreations: Walking, watching tennis, tai chi, music, films, theatre, mindfulness.

The Baroness Lister of Burtersett CBE, House of Lords, London SW1A 0PW
Tel: 020 7219 8984 *Email:* listerr@parliament.uk
Website: www.lboro.ac.uk/departments/socialsciences/staff/academicandresearch/lister-ruth.html

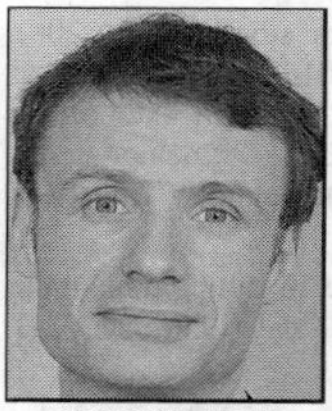

CROSSBENCH

LISTOWEL, EARL OF

LISTOWEL (6th Earl of, I), Francis Michael Hare; cr. 1822; 6th Viscount Ennismore and Listowel (I) 1816; 6th Baron Ennismore (I) 1800; 4th Baron Hare (UK) 1869. Born 28 June 1964; Son of 5th Earl.

Education: Westminster School; Queen Mary and Westfield College, London (BA English literature 1992).

Political career: *House of Lords:* First entered House of Lords 1997. Sits as Baron Hare; Elected hereditary peer 1999-. Member: House of Lords Offices Library and Computers Sub-committee 2000-02, European Union Sub-committee F (Home Affairs) 2003-07.

Political interests: Young under-privileged; Angola.

Other: Trustee, Michael Sieff Foundation; Patron: Voice, Who Cares? Trust, Caspari Foundation; Anna Freud Centre, Beanstalk. Hon. doctorate, University of East London; *Clubs:* Reform Club.

Recreations: Singing, music, art.

The Earl of Listowel, House of Lords, London SW1A 0PW
Tel: 020 7219 2247 *Email:* listowelf@parliament.uk
Email: francis.listowel@googlemail.com

CROSSBENCH

LISVANE, LORD

LISVANE (Life Baron), Robert James Rogers; cr 2014. Born 5 February 1950; Son of late Francis Barry Day Rogers and late Jeanne Turner Prichard Rogers; Married Revd Constance Jane Perkins 1981 (2 daughters).

Education: Tonbridge School (Scholar); Lincoln College, Oxford (Scholar and Judd exhibitioner, BA Anglo-Saxon, Norse and Celtic languages 1971, MA 1977; Rhodes Research Scholar 1971); French.

Non-political career: Ministry of Defence 1971; House of Commons 1972-2014: Assistant Clerk 1972, Various Procedural and Select Committee posts, Clerk of Select Committee on Defence 1983-89, Clerk of Private Members' Bills 1989-92, Clerk of the European Legislation Committee 1993-97, Principal Clerk 1997, Principal Clerk of Select Committees 1999-2001, Secretary to the House of Commons Commission 2001-03, Clerk of the Journals 2003-04, Principal Clerk of the Table Office 2004-06, Clerk of Legislation 2006-09, Clerk Assistant 2009-11, Clerk of the House and Chief Executive 2011-14.

Political career: *House of Lords:* Raised to the peerage as Baron Lisvane, of Blakemere in the County of Herefordshire and of Lisvane in the City and County of Cardiff 2014. Member, Parliamentary and Political Service Honours Committee 2014-. Member: Delegated Powers and Regulatory Reform 2015-, Ecclesiastical Committee 2015-. *Councils and public bodies:* Independent Chair, Standards Committee: Herefordshire Council 2002-09, Herefordshire and Worcestershire Fire and Rescue Authority 2002-09; West Mercia Police Authority: Member, Standards Committee 2002-09, Independent Chair, Selection Committee 2004-09; DL, Herefordshire 2015-; Independent Vice-President, Local Government Association 2016-; Chief Steward, City of Hereford 2016-.

Political interests: Constitution, Parliament and the judiciary, rural issues, heritage, the arts (especially music); Australia, France, Italy, Greece, Oman, New Zealand.

Other: Chair, Hereford Cathedral Perpetual Trust 2007-09; Vice-chair, Hereford Cathedral Fabric Committee 2016-; Honorary Fellow, Lincoln College, Oxford; Honorary Bencher, Middle Temple; Patron, Herefordshire Headway; Trustee: History of Parliament, Voces Cantabiles Music Foundation. Skinners' Company: Liveryman, Extra Member of the Court 2004-06; Renter Warden 2016; First Warden 2017. Freedom, City of London. *Spectator* Parliamentarian of the Year 2014. KCB 2013; *Clubs:* Travellers, Reform Club.

Publications: How Parliament Works (with Dr Rhodri Walters) (seventh edition 2015); Parliamentary Miscellanies: Order! Order! (2011); Who Goes Home? (2013).

Recreations: Music (church organist), cricket, sailing, shooting, natural history.

The Lord Lisvane KCB DL, House of Lords, London SW1A 0PW
Tel: 020 7219 5353 *Email:* lisvane@parliament.uk

LABOUR

LIVERMORE, LORD

LIVERMORE (Life Baron), Spencer Elliot Livermore; cr 2015. Born 12 June 1975; Married Seb Dance 2016 (MEP for London region).

Education: Beauchamps Comprehensive School, Wickford; London School of Economics (BSc economics 1996).

Non-political career: Labour Party: Economic Secretariat 1996-98, Senior adviser 1997, 2001 and 2005 general election campaigns, General election campaign director 2014-15; HM Treasury: Special adviser 1998-2003, Chief strategy adviser to Gordon Brown MP as Chancellor of the Exchequer 2003-07; Director of political strategy, Prime Minister's Office 2007-08; Senior strategist, Saatchi & Saatchi 2008-09; Head of strategy, Blue Rubicon 2009-14; Founder, Thirty Six Strategy 2012-14.

Political career: *House of Lords:* Raised to the peerage as Baron Livermore, of Rotherhithe in the London Borough of Southwark 2015. Member, Economic Affairs 2016-. *Other:* Patron, LGBT Labour.

Political interests: Economy and finance, business, industry and consumers, social mobility, education, employment and training, parliament, government and politics, election campaigns; Australia, China, European Union, India, Israel, United Kingdom, USA.

The Lord Livermore, House of Lords, London SW1A 0PW
Tel: 020 7219 3000 *Twitter:* @SpenceLivermore

CONSERVATIVE

LIVERPOOL, EARL OF

LIVERPOOL (5th Earl of, UK), Edward Peter Bertram Savile Foljambe; cr. 1905; Viscount Hawkesbury; 5th Baron Hawkesbury (UK) 1893. Born 14 November 1944; Son of Captain Peter George William Savile Foljambe; Married Lady Juliana Noel 1970 (divorced 1994) (2 sons); married Comtesse Marie-Ange de Pierredon 1995 (divorced 2001); married Georgina Lederman 2002.

Education: Shrewsbury School; Perugia University, Italy (Italian and Italian art 1963).

Non-political career: Melbourns Brewery Ltd, Stamford, Lincolnshire: Managing director 1971-76, Joint chair and managing director 1977-87; Director: Hilstone Developments Ltd 1986-91, Hart Hambleton plc 1986-92, Rutland Properties Ltd 1987-, J W Cameron & Co Ltd 1987-91; Chair and managing director, Maxador Ltd 1987-97; Chair, Rutland Management Ltd 1997-.

Political career: *House of Lords:* First entered House of Lords 1969; Elected hereditary peer 1999-. Member, EU Sub-committee B (Internal Market, Infrastructure and Employment) 2012-15.

Political interests: Environment, renewables, green energy, transport, IT, aviation.

Other: *Clubs:* Turf, Pratt's, Air Squadron Club.

Recreations: Flying, golf, shooting.

The Earl of Liverpool, House of Lords, London SW1A 0PW
Tel: 020 7219 5406 *Fax:* 020 7219 0318 *Email:* liverpoole@parliament.uk

CONSERVATIVE

LIVINGSTON OF PARKHEAD, LORD

LIVINGSTON OF PARKHEAD (Life Baron), Ian Paul Livingston; cr 2013. Born 28 July 1964; Married Debbie (1 son 1 daughter).

Education: Manchester University (BA economics).

Non-political career: Arthur Andersen 1984-87; Bank of America International 1987-88; 3i Group plc 1988-91; Senior management roles 1991-96; Chief finance officer, Dixons Group plc 1996-2002; BT Group plc: Chief finance director 2002-05, Chief executive officer, BT Retail 2005-08, Chief executive officer 2008-13; Dixons Carphone plc: Deputy Chair 2015-17, Chair 2017-; Chair, Man Group plc 2016-.

Political career: *House of Lords:* Raised to the peerage as Baron Livingston of Parkhead, of Parkhead in the City of Glasgow 2013. Minister of State for Trade and Investment and Government Spokesperson, Department for Business, Innovation and Skills and Foreign and Commonwealth Office 2013-15.

Other: Associate, Institute of Chartered Accountants; Non-executive director: Freeserve plc 1999-2001, Hilton Group plc 2003-06, Celtic Football Club 2007-17, Belmond Ltd 2015-, Jewish Care 2015-; Advisory board member, Livingbridge 2016-; Member, ICAEW (Institute of Chartered Accountants in England and Wales).

Recreations: Football, theatre.

The Lord Livingston of Parkhead, House of Lords, London SW1A 0PW
Tel: 020 7219 5353 *Email:* livingstoni@parliament.uk *Twitter:* @Lord_Livingston

CONSERVATIVE

LLEWELLYN OF STEEP, LORD

LLEWELLYN OF STEEP (Life Baron), Edward David Gerard Llewellyn; cr 2016. Born 23 September 1965; Married Anne (3 children).

Education: Eton College; New College, Oxford (BA modern languages).

Non-political career: Conservative Research Department 1988-92: Private Secretary to Margaret Thatcher (on secondment) 1990-91; Personal Adviser to Chris Patten as Governor of Hong Kong 1992-97; Office of UN High Representative, Sarajevo 1997-99; Cabinet of Chris Patten as EU Commissioner for External Relations 1999-2002; Chief of Staff to Lord Ashdown of Norton-sub-Hamdon as UN High Representative, Sarajevo 2002-05; Chief of Staff to David Cameron: as Leader of the Opposition 2005-10, as Prime Minister 2010-16; Ambassador to France 2016-.

Political career: *House of Lords:* Raised to the peerage as Baron Llewellyn of Steep, of Steep in the County of Hampshire 2016. Leave of absence November 2016-.

Other: MBE 1997; OBE 2006; PC 2015.

Rt Hon the Lord Llewellyn of Steep OBE, House of Lords, London SW1A 0PW
Tel: 020 7219 3000 *Twitter:* @EdLlewellynFCO

CONSERVATIVE

LLOYD-WEBBER, LORD

LLOYD-WEBBER (Life Baron), Andrew Lloyd Webber; cr. 1997. Born 22 March 1948; Son of late William Southcombe Lloyd Webber, CBE, DMus, FRCM, FRCO, and late Jean Hermione Johnstone; Married Sarah Tudor 1971 (divorced 1983) (1 son 1 daughter); married Sarah Brightman 1984 (divorced 1990); married Madeleine Gurdon 1991 (2 sons 1 daughter).

Education: Westminster School; Royal College of Music.

Non-political career: Composer: Requiem, a setting of the Latin Requiem Mass 1985, Variations (based on A minor Caprice No 24 by Paganini) 1977, symphonic version 1986, Joseph and the Amazing Technicolour Dreamcoat (with lyrics by Timothy Rice) 1968, rev 1973, 1991, 2007, Jesus Christ Superstar (with lyrics by Timothy Rice) 1970, rev 1996, Gumshoe (film score) 1971, The Odessa File (film score) 1974, Jeeves (with lyrics by Alan Ayckbourn) 1975, Evita (with lyrics by Timothy Rice) 1976, (stage version 1978, 2006), (film score additional music 1996), Tell Me On a Sunday (with lyrics by Don Black) 1980, 2003, Cats (based on poems by T. S. Eliot) 1981, Song and Dance (with lyrics by Don Black) 1982, Starlight Express (with lyrics by Richard Stillgoe) 1984, Requiem Mass 1985, The Phantom of the Opera (with lyrics by Charles Hart and Richard Stilgoe) 1986, Aspects of Love (with lyrics by Don Black and Charles Hart) 1989, Sunset Boulevard (with lyrics by Don Black and Christopher Hampton) 1993, By Jeeves (with lyrics by Alan Ayckbourn) 1996, Whistle Down The Wind (with lyrics by Jim Steinman) 1996, The Beautiful Game (with lyrics by Ben Elton) 2000, The Woman in White 2004, Phantom Vegas 2006, Love Never Dies 2009, Stephen Ward 2013; Producer: Joseph and the Amazing Technicolor Dreamcoat 1973, 1974, 1978, 1980, 1991, Jeeves Takes Charge 1975, Cats 1981, Song and Dance 1982,

Daisy Pulls it Off 1983, 2002, The Hired Man 1984, Starlight Express 1984, On Your Toes 1984, The Phantom of the Opera 1986, Café Puccini 1986, The Resistable Rise of Arturo Ui 1987, Lend Me a Tenor 1988, Aspects of Love 1989, Shirley Valentine (Broadway) 1989, La Bete 1992, Sunset Boulevard 1993, By Jeeves 1996, Jesus Christ Superstar 1996, 1998, Whistle Down the Wind 1996, 1998, The Beautiful Game 2000, Bombay Dreams 2002, The Phantom of the Opera (film) 2004, The Sound of Music 2006, Love Never Dies 2009, The Wizard of Oz 2011.

Political career: *House of Lords:* Raised to the peerage as Baron Lloyd-Webber, of Sydmonton in the County of Hampshire 1997.

Political interests: Art, architecture.

Other: FRCM 1988; Andrew Lloyd Webber Foundation. Hon DMus, Royal College of Music 2014. Star on the Hollywood Walk of Fame 1993; American Society of Composers, Authors and Publishers Triple Play Award 'First recipient'; Seven Tony Awards; Five Drama Desk Awards; Three Grammy Awards; Seven Laurence Olivier Awards; Praemium Imperiale Award for Music 1995; Richard Rodger's Award for contributions to excellence in Musical Theatre 1996; Oscar and Golden Globe for Best Original Song *You Must Love Me* from Evita the movie; London Critics' Circle Award for Best Musical *The Beautiful Game* 2000; Two International Emmys; Kennedy Center Honor 2006; BASCA Fellowship 2012. Kt 1992.

Publications: Evita (with Tim Rice) (1978); Cats the book of the musical (1981); Joseph and the Amazing Technicolor Dreamcoat (with Tim Rice) (1982); The Complete Phantom of the Opera (1987); The Complete Aspects of Love (1989); Sunset Boulevard: From Movie to Musical (1993); Aspects of Andrew Lloyd Webber, The Essential Songbook.

Recreations: Architecture, art, food and wine.

The Lord Lloyd-Webber, House of Lords, London SW1A 0PW
Tel: 020 7219 5353
Website: www.andrewlloydwebber.com *Twitter:* @OfficialALW

LOOMBA, LORD

NON-AFFILIATED

LOOMBA (Life Baron), Rajinder Paul Loomba; cr 2011. Born 13 November 1943; Son of late Shri Jagiri Lal Loomba and late Shrimati Pushpa Wati Loomba; Married Veena (2 daughters 1 son).

Education: D.A.V. College, Jalandhar, India; State University of Iowa, USA (1962); Hindi, Punjabi.

Non-political career: Founder and chairman: Rinku Group 1980-, The Loomba Group of Companies 1980-, The Loomba Foundation 1997-, India First Ltd 1999-.

Political career: *House of Lords:* Raised to the peerage as Baron Loomba, of Moor Park in the County of Hertfordshire 2011. *Other:* Left Liberal Democrats December 2016; now sits as Non-affiliated.

Political interests: Humanitarian causes, raise awareness of the plight of widows around the world, international development aid projects; South Asia, Bangladesh, Gabon, India, Kenya, Malawi, Nepal, Rwanda, South Africa, Sri Lanka, Uganda, UK, USA.

Other: Vice-patron, Gates 1998-; Member: Rotary Club of London 2001-, Royal Institute of International Affairs 2002-09; Patron, Children in Need, India 2002-12; Founding patron, World Punjabi Organisation 2002-; London First: Board member 2000-04, Member, President's Council 2004-06; Trustee, Maharajah Ranjit Singh Trust, India 2004-; Vice-president, Safer London Foundation 2006-12; Vice-president, Barnardo's 2005-; Chairman, Friends of the Three Faiths Forum 2007-; Member, Board of Governors, University of East London 2008-12; Member, Board of Development Oxfam 2008-11; Ambassador, Global Partnership Forum 2011-; Fellow, Royal Society of Arts; Director, V2R Investments Ltd; Honorary Fellowship, Northampton University 2014; Oxfam, Barnardo's, YBI, Virgin Unite. Freedom, City of London 2000. International Excellence Award 1991; Hind Rattan Award 1991; Asian of the Year Award 1997; Pride of India Gold Medal 1998; Highly Commended New Initiative, Beacon Prize 2004; Priyadarshni Academy Global Award 2006; Charity of the Year, The Asian Who's Who awards 2006. CBE 2008. Moor Park Golf Club.

Publications: Invisible Forgotten Sufferers: The Plight of Widows Around the World.

Recreations: Walking, reading, cooking.

The Lord Loomba CBE, House of Lords, London SW1A 0PW
Tel: 020 7219 3582 *Email:* loombar@parliament.uk
Loomba House, 622 Western Avenue, London W3 0TF *Tel:* 020 8102 0351
Email: raj@loomba.com *Website:* www.theloombafoundation.org

House of Lords Peers' Biographies

CONSERVATIVE

LOTHIAN, MARQUESS OF

LOTHIAN (13th Marquess of, S), Michael Andrew Foster Jude Kerr; cr 1701; 14th Earl of Lothian (S) 1606; 15th Earl of Ancram (S) 1633; Viscount of Briene (S) 1701; Lord Newbottle (S) 1591; Lord Jedburgh (S) 1622; Lord Kerr (S) 1633; 8th Baron Ker (UK) 1821; (Life) Baron Kerr of Monteviot 2010. Born 7 July 1945; Son of late 12th Marquess of Lothian, KCVO, DL; Married Lady Jane Fitzalan-Howard 1975, daughter of 16th Duke of Norfolk (2 daughters).

Education: Ampleforth College, Yorkshire; Christ Church, Oxford (BA history 1966, MA); Edinburgh University (LLB 1968); French.

Non-political career: Advocate, Scottish Bar 1970-79; QC (Scot) 1996.

Political career: *House of Commons:* Contested West Lothian 1970 general election. MP (Conservative) for Berwickshire and East Lothian February-October 1974. Contested Berwickshire and East Lothian October 1974 general election. MP for Edinburgh South 1979-87. Contested Edinburgh South 1987 general election. MP for Devizes 1992-2010. Parliamentary Under-Secretary of State, Scottish Office 1983-87; Northern Ireland Office: Parliamentary Under-Secretary of State 1993-94, Minister of State 1994-97; Member Shadow Cabinet 1997-2005: Frontbench Spokesperson for Constitutional Affairs, with overall responsibility for Scottish and Welsh issues 1997-98, Deputy Leader of the Opposition 2001-05; Shadow Secretary of State for: Foreign and Commonwealth Affairs 2001-05, International Affairs 2003-05, Defence 2005; Member, Intelligence and Security Committee 2006-10. Member: Energy 1980-83, Public Accounts 1992-93. Chair: Conservative Parliamentary Constitutional Committee 1992-93, Conservative Party Committee for Constitutional Affairs, Scotland and Wales 1997-98, Conservative Defence/Foreign Affairs Policy Committee 2001-05. *House of Lords:* Created a life peer as Baron Kerr of Monteviot, of Monteviot in Roxburghshire 2010. Member, Intelligence and Security Committee 2010-. *Other:* Chair, Conservative Party in Scotland 1980-83; Conservative Party: Deputy Chair June-October 1998, Chair 1998-2001, Contested leadership election 2001, Member, Policy Board 2001-05; Vice-President, Conservatives for Britain 2015-16. *Councils and public bodies:* DL, Roxburgh, Ettrick and Lauderdale 1990-.

Political interests: Housing, defence, agriculture; Middle East.

Other: Member, Board of Scottish Homes 1988-90; Chairman, Global Strategy Forum 2006-. Freedom: City of Gibraltar 2010-, Devizes Town 2011-. PC 1996; Grand Prior, Order of Saint Lazarus of Jerusalem 2013-; *Clubs:* New (Edinburgh), Whites, Beefsteak, Pratt's Club.

Publications: Numerous pamphlets published by Global Strategy Forum.

Recreations: Skiing, photography, folksinging.

Most Hon the Marquess of Lothian PC QC DL, House of Lords, London SW1A 0PW
Tel: 020 7219 5353 *Email:* lothianm@parliament.uk

CROSSBENCH

LOW OF DALSTON, LORD

LOW OF DALSTON (Life Baron), Colin MacKenzie Low; cr 2006. Born 23 September 1942; Son of Arthur Low and Catherine Cameron Low, née Anderson; Married Jill Irene Coton 1969 (1 son 1 daughter).

Education: Worcester College for the Blind; Queen's College, Oxford (BA jursiprudence 1965, MA); Churchill College, Cambridge (Diploma criminology 1966).

Non-political career: Law lecturer, Leeds University 1968-84; Director, Disability Resource Team (initially within GLC) 1984-94; City University, London: Senior research fellow 1994-2000, Visiting professor 2001-. Member: Association of University Teachers 1968-84, 1994-, NALGO/Unison 1984-94.

Political career: *House of Lords:* Raised to the peerage as Baron Low of Dalston, of Dalston in the London Borough of Hackney 2006. Member: Procedure 2007-12, Liaison 2016-. *Councils and public bodies:* Member: Special Educational Needs Tribunal 1994-, National Disability Council 1996-2000, Disability Rights Commission 2000-02; Independent member, House of Lords Appointment Commission 2014-.

Political interests: Disability, higher education, arts, music, broadcasting, crime and delinquency; Australia, South Africa, USA.

Other: Life member and holder of various offices, National Federation of the Blind 1969-92; Member and various positions, Association of Blind and Partially Sighted Teachers and Students 1970-; SKILL (National Bureau for Students with Disabilities): Member 1974-2011, Vice-president 2003-11; Disability Alliance: Chair 1991-97, President 1997-2010; Royal National Institute of the Blind: Chair 2000-09, Vice-President 2009-; President: European Blind Union 2003-11, International Council for the Education of all Visually Impaired People 2010-. Hon. doctorate, Open University 2011. CBE 2000.

Publications: Co-author: An Equal Say in Our Own Affairs (National Federation of the Blind of the United Kingdom [NFBUK] 1971), Educational Provision for the Visually Handicapped (NFBUK and Association of Blind and Partially Sighted Teachers and Students, 1973); Plus numerous articles on provision for the disabled, particularly education.

Recreations: Music, wine.

The Lord Low of Dalston CBE, House of Lords, London SW1A 0PW
Tel: 020 7219 4119 *Email:* lowc@parliament.uk

CONSERVATIVE

LUCAS OF CRUDWELL AND DINGWALL, LORD

LUCAS OF CRUDWELL (11th Baron, E) cr. 1663, and DINGWALL (de facto 8th Lord, 14th but for the attainder) (S) cr. 1609; Ralph Matthew Palmer. Born 7 June 1951; Son of late Major Hon. Robert Jocelyn Palmer, MC, and Anne Rosemary, Baroness Lucas of Crudwell (10th in line); Married Clarissa Lockett 1978 (divorced 1995) (1 son 1 daughter); married Amanda Atha 1995 (died 2000); married Antonia Rubinstein 2001 (1 daughter).

Education: Eton College; Balliol College, Oxford (BA physics 1972).

Non-political career: Articles with various firms once part of Arthur Andersen 1972-76; With S G Warburg & Co Ltd 1976-88; Director of various companies, principally those associated with the Good Schools Guide.

Political career: *House of Lords:* First entered House of Lords 1991; Government Whip 1994-97; Government Spokesperson for: Education 1994-95, Social Security and the Welsh Office 1994-97, Agriculture, Fisheries and Food and Environment 1995-97; Opposition Spokesperson for: Agriculture, Fisheries and Food 1997, Constitutional Affairs, Scotland and Wales (Wales) 1997, Environment, Transport and the Regions (Environment) 1997, International Development 1997-98; Elected hereditary peer 1999-. Member: Animals in Scientific Procedures 2001-02, Sub-committee on House of Lords' Offices Library and Computers, Information -2003; Co-opted Member, European Union Sub-committee E (Law and Institutions) 2006-07; Member: Merits of Statutory Instruments 2007-11, Science and Technology Sub-committee I 2012-13, Digital Skills 2014-15, Intellectual Property (Unjustified Threats) Bill 2016.

Political interests: Education, liberty, planning, finance, electronic government, copyright.

Other: Safe Ground; Fellow, Institute of Chartered Accountants in England and Wales; FCA. Liveryman, Mercers' Company.

The Lord Lucas of Crudwell and Dingwall, House of Lords, London SW1A 0PW
Tel: 020 7219 4177 *Email:* lucasr@parliament.uk *Twitter:* @LordLucasCD

CROSSBENCH

LUCE, LORD

LUCE (Life Baron), Richard Napier Luce; cr. 2000. Born 14 October 1936; Son of late Sir William Luce; Married Rose Nicholson 1961 (2 sons).

Education: Wellington College, Berkshire; Christ's College, Cambridge (BA history 1960); Wadham College, Oxford (overseas civil service course 1961).

Non-political career: Army national service 1955-57. District officer, Kenya 1961-63; Marketing manager: Gallaher Ltd 1963-65, Spirella 1965-67; Director, National Innovations Centre 1967-71; Vice-president, Institute of Patentees and Inventors 1974-79; Non-executive director, European Advisory Board, Corning Glass International SA 1976-79; Chair, Courtenay Stewart International Limited 1975-79; Non-executive director: Booker Tate 1991-96, Meridian Broadcasting 1991-97; Vice-chancellor, Buckingham University 1992-97; Governor and Commander-in-chief, Gibraltar 1997-2000; Lord Chamberlain of the Queen's Household 2000-06; Permanent Lord in Waiting to HM the Queen 2007-.

Political career: *House of Commons:* Contested Hitchin 1970 general election. MP (Conservative) for West Sussex, Arundel and Shoreham 1971 by-election to February 1974, for Shoreham February 1974-92. PPS to Geoffrey Howe as Minister for Trade and Consumer Affairs 1972-74; Opposition Whip 1974-75; Parliamentary Under-Secretary of State for Foreign and Commonwealth Affairs 1979-81; Minister of State, Foreign and Commonwealth Office 1981-82 (resigned April 1982 on Falklands issue) 1983-85; Minister for Arts and Civil Service, Privy Council Office 1985-90. *House of Lords:* Raised to the peerage as Baron Luce, of Adur in the County of West Sussex 2000. Member, Works of Art 2014-16. *Councils and public bodies:* DL, West Sussex 1991-; High Steward, Westminster Abbey 2011-16; Chair, Crown Nominations Commission for the See of Canterbury 2012; Chancellor, University of Gibraltar 2015-.

Political interests: International affairs, consumer affairs, constitutional affairs, the arts, civil service, higher education; Africa, Far East, Middle East.

Other: Chair: Atlantic Council of UK 1991-96, Commonwealth Foundation 1992-96; President, Voluntary Art Network 1993-2013; Trustee, Geographers' A-Z Map Trust 1993-2016; Emeritus trustee, Royal Academy of Arts; Member, court of governors, Royal Shakespeare Company 1994-2002; Trustee, Royal Collection Trust 2000-06; President: Royal Overseas League 2002-, King George V Fund for Actors and Actresses 2006-11; Patron, Sir William Luce Memorial Fund; President, Commonwealth Youth Orchestra and Choir 2010-13. Vice-chancellor, Buckingham University 1992-97; Chancellor, Gibraltar University 2015-. Honorary Fellow, Christ's College, Cambridge 2006; Honorary degree, Buckingham University 1998. PC 1986; Kt 1991; GCVO 2000; KG 2008; *Clubs:* RAC, Royal Overseas League Club.

Publications: Memoir, Ringing the Changes (Michael Russell, 2007).

Recreations: Walking, reading, piano, painting, swimming.

Rt Hon the Lord Luce KG GCVO DL, House of Lords, London SW1A 0PW
Tel: 020 7219 6147

LIBERAL DEMOCRAT

LUDFORD, BARONESS

Liberal Democrat Lords Spokesperson for Exiting the European Union

LUDFORD (Life Baroness), Sarah Ann Ludford; cr. 1997. Born 14 March 1951; Daughter of Joseph Campbell Ludford and Valerie Kathleen, née Skinner; Married Stephen Hitchins 1982.

Education: Portsmouth High School for Girls; London School of Economics (BSc Econ international history 1972; MSc Econ European studies 1977); Inns of Court School of Law; French, German.

Non-political career: Civil servant, Department of the Environment 1972-73; Independent Broadcasting Authority 1973-75; Called to the Bar, Gray's Inn 1979; Official, European Commission, Brussels 1979-85; European adviser, Lloyd's of London 1985-87; American Express Europe 1987-90; European affairs consultant 1990-99.

Political career: *House of Commons:* Contested (Liberal Democrat) Islington North 1992 and Islington South and Finsbury 1997 general elections. *House of Lords:* Raised to the peerage as Baroness Ludford, of Clerkenwell in the London Borough of Islington 1997. As an MEP, disqualified from participation 2009-14; Liberal Democrat Spokesperson for: Europe 2015-16, Exiting the European Union 2016-. Member, EU Justice Sub-committee 2015-. *Other:* European Parliament: Contested Hampshire East and Wight 1984 and London Central 1989 and 1994 elections, MEP for London region 1999-2014 (as Sarah Ludford): ALDE spokesperson on justice and home affairs, Rapporteur on anti-racism 2000-09, Vice-chair, Anti-racism and Diversity Intergroup, Co-ordinator, Kurdish Network, Contested London region 2014 election. Liberal Democrat Party: Member, Federal Policy Committee, Vice-president, Liberal Democrat LGBT Group; Council member, European Liberal Democrat and Reform Party; Vice-president, Liberal Democrat Friends of Israel. *Councils and public bodies:* Councillor, London Borough of Islington 1991-99.

Political interests: Europe, justice and home affairs, foreign affairs; Balkans, Cyprus, Middle East, Turkey, USA.

Other: Council member, Justice; Federal Trust; Member: Royal Institute of International Affairs (Chatham House), European Movement; Parliamentary Fellow, Institute of Public Affairs, London School of Economics.

Recreations: Theatre, ballet.

The Baroness Ludford, House of Lords, London SW1A 0PW
Tel: 020 7219 5353 *Email:* ludfords@parliament.uk *Twitter:* @SarahLudford

CONSERVATIVE

LUPTON, LORD

LUPTON (Life Baron), James Roger Crompton Lupton; cr 2015. Born 15 June 1955; Married Beatrice 1983 (3 daughters 1 son).

Education: Sedbergh School; Lincoln College, Oxford (BA law 1976); French.

Non-political career: Lovell White & King 1977-79; Qualified Solicitor 1979; S G Warburg & Co 1979-80; Deputy Chair, Barings Bank 1980-95; Managing director, Greenhill & Co 1998-; Chair, Greenhill Europe 2011-17; Non-executive director, Lloyds Banking Group plc 2017-.

Political career: *House of Lords:* Raised to the peerage as Baron Lupton, of Lovington in the County of Hampshire 2015. Member, Charities 2016-17. *Other:* Co-treasurer, Conservative Party 2013-16. *Councils and public bodies:* Governor, Downe House School 1998-2006; Trustee, British Museum 2012-17; Chairman, Dulwich Picture Gallery 2006-11.

Political interests: Child welfare, business, the City, the arts, responsible capitalism; France, Spain, UK.

Other: Advisory Board, Grange Park Opera 1997-2011; Member, international advisory board, Global Leadership Foundation 2008-; Chair, Lovington Foundation 2014-; Member, Law Society; Lovington Foundation, Kids Company, Emmaus Hampshire, Dulwich Picture Gallery, British Museum. CBE 2012; *Clubs:* Brooks' Club, 5 Hertford Street, City Capital Club.

Recreations: Opera, skiing, shooting, collecting art, music and family.

The Lord Lupton CBE, House of Lords, London SW1A 0PW
Tel: 020 7219 3000 *Email:* luptonj@parliament.uk

CROSSBENCH

LYTTON, EARL

LYTTON (5th Earl, UK), John Peter Michael Scawen Lytton; cr. 1880; Viscount Knebworth; 17th Baron Wentworth (E) 1529; 6th Baron Lytton (UK) 1866; 6th Bt of Knebworth (UK) 1838. Born 7 June 1950; Son of 4th Earl of Lytton; Married Ursula Alexandra (2 sons 1 daughter).

Education: Downside School, Somerset; College of Estate Management; Reading University (BSc estate management 1972).

Non-political career: Valuation officer, Inland Revenue 1975-81; Associate partner, Permutt Brown & Co 1982-86; Cubitt and West 1986-87; Founder, John Lytton & Co Chartered Surveyors 1988- (John Lytton & Co Ltd 2009-).

Political career: *House of Lords:* First entered House of Lords 1985; Sponsor Party Wall etc. Bill 1996; Elected hereditary peer 2011-. Member: Information 2012-15, Built Environment 2015-16. *Councils and public bodies:* President, National Association of Local Councils 1999-.

Political interests: Communities and local government finance, countryside conservation, agriculture, rural economy, town and country planning, property taxation.

Other: Council member, Country Landowners' Association 1993-; Horsham Chamber of Commerce: Chair 1993-95, President 1995-; Chairman: Leasehold Enfranchisement Advisory Service 1994-97, Leasehold Advisory Service 1997-; President: Newsted Abbey Byron Society, Institute of Heraldic and Genealogical Studies, 1st Shipley Scout Group, West Sussex, Sussex Association of Local Councils 1997-; Member, Countryside Alliance; Trustee, Shipley Windmill Trust; Hon. Fellow, Association of Building Engineers; Member, Chartered Institute of Arbitrators; FRICS; Elected member, Institute of Revenues, Rating and Valuation 1990.

The Earl of Lytton, House of Lords, London SW1A 0PW
Tel: 020 7219 5353 *Email:* lyttonj@parliament.uk
Website: home.btconnect.com/lytton

LAB/CO-OP

MCAVOY, LORD

Opposition Deputy Chief Whip; Opposition Spokesperson for Northern Ireland and Scotland

McAVOY (Life Baron), Thomas McLaughlin McAvoy; cr 2010. Born 14 December 1943; Son of late Edward McAvoy, steelworker, and late Frances McLaughlin McAvoy; Married Eleanor Kerr 1968 (4 sons).

Education: St Columbkilles Secondary School.

Non-political career: Hoover plc, Cambuslang 1974-87. USDAW: AEU shop steward 1974-87; Member, Unite 1974-.

Political career: *House of Commons:* MP (Lab/Co-op) for Glasgow Rutherglen 1987-2005, for Rutherglen and Hamilton West 2005-10. Opposition Whip 1991-93, 1996-97; Government Whip 1997-2010; Deputy Chief Whip 2008-10. Member: Northern Ireland Affairs 1994-96, Finance and Services 1997-2009, Selection 2008-10, Administration 2009, Members' Allowances 2009-10. PLP Departmental Committee on Northern Ireland: Member 1996-2010, Co-vice-chair 1996-97. *House of Lords:* Raised to the peerage as Baron McAvoy, of Rutherglen in the County of Lanarkshire 2010. Opposition Whip 2011-15; Opposition Spokesperson for: Northern Ireland 2012-, Scotland 2012-; Opposition Deputy Chief Whip 2015-. Member: Administration and Works 2012-15, Partnerships (Prosecution) (Scotland) Bill 2013. *Other:* Member, Co-operative Party. *Councils and public bodies:* Chair Rutherglen Community Council 1980-82; Councillor Strathclyde Regional Council 1982-87.

Political interests: Social services; Ireland, USA.

Other: PC 2003. South Lanarkshire Council, Eastfield Lifestyles.

Rt Hon the Lord McAvoy, House of Lords, London SW1A 0PW
Tel: 020 7219 5009 *Email:* mcavoyto@parliament.uk

CONSERVATIVE

MCCOLL OF DULWICH, LORD

McCOLL OF DULWICH (Life Baron), Ian McColl; cr. 1989. Born 6 January 1933; Son of late Frederick and Winifred McColl; Married Dr Jean Lennox, née McNair 1960 (1 son 2 daughters) (died 2012); married Dr Evy Lise Kaarvang 2015.

Education: Hutchesons' Grammar School, Glasgow; St Paul's School, London (Foundation Scholarship classics); London University (Master of Surgery 1965; MB BS 1957).

Non-political career: Honorary Group Captain, RAF, Armed Forces Parliamentary Scheme. Consultant surgeon and Sub Dean, St Bartholomew's Hospital 1967-71; Research fellow, Harvard Medical School 1967; Professor and Director of Surgery, Guy's Hospital 1971-98; Professor of Surgery, London University 1971-98; Consultant Surgeon to the Army 1980-98; Chair, Government Working Party on Artificial Limbs and Wheelchair Service (The McColl Report) 1984-86; Vice-chair, Disablement Services Authority 1987-91; Chair, Department of Surgery of the United Medical Schools of Guy's and St Thomas' Hospital 1988-92. BMA 1957-.

Political career: *House of Lords:* Raised to the peerage as Baron McColl of Dulwich, of Bermondsey in the London Borough of Southwark 1989. PPS to John Major as Prime Minister 1994-97; Deputy Speaker 1994-97, 1998-2002; Deputy Chairman of Committees 1994-97, 1998-2002; Opposition Spokesperson for Health 1997-2010. Member: European Communities Sub-committee F (Environment) 1991-94, Medical Ethics 1993-94, Science and Technology 2000-03, Science and Technology Sub-committees: IIA (Human Genetic Databases) 2000-01, II (Aircraft Cabin Environment) 2001, I (Systematic Biology and Biodiversity/Fighting Infection) 2002-03, I (Science and International Agreements) 2003-10, Patient-Assisted Dying for the terminally ill 2004, HIV and AIDS in the UK 2010-11, Joint Committee on the Draft Modern Slavery Bill 2014, Equality Act 2010 and Disability 2015-16, Long-Term Sustainability of the NHS 2016-17. *Other:* Member, governing council, Conservative Christian Fellowship.

Political interests: Disability, higher education, health service, forestry, medicine, health; Benin, Gambia, Ghana, Liberia, Madagascar, Malawi, Norway, Romania, Sierra Leone, Tanzania, Togo, Uganda.

Other: Commonwealth Parliamentary Association UK Branch: Member, executive committee 1999-2005, 2006-11, 2015-, Vice-chair 2011-15; Vice-chair, Inter-Parliamentary Union, British Group 2014-15; Chair, UK Board of Mercy Ships; Governor-at-large for England, Board of Governors, American College of Surgeons 1982-86; Mildmay Mission Hospital: President 1985-2000, Vice-President 2000-; Council member, Royal College of Surgeons 1986-94; President: Society of Minimally Invasive Surgery 1991-94, National Association of Limbless Disabled 1992-; Vice-President, John Groom's Association for Disabled People 1992-; President: Hospital Saving Association 1994-2001, Association of Endoscopic Surgery of Great Britain and Ireland 1994-96, Leprosy Mission 1996-; Royal College of Surgeons; FRCS 1962; FACS; FKC; MS; Shaftesbury Society, Mercyships, Livability, Bridge2Aid, Burrswood, British Home. Master, Worshipful Company of Barbers. Fellow, King's College, London 2001; Hon. FDS RCS 2007. George and Thomas Hutchesons Award 2000; Great Scot Award for medical charity work 2002; National Maritime Historical Society Distinguished service award 2002. CBE 1997; Order of Mercy 2007. Palace of Westminster; Jags of Dulwich.

Publications: Intestinal Absorption in Man (1976); NHS Data Book (1984); Government Report on Artificial Limb and Appliance Centre Service (1986); As well as articles in medical journals.

Recreations: Forestry, ornithology.

Professor the Lord McColl of Dulwich CBE, House of Lords, London SW1A 0PW
Tel: 020 7219 5141 *Fax:* 020 7219 6205 *Email:* mccolli@parliament.uk

LABOUR

MCCONNELL OF GLENSCORRODALE, LORD

McCONNELL OF GLENSCORRODALE (Life Baron), Jack Wilson McConnell; cr 2010. Born 30 June 1960; Son of William Wilson McConnell, tenant farmer, and Elizabeth McConnell; Married Bridget McLuckie 1990 (1 son 1 daughter).

Education: Arran High School, Isle of Arran; Stirling University (BSc mathematics; Dip Ed 1983).

Non-political career: Maths teacher, Lornshill Academy 1983-92; General secretary, Scottish Labour Party 1992-98; Education adviser, Clinton Hunter Development Initiative 2007-11; Prime Minister's Special Representative for Peace-Building 2008-10; Member, advisory board, PricewaterhouseCoopers. Member, Community.

Political career: *House of Commons:* Contested (Labour) Perth and Kinross 1987 general election. *House of Lords:* Raised to the peerage as Baron McConnell of Glenscorrodale, of the Isle of Arran in Ayrshire and Arran 2010. *Other:* Scottish Parliament: MSP for Motherwell and Wishaw

House of Lords Peers' Biographies

constituency 1999-2011: Scottish Labour: Minister for: Finance 1999-2000, Education, Europe and External Affairs 2000-01, First Minister 2001-07. Member, Labour Scottish Executive 1989-92; Scottish Labour Party: General Secretary 1992-98, Leader 2001-07. *Councils and public bodies:* Stirling District Council: Councillor 1984-93, Treasurer 1988-92, Council leader 1990-92; Member: Scottish Constitutional Convention 1989-98, Convention of Scottish Local Authorities 1990-92.

Political interests: Education, economic policy, international development, conflict and peace-building; China, EU, Japan, Malawi, Rwanda, USA.

Other: Member: Congress of Local and Regional Authorities in Europe 1999-2001, EU Committee of the Regions 2000-07; President, European Regions with Legislative Power 2004; Board Member, UK-Japan 21st Century Group 2010-; Ambassador: Action for Children, SSE's Scotland Sustainable Fund Panel; Pump Aid; Patron: Positive Women, Diana Awards; Advisory board, Institute for Cultural Diplomacy; Chair: Radio Clyde Cash for Kids, McConnell International Foundation, SSE Community Funding Panel 2013-; Patron, European Movement in Scotland 2016-; Fellow, 48 Group Club; Various charities supporting international development and vulnerable children. Honorary Doctorate, Stirling University 2008. Scottish Politician of the Year 2001; UK Public Health Champion 2005; Scottish Politics Lifetime Achievement Award 2010. PC 2001. Lamlash Golf Club.

Recreations: Golf, music, sports, gardening.

Rt Hon the Lord McConnell of Glenscorrodale, House of Lords, London SW1A 0PW
Tel: 020 7219 8913 *Email:* mcconnellj@parliament.uk *Twitter:* @LordMcConnell

MCDONAGH, BARONESS

LABOUR

McDONAGH (Life Baroness), Margaret Josephine McDonagh; cr. 2004. Born 26 June 1961; Daughter of Breda, née Doogue, psychiatric nurse, and Cumin McDonagh, building labourer.

Education: Holy Cross Secondary Modern, New Malden; Kingston College of Further Education, Surrey; Brunel University (BSc politics and modern history with statistics 1984); Kingston Business School (MA advanced marketing 1994); Harvard Business School, USA (advanced management programme 2002).

Non-political career: Labour Party 1987-2001: General election co-ordinator 1997, Secretary General 1998-2001; General manager, *Express* Newspapers 2001; Non-executive director: TBI plc 2004, Standard Life plc 2007. Amicus.

Political career: *House of Lords:* Raised to the peerage as Baroness McDonagh, of Mitcham and of Morden in the London Borough of Merton 2004. Member, House 2013-16.

The Baroness McDonagh, House of Lords, London SW1A 0PW
Tel: 020 7219 4438 *Email:* mcdonaghm@parliament.uk

MACDONALD OF RIVER GLAVEN, LORD

LIBERAL DEMOCRAT

MACDONALD OF RIVER GLAVEN (Life Baron), Kenneth Donald John Macdonald; cr 2010. Born 4 January 1953; Married Linda Zuck 1980 (2 sons 1 daughter).

Education: St Edmund Hall, Oxford (BA philosophy, politics and economics 1974).

Non-political career: Called to the Bar, Inner Temple 1978; Practising criminal lawyer 1978-; QC 1997; Recorder 2001-; Director of public prosecutions 2003-08; Bencher 2004; Member, Matrix Chambers 2008-; Visiting Professor of Law, London School of Economics 2009-; Warden, Wadham College, Oxford; Deputy High Court Judge 2010-.

Political career: *House of Lords:* Raised to the peerage as Baron Macdonald of River Glaven, of Cley-next-the-Sea in the County of Norfolk 2010. Member, Constitution 2012-13. *Councils and public bodies:* Member: Treasury Counsel Selection Committee, Central Criminal Court 2001-03, Sentencing Guidelines Council 2003-08, Criminal Procedure Rules Committee 2003-08, Independent Commission on Youth Crime 2008-; Trustee, Index on Censorship 2009-; Advisory board, Centre for Criminology, Oxford University.

Political interests: Security, criminal justice, civil liberties.

Other: Member, Bar Council 2000; Bar Public Affairs Group: Member 2001-03, Vice-chair 2001-02; Criminal Bar Association: Vice-chair 2002-03, Chair 2003-. Kt 2007.

The Lord Macdonald of River Glaven QC, House of Lords, London SW1A 0PW
Tel: 020 7219 5353

NON-AFFILIATED

MCFALL OF ALCLUITH, LORD

Senior Deputy Speaker

McFALL OF ALCLUITH (Life Baron), John Francis McFall; cr 2010. Born 4 October 1944; Son of late John and Jean McFall; Married Joan Ward 1969 (3 sons 1 daughter).

Education: St Patrick's Secondary School, Dumbarton; Paisley College of Technology (BSc chemistry 1974); Strathclyde University (MBA); Open University (BA education).

Non-political career: Mathematics and chemistry teacher; Depute head teacher 1983-87.

Political career: *House of Commons:* MP (Labour) for Dumbarton 1987-2005, for West Dunbartonshire 2005-10. Member Public Accounts Commission -2010; Opposition Whip 1989-91; Opposition Spokesperson for Scottish Affairs 1992-97; Government Whip 1997-98; Parliamentary Under-Secretary of State, Northern Ireland Office 1998-99 (Minister for Education, Training and Employment, Health and Community Relations 1998-99, for Economy and Education 1999). Chair, Treasury 2001-10; Member: Public Administration 2000-01, Treasury Sub-committee 2001-10, Liaison 2001-10, Liaison Sub-committee 2007-10. *House of Lords:* Raised to the peerage as Baron McFall of Alcluith, of Dumbarton in the County of Dunbartonshire 2010. Senior Deputy Speaker 2016-; Member, House of Lords Commission 2016-. Member: Economic Affairs Finance Bill Sub-Committee 2011, Joint Committee on the Draft Financial Services Bill 2011-12, Economic Affairs 2012-15, Parliamentary Commission on Banking Standards 2012-13, EU Financial Affairs Sub-committee 2015-16, European Union 2016; Chair: Privileges and Conduct 2016, Procedure 2016-, Liaison 2016-, Selection 2016-, Hybrid Instruments 2016-, Standing Orders (Private Bills) 2016-. *Other:* Member, Co-operative Party.

Political interests: Defence, education, economic policy, co-operative development, Third World; Latin America, Middle East, Romania.

Other: Fellow, Industry and Parliament Trust 1989, 2003. DUniv: Strathclyde University 2010, Glasgow University 2011, Stirling University 2011; Hon. doctorate of business administration, BPP Business School, London 2011; DUniv, West of Scotland University 2012. PC 2004.

Recreations: Jogging, golf, reading.

Rt Hon the Lord McFall of Alcluith, House of Lords, London SW1A 0PW
Tel: 020 7219 6000 *Email:* hlseniordeputyspeaker@parliament.uk

CONSERVATIVE

MACGREGOR OF PULHAM MARKET, LORD

MacGREGOR OF PULHAM MARKET (Life Baron), John Roddick Russell MacGregor; cr. 2001. Born 14 February 1937; Son of late Dr Norman MacGregor and Mary MacGregor, née Roddick; Married Jean Dungey 1962 (1 son 2 daughters).

Education: Merchiston Castle School, Edinburgh; St Andrews University (MA economics and history 1959); King's College, London University (LLB 1962).

Non-political career: Administrator, London University 1961-62; Editorial staff, *New Society* 1962-63; Special assistant to Sir Alec Douglas-Home as Prime Minister 1963-64; Head of private office of Edward Heath MP 1965-68; Business executive in the City 1968-79; Director, Hill Samuel Registrars Ltd 1971-79; Hill Samuel & Co Ltd: Director 1973-79, Deputy chair 1994-96; Director: Associated British Foods 1994-2007, Slough Estates/SEGRO 1995-2006, Unigate (now Uniq) 1996-2005, Friends Provident 1998-2007; Member, supervisory board, DAF Trucks NV 2000-09; Co-chair, UK Food and Agriculture Advisory Board, Rabobank International 2006-12; Chairman, pension fund trustees: SEGRO 2007-10, British Energy 2007-12, Anglian Water Group 2009-12, Eggborough Power Ltd 2011-16.

Political career: *House of Commons:* MP (Conservative) for South Norfolk February 1974-2001. Opposition Whip 1977-79; Government Whip (Lord Commissioner of the Treasury) 1979-81; Parliamentary Under-Secretary of State for Industry 1981-83; Minister of State, Ministry of Agriculture, Fisheries and Food 1983-85; Chief Secretary to the Treasury 1985-87; Minister of Agriculture, Fisheries and Food 1987-89; Secretary of State for Education and Science 1989-90; Lord President of the Council and Leader of the House of Commons 1990-92; Secretary of State for Transport 1992-94. *House of Lords:* Raised to the peerage as Baron MacGregor of Pulham Market, of Pulham Market in the County of Norfolk 2001. Member: Constitution 2002-05, 2015-, Regulators 2006-07; Economic Affairs: Member 2007-10, Chair 2010-14; Finance Bill Sub-committee: Member 2008-10, Chair 2010-14; Member, Leader's Group on Code of Conduct 2009; Chair: Audit 2011-13, Economic Affairs Finance Bill Sub-Committee 2011, 2012-15; Member, Joint Committee on National Security Strategy 2014-15. *Other:* Chairman: Young Conservative External Relations Committee 1959-62, Bow Group 1961-62; First President, Conservative and Christian Democratic Youth Community 1965; President, South Norfolk Conservative Association

2007-; Association of Conservative Peers: Vice-chair 2010-12, Chairman 2012-16. *Councils and public bodies:* Council member, Institute of Directors 1995-2007; Vice-President, Association of County Councils 1995-97; Trustee, Foundation of Business Responsibilities 1996-2004; Conservative nominee, Committee on Standards in Public Life 1997-2003; Deputy chair, Governing Bodies Association (now Association of Governing Bodies of Independent Schools) 1998-2006; Member, Independent Schools Council 1998-2005; Chair, St Andrew's (Ecumenical) Trust 2006-12; Norwich Cathedral: High Steward 2007-, Chair of Cathedral Council 2012-.

Political interests: Economic and financial matters, agriculture, education, industry, housing, countryside, rural affairs, transport, pensions, constitution; EU countries, USA.

Other: Member: Council of King's College, London 1996-2002, Inner Magic Circle; Patron, New London Orchestra; Vice-President, COBISEC; Royal Norfolk Agricultural Association: President 1988, Trustee 2004-10; Fellow, King's College, London. Hon. LLD, Westminster University. OBE 1971; PC 1985.

Recreations: Music, theatre, gardening, travel, conjuring.

Rt Hon the Lord MacGregor of Pulham Market OBE, House of Lords, London SW1A 0PW
Tel: 020 7219 4439

MCGREGOR-SMITH, BARONESS

CONSERVATIVE

MCGREGOR-SMITH (Life Baroness), Ruby McGregor-Smith; cr 2015. Born 22 February 1963; Married Graham (2 children).

Education: Lowlands Sixth Form College; Kingston Polytechnic (BA economics 1985).

Non-political career: BDO Stoy Hayward; Serco Group plc; Mitie Group: Group Finance Director 2002-05, Group Chief Operating Officer 2005-07, Chief Executive 2007-16.

Political career: *House of Lords:* Raised to the peerage as Baroness McGregor-Smith, of Sunninghill in the Royal County of Berkshire 2015. Member, EU Internal Market Sub-committee 2017-. *Councils and public bodies:* UK Business Ambassador for Professional and Business Services 2014-; Non-executive board member: Department for Culture, Media and Sport -2015, Department for Education 2015-.

Other: Non-executive director, PageGroup 2007-17; Chair: Public Services Strategy Board, Confederation of British Industry, Women's Business Council; Corporate board member, Great Ormond Street Hospital. Hon DLitt, Kingston University 2011. First Woman of Business Services, CBI 2007; Business Woman of the Year, Asian Woman of Achievement Awards 2008.

The Baroness McGregor-Smith CBE, House of Lords, London SW1A 0PW
Tel: 020 7219 3000 *Twitter:* @RubyMS

MCINNES OF KILWINNING, LORD

CONSERVATIVE

McINNES OF KILWINNING (Life Baron), Mark McInnes; cr 2016. Born 4 November 1976.

Education: Kilwinning Academy; Edinburgh University (MA 1998).

Non-political career: Director, Scottish Conservative and Unionist Party 2003-.

Political career: *House of Lords:* Raised to the peerage as Baron McInnes of Kilwinning, of Kilwinning in the County of Ayrshire 2016. *Councils and public bodies:* Councillor, Edinburgh City Council 2003-17; Governor, George Watson's College 2007-16.

Other: Curator of Patronage, Edinburgh University 2007-17; Director: Changeworks Resources for Life -2010, Eric Liddell Centre -2011, Better Together 2013-15, Trustee, Merchant Company Endowment Trust. CBE 2016.

The Lord McInnes of Kilwinning CBE, House of Lords, London SW1A 0PW
Tel: 020 7219 3000 *Email:* mcinnesm@parliament.uk *Twitter:* @Morningsidemark

MCINTOSH OF HUDNALL, BARONESS

LABOUR

McINTOSH OF HUDNALL (Life Baroness), Genista Mary McIntosh; cr. 1999. Born 23 September 1946; Daughter of late Geoffrey and Maire Tandy; Married Neil McIntosh 1971 (divorced 1990) (1 son 1 daughter).

Education: Hemel Hempstead Grammar School; York University (BA philosophy and sociology 1968).

Non-political career: Press Secretary, York Festival of Arts 1968-69; Royal Shakespeare Company: Casting director 1972-77, Planning controller 1977-84, Senior administrator 1986-90, Associate producer 1990; Executive director, Royal National Theatre 1990-January 1997, October 1997-2002; Chief executive, Royal Opera House, Covent Garden 1997; Principal, Guildhall School of Music and Drama 2002-03.

Political career: *House of Lords:* Raised to the peerage as Baroness McIntosh of Hudnall, of Hampstead in the London Borough of Camden 1999. Deputy Chairman of Committees 2007-; Deputy Speaker 2008-; Member: Consultative Panel on Parliamentary Security, House of Lords Commission 2016-. Member: Joint Scrutiny Committees on: Draft Mental Incapacity Bill 2003, Draft Charities Bill 2004, Draft Mental Health Bill 2004-05, Liaison 2005-09; Chair, London Local Authorities Bill 2006; Member: Communications 2007-10, 2016-, Administration and Works 2007-11, 2012-15, House 2010-12, HIV and AIDS in the UK 2010-11, Mental Capacity Act 2005 2013-14, Procedure 2013-16, Ecclesiastical Committee 2014-, Leader's Group on Governance 2015.

Political interests: Arts, public health, education, sustainable transport.

Other: Trustee: Roundhouse Trust 2000-, Southbank Sinfonia 2000-, National Opera Studio 2006-16; Board member, Royal Shakespeare Company 2010-17; Patron: Helena Kennedy Bursary Scheme, Cantate; Fellow, Royal Society of Arts; Childline, National Trust, Cancer Research. Three honorary degrees; Honorary fellowship, Goldsmith's College 2003.

Recreations: Gardening, music.

The Baroness McIntosh of Hudnall, House of Lords, London SW1A 0PW
Tel: 020 7219 8732 *Email:* mcintoshg@parliament.uk

MCINTOSH OF PICKERING, BARONESS

CONSERVATIVE

McINTOSH OF PICKERING (Life Baroness), Anne Caroline Ballingall McIntosh; cr 2015. Born 20 September 1954; Daughter of late Dr Alastair McIntosh, medical practitioner, and late Grethe-Lise McIntosh; Married John Harvey 1992.

Education: Harrogate Ladies' College; Edinburgh University (LLB 1977); Åarhus University, Denmark (European law 1978); French, Danish, Spanish, German, Italian.

Non-political career: Trainee, EEC Competition Directorate, Brussels 1978; Legal adviser, Didier & Associates, Brussels 1979-80; Apprentice, Scottish Bar, Edinburgh 1980-82; Admitted to Faculty of Advocates 1982-; Advocate, practising with European Community Law Office, Brussels 1982-83; Adviser, European Democratic Group, principally on Transport, Youth Education, Culture, Tourism, Relations with Scandinavia, Austria and Yugoslavia 1983-89; Strategic Adviser, Anne McIntosh Consulting Ltd 2015-.

Political career: *House of Commons:* Contested Workington 1987 general election. MP (Conservative) for Vale of York 1997-2010, for Thirsk and Malton 2010-15. Opposition Spokesperson for Culture, Media and Sport 2001-02; Shadow Minister for: Transport 2002-03, Environment and Transport 2003-05, Foreign Affairs 2005, Work and Pensions 2005-06, Children, Young People and Families 2006-07, Environment, Food and Rural Affairs 2007-10. Member: Environment, Transport and Regional Affairs 1999-2001, Environment, Transport and Regional Affairs (Transport Sub-Committee) 1999-2001, European Standing Committee C 1999-2001, European Scrutiny 2000-03, Transport, Local Government and the Regions (Transport Sub-Committee) 2001-02, Transport, Local Government and the Regions (Urban Affairs Sub-Committee) 2001-02, Transport, Local Government and the Regions 2001-02, Transport 2003-05; Environment, Food and Rural Affairs: Member 2007-10, Chair 2010-15; Member: Chairmen's Panel/Panel of Chairs 2010-15, Liaison 2010-15, Liaison (National Policy Statements Sub-committee) 2010-15. Joint Vice-chair, Conservative Party Committee for Social Security. *House of Lords:* Raised to the peerage as Baroness McIntosh of Pickering, of the Vale of York in the County of North Yorkshire 2015. Chair, Licensing Act 2003 2016-17. *Other:* European Parliament: MEP for: Essex North East 1989-94, Essex North and Suffolk South 1994-99: Bureau Member, European People's Party 1994-97. Executive Member, 1922 Committee 2000-01. *Councils and public bodies:* Member, Faculty of Advocates 1982-.

Political interests: Transport, tourism, legal affairs, environment, farming and animal husbandry; Central and Eastern Europe, Scandinavia.

Other: President, Anglia Enterprise in Europe 1989-99; Co-chair, European Transport Safety Council 1994-99; Member, Executive Committee, Commonwealth Parliamentary Association (UK Branch) 2014-15; President, Yorkshire First – Enterprise in Yorkshire; Member: Yorkshire Agricultural Society, Anglo-Danish Society; Vice-President, National Eye Research (Yorkshire) Advisory Board; Patron, Thirsk Museum Society; Fellow, Industry and Parliament Trust 1995; Graduate, Armed Forces Parliamentary Scheme, Royal Navy 2000; Vice-president, Association of Drainage Authorities 2014-; President, North Yorkshire Moore Railway 2016-; Vice-president: National Encephalitis Society 2016-, National Association of Child Contact Centres 2017-. Honorary Doctorate of Laws, Anglia Polytechnic University 1997; *Clubs:* Yorkshire Agricultural Society, Royal Over-seas League, Royal Automobile Club.

Recreations: Swimming, reading, cinema.

The Baroness McIntosh of Pickering, House of Lords, London SW1A 0PW
Tel: 020 7219 3000 *Email:* mcintoshac@parliament.uk *Twitter:* @AnneCMcIntosh

CONSERVATIVE

MACKAY OF CLASHFERN, LORD

MACKAY OF CLASHFERN (Life Baron), James Peter Hymers Mackay; cr. 1979. Born 2 July 1927; Son of late James Mackay, railwayman; Married Elizabeth Gunn Hymers 1958 (1 son 2 daughters).

Education: George Heriot's School, Edinburgh; Edinburgh University (MA mathematics and natural philosophy 1948; LLB 1955); Trinity College, Cambridge (BA maths 1952).

Non-political career: Lecturer in mathematics, St Andrews University 1948-50; Advocate 1955; QC (Scotland) 1965; Sheriff Principal, Renfrew and Argyll 1972-74; Dean, Faculty of Advocates 1976-79; Director, Stenhouse Holdings Ltd 1976-78; Judge of Supreme Court of Scotland 1984-85; Lord of Appeal in Ordinary 1985-87; Lord Clerk, Register of Scotland 2007-.

Political career: *House of Lords:* Raised to the peerage as Baron Mackay of Clashfern, of Eddrachillis in the District of Sutherland 1979. Lord Advocate 1979-84; Government Spokesperson for Legal Affairs in Scotland 1983-84; Lord of Appeal in Ordinary 1985-87; Lord High Chancellor 1987-97. Member, Privileges/Privileges and Conduct; Chair, Assisted Dying Bill; Member: Draft Human Tissue and Embryos Bill Joint Committee 2007, Joint Committee on the Draft Care and Support Bill 2013. *Other:* Chair, Conservative Party Constitutional Commission 1998-99.

Other: Vice-President, Commonwealth Parliamentary Association (UK Branch); Elder Brother, Trinity House; Part-time Member, Scottish Law Commission 1976-79; Member, Insurance Brokers' Registration Council 1978-79; Senator, College of Justice in Scotland 1984-85; Chair: Legal Reform Commission, Mauritius 1997-98, Legal Commission, Trinidad and Tobago 2000; Commissioner, Cambridge University 2003-16; Lord High Commission to General Assembly of Church of Scotland 2005, 2006; Royal College of Surgeons of Edinburgh 1989; Royal Society of Edinburgh; RICE; Royal College of Physicians Edinburgh 1990; Royal College of Obstetrics and Gynaecology; Chartered Institute of Taxation; Cancer UK, Barnardo's, Army Benevolent Fund, Mission Aviation Fellowship, Mercy Ships. Hon. Freeman, Woolman's Company. Chancellor, Heriot-Watt University 1991-2005. Hon. Fellow: Trinity College, Cambridge, Girton College, Cambridge; Several Honorary Degrees. PC 1979; KT 1997; *Clubs:* New (Edinburgh), Caledonian, Athenæum Club.

Publications: Senior Editor, Armour: Valuation for Rating (third edition, 1961); General Editor-in-chief, Halsbury's Laws of England 1999-2015.

Recreations: Walking, travel.

Rt Hon the Lord Mackay of Clashfern KT, House of Lords, London SW1A 0PW
Tel: 020 7219 6041 *Email:* mackayjp@parliament.uk

LABOUR

MACKENZIE OF CULKEIN, LORD

MACKENZIE OF CULKEIN (Life Baron), Hector Uisdean MacKenzie; cr. 1999. Born 25 February 1940; Son of late George MacKenzie, lighthouse keeper, and late Williamina Budge, née Sutherland; Married Anna Morrison 1961 (divorced 1991) (1 son 3 daughters).

Education: Isle of Erraid Public School, Argyll; Aird Public School, Isle of Lewis; Nicolson Institute, Stornoway, Isle of Lewis; Portree High School, Skye; Leverndale School of Nursing, Glasgow (RMN 1961); West Cumberland School of Nursing, Whitehaven (SRN 1966).

Non-political career: Student nurse, Leverndale Hospital 1958-61; Assistant lighthouse keeper, Clyde Lighthouses Trust 1961-64; West Cumberland Hospital: Student nurse 1964-66, Staff nurse 1966-69; Confederation of Health Service Employees: Assistant regional secretary 1969, Regional secretary, Yorkshire and East Midlands 1970-74, National officer 1974-83, Assistant General Secretary 1983-87, General Secretary 1987-93; Member, executive board, Public Services International 1987-2000; Associate General Secretary, Unison 1993-2000; Company secretary, UIA Insurance Ltd 1996-2000; TUC: President 1998-99, Senior Vice-President 1999-2000. Member, Unison.

Political career: *House of Lords:* Raised to the peerage as Baron MacKenzie of Culkein, of Assynt in Highland 1999. *Other:* Member, Labour Party Policy: Forum 1997-2000, Commission on Health 1998-2000.

Political interests: Health, nursing, defence, aviation, maritime affairs, land reform; Australia, Falkland Islands, USA.

Other: First Substitute Member, World Executive of Public Services International 1987-2000; Inter-Parliamentary Union (British Group); Trustee, COHSE 1974 Pension and Assurance Scheme; Governor member, RNLI; RGN; RMN. Lindsay Robertson Gold Medal for Nurse of the Year 1966; *Clubs:* St Elpheges, Wallington, Ruskin Club, Croydon.

Recreations: Reading, Celtic music, shinty, aviation, travel.

The Lord MacKenzie of Culkein, House of Lords, London SW1A 0PW
Tel: 020 7219 8515 *Fax:* 020 7219 8712 *Email:* mackenzieh@parliament.uk

NON-AFFILIATED

MACKENZIE OF FRAMWELLGATE, LORD

MACKENZIE OF FRAMWELLGATE (Life Baron), Brian Mackenzie; cr. 1998. Born 21 March 1943; Son of Frederick Mackenzie and Lucy Mackenzie, née Ward; Married Jean Seed 1965 (2 sons); married Deborah Glaister 2009 (divorced 2012).

Education: Eastbourne Boys' School, Darlington; London University (LLB 1974); FBI National Academy, Quantico, USA (Graduate 1985).

Non-political career: Durham Constabulary 1963-98: Chief Superintendent 1989-98. Member, Police Federation of England and Wales 1963-80; National President, Police Superintendents' Association 1995-98; Member, National Association of Retired Police Officers 1998-; Vice-President, BALPA 2003-.

Political career: *House of Lords:* Raised to the peerage as Baron Mackenzie of Framwellgate, of Durham in the County of Durham 1998. Suspended from membership December 2013-June 2014. EU Sub-committee F (Home Affairs): Co-opted member 2009-10, Member 2010-12; Member EU Sub-committee F (Home Affairs, Health and Education) 2012-13. *Other:* Labour Whip withdrawn June 2013.

Political interests: Police, home affairs, legal affairs; India, Poland, Russia, USA.

Other: Member: FBI National Academy Associates, International Association of Chiefs of Police; President/patron, various police, security, defence and hospice organisations; Honorary Billetmaster, City of Durham 1989-2004; Patron: Loomba Trust, Finchale Training College for Disabled, Durham; Managing Director, Mack Diligence Ltd; St Oswald's Hospice, Newcastle. OBE 1998; *Clubs:* Dunelm Club, Durham City.

Publications: Two Lives of Brian – From Policing to Politics (autobiography, Memoir Club, 2004).

Recreations: Herpetology, after-dinner speaking, swimming, fitness, singing.

The Lord Mackenzie of Framwellgate OBE, House of Lords, London SW1A 0PW
Tel: 020 7219 8632 *Email:* mackenzieb@parliament.uk
Website: lordbrianmackenzie.wixsite.com/website

LABOUR

MCKENZIE OF LUTON, LORD

Opposition Spokesperson for Work and Pensions

McKENZIE OF LUTON (Life Baron), William David McKenzie; cr. 2004. Born 24 July 1946; Son of Elsie May Doust and George McKenzie; Married Diane Joyce Angliss 1972.

Education: Reading School; Bristol University (BA economics and accounting 1967).

Non-political career: Articled clerk to salaried partner Martin Rata and Partners 1968-73; Price Waterhouse, London 1973-86: Senior to senior manager 1973-80, Partner 1980-86; Sundry consultancy projects 1986-92; Price Waterhouse, Hong Kong 1992-98: Consultant 1992-93, Partner 1993-98, Partner in charge, Vietnam 1996-98. Member, GMB 1980s-.

Political career: *House of Commons:* Contested (Labour) Luton South 1987 and 1992 general elections. *House of Lords:* Raised to the peerage as Baron McKenzie of Luton, of Luton in the County of Bedfordshire 2004. Government Spokesperson for: Trade and Industry 2005-07, Treasury 2005-07; Government Whip 2005-07; Parliamentary Under-Secretary of State and Government Spokesperson: Department for Work and Pensions 2007-10, Department for Communities and Local Government 2009-10; Opposition Spokesperson for: Communities and Local Government 2010-15, Work and Pensions 2010-13, 2015-. Member: Merits of Statutory Instruments 2005, Financial Exclusion 2016-17. *Other:* Various constituency party posts. *Councils and public bodies:* Luton Borough Council: Councillor 1976-92, 1999-2005, Leader 1999-2003.

Political interests: Local government, local government finance, taxation systems, education, airports.

Other: FCA 1979.

Recreations: Swimming, reading.

The Lord McKenzie of Luton, House of Lords, London SW1A 0PW
Tel: 020 7219 6339 *Email:* mckenziew@parliament.uk

CONSERVATIVE

MACLAURIN OF KNEBWORTH, LORD

MACLAURIN OF KNEBWORTH (Life Baron), Ian Charter MacLaurin; cr. 1996. Born 30 March 1937; Son of late Arthur George and Evelina Florence MacLaurin; Married Ann Margaret Collar 1961 (died 1999) (1 son 2 daughters); married Paula Brooke 2002 (2 stepdaughters).

Education: Malvern College.

Non-political career: National Service, RAF Flight Command 1956-58. Tesco plc 1959-97: Director 1970, Managing director 1973-85, Deputy chair 1983-85, Chair 1985-97; Director, Enterprise Oil 1984-90; Non-executive director: National Westminster Bank plc 1990-96, Gleneagles Hotels plc 1992-97; Vodafone Group plc: Non-executive director 1997-2006, Chair 1998-2006; Non-executive director: Whitbread plc 1997-2001, Evolution Group plc 2004-11, Fleet Support Group 2004-, Heineken NV 2006-10; Chair: Chartwell Group 2006-10, Vodafone Foundation 2006-09, Paperless Receipts 2012.

Political career: *House of Lords:* Raised to the peerage as Baron MacLaurin of Knebworth, of Knebworth in the County of Hertfordshire 1996. Member, Economic Affairs 2007-09. *Councils and public bodies:* DL, Hertfordshire 1992-2007; Chair, UK Sports Council (resigned 1997); DL, Wiltshire 2007-12.

Political interests: Industry, sports; Europe, UK.

Other: Chair, Food Policy Group, Retail Consortium 1980-84; Committee member, MCC 1986-95; President, Institute of Grocery Distribution 1989-92; Trustee, Royal Opera House Trust 1992; Chair, England and Wales Cricket Board (formerly Test and County Cricket Board) 1996-2002; Governor and Chairman of Council, Malvern College 2002-15; Chair, Hope for Tomorrow 2004-05; Trustee, Chance to Shine 2010; Chair, Sport Honours Committee 2011-15; President, MCC 2017-; Chartered director, Institute of Directors; FRSA 1986; FIM 1987; Hon. FCGI 1992. Liveryman, Carmen's Company 1982-. Freedom, City of London 1981. Chancellor, Hertfordshire University 1996-2005. Three honorary doctorates: Hertfordshire University, Stirling University, Bradford University; Hon. Fellow, University of Wales. Kt 1989; *Clubs:* Harry's Bar, Annabel's Club. Life President, Brocket Hall Golf; MCC; Royal and Ancient Golf Club; Royal St George's; Thurlestone.

Publications: Tiger by the Tail (1999).

Recreations: Golf, cricket, walking the dogs.

The Lord MacLaurin of Knebworth DL, House of Lords, London SW1A 0PW
Tel: 020 7219 5353

LIBERAL DEMOCRAT

MACLENNAN OF ROGART, LORD

MACLENNAN OF ROGART (Life Baron), Robert Adam Ross Maclennan; cr 2001. Born 26 June 1936; Son of late Sir Hector Maclennan; Married Mrs Helen Noyes 1968 (1 son 1 daughter 1 stepson).

Education: Glasgow Academy; Balliol College, Oxford (BA history 1958, MA); Trinity College, Cambridge (LLB 1962); Columbia University, New York.

Non-political career: Barrister.

Political career: *House of Commons:* MP for Caithness and Sutherland 1966-97, Caithness, Sutherland and Easter Ross 1997-2001 (Labour 1966-81, SDP 1981-88, Liberal Democrat 1988-2001). PPS to George Thomson: as Minister without Portfolio 1967-69, as Chancellor of the Duchy of Lancaster 1969-70; Additional Opposition Spokesperson for: Scottish Affairs 1970-71, Defence 1971-72; Parliamentary Under-Secretary of State, Department of Prices and Consumer Protection 1974-79; Opposition Frontbench Spokesperson for Foreign and Commonwealth Affairs 1980-81; SDP Spokesperson for: Agriculture, Fisheries and Food 1981-87, Home and Legal Affairs 1983-87, Northern Ireland 1983-87, Scotland (jointly) 1982-87; Alliance Spokesperson for Agriculture and Fisheries and Food 1987; Liberal Democrat Spokesperson for: Home Affairs and National Heritage 1988-94, Constitutional Affairs and Culture 1994-2001. *House of Lords:* Raised to the peerage as Baron Maclennan of Rogart, of Rogart in Sutherland 2001. Liberal Democrat Spokesperson for: Europe 2001-04, European Constitution 2004-05, Scotland 2004-09, Cabinet Office 2005-10, Constitutional Affairs 2007-10. Member: European Union 2005-09, 2010-15, EU Sub-committees: A (Economic and Financial Affairs and International Trade) 2005-08, E (Law and Institutions) 2008-10, Economic Affairs 2010, 2011, EU Sub-committee E (Justice and Institutions) 2010-12, Leader's Group on the Working Practices of the House of Lords 2010-11, EU Sub-committees: D (Agriculture, Fisheries, Environment and Energy) 2012-13, C (External Affairs) 2013-15, Constitution 2015-. Chair, Liberal Democrat Parliamentary Party Committees on: Constitutional and Political Reform (Cabinet Office) 2010-12, Scotland 2010-12. *Other:* Leader, SDP 1987-88; President, Liberal Democrat Party 1994-98.

Political interests: Constitutional reform, European Union, rural affairs, arts; all European countries, India, Pakistan, USA.

Other: Alternate National Parliamentary Representative, European Convention 2002-04; Director, Northlands Creative Glass -2017; Chair, North Highland Connections -2017. Freedom, Caithness. PC 1997; Légion d'Honneur (France) 2004; *Clubs:* Brooks's; Royal Automobile Club.

Publications: Librettos: The Lie (1992), Friend of The People (1999).

Recreations: Theatre, music, visual arts.

Rt Hon the Lord Maclennan of Rogart, House of Lords, London SW1A 0PW
Tel: 020 7219 4133 *Email:* maclennanr@parliament.uk

MCNALLY, LORD

LIBERAL DEMOCRAT

McNALLY (Life Baron), Tom McNally; cr. 1995. Born 20 February 1943; Son of late John and Elizabeth McNally; Married Eileen Powell 1970 (divorced 1990); married Juliet Lamy Hutchinson 1990 (2 sons 1 daughter).

Education: College of St Joseph, Blackpool; University College, London (BSc economics 1966) (President, Students Union 1965-66).

Non-political career: Political adviser to James Callaghan: as Secretary of State for Foreign and Commonwealth Affairs 1974-76, as Prime Minister 1976-79; Public affairs adviser, GEC 1983-84; Director and chief executive, British Retail Consortium 1985-87; Head of public affairs: Hill & Knowlton 1987-93, Shandwick 1993-96; Vice-chair, Weber Shandwick 1993-2004. Vice-President, National Union of Students 1966-67.

Political career: *House of Commons:* MP for Stockport South (Labour 1979-81, SDP 1981-83). Contested (SDP) Stockport 1983 general election. SDP Spokesperson for Education and Sport 1981-83. Member, Industry and Trade 1979-83. *House of Lords:* Raised to the peerage as Baron McNally, of Blackpool in the County of Lancashire 1995. Liberal Democrat Spokesperson for: Broadcasting and Trade and Industry 1996-97, Home Affairs 1998-2002, Broadcasting 2002-04, Home Office 2004; Liberal Democrat peers: Deputy Leader 2001-04, Leader 2004-13; Liberal Democrat Spokesperson for Constitutional Affairs 2006-10; Deputy Leader of the House of Lords 2010-13; Minister of State and Government Spokesperson, Ministry of Justice 2010-13. Member: Public Service 1996-97, Freedom of Information 1999, Draft Communications Bill Joint Committee 2002, Liaison 2005-13, Privileges/Privileges and Conduct 2005-13, Procedure 2005-13, Selection 2005-13, 2014, House 2005-13, Conventions Joint Committee 2006, Inheritance and Trustees' Powers Bill 2013, Insurance Bill 2014-15. *Other:* Labour Party Researcher 1967-68; International Secretary, Labour Party 1969-74. *Councils and public bodies:* Chairman, Youth Justice Board for England and Wales 2014-17.

Political interests: Penal reform, future of the BBC, media plurality; China, EU, India, Tunisia.

Other: Assistant General Secretary, Fabian Society 1966-67; Fellow, Industry and Parliament Trust 1981; Fellow, Chartered Institute of Public Relations (FCIPR) 2000; Fellow, University College, London 1995. Doctor of Law, Hertfordshire University 2011. PC 2004; *Clubs:* National Liberal Club.

Recreations: Watching sport, reading history.

Rt Hon the Lord McNally, House of Lords, London SW1A 0PW
Tel: 020 7219 5443 *Email:* mcnallyt@parliament.uk

MACPHERSON OF EARL'S COURT, LORD

CROSSBENCH

MACPHERSON OF EARL'S COURT (Life Baron), Nicholas Ian Macpherson; cr 2016. Born 14 July 1959; Son of Euen A. Macpherson and Nicolette (née Van der Bijl); Married Suky Jane Appleby 1983 (2 sons).

Education: Eton College; Balliol College, Oxford (BA philosophy, politics and economics 1981); University College, London (MSc economics of public policy 1982).

Non-political career: Economist, Confederation of British Industry 1982-83; Senior Analyst, Peat, Marwick and Mitchell Management Consultancy 1983-85; HM Treasury 1985-2016: Principal Private Secretary to Kenneth Clarke as Chancellor of the Exchequer 1993-97, Head, Work Incentives Policy 1997-98, Director, Budget and Public Finances 1998-2001, Managing Director: Public Services 2001-04, Budget and Public Finances Directorate 2004-05, Permanent Secretary 2005-16.

Political career: *House of Lords:* Raised to the peerage as Baron Macpherson of Earl's Court, of Earl's Court in the Royal Borough of Kensington and Chelsea 2016.

Political interests: Economy, public spending, European Union.

Other: Non-executive director, HM Revenue and Customs 2005-07; Chairman, C Hoare & Co 2016-; Non-executive director: Scottish American Investment Trust 2016-, British Land plc 2016-; Visiting Professor, King's College London University. KCB 2009; GCB 2015.

The Lord Macpherson of Earl's Court GCB, House of Lords, London SW1A 0PW
Tel: 020 7219 3000 *Email:* macphersonn@parliament.uk *Twitter:* @nickmacpherson2

LIBERAL DEMOCRAT

MADDOCK, BARONESS

MADDOCK (Life Baroness), Diana Margaret Maddock; cr. 1997. Born 19 May 1945; Daughter of late Reginald Derbyshire and Margaret Evans; Married Robert Maddock 1966 (2 daughters); married Alan Beith 2001 (MP 1973-2015, later Sir Alan, now Lord Beith (qv)).

Education: Brockenhurst Grammar School; Shenstone Training College (Cert Ed 1966); Portsmouth Polytechnic (Postgraduate Diploma linguistics 1978).

Non-political career: Geography teacher, Weston Park Girls' School, Southampton 1966-69; English as second language teacher: Extra-mural department, Stockholm University 1969-72, Sholing Girls' School, Southampton 1972-73, Anglo-Continental School of English, Bournemouth 1973-76, Greylands School of English (part time) 1990-91.

Political career: *House of Commons:* Contested Southampton Test 1992 general election. MP (Liberal Democrat) for Christchurch 29 July 1993 by-election to 1997. Liberal Democrat Spokesperson for Housing, Women's Issues and Family Policy 1994-97; Sponsored as Private Member's Bill, Home Energy Conservation Act 1995. *House of Lords:* Raised to the peerage as Baroness Maddock, of Christchurch in the County of Dorset 1997. Liberal Democrat Spokesperson for: Housing 1998-2004, Energy and Climate Change 2015. Member: European Union 2002-05, Merits of Statutory Instruments 2005-09, EU Sub-committee A: (Economic and Financial Affairs and International Trade) 2010-12, (Economic and Financial Affairs) 2012-14; Works of Art: Member 2012-13, Chair 2014-16; Chair, Lord Speaker's Advisory Panel on Works of Art 2017-. *Other:* President, Liberal Democrat Party 1998-2000. *Councils and public bodies:* Southampton City Council: Councillor 1984-93, Leader, Liberal Democrat Group; Member, Committee for Standards in Public Life 2003-09; Councillor: Northumberland County Council 2005-08, Berwick-upon-Tweed Borough Council 2007-09; Vice-President, Local Government Association 2010-.

Political interests: Education, local government, housing, environment; Denmark, Finland, Norway, Sweden.

Other: Vice-President: National Energy Action 2000-, National Home Improvement Council 2000-; President: Sustainable Energy Association, Anglo-Swedish Society; National Association of Almshouses, St Mungos (St Mungo Community Housing Association Ltd); *Clubs:* National Liberal, Northern Counties Club.

Recreations: Theatre, music, reading, travel.

The Baroness Maddock, House of Lords, London SW1A 0PW
Tel: 020 7219 1625 *Email:* maddockd@parliament.uk

CONSERVATIVE

MAGAN OF CASTLETOWN, LORD

MAGAN OF CASTLETOWN (Life Baron), George Morgan Magan; cr 2011. Born 14 November 1945; Son of Brigadier William Magan CBE and Maxine Mitchell; Married Wendy Chilton 1972 (2 sons 1 daughter).

Education: Winchester College.

Non-political career: Peat Marwick Mitchell 1964-70; Kleinwort Benson Ltd 1971-74; Director, Morgan Grenfell and Co Ltd 1974-88; Co-founder and chair, JO Hambro Magan 1988-96; Chair: Hawkpoint Partners 1997-2001, eMuse 2001-, Lion Capital Partners 2001-08, Mallett plc 2001-08, Morgan Shipley Ltd (Dubai) 2001-; Director: Edmiston and Co. 2001-, Allied Investment Partners (Abu Dhabi) 2007-12.

Political career: *House of Lords:* Raised to the peerage as Baron Magan of Castletown, of Kensington in the Royal Borough of Kensington and Chelsea 2011. Member: Works of Art 2015-16, Lord Speaker's Advisory Panel on Works of Art 2017-. *Other:* Conservative Party: Deputy treasurer 2002-03, Treasurer 2003, Board member 2003; Conservative Party Foundation: Director 2003-13, Deputy chairman 2009-13. *Councils and public bodies:* Royal Opera House, Covent Garden 1995-2001.

Other: Trustee: London Philharmonic Orchestra 1992-2006, British Museum Development Trust 1999-2003; *Clubs:* Royal Yacht Squadron Club.

The Lord Magan of Castletown, House of Lords, London SW1A 0PW
Tel: 020 7219 5353

INDEPENDENT ULSTER UNIONIST

MAGINNIS OF DRUMGLASS, LORD

MAGINNIS OF DRUMGLASS (Life Baron), Kenneth Wiggins Maginnis; cr 2001. Born 21 January 1938; Son of late Gilbert and Margaret Maginnis, née Wiggins; Married Joy Stewart 1961 (2 sons 2 daughters).

Education: Royal School, Dungannon; Stranmillis Teacher Training College, Belfast 1958.

Non-political career: Major (Rtd), 8 Battalion, Ulster Defence Regiment 1970-81. Teacher: Cookstown Secondary School 1959-60, Drumglass Primary School, Dungannon 1960-66; Principal, Pomeroy Primary School 1966-82.

Political career: *House of Commons:* Contested Fermanagh and South Tyrone August 1981 by-election. MP (UUP) for Fermanagh and South Tyrone 1983-2001 (Resigned December 1985 in protest against the Anglo-Irish Agreement; Re-elected 23 January 1986 by-election). UUP Spokesperson for: Defence and Home Office 1997-2000, Defence, Trade and Industry 2000-01. *House of Lords:* Raised to the peerage as Baron Maginnis of Drumglass, of Carnteel in the County of Tyrone 2001. *Other:* Member: Northern Ireland Assembly 1982, Northern Ireland Forum 1996-98. Treasurer, Ulster Unionist Council -2008; UUP Whip withdrawn June 2012; Resigned from UUP August 2012. *Councils and public bodies:* Councillor, Dungannon and South Tyrone Borough Council 1981-93, 2001-05; Member, Southern Health and Social Services Council 1989-93.

Political interests: Terrorism and internal security, defence, autism; Turkish Republic of Northern Cyprus.

Other: Chair: Moygashel Regeneration Group, Independent Review of Autism Services for DHSSPS(NI) 2008, Northern Ireland Regional ASD Reference Group 2009-11; Martin Residential Trust Belfast; *Clubs:* Ulster Reform Club. President, Dungannon Rugby Club 2001-02.

Recreations: Rugby.

The Lord Maginnis of Drumglass, House of Lords, London SW1A 0PW
Tel: 020 7219 8189 *Email:* maginnisk@parliament.uk
Email: ken.southtyrone@btinternet.com

CROSSBENCH

MAIR, LORD

MAIR (Life Baron), Robert James Mair; cr 2015. Born 20 April 1950; Married Margaret O'Connor 1981 (1 son 1 daughter).

Education: Clare College, Cambridge (engineering 1971; PhD tunnelling in soft ground 1979).

Non-political career: Engineer, London and Hong Kong 1971-76; Cambridge University: Research assistant, Department of Engineering 1976-79, Professor of geotechnical engineering and Head of civil and environmental engineering 1998-; Senior engineer, London 1980-83; Founding director, Geotechnical Consulting Group 1983-; Department of Civil Engineering, Nottingham University 1994-97; Master, Jesus College, Cambridge 2001-11; Chief engineering adviser to Laing O'Rourke Group 2011-; Principal investigator, Cambridge Centre for Smart Infrastructure and Construction 2011-; Recent international projects: Railway tunnels in Amsterdam, Barcelona, Bologna, Florence, Rome, Singapore and Warsaw, Motorway tunnels in Turkey; Closely involved with the design and construction of: Jubilee Line Extension for London Underground, Channel Tunnel Rail Link (now HS1), Crossrail projects.

Political career: *House of Lords:* Raised to the peerage as Baron Mair, of Cambridge in the County of Cambridgeshire 2015. Member, Science and Technology 2016-.

Other: Chair, international advisory board, Singapore Land Transport Authority; International Society of Soil Mechanics and Foundation Engineering: Board member, Chair, Technical Committee on Underground Construction in Soft Ground; Member, Crossrail's Engineering Expert Panel; Chair, Royal Society/Royal Academy of Engineering Review of Shale Gas Extraction in the UK (report published 2012); Fellow: Institution of Civil Engineers, Royal Society; Royal Academy of Engineering: Fellow, Senior vice-president 2008-11; Fellow, John's College, Cambridge 1998-2001. British Geotechnical Society Prize 1980; Institution of Civil Engineers: Geotechnical Research Medal 1994, Gold Medal 2004. CBE 2010.

Publications: Has published many papers, mainly on the geotechnical aspects of soft ground tunnelling and excavations.

Professor the Lord Mair CBE, House of Lords, London SW1A 0PW
Tel: 020 7219 3000

MALLALIEU, BARONESS

LABOUR

MALLALIEU (Life Baroness), Ann Mallalieu; cr. 1991. Born 27 November 1945; Daughter of late Sir William Mallalieu and Lady Mallalieu; Married Timothy Cassel 1979 (later Sir Timothy Bt) (divorced 2007) (2 daughters).

Education: Holton Park Girls' Grammar School, Wheatley; Newnham College, Cambridge (MA, LLM law 1968).

Non-political career: Called to the Bar, Inner Temple 1970; Elected Member, General Council of the Bar 1973-75; Recorder 1985-94; Bencher 1992; QC.

Political career: *House of Lords:* Raised to the peerage as Baroness Mallalieu, of Studdridge in the County of Buckinghamshire 1991. Opposition Spokesperson for: Home Affairs 1992-97, Legal Affairs 1992-97. Member Joint Committees on: Consolidation, Etc, Bills 1998-2005, 2006-, Statutory Instruments 2013-16. *Other:* Chair, Leave Country Sports Alone Labour Support Campaign 2000-. *Councils and public bodies:* Exmoor National Park Consultative Forum.

Political interests: Law, home affairs, agriculture, environment, animal welfare.

Other: Chair: Council, Ombudsman for Corporate Estate Agents 1993-2000, Suzy Lamplugh Trust 1996-2000; President: Countryside Alliance 1998-, British Hawking Association 1999-; Member, British Horseracing Board 2004-07; President, Horse Trust 2009-; Trustee: Racing Welfare 2009-, National Association of Stable Staff 2009-. Hon. Fellow, Newnham College, Cambridge 1992. Peer of the Year: *House Magazine* 2005, *Spectator* 2005.

Recreations: Hunting, poetry, sheep, fishing, racing.

The Baroness Mallalieu QC, House of Lords, London SW1A 0PW
Tel: 020 7219 2000

MALLOCH-BROWN, LORD

CROSSBENCH

MALLOCH-BROWN (Life Baron), George Mark Malloch-Brown; cr 2007. Born 16 September 1953; Son of late Robert Malloch-Brown and Ursula Malloch-Brown, née Pelly; Married Patricia Cronan 1989 (1 son 3 daughters).

Education: Marlborough College, Wiltshire; Magdalene College, Cambridge (BA history 1975); University of Michigan, USA (MA political science 1977).

Non-political career: Political correspondent, *Economist* 1977-79; Field operations for Cambodian refugees, Thailand 1979-81; Deputy chief emergency unit, UN High Commission for Refugees, Geneva 1981-83; Founder and editor, Economist Development Report 1983-86; Lead international partner, Sawyer-Miller Group 1986-94; World Bank 1994-99: Director, external affairs 1994-96, Vice-President, external affairs and UN affairs 1996-99; Administrator, UN Development Programme 1999-2005; UN 2005-06: Chef de Cabinet to Secretary-General Kofi Annan 2005-06, Deputy Secretary-General 2006; Vice-chair: Soros Fund Management 2007, Open Society Institute 2007, World Economic Forum 2009; Chair, EMEA operations, FTI Consulting 2010-16; Adviser, SouthWest Energy 2010-; Chair, SGO 2016-.

Political career: *House of Lords:* Raised to the peerage as Baron Malloch-Brown, of St Leonard's Forest in the County of West Sussex 2007. Minister of State for Africa, Asia and UN and Government Spokesperson, Foreign and Commonwealth Office (also attending Cabinet) 2007-09; On leave of absence June-December 2012, September 2015-October 2016.

Political interests: Development, foreign policy; Africa and Asia.

Other: Chair, Royal Africa Society; Board member: Open Society Institute, Save the Children International, Children's Investment Fund Foundation; Founder and board member, International Crisis Group 1995-; Board member: Centre for Global Development, Shell Foundation; Governor, Marlborough College. Honorary doctorates from three US and one Peruvian University; Honorary Fellow, Magdalene College, Cambridge. KCMG 2007; PC 2007.

Recreations: Reading, jogging, family.

Rt Hon the Lord Malloch-Brown KCMG, House of Lords, London SW1A 0PW
Tel: 020 7219 5353
Email: mark.malloch-brown@sgo.com

NON-AFFILIATED

MANCE, LORD

MANCE (Life Baron), Jonathan Hugh Mance; cr 2005. Born 6 June 1943; Son of Sir Henry and Lady Mance, née Joan Erica Robertson Baker; Married Mary Arden, later Rt Hon Dame Mary Arden, Lady Justice Arden 1973 (1 son 2 daughters).

Education: Charterhouse, Surrey; University College, Oxford (BA jurisprudence 1964, MA); French, German, mainly reading Spanish.

Non-political career: Called to the Bar, Middle Temple 1965; QC 1982; Bencher 1989; Recorder 1990-93; Judge commercial list High Court Queen's Bench Division 1993-99; Lord Justice of Appeal 1999-2005; Supreme Court of the United Kingdom: Justice 2009-17, Deputy President 2017-.

Political career: *House of Lords:* Raised to the peerage as Baron Mance, of Frognal in the London Borough of Camden 2005. Lord of Appeal in Ordinary 2005-09; As Justice of the Supreme Court, disqualified from participation 2009-. European Union Sub-committee E (Law and Institutions): Co-opted Member 2006-07, Chair 2007-09; Member, European Union 2007-09. *Councils and public bodies:* Chair, various Banking Appeals Tribunals 1992-93.

Countries of interest: Europe, Democratic Republic of the Congo.

Other: Council of Europe's Consultative Council of Judges: UK Representative Judge -2011, Chair 2000-03; Member, seven-person panel on the functioning of the European Union (established by the Lisbon Treaty, under Article 255 TFEU) 2010-14, 2014-; Member, Judicial Integrity Group; Chair, Lord Chancellor's Advisory Committee on Private International Law; Trustee, European Law Academy -2011; High Steward, Oxford University 2012-; Chair, International Law Association 2009-; President, British-German Jurists Association 2009-; Hon Fellow, American College of Trial Lawyers; Hampstead Counselling Service. Hon. Fellow: University College, Oxford, Wolfson College, Oxford, Liverpool John Moores University, John F Kennedy University, Buenos Aires, Argentina; Hon. Doc: Canterbury Church University, Oxford University. Kt 1993; PC 1999. Cumberland Lawn Tennis Club.

Publications: Editor and author various legal works and articles.

Recreations: Languages, music, tennis, skiing.

Rt Hon the Lord Mance, House of Lords, London SW1A 0PW
Tel: 020 7219 5353
Supreme Court of the United Kingdom, Parliament Square, London SW1P 3BD
Tel: 020 7960 1966 *Fax:* 020 7960 1961 *Email:* jackie.sears@supremecourt.uk

CONSERVATIVE

MANCROFT, LORD

MANCROFT (3rd Baron, UK), Benjamin Lloyd Stormont Mancroft; cr. 1937; 3rd Bt of Mancroft (UK) 1932. Born 16 May 1957; Son of 2nd Baron KBE TD and late Diana, née Lloyd; Married Emma Peart 1990 (2 sons 1 daughter).

Education: Eton College.

Non-political career: Chair: Inter Lotto (UK) Ltd 1995-, Scratch-n-Win Lotteries Ltd 1995-98; Non-executive director: St Martin's Magazines plc, Rok Corporation (and deputy chair) 2003-; Chair, New Media Lottery Services plc.

Political career: *House of Lords:* First entered House of Lords 1987; Elected hereditary peer 1999-. Member: Statutory Instruments Joint Committee 2002-07, Pre-legislative Scrutiny Committee on Draft Gambling Bill 2003-04, Administration and Works 2009-14, Licensing Act 2003 2016-17. *Other:* Member, Executive: National Union of Conservative Associations 1989-94, Association of Conservative Peers 1989-94, 1999-.

Political interests: Drug addiction, alcoholism, rural affairs.

Other: Joint Master, Vale of White Horse Fox Hounds 1987-89; Chair, Addiction Recovery Foundation 1989-; Phoenix House Housing Association: Director 1991-96, Vice-chairman 1992-96; Deputy chair, British Field Sports Society 1992-97; Chair, Drug and Alcohol Foundation 1994-; President, Alliance of Independent Retailers 1996-2000; Patron, Osteopathic Centre for Children 1996-; Lotteries Council: Executive Committee 1999-, President; Chair, Mentor (UK) 2001-; Vice-chair, Countryside Alliance 2005-; President, European Association for the Treatment of Addiction; Chair, Master of Foxhounds Association; *Clubs:* Pratt's Club.

Recreations: Hunting, stalking, shooting, fishing.

The Lord Mancroft, House of Lords, London SW1A 0PW
Tel: 020 7219 5353
Host Europe House, Kendal Avenue, London W3 0XA

MANDELSON, LORD

LABOUR

MANDELSON (Life Baron); Peter Benjamin Mandelson; cr 2008. Born 21 October 1953; Son of late George Mandelson and Hon Mary Joyce Morrison, daughter of late Baron Morrison of Lambeth.

Education: Hendon Grammar School; St Catherine's College, Oxford (BA philosophy, politics and economics 1976); French.

Non-political career: Producer, London Weekend Television 1982-85; Director, campaigns and communications, Labour Party 1985-90; Industrial consultant, SRU Group 1990-92; Economic department, Trade Union Congress (TUC) 1977-78; Commissioner for Trade, European Commission 2004-08; Chairman, Global Counsel LLP; Senior Adviser, Lazard Ltd. Member, GMB.

Political career: *House of Commons:* MP (Labour) for Hartlepool 1992-2004. Opposition Whip 1994-95; Opposition spokesperson: Civil service 1995-96, Election planning 1996-97; Minister without Portfolio 1997-98; Secretary of State for: Trade and Industry 1998, Northern Ireland 1999-2001. *House of Lords:* Raised to the peerage as Baron Mandelson, of Foy in the County of Herefordshire and Hartlepool in the County of Durham 2008. Secretary of State and Government Spokesperson for Business, Enterprise and Regulatory Reform/Business, Innovation and Skills 2008-10; First Secretary of State 2009-10; Lord President of the Council 2009-10. *Other:* Chair, PLP General Election Campaign (Planning) 1999-2001; Patron, LGBT Labour. *Councils and public bodies:* Councillor, London Borough of Lambeth 1979-82; High Steward, Hull 2013-.

Other: Chair, British Youth Council 1978-80; President, Central School of Speech and Drama 2001-; Chair, Policy Network 2001-; UK Chair, UK-Japan 21st century Group; President, Hartlepool United FC -2016; Board Member, Britain Stronger in Europe 2015-16; President: Great Britain-China Centre 2015-, Supervisory board, German British Forum; Chair, Design Museum 2017-. Chancellor, Manchester Metropolitan University 2016-. Hon Fellow, St Catherine's College, Oxford. Politicians' Politician, Channel 4 Political awards 2009. PC 1998; Grand Officer, Order of the Star of Italy 2016; Order of Légion d'Honneur (France) 2017.

Publications: Several books including: Broadcasting and Youth (1980), Labour's Next Steps: Tackling Social Exclusion (Fabian Society, 1997); Co-author: The Blair Revolution – Can New Labour Deliver? (Faber and Faber, 1996), The Blair Revolution Revisited (Politico's, 2004); Author, The Third Man (Harper Press, 2010); Contributor, The Purple Book (Progress, 2011).

Recreations: Cinema, theatre.

Rt Hon the Lord Mandelson, House of Lords, London SW1A 0PW
Tel: 020 7219 5353

MANNINGHAM-BULLER, BARONESS

CROSSBENCH

MANNINGHAM-BULLER (Life Baroness), Eliza(beth) Lydia Manningham-Buller; cr 2008. Born 14 July 1948; Daughter of 1st Viscount Dilhorne; Married.

Education: Northampton High School; Benenden School, Kent; Lady Margaret Hall, Oxford (BA English 1970).

Non-political career: Security Service 1974-2007: Deputy director-general 1997-2002, Director-general 2002-07.

Political career: *House of Lords:* Raised to the peerage as Baroness Manningham-Buller, of Northampton in the County of Northamptonshire 2008. Member, Privileges/Privileges and Conduct 2008-13; Sub-committee on Lords' Interests: Member 2008-09: Chair 2009-10; Member, Joint Committee on National Security Strategy 2010-13; Chair, Sub-committee on Lords' Conduct 2010-13; Member, Science and Technology 2013-16.

Political interests: National security, foreign policy, defence, health, higher education.

Other: Chair: Council, Imperial College London 2011-15, Wellcome Trust 2015-; Co-President, Chatham House 2016-. Honorary fellow: Lady Margaret Hall, Oxford, Northampton University, Cardiff University, City & Guilds; Five honorary doctorates: St Andrews University, Cranfield University, Open University, Oxford University, Leeds University 2012, Dundee University 2017. Women in Public Life Awards: Outstanding Achievement award 2007, Public Servant of the Year 2007. DCB 2005; LG 2014.

Publications: Securing Freedom (Based on 2011 Reith lectures) (Profile Books, 2012).

The Baroness Manningham-Buller LG DCB, House of Lords, London SW1A 0PW
Tel: 020 7219 5353

CONSERVATIVE

MANZOOR, BARONESS

MANZOOR (Life Baroness), Zahida Parveen Manzoor; cr 2013. Born 25 May 1958; Married Dr Madassar Manzoor 1984 (2 daughters).

Education: Leeds University (1982); New College, Durham University (Further Education Teaching Certificate 1984); Queen Elizabeth Hospital, Birmingham (State Certified Midwife 1984); Bradford University (MA applied social studies 1989).

Non-political career: West Suffolk Area Health Authority 1977-80: Student nurse, Staff nurse; Health visitor, Durham Area Health Authority 1983-84; Lecturer, Thomas Danby College 1984-86, 1987-88; North east regional programme director, Common Purpose Charitable Trust 1990-92; Intellisys Ltd: Director 1996-2003, Managing director, Property Development and Private Equity 2011-.

Political career: *House of Lords:* Raised to the peerage as Baroness Manzoor, of Knightsbridge in the Royal Borough of Kensington and Chelsea 2013. Liberal Democrat Spokesperson for: International Development 2015, Welfare, Work and Pensions 2015-16. Member: House 2015-16, EU External Affairs Sub-committee 2017-. *Other:* Member: Liberal Democrats -2016, Conservatives October 2016-. *Councils and public bodies:* Non-executive director, Bradford Hospitals NHS Trust 1991-92; Chair, Service Equity Committee 1991-92; Governor: Sheffield Hallam University 1991-93, Bradford and Airedale College of Health 1992-93; Chair, Bradford Health Authority 1992-97; Member of Court, Bradford University 1992-98; Deputy chair, Commission for Racial Equality 1993-98; Chair: CRE Complaints Committee 1994-98, CRE Audit Committee 1995-98; Governor, Keighley College 1994-95; Trustee, West Yorkshire Police Community Trust 1996-98; Policy board member, NHS England and Wales 1997-2001; Regional chair, Northern and Yorkshire Regions for the NHS Executive of England and Wales 1997-2001; Member, Race Equality Advisory Panel, Home Office 2003-; Legal Services Ombudsman for England and Wales 2003-11; Legal Services Complaints Commissioner 2004-10.

Other: Governor: Sheffield Hallam University 1991-93, Airedale College of Health 1992-93; Member, Bradford Congress 1992-96; Court Member, Bradford University 1992-98; Director, Bradford City Challenge 1993-96; Trustee: Uniting Britain Trust 1996-2000, West Yorkshire Police Charitable Trust 1996-98, NSPCC 1997-2003; Vice Patron, Regional Crime Stoppers 1998-2007; Patron, Ethnic Minority Disability Association 1999-; Independent Assessor, Foreign Office 1999-2013; Board Member: Diversity Focus Group for the Cabinet Office 1999-2000; Middle East Association 2013-; Chair, Middle East Technical Advisory Council for The Phoenix Partnership 2016-; Vice-patron, Regional Crime Stoppers 1998. Honorary Fellowship, Bolton Institute 1999 Honorary Doctorate: Bradford University 1999, Leeds Metropolitan University 2003, Bolton University 2010, Sheffield Hallam University 2016. Yorkshire Asian Business Personality of the Year 1992; National Asian Woman of the Year 1999; G22 National Leadership Award for Best Contribution to Public Services 2003; Lloyds Asian Jewel Award 2004; Top 100 most influential people in the UK in the Public Sector 2006; Top Three Most Successful Asian Women, Success Magazine 2007; One of the most influential Muslim women in the country, *The Times* and The Human Rights Commission 2009. CBE 1998.

The Baroness Manzoor CBE, House of Lords, London SW1A 0PW
Tel: 020 7219 3599 *Email:* manzoorz@parliament.uk

CROSSBENCH

MAR, COUNTESS OF

MAR (Countess of, 31st in line, S), Margaret of Mar; cr. 1114, precedence 1404; Lady Garioch (24th in line, S) 1320. Born 19 September 1940; Daughter of 30th Earl; Married Edwin Artiss 1959 (1 daughter) (divorced 1976); married John Salton 1976 (divorced 1981); married John Jenkin 1982.

Education: Kenya High School for Girls, Nairobi, Kenya; Lewes County Grammar School for Girls.

Non-political career: Civil service, clerical officer 1959-63; Sales superintendent, Post Office/British Telecom 1969-82; Farmer and cheesemaker 1982-2010; Farmer 2010-16. Vice-President, Association of Members of the Immigration Appeal Tribunal 2005-07.

Political career: *House of Lords:* First entered House of Lords 1975; Deputy Chair of Committees 1997-2007, 2010-12, 2014-; Deputy Speaker 1999-2007, 2011-; Elected hereditary peer 1999-; Contested Lord Speaker election 2006. Co-opted Member, European Communities Sub-committee C (Environment, Public Health and Consumer Protection) 1997-99; Member: EU Sub-committee D (Environment, Agriculture, Public Health and Consumer Protection/Environment and Agriculture) 2001-05, Refreshment 2005-09, Statutory Instruments Joint Committee 2007-10, Delegated Powers and Regulatory Reform 2013-16, Natural Environment and Rural Communities Act 2006 2017-.

Political interests: Health service, social security, agriculture, environment, pesticides, food standards; Africa.

Other: Numerous charitable organisations, especially ones involved in health; Chairman, Forward-Me. Laurent Perrier/Country Life Parliamentarian of the Year 1996; *BBC Wildlife Magazine* Green Ribbon Award 1997; *Spectator* Peer of the Year 1997; Honorary Associate: RCVS 2006, BVA 2006; Outstanding Achievement, Charity Champion Awards 2011. Holder of the Premier Earldom of Scotland; Recognised in the surname 'of Mar' by warrant of the Court of the Lord Lyon 1967, when she abandoned her second Christian name of Alison; *Clubs:* Farmers' Club.

Recreations: Gardening, reading, needlework.

The Countess of Mar, House of Lords, London SW1A 0PW
Tel: 020 7219 8627 *Fax:* 020 7219 1991 *Email:* marm@parliament.uk

LIBERAL DEMOCRAT

MARKS OF HENLEY-ON-THAMES, LORD

Liberal Democrat Shadow Lord Chancellor and Secretary of State for Justice

MARKS OF HENLEY-ON-THAMES (Life Baron), Jonathan Clive Marks; cr 2011. Born 19 October 1952; Son of late Geoffrey Marks and Patricia Marks, née Bowman; Married Sarah Russell 1982 (divorced 1991) (1 son 1 daughter); married Clementine Cafopoulous 1993 (3 sons 2 daughters).

Education: Harrow School; University College, Oxford (BA jurisprudence 1974); Inns of Court School of Law (1975); French, Greek.

Non-political career: Called to the Bar, Inner Temple 1975; Visiting lecturer in advocacy: Malaya University 1985, 1989-91, Mauritius University 1988, Sri Lanka University Law College 1992; QC 1995; Barrister, 4 Pump Court Chambers; Arbitrator and Family Law Arbitration.

Political career: *House of Commons:* Contested (SDP/All) Weston-Super-Mare 1983 and Falmouth and Camborne 1987 general elections. *House of Lords:* Raised to the peerage as Baron Marks of Henley-on-Thames, of Henley-on-Thames in the County of Oxfordshire 2011. Liberal Democrat: Spokesperson for Justice 2012-16, Shadow Lord Chancellor and Secretary of State for Justice 2016-. Member: Joint Committee on the Draft Defamation Bill 2011, Delegated Powers and Regulatory Reform 2012-15. Chair, Liberal Democrat Parliamentary Party Committee on Home Affairs, Justice and Equalities (Justice) 2012-15. *Other:* Contested Cornwall and Plymouth 1984 European Parliament election. Member, Liberal Democrat Committee for England 1988-89; Chair, Liberal Democrat Lawyers Association 2001-07; Member, Federal Policy Committee, Liberal Democrat 2004-10, 2012-.

Political interests: Justice issues, constitutional reform, human rights, education, health; Greece.

Other: Vice-patron, Jubilee; Sailing Trust; Fellow, Chartered Institute of Arbitrators 2012-. Worshipful Company of Pattenmakers; *Clubs:* Royal Automobile Club.

Recreations: Tennis, skiing, theatre, opera, travel.

The Lord Marks of Henley-on-Thames QC, House of Lords, London SW1A 0PW
Tel: 020 7219 6270 *Email:* marksj@parliament.uk
4 Pump Court, London EC4Y 7AN *Tel:* 020 7842 5555 *Email:* jmarks@4pumpcourt.com
Website: www.4pumpcourt.com

CONSERVATIVE

MARLAND, LORD

MARLAND (Life Baron), Jonathan Peter Marland; cr 2006. Born 14 August 1956; Son of Peter Greaves Marland and Audrey Joan Marland; Married Penelope Mary Lamb 1983 (2 sons 2 daughters).

Education: Shrewsbury School.

Non-political career: Director, Lloyd Thompson 1982-99; Partner, JLT Risk Solutions 1999-2006; Chair: Herriot Ltd 2000-10, Janspeed Performance Exhaust Systems Ltd 2002-10; Non-executive director, Clareville Capital LLP 2006-10; Director: Insurance Capital Partners LLP, Hunter Boot Ltd 2007-10; Chair, Jubilee/Appleclaim; Non-executive director: Essex Court Management, WH Ireland Ltd, Test Match Extra -2017.

Political career: *House of Commons:* Contested (Conservative) Somerset and Frome 2001 general election. *House of Lords:* Raised to the peerage as Baron Marland, of Odstock in the County of Wiltshire 2006. Opposition Whip 2009-10; Opposition Spokesperson for: Cabinet Office 2009-10, Energy and Climate Change 2009-10; Parliamentary Under-Secretary of State and Government Spokesperson, Department for: Energy and Climate Change 2010-12, Business, Innovation and Skills 2012-13. *Other:* Conservative Party: Treasurer 2003-07, Board member 2005-07; Director, C&UCO Properties (Party property company) 2006-05; Treasurer, Boris Johnson's London Mayoral Campaign 2007-08. *Councils and public bodies:* Royal Academy of Arts Development Committee 2008-10.

Political interests: Sport, arts, environment, business, finance.

Other: Advisory committee member, Airey Neave Trust 1992-; J P Marland Charitable Trust 1995-; Harnham Water Meadows Trust 2001-10; Trustee: Atlantic Partnership 2001-, Guggenheim (Museum) UK 2002-, Invercauld Estate 2002-15, Sports Nexus 2003-10; President, Salisbury FC 2008-10; International Churchill Society: Trustee 2009-, Chairman 2012-; Chairman: Tickets for Troops 2009-, Tricouni Brand Ltd 2014-, Commonwealth Enterprise and Investment Council 2014-; President, Commonwealth Youth Orchestra and Choir 2014; Chairman, Eco World Management and Advisory Services UK Ltd 2015-; FRSA 2008-; *Clubs:* RSA, MCC, Brooks's, Garrick Club.

Recreations: Sport, British art.

The Lord Marland, House of Lords, London SW1A 0PW
Tel: 020 7219 8738 *Email:* marland@parliament.uk
78 Belgrave Road, London SW1V 2BJ *Tel:* 020 7752 0177 *Email:* marland@odstock.net

CONSERVATIVE

MARLESFORD, LORD

MARLESFORD (Life Baron), Mark Shuldham Schreiber; cr. 1991. Born 11 September 1931; Son of late John Shuldham Schreiber, AE, DL and Maureen Schreiber, née Dent; Married Gabriella Federica 1969, daughter of Count Teodoro Veglio di Castelletto d'Uzzone (2 daughters).

Education: Eton College; Trinity College, Cambridge (BA economics 1956, MA); French.

Non-political career: National Service, Coldstream Guards, 2nd Lieutenant 1950-51. Fisons Ltd 1957-63; Conservative Research Department 1963-70; Special adviser: to HM Government 1970-74, to Leader of the Opposition 1974-75; *The Economist*: Editorial consultant 1974-91, Lobby correspondent 1976-91; Director, Eastern Group plc 1990-96; Adviser to Mitsubishi Corporation International NV 1990-2003; Independent national director, Times Newspaper Holdings 1991-2014; Adviser to Board, John Swire and Sons Ltd 1992-2009; Non-executive director, Baring New Russia Fund 1996-2007; Adviser, Sit Investment Associates, Minneapolis, USA 2001-; Non-executive director, Gave-Kal Research (Hong Kong) 2004-.

Political career: *House of Lords:* Raised to the peerage as Baron Marlesford, of Marlesford in the County of Suffolk 1991. Member, EU Sub-committee A: (Economic and Financial Affairs, Trade and External Relations/Economic and Financial Affairs) 2000-05, (Economic and Financial Affairs and International Trade) 2010-12, (Economic and Financial Affairs) 2012-14; Member, European Union 2003-07, 2012-14; EU Sub-committee F (Home Affairs): Member 2005-07, Co-opted member 2007-09. *Councils and public bodies:* Councillor, East Suffolk County Council 1968-70; Chair, Marlesford Parish Council 1978-; Member: Countryside Commission 1980-92, Rural Development Commission 1985-93; DL, Suffolk 1991-.

Political interests: Conservation, defence, EU economy; China, Egypt, Hong Kong, Iran.

Other: Chair, Council for the Protection of Rural England 1993-98; President: Suffolk ACRE 1995-2004, Suffolk Preservation Society 1997-; *Clubs:* Pratt's Club.

Recreations: Planting trees and hedges, collecting minerals.

The Lord Marlesford DL, House of Lords, London SW1A 0PW
Tel: 020 7219 5480 *Fax:* 020 7219 5979 *Email:* marlesford@parliament.uk
Marlesford Hall, Woodbridge, Suffolk IP13 0AU

CROSSBENCH

MARTIN OF SPRINGBURN, LORD

MARTIN OF SPRINGBURN (Life Baron), Michael John Martin; cr 2009. Born 3 July 1945; Son of Michael Martin, merchant seaman, and Mary McNeill, school cleaner; Married Mary McLay 1966 (1 son 1 daughter).

Education: St Patrick's Boys' School, Glasgow.

Non-political career: Metal worker, Rolls-Royce Engineering 1970-76; Full-time trades union official 1976-79. Shop steward, AUEW 1970-74; Trade union organiser, NUPE 1976-79; Member, AEEU (Craft Sector)/Unite; Sponsored as MP by AEEU.

Political career: *House of Commons:* MP for Glasgow Springburn 1979-2005, for Glasgow North East 2005-09 (Labour 1979-2000, Speaker 2000-09). PPS to Denis Healey as Deputy Leader of the Labour Party 1980-83; First Deputy Chairman, Ways and Means (Deputy Speaker) 1997-2000; Speaker 2000-09; Ex-officio chair House of Commons Commission 2000-09; Former chair

House of Lords
Peers' Biographies

Speaker's Committee on the Electoral Commission. Chair: Chairmen's Panel 1987-2000, Administration 1992-97, Liaison 1993-97; Member: Court of Referees 1997-2000, Unopposed Bills (Panel) 1997-2000, Standing Orders 1998-2000. *House of Lords:* Raised to the peerage as Baron Martin of Springburn, of Port Dundas in the City of Glasgow 2009; On leave of absence September 2017-. *Councils and public bodies:* Councillor: Glasgow Corporation 1973-74, Glasgow District Council 1974-79.

Political interests: Trade and industry, drug abuse, industrial relations, equal opportunities, care of the elderly, human rights, housing, apprenticeships; Canada, Italy, USA.

Other: Fellow, Industry and Parliament Trust 1984. Honorary doctorate, Glasgow University. PC 2000.

Recreations: Hillwalking, folk music, local history, playing the Highland Pipes (member of the College of Piping).

Rt Hon the Lord Martin of Springburn, House of Lords, London SW1A 0PW
Tel: 020 7219 1892 *Email:* martinm@parliament.uk

CROSSBENCH

MASHAM OF ILTON, BARONESS

MASHAM OF ILTON (Life Baroness), Susan Lilian Primrose Cunliffe-Lister; cr. 1970. Born 14 April 1935; Daughter of late Major Sir Ronald Sinclair, 8th Bt, TD, DL; Married Lord Masham, later 2nd Earl of Swinton 1959 (died 2006) (1 son 1 daughter both adopted).

Education: Heathfield School, Ascot; London Polytechnic.

Non-political career: Voluntary social work/health matters. Member, NFU.

Political career: *House of Lords:* Raised to the peerage as Baroness Masham of Ilton, of Masham in the North Riding of the County of Yorkshire 1970. Chair, Home Office Crime Prevention Working Group on Young People and Alcohol 1987. Member: Science and Technology Sub-committee I (Resistance to Anti-Microbial Agents) 1997-98, Administration and Works 2005-09, HIV and AIDS in the UK 2010-11. *Councils and public bodies:* Member: Peterlee and Newton Aycliffe Corporation 1973-85, Yorkshire Regional Health Authority 1982-90; DL, North Yorkshire 1991-; Member: North Yorkshire Family Health Service Authority 1990-96, Board of Visitors, Wetherby Young Offenders Institute.

Political interests: Health, disability, penal affairs and policy, drug abuse, farming, horticulture; Europe.

Other: North Yorkshire Red Cross: President 1963-88, Patron 1989-; Council member, Winston Churchill Trust 1980-2005; Hon. President, Ripon St Cecilia Orchestra 2008; Chair, Howard League Inquiry into Girls in Prison; Patron: International Spinal Research Trust, Northern Counties Trust for People Living with HIV/AIDS; Animal Health Trust; John Mordaunt Trust; Yorkshire Wildlife Trust; Highland Pony Society; Vice-President, Ponies UK; Former and current president, patron, chair, member of numerous charities, especially in areas of health and disability; Hon. Fellowship: RCGP 1981, Chartered Society of Physiotherapy 1996. Freedom: Ripon 1960, Harrogate 1989. Six honorary degrees; Four honorary fellowships. Rome Paralympics 1968: Gold 25m breaststroke swimming medal, Silver 25m backstroke swimming medal, Bronze women's doubles table tennis medal; Tokyo Paralympics 1964: Gold women's doubles table tennis medal, Silver 25m breaststroke swimming, 25m freestyle prone swimming, 25m freestyle supine swimming and women's singles table tennis medals; Tel Aviv Paralympics 1968: Silver women's doubles table tennis medal, Bronze women's singles table tennis medal.

Publications: The World Walks By (1986).

Recreations: Breeding Highland ponies, long haired dachshunds, gardening, swimming.

The Countess of Swinton, Baroness Masham of Ilton DL, House of Lords, London SW1A 0PW
Tel: 020 7219 3000 *Email:* mashams@parliament.uk
Dykes Hill House, Masham, Nr Ripon, North Yorkshire HG4 4NS *Tel:* 01765 689241
Fax: 01765 688184 *Email:* masham.swinton@gmail.com *Website:* mashamridingcentre.com

LABOUR

MASSEY OF DARWEN, BARONESS

MASSEY OF DARWEN (Life Baroness), Doreen Elizabeth Massey; cr. 1999. Born 5 September 1938; Daughter of late Jack and Mary Ann Hall, née Sharrock; Married Dr Leslie Massey 1966 (2 sons 1 daughter).

Education: Darwen Grammar School, Lancashire; Birmingham University (BA French 1961; DipEd 1962); London University (MA health education 1985); French, some Russian.

Non-political career: Graduate service overseas, Gabon 1962-63; French teacher, South Hackney School 1964-67; French and English teacher, Springside School, Philadelphia 1967-69; Running community playgroup 1970-77; Teacher/Head of year/Senior teacher in charge of health education, Walsingham School, London 1979-83; Director of training, Family Planning Association

(FPA) 1981-89; Adviser in personal, social and health education, Inner London Education Authority 1983-85; Director of Young People's Programme, Health Education Authority 1985-87; Director, FPA 1989-94; Independent consultant in health education 1994-2001; Chair, National Treatment Agency for Substance Misuse 2002-13. Former member: NUT, MSF.

Political career: *House of Lords:* Raised to the peerage as Baroness Massey of Darwen, of Darwen in the County of Lancashire 1999. Member: Selection 2005-08, Ecclesiastical Committee 2005-10, Works of Art 2007-11, Information 2010-15, Affordable Childcare 2014-15, EU Home Affairs Sub-committee 2015-. Vice-chair, PLP Departmental Group for Education 2010-15.

Political interests: Education, health, children and young people, sport, substance misuse; Central Asia, France, Russia, USA.

Other: Parliamentary Delegate, Council of Europe 2016-; President, Brook Advisory Centres; Patron, Family Planning Association; Advisory Council for Alcohol and Drug Education; Trust for the Study of Adolescence; Trustee, Unicef -2017; Patron: Women and Children First, Bedfordshire University Child Trafficking Unit; FRSA; ENO, Opera North, Tacade, Terrence Higgins Trust, Stonewall, Brook Advisory, Women and Children First. Fellow, University of Central Lancashire 2005; Honorary Doctorate, Birmingham University 2014; *Clubs:* Farmers Club, Lady Taverners Club.

Publications: Teaching About HIV/AIDS (1988); Co-author, Sex Education Factpack (1988); Sex Education: Why, What and How (1988); Editor, The Sex Education Source Book (1995); Lovers' Guide Encyclopaedia (1996); Articles on health education in a variety of journals.

Recreations: Theatre, opera, reading, walking, pilates, travel, sports.

The Baroness Massey of Darwen, House of Lords, London SW1A 0PW
Tel: 020 7219 8653 *Email:* masseyd@parliament.uk

CONSERVATIVE

MAUDE OF HORSHAM, LORD

MAUDE OF HORSHAM (Life Baron), Francis Anthony Aylmer Maude; cr 2015. Born 4 July 1953; Son of late Angus Maude (MP for Ealing South 1950-58 and Stratford-on-Avon 1963-83, later Lord Maude of Stratford-upon-Avon) and late Lady Maude; Married Christina Hadfield 1984 (2 sons 3 daughters).

Education: Abingdon School; Corpus Christi, Cambridge (MA history 1976) (Hulse Prize and Avory Studentship); College of Law (Forster Boulton Prize and Inner Temple Law Scholarship 1977).

Non-political career: Called to Bar, Inner Temple 1977; Practising barrister 1977-85; Head of global privatisation, Salomon Bros International 1992-93; Managing director, global privatisation, Morgan Stanley & Co Ltd 1993-97; Chair, Deregulation Task Force 1993-97; Benfield Group plc: Non-executive director 1999-, Deputy chair 2003-08; Non-executive director, Businesses for Sale Company plc 2000-02; Chair: Prestbury Holdings plc 2002-08, Jubilee Investment Trust plc 2003-07, The Mission Marketing Group 2006-09.

Political career: *House of Commons:* MP (Conservative) for North Warwickshire 1983-92. Contested North Warwickshire 1992 general election. MP for Horsham 1997-2010, for Horsham (revised boundary) 2010-15. PPS to Peter Morrison as Minister of State for Employment 1984; Government Whip 1985-87; Parliamentary Under-Secretary of State, Department of Trade and Industry 1987-89; Minister of State, Foreign and Commonwealth Office 1989-90; Financial Secretary to the Treasury 1990-92; Member, Shadow Cabinet 1997-2001: Shadow Secretary of State for: National Heritage 1997, Culture, Media and Sport 1997-98; Shadow Chancellor of the Exchequer 1998-2000; Shadow Secretary of State for Foreign and Commonwealth Affairs 2000-01; Shadow Minister for the Cabinet Office and Shadow Chancellor of the Duchy of Lancaster 2007-10; Minister for the Cabinet Office; Paymaster General 2010-15. Member, Public Accounts 1990-92. Member, Executive 1922 Committee 1997; Chair, Conservative Party Committees for: Culture, Media and Sport 1997-98, Finance 1998-2000, European Affairs 2000-01, Foreign and Commonwealth Affairs 2000-01. *House of Lords:* Raised to the peerage as Baron Maude of Horsham, of Shipley in the County of West Sussex 2015. Minister of State for Trade and Investment and Government Spokesperson, Department for Business, Innovation and Skills and Foreign and Commonwealth Office 2015-16. *Other:* Chair, Conservative Party 2005-07. *Councils and public bodies:* Councillor, Westminster City Council 1978-84; Chair of governors, Abingdon School 1994-2003.

Other: Advisory board member, Anvest Partners 2016-; Chair, Cogent Elliott Group Ltd 2016-; Senior adviser, Covington & Burling LLP 2016-; Advisory board member, OakNorth Bank 2016-; Chair, board, Brighton College International Schools 2017-. PC 1992.

Recreations: Skiing, reading, opera.

Rt Hon the Lord Maude of Horsham, House of Lords, London SW1A 0PW
Tel: 020 7219 3000

CONSERVATIVE

MAWHINNEY, LORD

MAWHINNEY (Life Baron), Brian Stanley Mawhinney; cr 2005. Born 26 July 1940; Son of Frederick and Coralie Mawhinney; Married Betty Oja 1965 (2 sons 1 daughter).

Education: Royal Belfast Academical Institution; Queen's University, Belfast (BSc physics 1963); Michigan University, USA (MSc radiation biology 1964); London University (PhD radiation biology 1968).

Non-political career: Assistant professor of radiation research, Iowa University, USA 1968-70; Lecturer (subsequently senior lecturer), Royal Free Hospital School of Medicine 1970-84. Life Member, AUT.

Political career: *House of Commons:* Contested Teesside Stockton October 1974 general election. MP (Conservative) for Peterborough 1979-97, for North West Cambridgeshire 1997-2005. PPS: to Barney Hayhoe as Minister of State, HM Treasury 1982-84, to Tom King as Secretary of State for: Employment 1983-85, Northern Ireland 1984-86; Northern Ireland Office: Parliamentary Under-Secretary of State 1986-90, Minister of State 1990-92; Minister of State, Department of Health 1992-94; Secretary of State for Transport 1994-95; Minister without Portfolio 1995-97; Shadow Home Secretary 1997-98. Chair, Conservative Party Committee for Home Affairs 1997-98. *House of Lords:* Raised to the peerage as Baron Mawhinney, of Peterborough in the County of Cambridgeshire 2005. Chair, Joint Committee on the Draft Defamation Bill 2011; Member: Joint Committee on Privacy and Injunctions 2011-12, Public Service and Demographic Change 2012-13, Long-Term Sustainability of the NHS 2016-17. *Other:* National President, Conservative Trade Unionists 1987-90; Chair, Conservative Party 1995-97; Member, governing council, Conservative Christian Fellowship. *Councils and public bodies:* Deputy chair, England 2018 World Cup Bid 2009-10.

Political interests: Health, Northern Ireland, Anglo-American relations, trade and industry; Middle East, USA.

Other: Member, British-Irish Parliamentary Assembly; Member: Medical Research Council 1979-83, National Council, National Society for Cancer Relief 1981-85; Fellow, Industry and Parliament Trust 1984; Member, General Synod of Church of England 1985-90; Review Committee of Privy Counsellors of the Anti-terrorism, Crime and Security Act 2002-; Football League: Chair 2003-10, Hon. President 2010-13; Director, Football Association 2006-08; Honorary member, Institute of Physics; Peterborough Association for the Blind, Evangelical Alliance Relief Fund, Macmillan Cancer Relief, More Than Gold. Freedom, Peterborough 2008. Visiting Parliamentary Fellow, St Anthony's College, Oxford 2004-05; Honorary LLD, Queen's University, Belfast 2008. PC 1994; Kt 1997. Member, Etton Furze Golf Club.

Publications: Co-author, Conflict and Christianity in Northern Ireland (1972); In the Firing Line – Politics, Faith, Power and Forgiveness (1999); Just a Simple Belfast Boy (autobiography) (Biteback Publishing, 2013).

Recreations: Sport, reading.

Rt Hon the Lord Mawhinney, House of Lords, London SW1A 0PW
Tel: 020 7219 5336

CROSSBENCH

MAWSON, LORD

MAWSON (Life Baron), Andrew Mawson; cr 2007. Born 8 November 1954; Son of Jack and Mary Mawson; Married Susan Barnes 1975 (1 daughter 2 sons).

Education: Hanson Boys' School, Bradford; Manchester University (BA theology 1979; MPhil urban spirituality 1990).

Non-political career: Ordained minister, United Reformed Church 1979; Founder and director, Church Action on Central America 1980-92; Founder, chief executive, chair, president, Bromley by Bow Centre (community and primary care facilities) 1984-; Co-founder, executive director, president, Community Action Network 1998-; Director: Andrew Mawson Partnerships 2007-, St Paul's Way CIC, Water City CIC 2011-, St Paul's Way Transformation Project; Founder: Poplar Harca, Leaside Regeneration; Non-executive director, Olympic Park Legacy Company 2009-.

Political career: *House of Lords:* Raised to the peerage as Baron Mawson, of Bromley-by-Bow in the London Borough of Tower Hamlets 2007. EU Sub-committee F (Home Affairs): Co-opted Member 2007-10, Member 2010-12; Member: Small- and Medium-Sized Enterprises 2012-13, Refreshment 2012-15, Joint Committee on the Draft Deregulation Bill 2013, Information 2014-16, European Union 2015-16, EU Internal Market Sub-committee 2015-.

Political interests: Public services, international affairs, health, education, enterprise; Europe, UK.

Other: Trustee, Legacy List 2015-; Chair, SS Robin Trust 2015-. Honorary doctorate. OBE 2000.

Publications: The Social Entrepreneur: Making Communities Work (2007).

Recreations: Music, walking, travel.

The Lord Mawson OBE, House of Lords, London SW1A 0PW
Tel: 020 7219 6197
c/o HLM Architects, Ground Floor, 46 Loman Street, London SE1 0EH *Tel:* 020 7620 6000
Email: andrew@amawsonpartnerships.com *Website:* www.amawsonpartnerships.com

LABOUR

MAXTON, LORD

MAXTON (Life Baron), John Alston Maxton; cr. 2004. Born 5 May 1936; Son of late John Maxton, agricultural economist, and late Jenny Maxton; Married Christine Waine 1970 (3 sons).

Education: Lord William's Grammar School, Thame; University College, Oxford (BA modern history 1960; DipEd 1961).

Non-political career: Teacher, Glasgow Academy 1961-70; Lecturer in social studies, Hamilton College 1970-79. Member: MSF, Educational Institute of Scotland.

Political career: *House of Commons:* MP (Labour) for Glasgow Cathcart 1979-2001. Opposition Scottish and Treasury Whip 1985; Opposition Frontbench Spokesperson for Scotland 1985-92. Chair PLP National Heritage/Culture, Media and Sport Committee, Member 1992-97. *House of Lords:* Raised to the peerage as Baron Maxton, of Blackwaterfoot in Ayrshire and Arran 2004. Member: Review of the BBC Charter 2005-06, Communications 2007-10, Information 2011-15, Science and Technology 2015-.

Political interests: Broadcasting, internet; France, Spain.

Other: Member: Association of Lecturers in Colleges of Education, Socialist Educational Association. Shiskine Golf and Tennis Club; Virgin Active; Hamilton Rugby Club.

Recreations: Listening to Jazz, fitness, holiday golf on the Isle of Arran, technology.

The Lord Maxton, House of Lords, London SW1A 0PW
Tel: 020 7219 6475 *Email:* maxtonj@parliament.uk
Email: maxtonj@yahoo.co.uk

CROSSBENCH

MEACHER, BARONESS

MEACHER (Life Baroness), Molly Christine Meacher; cr 2006. Born 15 May 1940; Daughter of William Frederick and Lucy Marie Reid; Married Michael Meacher 1962 (MP for Oldham West 1970-97 and Oldham West and Royton 1997-2015) (divorced 1987, died 2015) (2 sons 2 daughters); married Professor Richard Layard 1991, now Lord Layard (qv).

Education: Berkhamsted School for Girls; York University (BA economics 1970); London University (CQSW 1980); Russian and French.

Non-political career: Manager, National Association of Citizens Advice Bureaux 1982-84; Parliamentary officer, British Association of Social Workers 1984-86; Director, Campaign for Work 1986-91; Chief adviser to Russian Government on employment 1991-94; Member and deputy chair, Police Complaints Authority 1994-2002; Chair, Security Industry Authority 2002-04.

Political career: *House of Lords:* Raised to the peerage as Baroness Meacher, of Spitalfields in the London Borough of Tower Hamlets 2006. Alternate member, Procedure 2015-; Member, Joint Committee on Statutory Instruments 2015-. *Councils and public bodies:* Commissioner, Mental Health Act 1987-92; Non-executive director, Tower Hamlets Healthcare Trust 1994-98; Chair: Home Office Forum for Forensic Physicians 2002-04, Clinical Ethics Committee, Central and North West London Mental Health Trust 2004-08, East London NHS Foundation Trust 2004-13.

Political interests: Mental health, criminal justice, welfare benefits, social care; Russia.

Other: Chair, European Initiative on Drug Policy 2014-16; Chair, Dignity in Dying 2016-; President, Haemophilia Society; Russian European Trust, Taxaid. *Spectator* Peer of the Year 2015; Oldie Campaigner of the Year 2015. Hampstead Golf Club 2004-.

Publications: Scrounging on the Welfare (Hutchinson, 1972); To Him Who Hath (Penguin, 1977); New Methods of Mental Health Care (Penguin, 1979); Contributor: The Mentally Disordered Offender (Butterworth-Heinemann, 1991), Mental Health Services Today and Tomorrow (Radcliffe Publishing Oxford, 2008).

Recreations: Music, golf.

The Baroness Meacher, House of Lords, London SW1A 0PW
Tel: 020 7219 4081 *Email:* meachermc@parliament.uk

MENDELSOHN, LORD

LABOUR

Opposition Spokesperson for Business, Energy and Industrial Strategy and International Trade

MENDELSOHN (Life Baron), Jonathan Neil Mendelsohn; cr 2013. Born 30 December 1966.

Non-political career: Policy and communications adviser to Leader of the Opposition 1995-97; Business adviser and co-founder, LLM Communications 1997-2007; Financial Dynamics: Managing director 2005-07, Chair, Global Issues Division 2005-07; Partner, Oakvale Capital LLP.

Political career: *House of Lords:* Raised to the peerage as Baron Mendelsohn, of Finchley in the London Borough of Barnet 2013. Opposition Whip 2014-15; Opposition Spokesperson for: Business, Innovation and Skills 2015-16, Business, Energy and Industrial Strategy 2016-, International Trade 2016-. *Other:* Labour Party: Director of general election resources 2007-10, Assistant treasurer 2009-11.

The Lord Mendelsohn, House of Lords, London SW1A 0PW
Tel: 020 7219 3199

MILLER OF CHILTHORNE DOMER, BARONESS

LIBERAL DEMOCRAT

MILLER OF CHILTHORNE DOMER (Life Baroness), Susan Elisabeth Miller; cr. 1998. Born 1 January 1954; Daughter of Frederick Taylor and Norah Langham; Married John Miller 1980 (divorced 1998) (2 daughters 1 deceased); married Humphrey Temperley 1999.

Education: Sidcot School, Winscombe, Somerset; Oxford Polytechnic (book publishing 1975); French.

Non-political career: In publishing: David & Charles, Weidenfeld & Nicolson, Penguin Books 1975-79; Bookshop owner 1979-89; Vineyard owner 2009-.

Political career: *House of Lords:* Raised to the peerage as Baroness Miller of Chilthorne Domer, of Chilthorne Domer in the County of Somerset 1998. Liberal Democrat Spokesperson for: Agriculture and Rural Affairs 1999-2001, Environment, Food and Rural Affairs 2001-07, Home Affairs 2007-09. Member: European Union Sub-committee D (Environment and Agriculture) 2005-07, Draft Climate Change Bill Joint Committee 2007, Draft Marine Bill Joint Committee 2008. *Other:* Member, Liberal Democrat Federal Policy Committee. *Councils and public bodies:* South Somerset District Council: Councillor 1991-98, Leader 1996-98; Councillor, Somerset County Council 1997-2005.

Political interests: Environment, street children, human rights, nutrition and food, sovereignty, nuclear non proliferation and disarmament; Central and South America, France.

Other: Member: Inter-Parliamentary Union, Parliamentarians for Nuclear Non-proliferation and Disarmament (PNND); Vice-president: British Trust for Conservation Volunteers, Wildlife Link; Patron, ECOS Homes; TCF; President, Josephine Butler Society; Charlotte Miller Art Project, International Children's Trust (Juconi), Save the Children, Marine Conservation Society, Baby Milk Action, Wildlife Trusts, Oxfam, War on Want. Fellow, Joint University (Exeter and Bournemouth).

Publications: Stuck or Spiked – What Happened to eco-labelling in the UK (2002); Hungry for Change – A UK Food Policy (2004).

Recreations: Horse riding, reading, friends, gardening vegetables, wine.

The Baroness Miller of Chilthorne Domer, House of Lords, London SW1A 0PW
Tel: 020 7219 6042 *Email:* millers@parliament.uk

MITCHELL, LORD

NON-AFFILIATED

MITCHELL (Life Baron), Parry Andrew Mitchell; cr. 2000. Born 6 May 1943; Son of late Leon Mitchell and Rose Mitchell; Married Doreen Hargreaves 1972 (divorced) (1 daughter); married Hannah Lowy 1988 (twin sons).

Education: Christ's College Grammar School, London; London University (BSc economics 1964); Graduate School of Business, Columbia University, New York (MBA 1966).

Non-political career: Information technology entrepreneur; Chair and founder: United Leasing plc 1976-87, Syscap plc 1992-2006; Zuse Inc New York 2012-.

Political career: *House of Lords:* Raised to the peerage as Baron Mitchell, of Hampstead in the London Borough of Camden 2000. Opposition Spokesperson for Business, Innovation and Skills 2012-13. Member: House of Lords Offices Library and Computers Sub-committee 2001-03, Science and Technology Sub-committee II (Innovations in Computer Processors/Microprocessors/ Science and the Regional Development Agencies) 2002-03, Science and Technology Committee 2003-06; Chair, Science and Technology Sub-committee I (Science and International Agreements) 2003-04; Member, Science and Technology Sub-committee I (Scientific Aspects of Ageing) 2004-05; Co-opted Member: EU Sub-committee B (Internal Market) 2006-10, Science and Technology Sub-committee I (Nanotechnologies and food) 2009-10; Member: Small- and Medium-Sized Enterprises 2012, Joint Committee on National Security Strategy 2014-. *Other:* Labour's Business Ambassador 2013-16; Adviser to Shadow Ministerial Business, Innovation and Skills team 2013-16; Left the Labour Party September 2016; now sits as Non-affiliated.

Political interests: Information technology, small businesses, foreign affairs, education, alcohol abuse; Israel, USA.

Other: Trustee, Lowy Mitchell Foundation. Honorary fellow, College of Teachers 2011; *Clubs:* Players Club, New York Club.

Recreations: Scuba diving, theatre, jazz, opera.

The Lord Mitchell, House of Lords, London SW1A 0PW
Tel: 020 7219 8657 *Email:* mitchellp@parliament.uk *Twitter:* @lordparry

CONSERVATIVE

MOBARIK, BARONESS

MOBARIK (Life Baroness), Nosheena Shaheen Mobarik; cr 2014. Born 16 October 1957; Daughter of Tufail Shaheen; Married Iqbal (2 children).

Education: Glasgow Caledonian University (business); Open University; Strathclyde University (English literature and history).

Non-political career: Small business owner; Lecturer, Social policy in healthcare, Anniesland College; Co-founder, M Computer Technologies 1997-.

Political career: *House of Lords:* Raised to the peerage as Baroness Mobarik, of Mearns in the County of Renfrewshire 2014. Government Whip (Baroness in Waiting) 2016-17; On leave of absence September 2017-. Member: Refreshment 2015, EU Financial Affairs Sub-committee 2016, Intellectual Property (Unjustified Threats) Bill 2016. *Other:* European Parliament: Contested Scotland region 2014 European Parliament election. MEP for Scotland 2017-. *Councils and public bodies:* Governor, Craigholme School for Girls.

Other: Chair, CBI Scotland; Founder and trustee, Save the Bosnian People Campaign; Founder and convener, Scotland Pakistan Network; Member, Edinburgh Direct Aid; Chair, Pakistan Britain Trade and Investment Forum 2012-; Board member, Glasgow Film Theatre. OBE 2004; CBE 2014.

The Baroness Mobarik CBE MEP, House of Lords, London SW1A 0PW
Tel: 020 7219 5353
Website: www.nosheenamobarik.com

CROSSBENCH

MOGG, LORD

MOGG (Life Baron), John Frederick Mogg; cr 2008. Born 5 October 1943; Married Anne Smith 1967 (1 daughter 1 son).

Education: Bishop Vesey's Grammar School, Sutton Coldfield; Birmingham University (BA history 1965).

Non-political career: Rediffusion Ltd 1965-74; Principal: Office of Fair Trading 1974-76, Department of Trade 1976-79; First secretary, UK Permanent Representation to EC, Brussels 1979-82; Department of Trade and Industry 1982-89: Assistant secretary, minerals and metals division 1982-85, Principal private secretary to Secretaries of State Norman Tebbit, Leon Brittan and Paul Channon 1985-86, Under-secretary: European policy division 1986-87, Industrial materials market division 1987-89; Deputy head, European secretariat, Cabinet Office 1989-90; European Commission 1990-2003: Deputy director-general, DG III Internal Market and Industrial Affairs 1990-93, Director-general, DG XV, later DG Internal Market and Financial Services 1993-2003; Special adviser to President, Office for Harmonisation in the International Market 2009-12.

Political career: *House of Lords:* Raised to the peerage as Baron Mogg, of Queen's Park in the County of East Sussex 2008. On leave of absence September 2014-. *Councils and public bodies:* Gas and Electricity Markets Authority: Non-executive chair 2003-13, European adviser 2013-; Chair of Governors, Brighton University 2005-15.

Political interests: Business industry and consumers, economy and finance, education; European Union, USA.

Other: President, Council of European Energy Regulators 2003-; Chair: International Confederation of Energy Regulators 2010-15, Board of Regulators, Agency for the Co-operation of European Regulators 2011-, Advisory board, European Union Observatory on Infringements of Intellectual Property Rights 2012-; Trustee, Brighton Philharmonic Orchestra 2005-12; Member, advisory board, Electric Power Research Institute 2012-. KCMG 2003.

The Lord Mogg KCMG, House of Lords, London SW1A 0PW
Tel: 020 7219 5353 *Email:* moggj@parliament.uk
Tel: 020 7901 7203 *Fax:* 020 7901 7395 *Email:* john.mogg@ofgem.gov.uk

CONSERVATIVE

MONE, BARONESS

MONE (Life Baroness), Michelle Georgina Mone; cr 2015. Born 8 October 1971; Daughter of Duncan and Isobel Allan; Married Michael Mone (divorced 2013) (3 children).

Non-political career: Head of sales and marketing for Scotland, Labatt Brewers -1996; Founder: Ultimo 1996-2014, UTan 2012-.

Political career: *House of Lords:* Raised to the peerage as Baroness Mone, of Mayfair in the City of Westminster 2015. Leads a government review on supporting business start-ups in disadvantaged communities.

Political interests: Enterprise.

Other: Board of directors, Prince's Scottish Youth Business Trust; Princes Trust. Hon. Doctorate: Paisley University 2002, Hertfordshire University 2010. World Young Business Achiever Award 2000, USA; Business Woman of the Year, Corporate Elite Awards; Best Newcomer, British Apparel Export Awards. OBE 2010.

Publications: My Fight to the Top (autobiography, 2015).

The Baroness Mone OBE, House of Lords, London SW1A 0PW
Tel: 020 7219 3000 *Email:* monem@parliament.uk
MGM Media Limited, 86-90 Paul Street, London EC2A 4NE *Tel:* 020 3823 6900
Email: enquiries@michellemone.com
Website: michellemone.com *Twitter:* @MichelleMone

LABOUR

MONKS, LORD

MONKS (Life Baron), John Stephen Monks; cr 2010. Born 5 August 1945; Son of Charles Monks, parks superintendent, and Bessie Monks, teacher; Married Francine Schenk 1970 (2 sons 1 daughter).

Education: Ducie Technical High School, Manchester; Nottingham University (BA economic history 1967); French.

Non-political career: Trades Union Congress 1969-2003: Head of organisation and industrial relations department 1977-87, Deputy General Secretary 1987-93, General Secretary 1993-2003; General Secretary, European Trades Union Confederation 2003-11; Non-executive director, Thompsons' Solicitors 2010-; Special adviser to José Manuel Barroso as President, European Commission 2011-14; Trustee director, NOW: Pensions 2011-. President, British Airline Pilots' Association 2011-.

Political career: *House of Lords:* Raised to the peerage as Baron Monks, of Blackley in the County of Greater Manchester 2010. Member: Economic Affairs 2014-16, Economic Affairs Finance Bill Sub-committee 2015-16. *Councils and public bodies:* Council member, ACAS 1979-95; Vice-chair, Learning and Skills Council 2001-04; Chairman, Co-operative Commission 2000-01.

Countries of interest: Europe.

Other: Council member, Economic and Social Research Council 1988-91; People's History Museum: Trustee 1988-2016, Chair of Trustees 2004-16; President, British Airline Pilots Association 2011-. Honorary doctorates: Nottingham University, Salford University, Manchester University, Cranfield University, Cardiff University, Kingston University, Southampton University, Open University; Fellow, City & Guilds of London. Chevalier, Legion D'Honneur.

Recreations: Music, film, football, cricket, rugby (especially league).

The Lord Monks, House of Lords, London SW1A 0PW
Tel: 020 7219 6943 *Email:* monksj@parliament.uk

MONTROSE, DUKE OF

CONSERVATIVE

MONTROSE (8th Duke of, S), James Graham; cr. 1707; Marquis of Montrose (S) 1644; Marquess of Graham and Buchanan (S) 1707; Earl of Montrose (S) 1505; Earl of Kincardine (S) 1707; Earl Graham (GB) 1722; Viscount Dundaff (S) 1707; Lord Graham (S) 1445; Lord Aberuthven, Mugdock and Fintrie (S) 1707; Baron Graham (GB) 1722; 12th Bt of Braco (NA) 1625. Born 6 April 1935; Son of 7th Duke and late Isobel Sellar; Married Catherine MacDonnell, née Young 1970 (died 2014) (2 sons 1 daughter).

Education: Loretto School, Musselburgh; French.

Non-political career: Farmer, landowner.

Political career: *House of Lords:* First entered House of Lords 1996; Elected hereditary peer 1999-; Opposition Spokesperson for: Scotland 2001-10, Environment 2001-06, 2008-10, Food and Rural Affairs 2001-10; Opposition Whip 2001-10; Opposition Spokesperson for: Northern Ireland 2007, Wales 2007-08, 2009-10. Member: Partnerships (Prosecution) (Scotland) Bill 2013, Science and Technology 2015-16, EU Energy and Environment Sub-Committee 2016-. *Councils and public bodies:* Chair, Buchanan Community Council 1982-93; Vice-chair, Secretary of State's Working Party for Loch Lomond and the Trossachs.

Political interests: Europe, agriculture, rural affairs; Ethiopia, Sudan.

Other: Member: Inter-Parliamentary Union 1997-, Commonwealth Parliamentary Association 1997-; Queen's Bodyguard for Scotland (Royal Company of Archers): Member 1965-, Captain 2006-14; Hereditary Sheriff, Dunbartonshire; Member: Council of Scottish National Farmers Union 1981-90, Royal Scottish Pipers Society; President, Royal Highland and Agricultural Society 1997-98; Scottish Landowners Federation; President, National Sheep Association 2012; Royal Agricultural Benevolent Society. OStJ 1978; *Clubs:* Farmers Club.

Recreations: Walking, shooting, golf.

His Grace the Duke of Montrose, House of Lords, London SW1A 0PW
Tel: 020 7219 4487 *Fax:* 020 7219 5979 *Email:* montrosej@parliament.uk
Montrose Estates Ltd, Buchanan Castle, Drymen G63 0HY *Tel:* 01360 660307
Fax: 01360 660993

MOONIE, LORD

LAB/CO-OP

MOONIE (Life Baron), Lewis George Moonie; cr 2005. Born 25 February 1947; Son of late George Moonie, accountant, and Eva Moonie; Married Sheila Burt 1971 (2 sons).

Education: Grove Academy, Dundee; St Andrews University (MB, ChB 1970); Edinburgh University (DPM 1975; MRCPsych 1979; MSc community medicine 1981; MFCM 1984); French, Dutch.

Non-political career: Registrar training in psychiatry 1973-75; Full-time research clinical pharmacologist and medical adviser in pharmaceutical industry in Netherlands, Switzerland and Edinburgh 1975-80; Fife Health Board: Trainee community medicine 1980-84, Community medicine specialist 1984-87. Member: TGWU, MSF.

Political career: *House of Commons:* MP (Labour) for Kirkcaldy 1987-2005. Opposition Frontbench Spokesperson for: Technology, Trade and Industry 1989-92, Science and Technology 1992-94, Trade and Industry 1994-95, Broadcasting and Telecommunications 1995-97; Member House of Commons Commission 1997-2000; Parliamentary Under-Secretary of State (Minister for Veterans), Ministry of Defence 2000-03. *House of Lords:* Raised to the peerage as Baron Moonie, of Bennochy in Fife 2005. Member: Economic Affairs 2007-12, Finance Bill Sub-committee 2008-10, Economic Affairs Finance Bill Sub-Committee 2011. *Other:* Member, Co-operative Party. *Councils and public bodies:* Councillor, Fife Regional Council 1982-86.

Political interests: Industry, technology, economic policy, defence.

Other: RSPB, Oxfam.

Recreations: Fishing, walking, golf, bridge.

The Lord Moonie, House of Lords, London SW1A 0PW
Tel: 020 7219 4097 *Email:* mooniel@parliament.uk *Twitter:* @Moonie_1

MOORE OF LOWER MARSH, LORD

CONSERVATIVE

MOORE OF LOWER MARSH (Life Baron), John Edward Michael Moore; cr. 1992. Born 26 November 1937; Son of late Edward Moore; Married Sheila Tillotson 1962 (died 2008) (2 sons 1 daughter).

Education: Licensed Victuallers' School, Slough; London School of Economics (BSc Econ 1961).

Non-political career: Commissioned army national service with Royal Sussex Regiment in Korea 1955-57. Dean Witter (International) Ltd: Director 1968-79, Chair 1975-79; Advisory board member, Marvin and Palmer Inc 1989-; Director, Monitor Inc 1990-2006, Chair, European Executive Committee; Member, advisory board, Sir Alexander Gibb & Co 1990-95; Chair, Credit Suisse Asset Management 1992-2000; Director: Swiss American NY Inc 1992-96, GTECH 1993-2001, Blue Circle Industries plc 1993-2001, Camelot Holdings plc 1993-98; Rolls-Royce plc: Director 1994-2005, Deputy chair 1996-2003, Chair 2003-05; Supervisory board member, ITT Automotive Europe GMBH, Germany 1994-97; Director: Central European Growth Fund Ltd 1995-2000, BEA (NY) 1996-98, TIG Holdings Inc (NY) 1997-99, Private Client Bank (Zurich) 1999-2003.

Political career: *House of Commons:* MP (Conservative) for Croydon Central February 1974-92. Parliamentary Under-Secretary of State for Energy 1979-83; Economic Secretary to the Treasury 1983; Financial Secretary to the Treasury 1983-86; Secretary of State for: Transport 1986-87, Social Services 1987-88, Social Security 1988-89. *House of Lords:* Raised to the peerage as Baron Moore of Lower Marsh, of Lower Marsh in the London Borough of Lambeth 1992. *Other:* Chair: LSE Conservative Association 1958, Stepney Green Conservative Association 1968; Vice-chair (Youth), Conservative Party 1975-79. *Councils and public bodies:* Councillor, London Borough of Merton 1971-74; Member, Court of Governors, LSE 1977-2002.

Other: Council Member, Institute of Directors 1991-99; Energy Savings Trust: Chair 1992-95, President 1995-2001. PC 1986; *Clubs:* Royal Automobile Club.

Rt Hon the Lord Moore of Lower Marsh, House of Lords, London SW1A 0PW
Tel: 020 7219 5353

MORGAN, LORD

LABOUR

MORGAN (Life Baron), Kenneth Owen Morgan; cr. 2000. Born 16 May 1934; Son of late David Morgan and Margaret Morgan, née Owen; Married Jane Keeler 1973 (died 1992) (1 son 1 daughter); married Dr Elizabeth Gibson 2009.

Education: University College School, Hampstead; Oriel College, Oxford (BA modern history 1955, MA; DPhil 1958; DLitt 1985).

Non-political career: Lecturer, later senior lecturer in history, University College of Wales, Swansea 1958-66; Columbia University: Visiting Fellow 1962-63, Visiting Professor 1965; Fellow and praelector, modern history and politics, Queen's College, Oxford 1966-89; Visiting Professor, University of South Carolina 1972; O'Donnell lecturer, University of Wales 1981-82; Neale lecturer, University College, London 1986; Principal, then Vice-Chancellor, University College of Wales, Aberystwyth; University of Wales: Professor 1989-95, Senior Vice-Chancellor 1993-95, Emeritus Professor 1999; AH Dodd lecturer, University of Wales, Bangor 1992, 2004; Lloyd George Memorial lecturer 1993; Visiting lecturer, University of Texas (Austin) 1994, 1999, 2007, 2010, 2014; Faculty lecturer, Oxford University 1995-2000; BBC (Wales) annual lecturer 1995; Prothero lecturer, Royal Historical Society 1996; Callaghan lecturer, University College of Wales, Swansea 1996; Visiting Professor, Witwatersrand University, South Africa 1997, 1998, 2000; British Academy lecturer 1998; Benjamin Meaker Visiting Professor, Bristol University 2000; Merlyn-Rees lecturer, Glamorgan University 2002; Presidential lecturer, Rouen University 2003; Ford special lecturer, Oxford University 2005; London Guildhall lecturer 2006, 2007; Gresham College Lecturer 2007; Visiting Professor, King's College, London 2011-; Speaker's House lecture 2011; King's College London annual lecture 2012; SAES lecture, Limoges 2012; Visiting Lecturer: Texas University 2014, Riga University 2014. Member, AUT -1995.

Political career: *House of Lords:* Raised to the peerage as Baron Morgan, of Aberdyfi in the County of Gwynedd 2000. Member, Constitution 2001-04, 2015-; Joint Committee on Draft Constitutional Bill 2008.

Political interests: Education, Europe, foreign affairs, constitutional reform, civil liberties, children; France, India, South Africa, Wales, USA.

Other: Chair, Curatorium, Celtic Studies Centre, Tubingen University 1998-2005; President, Committee for Advanced Studies, Rouen University 2002-; Vice-President, Hon Society Cymmrodorion, Llafur, International Eisteddfod of Llangollen; Yr Academi Gymreig; Board member, Celtic Studies 1972-2003; Council member, Royal Historical Society 1983-86; Trustee, St Deiniol's, Hawarden 1989-96; Council member, National Library of Wales 1991-95; Academic assessor, Leverhulme Devolution project 1999-2002; Chair, Fabian Society Commission on the Monarchy 2002-03; Trustee, History of Parliament Trust 2002-; Chairman, University Committee on Student Radicalisation 2015; Fellow: Royal Historical Society 1964, British Academy 1983; Founding Fellow, Learned Society of Wales 2009; Hon. Fellow: Queen's College, Oxford 1992, Oriel College, Oxford 2003; Imperial Cancer Research, Royal Institute for the Deaf. Honorary doctorate: Wales University Glamorgan University Greenwich University. ACLS Fellowship, Columbia University 1962-63; Honorary Druid, Welsh National Eisteddfod 2008; Gold Medal for Lifetime Achievement, Honourable Society of Cymmrodorion 2009; Awards for Lifetime Achievement: Parliamentary Archives and History Group 2014, Welsh Parliamentarian of the Year 2014; *Clubs:* Reform Club. Member, Middlesex County Cricket Club.

Publications: Editor, Welsh History Review 1961-2003; Wales in British Politics 1868-1922 (1963, 1992); David Lloyd George: Welsh radical as world statesman (1963); Freedom or Sacrilege? (1967); Keir Hardie (1967); The Age of Lloyd George (1971); Editor, Lloyd George Family Letters (1973); Lloyd George (1974); Keir Hardie, Radical and Socialist (1975) (Arts Council prize); Consensus and Disunity (1979); Co-author, Portrait of a Progressive (1980); Rebirth of a Nation: Wales 1880-1980 (1981) (Arts Council prize); David Lloyd George (1981); Labour in Power, 1945-1951 (1984); Editor, The Oxford Illustrated History of Britain (1984, new updated edn, 2009); Labour People (1987); Editor, The Oxford History of Britain (1988, 2001, updated 2010); The Red Dragon and the Red Flag (1989); The People's Peace (1990, 2001); Co-editor, Twentieth Century British History (1994-99); Modern Wales: politics, places and people (1995); Britain and Europe (1995); Editor, The Young Oxford History of Britain and Ireland (1996, 2006); Callaghan: a life (1997); Co-editor, Crime, Protest and Police in Modern British Society (1999); The Twentieth Century (2000); The Great Reform Act (2001); 25 contributions to Oxford Dictionary of National Biography (2004) and supplements (2009) and (2014); Michael Foot: a Life (2007); Ages of Reform (2011); Editor, David Lloyd George (2013); Author and editor of many other works, as well as articles and reviews; Frequent broadcaster on history, politics and Welsh affairs; Revolution to Devolution (2014); My Histories (2015).

Recreations: Music, travel, sport (cricket), architectural history.

Professor the Lord Morgan, House of Lords, London SW1A 0PW
Tel: 020 7219 8616
Email: kenneth.morgan@hotmail.co.uk

MORGAN OF DREFELIN, BARONESS

CROSSBENCH

MORGAN OF DREFELIN (Life Baroness), Delyth Jane Morgan; cr. 2004. Born 30 August 1961; Daughter of David Elias Julian Morgan and Ann George, née Stedman; Married Jim Shepherd 1991 (1 daughter).

Education: Elliott Comprehensive, London; Putney College of Further Education; University College, London (BSc physiology 1986).

Non-political career: President, London University Union 1985-86; Campaigns organiser, Shelter 1986-88; Director, Workplace Nurseries Campaign 1988-92; Director of communications, National Asthma Campaign 1992-96; Chief executive: Breakthrough Breast Cancer 1996-2005, Breast Cancer Campaign 2011-15, Breast Cancer Now 2015-.

Political career: *House of Lords:* Raised to the peerage as Baroness Morgan of Drefelin, of Drefelin in the County of Dyfed 2004. Government Whip 2007-08; Government Spokesperson for: Communities and Local Government 2007-08, Work and Pensions 2007-08, Scotland 2007-08, Wales 2007-08; Parliamentary Under-Secretary of State (Intellectual Property and Quality) and Government Spokesperson, Department for Innovation, Universities and Skills 2008; Government Spokesperson for Cabinet Office 2008; Parliamentary Under-Secretary of State and Government Spokesperson, Department for Children, Schools and Families 2008-10; Opposition Spokesperson for Education 2010-11. Member: Merits of Statutory Instruments 2005-07, Draft Children (Contact and Adoption) Bill Joint Committee 2005. *Other:* Labour until July 2011 (on taking up position of chief executive of Breast Cancer Campaign); now sits as Crossbencher July 2011-.

Political interests: Science, health, women, children, voluntary sector; Wales.

Other: Chair, Childcare Umbrella 1989-92; Long Term Conditions Alliance: Trustee 1994-2000, Chair of trustees 1996-98; Member, Cancer Task Force 2000-05; Association of Medical Research Charities Trustee 2001-04; Member, NHS Modernisation Board 2002-05; Chair, Choice in Primary Care 2003-04; Patron, Sheila McKechnie Foundation 2004-; Chair of trustees, Foundations UK 2004-07; Trustee, Children with Leukaemia 2005-07; Chair, Patient Voices 2005-07; Member,

Ethics Committee, Royal College of Obstetricians and Gynaecologists 2006-07; Patron, Breast Cancer Campaign 2007; Chair, National Cancer Research Institute 2015-; Fellow: University College London, Cardiff University, Institute of Cancer Research, London University.

Recreations: Photography, singing, reading, watching rugby.

The Baroness Morgan of Drefelin, House of Lords, London SW1A 0PW
Tel: 020 7219 8727 *Email:* morgand@parliament.uk
Website: www.baronessmorgan.org.uk *Twitter:* @delythjmorgan

LABOUR

MORGAN OF ELY, BARONESS

MORGAN OF ELY (Life Baroness), Mair Eluned Morgan; cr 2011. Born 16 February 1967; Daughter of Rev Bob Morgan and Elaine Morgan; Married Rev Dr Rhys Jenkins 1996 (1 son 1 daughter).

Education: Atlantic College; Glantaf Welsh Language Comprehensive; Hull University (BA European studies); French, Spanish, Welsh.

Non-political career: Programme sales 1991; TV reporter 1992-93; Documentaries researcher, BBC 1993-94; Director of national business development, Wales, Scottish and Southern Energy plc 2009-13. Member, Unite.

Political career: *House of Lords:* Raised to the peerage as Baroness Morgan of Ely, of Ely in the City of Cardiff 2011. Opposition Whip 2013-16; Opposition Spokesperson for: Wales 2013-16, 2016-17, Foreign and Commonwealth Office 2014-16. *Other:* European Parliament: MEP for: Mid and West Wales 1994-99, Wales 1999-2009: Labour spokesperson on: Budgetary control, Energy, Industry; National Assembly for Wales: AM for Mid and West Wales region since 5 May 2016.

Political interests: European Union reform and economic development, devolution, tourism, minority languages, business, energy.

Other: Live Music Now Charity: Chair (Wales) 2012-16, Trustee (UK) 2012-16. Fellow, Trinity College Carmarthen; Cardiff University: Honorary Professor 2010-, Fellow.

Recreations: Walking, reading, having fun with family.

The Baroness Morgan of Ely, House of Lords, London SW1A 0PW
Tel: 020 7219 5353 *Email:* morganeluned@parliament.uk
National Assembly for Wales, Cardiff Bay, Cardiff CF99 1NA *Tel:* 0300 200 7264
Email: eluned.morgan@assembly.wales
Website: elunedmorgan.wales *Twitter:* @Eluned_Morgan

LABOUR

MORGAN OF HUYTON, BARONESS

MORGAN OF HUYTON (Life Baroness), Sally Morgan; cr. 2001. Born 28 June 1959; Daughter of Albert Morgan and Margaret Morgan; Married John Lyons 1984 (2 sons).

Education: Belvedere School for Girls, Liverpool; Van Mildert College, Durham University (BA geography 1980); King's College, London (PGCE 1981); Institute of Education, London (MA education 1988).

Non-political career: Secondary school geography teacher 1981-85; Labour Party: Student organiser 1985-88, Key seats organiser 1989-92, Director of campaigns and elections 1993-95, Head of party liaison to Tony Blair as Leader of the Opposition 1995-97; Prime Minister's Office 1997-2005: Political secretary to Tony Blair as Prime Minister 1997-2001, Director, government relations 2001-05; Adviser to ARK (Absolute Return for Kids) 2005-; Non-executive director, Carphone Warehouse plc 2005-; Member, advisory board, Virgin Holdings. Member, GMB.

Political career: *House of Lords:* Raised to the peerage as Baroness Morgan of Huyton, of Huyton in the County of Merseyside 2001. Cabinet Office: Minister of State 2001, Government Spokesperson for Women's Issues 2001. Co-opted Member, EU Sub-committee G (Social Policy and Consumer Affairs) 2006-09; Member: Public Service and Demographic Change 2012-13, Personal Service Companies 2013-14; Chair, Digital Skills 2014-15; Member, Science and Technology 2015-. *Councils and public bodies:* Councillor, Wandsworth Borough Council 1986-90; Trustee, Olympic Delivery Authority 2006-12; Chair, Office for Standards in Education (OFSTED) 2011-14.

Political interests: Equality issues, education, health.

Other: Chair, Future Leaders (head teacher training); Trustee, Mayor's Fund 2009-; Member, advisory board, Institute of Education, University of London; Children's charities.

Recreations: Gardening, family, cooking, theatre.

The Baroness Morgan of Huyton, House of Lords, London SW1A 0PW
Tel: 020 7219 5500 *Email:* morgan@parliament.uk

LABOUR

MORRIS OF ABERAVON, LORD

MORRIS OF ABERAVON (Life Baron), John Morris; cr. 2001. Born 5 November 1931; Son of late D W Morris and late M O A Lewis, formerly Morris; Married Margaret Lewis 1959 (3 daughters).

Education: Ardwyn School, Aberystwyth; University College of Wales, Aberystwyth (LLB 1952); Gonville and Caius College, Cambridge (LLM 1953); Gray's Inn (Holker Senior Exhibitioner); Welsh.

Non-political career: Commissioned Welch Regiment and served Royal Welch Fusiliers. Called to the Bar, Gray's Inn 1954; QC 1973; Recorder of Crown Court 1982-97; Bencher, Gray's Inn 1984. Member, GMB.

Political career: *House of Commons:* MP (Labour) for Aberavon 1959-2001. Parliamentary Secretary, Ministry of Power 1964-66; Joint Parliamentary Secretary, Ministry of Transport 1966-68; Minister of Defence for Equipment 1968-70; Secretary of State for Wales 1974-79; Shadow Attorney General and Principal Opposition Frontbench Spokesperson for Legal Affairs 1979-81, 1983-97; Attorney General 1997-99. *House of Lords:* Raised to the peerage as Baron Morris of Aberavon, of Aberavon in the County of West Glamorgan and of Ceredigion in the County of Dyfed 2001. Member: European Union Sub-committee C (Common Foreign and Security Policy/Foreign Affairs, Defence and Development Policy) 2002-05, Constitution 2006-09, Joint Committee on the Draft Defamation Bill 2011, EU Sub-committee E (Justice and Institutions) 2011-12, Inquiries Act 2005 2013-14, Procedure 2016-. *Councils and public bodies:* Chair: Joint Review of British Railways 1966-67, National Road Safety Advisory Council 1967-68; Committee member, Implementation of Nolan Report 1997; Member, Prime Minister's Advisory Committee on Business Appointments 2002-09; Lord Lieutenant, Dyfed 2002-06.

Political interests: Legal matters, armed forces, steel industry, agriculture; Spain.

Other: Member: UK Delegation, Consultative Assemblies Council of Europe and Western European Union 1963-64, 1982-83, UK Delegates to North Atlantic Assembly 1970, Executive Committee, Inter-Parliamentary Union, British Group, UK Delegation to US Senate (British-American Parliamentary Group) 2011; President, London Welsh Association 2001-08; Member, Prince's Trust Council (Cymru) 2002-08; Patron: London Welsh Lawyers Association 2010-, Edmund-Davies Charitable Trust. Freedom, Borough of Port Talbot 1992. Chancellor: Glamorgan University 2001-13, University of South Wales 2013-14. Hon. LLD: University of Wales, University of South Wales; Hon. Fellow: University College, Aberystwyth, Trinity College, Carmarthen, University College, Swansea, Gonville and Caius College, Cambridge, University College, Lampeter. Lifetime Achievement, *Wales Yearbook* awards 2011. PC 1970; Kt 1999; KG 2003.

Publications: Endowed Lecture, David Lloyd George Memorial (Hon. Society of Cymrodorion, London, 2005); Autobiography, Fifty Years in Politics and the Law (University of Wales Press, Cardiff, 2011); Youard Lecture, The Development by Attorney Generals of the Doctrine of Armed Intervention by States, without Security Council Authorisation, to Avert an Overwhelming Human Catastrophe (Swansea University, 2011); The Welsh and the United Kingdom (National Library of Wales Website, November 2013).

Recreations: Fishing, shooting.

Rt Hon the Lord Morris of Aberavon KG QC, House of Lords, London SW1A 0PW
Tel: 020 7219 3470/020 7219 3156 *Fax:* 020 7218 8602 *Email:* maggiestevenson@parliament.uk

CONSERVATIVE

MORRIS OF BOLTON, BARONESS

MORRIS OF BOLTON (Life Baroness), Patricia Morris; cr. 2004. Born 16 January 1953; Daughter of late James Sydney and Alice Whittaker; Married William Patrick Morris 1978 (1 daughter 1 son).

Education: Bolton School; Clifton and Didsbury Colleges of Education.

Non-political career: PA to: Northern Regional Director, Slater Walker Ltd 1974-75, Chevalier Dr Harry D. Schultz 1975; Fund manager, PPS 1975-77; Technical analyst: Foster & Braithwaite 1977-78, Charlton, Seal, Dimmock & Co 1979-83; Adviser to Abbot of Ampleforth 1998-2004; Policy and political adviser to Conservative MEP 1999-2001.

Political career: *House of Commons:* Contested (Conservative) Oldham Central and Royton 1992 general election. *House of Lords:* Raised to the peerage as Baroness Morris of Bolton, of Bolton in the County of Greater Manchester 2004. Opposition Whip 2004-10; Opposition Spokesperson for: Health 2004-06, 2009-10, Education and Skills 2004-07, Women 2005-10, Children, Schools and Families 2007-09, Work and Pensions 2009-10; Deputy Chairman of Committees 2010-; Deputy Speaker 2011-; Trade envoy to Jordan, Kuwait and Palestinian Territories 2012-. Member: Joint Committee on Human Rights 2010-11, Adoption Legislation 2012-13, Soft Power and the UK's

Influence 2013-14, Affordable Childcare 2014-15, European Union 2016; Chair, EU External Affairs Sub-committee 2016; Member, Services 2017-. *Other:* Conservative Party: Member, National Union Executive Committee 1991-96, Chair, North West Area Women's Committee 1993-96, Member: Conferences Committee 1998-2001, Field Operations Panel 1998-2001, Agents' Remuneration Panel 1998-2001, Vice-chair (Candidates) 2001-05. *Councils and public bodies:* Deputy chair, Salford Royal Hospitals NHS Trust 1993-97; DL, Greater Manchester 2008-.

Other: Chair, Bolton Cancer Research Campaign 1992-95; Trustee, Bolton Lads and Girls Club 1994-2002; Member, advisory board, Women 2 Win 2005-; President, National Benevolent Institution 2006-; Patron, Oxford Parent Infant Project (OXPIP) 2006-; Trustee: Agbis 2006-, Disability Partnership 2007-, Unicef UK 2007-; Co-chair, Women in Public Policy 2007-; Vice-president, Catholic Union of Great Britain 2008-; President, World Travel Market Advisory Council; Chair: Governance Group, Register of Providers of Cosmetic Injectable Treatments, Centre for Islamic Finance. OBE; *Clubs:* Special Forces Club.

Recreations: Music, reading, football (Bolton Wanderers FC).

The Baroness Morris of Bolton OBE DL, House of Lords, London SW1A 0PW
Tel: 020 7219 5353 *Email:* whitbycollinsa@parliament.uk *Twitter:* @MorrisofBolton

MORRIS OF HANDSWORTH, LORD

LABOUR

MORRIS OF HANDSWORTH (Life Baron), William (Bill) Manuel Morris; cr 2006. Born 19 October 1938; Son of William Morris and Una Cornwall; Married Minetta Smith 1957 (died 1990) (2 sons); partner Eileen Ware.

Education: Mizpah School, Manchester, Jamaica; Handsworth Technical College (day release mechanical engineering).

Non-political career: Hardy Spicers 1955-73: Transport and General Workers' Union 1958-2003: District Organiser, Nottingham/Derby 1973-76, District Secretary, Northampton 1976-79, National Secretary, Passenger Services Trade Group 1979-86, Deputy General Secretary 1986-91, General Secretary 1992-2003; Non-executive Director: Unity Trust Bank 1992-2003, Bank of England 1998-2006; Vice-chair, Jamaican National Money Services 2007-11; Chair, Midland Heart Housing Association 2007-14. Transport and General Workers' Union: Member 1958-, Shop steward at Hardy Spicers 1963-73; Member: T&G General Executive Council 1971-72, TUC General Council 1988-2003.

Political career: *House of Lords:* Raised to the peerage as Baron Morris of Handsworth, of Handsworth in the County of West Midlands 2006. Member: Joint Committee on Human Rights 2007-12, Adoption Legislation 2012-13, EU Sub-committee F (Home Affairs, Health and Education) 2013-15, EU Home Affairs Sub-committee 2015-16, Joint Committee on Statutory Instruments 2016-. *Other:* Chair: Conference Arrangements Committee, Labour Party/Trade Union Liaison Committee. *Councils and public bodies:* Chair, Morris Inquiry Metropolitan Police Authority 2004; Member: Commission for Racial Equality 1977-87, IBA General Advisory Council 1981-86, Road Transport Industries Training Board 1986-92, BBC General Advisory Council 1987-88, Employment Appeal Tribunal 1988-2008, ACAS (the Advisory Conciliation and Arbitration Service) 1997-2003, Royal Commission on House of Lords Reform 1999, Commission for Integrated Transport 1999-2005, Architects Registration Board 2001-05, Panel of Mergers and Take Overs 2005-; DL, Staffordshire 2008.

Political interests: Social justice, trade unions, the economy, international affairs, diversity.

Other: Member: Board International Transport Federation 1986-2003, EC Economic and Social Committee 1990-92; Member, Prince's Youth Business Trust 1987-90; Non-executive Director, England and Wales Cricket Board 2005-15; Trustee, Performance Birmingham Ltd 2008-15. Chancellor: University of Technology, Jamaica 2000-10, Staffordshire University 2004-11. Order of Jamaica (OJ) 2002; Kt 2003.

Recreations: Family life, walking, gardening, music.

The Lord Morris of Handsworth OJ, House of Lords, London SW1A 0PW
Tel: 020 7219 3485 *Email:* morrisw@parliament.uk
Website: www.billmorris.info

MORRIS OF YARDLEY, BARONESS

LABOUR

MORRIS OF YARDLEY (Life Baroness), Estelle Morris; cr 2005. Born 17 June 1952; Daughter of late Charles Morris (MP 1963-83) and Pauline Morris, née Dunn.

Education: Whalley Range High School, Manchester; Coventry College of Education, Warwick University (BEd 1974).

Non-political career: Teacher, Sidney Stringer School and Community College 1974-92. Member, CWU.

Political career: *House of Commons:* MP (Labour) for Birmingham Yardley 1992-2005. Opposition Whip 1994-95; Opposition Spokesperson for Education and Employment 1995-97; Department for Education and Employment/Skills 1997-2002: Parliamentary Under-Secretary of State 1997-98, Minister of State 1998-2001, Secretary of State for Education and Skills 2001-02; Minister of State (Minister for the Arts), Department for Culture, Media and Sport 2003-05. *House of Lords:* Raised to the peerage as Baroness Morris of Yardley, of Yardley in the County of West Midlands 2005. Member: Merits of Statutory Instruments/Secondary Legislation Scrutiny 2009-14, Social Mobility 2015-16, Citizenship and Civic Engagement 2017-. *Councils and public bodies:* Warwick District Council: Councillor 1979-91, Leader, Labour Group 1982-89.

Political interests: Education and training, political engagement, arts.

Other: Fellow, Industry and Parliament Trust 1994; Trustee: Hamlyn Foundation 2005-15, The Roundhouse 2008-15; Chair, Goldsmiths College, University of London 2012-; Trustee, National Poetry Archive 2013-. Seven honorary degrees. PC 1999.

Rt Hon the Baroness Morris of Yardley, House of Lords, London SW1A 0PW
Tel: 020 7219 3000 *Email:* morrise@parliament.uk

MORROW, LORD

DEMOCRATIC UNIONIST PARTY

MORROW (Life Baron), Maurice George Morrow; cr 2006. Born 27 September 1948; Son of Ernest and Eliza Jane Morrow; Married Jennifer Reid 1976 (2 daughters).

Education: Drumglass High School; East Tyrone College of Further and Higher Education.

Non-political career: Self-employed auctioneer, estate agent and valuer.

Political career: *House of Lords:* Raised to the peerage as Baron Morrow, of Clogher Valley in the County of Tyrone 2006. *Other:* Member, Northern Ireland Forum for Political Dialogue 1996-98; Northern Ireland Assembly: MLA for Fermanagh and South Tyrone 1998-2017 (as Maurice Morrow), Minister for Social Development 2000-01, 2016, DUP Chief Whip -2002, Member, Preparation for Government Committee 2006-07, Chair, Assembly Committees on: Procedures 2007-10, Justice 2010-11. Contested 2017 Fermanagh and South Tyrone Northern Ireland Assembly election. Chair, Democratic Unionist Party. *Councils and public bodies:* Councillor, Dungannon and South Tyrone Borough Council 1973-2017.

Countries of interest: Israel, USA.

Other: Alternate member, EU Committee of the Regions 2006-10; Member, Apprentice Boys of Derry; Director: Moygashel Development Association, Dungannon Enterprise Centre -2013.

Recreations: Field sports.

The Lord Morrow, House of Lords, London SW1A 0PW
Tel: 020 7219 5353
19 Church Street, Dungannon, Co Tyrone BT71 6AB *Tel:* 028 8775 2799 *Fax:* 028 8775 2802
Email: mauricemorrow@hotmail.com

MOUNTEVANS, LORD

CROSSBENCH

MOUNTEVANS (4th Baron, UK), Jeffrey Richard de Corban Evans; cr 1945. Born 13 May 1948; Son of 2nd Baron Mountevans; Married Hon Juliet Wilson 1972 (2 sons).

Education: Nautical College, Pangbourne; Pembroke College, Cambridge; Norwegian, French.

Non-political career: Honorary Commander, RNR 2015. Clarksons Platou: Shipbroker 1972-, Tanker broker 1972-79, Head, Gas and Specialised Tankers 2000-01, Managing director, Gas 2001-, Director 2014-17.

Political career: *House of Lords:* Elected hereditary peer 2015-. *Councils and public bodies:* City of London Corporation: Alderman 2007-, Sheriff 2012-13, Lord Mayor of London 2015-16.

Political interests: Maritime, international business, education.

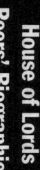

Other: Director and trustee, White Ensign Association; President, City of London Sea Cadets 2007-; Almoner and director, Christ's Hospital 2010-; Trustee: Seafarers UK 2011-, Mansion House Scholarship Scheme 2011-, St Paul's Chorister Trust 2013-; Chair: Maritime London 2013-, Maritime UK 2014-15, Maritime Growth Study: Keeping the UK Competitive; Younger Brother, Trinity House; Member, Institute of Chartered Shipbrokers; Lord Mayor's Appeal 2015-16, JDRF, Sea Cadets. Liveryman: Worshipful Company of Shipwrights 1979-, Worshipful Company of World Traders 2010-, Worshipful Company of Goldsmiths 2012-, Worshipful Company of Wheelwrights 2013-, Worshipful Company of Security Professionals 2013-. Freedom, City of London. Knight, Order of St John.

Recreations: Walking, skiing.

The Lord Mountevans, House of Lords, London SW1A 0PW
Tel: 020 7219 3000

MOYNIHAN, LORD

CONSERVATIVE

MOYNIHAN (4th Baron, UK), Colin Berkeley Moynihan; cr. 1929; 4th Bt of Carr Manor (UK) 1922. Born 13 September 1955; Son of 2nd Baron; Married Gaynor-Louise Metcalf 1992 (2 sons 1 daughter).

Education: Monmouth School (Music Scholar); University College, Oxford (BA philosophy, politics and economics 1977, MA 1982) (President of the Oxford Union); Brasenose College, Oxford (J A Fiddian Research Scholarship 1977); French.

Non-political career: Personal assistant to chair, Tate and Lyle Ltd 1978-80; Manager, Tate and Lyle Agribusiness 1980-82; Ridgways Tea and Coffee Merchants: Chief executive 1982-83, Chair 1983-87; Chair, CMA Consultants 1993-; Managing director, Independent Power Corporation plc 1996-2001; Director, Rowan Group of Companies 1996-2016; Chair and chief executive, Consort Resources Group of Companies 2000-03; Director, Clipper Windpower UK Ltd 2001-07, Executive chair, Clipper UK Ltd 2004-07, Chair, Clipper EU Ltd 2004-07; Non-executive chair, Pelamis Wave Energy Ltd 2005-11; Chair, British Olympic Association 2005-12; Director, London Organising Committee for Olympic Games (LOCOG) 2006-12; Member: International Olympic Committee (IOC) International Relations Commission 2008-12, IOC Candidature Acceptance Working Group for the 2016 Olympic Games 2008-16; Non-executive chair, Hydrodec 2012-.

Political career: *House of Commons:* MP (Conservative) for Lewisham East 1983-92. Contested Lewisham East 1992 general election. PPS to Kenneth Clarke MP: as Minister of Health 1985, as Paymaster-General 1985-87; Parliamentary Under-Secretary of State: Department of Environment (Minister for Sport) 1987-90, Department of Energy 1990-92. *House of Lords:* First entered House of Lords 1997; Senior Opposition Spokesperson for Foreign and Commonwealth Affairs 1997-2000; Elected hereditary peer 1999-; Shadow Minister for Sport 2003-05. Co-opted Member, European Union Sub-committee D (Environment and Agriculture) 2006-07; Member: Olympic and Paralympic Legacy 2013-14, The Arctic 2014-15, Delegated Powers and Regulatory Reform 2015-. *Councils and public bodies:* Governor, Sports Aid Foundation (London and South East) 1980-82.

Political interests: Foreign affairs, trade and industry, sport, inner cities, refugees, overseas aid and development.

Other: Member, Bow Group 1978-: Chair, Trade and Industry Standing Committee 1983-87; Director, Canterbury Festival 1999-2001; Executive council member, Association of National Olympic Committees (ANOC) 2006-12; Ex-officio member, Olympic Board; Spinal Injuries Association. Liveryman, Worshipful Company of Haberdashers 1981; Court of Assistants 2003-. Freedom, City of London 1978. Hon. doctorate, London Metropolitan University 2007. Oxford Double Blue, Rowing and Boxing 1976 and 1977; World Gold Medal for Lightweight Rowing, International Rowing Federation 1978; Silver Medal for Rowing at Moscow Olympic Games 1980; World Silver Medal for Rowing 1981; *Clubs:* Club at The Ivy, Le Beaujolais Club, Vincent's Club. London Rowing, Leander.

Recreations: Reading, sport, music.

The Lord Moynihan, House of Lords, London SW1A 0PW
Tel: 020 7219 5879 *Email:* moynihanc@parliament.uk
Westburn Business Centre, Westburn House, McNee Road, Prestwick KA9 2PB
Tel: 01292 471444 *Email:* e.owen@cmagroup.org.uk

CROSSBENCH

MURPHY, BARONESS

MURPHY (Life Baroness), Elaine Murphy; cr. 2004. Born 16 January 1947; Daughter of Roger Lawson, engineer, and Nell Lawson, née Allitt; Married John Murphy 1969 (divorced 2001); married Michael Robb 2001.

Education: West Bridgford Grammar School, Nottingham; Manchester University (MB ChB 1971, MD 1979); University College, London (PhD history of medicine 2000).

Non-political career: Professor of old age psychiatry, Guy's Hospital, United Medical Schools, University of London 1983-96; Chair: City and Hackney Community Services NHS Trust 1995-98, East London and City Health Authority 1998-2001, North East London Strategic Health Authority 2001-06, St George's Hospital Medical School, University of London 2006-10.

Political career: *House of Lords:* Raised to the peerage as Baroness Murphy, of Aldgate in the City of London 2004. Member: Science and Technology Sub-committee I (Scientific Aspects of Ageing) 2005, Leader's Group on Members Leaving the House 2010-11. *Councils and public bodies:* Commissioner, Commission on Assisted Dying 2010-.

Political interests: Mental health, NHS, learning disability, ageing, higher education; Italy.

Other: Vice-President, Alzheimer's Society; MRCPsych 1976; FRCPsych 1983; Oxfam. Three honorary doctorates.

Publications: 100-plus publications and books; After the Asylums (Faber, 1991); Co-author, The Falling Shadow (Duckworth, 1995); The Moated Grange (Book Guild, 2015).

Recreations: Italy, Norfolk, entertaining friends.

The Baroness Murphy, House of Lords, London SW1A 0PW
Tel: 020 7219 5353 *Email:* murphyel@parliament.uk

LABOUR

MURPHY OF TORFAEN, LORD

MURPHY OF TORFAEN (Life Baron), Paul Peter Murphy; cr 2015. Born 25 November 1948; Son of late Ronald Murphy and late Marjorie Murphy.

Education: St Francis School, Abersychan; West Monmouth School, Pontypool; Oriel College, Oxford (MA modern history 1970); French (basic).

Non-political career: Management trainee, CWS 1970-71; Lecturer in government, Ebbw Vale College of Further Education 1971-87; Visiting Parliamentary Fellow, St Anthony's College, Oxford 2006-07. Member, TGWU-Unite.

Political career: *House of Commons:* Contested Wells 1979 general election. MP (Labour) for Torfaen 1987-2015. Opposition Spokesperson on: Welsh Affairs 1988-94, Northern Ireland 1994-95, Foreign Affairs 1995, Defence, Disarmament and Arms Control 1995-97; Minister of State, Northern Ireland Office (Minister for Political Development) 1997-99; Secretary of State for: Wales 1999-2002, 2008-09, Northern Ireland 2002-05; Chairman, Intelligence and Security Committee 2005-08. Member, Joint Committee on National Security Strategy 2010-15. Chair, PLP Departmental Committee for Northern Ireland 2010-15. *House of Lords:* Raised to the peerage as Baron Murphy of Torfaen, of Abersychan in the County of Gwent 2015. Chair, Joint Committee on the Draft Investigatory Powers Bill 2015-16. *Other:* Secretary, Torfaen CLP 1971-87; Chair, Welsh Group, Labour MPs 1996-97. *Councils and public bodies:* Torfaen Borough Council: Councillor 1973-87, Chair, Finance Committee 1976-86; National Assembly for Wales Ambassador for Oxbridge 2013-14.

Political interests: Local and regional government, Wales, education, housing, foreign affairs; France, Ireland, Northern Ireland.

Other: Vice-chair, British-American Parliamentary Group 2004-05, 2007-09; British-Irish Parliamentary Assembly: Co-chair 2006-07, 2009-10, Vice-chair 2010-15; Vice-chair, Franco-British Friendship Group. Hon. Fellow, Oriel College, Oxford 2001; Parliamentary Visiting Fellow, St Antony's College, Oxford 2006-07; Hon. Fellow, Glyndŵr University, Wrexham 2009-; Hon. Doc. University of South Wales 2014. Knight of St Gregory (Papal Order); PC 1999; KCMCO; *Clubs:* Oxford and Cambridge Club.

Recreations: Classical music, cooking.

Rt Hon the Lord Murphy of Torfaen, House of Lords, London SW1A 0PW
Tel: 020 7219 6193 *Email:* murphypp@parliament.uk

CROSSBENCH

MYNERS, LORD

MYNERS (Life Baron), Paul Myners; cr 2008. Born 1 April 1948; Married 2nd Alison Macleod 1995 (1 son 1 daughter 3 daughters from previous marriage).

Education: Truro School, Cornwall; London University Institute of Education (BEd); Stanford Executive Program, Stanford School of Business, USA.

Non-political career: *Daily Telegraph* 1970-74; N M Rothschild & Sons Ltd 1974-85; Gartmore plc 1985-2001: Chief executive 1985-93, 1999-2000, Chair 1987-2001; Deputy chair, Powergen plc 1999-2001; Director, National Westminster Bank 1997-2000; Chair, Guardian Media Group 2000-08; Personal accounts delivery authority, Department for Work and Pensions 2007-09; Chair and managing partner, Cevian Capital 2011-; Chair, Edelman 2015-.

Political career: *House of Lords:* Raised to the peerage as Baron Myners, of Truro in the County of Cornwall 2008. Financial Services Secretary and Government Spokesperson, HM Treasury 2008-10. Member: Joint Committee on Privacy and Injunctions 2011-12, Works of Art 2012-13, Personal Service Companies 2013-14. Vice-chair, PLP Departmental Group for Treasury 2010-15. *Other:* Sat as Labour until January 2014, now sits as a Crossbencher. *Councils and public bodies:* Member: Financial Reporting Council 1995-2004, Company Law Review Consultative Committee 1998-2000; Court of Directors, Bank of England 2005-; Chair, Low Pay Commission 2006-.

Other: Trustee, Royal Academy Trust 2000-03; Tate Gallery: Trustee 2003-, Chair 2004-; Trustee: Glyndbourne 2003-, Smith Institute 2003-, National Gallery 2007-; Senior independent director, Co-operative Group Board 2014. Chancellor, Exeter University 2016-. CBE 2003.

The Lord Myners CBE, House of Lords, London SW1A 0PW
Tel: 020 7219 6760

CONSERVATIVE

NASEBY, LORD

NASEBY (Life Baron), Michael Wolfgang Laurence Morris; cr. 1997. Born 25 November 1936; Son of late Cyril Morris and Margaret Morris; Married Dr Ann Appleby 1960 (2 sons 1 daughter).

Education: Bedford School; St Catharine's College, Cambridge (BA economics 1960, MA); French.

Non-political career: National service pilot (RAF and NATO) 1955-57. Marketing manager, Reckitt and Colman Group 1960-64; Director: Service Advertising 1964-71, Benton & Bowles Ltd 1971-81; Chairman: Children's Mutual 1997-2005, Invesco Recovery Trust 2011 1995-2011; Non-executive director: Mansell Ltd 1998-2003, City Disputes Panel Ltd 2015-.

Political career: *House of Commons:* Contested Islington North 1966 general election. MP (Conservative) for Northampton South 1974-97. PPS to Hugh Rossi and Michael Alison as Ministers of State, Northern Ireland 1979-81; Deputy Speaker and Chairman of Ways and Means 1992-97. *House of Lords:* Raised to the peerage as Baron Naseby, of Sandy in the County of Bedfordshire 1997. Member: Standing Orders (Private Bills) 2003-, Administration and Works 2005-09; EU Sub-committee F (Home Affairs): Co-opted member 2009-10, Member 2010-11; Member, Joint Committee on the Draft Deregulation Bill 2013. *Councils and public bodies:* London Borough of Islington: Councillor 1968-74, Leader 1969-71, Alderman 1971-74.

Political interests: Energy, health service, exports, marketing, parliamentary procedure, financial services, questioning government of the day; Caribbean, Cayman Islands, Chile, France, India, Maldives, Singapore, Sri Lanka.

Other: Member, Council of Europe and Western European Union 1983-91; Trustee: Victoria County History Society Northamptonshire 1992-, Parliamentary Contributory Pension Fund 2005-; Patron, Naseby Battlefield Project Trust 2008-14; President, Lords and Commons Golf Society 2010-; Hon. Fellow in History, Northampton University; Bedford School Foundation, Northamptonshire VCH Trust, Northamptonshire County Cricket Club Youth Trust. Honorary fellow in history, Northampton University 2007. PC 1994; Sri Lanka Ratna 2005; Bernardo O'Higgins medal (Chile) 2013; *Clubs:* Carlton Club, Chamberlain, Ordre des Cofeaux de Champagne, Confrérie des Chevalier du Tasterin, Chevalier, Commanderie de Bordeaux à Londres, Chairman, Cofradia del Vino Chileno. President, Northamptonshire County Cricket; MCC; John O'Gaunt Golf Club; Port Stanley Golf; All England Lawn Tennis; Lords Taverners.

Publications: Helping The Exporter (1967); Co-author, Marketing Below The Line (1970); The Disaster of Direct Labour (1978).

Recreations: Golf, tennis, forestry, wine, cricket.

Rt Hon the Lord Naseby, House of Lords, London SW1A 0PW
Tel: 020 7219 5613
Email: amnaseby@btinternet.com

CONSERVATIVE

NASH, LORD

Parliamentary Under-Secretary of State for the School System and Government Spokesperson, Department for Education

NASH (Life Baron), John Alfred Stoddard; cr 2013. Born 22 March 1949; Son of John and Josephine Nash; Married Caroline 1983 (1 son 1 daughter).

Education: Milton Abbey School, Dorset; Corpus Christi College, Oxford (MA law 1971).

Non-political career: Barrister, Inner Temple 1972-74; William Brandts Sons & Co Ltd 1974-75; Lazard Brothers & Co Ltd 1975-83: Assistant director 1981-83; Advent Ltd 1983-88: Managing director 1987-88; Nash, Sells & Partners/Sovereign Capital Partners: Founder 1988, Chairman 1988-2010, Non-executive partner 2010-13; Non-executive director, Department for Education 2010-13.

Political career: *House of Lords:* Raised to the peerage as Baron Nash, of Ewelme in the County of Oxfordshire 2013. Department for Education: Government Spokesperson 2013-, Parliamentary Under-Secretary of State for: Schools 2013-16, School System 2016-.

Political interests: Education.

Other: Chair, British Venture Capital Association 1988-89; Corpus Christi College, Oxford: Foundation Fellow, Member, Investment Committee 2005-, Deputy Chair, Development Committee 2005-; Chair: Future (charity) 2005-, Pimlico Academy 2008-, Future Academies Trust 2008-; Board Member, Centre for Policy Studies 2003-13; Foundation fellow, Corpus Christi College, Oxford; *Clubs:* Athenæum Club, Turf Club. Sunningdale Golf Club; Pine Valley Golf Club, USA.

Recreations: Golf, tennis, skiing.

The Lord Nash, House of Lords, London SW1A 0PW
Tel: 020 7219 5353

CROSSBENCH

NEUBERGER, BARONESS

NEUBERGER (Life Baroness), Julia Babette Sarah Neuberger; cr. 2004. Born 27 February 1950; Daughter of late Walter Schwab, civil servant, and Alice Schwab, née Rosenthal, art collector; Married Anthony Neuberger 1973 (1 daughter 1 son).

Education: South Hampstead High School, London; Newnham College, Cambridge (BA Hebrew/Assyriology 1973, MA); Leo Baeck College, London (rabbinic ordination 1977).

Non-political career: Rabbi, author, broadcaster; Rabbi, South London Liberal Synagogue 1977-89; Visiting fellow: King's Fund Institute 1989-91, Harvard Medical School (Harkness fellowship) 1991-92; Chief executive, King's Fund 1997-2004; Consultant, Clore Duffield Foundation 2004-; Adviser to Trustees, Sainsbury Centre for Mental Health 2006-11; Bloomberg Professor, Harvard Divinity School, spring semester 2006; Senior Rabbi, West London Synagogue 2011-.

Political career: *House of Commons:* Contested (Liberal Democrat) Tooting 1983 general election. *House of Lords:* Raised to the peerage as Baroness Neuberger, of Primrose Hill in the London Borough of Camden 2004. Liberal Democrat Spokesperson for Health 2004-07; Prime Minister's Champion for Volunteering 2007-10. Member: EU Sub-committee G (Social Policy and Consumer Affairs) 2005-08, Draft Human Tissue and Embryos Bill Joint Committee 2007, Science and Technology Sub-committee I (Nanotechnologies and food) 2008-10, Science and Technology 2009-12; Chair, Science and Technology Sub-committee I (Behaviour Change) 2010-11; Member: Science and Technology Sub-committee I 2012-13, EU Justice Sub-committee 2015-. *Other:* Liberal Democrat until September 2011 (on taking up position of Senior Rabbi of West London Synagogue); Crossbench September 2011-. *Councils and public bodies:* Chair, Camden and Islington Community Health Services NHS Trust 1993-97; Civil Service Commissioner 2001-02; Member: Committee on Standards in Public Life 2001-04, One Housing Group 2008-12, Responsible Gambling Strategy Board 2008-11; Advisory Panel, Judicial Diversity 2009-10.

Political interests: Health, citizens' rights, asylum and refugees; Ireland.

Other: Patron, North London Hospice; Trustee: Imperial War Museum 1999-2006, Booker Prize Foundation 2002-11, British Council 2004-07, Liberal Democrats 2004-08, New Philanthropy Capital 2008-11, Van Leer Group Foundation 2012-; Board member and trustee, Social Market Foundation 2012-13; Chair, Review of How the Liverpool Care Pathway for Dying Patients is Used in Practice 2013-15; Trustee: Van Leer Jerusalem Institute 2012-, Rayne Foundation 2015-. Chancellor, Ulster University 1994-2000. Thirteen honorary doctorates; 5 honorary fellowships; Hon. Doctorate of Divinity, Cambridge University 2015. DBE 2004.

Publications: Caring for Dying Patients of Different Faiths (1986, 1994, 2004); The Story of Judaism (for children) (Dinosaur/Collins, 1987); Whatever's Happening to Women? (Kyle Cathie, 1991); Ethics and Healthcare: Research Ethics Committees in the UK (Kings Fund Institute, 1992); The Things That Matter; An Anthology of Women's Spiritual Poetry (Kyle Cathie, 1993);

On Being Jewish (Heinemann, 1996); Dying Well: a guide to enabling a good death (1999, 2004); The Moral State We're In (HarperCollins, 2006); Not Dead Yet: A Manifesto for Old Age (HarperCollins, 2008); Is That All There Is? (Rider, 2011); Frequent broadcaster and press contributor.

Recreations: Opera, gardening, Irish life, novels, food, sailing.

The Baroness Neuberger DBE, House of Lords, London SW1A 0PW
Tel: 020 7219 2716 *Email:* neubergerj@parliament.uk
West London Synagogue, 33 Seymour Place, London W1H 5AU *Tel:* 020 7535 0255
Fax: 020 7224 8258 *Email:* julia.neuberger@wls.org.uk *Website:* www.wls.org.uk

NEUBERGER OF ABBOTSBURY, LORD

NON-AFFILIATED

NEUBERGER OF ABBOTSBURY (Life Baron), David Edmond Neuberger; cr. 2006. Born 10 January 1948; Son of Prof Albert Neuberger CBE FRS and Lilian Dreyfus; Married Angela Holdsworth 1976 (2 sons 1 daughter).

Education: Westminster School; Christ Church, Oxford (BA chemistry 1970, MA); French.

Non-political career: NM Rothschild & Sons 1970-73; Called to the Bar, Lincoln's Inn 1974; QC 1987; Recorder 1990-96; Bencher 1993; High Court Judge, Chancery Division 1996-2004; Supervisory Chancery Judge, Midland, Wales and Chester, and Western Circuits 2001-04; Lord Justice of Appeal 2004-07; Judge in charge of Modernisation 2004-06; Lord of Appeal in Ordinary 2007-09; Master of the Rolls 2009-12; President of the Supreme Court 2012-17.

Political career: *House of Lords:* Raised to the peerage as Baron Neuberger of Abbotsbury, of Abbotsbury in the County of Dorset 2006. Lord of Appeal in Ordinary 2007-09; As a senior member of the judiciary, disqualified from participation 2009-17. *Councils and public bodies:* Chair, Advisory Committee on Spoliation of Art during the Holocaust 1997-; Governor, University of the Arts, London 2000-10.

Other: Chair, Schizophrenia Trust 2003-14; Patron, MHRUK 2014-. Freeman: Company of Drapers 2011, Chartered Surveyors Company 2015. Freedom, City of London. Kt 1996; PC 2004; *Clubs:* Garrick Club.

Rt Hon the Lord Neuberger of Abbotsbury, House of Lords, London SW1A 0PW
Tel: 020 7219 5353

NEVILLE-JONES, BARONESS

CONSERVATIVE

NEVILLE-JONES (Life Baroness), (Lilian) Pauline Neville-Jones; cr 2007. Born 2 November 1939; Daughter of Roland Neville-Jones and Cecilia Winn.

Education: Leeds Girls' High School; Lady Margaret Hall, Oxford (BA modern history 1961); French, German, some Spanish.

Non-political career: HM Diplomatic Service 1963-96: Third secretary, Salisbury, Rhodesia High Commission 1964-65, Third, second secretary, Singapore High Commission 1965-68, Foreign and Commonwealth Office, London (FCO) 1968-71, First secretary, Washington DC embassy 1971-75, FCO 1975-77, Member/chef de cabinet to European Commissioner Christopher Tugendhat, Brussels 1977-82, Head of planning staff, FCO 1983-87, Bonn embassy 1987-91: Minister (economics) 1987-88, Minister 1988-91, Seconded as Deputy Secretary to the Cabinet and Head of Defence and Overseas Secretariat, Cabinet Office 1991-94; Chair, Joint Intelligence Committee 1993-94; Political director, FCO 1994-96; Seconded as senior adviser to High Representative for Bosnia 1996; BBC International Governor 1998-2004; Chair: Information Assurance Advisory Council 2004-07, Qinetiq Group plc 2002-05.

Political career: *House of Lords:* Raised to the peerage as Baroness Neville-Jones, of Hutton Roof in the County of Cumbria 2007. Shadow Minister for Security and National Security Adviser to the Leader of the Opposition 2007-10; Minister of State for Security and Government Spokesperson, Home Office 2010-11; Special Representative to Business on Cyber Security 2011-14; Chair, Advisory Panel on Cyber Security, Bank of England 2015-. Member: Joint Committee on the National Security Strategy 2012-15, Joint Committee on the Draft Enhanced Terrorism Prevention and Investigation Measures Bill 2012-13, The Arctic 2014-15, Science and Technology 2015-. *Councils and public bodies:* BBC Governor 1997-2005; Member: City University Council 1997-2001, Oxford University Council 2001-04, Engineering and Physical Sciences Research Council 2013-, Lancaster University Council 2014-.

Political interests: National security issues, science and technology; Asia, Europe, Middle East.

Other: Cyclotion Trust, Unique. Freedom, City of London. Hon. doctorates: University of London, Open University, City University; Hon. fellow, Lady Margaret Hall, Oxford. CMG 1987; DCMG 1996; Légion d'Honneur (France) 2009; PC 2010.

Rt Hon the Baroness Neville-Jones DCMG, House of Lords, London SW1A 0PW
Tel: 020 7219 3208 *Email:* nevillejonesp@parliament.uk

CONSERVATIVE

NEVILLE-ROLFE, BARONESS

NEVILLE-ROLFE (Life Baroness), Lucy Jeanne Neville-Rolfe; cr 2013. Born 2 January 1953; Daughter of late Edmund and late Margaret Neville-Rolfe; Married Sir Richard Packer (4 sons).

Education: St Mary's Convent, Shaftesbury; Somerville College, Oxford (BA philosophy, politics and economics); Some French and German.

Non-political career: Ministry of Agriculture, Fisheries and Food 1973-92: Private Secretary to John Silkin as Minister of Agriculture, Fisheries and Food 1977-79, EC Sheepmeat and Milk 1979-86, Land Use 1986-88, Food Safety Act 1988-90, Head of Personnel 1990-92; Member, Prime Minister's Policy Unit 1992-94; Under Secretary 1994; Director, Deregulation Unit, Department of Trade and Industry/Better Regulation Unit, Cabinet Office 1995-97; Tesco plc: Group director of corporate affairs 1997-2006, Company Secretary 2003-06, Executive director, corporate and legal affairs 2006-12.

Political career: *House of Lords:* Raised to the peerage as Baroness Neville-Rolfe, of Chilmark in the County of Wiltshire 2013. Parliamentary Under-Secretary of State for Intellectual Property and Government Spokesperson: Department for Business, Innovation and Skills 2014-16, Department for Culture, Media and Sport 2015-16; Minister of State for Energy and Intellectual Property and Government Spokesperson, Department for Business, Energy and Industrial Strategy 2016; Commercial Secretary and Government Spokesperson, HM Treasury 2016-17. Member: Affordable Childcare 2014, Intellectual Property (Unjustified Threats) Bill 2016, European Union 2017-, EU Financial Affairs Sub-committee 2017-. *Councils and public bodies:* Governor, London Business School 2011-.

Political interests: Agriculture, animals, food, rural affairs, business, industry and consumers, culture, media and sport, European Union, international affairs, roll out of broadband, vocational education; China, Eastern Europe, Germany, India, South Asia.

Other: Non-executive director, John Laing Construction 1991-92; British Retail Consortium: Member, management board 1998-2012, Member, Economics and European Committee 1998-2013, Deputy chair 2003-12; EuroCommerce: Vice-president 1998-2008, President 2012-14; Board of Management, Foreign and Commonwealth Office 2000-05; Member, Deputy Prime Minister's Local Government Funding Committee 2003-04; Corporate Leaders Group on Climate Change 2005-13; Foresight Obesity Project 2005-07; China Britain Business Council 2005-13; Chair, Dobbies Garden Centres plc 2007-10; Non-executive director, Carbon Trust 2008-13; UK India Business Council 2008-13; Non-executive director, ITV plc 2010-14; Efficiency Board, Cabinet Office 2010-13; Strategic Advisory Group, UK Trade & Investment 2011-13; Member: PWC Advisory Board 2013-14, Supervisory Board of Metro AG 2013-14; Non-executive director: Boparan Ltd (2 Sisters Food Group) 2013-14, Hermes Equity Ownership Services 2013-14; Fellow, Institute of Chartered Secretaries; FCIS 2010. Hon. Fellow, Somerville College, Oxford. Women of Achievement Award 2007; PR Week Lifetime Achievement Award 2013. CMG 2005; DBE 2012.

Recreations: Gardening, art and architecture, racing, cricket, theatre.

The Baroness Neville-Rolfe DBE CMG, House of Lords, London SW1A 0PW
Tel: 020 7219 5353 *Email:* nevillerolfel@parliament.uk *Twitter:* @LNevilleRolfe

LIBERAL DEMOCRAT

NEWBY, LORD

Leader, Liberal Democrat Peers

NEWBY (Life Baron), Richard Mark Newby; cr 1997. Born 14 February 1953; Son of Frank and Kathleen Newby; Married Ailsa Ballantyne Thomson 1978 (2 sons).

Education: Rothwell Grammar School; St Catherine's College, Oxford (BA philosophy, politics and economics 1974, MA).

Non-political career: HM Customs and Excise: Administration trainee 1974, Private secretary to Permanent Secretary 1977-79, Principal, Planning Unit 1979-81; Secretary, SDP Parliamentary Committee 1981; SDP headquarters 1981-88: National Secretary 1983-88; Corporate affairs director, Rosehaugh plc 1988-92; Director: Matrix Communications Consultancy Ltd 1992-99, Flagship Group Ltd 1999-2001; Chair: Live Consulting 2001-12, Live Sport CIC 2009-12.

Political career: *House of Lords:* Raised to the peerage as Baron Newby, of Rothwell in the County of West Yorkshire 1997. Liberal Democrat Spokesperson for: Trade and Industry 1998-2000, Treasury 1998-2010; Sponsored Public Services (Social Value) Act 2012; Deputy Chief Whip (Captain of the Queen's Bodyguard of the Yeomen of the Guard) 2012-15; Government Spokesperson for Treasury 2012-15; Liberal Democrat: Chief Whip 2015-16, Leader, Liberal Democrat Peers 2016-; Member, House of Lords Commission 2016-. Member: Monetary Policy of the Bank of England/Economic Affairs 1998-2003, Ecclesiastical Committee 2002-12, Economic Affairs Sub-committee on Financial Bill 2004, Joint Committee on the Draft Financial Services Bill 2011-12, Administration and Works 2012-16, Privileges and Conduct 2012-, Procedure 2012-, Sub-committee on Leave of Absence 2012-13, Selection 2012-, Refreshment 2012-15, Joint Committee on Security 2012-15, Insurance Bill 2014-15, Finance 2016, Liaison 2016-. Chair, Liberal Democrat Parliamentary Party Committee on Treasury 2010-12. *Other:* Deputy Chair, Liberal Democrat General Election Team 1995-97; Liberal Democrat Campaigns and Communications Committee 1995-2006; Chief of Staff to Charles Kennedy as Leader of the Liberal Democrats 1999-2006; General Election Chief Whip in the House of Lords 2015.

Political interests: Europe, regional development; Eastern Caribbean, Pakistan, South Africa.

Other: The Prince's Trust. OBE 1990; PC 2014. MCC.

Recreations: Football, cricket, tennis.

Rt Hon the Lord Newby OBE, House of Lords, London SW1A 0PW
Tel: 020 7219 8501 *Email:* newbyr@parliament.uk *Twitter:* @RichardNewby3

NEWCASTLE, LORD BISHOP OF

NON-AFFILIATED

NEWCASTLE (12th Bishop of), Christine Elizabeth Hardman. Born 27 August 1951; Married Roger (2 daughters).

Education: Queen Elizabeth's Girls' Grammar School, Barnet; University of London (BSc (Econ) 1973); Oxford University (MTh applied theology 1994).

Non-political career: Articled clerk; Estate agency; Deaconess 1984; Curate, St John the Baptist, Markyate Street 1984-88; Ordained Deacon 1987; St Albans Ministerial Training Scheme/Oxford Ministry Course 1988-96: Tutor and course director, Director of Mission Studies; Ordained Priest 1994; Vicar, Holy Trinity and Christ the King, Stevenage 1996-2001; Rural Dean of Stevenage 1999-2001; Archdeacon of Lewisham and Greenwich 2001-12; Honorary Assistant Priest, Cathedral and Collegiate Church of St Saviour and St Mary Overie Southwark 2012-15; Bishop of Newcastle 2015-.

Political career: *House of Lords:* Entered House of Lords 2015. *Councils and public bodies:* Member: General Synod 1998-, Archbishops' Council 2010-15; Church Commissioner 2017-.

Political interests: Rural and urban issues; North East region, economic and business affairs; Botswana, Norway.

Other: Committee Member, Ecclesiastical Law Society.

Recreations: Theatre, being in the mountains, cycling.

Rt Rev the Lord Bishop of Newcastle, House of Lords, London SW1A 0PW
Tel: 020 7219 3000
Bishop's House, 29 Moor Road South, Gosforth, Newcastle upon Tyne NE3 1PA
Tel: 0191-285 2220 *Email:* bishop@newcastle.anglican.org
Website: www.newcastle.anglican.org *Twitter:* @BishopNewcastle

NEWLOVE, BARONESS

CONSERVATIVE

NEWLOVE (Life Baroness), Helen Margaret Newlove; cr 2010. Born 28 December 1961; Married Garry Newlove 1986 (died 2007) (3 daughters).

Non-political career: Campaigner against anti-social behaviour; Founder, Newlove Warrington 2009.

Political career: *House of Lords:* Raised to the peerage as Baroness Newlove, of Warrington in the County of Cheshire 2010. Government Champion for Active, Safer Communities: Home Office 2010-11, Department for Communities and Local Government 2011-12; Victims' Commissioner for England and Wales, Ministry of Justice 2013-. Member: EU Justice Sub-committee 2015-17, Citizenship and Civic Engagement 2017-.

Political interests: Community, policing, volunteering, anti-social behaviour, alcohol, victims, justice, national citizen service; Caribbean, Dubai, New Zealand, USA.

Other: Warrington Wolves Foundation, SAFE Place Merseyside, Fybromyalgia UK. Doctor of Laws, Bolton University 2017. Best Magazine Bravery Award 2008; Cheshire Woman of the Year 2009; Local Heroes Community Project of the Year 2009; Business Woman of the Year Achievement Award 2015.

The Baroness Newlove, House of Lords, London SW1A 0PW
Tel: 020 7219 6464 *Email:* newloveh@parliament.uk
102 Petty France, London SW1H 9AJ *Tel:* 020 3334 2908
Website: victimscommissioner.org.uk *Twitter:* @lady10newlove

CONSERVATIVE

NICHOLSON OF WINTERBOURNE, BARONESS

NICHOLSON OF WINTERBOURNE (Life Baroness), Emma Harriet Nicholson; cr. 1997. Born 16 October 1941; Daughter of late Sir Godfrey Nicholson, 1st and last Bt and late Lady Katharine Lindsay, daughter of 27th Earl of Crawford, KT, PC; Married Sir Michael Harris Caine 1987 (died 1999) (2 stepchildren).

Education: Portsdown Lodge School, Bexhill; St Mary's School, Wantage; Royal Academy of Music (LRAM 1962, ARCM); French.

Non-political career: ICL 1961-64; Computer consultant, John Tyzack and Partners 1964-69; Computer management consultant: McLintock Mann and Whinney Murray 1969-73, John Tyzack and Partners 1973-74; Save the Children Fund 1974-85: Director of Fundraising 1977-85; Consultant inter alia Dr Barnardos, Westminster Children's Hospital, The Duke of Edinburgh's Award Scheme, Foster Parents Plan, Association of Girl Guides and Scouts et al 1985-87; St Antony's College, Oxford: Visiting fellow 1995-96, Senior associate member 1997-98, 1998-99.

Political career: *House of Commons:* Contested (Conservative) Blyth 1979 general election. MP for Devon West and Torridge 1987-97 (Conservative 1987-95, Liberal Democrat 1995-97). PPS to Michael Jack as Minister of State: Home Office 1992-93, Ministry of Agriculture, Fisheries and Food 1993-95, Treasury 1995; Liberal Democrat Spokesperson for Overseas Development and Human Rights 1996-97. *House of Lords:* Raised to the peerage as Baroness Nicholson of Winterbourne, of Winterbourne in the Royal County of Berkshire 1997. Member, Liberal Democrat Foreign Affairs Team 1997-2016; Frontbench Spokesperson for Data Protection 1998-99; Trade Envoy to: Iraq 2014-, Azerbaijan and Turkmenistan 2016-, Kazakhstan 2017-. Member, Soft Power and the UK's Influence 2013-14; Chair, Sexual Violence in Conflict 2015-16. *Other:* European Parliament: MEP for South East region 1999-2009: Vice-chair, Foreign Affairs, Human Rights, Common Defence and Security Policy/Foreign Affairs Committee 1999-2007; Rapporteur for: Romania 1999-2007, Kashmir 2007-09; Chair, Interparliamentary Committee for Iraq; Deputy Chair, Euromed Committee for Women; Member, Committee for Finance, Sub-committee for Women's Affairs, Agriculture Committee; Member, Council for Lome Convention; Official observer including leader for 32 elections in Africa and Europe; Member, Monitoring Committee. Former treasurer, Positive European Group (Conservative); Vice-chair, Conservative Party 1983-87; Member, Federal Executive Committee, Liberal Democrats 1999-2003; Sat as Liberal Democrat in the Lords until September 2016; now sits as Conservative.

Political interests: Foreign and defence policy, human rights and the defence of freedom; Armenia, Azerbijan, France, Georgia, Germany, Iran, Iraq, Kazakhstan, Kuwait, Lebanon, Moldova, Romania, Saudi Arabia, Syria, Turkey, Turkmenistan, USA, Yemen.

Other: Member, UK Delegation to the Parliamentary Assembly of the Council of Europe 2011-15; Founder Chair, AMAR International Charitable Foundation; Founder President, Iraq-Britain Business Council; Vice President, Man Booker Prize for English Fiction; Chair, Booker Prize for Russian fiction; President, Caine Prize for African Writing; Chair, Children's High Level Group; Board member, GWPF; LRAM; ARCM; FRSA; Honorary D. Freeman, Worshipful Company of Information Technologists. Freedom, City of London. Honorary doctorate: Oklahoma City University, USA, Birmingham University, London Metropolitan University, Victor Babes University of Medicine and Pharmacy, Romania, Dimitrie Cantemir Christian University, Bucharest, Romania, Brigham Young University, USA 2017; *Clubs:* Reform, Royal Overseas League Club.

Publications: Why Does the West Forget? (1993); Secret Society – Inside and Outside the Conservative Party (1996); Co-editor, The Haqi Marshlands (2002).

The Baroness Nicholson of Winterbourne, House of Lords, London SW1A 0PW
Tel: 020 7219 5353
Website: emmanicholson.info

LAB/CO-OP

NICOL, BARONESS

NICOL (Life Baroness), Olive Mary Wendy Nicol; cr. 1982. Born 21 March 1923; Daughter of late James and Harriet Rowe-Hunter; Married Alexander Douglas Ian Nicol 1947 (died 2009) (2 sons 1 daughter).

Education: Cahir School, Co Tipperary, Ireland.

Non-political career: Clerical officer, Inland Revenue 1942-44; Inspector Admiralty 1944-48; Supplementary Benefits Tribunal 1976-78; Co-operative Board 1976-85: President 1981-85; Careers Service Consultative Panel 1978-81.

Political career: *House of Lords:* Raised to the peerage as Baroness Nicol, of Newnham in the County of Cambridge 1982. Member, Lord Chancellor's Advisory Committee 1982-88; Opposition Spokesperson for Green issues 1983-92; Opposition Whip 1983-87; Opposition Deputy Chief

Whip 1987-89; Opposition Spokesperson for Energy 1988-89; Deputy Speaker 1995-2002; Deputy Chair of Committees 1995-2002; Board Member, Parliamentary Office of Science and Technology (POST) 1998-2000; On leave of absence June 2012-June 2017. *Other:* Member, Co-operative Party. *Councils and public bodies:* JP, Cambridge Bench 1972-86; Cambridge City Council: Councillor 1972-82, Deputy Mayor 1974.

Political interests: Commerce, conservation, environment, energy, forestry.

Other: Various school governing bodies and other public service areas, including Granta Housing Association; Chair, United Charities 1967-86; Council member, RSPB 1989-94; Vice-President: Marine Conservation Society, RSPB, Council for National Parks; FRGS 1990-2001. Senior Member, Robinson College, Cambridge 1995-; Honorary Fellow, Institute of Wastes Management.

Recreations: Reading, walking, gardening.

The Baroness Nicol, House of Lords, London SW1A 0PW
Tel: 020 7219 5353

CONSERVATIVE

NOAKES, BARONESS

NOAKES (Life Baroness), Sheila Valerie Noakes; cr. 2000. Born 23 June 1949; Daughter of Albert and Iris Masters; Married (Colin) Barry Noakes 1985.

Education: Eltham Hill Grammar School; Bristol University (LLB 1970).

Non-political career: Peat Marwick Mitchell & Co/KPMG/KPMG Peat Marwick 1970-2000: Partner 1983-2000; Seconded to: HM Treasury 1979-81, Department of Health, as Director of Finance, NHS Management Executive 1988-91; Bank of England: Director 1994-2001, Senior non-executive director 1998-2001; Non-executive director: Carpetright plc 2001-14, SThree plc 2001-07, Hanson plc 2001-07, English National Opera 2001-08, John Laing plc 2002-04, Imperial Chemical Industries plc 2004-08, Severn Trent plc 2008-14, Royal Bank of Scotland Group plc 2011-.

Political career: *House of Lords:* Raised to the peerage as Baroness Noakes, of Goudhurst in the County of Kent 2000. Opposition Spokesperson for: Health 2001-03, Work and Pensions 2001-06, Treasury 2003-10. Member, Economic Affairs Finance Bill Sub-Committee 2012-13, 2016; Member: Audit 2011-14, Joint Committee on Voting Eligibilty (Prisoners) Bill 2013, Communications 2013-; Chair, Personal Service Companies 2013-14; Member: Economic Affairs 2013-14, Affordable Childcare 2014-15, Insurance Bill 2014-15, EU Internal Market Sub-committee 2015-. *Councils and public bodies:* Member: Inland Revenue Management Board 1992-99, NHS Policy Board 1992-95, Chancellor of the Exchequer's Private Finance Panel 1993-97; Commissioner, Public Works Loan Board 1995-2001; Member, Public Services Productivity Panel 1998-2000; Governor: London Business School 1998-2001, Eastbourne College 2000-04; Deputy Chairman, Ofcom 2014-.

Political interests: Health, public finance, trade and industry, public service management, horse racing, rural issues.

Other: Trustee, Thomson Reuters Founder Share Company 1998-2013; Board member, Social Market Foundation 2002-05; Institute of Chartered Accountants of England and Wales: Fellow, Council member 1987-2002, President 1999-2000; Board member, Companions, Institute of Management 1996-2002; FCA; Childrens Society, Dogs Trust, Cats Protection Society. Freedom, City of London. Three honorary doctorates. DBE 1996; *Clubs:* Farmers Club.

Recreations: Skiing, horse racing, opera, early classical music.

The Baroness Noakes DBE, House of Lords, London SW1A 0PW
Tel: 020 7219 5230 *Fax:* 020 7219 4215 *Email:* noakess@parliament.uk *Twitter:* @1SVN

NON-AFFILIATED

NORFOLK, DUKE OF

NORFOLK (18th Duke of, E), Edward William Fitzalan-Howard; cr. 1483; 29th Earl of Arundel (E) 1139/1289; Earl of Surrey (E) 1483; 16th Earl of Norfolk (E) 1644; 13th Baron Beaumont (E) 1309; 20th Baron Maltravers (E) 1330; 16th Baron FitzAlan, Clun, and Oswaldestre (E) 1627; 5th Baron Howard of Glossop (UK) 1869. Born 2 December 1956; Son of Major-General 17th Duke, KG, GCVO, CB, MC, DL; Married Georgina Susan Temple Gore 1987 (3 sons 2 daughters).

Education: Ampleforth College, Yorkshire; Lincoln College, Oxford (BA philosophy, politics and economics 1978, MA).

Non-political career: Chair: Sigas Ltd 1979-88, Parkwood Group Ltd 1989-2002.

Political career: *House of Lords:* Entered House of Lords 2002; On leave of absence June 2012-September 2016, April 2017-June 2017. *Councils and public bodies:* DL, West Sussex 2002-.

Other: Trustee: Tablet Trust, College of Arms Trust; Arundel and Littlehampton District Scouts; Arundel Branch, Royal British Legion; Friends of Arundel Cathedral; Oxford and Cambridge Catholic Education Board. Premier Duke and Earl of England; Earl Marshal and Hereditary Marshal and Chief Butler of England; *Clubs:* British Racing Drivers Club (Silverstone).

Recreations: Skiing, motor-racing, shooting.

His Grace the Duke of Norfolk DL, House of Lords, London SW1A 0PW
Tel: 020 7219 5353
Arundel Castle, Arundel, West Sussex BN18 9AB *Tel:* 01903 883400 *Fax:* 01903 884482

CROSSBENCH

NORTHBOURNE, LORD

NORTHBOURNE (5th Baron, UK), Christopher George Walter James; cr. 1884; 6th Bt of Langley Hall (GB) 1791. Born 18 February 1926; Son of 4th Baron and Katherine Louise, née Nickerson; Married Marie Sygne Aliki Claudel 1959 (3 sons 1 daughter).

Education: Eton College; Magdalen College, Oxford (MA 1959).

Non-political career: Farmer and businessman including overseas agriculture; Chair, Betteshanger Farms Ltd (UK); Nchima Tea and Tung Estates (Malawi).

Political career: *House of Lords:* First entered House of Lords 1982; Elected hereditary peer 1999-. *Councils and public bodies:* DL, Kent 1996-.

Political interests: Education, disadvantaged and excluded children, parents, family, agriculture, horticulture; Australia, France, Indonesia, Malawi.

Other: FRICS; Stepney Childrens' Fund (Toynbee); *Clubs:* Brooks's, Royal Yacht Squadron (Cowes), House of Lords Yacht Club.

Recreations: Painting, sailing, gardening.

The Lord Northbourne DL, House of Lords, London SW1A 0PW
Tel: 020 7219 3884 *Fax:* 020 7219 5933 *Email:* northbournec@parliament.uk

CONSERVATIVE

NORTHBROOK, LORD

NORTHBROOK (6th Baron, UK), Francis Thomas Baring; cr. 1866; 8th Bt of The City of London (GB) 1793. Born 21 February 1954; Son of 5th Baron; Married Amelia Taylor 1987 (divorced 2006) (3 daughters); married Charlotte Pike 2013.

Education: Winchester College; Bristol University (BA 1976).

Non-political career: Trainee accountant, Dixon Wilson & Co 1976-80; Credit and investment analyst/private client investment manager, Baring Bros & Co Ltd 1981-89; Senior investment manager, Taylor Young Investment Management Ltd 1990-93; Investment fund manager, Smith and Williamson 1993-95; Managing director, Northbrook Farms Ltd 1995-; Director, Mars Asset Management 1996-2006.

Political career: *House of Lords:* First entered House of Lords 1990; Elected hereditary peer 1999-; Opposition Whip 1999-2000. Member: Equality Act 2010 and Disability 2015-16, Financial Exclusion 2016-17.

Political interests: The City, agriculture, foreign affairs, constitution.

Other: Trustee, Fortune Forum 2006-; Member, advisory board, Iman Foundation 2016-; Royal Geographical Society. Freedom, City of London; *Clubs:* White's, Pratt's, Beefsteak, Gunmakers Club.

Recreations: Cricket, skiing, shooting.

The Lord Northbrook, House of Lords, London SW1A 0PW
Tel: 020 7219 4090 *Email:* northbrookf@parliament.uk

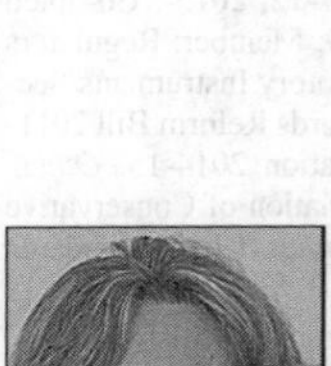

LIBERAL DEMOCRAT

NORTHOVER, BARONESS

Liberal Democrat Lords Spokesperson for Foreign and Commonwealth Affairs

NORTHOVER (Life Baroness), Lindsay Patricia Northover; cr. 2000. Born 21 August 1954; Daughter of Charles and Patricia Granshaw; Married John Northover 1988 (separated) (2 sons 1 daughter).

Education: Brighton and Hove High School; St Anne's College, Oxford (BA modern history 1976, MA); Bryn Mawr College, Pennsylvania University, USA (MA history and philosophy of science 1978; PhD 1981).

Non-political career: Research Fellow: University College London and St Mark's Hospital 1980-83, St Thomas's Hospital Medical School, London 1983-84; Lecturer, University College London 1984-91; Historian of twentieth century medicine, Wellcome Institute, London 1984-91. Member, AUT 1984-91.

Political career: *House of Commons:* Contested (as Lindsay Granshaw) (SDP/All) Welwyn Hatfield 1983 and 1987 and (Liberal Democrat) Basildon 1997 general elections. *House of Lords:* Raised to the peerage as Baroness Northover, of Cissbury in the County of West Sussex 2000. Liberal Democrat Spokesperson for: Health 2001-02, International Development 2002-10, Equality Bill 2009-10; Government Whip 2010-14; Government Spokesperson for: Advocate General for Scotland 2010, Law Officers 2010, Wales 2010, Justice 2010-12, Health 2010-13, Women and Equalities 2010-14; Department for International Development: Government Spokesperson 2010-15, Parliamentary Under-Secretary of State 2014-15; Government Spokesperson for: Environment, Food and Rural Affairs 2012-14, Culture, Media and Sport 2013-14, Education 2013-14; Liberal Democrat: Spokesperson for International Development 2015-16, Shadow Minister/Lords Spokesperson for Foreign and Commonwealth Affairs 2016-; Trade Envoy to Angola 2016-. Member: Stem Cell Research 2001-02, EU Sub-committee C (Foreign Affairs, Defence and Development Policy) 2003-04, Procedure 2005-09, EU Sub-committee A (Economic and Financial Affairs and International Trade) 2008-10. *Other:* Chair: SDP Health and Social Welfare Association 1987-88, Liberal Democrats' Parliamentary Candidates Association 1988-91, Women Liberal Democrats 1992-95; Trustee, Liberal Democrats 2009-11; President, Liberal Democrat Women 2014-.

Other: Vice-chair, Commonwealth Parliamentary Association 2008-10; Trustee, Bryn Mawr College Association, Great Britain; Council member, Overseas Development Institute 2005-10; Trustee: Tropical Health and Education Trust 2007-10, Unicef UK 2009-10; Honorary Associate Professor, Institute of Global Health Innovation, Imperial College, London 2016-; Member of Advisory Council, Wilton Park 2016-; Trustee, Malaria Consortium 2016-; Fellow, Royal Society of Arts 2013. English-Speaking Union award to study in USA 1972; St Anne's College Exhibition 1973; Herbert Plumer Bursary for postgraduate study overseas 1976; English-speaking Union Fellowship 1976-79; Mrs Giles Whiting Fellowship in the Humanities 1979-80. PC 2015.

Publications: Various academic publications.

Rt Hon the Baroness Northover, House of Lords, London SW1A 0PW
Tel: 020 7219 8623 *Email:* northoverl@parliament.uk *Twitter:* @LPNorthover

CONSERVATIVE

NORTON OF LOUTH, LORD

NORTON OF LOUTH (Life Baron), Philip Norton; cr. 1998. Born 5 March 1951; Son of late George and Ena Norton.

Education: King Edward VI Grammar School, Louth; Sheffield University (BA political theory and institutions 1972; PhD 1977) (Nalgo Prize); University of Pennsylvania (Thouron Scholar, MA political science 1975).

Non-political career: Hull University: Politics lecturer 1977-82, Senior lecturer 1982-84, Reader 1984-86, Professor of Government 1986-, Director, Centre of Legislative Studies 1992-, Head of Department of Politics and International Studies 2002-07; Associate editor, *Political Studies* 1987-93; Editor, *Journal of Legislative Studies* 1995-.

Political career: *House of Lords:* Raised to the peerage as Baron Norton of Louth, of Louth in the County of Lincolnshire 1998. Constitution: Chair 2001-04, Member 2007-12, 2015-; Co-opted member, EU Sub-committee E (Law and Institutions) 1999-2001, 2006-09; Member: Regulators 2006-07, Joint Committee on Draft Constitutional Bill 2008, Merits of Statutory Instruments/Secondary Legislation Scrutiny 2009-14, Joint Committee on Draft House of Lords Reform Bill 2011-12, Joint Committee on Voting Eligibilty (Prisoners) Bill 2013, Information 2014-15. *Other:* Chair, Conservative Academic Group 2000-; Executive Committee: Association of Conservative Peers 2001-14, Conservative History Group 2003-. *Councils and public bodies:* Chair, Standards Committee, Kingston-upon-Hull City Council 1999-2003.

Political interests: Constitutional affairs, parliamentary reform, legislatures, British politics, American politics, education.

Other: Executive committee member: Study of Parliament Group 1981-93, 2012-, Political Studies Association 1983-89; Member, Society and Politics Research Development Group, Economic and Social Research Council 1987-90; President, British Politics Group (USA) 1988-90; Warden, King Edward VI Grammar School, Louth 1990-93; President, Politics Association 1993-2008; Co-chair, Research Committee of Legislative Specialists, International Political Science Association 1994-2003; Hansard Society: Council member 1997-, Director of Studies 2002-; Chair, Commission to Strengthen Parliament 1999-2001; Vice-President, Political Studies Association

1999-; Trustee, History of Parliament Trust 1999-; Co-founder, Campaign for an Effective Second Chamber 2001; Trustee, Jo Carby-Hall Poland and Cyprus Scholarships/Fellowships 2009-; Member, advisory board, Opposition Studies Forum 2009-; Co-chair, Higher Education Commission 2012-; FRSA 1995; ACSS 2001. Hon. LLD, Lincoln University 2011; *Clubs:* Royal Overseas League Club.

Publications: Author or editor: Dissension in the House of Commons 1945-74 (1975); Conservative Dissidents (1978); Dissension in the House of Commons 1974-79 (1980); The Commons in Perspective (1981); Co-author, Conservatives and Conservatism (1981); The Constitution in Flux (1982); Law and Order and British Politics (1984); The British Polity (1984, 5th edition 2010); Parliament in the 1980s (1985); Co-editor, The Political Science of British Politics (1986); Legislatures (1990); Parliaments in Western Europe (1990); New Directions in British Politics? (1991); Co-editor, Parliamentary Questions (1993); Co-author, Back from Westminster (1993); Does Parliament Matter? (1993); National Parliaments and the European Union (1996); Co-editor, The New Parliaments of Central and Eastern Europe (1996); The Conservative Party (1996); Legislatures and Legislators (1998); Parliaments and Governments in Western Europe (1998); Parliaments and Pressure Groups in Western Europe (1998); Co-editor, Parliaments in Asia (1999); Parliaments and Citizens in Western Europe (2002); Co-editor: Post-Communist and Post-Soviet Legislatures: The Initial Decade (2007), The Internet and Parliamentary Democracy in Europe (2008); A Century of Constitutional Reform (2011); Eminent Parliamentarians (2012); Parliament in British Politics (2nd edition 2013); Co-author, Politics UK (8th edition 2013); The Voice of the Backbenches (2013).

Recreations: Table tennis, walking, writing.

Professor the Lord Norton of Louth, House of Lords, London SW1A 0PW
Tel: 020 7219 0669 *Fax:* 020 7219 1465 *Email:* nortonp@parliament.uk
Department of Politics, Hull University, Hull HU6 7RX *Tel:* 01482 465863 *Fax:* 01482 466208
Email: p.norton@hull.ac.uk
Websites: www2.hull.ac.uk/fass/politics/staff/professorphilipnorton.aspx
nortonview.wordpress.com lordsoftheblog.net/category/lord-norton
Twitter: @LordNortonLouth

NORWICH, LORD BISHOP OF

NON-AFFILIATED

NORWICH (71st Bishop of), Graham Richard James. Born 19 January 1951; Son of late Rev Lionel James and Florence James, née James; Married Julie Freemantle 1978 (1 daughter 1 son 1 daughter deceased).

Education: Northampton Grammar School; Lancaster University (BA history 1972); Oxford University (DipTh 1974); Cuddesdon Theological College, Oxford.

Non-political career: Deacon 1975; Assistant curate, Christ the Carpenter, Peterborough 1975-78; Priest 1976; Christ the King, Digswell, Hertfordshire 1979-83; Advisory Council for the Church's Ministry 1983-87: Selection Secretary and Secretary for Continuing Education 1983-85, Senior Selection Secretary 1985-87; Chaplain to Archbishop of Canterbury 1987-93; Bishop Suffragan of St Germans Diocese of Truro 1993-99; Bishop of Norwich 1999-.

Political career: *House of Lords:* Entered House of Lords 2004. Member, Communications 2011-15. *Councils and public bodies:* Member, Church of England General Synod 1995-; Chair, Rural Bishops Panel 2001-06; Board member: Countryside Agency 2001-06, Norfolk County Strategic Partnership 2003-11; Chair: Central Religious Advisory Committee, BBC 2004-08, Norfolk Community Foundation 2005-10; President, Royal Norfolk Agricultural Association 2005; Member, Archbishops' Council 2006-10; Chair: Ministry Division, Church of England 2006-12, Standing Conference on Religion and Belief, BBC 2009-11.

Political interests: Rural issues, media, education and training.

Other: Sponsor, Open Academy Norwich 2007-; Patron, President and Vice-President of around forty charities both locally and nationally. Hon. Doctorate: Civil Law, University of East Anglia 2015, Norwich University of the Arts 2016; *Clubs:* Athenæum, Strangers Club, Norwich.

Publications: Editor, New Soundings (DLT, 1997); The Lent Factor (Bloomsbury, 2014).

Recreations: Theatre, cricket, rugby, discovering second-hand bookshops.

Rt Rev the Lord Bishop of Norwich, House of Lords, London SW1A 0PW
Tel: 020 7219 5353
Bishop's House, Norwich NR3 1SB *Tel:* 01603 629001 *Email:* bishop@dioceseofnorwich.org
Website: www.dioceseofnorwich.org

LABOUR

NYE, BARONESS

NYE (Life Baroness), Susan Jane Nye; cr 2010. Born 17 May 1955; Married Gavyn Davies (2 sons 1 daughter).

Non-political career: Civil servant: Department of Employment 1974-76, Downing Street 1976-79; Office of the Leader of the Opposition 1979-92; Office manager to Gordon Brown MP as Shadow Chancellor of the Exchequer 1992-97; Political secretary to Gordon Brown MP as Chancellor of the Exchequer 1997-2007; Director of government relations, Downing Street 2007-10.

Political career: *House of Lords:* Raised to the peerage as Baroness Nye, of Lambeth in the London Borough of Lambeth 2010.

Other: Partner: Barnsham Barns (Norfolk) LLP, Machrie Golf LLP; General Partner, SPKRBM LP; Director: Actev II Ltd Trading Group, Machrie Golf Links and Hotel Ltd, Another Place Ltd; Board member, Burma Campaign UK; Trustee, Young Women's Trust.

The Baroness Nye, House of Lords, London SW1A 0PW
Tel: 020 7219 5353

NON-AFFILIATED

OAKESHOTT OF SEAGROVE BAY, LORD

OAKESHOTT OF SEAGROVE BAY (Life Baron), Matthew Alan Oakeshott; cr. 2000. Born 10 January 1947; Son of late Keith Oakeshott CMG, diplomat, and late Jill Oakeshott; Married Dr Philippa Poulton 1976 (2 sons 1 daughter).

Education: Charterhouse, Surrey (Senior Foundation Scholar); University and Nuffield Colleges, Oxford (BA philosophy, politics and economics 1968, MA); French, German, Spanish.

Non-political career: ODI/Nuffield Fellow, Kenya Ministry of Finance and Economic Planning 1968-70; Special adviser to Roy Jenkins MP 1972-76; Director, Warburg Investment Management 1976-81; Manager, Courtaulds Pension Fund 1981-85; Founder director, OLIM Ltd and Investment director, Value and Income Trust plc 1986-; Chairman, OLIM Property Ltd 2012-.

Political career: *House of Commons:* Contested (Labour) Horsham and Crawley October 1974 and (SDP/All) Cambridge 1983 general elections. *House of Lords:* Raised to the peerage as Baron Oakeshott of Seagrove Bay, of Seagrove Bay in the County of the Isle of Wight 2000. Liberal Democrat Spokesperson for: Treasury 2001-11, Work and Pensions 2002-10; Chair, Business Advisory Group to Vince Cable as Secretary of State for Business, Innovation and Skills 2010; On leave of absence May 2014-October 2015. Member: Economic Affairs 2001-04, House of Lords' Offices Finance and Staff Sub-committee 2001-02, Reform of House of Lords Joint Committee 2002-03, Economic Affairs 2007-08. *Other:* Member, SDP: National Committee 1981-82, National Economic Policy Committee 1981-85; Member, Liberal Democrat Taxation Group 2007-10; Resigned from Liberal Democrats May 2014; now sits as Non-affiliated. *Councils and public bodies:* Oxford City Councillor 1972-76.

Political interests: Economic policy, housing, overseas development; Brazil, Kenya.

Other: Governor, National Institute of Economic and Social Research; Chair, Coltstaple Trust; Coltstaple Trust.

Publications: Chapter in By-Elections in British Politics (1973).

Recreations: Music, elections, Arsenal FC.

The Lord Oakeshott of Seagrove Bay, House of Lords, London SW1A 0PW
Tel: 020 7219 3000 *Email:* oakeshottm@parliament.uk *Twitter:* @oakeshottm

LIBERAL DEMOCRAT

OATES, LORD

OATES (Life Baron), Jonathan Oates; cr 2015. Born 28 December 1969; Son of Revd Canon John Oates and Sylvia Mary West; Civil partner David Hill 2006.

Education: Marlborough College; Exeter University (BA politics).

Non-political career: Teaching in Zimbabwe 1988; Account manager, Westminster Strategy 1992-99; Political and media adviser, South African Parliament 1999-2001; Communications adviser, Youth Justice Board 2001; Associate, Mark Bolland Associates 2002-04; Bell Pottinger: Director 2004-07, Strategic media director 2008-09; Liberal Democrats: Director of policy and communications 2007-08, Director, general election communications 2009-10; Deputy communications director, Number 10 2010; Chief of Staff to Nick Clegg as the Deputy Prime Minister 2010-15; Director, H&O Communications Ltd.

Political career: *House of Lords:* Raised to the peerage as Baron Oates, of Denby Grange in the County of West Yorkshire 2015. On leave of absence September 2017-. Member, EU Justice Sub-committee 2016-17. *Other:* Election agent to: Ed Davey 1997, Jenny Tonge 2001; Campaign manager to Jeremy Browne 2005. *Councils and public bodies:* Kingston upon Thames Council: Councillor 1994-98, Deputy Leader 1997-98.

Political interests: International development, mental health, youth justice; Ethiopia, South Africa, Zimbabwe.

Other: Non-executive director, NHS Blood and Transplant 2017-; Member, governing council, Association of European Parliamentarians with Africa; External adviser, International Planned Parenthood Federation; *Clubs:* National Liberal Club.

Recreations: Poetry, football (Tottenham Hotspur FC), running.

The Lord Oates, House of Lords, London SW1A 0PW
Tel: 020 7219 3000

O'CATHAIN, BARONESS

CONSERVATIVE

O'CATHAIN (Life Baroness), Detta O'Cathain; cr. 1991. Born 3 February 1938; Daughter of late Caoimhghin and Margaret O'Cathain; Married William Bishop 1968 (died 2001).

Education: Laurel Hill, Limerick; University College, Dublin (BA economics, English and French 1961); French.

Non-political career: Assistant economist, Aer Lingus 1959-66; Group economist, Tarmac 1966-69; Economic adviser to Chair, Rootes Motors/Chrysler 1969-72; Senior economist, Carrington Viyella 1972; British Leyland: Economic adviser 1973-74, Director, Market Planning 1974-76; Corporate planning executive, Unigate plc 1976-81; Milk Marketing Board 1981-88: Managing director 1985-88; Managing director, Barbican Centre 1990-95; Numerous non-executive directorships.

Political career: *House of Lords:* Raised to the peerage as Baroness O'Cathain, of The Barbican in the City of London 1991. Member: Monetary Policy of the Bank of England/Economic Affairs 1998-2005, European Communities Sub-committee B (Energy, Industry and Transport) 1998-2002, European Union 1999-2001, 2010-15, Joint Committee on House of Lords Reform 2002-05, Constitution 2005-08; Co-opted Member, EU Sub-committee E (Law and Institutions) 2007-10; Chair EU Sub-committee B: (Internal Market, Energy and Transport) 2010-12, (Internal Market, Infrastructure and Employment) 2012-15; Member: Leader's Group on the Working Practices of the House of Lords 2010-11, Consumer Insurance (Disclosure and Representations) Bill 2011-12, Digital Skills 2014-15; Chair, Built Environment 2015-16; Member: High Speed Rail (London-West Midlands) Bill 2016, Joint Committee on Human Rights 2017-. *Other:* Chair, Conservative Friends of Azerbaijan. *Councils and public bodies:* Past President, Agricultural Section British Association for the Advancement of Science; Member: Design Council 1978-80, Engineering Council 1980-83; Council member, Industrial Society 1986-92; Patron, Women in Banking and Finance 2000-07.

Political interests: Arts, agriculture, industry, commerce, finance, retail industry, disabled, economic policy, family, energy; Azerbaijan, EU, Ireland, Israel, USA.

Other: Fellow: Royal Society of Arts 1986, Chartered Institute of Marketing 1987; Chair, Chichester Cathedral Council 2010-; President, Chartered Institute of Marketing 1998-2001; Fellow, Harris Manchester College, Oxford. Freedom, City of London. Honorary Fellow, Harris Manchester College, Oxford 2009. OBE 1983; Commander: Royal Norwegian Order 1993, Order of the Lion of Finland 1994, Order of Friends of Azerbaijan 2011; *Clubs:* Athenæum Club.

Recreations: Music, reading, swimming, walking, gardening.

The Baroness O'Cathain OBE, House of Lords, London SW1A 0PW
Tel: 020 7219 0662 *Email:* ocathaind@parliament.uk

O'DONNELL, LORD

CROSSBENCH

O'DONNELL (Life Baron), Augustine (Gus) Thomas O'Donnell; cr 2012. Born 1 October 1952; Son of late James O'Donnell and late Helen McLean; Married Melanie Timmis 1979 (1 daughter).

Education: Salesian College, Battersea; Warwick University (BA economics 1973); Nuffield College, Oxford (MPhil economics 1975).

Non-political career: Lecturer in Political Economy, Glasgow University 1975-79; HM Treasury 1979-2005: Economist 1979-85, First Secretary (Economic), Washington DC embassy 1985-88, Senior Economic Adviser 1988-89, Press Secretary to John Major: as Chancellor of Exchequer 1989-90, as Prime Minister 1990-94, Under Secretary, Monetary Group 1994-95, Deputy Director, Macroeconomic Policy and Prospects Directorate 1995-96, UK's Executive Director to IMF and World Bank 1997-98, Economic Minister, Washington DC embassy 1997-98, Director, Macroeconomic Policy and Prospects 1998-99, Head of Government Economic Service 1998-2003, Managing Director, Macroeconomic Policy and International Finance Directorate 1999-2002, Permanent Secretary and Chair HMT Management Board 2002-05; Secretary of the Cabinet and Head of the Home Civil Service, Cabinet Office 2005-11, Secretary of the Cabinet and Head of the Civil Service 2011; Chair, Main Honours Advisory Committee -2012; Senior fellow, Civil Service College, Singapore; Strategic Adviser to the chief executive, Toronto Dominion Bank 2012-; Chair, Frontier Economics 2013-; Non-executive Director and Strategic Adviser, Brookfield Asset Management 2013-; Chair, Public Interest Board, PwC 2016-; President of the Council, Institute for Fiscal Studies 2016-; Chair of Trustees, Pro Bono Economics 2016-.

Political career: *House of Lords:* Raised to the peerage as Baron O'Donnell, of Clapham in the London Borough of Wandsworth 2012.

Political interests: Public sector, especially the civil service, economic and financial issues, well-being, behavioural science; Bhutan, Canada, New Zealand, USA.

Other: Trustee, *The Tablet*; Member, Economist Trust; Chair, Commission on Wellbeing Policy, Legatum Institute 2012-; Member, Tech UK Brexit Advisory Panel; Society of Business Economists; Fellow, Institute for Government 2012; Hon. Fellow, British Academy 2014; Anchor House, Paul's Charity, Shine. Freedom, City of London. Honorary degrees from Glasgow and Warwick universities; Honorary fellow, Nuffield College, Oxford. CB 1994; KCB 2005; GCB 2011. Committee member, All England Lawn Tennis and Croquet Club.

Publications: Numerous articles on policy.

Recreations: Tennis, opera, golf.

The Lord O'Donnell GCB, House of Lords, London SW1A 0PW
Tel: 020 7219 5353 *Email:* odonnellg@parliament.uk
Frontier Economics, 71 High Holborn, London WC1V 6DA *Tel:* 020 7031 7000
Fax: 020 7031 7001 *Website:* www.frontier-economics.com *Twitter:* @Gus_ODonnell

O'LOAN, BARONESS

CROSSBENCH

O'LOAN (Life Baroness), Nuala Patricia O'Loan; cr 2009. Born 20 December 1951; Daughter of Gerard Herbert and Sara Herbert; Née St Clair-Herbert; Married Declan O'Loan (MLA 2007-11) 1975 (5 sons).

Education: Holy Child School, Harrogate; King's College, London (LLB 1973); College of Law, London (1976).

Non-political career: Articled clerk, Stephenson Harwood solicitors, London 1974-76; Law lecturer, Ulster Polytechnic 1976-80; Raised family in Kenya where her husband was teaching 1980-83: Teacher, St Patrick's School, Iten, Kenya 1982-83; Ulster University 1984-2000: Law lecturer, then senior lecturer 1984-92, Jean Monnet chair, European law 1992-2000; External examiner, Aberystwyth University, Trinity College Dublin and IPSERA 1996-2000; Visiting professor, School of Law, Ulster University; Member, Independent Group for Dialogue and Peace, Basque Country 2007-10; Ireland's roving ambassador for conflict resolution and special envoy to Timor Leste 2008-11; UN special envoy, women and peace-keeping 2009-11; Roving ambassador and special envoy of Ireland, women, peace and security 2009-11; Member, International Contact Group, Basque Country 2011-; Chair, Governing Authority, National University of Ireland, Maynooth.

Political career: *House of Lords:* Raised to the peerage as Baroness O'Loan, of Kirkinriola in the County of Antrim 2009. Member: Delegated Powers and Regulatory Reform 2010-15, EU Sub-committee E: (Justice and Institutions) 2011-12, (Justice, Institutions and Consumer Protection) 2012-15, Joint Committee on Human Rights 2012-15, Secondary Legislation Scrutiny 2015-. *Councils and public bodies:* Member: General Consumer Council, Northern Ireland 1991-96, UK Domestic Coal Consumers Council 1992-95, Ministerial Working Group on Green Economy 1993-95, Northern Health and Social Services Board 1993-97, Northern Ireland Police Authority 1997-2000; Chair, Northern Ireland Consumer Committee for Electricity 1997-2000; Strategy group 2010, Department for Economic Development 1998-99; Police Ombudsman for Northern Ireland 1999-2007; Special Commissioner, Commission for Racial Equality 2004-05; Chair, human rights inquiry, Equality and Human Rights Commission 2008-09; Independent Review for Home Office 2009-10; Chair: Governing Authority Maynooth University 2010, Daniel Morgan Independent Panel 2014; Member, BMA Ethics Committee 2014.

Countries of interest: Africa, South East Asia, Spain.

Other: Member, Consumers Consultative Council, European Commission 1994-95; Associate member, British-Irish Parliamentary Assembly; Member, Commonwealth Parliamentary Association; NetPLUSS, Club of Madrid; Member: Society of Public Teachers of Law 1992-2000, Irish

Association of Law Teachers 1992-2000, International Purchasing and Supply Educational Research Association 1992-2000; Patron: Living and Dying Well, Drumalis Retreat Centre, British Irish Association; Member, Royal Irish Academy 2013-; Chair, Catholic Council for Independent Inquiry into Child Sexual Abuse; Member: Law Society of England and Wales, Solicitor of Supreme Court England and Wales, Association of Women Solicitors; Trustee, CONCERN Worldwide 2008-12. Hon. Doctor of Laws: Ulster University 2008, National University of Ireland, Maynooth 2008, Higher Education and Technical Awards Council, Ireland, Queen's University, Belfast 2010. Outstanding Achievement Award, American Association for the Civilian Oversight of Law Enforcement 2007; Northern Ireland Woman of the Year, Irish Tatler Awards 2007; Person of the Year, RTE Awards 2008. DBE 2008.

Publications: Many (100+) in reviewed journals, books and papers; Review editor and member of editorial board, Public Procurement Law Review (Sweet and Maxwell) 1991-96.

Recreations: Reading.

The Baroness O'Loan DBE, House of Lords, London SW1A 0PW
Tel: 020 7219 8724 *Email:* oloann@parliament.uk
Email: nualaoloan@googlemail.com

O'NEILL OF BENGARVE, BARONESS

CROSSBENCH

O'NEILL OF BENGARVE (Life Baroness), Onora Sylvia O'Neill; cr. 1999. Born 23 August 1941; Daughter of late Hon. Sir Con O'Neill, GCMG and late Lady Garvey, née Pritchard; Married Edward Nell 1963 (divorced 1976) (2 sons).

Education: St Paul's Girls' School, London; Somerville College, Oxford (BA philosophy, psychology and physiology 1962, MA); Harvard University (PhD philosophy 1969); French, German.

Non-political career: Philosophy assistant, then associate professor, Barnard College, Columbia University 1970-77; Essex University: Philosophy lecturer 1977-78, Senior lecturer 1978-83, Reader 1983-87, Professor of philosophy 1987-92; Principal, Newnham College, Cambridge 1992-2006.

Political career: *House of Lords:* Raised to the peerage as Baroness O'Neill of Bengarve, of The Braid in the County of Antrim 1999. Member: Stem Cell Research 2002, BBC Charter Review 2005-06; Co-opted member: Science and Technology Sub-committee II (Genomic Medicine) 2008-09, Science and Technology Sub-committee I (Nanotechnologies and Food) 2009-10; Science and Technology Sub-committee I (Behavioural Change) 2010-11; Member: Sub-committee on Lords' Interests 2009-10, Sub-committee on Lords' Conduct 2010-, Political Polling and Digital Media 2017-. *Councils and public bodies:* Chair, Equalities and Human Rights Commission 2012-16.

Political interests: Constitutional reform, education especially higher education, medical ethics, languages, communication, copyright and publishing; Germany, Northern Ireland, Republic of Ireland.

Other: President, Aristotelian Society 1988-89; Fellow, Wissenschaftskolleg, Berlin 1989-90; Member, Animal Procedures Committee 1990-94; Nuffield Council on Bioethics: Member 1991-98, Chair 1996-98; Foreign Hon member, American Academy of Arts and Sciences 1993-; Human Genetics Advisory Commission: Member 1996-99, Chair 1998-99; Chair, Nuffield Foundation 1998-2010; Ditchley Foundation: Governor 2001-11, Council member 2003-11; Foreign Hon member, Austrian Academy of Sciences 2002-; Foreign member, American Philosophical Society 2003-; Hon member, Royal Irish Academy 2003-; President, Mind Association 2003-04; Trustee, Sense about Science 2004-14; Foreign member, Leopoldina 2004-; President, British Academy 2005-09; Trustee, American University of Sharjah 2005-; Foreign member, Norwegian Academy of Sciences 2006-; Board member, Medical Research Council 2012-; Trustee and Council Member, Foundation for Science and Technology; British Philosophical Association; FBA 1993, PBA 2005-09; F Med Sci 2002; Honorary FRS 2007. Over 20 honorary degrees. Kant Prize 2015; Holberg Prize 2017. CBE 1995; CH 2014; *Clubs:* Athenæum Club.

Publications: Faces of Hunger (1986); Constructions of Reason (1989), Towards Justice and Virtue (1996); Bounds of Justice (2000); Autonomy and Trust in Bioethics (2002); A Question of Trust (2002); Acting on Principle (2nd edition 2013); Co-author, Rethinking Informed Consent in Bioethics; Constructing Authorities: Reason, Politics and Interpretation in Kant's Philosophy (2016); Justice Across Boundaries: Whose Obligations? (2016).

Recreations: Walking and talking.

The Baroness O'Neill of Bengarve CH CBE, House of Lords, London SW1A 0PW
Tel: 020 7219 4120

LABOUR

O'NEILL OF CLACKMANNAN, LORD

O'NEILL OF CLACKMANNAN (Life Baron), Martin John O'Neill; cr 2005. Born 6 January 1945; Son of John O'Neill, fitter and turner; Married Elaine Samuel 1973 (2 sons).

Education: Trinity Academy, Edinburgh; Heriot-Watt University (BA economics); Moray House College of Education, Edinburgh; French (basic).

Non-political career: Insurance clerk 1963-67; President, Scottish Union of Students 1970-71; Open University Tutor.

Political career: *House of Commons:* Contested Edinburgh North October 1974 general election. MP (Labour) for Stirlingshire East and Clackmannan 1979-83, for Clackmannan 1983-97, for Ochil 1997-2005. Opposition Frontbench Spokesperson for: Scotland 1980-84, Defence and Disarmament and Arms Control 1984-88; Principal Opposition Frontbench Spokesperson for Defence 1988-92; Opposition Frontbench Spokesperson for Trade and Industry (Energy) 1992-95. Chair, Trade and Industry 1995-2005. *House of Lords:* Raised to the peerage as Baron O'Neill of Clackmannan, of Clackmannan in Clackmannanshire 2005. Member, Science and Technology 2006-07, 2007-10, 2012-15; Science and Technology Sub-committee I: Chair, Waste Reduction 2007-08, Member, Nanotechnologies and food 2008-10; Member, EU Home Affairs Sub-committee 2016-. *Other:* Held most party positions in constituency and local government organisations.

Political interests: Education, defence, trade and industry; Argentina.

Other: Chair, Nuclear Industry Association 2008-11. Honorary degree, Heriot-Watt University 2011.

Recreations: Cinema, jazz.

The Lord O'Neill of Clackmannan, House of Lords, London SW1A 0PW
Tel: 020 7219 5059 *Fax:* 020 7219 0528 *Email:* oneillm@parliament.uk

NON-AFFILIATED

O'NEILL OF GATLEY, LORD

O'NEILL OF GATLEY (Life Baron), Terence James (Jim) O'Neill; cr 2015. Born 17 March 1957.

Education: Sheffield University (BA economics 1978; MA); Surrey University (PhD 1982).

Non-political career: Economist: Bank of America 1982-83, Marine Midland Bank 1983-88; Swiss Bank Corporation 1988-95: Head of research 1991-95; Goldman Sachs 1995-2013: Head of Global Economics Research and chief currency economist 1995-2001, Chief economist 2001-10, Head of Global Economics, Commodities and Strategy Research 2008-10, Chair, Goldman Sachs Asset Management 2010-13.

Political career: *House of Lords:* Raised to the peerage as Baron O'Neill of Gatley, of Gatley in the County of Greater Manchester 2015. Commercial Secretary and Government Spokesperson, HM Treasury 2015-16. *Councils and public bodies:* Non-executive director, Department of Education -2015; Vice-president, Local Government Association 2017-.

Other: Honorary chair of economics, Manchester University; Visiting research fellow, Bruegel; Member, economic advisory board, IFC; Founding trustee, SHINE; Board member, Teach for All; Non-executive director, Manchester United FC; Chair, Cities Growth Commission 2013-14; Board member, Northern Powerhouse Partnership 2016-. Honorary degrees: Institute of Education, University of London, City University, Sheffield University.

The Lord O'Neill of Gatley, House of Lords, London SW1A 0PW
Tel: 020 7219 3000

CONSERVATIVE

OPPENHEIM-BARNES, BARONESS

OPPENHEIM-BARNES (Life Baroness), Sally Oppenheim-Barnes; cr. 1989. Born 26 July 1930; Daughter of late Mark Viner; Married Henry Oppenheim 1949 (died 1980) (1 son 2 daughters); married John Barnes 1984 (died 2004).

Education: Sheffield High School; Royal Academy of Dramatic Art.

Non-political career: Non-executive director, Boots Co plc 1981-93; Chair, National Consumer Council 1987-89; Director, Fleming High Income Trust plc 1989-97; Non-executive director, HFC Bank plc 1990-98; Former Vice-president, South Wales and West Fire Liaison Panel.

Political career: *House of Commons:* MP (Conservative) for Gloucester 1970-87. Opposition Spokesperson for Prices and Consumer Protection 1974-79; Member of the Shadow Cabinet 1975-79; Minister of State for Consumer Affairs 1979-82. *House of Lords:* Raised to the peerage as Baroness Oppenheim-Barnes, of Gloucester in the County of Gloucestershire 1989. Member, House of Lords' Offices 2000-02. *Other:* President, Conservative Club of Gloucester 1970. *Councils and* *public bodies:* Former National Vice-president, National Mobile Homes Residents' Association; Former Vice-president: National Union of Townswomen's Guilds 1973-79, Western Centre of Public Health Inspectors; President, National Waterways Trust -1990.

Political interests: Consumer affairs.

Other: MNDA, Dogs Trust. PC 1979; *Clubs:* House of Lords Bridge Club. Vanderbilt Racquet Club.

Recreations: Bridge, tennis.

Rt Hon the Baroness Oppenheim-Barnes, House of Lords, London SW1A 0PW
Tel: 020 7219 5353

O'SHAUGHNESSY, LORD

CONSERVATIVE

Parliamentary Under-Secretary of State and Government Spokesperson, Department of Health

O'SHAUGHNESSY (Life Baron), James Richard O'Shaughnessy; cr 2015. Born 26 March 1976; Married Lucy Sheppard 2005 (1 son 2 daughters).

Education: Wellington College; St Hugh's College, Oxford (BA philosophy, politics and economics 1998).

Non-political career: Conservative Party: Special adviser, Education and Skills 2001-03, Director of policy and research 2007-10; Head of research, LLM Communications 2003-04; Deputy director, Policy Exchange 2004-07; Director of policy to David Cameron as Prime Minister 2010-11; Head of group strategy, Wellington College 2012-14; Visiting fellow, Policy Exchange 2012-; Chief policy adviser, Portland Communications 2012-15; Director, Mayforth Consulting 2012-17; Honorary senior research fellow, Birmingham University 2012-17; Managing director, Floreat Education 2013-16; Founder and non-executive director, Edspace 2014-; Senior fellow, Legatum Institute 2016-17.

Political career: *House of Lords:* Raised to the peerage as Baron O'Shaughnessy, of Maidenhead in the Royal County of Berkshire 2015. Parliamentary Under-Secretary of State for Health and Government Spokesperson, Department of Health 2016-; Government Whip (Lord in Waiting) 2016-17. *Councils and public bodies:* Governor, Lena Gardens School 2013-; Chair of governors: Floreat Wandsworth Primary School -2016, Floreat Brentford Primary School -2017; Member, Department for Education Counter-Extremism Reference Group -2017.

The Lord O'Shaughnessy, House of Lords, London SW1A 0PW
Tel: 020 7219 3000 *Twitter:* @jamesosh

OUSELEY, LORD

CROSSBENCH

OUSELEY (Life Baron), Herman George Ouseley; cr 2001. Born 24 March 1945; Married Margaret (1 son 1 daughter).

Education: William Penn School, south London; Catford College (Diploma municipal administration).

Non-political career: Town planning administrator 1963-70; Homes for elderly management 1970-73; Community development policy co-ordinator 1970-81; Principal race relations adviser to Greater London Council 1981-84; London Borough of Lambeth: Assistant chief executive 1984-86, Chief executive 1990-93; Director of education and chief executive, Inner London Education Authority 1986-90; Chair and chief executive, Commission for Racial Equality 1993-2000; Director: Brooknight Security 1996-2005, Focus Consultancy Ltd 2000-11; Chair: Different Realities Partnership Ltd 2000-07, Solicitors Regulation Authority Advisory Group 2008-.

Political career: *House of Lords:* Raised to the peerage as Baron Ouseley, of Peckham Rye in the London Borough of Southwark 2001. *Councils and public bodies:* Local Government Association: President 2000-02, Vice-President 2010-.

Political interests: Public services, poverty, equality.

Other: Council member, Institute of Race Relations 1990-; Chair: Kick It Out 1994-, Policy Research Institute on Ageing and Ethnicity 1997-2011, PRESET education and employment charitable trust/Chandran Foundation 1997-; Council member, Football Association 2006-13; Trustee: Daneford Trust, Manchester United Foundation; Institute of Race Relations; Fellow, Chartered Institute of Personnel Development; Unicef. Thirteen honorary degrees. Kt 1997.

Publications: The System (1981).

The Lord Ouseley, House of Lords, London SW1A 0PW
Tel: 020 7219 8725 *Email:* ouseleyh@parliament.uk

INDEPENDENT SOCIAL DEMOCRAT

OWEN, LORD

OWEN (Life Baron), David Anthony Llewellyn Owen; cr. 1992. Born 2 July 1938; Son of late Dr John Owen, general practitioner, and Molly Owen, alderman; Married Deborah Schabert 1968 (2 sons 1 daughter).

Education: Bradfield College; Sidney Sussex College, Cambridge (BA natural sciences 1959; MB BChir 1962); St Thomas's Hospital, London 1956-61.

Non-political career: Various house appointments, St Thomas's Hospital 1962-64; Neurological and psychiatric registrar 1964-66; Research Fellow, Medical Unit 1966-68; Director, Deborah Owen Ltd 1972-2015; Non-executive director: New Crane Publishing 1992-2005, Coats Viyella 1994-2001; Executive chair, Global Natural Energy plc 1995-2006; Director, Abbott Laboratories plc 1995-2011; Chair, NEU Ltd 1999-2005; Non-executive chair, Europe-Steel Company 2000-15; Chair, Yukos International UK BV 2002-05; Member, Supervisory Council of Mazeikiu Nafta Oil Refinery, Lithuania 2002-05; Director: Intelligent Energy 2003-05, Hyperdynamics Corporation 2009-14.

Political career: *House of Commons:* Contested Torrington 1964 general election. MP for Plymouth Sutton 1966-74, for Plymouth Devonport 1974-92 (Labour 1966-81, SDP 1981-92). PPS to Gerry Reynolds as Minister of Defence 1966-68; Parliamentary Under-Secretary of State for Defence (Royal Navy) 1968-70; Opposition Spokesperson for Defence 1970-72; Parliamentary Under-Secretary of State, Department of Health and Social Security 1974, Minister of State 1974-76; Minister of State, Foreign Office 1976-77; Secretary of State for Foreign and Commonwealth Affairs 1977-79; Principal Opposition Spokesperson for Energy 1979-80. *House of Lords:* Raised to the peerage as Baron Owen, of the City of Plymouth 1992. *Other:* Social Democratic Party: Co-founder March 1981, Chairman, Parliamentary Committee 1981-82, Deputy Leader of the Party 1982-83, Leader 1983-87, Resigned over merger with Liberal Party; Re-elected SDP Leader 1988-90.

Political interests: International affairs (foreign and defence).

Other: Member: Palme Commission on Disarmament and Security Issues 1980-89, Independent Commission on International Humanitarian Issues 1983-88; EU Co-chair, International Conference on former Yugoslavia 1992-95; Carnegie Commission on Preventing Deadly Conflict 1994-99; Director, Center for International Humanitarian Co-operation 1996-; Eminent Persons Group on curbing illicit traffic in small arms and light weapons 1999-2001; Vice-President, Commonwealth Parliamentary Association (UK Branch); Patron: Social Market Foundation 1989-, James Callaghan Centre for Conflict Studies, University of Wales 2002-, Greenham Common Community Trust 2004-16; President, River Thames Society 2009-; Chairman of Trustees, Daedalus Trust 2010-17; Member, Campaign Committee, Vote Leave 2016; Founding Supporter, Change Britain 2016-; Fellow, Royal College of Physicians 2005. Freedom, City of Plymouth 2000. Chancellor, Liverpool University 1996-2009. Three honorary degrees. PC 1976; CH 1994.

Publications: A Unified Health Service (1968); The Politics of Defence (1972); In Sickness and in Health (1976); Human Rights (1978); Face the Future (1981); A Future that will Work (1984); A United Kingdom (1986); Personally Speaking (to Kenneth Harris) (1987); Our NHS (1988); Time to Declare (autobiography 1991); Seven Ages (poetry anthology 1992); Balkan Odyssey (1995); The Hubris Syndrome (2007); In Sickness and in Power: Illness in Heads of Government during the last 100 years (2008, revised editions 2011, 2016); Time to Declare: Second Innings (updated and abridged autobiography, 2009); Nuclear Papers (2009); Europe Restructured (2012, revised edition 2016); Bosnia and Herzegovina: The Vance Owen Peace Plan (2013); The Hidden Perspective: The Military Conversations of 1906-1914 (Haus, 2014); The Health of the Nation: NHS in Peril (Meuthen, 2014); Cabinet's Finest Hour: The Hidden Agenda of May 1940 (2016); British Foreign Policy After Brexit (2017).

Recreations: Sailing.

Rt Hon the Lord Owen CH, House of Lords, London SW1A 0PW
Tel: 01442 872617 *Fax:* 01442 876108 *Email:* davidowen@lorddavidowen.co.uk
Website: www.lorddavidowen.co.uk

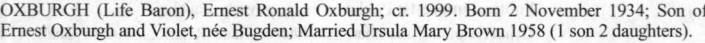

CROSSBENCH

OXBURGH, LORD

OXBURGH (Life Baron), Ernest Ronald Oxburgh; cr. 1999. Born 2 November 1934; Son of Ernest Oxburgh and Violet, née Bugden; Married Ursula Mary Brown 1958 (1 son 2 daughters).

Education: Liverpool Institute; Oxford University (BA natural sciences (geology) 1957, MA); Princeton University, USA (PhD geology 1960).

Non-political career: Oxford University: Departmental demonstrator 1960-61, Lecturer in geology 1961-78, Fellow, St Edmund Hall 1964-78, Emeritus Fellow 1978; California Institute of Technology: Visiting Professor 1967-68, Fairchild Fellow 1995-96; Visiting Professor, Stanford and Cornell Universities 1973-74; Cambridge University: Professor of mineralogy and petrology 1978-91, Head of Department of Earth Sciences 1980-88, Fellow of Trinity Hall 1978-82, President, Queens' College 1982-89, Professorial Fellow 1989-91; Chief scientific adviser, Ministry of Defence 1988-93; Rector, Imperial College of Science, Technology and Medicine, London 1993-2001; Chair: SETNET 2002-05, Shell Transport and Trading plc 2004-05, D1 Oils plc 2007-08, 20C 2007-17, Falck Renewables 2007-10; Adviser: Climate Change Capital 2005-10, Deutsche Bank 2008-12, McKinsey 2010-13; Non-executve director, Green Energy Options 2011-; Chair, Carbon-12 2017-.

Political career: *House of Lords:* Raised to the peerage as Baron Oxburgh, of Liverpool in the County of Merseyside 1999. Board member, Parliamentary Office of Science and Technology (POST) 2000-. Science and Technology: Member 1999-2005, 2016-, Chair 2001-05, Co-opted Member -2012; Member: Science and Technology Sub-committees: II (Science and Society) 1999-2000, II (Aircraft Cabin Environment) 2000-01; Chair, Science and Technology Sub-committee IIA (Human Genetic Databases) 2000-01; Member Science and Technology Sub-committees: I (Fighting Infection) 2002-03, II (Innovations in Computer Processors/Microprocessing/Science and the Regional Development Agencies) 2002-03, I (Science and International Agreements) 2003-04; Chair, Science and Technology Sub-committee II (Renewable Energy) 2003-04; Member Science and Technology Sub-committees: I (Scientific Aspects of Ageing) 2004-05, II (Energy Efficiency) 2004-05, Opposed Private Bills Committee (Broads) 2009; Co-opted Member, Science and Technology Sub-committee I (Radioactive Waste Management: a further update) 2010; Member: The Arctic 2014-15, Information 2015-16. *Councils and public bodies:* Member, National Committee of Inquiry into Higher Education (Dearing Committee) 1996-97; Council member, Foundation for Science and Technology; Chair, Scientific Programme Review Committee British Antarctic Survey.

Political interests: Higher education, health, energy, research and development, climate change; China, Singapore, USA.

Other: Member: ASTAR Singapore, SERC Singapore; President, European Union of Geosciences 1985-87; Member, geological and scientific academies and societies in USA, Germany, Austria, Australia and Venezuela; Natural History Museum: Trustee 1995-2002, Chairman 1999-2002; Vice-President, Globe UK; Council member, Winston Churchill Memorial Trust 1995-2008; President, Geological Society 1999-2001; Chair, Friends of Natural History Museum 2004-07; President, Carbon Capture and Storage Association 2006-16; Geological Society of London; Geological Society of America; Geologists' Association; American Geophysical Union; FRS 1978, Hon. FIMechE 1993, Hon. FCGI 1996, Hon. FREng 2000, Foreign Associate, US Academy of Sciences 2001, American Philosophical Society 2005. Hon. Fellow: Trinity Hall, Cambridge 1982, University College, Oxford 1983, St Edmund Hall, Oxford 1986; Queens' College, Cambridge 1992; Ten honorary doctorates. Bigsby Medal, Geological Society 1979. KBE 1992; Officier, Ordre des Palmes Académiques (France) 1995; Public Service Medal (Singapore) 2009; Honorary Citizen (Singapore) 2012; *Clubs:* Athenæum Club. Climbers, West Anglia Orienteering.

Publications: Contributor to geological, defence and scientific journals.

Recreations: Mountaineering, theatre, orienteering.

The Lord Oxburgh KBE, House of Lords, London SW1A 0PW
Tel: 020 7219 4341 *Fax:* 020 7219 5979 *Email:* oxburghe@parliament.uk

OXFORD, LORD BISHOP OF

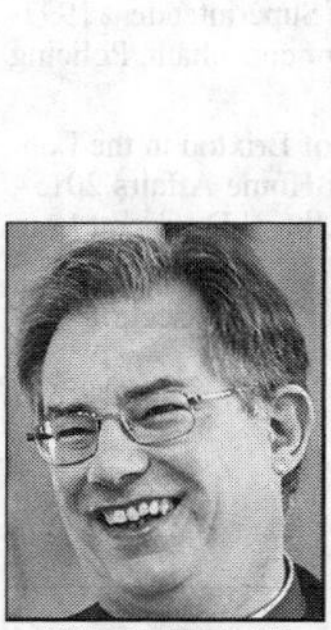

NON-AFFILIATED

OXFORD (43rd Bishop of), Steven John Lindsey Croft. Born 29 May 1957; Son of James and Marian Croft; Married Ann Baker 1978 (2 sons 2 daughters).

Education: Heath School, Halifax; Worcester College, Oxford (BA 1980, MA); St John's College, Durham (PhD 1984).

Non-political career: Ordained deacon 1983; Priest 1984; Curate, St Andrew's, Enfield 1983-87; Vicar, St George's, Ovenden 1987-96; Mission consultant, Diocese of Wakefield 1993-96; Priest-in-charge, St Augustine, Halifax 1994-96; Warden, Cranmer Hall, St John's College, Durham 1996-2004; Archbishop's Missioner and Team Leader, Fresh Expressions 2004-09; Bishop of: Sheffield 2009-16, Oxford 2016-.

Political career: *House of Lords:* First entered House of Lords as Bishop of Sheffield 2013-16; Entered House of Lords as Bishop of Oxford 2016. Member, Artificial Intelligence 2017-.

Other: Member, Archbishop's Council 2010-17.

Publications: The Identity of the Individual in the Psalms (1987); Growing New Christians (1993); Making New Disciples (1994); Co-author, Emmaus, The Way of Faith volumes one to six (1996), volumes seven to eight (1998); Man to Man: friendship and faith (1999); Co-author, Travelling Well (2000); The Lord is Risen (2001); Missionary Journeys, Missionary Church (2001); Transforming Communities: re-imagining the Church for the 21st-century (2002); Co-author, Learning for Ministry: making the most of study and training (2005); Moving On in a Mission-Shaped Church (2005); The Advent Calendar (2006); Editor: The Future of the Parish System (2006), Mission-shaped

Questions (2008); Jesus' People: what the church should do next (2009); Editor, Fresh Expressions in the Sacramental Tradition (2010); Exploring God's Mercy (2011); Exploring God's Love (2011); Pilgrim (2014); The Gift of Leadership, According to the Scriptures (2016).

Recreations: Walking, cooking, films.

Rt Rev the Lord Bishop of Oxford, House of Lords, London SW1A 0PW
Tel: 020 7219 3000
Church House Oxford, Langford Locks, Kidlington, Oxford OX5 1GF *Tel:* 01865 208222
Email: bishopoxon@oxford.anglican.org *Website:* www.oxford.anglican.org *Twitter:* @Steven_Croft

LIBERAL DEMOCRAT

OXFORD AND ASQUITH, EARL OF

OXFORD AND ASQUITH (3rd Earl of, UK), Raymond Benedict Bartholomew Michael Asquith; cr. 1925; Viscount Asquith. Born 24 August 1952; Son of 2nd Earl, KCMG; Married Clare 1978 (1 son 4 daughters).

Education: Ampleforth College; Balliol College, Oxford (MA); Russian, Ukrainian, French.

Non-political career: HM Diplomatic Service 1980-97: Moscow 1983-85, Cabinet Office 1985-92, British Embassy, Kiev 1992-97; Chair, Zander Corporation 2006-.

Political career: *House of Lords:* Elected hereditary peer 2014-. Member, EU External Affairs Sub-Committee 2015-.

Political interests: Energy, environment, foreign affairs; Eastern Europe, Iran, Middle East, Russia, Ukraine.

Other: Non-executive director: JKX Oil and Gas, Zander Corporation, Meteor; Director: Hansa Trust, British Ukrainian Society; Trustee, Ukrainian Catholic Foundation. OBE 1992.

The Earl of Oxford and Asquith OBE, House of Lords, London SW1A 0PW
Tel: 020 7219 5353 *Email:* oxfordr@parliament.uk

LIBERAL DEMOCRAT

PADDICK, LORD

Liberal Democrat Lords Spokesperson for Home Affairs

PADDICK (Life Baron), Brian Leonard Paddick; cr 2013. Born 24 April 1958; Married Mary 1983 (divorced); married Petter Belsvik 2009.

Education: Bec Grammar School, Tooting Bec, London; Sutton Manor High School, London; Queen's College, Oxford (BA philosophy, politics and economics 1986); Warwick Business School (MBA 1990); Fitzwilliam College, Cambridge (Diploma applied criminology and policing).

Non-political career: Metropolitan Police 1976-2007: Constable 1977-80, Sergeant 1980-83, Inspector 1983-89, Chief Inspector 1989-96, Superintendent 1996-97, Chief Superintendent 1997-2000, Commander 2001-03, Deputy Assistant Commissioner 2003-07; Senior consultant, Policing and Public Sector, Public Partners.

Political career: *House of Lords:* Raised to the peerage as Baron Paddick, of Brixton in the London Borough of Lambeth 2013. Liberal Democrat: Lords Spokesperson for Home Affairs 2015-, Shadow Home Secretary 2016-17. *Councils and public bodies:* Contested Liberal Democrat London mayoral candidacy 2008 and 2012.

Political interests: Crime, civil law, justice and rights, housing and planning, social security and pensions; Norway, South Africa, USA.

Publications: Line of Fire (Simon & Schuster UK, 2008).

The Lord Paddick, House of Lords, London SW1A 0PW
Tel: 020 7219 5353 *Email:* paddickb@parliament.uk
Website: www.brianpaddick.com *Twitter:* @brianpaddick

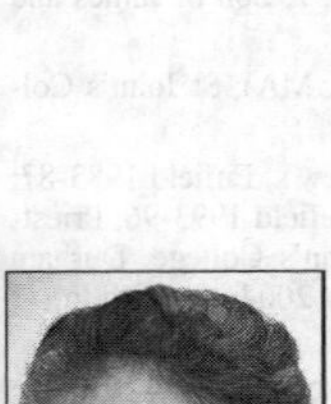

DEMOCRATIC UNIONIST PARTY

PAISLEY OF ST GEORGE'S, BARONESS

PAISLEY OF ST GEORGE'S (Life Baroness), Eileen Emily Paisley; cr 2006. Born 2 November 1931; Daughter of Thomas James and Emily Jane Cassells; Married Ian Paisley 1956 (MP for North Antrim 1970-85 and 1986-2010, MEP for Northern Ireland 1979-2004 and MLA for North Antrim 1998-2011, later Lord Bannside) (died 2014) (twin sons, including Ian Paisley (qv) MP for North Antrim, 3 daughters).

Education: Belfast Shorthand Institute and Business Training College.

Non-political career: Secretarial positions in several companies.

Political career: *House of Lords:* Raised to the peerage as Baroness Paisley of St George's, of St George's in the County of Antrim 2006. On leave of absence June 2013-May 2015, February

2016-June 2017. *Other:* Member: Northern Ireland Assembly 1973, Northern Ireland Convention 1975. Honorary Vice-President, DUP. *Councils and public bodies:* Councillor, Belfast Corporation 1967.

Political interests: Women, children, health, education.

Recreations: Gardening, reading, sewing, needlework.

The Baroness Paisley of St George's, House of Lords, London SW1A 0PW
Tel: 020 7219 5353

CROSSBENCH

PALMER, LORD

PALMER (4th Baron, UK), Adrian Bailie Nottage Palmer; cr. 1933; 4th Bt of Grosvenor Crescent (UK) 1916. Born 8 October 1951; Son of Colonel Hon Sir Gordon Palmer, KCVO and Hon Lady Palmer, DL; Married Cornelia Wadham 1977 (divorced 2004) (2 sons 1 daughter); married Loraine McMurrey 2006 (divorced 2013).

Education: Eton College; Edinburgh University (Certificate farming practice 1979); French.

Non-political career: Apprentice, Huntley and Palmers Ltd 1970-73; Sales manager, southern Belgium and Luxembourg 1974-77; Scottish representative to European Landowning Organisation 1986-91; Farmer. Member, National Farmers Union of Scotland.

Political career: *House of Lords:* First entered House of Lords 1990; Elected hereditary peer 1999-. Member: Advisory Panel on Works of Art 1995-98, 2000-02, 2005-09, Refreshment 1997-2000, 2003-05, Standing Orders (Private Bills) 2005-17; Co-opted Member, EU Sub-committee D (Environment and Agriculture) 2000-03, 2007-10; Procedure: Member 2007, Alternate Member 2007-10. *Councils and public bodies:* Member: Executive Council, Historic Houses Association 1981-99, Council, Scottish Landowners' Federation 1986-92; Secretary, Royal Caledonian Hunt 1989-2005; President, Palm Tree Silk Co (St Lucia) 1992-; Historic Houses Association for Scotland: Vice-chair 1993-94, Chair 1994-99; President: British Association of Biofuels and Oils 1999-, Renewable Energy Authority (transport division) 2006-.

Political interests: Agriculture, environment, heritage, media, tourism; St Lucia, Scotland, Zimbabwe.

Other: Member, Queen's Bodyguard for Scotland (Royal Company of Archers) 1990-96; Chair, Country Sports Defence Trust 1994-; Secretary, Scottish Peers Association 2007-; *Clubs:* New (Edinburgh), Pratt's, Chair, Lords and Commons Cigar Club. Patron, Manderston Cricket Club 1978-.

Recreations: Gardening.

The Lord Palmer, House of Lords, London SW1A 0PW
Tel: 020 7219 6452/020 7219 3156 *Fax:* 020 7219 5979 *Email:* palmerad@parliament.uk
Manderston, Duns, Borders TD11 3PP *Tel:* 01361 883450/01361 882636 *Fax:* 01361 882010
Email: palmer@manderston.co.uk

LIBERAL DEMOCRAT

PALMER OF CHILDS HILL, LORD

PALMER OF CHILDS HILL (Life Baron), Monroe Edward Palmer; cr 2011. Born 30 November 1938; Son of William and Sybil Polikoff; Married Susette Cardash 1962 (2 sons 1 daughter).

Education: Orange Hill Grammar School; Open University (BA 2005).

Non-political career: Chartered accountant 1963; Treasurer, Disablement Association, London Borough of Barnet 1971-88; Chair, Hendon Citizens Advice Bureau 1981-83; Barnet Citizens Advice Bureau: Vice-chair 1986-88, Chair 1988-90; Director, Barnet Homes 1994-2010.

Political career: *House of Commons:* Contested (Liberal) Hendon South 1979, (Liberal/All) 1983 and 1987 and (Liberal Democrat) Hastings and Rye 1992 and 1997 general elections. *House of Lords:* Raised to the peerage as Baron Palmer of Childs Hill, of Childs Hill in the London Borough of Barnet 2011. Liberal Democrat Spokesperson for: Defence 2011-15, Business, Innovation and Skills 2015-16; Party Lead Spokesperson on Small and Medium-sized Enterprises. Member: Refreshment 2012-15, Personal Service Companies 2013-14. Chair, Liberal Democrat Parliamentary Party Committee on International Affairs (Defence) 2012-15. *Other:* Joint Treasurer, Liberal Parliamentary Party 1977-83; Liberal Democrat Friends of Israel: Chair 1987-2010, Vice-President 2010-16, President 2016-; Treasurer, London Region, Liberal Democrats 2008-09. *Councils and public bodies:* London Borough of Barnet Council: Councillor 1986-94, 1998-2014, Chair, Audit Committee 2010-14.

Political interests: Business (including small businesses), taxation, local government, foreign affairs; Israel, Middle East, Palestine.

Other: Fellow, Institute of Chartered Accountants. OBE 1982; *Clubs:* National Liberal Club.

Recreations: Horse riding, reading, music.

The Lord Palmer of Childs Hill OBE, House of Lords, London SW1A 0PW
Tel: 020 7219 2561 *Email:* palmerm@parliament.uk *Twitter:* @palmermonroe

CONSERVATIVE

PALUMBO, LORD

PALUMBO (Life Baron), Peter Garth Palumbo; cr. 1991. Born 20 July 1935; Son of late Rudolph Palumbo and Elsie Palumbo; Married Denia Wigram 1959 (died 1986) (1 son, now Lord Palumbo of Southwark (qv), 2 daughters); married Hayat Morowa 1986 (1 son 2 daughters).

Education: Eton College; Worcester College, Oxford (MA law 1954).

Non-political career: Property developer.

Political career: *House of Lords:* Raised to the peerage as Baron Palumbo, of Walbrook in the City of London 1991. *Councils and public bodies:* Governor, London School of Economics and Political Science 1976-94; Chair: Tate Gallery Foundation 1986-87, Arts Council of Great Britain 1989-94; Serpentine Gallery: Chair 1994-2014, Chairman Emeritus 2014-; Council member, Royal Albert Hall 1995-99; Whitgift School: Governor 2002-10, Adviser emeritus to the Board of Governors 2010-.

Political interests: Arts, education, defence; Middle East, South America.

Other: Trustee: Mies van der Rohe Archive 1977-, Tate Gallery 1978-85, Whitechapel Arts Gallery Foundation 1981-87; Trustee and Hon treasurer, Writers and Scholars Educational Trust 1984-99; Chair, Painshill Park Trust Appeal 1986-96; Trustee: Natural History Museum 1994-2004, Design Museum 1995-2005; Governor, Royal Shakespeare Theatre 1995-2000; Chair, Pritzker Architecture Prize Jury 2004-; Hon. FRIBA; Hon. FFB 1994; Hon. FIStructE 1994. Liveryman, Salters' Company. Chancellor, Portsmouth University 1992-2007. Hon. DLitt, Portsmouth University 1993. Patronage of the Arts Award, Cranbrook Academy of Arts, Detroit, USA 2002. National Order of the Southern Cross (Brazil); *Clubs:* White's, Pratt's, Athenæum, Knickerbocker (New York), Garrick Club.

Recreations: Music, travel, gardening, reading.

The Lord Palumbo, House of Lords, London SW1A 0PW
Tel: 020 7219 5353
Email: peter@palumbomail.co.uk
Website: www.lordpeterpalumbo.com

LIBERAL DEMOCRAT

PALUMBO OF SOUTHWARK, LORD

PALUMBO OF SOUTHWARK (Life Baron), James Rudolph Palumbo; cr 2013. Born 6 June 1963; Son of Peter Garth Palumbo (now Lord Palumbo (qv)) and Denia Wigram; 1 son.

Education: Eton College; Worcester College, Oxford.

Non-political career: Property developer; Merchant banker: Merrill Lynch, Morgan Grenfell; Founder and chair, Ministry of Sound Group.

Political career: *House of Lords:* Raised to the peerage as Baron Palumbo of Southwark, of Southwark in the London Borough of Southwark 2013.

Publications: Tomas; Tancredi.

The Lord Palumbo of Southwark, House of Lords, London SW1A 0PW
Tel: 020 7219 5353

CROSSBENCH

PANNICK, LORD

PANNICK (Life Baron), David Philip Pannick; cr 2008. Born 7 March 1956; Son of late Maurice Pannick and late Rita Pannick; Married Denise Sloam 1978 (died 1999) (2 sons 1 daughter); married Nathalie Trager-Lewis 2003 (1 son 2 daughters).

Education: Bancroft's School, Essex; Hertford College, Oxford (MA 1977; BCL 1978); Gray's Inn, London.

Non-political career: Called to the Bar 1979; Barrister, Blackstone Chambers, Temple 1980-; Junior counsel to Crown (Common Law) 1988-92; QC 1992; Bencher, Gray's Inn 1998; Deputy High Court Judge 1998-2005.

Political career: *House of Lords:* Raised to the peerage as Baron Pannick, of Radlett in the County of Hertfordshire 2008. Member, Constitution 2008-13, 2016-.

Political interests: Legal matters; Israel, USA.

Other: Chair, British Legal Friends of the Hebrew University 2005-. Fellow, All Souls College, Oxford 1978-; Hon. fellow: Hertford College, Oxford, Hebrew University of Jerusalem; Hon. doctorate, Hertfordshire University.

Recreations: Cinema, theatre, Arsenal FC.

The Lord Pannick QC, House of Lords, London SW1A 0PW
Tel: 020 7219 5353
Blackstone Chambers, Temple, London EC4Y 9BW *Tel:* 020 7583 1770 *Fax:* 020 7822 7350
Email: davidpannick@blackstonechambers.com

LABOUR

PARE KH, LORD

PAREKH (Life Baron), Bhikhu Chhotalal Parekh; cr. 2000. Born 4 January 1935; Son of Chhotalal and Gajaraben Parekh; Married Pramila Dalal 1959 (3 sons).

Education: HDS High School, Amalsad, India; Bombay University (BA economics 1954; MA political science 1956); London University (PhD the idea of equality in English political thought 1966); Gujarati, Hindi.

Non-political career: London School of Economics: Politics tutor 1962-63, Centennial Professor 2001-03; Assistant lecturer in politics, Glasgow University 1963-64; Hull University: Politics lecturer, senior lecturer and reader 1964-82, Professor of political theory 1982-2001, Emeritus Professor 2000-; Visiting Professor: University of British Columbia, Canada 1967-68, Concordia University 1974-75, McGill University 1976-77, Harvard University 1996, Institute for Advanced Study, Vienna 1997, University of Pompeu Fabra, Barcelona 1997, University of Pennsylvania 1998, École des Hautes Études en Sciences Sociales 2000; Westminster University: Professor of political philosophy 2001-09, Emeritus Professor of Political Philosophy 2009-.

Political career: *House of Lords:* Raised to the peerage as Baron Parekh, of Kingston upon Hull in the East Riding of Yorkshire 2000. Member, Human Rights Joint Committee 2001-03. *Councils and public bodies:* Member, Rampton/Swann Committee of Inquiry into Educational Problems of Ethnic Minority Children 1978-82; Deputy chair, Commission for Racial Equality 1985-90; Vice-President, UK Council for Overseas Students Affairs 1989-99; Chair, Commission on Future of Multi-Ethnic Britain 1998-2001; President, British Association of South Asia Scholars 2004-07.

Political interests: Race relations, higher education, ethnic conflicts, global justice, international politics, multiculturalism; Canada, India, USA.

Other: Founding Member and Past President, Research Committee on Political Philosophy of International Political Science Association; Council Member, Policy Studies Institute 1985-90; Runnymede Trust: Trustee 1986-2003, Patron 2003; Gandhi Foundation: Trustee 1988, Patron 2002-, President 2012-; Council member, Institute for Public Policy Research 1990-96; Trustee: Anne Frank Educational Trust 1992-, Nirman Foundation 2000-; Fellow, Asiatic Society India 2003; Trustee: Rathbone Society 2003-, Black Umbrella 2005-; Patron: Institute of Advanced Study, Durham University 2008-10, Whistling Woods International, Mumbai 2008-; FRSA 1988; Fellow, British Academy 2003; President, Academy of Learned Societies for the Social Sciences 2004-08; Fellow, European Academy 2009; Cancer Research Society, Royal Society for the Blind, Barnardo's. Vice-chancellor, University of Baroda, India 1981-84. Sixteen honorary doctorates; Honorary Professor, University of Wales; Distinguished Professorial Fellow, Centre for the Study of Developing Societies, Delhi; Distinguished Visiting Professor, Cardozo Law School, New York; Distinguished Visiting Fellow, University of Maine, USA. British Asian of the Year 1991; Gujarati of the Year 1994; BBC's Special Lifetime Achievement Award for Asians 1999; Sir Isaiah Berlin Prize for Lifetime Contribution to Political Studies 2003; Pravasi Bharatiya Samman, by President of India 2005; Interdependence Prize, Campaign for Democracy, New York 2006; Pride of India 2006; Distinguished Global Thinker, India International Centre, Delhi 2006; Padma Bhushan, President of India 2007.

Publications: Politics and Experience (1968); Dissent and Disorder (1971); The Morality of Politics (1972); Knowledge and Belief in Politics (1973); Bentham's Political Thought (1973); Colour, Culture and Consciousness (1974); Jeremy Bentham: ten critical essays (1974); The Concept of Socialism (1975); Hannah Arendt and the Search for a new Political Philosophy (1981); Karl's Marx's Theory of Ideology (1982); Contemporary Political Thinkers (1982); Political Discourse (1986); Gandhi's Political Philosophy (1989); Colonialism, Tradition and Reform (1989); Jeremy Bentham: critical assessments (1993); The Decolonisation of Imagination (1995); Crisis and Change in Contemporary India (1995); Gandhi (1997); Race Relations in Britain (1998); Rethinking Multiculturalism (2000); The Future of Multi Ethnic Britain: The Parekh Report (2000); Culture and Economy in the Indian Diaspora (2003); A New Politics of Identity (2008); Conversations with Bhikhu Parekh (2012); Numerous articles in various learned journals.

Recreations: Reading, music, walking.

Professor the Lord Parekh, House of Lords, London SW1A 0PW
Tel: 020 7219 5353 *Fax:* 020 7219 5979
211 Victoria Avenue, Hull HU5 3EF *Tel:* 01482 345530 *Fax:* 01482 345530
Email: profparekh@gmail.com profparekh@profparekh.karoo.co.uk

LIBERAL DEMOCRAT

PARMINTER, BARONESS

Deputy Leader, Liberal Democrat Peers; Shadow Secretary of State for Environment, Food and Rural Affairs

PARMINTER (Life Baroness), Kathryn Jane Parminter; cr 2010. Born 24 June 1964; Daughter of James and June Parminter; Married Neil Sherlock 1994 (2 daughters).

Education: Millais School, West Sussex; Collyers Sixth Form College, Horsham; Lady Margaret Hall, Oxford (BA theology 1986, MA).

Non-political career: Graduate trainee, Nestle 1986-88; Parliamentary researcher to Simon Hughes MP 1988-89; Account executive, Juliette Hellman Public Relations 1989-90; Royal Society for the Prevention of Cruelty to Animals: Public relations officer 1990-92, Head of campaigns and events 1992-95, Head of public affairs 1995-96, Head of press and public affairs 1996-98; Chief executive, Campaign to Protect Rural England 1998-2004; Freelance consultant advising corporations and charities on CSR and charitable issues 2004-10.

Political career: *House of Lords:* Raised to the peerage as Baroness Parminter, of Godalming in the County of Surrey 2010. Deputy Leader, Liberal Democrat Peers 2015-; Liberal Democrat Spokesperson/Shadow Secretary of State for Environment, Food and Rural Affairs 2015-. Member, EU Sub-committee D: (Agriculture, Fisheries and Environment) 2010-12, (Agriculture, Fisheries, Environment and Energy) 2012-15; Member: European Union 2013-15, Built Environment 2015-16, Natural Environment and Rural Communities Act 2006 2017-. Chair, Liberal Democrat Policy Committees on: Energy and Climate Change; Environment, Food and Rural Affairs (Environment, Food and Rural Affairs) 2012, Environment, Food and Rural Affairs 2012-15. *Other:* Liberal Democrat: Policy Review Group 2005-07, Reform Commission 2008, Federal Executive 2008-10; Trustee, Liberal Democrat Party 2011-. *Councils and public bodies:* Councillor, Horsham District Council 1987-95.

Political interests: Environment, equality issues, food policy.

Other: Chair, Campaign for Protection of Hunted Animals 1997-98; Trustee, Institute for Public Policy Research 2007-; Advisory group, Every Child A Reader 2007-10; Vice-president, RSPCA 2011-15; Honorary Fellow, CIWEM; Meath Trust; *Clubs:* National Liberal Club.

Recreations: Walking.

The Baroness Parminter, House of Lords, London SW1A 0PW
Tel: 020 7219 4195 *Email:* parminterk@parliament.uk *Twitter:* @kateparminter

CROSSBENCH

PATEL, LORD

PATEL (Life Baron), Naren Babubhai Patel; cr. 1999. Born 11 May 1938; Son of Babubhai and Lalita Patel; Married Dr Helen Dally 1970 (twin sons 1 daughter).

Education: Government Secondary School, Dar Es Salaam, Tanzania; Harrow High School; St Andrews University (MB ChB 1964).

Non-political career: Consultant obstetrician, Ninewells Hospital, Dundee 1974-2003; Professor, Dundee University.

Political career: *House of Lords:* Raised to the peerage as Baron Patel, of Dunkeld in Perth and Kinross 1999. Board Member, Parliamentary Office of Science and Technology 2017-. Science and Technology: Member 1999-2003, 2005-09, 2010-15, Co-opted member 2015-16; Member: Science and Technology Sub-committees: II (Aircraft Cabin Environment) 2000-02, IIA (Human Genetic Databases) 2000-01, I (Fighting Infection) 2002-10, II (Innovations in Computer Processors/Microprocessing) 2002; Chair, Science and Technology Sub-committee II (Science and the Regional Development Agencies) 2003; Member, Science and Technology Sub-committee II: (Renewable Energy/Energy Efficiency) 2003-04, (Water Management) 2006, (Pandemic Influenza) 2006; Chair, Science and Technology Sub-committee II (Genomic Medicine) 2008-09; Member: Procedure 2012-15, Science and Technology Sub-committee I 2012-13, Affordable Childcare 2014-15, Social Mobility 2015-16; Chair: Long-Term Sustainability of the NHS 2016-17, Science and Technology 2017-. *Councils and public bodies:* President, Royal College of Obstetricians 1995-98; Chair, Academy of Medical Royal Colleges 1996-98; Council, General Medical Council 1998-2003; Chair: Specialist Training Authority of Medicine 1998-2001, NHS Quality Improvement, Scotland 1999-2006, Clinical Standards Board of Scotland 1999-2002; Member, Armed Forces Pay Review Body 2000-06; Chair: UK Stem Cell Oversight Committee 2005-10, National Patient Safety Agency 2006-10, Armed Forces Diversity and Equality Committee 2006-09, UK National Stem Cell Network 2007-09; Council member, Medical Research Council 2008-12.

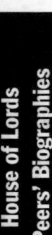

Political interests: Women's health, higher education, regulation of medicine, ethnic minority issues, standards in medicine, care of obstetric fistulas worldwide, NHS, medical research; France, India, South Africa, Sweden, Tanzania, USA.

Other: European Board of Obstetrics and Gynaecology 2000-03; Vice-President, International Federation of Obstetrics and Gynaecology 2000-03; President, European Association of Obstetricians and Gynaecologists 2005-07; FMedSci; FRCOG; FRSE; Fistula Fund, WellBeing, Safe Hands, South Asia Health Foundation. Chancellor, Dundee University 2006-. Numerous honorary degrees and fellowships from universities in the UK and worldwide. Kt 1997; KT 2010.

Publications: Several books, chapters, articles on maternal/foetal medicine, epidemiology, obstetrics, gynaecology, quality healthcare.

Recreations: Walking, travel.

The Lord Patel KT, House of Lords, London SW1A 0PW
Tel: 020 7219 8702

LABOUR

PATEL OF BLACKBURN, LORD

PATEL OF BLACKBURN (Life Baron), Adam Hafejee Patel; cr. 2000. Born 7 June 1940; Son of late Hafejee Ismail Patel and Aman Hafejee Patel; Married Ayesha Adam Bholabhai 1964 (4 sons 4 daughters).

Education: The Pioneer High School, Bharuch, Gujarat, India; MS Baroda University, India (BComm 1964); Gujarati, Hindi, Urdu.

Non-political career: Accountant, Ivan Jacques Chartered Accountants 1967-72; Newscaster (Gujrati), Blackburn Radio Inc 1971-74; Chief Internal Auditor, Zamtan, Zambia 1975-76; Director: Comet Cash and Carry 1977-97, Enterprise plc, Blackburn City Challenge, Blackburn Partnership 1977-95, East Lancashire Training Enterprise Council 1987-95, Lancashire Enterprises.

Political career: *House of Lords:* Raised to the peerage as Baron Patel of Blackburn, of Langho in the County of Lancashire 2000. *Councils and public bodies:* President: Indian Worker's Association 1968-2011, Lancashire Council of Mosques 1987-95; Vice-President, Blackburn Community Relations Council 1995; Counsellor, Muslim Council of Britain 1984-95; Magistrate, Blackburn 1984-95; Chair: Blackburn Racial Equality Council 1989-95, British Hajj Delegation and Committee 2001-10.

Political interests: Community and social work, education, race relations, economy and regeneration; Bangladesh, India, Kuwait, Pakistan, Qatar, Saudi Arabia, Swaziland, UAE, Zambia.

Other: Member, Commonwealth Parliamentary Association; Vice-President, Bopio; President, Lancashire Scouts 2005-; Bharuch Muslim Hospital. Hon. Doctorate of Social Science, Bolton University 2010; Honorary Fellowship: Bolton Institute, University of Central Lancashire. High Commissioner of India 2000; Lifetime achievement Jewel Award, Asian Jewel Awards 2005; Services to Muslim Community, Lancashire Council of Mosques 2008; Dedicated Services to Mankind, Ali Jauhar Foundation, Lucknow, India.

Recreations: Gardening, watching football and cricket, Blackburn Rovers FC, charity work, philanthropy.

The Lord Patel of Blackburn, House of Lords, London SW1A 0PW
Tel: 020 7219 5353 *Fax:* 020 7219 5979
36 Derwent House, Southern Grove, Mile End, London E3 4PU *Tel:* 020 8980 8252
Email: lordadampatel@hotmail.com

LABOUR

PATEL OF BRADFORD, LORD

PATEL OF BRADFORD (Life Baron), Kamlesh Kumar Patel; cr 2006. Born 28 September 1960; Son of Sudhindra Kumar and Savita Devi Patel; Married Yasmin Saloojee 1998 (2 sons 2 step-daughters).

Education: Belle Vue Boys Grammar School, Bradford; Huddersfield Polytechnic (CQSW 1987).

Non-political career: West Yorkshire Police Service 1981-91; Ambulanceman West Yorkshire Ambulance Service 1981-83; Bradford Social Services: Social worker 1983-87, Specialist case-worker (alcohol and drugs team) 1987-89; Manager, Bridge Project (drugs and mental health care organisation) 1989-95; University of Central Lancashire 1995-2010: Senior lecturer in social work 1995-97, Senior researcher in health 1997-98, Principal lecturer/research in health 1998-99, Professor and Head of Centre for Ethnicity and Health and of Institute for Philosophy, Diversity and Mental Health 1999-2008; Seconded as national strategic director, National Institute for Mental Health England 2003-04; Seconded as national director, Department of Health national delivering race equality mental health programme 2004-07; UK member, Unicef's Global Task Force on

Water, Sanitation and Hygiene 2006-10; Ministerial adviser to Hazel Blears as Secretary of State for Communities and Local Government 2008-09; Professor and Head of International School for Communities, Rights and Inclusion 2008-10; Professor, senior management team, De Montfort University March-October 2010; Director of strategic partnerships and senior adviser to the Vice-Chancellor, University of East London 2010-.

Political career: *House of Lords:* Raised to the peerage as Baron Patel of Bradford, of Bradford in the County of West Yorkshire 2006. Sat as Crossbench Peer 2006-08; Government Whip 2008-09; Opposition Spokesperson for Communities and Local Government 2010-11. Member, Mental Capacity Act 2005 2013-14. *Councils and public bodies:* Home Office Advisory Council for the Misuse of Drugs: Member, Criminal Justice Advisory Working Group 1990-96, Council member 1993-96; Mental Health Act Commission 1995-2008: Non-executive board member 1995-2001, Member 1995-2001, Vice-chair 2001-02, Chair 2002-08; Non-executive board member, Central Council for Education and Training and Social Work 1997-98; National Treatment Agency for Substance Misuse: Non-executive board member 2001-08, Chair, Audit and Risk Committee 2001-08; Non-executive board member, Healthcare Commission 2003-05; Commissioner and trustee, UK Drug Policy Commission 2007-09; Chair, National Prison Drug Treatment Review Group 2008-10; Leicestershire Partnership NHS Trust: Associate non-executive director 2008-, Adviser to Communities, Rights and Inclusion Programme 2008-, Chair, Communities, Rights and Inclusion Governance Committee 2010-; Chair, Integrated Equality and Human Rights Committee, Leicestershire County and Rutland NHS Trust 2010-; Vice President: Royal Society of Public Health London 2013-, Institute of Healthcare Management 2014-; Chair: Bradford Teaching Hospitals NHS Foundation Trust 2014-16; Bradford City Producer Board 2014-16; Board Director, England and Wales Cricket Board (ECB) 2015-.

Countries of interest: Africa, India, Middle East.

Other: UK Member, Unicef's Global Task Force on Water, Sanitation and Hygiene 2006-10; Patron: National Men's Health Forum 2003-, Sharing Voices 2007-12, Bridge Project 2008-; President, Bradford Magistrates Chaplaincy Service 2008-; Patron: Westminster Health Forum 2009-, British Muslim Heritage Centre 2009-, Equity Partnership 2009-, Bradford Cryrenians 2010-, Safe Inside – Safe Outside 2010-; Chair: International Deaf 2010-, International Forum for Community Innovations 2011-; Patron: Mental Health First Aid 2011-, Awaaz 2011-, Engage Communities 2012-, Lily Project 2012-, Intercultural Communication and Leadership School 2012-; Chair, Community Innovations Enterprise 2011-; President, National Appropriate Adult Network (NAAN) 2014-; Patron, Kala Sangam 2015-; Trustee: Milestone Group 2014-, Noon Memorial Legacy Trust 2016-; Chair, EDV 2015-16; Ambassador, Tutu Foundation 2015-; Patron, Yorkshire Enterprise Network 2015-; President, Asian Sports Foundation 2015-; Vice-President, Yorkshire Society 2015-; Paton: Maya Centre 2016-, Revolving Doors 2016-; Professorial fellow: Mental Health (Institute of Mental Health), Public Health (Royal Society of Public Health) 2012-. Two honorary doctorates. Long Service Medal, West Yorkshire Police 1991; Plaque of Recognition for Contributions to the Enhancement of Human Welfare and International Understanding, India High Commission, London 1999; Glory of India Award and Certificate of Excellence, India International Friendship Society 2009; Achievement Award for Services to Education, India International Foundation 2009; GG2 Man of the Year: Award for consistent lifetime achievement and contribution to public sector services, AMG Awards London 2015; Yorkshire Man of the Year: Award for lifetime contribution to the County of Yorkshire, Yorkshire Society 2016. OBE 1999. Northowram Fields Community Cricket Club.

Recreations: Member of several cricket clubs.

The Lord Patel of Bradford OBE, House of Lords, London SW1A 0PW
Tel: 020 7219 4557 *Email:* patelkk@parliament.uk *Twitter:* @LordKPatel

CONSERVATIVE

PATTEN, LORD

PATTEN (Life Baron), John Haggitt Charles Patten; cr. 1997. Born 17 July 1945; Son of late Jack Patten; Married Louise Alexandra Virginia Charlotte Rowe 1978 (1 daughter).

Education: Wimbledon College, London; Sidney Sussex College, Cambridge (MA; PhD).

Non-political career: Oxford University: University lecturer 1969-79, Fellow and tutor, Hertford College 1972-81, Supernumary Fellow, Hertford College 1981-94; Business adviser and company director 1995-.

Political career: *House of Commons:* MP (Conservative) for Oxford 1979-83, for Oxford West and Abingdon 1983-97. PPS to the Ministers of State at the Home Office 1980-81; Parliamentary Under-Secretary of State for: Northern Ireland 1981-83, Health 1983-85; Minister of State: Department of Environment 1985-87, Home Office 1987-92; Secretary of State for Education 1992-94. *House of Lords:* Raised to the peerage as Baron Patten, of Wincanton in the County of Somerset 1997. *Councils and public bodies:* Oxford City Councillor 1973-76.

House of Lords
Peers' Biographies

Other: Liveryman, Drapers' Company. Hon. Fellow, Harris Manchester College, Oxford. PC 1990.

Publications: Co-editor, The Conservative Opportunity (1976); Things to Come: The Tories in the 21st Century (1995) and other volumes.

Recreations: Talking with my wife and daughter.

Rt Hon the Lord Patten, House of Lords, London SW1A 0PW
Tel: 020 7219 1282

PATTEN OF BARNES, LORD

CONSERVATIVE

PATTEN OF BARNES (Life Baron), Christopher Francis Patten; cr 2005. Born 12 May 1944; Son of late Francis Patten, music publisher, and Joan McCarthy; Married Mary St Leger, née Thornton 1971 (3 daughters).

Education: St Benedict's School, West London; Balliol College, Oxford (BA modern history 1965, MA).

Non-political career: Conservative Research Department: Research officer 1966-70, Director 1974-79; Research officer: Cabinet Office 1970-72, Home Office 1972; Governor and Commander-in-Chief, Hong Kong 1992-97; Chair, Independent Commission on Policing in Northern Ireland 1998-99; Commissioner for External Relations, European Commission 1999-2004.

Political career: *House of Commons:* MP (Conservative) for Bath 1979-92. Contested Bath 1992 general election. PPS: to Norman St John Stevas as Leader of the House of Commons and Chancellor of the Duchy of Lancaster 1979-81, to Patrick Jenkin as Secretary of State for Social Services 1981; Parliamentary Secretary, Northern Ireland Office 1983-85; Minister of State: Department of Education and Science 1985-86, for Overseas Development, Foreign and Commonwealth Office 1986-89; Secretary of State for the Environment 1989-90; Chancellor of the Duchy of Lancaster 1990-92. *House of Lords:* Raised to the peerage as Baron Patten of Barnes, of Barnes in the London Borough of Richmond 2005. *Other:* Personal assistant to Chairman Conservative Party 1972-74; Chair, Conservative Party 1990-92; Patron, Tory Reform Group. *Councils and public bodies:* Chairman, BBC Trust 2011-14.

Other: Member, advisory council, Hague Institute for Global Justice, Netherlands 2012-. Chancellor: Newcastle University 1999-2009, Oxford University 2003-. Honorary Fellow: Balliol College, Oxford, St Antony's College, Oxford; Nine honorary doctorates. PC 1989; CH 1998.

Publications: The Tory Case (1983); East and West (1998); Not Quite the Diplomat (2005); What Next? Surviving the 21st Century (2008); First Confession – A Sort of Memoir (2017).

Rt Hon the Lord Patten of Barnes CH, House of Lords, London SW1A 0PW
Tel: 020 7219 8736 *Email:* pattenc@parliament.uk

PAUL, LORD

NON-AFFILIATED

PAUL (Life Baron), Swraj Paul; cr. 1996. Born 18 February 1931; Son of late Payare Paul and Mongwati Paul; Married Aruna Vij 1956 (2 sons 1 daughter 1 son and 1 daughter deceased).

Education: Foreman Christian College, Lahore, Pakistan; Punjab University (BSc physics, chemistry and maths 1949); Massachusetts Institute of Technology (BSc, MSc 1952, mechanical engineering); Hindi.

Non-political career: Partner in family firm in India, Apeejay Surrendra Group 1953; Came to the UK in 1966, establishing first business Natural Gas Tubes Ltd; Caparo Group Ltd: Formed 1978, Chairman 1978-.

Political career: *House of Lords:* Raised to the peerage as Baron Paul, of Marylebone in the City of Westminster 1996. Deputy Speaker 2008-10; Deputy Chairman of Committees 2008-10; Suspended from membership October 2010-February 2011. Member: European Communities Sub-committee B (Energy, Industry and Transport) 1997-2001, Monetary Policy of the Bank of England/Economic Affairs 2000, 2001-03, 2005-09, Science and Technology 2003-07, Science and Technology Sub-committee II (Energy Efficiency) 2004-05; EU Sub-committee B (Internal Market): Co-opted member 2007-08, Member 2008-10; Member: Finance Bill Sub-committee 2008-10, European Union 2008-10, EU Sub-committee B (Internal Market, Energy and Transport) 2010. *Other:* Resigned Labour Whip October 2010. *Councils and public bodies:* Member: London Development Agency 2000-08, London 2012 2003-05; Chairman, Olympic Delivery Committee 2005-11.

Political interests: Foreign affairs, economic affairs, education; Austria, China, Dubai, Germany, India, Poland, Spain, Switzerland, Turkey, USA.

Other: Founder and Chair, Ambika Paul Foundation 1978-; Chair: Piggy Bank Kids 2002-, Piggy Bank Kids Projects Ltd 2002-13, Theirworld 2013-15; Royal Society of Arts 1984-; Magic Bus, Chance to Shine, Hospices, ZSL. Freedom, City of London 1998. Thames Valley University: Pro-chancellor 1998-2000, Chancellor 2000-01; Chancellor: Wolverhampton University 1999-, Westminster University 2006-14. Fifteen honorary doctorates from England, Switzerland, Russia, USA and India. Corporate Leadership Award, MIT 1987. Padma Bhushan (Government of India) 1983; PC 2009. Royal Calcutta Turf; Royal Calcutta Golf; Cricket of India (Bombay); MCC.

Publications: Indira Gandhi (1984); Beyond Boundaries (autobiography, 1998).

Recreations: Grandchildren.

Rt Hon the Lord Paul, House of Lords, London SW1A 0PW
Tel: 020 7219 5353
Caparo Group Ltd, Caparo House, 103 Baker Street, London W1U 6LN *Tel:* 020 7486 1417
Fax: 020 7224 4109 *Email:* lp@caparogrp.com *Website:* www.caparo.com
Twitter: @RtHonLordPaulPC

PEARSON OF RANNOCH, LORD

UK INDEPENDENCE PARTY

PEARSON OF RANNOCH (Life Baron), Malcolm Everard MacLaren Pearson; cr. 1990. Born 20 July 1942; Son of late Colonel John MacLaren Pearson; Married Francesca Frua de Angeli 1965 (divorced 1970) (1 daughter); married Hon. Mary Charteris 1977 (divorced 1995) (2 daughters); married Caroline St Vincent Rose 1997.

Education: Eton College.

Non-political career: Founded PWS Group of reinsurance brokers 1964.

Political career: *House of Lords:* Raised to the peerage as Baron Pearson of Rannoch, of Bridge of Gaur in the District of Perth and Kinross 1990. Member, European Communities and Sub-committee on Social Affairs and the Environment 1992-96. *Other:* Leader, UKIP 2009-10. *Councils and public bodies:* Council for National Academic Awards: Member 1983-93, Hon. Treasurer 1986-93.

Political interests: European Union, intellectual impairment, Islamism, education.

Other: Co-founder, Global Britain; Patron, Register of Chinese Herbal Medicine; Founded Rannoch Charitable Trust 1984; Patron, RESCARE (Society for Children and Adults with Learning Disabilities and their Families) 1994-. Hon. LLD, CNAA 1992; *Clubs:* White's Club. Swinley Forest Golf.

Recreations: Stalking, fishing, shooting, golf.

The Lord Pearson of Rannoch, House of Lords, London SW1A 0PW
Tel: 020 7219 8686
Email: lordpearsonofrannoch@gmail.com

PEEL, EARL

Lord Chamberlain

CROSSBENCH

PEEL (3rd Earl, UK), William James Robert Peel; cr. 1929. 4th Viscount Peel (UK) 1895; Viscount Clanfield (UK) 1929; 8th Bt of Drayton Manor (GB) 1800. Born 3 October 1947; Son of 2nd Earl; Married Veronica Timpson 1973 (divorced 1987) (1 son 1 daughter); married Hon Charlotte Hambro 1989, née Soames (1 daughter).

Education: Ampleforth College, Yorkshire; Tours University, France; Royal Agricultural College, Cirencester.

Non-political career: Lord Chamberlain of the Queen's Household and Chancellor of the Royal Victorian Order 2006-.

Political career: *House of Lords:* First entered House of Lords 1979; Elected hereditary peer 1999-. Co-opted Member, European Union Sub-committee D (Environment and Agriculture Policy) 2003-06. *Councils and public bodies:* DL, North Yorkshire 1998-.

Other: Chair, North of England Grouse Research Project 1979-96; Member: Yorkshire Dales National Parks Committee 1981-87, Moorland Association Executive Committee 1988-2006; President, Yorkshire Wildlife Trust 1989-96; Council member, Nature Conservancy Council for England, then English Nature 1991-96; President, Gun Trade Association 1993-99; Duchy of Cornwall: Member, Prince's Council 1993-96, Lord Warden of the Stannaries 1994-2006; Game and Wildlife Conservation Trust: Chair 1994-2000, President 2000-08, Vice-president 2008-; Chair, Standing Conference on Country Sports 2001-06. GCVO 2006; PC 2006; *Clubs:* White's Club.

Recreations: Shooting, cricket, photography, ornithology.

Rt Hon the Earl Peel GCVO DL, House of Lords, London SW1A 0PW
Tel: 020 7219 5353
Lord Chamberlain, Buckingham Palace, London SW1A 1AA

PENDRY, LORD

LABOUR

PENDRY (Life Baron), Thomas Pendry; cr 2001. Born 10 June 1934; Son of late Leonard Pendry; Married Moira Smith 1966 (separated 1983) (1 son 1 daughter).

Education: St Augustine's School, Ramsgate; Plater Hall, Oxford University.

Non-political career: RAF national service 1955-57. Official, National Union of Public Employees 1960-70. Member, AEEU.

Political career: *House of Commons:* MP (Labour) for Stalybridge and Hyde 1970-2001. Opposition Whip 1971-74; Government Whip 1974-77 (resigned); Parliamentary Under-Secretary of State, Northern Ireland Office 1978-79; Opposition Frontbench Spokesperson for: Northern Ireland 1979-82, Overseas Development 1981-82, Regional Affairs and Devolution 1982-92, National Heritage (Sport and Tourism) 1992-97. *House of Lords:* Raised to the peerage as Baron Pendry, of Stalybridge in the County of Greater Manchester 2001. Member, Refreshment 2014-16. *Other:* Chair, Derby Labour Party 1966. *Councils and public bodies:* Councillor, Paddington Borough Council 1962-65.

Political interests: Industrial relations, housing, sport, recreation, finance, social security, environment; Hong Kong, Japan, Malta, USA.

Other: Member, Council of Europe and Western European Union 1973-75; President, Stalybridge Public Band; Patron, Football Supporter's Federation; Fellow, Industry and Parliament Trust 1979, 1988; President: Ramsgate FC, Stalybridge Labour Club; Football Foundation: Chair 2001-03, President 2003-; Patron, Teenage Cancer Trust. Freedom: Borough of Tameside, Lord Mottram of Longendale. Lordship of Mottram in Longendale 1995; PC 2001; Knight of Malta; Freeman, Tameside Borough Council; *Clubs:* Royal Air Force, Garrick Club; Stalybridge Labour Club. Boxed for Oxford University 1957-59; Middleweight Colonial boxing champion, Hong Kong 1957; Lord's Taverners; MCC; Vincent's, Oxford University.

Publications: Taking It on the Chin (autobiography) (Biteback Publishing, 2016).

Recreations: Watching all sport, meeting sportspersons, jazz.

Rt Hon the Lord Pendry, House of Lords, London SW1A 0PW
Tel: 020 7219 4590 *Fax:* 020 7219 4419 *Email:* pendryt@parliament.uk

PETERBOROUGH, LORD BISHOP OF

NON-AFFILIATED

PETERBOROUGH (38th Bishop of), Donald Spargo Allister. Born 27 August 1952; Son of Charles and Barbara Allister; Married Janice 1976 (3 children).

Education: Birkenhead School; Peterhouse, Cambridge (BA theology 1974); Trinity College, Bristol 1974.

Non-political career: Ordained deacon 1976; Curate: St George's, Hyde 1976-79, St Nicholas, Sevenoaks 1979-83; Part-time consultant editor, *Church of England Newspaper* 1976-83; Vicar, Christ Church, Birkenhead 1983-89; Rector, St Mary's, Cheadle 1989-2002; Rural Dean of Cheadle 1999-2002; Archdeacon of Chester 2002-10; Bishop of Peterborough 2010-; Assistant Bishop in the Diocese of Ely 2011-.

Political career: *House of Lords:* Entered House of Lords 2014. *Councils and public bodies:* Member: General Synod 2005-, Women Bishops Legislative Drafting Group 2006-08; Council for Christian Unity: Member 2006-13; Chair 2013-.

Political interests: Farming and rural affairs, prisons and criminal justice; Kenya, Korea (North and South).

Other: Honorary Doctorate in Theology, Chester University (2011); *Clubs:* Farmers Club.

Rt Rev the Lord Bishop of Peterborough, House of Lords, London SW1A 0PW
Tel: 020 7219 5353 *Email:* allisterd@parliament.uk
Bishop's Lodging, The Palace, Peterborough PE1 1YA *Tel:* 01733 562492
Email: bishop@peterborough-diocese.org.uk *Website:* www.peterborough-diocese.org.uk

CROSSBENCH

PHILLIPS OF WORTH MATRAVERS, LORD

PHILLIPS OF WORTH MATRAVERS (Life Baron), Nicholas Addison Phillips; cr. 1999. Born 21 January 1938; Son of Michael Pennington Phillips and Dora Phillips, née Hassid; Married Christylle Marie-Thérèse Rouffiac, née Doreau 1972 (2 daughters 1 stepson 1 stepdaughter).

Education: Bryanston School; King's College, Cambridge (BA law 1961, MA).

Non-political career: Royal Navy national service commissioned RNVR 1956-58. Called to the Bar, Middle Temple (Harmsworth Scholar) 1962; In practice at the Bar 1962-87; Junior Counsel to Ministry of Defence and to Treasury in Admiralty matters 1973-78; QC 1978; Recorder 1982-87; Judge of the High Court of Justice (Queen's Bench Division) 1987-95; Lord Justice of Appeal 1995-98; Chairman of the BSE Inquiry 1998-2000; Master of the Rolls 2000-05; Head of Civil Justice 2000-05; Lord Chief Justice 2005-08; President of the Supreme Court of the United Kingdom 2009-12; Visiting Professor: King's College London 2010-, Oxford University 2013-16.

Political career: *House of Lords:* Raised to the peerage as Baron Phillips of Worth Matravers, of Belsize Park in the London Borough of Camden 1999. Lord of Appeal in Ordinary 1999-2000; Senior Lord of Appeal in Ordinary 2008-09; As President of the Supreme Court, disqualified from participation 2009-12. Member: Joint Committee on Voting Eligibilty (Prisoners) Bill 2013, Selection 2015-16. *Councils and public bodies:* Member, Panel of Wreck Commissioners 1979; Chair: Law Advisory Committee, British Council 1991-97, Council of Legal Education 1992-97; Advisory Council of Institute of European and Comparative Law 1999-; Council of Management, British Institute of International and Comparative Law 1999-; Chair, Lord Chancellor's Advisory Committee on Public Records 2000-05; President, British Maritime Law Association 2005-; Chair: Sentencing Guidelines Council 2005-08, Criminal Procedure Rules Committee 2005-08.

Other: The Draper's Company; Worshipful Company of Shipwrights. Freedom, City of London. Chancellor, Bournemouth University 2009-. Honorary LLD, Exeter University 1998; Honorary Fellow, Society for Advanced Legal Studies 1999; Visitor: Nuffield College, Oxford 2000-05, University College, London 2000-05; Hon. Fellow, King's College, Cambridge 2003; Doctor of Civil Law, City University, London; Honorary LLD: London University, Birmingham University; Visitor, Darwin College, Cambridge 2005; International Maritime Law Institute 2007. Kt 1987; PC 1995; KG 2011; Officier of the Legion d'Honneur 2017; *Clubs:* Brooks's; Garrick Club.

Recreations: Sea, mountains.

Rt Hon the Lord Phillips of Worth Matravers KG, House of Lords, London SW1A 0PW
Tel: 020 7219 5353
Email: phillipsofworth@gmail.com

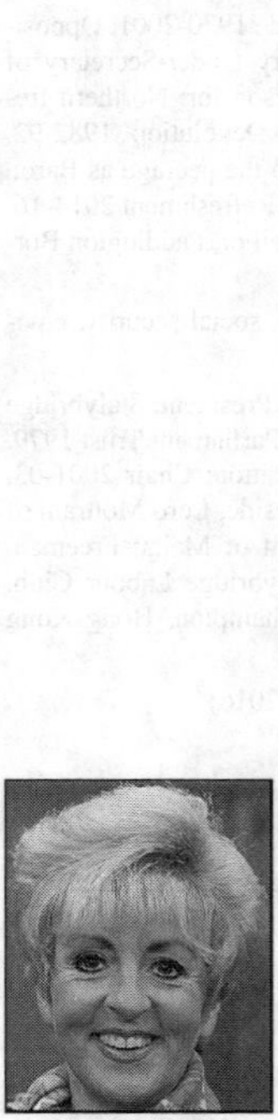

CONSERVATIVE

PIDDING, BARONESS

PIDDING (Life Baroness), Emma Samantha Pidding; cr 2015. Born 13 January 1966; Partner Tim Butcher.

Education: Dr Challoner's High School, Little Chalfont.

Non-political career: Lloyds Bank; Marketing and events manager, IT consultancy, Buckinghamshire; Owner, consultancy specialising in organising seminar and conferences.

Political career: *House of Lords:* Raised to the peerage as Baroness Pidding, of Amersham in the County of Buckinghamshire 2015. *Other:* Chair, Chesham and Amersham Young Conservatives 1991-94; Chesham and Amersham Conservative Association: Deputy chair 1997-2000, Chair 2000-03; Oxfordshire and Buckinghamshire Area Team: Deputy Chair (membership and fundraising) 2002-04, Area Chair 2004-06; National Convention: Vice-President 2006-09, President 2009-10, Chair 2012-15; President, Northern Ireland Conservatives 2007-; National volunteer by-election co-ordinator 2010-12; Deputy Chair, Conservative Party Board 2012-15. *Councils and public bodies:* Councillor, Chiltern District Council 1991-99.

Other: CBE 2014.

The Baroness Pidding CBE, House of Lords, London SW1A 0PW
Tel: 020 7219 3000
Email: emma.pidding@btinternet.com *Twitter:* @EmmaPidding

LIBERAL DEMOCRAT

PINNOCK, BARONESS

Liberal Democrat Lords Spokesperson for Communities and Local Government

PINNOCK (Life Baroness), Kathryn (Kath) Mary Pinnock; cr 2014. Born 25 September 1946.

Education: Keele University (Degree history and chemistry; Diploma teaching).

Non-political career: Secondary school teacher, various schools in Birmingham and West Yorkshire; Deputy Chief Examiner for GCE history.

Political career: *House of Commons:* Contested (Liberal Democrat) Batley and Spen 1997 and 2001 general elections. *House of Lords:* Raised to the peerage as Baroness Pinnock, of Cleckheaton in the County of West Yorkshire 2014. Liberal Democrat: Spokesperson for Children 2015, Shadow Secretary of State/Lords Spokesperson for Communities and Local Government 2016-. Member, EU Home Affairs Sub-committee 2015-. *Other:* Leader, Kirklees Liberal Democrats 1991-2014; President, Association of Liberal Democrat Councillors. *Councils and public bodies:* Kirklees Council: Councillor 1987-, Leader of the Council 2000-06; Governor, Whitcliffe Mount School, Cleckheaton; Board member, Yorkshire Forward 2001-11; Non-executive director, Yorkshire Water 2008-; Vice-President, Local Government Association 2015-.

Other: Association of West Yorkshire Authorities; Mayor of Borough of Kirklees Appeal Fund; CO2 Sense Limited; Council member, Huddersfield University.

The Baroness Pinnock, House of Lords, London SW1A 0PW
Tel: 020 7219 5353 *Twitter:* @KathPinnock

LABOUR

PITKEATHLEY, BARONESS

PITKEATHLEY (Life Baroness), Jill Elizabeth Pitkeathley; cr. 1997. Born 4 January 1940; Daughter of Roland and May Bisson; Married W. Pitkeathley 1961 (divorced 1978) (1 son 1 daughter); married David Emerson 2008.

Education: Ladies' College, Guernsey; Bristol University (BA economics 1960).

Non-political career: Social Worker 1961-68; Voluntary Service Co-ordinator, West Berkshire Health Authority 1970-83; National Consumer Council 1983-86; Director, National Council for Carers 1986 until merger with Association of Carers 1988; Carers National Association: Chief Executive 1988-98, Vice-President 2001-; Chair: Children and Families Court Advisory and Support Service 2003-08, Council for Health Care Regulatory Excellence/Professional Standards Authority 2009-15.

Political career: *House of Lords:* Raised to the peerage as Baroness Pitkeathley, of Caversham in the Royal County of Berkshire 1997. Deputy Speaker 2002-; Deputy Chair of Committees 2002-. Member: House of Lords' Offices Refreshment Sub-committee 2001-09, Information 2010-13, Joint Committee on the Draft Care and Support Bill 2013, Equality Act 2010 and Disability 2015-16; Chair, Charities 2016-17; Member, Citizenship and Civic Engagement 2017-. *Councils and public bodies:* Adviser to Griffith's Review of Community Care 1986-88; Community Council for Berkshire: Vice-President 1990-98, President 1998-2013; Chair: New Opportunities Fund 1998-2004, Future Builders Advisory Panel 2005-08, Advisory Board, Office of Third Sector 2008-10; Interim Chair, General Social Care Council 2008.

Political interests: Health, social care, voluntary sector, charities; Channel Islands.

Other: Vice-President, Carers UK 1998-; Trustee, Cumberland Lodge; Big Society Trust: Trustee 2011-14, Chair 2015-; Hon. RCGP; Hon. City and Guilds 2009; Carers UK. DL: Bristol 2002, London Metropolitan 2002. OBE 1993.

Publications: When I Went Home (1978); Mobilising Voluntary Resources (1984); Supporting Volunteers (1985); It's my duty, isn't it? (1989); Co-author: Age Gap Relationships (1996), Only Child (1994); Fiction: Cassandra and Jane (2004), Dearest Cousin Jane (2009).

Recreations: Gardening, grandchildren, writing.

The Baroness Pitkeathley OBE, House of Lords, London SW1A 0PW
Tel: 020 7219 0358 *Email:* pitkeathleyj@parliament.uk

LABOUR

PLANT OF HIGHFIELD, LORD

PLANT OF HIGHFIELD (Life Baron), Raymond Plant; cr. 1992. Born 19 March 1945; Son of late Stanley Plant and Marjorie Plant; Married Katherine Dixon 1967 (3 sons).

Education: Havelock School, Grimsby; King's College, London (BA philosophy 1966); Hull University (PhD political philosophy 1971); French, German.

Non-political career: Lecturer, then senior lecturer in philosophy, Manchester University 1967-79; Philosophy lecturer in several universities 1981-91; Professor of politics, Southampton University 1979-94; Master, St Catherine's College, Oxford 1994-2000; Professor of: European politics, Southampton University 2000-02, Law and philosophy, King's College, London 2002-: Head of Law School 2006-08; Visiting professor of law and philosophy, Institut d'Etudes Politiques, Paris 2008; Hon. professor of humanities, Winchester University; Part-time professor of law, Tallinn University, Estonia.

Political career: *House of Lords:* Raised to the peerage as Baron Plant of Highfield, of Weelsby in the County of Humberside 1992. Opposition Spokesperson for Home Affairs 1992-96. Member: Relations between Central and Local Government 1995-96, European Communities Sub-committee E 2000-03, Joint Committee on Human Rights 2003-07, Merits of Statutory Instruments/Secondary Legislation Scrutiny 2010-15, Joint Committee on the Draft Enhanced Terrorism Prevention and Investigation Measures Bill 2012-13, Inheritace and Trustees' Powers Bill 2013, Joint Committee on Able Marine Energy Park Development Consent Order 2014 2014-15, Ecclesiastical Committee 2014-, High Speed Rail (London-West Midlands) Bill 2016, Joint Committee on Consolidation, &c, Bills 2016-, Intellectual Property (Unjustified Threats) Bill 2016, Selection 2017-. *Other:* Chair, Labour Party Commission on Electoral Systems 1991-93.

Countries of interest: France, Germany, Portugal, Russia.

Other: President, National Council for Voluntary Organisations (NCVO) 1998-2002; Fellow, Industry and Parliament Trust 1998; Chair: Hope Medical Trust, Southampton 2000-06, Centrepoint 2001-04, Southampton University Development Trust 2007-08; FRSA 1992; ACSS (Academy of Learned Societies in the Social Sciences). Pro-Chancellor, Southampton University 1996-2000. Six honorary doctorates; Fellow: King's College, London, Catherine's College, Oxford, Cardiff University, Harris Manchester College, Oxford. Isiah Berlin prize 2010; *Clubs:* Athenæum Club.

Publications: Hegel (1974); Community and Ideology (1974); Political Philosophy and Social Welfare (1981); Philosophy, Politics and Citizenship (1984); Contributor to *The Times* (1988-91); Conservative Capitalism in Britain and the United States: a critical appraisal (1988); Modern Political Thought (1991); Politics, Theology and History (2001); The Neo-liberal State (OUP, 2009).

Recreations: Music, opera, reading.

Professor the Lord Plant of Highfield, House of Lords, London SW1A 0PW
Tel: 020 7219 5424
School of Law, King's College, Strand, London WC2R 2LS *Tel:* 020 7836 5454
Fax: 020 7848 2465 *Email:* raymond.plant@kcl.ac.uk

CONSERVATIVE

PLUMB, LORD

PLUMB (Life Baron), Charles Henry Plumb; cr. 1987. Born 27 March 1925; Son of late Charles Plumb; Married Marjorie Dunn 1947 (1 son 2 daughters 1 deceased).

Education: King Edward VI School, Nuneaton.

Non-political career: NFU: Council member 1959, Vice-President 1964-65, Deputy President 1966-69, President 1970-79; Non-executive director, Lloyds Bank, United Biscuits, Fisons 1979-94; Chair, Agricultural Mortgage Corporation 1994-95.

Political career: *House of Lords:* Raised to the peerage as Baron Plumb, of Coleshill in the County of Warwickshire 1987. EU Sub-committee D (Environment and Agriculture): Member 2005-06, 2007-08, Co-opted member 2006-07; Member: European Union 2008-12, EU Sub-committee B: (Internal Market) 2008-10, (Internal Market, Energy and Transport) 2010-12, (Internal Market, Infrastructure and Employment) 2012-13; Member, EU Sub-committee D: Agriculture, Fisheries, Environment and Energy 2013-15. *Other:* European Parliament: MEP (Conservative) for Cotswolds 1979-99: Chair: Agricultural Committee 1979-82, European Democratic Group 1982-87, 1994-99, President, European Parliament 1987-89, Honorary MEP 1999-; EU-ACP Joint Assembly: Co-president 1994-99, Honorary president 1999-; President, FMA (Former Members Association) 2001-07. President, North Warwickshire Conservative Association 1988-2000. *Councils and public bodies:* Member, Duke of Northumberland's Committee of Enquiry, Foot and Mouth Disease 1967-68; DL, Warwick 1977.

Political interests: Europe, agriculture, environment, international trade, farming; Africa, Commonwealth, USA.

Other: Chair, president numerous national and international organisations related to food, agriculture and environment: President, Comité des Organisations Professionnelles Agricoles de la CEE (COPA) 1975-77, Chair, British Agricultural Council 1975-79, President, Royal Agricultural Society of England 1977; Henry Plumb Trust; Royal Agricultural Benevolent Institute, Farm Africa. Master, Farmers' Company; Hon. Liveryman, Worshipful Company of Fruiterers. Freedom, City of London; Honorary Freedom of the Borough of North Warwickshire 2002. Chancellor, Coventry University 1995-2007. Hon. Fellow: Duchy College, Royal Agricultural College, Wye College 1995; Six honorary doctorates. RASE Gold Medal 1978. Kt 1973; Knight Commander's Cross of the Order of Merit (Federal Republic of Germany) 1976; Ordén de Merito (Portugal) 1987; Order of Merit (Luxembourg) 1988; Grand Cross of the Order of Civil Merit (Spain) 1989; Grand Order of the Phoenix (Greece) 1997; Medal Mediterraneum, European Institute, Florence (Italy) 1998; *Clubs:* St Stephen's Constitutional, Farmers' Club.

Publications: The Plumb Line (Greycoat Press, 2001).

Recreations: Shooting, country pursuits.

The Lord Plumb DL, House of Lords, London SW1A 0PW
Tel: 020 7219 1233 *Email:* plumbh@parliament.uk
Maxstoke, Coleshill, Warwickshire B46 2QJ *Tel:* 01675 464156 *Fax:* 01675 464156
Website: www.thehenryplumbfoundation.org.uk

CONSERVATIVE

POLAK, LORD

POLAK (Life Baron), Stuart Polak; cr 2015. Born 28 March 1961.

Non-political career: Youth Officer, United Synagogue; Conservative Friends of Israel: Director 1989-2015, Honorary President 2015-; Director, Markham Services Ltd; Senior consultant, Jardine Lloyd Thompson Group plc.

Political career: *House of Lords:* Raised to the peerage as Baron Polak, of Hertsmere in the County of Hertfordshire 2015. Member, EU Justice Sub-committee 2016-.

Other: Chair, TWC Associates; Senior consultant, Jardine Lloyd Thompson; Chair, European Friends of Israel; Trustee, Langdon Foundation; Director, Yavneh Foundation Trust; Board member, Europe Near East Forum. CBE 2015.

The Lord Polak CBE, House of Lords, London SW1A 0PW
Tel: 020 7219 3000

LABOUR

PONSONBY OF SHULBREDE, LORD

PONSONBY OF SHULBREDE (4th Baron, UK), Frederick Matthew Thomas Ponsonby; cr. 1930; (Life) Baron Ponsonby of Roehampton 2000. Born 27 October 1958; Son of 3rd Baron; Married Sarah Jackson 1995 (1 daughter 1 son).

Education: Holland Park Comprehensive School; University College, Cardiff (BSc physics 1980); Imperial College, London (MSc DIC petroleum engineering 1983).

Non-political career: Member, Unite.

Political career: *House of Lords:* Created a life peer as Baron Ponsonby of Roehampton, of Shulbrede in the County of West Sussex 2000. First entered House of Lords 1990; Opposition Spokesperson for Education 1992-97. Member: Science and Technology 1998-99, Science and Technology Sub-committee II (Science and Society) 1999, Constitution 2001. *Councils and public bodies:* Councillor, London Borough of Wandsworth 1990-94; JP: Westminster Bench 2005-11, Inner London Youth Panel 2008-11, Central London Bench 2012-, Central London Youth Panel 2012-, Greater London Family Panel 2012-.

Political interests: Foreign affairs.

Other: Delegate to: Council of Europe 1997-2001, Western European Union 1997-2001; Organisation for Security and Co-operation in Europe 2001-10; FIMM.

The Lord Ponsonby of Shulbrede, House of Lords, London SW1A 0PW
Tel: 020 7219 0071 *Email:* ponsonbyf@parliament.uk

CONSERVATIVE

POPAT, LORD

POPAT (Life Baron), Dolar Amarshi Popat; cr 2010. Born 14 June 1953; Son of Amarshibhai Haridas Popat and Parvatiben Amarshibhai Popat; Married Sandhya Popat 1980 (3 sons).

Education: Manjasi High School, Torono, Uganda; Kilburn Polytechnic; City of London Polytechnic, Moorgate; Chartered Institute of Management Accounting (management accounting 1977); Gujarati, Hindi, Swahili.

Non-political career: Practicing accountant 1980-82; Harrow Chamber of Commerce 1982-87; Chief executive, Fast Finance plc 1982-91; Founding Patron, Harrow Grange Hospice St Luke's Hospice 1984-; Founder and chief executive, TLC Group 1991-2010.

Political career: *House of Lords:* Raised to the peerage as Baron Popat, of Harrow in the London Borough of Harrow 2010. Government Whip 2013-15; Government Spokesperson: Business, Innovation and Skills 2013-15, Transport 2013-15, Communities and Local Government (Faith and Communities) 2014-15; Trade Envoy to Uganda and Rwanda 2016-; Conservative Party Whip 2015-. Member, Small- and Medium-Sized Enterprises 2012-13. *Other:* Secretary, Anglo-Asian Conservative Association; Chair, One Nation Forum, Barnet; President, Harrow East Conservative Association; Member, Conservative Ethnic Diversity Council; Co-chair, Conservative Friends of India 2012-13.

Political interests: International affairs, international development, small- and medium-sized businesses, banking and finance, community, exports; Africa, India, Kenya, Malawi, Tanzania, Uganda.

Other: Affiliate member, Institute of Chartered Management Accountants; Charities supported through the Lord Dolar Popat Foundation, St Luke's Hospice.

Recreations: Reading, tennis, walking, community work, travelling, Tottenham Hotspur FC.

The Lord Popat, House of Lords, London SW1A 0PW
Tel: 020 7219 0295 *Email:* popatd@parliament.uk
Website: www.lordpopat.com

CONSERVATIVE

PORTER OF SPALDING, LORD

PORTER OF SPALDING (Life Baron), Gary Andrew Porter; cr 2015. Born 8 September 1960; Married Karen (2 children).

Education: Collenswood School, Stevenage; De Montfort University (BA history and politics 2000); Canterbury Christ Church University (Postgraduate Certificate shared services 2011).

Non-political career: Industrial bakery; Labourer, warehouse building site; Contracts manager for a construction firm; Owner of small building firm.

Political career: *House of Lords:* Raised to the peerage as Baron Porter of Spalding, of Spalding in the County of Lincolnshire 2015. *Other:* Chair, Conservative Councillors Association 2013-16; Member, Conservative Party Board. *Councils and public bodies:* South Holland District Council: Councillor 2001-, Leader 2003-; Local Government Association: Chair, environment, housing and planning board 2009-11, Leader, Conservative Group and Vice-chair 2011-15, Chair 2015-.

Other: Director: South Holland Homes, Local Government Information House Ltd, Improvement and Development Agency for Local Government; Chair, District Council Network 2009-11.

The Lord Porter of Spalding CBE, House of Lords, London SW1A 0PW
Tel: 020 7219 3000
c/o Council Offices, Priory Road, Spalding PE11 2XE *Twitter:* @garyporterlga

NON-AFFILIATED

PORTSMOUTH, LORD BISHOP OF

PORTSMOUTH (9th Bishop of), Christopher Richard James Foster. Born 7 November 1953; Son of late Joseph James Frederick and late Elizabeth Foster, née Gibbs; Married Julia 1982 (died 2001) (1 son 1 daughter); married Sally 2006.

Education: Royal Grammar School, Guildford; Durham University (BA economics and politics 1975); Manchester University (MA (Econ) econometrics 1977); Trinity Hall, Cambridge (MA theology 1979); Westcott House, Cambridge.

Non-political career: Economics lecturer; Ordained deacon 1980; Assistant curate, Tettenhall Regis, Wolverhampton 1980-82; Chaplain, Wadham College, Oxford 1982-86; Assistant Priest, University Church of St Mary the Virgin 1982-86; Vicar, Christ Church, Southgate, London 1986-94; Director, CME, Edmonton Episcopal Area 1988-94; Sub-Dean and residentiary canon, St Albans Cathedral 1994-2001; Bishop of: Hertford 2001-10, Portsmouth 2010-.

Political career: *House of Lords:* Entered House of Lords 2014. *Councils and public bodies:* Hertfordshire University: Governor 2002-10, Chair, finance committee 2007-10; Council Member, Westcott House, Cambridge 2004-12; Member: Church Commissioners Pastoral Committee 2013-14, Dioceses Commission 2014-; Chair of Governors, Ripon College, Cuddesdon 2014-; Governor, Portsmouth University 2014-; Chair: Remuneration and Conditions of Service Committee, Archbishops' Council 2017-, Churches Funerals Group 2017-.

Countries of interest: Ghana.

Other: Director, Churches Together in England 2012-17. DLitt, Hertfordshire University 2011; *Clubs:* Athenæum, Royal Yacht Squadron Club.

Rt Rev the Lord Bishop of Portsmouth, House of Lords, London SW1A 0PW
Tel: 020 7219 5353 *Email:* fostercrj@parliament.uk
Bishopsgrove, 26 Osborn Road, Fareham PO16 7DQ *Tel:* 01329 280247
Email: bishop@portsmouth.anglican.org *Website:* www.portsmouth.anglican.org

CROSSBENCH

POWELL OF BAYSWATER, LORD

POWELL OF BAYSWATER (Life Baron), Charles David Powell; cr. 2000. Born 6 June 1941; Son of late Air Vice Marshal John Powell, OBE; Married Carla Bonardi 1964 (2 sons).

Education: Canterbury Cathedral Choir School; King's School, Canterbury; New College, Oxford (BA modern history 1963); Finnish, French, German, Italian.

Non-political career: Diplomatic Service 1963-83; Private Secretary to Prime Ministers: Margaret Thatcher 1983-90, John Major 1990-91; Director: Matheson & Co 1991-, Mandarin Oriental Hotel Group 1991-, Hong Kong Land Holdings 1991-2001, 2008-, Jardine Matheson Holdings 1991-2001, National Westminster Bank 1991-2000, J Rothschild Name Company 1992-2003, Said Holdings 1993-2000, Arjo Wiggins Appleton 1993-2000, Louis Vuitton Moët Hennessy 1995-, British Mediterranean Airways 1997-2007, Sagitta Asset Management 2001-05, Caterpillar Inc 2001-13, Textron Corporation 2001-17, Yell Group 2002-09, Schindler Holding 2003-14, Northern Trust Global Services 2004-14; Member, international advisory board: Phillips de Pury Luxembourg 2000-02, GEMS Private Equity 1999-2013, Thales UK 2004-, Alfa Capital 2005-10, Chubb Insurance 2006-, Barrick Gold 2006-; Chairman: International advisory board, Rolls Royce 2006-, Capital Generation Partners 2006-13, Magna Holdings International 2006-12, Bowmark 2008-; Northern Trust Corp 2014-.

Political career: *House of Lords:* Raised to the peerage as Baron Powell of Bayswater, of Canterbury in the County of Kent 2000. Co-opted Member, EU Sub-committee C (Common Foreign and Security Policy/Foreign Affairs, Defence and Development Policy) 2000-04; Member: Economic Affairs 2005-07, European Union 2006-10, EU Sub-committee B (Internal Market) 2006-10, Finance Bill Sub-committee 2006-11, Constitution 2010-15, Procedure 2015-, Joint Committee on the National Security Strategy 2016-. *Councils and public bodies:* Co-chairman, Asia Task Force 2007-14; UK Business Ambassador 2012-; Vice-president: Great Britain-China Centre, Asia House.

Political interests: Foreign affairs, defence, intelligence, trade; Asia, Europe, North America.

Other: Trustee, Aspen Institute, USA 1995-; Chair of Trustees, Oxford University Business School Foundation 1997-; President, China-Britain Business Council 1997-2007; Chair, Singapore British Business Council 1993-2001; Trustee, British Museum 2000-10; Chair, Atlantic Partnership 2000-; Trustee: Saïd Foundation 2008-, International Institute of Strategic Studies 2010-; Chair, British Museum Trust 2011-; Member, International Advisory Board, New York Council on Foreign Relations 2011-; Deputy chair, Fudan University School of Management Advisory Board 2012-; Honorary Fellow, Ashmolean Museum, Oxford; Foundation Fellow, Somerville College, Oxford; Honorary Fellow, King's College, London; Aspen Institute. KCMG 1990; Public Service Star (Singapore) 2001; *Clubs:* Turf Club.

Recreations: Walking.

The Lord Powell of Bayswater KCMG, House of Lords, London SW1A 0PW
Tel: 020 7219 5451
LVMH Clarendon House, 12 Clifford Street, London W1S 2LL *Tel:* 020 7399 1609
Fax: 020 7408 7428 *Email:* pa@charlespowell.com

CROSSBENCH

PRASHAR, BARONESS

PRASHAR (Life Baroness), Usha Kumari Prashar; cr. 1999. Born 29 June 1948; Daughter of late Naurhia Lal and Durga Devi Prashar; Married Vijay Kumar Sharma 1973.

Education: Duchess of Gloucester School, Nairobi, Kenya; Wakefield Girls' High School, Yorkshire; Leeds University (BA political science 1970); Glasgow University (Dip Soc Admin 1971); Hindi.

Non-political career: Conciliation officer, Race Relations Board 1971-75; Director, Runnymede Trust 1976-84; Research fellow, Policy Studies Institute 1984-86; Director, National Council of Voluntary Organisations 1986-91; National Literacy Trust: Deputy chair 1992-2000, Chair 2000-05; Executive chairman, Parole Board of England and Wales 1997-2000; First Civil Service Commissioner 2000-05; Non-executive director, Unite plc 2000-04; Chair, Judicial Appointments Commission 2005-10.

Political career: *House of Lords:* Raised to the peerage as Baroness Prashar, of Runnymede in the County of Surrey 1999. Member: Joint Committee on Human Rights 2000-04, 2008-10, Privileges 2008-09; Chair, Sub-committee on Lords' Interests 2008-09; EU Sub-committee F (Home Affairs, Health and Education): Member 2012-14, Chair 2014-15; Member, European Union 2014-17; Chair, EU Home Affairs Sub-committee 2015-17. *Councils and public bodies:* Member: Arts Council of Great Britain 1979-81, 1994-97, Study Commission on the Family 1980-83, Social Security Advisory Committee 1980-83, London Food Commission 1984-90, BBC Educational Broadcasting Council 1987-89, Solicitor's Complaints Bureau 1989-90, Royal Commission on Criminal Justice 1991-93; Part-time Civil Service Commissioner 1991-96; Member, Lord Chancellor's Advisory Committee on Legal Education and Conduct 1991-97; Non-executive director, Channel Four 1992-98; Chair: Royal Commonwealth Society 2002-08, ITV Board 2005-10; Member, Iraq Inquiry 2009-; British Council: Deputy chair 2012-, Acting chair 2016.

Political interests: Education, criminal justice, human rights, race relations, international affairs; Africa, Europe, India, Mauritius.

Other: Board member, Salzburg Seminar 2000-04; Member, executive committee, Child Poverty Action Group 1984-85; Hon. Vice-President, Council for Overseas Student Affairs 1986-; Trustee, Camelot Foundation 1995-2000; Governor, De Montfort University 1996-2006; Management Board, King's Fund 1997-2002; Trustee, Ethnic Minority Foundation 1997-2002; Tara Arts 1999-; Chair, National Literacy Trust 2000-05; Trustee, BBC World Service Trust 2002-05; Wise Thoughts 2002-; Ditchley Foundation: Governor and member, Management Committee 2003, Trustee 2004-; President: Community Foundation Network, National Literacy Trust; Trustee, Miriam Rothschild and John Foster Trust 2007-10; Cumberland Lodge 2007-; Senior Fellow, Salzberg Global Seminar; Companion, Chartered Management Institute; Fellow, Royal Society of Arts. Chancellor, De Montfort University 2000-06. Hon. Fellow, Goldsmith's College, London University; Ten honorary doctorates; Elected Master of the Bench of Inner Temple 2011. CBE 1994; PC 2009; *Clubs:* Royal Commonwealth Society Club. Foxhills Golf Club.

Publications: Contributor to several publications on health and race relations.

Recreations: Golf, music, art, reading.

Rt Hon the Baroness Prashar CBE, House of Lords, London SW1A 0PW
Tel: 020 7219 6792 *Email:* prasharu@parliament.uk

LABOUR

PRESCOTT, LORD

PRESCOTT (Life Baron), John Leslie Prescott; cr 2010. Born 31 May 1938; Son of late John Herbert Prescott, railway controller, and late Phyllis Prescott; Married Pauline Tilston 1961 (2 sons).

Education: Ellesmere Port Secondary Modern School; Ruskin College, Oxford (DipEcon/Pol 1965); Hull University (BSc (Econ) 1968).

Non-political career: Steward, Merchant Navy 1955-63; Union official, National Union of Seamen 1968-70. TU Official, National Union of Seamen, RMT (resigned 2002).

Political career: *House of Commons:* Contested Southport 1966 general election. MP (Labour) for Kingston-upon-Hull East 1970-83, for Hull East 1983-2010. PPS to Peter Shore as Secretary of State for Trade 1974-76; Opposition Spokesperson for: Transport 1979-81, Regional Affairs and Devolution 1981-83; Member Shadow Cabinet 1983-97: Shadow Secretary of State for: Transport 1983-84, 1988-93, Employment 1984-87, 1993-94, Energy 1987-89; Deputy Prime Minister 1997-2007; Secretary of State for the Environment, Transport and the Regions 1997-2001; First Secretary of State 2001-07. *House of Lords:* Raised to the peerage as Baron Prescott, of Kingston upon Hull in the County of East Yorkshire 2010. Adviser on climate change (unpaid) to Ed Miliband as Leader of the Opposition 2015. *Other:* Deputy Leader: Labour Party 1994-2007, Labour Party National Executive Committee 1997-2007; Contested Labour Party treasurer 2010.

Political interests: Climate change; China.

Other: Member, Council of Europe 1972-75; Delegate, EEC Parliamentary 1975; Leader: Labour Party Delegation to European Parliament 1976-79, UK Delegation Parliamentary Assembly of the Council of Europe/Western European Union 2007-; Rapporteur for the Committee on Social Affairs, Health and Sustainable Development for the Council of Europe. Hon. professor on Climate Change, Xiamen University; Hon. degree: Ningbo University, Nottingham University, Universiapolis, University in Agadir, Morocco. North of England Zoological Society Gold Medal 1999; Priyadarshni Award 2002; Political Tweeter of the Year, *PoliticsHome* awards 2012. PC 1994 (resigned July 2013).

Publications: Prezza: Pulling No Punches (2008).

Recreations: Jazz, theatre, music, aqua diving.

The Lord Prescott, House of Lords, London SW1A 0PW
Tel: 020 7219 5353 *Twitter:* @johnprescott

PRICE, LORD

CONSERVATIVE

PRICE (Life Baron), Mark Ian Price; cr 2016. Born 2 March 1961; Married Judith Bolt 1991 (2 daughters).

Education: Crewe County Grammar School for Boys; Lancaster University (BA archaeology and ancient history).

Non-political career: John Lewis 1982-98: Graduate trainee, Store manager: High Wycombe 1992-95, Cheadle 1995-98; Waitrose: Director of retail and marketing 1998-05, Managing director 2007-16, John Lewis Partnership: Director of Development 2005-07, Deputy chairman 2013-16.

Political career: *House of Lords:* Raised to the peerage as Baron Price, of Sturminster Newton in the County of Dorset 2016. Minister of State for Trade and Investment and Government Spokesperson, Department for Business, Innovation and Skills and Foreign and Commonwealth Office 2016; Minister of State for Trade Policy and Government Spokesperson, Department for International Trade 2016-17. *Councils and public bodies:* Deputy Chairman, Channel 4 2013-16; Non-executive member, Cabinet Office Board 2015-16.

Other: Chair: Prince's Countryside Fund 2010-16, Business in the Community 2011-15; Patron, Grocery Aid. Honorary degree: Lancaster University, Roehampton University; Fellowship: Aberystwyth University, Marketing Society. CVO 2014.

Publications: The Great British Picnic Guide (2008); The Food Lover's Handbook (2016); The Foolish King (2016); Fairness for All: Unlocking the Power of Employee Engagement (David Fickling Books, 2017); Workplace Fables: 145 True Life Stories (Stour Publishing, 2017).

Recreations: Writing, golf, ancient history.

The Lord Price CVO, House of Lords, London SW1A 0PW
Tel: 020 7219 3000

PRIMAROLO, BARONESS

LABOUR

PRIMAROLO (Life Baroness), Dawn Primarolo; cr 2015. Born 2 May 1954; Née Gasson; Married Michael Primarolo 1972 (divorced) (1 son); married Thomas Ducat 1990.

Education: Thomas Bennett Comprehensive School, Crawley; Bristol Polytechnic (BA social science 1984).

Non-political career: Secretary 1972-73; Secretary and advice worker, Law Centre, East London; Secretary, Avon County Council 1975-78; Voluntary work 1978-81; Mature student 1981-87. Member, Unison.

Political career: *House of Commons:* MP (Labour) for Bristol South 1987-2010, for Bristol South (revised boundary) 2010-15. Opposition Spokesperson for: Health 1992-94, Treasury and Economic Affairs 1994-97; HM Treasury: Financial Secretary 1997-99, Paymaster General 1999-2007; Minister of State: for Public Health, Department of Health 2007-09, for Children, Young People and Families, Department for Children, Schools and Families 2009-10; Shadow Minister for Children 2010; Second Deputy Chairman, Ways and Means and Deputy Speaker 2010-15. Member: Public Accounts 1997-98, Panel of Chairs 2010-15. *House of Lords:* Raised to the peerage as Baroness Primarolo, of Windmill Hill in the City of Bristol 2015. Member, Financial Exclusion 2016-17. *Councils and public bodies:* Councillor, Avon County Council 1985-87; Chair, Remuneration Board, National Assembly for Wales 2015-.

Political interests: Education, housing, social security, health, economic policy, equal opportunities.

Other: PC 2002; DBE 2014.

Rt Hon the Baroness Primarolo DBE, House of Lords, London SW1A 0PW
Tel: 020 7219 3000 *Email:* dawn.primarolo@parliament.uk

CONSERVATIVE

PRIOR OF BRAMPTON, LORD

Parliamentary Under-Secretary of State and Government Spokesperson, Department for Business, Energy and Industrial Strategy

PRIOR OF BRAMPTON (Life Baron), David Gifford Leathes Prior; cr 2015. Born 3 December 1954; Son of late James Prior (MP for Lowestoft 1959-83 and Waveney 1983-87, later Lord Prior) and Lady Prior; Married Caroline Holmes 1987 (1 son 1 daughter).

Education: Charterhouse School; Pembroke College, Cambridge (MA law 1976).

Non-political career: Called to the Bar, Gray's Inn 1977; Lehman Brothers and Lazard Freres, investment banks 1977-80; Senior executive, British Steel 1980-87; Investor and manager of various industrial businesses; Adviser to the health authority of Abu Dhabi.

Political career: *House of Commons:* MP (Conservative) for North Norfolk 1997-2001. Contested North Norfolk 2001 general election. *House of Lords:* Raised to the peerage as Baron Prior of Brampton, of Swannington in the County of Norfolk 2015. Parliamentary Under-Secretary of State and Government Spokesperson, Department of Health: (NHS Productivity) 2015-16, (Health) 2016, Parliamentary Under-Secretary of State and Government Spokesperson, Department for Business, Energy and Industrial Strategy 2016-. *Other:* Chair, Mid Norfolk Conservative Association 1995-96; Conservative Party: Vice-chairman 1998-99, Deputy chairman and chief executive 1999-2001. *Councils and public bodies:* Chair: NHS Workforce Race Equality Standard Strategic Advisory Group -2015, Norfolk and Norwich University Hospital 2002-13, Care Quality Commission 2013-15, Two free schools and an academy.

Other: Trustee, Inspiration Trust.

The Lord Prior of Brampton, House of Lords, London SW1A 0PW
Tel: 020 7219 3000

LABOUR

PROSSER, BARONESS

PROSSER (Life Baroness), Margaret Theresa Prosser; cr. 2004. Born 22 August 1937; Daughter of Frederick James and Lilian James, née Barry; Divorced (1 son 2 daughters).

Education: St Philomena's Convent, Carshalton, Surrey; North East London Polytechnic (Postgraduate Diploma housing, law and social security 1977).

Non-political career: Advice centre organiser, Southwark Community Development Project 1974-77; Legal adviser, Southwark Law Project 1977-83; Transport and General Workers' Union 1983-2002: District organiser 1983-84, National women's secretary 1984-92, National organiser 1992-98, Deputy secretary-general 1998-2002; President, Trades Union Congress 1995-96; Chair: Women's National Commission 2002-07, Women and Work Commission 2004-06. Member, Unite (T&G) 1977-.

Political career: *House of Lords:* Raised to the peerage as Baroness Prosser, of Battersea in the London Borough of Wandsworth 2004. Member, Information 2005-09; Co-opted member, EU Sub-committee G (Social Policy and Consumer Affairs) 2009-10; Member EU Sub-committees: G (Social Policies and Consumer Protection) 2010-12, A (Economic and Financial Affairs) 2012-13; Member: Soft Power and the UK's Influence 2013-14, Joint Committee on Human Rights 2015-. *Other:* National treasurer, Labour Party 1996-2001. *Councils and public bodies:* Member: Equal Opportunities Commission 1985-92, Low Pay Commission 2000-05; Deputy chair, Equality and Human Rights Commission 2006-12.

Political interests: World of work, equalities, equal pay; Middle East, USA.

Other: Fellow, Royal Society of Arts 1996-; Director, Trade Union Fund Managers 1998-; Non-executive director, Royal Mail Holdings 2004-10; Industry and Parliament Trust: Trustee 2012-16, Deputy Chair, board of trustees 2016-; Trustee: Involvement and Participation Association 2013-. Two honorary doctorates from London universities. OBE 1997.

Recreations: Walking, cooking.

The Baroness Prosser OBE, House of Lords, London SW1A 0PW
Tel: 020 7219 4694 *Fax:* 020 7219 0699 *Email:* prosserm@parliament.uk

LIBERAL DEMOCRAT

PURVIS OF TWEED, LORD

Liberal Democrat Lords Spokesperson for International Trade

PURVIS OF TWEED (Life Baron), Jeremy Purvis; cr 2013. Born 15 January 1974; Son of George Purvis, ambulance technician, and Eileen Purvis.

Education: Berwick-upon-Tweed High School; Brunel University (BSc politics and modern history 1996).

Non-political career: Research assistant to Sir David Steel MP, House of Commons 1993; Parliamentary assistant: Liberal International 1994, ELDR Group, European Parliament 1995; Personal assistant to Sir David Steel MP (later Lord Steel of Aikwood) 1996-98; Director: GJW Scotland 1998-2001, McEwan Purvis 2001-03; Policy and strategy adviser to Willie Rennie as Leader, Scottish Liberal Democrat; Leader, Devo Plus Group 2011-13; Director, Keep Scotland Beautiful 2012.

Political career: *House of Lords:* Raised to the peerage as Baron Purvis of Tweed, of East March in the Scottish Borders 2013. Liberal Democrat: Principal Spokesperson for Energy and Climate Change 2015, Shadow Minister/Lords Spokesperson for International Trade 2016-. Member, International Relations 2016-. *Other:* Scottish Parliament: MSP for Tweeddale, Ettrick and Lauderdale constituency 2003-11: Scottish Liberal Democrat Spokesperson for: Finance 2003-05, Justice 2005-07; Member, Scottish Parliament Arts Advisory Group 2007-11; Scottish Liberal Democrat: Shadow Cabinet Secretary for Education and Lifelong Learning 2007-08, Shadow Minister for Children and Early Years 2007-08, Spokesperson on Economy and Finance 2008-11, Contested Midlothian South, Tweeddale and Lauderdale constituency 2011 election.

Political interests: Economy and enterprise, Europe and foreign affairs, youth policies, rural development, design and architecture, Scottish affairs, democratic governance, constitutional reform.

Other: Member, Executive Committees: Commonwealth Parliamentary Association United Kingdom 2015-17, Inter-Parliamentary Union 2016-; Member, Amnesty International; Selkirk Merchant Company; Member, Scottish Parliament Commission on Parliamentary Reform 2016-.

Recreations: Classic cars, reading, painting.

The Lord Purvis of Tweed, House of Lords, London SW1A 0PW
Tel: 020 7219 5353
Website: www.jeremypurvis.org

LABOUR

PUTTNAM, LORD

PUTTNAM (Life Baron), David Terence Puttnam; cr. 1997. Born 25 February 1941; Son of late Leonard and Marie Puttnam; Married Patricia Jones 1961 (1 son 1 daughter).

Education: Minchenden Grammar School, London; City and Guilds 1958-62.

Non-political career: Advertising 1958-68; Film production 1968-98; Producer of films including: *Stardust*, 1974, *Bugsy Malone*, 1976 (four BAFTA Awards), *Midnight Express*, 1978 (two Academy Awards, three BAFTA Awards), *Chariots of Fire*, 1981 (four Academy Awards, three BAFTA Awards including awards for best film), *Local Hero*, 1982 (two BAFTA Awards); *The Killing Fields*, 1984 (three Academy Awards, seven nominations: eight BAFTA Awards including Best Film); *The Mission*, 1986 (Palme D'Or, Cannes, one Academy Award, seven nominations; three BAFTA Awards); *Memphis Belle*, 1990, as well as many others; Chair, Enigma Productions Ltd 1978-; Director: National Film Finance Corporation 1980-85, Anglia Television Group 1982-99; Visiting Professor, Bristol University 1984-96; Chair and chief executive officer, Columbia Pictures 1986-88; Village Roadshow plc 1988-98; Adviser, Department for Children, Schools and Families 1997-2005; Visiting lecturer, London School of Economics 1997-2002; Non-executive chair, Spectrum Strategy Consultants 1999-2006; Deputy chair, Channel 4 2006-12; Chair, Futurelab 2005-11; Non-executive director, Huntsworth plc 2007-12; Deputy chair, Profero 2010-14; Senior non-executive director, Promethean World 2006-15; Hon. Fellow of the Institute of Education, University of London 2007; Chairman, Atticus Education 2012-; Director, EMPGI Ireland. Hon. Member, BECTU.

Political career: *House of Lords:* Raised to the peerage as Baron Puttnam, of Queensgate in the Royal Borough of Kensington and Chelsea 1997. Trade envoy to: Vietnam, Laos and Cambodia 2012-17, Burma 2012-16. Chair, Draft Communications Bill Joint Committee 2002; Member, Information 2005-09; Chair, Draft Climate Change Bill Joint Committee 2007; Member, Artificial Intelligence 2017-. *Other:* Digital Champion, Republic of Ireland 2012-. *Councils and public bodies:* Chair, Film, Television and Video Advisory Committee, British Council 1992-2001; Member:

House of Lords
Peers' Biographies

British Screen Advisory Council 1988-98, Arts Council Lottery Panel 1995-98; Member, Education Standards Task Force 1997-2001; Chair: British Council Arts Advisory Committee 2001-03, Hansard Commission "Parliament in the Public Eye" 2004-05.

Political interests: Education, culture, environment; Ireland, USA.

Other: Fellow, World Economic Forum, Davos, Switzerland; President, Unicef UK 2002-09; National Film and Television School: Governor 1974-87, Chair 1987-96, Life President 2017; Chair, Producers and Directors Section ACTT 1975-77; Council for the Protection of Rural England: President 1986-92, Vice-President 1997-2007; Trustee: Sundance Institute 1985-90, Tate Gallery 1985-92; Governor, American Film Institute 1986-88; Trustee: National Aids Trust 1988-, Landscape Foundation; Chair, National Memorial Arboretum Trustees 1993-2003, Vice-President, BAFTA 1993-2002; Chair, National Museum of Photography, Film and Television 1994-2003; Trustee, Science Museum 1996-2004; Member, Court of Governors: London School of Economics 1997-2002, London Institute 1997-2002; Vice-President, Royal Geographical Society 1997-99; Trustee and fellow, World Economic Forum 1997-2008; Member: Academic Board, Bristol University, Arts and Humanities Research Board, UK-China Forum 1998-2002; Chair: Teaching Awards Trust 1998-2008, National Endowment for Science, Technology and Arts 1998-2003, General Teaching Council 1998-2001, BAFTA Trustees 2002-04; Trustee: Institute for Public Policy Reform, Thomson Foundation 2003-14; Chair, Sage Gateshead (North Music Trust) 2007-13; President, Film Distributors Association 2007-; Trustee: Eden Project 2009-13, Transformation Trust 2009-11, Baker Dearing Educational Trust 2010-13; Non-executive adviser, TSL Advisory Board 2010-; Chair, A Future for Public Service Television Inquiry 2015-16; Patron, Dublin Bid World Summit on Media for Children 2020/2023; FRGS; FRSA; FRPS; FCGI; BAFTA; National Film & Television School; Sam Spiegal Film School; Fellow: The British Film Institute, Royal Television Society; Unicef. Freedom, City of Sunderland 2007. Chancellor: Sunderland University 1998-2007, Open University 2006-14. Over 50 honorary degrees, diplomas and fellowships in UK and overseas. Ten Academy awards, 25 BAFTA awards and Ten Golden Globes, and numerous other awards, including: BAFTA Michael Balcon Award for outstanding contribution to British Film Industry 1982, RSA Benjamin Franklin Award 1996, World Economic Forum Crystal Award 1997, Honorary BECTU 1998, President's Medal, Royal Photographic Society 2003, BAFTA Fellowship 2006, RSA Bicentenary Medal 2007, New Media Consortium Fellows Award (USA) 2012. CBE 1983; Chevalier de l'Ordre des Arts et des Lettres (France) 1985; Officier de l'Ordre des Arts et des Lettres (France) 1992; Kt 1995; Commander de l'Ordre des Arts et des Lettres (France) 2006; *Clubs:* Chelsea Arts, Athenæum Club. Trustee, Sunderland AFC Foundation; MCC.

Publications: Contributor, The Third Age of Broadcasting (1982); Co-author, Rural England (1988); A Submission to the EC Think Tank on Audio-Visual Policy (1994); The Creative Imagination in 'What Needs to Change' (1996); The Undeclared War (1997); Movies and Money (1998); Members Only? Parliament in the Public Eye: Report of the Hansard Society Commission on the Communication of Parliamentary Democracy (Hansard Society, 2005); Parliament in the Public Eye 2006: Coming into Focus? (Hansard Society, 2006).

Recreations: Reading, cinema, landscape gardening.

The Lord Puttnam CBE, House of Lords, London SW1A 0PW
Tel: 020 7219 6822 *Fax:* 020 7219 5794 *Email:* puttnamd@parliament.uk
Website: www.davidputtnam.com *Twitter:* @Dputtnam

LABOUR

QUIN, BARONESS

QUIN (Life Baroness), Joyce Gwendolen Quin; cr. 2006. Born 26 November 1944; Daughter of late Basil Godfrey Quin, schoolmaster, and late Ida Quin, neé Ritson, teacher; Married (Francis) Guy MacMullen 2010.

Education: Whitley Bay Grammar School; Newcastle University (BA French 1967); London School of Economics (MSc international relations 1969); French, some Italian, German and Spanish.

Non-political career: Research officer, International Department, Labour Party HQ 1969-72; Lecturer in French, Bath University 1972-76; Tutor and lecturer in French and politics, Durham University 1976-79. Member, TGWU/Unite.

Political career: *House of Commons:* MP (Labour) for Gateshead East 1987-97, for Gateshead East and Washington West 1997-2005. Opposition Spokesperson for: Trade and Industry 1989-92, Employment 1992-93, Foreign and Commonwealth Affairs 1993-97; Minister of State: Home Office 1997-98, Foreign and Commonwealth Office 1998-99; Minister of State and Deputy Minister, Ministry of Agriculture, Fisheries and Food 1999-2001. Member, Joint Committee on House of Lords Reform 2003-05. Chair, PLP Regional Government Group 2001-05. *House of Lords:* Raised to the peerage as Baroness Quin, of Gateshead in the County of Tyne and Wear 2006.

Opposition Spokesperson for Environment, Food and Rural Affairs 2010-11. Member: Constitution 2007-10, EU Sub-committee C (External Affairs) 2013-14, European Union 2013-15; EU Justice, Institutions and Consumer Protection Sub-committee: Member 2014, Chair 2014-15; Member, Communications 2016-. *Other:* European Parliament: MEP for Tyne and Wear 1979-89. *Councils and public bodies:* Member, Review Committee of Privy Counsellors of Anti-terrorism, Crime and Security Act 2002-05.

Political interests: European affairs, industrial policy, regional policy; Europe (including Eastern Europe).

Other: Chair, Franco-British Council 2008-; President, Northumberland Pipers Society 2009-. Hon. Freedom, Borough of Gateshead 2006. Hon. Fellow: Sunderland Polytechnic 1986, St Mary's College, Durham University 1996. PC 1998; Officier de la Légion d'Honneur (France) 2010.

Publications: Author, The British Constitution – Continuity and Change (Northern Writers, 2010).

Recreations: North East local history, walking, music, reading, cycling, playing Northumbrian pipes.

Rt Hon the Baroness Quin, House of Lords, London SW1A 0PW
Tel: 020 7219 4009 *Email:* quinjg@parliament.uk

QUIRK, LORD

CROSSBENCH

QUIRK (Life Baron), Charles Randolph Quirk; cr. 1994. Born 12 July 1920; Son of late Thomas and Amy Randolph Quirk; Married Jean Williams 1946 (2 sons) (divorced 1979, died 1995); married Gabriele Stein 1984.

Education: Douglas High School, Isle of Man; University College, London (BA English 1947, MA; PhD; DLitt); Yale University, USA (Post-Doctoral Studies 1951-52).

Non-political career: Served RAF 1940-45. Lecturer in English, University College, London 1947-54; Commonwealth Fund Fellow, Yale University and University of Michigan 1951-52; Durham University: Reader in English language and literature 1954-58, Professor 1958-60; Professor, London University 1960-68; Quain Professor of English language and literature, University College, London 1968-81; President: Institute of Linguistics 1982-86, Royal College of Speech and Language Therapists 1987-91.

Political career: *House of Lords:* Raised to the peerage as Baron Quirk, of Bloomsbury in the London Borough of Camden 1994. Member: Science and Technology 1998-2003, Science and Technology Sub-committees: II (Science and Society) 1999-2000, I (Complementary and Alternative Medicine) 2000-01, I (Systematic Biology and Biodiversity) 2002, Hybrid Instruments 2005-17. *Councils and public bodies:* Chair, Committee of Enquiry in Speech Therapy Services 1969-72; Member of Senate, London University 1970-85; Governor, British Institute of Recorded Sound 1975-80; Member, BBC Archives Committee 1975-81; Board member, British Council 1983-91; Chair: Anglo-Spanish Foundation 1983-85, British Library Advisory Committee 1984-97; Member, RADA Council 1985-2004; President, British Academy 1985-89; Academic Governor, Richmond American University 1985-2006; Trustee: City Technology Colleges 1986-98, Wolfson Foundation 1987-2013; Royal Commissioner, 1851 Exhibition 1987-95; President, North of England Educational Conference 1989.

Political interests: Education, public communication, health, speech pathology, broadcasting, media.

Other: Member: Linguistic Society of America, Modern Language Association, Philological Society; FBA 1975; Academia Europaea; American Academy of Arts and Science; Royal Swedish Academy; Royal Belgian Academy of Science; Finnish Academy of Science. Vice-Chancellor, London University 1981-85. Hon LLD, DLitt, DSc from universities in the UK, USA and Europe. Jubilee Medal, Institute of Linguistics 1973. CBE 1975; Kt 1985; *Clubs:* Athenæum Club.

Publications: Co-author of several works on English, notably A Comprehensive Grammar of the English Language (1985); The Concessive Relation in Old English Poetry (1954); Essays on the English Language – Medieval and Modern (1968); The English Language and Images of Matter (1972); The Linguist and the English Language (1974); Style and Communication in the English Language (1984); Words at Work – Lectures on Textual Structures (1986); Grammatical and Lexical Variance in English (1995); Has contributed to conference proceedings and learned journals.

Professor the Lord Quirk CBE, House of Lords, London SW1A 0PW
Tel: 020 7219 2226 *Fax:* 020 7219 5979
University College London, Gower Street, London WC1E 6BT

LABOUR

RADICE, LORD

RADICE (Life Baron), Giles Heneage Radice; cr. 2001. Born 4 October 1936; Married Lisanne Koch 1971.

Education: Winchester College; Magdalen College, Oxford (BA history 1960); French.

Non-political career: Head of research department, General and Municipal Workers Union 1966-73. Member, GMB.

Political career: *House of Commons:* Contested Chippenham 1964 and 1966 general elections. MP (Labour) for Chester-le-Street 1 March 1973 by-election to 1983, for Durham North 1983-2001. PPS to Shirley Williams as Secretary of State for Education and Science 1978-79; Opposition Frontbench Spokesperson for: Foreign Affairs 1981, Employment 1982-83, Education 1983-87; Member, Shadow Cabinet 1983-87. Chair: Public Service 1996-97, Treasury 1997-2001. *House of Lords:* Raised to the peerage as Baron Radice, of Chester-le-Street in the County of Durham 2001. Member, European Union 2003-06; Chair, EU Sub-committee A (Economic and Financial Affairs, Trade and External Relations/Economic and Financial Affairs) 2003-06; Member EU Sub-committee C: (Foreign Affairs, Defence and Development Policy) 2010-12, (External Affairs) 2012-15.

Political interests: Economic and European affairs, Labour Party policy revision, foreign policy; France, Germany, India, Italy, Poland, Sweden.

Other: Chair: European Movement 1995-2001, Franco British Council 2002-07; Chair: British Association for Central and Eastern Europe 1997-2008, Policy Network 2007-09. Parliamentary Fellow, St Anthony's College Oxford 1994-95. Order of Merit (Germany) 1995, Légion d'Honneur (France) 2005. PC 1999.

Publications: Democratic Socialism (1965); Co-editor, More Power to People (1968); Co-author, Will Thorne (1974); The Industrial Democrats (1978); Co-author, Socialists in the Recession: a Survey of European Socialism (1986); Labour's Path to Power: the New Revisionism (1989); Offshore – Britain and the European Idea (1992); The New Germans (1995); Editor, What Needs to Change (1996); Friends and Rivals (2002); Diaries 1980-2001 (2004); The Tortoise and the Hares (2008); Trio: Blair, Brown and Mandelson (2010); Odd Couples (2015).

Recreations: Reading, tennis, gardening.

Rt Hon the Lord Radice, House of Lords, London SW1A 0PW
Tel: 020 7219 4194
Email: gh@radice.plus.com

LABOUR

RAMSAY OF CARTVALE, BARONESS

RAMSAY OF CARTVALE (Life Baroness), Meta Ramsay; cr. 1996. Born 12 July 1936; Daughter of Alexander Ramsay and Sheila, née Jackson.

Education: Hutchesons' Girls' Grammar School, Glasgow; Glasgow University (MA 1958; MEd 1961); Graduate Institute for International Affairs, Geneva 1967-68.

Non-political career: HM Diplomatic Service 1969-91: Stockholm embassy 1970-73, Helsinki embassy 1981-85, Counsellor, FCO London 1986-91; Foreign policy adviser to John Smith as Leader of the Labour Party 1992-94; Special adviser to John Cunningham as Shadow Secretary of State for Trade and Industry 1994-95. Member, GMB.

Political career: *House of Lords:* Raised to the peerage as Baroness Ramsay of Cartvale, of Langside in the City of Glasgow 1996. Government Spokesperson for: Culture, Media and Sport 1997-98, Health 1997-98, Scotland 1997-2001; Government Whip December 1997-2001; Member, Intelligence and Security Committee 1997, 2001-06; Government Spokesperson for Foreign Affairs and Europe 1998-2001; Deputy Speaker 2002-08. Member, Joint Committee on National Security Strategy 2010-14. *Other:* Member: Co-operative Party, Labour Finance and Industry Group, Labour Movement in Europe; Labour Friends of Israel. *Councils and public bodies:* Member, Lewisham Community Health Council 1992-94.

Political interests: Foreign affairs, defence, intelligence, women's affairs, Scotland; Finland, Israel, Sweden.

Other: Member, UK delegation to: Parliamentary Assembly of Organisation for Security and Co-operation in Europe 1997, NATO Parliamentary Assembly 2003-; Trustee, Smith Institute 1996-2008; Chair, Atlantic Council of the United Kingdom 1997, 2001-10; Member: Fabian Society, RIIA, Institute for Jewish Policy Research, 300 Group; Chair: Wyndham Deedes Trust, Kenneth

Lindsay Trust; FRSA; Blind Veterans UK. Three honorary doctorates: Bradford University 1997, Glasgow University 2004, Stirling University 2009. Commander of the Order of the White Rose of Finland 2002; *Clubs:* University Women's Club, Reform Club.

Recreations: Theatre, opera, ballet.

The Baroness Ramsay of Cartvale, House of Lords, London SW1A 0PW
Tel: 020 7219 3145 *Fax:* 020 7219 5979 *Email:* ramsaym@parliament.uk

CROSSBENCH

RAMSBOTHAM, LORD

RAMSBOTHAM (Life Baron), David John Ramsbotham; cr 2005. Born 6 November 1934; Son of late Rev John Alexander Ramsbotham, Bishop of Wakefield, and Eirian Morgan-Owen; Married Susan Dickinson 1958 (2 sons).

Education: Haileybury College, Hertford; Corpus Christi College, Cambridge (BA history 1957, MA 1971).

Non-political career: Army national service 1952-54; Rifle Brigade, UK and Germany 1957-62; Seconded to King's African Rifles 1962-63; Staff College 1964; Service in Far East 1965; 7 Armoured Brigade 1966-68; Royal Green Jackets, Germany 1968-71; Military assistant to Chief of the General Staff 1971-73; Commanding officer 2 Royal Green Jackets 1974-76; Commander, 39 Infantry Brigade 1978-80; Royal College of Defence Studies 1981; Director of Public Relations (Army) 1982-84; 4 Armoured Division, Germany 1976-78; Commander: 3 Armoured Division 1984-87, UK Field Army and Inspector General Territorial Army 1987-90; Adjutant General 1990-93; ADC General to HM the Queen 1990-93. Director of International Affairs, DSL Ltd 1994-99.

Political career: *House of Lords:* Raised to the peerage as Baron Ramsbotham, of Kensington in the Royal Borough of Kensington and Chelsea 2005. Member: Regulators 2006-07, Soft Power and the UK's Influence 2013-14, Joint Committee on National Security Strategy 2014-. *Councils and public bodies:* Chair, Hillingdon Hospital NHS Trust 1994-95; Chief Inspector of Prisons for England and Wales 1995-2001.

Political interests: Penal reform, youth justice, education and employment, UN peace keeping and reform, mental health particularly in prisons, post-conflict reconstruction, including demining.

Other: Advisory Board, Youth at Risk 1999-; Vice-chair: Prisoners Education Trust 2001-, President, UNLOCK (National Association of Ex-Prisoners) 2004-; Vice-chair, NAOPV (National Association of Official Prison Visitors) 2005-; Chair, Criminal Justice and Acquired Brain Injury Interest Group 2010-; Vice President, Centre for Mental Health 2010-; President, Institute of Food, Brain and Behaviour 2015-; Fellow: City and Guilds Institute 2001, Royal Society of Arts 2001, Royal College of Speech and Language Therapists 2013. Honorary Liveryman: Worshipful Company of Weavers 2008-, The Skinners' Company 2008-. Seven honorary doctorates; Honorary bencher, Grey's Inn 2001; Honorary fellow, Corpus Christi Cambridge 2001. OBE 1971; CBE 1980; KCB 1987; GCB 1993; *Clubs:* MCC, Beefsteak Club.

Publications: Prisongate (2003).

Recreations: Sailing, walking, arts, art history.

General the Lord Ramsbotham GCB CBE, House of Lords, London SW1A 0PW
Tel: 020 7219 8752 *Email:* ramsbothamd@parliament.uk

CONSERVATIVE

RANA, LORD

RANA (Life Baron), Diljit Singh Rana; cr. 2004. Born 20 September 1938; Son of Paras Ram Rana; Married Uma Kumari Passi 1966 (died 2002) (2 sons); married Shruti 2009 (divorced).

Education: AS High School, Khanna, Punjab, India; Punjab University (BA economics 1958); Hindi, Punjabi, Urdu.

Non-political career: Café and restaurant owner; Property developer, hotel owner, Belfast; Founder, Andras House Ltd office, hotel and retail property management company 1981; Founder and chair, Indian Business Forum 1985; President: Belfast Chamber of Trade 1991-92, Northern Ireland Chamber of Commerce 2004-06; Founder: Cordia Technologies Software Development, Europe India Chamber of Commerce; Indian Community Centre.

Political career: *House of Lords:* Raised to the peerage as Baron Rana, of Malone in the County of Antrim 2004.

Political interests: International development, global living wage, education, poverty alleviation, rural development, healthcare, human rights, non-violence, peaceful resolution of problems; India, Ireland, Mauritius, Namibia, Taiwan.

Other: Member, Confederation of British Industry; Northern Ireland Chamber of Commerce; Founder, Rana Charitable Trust 1996; Chair, Thanksgiving Square 2002-; JD Memorial Trust, India 2005-; President, Global Organisation for People of Indian Origin 2009-; Shardhanjali Trust, India; Member, Institute of Directors. Three honorary doctorates: Ulster University 1999, Queen's University, Belfast 2003, Bengal Engineering and Science University 2009. MBE 1996; Honorary Consul of India in Northern Ireland 2004; Non-resident Indian of the Year Award 2005; Samman Bharat Divas Award 2007; Honorary Consul of Namibia in Northern Ireland 2012.

Recreations: Community activities, charitable work, travel.

The Lord Rana MBE, House of Lords, London SW1A 0PW
Tel: 020 7219 3295 *Email:* ranad@parliament.uk
Andras House, 60 Great Victoria Street, Belfast BT2 7BB *Tel:* 028 9087 8787
Email: mail@andrashouse.co.uk
Website: www.diljitrana.com *Twitter:* @LordRana1

LIBERAL DEMOCRAT

RANDERSON, BARONESS

Liberal Democrat Shadow Secretary of State for Transport

RANDERSON (Life Baroness), Jennifer Elizabeth Randerson; cr 2011. Born 26 May 1948; Married Dr Peter Randerson 1970 (1 son 1 daughter).

Education: Wimbledon High School, London; Bedford College, London University (BA history 1969); London University Institute of Education (PGCE 1970); French, Welsh learner.

Non-political career: History, economics and politics teacher: Sydenham High School 1970-72, Spalding High School 1972-74, Llanishen High School, Cardiff 1974-76; Coleg Glan Hafren, Cardiff: Business studies lecturer 1976-, Manager 1994-99. Former branch chair and member, Association for College Management.

Political career: *House of Commons:* Contested (Liberal/All) Cardiff South and Penarth 1987 and (Liberal Democrat) Cardiff Central 1992 and 1997 general elections. *House of Lords:* Raised to the peerage as Baroness Randerson, of Roath Park in the City of Cardiff 2011. Parliamentary Under-Secretary of State and Government Spokesperson, Wales Office 2012-15; Government Spokesperson for Northern Ireland 2012-15; Liberal Democrat: Principal Spokesperson for Wales 2015, Spokesperson/Shadow Secretary of State for Transport 2015-. Member, EU Internal Market Sub-Committee 2015-. Chair, Liberal Democrat Parliamentary Party Committee on Wales 2011-12. *Other:* National Assembly for Wales: AM for Cardiff Central constituency 1999-2011: Welsh Liberal Democrat: Whip 1999-2000, Spokesperson for Education (under-16) 1999-2000, Minister for Culture, Sports and Welsh Language 2000-03, Acting Deputy First Minister 2001-02, Welsh Liberal Democrat: Spokesperson for: Economic Development, Finance and Transport 2003-05, Health and Finance/Health, Finance and Equal Opportunities 2005-07, Finance, Health and Well-being 2007-08, Shadow Minister for: Enterprise, Transport and Education 2008-09, Economy, Transport and Education 2009-10, Economy and Education 2010-11, Shadow Minister for Transport 2011. Former member: Welsh Campaigns and Candidates Committee, Federal Executive, Federal Policy Committee, Welsh Policy Committee; Contested Welsh Liberal Democrats leadership election 2008. *Councils and public bodies:* Cardiff City Council: Councillor 1983-2000, Opposition Leader 1995-99; JP (Supplemental list).

Political interests: Education, culture, the arts, local government, health, equal opportunities; Australia, Canada, Europe, France.

Other: Member: Friends of Synfonia Cymru, Friends of Nant Fawr, Institute of Welsh Affairs; Patron: Cardiff and Vale of Glamorgan Youth Wind Band 2010-, African Mothers' Foundation 2011-, Wales Council for Deaf People 2011-; Governor, Cardiff Metropolitan University 2011-12, 2015-17; RNID, British Deaf Association, Alzheimers Society, Mencap, Kidney Wales Foundation, The Living Room. Pro-Chancellor, Cardiff University 2017-. Honorary Fellowship, Cardiff University 2011; *Clubs:* National Liberal Club.

Recreations: Travel, concert and theatre going, walking, gardening.

The Baroness Randerson, House of Lords, London SW1A 0PW
Tel: 020 7219 2538 *Email:* randersonj@parliament.uk *Twitter:* @jennyranderson

CONSERVATIVE

RAWLINGS, BARONESS

RAWLINGS (Life Baroness), Patricia Elizabeth Rawlings; cr. 1994. Born 27 January 1939; Daughter of late Louis Rawlings and Mary Rawlings, née Boas de Winter; Married Sir David Wolfson 1962, now Lord Wolfson of Sunningdale (divorced 1967).

Education: Le Manoir, Lausanne, Switzerland; Oak Hall, Haslemere, Surrey; Florence University; University College, London (BA English 1979); London School of Economics (Postgraduate Diploma international relations 1983).

Non-political career: LEC Childrens Care Committee 1959-61; Nurse, Westminster Hospital; Director: California Dress Company 1969-82, Rheims and Laurent, French Fine Art Auctioneers 1969-71, Nigel Greenwood Inc 1969-86; Member: Peace through NATO Council 1985-88, British Video Classification Council 1986-89; Special adviser to Sir David Trippier as Minister for Inner Cities, Department of the Environment 1987-88; Board member, British Association for Central and Eastern Europe 1994-2008.

Political career: *House of Commons:* Contested (Conservative) Sheffield Central 1983 and Doncaster Central 1987 general elections. *House of Lords:* Raised to the peerage as Baroness Rawlings, of Burnham Westgate in the County of Norfolk 1994. Opposition Whip 1997-98; Opposition Spokesperson for: Culture, Media and Sport 1997-98, Foreign and Commonwealth Affairs December 1998-2010, International Development December 1998-2010; Government Whip (Baroness in Waiting) 2010-12; Government Spokesperson for: Scotland 2010-12, Culture, Olympics, Media and Sport (Arts, Culture, and Media) 2010-12, Attorney General's Office 2010-12, Advocate General for Scotland 2010-12. Member: House of Lords Offices Sub-committee (Advisory Panel on Works of Art) 2000-02, Information 2013-14, Works of Art 2014-16, Built Environment 2015-16, Lord Speaker's Advisory Panel on Works of Art 2017-. *Other:* European Parliament: MEP for Essex South West 1989-94, Contested Essex West and Hertfordshire East 1994 election. *Councils and public bodies:* Extra Baroness in Waiting, Lord Chamberlain's Office 2012-.

Political interests: International affairs, culture, heritage, media; Brazil, Bulgaria, Oman, Russia.

Other: British Red Cross Society: Member 1964-, Chair, London Branch, Hon. Vice-President 1988-; Director, English Chamber Orchestra and Music Society 1980-2001; Governor, American University in Bulgaria 1991-; Member, British Council 1997-; Council member, NACF; Member: European Academy of Sciences and Arts, Advisory Council, The Prince's Youth Business Trust; Chair of Council, King's College, London 1998-2007; Trustee, Chevening Estate 2002-; Patron, Afghan Mother and Child Health Care 2002; President: British Freight Forwarders Association, NCVO 2002-07, British Antique Dealers Association 2005-12; Chairman of Governors, English College in Prague 2008-16; President, Friends of BADA 2008-. Hon. DLitt, Buckingham University; Fellow: King's College, London, University College, London. National Badge of Honour, British Red Cross 1987. Order of the Rose (Silver) (Bulgaria) 1991; Grand Official, Order of the Southern Cross (Brazil) 1997; Hon Plaquette National Assembly of Republic of Bulgaria 2007. Royal West Norfolk Golf.

Recreations: Music, art, architecture, gardening, travel, golf.

The Baroness Rawlings, House of Lords, London SW1A 0PW
Tel: 020 7219 0664 *Email:* rawlingspe@parliament.uk

LIBERAL DEMOCRAT

RAZZALL, LORD

RAZZALL (Life Baron), Edward Timothy (Tim) Razzall; cr. 1997. Born 12 June 1943; Son of Leonard Razzall and Muriel Razzall; Married Deirdre Bourke 1982 (divorced 2003) (1 son 1 daughter from previous marriage); partner Baroness Bonham-Carter of Yarnbury (qv).

Education: St Paul's School, London; Open Scholar Worcester College, Oxford (BA jurisprudence 1965).

Non-political career: Teaching associate, North Western University, Chicago, USA 1965-66; Frere Cholmeley Bischoff, solicitors 1966-96: Partner 1973-96; Director, Cala plc 1973-99; Chair, Abaco Investments plc 1974-90; Partner, Argonaut Associates 1995-; Director, Erinaceous Group plc 2002-09; Chair, Boxhill Technologies plc 2010-; Director, Just Loans plc 2013-.

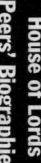

Political career: *House of Lords:* Raised to the peerage as Baron Razzall, of Mortlake in the London Borough of Richmond 1997. Liberal Democrat Spokesperson for: Trade and Industry/Business, Enterprise and Regulatory Reform 1998-2010, Civil Service and Public Sector Reform 2015-16, Manufacturing 2016-. Member: Joint Committee on Consolidation, Etc, Bills 1998-2005, 2006-, Delegated Powers and Regulatory Reform 2007-10, Communications 2010-15. Chair, Liberal Democrat Parliamentary Party Committee on: Business, Innovation and Skills 2010-14, Treasury 2014-15. *Other:* Treasurer, Liberal Party 1986-87; Liberal Democrats: Treasurer 1987-2000,

Member, Federal Executive Committee 1987-2010, Chair: General Election Campaign 1999-2006, Campaigns and Communications Committee 2000-06, Member, Campaigns and Communications Committee 2006-; President, Association of Liberal Democrat Councillors 1990-95. *Councils and public bodies:* London Borough of Richmond: Councillor 1974-98, Deputy Leader 1983-96.

Countries of interest: Greenland, Iceland, Sub-Saharan Africa.

Other: European Lawyer of the Year 1992. CBE 1993; *Clubs:* National Liberal, MCC, Soho House Club.

Publications: Chance Encounters: Tales from a Varied Life (autobiography) (Biteback Publishing, 2014).

Recreations: All sports.

The Lord Razzall CBE, House of Lords, London SW1A 0PW
Tel: 020 7219 5888

REA, LORD

LABOUR

REA (3rd Baron, UK), John Nicolas Rea; cr. 1937; 3rd Bt of Eskdale (UK) 1935. Born 6 June 1928; Son of late Hon. James Rea and Betty Rea, née Bevan; Married Elizabeth Robinson 1951 (divorced 1991) (4 sons); partner Jane Conniff (1 daughter); partner Katya Benjamin (1 daughter); married Judith Powell 1991.

Education: Dartington Hall School; Belmont Hill School, Massachusetts, USA; Dauntsey's School; Christ's College, Cambridge (MA natural sciences; MB, BChir 1954; MD 1969); University College Hospital, London (DObst, DCH, DPH 1956-65); Primitive French and Spanish.

Non-political career: Acting Sergeant, Suffolk Regiment, National Service 1946-48. Junior hospital posts 1954-57; Research fellow in paediatrics in Ibadan and Lagos, Nigeria 1962-65; Lecturer in social medicine, St Thomas' Hospital Medical School, London 1966-68; General practitioner, North London 1957-62, 1968-93. Member, Unite.

Political career: *House of Lords:* First entered House of Lords 1982; Deputy Opposition Spokesperson for Health and International Development 1992-97; Elected hereditary peer 1999-. Member: Science and Technology 1987-88, 1997-2002, Science and Technology Sub-committees: Non Food Crops/NHS Research and Development/Antibiotic Resistance/Medicinal Use of Cannabis 1997-2003, I (Complementary and Alternative Medicine) 2000, IIA (Human Genetic Databases) 2000-02, I (Systematic Biology and Biodiversity/Fighting Infection) 2002-03, I (Allergy) 2007, HIV and AIDS in the UK 2010-11. Vice-chair PLP Departmental Committee for International Development 2006-10.

Political interests: Health, food and nutrition, international development, human rights; Sub-saharan Africa, Latin America, Russia (Chechnya), Turkey (Kurdish question).

Other: Member: Inter-Parliamentary Union 1985-, Commonwealth Parliamentary Association 1985-; National Health Forum/UK Health Forum: Trustee 1986-, President 2015-; Chair, Healthlink Worldwide 1992-97; Member: Mary Ward Centre, Mother and Child Foundation, Caroline Walker Trust; Member, British Medical Association; FRCGP; FRSA; Oxfam, War on Want, VSO, World Development Movement. Honorary Degree, London Metropolitan University (formerly University of North London) 2002; *Clubs:* Royal Society of Medicine Club.

Publications: Papers on epidemiology, medical education etc in various medical journals 1970-97.

Recreations: Music (bassoon), gardening, photography.

The Lord Rea, House of Lords, London SW1A 0PW
Tel: 020 7219 5353 *Fax:* 020 7219 5969 *Email:* reajn@parliament.uk

REBUCK, BARONESS

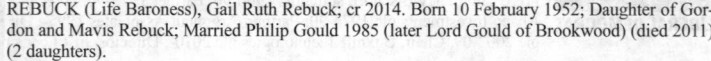

LABOUR

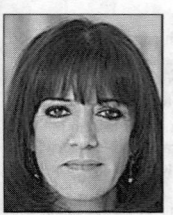

REBUCK (Life Baroness), Gail Ruth Rebuck; cr 2014. Born 10 February 1952; Daughter of Gordon and Mavis Rebuck; Married Philip Gould 1985 (later Lord Gould of Brookwood) (died 2011) (2 daughters).

Education: Sussex University (BA); Wharton Business School (Diploma); French, Spanish.

Non-political career: Production assistant, Grisewood & Dempsey 1975-76; Robert Nicholson Publications 1976-78: Editor, Publisher; Publisher, Hamlyn Paperbacks 1978-82; Publishing director, Century Publishing 1982-85; Publisher, Century Hutchinson 1985-89; Chair, Random Century 1989-91; Chair and Chief executive, Random House UK/Random House Group Ltd 1991-2013; Director, Penguin Random House 2013-.

Political career: *House of Lords:* Raised to the peerage as Baroness Rebuck, of Bloomsbury in the London Borough of Camden 2014.

Other: Member, Creative Industries Taskforce 1997-2000; Co-founder, World Book Day 1998; Royal College of Art: Trustee 1999-2014, Chair 2015-; Non-executive director: Work Foundation 2001-08, BskyB 2002-12; Chair, Quick Reads Charity 2006-; National Literacy Trust: Trustee 2007-14, Patron 2014-; Chair, Cheltenham Literature Festival 2013-17; Non-executive Director: Koovs plc 2014-, Belmond Ltd 2015-, The Guardian Media Group 2016-; Hon. Fellow, London Business School. Hon. doctorate: Sussex University, Essex University, Oxford Brookes University. CBE 2000; DBE 2009.

The Baroness Rebuck DBE, House of Lords, London SW1A 0PW
Tel: 020 7219 5353 *Email:* rebuckg@parliament.uk
Penguin Random House, 20 Vauxhall Bridge Road, London SW1V 2SA *Tel:* 020 7840 8877
Email: grebuck@penguinrandomhouse.co.uk *Twitter:* @gailrebuck

LIBERAL DEMOCRAT

REDESDALE, LORD

REDESDALE (6th Baron, UK), Rupert Bertram Mitford; cr. 1902; (Life) Baron Mitford 2000. Born 18 July 1967; Son of 5th Baron; Married Helen Shipsey 1998 (2 sons 2 daughters).

Education: Highgate School, London; Newcastle University (BA archaeology 1989).

Non-political career: Chairman: Anaerobic Digestion and Biogas Association 2009-, Carbon Management Association 2012-, Energy Managers Association 2012-.

Political career: *House of Lords:* Created a life peer as Baron Mitford, of Redesdale in the County of Northumberland 2000. First entered House of Lords 1991; Liberal Democrat Spokesperson for: Overseas Development 1994-99, Northern Ireland 1999, Tourism 2000, International Development 2000-01, Defence 2001-05, Energy 2005-09, Agriculture 2006-09; Contested Lord Speaker elections 2006, 2011.

Political interests: Environment, archaeology; Qatar.

Other: York Archaelogical Trust; Council member, Institute of Advanced Motorists 1994-2010; Fellow, Society of Antiquaries; Kids Kabin, Rainbow Trust.

Recreations: Caving, climbing, skiing.

The Lord Redesdale, House of Lords, London SW1A 0PW
Tel: 020 7219 4342 *Email:* redesdaler@parliament.uk

CONSERVATIVE

REDFERN, BARONESS

REDFERN (Life Baroness), Elizabeth Marie Redfern; cr 2015. Born 25 September 1947; Married Gordon 1974 (died 2009) (2 daughters).

Languages: French.

Non-political career: Former director, chemical and machinery company; Owner of a seed merchant business.

Political career: *House of Lords:* Raised to the peerage as Baroness Redfern, of the Isle of Axholme in the County of Lincolnshire 2015. Member: Long-Term Sustainability of the NHS 2016-17, Citizenship and Civic Engagement 2017-. *Other:* Chair, Brigg and Goole Conservative Association 1997-2002. *Councils and public bodies:* Member, Belton Parish Council 1987-2016; Councillor, Boothferry Borough Council 1992-96; North Lincolnshire Council: Councillor 1995-, Conservative group: Deputy Leader 1995-2006, Leader 2006-17, Deputy Council Leader 2003-06, Cabinet Member for: Adult Social Care 2003-07, Regeneration 2011-15, Devolution 2015-; Council Leader 2006-07, 2011-17; Member, Epworth Town Council 2007-16.

Other: Director: Humberside International Airport Board 2011-17, Greater Lincolnshire Local Enterprise Partnership 2011-17, Humber University Technology Ltd 2011-17; Chair, Humber Bridge Board 2012-14; Director, Rail North Limited 2013-17; Committee member, Epworth and District Agricultural Society. Chancellor, North Lincolnshire Children's University 2016-.

Recreations: Walking dogs, keen gardener, travel, theatre.

The Baroness Redfern, House of Lords, London SW1A 0PW
Tel: 020 7219 3000
c/o North Lincolnshire Council, Civic Centre, Ashby Road, Scunthorpe DN16 1AB
Tel: 01724 297556 *Email:* cllr.lizredfern@northlincs.gov.uk

CROSSBENCH

REES OF LUDLOW, LORD

REES OF LUDLOW (Life Baron), Martin John Rees; cr 2005. Born 23 June 1942; Son of late Reginald Jackson Rees and Joan Rees, née Bett; Married Professor Caroline Humphrey (later Dame) 1986.

Education: Shrewsbury School; Trinity College, Cambridge (BA mathematics 1963; PhD 1967).

Non-political career: Research associate, California Institute of Technology, USA 1967-68, 1971; Member, Institute for Advanced Study Princeton University, USA 1969-70; Professor, Sussex University 1972-73; Cambridge University: Professor of astronomy and experimental philosophy 1973-91, Professor of cosmology and astrophysics 2002-09, Master, Trinity College 2004-12; Royal Society: Research professor 1992-2003, President 2005-10; Astronomer Royal 1995-; Visiting professor, Leicester University and Imperial College, London 2000-.

Political career: *House of Lords:* Raised to the peerage as Baron Rees of Ludlow, of Ludlow in the County of Shropshire 2005. Member: Science and Technology 2010-15, Science and Technology Sub-committee I 2012-13, EU Internal Market Sub-committee 2015-.

Political interests: Science and technology, education, developing world, energy.

Other: Trustee: British Museum 1994-2000, Institute for Advanced Studies 1996-; Kennedy Memorial Trust 1999-2004; IPPR 2000-09; National Museum of Science and Industry 2002-; Gates Trust 2005-; Royal Institution 2008-09; FRS, Hon FBA Hon FAcad Med Sci; Hon FREng; Hon Fellow: Learned Society of Wales, City and Guilds, Four Cambridge University Colleges. Numerous honorary doctorates and fellowships; Hon. Member: US National Academy of Science, Russian Academy of Science, American Philosophical Society, Pontifical Academy of Science and other foreign academies. Numerous UK and international awards; Templeton Prize 2011. FRS 1979; Officer Order des Artes et lettres (France) 1991; Kt 1992; OM 2007; Order of the Rising Sun – Gold and Silver Star 2015 (Japan); *Clubs:* Athenæum Club; Oxford and Cambridge Club Hon, Walbrook Club.

Publications: Scientific and general articles, plus seven books.

Recreations: Writing, music, rural pursuits.

Professor the Lord Rees of Ludlow OM, House of Lords, London SW1A 0PW
Tel: 020 7219 5353
Trinity College, Cambridge CB2 1TQ *Tel:* 01223 338412/01223 369043 *Fax:* 01223 337520
Email: mjr36@cam.ac.uk

LABOUR

REID OF CARDOWAN, LORD

REID OF CARDOWAN (Life Baron), John Reid; cr 2010. Born 8 May 1947; Son of late Thomas Reid, postman, and late Mary Reid, factory worker; Married Cathie McGowan 1969 (died 1998) (2 sons); married Carine Adler 2002.

Education: St Patrick's Senior Secondary School, Coatbridge; Stirling University (MA history 1978; PhD economic history 1987); French.

Non-political career: Fellow, Armed Forces Parliamentary Scheme 1990-. Insurance clerk late 1960s; Scottish research officer, Labour Party 1979-83; Adviser to Neil Kinnock MP as Leader of Labour Party 1983-85; Scottish organiser, Trade Unionists for Labour 1985-87; Hon Professor, University College London; Director, John Reid Advisory Ltd. Member, TGWU.

Political career: *House of Commons:* MP (Labour) for Motherwell North 1987-97, for Hamilton North and Bellshill 1997-2005, for Airdrie and Shotts 2005-10. Deputy Opposition Spokesperson for: Children 1989-90, Defence, Disarmament and Arms Control 1990-97; Shadow Deputy Secretary of State for Defence 1995-97; Minister of State (Minister for the Armed Forces), Ministry of Defence 1997-98; Minister of State (Minister for Transport), Department of the Environment, Transport and the Regions 1998-99; Secretary of State for: Scotland 1999-2001, Northern Ireland 2001-02; Minister without Portfolio and Party Chair 2002-03; Leader of the House of Commons and President of the Council 2003; Secretary of State for: Health 2003-05, Defence 2005-06, the Home Department (Home Secretary) 2006-07. Chair, Modernisation of the House of Commons 2003. *House of Lords:* Raised to the peerage as Baron Reid of Cardowan, of Stepps in Lanarkshire 2010. Member, International Relations 2016-. *Other:* Member, Labour Party National Executive Committee 2002-03.

Political interests: Security, foreign affairs, defence, cyber.

Other: Chair, Institute for Security and Resilience Studies/Institute for Strategy, Resilience and Security, University College, London; Chair, advisory board, Shearwater Group plc. Hon doctorate, Stirling University 2009. Best Scot at Westminster 2001; Peace Person of the Year (Northern Ireland) 2002; Minister to Watch, *Spectator* 2005; Politician of the Year, *Spectator* 2006. PC 1998.

Publications: Co-author, Cyber Doctrine: Towards a framework for learning resilience (2011).

Recreations: Football, crosswords.

Rt Hon the Lord Reid of Cardowan, House of Lords, London SW1A 0PW
Tel: 020 7219 8537 *Email:* reidja@parliament.uk

CONSERVATIVE

RENFREW OF KAIMSTHORN, LORD

RENFREW OF KAIMSTHORN (Life Baron), Andrew Colin Renfrew; cr. 1991. Born 25 July 1937; Son of late Archibald and Helena Renfrew; Married Jane Margaret Ewbank 1965 (2 sons 1 daughter).

Education: St Albans School; St John's College, Cambridge (Exhibitioner, BA archaeology and anthropology 1962, MA; PhD 1965, ScD 1976); British School of Archaeology, Athens; French, Greek.

Non-political career: RAF national service 1956-58 . Sheffield University 1965-72: Lecturer in prehistory and archaeology 1965-70, Senior lecturer 1970-72, Reader 1972; Visiting lecturer, University of California 1967; Professor of archaeology, Southampton University 1972-81; Cambridge University: Disney Professor of Archaeology 1981-2004, Research director, McDonald Institute for Archaeological Research 2013; St John's College, Cambridge: Professional fellow 1981-86, Hon. fellow 2004-; Jesus College, Cambridge: Master 1986-97, Fellow 1986-2004, Honorary fellow 2004-, Emeritus fellow 2004-; Has lectured on archaeology in numerous British and American universities; Has excavated in Greece and the United Kingdom.

Political career: *House of Commons:* Contested (Conservative) Sheffield Brightside 1968 by-election. *House of Lords:* Raised to the peerage as Baron Renfrew of Kaimsthorn, of Hurlet in the District of Renfrew 1991. Chair, Library and Computing Sub-committee 1995-2003; Member: House 2003-07, Science and Technology 2017-. *Councils and public bodies:* Chair, Hampshire Archaeological Committee 1974-81; Member: Ancient Monuments Board for England 1974-84, Royal Commission for Historical Monuments (England) 1977-87; Vice-president, Royal Archaeological Institute 1982-85; Member: Historical Buildings and Monuments Commission for England 1984-86, Ancient Monuments Advisory Committee 1984-2001, UK National Commission for UNESCO 1984-86; Trustee, British Museum 1991-2000; Board member, Parliamentary Office of Science and Technology (POST) 1997-98; Member, executive committee, National Art Collections Fund Committee 2001-10.

Political interests: National heritage, arts, museums and galleries, education, foreign affairs; France, Greece, USA.

Other: Foreign associate, US National Academy of Sciences 1997; Corresponding Member: Austrian Academy of Sciences 2000, German Archaeological Institute 2004; Foreign member, Russian Academy of Sciences 2006; Trustee: Society of Antiquaries of London -2017, Antiquity Trust -2017; FSA; Hon FSA (Scotland); FBA 1980; Hon FRSE 2001. Freedom, City of London. Seven honorary doctorates. Huxley Memorial Medal 1991; Fyssen Prize 1996; European Science Foundation Latsis Prize 2003; Balzan Foundation Prize 2004; *Clubs:* Athenæum, United Oxford and Cambridge University Club.

Publications: The Emergence of Civilisation (1972); Editor The Explanation of Culture Change (1973); Before Civilisation (1973); Editor British Prehistory, a New Outline (1974); Investigations in Orkney (1979); Problems in European Prehistory (1979); An Island Polity (1982); Approaches to Social Archaeology (1984); The Prehistory of Orkney (1985); The Archaeology of Cult (1985); Archaeology and Language (1987); The Cycladic Spirit (1991); Loot, Legitimacy and Ownership: the Ethical Crisis in Archaeology (2000); Figuring It Out (2003); Prehistory, the Making of the Human Mind (2008); Collaboration with other authors on archaeological subjects, as well as contributions to archaeological journals.

Recreations: Contemporary art.

Professor the Lord Renfrew of Kaimsthorn, House of Lords, London SW1A 0PW
Tel: 020 7219 5353
McDonald Institute for Archaeological Research, Downing Street, Cambridge CB2 3ER
Tel: 01223 333521 *Fax:* 01223 333536 *Email:* acr10@cam.ac.uk

LIBERAL DEMOCRAT

RENNARD, LORD

RENNARD (Life Baron), Christopher John Rennard; cr. 1999. Born 8 July 1960; Son of late Cecil and Jean Rennard; Married Ann McTegart 1989.

Education: Liverpool Blue Coat School; Liverpool University (BA politics and economics 1982).

Non-political career: Liberal Party: Agent, Liverpool 1982-84, Regional Agent, East Midlands 1984-88; Social and Liberal Democrats Election Co-ordinator 1988-89; Liberal Democrats: Director of Campaigns and Elections 1989-2003, Chief Executive 2003-09; Consultant on management, campaigning, communications and fundraising 2009-; Director of Communications, British Healthcare Trades Association 2011-.

Political career: *House of Lords:* Raised to the peerage as Baron Rennard, of Wavertree in the County of Merseyside 1999. Liberal Democrat Spokesperson for: Communities and Local Government 2009-10, Constitutional Affairs 2009-10. Member: Information 2009-14, Constitution

2011-12, Political Polling and Digital Media 2017-. *Other:* Liberal Democrats: Overall responsibility for election campaigns 1989-2009, Member, Lords teams on: Constitutional and Political Reform, Health, Whip withdrawn March 2013-August 2014.

Political interests: Health, disability, public health, diabetes, constitutional and political reform, international democracy building, human rights.

Other: Member: Inter-Parliamentary Union, Commonwealth Parliamentary Association; Former Vice-President, Liberal International; Former Council Member, European Liberal Democrat and Reform Group; Chair: Commission on the Big Society (Association of Chief Executives of Voluntary Organisations) 2010-11, Primary Care Diabetes Society Commission on 'Keeping patients with diabetes out of hospital' 2011; Director and Trustee, Action on Smoking and Health 2011-14; Vice-president, Local Government Association 2011-13; Member and former Council Member, Electoral Reform Society. MBE 1989.

Recreations: Cooking, wine, France.

The Lord Rennard MBE, House of Lords, London SW1A 0PW
Tel: 020 7219 6717 *Fax:* 020 7219 2458 *Email:* rennardc@parliament.uk *Twitter:* @LordRennard

RENWICK OF CLIFTON, LORD

CROSSBENCH

RENWICK OF CLIFTON (Life Baron), Robin William Renwick; cr. 1997. Born 13 December 1937; Son of the late Richard and Clarice Renwick; Married Annie (1 son 1 daughter).

Education: St Paul's School, London; Jesus College, Cambridge (MA history 1962); University of Paris (Sorbonne); French.

Non-political career: Army national service 1956-58. Entered Foreign Service 1963; Dakar 1963-64; FO 1964-66; New Delhi 1966-70; Private Secretary to Minister of State, FCO 1970-72; First Secretary, Paris 1972-76; Counsellor, Cabinet Office 1976-78; Rhodesia Department, FCO 1978-80; Political Adviser to Governor of Rhodesia 1980; Head of Chancery, Washington 1981-84; Assistant Under-Secretary of State, FCO 1984-87; Ambassador to: South Africa 1987-91, USA 1991-95; Deputy Chair, Robert Fleming Holdings 1995-2000; Director: Compagnie Financiere Richemont AG 1995-, British Airways plc 1996-2005; Chair, Fluor Ltd 1996-2011; Director: Fluor Corporation 1997-2008, BHP Billiton plc 1997-2005, SAB Miller plc 1999-2008, Harmony Gold 1999-2004; Deputy Chair, Fleming Family and Partners 2000-15; Vice-chair, Investment Banking, JP Morgan Europe, JP Morgan Cazenove 2000-14; Director: Kazakhmys plc 2005-15, Gem Diamonds Ltd 2007-09, Bumi plc 2011-13; Senior Adviser: JP Morgan Europe 2014-16, Appian Capital; Director, Stonehage Fleming 2015-.

Political career: *House of Lords:* Raised to the peerage as Baron Renwick of Clifton, of Chelsea in the Royal Borough of Kensington and Chelsea 1997.

Political interests: Defence, foreign affairs; France, South Africa, USA.

Other: Trustee: The Economist 1996-2010, The Hakluyt Foundation 2000-07; FRSA. Visiting Fellow, Center for International Affairs, Harvard University 1980-81; Hon. DLitt, University of the Witwatersrand, South Africa 1990; Hon. Fellow, Jesus College 1992; Hon. DLitt: College of William and Mary, USA 1993, Oglethorpe University 1995. CMG 1980; KCMG 1988; *Clubs:* Brooks's Club. Queen's; Hurlingham.

Publications: Economic Sanctions (1981); Fighting with Allies (1996); Unconventional Diplomacy (1997); A Journey with Margaret Thatcher (2013); Helen Suzman (2014); Ready for Hillary? (2014); The End of Apartheid: Portrait of a Revolution (2015).

Recreations: Tennis, fly-fishing.

The Lord Renwick of Clifton KCMG, House of Lords, London SW1A 0PW
Tel: 020 7219 5353 *Email:* robin.renwick@parliament.uk
9 South Street, London W1K 2XA *Tel:* 020 7907 8500

RIBEIRO, LORD

CONSERVATIVE

RIBEIRO (Life Baron), Bernard Francisco Ribeiro; cr 2010. Born 20 January 1944; Son of late Miguel and Matilda Ribeiro; Married Elisabeth Orr 1968 (1 son 3 daughters including twins).

Education: Dean Close School, Cheltenham; Middlesex Hospital Medical School, London University (MBBS, LRCP 1967).

Non-political career: Drum Major, Combined Cadet Force 1958-62. Registrar, then Senior Registrar, Middlesex Hospital 1972-78; Lecturer in Urology, Ghana Medical School, Accra 1974; Consultant General Surgeon, Basildon University Hospital 1979-2008; Surgical Adviser to Expert Advisory Group on Aids (EAGA) and UK Advisory Panel for health care workers infected with blood-borne viruses (UKAP), Department of Health 1994-2003; President, Royal College of Surgeons of England 2005-08; Visiting Professor, University of North Carolina at Chapel Hill, USA 2006-07.

Political career: *House of Lords:* Raised to the peerage as Baron Ribeiro, of Achimota in the Republic of Ghana and of Ovington in the County of Hampshire 2010. Member: Refreshment 2015-16, EU Home Affairs Sub-committee 2015-, Long-Term Sustainability of the NHS 2016-17. *Other:* Member, Executive Committee, Association of Conservative Peers. *Councils and public bodies:* Member, Board of Visitors, HM Prison Chelmsford 1982-92; Council Member, Dean Close School, Cheltenham 2006-; President, Dean Close School Council 2016-; Chair, Independent Reconfiguration Panel 2012-.

Political interests: Health, education, prison reform; Africa (Ghana), USA.

Other: Royal College of Surgeons: Member 1967-, Fellow 1972-, Council member 1998-2008, Member, court of examiners 1998-2004, Chairman, Quality Assurance and Inspection 2000-05, Senior vice-president 2004-05, Chair, Honours Committee 2005-13, President 2005-08; Court of Patrons 2011-; Association of Surgeons of Great Britain and Ireland: Honorary secretary 1991-96, President 1999-2000, Chair, Distinction Awards Committee 2000-04; Consultant to advisory board, Health Policy Research Institute, American College of Surgeons 2000-10; Medical vice-chair, East of England Advisory Committee on Clinical Excellence Awards 2002-05; Member, Test and Itchen Association; Chair: Research Review Panel, Pelican Foundation 2009-, CORESS (Confidential Reporting System in Surgery) 2012-, Independent Reconfiguration Panel 2012-; Member: Royal Society of Medicine, British Medical Association; Honorary Fellow, American Association of Surgeons 2013-; Achimota Trust in London 2010-, Operation Hernia 2011-, Partnership in Health Information, Old Deacanians Society 2014-. Hon. Liveryman, Worshipful Company of Cutlers 2008-; Worshipful Company of Barbers: Middle Warden 2011-12, Upper Warden 2012-13, Master 2013-14, Deputy Master 2014-15. Freedom, City of London 1991. Fellow ad hominem, Royal College of Surgeons, Edinburgh 2000; Hon. Fellow, Ghana College of Physicians and Surgeons 2006; Fellow: Royal College of Physicians 2006, Academy of Medicine of Malaysia 2006; Hon. Fellow, Caribbean College of Surgeons 2007; Hon. Member, Académie Chirurgie de Paris 2008; Hon. Fellow: Royal College of Surgeons in Ireland 2008, Royal College of Physicians and Surgeons of Glasgow 2008, American College of Surgeons 2008; Fellow, College of Anaesthetists 2008; Hon. DSc, Anglia Ruskin University 2008; Hon. DEng, Bath University 2012. Charles Saint Medal, South Africa 2007; Arthur Li Oration, Hong Kong 2007. CBE 2004; Officer, Order of the Volta 2008; Kt 2009; *Clubs:* Surgical Sixty Club. Flyfishers' Club.

Publications: Chapters in surgical textbooks; Papers on rectal cancer and biliary manometry; Contributions to Royal College of Surgeons bulletins.

Recreations: Fishing, shooting, history of warfare.

The Lord Ribeiro CBE, House of Lords, London SW1A 0PW
Tel: 020 7219 4819 *Email:* ribeirob@parliament.uk

RICHARD, LORD

LABOUR

RICHARD (Life Baron), Ivor Seward Richard; cr. 1990. Born 30 May 1932; Son of Seward Thomas Richard; Married Geraldine Moore 1956 (divorced 1962) (1 son); married Alison Imrie 1962 (divorced) (1 son 1 daughter); married Janet Jones 1989 (1 son).

Education: St Michael's School, Bryn, Llanelly; Cheltenham College; Pembroke College, Oxford (Wightwick Scholar, BA jurisprudence 1953).

Non-political career: Called to the Bar, Inner Temple 1955; Bencher 1985; Practised in London 1955-74; QC 1971; UK Permanent Representative to UN 1974-79; EEC Commissioner 1981-85; Chair: World Trade Centre (Wales) Ltd 1985-97, World Trade Centre (London) Ltd 2010-17.

Political career: *House of Commons:* Contested South Kensington 1959 general election. MP (Labour) for Barons Court 1964-74. PPS to Denis Healey as Secretary of State for Defence 1966-67; Parliamentary Under-Secretary of State (Army), Ministry of Defence 1969-70; Opposition Spokesperson for Broadcasting, Posts and Telecommunications 1970-71; Deputy Spokesperson for Foreign Affairs 1971-74. *House of Lords:* Raised to the peerage as Baron Richard, of Ammanford in the County of Dyfed 1990. Opposition Spokesperson for: Home Office Affairs 1990-92, the Civil Service 1992-97, European Affairs 1992-97, the Treasury and Economic Affairs 1992-93; Leader of the Opposition 1992-97; Lord Privy Seal and Leader of the House of Lords 1997-98; Contested Lord Speaker election 2006. Chair, Constitutional Reform Bill 2004; Member: Liaison 2006-09, European Union 2008-13, EU Sub-committee F (Home Affairs) 2008-12; Chair: Barnett Formula 2008-09, Joint Committee on the Draft House of Lords Reform Bill 2011-12; Member: EU Sub-committee F (Home Affairs, Health and Education) 2012-13, Inquiries Act 2005 2013-14, EU Justice, Institutions and Consumer Protection Sub-committee 2014-15, EU Justice Sub-committee 2015-17, Trade Union and Party Funding 2016. *Councils and public bodies:* Chair, Commission on the Powers and Electoral Management of the NAW 2002-04.

Other: Hon. Fellow, Pembroke College, Oxford 1981. PC 1993.

Publications: Co-author, Europe or the Open Sea (1971); We, the British (1983); Co-author, Unfinished Business – the Reform of the House of Lords (1999); As well as articles in political journals.

Recreations: Music, talking.

Rt Hon the Lord Richard QC, House of Lords, London SW1A 0PW
Tel: 020 7219 1495/020 7219 6158 *Email:* richardi@parliament.uk

RICHARDS OF HERSTMONCEUX, LORD

CROSSBENCH

RICHARDS OF HERSTMONCEUX (Life Baron), David Julian Richards; cr 2014. Born 4 March 1952; Son of Colonel Jim and Pamela Richards; Married Caroline 1978 (2 daughters).

Education: Eastbourne College; University College, Cardiff (international relations 1974).

Non-political career: Commissioned into Royal Artillery 1971; Parachute and Commando trained; Chief of Staff, Berlin Infantry Brigade; Commanding Officer 3rd Regiment RHA; Instructor, Staff College, Camberley; Colonel, Army Plans, Ministry of Defence 1994-96; Commanding Officer 3rd Regiment RHA; Chief Joint Force Operations, Permanent Joint Headquarters 1998-2001; Chief of Staff, Allied Rapid Reaction Corps 2001-02; Assistant Chief of the General Staff 2002-05; Commander: Allied Rapid Reaction Corps 2005-06, International Stabilisation and Assistance Force Afghanistan 2006-07; Commander-in-Chief of UK Land Forces 2008-09; Chief of the General Staff 2009-10; Member, Defence Council 2009-13; Chief of the Defence Staff 2010-13; Senior adviser, International Institute for Strategic Studies 2013-; Executive Chairman, Equilibrium Global 2013-; Non-executive Chairman, Arturius International 2014-; Director, Palliser Associates Ltd; Visiting professor, Exeter University 2013-.

Political career: *House of Lords:* Raised to the peerage as Baron Richards of Herstmonceux, of Emsworth in the County of Hampshire 2014. *Councils and public bodies:* DL, Hampshire 2014.

Political interests: Defence, foreign policy; Middle East and Gulf, SW Asia, SE Asia, Africa.

Other: Deputy Grand President, Royal Commonwealth Ex-Services League; Member, European Leadership Foundation; Governor, Ditchley Foundation; Chair, Gurkha Welfare Trust 2007-11; Deputy grand president, Royal Commonwealth Ex-Services League 2013-; Vice-president, Blind Veterans UK 2014-; Member: European Leaders Network (ELN) 2014-, Advisory Panel, Homes for Heroes 2016-; President, Military Historical Society 2014-; Armed Forces Muslim Association, Lt Dougie Dalzell Memorial Trust, Afghan Appeal Fund, Sierra Leone Blind Schools Association, Combined Operations Pilotage Parties Trust, Garrison Military Re-enactment Group, Military Historical Society, Plant For Peace, Care After Combat, James Myatt Trust, Combined Services Polo Association, Speakers For Schools, Tickets 4 Troops, Forces Trust, Row2Recovery, L'Orchestre du Monde, Toe In The Water, London Taxi Benevolent Association for War Disabled. Freedom, City of London 2012. Fellow: Cardiff University 2013, Kings College London 2015. Annual Churchillian Award for Leadership, Churchillian Society of the UK 2011; Tufts University Boston Global Citizenship Award 2016. CBE 2000; DSO 2001; KCB 2007; GCB 2011; *Clubs:* Army and Navy, Cavalry and Guards Club. Royal Cruising Club; Royal Artillery Yacht Club; British Kiel Yacht Club; Royal Yacht Squadron.

Publications: Contributor: Oxford Handbook of Modern War (2012), Blair's Wars (2013); Taking Command (autobiography, 2014); Victory Among People (2011).

Recreations: Sailing, riding, military history.

General the Lord Richards of Herstmonceux GCB CBE DSO, House of Lords, London SW1A 0PW
Tel: 020 7219 5353 *Email:* richardsd@parliament.uk

RICHARDSON OF CALOW, BARONESS

CROSSBENCH

RICHARDSON OF CALOW (Life Baroness), Kathleen Margaret Richardson; cr. 1998. Born 24 February 1938; Daughter of Francis and Margaret Fountain; Married Ian Richardson 1964 (3 daughters).

Education: St Helena School, Chesterfield; Stockwell College (Teaching Certificate 1958); Wesley Deaconess College 1961-63; Wesley House, Cambridge (theological education 1977-79).

Non-political career: First Woman President of the Methodist Conference 1992-93; Moderator, Free Churches Council 1995-99; President, Churches Together In England 1995-99.

Political career: *House of Lords:* Raised to the peerage as Baroness Richardson of Calow, of Calow in the County of Derbyshire 1998. *Councils and public bodies:* Moderator of Churches Commission for Inter-faith Relations 2000-06.

Political interests: Church affairs, inter-faith relations.

Other: Chair: London Ecumenical Aids Trust 2000-11, British and Foreign Schools Society 2004-10; President, Christian Education 2004-10; Chair, Board of Management for Methodist Schools and Colleges 2004-11; Vice-President, Council of Christians and Jews; Ambassador, Action for Children; Langley House, Walsingham Homes, Methodist Homes. Three honorary doctorates. OBE 1994.

Recreations: Reading, needlework.

Rev the Baroness Richardson of Calow OBE, House of Lords, London SW1A 0PW
Tel: 020 7219 0314 *Email:* richardsonk@parliament.uk

RICKETTS, LORD

CROSSBENCH

RICKETTS (Life Baron), Peter Forbes Ricketts; cr 2016. Born 30 September 1952; Married Suzanne Julia Horlington 1980 (1 daughter 1 son).

Education: Bishop Vesey's Grammar School, Sutton Coldfield; Pembroke College, Oxford (MA).

Non-political career: HM Diplomatic Service 1974-2016: UK Mission to United Nations, New York 1974, Foreign and Commonwealth Office, London (FCO) 1975-76, Third Secretary, Singapore High Commission 1976-78, UK Delegation to North Atlantic Treaty Organisation (NATO) 1978-81, FCO 1981-85: Second Secretary, Near East and North African Department 1981-83, Assistant Private Secretary to Geoffrey Howe as Foreign Secretary 1983-85; First Secretary, Washington DC embassy 1986-89, FCO 1989-94: Deputy Head, Security Policy Department 1989-91, Head, Hong Kong Department 1991-94, Counsellor, Finance and Economic, Paris embassy 1994-97, FCO 1997-2003: Deputy Political Director 1997-99, Director, International Security 1999-2000, Chair, Joint Intelligence Committee, Cabinet Office (seconded to) 2000-01, Director-General, Political 2001-03, UK Permanent Representative to NATO 2003-06, Permanent Secretary and Head of the Diplomatic Service, FCO 2006-10, Prime Minister's National Security Adviser 2010-12, Ambassador to France 2012-16; Non-executive director, Engie Paris 2016-; Strategic adviser, Lockheed Martin 2016-.

Political career: *House of Lords:* Raised to the peerage as Baron Ricketts, of Shortlands in the County of Kent 2016.

Other: Visiting Professor, King's College London 2016-; Trustee: Royal Academy Development Fund 2016-, Leighton House Museum 2016-; Chair, Normandy Memorial Trust 2017-. Honorary Doctorate: Bath University, Kent University, London University. CMG 1999; KCMG 2003; GCMG 2011; GCVO 2014.

Recreations: Victorian art and literature, restoring Normandy farmhouse.

The Lord Ricketts GCMG GCVO, House of Lords, London SW1A 0PW
Tel: 020 7219 3000 *Twitter:* @LordRickettsP

RIDLEY, VISCOUNT

CONSERVATIVE

RIDLEY, (5th Viscount, UK) Matthew White Ridley; cr 1900; Baron Wensleydale; 9th Bt of Blagdon (GB) 1756. Born 7 February 1958; Son of 4th Viscount and Lady Anne Lumley; Married Anya Hurlbert 1989 (1 son 1 daughter).

Education: Eton College; Magdalen College, Oxford (BA zoology 1979; DPhil zoology 1983).

Non-political career: *The Economist* 1983-92: Science editor 1983-87, Washington correspondent 1987-90, American editor 1990-92; Columnist, *Daily Telegraph* and *Sunday Telegraph* 1993-2000; Northern Rock: Director 1994-2007, Non-executive chairman 2004-07; Director, Northern Investors 1994-2007; Founding chairman, International Centre for Life 1996-2003; Chairman, Northern 2 VCT 1999-2008; PA Holdings Ltd 1999-2008; Columnist: *Wall Street Journal*, *The Times*.

Political career: *House of Lords:* Elected hereditary peer 2013-. Member: Science and Technology 2014-17, Artificial Intelligence 2017-. *Other:* Vice-President, Conservatives for Britain 2015-16. *Councils and public bodies:* DL, Northumberland.

Other: Fellow: Royal Society of Literature, Academy of Medical Sciences; Foreign honorary member, American Academy of Arts and Sciences. Hon. DCL: Buckingham University 2003, Newcastle University 2007; Hon. DSc, Cold Spring Harbor Laboratory 2006.

Publications: Warts and All: The Men Who Would be Bush (Viking, 1989); The Red Queen: The Sex and the Evolution of Human Nature (Prentice Hall & IBD, 1994); The Origins of Virtue (Viking, 1996); Genome: The Auto-biography of a Species in 23 Chapters (Fourth Estate, 1999);

Nature via Nurture: Genes, Experience and What Makes us Human (Fourth Estate, 2003); Francis Crick: Discoverer of the Genetic Code (Harper Press, 2006); The Rational Optimist: How Prosperity Evolves (Fourth Estate, 2010); The Evolution of Everything (Fourth Estate, 2015).

The Viscount Ridley, House of Lords, London SW1A 0PW
Tel: 020 7219 5353 *Email:* ridleywm@parliament.uk
Blagdon Estate Office, Seaton Burn, Newcastle NE13 6DD *Tel:* 01670 789325
Website: www.mattridley.co.uk *Twitter:* @mattwridley

CONSERVATIVE

RISBY, LORD

RISBY (Life Baron), Richard John Grenville Spring; cr 2010. Born 24 September 1946; Son of late H J A Spring and late Marjorie Watson-Morris; Married Hon Jane Henniker-Major 1979 (divorced 1993) (1 son 1 daughter).

Education: Rondebosch, Cape Town, South Africa; University of Cape Town; Magdalene College, Cambridge (BA economics, MA); French.

Non-political career: Merrill Lynch Ltd 1971-86: Vice-President 1976-86; Deputy managing director, Hutton International Associates 1986-88; Executive director, Shearson Lehman Hutton 1988-90; Managing director, Xerox Furman Selz 1990-92.

Political career: *House of Commons:* Contested Ashton-Under-Lyne 1983 general election. MP (Conservative) for Bury St Edmunds 1992-97, for West Suffolk 1997-2010. PPS to: Sir Patrick Mayhew as Secretary of State for Northern Ireland 1994-95, Tim Eggar as Minister for Trade and Industry 1995-96, Nicholas Soames and James Arbuthnot as Ministers of State, Ministry of Defence 1996-97; Opposition Spokesperson for: Culture, Media and Sport November 1997-2000, Foreign Affairs 2000-04; Shadow Minister for the Treasury 2004-05. Member: Northern Ireland Affairs 1995-97, Health 1995-96, Deregulation 1997, Home Affairs 2006-07. *House of Lords:* Raised to the peerage as Baron Risby, of Haverhill in the County of Suffolk 2010. Trade envoy to Algeria 2012-. Member, EU External Affairs Sub-Committee 2015-. *Other:* Various offices in Westminster Conservative Association 1976-87, including CPC Chair 1990; Vice-chair: Conservative Industrial Fund 1993-96, Conservative Party (Business) 2005-10. *Councils and public bodies:* Member, Horserace Betting Levy Board 2016-.

Political interests: Treasury, small business, foreign affairs; China, Europe, Middle East, Pacific Rim, South Africa, USA.

Other: Deputy chair, Small Business Bureau 1992-; Fellow, Industry and Parliament Trust 1994; Governor, Westminster Foundation for Democracy 2001-10; Director, British Syria Society 2005-11; Chair, British-Ukrainian Society 2007-; President, Association for Decentralised Energy 2012; Patron: *London Magazine* 2013, Open Road 2013; *Clubs:* Boodle's Club.

Recreations: Country pursuits, tennis, swimming.

The Lord Risby, House of Lords, London SW1A 0PW
Tel: 020 7219 8996 *Email:* risbyr@parliament.uk

CONSERVATIVE

ROBATHAN, LORD

ROBATHAN (Life Baron), Andrew Robert George Robathan; cr 2015. Born 17 July 1951; Son of late Douglas Robathan and Sheena Robathan, née Gimson; Married Rachael Maunder 1991 (1 son 1 daughter).

Education: Merchant Taylors' School, Northwood; Oriel College, Oxford (BA modern history 1973, MA); RMA, Sandhurst; Army Staff College (psc 1984); French, German (colloquial).

Non-political career: Regular Army officer, Coldstream Guards and SAS 1974-89; Rejoined Army for Gulf War January-April 1991. BP 1991-92.

Political career: *House of Commons:* MP (Conservative) for Blaby 1992-2010, for South Leicestershire 2010-15. PPS to Iain Sproat as Minister of State, Department of National Heritage 1995-97; Shadow Minister for: Trade and Industry 2002-03, International Development 2003, Defence 2004-05; Opposition Deputy Chief Whip 2005-10; Ministry of Defence: Parliamentary Under-Secretary of State (Defence Personnel, Welfare and Veterans) 2010-12, Minister of State for the: Armed Forces 2012-13, Northern Ireland Office 2013-14. Member: International Development 1997-2002, 2003-04, Administration 2005-07, Selection 2006-10, Armed Forces Bill 2011, Joint Committee on Statutory Instruments 2014-15. Chair, Conservative Parliamentary Committee on Defence 1994-95; Vice-chair: Conservative Parliamentary Committee on Northern Ireland 1994-2002, Conservative Defence/Foreign Affairs Policy Committee 2001-02; Member, Executive, 1922 Committee 2001-02, 2003-04. *House of Lords:* Raised to the peerage as Baron Robathan, of Poultney in the County of Leicestershire 2015. Member, Trade Union and Party Funding 2016. *Councils and public bodies:* Councillor, London Borough of Hammersmith and Fulham 1990-92.

Political interests: International development, environment, transport, defence, Northern Ireland; Africa, Indian Sub-Continent, Middle East.

Other: Chairman, Halo Trust 2003-06. Freeman, Merchant Taylors' Company. Freedom, City of London. PC 2010; *Clubs:* Special Forces Club, Pratts Club.

Recreations: Mountain walking, skiing, wildlife, shooting.

Rt Hon the Lord Robathan, House of Lords, London SW1A 0PW
Tel: 020 7219 3550 *Email:* robathana@parliament.uk

ROBERTS OF LLANDUDNO, LORD

LIBERAL DEMOCRAT

ROBERTS OF LLANDUDNO (Life Baron), John Roger Roberts; cr. 2004. Born 23 October 1935; Son of Thomas Charles and Alice Ellen Roberts; Married Eirlys Ann 1962 (died 1995) (2 daughters 1 son).

Education: John Bright Grammar School, Llandudno; University College of North Wales (BA history, biblical history 1957); Handsworth Methodist College; Welsh.

Non-political career: Methodist Church 1959-: Superintendent minister: Llangollen 1965-70, Llandudno 1983-2002; Minister, Toronto Welsh Church 2003-04; Part-time lecturer, Llandrillo College.

Political career: *House of Commons:* Contested Conwy (Liberal) 1979, (Liberal/All) 1983, 1987, (Liberal Democrat) 1992 and 1997 general elections. *House of Lords:* Raised to the peerage as Baron Roberts of Llandudno, of Llandudno in the County of Gwynedd 2004. Liberal Democrat: Spokesperson for: International Development 2004-10, Wales 2004-10, Whip 2005-10. Member, Works of Art 2010-11, 2012-13, 2014-15. *Other:* Contested Wales 1999 European Parliament election. Chair, Union of University Liberal Societies 1956-57; Former President: Welsh Liberal Party, Welsh Liberal Democrats; Deputy President, Liberal Democrats. *Councils and public bodies:* Group leader, Aberconwy Borough Council 1976-87; Former Vice-President, Local Government Association.

Political interests: Human rights, international affairs, Welsh affairs, child welfare, asylum seekers, migrant workers; Canada, Israel, Poland, Uganda.

Other: President, Wales International Eisteddford 2008-14; Trustee, Fund for Human Need; Patron, Bite the Ballot; Chair, Grassroutes; Director, Commonwealth Carnival of Music; Vice-President, Llangollen International Music Eisteddford.

Publications: Author, Hel Tai (Gwasg y Bwthyn, 2010).

Recreations: Music, travel, walking.

The Lord Roberts of Llandudno, House of Lords, London SW1A 0PW
Tel: 020 7219 8739 *Email:* robertsr@parliament.uk
Website: lordrogerroberts.uk

ROBERTSON OF PORT ELLEN, LORD

LABOUR

ROBERTSON OF PORT ELLEN (Life Baron), George Islay MacNeill Robertson; cr. 1999. Born 12 April 1946; Son of late George Robertson, police inspector, and late Marion Robertson; Married Sandra Wallace 1970 (2 sons 1 daughter).

Education: Dunoon Grammar School, Argyll; Dundee University (MA economics 1968).

Non-political career: Hon. Regimental Colonel, London Scottish Regiment 2001-. Research Assistant, Tayside Study, Economics Group 1968-69; Scottish Organiser, GMWU 1969-78; Secretary-General, North Atlantic Treaty Organisation 1999-2003; Executive Deputy Chair, Cable and Wireless plc 2004-06; Chair, Cable and Wireless International 2006-08; Senior Counsellor, Cohen Group 2004-; Non-executive Director: Weir Group plc 2004-15, The Smiths Group 2004-06; Special Adviser, BP plc 2006-; Non-executive Director, Western Ferries (Clyde) Ltd 2006-13; Deputy Chair, TNK-BP 2006-13; Senior International Adviser, Cable and Wireless Communications plc 2008-15; Senior Adviser, Chatham House 2014-. Member, GMB 1965-.

Political career: *House of Commons:* MP (Labour) for Hamilton May 1978 by-election to 1997, for Hamilton South 1997 to 24 August 1999. PPS to David Ennals as Secretary of State for Social Services February-May 1979; Opposition Frontbench Spokesperson for: Scotland 1979-80, Defence 1980-81, Foreign and Commonwealth Affairs 1981-93, European and Community Affairs 1985-93; Shadow Secretary of State for Scotland 1993-97; Secretary of State for Defence 1997-99. *House of Lords:* Raised to the peerage as Baron Robertson of Port Ellen, of Islay in Argyll and Bute 1999. Secretary of State for Defence August-October 1999. *Other:* Chair, Scottish Labour Party 1977-78. *Councils and public bodies:* Vice-chair, British Council 1985-94; Chair: Commission on Global Road Safety 2006-15, Commission on National Security (IPPR) 2007-09.

Political interests: Foreign affairs, defence, road safety.

Other: Fellow, Industry and Parliament Trust 1983; Joint President, Royal Institute of International Affairs 2001-11; Elder Brother, Corporation of Trinity House 2002-; Chair: John Smith Memorial Trust 2004-08, Maggies (Cancer Care) Centre, Lanarkshire Appeal 2004-; Trustee, British Forces Foundation 2004-; Patron: Glasgow Islay Association 2004-, Alzheimer's Research UK 2004-; Member, advisory board: Centre for European Reform 2004-, European Council for Foreign Affairs 2007-; Museum of Islay Life 2008-; Patron, Islay Book Festival 2008-; Chair, Ditchley Foundation 2009-; Patron: Dunblane Centre 2010-, Disabilities Trust 2010-; Member, advisory board, International Institute for Strategic Studies 2013-; Chair, FIA Foundation 2016-; FRSA 1999; Hon FRSE 2003. Freedom: City of Glasgow 2012, City of London 2016. Chancellor, Order of St Michael and St George 2011-. Fourteen honorary doctorates from UK, Azerbaijan, Kyrgyzstan, Romania and Armenia; Hon. Professor, politics department, Stirling University 2009-. International Academy of Achievement, Golden Plate Award 2000; English Speaking Union Winston Churchill Medal of Honour 2003; Atlantic Council of USA Distinguished International Leadership Award 2003; Parliamentarian of the Year (Jt) 2003; Licentiate, Royal Photographic Society 2010. PC 1997; Honours from Italy, Germany, Poland, Hungary, Luxembourg, Netherlands, Spain, Belgium, Portugal, Lithuania, Romania, Bulgaria, Croatia, Estonia, Ukraine, Slovakia, Latvia, Slovenia; Presidential Medal of Freedom (USA) 2003; Distinguished Service Medal, US Department of Defence 2003; Golden Medal of Freedom, Kosovo 2016; KT 2004; GCMG 2004; *Clubs:* Army and Navy. Hamilton Rugby; Islay Golf; Dunblane New Golf.

Publications: Author, Islay and Jura: Photographs (Birlinn, 2006).

Recreations: Photography, golf, reading.

Rt Hon the Lord Robertson of Port Ellen KT GCMG, House of Lords, London SW1A 0PW
Tel: 020 7219 6235 *Email:* robertsong@parliament.uk

ROCHESTER, LORD BISHOP OF

NON-AFFILIATED

ROCHESTER (107th Bishop of), James Henry Langstaff. Born 27 June 1956; Son of Henry and Jillian Langstaff; Married Bridget Streatfeild 1977 (1 son 1 daughter).

Education: St Catherine's College, Oxford (BA philosophy, politics and economics 1977); Nottingham University (BA theology 1980); St John's College, Nottingham (Diploma pastoral studies).

Non-political career: Ordained deacon 1981; Assistant curate, St Peter, Farnborough 1981-86; Priest 1982; Vicar, St Matthew, Duddeston and St Clement, Nechells 1986-96; Rural dean, Birmingham City 1995-96; Chaplain to Bishop of Birmingham 1996-2000; Rector, Holy Trinity Sutton Coldfield 2000-04; Area Dean, Sutton Coldfield 2002-04; Bishop Suffragan of Lynn 2004-10; Bishop of Rochester 2010-; Bishop to Prisons 2013-.

Political career: *House of Lords:* Entered House of Lords 2014. *Councils and public bodies:* Non-executive director, Good Hope Hospital NHS Trust 2003-04; Member, East of England Regional Assembly 2006-10.

Other: Tutor, Aston Training Scheme 1987-97; Board member, FCH Housing and Care 1988-2002; Chair: Flagship Housing Group 2006-10, Housing Justice 2008-.

Rt Rev the Lord Bishop of Rochester, House of Lords, London SW1A 0PW
Tel: 020 7219 5353 *Email:* langstaffj@parliament.uk
Bishopscourt, 24 St Margaret's Street, Rochester, Kent ME1 1TS *Tel:* 01634 842721
Email: bishop.rochester@rochester.anglican.org *Website:* www.rochester.anglican.org
Twitter: @Jameslangstaff

ROCK, BARONESS

CONSERVATIVE

ROCK (Life Baroness), Kate Harriet Alexandra Rock; cr 2015. Born 9 October 1968; Married Caspar Rock 1999 (1 son 1 daughter).

Education: Sherborne School for Girls; Oxford Polytechnic (BA).

Non-political career: Retail and luxury brands team, College Hill 1996-2008; Conservative Party: Head of business development 2008-10, Director of business engagement 2010-15.

Political career: *House of Lords:* Raised to the peerage as Baroness Rock, of Stratton in the County of Dorset 2015. Member, Artificial Intelligence 2017-. *Other:* Vice-chair (business), Conservative Party 2015-16. *Councils and public bodies:* Governor, Burlington Danes Academy 2012-.

Political interests: Business, education.

Other: Non-executive director: First News (UK) Ltd 2014-, Imagination Technologies 2014-; Speaker, Speakers for Schools.

The Baroness Rock, House of Lords, London SW1A 0PW
Tel: 020 7219 3000

RODGERS OF QUARRY BANK, LORD

LIBERAL DEMOCRAT

RODGERS OF QUARRY BANK (Life Baron), William Thomas Rodgers; cr. 1992. Born 28 October 1928; Son of William and Gertrude Rodgers; Married Silvia Szulman 1955 (died 2006) (3 daughters).

Education: Sudley Road Council School; Quarry Bank High School, Liverpool; Magdalen College, Oxford (Open Exhibitioner, BA modern history 1951).

Non-political career: National Service 1947-49. General Secretary: Fabian Society 1953-60, Publishing 1960-64, 1970-72; Director-General, Royal Institute of British Architects 1987-94; Chair, Advertising Standards Authority 1995-2000.

Political career: *House of Commons:* Contested Bristol West 1957 by-election. MP for Stockton-on-Tees 1962-74, for Teesside, Stockton 1974-83 (Labour 1962-81, SDP 1981-83). Contested (SDP) Stockton North 1983 and (SDP/All) Milton Keynes 1987 general elections. Parliamentary Under-Secretary of State: Department of Economic Affairs 1964-67, Foreign Office 1967-68; Minister of State: Board of Trade 1968-69, HM Treasury 1969-70, Ministry of Defence 1974-76; Secretary of State for Transport 1976-79; Shadow Secretary of State for Defence 1979-80. *House of Lords:* Raised to the peerage as Baron Rodgers of Quarry Bank, of Kentish Town in the London Borough of Camden 1992. Liberal Democrat Spokesperson for Home Office Affairs 1994-97. Member: House of Lords' Offices 1998-2001, Liaison 1998-2001, Privileges 1998-2001, Procedure 1998-2001, Selection 1998-2001, House 2003-05, Constitution 2007-12, Standing Orders (Private Bills) 2013-. *Other:* Social Democratic Party: Joint founder 1981, Vice-president 1982-87; Leader, Liberal Democrat Peers 1998-2001. *Councils and public bodies:* Borough Councillor, St Marylebone 1958-62.

Other: Leader, UK Delegation to the Council of Europe and WEU 1967-68; Hon. FRIBA; Hon. FIStructE. Honorary LLD, Liverpool University; Honorary Fellow, Liverpool John Moore University. PC 1975.

Publications: Editor, Hugh Gaitskell 1906-1963 (1964); Co-author, The People into Parliament (1966); The Politics of Change (1982); Editor, Government and Industry (1986); Fourth Among Equals (2000).

Rt Hon the Lord Rodgers of Quarry Bank, House of Lords, London SW1A 0PW
Tel: 020 7219 3607

ROGAN, LORD

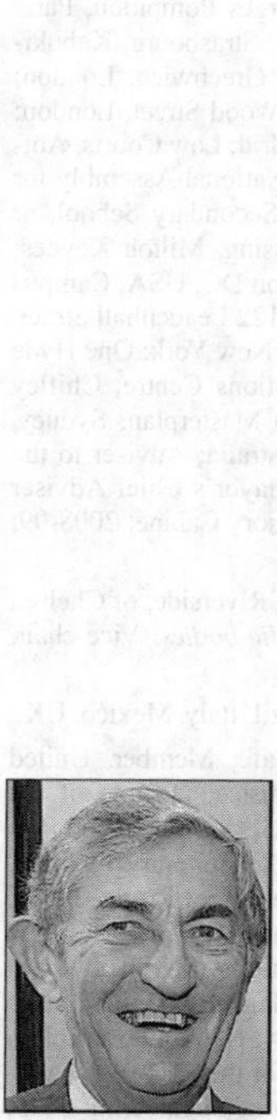

ULSTER UNIONIST PARTY

ROGAN (Life Baron), Dennis Robert David Rogan; cr. 1999. Born 30 June 1942; Son of late Robert Henderson Rogan; Married Lorna Colgan 1968 (2 sons).

Education: The Wallace High School; Belfast Institute of Technology; Open University (BA economics, politics 1976).

Non-political career: Hon. Colonel, 40 (Ulster) Signal Regiment (Volunteers) 2008-. Moygashel Ltd 1960-69; William Ewart & Sons Ltd 1969-72; Lamont Holdings plc 1972-78; Managing director, Dennis Rogan and Associates 1978-; Chair: Associated Processors Ltd 1985-, Events Management 2002-, Stakeholder Group 2005-; Council member, TLFCA-NI; Member, International Advisory Board, Parker Green International 2008-.

Political career: *House of Lords:* Raised to the peerage as Baron Rogan, of Lower Iveagh in the County of Down 1999. Leader in the Lords, Ulster Unionist Party 2001-. *Other:* Chair: Ulster Young Unionist Council 1968-69, South Belfast Constituency Association 1992-96; Ulster Unionist Party: Chair 1996-2001, Honorary secretary 2001-04, President 2004-06, Party officer 2012-. *Councils and public bodies:* Chair, Lisburn Unit of Management Health Board 1984-85; Member, Northern Ireland Police Fund 2001-05.

Political interests: Northern Ireland, trade and industry, defence.

Other: Member: CPA (UK) 2000-, IPU (UK) 2001-, British-Irish Parliamentary Assembly; Patron, Somme Association 1999-; Friend of the Salvation Army, Army Benevolent Fund; *Clubs:* Ulster Reform, Belfast, Army and Navy Club.

Recreations: Rugby football, oriental carpets, gardening, shooting.

The Lord Rogan, House of Lords, London SW1A 0PW
Tel: 020 7219 8625 *Email:* rogand@parliament.uk
31 Notting Hill, Malone Road, Belfast BT9 5NS *Tel:* 028 9066 2468

ROGERS OF RIVERSIDE, LORD

LABOUR

ROGERS OF RIVERSIDE (Life Baron), Richard George Rogers; cr. 1996. Born 23 July 1933; Son of Dada Geiringer and Nino Rogers; Married Su Brumwell 1961 (3 sons); married Ruth Elias 1973 (1 son 1 son deceased).

Education: Kingswood House School, Epsom, Surrey; Downs Lodge, Sutton; St John's School, Leatherhead; Architectural Association (AA Dip 1959); Yale University (MArch, Fulbright, Edward D. Stone and Yale Scholar 1961-62); RIBA; French, Italian.

Non-political career: Team 4 1963-67; Richard & Su Rogers 1968-70; Piano + Rogers 1970-78; Visiting professor, Yale University and University College, London 1978; Chair, Richard Rogers Architects Ltd 1978- (Rogers Stirk Harbour + Partners 2006-); Gave the BBC Reith Lectures entitled 'Cities for a Small Planet' 1995; Masterplans for many city centres, including Shanghai, Berlin, Mallorca, Paris and London; Buildings designed include: Centre Georges Pompidou, Paris (with Renzo Piano); Lloyd's of London; European Court of Human Rights, Strasbourg; Kabuki-Cho Tower, Tokyo; Channel 4 headquarters, London; Millennium Dome, Greenwich, London; Law Courts, Bordeaux, France; Lloyd's Registry of Shipping, London; 88 Wood Street, London; Broadwick House, Soho; Waterside, Paddington Basin; Barajas Airport, Madrid; Law Courts, Antwerp, Belgium; Hotel Hesperia and Conference Centre, Barcelona, Spain; National Assembly for Wales, Cardiff; Mossbourne City Academy, London; Minami Yamashiro Secondary School, nr Kyoto, Japan; Terminal 5, Heathrow Airport, London; Oxley Woods housing, Milton Keynes; Bodegas Protos winery, Penafiel, Spain; 300 New Jersey Avenue, Washington DC, USA; Campus Palmas Altas, Seville, Spain; Current projects include: Bullring, Barcelona; 122 Leadenhall Street, London; The Berkeley Hotel, London; Tower 3 on World Trade Centre site, New York; One Hyde Park, London; British Museum, London World Conservation and Exhibitions Centre; Chifley Square, Sydney, Australia; Canary Riverside South, London; Barangaroo Masterplan, Sydney, Australia; NEO Bankside Residential, London; Millers Point, Sydney, Australia; Adviser to the Mayor, Barcelona Urban Strategies Council; Greater London Authority: Mayor's Chief Adviser on Architecture and Urbanism 2000-08; Member, Mayor of London's Advisory Cabinet 2008-09; UK Business Ambassador 2008-.

Political career: *House of Lords:* Raised to the peerage as Baron Rogers of Riverside, of Chelsea in the Royal Borough of Kensington and Chelsea 1996. *Councils and public bodies:* Vice-chair, Arts Council of England 1994-96.

Political interests: Sustainable built environment, arts, New York City; Brazil, Italy, Mexico, UK.

Other: Member, Barcelona Urban Strategy Council; Director, River Cafe; Member, United Nations Architects' Committee; Patron, Society of Black Architects; Trustee, Doctors of the World, UK Board; Membre de l'Acadamie d'Architecture 1983; Member, RIBA Council and Policy Committees 1984-87; Chair, Board of Trustees, Tate Gallery 1984-88; Honorary member, Bund Deutscher Architekten 1989; President, National Communities Resource Centre 1991-; Chair, Architecture Foundation 1991-2001; Honorary Trustee, MOMA; Chair, Urban Task Force 1997-99; United Nations World Commissions on 21st Century Urbanisations; Member, Royal Institute of British Architects; Hon. Fellow: Royal Academy of Art, The Hague, American Institute of Architects 1983; Royal Academian, Royal Academy of London 1984; Hon. Fellow, Tokyo Society of Architects and Building Engineers 1996; Fellow, Royal Society for the Arts 1996; Academician, International Academy of Architecture; Fellow: Royal Academy of Engineering 2005, University of Wales Institute, Wales 2007; Maggie's Centres, Reprieve, Doctors of the World. Honorary degrees from British, Chinese, Czech and Spanish universities. International Union of Architects August Perret Prize for most outstanding international work (Centre Pompidon) 1975-78; Royal Gold Medal for Architecture 1985; American Academy and Institute of Arts and Letters, Arnold W Brunner Memorial Prize 1989; Friend of Barcelona 1997; Thomas Jefferson Memorial Foundation Medal in Architecture 1999; Japan Art Association Praemium Imperiale Award for Architecture 2000; Golden Lion for Lifetime Achievement 2006; Pritzker Architecture Prize Laureate 2007. Kt 1991; Chevalier l'Ordre National de la Légion d'Honneur (France) 1986; Officier de l'Ordre des Arts et des Lettres (France) 1995; CH 2008.

Publications: Richard Rogers + Architects (1985); A + U: Richard Rogers 1978-88 (1988); Architecture: A Modern View (1990); (jointly) A New London (1992); Richard Rogers (1995); Cities for a Small Planet (1997); Towards an Urban Renaissance (Urban Task Force, 1999); Richard Rogers, Complete Works, Vol 1 (1999); Paying for an Urban Renaissance (2000); Co-author Cities for a Small Country (2000); Richard Rogers, Complete Works, Vol 2 (2001); Delivering an Urban Renaissance (2002); Towards a Strong Urban Renaissance (2005); Richard Rogers, Architecture of the Future (2005); Richard Rogers, Complete Works, Vol 3 (2006); Richard Rogers + Architects, From the House to the City (2010); British Museum Word Conservation and Exhibitions Centre (2014).

Recreations: Friends, food, art, architecture, travel.

The Lord Rogers of Riverside CH, House of Lords, London SW1A 0PW
Tel: 020 7219 5353
Rogers Stirk Harbour and Partners, Thames Wharf, Rainville Road, London W6 9HA
Tel: 020 7385 1235 *Fax:* 020 7385 8409 *Email:* enquiries@rsh-p.com
Website: www.rsh-p.com

LABOUR

ROOKER, LORD

ROOKER (Life Baron), Jeffrey William Rooker; cr. 2001. Born 5 June 1941; Son of late William Rooker and Mary Rooker; Married Angela Edwards 1972 (died 2003); married Helen Hughes 2010.

Education: Aldridge Road Secondary Modern; Handsworth Technical School; Handsworth Technical College 1957-60; Aston University (BSc production engineering 1964); Warwick University (MA industrial relations 1972).

Non-political career: Apprentice toolmaker, Kings Heath Engineering Company 1957-63; Manager, Geo Salter & Co 1964-67; Production manager, Rola Celestion Ltd 1967-70; Lecturer, Lanchester Polytechnic, Coventry 1972-74. Member: Community 2010, GMB 2016-.

Political career: *House of Commons:* MP (Labour) for Birmingham Perry Barr February 1974-2001. PPS to Peter Archer as Solicitor General 1974-77; Opposition Frontbench Spokesperson for: Social Services 1979-80, Social Security 1980-83, Treasury and Economic Affairs 1983-84, Environment 1984-88, Community Care and Social Services 1990-92, Education 1992-93; Shadow Deputy Leader of the House of Commons 1994-97; Minister of State and Deputy Minister, Ministry of Agriculture, Fisheries and Food (Minister for Food Safety) 1997-99; Minister of State, Department of Social Security 1999-2001. *House of Lords:* Raised to the peerage as Baron Rooker, of Perry Barr in the County of West Midlands 2001. Minister of State and Government Spokesperson for: Home Office 2001-02, Office of the Deputy Prime Minister 2002-05; Minister of State, Northern Ireland Office 2005-06; Government Spokesperson for Northern Ireland 2005-08; Deputy Leader of the Lords 2005-08; Minister of State and Government Spokesperson, Department for Environment, Food and Rural Affairs 2006-08. Member: Procedure 2005-07, Barnett Formula 2008-09, Joint Committee on the Draft House of Lords Reform Bill 2011-12; Chair, Joint Committee on the Draft Deregulation Bill 2013; Member: EU Energy and Environment Sub-Committee 2015-, Charities 2016-17. *Councils and public bodies:* Birmingham Education Committee 1972-74; Council member, Institution of Production Engineers 1975-80; Lay Member of Council, Aston University 2008-10; Chair, Food Standards Agency 2009-13.

Political interests: Food, agriculture, planning, constitutional affairs, science and technology, housing, energy, fairness; New Zealand, Sweden.

Other: Chair, British Motorsport Training Trust 2011-; Fellow, Institution Engineering and Technology; Member, Institute of Management. DSc, Aston University 2001; DUniv, University of Central England 2002. Minister of the Year, *House Magazine* awards 2004; Peer of Year, Channel 4 2007; Lords Minister of the Year, *House Magazine* awards 2008. PC 1999.

Recreations: Walking, reading, motorsport (spectator).

Rt Hon the Lord Rooker, House of Lords, London SW1A 0PW
Tel: 020 7219 6469 *Email:* rookerj@parliament.uk

CONSERVATIVE

ROSE OF MONEWDEN, LORD

ROSE OF MONEWDEN (Life Baron), Stuart Alan Ransom Rose; cr 2014. Born 17 March 1949; Son of Harry and Margaret Rose; Married Jennifer Cook 1973 (divorced 2010) (1 daughter 1 son).

Education: Bootham School, York.

Non-political career: Marks & Spencer plc: Trainee 1971, Commercial director for Europe 1988-89, Chief Executive 2004-09, Chair 2009-10; Chief Executive: Burton Group 1989-97, Argos Plc 1998, Booker Plc 1998-2000, Iceland Group 2000, Arcadia Plc 2000-02; Ocado: Chair 2013-, Non-executive Director 2013-; Chair, Fat Face 2013-; Government Adviser on NHS leadership 2014.

Political career: *House of Lords:* Raised to the peerage as Baron Rose of Monewden, of Monewden in the County of Suffolk 2014.

Political interests: Business and sustainability.

Other: Non-executive Director: NSB Retail Systems plc 2000-04, Land Securities 2000-13; Chair, British Fashion Council 2003-08; Member, Advisory Committee, Bridgepoint 2010-; Non-

House of Lords
Peers' Biographies

executive Director, Woolworths Holdings 2011-; Oasis Dental Care 2013-; Chair, Britain Stronger in Europe 2015-16; Director, Soak & Sleep Holdings Ltd; Scar Free Foundation, Mvumi Secondary School. Hon. Degree: Leeds University, Aston University, Heriot Watt University, Suffolk University, York University. Kt 2008; *Clubs:* Groucho Club.

The Lord Rose of Monewden, House of Lords, London SW1A 0PW
Tel: 020 7219 5353

LABOUR

ROSSER, LORD

Opposition Spokesperson for Home Office and Transport

ROSSER (Life Baron), Richard Andrew Rosser; cr. 2004. Born 5 October 1944; Son of Gordon Rosser and Kathleen Rosser, née Moon; Married Sheena Denoon 1973 (2 sons 1 daughter).

Education: St Nicholas Grammar School for Boys, Northwood; University of London (BSc(Econ) economics 1970).

Non-political career: London Transport: Clerk 1962-65, PA to operating manager (railways) 1965-66; Transport Salaried Staffs' Association: Research officer 1966-76, Finance and organising officer 1976-77, London Midland regional division secretary 1977-82, Assistant general secretary 1982-89, General secretary 1989-2004; Non-executive director, Correctional Services Board/National Offender Management Service Board 2000-09; Chair, Prison Service/National Offender Management Service Audit Committee 2003-09. Transport Salaried Staffs' Association (TSSA) 1963-; GMB 1966-; Member, TUC general council 2000-04.

Political career: *House of Commons:* Contested (Labour) Croydon Central 1974 general election. *House of Lords:* Raised to the peerage as Baron Rosser, of Ickenham in the London Borough of Hillingdon 2004. Opposition Whip 2010-11; Opposition Spokesperson for: Home Office 2011-, Defence 2011-15, Transport 2011-. Member, Procedure 2005-09; Co-opted Member, EU Sub-committee E (Law and Institutions) 2007-10; Merits of Statutory Instruments: Member 2008-10, Chair 2009-10. Vice-chair, PLP Departmental Committee for Work and Pensions 2006-10. *Other:* Labour Party: Member, National Executive Committee 1988-98, Chair 1997-98. *Councils and public bodies:* London Borough of Hillingdon: Councillor 1971-78, Chair, Labour Group 1975-78; JP 1978.

Political interests: Transport, employment, criminal justice system, treatment of offenders; Taiwan.

Other: Honorary Vice-president, Ryman Isthmian Football League 2008-; Vice-president, Level Playing Field 2009-; Trustee, White Rose Children's Charity -2017; Chartered member, Institute of Logistics and Transport (formerly Institute of Transport) 1967.

Recreations: Walking, reading, going to non-league football matches.

The Lord Rosser, House of Lords, London SW1A 0PW
Tel: 020 7219 4589 *Email:* rosserr@parliament.uk

CROSSBENCH

ROSSLYN, EARL OF

ROSSLYN (7th Earl of, UK), Peter St Clair-Erskine; cr. 1801; 7th Baron Loughborough (GB) 1795; 11th Bt of Alva (NS) 1666. Born 31 March 1958; Son of 6th Earl; Married Helen Watters 1982 (2 sons 2 daughters).

Education: Eton College; Bristol University (BA Hispanic and Latin American studies 1980); Cambridge University (MSt applied criminology 2002).

Non-political career: Metropolitan Police 1980-94; Thames Valley Police 1994-2000; Commander, Metropolitan Police 2000-14: Royalty and diplomatic protection department 2003-14; Master of the Household to The Prince of Wales and The Duchess of Cornwall 2014-.

Political career: *House of Lords:* First entered House of Lords 1979; Elected hereditary peer 1999-.

Other: Member, Queen's Body Guard for Scotland, Royal Company of Archers; Trustee, Dunimarle Museum; Chair of Governors, Ludgrove School. QPM 2009; CVO 2014; *Clubs:* White's Club.

The Earl of Rosslyn CVO QPM, House of Lords, London SW1A 0PW
Tel: 020 7219 5353

CONSERVATIVE

ROTHERWICK, LORD

ROTHERWICK (3rd Baron, UK), Herbert Robin Cayzer; cr. 1939; 6th Bt of Gartmore (UK) 1904; 3rd Bt of Tylney (UK) 1924. Born 12 March 1954; Son of 2nd Baron; Married Sara Jane McAlpine 1982 (divorced 1994) (2 sons 1 daughter); married Tania Fox 2000 (1 son 1 daughter).

Education: Harrow School; RMA, Sandhurst; Royal Agricultural College, Cirencester (Diploma agriculture 1982).

Non-political career: Acting Captain, The Life Guards 1973-76; Household Cavalry, Territorial 1977-83; Member, Armed Forces Parliamentary Scheme 2010-12. Barings Bank 1976-78; Bristol Helicopters 1978-80; Farming and estate management 1982-.

Political career: *House of Lords:* First entered House of Lords 1996; Elected hereditary peer 1999-; Opposition Whip 2001-05; Opposition Spokesperson for: Education and Skills, Work and Pensions 2001-03, Environment, Food and Rural Affairs 2003-05, Transport 2004-05.

Political interests: Defence, aviation, agriculture.

Other: Member: Council of Europe 2000-01, Western European Union 2000-01; Vice-chair, Popular Flying Association 1999-2001; President, General Aviation Awareness Council; Board director, Cayzer Continuation PCC Ltd 2004-; Fellow, Industry and Parliamentary Trust 2005; Non-executive chair, Air Touring Ltd 2006-11; Director: Light Aviation Association, Cornbury Estates Company Limited, Cornbury Maintenance Company Limited. Succeeded his kinsman as 6th Bt of Gartmore 2012; *Clubs:* White's Club.

Recreations: Flying, Conservation.

The Lord Rotherwick, House of Lords, London SW1A 0PW
Tel: 020 7219 0660
Cornbury Park, Charlbury, Oxfordshire OX7 3EH *Tel:* 01608 811276 *Fax:* 01608 811252
Email: r@cpark.co.uk

CROSSBENCH

ROWE-BEDDOE, LORD

ROWE-BEDDOE (Life Baron), David Sydney Rowe-Beddoe; cr 2006. Born 19 December 1937; Son of late Sydney and Dolan Rowe-Beddoe, née Evans; Married Malinda Collison 1962 (divorced 1982) (3 daughters); married Madeleine Harrison 1984 (1 stepson 1 stepdaughter).

Education: Cathedral School, Llandaff; Stowe School, Buckinghamshire; St John's College, Cambridge (BA economics/law 1961, MA); Graduate School of Business Administration, Harvard University (PMD 1974); French, Spanish.

Non-political career: Sub-lieutenant, Royal Navy national service 1956-58; Lieutenant, Royal Naval Reserve 1958-66. Thomas De la Rue & Co 1961-76: Chief executive 1971-76, Executive director, De la Rue Co plc 1974-76; Revlon Inc 1976-81: President, Latin America and Caribbean 1976-77, President, Europe, Middle East and Africa 1977-81; President: GFTA Trendanalysen 1981-87, Morgan Stanley-GFTA Ltd 1983-91; Chair: Cavendish Services Ltd 1987-93, EHC International Ltd 2001-13; Deputy chair, Toye & Company plc 2002-14; Director: Mitel (Canada) 2002-06, Newport Networks Group plc 2004-09; Chair: GFTA – Euro/Dollar Technology Co Ltd 2005-14, Cardiff Wales Airport 2013-16.

Political career: *House of Lords:* Raised to the peerage as Baron Rowe-Beddoe, of Kilgetty in the County of Dyfed 2006. Co-opted member, EU Sub-committee B (Internal Market) 2007-10; Member: Barnett Formula 2008-09, Administration and Works 2009-14, EU Sub-committee B (Internal Market, Energy and Transport) 2010-12, Economic Affairs 2012-15, Sub-committee on Economic Affairs Finance Bill 2012-15, Procedure 2015-, Joint Committee on Statutory Instruments 2016-, Citizenship and Civic Engagement 2017-. *Councils and public bodies:* Chairman: Welsh Development Agency 1993-2001, Development Board for Rural Wales 1994-98; Wales Millennium Centre: Chairman 2001-10, Life President 2010-; Chairman, Representative Body of the Church in Wales 2002-13; Member, Governing Body, Church in Wales 2002-13; DL, Gwent 2003-; President, Royal Welsh College of Music and Drama 2004-; Deputy Chairman, UK Statistics Authority 2008-12; Chair, Office of National Statistics 2008-12.

Political interests: Arts and heritage, management, university, armed forces, faith and society; Argentina, Brazil, Central America, China, Mexico, North Korea, South America, UAE.

Other: Commonwealth Parliamentary Association; Inter-Parliamentary Union; President, British-Australia Society (Wales Branch); FRSA; Fellow, Institute of Welsh Affairs; Prince of Wales Trust, Church in Wales. Freedom, City of London. Pro-chancellor, University of South Wales 2007-. Honorary doctorates: University of Wales, University of Glamorgan/University of South Wales; Fellow: Cardiff University, Aberystwyth University, Newport University, Cardiff Metropolitan University. Beacon Prize 2004; Lifetime Achievement Award, *Western Mail* 2005;

Achievement Award, Worshipful Livery Company of Wales 2009. Kt 2000; Order of the Rising Sun, Gold Rays with Neck Ribbon (Japan) 2008; *Clubs:* Garrick, Cardiff and County, Brook Club (New York).

Recreations: Music, theatre, country pursuits.

The Lord Rowe-Beddoe DL, House of Lords, London SW1A 0PW
Tel: 020 7219 6255
Royal Welsh College of Music and Drama, Castle Grounds, Cathays Park, Cardiff CF10 3ER
Tel: 029 2039 1344 *Email:* david@rbinternet.com

LABOUR

ROWLANDS, LORD

ROWLANDS (Life Baron), Edward (Ted) Rowlands; cr. 2004. Born 23 January 1940; Son of William Samuel Rowlands, Clerk of Works; Married Janice Williams 1968 (died 2004) (2 sons 1 daughter).

Education: Rhondda Grammar School; Wirral Grammar, Cheshire; King's College, London (BA history 1962).

Non-political career: Research student 1962; Research assistant, History of Parliament Trust 1963-65; Lecturer: Modern history and government, Welsh College of Advanced Technology 1965-66, Law Department, London School of Economics 1972-74. Member: Association of University Teachers 1965-72, ASTMS 1972-2001.

Political career: *House of Commons:* MP (Labour) for Cardiff North 1966-70, for Merthyr Tydfil 13 April 1972 by-election to 1983, for Merthyr Tydfil and Rhymney 1983-2001. Parliamentary Under-Secretary of State (PUS), Welsh Office 1969-70, 1974-75; Foreign and Commonwealth Office 1975-79: PUS 1975-76, Minister of State 1976-79; Opposition Frontbench Spokesperson for: Foreign and Commonwealth Affairs 1979-80, Energy 1981-87. Member, Foreign Affairs 1987-2001; Former chair, Quadripartite Committee. *House of Lords:* Raised to the peerage as Baron Rowlands, of Merthyr Tydfil and Rhymney in the county of Mid Glamorgan 2004. Member: Constitution 2005-09, EU Sub-committee E: (Justice and Institutions) 2010-12, (Justice, Institutions and Consumer Protection) 2012-14, Extradition Law 2014-15, Joint Committee on Statutory Instruments 2015-, Secondary Legislation Scrutiny 2016-17, Delegated Powers and Regulatory Reform 2017-. *Councils and public bodies:* Member, Richard Commission 2003-04.

Political interests: International energy, constitution; Botswana, South Africa, former Soviet Eastern Europe.

Other: Fellow, Industry and Parliament Trust 1982; Judge, Booker McConnel Novel of the Year Competition 1984; Council member, Winston Churchill Memorial Trust 1989-2010; History of Parliamentary Trust: Chair 1993-2001, Trustee; President, National Training Federation for Wales; WaterAid. Honorary degree, Glamorgan University. CBE 2003.

Publications: 'Something Must be Done' South Wales v Whitehall 1921-1951 (TTC books); Robert Harley and the Battle for Power in Radnorshire 1690-1693 (Welsh History Review, 1990); A Golden Age – Peer Power in the Early Eighteenth Century (TTC Books, 2008).

Recreations: Gardening, golf.

The Lord Rowlands CBE, House of Lords, London SW1A 0PW
Tel: 020 7219 3842

LAB/CO-OP

ROYALL OF BLAISDON, BARONESS

ROYALL OF BLAISDON (Life Baroness), Janet Anne Royall; cr. 2004. Born 20 August 1955; Daughter of Basil and Myra Royall; Married Stuart Hercock 1980 (died 2010) (1 daughter 2 sons).

Education: Royal Forest of Dean Grammar School; Westfield College, London University (BA Spanish and French 1977); French, Spanish, some Italian.

Non-political career: Continental Farms (Europe) Ltd 1978; Secretary-General, British Labour Group, European Parliament 1979-85; Policy adviser/PA to Neil Kinnock MP as Leader of the Opposition 1986-92; Researcher/Press officer to Neil Kinnock MP 1992-95; Member, Cabinet of Neil Kinnock as: European Commissioner for Transport 1995-99, Vice-president of the Commission 1999-2001; Parliamentary co-ordinator, Press and communications directorate-general, European Commission 2001-03; Head of European Commission Office in Wales 2003-04. Member, USDAW.

Political career: *House of Lords:* Raised to the peerage as Baroness Royall of Blaisdon, of Blaisdon in the County of Gloucestershire 2004. Government Spokesperson for: Health 2005-08, International Development 2005-08, Foreign and Commonwealth Office 2005-08; Government Whip

2005-08; Chief Whip 2008; Leader of the House of Lords 2008-10; Lord President of the Council 2008-09; Government Spokesperson for: Equality 2008-10, Northern Ireland 2008-10, Cabinet Office 2009-10; Chancellor of the Duchy of Lancaster 2009-10; Shadow Leader of the House of Lords 2010-15; Opposition Spokesperson for: Cabinet Office 2010-12, Education 2010, Northern Ireland 2010-11, Work and Pensions 2010, Equalities Office 2010-12, International Development 2012-13. Member: Merits of Statutory Instruments 2005, Administration and Works 2008, Privileges/Privileges and Conduct 2008-15, Procedure 2008-15, Liaison 2008-15, House 2008-15, Selection 2008-15. *Other:* Member, Politics – Better Politics Policy Commission.

Political interests: Foreign policy, development, carers, democratic engagement, penal affairs, youth policies; Central and Latin America, Australia, Balkans, European Union, India, New Zealand, South Africa, USA.

Other: Vice-president, Party of European Socialists 2012-; Former Patron, Kidney Wales Foundation; Former President, Autism Cymru; Former Trustee: IPPR, National Botanic Garden of Wales, Generation Europe, Forest of Dean Crossroads, Better Learning Together – Our Co-operative Trust; Patron, ASHA Centre; Trustee, City Year UK; Chair: DRIVE, People's History Museum 2016-; Member Advisory Council, Step up to Serve; Principal, Somerville College, Oxford 2017-. Pro-chancellor, Bath University 2014-17. *The House Magazine* Peer of the Year, Dods Parliamentary Awards 2014. PC 2008.

Recreations: Reading, travel, gardening, swimming.

Rt Hon the Baroness Royall of Blaisdon, House of Lords, London SW1A 0PW
Tel: 020 7219 1435 *Email:* royallj@parliament.uk *Twitter:* @LabourRoyall

CROSSBENCH

RUSSELL OF LIVERPOOL, LORD

RUSSELL OF LIVERPOOL (3rd Baron, UK), Simon Gordon Jared Russell; cr 1919. Born 30 August 1952; Son of late Captain Hon Langley Gordon Haslingden Russell; Married Dr Gilda Albano 1984 (2 sons 1 daughter).

Education: Charterhouse; Trinity College, Cambridge; INSEAD, Fontainbleau, France; Italian, French.

Non-political career: Senior director, Spencer Stuart Management Consultants NV.

Political career: *House of Lords:* First entered House of Lords 1982; Elected hereditary peer 2014-.

Other: Trustee, Coram; Chair, Coram Life Education; Trustee, Perseverance Trust. Liveryman, Fishmongers' Company; *Clubs:* Brooks's Club.

The Lord Russell of Liverpool, House of Lords, London SW1A 0PW
Tel: 020 7219 5353

CONSERVATIVE

RYDER OF WENSUM, LORD

RYDER OF WENSUM (Life Baron), Richard Ryder; cr. 1997. Born 4 February 1949; Son of Stephen Ryder, JP, DL, farmer; Married Caroline Stephens (later CVO MBE) 1981 (1 daughter 1 son deceased).

Education: Radley College; Magdalene College, Cambridge (BA history 1971).

Non-political career: Former journalist; Director of family businesses in Suffolk; Political Secretary to Margaret Thatcher as Leader of the Opposition and Prime Minister 1975-81; Founding chair, Eastern Counties Radio 1997-2001; Chair: Institute of Cancer Research 2005-13, UCanDoIt 2011-14, Child Bereavement UK 2013-.

Political career: *House of Commons:* Contested Gateshead East February and October 1974 general elections. MP (Conservative) for Norfolk Mid 1983-97. PPS to: John Moore as Financial Secretary to the Treasury 1984, Geoffrey Howe as Foreign Secretary 1984-86; Government Whip 1986-88; Parliamentary Secretary, Ministry of Agriculture, Fisheries and Food 1988-89; HM Treasury: Economic Secretary 1989-90, Paymaster General July-November 1990; Government Chief Whip 1990-95. *House of Lords:* Raised to the peerage as Baron Ryder of Wensum, of Wensum in the County of Norfolk 1997. Co-opted Member, EU Sub-committee B (Internal Market) 2008-10; Member, EU Sub-committee B (Internal Market, Energy and Transport) 2010-12. *Other:* Chairman, Conservative Foreign and Commonwealth Council 1984-89. *Councils and public bodies:* BBC Governors: Vice-chair 2002-04, Acting chair 2004-05.

Other: OBE 1981; PC 1990.

Rt Hon the Lord Ryder of Wensum OBE, House of Lords, London SW1A 0PW
Tel: 020 7219 5353

CONSERVATIVE

SAATCHI, LORD

SAATCHI (Life Baron), Maurice Saatchi; cr. 1996. Born 21 June 1946; Son of Nathan and Daisy Saatchi; Married Josephine Hart 1984 (died 2011) (1 son 1 stepson).

Education: Tollington Grammar School, Muswell Hill, London; London School of Economics (BSc economics 1967); French.

Non-political career: Co-founder, Saatchi & Saatchi 1970; Partner, M & C Saatchi 1995-.

Political career: *House of Lords:* Raised to the peerage as Baron Saatchi, of Staplefield in the County of West Sussex 1996. Opposition Spokesperson for: Treasury 1999-2003, Cabinet Office 2001-03. *Other:* Co-chair, Conservative Party 2003-05. *Councils and public bodies:* Governor, London School of Economics 1985-.

Countries of interest: UK.

Other: Director, Museum of Garden History; Centre for Policy Studies: Director 1999-2013, Chair 2009-13.

Publications: The War of Independence (1999); Happiness Can't Buy Money (1999); The Bad Samaritan (2000); The Science of Politics (2001); Poor People! Stop Paying Tax! (2001); If this is Conservatism, I am a Conservative (2005); In Praise of Ideology (2007); Enemy of the People (2008); The Myth of Inflation Targeting (2009).

The Lord Saatchi, House of Lords, London SW1A 0PW
Tel: 020 7219 5353
M & C Saatchi plc, 36 Golden Square, London W1F 9EE *Tel:* 020 7543 4510 *Fax:* 020 7543 4502
Email: maurices@mcsaatchi.com

CROSSBENCH

SACKS, LORD

SACKS (Life Baron), Jonathan Henry Sacks; cr 2009. Born 8 March 1948; Son of late Louis David Sacks and late Louisa Frumkin; Married Elaine Taylor 1970 (1 son 2 daughters).

Education: Christ's College School, Finchley; Gonville and Caius College, Cambridge (BA 1972, MA); New College, Oxford; Jews' College, London (rabbinical ordination 1976); Yeshivat Etz Hayyim, London; London University (PhD 1981).

Non-political career: Moral philosophy lecturer, Middlesex Polytechnic 1971-73; Jews' College, London 1973-90: Jewish philosophy lecturer 1973-76, Talmud and philosophy lecturer 1976-82, First Chief Rabbi Sir Immanuel Jakobovits professor of modern Jewish thought 1982, Director, rabbinic faculty 1983-90, Principal 1984-90; Rabbi: Golders Green Synagogue 1978-82, Marble Arch Synagogue 1983-90; Chief Rabbi, United Hebrew Congregations of the Commonwealth 1991-2013; Professor of Jewish Thought, Kressel and Ephrat Family, Yeshiva University 2013-16; New York University: Ingeborg and Ira Rennert Global Distinguished Professor of Judaic Studies 2013-16, Ingeborg and Ira Rennert Global Distinguished Professor 2016-; King's College London: Professor of Law, Ethics and the Bible 2013-16, Emeritus Professor of Law, Ethics, and the Bible 2016-.

Political career: *House of Lords:* Raised to the peerage as Baron Sacks, of Aldgate in the City of London 2009. *Councils and public bodies:* Member, Central Advisory Committee, BBC and Independent Broadcasting Authority 1987-90.

Other: Nineteen honorary doctorates from UK, Israeli and US universities. Jerusalem Prize 1995. Kt 2005.

Publications: Numerous religious and philosophical works. Latest publications: The Home We Build Together: Recreating Society (Continuum, 2007); The Great Partnership: God, Science and the Search for Meaning (Hodder and Stoughton, 2011).

Rabbi the Lord Sacks, House of Lords, London SW1A 0PW
Tel: 020 7219 5353 *Email:* sacksj@parliament.uk
The Office of Rabbi Sacks, PO Box 72007, London NW6 6RW *Tel:* 020 7286 6391
Email: info@rabbisacks.org *Website:* www.rabbisacks.org *Twitter:* @rabbisacks

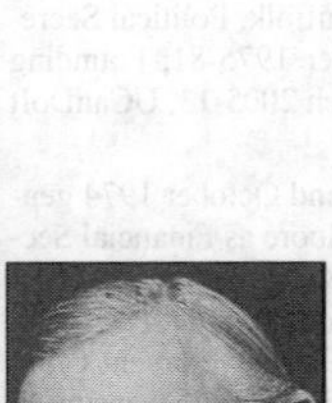

CONSERVATIVE

SAINSBURY OF PRESTON CANDOVER, LORD

SAINSBURY OF PRESTON CANDOVER (Life Baron), John Davan Sainsbury; cr. 1989. Born 2 November 1927; Son of late Lord Sainsbury (Life Peer); Married Anya Eltenton 1963 (2 sons 1 daughter).

Education: Stowe School, Buckinghamshire; Worcester College, Oxford (BA history).

Non-political career: Served Life Guards 1945-48. Joined J. Sainsbury in buying departments 1950: Director 1958-92, Vice-chair 1967-69, Chair and chief executive 1969-92, President 1992-; Director, *The Economist* 1972-80.

Political career: *House of Lords:* Raised to the peerage as Baron Sainsbury of Preston Candover, of Preston Candover in the County of Hampshire 1989. On leave of absence 2010-. Member, Joint

Parliamentary Scrutiny Committee on Draft Charities Bill 2004-05. *Councils and public bodies:* Member, National Committee for Electoral Reform 1976-85.

Political interests: Commerce, arts.

Other: Governor, Royal Ballet School 1965-76, 1987-91; Contemporary Arts Society: Honorary secretary 1965-71, Vice-chair 1971-74, Vice-President 1984-96, Vice-Patron 1998-2006; Royal Opera House, Covent Garden: Director 1969-85, Chair 1987-91, Hon. Vice-President 2009-; Chair, Council of Friends of Covent Garden 1969-81; Joint Hon. Treasurer, European Movement 1972-75; Director, Royal Opera House Trust 1974-84, 1987-97; Trustee: National Gallery 1976-83, Westminster Abbey Trust 1977-83; President's Committee, CBI 1982-84; Trustee: Tate Gallery 1982-83, Rhodes Trust 1984-98; Honorary Bencher, Inner Temple 1985; Chair, Benesh Institute of Choreology 1986-87; Royal Ballet: Governor 1987-2003, Chair of governors 1995-2003; President, Sparsholt College, Hampshire 1993-2000; Dulwich Picture Gallery: Chair of trustees 1994-2000, Patron 2004-; Director, Friends of the Nelson Mandela Children's Fund 1996-2000; Chair of trustees, Royal Opera House Endowment Fund 2001-05; Rambert School, chairman: Development committee 2002-03, Steering committee 2005-09; Visitor, Ashmolean Museum 2003-; Trustee, Saïd Business School Foundation 2003; Director, Rambert School of Ballet and Contemporary Dance 2003-05; Patron, Sir Harold Hillier Gardens and Arboretum 2005-; Chairman, Rambert School Trust 2005-10; Director, Centre for Policy Studies 2009-12; British Retail Consortium: Council member 1975-79, President 1993-97; Fellow, Institute of Grocery Distribution 1973-; Hon. FRIBA 1993. Hon. Fellow, Worcester College, Oxford 1982; Hon. DSc, Economics (London) 1985; Hon. DLitt, South Bank University 1992; Hon. LLD, Bristol University 1993; Hon. D.EconSc, Cape Town 2000; Hon. Fellow, British School at Rome 2002. Albert Medal, Royal Society of Arts 1989; Hadrian Award 2000; Prince of Wales Medal for Arts Philanthropy 2008; Sheldon Medal, Oxford University 2010; The Gjergi Kastrioti-Skenderbeg Presidential Award 2014. Kt 1980; KG 1992; *Clubs:* Garrick, Beefsteak Club.

The Lord Sainsbury of Preston Candover KG, House of Lords, London SW1A 0PW
Tel: 020 7219 5353

LABOUR

SAINSBURY OF TURVILLE, LORD

SAINSBURY OF TURVILLE (Life Baron), David John Sainsbury; cr 1997. Born 24 October 1940; Son of late Sir Robert and Lady Lisa Sainsbury; Married Susan Reid 1973 (3 daughters).

Education: Eton College; King's College, Cambridge (BA history and psychology 1963); Columbia University, New York (MBA 1971).

Non-political career: Joined J. Sainsbury plc 1963: Finance director 1973-90, Deputy chair 1988-92, Chief executive 1992-97, Chair 1992-98; Visiting Fellow, Nuffield College, Oxford 1987-95.

Political career: *House of Lords:* Raised to the peerage as Baron Sainsbury of Turville, of Turville in the County of Buckinghamshire 1997. Parliamentary Under-Secretary of State and Government Spokesperson, Department of Trade and Industry (Minister for Science and Innovation) 1998-2006; On leave of absence July 2013-. *Other:* Trustee, Social Democratic Party 1982-90. *Councils and public bodies:* Member, Committee of Review of Post Office (Carter Committee) 1975-77; London Business School: Member, governing body 1985-, Chair 1991-98.

Political interests: Science and innovation, policy, industry and education; Africa, China, India, USA.

Other: Settlor Gatsby Charitable Foundation; Chair, Institute for Government 2009-. Chancellor, Cambridge University 2011-. Honorary doctorate from Universities of Cambridge, Oxford and Manchester, and Imperial College; Hon. Fellowship, London Business School 1990; Hon. FREng 1994; Hon. FRS 2008; Hon. Fellow, Academy of Medical Sciences 2008. Andrew Carnegie Medal of Philanthropy (on behalf of Sainsbury Family) 2003.

Publications: Government and Industry: a new partnership (1981); Co-author, Wealth Creation and Jobs (1987); The Race to the Top – report for the Government on its science and innovation policies (2007); Progressive Capitalism: How to Achieve Economic Growth, Liberty and Social Justice (2013).

The Lord Sainsbury of Turville, House of Lords, London SW1A 0PW
Tel: 020 7219 5353

NON-AFFILIATED

ST ALBANS, LORD BISHOP OF

ST ALBANS (10th Bishop of), Alan Gregory Clayton Smith. Born 14 February 1957; Son of Frank Smith and Rosemary Smith.

Education: Trowbridge Grammar School for Boys; John of Gaunt School; Birmingham University (BA 1978; MA 1979); University of Wales, Bangor (PhD 2002).

Non-political career: Curate, Pudsey St Lawrence 1981-84; Chaplain, Lee Abbey Community 1984-90; Team vicar, St Matthew's, Walsall 1990-97; Diocesan Missioner 1990-97; Archdeacon, Stoke-on-Trent 1997-2001; Honorary canon, Lichfield Cathedral 1997-2001; Area Bishop, Shrewsbury 2001-09; Bishop of St Albans 2009-.

Political career: *House of Lords:* Entered House of Lords 2013. *Councils and public bodies:* Member, General Synod 1999-2001, 2009-.

Countries of interest: Caribbean, West and East Malaysia.

Other: Member: Amnesty International, Rural Bishops' Panel 2006-; Chair, Local Strategic Partnership, Shropshire. Hon DD, Birmingham University 2010.

Publications: Contributor: Changing Rural Life (2004), Celebrating Community: God's Gift for Today's World (2006); Growing up in Multifaith Britain: Explorations in Youth, Ethnicity and Religion (2007); God-Shaped Mission: A Perspective from the Rural Church (2007); The Reflective Leader (2011); Joint editor, Faith in the Future of the Countryside (2012); Saints and Pilgrims in the Diocese of St Albans (2013).

Recreations: Skiing, travelling, gardening, playing and listening to music.

Rt Rev Dr the Lord Bishop of St Albans, House of Lords, London SW1A 0PW
Tel: 020 7219 5353
Abbey Gate House, Abbey Mill Lane, St Albans AL3 4HD *Tel:* 01727 853305
Email: bishop@stalbans.anglican.org *Website:* www.stalbans.anglican.org
Twitter: @BishopStAlbans

CROSSBENCH

ST JOHN OF BLETSO, LORD

ST JOHN OF BLETSO (21st Baron, E), Anthony Tudor St John; cr. 1558; 18th Bt of Bletso (E) 1660. Born 16 May 1957; Son of 20th Baron, TD; Married Dr Helen Jane Westlake 1994 (divorced 2012) (2 sons 2 daughters); married Sabina McTaggart 2015.

Education: Diocesan College, Cape Town, South Africa; University of Cape Town (BSocSc 1977; BA law 1979; BProc law 1982); London University (LLM 1983); Afrikaans, German, Xhosa.

Non-political career: Solicitor; Financial Consultant; Attorney in South Africa 1983-85; Oil Analyst/Stockbroker, County Natwest 1985-88; Consultant to Merrill Lynch 1988-2008; Director, Albion VCT 2012-; Chair: GRIT Plc 2014-, Strand Hanson 2014-, IDH Plc 2015-; Advisory Board Member: Silicon Valley Bank 2015-, Betway 2015-.

Political career: *House of Lords:* First entered House of Lords 1978; Extra Lord in Waiting to HM The Queen 1998-; Elected hereditary peer 1999-. Member: European Communities/Union Sub-committee A (Economic and Financial Affairs, Trade and External Relations) 1997-2003, Library and Computers Sub-committee 1998-2000, European Union Sub-committee B (Internal Market) 2003-07, Information 2008-13, 2015-16, Communications 2009-14, Artificial Intelligence 2017-.

Political interests: Foreign affairs, finance, legal affairs, sport, information technology, environment; China, Egypt, Kenya, Mozambique, Sierra Leone, South Africa, Zimbabwe.

Other: Chair: Governing Board of Certification International, Sierra Leone Business Forum; Trustee: TUSK 1997-2012, Citizens-on-Line 2000-08, TVE (Television for the Environment) 2002-12, Life Neurological Trust 2004, M'Afrika Tikkun 2006-, Alexandra Rose Charities: Member 2008-14, Deputy Chair 2014-; Christel House, Co-existence Trust, Helen Feather Memorial Trust; Trustee, Emeritas TVE 2012-; Unicef; *Clubs:* Alfreds Club. Sunningdale Golf; Hurlingham; Royal Cape Golf.

Recreations: Skiing, golf, tennis, bridge.

The Lord St John of Bletso, House of Lords, London SW1A 0PW
Tel: 020 7219 3886 *Email:* stjohna@parliament.uk
Email: stjohn1957@gmail.com

SALISBURY, LORD BISHOP OF

NON-AFFILIATED

SALISBURY (78th Bishop of), Nicholas Roderick Holtam. Born 8 August 1954; Son of late Sydney Holtam and Kathleen Holtam; Married Helen Harris 1981 (3 sons 1 daughter).

Education: Latymer Grammar School; Collingwood College, Durham University (BA geography 1975); King's College London (BA divinity 1978); Durham University (MA theology 1989).

Non-political career: Ordained deacon 1979; Priest 1980; Assistant curate, St Dunstan and All Saints Stepney 1979-83; Tutor, Lincoln Theology College 1983-87; Vicar: Christ Church and St John with St Luke's, Isle of Dogs 1988-95, St Martin-in-the-Fields 1995-2011; Bishop of Salisbury 2011-.

Political career: *House of Lords:* Entered House of Lords 2014.

Political interests: Environment, disability, homelessness; Latvia, Scandinavia, South Africa, South Sudan, Sudan.

Other: Trustee, National Churches Trust 2008-; Vice-President, Royal School of Church Music 2012-; Honorary Fellow, Guild of Church Musicians 2013. Hon. DCL, Durham University 2005; FKC King's College London 2005; *Clubs:* Farmers Club.

Publications: A Room With a View: Ministry with the World at your Door (2008); The Art of Worship (2011).

Recreations: Theatre, museums, walking, cycling, reading, writing.

Rt Rev the Lord Bishop of Salisbury, House of Lords, London SW1A 0PW
Tel: 020 7219 5353 *Email:* holtamn@parliament.uk
South Canonry, 71 The Close, Salisbury, Wiltshire SP1 2ER *Tel:* 01722 334031
Email: bishop.salisbury@salisbury.anglican.org *Website:* www.salisbury.anglican.org

SANDERSON OF BOWDEN, LORD

CONSERVATIVE

SANDERSON OF BOWDEN (Life Baron), Charles Russell Sanderson; cr. 1985. Born 30 April 1933; Son of late Charles Plummer Sanderson; Married Elizabeth Macaulay 1958 (1 son 2 daughters 1 son deceased).

Education: St Mary's School, Melrose; Glenalmond College, Perthshire; Bradford Technical College (textile design and management); Scottish College of Textiles, Galashiels (HND design 1955); French.

Non-political career: Army national service 1951-53: Commissioned Royal Signals 1952; King's Own Scottish Borderers: Commissioned 1955-58, Trustee 2000-11. Partner, Charles P. Sanderson wool and yarn merchants 1958-87; Director: Johnston of Elgin 1980-87, Illingworth Morris 1982-87; Chair: Edinburgh Financial Trust plc 1983-87, Shires Investment plc 1983-87; Clydesdale Bank plc: Director 1986-2004, Chair 1999-2004; Hawick Cashmere Co: Chair 1991-2013, Director 2013-15; Scottish Mortgage and Trust plc: Director 1991-2003, Chair 1993-2003; Director: Woolcombers plc 1992-95, Edinburgh Woollen Mills 1992-97, United Auctions Ltd 1992-99, Watson-Philip plc 1993-99, Morrison Construction 1995-2001, Develica Deutschland plc 2006-09, Accsys Technologies plc 2007-.

Political career: *House of Lords:* Raised to the peerage as Baron Sanderson of Bowden, of Melrose in the District of Ettrick and Lauderdale 1985. Minister of State, Scottish Office 1987-90. *Other:* Scottish Conservative and Unionist Association: President 1977-79, Hon President 2010-; Vice-President, National Union of Conservative and Unionist Associations 1979-81; Chair: National Union Executive Committee 1981-86, Scottish Conservative Party 1990-93; Chair, Sanderson Commission, Scottish Conservative Party 2010. *Councils and public bodies:* Chair, Council of Glenalmond College 1994-2000; Member of Court, Napier University, Edinburgh 1994-2001; President, Royal Highland Agricultural Society of Scotland 2002-03; Roxburgh, Ettrick and Lauderdale: DL 1990-2003, Vice-Lieutenant 2003-08.

Political interests: Industry, textile industry, small businesses, Scottish affairs, housing, transport; China, Hong Kong.

Other: Chair, Scottish Peers Association 1998-2000; President: Royal Highland Agricultural Society 2002-03, Royal Highland Show 2002-03; Abbotsford Trust: Board member 2007-, Chair 2007-15; Friends of Bowden Kirk Trust Fund. Worshipful Company of Framework Knitters: Liveryman, Master 2005-06. Two honorary degrees: Glasgow University, Napier University. Kt 1981; *Clubs:* Caledonian Club. Hon. Company of Edinburgh Golfers.

Recreations: Golf, fishing.

The Lord Sanderson of Bowden, House of Lords, London SW1A 0PW
Tel: 020 7219 5353
Email: rsanderson235@gmail.com

SANDWICH, EARL OF

CROSSBENCH

SANDWICH (11th Earl of, E), John Edward Hollister Montagu; cr. 1660; Viscount Hinchingbrooke and Baron Montagu. Born 11 April 1943; Son of Rosemary Maud Peto and Victor Montagu (10th Earl, formerly Viscount Hinchingbrooke MP, who disclaimed the earldom and other honours for life in 1964); Married (Susan) Caroline Hayman 1968 (2 sons 1 daughter).

Education: Eton College; Trinity College, Cambridge (BA history and modern language Tripos 1965, MA); Open University (Certificate European studies 1973); French, German.

Non-political career: Assistant editor, Bodley Head 1966-68; Editor, India Tourism Development Corporation 1968-69; Christian Aid: Information officer 1974-85, Research officer 1985-86, Board 1999-2004; Joint owner/administrator, Mapperton Estate, Dorset 1982-; Consultant, CARE Britain 1987-93; Editor, Save the Children 1990-92. Former member, National Union of Journalists.

Political career: *House of Lords:* First entered House of Lords 1995; Elected hereditary peer 1999-. Member: Standing Orders (Private Bills) 2000-01, Library and Computers Sub-committee 2001-04, Constitution 2005-07; Co-opted Member, EU Sub-committee E (Law and Institutions) 2009-10; Member: European Union 2010-15, EU Sub-committee E: (Justice and Institutions) 2010-12, (Justice, Institutions and Consumer Protection) 2012-13, EU Sub-committee C (External Affairs) 2013-15.

Political interests: Aid and development, international affairs, national heritage; Afghanistan, India, Mozambique, Nepal, South Africa, Sudan, Uganda, Zimbabwe.

Other: President, Samuel Pepys Club 1985-; Associate, Care International 1993-; Trustee, Britain-Afghanistan Trust 1994-2001; Council, Anti-Slavery International 1997-2006; Vice-President, Worldaware 1997-2001; International Development Affairs Committee, Church House 1997-2001; Patron: Trust for Africa's Orphans 2000-, Haslar Visitors 2002-15; Independent Asylum Commission 2007-09; Dorset Expeditionary Society 2011-13; Member, British College Advisory Panel, Kathmandu 2013-.

Publications: Author or editor: The Book of the World (1971); Prospects for Africa (1988); Prospects for Africa's Children (1990); Children at Crisis Point (1992); Co-editor, Hinch: A Celebration (1997).

Recreations: Walking, tennis, sailing, skiing.

The Earl of Sandwich, House of Lords, London SW1A 0PW
Tel: 020 7219 3882 *Email:* sandwichj@parliament.uk

SASSOON, LORD

CONSERVATIVE

SASSOON (Life Baron), James Meyer Sassoon; cr 2010. Born 11 September 1955; Son of Hugh Sassoon and Marion Sassoon, née Schiff; Married Sarah Barnes 1981 (1 son 2 daughters).

Education: Eton College; Christ Church, Oxford (BA philosophy, politics and economics 1977, MA).

Non-political career: Thomson McLintock & Co (KPMG) 1977-86; S G Warburg & Co 1987-95: Director 1991-95; Warburg Dillon Read/UBS Warburg: Managing director 1995-2002, Vice-chair, Corporate Finance 2000-02; HM Treasury (HMT) 2002-08: Managing Director, Finance Regulation and Industry Directorate 2002-06, HMT Representative for Promotion of the City 2006-08; Member: Financial Stability Forum 2002-06, EU Financial Services Committee 2003-06; President, Financial Action Task Force 2007-08; Adviser to George Osborne MP as Shadow Chancellor of the Exchequer 2008-10; Member, Economic Recovery Committee, Shadow Cabinet 2009-10; Executive director, Jardine Matheson 2013-.

Political career: *House of Lords:* Raised to the peerage as Baron Sassoon, of Ashley Park in the County of Surrey 2010. Commercial Secretary and Government Spokesperson, HM Treasury 2010-13. Member, Consumer Insurance (Disclosure and Representations) Bill 2011-12. *Councils and public bodies:* Trustee, British Museum 2009-10, 2013-.

Political interests: Trade and investment, financial services; China, UK's major trading partners and inward/outward investors.

Other: Director, Partnerships UK 2002-06; Trustee, National Gallery Trust 2002-09; Merchants Trust plc: Director 2006-10, Chair 2010; Director, Nuclear Liabilities Fund 2008-10; Chair: ifs School of Finance 2009-10, China-Britain Business Council 2013-; Committee member, Hong Kong Association 2013-; Member, Global Advisory Board, Mitsubishi UFJ Financial Grpup 2013-; FCA. Kt 2008.

Publications: Author, The Tripartite Review (2009).

Recreations: Travel, the arts, gardening.

The Lord Sassoon, House of Lords, London SW1A 0PW
Tel: 020 7219 5353 *Email:* sassoonjm@parliament.uk
Matheson and Co Ltd, 3 Lombard Street, London, London EC3V 9AQ *Tel:* 020 7816 8100
Fax: 020 7623 5024 *Email:* jsassoon@matheson.co.uk

CROSSBENCH

SAVILLE OF NEWDIGATE, LORD

SAVILLE OF NEWDIGATE (Life Baron), Mark Oliver Saville; cr. 1997. Born 20 March 1936; Son of Kenneth and Olivia Saville; Married Jill Gray 1961 (2 sons).

Education: Rye Grammar School; Brasenose College, Oxford (Vinerian Scholar, BA law 1959; BCL 1960).

Non-political career: Second Lieutenant, Royal Sussex Regiment 1954-56. Called to the Bar, Middle Temple 1962; QC 1975; Bencher 1983; Judge of the High Court, Queen's Bench Division 1985-93; Lord Justice of Appeal 1994-97; Justice of the Supreme Court of the United Kingdom 2009-10.

Political career: *House of Lords:* Raised to the peerage as Baron Saville of Newdigate, of Newdigate in the County of Surrey 1997. Lord of Appeal in Ordinary 1997-2009; As Justice of the Supreme Court, disqualified from participation 2009-10. Chair, Intellectual Property (Unjustified Threats) Bill 2016.

Other: Two honorary law doctorates. Kt 1985; PC 1994; *Clubs:* Garrick Club.

Recreations: Sailing, flying, gardening, computers.

Rt Hon the Lord Saville of Newdigate, House of Lords, London SW1A 0PW
Tel: 020 7219 5353

LABOUR

SAWYER, LORD

SAWYER (Life Baron), Lawrence Sawyer; cr. 1998. Born 12 May 1943.

Education: Dodmire School; Eastbourne School; Darlington Technical School and College.

Non-political career: Engineering apprentice, Robert Stephenson and Hawthorne 1958-63; Engineering inspector, Lockhead Brakes, Leamington Spa 1963-65; Engineering inspection and work study officer, Cummins Engines, Darlington 1965-71; NUPE: Officer 1971-75, Northern Regional Officer 1975-81, Deputy General Secretary, NUPE/Unison 1981-94; Director: Investors in People UK 1998-2005, Reed Executive plc 1998-2001, Britannia Building Society 1999-2009; Visiting Professor, Cranfield Business School 1999-2013; Chair, Notting Hill Housing Association 1999-2004; Union Income Benefit Advisory Board 2000-; Royal Mail Partnership Board 2001-08; Reed Healthcare plc 2001-04; Thompsons Solicitors Supervisory Board 2001-10; Chair, Norlife 2004-. Member, Unison: Deputy General Secretary 1982-94.

Political career: *House of Lords:* Raised to the peerage as Baron Sawyer, of Darlington in the County of Durham 1998. Member: Affordable Childcare 2014-15, Refreshment 2015-16. *Other:* Labour Party: Member, National Executive 1982-94, 1998-2001, Chair, Labour Home Policy Committee 1989-94, Party Chair 1992, General Secretary 1994-98.

Political interests: Housing, employment, education, Royal Mail; Americas, Europe, South Africa.

Other: Member: Post Office Northern Advisory Board 1997-99, Nurses' and Midwives' Whitley Council 1997-99, NJIC for Manual Workers 1997-99; Cystic Fibrosis. Chancellor, Teesside University 2005-.

Recreations: Antiquarian book dealer and collector.

The Lord Sawyer, House of Lords, London SW1A 0PW
Tel: 020 7219 8668

LABOUR

SCOTLAND OF ASTHAL, BARONESS

SCOTLAND OF ASTHAL (Life Baroness), Patricia Janet Scotland; cr. 1997. Born 19 August 1955; Daughter of Arthur and Dellie Marie Scotland; Married Richard Mawhinney 1985 (2 sons).

Education: Walthamstow School for Girls; London University (LLB 1976).

Non-political career: Called to the Bar, Middle Temple 1977; Founding member, later head of chambers, 1 Gray's Inn Square 1979-; QC 1991; Assistant recorder 1992; Bencher 1997; Barrister specialising in family and administrative law 1997-91; Recorder 2000; Member, Bar of Antigua and Bar of the Commonwealth of Dominica; Secretary-General of the Commonwealth of Nations 2016-.

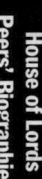

Political career: *House of Lords:* Raised to the peerage as Baroness Scotland of Asthal, of Asthal in the County of Oxfordshire 1997. Parliamentary Under-Secretary of State and Government Spokesperson for Foreign and Commonwealth Office 1999-2001; Parliamentary Secretary, Lord Chancellor's Department and Government Spokesperson for Law Officers' Department 2001-03; Minister of State and Government Spokesperson for Home Office 2003-07; Government Spokesperson for: Trade and Industry 2004-05, Women's Issues/Equal Agenda; Attorney General and Government Spokesperson for the Law Officers (attending cabinet) 2007-10; Shadow Attorney General 2010-11; Opposition Spokesperson for the Law Officers 2010-11; Trade envoy to South Africa 2012-16; On leave of absence March 2016-. Member: Privileges and Conduct 2012-16, Communications 2013-16. *Councils and public bodies:* Former member, Commission for Racial Equality; Alderman, Corporation of London 2014-.

Other: Alternate UK Government Representative, European Convention 2002-03; Member: Millennium Commission 1994-99, Thomas More Society, Lawyers' Christian Fellowship; Patron: Margaret Beaufort Institute, GAP; Vice-patron: CFAB, Almshouses Association. Chancellor, Greenwich University. Five honorary doctorates, Universities of Westminster, Buckingham, Leicester, East London and West Indies; Honorary Fellow: Wolfson College, Cambridge, Cardiff University. Peer of the Year, *House Magazine* awards 2004; Peer of the Year, Channel 4 2004; Parliamentarian of the Year, Political Studies Association 2004; Parliamentarian of the Year, *Spectator* 2005; Kathleen Carlin Justice Seekers award 2008; Lifetime Achievement award, Black Solicitors Network 2009; Female Personality of the Year award, GV Media Group 2009; Anti-corruption award, Doha 2009; European Women in Business Law Lifetime Achievement award, Euromoney Legal Media Group 2011. PC 2001.

Rt Hon the Baroness Scotland of Asthal QC, House of Lords, London SW1A 0PW
Tel: 020 7219 3000 *Twitter:* @PScotlandCSG

CONSERVATIVE

SCOTT OF BYBROOK, BARONESS

SCOTT OF BYBROOK (Life Baroness), Jane Antoinette Scott; cr 2015. Born 13 June 1947; Married (3 children).

Education: Lancashire College of Agriculture.

Non-political career: Dairy industry; Public relations; Marketing; Lecturer; Director, iESE Transformation Ltd.

Political career: *House of Lords:* Raised to the peerage as Baroness Scott of Bybrook, of Upper Wraxall in the County of Wiltshire 2015. Member, Natural Environment and Rural Communities Act 2006 2017-. *Councils and public bodies:* Wiltshire County Council: Councillor 1997-2009, Leader 2003-09; Wiltshire Council: Councillor 2009-, Leader 2009-; Member: Local Government Association, Court, Bath University; Member, independent taskforce, Royal Borough of Kensington recovery plan (following Grenville Tower fire) 2017-.

Other: Member: National Youth Agency, Wiltshire and Swindon Learning Skills Council; Chair, Wiltshire Strategic Board; Local Authority Inspector, Ofsted. OBE 2010.

The Baroness Scott of Bybrook OBE, House of Lords, London SW1A 0PW
Tel: 020 7219 3000
c/o Wiltshire Council, Bythesea Road, Trowbridge, Wiltshire BA14 8JN
Website: janescott.co.uk

LIBERAL DEMOCRAT

SCOTT OF NEEDHAM MARKET, BARONESS

SCOTT OF NEEDHAM MARKET (Life Baroness), Rosalind Carol Scott; cr. 2000. Born 10 August 1957; Daughter of Kenneth Vincent and Carol Leadbeater; Married Mark Valladares 2008 (1 son 1 daughter from previous marriage).

Education: Whitby Grammar School; Kent School; University of East Anglia (BA European studies 1999).

Political career: *House of Lords:* Raised to the peerage as Baroness Scott of Needham Market, of Needham Market in the County of Suffolk 2000. Liberal Democrat: Whip 2001-02, Deputy Chief Whip 2002, Spokesperson for: Transport, Local Government and the Regions 2001-02, Transport 2002-04, Office of the Deputy Prime Minister/Communities and Local Government 2004-09. Member: Liaison 2003-07, Delegated Powers and Regulatory Reform 2005-07, Communications 2007-10, Leader's Group on Members Leaving the House 2010-15, EU Sub-Committee G (Social Policies and Consumer Protection) 2011-12, Joint Committee on the Draft House of Lords Reform Bill 2011-12, European Union 2012-16, EU Sub-committee B (Internal Market, Infrastructure and Employment) 2012-13; Chair: EU Sub-committee D (Agriculture, Fisheries, Environment and Energy) 2013-15, EU Energy and Environment Sub-committee 2015-16; Member: Joint Committee on Statutory Instruments 2016-, Charities 2016-17, Natural Environment and Rural Communities Act 2006 2017-. *Other:* President, Liberal Democrat Party 2008-10; Vice-President, Alliance Liberal Democrats in Europe. *Councils and public bodies:* Councillor, Mid Suffolk District Council 1991-94; Suffolk County Council: Councillor 1993-2005, Vice-chair 1996-97, Chair, Transport Committee, Local Government Association 2002-04; Member, House of Lords Appointments Commission 2010-.

Political interests: Transport, Europe; Commonwealth, India, USA.

Other: Member: North Sea Commission 1997-2005, Council of European Municipalities and Regions 1997-2003, Congress of Local and Regional Authorities in Europe 1997-2003, EU Committee of the Regions 1998-2002, Inter-Parliamentary Union 2000-; Commonwealth Parliamentary Association 2000-; Trustee, Industry and Parliament Trust; Patron, ACE Anglia; Hon. Member, Chartered Institute Highways and Transportation; Suffolk Foundation; *Clubs:* Royal Commonwealth Society Club.

Recreations: Walking, political biography, genealogy.

The Baroness Scott of Needham Market, House of Lords, London SW1A 0PW
Tel: 020 7219 8660 *Email:* scottrc@parliament.uk *Twitter:* @BaronessRos

LIBERAL DEMOCRAT

SCRIVEN, LORD

SCRIVEN (Life Baron), Paul James Scriven; cr 2014. Born 7 February 1966; Partner.

Education: Rawthorpe High School, Huddersfield; Huddersfield Technical College; Manchester Polytechnic (BA); Sheffield University (Postgraduate Course health economics).

Non-political career: Senior manager, NHS; Director, Apps2Connect; Managing partner, Scriven Consulting 2010-.

Political career: *House of Commons:* Contested (Liberal Democrat) Sheffield Central 2010 general election. *House of Lords:* Raised to the peerage as Baron Scriven, of Hunters Bar in the City of Sheffield 2014. Member: EU Justice Sub-committee 2015-16, Long-Term Sustainability of the NHS 2016-17; Alternate Member, Procedure 2017-. *Councils and public bodies:* Sheffield City Council: Councillor 2000-12, 2016-, Leader of the Council 2008-11; Member, South Yorkshire Fire Authority 2001-12; Sheffield Executive Board 2006-11; Sheffield Local Enterprise Partnership 2010-11; Vice-president, Local Government Association 2017-.

Political interests: Local government, health, international LGBTI issues, civil liberties; Malaysia, Philippines, Singapore, Thailand.

Recreations: Walking, travel.

The Lord Scriven, House of Lords, London SW1A 0PW
Tel: 020 7219 5353 *Twitter:* @Paulscriven

CONSERVATIVE

SECCOMBE, BARONESS

SECCOMBE (Life Baroness), Joan Anna Dalziel Seccombe; cr. 1991. Born 3 May 1930; Daughter of late Robert Owen and Olive Barlow Owen; Married Henry Seccombe 1950 (died 2008) (2 sons).

Education: St Martin's, Solihull.

Political career: *House of Lords:* Raised to the peerage as Baroness Seccombe, of Kineton in the County of Warwickshire 1991. Opposition Whip 1997-2001; Opposition Deputy Chief Whip 2001-10; Opposition Spokesperson for: Education and Skills 2003-04, Legal Affairs 2003-06, Home Affairs 2004-07; Extra Baroness in Waiting to HM The Queen 2004-; Opposition Spokesperson for: Constitutional Affairs 2005-06, Constitutional and Legal Affairs/Justice 2006-10; Party Whip 2010-. Member: Information 2012-15, Consolidation, Etc, Bills Joint Committee 2014-, Liaison 2015-17. *Other:* Chairman: West Midlands Conservative Women's Committee 1975-78, Conservative Women's National Committee 1981-84; National Union of Conservative and Unionist Associations: Chairman 1987-88, Vice-chairman 1984-87, Member of Executive 1975-97; Chairman, Conservative Party Annual Conference, Blackpool 1987; Vice-chairman, Conservative Party with special responsibility for Women 1987-97. *Councils and public bodies:* JP, Solihull 1968-2000, Chairman of Bench 1981-84; Chairman, Lord Chancellor's Advisory Committee, Solihull 1975-93; Councillor, West Midlands County Council 1977-81, Chairman, Trading Standards Committee 1979-81; Member, Women's National Commission 1984-90; Governor, Nuffield Hospitals 1988-2001; Vice-President, Institute of Trading Standards Administration 1992-.

Political interests: Women's issues, family, criminal justice.

Other: Chair, Trustees of Nuffield Hospitals Pension Scheme 1992-2001; Trustee, Industry and Parliament Trust. DBE 1984. President, St Enedoc Golf Club 1992-.

Recreations: Golf, needlework.

The Baroness Seccombe DBE, House of Lords, London SW1A 0PW
Tel: 020 7219 4558 *Email:* seccombej@parliament.uk

House of Lords Peers' Biographies

CONSERVATIVE

SELBORNE, EARL OF

SELBORNE (4th Earl of, UK), John Roundell Palmer; cr. 1882; Viscount Wolmer; 4th Baron Selborne (UK) 1872. Born 24 March 1940; Son of Captain Viscount Wolmer (died on active service 1942), son of 3rd Earl, PC, CH; Married Joanna Van Antwerp, née James 1969 (3 sons 1 daughter).

Education: Eton College; Christ Church, Oxford (BA history 1961, MA).

Non-political career: Director: Lloyds Bank plc 1994-95, Lloyds TSB Group plc 1995-2004; Chair, Partners Board, Living with Environmental Change Programme 2008-12.

Political career: *House of Lords:* Succeeded the Peerage 1971; First entered House of Lords 1972; Elected hereditary peer 1999-; Board Member, Parliamentary Office of Science and Technology 2014-17. Chair, European Communities Sub-committee D 1991-93, 1999-2003; Science and Technology: Member 1992-97, 2005-14, Chair 1993-97; Member, European Union 1999-2003; Co-opted member, Science and Technology Sub-committee I (Systematic Biology and Biodiversity) 2002; Member, House of Lords Reform Joint Committee 2002-03; Chair, Science and Technology Sub-committee I (Water Management) 2005-07; Member: Draft Climate Change Bill Joint Committee 2007, Science and Technology Sub-committee I 2007-10 (Allergy/Waste Reduction 2007-08, Nanotechnologies and food 2008-10), Communications 2011-14; Chair, Science and Technology 2014-17. *Councils and public bodies:* Member, Apple and Pear Development Council 1969-73; Chair: Hops Marketing Board 1978-82, Agricultural and Food Research Council 1982-89; DL, Hampshire 1982; President: Royal Agricultural Society of England 1987-88, Royal Institute of Public Health and Hygiene 1991-97; Chair, Joint Nature Conservation Committee 1991-97; Member: NEDC Food Sector Group 1991-92, Royal Commission on Environmental Pollution 1993-98; President, Royal Geographical Society (with the Institute of British Geographers) 1997-2000; Chair, Foundation for Science and Technology 2006-.

Political interests: Science, agriculture, education, conservation; Azerbaijan, Kazakhstan.

Other: World Commission on the Ethics of Science and Technology, UNESCO 1999-2003; Chair of Trustees, Royal Botanic Gardens, Kew 2003-09; FRS 1991; FSB; Hon. Fellow, Linnean Society. Master, Mercers' Company 1989. Chancellor, Southampton University 1996-2006. Five honorary doctorates. KBE 1987; GBE 2011; *Clubs:* Travellers Club.

The Earl of Selborne GBE DL, House of Lords, London SW1A 0PW
Tel: 020 7219 6171 *Email:* selbornejr@parliament.uk
Email: selbornejr@gmail.com

CONSERVATIVE

SELKIRK OF DOUGLAS, LORD

SELKIRK OF DOUGLAS (Life Baron), James Alexander Douglas-Hamilton; cr. 1997. Born 31 July 1942; Son of late 14th Duke of Hamilton and Brandon, KT, PC, GCVO, AFC, DL, and late Lady Elizabeth Percy, OBE, DL, daughter of 8th Duke of Northumberland, KG, CBE, MVO; Married Hon Susan Buchan 1974 (4 sons including twins).

Education: Eton College; Balliol College, Oxford (BA modern history 1964) (Oxford Boxing Blue 1961-62); President, Oxford Union Society Summer 1964); Edinburgh University (LLB Scots law 1967).

Non-political career: Officer 6/7th Btn, Cameronians TA 1961-66; 2nd Btn Lowland Volunteers, TAVR 1971-74; Captain Cameronians TA 1973; Hon. Air Commodore No 2 (City of Edinburgh), Maritime Headquarters Unit 1995-99; Hon. Air Commodore No 603 (City of Edinburgh) Squadron 2000-15. Scots Advocate 1968-76; Depute Procurator Fiscal: Dumfries 1969, Edinburgh 1972; QC 1996.

Political career: *House of Commons:* MP (Conservative) for Edinburgh West 1974-97. Contested Edinburgh West 1997 general election. Opposition Whip 1976-79; Government Whip 1979-81; PPS to Malcolm Rifkind: as Minister of State, Foreign Office 1983-85, as Secretary of State for Scotland 1986-87; Scottish Office 1987-95: Parliamentary Under-Secretary of State 1987-95, Minister of State 1995-97. *House of Lords:* Raised to the peerage as Baron Selkirk of Douglas, of Cramond in the City of Edinburgh 1997. EU Sub-committee C (Foreign Affairs, Defence and Development Policy): Co-opted member 2008-10, Member 2011-12; Member Joint Committees on: Statutory Instruments 2012-15, Draft Deregulation Bill 2013; Member: EU Energy and Environment Sub-Committee 2015-, European Union 2016-. *Other:* Scottish Parliament: Contested Edinburgh West constituency 1999 and 2003 elections, MSP for Lothians region 1999-2007 (as Lord James Douglas-Hamilton): Member, Parliamentary Bureau 1999-2001, Business Manager/ Chief Whip, Conservative Group 1999-2001, Conservative Spokesperson for: Justice 2001-03, Education 2003-07. President, Oxford University Conservative Association Winter 1963. *Councils and public bodies:* Councillor, Edinburgh Corporation 1972-74; President: Royal Commonwealth Society in Scotland 1979-87, Scottish National Council, UN Association 1981-87; Member, Commission on Scottish Devolution (Calman Commission) 2008-09.

Political interests: Foreign affairs, defence, Scottish affairs, law reform, conservation, arts, housing, health, education, local government, environment, heritage; Africa, Asia, Australasia, Europe, Middle East, North America.

Other: Hon. President, Scottish Boxing Association 1975-98; President, International Rescue Corps 1995-; Edinburgh Support Group of Hope and Homes for Children: Chairman 2002-07, Patron 2007-; President: Scottish Veterans' Garden City Association 2007-, Trefoil Centre 2007; Chair, Scottish Advisory Committee, SkillForce; Member, Royal Company of Archers, Queen's Bodyguard for Scotland; Trustee, Selkirk Charitable Trust; Lord High Commissioner, General Assembly, Church of Scotland 2012-13; Chair, Scottish Peers' Association 2016-. Disclaimed the Earldom of Selkirk, November 1994; PC 1996; *Clubs:* Honorary Member, Royal Scots Club, Sloane Club. Member, Muirfield (Honorable Company of Edinburgh Golfers).

Publications: Motive for a Mission: The Story Behind Hess's Flight to Britain (1971); The Air Battle for Malta: The Diaries of a Fighter Pilot (1981); Roof of the World: Man's First Flight over Everest (1983); The Truth About Rudolf Hess (1993, new edition 2016); After You, Prime Minister (Stacey International, 2010).

Recreations: Golf, boxing, forestry, debating, history.

Rt Hon the Lord Selkirk of Douglas QC, House of Lords, London SW1A 0PW
Tel: 020 7219 2131 *Email:* selkirkj@parliament.uk

CONSERVATIVE

SELSDON, LORD

SELSDON (3rd Baron, UK), Malcolm McEacharn Mitchell-Thomson; cr. 1932; 4th Bt of Polmood (UK) 1900. Born 27 October 1937; Son of 2nd Baron, DSC.

Education: Winchester College; French, German.

Non-political career: Sub-Lieutenant RNVR, Royal Navy 1956-58. Plastics products manager, Universal Asbestos (UAM) 1959-63; Director, market analysis and research services, London Press Exchange Group 1964-72; European mergers and acquisitions, Singer & Friedlander (CT Bowring Group) 1972-76; Midland Bank Group 1976-90; International board member, Merloni Group, Italy 1978-98; Peasant farmer, Provence, France (vineyard and olive groves) 1987-; Deputy chairman, Comcap plc 1988-93; UK board member, Raab Karcher, Germany 1994-98; Director, MJ Gleeson Group plc 1996-2006; Director international banking, Samuel Montagu & Co; EU and public finance adviser.

Political career: *House of Lords:* First entered House of Lords 1963; Elected hereditary peer 1999-. Member: EC Sub-committee B (Internal Market, Energy and Transport) 1974-76, EC Sub-committee A (Economic and Financial Affairs and International Trade) 1974-84, Draft Human Tissue and Embryos Bill Joint Committee 2007, Information 2008-13. *Other:* Treasurer, Conservative Group on Europe. *Councils and public bodies:* Chair: Greater London and South East Council for Sport and Recreation 1977-83, Committee for Middle East Trade 1979-86; Member: British Overseas Trade Board 1983-86, East European Trade Council 1983-86.

Political interests: Trade and industry, foreign affairs, defence, economic and finance, health and technology, construction and planning; Africa, China, Commonwealth and overseas territories, EU, Middle East, Russia and former Soviet Union.

Other: British Delegate, Council of Europe and Western European Union 1972-78; President: British Exporters' Association 1992-98, Anglo Swiss Society 2001-. Secretary and treasurer, House of Lords Yacht Club; Member, MCC 1958-.

Recreations: Skiing, sailing, tennis, lawn tennis, golf.

The Lord Selsdon, House of Lords, London SW1A 0PW
Tel: 020 7219 6668 *Email:* selsdonm@parliament.uk

CONSERVATIVE

SHACKLETON OF BELGRAVIA, BARONESS

SHACKLETON OF BELGRAVIA (Life Baroness), Fiona Sara Shackleton; cr 2010. Born 26 May 1956; Daughter of late Jonathan Charkham CBE; Married Ian Shackleton (2 daughters).

Education: Francis Holland School; Benenden School; Exeter University (LLB 1977).

Non-political career: Articled clerk, Herbert Smith 1978-80; Admitted solicitor 1980; Partner: Brecher and Co. 1981-84, Farrer and Co. 1987-2000; Personal solicitor to: The Prince of Wales 1996-2005, Prince William of Wales 1996-, Prince Harry of Wales 1996-; Partner, Payne Hicks Beach Solicitors.

Political career: *House of Lords:* Raised to the peerage as Baroness Shackleton of Belgravia, of Belgravia in the City of Westminster 2010. Member, EU Justice Sub-committee 2015-. *Councils and public bodies:* Governor, Benenden School 1986-2007.

Other: Inaugural member, International Academy of Matrimonial Lawyers 1986-; Trustee: Broad Cairn Foundation, Glen Beg Foundation, Sir Frank Lowe's Football Trust -2017, Royal Opera House Endowment Fund; Director, Diana, Princess of Wales Memorial Fund Trustee Company -2017; Member, advisory council, London Philharmonic Orchestra. Hon. LLD, Exeter University 2010; Elected Master of the Bench, Inner Temple 2011. LVO 2005.

Publications: Co-author, The Divorce Handbook (1992).

The Baroness Shackleton of Belgravia LVO, House of Lords, London SW1A 0PW
Tel: 020 7219 5353
Email: fshackleton@phb.co.uk

LIBERAL DEMOCRAT

SHARKEY, LORD

SHARKEY (Life Baron), John Kevin Sharkey; cr 2010. Born 24 September 1947; Married (3 daughters).

Education: Manchester University (BSc mathematics 1968).

Non-political career: Benton & Bowles, KMP; Saatchi & Saatchi: Joined 1984, Deputy Chair 1986, Managing Director 1987; Chair, Broad Street Group, BDDP; Founder, Joint Chair and Chief Executive, Bainsfair Sharkey Trott/BST-BDDP 1990-97; Joint Chair, BDDP GGT 1997-98; Managing Director, Europe Manpower plc 1998; Chair, Sharkey Associates Ltd; Chief Operating Officer, Blue Arrow plc; Communications Adviser to Nick Clegg 2006-10.

Political career: *House of Lords:* Raised to the peerage as Baron Sharkey, of Niton Undercliff in the County of Isle of Wight 2010. Liberal Democrat Spokesperson for Personal Finances 2015-. Member: EU Sub-committee F (Home Affairs, Health and Education) 2012-15, Joint Committee on the Draft Deregulation Bill 2013, Information 2014-16, Economic Affairs 2015-. *Other:* Liberal Democrats: Chair, general election campaign 2010, Campaign director, YES to Fairer Votes for the 2011 Referendum.

Political interests: Finance, health, education, NW England, Isle of Wight; Cyprus, Middle East, Turkey.

Other: Non-executive Chair, Highland Partners Europe -2006; Hansard Society: Member 2004-, Hon Treasurer 2007-, Chair 2016-; Governor, Institute for Government 2013-; Chair, Association of Medical Research Charities 2015-; Director: New City Agenda 2014-, Full Fact Ltd 2015-; Chair: Specialised Healthcare Alliance 2017-, Member of Council, UCL 2017.

The Lord Sharkey, House of Lords, London SW1A 0PW
Tel: 020 7219 5353 *Email:* sharkeyjk@parliament.uk

CONSERVATIVE

SHARPLES, BARONESS

SHARPLES (Life Baroness), Pamela Sharples; cr. 1973. Born 11 February 1923; Daughter of late Lieutenant-Commander K W Newall, RN; Married Major Richard C Sharples, OBE, MC 1946 (later Sir Richard Sharples, Governor of Bermuda, assassinated 1973) (2 sons 2 daughters); married Patrick D de Laszlo 1977 (died 1980); married Robert Douglas Swan 1983 (died 1995).

Education: Southover Manor, Lewes; Florence University; French, some Italian.

Non-political career: WAAF 1941-46. Director, TVS 1982-93; Former publican.

Political career: *House of Lords:* Raised to the peerage as Baroness Sharples, of Chawton in the County of Hampshire 1973. Member, Leader's Group on Members Leaving the House 2010-15. *Councils and public bodies:* Member, Review Body on Armed Services Pay 1979-81.

Political interests: Small businesses, cheque-book journalism, prisoners' wives, pet quarantine, defence; South Africa.

Other: Member, Wessex Medical Trust 1997-2000. Defence Medal; War Medal; *Clubs:* Mid-Ocean Bermuda Club. Parliamentary Golf, Rushmoor Park.

Recreations: Golf, walking, gardening.

The Baroness Sharples, House of Lords, London SW1A 0PW
Tel: 020 7219 4456 *Email:* sharplesp@parliament.uk

LIBERAL DEMOCRAT

SHEEHAN, BARONESS

Liberal Democrat Shadow Secretary of State for International Development

SHEEHAN (Life Baroness), Shaista (Shas) Ahmad Sheehan; cr 2015. Born 29 July 1959; Married Patrick (3 children).

Education: Rosa Bassett Grammar School; University College London (BSc chemistry 1978); Imperial College (MSc environmental technology 1990).

Non-political career: Chemistry teacher; Nursing auxiliary, New Cross Hospital; Senior planner and buyer in advertising 1981-2005; Head of office to Susan Kramer MP 2005-08; Charity worker, Wimbledon Guild Daycentre and Faith in Action project for homeless people 2010-15.

Political career: *House of Commons:* Contested (Liberal Democrat) Wimbledon 2010 and 2015 general elections. *House of Lords:* Raised to the peerage as Baroness Sheehan, of Wimbledon in the London Borough of Merton and of Tooting in the London Borough of Wandsworth 2015. Liberal Democrat Shadow Secretary of State for International Development 2016-. Member, EU Energy and Environment Sub-committee 2015-. *Other:* Contested Londonwide region 2012 London Assembly election. Member, Green Lib Dems. *Councils and public bodies:* London Borough of Richmond upon Thames: Councillor 2006-10, Assistant Cabinet Member for Energy and Climate Change; Governor, Queen's CoE Primary School.

Other: Chair, Wimbledon Cancer Friendship Group; Trustee, Merton and Lambeth Citizen's Advice Bureau; Founding Member, 20's Plenty for Merton Steering Group; RSPB, Amnesty International, London Wildlife Trust.

Recreations: Spending time with family, walking, reading, cooking.

The Baroness Sheehan, House of Lords, London SW1A 0PW
Tel: 020 7219 3000 *Twitter:* @sheehanshas

CONSERVATIVE

SHEIKH, LORD

SHEIKH (Life Baron), Mohamed Iltaf Sheikh; cr 2006. Born 13 June 1941; Son of Mohamed Abdullah Sheikh and Kalsum Ara, née Bux; Married Shaida Begum Thantrey 1986 (1 daughter from previous marriage).

Education: Government Secondary School, Mbale, Uganda; City of London College (associateship Chartered Insurance Institute 1966); Holborn College (FCII 1968).

Non-political career: Section manager, Sun Alliance Insurance Co 1962-66; Accident underwriter, Household and General Insurance Company 1966-68; Principal officer, Guardian Royal Exchange 1968-78; Chair and chief executive, Camberford Law plc 1978-2008.

Political career: *House of Lords:* Raised to the peerage as Baron Sheikh, of Cornhill in the City of London 2006. Member, Communications 2016-17. *Other:* Conservative Muslim Forum: Chair 2004-14, President 2014-; Chair, Conservative Ethnic Diversity Council 2005-.

Political interests: Ethnic issues, environment, financial services, economy, home and international affairs, pensions.

Other: President, chair, council member several financial, especially insurance, bodies; British Insurance Brokers Association (BIBA): Regional chair 1991-92, 1996-97, Director; Director, South London Training and Enterprise Council 1998-99, 1999-2003. Freedom, City of London 1995.

Recreations: Keep-fit, walking, countryside, travel.

The Lord Sheikh, House of Lords, London SW1A 0PW
Tel: 020 7219 4542 *Email:* sheikhm@parliament.uk
Website: lordsheikh.com

CONSERVATIVE

SHEPHARD OF NORTHWOLD, BARONESS

SHEPHARD OF NORTHWOLD (Life Baroness), Gillian Patricia Shephard; cr 2005. Born 22 January 1940; Daughter of late Reginald and Bertha Watts; Married Thomas Shephard 1975 (2 stepsons).

Education: North Walsham Girls' High School; St Hilda's College, Oxford (BA modern languages 1961, MA); French, rusty German.

Non-political career: Education officer and schools inspector, Norfolk County Council 1963-75; Part-time lecturer, Workers' Educational Association and Cambridge Extra Mural Board 1965-87; Anglia TV 1975-77.

Political career: *House of Commons:* MP (Conservative) for South West Norfolk 1987-2005. PPS to Peter Lilley as Economic Secretary to the Treasury 1988-89; Parliamentary Under-Secretary of State, Department of Social Security 1989-90; Minister of State, HM Treasury 1990-92; Secretary of State for Employment and for Women's Issues 1992-93; Minister of Agriculture, Fisheries and Food 1993-94; Secretary of State for Education (and Employment) 1995-97; Shadow Leader of the House of Commons 1997-98; Member House of Commons Commission 1997-99; Shadow Chancellor of the Duchy of Lancaster 1997-98; Shadow Secretary of State for the Environment, Transport and the Regions 1998-99. *House of Lords:* Raised to the peerage as Baroness Shephard of Northwold, of Northwold in the County of Norfolk 2005. Member, Speakers' Working Group on All-Party Groups 2011-12. Member: Selection 2007-10, Procedure 2007-10, Joint Committee on the Draft House of Lords Reform Bill 2011-12, Public Service and Demographic Change 2012-13, Mental Capacity Act 2005 2013-14, Affordable Childcare 2014-15; Chair, Leader's Group on Governance 2015. *Other:* Conservative Party: Joint deputy chair 1991-92, Head, Candidates Development Unit 2001-03, Deputy chair 2002-03, Chair, Association of Conservative Peers 2007-12, Board member Board 2007-12. *Councils and public bodies:* JP 1973-; Norfolk County Council: Councillor 1977-89, Deputy Leader 1982-87; Government co-chair, Women's National Commission 1990; DL, Norfolk 2003-; Member, Committee on Standards in Public Life 2003-07; President, Norfolk Association of Local Councils 2009-; Deputy chair, Social Mobility Commission 2013-.

Political interests: Constitution, education, agriculture and rural affairs; Latin America, France.

Other: Member, Franco-British Council 2000-07; Oxford University: Council member 2002-06, Member, Continuing Education Board 2004-; Chair, Franco-British Society 2005-11; Member, Fawcett Commission 2005-; Patron, WEA 2006-; Royal Veterinary College: Chair of council 2006-, Fellow 2012-; Chair, Oxford University Society 2009-; Chair of council, Institute of Education 2010-; Council member, Royal Norfolk Agricultural Association; Trustee, Norwich Cathedral; Fellow, Royal Veterinary College; EDP We Care Appeal. Hon. fellow: St Hilda's College, Oxford, Queen Mary, University of London. PC 1992; Légion d'Honneur (France) 2009; *Clubs:* Norfolk Club.

Publications: Reforming Local Government (1999); Shephard's Watch (2000); Knapton Remembered (2007); Twentieth Century Village Voices (2011); The Real Iron Lady – Working with Margaret Thatcher (2013).

Recreations: Music, gardening, France.

Rt Hon the Baroness Shephard of Northwold, House of Lords, London SW1A 0PW
Tel: 020 7219 6241

SHERBOURNE OF DIDSBURY, LORD

CONSERVATIVE

SHERBOURNE OF DIDSBURY (Life Baron), Stephen Ashley Sherbourne; cr 2013. Born 15 October 1945; Son of the late Jack and Blanche Sherbourne.

Education: Burnage Grammar School, Manchester; St Edmund Hall, Oxford (MA philosophy, politics and economics); French, Italian.

Non-political career: Conservative Research Department: Head of economic section 1973-74, Assistant director 1974-75; Head of office for Edward Heath MP 1975-76; Special adviser to Patrick Jenkin as Secretary of State for Industry 1982-83; Political secretary to Margaret Thatcher as Prime Minister 1983-88; Senior corporate communications consultant, Lowe Bell Communications 1988-92; Managing director, Lowe Bell Consultants/Bell Pottinger Consultants 1992-99; Chair, Lowe Bell Political/Bell Pottinger Public Affairs 1994-2001; Director, Chime Communications plc 2001-03; Chief of Staff to Michael Howard as Leader of the Opposition 2003-05; Director: Smithfield Consultants 2006-, Newscounter 2007-10, Trufflenet 2010-; Chair, Interel Consulting UK 2012-13.

Political career: *House of Lords:* Raised to the peerage as Baron Sherbourne of Didsbury, of Didsbury in the City of Manchester 2013. Member: Communications 2014-17, Joint Committee on Statutory Instruments 2015-17, Trade Union and Party Funding 2016, Secondary Legislation Scrutiny 2017-.

Political interests: Economy, education, business; France, Germany, Italy, USA.

Other: Trustee, China Oxford Scholarship Fund 2006-11; Member, policy advisory board, Social Market Foundation 2007-. CBE 1988; Kt 2006.

Recreations: Cinema, music, theatre, tennis.

The Lord Sherbourne of Didsbury CBE, House of Lords, London SW1A 0PW
Tel: 020 7219 5353 *Email:* sherbournes@parliament.uk

House of Lords
Peers' Biographies

LABOUR

SHERLOCK, BARONESS

Opposition Senior Whip; Opposition Spokesperson for Work and Pensions

SHERLOCK (Life Baroness), Maeve Christina Mary Sherlock; cr 2010. Born 10 November 1960; Daughter of Roisin and William Sherlock.

Education: Our Lady's Senior School, Abingdon; Liverpool University (BA sociology 1984); Open University (MBA 1997); Durham University (MA theology 2007).

Non-political career: Treasurer, Liverpool University Guild 1984-85; National Union of Students: Executive officer 1985-86, Treasurer 1986-88, President 1988-90; Director, Endsleigh Insurance 1986-90; UKCOSA: Deputy director 1990-91, Director 1991-97; Director, National Council for One Parent Families 1997-2000; Special adviser to Gordon Brown MP as Chancellor of the Exchequer 2000-03; Chief executive, British Refugee Council 2003-06.

Political career: *House of Lords:* Raised to the peerage as Baroness Sherlock, of Durham in the County of Durham 2010. Opposition Whip 2013-15; Opposition Spokesperson for Work and Pensions 2013-; Opposition Senior Whip 2015-. *Councils and public bodies:* Member, Equality and Human Rights Commission 2007-10; Board member, Financial Ombudsman Service 2008-; Non-executive director, Child Maintenance and Enforcement Commission 2008-10; Member, Riot Communities and Victims Panel 2011-.

Political interests: Families with children, poverty, welfare state, health, communities, faith and politics.

Other: Court member, Warwick University 1993-95, Executive board member, European Association for International Education 1994-97, Assembly member, Greenwich University 1995-97; Governor, Sheffield Hallam University 1997-2000; Trustee: National Family and Parenting Institute 1999-2000, Demos 2004-07; Member: Advisory board, Naturalisation and Integration 2004-, National Refugee Integration Forum 2006-; Chair, National Students Forum 2008-10; Council member, St John's College, Durham University 2009-; NEPACS, Chapel Street. DUniv, Sheffield Hallam University; Hon. fellow, St Chad's College, Durham University. OBE 2000.

Recreations: Cookery, music, books.

The Baroness Sherlock OBE, House of Lords, London SW1A 0PW
Tel: 020 7219 8905 *Email:* sherlockm@parliament.uk *Twitter:* @maevesherlock

CONSERVATIVE

SHIELDS, BARONESS

SHIELDS (Life Baroness), Joanna Shields; cr 2014. Born 12 July 1962; Daughter of Kaye and Thomas Shields; Married Andy Stevenson (1 son).

Education: Pennsylvania State University (BSc 1984); George Washington University (MBA 1987); Hebrew.

Non-political career: Product manager, National Digital 1986-89; Vice-president, Electronics for Imaging, USA 1989-97: Chief executive officer, Veon, USA 1997-2000; Vice-president, International: Real Networks, USA 2000-02, Decru, USA 2002-03; Managing director, Syndication, Business Development, Google EMEA 2004-07; Chief executive officer, Bebo 2007-09; President, People Networks AOL 2010; Vice-president and managing director, Facebook EMEA 2010-13; Chair, TechCity UK 2013-15.

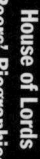

Political career: *House of Lords:* Raised to the peerage as Baroness Shields, of Maida Vale in the City of Westminster 2014. Adviser to the Prime Minister on Digital Economy 2014-15; Parliamentary Under-Secretary of State for Internet Safety and Security and Government Spokesperson: Department for Culture, Media and Sport and Home Office 2015-16, Home Office 2016-17; Prime Minister's Special Representative on: Internet Crime and Harms 2016-17, Internet Safety 2017-. *Councils and public bodies:* UK Business Ambassador for Digital Industries 2013-15; Founder and Member, WeProtect Global Alliance – End Child Sexual Exploitation Online (formerly US/UK Taskforce to combat child online abuse and exploitation) 2014-; Co-Chair, UK Council for Child Internet Safety; Member: Child Protection Implementation Taskforce, Tackling Extremism in Communities Implementation Taskforce, Inter-Ministerial Group on Violence Against Women and Girls, Inter-Ministerial Group on Child Sexual Abuse.

Political interests: Digital agenda, child online protection, cyber-security, counter-terrorism and extremism, conflict zones; USA.

Other: Trustee: NSPCC's There4Me 2005-09, Save the Children UK 2008-12, Prince's Trust Internet and Media Leadership Group, Women's Business Council, American School in London 2011-15; Member, EU Web Entrepreneurs Leaders' Club 2013-14; Non-executive director, London Stock Exchange Group 2014-15; Member, Advisory board, Elbi. Honorary doctorate, Public

Service and for the WeProtect Initiative, George Washington University. Most Influential Woman in the UK IT industry, *Computer Weekly* 2013; Lifetime Achievement Award, British Interactive Media Association 2013. OBE 2014.

The Baroness Shields OBE, House of Lords, London SW1A 0PW
Tel: 020 7219 5353 *Email:* shieldsj@parliament.uk
Website: www.joannashields.com *Twitter:* @joannashields

SHINKWIN, LORD

CONSERVATIVE

SHINKWIN (Life Baron) Kevin Joseph Maximilian Shinkwin; cr 2015. Born 7 June 1971.

Education: Hull University (BA British politics and legislative studies).

Non-political career: Parliamentary affairs manager, Macmillan Cancer Relief 2001-05; Cancer campaigns manager, Cancer Research UK 2005-08; Head of public affairs, Royal British Legion; Parliamentary and campaigns director, Wine and Spirits Trade Association 2013-15.

Political career: *House of Lords:* Raised to the peerage as Baron Shinkwin, of Balham in the London Borough of Wandsworth 2015. Member, Financial Exclusion 2016-17. *Councils and public bodies:* Commissioner, Equality and Human Rights Commission 2017-.

Other: Trustee, National Council for Palliative Care 2016-17.

The Lord Shinkwin, House of Lords, London SW1A 0PW
Tel: 020 7219 3000

SHIPLEY, LORD

LIBERAL DEMOCRAT

Liberal Democrat Lords Spokesperson for Housing

SHIPLEY (Life Baron), John Warren Shipley; cr 2010. Born 5 July 1946; Son of Edward Shipley and Grace Shipley, née Horton; Married Margaret Pattison 1969 (1 son 1 daughter).

Education: Whitby Grammar School; University College London (history 1969) (Union President 1968-69).

Non-political career: Brand management, Procter and Gamble 1969-71; Administrator, various roles then retired as regional director for the north of England and EU, Open University 1971-2005.

Political career: *House of Commons:* Contested (Liberal) Blyth February and October 1974, Hexham 1979, (Liberal/All) Newcastle upon Tyne North 1983 and 1987 general elections. *House of Lords:* Raised to the peerage as Baron Shipley, of Gosforth in the County of Tyne and Wear 2010. Liberal Democrat: Spokesperson for Decentralisation and the Northern Powerhouse 2015, Shadow Minister/Lords Spokesperson for Housing 2016-. Member: Economic Affairs 2010-15, Economic Affairs Finance Bill Sub-Committee 2011. *Other:* Member, Liberal Democrat Manifesto Working Group 2013-. *Councils and public bodies:* Newcastle City Council: Councillor 1975-2012, Opposition Leader 1988-98, Council Leader 2006-10; Member: Northumbria Police Authority 1980s, Tyne and Wear Passenger Transport Authority 1990s, 2004-06; Former board member, Newcastle International Airport Local Authority Holding Company 2004-06; Board member, One North East 2005-12; Vice-President, Local Government Association 2010-.

Political interests: Local government, regeneration; Central and eastern Europe.

Other: Former director: Northern Development Company 1990s, Tyne and Wear Development Company 1990s, 2004-08; Executive member, Universities for the North East; Former board member: NewcastleGateshead City Development Company (1NG), Newcastle Science City Company, Newcastle Local Strategic Partnership, Northern Way Transport Compact, Newcastle Theatre Royal Trust; Chair, Prince's Trust (North East). Doctor of Civil Law, Northumbria University 2011. OBE 1995.

Recreations: Classical music, theatre, First World War, Sunderland AFC.

The Lord Shipley OBE, House of Lords, London SW1A 0PW
Tel: 020 7219 5353 *Email:* shipleyj@parliament.uk

CONSERVATIVE

SHREWSBURY AND WATERFORD, EARL OF

SHREWSBURY (22nd Earl of, E), cr. 1442, AND WATERFORD (22nd Earl of, I), cr. 1446; Charles Henry John Benedict Crofton Chetwynd Chetwynd-Talbot; Earl Talbot and Viscount Ingestre (GB) 1784; Baron Talbot (GB) 1733. Born 18 December 1952; Son of 21st Earl; Married Deborah Hutchinson 1974 (2 sons 1 daughter).

Education: Harrow School.

Non-political career: Hon. Colonel, 'A' Squadron RMLY 2003-06. Joint Deputy Chairman, Britannia Building Society 1987-92; Director, Richmount Enterprise Zone Trust 1988-94; Director: PMI Limited 1996-98, Banafix Limited 1996-98, Minibusplus 1997-2001, Talbot Consulting Limited.

Political career: *House of Lords:* First entered House of Lords 1980; Elected hereditary peer 1999-; Assistant Party Whip 2013-. Member: Works of Art 2009-10, 2012-13, Services 2016-, Intellectual Property (Unjustified Threats) Bill 2016. *Other:* Member, Association of Conservative Peers. *Councils and public bodies:* DL, Staffordshire 1994-; Chair, Firearms Consultative Committee 1994-99.

Political interests: Agriculture, environment, construction industry, property, West Midlands, mineral extraction, firearms and shooting sports, fishing; Scotland.

Other: President and National Executive Director, British Institute of Innkeeping 1996-98; Hon. President, Gun Trade Association 2002-; British Shooting Sports Council: Chair 2002-08, President 2008-14; Deputy Chair, Standing Conference on Country Sports 2011-; President, Staffordshire Historic Churches Trust 2012-; High Steward, Sheffield Cathedral 2014-; President, Building Societies Association 1993-97; St Giles' Hospice, Lichfield. Member: Worshipful Company of Weavers, Worshipful Company of Gunmakers. Chancellor, Wolverhampton University 1993-99. Hon. LLD, Wolverhampton University 1994. Premier Earl on Rolls of both England and Ireland; Hereditary Lord High Steward of Ireland; *Clubs:* Army and Navy, Pratt's Club.

Recreations: Shooting, fishing.

The Earl of Shrewsbury and Waterford DL, House of Lords, London SW1A 0PW
Tel: 020 7219 3158 *Email:* shrewsburyc@parliament.uk
Throstles House, Birdsgrove Lane, Ashbourne, Derbyshire DE6 2BP

LIBERAL DEMOCRAT

SHUTT OF GREETLAND, LORD

SHUTT OF GREETLAND (Life Baron), David Trevor Shutt; cr. 2000. Born 16 March 1942; Son of late Edward Angus Shutt and Ruth Satterthwaite, née Berry; Married Margaret Pemberton 1965 (2 sons 1 daughter).

Education: Pudsey Grammar School.

Non-political career: Chartered accountant; Articled clerk, Smithson Blackburn and Company, Leeds 1959-66; Bousfield Waite and Company, Halifax: Taxation assistant, Partner 1970-94, Consultant 1994-2001; Non-executive director: Job Ownership Ltd 1978-85, Bradford Community Radio *Pennine Radio* 1984-89, Pluto Press Ltd 1985-86, New Society Ltd, *New Society* 1986-88, Statesman and Nation Publishing Company Ltd, *New Statesman* 1988-90, Gerald Duckworth and Co. Ltd 1990-95, Marcher Sound Ltd 1997-2000; Northern Broadsides 2002-10; X-Pert Health CIC 2007-10.

Political career: *House of Commons:* Contested (Liberal) Sowerby 1970, February and October 1974 and 1979, (Liberal/All) Calder Valley 1983 and 1987 and (Liberal Democrat) Pudsey 1992 general elections. *House of Lords:* Raised to the peerage as Baron Shutt of Greetland, of Greetland and Stainland in the County of West Yorkshire 2000. Liberal Democrat: Spokesperson for: Northern Ireland 2001-05, International Development 2001-04; Whip 2001-10: Deputy Chief Whip 2002-05, Chief Whip 2005-10; Deputy Chief Whip (Captain of the Queen's Bodyguard of the Yeomen of the Guard) 2010-12; Government Spokesperson for: Culture, Media and Sport 2010, Northern Ireland 2010-12, Transport 2010-12, Wales 2010-12. Member: European Union 2003-05, Administration and Works 2005-12, Privileges/Privileges and Conduct 2005-12, Procedure 2005-12, Selection 2005-12, Refreshment 2010-12, Joint Committee on Security 2010-12, Sub-committee on Leave of Absence 2011-12, Joint Committee on Parliamentary Privilege 2013; Chair, Inquiries Act 2005 2013-14; Member: EU Sub-committee A (Economic and Financial Affairs) 2014-15, Audit 2014-, EU Financial Affairs Sub-committee 2015-17. *Councils and public bodies:* Calderdale MBC: Councillor 1973-90, 1995-2003, Leader, Liberal Democrat Group 1979-82, 1995-2000, Mayor of Calderdale 1982-83.

Political interests: Transport, charities; Dependent territories, Ireland, Zimbabwe.

Other: Pennine Heritage 1976-2010; Historic Chapels Trust -2010; Member, Society of Friends (Quakers); Trustee: Joseph Rowntree Reform Trust Ltd 1975-2010, Joseph Rowntree Charitable Trust 1984-2010, The Irish Peace Institute 1990-2010; Chair and founder, Calderdale Community Foundation 1990-99; Treasurer, Institute for Citizenship Studies 1995-2001; Whitefield Regeneration Partnership 2005-10; Treasurer and trustee, Parliament Choir -2013; Fellow, Institute of Chartered Accountants in England and Wales; FCA. Freedom, Metropolitan Borough of Calderdale 2000. Citoyen d'Honneur de la Ville de Riorges (France) 1983; Paul Harris Fellow 1999. OBE 1992; PC 2009.

Recreations: Travel, transport.

Rt Hon the Lord Shutt of Greetland OBE, House of Lords, London SW1A 0PW
Tel: 020 7219 8624 *Email:* shuttd@parliament.uk
197 Saddleworth Road, Greetland, Halifax HX4 8LZ *Tel:* 01422 375276
Email: davidshutt@btinternet.com

LABOUR

SIMON, VISCOUNT

SIMON (3rd Viscount, UK), Jan David Simon; cr. 1940. Born 20 July 1940; Son of 2nd Viscount, CMG; Married Mary Elizabeth Burns 1969 (1 daughter).

Education: Westminster School; School of Navigation, Southampton University; Sydney Technical College.

Political career: *House of Lords:* First entered House of Lords 1993; Deputy Chairman of Committees 1998-; Deputy Speaker 1999-; Elected hereditary peer 1999-. Member: Dangerous Dogs (Amendment) Bill 1995-96, London Local Authorities Bill 1998, Procedure 1999-2002, Personal Bills 2004-09, Standing Orders (Private Bills) 2004-; Co-opted Member, Science and Technology Sub-committee I (Allergy) 2006-07.

Political interests: Disability, motor industry, police, road safety, science and technology, aviation; Australia, Qatar.

Other: Trustee, Guild of Experienced Motorists, Road Safety Charity 1999-; President: Driving Instructors Association 2000-13, GEM Motoring Assist 2004-; Younger Brother, Trinity House 2007-; Patron, Road Victims Trust 2010-; Graduate and Postgraduate, Police Service Parliamentary Scheme with Essex Police 2010-13; Trustee: Safety House 2015-16, Road Safety Trust 2015-16; Fellow, Hertfordshire University. Award, Police Federation of England and Wales 2013.

Recreations: Photography, baroque music.

The Viscount Simon, House of Lords, London SW1A 0PW
Tel: 020 7219 5353 *Email:* simonj@parliament.uk

CROSSBENCH

SINGH OF WIMBLEDON, LORD

SINGH OF WIMBLEDON (Life Baron); Indarjit Singh cr. 2011. Born 17 September 1932; Son of Dr Diwan Singh and Kundan Kaur; Married Dr Kanwaljit Kaur 1962 (2 daughters).

Education: Bishop Vesey's Grammar School, Sutton Coldfield; Birmingham University (MCom; MBA); MiminE CEng 1967; French, Hindi, Punjabi.

Non-political career: Head of Sikh Armed Services Chaplaincy. National Coal Board 1955-59, 1965-67; Mines manager, India 1959-65; Costain 1967-75; Management consultant, London 1975-2002; Editor, *Sikh Messenger* 1984-; Director, Network of Sikh Organisations UK 1995-; Founder Member, Interfaith Network UK.

Political career: *House of Lords:* Raised to the peerage as Baron Singh of Wimbledon, of Wimbledon in the London Borough of Merton 2011. Adviser to: Ministry of Justice on Sikhs in Prisons, Ministry of Defence on Sikhs in the Armed Services. *Councils and public bodies:* JP, Wimbledon 1984; Adviser, Commission for Racial Equality.

Political interests: Resolution of conflict, liaising with all political parties to ensure greater weightage of ethical considerations in decision-making; Canada, India, USA.

Other: Member, World Parliament of Religions and the Global Sikh Organisation; Contributor, Thought for the Day, BBC Radio 4 1984-; Prison Chaplaincy and Director, Sikh Chaplaincy Service UK 2004-; Member, Institution of Mining Engineers 1967; Amnesty International, Save the Children Fund, Unicef. Hon. DLitt, Coventry University 2002; Hon. DLaws, Leicester University 2004; Hon. DArts, Leeds Metropolitan University 2007; Hon. DLitt, York St Johns University 2014. Promotion of Inter-faith Understanding, UK Templeton Prize 1989; Inter-faith Medallion for Services to Religious Broadcasting 1991; Jewel of Punjab Award, World Punjabi Organisation. OBE 1996; CBE 2009.

The Lord Singh of Wimbledon CBE, House of Lords, London SW1A 0PW
Tel: 020 7219 8951

CONSERVATIVE

SKELMERSDALE, LORD

SKELMERSDALE (7th Baron, UK), Roger Bootle-Wilbraham; cr. 1828. Born 2 April 1945; Son of Brigadier 6th Baron and late Ann Quilter; Married Christine Morgan 1972 (1 son 1 daughter).

Education: Eton College; Lord Wandsworth College, Odiham; Somerset Farm Institute; Hadlow College of Agriculture and Horticulture; Dutch (rusty), French.

Non-political career: Voluntary Service Overseas, Zambia 1969-71; Horticulturist; Broadleigh Nurseries Ltd: Managing director 1972-81, Director 1991-; Parliamentary affairs adviser 1992-96.

Political career: *House of Lords:* Succeeded his father 1973; First entered House of Lords 1975; Government Whip 1981-86; Government Spokesperson on various topics 1981-86; Parliamentary Under-Secretary of State: Department of the Environment 1986-87, Department of Health and Social Security 1987-88, Department of Social Security 1988-89, Northern Ireland Office 1989-90; Deputy Chair of Committees 1991-94, 2010-15; Deputy Speaker 1994-2003, 2011-; Elected hereditary peer 1999-; Opposition Whip 2003-05; Opposition Spokesperson for: Health 2003-04, Work and Pensions 2003-09, Trade and Industry 2004-05, Home Office 2009-10. Co-opted Member, European Union Sub-committee B (Energy, Industry and Transport) 1997-2000, 2001-03; Member: Statutory Instruments Joint Committee 1998-2005, Procedure 1998-2000, 2014-17, Communications 2010-14, Leader's Group on the Working Practices of the House of Lords 2010-11, Refreshment 2015-16.

Political interests: Horticulture, Post Office, energy, environment, privatised utilities, health; Belize, Colombia, Zambia.

Other: Member, British-Irish Parliamentary Assembly; Vice-chair, Co-En-Co (Council for Environmental Conservation) 1979-81; President: British Naturalists Association 1979-95, Somerset Opera 1980-, Somerset Trust for Nature Conservation 1980-2014; Governor, Castle School, Taunton 1992-96; Chair of Council, Stroke Association 1993-2003; Trustee, Hestercombe Gardens Trust 2001-08; President, Somerset Contract Bridge Association 2007-; Royal Horticultural Society, Stroke Association, Somerset Opera, Voluntary Service Overseas. Former Liveryman, Worshipful Company of Gardeners.

Recreations: Bridge, gardening, reading, walking.

The Lord Skelmersdale, House of Lords, London SW1A 0PW
Tel: 020 7219 2450 *Fax:* 020 7219 5861 *Email:* skelmersdaler@parliament.uk
Broadleigh Gardens, Bishops Hull, Taunton TA4 1AE *Tel:* 020 7630 0088

CROSSBENCH

SKIDELSKY, LORD

SKIDELSKY (Life Baron), Robert Jacob Alexander Skidelsky; cr. 1991. Born 25 April 1939; Son of late Boris Skidelsky and Galia Skidelsky, née Sapelkin; Married Augusta Hope 1970 (2 sons 1 daughter).

Education: Brighton College; Jesus College, Oxford (BA modern history 1961); Nuffield College, Oxford (DPhil 1968).

Non-political career: Research fellow, Nuffield College, Oxford 1965-68; Associate professor, School of Advanced International Studies, Johns Hopkins University, Washington DC 1970-76; Head of department of history, philosophy and European studies, Polytechnic of North London 1976-78; Warwick University: Professor of: International studies 1978-90, Political economy 1990-2006; Director, Janus Capital 2001-11; Founder and chair, Centre for Global Studies 2002-; Director: Greater Europe Fund 2005-09, Sistema JSC 2008-10, Rusnano Capital 2010-. Member, AUT.

Political career: *House of Lords:* Raised to the peerage as Baron Skidelsky, of Tilton in the County of East Sussex 1991. Opposition Spokesperson for: Culture, Media and Sport 1997-98, the Treasury 1998-99. Member: Economic Affairs 2003-08, 2012-15, Refreshment 2009-14, EU Sub-committee G (Social Policies and Consumer Protection) 2010-12, Joint Committee on the Draft Financial Services Bill 2011-12, EU Financial Affairs Sub-committee 2015-. *Councils and public bodies:* Member: Lord Chancellor's Advisory Council on Public Records 1987-92, School Examinations and Assessment Council 1992-93; Governor, Portsmouth University 1994-97; Brighton College: Governor 1998-, Chair 2004-; Governor, Moscow School of Political Studies 1999-; Founder member, World Political Forum 2002-; Member, Academic Council, Wilton Park 2002-09.

Political interests: Education, economic policy, Europe, transition economies, arts; China, Russia.

Other: Member, Inter-Parliamentary Union; Fellow: Royal Historical Society 1973, Royal Society of Literature 1978, Chair: Charleston Trust 1987-92, Social Market Foundation 1991-2001; Fellow, British Academy 1994; Trustee, Daedatus Trust 2011-. Freedom, Knoxville, Tennessee, USA 1998. Hon DLitt, Buckingham University; Hon Fellow, Jesus College, Oxford 1997; Hon doctorate, University of Rome 2010; Hon DLitt, Warwick University 2011. Wolfson Prize for History 1992; Duff Cooper Prize for *Fighting for Britain, 1937-1946*, 2000; Lionel Gelber Prize for International Relations 2001; Council on Foreign Relations Prize 2002; James Tait Black Memorial Prize for *Fighting for Britain, 1937-1946*, 2002. Cavaliere di gran Croce (Italy) 2010; *Clubs:* Grillion's Club.

Publications: Includes: Politicians and the Slump (1967); English Progressive Schools (1969); Oswald Mosley (1975); Biographies of John Maynard Keynes: Hopes Betrayed, 1883-1920 (1983), The Economist as Saviour, 1920-1937 (1992), Fighting for Britain, 1937-1946 (2000), (abridged, single volume edition 2003); The World After Communism (1995); Keynes – The Return of the Master (2009); Co-author, How Much Is Enough? (Allen Lane, 2012); Britain Since 1900 – A Success Story? (Vintage, 2014).

Recreations: Opera, listening to music, tennis, table tennis, good conversation.

Professor the Lord Skidelsky, House of Lords, London SW1A 0PW
Tel: 020 7219 8721 *Email:* skidelskyr@parliament.uk
Room 207, Fielden House, 13 Little College Street, London SW1P 3SH
Website: www.skidelskyr.com

CROSSBENCH

SLIM, VISCOUNT

SLIM (2nd Viscount, UK), John Douglas Slim; cr. 1960. Born 20 July 1927; Son of Field Marshal 1st Viscount, KG, GCB, GCMG, GCVO, GBE, DSO, MC; Married Elisabeth Spinney 1958 (2 sons 1 daughter).

Education: Prince of Wales Royal Indian Military College, Dehra Dun; IMEDE, Switzerland (1971).

Non-political career: Regular Army 1944-72: Indian Army 6th Gurkha Rifles 1944, Argyll and Sutherland Highlanders 1948, Special Air Service 1952; Staff College Camberley 1961; Joint Services Staff College 1964. Morgan Crucible Company 1972-76; Peek plc: Chair 1976-91, Deputy chair 1991-96, Consultant 1996-2003; Director, Trailfinders Ltd 1985-2007, and other companies; Independent security consultant.

Political career: *House of Lords:* First entered House of Lords 1971; Founder member, House of Lords Defence Study Group 1971-; Elected hereditary peer 1999-. Member, Selection 2001-05; Procedure: Member 2005-07, Alternate Member 2007-10. *Councils and public bodies:* DL, Greater London 1988.

Political interests: Foreign affairs, defence, exports, industry, veterans and war widows.

Other: Foundation for Aviation and Sustainable Tourism (New Delhi); Parliamentary and Scientific Committee; Trustee, Royal Commonwealth Ex-Services League; President, Burma Star Association 1971-; Britain-Australia Society: Vice-President, Former chair; Vice-chair, Arab-British Chamber of Commerce 1977-96; Fellow, Royal Geographical Society 1983; SAS Association: President 2000-10, Patron 2010-; Patron, Prospect Burma; Clothworkers' Foundation; Indian Army Association; Burma Forces Welfare Association; Burma Children's Fund. Master, Clothworkers' Company 1995-96. Freedom, City of London 1953. Ebbe Munk Award, Denmark 1995; Shiramani Award, India 2002; Pingat Jasa, Malaysia 2007. OBE (Mil) 1973; *Clubs:* White's, Special Forces Club.

The Viscount Slim OBE DL, House of Lords, London SW1A 0PW
Tel: 020 7219 2122

LAB/CO-OP

SMITH OF BASILDON, BARONESS

Shadow Leader of the House of Lords; Opposition Spokesperson for Constitutional Affairs

SMITH OF BASILDON (Life Baroness), Angela Evans Smith; cr 2010. Born 7 January 1959; Daughter of Patrick Evans, retired factory worker, and Emily Evans, neé Russell, supervisor of church pre-school; Married Nigel Smith 1978.

Education: Chalvedon Comprehensive, Basildon; Leicester Polytechnic (BA public administration).

Non-political career: Trainee accountant, London Borough of Newham 1982-83; League Against Cruel Sports, finally head of political and public relations 1983-95; Research assistant to Alun Michael MP 1995-97. Member, Unite.

Political career: *House of Commons:* Contested Southend West 1987 general election. MP (Lab/Co-op) for Basildon 1997-2010. Contested South Basildon and East Thurrock 2010 general election. PPS to Paul Boateng as Minister of State, Home Office 1999-2001; Assistant Government Whip 2001-02; Parliamentary Under-Secretary of State: Northern Ireland Office 2002-06, Department for Communities and Local Government 2006-07; PPS to Gordon Brown as Prime Minister 2007-09; Minister of State, Cabinet Office 2009-10. Joint Vice-chair, PLP Departmental Committee for International Development 1999-2000. *House of Lords:* Raised to the peerage as Baroness Smith of Basildon, of Basildon in the County of Essex 2010. Opposition Spokesperson for: Energy and Climate Change 2010-13, Northern Ireland 2011-12, Home Office 2012-15; Opposition Deputy Chief Whip 2012-15; Shadow Leader of the House of Lords 2015-; Opposition Spokesperson for Constitutional Affairs 2015-; Member, House of Lords Commission 2016-. Member: Selection 2015-, House 2015, Liaison 2015, Privileges and Conduct 2015-, Procedure 2015-, Joint Committee on the Palace of Westminster 2015-16. *Councils and public bodies:* Essex County Council: Councillor 1989-97, Chief Whip 1993-96; Vice-President Local Government Association 2011-.

Political interests: Home affairs, animal welfare, international development, employment, third sector, fire service; Cuba, Germany, Ireland, Liechtenstein, Switzerland, USA.

Other: Patron, Basildon Women's Aid; Vice-chair, Cuba Solidarity Campaign; President, Basildon Ladies Football Club -2015; Vice-president, League Against Cruel Sports; Patron, Captive Animals Protection Society; Honorary President, St Clere's Co-op Academy Trust 2012-; Chair, Resolving Chaos 2012-14; Patron, Stanford and Corringham Schools Trust 2013-14; Chair, Production Exchange 2014-. Political Studies Association, Parliamentarian of the Year 2016. PC 2009.

Recreations: Swimming, reading, theatre, watching *Coronation Street*.

Rt Hon the Baroness Smith of Basildon, House of Lords, London SW1A 0PW
Tel: 020 7219 3237 *Email:* smithangela@parliament.uk *Twitter:* @LadyBasildon

SMITH OF CLIFTON, LORD

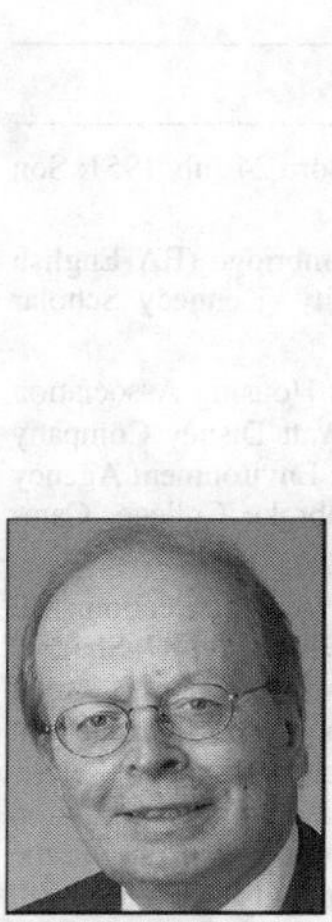

LIBERAL DEMOCRAT

SMITH OF CLIFTON (Life Baron), Trevor Arthur Smith; cr. 1997. Born 14 June 1937; Son of late Arthur Smith and late Vera Smith; Married Brenda Eustace 1960 (divorced 1973) (2 sons); married Julia Bullock 1979 (1 daughter).

Education: Hounslow College; Chiswick Polytechnic; London School of Economics (BSc economics 1958).

Non-political career: Secondary school teacher, London 1958-59; Temporary political science assistant lecturer, Exeter University 1959-60; Acton Society Trust: Research officer 1960-62, Trustee 1975-87; Lecturer in politics, Hull University 1962-67; Visiting associate professor, California State University, Los Angeles 1969; Queen Mary Westfield College, London: Head of department 1972-85, Dean of social studies 1979-82, Pro-principal 1983-87, Lecturer, senior lecturer, professor in political studies 1967-91, Senior pro-principal 1987-89, Senior vice-principal 1989-91; Director: Job Ownership Ltd 1978-85, New Society Ltd 1986-88; Statesman and Nation Publishing Company Ltd: Director 1988-90, Chair 1990; Director, Gerald Duckworth & Co 1990-95; Visiting Professor of Politics: York University 1999-2003, Portsmouth University 2000-01; Director, Democratic Audit Ltd 2007-11.

Political career: *House of Lords:* Raised to the peerage as Baron Smith of Clifton, of Mountsandel in the County of Londonderry 1997. Liberal Democrat Spokesperson for: Northern Ireland 2000-10, Constitutional Affairs 2007-10. Member, Science and Technology Sub-committee I (Complementary and Alternative Medicine) 1999-2000; Co-opted member, European Union Sub-committee E (Law and Institutions) 2000-; Chair, Animals in Scientific Procedures 2000-02; Member: Information 2003-07, Constitution 2005-08, Sub-committee on Lords' Interests 2006-08, Barnett Formula 2008-09, Works of Art 2009-10, Economic Affairs 2010-15. Chair, Liberal Democrat Policy Committee on Northern Ireland 2010-11. *Other:* Member, Liberal Party Executive 1958-59. *Councils and public bodies:* Member, Tower Hamlets District Health Authority 1987-91; Member of Senate, London University 1987-91; Non-executive director, North Yorkshire Regional Health Authority 2000-02.

Political interests: Northern Ireland, health, transport (aircraft), higher education, constitutional reform, corporate governance; China, Scandinavia.

Other: British-Irish Interparliamentary Assembly 2000-11; Joseph Rowntree Reform Trust Ltd: Director 1975-06, Chair 1987-99; Governor, University of Haifa, Israel 1985-91; Trustee, Employment Institute 1987-92; Political Studies Association of UK: Chair 1988-89, President 1991-93; Vice-chair, Board of Governors, Princess Alexandra and Newnham College of Nursing and Midwifery 1990-91; Institute of Citizenship 1991-2001; UK Socrates Council: Member 1993-99, Chair 1996-99; President, Belfast Civic Trust 1995-99; Member: Administrative Board, International Association of Universities 1995-96, Editorial Board, Government and Opposition 1995-2013, Board, A Taste of Ulster 1996-99; Chair, Hampden Trust 1999-2001; Stroke Association 2002-05; Board Member, Democratic Audit 2006-11; FRHistS; CCIM (CBIM 1992); FICPD; FRSA; AcSS; Intermediate Technology Development Group (now Practical Action), Blood Pressure Association, Diabetes UK, Camfed. Vice-chancellor, Ulster University 1991-99. Six honorary doctorates; Honorary Professor, Ulster University 1991; Honorary Fellow, Queen Mary Westfield College, London 2003. Kt 1996; *Clubs:* Reform Club. Easingwold CC.

Publications: Co-author: Training Managers (1962), Town Councillors (1964), Direct Action and Democratic Politics (1972); Town and County Hall (1966); Anti-Politics: consensus and reform (1972); The Politics of the Corporate Economy (1979); The Fixers (1996); Various articles and papers, book reviews and broadcasts.

Recreations: Water colour painting.

Professor the Lord Smith of Clifton, House of Lords, London SW1A 0PW
Tel: 020 7219 3563 *Fax:* 020 7219 5979 *Email:* smitht@parliament.uk

SMITH OF FINSBURY, LORD

NON-AFFILIATED

SMITH OF FINSBURY (Life Baron), Christopher Robert Smith; cr 2005. Born 24 July 1951; Son of Colin Smith, civil servant, and Gladys Smith, teacher.

Education: George Watson's College, Edinburgh; Pembroke College, Cambridge (BA English 1972; PhD 1979) (President, Cambridge Union 1972); Harvard University (Kennedy Scholar 1975-76); French, German (rusty).

Non-political career: Housing Corporation 1976-77; Shaftesbury Society Housing Association 1977-80; Society for Co-operative Dwellings 1980-83; Senior Adviser, Walt Disney Company 2001-07; Visiting Professor, University of the Arts London 2002-10; Chair: Environment Agency 2008-14, Immidtown Business Improvement District 2014; Master, Pembroke College, Cambridge 2015-. ASTMS: Branch secretary 1977-80, Branch chair 1980-83.

Political career: *House of Commons:* Contested Epsom and Ewell 1979 general election. MP (Labour) for Islington South and Finsbury 1983-2005. Opposition London Whip 1986-87; Shadow Treasury Minister 1987-92; Shadow Secretary of State for: Environmental Protection 1992-94, National Heritage 1994-95, Social Security 1995-96, Health 1996-97; Sponsored Environment and Safety Information Act 1988 (Private Member's Bill); Secretary of State for: National Heritage May-July 1997, Culture, Media and Sport July 1997-2001; Chair, Millennium Commission 1997-2001. *House of Lords:* Raised to the peerage as Baron Smith of Finsbury, of Finsbury in the London Borough of Islington 2005. *Other:* Chair, Labour Campaign for Criminal Justice 1985-88; Vice-President, Christian Socialist Movement 1987-; President, SERA 1992-2007; Patron, LGBT Labour. *Councils and public bodies:* Islington Borough Council: Councillor 1978-83, Chief Whip 1978-79, Chair of Housing 1981-83; Co-opted member, Council for National Parks 1980-89; Member: Committee on Standards in Public Life 2001-05, Review Committee of Privy Counsellors of the Anti-terrorism, Crime and Security Act 2002-03; Founding director, Clore Leadership Programme 2003-08; Chair: London Cultural Consortium 2004-08, Advertising Standards Authority 2007-17.

Political interests: Culture, media, sport, housing, local and regional government, foreign affairs, environment, civil liberties, criminal justice, economic policy, social security, health, higher education; Argentina, Australia, Brazil, China, Cyprus, Europe, Hong Kong, New Zealand, South Africa, USA.

Other: Tribune Group: Secretary 1984-88, Chair 1988-89, Chair of board, *Tribune* newspaper 1990-93; Member: Shelter Board 1986-92, Executive, National Council for Civil Liberties 1986-88; Sadlers Wells Theatre: Board member 1986-92, Governor 1992-97; Vice-President, Wildlife Link 1986-90; Fabian Society: Member, Executive 1990-98, Vice-chair 1995-96, Chair 1997-98; Trustee, John Muir Trust 1992-97; Chair of board, *New Century* Magazine 1993-96; Executive Committee, National Trust 1994-96; Senior associate, Judge Institute, Cambridge University 2001-06; Wordsworth Trust: Trustee 2001-17, Chair 2002-17, Honorary President 2017-; Board member, Royal National Theatre 2001-09; Chair, Classic FM Consumer Panel 2001-07; Donmar Warehouse: Board member 2001-15, Chair 2003-15; Board member: Terrence Higgins Trust 2001-05, Poetry Archive 2002-07; Chair of Judges, Man Booker Prize 2004; Governor, University of Arts, London 2005-08; Windsor Leadership Trust 2006-08; Board member, Phonographic Performance Ltd 2007-; International Advisory Committee, Russian State Museum, St Petersburg 2008-14; Chair of Judges, Museum of the Year Prize 2012; Trustee, The Sixteen 2013-; Chair, Art Fund 2014-; Non-executive Director, Spencer Ogden 2014-17. Freedom, London Borough of Islington 2011. Honorary fellow, Royal Institute of British Architects 2000; Honorary Doctor of Arts, City University 2003; Honorary fellow, Pembroke College, Cambridge 2004-; Senior Fellow, Royal College of Art 2007; Visiting fellow, Ashridge Business School 2007-10; Honorary fellow: King's College London 2008, Cumbria University 2010; Honorary doctorate, Lancaster University 2011; Honorary fellow, Royal Incorporation of Architects in Scotland 2012; Honorary doctorate: Westminster University 2015, London Metropolitan University 2016. PC 1997.

Publications: National Parks (Fabian Society, 1977); New Questions for Socialism (Fabian Society, 1996); Creative Britain (Faber, 1998); Co-author, Suicide of the West (Continuum, 2006).

Recreations: Mountaineering, literature, theatre, music, art.

Rt Hon the Lord Smith of Finsbury, House of Lords, London SW1A 0PW
Tel: 020 7219 5119
Pembroke College, Cambridge CB2 1RF *Tel:* 01223 338129 *Email:* master@pem.cam.ac.uk

LABOUR

SMITH OF GILMOREHILL, BARONESS

SMITH OF GILMOREHILL (Life Baroness), Elizabeth Margaret Smith; cr. 1995. Born 4 June 1940; Daughter of late Frederick William Moncrieff Bennett and late Elizabeth Waters Irvine Shanks; Married John Smith 1967 (MP 1970-94, Leader of the Labour Party 1992-94) (died 1994) (3 daughters).

Education: Hutchesons' Girls' Grammar School, Glasgow; Glasgow University (MA French and Russian 1962).

Non-political career: Chair, Lamda Development Board -2001; Non-executive director: Deutsche Bank, Scotland -2004, City Inn Ltd -2011; BP Advisory Board for Scotland -2004.

Political career: *House of Lords:* Raised to the peerage as Baroness Smith of Gilmorehill, of Gilmorehill in the District of the City of Glasgow 1995. Opposition Spokeswoman on National Heritage (Tourism) 1996-97. *Councils and public bodies:* Member, Press Complaints Commission 1995-2001; DL, City of Edinburgh 1996.

Political interests: Arts; Russia, Former Soviet Union.

Other: Executive Committee Member, Inter-Parliamentary Union British Group -2002; Board member, Edinburgh International Festival -1999; Council member, Britain in Europe Campaign; Member: British Heart Foundation -2000, Future of Europe Trust -2000, John Smith Memorial Trust, Know How Fund Advisory Board -2000; Trustee, Hakluyt Foundation -2001; Member: English Speaking Union, Russo-British Chamber of Commerce, Centre for European Reform -2004; 21st Century Trust -2008; President, Scottish Opera -2012; Chair, Edinburgh Festival Fringe -2012; Member: RIIA – Chatham House Mariinsky Theatre Trust; John Smith Memorial Trust, Dash Arts. Chancellor, Birkbeck College, London 1998-2003. Hon. LLD, University of Glasgow.

The Baroness Smith of Gilmorehill DL, House of Lords, London SW1A 0PW
Tel: 020 7219 5353 *Email:* smithlady@parliament.uk

CONSERVATIVE

SMITH OF HINDHEAD, LORD

SMITH OF HINDHEAD (Life Baron), Philip Roland Smith; cr 2015. Born 16 February 1966; Son of late John Smith and Ann Smith; Married Emma Clarke 1989 (1 son 1 daughter).

Education: Woolmer Hill School, Haslemere.

Non-political career: Association of Conservative Clubs: Joined 1987, Chief Executive 1999-.

Political career: *House of Lords:* Raised to the peerage as Baron Smith of Hindhead, of Hindhead in the County of Surrey 2015. Party Whip 2016-. Member: Licensing Act 2003 2016-17, Liaison 2017-, Political Polling and Digital Media 2017-. *Other:* Treasurer, Conservative Party 2001-; Chairman, National Conservative Draws Society 2001-; Financial Trustee, Conservative Agents' Benevolent Association (registered charity) 2014-; Trustee, Conservative Party Agents' Pension Fund 2014-; Member, Conservative Party's Finance and Audit Committee 2016-; Trustee, Conservative Party Archive 2017.

Political interests: Licensing, gambling, clubs, not-for-profit organisations.

Other: Chairman: Committee of Registered Clubs Associations, Best Bar None 2017-. Freedom, City of London 2007. CBE 2013; *Clubs:* Farnham Conservative, Carlton Club.

Publications: Club Law and Management (2008); Questions & Answers on Club Law and Management (2017).

The Lord Smith of Hindhead CBE, House of Lords, London SW1A 0PW
Tel: 020 7219 3000

CROSSBENCH

SMITH OF KELVIN, LORD

SMITH OF KELVIN (Life Baron), Robert Haldane Smith; cr 2008. Born 8 August 1944; Married Alison Bell 1969 (2 daughters).

Education: Allan Glen's School, Glasgow; Articles, Robb Ferguson & Co 1963-68; Qualified chartered accountant 1968.

Non-political career: Industrial and Commercial Finance Corporation 1968-82; Managing Director, National Commercial & Glyns Ltd 1983-85; General Manager, Corporate Finance Division, Royal Bank of Scotland plc; Managing Director, Charterhouse Development Capital Ltd 1985-89; Morgan Grenfell Development Capital Ltd 1989-2001: Chair 1989-2001, Chief Executive 1989-96; Chief Executive, Morgan Grenfell Asset Management Ltd 1996-2000; Member, Management Committee, Deutsche Bank AG 1996-2000; Deutsche Asset Management: Chief Executive 1999-2000, Vice-chair 2000-02; Chair, Weir Group plc 2002-13; Director, Standard Bank Group 2003-15; Chair: Scottish and Southern Energy plc 2005-16, Smith Group 2005-12; Member, Council of Economic Advisers to First Minister of Scotland 2007-11; Chair: IMI plc 2015-, Forth Ports Limited 2015-, Clyde Gateway 2015-, Alliance Trust plc 2016-.

Political career: *House of Lords:* Raised to the peerage as Baron Smith of Kelvin, of Kelvin in the City of Glasgow 2008. Chair, Smith Commission 2014. *Councils and public bodies:* Member, Museums Advisory Board 1983-85; National Museums of Scotland: Trustee 1985-2002, Chair, Board of Trustees 1993-2002; Museums and Galleries Commission: Commissioner 1988-98, Vice-chair 1997-98; Member, Financial Services Authority 1997-2000; BBC Governor and Chair, Broadcasting Council for Scotland 1999-2004; Financial Reporting Council: Member 2001-04, Chair, FRC Group on Audit Committees Combined Code of Guidance – The Smith Report 2003; Member, Judicial Appointments Board for Scotland 2002-07; Chair: Glasgow 2014 Commonwealth Games Organising Committee 2008-14, Code of Governance for Higher Education in Scotland 2012-13, UK Green Investment Bank 2012-.

Countries of interest: South Africa.

Other: Director and Treasurer, Sussex Heritage Trust 1975-82; Non-executive Director: Tip Europe plc 1987-89, MFI Furniture Group 1987-2000, Bank of Scotland plc 1998-2000; Deputy Chair, Bristow Helicopter Group 1991-95; President: British Association of Friends and Museums 1995-2005, Institute of Chartered Accountants of Scotland 1996-97; Statkis plc: Director 1997-99, Chair 1998-99; Non-executive Director: Network Rail 2002-03, Aegon UK plc 2002-09; Member, Board of Trustees, British Council 2002-05; Chair, BBC Children in Need 2003-04; Vice-chair: China Britain Business Council 2003-08, Kelvingrove Museum Appeal 2003-07; Non-executive Director, 3i Group plc 2004-09; Prince's Ambassador for CSR, Scottish Business in the Community 2006-07; Chair, Riverside Museum Appeal 2007-11; Patron, Foundation Scotland 2008-15; President, Royal Highland and Agricultural Society of Scotland 2010-11; Patron, Capital Appeal for Prince and Princess of Wales Hospice 2013-; Chair, International Public Policy Unit 2014-; Non-executive chair, British Business Bank 2017-; President, Institute of Chartered Accountants of Scotland 1996-97. Chancellor: University of the West of Scotland 2003-13, Strathclyde University 2013-. Honorary degree: Edinburgh University 1999, Glasgow University 2001, Paisley University 2003; Hon. Fellowship: Institute of Internal Auditors 2010, Royal College of Physicians and Surgeons of Glasgow 2014. British Venture Capital Association Hall of Fame 2006; Business Leader of the Year, Elite Insider 2008; Lifetime Achievement Award, Scottish Accounts Association 2010; Board Member of the Year, Scotland plc Award 2012; Outstanding Achievement, NED Awards 2012; Wallace Award, American Scottish Foundation 2012; Chairman's Award, Insitute of Directors 2014; Lifetime Achievement Award, Inspiring City: Glasgow 2014; Outstanding Achievement, Great London Scot Award 2014; Shackleton Medal, Royal Scottish Geographical Society 2015; Adam Smith Medal, Royal Society of Edinburgh 2015. Knighted 1999; KT 2014; CH 2016.

Publications: Co-author, Managing Your Company's Finances.

Recreations: Chanteclair Estate, guest house and vineyard in South Africa, highland cattle breeding.

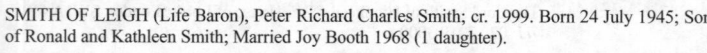

The Lord Smith of Kelvin KT CH, House of Lords, London SW1A 0PW *Tel:* 020 7219 5353

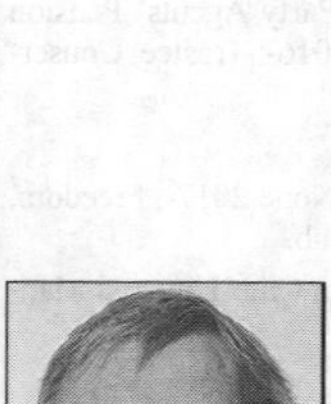

LABOUR

SMITH OF LEIGH, LORD

SMITH OF LEIGH (Life Baron), Peter Richard Charles Smith; cr. 1999. Born 24 July 1945; Son of Ronald and Kathleen Smith; Married Joy Booth 1968 (1 daughter).

Education: Bolton School; London School of Economics (BSc economics 1967); Garnett College, London University (CertEd(FE) 1969); Salford University (MSc urban studies 1983).

Non-political career: Lecturer: Walbrook College, London 1969-74, Manchester College of Art and Technology 1974-2000 (part-time 1991-2000); Manchester Airport plc: Board director 1986-2001, Chair 1989-90; Board director, Manchester Airport Group 2001-09. Member, NATFHE -2001.

Political career: *House of Lords:* Raised to the peerage as Baron Smith of Leigh, of Wigan in the County of Greater Manchester 1999. Vice-chair: PLP Departmental Committee for Office of the Deputy Prime Minister 2006-07, PLP Departmental Group for Communities and Local Government 2010-15. *Councils and public bodies:* Wigan Metropolitan Borough Council: Councillor 1978-, Chair, Finance Committee 1982-91, Council Leader 1991-; Member: Association of Metropolitan Authorities Policy Committee 1991-97, Local Government Association Policy and Strategy Committee 1997-2000; Vice-chair, Special Interest Group for Municipal Authorities 1997-; Member, Improvement and Development Agency 1999-2003; North West Regional Assembly: Chair 1999-2000, Executive Board 2005-09; Chair, Association of Greater Manchester Authorities 2000-17; Vice-President, Local Government Association 2010-; Chairman, Greater Manchester Combined Authority 2011-.

Political interests: Local government, regionalism, airports, health; Australia, France, New Zealand, USA.

Other: Oxfam, Wigan and Leigh Hospice. Freedom, Wigan Metropolitan Borough 2011. Doctor of Laws, Manchester Metropolitan University.

Recreations: Gardening, sport, jazz.

The Lord Smith of Leigh, House of Lords, London SW1A 0PW
Tel: 020 7219 8631 *Email:* smithprc@parliament.uk
Town Hall, Library Street, Wigan WN1 1YN *Tel:* 01942 827001 *Fax:* 01942 827365
Email: leader@wigan.gov.uk *Twitter:* @Lord_PeterSmith

SMITH OF NEWNHAM, BARONESS

LIBERAL DEMOCRAT

SMITH OF NEWNHAM (Life Baroness), Julie Elizabeth Smith; cr 2014. Born 1 June 1969; Daughter of Hugh Francis Smith and Eileen Elizabeth Smith, née Murphy.

Education: Merchant Taylor's School for Girls, Crosby; Brasenose College, Oxford (MA philosophy, politics and economics 1991); St Antony's College, Oxford (MPhil; DPhil politics 1995); French, German.

Non-political career: Fellow, Robinson College, Oxford 1997-; Head of European programme, Chatham House 1999-2003; Deputy director, Centre of International Studies, Cambridge University 2004-08; Senior lecturer of international relations, Department of Politics and International Studies (POLIS), Cambridge University 2009-.

Political career: *House of Lords:* Raised to the peerage as Baroness Smith of Newnham, of Crosby in the County of Merseyside 2014. Liberal Democrat Spokesperson for Defence 2015. Member, International Relations 2016-. *Other:* Vice-chair, Liberal Democrat Federal Policy Committee. *Councils and public bodies:* Cambridge City Council: Councillor 2003-15, Honorary Councillor 2015-.

Political interests: Europe, defence, higher education; France, Germany.

Other: Gladstone's Library Hawarden, Cambridge University Catholic Association.

Publications: Voice of the people: European Parliament in the 1990s (1995); Eminent Europeans: Personalities who shaped contemporary Europe (1996); A Sense of Liberty: A Short History of the Liberal International 1947-97 (1997); Democracy in the New Europe (1999); Europe's Elected Parliament (1999); The New Bilateralism: The UK's Bilateral Relations within the EU (2002); Co-editor, Through the Paper Curtain: Insiders and Outsiders in the New Europe (2003); Reinvigorating European Elections: the Implications of Electing the European Commission (2005); New Horizons in European Politics Series (2011-); Co-editor and contributor, Palgrave Handbook on National Parliaments and the European Union (2015).

Recreations: Yoga, ballet, travelling.

The Baroness Smith of Newnham, House of Lords, London SW1A 0PW
Tel: 020 7219 3214 *Email:* jes42@parliament.uk
Department of Politics and International Studies, Alison Richard Building, 7 West Road, Cambridge, Cambridgeshire CB3 9DT *Tel:* 01223 766259
Website: juliesmithcambridge.co.uk *Twitter:* @DrJulieSmith1

LABOUR

SNAPE, LORD

SNAPE (Life Baron), Peter Charles Snape; cr. 2004. Born 12 February 1942; Son of late Thomas Snape, Railway Chargeman; Married Winifred Grimshaw 1963 (divorced 1980) (2 daughters); married Janet Brenda Manley 2004.

Education: Dial Stone Secondary Modern School, Cheshire.

Non-political career: Regular Army service 1961-67: Royal Engineers 1961-64, Royal Corps of Transport 1964-67. British Railways/Rail: Railway signalman 1957-60, Goods guard 1967-70, Clerical officer 1970-74; Travel West Midlands: Non-executive director 1992-95, Chair 1995-2000; Transport consultant 2000-. National Union of Railwaymen: Member 1957-61, 1969-94, Branch chair 1970-74; Member, Rail Maritime and Transport Union 1994-.

Political career: *House of Commons:* MP (Labour) for West Bromwich East 1974-2001. Assistant Government Whip 1975-77; Government Whip 1977-79; Opposition Frontbench Spokesperson on: Defence 1979-82, Home Affairs 1982-84, Transport 1984-92. *House of Lords:* Raised to the peerage as Baron Snape, of Wednesbury in the County of West Midlands 2004. Member: Procedure 2005-07, Crossrail Bill 2008. *Councils and public bodies:* Bredbury and Romiley Urban District Council: Leader 1971-74, Chair, Finance Committee 1972-74.

Political interests: Transport.

Recreations: Golf, football.

The Lord Snape, House of Lords, London SW1A 0PW
Tel: 020 7219 5877

LABOUR

SOLEY, LORD

SOLEY (Life Baron), Clive Stafford Soley; cr 2005. Born 7 May 1939; Son of Joseph Soley and Doris Despard; Rosslyn Brown (1 son 1 daughter).

Education: Downshall Secondary Modern, Ilford; Newbattle Abbey Adult Education College (1963); Strathclyde University (BA politics and psychology 1968); Southampton University (Diploma applied social studies 1970).

Non-political career: RAF national service 1959-61. British Council, London and Madrid 1968-69; Probation Officer and Senior Probation Officer, Inner London Probation Service 1970-79; Chairman and Director, Good Governance Foundation 2011-15. Member, GMB.

Political career: *House of Commons:* MP (Labour) for Hammersmith North 1979-83, for Hammersmith 1983-97, for Ealing, Acton and Shepherds Bush 1997-2005. Opposition Spokesperson for: Northern Ireland 1982-85, Home Affairs 1985-87, Housing and Local Government 1987-89, Housing and Planning 1989-92. Chair, Northern Ireland Affairs 1995-97; Member: Joint Committee on House of Lords Reform 2002-05, Constitutional Affairs 2003-05. *House of Lords:* Raised to the peerage as Baron Soley, of Hammersmith in the London Borough of Hammersmith and Fulham 2005. Leader, Parliamentary Delegation to Bahrain 2014. Chair: Draft Children (contact) and Adoption Bill Joint Committee 2005, Intergovernmental Organisations 2007-08; Member: Delegated Powers and Regulatory Reform 2009-13, Inquiries Act 2005 2013-14, The Arctic 2014-15, EU Home Affairs Sub-committee 2015-. *Other:* Chair: Labour Campaign for Criminal Justice 1983-97, Parliamentary Labour Party 1997-2001; Member, Labour Party National Executive Committee 1998-2001; Chair, London Selection Board for Labour candidate for Mayor 1999. *Councils and public bodies:* Councillor, Hammersmith and Fulham Council 1974-78.

Political interests: Environment, civil liberties, foreign policy, aviation policy, good governance; China, South East Asia.

Other: International Observer at: First national elections in Mongolia 1990, Peruvian general election 1995; Leader, Westminster Foundation Group to Kosovo 1999; Chair, Alcohol Education Centre, Maudsley Hospital 1974-84; Fellow, Industry and Parliament Trust 1984; Chair: Mary Seacole Memorial Statue Appeal 2004-16, Arab-Jewish Forum 2005-14; Campaign Director, Future Heathrow 2005-10; Life Patron, Mary Seacole Trust 2016-; *Clubs:* Commonwealth Club.

Publications: 'The Politics of the Family' in Rewriting the Sexual Contract (Institute of Community Studies, 1997); Co-author: Regulating the Press (Pluto Press, 2000), A Statue for Mary: the Seacole Legacy, ed. Jean Gray (Mary Seacole Memorial Statue Appeal, 2016).

Recreations: Walking, photography, scuba diving.

The Lord Soley, House of Lords, London SW1A 0PW
Tel: 020 7219 5118 *Email:* soleyc@parliament.uk *Twitter:* @CliveSoley

CROSSBENCH

SOMERSET, DUKE OF

SOMERSET (19th Duke of, E), John Michael Edward Seymour; cr 1547; Baron Seymour; 17th bt of Berry Pomeroy (E) 1611. Born 30 December 1952; Son of 18th Duke; Married Judith-Rose 1984 (2 sons 2 daughters).

Education: Eton College; University of Neuchâtel; Royal Agricultural University.

Non-political career: Director, Duchy of Somerset Estates; Member, Witham Water LLP.

Political career: *House of Lords:* First entered House of Lords 1985; Elected hereditary peer 2014-. Member: Sub-committee D 1987-91, 1993-96, European Communities 1990-97, Sub-committee F 1992. *Councils and public bodies:* DL: Wiltshire 1993, Devon 1999-; Chair, advisory committee, Royal Agricultural University.

Political interests: Foreign affairs, accountability of the EU, rural society and economy, including conservation and heritage; Eastern Europe, India.

Other: Trustee: Motorsport Endeavour, Mount Edgcumbe Estate; Fellow, Royal Institute of Chartered Surveyors.

His Grace the Duke of Somerset DL, House of Lords, London SW1A 0PW
Tel: 020 7219 5353

NON-AFFILIATED

SOUTHWARK, LORD BISHOP OF

SOUTHWARK (10th Bishop of), Christopher Thomas James Chessun. Born 5 August 1956; Son of late Thomas Chessun and Joyce Chessun.

Education: Hampton Grammar School; University College, Oxford (BA modern history 1978); Trinity Hall, Cambridge (BA theology 1982); Westcott House Theology College, Cambridge.

Non-political career: Ordained Deacon 1983; Priest 1984; Assistant Curate, St Michael and All Angels Sandhurst 1983-87; Senior Curate, St Mary Portsea 1987-89; Chaplain and Minor Canon, St Paul's Cathedral 1989-93; Vocations Adviser, Diocese of London 1991-93; Rector, St Dunstan and All Saint's Stepney 1993-2001; Area Dean, Tower Hamlets 1997-2001; Archdeacon of Northolt 2001-05; Area Bishop of Woolwich 2005-11; Bishop of Southwark 2011-.

Political career: *House of Lords:* Entered House of Lords 2014. *Other:* Bishops Spokesperson on Immigration 2015-.

Political interests: Immigration, foreign affairs, international development; Israel, Palestine, Zimbabwe.

Other: Bishop for Urban Life and Faith 2010-14; Patron: Embrace the Middle East 2013-, Friends of the Holy Land 2013-. Freedom, City of London 1993; *Clubs:* Athenæum.

Rt Rev the Lord Bishop of Southwark, House of Lords, London SW1A 0PW
Tel: 020 7219 5353
Trinity House, 4 Chapel Court, Borough High Street, London SE1 1HW *Tel:* 020 7939 9420
Fax: 0843 290 6894 *Email:* bishop.christopher@southwark.anglican.org
Website: www.southwark.anglican.org

CONSERVATIVE

SPICER, LORD

SPICER (Life Baron), William Michael Hardy Spicer; cr 2010. Born 22 January 1943; Son of late Brigadier L H Spicer; Married Patricia Ann Hunter 1967 (1 son 2 daughters).

Education: Wellington College, Berkshire; Emmanuel College, Cambridge (MA economics 1964).

Non-political career: Assistant to the Editor, *The Statist* 1964-66; Conservative Research Department 1966-68; Director, Conservative Systems Research Centre 1968-70; Managing Director and Founder, Economic Models Limited 1970-80.

Political career: *House of Commons:* Contested Easington 1966 and 1970 general elections. MP (Conservative) for South Worcestershire 1974-97, for West Worcestershire 1997-2010. PPS to: Sally Oppenheim as Minister of State for Consumer Affairs 1979-82, Cecil Parkinson as Minister for Trade 1979-81; Parliamentary Under-Secretary of State for Transport 1984-87; Aviation Minister 1985-87; Parliamentary Under-Secretary of State, Department of Energy 1987-90; Minister of State, Housing and Planning, Department of Environment 1990. Chair, Parliamentary and Scientific Committee 1996-99; Member, Treasury 1997-2001; Chair, Treasury (Treasury Sub-Committee) 1999-2001. *House of Lords:* Raised to the peerage as Baron Spicer, of Cropthorne in the County of Worcestershire 2010. Chairman, Parliamentary and Political Service Honours Committee 2012-. *Other:* Conservative Party: Vice-chair 1981-83, Deputy Chair 1983-84, Board member 2001-; Chair 1922 Committee 2001-10; Chairman Conservative Party Finance and Audit Committee 2007-10. *Councils and public bodies:* President, Association of Electricity Producers 1991-2015; Governor, Wellington College 1992-2004; Member, UK Government Honours Main Committee.

Political interests: Economic policy; USA.

Other: Chair, European Research Group 1992-2001; Joint chairman, Congress of Democracy. Kt 1996; PC 2013; *Clubs:* Pratts, Garrick Club. Captain, Lords and Commons Tennis Club 1995-2005.

Publications: A Treaty Too Far: A New Policy For Europe (1992); The Challenge from the East: The Rebirth of the West (1996); The Spicer Diaries (Biteback, 2012); Six novels.

Recreations: Tennis, writing novels, painting, bridge.

Rt Hon the Lord Spicer, House of Lords, London SW1A 0PW
Tel: 020 7219 3000

STAIR, EARL OF

CROSSBENCH

STAIR (14th Earl of, S), John David James Dalrymple; cr. 1703; Viscount Dalrymple and Lord Newliston, Glenluce and Stranraer; 15th Viscount Stair and Lord Glenluce and Stranraer (S) 1690; 7th Baron Oxenfoord (UK) 1841; 15th Bt of Stair (S) 1664; 11th Bt of Killock (S) 1698. Born 4 September 1961; Son of 13th Earl; Married Hon Emily Stonor 2006 (1 son 1 daughter).

Education: Harrow School; Royal Military Academy, Sandhurst.

Non-political career: Commissioned Scots Guards 1982. Land management.

Political career: *House of Lords:* First entered House of Lords 1996; Elected hereditary peer 2008-. Member: EU Sub-committee F (Home Affairs, Health and Education) 2012-15, Refreshment 2015-16, EU Energy and Environment Sub-committee 2017-. *Councils and public bodies:* Board member: Scottish Enterprise Dumfries and Galloway 1999-2008, Scottish Environment Protection Agency 2002-09; Vice Lord-Lieutenant, Wigtown 2017-.

Political interests: Scottish affairs, agriculture, tourism, defence.

The Earl of Stair, House of Lords, London SW1A 0PW
Tel: 020 7219 5353 *Email:* dalrymplej@parliament.uk

STEDMAN-SCOTT, BARONESS

CONSERVATIVE

STEDMAN-SCOTT (Life Baroness), Deborah Stedman-Scott; cr 2010. Born 23 November 1955; Daughter of Jack Scott and Doreen-Margaret Scott; Civil partner Gabrielle Joy Stedman-Scott 2006.

Education: Ensham Secondary School for Girls; Southwark Technical College (1972).

Non-political career: Salvation Army 1978-83; Co-ordinator youth training scheme, Royal Tunbridge Wells Chamber of Commerce 1983-84; Tomorrow's People: Development manager 1984-86, Manager, Kent and Sussex 1986-88, South east regional manager 1988-93, Operations director 1993-95, Trust director 1995-2005, Chief executive 2005-15.

Political career: *House of Lords:* Raised to the peerage as Baroness Stedman-Scott, of Rolvenden in the County of Kent 2010. Deputy Chair of Committees 2014-. Member: Information 2011-15, Joint Committee on Parliamentary Privilege 2013, Social Mobility 2015-16, Charities 2016-17, Citizenship and Civic Engagement 2017-. *Councils and public bodies:* DL, East Sussex 2007-; Governor, Bexhill Academy 2015-.

Political interests: Unemployment, young people, education; New Zealand.

Other: Member, Advisory Board, International Centre for Drugs Policy 2004-07; Member, CBI: Employment Advisory Group 2004-09, Public Service Industry Forum; Employment Related Services Association: Founding Member, Chair 2007-09; Deputy Chair, Social Justice Policy Group; Trustee, New Philanthropy Capital 2011-17; Fellow, Centre for Social Justice, Trustee: Stefanou Foundation 2015-, Allia 2017-. Charity Principal of the Year 2005; Regional Entrepreneur of the Year, Ernst and Young 2010; Outstanding Leadership Award, Private Equity Foundation 2011; Women of The Year, Outstanding Achievement, Vitalise Woman of The Year Awards 2015. OBE 2008.

Recreations: Reading, travelling, art, particularly Lowry.

The Baroness Stedman-Scott OBE, House of Lords, London SW1A 0PW
Tel: 020 7219 8919 *Email:* stedmanscottd@parliament.uk

LIBERAL DEMOCRAT

STEEL OF AIKWOOD, LORD

STEEL OF AIKWOOD (Life Baron), David Martin Scott Steel; cr. 1997. Born 31 March 1938; Son of the late Very Rev. Dr David Steel, Moderator of the General Assembly of the Church of Scotland 1974-75; Married Judith MacGregor 1962 (2 sons 1 daughter).

Education: Prince of Wales School, Nairobi; George Watson's College, Edinburgh; Edinburgh University (MA 1960; LLB 1962); French, Swahili.

Non-political career: President, Edinburgh University Students' Representative Council 1961; Broadcaster; Journalist; BBC Television interviewer in Scotland 1964-65; Rector, Edinburgh University 1982-85.

Political career: *House of Commons:* Contested Roxburgh, Selkirk and Peebles October 1964 general election. MP (Liberal) for Roxburgh, Selkirk and Peebles 24 March 1965 by-election to 1983, for Tweeddale, Ettrick and Lauderdale 1983-97 (Liberal Democrat 1988-97). Sponsor, Abortion Act 1967; Liberal Chief Whip 1970-74. *House of Lords:* Raised to the peerage as Baron Steel of Aikwood, of Ettrick Forest in The Scottish Borders 1997. *Other:* Scottish Parliament: MSP for Lothians region 1999-2003 (as Sir David Steel): Presiding Officer 1999-2003. President, Edinburgh University Liberal Club 1960; Assistant Secretary, Scottish Liberal Party 1962-64; Leader, Liberal Party 1976-88; Joint Founder, Social and Liberal Democrats 1988. *Councils and public bodies:* DL, Roxburgh, Ettrick and Lauderdale 1990-2013.

Political interests: International democracy; Africa, China, Middle East, Taiwan.

Other: President, Liberal International 1992-94; President, Anti-Apartheid Movement in GB 1966-70; Chair, Scottish Advisory Council, Shelter 1968-72; President, Medical Aid for the Palestinians 1997-2004; Vice-President, Countryside Alliance 1998-99; President: Scottish Castles Association 2003-11, Jaguar Drivers' Club 2008-; Trustee, St Giles' Cathedral Restoration Trust; Visiting Fellow, St Antony's College, Oxford 2013; Hon. Fellow: Royal College of Obstetricians and Gynaecologists 2013, Royal Zoological Society of Scotland 2016; Scotland Prostate Cancer, Cancer Research International. Freedom: Tweeddale 1987, Ettrick and Lauderdale 1989. Ten honorary doctorates from British universities; Chubb fellow, Yale University, USA 1989. Queen's Lord High Commissioner to the General Assembly of the Church of Scotland 2003 and 2004. PC 1977; KBE 1990; Commander's Cross of the Order of Merit (Germany) 1992; Chevalier Légion d'Honneur (France) 2003; KT 2004; Honorary Knight of Order of St Georg Habsburg 2016; *Clubs:* National Liberal, Royal Overseas League Club.

Publications: No Entry, A House Divided; Editor, Partners in One Nation; David Steel's Border Country; Co-author, Mary Stuart's Scotland; Against Goliath (autobiography, 1989).

Recreations: Angling, classic car rallying.

Rt Hon the Lord Steel of Aikwood KT KBE, House of Lords, London SW1A 0PW
Tel: 020 7219 4433 *Email:* steeld@parliament.uk

LIBERAL DEMOCRAT

STEPHEN, LORD

STEPHEN (Life Baron), Nicol Ross Stephen; cr 2011. Born 23 March 1960; Son of Nicol Stephen, teacher, and Sheila Stephen, teacher; Married Caris Doig 1996 (2 sons 2 daughters).

Education: Robert Gordon's College, Aberdeen; Aberdeen University (LLB 1980); Edinburgh University (Diploma legal practice 1981); French.

Non-political career: Trainee solicitor, C & P H Chalmers 1981-83; Solicitor, Milne & Mackinnon 1983-88; Senior manager, Touche Ross Corporate Finance 1988-91; Director, Glassbox Ltd 1992-99.

Political career: *House of Commons:* Contested Kincardine and Deeside 1987 general election. MP (Liberal Democrat) for Kincardine and Deeside November 1991 by-election to 1992. Contested Kincardine and Deeside 1992 and Aberdeen South 1997 general elections. *House of Lords:* Raised to the peerage as Baron Stephen, of Lower Deeside in the City of Aberdeen 2011. Liberal Democrat Spokesperson for Scotland 2015-16. Member, Partnerships (Prosecution) (Scotland) Bill 2013. Chair, Liberal Democrat Parliamentary Party Committee on Scotland 2012-15. *Other:* Scottish Parliament: MSP for Aberdeen South constituency 1999-2011: Deputy Minister for Enterprise and Lifelong Learning 1999-2000, Minister for Higher Education 1999-2000, Deputy Minister for: Education, Europe and External Affairs 2000-01, Education and Young People 2001-03, Minister for Transport 2003-05, Deputy First Minister 2005-07, Minister for Enterprise and Lifelong Learning 2005-07. General election agent, Kincardine and Deeside 1983; Scottish Liberal Democrat Spokesperson for Health 1995-97; Party Spokesperson for Education and Heritage, Team Leader; Leader, Scottish Liberal Democrats 2005-08. *Councils and public bodies:* Councillor, Grampian Regional Council 1982-92.

Political interests: Economic development, education, health; China, India, Japan, USA.

Other: EU Committee of the Regions: Member 2002-05, Alternate member 2010-11; Former chair: CREATE (Campaign for Rail Electrification Aberdeen to Edinburgh), STAR Campaign (Save Tor-na-Dee Hospital and Roxburghe House); Founding director, Grampian Enterprise; Director, Grampion Youth Orchestra. Deeside Golf.

Recreations: Golf.

The Lord Stephen, House of Lords, London SW1A 0PW
Tel: 020 7219 2964 *Email:* stephenn@parliament.uk

CONSERVATIVE

STERLING OF PLAISTOW, LORD

STERLING OF PLAISTOW (Life Baron), Jeffrey Maurice Sterling; cr. 1991. Born 27 December 1934; Son of late Harry and Alice Sterling; Married Dorothy Smith 1985 (1 daughter).

Education: Reigate Grammar School; Preston Manor County School, Brent; Guildhall School of Music, London.

Non-political career: RAF National Service; Royal Naval Reserve: Honorary Captain 1991, Honorary Rear Admiral 2010, Honorary Vice Admiral 2015-. Paul Schweder and Co. (Stock Exchange) 1955-57; G Eberstadt & Co 1957-62; Financial director, General Guarantee Corporation 1962-64; Managing director, Gula Investments Ltd 1964-69; Chair, Sterling Guarantee Trust plc 1969, merging with P&O 1985; Board member, British Airways 1979-82; Executive chair, Peninsular and Oriental Steam Navigation Company 1983-2005; Special adviser: to Patrick Jenkin MP as Secretary of State for Industry 1982-83, to Secretaries of State for Trade and Industry 1983-90; P&O Princess Cruises plc: Chair 2000-03, Life President 2003-; Chair: Swan Hellenic 2007-, Hebridean Island Cruises 2009-.

Political career: *House of Lords:* Raised to the peerage as Baron Sterling of Plaistow, of Pall Mall in the City of Westminster 1991. Member: Joint Committee on National Security Strategy 2010-14, Sexual Violence in Conflict 2015-16.

Political interests: Shipping, economics, disability, arts, music, international affairs.

Other: Organisation for Rehabilitation through Training (ORT): Vice-President, British ORT 1978-; Deputy chair and Hon. treasurer, London Celebrations Committee, Queen's Silver Jubilee 1975-83; Chair, Young Vic Company 1975-83; Motability: Joint founder 1977, Chair 1994-; Chair of Governors, Royal Ballet School 1983-99; Governor, Royal Ballet 1986-99; Elder Brother, Trinity House 1991-; Chair: Board of Trustees, National Maritime Museum (which incorporates The Royal Observatory Greenwich and Royal Museums Greenwich) 2005-13, Cutty Sark Trust 2011-15; President, Ajex (Association of Jewish Ex-Servicemen and Women) 2012-; President: General Council, British Shipping 1990-91, European Community Shipowners' Associations 1992-94; Hon. Fellow: Institute of Marine Engineers 1991, Institute of Chartered Shipbrokers 1992; Hon. Member, Royal Institute of Chartered Surveyors 1993; Fellow, Incorporated Society of Valuers and Auctioneers 1995; Hon. Fellow, Royal Institute of Naval Architects 1997; Motability. Worshipful Company of Coopers. Freedom, City of London. Three honorary doctorates. Interfaith Medallion 2003. CBE 1977; Kt 1985; KStJ 1998; GCVO 2002; Grand Officer Order of May (Argentina) 2002; Officer's Cross Order of Merit (Germany) 2004; Officier de l'Ordre National de Légion d'Honneur (France) 2005; *Clubs:* Garrick, Hurlingham Club.

Recreations: Music, swimming, arts.

The Lord Sterling of Plaistow GCVO CBE, House of Lords, London SW1A 0PW
15 St James's Place, London SW1A 1NP *Tel:* 020 7647 8522 *Email:* pa@lordsterling.co.uk

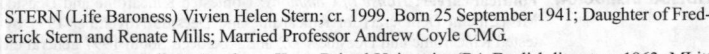

CROSSBENCH

STERN, BARONESS

STERN (Life Baroness) Vivien Helen Stern; cr. 1999. Born 25 September 1941; Daughter of Frederick Stern and Renate Mills; Married Professor Andrew Coyle CMG.

Education: Kent College, Pembury, Kent; Bristol University (BA English literature 1963; MLitt 1964; CertEd 1965).

Non-political career: Lecturer in education 1970; Principal officer, Community Relations Commission 1970-77; Director, NACRO 1977-96; Visiting fellow, Nuffield College, Oxford 1984-91; Senior research fellow, International Centre for Prison Studies, King's College London 1997-2010; Visiting professor, Essex University 2011-14.

Political career: *House of Lords:* Raised to the peerage as Baroness Stern, of Vauxhall in the London Borough of Lambeth 1999. Member: European Union 2000-03, Joint Committee on Human Rights 2004-08, Joint Committee on Statutory Instruments 2010-15, Inquiries Act 2005 2013-14, Secondary Legislation Scrutiny 2014-17. *Councils and public bodies:* Committee Member, Prison Disciplinary System 1984-85.

Political interests: Criminal justice, foreign affairs, human rights, international development, penal reform, prisons, rape and sexual violence, death penalty, violence against children; Afghanistan, Algeria, Argentina, Chile, Dominican Republic, Kazakhstan, Kenya, Kyrgyzstan, Tajikistan, Uzbekistan.

Other: Member: Special Programmes Board, Manpower Services Commission 1980-82, Youth Training Board 1982-88, General Advisory Council, IBA 1982-87; Penal Reform International: Honorary secretary-general 1989-2006, Honorary president 2006-; Member, Advisory Council, PSI 1993-96; Board member, Association for Prevention of Torture, Geneva 1993-2000; Trustee, Milton S Eisenhower Foundation, Washington 1993-2007; British Council: Member: Law Advisory Committee 1995-2000, Governance Advisory Committee 2002-06; Patron: Clean Break 1998-, Prisoners' Education Trust 1998-; President, New Bridge 2001-06; Vice-president, Comité de Soutien, Français Incarcérés au Loin (FIL) 2001-07; Convener, Scottish Consortium on Crime and Criminal Justice 2003-09; President, Association of Members of Independent Monitoring Boards 2005-; Patron, Amicus 2007-; Member, advisory council, Legal Policy Research Centre, Kazakhstan 2008-; International Legal Foundation, New York: Advisory Committee member 2009-14, Board member 2009-; Patron: Alternatives to Violence Project 2010-, Venture Trust 2010-, UK Network of Sex Work Projects 2011-, London Havens (Sexual Assault Referral Centres) 2012-; Survivors' Network, Brighton 2013; Co-chair, KNOW Violence Global Learning Initiative 2014-; Trustee: Institute for Criminal Policy Research 2014-, Redress 2015-. Six honorary doctorates; Hon. Fellow, LSE 1996. Peer of the Year, Women in Public Life Awards 2010. CBE 1992.

Publications: Bricks of Shame (1987); Imprisoned by Our Prisons (1989); Deprived of their Liberty, a report for Caribbean Rights (1990); A Sin Against the Future: imprisonment in the world (1998); Alternatives to Prison in Developing Countries (1999); Editor, Sentenced to Die: The Problems of TB in Prisons in Eastern Europe and Central Asia (2000); Creating Criminals: People and Prisons in a Market Society (2006); Report of an Independent Review into how rape complaints are handled by public authorities in England and Wales (The Stern Review, 2010).

The Baroness Stern CBE, House of Lords, London SW1A 0PW
Tel: 020 7219 5353 *Email:* sternvh@parliament.uk

CROSSBENCH

STERN OF BRENTFORD, LORD

STERN OF BRENTFORD (Life Baron), Nicholas Herbert Stern; cr 2007. Born 22 April 1946; Son of late Adalbert and Marion Stern, née Swann; Married Susan Ruth Chesterton 1968 (1 daughter 2 sons).

Education: Peterhouse, Cambridge (BA mathematics 1967); Nuffield College, Oxford (DPhil economics 1972); French.

Non-political career: Lecturer in industrial mathematics, Oxford, and Fellow in economics, St Catherine's College, Oxford 1970-77; Professor of economics, Warwick University 1978-85; London School of Economics and Political Science: Sir John Hicks Professor of Economics 1986-94, Professor of economics 1999-2003, IG Patel Chair 2007-; Chief Economist and Special Counsellor to the President, European Bank for Reconstruction and Development 1994-99; Chief Economist and Senior Vice-President, World Bank, Washington DC 2000-03; HM Treasury 2003-07: Managing director, Budget and Public Finance 2003-05, Second Permanent Secretary 2003-05, Head of Government Economic Service 2003-07, Adviser on Economics of Climate Change and Development (Stern Review) 2005-06.

Political career: *House of Lords:* Raised to the peerage as Baron Stern of Brentford, of Elsted in the County of West Sussex and of Wimbledon in the London Borough of Merton 2007. *Councils and public bodies:* Trustee, British Museum.

Other: Member, United Nations High Level Group on Development Strategy and Management of the Market Economy 1997; Fellow: British Academy, Econometric Society 1978. Eleven honorary doctorates. Foreign Honorary Member, American Academy of Arts and Sciences; Great Briton of the Year (Environment) 2006; Royal Geographical Society Patron's Royal Medal 2009; Asahi Glass Foundation Blue Planet Prize 2009. Kt 2004; CH 2017.

Publications: Crime, the Police and Criminal Statistics (1979); Editor, Journal of Public Economics 1981-97; Palanpur: The Economy of an Indian Village (1982); The Theory of Taxation for Developing Countries (World Bank, 1987); The Role of the State in Economic Development (1991); The Theory and Practice of Tax Reform in Developing Countries (1991); Economic Development in Palanpur over Five Decades (1998); A Case for Aid (World Bank, 2002); A Strategy for Development (World Bank, 2002); Co-author, Growth and Empowerment (2005); A Blueprint for a Safer Planet (2009).

Recreations: Walking, reading, football.

Professor the Lord Stern of Brentford CH, House of Lords, London SW1A 0PW
Tel: 020 7219 1300

CROSSBENCH

STEVENS OF KIRKWHELPINGTON, LORD

STEVENS OF KIRKWHELPINGTON (Life Baron), John Arthur Stevens; cr 2005. Born 21 October 1942; Married (2 sons 1 daughter).

Education: St Lawrence College, Ramsgate; Leicester University (LLB, LLD 2000); Southampton University.

Non-political career: Honorary Colonel, Northumbria Army Cadets 2006-; Honorary Air Commodore, No 3 (Royal Auxiliary) Air Force Police Squadron 2007-. Metropolitan Police 1963-83; Directing staff, Police Staff College 1983-84; Assistant Chief Constable, Hampshire Constabulary 1986-89; Deputy Chief Constable, Cambridgeshire Constabulary 1989-91; Chief Constable, Northumbria 1991-96; HM Inspector of Constabulary 1996-98; Metropolitan Police 1998-2005: Deputy Commissioner 1998-99, Commissioner 2000-05; Senior international security adviser to Prime Minister 2007-10; Chair: Border Policing Committee 2007, Independent Police Commission 2011.

Political career: *House of Lords:* Raised to the peerage as Baron Stevens of Kirkwhelpington, of Kirkwhelpington in the County of Northumberland 2005. *Other:* Chair, Independent Review into the Future of Policing in England and Wales 2011-. *Councils and public bodies:* Chair: Stevens Enquiries (into NI security forces and paramilitary collusion) 1989-92, 1999-2003, Joint Committee on Offender Profiling 1991, Inquiry into death of Princess Diana 2003-06, Strategic Advisory Panel, Interpol 2005-.

Other: Fellow, Wolfson College, Cambridge; Northumbria Youth Action, Newcastle Cathedral Restoration. Freedom, City of London 2002. Chancellor, Northumbria University 2005-15. QPM 1992; Kt 2000; Knight of St John 2002; Star of Romania; Emeritus Lay Cannon, Newcastle Cathedral; *Clubs:* RAF Club.

Publications: Not for the Faint Hearted (2005).

The Lord Stevens of Kirkwhelpington QPM, House of Lords, London SW1A 0PW
Tel: 020 7219 5488

UK INDEPENDENCE PARTY

STEVENS OF LUDGATE, LORD

STEVENS OF LUDGATE (Life Baron), David Robert Stevens; cr. 1987. Born 26 May 1936; Son of late A Edwin Stevens, CBE and Kathleen James; Married Patricia Rose 1961 (divorced 1971) (1 son 1 daughter); married Melissa Sadoff, née Milicevic 1977 (died 1989); married Meriza Giori, née Dzienciolsky 1990.

Education: Stowe School, Buckinghamshire; Sidney Sussex College, Cambridge (BA economics 1959, MA); French.

Non-political career: Second Lieutenant, Royal Artillery, National Service, Hong Kong 1954-56. Management trainee, Elliot Automation 1959; Hill Samuel Securities 1959-68; Drayton Group 1968-74; United News and Media plc (formerly United Newspapers): Director 1974-, Chair 1981-99; Chair: City and Foreign/Alexander Proudfoot 1976-95, Drayton Far East 1976-93, English and International 1976-89, Consolidated Venture 1979-93, Drayton Consolidated 1980-92, Drayton Japan 1980-88; MIM Britannia Ltd (formerly Montagu Investment Management Ltd): Chair and chief executive 1980-89, Chair 1989-93; Chair, Express Newspapers plc 1985-99; Deputy chair, Britannia Arrow Holdings plc 1987-89; Chair: Invesco MIM plc (formerly Britannia Arrow Holdings) 1989-92, Oak Industries 1989-95, Premier Asset Management 1997-2001, Personal Number Company 1998-2003; Express National Newspapers Ltd: Chair 1998-99, Deputy Chair 2014-.

Political career: *House of Lords:* Raised to the peerage as Baron Stevens of Ludgate, of Ludgate in the City of London 1987. *Other:* Member: Conservative Party 1987-2004, UK Independence Party 2013-; Sat as Conservative Independent 2004-13. *Councils and public bodies:* Chair, EDC for Civil Engineering 1984-86.

Political interests: European Union, tax and financial affairs; France, Italy, USA.

Other: Director, English National Opera 1980-87; Chair, Helicopter Emergency Rescue Services 1988-90; Patron, Royal College of Surgeons; National Association of Almshouses, Action Against Cancer, St George's Hospital (Cancer)Charity, Cancer Research. Hon. Fellow, Sidney Sussex College, Cambridge 1991. Grand Official, Order of the Southern Cross (Brazil) 1993; *Clubs:* White's Club. Sunningdale Golf, Swinley Forest Golf.

Recreations: Gardening, golf.

The Lord Stevens of Ludgate, House of Lords, London SW1A 0PW
Tel: 020 7219 5353 *Email:* stevensdavid@parliament.uk

LABOUR

STEVENSON OF BALMACARA, LORD

Opposition Whip

STEVENSON OF BALMACARA (Life Baron), Robert Wilfrid (Wilf) Stevenson; cr 2010. Born 19 April 1947; Son of late James Stevenson and late Elizabeth Macrae; Married Jennifer Antonio 1972 (divorced 1979); married Ann Minogue 1991 (1 son 2 daughters).

Education: Edinburgh Academy; University College, Oxford (BA natural sciences, chemistry, MA); Napier Polytechnic (FCCA).

Non-political career: Research officer, Edinburgh University Students' Association 1970-74; Secretary, Napier College, Edinburgh 1974-87; British Film Institute: Deputy Director 1987-88, Director 1988-97; Director, Smith Institute 1997-2008; Senior Policy Adviser, Prime Minister's Office 2008-10. Member, Unite 1974-.

Political career: *House of Lords:* Raised to the peerage as Baron Stevenson of Balmacara, of Little Missenden in the County of Buckinghamshire 2010. Opposition Whip 2011-; Opposition Spokesperson for: Business, Innovation and Skills 2011-16, Culture, Media and Sport 2011-17, Business, Energy and Industrial Strategy 2016-17, Higher Education 2016-17. Member: Communications 2011, Intellectual Property (Unjustified Threats) Bill 2016.

Political interests: Intellectual property, the Arts, Scotland; Burma, Eire, Iran, Turkey.

Other: Member, ACCA (retired); Hypospadias UK, Catalyst Trust. Hon DArts, Napier University 2008.

Publications: Editor: Gordon Brown Speeches (2006), Moving Britain Forward (2006), The Change We Choose: Speeches 2007-2009 (2010).

Recreations: Cinema, gardening, beekeeping.

The Lord Stevenson of Balmacara, House of Lords, London SW1A 0PW
Tel: 020 7219 8914/07778 465103 *Email:* stevensonw@parliament.uk
Email: wilf@wilfstevenson.co.uk *Twitter:* @missenden50

CROSSBENCH

STEVENSON OF CODDENHAM, LORD

STEVENSON OF CODDENHAM (Life Baron), Henry Dennistoun (Dennis) Stevenson; cr. 1999. Born 19 July 1945; Son of late Alexander and Sylvia Stevenson, née Ingleby; Married Charlotte Susan Vanneck 1972 (4 sons).

Education: Trinity College, Glenalmond; King's College, Cambridge (MA classics 1970).

Non-political career: Chair, SRU Group of Companies 1972-96; Non-executive director, Manpower Inc 1988-2006; Chair: Sinfonia 21 1989-99, Pearson plc 1996-05, Halifax plc 1999-2008, HBOS plc 2001-08, Non-executive director: Western Union Company 2006-, Culture and Sport Glasgow 2007-09, Loudwater Investment Partners Ltd 2007-.

Political career: *House of Lords:* Raised to the peerage as Baron Stevenson of Coddenham, of Coddenham in the County of Suffolk 1999. Member, Works of Art 2009-10, 2012-13. *Councils and public bodies:* Chair, House of Lords Appointments Commission 2000-08.

Countries of interest: Holland, Japan, Sierra Leone, USA.

Other: Chair: Government Working Party on role of voluntary movements and youth in the environment 1971, Newton Aycliffe and Peterlee New Town Development Corporation 1971-80, Independent Advisory Committee on Pop Festivals 1972-76, National Association of Youth Clubs 1973-81; Director, National Building Agency 1977-81; Adviser on agricultural marketing to Minister of Agriculture 1979-83; Director, London Docklands Development Corporation 1981-88; Chair: Intermediate Technology Development Group 1983-90, Trustees, Tate Gallery 1988-98; Member, Panel on Takeovers and Mergers 1992-2000; Board member, British Council 1996-2003; Governor: London School of Economics 1996-2002, London Business School 1996-2002; Director, Glyndebourne Productions 1998-; Hon. Member, Royal Society of Musicians of Great Britain 1998-; Trustee, Tate Gallery Foundation 1998-; Chair, Aldeburgh Music Ltd 2000-; Trustee, Horse's Mouth 2006-. Chancellor, University of the Arts, London 2000-10. CBE 1981; Kt 1998; *Clubs:* Brooks's, MCC Club.

Publications: Stevenson Commission Information and Communications Technology in UK Schools Report (1997).

The Lord Stevenson of Coddenham CBE, House of Lords, London SW1A 0PW
Tel: 020 7219 5353
Little Tufton House, 3 Dean Trench Street, London SW1P 3HB *Tel:* 020 7340 0650
Fax: 020 7340 0653 *Email:* dennis@hdstevenson.co.uk

CROSSBENCH

STEYN, LORD

STEYN (Life Baron), Johan van Zyl Steyn; cr. 1995. Born 15 August 1932; Son of Van Zyl Steyn and Janet Steyn; Married Susan Lewis 1977 (2 sons and 2 daughters from previous marriage; 1 stepson and 1 stepdaughter).

Education: Jan van Riebeeck School, Cape Town, South Africa; University of Stellenbosch, South Africa (BA law 1957; LLB 1957); Cape Province Rhodes Scholar 1955; University College, Oxford (MA law 1957).

Non-political career: Commenced practice at the South African Bar 1958; Senior Counsel of Supreme Court of South Africa 1970; English Bar 1973; QC 1979; Bencher, Lincoln's Inn 1985; Judge of the High Court, Queen's Bench Division 1985-91; Member, Supreme Court Rule Committee 1985-89; Departmental Advisory Committee on Arbitration Law 1986-89, Chair 1990-94; Chair, Race Relations Committee of the Bar 1987-88; Presiding Judge, Northern Circuit 1989-91; President, British Insurance Law Association 1992-94; Lord Justice of Appeal 1992-95; Chair: Advisory Council, Centre for Commercial Law Studies, Queen Mary and Westfield College, London 1993-94, Lord Chancellor's Advisory Committee on Legal Education and Conduct 1994-96, Appeal Board of the Takeover Panel 2006-14.

Political career: *House of Lords:* Raised to the peerage as Baron Steyn, of Swafield in the County of Norfolk 1995. Lord of Appeal in Ordinary 1995-2005.

Other: Hon. Member: American Law Institute 1999, Society of Legal Scholars 2002. Three honorary doctorates; Honorary fellow: University College, Oxford 1985, University College, London 2005. Kt 1985; PC 1992.

Publications: Democracy Through Law collected essays (Ashgate, 2004).

Rt Hon the Lord Steyn, House of Lords, London SW1A 0PW
Tel: 020 7219 5353

CROSSBENCH

STIRRUP, LORD

STIRRUP (Life Baron), Graham Eric (Jock) Stirrup; cr 2011. Born 4 December 1949; Son of William Stirrup and Jacqueline Stirrup, née Coulson; Married Mary Elliott 1976 (1 son).

Education: Merchant Taylors' School, Northwood; Royal Air Force College.

Non-political career: Qualified as flying instructor 1971; Service in the Sultan of Oman's Air Force 1973-75; Fighter reconnaissance pilot 1976-78; US Air Force 1978-81; Flight Commander 1982-84; Officer Commanding (OC) No II (Army Co-operation) Squadron 1985-87; Personal Staff Officer to Chief of the Air Staff 1987-90; OC RAF Marham 1990-92; Royal College of Defence Studies 1993; Director, Air Force Plans and Programmes, MoD 1994-97; Air OC No I 1997-98; Assistant Chief of Air Staff 1998-2000; Deputy Commander-in-Chief, Strike Command; Commander NATO Combined Air Operations Centre 9 and Director, European Air Group 2000-02; Deputy Chief of Defence Staff (Equipment Capability) 2002-03; Chief of the Air Staff 2003-06; Chief of the Defence Staff 2006-10.

Political career: *House of Lords:* Raised to the peerage as Baron Stirrup, of Marylebone in the City of Westminster 2011. Member: House 2013-16, EU External Affairs Sub-Committee 2015-. *Councils and public bodies:* Governor, Wellington College.

Countries of interest: Australia, Middle East, USA.

Other: Director, City of London Sinfonia; FRAeS; FIMgt. Hon. DSc, Cranfield University 2005. AFC 1982. CB 2000; KCB 2002; GCB 2005; KG 2013; *Clubs:* Royal Air Force, Beefsteak Club.

Recreations: History, music, theatre, golf.

Marshal of the Royal Air Force the Lord Stirrup KG GCB AFC ADC, House of Lords, London SW1A 0PW
Tel: 020 7219 5979 *Email:* stirrupg@parliament.uk

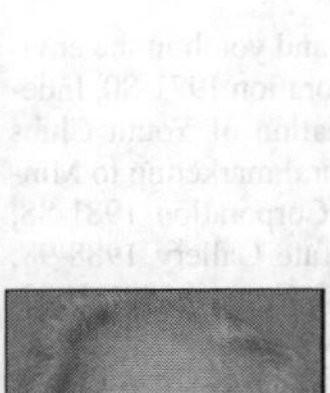

INDEPENDENT LABOUR

STODDART OF SWINDON, LORD

STODDART OF SWINDON (Life Baron), David Leonard Stoddart; cr. 1983. Born 4 May 1926; Son of Arthur Stoddart, coal miner, and Queenie Stoddart; Married 2nd Jennifer Percival-Alwyn 1961 (2 sons) (1 daughter from previous marriage).

Education: St Clement Danes Grammar School; Henley Grammar School.

Non-political career: British Railways; NHS; Power station clerical worker 1951-70. NALGO 1951-70; EETPU (later AEEU, now Unite) 1953-.

Political career: *House of Commons:* Contested Newbury 1959 and 1964 general elections. MP (Labour) for Swindon 1970-83. PPS to Reg Freeson as Minister for Housing and Construction 1974-75; Assistant Government Whip 1975-76; Government Whip 1976-77. *House of Lords:* Raised to the peerage as Baron Stoddart of Swindon, of Reading in the Royal County of Berkshire

1983. Opposition Spokesperson for Energy 1983-88; Opposition Whip 1983-88. *Councils and public bodies:* Reading County Borough Council: Councillor 1954-72, Council Leader 1967-72; Member, various boards including Thames Valley Water Board and Police Authority.

Political interests: Commonwealth, economic policy, energy, European Union, housing, industry, local government, transport.

Other: Member, Court and Council, Reading University 1964-68; Treasurer, Anzac Group 1985-2002; Chair: Campaign for an Independent Britain 1989-2007, Anti-Maastricht Alliance/Alliance against the European constitution 1991-2007; Founder member, Global Britain.

The Lord Stoddart of Swindon, House of Lords, London SW1A 0PW
Tel: 020 7219 5402 *Email:* stoddartd@parliament.uk

STONE OF BLACKHEATH, LORD

LABOUR

STONE OF BLACKHEATH (Life Baron), Andrew Zelig Stone; cr. 1997. Born 7 September 1942; Son of Sydney and Louise Stone; Married Vivienne Lee 1973 (1 son 2 daughters).

Education: Cardiff High School.

Non-political career: Marks and Spencer plc 1966-99: Personal assistant to chair 1978-80, Director 1990-, Joint managing director 1994-99; Director: N Brown 2002-13, Ted Baker plc 2002-04, McDonalds Advisory Board 2005-07, Deal Group Media plc 2005-07; Deputy chair, Sindicatum Carbon Capital Holdings Ltd 2005-09; Director, Falcon Power Holdings 2012-.

Political career: *House of Lords:* Raised to the peerage as Baron Stone of Blackheath, of Blackheath in the London Borough of Greenwich 1997. Departmental Liaison Peer to Baroness Jay as Leader of the House of Lords 1999-2001. Member, House of Lords Offices Refreshment Sub-committee 2000-02.

Political interests: Conflict resolution, art and science, health, ecology; China, Middle East.

Other: British Overseas Trade Board for Israel: Chair 1991-99, President 1995-2000; Governor, Weizmann Institute Foundation 1993-; Council member, Arts and Business 1994-2001; Member, national advisory committee, Creative and Cultural Education 1998-2000; Director, Science Media Centre 2001-05; Governor, Tel Aviv University 2001-04; Hon Vice-President, Movement for Reform Judaism; Chair, Dipex (Direct Patient Experiences) 2005-17; Trustee, Olive Tree Trust 2005-09; Governor, British University of Egypt 2006-; Member, Risk Commission (RSA); Chair, Sindicatum Climate Change Foundation 2009-11; Trustee, Prism the Gift Fund 2009-; Orphaids, Gauchers Association, DIPEX. Two honorary degrees.

Recreations: Reading, walking, thinking, meditating.

The Lord Stone of Blackheath, House of Lords, London SW1A 0PW
Tel: 020 7219 4556 *Fax:* 020 7219 5979 *Email:* stonea@parliament.uk

STONEHAM OF DROXFORD, LORD

Liberal Democrat Chief Whip in the Lords

LIBERAL DEMOCRAT

STONEHAM OF DROXFORD (Life Baron), Benjamin Russell Mackintosh Stoneham; cr 2011. Born 24 August 1948; Son of Major B J R Stoneham and Beryl Stoneham; Married Anne 1975 (2 sons 1 daughter).

Education: Harrow School; Christ's College, Cambridge (BA economics 1970); Warwick University (MA industrial relations 1971).

Non-political career: Research officer, Social and Administrative Studies Department, Oxford University 1971-74; NCB 1974-78; National officer, National Union of Railwaymen 1979-82; Portsmouth and Sunderland Newspapers 1982-89; Managing director, Portsmouth Publishing and Printing Ltd 1989-99; Group production and personnel director, News International 2000-03; Operations director, Liberal Democrat HQ 2003-10; Chair and director, First Wessex Housing Group Ltd 2007-12; Chair, Housing and Care 21 2011-.

Political career: *House of Commons:* Contested (Labour) Saffron Walden 1977 and 1979 and (SDP/All) Stevenage 1983 and 1987 general elections. *House of Lords:* Raised to the peerage as Baron Stoneham of Droxford, of the Meon Valley in the County of Hampshire 2011. Liberal Democrat: Whip 2011-15, Spokesperson for Business, Innovation and Skills 2015, Chief Whip in the Lords 2016-. Member: EU Sub-committee E (Justice, Institutions and Consumer Protection) 2012-15, Olympic and Paralympic Legacy 2013-14, Finance 2016-, Privileges and Conduct 2016-, Procedure 2016-, Selection 2016-. *Councils and public bodies:* Councillor, Hertfordshire County Council 1985-89.

Political interests: Pensions, housing and regeneration, media; France, South Africa, USA.

Other: Director, Make Votes Count; Trustee, Coltstaple Trust.

The Lord Stoneham of Droxford, House of Lords, London SW1A 0PW
Tel: 020 7219 8629

LIBERAL DEMOCRAT

STOREY, LORD

Liberal Democrat Lords Spokesperson for Education

STOREY (Life Baron), Michael John Storey; cr 2011. Born 25 May 1949; Married (1 daughter).

Education: Liverpool University (BEd).

Non-political career: Teacher: Prescot CoE Primary School 1972-77, New Hutte Primary School, Halewood 1977-82; Deputy headteacher, Halsnead Primary School, Whiston 1982-85; Headteacher: St Gabriel's CoE Primary School, Huyton 1985-90, Plantation County Primary School, Halewood 1990-2012.

Political career: *House of Lords:* Raised to the peerage as Baron Storey, of Childwall in the City of Liverpool 2011. Liberal Democrat: Whip 2011-14, Shadow Minister/Lords Spokesperson for Education 2015-. Member, Small- and Medium-Sized Enterprises 2012-13. Chair, Liberal Democrat Parliamentary Committee for Education, Families and Young People 2013-15. *Councils and public bodies:* Liverpool City Council: Councillor 1973-2011, Leader, Liberal Democrat opposition 1991-98, Council Leader 1998-2005, Lord Mayor of Liverpool 2009-10; Vice-president, Local Government Association 2017-.

Political interests: Education, regeneration, the arts, local authorities, Merseyside; France, Germany, Switzerland, USA.

Other: OBE 1994; CBE 2002.

Recreations: Reading, theatre, cinema, gardening.

The Lord Storey CBE, House of Lords, London SW1A 0PW
Tel: 020 7219 1972 *Email:* storeym@parliament.uk *Twitter:* @LordStorey

CONSERVATIVE

STOWELL OF BEESTON, BARONESS

STOWELL OF BEESTON (Life Baroness), Tina Wendy Stowell; cr 2011. Born 2 July 1967.

Education: Chilwell Comprehensive School; Broxtowe College of Further Education (1985).

Non-political career: Civil servant 1986-96: Ministry of Defence 1986-88, British Embassy, Washington DC 1988-91, Downing Street Press Office 1991-96; Private Sector (various, including Paradine Productions, Granada Media) 1996-98; Deputy Chief of Staff to William Hague MP as Leader of the Conservative Party 1998-2001; BBC: Deputy Secretary 2001-03, Head of communications to the Chairman and Board of Governors/BBC Trust 2003-08, Head of corporate affairs 2008-10; Consultant, Tina Stowell Associates 2010-11, 2016-; Director, ABTA Ltd 2016-.

Political career: *House of Lords:* Raised to the peerage as Baroness Stowell of Beeston, of Beeston in the County of Nottinghamshire 2011. Party Whip 2011; Government Whip 2011-13; Government Spokesperson for: Energy and Climate Change 2011-12, International Development 2011-12, Home Office 2011-13, Culture, Media and Sport 2012-13, Northern Ireland September-October 2012, Women and Equalities 2012-13, Work and Pensions 2012-13; Parliamentary Under-Secretary of State and Government Spokesperson, Department for Communities and Local Government 2013-14; Leader of the House of Lords and Lord Privy Seal 2014-16 (also attended Cabinet 2014-15, Cabinet member 2015-16). Member Joint Committees on: Human Rights 2011, Security 2012-13; Member: House 2014-16, Liaison 2014-16, Privileges and Conduct 2014-16, Procedure 2014-16, Selection 2014-16; Chair, Joint Committee on the Palace of Westminster 2015-16.

Political interests: Social mobility, political reform.

Other: Honorary Doctorate, Nottingham University 2016. MBE 1996; PC 2014.

Rt Hon the Baroness Stowell of Beeston MBE, House of Lords, London SW1A 0PW
Tel: 020 7219 5353 *Email:* stowellt@parliament.uk
Website: www.tinastowell.co.uk *Twitter:* @tinastowell

LIBERAL DEMOCRAT

STRASBURGER, LORD

STRASBURGER (Life Baron), Paul Cline Strasburger; cr 2011. Born 31 July 1946; Married.

Non-political career: IT and security industries; Property management.

Political career: *House of Lords:* Raised to the peerage as Baron Strasburger, of Langridge in the County of Somerset 2011. Member: Joint Committee on the Draft Communications Data Bill 2012-13, Information 2014-16, Joint Committee on the Draft Investigatory Powers Bill 2015-16.

Political interests: Civil liberties, the environment, unleashing potential, protecting citizens from the State and corporations.

Other: The Prince's Trust. MCC.

Recreations: All music (almost), sport, theatre, adventure.

The Lord Strasburger, House of Lords, London SW1A 0PW
Tel: 020 7219 5081 *Email:* strasburgerp@parliament.uk *Twitter:* @LordStras

STRATHCLYDE, LORD

CONSERVATIVE

STRATHCLYDE (2nd Baron, UK), Thomas Galloway Dunlop du Roy de Blicquy Galbraith; cr. 1955. Born 22 February 1960; Son of late Hon Sir Thomas Galbraith KBE (former MP, eldest son of 1st Baron, PC); Married Jane Skinner 1992 (3 daughters).

Education: Wellington College, Berkshire; University of East Anglia 1978-82; University of Aix-en-Provence 1981.

Non-political career: Lloyd's insurance broker; Bain Clarkson Ltd 1982-88; Chair, Trafalgar Capital Management Ltd 2001-10; Director: Scottish Mortgage Investment Trust plc 2004-10, Galena Asset Management Ltd 2004-10, Marketform Group Ltd 2004-10, Hampden Agencies Ltd 2008-10; Director, Trafigura Beheer BV Supervisory Board 2013-.

Political career: *House of Lords:* First entered House of Lords 1985; Government Whip 1988-89; Government Spokesperson for Trade and Industry, Treasury and Scotland 1988-89; Parliamentary Under-Secretary of State: Department of Employment (Tourism) 1989-90, Department of Environment 1990, 1992-93; Scottish Office (Agriculture and Fisheries) 1990-92; Department of Trade and Industry: Parliamentary Under-Secretary of State 1993-94, Minister of State 1994; Government Chief Whip 1994-97; Member, Shadow Cabinet 1997-2010; Opposition Chief Whip 1997-98; Deputy Speaker 1997-98; Deputy Chairman of Committees 1997-98; Leader of the Opposition 1998-2010; Opposition Spokesperson for Constitutional Affairs December 1998-2005; Elected hereditary peer 1999-; Leader of the House of Lords and Chancellor of the Duchy of Lancaster 2010-13. Member: Privileges/Privileges and Conduct 1994-2013, Procedure 1994-2013, Selection 1994-2013, Liaison 1998-2013, House 2002-13. *Other:* Contested Merseyside East 1984 European Parliament election. Chair: Commission on the Future Structure of the Scottish Conservative and Unionist Party 1997-98, Commission on the Future Governance of Scotland. *Councils and public bodies:* Governor, Wellington College 2010-.

Other: President, Quoted Companies Alliance 2003-09; Board Member, Centre for Policy Studies; Chair: Battersea Power Station Foundation 2015-, B & C (Bank) plc 2016-. Peer of 2000 Channel 4 and *The House Magazine*; Peer of the Year, *Spectator* 2004. PC 1995; CH 2013.

Publications: New Frontiers for Reform (CPS, 2001); Working in Harness: parliamentary government and the role of the Lords (Politeia, 2005).

Rt Hon the Lord Strathclyde CH, House of Lords, London SW1A 0PW
Tel: 020 7219 5353

STROUD, BARONESS

CONSERVATIVE

STROUD (Life Baroness), Philippa Claire Stroud; cr 2015. Born 2 April 1965; Married David Stroud 1989 (1 son twin daughters).

Education: St Catherine's School, Bramley; Birmingham University (BA French 1987); French, some knowledge of spoken Chinese.

Non-political career: Voluntary worker, drug rehabilitation centre, Hong Kong and Macau 1987-89; Founder, King's Arms Project, Bedford 1989-96; Director: Care Confidential -2004, Bridge Project Birmingham 2001-03; Executive Director, Centre for Social Justice 2004-10, 2015-; Special Adviser to Iain Duncan Smith MP as Secretary of State for Work and Pensions 2010-15.

Political career: *House of Commons:* Contested (Conservative) Birmingham Ladywood 2005 and Sutton and Cheam 2010 general elections. *House of Lords:* Raised to the peerage as Baroness Stroud, of Fulham in the London Borough of Hammersmith and Fulham 2015. *Councils and public bodies:* Former Governor, Blue Coat School.

Political interests: Social justice, education, health, crime, voluntary sector, family, social policy.

Other: Board member, SCOLA 2008-; Patron, Elevate 2008-; *Clubs:* United and Cecil Club.

Recreations: Travelling, eating out, movies, sport – especially skiing and sailing.

The Baroness Stroud, House of Lords, London SW1A 0PW
Tel: 020 7219 3000 *Email:* stroudp@parliament.uk
c/o Centre for Social Justice, 11 Belgrave Road, London SW1V 1RB *Tel:* 020 7592 1160

STUNELL, LORD

LIBERAL DEMOCRAT

STUNELL (Life Baron), Robert Andrew Stunell; cr 2015. Born 24 November 1942; Son of late Robert Stunell and Trixie Stunell; Married Gillian Chorley 1967 (3 sons 2 daughters).

Education: Surbiton Grammar School; Manchester University (architecture RIBA Pt. II exemption 1963); Liverpool Polytechnic; (Some) German, French.

Non-political career: Architectural assistant: CWS Manchester 1965-67, Runcorn New Town 1967-81; Freelance architectural assistant 1981-85; Association of Liberal Democrat Councillors: Various posts including political secretary 1985-97, Head of Service 1989-96. Member, NALGO: New Towns Whitley Council 1977-81.

Political career: *House of Commons:* Contested City of Chester 1979, 1983, 1987, Hazel Grove 1992 general elections. MP (Liberal Democrat) for Hazel Grove 1997-2010, for Hazel Grove (revised boundary) 2010-15. Liberal Democrat: Spokesperson for Energy 1997-2005, Deputy Chief Whip 1997-2001, Chief Whip 2001-06, Shadow Secretary of State for Office of the Deputy Prime Minister/Communities and Local Government 2006-07; Parliamentary Under-Secretary of State, Department for Communities and Local Government 2010-12. Member: Broadcasting 1997-2000, Modernisation of the House of Commons 1997-2006, Procedure 1997-2001, Unopposed Bills (Panel) 1997-2001, Standing Orders 1998-2001, Finance and Services 2001-06, Selection 2001-06, International Development 2009-10, Arms Export Controls 2009-10, Joint Committee on the Draft Modern Slavery Bill 2014. *House of Lords:* Raised to the peerage as Baron Stunell, of Hazel Grove in the County of Greater Manchester 2015. *Other:* Member, Liberal Democrat Federal: Executive Committee 2001-06, Conference Committee 2001-06; Chair, Local Election Campaign 2007-12. *Councils and public bodies:* Councillor: Chester City Council 1979-90, Cheshire County Council 1981-91; Vice-chair, Association of County Councils 1985-90; Councillor, Stockport Metropolitan Borough Council 1994-2002; Vice-president, Local Government Association 1997-2010; Member, Committee on Standards in Public Life 2016-.

Political interests: Local democracy and regional devolution, Third World, race relations, energy, climate change; North and Sub-Saharan Africa, European Union.

Other: President, Goyt Valley Rail Users Association; Vice-president, Macclesfield Canal Society 1998-2015; North West Constitutional Convention 1999-2001; Fellow, Industry and Parliament Trust 2000; Patron, Marple Civic Society 2012-; Governor, Westminster Foundation for Democracy 2013-15; Trustee, Mellor Archaeological Trust. OBE 1995; PC 2012; Kt 2013.

Publications: Budgeting For Real (1984, 1994, 1999); Life In The Balance (1986); Thriving In The Balance (1995); Open Active & Effective (1995); Local Democracy Guaranteed (1996); Energy – Clean and Green to 2050 (1999); Nuclear Waste – Cleaning up the Mess (2001).

Recreations: Theoretical astronomy, camping, table tennis.

Rt Hon the Lord Stunell OBE, House of Lords, London SW1A 0PW
Tel: 020 7219 3000 *Email:* andrew.stunell.hg@parliament.uk

SUGAR, LORD

NON-AFFILIATED

SUGAR (Life Baron), Alan Michael Sugar; cr 2009. Born 24 March 1947; Married Ann Simons 1968 (2 sons 1 daughter).

Non-political career: Amstrad and post-1997 successors Betacom and Viglen: Founder chair 1968-97, Chair 1991-2001, Chief executive 1998-2000; Presenter, *The Apprentice* BBC TV 2005-.

Political career: *House of Lords:* Raised to the peerage as Baron Sugar, of Clapton in the London Borough of Hackney 2009. Government Enterprise Champion 2009-10, 2016-.

Other: Kt 2000.

Publications: What You See Is What You Get: My Autobiography (2011); The Way I See It: Rants, Revelations And Rules For Life (2011); Unscripted: My Ten Years in Telly (2015).

The Lord Sugar, House of Lords, London SW1A 0PW
Tel: 020 7219 5353 *Twitter:* @Lord_Sugar

CONSERVATIVE

SUGG, BARONESS

Government Spokesperson, Department for International Trade; Whip (Baroness in Waiting)

SUGG (Life Baroness) Elizabeth Grace Sugg; cr 2016. Born 2 May 1977.

Education: Newcastle University (politics).

Non-political career: Sky News; Media, Conservative MEP Team; Aide to Ken Clarke MP; Prime Minister's Office 2005-16: Head of Operations, Director of Operations and Campaigns.

Political career: *House of Lords:* Raised to the peerage as Baroness Sugg, of Coldharbour in the London Borough of Lambeth 2016. Government Whip (Baroness in Waiting) 2017-; Government Spokesperson, Department for International Trade September 2017-.

Other: Board member, Cricket World Cup England and Wales 2019.

The Baroness Sugg CBE, House of Lords, London SW1A 0PW
Tel: 020 7219 3000

CONSERVATIVE

SURI, LORD

SURI (Life Baron), Ranbir Singh Suri; cr 2014. Born 10 February 1935.

Non-political career: Chair and Founder, Oceanic Jewellers 1976-.

Political career: *House of Lords:* Raised to the peerage as Baron Suri, of Ealing in the London Borough of Ealing 2014. *Other:* Chair, Anglo-Asian Conservative Association 1978-; British Asian Conservative Links: Founder, Chair 1997-2011; President, Conservative Ethnic Diversity Council. *Councils and public bodies:* Voluntary Associate: HM Prison Wormwood Scrubs 1982-85, Middlesex Probation Committee 1983-85; Member: Board of Visitors, HM Prison Pentonville 1985-2000, Advisory Council on Race Relations, Home Office 1988-92, Middlesex Probation Committee 1990-91, Local Review Committee, HM Prison Pentonville 1990-93; JP, Ealing 1991-2005; Member, Lord Chancellor's Advisory Committee on General Commissioners of Income Tax 2003-05.

Other: Honorary Correspndent to the British High Commissioner, Kenya 1973-74; Member, London Chamber of Commerce; Mentor, Prince's Youth Business Trust 1997-2003; Executive Committee Member, British Heart Foundation, Ealing 1995-96; Member, Institute of Directors 1991-2012; Friends of Shakespeare Globe; General Secretary, Board of British Sikhs 1991-92; Executive Committee Member, Bharatiya Vidya Bhavan; Adviser, Khalsa College 1988-89; Vice-President, Shepherd's Bush Gurdwara 1980-81. Shiromani Award 1979; Scroll of Honour 1985.

The Lord Suri, House of Lords, London SW1A 0PW
Tel: 020 7219 5353

CROSSBENCH

SUTHERLAND OF HOUNDWOOD, LORD

SUTHERLAND OF HOUNDWOOD (Life Baron), Stewart Ross Sutherland; cr 2001. Born 25 February 1941; Son of late George Sutherland and Ethel, née Masson; Married Sheena Robertson 1964 (2 daughters 1 son).

Education: Woodside School, Aberdeen; Robert Gordon's College, Aberdeen; Aberdeen University (MA philosophy 1963); Corpus Christi College, Cambridge (BA philosophy of religion 1965, MA).

Non-political career: Assistant lecturer, University College of North Wales, Bangor 1965-68; Lecturer, reader, Stirling University 1968-77; King's College, London: Professor of history and philosophy of religion 1977-85, Vice-principal 1981-85, Titular professor 1985-94, Principal 1985-90; Inspector of Schools and founder, Office for Standards in Education (OFSTED) 1992-94; Principal and Vice-chancellor, Edinburgh University 1994-2002; Non-executive director, NHP 2001-05; Chair: YTL Education (UK) Ltd 2003-, Frogtrade 2013-.

Political career: *House of Lords:* Raised to the peerage as Baron Sutherland of Houndwood, of Houndwood in the Scottish Borders 2001. Member, Science and Technology 2003-07; Chair: Science and Technology Sub-committee I (Scientific Aspects of Ageing) 2004-05, Science and Technology 2007-10; Member: Science and Technology Sub-committee I 2007-10 (Waste Reduction 2007-08, Nanotechnologies and food 2008-10, Radioactive Waste Management: a further update 2010), Science and Technology Sub-committee II (Genomic Medicine) 2008-09; Chair, Affordable Childcare 2014-15. *Councils and public bodies:* Member, Council for Science and Technology 1993-2000; Chair, Committee on Appeal Court Procedure (Scotland) 1994-96; Member, Higher Education Funding Council for England 1995-2001; Chair, Royal Commission on Long Term Care of the Elderly 1997-99; Provost, Gresham College 2002-08.

Political interests: Education, care of the elderly, research policy.

Other: Member, Hong Kong University Grants Committee 1995-2004; Hon. President, Alzheimer's and Dementia (Scotland) 2000-; Chair, Scottish Care 2001-; Hon. President, Saltire Society 2002-05; Chair, Quarry Products Association 2002-05; Board member, Courtauld Institute of Art 2002-07; President, Royal Society of Edinburgh 2002-05; Council member: British Academy 2002-05, Foundation for Science and Technology 2003-; President, David Hume Institute 2005-08; Chair, Associated Board of Royal Schools of Music 2006-12; Patron, University College London Centre for Dementia Care 2008-; Chair, Chartered Institute of Education Assessors 2009-11; FBA 1992; FRSE 1995; Eight honorary fellowships; Ethiopian Gemini Trust. Goldsmiths' Company: Court of Assistants 2000-, Prime Warden 2012-13. London University: Vice-chancellor 1990-94, Pro-chancellor 2006-08. Nineteen honorary degrees. Kt 1995; KT 2002; *Clubs:* New Club, Edinburgh.

Publications: Criminal Appeals and Alleged Miscarriages of Justice (1996); With Respect to Old Age (Royal Commission Report, 1999); Higher Education in Hong Kong (2003); Independent Review of Free Personal and Nursing Care in Scotland (2008); The Sutherland Inquiry into SATS (2009); Various books and academic articles.

Recreations: Rough gardening, jazz, Tassie Medallions, theatre.

The Lord Sutherland of Houndwood KT, House of Lords, London SW1A 0PW
Tel: 020 7219 1618 *Email:* sutherlands@parliament.uk

LIBERAL DEMOCRAT

SUTTIE, BARONESS

Liberal Democrat Lords Spokesperson for Northern Ireland

BARONESS SUTTIE (Life Baroness), Alison Mary Suttie; cr 2013. Born 27 August 1968; Daughter of late Dr Alastair M Suttie and Dr Gillian Suttie.

Education: Hawick High School; Heriot-Watt University (BA French and Russian 1990); French, Russian.

Non-political career: English Teacher, St Petersburg 1990-91; Liberal Democrat Adviser, House of Commons 1991-96; Adviser, ELDR group, European Parliament; Press Attaché and Adviser 1999-2001; Office of Pat Cox as President of the European Parliament; Press Secretary 2002-04; Head of Office to leaders of the Liberal Democrats Sir Menzies Campbell and Nick Clegg 2006-10; Deputy Chief of Staff, Office of Nick Clegg as the Deputy Prime Minister 2010-11; Consultant on democracy building projects specializing in the North Africa, Middle East and the countries of the former Soviet Union 2012; Training courses for UK civil servants, NGOs and charities 2012-; Associate, Global Partners Governance 2015-.

Political career: *House of Lords:* Raised to the peerage as Baroness Suttie, of Hawick in the Scottish Borders 2013. Liberal Democrat Shadow Secretary of State/Lords Spokesperson for Northern Ireland 2016-. Member: European Union 2015-, EU External Affairs Sub-Committee 2015-. *Other:* Liberal Democrats: Campaign Manager,2010 general election campaign, Co-ordinator, negotiation team leading to the establishment of the Coalition Government 2010, Party Whip 2013-, Member, Foreign Affairs Team 2013-.

Political interests: European affairs, international development (in particular global health and TB), political and constitutional reform, international relations, human rights; Middle East, North Africa, Russia and the countries of the former Soviet Union.

Other: Member, British-Irish Parliamentary Association 2017-; Trustee of Board, IPPR.

The Baroness Suttie, House of Lords, London SW1A 0PW
Tel: 020 7219 5353 *Email:* suttiea@parliament.uk

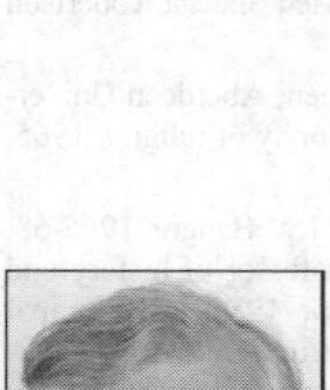

CONSERVATIVE

SWINFEN, LORD

SWINFEN (3rd Baron, UK), Roger Mynors Swinfen Eady; cr. 1919. Born 14 December 1938; Son of 2nd Baron; Married Patricia Blackmore 1962 (1 son 3 daughters).

Education: Westminster School; RMA, Sandhurst.

Non-political career: Lieutenant, The Royal Scots (The Royal Regiment). Director, Swinfen Charitable Trust 1998-.

Political career: *House of Lords:* First entered House of Lords 1977; Elected hereditary peer 1999-. Member: Greater Manchester Bill 1979, European Communities House of Lords: Sub-committees: C 1990-94, B 2004-05; Co-opted member: EU Sub-committees: B (Internal Market) 2005-06, C (Foreign Affairs, Defence and Development Policy) 2007-10; Member: Hybrid Instruments 2010-, Joint Committee on Consolidation, Etc, Bills 2010-15, Mental Capacity Act 2005 2013-14, Artificial Intelligence 2017-. *Councils and public bodies:* JP, Kent 1983-85.

Political interests: Disability, tele-medicine.

Other: President, South East Region, British Sports Association for the Disabled; Member, Direct Mail Services Standards Board 1983-97; Fellow, Industry and Parliament Trust 1983; Patron: Disablement Income Group 1988-, Labrador Rescue South East 1996-, World Orthopaedic Concern, MOET Iraq (Management of Obstetric Emergency Trauma), KunDe Foundation; Director, American Telemedicine Association 2009-13. Liveryman, Worshipful Company of Drapers. Honorary Research Fellow, Centre for Online Health, University of Queensland 2001-10. MBE 2015.

Publications: Co-author: An Evaluation of the First Year's Experience with a Low-cost Telemedicine Link in Bangladesh (2001), Store-and-Forward Teleneurology in Developing Countries (2001), Experience with a Low-cost Telemedicine System in Three Developing Countries (2001); Low Cost Telemedicine in the Developing World (2002); Telemedicine: The Way Ahead for Medicine in the Developing World (2003); Prospective Case Review of a Global E-health System for Doctors in Developing Countries (2004); Telemedicine Support for Iraq (2005); Low-cost Telemedicine in Iraq: analysis of referrals in the first 15 months (2005); Supporting Hospital Doctors in the Middle East by Email Telemedicine: Something the industrial world can do (2007).

Recreations: Gardening, painting, reading history.

The Lord Swinfen MBE, House of Lords, London SW1A 0PW
Tel: 020 7219 3500 *Email:* swinfenr@parliament.uk

LABOUR

SYMONS OF VERNHAM DEAN, BARONESS

SYMONS OF VERNHAM DEAN (Life Baroness), Elizabeth Conway Symons; cr. 1996. Born 14 April 1951; Daughter of Ernest Vize Symons and Elizabeth Megan, née Jenkins; Married Philip Bassett 2001 (1 son).

Education: Putney High School for Girls; Girton College, Cambridge (MA history 1974).

Non-political career: Research, Girton College, Cambridge 1972-74; Administration trainee, Department of the Environment 1974-77; Inland Revenue Staff Federation: Assistant secretary 1977-78, Deputy general secretary 1978-89; General secretary, Association of First Division Civil Servants 1989-97. Member, General Council, TUC 1989-96.

Political career: *House of Lords:* Raised to the peerage as Baroness Symons of Vernham Dean, of Vernham Dean in the County of Hampshire 1996. Parliamentary Under-Secretary of State, Foreign and Commonwealth Office 1997-99; Minister of State for: Defence Procurement, Ministry of Defence 1999-2001, International Trade and Investment, Foreign and Commonwealth Office and Department of Trade and Industry 2001-03; Government Spokesperson for: Foreign and Commonwealth Office 2001-05, Trade and Industry 2001-05; Deputy Leader of the Lords 2001-05; Minister of State for Middle East, Foreign and Commonwealth Office 2003-05; Opposition Spokesperson for Foreign and Commonwealth Office 2010-11. Member: EU Sub-committee C (Foreign Affairs, Defence and Development Policy): Co-opted member 2005-06, Member 2006-09; Member: Conventions Joint Committee 2006, European Union 2006-10; Co-opted Member, EU Sub-committee D (Environment and Agriculture) 2009-10; Member: National Security Strategy Joint Committee 2010, Joint Committee on the Draft House of Lords Reform Bill 2011-12, The Arctic 2014-15, EU External Affairs Sub-committee 2016-. *Other:* Member, Parliamentary Labour Party Parliamentary Committee 2001-10. *Councils and public bodies:* Governor: Polytechnic of North London 1989-94, London Business School 1993-97; Member, Employment Appeal Tribunal 1995-97; Board Member, Manchester Airports Group 2013-16.

Other: Council member, RIPA 1989-97; Hon. Associate, National Council of Women 1989; Member: Executive Council, Campaign for Freedom of Information 1989-97, Hansard Society Council 1992-97, Advisory Council, Civil Service College 1992-97; Council member: Industrial Society 1994-97, Open University 1994-97; FRSA. Lords Select Committee Member of the Year, *House Magazine* awards 2012. PC 2001.

Recreations: Reading, gardening.

Rt Hon the Baroness Symons of Vernham Dean, House of Lords, London SW1A 0PW
Tel: 020 7219 5837

CONSERVATIVE

TANLAW, LORD

TANLAW (Life Baron), Simon Brooke Mackay; cr. 1971. Born 30 March 1934; Son of late 2nd Earl of Inchcape; Married Joanna Susan Hirsch 1959 (1 son 2 daughters 1 son deceased); married Rina Siew Yong Tan 1976 (1 son 1 daughter).

Education: Eton College; Trinity College, Cambridge (BA medieval history, archaeology and anthropology 1957, MA).

Non-political career: Commissioned army national service, XII Royal Lancers, Malaya 1952-54. Inchcape Group of Companies, India and Far East 1960-66: Managing director 1967-71, Director 1971-92; Chair, Fandstan Group of Companies 1973-; Member, Executive Committee of the Great Britain-China Centre 1981-88.

Political career: *House of Commons:* Contested (Liberal) Galloway 1959, 1960 and 1964 general elections. *House of Lords:* Raised to the peerage as Baron Tanlaw, of Tanlawhill in the County of Dumfries 1971. *Councils and public bodies:* President, Sarawak Association 1973-75, 1997-99, 2012-; Member, Court of Governors, London School of Economics 1980-96.

Political interests: Time, space, countryside, daylight saving; Malaysia, Singapore.

Other: Hon. Treasurer, Scottish Peers Association 1979-86; Royal Observatory Greenwich Appeal Board 2004-05; Fellow: British Horological Institute, Royal Astronomical Society; President, Sarawak Association 2012-; Fellow, Buckingham University; Elizabeth Fitzroy Support, Tanlaw Foundation. Member: Worshipful Company of Fishmongers, Worshipful Company of Clockmakers. Chancellor, Buckingham University 2010-13. Hon. DUniversity, Buckingham University 1983; *Clubs:* White's, Oriental, Puffin's Club. Houghton Club.

Publications: Articles in Horological Journal.

Recreations: Fishing, horology.

The Lord Tanlaw, House of Lords, London SW1A 0PW
Tel: 020 7219 4613 *Email:* tanlaws@parliament.uk
Email: lordtanlaw@gmail.com

TAVERNE, LORD

LIBERAL DEMOCRAT

TAVERNE (Life Baron), Dick Taverne; cr. 1996. Born 18 October 1928; Son of late Dr N J M Taverne and Mrs L V Taverne; Married Janice Hennessey 1955 (2 daughters).

Education: Charterhouse School, Surrey; Balliol College, Oxford (MA literae humaniores 1951); Dutch.

Non-political career: Called to the Bar, Middle Temple 1954; QC 1965; Director, Equity & Law 1972-87; Institute for Fiscal Studies: Director 1970-79, Director-General 1979-81, Chair 1981-83; Director, BOC Group 1975-95; Director, Axa Equity & Law 1987-2001; PRIMA Europe Ltd: Director 1987-98, Chair 1991-93, President 1993-98; Chair, OLIM Investment Trust 1989-99; Deputy Chair, Central European Growth Fund 1994-2000; Chair, Axa Equity & Law Monitoring Board 2001-08; Founder and Chair, Sense about Science 2002-12; President, Research Defence Society 2003-08; Chair, IFG 2004-07.

Political career: *House of Commons:* Contested Wandsworth, Putney 1959 general election. MP (Labour) for Lincoln 1962-72 (resigned), (Democratic Labour) for Lincoln March 1973 by-election to September 1974. Contested (SDP) Southwark, Peckham 1982 by-election and Dulwich 1983 general election. Parliamentary Under-Secretary of State, Home Office 1966-68; HM Treasury: Minister of State 1968-69, Financial Secretary 1969-70. *House of Lords:* Raised to the peerage as Baron Taverne, of Pimlico in the City of Westminster 1996. Liberal Democrat Spokesperson for Treasury 1998-2005 (Euro 2001-05). Member: Monetary Policy of the Bank of England 2000-03, Animals in Scientific Procedures 2001-02, European Union Sub-committee A (Economic and Financial Affairs, Trade and External Relations/Economic and Financial Affairs) 2003-05; Science and Technology: Member 2004-09, Co-opted Member 2009; Member, Science and Technology Sub-committee II (Genomic Medicine) 2008-09. *Other:* Member: National Committee, Social Democratic Party 1981-87; Federal Policy Committee, Liberal Democrats 1989-90. *Councils and public bodies:* Chair: Public Policy Centre 1983-87, Alcohol and Drug Abuse Prevention and Treatment Ltd 1996-2008.

Political interests: Science and technology, European Union, crime and drugs, tax, economic policy.

Other: Member, International Independent Review Body to review workings of European Commission 1979; Honorary Fellow Mansfield College, Oxford; Refugee Council. Association of British Science Writers Parliamentary Science Communicator of the Year 2006.

Publications: The Future of the Left: Lincoln and after (1974); The March of Unreason – Science, Democracy and the New Fundamentalism (2005); Against the Tide (autobiography) (Biteback Publishing, 2014).

The Lord Taverne QC, House of Lords, London SW1A 0PW
Tel: 020 7219 3000
25 Tufton Court, Tufton Street, London SW1P 3QH *Tel:* 020 7233 2409
Email: dick.taverne@gmail.com

TAYLOR OF BOLTON, BARONESS

LABOUR

TAYLOR OF BOLTON (Life Baroness), Ann Taylor; cr 2005. Born 2 July 1947; Daughter of late John Walker and late Doreen Bowling; Married David Taylor 1966 (1 son 1 daughter).

Education: Bolton School; Bradford University (BSc politics and economic history 1969); Sheffield University (MA economic history 1970).

Non-political career: Part-time tutor, Open University 1971-74; Monitoring officer, Housing Corporation 1985-87; Member, Intelligence Review Committee 2004; Parliamentary Fellowship, St Anthony's College, Oxford; Member, advisory board, Thales UK 2010-. Member: Association of University Teachers, GMB.

Political career: *House of Commons:* Contested Bolton West February 1974 general election. MP (Labour) for Bolton West October 1974-83. Contested Bolton North East 1983 general election. MP for Dewsbury 1987-2005. PPS to Fred Mulley as Secretary of State for: Education and Science 1975-76, Defence 1976-77; Government Whip 1977-79; Opposition Frontbench Spokesperson for: Education 1979-81, Housing 1981-83, Home Office 1987-88, Environment 1988-92; Shadow Secretary of State for Education 1992-94; Shadow Chancellor of the Duchy of Lancaster 1994-95; Shadow Leader of the House 1994-97: Member House of Commons Commission 1994-98, President of the Council and Leader of the House of Commons 1997-98; Member Public Accounts Commission 1997-98; Government Chief Whip 1998-2001; Chair, Intelligence and Security Committee 2001-05. *House of Lords:* Raised to the peerage as Baroness Taylor of Bolton, of Bolton in the County of Greater Manchester 2005. Parliamentary Under-Secretary of State and Government Spokesperson: Ministry of Defence 2007-10 (Defence Equipment and Support 2007-08, International Defence and Security 2008-10), Foreign and Commonwealth Office 2009-10. Member: Joint Committee on National Security Strategy 2010-14, Constitution 2014-17, Leader's Group on Governance 2015, Lord Speaker's Committee on the Size of the House 2016-; Chair, Constitution 2017-. *Councils and public bodies:* Holmfirth UDC 1972-74.

Political interests: Education, Home Office, intelligence and security, defence.

Other: Member, UK Delegation to NATO Parliamentary Assembly 2014-15. Hon. Fellow, Birkbeck College, London University; Hon. Doctorate, Bradford University. PC 1997.

Publications: Choosing Our Future – Practical Politics of the Environment (1992).

Recreations: Bolton Wanderers FC.

Rt Hon the Baroness Taylor of Bolton, House of Lords, London SW1A 0PW
Tel: 020 7219 5183 *Email:* taylora@parliament.uk *Twitter:* @AnnTaylor_HoL

TAYLOR OF GOSS MOOR, LORD

LIBERAL DEMOCRAT

TAYLOR OF GOSS MOOR (Life Baron), Matthew Owen John Taylor; cr 2010. Born 3 January 1963; Son of late Ken Taylor, screenwriter, and Jill Taylor, née Black; Married Victoria Garner 2009 divorced 2017 (3 sons).

Education: Treliske School, Truro; University College School, London; Lady Margaret Hall, Oxford (BA philosophy, politics and economics 1986, MA).

Non-political career: Sabbatical President, Oxford University Student Union 1985-86; Economic policy researcher, Parliamentary Liberal Party, attached to David Penhaligon MP 1986-87; Director, Taylor & Garner Ltd (family business); Chair, National Housing Federation 2009-15; Non-executive director, South West Water 2010-; Chair, St Austell Ecotown Strategic Partnership Board 2010-; Non-executive director, Mayfield Towns Ltd 2013-; Chair, Bridgehall Real Estate 2013-; Chair, Kensa Group Ltd 2014-.

Political career: *House of Commons:* MP for Truro 12 March 1987 by-election to 1997, for Truro and St Austell 1997-2010 (Liberal/All 1987-88, Liberal Democrat 1988-2010). Liberal Spokesperson for Energy 1987-88; Liberal Democrat Spokesperson for: England (Local Government, Housing and Transport) 1988-89, Trade and Industry 1989-90, Education 1990-92, Citizen's Charter 1992-94; Principal Spokesperson for: Environment 1994-97, the Environment and Transport 1997-99, Economy 1999-2003, Cabinet Office and Social Exclusion 2006-07. Member: Broadcasting 1992-94, Environment 1996-97. *House of Lords:* Raised to the peerage as Baron Taylor of Goss Moor, of Truro in the County of Cornwall 2010. *Other:* Chair, Liberal Democrat: Campaigns and Communications 1989-95, Parliamentary Party 2003-05.

Political interests: Environment, economy, education, international development, rural communities, housing, sustainable development, planning.

Other: Honorary Member, Royal Town Planning Institute; Visiting Professor of Planning, Plymouth University.

Publications: Living Working Countryside (DCLG Review of Rural Housing and Rural Economy, 2008); The Rural Coalition (2010); Planning Practice Guidance Review (DCLG, 2013); Garden Villages (Policy Exchange, 2015).

The Lord Taylor of Goss Moor, House of Lords, London SW1A 0PW
Tel: 020 7219 5353 *Email:* taylormoj@parliament.uk

CONSERVATIVE

TAYLOR OF HOLBEACH, LORD

Chief Whip (Captain of the Honourable Corps of the Gentlemen-at-Arms)

TAYLOR OF HOLBEACH (Life Baron), John Derek Taylor; cr 2006. Born 12 November 1943; Son of late Percy Taylor and Ethel Taylor, née Brocklehurst; Married Julia Cunnington 1968 (2 sons).

Education: Bedford School; Conversational French and Dutch.

Non-political career: Director, Taylors Bulbs of Spalding 1968-2010. Member, NFU Bulb subcommittee 1982-87.

Political career: *House of Commons:* Contested (Conservative) Chesterfield February and October 1974 general elections. *House of Lords:* Raised to the peerage as Baron Taylor of Holbeach, of South Holland in the County of Lincolnshire 2006. Opposition Whip 2006-10; Opposition Spokesperson for: Environment 2006-07, Wales 2006-07, Work and Pensions 2006-10, Environment, Food and Rural Affairs 2007-10; Government Whip 2010-11; Government Spokesperson for: Cabinet Office 2010-11, Energy and Climate Change 2010-11, Work and Pensions 2010-11; Parliamentary Under-Secretary of State, Department for Environment, Food and Rural Affairs 2011-12; Parliamentary Under-Secretary of State (Criminal Information) and Government Spokesperson, Home Office 2012-14; Chief Whip (Captain of the Honourable Corps of the Gentlemen-at-Arms) 2014-; Deputy Chairman of Committees 2014-17. Member: Procedure 2014-, Privileges and Conduct 2014-, Selection 2014-, Administration and Works 2014-16, Services 2016-. *Other:* Contested Nottingham 1979 European Parliament election. Member, Executive Committee, East Midlands Conservative Council 1966-98; Chair, Candidates Committee 1997-98, 2002-05; Member, Conservative Board of: Finance 1985-89, Management 1996-98, 2000-03; President and Conservative Conference Chair 1997-98; Deputy chair, Conservative Party 2000-03; Chair: National Conservative Convention 2000-03, Conservatives Abroad 2001-09, Conservative Agents Superannuation Fund 2006-10. *Councils and public bodies:* Member, Horticulture Development Council 1986-91; Minister of Agriculture's Regional Panel: Eastern Region 1990-92, East Midlands Region 1992-96, Lincoln Diocesan Assets Committee 1995-2001, 2004-.

Political interests: Agriculture and horticulture, environment, energy, waste, freight, democracy and political parties; France, Netherlands, Slovenia.

Other: Chair, EC Working Party on European Bulb Industry 1982; Fellow, Royal Society of Arts 1994; Trustee, International Bomber Command Memorial Trust; Associate, Royal Agricultural Society 2012; Chartered Member, Institute of Horticulture 2015; Fellow, Chartered Institute of Horticulture 2014; Holbeach and East Elloe Hospital Trust. Liveryman: Worshipful Company of Farmers, Worshipful Company of Gardeners. Freedom, City of London. Peer of the Year, *House Magazine* awards 2011; Personality of the Year, *Farm Business Magazine* 2012. CBE 1992; PC 2014; *Clubs:* Farmers Club, Carlton Club.

Publications: Taylors Bulb Book.

Recreations: Travel, arts, literature, music.

Rt Hon the Lord Taylor of Holbeach CBE, House of Lords, London SW1A 0PW
Tel: 020 7219 3132 *Email:* holgovernmentwhips@parliament.uk taylorjl@parliament.uk

NON-AFFILIATED

TAYLOR OF WARWICK, LORD

TAYLOR OF WARWICK (Life Baron), John David Beckett Taylor; cr. 1996. Born 21 September 1952; Son of late Derief Taylor, Warwickshire professional cricketer, and Mrs Enid Taylor, nurse; Married 1981 (divorced 2005) (1 son 2 daughters); married Laura Colleen Taylor 2015 (1 son 4 daughters).

Education: Moseley Church of England School, Birmingham; Moseley Grammar School; Keele University (BA law 1977); Gray's Inn, Inns of Court School of Law.

Non-political career: Barrister-at-Law, called Gray's Inn 1978; Television and radio presenter; Author and Journalist; International Keynote Speaker; Special Adviser to the Home Secretary and Home Office Ministers 1990-91; Non-executive director: Currencies Direct Ltd -2010, Asia Now Resources Inc, Canada, International Small Business Congress; Bank Consultant; Judge 2001-06. Member, NUJ.

Political career: *House of Commons:* Contested (Conservative) Cheltenham 1992 general election. *House of Lords:* Raised to the peerage as Baron Taylor of Warwick, of Warwick in the County of Warwickshire 1996. Introduced the Criminal Evidence (Amendment) Bill which came into force March 1997 as the Criminal Evidence (Amendment) Act 1997; Suspended from membership May 2011-June 2012. Member, Information 2007-11. *Other:* Member, Association of Conservative Peers -2010; Resigned Conservative Whip July 2010. *Councils and public bodies:* Councillor, Solihull Borough Council 1986-91; Member: North West Thames Regional Health Authority 1992-93, Greater London Further Education Funding Council 1992-95; Vice-President, British Board of Film Classification 1998-; Member, Independent Football Commission 2002-03.

Political interests: International peace-making, diversity, immigration, media, business, trade, security and defence; Africa, China, Europe, Israel, Italy, Jamaica, Japan, USA.

Other: Member: International Trade Commission, Inter-Parliamentary Union, Commonwealth Parliamentary Association; Founder, Warwick Leadership Academy 1997-; Director, Warwick Leadership Foundation 1999-; Life Patron, West Indian Senior Citizens Association (WISCA); Patron: Parents Need Children Adoption Charity, Kidscape Charity; Executive Committee Member, Sickle Cell Anaemia Relief Charity; Member: Royal Television Society, Radio Academy; Vice-President, National Small Business Bureau; President, African Caribbean Westminster Business Initiative; Barker, Variety Club of Great Britain; Member, Industry and Parliament Trust; Member: Bar Council, Institute of Directors. Freedom: City of London 1998, City of Lexington, Kentucky, USA 2004, City of Las Vegas, USA 2007. Chancellor, Bournemouth University 2002-07. Honorary LLD: Warwick University 2001, Asbury College, Kentucky, USA 2004. Gray's Inn Advocacy Prize 1978. Hon. President, Ilford Town FC.

Publications: The System on Trial (BBC Publications, 1996); No Blacks, No Irish, No Dogs.

Recreations: Music, wife and family, sport, travel.

The Lord Taylor of Warwick, House of Lords, London SW1A 0PW
Tel: 020 7219 5604 *Email:* taylorjdb@parliament.uk
Website: www.lordtaylor.org *Twitter:* @LordJohnTaylor

TEBBIT, LORD

CONSERVATIVE

TEBBIT (Life Baron), Norman Beresford Tebbit; cr. 1992. Born 29 March 1931; Son of late Leonard Albert Tebbit; Married Margaret Daines 1956 (2 sons 1 daughter).

Education: Edmonton County Grammar School.

Non-political career: RAF pilot 1949-51, Commissioned; Served RAF 604 Squadron 1952-55. Journalist 1947-49; Publicist and publisher 1951-53; Airline pilot 1953-70; Assistant director of information, National Federation of Building Trades Employers 1975-79; Company director: Sears Holdings plc 1987-99, British Telecom 1987-96, BET 1987-96, Spectator (1828) Ltd 1989-2004; Political commentator on Sky Television's Target programme 1989-98; Company director, Onix Ltd 1990-92; Columnist: *The Sun* 1995-97, *Mail on Sunday* 1997-2001; Former director and adviser to JCB Excavators Ltd; Blogger, *Daily Telegraph* 2010-. Member and office holder, BALPA.

Political career: *House of Commons:* MP (Conservative) for Epping 1970-74, for Chingford 1974-92. PPS to Robin Chichester-Clarke as Minister of State, Department of Employment 1972-73; Parliamentary Under-Secretary of State, Department of Trade 1979-81; Minister of State for Industry 1981; Secretary of State for: Employment 1981-83, Trade and Industry and President of the Board of Trade 1983-85; Chancellor of the Duchy of Lancaster 1985-87. *House of Lords:* Raised to the peerage as Baron Tebbit, of Chingford in the London Borough of Waltham Forest 1992. *Other:* Chair, Conservative Party 1985-87; Vice-President, Conservatives for Britain 2015-16.

Political interests: Europe, industrial relations, aviation; UK.

Other: President, Air League 1994-98; Chair, Battle of Britain London Monument Appeal 2003-06; President: Nuffield Ortholics Appeal 2005-, Nuffield Orthopaedic Appeal 2005-; Member, Royal Aeronautical Society 2005-. Liveryman, Guild of Air Pilots and Air Navigators. Freedom, City of London. PC 1981; CH 1987; *Clubs:* Royal Air Force, Beefsteak, The Other Club.

Publications: Upwardly Mobile (1988); Unfinished Business (1991); The Game Cook (2009) (new edition 2017); Ben's Story (2014).

Recreations: Shooting.

Rt Hon the Lord Tebbit CH, House of Lords, London SW1A 0PW
Tel: 020 7219 3657 *Email:* tebbitn@parliament.uk

LABOUR

TEMPLE-MORRIS, LORD

TEMPLE-MORRIS (Life Baron), Peter Temple-Morris; cr 2001. Born 12 February 1938; Son of late His Hon Sir Owen Temple-Morris, QC; Married Tahere Alam 1964 (2 sons 2 daughters).

Education: Malvern College; St Catharine's College, Cambridge (BA law 1961, MA 1965); French.

Non-political career: Barrister, Inner Temple 1962-77; Second Prosecuting Council Inland Revenue, S.E. Circuit 1971-74; Solicitor 1989-; Consultant Solicitor 1989-2014.

Political career: *House of Commons:* Contested (Conservative) Newport 1964 and 1966, and Norwood Lambeth 1970 general elections. MP for Leominster February 1974-2001 (Conservative February 1974 to October 1997, Independent October 1997 to June 1998, Labour October 1998-2001). PPS to Norman Fowler as Minister of Transport 1979. *House of Lords:* Raised to the peerage as Baron Temple-Morris, of Llandaff in the County of South Glamorgan and of Leominister in the County of Herefordshire 2001. Member: Delegated Powers and Regulatory Reform 2003-07, EU Sub-committee E: (Justice and Institutions) 2010-12, (Justice, Institutions and Consumer Protection) 2012-13. *Other:* Chair, Cambridge University Conservative Association 1961; Society of Conservative Lawyers: Member, executive committee 1968-71, 1990-97, Chair 1995-97. *Councils and public bodies:* Member, governing council, Malvern College 1978-2002; Council, Wilton Park Conference Centre (FCO) 1990-97; Member, Lord Chancellor's Advisory Committee on National Records and Archives 2008-09; Chief Steward, City of Hereford 2009-16.

Political interests: Foreign affairs, Irish affairs, European Union, constitutional and legal affairs; Iran, Middle East, Netherlands.

Other: Executive British Branch, Inter-Parliamentary Union: Member 1977-97, Chair 1982-85; Member, Parliamentary Delegation to United Nations 1980, 1984 (Leader); Hon Vice-President, United Nations Association 1987-2005; British-Irish Parliamentary Body: Founding Co-chair 1990-97, Member 1997-2005; Commonwealth Parliamentary Association: Member, executive 1994-98, Vice-chair 1996; Member, Cambridge Afro-Asian Expedition 1961; Chair: Standing Committee on Home Affairs, Bow Group 1975-80, Afghanistan Support Committee 1981-82; Vice-chair, GB-USSR Association 1985-93; Fellow, Industry and Parliament Trust 1988; Chevalier du Tastevin (Chat. de Vougeot) 1988-2014, Honorary 2014-; Member, Academic Council, Wilton Park (FCO) 1990-97; Chair, Lords and Commons Solicitors Group 1992-97; Vice-chair, GB-Russia and Eastern Europe Centre 1993-98; President, Iran Society Council 1995-2009; Member, advisory council, British Institute of Persian Studies 1997-2009; Jurade De St Emilion 1999-; Chair, British-Iranian Chamber of Commerce 2002-04; President, St Catharine's College, Cambridge Society 2004; NSPCC. Freedom: City of London 1969, New Orleans, USA, Havana, Cuba. Honorary Citizen: New Orleans, USA, Havana, Cuba; Hon. Member, National Party of Australia, Queensland. Knight of the Order of Orange Nassau (Netherlands) 2007; *Clubs:* Cardiff and County (Cardiff), Reform Club.

Publications: Motoring Justice (1979); Across the Floor (2015).

Recreations: Wine and food, travel, theatre, cinema, art galleries.

The Lord Temple-Morris, House of Lords, London SW1A 0PW
Tel: 020 7219 4181 *Email:* templemorrisp@parliament.uk

LIBERAL DEMOCRAT

TEVERSON, LORD

TEVERSON (Life Baron), Robin Teverson; cr 2006. Born 31 March 1952; Son of Dr Crofton and Joan Teverson; Married Rosemary Young 1975 (2 daughters); married Terrye Lynn Jones 2006 (3 stepdaughters).

Education: Chigwell School, Essex; Waltham Forest Technical College; Exeter University (BA economics 1973).

Non-political career: Director, Exel Logistics 1986-89; Managing director: SPD Ltd 1986-89, Rationale Ltd supply chain consultancy 1989-2002; Chair, Finance South West Ltd 1999-2002; Chief executive, Finance Cornwall 2002-06; Director: Finance South West Ltd 2004-06, Devon and Cornwall Business Council 2006-16, KCS Print Ltd 2006-, UK-Japan 21st Century Group Ltd 2007-, Thornparks Ltd 2008-09; Chair, Wessex Investors Ltd 2008-.

Political career: *House of Commons:* Contested (Liberal Democrat) South East Cornwall 1992 general election. *House of Lords:* Raised to the peerage as Baron Teverson, of Tregony in the County of Cornwall 2006. Liberal Democrat: Whip 2006-09, Spokesperson for: Environment, Food and Rural Affairs 2006-08, Energy and Climate Change 2008-10, Principal Spokesperson for Transport 2015. Co-opted Member, EU Sub-committee F (Home Affairs) 2006-08; Member: Draft Climate Change Bill Joint Committee 2007, European Union 2008-13; Chair EU Sub-committee

C: (Foreign Affairs, Defence and Development Policy) 2008-12, (External Affairs) 2012-13; Chair, The Arctic 2014-15; Member: Economic Affairs 2015-16, Economic Affairs Finance Bill Sub-committee 2015-16, European Union 2016-; Chair, EU Energy and Environment Sub-Committee 2016-. Chair, Liberal Democrat Parliamentary Party Committees on: Environment, Food and Rural Affairs (Energy and Climate Change) 2010-12, Energy and Climate Change 2012-15. *Other:* European Parliament: MEP for Cornwall and West Plymouth 1994-99, Contested South West region 1999 election. Liberal Democrats: Chair, Federal Finance and Administration Committee 1999-2002, Member, Federal Executive 1999-2002, 2005-. *Councils and public bodies:* Member, Cornwall Council 2009-14.

Political interests: Business, transport, Europe, financial markets, international affairs; Australia, Chile, Denmark, India, Ireland.

Other: Member, Securities and Investment Institute (MSI).

Recreations: Running, history, science.

The Lord Teverson, House of Lords, London SW1A 0PW
Tel: 020 7219 3566 *Email:* teversonr@parliament.uk *Twitter:* @lordtev

THOMAS OF CWMGIEDD, LORD

NON-AFFILIATED

THOMAS OF CWMGIEDD (Life Baron), Roger John Laugharne Thomas; cr 2013. Born 22 October 1947; Son of Roger and Dinah Thomas; Married Elizabeth Ann.

Education: Rugby School; Trinity Hall, Cambridge (1969); University of Chicago Law School (JD 1970).

Non-political career: Assistant teacher 1965-66; Called to Bar, Gray's Inn 1969 (Bencher 1992); QC 1984; Recorder 1987-96; Judge: High Court of Justice 1996-2003, Commercial Court 1996-2003; Presiding Judge, Wales and Chester Circuit 1998-2001; Senior Presiding Judge, England and Wales 2003-06; Lord Justice of Appeal 2003-11; Queen's Bench Division: Vice-President 2008-11, President 2011-13; Deputy Head, Criminal Justice 2008-13; Lord Chief Justice of England and Wales 2013-17.

Political career: *House of Lords:* Raised to the peerage as Baron Thomas of Cwmgiedd, of Cwmgiedd in the County of Powys 2013. As a senior member of the judiciary, disqualified from participation 2013-17. *Councils and public bodies:* Chairman, Criminal Procedure Rule Committee 2013-17; President, Sentencing Council 2013-17.

Political interests: Administration of justice.

Other: DTI Inspector, Mirror Group Newspapers plc 1992; Vice-President, British Maritime Law Association 1996-; Deputy President, AIDA Reinsurance and Insurance Arbitration Society 1996-; Fellow, European Law Institute; President: British Insurance Law Association 2004-06, European Network of the Councils of the Judiciary 2008-10; Faculty fellow, Law School, Southampton Univeristy 1990; Lord Morris of Borth-y-Gest Lecturer, University of Wales 2000; Honorary fellow: Cardiff University, Aberystwyth University, Bangor University, Swansea University, Trinity Hall, Cambridge; Honorary LLD: University of South Wales, University of the West of England, Cardiff Metropolitan University; Fellow, Learned Society of Wales. Kt 1996; PC 2003.

Rt Hon the Lord Thomas of Cwmgiedd, House of Lords, London SW1A 0PW
Tel: 020 7219 5353

THOMAS OF GRESFORD, LORD

Liberal Democrat Shadow Attorney General

LIBERAL DEMOCRAT

THOMAS OF GRESFORD (Life Baron), Donald Martin Thomas; cr. 1996. Born 13 March 1937; Son of late Hywel Thomas and Olwen Thomas; Married Nan Thomas 1961, née Kerr (died 2000) (3 sons 1 daughter); married Baroness Walmsley (qv) 2005.

Education: Grove Park Grammar School, Wrexham; Peterhouse, Cambridge (MA classics; LLB).

Non-political career: Solicitor, Wrexham 1961-66; Lecturer in law 1966-68; Called to the Bar, Gray's Inn 1967, Bencher 1989; Barrister, Wales and Chester Circuit 1968-; Deputy Circuit Judge 1974-76; Recorder of the Crown Court 1976-2002; QC 1979; Deputy High Court Judge 1985-2009.

Political career: *House of Commons:* Contested (Liberal) West Flintshire 1964, 1966, 1970, and Wrexham February and October 1974, 1979, 1983, 1987 general elections. *House of Lords:* Raised to the peerage as Baron Thomas of Gresford, of Gresford in the County Borough of Wrexham 1996. Liberal Democrat: Spokesperson for: Welsh Affairs -2004, Home Office -2004; Shadow Attorney General 2004-06, 2007-10, 2015-, Shadow Lord Chancellor 2006-07, Spokesperson for: Justice

2007-10, Law Officers 2015-, Wales 2015-16. Member: Joint Committee on Privacy and Injunctions 2011-12, Delegated Powers and Regulatory Reform 2015-. Chair, Liberal Democrat Parliamentary Party Committees on Home Affairs, Justice and Equalities (Justice) 2010-12, Wales 2012-15. *Other:* Welsh Liberal Party: Vice-chair 1967-69, Chair 1969-74; President: Wrexham Liberal Association 1975-, Welsh Liberal Party 1977, 1978, 1979; Welsh Liberal Democrats: Vice-President 1991-93, President 1993. *Councils and public bodies:* Member, Criminal Injury Compensation Board 1985-93.

Political interests: Criminal justice; China, Hong Kong, Wales.

Other: Marcher Sound: Chair 1991-2000, Vice-chair 1983-91; President: Gresford Memorial Trust 1993-, London Welsh Chorale 2000-. OBE 1982; *Clubs:* Reform, Western (Glasgow) Club.

Recreations: Rugby football, rowing, golf, fishing, cooking, harp, piano, bagpipes, singing.

The Lord Thomas of Gresford OBE QC, House of Lords, London SW1A 0PW
Tel: 020 7219 5453 *Email:* thomasm@parliament.uk

THOMAS OF WINCHESTER, BARONESS

LIBERAL DEMOCRAT

THOMAS OF WINCHESTER (Life Baroness), Celia Marjorie Thomas; cr 2006. Born 14 October 1945; Daughter of David Thomas and Marjorie Thomas, née Best.

Education: St Swithun's School, Winchester.

Non-political career: Winchester Diocesan Board of Finance 1963-65; Winchester Cathedral Appeal 1965-66; The Pilgrims' School, Winchester 1967-72; Christ Church Cathedral School, Oxford 1972-74; Liberal/Liberal Democrat Lords Whips Office 1977-2006: Head of Office.

Political career: *House of Lords:* Raised to the peerage as Baroness Thomas of Winchester, of Winchester in the County of Hampshire 2006. Liberal Democrat Spokesperson for: Work and Pensions 2007-10, Disability 2015-. Member: Liaison 2007-10, Merits of Statutory Instruments 2007-10, Refreshment 2007-12; Procedure: Member 2007, 2009-13, 2017-, Alternate Member 2008-09; Chair, Delegated Powers and Regulatory Reform 2010-15; Member: Equality Act 2010 and Disability 2015-16, Joint Committee on Consolidation, &c, Bills 2015-. *Other:* Liberal/Liberal Democrat election agent: Winchester October 1974, Brecon and Radnor 1987 and 1992; President, Winchester Liberal Democrats.

Political interests: Disability, prisons, bee health, voting reform and machinery of government.

Other: Vice-president and trustee, Muscular Dystrophy; Patron: Winchester Churches Nightshelter, Avonbrook Projects Abroad, Thrive; Chair, Liberal Summer School, now Keynes Forum 2001-09; Vice-President, Lloyd George Society 2005-; Management Board, Centre Forum 2006-09; Patron, Pinotage Youth Development Academy, SA; Member, MCC Disability Access Group; Target Ovarian Cancer, Butterfly Conservation, Plantlife. Health Champion, Charity Champion awards 2012. MBE 1985.

Recreations: Music, theatre, gardening, butterfly conservation, watching cricket.

The Baroness Thomas of Winchester MBE, House of Lords, London SW1A 0PW
Tel: 020 7219 5353

THORNHILL, BARONESS

LIBERAL DEMOCRAT

THORNHILL (Life Baroness), Dorothy Thornhill; cr 2015. Born 26 May 1955; Married Dr Iain Sharpe (1 daughter 1 son).

Education: Park School, Preston; BEd English; MEd education of children with learning and behavioural difficulties.

Non-political career: Teacher for 25 years, including: Assistant head teacher, Queens School, Bushey 1995-2002.

Political career: *House of Commons:* Contested (Liberal Democrat) Watford 2015 general election. *House of Lords:* Raised to the peerage as Baroness Thornhill, of Watford in the County of Hertfordshire 2015. Liberal Democrat Spokesperson for Communities and Local Government 2015-16. *Councils and public bodies:* Watford Borough Council: Councillor 1992-2002, Directly Elected Mayor 2002-; Vice-president, Local Government Association 2017-.

Political interests: Housing, planning, education.

Other: Trustee, Work Place Matters. MBE 2011.

Recreations: Watching rugby, cycling, walking, reading, theatre, architecture.

The Baroness Thornhill MBE, House of Lords, London SW1A 0PW
Tel: 020 7219 3000 *Email:* thornhilld@parliament.uk
c/o Watford Borough Council, Hempstead Road, Town Hall, Watford WD17 3EX *Tel:* 01923 278371 *Email:* themayor@watford.gov.uk
Website: www.dorothythornhill.com *Twitter:* @MayorDorothy

LAB/CO-OP

THORNTON, BARONESS

THORNTON (Life Baroness), Dorothea Glenys Thornton; cr. 1998. Born 16 October 1952; Daughter of Peter and Jean Thornton; Married John Carr 1977 (1 son 1 daughter).

Education: Thornton Secondary School, Bradford; London School of Economics (BSc economics 1976).

Non-political career: National co-ordinator, Gingerbread 1977-79; Area officer, Citizens Advice Bureau 1979-81; Public affairs adviser, Co-operative Wholesale Society 1981-93; Director of development and general secretary, Fabian Society 1993-96; Chair, Pall Mall Consult 2001-08; Senior associate, Social Business International 2010-; Chief executive, Young Foundation 2015-17. Member, GMB.

Political career: *House of Lords:* Raised to the peerage as Baroness Thornton, of Manningham in the County of West Yorkshire 1998. Government Whip 2008-10; Government Spokesperson for: Work and Pensions 2008, Equality 2008, Health 2008, 2009-10; Parliamentary Under-Secretary of State, Department of Health 2010; Opposition Spokesperson for: Health 2010-12, Work and Pensions 2010, Equalities Office 2010-15, Culture, Media and Sport 2014-15. Member, EU Sub-committee C (Environment, Public Health and Consumer Protection) 1999-2000. *Other:* Member, Co-operative Party 1974-; Chair, Greater London Labour Party 1986-91; Labour Party Policy Forum 2005-08. *Councils and public bodies:* London School of Economics: Member, Court of Governors 1999-, Emeritus governor 2016-.

Political interests: Children, media, social enterprise, Yorkshire.

Other: RSA; NCH, Circusspace, One World Action, Theodora Childrens Trust, Patron Social Enterprise UK. Hon Doctorate, Bradford University 2015.

Recreations: Canoeing, hill-walking in Yorkshire.

The Baroness Thornton, House of Lords, London SW1A 0PW
Tel: 020 7219 8502 *Email:* thorntong@parliament.uk *Twitter:* @GlenysThornton

CROSSBENCH

THURLOW, LORD

THURLOW (9th Baron), Roualeyn Robert Hovell-Thurlow-Cumming-Bruce; cr 1792. Born 13 April 1952; Son of Lord Francis Thurlow, diplomat, and late Yvonne Wilson, artist; Married Bridget 1980 (2 sons 2 daughters).

Education: Milton Abbey School.

Non-political career: Chartered Surveyor, RICS 1979-2016; Jones Lang Wootton/Jones Lang LaSalle: Partner 1985-99, Managing director 1999-2007; Principal, RCB Advisors 2007-.

Political career: *House of Lords:* Elected hereditary peer 2015-. Member, Delegated Powers and Regulatory Reform 2016-. *Councils and public bodies:* Councillor, Mapledurham Parish Council 2000-.

Political interests: Europe, rural affairs, built environment, mental health; Commonwealth.

Other: Chair, Investors' Committee, UK Property Fund -2016; Senior Consultant and member, Investment Committee, Castleforge Partners; MRICS 1979; MIND, Charlie Waller Foundation; *Clubs:* White's, Pratt's Club. Friends of Hardwick Tennis Court.

Recreations: Country sports, golf.

The Lord Thurlow, House of Lords, London SW1A 0PW
Tel: 020 7219 3000 *Email:* thurlowr@parliament.uk

LIBERAL DEMOCRAT

THURSO, VISCOUNT

THURSO (3rd Viscount, UK) John Archibald Sinclair; cr 1952; 6th Bt of Ulbster (GB) 1786. Born 10 September 1953; Son of late Robin, 2nd Viscount Thurso, and late Margaret, née Robertson; Married Marion Ticknor, née Sage 1976 (2 sons 1 daughter).

Education: Eton College; Westminster Technical College (FIH Membership Exam 1974); French.

Non-political career: Managing Director: Lancaster Hotel 1981-85, Cliveden House Ltd 1985-93; Non-executive Director, Savoy Hotel plc 1993-98; Managing director, Fitness and Leisure Holdings Ltd 1995-2001; Chair: Thurso Fisheries Ltd 1995-, Scrabster Harbour Trust 1996-2001; Director: Profile Recruitment and Management Ltd 1996-2002, Walker Greenbank plc 1997-2002, Anton Mosiman Ltd 1997-2002; Chair, International Wine and Spirit Competition 1999-; Deputy Chair, Millennium and Copthorn's Hotels plc 2002-09.

Political career: *House of Commons:* MP (Liberal Democrat) for Caithness, Sutherland and Easter Ross 2001-05, for Caithness, Sutherland and Easter Ross (revised boundary) 2005-15. (First former hereditary member of House of Lords to become an MP). Liberal Democrat: Whip 2001-

02, Spokesperson for: Tourism 2001-05, Scotland 2001-03, Shadow Secretary of State for: Transport 2003-05, Scotland 2003-06, Business, Enterprise and Regulatory Reform 2008-09, Business, Innovation and Skills 2009-10; Member, House of Commons Commission 2010-15. Member: Culture, Media and Sport 2001-05, Administration 2005-10, Treasury 2006-15, Liaison 2010-15; Chair, Finance and Services 2010-15; Member: Joint Committee on the Draft House of Lords Reform Bill 2011-12, Parliamentary Commission on Banking Standards 2012-13. Chair, Liberal Democrat Parliamentary Party Committees on: Scotland 2010-15, Constitutional and Political Reform 2012-15. *House of Lords:* First entered House of Lords 1995: Liberal Democrat Spokesperson for: Tourism 1996-99, Food 1998-99; Elected hereditary peer 2016-. *Other:* Member, Liberal Democrat Party Federal Policy Committee 1999-2001. *Councils and public bodies:* Board member, Independent Parliamentary Standards Authority 2016; Chair, VisitScotland Board 2016-; Lord Lieutenant, Caithness 2017-.

Political interests: Tourism, House of Lords reform, treasury, financial services, banking reform, energy.

Other: Chair: Bucks Game Conservancy 1990-92, BHA Clubs Panel 1992-96, Master Innholders Association 1995-97; President, Licensed Victuallers Schools 1996-97; President and Fellow, Tourism Society 1999-; Patron: Hotel Catering and International Management Association 1997-2003, Institute of Management Services 1998-; President, Academy of Food and Wine Service 1998-; Chair, UK Springboard Festival Year 2000; Trustee: Castle of Mey Trust, La Foundation pour la Formation Hoteliere (Zurich); Chancellor, Wine Guild UK 2017-; FHCIMA 1991; FInstD 1997. Liveryman, Innholders' Company 1997. Freedom, City of London 1991. Hon. DBA, Oxford Brookes University 2004. PC 2014; *Clubs:* Brook's, New Edinburgh Club.

Publications: Tourism Tomorrow (1998).

Rt Hon the Viscount Thurso, House of Lords, London SW1A 0PW
Tel: 020 7219 3000

LAB/CO-OP

TOMLINSON, LORD

TOMLINSON (Life Baron), John Edward Tomlinson; cr. 1998. Born 1 August 1939; Son of Frederick and Doris Tomlinson; Married 2nd Paulette Fuller 1998.

Education: Westminster City School; Co-operative College, Loughborough (Diploma political, economic and social studies 1961); Brunel University (health services management 1974-76); Warwick University (MA industrial relations 1982).

Non-political career: Head of research, AUEW 1968-70; Senior lecturer in industrial relations and management, Solihull College of Technology 1979-84. Member, TGWU.

Political career: *House of Commons:* MP (Labour) for Meriden 1974-79. PPS to Harold Wilson as Prime Minister 1975-76; Parliamentary Under-Secretary of State, Foreign and Commonwealth Office 1976-79; Parliamentary Secretary, Ministry of Overseas Development 1977-79. *House of Lords:* Raised to the peerage as Baron Tomlinson, of Walsall in the County of West Midlands 1998. Member, European Union 1998-2002, 2005-08, 2010-15; EU Sub-committee A (Economic and Financial Affairs, Trade and External Relations): Member 1998-2002, Chair 2000-01; Member: House of Lords' Offices 2001-02, EU Sub-committee C (Foreign Affairs, Defence and Development Policy) 2003-07, Joint Committee on Conventions 2006; EU Sub-committee E (Law and Institutions): Member 2007-08, Co-opted member 2008-10; Member: EU Sub-committee F (Home Affairs) 2010-12, Audit 2011-13, EU Sub-committee F (Home Affairs, Health and Education) 2012-13, 2014-15, Insurance Bill 2014-15. *Other:* European Parliament: MEP for Birmingham West 1984-99. *Councils and public bodies:* Councillor, Sheffield City Council 1963-67; Dartford Borough Council: Councillor 1970-74, Deputy Leader.

Political interests: Finance, Europe, international development, foreign policy.

Other: House of Lords Representative on Convention on Future of Europe 2002-03; Member Parliamentary Assembly: Council of Europe, Western European Union; Vice-chair, Election of Judges Committee to the European Court of Human Rights; Industry and Parliament Trust: Trustee 1987, Chair of Trustees -2007; Vice-President, Hansard Society -2006; Chair, advisory board, London School of Commerce 2004-; President: British Fluoridation Society 2004-11, Association of Independent Higher Education Providers 2005-13; Anglia Ruskin University: Board of Governors 2008-, Chair 2010-; Chair of council, Association of Business Executives. Honorary doctorate, Birmingham University; Honorary Fellowship, University of Wales Institute, Cardiff 2007; *Clubs:* West Bromwich Labour Club.

Publications: Left, Right: The March of Political Extremism in Britain (Calders, 1981).

Recreations: Walking, reading, sport.

The Lord Tomlinson, House of Lords, London SW1A 0PW
Tel: 020 7219 3770 *Email:* tomlinsonj@parliament.uk

TONGE, BARONESS

NON-AFFILIATED

TONGE (Life Baroness), Jennifer Louise Tonge; cr 2005. Born 19 February 1941; Daughter of late Sidney Smith, school teacher, and late Violet Smith, school teacher; Married Keith Tonge 1964 (died 2013) (2 sons 1 daughter deceased).

Education: Dudley Girls' High School; University College, London (MB, BS 1964); French.

Non-political career: General practice/family planning 1968-78, 1987-92; Senior medical officer, Women's Services (Ealing) 1982-87; Manager, Community Health Services (Ealing) 1992-96. South West Thames Representative, BMA Public and Community Health Committee 1992-96.

Political career: *House of Commons:* Contested Richmond and Barnes 1992 general election. MP (Liberal Democrat) for Richmond Park 1997-2005. Liberal Democrat Spokesperson for International Development 1997-2003. *House of Lords:* Raised to the peerage as Baroness Tonge, of Kew in the London Borough of Richmond upon Thames 2005. Liberal Democrat Spokesperson for Health 2007-10. Co-opted Member, European Union Sub-committee F (Home Affairs) 2007-08; Member, HIV and AIDS in the UK 2010-11. *Other:* Chair, Richmond and Barnes Liberal Party 1978-80; Resigned the Liberal Democrat Whip February 2012; Sat as an Independent Liberal Democrat 2012-16; Resigned from Liberal Democrats October 2016; now sits as Non-affiliated. *Councils and public bodies:* London Borough of Richmond-on-Thames: Councillor 1981-90, Chair, Social Services 1983-87.

Political interests: Health, environment, international development; Afghanistan, Bangladesh, Colombia, Iraq, Palestine, Rwanda, Sudan.

Other: Organisation for Security and Co-operation in Europe: Parliamentary Assembly: Delegate 1998-2000, Deputy 2000-05; European Parliamentary Forum: Vice-chair 2009-, President 2013-; Kew Society; Chair, Welfare Association UK; Fellow, Royal Society for Public Health; HACAN ClearSkies; BMA; MFSRH; Fellow, Royal Society for Public Health; Visiting Parliamentary Fellow, St Anthony's College, Oxford 1999-2000; Hon Fellow, Royal College of Obstetricians and Gynaecologists 2015; Christian Aid, Welfare Association UK. Hon. Fellow, Faculty of Reproductive and Sexual Health, Royal College of Obstetricians and Gynaecologists. *ePolitix* Charity Award 2004. Hon member, Richmond Football Club (rugby).

Recreations: Birdwatching, looking after grandchildren.

The Baroness Tonge, House of Lords, London SW1A 0PW
Tel: 020 7219 4827 *Email:* tongej@parliament.uk

TOPE, LORD

LIBERAL DEMOCRAT

TOPE (Life Baron), Graham Norman Tope; cr. 1994. Born 30 November 1943; Son of late Leslie Tope; Married Margaret East 1972 (2 sons).

Education: Whitgift School, Croydon.

Non-political career: London Scottish TA 1962-64. Company secretary and insurance manager 1965-72; Deputy general secretary, Voluntary Action Camden 1975-90; Chair, Community Investors Ltd 1995-98.

Political career: *House of Commons:* MP (Liberal) Sutton and Cheam 7 December 1972 by-election to February 1974. Contested Sutton and Cheam February and October 1974 general elections. Liberal Spokesperson for Environment 1972-74. *House of Lords:* Raised to the peerage as Baron Tope, of Sutton in the London Borough of Sutton 1994. Liberal Democrat: Spokesperson for Education 1994-2000, Assistant Whip 1998-2000, Spokesperson for Communities and Local Government 2008-15, Spokesperson for London 2015-. Member: Relations between Central and Local Government 1995-96, EU Sub-committee F (Home Affairs) 2011-12, Public Service and Demographic Change 2012-13. Chair, Liberal Democrat Parliamentary Party Committee on Communities and Local Government 2010-15. *Other:* Member, Liberal Party National Council 1970-76; National League of Young Liberals: Vice-chair 1971-73, President 1973-75; President: London Liberal Democrats 1991-2000, Sutton Liberal Democrats 2014-. *Councils and public bodies:* London Borough of Sutton: Councillor 1974-2014, Leader, Liberal (later Liberal Democrat) Group 1974-99, Opposition Leader 1984-86, Council Leader 1986-99, Executive Councillor for Community Safety Leisure and Libraries 1999-2012; Member, London Fire and Civil Defence Authority 1995-97; Vice-president, Local Government Association 1997-2005, 2013-; Vice-chair, Association of London Government 1997-2000; London Assembly: Member 2000-08, Leader, Liberal Democrat Group 2000-06, Member, Metropolitan Police Authority 2000-08, Chair, Finance 2000-08, Mayor of London Cabinet 2000-04; Member: Croydon Strategic Partnership Board 2002-08, Sutton Strategic Partnership Board 2003-12, Safer Croydon Partnership Board 2004-08, Safer Sutton Partnership Board: Member 2004-12, Chair 2009-12; Chair, Local Government Group for Europe 2005-.

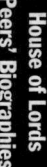

Political interests: Local government, Europe, London; Bermuda, EU, Western Balkans.

Other: EU Committee of the Regions: Member 1994-2014, Vice-chair, UK Delegation 1996-2014, Bureau member 1996-2014, President: European Liberal Democrat and Reform Group 1998-2002, Constitutional Affairs and European Governance Commission 2002-04, Political co-ordinator, ALDE Group 2007-14, Member, Political Monitoring Group 2008-10, Western Balkans Working Group 2008-14; Member, Congress of Local and Regional Authorities in Europe, Council of Europe 1996-2000; Rapporteur, Smarter Regulation 2010-11; Member, High Level Group of Independent Stakeholders on Administrative Burdens, European Commission. Member, Needle Makers Company. Freedom: City of London 1998, London Borough of Sutton 2014. CBE 1991.

Publications: Co-author: Liberals and the Community (1974), A Political Life (2011).

Recreations: Garden, history, walking, stamps.

The Lord Tope CBE, House of Lords, London SW1A 0PW
Tel: 020 7219 3098 *Fax:* 020 7219 0967 *Email:* topeg@parliament.uk

LAB/CO-OP

TOUHIG, LORD

Opposition Spokesperson for Defence

TOUHIG (Life Baron), James Donnelly (Don) Touhig; cr 2010. Born 5 December 1947; Son of late Michael and Catherine Touhig; Married Jennifer Hughes 1968 (died 2014) (2 sons 2 daughters).

Education: St Francis School, Abersychan; East Monmouth College.

Non-political career: Apprentice radio and tv engineer; Journalist 1968-76; Editor, Free Press of Monmouthshire 1976-90; General manager and editor-in-chief, Free Press Group of Newspapers 1988-92; General manager (business development): Bailey Group 1992-93, Bailey Print 1993-95. Member, TGWU.

Political career: *House of Commons:* Contested Richmond and Barnes 1992 general election. MP (Lab/Co-op) for Islwyn 16 February 1995 by-election to 2010. Public Interest Disclosure (Private Member's Bill) 1995; PPS to Gordon Brown as Chancellor of the Exchequer 1997-99; Assistant Government Whip 1999-2001; Parliamentary Under-Secretary of State, Wales Office 2001-05; Parliamentary Under-Secretary of State and Minister for Veterans, Ministry of Defence 2005-06; Member, Speaker's Committee for the Independent Parliamentary Standards Authority 2009-10. Member: European Standing Committee B 1995-96, Welsh Affairs 1996-97, Public Accounts 2006-10, Liaison 2009-10; Chair: Members' Allowances 2009-10. Hon. Secretary, PLP Welsh Regional Group 1995-99, 2007-08. *House of Lords:* Raised to the peerage as Baron Touhig, of Islwyn and Glansychan in the County of Gwent 2010. Opposition Whip 2015-16 Opposition Spokesperson for Defence 2015-. Member: Public Service and Demographic Change 2012, Liaison 2013-16. *Other:* Member, Labour Leadership Campaign Team (responsible for Devolution in Wales) 1996-97; Co-operative Party: Member, Chair, Parliamentary Group 1999, 2010. *Councils and public bodies:* Gwent County Council: Councillor 1973-95, Chair, Finance Committee 1992-94.

Political interests: Treasury, employment, health, education, local and regional government; France.

Other: Past President, South Wales Newspaper Society; Member: Mensa, Mencap, Amnesty International; President: Caerphilly County Borough Access Group, Caerphilly Citizens Advice Bureau, Newbridge and District Ladies Choir; Vice-president, National Autistic Society; Fellow, Industry and Parliament Trust 2003; Patron, Everyone's Child Romania. Freedom, City of London 2013. Papal Knight of the Order of St Sylvester 1991; PC 2006.

Recreations: Reading, cooking for family and friends, music, walking.

Rt Hon the Lord Touhig, House of Lords, London SW1A 0PW
Tel: 020 7219 7248 *Email:* touhigjd@parliament.uk

CROSSBENCH

TREES, LORD

TREES (Life Baron), Alexander John Trees; cr 2012. Born 12 June 1946; Son of John Trees, chemical engineer, and Margaret Trees, née Bell; Married Frances McAnally 1970 (1 daughter).

Education: Brigg Grammar School, Lincolnshire; Edinburgh University (BVMS 1969; PhD 1976); French, Italian.

Non-political career: Assistant in general veterinary practice, Derby 1970-71; Research assistant, Edinburgh University 1971-76; Elanco Products Ltd, Rome, Italy: Veterinary adviser 1977-80, Head of animal science 1980; Liverpool School of Tropical Medicine, Liverpool University: Lecturer, Department of Veterinary Parasitology 1980-91, Senior lecturer 1991-94, Head of: Veterinary Parasitology 1992-2001, Parasite and Vector Biology Division 1994-97, Professor of

Veterinary Parasitology 1994-2011; Liverpool University: Dean, Faculty of Veterinary Science 2001-08, Emeritus professor 2011-; Glasgow University: Visiting professor, School of Veterinary Medicine, Professor James McCall Memorial Lecture 2010; Editor-in-chief, *Veterinary Record* 2011-; Chair, Moredun Research Institute 2011-.

Political career: *House of Lords:* Raised to the peerage as Baron Trees, of The Ross in Perth and Kinross 2012. Member: EU Sub-committee D (Agriculture, Fisheries, Environment and Energy) 2014-15, European Union 2015-17, EU Energy and Environment Sub-Committee 2015-17.

Political interests: Veterinary matters, animal health and welfare, aspects of public health, tropical medicine and overseas development, higher education, professional regulation, the environment; Africa, Middle East.

Other: European Veterinary Parasitology College: Founding diplomate 2003, Vice-president 2006-09; Executive council, World Association of Veterinary Parasitology 2007-; British Society of Parasitology 1980-; Royal Society of Tropical Medicine and Hygiene: Fellow 1986-, Council 1997-2000; Hon. fellow, Myerscough College; Royal College of Veterinary Surgeons: Member 1969-, Council member 2000, Junior vice-president 2008-09, President 2009-10, Senior vice-president; President, Association of Veterinary Teachers and Research Workers 1996-97; British Veterinary Association: Member 1980-, Veterinary Policy Group 1997-2001, Chair, Education Group; Hon. FRSE. DVM, Royal Veterinary College, London University; DVMS, Glasgow University. Peter Bridge Award, BCVA; Selborne medal, Association of Veterinary Teachers and Research Workers 2005; Wooldridge lecture and medal, British Veterinary Association 2009; Amoroso award, British Small Animal Veterinary Association 2011; *Clubs:* Farmers Club.

Publications: 170+ papers in peer-reviewed academic journals.

Recreations: Natural history, outdoors, mountaineering, DIY.

Professor the Lord Trees, House of Lords, London SW1A 0PW
Tel: 020 7219 7278 *Fax:* 020 7219 1991 *Email:* treesa@parliament.uk

TREFGARNE, LORD

CONSERVATIVE

TREFGARNE (2nd Baron, UK), David Garro Trefgarne; cr. 1947. Born 31 March 1941; Son of 1st Baron; Married Rosalie Lane 1968 (2 sons 1 daughter).

Education: Haileybury College, Hertford; Princeton University, USA; French.

Non-political career: Non-executive director, Siebe plc 1991-98; Chairman: Engineering and Marine Training Authority (now SEMTA) 1994-2006, Scotty Group plc 2006-11.

Political career: *House of Lords:* First entered House of Lords 1962; Opposition Whip 1977-79; Government Whip 1979-80; Parliamentary Under-Secretary of State: Department of Trade 1980-81, Foreign and Commonwealth Office 1981-82, Department of Health and Social Security 1982-83, for the Armed Forces June 1983-85; Minister of State: for Defence Support 1985-86, for Defence Procurement 1986-89, Department of Trade and Industry (Minister for Trade) 1989-90; Elected hereditary peer 1999-. Member: Procedure 2000-03, Privileges 2002-05, Speakership of the House 2003; Co-opted Member, EU Sub-committee G (Social Policy and Consumer Affairs) 2006-08; Member: EU Sub-committee A (Economic and Financial Affairs and International Trade) 2010-11, Joint Committee on the Draft House of Lords Reform Bill 2011-12, Inquiries Act 2005 2013-14; Chair, Secondary Legislation Scrutiny 2015-. *Other:* Association of Conservative Peers: Treasurer 1997-2000, Chair 2000-04.

Political interests: Aviation, defence, constitutional reform; North Africa.

Other: President, Mechanical and Metal Trades Confederation 1990-2000; Governor, Guildford School of Acting 1992-2001; Member, Mary Rose Trust 1992-2001; Hon. President, Popular Flying Association 1992-2003; Life Governor and council member, Haileybury 1993-2001; Hon. President, British Association of Aviation Consultants 1993-; Vice-chair, Army Cadet Force 1993-2001; Patron, Catering Equipment Suppliers Association 2000-; Director, Arab-British Chamber of Commerce 2000-; Chair, Brooklands Museum Trust 2001-14; Director, UK Skills 2001-05; Libyan British Business Council: Chair 2003-13, President 2013-; President, TWI 2006; Honorary fellowship, IET. Hon. doctorate: Staffordshire University, University of Central Lancashire. Royal Aero Club Bronze Medal 1963. PC 1989; *Clubs:* RAF Club.

Recreations: Photography.

Rt Hon the Lord Trefgarne, House of Lords, London SW1A 0PW
Tel: 020 7219 5450 *Email:* trefgarned@parliament.uk
83 Victoria Street, London SW1H 0HW

CONSERVATIVE

TRENCHARD, VISCOUNT

TRENCHARD (3rd Viscount, UK), Hugh Trenchard; cr. 1936; 3rd Baron Trenchard (UK) 1930; 3rd Bt of Wolfeton (UK) 1919. Born 12 March 1951; Son of 2nd Viscount, MC and Patricia Bailey; Married Fiona 1975 (daughter of 2nd Baron Margadale) (2 sons 2 daughters).

Education: Eton College; Trinity College, Cambridge (BA archaeology and anthropology 1973); German, Japanese.

Non-political career: Captain, 4th Battalion, The Royal Green Jackets, TA 1972-80; Honorary Air Commodore, 600 (City of London) Squadron, Royal Auxiliary Air Force 2006-. Kleinwort Benson Ltd 1973-96: Chief Representative in Japan 1980-85, Director 1986-96; Director, Dover Japan Inc 1985-87; Kleinwort Benson International Inc: General manager (Tokyo branch) 1985-88, President 1988-95, Deputy chair 1995-96; Director, ACP Holdings Ltd 1990-94; Securities Committee, European Business Community in Japan: Chair 1993-95, Vice-chair of Council 1995; Director: Japan Securities Dealers Association 1994-95, Bond Underwriters Association of Japan 1994-95, Robert Fleming and Co Ltd 1996-98, Robert Fleming International Ltd 1998-2000; Non-executive director, Berkeley Technology Limited 1999-2011; Director, Westhall Capital Limited (formerly AC European Finance Limited) 2001-03; Non-executive chair, Dejima Fund Ltd 2001-09; Senior adviser, Prudential Financial Inc 2002-08; Non-executive director, Dryden Wealth Management Limited 2004-05; Stratton Street PCC Limited: Non-executive director 2005-, Chair 2009-, Director-general, European Fund and Asset Management Association 2006; Director, Standon Lordship Ltd 2006-; Managing director, Mizuho International plc 2007-12; Director: Bache Global Series 2008-15, UK Koyu Corporation Ltd 2009-, Lotte Chemical UK Ltd 2010-; Consultant and senior adviser, Mizuho Bank Ltd 2013-14; Consultant: Simon Robertson Associates LLP 2013-, Rolls-Royce Power Engineering plc 2014-15 Optum Health Solutions UK Ltd 2014-; Senior Adviser, Adamas Asset Management (HK) Ltd 2014-.

Political career: *House of Lords:* First entered House of Lords 1987; Elected hereditary peer 2004-. Member, Joint Committee on Financial Services and Markets 1999. *Other:* Chair, Conservatives Abroad in Japan 1986-88; President, North East Hertfordshire Conservative Association 2001-. *Councils and public bodies:* DL, Hertfordshire 2008-; Lieutenant, City of London 2014-.

Political interests: Financial services, defence, foreign affairs; China, Japan, Korea, USA.

Other: Member, Japan Association of Corporate Executives 1987-95; Chair, Japan Society 2000-04; RAF Benevolent Fund: Council and board of trustees 2006-13, Deputy chair of council 2014-; *Clubs:* Brooks's, Pratt's, Royal Air Force, Cavalry and Guards, Tokyo Club.

Recreations: Shooting, fishing, skiing.

The Viscount Trenchard DL, House of Lords, London SW1A 0PW
Tel: 020 7219 5353 *Email:* trenchardh@parliament.uk
Simon Robertson Associates LLP, 2 St James's Place, London SW1A 1NP *Tel:* 020 7318 8882
Email: hugh.trenchard@simonrobertsonassociates.com

CROSSBENCH

TREVETHIN AND OAKSEY, LORD

TREVETHIN (5th Baron, UK), cr 1921 AND OAKSEY (3rd Baron, UK), cr 1947; Patrick John Tristram Lawrence (known as Lord Oaksey). Born 29 June 1960; Son of 4th Baron, OBE JP; Married Lucinda 1987 (1 son 2 daughters).

Education: Christ Church, Oxford (philosophy, politics and economics).

Non-political career: Called to the Bar 1985; QC 2002; Barrister, 4 New Square.

Political career: *House of Lords:* Elected hereditary peer 2015-.

Other: Trustee, Associated Studios (charity).

The Lord Trevethin and Oaksey QC, House of Lords, London SW1A 0PW
Tel: 020 7219 3000

LABOUR

TRIESMAN, LORD

TRIESMAN (Life Baron), David Maxim Triesman; cr. 2004. Born 30 October 1943; Son of Michael Triesman and Rita Triesman, née Lubran; Married Lucy Hooberman 2004 (1 daughter).

Education: Stationers' Company's School, London; Essex University (BA social sciences 1968; MA philosophy of science 1969); King's College, Cambridge (postgraduate research 1970-73); French.

Non-political career: Senior researcher, addiction research unit, London University 1970-74; Senior lecturer and co-ordinator of postgraduate research, South Bank Polytechnic 1975-84; Non-executive chair, MCC (UBS) 1975-97; Visiting professor of economics, S Lawrence University, USA 1977; National negotiating secretary and deputy general secretary, NATFHE 1984-93; Chair, Victoria Management Ltd 1989-2001; General secretary and chief executive officer, Association of University Teachers 1993-2001; Visiting scholar in economics, Cambridge University 2000; Visiting fellow in economics, Wolfson College, Cambridge 2000-; Senior associate fellow, Manufacturing Group, Warwick University 2003-; Senior visiting fellow in politics, London School of Economics 2005-; Chairman, Football Association 2008-10; Director, Wembley National Stadium Ltd 2008-10; Chair, Board of Advisers, Templewood Merchant Bank 2010-13; Board member, Augur Buchler 2010-13; Chairman: Triesman Associates 2011-, International Board, Joule Africa 2011-, International Board, Hibernia College 2012-; Director: Havin Bank 2013-, Funding Affordable Homes Ltd 2013-, Salamanca Group Merchant Bank 2015-. AUT/University and College Union 1970-.

Political career: *House of Lords:* Raised to the peerage as Baron Triesman, of Tottenham in the London Borough of Haringey 2004. Government Spokesperson for: Education and Skills 2004-05, Trade and Industry 2004-05, Transport 2004, International Development 2004-05; Government Whip 2004-05; Foreign and Commonwealth Office: Government Spokesperson 2004-07, Parliamentary Under-Secretary of State 2005-07; Parliamentary Under-Secretary of State (Intellectual Property and Quality) and Government Spokesperson, Department for Innovation, Universities and Skills 2007-08; Opposition Spokesperson for: Business, Innovation and Skills 2010-11, Foreign and Commonwealth Office 2011-14. Member, EU External Affairs Sub-Committee 2015-. *Other:* General secretary, Labour Party 2001-03. *Councils and public bodies:* Member: Home Office Committee on Prison Education 1980-83, Greater London Manpower Board 1981-86; Chair, Burnham FHE Committee Teachers' Side 1985-86; Member: Bett Inquiry into Higher Education 1998-99, Ruskin College Governors 1999-2002, Better Regulations Task Force 2000-01; HM Treasury Public Services Productivity Panel 2000-02; Chair, National Inquiry into Housing Benefit (Cabinet Office) 2001; Member, England 2018/2022 FIFA World Cup bid -2010.

Political interests: Economics, industry, banking, foreign affairs, intelligence, broadcasting, higher education, public diplomacy, sports, arts, governance and ethics; Africa, the Americas, Caribbean, Cuba, China, Commonwealth, Europe, India, Middle East, UK Overseas Territories.

Other: British North American Committee; Chair, Usecolour Foundation 2000-02; Trustee: Public Management Foundation 2000-02; Football Foundation 2008-10; Patron, Tottenham Hotspurs Foundation 2008-; Fellow: Royal Statistical Society 1984, Royal Society of Arts 1992; One World Action, Amber Rocks. Freeman, Worshipful Company of Stationers and City of London 2016-. Fellow, Northampton University 1996; Honorary Doctor of Laws, London Southbank University 2009; Honorary Doctorate, Essex University 2010; *Clubs:* Reform Club. Tottenham Hotspur Supporters Club; Middlesex County Cricket Club.

Publications: Co-author, Football Mania (Ocean Books, 1972); Reconstructing Social Psychology (Penguin Books, 1974); Five Ring Circus: The Olympics (Pluto Press, 1984); College Administration (Longmans, 1988); c.50 academic papers in economics and epidemology.

Recreations: Family, football, blues and rock guitar, mountain walking, reading.

The Lord Triesman, House of Lords, London SW1A 0PW
Tel: 020 7219 6224 *Email:* triesmand@parliament.uk *Twitter:* @DavidTriesman

CONSERVATIVE

TRIMBLE, LORD

TRIMBLE (Life Baron), William David Trimble; cr 2006. Born 15 October 1944; Son of late William and Ivy Trimble; Married Daphne Orr 1978 (2 sons 2 daughters).

Education: Bangor Grammar School; Queen's University, Belfast (LLB 1968).

Non-political career: Queen's University, Belfast: Lecturer in Law 1968-77, Senior Lecturer 1977-90.

Political career: *House of Commons:* MP (UUP) for Upper Bann 1990 by-election to 2005. UUP Spokesperson for: Constitutional Affairs, Treasury 2002-05, Trade and Industry 2004-05, Work and Pensions 2004-05. *House of Lords:* Raised to the peerage as Baron Trimble, of Lisnagarvey in the County of Antrim 2006. EU Sub-committee A (Economic and Financial Affairs and International Trade): Co-opted member 2007-08, Member 2008-10; Member: European Union 2008-13, Barnett Formula 2008-09, EU Sub-committee C (Foreign Affairs, Defence and Development Policy) 2010-12, Joint Committee on the Draft House of Lords Reform Bill 2011-12, EU Sub-committee C (External Affairs) 2012-15, Inquiries Act 2005 2013-14, Delegated Powers and Regulatory Reform 2014-15, Joint Committee on the National Security Strategy 2015-, Joint Committee on Human Rights 2016-. *Other:* Member: Northern Ireland Constitutional Convention for South Belfast 1975-76, Northern Ireland Forum for Political Dialogue 1996-98; Northern Ireland Assembly: MLA for Upper Bann 1998-2007, First Minister 1998-July 2001, November 2001-03. Chair, Lagan Valley Unionist Association 1985-90; Leader, Ulster Unionist Party 1995-2005; Patron, Tory Reform Group; Sat in the Lords as Ulster Unionist 2006-07, now sits as Conservative 2007-.

Political interests: Legal affairs, arts and culture, foreign policy.

Other: Chair, Ulster Society 1985-90. Several honorary degrees. Nobel Peace Prize (jointly) 1998; Major Political Achievement House Award, Channel 4 and *The House* Magazine 1999; Parliamentarian of the Year, *Spectator* 2001; St Angela's Peace and Justice Group Award 2002. PC 1998; Légion d'Honneur (France) 2002.

Recreations: Music, reading.

Rt Hon the Lord Trimble, House of Lords, London SW1A 0PW
Tel: 020 7219 2421 *Fax:* 020 7219 5979

TRUE, LORD

CONSERVATIVE

TRUE (Life Baron), Nicholas Edward True; cr 2010. Born 31 July 1951; Son of Edward and Kathleen True; Married Anne-Marie Hood 1979 (2 sons 1 daughter).

Education: Nottingham High School; Peterhouse, Cambridge (BA 1973); Italian.

Non-political career: Member, Conservative Research Department 1975-82; Assistant to Conservative Party Deputy Leader 1978-82; Special adviser to Secretary of State for Health and Social Security 1982-86; Director, Public Policy Unit 1986-90; Deputy head, Prime Minister's Policy Unit 1991-95; Special adviser, Prime Minister's Office 1997; Private Secretary to Leader of the Opposition 1997-2010; Director, Opposition Whips' Office 1997-2010.

Political career: *House of Lords:* Raised to the peerage as Baron True, of East Sheen in the County of Surrey 2010. Procedure: Member 2011-12, 2015-, Alternate member 2012-15; Member, House 2012-15. *Other:* Conservative Councillors' Association. *Councils and public bodies:* Royal Borough of Richmond-upon-Thames Council: Councillor 1986-90, 1998-2017, Deputy Leader 2002-06, Opposition Leader 2006-10, Council Leader 2010-17; Board member, Royal Parks -2017; Vice-President, Local Government Association 2016-.

Political interests: Local government, education, constitution, arts; Guatemala, Italy.

Other: Olga Havel Foundation 1990-94; Sir Harold Hood's Charitable Trust 1996-; Richmond Civic Trust 2006-10; Venice in Peril Foundation. CBE 1993; *Clubs:* Beefsteak, Brook's, Traveller's Club.

Recreations: Books, history, art, gardens.

The Lord True CBE, House of Lords, London SW1A 0PW
Email: truen@parliament.uk
Leader's Office, c/o Democratic Services, York House, Twickenham TW1 3AA
Tel: 020 8487 5001 *Email:* cllr.lordtrue@richmond.gov.uk

TRUSCOTT, LORD

INDEPENDENT LABOUR

TRUSCOTT (Life Baron), Peter Derek Truscott; cr. 2004. Born 20 March 1959; Son of late Derek and Dorothy Truscott; Married Svetlana Chernikova 1991.

Education: Newton Abbot Grammar School; Knowles Hill Comprehensive School, Newton Abbot; Exeter College, Oxford (BA modern history 1981, MA; DPhil 1985).

Non-political career: Political organiser, Labour Party 1986-89; National Association for the Care and Resettlement of Offenders (NACRO) 1989-94; Author 1997-; Senior expert, European Commission 1999; Institute for Public Policy Research (IPPR): Visiting research fellow 1999-2000, Associate research fellow 2001-06; Associate fellow, Royal United Services Institute for Defence and Security Studies 2005-06, 2008-; Director: Energy Enterprises Ltd 2008-, Gulf Keystone Petroleum Ltd 2008-12, Eastern Petroleum Corporation 2008-11, African Minerals Ltd 2008-09; Associate Partner, Special Adviser and Chairman, advisory board, Opus Executive Partners 2008-11. Formerly TGWU, various posts in TU movement.

Political career: *House of Commons:* Contested (Labour) Torbay 1992 general election. *House of Lords:* Raised to the peerage as Baron Truscott, of St James's in the City of Westminster 2004. Parliamentary Under-Secretary of State for Energy and Government Spokesperson, Department of Trade and Industry 2006-07; Ministry of Defence Liaison Peer 2005-06; Suspended from membership May-November 2009. Member, EU Sub-committee C (Foreign Affairs, Defence and Development) 2007-09. *Other:* European Parliament: MEP for Hertfordshire 1994-99: Vice-president, Security Committee 1996-99, Contested Eastern region 1999 election. Labour Party: Member, NEC Domestic and International Policy Sub-committee 1997-99, Former National Membership Champion; Former member, Co-operative Party; Resigned Labour Party Whip 2009; now sits as Independent Labour. *Councils and public bodies:* Councillor, Colchester Borough Council 1988-92.

Political interests: Foreign affairs, defence, energy, international trade; Russia and former Soviet Union, EU.

Other: Election expert, Organisation for Security and Co-operation in Europe 1995, 1996, 1999, 2003; Parliamentary Ambassador for Russian Federation and Former Soviet Union, British Council; Fellow, Industry and Parliament Trust 2006; Children's Fire and Burn Trust.

Publications: Russia First (1997); European Defence (IPPR, 2000); Kursk: Russia's Lost Pride (Simon and Schuster, 2002); Putin's Progress (Simon and Schuster, 2004); The Ascendancy of Political Risk Management (RUSI, 2006); European Energy Security (RUSI, 2009); Numerous articles.

Recreations: Walking, swimming, theatre, travel.

The Lord Truscott, House of Lords, London SW1A 0PW
Tel: 020 7219 3241

CONSERVATIVE

TUGENDHAT, LORD

TUGENDHAT (Life Baron), Christopher Samuel Tugendhat; cr. 1993. Born 23 February 1937; Son of late Dr Georg and Mairé Tugendhat; Married Julia Dobson 1967 (2 sons).

Education: Ampleforth College, Yorkshire; Gonville and Caius College, Cambridge (BA history 1960, MA).

Non-political career: Army national service Essex Regiment 1955-57. Journalist, *Financial Times* 1960-70; Director: Sunningdale Oils 1971-76, Phillips Petroleum International (UK) Ltd 1972-76, EEC Commission: Commissioner for Budget and Financial Control, Financial Institutions Personnel and Administration 1977-85: Vice-President 1981-85; Director: National Westminster Bank 1985-91, The BOC Group 1985-96; Chair, Civil Aviation Authority 1986-91; Director, Commercial Union Assurance 1988-91; Deputy chair, National Westminster Bank 1990-91; Director, LWT (Holdings) plc 1991-94, Chairman: Abbey National plc 1991-2002, Blue Circle Industries plc 1996-2001; Board member, Eurotunnel plc 1991-2003; Director, Rio Tinto plc 1997-2004; Chairman: Lehman Brothers, Europe 2002-06, Lehman Brothers European Advisory Board 2006-07, Imperial College Healthcare NHS Trust 2007-11.

Political career: *House of Commons:* MP (Conservative) for Cities of London and Westminster 1970-74, for City of London and Westminster South 1974-76. *House of Lords:* Raised to the peerage as Baron Tugendhat, of Widdington in the County of Essex 1993. Member: Economic Affairs 2008-13, 2016-, Economic Affairs Finance Bill Sub-committee 2012-13, 2016-17, European Union 2013-16; Chair, EU Sub-committee C (External Affairs) 2013-16; Member, The Arctic 2014-15.

Political interests: Economy, foreign affairs, European Union.

Other: Chair, Royal Institute for International Affairs, Chatham House 1986-95; Governor, Council, Ditchley Foundation 1986-2010; Chair, European Policy Forum 1997-; Member, advisory board, OMFIF 2012-. Freedom, City of London. Chancellor, Bath University 1998-2013. Hon. LLD, Bath University 1998; Hon. DLitt, UMIST 2002. Kt 1990; *Clubs:* Athenæum Club.

Publications: Oil: the biggest business (1968); The Multinationals (1971); Making Sense of Europe (1986); Co-author Options for British Foreign Policy in the 1990s (1988).

Recreations: Family, reading, conversation.

The Lord Tugendhat, House of Lords, London SW1A 0PW
Tel: 020 7219 5353 *Email:* tugendhatc@parliament.uk

LABOUR

TUNNICLIFFE, LORD

Opposition Deputy Chief Whip; Opposition Spokesperson for Treasury and Defence

TUNNICLIFFE (Life Baron), Denis Tunnicliffe; cr 2004. Born 17 January 1943; Son of Harold and Nellie Tunnicliffe; Married Susan Dale 1968 (2 sons 1 deceased).

Education: Henry Cavendish School, Derby; University College, London (BSc mathematics 1965); College of Air Training, Hamble.

Non-political career: BOAC/British Airways 1966-86: Co-pilot 1966-72, Chief executive, International Leisure Group, Aviation Division 1986-88; London Underground Ltd: Managing director 1988-98, Chair 1998-2000; Chief executive, London Transport 1998-2000; Chair: United Kingdom Atomic Energy Authority 2002-04, Rail Safety and Standards Board 2003-08. Member, British Airline Pilots Association 1966-72.

House of Lords Peers' Biographies

Political career: *House of Lords:* Raised to the peerage as Baron Tunnicliffe, of Bracknell in the Royal County of Berkshire 2004. Government Whip 2008-10; Government Spokesperson for: International Development 2008-09, Work and Pensions 2008; Opposition Deputy Chief Whip 2010-; Opposition Spokesperson for: Defence 2010-11, 2016-, Business, Innovation and Skills 2012, Treasury 2014-. Member: Merits of Statutory Instruments 2005-08, Joint Committee on Security 2010-15, Refreshment 2013-14. *Councils and public bodies:* Councillor: Royal Borough of New Windsor 1972-75, Royal County of Berkshire 1974-78; Bracknell District Council: Councillor 1983-87, Leader 1985-87.

Political interests: Finance, justice, defence, climate change; Antigua.

Other: Trustee, Homerton College Cambridge 1998-2008; Council member, Royal Holloway College, University of London 2004-08; Board member, ACT (a property company that gives its profits to charity) 2004-08; Non-executive director, Defence Equipment and Support 2007-08. CBE 1993; *Clubs:* RAC, RAF Club.

Recreations: Theatre, boating, flying.

The Lord Tunnicliffe CBE, House of Lords, London SW1A 0PW
Tel: 020 7219 4326 *Email:* tunnicliffed@parliament.uk

LABOUR

TURNBERG, LORD

TURNBERG (Life Baron), Leslie Arnold Turnberg; cr. 2000. Born 22 March 1934; Son of Hyman and Dora Turnberg; Married Edna Barme 1968 (1 daughter 1 son deceased).

Education: Stand Grammar School, Whitefield; Manchester University (MB, ChB 1957; MD 1966).

Non-political career: Junior medical posts 1957-61, 1964-66: Manchester Jewish Hospital, Northern Hospital, Ancoats Hospital, Manchester Royal Infirmary; Registrar, University College Hospital, London 1961-64; Lecturer, Royal Free Hospital, London 1967; Research fellow, University of Texas South-Western Medical School, Dallas, Texas 1968; Manchester University: Lecturer, then senior lecturer 1968-73, Professor of medicine 1973-97, Dean, Faculty of medicine 1986-89; Scientific adviser, Association of Medical Research Charities 1997-.

Political career: *House of Lords:* Raised to the peerage as Baron Turnberg, of Cheadle in the County of Cheshire 2000. Science and Technology: Member 2001-06, Co-opted member 2013; Member: Science and Technology Sub-committees: I (Systematic Biology and Biodiversity/Fighting Infection) 2002-03, II (Renewable Energy) 2003-04, I (Scientific Aspects of Ageing) 2004-05, Draft Human Tissue and Embryos Bill Joint Committee 2007, Mental Capacity Act 2005 2013-14, Works of Art 2014-16, Long-Term Sustainability of the NHS 2016-17. *Other:* Member, Labour Friends of Israel. *Councils and public bodies:* Member: Salford Health Authority 1974-81, 1990-92, North West Regional Health Authority 1986-89; Chair: Conference of Medical Royal Colleges 1994-96, Specialist Training Authority 1996-98, Public Health Laboratory Service Board 1997-2002; President: Medical Council on Alcoholism 1997-2002, Medical Protection Society 1997-2007; Chair, Medical Advisory Board, Nations Healthcare 2004-07.

Political interests: Health service, medical education, research; Middle East, Israel.

Other: Trustee: Haddasah UK 1996-, Wolfson Foundation 1997-; Vice-president, Academy of Medical Sciences 1998-2004; Chair, Health Quality Service 1999-2004; President: British Society of Gastroenterology 1999-2000, Association of Physicians 2000; Trustee: Foulkes Foundation 2000-17, Dipex 2004-10; Chairman, National Centre for Replacement, Reduction and Refinement of use of Animals in Research 2004-07; Board member, Renovo 2006-11; Trustee: Ovarian Cancer Action 2007-, Weizmann UK 2010-; President, Royal College of Physicians 1992-97; MRCP 1961; FRCP 1973; FRCPE 1993; FRCP(I) 1993; Hon. Fellow: Academy of Medicine, Singapore 1994, College of Medicine, South Africa 1994; FRCPSGlas 1994; FCPPak 1994; Hong Kong College of Physicians 1995; FRAustCP 1995; FRCS 1996; FRCOphth 1996; FRCOG 1996; FRCPsych 1997; Malaysia College of Medicine 1997; FMedSci 1998; Physiological Society 2005. Four honorary doctorates. Kt 1994.

Publications: Author of publications on intestinal research and clinical gastroenterology.

Recreations: Reading, antiquarian books, painting, Chinese ceramics, walking.

The Lord Turnberg, House of Lords, London SW1A 0PW
Tel: 020 7219 5353 *Email:* turnbergl@parliament.uk

CROSSBENCH

TURNBULL, LORD

TURNBULL (Life Baron), Andrew Turnbull; cr 2005. Born 21 January 1945; Son of Anthony and Mary Turnbull; Married Diane Clarke 1967 (2 sons).

Education: Enfield Grammar School; Christ's College, Cambridge (BA economics 1967).

Non-political career: Economist, Government Republic of Zambia 1968-70; HM Treasury (HMT) 1970-94, 1998-2002: Seconded to International Monetary Fund 1976-78, Private Secretary (Economics) to Margaret Thatcher as Prime Minister 1983-85, Head, General Expenditure Policy Group 1985-88, Principal Private Secretary to Margaret Thatcher as Prime Minister 1988-92, Deputy Secretary, Public Finance and Monetary Policy 1992-93, Second Permanent Secretary, Public Expenditure 1993-94, Permanent Secretary 1998-2002; Permanent Secretary: Department of the Environment 1994-97, Department of Environment, Transport and the Regions 1997-98; Secretary of the Cabinet and Head of the Home Civil Service 2002-05; Non-executive director: Prudential plc 2006-15, British Land Company plc 2006-, Frontier Economics 2006-, BH Global Ltd (Chair) 2008-12.

Political career: *House of Lords:* Raised to the peerage as Baron Turnbull, of Enfield in the London Borough of Enfield 2005. Member: Audit 2011-13, Parliamentary Commission on Banking Standards 2012-13; Chair, Audit 2013-15; Member: Leader's Group on Governance 2015, Economic Affairs 2015-, Economic Affairs Finance Bill Sub-committee 2015-16, 2016-17. *Councils and public bodies:* Chair of Governors, Dulwich College 2009-15.

Political interests: Public services, the economy, financial services, energy, climate change; Zambia.

Other: Trustee, Global Warming Policy Foundation; Zambia Orphan Aid UK. Honorary doctorates: Middlesex University, Cranfield University; Honorary fellow, Christ's College, Cambridge. CB 1990; CVO 1992; KCB 1998; PC 2016.

Recreations: Golf, opera, sailing, walking, Tottenham Hotspur FC.

Rt Hon the Lord Turnbull KCB CVO, House of Lords, London SW1A 0PW
Tel: 020 7219 5353 *Email:* turnbulla@parliament.uk

CROSSBENCH

TURNER OF ECCHINSWELL, LORD

TURNER OF ECCHINSWELL (Life Baron), (Jonathan) Adair Turner; cr 2005. Born 5 October 1955; Son of Geoffrey Turner and Kathleen Turner, née Broadhurst; Married Orna Ni Chionna 1985 (2 daughters).

Education: Glenalmond School, Perthshire; Gonville and Caius College, Cambridge (BA history and economics 1978, MA) (Union President).

Non-political career: Economics Supervisor (part-time), Gonville and Caius College, Cambridge 1979-82; BP 1979; Chase Manhattan Bank 1979-82; McKinsey & Co 1982-95: Director 1994-95; Director-General, Confederation of British Industry 1995-99; Vice-chair, Merrill Lynch Europe 2000-06; Director: United Business Media 2000-08, Standard Chartered Bank 2006-08, Paternoster 2006-08; Chair: ESRC 2007-08, ODI 2007-10, Financial Services Authority 2008-13, Institute of New Economic Thinking (INET) 2013-, Centre for Financial Studies (Frankfurt) 2014-; Senior Independent Director, Oak North 2014-17; Non-Executive Director, Prudential plc 2015-; Chair, Energy Transitions Commission 2016-.

Political career: *House of Lords:* Raised to the peerage as Baron Turner of Ecchinswell, of Ecchinswell in the County of Hampshire 2005. Member, Economic Affairs 2007-08. *Councils and public bodies:* Chair: Low Pay Commission 2002-06, Pension Commission 2003-06, Committee on Climate Change 2008-12.

Countries of interest: China.

Other: Fellow, World Wide Fund for Nature (WWF) UK; Honorary Fellow, Royal Society of Edinburgh; Member, Advisory Council, People's Bank of China School of Finance, Tsighua University, Beijing 2014-; Trustee, British Museum 2014-; Fellow, Royal Society 2016-; Save the Children, WWF UK. Visiting professor: London School of Economics, Cass Business School; Honorary fellow, London Business School; Doctor of Law, Cambridge University 2017.

Publications: Author, Just Capital (MacMillan, 2001); Declining Populations in Philosophical Transactions of the Royal Society (2009); Economics After the Crisis (Lionel Robbins Memorial Lectures, MIT, 2012); Between Debt and the Devil: Money, Credit and Fixing Global Finance (Princeton University Press, 2015).

The Lord Turner of Ecchinswell, House of Lords, London SW1A 0PW
Tel: 020 7219 3000 *Twitter:* @AdairTurnerUK

LIBERAL DEMOCRAT

TYLER, LORD

Liberal Democrat Lords Spokesperson for Political and Constitutional Reform

TYLER (Life Baron), Paul Archer Tyler; cr 2005. Born 29 October 1941; Son of Oliver and Grace Tyler; Married Nicola Ingram 1970 (1 daughter 1 son).

Education: Sherborne School, Dorset; Exeter College, Oxford (BA modern history 1963, MA).

Non-political career: Director, public affairs, Royal Institute of British Architects 1972-73; Board member, Shelter: National Campaign for the Homeless 1975-76; Managing director, Cornwall Courier Newspaper Group 1976-81; Public affairs division, Good Relations plc: Chief executive 1984-86, Chair 1986-87, Senior consultant, Public Affairs 1987-92; Director, Western Approaches Public Relations Ltd 1987-92. National Union of Journalists 1973-82.

Political career: *House of Commons:* Contested Totnes 1966 and Bodmin 1970 general elections. MP (Liberal) for Bodmin February-October 1974. Contested Bodmin 1979 general election and Beaconsfield 1982 by-election. MP (Liberal Democrat) for North Cornwall 1992-2005. Liberal Democrat: Spokesperson for: Agriculture and Rural Affairs 1992-97, Agriculture, Tourism, Transport and Rural Affairs 1994-96, Food 1997-99, Chief Whip 1997-2001, Shadow Leader of the House 1997-2005, Spokesperson for Constitutional Reform 2001-05. *House of Lords:* Raised to the peerage as Baron Tyler, of Linkinhorne in the County of Cornwall 2005. Liberal Democrat: Spokesperson for: Constitutional Affairs 2006-10, Environment, Food and Rural Affairs 2008-09, Constitutional and Political Reform 2015-16, Shadow Minister/Lords Spokesperson for Political and Constitutional Reform 2016-. Member: Conventions Joint Committee 2006, Draft Constitutional Renewal Bill Joint Committee 2008, Procedure 2008-13, Joint Committee on the Draft House of Lords Reform Bill 2011-12, Delegated Powers and Regulatory Reform 2015-, Trade Union and Party Funding 2016. Chair, Liberal Democrat Parliamentary Party Committee on Constitutional and Political Reform 2010-15. *Other:* Contested (SLD) Cornwall and Plymouth 1989 European Parliament election. Chair: Devon and Cornwall Region Liberal Party 1981-82, Liberal Party National Executive Committee 1983-86; Campaign adviser to David Steel MP in 1983 and 1987 general elections. *Councils and public bodies:* Councillor, Devon County Council 1964-70; Member, Devon and Cornwall Police Authority 1965-70; Vice-chair, Dartmoor National Park Committee 1965-70; DL, Cornwall 2005-10.

Political interests: Tourism, rural affairs, constitutional reform; Australia, Canada, Finland, Germany, Sweden.

Other: Chair, Council for the Protection of Rural England Working Party on the future of the village 1974-81; Vice-President: British Resorts and Destinations Association 1995-, Youth Hostels Association 1996-2014; Director, Make Votes Count 2005-10; Chair, Faiths and Civil Society Unit, Goldsmiths College, London 2008-; Vice-chair, Hansard Society 2009-; Chair, advisory board, Interclimate Network 2010-; Patron, Joe Homan Charity 2011-; Ambassador, Concern Universal/United Purpose 2012-; Shelter. Parliamentarian of the Year, *Country Life* 1997. CBE 1985; PC 2014.

Publications: Co-author, Power to the Provinces (1968); A New Deal for Rural Britain (1978); Country Lives, Country Landscapes (1996); Britain's Democratic Deficit (2003); Co-author, Reforming the House of Lords – Breaking the Deadlock (2005); Co-author, Beating the Retreat – The Government's Flight from Constitutional Reform (2008); Constitutional Renewal Bill (2009); Lords Reform: A Guide for MPs (2012); Funding a Democracy: Breaking the Deadlock (2013); Who Decides? (2014).

Recreations: Sailing, gardening, walking.

Rt Hon the Lord Tyler CBE, House of Lords, London SW1A 0PW
Tel: 020 7219 6355 *Email:* tylerp@parliament.uk
Website: www.paultyler.libdems.org *Twitter:* @ptylerlords

LIBERAL DEMOCRAT

TYLER OF ENFIELD, BARONESS

Liberal Democrat Lords Spokesperson for Mental Health

TYLER OF ENFIELD (Life Baroness) Claire Tyler; cr 2011. Born 4 June 1957.

Education: Latymer Grammar School, Edmonton; Southampton University (BA law and politics); Diploma (management studies).

Non-political career: Greater London Council/Inner London Education Authority 1978-88; Department of Employment 1988-2000: Assistant Regional Director, Government Office for London, Head, 16-19 Policy Unit; Deputy Chief Executive, Connexions Service 2000-02; Director, Social Exclusion Unit, Office of the Deputy Prime Minister/Department for Communities and

Local Government 2002-06; Director, Vulnerable Children's Group, Department for Education and Skills 2006-07; Relate: Chief Executive 2007-12, Vice-president 2012-; President, National Children's Bureau 2012-; Chair, Making Every Adult Matter Coalition 2013-.

Political career: *House of Lords:* Raised to the peerage as Baroness Tyler of Enfield, of Enfield in the London Borough of Enfield 2011. Chair, Growing Giving Parliamentary Inquiry; Liberal Democrat Spokesperson for Mental Health 2015, 2017-. Member: Public Service and Demographic Change 2012-13, Affordable Childcare 2014-15, Social Mobility 2015-16; Chair, Financial Exclusion 2016-17. *Other:* Chair, Liberal Democrat Policy Working Group on Balanced Working; Vice-President, Liberal International Great Britain. *Councils and public bodies:* Chair, CAFCASS (Children and Family Court Advisory and Support Service) 2012-.

Political interests: Health and social care, welfare reform, social mobility, wellbeing, children and family policy, machinery of government, voluntary sector.

Other: Member, Joseph Rowntree Foundation Poverty and Disadvantage Committee 2002-06; Chair, Values-Based Child and Adolescent Mental Health System Commission -2016; Fellow, Chartered Institute for Personnel and Development.

The Baroness Tyler of Enfield, House of Lords, London SW1A 0PW
Tel: 020 7219 3606 *Email:* tylerc@parliament.uk

NON-AFFILIATED

UDDIN, BARONESS

UDDIN (Life Baroness), Pola Manzila Uddin; cr. 1998. Born 17 July 1959; Daughter of Mr and Mrs Khan; Married Komar Uddin 1976 (4 sons 1 daughter).

Education: Plashet School for Girls, Newham; Polytechnic of North London (Diploma social work 1990).

Non-political career: Youth and community worker, YWCA 1980-82; Liaison officer, Tower Hamlets Social Services 1982-84; Manager, Women's Health Project 1984-88; Asian Family Counselling Service 1989-90; Social worker, subsequently management consultant, Social Services Department, London Borough of Newham Council 1993-98; Non-executive director, Carlton Media Group 1999-2001; Project Leader, Addaction.

Political career: *House of Lords:* Raised to the peerage as Baroness Uddin, of Bethnal Green in the London Borough of Tower Hamlets 1998. Suspended from membership October 2010-May 2012. Co-opted Member, European Union Sub-committee G (Social Policy and Consumer Affairs) 2006-08. *Other:* Labour Whip suspended October 2010; now sits as Non-affiliated. *Councils and public bodies:* London Borough of Tower Hamlets: Councillor 1990-98, Deputy Leader 1994-96.

Political interests: Women, international affairs, human rights and equality; Bangladesh, Morocco, Qatar, Saudi Arabia, Tunisia, UAE.

Other: Patron: Bethnal Green and Victoria Park Housing Association, Social Action for Health, Women's Aid, Black Women's Health Project, Disability Trust, Student Partnership Worldwide, ORBIS International; NSPCC, East London Asian Family Counselling. Honorary degrees, universities of East London and Exeter.

The Baroness Uddin, House of Lords, London SW1A 0PW
Tel: 020 7219 8506 *Email:* uddinm@parliament.uk *Twitter:* @baroness_uddin

CONSERVATIVE

ULLSWATER, VISCOUNT

ULLSWATER (2nd Viscount, UK), Nicholas James Christopher Lowther; cr. 1921. Born 9 January 1942; Son of late Lieutenant John Lowther, MVO, RNVR, grandson of 1st Viscount, PC, GCB; Married Susan Weatherby 1967 (2 sons 2 daughters).

Education: Eton College; Trinity College, Cambridge (BA agriculture 1963, MA).

Non-political career: Captain, Royal Wessex Yeomanry, Retired. Chair, Wincanton Races Co Ltd 1986-93; Private Secretary and Comptroller to Princess Margaret, Countess of Snowdon 1998-2002.

Political career: *House of Lords:* First entered House of Lords 1963; Government Whip 1989-90; Parliamentary Under-Secretary of State, Department of Employment 1990-93; Government Chief Whip 1993-94; Minister of State, Department of the Environment (Construction and Planning) 1994-95; Elected hereditary peer 2003-; Deputy Speaker 2004-; Deputy Chair of Committees 2004-; Contested Lord Speaker election 2006. Co-opted Member, EU Sub-Committee F (Home Affairs) 2003-07; Member: Merits of Statutory Instruments 2003-05, Administration and Works 2005-09; Co-opted Member, EU Sub-committee D (Environment and Agriculture) 2006-10;

Member: Procedure 2009-, Liaison 2010-15, Privileges and Conduct 2013-, Delegated Powers and Regulatory Reform 2014-15; Chair, Joint Committee on Able Marine Energy Park Development Consent Order 2014 2014-15; Member: Selection 2015-, EU Energy and Environment Sub-Committee 2015-. *Councils and public bodies:* JP 1971-88; Councillor, King's Lynn and West Norfolk Borough Council 2003-11.

Other: Wiltshire Association of Boys Clubs: Chair 1966-74, Vice-President 1975-. PC 1994; LVO 2002; *Clubs:* Jockey (Newmarket), Pratt's Club.

Recreations: Racing, golf.

Rt Hon the Viscount Ullswater LVO, House of Lords, London SW1A 0PW
Tel: 020 7219 5219 *Email:* ullswatern@parliament.uk
Whiteacres, Cross Lane, Brancaster, King's Lynn, Norfolk PE31 8AE
Tel: 01485 210488

VADERA, BARONESS

NON-AFFILIATED

VADERA (Life Baroness), Shriti Vadera; cr 2007. Born 23 June 1962.

Non-political career: Executive director, UBS Warburg 1984-99; Adviser to the Chancellor of the Exchequer and member, Council of Economic Advisers, HM Treasury 1999-2007; Adviser on the Eurozone crisis, banking sector, debt restructuring and markets 2010-14; Chair, Santander UK plc 2015-.

Political career: *House of Lords:* Raised to the peerage as Baroness Vadera, of Holland Park in the London Borough of Kensington and Chelsea 2007. Parliamentary Under-Secretary of State and Government Spokesperson: Department for International Development 2007-08, Department for Business, Enterprise and Regulatory Reform/Business, Innovation and Skills (Minister for Economic Competitiveness, Small Business and Enterprise) 2008-09, Cabinet Office 2008-09; On leave of absence December 2011-. *Other:* Joined the House of Lords as Labour; now sits as Non-affiliated. *Councils and public bodies:* Adviser at Republic of Korea as Chair G20 2009-10.

Other: BHP Billiton: Non-executive director 2011-, Senior independent director 2015-; Non-executive director, AstraZeneca 2011-. PC 2009.

Rt Hon the Baroness Vadera, House of Lords, London SW1A 0PW
Tel: 020 7219 5353
Santander UK plc, Santander House, 2 Triton Square, Regent's Place, London NW1 3AN

VALENTINE, BARONESS

CROSSBENCH

VALENTINE (Life Baroness), Josephine (Jo) Clare Valentine; cr 2005. Born 8 December 1958; Daughter of Michael and Shirley Valentine; Married Simon Acland 1990 (2 daughters).

Education: St Paul's Girls' School, London; St Hugh's College, Oxford (BA maths and philosophy 1981); Casual French.

Non-political career: Manager, Barings 1981-88; Chief executive officer, Blackburn Partnership 1988-90; Senior manager, BOC Group 1990-95; Chief executive officer, Central London Partnership 1995-97; London First 1997-2016: Chief operating officer 2000-03, Chief executive officer 2003-16.

Political career: *House of Lords:* Raised to the peerage as Baroness Valentine, of Putney in the London Borough of Wandsworth 2005. Member: Works of Art 2009-10, 2012-13, EU Sub-committee B: (Internal Market, Energy and Transport) 2010-12, (Internal Market, Infrastructure and Employment) 2012-15. *Councils and public bodies:* Commissioner, National Lottery Commission 2000-05.

Political interests: Higher education, devolution, housing, transport and infrastructure, London, Europe, Blackpool, the Fylde Coast, Lancashire.

Other: Board member, Skill Festival Company 2005-16; Non-executive director, Peabody 2012-17; Board member: University College London 2014-, HS2 2014-; Honorary fellow: St Hugh's College, Oxford, Birkbeck College; Orchid Project, Aspired Futures. Honorary doctorate, Roehampton University; Honorary degree, University of London.

Recreations: Piano, bridge, travel.

The Baroness Valentine, House of Lords, London SW1A 0PW
Tel: 020 7219 5353

LIBERAL DEMOCRAT

VALLANCE OF TUMMEL, LORD

VALLANCE OF TUMMEL (Life Baron), Iain David Thomas Vallance; cr. 2004. Born 20 May 1943; Married Elizabeth McGonnigill 1967 (1 daughter 1 son).

Education: Edinburgh Academy; Dulwich College, London; Glasgow Academy; Brasenose College, Oxford (BA English language and literature 1965); London Business School (MSc business administration 1972).

Non-political career: Post Office 1966-81: Director: Central finance 1976-78, Telecommunications finance 1978-79, Materials department 1979-81; British Telecommunications (BT) 1981-2002: Chief of operations 1985-86, Chief executive 1986-95, Chair 1987-2001, President emeritus 2001-02; Vice-chair, Royal Bank of Scotland Group plc 1994-2005; Chair, European advisory committee, New York Stock Exchange 1995-2005; Director, Mobil Corporation 1996-99; Member, international advisory board, Allianz AG 1996-; Chair, European Services Forum 2003-08; Member: Supervisory board, Siemens AG 2003-13, European advisory council, Rothschild Group 2003-08.

Political career: *House of Lords:* Raised to the peerage as Baron Vallance of Tummel, of Tummel in Perth and Kinross 2004. Liberal Democrat Spokesperson for Trade and Industry/Business, Enterprise and Regulatory Reform 2005-10. Economic Affairs: Member 2005-07, Chair 2007-10; Chair, Finance Bill Sub-committee 2008-10; Member, EU Sub-committee A: (Economic and Financial Affairs and International Trade) 2010-12, (Economic and Financial Affairs) 2012-15; Member, Science and Technology 2015-. *Councils and public bodies:* CBI President's Committee: Member 1988-2002, President 2000-02; Board member, Scottish Enterprise 1998-2001; Deputy chair, Financial Reporting Council 2001-02.

Political interests: Business, economics, Europe.

Other: Member: European Foundation for Quality Management 1988-96, International advisory board, British-American Chamber of Commerce 1991-2002; Member, President's Committee, Business in the Community 1988-2002; Princess Royal Trust for Carers: Chair 1991-98, Vice-President 1999-2012; Chair: Nations Healthcare 2005-07, Amsphere Ltd 2006-, Royal Conservatoire of Scotland 2007-17; Chair, Edinburgh Business School 2017; Fellow, Chartered Institute of Bankers in Scotland. Honorary Fellow, Brasenose College, Oxford; Fellow: London Business School, Royal Society of Arts; Seven honorary doctorates. Kt 1994.

Recreations: Hill-walking, music.

The Lord Vallance of Tummel, House of Lords, London SW1A 0PW
Tel: 020 7219 2715 *Email:* vallancei@parliament.uk

CROSSBENCH

VAUX OF HARROWDEN, LORD

VAUX OF HARROWDEN (12th Baron, UK), Richard Hubert Gordon Gilbey; cr 1523. Born 16 March 1965; Son of 11th Baron; Married (2 children).

Education: Ampleforth College; Aberdeen University.

Non-political career: Chartered accountant, Price Waterhouse 1987-97; Investment banker, Indochina Asset Management 1997-2000; Chief financial officer, Reech Capital plc 2000-03; Managing director, corporate development, SunGard Data Systems Inc 2003-16; Self-employed consultant 2016-.

Political career: *House of Lords:* Elected hereditary peer 2017-.

Political interests: Renewable energy, farming; Scotland.

Other: Chairman, Fleet District Salmon Fishery Board; Trustee, Harrowden Chapel Trust.

The Lord Vaux of Harrowden, House of Lords, London SW1A 0PW
Tel: 020 7219 3000 *Email:* vaux@parliament.uk

CONSERVATIVE

VERE OF NORBITON, BARONESS

Government Whip (Baroness in Waiting)

VERE OF NORBITON (Life Baroness), Charlotte Sarah Emily Vere; cr 2016. Born 9 March 1969; Daughter of Colonel Roger Vere MBE RA and Mrs Karin Terry; Married (2 children from previous marriage).

Education: Stover School, Newton Abbot; University College London (BSc biochemical engineering 1989); Kellogg Graduate School of Management, Northwestern University, USA (MBA 1997).

Non-political career: Various positions, financial services 1989-99; Finance director, Recruit Media Ltd 2005-07; Chief executive, Big White Wall 2007-09; Founder and director, Women On... 2011-14; Executive director, Girls' Schools Association 2012-16; Independent Schools Council: Director 2012-16, Acting General-secretary 2014-15.

Political career: *House of Commons:* Contested Brighton Pavilion 2010 general election. *House of Lords:* Raised to the peerage as Baroness Vere of Norbiton, of Norbiton in the Royal London Borough of Kingston upon Thames 2016. Government Whip (Baroness in Waiting) 2016-. *Other:* Finance director, NO to AV 2010-11; Executive director, Conservatives In 2016. *Councils and public bodies:* Governor, Lovelace Primary School 2012-.

Political interests: Education, business, economy, mental health; Europe, South East Asia.

Other: Chair, Young Ambassadors with Samaritans 2003-07; Founder, Women On 2011-14; Trustee: Fatherhood Institute 2012-15, National Youth Arts Trust 2013-16, Shrewsbury House School Trust Ltd 2015-.

Recreations: Singing, running.

The Baroness Vere of Norbiton, House of Lords, London SW1A 0PW
Tel: 020 7219 3000 *Email:* verec@parliament.uk *Twitter:* @CharlotteV

LIBERAL DEMOCRAT

VERJEE, LORD

VERJEE (Life Baron), Rumi Verjee; cr 2013. Born 26 June 1957.

Education: Haileybury School; Downing College, Cambridge (law).

Non-political career: Lawyer, Middle Temple; Entrepreneur and philanthropist; Founder, Domino's Pizza UK; Chair, Thomas Goode & Co; Founder, Rumi Foundation 2006-.

Political career: *House of Lords:* Raised to the peerage as Baron Verjee, of Portobello in the Royal Borough of Kensington and Chelsea 2013. Member, Citizenship and Civic Engagement 2017-.

Other: Chair: Brompton Capital Ltd, Ipanema Properties; Member: World Presidents' Organization, Global Leadership Foundation, British Olympic Association advisory board for the 2012 Olympic Games; Convenor, MoreUnited.uk 2016-; Fellow, Downing College, Cambridge. CBE 2009.

The Lord Verjee CBE, House of Lords, London SW1A 0PW
Tel: 020 7219 5353
Website: rumifoundation.com

CONSERVATIVE

VERMA, BARONESS

VERMA (Life Baroness), Sandip Verma; cr 2006. Born 30 June 1959; Daughter of Shivcharan Singh Rana and Ravinder Rana; Married Ashok Kumar Verma 1977 (1 daughter 1 son).

Education: De Montfort University, Leicester (Deferred Degree business management); Hindi, Punjabi.

Non-political career: Managing Director, Domiciliary Care Services UK Ltd 2000-, Director, DCS Foods Ltd; Chair, Nexus Green Ltd; Global Chair, WWG; International Advisor to Amity University (India); Special Adviser to Sir John Cass Foundation; Non Executive, Renewal Energy Association.

Political career: *House of Commons:* Contested (Conservative) Hull East 2001 and Wolverhampton South West 2005 general elections. *House of Lords:* Raised to the peerage as Baroness Verma, of Leicester in the County of Leicestershire 2006. Opposition Whip 2006-10; Opposition Spokesperson for: Health 2006-07, Education and Skills 2006-07, Innovation, Universities and Skills 2007-09, Children, Schools and Families 2007-08, 2009-10, Universities and Skills 2009-10; Government Whip 2010-12; Government Spokesperson for: Cabinet Office 2010-12, International Development 2010-11, Women and Equalities 2010-12, Business, Innovation and Skills 2011-12; Parliamentary Under-Secretary of State and Government Spokesperson: Department of Energy and Climate Change 2012-15, Department for International Development 2015-16. Member, European Union 2016-; Chair, EU External Affairs Sub-committee 2016-. *Other:* Area chair, Conservative Women 2001-02; Area officer 2001-03; Executive National Conservative (Women) 2001-03; Chair, Leicester South Conservative Association 2006-08; President, City of Leicester Conservative Association 2008-09, 2010-11; Patron: Tory Reform Group, British Asian Conservative Link, Friends of Conservative Society of Indians; Vice-chair, Syston branch, Rutland Conservative Association.

Political interests: Health, education, overseas development, home affairs; Africa, Europe, South Asia.

Other: Patron: CST – Protecting the Jewish Community, India Association, The British Sikh Association, Bucks Punjabi Society, Pakistan-India and UK-Friendship Forum, Punjab Link Council; Extraordinary Champion, Roko Cancer (Breast Cancer); Board member, Football Foundation; NRI Institute, India; Punjab House Trust; Patron, Dil Trust UK; FRSA; Distinguished Fellowship, Institute of Directors, India. Freedom, City of London. Hon. Doctorate: Wolverhampton University, Amity University. Pravasi Bharatiya Saman, President of India 2011; Ellis Island Medal of Honour (USA).

Recreations: Socialising, walking, travel.

The Baroness Verma, House of Lords, London SW1A 0PW
Tel: 020 7219 5216 *Email:* vermas@parliament.uk *Twitter:* @Baroness_Verma

CONSERVATIVE

VINSON, LORD

VINSON (Life Baron), Nigel Vinson; cr. 1985. Born 27 January 1931; Son of late Ronald Vinson, farmer; Married Yvonne Collin 1972 (3 daughters).

Education: Nautical College, Pangbourne.

Non-political career: Lieutenant, Queen's Royal Regiment 1948-50. Founder, Plastic Coatings Ltd 1952 (floated on London Stock Exchange 1970); Director, British Airports Authority 1973-80; Co-founder and director, Centre for Policy Studies 1974-80; Director, Barclays Bank UK 1982-87; Deputy chair, Electra Investment Trust 1990-98; Chair: St Cuthbert's Newcastle Estates 1990-2000, Fleming Income and Growth Trust 1995-2000.

Political career: *House of Lords:* Raised to the peerage as Baron Vinson, of Roddam Dene in the County of Northumberland 1985. Member: Pollution 1997-98, Monetary Policy of the Bank of England/Economic Affairs 1998-2004, Draft Climate Change Bill Joint Committee 2007. *Other:* President, Berwick upon Tweed Conservative Association 2000-05. *Councils and public bodies:* Member: Crafts Advisory Committee 1971-77, Design Council 1973-80; President, Industrial Participation Association 1979-90; Chair, Rural Development Commission 1980-90; DL, Northumberland 1990.

Political interests: Small businesses, deregulation, tax, pensions; UK.

Other: CBI: Member, Grand Council 1975-, Deputy Chair, Smaller Firms Council 1979-84; Hon Director, Queen's Silver Jubilee Appeal 1976-78; Member, Regional Committee, National Trust 1977-84; Northumbrian National Parks: Member, Countryside Committee 1977-87, Chair, Rural Development Committee 1980-90; Member, Industry Year Steering Committee, Royal Society of Arts 1985; Institute of Economic Affairs: Chair of trustees 1988-95, Vice-President 1995-; Trustee, St George's House, Windsor 1990-96; Member, Foundation of Science and Technology 1991-; Chair: North East Civic Trust 1996-2001, Prince's Trust (NE) 1997-99; Trustee: Civitas 2003-, Chillingham Wild Cattle Association 2008; Council member, Freedom Association; Foundation Donor, Vinson Centre for Liberal Economics and Enterprise, Buckingham University 2017; CBIM; FRSA; Nigel Vinson Charitable Trust. Queen's Award to Industry 1971. LVO 1979; *Clubs:* Boodle's, Pratt's Club.

Publications: Personal Pensions for All (1984); Take Upon Retiring (Late Extra) (2005).

Recreations: Objets d'art, farming, horses.

The Lord Vinson LVO DL, House of Lords, London SW1A 0PW
Tel: 020 7219 5353
34 Kynance Mews, London SW7 4QR *Tel:* 020 7937 4183/01668 217230 *Fax:* 01668 217356
Email: roddamdene@btinternet.com

CONSERVATIVE

WAKEHAM, LORD

WAKEHAM (Life Baron), John Wakeham; cr. 1992. Born 22 June 1932; Son of late Major Walter John Wakeham; Married Anne Bailey 1965 (died 1984) (2 sons); married Alison Ward 1985 (1 son).

Education: Charterhouse School.

Non-political career: Army national service 1955-57, commissioned Royal Artillery. Chair: Genner Holdings 1994-, Press Complaints Commission 1995-2002, British Horseracing Board 1996-98.

Political career: *House of Commons:* Contested Coventry East 1966 and Putney 1970 general elections. MP (Conservative) for Maldon 1974-83, for South Colchester and Maldon 1983-92. Assistant Government Whip 1979-81; Government Whip 1981; Parliamentary Under-Secretary of State, Department of Industry 1981-82; Minister of State, HM Treasury 1982-83; Government Chief Whip 1983-87; Lord Privy Seal and Leader of the House of Commons 1987-88; Lord President of the Council and Leader of the House of Commons 1988-89; Secretary of State for Energy 1989-92; Given additional responsibility for co-ordinating the development and presentation of

Government policies 1990-92. *House of Lords:* Raised to the peerage as Baron Wakeham, of Maldon in the County of Essex 1992. Lord Privy Seal and Leader of the House of Lords 1992-94; Member, House of Lords Commission 2016-. Economic Affairs: Member 2003-09, Chair 2005-07; Member: Procedure 2003-07, 2010-15, Liaison 2007-10, House 2007-13, 2015-16, Finance Bill Sub-committee 2008-10, Selection 2010-15, Joint Committee on Security 2010-15, Economic Affairs Finance Bill Sub-Committee 2012-13, 2014, 2016-17, Lord Speaker's Committee on the Size of the House 2016-. *Councils and public bodies:* JP, Inner London 1972; DL, Hampshire 1997; Chair, Royal Commission on the Reform of the House of Lords 1999.

Political interests: Economic affairs, energy, reform of the constitution.

Other: Member, Governing Body, Charterhouse 1986-2004; Governor, Sutton's Hospital, Charterhouse 1992-; Trustee, RNLI: Management 1995-2003, Council 2003-05; Trustee: HMS Warrior 1860 1997-; President: GamCare 1997-2003, Brendoncare Foundation 1998-2011, Printers' Charitable Corporation 1998; Chair: Alexandra Rose Day 1998-2010, Cothill Education Trust 1998-2011; Chartered Accountant; FCA. Chancellor, Brunel University 1997-2012. Hon. PhD, Anglia Ruskin University 1992; Hon. DUniv, Brunel University 1998. PC 1983; *Clubs:* Buck's, St Stephen's Constitutional, Garrick, Royal Yacht Squadron (Cowes), Chair, Carlton Club 1992-98.

Recreations: Sailing, racing, reading.

Rt Hon the Lord Wakeham DL, House of Lords, London SW1A 0PW
Tel: 020 7219 3162 *Fax:* 020 7219 6807 *Email:* wakehamj@parliament.uk

CONSERVATIVE

WALDEGRAVE OF NORTH HILL, LORD

WALDEGRAVE OF NORTH HILL (Life Baron), William Arthur Waldegrave; cr. 1999. Born 15 August 1946; Son of 12th Earl Waldegrave, KG, GCVO, TD, DL and Mary Hermione Grenfell; Married Caroline Burrows OBE 1977 (1 son 3 daughters).

Education: Eton College; Corpus Christi College, Oxford (Open Scholar, BA literae humaniores 1969) (Union President 1968); Harvard University (Kennedy Scholar) 1969-70.

Non-political career: Fellow, All Souls, Oxford 1971-86, 1999-; Member: Central Policy Review Staff, Cabinet Office 1971-73, Political Staff at 10 Downing Street 1973-74; Leader of Opposition's Office 1974-75; With GEC Ltd 1975-81; Non-executive Director: Waldegrave Farms Ltd 1975-, Bristol and West plc (formerly Bristol and West Building Society) 1997-2006, Biotech Growth Trust plc (formerly Finsbury Life Sciences Investment Trust plc) 1997-2016, Henry Sotheran Ltd 1998-2015; Dresdner Kleinwort Wasserstein 1998-2003: Managing Director, Investment Banking, UBS; Vice-chairman and Managing Director, Investment Banking 2003-08; Non-executive Director, Bank of Ireland UK Holdings plc 2002-06; Member: International Advisory Board, Teijin Ltd 2006-08, Remuneration and Nomination Committee, Bergeson Worldwide Gas ASA 2006-08; Provost, Eton College 2009-; Chair: Biotech Growth Trust plc 2012-16, Coutts and Co 2014-, Coutts Foundation 2016-.

Political career: *House of Commons:* MP (Conservative) for Bristol West 1979-97. Parliamentary Under-Secretary of State: Department of Education and Science 1981-83, Department of Environment (DoE) 1983-85; Minister of State: DoE 1985-88, Foreign and Commonwealth Office 1988-90; Secretary of State for Health 1990-92; Chancellor of the Duchy of Lancaster and Minister for Public Service and Science 1992-94; Minister of Agriculture, Fisheries and Food 1994-95; Chief Secretary to HM Treasury 1995-97. *House of Lords:* Raised to the peerage as Baron Waldegrave of North Hill, of Chewton Mendip in the County of Somerset 1999. President Parliamentary and Scientific Committee 2000-03. Member, Joint Committee on National Security Strategy 2010-14. *Other:* Hon. Life member, Tory Reform Group. *Councils and public bodies:* JP, Inner London Juvenile Court 1975-79.

Other: Rhodes Trust: Trustee 1992-2011, Chair 2002-11; Trustee: Beit Memorial Fellowships 1998-2006, Strawberry Hill Trust 2002-14; Chair, National Museum of Science and Industry 2002-10; Trustee, Mandela Rhodes Foundation, South Africa 2003-11; President, Royal Bath and West Society 2006; Trustee, Cumberland Lodge, Windsor 2008-. Liveryman, Merchant Taylors' Company. Freedom: City of London, City of Bristol. Chancellor, Reading University 2016-. Hon. Fellow, Corpus Christi College, Oxford; Hon. DLitt, Reading University. Royal Society of Chemistry Parliamentary Award 2001. PC 1990; *Clubs:* Whites, Beefsteak, Pratt's, Clifton (Bristol), Leander Club. Eton Vikings.

Publications: The Binding of Leviathan (1978); A Different Kind of Weather (2015); Various pamphlets.

Rt Hon the Lord Waldegrave of North Hill, House of Lords, London SW1A 0PW
Tel: 020 7219 5353
Eton College, Windsor, Berkshire SL4 6DH *Tel:* 01753 671234 *Fax:* 01753 671283
Email: provostsecretary@etoncollege.org.uk

CROSSBENCH

WALKER OF ALDRINGHAM, LORD

WALKER OF ALDRINGHAM (Life Baron), Michael John Dawson Walker; cr. 2006. Born 7 July 1944; Son of William Walker and Dorothy Walker; Married Victoria Holme 1973 (2 sons 1 daughter).

Education: Milton School, Bulawayo, Zimbabwe; Woodhouse Grove School, Yorkshire; RMA Sandhurst (commissioned 1966).

Non-political career: Regimental and staff duties, Royal Anglian Regiment 1966-82; Military Assistant to Chief of the General Staff 1982-85; Commanding Officer, 1 Royal Anglian Regiment 1985-87; Commander, 20th Armoured Brigade 1987-89; Chief of Staff 1 (Br) Corps 1989-91; Colonel Commandant, Queen's Division 1991-2000; General Officer Commanding: North East District and Commander 2nd Infantry Division 1991-92, Eastern District 1992; Assistant Chief of the General Staff, Ministry of Defence 1992-94; Commander, Allied Command Europe Rapid Reaction Corps 1994-97; Colonel Commandant, Army Air Corps 1994-2004; Commander, Land Component Peace Implementation Force, Bosnia 1995-96; Commander-in-Chief, Land Command 1997-2000; Colonel, Royal Anglian Regiment 1997-2002; Aide de Camp General to the Queen 1997-2006; Chief of the General Staff 2000-03; Chief of the Defence Staff 2003-06; Governor, Royal Hospital Chelsea 2006-11.

Political career: *House of Lords:* Raised to the peerage as Baron Walker of Aldringham, of Aldringham in the County of Suffolk 2006. *Councils and public bodies:* DL, Greater London 2007-; Member, Prime Minister's Advisory Committee on Business Appointments.

Political interests: Defence, foreign affairs, international relations, country sports, sports; Africa, eastern Europe.

Other: Patron, British South Africa Police Association; Former chair, Army Benevolent Fund; Chair, Tutu Foundation UK; President, Sir Oswald Stoll Foundation. Hon. Doctor of Civil Law, University of East Anglia 2002; Hon. Doctor of Science in Social Science, Cranfield University 2003. OBE 1982; CBE 1990; KCB 1995; CMG 1997; Legion of Merit (USA) 1997; GCB 2000; Cross of Merit (Czechoslovakia) 2001.

Recreations: Golf, shooting, tennis, sailing, motorcycling, skiing.

The Lord Walker of Aldringham GCB CMG CBE DL, House of Lords, London SW1A 0PW
Tel: 020 7219 5353 *Email:* walkermjd@parliament.uk

CROSSBENCH

WALKER OF GESTINGTHORPE, LORD

WALKER OF GESTINGTHORPE (Life Baron), Robert Walker; cr. 2002. Born 17 March 1938; Son of late Ronald Robert Antony Walker and late Mary Helen Walker, née Welsh; Married Suzanne Diana Leggi 1962 (3 daughters 1 son).

Education: Downside School, Somerset; Trinity College, Cambridge (BA classics and law 1959); French, Italian.

Non-political career: 2nd Lieutenant R.A (National Service) 1959-61. Barrister, Lincoln's Inn 1960; QC 1982; High Court Judge, Chancery Division 1994-97; Lord Justice of Appeal 1997-2002; Justice of the Supreme Court of the United Kingdom 2009-13; Non-permanent Judge, Court of Final Appeal, Hong Kong 2009-.

Political career: *House of Lords:* Raised to the peerage as Baron Walker of Gestingthorpe, of Gestingthorpe in the County of Essex 2002. Lord of Appeal in Ordinary 2002-09; As Justice of the Supreme Court, disqualified from participation 2009-13. Chair, High Speed Rail (London-West Midlands) Bill 2016.

Other: Patron, International Advocacy Training Council. Honorary fellow, Trinity College, Cambridge 2006; Honorary doctorate, London Metropolitan University 2008. Kt 1994; PC 1997.

Publications: Articles in legal periodicals.

Recreations: Walking, gardening.

Rt Hon the Lord Walker of Gestingthorpe QC, House of Lords, London SW1A 0PW
Tel: 020 7219 5353

LIBERAL DEMOCRAT

WALLACE OF SALTAIRE, LORD

Liberal Democrat Lords Spokesperson for the Cabinet Office

WALLACE OF SALTAIRE (Life Baron), William John Lawrence Wallace; cr. 1995. Born 12 March 1941; Son of late William Edward Wallace and late Mary Agnes Tricks; Married Helen Rushworth 1968 (1 son 1 daughter).

Education: Westminster Abbey Choir School; St Edward's School, Oxford; King's College, Cambridge (BA history 1962); Cornell University, USA (PhD government 1968); Nuffield College, Oxford (MA 1965).

Non-political career: Lecturer in government, Manchester University 1967-77; Director of studies, Royal Institute of International Affairs 1978-90; Walter F. Hallstein Fellow, St Antony's College, Oxford 1990-95; London School of Economics 1995-: International relations reader 1995-99, Professor 1999-2005, Emeritus Professor 2005-.

Political career: *House of Lords:* Raised to the peerage as Baron Wallace of Saltaire, of Shipley in the County of West Yorkshire 1995. Liberal Democrat: Spokesperson for: Defence 1997-2001, Foreign and Commonwealth Affairs 1998-2010, Deputy Leader Liberal Democrat peers 2004-10, Spokesperson for Justice 2007-08; Government Whip 2010-15; Government Spokesperson for: Education (Higher Education) 2010, Foreign and Commonwealth Office 2010-15, Defence 2010-12, Business, Innovation and Skills 2010, Home Office (Security) 2010-11, Cabinet Office 2011-15; Liberal Democrat: Spokesperson for Foreign and Commonwealth Affairs 2015-16, Shadow Minister/Lords Spokesperson for the Cabinet Office 2016-. Member: Ecclesiastical Committee 1997-2010, European Union 1997-2000, 2001-02; Chair, European Union Sub-committee F (Social Affairs, Education and Home Affairs) 1997-2000; Member, European Union Sub-committee C (Common Foreign and Security Policy) 2001-02.

Political interests: Foreign affairs, defence, Europe, constitutional affairs; Armenia, EU member states, Georgia, Russia, Ukraine, USA.

Other: Voces Cantabiles Music/Gresham Centre 2004-; National Children's Choir of Great Britain -2017. Honorary doctorate, Université Libre de Bruxelles 1992. Chevalier, Ordre pour le Mérite (France) 1995; Légion d'Honneur (France) 2005; PC 2012. Saltaire Tennis Club.

Publications: The Foreign Policy Process in Britain (1977); The Transformation of Europe (1990); The Dynamics of European Integration (1990); Regional Integration – The West European Experience (1994); Policy-making in the European Union, with Helen Wallace (1996, 2000, 2005); Why Vote Liberal Democrat? (1997).

Recreations: Singing, swimming, walking, gardening.

Rt Hon the Lord Wallace of Saltaire, House of Lords, London SW1A 0PW
Tel: 020 7219 3125 *Email:* wallacew@parliament.uk

LIBERAL DEMOCRAT

WALLACE OF TANKERNESS, LORD

WALLACE OF TANKERNESS (Life Baron), James Robert Wallace; cr 2007. Born 25 August 1954; Son of John Fergus Thomson Wallace and Grace Wallace, née Maxwell; Married Rosemary Fraser 1983 (2 daughters).

Education: Annan Academy, Dumfriesshire; Downing College, Cambridge (BA economics and law 1975, MA); Edinburgh University (LLB law 1977).

Non-political career: Called to the Scottish Bar 1979; QC (Scot) 1997; Jim Wallace Consultancy Ltd 2007-10; Hon. Professor, Institute of Petroleum Engineering, Heriot-Watt University 2007-10; Advocate, Terra Firma Chambers, Edinburgh 2010; Hon. Bencher, Lincoln's Inn 2012.

Political career: *House of Commons:* Contested Dumfries 1979 general election. MP for Orkney and Shetland 1983-2001 (Liberal 1983-88, Liberal Democrat 1988-2001). *House of Lords:* Raised to the peerage as Baron Wallace of Tankerness, of Tankerness in Orkney 2007. Liberal Democrat Spokesperson for: Justice 2009-10, Scotland 2009-10, Equality Bill 2009-10; Advocate General for Scotland 2010-15; Government Spokesperson for: Scotland 2010-15, Wales 2010-12, Attorney General's Office/Law Officers 2010-15; Leader, Liberal Democrat Peers 2013-16; Deputy Leader of the House of Lords 2013-15; Member, House of Lords Commission 2016. Co-opted Member, EU Sub-committee D (Environment and Agriculture) 2008; Member: Constitution 2008-10, Partnerships (Prosecution) (Scotland) Bill 2013; House 2013-16, Liaison 2013-16, Privileges and Conduct 2013-16, Procedure 2013-16, Selection 2013-16, Joint Committee on the Palace of Westminster 2015-16. *Other:* Contested South Scotland 1979 European Parliament election; Scottish Parliament: MSP for Orkney 1999-2007: Deputy First Minister 1999-2005, Minister for: Justice 1999-2003, Enterprise and Lifelong Learning 2003-05. Scottish Liberal

Party: Member, Executive 1976-85, Vice-chair (policy) 1982-85; Hon. President, Scottish Young Liberals 1984-85; Leader, Scottish Liberal Democrats 1992-2005. *Councils and public bodies:* Member: Scottish Office Consultative Steering Group on Scottish Parliament 1998, Commission on Scottish Devolution 2008-09.

Political interests: Constitutional reform, Scottish home rule and federalism, Scottish law, rural development, energy conservation, shipping, Amnesty International, renewable energy; China, New Zealand, Norway, USA.

Other: Chair, Relationships Scotland 2008-10; Co-convener, Scottish Poverty Truth Commission 2009-10; Patron, European Movement in Scotland; Non-executive director, Water Retail Company 2017-; Member and chair of Regulation Board, Institute of Chartered Accountants of Scotland 2017-; Member, Faculty of Advocates; RNLI, Christian Aid, Amnesty International, British Red Cross. DLitt, Heriot-Watt University 2007; DUniv, Open University 2009; Doctor honoris causa, Edinburgh University 2009. Joint recipient Saltire Society's Andrew Fletcher Award for Services to Scotland 1998; Scottish Politician of the Year, *The Herald* 2000; Devolved Politician of the Year, Channel Four 2002; Lifetime Achievement Award, *The Herald* 2008. PC 2000; *Clubs:* Caledonian, Scottish Liberal Club. Orkney Golf Club.

Recreations: Golf, travel, music.

Rt Hon the Lord Wallace of Tankerness QC, House of Lords, London SW1A 0PW
Tel: 020 7219 3526 *Email:* wallacej@parliament.uk *Twitter:* @jrwallace54

LIBERAL DEMOCRAT

WALMSLEY, BARONESS

Liberal Democrat Lords Spokesperson for Health

WALMSLEY (Life Baroness), Joan Margaret Walmsley; cr. 2000. Born 12 April 1943; Daughter of Leo and Monica Watson; Married John Richardson 1966 (divorced 1980); married Christopher Walmsley 1986 (died 1995) (1 son 1 daughter 1 stepson 2 stepdaughters); married Lord Thomas of Gresford (qv) 2005 (3 stepsons 1 stepdaughter).

Education: Notre Dame High School, Liverpool; Liverpool University (BSc biology 1966); Manchester Polytechnic (PGCE 1979).

Non-political career: Cytologist, Christie Hospital, Manchester 1965-67; Teacher, Buxton College, Derbyshire 1979-86; Public relations consultant 1987-2003.

Political career: *House of Commons:* Contested (Liberal Democrat) Leeds South and Morley 1992 and Congleton 1997 general elections. *House of Lords:* Raised to the peerage as Baroness Walmsley, of West Derby in the County of Merseyside 2000. Liberal Democrat Spokesperson for: Early Years Education, Education and Skills 2001-03, Home Office 2003-04, Education and Children/Children, Schools and Families 2004-10, Education, Families and Young People 2010-13; Convener of the Liberal Democrat Peers 2014-15; Liberal Democrat Shadow Minister/Lords Spokesperson for Health 2015-. Member, Science and Technology 2000-05; Chair, Science and Technology Sub-committee I (Systematic Biology and Biodiversity) 2002; Member, Science and Technology Sub-committees: I (Fighting Infection) 2002-03, I (Science and International Agreements) 2003-04, I (Scientific Aspects of Ageing) 2004-05; Co-opted Member, Science and Technology 2008; Member: Adoption Legislation 2012-13, House 2014-15, Liaison 2014-15, Affordable Childcare 2014-15. Chair, Liberal Democrat Parliamentary Party Committee on Education, Families and Young People 2010-12. *Other:* Member, Liberal Democrat Conference Committee 2000-03; President, Women Liberal Democrats 2002-04; Member, Liberal Democrats Federal Executive 2003-04.

Political interests: Child protection, young offenders, prisoner education, environment, early years education.

Other: Patron: Family Planning Association, Helena Kennedy Trust; Infant Trust; WAVE Trust; Ambassador: NSPCC, 4Children; Honorary fellow, Unicef; Member, Parliament Choir; Amnesty International. Rex Boat Club.

Publications: Chaired report What on Earth? The threats to the Science Underpinning Conservation (2002).

Recreations: Music, theatre, gardening, rowing, good company, bee-keeping.

The Baroness Walmsley, House of Lords, London SW1A 0PW
Tel: 020 7219 6047 *Email:* walmsleyj@parliament.uk
Website: www.joanwalmsley.org.uk *Twitter:* @joan_walmsley

WARNER, LORD

CROSSBENCH

WARNER (Life Baron), Norman Reginald Warner; cr. 1998. Born 8 September 1940; Son of Albert and Laura Warner; Married Anne Lawrence 1961 (divorced 1981) (1 son 1 daughter); married Suzanne Reeve 1990 (1 son).

Education: Dulwich College, London; University of California, Berkeley (MPH) (Harkness Fellowship 1971-73).

Non-political career: Ministry of Health/DHSS 1959-85: Assistant private secretary: to Minister of Health 1967-68, to Secretary of State for Social Services 1968-69, Executive Councils Division 1969-71, NHS Reorganisation 1973-74, Principal private secretary to Secretary of State for Social Services 1974-76, Supplementary Benefits Division 1976-78, Management services 1979-81, Controller, Wales and South Western Region 1981-83, Under-Secretary, Supplementary Benefits Division 1984-85; Director of social services, Kent County Council 1985-91; Managing director, Warner Consultancy and Training Services Ltd 1991-97; Senior policy adviser to Home Secretary 1997-99; Chair: Youth Justice Board for England and Wales 1998-2003, London Sports Board 2003.

Political career: *House of Lords:* Raised to the peerage as Baron Warner, of Brockley in the London Borough of Lewisham 1998. Department of Health: Government Spokesperson 2003-06, Parliamentary Under-Secretary of State 2003-05, Minister of State: (NHS Delivery) 2005-06, (NHS Reform) 2006. Member: Science and Technology 2008-12, Science and Technology Sub-committee II (Genomic Medicine) 2008-09, Science and Technology Sub-committee I (Radioactive Waste Management: a further update) 2010, Adoption Legislation 2012-13; Member, Joint Committees on: the Draft Care and Support Bill 2013, the Draft Modern Slavery Bill 2014; Member, Long-Term Sustainability of the NHS 2016-17. *Other:* Resigned Labour Party and Whip October 2015; now sits as Crossbencher. *Councils and public bodies:* Chair: City and East London FHSA 1991-94, National Inquiry into Selection, Development and Management of Staff in Children's Homes 1991-92; Member, Local Government Commission 1995-96; Chair, NHS London Provider Agency 2007-09; Member, Commission on Funding of Care and Support (Dilnot Commission) 2010-11; Children's Commissioner, Birmingham City Council 2014-.

Political interests: Law and order, children, social and health care, end of life, Palestine; Commonwealth countries, North Africa/Middle East, USA.

Other: Member, Carers National Association 1991-94; Royal Philanthropic Society: Member 1991-, Chair 1993-98; Trustee: Leonard Cheshire Foundation 1994-96, MacIntyre Care 1994-97; Chair: Expert Panel for UK Harkness Fellowships 1994-97, Residential Forum, in Association with National Institute for Social Work 1994-97; National Council for Voluntary Organisations 2001-03; Harkness Fellowship 1971-73; Oxfam, Amnesty International, Samaritans. Gwilym Gibbon Fellow, Nuffield College, Oxford 1984. PC 2006.

Publications: Editor, Commissioning Community Alternatives in European Social and Health Care (1993); Articles in specialised journals and national newspapers; A Suitable Case for Treatment: The NHS and Reform (2011); Solving the NHS Care and Cash Crisis (2014).

Recreations: Reading, cinema, theatre, exercise, travel.

Rt Hon the Lord Warner, House of Lords, London SW1A 0PW
Tel: 020 7219 4540 *Email:* warnern@parliament.uk

WARSI, BARONESS

CONSERVATIVE

WARSI (Life Baroness), Sayeeda Hussain Warsi; cr 2007. Born 28 March 1971; Married (divorced) (1 daughter); Married Iftikhar (4 stepchildren).

Education: Dewsbury College; Leeds University (LLB 1992).

Non-political career: Trainee solicitor, Crown Prosecution Service 1994-96; Solicitor, Whitfield Hallam Goodall Solicitors 1996-97; Managing partner, George Warsi Solicitors 1997-2002; Legal draftsman, Ministry of Law, Pakistan 2002-03; Director, Shire Bed Company 2015-.

Political career: *House of Commons:* Contested (Conservative) Dewsbury 2005 general election. *House of Lords:* Raised to the peerage as Baroness Warsi, of Dewsbury in the County of West Yorkshire 2007. Shadow Minister for: Community Cohesion 2007-10, Social Action 2007-10; Minister without Portfolio 2010-12; Government Spokesperson for Cabinet Office 2011-12; Senior Minister of State (Faith and Communities) and Government Spokesperson, Department for Communities and Local Government and Foreign and Commonwealth Office 2012-14. Member, Sexual Violence in Conflict 2015-16. *Other:* Conservative Party: Vice-chairman (with responsibility for cities) 2005-07, Chairman 2010-12.

Political interests: Foreign affairs, faith, integration, freedom of religion, social action; Afghanistan, Central Asia, Bangladesh, Pakistan.

Other: Founder and chair, Savayra Foundation, UK 2003-. Pro Vice-Chancellor, Bolton University 2016-. Honorary Doctorate, University of Law. PC 2010.

Publications: The Enemy Within, A Tale of Muslim Britain.

Recreations: Writing, family life.

Rt Hon the Baroness Warsi, House of Lords, London SW1A 0PW
Tel: 020 7219 0262 *Email:* warsis@parliament.uk
Website: sayeedawarsi.com *Twitter:* @SayeedaWarsi

WARWICK OF UNDERCLIFFE, BARONESS

LABOUR

WARWICK OF UNDERCLIFFE (Life Baroness), Diana Warwick; cr. 1999. Born 16 July 1945; Daughter of Jack and Olive Warwick; Married Sean Bowes Young 1969.

Education: St Joseph's College, Bradford; Bedford College, London University (BA 1967).

Non-political career: Technical assistant to general secretary, NUT 1969-72; Assistant secretary, Civil and Public Services Association 1972-83; General secretary, Association of University Teachers 1983-92; Chief executive: Westminster Foundation for Democracy 1992-95, Universities UK (previously Committee of Vice-Chancellors and Principals/Universities UK) 1995-2009; Non-executive director: Lattice plc 2000-02, Universities Superannuation Scheme Ltd 2001-09; Chair: Human Tissue Authority 2010-, National Housing Federation 2015-. Member, TUC General Council 1989-92.

Political career: *House of Lords:* Raised to the peerage as Baroness Warwick of Undercliffe, of Undercliffe in the County of West Yorkshire 1999. Member: Science and Technology 1999-2005, Science and Technology Sub-committees: II (Aircraft Cabin Environment) 2000-01, (Stem Cell Research) 2001-02, II (Innovations in Computer Processors) 2001-02, I (Fighting Infection) 2002-03, (Science and International Agreements) 2003-04, Advisory Panel on Works of Art 2003-05, Joint Committee on the Draft Protection of Charities Bill 2014-15, Procedure 2016-. *Councils and public bodies:* Board member, British Council 1985-95; Member: Employment Appeal Tribunal 1987-99, Executive and Council, Industrial Society 1987-97, Commonwealth Institute 1988-95, Nolan/Neill Committee on Standards in Public Life 1994-99, OST Technology Foresight Steering Group 1997-2000.

Political interests: Higher education, science and technology, health, heritage, international development, pensions, corporate social responsibility.

Other: Member: Inter-Parliamentary Union 1999-, Commonwealth Parliamentary Association 1999-, British American Parliamentary Group 1999-; Trustee, Royal Anniversary Trust 1991-93; Council member, Duke of Edinburgh's Seventh Commonwealth Study Conference 1991; Voluntary Service Overseas: Chair 1994-2003, Life Vice-president 2003-; Member, RIIA 1995-; Trustee, St Catherine's Foundation, Windsor 1996-2008; Chair of trustee, International Students House 2000-; Chair, Modern Records Centre, Warwick University 2009-; Council member, University College London 2010-; Board member, Pensions Protection Fund 2011-; FRSA 1984; VSO, Womankind Worldwide. Five honorary doctorates.

Recreations: Theatre, opera, looking at pictures.

The Baroness Warwick of Undercliffe, House of Lords, London SW1A 0PW
Tel: 020 7219 5086 *Email:* warwickd@parliament.uk

WASSERMAN, LORD

CONSERVATIVE

WASSERMAN (Life Baron), Gordon Joshua Wasserman; cr 2011. Born 26 July 1938; Son of late John Wasserman QC and Prof Rachel Wasserman; Married Cressida Frances 1964.

Education: Westmount High School, Montreal, Canada; New College, Oxford (BA); McGill University, Canada (Rhodes Scholar 1959).

Non-political career: Senior research scholar, St Antony's College, Oxford 1961-64; Lecturer in economics, Merton College, Oxford 1963-64; Research Fellow, New College Oxford 1964-67; Home Office: Economic adviser 1967, Senior economic adviser 1972, Assistant secretary 1977-81; Head, Urban Deprivation Unit 1973-77; Civil service travelling fellowship, USA 1977-78; Under Secretary, Central Policy Review Staff, Cabinet Office 1981-83; Assistant Under Secretary of State, Home Office 1983-95; Special adviser (science and technology) to Police Commissioner, New York 1996-98; Chief of staff to Police Commissioner, New York 1998-2002; Special adviser to Police Commissioner, Philadelphia 1998-2003; Chair, ION Track Inc 2000-02; Chair and chief executive officer, Gordon Wasserman Group LLC 2003-.

Political career: *House of Lords:* Raised to the peerage as Baron Wasserman, of Pimlico in the City of Westminster 2011. Government Adviser on Policing and Criminal Justice 2011-. Member: EU Sub-committee F (Home Affairs, Health and Education) 2013-15, EU Home Affairs Sub-committee 2015-16.

Other: Vice-President, English Basketball Association 1983-86; Executive member, ELITE Group 1993-96; Board member, SEARCH Group Inc 1994-2000; Member, US Justice Department Advisory Panel on Science and Technology 1996-2003.

The Lord Wasserman, House of Lords, London SW1A 0PW
Tel: 020 7219 5353

CROSSBENCH

WATKINS OF TAVISTOCK, BARONESS

WATKINS OF TAVISTOCK (Life Baroness), Mary Jane Watkins; cr 2015. Born 5 March 1955; Married Roger Watkins 1981 (1 son 1 daughter).

Education: St Helen and St Katharine School, Abingdon; Wolfson School of Nursing, Westminster Hospital (qualified general nurse 1976); South London and Maudsley Nursing School (qualified mental health nurse 1979); Nightingale Scholar 1985; University of Wales (Masters nursing); King's College, University of London (PhD 1985).

Non-political career: Tutor, Nightingale School 1979-81; Nurse, Westminster Hospital London 1980; Tutor, Maudsley School of Nursing 1981-83; Academic director and senior tutor, Tor and South West College of Health; Plymouth University: Dean, Faculty of Health and Social Work, Emeritus Professor of Healthcare Leadership, Pro Vice-Chancellor, Health, Deputy Vice-Chancellor 2009-12; Nurse adviser to BUPA Medical Advisory Panel 2006-.

Political career: *House of Lords:* Raised to the peerage as Baroness Watkins of Tavistock, of Buckland Monachorum in the County of Devon 2015. Member: Licensing Act 2003 2016-17, Secondary Legislation Scrutiny 2017-. *Councils and public bodies:* Non-executive Director, Aster Housing Association 2010-; PenCLAHRC (NIHR Peninsula Collaboration for Leadership in Applied Health Research and Care) 2014-.

Political interests: Health, housing, higher education, secondary education.

Other: Member: UK Central Council for Nursing and Midwifery and Health Visiting 1996-2001, Council for Professions Supplementary to Medicine 1997-2001; Former nurse member, appraisal committee, National Institute for Health and Clinical Excellence 2001-07; Member, Royal College of Nursing; Nightingale Fellowship 1980. Honorary doctorate, Plymouth University 2012.

Publications: Published in the field of nursing education and leadership; Inaugural editor, Journal of Clinical Nursing.

Professor the Baroness Watkins of Tavistock, House of Lords, London SW1A 0PW
Email: watkinsm@parliament.uk
King's College London *Tel:* 020 7848 3325 *Email:* sadaf.qureshi@kcl.ac.uk

LABOUR

WATSON OF INVERGOWRIE, LORD

Opposition Spokesperson for Education

WATSON OF INVERGOWRIE (Life Baron), Michael (Mike) Goodall Watson; cr. 1997. Born 1 May 1949; Son of late Clarke and late Senga Watson, née Goodall; Married Lorraine McManus 1986 (divorced); married Clare Thomas 2004 (1 son).

Education: Dundee High School; Heriot-Watt University, Edinburgh (BA economics and industrial relations 1974); French.

Non-political career: Development officer, Workers Educational Association East Midlands District 1974-77; MSF: Full-time official 1977-89, Industrial officer 1977-79, Regional officer based in Glasgow 1979-89; Director, PS Communication Consultants Ltd, Edinburgh 1997-99; Associate director, Caledonia Consulting, Edinburgh 2007-12. Member, Unite 1975-.

Political career: *House of Commons:* MP (Labour) for Glasgow Central 1989-97. Chairman, Parliamentary Labour Party Committee on Overseas Development Aid 1991-97. *House of Lords:* Raised to the peerage as Baron Watson of Invergowrie, of Invergowrie in Perth and Kinross 1997. Opposition Spokesperson for Education 2015-. Member, Joint Committee on the Draft Protection of Charities Bill 2014-15. *Other:* Scottish Parliament: MSP for Glasgow Cathcart constituency 1999-2005 (as Mike Watson): Minister for Tourism, Culture and Sport 2001-03. Labour Party: Member, Scottish Executive Committee 1987-90, Party Whip suspended 2004, Re-admitted November 2012.

Political interests: Economy, social inclusion policy, overseas aid and development, extension of devolution throughout the UK; France.

Other: Fellow, Industry and Parliament Trust 1999; Visiting Research Fellow, Department of Government, Strathclyde University 1993-96, 1999-2002; Oxfam, Epilepsy Action Scotland, Shelter. Hon LLD, Abertay Dundee University 1998. Director, Dundee United Football Company Ltd 2003-05.

Publications: Rags to Riches: The Official History of Dundee United FC (1985); The Tannadice Encyclopedia (1997); Year Zero: An Inside View of the Scottish Parliament (2001).

Recreations: Dundee United FC, cycling, running.

The Lord Watson of Invergowrie, House of Lords, London SW1A 0PW
Tel: 020 7219 8731 *Email:* watsonm@parliament.uk

WATSON OF RICHMOND, LORD

LIBERAL DEMOCRAT

WATSON OF RICHMOND (Life Baron), Alan John Watson; cr. 1999. Born 3 February 1941; Son of Rev. John William Watson and Edna Mary, née Peters; Married Karen Lederer 1965 (2 sons).

Education: Diocesan College, Cape Town, South Africa; Kingswood School, Bath; Jesus College, Cambridge (Open Scholar history 1959; State Scholar 1959, MA 1963) (Vice-president, Cambridge Union); German.

Non-political career: Research assistant, Cambridge University 1962-64; BBC 1965-68: General trainee 1965-66, Reporter, *The Money Programme*, BBC TV 1966-68; Chief public affairs commentator, London Weekend Television 1969-70; Presenter: *Panorama*, BBC TV 1971-74, *The Money Programme* 1974-75; Head of TV, radio, audio-visual division, EEC, and Editor, European Community Newsreel service to Lomé Convention Countries 1975-79; Charles Barker City Ltd: Director 1980-85, Chief executive 1980-83; Deputy chair, Sterling Public Relations 1985-86; Chair: City and Corporate Counsel Ltd 1987-94, Threadneedle Publishing Group 1987-94, Corporate Vision Ltd 1989-98; Presenter: BBC 1 1990 *You and 92*, Documentary Series *The Germans*, Channel 4 1992; Chair, Corporate Television Networks 1992-; Member, Y&R Partnership Board; Chair: Burson-Marsteller UK 1994-2004, Burson-Marsteller Europe 1996-2007, Cola Cola Company European Advisory Board 2002-06, Raisin Social Ltd (Wine Importers) 2005-, Nexus Publishing 2007-, Havas Media/Havas Media Group 2008-.

Political career: *House of Commons:* Contested (Liberal) Richmond, Surrey 1974 and 1979 and (Liberal/All) Richmond and Barnes 1983 and 1987 general elections. *House of Lords:* Raised to the peerage as Baron Watson of Richmond, of Richmond in the London Borough of Richmond upon Thames 1999. Liberal Democrat Spokesperson for: Foreign and Commonwealth Affairs (Europe) 2000-01, 2002-05, Universities 2007-09. Member, EU Sub-committee C (Common Foreign and Security Policy) 2000-03; Co-opted Member, EU Sub-committee A (Economic and Financial Affairs) 2006-10. *Other:* President, Cambridge University Liberal Club 1961-; Chair, Liberal Party Parliamentary Association 1982-84; Member, Liberal Party National Executive 1982-86; President, Liberal Party 1984-85. *Councils and public bodies:* Chair of Governors, Westminster College, Oxford 1988-94.

Political interests: Worldwide use of English, EU enlargement, transatlantic relationship; Germany, Romania, Russia, USA.

Other: Member: Executive board, Unicef 1985-92, High Level EU-Romania Group 2000-02; Chair, Royal Television Society 1990-91; Visiting Fellow, Louvanium International Business Centre, Brussels 1990-95; Visiting Erasmus Professor in European studies, Louvain University 1990; President, Heathrow Association for Control of Aircraft Noise 1992-95; British-German Association: Chair 1992-2000; President 2000-; Vice-chair, European Movement 1995-2001; Prince of Wales Business Leaders Forum 1996-; Hon. Professor, German Studies, Birmingham University 1997-; Council member, British Studies Centre, Humboldt University, Berlin 1998-; Chair, Father Thames Trust 1999-; English Speaking Union: Chair 1999-2005, Chair, British Jamestown Committee 2005-07, International chair Emeritus 2006-, Vice-President 2012-; Trustee and Patron, Richmond Museum 2002-; Patron, Richmond Society 2002-; Visiting Fellow, Oriel College, Oxford 2003-; Chair: UK Steering Committee of Koenigswinter Conference 2003-10, Chemistry Advisory Board, Cambridge 2004-13; Hon. Fellow, Jesus College, Cambridge 2004-; Chair: Cambridge Foundation 2005-, Council of Commonwealth Societies 2005-12; FRSA; FIPR; FIVCA; FRTS; Marsh Memorial Homes, Cape Town, South Africa. High Steward (Deputy Chancellor), Cambridge University 2010-. Ten honorary doctorates from Russian, Romania, Moldovan, US and UK universities. Jean Monnet Prize for European TV coverage 1974; The Churchill Medal 2005. CBE 1985; Order of Merit (Germany) 1995; Grand Cross Order of Merit (Germany) 2001; Grand Cross Order of Merit (Romania) 2004; Knights Grand Cross (Germany) 2007; Order of the Red Eagle (Albania) 2014; *Clubs:* Brooks's, Royal Automobile Club, Kennel Club, Beefsteak Club. House of Lords Yacht Club.

Publications: Europe at risk (1972); The Germans: who are they now? (1992); Thatcher and Kohl: old rivalries revisited (1996); Jamestown: The Voyage of English (2007); The Queen and the USA (2012).

Recreations: Boating, wines, foreign travel, art.

The Lord Watson of Richmond CBE, House of Lords, London SW1A 0PW
Tel: 020 7219 8661

CTN Communications, 114 St Martin's Lane, London WC2N 4BE *Tel:* 020 7395 4485
Fax: 020 7395 4461 *Email:* alan.watson@ctn.co.uk
Website: www.lordalanwatson.co.uk

WATTS, LORD

LABOUR

WATTS (Life Baron), David Leonard Watts; cr 2015. Born 26 August 1951; Son of Leonard and Sarah Watts; Married Avril Davies 1972 (2 sons).

Education: Seel Road Secondary Modern School.

Non-political career: Labour Party organiser; Research assistant to: Angela Eagle MP 1992-93, John Evans MP 1993-97. Shop steward, United Biscuits AEU.

Political career: *House of Commons:* MP (Labour) for St Helens North 1997-2010, for St Helens North (revised boundary) 2010-15. PPS: to John Spellar: as Minister of State, Ministry of Defence 1999-2001, as Minister of Transport, Department for Transport, Local Government and the Regions 2001-02, as Minister of State, Department for Transport 2002-03, to John Prescott as Deputy Prime Minister 2003-05; Government Whip 2005-10; Opposition Whip 2010. Member: Finance and Services 1997-2001, 2005-06, Foreign Affairs 2010-12, Administration 2010-15, Arms Export Controls 2011-12, House of Commons Governance 2014-15. Chair: PLP North West Regional Group 2000-01, Parliamentary Labour Party 2012-15. *House of Lords:* Raised to the peerage as Baron Watts, of Ravenhead in the County of Merseyside 2015. Member, EU Home Affairs Sub-committee 2016-. *Councils and public bodies:* St Helens Metropolitan Borough Council: Councillor 1979-97, Leader 1993-97; Vice-chair, Association of Metropolitan Authorities.

Political interests: Regional policy, education, training.

Other: UK President, Euro Group of Industrial Regions 1989-93.

Recreations: Watching football and rugby, reading.

The Lord Watts, House of Lords, London SW1A 0PW
Tel: 020 7219 3000

WAVERLEY, VISCOUNT

CROSSBENCH

WAVERLEY (3rd Viscount, UK), John Desmond Forbes Anderson; cr. 1952. Born 31 October 1949; Son of 2nd Viscount.

Non-political career: Adviser to Chairman, CCC Group 1993-; Founder and Chairman, supplyfinder.com 2015-.

Political career: *House of Lords:* First entered House of Lords 1993; Elected hereditary peer 1999-; On leave of absence November 2013-March 2016.

Political interests: International affairs.

Other: Order of San Carlos (Grand Cross) (Colombia) 1998; Jubilee Medal (Kazakhstan) 2002; Chieftaincy (Yoruba) 2010; Anniversary Medal (Kyrgyzstan) 2010.

The Viscount Waverley, House of Lords, London SW1A 0PW
Tel: 020 7219 3174
Email: jd@lordwaverley.com
Website: lordwaverley.com

WEI, LORD

CONSERVATIVE

WEI (Life Baron), Nathanael Ming-Yan Wei; cr 2010. Born 19 January 1977; Son of Rev Edward Wei and Mrs Meggy Wei; Married Cynthia Wei 2003 (2 sons).

Education: Sir Frank Markham School, Milton Keynes; Jesus College, Oxford (BA modern languages 1999); Chinese (basic Mandarin and Cantonese), French, German.

Non-political career: Consultant, McKinsey 1999-2001; Co-founder: Teach First 2001-05, Future Leaders 2005-07, Challenge Network; Co-founder and partner, Shaftesbury Partnership 2006-10; Head of new ventures and strategic adviser, Absolute Return for Kids 2007-10; Community Foundation Network 2011-.

Political career: *House of Lords:* Raised to the peerage as Baron Wei, of Shoreditch in the London Borough of Hackney 2010. Government adviser, Big Society (unpaid), Cabinet Office 2010-11. Member, EU Internal Market Sub-committee 2015-. *Other:* Founding co-chair, Conservative Friends of the Chinese.

Countries of interest: East Asia (including China, Japan, Mongolia, South Korea) and South East Asia.

Other: Young Global Leader, World Economic Forum; Fellow, Young Foundation 2005-10; Board member, Asia House 2012-.

The Lord Wei, House of Lords, London SW1A 0PW
Tel: 020 7219 5353 *Email:* wein@parliament.uk
Website: natwei.com *Twitter:* @natwei

CONSERVATIVE

WELLINGTON, DUKE OF

WELLINGTON (9th Duke of, UK), Arthur Charles Valerian Wellesley; cr 1814; Marquess of Wellington (UK) 1812; Marquess of Douro (UK) 1814; Earl of Mornington (I) 1760; Earl of Wellington (UK) 1812; Viscount Wellesley (I) 1760; Viscount Wellington (UK) 1809; Baron Mornington (I) 1746; Baron Douro (UK) 1809. Born 19 August 1945; Son of 8th Duke; Married Princess Antonia Elizabeth Bridgid Luise OBE 1977 (daughter of HRH the late Prince Friedrich Georg Wilhelm Christoph of Prussia) (2 sons 3 daughters).

Education: Eton College; Christ Church, Oxford (MA PPE).

Non-political career: Deputy chair, Thames Valley Broadcasting 1975-84; Director: Antofagasta and Bolivia Railway 1977-80, Eucalyptus Pulp Mills 1979-88, Transatlantic Holdings 1983-95, Global Asset Management Worldwide 1984-2013; Deputy chair, Deltec Panamerica 1985-89; Chair, Deltec Securities 1985-89; Director, Continental and Industrial Trust 1987-90; Deputy chair, Guinness Mahon Holdings 1988-91; Chair: Dunhill Holdings 1991-93, Richemont Holdings 1993-, Framlington Group 1994-2005, Sun Life and Provincial Holdings 1995-2000; Director: Compagnie Financière Richemont 1999-2017, Sanofi 2002-14, Pernod Richard 2003-11, RIT Capital Partners 2010-.

Political career: *House of Commons:* Contested (Conservative) Islington North October 1974 general election. *House of Lords:* Succeeded his father to the dukedom of Ciudad Rodrigo 2010 and to the dukedom of Wellington and other honours 2014. Prince of Waterloo (Netherlands) 1815; Duke of Victoria and Marquess of Torres Vedras (Portugal); Count of Vimiero (Portugal) 1811; Duke of Ciudad Rodrigo and a Grandee of Spain (1st Class) (Spain) 1812. Elected hereditary peer 2015-. Member, EU Financial Affairs Sub-committee 2016-17. *Other:* European Parliament: MEP for: Surrey 1979-84, Surrey West 1984-89. *Councils and public bodies:* Councillor, Basingstoke Borough Council 1978-79; Member of council, Royal College of Art 1991-97; DL, Hampshire 1999; Chairman of council, King's College London 2007-16.

Other: Commissioner, English Heritage 2003-07. Freeman, City of London 2016. Hon D. Litt King's College London 2016. Order of Isabel the Catholic (Spain): Knight 1986, Grand Cross 2000; Grand Officer, Order of Merit (Portugal) 1987; OBE 1999; *Clubs:* Cavalry and Guards Club.

His Grace the Duke of Wellington OBE, House of Lords, London SW1A 0PW
Tel: 020 7219 3000 *Email:* wellington@parliament.uk

LABOUR

WEST OF SPITHEAD, LORD

WEST OF SPITHEAD (Life Baron), Alan William John West; cr 2007. Born 21 April 1948; Son of Walter West, Admiralty civil servant, and Jacqueline West, née Bliss; Married Rosemary Linington Childs 1973 (2 sons 1 daughter).

Education: Windsor Grammar School; Clydebank High School; Dartmouth (Britannia Royal Naval College); RN staff course 1978; Royal College of Defence Studies 1992; Higher Command and Staff course 1993; French (basic).

Non-political career: Active List, Royal Navy. Royal Navy 1965-2006: Seagoing posts 1966-73; Commanding officer (CO) HMS Yarnton 1973; HMSs Juno 1976, Ambuscade 1977, Norfolk 1979; CO HMS Ardent 1980; Naval Staff, Ministry of Defence (MoD) 1982; CO HMS Bristol 1987; Defence Intelligence Staff, MoD 1989; MoD 1993-96: Director Naval Staff Duties 1993, Naval Secretary 1994-96; Commander UK Task Group and of Anti-submarine Warfare Striking Force 1996-97; Chief of Defence Intelligence, MoD 1997-2001; Commander-in-Chief Fleet and East Atlantic and Commander Allied Naval Forces North 2001-02; Chief of Naval Staff and First Sea Lord, MoD 2002-06; Chairman, defence advisory board, QinetiQ 2006-07; Member, foreign advisory board, HSBC 2010-11; Strategic adviser, Primetake plc 2011-12; Chairman: Magic Industries Ltd 2012-13, Spearfish 2012-, MCM Solutions 2013-.

Political career: *House of Lords:* Raised to the peerage as Baron West of Spithead, of Seaview in the County of Isle of Wight 2007. Parliamentary Under-Secretary of State (Security and Counter-terrorism) and Government Spokesperson, Home Office 2007-10. Member, Joint Committee on National Security Strategy 2014-. *Councils and public bodies:* Trustee, Imperial War Museum 2007-16.

Political interests: Security, defence, foreign affairs, shipping/maritime; South West Asia, Horn of Africa, Gulf, Japan, Pakistan, Scandinavian countries, Ukraine.

Other: ELN; Younger Brother, Trinity House 1986-; President, Merchant Navy Medal Fund 2006-; Chairman, National Security Forum 2008-10; Member, RUSI; Master Mariner; President: Transport on Water, Great River Race, Merchant Navy Association; Member: Naval Review, Top Level Group, Global Strategy Fourm, Woodland Trust, UK National Defence Association, UK Defence Forum, Friends of the City Churches; St Anne's Lime House, Chauncy Maples, Bollington Sea Cadet Unit, Dockland Sinfonia, Medway Queen, Albert McKenzie Memorial Fund, Admiral Benbow Memorial Fund, Ardent Association. Liveryman, Honourable Company of Master Mariners; Company of Watermen and Lightermen of the River Thames. Chancellor, Southampton Solent University 2006-. Honorary doctorate 2006. Trench Gascoigne prize winner. DSC 1982; KCB 2000; ADC 2002; GCB 2004; PC 2010; *Clubs:* Navy Club of 1765 & 85, Royal Naval Club, Royal Yacht Squadron, St Barbara Association, British American Forces Dining Club, Anchorites, Britannia Association, Pepys Club, Destroyer Club, Pilgrims, Merchant Trading with the Continent, RNSA, Woodroffes, The Cachalots, The Old Gang Club.

Publications: Seaford House Paper (2002); Contributor, The Oxford Handbook of War.

Recreations: Boating, military history, OMRS.

Rt Hon Admiral the Lord West of Spithead GCB DSC, House of Lords, London SW1A 0PW
Tel: 020 7219 5953 *Email:* westaa@parliament.uk
Email: westbuzz1@btinternet.com

CONSERVATIVE

WHEATCROFT, BARONESS

WHEATCROFT (Life Baroness), Patience Jane Wheatcroft; cr 2010. Born 28 September 1951; Daughter of Anthony and Ruth Wheatcroft; Married Anthony Salter 1976 (2 sons 1 daughter).

Education: Wolverhampton High School for Girls; Queen Elizabeth's Grammar School, Tamworth; Birmingham University (LLB 1972).

Non-political career: Deputy city editor, *The Times* 1984-86; Assistant city editor, *Daily Mail* 1986-88; Editor, *Retail Week* 1988-93; Deputy city editor, *Mail on Sunday* 1994-97; Business and city editor, *The Times* 1997-2006; Editor, *Sunday Telegraph* 2006-07; Non-executive director: Barclays plc 2008-09, Shaftesbury plc 2008-09; Editor-in-chief, *Wall Street Journal Europe* 2009-10; Non-executive director: St James's Place plc, Fiat Chrysler Automobiles; Business consultant, DLA Piper.

Political career: *House of Lords:* Raised to the peerage as Baroness Wheatcroft, of Blackheath in the London Borough of Greenwich 2010. Member: EU Sub-committee G (Social Policies and Consumer Protection) 2011-12, Joint Committee on the Draft Financial Services Bill 2011-12, Constitution 2012-14, Economic Affairs Finance Bill Sub-committee 2012-13, 2014, 2015-16, Olympic and Paralympic Legacy 2013-14, Economic Affairs 2014-17. *Councils and public bodies:* Trustee, British Museum.

Political interests: Business, finance, economics, arts; China, India.

Other: Director, Association of Leading Visitor Attractions; Chair, *Financial Times* Complaints Commission; Action Aid, Samaritans. Hon. Doctorate, City University, London.

Recreations: Opera, skiing, theatre.

The Baroness Wheatcroft, House of Lords, London SW1A 0PW
Tel: 020 7219 5353
Email: patiencewheatcroft@googlemail.com

LABOUR

WHEELER, BARONESS

Opposition Senior Whip; Opposition Spokesperson for Health

WHEELER (Life Baroness), Margaret Eileen Joyce Wheeler; cr 2010. Born 25 March 1949; Partner.

Education: St Ursula's Convent School, Greenwich; Nottingham University (BA politics and psychology 1971).

Non-political career: Publishing/editorial trainee, Routledge and Kegan Paul 1971-73; Confederation of Health Service Employees 1973-93: Head of editorial department, Press officer, Campaigns strategies, Parliamentary and international officer 1973-88, Director of specialist and support services 1988-93; Unison: Director of organisation development 1993-97, Director of organisation and staff development 1997-2010; Natural carers strategy implementation team, Department of Health 2009-10. Member: National Union of Journalists 1972-2010, Unison 1997-2010.

Political career: *House of Lords:* Raised to the peerage as Baroness Wheeler, of Blackfriars in the City of London 2010. Opposition Whip 2010-13; Opposition Senior Whip 2013-; Opposition Spokesperson for Health 2015-. Member, Consumer Insurance (Disclosure and Representations) Bill 2011-12. *Councils and public bodies:* Former member: Commission on Social Justice, Enquiry panel into productivity and high performance, Department of Trade and Industry/Work Foundation; Investors in People Advisory Board, UK Commission for Employment and Skills.

Political interests: Health and social care; disabilities; China, India.

Other: Trustee and board member: One World Action, Carer Support, Elmbridge -2017; Chair and board member, Blackfriars Settlement; Christian Aid. MBE 2005.

Recreations: Walking, theatre, arts, music.

The Baroness Wheeler MBE, House of Lords, London SW1A 0PW
Tel: 020 7219 8909 *Email:* wheelerm@parliament.uk

LABOUR

WHITAKER, BARONESS

WHITAKER (Life Baroness), Janet Alison Whitaker; cr. 1999. Born 20 February 1936; Daughter of Alan Stewart and Ella Stewart, née Saunders; Married Ben Whitaker CBE 1964 (died 2014) (2 sons 1 daughter).

Education: Nottingham High School for Girls; Girton College, Cambridge (BA English 1957); Bryn Mawr College, USA (MA English 1959); Harvard University, USA (Radcliffe Fellow 1960); French.

Non-political career: Editor, André Deutsch (Publishers) 1961-66; Various posts, Health and Safety Executive 1974-88; Department of Education and Employment 1988-96: Head of sex equality branch 1992-96; Consultant: Commission for Racial Equality 1995-96, Commonwealth Secretariat 1996; Assessor, Citizens' Charter Chartermark 1996; Consultant, Committee of Reference, Friends Provident Group 2000-08; Chair, Department for Education Stakeholder Group for Gypsy, Roma and Traveller Education 2013. Member, FDA.

Political career: *House of Lords:* Raised to the peerage as Baroness Whitaker, of Beeston in the County of Nottinghamshire 1999. International Development Liaison Peer 1999-2007. Member: European Union Select Committee Sub-committee F (Social Affairs, Education and Home Affairs) 1999-2003, Joint Committee on Human Rights 2000-03, Joint Committee on Draft Corruption Bill 2003, Intergovernmental Organisations 2007-08, Joint Committee on Draft Bribery Bill 2009, Built Environment 2015-16, Natural Environment and Rural Communities Act 2006 2017-. *Councils and public bodies:* Magistrate 1985-2006; Member, Employment Tribunal 1995-2000; Deputy chair and chair, Camden Racial Equality Council 1996-99; Non-executive director, Tavistock and Portman NHS Trust 1997-2001; Member, Immigration Complaints Audit Committee 1998-99.

Political interests: Architecture and design, international development, race relations; Africa, Asia, Europe.

Other: Member: Inter-Parliamentary Union, Commonwealth Parliamentary Association, UK advisory panel, United Nations Association 2006-; Member/associate, Fabian Society 1962; Council member, SOS Sahel 1997-2011; Chair, Working Men's College for Men and Women 1998-2001; Advisory council, Transparency International (UK) 2001-09; Deputy chair, Independent Television Commission (ITC) 2001-03; Patron, Runnymede Trust 2001-; Overseas Development Institute: Council member 2003-11, Trustee 2006-09; Trustee, Unicef UK 2003-09; Patron, British Stammering Association 2003-; Practical Action (formerly Intermediate Technology Development Group) 2004-10; British Humanist Association: Vice-President 2004-, Patron 2014-; Patron, One World Trust 2004-; Member, Advisory Board, British Institute of Human Rights 2005-; Patron, Student Partnerships Worldwide 2005-10; President: South Downs Society 2012-16, Friends, Families and Travellers 2013-, Advisory Council for the Education of Romany and Other Travellers 2014-, Newhaven Historical Society 2016; Patron, Hillcrest Community Centre 2017; FRIBA; Fellow, Working Men's College; *Clubs:* Reform Club.

Recreations: Travel, walking, art, music, reading.

The Baroness Whitaker, House of Lords, London SW1A 0PW
Tel: 020 7219 5353 *Email:* whitakerj@parliament.uk

CONSERVATIVE

WHITBY, LORD

WHITBY (Life Baron), Michael John Whitby; cr 2013. Born 6 February 1948; Married Gaynor.

Education: James Watt Technical Grammar School, Birmingham; German.

Non-political career: Worked in the cultural sector in Liverpool; Lecturer in business and management studies; Chair and managing director, Skeldings Ltd.

Political career: *House of Commons:* Contested (Conservative) Delyn 1992 general election. *House of Lords:* Raised to the peerage as Baron Whitby, of Harborne in the City of Birmingham 2013. *Other:* Contested Midlands West 1987 European Parliament by-election. Member, Conservative Party 1979-; Board member, Conservative Councillors' Association. *Councils and public bodies:* Birmingham City Council: Councillor 1997-2014, Leader, Conservative Group 2003-14, Council Leader 2004-12; Member, West Midlands Police and Crime Panel; Governor, Baskerville School, Harborne, Birmingham; Vice-president, Local Government Association.

Other: Fellow, Institute of Directors; Director: Birmingham Science Park Aston Ltd, Marketing Birmingham Ltd; Member, Greater Birmingham and Solihull Local Enterprise Partnership; Board member: Advantage West Midlands, National Exhibition Centre; Committee member, THSH Trust.

The Lord Whitby, House of Lords, London SW1A 0PW
Tel: 020 7219 5353

LABOUR

WHITTY, LORD

WHITTY (Life Baron), John Lawrence (Larry) Whitty; cr. 1996. Born 15 June 1943; Son of late Frederick James and Kathleen May Whitty; Married Tanya Gibson 1969 (divorced 1986) (2 sons); married Angela Forrester 1993.

Education: Latymer Upper School, London; St John's College, Cambridge (BA economics 1965); French, German.

Non-political career: Hawker Siddeley Aviation 1960-62; Civil servant, Ministry of Aviation and Ministry of Technology 1965-70; Assistant secretary, Trades Union Congress 1970-73; Research officer, General, Municipal, Boilermakers and Allied Trade Union 1973-85; Chair, Cofeely East London Energy 2005-10. Member, GMB.

Political career: *House of Lords:* Raised to the peerage as Baron Whitty, of Camberwell in the London Borough of Southwark 1996. Government Whip 1997-98; Government Spokesperson for European Affairs, International Development, Foreign and Commonwealth Affairs, Education and Employment 1997-98; Parliamentary Under-Secretary of State and Government Spokesperson: Department of the Environment, Transport and the Regions (Minister for Roads and Road Safety) 1998-2001, Department for Environment, Food and Rural Affairs 2001-05. Member, Draft Climate Change Bill Joint Committee 2007; Co-opted member, EU Sub-committee B (Internal Market) 2007-10; Member EU Sub-committees: G (Social Policies and Consumer Protection) 2010-12, D (Agriculture, Fisheries, Environment and Energy) 2012-15; Member, European Union 2015-; Chair, EU Internal Market Sub-committee 2015-; Member, Trade Union and Party Funding 2016. Vice-chair, PLP Departmental Group for Energy and Climate Change 2010-15. *Other:* Labour Party: General Secretary 1985-94, European Co-ordinator 1994-97. *Councils and public bodies:* Chair, National Consumer Council 2006-08; Member, National Water Regulation Authority (Ofwat) 2006; Non-executive director, Environment Agency 2006-12; Chair, Consumer Focus 2008-10.

Political interests: Employment, energy, environment, food, Europe, consumers, education; China, France, Germany, Ireland, Italy, Japan.

Other: Member: Friends of the Earth, Fabian Society; President, Combined Heat and Power Association 2005-11; Chair: Housing Voice 2009-10, Cheshire Lehman Fund 2009-16, Road Safety Foundation 2014-; President, Environmental Protection UK 2016-; Alzheimer's Society. PC 2005.

Recreations: Theatre, cinema, swimming.

Rt Hon the Lord Whitty, House of Lords, London SW1A 0PW
Tel: 020 7219 3118 *Email:* whittyl@parliament.uk

WIGLEY, LORD

PLAID CYMRU

WIGLEY (Life Baron), Dafydd Wigley; cr 2011. Born 1 April 1943; Son of Elfyn and Myfanwy Wigley; Married Elinor Bennett 1967 (1 son 1 daughter 2 sons deceased).

Education: Caernarfon Grammar School; Rydal School, Colwyn Bay; Manchester University (BSc physics 1964); Welsh (fluent), French (modest).

Non-political career: Finance staff, Ford Motor Co 1964-67; Chief cost accountant and financial planning manager, Mars Ltd 1967-71; Financial controller, Hoover Ltd, Merthyr Plant 1971-74; Chair, Alpha-Dyffryn Ltd (Electronics) 1987-91; Board member, S4C 2003-06. Former member, Association of Scientific, Technical and Managerial Staffs (ASTMS).

Political career: *House of Commons:* Contested Merioneth 1970 general election. MP (Plaid Cymru) for Caernarfon February 1974-2001. Sponsor Disabled Persons Act 1981; Plaid Cymru: Whip 1987-91, Spokesperson for Constitutional Affairs 1997-2000. *House of Lords:* Raised to the peerage as Baron Wigley, of Caernarfon in the County of Gwynedd 2011. Member, Olympic and Paralympic Legacy 2013-14. *Other:* Contested North Wales region 1994 European Parliament election; National Assembly for Wales: AM for Caernarfon constituency 1999-2003: Shadow First Minister 1999-2000, Shadow Secretary for Finance 1999-2000, Contested North Wales region 2007 election. Leader and president, Plaid Cymru 1981-84, 1991-2000. *Councils and public bodies:* Councillor, Merthy Tydfil County Borough Council 1972-74; Vice-president, Local Government Association 2017-.

Political interests: Industry, employment, disability, Europe, minority languages; Argentina, Ireland, New Zealand, Slovenia, USA.

Other: Vice-President, Wales Council for the Disabled; President, Spastic Society for Wales 1985-90; Member, Mencap Profound Mental Handicap Study Committee 1987-97; Vice-President: Mencap in Wales 1990-, Federation of Economic Development Authorities (FEDA); Patron, Autism Wales 2003-; President: Gwynedd Family History Society 2005-, National Library of Wales 2008-12; Hon. member, Welsh Gorsedd of Bards; Honorary fellowship, Bangor University; NSPCC, Mencap Wales, Contact a Family. Freedom: Borough of Arfon 1996, Town of Caernarfon 2001. Pro-chancellor, University of Wales 2003-06. Hon. LLB University of Wales. National Federation of the Blind Grimshaw Memorial Award 1981. PC 1997; *Clubs:* Clwb y Castell Club, Caernarfon.

Publications: Co-author: An Economic Plan for Wales (1970), O Ddifri (1992), A Democratic Wales in an United Europe (1994), A Fair Choice for Wales (1996); Columnist, *Daily Post* 2009-.

Recreations: Chess, walking, soccer, Caernarfon Town FC, rugby, gardening.

Rt Hon the Lord Wigley, House of Lords, London SW1A 0PW
Tel: 020 7219 0780/020 7219 5021 *Email:* wigleyd@parliament.uk *Twitter:* @Dafydd_Wigley

WILCOX, BARONESS

CONSERVATIVE

WILCOX (Life Baroness), Judith Ann Wilcox; cr. 1996. Born 31 October 1940; Daughter of John and Elsie Freeman; Married Keith Davenport 1961 (divorced 1986) (1 son); married Sir Malcom Wilcox, CBE 1986 (died 1986).

Education: St Dunstan's Abbey, Devon; St Mary's Convent, Wantage; Plymouth University; French (basic).

Non-political career: Management of family business in Devon 1969-79; Founder/financial director, Capstan Fisheries Ltd, Devon 1979-84; Founder/chair, Channel Foods Ltd, Cornwall 1984-89; President Directeur-General, Pecheries de la Morinie, Boulogne-sur-Mer, France 1989-91; Chair: National Consumer Council 1990-96, Morinie et Cie, Boulogne-sur-Mer, France 1991-94; Board member, Automobile Association 1991-2001; Non-executive member, Inland Revenue Board 1992-95; Member, Prime Minister's Advisory Panel to Citizen's Charter Unit 1992-97; Commissioner, Local Government Commission 1992-95; Chair, Citizen's Charter Complaints Task Force 1993-95; Port of London Authority: Board member 1993-2000, Vice-chair 2000-05; Director: Cadbury Schweppes plc 1997-2007, Carpetright plc 1997-2010, Elexon Ltd 2000-02, Johnson Services plc 2003-09.

Political career: *House of Lords:* Raised to the peerage as Baroness Wilcox, of Plymouth in the County of Devon 1996. Opposition Whip 2002-05; Opposition Spokesperson for: the Treasury 2003-05, Cabinet Office 2005-06, Trade and Industry/Business, Enterprise and Regulatory Reform 2006-08; Energy and Climate Change 2008-10; Parliamentary Under-Secretary of State (Parliamentary Secretary for Business, Innovation and Skills) and Government Spokesperson, Department for Business, Innovation and Skills 2010-12. Member: EU Sub-committee D (Environment, Public Health and Consumer Protection) 1997-2000, Ecclesiastical Committee 1997-2010, Science and Technology Sub-committee II (Science and Society) 1999-2000, Science and Technology 2000-02, Science and Technology Sub-committee IIA (Human Genetic Databases) 2000-02; Chair, Science and Technology Sub-committee II (Aircraft Cabin Environment) 2000; Member: Liaison 2000-05, Science and Technology Sub-committees: I (Fighting Infection) 2002-03, II (Innovation in Computer Processors/Microprocessing) 2002-03, Ecclesiastical Standing Committee 2002-12, Extradition Law 2014-15, European Union 2015-, EU Energy and Environment Sub-Committee 2015-, Intellectual Property (Unjustified Threats) Bill 2016. *Councils and public bodies:* Member: General Advisory Council, BBC 1996-2000, Lord Chancellor's Review of the Court of Appeal 1996-97, Tax Law Review Committee 1996-2000; Governor: Imperial College 2006-12, Harris Westminster Sixth Form School 2014-.

Political interests: Fishing industry, mariculture, consumer affairs, finance, intellectual property; Australia, France.

Other: Council of Europe: Delegate 2013-, PACE 2013-, Equality 2013-, Rules 2014-; Council member, Institute of Directors 1991-98; Member, Governing Body, Institute of Food Research 1996-2002; President: National Federation of Consumer Groups, Institute of Trading Standards Administration (ITSA); Chair: London Diocesan Advisory Committee 2000-02, 2013-, Trustees, Community of St Mary the Virgin Wantage 2012-17; National Consumer Federation; FIMgt; FRSA; Royal National Mission to Deep Sea Fishermen, Children's Hospice South West. Liveryman, Fishmongers' Company 2006. Freedom, City of London. Hon. DSc Plymouth University 2004; *Clubs:* Athenæum, Nobody's Friends, Gardeners Club. St Mawes Sailing.

Recreations: Sailing, birdwatching, calligraphy.

The Baroness Wilcox, House of Lords, London SW1A 0PW
Tel: 020 7219 4458 *Email:* wilcoxj@parliament.uk

WILLETTS, LORD

CONSERVATIVE

WILLETTS (Life Baron), David Lindsay Willetts; cr 2015. Born 9 March 1956; Son of John and Hilary Willetts; Married Hon Sarah Butterfield 1986 (1 son 1 daughter).

Education: King Edward's School, Birmingham; Christ Church, Oxford (BA philosophy, politics and economics 1978); German (fluent).

Non-political career: HM Treasury 1978-84: Private secretary to Nicholas Ridley MP as Financial Secretary 1981-82, Principal, Monetary Policy Division 1982-84; Prime Minister's Downing Street Policy Unit 1984-86; Director of Studies, Centre for Policy Studies 1987-92; Consultant director, Conservative Research Department 1987-92; Director: Retirement Security Ltd 1988-94, Electra Corporate Ventures Ltd 1988-94; Governor, Ditchley Foundation 1998-; Visiting Fellow, Nuffield College, Oxford 1999-2006; Member, Global Commission on Ageing 2000-10; Visiting Fellow, Cass Business School 2004-07; Non-executive board member, National Council for Universities and Business 2015-; Executive chair, Resolution Foundation 2015-; Senior non-executive director, Surrey Satellite Technologies Ltd 2015-; Visiting Professor, King's College London; Honorary Fellow, Nuffield College, Oxford 2016-.

Political career: *House of Commons:* MP (Conservative) for Havant 1992-2010, for Havant (revised boundary) 2010-15. PPS to Sir Norman Fowler as Chairman of Conservative Party 1993-94; Assistant Government Whip 1994-95; Government Whip July-November 1995; Office of Public Service: Parliamentary Secretary 1995-96, Paymaster General July-December 1996; Opposition Spokesperson for Employment 1997-98; Shadow Secretary of State for: Education and Employment 1998-99, Social Security 1999-2001, Work and Pensions 2001-05, Welfare Reform 2004-05, Trade and Industry 2005, Education and Skills/Innovation, Universities and Skills 2005-09; Shadow Minister for Universities and Skills 2009-10; Minister of State for Universities and Science, Department for Business, Innovation and Skills 2010-14. Member, Social Security 1992-93. Member, Conservative Economic Affairs/Enterprise/Pensions/Social Affairs Policy Committee. *House of Lords:* Raised to the peerage as Baron Willetts, of Havant in the County of Hampshire 2015. *Other:* Conservative Party: Chair, Conservative Research Department 1997, Member, Policy Board, Head of policy co-ordination 2003-04. *Councils and public bodies:* Member: Lambeth and Lewisham Family Practitioners' Committee 1987-90, Parkside Health Authority 1988-90, Social Security Advisory Committee 1989-92; Trustee, Science Museum Group.

Political interests: Economic policy, health, social security, education, science; China, Germany, USA.

Other: Member, Competitiveness Council, Council of the European Union 2010-15; Board member, Biotech Industry Association 2015-; Non-executive director, Biotech Growth Trust 2015-; Chair, British Science Association 2015-; Trustee director, Francis Crick Institute 2015-; Honorary President, International Student Foundation 2016-. Honorary degree, Bath University 2017. PC 2010; *Clubs:* Hurlingham, Garrick Club.

Publications: Modern Conservatism (1992); Civic Conservatism (1994); Blair's Gurus (1996); Why Vote Conservative (1997); Welfare to Work (1998); After the Landslide (1999); Browned-off: What's Wrong with Gordon Brown's Social Policy (2000); Co-author, Tax Credits: Do They Add Up? (2002); Left Out, Left Behind (2003); Old Europe? Demographic Change and Pension Reform (2003); Conservatives in Birmingham (2008); The Pinch – How the baby boomers took their children's future – and why they should give it back (Atlantic Books, 2010).

Recreations: Swimming, reading, cycling.

Rt Hon the Lord Willetts, House of Lords, London SW1A 0PW
Tel: 020 7219 3000
Resolution Foundation, 2 Queen Anne's Gate, London SW1H 9AA

LABOUR

WILLIAMS OF ELVEL, LORD

WILLIAMS OF ELVEL (Life Baron), Charles Cuthbert Powell Williams; cr. 1985. Born 9 February 1933; Son of late Dr N P Williams, Lady Margaret Professor of Divinity at Oxford, and Muriel de Lérisson, née Cazenove; Married Jane Gillian Welby, née Portal 1975 (1 stepson, the Archbishop of Canterbury (qv)).

Education: Westminster School; Christ Church, Oxford (BA literae humaniores 1955, MA); London School of Economics (BSc Econ Part I 1964); French, German, Italian.

Non-political career: Army national service 1955-57, Subaltern KRRC (60th Rifles) HQ Battalion (Winchester) and 1st Battalion Derna (Libya). Various management posts, British Petroleum Co Ltd 1958-64; Personal assistant to manager, Guatemala branch, Bank of London and Montreal 1964-66; Manager, mergers and acquisitions, Eurofinance SA, Paris 1966-70; Baring Bros & Co Ltd 1970-77: Managing director 1971-77; Chair, Price Commission 1977-79; Managing director: Henry Ansbacher & Co Ltd 1979-82, Henry Ansbacher Holdings 1982-85; Director, Mirror Group Newspapers plc 1985-92.

Political career: *House of Lords:* Raised to the peerage as Baron Williams of Elvel, of Llansantffraed in Elvel in the County of Powys 1985. Opposition Spokesperson for Trade and Industry 1987-92; Deputy Leader of the Opposition 1989-92; Opposition Spokesperson for: Defence 1990-97, the Environment 1992-97. Member: Ecclesiastical Committee 1997-2013, European Union 1999-2002, EU Sub-committee C (Common Foreign and Security Policy) 1999-2003, Procedure 2005-08; EU Sub-committee C (Foreign Affairs, Defence and Development): Co-opted member 2009-10, Member 2010-12; Member EU Sub-committees: C (External Affairs) 2012-13, D (Agriculture, Fisheries, Environment and Energy) 2013-15; Member: Sexual Violence in Conflict 2015-16, Liaison 2016-.

Political interests: Banking, finance, environment; France, Germany, Italy, Russia, Spain.

Other: Chair, Academy of St Martin-in-the-Fields 1988-90; Busby Trustee, Westminster School 1989-99; Campaign for the Protection of Rural Wales: President 1989-95, Vice-President 1995-2012, President, Radnor Branch 1995-; Chair, Mid Wales Chamber Orchestra 2008-13; Macmillan Cancer Relief. CBE 1980; PC 2013; *Clubs:* Beefsteak, Reform Club. MCC.

Publications: The Last Great Frenchman: a life of General de Gaulle (1993); Bradman: an Australian Hero (1996); Adenauer: the Father of the New Germany (2000); Pétain (2005); Harold Macmillan (2009); Gentlemen and Players (2012).

Recreations: Cricket, music.

Rt Hon the Lord Williams of Elvel CBE, House of Lords, London SW1A 0PW
Tel: 020 7219 6054 *Email:* williamscc@parliament.uk

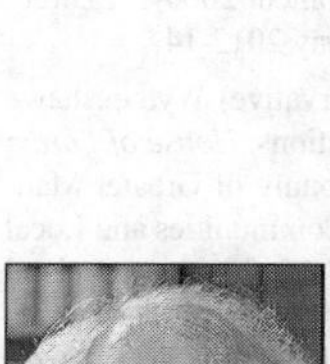

CROSSBENCH

WILLIAMS OF OYSTERMOUTH, LORD

WILLIAMS OF OYSTERMOUTH (Life Baron), Rowan Douglas Williams; cr 2013. Born 14 June 1950; Son of Aneurin and Delphine Williams; Married (Hilary) Jane Paul 1981 (1 son 1 daughter).

Education: Dynevor School, Swansea; Christ's College, Cambridge (BA theology 1971, MA); Christ Church and Wadham Colleges, Oxford (DPhil 1975; DD 1989); French, German, Welsh.

Non-political career: Lecturer, College of the Resurrection, Mirfield 1975-77; Tutor and director of studies, Westcott House, Cambridge 1977-80; Ordained priest 1978; Honorary curate, Chesterton St George, Ely 1980-83; Divinity lecturer, Cambridge 1980-86; Canon theologian, Leicester Cathedral 1981-82; Dean and Chaplain, Clare College, Cambridge 1984-86; Lady Margaret professor of divinity and canon of Christ Church, Oxford 1986-92; Bishop of Monmouth 1992-2002; Archbishop of Wales 1999-2002; Archbishop of Canterbury 2002-12.

Political career: *House of Lords:* Raised to the peerage as Baron Williams of Oystermouth, of Oystermouth in the City and County of Swansea 2013. First entered the House of Lords as Archbishop of Canterbury 2002.

Political interests: Children and family issues, development; Africa, Middle East.

Other: Fellow: British Academy 1990, Royal Society of Literature 2004, Learned Society of Wales 2010; Hon board member, Cardinal Willebrands Research Centre; Chair, Christian Aid. Hon. Liveryman, Worshipful Company of Wax Chandlers; Patron: The Stationers' Company, Parish Clerks. Freedom: City of Swansea 2010, City of Canterbury 2012. Chancellor, University of South Wales. Honorary fellow: Clare College, Cambridge, Wadham College, Oxford, Newport University, Swansea University; Honorary doctorates from German and US universities, plus: Aberdeen University, Cambridge University, Durham University, Exeter University, Kent University, King's College, London, Oxford University, Roehampton University, Wales University. Order of St. John of Jerusalem, Priory for Wales (Confrere); PC 2002; Royal Victorian Chain 2012; *Clubs:* Athenæum Club. Hon member, Kent County Cricket Club.

Publications: The Wound of Knowledge (1979); Resurrection (1982); The Truce of God (1983); Arius: heresy and tradition (1987); Editor The Making of Orthodoxy (1989); Teresa of Avila (1991); Open to Judgement (1994); Sergii Bulgakov (1999); On Christian Theology (2000); Lost Icons (2000); Christ on Trial (2000); Poems of Rowan Williams (2002); Ponder these things (2002); Writing in the Dust (2002); Silence and Honey Cakes (2003); The Dwelling of the Light (2003); Anglican Identities (2004); Grace and Necessity (2005); Why Study the Past? (2005); Tokens of Trust (2007); Wrestling with Angels (2007); Headwaters (poems 2008); Dostoevsky: Language, Faith and Fiction (2008); A Margin of Silence/Une Marge de Silence (2008); Co-editor, Crisis and Recovery: Ethics, Economics and Justice (Palgrave Macmillan, 2010); Co-author, For All That Has Been: Thanks: Growing a Sense of Gratitude (2010).

Recreations: Music, fiction, languages.

Most Rev and Rt Hon the Lord Williams of Oystermouth, House of Lords, London SW1A 0PW
Tel: 020 7219 5353
Magdalene College, Cambridge CB3 0AG *Tel:* 01223 332144 *Email:* jeh34@cam.ac.uk

CONSERVATIVE

WILLIAMS OF TRAFFORD, BARONESS

Minister of State for Countering Extremism and Government Spokesperson, Home Office; Government Spokesperson, Women and Equalities

WILLIAMS OF TRAFFORD (Life Baroness), Susan Frances Maria Williams; cr 2013. Born 16 May 1967; Daughter of John McElroy and Mary McElroy; Married Alex Williams 2005 (1 son 2 daughters).

Education: La Sagesse High School, Jesmond; Huddersfield Polytechnic (BSc applied nutrition 1989).

Non-political career: Nutritionist, Action and Research into Multiple Sclerosis (ARMS) 1992-2002; Leadership consultant, Local Government Improvement and Development 2006-12; Director, North West Rail Campaign 2011-14; Executive director, Atlantic Gateway 2012-14.

Political career: *House of Commons:* Contested (as Susan Fildes) (Conservative) Wythenshawe and Sale East 2001 and (as Susan Williams) Bolton West 2010 general elections. *House of Lords:* Raised to the peerage as Baroness Williams of Trafford, of Hale in the County of Greater Manchester 2013. Government Whip 2014-15; Government Spokesperson for: Communities and Local Government 2014-15, Home Office 2014-15, 2016-, Law Officers 2014-15, Northern Ireland 2014-15, Scotland 2014-15, Wales 2014, Education (Women and Equalities) 2015-16; Parliamentary Under-Secretary of State, Department for Communities and Local Government 2015-16; Government Spokesperson for Women and Equalities 2016-; Home Office: Minister of State 2016-17, Minister of State for Countering Extremism 2017-. *Councils and public bodies:* Trafford Metropolitan Borough Council: Councillor 1998-2011, Leader, Conservative group 2002-09, Council Leader 2004-09; Non-executive director, North West Development Agency 2007-11; Authority member, Greater Manchester Police Authority 2008-09.

Political interests: Local government, transport, foreign affairs.

Other: Board member, Central Salford Urban Regeneration Company 2008-10; Chair (North West), Heritage Lottery Fund.

Recreations: Walking, cycling, gardening.

The Baroness Williams of Trafford, House of Lords, London SW1A 0PW
Tel: 020 7219 5353 *Email:* williamssb@parliament.uk *Twitter:* @SusanBaroness

LIBERAL DEMOCRAT

WILLIS OF KNARESBOROUGH, LORD

WILLIS OF KNARESBOROUGH (Life Baron), Philip George Willis; cr 2010. Born 30 November 1941; Son of late George Willis, postman, and late Norah Willis, nurse; Married Heather Sellars 1974 (1 son 1 daughter).

Education: Burnley Grammar School; City of Leeds and Carnegie College (Cert Ed 1963); Birmingham University (BPhil education 1978); French.

Non-political career: Head teacher: Ormesby School, Cleveland 1978-82, John Smeaton Community High School, Leeds 1983-97. Member, Secondary Heads Association.

Political career: *House of Commons:* MP (Liberal Democrat) for Harrogate and Knaresborough 1997-2010. Liberal Democrat: Whip 1997-99, Spokesperson for Further, Higher and Adult Education 1997-99, Principal Spokesperson for Education and Employment 1999-2000, Shadow Secretary of State for Education and Skills 2000-05. Member: Education and Employment (Education Sub-Committee) 1999-2000, Education and Employment 1999-2000, Liaison 2005-10; Chair: Science and Technology 2005-07, Joint Committee on the Draft Human Tissue and Embryos Bill 2007, Innovation, Universities[, Science] and Skills/Science and Technology 2007-10. *House of Lords:* Raised to the peerage as Baron Willis of Knaresborough, of Harrogate in the County of North Yorkshire 2010. Science and Technology: Co-opted member 2010-11, Member 2011-15; Member: Science and Technology Sub-committee I 2012-13, Long-Term Sustainability of the NHS 2016-17. *Other:* Member, Association of Liberal Democrat Councillors. *Councils and public bodies:* Harrogate Borough Council: Councillor 1988-99, First Liberal Democrat Leader 1990-97; North Yorkshire County Council: Councillor 1993-97, Deputy Group Leader 1993-97; Vice-President, Local Government Association 2010-11.

Political interests: Inclusive education, health, local and regional government, science policy, higher education reform; Ireland.

Other: Council member: Foundation for Science and Technology, National Environment Research Council; President, AOC Charitable Trust; Chair: Association of Medical Research Charities -2016, NIHR Collaboration for Leadership in Applied Health Research and Care, Yorkshire and the Humber; Royal Society of Arts; Royal College of Nursing; National Children's Homes, St Michael's Hospice, Harrogate, Horticap, Bluecoat Wood Nursery, Harrogate Homeless Project. Doctor of Science, Salford University. Man of the Year, *Times Educational Supplement* 2002.

Publications: Quality and Compassion: the future of nursing (2012).

Recreations: Theatre, music, dance (especially ballet), football (Leeds United FC).

The Lord Willis of Knaresborough, House of Lords, London SW1A 0PW
Tel: 020 7219 5709 *Email:* willisg@parliament.uk

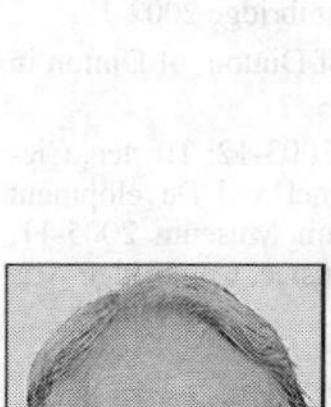

UK INDEPENDENCE PARTY

WILLOUGHBY DE BROKE, LORD

WILLOUGHBY DE BROKE (21st Baron, E), Leopold David Verney; cr. 1491. Born 14 September 1938; Son of 20th Baron, MC, AFC; Married Petra Aird 1965 (divorced 1989) (3 sons); married Mrs Alexandra du Luart 2003.

Education: Le Rosey, Switzerland; New College, Oxford (BA modern languages 1961).

Non-political career: Chair: St Martin's Magazines 1992-2008, SM Theatre Ltd 1992-; President, Heart of England Tourist Board 1999-2004.

Political career: *House of Lords:* First entered House of Lords 1986; Elected hereditary peer 1999-. Member: European Union 1997-2000, European Union Sub-committee D (Environment, Agriculture, Public Health and Consumer Protection) 1997-2001. *Other:* Vice-President, Conservatives Against a Federal Europe (CAFE) 1997-2007. *Councils and public bodies:* DL, Warwickshire 1999-.

Political interests: Rural affairs, EU; Europe, Hong Kong, Tibet.

Other: Patron, Warwickshire Association of Boys' Clubs 1990-04; Honorary governor, Royal Shakespeare Theatre 1992-; President, CPRE Warwickshire 2002-16; Chair, Warwickshire Hunt Ltd 2005-12. All England Lawn Tennis.

The Lord Willoughby de Broke DL, House of Lords, London SW1A 0PW
Tel: 020 7219 4941 *Email:* willoughbyl@parliament.uk
Ditchford Farm, Moreton in Marsh, Gloucestershire GL56 9RD *Tel:* 01608 661990
Fax: 01608 663565

LABOUR

WILLS, LORD

WILLS (Life Baron), Michael David Wills; cr 2010. Born 20 May 1952; Son of late Stephen Wills and Elizabeth Wills; Married Jill Freeman 1984 (3 sons 2 daughters).

Education: Haberdashers' Aske's, Elstree; Clare College, Cambridge (BA history 1973).

Non-political career: Third secretary, later second secretary, HM Diplomatic Service 1976-80; Researcher, later producer, London Weekend Television 1980-84; Director, Juniper Productions TV production company 1984-97. Member, TGWU.

Political career: *House of Commons:* MP (Labour) for North Swindon 1997-2010. Parliamentary Under-Secretary of State: Department of Trade and Industry (Minister for Small Firms, Trade and Industry) 1999, Department for Education and Employment 1999-2001; Parliamentary Secretary, Lord Chancellor's Department 2001-02; Parliamentary Under-Secretary of State, Home Office 2002-03: (for Criminal Justice System IT 2002, Information Technology in the Criminal Justice System 2003); Minister of State, Ministry of Justice 2007-10. *House of Lords:* Raised to the peerage as Baron Wills, of North Swindon in the County of Wiltshire and Woodside Park in the London Borough of Barnet 2010.

Other: Board member), Institute of Germanic and Romance Studies, University of London; President, Wiltshire Association of Local Councils; Member, advisory council, Transparency International UK. PC 2008.

Rt Hon the Lord Wills, House of Lords, London SW1A 0PW
Tel: 020 7219 5353

CROSSBENCH

WILSON OF DINTON, LORD

WILSON OF DINTON (Life Baron), Richard Thomas James Wilson; cr. 2002. Born 11 October 1942; Son of late Richard Ridley and Frieda Bell Wilson, née Finlay; Married Caroline Margaret Lee 1972 (1 son 1 daughter).

Education: Radley College; Clare College, Cambridge (BA law 1964; LLM 1965).

Non-political career: Called to Bar, Middle Temple 1965; Assistant principal, Board of Trade 1966-71; Principal, Cabinet Office 1971-73; Department of Energy 1974-86: Principal establishment and finance officer 1983-86; Seconded to Cabinet Office 1986-90: Head, economic secretariat 1987-90; Deputy secretary, industry, HM Treasury 1990-92; Permanent Secretary, Department of the Environment 1992-94; Permanent Under-Secretary, Home Office 1994-97; Cabinet Secretary and Head, Home Civil Service 1998-2002; Master of Emmanuel College, Cambridge 2002-12.

Political career: *House of Lords:* Raised to the peerage as Baron Wilson of Dinton, of Dinton in the County of Buckinghamshire 2002.

Other: Trustee, Ewing Foundation 1995-; Non-executive director, BSkyB 2003-12; Trustee, Cicely Saunders Foundation 2004-; President, Chartered Institute of Personnel and Development 2004-06; Chairman, Radley College 2004-10; Trustee, Syndic Fitzwilliam Museum 2005-11; Chairman: C Hoare & Co 2006-16, Prince's Teaching Institute 2006-09; Trustee, Cambridge Arts Theatre 2008-12. CB 1991; KCB 1997; GCB 2001.

Recreations: Home, garden.

The Lord Wilson of Dinton GCB, House of Lords, London SW1A 0PW
Tel: 020 7219 5353
Email: rw272@cam.ac.uk

CROSSBENCH

WILSON OF TILLYORN, LORD

WILSON OF TILLYORN (Life Baron), David Clive Wilson; cr. 1992. Born 14 February 1935; Son of late Rev. William Skinner Wilson and late Enid Wilson; Married Natasha Alexander 1967 (2 sons).

Education: Trinity College, Glenalmond; Keble College, Oxford (Scholar, BA history 1958, MA); London University (PhD modern Chinese history 1973); Chinese (Mandarin), French.

Non-political career: Army national service (Black Watch) 1953-55. Foreign Service 1958-68: Served Vientiane, Laos 1959-60, Language student, Hong Kong 1960-62, First Secretary, Peking Embassy 1963-65, FCO 1965-68; Editor, *China Quarterly* 1968-74; Visiting Scholar, Columbia University, New York 1972; Rejoined Diplomatic Service 1974-92: Seconded to Cabinet Office 1974-77, Political adviser, Hong Kong 1977-81, FCO 1981-87: Head of Southern European Department 1981-84, Assistant Under-Secretary of State 1984-87, Governor and Commander-in-Chief, Hong Kong 1987-92; Chair, Scottish Hydro Electric plc (now Scottish and Southern Energy plc) 1993-2000); Master, Peterhouse, Cambridge 2002-08; Deputy vice-chancellor, Cambridge University 2005-08.

Political career: *House of Lords:* Raised to the peerage as Baron Wilson of Tillyorn, of Finzean in the District of Kincardine and Deeside and of Fanling in Hong Kong 1992. Chair, Revised Red Deer Act (Scotland) 1996; Co-opted member, EU Sub-committee B (Energy, Industry and Transport) 2000-02; Member: EU Sub-committee B (Internal Market, Infrastructure and Employment) 2012-15, European Union 2013-15. *Councils and public bodies:* Board member, British Council 1993-2002; Chair, Scottish Committee of the British Council 1993-2002; Prime Minister's Advisory Committee on Public Appointments: Member 2000-09, Chair 2008-09.

Political interests: Scottish affairs, education; China (including Hong Kong SAR), East and South East Asia.

Other: Substitute Member, UK Delegation to Parliamentary Assembly of Council of Europe 2016-; Member: Oxford University Expedition to Somaliland 1957, British Mount Kongur Expedition (North West China) 1981; Council member, CBI Scotland 1993-2000; Member, Hopetoun House Preservation Trust 1993-98; President: Bhutan Society of the UK 1993-2008, Hong Kong Society 1994-2012, Hong Kong Association 1994-; Glenalmond College: Council member 1994-2005, Chair 2000-05; Vice-President, Royal Scottish Geographical Society 1996-; Scottish Peers Association: Vice-chair 1998-2000, Chair 2000-02; Trustee, Scotland's Churches Scheme (later Scotland's Churches Trust) 1999-2002, 2009-; Museums of Scotland: Trustee 1999-2006, Chair 2002-06; Member, Royal Society for Asian Affairs; Royal Society of Edinburgh: Council member 2000-04, President 2008-11; Carnegie Trust for the Universities of Scotland 2000-; Registrar, Order of Saint Michael and Saint George 2001-10; Chair, Advisory Council, St Paul's Cathedral 2009-; FRSE. Chancellor, Aberdeen University 1997-2013. Six honorary doctorates; Honorary Fellow: Keble College, Oxford 1987, Peterhouse, Cambridge 2008. CMG 1985; KCMG 1987; KStJ 1987; GCMG 1991; KT 2000; *Clubs:* Alpine, New (Edinburgh), Royal Northern and University (Aberdeen) Club.

Recreations: Mountaineering, reading, theatre.

The Lord Wilson of Tillyorn KT GCMG, House of Lords, London SW1A 0PW
Tel: 020 7219 5353 *Email:* wilsondc@parliament.uk

WINCHESTER, LORD BISHOP OF

NON-AFFILIATED

WINCHESTER (97th Bishop of), Tim Dakin. Born 6 February 1958; Married Sally (1 son 1 daughter).

Education: University College of Saint Mark and St John, Plymouth; King's College, London; Christ Church, Oxford.

Non-political career: Principal, Carlile College, Kenya 1993-2000; Curate, Nairobi Cathedral 1993-2000; General secretary, Church Mission Society 2000-12; Honorary Canon Theologian, Coventry Cathedral 2001-; Bishop of Winchester 2012-.

Political career: *House of Lords:* Entered House of Lords 2012.

Countries of interest: Burundi, Democratic Republic of Congo, Kenya, Rwanda, Uganda.

Recreations: Reading, walking, films.

Rt Revd Bishop of Winchester, House of Lords, London SW1A 0PW
Tel: 020 7219 5353 *Email:* dakint@parliament.uk
Wolvesey, Winchester SO23 9ND *Tel:* 01962 854050 *Email:* bishop.tim@winchester.anglican.org
Website: www.winchester.anglican.org

WINSTON, LORD

LABOUR

WINSTON (Life Baron), Robert Maurice Lipson Winston; cr. 1995. Born 15 July 1940; Son of late Laurence Winston and Ruth Winston-Fox, MBE; Married Lira Helen Feigenbaum 1973 (2 sons 1 daughter).

Education: St Paul's School, London; London Hospital Medical College, London University (MB, BS 1964).

Non-political career: Wellcome research senior lecturer, Institute of Obstetrics and Gynaecology 1974-78; Other posts in UK, Belgium and USA; Consultant obstetrician and gynaecologist, Hammersmith Hospital 1978-2005; Former Dean, Institute of Obstetrics and Gynaecology, Royal Postgraduate Medical School (RPMS), London; Former Chair, British Fertility Society; Institute of Obstetrics and Gynaecology, RPMS, London University: Professor of Fertility Studies 1987-2005, Professor Emeritus 2005-; President, British Association of Advancement of Science 2005; Professor of Science and Society, Imperial College, London 2008; Chair, Advisory Board, DeVOS Cohort Project, Singapore 2012-; Presenter: *Your Life in Their Hands*, BBC TV 1978-84; *An Eye for the Job*, ITV 1990; *Making Babies*, BBC TV 1995, *The Human Body*, BBC TV 1998, *Secret Life of Twins*, BBC TV 1999; *Millennium Babies*, BBC TV 1999; *Superhuman*, BBC TV 2000;

Child of our Time, BBC TV 2000-16, *Human Instinct*, BBC TV 2002, *Threads of Life*, BBC TV 2002, *Human Mind*, BBC TV 2003, *Walking with Cavemen*, BBC TV 2003, *The Story of God*, BBC TV 2005; *Superdoctors*, BBC TV 2010; *How Science Changed Our World*, BBC TV 2011; *My Favourite Things*, BBC/Sky Arts 2016; Various music programmes, BBC Radio 4, Radio 3. British Medical Association.

Political career: *House of Lords:* Raised to the peerage as Baron Winston, of Hammersmith in the London Borough of Hammersmith and Fulham 1995. Parliamentary Office of Science and Technology (POST): Member 1998-2006, Vice-chair 2006-. Science and Technology: Member 1996-2006, 2010-15, Chair 1998-2001; Member: Innovation Exploitation Barrier 1997, Science and Technology Sub-committees: II (Cannabis) 1998, II (Antibiotic Resistance) 1999-2000, I (Non-food Crops) 1999, II (Science and Society) 1999-2000, II (Aircraft Cabin Environment) 2000-01, IIA (Human Genetic Databases) 2000-01; Chair, Science and Technology Sub-committee I (Science in Schools) 2000-01; Member, Science and Technology Sub-committees: II (Renewable Energy) 2003-04, II (Science and RDAs) 2003, II (Energy Efficiency) 2004-08; Member, Draft Human Tissue and Embryos Bill Joint Committee 2007; Co-opted Member, Science and Technology Sub-committee II (Genomic Medicine) 2008-09; Member, Science and Technology Sub-committee I 2012-13.

Political interests: Health, science and technology, education, arts; New Zealand, Israel, Switzerland.

Other: Chair, Council, Royal College of Music; Commissioner, UK Pavilion Expo 2001; Council member: Cancer Research UK -2007, Surrey University, Engineering and Physical Sciences Research Council; Chair, Genesis Research Trust; Board Member, Twig, Educational Films; Trustee: Royal Institution, British Science Association, UK Stem Cell Foundation; Member, Cancer Research UK; DreamLearners Ltd; Patron, Euphonia; Academy of Medical Sciences; Royal Academy of Engineering; Hon FREng; FRCOG; FRCP; FRSA; FMedSci; FRCSE; FRCPS; FBS; FCGI; Natural History Museum, Cheltenham Festival, Royal College of Music, Glyndebourne Opera, Royal Opera House, Reach Out Lab Imperial College, Genesis Research Trust, Winston's Wish, Listening Books, Garsington Opera, Lyric Theatre, UJIA, Jewish Care, New Israel Fund, Traverse Theatre Edinburgh. Chancellor, Sheffield Hallam University 2001-. Hon. Fellow: Queen Mary Westfield College, Institute of Education, Endocrine Society; Twenty four honorary doctorates. Cedric Carter Medal, Clinical Genetics Society 1993; Victor Bonney Triennial Prize, Royal College of Surgeons of England 1993; Chief Rabbi's Award for Contribution to Community 1994; Gold Medal, Royal Society for Promotion of Health 1998; Michael Faraday Gold Medal, Royal Society 1999; Robert Menzies Medal 2001; BMA Gold Medal Book Prize, Human 2001 Edwin Stevens Medal, Royal Society of Medicine 2003; Gold Medal, North of England Zoological Society 2004; Peer of the Year, *House Magazine* 2008; Medallist, Olumuc Film Festival 2014; Science Book Prize, Royal Society 2005, 2013, 2016; *Clubs:* Athenæum, MCC, Garrick Club.

Publications: Reversibility of Sterilization (1978); Co-author Tubal Infertility (1981); Infertility, a Sympathetic Approach (1987); The IVF Revolution (1999); Superhuman (2000); Human Instinct (2002); Predictions (2002); The Human Mind (2003); The Story of God (2005); A Child Against All Odds (2006); Bad Ideas (2010); Science Year by Year (2013); Growing Up (2017); 16 illustrated books about science for children; Over 330 papers in scientific journals on human and experimental reproduction.

Recreations: Theatre, broadcasting, music, wine.

Professor the Lord Winston, House of Lords, London SW1A 0PW
Tel: 020 7219 6020 *Email:* winstonr@parliament.uk
11 Denman Drive, London NW11 6RE *Tel:* 020 8455 7475 *Email:* r.winston@imperial.ac.uk
Website: www.robertwinston.org *Twitter:* @ProfRWinston

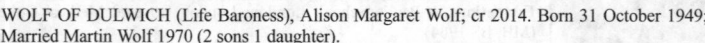

CROSSBENCH

WOLF OF DULWICH, BARONESS

WOLF OF DULWICH (Life Baroness), Alison Margaret Wolf; cr 2014. Born 31 October 1949; Married Martin Wolf 1970 (2 sons 1 daughter).

Education: Oxford High School; Oxford University (MA; MPhil); French (good), Italian (moderate to poor).

Non-political career: Research associate, National Institute of Education, Washington 1975-82; Institute of Education, University of London: Research officer 1983-85, Senior research officer 1985-95, Professor 1995-2004; King's College London: Sir Roy Griffiths Professor of Public Sector Management 2006-, Director, International Centre for University Policy Research 2012-.

Political career: *House of Lords:* Raised to the peerage as Baroness Wolf of Dulwich, of Dulwich in the London Borough of Southwark 2014. *Councils and public bodies:* Governor, King's College London Mathematics School; Member, King's College London Council.

Political interests: Training and skills policy, universities, medical workforce; Canada, France, Italy, Sweden, USA.

Other: Trustee: Abbeyfield Society, Newbury 2000-, Social Market Foundation 2013-16, King's College London Mathematics School; Academic Member, Council of King's College London; Abbeyfield (Newbury), Friends of King's College London Mathematics School. Sam Aaronovitch memorial prize 2008. CBE 2012.

Publications: Does Education Matter? (2002); The XX Factor: How Working Women are Creating a New Society (2013).

Professor the Baroness Wolf of Dulwich CBE, House of Lords, London SW1A 0PW
Tel: 020 7219 8619 *Email:* wolfa@parliament.uk
Department of Management, King's College London, 150 Stamford Street, London SE1 9NH
Website: www.kcl.ac.uk/sspp/departments/management/people/academic/wolf.aspx
Twitter: @XXFactorFacts

WOLFSON OF ASPLEY GUISE, LORD

CONSERVATIVE

WOLFSON OF ASPLEY GUISE (Life Baron), Simon Adam Wolfson; cr 2010. Born 27 October 1967; Son of David Wolfson, now Lord Wolfson of Sunningdale, and Susan Davis; Married Eleanor Shawcross 2012 (2 sons).

Education: Radley College; Trinity College, Cambridge (LLB 1989).

Non-political career: Next plc: Director 1997-, Managing director 1999-2001, Chief executive 2001-.

Political career: *House of Lords:* Raised to the peerage as Baron Wolfson of Aspley Guise, of Aspley Guise in the County of Bedfordshire 2010.

Political interests: Industry, economy.

Other: Trustee, Charles Wolfson Charitable Trust.

The Lord Wolfson of Aspley Guise, House of Lords, London SW1A 0PW
Tel: 020 7219 5353

WOOD OF ANFIELD, LORD

LABOUR

WOOD OF ANFIELD (Life Baron), Stewart Martin Wood; cr 2011. Born 25 March 1968; Son of Brian and Gisela Wood; Married Camilla Bustani 1998 (2 sons).

Education: Judd School, Tonbridge; University College, Oxford (BA philosophy, politics and economics); Harvard University (Fulbright Scholar, government department, PhD 1997); French, German.

Non-political career: Script consultant, BBC Documentaries 1995-2000; Junior research fellow, St John's College, Oxford 1996; Fellow in politics and lecturer, Magdalen College, Oxford 1996-2011; Special adviser to Gordon Brown: as Chancellor of the Exchequer 2001-07, as Prime Minister 2007-10; Adviser to Ed Miliband as Leader of the Opposition 2010-15. Member, Community.

Political career: *House of Lords:* Raised to the peerage as Baron Wood of Anfield, of Tonbridge in the County of Kent 2011. Opposition Spokesperson for Cabinet Office 2011-12, 2014-15; Shadow Minister without Portfolio, Cabinet Office 2011-15. Member, International Relations 2016-. *Other:* Ed Miliband Labour leadership campaign 2010; Member, Co-operative Party 2010-.

Political interests: Foreign policy, economic policy, sport, media and creative industries, Northern Ireland; China, EU, Germany, Russia, USA.

Other: Chair, United Nations Associations (UK) 2016-; Co-Founder and co-director, Nexus 1996-99; Member, British Film Institute; Board member, English Stage Company, Royal Court Theatre, London 2008-; Patron, Camden Psychotherapy Unit; Board member, YouGov/Cambridge; Fellow-In-Practice, Blavatnik School of Government, Oxford University 2016-.

Publications: Numerous articles and chapters on political economy, West European politics, education policy.

Recreations: Guitar, alt-country music, film and movie history, cricket, football (Liverpool FC).

The Lord Wood of Anfield, House of Lords, London SW1A 0PW
Tel: 020 7219 5854 *Email:* stewart.wood@parliament.uk *Twitter:* @StewartWood

CROSSBENCH

WOOLF, LORD

WOOLF (Life Baron), Harry Kenneth Woolf; cr. 1992. Born 2 May 1933; Son of late Alexander and Leah Woolf; Married Marguerite Sassoon 1961 (3 sons).

Education: Fettes College, Edinburgh; University College, London (LLB 1954).

Non-political career: Commissioned (National Service) 15/19th Royal Hussars 1954; Seconded to Army Legal Services 1954; Captain 1955. Called to Bar, Inner Temple 1954; Started practice at Bar 1956; Recorder of the Crown Court 1972-79; Junior Counsel, Inland Revenue 1973-74; First Treasury Junior Counsel (Common Law) 1974-79; Bencher 1976; Judge of the High Court of Justice, Queen's Bench Division 1979-86; Presiding Judge, South Eastern Circuit 1981-84; Member: Senate, Inns of Court and Bar 1981-85, Board of Management, Institute of Advanced Legal Studies 1985-93; Chair, Lord Chancellor's Advisory Committee on Legal Education 1986-90; Lord Justice of Appeal 1986-92; Chair, Board of Management, Institute of Advanced Legal Studies 1986-93; Held inquiry into: Prison disturbances 1990, part II with Judge Tumim, report 1991, Access to Justice 1994-96 (interim report 1995, final report and rules 1996); Master of the Rolls 1996-2000; Chair, Advisory Committee on Public Records 1996; Visitor: University College, London 1996-2000, Nuffield College, Oxford 1996-2000; Lord Chief Justice of England and Wales 2000-05; Visitor, Downing College, Cambridge 2005-; Judge of final appeal, Hong Kong; President, Qatar Financial Services Court; Chair of Council, University College London 2005-07; Chair, Woolf Committee 2007-08; President of the Civil and Commercial Court of Qatar.

Political career: *House of Lords:* Raised to the peerage as Baron Woolf, of Barnes in the London Borough of Richmond 1992. Lord of Appeal in Ordinary 1992-2006. Chair, Sub-committee on Lords' Interests 2006-08; Member: Constitution 2006-10, Privileges 2007-08, Inquiries Act 2005 2013-14; Chair, Insurance Bill 2014-15; Member, Joint Committee on Human Rights 2015-.

Other: President: Association of Law Teachers 1985-89, South West London Magistrates Association 1987-92, Central Council of Jewish Social Services 1989-99; Governor, Oxford Centre of Hebrew Studies (Emeritus) 1990-93; Butler Trust: Chair 1992-96, President 1996-; Trustee, St Mary's Hospital Special Trustees 1993-97; Mogen Dovid Adom 1995-; FBA. Honorary Liveryman, Drapers' Company. Pro-Chancellor, London University 1994-2002; Chancellor, Open University of Israel 2005-. Fellow: University College, London 1981, British Academy 2000; Twelve honorary doctorates; Hon. Fellow: Leeds Municipal University, Academy of Medical Sciences 2002-. Kt 1979; PC 1986; CH 2015; *Clubs:* Garrick, Royal Automobile Club.

Publications: Protection of the public: A New Challenge (Hamlyn lecture, 1990); Co-author: Zamir and Woolf: The Declaratory Judgement (2nd edition, 1993), De Smith, Woolf and Jowell (5th edition, 1995), Principles of Judicial Review; De Smith Administrative Law (6th edition, 2008); The Pursuit of Justice (Oxford University Press); Ethical Conduct in BAE Systems plc – The Way Forward.

Recreations: Theatre, music.

Rt Hon the Lord Woolf CH, House of Lords, London SW1A 0PW
Tel: 020 7219 1788/020 7219 3156 (PA) *Email:* maggiestevenson@parliament.uk

LABOUR

WOOLMER OF LEEDS, LORD

WOOLMER OF LEEDS (Life Baron), Kenneth John Woolmer; cr. 1999. Born 25 April 1940; Son of late Joseph Woolmer; Married Janice Chambers 1961 (3 sons).

Education: Kettering Grammar School; Leeds University (BA economics 1961).

Non-political career: Research Fellow, University of the West Indies 1961-62; Teacher, Friern Road Secondary Modern School, London 1963; Lecturer: Leeds University (economics) 1963-66, University of Ahmadu Bello, Nigeria 1966-68, Leeds University 1968-79; Halton Gill Associates: Principal 1979-96, Partner 1998-2009; Parliamentary adviser, Inland Revenue Staff Federation 1979-83; Leeds University Business School: Director of MBA Programmes 1991-97, Dean of External Relations 1997, Dean of Business School 1997-2000; Non-executive director, Thornfield Developments Ltd 1999-2002; Partner, Anderson McGraw 2001-06; Non-executive director: Courtcom Ltd 2001-03, Thornfield Ventures Ltd 2002-04. Member, AUT.

Political career: *House of Commons:* MP (Labour) for Batley and Morley 1979-83. Contested Batley and Spen 1983 and 1987 general elections. Frontbench Opposition Spokesperson for: Trade, Aviation, Shipping, Film Industry 1981-82, Prices and Consumer Protection 1982. *House of Lords:* Raised to the peerage as Baron Woolmer of Leeds, of Leeds in the County of West Yorkshire 1999. Chair, Yorkshire and Humber Regional Peers Group 2002-09. EU Sub-committee B (Energy, Industry and Transport/Internal Market): Member 1999-2002, Chair 2002-06; Member: European Union 2002-06, 2016-, Draft Climate Change Bill Joint Committee 2007; EU Sub-committee A (Economic and Financial Affairs and International Trade): Co-opted member 2007-10, Member 2010-12; Member: Secondary Legislation Scrutiny 2013-16, Personal Service Companies 2013-14, Built Environment 2015-16, EU Financial Affairs Sub-committee 2016-. *Councils and public bodies:* Leeds County Borough Council: Councillor 1970-74, Deputy Leader 1972-74; Councillor, Leeds Metropolitan District Council 1973-78; West Yorkshire Metropolitan County Council: Councillor 1973-80, Deputy Leader 1973-75, Leader 1975-77, Leader of the Opposition 1977-79; Chair: Planning and Transportation Committee, Association of Metropolitan Authorities 1974-77, Regional Energy Forum, Yorkshire Forward 2001-04.

Political interests: Energy, financial markets; China, EU accession states, India, Japan.

Other: Fellow, Industry and Parliament Trust 1980; Director: Leeds United AFC 1991-96, UK Japan 21st Century Group 2005-10; International Advisory Board, White Rose East Asia Centre 2007-; Chair, Board of Governors, Leeds Metropolitan University 2010-13; Warwick Business School Advisory Board 2012-14. Member, Yorkshire CCC.

Recreations: Football (Leeds United AFC supporter), cricket.

The Lord Woolmer of Leeds, House of Lords, London SW1A 0PW
Tel: 020 7219 8520 *Email:* woolmerk@parliament.uk

NON-AFFILIATED

WORCESTER, LORD BISHOP OF

WORCESTER (113th Bishop of), John Geoffrey Inge. Born 26 February 1955.

Education: Kent College, Canterbury; St Chads College, Durham (BSc chemistry); Keble College, Oxford (PGCE); College of the Resurrection, Mirfield, Yorkshire.

Non-political career: Chemistry teacher, Lancing College; Diocese of Chichester: Ordained deacon 1983, Ordained priest 1984; Chaplain: Lancing College, Harrow School; Vicar, St Luke's Church, Wallsend; Ely Cathedral: Residentiary Canon, Vice Dean 1999-2003; Bishop of Huntingdon 2003-08; Bishop of Worcester 2008-.

Political career: *House of Lords:* Entered House of Lords 2012. *Councils and public bodies:* Lord High Almoner to HM The Queen 2013-.

Other: Member: World Development Movement, Amnesty International; Trustee, Common Purpose.

Publications: A Christian Theology of Place (Ashgate, 2003); Living Love: In Conversation with the No. 1 Ladies' Detective Agency (Inspire, 2007).

Rt Rev the Lord Bishop of Worcester, House of Lords, London SW1A 0PW
Tel: 020 7219 5353
The Old Palace, Deansway, Worcester WR1 2JE *Tel:* 01905 20537
Email: generalinfo@cofe-worcester.org.uk *Website:* www.cofe-worcester.org.uk
Twitter: @BishopWorcester

NON-AFFILIATED

WORTHINGTON, BARONESS

WORTHINGTON (Life Baroness) Bryony Katherine Worthington; cr 2011. Born 19 September 1971; Married Dr Srivas Chennu 2010 (1 son).

Education: Queens' College, Cambridge (BA English literature 1993).

Non-political career: Fundraiser, Operation Raleigh; Wildlife and Countryside Link; Campaigner, Friends of the Earth; Department of Energy and Climate Change (on secondment); Policy adviser, Scottish and Southern Electricity; Founder and director, Sandbag 2008-.

Political career: *House of Lords:* Raised to the peerage as Baroness Worthington, of Cambridge in the County of Cambridgeshire 2011. Opposition Whip 2012-15; Opposition Spokesperson for Energy and Climate Change 2013-15. *Other:* Left the Labour group in the Lords April 2017; now sits as Non-Affiliated.

Political interests: Environment, climate change.

The Baroness Worthington, House of Lords, London SW1A 0PW
Tel: 020 7219 8987 *Email:* worthingtonb@parliament.uk *Twitter:* @bryworthington

LIBERAL DEMOCRAT

WRIGGLESWORTH, LORD

WRIGGLESWORTH (Life Baron), Ian William Wrigglesworth; cr 2013. Born 8 December 1939; Son of late Edward Wrigglesworth; Married Patricia Truscott 1967 (2 sons 1 daughter).

Education: Stockton Grammar School; Stockton-Billingham Technical College; College of St Mark and St John, Chelsea (Music and English Teaching Qualification 1966).

Non-political career: Personal assistant to Sir Ronald Gould as General Secretary of National Union of Teachers; Press and public affairs manager, National Giro; Divisional director, Smith's Industries 1976-2000; Deputy chair, John Livingston and Sons Ltd 1987-95; Director: CIT Holdings Ltd 1987-2003, Northern Development Co 1997-99, Tyne Tees TV 2002-06; Port of Tyne: Director 2003-05, Chair 2005-12; Chair, Bluehall Properties (now Durham Group) 2008-. Former Member: NUT; USDAW; NUJ.

Political career: *House of Commons:* MP for Teesside, Thornaby February 1974-83, for Stockton South 1983-87 (Labour/Co-op 1974-81, SDP/All 1981-87). Contested Stockton South 1987 general election. PPS to: Alex Lyon as Minister of State, Home Office March-November 1974, Roy Jenkins as Home Secretary 1974-76; Opposition Spokesperson on the Civil Service 1979-80; SDP Spokesperson on Economic Affairs and Taxation, Trade and Industry, Energy, Small Businesses and Consumer Affairs. *House of Lords:* Raised to the peerage as Baron Wrigglesworth, of Norton on Tees in the County of Durham 2013. Member: Economic Affairs Finance Bill Sub-committee 2014, 2017, Trade Union and Party Funding 2016. *Other:* Research officer, Co-operative Party; Member, Labour Party 1962-81; Founder member, Social Democrats 1981; Liberal Democrats: President 1988-90, Chair: Business Forum, National Trustees 2002-12, National Treasurer 2012-15. *Councils and public bodies:* Governor and Deputy Chair, Teesside University 1993-2002; DL, Tyne and Wear 2005-13; Deputy Chair, Regional Growth Fund Advisory Panel 2010-12.

Political interests: Economic, industrial and regional policy; India, USA.

Other: Chair: Northern region, CBI 1992-94, Northern Business Forum 1996-98, UK Land Estates 1995-2009, Government Policy Consultants Ltd 1998-2000, Newcastle-Gateshead Initiative 1999-2004, Baltic Centre for Contemporary Art 2004-09. Liveryman, Worshipful Company of Founders. Freedom, City of London 1995. Honorary Doctorate of: Music, Northumbria University 2011, Business Administration, Teesside University 2012. Kt 1991; *Clubs:* Groucho, Reform Club.

Recreations: Skiing, music, walking, cycling.

The Lord Wrigglesworth, House of Lords, London SW1A 0PW
Tel: 020 7219 8743 *Email:* wrigglesworthi@parliament.uk

CROSSBENCH

WRIGHT OF RICHMOND, LORD

WRIGHT OF RICHMOND (Life Baron), Patrick Richard Henry Wright; cr. 1994. Born 28 June 1931; Son of late Herbert and Rachel Wright; Married Virginia Gaffney 1958 (2 sons 1 daughter).

Education: Marlborough College, Wiltshire; Merton College, Oxford (BA literae humaniores 1955); Arabic, French.

Non-political career: Army national service (Royal Artillery) 1950-51. Diplomatic Service 1955-91: Middle East Centre for Arab Studies 1956-57, Third Secretary, Beirut Embassy 1958-60, Private Secretary and later First Secretary, Washington DC Embassy 1960-65, Private Secretary to Permanent Under-Secretary, Foreign Office 1965-67, First Secretary and Head of Chancery, Cairo Embassy 1967-70, Deputy Political Resident, Bahrain 1971-72, Head of Middle East Department, FCO 1972-74, Private Secretary (Overseas Affairs) to Prime Ministers Harold Wilson and James Callaghan 1974-77, Ambassador to: Luxembourg 1977-79, Syria 1979-81; Deputy Under-Secretary of State, FCO and chair, Joint Intelligence Committee 1982-84, Ambassador to Saudi Arabia 1984-86, Permanent Under-Secretary of State and Head of the Diplomatic Service 1986-91; Director: Barclays Bank plc 1991-96, British Petroleum Co (now BP plc) 1991-2001; De La Rue: Director 1991-2000, Consultant 2001-10; Advisory director, Unilever 1991-99; Director, BAA 1992-98; Member, Security Commission 1993-2002.

Political career: *House of Lords:* Raised to the peerage as Baron Wright of Richmond, of Richmond upon Thames in the London Borough of Richmond upon Thames 1994. EU Sub-committee F (Home Affairs): Member 2001-07, Chair 2004-07; Member: Science and Technology Sub-committee I (Science and International Agreements) 2003-04, European Union 2004-08, Conventions Joint Committee 2006; EU Sub-committee E (Law and Institutions): Member 2007-08, Co-opted Member 2008-10; Member, EU Sub-committee E (Justice and Institutions) 2010-11.

Political interests: Foreign affairs (particularly Middle East), public service; Middle East and Islamic world.

Other: Substitute Member, UK Delegation to Parliamentary Assembly of Council of Europe 2016; Governor: Ditchley Foundation 1986-2011, Wellington College 1991-2001; OStJ: Registrar 1991-95, Director of Overseas Relations 1995-97; Royal College of Music: Council member 1991-2001, Fellow 1994-; Council member, Atlantic College 1993-2000; Chair, Council, Royal Institute of International Affairs 1995-99; Home-Start International: Chairman 2004-07, Hon President 2008-11; Governor, Edward VII Hospital (Sister Agnes) 2005-07; Fellow, Wellington College 2009; St John Hospital, Medical Aid for Palestinians. Hon. Fellow, Merton College, Oxford 1987. Parliamentary Speech of the Year, *House Magazine* 2004. CMG 1978; KCMG 1984; GCMG 1989; KStJ 1990; *Clubs:* Oxford and Cambridge Club.

Publications: Contributor, The Arabists of Shemlan and Envoys to the Arab World (Stacey International).

Recreations: Piano duets, stamp collecting.

The Lord Wright of Richmond GCMG, House of Lords, London SW1A 0PW
Tel: 020 7219 5353
Email: prhwright@btinternet.com

CONSERVATIVE

WYLD, BARONESS

WYLD (Life Baroness), Laura Lee Wyld; cr 2017. Born 13 January 1978.

Education: Cambridge University (BA history).

Non-political career: Campaigns officer, Conservative Central Office; Research consultant, Quiller Consultants; Consultant, Lexington Communications 2003-07; Fishburn Hedges: Consultant 2007-09, Associate Director 2009-13; Head, Prime Minister's Appointments Unit 2013-16; Senior adviser, Strategic Communications Alliance.

Political career: *House of Lords:* Raised to the peerage as Baroness Wyld, of Gosforth in the City of Newcastle upon Tyne 2017.

Other: Council member, Institute of Directors; Board member, Urology Foundation 2017-.

The Baroness Wyld, House of Lords, London SW1A 0PW
Tel: 020 7219 3000

NON-AFFILIATED

YORK, LORD ARCHBISHOP OF

YORK (97th Archbishop of), John Mugabi Tucker Sentamu. Born 10 June 1949; Son of late John and Ruth Walakira; Married Margaret Wanambwa 1973.

Education: Kitante and Old Kampala Secondary Schools, Uganda; Makerere University, Uganda (LLB 1971); Diploma in legal practice, Uganda 1972; Selwyn College, Cambridge (BA 1976; PhD 1984); Ridley Hall, Cambridge.

Non-political career: Advocate, High Court of Uganda 1971-; Ordained 1979; Assistant chaplain, Selwyn College, Cambridge 1979; Chaplain, HM Remand Centre, Latchmere House 1979-82; Assistant curate: St Andrew, Ham 1979-82, St Paul, Herne Hill, London 1982-83; Holy Trinity and St Mathias, Tulse Hill London: Respectively priest and vicar 1983-84; Vicar 1985-96; Priest, St Saviour, Brixton Hill, London 1987-89; Honorary Canon, Southwark Cathedral 1993-96; Stepney Area Bishop, London 1996-2002; Bishop of Birmingham 2002-05; Archbishop of York 2005-; Hon. Master Bencher, Gray's Inn 2007-.

Political career: *House of Lords:* Entered House of Lords 2005. *Councils and public bodies:* Member, General Synod 1985-96, 2002-.

Political interests: Legal, community, young people, faith; Africa.

Other: Chair, Sickle Cell and Thalassaemia Screening Programme 2001-13; President: Youth for Christ 2004-, YMCA England 2005-; Sponsor, York Fairness Commission 2011-12; Fellow, Royal Society of Arts; Chair, Living Wage Commission 2013-14; Fellow: University College Christ Church, Canterbury 2001, Queen Mary College, University of London 2001; Honorary fellow, Selwyn College, Cambridge 2005; Visiting fellow, Harold Turner; Fellow, University of Otago, New Zealand 2014; Honorary fellow, St Margaret's College, Dunedin, New Zealand 2014. Freedom: City of London 2000, Montego Bay, Jamaica 2007. Chancellor: York St John University 2006-, Cumbria University 2007-. Twenty honorary doctorates from UK, Canada, Caribbean and US universities. Midlander of the Year 2003; Yorkshire Man of the Year 2007; Speaker of the Year 2007; York Ambassador, York Tourism Awards 2010. PC 2005.

Recreations: Cooking, music, rugby, football, athletics.

Most Rev and Rt Hon the Archbishop of York, House of Lords, London SW1A 0PW
Tel: 020 7219 5353
Bishopthorpe Palace, Bishopthorpe, York YO23 2GE *Tel:* 01904 707021 *Fax:* 01904 772389
Email: office@archbishopofyork.org
Website: www.archbishopofyork.org *Twitter:* @JohnSentamu

CONSERVATIVE

YOUNG OF COOKHAM, LORD

Government Spokesperson, Cabinet Office; Government Whip (Lord in Waiting)

YOUNG OF COOKHAM (Life Baron), George Samuel Knatchbull Young; cr 2015. Born 16 July 1941; Son of late Sir George Young, 5th Bt, CMG, and Elizabeth Young, née Knatchbull-Hugessen; Married Aurelia Nemon-Stuart 1964 (2 sons 2 daughters).

Education: Eton College; Christ Church, Oxford (BA philosophy, politics and economics 1963, MA); Surrey University (MPhil economics 1971).

Non-political career: Economic adviser, Post Office 1969-74.

Political career: *House of Commons:* MP (Conservative) for Ealing Acton February 1974-97, for North West Hampshire 1997-2010, for North West Hampshire (revised boundary) 2010-15. Opposition Whip 1976-79; Parliamentary Under-Secretary of State: Department of Health and Social Services 1979-81, Department of Environment 1981-86; Government Whip 1990; Department of Environment: Minister for Housing and Planning 1990-93, Minister for Housing, Inner Cities and Construction 1993-94; Financial Secretary, HM Treasury 1994-95; Secretary of State for Transport 1995-97; Shadow Secretary of State for Defence 1997-98; Shadow Leader of the House of Commons 1998-99, 2009-10; Member, House of Commons Commission 1998-99, 2009-12; Shadow Chancellor of the Duchy of Lancaster 1998-99; Shadow Leader of the House of Commons and Constitutional Affairs 1999-2000; Contested Speaker election 2000, 2009; Member, Speaker's Committee for the Independent Parliamentary Standards Authority 2009-12; Leader of the House of Commons, Lord Privy Seal 2010-12; Member, Public Accounts Commission 2010-12; Parliamentary Secretary to the Treasury; Chief Whip 2012-14; Member, Parliamentary and Political Service Honours Committee 2012-14. Member: Public Accounts 1994-95, Modernisation of the House of Commons 1998-2000, Selection 2001-09; Chair, Standards and Privileges 2001-09; Member: Liaison 2001-09, Liaison (Liaison Sub-Committee) 2002-09, Reform of the House of Commons 2009. Chair, Conservative Party: Committee for Defence 1997-98, Constitution Committee 1998-2000. *House of Lords:* Raised to the peerage as Baron Young of Cookham, of Cookham in the Royal County of Berkshire 2015. Government Whip (Lord in Waiting) 2016-; Government Spokesperson for: HM Treasury 2016, Cabinet Office 2016-. Member, Privileges and Conduct 2015-16. *Other:* Patron, Tory Reform Group; Former Vice-chair, Association of Conservative Peers. *Councils and public bodies:* Councillor: London Borough of Lambeth 1968-71, GLC 1970-73.

Political interests: Housing, disability, health education, constitutional reform.

Other: Trustee: Guinness Trust 1986-90, Foundations Independent Living Trust 2002-10. Backbencher of the Year, *Spectator* awards 1988; Resurrection of the Year, *Spectator* awards 2012. 6th Baronet, created 1813, succeeded his father 1960; PC 1993; CH 2012.

Publications: Tourism – Blessing or Blight (1970); I'm Keeping Young (2015).

Recreations: Bicycling, opera.

Rt Hon the Lord Young of Cookham CH, House of Lords, London SW1A 0PW
Tel: 020 7219 6665 *Email:* youngg@parliament.uk

CONSERVATIVE

YOUNG OF GRAFFHAM, LORD

YOUNG OF GRAFFHAM (Life Baron), David Ivor Young; cr. 1984. Born 27 February 1932; Son of late Joseph Young; Married Lita Marianne Shaw 1956 (2 daughters).

Education: Christ's College, Finchley; University College, London (LLB 1954).

Non-political career: Solicitor 1956; Executive, Great Universal Stores 1956-61; Chair: Eldonwall Ltd 1961-75, Manufacturers Hanover Property Services Ltd 1974-84; Industrial adviser/special adviser, Department of Industry 1979-82; Chair, Manpower Services Commission 1982-84; Fellow, University College London 1988; Executive Chair, Cable and Wireless plc 1990-95; Director, Salomon Inc 1990-94; Chair of several companies, including: Young Associates Ltd 1996-, Pixology Ltd 1997-, Newhaven Management Services 1997-, Spectrum Interactive plc, TSSI Ltd, Camcon Ltd; Director: Deeptek Ltd, Kashflow Software Ltd.

Political career: *House of Lords:* Raised to the peerage as Baron Young of Graffham, of Graffham in the County of West Sussex 1984. Cabinet Minister without Portfolio 1984-85; Secretary of State for: Employment 1985-87, Trade and Industry 1987-89; Adviser to the Prime Minister on: Health and Safety Law and Practice 2010, Enterprise 2010, 2011-. Member: Science and Technology 2003-06, Science and Technology Sub-committees: II (Science and the Regional Development Agencies) 2003, II (Renewable Energy) 2003-04, II (Energy Efficiency) 2004-. *Other:* Deputy chair, Conservative Party 1989-90. *Councils and public bodies:* DL, West Sussex 1999-.

Other: Chair, West Sussex Economic Forum 1993-2001; President, Institute of Directors 1993-2004; Chair of Council, University College, London 1995-2005; Chair, Chichester Festival Theatre Ltd 1997-; Prince's Trust: Chair, Development Board 2003-07, Trustees council member 2004-07; Chair and trustee, Peter Cruddas Foundation 2006-; Trustee, MBI AL Jaber Foundation 2007-; President and trustee, Chai Cancer Care 2007-. Honorary Doctorate of Science, Cranfield University 1986; Doctor of Laws, Honoris Causa, University College London 2006. PC 1984; CH 2015.

Publications: The Enterprise Years (1990).

Recreations: Photography, music, book collecting, fishing.

Rt Hon the Lord Young of Graffham CH DL, House of Lords, London SW1A 0PW
Tel: 020 7219 5353

YOUNG OF HORNSEY, BARONESS

CROSSBENCH

YOUNG OF HORNSEY (Life Baroness), Margaret Omolola (Lola) Young; cr. 2004. Born 1 June 1951; Daughter of Maxwell Fela Young and Yele Santos; Married Barrie Birch 1984 (1 son).

Education: Parliament Hill School for Girls, London; New College of Speech and Drama (Diploma dramatic art 1975; Teaching Certificate 1976); Middlesex Polytechnic/University (BA contemporary cultural studies 1988; PhD British film 1995).

Non-political career: Residential social worker, London Borough of Islington 1971-73; Professional actor 1976-84; Co-director and training and development manager, Haringey Arts Council 1985-89; Freelance lecturer and arts consultant 1989-91; Lecturer in media studies, Polytechnic of West London/Thames Valley University 1990-92; Middlesex University 1992-2001: Lecturer, Senior lecturer, Principal lecturer, Professor of cultural studies, Emeritus professor; Project director, Archives and Museum of Black Heritage 1997-2001; Head of culture, Greater London Authority 2002-04; Visiting professor, Birkbeck College, London; Founder, Cultural Brokers Arts and Heritage Consultancy 2004-.

Political career: *House of Lords:* Raised to the peerage as Baroness Young of Hornsey, of Hornsey in the London Borough of Haringey 2004. Co-opted Member, EU Sub-committee G (Social Policy and Consumer Affairs) 2007-10; Chair, EU Sub-committee G (Social Policies and Consumer Protection) 2010-12; Member: European Union 2010-13, Joint Committee on the Draft House of Lords Reform Bill 2011-12, EU Sub-committee C (External Affairs) 2012-15, Sexual Violence in Conflict 2015-16.

Political interests: Arts and culture, children and young people in care, mental health, equalities, London, North and South West England; Commonwealth, Sub-saharan Africa, USA.

Other: Commissioner, Royal Commission on Historical Manuscripts 2000-01; Board member: National Theatre 2000-03, South Bank Centre 2002-08; Chair: Arts Advisory Committee, British Council 2004-08, Nitro Theatre Company 2004-09; Patron, Post-adoption Centre 2004-; Council member, RSA 2005-08; Patron, Josephine Wolf Trust 2007-; Chair, Commonwealth group on Culture and Development 2008-12; Commissioner, English Heritage 2011-; FRSA 2000. Freeman, Tallow Chandlers Company. OBE 2001; *Clubs:* RSA, Hospital Club.

Publications: Numerous newspaper articles and radio and television broadcasts; Fear of the Dark: 'Race', Gender and Sexuality in Cinema (Routledge, 1996).

Recreations: Walking, cinema, theatre, visual arts, gardening, reading.

Professor the Baroness Young of Hornsey OBE, House of Lords, London SW1A 0PW
Tel: 020 7219 5991 *Email:* younglo@parliament.uk
Email: lola.young@culturalbrokers.co.uk *Twitter:* @LolaHornsey

YOUNG OF NORWOOD GREEN, LORD

LABOUR

YOUNG OF NORWOOD GREEN (Life Baron), Anthony Ian Young; cr. 2004. Born 16 April 1942; Son of late Henry and Sheila Young; Married Doreen Goodman (divorced 1984) (1 son 2 daughters); married Margaret Newnham 1985 (1 son 1 daughter).

Education: Harrow County Grammar School.

Non-political career: GPO (General Post Office) telecommunications apprentice 1958; Post Office Engineering Union: Union branch officer 1967, Member, National Executive Committee 1989-95; General secretary, National Communications Union 1989-95; Communication Workers' Union: Joint General secretary 1995-98, Senior deputy general secretary 1998-2002; Trades Union Council: Member, General Council 1989-2002, President 2001-02; Member, Communication Workers Union (CWU).

Political career: *House of Lords:* Raised to the peerage as Baron Young of Norwood Green, of Norwood Green in the London Borough of Ealing 2004. Parliamentary Under-Secretary of State (Skills and Apprenticeships 2008-09, Postal Affairs and Employment Relations 2009-10) and Government Spokesperson, Department for Innovation, Universities and Skills/Business, Innovation and Skills 2008-10; Government Whip 2008-10; Opposition Spokesperson for Business, Innovation and Skills 2010-15. Co-opted Member, European Union Sub-committee F (Home Affairs) 2007-08; Member: Crossrail Bill 2008, High Speed Rail (London-West Midlands) Bill 2016, EU Energy and Environment Sub-committee 2017-. *Councils and public bodies:* Member: Wilton Park Academic Council 1996-2005, Employment Tribunal Steering Board 1997-2003; Governor, BBC 1998-2002; Vice-chair, Ethical Trading Initiative; Chair, One World Broadcasting Trust 2002-09; Member, Armed Forces Pay Review Board -2008; Governor, Three Bridges Primary School.

Countries of interest: China, Italy, USA.

Other: Kt 2002.

Recreations: Cycling, tennis, table tennis, reading, gardening.

The Lord Young of Norwood Green, House of Lords, London SW1A 0PW
Tel: 020 7219 3176 *Email:* younga@parliament.uk

LABOUR

YOUNG OF OLD SCONE, BARONESS

YOUNG OF OLD SCONE (Life Baroness), Barbara Scott Young; cr. 1997. Born 8 April 1948; Daughter of late George Young and late Mary Young.

Education: Perth Academy; Edinburgh University (MA classics 1970); Strathclyde University (DipSocSci 1971); DipHSM 1974; Chartered Environmentalist 2005.

Non-political career: Sector administrator, Glasgow Health Board 1973-78; Director of planning and development, St Thomas' Health District, London 1978-79; District general administrator, Kensington and Chelsea and Westminster Area Health Authority 1979-82; District administrator, Haringey Health Authority (HA), London 1982-85; District general manager: Paddington and North Kensington HA 1985-88, Parkside HA 1988-91; Chief executive, Royal Society for the Protection of Birds 1991-98; Chair, English Nature 1998-2000; Non-executive director, Anglian Water 1998-2000; Chief executive: Environment Agency 2000-08, Diabetes UK 2010-15.

Political career: *House of Lords:* Raised to the peerage as Baroness Young of Old Scone, of Old Scone in Perth and Kinross 1997. Member: Built Environment 2015-16, Science and Technology 2016-. *Councils and public bodies:* BBC: Member, General Advisory Council 1985-88, Vice-chair 1998-2000; Committee member, Secretary of State for the Environment's Going for Green Initiative 1994-96; Member: UK Round Table on Sustainability 1995-2000, Commission on the Future of the Voluntary Sector 1995-97, Committee on the Public Understanding of Science 1996-97; Chair, Care Quality Commission 2008-09; Commissioner, Commission on Assisted Dying 2010-.

Political interests: Environment, broadcasting, health and social care, equality and rights.

Other: President, Institute of Health Services Management 1987-88; Patron, Institute of Ecological and Environment Management 1993-; Trustee, National Council for Voluntary Organisations 1994-98; Vice-President: Flora and Fauna International 1998-, World Council, Birdlife International 1999-, Plantlife 2000-15, RSPB 2000-; Trustee, Institute for Public Policy Research 2000-09; President: Beds, Cambs, Northants and Peterborough Wildlife Trust 2001-, British Trust of Ornithology 2004-13, South Georgia Heritage Trust 2008-; Bedfordshire Symphony Orchestra; Patron, Lantra; Chair: Environmentalists for Europe 2015-, Woodland Trust 2016-; Honorary member, RICS; Honorary fellow: Geologists Association, Linnean Society, Royal Society of Edinburgh; Eminent fellow, IAgrE; CIWEM Chartered Environmentalist; CIWM; Woodland Trust, RSPB, Action Aid, Plantlife, Dignity in Dying, Diabetes UK, Birdlife International, South Georgia Heritage Trust, Bedfordhsire, Cambridgeshire and Northamptonshire Wildlife Trust. Chancellor, Cranfield University 2010-. Fifteen honorary doctorates; Honorary Fellow, Sydney Sussex College.

Recreations: Cinema, gardening, dressage.

The Baroness Young of Old Scone, House of Lords, London SW1A 0PW
Tel: 020 7219 1000 *Email:* youngb@parliament.uk *Twitter:* @youngb48

CONSERVATIVE

YOUNGER OF LECKIE, VISCOUNT

Government Whip (Lord in Waiting)

YOUNGER OF LECKIE (5th Viscount, UK), James Edward George Younger; cr. 1923; 5th Bt of Leckie (UK) 1911. Born 11 November 1955; Son of 4th Viscount and Diana Tuck; Married Jennie Wootton 1988 (1 son 2 daughters).

Education: Cargilfield School, Edinburgh; Winchester College; St Andrews University (MA Hons medieval history 1979); Henley Management College (MBA 1993).

Non-political career: Personnel manager, Coats Patons 1979-84; Recruitment consultant, Angela Mortimer Ltd 1984-86; Executive search consultant, Stephens Consultancies 1986-92; Director, McInnes Younger 1992-94; Human Resources director, UBS Wealth Management 1994-2004; Director, Culliford Edmunds Associates 2004-07; Consultant, Eban Ltd 2007-10.

Political career: *House of Lords:* Elected Hereditary peer 2010-; Party Whip 2010-12; Government Whip (Lord in Waiting) 2012-13, 2015-; Government Spokesperson for: Culture, Olympics, Media and Sport/Culture, Media and Sport 2012-13, Scotland 2012-13, 2015-16, Attorney General's Office 2012, Advocate General for Scotland 2012, Law Officers 2012-13, 2 015-16, Transport 2012-13, 2015-16, Communities and Local Government 2015-16, Energy and Climate Change 2015-16, Northern Ireland 2015-16, Wales 2015-16, Higher Education 2016-17; Parliamentary Under-Secretary of State and Government Spokesperson, Department for Business, Innovation and Skills 2013-14. Member: Public Service and Demographic Change 2012, Joint Committee on the Draft Protection of Charities Bill 2014-15. *Other:* Chair, Buckingham Conservative Constituency Association 2006-10; Member, Association of Conservative Peers 2006-; Elected member, area board, Oxfordshire and Buckinghamshire Conservatives 2009-13; Chair, Milton Keynes Conservative Association 2010-13.

Political interests: Big Society, tourism, War Widows Association, localism, sports in schools, diversity and corporate responsibility, human resources, employment law, intergenerational; Scotland.

Other: Member, Queen's Bodyguard for Scotland, Royal Company of Archers; Highland Society of London: Director 2005-12, President 2012-; Member, Parliamentary Choir; President of Life Members, Kate Kennedy Club; Vice-president, War Widows Association; Trustee, Mrs W Wootton Trust; Patron: Almshouses Association, Garsington Opera, Brands Museum, Buckinghamshire County Museum; Trustee, Globe Run; London Committee Member, National Trust for Scotland; Member: Chartered Institute of Marketing, Association of MBAs; Pace Aylesbury, Aylesbury Museum. White Hunter Cricket Club.

Recreations: Sailing, cricket, skiing, running, tennis, DIY, highland dancing, country pursuits.

The Viscount Younger of Leckie, House of Lords, London SW1A 0PW
Tel: 020 7219 3527 *Email:* youngerj@parliament.uk

ANALYIS OF PEERS

Peers' Political Interests 988
Peers' Countries of Interest 1015
MPs who are now Peers 1028
Hereditary Peers 1032
Bishops 1033
Law Lords 1033
Peers on leave of absence 1034
Women Members 1034
Peers by Party 1045
Select Committees 1053
Principal Office Holders and Staff 1059
Political Offices 1060

Peers' Political Interests

For precise details of individuals' stated interests, see relevant biography. The interests listed are supplied by Peers themselves.

Animals

See also:
- Animal rights and welfare
- Horses

Business and industry

See also:
- Business
- Capital and financial markets
- Corporate governance
- Economics and finance
- Economy
- Enterprise
- EU economy
- Finance
- Financial services
- Personal finance
- Public finance
- Tax
- Trade

Children and Families

See also:
- Childcare
- Children
- Family

Communities, planning and local government

See also:
- Built environment
- Communities
- Construction industry
- Housing
- Local government
- Planning
- Urban communities

Culture, media and sport

See also:
- Architecture
- Arts
- Broadcasting
- Creative industries
- Culture
- Gambling and lotteries
- Heritage
- Media
- Music
- Performing arts
- Tourism
- Visual arts

Defence and security

See also:
- Armed Forces
- Defence
- Defence equipment and weapon systems
- Security

Disability

See also:
- Deaf children
- Disability rights
- Disabled children
- Learning disabilities

Education and skills

See also:
- Education
- Further and higher education
- Skills

Employment and welfare

See also:
- Employment
- Employment Law
- Equal opportunities and diversity
- Health and safety at work
- Unemployment and jobseeking
- Welfare

Energy and Utilities

See also:
- Energy
- Energy Conservation
- Energy Policy
- Gas Industry
- Utilites

Environment, agriculture and rural affairs

See also:
- Agriculture
- Countryside
- Environment
- Farming
- Fisheries
- Forestry
- Pollution
- Rural affairs
- Rural communities
- Sustainable development

European affairs

See also:
- European Union
- Regional policy

Government, politics and public administration

See also:
- Civil Service
- Constitutional Affairs
- Democracy and elections
- Devolved administrations
- Government
- Ireland
- Policy making

Political parties
Politics
Scotland

Health, wellbeing and care

See also:
Care
Food and drink
Health
Health and social care professionals
Medical ethics
Medicines
Mental health
National Health Service

Home affairs

See also:
Charities and volunteers
Consumer affairs
Crime
Crime prevention
Human rights
Immigration and nationality
Justice system
Law
Police
Prisons
Security
Social affairs
Social exclusion
Social inclusion
Social justice
Victims of crime
Youth justice

Information and communication

See also:
Communications
Communications industries
Freedom of information
Information and communication technology
Intellectual property

International affairs

See also:
Foreign policy
Human rights
International development and aid
Terrorism
Third World
Transatlantic relations

Religion

See also:
Church Affairs
Islam
Theology

Science, technology and research

See also:
Biotechnology
Engineering
Research and development
Science
Technology

Transport

See also:
Air transport
Aviation
Freight transport
Infrastructure
Public transport
Road safety
Road transport

Adoption

Baroness Gibson of Market Rasen	*Lab*	p693

Age discrimination

Baroness Barker	*Lib Dem*	p571

Agriculture

Baroness Bakewell of Hardington Mandeville	*Lib Dem*	p570
Lord Boswell of Aynho	*NA*	p590
Viscount Brookeborough	*CB*	p600
Lord Burnett	*Lib Dem*	p606
Baroness Byford	*Con*	p609
Lord Carlile of Berriew	*NA*	p615
Lord Cavendish of Furness	*Con*	p619
Lord Christopher	*Lab*	p624
Lord Colgrain	*Con*	p629
Earl of Courtown	*Con*	p635
Lord Curry of Kirkharle	*CB*	p644
Lord Dannatt	*CB*	p644
Lord Davies of Stamford	*Lab*	p648
Lord Dixon-Smith	*Con*	p655
Lord Framlingham	*Con*	p686
Lord Gardiner of Kimble	*Con*	p690
Lord Hague of Richmond	*Con*	p710
Lord Hanningfield	*NA*	p716
Lord Haskins	*CB*	p722
Earl of Home	*Con*	p736
Earl Howe	*Con*	p740
Lord Hughes of Woodside	*Lab*	p744
Lord Inglewood	*Con*	p750
Lord Kilclooney	*CB*	p766
Earl of Lindsay	*Con*	p786
Marquess of Lothian	*Con*	p793
Earl of Lytton	*CB*	p796
Lord MacGregor of Pulham Market	*Con*	p799
Baroness Mallalieu	*Lab*	p808
Countess of Mar	*CB*	p811

Duke of Montrose *Con* p821
Lord Morris of Aberavon *Lab* p825
Baroness Neville-Rolfe *Con* p833
Lord Northbourne *CB* p837
Lord Northbrook *Con* p837
Baroness O'Cathain *Con* p841
Lord Palmer *CB* p849
Lord Plumb *Con* p860
Lord Rooker *Lab* p887
Lord Rotherwick *Con* p889
Earl of Selborne *Con* p900
Baroness Shephard of Northwold *Con* p903
Earl of Shrewsbury and Waterford *Con* p907
Lord Taylor of Holbeach *Con* p934

Air transport

Lord Kirkhope of Harrogate *Con* p771

Airports

Lord McKenzie of Luton *Lab* p803
Lord Smith of Leigh *Lab* p914

Alcoholism

Lord Brooke of Alverthorpe *Lab* p599
Lord Mancroft *Con* p809
Lord Mitchell *NA* p818
Baroness Newlove *Con* p834

Animal rights and welfare

Lord Black of Brentwood *Con* p583
Baroness Fookes *Con* p681
Baroness Gale *Lab* p689
Baroness Howarth of Breckland *CB* p739
Baroness Mallalieu *Lab* p808
Lord Trees *CB* p942

Animals

Baroness Neville-Rolfe *Con* p833

Anti-social behaviour

Baroness Newlove *Con* p834

Apprenticeships

Lord Cotter *Lib Dem* p635
Lord Martin of Springburn *CB* p813

Architecture

Lord Beith *Lib Dem* p575
Lord Lloyd-Webber *Con* p791
Lord Purvis of Tweed *Lib Dem* p867
Baroness Whitaker *Lab* p967

Armed Forces

Lord Bilimoria *CB* p580
Lord Colgrain *Con* p629
Lord Harries of Pentregarth *CB* p718
Lord Morris of Aberavon *Lab* p825
Lord Rowe-Beddoe *CB* p889

Arts

Lord Aberdare *CB* p551
Lord Adebowale *CB* p552
Lord Archer of Weston-Super-Mare *NA* p562
Lord Armstrong of Ilminster *CB* p564
Baroness Bakewell *Lab* p569
Baroness Benjamin *Lib Dem* p576
Lord Bird *CB* p582
Baroness Blackstone *Lab* p584
Lord Bragg *Lab* p596
Lord Browne of Madingley *CB* p603
Lord Campbell of Pittenweem *Lib Dem* p612
Lord Carlile of Berriew *NA* p615
Earl of Clancarty *CB* p625
Lord Colwyn *Con* p631
Lord Cormack *Con* p633
Lord Crickhowell *Con* p640
Lord Davies of Oldham *Lab* p648
Lord Dobbs *Con* p655
Lord Donoughue *Lab* p656
Lord Eatwell *NA* p663
Viscount Eccles *Con* p663
Lord Grade of Yarmouth *Con* p702
Lord Hall of Birkenhead *CB* p713
Baroness Hamwee *Lib Dem* p714
Lord Howarth of Newport *Lab* p740
Lord Hoyle *Lab* p743
Lord Inglewood *Con* p750
Baroness Kidron *CB* p766
Earl of Kinnoull *CB* p770
Lord Knight of Weymouth *Lab/Co-op* p772
Lord Lisvane *CB* p789
Lord Lloyd-Webber *Con* p791
Lord Low of Dalston *CB* p793
Lord Luce *CB* p794
Lord Lupton *Con* p795
Baroness McIntosh of Hudnall *Lab* p800
Lord Maclennan of Rogart *Lib Dem* p804
Lord Marland *Con* p812
Baroness Morris of Yardley *Lab* p827
Baroness O'Cathain *Con* p841
Lord Palumbo *Con* p850
Baroness Randerson *Lib Dem* p872
Lord Renfrew of Kaimsthorn *Con* p877
Lord Rowe-Beddoe *CB* p889
Lord Selkirk of Douglas *Con* p900
Lord Skidelsky *CB* p909
Lord Sterling of Plaistow *Con* p920
Lord Stevenson of Balmacara *Lab* p923
Lord Storey *Lib Dem* p926
Lord Triesman *Lab* p944
Lord Trimble *Con* p945
Lord True *Con* p946
Baroness Wheatcroft *Con* p966
Lord Winston *Lab* p975

Asylum

Baroness Hamwee *Lib Dem* p714
Lord Hardie *CB* p717
Lord Hylton *CB* p749

Autism
Lord Clement-Jones *Lib Dem* p627
Lord Maginnis of Drumglass *Ind UU* p807

Aviation
Lord Brougham and Vaux *Con* p601
Lord Glenarthur *Con* p695
Earl of Liverpool *Con* p790
Lord MacKenzie of Culkein *Lab* p802
Lord Rotherwick *Con* p889
Viscount Simon *Lab* p908
Lord Smith of Clifton *Lib Dem* p911
Lord Soley *Lab* p916
Lord Tebbit *Con* p935
Lord Trefgarne *Con* p943

Banking and finance
Lord Lawson of Blaby *Con* p777
Lord Popat *Con* p862
Lord Williams of Elvel *Lab* p971

Banking services
Lord Triesman *Lab* p944

Big Society
Viscount Younger of Leckie *Con* p985

Biotechnology
Baroness Greenfield *CB* p705

Breast cancer
Baroness Falkender *Lab* p670

British film
Baroness Falkender *Lab* p670

Broadband
Baroness Neville-Rolfe *Con* p833

Broadcasting
Lord Birt *CB* p582
Lord Bragg *Lab* p596
Lord Crickhowell *Con* p640
Baroness Deech *CB* p651
Lord Eames *CB* p661
Lord Gordon of Strathblane *Lab* p699
Lord Griffiths of Fforestfach *Con* p709
Lord Hall of Birkenhead *CB* p713
Lord Holmes of Richmond *Con* p735
Baroness Jay of Paddington *Lab* p753
Lord Lipsey *Lab* p788
Lord Low of Dalston *CB* p793
Lord Maxton *Lab* p817
Lord Quirk *CB* p869
Lord Triesman *Lab* p944
Baroness Young of Old Scone *Lab* p984

Built environment
Lord Chidgey *Lib Dem* p623

Business
Lord Allen of Kensington *Lab* p557
Lord Bilimoria *CB* p580
Lord Blyth of Rowington *Con* p588
Lord Borwick *Con* p590
Baroness Bottomley of Nettlestone *Con* p591
Baroness Brady *Con* p596
Lord Cotter *Lib Dem* p635
Baroness Couttie *Con* p636
Lord Cromwell *CB* p641
Lord Drayson *Lab* p657
Lord Fox *Lib Dem* p685
Lord Grade of Yarmouth *Con* p702
Baroness Harding of Winscombe *Con* p718
Lord Hollick *Lab* p733
Lord Hunt of Wirral *Con* p747
Lord Jones of Cheltenham *Lib Dem* p756
Lord Kirkham *Con* p770
Lord Lupton *Con* p795
Lord Marland *Con* p812
Lord Mogg *CB* p819
Baroness Morgan of Ely *Lab* p824
Bishop of Newcastle *NA* p834
Baroness Nicol *Lab/Co-op* p835
Baroness O'Cathain *Con* p841
Lord Palmer of Childs Hill *Lib Dem* p849
Baroness Rock *Con* p884
Lord Rose of Monewden *Con* p887
Lord Taylor of Warwick *NA* p934
Lord Teverson *Lib Dem* p936
Lord Vallance of Tummel *Lib Dem* p953
Baroness Vere of Norbiton *Con* p953
Baroness Wheatcroft *Con* p966

Business and industry
Lord Ashdown of Norton-sub-Hamdon *Lib Dem* p565
Earl Attlee *Con* p567
Lord Bhattacharyya *Lab* p579
Lord Broers *CB* p599
Lord Cavendish of Furness *Con* p619
Lord Christopher *Lab* p624
Lord Davies of Stamford *Lab* p648
Baroness Dean of Thornton-le-Fylde *Lab* p649
Lord Deben *Con* p650
Lord Evans of Watford *Lab* p669
Viscount of Falkland *CB* p671
Lord Geddes *Con* p692
Baroness Golding *Lab* p698
Earl of Home *Con* p736
Lord Jones of Cheltenham *Lib Dem* p756
Lord Lee of Trafford *Lib Dem* p779
Lord Livermore *Lab* p790
Lord MacGregor of Pulham Market *Con* p799
Lord MacLaurin of Knebworth *Con* p804
Lord Mawhinney *Con* p816
Lord Moonie *Lab/Co-op* p821
Lord Moynihan *Con* p828
Lord Murphy of Torfaen *Lab* p829
Baroness Neville-Rolfe *Con* p833

Baroness Noakes *Con* p836
Baroness O'Cathain *Con* p841
Lord O'Neill of Clackmannan *Lab* p844
Baroness Quin *Lab* p868
Lord Rogan *UUP* p885
Lord Sainsbury of Turville *Lab* p893
Lord Selsdon *Con* p901
Lord Stoddart of Swindon *Ind Lab* p924
Lord Tebbit *Con* p935
Lord Triesman *Lab* p944
Lord Wigley *PlC* p969
Lord Willetts *Con* p970
Lord Wolfson of Aspley Guise *Con* p977

Cancer

Lord Clement-Jones *Lib Dem* p627

Capital and financial markets

Lord Bilimoria *CB* p580

Care

Baroness Barker *Lib Dem* p571
Baroness Emerton *CB* p667
Baroness Janke *Lib Dem* p752
Lord McAvoy *Lab/Co-op* p796
Lord Patel of Blackburn *Lab* p853
Baroness Royall of Blaisdon *Lab/Co-op* p890

Care for the elderly

Baroness Bakewell *Lab* p569
Lord Christopher *Lab* p624
Lord Lipsey *Lab* p788
Lord Martin of Springburn *CB* p813
Lord Sutherland of Houndwood *CB* p929

Charities and volunteers

Lord Allen of Kensington *Lab* p557
Earl of Arran *Con* p564
Baroness Chalker of Wallasey *Con* p621
Baroness Emerton *CB* p667
Lord Evans of Watford *Lab* p669
Lord Flight *Con* p680
Baroness Goudie *Lab* p700
Lord Howarth of Newport *Lab* p740
Lord Levy *Lab* p783
Baroness Morgan of Drefelin *CB* p823
Baroness Newlove *Con* p834
Baroness Pitkeathley *Lab* p859

Child poverty

Earl of Listowel *CB* p789

Child protection

Lord Bichard *CB* p580
Baroness Hughes of Stretford *Lab* p744
Baroness Shields *Con* p905
Baroness Walmsley *Lib Dem* p959

Children

Baroness Bakewell of Hardington Mandeville *Lib Dem* p570
Baroness Benjamin *Lib Dem* p576
Baroness Blood *Lab* p586
Lord Boateng *Lab* p588
Baroness Bottomley of Nettlestone *Con* p591
Baroness Butler-Sloss *CB* p609
Baroness Eaton *Con* p662
Baroness Gale *Lab* p689
Baroness Golding *Lab* p698
Baroness Goudie *Lab* p700
Lord Hardie *CB* p717
Lord Harrison *Lab* p721
Baroness Howarth of Breckland *CB* p739
Baroness Jowell *Lab* p759
Baroness Kidron *CB* p766
Baroness Kinnock of Holyhead *Lab* p769
Lord Kirkham *Con* p770
Baroness Lister of Burtersett *Lab* p788
Baroness Massey of Darwen *Lab* p814
Baroness Miller of Chilthorne Domer *Lib Dem* p818
Lord Morgan *Lab* p822
Baroness Morgan of Drefelin *CB* p823
Lord Northbourne *CB* p837
Baroness Paisley of St George's *DUP* p848
Baroness Stern *CB* p920
Baroness Thornton *Lab/Co-op* p939
Baroness Tyler of Enfield *Lib Dem* p950
Lord Warner *CB* p960
Lord Williams of Oystermouth *CB* p971

Children and Families

Bishop of Gloucester *NA* p696
Lord Hardie *CB* p717

Church Affairs

Baroness Richardson of Calow *CB* p880

Citizenship

Lord Alton of Liverpool *CB* p558
Lord Blunkett *Lab* p587

Civil Service

Lord Butler of Brockwell *CB* p608
Baroness Finn *Con* p679
Lord Hunt of Chesterton *Lab* p745
Lord Luce *CB* p794
Lord O'Donnell *CB* p841

Climate change

Baroness Altmann *Con* p558
Baroness Brown of Cambridge *CB* p601
Lord Duncan of Springbank *Con* p659
Baroness Featherstone *Lib Dem* p675
Lord Hannay of Chiswick *CB* p715
Lord Hunt of Kings Heath *Lab/Co-op* p746
Lord Jay of Ewelme *CB* p753
Lord Lawson of Blaby *Con* p777
Baroness Liddell of Coatdyke *Lab* p785
Lord Oxburgh *CB* p846
Lord Prescott *Lab* p864
Lord Stunell *Lib Dem* p928
Lord Turnbull *CB* p949

Commonwealth

Lord Craig of Radley	*CB*	p638
Lord Stoddart of Swindon	*Ind Lab*	p924

Communications

Lord Currie of Marylebone	*CB*	p643
Baroness Howe of Idlicote	*CB*	p741
Baroness O'Neill of Bengarve	*CB*	p843

Communities

Baroness Hanham	*Con*	p715
Earl of Lytton	*CB*	p796
Baroness Newlove	*Con*	p834
Lord Patel of Blackburn	*Lab*	p853
Lord Popat	*Con*	p862
Archbishop of York	*NA*	p981

Communities, planning and local government

Lord Arbuthnot of Edrom	*Con*	p562
Lord Cormack	*Con*	p633
Baroness Cumberlege	*Con*	p642
Lord Cunningham of Felling	*Lab*	p643
Baroness Jowell	*Lab*	p759
Baroness McIntosh of Pickering	*Con*	p801

Community Cohesion

Baroness Hussein-Ece	*Lib Dem*	p748

Community Development

Baroness Kennedy of Cradley	*Lab*	p762

Company law

Baroness Bowles of Berkhamsted	*Lib Dem*	p592

Conservation areas

Lord Marlesford	*Con*	p813
Baroness Nicol	*Lab/Co-op*	p835

Constituencies

Lord Howarth of Newport	*Lab*	p740

Constitutional Affairs

Lord Armstrong of Ilminster	*CB*	p564
Lord Beith	*Lib Dem*	p575
Lord Birt	*CB*	p582
Lord Bourne of Aberystwyth	*Con*	p591
Lord Brown of Eaton-under-Heywood	*CB*	p602
Lord Browne of Ladyton	*Lab*	p603
Lord Butler of Brockwell	*CB*	p608
Lord Carswell	*CB*	p617
Lord Cormack	*Con*	p633
Lord Darling of Roulanish	*Lab*	p645
Lord Dobbs	*Con*	p655
Lord Duncan of Springbank	*Con*	p659
Lord Dunlop	*Con*	p660
Lord Elis-Thomas	*NA*	p665
Baroness Falkner of Margravine	*Lib Dem*	p671
Lord Faulks	*Con*	p674
Lord Fellowes	*CB*	p676
Lord Forsyth of Drumlean	*Con*	p682
Lord German	*Lib Dem*	p692
Lord Gordon of Strathblane	*Lab*	p699
Baroness Gould of Potternewton	*Lab*	p701
Lord Hanningfield	*NA*	p716
Lord Hollick	*Lab*	p733
Lord Hunt of Kings Heath	*Lab/Co-op*	p746
Lord Inglewood	*Con*	p750
Lord Irvine of Lairg	*Lab*	p751
Baroness Jay of Paddington	*Lab*	p753
Earl of Kinnoull	*CB*	p770
Lord Lang of Monkton	*Con*	p776
Lord Lea of Crondall	*Lab*	p779
Lord Lisvane	*CB*	p789
Lord Luce	*CB*	p794
Lord MacGregor of Pulham Market	*Con*	p799
Lord Northbrook	*Con*	p837
Lord Norton of Louth	*Con*	p838
Lord Rooker	*Lab*	p887
Baroness Shephard of Northwold	*Con*	p903
Lord Temple-Morris	*Lab*	p936
Lord True	*Con*	p946
Lord Wallace of Saltaire	*Lib Dem*	p958

Constitutional reform

Lord Bird	*CB*	p582
Baroness Clark of Calton	*NA*	p625
Baroness Janke	*Lib Dem*	p752
Lord Lester of Herne Hill	*Lib Dem*	p782
Lord Lexden	*Con*	p784
Lord Maclennan of Rogart	*Lib Dem*	p804
Lord Marks of Henley-on-Thames	*Lib Dem*	p812
Lord Morgan	*Lab*	p822
Lord Norton of Louth	*Con*	p838
Baroness O'Neill of Bengarve	*CB*	p843
Lord Purvis of Tweed	*Lib Dem*	p867
Lord Rennard	*Lib Dem*	p877
Lord Smith of Clifton	*Lib Dem*	p911
Baroness Suttie	*Lib Dem*	p930
Lord Trefgarne	*Con*	p943
Lord Tyler	*Lib Dem*	p950
Lord Wakeham	*Con*	p955
Lord Wallace of Tankerness	*Lib Dem*	p958
Lord Young of Cookham	*Con*	p982

Construction industry

Baroness Chalker of Wallasey	*Con*	p621
Lord Selsdon	*Con*	p901
Earl of Shrewsbury and Waterford	*Con*	p907

Consumer affairs

Baroness Hayter of Kentish Town	*Lab/Co-op*	p725
Baroness Howarth of Breckland	*CB*	p739
Baroness Kennedy of Cradley	*Lab*	p762
Lord Luce	*CB*	p794
Baroness Neville-Rolfe	*Con*	p833
Lord Whitty	*Lab*	p968

Consumer rights

Baroness Altmann	*Con*	p558
Lord Deben	*Con*	p650

Lord Harris of Haringey *Lab* p719
Lord Mogg *CB* p819
Baroness Oppenheim-Barnes *Con* p844
Baroness Wilcox *Con* p969

Copyright

Lord Lucas of Crudwell and Dingwall *Con* p794
Baroness O'Neill of Bengarve *CB* p843

Corporate governance

Lord Smith of Clifton *Lib Dem* p911

Corporate Social Responsibility

Baroness Coussins *CB* p636
Baroness Warwick of Undercliffe *Lab* p961

Countryside

Lord Bragg *Lab* p596
Baroness Byford *Con* p609
Lord Cameron of Dillington *CB* p611
Lord Greaves *Lib Dem* p704
Lord Haskins *CB* p722
Lord MacGregor of Pulham Market *Con* p799

Countryside conservation

Earl of Lytton *CB* p796

Creative industries

Lord Black of Brentwood *Con* p583
Lord Clement-Jones *Lib Dem* p627
Lord Wood of Anfield *Lab* p977

Crime

Lord Bach *Lab* p568
Lord Birt *CB* p582
Baroness Evans of Bowes Park *Con* p668
Lord Low of Dalston *CB* p793
Lord Paddick *Lib Dem* p848
Baroness Stroud *Con* p927
Lord Taverne *Lib Dem* p932

Crime prevention

Lord Clement-Jones *Lib Dem* p627

Culture

Lord Aberdare *CB* p551
Lord Allen of Kensington *Lab* p557
Baroness Andrews *Lab* p561
Lord Bassam of Brighton *Lab/Co-op* p573
Baroness Benjamin *Lib Dem* p576
Lord Bilimoria *CB* p580
Lord Browne of Madingley *CB* p603
Earl of Clancarty *CB* p625
Baroness Doocey *Lib Dem* p656
Lord Dunlop *Con* p660
Lord Foster of Bath *Lib Dem* p683
Lord Hall of Birkenhead *CB* p713
Lord Holmes of Richmond *Con* p735
Baroness Hooper *Con* p736
Baroness Jones of Whitchurch *Lab* p757
Baroness Neville-Rolfe *Con* p833
Lord Puttnam *Lab* p867
Baroness Randerson *Lib Dem* p872
Baroness Rawlings *Con* p873
Lord Smith of Finsbury *NA* p912
Lord Trimble *Con* p945

Culture, media and sport

Lord Allen of Kensington *Lab* p557
Lord Holmes of Richmond *Con* p735
Lord Laming *CB* p774
Lord Lester of Herne Hill *Lib Dem* p782

Cycling

Lord Colwyn *Con* p631

Deaf children

Lord Bruce of Bennachie *Lib Dem* p605

Defence

Lord Arbuthnot of Edrom *Con* p562
Lord Ashdown of Norton-sub-Hamdon *Lib Dem* p565
Lord Astor of Hever *Con* p567
Earl Attlee *Con* p567
Lord Bach *Lab* p568
Lord Balfe *Con* p570
Lord Bilimoria *CB* p580
Viscount Brookeborough *CB* p600
Lord Burnett *Lib Dem* p606
Baroness Buscombe *Con* p607
Lord Campbell of Pittenweem *Lib Dem* p612
Lord Clark of Windermere *Lab* p625
Lord Cormack *Con* p633
Lord Craig of Radley *CB* p638
Lord Dannatt *CB* p644
Lord Davies of Stamford *Lab* p648
Baroness Dean of Thornton-le-Fylde *Lab* p649
Baroness Emerton *CB* p667
Earl of Erroll *CB* p668
Baroness Fookes *Con* p681
Lord Foulkes of Cumnock *Lab/Co-op* p684
Lord Fraser of Corriegarth *Con* p686
Lord Freeman *Con* p687
Lord Glenarthur *Con* p695
Lord Guthrie of Craigiebank *CB* p710
Lord Hamilton of Epsom *Con* p714
Lord Hayward *Con* p725
Baroness Helic *Con* p726
Lord Hutton of Furness *Lab* p749
Baroness Jolly *Lib Dem* p754
Lord Jones of Cheltenham *Lib Dem* p756
Lord Judd *Lab* p760
Lord Kirkhope of Harrogate *Con* p771
Lord Lee of Trafford *Lib Dem* p779
Baroness Liddell of Coatdyke *Lab* p785
Marquess of Lothian *Con* p793
Lord McFall of Alcluith *NA* p799
Lord MacKenzie of Culkein *Lab* p802
Lord Maginnis of Drumglass *Ind UU* p807

Baroness Manningham-Buller *CB* p810
Lord Marlesford *Con* p813
Lord Moonie *Lab/Co-op* p821
Baroness Nicholson of Winterbourne *Con* p835
Lord O'Neill of Clackmannan *Lab* p844
Lord Palumbo *Con* p850
Lord Powell of Bayswater *CB* p863
Baroness Ramsay of Cartvale *Lab* p870
Lord Reid of Cardowan *Lab* p876
Lord Richards of Herstmonceux *CB* p880
Lord Robathan *Con* p882
Lord Robertson of Port Ellen *Lab* p883
Lord Rogan *UUP* p885
Lord Rotherwick *Con* p889
Lord Selkirk of Douglas *Con* p900
Lord Selsdon *Con* p901
Baroness Sharples *Con* p902
Baroness Smith of Newnham *Lib Dem* p915
Baroness Taylor of Bolton *Lab* p933
Lord Taylor of Warwick *NA* p934
Lord Trefgarne *Con* p943
Viscount Trenchard *Con* p944
Lord Walker of Aldringham *CB* p957
Lord Wallace of Saltaire *Lib Dem* p958
Lord West of Spithead *Lab* p965

Defence and security

Lord Bach *Lab* p568

Defence equipment and weapon systems

Lord James of Blackheath *Con* p752

Democracy and elections

Lord Campbell-Savours *Lab* p613
Lord Greaves *Lib Dem* p704
Baroness Morris of Yardley *Lab* p827
Lord Purvis of Tweed *Lib Dem* p867
Baroness Royall of Blaisdon *Lab/Co-op* p890
Lord Steel of Aikwood *Lib Dem* p919
Lord Taylor of Holbeach *Con* p934

Dentists

Lord Colwyn *Con* p631

Development and education

Baroness D'Souza *CB* p658

Devolved administrations

Baroness Gale *Lab* p689

Devolved government

Lord Haskins *CB* p722
Baroness Morgan of Ely *Lab* p824
Lord Watson of Invergowrie *Lab* p962

Diabetes

Lord Kennedy of Southwark *Lab/Co-op* p763
Lord Rennard *Lib Dem* p877

Disability

Lord Addington *Lib Dem* p551
Baroness Brinton *Lib Dem* p598
Lord Browne of Ladyton *Lab* p603
Baroness Corston *Lab* p634
Baroness Doocey *Lib Dem* p656
Bishop of Ely *NA* p666
Baroness Gould of Potternewton *Lab* p701
Lord Hardie *CB* p717
Lord Howarth of Newport *Lab* p740
Lord Low of Dalston *CB* p793
Lord McColl of Dulwich *Con* p797
Baroness Masham of Ilton *CB* p814
Baroness O'Cathain *Con* p841
Lord Rennard *Lib Dem* p877
Bishop of Salisbury *NA* p895
Viscount Simon *Lab* p908
Lord Sterling of Plaistow *Con* p920
Baroness Thomas of Winchester *Lib Dem* p938
Lord Wigley *PlC* p969
Lord Young of Cookham *Con* p982

Disability rights

Baroness Campbell of Surbiton *CB* p612
Baroness Grey-Thompson *CB* p707

Disabled children

Baroness Flather *CB* p679

Drug-related crime

Lord Taverne *Lib Dem* p932

Drugs use and abuse

Lord Brooke of Alverthorpe *Lab* p599
Lord Mancroft *Con* p809
Lord Martin of Springburn *CB* p813
Baroness Masham of Ilton *CB* p814
Baroness Massey of Darwen *Lab* p814

Dyslexia

Lord Laird *NA* p774

Economic development

Baroness Brinton *Lib Dem* p598
Baroness Doocey *Lib Dem* p656

Economics and finance

Lord Blyth of Rowington *Con* p588
Lord Christopher *Lab* p624
Lord Darling of Roulanish *Lab* p645
Lord Dykes *CB* p661
Lord Eatwell *NA* p663
Lord Forsyth of Drumlean *Con* p682
Lord Foster of Bishop Auckland *Lab* p683
Lord Hague of Richmond *Con* p710
Lord Hayward *Con* p725
Lord Howell of Guildford *Con* p742
Lord Lamont of Lerwick *Con* p775
Lord Lawson of Blaby *Con* p777
Baroness Liddell of Coatdyke *Lab* p785
Lord McConnell of Glenscorrodale *Lab* p797
Lord McFall of Alcluith *NA* p799
Lord MacGregor of Pulham Market *Con* p799

Baroness McIntosh of Pickering *Con* p801
Lord Moonie *Lab/Co-op* p821
Lord Oakeshott of Seagrove Bay *NA* p840
Baroness O'Cathain *Con* p841
Lord Paul *NA* p855
Lord Radice *Lab* p870
Lord Redesdale *Lib Dem* p875
Lord Sterling of Plaistow *Con* p920
Lord Vallance of Tummel *Lib Dem* p953
Lord Wakeham *Con* p955
Baroness Wheatcroft *Con* p966

Economy

Lord Allen of Kensington *Lab* p557
Baroness Altmann *Con* p558
Bishop of Birmingham *NA* p582
Lord Blackwell *Con* p585
Lord Borwick *Con* p590
Lord Bourne of Aberystwyth *Con* p591
Lord Burnett *Lib Dem* p606
Lord Coe *Con* p628
Lord Cooper of Windrush *Con* p632
Baroness Couttie *Con* p636
Lord Crickhowell *Con* p640
Lord Currie of Marylebone *CB* p643
Lord Davies of Oldham *Lab* p648
Lord Desai *Lab* p653
Lord Dunlop *Con* p660
Viscount Eccles *Con* p663
Lord Empey *UUP* p667
Lord Flight *Con* p680
Lord Griffiths of Fforestfach *Con* p709
Viscount Hanworth *Lab* p717
Lord Hollick *Lab* p733
Lord Holmes of Richmond *Con* p735
Lord Horam *Con* p738
Lord Howarth of Newport *Lab* p740
Baroness Hughes of Stretford *Lab* p744
Lord Hunt of Wirral *Con* p747
Baroness Janke *Lib Dem* p752
Lord Kerr of Kinlochard *CB* p764
Lord Lang of Monkton *Con* p776
Lord Layard *Lab* p778
Lord Lea of Crondall *Lab* p779
Lord Livermore *Lab* p790
Lord Macpherson of Earl's Court *CB* p805
Lord Mogg *CB* p819
Lord Morris of Handsworth *Lab* p826
Bishop of Newcastle *NA* p834
Lord O'Donnell *CB* p841
Lord Patel of Blackburn *Lab* p853
Lord Purvis of Tweed *Lib Dem* p867
Lord Risby *Con* p882
Lord Selsdon *Con* p901
Lord Sheikh *Con* p903
Lord Skidelsky *CB* p909
Lord Smith of Finsbury *NA* p912
Lord Spicer *Con* p917
Lord Stephen *Lib Dem* p919
Lord Stoddart of Swindon *Ind Lab* p924
Lord Taverne *Lib Dem* p932
Lord Taylor of Goss Moor *Lib Dem* p933
Lord Touhig *Lab/Co-op* p942
Lord Triesman *Lab* p944
Lord Tugendhat *Con* p947
Lord Turnbull *CB* p949
Baroness Vere of Norbiton *Con* p953
Lord Watson of Invergowrie *Lab* p962
Lord Wolfson of Aspley Guise *Con* p977
Lord Wood of Anfield *Lab* p977
Lord Wrigglesworth *Lib Dem* p980

Education

Lord Aberdare *CB* p551
Lord Addington *Lib Dem* p551
Lord Ahmed *NA* p554
Lord Allan of Hallam *Lib Dem* p556
Baroness Andrews *Lab* p561
Baroness Armstrong of Hill Top *Lab* p563
Lord Baker of Dorking *Con* p568
Earl Baldwin of Bewdley *CB* p570
Lord Barker of Battle *Con* p572
Lord Bassam of Brighton *Lab/Co-op* p573
Lord Bates *Con* p573
Baroness Benjamin *Lib Dem* p576
Lord Bew *CB* p578
Lord Bhattacharyya *Lab* p579
Lord Bichard *CB* p580
Baroness Billingham *Lab* p581
Lord Black of Brentwood *Con* p583
Baroness Blackstone *Lab* p584
Lord Boswell of Aynho *NA* p590
Lord Bourne of Aberystwyth *Con* p591
Baroness Brinton *Lib Dem* p598
Lord Broers *CB* p599
Lord Browne of Belmont *DUP* p603
Lord Browne of Ladyton *Lab* p603
Lord Browne of Madingley *CB* p603
Baroness Browning *Con* p604
Baroness Butler-Sloss *CB* p609
Lord Campbell-Savours *Lab* p613
Earl of Clancarty *CB* p625
Baroness Clark of Calton *NA* p625
Lord Coe *Con* p628
Baroness Cohen of Pimlico *Lab* p629
Lord Cormack *Con* p633
Bishop of Coventry *NA* p637
Baroness Cox *CB* p637
Lord Cromwell *CB* p641
Baroness Cumberlege *Con* p642
Lord Darling of Roulanish *Lab* p645
Lord Davies of Coity *Lab/Co-op* p647
Lord Davies of Oldham *Lab* p648
Lord Desai *Lab* p653
Baroness Eaton *Con* p662
Viscount Eccles *Con* p663

Lord Elton	*Con*	p665
Bishop of Ely	*NA*	p666
Lord Empey	*UUP*	p667
Baroness Evans of Bowes Park	*Con*	p668
Lord Evans of Watford	*Lab*	p669
Lord Faulks	*Con*	p674
Baroness Finn	*Con*	p679
Lord Forsyth of Drumlean	*Con*	p682
Lord Foster of Bath	*Lib Dem*	p683
Lord Foster of Bishop Auckland	*Lab*	p683
Lord Fox	*Lib Dem*	p685
Baroness Garden of Frognal	*Lib Dem*	p690
Lord German	*Lib Dem*	p692
Bishop of Gloucester	*NA*	p696
Baroness Greenfield	*CB*	p705
Lord Griffiths of Burry Port	*Lab*	p708
Lord Griffiths of Fforestfach	*Con*	p709
Lord Hanningfield	*NA*	p716
Baroness Hayman	*CB*	p724
Lord Holmes of Richmond	*Con*	p735
Baroness Hooper	*Con*	p736
Lord Howarth of Newport	*Lab*	p740
Baroness Howe of Idlicote	*CB*	p741
Baroness Howells of St Davids	*Lab*	p742
Baroness Hughes of Stretford	*Lab*	p744
Lord Jones	*Lab*	p755
Baroness Jones of Whitchurch	*Lab*	p757
Lord Judd	*Lab*	p760
Baroness Kidron	*CB*	p766
Baroness King of Bow	*Lab*	p767
Baroness Kinnock of Holyhead	*Lab*	p769
Lord Krebs	*CB*	p773
Lord Levy	*Lab*	p783
Lord Lexden	*Con*	p784
Lord Lingfield	*Con*	p787
Lord Livermore	*Lab*	p790
Lord Lucas of Crudwell and Dingwall	*Con*	p794
Lord McConnell of Glenscorrodale	*Lab*	p797
Lord McFall of Alcluith	*NA*	p799
Lord MacGregor of Pulham Market	*Con*	p799
Baroness McIntosh of Hudnall	*Lab*	p800
Lord McKenzie of Luton	*Lab*	p803
Baroness Maddock	*Lib Dem*	p806
Lord Marks of Henley-on-Thames	*Lib Dem*	p812
Baroness Massey of Darwen	*Lab*	p814
Lord Mawson	*CB*	p816
Lord Mitchell	*NA*	p818
Lord Mogg	*CB*	p819
Lord Morgan	*Lab*	p822
Baroness Morgan of Huyton	*Lab*	p824
Baroness Morris of Yardley	*Lab*	p827
Lord Mountevans	*CB*	p827
Lord Murphy of Torfaen	*Lab*	p829
Lord Nash	*Con*	p831
Baroness Neville-Rolfe	*Con*	p833
Lord Northbourne	*CB*	p837
Lord Norton of Louth	*Con*	p838
Bishop of Norwich	*NA*	p839
Baroness O'Neill of Bengarve	*CB*	p843
Lord O'Neill of Clackmannan	*Lab*	p844
Baroness Paisley of St George's	*DUP*	p848
Lord Palumbo	*Con*	p850
Lord Patel of Blackburn	*Lab*	p853
Lord Paul	*NA*	p855
Lord Pearson of Rannoch	*UKIP*	p856
Baroness Prashar	*CB*	p864
Baroness Primarolo	*Lab*	p865
Lord Puttnam	*Lab*	p867
Lord Quirk	*CB*	p869
Lord Ramsbotham	*CB*	p871
Lord Rana	*Con*	p871
Baroness Randerson	*Lib Dem*	p872
Lord Rees of Ludlow	*CB*	p876
Lord Renfrew of Kaimsthorn	*Con*	p877
Baroness Rock	*Con*	p884
Lord Sainsbury of Turville	*Lab*	p893
Lord Sawyer	*Lab*	p897
Earl of Selborne	*Con*	p900
Lord Selkirk of Douglas	*Con*	p900
Lord Sharkey	*Lib Dem*	p902
Baroness Shephard of Northwold	*Con*	p903
Lord Skidelsky	*CB*	p909
Baroness Stedman-Scott	*Con*	p918
Lord Stephen	*Lib Dem*	p919
Lord Storey	*Lib Dem*	p926
Baroness Stroud	*Con*	p927
Lord Sutherland of Houndwood	*CB*	p929
Baroness Taylor of Bolton	*Lab*	p933
Lord Taylor of Goss Moor	*Lib Dem*	p933
Lord Touhig	*Lab/Co-op*	p942
Lord True	*Con*	p946
Baroness Vere of Norbiton	*Con*	p953
Baroness Verma	*Con*	p954
Lord Watts	*Lab*	p964
Lord Whitty	*Lab*	p968
Lord Willetts	*Con*	p970
Lord Willis of Knaresborough	*Lib Dem*	p973
Lord Wilson of Tillyorn	*CB*	p974
Lord Winston	*Lab*	p975

Education and skills

Lord Aberdare	*CB*	p551
Baroness Cox	*CB*	p637
Lord Flight	*Con*	p680
Baroness Garden of Frognal	*Lib Dem*	p690
Lord Geddes	*Con*	p692
Lord German	*Lib Dem*	p692
Lord Kirkhope of Harrogate	*Con*	p771
Lord Lea of Crondall	*Lab*	p779
Lord Redesdale	*Lib Dem*	p875
Baroness Thornhill	*Lib Dem*	p938
Baroness Watkins of Tavistock	*CB*	p962

Electoral reform

Lord Hain	*Lab*	p711
Baroness King of Bow	*Lab*	p767
Lord Lipsey	*Lab*	p788
Baroness Thomas of Winchester	*Lib Dem*	p938

Electoral services

Baroness Gould of Potternewton	*Lab*	p701
Lord Lexden	*Con*	p784

Employment

Lord Davies of Oldham	*Lab*	p648
Lord Holmes of Richmond	*Con*	p735
Lord Hoyle	*Lab*	p743
Baroness King of Bow	*Lab*	p767
Lord Layard	*Lab*	p778
Lord Lea of Crondall	*Lab*	p779
Lord Livermore	*Lab*	p790
Lord Ramsbotham	*CB*	p871
Lord Redesdale	*Lib Dem*	p875
Lord Rosser	*Lab*	p888
Lord Sawyer	*Lab*	p897
Lord Touhig	*Lab/Co-op*	p942
Lord Whitty	*Lab*	p968
Lord Wigley	*PlC*	p969

Employment and welfare

Lord Blunkett	*Lab*	p587
Lord Davies of Stamford	*Lab*	p648
Lord Forsyth of Drumlean	*Con*	p682
Lord MacGregor of Pulham Market	*Con*	p799
Lord Northbourne	*CB*	p837
Lord Northbrook	*Con*	p837
Lord Willetts	*Con*	p970

Employment Law

Lord Brookman	*Lab*	p600
Viscount Younger of Leckie	*Con*	p985

Energy

Lord Birt	*CB*	p582
Lord Black of Brentwood	*Con*	p583
Lord Broers	*CB*	p599
Lord Browne of Madingley	*CB*	p603
Lord Bruce of Bennachie	*Lib Dem*	p605
Earl Cathcart	*Con*	p618
Lord Cunningham of Felling	*Lab*	p643
Lord Deben	*Con*	p650
Lord Duncan of Springbank	*Con*	p659
Baroness Featherstone	*Lib Dem*	p675
Baroness Ford	*CB*	p681
Lord Foulkes of Cumnock	*Lab/Co-op*	p684
Baroness Gardner of Parkes	*Con*	p691
Lord Geddes	*Con*	p692
Lord Hannay of Chiswick	*CB*	p715
Viscount Hanworth	*Lab*	p717
Lord Hardie	*CB*	p717
Lord Haworth	*Lab*	p723
Baroness Hooper	*Con*	p736
Baroness Howarth of Breckland	*CB*	p739
Lord Howell of Guildford	*Con*	p742
Lord Hunt of Kings Heath	*Lab/Co-op*	p746
Lord Jay of Ewelme	*CB*	p753
Lord Lea of Crondall	*Lab*	p779
Baroness Liddell of Coatdyke	*Lab*	p785
Earl of Lindsay	*Con*	p786
Baroness Morgan of Ely	*Lab*	p824
Lord Naseby	*Con*	p830
Baroness Nicol	*Lab/Co-op*	p835
Baroness O'Cathain	*Con*	p841
Lord Oxburgh	*CB*	p846
Earl of Oxford and Asquith	*Lib Dem*	p848
Lord Rees of Ludlow	*CB*	p876
Lord Rooker	*Lab*	p887
Lord Skelmersdale	*Con*	p909
Lord Stoddart of Swindon	*Ind Lab*	p924
Lord Stunell	*Lib Dem*	p928
Lord Taylor of Holbeach	*Con*	p934
Viscount Thurso	*Lib Dem*	p939
Lord Turnbull	*CB*	p949
Lord Wakeham	*Con*	p955
Lord Whitty	*Lab*	p968
Lord Woolmer of Leeds	*Lab*	p978

Energy and Utilities

Lord Alderdice	*Lib Dem*	p555
Lord Birt	*CB*	p582
Baroness Fookes	*Con*	p681
Lord Geddes	*Con*	p692
Baroness Liddell of Coatdyke	*Lab*	p785
Lord Stunell	*Lib Dem*	p928
Baroness Young of Old Scone	*Lab*	p984

Energy Conservation

Lord Wallace of Tankerness	*Lib Dem*	p958

Engineering

Earl Attlee	*Con*	p567
Baroness Brown of Cambridge	*CB*	p601
Lord Fox	*Lib Dem*	p685
Lord Howie of Troon	*Lab*	p743
Lord Pendry	*Lab*	p857

Enterprise

Lord Mawson	*CB*	p816
Baroness Mone	*Con*	p820
Lord Purvis of Tweed	*Lib Dem*	p867

Environment

Lord Alton of Liverpool	*CB*	p558
Baroness Armstrong of Hill Top	*Lab*	p563
Baroness Bakewell of Hardington Mandeville	*Lib Dem*	p570
Earl Baldwin of Bewdley	*CB*	p570
Lord Barker of Battle	*Con*	p572
Lord Bassam of Brighton	*Lab/Co-op*	p573
Lord Beecham	*Lab*	p574
Lord Berkeley	*Lab*	p576
Lord Boateng	*Lab*	p588
Lord Bradshaw	*Lib Dem*	p595

Viscount Bridgeman	*Con*	p597
Lord Browne of Madingley	*CB*	p603
Lord Cameron of Dillington	*CB*	p611
Earl Cathcart	*Con*	p618
Lord Cavendish of Furness	*Con*	p619
Lord Clinton-Davis	*Lab*	p627
Lord Coe	*Con*	p628
Lord Colgrain	*Con*	p629
Earl of Courtown	*Con*	p635
Lord Crickhowell	*Con*	p640
Lord Cunningham of Felling	*Lab*	p643
Lord Deben	*Con*	p650
Lord Dixon-Smith	*Con*	p655
Lord Elis-Thomas	*NA*	p665
Earl of Erroll	*CB*	p668
Lord Forsyth of Drumlean	*Con*	p682
Lord Framlingham	*Con*	p686
Baroness Gale	*Lab*	p689
Lord Glentoran	*Con*	p696
Lord Graham of Edmonton	*Lab/Co-op*	p703
Lord Grantchester	*Lab*	p703
Lord Greaves	*Lib Dem*	p704
Baroness Hanham	*Con*	p715
Viscount Hanworth	*Lab*	p717
Lord Hardie	*CB*	p717
Lord Haworth	*Lab*	p723
Baroness Hilton of Eggardon	*Lab*	p730
Baroness Howarth of Breckland	*CB*	p739
Baroness Howe of Idlicote	*CB*	p741
Lord Hunt of Chesterton	*Lab*	p745
Lord Inglewood	*Con*	p750
Lord Jay of Ewelme	*CB*	p753
Lord Judd	*Lab*	p760
Baroness Kramer	*Lib Dem*	p773
Lord Krebs	*CB*	p773
Earl of Lindsay	*Con*	p786
Earl of Liverpool	*Con*	p790
Baroness McIntosh of Pickering	*Con*	p801
Baroness Maddock	*Lib Dem*	p806
Baroness Mallalieu	*Lab*	p808
Countess of Mar	*CB*	p811
Lord Marland	*Con*	p812
Baroness Miller of Chilthorne Domer	*Lib Dem*	p818
Baroness Nicol	*Lab/Co-op*	p835
Earl of Oxford and Asquith	*Lib Dem*	p848
Lord Palmer	*CB*	p849
Baroness Parminter	*Lib Dem*	p852
Lord Pendry	*Lab*	p857
Lord Plumb	*Con*	p860
Lord Puttnam	*Lab*	p867
Lord Redesdale	*Lib Dem*	p875
Lord Robathan	*Con*	p882
Lord St John of Bletso	*CB*	p894
Bishop of Salisbury	*NA*	p895
Lord Selkirk of Douglas	*Con*	p900
Lord Sheikh	*Con*	p903
Earl of Shrewsbury and Waterford	*Con*	p907
Lord Skelmersdale	*Con*	p909
Lord Smith of Finsbury	*NA*	p912
Lord Soley	*Lab*	p916
Lord Strasburger	*Lib Dem*	p926
Lord Taylor of Goss Moor	*Lib Dem*	p933
Lord Taylor of Holbeach	*Con*	p934
Baroness Tonge	*NA*	p941
Lord Trees	*CB*	p942
Baroness Walmsley	*Lib Dem*	p959
Lord Whitty	*Lab*	p968
Lord Williams of Elvel	*Lab*	p971
Baroness Young of Old Scone	*Lab*	p984

Environment, agriculture and rural affairs

Lord Birt	*CB*	p582
Lord Evans of Watford	*Lab*	p669
Lord Kirkhope of Harrogate	*Con*	p771
Lord McColl of Dulwich	*Con*	p797
Baroness McIntosh of Pickering	*Con*	p801
Baroness Mallalieu	*Lab*	p808
Lord Mitchell	*NA*	p818
Lord Morgan	*Lab*	p822
Baroness Noakes	*Con*	p836
Baroness Whitaker	*Lab*	p967
Lord Winston	*Lab*	p975
Baroness Young of Old Scone	*Lab*	p984

Equal opportunities and diversity

Baroness Afshar	*CB*	p553
Lord Ahmed	*NA*	p554
Baroness Bakewell	*Lab*	p569
Baroness Barker	*Lib Dem*	p571
Baroness Benjamin	*Lib Dem*	p576
Baroness Berridge	*Con*	p577
Baroness Blood	*Lab*	p586
Lord Boswell of Aynho	*NA*	p590
Baroness Bottomley of Nettlestone	*Con*	p591
Baroness Brady	*Con*	p596
Baroness Burt of Solihull	*Lib Dem*	p607
Baroness Campbell of Surbiton	*CB*	p612
Lord Cashman	*Lab*	p618
Lord Collins of Highbury	*Lab*	p630
Baroness Corston	*Lab*	p634
Baroness Coussins	*CB*	p636
Baroness Crawley	*Lab*	p640
Lord Davies of Abersoch	*NA*	p647
Baroness Dean of Thornton-le-Fylde	*Lab*	p649
Baroness Falkner of Margravine	*Lib Dem*	p671
Lord Faulkner of Worcester	*Lab*	p673
Baroness Finlay of Llandaff	*CB*	p678
Baroness Finn	*Con*	p679
Baroness Fookes	*Con*	p681
Baroness Gale	*Lab*	p689
Baroness Gibson of Market Rasen	*Lab*	p693
Bishop of Gloucester	*NA*	p696
Baroness Goudie	*Lab*	p700
Baroness Gould of Potternewton	*Lab*	p701

Baroness Greenfield *CB* p705
Baroness Grey-Thompson *CB* p707
Baroness Hayter of Kentish Town *Lab/Co-op* p725
Baroness Hodgson of Abinger *Con* p731
Baroness Hollis of Heigham *Lab* p734
Lord Holmes of Richmond *Con* p735
Baroness Howe of Idlicote *CB* p741
Baroness Hussein-Ece *Lib Dem* p748
Baroness King of Bow *Lab* p767
Baroness Kinnock of Holyhead *Lab* p769
Lord Layard *Lab* p778
Lord Lester of Herne Hill *Lib Dem* p782
Lord Martin of Springburn *CB* p813
Baroness Morgan of Huyton *Lab* p824
Lord Morris of Handsworth *Lab* p826
Lord Ouseley *CB* p845
Baroness Paisley of St George's *DUP* p848
Baroness Parminter *Lib Dem* p852
Baroness Primarolo *Lab* p865
Baroness Prosser *Lab* p866
Baroness Ramsay of Cartvale *Lab* p870
Baroness Randerson *Lib Dem* p872
Baroness Seccombe *Con* p899
Lord Taylor of Warwick *NA* p934

Equal pay

Baroness Altmann *Con* p558
Baroness Blood *Lab* p586
Baroness Prosser *Lab* p866

EU economy

Lord Marlesford *Con* p813

European affairs

Lord Deben *Con* p650
Viscount of Falkland *CB* p671
Baroness Falkner of Margravine *Lib Dem* p671
Lord Haskins *CB* p722
Baroness Henig *Lab* p727
Lord Hunt of Wirral *Con* p747
Baroness Hussein-Ece *Lib Dem* p748
Baroness King of Bow *Lab* p767
Lord Lawson of Blaby *Con* p777
Lord Lester of Herne Hill *Lib Dem* p782
Duke of Montrose *Con* p821
Lord Morgan *Lab* p822
Lord Newby *Lib Dem* p833
Lord Plumb *Con* p860
Lord Purvis of Tweed *Lib Dem* p867
Baroness Quin *Lab* p868
Lord Radice *Lab* p870
Baroness Randerson *Lib Dem* p872
Baroness Scott of Needham Market *Lib Dem* p898
Lord Skidelsky *CB* p909
Baroness Smith of Newnham *Lib Dem* p915
Baroness Suttie *Lib Dem* p930
Lord Tebbit *Con* p935
Lord Thurlow *CB* p939
Lord Tomlinson *Lab/Co-op* p940
Lord Tope *Lib Dem* p941
Baroness Valentine *CB* p952
Lord Vallance of Tummel *Lib Dem* p953
Lord Wallace of Saltaire *Lib Dem* p958
Lord Whitty *Lab* p968
Lord Wigley *PlC* p969

European Commission

Baroness Goudie *Lab* p700

European Union

Lord Ahmad of Wimbledon *Con* p554
Baroness Altmann *Con* p558
Lord Bilimoria *CB* p580
Lord Blackwell *Con* p585
Lord Boswell of Aynho *NA* p590
Lord Bowness *Con* p593
Baroness Crawley *Lab* p640
Lord Dykes *CB* p661
Lord Empey *UUP* p667
Lord Garel-Jones *Con* p691
Baroness Goudie *Lab* p700
Lord Hannay of Chiswick *CB* p715
Lord Harrison *Lab* p721
Baroness Hooper *Con* p736
Lord Inglewood *Con* p750
Lord Kalms *NA* p762
Lord Kilclooney *CB* p766
Lord Lamont of Lerwick *Con* p775
Lord Lea of Crondall *Lab* p779
Lord Liddle *Lab* p785
Lord Maclennan of Rogart *Lib Dem* p804
Lord Macpherson of Earl's Court *CB* p805
Baroness Morgan of Ely *Lab* p824
Baroness Neville-Rolfe *Con* p833
Lord Pearson of Rannoch *UKIP* p856
Lord Stoddart of Swindon *Ind Lab* p924
Lord Taverne *Lib Dem* p932
Lord Temple-Morris *Lab* p936
Lord Teverson *Lib Dem* p936
Lord Tugendhat *Con* p947
Lord Watson of Richmond *Lib Dem* p963
Lord Willoughby de Broke *UKIP* p973

Exports

Baroness Falkender *Lab* p670
Lord Naseby *Con* p830
Lord Popat *Con* p862

Faith schools

Baroness Warsi *Con* p960

Family

Baroness Blood *Lab* p586
Baroness Bottomley of Nettlestone *Con* p591
Baroness Butler-Sloss *CB* p609
Baroness Hanham *Con* p715
Lord Hardie *CB* p717
Baroness Hughes of Stretford *Lab* p744
Lord Knight of Weymouth *Lab/Co-op* p772

Baroness Miller of Chilthorne Domer	*Lib Dem*	p818
Lord Northbourne	*CB*	p837
Baroness O'Cathain	*Con*	p841
Baroness Seccombe	*Con*	p899
Baroness Stroud	*Con*	p927
Baroness Tyler of Enfield	*Lib Dem*	p950
Lord Williams of Oystermouth	*CB*	p971

Farming

Earl Cathcart	*Con*	p618
Lord Flight	*Con*	p680
Baroness McIntosh of Pickering	*Con*	p801
Countess of Mar	*CB*	p811
Baroness Masham of Ilton	*CB*	p814
Bishop of Peterborough	*NA*	p857
Lord Plumb	*Con*	p860
Lord Vaux of Harrowden	*CB*	p953

Film Industry

Viscount of Falkland	*CB*	p671

Finance

Lord Ahmad of Wimbledon	*Con*	p554
Lord Bilimoria	*CB*	p580
Lord Boswell of Aynho	*NA*	p590
Baroness Cohen of Pimlico	*Lab*	p629
Lord Davies of Stamford	*Lab*	p648
Lord Donoughue	*Lab*	p656
Lord Fraser of Corriegarth	*Con*	p686
Lord Hamilton of Epsom	*Con*	p714
Lord Higgins	*Con*	p729
Baroness Janke	*Lib Dem*	p752
Baroness Kramer	*Lib Dem*	p773
Lord Lawson of Blaby	*Con*	p777
Lord Lucas of Crudwell and Dingwall	*Con*	p794
Earl of Lytton	*CB*	p796
Lord Marland	*Con*	p812
Lord Mogg	*CB*	p819
Baroness O'Cathain	*Con*	p841
Lord O'Donnell	*CB*	p841
Lord Pendry	*Lab*	p857
Lord St John of Bletso	*CB*	p894
Lord Selsdon	*Con*	p901
Lord Sharkey	*Lib Dem*	p902
Lord Teverson	*Lib Dem*	p936
Lord Tomlinson	*Lab/Co-op*	p940
Baroness Wheatcroft	*Con*	p966
Baroness Wilcox	*Con*	p969
Lord Woolmer of Leeds	*Lab*	p978

Financial services

Baroness Altmann	*Con*	p558
Baroness Bowles of Berkhamsted	*Lib Dem*	p592
Lord Christopher	*Lab*	p624
Earl of Cork and Orrery	*CB*	p633
Earl of Kinnoull	*CB*	p770
Lord Naseby	*Con*	p830
Lord Sassoon	*Con*	p896
Lord Sheikh	*Con*	p903
Viscount Thurso	*Lib Dem*	p939
Viscount Trenchard	*Con*	p944
Lord Turnbull	*CB*	p949

Financial services regulation

Lord Foulkes of Cumnock	*Lab/Co-op*	p684

Fisheries

Lord Cameron of Dillington	*CB*	p611
Lord Duncan of Springbank	*Con*	p659
Baroness Golding	*Lab*	p698
Lord Hughes of Woodside	*Lab*	p744
Earl of Shrewsbury and Waterford	*Con*	p907
Baroness Wilcox	*Con*	p969

Food and drink

Lord Cameron of Dillington	*CB*	p611
Lord Curry of Kirkharle	*CB*	p644
Lord Haskins	*CB*	p722
Baroness Jones of Whitchurch	*Lab*	p757
Lord Krebs	*CB*	p773
Baroness Miller of Chilthorne Domer	*Lib Dem*	p818
Baroness Parminter	*Lib Dem*	p852
Lord Rea	*Lab*	p874
Lord Rooker	*Lab*	p887

Food industry

Earl of Lindsay	*Con*	p786
Baroness Neville-Rolfe	*Con*	p833
Lord Whitty	*Lab*	p968

Food Standards Agency

Countess of Mar	*CB*	p811

Foreign policy

Lord Balfe	*Con*	p570
Lord Bates	*Con*	p573
Lord Bew	*CB*	p578
Lord Craig of Radley	*CB*	p638
Lord Giddens	*Lab*	p694
Lord Hanningfield	*NA*	p716
Baroness Helic	*Con*	p726
Baroness Hodgson of Abinger	*Con*	p731
Lord Holmes of Richmond	*Con*	p735
Lord Hylton	*CB*	p749
Lord Jay of Ewelme	*CB*	p753
Lord Kirkhope of Harrogate	*Con*	p771
Baroness Manningham-Buller	*CB*	p810
Lord Palmer of Childs Hill	*Lib Dem*	p849
Lord Radice	*Lab*	p870
Lord Richards of Herstmonceux	*CB*	p880
Baroness Royall of Blaisdon	*Lab/Co-op*	p890
Lord Soley	*Lab*	p916
Baroness Stern	*CB*	p920
Lord Tomlinson	*Lab/Co-op*	p940
Lord Trimble	*Con*	p945
Lord Tugendhat	*Con*	p947
Baroness Williams of Trafford	*Con*	p972
Lord Wood of Anfield	*Lab*	p977

Forestry

Lord Cavendish of Furness	*Con*	p619
Lord Clark of Windermere	*Lab*	p625
Lord Framlingham	*Con*	p686
Lord McColl of Dulwich	*Con*	p797
Baroness Nicol	*Lab/Co-op*	p835

Freedom of information

Lord Cashman	*Lab*	p618
Lord Kirkwood of Kirkhope	*Lib Dem*	p771

Freight transport

Lord Taylor of Holbeach	*Con*	p934

Further and higher education

Lord Bilimoria	*CB*	p580
Baroness Bottomley of Nettlestone	*Con*	p591
Lord Bragg	*Lab*	p596
Baroness Brinton	*Lib Dem*	p598
Baroness Brown of Cambridge	*CB*	p601
Lord Butler of Brockwell	*CB*	p608
Baroness Butler-Sloss	*CB*	p609
Lord Clement-Jones	*Lib Dem*	p627
Baroness Deech	*CB*	p651
Lord Grabiner	*CB*	p701
Lord Hannay of Chiswick	*CB*	p715
Lord Haskins	*CB*	p722
Lord Howie of Troon	*Lab*	p743
Lord Liddle	*Lab*	p785
Lord Low of Dalston	*CB*	p793
Lord Luce	*CB*	p794
Lord McColl of Dulwich	*Con*	p797
Baroness Manningham-Buller	*CB*	p810
Baroness Murphy	*CB*	p829
Baroness O'Neill of Bengarve	*CB*	p843
Lord Oxburgh	*CB*	p846
Lord Parekh	*Lab*	p851
Lord Patel	*CB*	p852
Lord Rowe-Beddoe	*CB*	p889
Lord Smith of Clifton	*Lib Dem*	p911
Lord Smith of Finsbury	*NA*	p912
Baroness Smith of Newnham	*Lib Dem*	p915
Lord Trees	*CB*	p942
Lord Triesman	*Lab*	p944
Baroness Valentine	*CB*	p952
Baroness Warwick of Undercliffe	*Lab*	p961
Lord Willis of Knaresborough	*Lib Dem*	p973

Gambling and lotteries

Baroness Golding	*Lab*	p698
Lord Smith of Hindhead	*Con*	p913

Gardens

Baroness Masham of Ilton	*CB*	p814

Gas Industry

Lord Bruce of Bennachie	*Lib Dem*	p605

General economy

Baroness Bowles of Berkhamsted	*Lib Dem*	p592

Government

Lord Livermore	*Lab*	p790
Lord Triesman	*Lab*	p944

Government, politics and public administration

Lord Beith	*Lib Dem*	p575
Lord Boateng	*Lab*	p588
Lord Clement-Jones	*Lib Dem*	p627
Lord Darling of Roulanish	*Lab*	p645
Lord Denham	*Con*	p652
Baroness Falkner of Margravine	*Lib Dem*	p671
Lord Glentoran	*Con*	p696
Viscount Hailsham	*Con*	p711
Lord Haskins	*CB*	p722
Lord Higgins	*Con*	p729
Baroness Jowell	*Lab*	p759
Lord Kirkwood of Kirkhope	*Lib Dem*	p771
Lord Lester of Herne Hill	*Lib Dem*	p782
Lord McColl of Dulwich	*Con*	p797
Baroness Primarolo	*Lab*	p865
Baroness Randerson	*Lib Dem*	p872
Viscount Thurso	*Lib Dem*	p939
Lord Touhig	*Lab/Co-op*	p942

Health

Baroness Bakewell of Hardington Mandeville	*Lib Dem*	p570
Earl Baldwin of Bewdley	*CB*	p570
Baroness Barker	*Lib Dem*	p571
Lord Beecham	*Lab*	p574
Baroness Billingham	*Lab*	p581
Lord Black of Brentwood	*Con*	p583
Baroness Bottomley of Nettlestone	*Con*	p591
Lord Bourne of Aberystwyth	*Con*	p591
Lord Bradley	*Lab*	p595
Viscount Bridgeman	*Con*	p597
Baroness Brinton	*Lib Dem*	p598
Lord Brooke of Alverthorpe	*Lab*	p599
Viscount Brookeborough	*CB*	p600
Baroness Campbell of Surbiton	*CB*	p612
Lord Campbell-Savours	*Lab*	p613
Baroness Clark of Calton	*NA*	p625
Lord Coe	*Con*	p628
Lord Colwyn	*Con*	p631
Lord Cooper of Windrush	*Con*	p632
Baroness Cox	*CB*	p637
Lord Darling of Roulanish	*Lab*	p645
Lord Davies of Stamford	*Lab*	p648
Baroness Emerton	*CB*	p667
Baroness Falkender	*Lab*	p670
Lord Faulkner of Worcester	*Lab*	p673
Lord Fearn	*Lib Dem*	p674
Baroness Finlay of Llandaff	*CB*	p678
Baroness Fookes	*Con*	p681
Lord Forsyth of Drumlean	*Con*	p682
Baroness Gale	*Lab*	p689
Baroness Gardner of Parkes	*Con*	p691
Lord Glenarthur	*Con*	p695

Baroness Golding	*Lab*	p698
Baroness Hanham	*Con*	p715
Lord Harris of Haringey	*Lab*	p719
Lord Haworth	*Lab*	p723
Baroness Hayman	*CB*	p724
Baroness Healy of Primrose Hill	*Lab*	p726
Lord Horam	*Con*	p738
Earl Howe	*Con*	p740
Baroness Howells of St Davids	*Lab*	p742
Lord Hoyle	*Lab*	p743
Baroness Hughes of Stretford	*Lab*	p744
Lord Hughes of Woodside	*Lab*	p744
Baroness Hussein-Ece	*Lib Dem*	p748
Baroness Janke	*Lib Dem*	p752
Baroness Jay of Paddington	*Lab*	p753
Baroness Jolly	*Lib Dem*	p754
Baroness King of Bow	*Lab*	p767
Lord Kirkhope of Harrogate	*Con*	p771
Lord Kirkwood of Kirkhope	*Lib Dem*	p771
Lord Lansley	*Con*	p776
Lord McColl of Dulwich	*Con*	p797
Baroness McIntosh of Hudnall	*Lab*	p800
Lord MacKenzie of Culkein	*Lab*	p802
Baroness Manningham-Buller	*CB*	p810
Countess of Mar	*CB*	p811
Lord Marks of Henley-on-Thames	*Lib Dem*	p812
Baroness Masham of Ilton	*CB*	p814
Baroness Massey of Darwen	*Lab*	p814
Lord Mawhinney	*Con*	p816
Lord Mawson	*CB*	p816
Baroness Morgan of Drefelin	*CB*	p823
Baroness Morgan of Huyton	*Lab*	p824
Baroness Neuberger	*CB*	p831
Baroness Noakes	*Con*	p836
Lord Oxburgh	*CB*	p846
Baroness Paisley of St George's	*DUP*	p848
Baroness Pitkeathley	*Lab*	p859
Baroness Primarolo	*Lab*	p865
Lord Quirk	*CB*	p869
Lord Rana	*Con*	p871
Baroness Randerson	*Lib Dem*	p872
Lord Rea	*Lab*	p874
Lord Rennard	*Lib Dem*	p877
Lord Scriven	*Lib Dem*	p899
Lord Selkirk of Douglas	*Con*	p900
Lord Selsdon	*Con*	p901
Lord Sharkey	*Lib Dem*	p902
Lord Skelmersdale	*Con*	p909
Lord Smith of Clifton	*Lib Dem*	p911
Lord Smith of Finsbury	*NA*	p912
Lord Smith of Leigh	*Lab*	p914
Lord Stephen	*Lib Dem*	p919
Baroness Stroud	*Con*	p927
Baroness Suttie	*Lib Dem*	p930
Baroness Tonge	*NA*	p941
Lord Touhig	*Lab/Co-op*	p942
Lord Trees	*CB*	p942
Baroness Tyler of Enfield	*Lib Dem*	p950
Baroness Verma	*Con*	p954
Baroness Warwick of Undercliffe	*Lab*	p961
Lord Willetts	*Con*	p970
Lord Willis of Knaresborough	*Lib Dem*	p973
Lord Winston	*Lab*	p975

Health and safety at work

Baroness Gibson of Market Rasen	*Lab*	p693

Health and social care professionals

Lord Warner	*CB*	p960
Baroness Young of Old Scone	*Lab*	p984

Health, wellbeing and care

Baroness Finlay of Llandaff	*CB*	p678
Baroness Gardner of Parkes	*Con*	p691
Lord Hoyle	*Lab*	p743
Lord Hutton of Furness	*Lab*	p749
Baroness Quin	*Lab*	p868
Lord Robathan	*Con*	p882
Lord Sawyer	*Lab*	p897
Lord Stunell	*Lib Dem*	p928
Baroness Watkins of Tavistock	*CB*	p962

Heritage

Lord Aberdare	*CB*	p551
Lord Allan of Hallam	*Lib Dem*	p556
Baroness Andrews	*Lab*	p561
Lord Cormack	*Con*	p633
Lord Gardiner of Kimble	*Con*	p690
Baroness Hollis of Heigham	*Lab*	p734
Baroness Hooper	*Con*	p736
Lord Howarth of Newport	*Lab*	p740
Lord Lisvane	*CB*	p789
Lord Palmer	*CB*	p849
Baroness Rawlings	*Con*	p873
Lord Renfrew of Kaimsthorn	*Con*	p877
Lord Rowe-Beddoe	*CB*	p889
Lord Selkirk of Douglas	*Con*	p900
Duke of Somerset	*CB*	p917
Baroness Warwick of Undercliffe	*Lab*	p961

HIV and AIDS

Lord Fowler	*Lord Speaker*	p685

Home affairs

Lord Allan of Hallam	*Lib Dem*	p556
Lord Allen of Kensington	*Lab*	p557
Baroness Anelay of St Johns	*Con*	p561
Lord Bassam of Brighton	*Lab/Co-op*	p573
Lord Boateng	*Lab*	p588
Viscount Bridgeman	*Con*	p597
Lord Brooke of Alverthorpe	*Lab*	p599
Lord Carlile of Berriew	*NA*	p615
Lord Cavendish of Furness	*Con*	p619
Lord Dholakia	*Lib Dem*	p654
Baroness Hamwee	*Lib Dem*	p714
Lord Howard of Lympne	*Con*	p738
Lord Hutton of Furness	*Lab*	p749

Lord Irvine of Lairg *Lab* p751
Baroness Kennedy of Cradley *Lab* p762
Lord Kirkhope of Harrogate *Con* p771
Lord Mackenzie of Framwellgate *NA* p803
Baroness Mallalieu *Lab* p808
Lord Mancroft *Con* p809
Lord Martin of Springburn *CB* p813
Baroness Masham of Ilton *CB* p814
Lord Robertson of Port Ellen *Lab* p883
Lord Sheikh *Con* p903
Baroness Verma *Con* p954

Homelessness

Lord Fairfax of Cameron *Con* p670
Bishop of Salisbury *NA* p895

Horse racing

Viscount of Falkland *CB* p671
Baroness Golding *Lab* p698
Lord James of Blackheath *Con* p752
Lord Lipsey *Lab* p788
Baroness Noakes *Con* p836

Horses

Lord Higgins *Con* p729

House of Lords

Baroness D'Souza *CB* p658

Housing

Lord Alton of Liverpool *CB* p558
Baroness Andrews *Lab* p561
Baroness Bakewell of Hardington Mandeville *Lib Dem* p570
Lord Bassam of Brighton *Lab/Co-op* p573
Lord Best *CB* p578
Lord Bird *CB* p582
Lord Boateng *Lab* p588
Lord Bradley *Lab* p595
Lord Cameron of Dillington *CB* p611
Earl Cathcart *Con* p618
Earl of Courtown *Con* p635
Baroness Dean of Thornton-le-Fylde *Lab* p649
Baroness Doocey *Lib Dem* p656
Lord Filkin *NA* p677
Baroness Ford *CB* p681
Lord Gardiner of Kimble *Con* p690
Baroness Gardner of Parkes *Con* p691
Baroness Hanham *Con* p715
Baroness Hollis of Heigham *Lab* p734
Lord Hylton *CB* p749
Baroness Jones of Whitchurch *Lab* p757
Lord Kerslake *CB* p765
Baroness King of Bow *Lab* p767
Lord Knight of Weymouth *Lab/Co-op* p772
Marquess of Lothian *Con* p793
Lord MacGregor of Pulham Market *Con* p799
Baroness Maddock *Lib Dem* p806
Lord Martin of Springburn *CB* p813
Lord Murphy of Torfaen *Lab* p829
Lord Oakeshott of Seagrove Bay *NA* p840
Lord Paddick *Lib Dem* p848
Lord Pendry *Lab* p857
Baroness Primarolo *Lab* p865
Lord Rooker *Lab* p887
Lord Sawyer *Lab* p897
Lord Selkirk of Douglas *Con* p900
Earl of Shrewsbury and Waterford *Con* p907
Lord Smith of Finsbury *NA* p912
Lord Stoddart of Swindon *Ind Lab* p924
Lord Taylor of Goss Moor *Lib Dem* p933
Baroness Thornhill *Lib Dem* p938
Baroness Valentine *CB* p952
Baroness Watkins of Tavistock *CB* p962
Lord Young of Cookham *Con* p982

Human rights

Lord Ahmed *NA* p554
Lord Alton of Liverpool *CB* p558
Baroness Barker *Lib Dem* p571
Baroness Berridge *Con* p577
Lord Browne of Ladyton *Lab* p603
Baroness Campbell of Surbiton *CB* p612
Lord Cashman *Lab* p618
Lord Clinton-Davis *Lab* p627
Lord Cooper of Windrush *Con* p632
Lord Cormack *Con* p633
Baroness Corston *Lab* p634
Baroness Cox *CB* p637
Lord Dannatt *CB* p644
Baroness D'Souza *CB* p658
Lord Dubs *Lab* p658
Lord Faulkner of Worcester *Lab* p673
Lord Faulks *Con* p674
Lord Foulkes of Cumnock *Lab/Co-op* p684
Baroness Goudie *Lab* p700
Lord Greaves *Lib Dem* p704
Lord Hardie *CB* p717
Lord Harries of Pentregarth *CB* p718
Baroness Helic *Con* p726
Lord Hylton *CB* p749
Lord Judd *Lab* p760
Lord Kirkwood of Kirkhope *Lib Dem* p771
Lord Lester of Herne Hill *Lib Dem* p782
Lord Macdonald of River Glaven *Lib Dem* p798
Lord Marks of Henley-on-Thames *Lib Dem* p812
Lord Martin of Springburn *CB* p813
Baroness Miller of Chilthorne Domer *Lib Dem* p818
Lord Morgan *Lab* p822
Baroness Neuberger *CB* p831
Baroness Nicholson of Winterbourne *Con* p835
Lord Paddick *Lib Dem* p848
Baroness Prashar *CB* p864
Lord Rana *Con* p871

Lord Rea	*Lab*	p874
Lord Rennard	*Lib Dem*	p877
Lord Scriven	*Lib Dem*	p899
Lord Smith of Finsbury	*NA*	p912
Lord Soley	*Lab*	p916
Baroness Stern	*CB*	p920
Lord Strasburger	*Lib Dem*	p926
Baroness Suttie	*Lib Dem*	p930

Humanitarian aid

Lord Allen of Kensington	*Lab*	p557
Baroness Cox	*CB*	p637

Hunting

Earl of Shrewsbury and Waterford	*Con*	p907

Immigration and nationality

Lord Ahmed	*NA*	p554
Lord Dubs	*Lab*	p658
Lord Geddes	*Con*	p692
Lord Green of Deddington	*CB*	p704
Baroness Hamwee	*Lib Dem*	p714
Lord Hardie	*CB*	p717
Lord Hoyle	*Lab*	p743
Bishop of Southwark	*NA*	p917
Lord Taylor of Warwick	*NA*	p934

Information and communication technology

Lord Clement-Jones	*Lib Dem*	p627
Lord Inglewood	*Con*	p750

Infrastructure

Lord Hanningfield	*NA*	p716
Lord Thurlow	*CB*	p939
Baroness Valentine	*CB*	p952

Insurance

Lord Fairfax of Cameron	*Con*	p670
Earl of Kinnoull	*CB*	p770

Intellectual property

Baroness Bowles of Berkhamsted	*Lib Dem*	p592
Lord Clement-Jones	*Lib Dem*	p627
Lord Stevenson of Balmacara	*Lab*	p923
Baroness Wilcox	*Con*	p969

Intelligence Services

Lord Powell of Bayswater	*CB*	p863
Baroness Ramsay of Cartvale	*Lab*	p870
Baroness Taylor of Bolton	*Lab*	p933
Lord Triesman	*Lab*	p944

International affairs

Lord Ahmad of Wimbledon	*Con*	p554
Lord Arbuthnot of Edrom	*Con*	p562
Lord Ashdown of Norton-sub-Hamdon	*Lib Dem*	p565
Bishop of Birmingham	*NA*	p582
Baroness Blackstone	*Lab*	p584
Lord Bourne of Aberystwyth	*Con*	p591
Lord Browne of Ladyton	*Lab*	p603
Lord Campbell of Pittenweem	*Lib Dem*	p612
Lord Cavendish of Furness	*Con*	p619
Lord Chidgey	*Lib Dem*	p623
Lord Clinton-Davis	*Lab*	p627
Lord Coe	*Con*	p628
Lord Collins of Highbury	*Lab*	p630
Viscount Colville of Culross	*CB*	p631
Lord Cotter	*Lib Dem*	p635
Baroness Coussins	*CB*	p636
Bishop of Coventry	*NA*	p637
Lord Dobbs	*Con*	p655
Lord Foulkes of Cumnock	*Lab/Co-op*	p684
Baroness Gibson of Market Rasen	*Lab*	p693
Lord Glenarthur	*Con*	p695
Lord Griffiths of Burry Port	*Lab*	p708
Lord Hain	*Lab*	p711
Viscount Hanworth	*Lab*	p717
Baroness Henig	*Lab*	p727
Earl of Home	*Con*	p736
Lord Horam	*Con*	p738
Lord Howard of Lympne	*Con*	p738
Lord Howell of Guildford	*Con*	p742
Baroness Jolly	*Lib Dem*	p754
Lord Judd	*Lab*	p760
Lord Kerr of Kinlochard	*CB*	p764
Lord Lamont of Lerwick	*Con*	p775
Baroness Liddell of Coatdyke	*Lab*	p785
Lord Luce	*CB*	p794
Lord Mawson	*CB*	p816
Lord Mitchell	*NA*	p818
Lord Morgan	*Lab*	p822
Lord Morris of Handsworth	*Lab*	p826
Lord Moynihan	*Con*	p828
Lord Murphy of Torfaen	*Lab*	p829
Baroness Neville-Rolfe	*Con*	p833
Baroness Nicholson of Winterbourne	*Con*	p835
Lord Northbrook	*Con*	p837
Lord Owen	*Ind Soc Dem*	p846
Earl of Oxford and Asquith	*Lib Dem*	p848
Lord Parekh	*Lab*	p851
Lord Plumb	*Con*	p860
Lord Ponsonby of Shulbrede	*Lab*	p861
Lord Popat	*Con*	p862
Lord Powell of Bayswater	*CB*	p863
Baroness Prashar	*CB*	p864
Lord Purvis of Tweed	*Lib Dem*	p867
Baroness Ramsay of Cartvale	*Lab*	p870
Baroness Rawlings	*Con*	p873
Lord Reid of Cardowan	*Lab*	p876
Lord Renfrew of Kaimsthorn	*Con*	p877
Lord Risby	*Con*	p882
Lord Robertson of Port Ellen	*Lab*	p883
Lord St John of Bletso	*CB*	p894
Lord Selkirk of Douglas	*Con*	p900
Lord Selsdon	*Con*	p901
Lord Sheikh	*Con*	p903
Duke of Somerset	*CB*	p917
Bishop of Southwark	*NA*	p917

Lord Sterling of Plaistow *Con* p920
Baroness Suttie *Lib Dem* p930
Lord Temple-Morris *Lab* p936
Lord Teverson *Lib Dem* p936
Viscount Trenchard *Con* p944
Lord Triesman *Lab* p944
Lord Wallace of Saltaire *Lib Dem* p958
Baroness Warsi *Con* p960
Lord West of Spithead *Lab* p965
Lord Wright of Richmond *CB* p980

International and European affairs

Earl of Arran *Con* p564
Lord Bach *Lab* p568
Baroness Billingham *Lab* p581
Lord Campbell of Pittenweem *Lib Dem* p612
Lord Cunningham of Felling *Lab* p643
Lord Foster of Bath *Lib Dem* p683
Baroness Golding *Lab* p698
Lord Harrison *Lab* p721
Lord Hoyle *Lab* p743
Lord Jones of Cheltenham *Lib Dem* p756
Lord Knight of Weymouth *Lab/Co-op* p772
Lord Lipsey *Lab* p788
Lord Marland *Con* p812
Baroness Masham of Ilton *CB* p814
Baroness Massey of Darwen *Lab* p814
Baroness Noakes *Con* p836
Lord Pendry *Lab* p857
Lord Quirk *CB* p869
Lord Smith of Finsbury *NA* p912
Lord Touhig *Lab/Co-op* p942
Lord Walker of Aldringham *CB* p957

International development and aid

Lord Ahmad of Wimbledon *Con* p554
Baroness Andrews *Lab* p561
Baroness Armstrong of Hill Top *Lab* p563
Earl Attlee *Con* p567
Lord Barker of Battle *Con* p572
Lord Boateng *Lab* p588
Lord Cameron of Dillington *CB* p611
Baroness Chalker of Wallasey *Con* p621
Lord Chidgey *Lib Dem* p623
Lord Christopher *Lab* p624
Lord Clarke of Hampstead *Lab* p626
Lord Davies of Stamford *Lab* p648
Lord Foster of Bath *Lib Dem* p683
Lord Foulkes of Cumnock *Lab/Co-op* p684
Lord Freeman *Con* p687
Bishop of Gloucester *NA* p696
Lord Hannay of Chiswick *CB* p715
Lord Haskel *Lab* p721
Baroness Hodgson of Abinger *Con* p731
Lord Hughes of Woodside *Lab* p744
Baroness Jay of Paddington *Lab* p753
Baroness Kennedy of Cradley *Lab* p762
Baroness Kinnock of Holyhead *Lab* p769
Lord McConnell of Glenscorrodale *Lab* p797
Lord Moynihan *Con* p828
Lord Oakeshott of Seagrove Bay *NA* p840
Lord Oates *Lib Dem* p840
Lord Popat *Con* p862
Lord Rana *Con* p871
Lord Rea *Lab* p874
Lord Robathan *Con* p882
Bishop of Southwark *NA* p917
Baroness Stern *CB* p920
Baroness Suttie *Lib Dem* p930
Lord Taylor of Goss Moor *Lib Dem* p933
Lord Tomlinson *Lab/Co-op* p940
Baroness Tonge *NA* p941
Lord Trees *CB* p942
Baroness Verma *Con* p954
Baroness Warwick of Undercliffe *Lab* p961
Lord Watson of Invergowrie *Lab* p962
Baroness Whitaker *Lab* p967

International trade

Lord Radice *Lab* p870

Internet

Baroness Kidron *CB* p766
Lord Maxton *Lab* p817

Investment

Baroness Hughes of Stretford *Lab* p744
Lord Lee of Trafford *Lib Dem* p779
Lord Sassoon *Con* p896

Ireland

Lord Dubs *Lab* p658
Lord Kilclooney *CB* p766
Lord Temple-Morris *Lab* p936

Islam

Baroness Afshar *CB* p553
Lord Kalms *NA* p762
Lord Pearson of Rannoch *UKIP* p856

Journalism and journalists

Baroness Sharples *Con* p902

Justice system

Lord Bach *Lab* p568
Lord Beecham *Lab* p574
Lord Beith *Lib Dem* p575
Baroness Clark of Calton *NA* p625
Bishop of Gloucester *NA* p696
Baroness Hanham *Con* p715
Baroness Henig *Lab* p727
Baroness Hilton of Eggardon *Lab* p730
Baroness Kidron *CB* p766
Lord Kirkhope of Harrogate *Con* p771
Lord Macdonald of River Glaven *Lib Dem* p798
Lord McNally *Lib Dem* p805
Lord Marks of Henley-on-Thames *Lib Dem* p812
Baroness Meacher *CB* p817
Baroness Newlove *Con* p834
Lord Paddick *Lib Dem* p848

Baroness Prashar	*CB*	p864
Lord Rosser	*Lab*	p888
Baroness Seccombe	*Con*	p899
Lord Smith of Finsbury	*NA*	p912
Baroness Stern	*CB*	p920
Lord Thomas of Cwmgiedd	*NA*	p937
Lord Thomas of Gresford	*Lib Dem*	p937

Labour Party

Lord Davies of Abersoch	*NA*	p647
Baroness Healy of Primrose Hill	*Lab*	p726
Lord Jordan	*Lab*	p758
Lord Radice	*Lab*	p870

Law

Lord Arbuthnot of Edrom	*Con*	p562
Lord Brown of Eaton-under-Heywood	*CB*	p602
Lord Clinton-Davis	*Lab*	p627
Lord Hardie	*CB*	p717
Baroness Howe of Idlicote	*CB*	p741
Baroness Mallalieu	*Lab*	p808
Lord Selkirk of Douglas	*Con*	p900

Law and order

Baroness Buscombe	*Con*	p607
Lord Warner	*CB*	p960

Learning disabilities

Baroness Browning	*Con*	p604
Baroness Murphy	*CB*	p829

Legal affairs

Lord Browne of Ladyton	*Lab*	p603
Baroness Buscombe	*Con*	p607
Baroness Butler-Sloss	*CB*	p609
Lord Campbell of Pittenweem	*Lib Dem*	p612
Lord Carlile of Berriew	*NA*	p615
Lord Carswell	*CB*	p617
Lord Hutton of Furness	*Lab*	p749
Lord Inglewood	*Con*	p750
Lord Irvine of Lairg	*Lab*	p751
Baroness McIntosh of Pickering	*Con*	p801
Lord Mackenzie of Framwellgate	*NA*	p803
Lord Morris of Aberavon	*Lab*	p825
Lord Pannick	*CB*	p850
Lord St John of Bletso	*CB*	p894
Lord Temple-Morris	*Lab*	p936
Lord Trimble	*Con*	p945
Archbishop of York	*NA*	p981

Legal aid

Lord Beecham	*Lab*	p574

Local government

Lord Bach	*Lab*	p568
Baroness Bakewell of Hardington Mandeville	*Lib Dem*	p570
Lord Bassam of Brighton	*Lab/Co-op*	p573
Lord Beecham	*Lab*	p574
Bishop of Birmingham	*NA*	p582
Lord Blunkett	*Lab*	p587
Lord Bowness	*Con*	p593
Lord Bradley	*Lab*	p595
Viscount Bridgeman	*Con*	p597
Baroness Couttie	*Con*	p636
Baroness Cumberlege	*Con*	p642
Viscount Eccles	*Con*	p663
Lord Fearn	*Lib Dem*	p674
Lord Forsyth of Drumlean	*Con*	p682
Lord Graham of Edmonton	*Lab/Co-op*	p703
Lord Greaves	*Lib Dem*	p704
Baroness Hamwee	*Lib Dem*	p714
Baroness Hanham	*Con*	p715
Lord Hanningfield	*NA*	p716
Lord Harris of Haringey	*Lab*	p719
Baroness Hollis of Heigham	*Lab*	p734
Baroness Hughes of Stretford	*Lab*	p744
Baroness Hussein-Ece	*Lib Dem*	p748
Lord Inglewood	*Con*	p750
Baroness Janke	*Lib Dem*	p752
Lord Kerslake	*CB*	p765
Lord Lansley	*Con*	p776
Earl of Lytton	*CB*	p796
Lord McKenzie of Luton	*Lab*	p803
Baroness Maddock	*Lib Dem*	p806
Lord Murphy of Torfaen	*Lab*	p829
Lord Palmer of Childs Hill	*Lib Dem*	p849
Baroness Randerson	*Lib Dem*	p872
Lord Scriven	*Lib Dem*	p899
Lord Selkirk of Douglas	*Con*	p900
Lord Shipley	*Lib Dem*	p906
Lord Smith of Finsbury	*NA*	p912
Lord Smith of Leigh	*Lab*	p914
Lord Stoddart of Swindon	*Ind Lab*	p924
Lord Storey	*Lib Dem*	p926
Lord Tope	*Lib Dem*	p941
Lord Touhig	*Lab/Co-op*	p942
Lord True	*Con*	p946
Baroness Williams of Trafford	*Con*	p972
Lord Willis of Knaresborough	*Lib Dem*	p973

London economy

Baroness Valentine	*CB*	p952

Manufacturing

Lord Bhattacharyya	*Lab*	p579
Lord Bilimoria	*CB*	p580
Lord Brookman	*Lab*	p600
Baroness Burt of Solihull	*Lib Dem*	p607
Lord Fox	*Lib Dem*	p685
Lord Jones	*Lab*	p755
Lord Renfrew of Kaimsthorn	*Con*	p877
Lord Taylor of Goss Moor	*Lib Dem*	p933

Media

Lord Allen of Kensington	*Lab*	p557
Earl of Arran	*Con*	p564
Baroness Benjamin	*Lib Dem*	p576
Lord Black of Brentwood	*Con*	p583
Baroness Buscombe	*Con*	p607
Viscount Colville of Culross	*CB*	p631

Baroness Cumberlege *Con* p642
Lord Currie of Marylebone *CB* p643
Baroness Dean of Thornton-le-Fylde *Lab* p649
Lord Fowler *Lord Speaker* p685
Lord Grade of Yarmouth *Con* p702
Lord Grocott *Lab* p709
Lord Hollick *Lab* p733
Lord Holmes of Richmond *Con* p735
Lord Inglewood *Con* p750
Baroness Jay of Paddington *Lab* p753
Baroness Jones of Whitchurch *Lab* p757
Baroness Kidron *CB* p766
Lord Lester of Herne Hill *Lib Dem* p782
Baroness Liddell of Coatdyke *Lab* p785
Lord McNally *Lib Dem* p805
Baroness Neville-Rolfe *Con* p833
Bishop of Norwich *NA* p839
Lord Palmer *CB* p849
Lord Quirk *CB* p869
Baroness Rawlings *Con* p873
Lord Smith of Finsbury *NA* p912
Lord Taylor of Warwick *NA* p934
Baroness Thornton *Lab/Co-op* p939
Lord Wood of Anfield *Lab* p977

Medical ethics
Baroness Campbell of Surbiton *CB* p612
Baroness Finlay of Llandaff *CB* p678
Lord Guthrie of Craigiebank *CB* p710
Baroness O'Neill of Bengarve *CB* p843

Medical schools
Lord Turnberg *Lab* p948

Medicines
Earl Baldwin of Bewdley *CB* p570
Lord Faulks *Con* p674
Baroness Finlay of Llandaff *CB* p678
Lord McColl of Dulwich *Con* p797
Lord Patel *CB* p852

Medicines in the Third World
Lord Trees *CB* p942

Mental health
Lord Alderdice *Lib Dem* p555
Baroness Browning *Con* p604
Lord Carlile of Berriew *NA* p615
Bishop of Ely *NA* p666
Lord Fairfax of Cameron *Con* p670
Lord Layard *Lab* p778
Baroness Meacher *CB* p817
Baroness Murphy *CB* p829
Lord Oates *Lib Dem* p840
Lord Ramsbotham *CB* p871
Lord Thurlow *CB* p939
Baroness Vere of Norbiton *Con* p953

Middle East
Earl of Arran *Con* p564
Baroness Dean of Thornton-le-Fylde *Lab* p649
Lord Foster of Bath *Lib Dem* p683
Lord Grocott *Lab* p709
Lord Inglewood *Con* p750
Lord Low of Dalston *CB* p793
Baroness Young of Old Scone *Lab* p984

Mineral extraction
Earl of Shrewsbury and Waterford *Con* p907

Motor industry
Lord Brougham and Vaux *Con* p601
Viscount Simon *Lab* p908

Museums and galleries
Lord Armstrong of Ilminster *CB* p564
Viscount Eccles *Con* p663
Lord Renfrew of Kaimsthorn *Con* p877

Music
Baroness Jolly *Lib Dem* p754
Lord Lipsey *Lab* p788
Lord Low of Dalston *CB* p793
Lord Sterling of Plaistow *Con* p920

National Health Service
Baroness Cumberlege *Con* p642
Lord Davies of Coity *Lab/Co-op* p647
Lord Dubs *Lab* p658
Lord Grocott *Lab* p709
Lord James of Blackheath *Con* p752
Lord Jones *Lab* p755
Lord McColl of Dulwich *Con* p797
Baroness Murphy *CB* p829
Lord Naseby *Con* p830
Lord Patel *CB* p852
Lord Turnberg *Lab* p948

National security
Baroness Manningham-Buller *CB* p810
Baroness Neville-Jones *Con* p832

National Service
Baroness Newlove *Con* p834

NATO
Lord Cormack *Con* p633

Northern Ireland
Lord Alderdice *Lib Dem* p555
Lord Alton of Liverpool *CB* p558
Viscount Brookeborough *CB* p600
Lord Browne of Ladyton *Lab* p603
Lord Carswell *CB* p617
Lord Dunlop *Con* p660
Lord Eames *CB* p661
Lord Glentoran *Con* p696
Baroness Harris of Richmond *Lib Dem* p720
Lord Hylton *CB* p749

Lord Lexden *Con* p784
Lord Mawhinney *Con* p816
Lord Robathan *Con* p882
Lord Rogan *UUP* p885
Lord Smith of Clifton *Lib Dem* p911
Lord Wood of Anfield *Lab* p977

Nuclear weapons

Baroness Miller of Chilthorne Domer *Lib Dem* p818

Nursing

Baroness Cox *CB* p637
Lord MacKenzie of Culkein *Lab* p802

Osteoporosis

Baroness Burt of Solihull *Lib Dem* p607

Palliative care

Lord Cavendish of Furness *Con* p619

Parliamentary administration

Lord Lisvane *CB* p789
Lord Livermore *Lab* p790
Lord Naseby *Con* p830

Peacekeeping operations

Lord Taylor of Warwick *NA* p934

Pensions

Baroness Altmann *Con* p558
Baroness Bakewell *Lab* p569
Lord Blyth of Rowington *Con* p588
Lord Bradley *Lab* p595
Lord Christopher *Lab* p624
Baroness Clark of Calton *NA* p625
Lord Davies of Stamford *Lab* p648
Baroness Dean of Thornton-le-Fylde *Lab* p649
Lord Flight *Con* p680
Lord Freeman *Con* p687
Lord Grabiner *CB* p701
Baroness Hollis of Heigham *Lab* p734
Lord Holmes of Richmond *Con* p735
Lord Lipsey *Lab* p788
Lord MacGregor of Pulham Market *Con* p799
Lord Paddick *Lib Dem* p848
Lord Sheikh *Con* p903
Lord Vinson *Con* p955
Baroness Warwick of Undercliffe *Lab* p961

Performing arts

Earl of Glasgow *Lib Dem* p694

Personal finance

Baroness Altmann *Con* p558

Pet Travel Scheme (PETS)

Baroness Sharples *Con* p902

Planning

Baroness Andrews *Lab* p561
Baroness Billingham *Lab* p581
Lord Borwick *Con* p590
Lord Bradshaw *Lib Dem* p595
Baroness Burt of Solihull *Lib Dem* p607
Baroness Ford *CB* p681
Baroness Gardner of Parkes *Con* p691
Baroness Hamwee *Lib Dem* p714
Baroness Hanham *Con* p715
Lord Lucas of Crudwell and Dingwall *Con* p794
Earl of Lytton *CB* p796
Lord Paddick *Lib Dem* p848
Lord Rooker *Lab* p887
Lord Selsdon *Con* p901
Lord Taylor of Goss Moor *Lib Dem* p933
Baroness Thornhill *Lib Dem* p938

Police

Baroness Berridge *Con* p577
Lord Bradshaw *Lib Dem* p595
Lord Colgrain *Con* p629
Baroness Doocey *Lib Dem* p656
Lord Harris of Haringey *Lab* p719
Baroness Harris of Richmond *Lib Dem* p720
Baroness Henig *Lab* p727
Lord Imbert *CB* p750
Lord Mackenzie of Framwellgate *NA* p803
Baroness Newlove *Con* p834
Viscount Simon *Lab* p908

Policy making

Lord Sainsbury of Turville *Lab* p893

Political parties

Lord Taylor of Holbeach *Con* p934

Politics

Lord Norton of Louth *Con* p838

Postal Services

Earl of Kinnoull *CB* p770
Lord Sawyer *Lab* p897
Lord Skelmersdale *Con* p909

Poverty

Lord Adebowale *CB* p552
Lord Bird *CB* p582
Lord Bradley *Lab* p595
Lord Cashman *Lab* p618
Lord Harries of Pentregarth *CB* p718
Baroness Jolly *Lib Dem* p754
Baroness King of Bow *Lab* p767
Baroness Lister of Burtersett *Lab* p788
Lord Ouseley *CB* p845
Lord Rana *Con* p871

Prison reform

Lord Addington *Lib Dem* p551
Baroness Bottomley of Nettlestone *Con* p591
Lord Dubs *Lab* p658
Lord Fellowes *CB* p676
Lord Ramsbotham *CB* p871
Baroness Stern *CB* p920

Prisoners

Lord Hardie *CB* p717

Prisons

Baroness Burt of Solihull *Lib Dem* p607
Lord Christopher *Lab* p624
Baroness Gibson of Market Rasen *Lab* p693
Lord Glenarthur *Con* p695
Baroness Hamwee *Lib Dem* p714
Lord Hardie *CB* p717
Baroness Healy of Primrose Hill *Lab* p726
Earl Howe *Con* p740
Lord Hylton *CB* p749
Lord Judd *Lab* p760
Baroness Masham of Ilton *CB* p814
Bishop of Peterborough *NA* p857
Baroness Royall of Blaisdon *Lab/Co-op* p890
Baroness Stern *CB* p920
Baroness Thomas of Winchester *Lib Dem* p938

Private security services

Baroness Henig *Lab* p727

Public finance

Baroness Noakes *Con* p836

Public funding

Baroness Jowell *Lab* p759

Public sector pay and conditions

Lord O'Donnell *CB* p841

Public service reform

Lord Bichard *CB* p580
Baroness Jones of Whitchurch *Lab* p757

Public services

Lord Armstrong of Ilminster *CB* p564
Lord Blackwell *Con* p585
Lord Laming *CB* p774
Lord Mawson *CB* p816
Baroness Noakes *Con* p836
Lord Ouseley *CB* p845
Lord Turnbull *CB* p949
Lord Wright of Richmond *CB* p980

Rail transport

Lord Greaves *Lib Dem* p704

Rape

Baroness Stern *CB* p920

Recreation

Lord Pendry *Lab* p857

Refugees and asylum seekers

Lord Alton of Liverpool *CB* p558
Lord Greaves *Lib Dem* p704
Lord Judd *Lab* p760
Baroness Lister of Burtersett *Lab* p788
Lord Moynihan *Con* p828
Baroness Neuberger *CB* p831

Regeneration

Lord Adebowale *CB* p552
Lord Best *CB* p578
Baroness Ford *CB* p681
Lord Patel of Blackburn *Lab* p853
Lord Shipley *Lib Dem* p906
Lord Storey *Lib Dem* p926

Regional assemblies

Lord Dunlop *Con* p660
Lord Touhig *Lab/Co-op* p942

Regional government and policy

Lord Christopher *Lab* p624
Lord Darling of Roulanish *Lab* p645
Lord Flight *Con* p680
Lord Forsyth of Drumlean *Con* p682
Lord Foster of Bishop Auckland *Lab* p683
Lord Hague of Richmond *Con* p710
Lord Hamilton of Epsom *Con* p714
Lord Lansley *Con* p776
Baroness Liddell of Coatdyke *Lab* p785
Lord MacGregor of Pulham Market *Con* p799
Lord Moonie *Lab/Co-op* p821
Baroness O'Cathain *Con* p841
Lord Paul *NA* p855
Baroness Primarolo *Lab* p865
Lord Reid of Cardowan *Lab* p876
Lord Rowe-Beddoe *CB* p889
Lord Taylor of Goss Moor *Lib Dem* p933
Lord Willetts *Con* p970

Regional policy

Baroness Armstrong of Hill Top *Lab* p563
Lord Beecham *Lab* p574
Baroness Hughes of Stretford *Lab* p744
Lord Inglewood *Con* p750
Lord Jones *Lab* p755
Lord Kilclooney *CB* p766
Lord Liddle *Lab* p785
Lord Newby *Lib Dem* p833
Baroness Quin *Lab* p868
Lord Smith of Leigh *Lab* p914
Lord Wrigglesworth *Lib Dem* p980

Regulatory Reform

Baroness Bottomley of Nettlestone *Con* p591

Religion

Baroness Berridge *Con* p577
Lord Harries of Pentregarth *CB* p718
Lord Hylton *CB* p749
Archbishop of York *NA* p981

Renewables

Baroness Finn *Con* p679
Lord Hain *Lab* p711
Lord James of Blackheath *Con* p752
Earl of Liverpool *Con* p790
Lord Vaux of Harrowden *CB* p953
Lord Wallace of Tankerness *Lib Dem* p958

Research and development

Baroness Bowles of Berkhamsted *Lib Dem* p592
Lord Cashman *Lab* p618
Lord Haskel *Lab* p721
Lord Oxburgh *CB* p846
Lord Patel *CB* p852
Lord Rooker *Lab* p887
Lord Sutherland of Houndwood *CB* p929
Lord Turnberg *Lab* p948
Baroness Warwick of Undercliffe *Lab* p961
Lord Winston *Lab* p975

Retail industry

Baroness O'Cathain *Con* p841

Road safety

Lord Brougham and Vaux *Con* p601
Lord Robertson of Port Ellen *Lab* p883
Viscount Simon *Lab* p908

Royal Navy

Lord Haworth *Lab* p723

Rural affairs

Baroness Bakewell of Hardington Mandeville *Lib Dem* p570
Lord Cameron of Dillington *CB* p611
Earl Cathcart *Con* p618
Lord Elis-Thomas *NA* p665
Bishop of Ely *NA* p666
Lord Gardiner of Kimble *Con* p690
Lord Inglewood *Con* p750
Baroness Jolly *Lib Dem* p754
Earl of Kinnoull *CB* p770
Lord Knight of Weymouth *Lab/Co-op* p772
Earl of Lindsay *Con* p786
Lord Lisvane *CB* p789
Lord Maclennan of Rogart *Lib Dem* p804
Lord Mancroft *Con* p809
Duke of Montrose *Con* p821
Baroness Neville-Rolfe *Con* p833
Bishop of Newcastle *NA* p834
Baroness Noakes *Con* p836
Bishop of Norwich *NA* p839
Bishop of Peterborough *NA* p857
Lord Purvis of Tweed *Lib Dem* p867
Lord Rana *Con* p871
Baroness Shephard of Northwold *Con* p903
Lord Thurlow *CB* p939
Lord Tyler *Lib Dem* p950
Lord Wallace of Tankerness *Lib Dem* p958
Lord Willoughby de Broke *UKIP* p973

Rural communities

Lord Taylor of Goss Moor *Lib Dem* p933

Rural economy

Earl of Lytton *CB* p796

Science

Baroness Andrews *Lab* p561
Baroness Bowles of Berkhamsted *Lib Dem* p592
Baroness Brown of Cambridge *CB* p601
Viscount Colville of Culross *CB* p631
Lord Drayson *Lab* p657
Earl of Erroll *CB* p668
Baroness Greenfield *CB* p705
Lord Haskel *Lab* p721
Lord Hunt of Chesterton *Lab* p745
Lord Krebs *CB* p773
Baroness Morgan of Drefelin *CB* p823
Baroness Neville-Jones *Con* p832
Lord O'Donnell *CB* p841
Lord Rees of Ludlow *CB* p876
Lord Rooker *Lab* p887
Lord Sainsbury of Turville *Lab* p893
Earl of Selborne *Con* p900
Viscount Simon *Lab* p908
Lord Taverne *Lib Dem* p932
Baroness Warwick of Undercliffe *Lab* p961
Lord Willetts *Con* p970
Lord Willis of Knaresborough *Lib Dem* p973
Lord Winston *Lab* p975

Science and technology

Lord Hain *Lab* p711
Lord Hylton *CB* p749
Lord Kirkhope of Harrogate *Con* p771

Science, technology and research

Baroness Bowles of Berkhamsted *Lib Dem* p592
Lord Haskel *Lab* p721
Earl of Kinnoull *CB* p770

Scotland

Lord Dunlop *Con* p660
Earl of Erroll *CB* p668
Lord Foulkes of Cumnock *Lab/Co-op* p684
Lord Fraser of Corriegarth *Con* p686
Lord Glenarthur *Con* p695
Lord Gordon of Strathblane *Lab* p699
Earl of Home *Con* p736
Earl of Kinnoull *CB* p770
Earl of Lindsay *Con* p786
Lord Purvis of Tweed *Lib Dem* p867
Baroness Ramsay of Cartvale *Lab* p870
Lord Selkirk of Douglas *Con* p900
Lord Stevenson of Balmacara *Lab* p923
Lord Wilson of Tillyorn *CB* p974

Scottish Government

Lord Wallace of Tankerness *Lib Dem* p958

Scottish home rule

Lord Wallace of Tankerness *Lib Dem* p958

Security

Baroness Butler-Sloss *CB* p609
Lord Clark of Windermere *Lab* p625
Lord Dannatt *CB* p644
Lord Fairfax of Cameron *Con* p670
Baroness Liddell of Coatdyke *Lab* p785
Lord Macdonald of River Glaven *Lib Dem* p798

Lord Reid of Cardowan	*Lab*	p876
Baroness Taylor of Bolton	*Lab*	p933
Lord Taylor of Warwick	*NA*	p934
Lord West of Spithead	*Lab*	p965

Security

Lord Bach	*Lab*	p568
Lord Harris of Haringey	*Lab*	p719

Sexual abuse

Baroness Stern	*CB*	p920

Sexual health

Baroness Gould of Potternewton	*Lab*	p701

Sexually Transmitted Diseases

Baroness Barker	*Lib Dem*	p571

Skills

Lord Aberdare	*CB*	p551
Baroness Brinton	*Lib Dem*	p598
Lord Cotter	*Lib Dem*	p635
Baroness Garden of Frognal	*Lib Dem*	p690
Lord German	*Lib Dem*	p692
Lord Hall of Birkenhead	*CB*	p713
Lord Hunt of Wirral	*Con*	p747
Baroness Wolf of Dulwich	*CB*	p976

Slavery

Baroness Butler-Sloss	*CB*	p609
Baroness Goudie	*Lab*	p700

Small businesses

Lord Aberdare	*CB*	p551
Baroness Browning	*Con*	p604
Lord Cope of Berkeley	*Con*	p632
Lord Empey	*UUP*	p667
Lord Foster of Bishop Auckland	*Lab*	p683
Lord German	*Lib Dem*	p692
Earl of Glasgow	*Lib Dem*	p694
Lord Harrison	*Lab*	p721
Baroness Liddell of Coatdyke	*Lab*	p785
Baroness McIntosh of Pickering	*Con*	p801
Lord Mitchell	*NA*	p818
Lord Palmer of Childs Hill	*Lib Dem*	p849
Lord Popat	*Con*	p862
Lord Risby	*Con*	p882
Baroness Sharples	*Con*	p902
Lord Vinson	*Con*	p955

Smoking

Lord Faulkner of Worcester	*Lab*	p673
Baroness Gale	*Lab*	p689

Social affairs

Baroness Andrews	*Lab*	p561
Lord Beecham	*Lab*	p574
Lord Best	*CB*	p578
Lord Bichard	*CB*	p580
Baroness Blackstone	*Lab*	p584
Baroness Campbell of Surbiton	*CB*	p612
Lord Eames	*CB*	p661
Lord Griffiths of Fforestfach	*Con*	p709
Lord Redesdale	*Lib Dem*	p875

Social inclusion

Baroness Armstrong of Hill Top	*Lab*	p563
Lord Watson of Invergowrie	*Lab*	p962

Social justice

Lord Hain	*Lab*	p711
Lord Morris of Handsworth	*Lab*	p826
Baroness Stroud	*Con*	p927

Social workers

Baroness Brinton	*Lib Dem*	p598
Baroness Campbell of Surbiton	*CB*	p612
Lord Curry of Kirkharle	*CB*	p644
Baroness Howarth of Breckland	*CB*	p739
Baroness Meacher	*CB*	p817

Sport

Lord Addington	*Lib Dem*	p551
Lord Allen of Kensington	*Lab*	p557
Lord Archer of Weston-Super-Mare	*NA*	p562
Earl of Arran	*Con*	p564
Lord Bach	*Lab*	p568
Lord Bates	*Con*	p573
Baroness Benjamin	*Lib Dem*	p576
Baroness Billingham	*Lab*	p581
Lord Bradley	*Lab*	p595
Lord Brookman	*Lab*	p600
Lord Campbell of Pittenweem	*Lib Dem*	p612
Lord Colwyn	*Con*	p631
Lord Donoughue	*Lab*	p656
Baroness Doocey	*Lib Dem*	p656
Lord Dunlop	*Con*	p660
Baroness Evans of Bowes Park	*Con*	p668
Lord Faulkner of Worcester	*Lab*	p673
Lord Glentoran	*Con*	p696
Lord Grantchester	*Lab*	p703
Baroness Grey-Thompson	*CB*	p707
Lord Higgins	*Con*	p729
Lord Holmes of Richmond	*Con*	p735
Lord Hoyle	*Lab*	p743
Lord Jones of Cheltenham	*Lib Dem*	p756
Baroness Jowell	*Lab*	p759
Lord Knight of Weymouth	*Lab/Co-op*	p772
Lord MacLaurin of Knebworth	*Con*	p804
Lord Marland	*Con*	p812
Baroness Massey of Darwen	*Lab*	p814
Lord Moynihan	*Con*	p828
Baroness Neville-Rolfe	*Con*	p833
Lord Pendry	*Lab*	p857
Lord St John of Bletso	*CB*	p894
Lord Smith of Finsbury	*NA*	p912
Lord Triesman	*Lab*	p944
Lord Walker of Aldringham	*CB*	p957
Lord Wood of Anfield	*Lab*	p977

Steel industry

Lord Morris of Aberavon	*Lab*	p825

Stroke

Lord Lingfield	*Con*	p787

Sustainable development

Lord Taylor of Goss Moor	*Lib Dem*	p933

Tax

Lord Arbuthnot of Edrom	*Con*	p562
Lord Blackwell	*Con*	p585
Lord Dykes	*CB*	p661
Lord Flight	*Con*	p680
Earl of Lytton	*CB*	p796
Lord McKenzie of Luton	*Lab*	p803
Lord Palmer of Childs Hill	*Lib Dem*	p849
Lord Taverne	*Lib Dem*	p932
Lord Vinson	*Con*	p955

Technology

Lord Aberdare	*CB*	p551
Lord Allan of Hallam	*Lib Dem*	p556
Lord Ashdown of Norton-sub-Hamdon	*Lib Dem*	p565
Baroness Bowles of Berkhamsted	*Lib Dem*	p592
Earl of Erroll	*CB*	p668
Lord Fox	*Lib Dem*	p685
Lord Freeman	*Con*	p687
Lord Harris of Haringey	*Lab*	p719
Lord Haskel	*Lab*	p721
Lord Jones of Cheltenham	*Lib Dem*	p756
Earl of Liverpool	*Con*	p790
Lord Mitchell	*NA*	p818
Lord Moonie	*Lab/Co-op*	p821
Baroness Neville-Jones	*Con*	p832
Lord Rees of Ludlow	*CB*	p876
Lord Rooker	*Lab*	p887
Lord St John of Bletso	*CB*	p894
Lord Selsdon	*Con*	p901
Baroness Shields	*Con*	p905
Viscount Simon	*Lab*	p908
Lord Taverne	*Lib Dem*	p932
Baroness Warwick of Undercliffe	*Lab*	p961
Lord Winston	*Lab*	p975

Television

Earl of Glasgow	*Lib Dem*	p694

Terrorism

Lord Alderdice	*Lib Dem*	p555
Lord Maginnis of Drumglass	*Ind UU*	p807
Baroness Shields	*Con*	p905

Theology

Lord Alderdice	*Lib Dem*	p555

Third World

Viscount Eccles	*Con*	p663
Lord Judd	*Lab*	p760
Lord McFall of Alcluith	*NA*	p799
Lord Stunell	*Lib Dem*	p928

Tourism

Viscount Brookeborough	*CB*	p600
Lord Cotter	*Lib Dem*	p635
Baroness Doocey	*Lib Dem*	p656
Lord Fearn	*Lib Dem*	p674
Lord Foster of Bath	*Lib Dem*	p683
Lord Geddes	*Con*	p692
Earl of Glasgow	*Lib Dem*	p694
Lord Gordon of Strathblane	*Lab*	p699
Lord Harrison	*Lab*	p721
Lord Lee of Trafford	*Lib Dem*	p779
Baroness McIntosh of Pickering	*Con*	p801
Baroness Morgan of Ely	*Lab*	p824
Lord Palmer	*CB*	p849
Viscount Thurso	*Lib Dem*	p939
Lord Tyler	*Lib Dem*	p950
Viscount Younger of Leckie	*Con*	p985

Trade

Lord Aberdare	*CB*	p551
Lord Bruce of Bennachie	*Lib Dem*	p605
Baroness Chalker of Wallasey	*Con*	p621
Lord Davies of Abersoch	*NA*	p647
Lord Davies of Stamford	*Lab*	p648
Lord Evans of Watford	*Lab*	p669
Lord Haskel	*Lab*	p721
Lord Hoyle	*Lab*	p743
Lord Jones of Cheltenham	*Lib Dem*	p756
Lord Lansley	*Con*	p776
Lord Lee of Trafford	*Lib Dem*	p779
Lord Mawhinney	*Con*	p816
Lord Moynihan	*Con*	p828
Baroness Noakes	*Con*	p836
Lord O'Neill of Clackmannan	*Lab*	p844
Lord Plumb	*Con*	p860
Lord Redesdale	*Lib Dem*	p875
Lord Rogan	*UUP*	p885
Lord Selsdon	*Con*	p901
Lord Taylor of Warwick	*NA*	p934

Trade disputes

Lord Martin of Springburn	*CB*	p813

Trade Unions

Lord Balfe	*Con*	p570
Baroness Golding	*Lab*	p698
Baroness Hayter of Kentish Town	*Lab/Co-op*	p725
Lord Morris of Handsworth	*Lab*	p826

Transatlantic relations

Baroness Helic	*Con*	p726
Lord Watson of Richmond	*Lib Dem*	p963

Transport

Lord Alton of Liverpool	*CB*	p558
Earl Attlee	*Con*	p567
Lord Berkeley	*Lab*	p576
Lord Birt	*CB*	p582
Lord Borwick	*Con*	p590
Lord Brabazon of Tara	*Con*	p594
Lord Bradshaw	*Lib Dem*	p595
Lord Brougham and Vaux	*Con*	p601
Baroness Chalker of Wallasey	*Con*	p621
Lord Chidgey	*Lib Dem*	p623
Lord Clinton-Davis	*Lab*	p627
Lord Darling of Roulanish	*Lab*	p645

Lord Davies of Oldham	*Lab*	p648
Lord Dixon-Smith	*Con*	p655
Lord Dykes	*CB*	p661
Viscount of Falkland	*CB*	p671
Lord Faulkner of Worcester	*Lab*	p673
Lord Fearn	*Lib Dem*	p674
Lord Foster of Bath	*Lib Dem*	p683
Lord Foster of Bishop Auckland	*Lab*	p683
Baroness Gardner of Parkes	*Con*	p691
Lord Geddes	*Con*	p692
Lord Grantchester	*Lab*	p703
Lord Hanningfield	*NA*	p716
Viscount Hanworth	*Lab*	p717
Lord Haworth	*Lab*	p723
Lord Hayward	*Con*	p725
Lord Higgins	*Con*	p729
Lord Hollick	*Lab*	p733
Lord Horam	*Con*	p738
Lord Hughes of Woodside	*Lab*	p744
Lord Hunt of Kings Heath	*Lab/Co-op*	p746
Lord Jones of Cheltenham	*Lib Dem*	p756
Lord Kirkhope of Harrogate	*Con*	p771
Baroness Kramer	*Lib Dem*	p773
Earl of Liverpool	*Con*	p790
Lord MacGregor of Pulham Market	*Con*	p799
Baroness McIntosh of Hudnall	*Lab*	p800
Baroness McIntosh of Pickering	*Con*	p801
Lord Robathan	*Con*	p882
Lord Rogan	*UUP*	p885
Lord Rosser	*Lab*	p888
Lord Smith of Clifton	*Lib Dem*	p911
Lord Stoddart of Swindon	*Ind Lab*	p924
Lord Teverson	*Lib Dem*	p936
Baroness Valentine	*CB*	p952
Baroness Williams of Trafford	*Con*	p972

Tuberculosis

Baroness Suttie	*Lib Dem*	p930

Unemployment and jobseeking

Lord Colgrain	*Con*	p629
Baroness Stedman-Scott	*Con*	p918

United Nations

Lord Carlile of Berriew	*NA*	p615
Baroness Coussins	*CB*	p636
Lord Ramsbotham	*CB*	p871

Urban communities

Lord Griffiths of Burry Port	*Lab*	p708
Lord Northbrook	*Con*	p837

Utilites

Lord Skelmersdale	*Con*	p909

Venture capital

Lord Flight	*Con*	p680

Veterinary services

Lord Trees	*CB*	p942

Victims of crime

Baroness Newlove	*Con*	p834

Visual arts

Lord Freyberg	*CB*	p688

Waste policies and regulation

Lord Taylor of Holbeach	*Con*	p934

Welfare

Lord Bach	*Lab*	p568
Earl of Clancarty	*CB*	p625
Baroness Couttie	*Con*	p636
Lord Davies of Stamford	*Lab*	p648
Lord Giddens	*Lab*	p694
Baroness Healy of Primrose Hill	*Lab*	p726
Lord Hutton of Furness	*Lab*	p749
Lord Levy	*Lab*	p783
Lord Liddle	*Lab*	p785
Baroness Lister of Burtersett	*Lab*	p788
Countess of Mar	*CB*	p811
Baroness Meacher	*CB*	p817
Lord Paddick	*Lib Dem*	p848
Lord Smith of Finsbury	*NA*	p912

Welsh Assembly Government

Lord Carlile of Berriew	*NA*	p615

Young offenders

Lord Hardie	*CB*	p717
Baroness Walmsley	*Lib Dem*	p959

Youth justice

Lord Oates	*Lib Dem*	p840
Lord Ramsbotham	*CB*	p871

Youth services

Lord Purvis of Tweed	*Lib Dem*	p867

Peers' Countries of Interest

For precise details of individuals' stated interests, see relevant biography. The interests listed are supplied by Peers themselves.

Afghanistan

Lord Arbuthnot of Edrom	*Con*	p562
Lord Browne of Ladyton	*Lab*	p603
Baroness D'Souza	*CB*	p658
Baroness Featherstone	*Lib Dem*	p675
Baroness Hodgson of Abinger	*Con*	p731
Earl of Sandwich	*CB*	p896
Baroness Stern	*CB*	p920
Baroness Tonge	*NA*	p941
Baroness Warsi	*Con*	p960

Albania

Lord Bates	*Con*	p573

Algeria

Baroness Howells of St Davids	*Lab*	p742
Baroness Stern	*CB*	p920

Angola

Earl of Listowel	*CB*	p789

Argentina

Bishop of Carlisle	*NA*	p615
Lord Faulkner of Worcester	*Lab*	p673
Lord O'Neill of Clackmannan	*Lab*	p844
Lord Rowe-Beddoe	*CB*	p889
Lord Smith of Finsbury	*NA*	p912
Baroness Stern	*CB*	p920
Lord Wigley	*PlC*	p969

Armenia

Baroness Cox	*CB*	p637
Baroness Nicholson of Winterbourne	*Con*	p835
Lord Wallace of Saltaire	*Lib Dem*	p958

Australia

Lord Arbuthnot of Edrom	*Con*	p562
Lord Archer of Weston-Super-Mare	*NA*	p562
Lord Barker of Battle	*Con*	p572
Lord Bassam of Brighton	*Lab/Co-op*	p573
Lord Bird	*CB*	p582
Lord Broers	*CB*	p599
Lord Cooper of Windrush	*Con*	p632
Baroness Dean of Thornton-le-Fylde	*Lab*	p649
Lord Desai	*Lab*	p653
Lord Faulkner of Worcester	*Lab*	p673
Baroness Ford	*CB*	p681
Lord Gardiner of Kimble	*Con*	p690
Baroness Greenfield	*CB*	p705
Lord Harris of Haringey	*Lab*	p719
Lord Holmes of Richmond	*Con*	p735
Earl of Home	*Con*	p736
Lord Hoyle	*Lab*	p743
Lord Jones of Birmingham	*CB*	p755
Baroness Kingsmill	*Lab*	p768
Lord Kirkhope of Harrogate	*Con*	p771
Baroness Liddell of Coatdyke	*Lab*	p785
Baroness Lister of Burtersett	*Lab*	p788
Lord Lisvane	*CB*	p789
Lord Livermore	*Lab*	p790
Lord Low of Dalston	*CB*	p793
Lord MacKenzie of Culkein	*Lab*	p802
Lord Northbourne	*CB*	p837
Baroness Randerson	*Lib Dem*	p872
Baroness Royall of Blaisdon	*Lab/Co-op*	p890
Viscount Simon	*Lab*	p908
Lord Smith of Finsbury	*NA*	p912
Lord Smith of Leigh	*Lab*	p914
Lord Stirrup	*CB*	p924
Lord Teverson	*Lib Dem*	p936
Lord Tyler	*Lib Dem*	p950
Baroness Wilcox	*Con*	p969

Azerbaijan

Baroness Goudie	*Lab*	p700
Lord Haworth	*Lab*	p723
Baroness Nicholson of Winterbourne	*Con*	p835
Baroness O'Cathain	*Con*	p841
Earl of Selborne	*Con*	p900

Bahrain

Lord Jones of Cheltenham	*Lib Dem*	p756
Lord Jordan	*Lab*	p758

Bangladesh

Lord Ahmad of Wimbledon	*Con*	p554
Lord Bhatia	*NA*	p579
Lord Desai	*Lab*	p653
Baroness King of Bow	*Lab*	p767
Lord Loomba	*NA*	p792
Lord Patel of Blackburn	*Lab*	p853
Baroness Tonge	*NA*	p941
Baroness Uddin	*NA*	p951
Baroness Warsi	*Con*	p960

Belgium

Lord Astor of Hever	*Con*	p567

Belize

Lord Skelmersdale	*Con*	p909

Bermuda

Earl of Kinnoull	*CB*	p770
Lord Tope	*Lib Dem*	p941

Bosnia/Herzegovina

Lord Cormack	*Con*	p633
Lord Greaves	*Lib Dem*	p704

Botswana

Lord Jones of Cheltenham	*Lib Dem*	p756
Bishop of Newcastle	*NA*	p834
Lord Rowlands	*Lab*	p890

Brazil

Baroness Bakewell	*Lab*	p569
Lord Browne of Belmont	*DUP*	p603
Lord Desai	*Lab*	p653
Lord Gadhia	*NA*	p689
Lord Howarth of Newport	*Lab*	p740
Lord Oakeshott of Seagrove Bay	*NA*	p840
Baroness Rawlings	*Con*	p873
Lord Rogers of Riverside	*Lab*	p886
Lord Rowe-Beddoe	*CB*	p889
Lord Smith of Finsbury	*NA*	p912

Bulgaria

Baroness Gould of Potternewton	*Lab*	p701
Baroness Nicholson of Winterbourne	*Con*	p835
Baroness Rawlings	*Con*	p873

Burma

Lord Alton of Liverpool	*CB*	p558
Baroness Cox	*CB*	p637
Baroness Flather	*CB*	p679
Baroness Jones of Whitchurch	*Lab*	p757
Baroness Kinnock of Holyhead	*Lab*	p769
Lord Stevenson of Balmacara	*Lab*	p923

Burundi

Lord Browne of Ladyton	*Lab*	p603
Archbishop of Canterbury	*NA*	p613
Bishop of Durham	*NA*	p660
Bishop of Winchester	*NA*	p975

Cambodia

Lord Griffiths of Burry Port	*Lab*	p708
Lord Haworth	*Lab*	p723

Canada

Lord Armstrong of Ilminster	*CB*	p564
Lord Beith	*Lib Dem*	p575
Lord Black of Crossharbour	*NA*	p583
Lord Browne of Belmont	*DUP*	p603
Lord Bruce of Bennachie	*Lib Dem*	p605
Lord Desai	*Lab*	p653
Lord Empey	*UUP*	p667
Lord Faulkner of Worcester	*Lab*	p673
Baroness Fookes	*Con*	p681
Lord Harris of Haringey	*Lab*	p719
Baroness Harris of Richmond	*Lib Dem*	p720
Lord Holmes of Richmond	*Con*	p735
Baroness Howarth of Breckland	*CB*	p739
Lord Martin of Springburn	*CB*	p813
Lord O'Donnell	*CB*	p841
Lord Parekh	*Lab*	p851
Baroness Randerson	*Lib Dem*	p872
Lord Roberts of Llandudno	*Lib Dem*	p883
Lord Singh of Wimbledon	*CB*	p908
Lord Tyler	*Lib Dem*	p950
Baroness Wolf of Dulwich	*CB*	p976

Chile

Lord Bach	*Lab*	p568
Baroness Coussins	*CB*	p636
Lord Lamont of Lerwick	*Con*	p775
Lord Naseby	*Con*	p830
Baroness Stern	*CB*	p920
Lord Teverson	*Lib Dem*	p936

China

Lord Aberdare	*CB*	p551
Lord Ahmad of Wimbledon	*Con*	p554
Lord Ahmed	*NA*	p554
Lord Alton of Liverpool	*CB*	p558
Baroness Amos	*NA*	p559
Lord Bates	*Con*	p573
Lord Bhattacharyya	*Lab*	p579
Bishop of Birmingham	*NA*	p582
Lord Birt	*CB*	p582
Baroness Bottomley of Nettlestone	*Con*	p591
Lord Bradley	*Lab*	p595
Baroness Brown of Cambridge	*CB*	p601
Lord Christopher	*Lab*	p624
Lord Clement-Jones	*Lib Dem*	p627
Viscount Colville of Culross	*CB*	p631
Lord Cotter	*Lib Dem*	p635
Lord Cunningham of Felling	*Lab*	p643
Lord Davidson of Glen Clova	*Lab*	p646
Baroness Dean of Thornton-le-Fylde	*Lab*	p649
Lord de Mauley	*Con*	p652
Lord Desai	*Lab*	p653
Lord Dobbs	*Con*	p655
Lord Dunlop	*Con*	p660
Lord Dykes	*CB*	p661
Baroness Finlay of Llandaff	*CB*	p678
Baroness Finn	*Con*	p679
Lord Flight	*Con*	p680
Lord Foulkes of Cumnock	*Lab/Co-op*	p684
Lord Fraser of Corriegarth	*Con*	p686
Baroness Fritchie	*CB*	p688
Lord Gadhia	*NA*	p689
Baroness Gibson of Market Rasen	*Lab*	p693
Lord Giddens	*Lab*	p694
Lord Goddard of Stockport	*Lib Dem*	p697
Lord Gordon of Strathblane	*Lab*	p699
Baroness Gould of Potternewton	*Lab*	p701
Lord Grantchester	*Lab*	p703
Lord Griffiths of Fforestfach	*Con*	p709
Lord Hall of Birkenhead	*CB*	p713
Lord Hardie	*CB*	p717
Baroness Harding of Winscombe	*Con*	p718
Baroness Healy of Primrose Hill	*Lab*	p726
Baroness Henig	*Lab*	p727
Lord Howell of Guildford	*Con*	p742
Baroness Howells of St Davids	*Lab*	p742
Lord Inglewood	*Con*	p750
Baroness Jay of Paddington	*Lab*	p753
Baroness Jones of Whitchurch	*Lab*	p757
Baroness Jowell	*Lab*	p759
Lord Kerr of Kinlochard	*CB*	p764

Baroness Kidron	*CB*	p766
Baroness Kingsmill	*Lab*	p768
Lord Laming	*CB*	p774
Lord Leitch	*Lab*	p781
Baroness Liddell of Coatdyke	*Lab*	p785
Lord Livermore	*Lab*	p790
Lord McConnell of Glenscorrodale	*Lab*	p797
Lord McNally	*Lib Dem*	p805
Lord Marlesford	*Con*	p813
Baroness Neville-Rolfe	*Con*	p833
Lord Oxburgh	*CB*	p846
Lord Paul	*NA*	p855
Lord Prescott	*Lab*	p864
Lord Risby	*Con*	p882
Lord Rowe-Beddoe	*CB*	p889
Lord Sainsbury of Turville	*Lab*	p893
Lord St John of Bletso	*CB*	p894
Lord Sanderson of Bowden	*Con*	p895
Lord Sassoon	*Con*	p896
Lord Selsdon	*Con*	p901
Lord Skidelsky	*CB*	p909
Lord Smith of Clifton	*Lib Dem*	p911
Lord Smith of Finsbury	*NA*	p912
Lord Soley	*Lab*	p916
Lord Steel of Aikwood	*Lib Dem*	p919
Lord Stephen	*Lib Dem*	p919
Lord Stone of Blackheath	*Lab*	p925
Lord Taylor of Warwick	*NA*	p934
Lord Thomas of Gresford	*Lib Dem*	p937
Viscount Trenchard	*Con*	p944
Lord Triesman	*Lab*	p944
Lord Turner of Ecchinswell	*CB*	p949
Lord Wallace of Tankerness	*Lib Dem*	p958
Lord Wei	*Con*	p964
Baroness Wheatcroft	*Con*	p966
Baroness Wheeler	*Lab*	p966
Lord Whitty	*Lab*	p968
Lord Willetts	*Con*	p970
Lord Wood of Anfield	*Lab*	p977
Lord Woolmer of Leeds	*Lab*	p978
Lord Young of Norwood Green	*Lab*	p983

Colombia

Lord Alderdice	*Lib Dem*	p555
Lord Allan of Hallam	*Lib Dem*	p556
Lord Browne of Ladyton	*Lab*	p603
Baroness Coussins	*CB*	p636
Lord Skelmersdale	*Con*	p909
Baroness Tonge	*NA*	p941

Croatia

Lord Bates	*Con*	p573
Lord Browne of Belmont	*DUP*	p603
Lord Cormack	*Con*	p633
Lord Greaves	*Lib Dem*	p704

Cuba

Baroness Coussins	*CB*	p636
Baroness Smith of Basildon	*Lab/Co-op*	p910
Lord Triesman	*Lab*	p944

Cyprus

Lord Harris of Haringey	*Lab*	p719
Baroness Hussein-Ece	*Lib Dem*	p748
Lord Kilclooney	*CB*	p766
Baroness Ludford	*Lib Dem*	p795
Lord Maginnis of Drumglass	*Ind UU*	p807
Lord Sharkey	*Lib Dem*	p902
Lord Smith of Finsbury	*NA*	p912

Czech Republic

Lord Bruce of Bennachie	*Lib Dem*	p605
Baroness Finn	*Con*	p679

Democratic Republic of Congo

Lord Alton of Liverpool	*CB*	p558
Bishop of Birmingham	*NA*	p582
Archbishop of Canterbury	*NA*	p613
Lord Mance	*NA*	p809
Bishop of Winchester	*NA*	p975

Denmark

Lord Grantchester	*Lab*	p703
Baroness Maddock	*Lib Dem*	p806
Lord Teverson	*Lib Dem*	p936

Dominican Republic

Lord Griffiths of Burry Port	*Lab*	p708
Baroness Stern	*CB*	p920

East Timor

Baroness Cox	*CB*	p637

Ecuador

Lord Allan of Hallam	*Lib Dem*	p556

Egypt

Lord Alton of Liverpool	*CB*	p558
Baroness Berridge	*Con*	p577
Baroness Chalker of Wallasey	*Con*	p621
Lord Christopher	*Lab*	p624
Bishop of Coventry	*NA*	p637
Lord Dear	*CB*	p650
Lord Lansley	*Con*	p776
Lord Marlesford	*Con*	p813
Lord St John of Bletso	*CB*	p894

Ethiopia

Baroness Bonham-Carter of Yarnbury	*Lib Dem*	p589
Duke of Montrose	*Con*	p821
Lord Oates	*Lib Dem*	p840

Falkland Islands

Lord MacKenzie of Culkein	*Lab*	p802

Fiji

Lord Griffiths of Burry Port	*Lab*	p708

Finland

Lord Cormack	*Con*	p633
Baroness Maddock	*Lib Dem*	p806
Baroness Ramsay of Cartvale	*Lab*	p870
Lord Tyler	*Lib Dem*	p950

France

Baroness Afshar	*CB*	p553
Lord Anderson of Swansea	*Lab*	p560
Lord Arbuthnot of Edrom	*Con*	p562
Lord Armstrong of Ilminster	*CB*	p564
Lord Astor of Hever	*Con*	p567
Baroness Benjamin	*Lib Dem*	p576
Lord Birt	*CB*	p582
Baroness Blackstone	*Lab*	p584
Lord Blunkett	*Lab*	p587
Lord Bourne of Aberystwyth	*Con*	p591
Lord Bradley	*Lab*	p595
Lord Bragg	*Lab*	p596
Baroness Brinton	*Lib Dem*	p598
Lord Brougham and Vaux	*Con*	p601
Lord Browne of Belmont	*DUP*	p603
Archbishop of Canterbury	*NA*	p613
Earl of Clancarty	*CB*	p625
Baroness Cohen of Pimlico	*Lab*	p629
Baroness Coussins	*CB*	p636
Lord Donoughue	*Lab*	p656
Lord Drayson	*Lab*	p657
Viscount of Falkland	*CB*	p671
Baroness Finlay of Llandaff	*CB*	p678
Baroness Gibson of Market Rasen	*Lab*	p693
Lord Greaves	*Lib Dem*	p704
Lord Green of Hurstpierpoint	*Con*	p704
Baroness Greenfield	*CB*	p705
Viscount Hanworth	*Lab*	p717
Lord Harris of Haringey	*Lab*	p719
Lord Haskins	*CB*	p722
Baroness Hayter of Kentish Town	*Lab/Co-op*	p725
Lord Horam	*Con*	p738
Lord Hunt of Chesterton	*Lab*	p745
Lord Janvrin	*CB*	p752
Baroness King of Bow	*Lab*	p767
Lord Lansley	*Con*	p776
Lord Leitch	*Lab*	p781
Lord Liddle	*Lab*	p785
Lord Lisvane	*CB*	p789
Lord Lupton	*Con*	p795
Baroness Massey of Darwen	*Lab*	p814
Lord Maxton	*Lab*	p817
Baroness Miller of Chilthorne Domer	*Lib Dem*	p818
Lord Morgan	*Lab*	p822
Lord Murphy of Torfaen	*Lab*	p829
Lord Naseby	*Con*	p830
Baroness Nicholson of Winterbourne	*Con*	p835
Lord Northbourne	*CB*	p837
Lord Patel	*CB*	p852
Lord Plant of Highfield	*Lab*	p860
Lord Radice	*Lab*	p870
Baroness Randerson	*Lib Dem*	p872
Lord Renfrew of Kaimsthorn	*Con*	p877
Lord Renwick of Clifton	*CB*	p878
Baroness Shephard of Northwold	*Con*	p903
Lord Sherbourne of Didsbury	*Con*	p904
Lord Smith of Leigh	*Lab*	p914
Baroness Smith of Newnham	*Lib Dem*	p915
Lord Stevens of Ludgate	*UKIP*	p922
Lord Stoneham of Droxford	*Lib Dem*	p925
Lord Storey	*Lib Dem*	p926
Lord Taylor of Holbeach	*Con*	p934
Lord Touhig	*Lab/Co-op*	p942
Lord Watson of Invergowrie	*Lab*	p962
Lord Whitty	*Lab*	p968
Baroness Wilcox	*Con*	p969
Lord Williams of Elvel	*Lab*	p971
Baroness Wolf of Dulwich	*CB*	p976

Gambia

Lord Jones of Cheltenham	*Lib Dem*	p756
Lord McColl of Dulwich	*Con*	p797

Georgia

Lord Harries of Pentregarth	*CB*	p718
Lord Haworth	*Lab*	p723
Baroness Nicholson of Winterbourne	*Con*	p835
Lord Wallace of Saltaire	*Lib Dem*	p958

Germany

Lord Anderson of Swansea	*Lab*	p560
Lord Arbuthnot of Edrom	*Con*	p562
Lord Barker of Battle	*Con*	p572
Lord Browne of Belmont	*DUP*	p603
Earl of Clancarty	*CB*	p625
Baroness Cohen of Pimlico	*Lab*	p629
Bishop of Coventry	*NA*	p637
Baroness Eaton	*Con*	p662
Bishop of Ely	*NA*	p666
Lord Green of Hurstpierpoint	*Con*	p704
Viscount Hanworth	*Lab*	p717
Lord Horam	*Con*	p738
Lord Jones	*Lab*	p755
Lord Lansley	*Con*	p776
Bishop of Leeds	*NA*	p780
Lord Liddle	*Lab*	p785
Baroness Neville-Rolfe	*Con*	p833
Baroness Nicholson of Winterbourne	*Con*	p835
Baroness O'Neill of Bengarve	*CB*	p843
Lord Paul	*NA*	p855
Lord Plant of Highfield	*Lab*	p860
Lord Radice	*Lab*	p870
Lord Sherbourne of Didsbury	*Con*	p904
Baroness Smith of Basildon	*Lab/Co-op*	p910
Baroness Smith of Newnham	*Lib Dem*	p915
Lord Storey	*Lib Dem*	p926
Lord Tyler	*Lib Dem*	p950
Lord Watson of Richmond	*Lib Dem*	p963
Lord Whitty	*Lab*	p968
Lord Willetts	*Con*	p970
Lord Williams of Elvel	*Lab*	p971
Lord Wood of Anfield	*Lab*	p977

Gibraltar

Lord Hoyle	*Lab*	p743
Lord Kilclooney	*CB*	p766

Greece

Lord Bates	*Con*	p573
Lord Bourne of Aberystwyth	*Con*	p591
Lord Gardiner of Kimble	*Con*	p690
Lord Harris of Haringey	*Lab*	p719
Lord Lisvane	*CB*	p789
Lord Marks of Henley-on-Thames	*Lib Dem*	p812
Lord Renfrew of Kaimsthorn	*Con*	p877

Haiti

Lord Griffiths of Burry Port	*Lab*	p708

Hong Kong

Baroness Butler-Sloss	*CB*	p609
Baroness Finlay of Llandaff	*CB*	p678
Baroness Finn	*Con*	p679
Lord Geddes	*Con*	p692
Lord Marlesford	*Con*	p813
Lord Pendry	*Lab*	p857
Lord Sanderson of Bowden	*Con*	p895
Lord Smith of Finsbury	*NA*	p912
Lord Thomas of Gresford	*Lib Dem*	p937
Lord Willoughby de Broke	*UKIP*	p973
Lord Wilson of Tillyorn	*CB*	p974

Hungary

Lord Bruce of Bennachie	*Lib Dem*	p605

Iceland

Lord Inglewood	*Con*	p750
Lord Razzall	*Lib Dem*	p873

India

Baroness Afshar	*CB*	p553
Lord Ahmad of Wimbledon	*Con*	p554
Baroness Amos	*NA*	p559
Lord Arbuthnot of Edrom	*Con*	p562
Lord Archer of Weston-Super-Mare	*NA*	p562
Lord Bach	*Lab*	p568
Baroness Bakewell	*Lab*	p569
Baroness Barker	*Lib Dem*	p571
Lord Bassam of Brighton	*Lab/Co-op*	p573
Lord Bhatia	*NA*	p579
Lord Bhattacharyya	*Lab*	p579
Lord Bilimoria	*CB*	p580
Baroness Billingham	*Lab*	p581
Baroness Blackstone	*Lab*	p584
Lord Blair of Boughton	*CB*	p585
Baroness Bottomley of Nettlestone	*Con*	p591
Lord Bourne of Aberystwyth	*Con*	p591
Baroness Brown of Cambridge	*CB*	p601
Baroness Butler-Sloss	*CB*	p609
Bishop of Carlisle	*NA*	p615
Lord Clement-Jones	*Lib Dem*	p627
Baroness Corston	*Lab*	p634
Lord Crathorne	*Con*	p639
Lord Dear	*CB*	p650
Bishop of Derby	*NA*	p653
Lord Desai	*Lab*	p653
Lord Dholakia	*Lib Dem*	p654
Baroness D'Souza	*CB*	p658
Bishop of Ely	*NA*	p666
Lord Empey	*UUP*	p667
Lord Faulks	*Con*	p674
Baroness Featherstone	*Lib Dem*	p675
Baroness Finn	*Con*	p679
Lord Flight	*Con*	p680
Lord Gadhia	*NA*	p689
Baroness Gale	*Lab*	p689
Lord Glentoran	*Con*	p696
Bishop of Gloucester	*NA*	p696
Lord Gordon of Strathblane	*Lab*	p699
Baroness Goudie	*Lab*	p700
Lord Guthrie of Craigiebank	*CB*	p710
Lord Hardie	*CB*	p717
Baroness Harding of Winscombe	*Con*	p718
Lord Harries of Pentregarth	*CB*	p718
Lord Howell of Guildford	*Con*	p742
Lord Hunt of Chesterton	*Lab*	p745
Lord Janvrin	*CB*	p752
Lord Jay of Ewelme	*CB*	p753
Baroness Jay of Paddington	*Lab*	p753
Lord Jones of Birmingham	*CB*	p755
Lord Jordan	*Lab*	p758
Baroness Jowell	*Lab*	p759
Lord Kakkar	*CB*	p761
Baroness Kidron	*CB*	p766
Baroness Kingsmill	*Lab*	p768
Lord Leitch	*Lab*	p781
Lord Lester of Herne Hill	*Lib Dem*	p782
Lord Livermore	*Lab*	p790
Lord Loomba	*NA*	p792
Lord Mackenzie of Framwellgate	*NA*	p803
Lord Maclennan of Rogart	*Lib Dem*	p804
Lord McNally	*Lib Dem*	p805
Lord Morgan	*Lab*	p822
Lord Naseby	*Con*	p830
Baroness Neville-Rolfe	*Con*	p833
Lord Parekh	*Lab*	p851
Lord Patel	*CB*	p852
Lord Patel of Blackburn	*Lab*	p853
Lord Patel of Bradford	*Lab*	p853
Lord Paul	*NA*	p855
Lord Popat	*Con*	p862
Baroness Prashar	*CB*	p864
Lord Radice	*Lab*	p870
Lord Rana	*Con*	p871
Baroness Royall of Blaisdon	*Lab/Co-op*	p890
Lord Sainsbury of Turville	*Lab*	p893
Earl of Sandwich	*CB*	p896
Baroness Scott of Needham Market	*Lib Dem*	p898

Lord Singh of Wimbledon	*CB*	p908
Duke of Somerset	*CB*	p917
Lord Stephen	*Lib Dem*	p919
Lord Teverson	*Lib Dem*	p936
Lord Triesman	*Lab*	p944
Baroness Wheatcroft	*Con*	p966
Baroness Wheeler	*Lab*	p966
Lord Woolmer of Leeds	*Lab*	p978
Lord Wrigglesworth	*Lib Dem*	p980

Indonesia

Lord Ahmad of Wimbledon	*Con*	p554
Baroness Finn	*Con*	p679
Lord Northbourne	*CB*	p837

Iran

Baroness Afshar	*CB*	p553
Baroness D'Souza	*CB*	p658
Bishop of Durham	*NA*	p660
Lord Haworth	*Lab*	p723
Lord Lamont of Lerwick	*Con*	p775
Lord Marlesford	*Con*	p813
Baroness Nicholson of Winterbourne	*Con*	p835
Earl of Oxford and Asquith	*Lib Dem*	p848
Lord Stevenson of Balmacara	*Lab*	p923
Lord Temple-Morris	*Lab*	p936

Iraq

Lord Alton of Liverpool	*CB*	p558
Baroness Berridge	*Con*	p577
Lord Clement-Jones	*Lib Dem*	p627
Lord Foster of Bath	*Lib Dem*	p683
Lord Hylton	*CB*	p749
Baroness Nicholson of Winterbourne	*Con*	p835
Baroness Tonge	*NA*	p941

Ireland

Lord Bird	*CB*	p582
Lord Cotter	*Lib Dem*	p635
Earl of Courtown	*Con*	p635
Lord Donoughue	*Lab*	p656
Baroness Doocey	*Lib Dem*	p656
Lord Gardiner of Kimble	*Con*	p690
Lord Glentoran	*Con*	p696
Baroness Goudie	*Lab*	p700
Baroness Harris of Richmond	*Lib Dem*	p720
Lord Haskins	*CB*	p722
Baroness Healy of Primrose Hill	*Lab*	p726
Lord Kennedy of Southwark	*Lab/Co-op*	p763
Lord Kilclooney	*CB*	p766
Lord Lester of Herne Hill	*Lib Dem*	p782
Lord McAvoy	*Lab/Co-op*	p796
Lord Murphy of Torfaen	*Lab*	p829
Baroness Neuberger	*CB*	p831
Baroness O'Cathain	*Con*	p841
Baroness O'Neill of Bengarve	*CB*	p843
Lord Puttnam	*Lab*	p867
Lord Rana	*Con*	p871
Lord Shutt of Greetland	*Lib Dem*	p907
Baroness Smith of Basildon	*Lab/Co-op*	p910
Lord Stevenson of Balmacara	*Lab*	p923
Lord Teverson	*Lib Dem*	p936
Lord Whitty	*Lab*	p968
Lord Wigley	*PlC*	p969
Lord Willis of Knaresborough	*Lib Dem*	p973

Israel

Lord Ahmad of Wimbledon	*Con*	p554
Lord Arbuthnot of Edrom	*Con*	p562
Lord Beecham	*Lab*	p574
Baroness Burt of Solihull	*Lib Dem*	p607
Archbishop of Canterbury	*NA*	p613
Lord Carey of Clifton	*CB*	p614
Lord Clinton-Davis	*Lab*	p627
Bishop of Coventry	*NA*	p637
Baroness Deech	*CB*	p651
Bishop of Durham	*NA*	p660
Lord Graham of Edmonton	*Lab/Co-op*	p703
Baroness Greenfield	*CB*	p705
Lord Hylton	*CB*	p749
Lord Kalms	*NA*	p762
Lord Lansley	*Con*	p776
Lord Livermore	*Lab*	p790
Lord Mitchell	*NA*	p818
Lord Morrow	*DUP*	p827
Baroness O'Cathain	*Con*	p841
Lord Palmer of Childs Hill	*Lib Dem*	p849
Lord Pannick	*CB*	p850
Baroness Ramsay of Cartvale	*Lab*	p870
Lord Roberts of Llandudno	*Lib Dem*	p883
Bishop of Southwark	*NA*	p917
Lord Taylor of Warwick	*NA*	p934
Lord Turnberg	*Lab*	p948

Italy

Lord Adebowale	*CB*	p552
Lord Arbuthnot of Edrom	*Con*	p562
Lord Bach	*Lab*	p568
Lord Black of Brentwood	*Con*	p583
Baroness Bonham-Carter of Yarnbury	*Lib Dem*	p589
Lord Bourne of Aberystwyth	*Con*	p591
Lord Browne of Belmont	*DUP*	p603
Baroness Cohen of Pimlico	*Lab*	p629
Lord Donoughue	*Lab*	p656
Lord Hall of Birkenhead	*CB*	p713
Viscount Hanworth	*Lab*	p717
Lord Harris of Haringey	*Lab*	p719
Lord Haskins	*CB*	p722
Baroness Healy of Primrose Hill	*Lab*	p726
Baroness King of Bow	*Lab*	p767
Lord Leitch	*Lab*	p781
Lord Liddle	*Lab*	p785
Lord Lisvane	*CB*	p789
Lord Martin of Springburn	*CB*	p813
Baroness Murphy	*CB*	p829
Lord Radice	*Lab*	p870

Lord Rogers of Riverside *Lab* p886
Lord Sherbourne of Didsbury *Con* p904
Lord Stevens of Ludgate *UKIP* p922
Lord Taylor of Warwick *NA* p934
Lord Whitty *Lab* p968
Lord Williams of Elvel *Lab* p971
Baroness Wolf of Dulwich *CB* p976
Lord Young of Norwood Green *Lab* p983

Jamaica

Lord Faulkner of Worcester *Lab* p673
Lord Taylor of Warwick *NA* p934

Japan

Lord Bates *Con* p573
Lord Bird *CB* p582
Lord Birt *CB* p582
Baroness Bottomley of Nettlestone *Con* p591
Baroness Burt of Solihull *Lib Dem* p607
Viscount Colville of Culross *CB* p631
Lord Cunningham of Felling *Lab* p643
Baroness D'Souza *CB* p658
Baroness Finn *Con* p679
Lord Foster of Bishop Auckland *Lab* p683
Baroness Henig *Lab* p727
Lord Holmes of Richmond *Con* p735
Lord Howell of Guildford *Con* p742
Lord Lansley *Con* p776
Baroness Lister of Burtersett *Lab* p788
Lord McConnell of Glenscorrodale *Lab* p797
Lord Pendry *Lab* p857
Lord Stephen *Lib Dem* p919
Lord Stevenson of Coddenham *CB* p923
Lord Taylor of Warwick *NA* p934
Viscount Trenchard *Con* p944
Lord Wei *Con* p964
Lord West of Spithead *Lab* p965
Lord Whitty *Lab* p968
Lord Woolmer of Leeds *Lab* p978

Jordan

Baroness Chalker of Wallasey *Con* p621
Bishop of Coventry *NA* p637
Baroness D'Souza *CB* p658
Lord Jordan *Lab* p758

Kenya

Lord Aberdare *CB* p551
Lord Allan of Hallam *Lib Dem* p556
Lord Alton of Liverpool *CB* p558
Baroness Armstrong of Hill Top *Lab* p563
Baroness Barker *Lib Dem* p571
Baroness Butler-Sloss *CB* p609
Archbishop of Canterbury *NA* p613
Baroness Corston *Lab* p634
Lord Jones of Cheltenham *Lib Dem* p756
Lord Loomba *NA* p792
Lord Oakeshott of Seagrove Bay *NA* p840
Bishop of Peterborough *NA* p857
Lord Popat *Con* p862
Lord St John of Bletso *CB* p894
Baroness Stern *CB* p920
Bishop of Winchester *NA* p975

Korea, North

Lord Alton of Liverpool *CB* p558
Lord Bates *Con* p573
Baroness Cox *CB* p637
Lord Eames *CB* p661
Lord Fraser of Corriegarth *Con* p686
Lord Kerr of Kinlochard *CB* p764
Bishop of Peterborough *NA* p857
Lord Rowe-Beddoe *CB* p889
Viscount Trenchard *Con* p944

Korea, South

Lord Bates *Con* p573
Lord Eames *CB* p661
Lord Kerr of Kinlochard *CB* p764
Bishop of Peterborough *NA* p857
Viscount Trenchard *Con* p944
Lord Wei *Con* p964

Latvia

Bishop of Salisbury *NA* p895

Lesotho

Bishop of Durham *NA* p660
Lord Jones of Cheltenham *Lib Dem* p756

Libya

Lord James of Blackheath *Con* p752

Liechtenstein

Baroness Smith of Basildon *Lab/Co-op* p910

Lithuania

Lord Cormack *Con* p633

Malaysia

Lord Bourne of Aberystwyth *Con* p591
Baroness Butler-Sloss *CB* p609
Lord Desai *Lab* p653
Baroness Henig *Lab* p727
Lord Scriven *Lib Dem* p899
Lord Tanlaw *Con* p931

Maldives

Lord Naseby *Con* p830

Malta

Lord Judge *CB* p761
Lord Pendry *Lab* p857

Mauritius

Lord Desai *Lab* p653
Baroness Prashar *CB* p864
Lord Rana *Con* p871

Moldova

Lord German *Lib Dem* p692
Lord Hylton *CB* p749
Baroness Nicholson of Winterbourne *Con* p835

Mongolia

Lord Wei	*Con*	p964

Montenegro

Lord Browne of Belmont	*DUP*	p603

Morocco

Baroness Barker	*Lib Dem*	p571
Baroness Uddin	*NA*	p951

Nepal

Lord Davies of Oldham	*Lab*	p648
Baroness Featherstone	*Lib Dem*	p675
Lord Glentoran	*Con*	p696
Baroness Harris of Richmond	*Lib Dem*	p720
Lord Lea of Crondall	*Lab*	p779
Lord Loomba	*NA*	p792
Earl of Sandwich	*CB*	p896

Netherlands

Baroness Bottomley of Nettlestone	*Con*	p591
Earl of Clancarty	*CB*	p625
Lord Cormack	*Con*	p633
Viscount Craigavon	*CB*	p638
Baroness Finlay of Llandaff	*CB*	p678
Viscount Hanworth	*Lab*	p717
Lord Higgins	*Con*	p729
Lord Stevenson of Coddenham	*CB*	p923
Lord Taylor of Holbeach	*Con*	p934
Lord Temple-Morris	*Lab*	p936

New Zealand

Baroness Cohen of Pimlico	*Lab*	p629
Lord Faulkner of Worcester	*Lab*	p673
Baroness Fookes	*Con*	p681
Lord Freyberg	*CB*	p688
Baroness Fritchie	*CB*	p688
Baroness Hayter of Kentish Town	*Lab/Co-op*	p725
Lord Higgins	*Con*	p729
Lord Hoyle	*Lab*	p743
Baroness Kingsmill	*Lab*	p768
Lord Lisvane	*CB*	p789
Baroness Newlove	*Con*	p834
Lord O'Donnell	*CB*	p841
Lord Rooker	*Lab*	p887
Baroness Royall of Blaisdon	*Lab/Co-op*	p890
Lord Smith of Finsbury	*NA*	p912
Lord Smith of Leigh	*Lab*	p914
Baroness Stedman-Scott	*Con*	p918
Lord Wallace of Tankerness	*Lib Dem*	p958
Lord Wigley	*PlC*	p969

Nicaragua

Baroness King of Bow	*Lab*	p767

Nigeria

Lord Adebowale	*CB*	p552
Baroness Barker	*Lib Dem*	p571
Archbishop of Canterbury	*NA*	p613
Bishop of Coventry	*NA*	p637
Baroness Cox	*CB*	p637
Baroness Howells of St Davids	*Lab*	p742

Norway

Lord Anderson of Swansea	*Lab*	p560
Bishop of Carlisle	*NA*	p615
Lord Elton	*Con*	p665
Lord Faulkner of Worcester	*Lab*	p673
Lord McColl of Dulwich	*Con*	p797
Baroness Maddock	*Lib Dem*	p806
Bishop of Newcastle	*NA*	p834
Lord Paddick	*Lib Dem*	p848
Lord Wallace of Tankerness	*Lib Dem*	p958

Oman

Lord German	*Lib Dem*	p692
Lord Guthrie of Craigiebank	*CB*	p710
Baroness Jolly	*Lib Dem*	p754
Lord Lisvane	*CB*	p789
Baroness Rawlings	*Con*	p873

Pakistan

Lord Ahmad of Wimbledon	*Con*	p554
Lord Ahmed	*NA*	p554
Lord Arbuthnot of Edrom	*Con*	p562
Lord Bhatia	*NA*	p579
Baroness Butler-Sloss	*CB*	p609
Lord Desai	*Lab*	p653
Baroness Featherstone	*Lib Dem*	p675
Lord Guthrie of Craigiebank	*CB*	p710
Lord Maclennan of Rogart	*Lib Dem*	p804
Lord Newby	*Lib Dem*	p833
Lord Patel of Blackburn	*Lab*	p853
Baroness Warsi	*Con*	p960
Lord West of Spithead	*Lab*	p965

Poland

Baroness Cox	*CB*	p637
Baroness Deech	*CB*	p651
Lord Mackenzie of Framwellgate	*NA*	p803
Lord Paul	*NA*	p855
Lord Radice	*Lab*	p870
Lord Roberts of Llandudno	*Lib Dem*	p883

Portugal

Lord Bach	*Lab*	p568
Baroness Gibson of Market Rasen	*Lab*	p693
Lord Plant of Highfield	*Lab*	p860

Romania

Lord Lamont of Lerwick	*Con*	p775
Lord McColl of Dulwich	*Con*	p797
Lord McFall of Alcluith	*NA*	p799
Baroness Nicholson of Winterbourne	*Con*	p835
Lord Watson of Richmond	*Lib Dem*	p963

Russia

Lord Aberdare	*CB*	p551
Lord Ahmad of Wimbledon	*Con*	p554
Lord Ahmed	*NA*	p554

Lord Arbuthnot of Edrom	*Con*	p562
Lord Barker of Battle	*Con*	p572
Lord Bruce of Bennachie	*Lib Dem*	p605
Viscount Colville of Culross	*CB*	p631
Lord Cromwell	*CB*	p641
Lord Davies of Stamford	*Lab*	p648
Lord Dunlop	*Con*	p660
Bishop of Durham	*NA*	p660
Lord Fairfax of Cameron	*Con*	p670
Lord Foulkes of Cumnock	*Lab/Co-op*	p684
Lord Gadhia	*NA*	p689
Lord Giddens	*Lab*	p694
Lord Guthrie of Craigiebank	*CB*	p710
Lord Haworth	*Lab*	p723
Lord Hylton	*CB*	p749
Lord Imbert	*CB*	p750
Lord Kerr of Kinlochard	*CB*	p764
Bishop of Leeds	*NA*	p780
Lord Mackenzie of Framwellgate	*NA*	p803
Baroness Massey of Darwen	*Lab*	p814
Baroness Meacher	*CB*	p817
Earl of Oxford and Asquith	*Lib Dem*	p848
Lord Plant of Highfield	*Lab*	p860
Baroness Rawlings	*Con*	p873
Lord Rea	*Lab*	p874
Lord Selsdon	*Con*	p901
Lord Skidelsky	*CB*	p909
Baroness Smith of Gilmorehill	*Lab*	p913
Baroness Suttie	*Lib Dem*	p930
Lord Truscott	*Ind Lab*	p946
Lord Wallace of Saltaire	*Lib Dem*	p958
Lord Watson of Richmond	*Lib Dem*	p963
Lord Williams of Elvel	*Lab*	p971
Lord Wood of Anfield	*Lab*	p977

Rwanda

Lord Browne of Ladyton	*Lab*	p603
Lord Cotter	*Lib Dem*	p635
Bishop of Durham	*NA*	p660
Bishop of Ely	*NA*	p666
Baroness Gale	*Lab*	p689
Baroness King of Bow	*Lab*	p767
Lord Loomba	*NA*	p792
Lord McConnell of Glenscorrodale	*Lab*	p797
Baroness Tonge	*NA*	p941
Bishop of Winchester	*NA*	p975

Saudi Arabia

Baroness Howells of St Davids	*Lab*	p742
Baroness Nicholson of Winterbourne	*Con*	p835
Lord Patel of Blackburn	*Lab*	p853
Baroness Uddin	*NA*	p951

Scotland

Lord Fraser of Corriegarth	*Con*	p686
Baroness Goudie	*Lab*	p700
Lord Hope of Craighead	*CB*	p737
Lord Palmer	*CB*	p849
Earl of Shrewsbury and Waterford	*Con*	p907
Lord Vaux of Harrowden	*CB*	p953
Viscount Younger of Leckie	*Con*	p985

Serbia

Lord Browne of Belmont	*DUP*	p603

Sierra Leone

Lord Desai	*Lab*	p653
Lord Freeman	*Con*	p687
Lord Jones of Cheltenham	*Lib Dem*	p756
Lord McColl of Dulwich	*Con*	p797
Lord St John of Bletso	*CB*	p894
Lord Stevenson of Coddenham	*CB*	p923

Singapore

Lord Bhattacharyya	*Lab*	p579
Lord Bourne of Aberystwyth	*Con*	p591
Baroness Butler-Sloss	*CB*	p609
Lord Desai	*Lab*	p653
Baroness Finn	*Con*	p679
Lord Holmes of Richmond	*Con*	p735
Lord Naseby	*Con*	p830
Lord Oxburgh	*CB*	p846
Lord Scriven	*Lib Dem*	p899
Lord Tanlaw	*Con*	p931

Slovenia

Lord Taylor of Holbeach	*Con*	p934
Lord Wigley	*PlC*	p969

Somalia

Baroness Kidron	*CB*	p766

South Africa

Lord Anderson of Swansea	*Lab*	p560
Baroness Armstrong of Hill Top	*Lab*	p563
Baroness Benjamin	*Lib Dem*	p576
Lord Bird	*CB*	p582
Lord Birt	*CB*	p582
Lord Browne of Ladyton	*Lab*	p603
Lord Bruce of Bennachie	*Lib Dem*	p605
Lord Cashman	*Lab*	p618
Lord Clinton-Davis	*Lab*	p627
Baroness Coussins	*CB*	p636
Lord Cunningham of Felling	*Lab*	p643
Baroness Dean of Thornton-le-Fylde	*Lab*	p649
Bishop of Durham	*NA*	p660
Lord Dykes	*CB*	p661
Lord Faulkner of Worcester	*Lab*	p673
Lord Gadhia	*NA*	p689
Bishop of Gloucester	*NA*	p696
Lord Howarth of Newport	*Lab*	p740
Lord Hoyle	*Lab*	p743
Lord Hughes of Woodside	*Lab*	p744
Baroness Jay of Paddington	*Lab*	p753
Lord Jones of Birmingham	*CB*	p755
Baroness King of Bow	*Lab*	p767
Lord Lansley	*Con*	p776
Lord Lester of Herne Hill	*Lib Dem*	p782

Lord Loomba *NA* p792
Lord Low of Dalston *CB* p793
Lord Morgan *Lab* p822
Lord Newby *Lib Dem* p833
Lord Oates *Lib Dem* p840
Lord Paddick *Lib Dem* p848
Lord Patel *CB* p852
Lord Renwick of Clifton *CB* p878
Lord Risby *Con* p882
Lord Rowlands *Lab* p890
Baroness Royall of Blaisdon *Lab/Co-op* p890
Lord St John of Bletso *CB* p894
Bishop of Salisbury *NA* p895
Earl of Sandwich *CB* p896
Lord Sawyer *Lab* p897
Baroness Sharples *Con* p902
Lord Smith of Finsbury *NA* p912
Lord Smith of Kelvin *CB* p914
Lord Stoneham of Droxford *Lib Dem* p925

Spain

Lord Arbuthnot of Edrom *Con* p562
Lord Bach *Lab* p568
Lord Bassam of Brighton *Lab/Co-op* p573
Lord Brougham and Vaux *Con* p601
Lord Collins of Highbury *Lab* p630
Baroness Coussins *CB* p636
Baroness Finlay of Llandaff *CB* p678
Lord Garel-Jones *Con* p691
Baroness Gibson of Market Rasen *Lab* p693
Baroness Golding *Lab* p698
Lord Hain *Lab* p711
Baroness Healy of Primrose Hill *Lab* p726
Lord Leitch *Lab* p781
Lord Lupton *Con* p795
Lord Maxton *Lab* p817
Lord Morris of Aberavon *Lab* p825
Baroness O'Loan *CB* p842
Lord Paul *NA* p855
Lord Williams of Elvel *Lab* p971

Sri Lanka

Lord Bhatia *NA* p579
Baroness Cox *CB* p637
Lord Davies of Oldham *Lab* p648
Lord Desai *Lab* p653
Lord Faulks *Con* p674
Lord Hardie *CB* p717
Baroness Hayter of Kentish Town *Lab/Co-op* p725
Bishop of Leeds *NA* p780
Lord Loomba *NA* p792
Lord Naseby *Con* p830

Sudan

Lord Alton of Liverpool *CB* p558
Lord Carey of Clifton *CB* p614
Baroness Cox *CB* p637
Lord Curry of Kirkharle *CB* p644
Baroness Kinnock of Holyhead *Lab* p769
Bishop of Leeds *NA* p780
Duke of Montrose *Con* p821
Bishop of Salisbury *NA* p895
Earl of Sandwich *CB* p896
Baroness Tonge *NA* p941

Swaziland

Lord Jones of Cheltenham *Lib Dem* p756
Lord Patel of Blackburn *Lab* p853

Sweden

Lord Brooke of Alverthorpe *Lab* p599
Baroness Campbell of Surbiton *CB* p612
Bishop of Gloucester *NA* p696
Lord Liddle *Lab* p785
Baroness Maddock *Lib Dem* p806
Lord Patel *CB* p852
Lord Radice *Lab* p870
Baroness Ramsay of Cartvale *Lab* p870
Lord Rooker *Lab* p887
Lord Tyler *Lib Dem* p950
Baroness Wolf of Dulwich *CB* p976

Switzerland

Lord Brabazon of Tara *Con* p594
Earl of Courtown *Con* p635
Lord Leitch *Lab* p781
Lord Paul *NA* p855
Baroness Smith of Basildon *Lab/Co-op* p910
Lord Storey *Lib Dem* p926

Syria

Lord Alton of Liverpool *CB* p558
Bishop of Coventry *NA* p637
Baroness Cox *CB* p637
Baroness Nicholson of Winterbourne *Con* p835

Taiwan

Lord Arbuthnot of Edrom *Con* p562
Lord Faulkner of Worcester *Lab* p673
Baroness Gale *Lab* p689
Lord Grantchester *Lab* p703
Lord Hardie *CB* p717
Baroness Howells of St Davids *Lab* p742
Lord Kilclooney *CB* p766
Lord Rana *Con* p871
Lord Rosser *Lab* p888
Lord Steel of Aikwood *Lib Dem* p919

Tanzania

Baroness Armstrong of Hill Top *Lab* p563
Bishop of Gloucester *NA* p696
Lord Jones of Cheltenham *Lib Dem* p756
Bishop of Leeds *NA* p780
Lord McColl of Dulwich *Con* p797
Lord Patel *CB* p852
Lord Popat *Con* p862

Tunisia

Baroness Burt of Solihull *Lib Dem* p607
Lord McNally *Lib Dem* p805
Baroness Uddin *NA* p951

Turkey

Baroness Bakewell	*Lab*	p569
Lord Balfe	*Con*	p570
Lord Bhattacharyya	*Lab*	p579
Lord Cashman	*Lab*	p618
Lord Clement-Jones	*Lib Dem*	p627
Baroness Fritchie	*CB*	p688
Baroness Hussein-Ece	*Lib Dem*	p748
Lord Inglewood	*Con*	p750
Lord Kilclooney	*CB*	p766
Baroness Ludford	*Lib Dem*	p795
Baroness Nicholson of Winterbourne	*Con*	p835
Lord Paul	*NA*	p855
Lord Rea	*Lab*	p874
Lord Sharkey	*Lib Dem*	p902
Lord Stevenson of Balmacara	*Lab*	p923

Uganda

Lord Alton of Liverpool	*CB*	p558
Baroness Armstrong of Hill Top	*Lab*	p563
Baroness Cox	*CB*	p637
Bishop of Durham	*NA*	p660
Lord Freeman	*Con*	p687
Lord Howarth of Newport	*Lab*	p740
Lord Jones of Cheltenham	*Lib Dem*	p756
Lord Loomba	*NA*	p792
Lord McColl of Dulwich	*Con*	p797
Lord Popat	*Con*	p862
Lord Roberts of Llandudno	*Lib Dem*	p883
Earl of Sandwich	*CB*	p896
Bishop of Winchester	*NA*	p975

Ukraine

Earl of Oxford and Asquith	*Lib Dem*	p848
Lord Wallace of Saltaire	*Lib Dem*	p958
Lord West of Spithead	*Lab*	p965

United Arab Emirates

Lord Clement-Jones	*Lib Dem*	p627
Lord Jones of Cheltenham	*Lib Dem*	p756
Baroness Newlove	*Con*	p834
Lord Patel of Blackburn	*Lab*	p853
Lord Rowe-Beddoe	*CB*	p889
Baroness Uddin	*NA*	p951

United Kingdom

Lord Baker of Dorking	*Con*	p568
Viscount Brookeborough	*CB*	p600
Earl Cathcart	*Con*	p618
Lord Lee of Trafford	*Lib Dem*	p779
Lord Lexden	*Con*	p784
Lord Lingfield	*Con*	p787
Lord Livermore	*Lab*	p790
Lord Loomba	*NA*	p792
Lord Lupton	*Con*	p795
Lord MacLaurin of Knebworth	*Con*	p804
Lord Mawson	*CB*	p816
Lord Rogers of Riverside	*Lab*	p886
Lord Saatchi	*Con*	p892
Lord Tebbit	*Con*	p935
Lord Vinson	*Con*	p955

USA

Lord Aberdare	*CB*	p551
Lord Adebowale	*CB*	p552
Lord Ahmad of Wimbledon	*Con*	p554
Lord Ahmed	*NA*	p554
Lord Allan of Hallam	*Lib Dem*	p556
Lord Allen of Kensington	*Lab*	p557
Lord Arbuthnot of Edrom	*Con*	p562
Lord Armstrong of Ilminster	*CB*	p564
Lord Astor of Hever	*Con*	p567
Lord Bach	*Lab*	p568
Lord Balfe	*Con*	p570
Lord Barker of Battle	*Con*	p572
Lord Bassam of Brighton	*Lab/Co-op*	p573
Lord Bates	*Con*	p573
Baroness Benjamin	*Lib Dem*	p576
Lord Bilimoria	*CB*	p580
Baroness Billingham	*Lab*	p581
Lord Bird	*CB*	p582
Lord Birt	*CB*	p582
Baroness Blackstone	*Lab*	p584
Lord Blunkett	*Lab*	p587
Lord Blyth of Rowington	*Con*	p588
Lord Boateng	*Lab*	p588
Baroness Bonham-Carter of Yarnbury	*Lib Dem*	p589
Lord Borwick	*Con*	p590
Lord Bradley	*Lab*	p595
Lord Bragg	*Lab*	p596
Lord Broers	*CB*	p599
Lord Bruce of Bennachie	*Lib Dem*	p605
Lord Carrington of Fulham	*Con*	p616
Lord Cashman	*Lab*	p618
Lord Clinton-Davis	*Lab*	p627
Lord Cormack	*Con*	p633
Baroness Corston	*Lab*	p634
Lord Crathorne	*Con*	p639
Lord Cunningham of Felling	*Lab*	p643
Lord Davies of Stamford	*Lab*	p648
Baroness Dean of Thornton-le-Fylde	*Lab*	p649
Lord Dear	*CB*	p650
Baroness Deech	*CB*	p651
Lord Desai	*Lab*	p653
Lord Dobbs	*Con*	p655
Baroness Doocey	*Lib Dem*	p656
Lord Dunlop	*Con*	p660
Lord Dykes	*CB*	p661
Lord Eames	*CB*	p661
Lord Empey	*UUP*	p667
Lord Evans of Watford	*Lab*	p669
Lord Fairfax of Cameron	*Con*	p670
Baroness Falkner of Margravine	*Lib Dem*	p671
Lord Faulks	*Con*	p674
Baroness Featherstone	*Lib Dem*	p675

Lord Fellowes	*CB*	p676
Baroness Finn	*Con*	p679
Lord Flight	*Con*	p680
Baroness Ford	*CB*	p681
Lord Foster of Bishop Auckland	*Lab*	p683
Baroness Fritchie	*CB*	p688
Baroness Gale	*Lab*	p689
Bishop of Gloucester	*NA*	p696
Lord Goddard of Stockport	*Lib Dem*	p697
Baroness Goudie	*Lab*	p700
Baroness Gould of Potternewton	*Lab*	p701
Lord Graham of Edmonton	*Lab/Co-op*	p703
Baroness Hanham	*Con*	p715
Lord Harris of Haringey	*Lab*	p719
Lord Harrison	*Lab*	p721
Lord Haskel	*Lab*	p721
Lord Haskins	*CB*	p722
Baroness Healy of Primrose Hill	*Lab*	p726
Lord Higgins	*Con*	p729
Lord Holmes of Richmond	*Con*	p735
Lord Horam	*Con*	p738
Lord Howard of Lympne	*Con*	p738
Baroness Hughes of Stretford	*Lab*	p744
Lord Hunt of Chesterton	*Lab*	p745
Lord Hunt of Wirral	*Con*	p747
Baroness Jay of Paddington	*Lab*	p753
Lord Jones of Birmingham	*CB*	p755
Lord Kakkar	*CB*	p761
Lord Kerr of Kinlochard	*CB*	p764
Baroness Kidron	*CB*	p766
Baroness King of Bow	*Lab*	p767
Baroness Kingsmill	*Lab*	p768
Lord Kirkhope of Harrogate	*Con*	p771
Baroness Kramer	*Lib Dem*	p773
Lord Lansley	*Con*	p776
Lord Leitch	*Lab*	p781
Lord Lennie	*Lab*	p781
Lord Lester of Herne Hill	*Lib Dem*	p782
Baroness Liddell of Coatdyke	*Lab*	p785
Lord Liddle	*Lab*	p785
Baroness Lister of Burtersett	*Lab*	p788
Lord Livermore	*Lab*	p790
Lord Loomba	*NA*	p792
Lord Low of Dalston	*CB*	p793
Baroness Ludford	*Lib Dem*	p795
Lord McAvoy	*Lab/Co-op*	p796
Lord McConnell of Glenscorrodale	*Lab*	p797
Lord MacGregor of Pulham Market	*Con*	p799
Lord MacKenzie of Culkein	*Lab*	p802
Lord Mackenzie of Framwellgate	*NA*	p803
Lord Maclennan of Rogart	*Lib Dem*	p804
Lord Martin of Springburn	*CB*	p813
Baroness Massey of Darwen	*Lab*	p814
Lord Mawhinney	*Con*	p816
Lord Mitchell	*NA*	p818
Lord Mogg	*CB*	p819
Lord Morgan	*Lab*	p822
Lord Morrow	*DUP*	p827
Baroness Newlove	*Con*	p834
Baroness Nicholson of Winterbourne	*Con*	p835
Baroness O'Cathain	*Con*	p841
Lord O'Donnell	*CB*	p841
Lord Oxburgh	*CB*	p846
Lord Paddick	*Lib Dem*	p848
Lord Pannick	*CB*	p850
Lord Parekh	*Lab*	p851
Lord Patel	*CB*	p852
Lord Paul	*NA*	p855
Lord Pendry	*Lab*	p857
Lord Plumb	*Con*	p860
Baroness Prosser	*Lab*	p866
Lord Puttnam	*Lab*	p867
Lord Renfrew of Kaimsthorn	*Con*	p877
Lord Renwick of Clifton	*CB*	p878
Lord Ribeiro	*Con*	p878
Lord Risby	*Con*	p882
Baroness Royall of Blaisdon	*Lab/Co-op*	p890
Lord Sainsbury of Turville	*Lab*	p893
Baroness Scott of Needham Market	*Lib Dem*	p898
Lord Sherbourne of Didsbury	*Con*	p904
Baroness Shields	*Con*	p905
Lord Singh of Wimbledon	*CB*	p908
Baroness Smith of Basildon	*Lab/Co-op*	p910
Lord Smith of Finsbury	*NA*	p912
Lord Smith of Leigh	*Lab*	p914
Lord Spicer	*Con*	p917
Lord Stephen	*Lib Dem*	p919
Lord Stevens of Ludgate	*UKIP*	p922
Lord Stevenson of Coddenham	*CB*	p923
Lord Stirrup	*CB*	p924
Lord Stoneham of Droxford	*Lib Dem*	p925
Lord Storey	*Lib Dem*	p926
Lord Taylor of Warwick	*NA*	p934
Viscount Trenchard	*Con*	p944
Lord Wallace of Saltaire	*Lib Dem*	p958
Lord Wallace of Tankerness	*Lib Dem*	p958
Lord Warner	*CB*	p960
Lord Watson of Richmond	*Lib Dem*	p963
Lord Wigley	*PlC*	p969
Lord Willetts	*Con*	p970
Baroness Wolf of Dulwich	*CB*	p976
Lord Wood of Anfield	*Lab*	p977
Lord Wrigglesworth	*Lib Dem*	p980
Baroness Young of Hornsey	*CB*	p983
Lord Young of Norwood Green	*Lab*	p983

Uzbekistan

Baroness Stern	*CB*	p920

Vietnam

Baroness Brown of Cambridge	*CB*	p601
Lord Fraser of Corriegarth	*Con*	p686
Lord Haworth	*Lab*	p723
Lord Howarth of Newport	*Lab*	p740
Baroness Jowell	*Lab*	p759

Wales

Lord Aberdare	*CB*	p551
Lord Elis-Thomas	*NA*	p665
Lord Morgan	*Lab*	p822
Baroness Morgan of Drefelin	*CB*	p823
Lord Thomas of Gresford	*Lib Dem*	p937

Yemen

Baroness Nicholson of Winterbourne	*Con*	p835

Zambia

Lord Jones of Cheltenham	*Lib Dem*	p756
Lord Patel of Blackburn	*Lab*	p853
Lord Skelmersdale	*Con*	p909
Lord Turnbull	*CB*	p949

Zimbabwe

Lord Beith	*Lib Dem*	p575
Baroness Bonham-Carter of Yarnbury	*Lib Dem*	p589
Lord Bruce of Bennachie	*Lib Dem*	p605
Lord Gardiner of Kimble	*Con*	p690
Lord Jones of Cheltenham	*Lib Dem*	p756
Lord Oates	*Lib Dem*	p840
Lord Palmer	*CB*	p849
Lord St John of Bletso	*CB*	p894
Earl of Sandwich	*CB*	p896
Lord Shutt of Greetland	*Lib Dem*	p907
Bishop of Southwark	*NA*	p917

MPs who are now Peers

Irene Adams
Baroness Adams of Craigielea
Richard Allan
Lord Allan of Hallam
David Alton
Lord Alton of Liverpool
Michael Ancram
Marquess of Lothian
Donald Anderson
Lord Anderson of Swansea
James Arbuthnot
Lord Arbuthnot of Edrom
Jeffrey Archer
Lord Archer of Weston-Super-Mare
Hilary Armstrong
Baroness Armstrong of Hill Top
Paddy Ashdown
Lord Ashdown of Norton-sub-Hamdon
Kenneth Baker
Lord Baker of Dorking
Gregory Barker
Lord Barker of Battle
Michael Bates
Lord Bates
Alan Beith
Lord Beith
David Blunkett
Lord Blunkett
Paul Boateng
Lord Boateng
Betty Boothroyd
Baroness Boothroyd
Timothy Boswell
Lord Boswell of Aynho
Virginia Bottomley
Baroness Bottomley of Nettlestone
Keith Bradley
Lord Bradley
Des Browne
Lord Browne of Ladyton
Angela Browning
Baroness Browning
Malcolm Bruce
Lord Bruce of Bennachie
John Burnett
Lord Burnett
Lorely Burt
Baroness Burt of Solihull
Menzies Campbell
Lord Campbell of Pittenweem
Dale Campbell-Savours
Lord Campbell-Savours
Alexander Carlile
Lord Carlile of Berriew
Matthew Carrington
Lord Carrington of Fulham
Lynda Chalker
Baroness Chalker of Wallasey
David Chidgey
Lord Chidgey
David Clark
Lord Clark of Windermere
Lynda Clark
Baroness Clark of Calton
Stanley Clinton-Davis
Lord Clinton-Davis
Sebastian Coe
Lord Coe
John Cope
Lord Cope of Berkeley
Patrick Cormack
Lord Cormack
Jean Corston
Baroness Corston
Brian Cotter
Lord Cotter
Jack Cunningham
Lord Cunningham of Felling
Alistair Darling
Lord Darling of Roulanish
Bryan Davies
Lord Davies of Oldham
Quentin Davies
Lord Davies of Stamford
James Douglas-Hamilton
Lord Selkirk of Douglas
Alf Dubs
Lord Dubs
Hugh Dykes
Lord Dykes
Nicholas Edwards
Lord Crickhowell

Dafydd Elis-Thomas
Lord Elis-Thomas
Dafydd Elystan-Morgan
Lord Elystan-Morgan
Ronnie Fearn
Lord Fearn
Lynne Featherstone
Baroness Featherstone
Howard Flight
Lord Flight
Janet Fookes
Baroness Fookes
Michael Forsyth
Lord Forsyth of Drumlean
Derek Foster
Lord Foster of Bishop Auckland
Donald Foster
Lord Foster of Bath
George Foulkes
Lord Foulkes of Cumnock
Norman Fowler
Lord Fowler
Roger Freeman
Lord Freeman
Tristan Garel-Jones
Lord Garel-Jones
Llin Golding
Baroness Golding
Alastair Goodlad
Lord Goodlad
Edward Graham
Lord Graham of Edmonton
Bruce Grocott
Lord Grocott
John Gummer
Lord Deben
William Hague
Lord Hague of Richmond
Peter Hain
Lord Hain
Archie Hamilton
Lord Hamilton of Epsom
Helene Hayman
Baroness Hayman
Robert Hayward
Lord Hayward
Michael Heseltine
Lord Heseltine

Terence Higgins
Lord Higgins
Robin Hodgson
Lord Hodgson of Astley Abbotts
Douglas Hogg
Viscount Hailsham
John Horam
Lord Horam
Michael Howard
Lord Howard of Lympne
Alan Howarth
Lord Howarth of Newport
David Howell
Lord Howell of Guildford
William Howie
Lord Howie of Troon
Douglas Hoyle
Lord Hoyle
Beverley Hughes
Baroness Hughes of Stretford
Robert Hughes
Lord Hughes of Woodside
David Hunt
Lord Hunt of Wirral
John Hutton
Lord Hutton of Furness
Barry Jones
Lord Jones
Nigel Jones
Lord Jones of Cheltenham
Michael Jopling
Lord Jopling
Tessa Jowell
Baroness Jowell
Frank Judd
Lord Judd
Oona King
Baroness King of Bow
Tom King
Lord King of Bridgwater
Neil Kinnock
Lord Kinnock
Timothy Kirkhope
Lord Kirkhope of Harrogate
Archy Kirkwood
Lord Kirkwood of Kirkhope
Jim Knight
Lord Knight of Weymouth

Susan Kramer
Baroness Kramer
Norman Lamont
Lord Lamont of Lerwick
Ian Lang
Lord Lang of Monkton
Andrew Lansley
Lord Lansley
Nigel Lawson
Lord Lawson of Blaby
John Lee
Lord Lee of Trafford
Helen Liddell
Baroness Liddell of Coatdyke
Robert Lindsay
Earl of Crawford and Balcarres
Michael Lord
Lord Framlingham
Richard Luce
Lord Luce
Thomas McAvoy
Lord McAvoy
John McFall
Lord McFall of Alcluith
John MacGregor
Lord MacGregor of Pulham Market
Anne McIntosh
Baroness McIntosh of Pickering
David Maclean
Lord Blencathra
Robert Maclennan
Lord Maclennan of Rogart
Tom McNally
Lord McNally
Diana Maddock
Baroness Maddock
Ken Maginnis
Lord Maginnis of Drumglass
Peter Mandelson
Lord Mandelson
Michael Martin
Lord Martin of Springburn
Francis Maude
Lord Maude of Horsham
Brian Mawhinney
Lord Mawhinney
John Maxton
Lord Maxton

Lewis Moonie
Lord Moonie
John Moore
Lord Moore of Lower Marsh
Estelle Morris
Baroness Morris of Yardley
John Morris
Lord Morris of Aberavon
Michael Morris
Lord Naseby
Colin Moynihan
Lord Moynihan
Paul Murphy
Lord Murphy of Torfaen
Emma Nicholson
Baroness Nicholson of Winterbourne
Martin O'Neill
Lord O'Neill of Clackmannan
Sally Oppenheim-Barnes
Baroness Oppenheim-Barnes
David Owen
Lord Owen
Christopher Patten
Lord Patten of Barnes
John Patten
Lord Patten
Tom Pendry
Lord Pendry
John Prescott
Lord Prescott
Dawn Primarolo
Baroness Primarolo
David Prior
Lord Prior of Brampton
Joyce Quin
Baroness Quin
Giles Radice
Lord Radice
John Reid
Lord Reid of Cardowan
Ivor Richard
Lord Richard
Andrew Robathan
Lord Robathan
George Robertson
Lord Robertson of Port Ellen
William Rodgers
Lord Rodgers of Quarry Bank

Jeffrey Rooker
Lord Rooker
Ted Rowlands
Lord Rowlands
Richard Ryder
Lord Ryder of Wensum
Gillian Shephard
Baroness Shephard of Northwold
Angela Smith
Baroness Smith of Basildon
Chris Smith
Lord Smith of Finsbury
Peter Snape
Lord Snape
Clive Soley
Lord Soley
Michael Spicer
Lord Spicer
Richard Spring
Lord Risby
David Steel
Lord Steel of Aikwood
Nicol Stephen
Lord Stephen
David Stoddart
Lord Stoddart of Swindon
Andrew Stunell
Lord Stunell
Dick Taverne
Lord Taverne
Ann Taylor
Baroness Taylor of Bolton
John Taylor
Lord Kilclooney
Matthew Taylor
Lord Taylor of Goss Moor
Norman Tebbit
Lord Tebbit
Peter Temple-Morris
Lord Temple-Morris
John Thurso
Viscount Thurso
John Tomlinson
Lord Tomlinson
Jenny Tonge
Baroness Tonge
Graham Tope
Lord Tope
Don Touhig
Lord Touhig
David Trimble
Lord Trimble
Christopher Tugendhat
Lord Tugendhat
Paul Tyler
Lord Tyler
John Wakeham
Lord Wakeham
William Waldegrave
Lord Waldegrave of North Hill
Jim Wallace
Lord Wallace of Tankerness
Mike Watson
Lord Watson of Invergowrie
David Watts
Lord Watts
Dafydd Wigley
Lord Wigley
David Willetts
Lord Willetts
Phil Willis
Lord Willis of Knaresborough
Michael Wills
Lord Wills
Kenneth Woolmer
Lord Woolmer of Leeds
Ian Wrigglesworth
Lord Wrigglesworth
George Young
Lord Young of Cookham

Hereditary Peer Members

Under the 1999 House of Lords Act, which abolished the right of most hereditary peers to sit in the Upper Chamber, 92 hereditary peers retained their seats. These include two hereditary office holders, the Duke of Norfolk (Earl Marshal), and the Marquess of Cholmondeley (Lord Great Chamberlain).

Peers of Ireland are marked*, with their British honours in parenthesis.

A number of other peers sit under their hereditary titles, although they are members by virtue of life peerages, the titles of which appear in bold.

Lord Aberdare cr. 1873
Lord Addington cr. 1887
Earl of Arran cr. 1762* (Baron Sudley)
Lord Ashton of Hyde cr.1911
Viscount Astor cr. 1917
Lord Astor of Hever cr. 1956
Earl Attlee cr. 1955
Earl Baldwin of Bewdley cr. 1937
Lord Berkeley cr. 1421 (LP **Baron Gueterbock** 2000)
Lord Borwick cr. 1922
Lord Brabazon of Tara cr. 1942
Viscount Bridgeman cr. 1929
Viscount Brookeborough cr. 1952
Lord Brougham and Vaux cr. 1860
Earl of Caithness cr. 1455
Lord Carrington cr. 1796* (LP **Baron Carington of Upton** 1999) (Baron Carrington)
Earl Cathcart cr. 1814
Viscount Chandos cr. 1954 (LP **Baron Lyttelton of Aldershot** 2000)
Marquess of Cholmondeley cr. 1815
Earl of Clancarty cr. 1803* (Baron Trench)
Lord Colgrain cr. 1946
Viscount Colville of Culross cr. 1902
Lord Colwyn cr. 1917
Earl of Cork and Orrery cr. 1620/1660* (Baron Boyle of Marston)
Earl of Courtown cr. 1762* (Baron Saltersford)
Viscount Craigavon cr. 1927
Lord Crathorne cr. 1959
Earl of Crawford and Balcarres cr. 1398/1651 (LP **Baron Balniel** 1974)
Lord Cromwell cr. 1375
Lord de Mauley cr. 1838
Lord Denham cr. 1937
Earl of Dundee cr. 1660
Viscount Eccles cr. 1964
Lord Elton cr. 1934
Earl of Erroll cr. 1452
Lord Fairfax of Cameron cr. 1627
Viscount of Falkland cr. 1620
Lord Freyberg cr. 1951
Lord Geddes cr. 1942
Earl of Glasgow cr. 1703
Lord Glenarthur cr. 1918
Lord Glentoran cr. 1939
Viscount Goschen cr. 1900
Lord Grantchester cr. 1953
Lord Greenway cr. 1927
Viscount Hailsham cr. 1929 (LP **Baron Hailsham of Kettlethorpe** 2015)
Viscount Hanworth cr. 1936
Lord Henley cr. 1799* (Baron Northington)
Earl of Home cr. 1604
Earl Howe cr. 1821
Lord Hylton cr. 1866
Lord Inglewood cr. 1964
Earl of Kinnoull cr. 1633
Earl of Lindsay cr. 1633
Earl of Listowel cr. 1822* (Baron Hare)
Earl of Liverpool cr. 1905
Marquess of Lothian cr. 1701 (LP **Baron Kerr of Monteviot** 2010)
Lord Lucas of Crudwell and Dingwall cr. 1663/1609
Earl of Lytton cr. 1880
Lord Mancroft cr. 1937
Countess of Mar cr. 1114
Duke of Montrose cr. 1707
Lord Mountevans cr. 1945
Lord Moynihan cr. 1929
Duke of Norfolk cr. 1483
Lord Northbourne cr. 1884
Lord Northbrook cr. 1866
Earl of Oxford and Asquith cr. 1925
Lord Palmer cr. 1933
Earl Peel cr. 1929
Lord Ponsonby of Shulbrede cr. 1930 (LP **Baron Ponsonby of Roehampton** 2000)
Lord Rea cr. 1937
Lord Redesdale cr. 1902 (LP **Baron Mitford** 2000)
Viscount Ridley cr. 1900
Earl of Rosslyn cr. 1801
Lord Rotherwick cr. 1939
Lord Russell of Liverpool cr. 1919
Lord St John of Bletso cr. 1558
Earl of Sandwich cr. 1660
Earl of Selborne cr. 1882
Lord Selsdon cr. 1932
Earl of Shrewsbury and Waterford cr. 1442/1446
Viscount Simon cr. 1940
Lord Skelmersdale cr. 1828
Viscount Slim cr. 1960
Duke of Somerset cr. 1547

Earl of Stair cr. 1703
Lord Strathclyde cr. 1955
Lord Swinfen cr. 1919
Lord Thurlow cr. 1792
Viscount Thurso cr. 1952
Lord Trefgarne cr. 1947
Viscount Trenchard cr. 1936
Lord Trevethin and Oaksey cr. 1921/1947
Viscount Ullswater cr. 1921
Lord Vaux of Harrowden cr. 1523
Viscount Waverley cr. 1952
Duke of Wellington cr. 1814
Lord Willoughby de Broke cr. 1491
Viscount Younger of Leckie cr. 1923

Bishops

Since the mid-nineteenth century the number of bishops in the House (known as Lords Spiritual as opposed to Lords Temporal) has been limited by statute to 26. By ancient usage the two Anglican Archbishops and the Bishops of London, Durham and Winchester automatically have seats in the House of Lords. The remaining 21 diocesan bishops usually qualify for membership according to seniority. However until 2025, where there is a woman amongst those bishops awaiting a place in the Lords, she will be given priority in filling the vacancy under the terms of the Lords Spiritual (Women) Act 2015.

ARCHBISHOPS (2) AND DIOCESAN BISHOPS (3) EX-OFFICIO

Most Rev. and Rt Hon Justin Welby	Canterbury
Most Rev. and Rt Hon John Sentamu	York
Rt Rev. Paul Butler	Durham
Rt Rev. Tim Dakin	Winchester
To be appointed	London*

* The new Bishop of London is likely to be appointed by the end of 2017.

BISHOPS IN ORDER OF SENIORITY (21)†

		Entered Lords
Rt Rev. Peter Forster	Chester	2001
Rt Rev. Graham James	Norwich	2004
Rt Rev. Alastair Redfern	Derby	2010
Rt Rev. David Urquhart	Birmingham	2010
Rt Rev. John Inge	Worcester	2012
Rt Rev. Christopher Cocksworth	Coventry	2013
Rt Rev. Steven Croft	Oxford	2013
Rt Rev. Alan Smith	St Albans	2013
Rt Rev. James Newcome	Carlisle	2013
Rt Rev. Donald Allister	Peterborough	2014
Rt Rev. Christopher Foster	Portsmouth	2014
Rt Rev. Stephen Cottrell	Chelmsford	2014
Rt Rev. James Langstaff	Rochester	2014
Rt Rev. Stephen Conway	Ely	2014
Rt Rev. Christopher Chessun	Southwark	2014
Rt Rev. Nicholas Baines	Leeds	2014
Rt Rev. Nicholas Holtam	Salisbury	2014
Rt Rev. Rachel Treweek	Gloucester	2015
Rt Rev. Christine Hardman	Newcastle	2015
Rt Rev. Christopher Lowson	Lincoln	2017

†The Bishop of Bristol retired in October 2017, and will be replaced by the Bishop of Chichester.

Law Lords

Senior members of the judiciary are unable to sit or vote in the House of Lords until they retire.

Supreme Court Justices:
Baroness Hale of Richmond
Lord Kerr of Tonaghmore
Lord Mance

Senators of the College of Justice in Scotland: Lord Boyd of Duncansby, Baroness Clark of Calton

Peers on leave of absence (19)

Baroness Amos	*NA*
Baroness Ashton of Upholland	*NA*
Lord Black of Crossharbour	*NA*
Lord Blyth of Rowington	*Con*
Marquess of Cholmondeley	*NA*
Lord Clinton-Davis	*Lab*
Earl of Crawford and Balcarres	*Con*
Lord Graham of Edmonton	*Lab/Co-op*
Lord Hardie	*CB*
Baroness King of Bow	*Lab*
Lord Llewellyn of Steep	*Con*
Lord Martin of Springburn	*CB*
Baroness Mobarik	*Con*
Lord Mogg	*CB*
Lord Oates	*Lib Dem*
Lord Sainsbury of Preston Candover	*Con*
Lord Sainsbury of Turville	*Lab*
Baroness Scotland of Asthal	*Lab*
Baroness Vadera	*NA*

Women Members (216)

Women were first admitted into the House of Lords by the Life Peerage Act, 1958. Women peers by succession (indicated with an asterisk) were not admitted into the Upper House until 1963.

Baroness Adams of Craigielea	*Lab*
Baroness Afshar	*CB*
Baroness Altmann	*Con*
Baroness Amos	*NA*
Baroness Andrews	*Lab*
Baroness Anelay of St Johns	*Con*
Baroness Armstrong of Hill Top	*Lab*
Baroness Ashton of Upholland	*NA*
Baroness Bakewell	*Lab*
Baroness Bakewell of Hardington Mandeville	*Lib Dem*
Baroness Barker	*Lib Dem*
Baroness Benjamin	*Lib Dem*
Baroness Berridge	*Con*
Baroness Bertin	*Con*
Baroness Billingham	*Lab*
Baroness Blackstone	*Lab*
Baroness Blood	*Lab*
Baroness Bloomfield of Hinton Waldrist	*Con*
Baroness Bonham-Carter of Yarnbury	*Lib Dem*
Baroness Boothroyd	*CB*
Baroness Bottomley of Nettlestone	*Con*
Baroness Bowles of Berkhamsted	*Lib Dem*
Baroness Brady	*Con*
Baroness Brinton	*Lib Dem*
Baroness Brown of Cambridge	*CB*
Baroness Browning	*Con*
Baroness Burt of Solihull	*Lib Dem*
Baroness Buscombe	*Con*
Baroness Butler-Sloss	*CB*
Baroness Byford	*Con*
Baroness Campbell of Loughborough	*CB*
Baroness Campbell of Surbiton	*CB*
Baroness Cavendish of Little Venice	*NA*
Baroness Chakrabarti	*Lab*
Baroness Chalker of Wallasey	*Con*
Baroness Chisholm of Owlpen	*Con*
Baroness Clark of Calton	*NA*
Baroness Cohen of Pimlico	*Lab*
Baroness Corston	*Lab*
Baroness Coussins	*CB*
Baroness Couttie	*Con*
Baroness Cox	*CB*
Baroness Crawley	*Lab*
Baroness Cumberlege	*Con*
Baroness Dean of Thornton-le-Fylde	*Lab*
Baroness Deech	*CB*
Baroness Donaghy	*Lab*
Baroness Doocey	*Lib Dem*
Baroness Drake	*Lab*
Baroness D'Souza	*CB*
Baroness Eaton	*Con*
Baroness Eccles of Moulton	*Con*
Baroness Emerton	*CB*
Baroness Evans of Bowes Park	*Con*
Baroness Falkender	*Lab*
Baroness Falkner of Margravine	*Lib Dem*
Baroness Fall	*Con*
Baroness Farrington of Ribbleton	*Lab*
Baroness Featherstone	*Lib Dem*
Baroness Finlay of Llandaff	*CB*
Baroness Finn	*Con*
Baroness Flather	*CB*
Baroness Fookes	*Con*
Baroness Ford	*CB*
Baroness Fritchie	*CB*
Baroness Gale	*Lab*
Baroness Garden of Frognal	*Lib Dem*
Baroness Gardner of Parkes	*Con*
Baroness Gibson of Market Rasen	*Lab*
Bishop of Gloucester	*NA*
Baroness Goldie	*Con*
Baroness Golding	*Lab*
Baroness Goudie	*Lab*

Baroness Gould of Potternewton	*Lab*
Baroness Greenfield	*CB*
Baroness Greengross	*CB*
Baroness Grender	*Lib Dem*
Baroness Grey-Thompson	*CB*
Baroness Hale of Richmond	*NA*
Baroness Hamwee	*Lib Dem*
Baroness Hanham	*Con*
Baroness Harding of Winscombe	*Con*
Baroness Harris of Richmond	*Lib Dem*
Baroness Hayman	*CB*
Baroness Hayter of Kentish Town	*Lab/Co-op*
Baroness Healy of Primrose Hill	*Lab*
Baroness Helic	*Con*
Baroness Henig	*Lab*
Baroness Hilton of Eggardon	*Lab*
Baroness Hodgson of Abinger	*Con*
Baroness Hogg	*CB*
Baroness Hollins	*CB*
Baroness Hollis of Heigham	*Lab*
Baroness Hooper	*Con*
Baroness Howarth of Breckland	*CB*
Baroness Howe of Idlicote	*CB*
Baroness Howells of St Davids	*Lab*
Baroness Hughes of Stretford	*Lab*
Baroness Humphreys	*Lib Dem*
Baroness Hussein-Ece	*Lib Dem*
Baroness Janke	*Lib Dem*
Baroness Jay of Paddington	*Lab*
Baroness Jenkin of Kennington	*Con*
Baroness Jolly	*Lib Dem*
Baroness Jones of Moulsecoomb	*Green*
Baroness Jones of Whitchurch	*Lab*
Baroness Jowell	*Lab*
Baroness Kennedy of Cradley	*Lab*
Baroness Kennedy of The Shaws	*Lab*
Baroness Kidron	*CB*
Baroness King of Bow	*Lab*
Baroness Kingsmill	*Lab*
Baroness Kinnock of Holyhead	*Lab*
Baroness Kramer	*Lib Dem*
Baroness Lane-Fox of Soho	*CB*
Baroness Lawrence of Clarendon	*Lab*
Baroness Liddell of Coatdyke	*Lab*
Baroness Lister of Burtersett	*Lab*
Baroness Ludford	*Lib Dem*
Baroness McDonagh	*Lab*
Baroness McGregor-Smith	*Con*
Baroness McIntosh of Hudnall	*Lab*
Baroness McIntosh of Pickering	*Con*
Baroness Maddock	*Lib Dem*
Baroness Mallalieu	*Lab*
Baroness Manningham-Buller	*CB*
Baroness Manzoor	*Con*
Countess of Mar*	*CB*
Baroness Masham of Ilton	*CB*
Baroness Massey of Darwen	*Lab*
Baroness Meacher	*CB*
Baroness Miller of Chilthorne Domer	*Lib Dem*
Baroness Mobarik	*Con*
Baroness Mone	*Con*
Baroness Morgan of Drefelin	*CB*
Baroness Morgan of Ely	*Lab*
Baroness Morgan of Huyton	*Lab*
Baroness Morris of Bolton	*Con*
Baroness Morris of Yardley	*Lab*
Baroness Murphy	*CB*
Baroness Neuberger	*CB*
Baroness Neville-Jones	*Con*
Baroness Neville-Rolfe	*Con*
Bishop of Newcastle	*NA*
Baroness Newlove	*Con*
Baroness Nicholson of Winterbourne	*Con*
Baroness Nicol	*Lab/Co-op*
Baroness Noakes	*Con*
Baroness Northover	*Lib Dem*
Baroness Nye	*Lab*
Baroness O'Cathain	*Con*
Baroness O'Loan	*CB*
Baroness O'Neill of Bengarve	*CB*
Baroness Oppenheim-Barnes	*Con*
Baroness Paisley of St George's	*DUP*
Baroness Parminter	*Lib Dem*
Baroness Pidding	*Con*
Baroness Pinnock	*Lib Dem*
Baroness Pitkeathley	*Lab*
Baroness Prashar	*CB*
Baroness Primarolo	*Lab*
Baroness Prosser	*Lab*
Baroness Quin	*Lab*
Baroness Ramsay of Cartvale	*Lab*
Baroness Randerson	*Lib Dem*
Baroness Rawlings	*Con*
Baroness Rebuck	*Lab*
Baroness Redfern	*Con*
Baroness Richardson of Calow	*CB*
Baroness Rock	*Con*
Baroness Royall of Blaisdon	*Lab/Co-op*
Baroness Scotland of Asthal	*Lab*
Baroness Scott of Bybrook	*Con*
Baroness Scott of Needham Market	*Lib Dem*
Baroness Seccombe	*Con*
Baroness Shackleton of Belgravia	*Con*
Baroness Sharples	*Con*
Baroness Sheehan	*Lib Dem*
Baroness Shephard of Northwold	*Con*

Baroness Sherlock	*Lab*
Baroness Shields	*Con*
Baroness Smith of Basildon	*Lab/Co-op*
Baroness Smith of Gilmorehill	*Lab*
Baroness Smith of Newnham	*Lib Dem*
Baroness Stedman-Scott	*Con*
Baroness Stern	*CB*
Baroness Stowell of Beeston	*Con*
Baroness Stroud	*Con*
Baroness Sugg	*Con*
Baroness Suttie	*Lib Dem*
Baroness Symons of Vernham Dean	*Lab*
Baroness Taylor of Bolton	*Lab*
Baroness Thomas of Winchester	*Lib Dem*
Baroness Thornhill	*Lib Dem*
Baroness Thornton	*Lab/Co-op*
Baroness Tonge	*NA*
Baroness Tyler of Enfield	*Lib Dem*
Baroness Uddin	*NA*
Baroness Vadera	*NA*
Baroness Valentine	*CB*
Baroness Vere of Norbiton	*Con*
Baroness Verma	*Con*
Baroness Walmsley	*Lib Dem*
Baroness Warsi	*Con*
Baroness Warwick of Undercliffe	*Lab*
Baroness Watkins of Tavistock	*CB*
Baroness Wheatcroft	*Con*
Baroness Wheeler	*Lab*
Baroness Whitaker	*Lab*
Baroness Wilcox	*Con*
Baroness Williams of Trafford	*Con*
Baroness Wolf of Dulwich	*CB*
Baroness Worthington	*NA*
Baroness Wyld	*Con*
Baroness Young of Hornsey	*CB*
Baroness Young of Old Scone	*Lab*

Peers by Age

(Ages as at 1 October 2017)

	Conservative	%	*Labour*	%	*Lib Dem*	%	*CB*	%	*Other*	%	*Total*
30–39	2	0.8	0	0.0	0	0.0	0	0.0	0	0.0	2
40–49	21	8.2	5	2.5	4	4.0	3	1.7	3	3.6	36
50–59	35	13.6	17	8.3	14	13.9	19	10.6	12	14.5	97
60–69	72	28.0	51	25.0	34	33.7	50	27.9	37	44.6	244
70–79	83	32.3	91	44.6	37	36.6	69	38.5	25	30.1	305
80–89	38	14.8	36	17.6	12	11.9	34	19.0	5	6.0	125
Over 90	6	2.3	4	2.0	0	0.0	4	2.2	1	1.2	15
	257		204		101		179		83		824
Average age	**68.2**		**71.9**		**67.9**		**71.6**		**67.4**		

Baroness Bertin	39
Baroness Wyld	39
Lord McInnes of Kilwinning	40
Baroness Sugg	40
Lord Wei	40
Baroness Evans of Bowes Park	41
Lord O'Shaughnessy	41
Lord Livermore	42
Lord Purvis of Tweed	43
Lord Duncan of Springbank	44
Baroness Lane-Fox of Soho	44
Lord Holmes of Richmond	45
Baroness Mone	45
Baroness Berridge	45
Lord Freyberg	46
Lord Gadhia	46
Lord Shinkwin	46
Baroness Warsi	46
Baroness Worthington	46
Lord Oates	47
Lord Bridges of Headley	47
Baroness Rock	48
Baroness Brady	48
Baroness Chakrabarti	48
Baroness Grey-Thompson	48
Baroness Kennedy of Cradley	48
Baroness Smith of Newnham	48
Baroness Vere of Norbiton	48
Baroness Fall	49
Baroness Harding of Winscombe	49
Baroness King of Bow	49
Lord Wolfson of Aspley Guise	49
Lord Ahmad of Wimbledon	49
Baroness Cavendish of Little Venice	49
Baroness Finn	49
Baroness Helic	49
Baroness Suttie	49
Lord Wood of Anfield	49
Lord Mendelsohn	50
Baroness Morgan of Ely	50
Lord Redesdale	50
Baroness Stowell of Beeston	50
Baroness Williams of Trafford	50
Viscount Goschen	51
Lord Allan of Hallam	51
Lord Barker of Battle	51
Lord Caine	51
Lord Feldman of Elstree	51
Baroness Pidding	51
Lord Scriven	51
Lord Smith of Hindhead	51
Lord Alli	52
Lord Knight of Weymouth	52
Lord Llewellyn of Steep	52
Baroness Stroud	52
Lord Vaux of Harrowden	52
Lord Black of Brentwood	53
Lord Carter of Barnes	53
Lord Kakkar	53
Earl of Listowel	53
Lord Livingston of Parkhead	53
Baroness Parminter	53
Lord Kennedy of Southwark	54
Earl of Kinnoull	54
Lord Addington	54
Lord Adonis	54
Lord Cooper of Windrush	54
Lord Gilbert of Panteg	54
Bishop of Gloucester	54
Baroness McGregor-Smith	54
Lord Palumbo of Southwark	54
Lord Taylor of Goss Moor	54
Lord Bilimoria	55
Baroness Newlove	55

Lord Adebowale	55
Baroness Couttie	55
Lord Finkelstein	55
Baroness Grender	55
Baroness Shields	55
Baroness Vadera	55
Baroness Sherlock	56
Baroness Barker	56
Lord Bates	56
Lord Callanan	56
Lord Glasman	56
Lord Hague of Richmond	56
Baroness Kidron	56
Baroness McDonagh	56
Baroness Morgan of Drefelin	56
Lord Polak	56
Lord Price	56
Earl of Stair	56
Baroness Bloomfield of Hinton Waldrist	57
Marquess of Cholmondeley	57
Lord Cromwell	57
Lord Darzi of Denham	57
Lord Drayson	57
Lord Hill of Oareford	57
Lord McConnell of Glenscorrodale	57
Lord Patel of Bradford	57
Lord Porter of Spalding	57
Lord Rennard	57
Lord Stephen	57
Lord Strathclyde	57
Lord Trevethin and Oaksey	57
Bishop of Chichester	58
Lord Ponsonby of Shulbrede	58
Baroness Valentine	58
Baroness Campbell of Surbiton	58
Viscount Colville of Culross	58
Bishop of Coventry	58
Lord Dunlop	58
Lord Kestenbaum	58
Lord Leigh of Hurley	58
Lord Macpherson of Earl's Court	58
Baroness Morgan of Huyton	58
Baroness Sheehan	58
Baroness Smith of Basildon	58
Lord Truscott	58
Baroness Uddin	58
Baroness Verma	58
Baroness Bonham-Carter of Yarnbury	59
Bishop of Ely	59
Baroness Ford	59
Bishop of Leeds	59
Baroness Mobarik	59
Lord Ashton of Hyde	59
Bishop of Chelmsford	59
Lord Evans of Weardale	59
Lord Hastings of Scarisbrick	59
Baroness Manzoor	59
Lord Paddick	59
Viscount Ridley	59
Earl of Rosslyn	59
Bishop of Winchester	59
Earl Attlee	60
Lord Lansley	60
Duke of Norfolk	60
Lord Ahmed	60
Lord Allen of Kensington	60
Lord de Mauley	60
Lord Fink	60
Lord Fox	60
Lord Mancroft	60
Lord O'Neill of Gatley	60
Bishop of Oxford	60
Bishop of St Albans	60
Lord St John of Bletso	60
Baroness Scott of Needham Market	60
Baroness Tyler of Enfield	60
Lord Verjee	60
Baroness Jenkin of Kennington	61
Lord Jones of Birmingham	61
Earl of Lindsay	61
Baroness Stedman-Scott	61
Lord Turner of Ecchinswell	61
Viscount Younger of Leckie	61
Baroness Altmann	61
Baroness Ashton of Upholland	61
Archbishop of Canterbury	61
Lord Coe	61
Lord Deighton	61
Lord Fairfax of Cameron	61
Lord Gardiner of Kimble	61
Lord Haughey	61
Lord Hussain	61
Lord Marland	61
Lord Pannick	61
Bishop of Rochester	61
Baroness Shackleton of Belgravia	61
Bishop of Southwark	61
Lord Willetts	61
Lord Collins of Highbury	62
Lord Forsyth of Drumlean	62
Baroness Hodgson of Abinger	62
Lord Mawson	62
Lord Prior of Brampton	62
Lord Alderdice	62
Lord Borwick	62
Baroness Brinton	62
Bishop of Durham	62
Baroness Falkner of Margravine	62

Baroness Healy of Primrose Hill	62
Lord Hutton of Furness	62
Baroness Jones of Whitchurch	62
Lord Kerslake	62
Lord Lupton	62
Lord Moynihan	62
Baroness Nye	62
Baroness Royall of Blaisdon	62
Lord Sassoon	62
Baroness Scotland of Asthal	62
Baroness Thornhill	62
Baroness Watkins of Tavistock	62
Bishop of Worcester	62
Lord Darling of Roulanish	63
Lord Harris of Haringey	63
Lord Henley	63
Baroness Hussein-Ece	63
Lord Mandelson	63
Bishop of Portsmouth	63
Baroness Amos	63
Baroness Brown of Cambridge	63
Baroness Burt of Solihull	63
Baroness Buscombe	63
Earl of Courtown	63
Lord Keen of Elie	63
Baroness McIntosh of Pickering	63
Baroness Miller of Chilthorne Domer	63
Lord Northbrook	63
Baroness Northover	63
Baroness Primarolo	63
Lord Rotherwick	63
Bishop of Salisbury	63
Lord Wallace of Tankerness	63
Earl Cathcart	64
Lord Davies of Abersoch	64
Lord Goddard of Stockport	64
Baroness Lawrence of Clarendon	64
Lord Marks of Henley-on-Thames	64
Earl of Shrewsbury and Waterford	64
Duke of Somerset	64
Baroness Thornton	64
Lord Bassam of Brighton	64
Lord Blair of Boughton	64
Lord Blencathra	64
Baroness Bowles of Berkhamsted	64
Lord Boyd of Duncansby	64
Bishop of Carlisle	64
Viscount Chandos	64
Lord Lennie	64
Bishop of Lincoln	64
Lord Macdonald of River Glaven	64
Lord Malloch-Brown	64
Lord Maude of Horsham	64
Baroness Morris of Bolton	64

Baroness Neville-Rolfe	64
Lord Newby	64
Lord Popat	64
Viscount Thurso	64
Viscount Astor	65
Baroness Chisholm of Owlpen	65
Lord Falconer of Thoroton	65
Baroness Featherstone	65
Baroness O'Loan	65
Lord Palmer	65
Lord Arbuthnot of Edrom	65
Bishop of Birmingham	65
Lord Blackwell	65
Lord Bourne of Aberystwyth	65
Viscount Brookeborough	65
Lord Browne of Ladyton	65
Earl of Clancarty	65
Lord Crisp	65
Baroness Morris of Yardley	65
Lord O'Donnell	65
Earl of Oxford and Asquith	65
Bishop of Peterborough	65
Baroness Rebuck	65
Lord Richards of Herstmonceux	65
Lord Ricketts	65
Lord Russell of Liverpool	65
Lord Taylor of Warwick	65
Lord Teverson	65
Lord Thurlow	65
Lord Wills	65
Lord Cashman	66
Baroness Coussins	66
Lord Dannatt	66
Baroness Liddell of Coatdyke	66
Lord Alton of Liverpool	66
Lord Boateng	66
Lord Colgrain	66
Lord Gold	66
Lord Grantchester	66
Lord Hall of Birkenhead	66
Earl Howe	66
Lord Inglewood	66
Baroness Jolly	66
Lord Lucas of Crudwell and Dingwall	66
Baroness Ludford	66
Bishop of Newcastle	66
Lord Norton of Louth	66
Bishop of Norwich	66
Lord Robathan	66
Lord Smith of Finsbury	66
Baroness Symons of Vernham Dean	66
Viscount Trenchard	66
Lord True	66
Lord Watts	66

Baroness Wheatcroft	66
Baroness Young of Hornsey	66
Lord Cameron of Dillington	67
Lord Clement-Jones	67
Baroness Jones of Moulsecoomb	67
Lord Stirrup	67
Viscount Waverley	67
Baroness Wolf of Dulwich	67
Lord Bew	67
Lord Bradley	67
Bishop of Chester	67
Baroness Crawley	67
Lord Davidson of Glen Clova	67
Lord Elder	67
Lord Faulks	67
Lord Freud	67
Baroness Goldie	67
Lord Goldsmith	67
Baroness Greenfield	67
Lord Hain	67
Lord Hay of Ballyore	67
Baroness Hughes of Stretford	67
Baroness Kennedy of The Shaws	67
Baroness Kramer	67
Lord Lisvane	67
Earl of Lytton	67
Lord Mair	67
Baroness Neuberger	67
Lord Williams of Oystermouth	67
Earl of Caithness	68
Baroness Campbell of Loughborough	68
Lord Dobbs	68
Lord Green of Hurstpierpoint	68
Lord Murphy of Torfaen	68
Baroness Bakewell of Hardington Mandeville	68
Baroness Benjamin	68
Baroness Clark of Calton	68
Earl of Dundee	68
Lord Fellowes of West Stafford	68
Baroness Finlay of Llandaff	68
Baroness Hayman	68
Baroness Hayter of Kentish Town	68
Lord Hayward	68
Lord Hunt of Kings Heath	68
Baroness Lister of Burtersett	68
Lord Nash	68
Baroness Noakes	68
Lord Rose of Monewden	68
Lord Ryder of Wensum	68
Lord Storey	68
Lord Watson of Invergowrie	68
Baroness Wheeler	68
Archbishop of York	68
Baroness Adams of Craigielea	69
Lord Brabazon of Tara	69
Lord Browne of Belmont	69
Lord Carrington of Fulham	69
Lord Empey	69
Lord Leitch	69
Earl Peel	69
Lord Thomas of Cwmgiedd	69
Lord Touhig	69
Lord Berkeley of Knighton	69
Baroness Bottomley of Nettlestone	69
Lord Browne of Madingley	69
Lord Carlile of Berriew	69
Bishop of Derby	69
Baroness Doocey	69
Baroness Drake	69
Earl of Erroll	69
Lord Flight	69
Lord Haworth	69
Lord Jones of Cheltenham	69
Lord Kerr of Tonaghmore	69
Lord King of Lothbury	69
Lord Lipsey	69
Lord Lloyd-Webber	69
Baroness Manningham-Buller	69
Lord Morrow	69
Lord Mountevans	69
Lord Myners	69
Lord Neuberger of Abbotsbury	69
Baroness Prashar	69
Baroness Randerson	69
Lord Sacks	69
Lord Stoneham of Droxford	69
Lord West of Spithead	69
Lord Whitby	69
Baroness Young of Old Scone	69
Lord Bach	70
Baroness Browning	70
Lord Currie of Marylebone	70
Lord Elis-Thomas	70
Lord Fraser of Corriegarth	70
Lord Aberdare	70
Baroness Anelay of St Johns	70
Lord Bichard	70
Lord Blunkett	70
Lord Condon	70
Lord Foster of Bath	70
Baroness Hamwee	70
Lord Harrison	70
Lord Hennessy of Nympsfield	70
Baroness Humphreys	70
Baroness Janke	70
Baroness Jowell	70
Baroness Kingsmill	70
Lord Liddle	70

Lord Moonie	70
Baroness Murphy	70
Lord Oakeshott of Seagrove Bay	70
Baroness Redfern	70
Lord Reid of Cardowan	70
Baroness Scott of Bybrook	70
Lord Sharkey	70
Lord Stevenson of Balmacara	70
Lord Sugar	70
Baroness Taylor of Bolton	70
Baroness Armstrong of Hill Top	71
Lord Bamford	71
Earl of Cork and Orrery	71
Lord Magan of Castletown	71
Baroness Mallalieu	71
Lord Sherbourne of Didsbury	71
Baroness Thomas of Winchester	71
Lord Astor of Hever	71
Lord Bird	71
Lord Carter of Coles	71
Lord Faulkner of Worcester	71
Baroness Goudie	71
Viscount Hanworth	71
Lord Hardie	71
Baroness Hogg	71
Baroness Hollins	71
Lord Janvrin	71
Lord Jay of Ewelme	71
Lord Kirkwood of Kirkhope	71
Baroness McIntosh of Hudnall	71
Lord McKenzie of Luton	71
Baroness Pinnock	71
Lord Risby	71
Lord Robertson of Port Ellen	71
Lord Saatchi	71
Lord Shipley	71
Lord Stern of Brentford	71
Lord Strasburger	71
Lord Trees	71
Lord Waldegrave of North Hill	71
Lord Beecham	72
Lord Birt	72
Lord Bruce of Bennachie	72
Baroness Donaghy	72
Lord Farmer	72
Lord Glenarthur	72
Lord Kirkham	72
Earl of Liverpool	72
Lord McFall of Alcluith	72
Baroness Quin	72
Lord Rosser	72
Lord Trimble	72
Lord Best	72
Lord Burnett	72
Lord Eatwell	72
Lord German	72
Lord Grabiner	72
Viscount Hailsham	72
Baroness Hale of Richmond	72
Lord Hollick	72
Lord Kirkhope of Harrogate	72
Lord Krebs	72
Lord Lexden	72
Marquess of Lothian	72
Baroness Maddock	72
Lord Martin of Springburn	72
Lord Monks	72
Lord O'Neill of Clackmannan	72
Lord Ouseley	72
Lord Patten	72
Lord Plant of Highfield	72
Lord Skelmersdale	72
Lord Smith of Leigh	72
Lord Stevenson of Coddenham	72
Lord Turnbull	72
Baroness Warwick of Undercliffe	72
Duke of Wellington	72
Baroness Henig	73
Earl of Home	73
Lord Loomba	73
Lord McAvoy	73
Lord Mogg	73
Lord Taylor of Holbeach	73
Lord Tope	73
Lord Triesman	73
Baroness Afshar	73
Lord Balfe	73
Lord Black of Crossharbour	73
Lord Burns	73
Viscount Craigavon	73
Lord Curry of Kirkharle	73
Lord Davies of Stamford	73
Baroness D'Souza	73
Lord Filkin	73
Baroness Garden of Frognal	73
Baroness Harris of Richmond	73
Lord Howarth of Newport	73
Baroness Kinnock of Holyhead	73
Lord Laird	73
Lord Levy	73
Lord Patten of Barnes	73
Lord Ribeiro	73
Lord Smith of Kelvin	73
Lord Walker of Aldringham	73
Lord Boswell of Aynho	74
Lord Evans of Watford	74
Lord Stevens of Kirkwhelpington	74
Lord Stunell	74

Lord Wilson of Dinton	74
Baroness Andrews	74
Lord Beith	74
Lord Bowness	74
Lord Boyce	74
Lord Campbell-Savours	74
Lord Clarke of Stone-cum-Ebony	74
Baroness Cumberlege	74
Baroness Dean of Thornton-le-Fylde	74
Baroness Deech	74
Lord Goodlad	74
Lord Grade of Yarmouth	74
Lord Mackenzie of Framwellgate	74
Lord McNally	74
Lord Mance	74
Lord Mitchell	74
Lord Razzall	74
Earl of Sandwich	74
Lord Sawyer	74
Lord Spicer	74
Lord Tunnicliffe	74
Lord Vallance of Tummel	74
Baroness Walmsley	74
Lord Whitty	74
Lord Wigley	74
Lord Bell	75
Lord Cavendish of Furness	75
Lord Fellowes	75
Lord Griffiths of Fforestfach	75
Lord Hamilton of Epsom	75
Lord Levene of Portsoken	75
Baroness Nicholson of Winterbourne	75
Lord Tyler	75
Lord Willis of Knaresborough	75
Baroness Blackstone	75
Lord Brennan	75
Lord Brooke of Alverthorpe	75
Lord Chadlington	75
Baroness Chalker of Wallasey	75
Lord Chidgey	75
Lord Colwyn	75
Baroness Corston	75
Baroness Eaton	75
Lord Foulkes of Cumnock	75
Lord Freeman	75
Baroness Fritchie	75
Lord Glendonbrook	75
Lord Greaves	75
Lord Griffiths of Burry Port	75
Lord Harris of Peckham	75
Lord Hodgson of Astley Abbotts	75
Lord Hunt of Wirral	75
Lord Kerr of Kinlochard	75
Lord Kinnock	75
Lord Lamont of Lerwick	75
Lord Lee of Trafford	75
Lord Lingfield	75
Lord Low of Dalston	75
Lord Pearson of Rannoch	75
Lord Rees of Ludlow	75
Lord Rogan	75
Lord Selkirk of Douglas	75
Lord Shutt of Greetland	75
Lord Snape	75
Lord Stone of Blackheath	75
Viscount Ullswater	75
Lord Young of Norwood Green	75
Baroness Gale	76
Baroness Gibson of Market Rasen	76
Lord Grocott	76
Lord Sainsbury of Turville	76
Baroness Wilcox	76
Lord Ashdown of Norton-sub-Hamdon	76
Baroness Byford	76
Lord Campbell of Pittenweem	76
Lord Collins of Mapesbury	76
Lord Garel-Jones	76
Lord Green of Deddington	76
Lord Greenway	76
Lord Hameed	76
Baroness Hollis of Heigham	76
Lord Howard of Lympne	76
Lord Howard of Rising	76
Lord Hunt of Chesterton	76
Lord Judge	76
Baroness O'Neill of Bengarve	76
Lord Powell of Bayswater	76
Lord Puttnam	76
Lord Rooker	76
Lord Sheikh	76
Baroness Stern	76
Lord Sutherland of Houndwood	76
Baroness Tonge	76
Lord Trefgarne	76
Lord Wallace of Saltaire	76
Lord Watson of Richmond	76
Lord Young of Cookham	76
Lord Bragg	77
Lord Clark of Windermere	77
Lord Davies of Oldham	77
Lord Deben	77
Baroness Jay of Paddington	77
Baroness Neville-Jones	77
Lord Wrigglesworth	77
Lord Archer of Weston-Super-Mare	77
Lord Bhattacharyya	77
Lord Blyth of Rowington	77
Baroness Cohen of Pimlico	77

Lord Desai	77
Baroness Farrington of Ribbleton	77
Lord Hanningfield	77
Baroness Howarth of Breckland	77
Lord Irvine of Lairg	77
Lord Lang of Monkton	77
Lord MacKenzie of Culkein	77
Countess of Mar	77
Lord Mawhinney	77
Baroness Meacher	77
Lord Patel of Blackburn	77
Baroness Pitkeathley	77
Lord Rowlands	77
Earl of Selborne	77
Baroness Shephard of Northwold	77
Viscount Simon	77
Baroness Smith of Gilmorehill	77
Lord Warner	77
Lord Winston	77
Lord Woolmer of Leeds	77
Lord Framlingham	78
Lord Guthrie of Craigiebank	78
Lord Morris of Handsworth	78
Lord Palmer of Childs Hill	78
Lord Swinfen	78
Lord Anderson of Swansea	78
Lord Berkeley	78
Baroness Billingham	78
Lord Cormack	78
Lord Crathorne	78
Lord Cunningham of Felling	78
Lord Dykes	78
Earl of Glasgow	78
Baroness Hanham	78
Baroness Hooper	78
Lord Horam	78
Baroness Rawlings	78
Lord Skidelsky	78
Lord Soley	78
Lord Tomlinson	78
Lord James of Blackheath	79
Lord Kilclooney	79
Lord Lea of Crondall	79
Lord Moore of Lower Marsh	79
Lord Renwick of Clifton	79
Lord Rowe-Beddoe	79
Lord Selsdon	79
Earl of Arran	79
Earl Baldwin of Bewdley	79
Baroness Blood	79
Lord Broers	79
Lord Brougham and Vaux	79
Lord Butler of Brockwell	79
Lord Fowler	79
Lord Giddens	79
Lord Hope of Craighead	79
Lord Maginnis of Drumglass	79
Baroness Massey of Darwen	79
Baroness O'Cathain	79
Lord Owen	79
Lord Patel	79
Lord Phillips of Worth Matravers	79
Lord Prescott	79
Lord Rana	79
Baroness Richardson of Calow	79
Lord Steel of Aikwood	79
Lord Temple-Morris	79
Lord Walker of Gestingthorpe	79
Lord Wasserman	79
Lord Willoughby de Broke	79
Lord Luce	80
Lord Naseby	80
Lord Radice	80
Lord Brookman	80
Lord Brown of Eaton-under-Heywood	80
Lord Cope of Berkeley	80
Baroness Cox	80
Lord Dear	80
Lord Dholakia	80
Lord Eames	80
Lord Foster of Bishop Auckland	80
Lord Geddes	80
Lord Haskins	80
Lord Jones	80
Lord MacGregor of Pulham Market	80
Lord MacLaurin of Knebworth	80
Baroness Prosser	80
Lord Renfrew of Kaimsthorn	80
Lord Smith of Clifton	80
Lord Thomas of Gresford	80
Lord Tugendhat	80
Lord Carey of Clifton	81
Lord Cullen of Whitekirk	81
Lord Roberts of Llandudno	81
Lord Bradshaw	81
Lord Cotter	81
Baroness Fookes	81
Lord Gordon of Strathblane	81
Lord Harries of Pentregarth	81
Baroness Hilton of Eggardon	81
Lord Howell of Guildford	81
Lord Jordan	81
Lord Laming	81
Lord Lester of Herne Hill	81
Lord Maclennan of Rogart	81
Lord Maxton	81
Baroness Ramsay of Cartvale	81
Lord Saville of Newdigate	81

Lord Stevens of Ludgate	81
Baroness Whitaker	81
Lord Baker of Dorking	82
Lord Haskel	82
Lord Oxburgh	82
Lord Ramsbotham	82
Lord Sterling of Plaistow	82
Lord Davies of Coity	82
Baroness Emerton	82
Viscount of Falkland	82
Lord Glentoran	82
Baroness Greengross	82
Lord Hannay of Chiswick	82
Lord Judd	82
Baroness Masham of Ilton	82
Duke of Montrose	82
Lord Palumbo	82
Lord Parekh	82
Lord Suri	82
Lord Wilson of Tillyorn	82
Baroness Eccles of Moulton	83
Lord Carswell	83
Lord Crickhowell	83
Lord Dixon-Smith	83
Lord Donoughue	83
Baroness Flather	83
Lord Hoffmann	83
Lord Layard	83
Lord Morgan	83
Lord Pendry	83
Lord Tanlaw	83
Lord Turnberg	83
Lord Dubs	84
Lord Elystan-Morgan	84
Baroness Gould of Potternewton	84
Baroness Bakewell	84
Baroness Butler-Sloss	84
Baroness Golding	84
Lord Heseltine	84
Lord Imbert	84
Lord King of Bridgwater	84
Lord McColl of Dulwich	84
Lord Rogers of Riverside	84
Lord Sanderson of Bowden	84
Lord Williams of Elvel	84
Lord Woolf	84
Lord Kalms	85
Lord Morris of Aberavon	85
Baroness Paisley of St George's	85
Lord Alliance	85
Lord Bhatia	85
Lord Clarke of Hampstead	85
Baroness Falkender	85
Baroness Howe of Idlicote	85
Lord Hughes of Woodside	85
Lord Hylton	85
Lord Lawson of Blaby	85
Lord Richard	85
Lord Singh of Wimbledon	85
Lord Steyn	85
Lord Wakeham	85
Lord Young of Graffham	85
Viscount Bridgeman	86
Lord Jopling	86
Viscount Eccles	86
Lord Fearn	86
Baroness Howells of St Davids	86
Lord Hutton	86
Lord Marlesford	86
Lord Paul	86
Lord Tebbit	86
Lord Vinson	86
Lord Wright of Richmond	86
Baroness Boothroyd	87
Lord Elton	87
Lord Hoyle	87
Lord Kirkhill	87
Baroness Oppenheim-Barnes	87
Baroness Seccombe	87
Lord Clinton-Davis	88
Lord Rodgers of Quarry Bank	88
Lord Taverne	88
Lord Craig of Radley	88
Lord Denham	89
Lord Sainsbury of Preston Candover	89
Lord Higgins	89
Lord Rea	89
Lord Armstrong of Ilminster	90
Earl of Crawford and Balcarres	90
Baroness Gardner of Parkes	90
Lord Mackay of Clashfern	90
Viscount Slim	90
Lord Northbourne	91
Lord Stoddart of Swindon	91
Lord Christopher	92
Lord Graham of Edmonton	92
Lord Plumb	92
Lord Howie of Troon	93
Baroness Nicol	94
Baroness Sharples	94
Lord Quirk	97
Lord Carrington	98

Peers by Party

Conservative

AHMAD OF WIMBLEDON Lord
ALTMANN Baroness
ANELAY OF ST JOHNS Baroness
ARBUTHNOT OF EDROM Lord
ARRAN Earl of
ASHTON OF HYDE Lord
ASTOR Viscount
ASTOR OF HEVER Lord
ATTLEE Earl
BAKER OF DORKING Lord
BALFE Lord
BAMFORD Lord
BARKER OF BATTLE Lord
BATES Lord
BELL Lord
BERRIDGE Baroness
BERTIN Baroness
BLACK OF BRENTWOOD Lord
BLACKWELL Lord
BLENCATHRA Lord
BLOOMFIELD OF HINTON WALDRIST Baroness
BLYTH OF ROWINGTON Lord
BORWICK Lord
BOTTOMLEY OF NETTLESTONE Baroness
BOURNE OF ABERYSTWYTH Lord
BOWNESS Lord
BRABAZON OF TARA Lord
BRADY Baroness
BRIDGEMAN Viscount
BRIDGES OF HEADLEY Lord
BROUGHAM AND VAUX Lord
BROWNING Baroness
BUSCOMBE Baroness
BYFORD Baroness
CAINE Lord
CAITHNESS Earl of
CALLANAN Lord
CARRINGTON Lord
CARRINGTON OF FULHAM Lord
CATHCART Earl
CAVENDISH OF FURNESS Lord
CHADLINGTON Lord
CHALKER OF WALLASEY Baroness
CHISHOLM OF OWLPEN Baroness
COE Lord
COLGRAIN Lord
COLWYN Lord
COOPER OF WINDRUSH Lord
COPE OF BERKELEY Lord
CORMACK Lord
COURTOWN Earl of
COUTTIE Baroness
CRATHORNE Lord
CRAWFORD AND BALCARRES Earl of
CRICKHOWELL Lord
CUMBERLEGE Baroness
DEBEN Lord
DEIGHTON Lord
DE MAULEY Lord
DENHAM Lord
DIXON-SMITH Lord
DOBBS Lord
DUNCAN OF SPRINGBANK Lord
DUNDEE Earl of
DUNLOP Lord
EATON Baroness
ECCLES Viscount
ECCLES OF MOULTON Baroness
ELTON Lord
EVANS OF BOWES PARK Baroness
FAIRFAX OF CAMERON Lord
FALL Baroness
FARMER Lord
FAULKS Lord
FELDMAN OF ELSTREE Lord
FELLOWES OF WEST STAFFORD Lord
FINK Lord
FINKELSTEIN Lord
FINN Baroness
FLIGHT Lord
FOOKES Baroness
FORSYTH OF DRUMLEAN Lord
FRAMLINGHAM Lord
FRASER OF CORRIEGARTH Lord
FREEMAN Lord
FREUD Lord
GARDINER OF KIMBLE Lord
GARDNER OF PARKES Baroness
GAREL-JONES Lord
GEDDES Lord
GILBERT OF PANTEG Lord
GLENARTHUR Lord
GLENDONBROOK Lord
GLENTORAN Lord
GOLD Lord
GOLDIE Baroness
GOODLAD Lord
GOSCHEN Viscount
GRADE OF YARMOUTH Lord
GREEN OF HURSTPIERPOINT Lord
GRIFFITHS OF FFORESTFACH Lord
HAGUE OF RICHMOND Lord
HAILSHAM Viscount
HAMILTON OF EPSOM Lord
HANHAM Baroness

HARDING OF WINSCOMBE Baroness
HARRIS OF PECKHAM Lord
HAYWARD Lord
HELIC Baroness
HENLEY Lord
HESELTINE Lord
HIGGINS Lord
HILL OF OAREFORD Lord
HODGSON OF ABINGER Baroness
HODGSON OF ASTLEY ABBOTTS Lord
HOLMES OF RICHMOND Lord
HOME Earl of
HOOPER Baroness
HORAM Lord
HOWARD OF LYMPNE Lord
HOWARD OF RISING Lord
HOWE Earl
HOWELL OF GUILDFORD Lord
HUNT OF WIRRAL Lord
INGLEWOOD Lord
JAMES OF BLACKHEATH Lord
JENKIN OF KENNINGTON Baroness
JOPLING Lord
KEEN OF ELIE Lord
KING OF BRIDGWATER Lord
KIRKHAM Lord
KIRKHOPE OF HARROGATE Lord
LAMONT OF LERWICK Lord
LANG OF MONKTON Lord
LANSLEY Lord
LAWSON OF BLABY Lord
LEIGH OF HURLEY Lord
LEXDEN Lord
LINDSAY Earl of
LINGFIELD Lord
LIVERPOOL Earl of
LIVINGSTON OF PARKHEAD Lord
LLEWELLYN OF STEEP Lord
LLOYD-WEBBER Lord
LOTHIAN Marquess of
LUCAS OF CRUDWELL AND DINGWALL Lord
LUPTON Lord
McCOLL OF DULWICH Lord
MacGREGOR OF PULHAM MARKET Lord
McGREGOR-SMITH Baroness
McINNES OF KILWINNING Lord
McINTOSH OF PICKERING Baroness
MACKAY OF CLASHFERN Lord
MacLAURIN OF KNEBWORTH Lord
MAGAN OF CASTLETOWN Lord
MANCROFT Lord
MANZOOR Baroness
MARLAND Lord
MARLESFORD Lord
MAUDE OF HORSHAM Lord
MAWHINNEY Lord
MOBARIK Baroness
MONE Baroness
MONTROSE Duke of
MOORE OF LOWER MARSH Lord
MORRIS OF BOLTON Baroness
MOYNIHAN Lord
NASEBY Lord
NASH Lord
NEVILLE-JONES Baroness
NEVILLE-ROLFE Baroness
NEWLOVE Baroness
NICHOLSON OF WINTERBOURNE Baroness
NOAKES Baroness
NORTHBROOK Lord
NORTON OF LOUTH Lord
O'CATHAIN Baroness
OPPENHEIM-BARNES Baroness
O'SHAUGHNESSY Lord
PALUMBO Lord
PATTEN Lord
PATTEN OF BARNES Lord
PIDDING Baroness
PLUMB Lord
POLAK Lord
POPAT Lord
PORTER OF SPALDING Lord
PRICE Lord
PRIOR OF BRAMPTON Lord
RANA Lord
RAWLINGS Baroness
REDFERN Baroness
RENFREW OF KAIMSTHORN Lord
RIBEIRO Lord
RIDLEY Viscount
RISBY Lord
ROBATHAN Lord
ROCK Baroness
ROSE OF MONEWDEN Lord
ROTHERWICK Lord
RYDER OF WENSUM Lord
SAATCHI Lord
SAINSBURY OF PRESTON CANDOVER Lord
SANDERSON OF BOWDEN Lord
SASSOON Lord
SCOTT OF BYBROOK Baroness
SECCOMBE Baroness
SELBORNE Earl of
SELKIRK OF DOUGLAS Lord
SELSDON Lord
SHACKLETON OF BELGRAVIA Baroness
SHARPLES Baroness
SHEIKH Lord
SHEPHARD OF NORTHWOLD Baroness
SHERBOURNE OF DIDSBURY Lord

SHIELDS Baroness
SHINKWIN Lord
SHREWSBURY AND WATERFORD Earl of
SKELMERSDALE Lord
SMITH OF HINDHEAD Lord
SPICER Lord
STEDMAN-SCOTT Baroness
STERLING OF PLAISTOW Lord
STOWELL OF BEESTON Baroness
STRATHCLYDE Lord
STROUD Baroness
SUGG Baroness
SURI Lord
SWINFEN Lord
TANLAW Lord
TAYLOR OF HOLBEACH Lord
TEBBIT Lord
TREFGARNE Lord
TRENCHARD Viscount
TRIMBLE Lord
TRUE Lord
TUGENDHAT Lord
ULLSWATER Viscount
VERE OF NORBITON Baroness
VERMA Baroness
VINSON Lord
WAKEHAM Lord
WALDEGRAVE OF NORTH HILL Lord
WARSI Baroness
WASSERMAN Lord
WEI Lord
WELLINGTON Duke of
WHEATCROFT Baroness
WHITBY Lord
WILCOX Baroness
WILLETTS Lord
WILLIAMS OF TRAFFORD Baroness
WOLFSON OF ASPLEY GUISE Lord
WYLD Baroness
YOUNG OF COOKHAM Lord
YOUNG OF GRAFFHAM Lord
YOUNGER OF LECKIE Viscount

Labour

ADAMS OF CRAIGIELEA Baroness
ADONIS Lord
ALLEN OF KENSINGTON Lord
ALLI Lord
ANDERSON OF SWANSEA Lord
ANDREWS Baroness
ARMSTRONG OF HILL TOP Baroness
BACH Lord
BAKEWELL Baroness
BASSAM OF BRIGHTON Lord
BEECHAM Lord
BERKELEY Lord
BHATTACHARYYA Lord
BILLINGHAM Baroness
BLACKSTONE Baroness
BLOOD Baroness
BLUNKETT Lord
BOATENG Lord
BRADLEY Lord
BRAGG Lord
BRENNAN Lord
BROOKE OF ALVERTHORPE Lord
BROOKMAN Lord
BROWNE OF LADYTON Lord
CAMPBELL-SAVOURS Lord
CARTER OF COLES Lord
CASHMAN Lord
CHAKRABARTI Baroness
CHANDOS Viscount
CHRISTOPHER Lord
CLARK OF WINDERMERE Lord
CLARKE OF HAMPSTEAD Lord
CLINTON-DAVIS Lord
COHEN OF PIMLICO Baroness
COLLINS OF HIGHBURY Lord
CORSTON Baroness
CRAWLEY Baroness
CUNNINGHAM OF FELLING Lord
DARLING OF ROULANISH Lord
DARZI OF DENHAM Lord
DAVIDSON OF GLEN CLOVA Lord
DAVIES OF COITY Lord
DAVIES OF OLDHAM Lord
DAVIES OF STAMFORD Lord
DEAN OF THORNTON-LE-FYLDE Baroness
DESAI Lord
DONAGHY Baroness
DONOUGHUE Lord
DRAKE Baroness
DRAYSON Lord
DUBS Lord
ELDER Lord
EVANS OF WATFORD Lord
FALCONER OF THOROTON Lord
FALKENDER Baroness
FARRINGTON OF RIBBLETON Baroness
FAULKNER OF WORCESTER Lord
FOSTER OF BISHOP AUCKLAND Lord
FOULKES OF CUMNOCK Lord
GALE Baroness
GIBSON OF MARKET RASEN Baroness
GIDDENS Lord
GLASMAN Lord
GOLDING Baroness
GOLDSMITH Lord
GORDON OF STRATHBLANE Lord

GOUDIE Baroness
GOULD OF POTTERNEWTON Baroness
GRAHAM OF EDMONTON Lord
GRANTCHESTER Lord
GRIFFITHS OF BURRY PORT Lord
GROCOTT Lord
HAIN Lord
HANWORTH Viscount
HARRIS OF HARINGEY Lord
HARRISON Lord
HASKEL Lord
HAUGHEY Lord
HAWORTH Lord
HAYTER OF KENTISH TOWN Baroness
HEALY OF PRIMROSE HILL Baroness
HENIG Baroness
HILTON OF EGGARDON Baroness
HOLLICK Lord
HOLLIS OF HEIGHAM Baroness
HOWARTH OF NEWPORT Lord
HOWELLS OF ST DAVIDS Baroness
HOWIE OF TROON Lord
HOYLE Lord
HUGHES OF STRETFORD Baroness
HUGHES OF WOODSIDE Lord
HUNT OF CHESTERTON Lord
HUNT OF KINGS HEATH Lord
HUTTON OF FURNESS Lord
IRVINE OF LAIRG Lord
JAY OF PADDINGTON Baroness
JONES Lord
JONES OF WHITCHURCH Baroness
JORDAN Lord
JOWELL Baroness
JUDD Lord
KENNEDY OF CRADLEY Baroness
KENNEDY OF SOUTHWARK Lord
KENNEDY OF THE SHAWS Baroness
KESTENBAUM Lord
KING OF BOW Baroness
KINGSMILL Baroness
KINNOCK Lord
KINNOCK OF HOLYHEAD Baroness
KIRKHILL Lord
KNIGHT OF WEYMOUTH Lord
LAWRENCE OF CLARENDON Baroness
LAYARD Lord
LEA OF CRONDALL Lord
LEITCH Lord
LENNIE Lord
LEVY Lord
LIDDELL OF COATDYKE Baroness
LIDDLE Lord
LIPSEY Lord
LISTER OF BURTERSETT Baroness
LIVERMORE Lord
McAVOY Lord
McCONNELL OF GLENSCORRODALE Lord
McDONAGH Baroness
McINTOSH OF HUDNALL Baroness
MacKENZIE OF CULKEIN Lord
McKENZIE OF LUTON Lord
MALLALIEU Baroness
MANDELSON Lord
MASSEY OF DARWEN Baroness
MAXTON Lord
MENDELSOHN Lord
MONKS Lord
MOONIE Lord
MORGAN Lord
MORGAN OF ELY Baroness
MORGAN OF HUYTON Baroness
MORRIS OF ABERAVON Lord
MORRIS OF HANDSWORTH Lord
MORRIS OF YARDLEY Baroness
MURPHY OF TORFAEN Lord
NICOL Baroness
NYE Baroness
O'NEILL OF CLACKMANNAN Lord
PAREKH Lord
PATEL OF BLACKBURN Lord
PATEL OF BRADFORD Lord
PENDRY Lord
PITKEATHLEY Baroness
PLANT OF HIGHFIELD Lord
PONSONBY OF SHULBREDE Lord
PRESCOTT Lord
PRIMAROLO Baroness
PROSSER Baroness
PUTTNAM Lord
QUIN Baroness
RADICE Lord
RAMSAY OF CARTVALE Baroness
REA Lord
REBUCK Baroness
REID OF CARDOWAN Lord
RICHARD Lord
ROBERTSON OF PORT ELLEN Lord
ROGERS OF RIVERSIDE Lord
ROOKER Lord
ROSSER Lord
ROWLANDS Lord
ROYALL OF BLAISDON Baroness
SAINSBURY OF TURVILLE Lord
SAWYER Lord
SCOTLAND OF ASTHAL Baroness
SHERLOCK Baroness
SIMON Viscount
SMITH OF BASILDON Baroness
SMITH OF GILMOREHILL Baroness
SMITH OF LEIGH Lord
SNAPE Lord

SOLEY Lord
STEVENSON OF BALMACARA Lord
STONE OF BLACKHEATH Lord
SYMONS OF VERNHAM DEAN Baroness
TAYLOR OF BOLTON Baroness
TEMPLE-MORRIS Lord
THORNTON Baroness
TOMLINSON Lord
TOUHIG Lord
TRIESMAN Lord
TUNNICLIFFE Lord
TURNBERG Lord
WARWICK OF UNDERCLIFFE Baroness
WATSON OF INVERGOWRIE Lord
WATTS Lord
WEST OF SPITHEAD Lord
WHEELER Baroness
WHITAKER Baroness
WHITTY Lord
WILLIAMS OF ELVEL Lord
WILLS Lord
WINSTON Lord
WOOD OF ANFIELD Lord
WOOLMER OF LEEDS Lord
YOUNG OF NORWOOD GREEN Lord
YOUNG OF OLD SCONE Baroness

Crossbench

ABERDARE Lord
ADEBOWALE Lord
AFSHAR Baroness
ALTON OF LIVERPOOL Lord
ARMSTRONG OF ILMINSTER Lord
BALDWIN OF BEWDLEY Earl
BERKELEY OF KNIGHTON Lord
BEST Lord
BEW Lord
BICHARD Lord
BILIMORIA Lord
BIRD Lord
BIRT Lord
BLAIR OF BOUGHTON Lord
BOOTHROYD Baroness
BOYCE Lord
BROERS Lord
BROOKEBOROUGH Viscount
BROWN OF CAMBRIDGE Baroness
BROWN OF EATON-UNDER-HEYWOOD Lord
BROWNE OF MADINGLEY Lord
BURNS Lord
BUTLER OF BROCKWELL Lord
BUTLER-SLOSS Baroness
CAMERON OF DILLINGTON Lord
CAMPBELL OF LOUGHBOROUGH Baroness
CAMPBELL OF SURBITON Baroness
CAREY OF CLIFTON Lord
CARSWELL Lord
CLANCARTY Earl of
COLLINS OF MAPESBURY Lord
COLVILLE OF CULROSS Viscount
CONDON Lord
CORK AND ORRERY Earl of
COUSSINS Baroness
COX Baroness
CRAIG OF RADLEY Lord
CRAIGAVON Viscount
CRISP Lord
CROMWELL Lord
CULLEN OF WHITEKIRK Lord
CURRIE OF MARYLEBONE Lord
CURRY OF KIRKHARLE Lord
DANNATT Lord
DEAR Lord
DEECH Baroness
D'SOUZA Baroness
DYKES Lord
EAMES Lord
ELYSTAN-MORGAN Lord
EMERTON Baroness
ERROLL Earl of
EVANS OF WEARDALE Lord
FALKLAND Viscount of
FELLOWES Lord
FINLAY OF LLANDAFF Baroness
FLATHER Baroness
FORD Baroness
FREYBERG Lord
FRITCHIE Baroness
GRABINER Lord
GREEN OF DEDDINGTON Lord
GREENFIELD Baroness
GREENGROSS Baroness
GREENWAY Lord
GREY-THOMPSON Baroness
GUTHRIE OF CRAIGIEBANK Lord
HALL OF BIRKENHEAD Lord
HAMEED Lord
HANNAY OF CHISWICK Lord
HARDIE Lord
HARRIES OF PENTREGARTH Lord
HASKINS Lord
HASTINGS OF SCARISBRICK Lord
HAYMAN Baroness
HENNESSY OF NYMPSFIELD Lord
HOFFMANN Lord
HOGG Baroness
HOLLINS Baroness
HOPE OF CRAIGHEAD Lord
HOWARTH OF BRECKLAND Baroness

HOWE OF IDLICOTE Baroness
HUTTON Lord
HYLTON Lord
IMBERT Lord
JANVRIN Lord
JAY OF EWELME Lord
JONES OF BIRMINGHAM Lord
JUDGE Lord
KAKKAR Lord
KERR OF KINLOCHARD Lord
KERSLAKE Lord
KIDRON Baroness
KILCLOONEY Lord
KING OF LOTHBURY Lord
KINNOULL Earl of
KREBS Lord
LAMING Lord
LANE-FOX OF SOHO Baroness
LEVENE OF PORTSOKEN Lord
LISTOWEL Earl of
LISVANE Lord
LOW OF DALSTON Lord
LUCE Lord
LYTTON Earl
MACPHERSON OF EARL'S COURT Lord
MAIR Lord
MALLOCH-BROWN Lord
MANNINGHAM-BULLER Baroness
MAR Countess of
MARTIN OF SPRINGBURN Lord
MASHAM OF ILTON Baroness
MAWSON Lord
MEACHER Baroness
MOGG Lord
MORGAN OF DREFELIN Baroness
MOUNTEVANS Lord
MURPHY Baroness
MYNERS Lord
NEUBERGER Baroness
NORTHBOURNE Lord
O'DONNELL Lord
O'LOAN Baroness
O'NEILL OF BENGARVE Baroness
OUSELEY Lord
OXBURGH Lord
PALMER Lord
PANNICK Lord
PATEL Lord
PEEL Earl
PHILLIPS OF WORTH MATRAVERS Lord
POWELL OF BAYSWATER Lord
PRASHAR Baroness
QUIRK Lord
RAMSBOTHAM Lord
REES OF LUDLOW Lord
RENWICK OF CLIFTON Lord
RICHARDS OF HERSTMONCEUX Lord
RICHARDSON OF CALOW Baroness
RICKETTS Lord
ROSSLYN Earl of
ROWE-BEDDOE Lord
RUSSELL OF LIVERPOOL Lord
SACKS Lord
ST JOHN OF BLETSO Lord
SANDWICH Earl of
SAVILLE OF NEWDIGATE Lord
SINGH OF WIMBLEDON Lord
SKIDELSKY Lord
SLIM Viscount
SMITH OF KELVIN Lord
SOMERSET Duke of
STAIR Earl of
STERN Baroness
STERN OF BRENTFORD Lord
STEVENS OF KIRKWHELPINGTON Lord
STEVENSON OF CODDENHAM Lord
STEYN Lord
STIRRUP Lord
SUTHERLAND OF HOUNDWOOD Lord
THURLOW Lord
TREES Lord
TREVETHIN AND OAKSEY Lord
TURNBULL Lord
TURNER OF ECCHINSWELL Lord
VALENTINE Baroness
VAUX OF HARROWDEN Lord
WALKER OF ALDRINGHAM Lord
WALKER OF GESTINGTHORPE Lord
WARNER Lord
WATKINS OF TAVISTOCK Baroness
WAVERLEY Viscount
WILLIAMS OF OYSTERMOUTH Lord
WILSON OF DINTON Lord
WILSON OF TILLYORN Lord
WOLF OF DULWICH Baroness
WOOLF Lord
WRIGHT OF RICHMOND Lord
YOUNG OF HORNSEY Baroness

Liberal Democrat

ADDINGTON Lord
ALDERDICE Lord
ALLAN OF HALLAM Lord
ALLIANCE Lord
ASHDOWN OF NORTON-SUB-HAMDON Lord
BAKEWELL OF HARDINGTON MANDEVILLE Baroness

BARKER Baroness
BEITH Lord
BENJAMIN Baroness
BONHAM-CARTER OF YARNBURY Baroness
BOWLES OF BERKHAMSTED Baroness
BRADSHAW Lord
BRINTON Baroness
BRUCE OF BENNACHIE Lord
BURNETT Lord
BURT OF SOLIHULL Baroness
CAMPBELL OF PITTENWEEM Lord
CHIDGEY Lord
CLEMENT-JONES Lord
COTTER Lord
DHOLAKIA Lord
DOOCEY Baroness
FALKNER OF MARGRAVINE Baroness
FEARN Lord
FEATHERSTONE Baroness
FOSTER OF BATH Lord
FOX Lord
GARDEN OF FROGNAL Baroness
GERMAN Lord
GLASGOW Earl of
GODDARD OF STOCKPORT Lord
GREAVES Lord
GRENDER Baroness
HAMWEE Baroness
HARRIS OF RICHMOND Baroness
HUMPHREYS Baroness
HUSSAIN Lord
HUSSEIN-ECE Baroness
JANKE Baroness
JOLLY Baroness
JONES OF CHELTENHAM Lord
KIRKWOOD OF KIRKHOPE Lord
KRAMER Baroness
LEE OF TRAFFORD Lord
LESTER OF HERNE HILL Lord
LUDFORD Baroness
MACDONALD OF RIVER GLAVEN Lord
MACLENNAN OF ROGART Lord
McNALLY Lord
MADDOCK Baroness
MARKS OF HENLEY-ON-THAMES Lord
MILLER OF CHILTHORNE DOMER Baroness
NEWBY Lord
NORTHOVER Baroness
OATES Lord
OXFORD AND ASQUITH Earl of
PADDICK Lord
PALMER OF CHILDS HILL Lord
PALUMBO OF SOUTHWARK Lord
PARMINTER Baroness
PINNOCK Baroness
PURVIS OF TWEED Lord
RANDERSON Baroness
RAZZALL Lord
REDESDALE Lord
RENNARD Lord
ROBERTS OF LLANDUDNO Lord
RODGERS OF QUARRY BANK Lord
SCOTT OF NEEDHAM MARKET Baroness
SCRIVEN Lord
SHARKEY Lord
SHEEHAN Baroness
SHIPLEY Lord
SHUTT OF GREETLAND Lord
SMITH OF CLIFTON Lord
SMITH OF NEWNHAM Baroness
STEEL OF AIKWOOD Lord
STEPHEN Lord
STONEHAM OF DROXFORD Lord
STOREY Lord
STRASBURGER Lord
STUNELL Lord
SUTTIE Baroness
TAVERNE Lord
TAYLOR OF GOSS MOOR Lord
TEVERSON Lord
THOMAS OF GRESFORD Lord
THOMAS OF WINCHESTER Baroness
THORNHILL Baroness
THURSO Viscount
TOPE Lord
TYLER Lord
TYLER OF ENFIELD Baroness
VALLANCE OF TUMMEL Lord
VERJEE Lord
WALLACE OF SALTAIRE Lord
WALLACE OF TANKERNESS Lord
WALMSLEY Baroness
WATSON OF RICHMOND Lord
WILLIS OF KNARESBOROUGH Lord
WRIGGLESWORTH Lord

Non-Affiliated

AHMED Lord
AMOS Baroness
ARCHER OF WESTON-SUPER-MARE Lord
ASHTON OF UPHOLLAND Baroness
BHATIA Lord
BIRMINGHAM Lord Bishop of
BLACK OF CROSSHARBOUR Lord
BOSWELL OF AYNHO Lord
BOYD OF DUNCANSBY Lord
CANTERBURY Lord Archbishop of
CARLILE OF BERRIEW Lord
CARLISLE Lord Bishop of
CARTER OF BARNES Lord
CAVENDISH OF LITTLE VENICE Baroness

CHELMSFORD Lord Bishop of
CHESTER Lord Bishop of
CHICHESTER Lord Bishop of
CHOLMONDELEY Marquess of
CLARK OF CALTON Baroness
CLARKE OF STONE-CUM-EBONY Lord
COVENTRY Lord Bishop of
DAVIES OF ABERSOCH Lord
DERBY Lord Bishop of
DURHAM Lord Bishop of
EATWELL Lord
ELIS-THOMAS Lord
ELY Lord Bishop of
FILKIN Lord
GADHIA Lord
GLOUCESTER Lord Bishop of
HALE OF RICHMOND Baroness
HANNINGFIELD Lord
KALMS Lord
KERR OF TONAGHMORE Lord
LAIRD Lord
LEEDS Lord Bishop of
LINCOLN Lord Bishop of
LOOMBA Lord
McFALL OF ALCLUITH Lord
MACKENZIE OF FRAMWELLGATE Lord
MANCE Lord
MITCHELL Lord
NEUBERGER OF ABBOTSBURY Lord
NEWCASTLE Lord Bishop of
NORFOLK Duke of
NORWICH Lord Bishop of
OAKESHOTT OF SEAGROVE BAY Lord
O'NEILL OF GATLEY Lord
OXFORD Lord Bishop of
PAUL Lord
PETERBOROUGH Lord Bishop of
PORTSMOUTH Lord Bishop of
ROCHESTER Lord Bishop of
ST ALBANS Lord Bishop of
SALISBURY Lord Bishop of
SMITH OF FINSBURY Lord
SOUTHWARK Lord Bishop of
SUGAR Lord
TAYLOR OF WARWICK Lord
THOMAS OF CWMGIEDD Lord
TONGE Baroness
UDDIN Baroness
VADERA Baroness
WINCHESTER Lord Bishop of
WORCESTER Lord Bishop of
WORTHINGTON Baroness
YORK Lord Archbishop of

Democratic Unionist Party

BROWNE OF BELMONT Lord
HAY OF BALLYORE Lord
MORROW Lord
PAISLEY OF ST GEORGE'S Baroness

UK Independence Party

PEARSON OF RANNOCH Lord
STEVENS OF LUDGATE Lord
WILLOUGHBY DE BROKE Lord

Independent Labour

STODDART OF SWINDON Lord
TRUSCOTT Lord

Ulster Unionist Party

EMPEY Lord
ROGAN Lord

Green Party

JONES OF MOULSECOOMB Baroness

Independent Social Democrat

OWEN Lord

Independent Ulster Unionist

MAGINNIS OF DRUMGLASS Lord

Lord Speaker

FOWLER Lord

Plaid Cymru

WIGLEY Lord

Select Committees

Legislative Committees

Constitution

Examines constitutional implications of all public bills; reviews operation of the constitution.

Tel: 020 7219 5960 Fax: 020 7219 4931
Email: constitution@parliament.uk
www.parliament.uk/hlconstitution

Baroness Taylor of Bolton (Chair)	*Lab*
Lord Beith	*Lib Dem*
Baroness Corston	*Lab*
Baroness Drake	*Lab*
Lord Dunlop	*Con*
Lord Hunt of Wirral	*Con*
Lord Judge	*CB*
Lord MacGregor of Pulham Market	*Con*
Lord Maclennan of Rogart	*Lib Dem*
Prof. Lord Morgan	*Lab*
Prof. Lord Norton of Louth	*Con*
Lord Pannick	*CB*

Staff: Matt Korris (Clerk), Nadine McNally (Policy Analyst), Katy Durrans (Press Officer), Hadia Garwell (Committee Assistant)

Delegated Powers and Regulatory Reform

Reports whether the provisions of any bill inappropriately delegate legislative powers or whether they subject the exercise of legislative power to an inappropriate degree of parliamentary scrutiny.

Tel: 020 7219 3103 Fax: 020 7219 2571
Email: hldelegatedpowers@parliament.uk
www.parliament.uk/business/committees/committees-a-z/lords-select/delegated-powers-and-regulatory-reform-committee

Lord Blencathra (Chair)	*Con*
Baroness Dean of Thornton-le-Fylde	*Lab*
Lord Flight	*Con*
Lord Jones	*Lab*
Lord Lisvane	*CB*
Lord Moynihan	*Con*
Lord Rowlands	*Lab*
Lord Thomas of Gresford	*Lib Dem*
Lord Thurlow	*CB*
Lord Tyler	*Lib Dem*

Staff: Christine Salmon Percival (Clerk)

Hybrid Instruments

Tel: 020 7219 3231
www.parliament.uk/business/committees/committees-a-z/lords-select/hybrid-instruments-committee

Lord McFall of Alcluith (Chair)	*NA*
Lord Addington	*Lib Dem*
Lord Crickhowell	*Con*
Lord Dykes	*CB*
Lord Grantchester	*Lab*
Lord Harrison	*Lab*
Lord Swinfen	*Con*

Secondary Legislation Scrutiny

Tel: 020 7219 8821
Email: hlseclegscrutiny@parliament.uk
www.parliament.uk/business/committees/committees-a-z/lords-select/secondary-legislation-scrutiny-committee

Lord Trefgarne (Chair)	*Con*
Lord Faulkner of Worcester	*Lab*
Baroness Finn	*Con*
Lord Goddard of Stockport	*Lib Dem*
Baroness Gould of Potternewton	*Lab*
Lord Haskel	*Lab*
Lord Janvrin	*CB*
Lord Kirkwood of Kirkhope	*Lib Dem*
Baroness O'Loan	*CB*
Lord Sherbourne of Didsbury	*Con*
Prof. Baroness Watkins of Tavistock	*CB*

Staff: Emma Leach (Clerk)

Standing Orders (Private Bills)

Reviews compliance with standing orders.

Tel: 020 7219 3103
Email: prbohol@parliament.uk
www.parliament.uk/business/committees/committees-a-z/lords-select/standing-orders

Lord McFall of Alcluith (Chair)	*NA*
Lord Fellowes	*CB*
Lord Geddes	*Con*
Lord Goodlad	*Con*
Baroness Gould of Potternewton	*Lab*
Lord Naseby	*Con*
Lord Rodgers of Quarry Bank	*Lib Dem*
Viscount Simon	*Lab*

Ad Hoc Committees

Artificial Intelligence

Tel: 020 7219 4384 Fax: 20 7219 4931
Email: hlaiadhoc@parliament.uk
www.parliament.uk/business/committees/committees-a-z/lords-select/ai-committee

Lord Clement-Jones (Chair)	*Lib Dem*
Baroness Bakewell	*Lab*
Lord Giddens	*Lab*
Baroness Grender	*Lib Dem*
Lord Hollick	*Lab*

Lord Holmes of Richmond	*Con*
Lord Levene of Portsoken	*CB*
Rt Rev Bishop of Oxford	*NA*
Lord Puttnam	*Lab*
Viscount Ridley	*Con*
Baroness Rock	*Con*
Lord St John of Bletso	*CB*
Lord Swinfen	*Con*

Staff: Luke Hussey (Clerk), Ben Taylor (Policy Analyst), Dervish Mertcan (Press and Media Officer), Hannah Murdoch (Committee Assistant)

Citizenship and Civic Engagement

Tel: 020 7219 6075
Email: hlcitizenship@parliament.uk
www.parliament.uk/business/committees/committees-a-z/lords-select/citizenship-civic-engagement

Lord Hodgson of Astley Abbotts (Chair)	*Con*
Baroness Barker	*Lib Dem*
Lord Blunkett	*Lab*
Rt Rev Lord Harries of Pentregarth	*CB*
Baroness Lister of Burtersett	*Lab*
Baroness Morris of Yardley	*Lab*
Baroness Newlove	*Con*
Baroness Pitkeathley	*Lab*
Baroness Redfern	*Con*
Lord Rowe-Beddoe	*CB*
Baroness Stedman-Scott	*Con*
Lord Verjee	*Lib Dem*

Staff: Michael Collon (Clerk), Tim Stacey (Policy Analyst), Katy Durrans (Press Officer), Joanne Watson (Committee Assistant)

Natural Environment and Rural Communities Act 2006

Tel: 020 7219 4878 Fax: 020 7219 4931
Email: hlnercact@parliament.uk
www.parliament.uk/business/committees/committees-a-z/lords-select/nerc-act-committee

Lord Cameron of Dillington (Chair)	*CB*
Earl of Arran	*Con*
Baroness Byford	*Con*
Earl of Caithness	*Con*
Lord Faulkner of Worcester	*Lab*
Lord Foster of Bishop Auckland	*Lab*
Lord Harrison	*Lab*
Countess of Mar	*CB*
Baroness Parminter	*Lib Dem*
Baroness Scott of Bybrook	*Con*
Baroness Scott of Needham Market	*Lib Dem*
Baroness Whitaker	*Lab*

Staff: Matthew Smith (Clerk), Nathan Lechler (Policy Analyst), Anouska Russell (Press and Media Officer), James Thomas (Committee Assistant)

Political Polling and Digital Media

Tel: 020 7219 6968 Fax: 020 7219 4931
Email: hlpollingcommittee@parliament.uk
www.parliament.uk/business/committees/committees-a-z/lords-select/political-polling-digital-media

Lord Lipsey (Chair)	*Lab*
Baroness Couttie	*Con*
Baroness Fall	*Con*
Baroness Ford	*CB*
Lord Foulkes of Cumnock	*Lab/Co-op*
Lord Hayward	*Con*
Lord Howarth of Newport	*Lab*
Baroness Janke	*Lib Dem*
Baroness Jay of Paddington	*Lab*
Baroness O'Neill of Bengarve	*CB*
Lord Rennard	*Lib Dem*
Lord Smith of Hindhead	*Con*

Staff: Helena Peacock (Clerk), Beth Hooper (Policy Analyst), Owen Williams (Press Officer), Viv Roach (Committee Assistant)

Joint Committees

See Lords and Commons Joint Select Committees on p1062

Domestic Committees

Finance

To support the House of Lords Commission by considering expenditure on services provided from the Estimate for the House of Lords.
Tel: 020 7219 3736
Email: hlfinancecommittee@parliament.uk
www.parliament.uk/business/committees/committees-a-z/lords-select/finance-committee

Baroness Doocey (Chair)	*Lib Dem*
Lord Colgrain	*Con*
Lord Collins of Highbury	*Lab*
Lord Cope of Berkeley	*Con*
Earl of Courtown	*Con*
Lord Cromwell	*CB*
Lord Cunningham of Felling	*Lab*
Baroness Goudie	*Lab*

Lord Kerslake	*CB*
Lord Leigh of Hurley	*Con*
Lord Stoneham of Droxford	*Lib Dem*

Staff: Susannah Street (Clerk)

Services

To support the House of Lords Commission by agreeing day-to-day policy on member-facing services, providing advice on strategic policy decisions and overseeing the delivery and implementation of both.

Tel: 020 7219 3736
Email: hlservicescommittee@parliament.uk
www.parliament.uk/business/committees/committees-a-z/lords-select/services-committee

Lord Laming (Chair)	*CB*
Lord Bassam of Brighton	*Lab/Co-op*
Lord Campbell-Savours	*Lab*
Baroness Hollis of Heigham	*Lab*
Lord Hope of Craighead	*CB*
Baroness Humphreys	*Lib Dem*
Lord Kirkwood of Kirkhope	*Lib Dem*
Baroness Morris of Bolton	*Con*
Earl of Shrewsbury and Waterford	*Con*
Lord Taylor of Holbeach	*Con*

Staff: Susannah Street (Clerk)

Procedural Committees

Liaison

Co-ordinates and allocates resources for committee work.

Tel: 020 7219 6678 Fax: 020 7219 4931
Email: hlliaisoncmttee@parliament.uk
www.parliament.uk/business/committees/committees-a-z/lords-select/liaison-committee

Lord McFall of Alcluith (Chair)	*NA*
Baroness Evans of Bowes Park	*Con*
Lord Foulkes of Cumnock	*Lab/Co-op*
Baroness Garden of Frognal	*Lib Dem*
Baroness Hayter of Kentish Town	*Lab/Co-op*
Lord Hope of Craighead	*CB*
Lord Lang of Monkton	*Con*
Lord Low of Dalston	*CB*
Lord Newby	*Lib Dem*
Lord Smith of Hindhead	*Con*
Lord Williams of Elvel	*Lab*

Staff: Philippa Tudor (Clerk), Owen Williams (Press Officer), Heather Fuller (Committee Assistant)

Privileges and Conduct

Oversees the Code of Conduct for Members of the House of Lords, the Guide to the Code of Conduct and the Register of Lords' Interests.

Tel: 020 7219 8796
Email: mawsonc@parliament.uk
www.parliament.uk/business/committees/committees-a-z/lords-select/privileges-committee-for-privileges

Lord McFall of Alcluith (Chair)	*NA*
Lord Bassam of Brighton	*Lab/Co-op*
Lord Brown of Eaton-under-Heywood	*CB*
Earl Cathcart	*Con*
Lord Dear	*CB*
Rt Rev Lord Eames	*CB*
Baroness Evans of Bowes Park	*Con*
Lord Hope of Craighead	*CB*
Lord Irvine of Lairg	*Lab*
Baroness Jay of Paddington	*Lab*
Lord Mackay of Clashfern	*Con*
Lord Newby	*Lib Dem*
Baroness Smith of Basildon	*Lab/Co-op*
Lord Stoneham of Droxford	*Lib Dem*
Lord Taylor of Holbeach	*Con*
Viscount Ullswater	*Con*

Staff: Chloe Mawson (Clerk)

Procedure

Considers the operation of procedures for parliamentary business in the Lords.

Tel: 020 7219 8796
Email: mawsonc@parliament.uk
www.parliament.uk/business/committees/committees-a-z/lords-select/procedure-committee

Lord McFall of Alcluith (Chair)	*NA*
Lord Bassam of Brighton	*Lab/Co-op*
Lord Brabazon of Tara	*Con*
Baroness Evans of Bowes Park	*Con*
Baroness Farrington of Ribbleton	*Lab*
Lord Fowler	*Lord Speaker*
Lord Geddes	*Con*
Lord Hope of Craighead	*CB*
Baroness Humphreys	*Lib Dem*
Lord Morris of Aberavon	*Lab*
Lord Newby	*Lib Dem*
Lord Powell of Bayswater	*CB*
Lord Rowe-Beddoe	*CB*
Baroness Smith of Basildon	*Lab/Co-op*
Lord Stoneham of Droxford	*Lib Dem*
Lord Taylor of Holbeach	*Con*
Baroness Thomas of Winchester	*Lib Dem*
Lord True	*Con*
Baroness Warwick of Undercliffe	*Lab*

Alternate members:
Lord Brown of Eaton-under-Heywood *CB*
Baroness Browning *Con*
Lord Foulkes of Cumnock *Lab/Co-op*
Baroness Meacher *CB*
Lord Scriven *Lib Dem*
Staff: Chloe Mawson (Clerk)

Selection

Proposes members for select committees and other bodies.
Tel: 020 7219 3736
www.parliament.uk/business/committees/committees-a-z/lords-select/committeeofselection
Lord McFall of Alcluith (Chair) *NA*
Lord Bassam of Brighton *Lab/Co-op*
Lord Craig of Radley *CB*
Baroness Evans of Bowes Park *Con*
Lord Hope of Craighead *CB*
Lord Newby *Lib Dem*
Prof. Lord Plant of Highfield *Lab*
Baroness Smith of Basildon *Lab/Co-op*
Lord Stoneham of Droxford *Lib Dem*
Lord Taylor of Holbeach *Con*
Viscount Ullswater *Con*

Investigative Committees

Communications

Tel: 020 7219 8662 Fax: 020 7219 4931
Email: holcommunications@parliament.uk
www.parliament.uk/hlcommunications
Lord Henley (Chair) *Con*
Lord Allen of Kensington *Lab*
Baroness Benjamin *Lib Dem*
Baroness Bertin *Con*
Baroness Bonham-Carter of Yarnbury *Lib Dem*
Rt Rev Bishop of Chelmsford *NA*
Viscount Colville of Culross *CB*
Lord Finkelstein *Con*
Lord Gilbert of Panteg *Con*
Baroness Kidron *CB*
Baroness McIntosh of Hudnall *Lab*
Baroness Quin *Lab*
Lord Livermore *Lab*
Lord Sharkey *Lib Dem*
Lord Tugendhat *Con*
Lord Turnbull *CB*
Staff: Theodore Pembroke (Clerk), Anouska Russell (Press Officer), Rita Logan (Committee Assistant)

Staff: Ayeesha Waller (Clerk), Ben McNamee (Policy Analyst), Dervish Mertcan (Press Officer), Ali Day (Committee Assistant)

Economic Affairs

Tel: 020 7219 5358 Fax: 020 7219 4931
Email: economicaffairs@parliament.uk
www.parliament.uk/hleconomicaffairs
Twitter: @LordsEconCom
Lord Forsyth of Drumlean (Chair) *Con*
Baroness Bowles of Berkhamsted *Lib Dem*
Lord Burns *CB*
Lord Darling of Roulanish *Lab*
Baroness Harding of Winscombe *Con*
Lord Kerr of Kinlochard *CB*
Baroness Kingsmill *Lab*
Lord Lamont of Lerwick *Con*
Prof. Lord Layard *Lab*

European Union

Tel: 020 7219 6083 Fax: 020 7219 6715
Email: euclords@parliament.uk
www.parliament.uk/hleu
Twitter: @LordsEUCom
Lord Boswell of Aynho (Chair) *NA*
Baroness Armstrong of Hill Top *Lab*
Prof. Baroness Brown of Cambridge *CB*
Baroness Browning *Con*
Lord Crisp *CB*
Lord Cromwell *CB*
Baroness Falkner of Margravine *Lib Dem*
Lord Jay of Ewelme *CB*
Baroness Kennedy of The Shaws *Lab*
Earl of Kinnoull *CB*
Lord Liddle *Lab*
Baroness Neville-Rolfe *Con*
Lord Selkirk of Douglas *Con*
Baroness Suttie *Lib Dem*
Lord Teverson *Lib Dem*
Baroness Verma *Con*
Lord Whitty *Lab*
Baroness Wilcox *Con*
Lord Woolmer of Leeds *Lab*
Staff: Christopher Johnson (Principal Clerk), Stuart Stoner (Clerk), Owen Williams (Press Officer), Alice Delaney (Committee Assistant)

EU Energy and Environment Sub-committee

Tel: 020 7219 3015
Email: stenderuppetersenc@parliament.uk
www.parliament.uk/business/committees/committees-a-z/lords-select/eu-energy-environment-subcommittee

Lord Teverson (Chair) *Lib Dem*
Lord Curry of Kirkharle *CB*
Viscount Hanworth *Lab*
Prof. Lord Krebs *CB*
Duke of Montrose *Con*
Lord Rooker *Lab*
Lord Selkirk of Douglas *Con*
Baroness Sheehan *Lib Dem*
Earl of Stair *CB*
Viscount Ullswater *Con*
Baroness Wilcox *Con*
Lord Young of Norwood Green *Lab*
Staff: To be appointed (Clerk), Jennifer Mills (Policy Analyst), Anouska Russell (Press Officer), Breda Twomey (Committee Assistant)

EU External Affairs Sub-committee

Tel: 020 7219 6099
Email: georgee@parliament.uk
www.parliament.uk/hleuc

Baroness Verma (Chair) *Con*
Baroness Armstrong of Hill Top *Lab*
Prof. Baroness Brown of Cambridge *CB*
Lord Dubs *Lab*
Lord Horam *Con*
Baroness Manzoor *Con*
Earl of Oxford and Asquith *Lib Dem*
Lord Risby *Con*
Lord Stirrup *CB*
Baroness Suttie *Lib Dem*
Baroness Symons of Vernham Dean *Lab*
Lord Triesman *Lab*
Staff: Eva George (Clerk), Julia Ewert (Policy Analyst), Dervish Mertcan (Press Officer), Lauren Harvey (Committee Assistant)

EU Financial Affairs Sub-committee

Tel: 020 7219 3140
Email: turnerjd@parliament.uk
www.parliament.uk/business/committees/committees-a-z/lords-select/eu-financial-affairs-subcommittee

Baroness Falkner of Margravine (Chair) *Lib Dem*
Lord Bruce of Bennachie *Lib Dem*
Lord Butler of Brockwell *CB*
Lord de Mauley *Con*
Prof. Lord Desai *Lab*
Lord Fraser of Corriegarth *Con*
Lord Haskins *CB*
Baroness Liddell of Coatdyke *Lab*
Earl of Lindsay *Con*
Baroness Neville-Rolfe *Con*
Prof. Lord Skidelsky *CB*
Lord Woolmer of Leeds *Lab*
Staff: John Turner (Clerk), Holly Snaith (Policy Analyst), Dervish Mertcan (Press Officer), Claire Coast-Smith (Committee Assistant)

EU Home Affairs Sub-committee

Tel: 020 7219 4911
Email: labetaj@parliament.uk
www.parliament.uk/business/committees/committees-a-z/lords-select/eu-home-affairs-subcommittee

Lord Jay of Ewelme (Chair) *CB*
Baroness Browning *Con*
Lord Condon *CB*
Lord Crisp *CB*
Baroness Janke *Lib Dem*
Lord Kirkhope of Harrogate *Con*
Baroness Massey of Darwen *Lab*
Lord O'Neill of Clackmannan *Lab*
Baroness Pinnock *Lib Dem*
Lord Ribeiro *Con*
Lord Soley *Lab*
Lord Watts *Lab*
Staff: Tristan Stubbs (Clerk), Katie Barraclough (Policy Analyst), Anouska Russell (Press Officer), Samuel Lomas (Committee Assistant)

EU Internal Market Sub-committee

Tel: 020 7219 4840
Email: cunninghamal@parliament.uk
www.parliament.uk/business/committees/committees-a-z/lords-select/eu-internal-market-subcommittee

Lord Whitty (Chair) *Lab*
Lord Aberdare *CB*
Baroness Donaghy *Lab*
Lord German *Lib Dem*
Lord Lansley *Con*
Lord Liddle *Lab*
Baroness McGregor-Smith *Con*
Lord Mawson *CB*
Baroness Noakes *Con*
Baroness Randerson *Lib Dem*
Lord Rees of Ludlow *CB*
Lord Wei *Con*
Staff: Pippa Westwood (Clerk), Rosanna Barry (Policy Analyst), Dervish Mertcan (Press Officer), Anastasia Kvaskova (Committee Assistant)

EU Justice Sub-committee
Tel: 020 7219 3194
Email: davidsond@parliament.uk
www.parliament.uk/business/committees/committees-a-z/lords-select/eu-justice-subcommittee

Baroness Kennedy of The Shaws (Chair)	*Lab*
Lord Anderson of Swansea	*Lab*
Lord Cashman	*Lab*
Lord Cromwell	*CB*
Lord Gold	*Con*
Lord Judd	*Lab*
Earl of Kinnoull	*CB*
Baroness Ludford	*Lib Dem*
Baroness Neuberger	*CB*
Lord Polak	*Con*
Baroness Shackleton of Belgravia	*Con*

Staff: Christopher Clarke (Clerk), Tim Mitchell (Legal Adviser), Katy Durrans (Press Officer), Amanda McGrath (Committee Assistant)

International Relations
Tel: 020 7219 7412
Email: hlintlrelations@parliament.uk
www.parliament.uk/business/committees/committees-a-z/lords-select/international-relations-committee Twitter: @LordsIRCom

Lord Howell of Guildford (Chair)	*Con*
Lord Balfe	*Con*
Baroness Coussins	*CB*
Lord Grocott	*Lab*
Lord Hannay of Chiswick	*CB*
Baroness Helic	*Con*
Baroness Hilton of Eggardon	*Lab*
Lord Jopling	*Con*
Lord Purvis of Tweed	*Lib Dem*
Lord Reid of Cardowan	*Lab*
Baroness Smith of Newnham	*Lib Dem*
Lord Wood of Anfield	*Lab*

Staff: James Whittle (Clerk), Roshani Palamakumbura (Policy Analyst), Katy Durrans (Press and Media Officer), Sophie Taylor (Committee Assistant)

Science and Technology
Tel: 020 7219 5750 Fax: 020 7219 4931
Email: hlscience@parliament.uk
www.parliament.uk/hlscience
Twitter: @LordsSTCom

Lord Patel (Chair)	*CB*
Lord Borwick	*Con*
Lord Fox	*Lib Dem*
Lord Griffiths of Fforestfach	*Con*
Prof. Lord Hunt of Chesterton	*Lab*
Prof. Lord Kakkar	*CB*
Prof. Lord Mair	*CB*
Lord Maxton	*Lab*
Baroness Morgan of Huyton	*Lab*
Baroness Neville-Jones	*Con*
Lord Oxburgh	*CB*
Prof. Lord Renfrew of Kaimsthorn	*Con*
Lord Vallance of Tummel	*Lib Dem*
Baroness Young of Old Scone	*Lab*

Staff: Anna Murphy (Clerk), Daniel Rathbone (Policy Analyst), Anouska Russell (Press Officer), Cerise Burnett-Stuart (Committee Assistant)

Principal Office Holders and Staff

Lord Speaker: Rt Hon Lord Fowler 020 7219 6444 Email: lordspeaker@parliament.uk
Senior Deputy Speaker: Rt Hon Lord McFall of Alcluith 020 7219 6000
Email: hlseniordeputyspeaker@parliament.uk
Principal Deputy Chairman of Committees: Lord Boswell of Aynho 020 7219 7291
Email: boswellte@parliament.uk
Clerk of the Parliaments: Edward Ollard 020 7219 3171 Email: ollardec@parliament.uk
Clerk Assistant: Simon Burton 020 7219 3187 Email: burtons@parliament.uk
Reading Clerk and Clerk of the Overseas Office: Jake Vaughan 020 7219 3152
Email: vaughanj@parliament.uk
Gentleman Usher of the Black Rod: Lt Gen David Leakey CMG CBE 020 7219 3100
Email: leakeyd@parliament.uk
Commissioner for Standards: Lucy Scott-Moncrieff CBE 020 7219 7152
Email: lordsstandards@parliament.uk
Registrar of Members' Interests: Tom Wilson 020 7219 3112/020 7219 3120
Email: wilsont@parliament.uk
Clerk of Committees: Dr Philippa Tudor 020 7219 3130 Email: tudorfp@parliament.uk
Director of Facilities: Carl Woodall 020 7219 5501 Email: woodallc@parliament.uk
Finance Director: To be appointed
Director of Human Resources: Tom Mohan 020 7219 3185 Email: mohant@parliament.uk
Director of Parliamentary Digital Service: Tracey Jessup 020 7219 0745
Email: jessupt@parliament.uk
Clerk of Legislation: Andrew Makower 020 7219 3152 Email: makowera@parliament.uk
Examiners of Petitions for Private Bills: James Cooper 020 7219 3211 Email: cooperjj@parliament.uk, Daniel Greenberg 020 7219 5552 Email: greenbergd@parliament.uk, Colin Lee 020 7219 3255 Email: leecg@parliament.uk, Christine Salmon Percival 020 7219 3233 Email: salmonc@parliament.uk
Change Manager: Mary Ollard 020 7219 3828 Email: ollardm@parliament.uk
Clerks of the Journals (Job Share): Chloe Mawson 020 7219 8796 Email: mawsonc@parliament.uk, Kate Lawrence 020 7219 1624 Email: lawrenceks@parliament.uk
Director of Library Services: Patrick Vollmer 020 7219 5805 Email: vollmerp@parliament.uk
Director of the Parliamentary Archives: Adrian Brown 020 7219 3071
Email: brownad@parliament.uk
Director of Communications: Benet Hiscock 020 7219 0671 Email: hiscockb@parliament.uk
Editor of the Official Report: John Vice 020 7219 3397 Email: vicej@parliament.uk
Counsel to the Chairman of Committees: James Cooper 020 7219 3211
Email: cooperjj@parliament.uk
Deputy Counsel to the Chairman of Committees: Nicholas Beach 020 7219 3243
Email: beachn@parliament.uk
Assistant Counsel to the Chairman of Committees: John Crane 020 7219 3243
Email: cranejm@parliament.uk
Legal Adviser to the Human Rights Committee: To be appointed
Director of Parliamentary Procurement and Commercial Service: Veronica Daly 020 7219 0835
Email: dalyv@parliament.uk
Acting Head of Catering and Retail Services: Stephen Perkins 020 7219 4222
Email: perkinss@parliament.uk
Head of Property and Office Services: To be appointed
Head of Internal Audit: Paul Thompson 020 7219 3353 Email: thompsonp@parliament.uk
Internal Communications Manager: Sarah Burke 020 7219 4155 Email: burkes@parliament.uk
Freedom of Information and Data Protection Officer: Frances Grey 020 7219 0100
Email: greyf@parliament.uk
Private Secretary to the Lord Speaker: Patrick Milner 020 7219 6644 Email: milnerp@parliament.uk
Private Secretary to the Senior Deputy Speaker: Kate Meanwell 020 7219 6000
Email: hlseniordeputyspeaker@parliament.uk

Private Secretary to the Clerk of the Parliaments: Dominique Gracia 020 7219 4536
Email: graciad@parliament.uk
Principal Private Secretary to the Leader of the House and Government Chief Whip: Duncan Sagar 020 7219 6961 Email: sagard@parliament.uk
Private Secretary to the Leader of the House: Michael Torrance 020 7219 6782
Email: torrancem@parliament.uk
Principal Clerk of Select Committees: Christopher Johnson DPhil 020 7219 5458
Email: johnsonc@parliament.uk
Clerks of Select Committees: Nicolas Besly 020 7219 6072 Email: beslyn@parliament.uk, Sarah Jones 020 7219 3330 Email: jonessa@parliament.uk,
Deputy Head of Legislation Office: Christine Salmon Percival 020 7219 3233
Email: salmonc@parliament.uk

House of Lords Communications

Westminster, London SW1A 0PW
Tel: 020 7219 3107/Freephone: 0800 223 0855
Website: www.parliament.uk/lords

Director of Communications: Benet Hiscock 020 7219 0671 Email: hiscockb@parliament.uk
Head of Enquiry Service: Mark Simpson 020 7219 3107 Email: hlinfo@parliament.uk
Head of Marketing Communications: Seonaid Whitley 020 7219 5317 Email: whitleys@parliament.uk
Head of Press and Media: Owen Williams 020 7219 8659 Email: williamso@parliament.uk
Internal Communications Manager: Sarah Burke 020 7219 4155 Email: burkes@parliament.uk

Political Offices

Government

Tel: 020 7219 3131
Email: holgovernmentwhips@parliament.uk Website: www.lordswhips.org.uk

Leader of the House of Lords' Office 020 7219 3200
Government Whips' Office 020 7219 3131

Official Opposition

Leader's Office 020 7219 3237
Opposition Chief Whip's Office 020 7219 3237

Liberal Democrats

Leader's Office 020 7219 3178
Chief Whip's Office 020 7219 3114

Crossbenchers

Convenor: Rt Hon the Lord Hope of Craighead KT
Private Secretary: Joseph Topping 020 7219 1414 Email: lordscrossbenchconvenor@parliament.uk

PARLIAMENT

Joint Committees 1062
Statutory Committees 1062
Party Committees 1064
Privy Counsellors 1066
Political Parties 1069
Parliamentary Press Gallery 1073
Parliamentary Agents 1078

Joint Committees

Joint Committee on Consolidation, &c, Bills

These Bills fall into five categories: Consolidation Bills, whether public or private, which are limited to re-enacting existing law; Statute Law Revision Bills, which are limited to repeal of obsolete, spent, unnecessary or superseded enactments; Bills presented under the Consolidation of Enactments (Procedure) Act 1949, which include corrections and minor improvements to the existing law; Bills to consolidate any enactments with amendments to give effect recommendations made by the Law Commissions; Bills prepared by the Law Commissions to promote the reform of the Statute Law by the repeal of enactments which are no longer of practical utility.

Tel: 020 7219 3154
www.parliament.uk/business/committees/committees-a-z/joint-select/consolidation-committee

Baroness Andrews	*Lab*
Lord Armstrong of Ilminster	*CB*
Viscount Bridgeman	*Con*
Lord Carswell	*CB*
Rt Rev Lord Eames	*CB*
Viscount Eccles	*Con*
Viscount Hanworth	*Lab*
Baroness Mallalieu	*Lab*
Prof. Lord Plant of Highfield	*Lab*
Lord Razzall	*Lib Dem*
Baroness Seccombe	*Con*
Baroness Thomas of Winchester	*Lib Dem*

MPs still to be appointed

Joint Committee on Human Rights

Tel: 020 7219 2467
Email: jchr@parliament.uk
www.parliament.uk/jchr
Twitter: @UKParlJCHR

Baroness Hamwee	*Lib Dem*
Baroness Lawrence of Clarendon	*Lab*
Baroness O'Cathain	*Con*
Baroness Prosser	*Lab*
Lord Trimble	*Con*
Lord Woolf	*CB*

MPs still to be appointed

Staff: Robin James (Clerk, Commons), Megan Conway (Clerk, Lords), Liz Parratt (Media Officer)

Joint Committee on Statutory Instruments

Commons members of the Joint Committee also meet separately as the Select Committee on Statutory Instruments.

Tel: 020 7219 2026
Email: jcsi@parliament.uk
www.parliament.uk/jcsi

Baroness Bloomfied of Hinton Waldrist	*Con*
Lord Lexden	*Con*
Baroness Meacher	*CB*
Lord Morris of Handsworth	*Lab*
Lord Rowe-Beddoe	*CB*
Lord Rowlands	*Lab*
Baroness Scott of Needham Market	*Lib Dem*

MPs still to be appointed

Staff: Mike Winter (Clerk), Liz Booth (Committee Assistant)

Statutory Committees

These committees are not select committees or committees of Parliament, but statutory committees of parliamentarians, which are required by law to be made up of Members of the two Houses. Generally, however, they model their procedure closely on that of select committees, and, with the exception of the Intelligence and Security Committee and Parliamentary and Political Service Honours Committee, draw their secretariats from parliamentary staff.

Ecclesiastical Committee

This Committee examines draft Measures presented to it by the Legislative Committee of the General Synod of the Church of England. It reports to Parliament on whether or not it considers the measures to be expedient. The members of the Committee are appointed by the Speaker and Lord Speaker for the duration of each Parliament.

Tel: 020 7219 3152
Email: eccctte@parliament.uk
www.parliament.uk/business/committees/committees-a-z/other-committees/ecclesiastical-committee

Baroness Berridge	*Con*
Baroness Butler-Sloss	*CB*
Earl of Cork and Orrery	*CB*
Lord Cormack	*Con*
Lord Elton	*Con*

Lord Faulkner of Worcester	*Lab*
Lord Glenarthur	*Con*
Baroness Harris of Richmond	*Lib Dem*
Baroness Howarth of Breckland	*CB*
Lord Judd	*Lab*
Lord Lexden	*Con*
Lord Lisvane	*CB*
Baroness McIntosh of Hudnall	*Lab*
Prof. Lord Plant of Highfield	*Lab*

MPs still to be appointed

Staff: Jennifer Burch (Secretary, Commons), Christine Salmon Percival (Secretary, Lords)

Speaker's Committee on the Electoral Commission

The Speaker's Committee is a statutory body established under the Political Parties, Elections and Referendums Act 2000.

Of the appointed members, one is a Member of the House of Commons who is a Minister with responsibilities in relation to local government. This appointment is made by the Prime Minister. The other appointed members are Members of the House of Commons who are not Ministers and are appointed by the Speaker. Appointed members serve for the full length of the Parliament, unless they cease to be Members of the House, resign from the Committee, or another member is appointed in their place. They may be reappointed.

Tel: 020 7219 3351

Email: speakerscommittee@parliament.uk

www.parliament.uk/business/committees/committees-a-z/other-committees/speakers-committee-on-the-electoral-commission

John Bercow (Chair)	*Speaker*
Kirsty Blackman	*SNP*
Gloria De Piero	*Lab*
Nusrat Ghani	*Con*
Marcus Jones	*Con*
Bridget Phillipson	*Lab*

Staff: Michael Everett, Dr Robin James (Clerks), Sadie Smith (Media Officer), Jim Lawford (Committee Assistant)

Speaker's Committee for the Independent Parliamentary Standards Authority

The Committee considers the candidates proposed by the Speaker, following fair and open competition, for the posts of Chair and members of the Independent Parliamentary Standards Authority (IPSA). The candidates for these posts must then be considered by the House of Commons before their appointment by the Queen.

The Committee also reviews the IPSA's annual estimate of the resources it needs. The Speaker, the Leader of the House and the Chair of the Committees on Standards and Privileges are ex-officio members.

Tel: 020 7219 3351 Fax: 020 7219 2269

Email: scipsa@parliament.uk

www.parliament.uk/scipsa

Members still to be appointed

Staff: Michael Everett, Dr Robin James (Clerks), Sadie Smith (Media Officer), Jim Lawford (Committee Assistant)

Intelligence and Security Committee of Parliament

Tel: 020 7276 1215

isc.independent.gov.uk

Members still to be appointed

Parliamentary and Political Service Honours Committee

Tel: 020 7276 2777

Email: honours@cabinetoffice.gov.uk

Lord Spicer (Chair)	*Con*
Nick Brown	*Lab*
Lord Butler of Brockwell	*CB*
Lord Evans of Weardale	*CB*
Baroness Hayman	*CB*
Lord Lisvane	*CB*
Gavin Williamson	*Con*

Non-parliamentary Members:

Diane Bevan, Sir Paul Silk

Staff: Richard Tilbrook (Head of Honours and Appointments Secretariat)

Public Accounts Commission

The Commission's principal duties are to examine the National Audit Office Estimates, and (if satisfied) present them to the House of Commons, agree the National Audit Office (NAO)'s corporate strategy, appoint non-executive members of the NAO board (other than the chair) and consider value for money reports from the appointed auditor for the National Audit Office. The Leader of the House and Chair of the Public Accounts Committee are ex-officio members.

Tel: 020 7219 3275 Fax: 020 7219 2622

www.parliament.uk/business/committees/committees-a-z/other-committees/public-accounts-commission

Members still to be appointed

Staff: Helen Wood (Secretary), Ronnie Jefferson (Personal Assistant)

Party Committees

Conservative Party 1922 Committee

The 1922 Committee exists to give Conservative Backbench MPs a voice and as a mechanism for consultation between the backbenches and the Government.

The 1922 conducts the early stages of leadership elections in the Party and the Chairman has the role of the Returning Officer throughout the process, which includes a vote by the entire countrywide membership of the Conservative Party.

In Opposition, the membership extends to all members of the Parliamentary Party whether front or back benchers. Conservative Peers are invited to all 1922 meetings. When in Government, the 1922 is comprised of all the backbenchers of the Party; the Whips come to the weekly meetings by invitation, as do other Government Ministers.

Chairman: Graham Brady
Vice-chairmen: Cheryl Gillan, Charles Walker
Treasurer: Geoffrey Clifton-Brown
Secretaries: Bob Blackman, Nigel Evans
Members, Executive: Kemi Badenoch, Bernard Jenkin, John Lamont, Pauline Latham, Jeremy Lefroy, Sheryll Murray, Mark Pawsey, Antoinette Sandbach, Alec Shelbrooke, John Stevenson, Bill Wiggin, William Wragg

Parliamentary Labour Party Departmental Groups

Departmental Chairs' elections will take place shortly, details listed below were correct at the time of going to press.

Business, Energy and Industrial Strategy

Chair: Peter Kyle

Communities and Local Government

Chair: Lucy Powell

Culture, Media and Sport

Chair: Graham Jones

Defence

Chair: John Woodcock

Education

Chair: Ian Austin

Environment, Food and Rural Affairs

Chair: Barry Sheerman

Exiting the European Union

Chair: Emma Reynolds

Foreign Affairs

Chair: Mike Gapes

Health

Chair: Luciana Berger

Home Affairs

Chair: Steve McCabe

Housing and Planning
Chair: Julie Elliott

International Development
Chair: Ivan Lewis

International Trade
Chair: Catherine McKinnell

Justice
Chair: Shabana Mahmood

Northern Ireland
Chair: To be appointed

Transport
Chair: Gavin Shuker

Treasury
Chair: Chris Leslie

Women
Chair: Jess Phillips
Vice-chairs: Barbara Keeley *(Commons)*, Yasmin Qureshi *(Commons)*, Baroness Gale *(Lords)*, Baroness Lister of Burtersett *(Lords)*

Work and Pensions
Chair: Stephen Timms

Privy Counsellors

Privy Counsellors historically advised the monarch. The title is now largely honorary; it is given automatically to all cabinet members and the Speaker, the archbishops of Canterbury and York and the Bishop of London and to holders of certain judicial appointments. Leaders of the main political parties are conventionally nominated. The appointment is for life, unless withdrawn, and holders are addressed as 'Right Honourable' (Rt Hon).

The following lists members of the UK Parliaments and Assemblies who are Privy Counsellors.

Diane Abbott	2017
Lord Adonis	2009
Baroness Amos	2003
Lord Anderson of Swansea	2000
Baroness Anelay of St Johns	2009
Lord Arbuthnot of Edrom	1998
Baroness Armstrong of Hill Top	1999
Lord Ashdown of Norton-sub-Hamdon	1989
Baroness Ashton of Upholland	2006
Lord Astor of Hever	2015
Lord Baker of Dorking	1984
Lord Barker of Battle	2012
Sir Kevin Barron	2001
Lord Bassam of Brighton	2009
Lord Bates	2015
Margaret Beckett	1993
Lord Beith	1992
Hilary Benn	2003
Richard Benyon	2017
John Bercow	2009
Ian Blackford	2017
Baroness Blackstone	2001
Lord Blencathra	2001
Lord Blunkett	1997
Lord Boateng	1999
Baroness Boothroyd	1992
Baroness Bottomley of Nettlestone	1992
Lord Boyd of Duncansby	2000
Lord Brabazon of Tara	2013
Lord Bradley	2001
Karen Bradley	2016
Ben Bradshaw	2009
Tom Brake	2011
James Brokenshire	2015
Nick Brown	1997
Lord Brown of Eaton-under-Heywood	1992
Lord Browne of Ladyton	2005
Lord Bruce of Bennachie	2006
Alistair Burt	2013
Lord Butler of Brockwell	2004
Baroness Butler-Sloss	1988
Liam Byrne	2008
Alun Cairns	2016
Earl of Caithness	1990
Alan Campbell	2014
Lord Campbell of Pittenweem	1999
Most Rev Archbishop of Canterbury	2013
Rt Rev Lord Carey of Clifton	1991
Alistair Carmichael	2010
Lord Carrington	1959
Lord Carswell	1993
Baroness Chalker of Wallasey	1987
Greg Clark	2010
Baroness Clark of Calton	2013
Lord Clark of Windermere	1997
Kenneth Clarke	1984
Lord Clarke of Stone-cum-Ebony	1998
Lord Clinton-Davis	1998
Ann Clwyd	2004
Lord Collins of Mapesbury	2007
Yvette Cooper	2007
Lord Cope of Berkeley	1988
Jeremy Corbyn	2015
Baroness Corston	2003
Stephen Crabb	2014
Earl of Crawford and Balcarres	1972
Lord Crickhowell	1979
Lord Cullen of Whitekirk	1997
Lord Cunningham of Felling	1993
Lord Darling of Roulanish	1997
Prof. Lord Darzi of Denham	2009
Ruth Davidson	2016
Lord Davies of Oldham	2006
David Davis	1997
Baroness Dean of Thornton-le-Fylde	1998
Lord Deben	1985
Lord Denham	1981
Lord Dholakia	2010
Nigel Dodds	2010
Sir Jeffrey Donaldson	2007
Lord Drayson	2008
Baroness D'Souza	2009
Sir Alan Duncan	2010
Iain Duncan Smith	2001
Lord Elis-Thomas	2004
Tobias Ellwood	2017
Baroness Evans of Bowes Park	2016
David Evennett	2015
Lord Falconer of Thoroton	2003
Sir Michael Fallon	2012
Baroness Featherstone	2014
Lord Feldman of Elstree	2015
Lord Fellowes	1990
Frank Field	1997
Mark Field	2015
Caroline Flint	2008

Lord Forsyth of Drumlean	1995
Arlene Foster	2016
Lord Foster of Bath	2010
Lord Foster of Bishop Auckland	1993
Lord Foulkes of Cumnock	2002
Lord Fowler	1979
Dr Liam Fox	2010
Mark Francois	2010
Lord Freeman	1993
Lord Freud	2015
Baroness Garden of Frognal	2015
Lord Garel-Jones	1992
David Gauke	2016
Nick Gibb	2016
Cheryl Gillan	2010
Lord Goldsmith	2002
Lord Goodlad	1992
Michael Gove	2010
Lord Graham of Edmonton	1998
Chris Grayling	2010
Damian Green	2012
Justine Greening	2011
Dominic Grieve	2010
Lord Grocott	2002
Lord Hague of Richmond	1995
Viscount Hailsham	1992
Lord Hain	2001
Baroness Hale of Richmond	1999
Robert Halfon	2015
Lord Hamilton of Epsom	1991
Philip Hammond	2010
Matt Hancock	2014
Greg Hands	2014
David Hanson	2007
Lord Hardie	1997
Harriet Harman	1997
Mark Harper	2015
John Hayes	2013
Baroness Hayman	2000
Sir Oliver Heald	2016
John Healey	2008
Lord Henley	2013
Nick Herbert	2010
Lord Heseltine	1979
Lord Higgins	1979
Lord Hill of Oareford	2013
Margaret Hodge	2003
Lord Hoffmann	1992
Baroness Hollis of Heigham	1999
Lord Hope of Craighead	1989
Lord Howard of Lympne	1990
George Howarth	2005
Lord Howarth of Newport	2000
Earl Howe	2013
Lord Howell of Guildford	1979
Lindsay Hoyle	2013
Baroness Hughes of Stretford	2004
Jeremy Hunt	2010
Lord Hunt of Kings Heath	2009
Lord Hunt of Wirral	1980
Lord Hutton	1988
Lord Hutton of Furness	2001
Lord Irvine of Lairg	1997
Lord Janvrin	1998
Sajid Javid	2014
Baroness Jay of Paddington	1998
Boris Johnson	2016
Lord Jones	1999
Carwyn Jones	2010
David Jones	2012
Lord Jopling	1979
Baroness Jowell	1998
Lord Judge	1996
Prof. Lord Kakkar	2014
Lord Keen of Elie	2017
Lord Kerr of Tonaghmore	2003
Sadiq Khan	2009
Lord King of Bridgwater	1979
Lord Kinnock	1983
Sir Greg Knight	1995
Lord Knight of Weymouth	2008
Baroness Kramer	2014
Norman Lamb	2014
Lord Laming	2014
David Lammy	2008
Lord Lamont of Lerwick	1986
Lord Lang of Monkton	1990
Lord Lansley	2010
Lord Lawson of Blaby	1981
Andrea Leadsom	2016
Sir Oliver Letwin	2002
Brandon Lewis	2016
Dr Julian Lewis	2015
Baroness Liddell of Coatdyke	1998
David Lidington	2010
Lord Llewellyn of Steep	2015
Marquess of Lothian	1996
Lord Luce	1986
Lord McAvoy	2003
Lord McConnell of Glenscorrodale	2001
John McDonnell	2016
Pat McFadden	2008
Lord McFall of Alcluith	2004
Lord MacGregor of Pulham Market	1985
Ken Macintosh	2016
Lord Mackay of Clashfern	1979
Lord Maclennan of Rogart	1997
Sir Patrick McLoughlin	2005
Lord McNally	2005
Lord Malloch-Brown	2007
Lord Mance	1999
Lord Mandelson	1998
Lord Martin of Springburn	2000

Lord Maude of Horsham	1992
Lord Mawhinney	1994
Theresa May	2003
Ed Miliband	2007
Maria Miller	2012
Anne Milton	2015
Andrew Mitchell	2010
Lord Moore of Lower Marsh	1986
Nicky Morgan	2014
Lord Morris of Aberavon	1970
Baroness Morris of Yardley	1999
David Mundell	2010
Lord Murphy of Torfaen	1999
Lord Naseby	1994
Lord Neuberger of Abbotsbury	2004
Baroness Neville-Jones	2010
Lord Newby	2014
Baroness Northover	2015
Baroness Oppenheim-Barnes	1979
Lord Owen	1976
Priti Patel	2015
Owen Paterson	2010
Lord Patten	1990
Lord Patten of Barnes	1989
Lord Paul	2009
Earl Peel	2006
Lord Pendry	2000
Mike Penning	2014
Lord Phillips of Worth Matravers	1995
Baroness Prashar	2009
Baroness Primarolo	2002
Baroness Quin	1998
Lord Radice	1999
John Redwood	1993
Lord Reid of Cardowan	1998
Lord Richard	1993
Lord Robathan	2010
Lord Robertson of Port Ellen	1997
Lord Rodgers of Quarry Bank	1975
Lord Rooker	1999
Baroness Royall of Blaisdon	2008
Amber Rudd	2015
Joan Ryan	2007
Lord Ryder of Wensum	1990
Lord Saville of Newdigate	1994
Baroness Scotland of Asthal	2001
Lord Selkirk of Douglas	1996
Grant Shapps	2010
Baroness Shephard of Northwold	1992
Lord Shutt of Greetland	2009
Keith Simpson	2015
Baroness Smith of Basildon	2009
Lord Smith of Finsbury	1997
Sir Nicholas Soames	2011
Anna Soubry	2015
John Spellar	2001
Caroline Spelman	2010
Lord Spicer	2013
Sir Keir Starmer	2017
Lord Steel of Aikwood	1977
Lord Steyn	1992
Baroness Stowell of Beeston	2014
Lord Strathclyde	1995
Mel Stride	2017
Lord Stunell	2012
Nicola Sturgeon	2014
Sir Desmond Swayne	2011
Sir Hugo Swire	2010
Baroness Symons of Vernham Dean	2001
Baroness Taylor of Bolton	1997
Lord Taylor of Holbeach	2014
Lord Tebbit	1981
Lord Thomas of Cwmgiedd	2003
Emily Thornberry	2017
Viscount Thurso	2014
Stephen Timms	2006
Lord Touhig	2006
Lord Trefgarne	1989
Lord Trimble	1997
Elizabeth Truss	2014
Lord Turnbull	2016
Lord Tyler	2014
Viscount Ullswater	1994
Baroness Vadera	2009
Ed Vaizey	2016
Keith Vaz	2006
Theresa Villiers	2010
Lord Wakeham	1983
Lord Waldegrave of North Hill	1990
Lord Walker of Gestingthorpe	1997
Ben Wallace	2017
Lord Wallace of Saltaire	2012
Lord Wallace of Tankerness	2000
Lord Warner	2006
Baroness Warsi	2010
Admiral Lord West of Spithead	2010
John Whittingdale	2015
Lord Whitty	2005
Lord Wigley	1997
Lord Willetts	2010
Lord Williams of Elvel	2013
Most Rev Lord Williams of Oystermouth	2002
Gavin Williamson	2015
Lord Wills	2008
Rosie Winterton	2006
Lord Woolf	1986
Jeremy Wright	2014
Most Rev Archbishop of York	2005
Lord Young of Cookham	1993
Lord Young of Graffham	1984

Political Parties

Conservative and Unionist Party

4 Matthew Parker Street, London SW1H 9HQ
Tel: 020 7222 9000 Fax: 020 7222 1135
Email: chairman@conservatives.com Website: www.conservatives.com Twitter: @Conservatives

Leader: Theresa May MP
Party Chairman and Chairman of the Board: Sir Patrick McLoughlin MP
Chief Executive and Treasurer: Sir Mick Davis
Deputy Chairman: Amanda Sater
Deputy Chairman of the Board and Chair, National Conservative Convention: Rob Semple OBE
Chief Financial Officer: Simon Day
Chairs:
Conservative Councillors' Association: Rory Love
Scottish Conservative Party: Robert Forman MBE
Welsh Conservative Party: Jonathan Evans
Leader, Conservatives in the European Parliament: Ashley Fox MEP
Chairs:
Association of Conservative Peers: Lord Hunt of Wirral MBE
1922 Committee: Graham Brady MP
Vice-chairmen: Stephen Hammond MP, Dominic Johnson CBE, Anthea McIntyre MEP, Alec Shelbrooke MP
Secretary: Stephen Phillips OBE

Labour Party

Southside, 105 Victoria Street, London SW1E 6QT
Tel: 0345 092 2299/020 7783 1299 Fax: 020 7783 1234
Email: leader@labour.org.uk Website: www.labour.org.uk Twitter: @UKLabour

Leader: Jeremy Corbyn MP
Deputy Leader: Tom Watson MP
General Secretary: Iain McNicol
Treasurer: Diana Holland OBE

National Executive Committee

Leader: Jeremy Corbyn MP
Treasurer: Diana Holland OBE
Members:
Frontbench: Rebecca Long-Bailey MP, Jon Trickett MP, Kate Osamor MP
European Parliament Labour Party Leader: To be appointed
Ex-officio as General Secretary: Iain McNicol
Young Labour: Jasmin Beckett
Scottish Labour Representative: To be appointed
Welsh Labour Representative: Alun Davies AM

Division I - Trade Unions

Members:
BFAWU: Pauline McCarthy
CWU: Andy Kerr
GMB: Cath Speight
TSSA: Andi Fox
Ucatt: Jamie Bramwell, Jim Kennedy
Unison: Keith Birch, Wendy Nichols
Unite: Jennie Formby, Martin Mayer
Usdaw: Paddy Lillis

Division II - Socialist Societies

Members: James Asser, Keith Vaz MP

Division III - Constituency Labour Parties

Members: Ann Black, Christine Shawcroft, Claudia Webbe, Darren Williams, Peter Willsman, Rhea Wolfson

Division IV - Local Government

Members: Nick Forbes, Alice Perry

Division V - Parliamentary Labour Party/European Parliamentary Labour Party

Members: Margaret Beckett DBE MP, Shabana Mahmood MP, George Howarth MP

Parliamentary Labour Party

Chair: John Cryer MP
Secretary: Dan Simpson

Co-operative Party

65 St John Street, London EC1M 4AN
Tel: 020 7367 4150
Email: mail@party.coop Website: www.party.coop Twitter: @CoopParty

Chair: Gareth Thomas MP
Vice-chair: Cheryl Barrott
General Secretary: Claire McCarthy
Deputy General Secretary: Karen Wilkie
Chair, Parliamentary Group: Gavin Shuker MP

Scottish National Party

Gordon Lamb House, 3 Jackson's Entry, Edinburgh EH8 8PJ
Tel: 0800 633 5432 Fax: 0131-525 8901
Email: info@snp.org Website: www.snp.org Twitter: @theSNP

Leader: Nicola Sturgeon MSP
Depute Leader: Angus Robertson
President: Ian Hudghton MEP
Chief Executive: Peter Murrell 0131-525 8900 Email: peter.murrell@snp.org

Liberal Democrats

8-10 Great George Street, London SW1P 3AE
Tel: 020 7222 7999
Email: help@libdems.org.uk Website: www.libdems.org.uk Twitter: @LibDems

Leader: Sir Vince Cable MP Email: leader@libdems.org.uk
Deputy Leader: Jo Swinson MP
President: Baroness Brinton
Vice-Presidents: Steve Jarvis *(England)*, Sheila Thomson *(Scotland)*, Rodney Berman *(Wales)*
Treasurer: Lord German OBE
Acting Chief Executive: Sir Nick Harvey
Directors:
- *Communications:* Phil Reilly
- *Elections and Campaigns:* Shaun Roberts
- *Fundraising:* Emma Cherniavsky
- *People:* To be appointed
- *Operations:* Lucy Hope

Deputy Director, Elections and Campaigns: David McCobb
Leader's Chief of Staff: Ben Williams

Heads:
Compliance: David Allworthy
Conference: Lydia Dumont
Digital Operations: Stewart Christie
Finance: Tope Famaks
Content and Creative: Michael Wilkinson
International: Harriet Shone
Media: Jasper Gerard
Membership: Al Ghaff
Policy: Christian Moon
Training and Engagement: Dan Purchese
Parliamentary Adviser Unit: Giles Derrington
Commons Whip's Office: Jack Fletcher
Lords Whips' Office: Humphrey Amos

Democratic Unionist Party

91 Dundela Avenue, Belfast BT4 3BU
Tel: 028 9047 1155
Email: info@mydup.com Website: www.mydup.com Twitter: @duponline

Assembly Office, Room 207 Parliament Buildings, Stormont, Belfast BT4 3XX
Tel: 028 9052 1323

Leader: Arlene Foster MLA
Deputy Leader: Nigel Dodds OBE MP
Chair: Lord Morrow
Vice-chair: Dr William McCrea
Secretary: Michelle McIlveen MLA
Treasurer: Gregory Campbell MP
Press Officer: Clive McFarland 028 9065 4479 Email: clivemcfarland@dup.org.uk

Sinn Féin

Assembly Office:
Tel: 028 9052 1471/028 9052 1470 Fax: 028 9052 1476
Email: sfassembly@outlook.com Twitter: @sinnfeinireland

44 Parnell Square, Dublin 1, Ireland
Tel: +353 1 8726932 Fax: +353 1 8733441
Website: www.sinnfein.ie

53 Falls Road, Belfast BT12 4PD
Tel: 028 9034 7350 Fax: 028 9022 3001

President: Gerry Adams
Vice-President: Mary Lou McDonald
Chair: Declan Kearney MLA
General Secretary: Dawn Doyle
Treasurers: Pearse Doherty, Conor Murphy MLA
Director of Communications: Ciarán Quinn

Plaid Cymru (The Party of Wales)

Tŷ Gwynfor, Marine Chambers, Anson Court, Atlantic Wharf, Cardiff CF10 4AL
Tel: 029 2047 2272
Email: post@plaidcymru.org Website: www.plaid.cymru Twitter: @plaid_cymru

Assembly Office: Tel: 0300 200 7196

Leader: Leanne Wood AM
Chair: Alun Ffred Jones
Chief Executive: Gareth Clubb
Treasurer: Nigel Copner

Green Party

The Biscuit Factory, Unit 201, A Block, 100 Clements Road, London SE16 4DG
Tel: 020 3691 9400
Email: office@greenparty.org.uk Website: www.greenparty.org.uk Twitter: @TheGreenParty

Co-leaders: Jonathan Bartley, Dr Caroline Lucas MP
Deputy Leader: Amelia Womack

UK Independence Party

PO Box 408, Newton Abbot, Devon TQ12 9BG
Tel: 01626 831290 Fax: 01626 831348
Email: mail@ukip.org Website: www.ukip.org Twitter: @UKIP

Leader: Henry Bolton OBE
Deputy Leader: Peter Whittle
Party Chairman: Paul Oakden
Registered Treasurer: John Bickley
Deputy Treasurers: Christopher Mills, Andrew Love
General Secretary: Paul Oakley
Party Secretary: Adam Richardson
Senior Press Spokesperson: Gawain Towler

Parliamentary Press Gallery

The Parliamentary Lobby Journalists are those journalists authorised to work in Parliament.
Members of the Lobby are marked with an asterisk.
Tel 020 7219 4700; for individual desk numbers prefix 020 7219 in most cases.

Attendants 020 7219 5371
Press Bar 020 7219 4284
Website: www.pressgallery.org.uk

Press Gallery

Chairman	Matthew Chorley (The Times)	
Honorary Secretary	Tony Grew (Sunday Times)	
Honorary Treasurer	Robert Hutton (Bloomberg)	
Administrator	Elizabeth Johnson admin@pressgallery.org.uk	4395

Lobby

Chairman	Tom Newton Dunn (The Sun)	
Honorary Secretary	Joe Murphy (Evening Standard)	
Honorary Treasurer	Nigel Morris (The I)	4392

National Daily Newspapers

Daily Express
**Political Editor:* Macer Hall 3389
*Alison Little 3387
*David Maddox 6149 @DavidPBMaddox

Daily Mail
**Political Editor:* Jason Groves @JasonGroves1
**Deputy Political Editor:* John Stevens @johnestevens
*Larisa Brown 6561 @larisamlbrown
*Jack Doyle 3683 @jackwdoyle
Quentin Letts 020 7233 2413 @thequentinletts
*Daniel Martin 6561 @Daniel_J_Martin
Administrator: Nicole Worth 6894

Daily Mirror
**Political Editor:* Andrew Gregory @andrewgregory
*Ben Glaze @benglaze
*Kevin Maguire 6733 @Kevin_Maguire

Daily Record
*Torcuil Crichton 3336 @Torcuil

Evening Standard
**Political Editor:* Joe Murphy 5718 @JoeMurphyLondon
**Deputy Political Editor:* Nic Cecil 6730 @nicholascecil
**City Hall Editor:* Pippa Crerar @PippaCrerar
*Kate Proctor @KateProctorES
Administrator: Caroline Robertson

Financial Times
**Political Editor:* George Parker 4380 @GeorgeWParker
*Henry Mance @henrymance
*Jim Pickard 6892 @PickardJE
*Robert Wright @RKWinvisibleman

Guardian
**Political Editors:* Anushka Asthana @GuardianAnushka, Heather Stewart @GuardianHeather
**Deputy Political Editor:* Rowena Mason @rowenamason
John Crace @JohnJCrace
*Rajeev Syal 6738 @syalrajeev
*Peter Walker @peterwalker99
Administrator: Maria Remle

GUARDIAN UNLIMITED
Senior Political Correspondent: Andrew Sparrow 020 7886 9760 @AndrewSparrow

Herald
**Political Editor:* Mike Settle 0156 @settle_michael

The I
**Political Editor:* Nigel Morris @NigelpMorris

Independent
**Political Editor:* Joe Watts @JoeWatts_
**Political Commentators:* Andrew Grice, John Rentoul @JohnRentoul
*Ashley Cowburn @ashcowburn
*Rob Merrick @Rob_Merrick
*Jonathan Stone @joncstone
Sketch Writer: Tom Peck

Morning Star
Lamiat Sabin @LamiatSabin

Scotsman
Westminster Editor: Paris Gourtsoyannis 4370
@thistlejohn

Sun
**Political Editor:* Tom Newton Dunn 3337
@tnewtondunn
**Deputy Political Editor:* Steve Hawkes
@steve_hawkes
**Associate Editor:* Trevor Kavanagh 6144
@trevor_kavanagh
*Harry Cole @MrHarryCole
*Matthew Dathan @matt_dathan
*Lynn Davidson @ByLynnDavidson

Telegraph Media Group
**Political Editor:* Gordon Rayner
@gordonrayner
**Deputy Political Editor:* Steven Swinford
@Steven_Swinford
**Assistant Editor and Chief Political Correspondent:* Christopher Hope 4960
@christopherhope
Michael Deacon 4927 @MichaelPDeacon
*Emily Gosden @emilygosden
*Laura Hughes @Laura_K_Hughes
*Kate McCann @KateEMcCann
*Ben Riley-Smith @benrileysmith

The Times
**Political Editor:* Francis Elliott 5241
@elliotttimes
**Deputy Political Editor:* Sam Coates
@SamCoatesTimes
**Editor, Red Box:* Matthew Chorley
@MattChorley
**Policy Editor:* Oliver Wright @oliver_wright
*Lucy Fisher @LOS_Fisher
*Patrick Kidd @patrick_kidd
Henry Zeffman @hzeffman

National Sunday Newspapers

Mail on Sunday
**Political Editor:* Simon Walters 4531
*Brendan Carlin 3025
Dan Hodges @DPJHodges
*Glen Owen 4386

Observer
**Political Editor:* Toby Helm 3380 @tobyhelm
*Andrew Rawnsley @andrewrawnsley
Policy Editor: Michael Savage @michaelsavage

People
**Political Editor:* Nigel Nelson 6904
@NigelNelson

Sun on Sunday
**Political Editor:* David Wooding
@DavidWooding
*Ryan Sabey @ryansabey

Sunday Express
**Political Editor:* Camilla Tominey
@CamillaTominey
**Deputy Political Editor:* Kate Devlin
@_katedevlin
Adam Helliker @adamhelliker

Sunday Mirror
*Keir Mudie @mudiek

Sunday Times
**Political Editor:* Tim Shipman
@ShippersUnbound
**Deputy Political Editor:* Caroline Wheeler
@cazjwheeler
*Tony Grew @ayestotheright

Regional Press

Birmingham Evening Mail/Birmingham Post
*Jon Walker 3765 @jonwalker121

Eastern Daily Press
**Group Political Editor, Archant:* Richard Porritt
@Porritt

Local World
*Patrick Daly 4691 @thepatrickdaly

Press and Journal
*Lindsay Razaq 4390 @LJRazaq

Western Mail
**Political Editor:* David Williamson 4382
@dp_williamson

Yorkshire Post
Political Editor: Kathryn Langston

Magazines

Civil Service World
Acting Editor: Susannah Brecknell
020 7593 5618 @SusannahCSW

Economist
**Political Editor:* John Peet

House Magazine
Political Editor: Daniel Bond @DanBond1

New Statesman
*George Eaton @georgeeaton

Spectator
**Political Editor:* James Forsyth 3689
@JGForsyth
**Assistant Editor:* Isabel Hardman
@IsabelHardman
*Katy Balls @katyballs

Time Magazine
*Mark Leftly @Mleftly

Total Politics
Editor: David Singleton @singersz

Tribune
**Editor:* Chris McLaughlin 020 7433 6415
*David Hencke 2093 @davidhencke
Ian Hernon

News Agencies

Agence France Press (AFP)
*Alice Ritchie @alicejritchie

Associated Press
*Jill Lawless @JillLawless

Bloomberg News
*Robert Hutton 020 7222 5241 @RobDotHutton
Alex Morales @AlexJFMorales
*Svenja O'Donnell @SvenjaODonnell
*Thomas Penny 020 7233 3462
@ThomasWPenny
*Tim Ross @TimRoss_1

Dow Jones
*Jennifer Gross 1132 @jgginlondon

Parliament Today
*Mike Peters
*Julian Robinson

Press Association (PA News)
**Political Editor:* Andrew Woodcock
@AndyWoodcock
Parliamentary Editor: Richard Wheeler
@richard_kaputt
*Shaun Connolly
*Gavin Cordon @GavinCordon
*David Hughes @DavidHughesPA
*Sam Lister @sam_lister_
*Arjun Singh

Reuters
**Chief Political Correspondent:*
Elizabeth Piper 5389
*William James 5389 @WJames_Reuters
*Kylie MacLellan 5389 @kyliemaclellan

Broadcasting

BBC (British Broadcasting Corporation)

BBC POLITICAL PROGRAMMES
Head of BBC Westminster: To be appointed
Editor, Political News:
Katy Searle 020 7973 6016 @KatySearle
News Editor: Alison Macdonald
**Political Editor:* Laura Kuensberg @bbclaurak
**Deputy Political Editor:* John Pienaar
@Jponpolitics
**Assistant Political Editor:* Norman Smith
@BBCNormanS
**Chief Political Correspondent, BBC News Channel:* Victoria Young
Chief Political Correspondent, BBC Radio 5Live:
To be appointed
**Political Editor, BBC News Online:* Alex Hunt
@iAlexhunt
Diplomatic Correspondent: James Landale
@BBCJLandale
*Brian Wheeler (BBC News Online)

Political Correspondents
*Alex Forsyth @AlexForsythBBC
*Eleanor Garnier @BBCEleanorG
*Ross Hawkins @rosschawkins
*Chris Mason @ChrisMasonBBC
*Carole Walker @carolewalkercw
*Iain Watson @iainjwatson
*Ben Wright @BBCBenWright

English Regions

**Regional Political Editor:*
Bob Ledwidge 020 7973 6170
*Paul Rowley @PaulRowleyBBC

Regional Political Programmes

*Nina Warhurst (North West) @NinaWarhurst
*Patrick Burns (West Midlands) @PatrickBurnsBBC
*Paul Baltrop (West)
*Tim Donovan (London) @BBCTimDonovan
*Peter Henley (South) @BBCPeterH
*Tony Roe (East Midlands) @tonyroe
*Tim Iredale (North/Hull) @iredalepolitics
*Richard Moss (North East) @BBCRichardMoss
*Deborah McGurran (East) @GurranMc
*Martyn Oates (South West) @bbcmartynoates
Paul Siegert (South East)
Len Tingle (North) @Tinglepolitics
*Stephen Walker (NI)

National Regional Correspondents

David Cornock (Wales)
*Stephen Walker (NI)
David Porter (Scotland)

Parliamentary Correspondents

*Sean Curran
Mark D'Arcy @DArcyTiP
Susan Hulme @Susanh12
Rachel Byrne @rachelcbyrne

Channel 4 Television

CHANNEL 4 NEWS

**Political Editor:* Gary Gibbon 3334 @GaryGibbonBlog
*Michael Crick @MichaelLCrick
*Robert Hamilton
*Rob Thomson

Five News

Political Editor: Andy Bell 020 7705 3232 @andybell5news

Independent Television News

Tel: Press Gallery: 020 7219 3334/4387 News Desk (Gray's Inn Road): 020 7430 4551

ITV NEWS

**Political Editor:* Robert Peston @Peston
News Editor: To be appointed
*Carl Dinnen @carldinnen
*Chris Ship @chrisshipitv
*Adam Smith @adamtimsmith
*Libby Wiener @LibbyWienerITV
Producers: Claire Bidmead, *Dan Hewitt, @DanielHewittITV, Anne Lingley

Israel Radio

*Jerry Lewis 0452

ITV

GOOD MORNING BRITAIN

*Anne Alexander @Annemariealex

ITV ANGLIA

*Emma Hutchinson @ITVEmmaH

ITV CENTRAL

**Westminster News Editor of ITV Regions:*
Simon Mares 020 7233 0203 @SimonMaresITV
*Alison MacKenzie @Alison1mackITV

ITV GRANADA

*Dan Hewitt @DanielHewittITV

ITV MERIDIAN

*Phil Hornby 020 7976 3360 @philhornbyitv

ITV CYMRU WALES

**Political Editor:* Adrian Masters @adrianmasters84

ITV TYNE TEES/BORDER

*Peter MacMahon @petermacmahon

ITV WEST/WEST COUNTRY

*David Wood

ITV YORKSHIRE

*Joe Pike @joepike

London News Network

*Simon Harris @simonharrisitv

Scottish Television

**Westminster Correspondent:* Harry Smith @stvharry

Sky News

**Political Editor:* Faisal Islam 020 7705 5500 @faisalislam
*Adam Boulton @adamboultonSKY
*Tamara Cohen @tamcohen
*Jon Craig @joncraig
*Amber de Botton @AmberSkyNews
*Jason Farrell @JasonFarrellSky
Darren McCaffrey @DMcCaffreySKY
*Robert Nisbet Smith
Clare Parry
*Sophy Ridge @SophyRidgeSky
*Beth Rigby @BethRigby
Esme Wren @esmesky

UTV

*Ken Reid @KenReid_utv

Websites

Conservative Home
Editor: Paul Goodman @PaulGoodmanCH
**Contributing Editor:* Andrew Gimson @AndrewGimson

Huffington Post
**Executive Editor, Politics:* Paul Waugh @paulwaugh
*Owen Bennett @owenjbennett
*Ned Simons @nedsimons

Mail Online
Political Editor: James Tapsfield @JamesTapsfield
*Kate Ferguson @katefergusonCH4
*Tim Sculthorpe @timsculthorpe

Mirror Online
*Daniel Bloom @danbloom1
*Mikey Smith @mikeysmith

MLex
Matthew Holehouse @mattholehouse

Politicos
**Chief UK Political Correspondent:* Tom McTague @TomMcTague
*Jack Blanchard @Jack_Blanchard_
*Charlie Cooper @CharlieCooper8
*Annabelle Dickson @NewsAnnabelle

Politics.co.uk
**Editor:* Ian Dunt @IanDunt

PoliticsHome
**Editor:* Kevin Schofield @PolhomeEditor

International

Irish Times
*Denis Staunton @denisstaunton

New York Times
*Stephen Castle @_StephenCastle

RTE – Irish Broadcasting
**London Correspondent:* Fiona Mitchell @mitchefi

Parliamentary Agents

Parliamentary Agents provide general information on Parliament to both individuals and firms, fully reporting on progress of Bills. There are two types of Agent, those registered to propose and oppose bills on behalf of their clients and those who only oppose Bills.

Berwin Leighton Paisner LLP

Adelaide House, London Bridge, London EC4R 9HA
Tel: 020 3400 1000
Email: helen.kemp@blplaw.com tim.smith@blplaw.com Website: www.blplaw.com

Parliamentary Agent: Helen Kemp Email: helen.kemp@blplaw.com
Partner: Tim Smith Email: tim.smith@blplaw.com

Bircham Dyson Bell LLP

50 Broadway, London SW1H 0BL
Tel: 020 7783 3437
Email: enquirieslondon@bdb-law.co.uk Website: www.bdb-law.co.uk Twitter: @BDB_Law

Parliamentary Agents: Ian McCulloch, Paul Thompson, Nicholas Brown, David Mundy, Nicholas Evans
Partners: Shabana Anwar, Ian Cameron, Mark Challis, Sarah Clark, Tom Henderson, Matthew Smith, Angus Walker
Special Counsel: Jonathan Bracken 020 7783 3408 Email: jonathanbracken@bdb-law.co.uk
Head of Public Affairs: Stuart Thomson 020 7783 3439 Email: stuartthomson@bdb-law.co.uk
Principal Parliamentary Clerk: Pam Thompson 020 7783 3437
Email: pamthompson@bdb-law.co.uk

City Remembrancer

City Remembrancer's Office, PO Box 270, London EC2P 2EJ
Tel: 020 7332 1200
Email: rem.parliamentary@cityoflondon.gov.uk cityremembrancer@theguildhall.org.uk

City Remembrancer: Paul Double LVO

Eversheds Sutherland

1 Wood Street, London EC2V 7WS
Tel: 020 7497 9797 Fax: 020 7919 4919
Website: www.eversheds-sutherland.com Twitter: @ESgloballaw

Parliamentary Agents: Stephen Collings Email: stephencollings@eversheds-sutherland.com,
Monica Peto Email: monicapeto@eversheds-sutherland.com,
Joe Durkin Email: joedurkin@eversheds-sutherland.com
Partner: James O'Connor Email: jamesoconnor@eversheds-sutherland.com

Pinsent Masons LLP

30 Crown Place, Earl Street, London EC2A 4ES
Tel: 020 7418 7000
Email: robbie.owen@pinsentmasons.com Website: www.pinsentmasons.com

Parliamentary Agents (Partner): Robbie Owen 020 7490 6420
Email: robbie.owen@pinsentmasons.com
Parliamentary Agent (Legal Director): Richard Bull 020 7490 9284
Email: richard.bull@pinsentmasons.com *(Legal Director)*
Partner: Francis Tyrrell 020 7490 6994 Email: francis.tyrrell@pinsentmasons.com
Government Affairs and Legislation Clerk: Frances Ellis 020 7667 0164
Email: frances.ellis@pinsentmasons.com

Sharpe Pritchard LLP

Elizabeth House, Fulwood Place, London WC1V 6HG
Tel: 020 7405 4600
Email: alewis@sharpepritchard.co.uk Website: www.sharpepritchard.co.uk

Partners: Alastair Lewis Email: alewis@sharpepritchard.co.uk, Emyr Thomas Email: ethomas@sharpepritchard.co.uk

VWV

Barnards Inn, 86 Fetter Lane, London EC4A 1AD
Tel: 020 7405 1234 Fax: 020 7405 4171
Website: www.vwv.co.uk Twitter: @VWVLawFirm

Parliamentary Agent: Ronald Perry Email: rperry@vwv.co.uk

Winckworth Sherwood LLP

Minerva House, 5 Montague Close, London SE1 9BB
Tel: 020 7593 5000 Fax: 020 7593 5099
Email: agorlov@wslaw.co.uk pirving@wslaw.co.uk Website: www.wslaw.co.uk Twitter: @ws_law

Parliamentary Agents (Partners): Alison Gorlov, Paul Irving, *Parliamentary Agents (Consultants):* Chris Vine, Stephen Wiggs

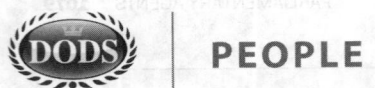

DEVOLVED PARLIAMENT AND ASSEMBLIES

Ministerial and Members' Salaries 1082

Scotland 1083

Scottish Government 1083

- Cabinet 1083
- Ministerial Responsibilities and Staff 1083

Opposition 1088

MSPs' Directory 1092

Parliamentary Committees 1111

Principal Officers and Officials 1114

Scottish Government Civil Service 1115

Political Parties 1118

Wales 1120

Welsh Government 1120

- Cabinet 1120
- Ministerial Responsibilities and Staff 1120

Opposition 1124

AMs' Directory 1125

Assembly Committees 1134

Principal Officers and Officials 1136

Welsh Government Civil Service 1137

Political Parties 1137

Northern Ireland 1139

Executive Committee of Ministers 1139

Ministerial Responsibilities and Staff 1139

MLAs' Directory 1142

Assembly Committees 1153

Principal Officers and Officials 1153

Northern Ireland Civil Service 1153

Political Parties 1156

Greater London Authority 1159

Mayoral Team 1159

London Assembly Members' Directory 1160

Assembly Committees 1162

Police and Crime Commissioners 1165

Combined Authorities 1170

Salaries

From 1 April 2017

	Annual salary (£)
Scottish Parliament	
MSP	61,778
MSP (dual mandate)	20,593

Members who hold any of the following offices are entitled to receive an additional annual salary:

First Minister	89,493
Cabinet Secretary	46,426
Minister	29,083
Presiding Officer	46,426
Deputy Presiding Officer	29,083
Lord Advocate	60,653
Solicitor General for Scotland	43,860

	Annual salary (£)
National Assembly for Wales	
AM	65,344

AMs who are also a Member of Parliament or Member of the European Parliament have their Assembly salary reduced by an amount equal to two thirds of the basic salary.

Members who hold any of the following offices are entitled to receive an additional annual salary:

First Minister	77,596
Cabinet Minister	36,756
Minister	21,441
Presiding Officer	41,861
Deputy Presiding Officer	21,441
Assembly Commissioners	13,273

	Annual salary (£)
Northern Ireland Assembly	
MLA	49,500

Members who hold any of the following offices are entitled to receive an additional annual salary:

First Minister	72,000
Deputy First Minister	72,000
Minister	38,000
Junior Minister	6,000
Speaker	38,000
Principal Deputy Speaker	6,000
Deputy Speaker	6,000

Scottish Government

Scottish Government, St Andrew's House, Regent Road, Edinburgh EH1 3DG
Switchboard: 0300 244 4000 Email: scottish.ministers@gov.scot
Website: www.gov.scot Twitter: @scotgov

Cabinet

First Minister	Rt Hon **Nicola Sturgeon**
Deputy First Minister and Cabinet Secretary for Education and Skills	**John Swinney**
Cabinet Secretary for Finance and Constitution	**Derek Mackay**
Cabinet Secretary for Health and Sport	**Shona Robison**
Cabinet Secretary for the Environment, Climate Change and Land Reform	**Roseanna Cunningham**
Cabinet Secretary for Culture, Tourism and External Affairs	**Fiona Hyslop**
Cabinet Secretary for Communities, Social Security and Equalities	**Angela Constance**
Cabinet Secretary for Justice	**Michael Matheson**
Cabinet Secretary for the Economy, Jobs and Fair Work	**Keith Brown**
Cabinet Secretary for the Rural Economy and Connectivity	**Fergus Ewing**

Also attending Cabinet

Minister for Parliamentary Business	**Joe FitzPatrick**
Minister for UK Negotiations on Scotland's Place in Europe	**Michael Russell**
Lord Advocate	Rt Hon **James Wolffe** QC
Solicitor General	**Alison di Rollo** QC

Ministerial Responsibilities and Staff

Office of the First Minister

St Andrew's House, Regent Road, Edinburgh EH1 3DG
Tel: 0300 244 4000
Email: firstminister@gov.scot Website: firstminister.gov.scot Twitter: @ScotGovFM

First Minister Rt Hon **Nicola Sturgeon** MSP

Head of the Scottish Government; responsible for development, implementation and presentation of Government policy; constitutional affairs; promoting and representing Scotland.

Parliamentary Liaison Officers	Ben Macpherson MSP	0131-348 5786
	Email: ben.macpherson.msp@parliament.scot	
	Gail Ross MSP	0131-348 5927
	Email: gail.ross.msp@parliament.scot	
Chief of Staff	Liz Lloyd	0131-244 5647
	Email: spads_admin@gov.scot	
Special Advisers		
Government Strategy, Europe and Constitution	Ewan Crawford	0131-244 7399
	Email: spads_admin@gov.scot	

Special Advisers continued.

	Callum McCaig Email: spads_admin@gov.scot	0131–244 4574
Head of Communications and Senior Political Spokesperson	Stuart Nicolson Email: spads_admin@gov.scot	0131-244 4779
Communications	Ross Ingebrigtsen Email: spads_admin@gov.scot	0131-244 2066
Head of Policy	Colin McAllister Email: spads_admin@gov.scot	0131-244 3248
	John MacInnes Email: spads_admin@gov.scot	0131-244 2066
	David Miller Email: spads_admin@gov.scot	0131-244 3361
Principal Private Secretary	John Somers Email: firstminister@gov.scot	0131-244 3757

Minister for UK Negotiations on Scotland's Place in Europe **Michael Russell** MSP

Private Secretary	Kirsty Hamilton Email: ministeruknspe@gov.scot	0131-244 2140

Education and Skills

St Andrew's House, Regent Road, Edinburgh EH1 3DG
Tel: 0131-556 8400
Email: dfmcse@gov.scot

Deputy First Minister and Cabinet Secretary for Education and Skills **John Swinney** MSP

Government Strategy; delivery and outcomes across portfolios; resilience; school standards; educational attainment and closing the attainment gap; National Improvement Framework; quality and improvement; teaching profession; school infrastructure and staffing; qualifications; behaviour; measures to combat bullying; Gaelic and Scots languages; modern languages; Historical Abuse Inquiry; named person scheme; cross-government co-ordination of public service reform; childcare implementation; early years; child protection; social services workforce; adoption and fostering; children's rights; looked-after children; children's hearings; protection of vulnerable groups; children's services; widening access; higher education and universities; further education and colleges; student funding; science and STEM; youth work; Skills Development Scotland; implementation of Wood recommendations.

Parliamentary Liaison Officer	Jenny Gilruth MSP Email: jenny.gilruth.msp@parliament.scot	0131-348 5793
Special Adviser	Colin McAllister Email: colin.mcallister@gov.scot	0131-244 3248
Private Secretary	Amy Harron Email: dfmcse@gov.scot	0131-244 5227

Minister for Childcare and Early Years **Mark McDonald** MSP

Private Secretary	Chris Inverarity Email: ministercey@gov.scot	0131-244 0953

Minister for Further Education, Higher Education and Science **Shirley-Anne Somerville** MSP

Private Secretary	Grant Moncur Email: ministerfehes@gov.scot	0131-244 1469

Finance and Constitution

St Andrew's House, Regent Road, Edinburgh EH1 3DG
Email: cabsecfc@gov.scot

Cabinet Secretary for Finance and Constitution **Derek Mackay** MSP

Scottish budget; fiscal policy; taxation; budgetary monitoring and reporting; Scottish public finances and their sustainability; public sector pay and pensions; Scottish Futures Trust; efficient government; public bodies policy; National Performance Framework; Registers of Scotland; government procurement; digital public services; constitution.

Parliamentary Liaison Officer	Kate Forbes MSP Email: kate.forbes.msp@parliament.scot	0131-348 6959
Senior Special Adviser	Colin McAllister Email: spads_admin@gov.scot	0131-244 3248
Special Adviser	Liz Lloyd Email: spads_admin@gov.scot	
Private Secretary	Alistair Paddison Email: cabsecfc@gov.scot	0131-244 4456

Minister for Parliamentary Business **Joe FitzPatrick** MSP

Private Secretary	Kevin Veitch Email: ministerpb@gov.scot	0131-348 5572

Health and Sport

St Andrew's House, Regent Road, Edinburgh EH1 3DG
Tel: 0131-244 2125 Email: cabsechs@gov.scot

Cabinet Secretary for Health and Sport **Shona Robison** MSP

NHS; elective centres; health care and social integration; carers; adult care and support; implementing 2020 Vision and National Clinical Strategy; patient services; NHS staff and pay; problem alcohol use and recovery; healthy working lives; national service planning; NHS performance; acute services; sporting events and legacy; patient safety; quality strategy; public health; health protection; sport and physical activity; primary care; mental health; allied healthcare services; dentistry; sexual health; medical records; health improvement; drugs policy; child and maternal health.

Parliamentary Liaison Officer	Fulton MacGregor MSP Email: fulton.macgregor.msp@parliament.scot	0131-348 5797
Special Adviser	David Hutchison Email: david.hutchison@gov.scot	0131-244 4892
Private Secretary	Lynn Lavery Email: cabsechs@gov.scot	0131-244 2125

Minister for Public Health and Sport **Aileen Campbell** MSP

Private Secretary	Craig Keddie Email: ministerphs@gov.scot	0131-244 6955

Minister for Mental Health **Maureen Watt** MSP

Private Secretary	Laura Hitchings Email: ministermh@gov.scot	0131-244 5539

Environment, Climate Change and Land Reform

St Andrew's House, Regent Road, Edinburgh EH1 3DG
Tel: 0131-244 1556 Email: cabsececclr@gov.scot

Cabinet Secretary for the Environment, Climate Change and Land Reform
Roseanna Cunningham MSP

Climate change; flood prevention; water quality; land reform; physical and marine environment; sustainable development; biodiversity; natural heritage; environmental protection; environmental and climate justice; national parks; Scottish Water.

Parliamentary Liaison Officer	Gillian Martin MSP Email: gillian.martin.msp@parliament.scot	0131-348 6953
Special Adviser	David Miller Email: david.miller@gov.scot	0131-244 3361
Private Secretary	David Johnston Email: cabsececclr@gov.scot	0131-244 1556

Culture, Tourism and External Affairs

St Andrew's House, Regent Road, Edinburgh EH1 3DG
Tel: 0131-244 7716 Email: cabsecctea@gov.scot

Cabinet Secretary for Culture, Tourism and External Affairs **Fiona Hyslop** MSP

Culture and the arts; broadcasting; architecture; built heritage; national identity; cross-government co-ordination on bringing major events to Scotland; national records; fair trade; tourism; international development; cross-government co-ordination on European Union and international relations; Scottish diaspora.

Parliamentary Liaison Officer	Ash Denham MSP Email: ash.denham.msp@parliament.scot	0131-348 5923
Special Adviser	Katy Bowman Email: katy.bowman@gov.scot	0131-244 2016
Private Secretary	Christopher Nicholson Email: chris.nicholson@gov.scot cabsecctea@gov.scot	0131-244 7716

Minister for International Development and Europe Dr **Alasdair Allan** MSP

Private Secretary	Amy Brown Email: ministeride@gov.scot	0131-244 5618

Communities, Social Security and Equalities

St Andrew's House, Regent Road, Edinburgh EH1 3DG
Tel: 0131-556 8400 Email: cabseccsse@gov.scot

Cabinet Secretary for Communities, Social Security and Equalities **Angela Constance** MSP

Welfare policy; community empowerment; devolution to communities and reform of local government; equalities; religious and faith organisations; protection and development of social and human rights; third sector and social economy; democratic renewal; local government; housing; homelessness; community planning; planning; business improvement districts; town centres; building standards; social security; implementation of new powers; measures against poverty; disabilities; older people.

Parliamentary Liaison Officer	Mairi Gougeon MSP Email: mairi.gougeon.msp@parliament.scot	0131-348 6947
Special Adviser	Jeanette Campbell Email: jeanette.campbell@gov.scot	0131-244 5190
Private Secretary	Stuart McLean Email: cabseccsse@gov.scot	0131-244 2513

Minister for Local Government and Housing **Kevin Stewart** MSP

Private Secretary	Marissa Gallagher Email: ministerlgh@gov.scot	0131-244 4425

Minister for Social Security **Jeane Freeman** MSP

Private Secretary	Gavin McDougall Email: ministersocsec@gov.scot	0131-244 5027

Justice

St Andrew's House, Regent Road, Edinburgh EH1 3DG
Tel: 0131-556 8400 Email: cabinetsecretaryforjustice@gov.scot

Cabinet Secretary for Justice **Michael Matheson** MSP

Justice system; criminal law procedure; civil law; family and property law; police, fire and rescue services; mountain rescue; legal profession; violence reduction; anti-sectarianism; courts; sentencing; security; human rights; human trafficking; access to justice; community safety; anti-social behaviour; prisons and prisoners; female offenders; criminal justice social work; victims and witnesses; reducing re-offending; youth justice; liquor licensing.

Parliamentary Liaison Officer	Tom Arthur MSP Email: tom.arthur.msp@parliament.scot	0131-348 5863
Special Adviser	John McFarlane Email: john.mcfarlane@gov.scot	0131-244 1811
Private Secretary	Kevin McGowan Email: cabinetsecretaryforjustice@gov.scot	0131-244 4091

Minister for Community Safety **Annabelle Ewing** MSP

Private Secretary	Steven Day Email: ministercsla@gov.scot	0131-244 4579

Economy, Jobs and Fair Work

St Andrew's House, Regent Road, Edinburgh EH1 3DG
Tel: 0131-244 0585 Email: cabsecejfw@gov.scot

Cabinet Secretary for the Economy, Jobs and Fair Work **Keith Brown** MSP

The Scottish Economy; infrastructure investment policy; Scottish Enterprise; trade and inward investment; innovation; internationalisation; increasing productivity; fair work and inclusive growth; labour market strategy; living wage; European Structural funds; infrastructure investment policy; consumer advocacy and advice; employment policy; trade unions; bankruptcy policy and Accountant in Bankruptcy; business, industry and manufacturing; cities; energy and energy consent; Regional Economic Forums; life sciences; financial services; low carbon economy; renewable energy industries; youth and women's employment; employability programmes.

Parliamentary Liaison Officer	Ivan McKee MSP Email: ivan.mckee.msp@parliament.scot	0131-348 6950
Special Adviser	Stewart Maxwell Email: stewart.maxwell2@gov.scot	
Private Secretary	Simon Forrest Email: cabsecejfw@gov.scot	0131-244 0585

Minister for Business, Innovation and Energy **Paul Wheelhouse** MSP

Private Secretary	Antonia Farrell Email: ministerbie@gov.scot	0131-244 1271

Minister for Employability and Training **Jamie Hepburn** MSP

Private Secretary	Steven Turnbull Email: ministeret@gov.scot	0131-244 2135

Rural Economy and Connectivity

St Andrew's House, Regent Road, Edinburgh EH1 3DG
Tel: 0131-244 2189 Email: cabsecrec@gov.scot

Cabinet Secretary for the Rural Economy and Connectivity **Fergus Ewing** MSP

Rural Scotland; Highlands Islands Enterprise; agriculture; forestry; fisheries; aquaculture; food and drink; crofting; transport; connectivity, including 100 per cent broadband.

Parliamentary Liaison Officer	Emma Harper MSP Email: emma.harper.msp@parliament.scot	0131-348 6965
Special Advisers	Kate Higgins Email: kate.higgins@gov.scot	0131-244 3460
	John McFarlane Email: john.mcfarlane@gov.scot	0131-244 1811
Private Secretary	Fiona MacKenzie Email: cabsecrec@gov.scot	0131-244 2492
Minister for Transport and Islands	**Humza Yousaf** MSP	
Private Secretary	Mariella Matheson Email: transportminister@gov.scot	0131- 244 4426

Whips

Chief Whip	**Bill Kidd**
Depute Whips	**George Adam** **Ruth Maguire** **Maree Todd**

Opposition

Scottish Conservatives

Shadow Cabinet

Leader	Rt Hon **Ruth Davidson**
Chief Whip and Business Manager; Spokesperson for the Low Carbon Economy	**Maurice Golden**
Deputy Leader and Shadow Cabinet Secretary for Europe and External Affairs	**Jackson Carlaw**
Shadow Cabinet Secretary for Finance	**Murdo Fraser**
Shadow Cabinet Secretary for Economy, Jobs and Fair Work	**Dean Lockhart**
Shadow Cabinet Secretary for Health and Sport	**Miles Briggs**
Shadow Cabinet Secretary for Education and Skills	**Liz Smith**
Shadow Cabinet Secretary for Climate Change, Environment and Land Reform; 2021 Policy Co-ordinator	**Donald Cameron**
Shadow Cabinet Secretary for Rural Economy and Connectivity	**Peter Chapman**
Shadow Cabinet Secretary for Communities, Social Security, Constitution and Equalities	Prof **Adam Tomkins**
Shadow Cabinet Secretary for Justice	**Liam Kerr**
Shadow Cabinet Secretary for Culture and Tourism	**Rachael Hamilton**

Shadow Ministers

Shadow Minister for Transport and Infrastructure	**Jamie Greene**
Shadow Minister for Taxation	**Bill Bowman**
Shadow Minister for Financial Sustainability	**Tom Mason**
Shadow Minister for Business, Innovation and Energy; Deputy Business Manager	**Alexander Burnett**

Shadow Minister for Jobs, Employability and Training	**Jamie Halcro Johnston**
Shadow Minister for Mental Health, Public Health and Equalities	**Annie Wells**
Shadow Minister for Health Education, Lifestyle and Sport	**Brian Whittle**
Shadow Minister for Further Education, Higher Education and Science	**Oliver Mundell**
Shadow Minister for Childcare and Early Years	**Michelle Ballantyne**
Shadow Minister for Biodiversity, Animal Welfare and the Digital Economy	**Finlay Carson**
Shadow Minister for Rural Affairs	**Edward Mountain**
Shadow Minister for Farming	**John Scott**
Shadow Minister for Welfare Reform	**Jeremy Balfour**
Shadow Minister for Housing and Communities	**Graham Simpson**
Shadow Minister for Local Government	**Alexander Stewart** MBE
Shadow Minister for Legal Affairs	**Gordon Lindhurst**
Shadow Minister for Community Safety and Veterans' Affairs	**Maurice Corry**
Shadow Minister for Tourism and Small Business	**Alison Harris**

Scottish Labour

Spokespeople

Leader	**To be appointed on 18 November**
Deputy Leader; Spokesperson for Community, Social Security and Equalities	**Alex Rowley**
Spokesperson for Education, Skills and Science	**Iain Gray**
Spokesperson for Finance	**Kezia Dugdale**
Spokesperson for Health	**Anas Sarwar**
Spokesperson for Culture, Sport, Tourism and External Affairs	**Lewis Macdonald**
Spokesperson for Environment, Climate Change and Land Reform	**Claudia Beamish**
Spokesperson for Rural Economy and Connectivity	**Rhoda Grant**
Spokesperson for Economy, Fair Work and Jobs	**Jackie Baillie**
Spokesperson for Justice	**Claire Baker**
Parliamentary Business Manager; Minister without Portfolio	**James Kelly**

(Ian Murray MP attends Shadow Cabinet as Westminster Spokesperson for Scottish Labour)

Shadow Ministers

Shadow Minister for Social Security; Whip	**Mark Griffin**
Shadow Minister for Community, Housing and Social Justice	**Pauline McNeill**
Shadow Minister for Education	**Daniel Johnson**
Shadow Minister for Health; Whip	**Colin Smyth**
Shadow Minister for Inequality	**Monica Lennon**

Devolved Parliament and Assemblies

Shadow Minister for Environment, Climate Change and Land Reform	**David Stewart**
Shadow Minister for Transport and Town Centres	**Neil Bibby**
Shadow Minister for Economy	**Richard Leonard**
Shadow Minister for Justice	**Mary Fee**

Scottish Green Party

Co-convener and Spokesperson for Finance, Economy, Fair Work and Equalities	**Patrick Harvie**
Spokesperson for Justice, Transport, Tourism and Rural and Island Communities	**John Finnie**
Spokesperson for Health and Sport, Social Security and Children and Young People	**Alison Johnstone**
Spokesperson for Communities, Housing, Land Reform and Local Government	**Andy Wightman**
Spokesperson for Climate, Energy, Environment, Food and Farming	**Mark Ruskell**
Spokesperson for International Development and External Affairs, Education and Skills and Culture and Media	**Ross Greer**

Scottish Liberal Democrats

Leader; Spokesperson for Finance	**Willie Rennie**
Spokesperson for Education and Sport	**Tavish Scott**
Spokesperson for Health	**Alexander Cole-Hamilton**
Spokesperson for Justice and Energy	**Liam McArthur**
Spokesperson for Rural Affairs and Business Manager	**Mike Rumbles**

Scottish Parliament

Scottish Parliament, Edinburgh EH99 1SP
Tel: 0131-348 5000/0800 092 7500 Textphone: 0800 092 7100
Email: sp.info@scottish.parliament.uk Website: www.parliament.scot Twitter: @scotparl

Members (MSPs)

State of the Parties (October 2017)

	Constituency	*Regional*	*Total*
Scottish National Party	59*	4	63
Scottish Conservative and Unionist Party	7	24	31
Scottish Labour Party (includes Scottish Labour/Co-operative Party)	3	20†	23
Scottish Green Party	0	6	6
Scottish Liberal Democrats	4	1	5
Presiding Officer	0	1	1
	73	**56**	**129 seats**

* Includes two Deputy Presiding Officer who can participate and vote fully in the Parliament when not in the chair.

† Excludes the Presiding Officer who has no party allegiance while in post.

Changes since 2016 Scottish Parliament election

RESIGNATIONS

Rachael Hamilton	South Scotland – *Con*	2 May 2017
John Lamont	Ettrick, Roxburgh and Berwickshire – *Con*	4 May 2017
Douglas Ross	Highlands and Islands – *Con*	11 June 2017
Ross Thomson	North East Scotland – *Con*	12 June 2017

DEATHS

Alex Johnstone	North East Scotland – *Con*	7 December 2016

REPLACEMENTS

Bill Bowman	North East Scotland – *Con*	Returned 9 December 2016 following the death of Alex Johnstone
Michelle Ballantyne	South Scotland – *Con*	Returned 17 May 2017 following the resignation of Rachael Hamilton
Tom Mason	North East Scotland – *Con*	Returned 15 June 2017 following the resignation of Ross Thomson
Jamie Halcro Johnston	Highlands and Islands – *Con*	Returned 16 June 2017 following the resignation of Douglas Ross

BY-ELECTIONS

ETTRICK, ROXBURGH AND BERWICKSHIRE

8 June 2017 due to the resignation of the Conservative MSP John Lamont

Con	Rachael Hamilton	20,658
SNP	Gail Hendry	11,320
Lab	Sally Prentice	3,406
Lib Dem	Catriona Bhatia	3,196

Con majority 9,338 – Con hold (0.42% from SNP to Con)
Electorate 55,395 – Total vote 38,653 – Turnout 69.78%

MSPs' Directory

Con	Conservative
Green	Green Party
Lab	Labour
Lab/Co-op	Labour/Co-operative
Lib Dem	Liberal Democrat
Pres Off	Presiding Officer
SNP	Scottish National Party

ADAM, Mr George *SNP* **Paisley**
Depute Whip
Tel: 0131-348 5869 Email: george.adam.msp@parliament.scot
Constituency office: 4 Johnston Street, Paisley PA1 1XG
Tel: 0141-887 8075
Website: www.paisleysmsp.org Twitter: @georgeadam

ADAMSON, Ms Clare *SNP* **Motherwell and Wishaw**
Tel: 0131-348 6377 Email: clare.adamson.msp@parliament.scot
Constituency office: Suite G2, Dalziel Building, 7 Scott Street, Motherwell ML1 1PN
Tel: 01698 337540
Website: www.clareadamsonmsp.scot Twitter: @ClareAdamsonSNP

ALLAN, Dr Alasdair *SNP* **Na h-Eileanan an Iar**
Minister for International Development and Europe
Email: alasdair.allan.msp@parliament.scot
Ministerial office: Scottish Government, St Andrews House, Regent Road, Edinburgh EH1 3DG
Tel: 0300 244 4000
Constituency office: 20 Kenneth Street, Stornoway HS1 2DR
Tel: 01851 700357
Website: alasdairallan.scot Twitter: @alasdairallan

ARTHUR, Mr Tom *SNP* **Renfrewshire South**
Parliamentary Liaison Officer to Michael Matheson as Cabinet Secretary for Justice
Tel: 0131-348 5863 Email: tom.arthur.msp@parliament.scot
Constituency office: 49 High Street, Johnstone PA5 8AJ
Tel: 01505 331990
Website: www.tomarthursnp.scot Twitter: @ThomasCArthur

BAILLIE, Ms Jackie *Lab* **Dumbarton**
Scottish Labour Spokesperson for Economy, Fair Work and Jobs
Tel: 0131-348 5905 Email: jackie.baillie.msp@parliament.scot
Constituency office: 6 Church Street, Dumbarton G82 1QL
Tel: 01389 734214
Website: www.jackiebaillie.co.uk Twitter: @jackiebmsp

BAKER, Mrs Claire *Lab* **Mid Scotland and Fife**
Scottish Labour Spokesperson for Justice
Tel: 0131-348 6769 Fax: 0131-348 6761 Email: claire.baker.msp@parliament.scot
Regional office: Ore Valley Business Centre, 93 Main Street, Lochgelly, Fife KY5 9AF
Tel: 01592 786726 Email: claire-baker@live.co.uk
Website: www.clairebaker.org Twitter: @clairebakermsp

BALFOUR, Mr Jeremy *Con* **Lothian**
Shadow Minister for Welfare Reform
Tel: 0131-348 5961 Email: jeremy.balfour.msp@parliament.scot
Regional office: No regional office publicised
Website: www.jeremybalfour.org.uk

BALLANTYNE, Ms Michelle *Con* **South Scotland**
Shadow Minister for Childcare and Early Years
Tel: 0131-348 5661 Email: michelle.ballantyne.msp@parliament.scot
Regional office: Lower Langbrae, Main Street, St Boswells TD6 0AP
Website: www.michelleballantyne.org.uk Twitter: @MBallantyneMSP

BEAMISH, Ms Claudia *Lab/Co-op* **South Scotland**
Scottish Labour Spokesperson for Environment, Climate Change and Land Reform
Tel: 0131-348 6889 Email: claudia.beamish.msp@parliament.scot
Regional office: 12 St Vincent Place, Lanark ML11 7LA
Tel: 01555 664065
Website: www.claudiabeamish.com Twitter: @claudiabeamish

BEATTIE, Mr Colin *SNP* **Midlothian North and Musselburgh**
Tel: 0131-348 6373 Email: colin.beattie.msp@parliament.scot
Constituency office: 164 High Street, Dalkeith EH22 1AY
Tel: 0131-454 0204
Website: colinbeattiemsp.org Twitter: @uartlach

BIBBY, Mr Neil *Lab/Co-op* **West Scotland**
Scottish Labour Shadow Minister for Transport and Town Centres
Tel: 0131-348 6385 Email: neil.bibby.msp@parliament.scot
Regional office: 4 St Mirren Street, Paisley PA1 1UA
Tel: 0141-889 0457 Fax: 0141-840 2510 Twitter: @neilbibby

BOWMAN, Mr Bill *Con* **North East Scotland**
Shadow Minister for Taxation
Tel: 0131-348 5649 Email: bill.bowman.msp@parliament.scot
Constituency offices: 190 East High Street, Forfar, Angus DD8 2HG
80 Rosemount Place, Aberdeen AB25 2XN Twitter: @billabowman

BRIGGS, Mr Miles *Con* **Lothian**
Shadow Cabinet Secretary for Health and Sport
Tel: 0131-348 5945 Email: miles.briggs.msp@parliament.scot
Regional office: 29 Roseburn Terrace, Edinburgh EH12 5NQ
Tel: 0131-337 9764
Website: www.milesbriggs.scot Twitter: @MilesBriggsMSP

BROWN, Mr Keith *SNP* **Clackmannanshire and Dunblane**
Cabinet Secretary for the Economy, Jobs and Fair Work
Email: keith.brown.msp@parliament.scot
Ministerial office: Scottish Government, St Andrews House, Regent Road, Edinburgh EH1 3DG
Tel: 0300 244 4000
Constituency office: Unit 4, Townhead Institute, 39 Drysdale Street, Alloa FK10 1JA
Tel: 01259 219333
Website: www.keithbrownmsp.org Twitter: @KeithBrownSNP

BURNETT, Mr Alexander *Con* **Aberdeenshire West**
Shadow Minister for Business, Innovation and Energy; Deputy Business Manager
Tel: 0131-348 5642 Email: alexander.burnett.msp@parliament.scot
Constituency office: No constituency office publicised
Website: www.alexanderburnett.com Twitter: @AJABurnett

CAMERON, Mr Donald *Con* **Highlands and Islands**
Shadow Cabinet Secretary for Climate Change, Environment and Land Reform; 2021 Policy Co-ordinator
Tel: 0131-348 6989 Email: donald.cameron.msp@parliament.scot
Regional office: No regional office publicised
Website: www.donaldcameron.org.uk Twitter: @dajcameron

CAMPBELL, Ms Aileen *SNP* **Clydesdale**
Minister for Public Health and Sport
Tel: 0131-348 6707 Email: aileen.campbell.msp@parliament.scot
Ministerial office: Scottish Government, St Andrews House, Regent Road, Edinburgh EH1 3DG
Tel: 0300 244 4000
Constituency office: Room 9, Kirkton Chambers, 12 Kirkton Street, Carluke ML8 4AB
Tel: 01555 750249
Website: www.aileencampbell.com Twitter: @clydesdaileen

CARLAW, Mr Jackson *Con* **Eastwood**
Deputy Leader, Scottish Conservatives; Shadow Cabinet Secretary for Europe and External Affairs
Tel: 0131-348 6800 Email: jackson.carlaw.msp@parliament.scot
Constituency office: Spiersbridge House, 1 Spiersbridge Way, Thornliebank, Glasgow G46 8NG
Tel: 0141-465 6611 Twitter: @Carlaw4Eastwood

CARSON, Mr Finlay *Con* **Galloway and West Dumfries**
Shadow Minister for Biodiversity, Animal Welfare and the Digital Economy
Tel: 0131-348 5890 Email: kyle.macintyre.msp@parliament.scot finlay.carson.msp@parliament.scot
Constituency office: 107 King Street, Castle Douglas DG7 1LZ
Tel: 01556 504991 Email: gillian.dykes@parliament.scot
Website: www.finlaycarson.co.uk Twitter: @fincarson

CHAPMAN, Mr Peter *Con* **North East Scotland**
Shadow Cabinet Secretary for Rural Economy and Connectivity
Tel: 0131-348 6150 Email: peter.chapman.msp@parliament.scot
Regional office: 80 Rosemount Place, Aberdeen AB25 2XN
Email: peter.chapman@scottishconservatives.com
Website: www.peter-chapman.org.uk Twitter: @PeterChapmanMSP

COFFEY, Mr Willie *SNP* **Kilmarnock and Irvine Valley**
Tel: 0131-348 6515 Fax: 0131-348 6517 Email: willie.coffey.msp@parliament.scot
Constituency office: 62 John Finnie Street, Kilmarnock KA1 1BS
Tel: 01563 537300 Fax: 01563 537300 Email: willie.coffey@msp-office.co.uk

COLE-HAMILTON, Mr Alexander *Lib Dem* **Edinburgh Western**
Scottish Liberal Democrats Spokesperson for Health
Tel: 0131-348 5821 Email: alex.cole-hamilton.msp@parliament.scot
Constituency office: 185 St John's Road, Edinburgh EH12 7SL
Tel: 0131-334 1814
Website: www.alexcolehamilton.org.uk Twitter: @agcolehamilton

CONSTANCE, Ms Angela *SNP* **Almond Valley**
Cabinet Secretary for Communities, Social Security and Equalities
Email: angela.constance.msp@parliament.scot
Ministerial office: Scottish Government, St Andrews House, Regent Road, Edinburgh EH1 3DG
Tel: 0300 244 4000
Constituency office: Unit 4, Ochil House, Beveridge Square, Livingston EH54 6QF
Tel: 01506 460403 Twitter: @AConstanceSNP

CORRY, Mr Maurice *Con* **West Scotland**
Shadow Minister for Community Safety and Veterans' Affairs
Tel: 0131-348 6155 Email: maurice.corry.msp@parliament.scot
Regional office: Suite 4, Kirkhouse, Kirkroad, Bearsden G61 3RG
Tel: 0141-942 4942

CRAWFORD, Mr Bruce *SNP* **Stirling**
Tel: 0131-348 5687 Email: bruce.crawford.msp@parliament.scot
Constituency office: Office 16, John Player Building, Stirling Enterprise Park, Stirling FK7 7RP
Tel: 01786 471899
Website: www.brucecrawfordmsp.scot Twitter: @rhbrucecrawford

CUNNINGHAM, Ms Roseanna *SNP* **Perthshire South and Kinross-shire**
Cabinet Secretary for the Environment, Climate Change and Land Reform
Tel: 0131-348 5697 Fax: 0131-348 5563 Email: roseanna.cunningham.msp@parliament.scot
Ministerial office: Scottish Government, St Andrews House, Regent Road, Edinburgh EH1 3DG
Tel: 0300 244 4000
Constituency office: 63 Glasgow Road, Perth PH2 0PE
Tel: 01738 620540
Website: www.roseannacunningham.com Twitter: @strathearnrose

DAVIDSON, Rt Hon Ruth *Con* **Edinburgh Central**
Leader, Scottish Conservative and Unionist Party
Tel: 0131-348 6370 Email: ruth.davidson.msp@parliament.scot
Constituency office: No constituency office publicised Twitter: @ruthdavidsonmsp

DENHAM, Ms Ash *SNP* **Edinburgh Eastern**
Parliamentary Liaison Officer to Fiona Hyslop as Cabinet Secretary for Culture, Tourism and External Affairs
Tel: 0131-348 5923 Email: ash.denham.msp@parliament.scot
Constituency office: SPACE, 11 Harewood Road, Edinburgh EH16 4NT
Tel: 0131-659 4707
Website: www.ashdenham.scot Twitter: @ashtenRD

DEY, Mr Graeme *SNP* **Angus South**
Tel: 0131-348 6292 Email: graeme.dey.msp@parliament.scot
Constituency office: 282-284 High Street, Arbroath, Angus DD11 1JF
Tel: 01241 873058
Website: www.graemedey.info

DORIS, Mr Bob *SNP* **Glasgow Maryhill and Springburn**
Tel: 0131-348 6547 Fax: 0131-348 6549 Email: bob.doris.msp@parliament.scot
Constituency office: Maryhill Burgh Halls, 10-24 Gairbraid Avenue, Glasgow G20 8YE
Tel: 0141-946 7700
Website: www.bobdoris.com Twitter: @BobDorisSNP

DORNAN, Mr James *SNP* **Glasgow Cathcart**
Tel: 0131-348 5683 Email: james.dornan.msp@parliament.scot
Constituency office: 2 Clarkston Road, Glasgow G44 4EQ
Tel: 0141-632 5238
Website: www.jamesdornanmsp.org Twitter: @glasgowcathcart

DUGDALE, Ms Kezia *Lab/Co-op* **Lothian**
Scottish Labour Spokesperson for Finance
Tel: 0131-348 6894 Email: kezia.dugdale.msp@parliament.scot
Regional office: 4 Northfield Court, West Calder EH55 8DS
Tel: 01506 873242
Website: www.keziadugdale.com Twitter: @kezdugdale

EWING, Ms Annabelle *SNP* **Cowdenbeath**
Minister for Community Safety
Tel: 0131-348 6290 Email: annabelle.ewing.msp@parliament.scot
Ministerial office: Scottish Government, St Andrews House, Regent Road, Edinburgh EH1 3DG
Tel: 0300 244 4000
Constituency office: 253-257 High Street, Cowdenbeath KY4 9QF
Tel: 01383 611067 Twitter: @aewingmsp

EWING, Mr Fergus *SNP* **Inverness and Nairn**
Cabinet Secretary for the Rural Economy and Connectivity
Tel: 0131-348 5732 Email: fergus.ewing.msp@parliament.scot
Ministerial office: Scottish Government, St Andrews House, Regent Road, Edinburgh EH1 3DG
Tel: 0300 244 4000
Constituency office: 112 Church Street, Inverness IV1 1EP
Tel: 01463 713004 Email: fergus@fergusewing.com
Website: www.fergusewing.com Twitter: @fergusewingmsp

FABIANI, Ms Linda *SNP* **East Kilbride**
Deputy Presiding Officer
Tel: 0131-348 5698 Fax: 0131-348 6473 Email: linda.fabiani.msp@parliament.scot
Constituency office: 1/3 Strathmore House, East Kilbride G74 1LF
Tel: 01355 232800 Fax: 01355 232770
Website: www.lindafabiani.scot Twitter: @lindafabianisnp

FEE, Ms Mary *Lab* **West Scotland**
Scottish Labour Shadow Minister for Justice
Tel: 0131-348 6391 Email: mary.fee.msp@parliament.scot
Regional office: 4 St Mirren Street, Paisley PA1 1UA
Tel: 0141-889 4828 Fax: 0141-840 2510
Website: maryfeemsp.com Twitter: @MaryFeeMSP

FINDLAY, Mr Neil *Lab* **Lothian**
Tel: 0131-348 6896 Email: neil.findlay.msp@parliament.scot
Regional office: 4 Northfield Court, West Calder EH55 8DS
Tel: 01506 873242
Website: www.neilfindlaymsp.com Twitter: @NeilFindlay_MSP

FINNIE, Mr John *Green* **Highlands and Islands**
Scottish Green Party Spokesperson for Justice, Transport, Tourism and Rural and Island Communities
Tel: 0131-348 6898 Email: john.finnie.msp@parliament.scot
Regional office: 16/22 Market Hall, Victorian Market, Inverness IV1 1PJ
Tel: 01463 710194
Website: johnfinnie.scot Twitter: @JohnFinnieHI

FitzPATRICK, Mr Joe *SNP* **Dundee City West**
Minister for Parliamentary Business
Email: joe.fitzpatrick.msp@parliament.scot
Ministerial office: Scottish Government, St Andrews House, Regent Road, Edinburgh EH1 3DG
Tel: 0300 244 4000
Constituency office: 37 Dock Street, Dundee DD1 3DR
Tel: 01382 843244
Website: www.joe.fitzpatrick.scot Twitter: @joefitzsnp

FORBES, Ms Kate *SNP* **Skye, Lochaber and Badenoch**
Parliamentary Liaison Officer to Derek Mackay as Cabinet Secretary for Finance and Constitution
Tel: 0131-348 6959 Email: kate.forbes.msp@parliament.scot
Constituency office: 12 High Street, Dingwall IV15 9RU
Tel: 01349 863888
Website: www.kateforbes.scot Twitter: @kateforbesmsp

FRASER, Mr Murdo *Con* **Mid Scotland and Fife**
Shadow Cabinet Secretary for Finance
Tel: 0131-348 5293 Email: murdo.fraser.msp@parliament.scot
Regional office: Control Tower, Perth Airport, Scone, Perth PH2 6PL
Tel: 01738 553990 Email: pkconservatives@gmail.com
Website: www.murdofraser.com Twitter: @murdo_fraser

FREEMAN, Ms Jeane *SNP* **Carrick, Cumnock and Doon Valley**
Minister for Social Security
Tel: 0131-348 6745 Email: jeane.freeman.msp@parliament.scot
Ministerial office: Scottish Government, St Andrews House, Regent Road, Edinburgh EH1 3DG
Tel: 0300 244 4000
Constituency office: 46-48 Glaisnock Street, Cumnock KA18 1BY
Tel: 01290 425876
Website: www.jeanefreeman.scot Twitter: @JeaneF1MSP

GIBSON, Mr Kenneth *SNP* **Cunninghame North**
Tel: 0131-348 6536 Fax: 0131-348 6539 Email: kenneth.gibson.msp@parliament.scot
Constituency office: 15 Main Street, Dalry KA24 5DL
Tel: 01294 833687
Website: www.kennethgibson.org

GILRUTH, Ms Jenny *SNP* **Mid Fife and Glenrothes**
Parliamentary Liaison Officer to John Swinney as Deputy First Minister and Cabinet Secretary for Education and Skills
Tel: 0131-348 5793 Email: jenny.gilruth.msp@parliament.scot
Constituency office: 12 Commercial Street, Markinch KY7 6DE
Tel: 01592 764815
Website: www.jennygilruthmsp.scot Twitter: @JennyGilruth

GOLDEN, Mr Maurice *Con* **West Scotland**
Chief Whip; Spokesperson for the Low Carbon Economy
Tel: 0131-348 6146 Email: maurice.golden.msp@parliament.scot
Regional office: 4 Kirk House, Kirk Road, Bearsden, Glasgow G61 3RG
Tel: 0141-942 4942
Website: www.mauricegolden.com Twitter: @mgoldenmsp

GOUGEON, Ms Mairi *SNP* **Angus North and Mearns**
Parliamentary Liaison Officer to Angela Constance as Cabinet Secretary for Communities, Social Security and Equalities
Tel: 0131-348 6947 Email: mairi.gougeon.msp@parliament.scot
Constituency office: 14-18 Swan Street, Brechin DD9 6EF Twitter: @MairiEvans

GRAHAME, Ms Christine *SNP* **Midlothian South, Tweeddale and Lauderdale**
Deputy Presiding Officer
Tel: 0131-348 5729 Email: christine.grahame.msp@parliament.scot
Constituency office: 46 High Street, Galashiels TD1 1SE
Tel: 01896 759575
Website: www.christinegrahame.com

GRANT, Mrs Rhoda *Lab/Co-op* **Highlands and Islands**
Scottish Labour Spokesperson for Rural Economy and Connectivity
Tel: 0131-348 5766 Email: rhoda.grant.msp@parliament.scot
Regional office: 3 Gordon Terrace, Inverness IV2 3HD
Tel: 01463 716299
Website: www.himsps.org.uk/rhodagrant Twitter: @rhodagrant

GRAY, Mr Iain *Lab* **East Lothian**
Scottish Labour Spokesperson for Education, Skills and Science
Tel: 0131-348 5839 Fax: 0131-348 6359 Email: iain.gray.msp@parliament.scot
Constituency office: Prestongrange House, West Wing, Royal Musselburgh Golf Club, Prestonpans, East Lothian EH32 9RP
Tel: 01875 818415 Email: eastlothianlabour@btconnection.com
Website: www.iaingraymsp.co.uk Twitter: @IainGrayMSP

GREENE, Mr Jamie *Con* **West Scotland**
Shadow Minister for Transport and Infrastructure
Tel: 0131-348 6137 Email: jamie.greene.msp@parliament.scot
Regional office: No regional office publicised
Website: jamiegreene.uk Twitter: @jamiegreeneuk

GREER, Mr Ross *Green* **West Scotland**
Scottish Green Party Spokesperson for International Development and External Affairs, Education and Skills and Culture and Media
Tel: 0131-348 6347 Email: ross.greer.msp@parliament.scot
Regional office: No regional office publicised Twitter: @ross_greer

GRIFFIN, Mr Mark *Lab* **Central Scotland**
Scottish Labour Shadow Minister for Social Security; Whip
Tel: 0131-348 6397 Email: mark.griffin.msp@parliament.scot
Regional office: Unit 32, Coatbridge Business Centre, 204 Main Street, Coatbridge ML5 3RB
Tel: 01236 423555
Website: www.markgriffinmsp.org.uk Twitter: @MarkGriff1n

HALCRO JOHNSTON, Mr Jamie *Con* **Highlands and Islands**
Shadow Minister for Jobs, Employability and Training
Tel: 0131-348 6140 Email: jamie.halcrojohnston.msp@parliament.scot
Regional office: Details still to be confirmed
Website: www.jamiehalcrojohnston.org.uk Twitter: @jhalcrojohnston

HAMILTON, Ms Rachael *Con* **Ettrick, Roxburgh and Berwickshire**
Shadow Cabinet Secretary for Culture and Tourism
Tel: 0131-348 6971 Email: rachael.hamilton.msp@parliament.scot
Constituency office: 25 High Street, Hawick TD9 9BU
Tel: 01450 375948
Website: www.rachaelhamilton.co.uk Twitter: @Rachael2Win

HARPER, Ms Emma *SNP* **South Scotland**
Parliamentary Liaison Officer to Fergus Ewing as Cabinet Secretary for the Rural Economy and Connectivity
Tel: 0131-348 6965 Email: emma.harper.msp@parliament.scot
Regional office: Unit 7, Loreburne Centre, High Street, Dumfries DG1 2BD
Tel: 01387 255334 Twitter: @emmasnpharper

HARRIS, Ms Alison *Con* **Central Scotland**
Shadow Minister for Tourism and Small Business
Tel: 0131-348 6152 Email: alison.harris.msp@parliament.scot
Regional office: Suite 4B, 91 Bothwell Road, Hamilton ML3 0DW
Tel: 01698 517011 Twitter: @AlisonHarrisMSP

HARVIE, Mr Patrick *Green* **Glasgow**
Co-convener, Scottish Green Party; Spokesperson for Finance, Economy, Fair Work and Equalities
Tel: 0131-348 6363 Fax: 0131-348 5972 Email: patrick.harvie.msp@parliament.scot
Regional office: 19 Argyle Court, 1103 Argyle Street, Glasgow G3 8ND
Tel: 0141-221 6999
Website: www.patrickharviemsp.com Twitter: @patrickharvie

HAUGHEY, Ms Clare *SNP* **Rutherglen**
Tel: 0131-348 5756 Email: clare.haughey.msp@parliament.scot
Constituency office: 85 Main Street, Rutherglen, Glasgow G73 2JQ
Tel: 0141-561 5131
Website: clarehaughey.scot Twitter: @haughey_clare

HEPBURN, Mr Jamie *SNP* **Cumbernauld and Kilsyth**
Minister for Employability and Training
Tel: 0131-348 6574 Fax: 0131-348 6575 Email: jamie.hepburn.msp@parliament.scot
Ministerial office: Scottish Government, St Andrews House, Regent Road, Edinburgh EH1 3DG
Tel: 0300 244 4000
Constituency office: 13 The Wynd, Cumbernauld G67 2ST
Tel: 01236 453969
Website: jamiehepburn.net Twitter: @jamiehepburn

HYSLOP, Ms Fiona *SNP* **Linlithgow**
Cabinet Secretary for Culture, Tourism and External Affairs
Tel: 0131-348 5921 Email: fiona.hyslop.msp@parliament.scot
Ministerial office: Scottish Government, St Andrews House, Regent Road, Edinburgh EH1 3DG
Tel: 0300 244 4000
Constituency office: 59 West Main Street, Whitburn, West Lothian EH47 0QD
Tel: 01501 749941 Email: allistair.tatton@parliament.scot
Website: www.fionahyslop.com Twitter: @fionahyslop

JOHNSON, Mr Daniel *Lab* **Edinburgh Southern**
Scottish Labour Shadow Minister for Education
Tel: 0131-348 6462 Email: daniel.johnson.msp@parliament.scot
Constituency office: 134 Comiston Road, Edinburgh EH10 5QN
Tel: 0131-541 2145
Website: www.danieljohnson.org.uk Twitter: @DJohnsonMSP

JOHNSTONE, Ms Alison *Green* **Lothian**
Scottish Green Party Spokesperson for Health and Sport, Social Security and Children and Young People
Tel: 0131-348 6364 Email: alison.johnstone.msp@parliament.scot
Regional office: No regional office
Website: alisonjohnstonemsp.com Twitter: @alisonjohnstone

KELLY, Mr James *Lab/Co-op* **Glasgow**
Scottish Labour Parliamentary Business Manager and Minister without Portfolio
Tel: 0131-348 6510 Fax: 0131-348 6513 Email: james.kelly.msp@parliament.scot
Regional office: Bellahouston Business Centre, 423 Paisley Road West, Glasgow G51 1PZ
Tel: 0141-465 9936 Twitter: @JamesKellyLab

KERR, Mr Liam *Con* **North East Scotland**
Shadow Cabinet Secretary for Justice
Tel: 0131-348 6973 Email: liam.kerr.msp@parliament.scot
Regional offices: 190 East High Street, Forfar, Aberdeenshire DD8 2HG
80 Rosemount Place, Aberdeen AB25 2XN
Website: www.liamkerr.org.uk Twitter: @liamkerrmsp

KIDD, Mr Bill *SNP* **Glasgow Anniesland**
SNP Chief Whip
Tel: 0131-348 5691/0131-348 6593 Email: bill.kidd.msp@parliament.scot
Constituency office: 476 Crow Road, Glasgow G11 7DR
Tel: 0141-339 3277
Website: www.billkiddmsp.org Twitter: @BillKiddSNP

LAMONT, Ms Johann *Lab/Co-op* **Glasgow**
Tel: 0131-348 5847 Email: johann.lamont.msp@parliament.scot
Regional office: Bellahouston Business Centre, 423 Paisley Road West, Glasgow G51 1PZ
Tel: 0141-465 9937 Twitter: @johannlamont

LENNON, Ms Monica *Lab* **Central Scotland**
Scottish Labour Shadow Minister for Inequality
Tel: 0131-348 6484 Email: monica.lennon.msp@parliament.scot
Regional office: No regional office publicised Twitter: @monicalennon7

LEONARD, Mr Richard *Lab* **Central Scotland**
Scottish Labour Shadow Minister for Economy
Tel: 0131-348 6465 Email: richard.leonard.msp@parliament.scot
Regional office: No regional office publicised
Website: www.richardleonard.org.uk

LINDHURST, Mr Gordon *Con* **Lothian**
Shadow Minister for Legal Affairs
Tel: 0131-348 5948 Email: gordon.lindhurst.msp@parliament.scot
Regional office: 29 Roseburn Terrace, Edinburgh EH12 5NQ
Website: www.gordonlindhurst.com Twitter: @GLindhurstMSP

LOCHHEAD, Mr Richard *SNP* **Moray**
Tel: 0131-348 5712 Fax: 0131-348 5737 Email: richard.lochhead.msp@parliament.scot
Constituency office: Office 2, Gairland Business Centre, 8 West Street, Fochabers, Moray IV32 7DJ
Tel: 01343 545077
Website: www.richardlochhead.org Twitter: @richardlochhead

LOCKHART, Mr Dean *Con* **Mid Scotland and Fife**
Shadow Cabinet Secretary for Economy, Jobs and Fair Work
Tel: 0131-348 5993 Email: dean.lockhart.msp@parliament.scot
Regional office: Canmore House, 31 Canmore Street, Dunfermline KY12 7NU
Tel: 01383 720530
Website: www.deanlockhart.org.uk Twitter: @DeanLockhartMSP

LYLE, Mr Richard *SNP* **Uddingston and Bellshill**
Tel: 0131-348 6394 Fax: 0131-348 6798 Email: richard.lyle.msp@parliament.scot
Constituency office: 188 Main Street, Bellshill, North Lanarkshire ML4 1AE
Tel: 01698 479900
Website: www.richardlylemsp.org Twitter: @richardlylesnp

McALPINE, Ms Joan *SNP* **South Scotland**
Tel: 0131-348 6885 Email: joan.mcalpine.msp@parliament.scot
Regional office: Unit 7, Loreburne Shopping Centre, High Street, Dumfries DG1 2BD
Tel: 01387 255334
Website: www.joanmcalpine.com Twitter: @joanmcalpine

McARTHUR, Mr Liam *Lib Dem* **Orkney Islands**
Scottish Liberal Democrats Spokesperson for Justice and Energy
Tel: 0131-348 5815 Fax: 0131-348 5807 Email: liam.mcarthur.msp@parliament.scot
Constituency office: 14 Palace Road, Kirkwall, Orkney KW15 1PA
Tel: 01856 876541 Fax: 01856 876162 Email: msp@msporkney.com
Website: www.liammcarthur.org.uk Twitter: @Liam4Orkney

MacDONALD, Mr Angus *SNP* **Falkirk East**
Tel: 0131-348 5489 Email: angus.macdonald.msp@parliament.scot
Constituency office: 2 York Arcade, Grangemouth FK3 8BA
Tel: 01324 482100
Website: www.angusmacdonald.info Twitter: @AngusMacDonaldSNP

MacDONALD, Mr Gordon *SNP* **Edinburgh Pentlands**
Tel: 0131-348 5741 Email: gordon.macdonald.msp@parliament.scot
Constituency office: 9 Kingsknowe Park, Edinburgh EH14 2JQ
Tel: 0131-443 0595 Twitter: @GMacdonaldSNP

MACDONALD, Mr Lewis *Lab* **North East Scotland**
Scottish Labour Spokesperson for Culture, Sport, Tourism and External Affairs
Tel: 0131-348 5915 Fax: 0131-348 5958 Email: lewis.macdonald.msp@parliament.scot
Regional office: 70 Rosemount Place, Aberdeen AB25 2XJ
Tel: 01224 646333 Fax: 01224 645450
Website: www.lewismacdonald.co.uk Twitter: @LewisMacdMSP

McDONALD, Mr Mark *SNP* **Aberdeen Donside**
Minister for Childcare and Early Years
Tel: 0131-348 6522 Email: mark.mcdonald.msp@parliament.scot
Ministerial office: Scottish Government, St Andrews House, Regent Road, Edinburgh EH1 3DG
Tel: 0300 244 4000
Constituency office: Unit 12a, Mastrick Shopping Centre, Greenfern Place, Aberdeen AB16 6JR
Tel: 01224 789457
Website: www.markmcdonald.org Twitter: @markmcdsnp

MacGREGOR, Mr Fulton *SNP* **Coatbridge and Chryston**
Parliamentary Liaison Officer to Shona Robison as Cabinet Secretary for Health and Sport
Tel: 0131-348 5797 Email: fulton.macgregor.msp@parliament.scot
Constituency office: Coatbridge Business Centre, 204 Main Street, Coatbridge ML5 3RB
Tel: 01236 897540 Twitter: @fultonsnp

MACINTOSH, Rt Hon Ken *Pres Off* **West Scotland**
Presiding Officer
Tel: 0131-348 5324/0131-348 5896 Email: ken.macintosh.msp@parliament.scot
Regional office: 1 Spiersbridge Way, Thornliebank, East Renfrewshire G46 8NG
Tel: 0141-620 6310
Website: www.kenmacintosh.scot Twitter: @KenMacintoshMSP

MACKAY, Mr Derek *SNP* **Renfrewshire North and West**
Cabinet Secretary for Finance and Constitution
Email: derek.mackay.msp@parliament.scot
Ministerial office: Scottish Government, St Andrews House, Regent Road, Edinburgh EH1 3DG
Tel: 0300 244 4000
Constituency office: 37 Hairst Street, Renfrew PA4 8QU
Tel: 0141-885 2076
Website: www.derekmackaymsp.org Twitter: @DerekMackaySNP

MACKAY, Ms Rona *SNP* **Strathkelvin and Bearsden**
Tel: 0131-348 5789 Email: rona.mackay.msp@parliament.scot
Constituency office: 78 Townhead, Kirkintilloch G82 1QS
Tel: 0141-776 1561
Website: ronamackay.scot Twitter: @ronamackaymsp

McKEE, Mr Ivan *SNP* **Glasgow Provan**
Parliamentary Liaison Officer to Keith Brown as Cabinet Secretary for the Economy, Jobs and Fair Work
Tel: 0131-348 6950 Email: ivan.mckee.msp@parliament.scot
Constituency office: 12 Hillfoot Street, Glasgow G31 2LF
Tel: 0141-556 4441
Website: www.ivanmckee.scot Twitter: @ivan_mckee

McKELVIE, Ms Christina *SNP* **Hamilton, Larkhall and Stonehouse**
Tel: 0131-348 6680 Fax: 0131-348 6683 Email: christina.mckelvie.msp@parliament.scot
Constituency office: Barncluith Business Centre, Townhead Street, Hamilton ML3 7DP
Tel: 01698 403311 Fax: 01698 403313
Website: www.christina-mckelvie.org Twitter: @christinasnp

McMILLAN, Mr Stuart *SNP* **Greenock and Inverclyde**
Tel: 0131-348 6810 Email: stuart.mcmillan.msp@parliament.scot
Constituency office: 26 Grey Place, Greenock PA15 1YF
Tel: 01475 720930
Website: www.stuartmcmillansnp.wordpress.com Twitter: @stumcmillansnp

McNEILL, Ms Pauline *Lab* **Glasgow**
Scottish Labour Shadow Minister for Community, Housing and Social Justice
Tel: 0131-348 6475 Email: pauline.mcneill.msp@parliament.scot
Regional office: Suite 1-11, Bellahouston Business Park, 423 Paisley Road West, Glasgow G51 1PZ
Tel: 0141-465 9932
Website: www.paulinemcneilldotcom.wordpress.com Twitter: @Pauline_McNeill

MACPHERSON, Mr Ben *SNP* **Edinburgh Northern and Leith**
Parliamentary Liaison Officer to Nicola Sturgeon as First Minister
Tel: 0131-348 5786 Email: ben.macpherson.msp@parliament.scot
Constituency office: 34 Constitution Street, Edinburgh EH6 6RS
Tel: 0131-600 0134
Website: www.benmacpherson.scot Twitter: @benmacpherson

MAGUIRE, Ms Ruth *SNP* **Cunninghame South**
Depute Whip
Tel: 0131-348 6953 Email: ruth.maguire.msp@parliament.scot
Constituency office: 14 Eglinton Street, Irvine KA12 8AS
Tel: 01294 276730
Website: ruthmaguire.scot Twitter: @rbfmaguire

MARRA, Ms Jenny *Lab* **North East Scotland**
Tel: 0131-348 6427 Email: jenny.marra.msp@parliament.scot
Regional office: Office 5/2, Whitehall House, 33 Yeaman Shore, Dundee DD1 4BJ
Tel: 01382 202584 Email: jenny@jennymarra.com
Website: www.jennymarra.com Twitter: @jennymarra
(currently on maternity leave)

MARTIN, Ms Gillian *SNP* **Aberdeenshire East**
Parliamentary Liaison Officer to Roseanna Cunningham as Cabinet Secretary for Environment, Climate Change and Land Reform
Tel: 0131-348 6953 Email: gillian.martin.msp@parliament.scot
Constituency office: 20-22 Market Place, Inverurie, Aberdeenshire AB51 3XN
Tel: 01467 621647
Website: missymartin.blogspot.co.uk Twitter: @GillianGMartin

MASON, Mr John *SNP* **Glasgow Shettleston**
Tel: 0141-550 4327 Email: john.mason.msp@parliament.scot
Constituency office: 1335 Gallowgate, Parkhead Cross, Glasgow G31 4DN
Tel: 0141-550 4327
Website: www.john-mason.org Twitter: @johnmasonmsp

MASON, Mr Tom *Con* **North East Scotland**
Shadow Minister for Financial Sustainability
Tel: 0131-348 6981 Email: tom.mason.msp@parliament.scot
Regional office: Details still to be confirmed Twitter: @TomMasonMSP

MATHESON, Mr Michael *SNP* **Falkirk West**
Cabinet Secretary for Justice
Email: michael.matheson.msp@parliament.scot
Ministerial office: Scottish Government, St Andrews House, Regent Road, Edinburgh EH1 3DG
Tel: 0300 244 4000
Constituency office: 15a East Bridge Street, Falkirk FK1 1YB
Tel: 01324 629271 Fax: 01324 635576 Email: andrew.maclachlan@parliament.scot
Website: michaelmatheson.org Twitter: @mathesonmichael

MITCHELL, Ms Margaret *Con* **Central Scotland**
Tel: 0131-348 5639 Email: margaret.mitchell.msp@parliament.scot
Regional office: Suite 4B, 91 Bothwell Road, Hamilton ML3 0DW
Tel: 01698 282815 Email: liz.mclean@parliament.scot
Website: www.margaretmitchellmsp.scot

MOUNTAIN, Mr Edward *Con* **Highlands and Islands**
Shadow Minister for Rural Affairs
Tel: 0131-348 6953 Email: edward.mountain.msp@parliament.scot
Regional office: No regional office publicised Twitter: @1edmountain

MUNDELL, Mr Oliver *Con* **Dumfriesshire**
Shadow Minister for Further Education, Higher Education and Science
Tel: 0131-348 5631 Email: oliver.mundell.msp@parliament.scot
Constituency office: 78 High Street, Lockerbie DG11 2EU
Tel: 01576 203910
Website: www.olivermundell.com Twitter: @olivermundell

NEIL, Mr Alex *SNP* **Airdrie and Shotts**
Tel: 0131-348 5703 Fax: 0131-348 5895 Email: alex.neil.msp@parliament.scot
Constituency office: Office 15, Airdrie Business Centre, 1 Chapel Lane, Airdrie ML6 6GX
Tel: 01236 439610 Twitter: @alexneilsnp

PATERSON, Mr Gil *SNP* **Clydebank and Milngavie**
Tel: 0131-348 6812 Fax: 0131-348 6814 Email: gil.paterson.msp@parliament.scot
Constituency office: Suite 1-6, Titan Enterprise Centre, 1 Aurora Avenue, Queens Quay, Clydebank G81 1BF
Tel: 0141-952 9677 Fax: 0141-952 9677
Website: www.gilmsp.com Twitter: @GilMPaterson

RENNIE, Mr Willie *Lib Dem* **North East Fife**
Leader, Scottish Liberal Democrats; Spokesperson for Finance
Tel: 0131-348 5803 Email: willie.rennie.msp@parliament.scot
Constituency office: G3, Granary Business Centre, Cupar, Fife KY15 5YQ
Tel: 01334 656361 Email: willie.c.rennie@gmail.com Twitter: @willie_rennie

ROBISON, Ms Shona *SNP* **Dundee City East**
Cabinet Secretary for Health and Sport
Fax: 0131-348 4017 Email: shona.robison.msp@parliament.scot
Ministerial office: Scottish Government, St Andrews House, Regent Road, Edinburgh EH1 3DG
Tel: 0300 244 4000
Constituency office: The Factory Skate Park, 15 Balunie Drive, Dundee DD4 8PS
Tel: 01382 903219 Email: dundee@shona.robison.scot
Website: www.robison.scot Twitter: @shonarobison

ROSS, Ms Gail *SNP* **Caithness, Sutherland and Ross**
Parliamentary Liaison Officer to Nicola Sturgeon as First Minister
Tel: 0131-348 5927 Email: gail.ross.msp@parliament.scot
Constituency office: 106 High Street, Invergordon, Ross-shire IV18 0DR
Tel: 01349 888255
Website: www.gailrosssnp.org Twitter: @gailrosssnp

ROWLEY, Mr Alex *Lab* **Mid Scotland and Fife**
Deputy Leader, Scottish Labour Party; Spokesperson for Community, Social Security and Equalities
Tel: 0131-348 6827 Email: alex.rowley.msp@parliament.scot
Regional office: Ore Valley Business Centre, 93 Main Street, Lochgelly KY5 9AF
Tel: 01592 786725
Website: www.alexrowley.org Twitter: @Alex_RowleyMSP

RUMBLES, Mr Mike *Lib Dem* **North East Scotland**
Scottish Liberal Democrats Spokesperson for Rural Affairs and Business Manager
Tel: 0131-348 5816 Email: mike.rumbles.msp@parliament.scot
Regional office: Bluesky Business Space, Westpoint House, Arnhall Business Park, Westhill, Aberdeenshire AB32 6FS
Tel: 01224 766959

RUSKELL, Mr Mark *Green* **Mid Scotland and Fife**
Scottish Green Party Spokesperson for Climate, Energy, Environment, Food and Farming
Tel: 0131-348 6468 Email: mark.ruskell.msp@parliament.scot
Regional office: 67a King Street, Stirling FK8 1BN
Tel: 01786 448203 Twitter: @markruskell

RUSSELL, Mr Michael *SNP* **Argyll and Bute**
Minister for UK Negotiations on Scotland's Place in Europe
Tel: 0131-348 5738 Email: michael.russell.msp@parliament.scot
Ministerial office: Scottish Government, St Andrews House, Regent Road, Edinburgh EH1 3DG
Tel: 0300 244 4000
Constituency office: 81 Argyll Street, Dunoon, Argyll PA23 7DH
Tel: 01369 702011
Website: michaelrussellmsp.scot Twitter: @feorlean

SARWAR, Mr Anas *Lab* **Glasgow**
Scottish Labour Spokesperson for Health
Tel: 0131-348 5830 Email: anas.sarwar.msp@parliament.scot
Regional office: Suite 1-11, Bellahouston Business Park, 423 Paisley Road West, Glasgow G5 1PZ
Tel: 0141-465 9933
Website: www.anassarwar.org Twitter: @AnasSarwar

SCOTT, Mr John *Con* **Ayr**
Shadow Minister for Farming
Tel: 0131-348 5664 Fax: 0131-348 5617 Email: john.scott.msp@parliament.scot
Constituency office: 17 Wellington Square, Ayr KA7 1EZ
Tel: 01292 286251 Fax: 01292 280480

SCOTT, Mr Tavish *Lib Dem* **Shetland Islands**
Scottish Liberal Democrats Spokesperson for Education and Sport
Tel: 0131-348 6296 Fax: 0131-348 5807 Email: tavish.scott.msp@parliament.scot
Constituency office: 171 Commercial Street, Lerwick, Shetland ZE1 0HX
Tel: 01595 690044 Fax: 01595 690055 Email: tscott@supanet.com
Website: www.tavishscott.com Twitter: @tavishscott

SIMPSON, Mr Graham *Con* **Central Scotland**
Shadow Minister for Housing and Communities
Tel: 0131-348 6983 Email: graham.simpson.msp@parliament.scot
Regional office: No regional office publicised
Website: grahamsimpson.yourcllr.com Twitter: @GrahamSMSP

SMITH, Ms Elaine *Lab* **Central Scotland**
Tel: 0131-348 5824 Fax: 0131-348 6942 Email: elaine.smith.msp@parliament.scot
Regional office: Unit 32, Coatbridge Business Centre, 204 Main Street, Coatbridge ML5 3RB
Tel: 01236 423555 Twitter: @elainesmithmsp

SMITH, Miss Liz *Con* **Mid Scotland and Fife**
Shadow Cabinet Secretary for Education and Skills
Tel: 0131-348 6762 Fax: 0131-348 6764 Email: elizabeth.smith.msp@parliament.scot
Regional office: Control Tower, Perth Airport, Scone, Perth PH2 6PL
Tel: 01738 553990 Fax: 01738 553967 Email: pkconservatives@gmail.com
Website: www.ospconservatives.com Twitter: @MSPliz

SMYTH, Mr Colin *Lab* **South Scotland**
Scottish Labour Shadow Minister for Health; Whip
Tel: 0131-348 6986 Email: colin.smyth.msp@parliament.scot
Regional office: 17 Buccleuch Street, Dumfries DG1 2AT
Tel: 01387 279205 Twitter: @ColinSmythMSP

SOMERVILLE, Ms Shirley-Anne *SNP* **Dunfermline**
Minister for Further Education, Higher Education and Science
Tel: 0131-348 5778 Email: shirley-anne.somerville.msp@parliament.scot
Ministerial office: Scottish Government, St Andrews House, Regent Road, Edinburgh EH1 3DG
Tel: 0300 244 4000
Constituency office: 34 Chalmers Street, Dunfermline KY12 8DF
Tel: 01383 249200 Twitter: @s_a_somerville

STEVENSON, Mr Stewart *SNP* **Banffshire and Buchan Coast**
Email: stewart.stevenson.msp@parliament.scot
Constituency office: Unit 8, Burnside Business Centre, Burnside Road, Peterhead, Aberdeenshire AB42 3AW
Tel: 01779 470444 Fax: 01779 822025 Email: msp@stewartstevenson.scot
Website: www.stewartstevenson.scot Twitter: @zsstevens

STEWART, Mr Alexander, MBE *Con* **Mid Scotland and Fife**
Shadow Minister for Local Government
Tel: 0131-348 6134 Email: alexander.stewart.msp@parliament.scot
Regional office: 31 Canmore Street, Dunfermline KY12 5NU
Tel: 01383 720530
Website: www.alexanderstewart.org.uk

STEWART, Mr David *Lab/Co-op* **Highlands and Islands**
Scottish Labour Shadow Minister for Environment, Climate Change and Land Reform
Tel: 0131-348 5766 Email: david.stewart.msp@parliament.scot
Regional office: 3 Gordon Terrace, Inverness IV2 3HD
Tel: 01463 716299 Twitter: @Davidstewartmsp

STEWART, Mr Kevin *SNP* **Aberdeen Central**
Minister for Local Government and Housing
Tel: 0131-348 6382 Email: kevin.stewart.msp@parliament.scot
Ministerial office: Scottish Government, St Andrews House, Regent Road, Edinburgh EH1 3DG
Tel: 0300 244 4000
Constituency office: Third Floor, 27 John Street, Aberdeen AB25 1BT
Tel: 01224 624719 Twitter: @KevinStewartSNP

STURGEON, Rt Hon Nicola *SNP* **Glasgow Southside**
First Minister; Leader, Scottish National Party
Tel: 0131-348 5695 Email: nicola.sturgeon.msp@parliament.scot
Ministerial office: Scottish Government, St Andrews House, Regent Road, Edinburgh EH1 3DG
Tel: 0300 244 4000
Constituency office: Unit 3, Govanhill Workspace, 69 Dixon Road, Glasgow G42 8AT
Tel: 0141-424 1174 Twitter: @nicolasturgeon

SWINNEY, Mr John *SNP* **Perthshire North**
Deputy First Minister; Cabinet Secretary for Education and Skills
Tel: 0131-348 5717 Email: john.swinney.msp@parliament.scot
Ministerial office: Scottish Government, St Andrews House, Regent Road, Edinburgh EH1 3DG
Tel: 0300 244 4000
Constituency office: 17-19 Leslie Street, Blairgowrie PH10 6AH
Tel: 01250 876576
Website: www.johnswinney.scot Twitter: @johnswinney

TODD, Ms Maree *SNP* **Highlands and Islands**
Depute Whip
Tel: 0131-348 5784 Email: maree.todd.msp@parliament.scot
Regional office: 12 High Street, Dingwall, Ross-Shire IV15 9RU
Tel: 01349 863888
Website: www.mareetodd.scot Twitter: @mareetoddsnp

TOMKINS, Prof Adam *Con* **Glasgow**
Shadow Cabinet Secretary for Communities, Social Security, Constitution and Equalities
Tel: 0131-348 5963 Email: adam.tomkins.msp@parliament.scot
Regional office: 1018 Maryhill Road, Glasgow G20 9TE Twitter: @ProfTomkins

TORRANCE, Mr David *SNP* **Kirkcaldy**
Tel: 0131-348 6892 Email: david.torrance.msp@parliament.scot
Constituency office: 53 Kirk Wynd, Kirkcaldy, Fife KY1 1EH
Tel: 01592 200349
Website: davidtorrancemsp.scot Twitter: @DavidHTorrance

WATT, Ms Maureen *SNP* **Aberdeen South and North Kincardine**
Minister for Mental Health
Tel: 0131-348 6675 Email: maureen.watt.msp@parliament.scot
Ministerial office: Scottish Government, St Andrews House, Regent Road, Edinburgh EH1 3DG
Tel: 0300 244 4000
Constituency office: 51 Victoria Road, Torry, Aberdeen AB11 9LS
Tel: 01224 876743 Twitter: @maureenSNP

WELLS, Ms Annie *Con* **Glasgow**
Shadow Minister for Mental Health, Public Health and Equalities
Tel: 0131-348 5991 Email: annie.wells.msp@parliament.scot
Regional office: 1018 Maryhill Road, Glasgow G20 9TE
Tel: 0141-945 6465 Twitter: @AnnieWellsMSP

WHEELHOUSE, Mr Paul *SNP* **South Scotland**
Minister for Business, Innovation and Energy
Tel: 0131-348 6891 Email: paul.wheelhouse.msp@parliament.scot
Ministerial office: Scottish Government, St Andrews House, Regent Road, Edinburgh EH1 3DG
Tel: 0300 244 4000
Regional office: 8 Sandbed, Hawick, Roxburghshire TD9 0HE
Tel: 01450 379572
Website: www.paul-wheelhouse.scot Twitter: @paulwheelhouse

WHITE, Ms Sandra *SNP* **Glasgow Kelvin**
Tel: 0131-348 5688 Fax: 0131-348 5945 Email: sandra.white.msp@parliament.scot
Constituency office: 1274 Argyle Street, Glasgow G3 8AA
Tel: 0141-339 7693
Website: sandrawhitemsp.scot Twitter: @sandrawhitesnp

WHITTLE, Mr Brian *Con* **South Scotland**
Shadow Minister for Health Education, Lifestyle and Sport
Tel: 0131-348 5623 Email: brian.whittle.msp@parliament.scot
Regional office: 25 Portland Road, Kilmarnock KA1 2BT
Tel: 01563 544399
Website: www.brianwhittle.org.uk Twitter: @brianwhittle

WIGHTMAN, Mr Andy *Green* **Lothian**
Scottish Green Party Spokesperson for Communities, Housing, Land Reform and Local Government
Tel: 0131-348 6368 Email: andy.wightman.msp@parliament.scot
Regional office: No regional office publicised
Website: www.andywightman.com Twitter: @andywightman

YOUSAF, Mr Humza *SNP* **Glasgow Pollok**
Minister for Transport and Islands
Tel: 0131-348 6209 Email: humza.yousaf.msp@parliament.scot
Ministerial office: Scottish Government, St Andrews House, Regent Road, Edinburgh EH1 3DG
Tel: 0300 244 4000
Constituency office: 1612-1614 Paisley Road West, Cardonald, Glasgow G52 3QN
Tel: 0141-882 4647
Website: www.humzayousaf.org Twitter: @humzayousaf

Women MSPs (46)

ADAMSON Clare	*SNP*
BAILLIE Jackie	*Lab*
BAKER Claire	*Lab*
BALLANTYNE Michelle	*Con*
BEAMISH Claudia	*Lab/Co-op*
CAMPBELL Aileen	*SNP*
CONSTANCE Angela	*SNP*
CUNNINGHAM Roseanna	*SNP*
DAVIDSON Ruth	*Con*
DENHAM Ash	*SNP*
DUGDALE Kezia	*Lab/Co-op*
EWING Annabelle	*SNP*
FABIANI Linda	*SNP*
FEE Mary	*Lab*
FORBES Kate	*SNP*
FREEMAN Jeane	*SNP*
GILRUTH Jenny	*SNP*
GOUGEON Mairi	*SNP*
GRAHAME Christine	*SNP*
GRANT Rhoda	*Lab/Co-op*
HAMILTON Rachael	*Con*
HARPER Emma	*SNP*
HARRIS Alison	*Con*
HAUGHEY Clare	*SNP*
HYSLOP Fiona	*SNP*
JOHNSTONE Alison	*Green*
LAMONT Johann	*Lab/Co-op*
LENNON Monica	*Lab*
McALPINE Joan	*SNP*
MACKAY Rona	*SNP*
McKELVIE Christina	*SNP*
McNEILL Pauline	*Lab*
MAGUIRE Ruth	*SNP*
MARRA Jenny	*Lab*
MARTIN Gillian	*SNP*
MITCHELL Margaret	*Con*
ROBISON Shona	*SNP*
ROSS Gail	*SNP*
SMITH Elaine	*Lab*
SMITH Liz	*Con*
SOMERVILLE Shirley-Anne	*SNP*
STURGEON Nicola	*SNP*
TODD Maree	*SNP*
WATT Maureen	*SNP*
WELLS Annie	*Con*
WHITE Sandra	*SNP*

Constituencies

			Majority	*%*
Aberdeen Central	Kevin Stewart	SNP	4,349	16.2
Aberdeen Donside	Mark McDonald	SNP	11,630	37.4
Aberdeen South and North Kincardine	Maureen Watt	SNP	2,755	8.48
Aberdeenshire East	Gillian Martin	SNP	5,837	16.74
Aberdeenshire West	Alexander Burnett	Con	900	2.55
Airdrie and Shotts	Alex Neil	SNP	6,192	23.21
Almond Valley	Angela Constance	SNP	8,393	23.98
Angus North and Mearns	Mairi Gougeon	SNP	2,472	8.38
Angus South	Graeme Dey	SNP	4,304	13.43
Argyll and Bute	Michael Russell	SNP	5,978	20.2
Ayr	John Scott	Con	750	1.99
Banffshire and Buchan Coast	Stewart Stevenson	SNP	6,583	22.84
Caithness, Sutherland and Ross	Gail Ross	SNP	3,913	12.1
Carrick, Cumnock and Doon Valley	Jeane Freeman	SNP	6,006	18.89
Clackmannanshire and Dunblane	Keith Brown	SNP	6,721	22.51
Clydebank and Milngavie	Gil Paterson	SNP	8,432	25.58
Clydesdale	Aileen Campbell	SNP	5,979	17.69

			Majority	*%*
Coatbridge and Chryston	Fulton MacGregor	SNP	3,779	13.3
Cowdenbeath	Annabelle Ewing	SNP	3,041	10.21
Cumbernauld and Kilsyth	Jamie Hepburn	SNP	9,478	33.37
Cunninghame North	Kenneth Gibson	SNP	8,724	27.16
Cunninghame South	Ruth Maguire	SNP	5,693	22.07
Dumbarton	Jackie Baillie	Lab	109	0.32
Dumfriesshire	Oliver Mundell	Con	1,230	3.38
Dundee City East	Shona Robison	SNP	10,898	38.18
Dundee City West	Joe FitzPatrick	SNP	8,828	31.64
Dunfermline	Shirley-Anne Somerville	SNP	4,558	13.84
East Kilbride	Linda Fabiani	SNP	10,979	31.58
Eastwood	Jackson Carlaw	Con	1,610	4.43
Edinburgh Central	Ruth Davidson	Con	610	1.78
Edinburgh Eastern	Ash Denham	SNP	5,087	14.28
Edinburgh Northern and Leith	Ben Macpherson	SNP	6,746	18.06
Edinburgh Pentlands	Gordon MacDonald	SNP	2,456	7.33
Edinburgh Southern	Daniel Johnson	Lab	1,123	2.92
Edinburgh Western	Alexander Cole-Hamilton	Lib Dem	2,960	7.42
Ettrick, Roxburgh and Berwickshire	Rachael Hamilton	Con	9,338	24.16
Falkirk East	Angus MacDonald	SNP	8,312	25.47
Falkirk West	Michael Matheson	SNP	11,280	35.03
Mid Fife and Glenrothes	Jenny Gilruth	SNP	8,276	28.92
North East Fife	Willie Rennie	Lib Dem	3,465	10.14
Galloway and West Dumfries	Finlay Carson	Con	1,514	4.53
Glasgow Anniesland	Bill Kidd	SNP	6,153	21.07
Glasgow Cathcart	James Dornan	SNP	9,390	30.47
Glasgow Kelvin	Sandra White	SNP	4,048	14.18
Glasgow Maryhill and Springburn	Bob Doris	SNP	5,602	23.59
Glasgow Pollok	Humza Yousaf	SNP	6,482	23.08
Glasgow Provan	Ivan McKee	SNP	4,783	19.73
Glasgow Shettleston	John Mason	SNP	7,323	28.71
Glasgow Southside	Nicola Sturgeon	SNP	9,593	38.09
Greenock and Inverclyde	Stuart McMillan	SNP	8,230	25.85
Hamilton, Larkhall and Stonehouse	Christina McKelvie	SNP	5,437	18.75
Inverness and Nairn	Fergus Ewing	SNP	10,857	28.17
Kilmarnock and Irvine Valley	Willie Coffey	SNP	11,194	32.45
Kirkcaldy	David Torrance	SNP	7,395	23.65
Linlithgow	Fiona Hyslop	SNP	9,335	24.22
East Lothian	Iain Gray	Lab	1,127	2.96
Midlothian North and Musselburgh	Colin Beattie	SNP	7,035	20.2
Midlothian South, Tweeddale and Lauderdale	Christine Grahame	SNP	5,868	16.42
Moray	Richard Lochhead	SNP	2,875	8.57
Motherwell and Wishaw	Clare Adamson	SNP	6,223	21.28
Na h-Eileanan an Iar	Alasdair Allan	SNP	3,496	26.36
Orkney Islands	Liam McArthur	Lib Dem	4,534	42.93
Paisley	George Adam	SNP	5,199	17.57
Perthshire North	John Swinney	SNP	3,336	9.77
Perthshire South and Kinross-shire	Roseanna Cunningham	SNP	1,422	3.92

			Majority	%
Renfrewshire North and West	Derek Mackay	SNP	7,373	23.88
Renfrewshire South	Tom Arthur	SNP	4,408	14.79
Rutherglen	Clare Haughey	SNP	3,743	11.31
Shetland Islands	Tavish Scott	Lib Dem	4,895	44.15
Skye, Lochaber and Badenoch	Kate Forbes	SNP	9,043	24.68
Stirling	Bruce Crawford	SNP	6,718	19.58
Strathkelvin and Bearsden	Rona Mackay	SNP	8,100	20.58
Uddingston and Bellshill	Richard Lyle	SNP	4,809	16.18

Regions

			Count elected on
Central Scotland	Mark Griffin	Lab	4
Central Scotland	Alison Harris	Con	7
Central Scotland	Monica Lennon	Lab	3
Central Scotland	Richard Leonard	Lab	1
Central Scotland	Margaret Mitchell	Con	2
Central Scotland	Graham Simpson	Con	5
Central Scotland	Elaine Smith	Lab	6
Glasgow	Patrick Harvie	Green	4
Glasgow	James Kelly	Lab/Co-op	5
Glasgow	Johann Lamont	Lab/Co-op	2
Glasgow	Pauline McNeill	Lab	6
Glasgow	Anas Sarwar	Lab	1
Glasgow	Adam Tomkins	Con	3
Glasgow	Annie Wells	Con	7
Highlands and Islands	Donald Cameron	Con	4
Highlands and Islands	John Finnie	Green	5
Highlands and Islands	Rhoda Grant	Lab/Co-op	2
Highlands and Islands	Jamie Halcro Johnston	Con	–
Highlands and Islands	Edward Mountain	Con	3
Highlands and Islands	David Stewart	Lab/Co-op	7
Highlands and Islands	Maree Todd	SNP	6
Lothian	Jeremy Balfour	Con	6
Lothian	Miles Briggs	Con	1
Lothian	Kezia Dugdale	Lab/Co-op	3
Lothian	Neil Findlay	Lab	5
Lothian	Alison Johnstone	Green	2
Lothian	Gordon Lindhurst	Con	4
Lothian	Andy Wightman	Green	7
Mid Scotland and Fife	Claire Baker	Lab	4
Mid Scotland and Fife	Murdo Fraser	Con	1
Mid Scotland and Fife	Dean Lockhart	Con	5
Mid Scotland and Fife	Alex Rowley	Lab	2
Mid Scotland and Fife	Mark Ruskell	Green	7
Mid Scotland and Fife	Liz Smith	Con	3
Mid Scotland and Fife	Alexander Stewart	Con	6
North East Scotland	Bill Bowman	Con	–
North East Scotland	Peter Chapman	Con	4
North East Scotland	Liam Kerr	Con	7
North East Scotland	Lewis Macdonald	Lab	5
North East Scotland	Jenny Marra	Lab	2
North East Scotland	Tom Mason	Con	–
North East Scotland	Mike Rumbles	Lib Dem	6

			Count elected on
South Scotland	Michelle Ballantyne	Con	–
South Scotland	Claudia Beamish	Lab/Co-op	1
South Scotland	Emma Harper	SNP	4
South Scotland	Joan McAlpine	SNP	2
South Scotland	Colin Smyth	Lab	5
South Scotland	Paul Wheelhouse	SNP	6
South Scotland	Brian Whittle	Con	7
West Scotland	Neil Bibby	Lab/Co-op	1
West Scotland	Maurice Corry	Con	6
West Scotland	Mary Fee	Lab	3
West Scotland	Maurice Golden	Con	4
West Scotland	Jamie Greene	Con	2
West Scotland	Ross Greer	Green	7
West Scotland	Ken Macintosh	Pres Off	5

Parliamentary Committees

Conveners Group

The Conveners Group comprises the conveners of the mandatory and subject committees of the Parliament but is not itself a Parliamentary committee

Tel: 0131-348 5202
Email: vikki.little@parliament.scot
www.scottish.parliament.uk/parliamentary business/21516.aspx

Clare Adamson *SNP*
Jackie Baillie *Lab*
Bruce Crawford *SNP*
Graeme Dey *SNP*
Bob Doris *SNP*
James Dornan *SNP*
Neil Findlay *Lab*
Christine Grahame *SNP*
Johann Lamont *Lab/Co-op*
Gordon Lindhurst *Con*
Joan McAlpine *SNP*
Christina McKelvie *SNP*
Margaret Mitchell *Con*
Edward Mountain *Con*
John Scott *Con*
Sandra White *SNP*
Staff: Susan Duffy (Clerk)

Mandatory Committees

Culture, Tourism, Europe and External Relations

Tel: 0131-348 5234
Email: europe@parliament.scot
www.parliament.scot/parliamentarybusiness/currentcommittees/european-committee.aspx
Twitter: @SP_European

Joan McAlpine (Convener) *SNP*
Lewis Macdonald (Deputy Convener) *Lab*
Jackson Carlaw *Con*
Mairi Gougeon *SNP*
Ross Greer *Green*
Rachael Hamilton *Con*
Richard Lochhead *SNP*
Stuart McMillan *SNP*
Tavish Scott *Lib Dem*
Staff: Katy Orr (Clerk)

Delegated Powers and Law Reform

Tel: 0131-348 5212
Email: dplr.committee@parliament.scot
www.parliament.scot/parliamentarybusiness/currentcommittees/delegated-powers-committee.aspx Twitter: @SP_subleg

Graham Simpson (Convener) *Con*
Stuart McMillan (Deputy Convener) *SNP*
Alison Harris *Con*
Monica Lennon *Lab*
David Torrance *SNP*
Staff: Euan Donald (Clerk)

Equalities and Human Rights

Tel: 0131-348 5223
Email: equalities.humanrights@parliament.scot
www.parliament.scot/parliamentarybusiness/currentcommittees/equalities-human-rights-committee.aspx Twitter: @SP_EHRiC

Christina McKelvie (Convener) *SNP*
Alexander Cole-Hamilton (Deputy Convener) *Lib Dem*
Mary Fee *Lab*
Jamie Greene *Con*
Gail Ross *SNP*
David Torrance *SNP*
Annie Wells *Con*
Staff: Claire Menzies (Clerk)

Finance and Constitution

Tel: 0131-348 5215
Email: finance.constitution@parliament.scot
www.parliament.scot/parliamentarybusiness/currentcommittees/finance-constitution-committee.aspx Twitter: @SP_FinCon

Bruce Crawford (Convener) *SNP*
Adam Tomkins (Deputy Convener) *Con*
Neil Bibby *Lab/Co-op*
Alexander Burnett *Con*
Willie Coffey *SNP*
Ash Denham *SNP*
Murdo Fraser *Con*
Patrick Harvie *Green*
James Kelly *Lab/Co-op*
Ivan McKee *SNP*
Maree Todd *SNP*
Staff: James Johnston (Clerk)

Public Audit and Post-Legislative Scrutiny

Tel: 0131-348 5390
Email: papls.committee@parliament.scot
www.parliament.scot/parliamentarybusiness/currentcommittees/public-audit-committee.aspx
Twitter: @SP_PAPLS

Jackie Baillie (Acting Convener) *Lab*
Jenny Marra (Convener – on maternity leave) *Lab*
Liam Kerr (Deputy Convener) *Con*
Colin Beattie *SNP*
Bill Bowman *Con*
Willie Coffey *SNP*
Monica Lennon *Lab*
Alex Neil *SNP*
Staff: Terry Shevlin (Clerk)

Public Petitions

Tel: 0131-348 5254
Email: petitions@parliament.scot
www.parliament.scot/parliamentarybusiness/currentcommittees/petitions-committee.aspx
Twitter: @sp_petitions

Johann Lamont (Convener) *Lab/Co-op*
Angus MacDonald (Deputy Convener) *SNP*
Michelle Ballantyne *Con*

Subject Committees

Economy, Jobs and Fair Work

Tel: 0131-348 5403
Email: economyjobsandfairwork@parliament.scot
www.parliament.scot/parliamentarybusiness/currentcommittees/economy-committee.aspx
Twitter: @SP_Economy

Gordon Lindhurst (Convener) *Con*
John Mason (Deputy Convener) *SNP*
Jackie Baillie *Lab*
Ash Denham *SNP*
Jamie Halcro Johnston *Con*
Richard Leonard *Lab*
Dean Lockhart *Con*
Gordon MacDonald *SNP*
Gillian Martin *SNP*
Gil Paterson *SNP*
Andy Wightman *Green*
Staff: Alison Walker (Clerk)

Education and Skills

Tel: 0131-348 6225
Email: es.committee@parliament.scot
www.parliament.scot/parliamentarybusiness/currentcommittees/education-committee.aspx
Twitter: @SP_EduSkills

James Dornan (Convener) *SNP*
Johann Lamont (Deputy Convener) *Lab/Co-op*
Colin Beattie *SNP*
Ross Greer *Green*
Clare Haughey *SNP*
Daniel Johnson *Lab*
Ruth Maguire *SNP*
Gillian Martin *SNP*
Oliver Mundell *Con*
Tavish Scott *Lib Dem*
Liz Smith *Con*
Staff: Roz Thomson (Clerk)

Rona Mackay *SNP*
Brian Whittle *Con*
Staff: Catherine Ferguson (Clerk)

Standards, Procedures and Public Appointments

Tel: 0131-348 6924
Email: sppa.committee@parliament.scot
www.parliament.scot/parliamentarybusiness/currentcommittees/standards-committee.aspx

Clare Adamson (Convener) *SNP*
Patrick Harvie (Deputy Convener) *Green*
Tom Arthur *SNP*
Jamie Halcro Johnston *Con*
Emma Harper *SNP*
Daniel Johnson *Lab*
Alexander Stewart *Con*
Staff: Dougie Wands (Clerk)

Environment, Climate Change and Land Reform

Tel: 0131-348 5240
Email: ecclr.committee@parliament.scot
www.parliament.scot/parliamentarybusiness/currentcommittees/environment-committee.aspx
Twitter: @SP_ECCLR

Graeme Dey (Convener) *SNP*
John Scott (Deputy Convener) *Con*
Claudia Beamish *Lab/Co-op*
Donald Cameron *Con*
Finlay Carson *Con*
Kate Forbes *SNP*
Emma Harper *SNP*
Richard Lyle *SNP*
Angus MacDonald *SNP*
Mark Ruskell *Green*
David Stewart *Lab/Co-op*
Staff: Lynn Tullis (Clerk)

Health and Sport

Tel: 0131-348 5210
Email: healthandsport@parliament.scot
www.parliament.scot/parliamentarybusiness/currentcommittees/health-committee.aspx
Twitter: @sp_healthsport

Neil Findlay (Convener) *Lab*
Clare Haughey (Deputy Convener) *SNP*
Tom Arthur *SNP*
Miles Briggs *Con*
Alexander Cole-Hamilton *Lib Dem*
Jenny Gilruth *SNP*
Alison Johnstone *Green*
Ivan McKee *SNP*
Colin Smyth *Lab*

Maree Todd *SNP*
Brian Whittle *Con*
Staff: David Cullum (Clerk)

Justice
Tel: 0131-348 5047
Email: justicecommittee@parliament.scot
www.parliament.scot/parliamentarybusiness/currentcommittees/justice-committee.aspx
Twitter: @SP_Justice

Margaret Mitchell (Convener) *Con*
Rona Mackay (Deputy Convener) *SNP*
Maurice Corry *Con*
Mary Fee *Lab*
John Finnie *Green*
Mairi Gougeon *SNP*
Liam Kerr *Con*
Liam McArthur *Lib Dem*
Fulton MacGregor *SNP*
Ben Macpherson *SNP*
Stewart Stevenson *SNP*
Staff: Peter McGrath (Clerk)

Justice Sub-committee on Policing
Tel: 0131-348 5220
Email: justice.committee@scottish.parliament.uk
www.scottish.parliament.uk/parliamentarybusiness/currentcommittees/61065.aspx

Mary Fee (Convener) *Lab*
Margaret Mitchell (Deputy Convener) *Con*
John Finnie *Green*
Liam McArthur *Lib Dem*
Rona Mackay *SNP*
Ben Macpherson *SNP*
Stewart Stevenson *SNP*
Staff: Diane Barr (Clerk)

Local Government and Communities
Tel: 0131-348 6037
Email: lgccommittee@parliament.scot
www.parliament.scot/parliamentarybusiness/currentcommittees/local-govt-committee.aspx
Twitter: @SP_LocalGovt

Bob Doris (Convener) *SNP*
Elaine Smith (Deputy Convener) *Lab*
Kenneth Gibson *SNP*
Jenny Gilruth *SNP*
Graham Simpson *Con*
Alexander Stewart *Con*
Andy Wightman *Green*
Staff: Jane Williams (Clerk)

Rural Economy and Connectivity
Tel: 0131-348 5211
Email: rec.committee@parliament.scot
www.parliament.scot/parliamentarybusiness/currentcommittees/rural-committee.aspx
Twitter: @SP_RECcttee

Edward Mountain (Convener) *Con*
Gail Ross (Deputy Convener) *SNP*
Peter Chapman *Con*
John Finnie *Green*
Rhoda Grant *Lab/Co-op*
Jamie Greene *Con*
Richard Lyle *SNP*
Fulton MacGregor *SNP*
John Mason *SNP*
Mike Rumbles *Lib Dem*
Stewart Stevenson *SNP*
Staff: Steve Farrell (Clerk)

Social Security
Tel: 0131-348 5228
Email: socialsecuritycommittee@parliament.scot
www.parliament.scot/parliamentarybusiness/currentcommittees/social-security-committee.aspx Twitter: @SP_SocialSecur

Sandra White (Convener) *SNP*
Pauline McNeill (Deputy Convener) *Lab*
George Adam *SNP*
Jeremy Balfour *Con*
Mark Griffin *Lab*
Alison Johnstone *Green*
Ben Macpherson *SNP*
Ruth Maguire *SNP*
Adam Tomkins *Con*
Staff: Simon Watkins (Clerk)

Scottish Commission for Public Audit
The Scottish Commission for Public Audit is not formally a parliamentary committee. The Commission was established under section 12 of the Public Finance and Accountability (Scotland) Act 2000 and is made up of five MSPs.
Tel: 0131-348 6526 Email: scpa@parliament.scot
www.scottish.parliament.uk/parliamentarybusiness/1704.aspx

Colin Beattie (Convener) *SNP*
Bill Bowman *Con*
Alison Johnstone *Green*
Rona Mackay *SNP*
Staff: Stephen Herbert (Secretary)

Principal Officers and Officials

Office of the Presiding Officer

Presiding Officer Rt Hon **Ken Macintosh** MSP

Principal Private Secretary Joanne McNaughton 0131-348 5302
Email: joanne.mcnaughton@parliament.scot

Deputy Presiding Officers **Linda Fabiani** MSP (SNP), **Christine Grahame** MSP (SNP)

Scottish Parliamentary Corporate Body

(responsible for administration)

Chair Rt Hon Ken Macintosh (Pres Off)
Members Jackson Carlaw (Con)
Liam McArthur (Lib Dem)
Gordon MacDonald (SNP)
David Stewart (Lab/Co-op)
Andy Wightman (Green)

Secretariat

Officer Judith Proudfoot 0131-348 5307
Email: judith.proudfoot@parliament.scot

Parliamentary Bureau

(responsible for all-party business programme and forward planning)

Chair Rt Hon Ken Macintosh (Pres Off)
Members Joe FitzPatrick (SNP)
Maurice Golden (Con)
Patrick Harvie (Green)
James Kelly (Lab/Co-op)
Mike Rumbles (Lib Dem)

Leadership Group

Clerk/Chief Executive Sir Paul Grice 0131-348 5255
Email: paul.grice@parliament.scot

Head, Legal Services, Procurement and Audit Judith Morrison 0131-348 6649
Email: judith.morrison@parliament.scot

Assistant Clerks/Chief Executives Michelle Hegarty 0131-348 6070
Email: michelle.hegarty@parliament.scot
Ken Hughes 0131-348 5168
Email: ken.hughes@parliament.scot
David McGill 0131-348 5161
Email: david.mcgill@parliament.scot

Heads

Digital Services Alan Balharrie 0131-348 6535
Email: alan.balharrie@parliament.scot

Human Resources and Facilities Management Colin Chisholm 0131-348 6630
Email: colin.chisholm@parliament.scot

Finance and Security Derek Croll 0131-348 6819
Email: derek.croll@parliament.scot

Research, Communications and Public Engagement Callum Thomson 0131-348 5253
Email: callum.thomson@parliament.scot

Committees and Outreach Susan Duffy 0131-348 5201
Email: susan.duffy@parliament.scot

Chamber, Reporting and Broadcasting Tracey White 0131-348 5173
Email: tracey.white@parliament.scot

Scottish Government Civil Service

Permanent Secretary's Office
St Andrew's House, Regent Road, Edinburgh EH1 3DG
Tel: 0131-556 8400/0845 774 1741
Email: ceu@gov.scot Website: www.gov.scot Twitter: @PermSecScot
Permanent Secretary: Leslie Evans 0131-244 5148 Email: permanentsecretary@gov.scot

Constitution and External Affairs Directorate-General
St Andrew's House, Regent Road, Edinburgh EH1 3DG
Tel: 0131-244 0170
Director-General: Ken Thomson 0131-244 6923 Email: dgcea@gov.scot

Economy Directorate-General
St Andrew's House, Regent Road, Edinburgh EH1 3DG
Email: dgeconomy@gov.scot
Director-General: Liz Ditchburn Email: dgeconomy@gov.scot

Education, Communities and Justice Directorate-General
St Andrew's House, Regent Road, Edinburgh EH1 3DG
Tel: 0131-244 2814 Twitter: @PaulJScotGov
Director-General: Paul Johnston 0131-244 2835 Email: dgecj@scot.gov

Finance Directorate-General
Victoria Quay, Edinburgh EH6 6QQ
Tel: 0131-244 4000
Email: dgfinance@gov.scot
Director-General: Alyson Stafford CBE 0131-244 5692 Email: dgfinance@gov.scot

Health and Social Care Directorate-General
St Andrew's House, Regent Road, Edinburgh EH1 3DG
Tel: 0131-244 2790
Email: dghsc@gov.scot Website: www.gov.scot Twitter: @scotgovhealth
Director-General: Paul Gray 0131-244 2790 Email: paul.gray@gov.scot

Organisational Development and Operations Directorate-General
St Andrews House, Edinburgh EH1 3DG
Tel: 0131-244 6021
Email: dgodo@gov.scot Twitter: @SPDA
Director-General: Sarah Davidson 0131-244 6021 Email: dgodo@gov.scot

Crown Office and Procurator Fiscal Service
25 Chambers Street, Edinburgh, Midlothian EH1 1LA
Tel: 01389 739557 Fax: 0844 561 4069
Email: enquirypoint@copfs.gsi.gov.uk Website: www.copfs.gov.uk
Lord Advocate: Rt Hon James Wolffe QC 0131-243 3108 Email: lordadvocate@gov.scot
Solicitor General for Scotland: Alison di Rollo QC 0131-243 3110 Email: solicitorgeneral@gov.scot
Crown Agent and Chief Executive: David Harvie 0131-243 3399
Email: pscrownagent@copfs.gsi.gov.uk

Executive Agencies

Accountant in Bankruptcy

1 Pennyburn Road, Kilwinning, Ayrshire KA13 6SA
Tel: 0300 200 2600 Fax: 0300 200 2601
Email: aib@aib.gsi.gov.uk Website: www.aib.gov.uk Twitter: @AiB_updates

Number of staff: 145

Chief Executive: Dr Richard Dennis 0300 200 2900 Email: ce@aib.gsi.gov.uk

Sponsored by: Economy Directorate-General, Scottish Government

Disclosure Scotland

1 Pacific Quay, Glasgow G51 1DZ
Tel: 0300 020 0040 Email: info@disclosurescotland.co.uk
Website: www.mygov.scot/organisations/disclosure-scotland/ Twitter: @disclosurescot

PO Box 250, Glasgow G51 1YU

Number of staff: 322

Chief Executive: Lorna Gibbs Email: dsadmin@disclosurescotland.gsi.gov.uk

Sponsored by: Education, Communities and Justice Directorate-General, Scottish Government

Education Scotland

Denholm House, Almondvale Business Park, Almondvale Way, Livingston EH54 6GA
Tel: 0131-244 4330 Email: enquiries@educationscotland.gov.gsi.uk
Website: www.education.gov.scot Twitter: @EducationScot

Number of staff: 310

Interim Chief Executive: Karen Reid

Sponsored by: Education, Communities and Justice Directorate-General, Scottish Government

Scottish Prison Service

Calton House, 5 Redheughs Rigg, Edinburgh, Lothian EH12 9HW
Tel: 0131-330 3500
Email: gaolinfo@sps.pnn.gov.uk Website: www.sps.gov.uk

Number of staff: 4,563

Chief Executive: Colin McConnell 0131-330 3601 Email: sharon.lawson@sps.pnn.gov.uk

Sponsored by: Education, Communities and Justice Directorate-General, Scottish Government

Scottish Public Pensions Agency

7 Tweedside Park, Tweedbank, Galashiels TD1 3TE
Tel: 01896 893000 Fax: 01896 893214
Website: www.sppa.gov.uk

Number of staff: 297

Chief Executive: Penelope Cooper 01896 893232 Email: sppachiefexecutive@gov.scot

Sponsored by: Finance Directorate-General, Scottish Government

Student Awards Agency Scotland

Saughton House, Broomhouse Drive, Edinburgh EH11 3UT
Tel: 0300 555 0505
Email: saasce@gov.scot Website: www.saas.gov.uk Twitter: @saastweet

Number of staff: 284

Chief Executive: Paul Lowe 0131-244 5867 Email: saasce@gov.scot

Transport Scotland
Buchanan House, 58 Port Dundas Road, Glasgow G4 0HF
Tel: 0141-272 7100
Email: info@transport.gov.scot Website: www.transport.gov.scot Twitter: @transcotland
Number of staff: 385
Chief Executive: Roy Brannen 0141-272 7110 Email: chiefexecutive@transport.gov.scot
Sponsored by: Economy Directorate-General, Scottish Government

Non-Ministerial Departments

Food Standards Scotland
4th Floor, Pilgrim House, Aberdeen AB11 5RL
Tel: 01224 285100
Email: enquiries@fss.scot Website: foodstandards.gov.scot Twitter: @fsscot
Number of staff: 184
Chief Executive: Geoff Ogle Email: geoff.ogle@fss.scot
Chair: Ross Finnie Email: ross.finnie@fss.scot

National Records of Scotland
HM General Register House, 2 Princes Street, Edinburgh EH1 3YY
Tel: 0131-535 1314
Email: rg-keeper@nrscotland.gov.uk Website: www.nrscotland.gov.uk Twitter: @NatRecordsScot
Ladywell House, Ladywell Road, Edinburgh EH12 7TF
Tel: 0131-334 0380
Number of staff: 397
Registrar General for Scotland and Keeper of the Records of Scotland: Tim Ellis 0131-535 1312
Email: rg-keeper@nrscotland.gov.uk

Registers of Scotland
Meadowbank House, 153 London Road, Edinburgh EH8 7AU
Tel: 0800 169 9391 Fax: 0131-479 3688
Email: customer.services@ros.gov.uk Website: www.ros.gov.uk Twitter: @registersofscot
Number of staff: 1,014
Keeper of the Registers of Scotland and Chief Executive: Sheenagh Adams 0131-659 6111 ext 3299
Email: sheenagh.adams@ros.gov.uk

Revenue Scotland
PO Box 24068, Victoria Quay, Edinburgh EH6 9BR
Tel: 030 0020 0310
Email: info@revenue.scot Website: www.revenue.scot Twitter: @revenuescotland
Number of staff: 57
Chair: Dr Keith Nicholson
Chief Executive: Elaine Lorimer 030 0020 0310 Email: info@revenue.scot

Office of the Scottish Charity Regulator
Second Floor, Quadrant House, 9 Riverside Drive, Dundee DD1 4NY
Tel: 01382 220446 Fax: 01382 220314
Email: info@oscr.org.uk Website: www.oscr.org.uk Twitter: @ScotCharityReg
Number of staff: 54
Chair: Very Rev Dr Graham Forbes CBE
Chief Executive: David Robb 01382 346868 Email: david.robb@oscr.org.uk

Scottish Courts and Tribunal Service

Saughton House, Broomhouse Drive, Edinburgh, Midlothian EH11 3XD
Tel: 0131-444 3352 Fax: 0131-443 2610
Email: enquiries@scotcourts.gov.uk Website: www.scotcourts.gov.uk Twitter: @SCTScourtstribs

Number of staff: 1,733

Chair: Rt Hon Lord Colin Carloway
Chief Executive: Eric McQueen 0131-244 3306 Email: emcqueen@scotcourts.gov.uk

Scottish Fiscal Commission

Governor's House, Regent Road, Edinburgh EH1 3DE
Email: info@fiscalcommission.scot Website: www.fiscalcommission.scot Twitter: @scotfisccomm

Number of staff: 19

Chair: Lady Susan Rice CBE 01312 440738 Email: susan.rice@fiscalcommission.scot
Chief Executive: John Ireland 01312 440738 Email: john.ireland@fiscalcommission.scot

Scottish Housing Regulator

Buchanan House, 58 Port Dundas Road, Glasgow G4 0HF
Tel: 0141-242 5642 Email: shr@scottishhousingregulator.gsi.gov.uk
Website: www.scottishhousingregulator.gov.uk Twitter: @SHR_news

Number of staff: 49

Chief Executive: Michael Cameron 0141-242 5565
Email: sharon.campbell@scottishhousingregulator.gsi.gov.uk
Chair: George Walker 0141-242 5642 Email: shr@scottishhousingregulator.gsi.gov.uk

Political Parties

Scottish National Party

Gordon Lamb House, 3 Jackson's Entry, Edinburgh EH8 8PJ
Tel: 0800 633 5432 Fax: 0131-525 8901
Email: info@snp.org Website: www.snp.org Twitter: @theSNP

Leader: Nicola Sturgeon MSP
Depute Leader: Angus Robertson
President: Ian Hudghton MEP
Chief Executive: Peter Murrell 0131-525 8900 Email: peter.murrell@snp.org

Scottish Conservative and Unionist Party

67 Northumberland Street, Edinburgh EH3 6JG
Tel: 0131-524 0030 Website: www.scottishconservatives.com Twitter: @scottories

Leader: Ruth Davidson MSP
Chairman: Robert Forman MBE
Conference Convener: Richard Wilkinson
Director: Lord McInnes of Kilwinning CBE
Treasurer: Bryan Johnston
Director of Strategy and Communications: Eddie Barnes

Scottish Labour

290 Bath Street, Glasgow G2 4RE
Tel: 0141-572 6900
Email: scotland@labour.org.uk Website: www.scottishlabour.org.uk Twitter: @scottishlabour

Acting Leader: Alex Rowley MSP (The new leader will be announced 18 November 2017)
Deputy Leader: Alex Rowley MSP
Chair: Linda Stewart
General Secretary: Brian Roy 0141-572 6900

Scottish Green Party

Bonnington Mill, 72 Newhaven Road, Edinburgh EH6 5QG
Tel: 0870 077 2207
Email: office@scottishgreens.org.uk Website: greens.scot Twitter: @scotgp
Co-conveners: Maggie Chapman, Patrick Harvie MSP
Head of Media: Jason Rose 0131-348 6360 Email: press@scottish.parliament.uk
Senior Party Administrator: Scott Lamb Email: scott@scottishgreens.org.uk
Operations Manager: Pete Morrison Email: ops.manager@scottishgreens.org.uk
Finance Officer: Louise Jaundrell Email: finance@scottishgreens.org.uk

Scottish Liberal Democrats

4 Clifton Terrace, Edinburgh EH12 5DR
Tel: 0131-337 2314
Email: hq@scotlibdems.org.uk Website: www.scotlibdems.org.uk Twitter: @scotlibdems
Leader: Willie Rennie MSP
Deputy Leader: Alistair Carmichael MP
President: Eileen McCartin MBE
Party Manager: Linda Wilson 0131-337 2314 Email: linda.wilson@scotlibdems.org.uk
Chief of Staff, Scottish Parliament: Matthew Clark 0131-348 5818
Email: matthew.clark@parliament.scot
Press Officer: Tim Hustler 0131-348 5812 Email: tim.hustler@parliament.scot

Welsh Government

Llywodraeth Cymru

Welsh Government, Fifth Floor, Tŷ Hywel, Cardiff Bay CF99 1NA
Switchboard: 0300 060 3300 Email: customerhelp@wales.gsi.gov.uk
Website: www.gov.wales Twitter: @WelshGovernment

Cabinet

First Minister	Rt Hon **Carwyn Jones** (Lab)
Cabinet Secretary for Economy and Infrastructure	**Ken Skates** (Lab)
Cabinet Secretary for Health, Wellbeing and Sport	**Vaughan Gething** (Lab/Co-op)
Cabinet Secretary for Finance and Local Government	**Mark Drakeford** (Lab)
Cabinet Secretary for Education	**Kirsty Williams** CBE (Lib Dem)
Cabinet Secretary for Environment and Rural Affairs	**Lesley Griffiths** (Lab)
Cabinet Secretary for Communities and Children	**Carl Sargeant** (Lab)
Leader of the House and Chief Whip	**Jane Hutt** (Lab)

Also attending Cabinet
Counsel General — **Mick Antoniw** (Lab/Co-op)

Ministerial Responsibilities and Staff

Office of the First Minister

First Minister Rt Hon **Carwyn Jones** AM (Lab)

Exercise of functions by the Welsh Government; constitutional affairs; strategic and corporate planning in the Welsh Government; strategic communications; legislative programme; policy development and co-ordination of policy; international affairs, including strategic direction on EU withdrawal, international relations and Welsh Government presence abroad; overall responsibility for openness in Government, including Freedom of Information; civil contingencies, including chairing the Wales Resilience Forum; oversight of the Welsh Government's relationship with the Wales Audit Office; staffing, including the terms and conditions of Special Advisers and Welsh Government civil servants, but not members of the Senior Civil Service; overall responsibility for public appointments; Ministerial Code; tribunals.

Special Adviser	Matt Greenough Email: matt.greenough@gov.wales	0300 025 8690
Principal Private Secretary	Desmond Clifford Email: desmond.clifford@gov.wales	0300 025 7765 Fax: 0300 025 1879
Senior Private Secretary	Rose Stewart Email: ps.firstminister@gov.wales	0300 025 8764 Fax: 0300 025 1879

Economy and Infrastructure

Cabinet Secretary for Economy and Infrastructure **Ken Skates** AM (Lab)

Support and advice to assist the establishment, growth, modernisation or development of business in Wales; promotion of Wales as a location for business and investment; promotion of Welsh exports; entrepreneurship, enterprise and business information; Finance Wales, Development Bank, Steel; environmental improvements in relation to industrial and commercial developments; economic advisory panels; social enterprise and the social economy; property assets held with the Economy Development portfolio and supporting the delivery of property infrastructure (sites and premises);

National Infrastructure Commission; transport; road safety; road transport; rail services; funding of programmes to local authorities and bodies delivering transport services; ports; Welsh tourism; major events; elite sports; historic environment and culture in Wales; National Botanic Garden of Wales; Creative Wales; cultural property legislation and tax relief; lottery funding.

Special Adviser	Andrew Johnson Email: andrew.johnson@gov.wales	0300 025 8673
Private Secretary	Janine Boyer-Day Email: ps.cabsececonandi@gov.wales	0300 025 8768

Health, Wellbeing and Sport

Cabinet Secretary for Health, Wellbeing and Sport **Vaughan Gething** AM (Lab/Co-op)

Ooversight of all aspects of NHS delivery and performance in Wales, including performance against NHS Outcomes and Delivery Framework targets; all aspects of the NHS in Wales other than other than oversight of the medical professions, policy on surrogacy, xenotransplantation, embryology and human genetics and licensing of medicines; delivery of the new outcome measures; scrutiny of NHS organisations' performance against their 3-year plans; oversight of the escalation procedures in the NHS; charges for NHS services; provision of services to the mentally ill; receipt of, response to and direction of reports from, the Health Care Inspectorate for Wales; oversight of the Wales Audit Office's activities so far as relating to the NHS in Wales; research and development in health and social care; post-graduate medical education.

Special Adviser	Jane Runeckles Email: jane.runeckles@gov.wales	0300 025 8611
Senior Private Secretary	Rory Powell Email: ps.cabsechealthwands@gov.wales	0300 025 8386

Minister for Social Services and Public Health **Rebecca Evans** AM (Lab/Co-op)

Policy and oversight of the provision of all social services activities of local authorities in Wales; care in the community; Care Council for Wales; regulation of residential, domiciliary, adult placements, foster care, under eight's care provision and private healthcare; inspection of, and reporting on, the provision of social services by local authorities in Wales; Older People's Commissioner for Wales; Public Health Wales Bill; public health and health protection; food safety and drinking water; community sport, physical activity and active recreation; promotion of walking and cycling; GM food, excluding cultivation of crops; prison health service; substance misuse; armed forces and veterans' health.

Private Secretary	Ruth Parness Email: ps.minssandph@gov.wales	0300 025 8631

Finance and Local Government

Cabinet Secretary for Finance and Local Government **Mark Drakeford** AM (Lab)

Provision of strategic financial direction and management of the resources of the Welsh Government; development of a Welsh Treasury; tax policy including local taxes; administration and operation for taxes; publication and consultation on the Welsh Government's budget proposals; strategic investment decisions in line with the Wales Infrastructure Investment Plan; Invest to Save Fund; City Deals; oversight of financial accounting and audit; budget monitoring and management; value for money and effectiveness of governmental spend; devolved funding settlement and the Statement of Funding Policy; Value Wales and the National Procurement Service; oversight and implementation of the Well-being of Future Generations (Wales) Act; co-ordination of National Statistics and Census in Wales; EU structural funds, related programmes except the CAP; reform of local authorities; Local Government Partnership Council; Local government constitutional matters, scrutiny arrangements, cabinets, elected mayors, role of councillors, diversity, conduct and remuneration; local government elections; local government finance policy; council tax, non-domestic rates and council tax reduction; sponsorship of the Valuation Office Agency and the Valuation Tribunal Service.

Special Advisers

Finance	Madeleine Brindley Email: madeleine.brindley@gov.wales	0300 025 8965
Local Government	Alex Rawlin Email: alex.rawlin@gov.wales	0300 025 8591
Europe	Gareth Williams Email: gareth.williams32@gov.wales	0300 025 8577
Senior Private Secretary	Rebecca Lewis Email: ps.cabsecfinanceandlg@gov.wales	0300 025 8467

Education

Cabinet Secretary for Education **Kirsty Williams** CBE AM (Lib Dem)

School governance, organisation and admissions; school standards, improvement and pupil attainment; Estyn work programme; school funding; curriculum, assessment and qualifications; safeguarding and inclusion in schools; bilingual education; complaints against Local Education Authorities and school governing bodies; 21st Century Schools and Education programme; Schools Challenge Cymru; Qualifications Wales; higher education policy, strategy and funding; education workforce training and development; teacher training; medical education.

Special Adviser	Tom Woodward Email: tom.woodward@gov.wales	0300 025 8141
Senior Private Secretary	Helen Childs Email: ps.cabseceducation@gov.wales	0300 025 8783

Minister for Lifelong Learning and Welsh Language **Alun Davies** AM (Lab/Co-op)

Early years; foundation phase; additional learning needs; dyslexia at all ages; Additional Learning Needs Bills; further education; further education student support, Education Maintenance Allowance and Welsh Government Learning Grant; revenue funding of sixth forms, further education colleges and adult community learning; Digital Learning Strategy; Welsh medium and bilingual education; Welsh language; vocational, key and essential skills qualifications for all ages; Credit and Qualifications Framework for Wales; prisoner learning; broadcasting policy; youth work policy.

Private Secretary	Matthew Mithan Email: ps.minllandwl@gov.wales	0300 025 8717

Minister for Skills and Science **Julie James** AM (Lab)

Apprenticeship and Skillbuild; youth and adult employability policy and delivery; work-based learning providers; sector skills; Wales Employment and Skills Board and Commission for Employment and Skills; workforce skills development; core funding for Chwarae Teg; European Structural Funds relating to skills and employment; simplification and integration of business skills and business development services; development of science policy; research and innovation; development, retention and attraction of higher level research students; maximisation of economic benefits of higher education research and development; digital infrastructure, including broadband and mobile; digital service transformation for the Welsh public sector; digital inclusion; careers advice.

Private Secretary	Kate Bacon Email: ps.minskillsands@gov.wales	0300 025 8769

Environment and Rural Affairs

Cabinet Secretary for Environment and Rural Affairs **Lesley Griffiths** AM (Lab)

Strategy and policy for Natural Resources Management; overseeing Environment (Wales) Act and Natural Resources Wales; cross-cutting measures of mitigation and adaptation in relation to climate change; strategy and policy for water; sustainable resource and waste management; energy policy; reduction of fuel poverty; access to the countryside, coast and rights of way and Areas of Outstanding Natural Beauty and National Parks; biodiversity; forestry; inland, coastal and sea fisheries; Common Fisheries Policy; marine and fresh water planning, biodiversity, conservation and licensing; oversight and implementation of the

Planning Acts; planning policy; Developments of National Significance; building regulations; Wales Spatial Plan and National Development Framework; allotments and urban green infrastructure; local environment quality; Rural Development Programme; Common Agricultural Policy; agriculture development; agri-food sector development; animal health and welfare; Bovine TB Eradication Plan; livestock policy; Holding Registration Policy; protection and management of wildlife; GM crops; crop price information provision; Best and Most Versatile Land policy and mineral site restoration advice; Agricultural Land Classification and implementation of the EIA (Agriculture) Regulations.

Special Adviser	Alex Rawlin Email: alex.rawlin@gov.wales	0300 025 8591
Private Secretary	Mandy Lewis Email: ps.cabsecenvandra@gov.wales	029 2089 8453

Communities and Children

Cabinet Secretary for Communities and Children **Carl Sargeant** AM (Lab)

Children's and young people's rights and entitlements; childcare; legislation relating to the removal of the offence of Reasonable Chastisement; Flying Start; Families First; adoption and fostering; children and young people's advocacy; information sharing under Children Act 2004; CAFCASS; Communities First; welfare reform; financial inclusion; regeneration; housing activities of Local Authorities and housing associations; allocation of housing; supply and quality of market, social and affordable housing; homelessness and housing support, excluding Housing Benefit payment; private rentals; aids and adaptations; co-ordination of issues relating to Gypsies and Travellers, asylum-seekers, immigration, migrant workers and community cohesion; crime and justice policy; community safety; fire and rescue; armed forces and veterans; volunteering; Post Office and Royal Mail; anti-slavery, domestic abuse, gender-based violence and sexual violence; equalities (covering the protected characteristics under the Equality Act 2010) and human rights in relation to UN and EU Conventions

Special Adviser	David Costa Email: david.costa@gov.wales	029 2089 8496
Senior Private Secretary	Imelda Francombe Email: ps.cabseccommsandc@gov.wales	0300 025 9107

Leader of the House

Leader of the House and Chief Whip **Jane Hutt** AM (Lab)

Managing Government Business in the Assembly in line with Standing Orders; delivery of the weekly Business Statement; represents the Government in the Business Committee; liaison with other Parties on the Government's Legislative Programme, but not individual Bills which remain the responsibility of the lead Cabinet Secretary.

Private Secretary	Mandy Williams Email: ps.leaderofhouseandcw@gov.wales	0300 025 8774

Counsel General

Counsel General **Mick Antoniw** AM (Lab/Co-op)

Provide legal advice to the government; oversee the work of the Legal Services Department which provides legal services to the Welsh Government; oversee prosecutions on behalf of the Welsh Government; oversee representation of the Welsh Government in the courts; consider whether bills passed by the Assembly need to be referred to the Supreme Court for determination as to whether they are within the Assembly's competence; answer questions about his work in the Assembly; perform other functions in the public interest including, where the Counsel General considers it appropriate, institute, defend or appear in any legal proceedings relating to functions of the Welsh Government.

Senior Private Secretary	David Rich Email: pscounselgeneral@gov.wales	0300 025 8767

Opposition

Plaid Cymru

Leader	**Leanne Wood**
Shadow Cabinet Secretary for Health and Social Care	**Rhun ap Iorwerth**
Shadow Cabinet Secretary for Education, Children, Skills and Lifelong Learning	**Llyr Gruffydd**
Shadow Cabinet Secretary for Business, Economy and Finance	**Adam Price**
Shadow Cabinet Secretary for Sustainable Communities, Energy and Rural Affairs	**Simon Thomas**
Shadow Cabinet Secretary for Local Government, Welsh Language, Equalities and Planning	**Siân Gwenllian**
Shadow Cabinet Secretary for Housing, Poverty, Communities and Steel	**Bethan Jenkins**
Shadow Cabinet Secretary for Sports and Tourism	**To be appointed**
Shadow Cabinet Secretary for Culture and Infrastructure; Chair, Assembly Group	**Dr Dai Lloyd**
Shadow Cabinet Secretary for External Affairs, Non-Devolved Matters, Police, Criminal Justice System and Social Protection	**Steffan Lewis**

Welsh Conservatives

Leader, Welsh Conservatives in the National Assembly	**Andrew R T Davies**
Deputy Leader, Welsh Conservatives in the National Assembly; Chief Whip; Group Business Manager; Spokesperson for Rural Affairs	**Paul Davies**
Spokesperson for Skills	**Mohammad Asghar**
Spokesperson for Health; Campaigns Director	**Angela Burns**
Spokesperson for Social Services and Older People's Champion, Welsh Language, Swansea Bay City Deal and Broadcasting	**Suzy Davies**
Spokesperson for Local Government	**Janet Finch-Saunders**
Spokesperson for Economy, Transport and Sport	**Russell George**
Spokesperson for Communities, Europe and North Wales Growth Deal	**Mark Isherwood**
Spokesperson for Environment and Sustainability, Planning, Housing and Wales Bill	**David Melding**
Spokesperson for Education and Children; Policy Director	**Darren Millar**
Spokesperson for Finance	**Nick Ramsay**

UK Independence Party

Leader, Assembly Group; Spokesperson for for Culture, Finance, Agriculture and Environment	**Neil Hamilton**
Spokesperson for Health and Social Care	**Caroline Jones**
Spokesperson for Local Government, Housing, Communities and Sport; Business Manager	**Gareth Bennett**
Spokesperson for Education, Childcare and Training	**Michelle Brown**
Spokesperson for Transport, Infrastructure and Skills	**David Rowlands**

National Assembly for Wales (Cynulliad Cenedlaethol Cymru)

Cardiff Bay, Cardiff CF99 1NA
Tel: 0300 200 6565
Email: contact@assembly.wales Website: www.assembly.wales Twitter: @assemblywales

Members (AMs)

State of the Parties (October 2017)

	Constituency	*Regional*	*Total*
Labour (includes Labour/Co-operative Party)	27*	2	29
Conservative	6	5	11
Plaid Cymru	4†	5	9
UK Independence Party	0	5	5
Independent	1	3	4
Liberal Democrat	1	0	1
Presiding Officer	1	0	1
	40	20	60 seats

*Includes a Deputy Presiding Officer who can participate and vote fully in the Assembly when not in the chair.
†Excludes the Presiding Officer who has no party allegiance while in post.

Changes since 2016 National Assembly for Wales election

CHANGE OF PARTY

Nathan Gill	North Wales	Left UKIP Assembly group August 2016, now Independent
Dafydd Elis-Thomas	Dwyfor Meirionnydd	Left Plaid Cymru October 2016, now Independent
Mark Reckless	South Wales East	Left UK Independence Party April 2017, now Independent
Neil McEvoy	South Wales Central	Left Plaid Cymru September 2017, now Independent

AMs' Directory

Con	Conservative
Ind	Independent
Lab	Labour
Lab/Co-op	Labour/Co-operative
Lib Dem	Liberal Democrat
PlC	Plaid Cymru
Pres Off	Presiding Officer
UKIP	UK Independence Party

ANTONIW, Mr Mick *Lab/Co-op* **Pontypridd**
Counsel General
Tel: 0300 200 7116 Email: mick.antoniw@assembly.wales
Ministerial office: Welsh Government, Fifth Floor, Tŷ Hywel, Cardiff Bay CF99 1NA
Tel: 0300 060 4400
Constituency office: 10 Market Street, Pontypridd CF37 2ST
Tel: 01443 406400 Fax: 01443 406402
Website: www.mickantoniw.co.uk Twitter: @MickAntoniw1

AP IORWERTH, Mr Rhun *PlC* **Ynys Môn**
Plaid Cymru Shadow Cabinet Secretary for Health and Social Care
Tel: 0300 200 7181 Email: rhun.apiorwerth@assembly.wales
Constituency office: 1B Church Street, Llangefni, Ynys Môn LL77 7DU
Tel: 01248 723599 Website: www.rhunapiorwerth.wales Twitter: @Rhunapiorwerth

ASGHAR, Mr Mohammad *Con* **South Wales East**
Welsh Conservatives Spokesperson for Skills
Tel: 0300 200 7239 Email: mohammad.asghar@assembly.wales
Regional office: Unit 1, Fairoak House, 15-17 Church Road, Newport, Gwent NP19 7EJ
Tel: 01633 220022 Fax: 01633 220611
Website: www.mohammadasgharam.org.uk Twitter: @mohammadasghar

BENNETT, Mr Gareth *UKIP* **South Wales Central**
Welsh UKIP Spokesperson for Local Government, Housing, Communities and Sport; Business Manager
Tel: 0300 200 7263 Email: gareth.bennett@assembly.wales
Regional office: No regional office publicised
Website: bennettukip.co.uk Twitter: @GarethBennettAM

BLYTHYN, Ms Hannah *Lab* **Delyn**
Tel: 0300 200 7132 Email: hannah.blythyn@assembly.wales
Constituency office: No constituency office publicised
Website: www.hannahblythyn.wales Twitter: @hannahblythyn

BOWDEN, Ms Dawn *Lab* **Merthyr Tydfil and Rhymney**
Tel: 0300 200 7170 Email: dawn.bowden@assembly.wales
Constituency office: 110 High Street, Merthyr Tydfil CF47 8AP
Tel: 01685 386672
Website: www.dawnbowdenam.co.uk Twitter: @Dawn_Bowden

BROWN, Ms Michelle *UKIP* **North Wales**
Welsh UKIP Spokesperson for Education, Childcare and Training
Tel: 0300 200 7267 Email: michelle.brown@assembly.wales
Regional office: No regional office publicised
Website: voicesofreason.wix.com/michellebrownukip Twitter: @MBrownAM

BRYANT, Ms Jayne *Lab* **Newport West**
Tel: 0300 200 7104 Email: jayne.bryant@assembly.wales
Constituency office: No constituency office publicised
Website: www.jaynebryant.wales Twitter: @JBryantWales

BURNS, Mrs Angela *Con* **Carmarthen West and South Pembrokeshire**
Welsh Conservatives Spokesperson for Health; Campaigns Director
Tel: 0300 200 7243 Email: angela.burns@assembly.wales
Constituency office: County Chambers, Warren Street, Tenby, Pembrokeshire SA70 7JS
Tel: 01834 843052
Website: www.angelaburns.org.uk Twitter: @angelaburnsam

DAVID, Dr Hefin *Lab* **Caerphilly**
Tel: 0300 200 7154 Email: hefin.david@assembly.wales
Constituency office: Bargoed YMCA, Gilfach, Bargoed CF81 8JA
Tel: 01443 838542 Twitter: @hef4caerphilly

DAVIES, Mr Alun *Lab/Co-op* **Blaenau Gwent**
Minister for Lifelong Learning and Welsh Language
Tel: 0300 200 7145 Fax: 029 2089 8302 Email: alun.davies@assembly.wales
Ministerial office: Welsh Government, Fifth Floor, Tŷ Hywel, Cardiff Bay CF99 1NA
Tel: 0300 060 4400
Constituency office: 23 Beaufort Street, Brynmawr, Blaenau Gwent NP23 4AQ
Tel: 01495 311160
Website: www.alundaviesam.org Twitter: @alundaviesam

DAVIES, Mr Andrew R T *Con* **South Wales Central**
Leader, Welsh Conservatives in the National Assembly
Tel: 0300 200 7227 Email: andrewrt.davies@assembly.wales
Regional office: 79 Eastgate, Cowbridge, Vale of Glamorgan CF71 7AA
Website: www.andrewrtdavies.co.uk Twitter: @andrewrtdavies

DAVIES, Mr Paul *Con* **Preseli Pembrokeshire**
Deputy Leader, Welsh Conservatives in the National Assembly; Chief Whip; Business Manager; Welsh Conservative Spokesperson for Rural Affairs
Tel: 0300 200 7216 Email: paul.davies@assembly.wales
Constituency office: 20 Upper Market Street, Haverfordwest SA61 1QA
Tel: 01437 766425 Fax: 01437 766425
Website: www.pauldaviesam.co.uk

DAVIES, Mrs Suzy *Con* **South Wales West**
Welsh Conservatives Spokesperson for Social Services and Older People's Champion, Welsh Language, Swansea Bay City Deal and Broadcasting
Tel: 0300 200 7208 Fax: 029 2089 8391 Email: suzy.davies@assembly.wales
Regional offices: Cornhill Chambers, 8 Christina Street, Swansea SA1 4EW
1a Station Hill, Bridgend CF31 1EA
Website: suzydavies.wales Twitter: @suzydaviesam

DRAKEFORD, Mr Mark *Lab* **Cardiff West**
Cabinet Secretary for Finance and Local Government
Tel: 0300 200 7158 Email: mark.drakeford@assembly.wales
Ministerial office: Welsh Government, Fifth Floor, Tŷ Hywel, Cardiff Bay CF99 1NA
Tel: 0300 060 4400
Constituency office: 395 Cowbridge Road East, Canton, Cardiff CF5 1JG
Tel: 029 2022 3207
Website: www.markdrakeford.com Twitter: @markdrakeford

ELIS-THOMAS, Rt Hon Dafydd *Ind* **Dwyfor Meirionnydd**
Tel: 0300 200 7175 Email: dafydd.elis-thomas@assembly.wales
Constituency office: 7 Bank Place, Porthmadog, Gwynedd LL49 9AA
Tel: 01766 515028
Website: www.dafyddelisthomas.org Twitter: @ElisThomasD

EVANS, Mrs Rebecca *Lab/Co-op* **Gower**
Minister for Social Services and Public Health
Tel: 0300 200 7160 Email: rebecca.evans@assembly.wales
Ministerial office: Welsh Government, Fifth Floor, Tŷ Hywel, Cardiff Bay CF99 1NA
Tel: 0300 060 4400
Constituency office: 9 Pontardulais Road, Gorseinon SA4 4FE
Tel: 01792 899081
Website: www.rebeccaevans4gower.com Twitter: @rebeccaevansam

FINCH-SAUNDERS, Mrs Janet *Con* **Aberconwy**
Welsh Conservatives Spokesperson for Local Government
Tel: 0300 200 7247 Email: janet.finchsaunders@assembly.wales
Constituency office: 29 Madoc Street, Llandudno LL30 2TL
Tel: 01492 871198
Website: www.janetfinchsaunders.org.uk Twitter: @jfinchsaunders

GEORGE, Mr Russell *Con* **Montgomeryshire**
Welsh Conservatives Spokesperson for Economy, Transport and Sport
Tel: 0300 200 7206 Email: russell.george@assembly.wales
Constituency office: 13 Parker's Lane, Newtown, Powys SY16 2LT
Tel: 01686 610887
Website: www.russellgeorge.com Twitter: @russ_george

GETHING, Mr Vaughan *Lab/Co-op* **Cardiff South and Penarth**
Cabinet Secretary for Health, Wellbeing and Sport
Tel: 0300 200 7150 Email: vaughan.gething@assembly.wales
Ministerial office: Welsh Government, Fifth Floor, Tŷ Hywel, Cardiff Bay CF99 1NA
Tel: 0300 060 4400
Constituency office: Ground Floor, Mount Stuart House, Mount Stuart Square, Butetown, Cardiff CF10 5FQ
Website: www.vaughangething.co.uk Twitter: @vaughangething

GILL, Mr Nathan *Ind* **North Wales**
Tel: 0300 200 7521 Email: nathan.gill@assembly.wales
Regional office: 10 Bridge Street, Menai Bridge LL59 5DW
Tel: 01248 717052
Website: nathangill.wales Twitter: @NathanGillMEP

GRIFFITHS, Mr John *Lab/Co-op* **Newport East**
Tel: 0300 200 7121 Email: john.griffiths@assembly.wales
Constituency office: Seventh Floor, Clarence House, Clarence Place, Newport NP19 7AA
Tel: 01633 222302
Website: www.johngriffithslabour.wordpress.com Twitter: @JGriffithsLab

GRIFFITHS, Mrs Lesley *Lab* **Wrexham**
Cabinet Secretary for Environment and Rural Affairs
Tel: 029 2089 8536 Email: lesley.griffiths@assembly.wales
Ministerial office: Welsh Government, Fifth Floor, Tŷ Hywel, Cardiff Bay CF99 1NA
Tel: 0300 060 4400
Constituency office: Vernon House, 41 Rhosddu Road, Wrexham LL11 2NS
Tel: 01978 355743
Website: www.lesleygriffiths.org Twitter: @lesley4wrexham

GRUFFYDD, Mr Llyr *PlC* **North Wales**
Plaid Cymru Shadow Cabinet Secretary for Education, Children, Skills and Lifelong Learning
Email: llyr.gruffydd@assembly.wales
Regional office: Office 3, Ground Floor, Birch House Business Centre, Hen Lon Parcwr, Rhuthun, Denbighshire LL15 1HA
Tel: 01824 703593
Website: www.llyrgruffydd.cymru Twitter: @llyrgruffydd

GWENLLIAN, Ms Siân *PlC* **Arfon**
Plaid Cymru Shadow Cabinet Secretary for Local Government, Welsh Language, Equalities and Planning
Tel: 0300 200 7192 Email: sian.gwenllian@assembly.wales
Constituency office: 8 Castle Street, Caernarfon LL55 1SE Twitter: @siangwenfelin

HAMILTON, Mr Neil *UKIP* **Mid and West Wales**
Leader, UKIP Assembly Group; Welsh UKIP Spokesperson for Culture, Finance, Agriculture and Environment
Tel: 0300 200 7422 Email: neil.hamilton@assembly.wales
Regional office: No regional office details publicised
Website: neilhamiltonukip.com Twitter: @NeilUKIP

HEDGES, Mr Mike *Lab* **Swansea East**
Tel: 0300 200 7140 Email: mike.hedges@assembly.wales
Constituency office: 97 Pleasant Street, Morriston, Swansea SA6 6HJ
Tel: 01792 790621 Fax: 01792 794802
Website: www.mikehedges.org.uk Twitter: @mikehedgesam

HOWELLS, Ms Vikki *Lab* **Cynon Valley**
Tel: 0300 200 7163 Email: vikki.howells@assembly.wales
Constituency office: 27 High Street, Aberdare CF44 7AA
Tel: 01685 881388
Website: www.vikkihowells.com Twitter: @VikkiHowells

HUTT, Ms Jane *Lab* **Vale of Glamorgan**
Leader of the House and Chief Whip
Tel: 0300 200 7110 Fax: 029 2089 8129 Email: jane.hutt@assembly.wales
Ministerial office: Welsh Government, Fifth Floor, Tŷ Hywel, Cardiff Bay CF99 1NA
Tel: 0300 060 4400
Constituency office: 115 High Street, Barry CF62 7DT
Tel: 01446 740981 Fax: 01446 747106
Website: www.janehutt.co.uk Twitter: @janehutt

IRRANCA-DAVIES, Mr Huw *Lab/Co-op* **Ogmore**
Tel: 0300 200 7105 Email: huw.irranca-davies@assembly.wales
Constituency office: Unit 2, 112-113 Commercial Street, Maesteg CF34 9DL
Tel: 01656 737777
Website: www.huwirranca-davies.org.uk Twitter: @huw4ogmore

ISHERWOOD, Mr Mark *Con* **North Wales**
Welsh Conservatives Spokesperson for Communities, Europe and North Wales Growth Deal
Tel: 0300 200 7217 Email: mark.isherwood@assembly.wales
Regional office: 5 Halkyn Street, Holywell CH8 7TX
Tel: 01352 710232 Fax: 01352 714074
Website: www.markisherwood.co.uk Twitter: @MarkIsherwoodAM

JAMES, Ms Julie *Lab* **Swansea West**
Minister for Skills and Science
Tel: 0300 200 7137 Email: julie.james@assembly.wales
Ministerial office: Welsh Government, Fifth Floor, Tŷ Hywel, Cardiff Bay CF99 1NA
Tel: 0300 060 4400
Constituency office: First Floor, 11 Wind Street, Swansea SA1 1DP
Tel: 01792 460836 Website: swanseawest.wales
Website: juliejamesam.co.uk Twitter: @juliejamesam

JENKINS, Ms Bethan *PlC* **South Wales West**
Plaid Cymru Shadow Cabinet Secretary for Housing, Poverty, Communities and Steel
Tel: 0300 200 7185 Email: bethan.jenkins@assembly.wales
Regional office: Unit 2, Brunel Way, Baglan Energy Park, Port Talbot SA11 2FP
Tel: 01639 820530 Email: philippa.richards@wales.gov.uk
Website: www.bethanjenkins.plaidcymru.org Twitter: @bethanjenkins

JONES, Ms Ann *Lab/Co-op* **Vale of Clwyd**
Deputy Presiding Officer
Tel: 0300 200 7173 Email: ann.jones@assembly.wales
Constituency office: The Hub, 69-75 Wellington Road, Rhyl, Denbighshire LL18 1BE
Tel: 01745 332813
Website: www.annjones.org.uk Twitter: @ann_jonesam

JONES, Ms Caroline *UKIP* **South Wales West**
Welsh UKIP Spokesperson for Health and Social Care
Email: caroline.jones@assembly.wales
Regional office: No regional office publicised
Website: www.carolinejones.wales Twitter: @carolineUKIP

JONES, Rt Hon Carwyn *Lab* **Bridgend**
First Minister; Leader, Welsh Labour
Tel: 0300 200 7095 Email: carwyn.jones@assembly.wales
Ministerial office: Welsh Government, Fifth Floor, Tŷ Hywel, Cardiff Bay CF99 1NA
Tel: 0300 060 4400
Constituency office: First and Second Floor Suites, 3 Cross Street, Bridgend CF31 1EX
Tel: 01656 664320 Email: christopher.mainwaring@assembly.wales
Website: www.carwynjonesam.com Twitter: @AMCarwyn

JONES, Ms Elin *Pres Off* **Ceredigion**
Presiding Officer
Email: elin.jones@assembly.wales
Constituency office: Ty Goronwy, 32 Heol y Wig, Aberystwyth, Ceredigion SY23 2LN
Tel: 01970 624516 Fax: 01970 624473
Website: www.elinjones.wales Twitter: @elinceredigion

LEWIS, Mr Steffan *PlC* **South Wales East**
Plaid Cymru Shadow Cabinet Secretary for External Affairs, Non-Devolved Matters, Police, Criminal Justice System and Social Protection
Tel: 0300 200 7188 Email: steffan.lewis@assembly.wales
Regional office: 1a Griffiths Blds, Victoria Terrace, Newbridge, Caerphilly NP11 4EW
Tel: 01495 241100 Twitter: @steffanlewis

LLOYD, Dr Dai *PlC* **South Wales West**
Plaid Cymru Shadow Cabinet Secretary for Culture and Infrastructure; Chair, Assembly Group
Tel: 0300 200 7255 Email: dai.lloyd@assembly.wales
Regional office: Uned 2, Ffordd Brunel, Parc Ynni Baglan, Baglan SA11 2FP
Tel: 01639 820530 Twitter: @DaiLloydSwansea

McEVOY, Mr Neil *Ind* **South Wales Central**
Email: neil.mcevoy@assembly.wales
Regional office: 321 Cowbridge Road, Cardiff CF5 1JD Twitter: @neiljmcevoy

MELDING, Mr David *Con* **South Wales Central**
Welsh Conservatives Spokesperson for Environment and Sustainability, Planning, Housing and Wales Bill
Tel: 0300 200 7220 Email: david.melding@assembly.wales
Regional office: Office 2, 20 Pantbach Road, Birchgrove, Cardiff CF14 1UA
Tel: 029 2062 3088 Email: sarah.sharpe@assembly.wales
Website: www.davidmelding.wales Twitter: @DavidMeldingAM

MILES, Mr Jeremy *Lab/Co-op* **Neath**
Tel: 0300 200 7107 Email: jeremy.miles@assembly.wales
Constituency office: 7 High Street, Pontardawe, Swansea SA8 4HU
Tel: 01792 869993
Website: jeremymiles.cymru Twitter: @Jeremy_Miles

MILLAR, Mr Darren *Con* **Clwyd West**
Welsh Conservatives Spokesperson for Education and Children; Policy Director
Tel: 0300 200 7214 Email: darren.millar@assembly.wales
Constituency office: North Wales Business Park, Abergele LL22 8LJ
Tel: 01745 839117
Website: www.darrenmillar.wales Twitter: @darrenmillaram

MORGAN, Mrs Julie *Lab* **Cardiff North**
Tel: 0300 200 7362 Email: julie.morgan@assembly.wales
Constituency office: 17 Plasnewydd, Whitchurch, Cardiff CF14 1NR
Tel: 029 2061 4577
Website: www.juliemorgan.org.uk Twitter: @juliemorganlab

MORGAN, Eluned *Lab* **Mid and West Wales**
Tel: 0300 200 7264 Email: eluned.morgan@assembly.wales
Regional office: 19 Cartlett, Haverfordwest, Pembrokeshire SA61 2LH
Website: elunedmorgan.wales Twitter: @Eluned_Morgan

NEAGLE, Ms Lynne *Lab/Co-op* **Torfaen**
Tel: 0300 200 7168 Email: lynne.neagle@assembly.wales
Constituency office: 73 Upper Trosnant Street, Pontypool, Torfaen NP4 8AU
Tel: 01495 740022 Fax: 01495 755776 Twitter: @lynne_neagle

PASSMORE, Ms Rhianon *Lab/Co-op* **Islwyn**
Tel: 0300 200 7097 Email: rhianon.passmore@assembly.wales
Constituency office: 208 High Street, Blackwood NP12 1AJ
Tel: 01495 225162 Twitter: @rhi4islwyn

PRICE, Mr Adam *PlC* **Carmarthen East and Dinefwr**
Plaid Cymru Shadow Cabinet Secretary for Business, Economy and Finance
Tel: 0300 200 7177 Email: adam.price@assembly.wales
Constituency office: 37 Wind Street, Ammanford SA18 3DN
Tel: 01269 597677 Twitter: @_Adam_Price

RAMSAY, Mr Nick *Con* **Monmouth**
Welsh Conservatives Spokesperson for Finance
Tel: 0300 200 7211 Email: nicholas.ramsay@assembly.wales
Constituency office: The Grange, 16 Maryport Street, Usk, Monmouthshire NP15 1AB
Tel: 01291 674898 Email: katherine.jordan@assembly.wales
Website: www.nickramsay.org.uk Twitter: @nickramsayam

RATHBONE, Ms Jenny *Lab* **Cardiff Central**
Tel: 0300 200 7134 Email: jenny.rathbone@assembly.wales
Constituency office: 165 Albany Road, Cardiff CF24 3NT
Tel: 029 2025 6255
Website: jennyrathbone.com Twitter: @jennyrathbone

RECKLESS, Mr Mark *Ind* **South Wales East**
Tel: 0300 200 7204 Email: mark.reckless@assembly.wales
Regional office: 20 Commercial Street, Pontypool NP4 6SA
Website: www.markreckless.com Twitter: @MarkReckless

REES, Mr David *Lab* **Aberavon**
Tel: 0300 200 7128 Fax: 029 2089 8383 Email: david.rees@assembly.wales
Constituency office: Unit 6, Water Street Business Centre, Gwyn Terrace, Aberafan, Port Talbot SA12 6LG
Tel: 01639 870779 Fax: 01639 870779
Website: david-rees.com Twitter: @davidreesam

ROWLANDS, Mr David *UKIP* **South Wales East**
Welsh UKIP Spokesperson for Transport, Infrastructure and Skills
Tel: 0300 200 7235 Email: davidj.rowlands@assembly.wales
Regional office: 20 Commercial Street, Pontypool, Torfaen NP4 6JS Twitter: @DavidRowlandsUK

SARGEANT, Mr Carl *Lab* **Alyn and Deeside**
Cabinet Secretary for Communities and Children
Tel: 0300 200 7139 Email: carl.sargeant@assembly.wales
Ministerial office: Welsh Government, Fifth Floor, Tŷ Hywel, Cardiff Bay CF99 1NA
Tel: 0300 060 4400
Constituency office: 70 High Street, Connah's Quay, Flintshire CH5 4DD
Tel: 01244 823547 Fax: 01244 823547 Twitter: @Carl4AandD

SKATES, Mr Ken *Lab* **Clwyd South**
Cabinet Secretary for Economy and Infrastructure
Tel: 0300 200 7114 Email: ken.skates@assembly.wales
Ministerial office: Welsh Government, Fifth Floor, Tŷ Hywel, Cardiff Bay CF99 1NA
Tel: 0300 060 4400
Constituency office: Unit 19, The Malthouse Business Centre, Regent Street, Llangollen LL20 8RP
Tel: 01978 869058
Website: www.kenskates.co.uk Twitter: @KenSkatesAM

THOMAS, Mr Simon *PlC* **Mid and West Wales**
Plaid Cymru Shadow Cabinet Secretary for Sustainable Communities, Energy and Rural Affairs
Tel: 0300 200 7190 Email: simon.thomas@assembly.wales
Regional office: 32 Heol y Wig, Aberystwyth SY23 2LN
Tel: 01970 624984
Website: www.simonthomas.plaidcymru.org Twitter: @SimonThomasAC

WATERS, Mr Lee *Lab/Co-op* **Llanelli**
Tel: 0300 200 7101 Email: lee.waters@assembly.wales
Constituency office: 43 Pottery Street, Llanelli, Carmarthenshire SA15 1SU
Tel: 01554 774902
Website: leeforllanelli.wales Twitter: @Amanwy

WATSON, Mrs Joyce *Lab* **Mid and West Wales**
Tel: 0300 200 7093 Fax: 029 2089 8419 Email: joyce.watson@assembly.wales
Regional office: 3 Red Street, Carmarthen SA31 1QL
Tel: 01267 233448
Website: www.joycewatson.co.uk Twitter: @JoyceWatsonam

WILLIAMS, Ms Kirsty, CBE *Lib Dem* **Brecon and Radnorshire**
Cabinet Secretary for Education
Tel: 0300 200 7277 Email: kirsty.williams@assembly.wales
Ministerial office: Welsh Government, Fifth Floor, Tŷ Hywel, Cardiff Bay CF99 1NA
Tel: 0300 060 4400
Constituency office: 4 Water Gate, Brecon, Powys LD3 9AN
Tel: 01874 625739
Website: www.kirstywilliams.org.uk Twitter: @kirsty_williams

WOOD, Ms Leanne *PlC* **Rhondda**
Leader, Plaid Cymru
Tel: 0300 200 7202 Email: leanne.wood@assembly.wales
Constituency office: 68 Heol Pontypridd, Porth CF39 9PL
Tel: 01443 681420
Website: www.leannewood.org Twitter: @leannewood

Women AMs (25)

BLYTHYN Hannah	*Lab*	JENKINS Bethan	*PlC*
BOWDEN Dawn	*Lab*	JONES Ann	*Lab/Co-op*
BROWN Michelle	*UKIP*	JONES Caroline	*UKIP*
BRYANT Jayne	*Lab*	JONES Elin	*Pres Off*
BURNS Angela	*Con*	MORGAN Julie	*Lab*
DAVIES Suzy	*Con*	MORGAN Eluned	*Lab*
EVANS Rebecca	*Lab/Co-op*	NEAGLE Lynne	*Lab/Co-op*
FINCH-SAUNDERS Janet	*Con*	PASSMORE Rhianon	*Lab/Co-op*
GRIFFITHS Lesley	*Lab*	RATHBONE Jenny	*Lab*
GWENLLIAN Siân	*PlC*	WATSON Joyce	*Lab*
HOWELLS Vikki	*Lab*	WILLIAMS Kirsty	*Lib Dem*
HUTT Jane	*Lab*	WOOD Leanne	*PlC*
JAMES Julie	*Lab*		

Constituencies

			Majority	*%*
Aberavon	David Rees	Lab	6,402	30.51
Aberconwy	Janet Finch-Saunders	Con	754	3.39
Alyn and Deeside	Carl Sargeant	Lab	5,364	24.56
Arfon	Siân Gwenllian	PlC	4,162	20.63
Blaenau Gwent	Alun Davies	Lab/Co-op	650	3.04
Brecon and Radnorshire	Kirsty Williams	Lib Dem	8,170	26.78
Bridgend	Carwyn Jones	Lab	5,623	20.85
Caerphilly	Hefin David	Lab	1,575	5.79
Cardiff Central	Jenny Rathbone	Lab	817	3.12
Cardiff North	Julie Morgan	Lab	3,667	9.76
Cardiff South and Penarth	Vaughan Gething	Lab/Co-op	6,921	22.71
Cardiff West	Mark Drakeford	Lab	1,176	3.66

			Majority	%
Carmarthen East and Dinefwr	Adam Price	PlC	8,700	29.11
Carmarthen West and South Pembrokeshire	Angela Burns	Con	3,373	11.49
Ceredigion	Elin Jones	Pres Off*	2,408	8.14
Clwyd South	Ken Skates	Lab	3,016	13.54
Clwyd West	Darren Millar	Con	5,063	19.23
Vale of Clwyd	Ann Jones	Lab/Co-op	768	3.17
Cynon Valley	Vikki Howells	Lab	5,994	31.01
Delyn	Hannah Blythyn	Lab	3,582	15.36
Dwyfor Meirionnydd	Dafydd Elis-Thomas	Ind*	6,406	31.41
Vale of Glamorgan	Jane Hutt	Lab	777	2.05
Gower	Rebecca Evans	Lab/Co-op	1,829	6.02
Islwyn	Rhianon Passmore	Lab/Co-op	5,106	22.75
Llanelli	Lee Waters	Lab/Co-op	382	1.35
Merthyr Tydfil and Rhymney	Dawn Bowden	Lab	5,486	26.34
Monmouth	Nick Ramsay	Con	5,147	16.32
Montgomeryshire	Russell George	Con	3,339	14.06
Neath	Jeremy Miles	Lab/Co-op	2,923	11.47
Newport East	John Griffiths	Lab/Co-op	4,896	23.51
Newport West	Jayne Bryant	Lab	4,115	14.75
Ogmore	Huw Irranca-Davies	Lab/Co-op	9,468	40.3
Pontypridd	Mick Antoniw	Lab/Co-op	5,327	20.9
Preseli Pembrokeshire	Paul Davies	Con	3,930	13.78
Rhondda	Leanne Wood	PlC	3,459	14.66
Swansea East	Mike Hedges	Lab	7,452	35.98
Swansea West	Julie James	Lab	5,080	22.73
Torfaen	Lynne Neagle	Lab/Co-op	4,498	19.46
Wrexham	Lesley Griffiths	Lab	1,325	6.48
Ynys Môn	Rhun ap Iorwerth	PlC	9,510	37.63

Regions

			Count elected on
Mid and West Wales	Neil Hamilton	UKIP	1
Mid and West Wales	Eluned Morgan	Lab	4
Mid and West Wales	Simon Thomas	PlC	3
Mid and West Wales	Joyce Watson	Lab	2
North Wales	Michelle Brown	UKIP	4
North Wales	Nathan Gill	Ind†	1
North Wales	Llyr Gruffydd	PlC	2
North Wales	Mark Isherwood	Con	3
South Wales Central	Gareth Bennett	UKIP	3
South Wales Central	Andrew R T Davies	Con	1
South Wales Central	Neil McEvoy	Ind*	2
South Wales Central	David Melding	Con	4
South Wales East	Mohammad Asghar	Con	4
South Wales East	Steffan Lewis	PlC	2
South Wales East	Mark Reckless	Ind†	1
South Wales East	David Rowlands	UKIP	3
South Wales West	Suzy Davies	Con	2
South Wales West	Bethan Jenkins	PlC	1
South Wales West	Caroline Jones	UKIP	3
South Wales West	Dai Lloyd	PlC	4

* Elected as Plaid Cymru
† Elected as UKIP

Assembly Committees

Chairs' Forum

Tel: 0300 200 6565
Email: coordinationunit@assembly.wales
senedd.assembly.wales/
mgcommitteedetails.aspx?id=462

Elin Jones (Chair)	*Pres Off*
Jayne Bryant	*Lab*
Russell George	*Con*
John Griffiths	*Lab/Co-op*
Mike Hedges	*Lab*
Huw Irranca-Davies	*Lab/Co-op*
Bethan Jenkins	*PlC*
Ann Jones	*Lab/Co-op*
Dai Lloyd	*PlC*
Lynne Neagle	*Lab/Co-op*
Nick Ramsay	*Con*
Mark Reckless	*Ind*
David Rees	*Lab*
David Rowlands	*UKIP*
Simon Thomas	*PlC*

Staff: Chris Warner (Clerk)

Business

Email: seneddchamber@assembly.wales
www.assembly.wales/seneddbusiness

Elin Jones (Chair)	*Pres Off*
Rhun ap Iorwerth	*PlC*
Gareth Bennett	*UKIP*
Paul Davies	*Con*
Jane Hutt	*Lab*

Staff: Aled Elwyn Jones (Clerk)

Children, Young People and Education

Email: seneddcype@assembly.wales
www.assembly.wales/seneddcype
Twitter: @SeneddCYPE

Lynne Neagle (Chair)	*Lab/Co-op*
Michelle Brown	*UKIP*
Hefin David	*Lab*
John Griffiths	*Lab/Co-op*
Llyr Gruffydd	*PlC*
Darren Millar	*Con*
Julie Morgan	*Lab*
Mark Reckless	*Ind*

Staff: Llinos Madeley (Clerk)

Climate Change, Environment and Rural Affairs

Email: seneddccera@assembly.wales
www.assembly.wales/seneddccera
Twitter: @SeneddCCERA

Mike Hedges (Chair)	*Lab*
Gareth Bennett	*UKIP*
Jayne Bryant	*Lab*
Siân Gwenllian	*PlC*
Huw Irranca-Davies	*Lab/Co-op*
David Melding	*Con*
Jenny Rathbone	*Lab*
Simon Thomas	*PlC*

Staff: Marc Wyn Jones (Clerk)

Constitutional and Legislative Affairs

Email: seneddcla@assembly.wales
www.assembly.wales/seneddcla
Twitter: @SeneddCLA

Huw Irranca-Davies (Chair)	*Lab/Co-op*
Dafydd Elis-Thomas	*Ind*
Nathan Gill	*Ind*
Dai Lloyd	*PlC*
David Melding	*Con*

Staff: Gareth Williams (Clerk)

Culture, Welsh Language and Communications

Email: seneddcwlc@assembly.wales
www.assembly.wales/seneddswlc
Twitter: @SeneddCWLC

Bethan Jenkins (Chair)	*PlC*
Hannah Blythyn	*Lab*
Dawn Bowden	*Lab*
Suzy Davies	*Con*
Neil Hamilton	*UKIP*
Dai Lloyd	*PlC*
Jeremy Miles	*Lab/Co-op*
Lee Waters	*Lab/Co-op*

Staff: Steve George (Clerk)

Economy, Infrastructure and Skills

Email: seneddeis@assembly.wales
www.assembly.wales/seneddeis
Twitter: @SeneddEIS

Russell George (Chair)	*Con*
Hannah Blythyn	*Lab*
Hefin David	*Lab*
Vikki Howells	*Lab*
Mark Isherwood	*Con*
Jeremy Miles	*Lab/Co-op*
Adam Price	*PlC*
David Rowlands	*UKIP*

Staff: Gareth Price (Clerk)

Equality, Local Government and Communities

Email: seneddcommunities@assembly.wales
www.assembly.wales/seneddcommunities
Twitter: @SeneddELGC

John Griffiths (Chair)	*Lab/Co-op*
Gareth Bennett	*UKIP*
Janet Finch-Saunders	*Con*
Siân Gwenllian	*PlC*
Bethan Jenkins	*PlC*
Rhianon Passmore	*Lab/Co-op*
Jenny Rathbone	*Lab*
Joyce Watson	*Lab*

Staff: Naomi Stocks (Clerk)

External Affairs and Additional Legislation

Email: seneddeaal@assembly.wales
www.assembly.wales/seneddeaal
Twitter: @SeneddEAAL

David Rees (Chair)	*Lab*
Dawn Bowden	*Lab*
Michelle Brown	*UKIP*
Suzy Davies	*Con*
Mark Isherwood	*Con*
Steffan Lewis	*PlC*
Jeremy Miles	*Lab/Co-op*
Eluned Morgan	*Lab*

Staff: Alun Davidson (Clerk)

Finance

Email: seneddfinance@assembly.wales
www.assembly.wales/seneddfinance
Twitter: @SeneddFinance

Simon Thomas (Chair)	*PlC*
Neil Hamilton	*UKIP*
Mike Hedges	*Lab*
Steffan Lewis	*PlC*
Eluned Morgan	*Lab*
Nick Ramsay	*Con*
David Rees	*Lab*

Staff: Bethan Davies (Clerk)

Health, Social Care and Sport

Email: seneddhealth@assembly.wales
www.assembly.wales/seneddhealth
Twitter: @seneddhealth

Dai Lloyd (Chair)	*PlC*
Rhun ap Iorwerth	*PlC*
Dawn Bowden	*Lab*
Jayne Bryant	*Lab*
Angela Burns	*Con*
Caroline Jones	*UKIP*
Julie Morgan	*Lab*
Lynne Neagle	*Lab/Co-op*

Staff: Sian Thomas (Clerk)

Petitions

Email: seneddpetitions@assembly.wales
www.assembly.wales/seneddpetitions
Twitter: @SeneddPetitions

David Rowlands (Chair)	*UKIP*
Janet Finch-Saunders	*Con*
Mike Hedges	*Lab*

Staff: Graeme Francis (Clerk)

Public Accounts

Email: seneddpac@assembly.wales
www.assembly.wales/seneddpac
Twitter: @SeneddPAC

Nick Ramsay (Chair)	*Con*
Mohammad Asghar	*Con*
Neil Hamilton	*UKIP*
Vikki Howells	*Lab*
Rhianon Passmore	*Lab/Co-op*
Lee Waters	*Lab/Co-op*

Staff: Fay Buckle (Clerk)

Scrutiny of the First Minister

Email: scrutinyfm@assembly.wales
www.assembly.wales/scrutinyfm

Ann Jones (Chair)	*Lab/Co-op*
Jayne Bryant	*Lab*
Russell George	*Con*
John Griffiths	*Lab/Co-op*
Mike Hedges	*Lab*
Huw Irranca-Davies	*Lab/Co-op*
Bethan Jenkins	*PlC*
Dai Lloyd	*PlC*
Lynne Neagle	*Lab/Co-op*
Nick Ramsay	*Con*
David Rees	*Lab*
David Rowlands	*UKIP*
Simon Thomas	*PlC*

Staff: Graeme Francis (Clerk)

Standards of Conduct

Email: seneddstandards@assembly.wales
www.assembly.wales/seneddstandards

Jayne Bryant (Chair)	*Lab*
Gareth Bennett	*UKIP*
Paul Davies	*Con*
Llyr Gruffydd	*PlC*

Staff: Meriel Singleton (Clerk)

Principal Officers and Officials

Office of the Presiding Officer

Presiding Officer **Elin Jones** AM

Head, Private Office — Gwion Evans — 0300 200 7403
Email: gwion.evans@assembly.wales

Deputy Presiding Officer **Ann Jones** AM (Lab/Co-op)

Assembly Commission

Chair	Elin Jones (Pres Off)
Members	Suzy Davies (Con)
	Caroline Jones (UKIP)
	Adam Price (PlC)
	Joyce Watson (Lab)

Senior Management Team

Chief Executive and Clerk of the Assembly — Manon Antoniazzi 0300 200 6230
Email: manon.antoniazzi@assembly.wales

Directors

Business	Adrian Crompton 0300 200 6228 Email: adrian.crompton@assembly.wales
Resources	Dave Tosh 0300 200 6497 Email: david.tosh@assembly.wales
Commission Services	Craig Stephenson 0300 200 6229 Email: craig.stephenson@assembly.wales
Chief Legal Adviser	Elisabeth Jones 0300 200 6432 Email: elisabeth.jones@assembly.wales

Heads

Communications	Non Gwilym 0300 200 6266 Email: non.gwilym@assembly.wales
Chamber and Committee Services	Siân Wilkins 0300 200 6380 Email: sian.wilkins@assembly.wales
Commission and Member Support Service	Sulafa Thomas 0300 200 6227 Email: sulafa.thomas@assembly.wales
Policy and Legislation Committee Service	Chris Warner 0300 200 6320 Email: christopher.warner@assembly.wales
Research Service	Kathryn Potter 0300 200 6587 Email: kathryn.potter@assembly.wales
Financial Services	Nia Morgan 0300 200 6530 Email: nia.morgan@assembly.wales
Translation and Reporting Service	Mair Parry-Jones 0300 200 6391 Email: mair.parry-jones@assembly.wales
Strategic Transformation Service	Anna Daniel 0300 200 6329 Email: anna.daniel@assembly.wales
ICT	Mark Neilson 0300 200 7399 Email: mark.neilson@assembly.wales
Legal Services	Matthew Richards 0300 200 6435 Email: matthew.richards@assembly.wales
Human Resources	Lowri Williams 0300 200 6461 Email: lowri.wiliams@assembly.wales
Governance and Audit	Gareth Watts 0300 200 6537 Email: gareth.watts@assembly.wales

Welsh Government Civil Service

Welsh Government, Cathays Park, Cardiff, South Glamorgan CF10 3NQ
Tel: 0300 060 4400
Email: [firstname.surname]@wales.gsi.gov.uk Website: www.gov.wales

Llywodraeth Cymru, Parc Cathays, Caerdydd, South Glamorgan CF10 3NQ
Tel: 0300 060 4400

Office of the Permanent Secretary

Permanent Secretary: Dame Shan Morgan DCMG

Office of the First Minister and Cabinet Office

Head of Office of the First Minister: Desmond Clifford 0300 025 7765
Email: desmond.clifford@gov.wales

Education and Public Services Group

Deputy Permanent Secretary: Owen Evans 029 2082 5381 Email: owen.evans3@wales.gsi.gov.uk

Health and Social Services Group

Director-General, Health and Social Services/NHS Wales Chief Executive:
Dr Andrew Goodall 029 2080 1182 Email: andrew.goodall@wales.gsi.gov.uk

Economy, Skills and Natural Resources Group

Deputy Permanent Secretary: James Price 029 2082 6646 Email: james.price@wales.gsi.gov.uk

Non-Ministerial Department

Estyn – HM Inspectorate for Education and Training in Wales

Anchor Court, Keen Road, Cardiff CF24 5JW
Tel: 029 2044 6446
Email: enquiries@estyn.gov.wales Website: www.estyn.gov.wales Twitter: @EstynHMI

Llys Angor, Heol Keen, Caerdydd CF24 5JW
Tel: 029 2044 6446
Email: ymholiadau@estyn.llyw.cymru Website: www.estyn.llyw.cymru

Number of staff: 120
HM Chief Inspector of Education and Training in Wales: Meilyr Rowlands 029 2044 6523
Email: chief-inspector@estyn.gov.wales

Political Parties

Welsh Labour (Llafur Cymru)

Unite the Union Building, 1 Cathedral Road, Cardiff CF11 9HA
Tel: 029 2087 7700 Fax: 029 2022 1153
Email: wales@labour.org.uk Website: www.welshlabour.org.uk Twitter: @welshlabour

Labour Group Office:
Tel: 029 2087 7700
Email: wales@labour.org.uk

First Minister and Leader of Welsh Labour: Carwyn Jones AM
General Secretary: David Hagendyk
Press Officer: Rhiannon Evans

Welsh Conservatives (Ceidwadwyr Cymreig)

Welsh Conservative Campaign Headquarters, Unit 5, Pro-copy Business Centre, Parc Ty Glas, Cardiff CF14 5DU
Tel: 029 2073 6562
Email: info@welshconservatives.com Website: www.welshconservatives.com
Twitter: @welshconserv

Chairman: Byron Davies
Deputy Chairmen: Lyndon Jones MBE 01792 875553 Email: lyndon.jones@welshconservatives.com, Paul Morris 01792 455520
Director: Richard Minshull 029 2073 6562 Email: richard.minshull@welshconservatives.com
Head of Media: Tomas Barrett 0300 200 7223 Email: tomas.barrett@assembly.wales
Senior Press Officer, Assembly: Vincent Bailey 0300 200 7279 Email: vincent.bailey@assembly.wales
Media Officer, Welsh Conservative Party: Denise Howard 029 2073 6562
Email: denise.howard@conservatives.com

Plaid Cymru (The Party of Wales)

Tŷ Gwynfor, Marine Chambers, Anson Court, Atlantic Wharf, Cardiff CF10 4AL
Tel: 029 2047 2272
Email: post@plaidcymru.org Website: www.plaid.cymru Twitter: @plaid_cymru

Assembly Office:
Tel: 0300 200 7196

Leader: Leanne Wood AM
Chair: Alun Ffred Jones
Chief Executive: Gareth Clubb
Treasurer: Nigel Copner

UK Independence Party Wales

Tel: 0300 200 7422
Email: neil.hamilton@assembly.wales Website: ukipwales.cymru Twitter: @UKIPinWales
Leader, Assembly Group: Neil Hamilton AM
Chief of Staff: Robin Hunter-Clarke

Welsh Liberal Democrats (Democratiaid Rhyddfrydol Cymru)

38 The Parade, Cardiff CF24 3AD
Tel: 029 2031 3400
Email: enquiries@welshlibdems.wales Website: www.welshlibdems.wales Twitter: @welshlibdems
Leader: Mark Williams
Communications and Policy Officer: Rhys Taylor Email: rhys.taylor@welshlibdems.org.uk
Campaigns and Local Parties Coordinator: Matthew Palmer
Email: matt.palmer@welshlibdems.org.uk

Northern Ireland Assembly

Parliament Buildings, Stormont, Belfast BT4 3XX
Tel: 028 9052 1137/Textphone: 028 9052 1209 Fax: 028 9052 1961
Email: info@niassembly.gov.uk Website: www.niassembly.gov.uk Twitter: @niassembly

Executive Committee of Ministers

Talks between the Parties have still not led to an agreement on the appointment of a First Minister, Deputy First Minister or Executive.

Ministerial Responsibilities and Staff

Executive Office

GD36 Stormont Castle, Stormont Estate, Belfast BT4 3TT
Tel: 028 9037 8158 Email: ps.ministers@executiveoffice-ni.gov.uk
Website: www.executiveoffice-ni.gov.uk Twitter: @niexecutive

Delivering social change through a framework co-ordinating key actions across government; strategic investment and regeneration through the Social Investment Fund and the Maze Long Kesh site; making Government work through the Programme for Government and support for the Executive; co-operation through the British/Irish, Joint Ministerial Committee, North/South Ministerial Council, European Policy and Co-ordination; promoting international relations through the NI Bureaus in Washington, China and the Office of the Northern Ireland Executive in Brussels; policy responsibility for equality, victims and survivors, human rights, social change, good relations and building a united community.

First Minister **To be appointed**

Principal Private Secretary	Jeremy Gardner	028 9037 8080

Deputy First Minister **To be appointed**

Junior Minister **To be appointed**

Private Secretary	Laura Parkhill	028 9037 8097

Junior Minister **To be appointed**

Private Secretary	Kathy Monaghan	028 9037 8125

Department of Agriculture, Environment and Rural Affairs

Dundonald House, Upper Newtownards Road, Ballymiscaw, Belfast BT4 3SB
Tel: 0300 200 7852
Email: daera.helpline@daera-ni.gov.uk Website: www.daera-ni.gov.uk Twitter: @daera_ni

Food; farming; environmental; fisheries; forestry and sustainability policy and the development of the rural sector in Northern Ireland; assists the sustainable development of the agri-food, environmental, fishing and forestry sectors of the Northern Ireland economy; having regard for the needs of the consumers; the protection of human, animal and plant health; welfare of animals; conservation and enhancement of the environment.

Minister of Agriculture, Environment and Rural Affairs To be appointed

Private Secretary	Ruth Galwey	028 9052 4011/028 9052 4140 Email: private.office@daera-ni.gov.uk

Department for Communities

Causeway Exchange, 1-7 Bedford Street, Belfast, Co Antrim BT2 7EG
Tel: 028 9082 3000 Email: private.office@communities-ni.gov.uk
Website: www.communities-ni.gov.uk Twitter: @CommunitiesNI

Housing; urban regeneration; sport; benefits and pensions; finding employment; finding staff; arts and culture; museums and libraries; support for children; historic environment; voluntary and community; languages; statistics and research; social inclusion; law and legislation; appeals service; local government; Public Record Office.

Minister for Communities **To be appointed**

Private Secretary	Pamela Baxter Email: pamela.baxter@communities-ni.gov.uk	028 9082 3327

Department for the Economy

Netherleigh, Massey Avenue, Belfast BT4 2JP
Tel: 028 9052 9900 Email: private.office@economy-ni.gov.uk
Website: www.economy-ni.gov.uk Twitter: @Economy_NI

Economic development policy, including business development; energy; telecoms; tourism; assured skills, apprenticeships and youth training, higher education policy; careers; promoting good employment practice; consumer affairs; health and safety at work; Insolvency Service; labour market and economic statistics services; Invest NI; InterTrade Ireland and Tourism Ireland; Health and Safety Executive for NI; the Consumer Council for NI.

Minister for the Economy **To be appointed**

Private Secretary	Siobhan Tweedie Email: siobhan.tweedie@economy-ni.gov.uk	028 9052 9452

Devolved Parliament and Assemblies

Department of Education

Rathgael House, Balloo Road, Rathgill, Bangor BT19 7PR
Tel: 028 9127 9279 Email: private.office@education-ni.gov.uk
Website: www.education-ni.gov.uk Twitter: @Education_NI

Curriculum and learning; pupils and parents; teaching staff; non-teaching staff; schools and infrastructure; support and development; statistics and research; equality and good relations.

Minister of Education **To be appointed**

Private Secretary To be appointed

Department of Finance

Clare House, 303 Airport Road, Belfast BT3 9ED
Email: private.office@finance-ni.gov.uk Website: www.finance-ni.gov.uk Twitter: @dptfinance

Finance; working in the Northern Ireland Civil Service; procurement; programme and project management and assurance; property rating; property valuation; land registration; mapping and geographic information; building regulations and energy efficiency of buildings; Civil law reform; Account NI; Public Sector Reform Division; statistics and research; Government Legal Service for Northern Ireland.

Minister of Finance **To be appointed**

Private Secretary	Sean Kerr Email: sean.kerr@finance-ni.gov.uk	028 9081 6711

Department of Health

C5.10, Castle Buildings, Stormont, Belfast BT4 3SQ
Tel: 028 9052 0643 Website: www.health-ni.gov.uk Twitter: @Healthdpt

Dentistry; finance, procurement and support services; good management, good records; health workforce policy and management; nursing and allied health professionals; governance in health and social care; mental health and learning disabilities; safety and quality standards; public health policy and advice; professional medical and environmental health advice; pharmacy; social services; health policy; DoH statistics and research.

Minister of Health **To be appointed**

Private Secretary   Paula Magill   028 9052 0643
Email: private.office@health-ni.gov.uk

Department for Infrastructure

Clarence Court, 10-18 Adelaide Street, Belfast BT2 8GB
Tel: 028 9054 0540
Website: www.infrastructure-ni.gov.uk Twitter: @deptinfra

Road improvement schemes; transport initiatives; roads; public transport; active travel; waterways; TransportNI procurement; road users; water and sewerage services; ports; statistics and research; regional development; planning; rivers and flooding.

Minister for Infrastructure **To be appointed**

Private Secretary   Lynda More   028 9054 0105
Email: private.office@infrastructure-ni.gov.uk

Department of Justice

Block B, Castle Buildings, Stormont Estate, Belfast BT4 3SG
Tel: 028 9076 3000
Email: private.office@justice-ni.x.gsi.gov.uk Website: www.justice-ni.gov.uk Twitter: @Justice_NI

Justice and the law; legal aid; prisons; youth justice; forensic science; policing and community safety; statistics and research.

Minister of Justice **To be appointed**

Acting Private Secretary   Barbara Smallwoods   028 9052 8121
Email: barbara.smallwoods@justice-ni.x.gsi.gov.uk

Members (MLAs)

State of the Parties (October 2017)

	Total
Democratic Unionist Party	28
Sinn Féin	27
Social Democratic and Labour Party	12
Ulster Unionist Party	10
Alliance	8
Green Party	2
Independent	1
People Before Profit Alliance	1
Traditional Unionist Voice	1
	90 seats

Changes since 2017 Northern Ireland Assembly election

RESIGNATIONS

Paul Girvan	South Antrim – *DUP*	8 June 2017
Michelle Gildernew	Fermanagh and South Tyrone – *Sinn Féin*	8 June 2017
Chris Hazzard	South Down – *Sinn Féin*	8 June 2017
Elisha McCallion	Foyle – *Sinn Féin*	8 June 2017
Barry McElduff	West Tyrone – *Sinn Féin*	8 June 2017

REPLACEMENTS

Colm Gildernew	Fermanagh and South Tyrone – *Sinn Féin*	Returned 20 June 2017 following the resignation of Michelle Gildernew
Catherine Kelly	West Tyrone – *Sinn Féin*	Returned 20 June 2017 following the resignation of Barry McElduff
Karen Mullan	Foyle – *Sinn Féin*	Returned 20 June 2017 following the resignation of Elisha McCallion
Emma Rogan	South Down – *Sinn Féin*	Returned 20 June 2017 following the resignation of Chris Hazzard
Trevor Clarke	South Antrim – *DUP*	Returned 28 June 2017 following the resignation of Paul Girvan

MLAs' Directory

All	Alliance
DUP	Democratic Unionist Party
Green	Green Party
Ind	Independent
PBPA	People Before Profit Alliance
SDLP	Social Democratic and Labour Party
TUV	Traditional Unionist Voice
UUP	Ulster Unionist Party

AGNEW, Mr Steven *Green* **North Down**
Leader, Green Party in Northern Ireland
Tel: 028 9052 1790 Email: steven.agnew@mla.niassembly.gov.uk
Constituency office: 76 Abbey Street, Bangor, Co Down BT20 4JB
Tel: 028 9145 9110 Email: stevenagnewgpni@hotmail.co.uk
Website: www.stevenagnew.net Twitter: @stevenagnew

AIKEN, Mr Stephen *UUP* **South Antrim**
Tel: 028 9041 8367 Email: steve.aiken@mla.niassembly.gov.uk
Constituency office: 3 The Square, Ballyclare BT39 9BB
Tel: 028 9334 4966 Twitter: @SteveAikenUUP

ALLEN, Mr Andy *UUP* **Belfast East**
Email: andy.allen@mla.niassembly.gov.uk
Constituency office: 174 Albertbridge Road, Belfast BT5 4GS
Tel: 028 9046 3900 Twitter: @AndyAllen88

ALLISTER, Mr Jim *TUV* **North Antrim**
Leader, Traditional Unionist Voice
Tel: 028 9052 1175 Email: jim.allister@mla.niassembly.gov.uk
Constituency offices: 38 Henry Street, Ballykeel, Ballymena, Co Antrim BT42 3AH
Tel: 028 2564 0250 Email: info@jimallister.org
1 Charles Street, Ballymoney, Co Antrim BT53 6DX
Tel: 028 2723 8393
Website: www.jimallister.org Twitter: @jimallister

ARCHIBALD, Ms Caoimhe *Sinn Féin* **East Londonderry**
Email: caoimhe.archibald@mla.niassembly.gov.uk
Constituency office: 81 Main Street, Dungiven BT47 4LE
Tel: 028 7774 2488 Twitter: @carchibald_sf

ARMSTRONG, Mrs Kellie *All* **Strangford**
Tel: 028 9052 0308 Email: kellie.armstrong@mla.niassembly.gov.uk
Constituency office: 14 South Street, Newtownards BT23 4JT
Tel: 028 9181 1414 Email: kellie.armstrong@allianceparty.org Twitter: @Kelmba

BAILEY, Ms Clare *Green* **Belfast South**
Tel: 028 9052 1504 Email: clare.bailey@mla.niassembly.gov.uk
Constituency office: No constituency office publicised Twitter: @ClareBaileyGPNI

BARTON, Ms Rosemary *UUP* **Fermanagh and South Tyrone**
Email: rosemary.barton@mla.niassembly.gov.uk
Constituency office: 1 Regal Pass, Enniskillen BT74 7NT Twitter: @RosemaryBarton1

BEATTIE, Mr Doug, MC *UUP* **Upper Bann**
Email: doug.beattie@mla.niassembly.gov.uk
Constituency office: 103 Bridge Street, Portadown BT63 5WU Twitter: @beattiedoug

BEGGS, Mr Roy *UUP* **East Antrim**
Tel: 028 9052 1546 Email: roy.beggs@mla.niassembly.gov.uk
Constituency offices: 3 St Brides Street, Carrickfergus, Co Antrim BT38 8AF
Tel: 028 9336 2995 Email: roybeggs.office@btopenworld.com
41 Station Road, Inver, Larne, Co Antrim BT40 3AA
Tel: 028 2827 3258 Fax: 028 2827 3258 Email: roybeggs.office3@btopenworld.com
Website: www.roybeggs.co.uk Twitter: @roybeggs

BOYLAN, Mr Cathal *Sinn Féin* **Newry and Armagh**
Tel: 028 9041 8351 Email: cathal.boylan@mla.niassembly.gov.uk
Constituency office: 59 Thomas Street, Armagh, Co Armagh BT61 7QB
Tel: 028 3751 1797 Email: armaghsinnfein@gmail.com Website: www.newryarmaghsf.com
Twitter: @cathalboylansf

BOYLE, Ms Michaela *Sinn Féin* **West Tyrone**
Tel: 028 9041 8383 Email: michaela.boyle@mla.niassembly.gov.uk
Constituency office: 1a Melvin Road, Ballycolman, Strabane, Co Tyrone BT82 9PP
Tel: 028 7188 6464 Email: micheala.boyle@sinn-fein.ie Twitter: @michaelaboylesf

BRADLEY, Mr Maurice *DUP* **East Londonderry**
Email: maurice.bradley@mla.niassembly.gov.uk
Constituency office: 2 Park Street, Coleraine BT52 1BD

BRADLEY, Ms Paula *DUP* **Belfast North**
Tel: 028 9052 1335 Email: paula.bradley@mla.niassembly.gov.uk
Constituency office: 3 Portland Avenue, Glengormley, Newtownabbey BT36 5EY
Tel: 028 9083 0066 Twitter: @PaulaBradleyMLA

BRADLEY, Ms Sinéad *SDLP* **South Down**
Email: sinead.bradley@mla.niassembly.gov.uk
Constituency office: 11-14 Newry Street, Ringmackilroy, Warrenpoint BT34 3JZ
Twitter: @sineadbradleysd

BRADSHAW, Ms Paula *All* **Belfast South**
Tel: 028 9052 1560 Email: paula.bradshaw@mla.niassembly.gov.uk
Constituency office: 100 University Street, Belfast BT7 1HE
Tel: 028 9032 8162 Email: paula.bradshaw@allianceparty.org Twitter: @PaulaJaneB

BUCHANAN, Mr Keith *DUP* **Mid Ulster**
Email: keith.buchanan@mla.niassembly.gov.uk
Constituency office: 2 Queens Avenue, Magherafelt BT45 6BU
Tel: 028 7930 0295/028 7930 0296 Twitter: @buchanan_dup

BUCHANAN, Mr Thomas *DUP* **West Tyrone**
Tel: 028 9052 1128 Email: thomas.buchanan@mla.niassembly.gov.uk
Constituency office: 5 Dublin Road, Omagh, Co Tyrone BT78 1ES
Tel: 028 8224 7702 Email: tombuchananmla@hotmail.co.uk

BUCKLEY, Mr Jonathan *DUP* **Upper Bann**
Email: jonathan.buckley@mla.niassembly.gov.uk
Constituency office: No constituency office publicised Twitter: @JBuckleyMLA

BUNTING, Ms Joanne *DUP* **Belfast East**
Tel: 028 9052 1748 Email: joanne.bunting@co.niassembly.gov.uk
Constituency office: No constituency office publicised Twitter: @joanne_bunting

BUTLER, Mr Robbie *UUP* **Lagan Valley**
Email: robbie.butler@mla.niassembly.gov.uk
Constituency office: 59 Bridge Street, Lisburn BT28 1XZ Twitter: @t3robbie

CAMERON, Mrs Pam *DUP* **South Antrim**
Tel: 028 9052 1816 Email: pam.cameron@mla.niassembly.gov.uk
Constituency office: 12a Beverley Road, Newtownabbey BT36 6QD
Website: www.pamcameron.org Twitter: @PamCameronMLA

CARROLL, Mr Gerry *PBPA* **Belfast West**
Email: gerry.carroll@mla.niassembly.gov.uk
Constituency office: 208 Falls Road, Belfast BT12 6AH

CATNEY, Mr Pat *SDLP* **Lagan Valley**
Email: pat.catney@mla.niassembly.gov.uk
Constituency office: No constituency office publicised Twitter: @PatCatney

CHAMBERS, Mr Alan *UUP* **North Down**
Email: alan.chambers@mla.niassembly.gov.uk
Constituency office: No constituency office publicised Twitter: @alcham49

CLARKE, Mr Trevor *DUP* **South Antrim**
Email: trevor.clarke@mla.niassembly.gov.uk
Constituency office: No constituency office publicised Twitter: @trevorclarkemla

DALLAT, Mr John *SDLP* **East Londonderry**
Email: john.dallat@mla.niassembly.gov.uk
Constituency office: No constituency office publicised Twitter: @johndallat

DICKSON, Mr Stewart *All* **East Antrim**
Tel: 028 9052 1315 Email: stewart.dickson@mla.niassembly.gov.uk
Constituency offices: 8 West Street, Carrickfergus, Co Antrim BT38 7AR
Tel: 028 9335 0286
97c Main Street, Larne BT40 1HJ
Website: stewartdicksonmla.com Twitter: @stewartcdickson

DILLON, Ms Linda *Sinn Féin* **Mid Ulster**
Email: linda.dillon@mla.niassembly.gov.uk
Constituency office: No constituency office publicised Twitter: @LindaDillon81

DOLAN, Ms Jemma *Sinn Féin* **Fermanagh and South Tyrone**
Email: jemma.dolan@mla.niassembly.gov.uk
Constituency office: 7 Market Street, Ennskillen BT74 7DS
Tel: 028 6632 8214 Twitter: @jemma_dolan

DUNNE, Mr Gordon, MBE *DUP* **North Down**
Tel: 028 9042 3322 Email: gordon.dunne@mla.niassembly.gov.uk
Constituency office: 8 Church Road, Holywood, Co Down BT18 9BU
Tel: 028 9042 3322 Email: info@gordondunne.org
Website: www.gordondunne.org Twitter: @gordondunnemla

DURKAN, Mr Mark H *SDLP* **Foyle**
Tel: 028 9041 8354 Email: markh.durkan@mla.niassembly.gov.uk
Constituency office: 141h Strand Road, Derry, Co Derry BT48 7PB
Tel: 028 7136 5516 Email: mhdurkan@sdlp.ie
Website: www.markhdurkan.com Twitter: @markhdurkan

EASTON, Mr Alex *DUP* **North Down**
Tel: 028 9058 8379 Email: alex.easton@mla.niassembly.gov.uk
Constituency office: 7 High Street, Donaghadee, Co Down BT21 0AA
Tel: 028 9188 9620 Website: www.nddup.org.uk
Website: alexeastonmla.org

EASTWOOD, Mr Colum *SDLP* **Foyle**
Leader, Social Democratic and Labour Party
Tel: 028 9041 8357 Email: colum.eastwood@mla.niassembly.gov.uk
Constituency office: Northside Village Centre, Glengalliagh Road, Derry BT48 8NN
Tel: 028 7135 0045 Email: colum.eastwood@sdlp.ie Twitter: @columeastwood

ENNIS, Ms Sinéad *Sinn Féin* **South Down**
Email: sinead.ennis@mla.niassembly.gov.uk
Constituency office: No constituency office publicised Twitter: @EnnisSinead

FARRY, Dr Stephen *All* **North Down**
Tel: 028 9052 1314 Email: stephen.farry@mla.niassembly.gov.uk
Constituency office: 58 Abbey Street, Bangor BT20 4JB
Tel: 028 9185 9475 Email: stephen.farry@allianceparty.org Twitter: @StephenFarryMLA

FEARON, Ms Megan *Sinn Féin* **Newry and Armagh**
Tel: 028 9041 8305/028 3086 1948 Email: megan.fearon@mla.niassembly.gov.uk
Constituency office: 1 Kilmorey Terrace, Patrick Street, Ballinlare, Newry BT35 8DW
Tel: 028 3026 1693 Twitter: @mfearonsf

FLYNN, Ms Órlaithí *Sinn Féin* **Belfast West**
Email: orlaithi.flynn@mla.niassembly.gov.uk
Constituency office: No constituency office publicised Twitter: @Orlaithi

FORD, Mr David *All* **South Antrim**
Tel: 028 9052 1314 Fax: 028 9052 1313 Email: david.ford@mla.niassembly.gov.uk
Constituency office: Unit 2, 21a Carnmoney Road, Newtownabbey, Co Antrim BT36 6HL
Tel: 028 9084 0930 Fax: 028 9083 7774 Email: south.antrim@davidford.org
Website: www.davidford.org Twitter: @DavidFordMLA

FOSTER, Rt Hon Arlene *DUP* **Fermanagh and South Tyrone**
Leader, Democratic Unionist Party
Tel: 028 9041 8366 Email: arlene.foster@mla.niassembly.gov.uk
Constituency office: 27 East Bridge Street, Enniskillen, Co Fermanagh BT74 7BW
Tel: 028 6632 0722 Email: arlene@arlenefoster.org.uk
Website: www.arlenefoster.org.uk Twitter: @DUPleader

FREW, Mr Paul *DUP* **North Antrim**
Tel: 028 9041 8392 Email: paul.frew@mla.niassembly.gov.uk
Constituency office: 9-11 Church Street, Ballymena, Co Antrim BT43 6DD
Tel: 028 2564 1421 Fax: 028 2565 7296 Email: frew637@btinternet.com
Website: www.paulfrew.co.uk Twitter: @paulfrewDUP

GILDERNEW, Mr Colm *Sinn Féin* **Fermanagh and South Tyrone**
Email: colm.gildernew@mla.niassembly.gov.uk
Constituency office: No constituency office publicised Twitter: @GildernewColm

GIVAN, Mr Paul *DUP* **Lagan Valley**
Tel: 028 9041 8389 Email: paul.givan@mla.niassembly.gov.uk
Constituency office: The Old Town Hall, 29 Castle Street, Lisburn, Co Antrim BT27 4DH
Tel: 028 9266 1100 Email: paul@laganvalley.net Twitter: @paulgivan

HAMILTON, Mr Simon *DUP* **Strangford**
Email: simon.hamilton@mla.niassembly.gov.uk
Constituency office: 7 The Square, Comber, Co Down BT23 5DX
Tel: 028 9187 0900 Email: simonhamilton@dup.org.uk
Website: www.simonhamilton.org Twitter: @simonhamilton

HANNA, Ms Claire *SDLP* **Belfast South**
Tel: 028 9052 0369 Email: claire.hanna@mla.niassembly.gov.uk
Constituency office: No constituency office publicised
Email: info@clairehanna.org
Website: clairehanna.org Twitter: @ClaireHanna

HILDITCH, Mr David *DUP* **East Antrim**
Tel: 028 9052 1322 Email: david.hilditch@mla.niassembly.gov.uk
Constituency office: 31 Lancasterian Street, Carrickfergus, Co Antrim BT38 7AB
Tel: 028 9332 9980 Email: davyhilditch.mla@gmail.com
Website: www.davidhilditch.org

HUMPHREY, Mr William *DUP* **Belfast North**
Tel: 028 9052 1322 Email: william.humphrey@mla.niassembly.gov.uk
Constituency office: Park Gate House, 35 Woodvale Road, Belfast BT13 3BN
Tel: 028 9074 4008 Email: williamhy@dup-belfast.co.uk

IRWIN, Mr William *DUP* **Newry and Armagh**
Tel: 028 9052 0313 Email: william.irwin@mla.niassembly.gov.uk
Constituency office: 18 Main Street, Richhill, Co Antrim BT61 9PW
Tel: 028 3887 0500 Fax: 028 3887 0054

KEARNEY, Mr Declan *Sinn Féin* **South Antrim**
Email: declan.kearney@mla.niassembly.gov.uk
Constituency office: Unit 1, 2 Main Street, Randalstown, Co Antrim BT41 3AB
Tel: 028 9447 3972 Twitter: @declankearneysf

KELLY, Ms Catherine *Sinn Féin* **West Tyrone**
Email: catherine.kelly@mla.niassembly.gov.uk
Constituency office: No constituency office publicised Twitter: @kelly_caitk16

KELLY, Mrs Dolores *SDLP* **Upper Bann**
Email: dolores.kelly@mla.niassembly.gov.uk
Constituency office: No constituency office publicised Twitter: @doloreskelly

KELLY, Mr Gerry *Sinn Féin* **Belfast North**
Tel: 028 9052 1471 Email: gerry.kelly@mla.niassembly.gov.uk
Constituency office: 545 Antrim Road, Belfast BT15 3BU
Tel: 028 9521 5649 Email: gerry.kelly@sinn-fein.ie Twitter: @gerrykellymla

LOCKHART, Ms Carla *DUP* **Upper Bann**
Email: carla.lockhart@mla.niassembly.gov.uk
Constituency office: 50a High Street, Lurgan, Co Armagh BT66 8AU
Tel: 028 3831 0088 Twitter: @carlalockhart

LONG, Mrs Naomi *All* **Belfast East**
Leader, Alliance Party
Tel: 028 9052 0351 Email: naomi.long@mla.niassembly.gov.uk
Constituency office: 56 Upper Newtownards Road, Belfast BT4 3EL
Tel: 028 9047 2004 Email: naomilong@allianceparty.org
Website: www.naomilong.com Twitter: @naomi_long

LUNN, Mr Trevor *All* **Lagan Valley**
Tel: 028 9052 1139 Email: trevor.lunn@mla.niassembly.gov.uk
Constituency office: 17 Graham Gardens, Lisburn, Co Antrim BT28 1XE
Tel: 028 9267 1177 Fax: 028 9267 1157 Email: trevor.lunn@allianceparty.org
Twitter: @TrevorLunnLV

LYNCH, Mr Seán *Sinn Féin* **Fermanagh and South Tyrone**
Tel: 028 9052 0350 Email: sean.lynch@mla.niassembly.gov.uk
Constituency office: 115 Main Street, Lisnaskea, Co Fermanagh BT92 0JE
Tel: 028 6772 1642 Email: sean.lynch@sinn-fein.ie Twitter: @seanlynch122

LYONS, Mr Gordon *DUP* **East Antrim**
Tel: 028 2826 7722 Email: gordon.lyons@mla.niassembly.gov.uk
Constituency office: 116 Main Street, Larne BT40 1RG
Tel: 028 2826 7722 Twitter: @gordonlyons1

LYTTLE, Mr Chris *All* **Belfast East**
Tel: 028 9052 1314 Email: chris.lyttle@mla.niassembly.gov.uk
Constituency office: 56 Upper Newtownards Road, Belfast, Co Down BT4 3EL
Tel: 028 9047 2004 Fax: 028 9065 6408 Email: chris.lyttle.co@niassembly.gov.uk
Website: www.chrislyttle.com Twitter: @chris_lyttle

McALEER, Mr Declan *Sinn Féin* **West Tyrone**
Tel: 028 9052 1470 Email: declan.mcaleer@mla.niassembly.gov.uk
Constituency office: 4-5 James Street, Omagh BT78 1DH
Tel: 028 8225 3040 Fax: 028 8225 3041 Email: declanmcaleer@ymail.com Twitter: @mc_mla

McCANN, Mr Fra *Sinn Féin* **Belfast West**
Tel: 028 9052 1471 Email: fra.mccann@mla.niassembly.gov.uk
Constituency office: 51-55 Falls Road, Belfast, Co Antrim BT12 4PD
Tel: 028 9050 8989 Fax: 028 9050 8988 Email: framccann@hotmail.com Twitter: @framccannmla

McCARTNEY, Mr Raymond *Sinn Féin* **Foyle**
Tel: 028 9052 0322 Email: raymond.mccartney@mla.niassembly.gov.uk
Constituency office: Ráth Mór Business Park, Eastway Road, Derry BT48 0LZ
Tel: 028 7137 7551 Email: foyleassembly@gmail.com Twitter: @RaymondMcCartn1

McCROSSAN, Mr Daniel *SDLP* **West Tyrone**
Email: daniel.mccrossan@mla.niassembly.gov.uk
Constituency office: SDLP Advice Centre, 5 Butcher Street, Strabane BT82 8BJ
Tel: 028 7188 2828 Email: strabaneoffice@sdlp.ie Twitter: @McCrossanMLA

McGLONE, Mr Patsy *SDLP* **Mid Ulster**
Tel: 028 9052 0347
Constituency office: 54a William Street, Cookstown, Co Tyrone BT80 8NB
Tel: 028 8675 8175 Fax: 028 8676 4611 Email: ask@patsymcglone.com patsymcglonemla@yahoo.ie
Website: www.patsymcglone.com Twitter: @patsymcglone

McGRATH, Mr Colin *SDLP* **South Down**
Email: colin.mcgrath@mla.niassembly.gov.uk
Constituency office: 97a Main Street, Ballaghbeg, Co Down BT33 0AE
Tel: 028 4379 8350
Website: colinmcgrath.net Twitter: @colinsdlp

McGUIGAN, Mr Philip *Sinn Féin* **North Antrim**
Email: philip.mcguigan@mla.niassembly.gov.uk
Constituency office: No constituency office publicised Twitter: @mcguigan_philip

McILVEEN, Miss Michelle *DUP* **Strangford**
Tel: 028 9052 1557 Email: michelle.mcilveen@mla.niassembly.gov.uk
Constituency office: 7 The Square, Comber, Co Down BT23 5DX
Tel: 028 9187 1441 Email: mail@michellemcilveen.org.uk
Website: www.michellemcilveen.org.uk Twitter: @mmcilveenmla

McNULTY, Mr Justin *SDLP* **Newry and Armagh**
Email: justin.mcnulty@mla.niassembly.gov.uk
Constituency office: 15 Trevor Hill, Carneyhough, Newry BT34 1DN
Tel: 028 3026 7933
Website: www.justinmcnulty.ie Twitter: @JustinMcNu1ty

MALLON, Ms Nichola *SDLP* **Belfast North**
Tel: 028 9515 0100 Email: nichola.mallon@mla.niassembly.gov.uk
Constituency office: 162c Antrim Road, Belfast BT15 2AH Twitter: @nicholamallon

MASKEY, Mr Alex *Sinn Féin* **Belfast West**
Tel: 028 9052 1224 Email: alex.maskey@mla.niassembly.gov.uk
Constituency office: 147 Andersonstown Road, Ballydownfine, Belfast, Co Antrim BT11 9BW
Tel: 028 9080 8404 Twitter: @AlexMaskeyMLA

MIDDLETON, Mr Gary *DUP* **Foyle**
Email: gary.middleton@mla.niassembly.gov.uk
Constituency office: First Floor, Waterside Centre, Waterside, Co Londonderry BT47 6BG
Tel: 028 7134 6271 Twitter: @Gary_Middleton

MILNE, Mr Ian *Sinn Féin* **Mid Ulster**
Email: ian.milne@mla.niassembly.gov.uk
Constituency office: 79 Quarry Road, Gulladuff, Co Derry BT45 8NT
Tel: 028 7964 4550 Twitter: @Ianmilnesf

MULLAN, Ms Karen *Sinn Féin* **Foyle**
Email: karen.mullan@mla.niassembly.gov.uk
Constituency office: Sinn Fein Centre, Ráth Mór Business Park, Eastway Road, Derry BT48 0LZ
Twitter: @k_mullan

MURPHY, Mr Conor *Sinn Féin* **Newry and Armagh**
Email: conor.murphy@mla.niassembly.gov.uk
Constituency office: 10 Newry Street, Crossmaglen BT35 9JH
Tel: 028 3086 1948 Twitter: @conormurphysf

NESBITT, Mr Mike *UUP* **Strangford**
Tel: 028 9052 1861 Email: mike.nesbitt@mla.niassembly.gov.uk
Constituency office: 16 South Street, Newtownards, Co Down BT23 4JT
Tel: 028 9182 1587 Twitter: @mikenesbittni

NEWTON, Mr Robin, MBE *DUP* **Belfast East**
Tel: 028 9052 1322 Email: robin.newton@mla.niassembly.gov.uk
Constituency office: 13 Castlereagh Road, Belfast BT5 5FB
Tel: 028 9045 9500 Fax: 028 9052 1912 Email: mail@robinnewton.co.uk
Website: www.robinnewton.co.uk Twitter: @RobinNewton4MLA

NÍ CHUILÍN, Ms Carál *Sinn Féin* **Belfast North**
Tel: 028 9052 1471 Email: caral.nichuilin@mla.niassembly.gov.uk
Constituency office: 545 Antrim Road, Belfast, Co Antrim BT15 3BU
Tel: 028 9521 5649 Email: caral.nichuilin@sinn-fein.ie Twitter: @CaralNiChuilin

O'DOWD, Mr John *Sinn Féin* **Upper Bann**
Tel: 028 9052 1471 Email: john.odowd@mla.niassembly.gov.uk
Constituency office: 77 North Street, Lurgan, Co Armagh BT67 9AH
Tel: 028 3834 9675 Fax: 028 3832 2610 Email: johnodowd@hotmail.com
Website: www.upperbannsf.com Twitter: @johnodowdsf

Ó MUILLEOIR, Mr Máirtín *Sinn Féin* **Belfast South**
Email: mairtin.omuilleoir@mla.niassembly.gov.uk
Constituency office: 178 Ormeau Road, Belfast BT7 2ED
Email: sandebelfast@sinn-fein.ie
Website: newbelfast.com Twitter: @newbelfast

O'NEILL, Ms Michelle *Sinn Féin* **Mid Ulster**
Tel: 028 9052 0463 Email: michelle.oneill@mla.niassembly.gov.uk
Constituency office: 79 Quarry Road, Gulladuff, Co Derry BT45 8NP
Tel: 028 7964 4550 Fax: 028 8774 6903 Email: michelle.oneill@dstbc.org Twitter: @moneillsf

POOTS, Mr Edwin *DUP* **Lagan Valley**
Tel: 028 9052 1114 Email: edwin.poots@mla.niassembly.gov.uk
Constituency offices: The Old Town Hall, 29 Castle Street, Lisburn, Co Antrim BT27 4DH
Tel: 028 9260 3003 Fax: 028 9267 1845 Email: edwin@edwinpoots.co.uk
3 Church Street, Dromore, Co Down BT25 1AA
Tel: 028 9269 8866
Website: www.edwinpoots.co.uk

ROBINSON, Mr George, MBE *DUP* **East Londonderry**
Tel: 028 9052 1322 Email: george.robinson@mla.niassembly.gov.uk
Constituency office: 6-8 Catherine Street, Limavady, Co Londonderry BT49 9DB
Tel: 028 7776 9191 Fax: 028 7776 9111 Email: limavadyhq@dup.org.uk Twitter: @g_rob44

ROGAN, Ms Emma *Sinn Féin* **South Down**
Email: emma.rogan@mla.niassembly.gov.uk
Constituency office: Details still to be confirmed Twitter: @emmarogan12

SHEEHAN, Mr Pat *Sinn Féin* **Belfast West**
Tel: 028 9052 1471 Email: pat.sheehan@mla.niassembly.gov.uk
Constituency office: 2a Monagh Crescent, Turf Lodge, Belfast, Co Antrim BT11 8EB
Tel: 028 9061 3894 Email: patsheehan@ymail.com Twitter: @PatSheehanMLA

STALFORD, Mr Christopher *DUP* **Belfast South**
Email: christopher.stalford@mla.niassembly.gov.uk
Constituency office: 127/145 Sandy Row, Belfast BT12 5ET
Tel: 028 9031 5329 Twitter: @cdmstalforddup

STEWART, Mr John *UUP* **East Antrim**
Email: john.stewart@mla.niassembly.gov.uk
Constituency office: No constituency office publicised
Website: johnstewartuup.blogspot.co.uk Twitter: @JohnStewart1983

STOREY, Mr Mervyn *DUP* **North Antrim**
Tel: 028 9052 1322 Email: mervyn.storey@mla.niassembly.gov.uk
Constituency office: 3 Market Street, Ballymoney BT53 6EA
Tel: 028 2766 9753 Fax: 028 2766 6143 Email: mervynstoreymla@gmail.com

SUGDEN, Ms Claire *Ind* **East Londonderry**
Tel: 028 9052 0310 Email: claire.sugden@mla.niassembly.gov.uk
Constituency office: 1 Upper Abbey Street, Coleraine BT52 1BF
Tel: 028 7032 7294
Website: www.clairesugden.co.uk Twitter: @ClaireSugden

SWANN, Mr Robin *UUP* **North Antrim**
Leader, Ulster Unionist Party
Tel: 028 9052 1766 Email: robin.swann@mla.niassembly.gov.uk
Constituency office: 13-15 Queen Street, Harryville, Ballymena, Co Antrim BT42 2BB
Tel: 028 2565 9595 Email: robin.swannmla@gmail.com
Website: www.robinswannmla.com Twitter: @RobinSwannUUP

WEIR, Mr Peter *DUP* **Strangford**
Tel: 028 9052 1296 Fax: 028 9052 1287 Email: peter.weir@mla.niassembly.gov.uk
Constituency office: No constituency office publicised
Email: pjweir@hotmail.com
Website: www.peterweir.net Twitter: @peterweirmla

WELLS, Mr Jim *DUP* **South Down**
Tel: 028 9052 1110 Fax: 028 9052 1820
Constituency office: 12 Bridge Street, Kilkeel, Co Down BT34 4AD
Tel: 028 4176 9900 Fax: 028 3832 1837 Email: jimwells6@gmail.com Twitter: @jim_wells_mla

Women MLAs (28)

ARCHIBALD Caoimhe	*Sinn Féin*	FLYNN Órlaithí	*Sinn Féin*
ARMSTRONG Kellie	*All*	FOSTER Arlene	*DUP*
BAILEY Clare	*Green*	HANNA Claire	*SDLP*
BARTON Rosemary	*UUP*	KELLY Catherine	*Sinn Féin*
BOYLE Michaela	*Sinn Féin*	KELLY Dolores	*SDLP*
BRADLEY Paula	*DUP*	LOCKHART Carla	*DUP*
BRADLEY Sinéad	*SDLP*	LONG Naomi	*All*
BRADSHAW Paula	*All*	McILVEEN Michelle	*DUP*
BUNTING Joanne	*DUP*	MALLON Nichola	*SDLP*
CAMERON Pam	*DUP*	MULLAN Karen	*Sinn Féin*
DILLON Linda	*Sinn Féin*	NÍ CHUILÍN Carál	*Sinn Féin*
DOLAN Jemma	*Sinn Féin*	O'NEILL Michelle	*Sinn Féin*
ENNIS Sinéad	*Sinn Féin*	ROGAN Emma	*Sinn Féin*
FEARON Megan	*Sinn Féin*	SUGDEN Claire	*Ind*

Constituencies

			Count elected on
East Antrim	Roy Beggs	UUP	6th
East Antrim	Stewart Dickson	All	6th
East Antrim	David Hilditch	DUP	3rd
East Antrim	Gordon Lyons	DUP	8th
East Antrim	John Stewart	UUP	9th

			Count elected on
North Antrim	Jim Allister	TUV	7th
North Antrim	Paul Frew	DUP	7th
North Antrim	Philip McGuigan	Sinn Féin	6th
North Antrim	Mervyn Storey	DUP	7th
North Antrim	Robin Swann	UUP	6th
South Antrim	Stephen Aiken	UUP	5th
South Antrim	Pam Cameron	DUP	8th
South Antrim	Trevor Clarke	DUP	–
South Antrim	David Ford	All	7th
South Antrim	Declan Kearney	Sinn Féin	4th
Belfast East	Andy Allen	UUP	9th
Belfast East	Joanne Bunting	DUP	9th
Belfast East	Naomi Long	All	1st
Belfast East	Chris Lyttle	All	8th
Belfast East	Robin Newton	DUP	11th
Belfast North	Paula Bradley	DUP	6th
Belfast North	William Humphrey	DUP	6th
Belfast North	Gerry Kelly	Sinn Féin	7th
Belfast North	Nichola Mallon	SDLP	7th
Belfast North	Carál Ní Chuilín	Sinn Féin	7th
Belfast South	Clare Bailey	Green	9th
Belfast South	Paula Bradshaw	All	6th
Belfast South	Claire Hanna	SDLP	6th
Belfast South	Máirtín Ó Muilleoir	Sinn Féin	1st
Belfast South	Christopher Stalford	DUP	9th
Belfast West	Gerry Carroll	PBPA	3rd
Belfast West	Órlaithí Flynn	Sinn Féin	1st
Belfast West	Fra McCann	Sinn Féin	4th
Belfast West	Alex Maskey	Sinn Féin	3rd
Belfast West	Pat Sheehan	Sinn Féin	4th
North Down	Steven Agnew	Green	7th
North Down	Alan Chambers	UUP	1st
North Down	Gordon Dunne	DUP	2nd
North Down	Alex Easton	DUP	1st
North Down	Stephen Farry	All	1st
South Down	Sinéad Bradley	SDLP	3rd
South Down	Sinéad Ennis	Sinn Féin	1st
South Down	Colin McGrath	SDLP	7th
South Down	Emma Rogan	Sinn Féin	–
South Down	Jim Wells	DUP	5th
Fermanagh and South Tyrone	Rosemary Barton	UUP	4th
Fermanagh and South Tyrone	Jemma Dolan	Sinn Féin	3rd
Fermanagh and South Tyrone	Arlene Foster	DUP	2nd
Fermanagh and South Tyrone	Colm Gildernew	Sinn Féin	–
Fermanagh and South Tyrone	Seán Lynch	Sinn Féin	4th
Foyle	Mark H Durkan	SDLP	5th
Foyle	Colum Eastwood	SDLP	3rd
Foyle	Raymond McCartney	Sinn Féin	2nd
Foyle	Gary Middleton	DUP	6th
Foyle	Karen Mullan	Sinn Féin	–
Lagan Valley	Robbie Butler	UUP	7th
Lagan Valley	Pat Catney	SDLP	8th
Lagan Valley	Paul Givan	DUP	1st
Lagan Valley	Trevor Lunn	All	7th
Lagan Valley	Edwin Poots	DUP	8th

			Count elected on
East Londonderry	Caoimhe Archibald	Sinn Féin	12th
East Londonderry	Maurice Bradley	DUP	9th
East Londonderry	John Dallat	SDLP	12th
East Londonderry	George Robinson	DUP	9th
East Londonderry	Claire Sugden	Ind	8th
Newry and Armagh	Cathal Boylan	Sinn Féin	1st
Newry and Armagh	Megan Fearon	Sinn Féin	2nd
Newry and Armagh	William Irwin	DUP	1st
Newry and Armagh	Justin McNulty	SDLP	2nd
Newry and Armagh	Conor Murphy	Sinn Féin	3rd
Strangford	Kellie Armstrong	All	4th
Strangford	Simon Hamilton	DUP	5th
Strangford	Michelle McIlveen	DUP	9th
Strangford	Mike Nesbitt	UUP	9th
Strangford	Peter Weir	DUP	11th
West Tyrone	Michaela Boyle	Sinn Féin	1st
West Tyrone	Thomas Buchanan	DUP	1st
West Tyrone	Catherine Kelly	Sinn Féin	–
West Tyrone	Declan McAleer	Sinn Féin	5th
West Tyrone	Daniel McCrossan	SDLP	5th
Mid Ulster	Keith Buchanan	DUP	1st
Mid Ulster	Linda Dillon	Sinn Féin	2nd
Mid Ulster	Patsy McGlone	SDLP	5th
Mid Ulster	Ian Milne	Sinn Féin	2nd
Mid Ulster	Michelle O'Neill	Sinn Féin	1st
Upper Bann	Doug Beattie	UUP	5th
Upper Bann	Jonathan Buckley	DUP	4th
Upper Bann	Dolores Kelly	SDLP	6th
Upper Bann	Carla Lockhart	DUP	1th
Upper Bann	John O'Dowd	Sinn Féin	5th

Assembly Committees

Committees will be appointed following the formation of the Executive.

Principal Officers and Officials

Office of the Speaker

Speaker **To be appointed**

Private Secretary	Frances Leneghan Email: frances.leneghan@niassembly.gov.uk	028 9052 1377
Adviser	Robin Ramsey Email: robin.ramsey@niassembly.gov.uk	028 9052 1551

Principal Deputy Speaker **To be appointed**

Deputy Speakers **To be appointed**

Assembly Commission

Chair and members still to be appointed

Principal Officers

Clerk/Chief Executive	Lesley Hogg
Directors	
Corporate Services	Richard Stewart
Facilities	Stephen Welch
Legal and Governance Services	Tara Caul
Parliamentary Services	Dr Gareth McGrath
Examiner of Statutory Rules	Angela Kelly
Clerk Assistants	Paul Gill Damien Martin
Editor of Debates	Simon Burrowes
Adviser to the Speaker/Head of Corporate Support	Robin Ramsey
Comptroller and Auditor General	Kieran Donnelly

Northern Ireland Civil Service

Executive Office

GD36 Stormont Castle, Stormont Estate, Belfast BT4 3TT
Tel: 028 9052 8400 Email: info.imcab@executiveoffice-ni.gov.uk
Website: www.executiveoffice-ni.gov.uk Twitter: @niexecutive
Interim Head of Northern Ireland Civil Service and Secretary to the Executive:
David Sterling 02890 378133 Email: hocs@executiveoffice-ni.gov.uk

Department of Agriculture, Environment and Rural Affairs

Dundonald House, Upper Newtownards Road, Ballymiscaw, Belfast BT4 3SB
Tel: 0300 200 7852 Email: daera.helpline@daera-ni.gov.uk
Website: www.daera-ni.gov.uk Twitter: @daera_ni
Permanent Secretary: Noel Lavery 028 9052 4608 Email: noel.lavery@daera-ni.gov.uk

Department for Communities

Causeway Exchange, 1-7 Bedford Street, Belfast BT2 7EG
Tel: 028 9082 9000 Email: private.office@communities-ni.gov.uk
Website: www.communities-ni.gov.uk Twitter: @CommunitiesNI
Permanent Secretary: Leo O'Reilly CB 028 9082 3301 Email: leo.oreilly@communities-ni.gov.uk

Department for the Economy

Netherleigh, Massey Avenue, Belfast BT4 2JP
Tel: 028 9052 9900 Email: dfemail@economy-ni.gov.uk
Website: www.economy-ni.gov.uk Twitter: @Economy_NI

Permanent Secretary: Dr Andrew McCormick 028 9052 9441
Email: andrew.mccormick@economy-ni.gov.uk

Department of Education

Rathgael House, Balloo Road, Rathgill, Bangor BT19 7PR
Tel: 028 9127 9279 Email: de.dewebmail@education-ni.gov.uk
Website: www.education-ni.gov.uk Twitter: @Education_NI

Permanent Secretary: Derek Baker 028 9127 9309 Email: derek.baker@education-ni.gov.uk

Department of Finance

Clare House, 303 Airport Road, Belfast BT3 9ED
Tel: 028 9081 6933 Fax: dof.enquiries@finance-ni.gov.uk
Website: www.finance-ni.gov.uk Twitter: @dptfinance

Interim Permanent Secretary: Hugh Widdis 028 9081 6590 Email: hugh.widdis@finance-ni.gov.uk

Department of Health

C5.20, Castle Buildings, Stormont Estate, Belfast BT4 3SQ
Tel: 028 9052 0500 Email: webmaster@health-ni.gov.uk
Website: www.health-ni.gov.uk Twitter: @HealthServiceNI

Permanent Secretary: Richard Pengelly Email: richard.pengelly@health-ni.gov.uk

Department for Infrastructure

Clarence Court, 10-18 Adelaide Street, Belfast BT2 8GB
Tel: 028 9054 0540 Email: dcu@infrastructure-ni.gov.uk
Website: www.infrastructure-ni.gov.uk Twitter: @deptinfra

Permanent Secretary: Peter May 028 9054 1175 Email: peter.may@infrastructure-ni.gov.uk

Department of Justice

Block B, Castle Buildings, Stormont Estate, Belfast BT4 3SG
Tel: 028 9076 3000/028 9052 7668 (text phone)
Website: www.justice-ni.gov.uk Twitter: @Justice_NI

Permanent Secretary: Nick Perry 028 9052 2992 Email: nick.perry@justice-ni.gov.uk

Office of the Attorney General for Northern Ireland

PO Box 1272, Belfast BT1 9LU
Tel: 028 9072 5333 Email: contact@attorneygeneralni.gov.uk
Website: www.attorneygeneralni.gov.uk

Attorney General for Northern Ireland: John F Larkin QC

Executive Agencies

Northern Ireland Courts and Tribunals Service

Laganside House, 23-27 Oxford Street, Belfast BT1 3LA
Tel: 0300 200 7812
Website: www.courtsni.gov.uk

Number of staff: 762

Acting Chief Executive: Peter Luney Email: peter.luney@courtsni.gov.uk

Sponsored by: Department of Justice, Northern Ireland Civil Service

Driver and Vehicle Agency
148-158 Corporation Street, Belfast BT1 3DH
Tel: 0300 200 7861 Email: dva@infrastructure-ni.gov.uk
Website: www.infrastructure-ni.gov.uk/driver-and-vehicle-agency

66 Balmoral Road, Belfast BT12 6QL
Tel: 0300 200 7861

County Hall, Castlerock Road, Coleraine, Co Londonderry BT51 3HS
Tel: 0300 200 7861

Number of staff: 792

Chief Executive: Paul Duffy 028 9025 4125 Email: chief.executivedva@infrastructure-ni.gov.uk
Sponsored by: Department for Infrastructure, Northern Ireland Civil Service

Northern Ireland Environment Agency
Klondyke Building, Gasworks Business Park, Lower Ormeau Road, Belfast BT7 2JA
Tel: 028 9056 9381 Email: nieaboardsecretariat@daera-ni.gov.uk
Website: www.daera-ni.gov.uk/northern-ireland-environment-agency

Number of staff: 460

Chief Executive: David Small Email: david.small@daera-ni.gov.uk
Sponsored by: Department of Agriculture, Environment and Rural Affairs, Northern Ireland Civil Service

Forensic Science Northern Ireland
151 Belfast Road, Carrickfergus BT38 8PL
Tel: 028 9036 1888 Fax: 028 9036 1900 Email: forensic.science@fsni.x.gsi.gov.uk
Website: www.justice-ni.gov.uk/fsni

Number of staff: 181

Chief Executive: Stan Brown 028 9036 1801 Email: generalenquiries@fsni.x.gsi.gov.uk
Sponsored by: Department of Justice, Northern Ireland Civil Service

Forest Service
Inishkeen House, Killyhevlin Ind Estate, Enniskillen, Co Fermanagh BT74 4EJ
Tel: 028 6634 3165
Email: customer.forestservice@daera-ni.gov.uk Website: www.daera-ni.gov.uk/forest-service

Number of staff: 210

Chief Executive: Malcolm Beatty 028 6634 3086 Email: malcolm.beatty@daera-ni.gov.uk
Sponsored by: Department of Agriculture, Environment and Rural Affairs, Northern Ireland Civil Service

Invest Northern Ireland
Bedford Square, Bedford Street, Belfast BT2 7ES
Tel: 0800 181 4422 Fax: 028 9043 6536
Email: enquiry@investni.com Website: www.investni.com Twitter: @InvestNINews

Number of staff: 619

Chair: Mark Ennis 028 9069 8255 Email: mark.ennis@investni.com
Chief Executive: Alastair Hamilton 028 9069 8260 Email: alastair.hamilton@investni.com
Sponsored by: Department for the Economy, Northern Ireland Civil Service

Legal Services Agency Northern Ireland
2nd Floor, Waterfront Plaza, 8 Langanbank Road, Mays Meadow, Belfast BT1 3BN

Number of staff: 130

Chief Executive: Paul Andrews Email: paul.andrews@justice-ni.gov.uk
Sponsored by: Department of Justice, Northern Ireland Civil Service

Northern Ireland Prison Service

Dundonald House, Upper Newtownards Road, Belfast BT4 3SU
Tel: 028 9052 2922 Email: info@niprisonservice.gov.uk
Website: www.justice-ni.gov.uk/topics/prisons Twitter: @NIPSofficial

Number of staff: 1,728

Director, Reducing Offending: Ronnie Armour 028 9052 5147
Email: ronnie.armour@justice-ni.x.gsi.gov.uk

Sponsored by: Department of Justice, Northern Ireland Civil Service

Northern Ireland Statistics and Research Agency

Colby House, Stranmillis Court, Belfast BT9 5RR
Tel: 028 9038 8400
Email: info@nisra.gov.uk Website: www.nisra.gov.uk Twitter: @NISRA

Number of staff: 455

Registrar General and Chief Executive: Siobhan Carey 028 9034 8102
Email: siobhan.carey@finance-ni.gov.uk

Sponsored by: Department of Finance, Northern Ireland Civil Service

Youth Justice Agency

41 Waring Street, Belfast BT1 2DY
Tel: 028 9031 6400 Fax: 028 9031 6402/3 Email: info@yjani.gov.uk
Website: www.justice-ni.gov.uk/topics/youth-justice Twitter: @Y_J_Agency

Number of staff: 250

Chief Executive: Declan McGeown 028 9031 6452 Email: declan.mcgeown@justice-ni.x.gsi.gov.uk

Sponsored by: Department of Justice, Northern Ireland Civil Service

Non-Ministerial Department

Public Prosecution Service for Northern Ireland

Headquarters, Belfast Chambers, 93 Chichester Street, Belfast BT1 3JR
Tel: 028 9089 7100
Email: info@ppsni.gsi.gov.uk Website: www.ppsni.gov.uk
Director of Public Prosecutions for Northern Ireland: Barra McGrory QC 028 9089 7181
Email: barra.mcgrory@ppsni.gsi.gov.uk

Political Parties

Democratic Unionist Party

91 Dundela Avenue, Belfast BT4 3BU
Tel: 028 9047 1155
Email: info@mydup.com Website: www.mydup.com Twitter: @duponline
Assembly Office, Room 207 Parliament Buildings, Stormont, Belfast BT4 3XX
Tel: 028 9052 1323

Leader: Arlene Foster MLA
Deputy Leader: Nigel Dodds OBE MP
Chair: Lord Morrow
Vice-chair: Dr William McCrea
Secretary: Michelle McIlveen MLA
Treasurer: Gregory Campbell MP
Press Officer: Clive McFarland 028 9065 4479 Email: clivemcfarland@dup.org.uk

Sinn Féin

Assembly Office:
Tel: 028 9052 1471/028 9052 1470 Fax: 028 9052 1476
Email: sfassembly@outlook.com Twitter: @sinnfeinireland

44 Parnell Square, Dublin 1, Ireland
Tel: +353 1 8726932 Fax: +353 1 8733441
Website: www.sinnfein.ie

53 Falls Road, Belfast BT12 4PD
Tel: 028 9034 7350 Fax: 028 9022 3001

President: Gerry Adams
Vice-President: Mary Lou McDonald
Chair: Declan Kearney MLA
General Secretary: Dawn Doyle
Treasurers: Pearse Doherty, Conor Murphy MLA
Director of Communications: Ciarán Quinn

Social Democratic and Labour Party

121 Ormeau Road, Belfast BT7 1SH
Tel: 028 9024 7700 Fax: 028 9023 6699
Email: info@sdlp.ie Website: www.sdlp.ie Twitter: @sdlplive

Assembly Office: Tel: 028 9052 1319

Press Office: Tel: 028 9052 1837

Leader: Colum Eastwood MLA
Deputy Leader: Fearghal McKinney
Chair: Ronan McCay
Vice-chair: Gerard McDonald
General Secretary: Gerry Cosgrove Email: gerry.cosgrove@sdlphq.ie
International Secretary: Dr Naomh Gallagher

Ulster Unionist Party

Strandtown Hall, 2-4 Belmont Road, Belfast BT4 2AN
Tel: 028 9047 4630 Fax: 028 9065 2149
Email: uup@uup.org Website: www.uup.org Twitter: @uuponline

Assembly Office, Room 214 Parliament Buildings, Stormont, Belfast BT4 3XX
Tel: 028 9052 1423 Fax: 028 9052 1883

Policy Unit: Tel: 028 9052 1892

Leader: Robin Swann MLA
Chair: Lord Empey OBE
Vice-chair: Roy McCune
Treasurer: Mark Cosgrove
Party Officers: Stephen Aiken MLA, Tom Elliott, James Nicholson MEP, Sandra Overend, Jenny Palmer, Alexander Redpath, Lord Rogan, George White, Trevor Wilson
Communications and Policy Co-ordinator: John Moore 028 9052 1328 Email: john.moore@uup.org
Press Officer: Stephen Barr 028 9052 1890 Email: stephen.barr@party.niassembly.gov.uk

Alliance

88 University Street, Belfast BT7 1HE
Tel: 028 9032 4274 Fax: 028 9033 3147
Email: alliance@allianceparty.org Website: www.allianceparty.org Twitter: @allianceparty

Assembly Office, Room 220 Parliament Buildings, Stormont, Belfast BT4 3XX
Tel: 028 9052 1314 Fax: 028 9052 1313
Email: stormont@allianceparty.org

Leader: Naomi Long MLA
Chair: Dr Duncan Morrow Email: duncan.morrow@allianceparty.org
General Secretary: Sharon Lowry Email: sharon.lowry@allianceparty.org
Joint Hon Treasurers: Alan McBride Email: a.mcbride@wavetrauma.org, Billy Webb Email: billy.webb@allianceparty.org
Press Officer: Scott Jamison Email: scott.jamison@allianceparty.org

Green Party

PO Box 369, Bangor BT20 9FJ
Tel: 028 9145 9110
Email: info@greenpartyni.org Website: www.greenpartyni.org Twitter: @greenpartyni

Assembly Office:
Tel: 028 9052 1790

Leader, Green Party in Northern Ireland: Steven Agnew MLA
Chair: Ricky Bamford
Press Officer: Sinead McIvor 028 9052 1141 Email: sinead.mcivor@party.niassembly.gov.uk

People Before Profit

c/o Sarsfield Road, Dublin 10, Ireland
Tel: 028 9041 8355
Email: info@peoplebeforeprofit.ie Website: peoplebeforeprofit.ie Twitter: @pb4p

Traditional Unionist Voice

38 Henry Street, Ballymena BT42 3AH
Tel: 028 2564 0250
Website: www.tuv.org.uk

Assembly Office:
Tel: 028 9052 1461

Leader: Jim Allister MLA
President: William Ross
Chair: Ivor McConnell
Party Secretary: Joel Johnston
Treasurer: Kenny Loughrin
Press Officer: Samuel Morrison

Greater London Authority

City Hall, The Queens Walk, London SE1 2AA
Tel: 020 7983 4000 Fax: 020 7983 4057 Email: assembly@london.gov.uk
Website: www.london.gov.uk Twitter: @MayorofLondon/@LondonAssembly

Mayoral Team

Mayor of London Rt Hon **Sadiq Khan** (Lab)
Tel: 020 7983 5646 Email: mayor@london.gov.uk

Statutory Deputy Mayor; Deputy Mayor for Education and Childcare:
Joanne McCartney AM (Lab/Co-op)
Tel: 020 7983 5504 Email: joanne.mccartney@london.gov.uk

Deputy Mayor for Housing and Residential Development: James Murray
Tel: 020 7983 4343 Email: james.murray@london.gov.uk

Deputy Mayor for Planning, Regeneration and Skills: Jules Pipe
Tel: 020 7983 4190 Email: jules.pipe@london.gov.uk

Deputy Mayor for Culture and Creative Industries: Justine Simons OBE
Tel: 020 7983 5853 Email: justine.simons@london.gov.uk

Deputy Mayor for Social Integration, Social Mobility and Community Engagement: Matthew Ryder QC
Tel: 020 7983 4015 Email: matthew.ryder@london.gov.uk

Deputy Mayor for Business: Rajesh Agrawal
Tel: 020 7983 4516 Email: rajesh.agrawal@london.gov.uk

Deputy Mayor for Environment and Energy: Shirley Rodrigues
Tel: 020 7983 4384 Email: shirley.rodrigues@london.gov.uk

Deputy Mayor for Policing and Crime: Sophie Linden
Tel: 020 7983 5696 Email: sophie.linden@mopac.london.gov.uk

Deputy Mayor for Transport and Deputy Chair of Transport for London: Val Shawcross CBE
Tel: 020 7983 4099 Email: val.shawcross@london.gov.uk

Chief of Staff: David Bellamy
Tel: 020 7983 4538 Email: david.bellamy@london.gov.uk

Mayoral Director of Policy: Nick Bowes
Tel: 020 7983 4030 Email: nick.bowes@london.gov.uk

Mayoral Director of Communications: Patrick Hennessy
Tel: 020 7983 4069 Email: patrick.hennessy@london.gov.uk

Mayoral Director for External and International Affairs: Leah Kreitzman
Tel: 020 7983 4030 Email: leah.kreitzman@london.gov.uk

Mayoral Director for Political and Public Affairs: Jack Stenner
Tel: 020 7983 4069 Email: jack.stenner@london.gov.uk

Chief Digital Officer: Theo Blackwell

Chair, London Fire and Emergency Planning Authority: Fiona Twycross AM (Lab)
Tel: 020 7983 5545 Email: fiona.twycross@london.gov.uk

Chair, Night Time Commission: Philip Kolvin QC
Tel: 020 7983 5853 Email: philip.kolvin@london.gov.uk

Night Czar: Amy Lamé
Tel: 020 7983 4538 Email: amy.lame@london.gov.uk

Commissioner for Walking and Cycling: Dr Will Norman
Tel: 020 3054 1155 Email: willnorman@tfl.gov.uk

Victims Commissioner: Claire Waxman
Tel: 020 7983 4646 Email: claire.waxman@mopac.london.gov.uk

Spokespeople

Labour Group

Leader, Labour Group on the London Assembly; Spokesperson on Budget and Performance: Len Duvall OBE
Deputy Leader, Labour Group on the London Assembly; Spokesperson on Economics: Fiona Twycross
Spokesperson on Transport (on maternity leave): Florence Eshalomi
Spokesperson on Police and Crime: Unmesh Desai
Spokesperson on Housing; Spokesperson on Transport (maternity cover): Tom Copley
Spokesperson on Health: Dr Onkar Sahota
Spokesperson on Education: Jennette Arnold OBE
Spokesperson on Planning: Nicky Gavron
Spokesperson on Environment: Leonie Cooper
Spokesperson on Regeneration: Navin Shah

Conservative Group

Leader, Conservative Group on the London Assembly; Spokesperson for Budget and Oversight: Gareth Bacon
Spokesperson on Planning: Tony Devenish
Spokesperson on Health, Environment and Regeneration: Shaun Bailey
Spokesperson on Housing: Andrew Boff
Spokesperson on Police and Crime: Steve O'Connell
Spokesperson on Transport: Keith Prince

London Assembly Members' Directory

ARBOUR, Mr Tony, JP *Con* **South West**
Deputy Chair, London Assembly
Tel: 020 7983 4116 Email: tony.arbour@london.gov.uk

ARNOLD, Ms Jennette, OBE *Lab/Co-op* **North East**
Chair, London Assembly; Labour Spokesperson on Education
Tel: 020 7983 4349 Email: jennette.arnold@london.gov.uk
Website: jennettearnold.com Twitter: @JennetteArnold

BACON, Mr Gareth *Con* **Bexley and Bromley**
Leader, Conservative Group on the Assembly; Conservative Spokesperson for Budget and Oversight
Tel: 020 7983 5784 Email: gareth.bacon@london.gov.uk

BAILEY, Mr Shaun *Con* **Londonwide**
Conservative Spokesperson on Health, Environment and Regeneration
Tel: 020 7983 4354 Email: shaun.bailey@london.gov.uk Twitter: @ShaunBaileyUK

BERRY, Ms Sian *Green* **Londonwide**
Leader, Green Party Group on the Assembly
Tel: 020 7983 4391 Fax: 020 7983 4398 Email: sian.berry@london.gov.uk Twitter: @sianberry

BOFF, Mr Andrew *Con* **Londonwide**
Conservative Spokesperson on Housing
Tel: 020 7983 4366 Email: andrew.boff@london.gov.uk Twitter: @AndrewBoff

COOPER, Ms Leonie *Lab* **Merton and Wandsworth**
Labour Spokesperson on Environment
Email: leonie.cooper@london.gov.uk

COPLEY, Mr Tom *Lab* **Londonwide**
Labour Spokesperson on Housing and on Transport (maternity cover)
Tel: 020 7983 5545 Email: tom.copley@london.gov.uk
Website: tomcopley.com Twitter: @tomcopley

DESAI, Mr Unmesh *Lab* **City and East**
Labour Spokesperson on Police and Crime
Tel: 020 7983 4430 Email: unmesh.desai@london.gov.uk Twitter: @unmeshdesai

DEVENISH, Mr Tony *Con* **West Central**
Conservative Spokesperson on Planning
Email: tony.devenish@london.gov.uk

DISMORE, Mr Andrew *Lab* **Barnet and Camden**
Tel: 020 7983 5529 Email: andrew.dismore@london.gov.uk
Website: www.andrewdismore.org.uk Twitter: @Andrew_Dismore

DUVALL, Mr Len, OBE *Lab/Co-op* **Greenwich and Lewisham**
Leader, Labour Group on the London Assembly; Labour Spokesperson on Budget and Performance
Tel: 020 7983 4517 Email: len.duvall@london.gov.uk Twitter: @Len_Duvall

ESHALOMI, Ms Florence *Lab* **Lambeth and Southwark**
Labour Spokesperson on Transport (on maternity leave)
Tel: 020 7983 4427 Email: florence.eshalomi@london.gov.uk Twitter: @FloEshalomi

GAVRON, Ms Nicky *Lab/Co-op* **Londonwide**
Labour Spokesperson on Planning
Tel: 020 7983 4509 Email: nicky.gavron@london.gov.uk
Website: www.nickygavron.co.uk Twitter: @nickygavron

HALL, Ms Susan *Con* **Londonwide**
Email: susan.hall@london.gov.uk Twitter: @Councillorsuzie

KURTEN, Mr David *UKIP* **Londonwide**
Email: david.kurten@london.gov.uk
Website: www.davidkurten.net Twitter: @davidkurten

McCARTNEY, Ms Joanne *Lab/Co-op* **Enfield and Haringey**
Statutory Deputy Mayor; Deputy Mayor for Education and Childcare
Tel: 020 7983 5524 Email: joanne.mccartney@london.gov.uk
Website: joannemccartney.co.uk Twitter: @JoanneMcCartney

O'CONNELL, Mr Steve *Con* **Croydon and Sutton**
Conservative Spokesperson on Police and Crime
Tel: 020 7983 4405 Email: steve.o'connell@london.gov.uk
Website: www.steveoconnell.org

PIDGEON, Ms Caroline, MBE *Lib Dem* **Londonwide**
Leader, Liberal Democrat Group on the London Assembly
Tel: 020 7983 4362 Email: caroline.pidgeon@london.gov.uk
Website: www.carolinepidgeon.org Twitter: @CarolinePidgeon

PRINCE, Mr Keith *Con* **Havering and Redbridge**
Conservative Spokesperson on Transport
Tel: 020 7983 4955 Email: keith.prince@london.gov.uk
Website: www.keithprince.london Twitter: @KeithPrinceAM

RUSSELL, Ms Caroline *Green* **Londonwide**
Email: caroline.russell@london.gov.uk Twitter: @CarolineRussell

SAHOTA, Dr Onkar *Lab* **Ealing and Hillingdon**
Labour Spokesperson on Health
Tel: 020 7983 6558 Email: onkar.sahota@london.gov.uk
Website: www.dronkarsahota.com Twitter: @DrOnkarSahota

SHAH, Mr Navin *Lab* **Brent and Harrow**
Labour Spokesperson on Regeneration
Tel: 020 7983 4876 Email: navin.shah@london.gov.uk
Website: www.navinshah.com Twitter: @NavinShahAM

TWYCROSS, Ms Fiona *Lab* **Londonwide**
Deputy Leader, Labour Group on the London Assembly; Labour Spokesperson on Economics
Tel: 020 7983 5545 Email: fiona.twycross@london.gov.uk
Website: www.fionatwycross.org Twitter: @fionatwycross

WHITTLE, Mr Peter *UKIP* **Londonwide**
Leader, UKIP Group on the Assembly; Deputy Leader, UK Independence Party
Email: peter.whittle@london.gov.uk Twitter: @prwhittle

Constituencies

Barnet and Camden	Andrew Dismore	Lab
Bexley and Bromley	Gareth Bacon	Con
Brent and Harrow	Navin Shah	Lab
City and East	Unmesh Desai	Lab
Croydon and Sutton	Steve O'Connell	Con
Ealing and Hillingdon	Onkar Sahota	Lab
Enfield and Haringey	Joanne McCartney	Lab/Co-op
Greenwich and Lewisham	Len Duvall	Lab/Co-op
Havering and Redbridge	Keith Prince	Con
Lambeth and Southwark	Florence Eshalomi	Lab
Merton and Wandsworth	Leonie Cooper	Lab
North East	Jennette Arnold	Lab/Co-op
South West	Tony Arbour	Con
West Central	Tony Devenish	Con

Londonwide list

Shaun Bailey	Con
Sian Berry	Green
Andrew Boff	Con
Tom Copley	Lab
Nicky Gavron	Lab/Co-op
Susan Hall	Con
David Kurten	UKIP
Caroline Pidgeon	Lib Dem
Caroline Russell	Green
Fiona Twycross	Lab
Peter Whittle	UKIP

Assembly Committees

Budget and Performance

Tel: 020 7983 5526
Email: laura.pelling@london.gov.uk
www.london.gov.uk/moderngov/mgcommitteedetails.aspx?id=129

Gareth Bacon (Chair) *Con*
Len Duvall (Deputy Chair) *Lab/Co-op*
Sian Berry *Green*
Leonie Cooper *Lab*
Unmesh Desai *Lab*
Caroline Pidgeon *Lib Dem*
Keith Prince *Con*
Staff: Laura Pelling (Principal Committee Manager)

Budget Monitoring Sub-committee

Tel: 020 7983 4383
Email: laura.francis@london.gov.uk
www.london.gov.uk/moderngov/mgcommitteedetails.aspx?id=130

Gareth Bacon (Chair) *Con*
Len Duvall (Deputy Chair) *Lab/Co-op*
Jennette Arnold *Lab/Co-op*
Staff: Laura Francis (Committee Assistant)

Confirmation Hearings

Tel: 020 7983 6559
Email: teresa.young@london.gov.uk
www.london.gov.uk/moderngov/mgcommitteedetails.aspx?id=135

Andrew Boff (Chair) *Con*
Jennette Arnold *Lab/Co-op*
Tom Copley *Lab*
Steve O'Connell *Con*
Caroline Russell *Green*
Onkar Sahota *Lab*
Peter Whittle *UKIP*
Staff: Teresa Young (Senior Committee Officer)

Economy

Tel: 020 7983 4616
Email: clare.bryant@london.gov.uk
www.london.gov.uk/moderngov/mgcommitteedetails.aspx?id=255

Caroline Russell (Chair) *Green*
Jennette Arnold *Lab/Co-op*
Shaun Bailey *Con*
Andrew Dismore *Lab*
Susan Hall *Con*
Fiona Twycross *Lab*
Staff: Clare Bryant (Committee Officer)

Environment

Tel: 020 7983 4616
Email: clare.bryant@london.gov.uk
www.london.gov.uk/moderngov/mgcommitteedetails.aspx?id=305

Leonie Cooper (Chair) *Lab*
Caroline Russell (Deputy Chair) *Green*
Tony Arbour *Con*
Jennette Arnold *Lab/Co-op*
Shaun Bailey *Con*
David Kurten *UKIP*
Joanne McCartney *Lab/Co-op*
Staff: Clare Bryant (Committee Officer)

Fire, Resilience and Emergency Planning

Gareth Bacon *Con*
Leonie Cooper *Lab*
Andrew Dismore *Lab*
Florence Eshalomi *Lab*
David Kurten *UKIP*

GLA Oversight

Tel: 020 7983 4425
Email: vishal.seegoolam@london.gov.uk
www.london.gov.uk/moderngov/mgcommitteedetails.aspx?id=254

Len Duvall (Chair) *Lab/Co-op*
Gareth Bacon (Deputy Chair) *Con*
Sian Berry *Green*
Tom Copley *Lab*
Steve O'Connell *Con*
Keith Prince *Con*
Onkar Sahota *Lab*
Navin Shah *Lab*
Peter Whittle *UKIP*
Staff: Vishal Seegoolam (Principal Committee Manager)

Health

Tel: 020 7983 4616
Email: clare.bryant@london.gov.uk
www.london.gov.uk/moderngov/mgcommitteedetails.aspx?id=304

Onkar Sahota (Chair) *Lab*
Andrew Boff *Con*
Unmesh Desai *Lab*
Susan Hall *Con*
Fiona Twycross *Lab*
Staff: Clare Bryant (Committee Officer)

Housing

Tel: 020 7983 4616
Email: clare.bryant@london.gov.uk
www.london.gov.uk/moderngov/mgcommitteedetails.aspx?id=302

Sian Berry (Chair) *Green*
Andrew Boff (Deputy Chair) *Con*
Leonie Cooper *Lab*
Tom Copley *Lab*
Tony Devenish *Con*
Nicky Gavron *Lab/Co-op*
David Kurten *UKIP*
Staff: Clare Bryant (Committee Officer)

Planning

Tel: 020 7983 4926
Email: john.johnson@london.gov.uk
www.london.gov.uk/moderngov/mgcommitteedetails.aspx?id=258

Nicky Gavron (Chair) *Lab/Co-op*
Andrew Boff (Deputy Chair) *Con*
Tom Copley *Lab*
Tony Devenish *Con*
Navin Shah *Lab*
Staff: John Johnson (Committee Officer)

Police and Crime

Tel: 020 7983 6559
Email: teresa.young@london.gov.uk
www.london.gov.uk/moderngov/mgcommitteedetails.aspx?id=240

Steve O'Connell (Chair) *Con*
Sian Berry (Deputy Chair) *Green*
Tony Arbour *Con*
Unmesh Desai *Lab*
Andrew Dismore *Lab*
Len Duvall *Lab/Co-op*
Florence Eshalomi *Lab*
Caroline Pidgeon *Lib Dem*
Peter Whittle *UKIP*
Staff: Teresa Young (Senior Committee Officer)

Regeneration
Tel: 020 7983 6559
Email: teresa.young@london.gov.uk
www.london.gov.uk/moderngov/mgcommitteedetails.aspx?id=303
Navin Shah (Chair) *Lab*
Shaun Bailey (Deputy Chair) *Con*
Tony Devenish *Con*
Andrew Dismore *Lab*
Nicky Gavron *Lab/Co-op*
Staff: Teresa Young (Senior Committee Officer)

Transport
Tel: 020 7983 5526
Email: laura.pelling@london.gov.uk
www.london.gov.uk/moderngov/mgcommitteedetails.aspx?id=173
Keith Prince (Chair) *Con*
Caroline Pidgeon (Deputy Chair) *Lib Dem*
Tom Copley *Lab*
Florence Eshalomi *Lab*
David Kurten *UKIP*
Joanne McCartney *Lab/Co-op*
Steve O'Connell *Con*
Caroline Russell *Green*
Navin Shah *Lab*
Staff: Laura Pelling (Principal Committee Manager)

Audit Panel
Tel: 020 7983 5520
Email: polly.hanford@london.gov.uk
www.london.gov.uk/moderngov/mgcommitteedetails.aspx?id=128
Peter Whittle (Chair) *UKIP*
Keith Prince (Deputy Chair) *Con*
Leonie Cooper *Lab*
Tom Copley *Lab*
Staff: Polly Hanford (Committee Assistant)

Education Panel
Tel: 020 7983 4383
Email: laura.francis@london.gov.uk
www.london.gov.uk/moderngov/mgcommitteedetails.aspx?id=322
Jennette Arnold (Chair) *Lab/Co-op*
Tony Arbour *Con*
Susan Hall *Con*
David Kurten *UKIP*
Fiona Twycross *Lab*
Staff: Laura Francis (Committee Assistant)

Devolution Working Group
Tel: 020 7983 4425
Email: vishal.seegoolam@london.gov.uk
www.london.gov.uk/moderngov/mgcommitteedetails.aspx?id=359
Len Duvall (Chair) *Lab/Co-op*
Sian Berry *Green*
Andrew Boff *Con*
Peter Whittle *UKIP*
Staff: Vishal Seegoolam (Principal Committee Manager)

EU Exit Working Group
Tel: 020 7983 4425
Email: vishal.seegoolam@london.gov.uk
www.london.gov.uk/moderngov/mgCommitteeDetails.aspx?ID=421
Len Duvall (Chair) *Lab/Co-op*
Gareth Bacon (Deputy Chair) *Con*
Caroline Pidgeon *Lib Dem*
Caroline Russell *Green*
Peter Whittle *UKIP*
Staff: Vishal Seegoolam (Principal Committee Manager)

Police and Crime Commissioners

Avon and Somerset

OPCC, Police Headquarters, Valley Road, Portishead BS20 8JJ
Tel: 01275 816377 Fax: 01275 816388 Email: pcc@avonandsomerset.pnn.police.uk
Website: www.avonandsomerset-pcc.gov.uk Twitter: @AandSPCC

Police and Crime Commissioner: Sue Mountstevens (Ind)

Bedfordshire

OPCC, Bridgebury House, Woburn Road, Kempston, Bedfordshire MK43 9AX
Tel: 01234 842064 Email: pcc@bedfordshire.pnn.police.uk
Website: www.bedfordshire.pcc.police.uk Twitter: @BedsPCC

Police and Crime Commissioner: Kathryn Holloway (Con)

Cambridgeshire

OPCC, PO Box 688, Huntingdon PE29 9LA
Tel: 0300 333 3456 Email: cambs-pcc@cambs.pnn.police.uk
Website: www.cambridgeshire-pcc.gov.uk Twitter: @PCCCambs

Police and Crime Commissioner: Jason Ablewhite (Con)

Cheshire

OPCC, Clemonds Hey, Oakmere Road, Winsford, Cheshire CW7 2UA
Tel: 01606 364000 Email: police.crime.commissioner@cheshire.pnn.police.uk
Website: www.cheshire-pcc.gov.uk Twitter: @CheshirePCC

Police and Crime Commissioner: David Keane (Lab)

Cleveland

OPCC, Police Headquarters, Ladgate Lane, Middlesbrough TS8 9EH
Tel: 01642 301653 Email: pcc@cleveland.pnn.police.uk
Website: www.cleveland.pcc.police.uk Twitter: @Cleveland_PCC

Police and Crime Commissioner: Barry Coppinger (Lab)

Cumbria

OPCC, Carleton Hall, Penrith, Cumbria CA10 2AU
Tel: 01768 217734 Email: commissioner@cumbria-pcc.gov.uk
Website: cumbria-pcc.gov.uk Twitter: @cumbriapcc

Police and Crime Commissioner: Peter McCall (Con)

Derbyshire

OPCC, Butterley Hall, Ripley, Derbyshire DE5 3RS
Tel: 0300 122 6000 Email: pccoffice@derbyshire.pnn.police.uk
Website: www.derbyshire-pcc.gov.uk Twitter: @DerbysPCC

Police and Crime Commissioner: Hardyal Dhindsa (Lab)

Devon and Cornwall

OPCC, Alderson Drive, Exeter EX2 7RP
Tel: 01392 225555
Email: opcc@devonandcornwall.pnn.police.uk Website: www.devonandcornwall-pcc.gov.uk
Twitter: @DC_PCC

Police and Crime Commissioner: Alison Hernandez (Con)

Dorset
OPCC, Force Headquarters, Winfrith, Dorchester, Dorset DT2 8DZ
Tel: 01305 229084/01202 229084
Email: pcc@dorset.pnn.police.uk Website: www.dorset.pcc.police.uk Twitter: @PCCDorset
Police and Crime Commissioner: Martyn Underhill (Ind)

Durham
OPCC, Durham Police Headquarters, Aykley Heads, Durham DH1 5TT
Tel: 0191-375 2001
Email: general.enquiries@durham.pcc.pnn.gov.uk Website: www.durham-pcc.gov.uk
Twitter: @DurhamPCC
Police and Crime Commissioner: Ron Hogg (Lab)

Dyfed-Powys
OPCC, PO Box 99, Llangunnor, Carmarthen SA31 2PF
Tel: 01267 226440
Email: opcc@dyfed-powys.pnn.police.uk Website: www.dyfedpowys-pcc.org.uk
Twitter: @DPOPCC
Police and Crime Commissioner: Dafydd Llywelyn (PlC)

Essex
OPCC, 3 Hoffmanns Way, Chelmsford, Essex CM1 1GU
Tel: 01245 291600
Email: pcc@essex.pnn.police.uk Website: www.essex.pcc.police.uk Twitter: @EssexPCC
Police and Crime Commissioner: Roger Hirst (Con)

Gloucestershire
OPCC, 1 Waterwells, Waterwells Drive, Quedgeley, Gloucestershire GL2 2AN
Tel: 01452 754348
Email: pcc@gloucestershire.pnn.police.uk Website: www.gloucestershire-pcc.gov.uk
Twitter: @GlosPCC
Police and Crime Commissioner: Martin Surl (Ind)

Gwent
OPCC, Police Headquarters, Cwmbran, Torfaen, Gwent NP44 2XJ
Tel: 01633 642200 Email: commissioner@gwent.pnn.police.uk
Website: www.gwent.pcc.police.uk Twitter: @GwentPCC
Police and Crime Commissioner: Jeff Cuthbert (Lab)

Hampshire
OPCC, St George's Chambers, St George's Street, Winchester, Hampshire SO23 8AJ
Tel: 01962 871595
Email: opcc@hampshire.pnn.police.uk Website: www.hampshire-pcc.gov.uk Twitter: @HantsPCC
Police and Crime Commissioner: Michael Lane (Con)

Hertfordshire
OPCC, Harpenden Police Station, 15 Vaughan Road, Harpenden, Hertfordshire AL5 4GZ
Tel: 01707 806100 Email: commissioner@herts.pnn.police.uk
Website: www.hertscommissioner.org Twitter: @HertsPCC
Police and Crime Commissioner: David Lloyd (Con)

Humberside

OPCC, The Lawns, Harland Way, Cottingham HU16 5SN
Tel: 01482 220787
Email: pcc@humberside.pnn.police.uk Website: www.humberside-pcc.gov.uk
Twitter: @HumbersidePCC
Police and Crime Commissioner: Keith Hunter (Lab)

Kent

OPCC, Kent Police Headquarters, Sutton Road, Maidstone ME15 9BZ
Tel: 01622 677055
Email: contactyourpcc@pcc.kent.pnn.police.uk Website: www.kent-pcc.gov.uk Twitter: @PCCKent
Police and Crime Commissioner: Matthew Scott (Con)

Lancashire

OPCC, PO Box 100, County Hall, Preston PR1 0LD
Tel: 01772 533587
Email: commissioner@lancashire-pcc.gov.uk Website: www.lancashire-pcc.gov.uk
Twitter: @LancsPCC
Police and Crime Commissioner: Clive Grunshaw (Lab)

Leicestershire

OPCC, Leicestershire Police Force Headquarters, St Johns, Enderby, Leicestershire LE19 2BX
Tel: 0116-229 8980/0116-248 2312 (media enquiries)
Email: police.commissioner@leics.pcc.pnn.gov.uk Website: www.leics.pcc.police.uk
Twitter: @LeicsPCC
Police and Crime Commissioner: Lord Bach (Lab)

Lincolnshire

OPCC, Lincolnshire Police Headquarters, Deepdale Lane, Nettleham, Lincoln, Lincolnshire LN2 2LT
Tel: 01522 947192 Email: lincolnshire-pcc@lincs.pnn.police.uk
Website: www.lincolnshire-pcc.gov.uk Twitter: @LincolnshirePCC
Police and Crime Commissioner: Marc Jones (Con)

Merseyside

OPCC, Allerton Police Station, Rose Lane, Liverpool L18 6JE
Tel: 0151-777 5155
Email: info@merseysidepcc.info Website: www.merseysidepcc.info Twitter: @MerseysidePCC
Police and Crime Commissioner: Rt Hon Jane Kennedy (Lab)

Norfolk

OPCC, Building 8, Jubilee House, Falconers Chase, Wymondam, Norfolk NR18 0WW
Tel: 01953 424455
Email: opccn@norfolk.pnn.police.uk Website: www.norfolk-pcc.gov.uk Twitter: @NorfolkPCC
Police and Crime Commissioner: Lorne Green (Con)

Northamptonshire

OPCC, The West Wing, Force Headquarters, Wootton Hall, Northampton, Northamptonshire NN4 0JQ
Tel: 01604 888113 Email: commissioner@northantspcc.pnn.police.uk
Website: www.northantspcc.org.uk Twitter: @NorthantsOPCC
Police and Crime Commissioner: Stephen Mold (Con)

Northumbria

OPCC, Second Floor, Victory House, Balliol Business Park, Benton Lane, Newcastle upon Tyne NE12 8EW
Tel: 0191-221 9800
Email: enquiries@northumbria-pcc.gov.uk Website: www.northumbria-pcc.gov.uk
Twitter: @NorthumbriaPCC

Police and Crime Commissioner: Dame Vera Baird DBE QC (Lab)

Nottinghamshire

OPCC, Arnot Hill House, Arnot Hill Park, Arnold, Nottingham NG5 6LU
Tel: 0115-844 5998 Fax: 0115-844 5081
Email: nopcc@nottinghamshire.pnn.police.uk Website: www.nottinghamshire.pcc.police.uk
Twitter: @NottsPCC

Police and Crime Commissioner: Paddy Tipping (Lab)

Staffordshire

OPCC, Staffordshire Police HQ (Block 9), Weston Road, Stafford ST18 0YY
Tel: 01785 232385 Email: pcc@staffordshire.pcc.pnn.gov.uk
Website: www.staffordshire-pcc.gov.uk Twitter: @StaffsPCC

Police and Crime Commissioner: Matthew Ellis (Con)

Suffolk

OPCC, Police Headquarters, Portal Avenue, Martlesham Heath, Ipswich IP5 3QS
Tel: 01473 782773
Email: spcc@suffolk.pnn.police.uk Website: www.suffolk-pcc.gov.uk Twitter: @TimSPCC

Police and Crime Commissioner: Tim Passmore (Con)

Surrey

OPCC, PO Box 412, Guildford, Surrey GU3 1YJ
Tel: 01483 630200 Fax: 01483 634502
Email: surreypcc@surrey.police.uk Website: www.surrey-pcc.gov.uk Twitter: @SurreyPCC

Police and Crime Commissioner: David Munro (Con)

Sussex

OPCC, Sackville House, Brooks Close, Lewes, East Sussex BN7 2FZ
Tel: 01273 481561
Email: pcc@sussex-pcc.gov.uk Website: www.sussex-pcc.gov.uk Twitter: @Sussexpcc

Police and Crime Commissioner: Katy Bourne (Con)

Thames Valley

OPCC, The Farmhouse, Thames Valley Police Headquarters, Oxford Road, Kidlington, Oxon OX5 2NX
Tel: 01865 846780
Email: pcc@thamesvalley.pnn.police.uk Website: www.thamesvalley-pcc.gov.uk Twitter: @TV_PCC

Police and Crime Commissioner: Anthony Stansfeld (Con)

North Wales

OPCC, Police Headquarters, Glan y Don, Colwyn Bay, Conwy LL29 8AW
Tel: 01492 805486 Email: opcc@nthwales.pnn.police.uk
Website: www.northwales-pcc.gov.uk Twitter: @NorthWalesPCC

Police and Crime Commissioner: Arfon Jones (PlC)

South Wales

OPCC, Police Headquarters, Bridgend CF31 3SU
Tel: 01656 869366
Email: commissioner@south-wales.pnn.police.uk Website: commissioner.south-wales.police.uk
Twitter: @commissionersw

Police and Crime Commissioner: Rt Hon Alun Michael (Lab/Co-op)

Warwickshire

OPCC, 3 Northgate Street, Warwick CV34 4SP
Tel: 01926 412322
Email: opcc@warwickshire.gov.uk Website: www.warwickshire-pcc.gov.uk
Twitter: @WarwickshirePCC

Police and Crime Commissioner: Philip Seccombe (Con)

West Mercia

OPCC, West Mercia Police, Hindlip Hall, Worcester WR3 8SP
Tel: 01905 331656 Email: opcc@westmercia.pnn.police.uk
Website: www.westmercia-pcc.gov.uk Twitter: @westmerciapcc

Police and Crime Commissioner: John Campion (Con)

West Midlands

OPCC, Lloyd House, Colmore Circus Queensway, Birmingham B4 6NQ
Tel: 0121-626 6060 Email: wmpcc@west-midlands.pnn.police.uk
Website: www.westmidlands-pcc.gov.uk Twitter: @WestMidsPCC

Police and Crime Commissioner: David Jamieson (Lab)

Wiltshire

OPCC, London Road, Devizes, Wiltshire SN10 2RD
Tel: 01380 734022 Email: pcc@wiltshire.pcc.pnn.gov.uk
Website: www.wiltshire-pcc.gov.uk Twitter: @PCCWiltsSwindon

Police and Crime Commissioner: Angus Macpherson (Con)

North Yorkshire

OPCC, 12 Granby Road, Harrogate, North Yorkshire HG1 4ST
Tel: 01423 569562 Email: info@northyorkshire-pcc.gov.uk
Website: www.northyorkshire-pcc.gov.uk Twitter: @northyorkspcc

Police and Crime Commissioner: Julia Mulligan (Con)

South Yorkshire

OPCC, South Yorkshire Police HQ, Ground Floor, Carbrook House, Carbrook Hall Road, Sheffield, South Yorkshire S9 2EH
Tel: 0114-296 4150
Email: info@southyorkshire-pcc.gov.uk Website: www.southyorkshire-pcc.gov.uk Twitter: @SYPCC

Police and Crime Commissioner: Dr Alan Billings (Lab)

West Yorkshire

OPCC, Ploughland House, 62 George Street, Wakefield WF1 1DL
Tel: 01924 294000 Email: contact@westyorkshire.pcc.pnn.gov.uk
Website: www.westyorkshire-pcc.gov.uk Twitter: @WestYorksOPCC

Police and Crime Commissioner: Mark Burns-Williamson (Lab)

Combined Authorities

Elections took place on 4 May 2017 to elect Mayors to six newly-created Combined Authorities.

Cambridgeshire and Peterborough Combined Authority

Tel: 01473 276126
Email: info@gcgp.co.uk Website: cambspboroca.org Twitter: @CambsPboroCA
Mayor: James Palmer (Con)

Liverpool City Region Combined Authority

No 1 Mann Island, Liverpool L3 1BP
Email: info@liverpoolcityregion-ca.gov.uk Website: www.liverpoolcityregion-ca.gov.uk
Twitter: @LiverpoolCRCA
Mayor: Steve Rotheram (Lab)

Greater Manchester Combined Authority

Churchgate House, 56 Oxford Street, Manchester M1 6EU
Tel: 0161-778 7000
Email: enquiries@greatermanchester-ca.gov.uk Website: www.greatermanchester-ca.gov.uk
Twitter: @greatermcr
Mayor: Rt Hon Andy Burnham (Lab)

Tees Valley Combined Authority

Cavendish House, Teesdale Business Park, Stockton-on-Tees, Tees Valley TS17 6QY
Tel: 01642 524400
Email: info@teesvalley-ca.gov.uk Website: teesvalley-ca.gov.uk Twitter: @TeesValleyCA
Mayor: Ben Houchen (Con)

West of England Combined Authority

Engine Shed, Station Approach, Temple Meads, Bristol BS1 6QH
Tel: 0117-903 6868
Email: info@westofengland-ca.org.uk Website: www.westofengland-ca.org.uk
Twitter: @WestYorkshireCA
Mayor: Tim Bowles (Con)

West Midlands Combined Authority

16 Summer Lane, Birmingham B19 3SD
Tel: 0121-200 2787
Email: andy.street@wmca.org.uk Website: www.wmca.org.uk Twitter: @WestMids_CA
Mayor: Andy Street (Con)

EUROPEAN UNION 1172

European Parliament 1172

Cabinet of the President 1172

State of National Parties 1173

State of European Party Groups 1173

UK MEPs' Directory 1173

European Commission 1184

College of Commissioners 1184

European Council 1185

Council of the European Union 1186

Permanent Representatives 1187

General Secretariat 1189

European Parliament

Rue Wiertz 60, 1047 Brussels, Belgium
Tel: +32 2 284 21 11 Fax: +32 2 284 92 01
Email: [firstname.surname]@europarl.europa.eu Website: www.europarl.europa.eu
Twitter: @europarl_en

Allée du Printemps, 67070 Strasbourg Cedex, France
Tel: +33 3 88 17 40 01 Fax: +33 3 88 17 92 01

Plateau du Kirchberg, 2929 Luxembourg
Tel: +352 4300 1 Fax: +352 4300 24842

United Kingdom Offices

Europe House, 32 Smith Square, London SW1P 3EU
Tel: 020 7227 4300 Fax: 020 7227 4302
Email: eplondon@europarl.europa.eu Website: www.europarl.org.uk

Head of UK Office: Björn Kjellström
Tel: 020 7227 4325 Email: bjorn.kjellstrom@europarl.europa.eu

Outreach: Elisabeth Sweeney
Tel: 020 7227 4328 Email: elisabeth.sweeney@europarl.europa.eu

Cabinet of the President

Rue Wiertz 60, 1047 Brussels, Belgium
Tel: +32 2 284 21 11 Fax: +32 2 284 92 01
Email: [firstname.surname]@europarl.europa.eu Website: www.europarl.europa.eu

President	Antonio Tajani (Ita)	
Head of Cabinet	Diego Canga Fano	+32 2 283 42 31/+33 388 1 64 942
Deputy Heads of Cabinet		
Internal Affairs	Alessandro Chiocchetti	+32 2 284 07 54/+33 388 1 734 61
External Relations, Spokesperson	Carlo Corazza	+32 2 284 40 90/+33 388 1 735 88
Adviser	Gonzalo De Mendoza Asensi	+32 2 283 05 26/+33 388 1 728 19
Head of Private Office	Chiara Salvelli	+32 2 485 77 50/+33 388 1 754 12
Legislation		
Team Leader	Michael Weiss	+32 2 284 15 66/+33 388 1 728 54
Advisers	Markus Warasin	+32 2 283 10 74/+33 388 1 642 25
	Valérie Glatigny	+32 2 283 23 70/+33 388 1 726 36
	Angelika Chomicka	+32 2 283 12 50/+33 388 17 34 24
	Lauro Panella	+32 2 283 15 49/+33 388 1 726 36
External Policies		
Team Leader	Jesper Haglund	+32 2 284 37 38/+33 388 1 738 03
Advisers	Guglielmo di Cola	+32 2 284 34 70/+33 388 1 786 24
	Urszula Mojkowska	+32 2 289 27 69/+33 388 1 738 76
	François Gabriel	+32 2 283 24 58/+33 388 1 738 82
Communication		
Team Leader	Delia Vlase	+32 2 283 25 51/+33 388 1 770 90
Advisers	Nicholas Simoncini	+32 2 283 24 17/+33 388 1 738 77
	Peter Agius	+32 2 284 06 45/+33 388 1 745 68
Bureau and Administration		
Advisers	Fabrizio Capogrosso	+32 2 283 87 50/+33 388 1 787 50
	Boglárka Bólya	+32 2 284 21 16/+33 3 88 17 24 92

UK Members (MEPs)

State of National Parties (October 2017)

	Total
Labour	20
Conservative	20
UK Independence Party	19
Independent	4
Green Party	3
Scottish National Party	2
Democratic Unionist Party	1
Liberal Democrat	1
Plaid Cymru	1
Sinn Féin	1
Ulster Unionist Party	1
	73 seats

State of European Party Groups (October 2017)

	Total
European Conservatives and Reformists Group (ECR)	21
Europe of Freedom and Direct Democracy Group (EFDD)	20
Progressive Alliance of Socialists and Democrats (S&D)	20
Greens-European Free Alliance (Greens-EFA)	6
Non-attached Group (NA)	3
Alliance of Liberals and Democrats for Europe (ALDE)	1
Europe of Nations and Freedom (ENF)	1
European United Left-Nordic Green Left Confederal Group (GUE-NGL)	1
	73 seats

UK MEPs' Directory

Within the MEP contact directory we have only included MEPs' room numbers and buildings for the Parliaments' offices in Brussels and Strasbourg, but not the remainder of the addresses, which do not vary and are as follows:

Brussels: European Parliament, 60 Rue Wiertz, 1047 Brussels, Belgium

Strasbourg: European Parliament, Avenue du Président Robert Schuman 1, CS 91024, 67070 Strasbourg Cedex, France

ALDE	Alliance of Liberals and Democrats for Europe
ECR	European Conservatives and Reformists Group
EFDD	Europe of Freedom and Direct Democracy Group
ENF	Europe of Nations and Freedom
Greens-EFA	Greens-European Free Alliance
GUE-NGL	European United Left-Nordic Green Left Confederal Group
NA	Non-attached Group
S&D	Progressive Alliance of Socialists and Democrats

AGNEW, Mr Stuart *UKIP/EFDD* **Eastern**

UK office: 25 Regent Street, Great Yarmouth NR30 1RL

Tel: 01493 856744 Email: ukipeastadmin@intamail.com eastern@ukip.org

Website: www.stuartagnewmep.co.uk

Brussels office: 03E252, Bâtiment Altiero Spinelli

Tel: +32 2 284 54 04 Fax: +32 2 284 94 04 Email: johnstuart.agnew@europarl.europa.eu

Strasbourg office: T08036, Bâtiment Louise Weiss

Tel: +33 3 88 17 54 04 Fax: +33 3 88 17 94 04

AKER, Mr Tim *UKIP/EFDD* **Eastern**
UK office: 64a Orsett Road, Grays, Thurrock RM17 5EB
Email: tim.aker@ukip.org Website: www.timakermep.org Twitter: @Tim_Aker
Brussels office: 03F258, Bâtiment Altiero Spinelli
Tel: +32 2 284 51 09 Fax: +32 2 284 91 09 Email: tim.aker@europarl.europa.eu
Strasbourg office: T08048, Bâtiment Louise Weiss
Tel: +33 3 88 17 51 09 Fax: +33 3 88 17 91 09

ANDERSON, Ms Lucy *Lab/S&D* **London**
UK office: 20 Hanson Street, London W1W 6UF
Email: office@lucyanderson.org Website: www.lucyanderson.org Twitter: @LucyAndersonMEP
Brussels office: 01G201, Bâtiment Altiero Spinelli
Tel: +32 2 284 54 96 Fax: +32 2 284 94 96 Email: lucy.anderson@europarl.europa.eu
Strasbourg office: T07046, Bâtiment Louise Weiss
Tel: +33 3 88 17 54 96 Fax: +33 3 88 17 94 96

ANDERSON, Ms Martina *Sinn Féin/GUE-NGL* **Northern Ireland**
UK office: Unit 2, Spencer House, 18-22 Spencer Road, Derry BT47 6QA
Tel: 028 7131 8683 Website: martinamep.eu Twitter: @mepstandingup4u
Brussels office: 02M121, Bâtiment Willy Brandt
Tel: +32 2 284 52 22 Fax: +32 2 284 92 22 Email: martina.anderson@europarl.europa.eu
Strasbourg office: T05145, Bâtiment Louise Weiss
Tel: +33 3 88 17 52 22 Fax: +33 3 88 17 92 22

ARNOTT, Mr Jonathan *UKIP/EFDD* **North East**
UK office: 41 Elwick Road, Hartlepool TS26 9AE Website: www.jonathanarnott.co.uk
Twitter: @JonathanArnott
Brussels office: 03E258, Bâtiment Altiero Spinelli
Tel: +32 2 284 53 30 Fax: +32 2 284 93 30 Email: jonathan.arnott@europarl.europa.eu
Strasbourg office: T08038, Bâtiment Louise Weiss
Tel: +33 3 88 17 53 30 Fax: +33 3 88 17 93 30

ASHWORTH, Mr Richard *Con/ECR* **South East**
UK office: 5 Hazelgrove Road, Haywards Heath RH16 3PH
Tel: 01444 474858 Website: www.richardashworth.org Twitter: @richardashmep
Brussels office: 06M105, Bâtiment Willy Brandt
Tel: +32 2 284 53 09 Fax: +32 2 284 93 09 Email: richard.ashworth@europarl.europa.eu
Strasbourg office: T11028, Bâtiment Louise Weiss
Tel: +33 3 88 17 53 09 Fax: +33 3 88 17 93 09

ATKINSON, Ms Janice *Ind/ENF* **South East**
UK office: Whitehall Suite, Seven Henrietta Street, London WC2E 8PS
Tel: 020 3829 3481 Email: contact@janiceatkinson.co.uk Website: www.janiceatkinson.co.uk
Twitter: @Janice4Brexit
Brussels office: 06G351, Bâtiment Altiero Spinelli
Tel: +32 2 284 55 37 Fax: +32 2 284 95 37 Email: janice.atkinson@europarl.europa.eu
Strasbourg office: T10087, Bâtiment Louise Weiss
Tel: +33 3 88 17 55 37 Fax: +33 3 88 17 95 37

BASHIR, Mr Amjad *Con/ECR* **Yorkshire & Humber**
Brussels office: 06M121, Bâtiment Willy Brandt
Tel: +32 2 284 53 19 Fax: +32 2 284 93 19 Email: amjad.bashir@europarl.europa.eu
Strasbourg office: T11027, Bâtiment Louise Weiss
Tel: +33 3 88 17 53 19 Fax: +33 3 88 17 93 19

BATTEN, Mr Gerard *UKIP/EFDD* **London**
UK office: PO Box 2959, Romford RM7 1QZ
Tel: 020 7403 7174/020 7403 7175 Email: gbmepoffice@btinternet.com
Website: www.gerardbattenmep.co.uk Twitter: @gerardbattenmep
Brussels office: 03F343, Bâtiment Altiero Spinelli
Tel: +32 2 284 59 20 Fax: +32 2 284 99 20 Email: gerard.batten@europarl.europa.eu
Strasbourg office: T08063, Bâtiment Louise Weiss
Tel: +33 3 88 17 59 20 Fax: +33 3 88 17 99 20

BEARDER, Ms Catherine *Lib Dem/ALDE* **South East**
Quaestor, European Parliament
UK office: Second Floor, 8-10 Great George Street, London SW1P 3AE
Tel: 020 7340 4935 Email: catherine@bearder.eu Website: www.bearder.eu Twitter: @catherinemep
Brussels office: 10G138, Bâtiment Altiero Spinelli
Tel: +32 2 284 56 32 Fax: +32 2 284 96 32 Email: catherine.bearder@europarl.europa.eu
Strasbourg office: T12028, Bâtiment Louise Weiss
Tel: +33 3 88 17 56 32 Fax: +33 3 88 17 96 32

BOURS, Ms Louise *UKIP/EFDD* **North West**
UK office: 4a Wexford Road, Oxton, Wirrall CH43 9TB
Tel: 0151-375 9662 Website: www.louiseboursmep.co.uk
Brussels office: 03F247, Bâtiment Altiero Spinelli
Tel: +32 2 284 55 52 Fax: +32 2 284 95 52 Email: louise.bours@europarl.europa.eu
Strasbourg office: T08087, Bâtiment Louise Weiss
Tel: +33 3 88 17 55 52 Fax: +33 3 88 17 95 52

BRANNEN, Mr Paul *Lab/S&D* **North East**
UK office: Labour Central, Kings Manor, Newcastle upon Tyne NE1 6PA
Tel: 0191-246 5276 Email: info@paulbrannen.co.uk Website: www.paulbrannen.co.uk
Twitter: @PaulBrannenNE
Brussels office: 13G209, Bâtiment Altiero Spinelli
Tel: +32 2 284 57 95 Fax: +32 2 284 97 95 Email: paul.brannen@europarl.europa.eu
Strasbourg office: T07042, Bâtiment Louise Weiss
Tel: +33 3 88 17 57 95 Fax: +33 3 88 17 97 95

BULLOCK, Mr Jonathan *UKIP/EFDD* **East Midlands**
Brussels office: 03E240, Bâtiment Altiero Spinelli
Tel: +32 2 284 57 64 Fax: +32 2 284 97 64 Email: jonathan.bullock@europarl.europa.eu Twitter: @JonathanMEP
Strasbourg office: T08052, Bâtiment Louise Weiss
Tel: +33 3 88 17 57 64 Fax: +33 3 88 17 97 64

CAMPBELL BANNERMAN, Mr David *Con/ECR* **Eastern**
UK office: 153 St Neots Road, Hardwick CB23 7QJ
Tel: 01954 210333 Email: office@dcbmep.org Website: www.dcbmep.org Twitter: @dcbmep
Brussels office: 07M083, Bâtiment Willy Brandt
Tel: +32 2 284 57 33 Fax: +32 2 284 97 33 Email: david.campbellbannerman@europarl.europa.eu
Strasbourg office: T11036, Bâtiment Louise Weiss
Tel: +33 3 88 17 57 33 Fax: +33 3 88 17 97 33

CARVER, Mr James *UKIP/EFDD* **West Midlands**
UK office: Unit 1, 12 Lisle Avenue, Kidderminster DY11 7DL
Tel: 01562 216020 Email: mep@jamescarver.org Website: www.jamescarver.org
Twitter: @JamesJimCarver
Brussels office: 03F158, Bâtiment Altiero Spinelli
Tel: +32 2 284 57 44 Fax: +32 2 284 97 44 Email: james.carver@europarl.europa.eu
Strasbourg office: T08085, Bâtiment Louise Weiss
Tel: +33 3 88 17 57 44 Fax: +33 3 88 17 97 44

COBURN, Mr David *UKIP/EFDD* **Scotland**
UK office: 1 St Colme Street, Edinburgh EH3 6AA
Tel: 0131-220 8289 Email: info@davidcoburnmep.com Website: www.davidcoburnmep.co.uk
Twitter: @DavidCoburnUKip
Brussels office: 03F171, Bâtiment Altiero Spinelli
Tel: +32 2 284 54 81 Fax: +32 2 284 94 81 Email: david.coburn@europarl.europa.eu
Strasbourg office: T08089, Bâtiment Louise Weiss
Tel: +33 3 88 17 54 81 Fax: +33 3 88 17 94 81

COLLINS, Ms Jane *UKIP/EFDD* **Yorkshire & Humber**
UK office: Wallingfen Lodge, Main Road, Newport HU15 2RH
Tel: 01430 449 666 Email: contact@jane-collins.org Website: www.jane-collins.org
Twitter: @Jane_CollinsMEP
Brussels office: 03F349, Bâtiment Altiero Spinelli
Tel: +32 2 284 51 04 Fax: +32 2 284 91 04 Email: jane.collins@europarl.europa.eu
Strasbourg office: T08069, Bâtiment Louise Weiss
Tel: +33 3 88 17 51 04 Fax: +33 3 88 17 91 04

CORBETT, Mr Richard *Lab/S&D* **Yorkshire & Humber**
UK office: Unity Business Centre, 26 Roundhay Road, Leeds LS7 1AB
Tel: 0113-243 0554 Email: richard@richardcorbett.org.uk Website: www.richardcorbett.org.uk
Twitter: @RCorbettMEP
Brussels office: 13G165, Bâtiment Altiero Spinelli
Tel: +32 2 284 54 84 Fax: +32 2 284 94 84 Email: richard.corbett@europarl.europa.eu
Strasbourg office: T07038, Bâtiment Louise Weiss
Tel: +33 3 88 17 54 84 Fax: +33 3 88 17 94 84

DALTON, Mr Daniel *Con/ECR* **West Midlands**
UK office: Office S4, Berkeley House, 6-8 The Square, Kenilworth CV8 1EB
Tel: 01926 930683 Email: daniel@danieldaltonmep.co.uk Website: www.danieldaltonmep.co.uk
Twitter: @DDalton40
Brussels office: 05M075, Bâtiment Willy Brandt
Tel: +32 2 284 58 97 Fax: +32 2 284 98 97 Email: daniel.dalton@europarl.europa.eu
Strasbourg office: T11032, Bâtiment Louise Weiss
Tel: +33 3 88 17 58 97 Fax: +33 3 88 17 98 97

DANCE, Mr Seb *Lab/S&D* **London**
UK office: 46 Tower Bridge Road, London SE1 4TR
Tel: 020 7231 2308 Website: www.sebdance.com Twitter: @SebDance
Brussels office: 13G318, Bâtiment Altiero Spinelli
Tel: +32 2 284 58 33 Fax: +32 2 284 98 33 Email: seb.dance@europarl.europa.eu
Strasbourg office: T07050, Bâtiment Louise Weiss
Tel: +33 3 88 17 58 33 Fax: +33 3 88 17 98 33

DARTMOUTH, Mr William *UKIP/EFDD* **South West**
UK office: PO Box 410, Newton Abbot TQ12 9BJ Website: www.williamdartmouth.com
Brussels office: 03F361, Bâtiment Altiero Spinelli
Tel: +32 2 284 57 35 Fax: +32 2 284 97 35 Email: william.dartmouth@europarl.europa.eu
Strasbourg office: T08073, Bâtiment Louise Weiss
Tel: +33 3 88 17 57 35 Fax: +33 3 88 17 97 35

DEVA, Mr Nirj *Con/ECR* **South East**
UK office: 98 Admiralty Close, West Drayton UB7 9NJ
Tel: 018 9544 8553 Email: office@nirjdeva.com Website: www.nirjdeva.com Twitter: @nirjdeva
Brussels office: 04M019, Bâtiment Willy Brandt
Tel: +32 2 284 52 45 Fax: +32 2 284 92 45 Email: nirj.deva@europarl.europa.eu
Strasbourg office: T11038, Bâtiment Louise Weiss
Tel: +33 3 88 17 52 45 Fax: +33 3 88 17 92 45

DODDS, Ms Diane *DUP/NA* **Northern Ireland**
UK office: DUP European Office, Garvey Studios, Longstone Street, Lisburn BT28 1TP
Tel: 028 9266 7733 Email: diane@dianedodds.co.uk Website: www.dianedodds.co.uk
Twitter: @dianedoddsmep
Brussels office: 11G206, Bâtiment Altiero Spinelli
Tel: +32 2 284 57 70 Fax: +32 2 284 97 70 Email: diane.dodds@europarl.europa.eu
Strasbourg office: T06045, Bâtiment Louise Weiss
Tel: +33 3 88 17 57 70 Fax: +33 3 88 17 97 70

ETHERIDGE, Mr Bill *UKIP/EFDD* **West Midlands**
UK office: Unit 4, 4-7, Victoria Works, Victoria Passage, Wolverhampton WV1 4LG
Tel: 01902 238060 Email: info.etheridgemep@gmail.com Website: www.billetheridge.co.uk
Twitter: @BillUKIP
Brussels office: 03F142, Bâtiment Altiero Spinelli
Tel: +32 2 284 54 53 Fax: +32 2 284 94 53 Email: bill.etheridge@europarl.europa.eu
Strasbourg office: T08065, Bâtiment Louise Weiss
Tel: +33 3 88 17 54 53 Fax: +33 3 88 17 94 53

EVANS, Ms Jill *PlC/Greens-EFA* **Wales**
UK office: 45 Gelligaled Road, Ystrad, Rhondda Cynon Taf CF41 7RQ
Tel: 014 4344 1395 Fax: 014 4344 0999 Email: post@jillevans.net Website: www.jillevans.net
Twitter: @jillevansmep
Brussels office: 04F374, Bâtiment Altiero Spinelli
Tel: +32 2 284 51 03 Fax: +32 2 284 91 03 Email: jill.evans@europarl.europa.eu
Strasbourg office: T05051, Bâtiment Louise Weiss
Tel: +33 3 88 17 51 03 Fax: +33 3 88 17 91 03

FARAGE, Mr Nigel *UKIP/EFDD* **South East**
UK office: The Old Grain Store, Church Lane, Lyminster BN17 7QJ
Tel: 01903 885573 Fax: 01903 885574 Email: ukipse@ukip.org Twitter: @nigel_farage
Brussels office: 07F367, Bâtiment Altiero Spinelli
Tel: +32 2 284 58 55 Fax: +32 2 284 98 55 Email: nigel.farage@europarl.europa.eu
Strasbourg office: T06007, Bâtiment Louise Weiss
Tel: +33 3 88 17 58 55 Fax: +33 3 88 17 98 55

FINCH, Mr Ray *UKIP/EFDD* **South East**
UK office: Old Grain Store, Church Lane, Lyminster BN17 7QJ
Tel: 01903 885 573 Twitter: @raymondfinch
Brussels office: 03F266, Bâtiment Altiero Spinelli
Tel: +32 2 284 55 94 Fax: +32 2 284 95 94 Email: raymond.finch@europarl.europa.eu
Strasbourg office: T08071, Bâtiment Louise Weiss
Tel: +33 3 88 17 55 94 Fax: +33 3 88 17 95 94

FLACK, Mr John *Con/ECR* **Eastern**
Brussels office: 04M083, Bâtiment Willy Brandt
Tel: +32 2 284 56 72 Fax: +32 2 284 96 72 Email: john.flack@europarl.europa.eu
Strasbourg office: T08057, Bâtiment Louise Weiss
Tel: +33 3 88 17 56 72 Fax: +33 3 88 17 96 72

FOSTER, Ms Jacqueline *Con/ECR* **North West**
UK office: Maritime Knowledge Hub, 3 Vanguard Way, Birkenhead CH41 9HX
Tel: 015 1231 2952 Email: office@jacquelinefostermep.com Website: www.jacquelinefostermep.com
Twitter: @jfostermep
Brussels office: 06M113, Bâtiment Willy Brandt
Tel: +32 2 284 56 74 Fax: +32 2 284 96 74 Email: jacqueline.foster@europarl.europa.eu
Strasbourg office: T11044, Bâtiment Louise Weiss
Tel: +33 3 88 17 56 74 Fax: +33 3 88 17 96 74

FOX, Mr Ashley *Con/ECR* **South West**
UK office: 5 Westfield Park, Bristol BS6 6LT
Tel: 0117-973 7050 Email: ashley@ashleyfoxmep.co.uk Website: www.ashleyfoxmep.co.uk
Twitter: @Ashleyfoxmep
Brussels office: 05M009, Bâtiment Willy Brandt
Tel: +32 2 283 76 77 Fax: +32 2 283 96 77 Email: ashley.fox@europarl.europa.eu
Strasbourg office: T11046, Bâtiment Louise Weiss
Tel: +33 3 88 17 56 77 Fax: +33 3 88 17 96 77

GILL, Mr Nathan *Ind/EFDD* **Wales**
UK office: 10 Bridge Street, Menai Bridge LL59 5DW
Tel: 012 4871 7052 Email: nathan.gill@ukipwales.org Twitter: @NathanGillMEP
Brussels office: 03F155, Bâtiment Altiero Spinelli
Tel: +32 2 284 53 41 Fax: +32 2 284 93 41 Email: nathan.gill@europarl.europa.eu
Strasbourg office: T08091, Bâtiment Louise Weiss
Tel: +33 3 88 17 53 41 Fax: +33 3 88 17 93 41

GILL, Ms Neena, CBE *Lab/S&D* **West Midlands**
UK office: Terry Duffy House, 1 Thomas Street, West Bromwich B70 6NT
Tel: 0121-569 1918 Email: neenagillmep@gmail.com Twitter: @MEPNeenaGill
Brussels office: 13G265, Bâtiment Altiero Spinelli
Tel: +32 2 284 51 93 Fax: +32 2 284 91 93 Email: neena.gill@europarl.europa.eu
Strasbourg office: T07034, Bâtiment Louise Weiss
Tel: +33 3 88 17 51 93 Fax: +33 3 88 17 91 93

GIRLING, Ms Julie *Con/ECR* **South West**
UK office: PO Box 308, Evesham WR11 9EJ
Tel: 01386 882491 Email: linda@juliegirling.com Website: www.juliegirling.com
Twitter: @juliegirling
Brussels office: 06M089, Bâtiment Willy Brandt
Tel: +32 2 284 56 78 Fax: +32 2 284 96 78 Email: julie.girling@europarl.europa.eu
Strasbourg office: T11048, Bâtiment Louise Weiss
Tel: +33 3 88 17 56 78 Fax: +33 3 88 17 96 78

GRIFFIN, Ms Theresa *Lab/S&D* **North West**
UK office: Unit 303, Vanilla Factory, 39 Fleet Street, Liverpool L1 4AR
Tel: 0151-709 9987 Email: theresa@theresagriffin.eu Website: www.theresagriffin.eu
Twitter: @TheresaMEP
Brussels office: 13G310, Bâtiment Altiero Spinelli
Tel: +32 2 284 52 71 Fax: +32 2 284 92 71 Email: theresa.griffin@europarl.europa.eu
Strasbourg office: T07067, Bâtiment Louise Weiss
Tel: +33 3 88 17 52 71 Fax: +33 3 88 17 92 71

HANNAN, Mr Daniel *Con/ECR* **South East**
UK office: PO Box 99, Hassocks BN6 0DY
Email: office@hannan.co.uk Website: www.hannan.co.uk Twitter: @DanielJHannan
Brussels office: 04M045, Bâtiment Willy Brandt
Tel: +32 2 284 51 37 Fax: +32 2 284 91 37 Email: daniel.hannan@europarl.europa.eu
Strasbourg office: T11050, Bâtiment Louise Weiss
Tel: +33 3 88 17 51 37 Fax: +33 3 88 17 91 37

HONEYBALL, Ms Mary *Lab/S&D* **London**
UK office: 4G Shirland Mews, London W9 3DY
Tel: 020 8964 9815 Fax: 020 8960 0150 Email: mary@maryhoneyball.net
Website: thehoneyballbuzz.com Twitter: @maryhoneyball
Brussels office: 13G258, Bâtiment Altiero Spinelli
Tel: +32 2 284 52 09 Fax: +32 2 284 92 09 Email: mary.honeyball@europarl.europa.eu
Strasbourg office: T07048, Bâtiment Louise Weiss
Tel: +33 3 88 17 52 09 Fax: +33 3 88 17 92 09

HOOKEM, Mr Mike *UKIP/EFDD* **Yorkshire & Humber**
UK office: Wallingfen Lodge, Main Road, Newport HU15 2RH
Email: contact@mike-hookem.org Website: www.mike-hookem.org Twitter: @MikeHookemMEP
Brussels office: 03F353, Bâtiment Altiero Spinelli
Tel: +32 2 284 55 61 Fax: +32 2 284 95 61 Email: mike.hookem@europarl.europa.eu
Strasbourg office: T08067, Bâtiment Louise Weiss
Tel: +33 3 88 17 55 61 Fax: +33 3 88 17 95 61

HOWARTH, Mr John *Lab/S&D* **South East**
UK office: Unit A Bishops Mews, Transport Way, Oxford OX4 6HD
Email: contact@johnhowarthmep.uk Website: www.johnhowarthmep.uk
Twitter: @JohnHowarth1958
Brussels office: 13G265, Bâtiment Altiero Spinelli
Tel: +32 2 284 52 73 Fax: +32 2 284 92 73 Email: john.howarth@europarl.europa.eu
Strasbourg office: T07028, Bâtiment Louise Weiss
Tel: +33 3 88 17 52 73 Fax: +33 3 88 17 92 73

HUDGHTON, Mr Ian *SNP/Greens-EFA* **Scotland**
UK office: 8 Old Glamis Road, Dundee DD3 8HP
Tel: 01382 623200 Fax: 01382 903205 Website: www.hudghtonmep.com
Twitter: @hudghtonmepSNP
Brussels office: 04F353, Bâtiment Altiero Spinelli
Tel: +32 2 284 54 99 Fax: +32 2 284 94 99 Email: ian.hudghton@europarl.europa.eu
Strasbourg office: T05049, Bâtiment Louise Weiss
Tel: +33 3 88 17 54 99 Fax: +33 3 88 17 94 99

JAMES, Ms Diane *Ind/NA* **South East**
UK office: 83 South Street, Dorking RH4 2JU
Tel: 01306 867198 Twitter: @DianeJamesMEP
Brussels office: 07F362, Bâtiment Altiero Spinelli
Tel: +32 2 284 55 41 Fax: +32 2 284 95 41 Email: diane.james@europarl.europa.eu
Strasbourg office: T08046, Bâtiment Louise Weiss
Tel: +33 3 88 17 55 41 Fax: +33 3 88 17 95 41

KAMALL, Mr Syed *Con/ECR* **London**
Chair, European Conservatives and Reformists Group
UK office: 161 Brigstock Road, Croydon CR7 7JP
Tel: 020 7041 9025 Website: www.syedkamall.co.uk Twitter: @syedkamall
Brussels office: 06M099, Bâtiment Willy Brandt
Tel: +32 2 284 57 92 Fax: +32 2 284 97 92 Email: syed.kamall@europarl.europa.eu
Strasbourg office: T06053, Bâtiment Louise Weiss
Tel: +33 3 88 17 57 92 Fax: +33 3 88 17 97 92

KARIM, Mr Sajjad *Con/ECR* **North West**
UK office: 442 Barlow Moor Road, Manchester M21 0BQ
Email: info@sajjadkarim.eu Website: www.sajjadkarim.eu Twitter: @shkmep
Brussels office: 07M081, Bâtiment Willy Brandt
Tel: +32 2 284 56 40 Fax: +32 2 284 96 40 Email: sajjad.karim@europarl.europa.eu
Strasbourg office: T11054, Bâtiment Louise Weiss
Tel: +33 3 88 17 56 40 Fax: +33 3 88 17 96 40

KHAN, Mr Wajid *Lab/S&D* **North West**
Brussels office: 13G342, Bâtiment Altiero Spinelli
Tel: +32 2 284 54 37 Fax: +32 2 284 94 37 Email: wajid.khan@europarl.europa.eu
Strasbourg office: T07071, Bâtiment Louise Weiss
Tel: +33 3 88 17 54 37 Fax: +33 3 88 17 94 37

KIRTON-DARLING, Ms Jude *Lab/S&D* **North East**
UK office: Labour Central, Kings Manor, Newcastle upon Tyne NE1 6PA
Tel: 0191-620 0105 Email: office@northeastlabour.eu Website: www.northeastlabour.eu
Twitter: @Jude_KD
Brussels office: 13G210, Bâtiment Altiero Spinelli
Tel: +32 2 284 51 05 Fax: +32 2 284 91 05 Email: jude.kirton-darling@europarl.europa.eu
Strasbourg office: T07052, Bâtiment Louise Weiss
Tel: +33 3 88 17 51 05 Fax: +33 3 88 17 91 05

LAMBERT, Ms Jean *Green/Greens-EFA* **London**
UK office: CAN Mezzanine, 49-51 East Road, London N1 6AH
Tel: 020 7250 8416 Email: jeanlambert@greenmeps.org.uk Website: www.jeanlambertmep.org.uk
Twitter: @greenjeanmep
Brussels office: 04F167, Bâtiment Altiero Spinelli
Tel: +32 2 284 55 07 Fax: +32 2 284 95 07 Email: jean.lambert@europarl.europa.eu
Strasbourg office: T05087, Bâtiment Louise Weiss
Tel: +33 3 88 17 55 07 Fax: +33 3 88 17 95 07

McAVAN, Ms Linda *Lab/S&D* **Yorkshire & Humber**
UK office: Labour Constituency Office, 79 High Street, Wath upon Dearne S63 7QB
Tel: 01709 875665 Email: lindamcavan@lindamcavanmep.org.uk
Website: www.lindamcavanmep.org.uk Twitter: @lindamcavanmep
Brussels office: 13G346, Bâtiment Altiero Spinelli
Tel: +32 2 284 54 38 Fax: +32 2 284 94 38 Email: linda.mcavan@europarl.europa.eu
Strasbourg office: T07040, Bâtiment Louise Weiss
Tel: +33 3 88 17 54 38 Fax: +33 3 88 17 94 38

McCLARKIN, Ms Emma *Con/ECR* **East Midlands**
UK office: Three Crowns Yard, High Street, Market Harborough LE16 7AF
Tel: 01858 419709 Fax: 01858 432855 Email: emmamcclarkin@eastmidsmeps.co.uk
Website: www.emmamcclarkin.com Twitter: @emmamcclarkin
Brussels office: 04M009, Bâtiment Willy Brandt
Tel: +32 2 284 56 84 Fax: +32 2 284 96 84 Email: emma.mcclarkin@europarl.europa.eu
Strasbourg office: T11055, Bâtiment Louise Weiss
Tel: +33 3 88 17 56 84 Fax: +33 3 88 17 96 84

McINTYRE, Ms Anthea *Con/ECR* **West Midlands**
UK office: The Chapel, Wythall Estate, Walford, Ross-on-Wye HR9 5SD
Tel: 01989 769544 Email: anthea@antheamcintyre.com Website: www.antheamcintyre.com
Twitter: @anthea_mcintyre
Brussels office: 05M081, Bâtiment Willy Brandt
Tel: +32 2 284 51 06 Fax: +32 2 284 91 06 Email: anthea.mcintyre@europarl.europa.eu
Strasbourg office: T11034, Bâtiment Louise Weiss
Tel: +33 3 88 17 71 06 Fax: +33 3 88 17 91 06

MARTIN, Mr David *Lab/S&D* **Scotland**
UK office: Midlothian Innovation Centre, Pentlandfield, Roslin, Midlothian EH25 9RE
Tel: 0131-440 9040 Email: david@martinmep.com Website: www.martinmep.com
Twitter: @davidmartinmep
Brussels office: 13G157, Bâtiment Altiero Spinelli
Tel: +32 2 284 55 39 Fax: +32 2 284 95 39 Email: david.martin@europarl.europa.eu
Strasbourg office: T07036, Bâtiment Louise Weiss
Tel: +33 3 88 17 55 39 Fax: +33 3 88 17 95 39

MATTHEWS, Mr Rupert *Con/ECR* **East Midlands**
UK office: Email: rupert@rupertmatthews.com Website: www.rupertmatthews.com
Twitter: @RMatthewsMEP
Brussels office: 04M089, Bâtiment Willy Brandt
Tel: +32 2 284 55 98 Fax: +32 2 284 95 98 Email: rupert.matthews@europarl.europa.eu
Strasbourg office: T11052, Bâtiment Louise Weiss
Tel: +33 3 88 17 55 98 Fax: +33 3 88 17 95 98

MAYER, Ms Alex *Lab/S&D* **Eastern**
UK office: European Office, Unit 5, ESpace South, 26 St Thomas Place, Ely CB7 4EX
Tel: 01353 644045 Email: contact@alexmayer.eu Website: www.alexmayer.eu Twitter: @alexlmayer
Brussels office: 13G317, Bâtiment Altiero Spinelli
Tel: +32 2 284 54 77 Fax: +32 2 284 94 77 Email: alex.mayer@europarl.europa.eu
Strasbourg office: T07044, Bâtiment Louise Weiss
Tel: +33 3 88 17 54 77 Fax: +33 3 88 17 94 77

MOBARIK, Baroness, CBE *Con/ECR* **Scotland**
Brussels office: 06M087, Bâtiment Willy Brandt
Tel: +32 2 284 52 49 Fax: +32 2 284 92 49
Email: nosheena.mobarik@europarl.europa.eu
Strasbourg office: T11042, Bâtiment Louise Weiss
Tel: +33 3 88 17 52 49 Fax: +33 3 88 17 92 49

MOODY, Ms Clare *Lab/S&D* **South West**
UK office: Unit 32, Base Point Business Centre, Jubilee Close, Weymouth DT4 7BS
Tel: 01305 858285 Email: clare@claremoodymep.com Website: www.claremoodymep.com
Twitter: @ClareMoodyMEP
Brussels office: 13G309, Bâtiment Altiero Spinelli
Tel: +32 2 284 53 08 Fax: +32 2 284 93 08 Email: clare.moody@europarl.europa.eu
Strasbourg office: T07073, Bâtiment Louise Weiss
Tel: +33 3 88 17 53 08 Fax: +33 3 88 17 93 08

MORAES, Mr Claude *Lab/S&D* **London**
Chair, Civil Liberties, Justice and Home Affairs Committee
UK office: 65 Barnsbury Street, London N1 1EJ
Tel: 020 7609 5005 Email: office@claudemoraes.com Website: www.claudemoraes.com
Twitter: @claudemoraesmep
Brussels office: 13G205, Bâtiment Altiero Spinelli
Tel: +32 2 284 75 53 Fax: +32 2 284 95 53 Email: claude.moraes@europarl.europa.eu
Strasbourg office: T07040, Bâtiment Louise Weiss
Tel: +33 3 88 17 55 53 Fax: +33 3 88 17 95 53

NICHOLSON, Mr James *UUP/ECR* **Northern Ireland**
UK office: Strandtown Hall, 2-4 Belmont Road, Belfast BT4 2AN
Tel: 028 9047 4630 Fax: 028 9065 2149 Email: jim.nicholson@uup.org
Website: www.jim-nicholson.eu Twitter: @jnicholsonmep
Brussels office: 04M047, Bâtiment Willy Brandt
Tel: +32 2 284 59 33 Fax: +32 2 284 99 33 Email: james.nicholson@europarl.europa.eu
Strasbourg office: T11057, Bâtiment Louise Weiss
Tel: +33 3 88 17 59 33 Fax: +33 3 88 17 99 33

NUTTALL, Mr Paul *UKIP/EFDD* **North West**
UK office: UKIP North West, PO Box 2034, Liverpool L69 2DG
Tel: 0151-375 9660 Website: www.paulnuttallmep.com Twitter: @paulnuttallukip
Brussels office: 03F254, Bâtiment Altiero Spinelli
Tel: +32 2 284 57 40 Fax: +32 2 284 97 40 Email: paul.nuttall@europarl.europa.eu
Strasbourg office: T08093, Bâtiment Louise Weiss
Tel: +33 3 88 17 57 40 Fax: +33 3 88 17 97 40

O'FLYNN, Mr Patrick *UKIP/EFDD* **Eastern**
UK office: 90a Bridge Street, Peterborough PE1 1DY
Tel: 017 3389 1640 Twitter: @oflynnmep
Brussels office: 03F163, Bâtiment Altiero Spinelli
Tel: +32 2 284 53 37 Fax: +32 2 284 93 37 Email: patrick.oflynn@europarl.europa.eu
Strasbourg office: T08050, Bâtiment Louise Weiss
Tel: +33 3 88 17 53 37 Fax: +33 3 88 17 93 37

PALMER, Mr Rory *Lab/S&D* **East Midlands**
Contact details still to be confirmed at time of going to press
Twitter: @Rory_Palmer

PARKER, Ms Margot *UKIP/EFDD* **East Midlands**
UK office: 44b High Street, Old Village, Corby NN17 1UU
Tel: 01536 204503 Email: margot.parker@ukip.org Website: www.margotparkermep.uk
Twitter: @MargotLJParker
Brussels office: 03F265, Bâtiment Altiero Spinelli
Tel: +32 2 284 51 82 Fax: +32 2 284 91 82 Email: margot.parker@europarl.europa.eu
Strasbourg office: T08056, Bâtiment Louise Weiss
Tel: +33 3 88 17 51 82 Fax: +33 3 88 17 91 82

PROCTER, Mr John *Con/ECR* **Yorkshire & Humber**
Brussels office: 07M059, Bâtiment Willy Brandt
Tel: +32 2 284 53 21 Fax: +32 2 284 93 21 Email: john.procter@europarl.europa.eu
Strasbourg office: T11030, Bâtiment Louise Weiss
Tel: +33 3 88 17 53 21 Fax: +33 3 88 17 93 21

REID, Ms Julia *UKIP/EFDD* **South West**
UK office: 40 Market Place, Chippenham SN15 3HT
Tel: 01249 445653 Email: julia.reid@ukip.org Website: www.juliareid.co.uk Twitter: @Julia_reid
Brussels office: 03F259, Bâtiment Altiero Spinelli
Tel: +32 2 284 57 41 Fax: +32 2 284 97 41 Email: julia.reid@europarl.europa.eu
Strasbourg office: T08058, Bâtiment Louise Weiss
Tel: +33 3 88 17 57 41 Fax: +33 3 88 17 97 41

SCOTT CATO, Dr Molly *Green/Greens-EFA* **South West**
UK office: Unit 216 Brunswick Court, Brunswick Street, Bristol BS2 8PE
Tel: 0117-916 6598 Email: office@mollymep.org.uk Website: www.mollymep.org.uk
Twitter: @MollyScottCato
Brussels office: 04F146, Bâtiment Altiero Spinelli
Tel: +32 2 284 57 37 Fax: +32 2 284 97 37 Email: molly.scottcato@europarl.europa.eu
Strasbourg office: T05085, Bâtiment Louise Weiss
Tel: +33 3 88 17 57 37 Fax: +33 3 88 17 97 37

SEYMOUR, Ms Jill *UKIP/EFDD* **West Midlands**
UK office: Independence House, 27 Bridge Road, Wellington, Telford TF6 1ED
Tel: 01952 924040 Email: enquiries@jseymourmep.co.uk Website: jillseymourukip.org
Twitter: @JSeymourUKIP
Brussels office: 03F154, Bâtiment Altiero Spinelli
Tel: +32 2 284 58 03 Fax: +32 2 284 98 03 Email: jill.seymour@europarl.europa.eu
Strasbourg office: T08044, Bâtiment Louise Weiss
Tel: +33 3 88 17 58 03 Fax: +33 3 88 17 98 03

SIMON, Mr Siôn *Lab/S&D* **West Midlands**
UK office: Terry Duffy House, Thomas Street, West Bromwich B70 6NT
Tel: 0121-569 1911 Email: sionsimon@sion-simon.org.uk Website: www.sion-simon.org.uk
Twitter: @sionsimon
Brussels office: 13G169, Bâtiment Altiero Spinelli
Tel: +32 2 284 55 05 Fax: +32 2 284 95 05 Email: sion.simon@europarl.europa.eu
Strasbourg office: T12038, Bâtiment Louise Weiss
Tel: +33 3 88 17 55 05 Fax: +33 3 88 17 95 05

SMITH, Mr Alyn *SNP/Greens-EFA* **Scotland**
UK office: TechCube, 1 Summerhall, Edinburgh EJ9 1PL
Tel: 0131-290 2149 Website: www.alynsmith.eu Twitter: @alynsmithmep
Brussels office: 04F343, Bâtiment Altiero Spinelli
Tel: +32 2 284 51 87 Fax: +32 2 284 91 87 Email: alyn.smith@europarl.europa.eu
Strasbourg office: T05053, Bâtiment Louise Weiss
Tel: +33 3 88 17 51 87 Fax: +33 3 88 17 91 87

STIHLER, Ms Catherine *Lab/S&D* **Scotland**
Brussels office: 13G351, Bâtiment Altiero Spinelli
Tel: +32 2 284 54 62 Fax: +32 2 284 94 62 Email: catherine.stihler@europarl.europa.eu
Strasbourg office: T07032, Bâtiment Louise Weiss
Tel: +33 3 88 17 54 62 Fax: +33 3 88 17 94 62

SWINBURNE, Ms Kay *Con/ECR* **Wales**
UK office: Unit 5, Heol Llanishen Fach, Rhiwbina, Cardiff CF14 6RG
Tel: 029 2054 0895 Email: kayswinburnemep@welshconservatives.com
Website: www.kayswinburne.wales Twitter: @KaySwinburneMEP
Brussels office: 05M065, Bâtiment Willy Brandt
Tel: +32 2 284 56 87 Fax: +32 2 284 96 87 Email: kay.swinburne@europarl.europa.eu
Strasbourg office: T11061, Bâtiment Louise Weiss
Tel: +33 3 88 17 56 87 Fax: +33 3 88 17 96 87

TANNOCK, Mr Charles *Con/ECR* **London**
UK office: Conservative-London Region, 4 Greyhound Road, London W6 8NX
Tel: 020 8962 1286 Email: charles@charlestannock.com Website: www.charlestannock.com
Twitter: @charlestannock
Brussels office: 04M081, Bâtiment Willy Brandt
Tel: +32 2 284 58 70 Fax: +32 2 284 98 70 Email: charles.tannock@europarl.europa.eu
Strasbourg office: T11065, Bâtiment Louise Weiss
Tel: +33 3 88 17 58 70 Fax: +33 3 88 17 98 70

TAYLOR, Mr Keith *Green/Greens-EFA* **South East**
UK office: Office of the Green MEPs, CAN Mezzanine, 49-51 East Road, London N1 6AH
Tel: 020 7250 8415 Email: keithoffice@greenmeps.org.uk Website: www.keithtaylormep.org.uk
Twitter: @greenkeithmep
Brussels office: 04F136, Bâtiment Altiero Spinelli
Tel: +32 2 284 51 53 Fax: +32 2 284 91 53 Email: keith.taylor@europarl.europa.eu
Strasbourg office: T05089, Bâtiment Louise Weiss
Tel: +33 3 88 17 51 53 Fax: +33 3 88 17 91 53

VAN ORDEN, Mr Geoffrey *Con/ECR* **Eastern**
UK office: Conservative Office, 88 Rectory Lane, Chelmsford CM1 1RF
Tel: 01245 345188 Fax: 01245 269757 Website: www.geoffreyvanorden.com Twitter: @GVOMEP
Brussels office: 06M049, Bâtiment Willy Brandt
Tel: +32 2 284 53 32 Fax: +32 2 284 93 32 Email: geoffrey.vanorden@europarl.europa.eu
Strasbourg office: T11067, Bâtiment Louise Weiss
Tel: +33 3 88 17 53 32 Fax: +33 3 88 17 93 32

VAUGHAN, Mr Derek *Lab/S&D* **Wales**
UK office: Fourth Floor, Transport House, 1 Cathedral Road, Cardiff CF11 9SD
Tel: 029 2022 7660 Email: contact@derekvaughanmep.org.uk
Website: www.derekvaughanmep.org.uk Twitter: @derekvaughan
Brussels office: 13G257, Bâtiment Altiero Spinelli
Tel: +32 2 284 54 19 Fax: +32 2 284 94 19 Email: derek.vaughan@europarl.europa.eu
Strasbourg office: T07030, Bâtiment Louise Weiss
Tel: +33 3 88 17 54 19 Fax: +33 3 88 17 94 19

WARD, Ms Julie *Lab/S&D* **North West**
UK office: B.02 Jactin House, 24 Hodd Street, Manchester M4 6WX
Email: contact@juliewardmep.eu Website: www.juliewardmep.eu Twitter: @julie4nw
Brussels office: 13G306, Bâtiment Altiero Spinelli
Tel: +32 2 284 57 02 Fax: +32 2 284 97 02 Email: julie.ward@europarl.europa.eu
Strasbourg office: T07069, Bâtiment Louise Weiss
Tel: +33 3 88 17 57 02 Fax: +33 3 88 17 97 02

WOOLFE, Mr Steven *Ind/NA* **North West**
UK office: 62 Northgate Street, Chester CH1 2HT
Tel: 01244 630200 Email: office@stevenwoolfe.co.uk Website: www.stevenwoolfe.co.uk
Twitter: @Steven_Woolfe
Brussels office: 03F243, Bâtiment Altiero Spinelli
Tel: +32 2 284 51 15 Fax: +32 2 284 91 15 Email: steven.woolfe@europarl.europa.eu
Strasbourg office: T05008, Bâtiment Louise Weiss
Tel: +33 3 88 17 51 15 Fax: +33 3 88 17 91 15

European Commission

European Commission, 1049 Brussels, Belgium
Tel: +32 2 299 11 11
Email: [firstname.surname]@ec.europa.eu Website: www.ec.europa.eu Twitter: @eu_commission

United Kingdom

32 Smith Square, London SW1P 3EU, United Kingdom
Tel: 020 7973 1992 Fax: 020 7973 1900 Email: comm-rep-london@ec.europa.eu
Website: ec.europa.eu/unitedkingdom Twitter: @eulondonrep
Acting Head of Representation, London: Christine Dalby
Press Officer, London: Mark English

9 Alva Street, Edinburgh EH2 4PH, United Kingdom
Tel: 0131-225 2058 Fax: 0131-226 4105
Head of Representation, Edinburgh: Graham Blythe
Press Officer, Edinburgh: Külli Nurk

74-76 Dublin Road, Belfast BT2 7HP, United Kingdom
Tel: 028 9024 0708 Fax: 028 9024 8241
Head of Representation, Belfast: Colette Fitzgerald
Press Officer, Belfast: Catherine McShane

2 Caspian Point, Caspian Way, Cardiff CF10 4QQ, United Kingdom
Tel: 029 2089 5020 Fax: 029 2089 5035
Head of Representation, Cardiff: David Hughes
Press Officer, Cardiff: Rachael Davies

College of Commissioners

President of the European Commission	Jean-Claude Juncker (Lux)
Better Regulation, Interinstitutional Relations, the Rule of Law and the Charter of Fundamental Rights	Frans Timmermans (Nth)
External Relations	Federica Mogherini (Ita)
Digital Single Market	Andrus Ansip (Est)
Energy Union	Maroš Šefčovič (Slk)

Euro and Social Dialogue	Valdis Dombrovskis (Lat)
Jobs, Growth, Investment and Competitiveness	Jyrki Katainen (Fin)
Budget and Human Resources	Günther Oettinger (Ger)
Security Union	Julian King (UK)
Digital Economy and Society	Mariya Gabriel (Bul)
European Neighbourhood Policy and Enlargement Negotiations	Johannes Hahn (Aut)
Trade	Cecilia Malmström (Swe)
International Co-operation and Development	Neven Mimica (Cro)
Climate Action and Energy	Miguel Arias Cañete (Spa)
Environment, Maritime Affairs and Fisheries	Karmenu Vella (Mal)
Health and Food Safety	Vytenis Andriukaitis (Lit)
Migration, Home Affairs and Citizenship	Dimitris Avramopoulos (Gre)
Employment, Social Affairs, Skills and Labour Mobility	Marianne Thyssen (Bel)
Economic and Financial Affairs, Taxation and Customs	Pierre Moscovici (Fra)
Humanitarian Aid and Crisis Management	Christos Stylianides (Cyp)
Agriculture and Rural Development	Phil Hogan (Irl)
Transport	Violeta Bulc (Sln)
Internal Market, Industry, Entrepreneurship and SMEs	Elżbieta Bieńkowska (Pol)
Justice, Consumers and Gender Equality	Věra Jourová (Cze)
Education, Culture, Youth and Sport	Tibor Navracsics (Hun)
Regional Policy	Corina Crețu (Rom)
Competition	Margrethe Vestager (Den)
Research, Science and Innovation	Carlos Moedas (Por)

European Council and the Council of the EU

European Council

Rue de la Loi 175, 1048 Brussels, Belgium
Tel: +32 2 281 61 11 Fax: +32 2 281 69 99
Email: donald.tusk@consilium.europa.eu Website: www.consilium.europa.eu/en/european-council
Twitter: @eucouncilpress @EUCouncil

Since the implementation of the Lisbon Treaty in 2009, the Council is chaired by the permanent president of the European Council; the head of government or state of the country holding the rotating Council presidency deputises for the president in his absence.

President: Donald Tusk (Pol)

Heads of Government and Heads of State sitting on the Council

Austria	Federal Chancellor Christian Kern*
Belgium	Prime Minister Charles Michel
Bulgaria	Prime Minister Boyko Borisov
Croatia	Prime Minister Andrej Plenković

Cyprus	President Nicos Anastasiades
Czech Republic	Prime Minister Bohuslav Sobotka†
Denmark	Prime Minister Lars Løkke Rasmussen
Estonia	Prime Minister Jüri Ratas
Finland	Prime Minister Juha Sipilä
France	President Emmanuel Macron
Germany	Federal Chancellor Angela Merkel
Greece	Prime Minister Alexis Tsipras
Hungary	Prime Minister Viktor Orbán
Ireland	Prime Minister Leo Varadkar
Italy	Prime Minister Paolo Gentiloni
Latvia	Prime Minister Māris Kučinskis
Lithuania	President Dalia Grybauskaitė
Luxembourg	Prime Minister Xavier Bettel
Malta	Prime Minister Joseph Muscat
Netherlands	Prime Minister Mark Rutte
Poland	Prime Minister Beata Szydło
Portugal	Prime Minister António Costa
Romania	President Klaus Iohannis
Slovakia	Prime Minister Robert Fico
Slovenia	Prime Minister Miro Cerar
Spain	Prime Minister Mariano Rajoy
Sweden	Prime Minister Stefan Löfven
United Kingdom	Prime Minister Theresa May

*Elections to be held on 15 October

†Elections to be held on 20-21 October

Presidency of the Council

Website: www.eu2017.ee Twitter: @EU2017EE

Each Member State presides over the Council for a period of six months in turn, in partnership with the permanent President of the Council, in accordance with a pre-established rota. The Presidency of the Council organises the work of the institution and organises and chairs all meetings. It facilitates legislative and political decision-making and brokers compromises between the Member States.

For the period 2017-18, the order of succession is:

2017

Second half:	Estonia

2018

First half:	Bulgaria
Second half:	Austria

Council of the European Union

Rue de la Loi 175, 1048 Brussels, Belgium
Tel: +32 2 281 61 11 Fax: +32 2 281 69 99
Email: public.info@consilium.europa.eu Website: www.consilium.europa.eu
Twitter: @EUCouncilPress

The Council of Ministers has one representative from each Member State. Ministers who attend its meetings vary depending on the subject under discussion: finance ministers on financial affairs, agricultural ministers on agricultural matters, etc.

The Council meetings and deliberations are prepared by the Committee of Representatives (Coreper), which is composed of the Member States' ambassadors to the Union. A staff of national civil servants assists each ambassador.

Permanent Representatives

Austria
Avenue de Cortenbergh 30, 1040 Brussels
Tel: +32 2 234 51 00 Fax: +32 2 235 63 00
Email: bruessel-ov@bmeia.gv.at
www.bmeia.gv.at/en/austrian-representation-brussels Twitter: @AustriaatEU

Permanent Representative: Nikolaus Marschik

Belgium
Rue de la Loi 61-63, 1040 Brussels
Tel: +32 2 233 21 11 Fax: +32 2 231 10 75
Email: dispatch.belgoeurop@diplobel.fed.be
www.diplomatie.belgium.be/belgium_eu
Twitter: @BelgiumEU

Permanent Representative: François Roux

Bulgaria
Square Marie-Louise 49, 1000 Brussels
Tel: +32 2 235 83 00 Fax: +32 2 374 91 88
Email: mission.brusselseu@bg-permrep.eu
www.mfa.bg/embassies/belgiumpp

Permanent Representative: Dimiter Tzantchev

Croatia
Avenue des Arts 50, 1000 Brussels
Tel: +32 2 507 54 11 Fax: +32 2 646 56 64
Email: hr.perm.rep@mvep.hr
eu.mfa.hr/en

Permanent Representative: Mato Škrabalo

Cyprus
Avenue de Cortenbergh 61, 1000 Brussels
Tel: +32 2 739 51 11 Fax: +32 2 735 45 52
Email: cy.perm.rep@mfa.gov.cy
www.mfa.gov.cy/permrepeu
Twitter: @CyprusinEU

Permanent Representative: Nicholas Emiliou

Czech Republic
Rue Caroly 15, 1050 Brussels
Tel: +32 2 213 91 11 Fax: +32 2 213 91 85
Email: eu.brussels@embassy.mzv.cz
www.mzv.cz/representation_brussels/en/index.html

Permanent Representative: Martin Povejšil

Denmark
Rue d'Arlon 73, 1040 Brussels
Tel: +32 2 233 08 11 Fax: +32 2 230 93 84
Email: brurep@um.dk
eu.um.dk/en.aspx Twitter: @DKinEU

Permanent Representative: Kim Jørgensen

Estonia
Rue Guimard 11-13, 1040 Brussels
Tel: +32 2 227 39 10 Fax: +32 2 227 39 25
Email: permrep.eu@mfa.ee
www.eu.estemb.be/eng

Permanent Representative: Kaja Tael

Finland
Avenue de Cortenbergh 80, 1000 Brussels
Tel: +32 2 287 84 11 Fax: +32 2 287 84 00
Email: sanomat.eue@formin.fi
www.finland.eu Twitter: @finpermrepeu

Permanent Representative: Marja Rislakki

France
Place de Louvain 14, 1000 Brussels
Tel: +32 2 229 82 11 Fax: +32 2 229 82 82
Email: presse.bruxelles-dfra@diplomatie.gouv.fr
www.rpfrance.eu Twitter: @rpuefrance

Permanent Representative: Pierre Sellal

Germany
Rue Jacques de Lalaing 8-14, 1040 Brussels
Tel: +32 2 787 10 00 Fax: +32 2 787 20 00
Email: info@bruessel-eu.diplo.de
www.bruessel-eu.diplo.de
Twitter: @GermanyintheEU

Permanent Representative: Reinhard Silberberg

Greece
Rue Jacques De Lalaing 19-21, 1040 Brussels
Tel: +32 2 551 56 11 Fax: +32 2 551 56 51
Email: mea.bruxelles@rp-grece.be
www.gr2014.eu

Permanent Representative: Andreas Papastavrou

Hungary
Rue de Trèves 92-98, 1040 Brussels
Tel: +32 2 234 12 00 Fax: +32 2 372 07 84
Email: sec.beu@mfa.gov.hu
eu-brusszel.mfa.gov.hu/eng

Permanent Representative: Olivér Várhelyi

Ireland
Rue Froissart 50, 1040 Brussels
Tel: +32 2 230 85 80 Fax: +32 2 230 32 03
Email: irlprb@dfa.ie
www.irelandrepbrussels.be
Twitter: @irelandrepbru

Permanent Representative: Declan Kelleher

Italy
Rue du Marteau 7-15, 1000 Brussels
Tel: +32 2 220 04 11 Email: rpue@rpue.esteri.it
www.italiaue.esteri.it/rapp_ue/en
Twitter: @ItalyinEU
Permanent Representative: Maurizio Massari

Latvia
Avenue des Arts 23, 1000 Brussels
Tel: +32 2 238 31 00 Fax: +32 2 238 32 50
Email: permrep.eu@mfa.gov.lv
www.mfa.gov.lv/en/brussels Twitter: @LVinEU
Permanent Representative:
Sanita Pavļuta-Deslandes

Lithuania
Rue Belliard 41-43, 1040 Brussels
Tel: +32 2 771 01 40 Fax: +32 2 771 45 97
Email: office@eu.mfa.lt
eu.mfa.lt Twitter: @eu2013ltpress
Permanent Representative: Jovita Neliupšienė

Luxembourg
Avenue de Cortenbergh 75, 1000 Brussels
Tel: +32 2 737 56 00 Fax: +32 2 737 56 10
Email: bruxelles.rpue@mae.etat.lu
bruxelles-rpue.mae.lu/en Twitter: @RPUE_LU
Permanent Representative: Georges Friden

Malta
Rue Archimède 25, 1000 Brussels
Tel: +32 2 343 01 95 Fax: +32 2 343 01 06
Email: maltarep@gov.mt www.odpm.gov.mt
Permanent Representative: Marlene Bonnici

Netherlands
Avenue de Cortenbergh 4-10, 1040 Brussels
Tel: +32 2 679 15 11 Fax: +32 2 679 17 75
Email: bre@minbuza.nl
www.permanentrepresentations.nl
Twitter: @NLatEU
Permanent Representative: Robert de Groot

Poland
Rue Stevin 139, 1000 Brussels
Tel: +32 2 780 42 00 Fax: +32 2 780 42 97
Email: bebrustpe@msz.gov.pl
brukselaue.msz.gov.pl Twitter: @plpermrepeu
Permanent Representative: Jarosław Starzyk

Portugal
Avenue de Cortenbergh 12, 1040 Brussels
Tel: +32 2 286 42 11 Fax: +32 2 231 00 26
Email: reper@reper-portugal.be
www.ue.missaoportugal.mne.pt/en
Permanent Representative: Nuno Brito

Romania
Rue Montoyer 12, 1000 Brussels
Tel: +32 2 700 06 40 Fax: +32 2 700 06 41
Email: bru@rpro.eu
ue.mae.ro/en Twitter: @ROPermRepEU
Permanent Representative:
Luminița Teodora Odobescu

Slovakia
Avenue de Cortenbergh 79, 1000 Brussels
Tel: +32 2 743 68 11 Fax: +32 2 743 68 88
Email: eu.brussels@mzv.sk
www.eubrussels.mfa.sk
Twitter: @SLOVAKIAinEU
Permanent Representative: Peter Javorčík

Slovenia
Rue du Commerce 44, 1000 Brussels
Tel: +32 2 213 63 00
Email: slomission.eu@gov.si
brussels.representation.si Twitter: @SLOtoEU
Permanent Representative: Janez Lenarčič

Spain
Boulevard du Régent 52, 1000 Brussels
Tel: +32 2 509 86 11
Fax: +32 2 511 19 40/+32 2 511 26 30
Email: reper.bruselasue@reper.maec.es
representacionpermanente.eu
Twitter: @UeEspana
Permanent Representative:
Juan Pablo Garcia-Berdoy y Cerezo

Sweden
Square de Meeûs, 1000 Brussels
Tel: +32 2 289 56 11 Fax: +32 2 289 56 00
Email: representationen.bryssel@gov.se
www.government.se/sweden-in-the-eu/permanent-representation-of-sweden-to-the-eu
Twitter: @SwedeninEU
Permanent Representative: Lars Danielsson

United Kingdom
Avenue d'Auderghem 10, 1040 Brussels
Tel: +32 2 287 82 11 Fax: +32 2 287 83 98
Email: ukrep@fco.gov.uk
www.gov.uk/government/world/organisations/uk-representation-to-the-eu Twitter: @ukineu
Permanent Representative:
Tim Barrow KCMG LVO MBE

General Secretariat

Rue de la Loi 175, 1048 Brussels, Belgium
Tel: +32 2 281 61 11 Fax: +32 2 281 69 34
Email: press.office@consilium.europa.eu Website: www.consilium.europa.eu

Secretary-General: Jeppe Tranholm-Mikkelsen Email: jeppe.tranholm-mikkelsen@consilium.europa.eu

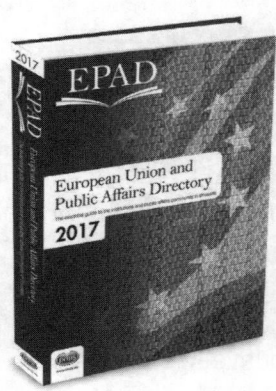

GOVERNMENT AND PUBLIC OFFICES

Permanent Secretaries 1192
Departments of State 1193
- Prime Minister's Office 1193
- Department for Business, Energy and Industrial Strategy 1193
- Cabinet Office 1193
- Department for Communities and Local Government 1194
- Ministry of Defence 1195
- Department for Digital, Culture, Media and Sport 1195
- Department for Education 1196
- Department for Environment, Food and Rural Affairs 1197
- Department for Exiting the European Union 1197
- Foreign and Commonwealth Office 1198
- Department of Health 1199
- Home Office 1199
- Department for International Development 1200
- Department for International Trade 1200
- Ministry of Justice 1201
- Law Officers 1201
- Northern Ireland Office 1202
- Privy Council Office 1202
- Scotland Office 1202
- Department for Transport 1203
- HM Treasury 1203
- Office of the Secretary of State for Wales 1204
- Department for Work and Pensions 1204

Executive Agencies 1205
Non-Ministerial Departments 1212
Ombudsmen and Complaint-Handling Bodies 1216
Political and Parliamentary Organisations 1221

Permanent Secretaries

Departments of State

Business, Energy and Industrial Strategy
Permanent Secretary
Alex Chisholm

Cabinet Office
Chief Executive
John Manzoni
Cabinet Secretary
Sir Jeremy Heywood KCB CVO

Communities and Local Government
Permanent Secretary
Melanie Dawes CB

Defence
Permanent Secretary
Stephen Lovegrove CB

Digital, Culture, Media and Sport
Permanent Secretary
Sue Owen CB

Education
Permanent Secretary
Jonathan Slater

Environment, Food and Rural Affairs
Permanent Secretary
Clare Moriarty CB

Exiting the European Union
Permanent Secretary
Dr Philip Rycroft CB

Foreign and Commonwealth Office
Permanent Under-Secretary of State
Sir Simon McDonald KCMG KCVO

Health
Permanent Secretary
Sir Chris Wormald KCB

Home Office
Permanent Secretary
Philip Rutnam
Second Permanent Secretary
Patsy Wilkinson CB

International Development
Acting Permanent Secretary (until end of December 2017)
Nick Dyer
Permanent Secretary (from January 2018)
Matthew Rycroft

International Trade
Permanent Secretary
Antonia Romeo
Second Permanent Secretary
Crawford Falconer

Justice
Permanent Secretary
Richard Heaton CB

Northern Ireland Office
Permanent Secretary
Sir Jonathan Stephens KCB

Transport
Permanent Secretary
Bernadette Kelly CB

Treasury
Permanent Secretary
Sir Tom Scholar KCB
Second Permanent Secretary
Charles Roxburgh

Work and Pensions
Permanent Secretary
Sir Robert Devereux KCB

Devolved Parliament and Assemblies

Northern Ireland Executive
Interim Head of Northern Ireland Civil Service and Secretary to the Executive
David Sterling

Scottish Government
Permanent Secretary
Leslie Evans

Welsh Government
Permanent Secretary
Dame Shan Morgan DCMG

Departments of State

Prime Minister's Office

10 Downing Street, London SW1A 2AA
Tel: 020 7930 4433
Website: www.gov.uk/number10 Twitter: @number10gov
Prime Minister, First Lord of the Treasury and Minister for the Civil Service: Rt Hon **Theresa May** MP
For staff see p13

Department for Business, Energy and Industrial Strategy

1 Victoria Street, London SW1H 0ET
Tel: 020 7215 5000
Email: enquiries@beis.gov.uk Website: www.gov.uk/beis Twitter: @beisgovuk

MINISTERS

Secretary of State: Rt Hon Greg Clark MP
Minister of State for Climate Change and Industry: Claire Perry MP
Minister of State for Universities, Science, Research and Innovation: Jo Johnson MP
Parliamentary Under-Secretary of State (Minister for Small Business, Consumers and Corporate Responsibility): Margot James MP
Parliamentary Under-Secretary of State (Minister for Energy and Industry): Richard Harrington MP
Parliamentary Under-Secretary of State: Lord Prior of Brampton

Head of Parliamentary Unit: Oliver Bennett 020 7215 6630
***House of Lords Spokesperson:* Lord Prior of Brampton**

CIVIL SERVANTS

Permanent Secretary: Alex Chisholm 020 7215 5914 Email: permanentsecretary@beis.gov.uk
Director-General, Energy and Security: Jeremy Pocklington 0300 068 5668
Email: jeremy.pocklington@beis.gov.uk
Director-General, Energy Transformation: Clive Maxwell 030 0068 8181
Email: clive.maxwell@beis.gov.uk
Director-General, Market Frameworks: Jaee Samant 020 7215 5628 Email: jaee.samant@beis.gov.uk
Director-General, Finance and Corporate Services: Angie Ridgwell 0300 068 5115
Email: angie.ridgwell@beis.gov.uk
Director-General, Business and Science: Gareth Davies 020 7215 1219
Email: gareth.davies@beis.gov.uk
Director-General, International, Growth and Analysis: Sam Beckett OBE 020 7215 5330
Email: sam.beckett@beis.gov.uk

Executive Agencies: Companies House; Insolvency Service; Intellectual Property Office; Met Office; UK Space Agency

Cabinet Office

70 Whitehall, London SW1A 2AS
Tel: 020 7276 1234 Email: publiccorrespondence@cabinetoffice.gov.uk
Website: www.gov.uk/cabinet-office Twitter: @cabinetofficeuk

MINISTERS

First Secretary of State; Minister for the Cabinet Office: Rt Hon Damian Green MP
Parliamentary Secretary (Minister for the Constitution): Chris Skidmore MP
Parliamentary Secretary (Minister for Government Resilience and Efficiency): Caroline Nokes MP
Chancellor of the Duchy of Lancaster: Rt Hon Sir Patrick McLoughlin MP

Parliamentary Clerk: Kevin Candy 020 7276 1208
***House of Lords Spokesperson:* Lord Young of Cookham**

CIVIL SERVANTS

Chief Executive of the Civil Service and Permanent Secretary : John Manzoni 020 7271 8822
Email: chief.executive@cabinetoffice.gov.uk
Cabinet Secretary and Head of the Civil Service: Sir Jeremy Heywood KCB CVO 020 7276 0101
Email: cabinet.secretary@cabinetoffice.gov.uk
Second Permanent Secretary and Head of UK Governance Group:
Dr Philip Rycroft CB 020 7276 8944 Email: philip.rycroft@cabinetoffice.gov.uk
First Parliamentary Counsel: Elizabeth Gardiner CB 020 7276 6541
Email: 1pc@cabinetoffice.gov.uk
Acting Director-General, UK Governance: Lucy Smith 07768 646220
Email: lucy.smith@cabinetoffice.gov.uk
Director-General, Propriety and Ethics and Head of Private Offices: Sue Gray 020 7276 2470
Email: sue.gray@cabinetoffice.gov.uk
Director-General, Government Digital Service: Kevin Cunnington
Email: kevin.cunnington@digital.cabinet-office.gov.uk
Chief People Officer: Rupert McNeil 020 7271 6858 Email: rupert.mcneil@cabinetoffice.gov.uk
Chief Commercial Officer: Gareth Rhys Williams Email: andrew.barton@cabinetoffice.gov.uk
Chair, Joint Intelligence Committee and Professional Head of Intelligence Analysis:
Charles Farr CMG OBE
Prime Minister's National Security Adviser: Mark Sedwill CMG
Email: mark.sedwill@cabinetoffice.gov.uk
Chief Executive, Infrastructure and Projects Authority: Tony Meggs
Email: ruhana.choudhury@ipa.gov.uk
Executive Director, Government Communications: Alex Aiken 020 7276 6009
Email: alex.aiken@cabinetoffice.gov.uk
Executive Director, Implementation Group: James Quinault CBE 07584 886452
Email: james.quinault@cabinetoffice.gov.uk
Finance Director: Guy Lester 020 7276 0530 Email: guy.lester@cabinetoffice.gov.uk
Executive Agency: Crown Commercial Service

Department for Communities and Local Government

2 Marsham Street, London SW1P 4DF
Tel: 0303 444 0000
Email: contactus@communities.gsi.gov.uk Website: www.gov.uk/dclg Twitter: @communitiesuk

MINISTERS

Secretary of State: Rt Hon Sajid Javid MP
Minister of State for Housing and Planning: Alok Sharma MP
Parliamentary Under-Secretary of State (Minister for the Northern Powerhouse and Local Growth):
Jake Berry MP
Parliamentary Under-Secretary of State (Minister for Local Government): Marcus Jones MP
Parliamentary Under-Secretary of State (Minister for Faith): Lord Bourne of Aberystwyth
Parliamentary Clerk: Paul B Smith 030 3444 3407
***House of Lords Spokesperson:* Lord Bourne of Aberystwyth**

CIVIL SERVANTS

Permanent Secretary: Melanie Dawes CB 0303 444 2785
Email: psmelaniedawes@communities.gsi.gov.uk
Director-General, Local Government and Public Services: Dr Jo Farrar OBE
Email: jo.farrar@communities.gsi.gov.uk
Director-General, Housing and Planning: Helen MacNamara
Email: helen.macnamara@communities@gsi.gov.uk

Director-General, Decentralisation and Growth : Simon Ridley 0303 444 4258
Email: simon.ridley@communities.gsi.gov.uk
Director, Strategy, Communications and Private Office: Lise-Anne Boissiere
Email: lise-anne.boissiere@communities.gsi.gov.uk
Director, Finance: Jacinda Humphry 0303 444 2196
Email: jacinda.humphry@communities.gsi.gov.uk
Director, People, Capability and Change: Christine Hewitt
Email: christine.hewitt@communities.gsi.gov.uk
Executive Agencies: Planning Inspectorate; Queen Elizabeth II Centre

Ministry of Defence

Main Building, Whitehall, London SW1A 2HB
Tel: 020 7218 9000
Website: www.gov.uk/mod Twitter: @defenceHQ

MINISTERS

Secretary of State: Rt Hon Sir Michael Fallon KCB MP
Minister of State and Deputy Leader of the House of Lords: Rt Hon Earl Howe
Minister of State for the Armed Forces: Mark Lancaster TD MP
Parliamentary Under-Secretary of State (Defence Procurement): Harriett Baldwin MP
Parliamentary Under-Secretary of State (Defence People and Veterans): Rt Hon Tobias Ellwood MP
Parliamentary Clerk: Teresa Andrews 020 7218 1991
House of Lords Spokesperson: **Earl Howe**

CIVIL SERVANTS

Permanent Secretary: Stephen Lovegrove CB
Chief of the Defence Staff: Air Chief Marshal Sir Stuart Peach GBE KCB ADC DL 020 7218 6190
Email: cds-privateoffice@mod.uk
Director-General, Finance: Louise Tulett CBE 020 7807 8947 Email: dgfinance-pa@mod.uk
Director-General, Security Policy: Peter Watkins CBE 020 7218 3830
Email: peter.watkins262@mod.uk
Director-General, Head Office and Commissioning Services: Julie Taylor 020 7218 4077
Email: dghocs-pa@mod.uk
Director-General, Nuclear: Julian Kelly
Chief of the Air Staff: Air Chief Marshal Sir Stephen Hillier KCB CBE DFC ADC
Email: cas-outeroffice@mod.uk
Chief of Defence People: Lt Gen Richard Nugee CVO CBE
First Sea Lord and Chief of the Naval Staff: Admiral Sir Philip Jones KCB ADC 020 7218 6193
Email: navy-1slcnsgroup@mod.uk
Chief of the General Staff: General Sir Nicholas Carter KCB CBE DSO ADC Gen 020 7218 6153
Email: armycgs-privateoffice-shared@mod.uk
Commander, Joint Forces Command: General Sir Chris Deverell KCB MBE ADC Gen 01923 958529
Email: jfc-comd-outeroffice@mod.uk
Chief Executive, Defence Infrastructure Organisation: Graham Dalton
Chief Executive, Defence Equipment and Support: Tony Douglas 0117 913 0004
Email: DESCEO-OuterOffice@mod.uk
Executive Agencies: Defence Electronics and Components Agency; Defence Science and Technology Laboratory; UK Hydrographic Office

Department for Digital, Culture, Media and Sport

100 Parliament Street, London SW1A 2BQ
Tel: 020 7211 6000
Email: enquiries@culture.gov.uk Website: www.gov.uk/dcms Twitter: @dcms

MINISTERS

Secretary of State: Rt Hon Karen Bradley MP
Minister of State for Digital: Rt Hon Matt Hancock MP
Parliamentary Under-Secretary of State for Sport and Civil Society: Tracey Crouch MP
Parliamentary Under-Secretary of State for Arts, Heritage and Tourism: John Glen MP
Parliamentary Under-Secretary of State: Lord Ashton of Hyde
Parliamentary Clerk: Ed Little
House of Lords Spokesperson: **Lord Ashton of Hyde**

CIVIL SERVANTS

Permanent Secretary: Sue Owen CB 020 7211 6254 Email: permanent.secretary@culture.gov.uk
Director-General, Performance and Strategy: Helen Judge 020 7211 6131
Email: helen.judge@culture.gov.uk
Director-General, Digital and Media: Matthew Gould CMG MBE 07738 112418
Email: matthew.gould@culture.gov.uk
Director, Culture and Sport: Clare Pillman 020 7211 6000 Email: clare.pillman@culture.gov.uk
Director, Finance: Tim Sparrow 020 7211 6229 Email: tim.sparrow@culture.gov.uk
Director, Office for Civil Society and Innovation: David Rossington 020 7211 6266
Email: david.rossington@culture.gov.uk
Director, Corporate Strategy: Kate Joseph 020 7211 6415 Email: kenyatta-joseph@culture.gov.uk
Director, Legal: Caroline Croft 020 7211 2429 Email: caroline.croft@culture.gov.uk
Director, Digital Economy and Technology: Gila Sacks 020 7211 2163
Email: gila.sacks@culture.gov.uk
Director, Telecoms: Dr Joe Butler 020 7211 2163 Email: joe.butler@culture.gov.uk
Director, Cyber Security and Data Protection: Yasmin Brooks 020 7211 2848
Email: yasmin.brooks@culture.gov.uk
Director, Media: Andrea Young 020 7211 6370 Email: andrea.young@culture.gov.uk
Director, International and Internet: Sarah Connolly 020 7211 6682
Email: sarah.connolly@culture.gov.uk
Director, EU Trade and Capability: Dr Rosemary Pratt 020 7211 6723
Email: rosemary.pratt@culture.gov.uk
Director, Corporate Strategy: Claudia Kenyatta 020 7211 6415 Email: kenyatta-joseph@culture.gov.uk
Chief Executive, Broadband Delivery UK: William Priest 020 7211 6380
Email: william.priest@culture.gov.uk
Executive Agency: Royal Parks

Department for Education

Sanctuary Buildings, Great Smith Street, London SW1P 3BT
Tel: 0370 000 2288
Email: [firstname.surname]@education.gov.uk Website: www.gov.uk/dfe
Twitter: @EducationGovUK

MINISTERS

Secretary of State: Rt Hon Justine Greening MP
Minister of State for School Standards; Minister for Equalities: Rt Hon Nick Gibb MP
Minister of State for Children and Families: Robert Goodwill MP
Minister of State for Universities, Science, Research and Innovation: Jo Johnson MP
Minister of State for Apprenticeships and Skills; Minister for Women: Rt Hon Anne Milton MP
Parliamentary Under-Secretary of State for the School System: Lord Nash
Parliamentary Clerk: Amy Ross
House of Lords Spokesperson: **Lord Nash**

CIVIL SERVANTS

Permanent Secretary: Jonathan Slater 020 7340 7414 Email: permanent.secretary@education.gov.uk secretary-diary.permanent@education.gov.uk
Director-General, Infrastructure and Funding: Andrew McCully 020 7340 8075
Email: andrew.mccully@education.gov.uk
Director-General, Social Care, Mobility and Equalities: Indra Morris 020 7340 7342
Email: indra.morris@education.gov.uk
Director-General, Insight, Resources and Transformation: Howard Orme 020 7340 7356
Email: howard.orme@education.gov.uk
Director-General, Education Standards: Paul Kett 020 7783 8095 Email: paul.kett@education.gov.uk
Director-General, Tertiary Education: Philippa Lloyd 07785 387031
Email: philippa.lloyd@education.gov.uk
Director, Government Equalities Office: Hilary Spencer 020 7783 8574
Email: hilary.spencer@geo.gov.uk hilary.spencer@education.gov.uk
Chief Executive, Education and Skills Funding Agency: Eileen Milner
Email: eileen.milner@education.gov.uk

Executive Agencies: Education and Skills Funding Agency; National College for Teaching and Leadership; Standards and Testing Agency

Department for Environment, Food and Rural Affairs

Nobel House, 17 Smith Square, London SW1P 3JR
Tel: 020 7238 6000 Fax: 0345 933 5577
Email: defra.helpline@defra.gsi.gov.uk Website: www.gov.uk/defra Twitter: @DefraGovUK

MINISTERS

Secretary of State: Rt Hon Michael Gove MP
Minister of State for Agriculture, Fisheries and Food: George Eustice MP
Parliamentary Under-Secretary of State for Environment: Dr Therese Coffey MP
Parliamentary Under-Secretary of State for Rural Affairs and Biosecurity: Lord Gardiner of Kimble
Parliamentary Clerk: Deirdre Kennedy MBE 020 8026 3042

***House of Lords Spokesperson:* Lord Gardiner of Kimble**

CIVIL SERVANTS

Permanent Secretary: Clare Moriarty CB
Director-General, Food, Farming and Biodiversity: David Kennedy
Email: david.kennedy@defra.gsi.gov.uk
Director-General, Strategy, EU Exit and Finance: Nick Joicey 020 8225 7329
Email: nick.joicey@defra.gsi.gov.uk
Director-General, Marine, Natural Environment and Rural: Sonia Phippard 020 8026 4112
Email: sonia.phippard@defra.gsi.gov.uk
Chief Operating Officer: Betsy Bassis 020 7238 4831 Email: betsy.bassis@defra.gsi.gov.uk
Chief Scientific Adviser: Prof Ian Boyd FSB FRSE 020 7238 1645 Email: ian.boyd@defra.gsi.gov.uk
Chief Finance Officer: Mark McLaughlin Email: mark.mclauglin@defra.gsi.gov.uk

Executive Agencies: Animal and Plant Health Agency; Centre for Environment, Fisheries and Aquaculture Science; Rural Payments Agency; Veterinary Medicines Directorate

Department for Exiting the European Union

9 Downing Street, London SW1A 2AS
Tel: 020 7276 0432 Website: www.gov.uk/dexeu Twitter: @dexeugov

MINISTERS

Secretary of State: Rt Hon David Davis MP
Minister of State: Rt Hon Baroness Anelay of St Johns DBE
Parliamentary Under-Secretary of State: Robin Walker MP
Parliamentary Under-Secretary of State: Steve Baker MP
***House of Lords Spokesperson:* Baroness Anelay of St Johns**
Parliamentary Clerk: Bertie Archer

CIVIL SERVANTS

Permanent Secretary: Dr Philip Rycroft CB
Director-General: Alex Ellis
Director-General: Sarah Healey
Director, Negotiation Co-ordination Unit: Matt Baugh OBE
Director, Market Access and Budget: Catherine Webb
Director, Justice, Security and Migration: Chris Jones 07808 024882
Email: chris.jones@dexeu.gov.uk
Director, Cross-Government Policy and Coordination: Tom Shinner
Director, Engagement and Corporate Strategy: Joanna Key
Director, Trade and Partnerships/ NSS Link: Antony Phillipson
Director, Planning and Analysis (job share): Susannah Storey 07753 277818
Email: susannah.storey@dexeu.gov.uk
Director, Planning and Analysis (job share): Jo Shanmugalingam

Foreign and Commonwealth Office

King Charles Street, London SW1A 2AH
Tel: 020 7008 1500
Email: fcocorrespondence@fco.gov.uk Website: www.gov.uk/fco Twitter: @ForeignOffice

Government and Public Offices

MINISTERS

Secretary of State: Rt Hon Boris Johnson MP
Minister of State for Europe and the Americas: Rt Hon Sir Alan Duncan KCMG MP
Minister of State for Africa: Rory Stewart OBE MP
Minister of State for the Middle East: Rt Hon Alistair Burt MP
Minister of State for the Commonwealth and the UN: Lord Ahmad of Wimbledon
Minister of State for Asia and the Pacific: Rt Hon Mark Field MP
Parliamentary Clerk: Nat Dawbarn 020 7008 4005
***House of Lords Spokesperson:* Lord Ahmad of Wimbledon**

CIVIL SERVANTS

Permanent Under-Secretary of State and Head of HM Diplomatic Service:
Sir Simon McDonald KCMG KCVO 020 7008 2150 Email: pus.action@fco.gov.uk
Director-General, Chief Operating Officer: Peter Jones 020 7008 0410
Email: peter.jones@fco.gov.uk
Director-General, Consular and Security: Philip Barton CMG 020 7008 2176
Email: philip.barton@fco.gov.uk
Director-General, Political: Karen Pierce CMG 020 7008 2176 Email: karen.pierce@fco.gov.uk
Director-General, Legal: Sir Iain Macleod KCMG 020 7008 3052
Email: gary.hellen@fco.gov.uk
Director-General, Economic and Global Issues: Deborah Bronnert CMG 020 7008 2208
Email: deborah.bronnert@fco.gov.uk
Director-General, EU Exit: Lindsay Croisdale-Appleby 020 7008 7973
Email: lindsay.appleby@fco.gov.uk
Director, Communications: Helen Bower-Easton CBE 020 7008 2382
Email: helen.bowereaston@fco.gov.uk
Director, Strategy and Strategic Programmes Coordinator: Dr Liane Saunders 020 7008 2882
Email: liane.saunders@fco.gov.uk
Director, Finance: Andrew Sanderson 020 7008 0595 Email: andrew.sanderson@fco.gov.uk
Director, Human Resources: Jill Gallard 020 7008 0580 Email: jill.gallard@fco.gov.uk
Management Board Overseas Network Representative: Her Excellency Alison Blake
Executive Agencies: FCO Services; Wilton Park

Department of Health

Richmond House, 79 Whitehall, London SW1A 2NS
Tel: 020 7210 4850
Website: www.gov.uk/dh Twitter: @dhgovuk

MINISTERS

Secretary of State: Rt Hon Jeremy Hunt MP
Minister of State for Health: Philip Dunne MP
Parliamentary Under-Secretary of State (Care and Mental Health): Jackie Doyle-Price MP
Parliamentary Under-Secretary of State (Public Health and Primary Care): Steve Brine MP
Parliamentary Under-Secretary of State for Health (Lords): Lord O'Shaughnessy
Parliamentary Clerk: Tom Powell

House of Lords Spokesperson: **Lord O'Shaughnessy**

CIVIL SERVANTS

Permanent Secretary: Sir Chris Wormald KCB 020 7972 2918 Email: chris.wormald@dh.gsi.gov.uk
Chief Commercial Officer: Steve Oldfield Email: steve.oldfield@dh.gsi.gov.uk
Chief Medical Officer: Prof Dame Sally Davies DBE 020 7210 5151
Email: sally.davies@dh.gsi.gov.uk
Chief Scientific Adviser: Prof Chris Whitty 020 7210 5489
Director-General, Finance and Group Operations: David Williams 020 7210 5685
Email: david.williams@dh.gsi.gov.uk
Director-General, Acute Care and Workforce: Lee McDonough 020 7210 5368
Email: lee.mcdonough@dh.gsi.gov.uk
Director-General, Community Care: Tamara Finkelstein 020 7210 4369
Email: tamara.finkelstein@dh.gsi.gov.uk
Director-General, Global and Public Health: Clara Swinson 020 7210 5691
Email: clara.swinson@dh.gsi.gov.uk

Executive Agencies: Medicines and Healthcare Products Regulatory Agency; Public Health England

Home Office

2 Marsham Street, London SW1P 4DF
Tel: 020 7035 4848 Fax: 020 7035 4745
Email: public.enquiries@homeoffice.gsi.gov.uk Website: www.gov.uk/home-office
Twitter: @ukhomeoffice

MINISTERS

Secretary of State: Rt Hon Amber Rudd MP
Minister of State for Immigration: Rt Hon Brandon Lewis MP
Minister of State for Security: Rt Hon Ben Wallace MP
Minister of State for Policing and the Fire Service: Nick Hurd MP
Minister of State for Countering Extremism: Baroness Williams of Trafford
Parliamentary Under-Secretary of State for Crime, Safeguarding and Vulnerability:
Sarah Newton MP
Parliamentary Clerk: Benjamin Pugsley 020 7035 8838

House of Lords Spokesperson: **Baroness Williams of Trafford**

CIVIL SERVANTS

Permanent Secretary: Philip Rutnam 020 7035 0197
Email: permanentsecretary.submissions@homeoffice.gsi.gov.uk
Second Permanent Secretary: Patsy Wilkinson CB 020 7035 0503
Email: secondpermanentsecretary@homeoffice.gsi.gov.uk
Director-General, Office for Security and Counter-Terrorism: Tom Hurd OBE 020 7035 8882
Email: dg.osct@homeoffice.x.gsi.gov.uk

Director-General, Border Force: Paul Lincoln 020 7035 8606
Email: dgborderforce.submissions@homeoffice.gsi.gov.uk
Director-General, HM Passport Office: Mark Thomson 020 7752 7040
Email: mark.thomson@hmpo.gsi.gov.uk
Director-General, UK Visas and Immigration: Mark Thomson 020 7752 7040
Email: mark.thomson@hmpo.gsi.gov.uk
Director-General, Capabilities and Resources: Mike Parsons 020 7035 0989
Email: michael.parsons2@homeoffice.gsi.gov.uk
Director-General, Immigration Enforcement: Hugh Ind 020 7035 1205
Email: hugh.ind@homeoffice.gsi.gov.uk
Director-General, Crime, Policing and Fire: To be appointed
Director-General, Legal: Peter Fish 020 7035 1393 Email: peter.fish@homeoffice.gsi.gov.uk
Director, Communications: Simon Wren CBE 020 7035 4102
Email: simon.wren2@homeoffice.gsi.gov.uk
Chief People Officer: Paula Leach Email: paula.leach@homeoffice.gsi.gov.uk

Department for International Development

22 Whitehall, London SW1A 2EG
Tel: 020 7023 0000
Email: enquiry@dfid.gov.uk Website: www.gov.uk/dfid Twitter: @dfid_uk
Abercrombie House, Eaglesham Road, East Kilbride, Glasgow G75 8EA
Tel: 01355 844000 Fax: 01355 844099

MINISTERS

Secretary of State: Rt Hon Priti Patel MP
Minister of State: Rory Stewart OBE MP
Minister of State: Rt Hon Alistair Burt MP
Minister of State: Rt Hon Lord Bates
Parliamentary Clerk: Ailish McAllister 020 7023 0559
***House of Lords Spokesperson:* Lord Bates**

CIVIL SERVANTS

Acting Permanent Secretary (until the end of December 2017): Nick Dyer 020 7023 0850
Email: pspermsec@dfid.gov.uk
Permanent Secretary (from January 2018): Matthew Rycroft 020 7023 0850
Email: pspermsec@dfid.gov.uk
Director-General, Policy and Global Programmes: Nick Dyer 020 7023 0905
Email: n-dyer@dfid.gov.uk
Director-General, Country Programmes: Lindy Cameron 020 7023 0415
Email: l-cameron@dfid.gov.uk
Director-General, Finance and Corporate Performance: Joy Hutcheon 020 7023 0407
Email: j-hutcheon@dfid.gov.uk
Acting Director-General, Economic Development: Rachel Turner Email: r-turner@dfid.gov.uk

Department for International Trade

King Charles Street, Whitehall, London SW1A 2AH
Tel: 020 7215 5000
Email: enquiries@trade.gsi.gov.uk Website: www.gov.uk/dit Twitter: @tradegovuk

MINISTERS

Secretary of State: Rt Hon Dr Liam Fox MP
Minister of State for Trade Policy: Rt Hon Greg Hands MP
Parliamentary Under-Secretary of State for Investment: Mark Garnier MP
Parliamentary Clerk: Debbie Goodier
***House of Lords Spokesperson:* Baroness Sugg**

CIVIL SERVANTS

Permanent Secretary: Antonia Romeo Email: perm.sec@trade.gsi.gov.uk
Second Permanent Secretary and Chief Trade Negotiation Adviser: Crawford Falconer
Email: secondperm.sec@trade.gsi.gov.uk
Director-General, International Trade and Investment: Dr Catherine Raines FRSA
Email: chief.executive@trade.gov.uk
Director-General, Trade Policy: John Alty CB Email: tpg-directorgeneral@trade.gov.uk
Director-General, Chief Operating Officer: Catherine Vaughan
Email: catherine.vaughan@trade.gov.uk
Director-General, Chief Executive, UK Export Finance: Louis Taylor
Email: ChiefExecutiveOffice@ukexportfinance.gov.uk
Director, Transition Programme: Paul McComb Email: paul.mccomb@trade.gsi.gov.uk
Director, Finance and Corporate Services: Alison Currie Email: alison.currie@trade.gsi.gov.uk
Director, Ministerial Strategy: Darren Tierney 07702 162699 Email: darren.tierney@trade.gsi.gov.uk
Director, Human Resources and Organisational Development: James Norton 020 7215 0880
Email: james.norton@trade.gsi.gov.uk
Director, Communications: Toby Orr 020 7215 3069 Email: toby.orr@trade.gsi.gov.uk

Ministry of Justice

102 Petty France, London SW1H 9AJ
Tel: 020 3334 3555
Email: general.queries@justice.gsi.gov.uk Website: www.gov.uk/moj Twitter: @MoJgovuk

MINISTERS

Lord Chancellor and Secretary of State for Justice: Rt Hon David Lidington CBE MP
Minister of State: Dominic Raab MP
Parliamentary Under-Secretary of State for Prisons and Probation: Sam Gyimah MP
Parliamentary Under-Secretary of State for Youth Justice, Victims, Female Offenders and Offender Health: Dr Phillip Lee MP
Spokesperson in the Lords: Lord Keen of Elie QC
Parliamentary Clerk: Rob Evans

CIVIL SERVANTS

Permanent Secretary: Richard Heaton CB Email: richard.heaton@justice.gov.uk
Chief Operating Officer: Matthew Coats Email: matthew.coats@justice.gov.uk
Chief Financial Officer and Head of Government Finance Function: Mike Driver
Email: mike.driver@justice.gov.uk
Acting Director-General, Justice and Courts Policy Group : Scott McPherson
Email: scott.mcpherson@justice.gov.uk
Director-General, Prison Reform, Offender and Youth Justice Policy Group:
Justin Russell 07920 757829 Email: justin.russell@justice.gov.uk
Chief Executive, National Offender Management Service: Michael Spurr 0300 047 6325
Email: ceohmpps@noms.gov.uk

Executive Agencies: HM Courts & Tribunals Service; Criminal Injuries Compensation Authority; Legal Aid Agency; HM Prison and Probation Service; HM Prison Service; Office of the Public Guardian

Law Officers

Attorney General's Office, 5-8 The Sanctuary, London SW1P 3JS
Tel: 020 7271 2492 Fax: 020 7271 2453
Email: [firstname.surname]@attorneygeneral.gsi.gov.uk Website: www.gov.uk/ago

Office of the Advocate General for Scotland, Dover House, 66 Whitehall, London SW1A 2AU
Tel: 020 7270 6720
Email: privateoffice@advocategeneral.gsi.gov.uk [firstname.surname]@advocategeneral.gsi.gov.uk
Website: www.gov.uk/oag

MINISTERS

Attorney General: Rt Hon Jeremy Wright QC MP
Solicitor General: Robert Buckland QC MP
Advocate General for Scotland: Lord Keen of Elie QC
***House of Lords Spokesperson:* Lord Keen of Elie**

CIVIL SERVANTS

Director and Solicitor to the Advocate General for Scotland: Neil Taylor
Email: neil.taylor@advocategeneral.gsi.gov.uk
Director-General, Attorney General's Office: Rowena Collins-Rice 020 7271 2401
Email: rowena.collins-rice@attorneygeneral.gsi.gov.uk

Northern Ireland Office

1 Horseguards Road, Whitehall, London SW1A 2HQ
Tel: 020 7210 0820 Email: enquiries@nio.gov.uk Website: www.gov.uk/nio Twitter: @niopressoffice
Stormont House, Stormont Estate, Belfast BT4 3ST
Tel: 028 9052 0700/028 9052 7668 (Textphone)

MINISTERS

Secretary of State: Rt Hon James Brokenshire MP
Parliamentary Under-Secretary of State: Chloe Smith MP
Parliamentary Under-Secretary of State: Lord Bourne of Aberystwyth
Parliamentary Clerk: Louise Newby 020 7210 6575
***House of Lords Spokesperson:* Lord Bourne of Aberystwyth**

CIVIL SERVANTS

Permanent Secretary: Sir Jonathan Stephens KCB

Privy Council Office

Room G/04, 1 Horse Guards Road, London SW1A 2HQ
Tel: 020 7271 3292 Email: enquiries@pco.gov.uk Website: privycouncil.independent.gov.uk

MINISTERS

Lord President of the Council; Leader of the House of Commons: Rt Hon Andrea Leadsom MP

CIVIL SERVANTS

Clerk of the Council: Richard Tilbrook 020 7271 3292 Email: enquiries@pco.gov.uk
Head of Secretariat and Deputy Clerk of the Council: Ceri King 020 7271 3294
Email: ceri.king@pco.gov.uk
Deputy Clerk: Christopher Berry 020 7271 1406 Email: christopher.berry@pco.gov.uk
Secretariat and Parliamentary Business Manager: Niall Clarke-Petty 020 7271 1418
Email: niall.clarke-petty@pco.gov.uk

Scotland Office

Dover House, Whitehall, London SW1A 2AU
Tel: 020 7270 6754 Email: [firstname.surname]@scotlandoffice.gsi.gov.uk
Website: www.gov.uk/scotland-office Twitter: @UKGovScotland

MINISTERS

Secretary of State: Rt Hon David Mundell MP
Parliamentary Under-Secretary of State: Lord Duncan of Springbank
Parliamentary Clerk: Louise Newby 020 7210 6575
***House of Lords Spokesperson:* Lord Duncan of Springbank**

CIVIL SERVANTS

Director: Gillian McGregor Email: gillian.mcgregor@scotlandoffice.gsi.gov.uk

Department for Transport

Great Minster House, 33 Horseferry Road, London SW1P 4DR
Tel: 0300 330 3000
Email: [firstname.surname]@dft.gsi.gov.uk Website: www.gov.uk/dft Twitter: @TransportGovUK

MINISTERS

Secretary of State: Rt Hon Chris Grayling MP
Minister of State for Transport Legislation and Maritime: Rt Hon John Hayes CBE MP
Parliamentary Under-Secretary of State for Rail, Accessibility and HS2: Paul Maynard MP
Parliamentary Under-Secretary of State for Roads, Local Transport and Devolution: Jesse Norman MP
Parliamentary Under-Secretary of State for Aviation, International and Security: Lord Callanan
Parliamentary Clerk: James Langston 020 7944 4472

House of Lords Spokesperson: **Lord Callanan**

CIVIL SERVANTS

Permanent Secretary: Bernadette Kelly CB 020 7944 3017 Email: bernadette.kelly@dft.gsi.gov.uk
Director-General, International, Security and Environment Group: Lucy Chadwick 020 7944 6948
Email: lucy.chadwick@dft.gsi.gov.uk
Director-General, Roads, Devolution and Motoring Group: Tricia Hayes 020 7944 2400
Email: patricia.hayes@dft.gsi.gov.uk
Director-General, Resources and Strategy Group: Jonathan Moor CBE 020 7944 4597
Email: jonathan.moor@dft.gsi.gov.uk
Director-General, High Speed Rail Group: Michael Hurn 020 7944 2112
Email: michael.hurn@dft.gsi.gov.uk
Director-General, Rail Group: Nick Joyce 020 7944 4190 Email: nick.joyce@dft.gsi.gov.uk
Chief Scientific Adviser: Phil Blythe 07920 581420 Email: philip.blythe@dft.gsi.gov.uk
General Counsel: Nick Olley 020 7944 4770 Email: nick.olley@dft.gsi.gov.uk

Executive Agencies: Driver and Vehicle Licensing Agency; Driver and Vehicle Standards Agency; Maritime and Coastguard Agency; Vehicle Certification Agency

HM Treasury

1 Horse Guards Road, London SW1A 2HQ
Tel: 020 7270 5000 Fax: 020 7270 5148
Email: public.enquiries@hmtreasury.gsi.gov.uk Website: www.gov.uk/treasury Twitter: @hmtreasury

MINISTERS

Chancellor of the Exchequer: Rt Hon Philip Hammond MP
Chief Secretary to the Treasury: Rt Hon Elizabeth Truss MP
Financial Secretary; Paymaster General: Rt Hon Mel Stride MP
Economic Secretary: Steve Barclay MP
Exchequer Secretary: Andrew Jones MP
Parliamentary Clerk: Simon Turrell 020 7270 4520

House of Lords Spokesperson: **Lord Bates**

CIVIL SERVANTS

Permanent Secretary: Sir Tom Scholar KCB 020 7270 5743
Email: action.permsec@hmtreasury.gsi.gov.uk
Second Permanent Secretary: Charles Roxburgh Email: charles.roxburgh@hmtreasury.gsi.gov.uk
Director-General, Financial Services: Katharine Braddick 020 7270 4448
Email: katharine.braddick@hmtreasury.gsi.gov.uk
Director-General, Public Spending and Finance: James Bowler CB
Email: james.bowler@hmtreasury.gsi.gov.uk
Director-General, International and EU: Mark Bowman 020 7270 6637
Email: mark.bowman@hmtreasury.gsi.gov.uk
Director-General, Economics: Sir David Ramsden CBE 020 7270 4318
Email: dave.ramsden@hmtreasury.gsi.gov.uk

Director-General, Tax and Welfare: Beth Russell 020 7270 6259
Email: beth.russell@hmtreasury.gsi.gov.uk
Chief Financial Officer and Head of Government Finance Function: Mike Driver
Email: mike.driver@justice.gov.uk

Executive Agencies: Government Internal Audit Agency; National Infrastructure Commission; UK Debt Management Office

Office of the Secretary of State for Wales

Gwydyr House, Whitehall, London SW1A 2NP
Tel: 020 7270 6137 Email: correspondence@walesoffice.gsi.gov.uk
Website: www.gov.uk/wales-office Twitter: @ukgovwales

1 Caspian Point, Caspian Way, Cardiff CF10 4DQ
Tel: 029 2092 4228

MINISTERS

Secretary of State: Rt Hon Alun Cairns MP
Parliamentary Under-Secretary of State: Guto Bebb MP
Parliamentary Under-Secretary of State: Lord Duncan of Springbank
Parliamentary Clerk: Louise Newby 020 7270 0584/020 7210 6551

House of Lords Spokesperson: **Lord Duncan of Springbank**

CIVIL SERVANTS

Director: Glynne Jones 020 7270 0559 Email: glynne.jones@walesoffice.gsi.gov.uk

Department for Work and Pensions

Caxton House, Tothill Street, London SW1H 9DA
Email: freedom-of-information-request@dwp.gsi.gov.uk ministers@dwp.gsi.gov.uk
Website: www.gov.uk/dwp Twitter: @DWP

MINISTERS

Secretary of State: Rt Hon David Gauke MP
Minister of State for Employment: Damian Hinds MP
Minister of State for Disabled People, Health and Work: Penny Mordaunt MP
Parliamentary Under-Secretary of State for Pensions and Financial Inclusion: Guy Opperman MP
Parliamentary Under-Secretary of State for Family Support, Housing and Child Maintenance: Caroline Dinenage MP
Parliamentary Under-Secretary of State (Lords): Baroness Buscombe
Parliamentary Clerk: Howard Sargent 020 3267 5053

House of Lords Spokesperson: **Baroness Buscombe**

CIVIL SERVANTS

Permanent Secretary: Sir Robert Devereux KCB 020 3267 5013
Email: robert.devereux@dwp.gsi.gov.uk
Director-General, Finance: Peter Schofield 020 7449 5780 Email: peter.schofield1@dwp.gsi.gov.uk
Director-General, Universal Credit Operations: Susan Park 020 7340 4463
Email: susan.park@dwp.gsi.gov.uk
Director-General, Strategy: Jonathan Mills 020 7449 5516 Email: jonathan.mills@dwp.gsi.gov.uk
Director-General, Human Resources: Debbie Alder 020 7340 4193
Email: debbie.alder@dwp.gsi.gov.uk
Director-General, Universal Credit Programme: Neil Couling CBE 020 7245 3844
Email: neil.couling@dwp.gsi.gov.uk
Director-General, Chief Digital and Information Officer: Mayank Prakash 020 7449 7892
Email: mayank.prakash@dwp.gsi.gov.uk
Director-General, Operations: Andrew Rhodes 020 7449 7512
Email: andrew.rhodes@dwp.gsi.gov.uk

Executive Agencies

Animal and Plant Health Agency

Corporate Headquarters, Woodham Lane, Addlestone, Surrey KT15 3NB
Tel: 01932 341111
Email: apha.corporatecorrespondence@apha.gsi.gov.uk Website: www.gov.uk/apha
Twitter: @APHAgovuk

Number of staff: 2,252

Chief Executive: Chris Hadkiss 01932 341111 Email: apha.corporatecorrespondence@apha.gsi.gov.uk

Sponsored by: Department for Environment, Food and Rural Affairs, Scottish Government, Welsh Government

Centre for Environment, Fisheries and Aquaculture Science

Lowestoft Laboratory, Pakefield Road, Lowestoft, Suffolk NR33 0HT
Tel: 01502 562244 Fax: 01502 513865
Email: cmboffice@cefas.co.uk
Website: www.cefas.co.uk Twitter: @CefasGovUK

Weymouth Laboratory, The Nothe, Barrack Road, Weymouth, Dorset DT4 8UB
Tel: 01305 206600 Fax: 01305 206601

Number of staff: 535

Chief Executive: RAdm Tom Karsten 01502 562244 Email: tom.karsten@cefas.co.uk

Sponsored by: Department for Environment, Food and Rural Affairs

Companies House

Crown Way, Cardiff CF14 3UZ
Tel: 0303 1234 500 Fax: 029 2038 0517
Email: enquiries@companies-house.gov.uk
Website: www.gov.uk/companies-house Twitter: @CompaniesHouse

Number of staff: 890

Non-Executive Chair: Lesley Cowley OBE
Chief Executive and Registrar of Companies for England and Wales: Louise Smyth
Email: lsmyth@companieshouse.gov.uk

Sponsored by: Department for Business, Energy and Industrial Strategy

HM Courts & Tribunals Service

102 Petty France, London SW1H 9AJ
Tel: 020 3334 3555
Website: www.gov.uk/hmcts Twitter: @HMCTSgovuk

Number of staff: 17,000

Chief Executive: Susan Acland-Hood 020 3334 3012 Email: hmcts.chiefexecutive@hmcts.gov.uk

Sponsored by: Ministry of Justice

Criminal Injuries Compensation Authority

Alexander Bain House, Atlantic Quay, 15 York Street, Glasgow G2 8JQ
Tel: 0300 003 3601
Website: www.gov.uk/cica Twitter: @CICAgov

Number of staff: 300

Chief Executive: Carole Oatway CBE Email: carole.oatway@cica.gsi.gov.uk

Sponsored by: Ministry of Justice

Crown Commercial Service
Aviation House, 125 Kingsway, London WC2B 6NH
Tel: 03454 102222
Email: info@crowncommercial.gov.uk
Website: www.gov.uk/ccs Twitter: @gov_procurement
Ninth Floor, The Capital, Old Hall Street, Liverpool L3 9PP
Email: info@crowncommercial.gov.uk Website: www.gov.uk/ccs
Rosebery Court, St Andrews Business Park, Norwich NR7 0HS
Email: info@crowncommercial.gov.uk Website: www.gov.uk/ccs
Concept House, Cardiff Road, Newport NP10 8QQ
Email: info@crowncommercial.gov.uk Website: www.gov.uk/ccs
Number of staff: 800
Chair: Tony van Kralingen
Chief Executive and Accounting Officer: Malcolm Harrison
Sponsored by: Cabinet Office

Defence Electronics and Components Agency
Welsh Road, Sealand, Deeside, Flintshire CH5 2LS
Tel: 01244 847 694
Email: decainfo@deca.mod.uk Website: www.gov.uk/deca
Number of staff: 430
Chief Executive: Geraint Spearing 01244 847701 Email: judith.lee@deca.mod.uk
Sponsored by: Ministry of Defence

Defence Science and Technology Laboratory
Porton Down, Salisbury, Wiltshire SP4 0JQ
Tel: 01980 950000
Email: central-enquiries@dstl.gov.uk Website: www.gov.uk/dstl Twitter: @dstlmod
Number of staff: 3,650
Chair: Sir David Pepper KCMG
Chief Executive: Jonathan Lyle CB 01980 957419 Email: jhlyle@dstl.gov.uk
Sponsored by: Ministry of Defence

Driver and Vehicle Licensing Agency
Longview Road, Morriston, Swansea SA6 7JL
Tel: 0300 790 6801 (Drivers)/0300 790 6802 (Vehicles)
Website: www.gov.uk/dvla Twitter: @dvlagovuk
Number of staff: 6,042
Chief Executive: Oliver Morley 01792 384538 Email: chief.executive@dvla.gsi.gov.uk
Sponsored by: Department for Transport

Driver and Vehicle Standards Agency
2nd Floor, Berkeley House, Croydon Street, Bristol BS5 0DA
Tel: 0117-954 3200
Email: corporatereputation@dvsa.gov.uk
Website: www.gov.uk/dvsa Twitter: @DVSAgovuk
Number of staff: 4,470
Non-Executive Chair: Bridget Rosewell OBE 020 8878 6333 Email: brosewell@volterra.co.uk
Chief Executive: Gareth Llewellyn 0117-954 3211 Email: gareth.llewellyn@dvsa.gov.uk
Sponsored by: Department for Transport

Education and Skills Funding Agency

53-55 Butts Park Road, Earlsdon, Coventry CV1 3BH
Tel: 0370 000 2288
Website: www.gov.uk/esfa Twitter: @esfagov
Number of staff: 730
Chief Executive: Eileen Milner 02476 660320 Email: eileen.milner@education.gov.uk
Sponsored by: Department for Education

FCO Services

Hanslope Park, Milton Keynes MK19 7BH
Tel: 01908 515789
Email: fco.services@fco.gov.uk Website: www.fcoservices.gov.uk
Number of staff: 1,300
Chief Executive: Danny Payne 01908 515993 Email: danny.payne@fco.gov.uk
Sponsored by: Foreign and Commonwealth Office

Forest Enterprise England

620 Bristol Business Park, Coldharbour Lane, Bristol BS16 1EJ
Tel: 0117-906 6000 Fax: 0117-931 2859
Email: fe.england@forestry.gsi.gov.uk
Website: www.forestry.gov.uk/englandsforests
Number of staff: 938
Chief Executive: Simon Hodgson 0300 067 4001 Email: simon.hodgson@forestry.gsi.gov.uk
Sponsored by: Forestry Commission

Forest Research

Alice Holt Lodge Research Station, Farnham, Surrey GU10 4LH
Tel: 0300 067 5600/01420 22255
Email: research.info@forestry.gsi.gov.uk
Website: www.forestry.gov.uk/forestresearch
Twitter: @Forest_Research
Northern Research Station, Roslin, Midlothian EH25 9SY
Tel: 0300 067 5903 Fax: 0131-445 5124
Email: nrs@forestry.gsi.gov.uk
Forest Research in Wales, Asiantaeth Ymchwil Goedwig / Forest Research Agency, Adeilad Thoday / Thoday Building, Ffordd Deiniol / Deiniol Road, Bangor LL57 2UW
Tel: 0300 067 5774/01248 382291
Email: fcwenquiries@forestry.gsi.gov.uk
Number of staff: 231
Chief Executive: Professor James Pendlebury 0300 067 5971
Email: james.pendlebury@forestry.gsi.gov.uk
Sponsored by: Forestry Commission

Government Internal Audit Agency

1 Horse Guards Road, London SW1A 2HQ
Email: correspondence@giaa.gsi.gov.uk
Website: www.gov.uk/giaa
Number of staff: 450
Chief Executive Officer: Jon Whitfield Email: correspondence@giaa.gsi.gov.uk
Sponsored by: HM Treasury

The Insolvency Service

4 Abbey Orchard Street, London SW1P 2HT
Tel: 0300 678 0015/020 7637 1110
Email: insolvency.enquiryline@insolvency.gsi.gov.uk
Website: www.gov.uk/insolvency-service
Twitter: @insolvencygovuk

Number of staff: 1,420

Chair: Stephen Allinson
Chief Executive and Inspector General: Sarah Albon 020 7291 6713
Email: sarah.albon@insolvency.gsi.gov.uk

Sponsored by: Department for Business, Energy and Industrial Strategy

Intellectual Property Office

Concept House, Cardiff Road, Newport NP10 8QQ
Tel: 0300 300 2000 Fax: 01633 817777
Email: information@ipo.gov.uk Website: www.gov.uk/ipo Twitter: @The_IPO

Number of staff: 1,169

Chair: Bob Gilbert CBE 01633 814423 Email: bob.gilbert@ipo.gov.uk
Chief Executive and Comptroller General: Tim Moss CBE Email: tim.moss@ipo.gov.uk

Sponsored by: Department for Business, Energy and Industrial Strategy

Legal Aid Agency

Legal Aid Agency, 102 Petty France, London SW1H 9AL
Tel: 0300 200 2020/0845 345 4345
Email: contactcivil@legalaid.gsi.gov.uk
Website: www.gov.uk/government/organisations/legal-aid-agency
Twitter: @LegalAidAgency

Number of staff: 1,287

Chief Executive: Shaun McNally CBE 0151-235 6949 Email: shaun.mcnally@justice.gsi.gov.uk

Sponsored by: Ministry of Justice

Maritime and Coastguard Agency

Spring Place, 105 Commercial Road, Southampton, Hampshire SO15 1EG
Tel: 020 3817 2000
Email: infoline@mcga.gov.uk Website: www.gov.uk/mca Twitter: @MCA_media

Number of staff: 1,038

Non-Executive Chairman: Michael Parker 020 3817 2167 Email: michael.parker@mcga.gov.uk
Chief Executive: Vice Admiral (Retd) Sir Alan Massey KCB CBE 020 3817 2385
Email: alan.massey@mcga.gov.uk

Sponsored by: Department for Transport

Medicines and Healthcare Products Regulatory Agency

151 Buckingham Palace Road, London SW1W 9SZ
Tel: 020 3080 6000
Email: info@mhra.gov.uk
Website: www.gov.uk/mhra Twitter: @MHRAgovuk

Number of staff: 1,200

Chair: Sir Michael Rawlins GBE 020 3080 6875 Email: michael.rawlins@mhra.gov.uk
Chief Executive: Dr Ian Hudson 020 3080 6100 Email: ian.hudson@mhra.gov.uk

Sponsored by: Department of Health

Met Office
FitzRoy Road, Exeter, Devon EX1 3PB
Tel: 0370 900 0100/01392 885680 Fax: 0370 900 5050/01392 885681
Email: enquiries@metoffice.gov.uk Website: www.metoffice.gov.uk Twitter: @metoffice
Number of staff: 2,000
Chief Executive: Rob Varley 01392 884621 Email: rob.varley@metoffice.gov.uk
Sponsored by: Department for Business, Energy and Industrial Strategy

National College for Teaching and Leadership
Sanctuary Buildings, 20 Great Smith Street, London SW1P 3BT
Tel: 037 0000 2288
Email: www.education.gov.uk/help/contactus Website: www.gov.uk/nctl Twitter: @the_college
Number of staff: 350
Chair: Roger Pope Email: roger.pope@education.gov.uk
Sponsored by: Department for Education

National Infrastructure Commission
5th Floor, 11 Philpot Lane, London EC3M 8UD
Website: www.nic.org.uk
Chair: Rt Hon Lord Adonis
Chief Executive: Philip Graham
Sponsored by: HM Treasury

Planning Inspectorate
Temple Quay House, 2 The Square, Temple Quay, Bristol BS1 6PN
Tel: 030 3444 5000 Email: enquiries@pins.gsi.gov.uk
Website: www.gov.uk/pins Twitter: @PINSgov
Number of staff: 700
Chair, Planning Inspectorate Board: Sara Weller CBE
Chief Executive: Sarah Richards Email: sarah.richards@pins.gsi.gov.uk
Sponsored by: Welsh Government
Sponsored by: Department for Communities and Local Government

HM Prison and Probation Service
5th Floor, 102 Petty France, London SW1H 9AJ
Tel: 020 3193 5921 Email: public.enquiries@noms.gsi.gov.uk
Website: gov.uk/hmpps Twitter: @hmpps
Number of staff: 43,530
Chief Executive: Michael Spurr 0300 047 6325 Email: ceohmpps@noms.gov.uk
Sponsored by: Ministry of Justice

HM Prison Service
Clive House, 70 Petty France, London SW1H 9EX
Tel: 0300 047 6325 Email: public.enquiries@noms.gsi.gov.uk
Website: www.gov.uk/government/organisations/hm-prison-service
Chief Executive: Michael Spurr
Sponsored by: Ministry of Justice

Office of the Public Guardian
PO Box 16185, Birmingham B2 2WH
Tel: 0300 456 0300 Fax: 0870 739 5780 Email: customerservices@publicguardian.gsi.gov.uk
Website: www.gov.uk/opg Twitter: @OPGDigital

Number of staff: 1,300

Chief Executive and Public Guardian: Alan Eccles CBE 0121-631 6845
Email: alan.eccles@publicguardian.gsi.gov.uk
Sponsored by: Ministry of Justice

Public Health England

Wellington House, 133-155 Waterloo Road, London SE1 8UG
Tel: 020 7654 8000 Email: enquiries@phe.gov.uk Website: www.gov.uk/phe Twitter: @PHE_uk

Number of staff: 5,000

Interim Chair: Sir Derek Myers
Chief Executive: Duncan Selbie Email: duncan.selbie@phe.gov.uk
Sponsored by: Department of Health

Queen Elizabeth II Centre

Broad Sanctuary, Westminster, London SW1P 3EE
Tel: 020 7798 4000 Fax: 020 7798 4200
Email: info@qeiicentre.london Website: www.qeiicentre.london Twitter: @QEIICentre

Number of staff: 46

Chief Executive: Mark Taylor 020 7798 4010 Email: mark.taylor@qeiicentre.london
Sponsored by: Department for Communities and Local Government

The Royal Parks

The Old Police House, Hyde Park, London W2 2UH
Tel: 0300 061 2001 Fax: 020 7298 2005
Email: hq@royalparks.gsi.gov.uk Website: www.royalparks.org.uk Twitter: @theroyalparks

Number of staff: 120

Chief Executive: Andrew Scattergood Email: chiefexecutive@royalparks.gsi.gov.uk
Chairman: Loyd Grossman CBE FSA 0300 061 2007 Email: chairman@royalparks.gsi.gov.uk
Sponsored by: Department for Digital, Culture, Media and Sport

Rural Payments Agency

Northgate House, 21-23 Valpy Street, PO Box 69, Reading, Berkshire RG1 1AF
Tel: 03000 200301
Email: ruralpayments@defra.gsi.gov.uk Website: www.gov.uk/rpa Twitter: @Ruralpay

Number of staff: 2,107

Chief Executive: Paul Caldwell 01228 640314 Email: paul.caldwell@rpa.gsi.gov.uk
Sponsored by: Department for Environment, Food and Rural Affairs

Standards and Testing Agency

53-55 Butts Road, Earlsdon Park, Coventry CV1 3BH
Tel: 0370 000 2288 Email: assessments@education.gov.uk Website: www.gov.uk/sta

Number of staff: 115

Chief Executive: Claire Burton 020 7340 7378 Email: ceooffice.sta@education.gov.uk
Sponsored by: Department for Education

UK Debt Management Office

Eastcheap Court, 11 Philpot Lane, London EC3M 8UD
Tel: 020 7862 6500 Email: [firstname.surname]@dmo.gsi.gov.uk Website: www.dmo.gov.uk

Number of staff: 121

Chief Executive: Sir Robert Stheeman 020 7862 6519 Email: robert.stheeman@dmo.gsi.gov.uk
Sponsored by: HM Treasury

UK Hydrographic Office
Admiralty Way, Taunton TA1 2DN
Tel: 01823 484444
Email: customerservices@ukho.gov.uk
Website: www.gov.uk/ukho Twitter: @UKHO_Online

Number of staff: 950

Non-Executive Chair: Adam Singer
Chief Executive: John Humphrey 01823 483505 Email: john.humphrey@ukho.gov.uk
Sponsored by: Ministry of Defence

UK Space Agency
Polaris House, North Star Avenue, Swindon SN2 1SZ
Tel: 020 7215 5000
Email: info@ukspaceagency.bis.gsi.gov.uk Website: www.gov.uk/uksa Twitter: @spacegovuk

Number of staff: 76

Chief Executive: Graham Turnock
Sponsored by: Department for Business, Energy and Industrial Strategy

Valuation Office Agency
Wingate House, 93-107 Shaftesbury Avenue, London W1D 5BU
Tel: 0300 050 1501/0300 050 5505 (Wales) Fax: 0300 050 0690
Email: customerservices@voa.gsi.gov.uk
Website: www.voa.gov.uk Twitter: @VOAgovuk

Number of staff: 3,600

Chief Executive: Melissa Tatton CBE Email: melissa.tatton@voa.gsi.gov.uk
Sponsored by: HM Revenue & Customs

Vehicle Certification Agency
1 The Eastgate Office Centre, Eastgate Road, Bristol BS5 6XX
Tel: 0300 330 5797 Email: enquiries@vca.gov.uk Website: www.dft.gov.uk/vca

Number of staff: 150

Chief Executive: Pia Wilkes Email: pia.wilkes@vca.gov.uk
Sponsored by: Department for Transport

Veterinary Medicines Directorate
Woodham Lane, New Haw, Addlestone, Surrey KT15 3LS
Tel: 01932 336911 Email: postmaster@vmd.defra.gsi.gov.uk Website: www.gov.uk/vmd

Number of staff: 160

Chief Executive: Prof Peter Borriello 01932 338302 Email: p.borriello@vmd.defra.gsi.gov.uk
Sponsored by: Department for Environment, Food and Rural Affairs

Wilton Park
Wiston House, Steyning BN44 3DZ
Tel: 01903 815020 Fax: 01903 816373
Email: admin@wiltonpark.org.uk
Website: www.wiltonpark.org.uk Twitter: @wiltonpark

Number of staff: 70

Chairman: Iain Ferguson CBE 01903 817766 Email: iain.ferguson@wiltonpark.org.uk
Acting Chief Executive: Myles Wickstead CBE Email: myles.wickstead@wiltonpark.org.uk
Sponsored by: Foreign and Commonwealth Office

Non-Ministerial Departments

Non-Ministerial Departments are headed by office-holders, boards or Commissioners with specific statutory responsibilities

Charity Commission

Second Floor, 1 Drummond Gate, London SW1V 2QQ
Tel: 0300 066 9197
Email: see forms on website Website: www.charitycommission.gov.uk Twitter: @ChtyCommission

Number of staff: 300

Chair: William Shawcross CVO 030 0065 2159
Email: william.shawcross@charitycommission.gsi.gov.uk
Chief Executive: Helen Stephenson Email: helen.stephenson@charitycommission.gsi.gov.uk

Competition and Markets Authority

Victoria House, 37 Southampton Row, London WC1B 4AD
Tel: 020 3738 6000
Email: general.enquiries@cma.gsi.gov.uk Website: www.gov.uk/cma Twitter: @CMAgovUK

Number of staff: 600

Chair: Professor Lord Currie of Marylebone 020 3738 6000 Email: david.currie@cma.gsi.gov.uk
Chief Executive: Dr Andrea Coscelli 020 3738 6286 Email: andrea.coscelli@cma.gsi.gov.uk

Crown Prosecution Service

Rose Court, 2 Southwark Bridge, London SE1 9HS
Tel: 020 3357 0899
Email: enquiries@cps.gsi.gov.uk Website: www.cps.gov.uk Twitter: @cpsuk

Number of staff: 5,974

Director of Public Prosecutions: Alison Saunders CB
Chief Executive: Nick Folland

Food Standards Agency

Aviation House, 125 Kingsway, London WC2B 6NH
Tel: 020 7276 8000
Email: helpline@foodstandards.gsi.gov.uk Website: www.food.gov.uk Twitter: @foodgov

Number of staff: 1,073

Chair: Heather Hancock 020 7276 8120 Email: david.self@foodstandards.gsi.gov.uk
Chief Executive: Jason Feeney CBE 020 7276 8616 Email: chiefexecutive@foodstandards.gsi.gov.uk

Forestry Commission

Forestry Commission Head Office, Silvan House, 231 Corstorphine Road, Edinburgh EH12 7AT
Tel: 0300 067 5000
Email: enquiries@forestry.gsi.gov.uk Website: www.forestry.gov.uk Twitter: @ForestryCommEng

Number of staff: 3,000

Chair: Sir Harry Studholme

Office of Gas and Electricity Markets

9 Millbank, London SW1P 3GE
Tel: 020 7901 7000 Fax: 020 7901 7066 Website: www.ofgem.gov.uk Twitter: @ofgem

Number of staff: 761

Chair of the Gas and Electricity Markets Authority: David Gray 020 7901 7203
Email: chairman@ofgem.gov.uk
Chief Executive: Dermot Nolan 020 7901 7357 Email: dermot.nolan@ofgem.gov.uk

Government Actuary's Department

Finlaison House, 15-17 Furnival Street, London EC4A 1AB
Tel: 020 7211 2601 Fax: 020 7211 2650
Email: enquiries@gad.gov.uk Website: www.gov.uk/gad

Number of staff: 160

Government Actuary: Martin Clarke CB 020 7211 2620 Email: enquiries@gad.gov.uk
Deputy Government Actuary: Colin Wilson

Government Legal Department

One Kemble Street, London WC2B 4TS
Tel: 020 7210 3000
Email: thetreasurysolicitor@governmentlegal.gov.uk Website: www.gov.uk/gld

Number of staff: 1,873

HM Procurator-General and Treasury Solicitor and Head of the Government Legal Service: Jonathan Jones 020 7210 3050 Email: jonathan.jones@governmentlegal.gov.uk

HM Land Registry

Head Office, Trafalgar House, 1 Bedford Park, Croydon, London CR0 2AQ
Tel: 0300 006 0004
Email: customersupport@landregistry.gov.uk
Website: www.gov.uk/land-registry Twitter: @LandRegGov

Number of staff: 4,915

Non-Executive Chair: Michael Mire Email: michael.mire@landregistry.gov.uk
Chief Executive and Chief Land Registrar: Graham Farrant 0300 006 7457
Email: graham.farrant@landregistry.gov.uk

The National Archives

Kew, Richmond TW9 4DU
Tel: 020 8876 3444 Fax: 020 8878 8905
Website: www.nationalarchives.gov.uk Twitter: @UkNatArchives

Number of staff: 536

Chief Executive and Keeper: Jeff James 020 8392 5220 Email: jeff.james@nationalarchives.gsi.gov.uk

National Crime Agency

1-6 Citadel Place, Tinworth Street, London SE11 5EF
Tel: 0370 496 7622
Email: communication@nca.x.gsi.gov.uk
Website: www.nationalcrimeagency.gov.uk
Twitter: @NCA_UK
Director-General: Lynne Owens CBE QPM
Deputy Directors-General: Matthew Horne, Nina Cope

National Savings and Investments

1 Drummond Gate, Pimlico, London SW1V 2QX
Tel: 020 7932 6600
Website: www.nsandi.com Twitter: @nsandi

Number of staff: 180

Non-Executive Director and Chairman of the Board: Ed Anderson
Chief Executive: Ian Ackerley 020 7932 6602 Email: ian.ackerley@nsandi.com

Government and Public Offices

Ordnance Survey

Explorer House, Adanac Drive, Southampton, Hampshire SO16 0AS
Tel: 034 5605 0505
Email: customerservices@os.uk Website: www.os.uk Twitter: @OrdnanceSurvey

Number of staff: 1,100

Chief Executive: Nigel Clifford FRGS FRICS 023 8005 6001 Email: nigel.clifford@os.uk

Office of Qualifications and Examinations Regulation

Spring Place, Coventry Business Park, Herald Avenue, Coventry CV5 6UB
Tel: 0300 303 3344 Fax: 0300 303 3348
Email: public.enquiries@ofqual.gov.uk Website: www.gov.uk/ofqual Twitter: @ofqual

Number of staff: 191

Chair: Roger Taylor 02476 716741 Email: roger.taylor@ofqual.gov.uk
Chief Regulator: Sally Collier 02476 671809 Email: sally.collier@ofqual.gov.uk

Office of Rail and Road

One Kemble Street, London WC2B 4AN
Tel: 020 7282 2000 Fax: 020 7282 2040
Email: contact.cct@orr.gov.uk Website: www.orr.gov.uk Twitter: @railandroad

Number of staff: 286

Chair: Professor Stephen Glaister CBE 020 7282 2178 Email: stephen.glaister@orr.gov.uk
Chief Executive: Joanna Whittington 020 7282 2117 Email: joanna.whittington@orr.gov.uk

HM Revenue & Customs

100 Parliament Street, London SW1A 2BQ
Tel: 0300 058 9668
Email: correspondence-team.mincom@hmrc.gsi.gov.uk
Website: www.gov.uk/hmrc Twitter: @HMRCgovuk

Number of staff: 59,700

Executive Chair and Permanent Secretary: Edward Troup Email: edward.troup@hmrc.gsi.gov.uk
Chief Executive and Permanent Secretary: Jon Thompson Email: chief.executive@hmrc.gsi.gov.uk

Serious Fraud Office

2-4 Cockspur Street, London SW1Y 5BS
Tel: 020 7239 7272
Email: public.enquiries@sfo.gsi.gov.uk
Website: www.sfo.gov.uk

Number of staff: 400

Director: David Green CB QC 020 7239 7045 Email: chris.drake@sfo.gsi.gov.uk
General Counsel: Alun Milford 020 7239 7116 Email: alun.milford@sfo.gsi.gov.uk

Office for Standards in Education, Children's Services and Skills

Aviation House, 125 Kingsway, London WC2B 6SE
Tel: 0300 123 1231
Email: enquiries@ofsted.gov.uk
Website: www.gov.uk/ofsted Twitter: @Ofstednews

Number of staff: 1,510

Chair: Prof Julius Weinberg 0300 0131 521 Email: julius.weinberg@ofsted.gov.uk
HM Chief Inspector of Education, Children's Services and Skills: Amanda Spielman 030 0013 1993
Email: amanda.spielman@ofsted.gov.uk

UK Statistics Authority/Office for National Statistics

1 Drummond Gate, London SW1V 2QQ
Tel: 0845 604 1857 (Authority)/0845 601 3034 (ONS)
Email: authority.enquiries@statistics.gsi.gov.uk info@ons.gsi.gov.uk
Website: www.statisticsauthority.gov.uk www.ons.gov.uk Twitter: @UKStatsAuth

Number of staff: 40

Chair: Sir David Norgrove
National Statistician and ONS Chief Executive: John Pullinger CB 020 7592 8663
Email: national.statistician@statistics.gsi.gov.uk

UK Supreme Court

Parliament Square, London SW1P 3BD
Tel: 020 7960 1900/020 7960 1500 Fax: 020 7960 1901
Email: enquiries@supremecourt.uk Website: www.supremecourt.uk Twitter: @UKSupremeCourt

Number of staff: 40

Chief Executive: Mark Ormerod 020 7960 1906 Email: mark.ormerod@supremecourt.uk
President of the Supreme Court: Rt Hon Baroness Hale of Richmond DBE

Water Services Regulation Authority

Ofwat Birmingham Office, Centre City Tower, 7 Hill Street, Birmingham, West Midlands B5 4UA
Tel: 0121-644 7500
Email: mailbox@ofwat.gsi.gov.uk Website: www.ofwat.gov.uk Twitter: @Ofwat

Number of staff: 196

Chair: Jonson Cox 0121-644 7500 Email: jonson.cox@ofwat.gsi.gov.uk
Chief Executive: Cathryn Ross 0121-644 7500 Email: cathryn.ross@ofwat.gsi.gov.uk

Government and Public Offices

Ombudsmen and Complaint-handling Bodies

Adjudicator's Office

Adjudicator's Office, PO Box 10280, Nottingham NG2 9PF
Tel: 0300 057 1111 Fax: 0300 059 4513
Website: www.adjudicatorsoffice.gov.uk

Number of staff: 131

Adjudicator: Helen Megarry
Head of Office: Margaret Allcock 0300 057 1781

Advertising Standards Authority

Mid City Place, 71 High Holborn, London WC1V 6QT
Tel: 020 7492 2222 Fax: 020 7242 3696
Website: www.asa.org.uk Twitter: @ASA_UK

Number of staff: 115

Chair: Rt Hon Lord Smith of Finsbury
Chief Executive: Guy Parker

Children and Young People's Commissioner Scotland

Rosebery House, 9 Haymarket Terrace, Edinburgh EH12 5EZ
Tel: 0131-346 5350
Email: info@cypcs.org.uk
Website: www.cypcs.org.uk Twitter: @cypcs

Number of staff: 15

Commissioner: Bruce Adamson Email: bruce.adamson@cypcs.org.uk

---

Commissioner for Public Appointments Northern Ireland

Dundonald House, Annexe B, Stormont Estate, Upper Newtownards Road, Belfast BT4 3SB
Tel: 028 9052 4820
Email: info@publicappointmentsni.org Website: www.publicappointmentsni.org

Number of staff: 2

Commissioner: Judena Leslie 028 9052 4820 Email: info@publicappointmentsni.org

---

Commissioner for Ethical Standards in Public Life in Scotland

Thistle House, 91 Haymarket Terrace, Edinburgh, Lothian EH12 5HE
Tel: 0300 011 0550
Email: info@ethicalstandards.org.uk
Website: www.ethicalstandards.org.uk

Number of staff: 18

Commissioner for Ethical Standards in Public Life in Scotland: Bill Thomson 0300 011 0550
Email: info@ethicalstandards.org.uk

European Ombudsman

Avenue du Président Robert Schuman 1, CS 30403, 67001 Strasbourg Cedex, France
Tel: +33 3 88 17 23 13
Email: eo@ombudsman.europa.eu
Website: www.ombudsman.europa.eu Twitter: @EUOmbudsman

Number of staff: 76

Ombudsman: Emily O'Reilly +33 3 88 17 23 13 Email: eo@ombudsman.europa.eu
Secretary-General: Beate Gminder +32 2 296 56 94 Email: beate.gminder@ombudsman.europa.eu

Financial Ombudsman Service

Exchange Tower, London E14 9SR
Tel: 020 7964 1000/0800 023 4567 (consumer) Fax: 020 7964 1001
Email: complaint.info@financial-ombudsman.org.uk Website: www.financial-ombudsman.org.uk
Twitter: @Financialombuds

Number of staff: 4,000

Chair: Sir Nicholas Montagu KCB
Chief Executive and Chief Ombudsman: Caroline Wayman 020 7964 0642
Email: caroline.wayman@financial-ombudsman.org.uk

Financial Services Ombudsman Scheme for the Isle of Man

Thie Slieau Whallian, Foxdale Road, St John's, Isle of Man IM4 3AS
Tel: 01624 686500 Fax: 01624 686504
Email: ombudsman@iomoft.gov.im Website: www.gov.im/oft/ombudsman

Number of staff: 3

Senior Adjudicator: Norman Teare

Gibraltar Public Services Ombudsman

Office of the Ombudsman, 10 Governor's Lane, Gibraltar
Tel: +350 200 46001 Fax: +350 200 46002
Email: info@ombudsman.gi Website: www.ombudsman.org.gi Twitter: @GibraltarOmbuds

Number of staff: 7

Ombudsman: Dilip Dayaram Tirathdas MBE +350 200 46001
Email: dilip.dayaram.tirathdas@ombudsman.gi

Groceries Code Adjudicator

Victoria House, Southampton Row, London WC1B 4DA
Tel: 020 3738 6537
Email: enquiries@gca.gsi.gov.uk Website: www.gov.uk/gca Twitter: @UKGCA

Number of staff: 5

Adjudicator: Christine Tacon CBE 020 3738 6535 Email: enquiries@gca.gsi.gov.uk

Independent Case Examiner

PO Box 209, Bootle, Merseyside L20 7WA
Tel: 0345 606 0777 Fax: 0151-221 6601
Email: ice@dwp.gsi.gov.uk Website: www.gov.uk/ice

Number of staff: 78

Independent Case Examiner: Joanna Wallace 0345 606 0777 Email: ice@dwp.gsi.gov.uk

Independent Complaints Reviewer

1 Victoria Street, London SW1H 0ET
Tel: 020 7930 0749
Email: enquiries@icrev.org.uk Website: www.icrev.org.uk

Number of staff: 5

Independent Complaints Reviewer for the National Archives, the Children's Commissioner for Wales and Joint Independent Complaints Reviewer for the Youth Justice Agency Northern Ireland:
Jodi Berg OBE 020 7930 0749 Email: enquiries@icrev.org.uk
Independent Complaints Reviewer for Land Registry and Joint Independent Complaints Reviewer for the Youth Justice Agency Northern Ireland:
Elizabeth Derrington 020 7930 0749 Email: enquiries@icrev.org.uk

Judicial Appointments and Conduct Ombudsman

9.53, Ninth Floor, The Tower, 102 Petty France, London SW1H 9AJ
Tel: 020 3334 2900
Email: headofoffice@jaco.gsi.gov.uk
Website: www.gov.uk/government/organisations/judicial-appointments-and-conduct-ombudsman

Number of staff: 8

Judicial Appointments and Conduct Ombudsman: Paul Kernaghan CBE QPM

Legal Ombudsman

For Legal Complaints:, PO Box 6806, Wolverhampton WV1 9WJ
Tel: 0300 555 0333
Email: enquiries@legalombudsman.org.uk Website: www.legalombudsman.org.uk
Twitter: @Legal_Ombudsman

Number of staff: 253

Chief Ombudsman: Kathryn Stone OBE 0121-245 3487
Email: elizabeth.woodall@legalombudsman.org.uk
Chief Executive: Rob Powell 0121-245 3100 Email: kay.kershaw@legalombudsman.org.uk

Local Government and Social Care Ombudsman

PO Box 4771, Coventry CV4 0EH
Tel: 0300 061 0614
Website: www.lgo.org.uk Twitter: @LGOmbudsman

Number of staff: 173

Chair and Ombudsman: Michael King 0330 403 4089 Email: s.elford@lgo.org.uk
Chief Executive: Nigel Ellis 0330 403 4089 Email: s.elford@lgo.org.uk

Northern Ireland Public Services Ombudsman

Progressive House, 33 Wellington Place, Belfast BT1 6HN
Tel: 028 9023 3821/0800 343 424 Fax: 028 9023 4912
Email: nipso@nipso.org.uk
Website: www.nipso.org.uk Twitter: @NIPSO_Comms

Number of staff: 35

Ombudsman: Marie Anderson 028 9089 7773 Email: marie.anderson@nipso.org.uk

Office of the Independent Adjudicator for Higher Education

Second Floor, Abbey Gate, 57-75 Kings Road, Reading, Berkshire RG1 3AB
Tel: 0118-959 9813 Fax: 0118-958 8029
Email: enquiries@oiahe.org.uk
Website: www.oiahe.org.uk Twitter: @oiahe

Number of staff: 60

Independent Adjudicator and Chief Executive: Judy Clements OBE 0118 959 9813
Email: leadershipoffice@oiahe.org.uk

Office of the Schools Adjudicator

Bishopsgate House, Feethams, Darlington DL1 5QE
Tel: 01325 340 402
Email: osa.team@osa.gsi.gov.uk
Website: www.gov.uk/government/organisations/office-of-the-schools-adjudicator

Number of staff: 18

Chief Schools Adjudicator: Shan Scott 01325 340 402 Email: osa.team@osa.gsi.gov.uk

Ombudsman Association

Tel: 020 8642 6143
Email: oasupport@ombudsmanassociation.org Website: www.ombudsmanassociation.org
Twitter: @OmbudAssoc

Number of staff: 2

Director: Donal Galligan 020 8642 6143 Email: donal.galligan@ombudsmanassociation.org

Ombudsman Services

The Brew House, Wilderspool Park, Greenall's Avenue, Warrington, Cheshire WA4 6HL
Tel: 0330 440 1624/01925 530263
Email: enquiries@os-communications.org Website: www.ombudsman-services.org
Twitter: @ombudservices

Chair: Lord Clement-Jones CBE
Chief Ombudsman: Lewis Shand Smith

Parliamentary and Health Service Ombudsman

Millbank Tower, 21-24 Millbank, London SW1P 4QP
Tel: 0345 015 4033 Fax: 0300 061 4000
Email: phso.enquiries@ombudsman.org.uk Website: www.ombudsman.org.uk
Twitter: @PHSOmbudsman

Number of staff: 450

Chief Executive: Amanda Campbell 0300 015 4033
Ombudsman: Rob Behrens CBE

The Pensions Ombudsman

Sixth Floor, 11 Belgrave Road, London SW1V 1RB
Tel: 020 7630 2200 Fax: 020 7821 0065
Email: enquiries@pensions-ombudsman.org.uk Website: www.pensions-ombudsman.org.uk
Twitter: @PensionsOmbuds

Number of staff: 60

Ombudsman: Anthony Arter
Deputy Ombudsman: Karen Johnston

Police Ombudsman for Northern Ireland

New Cathedral Buildings, 11 Church Street, Belfast BT1 1PG
Tel: 028 9082 8600 Fax: 028 9082 8659
Email: info@policeombudsman.org
Website: www.policeombudsman.org Twitter: @ponipressoffice

Number of staff: 150

Police Ombudsman for Northern Ireland: Dr Michael Maguire 028 9082 8727
Email: maria.quinn@policeombudsman.org
Chief Executive: Adrian McAllister 028 9082 8680 Email: adrian.mcallister@policeombudsman.org

Prisons and Probation Ombudsman for England and Wales

PO Box 70769, London SE1P 4XY
Tel: 020 7633 4100 Fax: 020 7633 4141
Email: mail@ppo.gsi.gov.uk
Website: www.ppo.gov.uk Twitter: @PPOmbudsman

Number of staff: 112

Acting Ombudsman: Elizabeth Moody 020 7633 4027 Email: elizabeth.moody@ppo.gsi.gov.uk

The Property Ombudsman
Milford House, 43-55 Milford Street, Salisbury SP1 2BP
Tel: 01722 333306
Email: admin@tpos.co.uk Website: www.tpos.co.uk Twitter: @TPOmb

Number of staff: 75

Ombudsman: Katrine Sporle CBE MSc 01722 333306 Email: katrine.sporle@tpos.co.uk

Public Services Ombudsman for Wales
1 Ffordd yr Hen Gae, Pencoed, Bridgend CF35 5LJ
Tel: 0300 790 2003 Fax: 01656 641199
Email: ask@ombudsman-wales.org.uk Website: www.ombudsman-wales.org.uk
Twitter: @OmbudsmanWales

Number of staff: 55

Public Services Ombudsman for Wales: Nick Bennett

Scottish Information Commissioner
Kinburn Castle, Doubledykes Road, St Andrews, Fife KY16 9DS
Tel: 01334 464610 Fax: 01334 464611
Email: enquiries@itspublicknowledge.info Website: www.itspublicknowledge.info
Twitter: @FOIScotland

Number of staff: 23

Commissioner: Daren Fitzhenry 01334 464610 Email: sic@itspublicknowledge.info

The Scottish Legal Complaints Commission
The Stamp Office, 10-14 Waterloo Place, Edinburgh EH1 3EG
Tel: 0131-201 2130 Fax: 0131-201 2131
Email: enquiries@scottishlegalcomplaints.org.uk Website: www.scottishlegalcomplaints.org.uk

Number of staff: 44

Chair: Bill Brackenridge
Chief Executive: Neil Stevenson

Scottish Public Services Ombudsman
4 Melville Street, Edinburgh EH3 7NS
Tel: 0131-225 5300/0800 377 7330 Fax: 0800 377 7331
Website: www.spso.org.uk Twitter: @spso_ombudsman

Number of staff: 50

Ombudsman: Rosemary Agnew

Service Complaints Ombudsman for the Armed Forces
SCC PO Box 72252, London SW1P 9ZZ
Tel: 020 7877 3450
Email: contact@servicecomplaintsombudsman.gsi.gov.uk
Website: www.servicecomplaintsombudsman.org.uk Twitter: @SCOAF_UK

Number of staff: 25

Service Complaints Ombudsman to the Armed Forces: Nicola Williams

Political and Parliamentary Organisations

Armed Forces Parliamentary Scheme

13 Cowley Street, London SW1P 3LZ
Tel: 020 7222 0480 Fax: 020 7222 7783
Email: lesley.snape1@btinternet.com Website: www.af-ps.info
Chair: Sir Neil Thorne OBE TD DL

Audit Scotland

Fourth Floor, 102 West Port, Edinburgh EH3 9DN
Tel: 0131-625 1500
Email: info@audit-scotland.gov.uk Website: www.audit-scotland.gov.uk Twitter: @auditscotland
Auditor General for Scotland: Caroline Gardner
Chair: Ian Leitch CBE

Boundary Commission for England

First Floor, 35 Great Smith Street, London SW1P 3BQ
Tel: 020 7276 1102
Email: information@boundarycommissionengland.gov.uk
Website: boundarycommissionforengland.independent.gov.uk www.bce2018.org.uk
Twitter: @BCE2018
Chair: Rt Hon John Bercow MP
Deputy Chair: Hon Mr Justice Andrew Nicol
Secretary: Sam Hartley 020 7276 1538 Email: sam.hartley@boundarycommissionengland.gov.uk

Boundary Commission for Northern Ireland

The Bungalow, Stormont House, Stormont Estate, Belfast BT4 3SH
Email: contact@boundarycommission.org.uk Website: www.boundarycommission.org.uk
Twitter: @BCNI2018
Chairman: Rt Hon John Bercow MP
Deputy Chairman: Hon Madam Justice Denise McBride DBE QC
Secretary: Eamonn McConville 028 9052 7821

Boundary Commission for Scotland

Thistle House, 91 Haymarket Terrace, Edinburgh EH12 5HD
Tel: 0131-244 2001
Email: bcs@scottishboundaries.gov.uk Website: www.bcomm-scotland.independent.gov.uk
Twitter: @BCommScot
Chairman: Rt Hon John Bercow MP
Deputy Chairman: Hon Lord Hugh Matthews
Secretary: Isabel Drummond-Murray Email: sbc@scottishboundaries.gov.uk

Boundary Commission for Wales

Hastings House, Fitzalan Court, Cardiff CF24 0BL
Tel: 029 2046 4819 Fax: 029 2046 4823
Email: bcomm.wales@wales.gsi.gov.uk
Website: www.bcomm-wales.gov.uk www.bcw2018.org.uk
Twitter: @BCommWales
Chairman: Rt Hon John Bercow MP
Deputy Chairman: Sir Clive Lewis
Secretary: Steve Halsall

Commonwealth Parliamentary Association United Kingdom

Westminster Hall, Houses of Parliament, London SW1A 0AA
Tel: 020 7219 5373 Fax: 020 7233 1202
Email: cpauk@parliament.uk Website: www.uk-cpa.org Twitter: @CPA_UK

Joint Presidents: Rt Hon John Bercow MP, Rt Hon Lord Fowler
Chairman of the Branch: Rt Hon Theresa May MP
Chair of the Executive Committee: James Duddridge MP
Vice-chairs: Nigel Evans MP, Rt Hon David Hanson MP, Rt Hon Lord Foulkes of Cumnock
Honorary Treasurer: Dr Roberta Blackman-Woods MP
Members, Executive Committee: Baroness Berridge, Rt Hon Baroness Corston, Rt Hon Lord Dholakia OBE DL, Rt Hon Baroness D'Souza CMG, Nusrat Ghani MP, Chris Law MP, Ian Liddell-Grainger MP, Professor Lord McColl of Dulwich CBE, Rt Hon Maria Miller MP, Madeleine Moon MP, Ian Murray MP, Andrew Rosindell MP, Shailesh Vara MP, Rt Hon Keith Vaz MP, Valerie Vaz MP
Chief Executive and Secretary: Jon Davies
Deputy Chief Executive: Helen Haywood
Head of Multilateral Projects: Ann Hodkinson
Head of International Outreach: Susie Latta

Confederation of British Industry

CBI, Cannon Place, 78 Cannon Street, London EC4N 6HN
Tel: 020 7379 7400
Email: enquiries@cbi.org.uk Website: www.cbi.org.uk Twitter: @CBItweets

President: Paul Drechsler CBE
Director-General: Carolyn Fairbairn
Senior Campaigns Adviser: Peter McManus 07469 155294 Email: peter.mcmanus@cbi.org.uk

Electoral Commission

3 Bunhill Row, London EC1Y 8YZ
Tel: 0333 103 1928 Fax: 020 7271 0505 Email: info@electoralcommission.org.uk
Website: www.electoralcommission.org.uk www.aboutmyvote.org.uk Twitter: @ElectoralCommUK

Chair of Commission Board: Sir John Holmes GCVO KBE CMG
Commissioners: Dame Susan Bruce DBE, Anna Carragher, Prof Elan Closs Stephens CBE, Tony Hobman *(until 31 December 2017),* Lord Horam, David Howarth, Alasdair Morgan, Bridget Prentice, Robert Vincent CBE
Chief Executive: Claire Bassett
Secretary to the Commission Board: Kairen Zonena

Electoral Office for Northern Ireland

St Anne's House, 15 Church Street, Belfast BT1 1ER
Tel: 0800 432 0712
Email: [firstname.surname]@eoni.org.uk Website: www.eoni.org.uk Twitter: @eoni_official
Chief Electoral Officer: Virginia McVea Email: virginia.mcvea@eoni.org.uk

Electoral Reform Society

2-6 Boundary Row, London SE1 8HP
Tel: 020 3714 4070
Email: ers@electoral-reform.org.uk Website: www.electoral-reform.org.uk Twitter: @electoralreform

Chair: Jon Walsh
Vice-chair: Justina Cruikshank
Chief Executive: Darren Hughes Email: darren.hughes@electoral-reform.org.uk
Treasurer: Clare Coatman

Electoral Reform Society Cymru

Baltic House, Mount Stuart Square, Cardiff CF10 5FH
Tel: 029 2049 6613
Email: wales@electoral-reform.org.uk Website: www.electoral-reform.org.uk/ers-cymru
Director: Jess Blair

Electoral Reform Society Scotland

12 South Charlotte Street, Edinburgh EH2 4AX
Tel: 0131-624 9853
Email: scotland@electoral-reform.org.uk Website: www.electoral-reform.org.uk/ers-scotland
Director: Willie Sullivan

Fire Service Parliamentary Scheme

13 Cowley Street, London SW1P 3LZ
Tel: 020 7222 0480 Fax: 020 7222 7783
Email: lesley.snape1@btinternet.com Website: www.af-ps.info
Chair: Sir Neil Thorne OBE TD DL

Hansard Society

Fifth Floor, 9 King Street, London EC2V 8EA
Tel: 020 7710 6070 Fax: 020 7710 6088
Email: contact@hansardsociety.org.uk Website: www.hansardsociety.org.uk
Twitter: @HansardSociety
Chairman: Lord Sharkey
Honorary Treasurer: Shirley Cameron
Director and Head of Research: Dr Ruth Fox 020 7710 6070 Email: ruth.fox@hansardsociety.org.uk

Independent Parliamentary Standards Authority

Fourth Floor, 30 Millbank, London SW1P 4DU
Tel: 020 7811 6400
Email: info@theipsa.org.uk Website: www.theipsa.org.uk
Twitter: @ipsaUK
Chair: Ruth Evans
Chief Executive: Marcial Boo
Board Members: Sir Robert Owen, Elizabeth Padmore, Anne Whitaker, Rt Hon Jenny Willott
Directors
Regulation: John Sills
MP Support Services: Victoria Cox
Corporate Services: Alastair Bridges

Industry and Parliament Trust

Suite 101, 3 Whitehall Court, London SW1A 2EL
Tel: 020 7839 9400 Fax: 020 7839 9401
Email: enquiries@ipt.org.uk Website: www.ipt.org.uk
Twitter: @indparltrust
Presidents: Rt Hon John Bercow MP, Rt Hon Lord Fowler
Chairmen
Board of Trustees: Sir David Amess MP
Management Board: Sharon Davies
Chief Executive: Nick Maher

Government and Public Offices

British Group Inter-Parliamentary Union

Palace of Westminster, London SW1A 0AA
Tel: 020 7219 3011/2/3 Fax: 020 7219 8780
Email: bgipu@parliament.uk Website: www.bgipu.org Twitter: @BGIPU

Honorary Presidents: Rt Hon John Bercow MP, Rt Hon Lord Fowler
Chair: Nigel Evans MP
Vice-chairs: Rt Hon Lord Anderson of Swansea, Rt Hon Ann Clwyd MP, Ian Liddell-Grainger MP
Treasurer: Nic Dakin MP
Director: Rick Nimmo

National Audit Office

157-197 Buckingham Palace Road, Victoria, London SW1W 9SP
Tel: 020 7798 7000/020 7798 7400 (Press Office) Fax: 020 7828 7070
Email: enquiries@nao.gsi.gov.uk Website: www.nao.org.uk Twitter: @NAOorguk

Chair: Lord Bichard KCB
Comptroller and Auditor General: Sir Amyas Morse KCB
Executive Leaders: Adbool Kara, Daniel Lambauer, Kate Mathers, Rebecca Sheeran, Stephen Smith, John Thorpe, Max Tse
Director, Parliamentary Relations: Adrian Jenner 020 7798 7461
Email: adrian.jenner@nao.gsi.gov.uk

Police Service Parliamentary Scheme

13 Cowley Street, London SW1P 3LZ
Tel: 020 8501 1673 Fax: 020 8500 6854
Email: ej_hunt@hotmail.com Website: www.af-ps.info

Chair: Sir Neil Thorne OBE TD DL

Committee on Standards in Public Life

Room GC.05, 1 Horse Guards Road, London SW1A 2HQ
Tel: 020 7271 2948
Email: public@public-standards.gov.uk Website: www.gov.uk/public-standards
Twitter: @PublicStandards

Chair: Lord Bew
Members: Rt Hon Dame Margaret Beckett DBE MP, Sheila Drew Smith OBE, Simon Hart MP, Dr Jane Martin CBE, Jane Ramsey, Monisha Shah, Rt Hon Lord Stunell OBE
Secretary: Lesley Bainsfair

Trades Union Congress

Congress House, Great Russell Street, London WC1B 3LS
Tel: 020 7636 4030
Email: info@tuc.org.uk Website: www.tuc.org.uk Twitter: @tucnews

President: Sally Hunt
General Secretary: Frances O'Grady
Deputy General Secretary: Paul Nowak
Heads
Campaigns and Communications Department: Antonia Bance Email: abance@tuc.org.uk
Economic and Social Affairs Department: Kate Bell
Equality and Strategy Department: Sam Gurney
Management Services and Administration Department: Matilda Quiney
Organisation and Services Department and Director of unionlearn: Kevin Rowan
European Union and International Relations Department: Owen Tudor

Wales Audit Office

24 Cathedral Road, Cardiff CF11 9LJ
Tel: 029 2032 0500 Fax: 029 2032 0600
Email: info@audit.wales Website: www.audit.wales Twitter: @WalesAudit
Auditor-General for Wales: Huw Vaughan Thomas

The Whitehall & Industry Group

80 Petty France, London SW1H 9EX
Tel: 020 7222 1166 Fax: 020 7222 1167
Email: info@wig.co.uk Website: www.wig.co.uk Twitter: @wiguk
Chief Executive: Peter Unwin CB

DIPLOMATIC REPRESENTATION

DIPLOMATIC REPRESENTATION 1228
British Embassies and High Commissions 1228
UK Permanent Representation 1250
London Embassies and High Commissions 1251
Royal Households 1275
HM Lord Lieutenants 1276
British Overseas Territories 1278
The Commonwealth 1278

Diplomatic Representation

British Embassies and High Commissions

Afghanistan
British Embassy, 15th Street, Roundabout Wazir Akbar Khan, PO Box 334, Kabul
Tel: +93 700 102 000 Fax: +93 700 102 250
Website: www.gov.uk/government/world/organisations/british-embassy-kabul
Ambassador: HE Sir Nicholas Kay KCMG

Albania
British Embassy, Rruga Skenderbeg 12, Tirana
Tel: +355 4 223 4973 Fax: +355 4 224 7697
Email: british.embassytirana@fco.gov.uk
Website: www.gov.uk/government/world/organisations/british-embassy-tirana
Ambassador: HE Duncan Norman MBE

Algeria
British Embassy, 3 Chemin Capitaine Hocine Slimane (ex Chemin des Glycines), Algiers
Tel: +213 770 085 000 Fax: +213 770 085 099
Email: britishembassy.algiers@fco.gov.uk
Website: www.gov.uk/government/world/organisations/british-embassy-algiers Twitter: @ukinalgeria
Ambassador: HE Barry Lowen

Andorra – see Spain

Angola
Non-resident: São Tomé and Príncipe
British Embassy, Rua 17 de Setembro, No 4, Caixa, 1244 Luanda
Tel: +244 222 334 582 Fax: +244 222 333 331
Email: postmaster.luand@fco.gov.uk
Website: www.gov.uk/government/world/organisations/british-embassy-luanda
Ambassador (until February 2018): HE John Dennis
Ambassador (from February 2018): HE Jessica Hand

Antigua and Barbuda – see Barbados

Argentina
British Embassy, Dr Luis Agote 2412, 1425 Buenos Aires
Tel: +54 11 4808 2200 Fax: +54 11 4808 2274
Email: askinformation.baires@fco.gov.uk
Website: www.gov.uk/government/world/organisations/british-embassy-buenos-aires
Ambassador: HE Mark Kent

Armenia
British Embassy, 34 Baghramyan Avenue, 0019 Yerevan
Tel: +374 10 264 301 Fax: +374 10 264 318
Email: enquiries.yerevan@fco.gov.uk
Website: www.gov.uk/government/world/organisations/british-embassy-armenia
Ambassador: HE Judith Farnworth

Australia

British High Commission, Commonwealth Avenue, Yarralumla, Canberra ACT 2600
Tel: +61 2 6270 6666 Fax: +61 2 6273 3236 Email: australia.enquiries@fco.gov.uk
Website: www.gov.uk/government/world/organisations/british-high-commission-canberra
Twitter: @ukinaustralia

High Commissioner: HE Menna Rawlings CMG

Austria

British Embassy, Jaurèsgasse 12, 1030 Vienna
Tel: +43 1 716130 Fax: +43 1 71613 2900 Email: press@britishembassy.at
Website: www.gov.uk/government/world/organisations/british-embassy-vienna

Ambassador: HE Leigh Turner CMG

Azerbaijan

British Embassy, 45 Khagani Street, AZ1010 Baku
Tel: +994 12 4377878 Fax: +994 12 4977434
Email: generalenquiries.baku@fco.gov.uk
Website: www.gov.uk/government/world/organisations/british-embassy-baku
Twitter: @ukinazerbaijan

Ambassador: HE Dr Carole Crofts

Bahamas – see Jamaica

Bahrain

British Embassy, 21 Government Avenue, PO Box 114, Manama 306
Tel: +973 17574100 Fax: +973 17574161
Website: www.gov.uk/government/world/organisations/british-embassy-manama
Twitter: @ukinbahrain

Ambassador: HE Simon Martin

Bangladesh

British High Commission, United Nations Road, Baridhara, PO Box 6079, Dhaka 1212
Tel: +880 2 55668700
Email: dhaka.press@fco.gov.uk
Website: www.gov.uk/government/world/organisations/british-high-commission-dhaka
Twitter: @ukinbangladesh

High Commissioner: HE Alison Blake

Barbados

Non-resident: Antigua and Barbuda, Commonwealth of Dominica, Grenada, St Kitts and Nevis, St Lucia, St Vincent and the Grenadines

British High Commission, Lower Collymore Rock, PO Box 676, Bridgetown
Tel: +1 246 430 7800 Email: ukinbarbados@fco.gov.uk
Website: www.gov.uk/government/world/organisations/british-high-commission-barbados

High Commissioner: HE Janet Douglas CMG

Belarus

British Embassy, 37 Karl Marx Street, 220030 Minsk
Tel: +375 17 229 8200 Fax: +375 17 229 8206 Email: ukin.belarus@fco.gov.uk
Website: www.gov.uk/government/world/organisations/british-embassy-minsk

Ambassador: HE Fionna Gibb

Belgium

British Embassy, Avenue d'Auderghem 10, 1040 Brussels
Tel: +32 2 287 62 11 Fax: +32 2 287 62 50
Email: public.brussels@fco.gov.uk
Website: www.gov.uk/government/world/organisations/british-embassy-brussels
Twitter: @ukinbelgium

Ambassador: HE Alison Rose

Belize

British High Commission, North Ring Road/Melhado Parade, PO Box 91, Belmopan
Tel: +501 822 2146
Email: brithicom@btl.net
Website: www.gov.uk/government/world/organisations/british-high-commission-belmopan

High Commissioner: HE Peter Hughes OBE

Benin – see Ghana

Bolivia

British Embassy, Avenida Arce 2732, La Paz
Tel: +591 2 243 3424 Fax: +591 2 243 1073
Email: belapaz@fco.gov.uk
Website: www.gov.uk/government/world/organisations/british-embassy-bolivia Twitter: @ukinbolivia

Ambassador: HE James Thornton

Bosnia and Herzegovina

British Embassy, 39a Hamdije Cemerlica Street, 71000 Sarajevo
Tel: +387 33 282 200 Fax: +387 33 282 203
Email: britemb@bih.net.ba
Website: www.gov.uk/government/world/organisations/british-embassy-sarajevo

Ambassador: HE Edward Ferguson

Botswana

British High Commission, Plot 1079-1084 Main Mall, off Queens Road, Gaborone
Tel: +267 395 2841 Fax: +267 395 6105
Email: ukinbotswana@gmail.com
Website: www.gov.uk/government/world/organisations/british-high-commission-gaborone

High Commissioner: HE Katharine Ransome

Brazil

British Embassy, Quadra 801 – Conjunto K – Lote 8, Av. das Nações – Asa Sul, CEP 70408-900, Brasilia
Tel: +55 61 3329 2300 Fax: +55 61 3329 2369
Email: press.brasilia@fco.gov.uk
Website: www.gov.uk/government/world/organisations/british-embassy-brazil Twitter: @ukinbrazil

Ambassador: HE Dr Vijay Rangarajan CMG

Brunei

British High Commission, 2.01, Second Floor, Block D, Kompleks Bangunan Yayasan Sultan Haji, Hassanal Bokiah, BS8711 Bandar Seri Begawan
Tel: +673 2 222231 Fax: +673 2 234315 Email: brithc@brunet.bn
Website: www.gov.uk/government/world/organisations/british-high-commission-bandar-seri-begawan
Twitter: @ukinbrunei

High Commissioner: HE Richard Lindsay

Bulgaria
British Embassy, 9 Moskovska Street, 1000 Sofia
Tel: +359 2 933 9222 Fax: +359 2 933 9250
Email: britishembassysofia@fco.gov.uk
Website: www.gov.uk/government/world/organisations/british-embassy-sofia Twitter: @ukinbulgaria
Ambassador: HE Emma Hopkins OBE

Burkina Faso – see Ghana

Burma (Myanmar)
British Embassy, 80 Strand Road, PO Box No 638, Rangoon
Tel: +95 1 370865 Fax: +95 1 370866
Website: www.gov.uk/government/world/organisations/british-embassy-rangoon Twitter: @ukinburma
Ambassador: HE Andrew Patrick

Burundi – see Rwanda

Cabo Verde – see Senegal

Cambodia
British Embassy, 27-29 Street 75, Sangkat Srah Chak, Khan Daun Penh, 12201 Phnom Penh
Tel: +855 23 427 124 Fax: +855 23 427 125
Email: ukincambodia@fco.gov.uk
Website: www.gov.uk/government/world/organisations/british-embassy-phnom-penh
Ambassador: HE Bill Longhurst

Cameroon
Non-resident: Chad, Equatorial Guinea, Gabon
British High Commission, Avenue Winston Churchill, BP 547, Yaoundé
Tel: +237 22 22 07 96 Fax: +237 2222 01 48
Email: bhc.yaounde@fco.gov.uk
Website: www.gov.uk/government/world/organisations/british-high-commission-yaounde
Twitter: @ukincameroon
High Commissioner: HE Rowan Laxton

Canada
British High Commission, 80 Elgin Street, Ottawa K1P 5K7
Tel: +1 613 237 1530 Fax: +1 613 237 7980
Email: ukincanada@fco.gov.uk
Website: www.gov.uk/government/world/organisations/british-high-commission-ottawa
blogs.fco.gov.uk/ukincanada Twitter: @ukincanada
High Commissioner: HE Susan le Jeune d'Allegeershecque CMG

Chad – see Cameroon

Chile
British Embassy, Avda El Bosque Norte 0125, Las Condes, Santiago
Tel: +56 2 370 4100 Fax: +56 2 370 4160
Email: embsan@britemb.cl
Website: www.gov.uk/government/world/organisations/british-embassy-chile Twitter: @ukinchile
Ambassador: HE Fiona Clouder

China
British Embassy, 11 Guang Hua Lu, Jian Guo Men Wai, 100 600 Beijing
Tel: +86 10 5192 4000 Fax: +86 10 5192 4239
Website: www.gov.uk/government/world/organisations/british-embassy-beijing Twitter: @ukinchina
Ambassador: HE Dame Barbara Woodward DCMG OBE

Colombia
British Embassy, Carrera 9 No 76-49, Piso 8, Edificio ING Barings, Bogotá
Tel: +57 1 326 8300 Email: embajadabritanica.bogota@fco.gov.uk
Website: www.gov.uk/government/world/organisations/british-embassy-colombia
Twitter: @ukincolombia
Ambassador: HE Dr Peter Tibber

Comoros – see Mauritius

Democratic Republic of Congo
Non-resident: Republic of Congo
British Embassy, 83 Avenue Roi Baudoin, Gombe, Kinshasa
Tel: +243 81 556 6200 Fax: +243 81 346 4291
Email: ambassade.britannique@fco.gov.uk
Website: www.gov.uk/government/world/organisations/british-embassy-kinshasa Twitter: @ukindrc
Ambassador: HE Dr John Murton

Republic of Congo – see Democratic Republic of Congo

Costa Rica
Non-resident: Nicaragua
British Embassy, Edificio Centro Colón, Paseo Colón and Streets 38 and 40, San José
Tel: +506 2258 2025 Fax: +506 2233 9938
Email: ukin.costarica@fco.gov.uk
Website: www.gov.uk/government/world/organisations/british-embassy-in-costa-rica
Ambassador: HE Ross Denny

Côte d'Ivoire
British Embassy, Quartier Ambassades, Impasse du Belier, Rue A58, 01 BP 2581 Abidjan 01
Tel: +225 22 44 26 69 Fax: +225 22 48 95 48
Email: british.embassy.abidjan@fco.gov.uk
Website: www.gov.uk/government/world/organisations/british-embassy-abidjan
Ambassador: HE Josephine Gauld

Croatia
British Embassy, Ivana Lučića 4, 10000 Zagreb
Tel: +385 1 6009 100 Fax: +385 1 6009 111
Website: www.gov.uk/government/world/organisations/british-embassy-zagreb Twitter: @ukincroatia
Ambassador: HE Andrew Dalgleish

Cuba
British Embassy, Calle 34 no. 702e/7ma, Miramar, Playa, 11300 La Habana
Tel: +537 214 2200 Email: ukincuba@fco.gov.uk
Website: www.gov.uk/government/world/organisations/british-embassy-havana
Ambassador: HE Dr Antony Stokes LVO

Cyprus

British High Commission, Alexander Pallis Street, PO Box 21978, Nicosia 1587
Tel: +357 2 861100 Fax: +357 2 861125
Email: ukincyprus@fco.gov.uk
Website: www.gov.uk/government/world/organisations/british-high-commission-nicosia
Twitter: @ukincyprus

High Commissioner (until spring 2018): HE Matthew Kidd CMG
High Commissioner (from spring 2018): HE Stephen Lillie CMG

Czech Republic

British Embassy, Thunovská 14, 118 00 Prague 1
Tel: +420 257 402 111 Fax: +420 257 402 296
Email: ukinczechrepublic@fco.gov.uk
Website: www.gov.uk/government/world/organisations/british-embassy-prague

Ambassador: HE Jan Thompson OBE

Denmark

British Embassy, Kastelsvej 36-40, 2100 Copenhagen Ø
Tel: +45 35 44 52 00
Email: enquiry.copenhagen@fco.gov.uk
Website: www.gov.uk/government/world/organisations/british-embassy-copenhagen

Ambassador: HE Dominic Schroeder

Djibouti – see Ethiopia

Dominica – see Barbados

Dominican Republic

British Embassy, Ave 27 de Febrero No 233, Edificio Corominas Pepin, Santo Domingo
Tel: +1 809 472 7111
Email: uk.indominicanrepublic@fco.gov.uk
Website: www.gov.uk/government/world/organisations/british-embassy-santo-domingo
Twitter: @ukindomrep

Ambassador: HE Christopher Campbell

East Timor – see Indonesia

Ecuador

British Embassy, 14th Floor, Citiplaza Building, Naciones Unidas Avenue and República de El Salvador, PO Box 17-17-830, Quito
Tel: +593 2 3972 200
Email: britishembassy.quito@fco.gov.uk
Website: www.gov.uk/government/world/organisations/british-embassy-in-ecuador
Twitter: @ukinecuador

Ambassador: HE Katherine Ward LVO

Egypt

British Embassy, 7 Ahmed Ragheb Street, Garden City, Cairo
Tel: +20 2 2791 6000 Fax: +20 2 2791 6132
Email: cairo.press@fco.gov.uk
Website: www.gov.uk/government/world/organisations/british-embassy-cairo Twitter: @ukinegypt

Ambassador: HE John Casson CMG

El Salvador

British Embassy, Torre Futura, 14th Floor, Colonia Escalón, San Salvador
Tel: +503 2511 5757 Email: britishembassy.elsalvador@fco.gov.uk
Website: www.gov.uk/government/world/organisations/british-embassy-san-salvador
Twitter: @ukinelsalvador

Ambassador: HE Bernhard Garside

Equatorial Guinea – see Cameroon

Eritrea

British Embassy, 66-68 Mariam Ghimbi Street, Zip Code 174, PO Box 5584, Asmara
Tel: 01908 516666 Fax: +291 112 01 04 Email: asmara.enquiries@fco.gov.uk
Website: www.gov.uk/government/world/organisations/british-embassy-asmara

Ambassador: HE Ian Richards

Estonia

British Embassy, Wismari 6, 15098 Tallinn
Tel: +372 667 4700 Fax: +372 667 4755 Email: infotallinn@fco.gov.uk
Website: www.gov.uk/government/world/organisations/british-embassy-tallin

Ambassador: HE Theresa Bubbear

Ethiopia

Non-resident: Djibouti

British Embassy, Comoros Street, 858, Addis Ababa
Tel: +251 11 661 2354 Fax: +251 11 661 0588
Email: britishembassy.addisababa@fco.gov.uk
Website: www.gov.uk/government/world/organisations/british-embassy-addis-ababa

Ambassador: HE Susanna Moorehead

Fiji

Non-resident: Kiribati, Marshall Islands, Micronesia, Tonga and Tuvalu

British High Commission, 47 Gladstone Road, Suva
Tel: +679 322 9100 Fax: +679 322 9132
Email: publicdiplomacysuva@fco.gov.uk
Website: www.gov.uk/government/world/organisations/british-high-commission-suva

High Commissioner: HE Melanie Hopkins

Finland

British Embassy, Itäinen Puistotie 17, 00140 Helsinki
Tel: +358 9 2286 5100 Fax: +358 9 2286 5284
Email: info.helsinki@fco.gov.uk
Website: www.gov.uk/government/world/organisations/british-embassy-helsinki
Twitter: @ukinfinland

Ambassador: HE Sarah Price

France

Non-resident: Monaco

British Embassy, 35 rue du Faubourg St Honoré, 75363 Paris Cedex 08
Tel: +33 1 44 51 31 00 Fax: +33 1 44 51 31 09 Email: france.enquiries@fco.gov.uk
Website: www.gov.uk/government/world/organisations/british-embassy-paris Twitter: @ukinfrance

Ambassador: HE Lord Llewellyn of Steep OBE

Gabon – see Cameroon

The Gambia

British Embassy, 48 Atlantic Road, Fajara, PO Box 507, Banjul
Tel: +220 4495134 Email: ukinthegambia@fco.gov.uk
Website: www.gov.uk/government/world/organisations/british-high-commission-banjul
Ambassador: HE Sharon Wardle

Georgia

British Embassy, 51 Krtsanisi Street, Tbilisi 0114
Tel: +995 32 2274747 Fax: +995 32 2274792
Email: british.embassy.tbilisi@fco.gov.uk
Website: www.gov.uk/government/world/organisations/british-embassy-tbilisi
Ambassador: HE Justin McKenzie Smith

Germany

British Embassy, Wilhelmstrasse 70, 10117 Berlin
Tel: +49 30 204570 Email: ukingermany@fco.gov.uk
Website: www.gov.uk/government/world/organisations/british-embassy-berlin Twitter: @ukingermany
Ambassador: HE Sir Sebastian Wood KCMG

Ghana

Non-resident: Benin, Burkina Faso, Togo
British High Commission, Julius Nyerere Link, off Gamel Abdul Nasser Avenue, PO Box 296, Accra
Tel: +233 302 213 250 Fax: +233 302 213 274
Email: high.commission.accra@fco.gov.uk
Website: www.gov.uk/government/world/organisations/british-high-commission-accra
Twitter: @ukinghana
High Commissioner: HE Iain Walker

Greece

British Embassy, 1 Ploutarchou Street, 106 75 Athens
Tel: +30 1 7272 600 Email: information.athens@fco.gov.uk
Website: www.gov.uk/government/world/organisations/british-embassy-athens Twitter: @ukingreece
Ambassador: HE Kate Smith CMG

Grenada – see Barbados

Guatemala

British Embassy, Edificio Torre Internacional, Nivel 11, 16 Calle 0-55, Zona 10, Guatemala City
Tel: +502 2380 7300 Email: embajadabritanicagt@gmail.com
Website: www.gov.uk/government/world/organisations/british-embassy-guatemala
Twitter: @ukinguatemala
Ambassador: HE Thomas Carter

Guinea

British Embassy, Villa 1, Residence 2000, Corniche Sud, Conakry
Tel: +224 63 35 53 29
Email: britembconakry@hotmail.com
Website: www.gov.uk/government/world/organisations/british-embassy-conakry
Ambassador: HE Catherine Inglehearn

Guinea-Bissau – see Senegal

Guyana

Non-resident: Suriname

British High Commission, 44 Main Street, Georgetown
Tel: +592 226 5881 Fax: +592 225 3555 Email: bhcguyana@networksgy.com
Website: www.gov.uk/government/world/organisations/british-high-commission-georgetown

High Commissioner: HE Greg Quinn

Haiti

Ambassador resident in Dominican Republic

British Embassy, Entre 73 et 75 Delmas, Port-au-Prince
Tel: +509 2812 9191
Website: www.gov.uk/government/world/organisations/british-embassy-port-au-prince

Non-resident Ambassador: HE Sharon Campbell

Holy See

British Embassy, Via XX Settembre 80a, 00187 Rome
Tel: +39 06 4220 4000 Fax: +39 06 4220 4205
Email: holysee@fco.gov.uk
Website: www.gov.uk/government/world/organisations/british-embassy-holy-see
Twitter: @ukinholysee

Ambassador: HE Sally Axworthy MBE

Honduras

Ambassador resident in Guatemala

c/o British Embassy Guatemala City, Edificio Torre Internacional, Nivel 11, 16 Calle 0-55, Zona 10, Guatemala City, Guatemala
Tel: +502 2380 7300
Website: www.gov.uk/government/world/organisations/british-embassy-honduras

Non-resident Ambassador: HE Carolyn Davidson

Hungary

British Embassy, Füge utca 5-7, 1022 Budapest
Tel: +36 1 266 2888 Fax: +36 1 266 0907
Email: info@britemb.hu
Website: www.gov.uk/government/world/organisations/british-embassy-budapest
Twitter: @ukinhungary

Ambassador: HE Iain Lindsay OBE

Iceland

British Embassy, Laufásvegur 31, 101 Reykjavik
Tel: +354 550 5100 Fax: +354 550 5105 Email: info@britishembassy.is
Website: www.gov.uk/government/world/organisations/british-embassy-reykjavik

Ambassador: HE Michael Nevin

India

British High Commission, Shantipath, Chanakyapuri, New Delhi 110021
Tel: +91 11 2419 2100 Fax: +91 11 2419 2411 Email: web.newdelhi@fco.gov.uk
Website: www.gov.uk/government/world/organisations/british-high-commission-new-delhi
Twitter: @ukinindia

High Commissioner: HE Sir Dominic Asquith KCMG

Indonesia

Non-resident: Timor-Leste

British Embassy, Jalan M H Thamrin No 75, Jakarta 10310
Tel: +62 21 2356 5200 Fax: +62 21 2356 5351
Email: jakarta.mcs@fco.gov.uk
Website: www.gov.uk/government/world/organisations/british-embassy-jakarta
Twitter: @ukinindonesia

Ambassador: HE Moazzam Malik

Iran

British Embassy, 198 Ferdowsi Avenue, 11316-91144 Tehran
Tel: +98 21 6405 2000
Website: www.gov.uk/government/world/organisations/uk-for-iranians

Ambassador: HE Nicholas Hopton

Iraq

British Embassy, International Zone, Baghdad
Tel: +964 790 192 6280
Website: www.gov.uk/government/world/organisations/british-embassy-baghdad
Twitter: @ukiniraq

Ambassador: HE Jonathan Wilks CMG

Ireland

British Embassy, 29 Merrion Road, Ballsbridge, Dublin 4
Tel: +353 1 205 3700 Fax: +351 1 205 3885
Website: www.gov.uk/government/world/organisations/british-embassy-dublin
Twitter: @britembdublin

Ambassador: HE Robin Barnett CMG OBE

Israel

British Embassy, 192 Hayarkon Street, 6340502 Tel Aviv
Tel: +972 3 725 1222 Fax: +972 3 725 1203
Email: webmaster.telaviv@fco.gov.uk
Website: www.gov.uk/government/world/organisations/british-embassy-tel-aviv Twitter: @ukinisrael

Ambassador: HE David Quarrey CMG

Italy

Non-resident: San Marino

British Embassy, Via XX Settembre 80/a, 00187 Rome
Tel: +39 6 4220 0001 Email: inforome@fco.gov.uk
Website: www.gov.uk/government/world/organisations/british-embassy-rome Twitter: @ukinitaly

Ambassador: HE Jill Morris CMG

Ivory Coast – see Côte d'Ivoire

Jamaica

Non-resident: Bahamas

British High Commission, PO Box 575, 28 Trafalgar Road, Kingston 10
Tel: +1 876 936 0700 Fax: +1 876 510 0737 Email: ppa.kingston@fco.gov.uk
Website: www.gov.uk/government/world/organisations/british-high-commission-jamaica
Twitter: @ukincaribbean

High Commissioner: HE Asif Ahmad CMG

Japan

British Embassy, No 1 Ichiban-cho, Chiyoda-ku, 102-8381 Tokyo
Tel: +81 3 5211 1100 Fax: +81 3 5275 3164
Email: public-enquiries.tokyo@fco.gov.uk
Website: www.gov.uk/government/world/organisations/british-embassy-tokyo Twitter: @ukinjapan

Ambassador: HE Paul Madden CMG

Jordan

British Embassy, (PO Box 87) Abdoun, 11118 Amman
Tel: +962 6 590 9200 Fax: +962 6 590 9279
Email: amman.enquiries@fco.gov.uk
Website: www.gov.uk/government/world/organisations/british-embassy-amman Twitter: @ukinjordan

Ambassador: HE Edward Oakden CMG

Kazakhstan

British Embassy, 62 Kosmonavtov Street, Astana 010000
Tel: +7 7172 556200 Fax: +7 7272 556211
Email: ukinkz@fco.gov.uk
Website: www.gov.uk/government/world/organisations/british-embassy-astana Twitter: @ukinkz

Ambassador (until early 2018): HE Dr Carolyn Browne CMG
Ambassador (from early 2018): HE Michael Gifford

Kenya

British High Commission, Upper Hill Road, PO Box 30465-00100, Nairobi
Tel: +254 20 287 3000 Email: nairobi.enquiries@fco.gov.uk
Website: www.gov.uk/government/world/organisations/british-high-commission-nairobi
Twitter: @ukinkenya

High Commissioner: HE Nic Hailey

Kiribati – see Fiji

Democratic People's Republic of Korea (North)

British Embassy, Munsu-dong Diplomatic Compound, Pyongyang
Tel: +850 2 381 7982 Fax: +850 2 381 7985
Email: pyongyang.enquiries@fco.gov.uk
Website: www.gov.uk/government/world/organisations/british-embassy-pyonyang

Ambassador: HE Alastair Morgan

Republic of Korea (South)

British Embassy, Sejong-daero 19-gil 24, 04519 Seoul Jung-gu
Tel: +82 2 3210 5500 Fax: +82 2 725 1738
Email: enquiry.seoul@fco.gov.uk
Website: www.gov.uk/government/world/organisations/british-embassy-seoul Twitter: @ukinkorea

Ambassador (until March 2018): HE Charles Hay MVO
Ambassador (from March 2018): HE Simon Smith CMG

Kosovo

British Embassy, Lidhja e Pejes 177, 10000 Pristina
Tel: +381 38 254 700 Fax: +381 38 606 662
Email: britishembassy.pristina@fco.gov.uk
Website: www.gov.uk/government/world/organisations/british-embassy-pristina

Ambassador: HE Ruairí O'Connell

Kuwait

British Embassy, PO Box 2, 13001, Safat
Tel: +965 2259 4320 Fax: +965 2259 4339
Email: kuwait.generalenquiries@fco.gov.uk
Website: www.gov.uk/government/world/organisations/british-embassy-kuwait Twitter: @ukinkuwait
Ambassador: HE Michael Davenport MBE

Kyrgyzstan

British Embassy, 21 Erkindik Boulevard, Office 404, 720040 Bishkek
Tel: +996 312 303637
Email: ukin.kyrgyzrepublic@fco.gov.uk
Website: www.gov.uk/government/world/organisations/british-embassy-bishkek
Ambassador: HE Robin Ord-Smith MVO

Laos

British Embassy, Rue Yokkabat, Phonexay, Saysettha District, Vientaine
Tel: +856 30 777 1065
Email: britishembassy.vientiane@fco.gov.uk
Website: www.gov.uk/government/world/organisations/british-embassy-vientiane Twitter: @ukinlaos
Ambassador: HE Hugh Evans

Latvia

British Embassy, 5 J Alunana Street, LV-1010 Riga
Tel: +371 6774 4700 Fax: +371 6777 4707
Email: britishembassy.riga@fco.gov.uk
Website: www.gov.uk/government/world/organisations/british-embassy-riga Twitter: @ukinlatvia
Ambassador: HE Keith Shannon

Lebanon

British Embassy, Embassies Complex, Armies Street, Zkak Al-Blat, Serail Hill, PO Box 11-471 Beirut
Tel: +961 1 960800 Fax: +961 1 960855
Website: www.gov.uk/government/world/organisations/british-embassy-beirut Twitter: @ukinlebanon
Ambassador: HE Hugo Shorter

Lesotho – see South Africa

Liberia

Leone Compound, 12th Street Beach-side, Sinkor, Monrovia
Tel: +231 77530320
Email: ukemb.liberia@gmail.com
Website: www.gov.uk/government/world/organisations/british-embassy-monrovia
Ambassador: HE David Belgrove OBE

Libya

(Operations suspended since 4 August 2014)
c/o British Embassy in Tunisia, Rue du Lac Windermere, Les Berges du Lac, 1053 Tunis
Tel: +216 71 108 700
Website: www.gov.uk/government/world/organisations/british-embassy-tripoli Twitter: @ukinlibya
Ambassador: HE Peter Millett CMG

Liechtenstein – see Switzerland

Lithuania
British Embassy, Antakalnio str. 2, LT-10308 Vilnius
Tel: +370 5 246 2900 Fax: +370 5 246 2901
Email: be-vilnius@britain.lt
Website: www.gov.uk/government/world/organisations/british-embassy-vilnius

Ambassador: To be appointed
Chargé d'Affaires: Andrew Pearce OBE

Luxembourg
British Embassy, Boulevard Joseph II 5, 1840 Luxembourg
Tel: +352 22 98 64 Fax: +352 22 98 67
Email: britemb@internet.lu
Website: www.gov.uk/government/world/organisations/british-embassy-in-luxembourg

Ambassador: HE John Marshall

Former Yugoslav Republic of Macedonia
British Embassy, Todor Aleksandrov No. 165, 1000 Skopje
Tel: +389 2 3299 299 Fax: +389 2 3179 726
Email: britishembassyskopje@fco.gov.uk
Website: www.gov.uk/government/world/organisations/british-embassy-skopje
Twitter: @ukinmacedonia

Ambassador: HE Charles Garrett

Madagascar
British Embassy, Ninth Floor Tour Zital, Ravoninahitriniarivo Street, Ankorondrano, Antananarivo 101
Tel: +261 2022 33053 Email: beantananarivo@moov.mg
Website: www.gov.uk/government/world/organisations/british-embassy-antananarivo

Ambassador (until late 2017): HE Timothy Smart
Ambassador (from late 2017): HE Dr Phil Boyle

Malawi
British High Commission, PO Box 30042, Lilongwe 3
Tel: +265 772 400 Fax: +265 772 657 Email: bhclilongwe@fco.gov.uk
Website: www.gov.uk/government/world/organisations/british-high-commission-lilongwe

High Commissioner: HE Holly Tett

Malaysia
British High Commission, Level 27 Menara Binjai, 2 Jalan Binjai, 50450 Kuala Lumpur
Tel: +60 3 2170 2200 Fax: +60 3 2170 2370
Email: press.kualalumpur@fco.gov.uk
Website: www.gov.uk/government/world/organisations/british-high-commission-kuala-lumpur
Twitter: @ukinmalaysia

High Commissioner: HE Victoria Treadell CMG MVO

Maldives – see Sri Lanka

Mali
Non-resident: Niger

British Embassy, Cité du Niger II, Bamako
Tel: +223 44 97 69 13 Fax: +223 44 97 69 11 Email: bebamako@fco.gov.uk
Website: www.gov.uk/government/world/organisations/british-embassy-bamako

Ambassador: HE the Hon Alice Walpole OBE

Malta

British High Commission, Whitehall Mansions, Ta'Xbiex Seafront, Ta'Xbiex XBX 1026
Tel: +356 2323 0000 Fax: +356 2323 2216
Email: malta.consulate@fco.gov.uk
Website: www.gov.uk/government/world/organisations/british-high-commission-malta
High Commissioner: HE Stuart Gill OBE

Marshall Islands – see Fiji

Mauritania – see Morocco

Mauritius

Non-resident: Comoros
British High Commission, Seventh Floor, Les Cascades Building, Edith Cavell Street, Port Louis
Tel: +230 202 9400 Fax: +230 202 9408
Email: bhc@intnet.mu
Website: www.gov.uk/government/world/organisations/british-high-commission-port-louis
High Commissioner: HE Keith Allan

Mexico

British Embassy, Río Lerma 71, Col Cuauhtémoc, 06500 Mexico City
Tel: +52 55 1670 3200 Fax: +52 55 1670 3217
Email: ukinmexico@fco.gov.uk
Website: www.gov.uk/government/world/organisations/british-embassy-mexico-city
Twitter: @ukinmexico
Ambassador: HE Duncan Taylor CBE

Micronesia – see Fiji

Moldova

British Embassy, 18 Nicolae Iorga Str., MD-2012 Chisinau
Tel: +373 22 22 59 02 Fax: +373 22 25 18 59
Email: enquiries.chisinau@fco.gov.uk
Website: www.gov.uk/government/world/organisations/british-embassy-chisinau
Twitter: @ukinmoldova
Ambassador: HE Lucy Joyce OBE

Monaco – see France

Mongolia

British Embassy, Peace Avenue 30, Bayanzurkh District, Ulaanbaatar ZIP 13381
Tel: +976 11 458133 Fax: +976 11 458036
Email: enquiries.mongolia@fco.gov.uk
Website: www.gov.uk/government/world/organisations/british-embassy-ulaanbaatar
Ambassador: HE Catherine Arnold

Montenegro

British Embassy, Ulcinjska 8, Gorica C, 81000 Podgorica
Tel: +382 20 420 100 Fax: +382 20 420 140
Email: podgorica@fco.gov.uk
Website: www.gov.uk/government/world/organisations/british-embassy-podgorica
Twitter: @ukinmontenegro
Ambassador: HE Alison Kemp

Morocco

Non-resident: Mauritania

British Embassy, 28 Avenue S.A.R. Sidi Mohammed, Souissi, 10105 (BP 45) Rabat
Tel: +212 537 63 33 33 Fax: +212 537 75 87 09
Website: www.gov.uk/government/world/organisations/british-embassy-rabat

Ambassador: HE Thomas Reilly

Mozambique

British High Commission, Avenida Vladimir Lenine 310, PO Box 55, Maputo
Tel: +258 21 356 000 Fax: +258 21 356 060
Email: maputo.consularenquiries@fco.gov.uk
Website: www.gov.uk/government/world/organisations/british-high-commission-maputo

High Commissioner: HE Joanna Kuenssberg

Myanmar – see Burma

Namibia

British High Commission, 116 Robert Mugabe Avenue, PO Box 22202, Windhoek
Tel: +264 61 274800 Fax: +264 61 228895
Email: general.windhoek@fco.gov.uk
Website: www.gov.uk/government/world/organisations/british-high-commission-windhoek

High Commissioner: HE Jo Lomas

Nauru – see Solomon Islands

Nepal

British Embassy, PO Box 106, Lainchaur, Kathmandu
Tel: +977 1 4237100 Fax: +977 1 4411789
Email: bekathmandu@fco.gov.uk
Website: www.gov.uk/government/world/organisations/british-embassy-kathmandu
Twitter: @ukinnepal

Ambassador: HE Richard Morris

Netherlands

British Embassy, Lange Voorhout 10, 2514 ED The Hague
Tel: +31 70 4270 427
Email: ukinnl@fco.gov.uk
Website: www.gov.uk/government/world/organisations/british-embassy-the-hague Twitter: @ukinnl

Ambassador: HE Peter Wilson CMG

New Zealand

Non-resident: Samoa; Governor: Pitcairn, Henderson, Ducie and Oeno Islands

British High Commission, 44 Hill Street, Wellington 6011
Tel: +64 4 924 2888 Fax: +64 4 473 4982
Website: www.gov.uk/government/world/organisations/british-high-commission-wellington
Twitter: @ukinnz

High Commissioner (until January 2018): HE Jonathan Sinclair LVO
High Commissioner (from January 2018): HE Laura Clarke

Nicaragua – see Costa Rica

Niger – see Mali

Nigeria

British High Commission, Plot 1137, Diplomatic Drive, Central Business District, Abuja
Tel: +234 9 462 2200 Fax: +234 9 462 2263
Email: ppainformation.abuja@fco.gov.uk
Website: www.gov.uk/government/world/organisations/british-high-commission-abuja
Twitter: @ukinnigeria
High Commissioner: HE Paul Arkwright CMG

Norway

British Embassy, Thomas Heftyesgate 8, 0264 Oslo
Tel: +47 23 13 27 00 Fax: +47 23 13 27 41
Email: ukinnorway@fco.gov.uk
Website: www.gov.uk/government/world/organisations/british-embassy-oslo Twitter: @ukinnorway
Ambassador (until summer 2018): HE Sarah Gillett CMG CVO
Ambassador (from summer 2018): HE Richard Wood

Oman

British Embassy, PO Box 185, 116 Mina Al Fahal, Muscat
Tel: +968 2460 9000 Fax: +968 2460 9010
Email: muscat.enquiries@fco.gov.uk
Website: www.gov.uk/government/world/organisations/british-embassy-muscat Twitter: @ukinoman
Ambassador: HE Hamish Cowell CMG

Pakistan

British High Commission, Diplomatic Enclave, Ramna-5, PO Box 1122, Islamabad
Tel: +92 51 201 2000
Email: islamabad-general.enquiries@fco.gov.uk
Website: www.gov.uk/government/world/organisations/british-high-commission-islamabad
Twitter: @ukinpakistan
High Commissioner: HE Thomas Drew CMG

Palau – see Philippines

Panama

British Embassy, Fourth Floor, Humboldt Tower, Calle 53, Marbella, Panama City
Tel: +507 297 6550 Fax: +507 297 6588
Website: www.gov.uk/government/world/organisations/british-embassy-panama-city
Twitter: @ukinpanama
Ambassador: HE Damion Potter

Papua New Guinea

British High Commission, Sec 411, Lot 1 and 2, Kiroki Street, Waigani, National Capital District, Port Moresby
Tel: +675 303 7600 Fax: +675 325 3547 Email: uk.inpng@fco.gov.uk
Website: www.gov.uk/government/world/organisations/british-high-commission-port-moresby
High Commissioner: HE Simon Tonge

Paraguay

British Embassy, Edificio Citicenter Piso 5, Av. Mariscal López y Cruz del Chaco, Asuncion
Tel: +595 21 614 588 Email: be-asuncion.enquiries@fco.gov.uk
Website: www.gov.uk/government/world/organisations/british-embassy-asuncion
Ambassador: HE Matthew Hedges

Peru

British Embassy, Torre Parque Mar (Piso 22), Avenida José Larco, 1301 Miraflores, Lima
Tel: +51 1 617 3000 Fax: +51 1 617 3100
Email: belima@fco.gov.uk
Website: www.gov.uk/government/world/organisations/british-embassy-peru Twitter: @ukinperu
Ambassador (until spring 2018): HE Anwar Choudhury
Ambassador (from spring 2018): HE Kate Harrisson

Philippines

Non-resident: Palau

British Embassy, 120 Upper McKinley Road, McKinley Hill, Taguig City, 1634 Manila
Tel: +63 2 858 2200 Fax: +63 2 858 2313
Email: ukinthephilippines@fco.gov.uk
Website: www.gov.uk/government/world/organisations/british-embassy-manila
Twitter: @ukinphilippines
Ambassador: HE Daniel Pruce

Poland

British Embassy, ul. Kawalerii 12, 00-468 Warsaw
Tel: +48 22 311 00 00 Fax: +48 22 311 03 13
Email: info@britishembassy.pl
Website: www.gov.uk/government/world/organisations/british-embassy-warsaw Twitter: @ukinpoland
Ambassador: HE Jonathan Knott

Portugal

British Embassy, Rua de São Bernardo 33, 1249-082 Lisbon
Tel: +351 21 392 40 00 Fax: +351 21 392 41 84
Email: ppa.lisbon@fco.gov.uk
Website: www.gov.uk/government/world/organisations/british-embassy-lisbon Twitter: @ukinportugal
Ambassador: HE Kirsty Hayes

Qatar

British Embassy, West Bay, Dafna Area, Onaiza Zone 66, Al Shabab Street, PO Box 3 Doha
Tel: +974 496 2000 Fax: +974 496 2086
Email: embassy.doha@fco.gov.uk
Website: www.gov.uk/government/world/organisations/british-embassy-doha Twitter: @ukinqatar
Ambassador: HE Ajay Sharma CMG

Romania

British Embassy, 24 Strada Jules Michelet, 010463 Bucharest
Tel: +40 21 201 7200 Email: britishembassy.bucharest@fco.gov.uk
Website: www.gov.uk/government/world/organisations/british-embassy-bucharest
Twitter: @ukinromania
Ambassador: HE Paul Brummell CMG

Russia

British Embassy, Smolenskaya Naberezhnaya 10, 121099 Moscow
Tel: +7 495 956 7200 Fax: +7 495 956 7481 Email: ukinrussia@fco.gov.uk
Website: www.gov.uk/government/world/organisations/british-embassy-moscow Twitter: @ukinrussia
Ambassador: HE Dr Laurie Bristow CMG

Rwanda

Non-resident Ambassador: Burundi

British High Commission, Parcelle No 1131, Boulevard de l'Umuganda, Kacyiru-Sud, BP 576, Kigali
Tel: +250 252 556 000 Fax: +250 252 582 044 Email: bhc.kigali@fco.gov.uk
Website: www.gov.uk/government/world/organisations/british-high-commission-kigali
Twitter: @ukinrwanda

High Commissioner: HE William Gelling OBE

St Kitts and Nevis – see Barbados

St Lucia – see Barbados

St Vincent and the Grenadines – see Barbados

Samoa – see New Zealand

San Marino – see Italy

São Tomé and Príncipe – see Angola

Saudi Arabia

British Embassy, PO Box 94351, Riyadh 11693
Tel: +966 1 4819 100 Fax: +966 1 481 9350
Website: www.gov.uk/government/world/organisations/british-embassy-riyadh
Twitter: @ukinsaudiarabia

Ambassador: HE Simon Collis CMG

Senegal

Non-resident: Cabo Verde, Guinea-Bissau

British Embassy, 20 Rue du Docteur Guillet, BP 6025, Dakar
Tel: +221 33 823 73 92 Fax: +221 33 823 27 66 Email: britembe@orange.sn
Website: www.gov.uk/government/world/organisations/british-embassy-dakar

Ambassador: HE George Hodgson

Serbia

British Embassy, Resavska 46, 11000 Belgrade
Tel: +381 11 3060 900 Fax: +381 11 3061 070 Email: belgrade.ppd@fco.gov.uk
Website: www.gov.uk/government/world/organisations/british-embassy-belgrade

Ambassador: HE Denis Keefe CMG

Seychelles

British High Commission, Third Floor, Oliaji Trade Centre, Francis Rachel Street, Victoria, Mahé
Tel: +248 283 666 Fax: +248 283 657 Email: bhcvictoria@fco.gov.uk
Website: www.gov.uk/government/world/organisations/high-commission-victoria

High Commissioner: HE Caron Röhsler

Sierra Leone

British High Commission, 6 Spur Road, Freetown
Tel: +232 76541386
Email: freetown.general.enquiries@fco.gov.uk
Website: www.gov.uk/government/world/organisations/british-high-commission-freetown

High Commissioner: HE Guy Warrington

Singapore

British High Commission, 100 Tanglin Road, 247919 Singapore
Tel: +65 6424 4200 Email: enquiries.singapore@fco.gov.uk
Website: www.gov.uk/government/world/organisations/british-high-commission-singapore
Twitter: @ukinsingapore

High Commissioner: HE Scott Wightman CMG

Slovakia

British Embassy, Panská 16, 811 01 Bratislava
Tel: +421 2 5998 2000 Fax: +421 2 5998 2237
Email: britishembassybratislava@fco.gov.uk
Website: www.gov.uk/government/world/organisations/british-embassy-bratislava

Ambassador: HE Andrew Garth

Slovenia

British Embassy, Fourth Floor, Trg Republike 3, 1000 Ljubljana
Tel: +386 1 200 3910 Fax: +386 1 425 0174
Email: info@british-embassy.si
Website: www.gov.uk/government/world/organisations/british-embassy-ljubljana
Twitter: @ukinslovenia

Ambassador: HE Sophie Honey

Solomon Islands

Non-resident: Vanuatu and Nauru

British High Commission, Gallery 3 and 4, First Floor, Heritage Park Hotel Ltd, Mendana Avenue, 676 Honiara
Tel: +677 21705 Fax: +677 21549 Email: bhc@solomon.com.sb
Website: www.gov.uk/government/world/organisations/british-high-commission-honiara

High Commissioner: HE David Ward

Somalia

British Embassy Mogadishu, Mogadishu
Email: somalia.enquiries@fco.gov.uk
Website: www.gov.uk/government/world/organisations/british-embassy-mogadishu
Twitter: @ukinsomalia

Ambassador: HE David Concar

South Africa

Non-resident: Lesotho, Swaziland

British High Commission, 255 Hill Street, Arcadia, Pretoria, 0002 Gauteng
Tel: +27 12 421 7500
Website: www.gov.uk/government/world/organisations/british-high-commission-pretoria
Twitter: @ukinsouthafrica

High Commissioner: HE Nigel Casey CMG MVO

South Sudan

British Embassy, EU Compound, Kololo Road, Thom Ping, Juba
Tel: +211 91 232 3712 Email: ukin.southsudan@fco.gov.uk
Website: www.gov.uk/government/world/organisations/british-embassy-juba
Twitter: @ukinsouthsudan

Ambassador: HE Alison Blackburne

Spain

Non-resident: Andorra

British Embassy, Torre Espacio, Paseo de la Castellana 259D, 28046 Madrid
Tel: +34 91 714 63 00 Fax: +34 91 714 63 01
Website: www.gov.uk/government/world/organisations/british-embassy-madrid Twitter: @ukinspain

Ambassador: HE Simon Manley CMG

Sri Lanka

Non-resident Ambassador: Maldives

British High Commission, 389 Bauddhaloka Mawatha, Colombo 7
Tel: +94 11 5390639 Fax: +94 11 5390692
Email: colombo.general@fco.gov.uk
Website: www.gov.uk/government/world/organisations/british-high-commission-colombo
Twitter: @ukinsrilanka

High Commissioner: HE James Dauris

Sudan

British Embassy, off Sharia Al Baladia, Khartoum East, PO Box No 801
Tel: +249 156 775500 Fax: +249 183 776457
Email: information.khartoum@fco.gov.uk
Website: www.gov.uk/government/world/organisations/british-embassy-khartoum

Ambassador: HE Michael Aron

Suriname – see Guyana

Swaziland – see South Africa

Sweden

British Embassy, Skarpögatan 6-8, Box 27819, 115 93 Stockholm
Tel: +46 8 671 3000 Fax: +46 8 662 9989
Email: stockholm@fco.gov.uk
Website: www.gov.uk/government/world/organisations/british-embassy-stockholm
Twitter: @ukinsweden

Ambassador: HE David Cairns

Switzerland

Non-resident: Liechtenstein

British Embassy, Thunstrasse 50, 3005 Berne
Tel: +41 31 359 77 00 Fax: +41 31 359 77 01
Email: info.berne@fco.gov.uk
Website: www.gov.uk/government/world/organisations/british-embassy-berne

Ambassador (until January 2018): HE David Moran
Ambassador (from January 2018): HE Jane Owen

Tajikistan

British Embassy, 65 Mirzo Tursunzade Street, 734002 Dushanbe
Tel: +992 372 24 2221 Fax: +992 372 27 1726
Email: dushanbe.reception@fco.gov.uk
Website: www.gov.uk/government/world/organisations/british-embassy-dushanbe
blogs.fco.gov.uk/ukintajikistan Twitter: @ukintajikistan

Ambassador: HE Hugh Philpott

Tanzania

British High Commission, Umoja House, Hamburg Avenue, PO Box 9200, Dar es Salaam
Tel: +255 22 229 0000 Fax: +225 22 211 0102 Email: bhc.dar@fco.gov.uk
Website: www.gov.uk/government/world/organisations/british-high-commission-dar-es-salaam
Twitter: @ukintanzania

High Commissioner: HE Sarah Cooke

Thailand

British Embassy, 14 Wireless Road, Lumpini, Pathumwan, 10330 Bangkok
Tel: +66 2 305 8333 Fax: +66 2 255 9278 Email: info.bangkok@fco.gov.uk
Website: www.gov.uk/government/world/organisations/british-embassy-bangkok
Twitter: @ukinthailand

Ambassador: HE Brian Davidson

Togo – see Ghana

Tonga – see Fiji

Trinidad and Tobago

British High Commission, 19 St Clair Avenue, St Clair, Port of Spain
Tel: +1 868 350 0444 Fax: +1 868 350 0425 Email: generalenquiries.ptofs@fco.gov.uk
Website: www.gov.uk/government/world/organisations/british-high-commission-trinidad-and-tobago
Twitter: @ukintt

High Commissioner: HE Tim Stew MBE

Tunisia

British Embassy, Rue du Lac Windermere, Les Berges du Lac, 1053 Tunis
Tel: +216 71 108 700 Fax: +216 71 108 749 Email: britishembassytunis@fco.gov.uk
Website: www.gov.uk/government/world/organisations/british-embassy-tunis Twitter: @ukintunisia

Ambassador: HE Louise De Sousa

Turkey

British Embassy, Şehit Ersan Caddesi 46/A, Çankaya, Ankara
Tel: +90 312 455 3344 Fax: +90 312 455 3352 Email: info.officer@fco.gov.uk
Website: www.gov.uk/government/world/organisations/british-embassy-ankara Twitter: @ukinturkey

Ambassador (until Janaury 2018): HE Richard Moore CMG
Ambassador (from Janaury 2018): HE Dominick Chilcott CMG

Turkmenistan

British Embassy, Third Floor Office Building, Four Points Ak Altin Hotel, 744001 Ashgabat
Tel: +993 12 363462 Fax: +993 12 363465
Email: ukembassy.ashgabat@fco.gov.uk
Website: www.gov.uk/government/world/organisations/british-embassy-ashgabat

Ambassador: HE Thorhilda Abbott-Watt OBE

Tuvalu – see Fiji

Uganda

British High Commission, 4 Windsor Loop, PO Box 7070, Kampala
Tel: +256 31 2312000 Fax: +256 41 4257304 Email: kampala.bhcinfo@fco.gov.uk
Website: www.gov.uk/government/world/organisations/british-high-commission-kampala
Twitter: @ukinuganda

High Commissioner: HE Peter West CMG

Ukraine

British Embassy, 9 Desyatynna Street, 01025 Kyiv
Tel: +380 44 490 3660 Fax: +380 44 490 3662 Email: ukembinf@gmail.com
Website: www.gov.uk/government/world/organisations/british-embassy-kyiv
Ambassador: HE Judith Gough

United Arab Emirates

British Embassy, Khalid bin Al Waleed Street (Street 22), PO Box 248, Abu Dhabi
Tel: +971 2 610 1100 Fax: +971 2 610 1586
Website: www.gov.uk/government/world/organisations/british-embassy-abu-dhabi Twitter: @ukinuae

British Embassy, Al Seef Street, PO Box 65, Dubai
Tel: +971 4 309 4444 Fax: +971 4 309 4301
Website: www.gov.uk/government/world/organisations/british-embassy-dubai
Ambassador: HE Philip Parham

United States of America

British Embassy, 3100 Massachusetts Avenue NW, Washington DC 20008
Tel: +1 202 588 6500 Email: britishembassyenquiries@gmail.com
Website: www.gov.uk/government/world/organisations/british-embassy-washington
Twitter: @ukinusa
Ambassador: HE Sir Kim Darroch KCMG

Uruguay

British Embassy, Calle Marco Bruto 1073, 11300 Montevideo
Tel: +598 2622 3630 Fax: +598 2622 7815 Email: ukinuruguay@adinet.com.uy
Website: www.gov.uk/government/world/organisations/british-embassy-montevideo
Twitter: @ukinuruguay
Ambassador: HE Ian Duddy

Uzbekistan

British Embassy, 67 Gulyamov Street, 100000 Tashkent
Tel: +99 871 120 1500 Email: ukin.uzbekistan@fco.gov.uk
Website: www.gov.uk/government/world/organisations/british-embassy-tashkent
Twitter: @ukinuzbekistan
Ambassador: HE Christopher Allan

Vanuatu – see Solomon Islands

Venezuela

British Embassy, Torre La Castellana, Piso 11, Avenida La Principal de la Castellana, (Av Eugenio Mendoza) La Castellana, 1061 Caracas
Tel: +58 21 2 319 5800 Fax: +58 21 2 267 1275 Email: ukinvenezuela@fco.gov.uk
Website: www.gov.uk/government/world/organisations/british-embassy-venezuela
Twitter: @ukinvenezuela
Ambassador: HE Andrew Soper

Vietnam

British Embassy, Fourth Floor, 31 Hai Ba Trung, Hanoi
Tel: +84 4 936 0500 Fax: +84 4 936 0561 Email: generalenquiries.vietnam@fco.gov.uk
Website: www.gov.uk/government/world/organisations/british-embassy-hanoi
Ambassador: HE Giles Lever

Yemen

(Operations suspended since 11 February 2015)

British Embassy, 938 Thahr Himyar Street, East Ring Road, near Mövenpick Hotel, Sana'a
Tel: 020 7008 1500
Website: www.gov.uk/government/world/organisations/british-embassy-sana-a Twitter: @ukinyemen
Ambassador: HE Simon Shercliff OBE

Zambia

British High Commission, 5210 Independence Avenue, PO Box 50050, 15101 Ridgeway, 10101 Lusaka
Tel: +260 211 423200 Fax: +260 211 423278
Email: lusakageneralenquiries@fco.gov.uk
Website: www.gov.uk/government/world/organisations/british-high-commission-lusaka
Twitter: @ukinzambia
High Commissioner: HE Fergus Cochrane-Dyet OBE

Zimbabwe

British Embassy, 3 Norfolk Road, Mount Pleasant, Harare
Tel: +263 4 8585 5200 Fax: +263 4 8585 5284
Email: ukinfo.harare@fco.gov.uk
Website: www.gov.uk/government/world/organisations/british-embassy-harare
Ambassador: HE Catriona Laing CB

UK Permanent Representations

UK Delegation to the Council of Europe

Rue Gottfried 18, 67000 Strasbourg, France
Tel: +33 3 88 35 00 78 Fax: +33 3 88 36 74 39 Email: ukdelstrasbourg@fco.gov.uk
Website: www.gov.uk/government/world/organisations/uk-delegation-to-the-council-of-europe
Twitter: @UKDelCoE

UK Permanent Representative: HE Christopher Yvon

UK Permanent Representation to the EU

Avenue d'Auderghem 10, 1040 Brussels, Belgium
Tel: +32 2 287 82 11 Email: ukrep@fco.gov.uk
Website: www.gov.uk/government/world/organisations/uk-representation-to-the-eu Twitter: @ukineu
UK Permanent Representative: HE Sir Tim Barrow KCMG LVO MBE

Political and Security Committee

UK Permanent Representative: HE Paul Johnston

UK Joint Delegation to NATO

NATO, Boulevard Leopold III, 1110 Brussels, Belgium
Tel: +32 2 707 75 01 Fax: +32 2 707 75 96 Email: ukdel.natogeneralenquiries@fco.gsi.gov.uk
Website: www.gov.uk/government/world/organisations/uk-joint-delegation-to-nato Twitter: @uknato
UK Permanent Representative to the North Atlantic Council: HE Sarah Macintosh CMG

UK Delegation to the OECD

Rue du Faubourg Saint-Honoré 35, 75363 Paris CEDEX, France
Tel: +33 1 44 51 31 00 Fax: +33 1 44 51 31 83 Email: fennel.waters@fco.gov.uk
Website: www.gov.uk/government/world/organisations/uk-permanent-delegation-to-the-oecd
Twitter: @ukoecd
Ambassador: HE Christopher Sharrock

UK Delegation to the OSCE
Jaurèsgasse 12, 1030 Vienna, Austria
Tel: +43 1 716 130 Email: ukdel@britishembassy.at
Website:
www.gov.uk/government/world/organisations/organisation-for-security-and-co-opertation-in-europe
Twitter: @ukosce

Head of UK Delegation: HE Sian MacLeod OBE

UK Mission to the UN and other International Organisations (Geneva)
Avenue Louis Casaï 58, Case Postale 6, 1216 Cointrin, Geneva, Switzerland
Tel: +41 22 918 23 00 Fax: +41 22 918 23 33
Website: www.gov.uk/government/world/organisations/uk-mission-to-the-united-nations-geneva
Twitter: @ukmissiongeneva

UK Permanent Representative: HE Julian Braithwaite

Conference on Disarmament
UK Permanent Representative: HE Dr Matthew Rowland

UK Mission to the UN (New York)
One Dag Hammarskjöld Plaza, 885 Second Avenue, New York 10017, USA
Tel: +1 212 745 9200 Fax: +1 212 745 9316
Website: www.gov.uk/government/world/organisations/uk-mission-to-un-in-new-york
Twitter: @ukun_newyork

Ambassador and Permanent Representative: HE Matthew Rycroft CBE

UK Mission to the UN and other International Organisations (Vienna)
Jaurèsgasse 12, 1030 Vienna, Austria
Tel: +43 1 716 130 Fax: +43 1 716 134 900 Email: ukmis.vienna@fco.gov.uk
Website: www.gov.uk/government/world/organisations/united-kingdom-mission-to-the-united-nations
Twitter: @ukmissionvienna

UK Permanent Representative: HE Leigh Turner CMG
UK Permanent Representative to the International Atomic Energy Agency: HE Dr David Hall

London Embassies and High Commissions

Afghanistan
Embassy of the Islamic Republic of Afghanistan, 31 Prince's Gate, Exhibition Road, London SW7 1QQ
Tel: 020 3609 8021
Email: ea@afghanistanembassy.org.uk Website: www.afghanistanembassy.org.uk

Ambassador: HE Said Tayeb Jawad

Albania
Embassy of the Republic of Albania, 33 St George's Drive, London SW1V 4DG
Tel: 020 7828 8897 Fax: 020 7828 8869
Email: embassy.london@mfa.gov.al Website: www.ambasadat.gov.al/united-kingdom/en
Twitter: @AlEmbassyUK

Ambassador: HE Qirjako Qirko

Algeria
Embassy of the People's Democratic Republic of Algeria, 1-3 Riding House Street,
London W1W 7DR
Tel: 020 7299 7077 Fax: 020 7299 7076
Email: info@algerianembassy.org.uk Website: www.algerianembassy.org.uk

Ambassador: HE Amar Abba

Angola

Embassy of the Republic of Angola, 22 Dorset Street, London W1U 6QY
Tel: 020 7299 9850 Fax: 020 7486 9397
Email: embassy@angola.org.uk Website: www.angola.org.uk

Ambassador: HE Miguel Fernandes Neto

Antigua and Barbuda

High Commission for Antigua and Barbuda, Second Floor, 45 Crawford Place, London W1H 4LP
Tel: 020 7258 0070 Fax: 020 7258 7486
Email: highcommission@antigua-barbuda.com Website: www.antigua-barbuda.com

High Commissioner: HE Karen-Mae Hill

Argentina

Embassy of the Argentine Republic, 65 Brook Street, London W1K 4AH
Tel: 020 7318 1300 Fax: 020 7318 1301
Email: info@argentine-embassy-uk.org Website: www.argentine-embassy-uk.org

Ambassador: HE Carlos Sersale di Cerisano

Armenia

Embassy of the Republic of Armenia, 25a Cheniston Gardens, London W8 6TG
Tel: 020 7938 5435 Fax: 020 7938 2595
Email: armembassyuk@mfa.am Website: www.uk.mfa.am/en

Ambassador: HE Dr Armen Sarkissian

Australia

Australian High Commission, Australia House, Strand, London WC2B 4LA
Tel: 020 7379 4334 Fax: 020 7240 5333
Email: generalenquiries.lhlh@dfat.gov.au Website: www.uk.embassy.gov.au
Twitter: @aushouselondon

High Commissioner: HE Alexander Downer AC

Austria

Embassy of Austria, 18 Belgrave Mews West, London SW1X 8HU
Tel: 020 7344 3250 Fax: 020 7344 0292
Email: london-ob@bmeia.gv.at Website: www.bmeia.gv.at/en/austrian-embassy-london
Twitter: @austriainuk

Ambassador: HE Martin Eichtinger

Azerbaijan

Embassy of the Republic of Azerbaijan, 4 Kensington Court, London W8 5DL
Tel: 020 7938 3412 Fax: 020 7937 1783
Email: london@mission.mfa.gov.az Website: www.azembassy.org.uk Twitter: @AzEmbUK

Ambassador: HE Tahir Taghizadeh

Bahamas

High Commission of the Commonwealth of the Bahamas, 10 Chesterfield Street, London W1J 5JL
Tel: 020 7408 4488 Fax: 020 7499 9937
Email: information@bahamashclondon.net Website: www.bahamashclondon.net
Twitter: @BahamasHCLondon

Acting High Commissioner: Allison Booker

Bahrain
Embassy of the Kingdom of Bahrain, 30 Belgrave Square, London SW1X 8QB
Tel: 020 7201 9170 Fax: 020 7201 9183
Email: information@bahrainembassy.co.uk Website: www.bahrainembassy.co.uk

Ambassador: HE Shaikh Fawaz bin Mohammed Al Khalifa

Bangladesh
High Commission for the People's Republic of Bangladesh, 28 Queen's Gate, London SW7 5JA
Tel: 020 7584 0081 Fax: 020 7581 7477
Email: bhclondon@btconnect.com Website: www.bhclondon.org.uk

High Commissioner: HE Dr Nazmul Quaunine

Barbados
Barbados High Commission, 1 Great Russell Street, London WC1B 3ND
Tel: 020 7631 4975 Fax: 020 7323 6872 Email: london@foreign.gov.bb

High Commissioner: HE Guy Hewitt

Belarus
Embassy of the Republic of Belarus, 6 Kensington Court, London W8 5DL
Tel: 020 7937 3288 Fax: 020 7361 0005 Email: uk.london@mfa.gov.by Website: uk.mfa.gov.by/en

Ambassador: HE Sergei Aleinik

Belgium
Embassy of Belgium, 17 Grosvenor Crescent, London SW1X 7EE
Tel: 020 7470 3700 Fax: 020 7470 3795
Email: london@diplobel.fed.be Website: countries.diplomatie.belgium.be/en/united_kingdom

Ambassador: HE Rudolf Huygelen

Belize
Belize High Commission, Third Floor, 45 Crawford Place, London W1H 4LP
Tel: 020 7723 3603 Fax: 020 7723 9637
Email: info@belizehighcommission.co.uk Website: www.belizehighcommission.co.uk

High Commissioner: HE Perla Perdomo

Benin
No London Embassy
Embassy of the Republic of Benin, 87 Avenue Victor Hugo, 75116 Paris, France
Tel: +33 1 45 00 98 82 Fax: +33 1 45 01 82 02
Email: contact@ambassade-benin.fr Website: www.ambassade-benin.fr

Ambassador: HE Jules-Armand Aniambossou

UK Consulate
Millennium House, Humber Road, London NW2 6DW
Tel: 020 8830 8612 Fax: 020 7435 0665
Email: beninconsulate@hotmail.co.uk Website: beninconsulate.co.uk/index.html

Honorary Consul: To be appointed

Bhutan
No London Embassy

UK Consulate
2 Windacres Warren Road, Guildford GU1 2HG
Tel: 01483 538189 Email: mrutland@aol.com

Honorary Consul: Michael Rutland

Bolivia

Embassy of Bolivia, 106 Eaton Square, London SW1W 9AD
Tel: 020 7235 4248 Fax: 020 7235 1286
Email: embol@bolivianembassy.co.uk Website: www.bolivianembassy.co.uk Twitter: @boliviaenuk

Ambassador: HE Roberto Calzadilla Sarmiento

Bosnia and Herzegovina

Embassy of Bosnia and Herzegovina, 5-7 Lexham Gardens, London W8 5JJ
Tel: 020 7373 0867 Fax: 020 7373 0871
Email: embassy@bhembassy.co.uk Website: www.bhembassy.co.uk

Ambassador: HE Branko Nešković

Botswana

Botswana High Commission, 6 Stratford Place, London W1C 1AY
Tel: 020 7499 0031 Fax: 020 7495 8595
Email: bohico@govbw.com

High Commissioner: HE Roy Blackbeard

Brazil

Embassy of Brazil, 14-16 Cockspur Street, London SW1Y 5BL
Tel: 020 7747 4533 Fax: 020 7747 4555
Email: info.london@itamaraty.gov.br Website: londres.itamaraty.gov.br/en-us
Twitter: @BrazilEmbassyUK

Ambassador: HE Eduardo dos Santos

Brunei

Brunei Darussalam High Commission, 19-20 Belgrave Square, London SW1X 8PG
Tel: 020 7581 0521 Fax: 020 7235 9717
Email: info@bdhcl.co.uk

High Commissioner: HE Major General Dato Paduka Seri Haji Aminuddin Ihsan Bin Pehin

Bulgaria

Embassy of the Republic of Bulgaria, 186-188 Queen's Gate, London SW7 5HL
Tel: 020 7581 3144 Fax: 020 7584 4948
Email: info@bulgarianembassy.org.uk Website: www.bulgarianembassy-london.org

Ambassador: HE Konstantin Dimitrov

Burkina Faso

No London Embassy

Embassy of the Republic of Burkina Faso, Place Guy d'Arezzo 16, 1180 Brussels, Belgium
Tel: +32 2 345 99 12 Fax: +32 2 345 06 12
Email: ambassade.burkina@skynet.be Website: www.ambassadeduburkina.be

Ambassador: To be appointed
Chargé d'Affaires: Dieudonné Kere

UK Consulate

The Lilacs, Stane Street, Ockley, Surrey RH5 5LU
Tel: 01306 627225
Email: consul@colinseelig.co.uk
Website: www.burkinafasovisa.co.uk

Honorary Consul: Colin Seelig

Burma (Myanmar)
Embassy of the Republic of the Union of Myanmar, 19a Charles Street, London W1J 5DX
Tel: 020 7148 0740 Fax: 020 7409 7043
Email: general@myanmarembassylondon.com Website: www.myanmarembassylondon.com
Ambassador: HE U Kyaw Zwar Minn

Burundi
Embassy of the Republic of Burundi, Second Floor, Uganda House, 58-59 Trafalgar Square, London WC2N 5DX
Tel: 020 7930 4958 Fax: 020 7930 4957
Website: www.burundiembassy.org.uk
Ambassador: HE Ernest Ndabashinze

Cabo Verde
No London Embassy
Embassy of the Republic of Cabo Verde, Avenue Jeane 29, 1050 Brussels, Belgium
Tel: +32 2 643 62 70 Fax: +32 2 646 33 85 Email: emb.caboverde@skynet.be
Ambassador: To be appointed

UK Consulate
33 Buckthorne Road, London SE4 2DG
Email: a.diasborges@googlemail.com
Honorary Consul: Anne-Marie Dias Borges

Cambodia
Royal Embassy of Cambodia, 64 Brondesbury Park, Willesden Green, London NW6 7AT
Tel: 020 8451 7850 Fax: 020 8451 7594
Email: cambodianembassy@btconnect.com Website: www.cambodianembassy.org.uk
Ambassador: HE Dr Soeung Rathchavy

Cameroon
High Commission for the Republic of Cameroon, 84 Holland Park, London W11 3SB
Tel: 020 7727 0771 Fax: 020 7792 9353
Email: info@cameroonhighcommission.co.uk Website: www.cameroonhighcommission.co.uk
High Commissioner: HE Nkwelle Ekaney

Canada
Canadian High Commission, Canada House, Trafalgar Square, London SW1Y 5BJ
Tel: 0207 004 6000 Fax: 0207 004 6050
Email: ldn@international.gc.ca Website: www.unitedkingdom.gc.ca Twitter: @CanadianUK
High Commissioner: HE Janice Charette

Central African Republic
No London Embassy
Embassy of the Central African Republic, 30 rue des Perchamps, 75016 Paris, France
Ambassador: To be appointed

Chad
No London Embassy
Embassy of the Republic of Chad, Boulevard Lambermont 52, 1030 Brussels, Belgium
Tel: +32 2 215 19 75 Fax: +32 2 216 35 26 Email: ambassade.tchad@chello.be
Ambassador: HE Ousmane Matar Breme

Chile

Embassy of Chile, 37-41 Old Queen Street, London SW1H 9JA
Tel: 020 7222 2361 Fax: 020 7222 0861
Email: embachile@embachile.co.uk Website: chileabroad.gov.cl/reino-unido/en
Twitter: @Chile_in_the_UK

Ambassador: HE Rolando Drago Rodríguez

China

Embassy of the People's Republic of China, 49-51 Portland Place, London W1B 1JL
Tel: 020 7299 4049
Website: www.chinese-embassy.org.uk

Ambassador: HE Liu Xiaoming

Colombia

Embassy of Colombia, 3 Hans Crescent, London SW1X 0LN
Tel: 020 7589 9177
Email: elondres@cancilleria.gov.co Website: reinounido.embajada.gov.co
Twitter: @colombianembuk

Ambassador: HE Néstor Osorio Londoño

Comoros

No London Embassy

UK Consulate

11 Park Place, London SW1A 1LP
Tel: 07768 821888
Email: kchehabi@gmail.com

Honorary Consul: Khaled Chehabi

Democratic Republic of Congo

Embassy of the Democratic Republic of Congo, 45-49 Great Portland Street, London W1W 7LD
Tel: 020 7580 3931 Fax: 020 7580 8713
Email: missionrdclondres@gmail.com

Ambassador: HE Marie Ndjeka Opombo

Republic of Congo

No London Embassy
Embassy of the Republic of Congo, 37 bis Rue Paul Valéry, 75116 Paris, France
Tel: +33 1 45 00 60 57 Fax: +33 1 40 67 17 33

Ambassador: HE Henri Marie Joseph Lopes

UK Consulate

Third Floor, Holborn Gate, 26 Southampton Buildings, London WC2A 1PN
Tel: 020 7922 0695 Fax: 020 7401 2566
Website: consulateofthecongobrazzaville.webs.com

Honorary Consul: Louis Muzzu

Costa Rica

Embassy of Costa Rica, 14 Lancaster Gate, London W2 3LH
Tel: 020 7706 8844 Fax: 020 7706 8655
Email: info@costaricanembassy.co.uk Website: www.costaricanembassy.co.uk

Ambassador: HE Jose Enrique Castillo Barrantes

Côte d'Ivoire
Embassy of the Republic of Côte d'Ivoire, 2 Upper Belgrave Street, London SW1X 8BJ
Tel: 020 7235 6991 Fax: 020 7259 5320
Ambassador: HE Georges Aboua

Croatia
Embassy of the Republic of Croatia, 21 Conway Street, London W1T 6BN
Tel: 020 7387 2022 Fax: 020 7387 0310
Email: croemb.london@mvep.hr Website: uk.mfa.hr Twitter: @CROinUK
Ambassador: HE Igor Pokaz

Cuba
Embassy of the Republic of Cuba, 167 High Holborn, London WC1V 6PA
Tel: 020 7240 2488 Fax: 020 7836 2602 Email: secembajador@uk.embacuba.cu
Website: misiones.minrex.gob.cu/en/united-kingdom/embassy-cuba-united-kingdom
Ambassador: HE Teresita de Jesús Vincente Sotolongo

Cyprus
High Commission of the Republic of Cyprus, 13 St James's Square, London SW1Y 4LB
Tel: 020 7321 4100 Fax: 020 7321 4164 Email: cyprusinuk@mfa.gov.cy
Website: www.mfa.gov.cy/mfa/highcom/london.nsf/index_en/index_en?opendocument
High Commissioner: HE Euripides Evriviades

Czech Republic
Embassy of the Czech Republic, 26 Kensington Palace Gardens, London W8 4QY
Tel: 020 7243 1115 Fax: 020 7243 7926
Email: london@embassy.mzv.cz Website: www.mzv.cz/london/en/index.html
Ambassador: HE Libor Sečka

Denmark
Royal Danish Embassy, 55 Sloane Street, London SW1X 9SR
Tel: 020 7333 0200 Fax: 020 7333 0270
Email: lonamb@um.dk Website: storbritannien.um.dk Twitter: @denmarkinuk
Ambassador: HE Lars Thuesen

Djibouti
No London Embassy
Embassy of the Republic of Djibouti, 26 Rue Emilie Ménier, 75116 Paris, France
Tel: +33 1 47 27 49 22 Fax: +33 1 45 53 50 53 Email: webmaster@amb-djibouti.org
Ambassador: HE Ayeid Mousseid Yahya

Dominica
High Commission for the Commonwealth of Dominica, 1 Collingham Gardens, London SW5 0HW
Tel: 020 7370 5194 Fax: 020 7373 8743
Email: info@dominicahighcommission.co.uk Website: www.dominicahighcommission.co.uk
Acting High Commissioner: Janet Charles

Dominican Republic
Embassy of the Dominican Republic, 8 Gloucester Square, London W2 2TJ
Tel: 020 7727 7091 Fax: 020 7727 3693
Email: pa@dominicanembassy.org.uk Website: www.dominicanembassy.org.uk
Ambassador: HE Dr Federico Alberto Cuello Camilo

Ecuador

Embassy of Ecuador, Flat 3b, 3 Hans Crescent, London SW1X 0LS
Tel: 020 7584 1367 Fax: 020 7590 2509
Email: eecugranbretania@mmrree.gov.ec Website: reinounido.embajada.gob.ec
Twitter: @EmbajadaEcuUK

Ambassador: HE Carlos Abad Ortiz

Egypt

Embassy of the Arab Republic of Egypt, 26 South Street, London W1K 1DW
Tel: 020 7499 3304 Fax: 020 7491 1542
Email: eg.emb_london@mfa.gov.eg Website: www.egyptembassyuk.org Twitter: @egyptconsulatuk

Ambassador: HE Nasser Kamel

El Salvador

Embassy of El Salvador, 8 Dorset Square, London NW1 6PU
Tel: 020 7224 9800 Fax: 020 7224 9878
Email: embajadalondres@rree.gob.sv Twitter: @elsembassy

Ambassador: HE Lidia Hayek-Weinmann

Equatorial Guinea

Embassy of the Republic of Equatorial Guinea, 13 Park Place, London SW1A 1LP
Tel: 020 7499 6867 Fax: 020 7499 6782 Email: embarege-londres@embarege-londres.org

Ambassador: HE Maricruz Evuna Andeme

Eritrea

Embassy of the State of Eritrea, 96 White Lion Street, London N1 9PF
Tel: 020 7713 0096 Fax: 020 7713 0161 Email: eriemba@eriembauk.com

Ambassador: HE Estifanos Habtemariam Ghebreyesus

Estonia

Embassy of the Republic of Estonia, 44 Queen's Gate Terrace, London SW7 5PJ
Tel: 020 7589 3428 Fax: 020 7589 3430
Email: london@mfa.ee Website: www.london.vm.ee Twitter: @estembassyuk

Ambassador: HE Tiina Intelmann

Ethiopia

Embassy of the Federal Democratic Republic of Ethiopia, 17 Prince's Gate, London SW7 1PZ
Tel: 020 7589 7212 Fax: 020 7584 7054
Email: info@ethioembassy.org.uk Website: www.ethioembassy.org.uk Twitter: @EthioEmbassyUK

Ambassador: HE Dr Hailemichael Aberra Afework

Fiji

High Commission of the Republic of the Fiji Islands, 34 Hyde Park Gate, London SW7 5DN
Tel: 020 7584 3661 Fax: 020 7584 2838
Email: mail@fijihighcommission.org.uk Website: www.fijihighcommission.org.uk

High Commissioner: HE Jitoko Cakacakabalavu Tikolevu

Finland

Embassy of Finland, 38 Chesham Place, London SW1X 8HW
Tel: 020 7838 6200 Fax: 020 7235 3680
Email: sanomat.lon@formin.fi Website: www.finemb.org.uk Twitter: @finlandinuk

Ambassador: HE Päivi Luostarinen

France

Embassy of France, 58 Knightsbridge, London SW1X 7JT
Tel: 020 7073 1000 Fax: 020 7073 1004
Website: www.ambafrance-uk.org Twitter: @FranceintheUK
Ambassador: HE Jean-Pierre Jouyet

Gabon

Embassy of the Gabonese Republic, 27 Elvaston Place, London SW7 5NL
Tel: 020 7823 9986 Fax: 020 7584 0047 Email: gabonembassyuk@gmail.com
Ambassador: HE Aichatou Sanni Aoudou

The Gambia

Embassy of The Gambia, 92 Ledbury Road, London W11 2AH
Tel: 020 7229 8066 Fax: 020 7229 9225
Email: info@gambiaembassy.org.uk Website: www.gambiaembassy.org.uk
Ambassador: To be appointed

Georgia

Embassy of Georgia, 4 Russell Gardens, London W14 8EZ
Tel: 020 7348 1941 Fax: 020 7603 6682
Email: london.emb@mfa.gov.ge Website: www.uk.mfa.gov.ge
Ambassador: HE Tamar Beruchashvili

Germany

Embassy of the Federal Republic of Germany, 23 Belgrave Square, London SW1X 8PZ
Tel: 020 7824 1300 Fax: 020 7824 1449
Email: info@london.diplo.de Website: www.london.diplo.de Twitter: @germanembassy
Ambassador: HE Dr Peter Ammon

Ghana

High Commission for Ghana, 13 Belgrave Square, London SW1X 8PN
Tel: 020 7201 5921 Fax: 020 7245 9552
Email: gh.donlon@gmail.com Website: www.ghanahighcommissionuk.com
High Commissioner: HE Papa Owusu-Ankomah

Greece

Embassy of Greece, 1a Holland Park, London W11 3TP
Tel: 020 7229 3850 Fax: 020 7229 7221
Email: gremb.lon@mfa.gr Website: www.mfa.gr/uk/en Twitter: @GreeceinUK
Ambassador: HE Dimitris Caramitsos-Tziras

Grenada

High Commission for Grenada, The Chapel, Archel Road, London W14 9QH
Tel: 020 7385 4415 Fax: 020 7381 4807
Email: office@grenada-highcommission.co.uk Twitter: @grenadahcuk
High Commissioner: HE Karl Hood

Guatemala

Embassy of Guatemala, First floor, Suite 1, 105a Westbourne Grove, London W2 4UW
Tel: 020 7221 1525 Email: info@guatemalanembassy.co.uk
Ambassador: HE Acisclo Valladares Molina

Guinea

Embassy of the Republic of Guinea, 42 Upper Berkeley Street, London W1H 5PW
Tel: 020 3752 6624 Email: embassyofguinea@gmail.com
Ambassador: To be appointed

Guinea-Bissau

No London Embassy
Embassy of the Republic of Guinea-Bissau, Rue St Lazare 94, 75009 Paris, France
Tel: +33 1 48 74 36 39
Ambassador: To be appointed

Guyana

High Commission for Guyana, 3 Palace Court, Bayswater Road, London W2 4LP
Tel: 020 7229 7684 Fax: 020 7727 9809
Email: guyanahc1@btconnect.com Website: www.guyanahclondon.co.uk
High Commissioner: HE Frederick Hamley Case

Haiti

Embassy of the Republic of Haiti, 21 Bloomsbury Way, London WC1A 2TH
Tel: 020 3771 1427 Fax: 020 7637 8980 Email: amb.royaumeuni@diplomatie.ht
Ambassador: To be appointed
Chargé d'Affaires: Bocchit Edmond

Holy See

Apostolic Nunciature, 54 Parkside, London SW19 5NE
Tel: 020 8944 7189 Fax: 020 8947 2494 Email: nuntius@globalnet.co.uk
Apostolic Nuncio: HE Edward Adams

Honduras

Embassy of Honduras, Fourth Floor, 136 Baker Street, London W1U 6UD
Tel: 020 7486 4880 Fax: 020 7486 4550
Email: hondurasuk@lineone.net
Ambassador: HE Ivan Romero-Martinez

Hungary

Embassy of Hungary, 35 Eaton Place, London SW1X 8BY
Tel: 020 7204 3440 Fax: 020 7823 1348
Email: mission.lon@mfa.gov.hu Website: www.mfa.gov.hu/emb/london
Ambassador: HE Kristóf Szalay-Bobrovniczky

Iceland

Embassy of Iceland, 2a Hans Street, London SW1X 0JE
Tel: 020 7259 3999 Fax: 020 7245 9649
Email: emb.london@mfa.is Website: www.iceland.is/iceland-abroad/uk Twitter: @icelandinuk
Ambassador: HE Thórdur Aegir Óskarsson

India

High Commission for India, India House, Aldwych, London WC2B 4NA
Tel: 020 7836 8484 Fax: 020 7836 4331
Email: hc.office@hcilondon.in Website: hcilondon.in Twitter: @HCI_London
High Commissioner: HE Yashvardhan Kumar Sinha

Indonesia

Embassy of the Republic of Indonesia, 30 Great Peter Street, London SW1P 2BU
Tel: 020 7499 7661 Fax: 020 7491 4993
Email: kbri@btconnect.com Website: www.indonesianembassy.org.uk Twitter: @KbriLondon

Ambassador: HE Dr Rizal Sukma

Iran

Embassy of the Islamic Republic of Iran, 16 Prince's Gate, London SW7 1PT
Tel: 020 7225 4208 Email: iranemb.lon@mfa.gov.ir

Ambassador: HE Hamid Baeidinejad

Iraq

Embassy of the Republic of Iraq, 21 Queen Gate, London SW7 5JE
Tel: 020 7590 7650 Fax: 020 7590 7679
Email: lonemb@mofa.gov.iq Website: mofamission.gov.iq/en/uklondon

Ambassador: HE Dr Salih Husain Ali

Ireland

Embassy of Ireland, 17 Grosvenor Place, London SW1X 7HR
Tel: 020 7235 2171 Fax: 020 7589 8450
Email: londonembassymail@dfa.ie Website: www.embassyofireland.co.uk Twitter: @irelandembgb

Ambassador: HE Adrian O'Neill

Israel

Embassy of Israel, 2 Palace Green, London W8 4QB
Tel: 020 7957 9500 Fax: 020 7957 9555
Email: info@london.mfa.gov.il Website: embassies.gov.il/london Twitter: @israelinuk

Ambassador: HE Mark Regev

Italy

Embassy of Italy, 14 Three Kings Yard, Davies Street, London W1K 4EH
Tel: 020 7312 2200 Fax: 020 7312 2230
Email: ambasciata.londra@esteri.it Website: www.amblondra.esteri.it Twitter: @ItalyinUK

Ambassador: HE Pasquale Terracciano

Ivory Coast – see Côte d'Ivoire

Jamaica

Jamaican High Commission, 1-2 Prince Consort Road, London SW7 2BZ
Tel: 020 7823 9911 Fax: 020 7589 5154 Email: jamhigh@jhcuk.com Website: www.jhcuk.org

High Commissioner: HE Seth Ramocan

Japan

Embassy of Japan, 101-104 Piccadilly, London W1J 7JT
Tel: 020 7465 6500 Fax: 020 7491 9348
Email: info@ld.mofa.go.jp Website: www.uk.emb-japan.go.jp Twitter: @japaninuk

Ambassador: HE Koji Tsuruoka

Jordan

Embassy of the Hashemite Kingdom of Jordan, 6 Upper Phillimore Gardens, London W8 7HA
Tel: 020 7937 3685 Fax: 020 7937 8795 Email: london@fm.gov.jo

Ambassador: To be appointed
Chargé d'Affaires: Daifallah Al-Fayez

Kazakhstan

Embassy of the Republic of Kazakhstan, 33 Thurloe Square, London SW7 2DS
Tel: 020 7925 1757 Fax: 020 7930 8990
Email: london@kazembassy.org.uk Website: www.kazembassy.org.uk Twitter: @KazEmbassyUK
Ambassador: HE Erlan Idrissov

Kenya

Kenya High Commission, 45 Portland Place, London W1B 1AS
Tel: 020 7636 2371 Fax: 020 7323 6717
Email: info@kenyahighcom.org.uk Website: www.kenyahighcom.org.uk
Twitter: @KenyaMissionUK
High Commissioner: HE Lazarus Amayo

Kiribati

No London High Commission
Kiribati High Commissioner, c/o Office of the President, PO Box 68, Bairiki, Tarawa, Kiribati
Acting High Commissioner: Makurita Baaro

UK Consulate

The Great House, Llandewi Rydderch, Monmouthshire NP7 9UY
Tel: 01873 840375 Fax: 01873 840375
Email: mravellwalsh@btopenworld.com
Honorary Consul: Michael Ravell Walsh

Democratic People's Republic of Korea (North)

Embassy of the Democratic People's Republic of Korea, 73 Gunnersbury Avenue, London W5 4LP
Tel: 020 8992 4965 Fax: 020 8992 2053
Email: dprkrepmission@yahoo.co.uk
Ambassador: HE Il Choe

Republic of Korea (South)

Embassy of the Republic of Korea, 60 Buckingham Gate, London SW1E 6AJ
Tel: 020 7227 5500 Fax: 020 7227 5503
Email: koreanembinuk@mofat.go.kr Website: gbr.mofat.go.kr/english/eu/gbr/main/index.jsp
Twitter: @KoreanEmbassyUK
Ambassador: HE Joonkook Hwang

Kosovo

Embassy of the Republic of Kosovo, 8 John Street, London WC1N 2ES
Tel: 020 7405 1010 Email: embassy.uk@ks-gov.net Website: www.kosovoembassy.org.uk
Ambassador: HE Lirim Greiçevci

Kuwait

Embassy of the State of Kuwait, 2 Albert Gate, London SW1X 7JU
Tel: 020 7590 3400 Fax: 020 7823 1712
Ambassador: HE Khaled Al Duwaisan GCVO

Kyrgyzstan

Embassy of the Kyrgyz Republic, Ascot House, 119 Crawford Street, London W1U 6BJ
Tel: 020 7935 1462 Fax: 020 7935 7449 Email: mail@kyrgyz-embassy.org.uk
Website: www.kyrgyz-embassy.org.uk Twitter: @kyrgyzembassy
Ambassador: HE Gulnara Iskakova

Laos

Embassy of the Lao People's Democratic Republic, 49 Porchester Terrace, London W2 3TS
Tel: 020 7402 3770 Fax: 020 7262 1994 Email: laosemblondon@gmail.com
Ambassador: HE Sayakane Sisaouvong

Latvia

Embassy of the Republic of Latvia, 45 Nottingham Place, London W1U 5LY
Tel: 020 7312 0041 Fax: 020 7312 0042
Email: embassy.uk@mfa.gov.lv Website: www.london.mfa.gov.lv Twitter: @LVembassyUK
Ambassador: HE Baiba Braže

Lebanon

Embassy of Lebanon, 21 Palace Gardens Mews, London W8 4QN
Tel: 020 7229 7265 Fax: 020 7243 1699
Email: emb.leb@btinternet.com Website: lebaneseembassyuk.org
Ambassador: HE Inaam Osseiran

Lesotho

High Commission of the Kingdom of Lesotho, 7 Chesham Place, London SW1X 8HN
Tel: 020 7235 5686 Fax: 020 7235 5023
Email: lhc@lesotholondon.org.uk Website: www.lesotholondon.org.uk
High Commissioner: HE Dr John Oliphant

Liberia

Embassy of the Republic of Liberia, 23 Fitzroy Square, London W1 6EW
Tel: 020 7388 5489 Fax: 020 7388 2899 Email: info@embassyofliberia.org.uk
Ambassador: HE Dr Mohammed Sheriff

Libya

Embassy of Libya, 15 Knightsbridge, London SW1X 7LY
Tel: 020 7201 8280 Fax: 020 7245 0588 Website: english.libyanembassy.org
Ambassador: To be appointed
Chargé d'Affaires: Mohamed A E Elkoni

Lithuania

Embassy of the Republic of Lithuania, Lithuania House, 2 Bessborough Gardens, London SW1V 2JE
Tel: 020 7592 2840 Fax: 020 7592 2864
Email: amb.uk@urm.lt Website: uk.mfa.lt Twitter: @LTEMBASSYUK
Ambassador: HE Renatas Norkus

Luxembourg

Embassy of Luxembourg, 27 Wilton Crescent, London SW1X 8SD
Tel: 020 7235 6961 Fax: 020 7235 9734 Email: londres.amb@mae.etat.lu Website: londres.mae.lu/en
Ambassador: HE Jean Olinger

Former Yugoslav Republic of Macedonia

Embassy of the Republic of Macedonia, Suites 2.1-2.2, Buckingham Court, 75-83 Buckingham Gate, London SW1E 6PE
Tel: 020 7066 0535 Fax: 020 7976 0539 Email: info@macedonianembassy.org.uk
Ambassador: To be appointed
Chargé d'Affaires: Jasmin Kjahil

Madagascar

No London Embassy
Embassy of the Republic of Madagascar, 4 Avenue Raphael, 75016 Paris, France
Tel: +33 1 45 04 62 11 Fax: +33 1 45 03 58 70
Email: accueil@ambassade-madagascar.fr

Ambassador: To be appointed

Malawi

High Commission for the Republic of Malawi, 36 John Street, London WC1N 2AT
Tel: 020 7421 6010 Fax: 020 7831 9273
Email: malawi@malawihighcommission.co.uk Website: www.malawihighcommission.co.uk
Twitter: @MalawiinUK

High Commissioner: HE Kena Mphonda

Malaysia

Malaysian High Commission, 52 Bedford Row, London WC1R 4LR
Tel: 020 7242 4308 Fax: 020 7404 2523
Email: mwlondon@kln.gov.my Website: www.kln.gov.my/web/gbr_london
High Commissioner: HE Dato Ahmad Rasidi Hazizi

Maldives

Embassy of the Republic of Maldives, 22 Nottingham Place, London W1U 5NJ
Tel: 020 7224 2135 Fax: 020 7224 2157
Email: info@maldivesembassy.uk Website: www.maldivesembassy.uk Twitter: @maldiveshcuk
Ambassador: HE Ahmed Shiaan

Mali

No London Embassy
Embassy of the Republic of Mali, Avenue Molière 487, 1050 Brussels, Belgium
Tel: +32 2 345 74 32 Fax: +32 2 344 57 00
Email: info@amba-mali.be Website: www.amba-mali.be
Ambassador: HE Sékou Dit Gaoussou Cissé

Malta

Malta High Commission, Malta House, 36-38 Piccadilly, London W1J 0LE
Tel: 020 7292 4800 Fax: 020 7292 4803 Email: maltahighcommission.london@gov.mt
Website: foreignaffairs.gov.mt/en/embassies/hc_london/pages/hc-london.aspx
High Commissioner: HE Norman Hamilton

Mauritania

Embassy of the Islamic Republic of Mauritania, Carlyle House, 235-237 Vauxhall Bridge Road, London SW1V 1EJ
Tel: 020 7233 6158
Ambassador: To be appointed
Chargé d'Affaires: Mohamed Yahya Sidi Haiba

Mauritius

Mauritius High Commission, 32-33 Elvaston Place, London SW7 5NW
Tel: 020 7581 0294 Fax: 020 7823 8437
Email: londonhc@govmu.org
High Commissioner: HE Girish Nunkoo

Mexico

Embassy of Mexico, 16 St George Street, London W1S 1FD
Tel: 020 7499 8586 Fax: 020 7495 4035
Email: embgbretana@sre.gob.mx Website: embamex.sre.gob.mx/reinounido/index.php/en
Twitter: @embamexru
Ambassador: HE Julián Ventura

Moldova

Embassy of the Republic of Moldova, 5 Dolphin Square, Edensor Road, London W4 2ST
Tel: 020 8995 6818 Fax: 020 8995 6927
Email: embassy.london@mfa.md Website: britania.mfa.gov.md/activitatea-curenta-en
Ambassador: To be appointed
Chargé d'Affaires: Vilen Murzac

Monaco

Embassy of the Principality of Monaco, 7 Upper Grosvenor Street, London W1K 2LX
Tel: 020 7318 1081 Fax: 020 7493 4563 Email: embassy.uk@gouv.mc
Website: embassy-to-uk.gouv.mc/en/monaco-embassy-to-united-kingdom
Ambassador: HE Evelyne Genta

Mongolia

Embassy of Mongolia, 7 Kensington Court, London W8 5DL
Tel: 020 7937 0150 Fax: 020 7937 1117
Email: office@embassyofmongolia.co.uk Website: www.embassyofmongolia.co.uk
Twitter: @MnEmbassyInUK
Ambassador: HE Sanjaa Bayar

Montenegro

Embassy of Montenegro, 47 De Vere Gardens, London W8 5AW
Tel: 020 3302 7227 Fax: 020 7243 9358 Email: unitedkingdom@mfa.gov.me
Ambassador: HE Borislav Banović

Morocco

Embassy of the Kingdom of Morocco, 49 Queen's Gate Gardens, London SW7 5NE
Tel: 020 7581 5001 Fax: 020 7225 3862 Email: ambalondres@maec.gov.ma
Website: www.moroccanembassylondon.org.uk Twitter: @MOROCCOinUK
Ambassador: HE Abdesselam Aboudrar

Mozambique

High Commission for the Republic of Mozambique, 21 Fitzroy Square, London W1T 6EL
Tel: 020 7383 3800 Fax: 020 7383 3801
Website: www.mozambiquehighcommission.org.uk
High Commissioner: HE Filipe Chidumo

Myanmar – see Burma

Namibia

High Commission for the Republic of Namibia, 6 Chandos Street, London W1G 9LU
Tel: 020 7636 6244 Fax: 020 7637 5694
Email: info@namibiahc.org.uk Website: www.namibiahc.org.uk
High Commissioner: HE Steve Vemunavi Katjiuanjo

Nauru

No London High Commission
High Commissioner: To be appointed

UK Consulate

Romshed Courtyard, Underriver, nr Sevenoaks, Kent TN15 0SD
Tel: 01732 746061 Fax: 01732 746062 Email: nauru@weald.co.uk
Honorary Consul: Martin Weston

Nepal

Embassy of Nepal, 12a Kensington Palace Gardens, London W8 4QU
Tel: 020 7229 1594 Fax: 020 7792 9861
Email: eon@nepembassy.org.uk Website: www.nepembassy.org.uk
Ambassador: HE Dr Durga Bahadur Subedi

Netherlands

Embassy of the Kingdom of the Netherlands, 38 Hyde Park Gate, London SW7 5DP
Tel: 020 7590 3200 Email: lon@minbuza.nl
Website: www.netherlandsworldwide.nl/countries/united-kingdom/about-us/embassy-in-london
Twitter: @NLinUK
Ambassador: HE Simon Smits

New Zealand

New Zealand High Commission, New Zealand House, 80 Haymarket, London SW1Y 4TQ
Tel: 020 7930 8422 Fax: 020 7839 4580
Email: aboutnz@newzealandhc.org.uk Website: www.mfat.govt.nz/uk
High Commissioner: HE Rt Hon Sir Jerry Mateparae

Nicaragua

Embassy of Nicaragua, Suite 31, Vicarage House, 58-60 Kensington Church Street, London W8 4DB
Tel: 020 7938 2373 Fax: 020 7937 0952
Email: embaniclondon@btconnect.com
Ambassador: HE Guisell Morales-Echaverry

Niger

No London Embassy
Embassy of the Republic of Niger, 154 Rue de Longchamp, 75116 Paris, France
Tel: +33 1 45 04 80 60 Fax: +33 1 45 04 79 73
Website: ambassadeniger-fr.org
Ambassador: To be appointed

UK Consulate

MPC House, 15 Maple Mews, London NW6 5UZ
Tel: 020 7328 8180 Fax: 020 7328 8120
Email: consulate@nigerconsulateuk.org Website: www.nigerconsulateuk.org
Honorary Consul: Muhammadu Dikko Ladan

Nigeria

High Commission for the Federal Republic of Nigeria, Nigeria House, 9 Northumberland Avenue, London WC2N 5BX
Tel: 020 7839 1244 Fax: 020 7839 8746
Email: information@nigeriahc.org.uk Website: www.nigeriahc.org.uk
Acting High Commissioner: Kabiru Bala

Royal Norwegian Embassy, 25 Belgrave Square, London SW1X 8QD
Tel: 020 7591 5500 Fax: 020 7245 6993
Email: emb.london@mfa.no Website: www.norway.org.uk Twitter: @norwayinuk
Ambassador: HE Mona Juul

Oman

Embassy of the Sultanate of Oman, 167 Queen's Gate, London SW7 5HE
Tel: 020 7225 0001 Fax: 020 7589 2505 Email: theembassy@omanembassy.org.uk
Ambassador: HE Abdul Aziz Al Hinai

Pakistan

High Commission for the Islamic Republic of Pakistan, 35-36 Lowndes Square, London SW1X 9JN
Tel: 020 7664 9200 Fax: 020 7664 9224
Email: protocol@phclondon.org Website: www.phclondon.org Twitter: @phclondon
High Commissioner: HE Syed Ibne Abbas

Palau

No London Embassy

UK Consulate

Bankfoot Square, Bankfoot Street, Batley WF17 5LH
Tel: 01924 470786 Fax: 01924 474747 Website: palauconsulate.org.uk
Honorary Consul: Mr Q Mohammed

Panama

Embassy of Panama, 40 Hertford Street, London W1J 7SH
Tel: 020 7493 4646 Fax: 020 7493 4333
Email: panama1@btconnect.com Website: www.panamaconsul.co.uk
Ambassador: HE Daniel Eduardo Fábrega Venier

Papua New Guinea

Papua New Guinea High Commission, Ground Floor, 14 Waterloo Place, London SW1Y 4AR
Tel: 020 7930 0922 Fax: 020 7930 0828 Email: info@png.org.uk Website: www.pnghighcomm.org.uk
High Commissioner: HE Winnie Kiap

Paraguay

Embassy of the Republic of Paraguay, Third Floor, 344 Kensington High Street, London W14 8NS
Tel: 020 7610 4180 Fax: 020 7371 4297
Email: embaparuk@paraguayembassy.co.uk Website: www.paraguayembassy.co.uk
Ambassador: HE Genaro Vicente Pappalardo Ayala

Peru

Embassy of Peru, 52 Sloane Street, London SW1X 9SP
Tel: 020 7235 1917 Fax: 020 7235 4463
Email: postmaster@peruembassy-uk.com Website: www.peruembassy-uk.com
Ambassador: HE Claudio de la Puente

Philippines

Embassy of the Republic of the Philippines, 6-8 Suffolk Street, London SW1Y 4HG
Tel: 020 7451 1780 Fax: 020 7930 9787
Email: embassy@philemb.co.uk Website: londonpe.dfa.gov.ph Twitter: @philemblondon
Ambassador: HE Antonio Lagdameo

Poland
Embassy of the Republic of Poland, 47 Portland Place, London W1B 1JH
Tel: 020 7291 3520 Fax: 020 7291 3575
Email: london@msz.gov.pl Website: london.mfa.gov.pl/en Twitter: @polishembassyuk
Ambassador: HE Arkady Rzegocki

Portugal
Embassy of Portugal, 11 Belgrave Square, London SW1X 8PP
Tel: 020 7235 5331 Fax: 020 7245 1287 Email: londres@me.pt
Ambassador: HE Manuel Lobo Antunes

Qatar
Embassy of the State of Qatar, 1 South Audley Street, London W1K 1NB
Tel: 020 7493 2200 Fax: 020 7493 2819
Email: amblondon@mofa.gov.qa Website: london.embassy.qa/en Twitter: @QatarEmbassyUK
Ambassador: HE Yousef Ali Al-Khater

Romania
Embassy of Romania, Arundel House, 4 Palace Green, London W8 4QD
Tel: 020 7937 9666 Fax: 020 7937 8069
Email: roemb@roemb.co.uk Website: londra.mae.ro
Ambassador: HE Dan Mihalache

Russia
Embassy of the Russian Federation, 6-7 Kensington Palace Gardens, London W8 4QP
Tel: 020 7229 6412 Fax: 020 7727 8625
Email: info@rusemb.org.uk Website: www.rusemb.org.uk Twitter: @russianembassy
Ambassador: HE Alexander Yakovenko

Rwanda
High Commission for the Republic of Rwanda, 120-122 Seymour Place, London W1H 1NR
Tel: 020 7224 9832 Fax: 020 7724 8642
Email: uk@ambarwanda.org.uk Website: www.rwandahc.org Twitter: @rwandahcuk
High Commissioner: HE Yamina Karitanyi

St Kitts and Nevis
High Commission for Saint Christopher and Nevis, 10 Kensington Court, London W8 5DL
Tel: 020 7937 9718 Fax: 020 7937 7484
Email: info@sknhc.co.uk Website: www.stkittsnevisuk.com Twitter: @sknhcuk
High Commissioner: HE Kevin Isaac

St Lucia
High Commission for Saint Lucia, 1 Collingham Gardens, London SW5 0HW
Tel: 020 7370 7123 Fax: 020 7370 1905 Email: enquiries@stluciahcuk.org
High Commissioner: HE Guy Mayers

St Vincent and the Grenadines
High Commission for Saint Vincent and the Grenadines, 10 Kensington Court, London W8 5DL
Tel: 020 7460 1256 Fax: 020 7937 6040
Email: info@svghighcom.co.uk Website: www.svghighcom.co.uk Twitter: @svghighcom
High Commissioner: HE Cenio Lewis

Samoa

No London High Commission
Embassy of Samoa, Avenue Commandant Lothaire 1, 1040 Brussels, Belgium
Tel: +32 2 660 84 54 Fax: +32 2 675 03 36 Email: samoaembassy@skynet.be

High Commissioner: HE Fatumanava Dr Pa'olelei Luteru

UK Consulate

Church Cottage, Pedlinge, nr Hythe, Kent CT21 5JL
Tel: 01303 260541 Fax: 01303 238058
Honorary Consul: Prunella Scarlett LVO

San Marino

No London Embassy
Embassy of the Republic of San Marino, Department of Foreign Affairs, Palazzo Begni – Contrada Omerelli, 47890 San Marino, San Marino
Tel: +378 0549 882422 Email: dipartimentoaffariesteri@pa.sm

Ambassador: HE Federica Bigi

UK Consulate

Flat 51, 162 Sloane Street, London SW1X 9BS
Tel: 020 7259 9754 Fax: 01268 292629
Email: consolato.londra.sm@gmail.com

Honorary Consul: Eduardo Teodorani-Fabbri

São Tomé and Príncipe

No London Embassy
Embassy of São Tomé and Principé, Avenue de Tervuren 175, 1150 Brussels, Belgium
Tel: +32 2 734 89 66 Fax: +32 2 734 88 15 Email: ambassade@saotomeprincipe.be

Ambassador: To be appointed
Chargé d'Affaires: Armindo de Brito Fernandes

UK Consulate

Flat 8, Marsham Court, 58 Victoria Drive, London SW19 6BB
Tel: 020 8788 6139

Honorary Consul: Nathalie Galland-Burkl

Saudi Arabia

Royal Embassy of Saudi Arabia, 30 Charles Street, London W1J 5DZ
Tel: 020 7917 3000
Email: ukemb@mofa.gov.sa Website: www.saudiembassy.org.uk Twitter: @SaudiEmbassyUK
Ambassador: HE HRH Prince Mohammed bin Nawaf Al Saud

Senegal

Embassy of the Republic of Senegal, 39 Marloes Road, London W8 6LA
Tel: 020 7938 4048 Fax: 020 7938 2546 Email: senegalembassy@hotmail.co.uk

Ambassador: HE Prof Cheikh Ahmadou Dieng

Serbia

Embassy of the Republic of Serbia, 28 Belgrave Square, London SW1X 8QB
Tel: 020 7235 9049 Fax: 020 7235 7092
Email: london@serbianembassy.org.uk Website: www.serbianembassy.org.uk
Ambassador: To be appointed
Chargé d'Affaires: Nataša Marić

Seychelles

High Commission of the Republic of Seychelles, Fourth Floor, 130-132 Buckingham Palace Road, London SW1W 9SA
Tel: 020 7245 0680 Fax: 020 7730 0087 Email: seyhc.london@btconnect.com

High Commissioner: HE Derick Ally

Sierra Leone

Sierra Leone High Commission, 41 Eagle Street, London WC1R 4TL
Tel: 020 7404 0140 Fax: 020 7430 9862 Email: info@slhc-uk.org.uk Website: www.slhc-uk.org

High Commissioner: HE Edward Turay

Singapore

High Commission for the Republic of Singapore, 9 Wilton Crescent, London SW1X 8SP
Tel: 020 7235 8315 Fax: 020 7245 6583
Email: singhc_lon@sgmfa.gov.sg Website: www.mfa.gov.sg/london Twitter: @shclon

High Commissioner: HE Chi Hsia Foo

Slovakia

Embassy of the Slovak Republic, 25 Kensington Palace Gardens, London W8 4QY
Tel: 020 7313 6470 Fax: 020 7313 6481
Email: emb.london@mzv.sk Website: www.mzv.sk/web/londyn-en

Ambassador: HE L'ubomír Rehák

Slovenia

Embassy of the Republic of Slovenia, 17 Dartmouth Street, London SW1H 9BL
Tel: 020 7222 5700 Fax: 020 7222 5277
Email: vlo@gov.si Website: www.london.embassy.si Twitter: @SLOinUK

Ambassador: HE Tadej Rupel

Solomon Islands

High Commission for the Solomon Islands, Room 229-230, 10 Greycoat Place, London SW1P 1SB

High Commissioner (Non-Resident): HE Moses Kouni Mose

South Africa

High Commission of the Republic of South Africa, South Africa House, Trafalgar Square, London WC2N 5DP
Tel: 020 7451 7299 Fax: 020 7839 5670
Email: london.general@foreign.gov.za Website: www.southafricahouseuk.com

High Commissioner: HE Thembinkosi Obed Mlaba

South Sudan

Embassy of the Republic of South Sudan, Winchester House, 259-269 Old Maryleborne Road, London NW1 5RA
Tel: 020 7339 3100 Email: info@embrss.org.uk Website: embrss.org.uk

Ambassador: HE Sabit Abbe Alley

Spain

Embassy of Spain, 39 Chesham Place, London SW1X 8SB
Tel: 020 7235 5555 Fax: 020 7259 5392 Email: emb.londres@maec.es
Website: www.exteriores.gob.es/embajadas/londres/en Twitter: @EmbSpainUK

Ambassador: HE Carlos Bastarreche

Sri Lanka

High Commission for the Democratic Socialist Republic of Sri Lanka, 13 Hyde Park Gardens, London W2 2LU
Tel: 020 7262 1841 Fax: 020 7262 7970
Email: mail@slhc-london.co.uk Website: www.srilankahighcommission.co.uk
High Commissioner: HE Amari Mandika Wijewardine

Sudan

Embassy of the Republic of the Sudan, 3 Cleveland Row, London SW1A 1DD
Tel: 020 7839 8080 Fax: 020 7839 7560 Email: admin@sudanembassy.co.uk
Ambassador: HE Mohammed Abdalla Ali Eltom

Suriname

No London Embassy
Embassy of the Republic of Suriname, rue du Ranelagh 91, 75016 Paris, France
Tel: +33 01 45 25 93 00 Email: secretariat@ambassadesurinamefr.org
Ambassador: HE Harvey Naarendorp

UK Consulate

127 Pier House, 31 Cheyne Walk, London SW3 5HN
Tel: 020 3084 7143 Email: ajethu@honoraryconsul.info
Honorary Consul: Dr Amwedhkar Jethu

Swaziland

Kingdom of Swaziland High Commission, 20 Buckingham Gate, London SW1E 6LB
Tel: 020 7630 6611 Fax: 020 7630 6564 Email: enquiries@swaziland.org.uk
High Commissioner: HE Christian Muzie Nkambule

Sweden

Embassy of Sweden, 11 Montagu Place, London W1H 2AL
Tel: 020 7917 6400 Fax: 020 7724 4174
Email: ambassaden.london@gov.se Website: www.swedenabroad.com/london Twitter: @swedeninuk
Ambassador: HE Torbjörn Sohlström

Switzerland

Embassy of Switzerland, 16-18 Montagu Place, London W1H 2BQ
Tel: 020 7616 6000 Fax: 020 7724 7001
Email: lon.vertretung@eda.admin.ch Website: www.eda.admin.ch/london Twitter: @swissembassyuk
Ambassador: HE Alexandre Fasel

Tajikistan

Embassy of the Republic of Tajikistan, Suite 309, 3 Shortlands, Hammersmith, London W6 8DA
Tel: 020 8834 1003 Fax: 020 8834 1100
Email: tajemblondon@mfa.tj Website: www.tajembassy.org.uk
Ambassador: To be appointed
Chargé d'Affaires: Asliddin Rakhmatov

Tanzania

High Commission for the United Republic of Tanzania, 3 Stratford Place, London W1C 1AS
Tel: 020 7569 1470 Fax: 020 7491 3710
Email: balozi@tanzaniahighcomm.co.uk Website: tanzaniahighcomm.co.uk
High Commissioner: HE Dr Asha-Rose Migiro

Thailand

Royal Thai Embassy, 29-30 Queen's Gate, London SW7 5JB
Tel: 020 7589 2944 Fax: 020 7823 7492
Email: thaiduto@btinternet.com Website: www.thaiembassyuk.org.uk

Ambassador: HE Pisanu Suvanajata

East Timor

Embassy of the Democratic Republic of East Timor, Portland House, Bresenden Place, London SW1E 5RS
Tel: 020 3440 9025

Ambassador: HE Joaquim Lopes da Fonseca

Togo

Embassy of the Republic of Togo, Unit 3, 7 and 8 Lysander Mews, Lysander Grove, London N19 3QP
Tel: 020 3198 9579

Ambassador: To be appointed
Chargé d'Affaires: Abra Dackey

Tonga

Tonga High Commission, 36 Molyneux Street, London W1H 5BQ
Tel: 020 7724 5828 Fax: 020 7723 9074

Acting High Commissioner: Sione Sonata Tupou

Trinidad and Tobago

High Commission of the Republic of Trinidad and Tobago, 42 Belgrave Square, London SW1X 8NT
Tel: 020 7245 9351 Fax: 020 7823 1065 Email: hclondon@foreign.gov.tt Twitter: @tnt_london

High Commissioner: HE Orville London

Tunisia

Embassy of Tunisia, 29 Prince's Gate, London SW7 1QG
Tel: 020 7584 8117 Fax: 020 7584 3205
Email: london@tunisianembassy.co.uk Website: www.at-londres.diplomatie.gov.tn

Ambassador: To be appointed
Chargé d'Affaires: Anouar Ben Youssef

Turkey

Embassy of the Republic of Turkey, 43 Belgrave Square, London SW1X 8PA
Tel: 020 7393 0202 Fax: 020 7393 0066
Email: embassy.london@mfa.gov.tr Website: london.emb.mfa.gov.tr Twitter: @TurkEmbLondon
Ambassador: HE Abdurrahman Bilgiç

Turkmenistan

Embassy of Turkmenistan, 131 Holland Park Avenue, London W11 4UT
Tel: 020 7610 5239 Fax: 020 7751 1903
Email: tkm-embassy-uk@btconnect.org.uk Website: uk.tmembassy.gov.tm/en
Ambassador: HE Yazmurad Seryaev

Tuvalu

No London High Commission
High Commissioner: To be appointed
UK Consulate

Tuvalu House, 230 Worple Road, London SW20 8RH
Tel: 020 8879 0985 Fax: 020 8879 0985 Email: tuvaluconsulate@netscape.net

Honorary Consul: Sir Iftikhar Ayaz KBE

Uganda
Uganda High Commission, Uganda House, 58-59 Trafalgar Square, London WC2N 5DX
Tel: 020 7839 5783 Fax: 020 7839 8925
Email: info@ugandahighcommission.co.uk Website: london.mofa.go.ug
High Commissioner: HE Julius Peter Moto

Ukraine
Embassy of Ukraine, 60 Holland Park, London W11 3SJ
Tel: 020 7727 6312 Fax: 020 7792 1708
Email: emb_gb@mfa.gov.ua Website: uk.mfa.gov.ua/en Twitter: @UkrEmbLondon
Ambassador: HE Natalia Galibarenko

United Arab Emirates
Embassy of the United Arab Emirates, 30 Prince's Gate, London SW7 1PT
Tel: 020 7581 1281 Fax: 020 7581 9616
Email: informationuk@mofa.gov.ae Website: www.uae-embassy.ae
Ambassador: HE Sulaiman Hamid Almazroui

United States of America
American Embassy, 24 Grosvenor Square, London W1K 6AH
Tel: 020 7499 9000 Website: uk.usembassy.gov Twitter: @usainuk
Ambassador: HE Robert Wood Johnson

Uruguay
Embassy of Uruguay, Fourth Floor, 150 Brompton Road, Knightsbridge, London SW3 1HX
Tel: 020 7584 4200 Fax: 020 7584 2947
Email: urureinounido@mrree.gub.uy
Ambassador: HE Fernando López-Fabregat

Uzbekistan
Embassy of the Republic of Uzbekistan, 41 Holland Park, London W11 3RP
Tel: 020 7229 7679 Fax: 020 7229 7029
Email: info@uzbekembassy.org Website: www.uzbekembassy.org Twitter: @uzbekembassy
Ambassador: HE Alisher Shaykhov

Vanuatu
No London High Commission
High Commission of Vanuatu, Avenue de Tervueren 380, Chemin de Ronde, 1150 Brussels, Belgium
Tel: +32 2 771 74 94 Fax: +32 2 771 74 94 Email: info@vanuatuembassy.net
High Commissioner: HE Roy Mickey Joy

Venezuela
Embassy of the Bolivarian Republic of Venezuela, 1 Cromwell Road, London SW7 2HW
Tel: 020 7584 4206 Fax: 020 7589 8887 Website: reinounido.embajada.gob.ve
Ambassador: HE Rocío Maneiro

Vietnam
Embassy of the Socialist Republic of Vietnam, 12-14 Victoria Road, London W8 5RD
Tel: 020 7937 1912 Fax: 020 7937 6108
Email: vanphong@vietnamembassy.org.uk Website: www.vietnamembassy.org.uk
Ambassador: HE Nguyen Van Thao

Yemen

Embassy of the Republic of Yemen, 57 Cromwell Road, London SW7 2ED
Tel: 020 7584 6607
Email: admin@yemenembassy.co.uk

Ambassador: HE Dr Yassin Saeed Ahmed Noman

Zambia

High Commission for the Republic of Zambia, Zambia House, 2 Palace Gate, London W8 5NG
Tel: 020 7581 2142 Fax: 020 7581 1353
Email: info@zambiahc.org.uk Website: www.zambiahc.org.uk

High Commissioner: HE Muyeba Schicapwa Chikonde

Zimbabwe

Embassy for the Republic of Zimbabwe, Zimbabwe House, 429 Strand, London WC2R 0JR
Tel: 020 7836 7755 Fax: 020 7379 1167
Email: zimebassy@zimlondon.gov.zw

Ambassador: To be appointed
Chargé d'Affaires: Cecil T Chinenere

Royal Households

HER MAJESTY'S HOUSEHOLD
Buckingham Palace, London SW1A 1AA Tel: 020 7930 4832
Website: www.royal.uk Twitter: @RoyalFamily
Private Secretary to HM The Queen: Edward Young CVO

HRH THE PRINCE PHILIP, DUKE OF EDINBURGH
Buckingham Palace, London SW1A 1AA Tel: 020 7930 4832
Private Secretary and Treasurer: Brig. Archie Miller-Bakewell

TRH THE PRINCE OF WALES AND THE DUCHESS OF CORNWALL
Clarence House, London SW1A 1BA Tel: 020 7930 4832
Website: www.princeofwales.gov.uk Twitter: @ClarenceHouse
Principal Private Secretary: Clive Alderton LVO

TRH THE DUKE AND DUCHESS OF CAMBRIDGE
Kensington Palace, London W8 4PU Tel: 020 7930 4832
Website: www.dukeandduchessofcambridge.org Twitter: @KensingtonRoyal
Private Secretary to The Duke of Cambridge: Miguel Head LVO
Private Secretary to The Duchess of Cambridge: Catherine Quinn

HRH PRINCE HENRY OF WALES
Kensington Palace, London W8 4PU Tel: 020 7930 4832
Website: www.princehenryofwales.org
Private Secretary: Ed Lane-Fox

HRH THE DUKE OF YORK
Buckingham Palace, London SW1A 1AA Tel: 020 7930 4832
Website: thedukeofyork.org Twitter: @TheDukeofYork
Private Secretary and Treasurer: Amanda Thirsk LVO

TRH THE EARL AND COUNTESS OF WESSEX
Bagshot Park, Bagshot, Surrey GU19 5PL Tel: 020 7930 4832
Private Secretary: Tim Roberts

HRH THE PRINCESS ROYAL
Buckingham Palace, London SW1A 1AA Tel: 020 7930 4832
Private Secretary: Capt. Nick Wright CVO RN

TRH THE DUKE AND DUCHESS OF GLOUCESTER
Kensington Palace, London W8 4PU Tel: 020 7930 4832
Private Secretary and Comptroller: Lt Col Alastair Todd

HRH THE DUKE OF KENT
St James's Palace, London SW1A 1BQ Tel: 020 7930 4872
Private Secretary: Nicholas Marden

HRH THE DUCHESS OF KENT
Wren House, Palace Green, London W8 4PY Tel: 020 7937 2730
Secretary: Pauline Verbe

TRH PRINCE AND PRINCESS MICHAEL OF KENT
Kensington Palace, London W8 4PU
Website: www.princemichael.org.uk
Private Secretary: Camilla Rogers

HRH PRINCESS ALEXANDRA, THE HONOURABLE LADY OGILVY
Buckingham Palace, London SW1A 1AA Tel: 020 7930 4832
Private Secretary and Comptroller: Diane Duke LVO

HM Lord Lieutenants

ENGLAND

Bedfordshire	Helen Nellis
Berkshire	James Puxley
City and County of Bristol	Peaches Golding OBE
Buckinghamshire	Sir Henry Aubrey-Fletcher Bt
Cambridgeshire	Julie Spence OBE QPM
Cheshire	David Briggs MBE
Cornwall	Col Edward Bolitho OBE
County Durham	Susan Snowdon
Cumbria	Claire Hensman
Derbyshire	William Tucker
Devon	David Fursdon
Dorset	Angus Campbell
East Riding of Yorkshire	Hon Susan Cunliffe-Lister
East Sussex	Peter Field JP
Essex	Jennifer Tolhurst
Gloucestershire	Dame Janet Trotter DBE
Greater London	Kenneth Olisa OBE
Greater Manchester	Warren Smith JP
Hampshire	Nigel Atkinson
Herefordshire	Dowager Countess of Darnley JP
Hertfordshire	Robert Voss CBE
Isle of Wight	Major General Martin White CB CBE
Kent	Viscount De L'Isle MBE
Lancashire	Lord Shuttleworth KG KCVO
Leicestershire	Lady Gretton DCVO JP
Lincolnshire	Toby Dennis
Merseyside	Mark Blundell
Norfolk	Richard Jewson JP
North Yorkshire	Barry Dodd CBE
Northamptonshire	David Laing
Northumberland	Duchess of Northumberland
Nottinghamshire	Sir John Peace
Oxfordshire	Tim Stevenson OBE
Rutland	Dr Laurence Howard OBE JP
Shropshire	Sir Algernon Heber-Percy KCVO JP
Somerset	Annie Maw
South Yorkshire	Andrew Coombe
Staffordshire	Ian Dudson CBE
Suffolk	Countess of Euston
Surrey	Michael More-Molyneux
Tyne and Wear	Susan Winfield OBE
Warwickshire	Timothy Cox
West Midlands	John Crabtree OBE
West Sussex	Susan Pyper
West Yorkshire	Dame Ingrid Roscoe
Wiltshire	Sarah Troughton
Worcestershire	Lt Col Patrick Holcroft LVO OBE

SCOTLAND

City of Aberdeen*	Lord Provost Barney Crockett
Aberdeenshire	James Ingleby
Angus	Georgiana Osborne
Argyll and Bute	Patrick Stewart MBE
Ayrshire and Arran	John Duncan QPM
Banffshire	Clare Russell
Berwickshire	Jeanna Swan
Caithness	Viscount Thurso
Clackmannanshire	Lt Col Johnny Stewart
Dumfries	Fiona Armstrong
Dunbartonshire	Real Admiral Michael Gregory OBE
City of Dundee*	Lord Provost Ian Borthwick
East Lothian	Major Michael Williams MBE
City of Edinburgh*	Lord Provost Frank Ross
Fife	Robert Balfour
City of Glasgow*	Lord Provost Eva Bolander
Inverness	Donald Cameron of Lochiel (the Younger)
Kincardineshire	Carol Kinghorn
Lanarkshire	Mushtaq Ahmad OBE
Midlothian	Sir Robert Clerk Bt OBE
Moray	Lt Col Sir Grenville Johnston OBE TD
Nairn	Ewen Brodie of Lethen CVO
Orkney	Bill Spence
Perth and Kinross	Brig Melville Jameson CBE
Renfrewshire	Guy Clark JP
Ross and Cromarty	Janet Bowen
Roxburgh, Ettrick and Lauderdale	Duke of Buccleuch and Queensberry
Shetland	Robert Hunter
Stewartry of Kirkcudbright	Lt Col Sir Malcom Ross GVO OBE
Stirling and Falkirk	Alan Simpson OBE
Sutherland	Dr Monica Main
Tweeddale	Professor Sir Hew Strachan
West Lothian	Moira Niven MBE
Western Isles	Donald Martin
Wigtown	John Ross CBE

**The Lord Provosts of the four City Districts (Aberdeen, Dundee, Edinburgh and Glasgow) are ex-officio Lord Lieutenants.*

WALES

Clwyd	Henry Fetherstonhaugh OBE
Dyfed	Sara Edwards
Gwent	Brig Robert Aitken CBE
Gwynedd	Edmund Bailey
Mid Glamorgan	Kathrin Thomas CVO JP
Powys	Hon Dame Shân Legge-Bourke DCVO
South Glamorgan	Morfudd Meredith
West Glamorgan	Byron Lewis

NORTHERN IRELAND

County Antrim	Joan Christie OBE
County Armagh	Earl of Caledon KCVO
County Borough of Belfast	Fionnuala Jay-O'Boyle CBE
County Borough of Londonderry	Dr Angela Garvey
County Down	David Lindsay
County Fermanagh	Viscount Brookeborough
County Londonderry	Denis Desmond CBE
County Tyrone	Robert Scott OBE JP

Association of Lord Lieutenants
Chairman: Lord Shuttleworth KG KCVO
Secretary: Tom Wilson Email: office@lord-lieutenants.uk

British Overseas Territories Governors and Commanders-in-Chief

Anguilla	HE Tim Foy OBE *(Governor)*
Bermuda	HE John Rankin CMG *(Governor)*
British Antarctic Territory	Ben Merrick *(Commissioner)* (Non-resident)
British Indian Ocean Territory	Ben Merrick *(Commissioner)* (Non-resident)
British Virgin Islands	HE Gus Jaspert *(Governor)*
Cayman Islands	HE Helen Kilpatrick CB *(Governor until March 2018)* HE Anwar Choudhury *(Governor from March 2018)*
Falkland Islands	HE Nigel Phillips CBE *(Governor)*
Gibraltar	HE Lt Gen Edward Davis CB CBE *(Governor)*
Montserrat	HE Elizabeth Carriere *(Governor)*
Pitcairn, Henderson, Ducie and Oeno Islands	HE Jonathan Sinclair LVO *(Governor until January 2018)*, HE Laura Clarke *(Governor from January 2018)* (Non-resident) see New Zealand – British Embassies and High Commissions section
St Helena and Dependencies	HE Lisa Phillips CBE *(Governor)*
South Georgia and South Sandwich Islands	HE Nigel Phillips CBE *(Commissioner)* (Non-resident)
Turks and Caicos Islands	HE Dr John Freeman CMG *(Governor)*

The Commonwealth

Of the 54 member countries of the Commonwealth, Queen Elizabeth II is Head of State of 16 (including the United Kingdom), 33 are republics, and 5 are monarchies with other sovereigns. The Queen remains symbolically Head of the Commonwealth.

GOVERNORS-GENERAL

In the overseas realms of which she is Queen, Her Majesty is represented by a Governor-General.

Antigua and Barbuda	HE Sir Rodney Williams GCMG *Prime Minister:* Hon Gaston Browne
Australia	HE Gen Sir Peter Cosgrove AK MC *Prime Minister:* Hon Malcolm Turnbull
Bahamas	HE Dame Marguerite Pindling *Prime Minister:* Hubert Minnis

Barbados	HE Sir Philip Marlowe Greaves *Prime Minister:* HE Freundel Stuart
Belize	HE Sir Colville Young GCMG MBE *Prime Minister:* HE Dean Barrow
Canada	HE Julie Payette *Prime Minister:* HE Justin Trudeau
Grenada	HE Dame Cecile La Grenade GCMG OBE *Prime Minister:* Rt Hon Dr Keith Mitchell
Jamaica	HE Sir Patrick Allen ON GCMG *Prime Minister:* Most Hon Andrew Holness ON
New Zealand	HE Rt Hon Dame Patsy Reddy GNZM QSO *Prime Minister:* HE Bill English
Papua New Guinea	HE Sir Michael Ogio GCMG CBE *Prime Minister:* Hon Peter O'Neill CMG
St Christopher and Nevis*	HE Sir Tapley Seaton GCMG CVO QC *Prime Minister:* Hon Dr Timothy Harris
St Lucia*	HE Dame Pearlette Louisy GCMG *Prime Minister:* Hon Allen M Chastanet
St Vincent and The Grenadines*	HE Sir Frederick Ballantyne *Prime Minister:* Hon Dr Ralph Gonsalves
Solomon Islands	HE Sir Frank Kabui GCMG OBE *Prime Minister:* Manasseh Sogavare
Tuvalu	HE Sir Iakoba Italeli GCMG *Prime Minister:* Enele Sopoaga

*Eastern Caribbean States.

REPUBLICS AND OTHER COMMONWEALTH MONARCHIES HEADS OF STATE AND HEADS OF GOVERNMENT

Bangladesh	*President and Head of State:* HE Abdul Hamid *Prime Minister:* Hon Sheikh Hasina
Botswana	*President and Head of State:* HE Lt Gen Seretse Khama Ian Khama
Brunei Darussalam	*Sultan and Head of Government:* HM Sultan Hassanal Bolkiah of Brunei
Cameroon	*President and Head of State:* HE Paul Biya *Prime Minister and Head of Government:* Philémon Yang
Cyprus	*President and Head of State:* Nicos Anastasiades
Dominica	*President and Head of State:* HE Charles Savarin *Prime Minister and Head of Government:* Hon Roosevelt Skerrit
Fiji Islands	*President and Head of State:* HE Major General Jioji Konrote *Prime Minister and Head of Government:* Rear Admiral Josaia Voreqe Bainimarama
Ghana	*President and Head of State:* HE Nana Akufo-Addo
Guyana	*President and Head of State:* HE David Granger *Prime Minister and Head of Government:* Hon Moses Nagamootoo
India	*President and Head of State:* HE Shri Ram Nath Kovind *Prime Minister and Head of Government:* Hon Narendra Modi
Kenya	*President and Head of State:* HE Uhuru Kenyatta
Kiribati	*President and Head of State:* HE Taneti Maamau

Lesotho *Head of State:* His Majesty King Letsie III
Prime Minister and Head of Government: Thomas Thabane

Malawi *President and Head of State:* HE Peter Mutharika

Malaysia *Head of State (King of Malaysia):* HM Sultan Muhammad V
Prime Minister and Head of Government: Hon Dato' Sri Mohd Najib

Malta *President and Head of State:* Marie-Louise Coleiro Preca
Prime Minister and Head of Government: Joseph Muscat

Mauritius *President and Head of State:* HE Ameenah Gurib-Fakim
Prime Minister and Head of Government: Pravind Jugnauth

Mozambique *President and Head of State:* HE Filipe Nyusi

Namibia *President and Head of State:* HE Dr Hage Geingob

Nauru *President and Head of Government:* HE Baron Waqa

Nigeria *President and Head of State:* HE Muhammadu Buhari

Pakistan *President and Head of State:* HE Mamnoon Hussain
Prime Minister and Head of Government: Shahid Khaqan Abbas

Rwanda *President and Head of State:* HE Paul Kagame
Prime Minister and Head of Government: Edouard Ngirente

Samoa *Head of State:* HE Tuimalealiifano Vaaletoa Sualauvi II
Prime Minister Head of Government: Tuilaepa Aiono Sailele Malielegaoi

Seychelles *President and Head of State:* HE Danny Faure

Sierra Leone *President and Head of Government:* HE Dr Ernest Bai Koroma

Singapore *President and Head of State:* HE Halimah Yacob
Prime Minister and Head of Government: Lee Hsien Loong

South Africa *President and Head of State:* HE Jacob Zuma

Sri Lanka *President and Head of State:* HE Maithripala Sirisena
Prime Minister and Head of Government: Hon Ranil Wickremesinghe

Swaziland *Head of State:* HM King Mswati III
Prime Minister and Head of Government: Dr Sibusiso Barnabas Dlamini

Tanzania *President and Head of State:* HE Dr John Magufuli
Prime Minister and Head of Government: Kassim Majaliwa

Tonga *Head of State:* HM King George Tupou VI
Prime Minister and Head of Government: Hon Samuela 'Akilisi Pohiva

Trinidad and Tobago *President and Head of State:* HE Anthony Carmona
Prime Minister and Head of Government: Hon Dr Keith Rowley

Uganda *President and Head of State:* HE Yoweri Museveni
Prime Minister and Head of Government: Dr Ruhakana Rugunda

Vanuatu *President and Head of State:* HE Tallis Obed Moses
Prime Minister and Head of Government: Charlot Salwai

Zambia *President and Head of State:* HE Edgar Lungu

Forms of Address

Formal modes of address become less formal every year but there are occasions when a person may want to address someone with strict formality. The first form of address given is that which should always be used on the envelope, the second is the formal salutation and conclusion and the third is the less formal salutation and conclusion, respectively (1), (2) and (3).

The honorific prefix 'The Right Honourable' is not now generally used for Peers other than Privy Counsellors.

The courtesy titles Honourable, Lady and Lord to which sons and daughters of Peers (depending on the rank of their father) are not prefixed by the definite article. These are the practices adopted by the Earl Marshal's Office and that of the Lord Chamberlain of the Household and consequently have been followed here.

In the formal mode of address the conclusion '... Obedient Servant' has been used. This is a matter of choice as it can be 'humble and obedient servant' or simply 'I am, Sir (my Lord et al) Yours faithfully'.

AMBASSADOR—(1) His Excellency Mr., Dr., etc. as appropriate, (Esquire is never used), Ambassador of the Italian Republic, (the name of the country in full i.e. not The Italian Ambassador). (2) Your Excellency, conclude I am Your Excellency's Obedient Servant. (3) Dear Mr Ambassador, conclude Yours sincerely. A list of Ambassadors is available on p1292. In conversation an Ambassador is addressed as 'Your Excellency', but once is sufficient, thereafter 'Sir' is normal.

AMBASSADOR'S PARTNER—(1) As the married partner of the Ambassador they are not 'Your Excellency' nor in the case of a wife 'Ambassadress'.

ARCHBISHOP—(1) The Most Rev The Lord Archbishop of York. Or, The Most Rev John Smith, Lord Archbishop of York. (2) Your Grace or My Lord Archbishop, conclude I am Your Grace's Obedient Servant. (3) Dear Archbishop, conclude Yours sincerely. The Archbishops of Canterbury and York are Privy Counsellors and are therefore addressed as The Most Reverend and Right Honourable.

BARON—(1) The Lord Barton. (2) My Lord, conclude I am, My Lord, Your Obedient Servant. (3) Dear Lord Barton, conclude Yours sincerely.

BARONESS IN HER OWN RIGHT OR BARON'S WIFE —(1) The Lady Barton or, in the case of Baronesses in their own right, most prefer to be styled The Baroness Barton (see biographies of Members of the House of Lords p570). (2) Dear Madam, conclude Yours faithfully. (3) Dear Lady Barton or Dear Baroness Barton, conclude Yours sincerely.

BARONETS—(1) Sir John Smith, Bt. (the abbreviation Bart. is not much used today but is not incorrect). (2) Dear Sir, conclude Yours faithfully. (3) Dear Sir John, conclude Yours sincerely.

BISHOP WITH A SEAT IN THE HOUSE OF LORDS—(1) The Right Reverend The Lord Bishop of Buxton. Or, The Right Reverend John Smith, Lord Bishop of Buxton. (2) My Lord Bishop, conclude I am, My Lord, Your Obedient Servant. (3) Dear Lord Bishop, Dear Bishop or Dear Bishop of Buxton, conclude Yours sincerely. The Lord is not used for Bishops not sitting in the Lords. Bishops suffragan are addressed by courtesy in the same way as diocesan bishops.

COUNTESS—(1) The Countess of Poole. (2) Dear Madam, conclude Yours faithfully. (3) Dear Lady Poole, conclude Yours sincerely.

DAME—(1) Dame Mary Smith, followed by appropriate post-nominal letters (e.g. DBE). (2) Dear Madam, conclude Yours faithfully. (3) Dear Dame Mary, conclude Yours sincerely.

DUCHESS—(1) Her Grace The Duchess of Avon. (2) Your Grace, conclude I am, Your Grace's Obedient Servant. (3) Dear Duchess of Avon, conclude Yours sincerely.

DUKE—(1) His Grace The Duke of Avon. (2) Your Grace, or My Lord Duke, conclude I am, Your Grace's Obedient Servant. (3) Dear Duke of Avon, conclude Yours sincerely.

EARL—(1) The Earl of Hethe. (2) My Lord, conclude I am my Lord Your Obedient Servant. (3) Dear Lord Hethe, conclude Yours sincerely.

GOVERNORS GENERAL, GOVERNORS AND LIEUTENANT GOVERNORS—As for Ambassadors but followed by description of office, such as Governor General and Commander-in-Chief of New Zealand. (3) Dear Governor General, Governor or Lieutenant-Governor, conclude Yours sincerely. The Lieutenant-Governors of Guernsey, Jersey and the Isle of Man enjoy this style. The Governor General of Canada has the style 'The Right Honourable' for life and a Lieutenant-Governor of a Canadian Province is 'His Honour' for life.

JUDGE (LORD JUSTICE OF APPEAL)—(1) The Right Honourable Sir John Smith, as he is invariably a Privy Counsellor and a Knight, or the Right Honourable Lord Justice Smith. (2) My Lord, conclude I am My Lord, Your Obedient Servant. (3) Dear Sir John, conclude Yours sincerely.

JUDGE (JUSTICE OF THE HIGH COURT)—(1) The Honourable Sir John Smith, as he is invariably a Knight, or The Honourable Mr Justice Smith. (2) and (3) as for a Lord Justice of Appeal.

JUDGE (CIRCUIT JUDGE)—(1) His Honour Judge Smith. (2) Your Honour, conclude I have the honour to be Your Honour's Obedient Servant. (3) Dear Sir (or Judge Smith), conclude Yours sincerely.

JUDGE (WOMEN JUDGES)—(1) The Right Honourable Dame Ann Smith, DBE (if a Lord of Appeal), The Honourable Dame Anne Smith, DBE (if a High Court Judge). (2) and (3) as for a male Judge with suitable gender changes.

KNIGHT—(1) Sir John Smith, if a Knight Bachelor there is no post-nominal addition in this respect but if a Knight or Knight Grand Cross or Grand Commander of an Order of Chivalry the appropriate post-nominal letters should be added. A Knight may be so addressed when his knighthood is announced, there is now no need to wait for the accolade to have been conferred. (2) Dear Sir, conclude Yours faithfully. (3) Dear Sir John, conclude Yours sincerely.

LORD LIEUTENANT—(1) The normal form of address, followed by, for courtesy, H.M.'s Lord Lieutenant for the County of Newshire. (2) My Lord Lieutenant, conclude I have the honour to be my Lord Lieutenant, Your Obedient Servant. (3) Dear Lord (Sir John or Mr. as appropriate), conclude Yours sincerely.

LORD OF SESSION IN SCOTLAND—(1) The Honourable (or Right Honourable if a Privy Counsellor), Lord Glentie. (2) My Lord, conclude I have the honour to be My Lord, Your Obedient Servant. (3) Dear Lord Glentie, conclude Yours sincerely. Note: The wife of a Lord of Session is styled as the wife of a Baron but her children have no courtesy titles. The Lord Justice General or Lord Justice Clerk is usually so addressed in correspondence, rather than by his juridical title.

MEMBER OF NATIONAL ASSEMBLY FOR WALES—Address according to rank with the addition of the letters AM after the name.

MEMBER OF NORTHERN IRELAND ASSEMBLY—Address according to rank with the addition of the letters MLA after the name.

MEMBER OF PARLIAMENT—(1) Address according to rank with the addition of the letters MP after the name. Privy Counsellors have the prefix 'The Right Honourable'. Letters to Ministers may start Dear Minister.

MEMBER OF SCOTTISH PARLIAMENT—Address according to rank with the addition of the letters MSP after the name.

PRIME MINISTER—The Prime Minister has the prefix 'The Right Honourable', as a Member of the Privy Council and the letters MP after the name, as a Member of Parliament. Letters to the Prime Minister may start Dear Prime Minister.

PRINCE—(1) HRH The Prince Henry of Wales or, if a Duke, HRH The Duke of Kent; the children of the Sovereign use the definite article before Prince (e.g. The Prince Edward). (2) Your Royal Highness or Sir, conclude I have the honour to be Your Royal Highness's Obedient Servant. In conversation address as Your Royal Highness but once is sufficient, thereafter Sir is normal.

PRINCESS—(1) HRH Princess Beatrice of York, or, if the wife of a Royal Duke, HRH The Duchess of Kent; a daughter of the Sovereign uses the definite article before Princess (e.g. The Princess Anne). (2) Your Royal Highness or Madam, conclude I have the honour to be Your Royal Highness's Obedient Servant. In conversation address as Your Royal Highness but once is sufficient, thereafter Ma'am (pronounced so as to rhyme with lamb) is normal.

PRIVY COUNSELLOR—(1) The Right Honourable prefixes the name and style except in respect of Marquesses and Dukes when the letters PC are placed after the name. The letters follow those indicating membership of Orders of Chivalry. (2) Address according to rank. (See also Member of Parliament).

QUEEN—(1) Her Majesty the Queen, although letters are usually addressed to The Private Secretary to Her Majesty the Queen. (2) Your Majesty or 'May it please your Majesty', conclude I have the honour to be Your Majesty's Obedient Subject. (3) Madam, conclude With my humble duty to Your Majesty. In conversation address as Your Majesty at first thereafter as Ma'am (see Princess).

Parliamentary Terms and Proceedings

For further details see Dod's *Handbook of House of Commons Procedure* by Paul Evans (8th edition, 2012) and Dod's *Handbook of House of Lords Procedure* by Mary Robertson and Thomas Elias (2nd edition, 2006).

References in ***bold italics*** have entries of their own.

accounting officer: the person (usually the permanent secretary of a government department or chief executive of an agency) responsible for accounting to Parliament, in respect of each of the ***Estimates*** (or part of such Estimate), for the resources voted by Parliament for the public service.

address: a motion for an address usually involves either House asking for some matter or request to be communicated to the sovereign.

adjournment motion: although technically a motion moved for the purpose of bringing to a conclusion a sitting, when it is rarely debated, such a motion is often used as a procedural device in the Commons for enabling a debate to take place without having to come to a conclusion in terms (see also ***general debate***).

adjournment debate: a debate on an ***adjournment motion*** (see also ***daily adjournment*** and ***general debate***).

affirmation: see ***oath***.

allocation of time motion: see ***guillotine***.

allotted days: in the Commons, the days allotted to debate a bill under a programme order or a guillotine, also the 20 days allotted each session as opposition days and the 35 days allotted in each session to **backbench business.**

ambit: the description of the scope of expenditure covered by an ***Estimate*** for moneys voted by Parliament for the public services (see also ***appropriation*** and ***Estimates***).

amendment: a proposal to change the terms of a motion or to alter a ***bill***.

annunciator: the television screens situated around Parliament and its precincts on which details of the current proceedings and future business of either House are shown.

appropriation: the allocation of money by Parliament to specified purposes. The Resource Accounts are the ***Comptroller & Auditor General***'s audited accounts showing that money has been spent in accordance with Parliament's instructions embodied in the ***Supply and Appropriation Acts*** (see also ***Consolidated Fund*** and ***Estimates***).

backbench: the backbenches are the places where Members who are not government Ministers or official opposition ***shadows*** sit in each Chamber, hence *backbencher*, the term used to describe a Member who holds no official position in government or in his or her party and who is therefore not bound by the convention of collective responsibility: such a Member may more formally be referred to as a private Member though, strictly speaking, this term applies to any Member not in receipt of a ministerial salary.

backbench business: in the Commons there are 35 days in each session allotted to business which is chosen by the ***Backbench Business Committee*** (27 in the main Chamber and 8 – in the form of 16 Thursday afternoon sessions – in Westminster Hall) which is not government business, ***opposition days*** or private Members' business.

Backbench Business Committee: the committee of the Commons of seven ***backbench*** Members elected by secret ballot of the whole House which is charged with choosing the business to be taken on the days allotted to ***backbench business***.

ballot: the term is used in the House of Commons to refer to the draw for private Members' bills. There is also provision for secret ballots in the House's proceedings relating to the election of its ***Speaker***, the ***Deputy Speakers***, the ***Backbench Business Committee*** and the Chairs of the principal ***select committees***.

Bar of the House: in the Commons, the line across the floor of the Chamber which marks its formal threshold: the Bar is also marked by a rail (now invariably retracted) to which, in former times, ***strangers*** might be summoned to address the House or to be arranged before it: in the Lords, this bar (about waist height) is where Members of the Commons stand to hear the **Queen's Speech** at the State Opening and on **prorogation**.

bill: a proposal for legislation formally presented to either House of Parliament; a bill may be a ***private bill*** or a ***public bill***.

Black Rod: the Gentleman Usher of the Black Rod, a member of the royal household, the broad equivalent in the Lords of the ***Serjeant at Arms***, responsible for the security of the House and sent to summon the Commons to the Lords at the opening and closing of ***sessions***.

book entry: in the Commons, an entry in the ***Votes and Proceedings*** which records as a procedural event something which occurred without any actual proceedings taking place on the floor of the House.

breach of privilege: an abuse of one of the privileges of either House or an attempt to impede or frustrate either House or one of their Members in the exercise of one of their privileges.

budget resolutions: the series of financial resolutions, passed by the House of Commons at the conclusion of the debate on the ***budget statement***, on which the ***Finance Bill*** is founded.

budget statement: the annual statement made by the Chancellor of the Exchequer (usually in March or April) setting out the government's tax and spending plans and proposals for their reconciliation for the forthcoming financial year: at the end of the debate on the budget, the ***budget resolutions*** are passed and the ***Finance Bill*** is introduced.

business motion: a motion proposing to regulate the time available to the Commons for consideration of a specified item of business at a specified sitting; in the Lords, a business of the House motion is moved by the Leader of the House to allow its standing orders to be suspended or varied or to make other arrangements for organising debates.

business question: in the Commons, the question addressed each Thursday to the ***Leader of the House*** under the urgent question procedure in reply to which the main items of business to be taken on each sitting day for the next week or so are announced.

by-election: an election in a single constituency to fill a vacancy caused by the death or ***disqualification***, etc. of a Member of Parliament (or in the Lords, to fill a vacancy amongst the elected hereditary peers).

C&AG: see ***Comptroller & Auditor General***.

Cabinet: the inner circle of the government to which the Minister in charge of each government department belongs (and certain other Ministers), presided over by the ***Prime Minister***.

casting vote: in the Commons, where any ***division*** (either in the House or in a ***general committee***) results in a tie, it is decided on the vote of the occupant of the Chair, which is given in accordance with precedent.

Central Lobby: the main public area of the Palace of Westminster, equidistant from the two Houses of Parliament, where members of the public are received by Members.

Chairman of Committees: in the Lords, the first Deputy Speaker and chairman of the panel of deputy speakers; also chairs the Committee of Selection, the Liaison Committee and the Procedure Committee, and has special responsibilities for ***private business*** and committees of the whole House.

Chairman of Ways and Means: in the Commons, the first Deputy Speaker, with particular responsibilities for ***private business*** and ***committees of the whole House*** and ***sittings in Westminster Hall***.

Chief Whip: the senior ***Whip*** in each party in each House: the government chief whips attend meetings of the Cabinet.

Chiltern Hundreds: the steward or bailiff of the three Chiltern Hundreds is the mythical 'office of profit under the Crown' to which Members of the Commons are appointed when wishing to resign their seats by disqualifying themselves from membership of the House (see ***disqualification***): the Stewardship of the Manor of Northstead is also used for this purpose.

Clandestine Outlawries Bill: the bill presented *proforma* in the Commons on the first day of each session; in the Lords the Select Vestries Bill; they each signify the right of Parliament to legislate on matters not included in the Queen's Speech.

Clerk Assistant: in each House, the second ***Clerk at the Table***, and first deputy to the ***Clerk of the House*** and the ***Clerk of the Parliaments***.

Clerks at the Table: the senior clerks in each Clerk of the House's Department who sit at the ***Table*** of the House.

Clerk of the House: the principal permanent officer of the House of Commons and principal adviser to the Speaker on the law, procedure and practice of the Commons; also the ***accounting officer*** for the House of Commons Vote.

Clerk of the Parliaments: the principal permanent officer of the House of Lords, and principal adviser to the Lord Speaker on the law, procedure and practice of the Lords. Also the House's ***accounting officer***.

closure: a procedural device for bringing a debate to a conclusion.

code of conduct: the codes adopted by each House to guide Members on questions relating to the interpretation of its resolutions in respect of the declarations in the ***Register of Members' Interests*** (***Register of Members' Financial Interests*** in the Commons), relating to financial and other relationships with outside persons and bodies.

command paper: a government publication (more often than not a ***White Paper***) presented to Parliament by 'command of Her Majesty'.

Commissioner for Standards: the officer of each House appointed to supervise the ***Register of Members' Financial Interests***, to advise Members on the interpretation of the ***code of conduct*** and to assist the ***Committee on Standards and Privileges*** in its work.

committal: the act of sending a ***bill*** to a committee of one kind or another after it has received a ***second reading***; in the Lords also called 'commitment'.

committee: see ***committee of the whole House, general committee, grand committee, joint committee, public bill committee, select committee***.

Committee for Privileges: in the Lords, the Committee which investigates allegations of breaches of privilege or contempts and peerage claims; it has a sub-committee on Lords' Interests.

Committee of Selection: in the Commons, the committee which appoints Members to ***general committees*** and proposes Members to ***select committees***; in the Lords the committee which proposes Members to most select committees.

Committee on Standards and Privileges: in the Commons, the select committee which investigates allegations of ***breaches of privilege***, ***contempts*** and, with the assistance of the ***Commissioner for Standards***, matters relating to the ***code of conduct***, in particular complaints about Members in relation to outside financial interests and related matters.

committee of the whole House: either House forms itself into a committee of all its Members when it decides to take the committee stage of a ***bill*** on the floor of the House.

committee stage: the next stage of a bill's progress after it has been given a ***second reading*** and committed; it is the stage at which a bill receives the most detailed examination. In the Commons, this generally takes place in a ***public bill committee***, sometimes in ***committee of the whole House***, and very occasionally in another type of committee. In the Lords, this may take place in committee of the whole House or in a Grand Committee, or very occasionally some other type of committee. After a bill has completed its committee stage it is reported back to the House for its ***report stage***.

Commons Amendments: amendments proposed by the Commons to a ***bill*** which has been sent to it by the Lords.

Comptroller & Auditor General: the officer of the House of Commons responsible for the running of the ***National Audit Office*** and for assisting the ***Public Accounts Committee*** in its scrutiny of public expenditure.

consideration: the more formal title for the ***report stage*** of a bill.

Consolidated Fund: the general fund into which almost all government receipts (in the form of taxes, duties, etc.) are paid (under section 10 of the Exchequer and Audit Act 1866) and out of which almost all government expenditure is met: Parliament passes the regular *Supply & Appropriation Bills* which appropriate to the government service out of the Fund the total sums voted for particular purposes by way of the ***Estimates***.

consolidation bill: a ***bill*** which consolidates much of the existing law on a particular subject into one convenient statute: because such bills do not (except within strict and very narrow limits) change the law, they are subject to special procedures distinct from the general procedures applying to public bills.

constituency: each Member of Parliament is elected by the voters in a single geographical division of the UK which is known as a constituency: each has a unique name given by the Boundary Commission, which also recommends the boundaries of each constituency and periodically reviews these. At present each has generally between 60,000 and 80,000 electors (though at the extremes there are wide variations for historical and geographical reasons. At present the UK is divided into 650 constituencies.

contempt: disobedience to, or defiance of, an order of either House, or some other insult to either House or its dignity or a ***breach of privilege***.

Crossbenches: Peers who do not take the Whip of any party in the House of Lords, otherwise 'independents', sit on the crossbenches which face the throne, and are known as 'Crossbench Peers'; however, not all independent peers join the group, which works as an administrative but not political collective. In the Commons those sitting on the few crossbenches are not recognised to speak by the Chair.

crown prerogative: essentially, prerogative actions are those which the executive may take without the sanction of Parliament: they include ***prorogation*** and ***dissolution*** of Parliament (though the latter is a statutory matter under the provisions in the 2011 Fixed-term Parliaments Act), the grant of honours, the declaration of war and, in some circumstances, the making of treaties with foreign governments.

CWH: see ***committee of the whole House***.

daily adjournment: the half-hour debate at the end of each day's sitting in the House of Commons at which a ***backbench*** Member has the opportunity to raise a matter with a Minister.

delegated legislation: legislation made by Ministers under powers granted to them in Acts of Parliament, usually by means of a ***statutory instrument***.

delegated legislation committees: in the Commons, the ***general committees*** which consider items of ***delegated legislation*** referred to them by the House.

departmental select committees: the select committees of the House of Commons established under standing orders to oversee the work of individual government departments.

Deputy Chairmen: the First and Second Deputy Chairmen of Ways and Means in the Commons, who with the ***Chairman of Ways and Means*** share with the ***Speaker*** the duties of presiding over the House. In the Lords, there is a panel of Deputy Chairmen who assist the ***Chairman of Committees***. There is a First Deputy Chairman, who chairs the European Union Committee.

Deputy Speakers: see **Chairman of Ways** and Means and **Deputy Chairmen.**

despatch box: two despatch boxes are situated at either side of the ***Table*** in each House and serve as lecterns for those leading debate (or answering questions) from the government and official opposition frontbenches.

dilatory motion: in the Commons a motion for the adjournment of debate or for the adjournment of the House or a committee moved for the purpose of superseding the business in hand.

Director General of the House of Commons: the officer responsible for the delivery of services to Members and the public.

Director of Parliamentary Broadcasting: the officer of both Houses responsible for day to day oversight of the broadcasting of their proceedings.

disqualification: there are a large number of offices the holding of which disqualify a person from sitting as a Member of the House of Commons. Broadly speaking these fall within the general disqualifying category of 'offices of profit under the Crown', though the holders of ministerial office (up to a maximum of 95) are exempt (see also ***Chiltern Hundreds***). There are also general disqualifications for civil servants, police officers, members of the armed forces, some judges and members of non-Commonwealth overseas legislatures. Also disqualified, in general terms, are persons ineligible to vote in a general election, for example Peers entitled to sit in the House of Lords, aliens, persons under the age of 18, sentenced prisoners and persons detained under the Mental Health Act. So too are bankrupts, under the Insolvency Act 1986. Members may also be disqualified after an election for breach of electoral law. In the Lords, peers under the age of 21, aliens, bankrupts and those convicted of treason are disqualified from membership.

dissolution: under the terms of the fixed-term Parliaments Act of 2011 dissolution normally takes place 17 days before the date fixed by statute for the next general election (the first Thursday in May in the fifth year following the last general election) unless an earlier dissolution is triggered by either a vote of two-thirds of the Members of the House of Commons or a vote of no confidence in the government followed by a failure to express confidence in a new government within a fortnight.

division: a vote, that is the means by which either House or one of their committees ascertains the number of Members for and against a proposition before it when the Chair's opinion as to which side is in the majority on a ***Question*** is challenged. A division in the House of Commons on a question which might otherwise take place after the moment of interruption may, in certain circumstances, be automatically deferred; deferred divisions are then taken by collecting voting papers from members on the following Wednesday afternoon.

division bell area: the area from within which it is deemed to be possible to reach the ***division lobbies*** within the period from the ringing of the ***division bells*** to the closing of the lobby doors during a ***division***.

division bells: the bells, situated in the House and its precincts and outbuildings which are rung to summon Members to vote in a ***division***. Their function has been largely superseded off the premises by electronic devices, activated by the ***Whips*** offices.

division lobbies: the lobbies running down either side of each Chamber through which Members must pass to register their votes in a ***division***.

draft bill: a bill presented to Parliament, and published more generally, in draft form (usually as a ***command paper***), to enable consultation on its form and contents to take place before a **bill** is formally introduced into one or other House; the number published has increased in recent years though not steadily; they are now regularly referred to a joint committee or taken up by a select committee for consideration and report.

early day motions: expressions of opinion by Members of the Commons on almost any subject which are published in the form of motions printed in the Notice Paper part of the ***Vote Bundle***, to which other Members may add their names to indicate support. They are not debated.

Ecclesiastical Committee: the statutory committee of Members of both Houses which considers Church of England ***Measures***.

Editor: the officer of the House of Commons in charge of the publication of the ***Official Report*** of debates in the Chamber and in ***general committees*** (aka ***Hansard***). The Lords has its own Hansard, overseen by the Editor of Debates.

EDM: see ***early day motions***.

Electoral Commission*:* the statutory body established under the Political Parties, Elections and Referendums Act 2000 which has wide-ranging responsibilities in respect of the conduct of elections and referendums and the registration of political parties and related matters. Its funding and work are overseen by a statutory committee of elected parliamentarians called the Speaker's Committee on the Electoral Commission.

English Votes for English Laws (EVEL): To account for the discrepancies caused by devolution and the so-called West Lothian question, a law was passed allowing a committee of MPs from English (or English and Welsh) constituencies to consent to or veto any Bills which would only affect England (or England and Wales).

Erskine May: Erskine May's *Treatise on the Law, Privileges, Proceedings and Usage of Parliament*, first published by the-then Assistant Librarian and subsequently ***Clerk of the House***, Thomas Erskine May in 1844, and revised by his successors as Clerk ever since: it is acknowledged as the authoritative text book on the law and practice of both Houses of Parliament: the latest edition is the 24th, edited by Sir Malcolm Jack (LexisNexis, London, 2011).

Estimates: the form in which the government presents, for approval by the Commons, its requests for the resources needed to cover recurring public expenditure.

Estimates days: the three days in each session set aside in the Commons for consideration of the Estimates, in practice used for debate on one or more select committee reports chosen by the ***Liaison Committee***.

European Committees: in the Commons, the group of ***general committees*** which consider documents referred to them by the European Scrutiny Committee relating to the EU.

Examiner of Petitions: the officer of each House with responsibility for examining certain matters relating to private bills and hybrid bills for compliance with the standing orders relating to ***private business***.

exempted business: business which, under standing orders or under a specific order of the House of Commons, may be carried on after the ***moment of interruption***.

Father of the House: see ***Senior Member***.

Finance Bill: the annual bill, founded on the ***budget resolutions***, which embodies the government's statutory power to levy most taxes and duties, and which may include other provisions relating to taxes management.

financial privilege: the right to approve proposals for taxation or for government expenditure which the Commons asserts as its exclusive privilege, not shared with the Lords.

financial resolutions: the collective term for ***money resolutions***, ***ways and means resolutions***, and ***supply resolutions***.

first reading: the formal first stage of a ***bill***'s progress, which occurs without debate or vote after it has been introduced to either House.

frontbench: the frontbenches are where Ministers and their official opposition ***shadows*** sit in each Chamber, hence *frontbencher* or *frontbench spokesman* (in the Commons the government frontbench is also known as the *Treasury Bench*).

general committees: the family of committees in the Commons (known until recently as ''standing committees'') which proceed principally by debate rather than inquiry; it includes ***delegated legislation committees***, ***European Committees***, ***grand committees*** and ***public bill committees***.

general debate: debates of a general nature which take place on the motion "that this House has considered [a specified matter]"; the motion is not amendable.

general election: an event initiated by the ***dissolution*** of Parliament under the provisions within the Fixed-term Parliaments Act 2011, when all seats are automatically vacated and elections must be held in each ***constituency*** to elect a Member of Parliament.

grand committees: in the Commons there are three grand committees for Scotland, Wales and Northern Ireland; they are general committees on which all Members having their constituency in the relevant country have an automatic place; in the case of Wales and Northern Ireland additional members from outside those countries may be added; the grand committees generally debate matters (including legislative proposals) relevant to the specific country; they may also conduct other types of proceedings including oral questions and statements. They sometimes meet away from Westminster. The term has a different meaning in the House of Lords, where it is applied to any proceedings of a ***committee of the whole House*** held in parallel with sittings in the main chamber.

guillotine: an order of the House of Commons which limits the time available to debate any stage or stages of a bill, now largely superseded by ***programme*** orders.

Hansard: the colloquial name for the ***Official Report***, the publication containing the accurate and full (though not strictly verbatim as often claimed) reports of what is said and done in the debates of each House and their committees (other than select committees).

health service commissioner: the officer of the House of Commons who acts as the ombudsman for the NHS in England who also holds the office of ***PCA*** and who reports to the Public Administration Select Committee: there are separate commissioners for Wales and Scotland reporting to the devolved legislatures.

House of Commons Commission: the executive body of Members responsible for the running of the House.

Individual Voter Registration: Under old rules one person per household registered everyone in the house to vote, but the new law means each person is responsible for registering themselves, and have to provide identifying information such as national insurance number for verification during the process.

insistence: when one House insists on its own version of the text of a bill or amendment during the exchange of messages ('ping pong') without offering an alternative or compromise.

instruction: after ***committal*** of a bill, either House may give an instruction to any committee to which it is committed to do certain things that the committee might not otherwise be empowered to do.

Joint Committee on Human Rights: a joint select committee of both Houses charged with examining bills, ***remedial orders*** and other matters relating to human rights in the UK.

joint committees: select committees which include Members of both Houses.

Journals: the ***Votes and Proceedings*** of the House of Commons and the ***Minute*** of the House of Lords are each consolidated into the Journals on a sessional basis and these form the authoritative record of the decisions of each House.

law commissions: the law commissions for England and Wales and for Scotland prepare proposals for reform of the law and also for its rationalisation by means of ***consolidation bills*** and statute law repeal bills.

Leader of the House: the Cabinet Minister charged with special responsibility for the management of the House of Commons and its business, part of the ***usual channels***. He or she is a member, *ex officio*, of the ***House of Commons Commission***. He or she also has responsibility for the cabinet committees dealing with the management of the Government's legislative programme. His or her name will frequently appear on motions relating to the business of the House, and he or she will initiate government proposals for the reform of its procedures. His or her most public role is the period of questioning which, each Thursday, follows the ***business question***. The Leader of the House of Lords is also a minister in the Cabinet and has similar responsibilities to those of the Leader of the Commons except that he or she also has a responsibility to the House as well as a responsibility to the Government.

leader of the opposition: the person elected leader of the second largest party in the House of Commons is the leader of the official opposition. He or she receives official recognition in this role in the receipt of a ministerial salary and appointment to the Privy Council. The leader of the opposition has certain well-entrenched conventional rights to initiate certain kinds of business, in particular to demand, and to expect in most circumstances to receive, an opportunity to move a motion of no confidence in the Government. He also has certain rights under standing orders (see ***official opposition***). In the Lords, the Leader of the Opposition is the leader of the second largest party in the Commons. He or she receives a salary.

leave: there are a number of types of proceeding which may only be done by leave of the House (or a committee). These include to speak more than once to a Question other than in committee, to withdraw a motion before the House or a committee and to move certain types of motion. Generally leave must be unanimous, that is, any single objection from any Member in the House or in a committee means that leave is thereby denied.

Liaison Committee: in the Commons the select committee consisting mainly of the Chairs of other select committees, which under standing orders has certain powers and duties in relation to the proceedings of the House, as well as a more informal role exercising oversight of the work, and as an advocate of the interests, of select committees in general. It also has a power to examine the Prime Minister on matters of public policy, and certain duties relating to National Policy Statements proposed to be made under the Planning Act 2008. The Lords also has a Liaison Committee, chaired by the Chairman of Committees, which oversees the work of its committees.

lobby correspondents: certain representatives of the various news media who have the authority of the ***Serjeant at Arms*** to enter the ***Members' Lobby*** when the House of Commons is sitting and who enjoy certain other privileges of access to areas of the Palace otherwise closed to persons apart from Members and permanent staff. They also subscribe to a code of conduct relating to the disclosure of the sources of their information (hence the expression 'on lobby terms').

Lord Speaker: Speaker of the House of Lords, having taken the role over from the Lord Chancellor in 2006. Elected by the House from amongst its Members.

Lords Amendments: the amendments proposed by the Lords to a ***bill*** which has been passed by the Commons.

Lords Commissioners: the Peers appointed by the Queen to deliver her ***proclamation*** proroguing Parliament and her ***royal assent*** to Acts agreed just before ***prorogation*** and any other Commission she chooses to send.

Loyal Address: the motion moved in reply to the ***Queen's Speech*** on which the debate on the Queen's Speech takes place.

Mace: the symbol of the Crown's authority in Parliament, which is displayed in each House whenever the House is in session.

maiden speech: the first speech delivered by a Member after he or she first enters the House. By convention, in the Commons, it includes a tribute to his or her predecessor, an encomium to his or her ***constituency***, and avoids controversy (though this latter tradition shows signs of dying out). Also, by tradition, it is heard without interruption from other Members. The latter two points apply also to maiden speeches in the House of Lords.

manuscript amendment: an amendment of which no ***notice*** has been given, which (in the Commons) is presented to the Chair during debate or (in the Lords) is circulated to Members in manuscript or typescript form.

marshalled list: a list of ***amendments*** proposed to a ***bill*** which has been arranged in the order in which the amendments will be considered at ***committee stage***, ***report stage*** or, in the Lords, third reading, rather than in the order in which they were received.

Measure: legislation made by the General Synod of the Church of England.

Member in charge: the Member in charge of a bill is the one who introduces it to the House, and he or she has certain prerogatives in relation to that bill. In the case of a government bill, any Minister (including a ***Whip***) may exercise the rights of the Member in charge.

Members' lobby: the area immediately outside the Commons Chamber generally reserved to Members and ***lobby correspondents*** and staff of the House when the House is sitting. The equivalent in the Lords is the 'Peers Lobby'.

Minister: a member of the government, usually entitled to receive a ministerial salary and bound by the convention of collective responsibility for decisions of government. For procedural purposes, the members of the government (including ***Whips***) are each regarded as being able to act on behalf of any other Minister.

Minute: the document produced after each sitting of the House of Lords recording decisions taken at that sitting and also setting out future business, questions for written answers and other information on the progress of procedural business.

moment of interruption: the time set by standing orders in the House of Commons at which the main business of a day's sitting normally ends after which business may only be taken if it is ***exempted business*** or unopposed business. Currently the moment of interruption is 10 pm on Mondays and Tuesdays, 7 pm on Wednesdays, 6 pm on Thursdays and 2.30 pm on Fridays.

money bill: a bill which is concerned exclusively with raising or spending public money and which, under the terms of the ***Parliament Acts***, cannot be amended by the Lords.

money resolution: a ***resolution*** of the House of Commons, agreed on a motion which may only be moved by a ***Minister***, authorising the provisions of a ***bill*** which entail novel forms of public expenditure.

naming: a Member who persistently defies the authority of the Chair in the House of Commons ma *named* by the Chair, which immediately causes a motion to be moved to suspend the Member fron service of the House.

National Audit Office: the office under the direction of the ***Comptroller & Auditor General*** w audits the expenditure of government departments.

National Policy Statement Committee: a select committee designated by the Commons ***Li Committee*** to consider a proposal for a National Policy Statement which a Minister has laid befo House under 5.9 of the Planning Act 2008. It has between 7 and 14 members drawn fro Communities and Local Government; Energy and Climate Change; Environment, Food and Affairs; Transport and Welsh Affairs Committees.

Northstead, Manor of: see ***Chiltern Hundreds***.

notice: where it is a requirement of standing orders or the rules of the House that a motion r notice, it means that such a motion cannot be moved unless it appears on the ***Order Paper***. I circumstances, the latest time for giving notice of a motion to appear on a Paper for the next sitt is the rising of the House on the previous day. While there is no formal requirement for n amendments to bills in committee or on report, the Chair will generally not select ***mar amendments*** or ***starred amendments*** for debate. This does not apply in the Lords where ma amendments may be moved on Committee and at Report stage without notice. Written notice is of oral and written ***PQ***s except ***urgent questions*** (Private Notice Questions in the Lords) anc ***questions*** in the Commons. In the Commons, but not in the Lords, notice is required of presen bills.

Notice Paper: the blue pages of the **Vote Bundle** include the Notice Papers for notices of c notices of motions for future days, notices of early day motions and notices of amendments to

oath: on their election at a general election or a ***by-election***, each Member of the Commons i to take the parliamentary oath or to make the required affirmation before taking his or Witnesses before a committee of the House may also be required to take an oath before giving though this requirement is generally only imposed on witnesses before a private bill commit Lords, Members take the oath on their first introduction and at the start of each ***session***.

official opposition: the Party with the second largest number of Members in the House of C the official opposition, a status which gains it certain privileges by long-standing conventi the right of its official spokespeople to sit on the ***frontbench*** and to address the House from th ***box***) as well as certain rights under the standing orders (to initiate debate on the majority of ***days***) and by statute (such as for certain of its officers to receive ministerial salaries). To a privileges are shared by members of that same party in the House of Lords.

Official Report: see ***Hansard***.

ombudsman: see ***Parliamentary Commissioner for Administration***.

opposition days: the 20 days each session set aside under standing orders of the House of which the opposition parties have the right to choose the business for debate.

oral question: see ***PQ***.

order: when either House agrees a motion that something should happen (such as a bill b for a second reading or for consideration) it becomes an order of the House (see also ***re*** word is also commonly used in the House of Commons to connote procedural regula expression 'in order') or to correct parliamentary behaviour (as in the Chair's call of which is also used as a form of oral procedural 'punctuation'). In the Lords the word "u the same meaning as "out of Order" in the Commons.

Order Paper: the paper, published each sitting day (except the first day of a ***session***), business of each House and for any sitting in Westminster Hall (or in a Grand Committ for that day, as well as ***parliamentary questions*** (PQs) for oral answer to be asked th written answer that day, and certain other items such as notices of ***written statem*** notices, ***remaining orders*** (in the Commons) and lists of future business.

Outlawries Bill: see ***Clandestine Outlawries Bill***.

PAC: see ***Public Accounts Committee***.

Parliament Acts: the Parliament Act 1911 as amended and supplemented by the Parliament Act 1949 restrict the powers of the Lords to amend ***money bills*** or reject or delay other ***bills*** agreed by the Commons.

Panel of Chairs: in the Commons, the body of Members appointed by the ***Speaker*** from among whom he chooses the Chair of each ***general committee***. They receive an additional payment for this work. In the Lords, there is a panel of Deputy Chairmen who assist the ***Chairman of Committees***.

Parliamentary Commissioner for Administration: the officer of the House of Commons appointed under statute to investigate complaints of maladministration leading to injustice in the public service, commonly known as the ombudsman. His or her work is overseen by the Public Administration Select Committee (see also ***health service commissioner***).

Parliamentary Commissioner for Standards: see ***Commissioner for Standards***.

Parliamentary Counsel: the civil servants (all lawyers) who draft ***bills*** on the instruction of the government, not to be confused with the ***Speaker's Counsel*** or Counsel of the Chairman of Committees or other lawyers working directly to either House.

parliamentary question: a question addressed (generally) to a Minister for answer orally on the floor of the House at question time, or in writing in ***Hansard***.

PCA: see ***Parliamentary Commissioner for Administration***.

PNQ: see ***urgent question***.

PQ: see ***parliamentary question***.

point of order: properly, a request by a Member of the Commons to the Chair for elucidation of, or a ruling on, a question of procedure, but not infrequently misused by Members who do not have the floor of the House or of a committee to interrupt proceedings for other purposes.

prayers: each sitting of each House begins with prayers, conducted by the Speaker's Chaplain in the Commons or a Bishop in the Lords. The term is also used colloquially to describe a motion to annul a ***statutory instrument*** subject to negative resolution procedure; and to designate the final paragraph of a ***public petition***.

prerogative: see ***Crown prerogative***.

press gallery: the gallery of the Chamber of the Commons above and behind the Speaker's Chair reserved to accredited representatives of the various news media, also used more generally to describe the large area outside and behind this gallery given over to the use of journalists etc. and also to describe collectively the accredited members of the press gallery (see also ***lobby correspondents***). In the Lords there is a much smaller Press Gallery, at the far end from the Throne.

Prime Minister: the First Lord of the Treasury and the head of the government; the person who is elected the leader of the party which can sustain a majority (either alone or in coalition) in the Commons.

Prince of Wales's consent: see ***Queen's consent***.

private bill: a bill to confer on individuals, or more commonly corporate bodies of one kind or another, powers in excess of or in contradiction to the general law.

private business: the business of each House for the most part relating directly or indirectly to ***private bills***.

Private Member's bill: a ***public bill*** introduced to either House by a Member who is not a ***Minister***.

private notice question: the former name for what is now called an ***urgent question*** in the Commons. The term is still used in the House of Lords.

privilege: a privilege enjoyed by either House collectively or its Members individually in excess of the general law, which enables it or them to fulfil the functions and duties of the House.

Privy Counsellor: a Member of the Queen's Privy Council, the body of senior royal advisers whicl former times was something equivalent to the ***Cabinet***, membership of which is now confe automatically on Cabinet Ministers and also on certain senior judges; it is also by convention grante the leaders of parties of any size in the Commons and is occasionally conferred as a mark of honou senior backbenchers and occasionally others outside these circles. The Council retains certain jud functions and residual executive functions. Membership once conferred is for life, unless withdraw entitles the holder to the courtesy of the title 'Right Honourable' as in 'the Right Honourable Me for Witney'. In written form this is usually abbreviated to 'Rt Hon'.

Procedure Committee: ***select committees*** of each House appointed to consider proposals fo reform of their procedures.

proclamation: the Queen issues proclamations for the **prorogation** and summoning Parliament.

programme: an order made by the House of Commons after a ***bill***'s ***second reading*** to timetab subsequent proceedings on that bill.

prorogation: the end of a ***session***.

Public Accounts Commission: the statutory committee of elected parliamentarians whi oversight of the ***National Audit Office***.

Public Accounts Committee: the ***select committee*** of the House of Commons, which works with the ***Comptroller & Auditor General*** and the ***National Audit Office***, with particular respo for ensuring propriety, efficiency, economy and effectiveness in the spending of public money.

public bill: a proposal for legislation to change the general law; most bills introduced into eithe by the government or by private Members are public bills; a minority are ***private bills***.

public bill committee: in the Commons the ***committee stage*** of proceedings on a public bill i taken in a public bill committee (until recently a 'standing committee'). Each committee is app *hoc* to consider each bill and ceases to exist once that bill is reported back to the House. P committees are ***general committees***, but exceptionally in this category, they have power to tal and oral evidence from witnesses, in the manner of ***select committees***, at some of their sittings

Public Bill Office: the office in each House with particular responsibility for the mana legislation and (in the Commons) for clerking the ***public bill committees*** and other ***general c*** of the House.

public gallery: the gallery of each Chamber in which members of the public may sit to proceedings; there is also an area designated for the same purpose in each committee r ***sittings in Westminster Hall***.

public petition: a petition to either House (but generally to the Commons) for redress of a g other relief.

Queen's consent: where the legislation proposed in a ***bill*** touches on the prerogative interests of the Crown, her consent is required for the bill to proceed: this may be required either before the ***second reading*** or ***third reading*** (or, conceivably, before ***first reading***), d the nature of the interest and the extent to which it is fundamental to the bill's purposes. C be obtained from the Queen by a Minister and must be signified at the appropriate tim ***Counsellor***. The Prince of Wales's consent may also be required, as the heir to the throne, l bills may be debated at certain stages.

Queen's recommendation: only the government can propose increases in public expen recommendation of the 'Crown' is therefore required for a motion in the Commons whic increase or widen the scope of public expenditure: such a motion can therefore be mo Minister.

Queen's Speech: the speech read by the Queen from her throne in the Lords Chamber on each ***session*** setting out, among other matters, details of the government's propo programme.

question: see ***parliamentary question***.

Question: in procedural jargon, the matter before either House or a committee awaiting time.

Questions Book: a daily publication of the House of Commons divided into two parts: Part 1 lists all questions for written answer on that day, Part 2 lists all outstanding PQs for oral or written answer on future days.

question time: the period set aside for ***PQ***s to be asked and answered orally on the floor of either House.

quorum: The minimum number of members needed to be present at a sitting to make proceedings valid. The quorum of the House of Commons is 40 but only for divisions; the quorum for a ***sitting in Westminster Hall*** is three; the quorum of a ***general committee*** (except a ***European Committee***) is one-third of its members, with fractions rounded up; the quorum of a European Committee is three of its appointed members, not including the Chair; the quorum of a ***select committee*** is one-third of its membership or three, whichever is the greater, unless otherwise set out in the standing orders or its order of appointment. The quorum of the Lords is 30 for legislative business or otherwise three.

reasoned amendment: an amendment proposed to the motion to give a ***bill*** a ***second reading*** or ***third reading***.

recess: strictly speaking, the period when Parliament is prorogued; now used to refer to either House's regular holiday adjournments at Christmas, in February, at Easter, at Whitsun and in the summer.

Register of Members' Financial Interests: (in the Lords, Register of Members' Interests) the registers, published annually, in which Members of either House record their outside financial interests and the receipt of gifts, free travel, etc.

Registrar of Members' Financial Interests: (in the Lords, Registrar of Members' Interests) the officers of each House responsible for the maintenance of the ***Register of Members' Financial Interests***.

remaining orders: the list of forthcoming government business published with the ***Order Paper*** of the House of Commons each day.

remedial order: a form of ***delegated legislation*** which remedies an incompatibility between UK law and the European Convention on Human Rights.

report stage: the stage of a ***bill***'s progress in each House between its ***committee stage*** and its ***third reading***, at which further detailed amendments may be made.

resolution: when a motion is agreed by either House, it becomes a resolution (unless it is an ***order***).

resource accounts: the audited accounts of ***voted expenditure*** authorised by the ***Estimates***.

return: an answer or response to an address from either House for the deposit of same document.

royal assent: the Queen's assent to a ***bill*** agreed to by both Houses of Parliament is the final act which makes that bill an Act of Parliament.

royal recommendation: see ***Queen's recommendation***.

seconder: no seconder is required for a motion to be proposed to either House, but by tradition the motion for the ***Loyal Address*** is seconded.

second reading: the first stage at which a ***bill*** is debated (and possibly voted on) in each House.

select committees: committees established by either House to inquire into particular matters or subject areas and to report back their findings and recommendations. In the Commons most are appointed permanently, and have members who remain on them for a Parliament unless replaced (and for most of them their Chairs are separately elected by secret ballot of the whole House); some are appointed ad hoc and cease to exist once they have reported on the matter which the House has referred to them. In the Lords most committees are appointed each session. Members remain on them for several ***sessions*** but are subject to a rotation rule.

Select Vestries Bill – see ***Clandestine Outlawries Bill***.

Senior Member: the Member of the House of Commons who has the longest *continuous* period of service in the House, also known as the ***Father of the House***.

Serjeant at Arms: the officer of the House of Commons responsible for security and ceremonial.

session: the period between the state opening of Parliament and its prorogation or dissolution, in t past this has generally been a year running from November to November, but was often altered by t timing of general elections; the present government has indicated its intention to run sessions norma from May to April.

shadow: broadly speaking, the official opposition appoints or elects Members of its party to 'shadc each government Minister, that is, to take particular responsibility for presenting in and out Parliament the policies of the opposition for the areas which are that ***Minister***'s responsibility, he 'Shadow Home Secretary' etc (also called *frontbench spokesmen or spokeswomen or spokesperson*

shuffle: the process by which the ***PQ***s for oral answer in the Commons are randomly sorte determine which Members' questions will be printed on the ***Order Paper*** on any given day, and in order.

sitting: a single meeting of either House or one of their committees.

sittings in Westminster Hall: the 'parallel chamber' of the House of Commons which meets i Grand Committee Room off Westminster Hall on Tuesdays, Wednesdays and Thursdays. On Tue and Wednesdays it debates subjects chosen by ***backbench*** Members in timed slots of either an and-a-half or half-an-hour; on Thursdays it debates reports from ***select committees*** chosen b ***Liaison Committee***, or subjects selected by the ***Backbench Business Committee***, for three hou decisions are taken at sittings in Westminster Hall, and all its proceedings take place as ***adjour debates***.

Speaker: the impartial presiding officer of the House of Commons: in the Lords the Lord Speak their deputies have far fewer formal powers than their Commons equivalents.

Speaker's Counsel: officers of the House who head its **legal services office**, including those providing legal advice to the **Speaker** and to certain of the committees of the House.

standing committee: see ***general committees***.

standing orders: the rules formulated by each House to regulate their own proceedings.

starred amendment: an amendment to a bill which has not appeared on a notice paper suf before the sitting at which it is to be considered; as a rule, the Chair in the Commons will not se an amendment for debate (see also ***notice***). No such problem arises in the Lords.

state opening: the occasion on the first day of each ***session*** on which the Queen usually atter House of Lords to deliver the ***Queen's Speech***.

statutory instruments: the form in which most ***delegated legislation*** is made.

strangers: the traditional and now obsolete appellation for anyone who is not a Member, official of the House.

Supply and Appropriation Bills/Acts: the twice yearly Acts of Parliament which giv authority to the appropriations made by the House of Commons in agreeing the ***Estimates***.

supply resolution: one of the ***resolutions*** on which the ***Supply and Appropriation bills*** are f

Table: the Table of the House, situated between the government and opposition ***frontbencl*** House; in former times this was the place where motions, questions, reports etc. were delive possession of the House *via* the Clerks, hence 'tabled' or 'laid upon the Table'.

Table Office: in the Commons the office, situated outside the Chamber of the Common Speaker's Chair, in which ***PQ***s and ***EDM***s are tabled; it also deals with all matters rel business on the floor of the House other than legislation. In the Lords, the office situa Prince's Chamber where all business is tabled (including questions) and where the ***Minute***

ten-minute-rule bill: a ***bill*** introduced into the Commons where the Member seeking the House to introduce the bill, and a Member who opposes granting it, may each make a before the House comes to a decision on whether to allow the bill to proceed.

Test Roll: the Test Roll must be signed by each new Member after he or she has take affirmed after being elected or appointed to either House.

third reading: the final stage of a whole ***bill***'s passage through either House, Amendments or Commons Amendments to the bill may subsequently be considered.

topical debate: a debate on a motion "That this House has considered [a specified matter]", on a topic chosen by the ***Backbench Business Committee***. It may last no more than 90 minutes and both frontbench and backbench speeches are time-limited.

topical questions: a procedure whereby the last few minutes of oral question time to particular Ministers are devoted to questions of which no notice needs to be given of the terms of the question; the choice of Members who have the opportunity to ask a topical question is determined by an electronic ballot (see ***shuffle***) of those who have entered their names for a particular question time in advance.

urgent question: an oral parliamentary question in the Commons asked with the consent of the Speaker without published ***notice*** relating to an urgent and important matter. In the Lords, called a ***Private Notice Question***, or PNQ.

usual channels: the colloquial name for the discussions about the business of each House which take place between the ***Whips*** and the Leaders of each House, and in the Lords sometimes (but not always) including the Convenor of the Crossbench Peers.

voted expenditure: the Commons' agreement to an ***Estimate*** followed by a ***Supply and Appropriation Act*** represents the detailed ***appropriation*** of public money to the public service by Parliament.

Votes and Proceedings: the daily minute of the Commons' proceedings.

Vote Bundle: the papers published each day on which the House of Commons sits, including among other things the ***Order Paper***, the ***remaining orders***, the ***Votes and Proceedings***, and the ***notice*** papers (in the Lords the ***Minute*** serves the same general purpose).

ways and means resolution: a ***resolution*** authorising a charge on the people, that is, for the most part, taxes and duties: the ***Finance Bill*** is founded on ways and means resolutions.

Westminster Hall: the oldest remaining part of the Palace of Westminster, now used solely as a public area and for occasional ceremonial purposes (see also ***sittings in Westminster Hall***.)

Whips: the officers of each party in each House with particular responsibilities for party management and organisation of the business of the House and its committees.

White Paper: a ***command paper*** embodying some statement of government policy, often including proposals for legislation.

writ: the issue of a writ is the formal process for initiating a **by-election** (or indeed a general election) in the Commons. In the Lords, new Members are summoned by writ, and all Members receive a writ of summons at the beginning of a new Parliament.

written statement: a vehicle which may be used by a ***minister*** to inform either House on various types of matter relating to his or her responsibilities; they are published in ***Hansard***.

Abbreviations

ABRO	Army Base Repair Organisation
ACA	Associate, Institute of Chartered Accountants
ACAS	Advisory, Conciliation and Arbitration Service
ACPO	Association of Chief Police Officers
ACRE	Action with Communities in Rural England
AcSS	Academy of Learned Societies for the Social Statistics
ADC	Aide-de-camp
AEEU	Amalgamated Engineering and Electrical Union
AEF	Amalgamated Union of Engineering and Foundry Workers
AEU	Amalgamated Engineering Union
AFC	Air Force Cross
AIB	Associate, Institute of Bankers
AIESC	Association Internationale des Étudiants en Sciences Économiques et Commerciales
ALDE	Alliance of Liberals and Democrats for Europe
All	Alliance Party of Northern Ireland
AM	Assembly Member (National Assembly for Wales) (London Assembly)
AMP	Advanced Management Program; Air Member for Personnel
AO	Officer, Order of Australia
APEX	Association of Professional, Executive, Clerical and Computer Staff
ARA	Associate, Royal Academy
ARCM	Associate, Royal College of Music
ARCS	Associate, Royal College of Science
ARICS	Professional Associate, Royal Institution of Chartered Surveyors
ASBAH	Association for Spina Bifida and Hydrocephalus
ASLEF	Associated Society of Locomotive Engineers and Firemen
ATII	Associate Member, Incorporated Institute of Taxation
AUEW	Amalgamated Union of Engineering Workers
BA	Bachelor of Arts
BAFTA	British Academy of Film and Television Arts
BALPA	British Air Line Pilots' Association
BAOR	British Army on the Rhine
BChir	Bachelor of Surgery
BCL	Bachelor of Civil Law
BCom	Bachelor of Commerce
BD	Bachelor of Divinity
BDS	Business Development Service
BE	Bachelor of Engineering
BEc	Bachelor of Economics
BECTU	Broadcasting, Entertainment, Cinematograph and Theatre Union
BEd	Bachelor of Education
BEM	British Empire Medal
BFI	British Film Institute
BIC	British-Irish Council
BIGC	British-Irish Governmental Conference
BIS	Department for Business, Innovation and Skills
BLitt	Bachelor of Literature
BMA	British Medical Association
BMus	Bachelor of Music
BNP	British National Party
BOAC	British Overseas Airways Corporation
BP	British Petroleum
BS	Bachelor of Surgery

BSocSci	Bachelor of Social Science
Bt	Baronet
BT	British Telecom
Bus-Pass	Bus Pass Elvis Party
BVC	Bar Vocational Course
CAFCASS	Children and Family Court Advisory and Support Service
CAFOD	Catholic Aid Fund for Overseas Development
CAMRA	Campaign for Real Ale
CAP	Common Agricultural Policy
CB	Companion of the Order of the Bath; Crossbench
CBC	County Borough Council
CBE	Commander of the Order of the British Empire
CBI	Confederation of British Industry
CBIM	Companion, British Institute of Management
CBRN	Chemical, Biological, Radiological and Nuclear
CCHQ	Conservative Party Campagn Headquarters
CCIM	Certified Commercial Investment Member
CCS	Carbon Capture and Storage
CDipAF	Certified Diploma in Accounting and Finance
CEFAS	Centre for Environment, Fisheries and Aquaculture Science
CEng	Chartered Engineer
CEOP	Child Exploitation and Online Protection
CERT	Carbon Emissions Reduction Target
Cert Ed	Certificate of Education
CESP	Community Energy Saving Programme
CFP	Common Fisheries Policy
CH	Companion of Honour
ChB	Bachelor of Surgery
ChM	Master of Surgery
CIE	Companion of the Order of the Indian Empire
CIMA	Chartered Institute of Management Accountants
CIMgt	Companion, Institute of Management
CIPFA	Chartered Institute of Public Finance and Accountancy
CIS	Institute of Chartered Secretaries and Administrators
CLP	Constituency Labour Party
CMEC	Child Maintenance and Enforcement Commission
CMG	Companion of the Order of St Michael and St George
CND	Campaign for Nuclear Disarmament
CoE	Church of England
COI	Central Office of Information
Con	Conservative Party
COPD	Chronic Obstructive Pulmonary Disease
PA	Commonwealth Parliamentary Association; Christian Peoples Alliance
PE	Common Professional Examination
Phys	Chartered Physicist
PRE	Campaign to Protect Rural England
PS	Crown Prosecution Service
Psychol	Chartered Psychologist
QSW	Certificate of Qualification in Social Work
	Created
A	Child Support Agency; Chief Scentific Adviser
SCE	Conference on Security and Co-operation in Europe
SI	Committee on the Intelligence Services; Companion of the Order of the Star of India
SL	Central Science Laboratory

CStJ	Commander, Most Venerable Order of the Hospital of St. John of Jerusalem
CVO	Commander of the Royal Victorian Order
CWU	Communication Workers Union
DARA	Defence Aviation Repair Agency
DASA	Defence Analytical Services Agency
DBA	Doctor of Business Administration
DBE	Dame Commander of the Order of the British Empire
DCB	Dame Commander of the Order of the Bath
DCL	Doctor of Civil Law
DCLG	Department for Communities and Local Government
DCM	Distinguished Conduct Medal
DCMG	Dame Commander of the Order of St Michael and St George
DCMS	Department for Culture, Media and Sport/Digital, Culture, Media and Sport
DCSA	Defence Communication Services Agency
DCSF	Department for Children, Schools and Families
DCVO	Dame Commander of the Royal Victorian Order
DD	Doctor of Divinity
DECC	Department of Energy and Climate Change
DEFRA	Department of the Environment, Food and Rural Affairs
DFC	Distinguished Flying Cross
DExEU	Department for Exiting the European Union
DFID	Department for International Development
DFM	Distinguished Flying Medal
DfT	Department for Transport
DH	Department of Health
DHSS	Department of Health and Social Security
DipAgriSci	Diploma in Agricultural Science
DipEd	Diploma in Education
DipObst	Diploma in Obstetrics
DIUS	Department for Innovation, Universities and Skills
DIT	Department for International Trade
DL	Deputy Lieutenant
Dlitt	Doctor of Letters; Doctor of Literature
DMS	Diploma in Management Studies
DoE	Department of Environment
DoJ	Department of Justice (Northern Ireland)
DPH	Diploma in Public Health
DPhil	Doctor of Philosophy
DPM	Diploma, Personnel Management; Diploma, Psychological Medicine
DSC	Distinguished Service Cross
DSc	Doctor of Science
DSDA	Defence Storage and Distribution Agency
DSO	Distinguished Service Order
DSocSci	Doctor of Social Science
DST	Defence Science and Technology
DStJ	Dame of Grace/or Dame of Justice, Order of the Hospital of St John Jerusalem
Dstl	Defence Science and Technology Laboratory
DTI	Department of Trade and Industry
DTMA	Defence Transport and Movements Agency
DU	Doctor of the University
DUniv	Doctor of the University
DUP	Democratic Unionist Party
DVA	Defence Vetting Agency
DWP	Department for Work and Pensions

EC	European Community
ECGD	Export Credits Guarantee Department
ECHR	European Convention on Human Rights
ECO	Energy Company Obligation
Econ	Economics
ECR	European Conservatives and Reformists Group
EdD	Doctor of Education
EFCW	European Forum for Child Welfare
EFD	Europe of Freedom and Democracy Group
EIA	Environmental Investigation Agency
EMR	Electricity Market Reform
EMU	Economic and Monetary Union
Eng Dem	English Democrats
EPLP	European Parliament Labour Party
ERD	Emergency Reserve Decoration (Army)
ESRC	Economic and Social Research Council
ETS	Emissions Trading System; Employment Tribunals Service
ETUC	European Trade Union Confederation
EU	European Union
EUL-NGL	European United Left-Nordic Green Left Confederal Group
FACS	Fellow, American College of Surgeons
FArbA	Fellow, Arboricultural Association
FBA	Fellow, British Academy
FBIM	Fellow, British Institute of Management
FC	Football Club
FCA	Fellow, Chartered Accountant
FCCA	Fellow, Chartered Association of Certified Accountants
FCGI	Fellow, City and Guilds
FCILT	Fellow, Chartered Institute of Logistics and Transport
FCIM	Fellow, Chartered Institute of Marketing
FCIPS	Fellow, Chartered Institute of Purchasing and Supply
FCIT	Fellow, Chartered Institute of Transport
FCMA	Fellow, Chartered Institute of Management Accountants
FCO	Foreign and Commonwealth Office
FCP	Fellow, College of Physicians
FCPA	Fellow, Australian Society of Certified Practising Accountants
FCPaed	Fellow, College of Paediatrics
FCPsych	Fellow, College of Psychiatrists
FDA	Association of First Division Civil Servants
FE	Further Education
FHCIMA	Fellow, Hotel, Catering and Institutional Management Association
FICE	Fellow, Institution of Civil Engineers
FICPD	Fellow, Institute of Continuing Professional Development
FIEE	Fellow, Institution of Electrical Engineers
FILA	Fellow, Institute of Landscape Architects
FIMechE	Fellow, Institution of Mechanical Engineers
FIMgt	Fellow, Institute of Management
FIMI	Fellow, Institute of the Motor Industry
FIMM	Fellow, Institute of Mining and Metallurgy
FIMT	Fellow, Institute of the Motor Trade
FInstD	Fellow, Institute of Directors
FInstM	Fellow, Institute of Marketing
FInstP	Fellow, Institute of Physics
FInstPet	Fellow, Institute of Petroleum
FInstPS	Fellow, Institute of Purchasing and Supply

FIPA	Fellow, Institute of Practitioners in Advertising
FIPR	Fellow, Institute of Public Relations
FIQA	Fellow, Institute of Quality Assurance
FIRTE	Fellow, Institute of Road Transport Engineers
FITs	Feed-in Tariffs
FKC	Fellow, King's College, London
FLA	Fellow, Library Association
FMA	Fellow, Museums Association
FMedSci	Fellow, Academy of Medical Sciences
FMI	Foundation for Manufacturing and Industry
FO	Foreign Office
FRAeS	Fellow, Royal Aeronautical Society
FRAM	Fellow, Royal Academy of Music
FRAME	Fund for the Replacement of Animals in Medical Experiments
FRCA	Fellow, Royal College of Anaesthetists; Fellow, Royal College of Art
FRCN	Fellow, Royal College of Nursing
FRCOG	Fellow, Royal College of Obstetricians and Gynaecologists
FRCOphth	Fellow, Royal College of Ophthalmologists
FRCP	Fellow, Royal College of Physicians
FRCPath	Fellow, Royal College of Pathologists
FRCPCH	Fellow, Royal College of Paediatrics and Child Health
FRCPSGlas	Fellow, Royal College of Physicians and Surgeons, Glasgow
FRCPsych	Fellow, Royal College of Psychiatrists
FRCS	Fellow, Royal College of Surgeons of England
FRCVS	Fellow, Royal College of Veterinary Surgeons
FREng	Fellow, Royal Academy of Engineering
FRGS	Fellow, Royal Geographical Society
FRHistS	Fellow, Royal Historical Society
FRIBA	Fellow, Royal Institute of British Architects
FRPS	Fellow, Royal Photographic Society
FRRME	Foundation for Relief and Reconciliation in the Middle East
FRS	Fellow, The Royal Society
FRSA	Fellow, Royal Society of Arts
FRSE	Fellow, Royal Society of Edinburgh
FRSH	Fellow, Royal Society for the Promotion of Health
FRSS	Fellow, Royal Statistical Society
FSA	Fellow, Society of Antiquaries; Financial Services Authority
FSAA	Fellow, Society of Incorporated Accountants and Auditors
FSB	Fellow, Society of Biology
GBE	Knight or Dame Grand Cross of the Order of the British Empire
GC	George Cross
GCB	Knight or Dame Grand Cross of the Order of the Bath
GCFO	Group Chief Financial Officer
GCHQ	Government Communication Headquarters
GCIE	Knight Grand Commander, Order of the Indian Empire
GCMG	Knight or Dame Grand Cross of the Order of St Michael and St George
GCSI	Knight Grand Commander, Order of the Star of India
GCVO	Knight or Dame Grand Cross of the Royal Victorian Order
GLC	Greater London Council
GMB	General Municipal Boilermakers Union
GMBATU	General, Municipal, Boilermakers and Allied Trades Union (see GMB)
GMES	Global Monitoring of Environmental Security
GMOs	Genetically Modified Organisms
GMW	General Municipal Boilermakers and Allied Trades Union
GMWU	General Municipal Workers' Union

GNN	Government News Network
GPMU	Graphical, Paper, Media Union
GPO	General Post Office
Green	Green Party
Greens-EFA	Greens-European Free Alliance
GSM	General Service Medal
HCIMA	Hotel and Catering International Management Association
HE	His/Her Excellency; Higher Education
HEFCE	Higher Education Funding Council for England
HMCI	Her Majesty's Chief Inspector
HMMTB	Her Majesty's Motor Torpedo Boat
HMT	Her Majesty's Treasury
Hon	Honorary; Honourable
HP	Hereditary Peer
IAG	Information, Advice and Guidance
IB	Incapacity Benefit
ICAEW	Institute of Chartered Accountants in England and Wales
ICFTU	International Confederation of Free Trade Unions
ICI	Imperial Chemical Industries
ICT	Information Communications Technology
IDeA	Improvement and Development Agency for Local Government
IFAW	International Fund for Animal Welfare
IISS	International Institute of Strategic Studies
ILEA	Inner London Education Authority
IMEDE	Institut pour l'Etude des Methodes de Direction de l'Entreprise
IMF	International Monetary Fund
Ind	Independent
Ind Con	Independent Conservative
Ind Lab	Independent Labour
Ind Lib Dem	Independent Liberal Democrat
Ind Soc Dem	Independent Social Democrat
Ind UU	Independent Ulster Unionist
INSEAD	Institut Européen d'Administration des Affaires
IPP	Immigrants Political Party
IPSA	Independent Parliamentary Standards Authority
IPU	Inter-Parliamentary Union
ITU	International Telecommunication Union (UN)
JCR	Junior Common Room
JIC	Joint Intelligence Committee
JMC	Joint Ministerial Committee
JNCC	Joint Nature Conservation Committee
JP	Justice of the Peace
JSD	Doctor of Juristic Science
KBE	Knight Commander of the Order of the British Empire
KCB	Knight Commander of the Order of the Bath
KCIE	Knight Commander of the Order of the Indian Empire
KCMG	Knight Commander of the Order of St Michael and St George
KCSI	Knight Commander of the Order of the Star of India
KCVO	Knight Commander of the Royal Victorian Order
KG	Knight of the Order of the Garter
KM	Knight of Malta
KP	Knight, Order of St Patrick
KRRC	King's Royal Rifle Corps
KStJ	Knight of the Most Venerable Order of the Hospital of St John of Jerusalem
KT	Knight of the Order of the Thistle

Kt	Knight Bachelor; knighted
Lab	Labour Party
Lab/Co-op	Labour Co-operative
LAMDA	London Academy of Music and Dramatic Art
LAPADA	Association for Professional Art and Antiques Dealers
LCC	London County Council
LCO	Legislative Competence Order
LDS	Licentiate in Dental Surgery
LEA	Local Education Authority
LEAF	Linking Environment And Farming
LG	Lady Companion, Order of the Garter
LGIU	Local Government Information Unit
LGSM&D	Licentiate, Guildhall School of Music and Drama
Lib Dem	Liberal Democrat
LIBiol	Licentiate, Institute of Biology
LLB	Bachelor of Laws
LLD	Doctor of Laws
LLM	Master of Laws
LLP	Limited Liability Partnership
LOL	Loyal Orange Lodge
LP	Life Peer
LRAM	Licentiate, Royal Academy of Music
LRCP	Licentiate, Royal College of Physicians, London
LSE	London School of Economics
Lt	Lieutenant
LVO	Lieutenant of the Royal Victorian Order
MA	Master of Arts
MAFF	Ministry of Agriculture, Fisheries and Food
MALD	Master of Arts in Law and Diplomacy
MB	Bachelor of Medicine
MBA	Master of Business Administration
MBC	Metropolitan Borough Council
MBE	Member of the Order of the British Empire
MBL	Master in Business Leadership
MC	Military Cross
MCC	Marylebone Cricket Club
MD	Doctor of Medicine
MDC	Metropolitan District Council
ME	Myalgic Encephalomyelitis
MEd	Master of Education
MENA	Middle East North Africa
MENCAP	Royal Society for Mentally Handicapped Children and Adults
MEP	Member of the European Parliament
MFCM	Member, Faculty of Community Medicine
MIBiol	Member, Institute of Biology
MICE	Member, Institution of Civil Engineers
MIMechE	Member, Institution of Mechanical Engineers
MIMinE	Member, Institution of Mining Engineers
MInstP	Member, Institute of Physics
MIPD	Member, Institute of Personnel and Development
MLA	Member of Legislative Assembly (Northern Ireland Assembly)
Mlitt	Master of Letters
MM	Military Medal
MoD	Ministry of Defence
MoJ	Ministry of Justice

MP	Member of Parliament
MPH	Master of Public Health
MPhil	Master of Philosophy
MRCGP	Member, Royal College of General Practitioners
MRCP	Member, Royal College of Physicians
MRCPsych	Member, Royal College of Psychiatrists
MRCS	Member, Royal College of Surgeons
MS	Master of Surgery
MSF	Manufacturing Science Finance Union
MSP	Member of Scottish Parliament
MTh	Master of Theology
MVO	Member of the Royal Victorian Order
NA	Non-Affiliated; Non-attached Group; National Academician (USA)
NACF	National Art Collections Fund
NAO	National Audit Office
NATO	North Atlantic Treaty Organisation
NATS	National Air Traffic Services
NCB	National Coal Board
NCVO	National Council for Voluntary Organisations
NCVQ	National Council for Vocational Qualifications
NDA	Nuclear Decommissioning Agency
NDPB	Non-Departmental Public Body
NEC	National Executive Committee
NEDC	National Economic Development Council
NEET	Not in Education, Employment or Training
NESTA	National Endowment for Science, Technology and the Arts
NFU	National Farmers' Union
NGO	Non-governmental Organisation
NHA	National Health Action Party
NHS LIFT	NHS Local Improvement Finance Trust
NHSPASA	NHS Purchasing and Supply Agency
NI	Northern Ireland
NICE	National Institute for Health and Clinical Excellence
NICS	Northern Ireland Civil Service
NINOs	National Insurance Numbers
NIO	Northern Ireland Office
NIPS	Northern Ireland Prison Service
NOMS	Naitional Offender Management Service
nr	near
NSPCC	National Society for Prevention of Cruelty to Children
NUJ	National Union of Journalists
NUM	National Union of Mineworkers
NUR	National Union of Railwaymen
NUT	National Union of Teachers
NVQ	National Vocational Qualification
OBE	Officer of the Order of the British Empire
OC	Officer, Order of Canada
OCSC	Office of the Civil Service Commissioners
ODI	Overseas Development Institute
OECD	Organisation for Economic Co-Operation and Development
OFCOM	Office of Communications
Ofgem	Office of Gas and Electricity Markets
OfMDFM	Office of the First Minister and Deputy First Minister
Ofqual	Office of Qualifications and Examinations Regulator
OFSTED	Office for Standards in Education

OFT	Office of Fair Trading
OFWAT	Office of Water Services
OGC	Office of Government Commerce
OJ	Order of Jamaica
OM	Order of Merit
OSCE	Organisation on Security and Co-operation in Europe
OStJ	Officer of the Most Venerable Order of the Hospital of St John of Jerusalem
OUP	Oxford University Press
PC	Privy Counsellor
PCC	Press Complaints Commission
PFI	Private Finance Initiative
PGCE	Post Graduate Certificate of Education
PhD	Doctor of Philosophy
PlC	Plaid Cymru
PLP	Parliamentary Labour Party
PMOS	Prime Minister's Official Spokesman
POST	Parliamentary Office of Science and Technology
PPP	Public Private Partnerships
PPS	Parliamentary Private Secretary; Principal Private Secretary
PR	Proportional Representation; public relations
PSA	Public Services Agreement
PUS	Parliamentary Under-Secretary; Permanent Under-Secretary
QC	Queen's Counsel
QCDA	Qualifications and Curriculum Development Agency
QIPP	Quality, Innovation, Productivity and Prevention
QPM	Queen's Police Medal
QSO	Queen's Service Order (New Zealand)
RA	Royal Academician; Royal Regiment of Artillery
RAC	Royal Automobile Club; Royal Agricultural College; Royal Armoured Corps
RADA	Royal Academy of Dramatic Art
RAFVR	Royal Air Force Volunteer Reserve
RAMC	Royal Army Medical Corps
RC	Roman Catholic
RCAC	Royal Canadian Armoured Corps
RCDS	Royal College of Defence Studies
RCVS	Royal College of Veterinary Surgeons
RD	Royal Naval and Royal Marine Forces Reserve Decoration
RDC	Rural District Council
RDPE	Rural Development Programme for England
RFC	Rugby Football Club
RGS	Royal Geographical Society
RHI	Renewable Heat Incentive
RICS	Royal Institution of Chartered Surveyors
RIIA	Royal Institute of International Affairs
RLFC	Rugby League Football Club
RMA	Royal Military Academy
RMN	Registered Mental Nurse
RMT	Rail, Maritime and Transport Union
RN	Royal Navy
RNLI	Royal National Lifeboat Institute
RNR	Royal Navy Reserve
RNVR	Royal Naval Volunteer Reserve
RoSPA	Royal Society for the Prevention of Accidents
RPA	Rural Payments Agency
RPA	Raising Participation Age

RPMS	Royal Postgraduate Medical School
RSA	Royal Society of Arts
RSC	Royal Society of Chemistry
RSO	Resident Surgical Officer
RSPCA	Royal Society for Prevention of Cruelty to Animals
Rt Hon	Right Honourable
RTS	Royal Television Society
RUFC	Rugby Union Football Club
RUSI	Royal United Services Institute
S&D	Progressive Alliance of Socialists and Democrats
SBS	Small Business Service
SCAA	School Curriculum and Assessment Authority
SCCRC	Scottish Criminal Cases Review Commission
ScD	Doctor of Science
SCE	Service Children's Education
SCS	Senior Civil Servant
SDA	Scottish Development Agency
SDLP	Social Democratic and Labour Party
SDSR	Strategic Defence and Security Review
SEN	Special Education Needs
SF	Sinn Féin
SFO	Serious Fraud Office
SMEs	Small and Medium Enterprises
SNP	Scottish National Party
SOCA	Serious Organised Crime Agency
SOGAT	Society of Graphical and Allied Trades
SpAds	Special Advisers
SQA	Scottish Qualifications Authority
SRB	Single Regeneration Budget
SRC	Science Research Council
SSA	Standard Spending Assessment
SSAFA	Soldiers, Sailors, Airmen and Families Association
SSC	Solicitor before Supreme Court (Scotland)
SSRC	Social Science Research Council
STV	Single Transferable Vote
SVQ	Scottish Vocational Qualification
TA	Territorial Army
TD	Territorial Efficiency Decoration
TGWU	Transport and General Workers Union
TLB	Top Level Budget
TSSA	Transport Salaried Staffs' Association
TUC	Trades Union Congress
TUSC	Trade Unionist and Socialist Coalition
TUV	Traditional Unionist Voice Party
UAE	United Arab Emirates
UCATT	Union of Construction, Allied Trades and Technicians
UDC	Urban District Council
UKIP	UK Independence Party
UKTI	United Kingdom Trade and Investment
UMIST	University of Manchester Institute of Science and Technology
UNA	United Nations Association
UNCRC	United Nations Convention on the Rights of the Child
UNCTAD	United Nations Conference on Trade and Development
UNDP	United Nations Development Programme
UNEP	United Nations Environment Programme

UNESCO	United Nations Educational, Scientific and Cultural Organisation
UNHCR	United Nations High Commissioner for Refugees
UNICEF	United Nations Children's Fund
UNISON	(an amalgamation of COHSE, NALGO and NUPE)
Unite	(an amalgamation of Amicus and the Transport and General Workers' Union)
UPW	Union of Postal Workers
USDAW	Union of Shop Distributive and Allied Workers
UTC	University Teaching Colleges
UUP	Ulster Unionist Party
UUUC	United Ulster Unionist Coalition
UWP	University of Wales Press
VAT	Value Added Tax
VC	Victoria Cross
VFR	Victims Final Right Party
VR	Volunteer Reserve
VRD	Royal Naval Volunteer Reserve Officers' Decoration
VSO	Voluntary Service Overseas
WAAF	Women's Auxiliary Air Force
WEA	Workers' Educational Association
WEU	Western European Union
WHO	World Health Organisation (UN)
WMO	World Meteorological Organisation (UN)
WS	Writer to the Signet
WWF	World Wide Fund for Nature
YF	Yorkshire First
YMCA	Young Men's Christian Association
YPLA	Young People's Learning Agency

Index of Members of Parliaments and Assemblies

Abbott, Diane *(Lab)* MP 63
Abrahams, Debbie *(Lab)* MP 63
Adam, George *(SNP)* MSP 1092
Adams, Nigel *(Con)* MP 64
Adamson, Clare *(SNP)* MSP 1092
Afolami, Bim *(Con)* MP 64
Afriyie, Adam *(Con)* MP 64
Agnew, Steven *(Green)* MLA 1142
Aiken, Stephen *(UUP)* MLA 1143
Aldous, Peter *(Con)* MP 65
Alexander, Heidi *(Lab)* MP 65
Ali, Rushanara *(Lab)* MP 66
Allan, Alasdair *(SNP)* MSP 1092
Allan, Lucy *(Con)* MP 66
Allen, Andy *(UUP)* MLA 1143
Allen, Heidi *(Con)* MP 66
Allin-Khan, Rosena *(Lab)* MP 67
Allister, Jim *(TUV)* MLA 1143
Amesbury, Mike *(Lab)* MP 67
Amess, David *(Con)* MP 67
Andrew, Stuart *(Con)* MP 68
Antoniazzi, Tonia *(Lab)* MP 68
Antoniw, Mick *(Lab/Co-op)* AM 1125
ap Iorwerth, Rhun *(PlC)* AM 1125
Archibald, Caoimhe *(Sinn Féin)* MLA 1143
Argar, Edward *(Con)* MP 69
Armstrong, Kellie *(All)* MLA 1143
Arthur, Tom *(SNP)* MSP 1092
Asghar, Mohammad *(Con)* AM 1126
Ashworth, Jon *(Lab/Co-op)* MP 69
Atkins, Victoria *(Con)* MP 70
Austin, Ian *(Lab)* MP 70

Bacon, Richard *(Con)* MP 70
Badenoch, Kemi *(Con)* MP 71
Bailey, Adrian *(Lab/Co-op)* MP 71
Bailey, Clare *(Green)* MLA 1143
Baillie, Jackie *(Lab)* MSP 1092
Baker, Claire *(Lab)* MSP 1092
Baker, Steve *(Con)* MP 72
Baldwin, Harriett *(Con)* MP 72
Balfour, Jeremy *(Con)* MSP 1092
Ballantyne, Michelle *(Con)* MSP 1093
Barclay, Steve *(Con)* MP 73
Bardell, Hannah *(SNP)* MP 73
Baron, John *(Con)* MP 74
Barron, Kevin *(Lab)* MP 74
Barton, Rosemary *(UUP)* MLA 1143
Beamish, Claudia *(Lab/Co-op)* MSP 1093
Beattie, Colin *(SNP)* MSP 1093
Beattie, Doug *(UUP)* MLA 1143
Bebb, Guto *(Con)* MP 75
Beckett, Margaret *(Lab)* MP 75
Beggs, Roy *(UUP)* MLA 1143
Bellingham, Henry *(Con)* MP 76
Benn, Hilary *(Lab)* MP 76
Bennett, Gareth *(UKIP)* AM 1126
Benyon, Richard *(Con)* MP 77
Bercow, John *(Speaker)* MP 78
Beresford, Paul *(Con)* MP 79
Berger, Luciana *(Lab/Co-op)* MP 79
Berry, Jake *(Con)* MP 80
Betts, Clive *(Lab)* MP 80
Bibby, Neil *(Lab/Co-op)* MSP 1093
Black, Mhairi *(SNP)* MP 81
Blackford, Ian *(SNP)* MP 81
Blackman, Bob *(Con)* MP 81
Blackman, Kirsty *(SNP)* MP 82
Blackman-Woods, Roberta *(Lab)* MP 82
Blomfield, Paul *(Lab)* MP 83
Blunt, Crispin *(Con)* MP 83
Blythyn, Hannah *(Lab)* AM 1126
Boles, Nick *(Con)* MP 84
Bone, Peter *(Con)* MP 84
Bottomley, Peter *(Con)* MP 85
Bowden, Dawn *(Lab)* AM 1126
Bowie, Andrew *(Con)* MP 85
Bowman, Bill *(Con)* MSP 1093
Boylan, Cathal *(Sinn Féin)* MLA 1143
Boyle, Michaela *(Sinn Féin)* MLA 1143
Brabin, Tracy *(Lab/Co-op)* MP 86
Bradley, Ben *(Con)* MP 86
Bradley, Karen *(Con)* MP 86
Bradley, Maurice *(DUP)* MLA 1144
Bradley, Paula *(DUP)* MLA 1144
Bradley, Sinéad *(SDLP)* MLA 1144
Bradshaw, Ben *(Lab)* MP 87
Bradshaw, Paula *(All)* MLA 1144
Brady, Graham *(Con)* MP 87
Brady, Mickey *(Sinn Féin)* MP 88
Brake, Tom *(Lib Dem)* MP 88
Brennan, Kevin *(Lab)* MP 89
Brereton, Jack *(Con)* MP 89
Bridgen, Andrew *(Con)* MP 90
Briggs, Miles *(Con)* MSP 1093
Brine, Steve *(Con)* MP 90
Brock, Deidre *(SNP)* MP 91
Brokenshire, James *(Con)* MP 91
Brown, Alan *(SNP)* MP 91
Brown, Keith *(SNP)* MSP 1093
Brown, Lyn *(Lab)* MP 92
Brown, Michelle *(UKIP)* AM 1126
Brown, Nick *(Lab)* MP 92
Bruce, Fiona *(Con)* MP 93
Bryant, Chris *(Lab)* MP 93
Bryant, Jayne *(Lab)* AM 1126
Buchanan, Keith *(DUP)* MLA 1144
Buchanan, Thomas *(DUP)* MLA 1144
Buck, Karen *(Lab)* MP 94
Buckland, Robert *(Con)* MP 94
Buckley, Jonathan *(DUP)* MLA 1144
Bunting, Joanne *(DUP)* MLA 1144
Burden, Richard *(Lab)* MP 95
Burghart, Alex *(Con)* MP 96
Burgon, Richard *(Lab)* MP 96
Burnett, Alexander *(Con)* MSP 1093
Burns, Angela *(Con)* AM 1126
Burns, Conor *(Con)* MP 96
Burt, Alistair *(Con)* MP 97
Butler, Dawn *(Lab)* MP 97
Butler, Robbie *(UUP)* MLA 1144
Byrne, Liam *(Lab)* MP 98

Cable, Vince *(Lib Dem)* MP 99
Cadbury, Ruth *(Lab)* MP 99
Cairns, Alun *(Con)* MP 100
Cameron, Donald *(Con)* MSP 1093
Cameron, Lisa *(SNP)* MP 100
Cameron, Pam *(DUP)* MLA 1144
Campbell, Aileen *(SNP)* MSP 1094

Campbell, Alan *(Lab)*	MP	101
Campbell, Gregory *(DUP)*	MP	101
Campbell, Ronnie *(Lab)*	MP	102
Carden, Dan *(Lab)*	MP	102
Carlaw, Jackson *(Con)*	MSP	1094
Carmichael, Alistair *(Lib Dem)*	MP	102
Carroll, Gerry *(PBPA)*	MLA	1144
Carson, Finlay *(Con)*	MSP	1094
Cartlidge, James *(Con)*	MP	103
Cash, Bill *(Con)*	MP	103
Catney, Pat *(SDLP)*	MLA	1144
Caulfield, Maria *(Con)*	MP	104
Chalk, Alex *(Con)*	MP	104
Chambers, Alan *(UUP)*	MLA	1144
Champion, Sarah *(Lab)*	MP	104
Chapman, Douglas *(SNP)*	MP	105
Chapman, Jenny *(Lab)*	MP	105
Chapman, Peter *(Con)*	MSP	1094
Charalambous, Bambos *(Lab)*	MP	105
Cherry, Joanna *(SNP)*	MP	106
Chishti, Rehman *(Con)*	MP	106
Chope, Christopher *(Con)*	MP	106
Churchill, Jo *(Con)*	MP	107
Clark, Colin *(Con)*	MP	107
Clark, Greg *(Con)*	MP	108
Clarke, Kenneth *(Con)*	MP	108
Clarke, Simon *(Con)*	MP	109
Clarke, Trevor *(DUP)*	MLA	1144
Cleverly, James *(Con)*	MP	109
Clifton-Brown, Geoffrey *(Con)*	MP	110
Clwyd, Ann *(Lab)*	MP	110
Coaker, Vernon *(Lab)*	MP	111
Coffey, Ann *(Lab)*	MP	111
Coffey, Therese *(Con)*	MP	112
Coffey, Willie *(SNP)*	MSP	1094
Cole-Hamilton, Alexander *(Lib Dem)*	MSP	1094
Collins, Damian *(Con)*	MP	112
Constance, Angela *(SNP)*	MSP	1094
Cooper, Julie *(Lab)*	MP	113
Cooper, Rosie *(Lab)*	MP	113
Cooper, Yvette *(Lab)*	MP	114
Corbyn, Jeremy *(Lab)*	MP	114
Corry, Maurice *(Con)*	MSP	1094
Costa, Alberto *(Con)*	MP	115
Courts, Robert *(Con)*	MP	115
Cowan, Ronnie *(SNP)*	MP	116
Cox, Geoffrey *(Con)*	MP	116
Coyle, Neil *(Lab)*	MP	116
Crabb, Stephen *(Con)*	MP	117
Crausby, David *(Lab)*	MP	117
Crawford, Bruce *(SNP)*	MSP	1094
Crawley, Angela *(SNP)*	MP	118
Creagh, Mary *(Lab)*	MP	118
Creasy, Stella *(Lab/Co-op)*	MP	119
Crouch, Tracey *(Con)*	MP	119
Cruddas, Jon *(Lab)*	MP	120
Cryer, John *(Lab)*	MP	120
Cummins, Judith *(Lab)*	MP	121
Cunningham, Alex *(Lab)*	MP	121
Cunningham, Jim *(Lab)*	MP	122
Cunningham, Roseanna *(SNP)*	MSP	1095
Dakin, Nic *(Lab)*	MP	122
Dallat, John *(SDLP)*	MLA	1145
Davey, Ed *(Lib Dem)*	MP	122
David, Hefin *(Lab)*	AM	1126
David, Wayne *(Lab)*	MP	123
Davidson, Ruth *(Con)*	MSP	1095
Davies, Alun *(Lab/Co-op)*	AM	1126
Davies, Andrew R T *(Con)*	AM	1127
Davies, Chris *(Con)*	MP	124
Davies, David *(Con)*	MP	124
Davies, Geraint *(Lab/Co-op)*	MP	125
Davies, Glyn *(Con)*	MP	125
Davies, Mims *(Con)*	MP	126
Davies, Paul *(Con)*	AM	1127
Davies, Philip *(Con)*	MP	126
Davies, Suzy *(Con)*	AM	1127
Davis, David *(Con)*	MP	126
Day, Martyn *(SNP)*	MP	127
Debbonaire, Thangam *(Lab)*	MP	127
De Cordova, Marsha *(Lab)*	MP	128
Denham, Ash *(SNP)*	MSP	1095
Dent Coad, Emma *(Lab)*	MP	128
De Piero, Gloria *(Lab)*	MP	128
Dey, Graeme *(SNP)*	MSP	1095
Dhesi, Tanmanjeet Singh *(Lab)*	MP	129
Dickson, Stewart *(All)*	MLA	1145
Dillon, Linda *(Sinn Féin)*	MLA	1145
Dinenage, Caroline *(Con)*	MP	129
Djanogly, Jonathan *(Con)*	MP	129
Docherty, Leo *(Con)*	MP	130
Docherty-Hughes, Martin *(SNP)*	MP	130
Dockerill (*now* Lopez), Julia *(Con)*	MP	131
Dodds, Anneliese *(Lab/Co-op)*	MP	131
Dodds, Nigel *(DUP)*	MP	132
Dolan, Jemma *(Sinn Féin)*	MLA	1145
Donaldson, Jeffrey *(DUP)*	MP	132
Donelan, Michelle *(Con)*	MP	133
Doris, Bob *(SNP)*	MSP	1095
Dornan, James *(SNP)*	MSP	1095
Dorries, Nadine *(Con)*	MP	133
Double, Steve *(Con)*	MP	134
Doughty, Stephen *(Lab/Co-op)*	MP	134
Dowd, Peter *(Lab)*	MP	134
Dowden, Oliver *(Con)*	MP	135
Doyle-Price, Jackie *(Con)*	MP	135
Drakeford, Mark *(Lab)*	AM	1127
Drax, Richard *(Con)*	MP	135
Drew, David *(Lab/Co-op)*	MP	136
Dromey, Jack *(Lab)*	MP	136
Duddridge, James *(Con)*	MP	137
Duffield, Rosie *(Lab)*	MP	137
Dugdale, Kezia *(Lab/Co-op)*	MSP	1095
Duguid, David *(Con)*	MP	138
Duncan, Alan *(Con)*	MP	138
Duncan Smith, Iain *(Con)*	MP	139
Dunne, Gordon *(DUP)*	MLA	1145
Dunne, Philip *(Con)*	MP	139
Durkan, Mark H *(SDLP)*	MLA	1145
Eagle, Angela *(Lab)*	MP	140
Eagle, Maria *(Lab)*	MP	140
Easton, Alex *(DUP)*	MLA	1145
Eastwood, Colum *(SDLP)*	MLA	1145
Edwards, Jonathan *(PlC)*	MP	141
Efford, Clive *(Lab)*	MP	141
Elis-Thomas, Dafydd *(Ind)*	AM	1127
Elliott, Julie *(Lab)*	MP	142
Ellis, Michael *(Con)*	MP	142
Ellman, Louise *(Lab/Co-op)*	MP	143
Ellwood, Tobias *(Con)*	MP	143
Elmore, Chris *(Lab)*	MP	144
Elphicke, Charlie *(Con)*	MP	144
Ennis, Sinéad *(Sinn Féin)*	MLA	1145
Esterson, Bill *(Lab)*	MP	145
Eustice, George *(Con)*	MP	145

Evans, Chris *(Lab/Co-op)* MP 146
Evans, Nigel *(Con)* MP 146
Evans, Rebecca *(Lab/Co-op)* AM 1127
Evennett, David *(Con)* MP 147
Ewing, Annabelle *(SNP)* MSP 1095
Ewing, Fergus *(SNP)* MSP 1096

Fabiani, Linda *(SNP)* MSP 1096
Fabricant, Michael *(Con)* MP 148
Fallon, Michael *(Con)* MP 148
Farrelly, Paul *(Lab)* MP 149
Farron, Tim *(Lib Dem)* MP 150
Farry, Stephen *(All)* MLA 1145
Fearon, Megan *(Sinn Féin)* MLA 1145
Fee, Mary *(Lab)* MSP 1096
Fellows, Marion *(SNP)* MP 150
Fernandes, Suella *(Con)* MP 150
Field, Frank *(Lab)* MP 151
Field, Mark *(Con)* MP 151
Finch-Saunders, Janet *(Con)* AM 1127
Findlay, Neil *(Lab)* MSP 1096
Finnie, John *(Green)* MSP 1096
Fitzpatrick, Jim *(Lab)* MP 152
FitzPatrick, Joe *(SNP)* MSP 1096
Fletcher, Colleen *(Lab)* MP 153
Flint, Caroline *(Lab)* MP 153
Flynn, Órlaithí *(Sinn Féin)* MLA 1145
Flynn, Paul *(Lab)* MP 154
Forbes, Kate *(SNP)* MSP 1096
Ford, David *(All)* MLA 1146
Ford, Vicky *(Con)* MP 154
Foster, Arlene *(DUP)* MLA 1146
Foster, Kevin *(Con)* MP 155
Fovargue, Yvonne *(Lab)* MP 155
Fox, Liam *(Con)* MP 155
Foxcroft, Vicky *(Lab)* MP 156
Francois, Mark *(Con)* MP 156
Fraser, Murdo *(Con)* MSP 1096
Frazer, Lucy *(Con)* MP 157
Freeman, George *(Con)* MP 157
Freeman, Jeane *(SNP)* MSP 1097
Freer, Mike *(Con)* MP 158
Frew, Paul *(DUP)* MLA 1146
Frith, James *(Lab)* MP 158
Furniss, Gill *(Lab)* MP 159
Fysh, Marcus *(Con)* MP 159

Gaffney, Hugh *(Lab)* MP 159
Gale, Roger *(Con)* MP 160
Gapes, Mike *(Lab/Co-op)* MP 160
Gardiner, Barry *(Lab)* MP 161
Garnier, Mark *(Con)* MP 162
Gauke, David *(Con)* MP 162
George, Russell *(Con)* AM 1127
George, Ruth *(Lab)* MP 163
Gething, Vaughan *(Lab/Co-op)* AM 1128
Gethins, Stephen *(SNP)* MP 163
Ghani, Nusrat *(Con)* MP 163
Gibb, Nick *(Con)* MP 164
Gibson, Kenneth *(SNP)* MSP 1097
Gibson, Patricia *(SNP)* MP 164
Gildernew, Colm *(Sinn Féin)* MLA 1146
Gildernew, Michelle *(Sinn Féin)* MP 164
Gill, Nathan *(Ind)* AM 1128
Gill, Preet Kaur *(Lab/Co-op)* MP 165
Gillan, Cheryl *(Con)* MP 165
Gilruth, Jenny *(SNP)* MSP 1097
Girvan, Paul *(DUP)* MP 166
Givan, Paul *(DUP)* MLA 1146
Glen, John *(Con)* MP 166
Glindon, Mary *(Lab)* MP 167
Godsiff, Roger *(Lab)* MP 167
Golden, Maurice *(Con)* MSP 1097
Goldsmith, Zac *(Con)* MP 168
Goodman, Helen *(Lab)* MP 168
Goodwill, Robert *(Con)* MP 169
Gougeon, Mairi *(SNP)* MSP 1097
Gove, Michael *(Con)* MP 169
Grady, Patrick *(SNP)* MP 170
Graham, Luke *(Con)* MP 170
Graham, Richard *(Con)* MP 170
Grahame, Christine *(SNP)* MSP 1097
Grant, Bill *(Con)* MP 171
Grant, Helen *(Con)* MP 171
Grant, Peter *(SNP)* MP 172
Grant, Rhoda *(Lab/Co-op)* MSP 1097
Gray, Iain *(Lab)* MSP 1097
Gray, James *(Con)* MP 172
Gray, Neil *(SNP)* MP 173
Grayling, Chris *(Con)* MP 173
Green, Chris *(Con)* MP 174
Green, Damian *(Con)* MP 174
Green, Kate *(Lab)* MP 175
Greene, Jamie *(Con)* MSP 1098
Greening, Justine *(Con)* MP 175
Greenwood, Lilian *(Lab)* MP 176
Greenwood, Margaret *(Lab)* MP 176
Greer, Ross *(Green)* MSP 1098
Grieve, Dominic *(Con)* MP 177
Griffin, Mark *(Lab)* MSP 1098
Griffith, Nia *(Lab)* MP 177
Griffiths, Andrew *(Con)* MP 178
Griffiths, John *(Lab/Co-op)* AM 1128
Griffiths, Lesley *(Lab)* AM 1128
Grogan, John *(Lab)* MP 178
Gruffydd, Llyr *(PlC)* AM 1128
Gwenllian, Siân *(PlC)* AM 1128
Gwynne, Andrew *(Lab)* MP 179
Gyimah, Sam *(Con)* MP 179

Haigh, Louise *(Lab)* MP 180
Hair, Kirstene *(Con)* MP 180
Halcro Johnston, Jamie *(Con)* MSP 1098
Halfon, Robert *(Con)* MP 180
Hall, Luke *(Con)* MP 181
Hamilton, Fabian *(Lab)* MP 181
Hamilton, Neil *(UKIP)* AM 1128
Hamilton, Rachael *(Con)* MSP 1098
Hamilton, Simon *(DUP)* MLA 1146
Hammond, Philip *(Con)* MP 182
Hammond, Stephen *(Con)* MP 182
Hancock, Matt *(Con)* MP 183
Hands, Greg *(Con)* MP 184
Hanna, Claire *(SDLP)* MLA 1146
Hanson, David *(Lab)* MP 184
Hardy, Emma *(Lab)* MP 185
Harman, Harriet *(Lab)* MP 185
Harper, Emma *(SNP)* MSP 1098
Harper, Mark *(Con)* MP 185
Harrington, Richard *(Con)* MP 186
Harris, Alison *(Con)* MSP 1098
Harris, Carolyn *(Lab)* MP 186
Harris, Rebecca *(Con)* MP 187
Harrison, Trudy *(Con)* MP 187
Hart, Simon *(Con)* MP 187
Harvie, Patrick *(Green)* MSP 1098

Haughey, Clare *(SNP)*	MSP	1098
Hayes, Helen *(Lab)*	MP	188
Hayes, John *(Con)*	MP	188
Hayman, Sue *(Lab)*	MP	189
Hazzard, Chris *(Sinn Féin)*	MP	190
Heald, Oliver *(Con)*	MP	190
Healey, John *(Lab)*	MP	190
Heappey, James *(Con)*	MP	191
Heaton-Harris, Chris *(Con)*	MP	191
Heaton-Jones, Peter *(Con)*	MP	192
Hedges, Mike *(Lab)*	AM	1128
Henderson, Gordon *(Con)*	MP	192
Hendrick, Mark *(Lab/Co-op)*	MP	193
Hendry, Drew *(SNP)*	MP	193
Hepburn, Jamie *(SNP)*	MSP	1099
Hepburn, Stephen *(Lab)*	MP	194
Herbert, Nick *(Con)*	MP	194
Hermon, Sylvia *(Ind)*	MP	194
Hilditch, David *(DUP)*	MLA	1146
Hill, Mike *(Lab)*	MP	195
Hillier, Meg *(Lab/Co-op)*	MP	195
Hinds, Damian *(Con)*	MP	196
Hoare, Simon *(Con)*	MP	196
Hobhouse, Wera *(Lib Dem)*	MP	197
Hodge, Margaret *(Lab)*	MP	197
Hodgson, Sharon *(Lab)*	MP	198
Hoey, Kate *(Lab)*	MP	198
Hollern, Kate *(Lab)*	MP	199
Hollingbery, George *(Con)*	MP	199
Hollinrake, Kevin *(Con)*	MP	200
Hollobone, Philip *(Con)*	MP	200
Holloway, Adam *(Con)*	MP	200
Hopkins, Kelvin *(Lab)*	MP	201
Hosie, Stewart *(SNP)*	MP	201
Howarth, George *(Lab)*	MP	202
Howell, John *(Con)*	MP	202
Howells, Vikki *(Lab)*	AM	1128
Hoyle, Lindsay *(Lab)*	MP	203
Huddleston, Nigel *(Con)*	MP	203
Hughes, Eddie *(Con)*	MP	204
Humphrey, William *(DUP)*	MLA	1146
Hunt, Jeremy *(Con)*	MP	204
Huq, Rupa *(Lab)*	MP	204
Hurd, Nick *(Con)*	MP	205
Hussain, Imran *(Lab)*	MP	205
Hutt, Jane *(Lab)*	AM	1129
Hyslop, Fiona *(SNP)*	MSP	1099
Irranca-Davies, Huw *(Lab/Co-op)*	AM	1129
Irwin, William *(DUP)*	MLA	1146
Isherwood, Mark *(Con)*	AM	1129
Jack, Alister *(Con)*	MP	206
James, Julie *(Lab)*	AM	1129
James, Margot *(Con)*	MP	206
Jardine, Christine *(Lib Dem)*	MP	206
Jarvis, Dan *(Lab)*	MP	207
Javid, Sajid *(Con)*	MP	207
Jayawardena, Ranil *(Con)*	MP	208
Jenkin, Bernard *(Con)*	MP	208
Jenkins, Bethan *(PlC)*	AM	1129
Jenkyns, Andrea *(Con)*	MP	209
Jenrick, Robert *(Con)*	MP	209
Johnson, Boris *(Con)*	MP	209
Johnson, Caroline *(Con)*	MP	210
Johnson, Daniel *(Lab)*	MSP	1099
Johnson, Diana *(Lab)*	MP	210
Johnson, Gareth *(Con)*	MP	211
Johnson, Jo *(Con)*	MP	211
Johnstone, Alison *(Green)*	MSP	1099
Jones, Andrew *(Con)*	MP	212
Jones, Ann *(Lab/Co-op)*	AM	1129
Jones, Caroline *(UKIP)*	AM	1129
Jones, Carwyn *(Lab)*	AM	1129
Jones, Darren *(Lab)*	MP	212
Jones, David *(Con)*	MP	213
Jones, Elin *(Pres Off)*	AM	1130
Jones, Gerald *(Lab)*	MP	213
Jones, Graham *(Lab)*	MP	213
Jones, Helen *(Lab)*	MP	214
Jones, Kevan *(Lab)*	MP	214
Jones, Marcus *(Con)*	MP	215
Jones, Sarah *(Lab)*	MP	215
Jones, Susan Elan *(Lab)*	MP	216
Kane, Mike *(Lab)*	MP	216
Kawczynski, Daniel *(Con)*	MP	216
Kearney, Declan *(Sinn Féin)*	MLA	1146
Keegan, Gillian *(Con)*	MP	217
Keeley, Barbara *(Lab)*	MP	217
Kelly, Catherine *(Sinn Féin)*	MLA	1147
Kelly, Dolores *(SDLP)*	MLA	1147
Kelly, Gerry *(Sinn Féin)*	MLA	1147
Kelly, James *(Lab/Co-op)*	MSP	1099
Kendall, Liz *(Lab)*	MP	218
Kennedy, Seema *(Con)*	MP	218
Kerr, Liam *(Con)*	MSP	1099
Kerr, Stephen *(Con)*	MP	219
Khan, Afzal *(Lab)*	MP	219
Kidd, Bill *(SNP)*	MSP	1099
Killen, Gerard *(Lab/Co-op)*	MP	219
Kinnock, Stephen *(Lab)*	MP	220
Knight, Greg *(Con)*	MP	220
Knight, Julian *(Con)*	MP	221
Kwarteng, Kwasi *(Con)*	MP	221
Kyle, Peter *(Lab)*	MP	222
Laing, Eleanor *(Con)*	MP	222
Laird, Lesley *(Lab)*	MP	223
Lake, Ben *(PlC)*	MP	223
Lamb, Norman *(Lib Dem)*	MP	223
Lammy, David *(Lab)*	MP	224
Lamont, Johann *(Lab/Co-op)*	MSP	1099
Lamont, John *(Con)*	MP	225
Lancaster, Mark *(Con)*	MP	225
Latham, Pauline *(Con)*	MP	226
Lavery, Ian *(Lab)*	MP	226
Law, Chris *(SNP)*	MP	227
Leadsom, Andrea *(Con)*	MP	227
Lee, Karen *(Lab)*	MP	227
Lee, Phillip *(Con)*	MP	228
Lefroy, Jeremy *(Con)*	MP	228
Leigh, Edward *(Con)*	MP	229
Lennon, Monica *(Lab)*	MSP	1100
Leonard, Richard *(Lab)*	MSP	1100
Leslie, Chris *(Lab/Co-op)*	MP	229
Letwin, Oliver *(Con)*	MP	230
Lewell-Buck, Emma *(Lab)*	MP	230
Lewer, Andrew *(Con)*	MP	231
Lewis, Brandon *(Con)*	MP	231
Lewis, Clive *(Lab)*	MP	231
Lewis, Ivan *(Lab)*	MP	232
Lewis, Julian *(Con)*	MP	232
Lewis, Steffan *(PlC)*	AM	1130
Liddell-Grainger, Ian *(Con)*	MP	233
Lidington, David *(Con)*	MP	233
Linden, David *(SNP)*	MP	234

Lindhurst, Gordon *(Con)*	MSP	1100
Little Pengelly, Emma *(DUP)*	MP	234
Lloyd, Dai *(PlC)*	AM	1130
Lloyd, Stephen *(Lib Dem)*	MP	235
Lloyd, Tony *(Lab)*	MP	235
Lochhead, Richard *(SNP)*	MSP	1100
Lockhart, Carla *(DUP)*	MLA	1147
Lockhart, Dean *(Con)*	MSP	1100
Long, Naomi *(All)*	MLA	1147
Long-Bailey, Rebecca *(Lab)*	MP	236
Lopez *(née* Dockerill*)*, Julia *(Con)*	MP	131
Lopresti, Jack *(Con)*	MP	236
Lord, Jonathan *(Con)*	MP	236
Loughton, Tim *(Con)*	MP	237
Lucas, Caroline *(Green)*	MP	238
Lucas, Ian C *(Lab)*	MP	238
Lunn, Trevor *(All)*	MLA	1147
Lyle, Richard *(SNP)*	MSP	1100
Lynch, Holly *(Lab)*	MP	239
Lynch, Seán *(Sinn Féin)*	MLA	1147
Lyons, Gordon *(DUP)*	MLA	1147
Lyttle, Chris *(All)*	MLA	1147
McAleer, Declan *(Sinn Féin)*	MLA	1147
McAlpine, Joan *(SNP)*	MSP	1100
McArthur, Liam *(Lib Dem)*	MSP	1100
McCabe, Steve *(Lab)*	MP	239
McCallion, Elisha *(Sinn Féin)*	MP	240
McCann, Fra *(Sinn Féin)*	MLA	1147
McCarthy, Kerry *(Lab)*	MP	240
McCartney, Raymond *(Sinn Féin)*	MLA	1147
McCrossan, Daniel *(SDLP)*	MLA	1148
McDonagh, Siobhain *(Lab)*	MP	241
McDonald, Andy *(Lab)*	MP	241
MacDonald, Angus *(SNP)*	MSP	1100
MacDonald, Gordon *(SNP)*	MSP	1100
Macdonald, Lewis *(Lab)*	MSP	1101
McDonald, Mark *(SNP)*	MSP	1101
McDonald, Stewart Malcolm *(SNP)*	MP	241
McDonald, Stuart C *(SNP)*	MP	242
McDonnell, John *(Lab)*	MP	242
McElduff, Barry *(Sinn Féin)*	MP	243
McEvoy, Neil *(Ind)*	AM	1130
McFadden, Pat *(Lab)*	MP	243
McGinn, Conor *(Lab)*	MP	243
McGlone, Patsy *(SDLP)*	MLA	1148
McGovern, Alison *(Lab)*	MP	244
McGrath, Colin *(SDLP)*	MLA	1148
MacGregor, Fulton *(SNP)*	MSP	1101
McGuigan, Philip *(Sinn Féin)*	MLA	1148
McIlveen, Michelle *(DUP)*	MLA	1148
McInnes, Liz *(Lab)*	MP	244
Macintosh, Ken *(Pres Off)*	MSP	1101
Mackay, Derek *(SNP)*	MSP	1101
Mackay, Rona *(SNP)*	MSP	1101
McKee, Ivan *(SNP)*	MSP	1101
McKelvie, Christina *(SNP)*	MSP	1101
Mackinlay, Craig *(Con)*	MP	245
McKinnell, Catherine *(Lab)*	MP	245
Maclean, Rachel *(Con)*	MP	245
McLoughlin, Patrick *(Con)*	MP	246
McMahon, Jim *(Lab/Co-op)*	MP	246
McMillan, Stuart *(SNP)*	MSP	1102
McMorrin, Anna *(Lab)*	MP	247
McNally, John *(SNP)*	MP	247
MacNeil, Angus *(SNP)*	MP	247
McNeill, Pauline *(Lab)*	MSP	1102
McNulty, Justin *(SDLP)*	MLA	1148
McPartland, Stephen *(Con)*	MP	248
Macpherson, Ben *(SNP)*	MSP	1102
McVey, Esther *(Con)*	MP	248
Madders, Justin *(Lab)*	MP	249
Maguire, Ruth *(SNP)*	MSP	1102
Mahmood, Khalid *(Lab)*	MP	249
Mahmood, Shabana *(Lab)*	MP	249
Main, Anne *(Con)*	MP	250
Mak, Alan *(Con)*	MP	250
Malhotra, Seema *(Lab/Co-op)*	MP	251
Mallon, Nichola *(SDLP)*	MLA	1148
Malthouse, Kit *(Con)*	MP	251
Mann, John *(Lab)*	MP	252
Mann, Scott *(Con)*	MP	252
Marra, Jenny *(Lab)*	MSP	1102
Marsden, Gordon *(Lab)*	MP	252
Martin, Gillian *(SNP)*	MSP	1102
Martin, Sandy *(Lab)*	MP	253
Maskell, Rachael *(Lab/Co-op)*	MP	253
Maskey, Alex *(Sinn Féin)*	MLA	1148
Maskey, Paul *(Sinn Féin)*	MP	254
Mason, John *(SNP)*	MSP	1102
Mason, Tom *(Con)*	MSP	1102
Masterton, Paul *(Con)*	MP	254
Matheson, Chris *(Lab)*	MP	254
Matheson, Michael *(SNP)*	MSP	1102
May, Theresa *(Con)*	MP	255
Maynard, Paul *(Con)*	MP	255
Mearns, Ian *(Lab)*	MP	256
Melding, David *(Con)*	AM	1130
Menzies, Mark *(Con)*	MP	256
Mercer, Johnny *(Con)*	MP	257
Merriman, Huw *(Con)*	MP	257
Metcalfe, Stephen *(Con)*	MP	257
Middleton, Gary *(DUP)*	MLA	1148
Miles, Jeremy *(Lab/Co-op)*	AM	1130
Miliband, Ed *(Lab)*	MP	258
Millar, Darren *(Con)*	AM	1130
Miller, Maria *(Con)*	MP	258
Milling, Amanda *(Con)*	MP	259
Mills, Nigel *(Con)*	MP	259
Milne, Ian *(Sinn Féin)*	MLA	1148
Milton, Anne *(Con)*	MP	260
Mitchell, Andrew *(Con)*	MP	260
Mitchell, Margaret *(Con)*	MSP	1103
Molloy, Francie *(Sinn Féin)*	MP	261
Monaghan, Carol *(SNP)*	MP	261
Moon, Madeleine *(Lab)*	MP	261
Moore, Damien *(Con)*	MP	262
Moran, Layla *(Lib Dem)*	MP	262
Mordaunt, Penny *(Con)*	MP	262
Morden, Jessica *(Lab)*	MP	263
Morgan, Julie *(Lab)*	AM	1130
Morgan, Nicky *(Con)*	MP	263
Morgan, Eluned *(Lab)*	AM	1130
Morgan, Stephen *(Lab)*	MP	264
Morris, Anne Marie *(Ind)*	MP	264
Morris, David *(Con)*	MP	265
Morris, Grahame *(Lab)*	MP	265
Morris, James *(Con)*	MP	266
Morton, Wendy *(Con)*	MP	266
Mountain, Edward *(Con)*	MSP	1103
Mullan, Karen *(Sinn Féin)*	MLA	1148
Mundell, David *(Con)*	MP	267
Mundell, Oliver *(Con)*	MSP	1103
Murphy, Conor *(Sinn Féin)*	MLA	1148
Murray, Ian *(Lab)*	MP	267
Murray, Sheryll *(Con)*	MP	268
Murrison, Andrew *(Con)*	MP	268

Nandy, Lisa *(Lab)* MP 269
Neagle, Lynne *(Lab/Co-op)* AM 1130
Neil, Alex *(SNP)* MSP 1103
Neill, Robert *(Con)* MP 269
Nesbitt, Mike *(UUP)* MLA 1149
Newlands, Gavin *(SNP)* MP 270
Newton, Robin *(DUP)* MLA 1149
Newton, Sarah *(Con)* MP 270
Ní Chuilín, Carál *(Sinn Féin)* MLA 1149
Nokes, Caroline *(Con)* MP 270
Norman, Jesse *(Con)* MP 271
Norris, Alex *(Lab/Co-op)* MP 272

O'Brien, Neil *(Con)* MP 272
O'Dowd, John *(Sinn Féin)* MLA 1149
Offord, Matthew *(Con)* MP 272
O'Hara, Brendan *(SNP)* MP 273
O'Mara, Jared *(Lab)* MP 273
Ó Muilleoir, Máirtín *(Sinn Féin)* MLA 1149
Onasanya, Fiona *(Lab)* MP 273
O'Neill, Michelle *(Sinn Féin)* MLA 1149
Onn, Melanie *(Lab)* MP 273
Onwurah, Chi *(Lab)* MP 274
Opperman, Guy *(Con)* MP 274
Osamor, Kate *(Lab/Co-op)* MP 275
Owen, Albert *(Lab)* MP 275

Paisley, Ian *(DUP)* MP 276
Parish, Neil *(Con)* MP 276
Passmore, Rhianon *(Lab/Co-op)* AM 1131
Patel, Priti *(Con)* MP 277
Paterson, Gil *(SNP)* MSP 1103
Paterson, Owen *(Con)* MP 277
Pawsey, Mark *(Con)* MP 278
Peacock, Stephanie *(Lab)* MP 278
Pearce, Teresa *(Lab)* MP 278
Penning, Mike *(Con)* MP 279
Pennycook, Matthew *(Lab)* MP 279
Penrose, John *(Con)* MP 280
Percy, Andrew *(Con)* MP 280
Perkins, Toby *(Lab)* MP 281
Perry, Claire *(Con)* MP 281
Phillips, Jess *(Lab)* MP 282
Phillipson, Bridget *(Lab)* MP 282
Philp, Chris *(Con)* MP 282
Pidcock, Laura *(Lab)* MP 283
Pincher, Christopher *(Con)* MP 283
Platt, Jo *(Lab/Co-op)* MP 283
Pollard, Luke *(Lab/Co-op)* MP 284
Poots, Edwin *(DUP)* MLA 1149
Poulter, Dan *(Con)* MP 284
Pound, Stephen *(Lab)* MP 285
Pow, Rebecca *(Con)* MP 285
Powell, Lucy *(Lab/Co-op)* MP 286
Prentis, Victoria *(Con)* MP 286
Price, Adam *(PlC)* AM 1131
Prisk, Mark *(Con)* MP 286
Pritchard, Mark *(Con)* MP 287
Pursglove, Tom *(Con)* MP 288

Quin, Jeremy *(Con)* MP 288
Quince, Will *(Con)* MP 288
Qureshi, Yasmin *(Lab)* MP 289

Raab, Dominic *(Con)* MP 289
Ramsay, Nick *(Con)* AM 1131
Rashid, Faisal *(Lab)* MP 290
Rathbone, Jenny *(Lab)* AM 1131
Rayner, Angela *(Lab)* MP 290
Reckless, Mark *(Ind)* AM 1131
Redwood, John *(Con)* MP 290
Reed, Steve *(Lab/Co-op)* MP 291
Rees, Christina *(Lab/Co-op)* MP 292
Rees, David *(Lab)* AM 1131
Rees-Mogg, Jacob *(Con)* MP 292
Reeves, Ellie *(Lab)* MP 292
Reeves, Rachel *(Lab)* MP 293
Rennie, Willie *(Lib Dem)* MSP 1103
Reynolds, Emma *(Lab)* MP 293
Reynolds, Jonathan *(Lab/Co-op)* MP 294
Rimmer, Marie *(Lab)* MP 294
Robertson, Laurence *(Con)* MP 295
Robinson, Gavin *(DUP)* MP 295
Robinson, Geoffrey *(Lab)* MP 296
Robinson, George *(DUP)* MLA 1149
Robinson, Mary *(Con)* MP 296
Robison, Shona *(SNP)* MSP 1103
Rodda, Matt *(Lab)* MP 296
Rogan, Emma *(Sinn Féin)* MLA 1149
Rosindell, Andrew *(Con)* MP 297
Ross, Douglas *(Con)* MP 297
Ross, Gail *(SNP)* MSP 1103
Rowlands, David *(UKIP)* AM 1131
Rowley, Alex *(Lab)* MSP 1103
Rowley, Danielle *(Lab)* MP 298
Rowley, Lee *(Con)* MP 298
Ruane, Chris *(Lab)* MP 298
Rudd, Amber *(Con)* MP 299
Rumbles, Mike *(Lib Dem)* MSP 1104
Ruskell, Mark *(Green)* MSP 1104
Russell, Michael *(SNP)* MSP 1104
Russell-Moyle, Lloyd *(Lab/Co-op)* MP 299
Rutley, David *(Con)* MP 300
Ryan, Joan *(Lab)* MP 300

Sandbach, Antoinette *(Con)* MP 301
Sargeant, Carl *(Lab)* AM 1131
Sarwar, Anas *(Lab)* MSP 1104
Saville Roberts, Liz *(PlC)* MP 301
Scott, John *(Con)* MSP 1104
Scott, Tavish *(Lib Dem)* MSP 1104
Scully, Paul *(Con)* MP 302
Seely, Bob *(Con)* MP 302
Selous, Andrew *(Con)* MP 302
Shah, Naz *(Lab)* MP 303
Shannon, Jim *(DUP)* MP 303
Shapps, Grant *(Con)* MP 304
Sharma, Alok *(Con)* MP 304
Sharma, Virendra *(Lab)* MP 305
Sheehan, Pat *(Sinn Féin)* MLA 1149
Sheerman, Barry *(Lab/Co-op)* MP 305
Shelbrooke, Alec *(Con)* MP 306
Sheppard, Tommy *(SNP)* MP 306
Sherriff, Paula *(Lab)* MP 306
Shuker, Gavin *(Lab/Co-op)* MP 307
Siddiq, Tulip *(Lab)* MP 307
Simpson, David *(DUP)* MP 308
Simpson, Graham *(Con)* MSP 1104
Simpson, Keith *(Con)* MP 308
Skates, Ken *(Lab)* AM 1131
Skidmore, Chris *(Con)* MP 309
Skinner, Dennis *(Lab)* MP 309
Slaughter, Andy *(Lab)* MP 310
Smeeth, Ruth *(Lab)* MP 310
Smith, Angela *(Lab)* MP 311
Smith, Cat *(Lab)* MP 311
Smith, Chloe *(Con)* MP 312
Smith, Elaine *(Lab)* MSP 1104
Smith, Eleanor *(Lab)* MP 312

Smith, Henry *(Con)* MP 312
Smith, Jeff *(Lab)* MP 313
Smith, Julian *(Con)* MP 313
Smith, Laura *(Lab)* MP 314
Smith, Liz *(Con)* MSP 1104
Smith, Nick *(Lab)* MP 314
Smith, Owen *(Lab)* MP 314
Smith, Royston *(Con)* MP 315
Smyth, Colin *(Lab)* MSP 1105
Smyth, Karin *(Lab)* MP 315
Snell, Gareth *(Lab/Co-op)* MP 315
Soames, Nicholas *(Con)* MP 316
Sobel, Alex *(Lab/Co-op)* MP 316
Somerville, Shirley-Anne *(SNP)* MSP 1105
Soubry, Anna *(Con)* MP 317
Spellar, John *(Lab)* MP 317
Spelman, Caroline *(Con)* MP 318
Spencer, Mark *(Con)* MP 318
Stalford, Christopher *(DUP)* MLA 1149
Starmer, Keir *(Lab)* MP 319
Stephens, Chris *(SNP)* MP 319
Stephenson, Andrew *(Con)* MP 320
Stevens, Jo *(Lab)* MP 320
Stevenson, John *(Con)* MP 321
Stevenson, Stewart *(SNP)* MSP 1105
Stewart, Alexander *(Con)* MSP 1105
Stewart, Bob *(Con)* MP 321
Stewart, David *(Lab/Co-op)* MSP 1105
Stewart, Iain *(Con)* MP 321
Stewart, John *(UUP)* MLA 1150
Stewart, Kevin *(SNP)* MSP 1105
Stewart, Rory *(Con)* MP 322
Stone, Jamie *(Lib Dem)* MP 323
Storey, Mervyn *(DUP)* MLA 1150
Streeter, Gary *(Con)* MP 323
Streeting, Wes *(Lab)* MP 324
Stride, Mel *(Con)* MP 324
Stringer, Graham *(Lab)* MP 325
Stuart, Graham *(Con)* MP 325
Sturdy, Julian *(Con)* MP 326
Sturgeon, Nicola *(SNP)* MSP 1105
Sugden, Claire *(Ind)* MLA 1150
Sunak, Rishi *(Con)* MP 326
Swann, Robin *(UUP)* MLA 1150
Swayne, Desmond *(Con)* MP 326
Sweeney, Paul *(Lab/Co-op)* MP 327
Swinney, John *(SNP)* MSP 1105
Swinson, Jo *(Lib Dem)* MP 327
Swire, Hugo *(Con)* MP 328
Syms, Robert *(Con)* MP 328

Tami, Mark *(Lab)* MP 329
Thewliss, Alison *(SNP)* MP 329
Thomas, Derek *(Con)* MP 329
Thomas, Gareth *(Lab/Co-op)* MP 330
Thomas, Simon *(PlC)* AM 1131
Thomas-Symonds, Nick *(Lab)* MP 330
Thomson, Ross *(Con)* MP 331
Thornberry, Emily *(Lab)* MP 331
Throup, Maggie *(Con)* MP 332
Timms, Stephen *(Lab)* MP 332
Todd, Maree *(SNP)* MSP 1106
Tolhurst, Kelly *(Con)* MP 333
Tomkins, Adam *(Con)* MSP 1106
Tomlinson, Justin *(Con)* MP 333
Tomlinson, Michael *(Con)* MP 334
Torrance, David *(SNP)* MSP 1106
Tracey, Craig *(Con)* MP 334
Tredinnick, David *(Con)* MP 334
Trevelyan, Anne-Marie *(Con)* MP 335
Trickett, Jon *(Lab)* MP 335
Truss, Elizabeth *(Con)* MP 336
Tugendhat, Tom *(Con)* MP 336
Turley, Anna *(Lab/Co-op)* MP 337
Turner, Karl *(Lab)* MP 337
Twigg, Derek *(Lab)* MP 337
Twigg, Stephen *(Lab/Co-op)* MP 338
Twist, Liz *(Lab)* MP 338

Umunna, Chuka *(Lab)* MP 339

Vaizey, Ed *(Con)* MP 339
Vara, Shailesh *(Con)* MP 340
Vaz, Keith *(Lab)* MP 340
Vaz, Valerie *(Lab)* MP 341
Vickers, Martin *(Con)* MP 341
Villiers, Theresa *(Con)* MP 342

Walker, Charles *(Con)* MP 342
Walker, Robin *(Con)* MP 343
Walker, Thelma *(Lab)* MP 343
Wallace, Ben *(Con)* MP 343
Warburton, David *(Con)* MP 344
Warman, Matt *(Con)* MP 345
Waters, Lee *(Lab/Co-op)* AM 1132
Watling, Giles *(Con)* MP 345
Watson, Joyce *(Lab)* AM 1132
Watson, Tom *(Lab)* MP 345
Watt, Maureen *(SNP)* MSP 1106
Weir, Peter *(DUP)* MLA 1150
Wells, Annie *(Con)* MSP 1106
Wells, Jim *(DUP)* MLA 1150
West, Catherine *(Lab)* MP 346
Western, Matt *(Lab)* MP 346
Whately, Helen *(Con)* MP 347
Wheeler, Heather *(Con)* MP 347
Wheelhouse, Paul *(SNP)* MSP 1106
White, Sandra *(SNP)* MSP 1106
Whitehead, Alan *(Lab)* MP 348
Whitfield, Martin *(Lab)* MP 348
Whitford, Philippa *(SNP)* MP 348
Whittaker, Craig *(Con)* MP 349
Whittingdale, John *(Con)* MP 349
Whittle, Brian *(Con)* MSP 1106
Wiggin, Bill *(Con)* MP 350
Wightman, Andy *(Green)* MSP 1106
Williams, Hywel *(PlC)* MP 350
Williams, Kirsty *(Lib Dem)* AM 1132
Williams, Paul *(Lab)* MP 351
Williamson, Chris *(Lab)* MP 351
Williamson, Gavin *(Con)* MP 352
Wilson, Phil *(Lab)* MP 352
Wilson, Sammy *(DUP)* MP 353
Winterton, Rosie *(Lab)* MP 353
Wishart, Pete *(SNP)* MP 354
Wollaston, Sarah *(Con)* MP 354
Wood, Leanne *(PlC)* AM 1132
Wood, Mike *(Con)* MP 355
Woodcock, John *(Lab/Co-op)* MP 355
Wragg, William *(Con)* MP 356
Wright, Jeremy *(Con)* MP 356

Yasin, Mohammad *(Lab)* MP 356
Yousaf, Humza *(SNP)* MSP 1107

Zahawi, Nadhim *(Con)* MP 357
Zeichner, Daniel *(Lab)* MP 357

Index

1922 Committee 1064

abbreviations 1297–1307
accommodation allowance, MPs 58
Accommodation and Logistics Services, House of Commons 458
Accountant in Bankruptcy, Scotland 1116
Adjudicator's Office 1216
Administration, Commons Select Committee 453
Advertising Standards Authority 1216
Advocate General for Scotland 5, 30, 1202
age
  of MPs 435–441
  of Peers 1037–1044
Agriculture, Environment and Rural Affairs, Northern Ireland Executive 1139
Alliance Party
  headquarters 1157
  state of parties, Northern Ireland Assembly 1142
allowances, MPs 58–59
ambassadors
  British Embassies and High Commissions 1228–1250
  London Embassies and High Commissions 1251–1274
AMs
  change of party 1125
  changes since 2016 election 1125
  constituencies and majorities 1132–1133
  contact directory 1125–1132
  regions 1133
  salaries 1082
  women 1132
Animal and Plant Health Agency 1205
Archbishops 548, 549, 1033
Armed Forces Parliamentary Scheme 1221
Artificial Intelligence, Lords Select Committee 1053
Assembly Members *see* AMs
Attorney General 2, 5, 29, 1202
Audit Scotland 1221

Backbench Business, Commons Select Committee 453
Berwin Leighton Paisner LLP 1078
biographies
  MPs 63–357
  Peers 551–985
Bircham Dyson Bell LLP 1078
Bishops 548, 549, 1033
Black Rod, House of Lords 1059
Boundary Commission
  England 1221
  Northern Ireland 1221
  Scotland 1221
  Wales 1221
British Embassies and High Commissions 1228–1250
British Group Inter-Parliamentary Union 1224
British Overseas Territories, Governors and Commanders-in-Chief 1278
Broadcasting, Press Gallery 1075–1076
Business, Energy and Industrial Strategy
  Commons Select Committee 447
  Department for 3, 13–15, 1193
by-elections
  rules 464
  Scotland 1091

Cabinet Office 3, 15–16, 1193–1194
Cabinets
  Executive Committee of Ministers, Northern Ireland 1139
  Scottish Government 1083
  Welsh Government 1120
  Westminster 2
  see also Shadow Cabinets

candidates
2017 General Election 465–531
election rules 464
parties contesting 2017 General Election 465
Catering Services, House of Commons 457
Centre for Environment, Fisheries and Aquaculture Science 1205
Chairman of Committees, House of Lords 548
Chairman of Ways and Means 62
Chamber and Committees Team, House of Commons 455–456
Chamber Business Team, House of Commons 455
Chancellor of the Duchy of Lancaster 3, 16, 1193
changes of party
AMs 1125
MPs 62
Peers 550
Charity Commission 1212
Chief Secretary to the Treasury 2, 5, 34, 1203
Chief Whip
Government
House of Commons 2, 6, 461
House of Lords 6
Opposition
House of Commons 47, 461
House of Lords 47
salaries 57
Children and Young People's Commissioner Scotland 1216
Citizenship and Civic Engagement, Lords Select Committee 1054
City Remembrancer 1078
Civil Service
Northern Ireland 1153–1154
Scotland 1115
UK Departments of State 1193–1204
UK Permanent Secretaries 1192
Wales 1137
Clerk of the House 455
Combined Authorities 1170
Commissioner for Ethical Standards in Public Life in Scotland 1216
Commissioner for Public Appointments Northern Ireland 1216
Committee Office, House of Commons 456
Committee on Standards in Public Life 1224
Committees
Cabinet 38
House of Commons Select 447–454
Committees on Private Bills 451–452
Departmental Committees 447–451
Internal Committees 453–454
Other Committees 452–453
House of Lords Select 1053–1058
Ad Hoc Committees 1053–1054
Domestic Committees 1054–1055
Investigative Committees 1056–1058
Legislative Committees 1053
Procedural Committees 1055–1056
Implementation Taskforces 38
Joint Westminster 1062
London Assembly 1162–1164
National Assembly for Wales 1134–1135
Northern Ireland Assembly 1153
political party, Westminster 1064–1065
Scottish Parliament 1111–1113
Statutory Committees, Westminster 1062–1063
Commons Reference Group on Representation and Inclusion, Commons Select Committee 454
Commonwealth 1278–1280
Governors-General 1278–1279
Heads of State and Heads of Government 1279–1280
Commonwealth Parliamentary Association United Kingdom 1222

Communications Office, House of Commons 457
Communications, Lords Select Committee 1056
Communities and Children, Welsh Government 1123
Communities and Local Government
  Commons Select Committee 447
  Department for 3, 16–17, 1194–1195
Communities, Northern Ireland Executive 1139
Communities, Social Security and Equalities, Scottish Government 1086
Companies House 1205
Competition and Markets Authority 1212
Complaint-handling Bodies 1216–1220
Confederation of British Industry 1222
Conservative Party
  1922 Committee 1064
  2017 general election results in vulnerable seats 537–539
  headquarters 1069
  London Assembly Spokespeople 1159
  Political Offices
    House of Commons 461
    House of Lords 1060
  state of parties
    European Parliament 1173
    House of Commons 62
    House of Lords 549
    National Assembly for Wales 1125
    Scottish Parliament 1091
  see also Scottish Conservatives, Welsh Conservatives
Consolidation, &c, Bills, Joint Committee 1062
constituencies
  50 safest after 2017 election 428–429
  House of Commons 411–429
  London Assembly 1162
  most vulnerable after 2017 election 424–428
  National Assembly for Wales 1132–1133
  Northern Ireland Assembly 1150–1152
  polling results, 2017 election 465–531
  Scottish Parliament 1107–1109
Constitution, Lords Select Committee 1053
contact directories
  AMs 1125–1132
  London Assembly members 1160–1162
  MLAs 1142–1150
  MPs 62
  MSPs 1092–1107
  UK MEPs 1173–1184
  see also biographies
Co-operative Party
  headquarters 1070
Corporate Services, House of Commons 458
correspondence
  forms of address 1281–1282
  to MPs 62
  to Peers 548
Council of the European Union 1186–1189
  General Secretariat 1188–1189
  Permanent Representatives 1187–1188
Counsel General, Welsh Government 1123
countries of interest
  MPs 386–395
  Peers 1015–1027
Court of Referees, Commons Select Committee 451
Courts & Tribunals Service, HM 1205
Criminal Injuries Compensation Authority 1205
Crossbenchers
  Opposition, Westminster 56
  state of parties, House of Lords 549
  Political Offices, House of Lords 1060

Crown Commercial Service 1206
Crown Prosecution Service 1212
Culture, Tourism and External Affairs, Scottish Government 1086
Curator's Office, House of Commons 457

deaths
  MSPs 1091
  Peers 550
Debt Management Office, UK 1210
Defence
  Commons Select Committee 447
  Ministry of 3, 17–18, 1195
Defence Electronics and Components Agency 1206
Defence Science and Technology Laboratory 1206
Delegated Powers and Regulatory Reform, Lords Select Committee 1053
Democratic Unionist Party
  2017 general election results in vulnerable seats 541
  headquarters 1071, 1156
  Opposition, Westminster 55
  Political Offices, House of Commons 461
  state of parties
    European Parliament 1173
    House of Commons 62
    House of Lords 549
    Northern Ireland Assembly 1142
Departments of State 3–6, 1193–1204
  Business, Energy and Industrial Strategy 3, 13–15, 1193
  Cabinet Office 3, 15–16, 1193–1194
  Communities and Local Government 3, 16–17, 1194–1195
  Defence 3, 17–18, 1195
  Digital, Culture, Media and Sport 3, 18–19, 1195–1196
  Education 3, 19–21, 1196–1197
  Environment, Food and Rural Affairs 4, 21, 1197
  Exiting the European Union 4, 21–22, 1197–1198
  Foreign and Commonwealth Office 4, 22–24, 1198
  Health 4, 24–25, 1199
  Home Office 4, 25–26, 1199–1200
  International Development 4, 26–27, 1200
  International Trade 4, 27–28, 1200–1201
  Justice 5, 28–29, 1201
  Law Officers 5, 29–30, 1201–1202
  Leader of the House of Commons 5, 30
  Leader of the House of Lords 5, 30–31
  Northern Ireland Office 5, 31–32, 1202
  Prime Minister's Office 3, 13, 1193
  Privy Council Office 5, 32, 1202
  Scotland Office 5, 32, 1202
  Transport 5, 33, 1203
  Treasury 5, 33–35, 1203–1204
  Wales Office/Office of the Secretary of State for Wales 6, 35–36, 1204
  Work and Pensions 6, 36–37, 1204
Deputy Leader of the House of Lords 5, 31
Deputy Speakers
  House of Commons 62
  House of Lords 548
Digital, Culture, Media and Sport
  Commons Select Committee 447
  Department for 3, 18–19, 1195–1196
Digital, Implementation Taskforce 38
Diplomatic Representation
  British Embassies and High Commissions 1228–1250
  London Embassies and High Commissions 1251–1274
  UK Permanent Representations 1250–1251
Disclosure Scotland 1116
Driver and Vehicle Agency, Northern Ireland 1155
Driver and Vehicle Licensing Agency 1206
Driver and Vehicle Standards Agency 1206
Duchy of Lancaster, Chancellor of 3, 16, 1193

Earl Marshal 548, 1032
Ecclesiastical Committee, Statutory Committee 1062
Economic Affairs, Lords Select Committee 1056
Economy, Northern Ireland Executive 1140
Economy and Industrial Strategy, Cabinet Committee 38
Economy and Infrastructure, Welsh Government 1120
Economy, Jobs and Fair Work, Scottish Government 1087
Education
  Commons Select Committee 448
  Department for 3, 19–21, 1196–1197
  Northern Ireland Executive 1140
  Welsh Government 1122
Education and Skills Funding Agency 1207
Education and Skills, Scottish Government 1084
Education Scotland 1116
elections
  2015 and 2017 general election results comparison 532
  electoral register 464
  rules and timetable for 464
  see also by-elections, constituencies, General Election 2017
Electoral Commission 1222
Electoral Office for Northern Ireland 1222
Electoral Reform Society 1222
Electoral Reform Society Cymru 1223
Electoral Reform Society Scotland 1223
Embassies
  British Embassies and High Commissions 1228–1250
  London Embassies and High Commissions 1251–1274
Employment and Skills, Implementation Taskforce 38
Environment and Rural Affairs, Welsh Government 1122
Environment, Climate Change and Land Reform, Scottish Government 1085
Environment, Food and Rural Affairs
  Commons Select Committee 448
  Department for 4, 21, 1197
Environmental Audit, Commons Select Committee 452
Estyn – HM Inspectorate for Education and Training in Wales 1137
Ethical Standards in Public Life in Scotland, Commissioner for 1216
European Commission 1184–1185
European Council 1185–1186
  Presidency 1185
European Ombudsman 1216
European Parliament 1172–1184
  Cabinet of the President 1172
  political groups 1173
  UK Members' contact directory 1173–1184
  UK national parties 1173
  UK offices of 1172
European Scrutiny, Commons Select Committee 452
European Union Exit and Trade, Cabinet Committee 38
European Union, Lords Select Committee 1056
Eversheds Sutherland 1078
Executive Agencies
  Northern Ireland 1154–1156
  Scotland 1116–1117
  UK 1205–1211
Executive Office, Northern Ireland Executive 1139
Exiting the European Union
  Commons Select Committee 448
  Department for 4, 21–22, 1197–1198

FCO Services 1207
Finance and Constitution, Scottish Government 1085
Finance and Local Government, Welsh Government 1121
Finance
  Commons Select Committee 454
  Lords Select Committee 1054
  Northern Ireland Executive 1140

Financial Ombudsman Service 1217
Financial Services Ombudsman Scheme for the Isle of Man 1217
Fire Service Parliamentary Scheme 1223
First Lord of the Treasury 2, 13
First Minister
  Scotland 1083
  Wales 1120
Fixed-Term Parliaments Act 2011 464
Food Standards Agency 1212
Food Standards Scotland 1117
Foreign Affairs, Commons Select Committee 448
Foreign and Commonwealth Office 4, 22–24, 1198
Foreign Secretary 2, 4, 23, 1198
Forensic Science Northern Ireland 1155
Forest Enterprise England 1207
Forest Research 1207
Forest Service, Northern Ireland 1155
Forestry Commission 1212

Gas and Electricity Markets, Office of 1212
General Election 2017 464–546
  2015 and 2017 outcomes 532
  defeated MPs 544–546
  new MPs 543–544
  parties with candidates in the General Election 465
  parties with seats in the House of Commons 465
  results by constituency 465–531
  results compared with 2015 532
  results in vulnerable seats 537–542
  retired MPs 546
  rules and timetable for 464
  seats which changed parties 536–537
  share of the vote 532
  share of the vote by region 532–536
Gentleman Usher of the Black Rod, House of Lords 1059
Gibraltar Public Services Ombudsman 1217
Governance Office, House of Commons 455
Government 2–46
  Political Office, House of Commons 461
  Political Office, House of Lords 1060
Government Actuary's Department 1213
Government Internal Audit Agency 1207
Government Legal Department 1213
Greater London Authority 1159–1164
Green Party
  2017 general election results in vulnerable seats 542
  headquarters 1072, 1158
  state of parties
    European Parliament 1173
    House of Commons 62
    House of Lords 549
    Northern Ireland Assembly 1142
    Scottish Parliament 1091
Groceries Code Adjudicator 1217

Hansard Society 1223
Health
  Commons Select Committee 449
  Department of 4, 24–25, 1199
  Northern Ireland Executive 1140
Health and Sport, Scottish Government 1085
Health, Wellbeing and Sport, Welsh Government 1121
Hereditary Peers 464, 548, 549, 1032–1033
High Commissions
  British High Commissions 1228–1250
  London High Commissions 1251–1274
Historic Collections Team, House of Commons 458

HM Courts & Tribunals Service 1205
HM Land Registry 1213
HM Lord Lieutenants 1276–1278
HM Prison and Probation Service 1209
HM Prison Service 1209
HM Revenue & Customs 1214
HM Treasury 5, 33–35, 1203–1204
Home Affairs, Commons Select Committee 449
Home Office 4, 25–26, 1199–1200
Home Secretary 2, 4, 25, 1199
House of Commons
  administration 62, 455–460
    Accommodation and Logistics Services 458
    Catering Services 457
    Chamber and Committees Team 455–456
    Chamber Business Team 455
    Clerk of the House 455
    Commission 62
    Committee Office 456
    Communications Office 457
    Corporate Services 458
    Curator's Office 457
    Governance Office 455
    Historic Collections Team 458
    House of Commons Enquiry Service 458
    House of Commons Library 459
    Houses of Parliament Shop 459
    In-House Services 457–458
    Journal Office 456
    Media and Communications Service (Select Committees) 455
    Members Estimate Committee 62
    National Parliament Office, Brussels 455
    Office of Speaker's Counsel 456
    Official Report (Hansard) 456
    Overseas Office 455
    Parliamentary Audio Visual 456
    Parliamentary Commissioner for Standards 460
    Parliamentary Digital Service 458
    Parliamentary Maintenance Services Team 457
    Parliamentary Office of Science and Technology (POST) 459
    Parliamentary Security Department 458
    Participation Team 458–459
    Private Bill Office 456
    Public Bill Office 455
    Research and Information Team 459
    Research Sections 459
    Serjeant at Arms Office 457
    Strategic Estates 460
    Table Office 456
    Vote Office 456
  changes since 2017 general election 62
  committees 447–454
    Committees on Private Bills 451–452
    Departmental Committees 447–451
    Internal Committees 453–454
    Other Committees 452–453
  constituencies, MPs and majorities 411–429
  elections
    constituencies, MPs and majorities 411–429
    state of parties 62, 532
    see also General Election 2017
  Members' contact directory 62
  office holders
    Chairman of Ways and Means 62
    Deputy Speakers 62
    Leader of the House 5, 30

House of Commons, office holders continued...
Leader of the Opposition 47
Opposition Whips 461
Prime Minister 2, 13
Speaker 62
Whips 461
political parties
Political Offices 461
state of parties 62
Speaker and Deputy Speakers 62
House of Commons Enquiry Service, House of Commons 458
House of Commons Library, House of Commons 459
House of Lords
Appointments Commssion 549
changes since last edition 550
Commission 549
committees 1053–1058
Ad Hoc Committees 1053–1054
Domestic Committees 1054–1055
Investigative Committees 1056–1058
Legislative Committees 1053
Procedural Committees 1055–1056
office holders
Chairman and Deputy Chairmen 548, 1059
Deputy Speakers 548
Gentleman Usher of the Black Rod 1059
Leader of the House 2, 5, 31
Lord Speaker 548, 1059
Senior Deputy Speaker 1059
Whips 1060
political parties
Political Offices 1060
state of parties 549
House of Lords Act (1999) 548, 1032
House of Lords Information Office 1060
Houses of Parliament Shop, House of Commons 459
Housing, Implementation Taskforce 38
Human Rights, Joint Committee 1062
Hybrid Instruments, Lords Select Committee 1053
Hydrographic Office, UK 1211

Immigration, Implementation Taskforce 38
Implementation Taskforces 38
Independent Adjudicator for Higher Education, Office of the 1218
Independent Case Examiner 1217
Independent Complaints Reviewer 1217
Independent Parliamentary Standards Authority 1223
Speaker's Committee for the, Statutory Committee 1063
Independents
state of parties 1125
European Parliament 1173
House of Commons 62
National Assembly for Wales 1125
Northern Ireland Assembly 1142
Industry and Parliament Trust 1223
Infrastructure, Northern Ireland Executive 1141
In-House Services, House of Commons 457–458
Insolvency Service 1208
Intellectual Property Office 1208
Intelligence and Security Committee of Parliament, Statutory Committee 1063
International Development
Commons Select Committee 449
Department for 4, 26–27, 1200
International Relations, Lords Select Committee 1058
International Trade
Commons Select Committee 449
Department for 4, 27–28, 1200–1201

International, Press Gallery 1077
Invest Northern Ireland 1155
Irish Peerages 1032–1033

Joint Westminster Committees 1062
Journal Office, House of Commons 456
Judicial Appointments and Conduct Ombudsman 1218
Justice
  Commons Select Committee 450
  Ministry of 5, 28–29, 1201
  Northern Ireland Executive 1141
  Scottish Government 1087
Justices of the Supreme Court 548

Labour Party
  2017 general election results in vulnerable seats 539–540, 541
  headquarters 1069
  London Assembly Spokespeople 1159
  Opposition, Westminster 47–52
  Parliamentary Labour Party
    Departmental Groups 1064–1065
  Political Offices
    House of Commons 461
    House of Lords 1060
  state of parties
    European Parliament 1173
    House of Commons 62
    House of Lords 549
    National Assembly for Wales 1125
    Scottish Parliament 1091
  see also Scottish Labour, Welsh Labour
Lancaster, Chancellor of the Duchy of 3, 16, 1193
Land Registry, HM 1213
Law Lords 548, 1033
Law Officers 5, 29–30, 1201–1202
Leader of the House of Commons 5, 30
Leader of the House of Lords 2, 5, 30–31
Leader of the House, Welsh Government 1123
Leader of the Opposition, House of Commons 47
Legal Aid Agency 1208
Legal Ombudsman 1218
Legal Services Agency Northern Ireland 1155
Liaison
  Commons Select Committee 454
  Lords Select Committee 1055
Liberal Democrats
  2017 general election results in vulnerable seats 541
  headquarters 1070
  Opposition, Westminster 54
  Political Offices
    House of Commons 461
    House of Lords 1060
  state of parties
    European Parliament 1173
    House of Commons 62
    House of Lords 549
    National Assembly for Wales 1125
    Scottish Parliament 1091
  see also Scottish Liberal Democrats, Welsh Liberal Democrats
Life Peers 548, 549, 1032–1033
Lobby Correspondents 1073–1077
Local Government and Social Care Ombudsman 1218
London Assembly
  committees 1162–1164
  constituencies and Londonwide list 1162
  Members' contact directory 1160–1162
  spokespeople 1159

London Embassies and High Commissions 1251–1274
Lord Chancellor 2, 5, 28, 1201
Lord Great Chamberlain 548, 1032
Lord President of the Council 5, 30, 1202
Lord Privy Seal 2, 5, 31
Lord Speaker, House of Lords 548, 1059
Lords of Appeal in Ordinary (Law Lords) 548
Lords Spiritual 548, 1033

Magazines, Press Gallery 1075
majorities
  AMs' 1132–1133
  MPs' 411–429
  MSPs' 1107–1109
Maritime and Coastguard Agency 1208
Mayor of London 1159
  Mayoral Team 1159
  see also Greater London Authority, London Assembly
Media and Communications Service (Select Committees), House of Commons 455
Medicines and Healthcare Products Regulatory Agency 1208
Members Estimate Committee, House of Commons 62
Members of Parliament *see* MPs
Members of the European Parliament, contact directory 1173–1184
Members of the London Assembly *see* London Assembly
Members of the Northern Ireland Assembly *see* MLAs
Members of the Scottish Parliament *see* MSPs
Members of the Welsh Assembly see AMs
MEPs, contact directory 1173–1184
Met Office 1209
Ministers
  attending UK Cabinet 2
  Government 3–6, 13–37
  responsibilities and staff
    Northern Ireland Executive 1139–1141
    Scottish Government 1083–1088
    UK 3–6, 13–37
    Welsh Government 1120–1123
  salaries 57
    salaries of devolved 1082
  see also Shadow Ministers
Ministry of Defence 3, 17–18, 1195
Ministry of Justice 5, 28–29, 1201
MLAs
  changes since 2017 election 1142
  constituencies 1150–1152
  contact directory 1142–1150
  replacements 1142
  resignations 1142
  salaries 1082
  women 1150
MPs
  accommodation allowance 58
  allowances 58–59
  biographies 63–357
  by age 435–441
  by party 442–446
  by region 396–408
  change of party 62
  changes since 2017 general election 62
  constituencies and majorities 411–429
  contact directory 62
  correspondence to 1282
  countries of interest 386–395
  defeated in 2017 544–546
  new in 2017 543–544
  now Peers 1028–1031
  office costs allowance 58

MPs continued...
pensions 58
political interests 360–385
retired in 2017 546
salaries 57
severance pay 59
staffing costs allowance 58
starting-up allowance 58
travel allowance 58
winding-up allowance 58
women 430–434
MSPs
by-elections 1091
changes since 2016 election 1091
constituencies and majorities 1107–1109
contact directory 1092–1107
deaths 1091
regions 1109–1110
replacements 1091
resignations 1091
salaries 1082
women 1107

National Archives 1213
National Assembly for Wales 1124–1133
changes since 2016 election 1125
committees 1134–1135
constituencies 1132–1133
Members' contact directory 1125–1132
Officers and Officials 1135–1136
Opposition Spokespeople 1124
Opposition Whips 1124
political parties 1137–1138
Presiding Officer 1125, 1136
regions 1133
salaries 1082
Shadow Ministers 1124
state of parties 1125
See also AMs, Welsh Government
National Audit Office 1224
National College for Teaching and Leadership 1209
National Crime Agency 1213
National Daily Newspapers, Press Gallery 1073–1074
National Infrastructure Commission 1209
National Parliament Office, Brussels, House of Commons 455
National Records of Scotland 1117
National Savings and Investments 1213
National Security Council, Cabinet Committee 38
National Sunday Newspapers, Press Gallery 1074
Natural Environment and Rural Communities Act 2006, Lords Select Committee 1054
News Agencies, Press Gallery 1075
Non-Ministerial Departments
Northern Ireland 1156
Scotland 1117–1118
UK 1212–1215
Wales 1137
Northern Ireland Affairs, Commons Select Committee 450
Northern Ireland Assembly 1139–1153
changes since 2017 election 1142
committees 1153
constituencies 1150–1152
Members' contact directory 1142–1150
Officers and Officials 1153
political parties 1156–1158
salaries 1082
state of parties 1142
see also MLAs

Northern Ireland Courts and Tribunals Service 1154
Northern Ireland Environment Agency 1155
Northern Ireland Executive
  Civil Service 1153–1154
  Executive Agencies 1154–1156
  Executive Committee of Ministers 1139
  Ministerial responsibilities and staff 1139–1141
  Non-Ministerial Departments 1156
Northern Ireland Office 5, 31–32, 1202
Northern Ireland Prison Service 1156
Northern Ireland Public Services Ombudsman 1218
Northern Ireland Statistics and Research Agency 1156

office costs allowance, MPs 58
Office for Standards in Education, Children's Services and Skills 1214
Office of Gas and Electricity Markets 1212
Office of Qualifications and Examinations Regulation 1214
Office of Rail and Road 1214
Office of Speaker's Counsel, House of Commons 456
Office of the Independent Adjudicator for Higher Education 1218
Office of the Public Guardian 1209
Office of the Schools Adjudicator 1218
Office of the Scottish Charity Regulator 1117
Office of the Secretary of State for Wales 1204
Officers and Officials
  House of Commons 455–460
  House of Lords 1059
  National Assembly for Wales 1135–1136
  Northern Ireland Assembly 1153
  Scottish Parliament 1113–1114
Official Report (Hansard), House of Commons 456
Ombudsman Association 1219
Ombudsman Services 1219
Ombudsmen 1216–1220
Opposition
  House of Commons 47–56
  House of Lords 51–56
  National Assembly for Wales 1124
  Political Offices, Westminster 461
  Scottish Parliament 1088–1090
  Shadow Cabinet (UK) 47
  Shadow Ministers (UK) 48–51
Opposition Whips
  House of Commons 47, 461
  House of Lords 47
  National Assembly for Wales 1124
  Official Opposition 461
  Scottish Parliament 1088–1090
Ordnance Survey 1214
Overseas Office, House of Commons 455

Panel of Chairs, Commons Select Committee 454
Parliamentary Agents 1078
Parliamentary and Health Service Ombudsman 1219
Parliamentary and Political Service Honours, Statutory Committee 1063
Parliamentary Audio Visual, House of Commons 456
Parliamentary Business and Legislation, Cabinet Committee 38
Parliamentary Commissioner for Standards, House of Commons 460
Parliamentary Digital Service, House of Commons 458
parliamentary franchise 464
Parliamentary Maintenance Services Team, House of Commons 457
Parliamentary Office of Science and Technology (POST), House of Commons 459
Parliamentary Press Gallery 1073–1077
Parliamentary Private Secretaries 39–42
Parliamentary Security Department, House of Commons 458
Participation Team, House of Commons 458–459
pay *see* salaries

Peers
  Archbishops 548, 549, 1033
  biographies 551–985
  Bishops 548, 549, 1033
  by age 1037–1044
  by party 1045–1052
  change of party 550
  changes since last edition 550
  countries of interest 1015–1027
  deaths 550
  Government spokespeople 7
  Hereditary 548, 549, 1032–1033
  Hereditary and voting rights 464
  Irish 1032–1033
  Law Lords 548, 1033
  Life 548, 549, 1032–1033
  Lords Spiritual 548, 1033
  new members 550
  non-attending 550
  on leave of absence 1034
  Opposition spokespeople 51
  party affiliations 549
  peerages pending 550
  political interests 988–1014
  retirements 550
  salaries 57
  who were MPs 1028–1031
  women 1034–1036
Pensions Ombudsman 1219
pensions, MPs 58
People Before Profit Alliance
  headquarters 1158
  state of parties, Northern Ireland Assembly 1142
Permanent Representations
  Council of the EU 1187–1188
  to international bodies (UK) 1250–1251
Permanent Secretaries 1192
Petitions, Commons Select Committee 452
Pinsent Masons LLP 1078
Plaid Cymru (The Party of Wales)
  2017 general election results in vulnerable seats 541
  headquarters 1071, 1138
  opposition 56, 1124
  Political Offices, House of Commons 461
  state of parties
    European Parliament 1173
    House of Commons 62
    House of Lords 549
    National Assembly for Wales 1125
Planning Inspectorate 1209
Police and Crime Commissioners 1165–1169
Police Ombudsman for Northern Ireland 1219
Police Service Parliamentary Scheme 1224
policy committees 1064–1065
Political and Parliamentary Organisations 1221–1225
political interests
  MPs 360–385
  Peers 988–1014
Political Offices
  House of Commons 461
  House of Lords 1060
political parties
  National Assembly for Wales 1124, 1137–1138
    Independents 1125
    Plaid Cymru 1124, 1125, 1138
    UK Independence Party 1138, 1124

political parties, National Assembly for Wales continued...
Welsh Conservatives 1124, 1125, 1138
Welsh Labour 1125, 1137
Welsh Liberal Democrats 1125, 1138
Northern Ireland Assembly 1156–1158
Alliance 1157
Democratic Unionist Party 1156
Green Party 1158
People Before Profit 1158
Sinn Féin 1157
Social Democratic and Labour Party 1157
Traditional Unionist Voice 1158
Ulster Unionist Party 1157
Party Committees, Westminster 1064–1065
Scottish Parliament 1088–1090, 1118–1119
Scottish Conservatives 1088, 1091, 1118
Scottish Green Party 1090, 1091, 1119
Scottish Labour 1089, 1091, 1118
Scottish Liberal Democrats 1090, 1091, 1119
Scottish National Party 1091, 1118
Westminster 47–56, 1069–1072
Conservative and Unionist Party 1069
Co-operative Party 1070
Democratic Unionist Party 1071
Green Party 1072
Labour Party 1069
Liberal Democrats 1070
MPs, by party 442–446
parties with candidates in the General Election 465
parties with seats in the House of Commons 465
Peers, by party 1045–1052
Plaid Cymru 1071
Scottish National Party 1070
Sinn Féin 1071
UK Independence Party 1072
Political Polling and Digital Media, Lords Select Committee 1054
Presiding Officer
National Assembly for Wales 1125, 1136
Scottish Parliament 1091, 1114
Press Gallery, Parliamentary 1073–1077
Prime Minister 2, 13, 57
Prime Minister's Office 3, 13, 1193
Prison and Probation Service, HM 1209
Prison Service, HM 1209
Prisons and Probation Ombudsman for England and Wales 1219
Private Bill Office, House of Commons 456
Privileges and Conduct, Lords Select Committee 1055
Privileges, Commons Select Committee 452
Privy Council Office 5, 32, 1202
Privy Counsellors 1066–1068, 1281, 1282
Procedure
Commons Select Committee 452
Lords Select Committee 1055
Property Ombudsman 1220
Public Accounts Commission, Statutory Committee 1063
Public Accounts, Commons Select Committee 453
Public Administration and Constitutional Affairs, Commons Select Committee 453
Public Appointments Northern Ireland, Commissioner for 1216
Public Bill Office, House of Commons 455
Public Guardian, Office of the 1209
Public Health England 1210
Public Prosecution Service for Northern Ireland 1156
Public Services Ombudsman for Wales 1220

Qualifications and Examinations Regulation, Office of 1214
Queen Elizabeth II Centre 1210

Rail and Road, Office of 1214
Regional Press, Press Gallery 1074
regions
2017 general election results 532–536
MPs listed by 396–408
National Assembly for Wales 1133
Scottish Parliament 1109–1110
Registers of Scotland 1117
Regulatory Reform, Commons Select Committee 453
replacements
MLAs 1142
MSPs 1091
Research and Information Team, House of Commons 459
Research Sections, House of Commons 459
resignations
MLAs 1142
MSPs 1091
Revenue & Customs, HM 1214
Revenue Scotland 1117
Royal Households 1275
Royal Parks 1210
Rural Economy and Connectivity, Scottish Government 1087
Rural Payments Agency 1210

salaries
AMs 1082
devolved ministerial 1082
MLAs 1082
MPs 57
MSPs 1082
severance payments, MPs 57
Westminster ministerial 57
Whips 57
Schools Adjudicator, Office of the 1218
Science and Technology
Commons Select Committee 450
Lords Select Committee 1058
Scotland Office 5, 32, 1202
Scottish Affairs, Commons Select Committee 450
Scottish Charity Regulator, Office of the 1117
Scottish Conservatives
headquarters 1118
opposition 1088
state of parties 1091
Scottish Courts and Tribunal Service 1118
Scottish Fiscal Commission 1118
Scottish Government 1083–1088
Cabinet 1083
Civil Service 1115
Executive Agencies 1116–1117
First Minister 1083
Ministerial responsibilities and staff 1083–1088
Non-Ministerial Departments 1117–1118
Whips 1088
Scottish Green Party
headquarters 1119
opposition 1090
state of parties 1091
Scottish Housing Regulator 1118
Scottish Information Commissioner 1220
Scottish Labour
headquarters 1118
opposition 1089
state of parties 1091
Scottish Legal Complaints Commission 1220

Scottish Liberal Democrats
headquarters 1119
opposition 1090
state of parties 1091
Scottish National Party
2017 general election results in vulnerable seats 541
headquarters 1070, 1118
Opposition, Westminster 53
Political Offices, House of Commons 461
state of parties
European Parliament 1173
House of Commons 62
Scottish Parliament 1091
Scottish Parliament 1088–1110
by-elections 1091
changes since 2016 election 1091
committees 1111–1113
constituencies 1107–1109
Members' contact directory 1092–1107
Officers and Officials 1113–1114
Opposition 1088–1090
political parties 1118–1119
Presiding Officer 1091, 1114
regions 1109–1110
salaries 1082
Shadow Cabinet 1088
Shadow Ministers 1088
state of parties 1091
see also MSPs, Scottish Government
Scottish Prison Service 1116
Scottish Public Pensions Agency 1116
Scottish Public Services Ombudsman 1220
Secondary Legislation Scrutiny, Lords Select Committee 1053
Selection
Commons Select Committee 453
Lords Select Committee 1056
Serious Fraud Office 1214
Serjeant at Arms Office, House of Commons 457
Service Complaints Ombudsman for the Armed Forces 1220
Services, Lords Select Committee 1055
severance payments, MPs 59
Shadow Cabinets
House of Commons 47
Scottish Parliament 1088
Shadow Ministers
House of Commons 48–51
National Assembly for Wales 1124
Scottish Parliament 1088
See also Opposition
Sharpe Pritchard LLP 1079
Sinn Féin
2017 general election results in vulnerable seats 542
headquarters 1071, 1157
state of parties
European Parliament 1173
House of Commons 62
Northern Ireland Assembly 1142
Social Democratic and Labour Party
2017 general election results in vulnerable seats 541
headquarters 1157
state of parties, Northern Ireland Assembly 1142
Social Reform, Cabinet Committee 38
Solicitor General 5, 30, 1202
Space Agency, UK 1211

Speaker
House of Commons 62
House of Lords (Lord Speaker) 548, 1059
see also Presiding Officer
Speaker's Committee on the Electoral Commission, Statutory Committee 1063
Special Advisers 43–46
staffing costs allowance, MPs 58
Standards and Testing Agency 1210
Standards in Education, Children's Services and Skills, Office for 1214
Standards in Public Life, Committee on 1224
Standards, Commons Select Committee 453
Standing Orders (Private Bills), Lords Select Committee 1053
Standing Orders, Commons Select Committee 452
starting-up allowance, MPs 58
state of parties
European Parliament 1173
House of Commons 62
House of Lords 549
National Assembly for Wales 1125
Northern Ireland Assembly 1142
Scottish Parliament 1091
Statistics Authority/Office for National Statistics, UK 1215
Statutory Committees, Westminster 1062–1063
Statutory Instruments, Joint Committee 1062
Strategic Estates, House of Commons 460
Student Awards Agency Scotland 1116
Supreme Court
Justices 548, 1033
UK 1215

Table Office, House of Commons 456
Tackling Modern Slavery and People Trafficking, Implementation Taskforce 38
Trades Union Congress 1224
Traditional Unionist Voice
headquarters 1158
state of parties, Northern Ireland Assembly 1142
Transport
Commons Select Committee 450
Department for 5, 33, 1203
Transport Scotland 1117
travel allowance, MPs 58
Treasury
Commons Select Committee 451
HM 5, 33–35, 1203–1204

UK Debt Management Office 1210
UK Hydrographic Office 1211
UK Independence Party
2017 general election results in vulnerable seats 542
headquarters 1138, 1072
opposition 1124
state of parties
European Parliament 1173
House of Lords 549
UK Permanent Representations to international bodies 1250–1251
UK Space Agency 1211
UK Statistics Authority/Office for National Statistics 1215
UK Supreme Court 1215
Justices 548, 1033
Ulster Unionist Party
2017 general election results in vulnerable seats 542
headquarters 1157
state of parties
European Parliament 1173
House of Lords 549
Northern Ireland Assembly 1142

Valuation Office Agency 1211
Vehicle Certification Agency 1211
Veterinary Medicines Directorate 1211
Vote Office, House of Commons 456
voters, number of 464
VWV 1079

Wales Audit Office 1225
Wales Office/Office of the Secretary of State for Wales 6, 35–36, 1204
Water Services Regulation Authority 1215
Websites, Press Gallery 1077
Welsh Affairs, Commons Select Committee 451
Welsh Conservatives
  headquarters 1138
  opposition 1124
  state of parties 1125
Welsh Government 1120–1123
  Cabinet 1120
  Civil Service 1137
  First Minister 1120
  Ministerial responsibilities and staff 1120–1123
  Non-Ministerial Department 1137
  Whips 1120
Welsh Labour
  headquarters 1137
  state of parties 1125
Welsh Liberal Democrats
  headquarters 1138
  state of parties 1125
Whips
  Government (UK) 6
  House of Commons 2, 51, 461
  House of Lords 52
  Opposition, Westminster 51–52, 461
  Scottish Government 1088
  Welsh Government 1120
Whitehall & Industry Group 1225
Wilton Park 1211
Winckworth Sherwood LLP 1079
winding-up allowance, MPs 58
women
  AMs 1132
  MLAs 1150
  MPs 430–434
  MPs (1945-2017) 430
  MSPs 1107
  Peers 1034–1036
Women and Equalities, Commons Select Committee 451
Work and Pensions
  Commons Select Committee 451
  Department for 6, 36–37, 1204

Youth Justice Agency, Northern Ireland 1156